Psychopharmacology
Drugs, the Brain, and Behavior
FOURTH EDITION

Psychopharmacology

Drugs, the Brain, and Behavior

Fourth Edition

Jerrold S. Meyer
University of Massachusetts

Andrew M. Farrar
University of Massachusetts

Dominik Biezonski
Prevail Therapeutics,
a wholly owned subsidiary of Eli Lilly and Company

Jennifer R. Yates
Lander University

 SINAUER ASSOCIATES

NEW YORK   OXFORD
OXFORD UNIVERSITY PRESS

About the cover

Anonymous, *Mescaline Painting – Blue and Red Abstract* (c. 1938). This striking painting was a product of a 1930s British psychiatric experiment to study artistic self-expression under the influence of mescaline, which at the time was purported to induce a schizophrenia-like state. Courtesy Bethlem Museum of the Mind.

Psychopharmacology
Drugs, the Brain, and Behavior, Fourth Edition

Oxford University Press is a department of the University of Oxford. It furthers the University's objective of excellence in research, scholarship, and education by publishing worldwide. Oxford is a registered trade mark of Oxford University Press in the UK and certain other countries.

Published in the United States of America by Oxford University Press
198 Madison Avenue, New York, NY 10016, United States of America.

© 2023, 2018, 2013, 2004 Oxford University Press

For titles covered by Section 112 of the US Higher Education Opportunity Act, please visit www.oup.com/us/he for the latest information about pricing and alternate formats.

Address editorial correspondence to:

Sinauer Associates
23 Plumtree Road
Sunderland, MA 01375 U.S.A.

ACCESSIBLE COLOR CONTENT   Every opportunity has been taken to ensure that the content herein is fully accessible to those who have difficulty perceiving color. Exceptions are cases where the colors provided are expressly required because of the purpose of the illustration.

NOTICE OF TRADEMARKS   Throughout this book trademark names have been used, and in some instances, depicted. In lieu of appending the trademark symbol to each occurrence, the authors and publisher state that these trademarks are used in an editorial fashion, to the benefit of the trademark owners, and with no intent to infringe upon the trademarks. Every effort has been made to determine and contact copyright holders. In the case of any omissions, the publisher will be pleased to make suitable acknowledgement in future editions.

Library of Congress Cataloging-in-Publication Data

Names: Meyer, Jerrold S., 1947- author.

Title: Psychopharmacology: drugs, the brain, and behavior / Jerrold S. Meyer, Andrew M. Farrar, Dominik Biezonski, and Jennifer R. Yates.

Description: Fourth edition. | Sunderland, Massachusetts, USA : Oxford University Press, [2023] | Includes bibliographical references and index.

Identifiers: LCCN 2017049700 | (hardcover) ISBN 9781605359878, (ebook) ISBN 9781605359892.

Subjects: LCSH: Psychotropic drugs--Pharmacokinetics. | Psychotropic drugs--Therapeutic use.

Classification: LCC RM315 .M478 2019 | DDC 615.7/88--dc23

LC record available at https://lccn.loc.gov/2017049700

The *Diagnostic and Statistical Manual of Mental Disorders, DSM, DSM-IV, DSM-IV-TR,* and *DSM-5* are registered trademarks of the American Psychiatric Association. Oxford University Press is not associated with the American Psychiatric Association or with any of its products or publications, nor do the views expressed herein represent the policies and opinions of the American Psychiatric Association.

Printed in the United States of America

Jerrold Meyer *dedicates his contribution to the book to his lovely wife and colleague, Dr. Melinda Novak, for her unwavering patience and support during the countless hours he was squirreled away in his home office working on the project.*

Andrew Farrar *dedicates his contribution to the book to his wife and partner in all endeavors, Dr. Mariana Pereira, for her patience, dedication and support.*

Dominik Biezonski *dedicates his contribution to the book to his incredible wife, Patty Biezonski, and to his loving parents, John and Margaret Biezonski.*

Jennifer Yates *dedicates her contribution to the book to Dr. James C. Walton, for supporting her, always.*

Brief Contents

Contents

3 Chemical Signaling by Neurotransmitters and Hormones 75

4 Methods of Research in Psychopharmacology 107

10   Alcohol   289

11   The Opioids   330

12 Psychomotor Stimulants: Cocaine, Amphetamine, and Related Drugs   368

13 Nicotine and Caffeine   406

14 Marijuana and the Cannabinoids 445

15 Psychedelic and Hallucinogenic Drugs, PCP, and Ketamine 483

18   Affective Disorders: Antidepressants and Mood Stabilizers   587

19   Schizophrenia: Antipsychotic Drugs   619

20 Neurodegenerative Diseases 654

Preface

Jerrold Meyer and Linda Quenzer were approached by Sinauer Associates about 20 years ago to develop a new undergraduate textbook on psychopharmacology. We were already co-authors with Robert Feldman on a massive, 900-page-long graduate level textbook entitled *Principles of Neuropsychopharmacology*, but our Sinauer editor wanted something more than just a condensed and simplified version of the "big book." Our charge was to engage the interest of undergraduate students in learning about psychoactive drugs and their mechanisms of action, while maintaining the more advanced textbook's high standard of comprehensive and up-to-date coverage. The fact that Sinauer has now published the Fourth Edition of *Psychopharmacology: Drugs, the Brain, and Behavior*, indicates that we have had some success in fulfilling that charge.

In the preface to the first edition of this work, the authors commented on the long history of human use of mind-altering substances that eventually led to the need for a science of psychopharmacology. This field of study was already exploding by the late 20th and early 21st centuries, and nothing has happened since then to slow down this remarkable growth. However, new trends are always emerging in any vibrant area of scholarship, and psychopharmacology is no exception in that regard. One such trend particularly worth noting is the impact of changing attitudes toward formerly disparaged substances, at least within Western societies. This impact can be seen in two significant developments. First, many countries or smaller political districts (i.e., states, provinces, or cities), especially within North America and Western Europe, are decriminalizing the personal use of various recreational drugs. Some drugs, like cannabis, have even been fully legalized for such use. Although the politics of decriminalization and legalization remain contentious, a clear trend is in place. Second, we are seeing a remarkable development of therapeutic applications using mind-altering drugs like psilocybin, LSD, MDMA (ecstasy), and ketamine, that until recently were deemed highly addictive and (except for ketamine) without legitimate medical use. Again, this development is not without controversy; however, we are convinced that the growing empirical evidence for therapeutic benefits derived from careful use of psychedelic medications will cement their place in the therapeutic domain.

In accordance with pharmacology being a medical discipline, this new edition continues to emphasize the known or potential therapeutic applications of every compound mentioned in the textbook. However, it's important for readers to recognize not only the advances being made in medications development for some CNS disorders, but also the areas where progress has been frustratingly slow. For example, the introduction of new and exciting psychedelic medications promises to benefit mood-, anxiety-, and trauma-related disorders, but these drugs are less likely to help patients recover from neurodegenerative disorders like Alzheimer's disease, multiple sclerosis, or amyotrophic lateral sclerosis. Drug addiction and autism spectrum disorders are two other important areas where advances in pharmacotherapy have lagged. Therefore, throughout the book we have tried to identify the specific therapeutic benefits and limitations (where appropriate) of each successful medication, failures of medications that seemed promising at one time, and gaps where new medications are sorely needed.

Every chapter in this Fourth Edition is fully updated, with many citations from 2020 and 2021. Special attention is given to recent developments and emerging trends in psychopharmacology while retaining the same organization as in previous editions. The first four chapters provide extensive foundation materials, including the basic principles of pharmacology, neurophysiology and neuroanatomy, cell signaling in the nervous and endocrine systems, and current methods in behavioral assessment and neuropharmacology. The new Case Studies box feature is used in Chapter 1 (Principles of Pharmacology) and in Chapter 2 (Structure and Function of the Nervous System) to demonstrate how the basic concepts of pharmacology and neuroscience are applied in clinical practice. Among the highlights of Chapter 3 (Chemical Signaling by Neurotransmitters and Hormones) are expanded coverage of oxytocin and vasopressin regulation of social behaviors and current evidence on the use of oxytocin to treat the social communication deficits present in autism spectrum disorder. Chapter 4 (Methods of Research in Psychopharmacology) is updated with examples of state-of-the-art techniques, including examples from genetic engineering and artificial intelligence, to illustrate how these technologies are being used to better understand drug effects on behavior and the complex genetic basis of drug-organism interactions. The next four chapters, Chapter 5 (Catecholamines), Chapter 6 (Serotonin), Chapter 7 (Acetylcholine), and Chapter 8 (Glutamate and GABA), describe the key features of neurotransmitter systems that are particularly important to psychopharmacologists. Information about the neurochemistry, anatomy, and behavioral functions of these transmitters not only lays the groundwork for the chapters that follow, but this new edition places increased emphasis on clinical applications of neurotransmitter-targeted drugs. The next eight chapters focus on recreational drugs and their potential for misuse. Chapter 9 (Drug Misuse and Addiction) covers the current theories and mechanisms of drug addiction, which is followed by seven chapters devoted to specific recreational drugs. Chapter 10 (Alcohol) discusses the pharmacology of alcohol, the features of alcohol use disorder (previously called alcoholism), and both current and emerging treatments for this disorder. Chapter 11 (The Opioids) describes the features of the endogenous opioid system, opioid use disorder, and novel treatments for that disorder. The chapter has been updated to reflect the increasing severity of the opioid epidemic and the array of harm-reduction strategies being employed to combat it. This section of the book continues with Chapter 12 (Psychomotor Stimulants: Cocaine, Amphetamine, and Related Drugs), Chapter 13 (Nicotine and Caffeine), Chapter 14 (Marijuana and the Cannabinoids), Chapter 15 (Psychedelic and Hallucinogenic Drugs, PCP, and Ketamine), and Chapter 16 (Inhalants, GHB, and Anabolic-Androgenic Steroids). Among the highlights of these chapters are greatly expanded coverage of e-cigarettes and vaping (Chapter 13), new discussions of cannabis legalization and emerging therapeutic applications of cannabidiol (CBD) and other cannabinoids (Chapter 14), and the mechanisms by which entactogens and psychedelic drugs (MDMA, psilocybin, and LSD) are thought to work when used in drug-assisted psychotherapy for mood- and trauma-related disorders (Chapter 15). The final four chapters consider the neurobiology of neuropsychiatric and neurodegenerative disorders and the drugs used to treat these disorders. Chapter 17 (Disorders of Anxiety and Impulsivity and the Drugs Used to Treat Them) and Chapter 18 (Affective Disorders: Antidepressants and Mood Stabilizers) cover not only classical pharmacotherapies such as benzodiazepines and selective serotonin reuptake inhibitors (SSRIs) but also novel approaches using more "non-traditional" substances such as ketamine and psilocybin, that are discussed in prior chapters on recreational drugs. We highlight ongoing studies on these substances that seek to determine optimal dosing regimens, tolerability, durability, and mechanisms of action, the latter which may lead to the generation of novel compounds with reduced side effects. Chapter 19 (Schizophrenia: Antipsychotic Drugs) has been updated with examples of recent studies demonstrating the promise of pharmacogenetics in optimizing treatment efficacy while reducing side effects, such as tardive dyskinesia. Finally, Chapter 20 (Neurodegenerative Diseases) updates our discussion of the symptoms, clinical trials, FDA-approved therapies, and diagnostic tools, including advances in neuroimaging, for all disorders covered in the chapter. It additionally introduces novel developments such as a new symptom (unusual body odor) that helps diagnose Parkinson's disease and a recently developed technology (focused ultrasound) for treating Alzheimer's disease.

Several features of *Psychopharmacology: Drugs, the Brain, and Behavior* distinguish it from its many competitors. Full-color photos depict pharmacologically relevant plant species, drugs in crystalline form, and drug-related paraphernalia. Beautifully rendered four-color illustrations present data from important experiments and portray models of drug action, including neural pathways thought to mediate the psychological and behavioral effects of specific substances. Bulleted interim summaries highlight the key points made in each part of the chapter, and study questions are provided at the end of each chapter to assist students in reviewing the most important material. A new feature for this edition is the inclusion of learning objectives at the beginning of each section to help direct students and instructors towards the main content to be covered. Breakout boxes (printed and on the web) categorized by the themes of Pharmacology in Action, The Cutting Edge, Of Special Interest, Clinical Applications, Case Studies, and History of Psychopharmacology highlight topics of particular importance. Finally, the new Enhanced e-book offers access to Web Boxes, study resources such as self assessment at the end of each section, flashcards, weblinks and animations that visually illustrate key neurophysiological and neurochemical processes important for Psychopharmacology.

Finally, the new Enhanced e-book offers access to Web Boxes, study resources such as self assessment at the end of each section, flashcards, weblinks and animations that visually illustrate key neurophysiological and neurochemical processes important for psychopharmacology.

Readers familiar with previous editions of this textbook may notice that the long-standing co-author Linda Quenzer was not involved in preparing this new edition. Although Linda has retired from textbook writing, she has been ably replaced by new co-authors Andrew Farrar and Dominik Biezonski. We are confident that this new team, which includes previous contributor Jennifer Yates, has produced a worthy successor to previous editions of the textbook. We hope that you, the reader, will ultimately agree with that assessment.

Acknowledgments

This book is the culmination of the efforts of many dedicated people who contributed their ideas and hard work to the project. We'd like to thank and acknowledge the outstanding editorial team at Sinauer Associates/Oxford University Press: Jessica Fiorillo (Executive Editor), Johannah Walkowicz (Production Editor), and Malinda Labriola (Editorial Assistant). Thank you all for your help in putting together the Fourth Edition, your guidance in making the transition to Oxford University Press, and not least your patience throughout the process of writing, revising, and revising again when necessary. You had a vision for this project that kept us moving forward in our goal of producing the best possible psychopharmacology textbook. Mark Siddall continues to do a fantastic job of seeking out just the right photographs for the book. We are indebted to other key staff members of Oxford University Press who worked on this project, including Joan Gemme, Meg Britton Clark, Michele Beckta, Suzanne Carter, and Sean Hynd. We also thank Wendy Walker and Danna Lockwood for their help with editing, and Melissa Flamson for assisting with permissions. And we must acknowledge Dragonfly Media Group for the beautiful job rendering the illustrations.

The following reviewers contributed many excellent suggestions for improving the book:

Joel Alexander, Western Oregon University
Sage Andrew, University of Missouri
Chiye Aoki, New York University
Susan Barron, University of Kentucky
Ethan Block, University of Pittsburgh
Evan Caldbick, Simon Fraser University
Leighann R. Chaffee, University of Washington, Tacoma
Kirstein Cheryl, University of South Florida
Matt Clasen, American University
Patricia DiCiano, The Centre for Addiction and Mental Health and Seneca College

Henry Gorman, Austin College
Bill Griesar, Portland State University
Joshua Gulley, University of Illinois at Urbana-Champaign
Matt Holahan, Carleton University
Phillip Holmes, University of Georgia
Adam Howorko, PhD; Athabasca University, Concordia University Edmonton
Michael Kane, University of Pennsylvania
Thomas Lanthorn, Sam Houston State University
Jeffrey Lamoureux, Boston College
Lauren Liets, University of California, Davis
Ilyssa Loiacono, Queens College
Margaret Martinetti, The College of New Jersey
Janice McMurray, University of Nevada, Las Vegas
M. Foster, Olive Arizona State University
Robert Patrick, Brown University
Anna Rissanen, Memorial University, Newfoundland
Margaret Ruddy, The College of New Jersey
Jeffrey Rudski, Muhlenberg College
Lawrence Ryan, Oregon State University
Fred Shaffer, Truman State University
Marek Schwendt, University of Florida
Bob Stewart, Washington and Lee University
Evan Zucker, Loyola University

Lastly, we would like to acknowledge and thank the many adopters of this textbook and their students. To new adopters, we appreciate your selection and trust that you will still be happy with that selection after having used the book in your classroom. If you are a previous adopter, we thank you for your continued loyalty that has made it possible to reach this Fourth Edition of the book. Finally, if you are a student, we hope that reading our book and studying the field of psychopharmacology might inspire you to choose this exciting and dynamic field for your own career so that in the years to come, your name might be among the researchers cited in a future edition of *Psychopharmacology: Drugs, the Brain, and Behavior.*

Digital Resources

for *Psychopharmacology*, Fourth Edition

For the Instructor
(Available at **oup.com/he/meyer4e**)

Instructors using *Psychopharmacology*, Fourth Edition, have access to a wide variety of resources to aid in course planning, lecture development, and student assessment.

Content includes:

- **PowerPoint Presentations** Two different PowerPoint presentations are provided for each chapter of the textbook:

  □ *Figures & Tables*: All of the figures and tables from the chapter, with figure numbers and titles on each slide, complete captions in the Notes field, and alt text embedded for accessibility. All the artwork has been reformatted and optimized for exceptional image quality when projected in class.

  □ *Lecture*: A complete lecture outline with selected figures and tables.

- **Test Bank** Revised and updated for the Fourth Edition, the Test Bank consists of a broad range of questions covering key facts and concepts in each chapter. Both multiple-choice and short-answer questions are provided. All questions are ranked according to Bloom's Taxonomy, aligned to new Learning Objectives, and referenced to specific textbook sections. Available in multiple formats, including MS Word and Common Cartridge (for import into learning management systems).

Enhanced E-Book for the Student
(ISBN 9781605359892)

Ideal for self-study, the *Psychopharmacology*, Fourth Edition, enhanced e-book delivers the full suite of digital resources in a format independent from any courseware or learning management system platform, making *Psychopharmacology*'s online resources more accessible for students.

The enhanced e-book is available via RedShelf, VitalSource, and other leading higher education e-book vendors and includes the following student resources:

- *Learning Objectives* outline the important takeaways of every major section.

- *Animations* give students detailed, narrated depictions of some of the complex processes described in the textbook.

- *Self-Assessment Quizzes* following each major section allow students to gauge their understanding of key concepts before proceeding. **NEW** for this edition.

- *Web Boxes* include coverage of novel and cutting-edge topics useful for special discussion.

- *Web Links* list suggested websites and other online resources related to each chapter.

- *Recommended Readings* provide additional references and readings for each chapter.

- *Flashcards* help students master the hundreds of new terms introduced in the textbook.

The Web Boxes are also available to students using the print book. Go to **oup.com/he/meyer4e**.

Principles of Pharmacology

WILLIAM S. BAER (1872–1931) WAS AN ORTHOPEDIC SURGEON at Johns Hopkins University, where he established the orthopedic department and led it for most of his life, training many of the outstanding orthopedists of the day. During World War I Baer observed that soldiers who had severe and deep flesh wounds did not have the fever associated with infection and showed little of the expected necrotic (dead) tissue damage if there was a significant presence of maggots (fly larvae) in the wounds. Although it had been believed that early peoples (Australian aborigines and Mayan Indian tribes) and others throughout history had used maggots to clean wounds, it was Baer who once again recognized their importance, especially in tense battlefield conditions where infection was especially hard to treat. Apparently the maggots ingested the dying tissue but left healthy tissue intact. Baer, upon doing further "pharmacological" experiments, showed that his hospitalized patients with severe and chronic bone infections showed remarkable recovery after being treated with maggots—the inflamed and dying tissue was ingested, leaving wounds clean and healthy, and new tissue formed. As long as the maggots were sterilized, secondary infections were avoided. After his research, "maggot therapy" became popular and was used throughout the 1930s and 1940s until penicillin was established as an easier treatment for infection. However, it has been suggested that in modern times, maggot therapy will be reintroduced to treat those wounds infected with antibiotic-resistant bacteria. At present in the European Union, Japan, and Canada, maggots are considered "medicinal drugs," and in 2005 the U.S. Food and Drug Administration approved the use of maggots as a medical "device."

What actually causes the amazing healing process is not entirely clear, but pharmacologists are beginning to understand that maggot secretions suppress the immune system and reduce inflammation, and they may also enhance cell growth and increase oxygen concentration in the wound. This is certainly not the first time pharmacology has returned to earlier forms of therapeutics, but the science now can isolate and identify those components that lead to healing. ■

Maggot therapy can be used to clean wounds and prevent infection.

1.1 Pharmacology: The Science of Drug Action

Pharmacology is the scientific study of the actions of drugs and their effects on a living organism. Until the beginning of the last century, pharmacologists studied drugs that were almost all naturally occurring substances. The importance of plants in the lives of ancient humans is well documented. Writings from as early as 1500 BCE describe plant-based medicines used in Egypt and in India. The Ebers Papyrus describes the preparation and use of more than 700 remedies for ailments as varied as crocodile bites, baldness, constipation, headache, and heart disease. Of course, many of these treatments included elements of magic and incantation, but there are also references to some modern drugs such as castor oil and opium. The Chinese also have a very long and extensive tradition in the use of herbal remedies that continues today. World Health Organization estimates suggest that in modern times, as many as 80% of the people in developing countries are totally dependent on herbs or plant-derived medicinals. And in 1999, in the United States, modern herbal medicines and drugs based on natural products represented half of the top 20 drugs on the market (Hollinger, 2008). Many Americans are enamored with herbal medications despite limited clinical support for their effectiveness, because they believe these treatments are more "natural." Nevertheless, serious dangers have been associated with some of them. **WEB BOX 1.1** discusses the benefits and dangers of herbal remedies.

When placed in historical context, it can be seen that drug development in the United States is in its infancy. The rapid introduction of many new drugs by the pharmaceutical industry has forced the development of several specialized areas of pharmacology. Two of these areas are of particular interest to us. **Neuropharmacology** is concerned with drug-induced changes in the functioning of cells in the nervous system, and **psychopharmacology** emphasizes drug-induced changes in mood, thinking, and behavior. In combination, the goal of **neuropsychopharmacology** is to identify chemical substances that act on the nervous system to alter behavior that is disturbed because of injury, disease, or environmental factors. Additionally, neuropsychopharmacologists are interested in using chemical agents as probes to gain an understanding of the neurobiology of behavior.

When we speak of **drug action**, we are referring to the specific molecular changes produced by a drug when it binds to a particular target site or receptor. These molecular changes lead to more widespread alterations in physiological or psychological functions, which we consider **drug effects**. The site of drug action may be very different from the site of drug effect. For example, atropine is a drug used in ophthalmology to dilate the pupil of the eye before eye examinations. Atropine has a site of action (the eye muscles of the iris) that is close to the site of its ultimate effect (widening the pupil), so it is administered directly to the eye. In comparison, morphine applied to the eye itself has no effect. Yet when it is taken internally, the drug's action on the brain leads to "pinpoint" pupils. Clearly, for morphine, the site of effect is far distant from the site of its initial action.

Keep in mind that because drugs act at a variety of target sites, they always have multiple effects. Some may be **therapeutic effects**, meaning that the drug–receptor interaction produces desired physical or behavioral changes. All other effects produced are referred to as **side effects**, and they vary in severity from mildly annoying to distressing and dangerous. For example, amphetamine-like drugs produce alertness and insomnia, increased heart rate, and decreased appetite. Drugs in this class reduce the occurrence of spontaneous sleep episodes characteristic of the disorder called *narcolepsy*, but they produce anorexia (loss of appetite) as the primary side effect. In contrast, the same drug may be used as a prescription diet control in weight-reduction programs. In such cases, insomnia and hyperactivity are frequently disturbing side effects. Thus therapeutic and side effects can change, depending on the desired outcome.

It is important to keep in mind that there are no "good" or "bad" drugs, because all drugs are just chemicals. It is the way a drug is procured and used that determines its character. Society tends to think of "good" drugs as those purchased at a pharmacy and taken at the appropriate dosage for a particular medicinal purpose, and "bad" drugs as those acquired in an illicit fashion and taken recreationally to achieve a desired psychological state. Even with this categorization, the differences are blurred because many people consider alcohol to be "bad" even though it is purchased legally. Morphine and cocaine have legitimate medicinal uses, making them "good" drugs under some conditions, although they can, when misused, lead to dangerous consequences and addiction, making the same drugs "bad." Finally, many "good" prescription drugs are acquired illicitly or are misused by increasing the dose, prolonging use, or sharing the drug with other individuals, leading to "bad" outcomes. As you will read in later chapters, the ideas of Americans about appropriate drug use have changed dramatically over time (see the sections on the history of the use of narcotics in Chapter 11 and cocaine in Chapter 12).

Many of the drug effects we have described so far have been **specific drug effects**, defined as those based on the physical and biochemical interactions of a drug with a target site in living tissue. In contrast, **nonspecific drug effects** are those that are based not on the chemical activity of a drug–receptor interaction, but on certain unique characteristics of the individual. It is clear that an individual's background (e.g., drug-taking experience), present mood, expectations of drug effect, perceptions of the drug-taking situation, attitude toward the person administering the drug, and other factors influence the outcome of drug use. Nonspecific drug effects help to explain why the same individual self-administering the same amount of ethyl alcohol may experience a sense of being lighthearted and gregarious on one occasion, and depressed and melancholy on another. The basis for such a phenomenon may well be the varied neurochemical states existing within the individual at different times, with which specific drug effects interact.

Placebo effect

Common examples of nonspecific effects are the multiple outcomes that result from taking a **placebo**. Many of you automatically think of a placebo as a "fake" pill. A placebo *is* in fact a pharmacologically inert compound administered to an individual; however, in many instances it has not only therapeutic effects, but side effects as well. Just as many of the symptoms of illness may have psychogenic or emotional origins, belief in a drug may produce real physiological effects despite the lack of chemical activity. These effects are not limited to the individual's subjective evaluation of relief but include measurable physiological changes such as altered gastric acid secretion, blood vessel dilation, hormonal changes, and so forth.

In a classic study, two groups of patients with ulcers were given a placebo. In the first group, the medication was provided by a physician, who assured the patients that the drug would provide relief. The second group also received the placebo, but it was administered by a nurse, who described it as experimental in nature. In group 1, 70% of the patients found significant relief, but in group 2, only 25% were helped by the "drug" (Levine, 1973). Based on these results, it is clear that a sugar pill is not a drug that can heal ulcers, but rather its effectiveness depends on the ritual of the therapeutic treatment that can have both neurobiological and behavioral effects that influence the outcome. It is a perfect example of mind–body interaction, and there has been increasing interest in understanding the mechanism responsible for the placebo effect as a means to enhance the therapeutic effectiveness of drug treatments. Although some consider deliberate prescription of placebos to patients unethical because of the deception involved, other physicians and ethicists have identified appropriate uses for placebos that represent an inexpensive treatment that avoids unnecessary medications.

Placebo effects may in part be explained by Pavlovian conditioning in which symptom improvement in the past has been associated with particular characteristics of a medication, for example its taste, color, shape, and size; a particular recommending clinician, with her white coat, reassuring tone of voice, or attitude; or aspects of the medical facility. Since a placebo effect has been demonstrated many times in animal models, cues in the environment are apparently sufficient, and verbal reassurances are not necessary. In fact, patients have been shown to benefit even if they are told that the medication is a placebo, so deception is apparently not a necessity; however, verbal suggestion interacts with conditioning (see Colagiuri et al., 2015).

A second possible explanation for the placebo effect is that of conscious, explicit expectation of outcomes. For example, those individuals who anticipate relief may show an enhanced placebo response. Of great interest are the placebo-induced neurobiological effects within the brain. Research has shown that when placebos effectively reduce pain, those individuals who are responders have significantly higher levels of natural pain-relieving opioid neuropeptides in their cerebrospinal fluid than those individuals who do not show a response to the placebo. Further, the subjects who anticipate pain relief show reduced neural activity in pain-related brain regions (see Benedetti et al., 2011).

While Pavlovian conditioning and conscious expectation both contribute to the placebo effect, other factors may also have a part (see Murray and Stoessl, 2013; Carlino et al., 2016). Placebo effects may involve social learning. That is, observing another individual anticipating a positive outcome can be a more powerful inducer of the placebo effect than direct conditioning or verbal suggestions. Others have found that anticipating a successful outcome reduces anxiety and activates reward networks in the brain. Finally, a number of genetic variants have been found that influence the placebo effect. Understanding more about which genes identify patients who will respond to placebo could allow treatment to be adjusted to maximize outcome (Colagiuri et al., 2015). This is one step toward personalized medicine (see the last section of this chapter).

In contrast to placebos, negative expectations may increase the level of anxiety experienced, which may also influence the outcome of treatment. Expecting treatment failure when an inert substance is given along with verbal suggestions of negative outcome, such as increased pain or another aversive event, would increase anxiety as well as cause an accompanying change in neural mechanisms, including increases in stress hormones. This is the **nocebo** effect, and both the nocebo-induced increase in pain reported and the hormonal stress response can be reduced by treatment with an antianxiety drug, demonstrating that expectation-induced anxiety plays a part in the nocebo effect. Nocebos are important to study because warnings about potential side effects can lead to greater side-effect occurrence. Unfortunately, because drug companies are required by law to provide a comprehensive listing of all possible side effects, many individuals have negative expectations, leading to increased side effects.

BOX 1.1 ■ PHARMACOLOGY IN ACTION

Naming Drugs

Drug names can be a confusing issue for many people because drugs that are sold commercially, by prescription or over the counter, usually have four or more different kinds of names.

All drugs have a *chemical name* that is a complete chemical description suitable for synthesizing by an organic chemist. Chemical names are rather clumsy and are rarely used except in a laboratory setting. In contrast, *generic* or *nonproprietary names* are official names of drugs that are listed in the United States Pharmacopeia. The generic name is a much shorter form of the chemical name but is still unique to that drug. For example, one popular antianxiety drug has the chemical name 7-chloro-1,3-dihydro-1-methyl-5-phenyl-2H-1,4-benzodiazepin-2-one and the generic name diazepam. The *brand name*, or *trade name*, of that drug (Valium) specifies a particular manufacturer and a formulation. A brand name is trademarked and copyrighted by an individual company, which means that the company has an exclusive right to advertise and sell that drug.

Slang or *street names* of commonly abused drugs are another way to identify a particular chemical. Unfortunately, these names change over time and vary with geographical location and particular groups of people. In addition, there is no way to know the chemical characteristics of the substance in question. Some terms are used in popular films or television and become more generally familiar, such as "crack" or "ice," but most disappear as quickly as they appear.

In pharmacology, the placebo is essential in the design of experiments conducted to evaluate the effectiveness of new medications, because it eliminates the influence of expectation on the part of the experiment's participants. The control group is identical to the experimental group in all ways and is unaware of the substitution of an inactive substance (e.g., sugar pill, saline injection) for the test medication. Comparison of the two groups provides information on the effectiveness of the drug beyond the expectations of the participants. Of course, drugs with strong subjective effects or prominent side effects make placebo testing more challenging because the experimental group will be aware of the effects while those experiencing no effects will conclude they are the control group. To avoid that problem, some researchers may use an "active" placebo, which is a drug (unrelated to the drug being tested) that produces some side effects that suggest to the control participants that they are getting the active agent. In other cases clinical researchers may feel that it is unethical to leave the placebo group untreated if there is an effective agent available. In that case the control group will be given the older drug, and effectiveness of the new drug will be compared with it rather than with a placebo.

The large contribution of nonspecific factors and the high and variable incidence of placebo responders make the **double-blind experiment** highly desirable. In these experiments, neither the patient nor the observer knows what treatment the participant has received. Such precautions ensure that the results of any given treatment will not be biased on the part of the participant or the observer. If you would like to read more about the use of placebos in both clinical research and therapeutics and the associated ethical dilemmas, refer to the articles by Brown (1998) and Louhiala (2009).

Throughout this chapter, we present examples that include both therapeutic and recreational drugs that affect mood and behavior. Since there are usually several names for the same substance, it may be helpful for you to understand how drugs are named (**BOX 1.1**).

Pharmacokinetic factors determining drug action

Although it is safe to assume that the chemical structure of a drug determines its action, it quickly becomes clear that additional factors are also powerful contributors. The dose of the drug administered is clearly important, but more important is the amount of drug in the blood that is free to bind at specific target sites (**bioavailability**) to elicit drug action. The following sections of this chapter describe in detail the dynamic factors that contribute to bioavailability. Collectively, these factors constitute the **pharmacokinetic** component of drug action; they are listed below and illustrated in **FIGURE 1.1**.

1. *Routes of administration.* How and where a drug is administered determines how quickly and how completely the drug is absorbed into the blood.

2. *Absorption and distribution.* Because a drug rarely acts where it initially contacts the body, it must pass through a variety of cell membranes and enter the blood plasma, which transports the drug to virtually all of the cells in the body.

3. *Binding.* Once in the blood plasma, some drug molecules move to tissues to bind to active target sites (receptors). While in the blood, a drug may

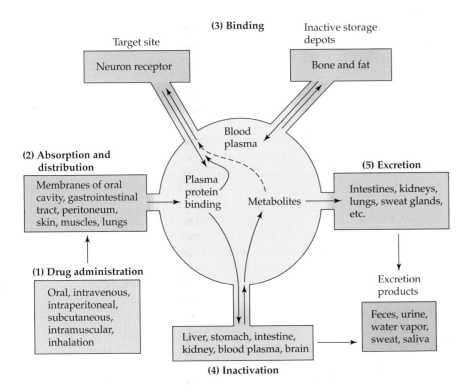

(3) Binding

Target site

Neuron receptor

Inactive storage depots

Bone and fat

Blood plasma

(2) Absorption and distribution

Membranes of oral cavity, gastrointestinal tract, peritoneum, skin, muscles, lungs

Plasma protein binding

Metabolites

(5) Excretion

Intestines, kidneys, lungs, sweat glands, etc.

(1) Drug administration

Oral, intravenous, intraperitoneal, subcutaneous, intramuscular, inhalation

Liver, stomach, intestine, kidney, blood plasma, brain

(4) Inactivation

Excretion products

Feces, urine, water vapor, sweat, saliva

FIGURE 1.1 Pharmacokinetic factors that determine bioavailability of drugs From the site of administration (1), the drug moves through cell membranes to be absorbed into the blood (2), where it circulates to all cells in the body. Some of the drug molecules may bind to inactive sites such as plasma proteins or storage depots (3), and others may bind to receptors in target tissue. Bloodborne drug molecules also enter the liver (4), where they may be transformed into metabolites and travel to the kidneys and other discharge sites for ultimate excretion (5) from the body.

also bind (**depot binding**) to plasma proteins or may be stored temporarily in bone or fat, where it is inactive.

4. *Inactivation.* Drug inactivation, or **biotransformation**, occurs primarily as a result of metabolic processes in the liver as well as other organs and tissues. The amount of drug in the body at any one time is dependent on the dynamic balance between absorption and inactivation. Therefore, inactivation influences both the intensity and the duration of drug effects.

5. *Excretion.* The drug metabolites are eliminated from the body with the urine or feces. Some drugs are excreted in an unaltered form by the kidneys.

Although these topics are discussed sequentially in the following pages, keep in mind that in the living organism, these factors are at work simultaneously. In addition to bioavailability, the drug effect experienced will also depend on how rapidly the drug reaches its target, the frequency and history of prior drug use (see the discussion on tolerance later in the chapter), and nonspecific factors that are characteristics of individuals and their environments.

Methods of drug administration influence the onset of drug action

The route of administration of a drug determines how much drug reaches its site of action and how quickly the drug effect occurs. There are two major categories of administration methods. **Systemic** routes of administration refer to methods in which drugs distribute throughout the entire body, thus reaching the target tissue through general circulation. Within the broad category of systemic administration, **enteral** methods of administration use the gastrointestinal (GI) tract (*enteron* is the Greek word for "gut"); agents administered by these methods are generally slow in onset and produce highly variable blood levels of drug. The most common enteral method of administration is oral, but rectal administration with the use of suppositories is another enteral route. Other systemic routes of administration are **parenteral** and include those that do not use the alimentary canal, such as injection or pulmonary administration.

Oral administration (**PO**) is the most commonly used route for taking drugs, because it is safe, self-administered, and economical, and it avoids the complications and discomfort of injection methods. Drugs that are taken orally come in the form of capsules, pills, tablets, or liquid, but to be effective, the drug must dissolve in stomach fluids and pass through the stomach or intestine wall to reach blood capillaries. In addition, the drug must be resistant to destruction by stomach acid and stomach enzymes that are important for normal digestion.

Movement of the drug from the site of administration to the blood circulation is called **absorption**. Although some drugs are absorbed from the stomach, most drugs are not fully absorbed until they reach the small intestine. Many factors influence how quickly the stomach empties its contents into the small intestine and hence determine the ultimate rate of absorption. For example, food in the stomach, particularly if it is fatty, slows the movement of the drug into the intestine, thereby delaying absorption into the blood. The amount of food consumed, the level of physical activity of the individual, and many other factors make it difficult to predict how quickly the drug will reach the intestine. In addition, many drugs undergo extensive first-pass metabolism. **First-pass metabolism** is an evolutionarily beneficial function because potentially harmful chemicals and toxins that are ingested pass via the portal vein to the liver, where they are chemically altered by a variety of enzymes before passing to the heart for circulation throughout the body (**FIGURE 1.2**). Unfortunately, some therapeutic drugs taken orally may undergo extensive metabolism (more than 90%), reducing their bioavailability. Drugs that show extensive first-pass effects must be administered at higher doses or in an alternative manner, such as by injection. Because of these many factors, oral administration produces drug plasma levels that are more irregular and unpredictable and rise

more slowly than those produced by other methods of administration.

Rectal administration requires the placement of a drug-filled suppository in the rectum, where the suppository coating gradually melts or dissolves, releasing the drug, which will be absorbed into the blood. Depending on the placement of the suppository, the drug may avoid some first-pass metabolism. Drug absorbed from the lower rectum into the hemorrhoidal vein bypasses the liver. However, deeper placement means that the drug is absorbed by veins that drain into the portal vein, going to the liver before the general circulation. Bioavailability of drugs administered in this way is difficult to predict, because absorption is irregular (**BOX 1.2**). Although rectal administration is not used as commonly as oral administration, it is an effective

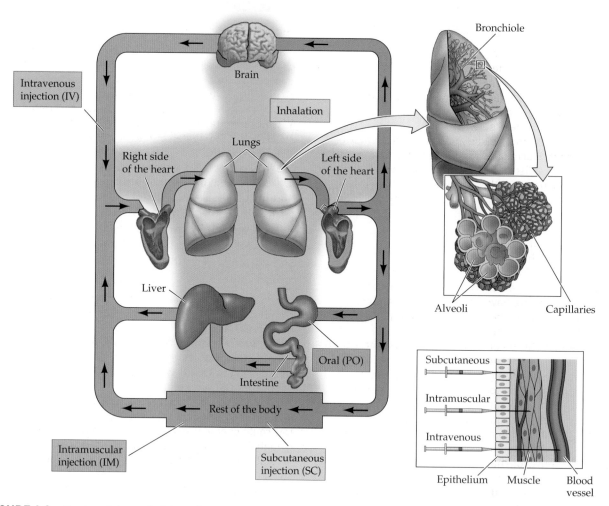

FIGURE 1.2 **Routes of drug administration** First-pass effect. Drugs administered orally are absorbed into the blood and must pass through the liver before reaching the general circulation. Some drug molecules may be destroyed in the liver before they can reach target tissues. The arrows indicate the direction of blood flow in the arteries (red) and veins (blue). (Top inset) Pulmonary absorption through capillaries in the alveoli. Rapid absorption occurs after inhalation because the large surface area of the lungs and the rich capillary networks provide efficient exchange of gases to and from the blood. (Bottom inset) Methods of administration by injection. The speed of absorption of drug molecules from administration sites depends on the amount of blood circulating to that area.

route in infants and in individuals who are vomiting, unconscious, or unable to take medication orally.

Intravenous (IV) injection is the most rapid and accurate method of drug administration in that a precise quantity of the agent is placed directly into the blood and passage through barriers such as the stomach wall is eliminated (see Figure 1.2). However, the quick onset of drug effect with IV injection is also a potential hazard. An overdose or a dangerous allergic reaction to the drug leaves little time for corrective measures, and the drug cannot be removed from the body as it can be removed from the stomach by stomach pumping.

For drug abusers, IV administration provides a more dramatic subjective drug experience than self-administration in other ways, because the drug reaches the brain almost instantly. Drug users report that intravenous injection of a cocaine solution usually produces an intense "rush" or "flash" of pure pleasure that lasts for approximately 10 minutes. This experience rarely occurs when cocaine is taken orally or is taken into the nostrils (snorting; see the discussion on topical administration). However, IV use of street drugs poses several special hazards. First, drugs that are impure or of unknown quality provide uncertain doses, and toxic reactions are common. Second, lack of sterile injection equipment and aseptic technique can lead to infections such as hepatitis, human immunodeficiency virus (HIV), and endocarditis (inflammation of the lining of the heart). Fortunately, many cities have implemented free needle programs, which significantly reduce the

BOX 1.2 ■ CASE STUDIES

The Perils of Alcohol Taken by an Unconventional Route of Administration

As described in this chapter, pharmacokinetic factors play a significant role in drug bioavailability and hence drug effects. With respect to drugs of abuse, many drug users experiment with alternative routes of administration in order to avoid unpleasant side effects or enhance the desired effects of a given drug. Ethyl alcohol, or ethanol, is consumed almost exclusively orally, in the form of a fermented drink, like beer or wine, or as a distilled spirit, like vodka or whiskey. When consumed by the oral route of administration, ethanol has relatively high bioavailability. However, because most ethanol is absorbed in the intestines, the stomach contents, and thus the rate of gastric emptying, can powerfully influence ethanol absorption and bioavailability.

Even though nearly all ethanol is consumed orally, even in cases of excessive consumption and abuse, some individuals have engaged in the dangerous practice of administering ethanol-containing drinks rectally, as an alcohol enema. The practice of rectally administering alcohol is highly risky for a couple of notable reasons. Alcohol, particularly at higher concentrations, is highly irritating to the sensitive mucosa of the colon, and as such, exposure to alcohol-containing drinks has resulted in numerous cases of severe colitis, requiring hospitalization. More seriously, the colon absorbs alcohol very rapidly, and unlike the stomach, the colon does not contain alcohol dehydrogenase (ADH), which normally begins the biotransformation of ethanol in the stomach before it is absorbed into the bloodstream. Moreover, ethanol absorbed through the colon does not undergo first-pass metabolism, further contributing to its elevated bioavailability. The more rapid absorption and hence higher bioavailability of ethanol through rectal administration can result in a blood-alcohol concentration that is significantly higher than if the same amount of ethanol were consumed orally. The higher bioavailability and thus more pronounced intoxicating effect of alcohol is likely chief among the reasons that some individuals choose to administer alcohol rectally. Other reasons may include avoidance of vomiting as well as the false belief that rectally administered alcohol would be undetectable on the breath.

Peterson and colleagues (2014) present the case of a 52-year-old man who was found deceased in his home following rectal administration of wine. At the time of autopsy, the decedent's blood-alcohol concentration was 350 mg/dL, while the vitreous ethanol concentration was 410 mg/dL. Determining postmortem alcohol content from the vitreous fluid of the eye is thought to reflect alcohol concentration more accurately at the time of death, since blood levels of alcohol tend to vary quite widely and decrease in the postmortem period. In any event, it is likely that the blood-alcohol concentration in the decedent was at least in the range of 350 to 410 mg/dL at the time of death, which is well within the range at which most people would suffer the fatal effects of ethanol.

While accidental ethanol overdoses resulting in death are relatively common, it is unusual that these fatal overdoses are the result of rectal administration. Given the high bioavailability of ethanol from this route of administration and hence the elevated potential for unintentional overdose, the small number of fatal overdoses likely reflects the fact that while dangerous, alcohol enema is a far less commonly used method of administration than oral consumption. As discussed in Chapter 10, alcohol overdose by any route of administration represents a fraction of the total number of alcohol-related fatalities, which can include fatalities caused by other dangerous behaviors, including motor vehicle accidents.

probability of cross-infection. Third, many drug abusers attempt to dissolve drugs that have insoluble filler materials, which, when injected, may become trapped in the small blood vessels in the lungs, leading to reduced respiratory capacity or death.

An alternative to the IV procedure is **intramuscular (IM)** injection, which provides the advantage of slower, more even absorption over a period of time. Drugs administered by this method are usually absorbed within 10 to 30 minutes. Absorption can be slowed down by combining the drug with a second drug that constricts blood vessels, because the rate of drug absorption is dependent on the rate of blood flow to the muscle (see Figure 1.2). To provide slower, sustained action, the drug may be injected as a suspension in vegetable oil. For example, IM injection of medroxyprogesterone acetate (Depo-Provera) provides effective contraception for 3 to 6 months without the need to take daily pills. One disadvantage of IM administration is that in some cases, the injection solution can be highly irritating, causing significant muscle discomfort.

Intraperitoneal (IP) injection is rarely used with humans, but it is the most common route of administration for small laboratory animals. The drug is injected through the abdominal wall into the peritoneal cavity—the space that surrounds the abdominal organs. IP injection produces rapid effects, but not as rapid as those produced by IV injection. Variability in absorption occurs, depending on where (within the peritoneum) the drug is placed.

In **subcutaneous (SC)** administration, the drug is injected just below the skin (see Figure 1.2) and is absorbed at a rate that is dependent on blood flow to the site. Absorption is usually fairly slow and steady, but there can be considerable variability. Rubbing the skin to dilate blood vessels in the immediate area increases the rate of absorption. Injection of a drug in a nonaqueous solution (such as peanut oil) or implantation of a drug pellet or delivery device further slows the rate of absorption. Subcutaneous implantation of drug-containing pellets is most often used to administer hormones. Implanon and Nexplanon are two contraceptive implants now available in the United States. The hormones are contained in a single small rod about 40 mm (1.5 inches) long that is implanted through a small incision just under the skin of the upper arm. A woman is protected from pregnancy for a 3-year period unless the device is removed. Recent technological advances allow drug solutions to be injected in a liquid form, which, upon contact with subcutaneous tissue fluid, forms a biodegradable solid or gel that slowly releases active drug over a period of up to 1 month. This technology has been used to administer buprenorphine, which acts as a partial agonist or antagonist at opioid receptors. This mechanism of action is thought to help individuals overcome opioid use disorder by

reducing drug withdrawal and promoting treatment compliance due to the long duration of effect (see Ling et al., 2019; Rosenthal, 2019, for detailed reviews of the effectiveness of these novel formulations). Also, refer to Chapter 11 for information about the endogenous opioid system and drugs that act upon it.

Inhalation of drugs, such as those used to treat asthma attacks, allows drugs to be absorbed into the blood by passing through the lungs. Absorption is very rapid because the area of the pulmonary absorbing surfaces is large and rich with capillaries (see Figure 1.2). The effect on the brain is very rapid because blood from the capillaries of the lungs travels only a short distance back to the heart before it is pumped quickly to the brain via the carotid artery, which carries oxygenated blood to the head and neck. The psychoactive effects of inhaled substances can occur within a matter of seconds.

Inhalation is the method preferred for self-administration in cases when oral absorption is too slow and much of the active drug would be destroyed in the GI tract before it reached the brain. Nicotine released from the tobacco of a cigarette by heat into the smoke produces a very rapid rise in blood level and rapid central nervous system (CNS) effects, which peak in a matter of minutes. Tetrahydrocannabinol (THC), an active ingredient of marijuana, and crack cocaine are also rapidly absorbed after smoking. In addition to the inherent dangers of the drugs themselves, disadvantages of inhalation include irritation of the nasal passages and damage to the lungs caused by small particles that may be included in the inhaled material.

Topical application of drugs to mucous membranes, such as the conjunctiva of the eye, the oral cavity, nasopharynx, vagina, colon, and urethra, generally provides local drug effects. Because topically applied drugs are typically intended to act locally, this method of drug administration is generally not considered a systemic route of administration. However, some topically administered drugs can nevertheless be readily absorbed into the general circulation, leading to widespread effects. A related delivery method is **sublingual administration**, which involves placing the drug under the tongue, where it contacts the mucous membrane and is absorbed rapidly into a rich capillary network. Sublingual administration has several advantages over oral administration, because the drug is not broken down by gastric acid or gastric enzymes. Further, its absorption is faster because it is absorbed directly into the blood and is not dependent on those factors that determine how quickly the stomach empties its contents into the small intestine. Additionally, since the drug is not absorbed from the GI tract, it avoids first-pass metabolism. **Intranasal administration** is of special interest because it causes local effects such as relieving nasal congestion and treating allergies, but it can also have systemic effects, in which case the drug moves very rapidly across a single epithelial cell layer into the bloodstream, avoiding first-pass liver metabolism and producing higher bioavailability than if given orally. The approach is noninvasive, painless, and easy to use, and hence it enhances compliance. Even more important is the fact that intranasal administration allows the blood–brain barrier to be bypassed, perhaps by achieving direct access to the fluid that surrounds the brain (**cerebrospinal fluid [CSF]**) and moving from there to extracellular fluid found in the intercellular spaces between neurons. (For a discussion of the potential mechanisms by which intranasal administration can bypass the blood–brain barrier, see Crowe et al., 2018.) A large number of drugs, hormones, steroids, proteins, peptides, and other large molecules are available in nasal spray preparations for intranasal delivery, although not all drugs can be atomized. Hence, neuropeptides such as the hormone oxytocin can be administered by intranasal sprays to achieve significant concentrations in the brain. **WEB BOX 1.2** describes a study that evaluated the effects of intranasal oxytocin administration on social behavior in autistic adults.

Intranasal absorption can also be achieved without dissolving the drug. Direct application of finely powdered cocaine to the nasal mucosa by sniffing leads to rapid absorption, which produces profound effects on the CNS that peak in about 15 to 30 minutes. One side effect of "snorting" cocaine is the formation of perforations in the nasal septum, the cartilage that separates the two nostrils. This damage occurs because cocaine is a potent vasoconstrictor. Reducing blood flow deprives the underlying cartilage of oxygen, leading to necrosis. Additionally, contaminants in the cocaine act as chemical irritants, causing tissue inflammation. Cocaine addicts whose nasal mucosa has been damaged by chronic cocaine "snorting" may resort to application of the drug to the rectum, vagina, or penis.

Although the skin provides an effective barrier to the diffusion of water-soluble drugs, certain lipid-soluble substances (i.e., those that dissolve in fat) are capable of penetrating slowly. Accidental absorption of industrial and agricultural chemicals such as tetraethyl lead, organophosphate insecticides, and carbon tetrachloride through the skin produces toxic effects on the nervous system and on other organ systems. **Transdermal** (i.e., through the skin) drug administration with skin patches provides controlled and sustained delivery of drug at a preprogrammed rate. The method is convenient because the individual does not have to remember to take a pill, and it is painless without the need for injection. It also provides the advantage of avoiding the first-pass effect. In cases of mass vaccination campaigns, transdermal delivery is much quicker than other methods, and it reduces the dangers of accidental needle sticks of health care workers and unsafe disposal of used needles. Conventional patches consist of a polymer matrix embedded with the drug in high concentration. Transdermal delivery is now a common way to prevent motion sickness with scopolamine, reduce cigarette craving with nicotine, relieve angina pectoris with nitroglycerin, and provide hormones after menopause or for contraceptive purposes. The major disadvantage of transdermal delivery is that because skin is designed to prevent materials from entering the body, a limited number of drugs are able to penetrate. However, techniques are continuing to be developed to increase skin permeability through a variety of methods. For instance, handheld ultrasound devices that send low-intensity sound energy waves through surrounding fluid in the tissue temporarily increase the size of the pores in the skin, allowing absorption of large molecules from a skin patch. Other "active" patch systems that help to move large molecules through the skin use iontophoresis, which involves applying a small electrical current with tiny batteries to the reservoir or the patch. The electrical charge repels drug molecules with a similar charge and forces them through the skin at a predetermined rate. If the amount and duration of current are changed, drug delivery can be restricted to the skin for local effects or can be forced more deeply into the blood. This process is also capable of pulling molecules out through the skin for monitoring. Such monitoring might be used by diabetic individuals to more frequently and painlessly evaluate levels of blood glucose. An additional approach uses mechanical disruption of the skin. Small arrays of microneedles about 1 µm in diameter and 100 µm long and coated with drug or vaccine are placed on the skin. The needles penetrate the superficial layer of the skin—the stratum corneum—where the drug is delivered without stimulating underlying pain receptors. This method provides the opportunity for painless vaccinations and drug injections that can be self-administered. These and other developing techniques have been described by Langer (2003), Banga (2009), and Waghule and colleagues (2019).

Special injection methods must be used for some drugs that act on nerve cells, because a cellular barrier, the blood–brain barrier (discussed later in the chapter), prevents or slows passage of these drugs from the blood into neural tissue. To directly bypass the blood–brain barrier, **central** routes of administration may be used. For example, **intrathecal** injection is used when spinal anesthetics are administered directly into the CSF in the subarachnoid space surrounding the spinal cord, whereas **epidural** infusion, in which a catheter is implanted in the epidural space just outside of the dura mater, is commonly used during childbirth, bypassing the blood–brain barrier (**FIGURE 1.3**). In animal experiments, a microsyringe or a cannula enables precise drug infusion into discrete areas of brain tissue (**intracranial**) or into

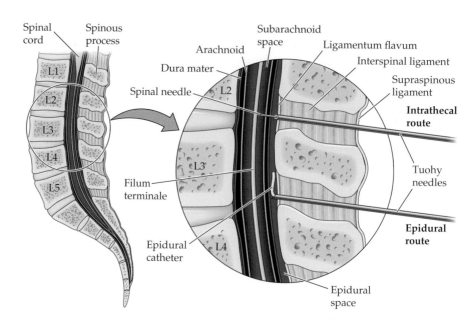

FIGURE 1.3 Anatomical diagram of intrathecal and epidural routes of administration (Left) Cross-section of the lumbar spine, illustrating the typical spinal level selected for intrathecal and epidural routes of administration. (Right) The intrathecal route of administration requires that the tip of the infusion catheter penetrate the dura mater and arachnoid membranes, allowing for drug to be infused directly into the subarachnoid space. In contrast, the epidural route uses a flexible catheter that targets the space outside of the dura mater (epidural space). (After F. Cox [Ed.]. 2009. *Perioperative Pain Management*. Wiley-Blackwell: Oxford.)

the CSF-filled chambers, the ventricles (**intracerebro-ventricular**). In this way, experimenters can study the electrophysiological, biochemical, or behavioral effects of drugs on particular nerve cell groups. This method is described in Chapter 4. Animal research has evolved into potentially important treatment methods for human conditions such as cerebral meningitis (inflammation of one of the protective membranes covering the brain). An **infusion pump** implanted under the skin of the scalp can be programmed to deliver a constant dose of antibiotic into the cerebral ventricles; this device permits treatment of brain infection and is useful because antibiotics are normally prevented from passing the blood–brain barrier. These infusion pumps have important uses in delivering drugs systemically as well. With appropriate software, it is possible to provide pulsed administration of an agent that mimics the normal biological rhythm, for example, of hormones. An exciting development has been the addition of feedback regulation of these pumps, which includes a sensor element that monitors a substance such as blood glucose in a diabetic individual and responds with an appropriate infusion of insulin delivered from an implantable pump that acts much like an artificial pancreas. The downside to these pumps is the risk of infection and frequent clogging, which reduces their usefulness in maintaining stable drug concentrations over prolonged periods.

Many disorders of the CNS are characterized by abnormal changes in gene activity, which alter the manufacture of an essential protein such as an enzyme or a receptor. **Gene therapy** refers to the application of deoxyribonucleic acid (DNA), which encodes a specific protein, to a particular target site. DNA can be used to increase or block expression of the gene product to correct the clinical condition. One significant difficulty in the application of gene therapy involves creating the

appropriate gene delivery system. Such a delivery system, which is called a *vector*, is needed to carry the gene into the nuclei of target cells to alter protein synthesis. Administering gene therapy is clearly more challenging when disorders of the CNS, rather than disorders of any other part of the body, are treated. Vectors are usually injected directly into the brain region targeted for modification. **Viral vectors** are frequently considered for this delivery system because of the special ability of viruses to bind to and enter cells and their nuclei, where they insert themselves into the chromosomes to alter DNA. Because viruses vary in terms of binding, cell entry proteins, and other properties, a variety of viruses are being evaluated.

Lim and colleagues (2010) provide a review of viral vector delivery as an approach to treating diseases of the CNS. Human trials have been increasing in number, but much research remains to be done before the safety and usefulness of gene therapy are fully demonstrated. Concerns expressed by researchers include the following: that an immune response may be initiated by the introduction of foreign material, that the viral vector may recover its ability to cause disease once it is placed in the human cell, and that inserting the vector in the wrong place may induce tumor growth. Nevertheless, many animal studies are highly encouraging, and gene therapy is believed to have enormous potential for the treatment of debilitating disorders of the nervous system such as stroke-induced damage, spinal cord injury, chronic pain conditions, and neurodegenerative disorders such as Alzheimer's disease, Parkinson's disease, and Huntington's disease.

IMPACT ON BIOAVAILABILITY Because the route of administration significantly alters the rate of absorption, blood levels of the same dose of a drug

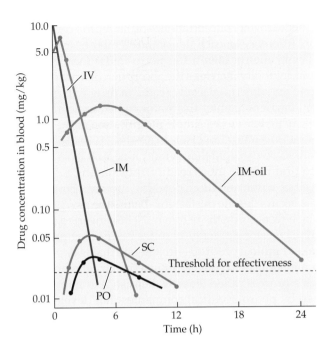

FIGURE 1.4 **The time course of drug blood level depends on route of administration** The blood level of the same amount of drug administered by different procedures to the same individual varies significantly. Intravenous (IV) administration produces an instantaneous peak when the drug is placed in the blood, followed by a rapid decline. Intramuscular (IM) administration produces rapid absorption and rapid decline, although IM administration in oil (IM-oil) shows slower absorption and gradual decline. Slow absorption after subcutaneous (SC) administration means that some of the drug is metabolized before absorption is complete. For this reason, no sharp peak occurs, and overall blood levels are lower. Oral (PO) administration produces the lowest blood levels and a relatively short time over threshold for effectiveness in this instance. (After R. R. Levine. 1973. *Pharmacology: Drug Actions and Reactions*. Little, Brown, and Co.: Boston; D. F. Marsh. 1951. *Outlines of Fundamental Pharmacology*. Charles C. Thomas: Springfield, IL.)

administered by different routes vary significantly. **FIGURE 1.4** compares drug concentrations in blood over time for various routes of administration. Keep in mind that the peak level for each method reflects not only differences in absorption rate, but also the fact that slow absorption provides the opportunity for liver metabolism to act on some of the drug molecules before absorption is complete. Advantages and disadvantages of selected methods of administration are summarized in **TABLE 1.1.**

Multiple factors modify drug absorption

Once the drug has been administered, it is absorbed from the site of administration into the blood to be circulated throughout the body and ultimately to the brain, which is the primary target site for **psychoactive drugs** (i.e., those drugs that have an effect on thinking, mood, and behavior). We have already shown that the rate of absorption is dependent on several factors. Clearly, the route of administration alters absorption because it determines the area of the absorbing surface, the number of cell layers between the site of administration and the blood, the amount of drug destroyed by metabolism or digestive processes, and the extent of binding to food or inert complexes. Absorption is also dependent on drug concentration, which is determined

TABLE 1.1 Advantages and Disadvantages of Selected Routes of Drug Administration		
Route of administration	**Advantages**	**Disadvantages**
Oral (PO)	Safe; self-administered; economical; no needle-related complications	Slow and highly variable absorption; subject to first-pass metabolism; less-predictable blood levels
Intravenous (IV)	Most rapid; most accurate blood concentration	Overdose danger; cannot be readily reversed; requires sterile needles and medical technique
Intramuscular (IM)	Slow and even absorption	Localized irritation at site of injection; needs sterile equipment
Subcutaneous (SC)	Slow and prolonged absorption	Variable absorption depending on blood flow
Inhalation	Large absorption surface; very rapid onset; no injection equipment needed	Irritation of nasal passages; inhaled small particles may damage lungs
Topical	Localized action and effects; easy to self-administer	May be absorbed into general circulation
Transdermal	Controlled and prolonged absorption	Local irritation; useful only for lipid-soluble drugs
Epidural	Bypasses blood–brain barrier; very rapid effect on CNS	Not reversible; needs trained anesthesiologist; possible nerve damage
Intranasal	Ease of use; local or systemic effects; very rapid; no first-pass metabolism; bypasses blood–brain barrier	Not all drugs can be atomized; potential irritation of nasal mucosa

in part by individual differences in age, sex, and body size. Finally, absorption is dependent on the solubility and ionization of the drug.

TRANSPORT ACROSS MEMBRANES

Perhaps the single most important factor in determining plasma drug levels is the rate of passage of the drug through the various cell layers (and their respective membranes) between the site of administration and the blood. To understand this process, we need to look more carefully at cell membranes.

Cell membranes are made up primarily of complex lipid (fat) molecules called **phospholipids**, which have a negatively charged phosphate region (the head) at one end and two uncharged lipid tails (**FIGURE 1.5A**). These molecules are arranged in a bilayer, with their phosphate ends forming two almost continuous sheets filled with fatty material (**FIGURE 1.5B**). This configuration occurs because the polar heads are attracted to the polar water molecules. Hence, the charged heads are in contact with both the aqueous intracellular fluid and the aqueous extracellular fluid. Proteins that are found inserted into the phospholipid bilayer have functions that will be described later (see Chapter 3). The molecular characteristics of the cell membrane prevent most molecules from passing through unless they are soluble in fat.

LIPID-SOLUBLE DRUGS

Drugs with high lipid solubility move through cell membranes by **passive diffusion**, leaving the water in the blood or stomach juices and entering the lipid layers of membranes. Movement across the membranes is always in a direction from higher to lower concentration. The larger the concentration difference on each side of the membrane (called the **concentration gradient**), the more rapid is the diffusion. Lipid solubility increases the absorption of drug into the blood and determines how readily a drug will pass the lipid barriers to enter the brain. For example, the narcotic drug heroin is a simple modification of the parent compound morphine. Heroin, or diacetylmorphine, is more soluble in lipid than is morphine, and it penetrates into brain tissue more readily, thus having a quicker onset of action and more potent reinforcing properties. This occurs despite the fact that before the psychotropic drug effects occur, the heroin must be converted to morphine by esterase enzymes in the brain. That property makes heroin a prodrug—that is, one that is dependent on metabolism to convert an inactive drug to an active one, a process called **bioactivation**. This strategy is one used by pharmaceutical companies that develop prodrugs that cross the blood–brain barrier (see the section Drug Distribution Is Limited by Selective Barriers) if the active drug cannot penetrate easily.

IONIZED DRUGS

Most drugs are not readily lipid soluble, because they are weak acids or weak bases that can become ionized when dissolved in water. Just as common table salt (NaCl) produces positively charged ions (Na^+) and negatively charged ions (Cl^-) when dissolved in water, many drugs form two charged (ionized) particles when placed in water. Although NaCl is a strong electrolyte, which causes it to almost entirely dissociate in water, most drugs are only partially ionized when dissolved in water. The extent of **ionization**

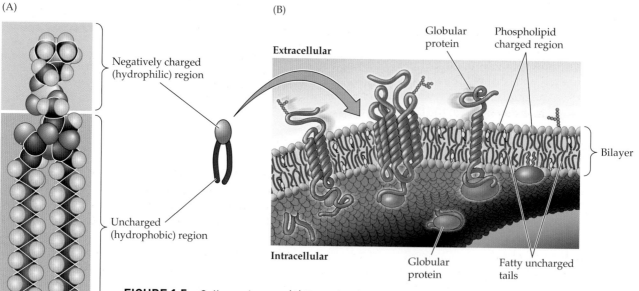

(A)

Negatively charged (hydrophilic) region

Uncharged (hydrophobic) region

(B)

Extracellular

Globular protein

Phospholipid charged region

Bilayer

Intracellular

Globular protein

Fatty uncharged tails

FIGURE 1.5 **Cell membranes** (A) Example of a phospholipid molecule with a negatively charged group (PO_4^-) at one end (hydrophilic) and two fatty uncharged tails (hydrophobic). (B) The arrangement of individual phospholipid molecules forms a bilayer, with negatively charged heads attracted to the water molecules of both intracellular and extracellular fluids. The fatty tails of the molecules are tucked within the two charged layers and have no contact with aqueous fluid. Embedded in the bilayer are protein molecules that serve as receptors or channels.

TABLE 1.2	pH of Body Fluids
Fluid	**pH**
Stomach	1.35–3.5
Blood	7.35–7.4
Kidney urine	4.6–8.0
Cerebrospinal fluid (CSF)	7.3

Source: After G. K. Schwalfenberg. 2012. *J Environ Public Health* 2012: 727630.

depends on two factors: the relative acidity/alkalinity (pH) of the solution, and an intrinsic property of the molecule (pK$_a$).

Acidity or alkalinity is expressed as pH, which is described on a scale of 1 to 14, with 7 being neutral. Acidic solutions have a lower pH, and alkaline (basic) solutions have a pH greater than 7.0. Drugs are dissolved in body fluids that differ in pH (**TABLE 1.2**), and these differences play a role in drug ionization and movement from one body fluid compartment to another, for example from the stomach to the bloodstream, or from the bloodstream into the kidney urine.

The second factor determining ionization is a characteristic of the drug molecule. The pK$_a$ of a drug represents the pH of the aqueous solution in which that drug would be 50% ionized and 50% non-ionized. In general, drugs that are weak acids ionize more readily in an alkaline environment and become less ionized in an acidic environment. The reverse is true of drugs that are weak bases. If we put the weak acid aspirin (acetylsalicylic acid) into stomach acid, it will remain primarily in a non-ionized form (**FIGURE 1.6**). The lack of electrical charge makes the drug more lipid soluble and hence readily absorbed from the stomach to the blood. In the intestine, where the pH is around 5.0 to 6.0, ionization increases and absorption through that membrane is reduced compared with that of the stomach.

This raises the question of why aspirin molecules do not move from the stomach to the blood and back to the stomach again. In our example, aspirin in the acidic gastric fluid is primarily in non-ionized form and thus passes through the stomach wall into the blood. In blood (pH 7.4), however, aspirin becomes more ionized; it is said to be "trapped" within the blood and does not return to the stomach. Meanwhile, the circulation moves the aspirin molecules away from their concentrated site at the stomach to maintain a concentration gradient that favors drug absorption. Hence, although passive diffusion would normally cease when drug concentration approached a 50:50 equilibrium, the combination of ion trapping and blood circulation of the drug away from the absorbing surface means that absorption from oral administration can be quite high. Keep in mind that although the acidic stomach favors absorption of weak acids, much of the aspirin

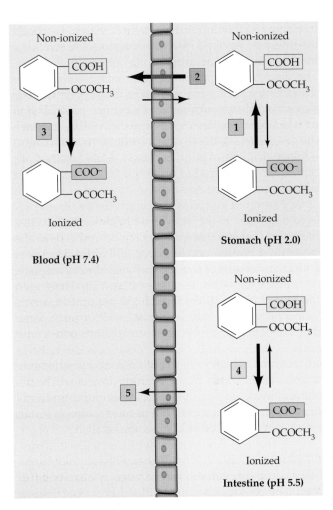

FIGURE 1.6 **Effect of ionization on drug absorption** On the right side of the cell barrier in stomach acid (pH 2.0), aspirin molecules tend to remain in the non-ionized form (1), which promotes the passage of the drug through the cell walls (2) to the blood. Once the intact aspirin molecules reach the blood (pH 7.4), they ionize (3) and are "trapped" in the blood to be circulated throughout the body. In the lower portion of the figure, when the aspirin has reached the intestine, it tends to dissociate to a greater extent (4) in the more basic pH. Its more ionized form reduces passage (5) through the cells to the blood, so absorption from the intestine is slower than from the stomach.

is absorbed in the small intestine because absorption is also determined by the length of time the drug is in contact with the absorptive membrane.

Drugs that are highly charged in both acidic and basic environments are very poorly absorbed from the GI tract and cannot be administered orally. This explains why South American hunters readily eat the flesh of game killed with curare-poisoned arrows. Curare is highly ionized in both the acidic stomach and the alkaline intestine, so the drug does not leave the digestive system to enter their blood.

OTHER FACTORS Factors other than ionization have a significant influence on absorption as well. For instance, the much larger surface area of the small intestine and the slower movement of material through the intestine, as compared with the stomach, provide a much greater opportunity for absorption of all drugs. Therefore, the rate at which the stomach empties into the intestine very often is the significant rate-limiting factor. For this reason, medication is often prescribed to be taken before meals and with sufficient fluid to move the drug through the stomach and into the intestine.

Since drug absorption is closely related to the concentration of the drug in body fluids (e.g., stomach), it should certainly be no surprise to you that the drug dosage required to achieve a desired effect is directly related to the size of the individual. In general, the larger the individual, the more diluted the drug will be in the larger fluid volume, and less drug will reach target sites within a given unit of time. The average dose of a drug is typically based on the response of individuals between the ages of 18 and 65 who weigh 150 pounds. However, for people who are very lean or obese, the average dose may be inappropriate because of variations in the ratio of fat to water in the body. For these individuals, body surface area, which reflects both size and weight, may serve as a better basis for determining drug dose. The sex of the individual also plays a part in determining plasma drug level: in women, adipose tissue, relative to water, represents a larger proportion of the total body weight. Overall, the total fluid volume, which contains the drug, is relatively smaller in women than in men, producing a higher drug concentration at the target site in women. It should be obvious also that in the smaller fluid volume of a child, a standard dose of a drug will be more concentrated and therefore will produce a greater drug effect.

Drug distribution is limited by selective barriers

Regardless of the route of administration, once the drug has entered the blood, it is carried throughout the body within 1 or 2 minutes and can have an action at any number of receptor sites. In general, those parts of the body in which blood flow is greatest will have the highest concentration of drug. Since blood capillaries have numerous pores, most drugs can move from blood and enter body tissues regardless of lipid solubility, unless they are bound to protein (see the discussion on depot binding later in this chapter). Quite rapidly, high concentrations of drugs will be found in the heart, brain, kidneys, and liver. Other tissues with less vasculature will more slowly continue to absorb the drug from the plasma, causing plasma levels to fall gradually. As plasma levels fall, the concentration of drug in the highly vascularized organs will be greater than that in the blood, so the drug will move from those organs back into the plasma to maintain equilibrium. Hence, those organs will have an initial high concentration of drug, and then **drug redistribution** will reduce drug concentration there. Ultimately drug concentration will be in equilibrium in all tissues. Drug redistribution may be responsible for terminating the action of a drug, as in the case of the rapid-acting CNS depressant thiopental. Thiopental, a barbiturate used for intravenous anesthesia, is highly lipid soluble; therefore, rapid onset of sedation is caused by entry of the drug into the brain. Deep sedation does not last very long, because the blood level falls rapidly as a result of redistribution of the drug to other tissues, causing thiopental to move from the brain to the blood to maintain equilibrium. High levels of thiopental can be found in the brain 30 seconds after IV infusion. However, within 5 minutes, brain levels of the drug drop to threshold anesthetic concentrations. In this way, thiopental induces sleep almost instantaneously but is effective for only about 5 minutes, followed by rapid recovery.

Because the brain receives about 20% of the blood that leaves the heart, lipid-soluble drugs are readily distributed to brain tissue. However, the blood–brain barrier limits the movement of ionized molecules from the blood to the brain.

BLOOD–BRAIN BARRIER   Blood plasma is supplied by a dense network of blood vessels that permeate the entire brain. This system supplies brain cells with oxygen, glucose, and amino acids, and it carries away carbon dioxide and other waste products. Despite the vital role that blood circulation plays in cerebral function, many substances found in blood fluctuate significantly and would have disruptive effects on brain cell activity if materials were transferred freely between blood and brain (and the brain's associated CSF).

CSF is a clear, colorless liquid that fills the subarachnoid space that surrounds the entire bulk of the brain and spinal cord and also fills the hollow spaces (ventricles) and their interconnecting channels (aqueducts), as well as the centrally located cavity that runs longitudinally through the length of the spinal cord (central canal) (**FIGURE 1.7A**). CSF is manufactured by cells of the choroid plexus, which line the cerebral ventricles. In contrast to the wide fluctuations that occur in the blood plasma, the contents of the CSF remain quite stable. Many substances that diffuse out of the blood and affect other organs in the body do not seem to enter the CSF, nor do they affect brain tissue. This separation between brain capillaries and the brain/CSF constitutes what we call the blood–brain barrier. **FIGURE 1.7B** shows an enlargement of the relationship between the cerebral blood vessels and the CSF.

The principal component of the blood–brain barrier is the distinct morphology of brain capillaries. **FIGURE 1.8** shows a comparison between typical capillaries found throughout the body (Figure 1.8A) and capillaries that serve the CNS (Figure 1.8B). Because the job of blood vessels is to deliver nutrients to cells while removing waste, the walls of typical capillaries are made up of endothelial cells that have both small gaps (**intercellular clefts**)

FIGURE 1.7 Distribution of cerebrospinal fluid (A) Cerebrospinal fluid (CSF; blue) is manufactured by the choroid plexus within the cerebral ventricles. In addition to filling the ventricles and their connecting aqueducts, CSF fills the space between the arachnoid membrane and the pia mater (subarachnoid space) to cushion the brain against trauma. (B) The enlarged diagram shows detail of CSF-filled subarachnoid space and its relationship to cerebral blood vessels. Note how the blood vessels penetrate the brain tissue.

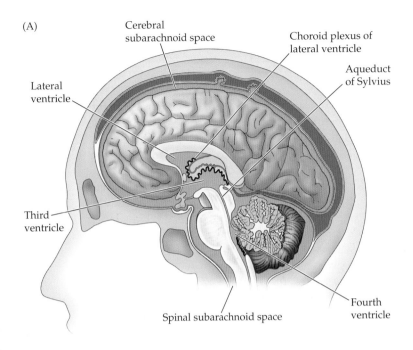

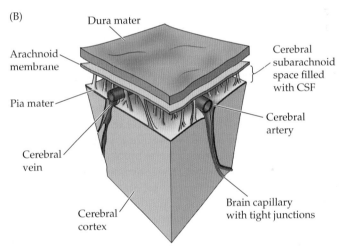

and larger openings (**fenestrations**) through which molecules can pass. In addition, general capillaries have **pinocytotic vesicles** that envelop and transport larger molecules through the capillary wall. In contrast, in brain capillaries, the intercellular clefts are closed because adjoining edges of the endothelial cells are fused, forming **tight junctions**. Also, fenestrations are absent and pinocytotic vesicles are rare. Although lipid-soluble materials can pass through the walls of the blood vessels, most materials are moved from the blood of brain capillaries by special transporters. Surrounding brain capillaries are numerous glial feet—extensions of the glial cells called **astrocytes** or **astroglia**. It is becoming apparent that these astrocytic glial feet contribute to both postnatal formation and maintenance of the blood–brain barrier throughout adulthood. It has been shown that blood–brain barrier characteristics depend on the CNS environment, because if the endothelial cells are removed and cultured without astroglia, they lose their barrier function. Conversely, blood–brain barrier characteristics can be induced in non-CNS endothelial cells that are cultured with astrocytes (see Alvarez et al., 2013). By filling in the extracellular space around capillaries and releasing secretion factors, these astroglia apparently help maintain the endothelial tight junctions. Also, it is likely that the close interface of astrocytes with both nerve cells and brain capillaries provides the astrocytes with a unique opportunity to coordinate the delivery of oxygen and glucose in the blood with the energy required by activated neurons. There is more discussion of the many functions of astrocytes in Chapter 2.

Before we go on, we should emphasize that the blood–brain barrier is selectively permeable, not impermeable. Although the barrier does reduce diffusion of water-soluble (i.e., ionized) molecules, it does not impede lipid-soluble molecules.

Finally, the blood–brain barrier is not complete. Several brain areas are not isolated from materials in the blood, and a limited blood–brain barrier exists in other regions of the brain wherever a functional interaction (e.g., blood monitoring) is required between blood and neural tissue. For example, the area postrema, or chemical trigger zone, is a cluster of cells in the brainstem that responds to toxins in the blood and induces vomiting.

The limited permeability of the blood–brain barrier is important in psychopharmacology because we need to know which drugs remain non-ionized at plasma pH and readily enter the CNS, and which drugs only circulate throughout the rest of the body. Minor differences in drug molecules are responsible for the relative selectivity of drug action. For example, physostigmine readily crosses the blood–brain barrier and is useful for treating the intoxication caused by some agricultural pesticides. It does so by increasing the availability of the neurotransmitter acetylcholine.

(A) Typical capillary

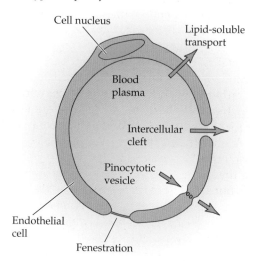

(B) Brain capillary

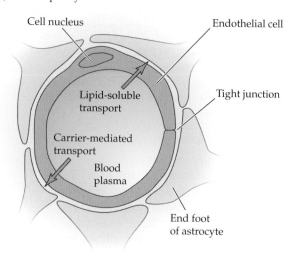

FIGURE 1.8 **Cross-section of typical capillaries and brain capillaries** (A) Capillaries found throughout the body have characteristics that encourage movement of materials between the blood and surrounding cells. (B) Brain capillaries minimize movement of water-soluble molecules through the blood vessel wall because there are essentially no large or small clefts or pinocytotic sites. (After W. H. Oldendorf. 1977. *Exp Eye Res* 25: 177–190. © 1977. Reprinted with permission from Elsevier.)

In contrast, the structurally related but highly ionized drug neostigmine is excluded from the brain and increases acetylcholine only peripherally. Its restriction by the blood–brain barrier means that neostigmine can be used to treat the muscle disease myasthenia gravis without significant CNS side effects, but it would not be effective in treating pesticide-induced intoxication. As mentioned earlier in this section, because many drugs that are ionized do not pass through the blood–brain barrier, direct delivery of the drug into brain tissue by intracranial injection may be necessary, although at least some drugs can be atomized and delivered intranasally to bypass the blood–brain barrier. A second approach is to develop a prodrug that is lipid soluble and becomes bioactivated by brain enzymes.

PLACENTAL BARRIER A second barrier, unique to women, is found between the blood circulation of a pregnant mother and that of her fetus. The placenta, which connects the fetus with the mother's uterine wall, is the means by which nutrients obtained from the digestion of food, O_2, CO_2, fetal waste products, and drugs are exchanged. As is true for other cell membranes, lipid-soluble substances diffuse easily, and water-soluble substances pass less easily. The potential for transfer of drugs from mother to fetus has very important implications for the health and well-being of the developing child. Potentially damaging effects on the fetus can be divided into two categories: acute toxicity and teratogenic effects.

The fetus may experience acute toxicity in utero after exposure to the disproportionately high drug blood level of its mother. In addition, after birth, any drug remaining in the newborn's circulation is likely to have a dramatic and prolonged action because of slow and incomplete metabolism. It is well known that opiates such as heroin readily reach the fetal circulation and that newborn infants of heroin- or methadone-addicted mothers experience many of the signs of opiate withdrawal. Certain tranquilizers, gaseous anesthetics, alcohol, many barbiturates, and cocaine all readily pass into the fetal circulation to cause acute toxicity. In addition, alcohol, cocaine, and the carbon monoxide in cigarette smoke all deprive the fetus of oxygen. Such drugs pose special problems because they are readily accessible and are widely used.

Teratogens are agents that induce developmental abnormalities in the fetus. The effects of teratogens such as drugs (both therapeutic and illicit), exposure to X-rays, and some maternal infections (e.g., German measles) are dependent on the timing of exposure. The fetus is most susceptible to damaging effects during the first trimester of pregnancy, because it is during this period that many of the fetal organ systems are formed. Each organ system is maximally sensitive to damaging effects during its time of cell differentiation (**TABLE 1.3**). Many drugs can have damaging effects on the fetus despite minimal adverse effects in the mother. For example, the vitamin A–related substance isotretinoin, which is a popular prescription acne medication (Accutane), produces serious birth defects and must be avoided by sexually active young women. Experience has taught us that evaluation of drug safety must consider potential fetal effects, as well as effects on adults. Furthermore, because teratogenic effects are most severe during the time before pregnancy is typically recognized, the use of any drug known to be teratogenic in animals should be avoided by women of childbearing age.

TABLE 1.3   Critical Periods of Teratogenic Sensitivity for Several Organ Systems in the Human Fetus

Organ system	Weeks after fertilization
Brain	3–16
Eye	4–8
Genitalia	7–9
Heart	3–6
Limbs	4–6

Depot binding alters the magnitude and duration of drug action

We already know that after a drug has been absorbed into the blood from its site of administration, it circulates throughout the body. Thus, high concentrations of drug may be found in all organs that are well supplied with blood until the drug gradually redistributes to all tissues in the body. Drug binding occurs at many inactive sites, where no measurable biological effect is initiated. Such sites, called **drug depots** or **silent receptors**, include several plasma proteins, with albumin being most important. Any drug molecules bound to these depots cannot reach active sites, nor can they be metabolized by the liver. However, the drug binding is reversible, so the drug remains bound only until the blood level drops, causing it to unbind gradually and circulate in the plasma.

The binding of a drug to inactive sites—called **depot binding**—has significant effects on the magnitude and duration of drug action. Some of these effects are summarized in **TABLE 1.4**. First, depot binding reduces the concentration of drug at its sites of action because only freely circulating (unbound) drug can pass across membranes. Onset of action of a drug that binds readily to depot sites may be delayed and its effects reduced because the number of drug molecules reaching the target tissue is dependent on its release from inactive sites. Individual differences in the amount of depot binding explain in part why some people are more sensitive than others to a particular drug.

Second, because binding to albumin, fat, and muscle is rather nonselective, many drugs with similar physiochemical characteristics compete with each other for these sites. Such competition may lead to a much-higher-than-expected free drug blood level of the displaced drug, producing a drug overdose. For example, the antiseizure drug phenytoin is highly protein bound, but aspirin can displace some of the phenytoin molecules from the binding sites because aspirin binds more readily. When phenytoin is displaced from plasma protein by aspirin, the elevated drug level may be responsible for unexpected side effects. Many psychoactive drugs, including the antidepressant fluoxetine (Prozac) and the tranquilizer diazepam (Valium), show extensive (more than 90% of the drug molecules) plasma protein binding and may contribute to drug interactions in some cases.

Third, bound drug molecules cannot be altered by liver enzymes, because the drug is not free to leave the blood to enter liver cells for metabolism. For this reason, depot binding frequently prolongs the time that the drug remains in the body. This phenomenon explains why some drugs, such as THC, which is stored in fat and is only slowly released, can be detected in urine for many days after a single dose. Such slow release means that an individual could test positive for urinary THC (one active ingredient in marijuana) without experiencing cognitive effects at that time. The prolonged presence of drugs in body fat and inert depots makes pre-employment and student drug testing possible.

Finally, as mentioned previously, redistribution of a drug from highly vascularized organs (e.g., brain) to tissues with less blood flow will reduce drug concentrations in those organs. The redistribution occurs more rapidly for highly lipid-soluble drugs that reach the

TABLE 1.4   Effects of Drug Depot Binding on Therapeutic Outcome

Depot-binding characteristics	Therapeutic outcome
Rapid binding to depots before reaching target tissue	Slower onset and reduced effects
Individual differences in amount of binding	Varying effects: High binding means less free drug, so some people seem to need higher doses. Low binding means more free drug, so these individuals seem more sensitive.
Competition among drugs for depot-binding sites	Higher-than-expected blood levels of the displaced drug, possibly causing greater side effects, even toxicity
Unmetabolized bound drug	Drug remaining in the body for prolonged action
Redistribution of drug to less vascularized tissues and inactive sites	Termination of drug action

brain very quickly but also redistribute readily because of the ease of movement through membranes. Those drugs have a rapid onset but short duration of action.

Biotransformation and elimination of drugs contribute to bioavailability

Drugs are eliminated from the body through the combined action of several mechanisms, including biotransformation (metabolism) of the drug and excretion of metabolites that have been formed. Drug clearance reduces blood levels and in large part determines the intensity and duration of drug effects. The easiest way to assess the rate of elimination consists of intravenously administering a drug to establish a peak plasma drug level, then collecting repeated blood samples. The decline in plasma drug concentration provides a direct measure of the clearance rate without complication by absorption kinetics.

DRUG CLEARANCE Drug clearance from the blood usually occurs exponentially and is referred to as **first-order kinetics**. Exponential elimination means that a constant *fraction* (50%) of free drug in the blood is removed during each time interval. The exponential function occurs because even at relatively high drug concentrations, surplus clearance sites are available, so the rate is concentration-dependent. Hence, when blood levels are high, clearance occurs more rapidly, and as blood levels drop, the rate of clearance is reduced. The amount of time required for removal of 50% of the drug in blood is called the **half-life**, or $t_{1/2}$. **FIGURE 1.9** provides an example of half-life determination for the stimulant dextroamphetamine (Dexedrine), a drug used to treat attention-deficit/hyperactivity disorder (ADHD). Although all drugs are essentially eliminated after six half-lives, many psychoactive drugs have half-lives of several days, so clearance may take weeks after even a single dose. A list of the half-lives of some common drugs is provided in **TABLE 1.5**. Keep in mind that clearance from the blood is also dependent on biotransformation rate as well as depot binding and storage in reservoirs such as fat.

The principal goal of any drug regimen is to maintain the plasma concentration of the drug at a constant desired level for a therapeutic period. The therapeutic window is the range of plasma drug levels that are high enough to be effective, but not so high that they cause toxic or otherwise intolerable side effects. For some drugs, such as stimulants used to treat ADHD, or hypnotic drugs used to promote sleep, the therapeutic period is only part of each day, so a single daily dose of a drug with a relatively short half-life would be required to avoid disruptive effects at other times of day. However, in many cases the target therapeutic concentration is achieved only after multiple administrations. For instance, as **FIGURE 1.10** shows, a predictable fluctuation in blood level occurs over

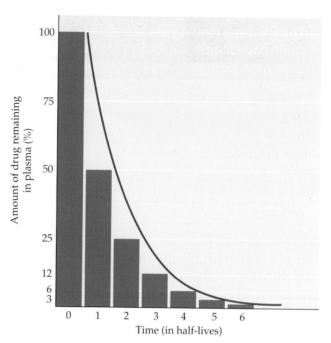

FIGURE 1.9 **First-order kinetics of drug clearance** Exponential elimination of drug from the blood occurs when clearance during a fixed time interval is always 50% of the drug remaining in blood. For example, the half-life of orally administered dextroamphetamine (Dexedrine) is approximately 10 hours. Therefore, 10 hours (one half-life) after the peak plasma concentration has been reached, the drug concentration is reduced to about 50% of its initial value. After 20 and 30 hours (i.e., two and three half-lives) have elapsed, the concentration is reduced to 25% and 12.5%, respectively. After six half-lives, the drug is essentially eliminated, with 1.6% remaining. The curve representing the rate of clearance is steeper early on, when the rate is more rapid, and becomes more shallow as the rate of clearance decreases.

time as a result of the dynamic balance between absorption and clearance. After oral administration at time A, the plasma level of a drug gradually increases to its peak (peak 1) followed by a decrease because of drug biotransformation, elimination, or storage at inactive sites. If first-order kinetics is assumed, after one half-life (time B), the plasma drug level has fallen to half its peak value. Half-life determines the time needed to reach the **steady state plasma level**, which is the desired blood concentration of drug achieved when the absorption/distribution phase is equal to the metabolism/excretion phase. For any given daily dose of a drug, the steady state plasma level is approached after a period of time equal to five half-lives (time C), at which point only 3.125% of the initial dose theoretically remains, minimally contributing to the total drug concentration achieved with subsequent doses. Hence, for a given dosing interval, the shorter the half-life of a drug, the more rapidly the therapeutic level of the drug will be achieved. Drugs with longer half-lives will take longer to reach consistent blood

TABLE 1.5 Half-Lives of Some Common Drugs

Drug	Half-life
Cocaine	0.7–1.5 hours[a]
Morphine	2–3.52 hours[b]
Nicotine	2 hours[c]
Methylphenidate	2–3 hours[d]
THC	20–30 hours[e]
Ibuprofen	1.8–2 hours[f]
Sertraline	22–36 hours[g]

Sources: Based on data in [a]J. L. Zimmerman. 2012 *Crit Care Clin* 28: 517–526; [b]C. E. Inturrisi. 2002. *Clin J of Pain* 18: S3; [c]N. L. Benowitz et al. 1982. *J Pharmacol Exp Ther* 221: 368–372; [d]H. C. Kimko et al. 1999. *Clin Pharmacokinet* 37: 457–470; [e]F. Grotenhermen. 2003. *Clin Pharmacokinet* 42: 327–360; [f]R. Bushra and N. Aslam 2010. *Oman Med J* 25: 55–1661; and [g]C. L. DeVane et al. 2002. *Clin Pharmacokinet* 41: 1247–1266.

levels. For example, if we needed the blood level of drug X with a half-life of 4 hours to be 1000 mg, we might administer 500 mg at the outset. After 4 hours, the blood level would have dropped to 250 mg, at which time we could administer another 500 mg, raising the blood level to 750 mg. Four hours later, another 500 mg could be added to the current blood level of 375 mg, bringing the new value to 875 mg, and so forth. The amount of drug would continue to rise until a maximum of 1000 mg was reached because more drug was given than was metabolized. However, as we reached the steady state level after approximately five half-lives, the amount administered would approximate the amount metabolized (500 mg).

Although most drugs are cleared from the blood by first-order kinetics, under certain conditions some drugs are eliminated according to the zero-order model. **Zero-order kinetics** means that drug molecules are cleared at a constant rate regardless of drug concentration; this is graphically represented as a straight line (**FIGURE 1.11**). It happens when drug levels are high and routes of metabolism or elimination are saturated (i.e., more drug molecules are available than sites). A classic example of a drug that is eliminated by zero-order kinetics is high-dose ethyl alcohol. When two or more drinks of alcohol are consumed in a relatively short time, alcohol molecules saturate the enzyme-binding sites, and metabolism occurs at its maximum rate of approximately 10 to 15 ml/hour, or 1.0 ounce of 100-proof alcohol per hour regardless of concentration. This rate is determined by the number of enzyme molecules. Any alcohol consumption that occurs after saturation of the enzyme will raise blood levels dramatically and produce intoxication. Although zero-order biotransformation occurs at high levels of alcohol, the biotransformation rate shifts to first-order kinetics as blood levels are reduced (see Figure 1.11).

BIOTRANSFORMATION BY LIVER MICROSOMAL ENZYMES Most drugs are chemically altered by the body before they are excreted. These chemical changes

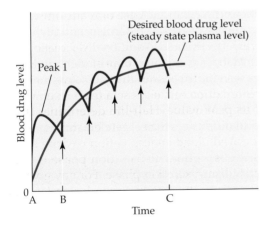

FIGURE 1.10 **Achieving steady state plasma levels of drug** The scalloped line shows the pattern of accumulation during repeated administration of a drug. The arrows represent the times of administration. The shape of the scallop is dependent on both the rate of absorption and the rate of elimination. The smooth line represents drug accumulation in the blood during continuous intravenous infusion of the same drug.

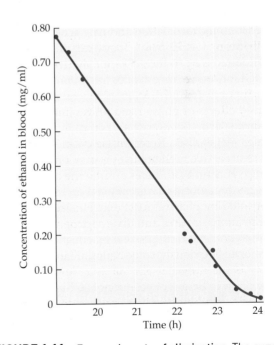

FIGURE 1.11 **Zero-order rate of elimination** The curve shows the decline of ethanol content in blood after intravenous administration of a large dose to laboratory animals. The *x*-axis represents the time beginning 19 hours after administration. Plotted data show the change from zero-order to first-order kinetics when low concentrations are reached between 23 and 24 hours after administration. (After E. K. Marshall, Jr. 1953. *J Pharmacol Exp Ther* 109: 431.)

are catalyzed by enzymes and can occur in many tissues and organs, including the stomach, intestine, blood plasma, kidney, and brain. However, the greatest number of chemical changes, which we call *drug metabolism* or biotransformation, occur in the liver.

There are two major types of biotransformation. Type I biotransformations are sometimes called phase I because these reactions often occur before a second metabolic step. Phase I changes involve *nonsynthetic* modification of the drug molecule by oxidation, reduction, or hydrolysis. Oxidation is by far the most common reaction; it usually produces a metabolite that is less lipid soluble and less active, but it may produce a metabolite with equal or even greater activity than the parent drug. Type II, or phase II, modifications are *synthetic* reactions that require the combination (called *conjugation*) of the drug with some small molecule such as glucuronide, sulfate, or methyl groups. Glucuronide conjugation is particularly important for inactivating psychoactive drugs. These metabolic products are less lipid soluble because they are highly ionized and are almost always biologically inactive. In summary, the two phases of drug biotransformation ultimately produce one or more inactive metabolites, which are water soluble, so they can be excreted more readily than the parent drug. Metabolites formed in the liver are returned to the circulation and are subsequently filtered out by the kidneys, or they may be excreted into bile and eliminated with the feces. Metabolites that are active return to the circulation and may have additional action on target tissues before they are further metabolized into inactive products. Obviously, drugs that are converted into active metabolites have a prolonged duration of action. **TABLE 1.6** shows several examples of the varied effects of phase I and phase II metabolism. The sedative drug phenobarbital is rapidly inactivated by phase I metabolism. In contrast, aspirin is converted at first to an active metabolite by phase I metabolism, but phase II action produces an inactive compound. Morphine does not undergo phase I metabolism but is inactivated by phase II reactions. Finally, diazepam (Valium), a long-lasting antianxiety drug, has several active metabolites before phase II inactivation. Further, as mentioned previously, some drugs are inactive until

they are metabolized. For example, the inactive drug codeine is metabolized in the body to the active drug morphine, making codeine a prodrug.

The liver enzymes primarily responsible for metabolizing psychoactive drugs are located on the smooth endoplasmic reticulum, which is a network of tubules within the liver cell cytoplasm. These enzymes are often called **microsomal enzymes** because they exhibit particular characteristics on biochemical analysis. Microsomal enzymes lack strict specificity and can metabolize a wide variety of xenobiotics (i.e., chemicals that are foreign to the living organism), including toxins ingested with food, environmental pollutants, and carcinogens, as well as drugs. Among the most important liver microsomal enzymes is the **cytochrome P450 (CYP450)** enzyme family. Members of this class of enzyme, which number more than 50, are responsible for oxidizing most psychoactive drugs, including antidepressants, morphine, and amphetamines. Although they are primarily found in the liver, cytochrome enzymes are also located in the intestine, kidney, lungs, and nasal passages, where they alter foreign molecules. Enzymes are classified into families and subfamilies by their amino acid sequences, as well as by the genes encoding them, and they are designated by a number—letter—number sequence such as 2D6. Among the cytochrome enzymes that are particularly important for psychotropic drug metabolism are CYP450 1A2, 3A4, 2D6, and several in the 2C subfamily.

FACTORS INFLUENCING DRUG METABOLISM The enzymes of the liver are of particular interest to psychopharmacologists because several factors significantly influence the rate of biotransformation. These factors alter the magnitude and duration of drug effects and are responsible for significant drug interactions. These drug interactions can either increase bioavailability, causing adverse effects, or reduce blood levels, which may reduce drug effectiveness. Additionally, variations in the rate of metabolism explain many of the individual differences seen in response to drugs. Factors that modify biotransformation capacity include (1) enzyme induction, (2) enzyme inhibition, (3) drug competition, and (4) individual differences in age, gender, and genetics.

TABLE 1.6	Varied Effects of Phase I and Phase II Metabolism		
Active drug	**Active metabolites and inactive metabolites**[a]		
Phenobarbital	Phase I ⟶ Hydroxy-phenobarbital		
Aspirin	Phase I ⟶ **Salicylic acid** — Phase II ⟶ Salicylic-glucuronide		
Morphine	Phase II ⟶ Morphine-6-glucuronide		
Diazepam	Phase I ⟶ **Desmethyldiazepam** — Phase II ⟶ **Oxazepam** — Phase II ⟶ Oxazepam-glucuronide		

[a]Bold terms indicate active metabolites.

Many psychoactive drugs, when used repeatedly, cause an increase in a particular liver enzyme (called **enzyme induction**). Increased numbers of enzyme molecules not only cause the drugs to speed up their own rate of biotransformation two- to threefold but also can increase the rate of metabolism of all other drugs modified by the same enzyme. For example, repeated use of the antiseizure drug carbamazepine (Tegretol) increases the number of CYP450 3A4 enzyme molecules, leading to more rapid metabolism of carbamazepine and many other drugs, producing a lower blood level and a reduced biological effect. Among the drugs metabolized by the same enzyme are oral contraceptives. For this reason, if carbamazepine is prescribed to a woman who is taking oral contraceptives, she will need an increased hormone dose or an alternative means of birth control (Zajecka, 1993). When drug use is terminated, there is a gradual return to normal levels of metabolism.

Another common example is cigarette smoke, which increases CYP450 1A2 enzymes. People who are heavy smokers may need higher doses of drugs such as antidepressants and caffeine that are metabolized by the same enzyme. Such changes in drug metabolism and elimination explain in part why some drugs lose their effectiveness with repeated use, a phenomenon known as *tolerance* (see the discussion on tolerance later in the chapter); these changes also cause a reduced effect of other drugs that are metabolized by the same enzyme (cross-tolerance). Clearly, drug-taking history can have a major impact on the effectiveness of the drugs that an individual currently takes.

In contrast to drug-induced induction of liver enzymes, some drugs directly inhibit the action of enzymes (**enzyme inhibition**); this reduces the metabolism of other drugs taken at the same time that are metabolized by the same enzyme. In such cases, one would experience a much more intense or prolonged drug effect and increased potential for toxicity. Monoamine oxidase inhibitors (MAOIs), used to treat depression, act in the brain by preventing the destruction of certain neurotransmitters by the enzyme monoamine oxidase (MAO). The same enzyme is found in the liver, where it normally metabolizes amines such as tyramine, which is found in red wine, beer, some cheeses, and other foods. When individuals who are taking these antidepressants eat foods rich in tyramine, dangerous high blood pressure and cardiac arrhythmias can occur, making normal foods potentially life-threatening. Further detail on this side effect of MAOIs is provided in Chapter 18.

In addition, because MAOIs are not specific for MAO, they have the potential to cause adverse effects unrelated to MAO function. They inhibit several microsomal enzymes of the CYP450 family, producing elevated blood levels of many drugs and potentially causing increased side effects or unexpected toxicity.

A second drug–food interaction involves the ingestion of grapefruit juice, which significantly inhibits the biotransformation of many drugs metabolized by CYP450 3A4, including numerous psychiatric medications. A single glass (5 ounces) of grapefruit juice elevates the blood levels of those drugs significantly by inhibiting their first-pass metabolism. The effect is caused by chemicals in grapefruit that are not found in oranges, such as bergamottin. Inhibition persists for 24 hours and dissipates gradually after several days, but it can be a hazard for those taking medications daily, because it causes significant drug accumulation.

A second type of inhibition, based on **drug competition** for the enzyme, occurs for drugs that share a metabolic system. Because the number of enzyme molecules is limited, an elevated concentration of either drug reduces the metabolic rate of the second, causing potentially toxic levels. CYP450 metabolism of alcohol leads to higher-than-normal brain levels of other sedative–hypnotics (e.g., barbiturates or Valium) when administered at the same time, producing a potentially dangerous drug interaction.

Finally, differences in drug metabolism due to genetic and environmental factors can explain why some individuals seem to be extremely sensitive to certain drugs, but others may need much higher doses than normal to achieve an effect. Over 40 years ago, the first **genetic polymorphisms** (genetic variations among individuals that produce multiple forms of a given protein) for drug-metabolizing enzymes were identified. Large variations, for instance, were found in the rate of acetylation of isoniazid, a drug used to treat tuberculosis and subsequently found to relieve depression. Acetylation is a conjugation reaction in which an acetyl group is attached to the drug. These genetic polymorphisms that determine acetylation rate vary across populations. For instance, 44% to 54% of American Caucasians and African Americans, 60% of Europeans, 10% of Asians, and only 5% of Inuit are slow inactivators (Levine, 1973).

The enzymes that have been studied most are in the CYP450 family, and each has multiple polymorphisms. In that family, CYP2D6 (i.e., CYP450 2D6) is of great interest because it is responsible for metabolizing numerous psychotropic drugs, including many antidepressants, antipsychotics, antihistamines, muscle relaxants, opioid analgesics, and others. In a recent study, swabs of epithelial cells from the cheek linings of 31,563 individuals were taken and analyzed for the number of copies of the gene for CYP2D6. **FIGURE 1.12A** shows the distribution of samples based on the number (zero, one, two, or three or more) of normal CYP2D6 genes (Beoris et al., 2016; see Taylor et al., 2020, for review). A small percentage of individuals (0.14%) are very poor metabolizers and have multiple copies of a polymorphism that is ineffective in metabolizing substrates for the CYP2D6 enzyme. Intermediary metabolizers make up 7.25% of

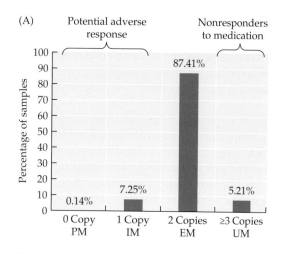

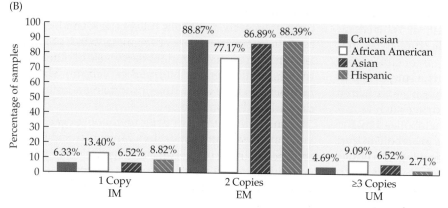

FIGURE 1.12 Four genetic populations based on the number of normal CYP2D6 genes (A) Percentage of samples containing zero, one, two, and three or more copies of the normal CYP2D6 gene from 31,563 individuals. PM, poor metabolizers; IM, intermediary metabolizers; EM, extensive metabolizers; UM, ultrarapid metabolizers. (B) Percentage of samples containing one, two, and three or more copies of the normal CYP2D6 gene in self-reported ethnic groups: Caucasians (yellow), African Americans (no-fill), Asians (red hatch marks), Hispanics (blue hatch marks). (After M. Beoris et al. 2016. *Pharmacogenet Genomics* 26 [2]: 96–99. doi.org/10.1097/FPC.0000000000000188)

the population tested and have one deficient allele and one normal allele. These two clusters of individuals having poorer metabolism would be expected to have greater bioavailability of those drugs, which may be responsible for adverse drug reactions or toxicity. These individuals would benefit from a reduction in drug dosage. Approximately 87% of the individuals are extensive metabolizers and have two normal alleles. They are considered extensive metabolizers because the normal enzyme is highly functional and efficient. The fourth group (5.21% of the population tested) are ultrarapid metabolizers and have multiple (three or more) normal gene copies. The ultrarapid group would be expected to have significantly lower blood levels of drug than normal, which may make them nonresponders to the medication. Hence, these individuals would benefit from higher drug dosage. Such differences are significant because there may be as much as a 1000-fold difference in rate of metabolism for a particular drug among these individuals. In addition, the data showed there are different distributions of these genotypes in different populations. **FIGURE 1.12B** shows the data for one or more copies of the normal gene (the samples with zero copies are not shown) broken down by self-reported ethnicity (about two-thirds of the individuals provided data on ethnicity). The data show that the frequency of individuals with two copies of CYP2D6 was significantly lower

in African Americans than in the other ethnic groups and that the percentage of individuals with one copy was 1.5 to 2.1 times higher in that group. Additionally, the percentage of individuals with three or more copies among African American was 1.4 to 3.4 times higher. These differences indicate greater variation in CYP2D6 metabolism in African Americans, which puts some at greater risk for adverse side effects and others at risk for inadequate response to psychotropic medications. Further discussion of this topic can be found at the end of the chapter in the section Pharmacogenetics and Personalized Medicine.

Other enzymes also show wide genetic differences. For example, approximately 50% of certain Asian groups (Chinese, Japanese, and Koreans) have reduced capacity to metabolize acetaldehyde, which is an intermediary metabolic step in the breakdown of alcohol. The resulting elevation in acetaldehyde causes facial flushing, tachycardia, a drop in blood pressure, and sometimes nausea and vomiting. The reduced metabolic capacity is caused by a specific mutation in the gene for aldehyde dehydrogenase (Wall and Ehelers, 1995).

Along with variations in genes, other individual differences may influence metabolism. Significant changes in nutrition or in liver function, which accompany various diseases, lead to significantly higher drug blood levels and prolonged and exaggerated effects. Advanced age is often accompanied by a reduced ability to metabolize drugs, while children under age 2 also have insufficient metabolic capacity and are vulnerable to drug overdose. In addition, both the young and the elderly have reduced kidney function, so clearance of drugs for them is much slower. Sex differences in drug metabolism also exist. For example, the stomach enzymes that metabolize alcohol before it reaches the bloodstream are far less effective in women than in men. This means that for an identical dose, a woman will have a much higher concentration of alcohol reaching her blood to produce biological effects. If you would like to read more about some of the clinical concerns related to differences in drug metabolism, see Applegate (1999).

RENAL EXCRETION Although drugs can be excreted from the body in the breath, sweat, saliva, feces, or breast milk, the most important route of elimination is the urine. Therefore, the primary organ of elimination is the kidney. The kidneys are a pair of organs, each about the size of a fist. They are responsible for filtering materials out of the blood and excreting waste products. As filtered materials pass through the kidney tubules, necessary substances such as water, glucose, sodium, potassium, and chloride are reabsorbed into the blood.

Most drugs are readily filtered by the kidney unless they are bound to plasma proteins or are of large molecular size. However, because reabsorption of water from the tubules makes the drug concentration greater in the tubules than in the surrounding blood vessels, many drug molecules are reabsorbed back into the blood. Ionization of drugs reduces reabsorption because it makes the drugs less lipid soluble. Liver biotransformation of drugs into ionized (water-soluble) molecules traps the metabolites in the kidney tubules, so they can be excreted along with waste products in the urine.

Reabsorption from the tubules, similar to diffusion across other membranes (discussed earlier), is pH-dependent. When tubular urine is made more alkaline, weak acids are excreted more rapidly because they become more ionized and are not reabsorbed as well; that is, they are "trapped" in the tubular urine. If the urine is acidic, the weakly acidic drug will be less ionized and more easily reabsorbed; thus, excretion will be less. The opposite is true for a weakly basic drug, which will be excreted more readily when tubular urine is acidic rather than basic. This principle of altering urinary pH is frequently used in the treatment of drug toxicity, when it is highly desirable to remove the offending drug from the body as quickly as possible. In the case of phenobarbital poisoning, for example, kidney excretion of this weakly acidic substance is greatly enhanced by alkalinization of the urine with sodium bicarbonate. This treatment leads to ionization and trapping of the drug within the tubules, from whence it is readily excreted. Acidifying the urine by administering IV ammonium chloride increases the percentage of ionization of weakly basic drugs, which enhances their excretion. For example, acidifying the urine increases the rate of excretion of amphetamine and shortens the duration of a toxic overdose episode.

Therapeutic drug monitoring

For a drug to be clinically effective while producing minimal side effects, optimal blood levels and hence drug concentration at the target site must be maintained throughout the treatment period. The difficulties in determining the appropriate drug dosage for initial clinical trials with humans and for veterinary medical treatment based on preclinical laboratory animal testing are described in **BOX 1.3**. Optimal blood levels must be determined in clinical trials before Food and Drug Administration (FDA) approval. However, wide variation in rates of absorption, metabolism, and elimination among individuals because of differences in gender, age, genetic profile, disease state, and drug interactions can lead to significant differences in blood levels. Blood levels that are too low prevent desired clinical outcomes, and for individuals with higher-than-normal blood levels, unwanted side effects and toxicity may occur. In the future, pharmacogenetic screening of individuals (see the section Pharmacogenetics and Personalized Medicine in Psychiatry) will allow personalized prescription of drug doses, but at present, the appropriate dosage of a drug is determined most often by the clinical response of a given individual. Under some conditions, such as for drugs with serious side effects, multiple blood samples are taken after drug administration to determine plasma levels of drug or to monitor a biological process (i.e., **biomarker**) for a toxic response (**therapeutic drug monitoring**). Short-term blood sampling may be done to establish the optimal dosage for a patient taking a new medication. After each dosage correction by the physician, it may take some time to reach steady state (approximately five half-lives), so monitoring may continue for several days or weeks, until the optimal dosage has been determined. For drugs that must be taken over the life span, periodic monitoring may be performed regularly. Monitoring detects changes in pharmacokinetics due to aging, hormonal changes during pregnancy and menopause, stress, changes in medical condition, or addition of new medications. Many of the monitored psychotropic drugs, such as antiepileptic drugs, including carbamazepine, some antidepressants, and drugs used as mood stabilizers such as lithium and valproic acid, are taken on a long-term basis.

Therapeutic drug monitoring is especially important for drugs that have a narrow therapeutic index (i.e., the dose needed for effectiveness is very similar to the dose that causes serious side effects; see section 1.2 Pharmacodynamics). Because blood levels rise to a peak and then fall to a trough just before the next administration (see Figure 1.10), drug monitoring can ensure that the peak remains below the blood level associated with toxic effects, while the trough remains in the therapeutic range to maintain adequate symptom relief. Modifying the dosage for a given individual can optimize treatment. In addition, drug monitoring can be used to determine whether the individual is taking the drug according to the prescribed regimen. Failure to comply with the drug treatment protocol often can be corrected by further patient education. The American Association for Clinical Chemistry (2020) provides additional information on therapeutic drug monitoring at https://labtestsonline.org/tests/therapeutic-drug-monitoring.

BOX 1.3 ■ PHARMACOLOGY IN ACTION

Interspecies Drug Dose Extrapolation

Interspecies drug dose extrapolation means converting or scaling the appropriate dose in one species to another species. It is vital not only in veterinary medicine, but also in drug development when the initial clinical trials with humans are based on preclinical testing in laboratory animals. It is also significant in the laboratory in order to replicate results from one species in another. The goal of dose extrapolation is to find the optimal dose for effectiveness and safety. See Sharma and McNeill (2009) for a full discussion.

© iStock.com/Oppdowngalon

Comparing the sizes of the animals is the most obvious approach to scaling a drug dose to a different species, but it is not the only factor. Using size alone can have disastrous consequences, as shown by the tragic outcome in Tusko, a 14-year-old Asiatic elephant housed in the Lincoln Park Zoo in Oklahoma City (West et al., 1962). The researchers used only the difference in weight to scale the dose for the elephant from previous experiments with cats. If the elephant's sensitivity to the hallucinogenic lysergic acid diethylamide (LSD) resembled that of humans, the 297 mg given to the elephant would have been an enormous overdose. Almost immediately after the drug was injected into the rump of the 3.5-ton elephant with a dart rifle, he stormed around his pen, appearing uncoordinated before he collapsed, defecated, and had continuous seizures. His tongue turned blue and he struggled to breathe, dying shortly later of strangulation. There were efforts to save him, but the drugs used may have instead contributed to his death. One must conclude that the elephant's sensitivity to LSD more closely resembled that of humans than of felines.

There are many pharmacokinetic and pharmacodynamic factors that are unrelated to size yet vary significantly among species. For example, protein binding at silent depots varies greatly among species because of differences in affinity to and number of binding sites. Hence, for any drug that shows high depot binding in one species, using weight alone to determine dose would be ineffective, whereas correction for the extent of protein binding would increase accuracy. Complex interspecies differences in drug metabolism are also key factors in differences in bioavailability of a given drug. For example, there are major variations among species in the CYP450 enzyme family amino acid sequences. The varied enzyme structures determine which drug substrates are acted upon by the enzyme. Another example of varied metabolism is conjugation with glucuronide, which is important and efficient in humans, while cats lack glucuronidation. Rats are very efficient acetylators, but dogs lack acetylation, while humans are intermediate between the two. It is clear that these differences will lead to variations in the blood levels of drug in different species.

In addition to differences in weight and pharmacokinetic factors, drug targets also contribute to variations in interspecies response to administered drugs. CNS neurotransmitters are differentially distributed in the brains of various species, and differences in the number, affinity, distribution, and regulation of receptors likely explain dramatic differences in drug response. For example, opiate analgesics such as morphine cause CNS depression in primates, dogs, and rats but induce excitation in horses and cats. These pharmacodynamic factors are not related to the size of the animal, so to adequately convert the drug dose, one should have some understanding of the receptor characteristics of each species.

SECTION SUMMARY

- A placebo is an inert substance that produces an effective therapeutic response and side effects. Placebo response depends on the ritual of the therapeutic treatment, which has neurobiological and behavioral effects. The multiple explanations for the effectiveness of placebos include Pavlovian conditioning and expectation of outcome.

- A double-blind experimental design ensures that observed drug effects are not influenced by expectations of the participants or experimenter.

- The effects of a drug are determined by (1) how much of the drug reaches its target sites, where it has biological action, and (2) how quickly the drug reaches those sites.

- Interacting pharmacokinetic factors that determine how much free drug is in the blood (bioavailability) include method of administration, rate of absorption and distribution, binding at inactive sites, biotransformation, and excretion.

- The route of administration determines both onset and duration of drug action.

- The method of administration influences absorption of the drug because it determines the area of the absorbing surface, the number of cell layers through which the drug must pass, and the extent of first-pass metabolism.

- Oral and rectal routes of administration are enteral because they involve the gastrointestinal tract; all other methods are called parenteral.

- Each method of administration provides distinct advantages and disadvantages involving rate of onset, blood level of drug achieved, duration of action, convenience, safety, and special uses.

- Absorption is dependent on method of administration, solubility and ionization of the drug, and individual differences in age, sex, and body size.

- Fat-soluble drugs are not ionized and readily pass through lipid membranes at a rate dependent on the concentration gradient.

- Drugs that are weak acids tend to remain non-ionized (lipid soluble) in acidic body fluids such as stomach juices; they are more readily absorbed there than in the more alkaline intestinal fluid. Drugs that are weak bases are more ionized in the acidic stomach fluid, so they are absorbed less readily there than from the more basic intestine, where ionization is reduced.

- Drug distribution is determined by the volume of blood flow to the tissue, but drug concentration in the central nervous system is limited by the blood–brain barrier that is formed by specialized brain capillaries that have few pores to allow drugs to leave the circulation. Only lipid-soluble drugs readily enter the brain.

- The placental barrier separates maternal circulation from fetal circulation, but it does not impede passage of most drug molecules.

- Drug molecules bound to inactive depots, including plasma proteins, cannot act at target sites, nor can they be metabolized, so the magnitude, onset, and duration of drug action are affected.

- Drug clearance from the blood usually occurs by first-order kinetics such that a constant fraction (50%) of the free drug is removed during each time interval. This interval is called the drug half-life. Some drugs are cleared according to zero-order kinetics, in which clearance occurs at a constant rate regardless of drug concentration.

- The steady state plasma level is the stable blood concentration of drug achieved when the absorption/distribution phase is equal to the metabolism/excretion phase. The steady state plasma level is approached after a period of time equal to five half-lives.

- Enzymatic drug metabolism or biotransformation occurs primarily in the liver and produces chemical changes in the drug molecule that make it inactive and more water soluble. The cytochrome P450 family of enzymes consists of the most important type of liver enzyme for transforming psychotropic drugs.

- Drug metabolism occurs in two steps. Phase I consists of oxidation, reduction, or hydrolysis and produces an ionized metabolite that may be inactive or as active as or more active than the parent drug. Phase II metabolism involves conjugation of the drug with a simple molecule provided by the body, such as glucuronide or sulfate. Products of phase II metabolism are always inactive and are more water soluble.

- The kidney is most often responsible for filtration of metabolites from the blood before excretion in the urine. Alternatively, metabolites may be excreted into bile and eliminated with the feces.

- Factors that change the biotransformation rate may alter the magnitude and duration of drug effects or cause drug interactions, and they may explain variability in individual response to drugs. Chronic use of some drugs can induce (increase) the quantity of liver enzymes, thereby decreasing bioavailability. Drugs that inhibit liver enzymes increase the blood levels of a drug, enhancing its action. Competition among drugs for metabolism by the same enzyme increases blood levels of one or both drugs. Genetic differences and individual differences in age, sex, nutrition, and organ function may influence the rate of drug metabolism.

- Therapeutic drug monitoring involves taking multiple blood samples to directly measure plasma levels of drug or another biomarker after a drug has been administered. Monitoring is done to identify the optimal dosage for a patient to maximize therapeutic benefit and minimize side effects. It is especially important for drugs with serious side effects and when there are changes in an individual's pharmacokinetics due to aging, hormonal changes, stress, the addition of new medications, or other events.

1.2 Pharmacodynamics: Drug–Receptor Interactions

Pharmacodynamics is the study of the physiological and biochemical interaction of drug molecules with target tissue that is responsible for the ultimate effects of a drug. Drugs can be classified into a wide variety of categories (**BOX 1.4**), but all the drugs that we are concerned with affect cell function in target tissue by acting on specific molecular targets, including enzymes, transporter proteins, receptors, and others. Knowing which targets a drug acts on and where these targets are located is crucial for understanding what actions and side effects will be produced.

Receptors can be more selectively defined as large protein molecules located on the cell surface or within cells that are the initial sites of action of biologically active agents such as neurotransmitters, hormones, and drugs (all referred to as ligands). A **ligand** is defined as any molecule that binds to a receptor with some selectivity. Because most drugs do not readily cross neural cell membranes, neuropharmacology most often is interested in receptors found on the cell surface that relay information through the membrane to affect intracellular processes (**FIGURE 1.13A**). Which of the many possible intracellular changes occurs depends on whether the receptor is coupled with an ion channel to alter the membrane potential or with a G protein to produce longer-lasting changes such as activation of an enzyme (see Chapter 3). The essential goal of neuropharmacology is to identify drugs that can influence neurotransmission, to enhance or reduce normal functioning of the cell and bring about a clinically useful effect.

The second type of receptor is found within the target cell, either in the cytoplasm (e.g., glucocorticoids) or in the nucleus (e.g., sex steroid receptors). Most of the hormones that act on the brain to influence neural events use this type of receptor. Hormonal binding to intracellular receptors alters cell function by triggering changes in expression of genetic material within the nucleus, producing differences in protein synthesis (**FIGURE 1.13B**). Sex hormones act in this way to facilitate mating behavior and other activities related to reproduction, such as lactation. This mechanism is described more fully in Chapter 3.

Extracellular and intracellular receptors have several common features

Several characteristics are common among receptors in general. The ability to recognize specific molecular shapes is one very important characteristic. The usual analogy of a lock and key suggests that only a limited group of neurochemicals or drugs can bind to a particular receptor protein to initiate a cellular response. These neurochemicals are called **receptor agonists**. Molecules that have the best chemical "fit" (i.e., have the highest **affinity**) attach most readily to the receptor.

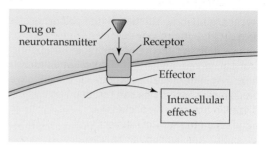

(A)

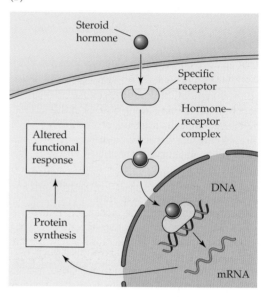

(B)

FIGURE 1.13 **Two principal types of receptors** (A) Most drugs and neurotransmitters remain outside the cell and bind to receptors on the exterior cell surface. When these receptors are activated, they initiate changes in an effector, causing intracellular changes such as movement of ions or changes in enzyme activity. (B) Many hormones are capable of entering the cell before acting on an intracellular receptor that changes the expression of specific genes within the nucleus. The altered protein synthesis in turn leads to changes in cell function that may include altering gluconeogenesis, modulating the menstrual cycle, and others.

However, just as one may put a key in a lock but may not be able to turn the key, so too a ligand may be recognized by a receptor, but it may not initiate a biological action. Such ligands are considered to have low intrinsic **efficacy**. These molecules are called **receptor antagonists** because not only do they produce no cellular effect after binding, but by binding to the receptor, they also prevent an "active" ligand from binding; hence, they "block" the receptor (**FIGURE 1.14**). **Partial agonists** demonstrate efficacy that is less than that of full agonists but more than that of an antagonist at a given receptor. Finally, when **inverse agonists** bind to a receptor, they initiate a biological action, but it is an action that is opposite to that produced by an agonist. Conceptually, inverse agonism relies on the discovery

BOX 1.4 ■ PHARMACOLOGY IN ACTION

Drug Categories

As we learned earlier in this chapter, all drugs have multiple effects, which vary with dose and bioavailability, the nature of the receptors occupied, and the drug-taking history (e.g., tolerance) of the individual. For these reasons, drugs can be categorized in any of several classes, depending on the trait of interest. One might classify drugs according to chemical structure, medical use, legal status, neurochemical effects, abuse potential, behavioral effects, and many other categories. Amphetamine may be described as a CNS stimulant (based on increased brain activity and behavioral arousal), an anorectic used for diet control (medical use), a sympathomimetic (because it neurochemically mimics the effects of the sympathetic nervous system), or a Schedule III drug (a controlled substance based on the federal government's assessment of abuse potential). Because we are particularly interested in brain function and behavior, the classification used in this text emphasizes CNS action and behavioral effects.

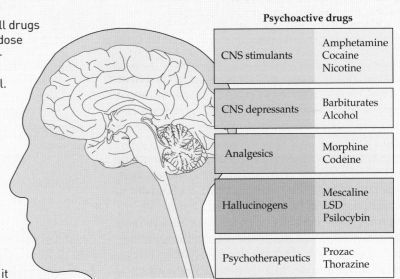

Psychoactive drugs

CNS stimulants	Amphetamine Cocaine Nicotine
CNS depressants	Barbiturates Alcohol
Analgesics	Morphine Codeine
Hallucinogens	Mescaline LSD Psilocybin
Psychotherapeutics	Prozac Thorazine

CNS stimulants produce increased behavioral arousal, alertness, and a sense of well-being in the individual. Among drugs in this class are amphetamine, cocaine, and methylphenidate (Ritalin), as well as the methylxanthines, which include caffeine, theophylline, and theobromine. Nicotine may also be included here because of its mild activating effect, although for some individuals, the drug clearly has a calming effect. Classification is complicated by the fact that drug effects are dose-dependent, and drugs occasionally produce dramatically different effects at different doses. Low and moderate doses of amphetamine, for example, stimulate physical activity, but at high doses, locomotion may be reduced and replaced by meaningless stereotyped, repetitive acts that have clear psychotic characteristics.

CNS depressants include a variety of drugs that depress CNS function and behavior to cause a sense of relaxation and drowsiness. Some of the sedative–hypnotics are useful for these sedating qualities and for their ability to induce sleep. At high doses, more profound mental clouding occurs, along with loss of coordination, intoxication, and coma. Significant drugs in this group include the barbiturates (such as Seconal), the benzodiazepines (including Valium), and ethyl alcohol, all of which will be considered in later chapters. Some might include marijuana in this class because of its relaxing and depressant qualities at low doses, although at higher doses, hallucinogenic characteristics may occur.

Analgesics are drugs that frequently have CNS-depressant qualities, although their principal effect is to reduce the perception of pain. The most important drugs in this class are the narcotics. Narcotics, or opiates, such as morphine or codeine are derived from the opium poppy; the synthetic narcotics (sometimes called *opioids*) include heroin, meperidine (Demerol), methadone, and fentanyl. All opiate-like drugs produce relaxation and sleep, as well as analgesia. Under some circumstances, these drugs also produce a powerful sense of euphoria. Non-narcotic analgesics also belong in this class but have little effect on behavior and do not produce relaxation or sleep. They include aspirin, acetaminophen (Tylenol), and ibuprofen (Motrin).

Hallucinogens are often called "psychedelics" because their primary effect is to induce vivid perceptual distortions. As a group, these drugs produce a wide variety of effects on brain chemistry and neural activity. They include many naturally occurring substances such as mescaline and psilocybin. Certainly, LSD belongs in this class, as does MDMA. The drug PCP and its analog ketamine, which is used as an animal anesthetic, might belong in the class of CNS depressants, but their ability to cause profound hallucinogenic experiences and their use as models for psychotic behavior prompt their placement in this category.

Psychotherapeutic drugs as a classification is intended to suggest that some psychoactive drugs are used almost exclusively to treat clinical disorders of mood or behavior. Antipsychotics reduce symptoms of schizophrenia, including hallucinations and bizarre behavior. Examples include haloperidol (Haldol) and chlorpromazine (Thorazine). Antidepressants also belong in this classification; they are used to treat disorders of mood. Among the most familiar are duloxetine (Cymbalta), sertraline (Zoloft), and fluoxetine (Prozac). Finally, mood stabilizers reduce the dramatic mood swings between mania and depression that characterize bipolar disorder. Lithium carbonate (Lithonate) is still most often prescribed, but valproate (Depakote) and carbamazepine (Tegretol) are increasingly popular. Each of these types of drugs will be described in subsequent chapters of this text.

FIGURE 1.14 **Agonist and antagonist interactions with receptors** The agonist molecule has an excellent fit for the receptor (high affinity) and produces a significant biological response (high efficacy). The antagonist in this case fits less well and has very low efficacy. Note that if both the agonist and the antagonist are present simultaneously, they will compete to fit into the same receptor, producing a partial drug effect. (After C. R. Carroll. 1996. *Drugs in Modern Society*, 4th ed., Brown and Benchmark: Guilford, CT.)

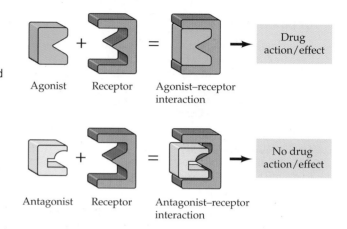

that many neurotransmitter receptors can be active even in the absence of a neurotransmitter or drug agonist. This baseline receptor function, known as **constitutive activity**, is unaffected by neutral antagonists, but can be reduced by inverse agonists (see Berg and Clarke, 2018, for a discussion of inverse agonism). Hence, drug action can vary in efficacy along a continuum ranging from full agonist action with maximal efficacy, to partial agonist action to the inactive antagonist, to partial inverse agonist action with some inverse efficacy, to full inverse agonist action that shows maximal inverse efficacy (**FIGURE 1.15**). The importance of these distinctions will become apparent in later chapters as we discuss specific drug classes. Interested readers may also enjoy the article by Neubig and colleagues (2003) for an authoritative review of receptor and ligand terminology.

We should mention here that many drugs exert their effects in ways other than by directly binding to and activating a receptor. For instance, some drugs can enhance synaptic function by increasing neurotransmitter synthesis or release or by prolonging the action of the neurotransmitter within the synapse. Alternatively, other drugs interfere with synaptic function by reducing neurotransmitter synthesis or release or by terminating the action of the neurotransmitter more quickly. These actions will be described more fully in Chapter 3.

A second significant feature of receptors is that binding or attachment of the specific ligand is temporary. When the ligand dissociates (i.e., separates) from the receptor, it has opportunities to attach once again. Likewise, the momentarily unbound receptor is available for other receptor ligands, such as endogenous neurotransmitters or other drugs (e.g., agonists or antagonists).

Third, ligands binding to the receptor produce a physical change in the three-dimensional shape of the

protein, thus initiating a series of intracellular events that ultimately generate a biobehavioral effect. How much intracellular activity occurs depends on the number of interactions with the receptor and the ability of the ligand to alter the shape of the receptor, which reflects its efficacy.

Fourth, although we tend to think about receptors as a permanent characteristic of cells, these proteins in fact have a life cycle, just as other cell proteins do. Not only is there a normal life span for receptors, but receptors are also modified both in number (long-term regulation) and in sensitivity (more rapid regulation via second messengers). Long-term regulation, called **up-regulation** when receptor numbers increase and **down-regulation** when receptors are reduced in number, reflects compensatory changes after prolonged absence of receptor agonists or chronic activation of the receptor, respectively. For instance, chronic use of receptor antagonists leads to subsequent up-regulation of receptors. Likewise, drugs that act as agonists at the receptor cause a reduction in receptor proteins if they are administered repeatedly. In each case, the change in receptor number requires 1 to 2 weeks of altered activity. Change in sensitivity due to second messenger–induced function is far more rapid. These changes will be discussed more fully in Chapter 3.

Finally, we have already learned that once drugs are absorbed, they are distributed throughout the body, where multiple sites of action (receptors) mediate different biobehavioral effects. However, the receptor proteins for a given drug or neurotransmitter may have different characteristics in different target

FIGURE 1.15 **Continuum of drug efficacy** Independent of affinity, drugs can vary in efficacy along a continuum from full agonist action having maximum efficacy to antagonist action with no efficacy to full inverse agonist efficacy. Partial agonists and partial inverse agonists fall in between.

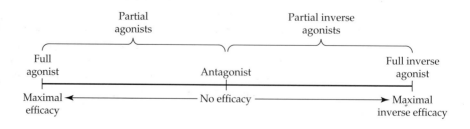

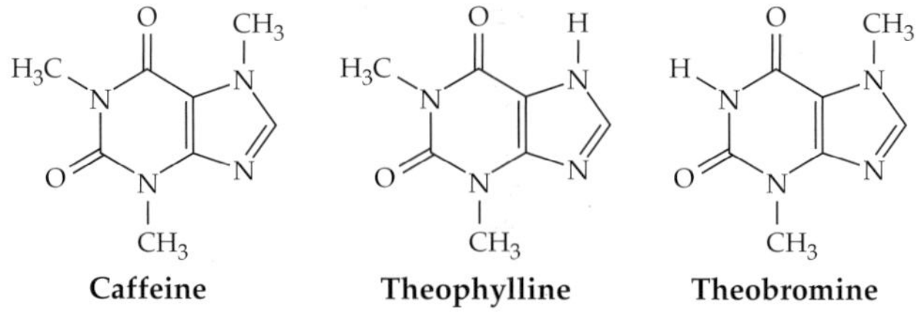

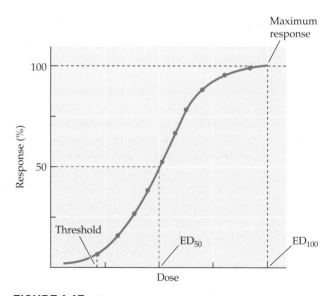

FIGURE 1.16 Chemical structures of the xanthines caffeine, theophylline, and theobromine

tissues. These varied receptors, called **receptor subtypes**, will be discussed more extensively later in the book. **FIGURE 1.16** shows the three mildly stimulant drugs caffeine, theophylline, and theobromine, all of which belong to the xanthine class and act as adenosine receptor antagonists, but preferentially bind to different adenosine receptor subtypes. Subtle differences in structure are responsible for differences in the magnitude of biological effects, depending on which adenosine receptor subtypes they bind to most effectively. You can see in **TABLE 1.7** that caffeine is more effective at the adenosine receptor subtype in the CNS to produce alertness than are xanthines found in tea (theophylline) or cocoa (theobromine). In contrast, theophylline is the most active of the three in stimulating the heart and causing increased urine output (diuresis).

Dose–response curves describe receptor activity

One important method used to evaluate drug–target activity is the **dose–response curve**, which describes the extent of biological or behavioral effect (mean response in a population) produced by a given

drug concentration (dose). A typical curve is shown in **FIGURE 1.17**. When plotted on a semi-log scale, the curve takes on a classic S-shape. At low doses, the drug-induced effect is slight because very few receptors are occupied. As the dose of the drug is increased, more receptors are occupied, and a greater biobehavioral response occurs. The 50% effective dose (ED_{50}) is the dose that produces half the maximal effect, and maximal response occurs at a dose at which we assume the receptors are fully occupied* (we might call it the ED_{100}). Nonetheless, when considering dose–response relationships, particularly in the context of behavioral pharmacology, it is important to keep in mind that whether a drug exerts intrinsic biochemical efficacy at a receptor does not always correspond to the ability of the drug to produce behavioral changes, or behavioral efficacy. There are numerous examples of receptor antagonists that produce pronounced behavioral and physiological effects on their own, including the example of adenosine receptor antagonists mentioned above.

If we were to graph the effects of several pain-relieving drugs, we might find a relationship similar to the one shown in **FIGURE 1.18**. The first three curves show the dose–response characteristics for hydromorphone, morphine, and codeine—all drugs from the

---

*This assumption is not warranted in all cases, however, as can be seen in those models of receptor pharmacology that describe "spare receptors." Readers interested in the complexities of receptor occupancy theory should refer to a standard textbook in pharmacology.

TABLE 1.7 Relative Biological Activity[a] of Xanthines[b]			
Biological effects	Caffeine	Theophylline	Theobromine
CNS stimulation	1	2	3
Cardiac stimulation	3	1	2
Respiratory stimulation	1	2	3
Skeletal muscle stimulation	1	2	3
Diuresis	3	1	2

Source: J. M. Ritchie. 1975. In *The Pharmacological Basis of Therapeutics* (5th ed.), L. Goodman and Gilman (Eds.), pp. 367–378. Macmillan: New York

[a] Each drug acts more effectively on some xanthine receptor subtypes than others. 1 = most active; 3 = least active.

[b] Derivatives of xanthine are a group of alkaloids used as mild stimulants and bronchodilators.

FIGURE 1.17 **Dose–response curve** The classic S-shape describes the gradual increase in biological response that occurs with increasing doses of a drug (drug–receptor activation). Threshold is the dose that produces the smallest measurable response. The dose at which the maximum response is achieved is the ED_{100} (100% effective dose), and the ED_{50} is the dose that effectively produces 50% of the maximum response.

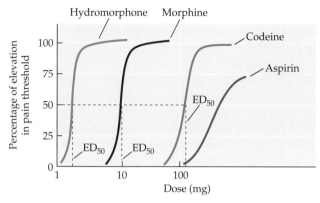

FIGURE 1.18   Dose–response curves for four analgesic agents   Each curve represents the increase in pain threshold (the magnitude of painful stimulus required to elicit a withdrawal response) as a function of dose. Knowing the ED_{50} doses for hydromorphone, morphine, and codeine helps when comparing their potency. The linear portions of the curves for the opiate analgesics are parallel, suggesting that they work through the same mechanism. Aspirin is not an opiate and relieves pain by a very different mechanism of action, so the shape of the curve is distinct. In addition, the maximum effectiveness of aspirin never reaches the level of the opiates. (After R. R. Levine, 1973. *Pharmacology: Drug Actions and Reactions*, 1st ed. Little, Brown, and Co.: Boston. © 1973 by Little, Brown and Company, Inc.)

opiate analgesic class. For each drug, increasing the concentration produces greater analgesia (elevation in pain threshold) until the maximal response is achieved. The amount of drug necessary to produce a specific effect indicates the **potency** of the drug. Differences in potency among these three drugs can be seen by comparing the ED_{50} across all of them. To achieve the same effect, hydromorphone requires approximately 2 mg, morphine 10 mg, and codeine more than 100 mg. Therefore, morphine is more potent than codeine, and hydromorphone is more potent than either. The relative position of the curves on the *x*-axis indicates potency and reflects the affinity of each drug for the receptor that mediates the measured response. Although the three differ in affinity for the receptor, each reaches the same maximum on the *y*-axis, indicating that they have identical efficacy. The fact that the linear portions of the curves are parallel to one another indicates that they are working by the same mechanism. Although the concept of potency provides some means of comparison, its practical use is limited. As you can see, a lower-potency drug is frequently just as effective and requires only a somewhat higher dose. If the low-potency drug also produces fewer side effects or is less expensive, then it may in fact be the preferred drug.

Figure 1.18 also shows the dose–response curve for aspirin. In contrast to the first three drugs, aspirin is not an opioid, and the distinctive shape of its dose–response curve indicates that although aspirin may relieve pain, it does not act on the same receptors or work by the same mechanism. In addition, regardless of how much aspirin is administered, it never achieves the same efficacy as the opiates.

The therapeutic index calculates drug safety

A second type of dose–response curve does not look at the mean response to a range of drug doses in a group of recipients but instead looks at the cumulative percentage of the population experiencing a particular drug-induced response. This type of curve is used to calculate drug safety. Among the multiple responses to any drug, some are undesirable or even dangerous side effects that need to be evaluated carefully in a therapeutic situation. For example, **FIGURE 1.19** depicts three distinct pharmacological effects produced by drug A, which is prescribed to reduce anxiety. The blue curve shows the percentage of individuals who experience reduced anxiety at various doses of the drug. You can see that even at low doses, some subjects will show reduced anxiety. At somewhat higher doses, the same individuals will respond to the drug and other subjects will begin to respond as well. Ultimately there will be a dose to which 100% of the subjects respond. The purple curve shows the percentage of persons suffering respiratory depression (a toxic effect) from various doses of the same drug. By comparing the ED_{50} for relieving anxiety (i.e., the dose at which 50% of the population shows reduced anxiety) and the TD_{50} (the dose at which 50% of the population experiences a particular toxic effect) for respiratory depression, you can see that for most individuals, the toxic dose is much higher than the dose that produces the desired effect. An alternative interpretation is that at the dose needed to provide significant clinical relief for many patients (50%), none of the patients would be likely to experience respiratory depression. Therefore, pharmacologists would say that the drug has a relatively favorable **therapeutic index** ($TI = TD_{50}/ED_{50}$). In contrast, the dose of drug A that produces sedation and mental clouding (red curve) is not very different from the ED_{50}. This small difference means that the probability is high that a dose that is effective in reducing anxiety is likely to also produce significant mental clouding and sedation, which may represent serious side effects for many people who might use the drug. Another index is the certain safety factor index, defined as the dose of drug that is lethal to 1% of the population compared with the dose that is therapeutically effective in 99% of the population (LD_1/ED_{99}). This index is not used very often, because significant ethical limitations do not allow the lethal doses in humans to be readily determined.

Receptor antagonists compete with agonists for binding sites

We have already introduced the concept of receptor antagonists as those drugs that compete with agonists to bind to receptors but fail to initiate an intracellular effect, thereby reducing the effects of the agonists. These are called **competitive antagonists**. As the name implies, they can be displaced from those sites by an excess of the agonist, because an increased concentration of active

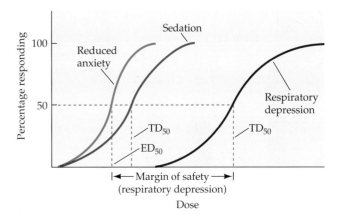

FIGURE 1.19   Comparison of ED_{50} and TD_{50} The therapeutic index (TI) is calculated by comparing the dose of drug required to produce a toxic effect in 50% of individuals (TD_{50}) with the dose that is effective for 50% (ED_{50}). Each drug may have several therapeutic indices based on its toxic effects or side effects of concern. Because the optimum condition is to have a drug that is effective at a low dose with no toxicity except at very high doses, the TI will be large for a safer drug. The figure shows a large margin of safety for an antianxiety drug that can produce respiratory depression.

drug can compete more effectively for the fixed number of receptors. A simple example will clarify. If we assume that the agonist and the antagonist have similar affinities for the receptor, then if both 100 molecules of drug and 100 molecules of antagonist were present at the receptor, the probability of an agonist acting on the receptor would be 1 to 1. If agonist molecules were increased to 1000, the odds of agonist binding would rise to 10 to 1; at 1,000,000 agonist molecules, the odds would favor agonist binding by 10,000 to 1. Certainly at this point, the presence of the antagonist is of no consequence for the biobehavioral effect as measured.

FIGURE 1.20A illustrates the effect of a competitive antagonist, naloxone, on the analgesic effect of morphine. The blue line shows a typical dose–response curve for the analgesic effect of morphine. When participants were pretreated with naloxone, the dose–response curve shifted to the right (red line), demonstrating that for any given dose of morphine, naloxone-pretreated subjects showed less analgesia. The addition of naloxone diminished the potency of morphine. The figure also shows that the inhibitory action of naloxone was overcome by increasing the amount of morphine administered; that is, the same maximum effect (analgesia) was achieved, but more morphine was required. If you look at the chemical structures of the two drugs in Figure 11.3, you will see the striking similarity and will understand how the two drugs compete to be recognized by the same receptor protein.

We have emphasized receptor antagonism because, in combination with the concept of dose dependency, it is a vital tool in pharmacology. If we want to know whether a specific ligand–receptor interaction is responsible for a particular biological effect, the biological effect must be shown to occur in proportion to the amount of ligand present (dose) and, furthermore, the effect must be reduced in the presence of a competitive antagonist.

Of course, other types of antagonism can occur. **Non-competitive antagonists** are drugs that reduce the effects of agonists in ways other than competing for the receptor. For example, a noncompetitive antagonist may impair agonist action by binding to a portion of the receptor other than the agonist-binding site, by disturbing the cell membrane supporting the receptor, or in some cases by interfering with the intracellular processes that were initiated by the agonist–receptor association. **FIGURE 1.20B** illustrates the effect of a noncompetitive antagonist on the analgesic effect of morphine. In general, the

shape of the dose–response curve will be distorted, and the same maximum effect is not likely to be reached.

Furthermore, although pharmacologists are concerned with molecular actions at the receptor, biobehavioral interactions can result in several different possible outcomes. **Physiological antagonism (FIGURE 1.21A)** involves two drugs that act in two distinct ways but

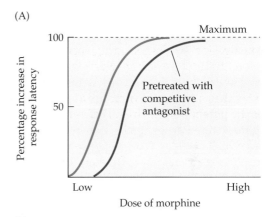

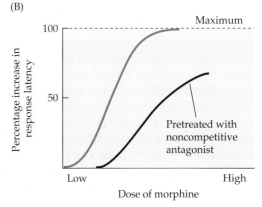

FIGURE 1.20   Drug antagonism (A) The effect of a competitive antagonist (naloxone) on the analgesic effect of morphine. The addition of a competitive antagonist essentially reduces the potency of the agonist, as is shown by the parallel shift of the dose–response curve to the right. (B) In contrast, adding a noncompetitive antagonist usually produces a distinct change in the shape of the dose–response curve, indicating that it does not act at the same receptor site. Also, regardless of the increase in morphine, the maximum efficacy is never reached.

(A) Physiological antagonism

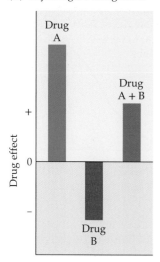

FIGURE 1.21 **Possible results of the interaction of two drugs** (A) Physiological antagonism results when two drugs produce opposite effects and reduce each other's effectiveness. (B) Additive effects are seen when the combined drug effect equals the sum of each drug alone. (C) Potentiation is said to occur when combined drug effects are greater than the sum of individual drug effects.

(B) Additive effects

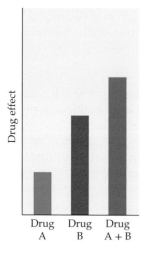

(C) Potentiation

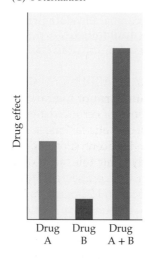

administered), changes in the magnitude of response to the drug often occur. Typically, the response diminishes with chronic use (tolerance), but occasionally the effects are increased (sensitization). In some cases, selected effects of a particular drug decrease while others increase in magnitude, as is true for the stimulant drug amphetamine. It should be clear that an individual's drug-taking history has a significant influence on drug action.

Repeated drug exposure can cause tolerance

Drug **tolerance** is defined as a diminished response to drug administration after repeated exposure to that drug. In other words, tolerance has developed when increasingly larger doses of a given drug must be administered to obtain the same magnitude of biological effect that occurred with the original dose. Development of tolerance to one drug can diminish the effectiveness of a second drug. This phenomenon, called **cross-tolerance**, serves as the basis for a number of drug interactions. For example, the effective anticonvulsant dose of phenobarbital is significantly larger in a patient who has a history of chronic alcohol use than in a patient who has not developed tolerance to alcohol.

CHARACTERISTICS OF TOLERANCE Although the appearance of tolerance varies, several general features are worth mentioning. These characteristics are summarized in **TABLE 1.8**. First, as is true for biological processes in general, tolerance is reversible; that is, it gradually diminishes if use of the drug is stopped. Additionally, the extent of tolerance that develops is dependent on the pattern of drug administration—that is, the dose and frequency of drug use, as well as the environment in which it occurs. Chronic heroin users may take as much as 1800 mg without ill effects, despite the fact that the lethal range for a novice heroin user is 200 to 400 mg.

However, regardless of dose and frequency, some drugs induce tolerance relatively rapidly (e.g., LSD), while others require weeks of chronic use (barbiturates) or never cause significant tolerance (antipsychotics). In some cases, tolerance develops during just a single administration, as when an individual experiences significantly greater effects of alcohol as his blood level rises than he experiences several hours later, when his blood level has fallen to the same point. This form of tolerance is called **acute tolerance**.

It is important to be aware that not all biobehavioral effects of a particular drug demonstrate tolerance

interact in such a way that they reduce each other's effectiveness in the body. For example, one drug may act on receptors in the heart to increase heart rate, and the second may act on distinct receptors in the brainstem to slow heart rate. Clearly, two agents may have **additive effects** if the outcome exceeds the effect of either drug alone (**FIGURE 1.21B**). Finally, **potentiation** refers to the situation in which the combination of two drugs produces effects that are greater than the sum of their individual effects (**FIGURE 1.21C**). Potentiation often involves issues of pharmacokinetics such as altered metabolic rate or competition for depot binding, which may elevate free drug blood levels in unexpected ways.

Biobehavioral effects of chronic drug use

Many prescription and over-the-counter drugs are taken on a regular basis for chronic medical or psychiatric conditions. These drugs are taken for periods of weeks, months, or even years. Recreational drugs are most often used repeatedly rather than on only a single occasion. When a drug is used frequently (i.e., chronically

TABLE 1.8 Significant Characteristics of Tolerance

It is reversible when drug use stops.

It is dependent on dose and frequency of drug use and the drug-taking environment.

It may occur rapidly, after long periods of chronic use, or never.

Not all effects of a drug show the same degree of tolerance.

Several different mechanisms explain multiple forms of tolerance.

TABLE 1.9 Types of Tolerance Exhibited by Selected Drugs

Drug or drug class	Metabolic tolerance	Pharmacodynamic tolerance	Behavioral tolerance
Barbiturates	+	+	+
Alcohol	+	+	+
Morphine	+	+	+
Amphetamine	–	+	+
Cocaine	–	+	+
Caffeine	–	+	?
Nicotine	–	+	?
LSD	–	+	–

Note: + indicates that the drug produces the type of tolerance indicated; – indicates that the drug does not produce the indicated type of tolerance; ? indicates that evidence is mixed regarding whether the drug produces the indicated type of tolerance.

equally. For example, morphine-induced nausea and vomiting show rapid development of tolerance, but the constipating effects of the drug rarely diminish even after long-term use. Sometimes the uneven development of tolerance is beneficial, as when tolerance develops for the side effects of a drug but not for its therapeutic effects. At other times, the uneven development of tolerance poses a hazard, as when the desired effects of a drug diminish, requiring increased doses, but the lethal or toxic effects do not show tolerance. Chronic barbiturate use is one such example. As more drug is taken to achieve the desired effect, the dose gets increasingly close to the lethal dose that causes respiratory depression.

Finally, several types of tolerance may occur and have distinct mechanisms. Although some drugs never induce tolerance at all, others may cause several types of tolerance, as shown in **TABLE 1.9**. The three principal forms are metabolic tolerance, pharmacodynamic tolerance, and behavioral tolerance. A fourth type, called acute tolerance, was described above with respect to alcohol.

METABOLIC TOLERANCE (DRUG DISPOSITION TOLERANCE)

Drug disposition tolerance, or **metabolic tolerance**, occurs when repeated use of a drug reduces the amount of that drug that is available at the target tissue. The most common form of drug disposition tolerance occurs when drugs increase their own rate of metabolism. It is clear that many drugs are capable of liver microsomal enzyme induction (see the discussion on biotransformation earlier in this chapter), which results in increased metabolic capacity. A more efficient metabolism reduces the amount of drug available to target tissue and diminishes drug effects. All drugs metabolized by the induced enzyme family will likewise show a reduced effect (cross-tolerance). Drug disposition tolerance requires repeated administration over time for protein synthesis to build new enzyme proteins. Well-documented examples of inducers of liver enzymes such as CYP450 include drugs from many classes, including the sedative phenobarbital,

the antibiotic rifampicin, the antiseizure medication phenytoin, cigarette smoke, and anabolic steroids.

PHARMACODYNAMIC TOLERANCE

The most dramatic form of tolerance that develops to the central actions of certain drugs cannot be explained by pharmacokinetic factors, such as altered metabolism or altered concentration of drug reaching the brain. **Pharmacodynamic tolerance** occurs when changes in neural function compensate for continued presence of the drug. In section 1.2 Pharmacodynamics, we described the normal response to chronic receptor activation as receptor down-regulation. Once receptors have down-regulated, a given amount of drug will have fewer receptors to act on and therefore will produce less of a biological effect. Compensatory up-regulation (increased receptor number) occurs in cases in which receptor activation is chronically reduced, such as when receptor activation is blocked by a competitive antagonist. Other compensatory cellular adjustments to chronic drug use will be described in later chapters that focus on individual agents such as ethanol, amphetamine, caffeine, and others. These drug-induced compensatory changes also help to explain the **withdrawal syndrome** that occurs when chronic drug users abruptly stop using the drug. Because the adaptive mechanism produces effects opposite to the initial drug effects, when the drug is no longer present, the adaptive mechanism remains functioning and so causes a rebound withdrawal syndrome, overshooting basal levels. For example, alcohol has sedating effects and depresses CNS function, while withdrawal is characterized by a hyperexcitable state. The occurrence of the withdrawal or abstinence syndrome is the hallmark of **physical dependence**, which is defined as a physiological state in which the body adapts to the chronic presence of a drug and elicits a drug-specific withdrawal syndrome if the drug is abruptly stopped or dosage is reduced. Chapter 11 on opioids and Chapter 9 on drug misuse provide a more complete discussion along with examples.

BEHAVIORAL TOLERANCE Although many instances of tolerance can be attributed to cell physiology and chemistry, a behavioral component involving learning and adaptation has been demonstrated by numerous investigators. **Behavioral tolerance** (sometimes called *context-specific tolerance*) is seen when tolerance occurs in the same environment in which the drug was administered, but tolerance is not apparent or is much reduced in a novel environment. Several types of learning (classical conditioning and operant conditioning) may play a part in the development of behavioral tolerance, as well as in the withdrawal syndrome characteristic of physical dependence (see Chapter 9).

Pavlovian conditioning, or **classical conditioning**, plays an important role in drug use and in tolerance. In the original experiments with Pavlov's dogs, the meaningless bell (neutral stimulus) was presented immediately before the meat (unconditioned stimulus) was presented, which elicited reflexive salivation (unconditioned response). After repeated pairings, the bell took on the characteristic of a conditioned stimulus, because when presented alone, it could elicit salivation—now a conditioned response. Hence the bell was a cue that predicted what was about to happen. Since many psychoactive drugs elicit unconditioned effects such as cortical arousal, elevated blood pressure, or euphoria, they can act as unconditioned stimuli, and the drug-taking procedure or stimuli in the environment may become conditioned stimuli that elicit a conditioned response even before the drug is administered (**FIGURE 1.22**). These associations with the drug may explain why the various rituals and procedures of drug procurement and use may elicit effects similar to those produced by the drug itself and remind the individual of how the drug feels, causing intense craving. Anticipation of drug effects may also explain behavioral tolerance.

Siegel (1985) suggests that tolerance is due at least in part to the learning of an association between the effects of a given drug and the environmental cues that reliably precede the drug effects. For development of tolerance, the "anticipatory" response (conditioned response) must be compensatory in nature; that is, the environment associated with administration of the drug elicits physiological responses *opposite* to the effect of the drug. For instance, in animals repeatedly experiencing the hyperthermic effects of injected morphine, the injection procedure alone *in the same environment* leads to a compensatory drop in body temperature. **FIGURE 1.23** shows the results of a study of two groups of rats given an identical course of morphine injections (5 mg/kg SC for 10 days), which would normally produce evidence of tolerance to

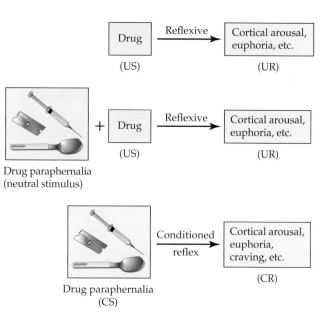

FIGURE 1.22 Classical conditioning of drug-related cues Although drug-taking equipment and the immediate environment initially serve as meaningless stimuli for the individual, their repeated pairing with the drug (unconditioned stimulus; US), which naturally elicits euphoria, arousal, or other desirable effects (unconditioned response; UR), gives the drug-taking equipment new meaning. Ultimately, the equipment and the environment alone (now a conditioned stimulus; CS) could elicit drug effects (conditioned response; CR) in the absence of the drug.

the hyperthermic effect. On the test day, rats given morphine in the identical environment (the "same" animals) showed the expected decrease in hyperthermia—an indication of tolerance. However, animals given morphine in a novel environment (the "different" animals) did not show the same extent of tolerance. The conclusion drawn is that classically conditioned environmental responses contribute to the development of tolerance to morphine. Some researchers believe that environmentally induced tolerance may explain why drug-dependent individuals who use their drug in a new environment or who alter their drug-taking routine may suddenly show a much greater response to the same dose of the drug they had used the day before. This phenomenon may explain at least some of the fatal drug overdoses that occur each year. Although environment is clearly significant in drug tolerance, keep in mind that neural changes that underlie learning or behavioral tolerance reflect subtle alterations in physiology that may be similar to pharmacodynamic tolerance.

The appearance of tolerance to a psychoactive drug is often manifested in a task in which **operant conditioning** plays some part. For example, Leblanc and colleagues (1976) showed that administration of alcohol (2.5 g/kg IP) to rats initially disrupted the performance of traversing a moving belt, but repeated administrations had less effect. The improved performance could be identified as a type of tolerance, but the apparent tolerance could be due to learning of a new skill (the ability to run on a treadmill while under the influence

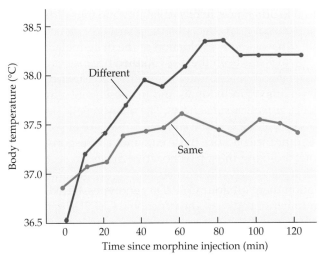

FIGURE 1.23 **Tolerance to morphine-induced hyperthermia** After an identical series of prior morphine injections (5 mg/kg SC for 10 days), rats were tested with a morphine injection, and changes in body temperature were measured for the next 2 hours. One group of rats was given morphine in the same environment in which they were previously treated ("same"), and the second group was tested in a novel environment ("different"). Animals treated in the same environment show much less hyperthermia; this indicates tolerance. (After S. Siegel. 1978. In *Behavioral Tolerance: Research and Treatment Implications*. N. A. Krasnegor (Ed.), NIDA Research Monograph 18. U.S. Department of Health, Education and Welfare, Public Health Service, National Institute of Drug Abuse: Washington DC.)

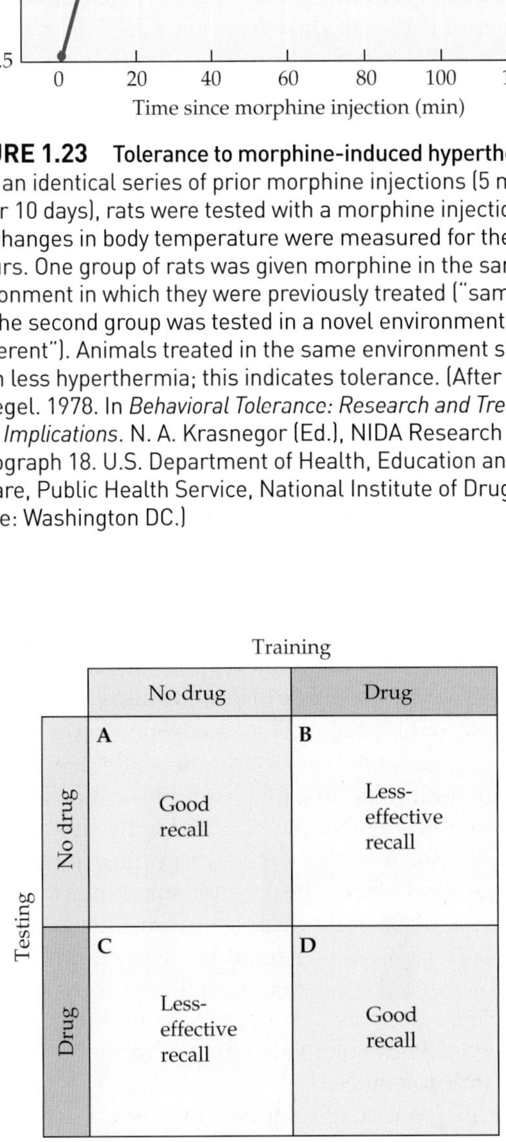

	Training	
	No drug	**Drug**
No drug	**A** Good recall	**B** Less-effective recall
Drug	**C** Less-effective recall	**D** Good recall

(left axis label: Testing)

FIGURE 1.24 **Experimental design to test state-dependent learning** Four different conditions show the difficulties involved in transferring learning from one drug state to another. Individuals trained without drug and tested without drug (A) show maximum performance that is not much different from the performance of those trained and tested under the influence of the drug (D). However, subjects asked to perform in a state different from the training condition (B and C) showed recall that was less efficient.

of the drug), which would be expected to improve with practice. How can we know that the improvement was not due to changes in metabolic rate or to pharmacodynamic tolerance? The answer can be found by adding a second group of animals that have the same number of alcohol treatments and the same number of practice sessions on the treadmill but receive the drug *after* each practice session. If tolerance in the first group was due to metabolic changes, the extent of tolerance in the two groups should be identical, but in fact, the second group in such trials has shown significantly less tolerance. The same type of tolerance is demonstrated by the individual with alcohol use disorder who learns to maneuver fairly efficiently while highly intoxicated, to avoid detection, whereas a less experienced alcohol abuser with the same blood-alcohol level may appear behaviorally to be highly intoxicated. Young and Goudie (1995) is an excellent source for additional details on the role of classical and operant conditioning in the development of tolerance to the behavioral effects of drugs.

STATE-DEPENDENT LEARNING **State-dependent learning** is a concept that is closely related to behavioral tolerance. Tasks learned under the influence of a psychoactive drug may subsequently be performed better in the drugged state than in the nondrugged state. Conversely, learning acquired in the nondrugged state may be more available in the nondrugged state. This phenomenon illustrates the difficulty in transferring learned performance from a drugged to a non-drugged condition (**FIGURE 1.24**). An example of this is the alcohol abuser who while intoxicated hides his supply of liquor for later consumption but is unable to find it while sober. Once he has returned to the intoxicated state, he can readily locate his cache.

One explanation for state dependency is that the internal stimulus properties of the drug effect may act as environmental cues. A drugged subject learns to perform a particular task in relation to all internal and external cues in the environment, including drug-related cues. Thus, in the absence of drug-related cues, performance deteriorates in much the same way as it would if the test apparatus were altered. It has been shown in animal studies that the decrease in performance is very much related to the change in environmental cues and that a particular drug state does provide readily discriminable stimuli. A comparison of state-dependent learning with the cuing properties of drugs as discriminative stimuli (see Chapter 4) is provided by Koek (2011).

Chronic drug use can cause sensitization

Despite the fact that repeated drug administration produces tolerance for many effects of a given drug, sensitization can occur for other effects of the same drug. **Sensitization**, sometimes called *reverse tolerance*, is the enhancement of particular drug effects after repeated administration of the same dose of drug. For instance, prior administration of cocaine to animals significantly increases motor activity and stereotypy (continual repetition of a simple action such as head bobbing) produced by subsequent stimulant administration. Chronic administration of higher doses of cocaine has been shown to produce an increased susceptibility to cocaine-induced catalepsy, in which the animal remains in abnormal or distorted postures for prolonged intervals, as well as hyperthermia and convulsions (Post and Weiss, 1988). Cocaine and amphetamine are examples of drugs that induce tolerance for some effects (euphoria) and sensitization for others (see Chapter 12).

As is true for tolerance, the development of sensitization is dose-dependent, and the interval between treatments is important. Further, cross-sensitization with other psychomotor stimulants has been documented. Conditioning also plays a significant role in the appearance of sensitization. Pretreatment with the stimulant followed by testing in novel environments yields significantly more sensitization than occurs in the identical environment. However, in contrast to drug tolerance, the augmentation of response to drug challenge tends to persist for long periods of abstinence, indicating that long-term physiological changes may occur as a result of stimulant administration. Further discussion of sensitization will be provided in Chapter 12.

Pharmacogenetics and personalized medicine in psychiatry

Pharmacogenetics (sometimes called *pharmacogenomics*) is the study of the genetic basis for variability in drug response among individuals. Its goals are to identify genetic factors that confer susceptibility to specific side effects and to predict good or poor therapeutic response. By referring to genetic information on each patient, it should be possible for the clinician to select the most appropriate drug for that individual—the ultimate in personalized medicine.

Variability in response to a given drug among individuals may be explained by heritability of pharmacokinetic or pharmacodynamic factors. Genetic variation in pharmacokinetic factors can

lead to differences in bioavailability and thus differences in biobehavioral effects. Of the pharmacokinetic factors, pharmacogenetic evaluation of the drug-metabolizing enzymes has been the most studied because variations in metabolic rate produce large differences in drug blood level among individuals and in subsequent clinical effects, as well as side effects. The many genetic polymorphisms of the CYP450 enzyme family are of particular significance because those enzymes are responsible for metabolizing most psychoactive drugs. In section 1.1 Pharmacology you learned that in the general population there are four CYP2D6 genotypes, based on the number of copies of the functional CYP2D6 gene, that correspond to poor, intermediary, extensive, and ultrarapid metabolizers (see Figure 1.12). Genetic knowledge of an individual's metabolic function can be used to adjust the dose of drug to achieve the optimal blood level and the subsequent optimal therapeutic response without adverse side effects (Kirchheiner and Seeringer, 2007). An example of this principle can be seen in **FIGURE 1.25**. The top of the figure shows the standard dose of a drug metabolized by CYP450 enzymes and the estimated dosages appropriate for the four genotypes, shown in the middle. The bottom of the figure shows four sets of plasma concentration time courses, one set for each genotype. The dotted curves show the plasma levels without dosage correction. The solid curves represent the target concentrations with dosage adjusted for genotype. Plasma levels above the dashed line indicate a potential for adverse side effects. Plasma levels below the solid curve indicate inadequate drug concentration for effective therapeutics. Hence, for individuals who have an identified polymorphism for poor metabolism, a significantly lower dose should be administered to achieve

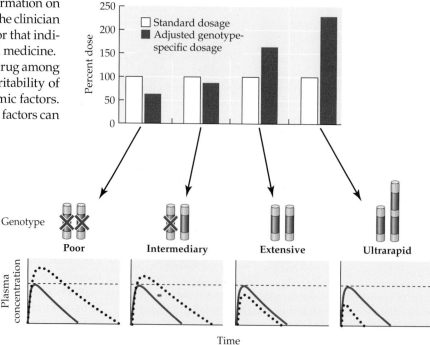

FIGURE 1.25 Drug dosage adjustments based on genotype Compared with standard dosages (open), theoretical dosages (solid red) were estimated based on drug-metabolizing genotype in order to achieve equal drug plasma concentration time courses to maximize therapeutic efficacy and avoid unwanted adverse effects. See text for details. (After J. Kirchheiner and A. Seeringer. 2007. *Biochim Biophys Acta* 1770: 489–494. © 2006. Reprinted with permission from Elsevier.)

the desired blood level. The intermediary metabolizers, with one normal allele and one inactive polymorphism, would also be administered a slightly reduced dosage to optimize plasma concentration. In contrast, individuals with two highly functional genes (extensive metabolizers) should be administered a higher-than-normal dosage to ensure therapeutic effectiveness. Finally, the ultra-rapid metabolizers, having additional high-functioning polymorphisms, would need a still higher dosage to reach adequate plasma concentrations for effective treatment. Hence, knowing the genetic variation in metabolizing enzymes in individuals helps to predict the bioavailability of a given drug so that the optimal therapeutic dose that avoids side effects can be administered.

Knowing the inherited level of function of a drug-metabolizing enzyme is clearly useful in determining the correct dose of a drug for a given individual, but it is important to recall that multiple genetic factors, demographic factors (e.g., gender, ethnicity, and age), environmental factors including diet, cigarette smoking, and concomitant use of multiple medications also alter drug metabolism (Arranz and Kapur, 2008). For this reason, recent research aims to examine how drug effects vary in response to the combined influence of genetic and environmental factors. The emerging field of **pharma-coepigenetics** thus builds on the principles of pharmacogenetics, taking into account the role of **epigenetic** modifications that can alter gene function and arise from environmental and behavioral factors (Peedicayil, 2019).

Genetic polymorphisms may also influence pharmacodynamic drug targets (i.e., sites of action of the agent). These sites include receptors, transporters, and other membrane proteins, as well as downstream intracellular signaling cascades. Pharmacogenomic studies of drug response typically examine the association between drug effects and polymorphisms in genes suspected to have a role in the mechanism of action of that drug or in the pathophysiology of the disorder. Efforts are made to correlate the gene variant with the therapeutic or side effects of a given drug. One example involves antidepressants that inhibit the serotonin transporter to increase the function of serotonin. Several studies have shown that individuals with the long variant of the gene for the serotonin transporter have a better response to treatment with particular drugs and are more likely to show remission (i.e., complete elimination of symptoms of depression) than individuals with the short allele, at least in Caucasian populations (Schosser and Kasper, 2009).

It is anticipated that routine genetic screening of patients will provide several advantages. Predicting how patients with distinct genetic profiles will respond to a particular medication before treatment begins would avoid the current costly and time-consuming method of trial and error to determine the best drug and the appropriate dose. Additionally, it is anticipated that genotyping will identify those individuals who are most susceptible to dangerous or debilitating side effects.

Minimizing side effects and serious toxic reactions not only would protect patients, but also should increase compliance with the drug regimen, and this would lead to fewer instances of relapse.

Despite encouraging basic biomedical research showing the potential of genomic screening, multiple challenges remain for the routine application of pharmacogenomics in clinical practice. One major challenge is that patients are not routinely genotyped, so a database of genetic information that can predict clinically meaningful treatment response outcomes remains to be built. Performing such studies for the database is difficult, expensive, and labor intensive because they require a large sample size for statistical validity and prolonged periods of monitoring therapeutic outcomes and side effects. However, Urban and Goldstein (2014) suggest including genetic screening in several phases of clinical trials leading to FDA approval of new drugs (see Chapter 4 for a discussion of the testing phases). Such screening would enhance the database and potentially detect markers that predict drug efficacy or adverse drug reactions, which might help pharmaceutical companies identify individuals for the final phase of testing. Although genotyping can be relatively expensive at this point in time, it is anticipated that with increased use, the costs will continue to diminish and genetic screening may become a routine procedure. Thus far, clinical use of genetic screening has been limited to selecting specialized drugs for unusual patients and regulating the dosage of drugs when the therapeutic index is narrow. It must be concluded that pharmacogenetics holds great promise for better psychiatric treatment, but further development will be needed if it is to reach its clinical potential. For more information you might want to check out a National Institutes of Health (NIH) website such as www.genome.gov/27530645.

SECTION SUMMARY

- Drugs have biological effects because they interact with receptors on target tissues.

- Agonists are drugs or ligands that bind and are capable of changing the shape of the receptor protein and subsequently altering cell function.

- Ligands that attach most readily are said to have high affinity for the receptor.

- Antagonists are capable of binding and may have high affinity while producing no physiological change; hence, they have little or no efficacy. Antagonists "block" agonist activity by preventing agonists from binding to the receptor at the same moment.

- Inverse agonists bind to a receptor and initiate a biological action that is opposite that produced by an agonist.

- In general, binding of the specific ligand to a receptor is reversible.

- Receptor number changes to compensate for either prolonged stimulation (causing down-regulation) or absence of receptor stimulation (causing up-regulation).

■ Dose–response curves show that with increasing doses, the effect increases steadily until the maximum effect is reached.

■ The ED_{50} is the dose that produces a half-maximal (50%) effect. The more potent drug is the one that has the lower ED_{50}.

■ Comparison of the TD_{50} (50% toxic dose) with the ED_{50} (50% effective dose) for a single drug provides the therapeutic index, which is a measurement of drug safety.

■ Competitive receptor antagonists reduce the potency of an agonist; this is shown by a parallel shift of the dose–response curve to the right with no change in the maximum effect.

■ Biobehavioral interactions of drugs can produce physiological antagonism, additive effects, or potentiation.

■ Chronic drug use may lead to a reduction in biobehavioral effects (tolerance), but in some circumstances, drug effects increase with repeated use (sensitization).

■ Cross-tolerance may occur if repeated use of one drug reduces the effectiveness of a second drug.

■ Tolerance is generally a reversible condition that depends on dose, frequency of use, and the drug-taking environment. Not all drugs induce tolerance, and not all effects of a given drug undergo tolerance to the same extent or at the same rate.

■ Metabolic tolerance occurs when drugs increase the quantity of the liver's metabolizing enzymes; this more rapidly reduces the effective blood level of the drug.

■ Pharmacodynamic tolerance depends on adaptation of the nervous system to continued presence of the drug by increasing or decreasing receptor number or by producing other compensatory intracellular processes.

■ Behavioral tolerance occurs when learning processes and environmental cues contribute to the reduction in drug effectiveness. Pavlovian conditioning and operant conditioning can contribute to the change in drug response.

■ Sensitization is dependent on dose, intervals between treatments, and the drug-taking environment. Cross-sensitization with other drugs in the same class can occur. Unlike tolerance, sensitization is not readily reversible, and it persists for long periods of abstinence caused by long-term physiological changes to cells.

■ Pharmacogenetics strives to identify genetic polymorphisms in individuals that predict a good or poor therapeutic response to a specific drug or susceptibility to specific side effects. Genetic variation in pharmacokinetic factors such as rate of drug metabolism is responsible for determining drug blood level and subsequent biobehavioral effects. Genetic polymorphisms and epigenetic changes may influence the targets for drugs such as receptors and transporters.

STUDY QUESTIONS

1. What is the placebo effect? Discuss several possible explanations for the placebo effect. How might it be used clinically and in research?

2. What are the principal pharmacokinetic factors? Explain how they determine bioavailability.

3. Discuss the advantages and disadvantages of several methods of administering drugs. How might these factors be weighed when deciding on the optimal route of administration?

4. Describe the factors that influence the absorption of lipid-soluble and ionized drugs.

5. What is the blood–brain barrier, and why is it important to psychopharmacology?

6. What is depot binding? Discuss three ways that it can alter the magnitude and duration of drug action.

7. Compare and contrast synthetic and nonsynthetic biotransformations. Why are these metabolic changes to the drug molecule necessary for excretion?

8. What are the factors that modify biotransformation?

9. What is a drug receptor? Provide several characteristics that are common among receptors in general.

10. Define agonist, antagonist, partial agonist, and inverse agonist as they relate to drug–receptor interactions.

11. What is a dose–response curve? How does the curve show threshold response, ED50, and maximum response? Draw and label an example curve to show your thinking.

12. What is the difference between potency and efficacy? How is that shown graphically?

13. What is the therapeutic index? Why is it important?

14. What effect does a competitive antagonist have when co-administered with an agonist of the same receptor? Compare its effect on potency and efficacy. How would a noncompetitive antagonist differ?

15. Define drug tolerance and describe three types of tolerance and their mechanisms. Compare tolerance with sensitization.

16. Describe pharmacogenetics and its role in personalized medicine. Give one example of its potential use in clinical treatment.

Structure and Function of the Nervous System

MICHELLE WAS A FIRST-SEMESTER SENIOR ENGLISH MAJOR when she first noticed that she was unusually fatigued and often felt dizzy and weak, barely able to lift her legs to climb stairs. She said it felt as though she were walking through oatmeal. As the semester wore on, Michelle found she had increasing trouble reading her assignments because of blurred vision and a sense that the words were moving on the page. Although these symptoms disappeared temporarily, they recurred with greater intensity just a few weeks later. When she realized she was almost too weak to walk and began slurring her speech, she made an appointment to see her hometown doctor. After a series of tests, Michelle's doctor told her she had multiple sclerosis (MS)—a progressive, degenerative autoimmune disease in which the immune system attacks the nerve cells in the brain and spinal cord, producing sensory and motor deficits. The doctor tried to reassure her. He said that MS is a disease that is characterized by remissions (absence of symptoms) and relapses and that some people go years before experiencing another episode. During remission, many people lead perfectly normal lives. However, it is a disease that can be treated but not cured. Fortunately, there are disease-modifying drugs that reduce the relapse rate and subsequently slow the progression of MS. This chapter describes nervous system structure and function. By the end of the chapter, you should have a good idea of what causes MS and of why Michelle experienced the particular symptoms she did.

As we already know, psychopharmacology is the study of how drugs affect emotion, memory, thinking, and behavior. Drugs can produce these widespread effects because they modify the function of the human brain, most often by altering the chemical nature of the nervous system. To gain an understanding of drug action, we first need to know a bit about individual nerve cell structure and electrochemical function. Second, we need to have an essential understanding of how these individual cells form the complex circuits that represent the anatomical basis for behavior. We hope that for most readers, Chapter 2 will be a review of the (1) structure of nerve cells, (2) electrochemical properties of neurons, and (3) anatomy of the nervous system, as we put the

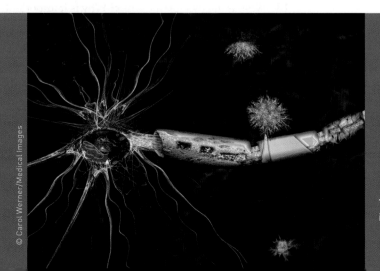

The myelin sheath of a neuron damaged by MS is being repaired by an oligodendrocyte.

individual neurons together into functional units. Chapter 3 follows up with greater detail on the chemical nature of nerve cell function. ◼

2.1 Cells of the Nervous System

All tissues in the body are composed of cells, and the special characteristics of different types of cells determine the structures and functions of the tissues and the organs. Understanding how those cells became specialized (differentiated) is of tremendous importance to basic science as well as clinical research. **BOX 2.1** describes embryonic stem cells and their potential in research and therapeutics. Embryonic stem cells destined to form the nervous system become two primary types of cells: nerve cells called **neurons** and supporting cells called **glial cells** that provide metabolic support, protection, and insulation for neurons (see the section Glial Cells Provide Vital Support for Neurons). The principal function of neurons is to transmit information in the form of electrical signaling over long distances. **Sensory neurons**, which are sensitive to environmental stimuli, convert physical stimuli in the world around us and in our internal environment into an electrical signal and transmit that information to circuits of **interneurons**, which are nerve cells within the brain and spinal cord. Interneurons form complex interacting neural circuits and are responsible for conscious sensations, recognition, memory, decision making, and cognition. In turn, **motor neurons** direct a biobehavioral response appropriate for the situation. Although these neurons have common features, their structural arrangements and sizes vary according to their specific functions. **FIGURE 2.1** provides some examples of the many possible shapes of neurons that were first described by the 19th-century histological studies of the Spanish neuroanatomist Ramón y Cajal. For much of the 20th century, neuroscientists relied

on the same set of techniques developed by early neuroanatomists to describe and categorize the diversity of cell types in the nervous system.

Histological methods that prepare tissue for microscopic study involve preparing very thin slices of the brain after it has been perfused with a salt solution to remove the blood, and treating the tissue with fixative that kills potentially damaging microorganisms, stops enzymatic damage, and hardens normally soft tissue. After slicing, one of several types of stain is applied to make fine cellular details visible. The Golgi technique, developed in 1873 by the Italian scientist Camillo Golgi, stains only a few cells in their entirety for detailed visualization of individual neurons (see Figure 2.1); others selectively stain myelin to view bundles of axons. Still others selectively stain cell bodies or degenerating axons that identify damaged cells. After the tissue is stained, slices are examined with light or electron microscopy. Although variations on this basic technique are still used, new technologies (see Chapter 4) in cell biology and molecular biology provide investigators with many additional tools with which to identify minute differences in the structural features of neurons, trace their multiple connections, and evaluate physiological responses.

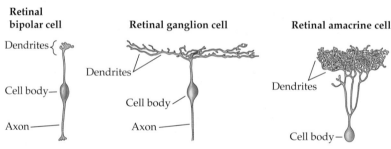

FIGURE 2.1   Varied shapes of neurons These drawings are from actual nerve cells stained by the Golgi technique. Neurons are drawn to different scales to show their varied structures.

BOX 2.1 ■ THE CUTTING EDGE

Embryonic Stem Cells

Stem cells are undifferentiated (i.e., unspecialized) cells that have the ability to proliferate; that is, they replicate themselves over long periods of time by cell division. A second distinguishing feature is that although they are unspecialized, stem cells have the capacity to become any specific tissue or organ cell type, such as red blood cell, muscle, or neuron, each with its unique structure and functions. This is possible because all cells of the body have identical genetic material, but some genes are activated and others are silenced to produce a cell type with all the appropriate proteins to perform its specialized functions. Hence in a nerve cell, particular genes are silenced, and in a heart cell, other genes are silenced. Embryonic stem cells are derived primarily from a portion of very-early-stage embryos that would normally become the three germ layers that ultimately develop into all the different tissues of the body. The cells are maintained in a laboratory cell culture dish and multiply, potentially yielding millions of embryonic stem cells (see **FIGURE**). If, after 6 months, the cells have not differentiated into specific tissue cells, they are considered pluripotent, having more than one potential outcome. Scientists attempt to control differentiation to a specific cell type by changing the chemicals in the culture dish or by inserting specific genes into the cells to provide direction.

There are several potential benefits from stem cell research. First, in the laboratory, the differentiated cells can be used to develop model systems to improve our understanding of how an organism develops from a single cell. Understanding what genes and molecular controls direct normal differentiation may provide important clues about the nature of disease-causing aberrations and the causes of cancer and birth defects, both of which are due to abnormal cell differentiation and cell division. This understanding can lead to new strategies for treatment. Second, drug development can be more efficient if multiple cell lines are used to screen new drugs for potential toxic effects on various cell types from multiple organs. Such preliminary testing would also reduce harm to animals or humans.

Third, the most publicized potential application of stem cell research is the use of stem cells for cell transplantation therapies for degenerative diseases or diseased organs. Promising results from initial research with stem cells involved animal models of Parkinson's disease, which showed that administered stem cells migrate to the damaged area of the brain and replace lost dopamine neurons, producing significant improvement in motor function. Others used the cells to replace lost oligodendroglial cells that provide myelin in a rat model of human demyelinating disease (Brüstle et al., 1999). Stem cells can also be directed to form specific classes of CNS neurons. For example, by providing appropriate inductive signals and transcription factors, stem cells can be directed to become motor neurons. These cells replicate in the spinal cord, extend axons, and form synapses with target muscle (Wichterle et al., 2002).

Successes with rat models have encouraged early trials in human patients. Efforts have been made to replace inactive pancreatic β-cells in individuals with type 1 diabetes to restore normal levels of insulin. Additional trials have been initiated to evaluate stem cell use in Parkinson's disease, amyotrophic lateral sclerosis (ALS), macular degeneration, and severe burns. The first trials to treat patients with paraplegia after injury to the thoracic region of the spinal cord are under way. The list of neurodegenerative disorders that might someday be tackled by stem cell transplantation is long and includes Alzheimer's disease, ALS, stroke, brain trauma and tumors, MS, Tay-Sachs disease, Duchenne muscular dystrophy, and many others. Evidence also suggests that there is reduced proliferation of brain stem cells in patients with schizophrenia, depression, and bipolar disorder, which may someday be corrected by stem cell transplantation. The potential for this type of treatment is enormous, but whether results in humans will resemble those of the animal research must still be determined. Among the hurdles remaining is the need

(Continued)

(A)

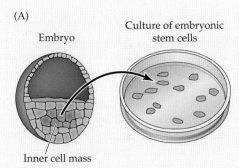

Embryo

Culture of embryonic stem cells

Inner cell mass

(B)

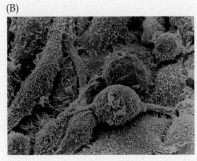

© Dr. Yorgos Nikas/Science Source

Culture of embryonic stem cells (A) Embryonic stem cells are cultured from the inner cell mass of an early-stage embryo. (B) Scanning electron micrograph of cultured embryonic stem cells.

BOX 2.1 ■ THE CUTTING EDGE (continued)

to increase basic research into the cellular events that lead to differentiation of pluripotent stem cells into the specific types of cells needed. In addition, steps may be needed to modify the stem cells to avoid immune rejection of the tissue. Finally, methods of delivery of the cells into the appropriate part of the body will need to be developed for each type of cell therapy. Clearly, treatment of brain disorders is particularly challenging.

A second approach to cell therapy is to use adult stem cells, which are found in many tissues, including brain, blood, skin, and heart. These cells normally function to repair the damaged tissue of the organ in which they reside and so are not pluripotent but are limited in differentiation to cell types within that organ. In general, adult stem cells are considered much more limited in their therapeutic potential than those derived from embryos. A second limitation with adult stem cells is that each tissue has only a small number of stem cells, so isolating them is difficult. Furthermore, once they are removed from the body, their ability to divide is limited, so it is more difficult to make the large quantities needed for transplantation. The number of adult cells further decreases with age, and the older cells may have more DNA damage, which may explain their shorter life span compared with pluripotent stem cells. One potential advantage of using adult stem cells is that there might be less risk of immune rejection, because the patient's cells would be isolated, multiplied in cell culture, and then readministered to that same patient.

Neuroscientists are interested in neural stem cells that are found in only two brain areas: the subventricular zone that lines the lateral ventricles and the hippocampal dentate gyrus. These cells support neurogenesis—the birth of new nerve cells throughout the life span—but also differentiate into oligodendroglia and astrocytes. The importance of neurogenesis in the hippocampus has become an important focus of research into the mechanism of action of antidepressants—a topic that will be discussed further in Chapter 18.

In an effort to overcome the ethical and political hurdles imposed on embryonic stem cell research that have restricted government funding, scientists have developed *induced* pluripotent stem cells (IPS cells). IPS cells are created by genetically reprogramming mature cells to develop the characteristics of the embryonic stem cell, essentially reversing the cell's differentiated fate. These cells have the cell markers of embryonic cells, reproduce in cell culture, and can develop into a wide variety of cells. Further, they avoid the controversial use of human embryos. IPS cells have been useful in drug development and testing and basic research, and a few small studies have been performed in human patients who were undergoing heart surgery. Stem cells injected into the blood or directly into the injured heart seemed to help heart function. However, these studies, although encouraging, are very preliminary. Another advantage of IPS cells is that they would be a match to the cell donor, so they should not be rejected by the immune system. However, a significant downside is that genetic reprogramming requires the use of viral vectors to get the genetic material into the adult cells. Since the use of the retrovirus may produce cancers, alternative nonviral techniques must be developed. Furthermore, more careful evaluation and comparison of IPS cells with embryonic stem cells and adult stem cells are needed to promote understanding of how they differentiate and to evaluate the potential for causing genetic errors. Recent findings suggest that selection of high-quality, fully differentiated cell lines that are free of cancer-causing mutations may significantly reduce this risk (e.g., Kikuchi et al., 2017), although the costs associated with generating such lines and producing transplantable cells remains an obstacle (Sonntag et al., 2018). While several clinical trials are under way, it is clear that much more research is needed before these cells will be useful therapeutically. A good source of further information is the NIH website Stem Cell Information (NIH, n.d.).

Neurons have three major external features

Although neurons come in a variety of shapes and sizes and utilize various neurochemicals, they have several principal morphological features in common (**FIGURE 2.2**). These features include (1) the **soma**, or cell body, which contains the nucleus and other organelles that maintain cell metabolic function; (2) the **dendrites**, which are treelike projections from the soma that receive information from other cells; and (3) the **axon**, the single tubular extension that conducts the electrical signal from the cell body to the terminal buttons on the axon terminals. Like all other cells, neurons are enclosed by a semipermeable membrane and are filled with a salty, gelatinous fluid—the **cytoplasm**. Neurons are also surrounded by salty fluid (**extracellular fluid**), from which they take oxygen, nutrients, and drugs, and into which they secrete metabolic waste products that ultimately reach the blood and then are filtered out by the kidneys (see Chapter 1). Like other cells, neurons have **mitochondria**, which are responsible for generating energy from glucose in the form of adenosine triphosphate (ATP). The assumption that the rate of ATP synthesis reflects neuron activity is an underlying premise of several techniques that enable us to

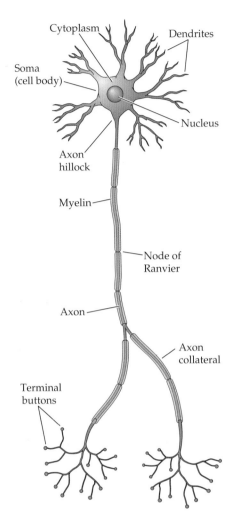

FIGURE 2.2 **Principal parts of neurons** Despite differences in size and shape, most neurons have numerous features in common.

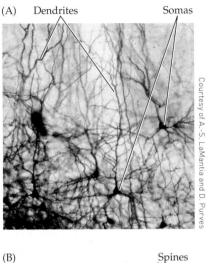

Courtesy of A.-S. LaMantia and D. Purves

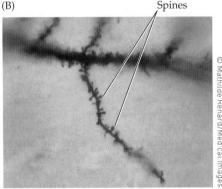

© Mathilde Renard/Med cal Images

FIGURE 2.3 **Dendritic trees with spines** (A) Light micrograph of neurons in the human cerebral cortex. Branching dendrites are clearly visible. (B) Higher magnification shows multiple spines all along the dendrite.

visualize the functioning of brain cells (see Chapter 4 for a discussion of positron emission tomography [PET] and functional magnetic resonance imaging [fMRI]).

DENDRITES The general pattern of neuron function involves the dendrites and soma receiving information from other cells across the gap between them, called the **synapse**. On the dendrites of a single neuron, as well as on the soma, there may be thousands of receptors that selectively respond to neurochemicals released by other neurons. Depending on the changes produced in the receiving cell, the overall effect may be either excitatory or inhibitory. Notably, each neuron receives and integrates a vast amount of information from many cells; this function is called **convergence**. The integrated information in turn can be transmitted to a few neurons or to thousands of other neurons; this process is known as **divergence**. If we look more closely using higher magnification, we see that dendrites are usually covered with short **dendritic spines** (**FIGURE 2.3**) that

dramatically increase the receiving surface area. The complex architecture of the dendritic tree reflects the complexity of synaptic connections with other neurons and determines brain function. Dendrites and their spines exhibit the special feature of being constantly modified and can change shape rapidly in response to changes in synaptic transmission (Fischer et al., 1998). Long-lasting changes in synaptic activity change the size and number as well as the shape of dendritic spines from thin to mushroom shaped; this apparently serves as the basis for more efficient signaling. These changes occur throughout life and permit us to continue to learn new associations as we interact with our environment.

Evidence suggesting the importance of dendritic spines to learning comes from studies of human patients and animal models of mental impairment. Individuals with intellectual disabilities have dendritic spines that are unusually small and immature looking; this may result from either a failure of maturation of small spines into larger spines or an inability to maintain spine structure. It is impossible to retain knowledge acquired during development without the large spines, and that failure manifests as intellectual deficiencies. In contrast, individuals with schizophrenia have dendritic spines of a normal *size* but reduced spine *density*, particularly in the prefrontal cortex. Although their intelligence is in the normal range, cognitive and negative symptoms of the disorder include poor working memory, lack of attention, poor episodic memory, and low motivation—all of which may be explained by poor connectivity between neurons. For further details on dendritic spine dynamics, the reader is directed to a review by Runge and colleagues (2020).

AXONS AND TERMINAL BUTTONS The single long extension from the soma is the axon. Axons are tubular in structure and are filled with axoplasm (i.e., cytoplasm within the axon). Axons vary significantly in both length and diameter. Their function is to transmit the electrical signal (action potential) that is generated at the **axon hillock** down the length of the axon to the terminals. The axon hillock is that portion of the axon that is adjacent to the cell body.

Although there is usually only one axon for a given neuron, axons split or bifurcate into numerous branches called **axon collaterals**, providing the capacity to influence many more cells. At the ends of the axons are small enlargements called **terminal buttons**, which are located near the dendrites or somas of other cells. Terminal buttons are also called *boutons* or *axon terminals*. Terminal buttons contain small packets (**synaptic vesicles**) of neurochemicals (called **neurotransmitters**) that provide the capacity for chemical transmission of information across the synapse to adjacent cells or to the target organ. Neurons are frequently named according to the neurotransmitter that they synthesize and release. Hence cells that release dopamine are dopaminergic neurons, those that release serotonin are serotonergic, and so forth.

Most axons are wrapped with a fatty insulating coating, called **myelin**, created by concentric layers of glial cells (**FIGURE 2.4A**). There are two types of glial cells that form the myelin sheath: Schwann cells, which myelinate peripheral nerves that serve muscles, organs, and glands; and oligodendroglia, which myelinate

nerves within the brain and spinal cord. The myelin sheath provided by both types of glial cells is not continuous along the axon but has breaks in it where the axon is bare to the extracellular fluid. These bare spots, called **nodes of Ranvier** (**FIGURE 2.4B**), are the sites at which the action potential is regenerated during conduction of the electrical signal along the length of the axon. The myelin sheath increases the speed of conduction along the axon; in fact, the thicker the myelin, the quicker the conduction. While a small number of neurons are unmyelinated and conduct slowly, others are thinly wrapped, and some rapidly conducting neurons may have a hundred or more wraps. Myelination also reduces the energy required to restore the neuron to its resting state after transmission of the electrical signal.

The best example of the importance of myelin to neuron function comes from multiple sclerosis (MS), the disease that was introduced in the chapter opener. MS is an autoimmune disease in which the immune system attacks a protein in the myelin produced by oligodendrocytes (but not Schwann cells), so the myelin loss is confined to the brain, spinal cord, and optic nerves. The particular symptoms depend on which neurons have lost their myelin sheath, and they vary greatly from person to person and even within the same person over time. Among the most common symptoms are fatigue; numbness; poor coordination and balance; vision problems; bladder, bowel, and sexual dysfunction; cognitive problems; and depression. Although myelin can be repaired by oliogodendroglia, the repair is slow and not very effective in MS. However, researchers are hopeful that new drugs will be developed that reverse nerve damage by facilitating remyelination to improve symptoms (e.g., Dombrowski et al., 2017). Currently available pharmacotherapies and more details on MS are provided in Chapter 20.

SOMA The cell body is responsible for the metabolic care of the neuron. Among its important functions is the synthesis of proteins that are needed throughout the cell for growth and maintenance. These proteins include such things as enzymes, receptors, and components of the cell membrane. Within the nucleus are pairs of chromosomes that we inherited from our parents. **Chromosomes** are long strands of deoxyribonucleic acid (DNA), and **genes** are small portions of chromosomes that code for the manufacture of a specific protein molecule. Hence the **coding region** of a gene provides the "recipe" for a specific protein such as a receptor or an enzyme. Although every cell in the body contains

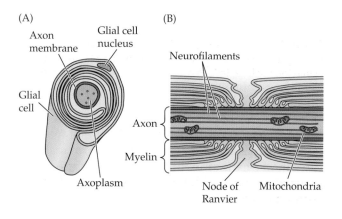

(A)

Axon membrane

Glial cell nucleus

Glial cell

Axoplasm

(B)

Neurofilaments

Axon

Myelin

Node of Ranvier

Mitochondria

FIGURE 2.4 Myelin sheath (A) Cross-section of an axon with multiple layers of glial cell wraps forming the myelin sheath. (B) Longitudinal drawing of a myelinated axon at a node of Ranvier.

the full genetic library of information, each cell type manufactures only those proteins needed for its specific function. Hence liver cells manufacture enzymes to metabolize toxins, and neurons manufacture enzymes needed to synthesize neurotransmitters and carry out functions necessary for neural transmission. In addition, which specific genes are activated is determined in part by our day-to-day experience. Neurobiologists are finding that experiences such as prolonged stress and chronic drug use may turn on or turn off the production of particular proteins by modifying transcription factors. **Transcription factors** are nuclear proteins that direct protein production. Transcription factors such as CREB bind to the **promoter region** of the gene adjacent to the coding region, modifying its rate of transcription.

Transcription occurs in the nucleus, where messenger RNA (mRNA) makes a complementary copy of the active gene. After moving from the nucleus to the cytoplasm, mRNA attaches to organelles called **ribosomes**, which decode the recipe and link the appropriate amino acids together to form the protein. This process is called **translation**. Some of the basic steps in protein synthesis are shown in **FIGURE 2.5**.

EPIGENETICS   We already said that environmental events can alter the rate of gene expression through induction of transcription factors. In addition, there are longer-lasting environmentally induced epigenetic modifications that determine which genes will be turned on or off and how much gene expression occurs. These changes may persist through the lifetime of the organism and may even be passed on to future generations if modifications are present in the germ cell line (i.e., eggs and sperm). These events occur despite the fact that the basic structure of the DNA is not altered. Instead, the simple covalent attachment of methyl groups (**DNA methylation**) to particular locations on a gene usually decreases expression of that gene. A second type of modification is **chromatin remodeling.** Chromatin is a complex of small spherical histone proteins around which the DNA wraps (**FIGURE 2.6A**). Environmentally induced acetylation, methylation, or phosphorylation of the lysine residues of histone tails can loosen the chromatin structure, allowing transcription factors to bind to the DNA and activate expression of the gene (**FIGURE 2.6B**). In other cases, chemical modification of the histone tails makes the chromatin more tightly packed, which represses gene expression by physically limiting the access of transcription factors (**FIGURE 2.6C**).

Epigenetic modification of gene expression has been understood since the 1970s because the phenomenon is central to cell differentiation in the developing fetus. Because all cells in the organism have identical DNA, they differentiate into organ-specific cells only when epigenetic processes turn on some of the genes and turn off others in utero. However,

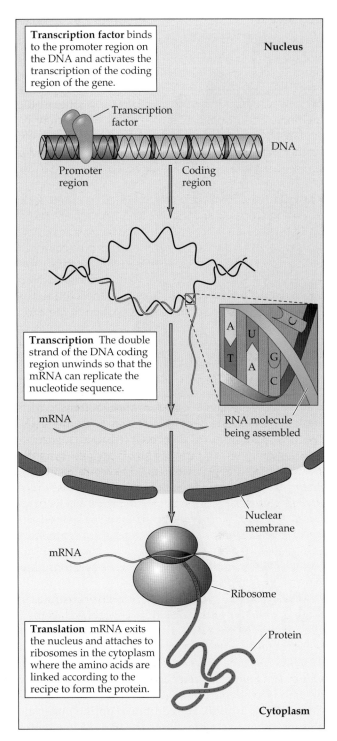

FIGURE 2.5 **Stages of protein synthesis** Activation of a gene by a transcription factor initiates the formation of mRNA within the nucleus, followed by translation into a protein on the ribosomes in the cytoplasm.

pre- or postnatal epigenetic modification can also occur in response to environmental factors such as starvation or overabundance of food, stress, poor prenatal nutrition, childhood abuse and neglect, exposure to environmental toxins, and so forth. A brief

(A) **Chromatin**

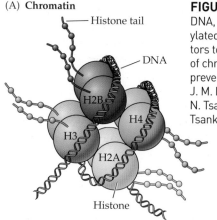

- Histone tail
- DNA
- H2B
- H4
- H3
- H2A
- Histone

FIGURE 2.6 Epigenetic regulation of gene transcription (A) Chromatin is a complex of DNA, histone proteins, and nonhistone proteins (not shown). (B) When histone tails are acetylated, charges open up the chromatin, creating an active state that allows transcription factors to bind to the promoter region of a gene to enhance transcription. (C) The inactive state of chromatin is caused by methylation of histone tails, which pulls the chromatin tighter and prevents the binding of transcription factors, reducing transcription of the gene. (A after J. M. Levenson and J. D. Sweatt. 2005. *Nat Rev Neurosci* 6: 108–118. doi.org/10.1038/nrn1604; N. Tsankova, et al. 2007. *Nat Rev Neurosci* 8: 355–367. doi.org/10.1038/nrn2132; B,C after N. Tsankova, et al. 2007. *Nat Rev Neurosci* 8: 355–367. doi.org/10.1038/nrn2132.)

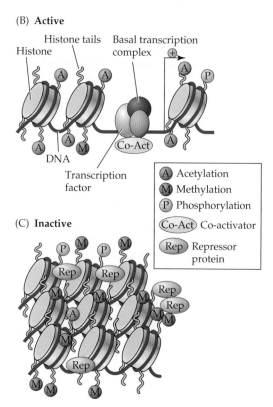

(B) **Active**

- Histone
- Histone tails
- Basal transcription complex
- Transcription factor
- DNA

Ⓐ	Acetylation
Ⓜ	Methylation
Ⓟ	Phosphorylation
Co-Act	Co-activator
Rep	Repressor protein

(C) **Inactive**

cause persistent neuroadaptive changes despite years of abstinence. One explanation may be that drugs of abuse enhance histone acetylation of multiple genes, which would produce persistent changes in gene expression. The potential for clinical use of epigenetic manipulations in drug treatment programs is suggested by a study showing that inhibition of an enzyme that removes acetyl groups from histone, which increased acetylation in nucleus accumbens, reduced drug-seeking behavior in laboratory animals and also reduced the probability of relapse when the mice were re-exposed to cocaine (Malvaez et al., 2010; see Werner et al., 2021, for a review of the epigenetic mechanisms involved in drug relapse).

An additional potentially significant role for epigenetic mechanisms may help to explain the etiology of many complex disorders, such as anxiety and depression, that have not shown a strong genetic link despite the newest sophisticated molecular genetic techniques. For these and other psychiatric disorders, the genetic polymorphisms identified so far contribute only about 1% of the risk for developing the disease. Hence the environment along with epigenetic mechanisms may have a greater part in initiating the disorder. Epigenetic changes may also help to explain why some disorders, such as autism and many neurological disorders, appear to run in families and yet have no classic genetic transmission (Sweatt, 2013). Finally, epigenetic mechanisms may also help us understand the link between early life events such as abuse or neglect and the increased occurrence of clinical depression (see Chapter 18) and anxiety disorders (see Chapter 17) later in life.

A major goal of neuropharmacology research is to develop drugs that can be used to manipulate epigenetic factors—for example, to deacetylate histone or increase methylation of DNA to treat psychiatric disorders that have genetic components, such as autism, schizophrenia, depression, Alzheimer's disease, and others. In essence, the drug could be used to enhance gene expression that may have been suppressed by the disorder or turn off expression of genes that are associated with the development of symptoms.

AXOPLASMIC TRANSPORT Having said that proteins are synthesized within the soma and knowing that proteins are needed throughout the neuron, we must consider how these proteins are moved to the

video, *The Epigenome at a Glance*, from the University of Utah is available online (Genetic Science Learning Center, 2013, July 15). For additional online materials and interactive activities, go to the parent site: Learn. genetics.utah.edu/content/epigenetics/.

Epigenetic mechanisms became a major focus of research when it became clear that epigenetic differences caused by environmental factors could explain previously unanswered questions. For instance, it may explain why monozygotic twins who have identical genes do not necessarily develop the same disorders, such as schizophrenia or bipolar disorder, cancer, or diabetes. Epigenetic events may also help to explain the persistence of the drug-taking behavior characteristic of addiction (see Chapter 9). Drugs of abuse can

required destination. The process is called **axoplasmic transport**, and it depends on structures of the cytoskeleton. The **cytoskeleton**, as the name suggests, is a matrix composed of tubular structures, which include microtubules and neurofilaments that form a mesh-like mass that provides shape for the cell. In addition, the microtubules, which run longitudinally down the axon, provide a stationary track along which small packets of newly synthesized protein are carried by specialized motor proteins (**FIGURE 2.7**). Movement of materials occurs in both directions. Newly synthesized proteins are packaged in the soma and transported in an anterograde direction toward the axon terminals. At the terminals, the contents are released, and retrograde axonal transport carries waste materials from the axon terminals back to the soma for recycling.

Abnormalities of the cytoskeleton constitute one of several pathological features of the brain in people with Alzheimer's disease—the neurofibrillary tangles. These tangles are made up of long, paired, spiral neurofilaments braided together. The neurofilament proteins, called tau, are normally important in keeping the microtubules running parallel and longitudinally directed down the axon. Tau normally has phosphate molecules attached to it, but in Alzheimer's disease a large number of additional phosphate groups attach. This hyperphosphorylation causes tau to separate from the microtubules, and tau becomes twisted together to form tangles and accumulates as a mass in the soma. The microtubules disintegrate, destroying the material transport system, and the axons shrivel up so neurons can no longer communicate with each other. The number of such tangles is directly related to the extent of cognitive impairment, which demonstrates clearly the importance of the cytoskeleton to brain function. Alzheimer's disease is discussed in detail in Chapter 20.

Characteristics of the cell membrane are critical for neuron function

One of the more important characteristics of neurons is the cell membrane. In Chapter 1 we learned that the neuronal membrane is essentially a phospholipid bilayer that prevents most materials from freely passing (see Figure 1.5), unless they are lipid soluble. In addition to phospholipids, membranes have proteins inserted into the bilayer. Many of these proteins are **receptors**—large molecules that are the initial sites of action of neurotransmitters, hormones, and drugs. Details of these receptors and their functions are described in Chapter 3. Other important proteins associated with the membrane are enzymes that catalyze biochemical reactions in the cell. A third important group of proteins consists of ion channels and transporters. Because the membrane is not readily permeable to charged molecules, special devices are needed to move molecules such as amino acids, glucose, and metabolic products across the membrane. Movement of these materials is achieved by transporter proteins, which are described further in Chapter 3. In addition, charged particles (ions), such as potassium (K^+), sodium (Na^+), chloride (Cl^-), and calcium (Ca^{2+}), that are needed for neuron function can be moved through the membrane only via ion channels. These channels are protein molecules that penetrate through the cell membrane and have a water-filled pore through which ions can pass.

Ion channels have several important characteristics. First, they are relatively specific for particular ions, although some allow more than one type of ion to pass through. Second, most channels are not normally open to allow free passage of the ions, but are in a closed configuration that can be opened momentarily by specific stimuli. These channels are referred to as **gated channels**. Two types of channels of immediate interest to us are **ligand-gated channels** and **voltage-gated channels**. Looking at the ligand-gated channel in **FIGURE 2.8A**, you can see that when a drug, hormone, or neurotransmitter binds to a receptor that recognizes the ligand, the channel protein changes shape and opens the gate, allowing flow of a specific ion either into or out of the cell. The direction in which an ion moves is determined by its relative concentration; it always travels from high to low concentration. Hence, given an open gate, Na^+,

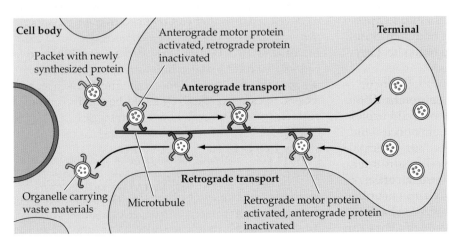

Cell body
Packet with newly synthesized protein
Anterograde motor protein activated, retrograde protein inactivated
Anterograde transport
Terminal
Retrograde transport
Organelle carrying waste materials
Microtubule
Retrograde motor protein activated, anterograde protein inactivated

FIGURE 2.7 Axoplasmic transport The movement of newly synthesized proteins from the soma to the axon terminals (anterograde) is powered along the microtubules by a motor protein called kinesin. Old proteins are carried from the terminals to the soma (retrograde) by the motor protein dynein.

(A)

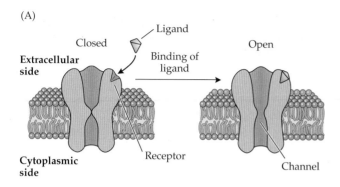

FIGURE 2.8 Ion channels (A) When a ligand (neurotransmitter, hormone, or drug) binds to a receptor on the channel, the ligand-gated channel protein changes shape and opens the gate, allowing passage of a specific ion. (B) A voltage-gated channel is opened when the electrical potential across the membrane near the channel is altered. (C) Modification of a channel by a second messenger, which produces intracellular phosphorylation (addition of a phosphate group) and regulates the state of the channel. (After S. A. Siegelbaum and J. Koester. 2000. In *Principles of Neural Science*, 4th ed., E. R. Kandel et al. [Eds.], pp.105–124. McGraw-Hill: New York. © McGraw-Hill.)

(B)

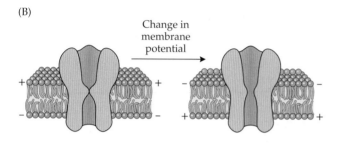

(C)

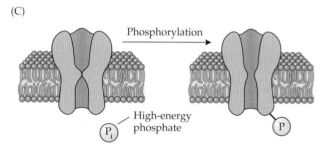

cells and oligodendroglia differ in several ways in addition to their location in the nervous system. Schwann cells (**FIGURE 2.9A**) are dedicated to a single neuron, and these PNS axons, when damaged, are prompted to regenerate axons because of the Schwann cell response. First, the Schwann cells release growth factors, and second, they provide a pathway for regrowth of the axon toward the target tissue. Oligodendroglia (**FIGURE 2.9B**), in contrast, send out multiple paddle-shaped "arms," which wrap many different axons to produce segments of the myelin sheath. In addition, they do not provide nerve growth factors when an axon is damaged, nor do they provide a path for growth.

Two other significant types of glial cells are the astrocytes and microglia. **Astrocytes** are large, star-shaped cells that have numerous extensions. They intertwine with neurons and provide structural support; in addition, they help to maintain the ionic environment around

Cl⁻, and Ca^{2+} will move into the cell, while K^+ moves out (see details on local potentials in the next section). A second type of channel, which will be of importance later in this chapter, is the type that is opened by voltage differences across the membrane. These voltage-gated channels are opened not by ligands, but by the application of a small electrical charge to the membrane surrounding the channel (**FIGURE 2.8B**). Other channels are modified by second messengers (**FIGURE 2.8C**), but discussion of these will have to wait until Chapter 3. Regardless of the stimulus opening the channel, it opens only briefly and then closes again, limiting the total amount of ion flux.

Glial cells provide vital support for neurons

Glial cells have a significant role in neuron function because they provide physical support to neurons, maintain the chemical environment of neurons, and provide immunological function. The four principal types are oligodendroglia, Schwann cells, astrocytes, and microglia. **Schwann cells** and **oligodendroglia**, described earlier, produce the myelin sheath on neuronal axons of the peripheral nervous system (PNS) and the central nervous system (CNS), respectively. Schwann

(A)

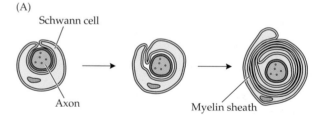

(B)

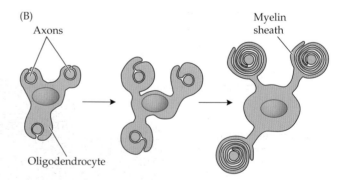

FIGURE 2.9 Glial cells forming myelin (A) Schwann cells in the PNS dedicate themselves to a single axon and wrap many times to form the myelin for one segment. (B) Each oligodendrocyte in the CNS sends out multiple sheetlike arms that wrap around segments of multiple nearby axons to form the myelin sheath.

neurons and modulate the chemical environment by taking up excess neurochemicals that might otherwise damage cells. Because astrocytes have a close relationship with both blood vessels and neurons, it is likely that they aid the movement of necessary materials from the blood to nerve cells. Greater detail on astrocyte function is provided in **BOX 2.2**. **Microglia** are far smaller than astrocytes and act as scavengers that collect at sites of neuron damage to remove dying cells. In addition to their phagocytotic function, microglia are the primary source of immune response in the CNS and are responsible for the inflammation reaction that occurs after brain damage. Chapter 19 describes their potential role in the etiology of schizophrenia. **TABLE 2.1** summarizes the functions of glial cells.

TABLE 2.1	Functions of Glial Cells
Cell	**Function**
Astrocytes	Provide structural support
	Maintain ionic and chemical environment
	Store nutrients to provide energy for neurons
	Perform gliosis
	Regulate CNS blood flow
	Coordinate reciprocal glia–neuron activity
Microglia	Perform phagocytosis
	Provide immune system function
Schwann cells	Form myelin sheath on a single axon in the PNS
	Release growth factors following neuron damage
	Provide a channel to guide axons to targets
Oligodendroglia	Form myelin sheath on multiple axons in the CNS
	Inhibit regrowth of axons following neuron damage

BOX 2.2 ■ OF SPECIAL INTEREST

Astrocytes

Although astrocytes were previously believed to act merely as a "brain glue" by providing support for the all-important neurons, in the last 30 years many new vital functions have been identified for these cells. Their importance to nervous system function is suggested by the fact that the ratio of astroglia to neurons increases with the complexity of brain function. In worms, there is one astrocyte for every six neurons (1:6), the ratio in rodent cortex is 1:3, and in human cortex there are slightly more astrocytes than neurons (1.4:1) (Sofroniew and Vinters, 2010). Not only does the ratio of astrocytes to neurons change, but the astrocyte domain (soma plus processes) increases with increasing complexity of brain function (see **FIGURE**).

Much of the research has been focused on how the glial cells respond to tissue damage, because they are potentially novel therapeutic targets for many diseases of the nervous system that involve gliosis (activation and accumulation of glial cells in response to CNS injury). These diseases include Alzheimer's disease, neuropathic pain, multiple sclerosis (MS), Parkinson's disease, seizure disorders, migraine, and many others. The response to CNS injury begins with the arrival of microglia, which provide a rapid response to inflammatory signals caused by brain damage. The arrival of microglia initiates the action of astrocytes, called astrogliosis. Gliosis, a reactive change in glial cells following CNS damage, is characterized by an increase in filaments of the cytoskeleton, leading to cell enlargement and build-up of scar tissue. Depending on the nature and extent of damage, astroglia can have either beneficial or detrimental effects. For instance, in some cases they release anti-inflammatory molecules, but in other circumstances they may release pro-inflammatory neurotoxic substances, which may contribute further to inflammatory disorders such as MS. Additionally, while astroglia protect against programmed cell death, in other cases the astroglial scar

(Continued)

Astrocytes in cortex of an adult mouse, a rhesus monkey, and a human Although all show a bushy morphology, the size of the astrocyte increases with increasing complexity of brain function.

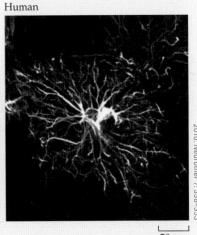

Mouse

Rhesus monkey

Human

50 µm   50 µm   50 µm

From H. K. Kimelberg and M. Nedergaard. 2010. *Neurother* 7: 338–353

BOX 2.2 ■ OF SPECIAL INTEREST *(continued)*

tissue prevents the regeneration of axons. Although the scar tissue may impair recovery, in other cases it may prevent the spreading of an infectious agent to healthy brain tissue by creating a physical barrier (see Sofroniew and Vinters, 2010).

Astroglia do not have electrical excitability, as neurons do, but are capable of communicating with nearby cells (both neurons and other glia) by altering their intracellular calcium concentration. Neurons can signal to the astrocytes by releasing neurotransmitters, including glutamate, GABA (γ-aminobutyric acid), acetylcholine, and norepinephrine. The astrocytes can reciprocally influence the function of neighboring neurons, so there is a coordinated network of glial–neuron activity.

Furthermore, astroglia have proteins in their membranes, called transporters, that remove certain neurotransmitters from the synapse, hence terminating their synaptic action. This function is especially important for the amino acid neurotransmitter glutamate. Uptake of glutamate by astrocytes has several functions. After glutamate is taken up, the astrocyte converts it to glutamine. Glutamine can be transported back into neurons, where it can be converted back into glutamate for neurotransmission (Boison et al., 2010). The uptake of glutamate by astrocytes is also important when synaptic glutamate levels are high for prolonged periods, because glutamate can have damaging effects (excitotoxicity) on neurons (see Chapter 8). Impaired uptake of glutamate by astrocytes has been implicated in some neurodegenerative diseases, such as amyotrophic lateral sclerosis (ALS), and also disorders associated with severe energy failure, such as severe head trauma or status epilepticus, which is characterized by prolonged, uncontrolled seizures. Multiple studies have shown structural and physiological abnormalities in astrocytes in epileptic tissue such as in the hippocampus. Others have found that animals that have been genetically modified to prevent glutamate uptake have been highly susceptible to excitotoxicity and many have developed epileptic seizures (see Peterson and Binder, 2020). Failure of astroglia function not only prevents glutamate uptake but also impairs the ability to remove excess synaptic K+ and maintain the appropriate salt–water balance and extracellular pH.

In addition to the significant role of astrocytes in responding to tissue damage, modulating synaptic function, and maintaining the extracellular fluid, astrocytes also surround all the blood vessels in the brain (see Figure 1.8) and thus play a large role in regulating CNS blood flow. They respond to the neurotransmitters released by adjacent neurons by increasing their intracellular Ca^{2+}. This in turn causes the release of vasoactive chemicals, such as prostaglandins, that produce vasodilation. They regulate the amount of blood flow in a given brain region based on the level of synaptic activity of hundreds of neurons. In this way astroglia can coordinate the availability of oxygen and glucose in the blood with the amount of neural activity. As you will see in Chapter 4, that principle is the basis for fMRI, which scans the brain for increased blood flow and oxygenation to identify those areas that are most metabolically active. Although it is unclear what the precise chemical mediators between the astrocytes and blood vessels are, much more research is ongoing (Filosa et al., 2016).

Additionally, because astrocytes bridge the gap between blood vessels and neurons, they are able to take up glucose from the blood and store it in the form of glycogen. During times when blood glucose is low and/or neurons show enhanced electrical activity, the astrocytes convert glycogen to lactate and transfer it to neurons to provide energy to the cells. Several excellent reviews on astrocyte function and their role in CNS disorders and brain pathology are available (Acioglu et al., 2021; Escartin et al., 2021).

SECTION SUMMARY

■ Neurons are surrounded by a cell membrane and are filled with cytoplasm and the organelles needed for optimal functioning.

■ Among the most important organelles are the mitochondria, which provide energy for the metabolic work of the cell.

■ The principal external features of a neuron are the soma, treelike dendrites, and a single axon extending from the soma that carries the electrical signal all the way to the axon terminals.

■ Axon terminals contain synaptic vesicles filled with neurotransmitter molecules that are released into the synapse between cells when the action potential arrives.

■ The dendrites of a neuron are covered with minute spines that increase the receiving surface area of the cell. These spines are reduced in size in individuals with intellectual impairment and reduced in number in those with schizophrenia.

■ Thousands of receptors that respond to neurotransmitters released by other neurons are found on the dendrites, dendritic spines, and soma of the cell.

■ The axon hillock is located at the juncture of soma and axon and is responsible for summation (or integration) of the multiple signals required to generate an action potential.

■ Conduction of the action potential along the axon is enhanced by the insulating property of the myelin created by nearby glial cells.

- The nucleus of the cell is located within the soma, and protein synthesis occurs there. Transcription of the genetic code for a specific protein by mRNA occurs within the nucleus, and translation of the "recipe," carried by the mRNA, occurs on the ribosomes in the cytoplasm. Ribosomes link together appropriate amino acids to create the protein.

- Changes in synaptic activity increase or decrease the production of particular proteins by activating transcription factors in the nucleus.

- Epigenetics is the study of how environmental factors turn on or turn off the expression of specific genes. Although epigenetic markers do not modify DNA, they can last a lifetime and may be transmitted to future generations. Two common markers are DNA methylation and chromatin remodeling.

- Future drug development will target epigenetic factors to treat psychiatric disorders that have genetic components by turning on protective genes or turning off genes associated with pathology.

- Newly manufactured proteins are packaged into vesicles in the soma and are moved by motor proteins that slide along the neuron's microtubules (part of the cytoskeleton) to the terminals (anterograde transport). Protein waste and cell debris are transported from the terminals back to the soma (retrograde transport) for recycling.

- The cell membrane is a phospholipid bilayer that prevents most materials from passing through, unless the material is lipid soluble. Special transporters carry other essential materials, such as glucose, amino acids, and neurotransmitters into the cell. Ion channels allow ions such as Na^+, K^+, Cl^-, and Ca^{2+} to move across the membrane. Other proteins associated with the membrane include receptors and enzymes.

- Four types of glial cells are found in the nervous system. Schwann cells and oligodendroglia produce the myelin sheath on PNS and CNS neurons, respectively. Astrocytes regulate the extracellular environment of the neurons, regulate CNS blood flow, and provide physical support and nutritional assistance. Microglia act as phagocytes to remove cellular debris and provide immune function.

2.2 Electrical Transmission within a Neuron

The transmission of information within a single neuron is an electrical process and depends on the semipermeable nature of the cell membrane. When the normal resting electrical charge of a neuron is disturbed sufficiently by signals from other cells, a threshold is reached that initiates the electrical signal (action potential) that conveys the message along the entire length of the axon to the axon terminals. This section of the chapter examines each of the stages: resting membrane potential, local potentials, threshold, and action potential.

Ion distribution is responsible for the cell's resting potential

All neurons have a difference in electrical charge between the interior and exterior of the cell, called the **resting membrane potential**. This can be measured by placing one electrode on the exterior of the cell in the extracellular fluid and a second, much finer microelectrode into the intracellular fluid inside the cell (**FIGURE 2.10**). The inside of the neuron is more negative than the outside, and a voltmeter would tell us that the difference is approximately –70 millivolts (mV), making the neuron **polarized** in its resting state.

Selective permeability of the membrane and uneven distribution of ions inside and outside the cell are responsible for the membrane potential. This means that when the cell is at rest, there are more negatively

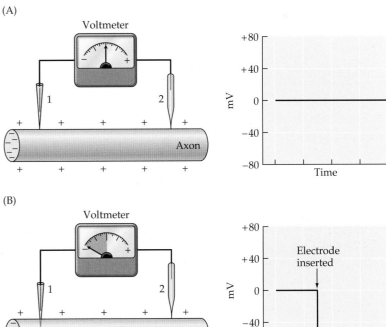

FIGURE 2.10 Membrane potential recording from a squid axon (A) When both electrodes are applied to the outside of the membrane, no difference in potential is recorded. (B) When the microelectrode is inserted into the axoplasm, a voltage difference between inside and outside is recorded. The graph shows the voltage change when one electrode penetrates the cell.

charged particles (ions) inside the cell and more positively charged ions outside the cell. **FIGURE 2.11** shows the relative concentration of different ions on either side of the membrane. Inside we find many large, negatively charged molecules, such as proteins and amino acids, which cannot leave the cell. Potassium is also in much higher concentration (perhaps 20 times higher) inside the cell than outside. In contrast, Na^+ and Cl^- are present in greater concentration outside the cell than inside.

Several forces are responsible for this ion distribution and membrane potential. The concentration gradient and electrostatic pressure for the K^+ ion are particularly important; K^+ moves more freely through the membrane than other ions because some of its channels are not gated at the resting potential. Recall that ions move through relatively specific channels and that most are gated, meaning that they are normally held closed until opened by a stimulus. Since the inside of the cell normally has numerous large, negatively charged materials that do not move through the membrane, the positively charged K^+ ion is pulled into the cell because it is attracted to the internal negative charge—that is, by **electrostatic pressure** (see Figure 2.11). However, as the concentration of K^+ inside rises, K^+ responds to the concentration gradient by moving out of the cell. The concentration gradient is a force that equalizes the amount or concentration of material across a biological barrier. When the two forces on K^+ (inward electrostatic pressure and outward concentration gradient) are balanced at what is called the **equilibrium potential for potassium**, the membrane potential is still more negative inside (–70 mV). In addition, because small amounts

of Na^+ leak into the cell, an energy-dependent pump contributes to the resting potential by exchanging Na^+ for K^+ across the membrane. For every three ions of Na^+ pumped out by this **Na^+–K^+ pump**, two K^+ ions are pumped in, keeping the inside of the cell negative.

In summary, all cells are polarized at rest, having a difference in charge across their membranes. The potential is due to the uneven distribution of ions across the membrane, which occurs because ions move through relatively specific channels that normally are not open. K^+ has greater ability to move freely through ungated channels. Although all cells are polarized, what makes neurons different is that rapid changes in the membrane potential provide the means for neurons to conduct information; this, in turn, influences hundreds of other cells in the nervous system. The rapid change in membrane potential that is propagated down the length of the axon is called the **action potential**. For a cell to generate an action potential, the membrane potential must be changed from resting (–70 mV) to the **threshold** for firing (–50 mV). At –50 mV, voltage-gated Na^+ channels open, generating a rapid change in membrane potential. Before we look closely at the action potential, let's see what happens to a neuron to cause the membrane potential to change from resting to threshold.

Local potentials are small, transient changes in membrane potential

Although the membrane potential at rest is –70 mV, various types of stimuli that disturb the membrane can open ion channels momentarily, causing small, local changes in ion distribution and hence electrical

	● Na^+	◉ K^+	○ Cl^-	○ Ca^{2+}	● Protein
Concentration outside cell	440	20	560	10	Few
Concentration inside cell	50	400	40–150	0.0001	Many

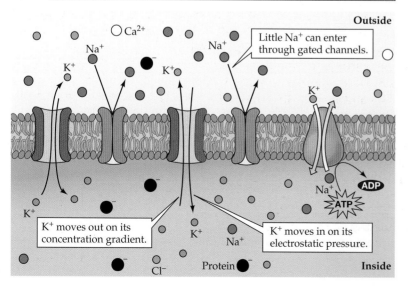

FIGURE 2.11 Distribution of ions inside and outside a neuron at resting potential Na^+ and Cl^- are more concentrated outside the cell and cannot move in freely through their gated channels. Some K^+ channels are not gated, allowing the concentration of the ion to force K^+ outward while electrostatically it is pulled in. At –70 mV, equilibrium between the two forces is reached. The Na^+–K^+ pump helps to maintain the ion distribution. It requires significant energy (ATP) to move ions against their concentration gradients.

potential differences called **local potentials**. To visualize the small changes in membrane potential, we attach our electrodes to an amplifier and to a computer that measures and records the changing voltage over time (**FIGURE 2.12**). For instance, applying a small, positive electrical current or momentarily opening gated Na$^+$ channels allows a relatively small number of Na$^+$ ions to enter the cell. These ions enter because Na$^+$ is more concentrated outside than inside, so the concentration gradient drives the ions in. The oscilloscope shows that positively charged ions make the inside of the cell slightly more positive in a small, localized area of the membrane, bringing the membrane potential a tiny bit closer to the threshold for firing. This change is called a local **depolarization** and is excitatory. Other stimuli may open Cl$^-$ channels, which allow Cl$^-$ into the cell because the ion's concentration is greater on the outside of the cell. The local increase in the negatively charged ion makes the cell slightly more negative inside and brings the resting potential farther away from threshold. This **hyperpolarization** of the membrane is inhibitory. Finally, if gated K$^+$ channels are opened by a stimulus, K$^+$ is driven outward locally on the basis of its concentration gradient. Because positively charged ions leave the cell, it becomes just slightly more negative inside, making the membrane potential farther from threshold and causing local hyperpolarization. These local potentials are of significance to psychopharmacology because when drugs or neurotransmitters bind to particular receptors in the nervous system, they may momentarily open specific ion channels (see Figure 2.8), causing an excitatory or inhibitory effect. Because neurotransmitters act on the postsynaptic membrane, the effects are called **excitatory postsynaptic potentials (EPSPs)** or **inhibitory postsynaptic potentials (IPSPs)**.

These local potentials (hyperpolarizations and depolarizations), generated on the dendrites and cell body, have several significant characteristics. First, they are graded, meaning that the larger the stimulus, the greater is the magnitude of hyperpolarization or depolarization. Also, as soon as the stimulus stops, the ion channels close and the membrane potential returns to resting levels. These local potentials decay rapidly as they passively travel along the cell membrane. Finally, local potentials show summation, sometimes called **integration**, meaning that several small depolarizations can add up

(A)

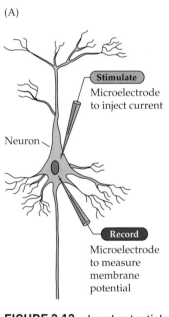

(B)

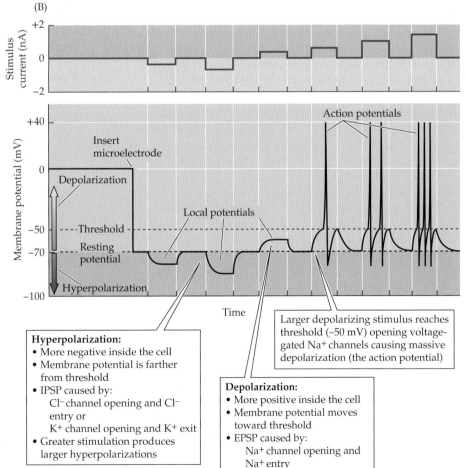

FIGURE 2.12 Local potentials and action potentials (A) Experimental method of stimulating and recording membrane potentials. (B) The magnitudes of negative and positive stimuli applied are shown in the upper panel, and the corresponding electrical recording is shown in the lower panel. The stimulus current is in nanoamperes (nA).

to larger changes in membrane potential, as several hyperpolarizations can produce larger inhibitory changes. When hyperpolarizations and depolarizations occur at the same time, they cancel each other out. The receptor areas of a neuron involved in local potential generation receive information from thousands of synaptic connections from other neurons that at any given instant produce IPSPs or EPSPs (as well as other biochemical changes to be described in Chapter 3). Integration of EPSPs and IPSPs occurs in the axon hillock (**FIGURE 2.13**) and is responsible for generation of the action potential if the threshold for activation is reached.

Sufficient depolarization at the axon hillock opens voltage-gated Na⁺ channels, producing an action potential

The summation of local potentials at the axon hillock is responsible for generation of the action potential. The –50 mV membrane potential (threshold) is responsible for opening large numbers of Na⁺ channels that are voltage gated—that is, the change in voltage across the membrane near these channels is responsible for opening them (**FIGURE 2.14**). Because Na⁺ is much more concentrated outside the cell, its concentration gradient moves it inward; in addition, since the cell at threshold is still negative inside, Na⁺ is driven in by the electrostatic pressure. These two forces move large numbers of Na⁺ ions into the cell very quickly, causing the rapid change in membrane potential from –50 mV to +40 mV (called *the rising phase of the action potential*) before the Na⁺ channels close and remain closed for a fixed period of time while they reset. The time during which the Na⁺ channels are closed and cannot be opened, regardless of the amount of excitation, prevents the occurrence of another action potential and is called the **absolute refractory period**. The closing of Na⁺ channels explains why the maximum number of action potentials that can occur is about 1200 impulses per second. The action potential is a rapid change in membrane potential that lasts only about 1 millisecond. When the membrane potential approaches resting levels, the Na⁺ channels are reset and ready to open.

Meanwhile, during the rising phase, the changing membrane potential due to Na⁺ entry causes voltage-gated K⁺ channels to open, and K⁺ moves out of the cell. K⁺ channels remain open after Na⁺ channels have closed, causing the membrane potential to return to resting levels. The membrane potential actually overshoots the resting potential, so the membrane remains hyperpolarized for a short time until the excess K⁺ diffuses away or is exchanged for Na⁺ by the Na⁺–K⁺ pump. Because the membrane is more polarized than normal, it is more difficult to generate an action potential. The brief hyperpolarizing phase is called the **relative refractory period** because it takes more excitation

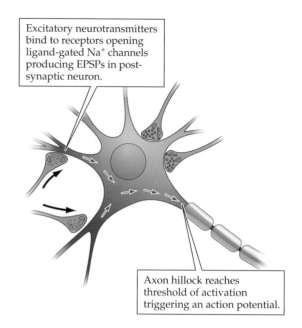

Excitatory neurotransmitters bind to receptors opening ligand-gated Na⁺ channels producing EPSPs in post-synaptic neuron.

Axon hillock reaches threshold of activation triggering an action potential.

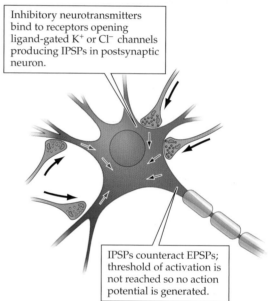

Inhibitory neurotransmitters bind to receptors opening ligand-gated K⁺ or Cl⁻ channels producing IPSPs in postsynaptic neuron.

IPSPs counteract EPSPs; threshold of activation is not reached so no action potential is generated.

FIGURE 2.13 **Summation of local potentials** Many inhibitory and excitatory synapses influence each neuron, causing local electrical potentials (IPSPs and EPSPs) as well as biochemical changes. At each instant in time, the electrical potentials summate and may reach the threshold for firing. Integration of electrical events occurs at the axon hillock, where the action potential is first generated. The action potential is then conducted along the axon to the axon terminals.

to first reach resting potential and further depolarization to reach threshold. The relative refractory period explains why the intensity of stimulation determines the rate of firing. Low levels of excitation cannot overcome the relative refractory period, but with increasing excitation, the neuron will fire again as soon as the absolute refractory period has ended.

If the threshold is reached, an action potential occurs (first at the hillock). Its size is unrelated to the amount of stimulation; hence it is considered *all-or-none*. Reaching

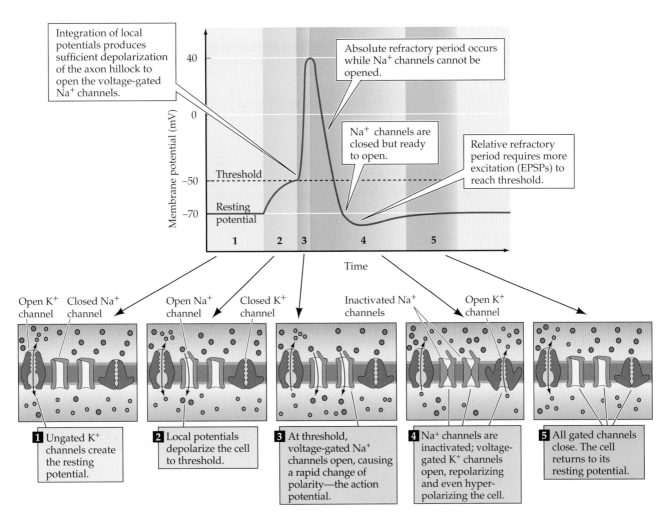

FIGURE 2.14 **Stages of the action potential** Opening and closing of Na⁺ and K⁺ channels are responsible for the characteristic shape of the action potential.

the threshold will generate the action potential, but more excitatory events (EPSPs) will not make it larger; fewer excitatory events will not generate an action potential at all. The action potential moves along the axon because positively charged Na⁺ ions spread passively to nearby regions of the axon, which changes the membrane potential to threshold and causes the opening of other voltage-gated Na⁺ channels (**FIGURE 2.15**). The regeneration process of the axon potential continues sequentially along the entire axon and does not decrease in size; hence it is called *nondecremental* (i.e., it does not decay). In myelinated axons, the speed of conduction is as much as 15 times quicker than in nonmyelinated axons because regeneration of the action potential occurs only at the nodes of Ranvier. This characteristic makes the conduction seem to jump along the axon, so it is called **saltatory conduction**. In addition, myelinated axons use less energy because the Na⁺–K⁺ pump, which uses large amounts of ATP, has to work only at the nodes rather than all along the axon.

Now that we understand normal neuron firing, it is worth a look at **WEB BOX 2.1**, which describes abnormal firing during epileptic seizures. **TABLE 2.2** lists characteristics specific to local and action potentials.

TABLE 2.2 **Characteristics of Local Potentials and Action Potentials**

Local potentials	Action potentials
Graded	All-or-none
Decremental	Nondecremental
Spatial and temporal summation	Intensity of stimulus coded by rate of firing
Produced by opening of ligand-gated channels	Produced by opening of voltage-gated channels
Depolarization or hyperpolarization	Depolarization

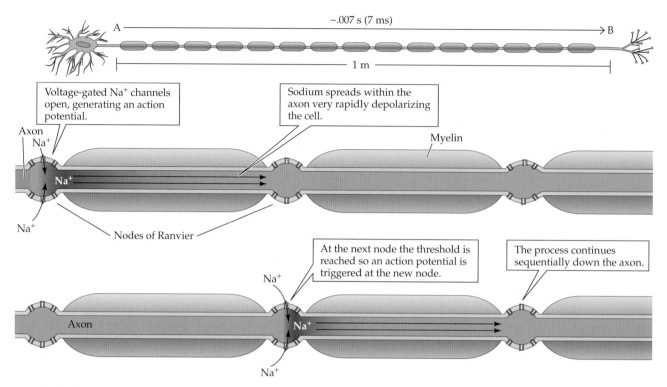

FIGURE 2.15 **Conduction along myelinated axons** The generation of the action potential at one node spreads depolarization along the axon, which in turn changes the membrane potential to threshold and opens voltage-gated Na+ channels at the next node of Ranvier.

Drugs and poisons alter axon conduction

As we will learn, most drugs act at synapses to modify chemical transmission. However, a few alter action potential conductance along the axon. Drugs that act as local anesthetics, such as procaine (Novocaine), lidocaine (Xylocaine), and benzocaine (found in Anbesol), impair axonal conduction by blocking voltage-gated Na$^+$ channels. It should be apparent that if voltage-gated Na$^+$ channels cannot open, an action potential cannot occur, and transmission of the pain signal cannot reach the brain. Hence the individual is not aware of the damaging stimulus. Several antiepileptic drugs also block voltage-gated Na$^+$ channels but in a more subtle manner. One such drug is phenytoin (Dilantin), which apparently reduces Na$^+$ conduction during rapid, repeated, and sustained neuronal firing, a condition that characterizes seizure activity. This selectivity can occur because rather than blocking the channel, phenytoin selectively binds to closed Na$^+$ channels. Since it takes time for the drug to unbind, its presence prolongs the refractory state of the channel, slowing down the firing rate.

Neurotoxins that bind to Na$^+$ channels have much more striking effects. One of these is saxitoxin, which is a poison that blocks voltage-gated Na$^+$ channels throughout the nervous system when it is ingested. Saxitoxin is found in shellfish exposed to "red tide," a common event along the nation's coastlines that is caused by large concentrations of microscopic red dinoflagellates of the species *Gonyaulax*, a marine plankton that

produces the neurotoxin. Oral ingestion circulates the toxin throughout the body and causes conduction failure and subsequent death due to suffocation. It is a hazard not only for humans but also for fish, birds, and animals such as manatees. A second toxin, tetrodotoxin, is also found in several types of fish, including the Japanese puffer fish, which is considered one of the most poisonous vertebrates in the world. However, it is considered a delicacy in Japan, where chefs are specially trained in the art of preparing the fish without the toxic liver, gonads, and skin. Nevertheless, there are numerous poisonings each year caused by the binding of tetrodotoxin to the voltage-gated Na$^+$ channels, which prevents action potentials. Symptoms include facial numbness, nausea, vomiting, and abdominal pain followed by increasing paralysis, first of the limbs and then of the respiratory muscles. Cardiac dysfunction and coma can occur if the individual survives long enough. Death, which occurs in 50% of cases, can occur as soon as 4 to 6 hours after ingestion (Benzer, 2015).

SECTION SUMMARY

- At rest, neurons have an electrical charge across the membrane of –70 mV (resting potential), with the inside being more negative than the outside.

- The resting potential results from the balance between two competing forces on K$^+$ ions. Electrostatic pressure moves K$^+$ inward because it is attracted by negatively charged molecules trapped inside the cell. The concentration gradient for K$^+$ pushes ions out of the cell in an effort to distribute them evenly.

- The Na$^+$–K$^+$ pump also helps to maintain the negative membrane potential by exchanging three Na$^+$ ions (moved out of the cell) for two K$^+$ ions (taken in).

- Excitatory postsynaptic potentials (EPSPs), or depolarizations, occur when ligand-gated Na$^+$ channels open and allow Na$^+$ to enter the cell on its concentration gradient, making the cell slightly more positive and bringing the membrane potential closer to the threshold for firing. Opening Cl$^-$ channels allows Cl$^-$ to enter on its concentration gradient, making the cell more negative and farther from the threshold, causing hyperpolarizations called inhibitory postsynaptic potentials (IPSPs).

- The temporal and spatial summation of EPSPs and IPSPs occurs at the axon hillock. If the threshold (−50 mV) is reached, voltage-gated Na$^+$ channels open, allowing large amounts of Na$^+$ to enter the cell to produce the massive depolarization known as the action potential.

- At the peak of the action potential (+40 mV), voltage-gated Na$^+$ channels close and cannot be opened until they reset at the resting potential, so no action potential can occur during this time (the absolute refractory period).

- As the cell becomes more positive inside, voltage-gated K$^+$ channels open and K$^+$ exits from the cell, bringing the membrane potential back toward resting levels. The overshoot by K$^+$ causes the cell to be more polarized than normal, so it is more difficult to reach the threshold to generate another action potential (relative refractory period).

- The action potential moves down the length of the axon by sequential opening of voltage-gated Na$^+$ channels.

- In myelinated axons, regeneration of the action potential occurs only at the nodes of Ranvier, producing a rapid, saltatory conduction that is more energy efficient because the Na$^+$–K$^+$ pump needs to exchange ions only at the nodes.

2.3 Organization of the Nervous System

Thus far we have described the structure of individual neurons and their ability to conduct electrical signals. Clearly, neurons never function individually but form interacting circuits referred to as *neural networks*. Such complexity allows us to make coordinated responses to changes in the environment. For example, as we perceive a potential danger, we suddenly become vigilant and more acutely aware of our surroundings. Meanwhile, internal organs prepare us for action by elevating heart rate, blood pressure, available energy sources, and so forth. Most of us will also calculate the probable outcome of fighting or running before taking a defensive or aggressive stance. Even simple responses require complex coordination of multiple nuclei in the brain and spinal cord. The following section describes the organization of neurons into brain regions that serve specific functions. This section provides only the highlights of functional neuroanatomy and emphasizes those brain structures that receive more attention in subsequent chapters. **BOX 2.3** provides a quick review of the terms used to describe the location of structures in the nervous system.

BOX 2.3 ■ THE CUTTING EDGE

Finding Your Way in the Nervous System

To discuss anatomical relationships, a systematic method to describe location in three dimensions is needed. The directions are based on the **neuraxis**, an imaginary line beginning at the base of the spinal cord and ending at the front of the brain. For most animals, the neuraxis is a straight line; however, because humans walk upright, the neuraxis bends, changing the relationship of the brain to the spinal cord (**FIGURE A**). For this reason, both the top of the head and the back of the body are called **dorsal**; **ventral** refers to the underside of the brain and the front surface of the body. To avoid confusion, sometimes the top of the human brain is described as **superior** and the bottom as **inferior**. In addition, the head end of the nervous system is **anterior** or **rostral**, and the tail end is **posterior** or **caudal**. Finally, **medial** means "toward the center or midline of the body," and **lateral** means "toward the side." We can

describe the location of any brain area using three pairs of dimensional descriptors: dorsal/ventral, anterior/posterior, and medial/lateral.

Much of our knowledge about the structure of the nervous system comes from examining two-dimensional slices (**FIGURE B**). The orientation of the slice (or **section**) is typically in any one of three different planes:

- **Horizontal** sections are slices parallel to the horizon.

- **Sagittal** sections are cut on the plane that bisects the nervous system into right and left halves. The **midsagittal** section is the slice that divides the brain into left and right symmetrical pieces.

- **Coronal** (or **frontal**) sections are cut parallel to the face.

(Continued)

BOX 2.3 ■ THE CUTTING EDGE *(continued)*

Identifying specific structures in these different views takes a good deal of experience. However, computer-assisted evaluation allows us to visualize the brain of a living human in far greater detail than was previously possible. Magnetic resonance imaging (MRI) and computerized tomography (CT) not only provide detailed anatomical images of brain slices but also reconstruct three-dimensional images of the brain using mathematical techniques. Positron emission tomography (PET) and functional MRI (fMRI) provide a view of the functioning brain by mapping blood flow or glucose utilization in various disease states, after drug administration, and during other experimental manipulations. These visualization techniques are described in Chapter 4, the chapter on methods in research.

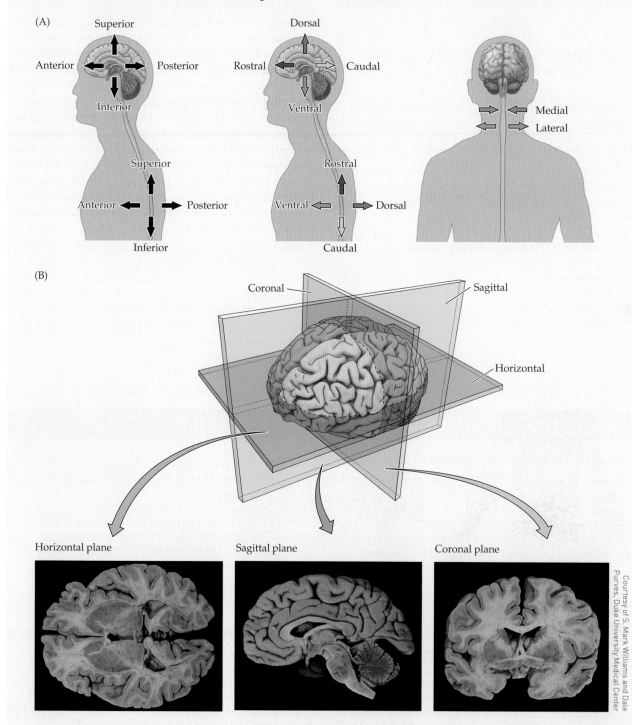

The nervous system comprises the central and peripheral divisions

The nervous system includes the central nervous system, or CNS (the brain and spinal cord) and the peripheral nervous system, or PNS (all nerves outside the CNS) (**FIGURE 2.16A**). The PNS in turn can be further divided into the somatic system, which controls voluntary muscles with both spinal nerves and cranial nerves, and the autonomic nervous system, which consists of autonomic nerves and some cranial nerves that control the function of organs and glands. The autonomic nervous system has both sympathetic and parasympathetic divisions, which help the organism to respond to changing energy demands. **FIGURE 2.16B** provides an overall view of the divisions of the nervous system. We begin by looking more closely at the PNS.

SOMATIC NERVOUS SYSTEM Each spinal nerve consists of many neurons, some of which carry sensory information and others motor information; hence they are called *mixed nerves*. Within each mixed nerve, sensory information is carried from the surface of the

body and from muscles into the dorsal horn of the spinal cord by neurons that have their cell bodies in the dorsal root ganglia (**FIGURE 2.17**). These signals going into the spinal cord are called **sensory afferents**. Mixed nerves also have motor neurons, which are cells beginning in the ventral horn of the spinal cord and ending on skeletal muscles. These are called **motor efferents** and are responsible for voluntary movements.

The 12 pairs of cranial nerves that project from the brain provide functions similar to those provided by the spinal nerves, except that they serve primarily the head and neck; hence they carry sensory information such as vision, touch, and taste into the brain and control muscle movement needed for things like chewing and laughing. They differ from the spinal nerves in that they are not all mixed nerves; several are dedicated to only sensory or only motor function. In addition, several of the cranial nerves innervate glands and organs rather than skeletal muscles; this means that they are part of the autonomic nervous system (see the next section). The vagus nerve (cranial nerve X) is unique among the cranial nerves because it communicates with numerous organs in the viscera, including

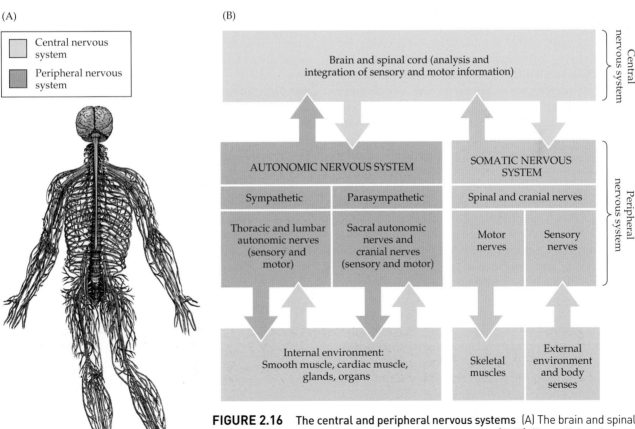

FIGURE 2.16 The central and peripheral nervous systems (A) The brain and spinal cord, shown in yellow, make up the central nervous system (CNS). The peripheral nervous system (PNS), shown in purple, connects all parts of the body to the CNS. (B) Organization of the nervous system: internal and external environments send sensory information by way of peripheral nerves to the CNS, where neural circuits analyze and integrate the information before sending signals to regulate muscle and internal organ function.

FIGURE 2.17 Spinal nerves of the peripheral nervous system (PNS) Cross-section of the spinal cord shows mixed spinal nerves with sensory afferents entering the dorsal horn and motor efferents leaving the ventral horn to innervate skeletal muscles. Note that the soma for the afferent neuron is in the dorsal root ganglion.

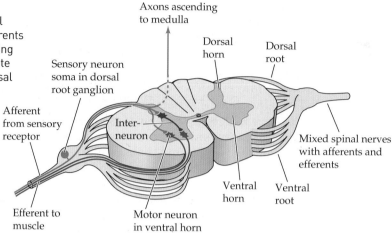

the heart, lungs, and gastrointestinal tract. The vagus nerve consists of both sensory and motor neurons.

AUTONOMIC NERVOUS SYSTEM The autonomic nerves, collectively called the *autonomic nervous system* (ANS), regulate the internal environment by innervating smooth muscles such as those in the heart, intestine, urinary bladder, and glands, including the adrenal and salivary glands. The purpose of the ANS is to control digestive processes, blood pressure, body temperature, and other functions that provide or conserve energy appropriate to the environmental needs of the organism. The ANS is divided into two components, the sympathetic and parasympathetic divisions, and both divisions serve most organs of the body (**FIGURE 2.18**). Although their functions usually work in opposition to one another, control of our internal environment is not an all-or-none affair. Instead, activity of the **sympathetic** division predominates when energy expenditure is necessary, such as during times of stress, excitement, and exertion; hence its nickname is the "fight-or-flight" system. This system increases heart rate and blood pressure, stimulates secretion of adrenaline, and increases blood flow to skeletal muscles, among other effects. The **parasympathetic** division predominates at times when energy reserves can be conserved and stored for later use; hence this system increases salivation, digestion, and storage of glucose and other nutrients and also slows heart rate and decreases respiration.

In addition to contrasting functions, the two branches of the ANS have anatomical differences, including points of origin in the CNS. The cell bodies of the efferent sympathetic neurons are in the ventral horn of the spinal cord at the thoracic and lumbar regions (see Figure 2.18). Their axons project for a relatively short distance before they synapse with a cluster of cell bodies called *sympathetic ganglia*. Some of these ganglia are lined up very close to the spinal cord; others, such as the celiac ganglion, are located somewhat farther away. These preganglionic fibers release the neurotransmitter

acetylcholine onto cell bodies in the ganglia. These postganglionic cells project their axons for a relatively long distance to the target tissues, where they release the neurotransmitter norepinephrine.

In contrast, the cell bodies of the efferent parasympathetic neurons are located either in the brain (cranial nerves III, VII, IX, and X) or in the ventral horn of the spinal cord at the sacral region. Preganglionic neurons travel long distances to synapse on cells in the parasympathetic ganglia that are not neatly lined up along the spinal cord but are close to individual target organs. The preganglionic fibers release acetylcholine, just as the sympathetic preganglionics do. However, parasympathetic postganglionic neurons, which are quite short, also release acetylcholine. Understanding the autonomic nervous system is especially important for psychopharmacologists because many psychotherapeutic drugs alter either norepinephrine or acetylcholine in the brain to relieve symptoms, but by altering those same neurotransmitters in the peripheral nerves, these drugs often produce annoying or dangerous side effects, such as elevated blood pressure, dry mouth, and urinary problems (all related to autonomic function; **BOX 2.4**). **TABLE 2.3** summarizes the differences between the two divisions of the ANS.

FIGURE 2.18 Autonomic nervous system (ANS) ▶ The internal organs, smooth muscles, and glands served by the ANS have both sympathetic and parasympathetic regulation. The two divisions have opposing effects on the organs; the sympathetic effects prepare the individual for action, and the parasympathetic effects serve to generate and store energy and reduce energy expenditure. Acetylcholine is the neurotransmitter released in all autonomic ganglia because preganglionic fibers are cholinergic neurons. At the target organs, the parasympathetic neurons release acetylcholine once again, while sympathetic neurons (noradrenergic neurons) release norepinephrine. Their anatomical and neurotransmitter differences are described in the text and are summarized in Table 2.3.

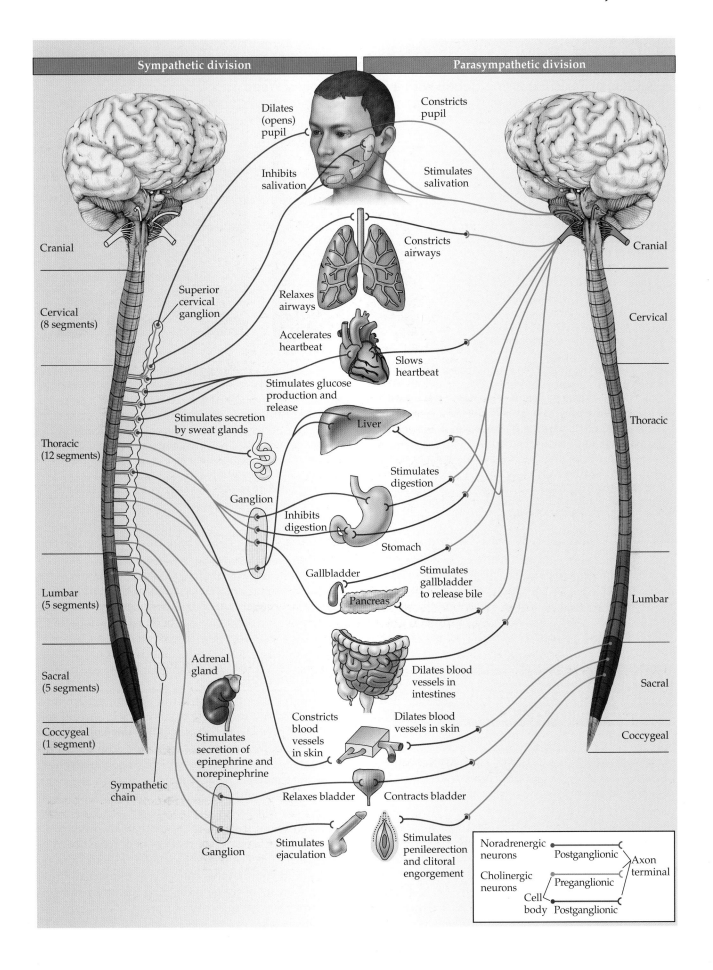

Sympathetic division

Parasympathetic division

Dilates (opens) pupil

Inhibits salivation

Constricts pupil

Stimulates salivation

Cranial

Cervical (8 segments)

Thoracic (12 segments)

Lumbar (5 segments)

Sacral (5 segments)

Coccygeal (1 segment)

Superior cervical ganglion

Stimulates secretion by sweat glands

Ganglion

Adrenal gland

Stimulates secretion of epinephrine and norepinephrine

Sympathetic chain

Ganglion

Relaxes airways

Accelerates heartbeat

Stimulates glucose production and release

Inhibits digestion

Gallbladder

Pancreas

Constricts blood vessels in skin

Relaxes bladder

Stimulates ejaculation

Constricts airways

Slows heartbeat

Liver

Stimulates digestion

Stomach

Stimulates gallbladder to release bile

Dilates blood vessels in intestines

Dilates blood vessels in skin

Contracts bladder

Stimulates penile erection and clitoral engorgement

Cranial

Cervical

Thoracic

Lumbar

Sacral

Coccygeal

Noradrenergic neurons

Postganglionic

Cholinergic neurons

Preganglionic

Cell body Postganglionic

Axon terminal

BOX 2.4 ■ CASE STUDIES

A Case of Toxic Experimentation with a Garden-Variety Weed

It is widely known that a large variety of plants contain psychoactive compounds. As will be described in later chapters, many such plants are cultivated specifically for their psychoactive properties, including cannabis, tobacco, coffee, coca, and several others. In addition to these well-known psychoactive plants, there are numerous other plants that grow in the wild and contain psychoactive compounds. In many cases, these wild psychoactive plants have been used in traditional medicine, but their use has largely been discontinued with advances in medical knowledge and the development of selective pharmacological agents.

(A)

(B)

Taka/CC BY-SA 3.0

Agnieszka Kwiecień (Nova)/CC BY 3.0

One such plant is jimsonweed (*Datura stramonium*; also known as thorn apple, moonflower, devil's snare, and others; **FIGURE**), which is an herbaceous plant that grows wild in most temperate climates around the world. When ingested, jimsonweed is known to produce hallucinations, and is frequently consumed for this purpose by curious adolescents. All parts of the jimsonweed plant contain atropine, hyoscyamine and scopolamine, with the highest concentrations found in the leaves and seeds (Figure A and B, respectively). All of these compounds are antagonists for the muscarinic subtype of acetylcholine receptor (see Chapter 7) and thereby act as hallucinogens of the anticholinergic type (sometimes referred to as "deliriants" to distinguish them from the psychedelic hallucinogens described in Chapter 15). Ingestion of jimsonweed typically results in the onset of effects within 30 to 60 minutes

of consumption. In addition to hallucinations, which reflect the effects of muscarinic acetylcholine receptor antagonism in the brain, jimsonweed produces a range of physiological responses in the periphery though actions on the parasympathetic division of the autonomic nervous system, which as mentioned earlier in this chapter, also uses acetylcholine as a neurotransmitter at muscarinic receptors.

Chan (2002) describes the case of a 15-year-old boy who was brought to the hospital by his mother, who had observed unusual behavior, including hallucinations. Upon discovering her son, the patient's mother observed several white flowers in his bedroom and brought them to the hospital. Emergency room staff noted that the boy was mumbling and appeared confused, reacting to nonexistent stimuli by reaching into the air as if to catch something. Toxicology screening

TABLE 2.3 Characteristics of the Sympathetic and Parasympathetic Divisions of the ANS	
Sympathetic	**Parasympathetic**
Energy mobilization	Energy conservation and storage
Origin in thoracic and lumbar spinal cord	Origin in the brain and sacral spinal cord
Relatively short preganglionic fibers; long postganglionics	Long preganglionic fibers ending near organs; short postganglionics
Releases acetylcholine in ganglia and norepinephrine at target	Releases acetylcholine at both ganglia and target

CNS functioning is dependent on structural features

The tough bone of the skull and vertebrae maintains the integrity of the delicate tissue of the brain and spinal cord. Three layers of tissue called **meninges** lie just within the bony covering and provide additional protection. The outermost layer, which is also the toughest, is the **dura mater**. The **arachnoid**, just below the dura, is a membrane with a weblike sublayer (subarachnoid space) filled with cerebrospinal fluid (CSF). Finally, the **pia mater** is a thin layer of tissue that sits directly on the nervous tissue. Some readers may have heard of the type of cancer called meningioma. It should now be apparent to you that this cancer is a tumor that forms on these layers of tissue protecting the brain and spinal cord. The vast majority of tumors of this type are

BOX 2.4 ■ CASE STUDIES (continued)

indicated the absence of common drugs of abuse, while blood and urine tests were also normal. Notably, physical examination indicated that the patient's pupils were dilated to 8 mm (3–5 mm is normal), mucous membranes were dry, and bowel motility was decreased. These signs, among others, are collectively indicative of an anticholinergic effect on the parasympathetic division of the autonomic nervous system, giving rise to the mnemonic commonly used by medical professionals for recognizing anticholinergic syndrome: "blind as a bat, dry as a bone, red as a beet, mad as a hatter, and hot as a hare."

Upon observing the pattern of clinical signs in combination with the reported ingestion of a wild plant, the emergency room physician suspected that the patient was exhibiting signs of jimsonweed toxicity and commenced treatment with a benzodiazepine for agitation, while admitting the patient for observation. Once the patient stabilized and his mental status improved, he confirmed that he had consumed jimsonweed for its hallucinogenic properties.

While the hallucinations produced by jimsonweed and other anticholinergics are frequently described as frightening or even "nightmarish," the toxic anticholinergic syndrome caused by jimsonweed can include seizures, CNS depression, respiratory failure, and cardiac abnormalities, all of which can be life-threatening. Aside from supportive measures and monitoring,

treatment for severe anticholinergic syndrome may include physostigmine (e.g., Glatstein et al., 2012), an acetylcholinesterase inhibitor that acts to increase extracellular levels of acetylcholine by preventing enzymatic inactivation, thus displacing anticholinergic compounds from muscarinic acetylcholine receptors.

The medical literature, as well as the popular press, contain numerous reports of adolescents and young adults requiring hospitalization due to jimsonweed toxicity. Many young people who are curious about drug experimentation may be drawn to jimsonweed given its legality and wide availability. In their presentation of a similar case of jimsonweed poisoning, Benyon and Chaturvedi (2018) suggested that the availability of information about jimsonweed on the internet, including how to obtain and prepare jimsonweed for recreational use, as well as the ability to purchase seeds from online vendors (see Vearrier and Greenberg, 2010, for another case study), may play a significant role in influencing young people to experiment with jimsonweed, without necessarily providing adequate information about the risks. While experimental use of jimsonweed rarely escalates to chronic abuse, the acute danger of jimsonweed toxicity is significant. Educating adolescents and young adults about the serious risks associated with consumption of jimsonweed and related plant species is essential to deterring young people from this dangerous form of experimentation.

---

benign (i.e., nonmalignant) and slow growing and often require no treatment unless their growth causes significant symptoms such as headaches, double vision, loss of smell, or weakness.

The CSF not only surrounds the brain and spinal cord but also fills the irregularly shaped cavities within the brain, called **cerebral ventricles**, and the channel that runs the length of the spinal cord, called the **central canal**. CSF is formed by the choroid plexus within the lateral ventricle of each hemisphere and flows to the third and fourth ventricles before moving into the subarachnoid space to bathe the exterior of the brain and spinal cord (see Figure 1.7A). Additionally, CSF helps in the exchange of nutrients and waste products between the brain and the blood. This exchange is possible because the capillaries found in the choroid plexus do not have the tight junctions typical of capillaries in the brain that form the blood–brain barrier, as described in Chapter 1. When the flow of CSF is impeded by a tumor, infection, or congenital abnormalities, the fluid builds up in the brain, causing compression of the delicate neural tissue surrounding the ventricles. This condition is called hydrocephalus

and produces a variety of symptoms, including nausea and vomiting, blurred vision, problems with balance and coordination, drowsiness, and memory loss. For a thorough description of the disorder, see the NIH *Hydrocephalus Fact Sheet* (NIH, 2020). A brief video from the Boston Children's Hospital describes hydrocephalus and the common neurosurgical treatment (Warf, 2011).

The CNS has six distinct regions reflecting embryological development

The six anatomical divisions of the adult CNS are evident in the developing embryo. It is important to know about the development of the brain because exposure to harmful events, including therapeutic and illicit drugs, environmental toxins, and stress, will have different outcomes depending on the timing of the insult and the developmental event occurring at that time. You will read more about this in later chapters on clinical disorders and in the chapter on alcohol. The CNS starts out as a fluid-filled tube that soon develops three enlargements at one end that become the adult hindbrain, midbrain, and forebrain, while the remainder of the

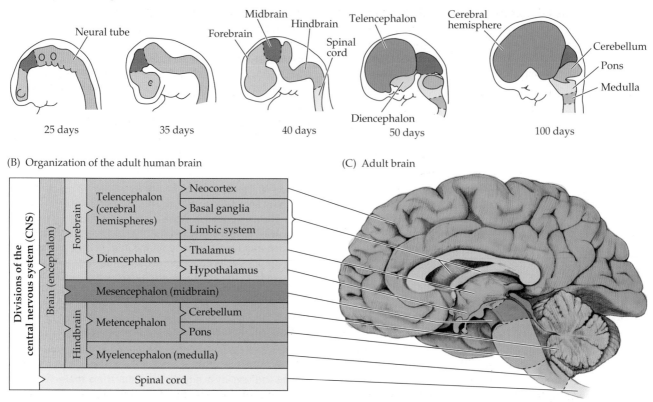

(A) Embryonic development of the human brain

Neural tube — 25 days

35 days

Midbrain
Forebrain
Hindbrain
Spinal cord — 40 days

Telencephalon
Diencephalon — 50 days

Cerebral hemisphere
Cerebellum
Pons
Medulla — 100 days

(B) Organization of the adult human brain

(C) Adult brain

Divisions of the central nervous system (CNS)	Brain (encephalon)	Forebrain	Telencephalon (cerebral hemispheres)	Neocortex
				Basal ganglia
				Limbic system
			Diencephalon	Thalamus
				Hypothalamus
		Mesencephalon (midbrain)		
	Hindbrain	Metencephalon	Cerebellum	
			Pons	
		Myelencephalon (medulla)		
	Spinal cord			

FIGURE 2.19 **Divisions of the central nervous system (CNS)** (A) Beginning with the primitive neural tube in the human embryo, the CNS develops rapidly. By day 50 of gestation, the six divisions of the adult CNS are apparent in the fetus. (B) The organization of the CNS (brain and spinal cord) presented in the table is color-coded to match the divisions shown in the adult brain (sagittal section) (C).

neural tube becomes the spinal cord (**FIGURE 2.19A**). The structural organization of these regions reflects the hierarchical nature of their functions. Each level has overlapping functions, and higher levels partially replicate the functions of lower ones but provide increased behavioral complexity and refined nervous system control. The fluid-filled chamber itself becomes the ventricular system in the brain and the central canal in the spinal cord. Within 2 months of conception, further subdivisions occur: the hindbrain enlargement develops two swellings, as does the forebrain. These divisions, in ascending order, are the spinal cord, myelencephalon, metencephalon, mesencephalon, diencephalon, and telencephalon. Each region can be further subdivided into clusters of cell bodies, called **nuclei**, and their associated bundles of axons, called **tracts**. (In the PNS, they are called **ganglia** and **nerves**, respectively.) These interconnecting networks of cells will be the focus of much of the remainder of this book, because drugs that alter brain function (that is, psychotropic drugs) modify the interactions of these neurons. The principal divisions of the CNS are summarized in **FIGURE 2.19B,C**. .

NEUROTROPHIC FACTORS Neurotrophic factors are proteins that influence not only neuron growth but also cell differentiation and survival. Nervous system development and maintenance of synaptic connections over the life span are dependent on the presence of neurotrophic factors such as nerve growth factor (NGF), brain-derived neurotrophic factor (BDNF), neurotrophin-3, and neurotrophin-4/5. Although similar in structure and general function, neurotrophins show some specificity. For example, NGF, the first neurotrophic factor to be discovered, is synthesized and secreted by peripheral target organs and guides the development of axonal processes of nearby neurons to establish synaptic connections with the target organ. Additionally, the presence of neurotrophic factors determines which neuronal connections survive and which are unnecessary and are eliminated by cell death. Apparently, the large population of neurons competes for the limited amount of neurotrophic factor in the target tissue, and those that are not supported by access to neurotrophins die, while those that respond to NGF establish appropriate synaptic connections. This process ensures that the number of connections is appropriate for the target tissue. NGF guides the growth of sympathetic neurons and a subpopulation of sensory ganglion cells. Other neurotrophins aid the survival of other subsets of peripheral sensory neurons. It is also clear that glial Schwann cells, which myelinate neurons of the PNS, release a growth factor when their axon is damaged. The growth factor in this case leads to regeneration of the damaged axon. In the CNS, neurotrophins like BDNF may be released by target neurons to maintain appropriate synaptic connections, but in some cases, the neurotrophin acts on the same neuron that produces it for autoregulation. Additionally, in some cases, neurotrophic factors are transported from the soma to the axon terminals, where their release modifies nearby cell bodies or nerve terminals of other neurons. For example, neurotrophins determine which of the cell dendrites grow and which retract, a process that influences synaptic activity and plasticity, quite independent of their role in cell survival. Research into the involvement of neurotrophic factors in mood disorders has suggested the neurotrophic hypothesis of depression and other psychiatric disorders. The importance of neurotrophic factors as potential therapeutic agents for neurodegenerative diseases such as Alzheimer's disease (see Chapter 20) and psychiatric disorders (see Chapter 18) will be discussed further in later chapters.

SPINAL CORD   The spinal cord is made up of gray and white matter. The former appears butterfly shaped in cross-section (**FIGURE 2.20A**) and is called *gray matter* because the large numbers of cell bodies in this region appear dark on histological examination. The cell bodies in the dorsal horn receive information from sensory afferent neurons entering the spinal cord, and cell bodies of motor neurons in the ventral horn send efferents to skeletal muscles. The white matter surrounding the butterfly-shaped gray matter is made up of myelinated axons of ascending pathways that conduct sensory information to the brain, as well as myelinated axons of descending pathways from higher centers to the motor neurons that initiate muscle contraction (**FIGURE 2.20B**).

As we move up the spinal cord and enter the skull, the spinal cord enlarges and becomes the **brainstem**. Examination of the ventral surface of the brain (**FIGURE 2.21A**) shows that the brainstem with its three principal parts—medulla, pons, and midbrain—is clearly visible. The brainstem contains the reticular formation, a large network of cells and interconnecting fibers that extends up the core of the brainstem for most of its length (described later in the section Metencephalon). Additionally, the brainstem is the origin of numerous cranial nerves that receive sensory information from the skin and joints of the face, head, and neck, as well as providing motor control to the muscles in that region. A significant volume of the brainstem is made up of ascending and descending axons coursing between the spinal cord and higher brain regions. The relationships of the structures of the brainstem are apparent in the midsagittal view (**FIGURE 2.21B**).

(A)

White matter
Gray matter
Motor efferents (PNS)
Subarachnoid space

Spinal nerve
Sensory afferents (PNS)
Pia mater
Arachnoid
Dura mater
Vertebra

The membranes (meninges) that surround the spinal cord

FIGURE 2.20   Spinal cord   (A) A view of the spinal cord showing its relationship to the protective layers of meninges and the bony vertebrae. Note the clearly defined gray matter and white matter in cross-section. (B) Schematic diagram of the ascending sensory tracts (blue) and the descending motor tracts (red).

(B)

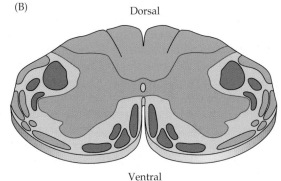

Dorsal

Ventral

(A) Ventral view

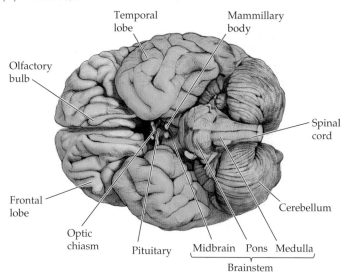
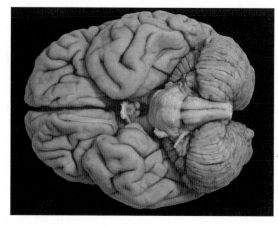

(B) Midsagittal view

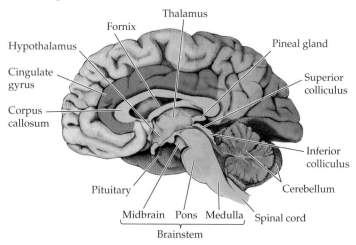
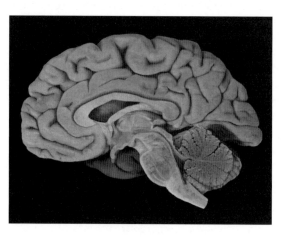

FIGURE 2.21 **Two views of the human brain** The drawings on the left in each panel label the structural features that are visible on the ventral external surface (A) and the midsagittal (midline) section (B). The right side of each panel shows the same view of a human postmortem brain specimen.

MYELENCEPHALON The first major structure of the brainstem that we encounter is the myelencephalon, or medulla. Within the **medulla**, multiple cell groups regulate vital functions, including heart rate, digestion, respiration, blood pressure, coughing, and vomiting. When an individual dies from a drug overdose, the cause is most often depression of the respiratory center in the medulla. Also located in the medulla is the **area postrema**, or the vomiting center, described in Chapter 1 as a cluster of cells with a reduced blood–brain barrier that initiates vomiting in response to toxins in the blood. Drugs in the opioid class such as morphine act on the area postrema and produce vomiting, a common unpleasant side effect of treatment for pain. The nuclei for cranial nerves XI and XII, which control the muscles of the neck and tongue, are also located in the medulla.

One portion of the medulla contains the medullary pyramids. These pyramids (two ridgelike structures) contain motor fibers that start in the motor region of the cerebral cortex and descend to the spinal cord, so they are named the corticospinal tract. These neurons synapse on spinal motor neurons described earlier. From 80% to 90% of the corticospinal neurons cross to the other side of the brain in the pyramids, explaining why the left motor cortex controls all voluntary movement on the right side of the body while the right motor cortex controls the left.

METENCEPHALON Two large structures within the metencephalon are the pons and the cerebellum (see Figure 2.21). Within the central core of the pons and extending rostrally into the midbrain and caudally into the medulla is the **reticular formation**. The reticular formation is not really a structure but a collection of perhaps 100 small nuclei forming a network that plays an important role in arousal, attention, sleep, and muscle tone, as well as in some cardiac and respiratory reflexes. One nucleus, called the **locus coeruleus**, is of particular importance to psychopharmacology because it is a cluster of cell bodies that distribute their axons to many areas of the forebrain. These cells are the principal source of all neurons that release the neurotransmitter norepinephrine from their terminals. When active, these cells cause arousal, increased vigilance, and attention. Drugs such as amphetamine enhance their function, causing sleeplessness and enhanced alertness.

Other cell groups within the pons that also belong to the reticular formation are the **dorsal** and **median raphe nuclei**. These two clusters of cells are the source of most of the neurons in the CNS that use serotonin as their neurotransmitter. Together, cell bodies in the dorsal and median raphe send axons releasing serotonin to virtually all forebrain areas and function in the regulation of diverse processes, including sleep, aggression and impulsiveness, neuroendocrine functions, and emotion. Because it has a generally inhibitory effect on CNS function, serotonin may maintain behaviors within specific limits. Drugs such as LSD (lysergic acid diethylamide) produce their dramatic hallucinogenic effects by inhibiting the inhibitory functions of the raphe nuclei (see Chapter 15).

The **cerebellum** is a large foliated structure on the dorsal surface of the brain that connects to the pons by several large bundles of axons called **cerebellar peduncles**. The cerebellum is a significant sensorimotor center and receives visual, auditory, and somatosensory input, as well as information about body position and balance, from the vestibular system. By coordinating sensory information with motor information received from the cerebral cortex, the cerebellum coordinates movements by timing and patterning skeletal muscle contractions. In addition, the cerebellum allows us to make corrective movements to maintain our balance and posture. Damage to the cerebellum produces poor coordination and jerky movements. Drugs such as alcohol at moderate doses inhibit the function of the cerebellum and cause slurred speech and staggering.

MESENCEPHALON The midbrain has two divisions: the tectum and the tegmentum. The tectum, the dorsalmost structure, consists of the superior colliculi, which are part of the visual system, and the inferior colliculi, which are part of the auditory system (see Figure 2.21B). These nuclei are involved in reflexes such as the pupillary reflex to light, eye movement, and reactions to moving stimuli.

Within the **tegmentum** are several structures that are particularly important to psychopharmacologists.

The first is the **periaqueductal gray** (**PAG**), which surrounds the cerebral aqueduct that connects the third and fourth ventricles. The PAG is one of the areas that are important for the modulation of pain. Local electrical stimulation of these cells produces analgesia but no change in the ability to detect temperature, touch, or pressure. The PAG is rich in opioid receptors, making it an important site for morphine-induced analgesia. Chapter 11 describes the importance of natural opioid neuropeptides and the PAG in pain regulation. The PAG is also important in sequencing species-specific actions, such as defensive rage and predation.

The **substantia nigra** is a cluster of cell bodies whose relatively long axons innervate the striatum, a component of the basal ganglia (**FIGURE 2.22**). These cells constitute one of several important neural pathways that utilize dopamine as their neurotransmitter. This pathway is called the nigrostriatal tract. (The names of neural pathways often combine the site of origin of the fibers with their termination site, hence *nigrostriatal*, meaning "substantia nigra to striatum.") This neural circuit is critical for the initiation and modulation of movement. Cell death in the substantia nigra is the cause of Parkinson's disease—a disorder characterized by tremor, rigidity, and inability to initiate movements. An adjacent cluster of dopaminergic cells in the midbrain is the **ventral tegmental area** (**VTA**). Some of these cells project axons to the septum, olfactory tubercle, nucleus accumbens, amygdala, and other limbic structures in the forebrain (see the section on the telencephalon below). Hence these cells form the mesolimbic tract (note that *meso* refers to "midbrain"). Other cells in the VTA project to structures in the prefrontal

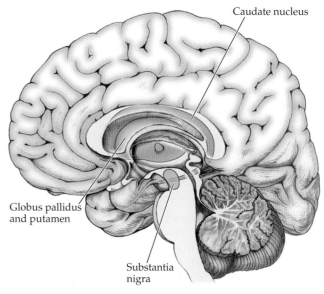

FIGURE 2.22 **The basal ganglia** These four structures form neural pathways that utilize dopamine as their neurotransmitter. These neural circuits constitute a system for motor control.

cortex, cingulate cortex, and entorhinal areas and are considered the mesocortical tract. All three of these dopamine pathways are of significance in our discussions of Parkinson's disease (see Chapter 20), drug addiction (see Chapter 9), and schizophrenia (see Chapter 19).

DIENCEPHALON The two major structures in the diencephalon are the thalamus and the hypothalamus. The **thalamus** is a cluster of nuclei that first process and then distribute sensory and motor information to the appropriate portion of the cerebral cortex. For example, the lateral geniculate nucleus of the thalamus receives visual information from the eyes before projecting it to the primary visual cortex. Most incoming signals are integrated and modified before they are sent on to the cortex. The functioning of the thalamus helps the cortex to direct its attention to selectively important sensory messages while diminishing the significance of others; hence the thalamus helps to regulate levels of awareness.

The second diencephalic structure, the **hypothalamus**, lies ventral to the thalamus at the base of the brain. Although it is much smaller than the thalamus, it is made up of many small nuclei that perform functions critical for survival (**FIGURE 2.23**). The hypothalamus receives a wide variety of information about the internal environment and, in coordination with closely related structures in the limbic system (see the section on the telencephalon below), initiates various mechanisms important for limiting the variability of the body's internal states (i.e., they are responsible for homeostasis). Several nuclei are involved in maintaining body temperature and salt–water balance. Other nuclei modulate hunger, thirst, energy metabolism, reproductive behaviors, and emotional responses such as aggression. The hypothalamus directs behaviors for adjusting to these changing needs by controlling both the autonomic nervous system and the endocrine system and organizing behaviors in coordination with other brain areas. Axons from nuclei in the hypothalamus descend into the brainstem to the nuclei of the cranial nerves that provide parasympathetic control.

Additionally, other axons descend farther into the spinal cord to influence sympathetic nervous system function. Other hypothalamic nuclei communicate with the contiguous pituitary gland by two methods: neural control of the posterior pituitary and hormonal control of the anterior pituitary. By regulating the endocrine hormones, the hypothalamus has widespread and prolonged effects on body physiology. Of particular significance to psychopharmacology is the role of the paraventricular nucleus in regulating the hormonal response to stress, because stress has a major impact on our behavior and vulnerability to psychiatric disorders. **BOX 2.5** describes the neuroendocrine response to stress and previews its significance for psychiatric ills and their treatment.

TELENCEPHALON The cerebral hemispheres make up the largest region of the brain and include the external cerebral cortex, the underlying white matter, and subcortical structures belonging to the basal ganglia and limbic system. The **basal ganglia** include the caudate, putamen, and globus pallidus and, along with the substantia nigra in the midbrain, make up a system for motor control (see Figure 2.22). Drugs administered to control symptoms of Parkinson's disease act on this group of structures.

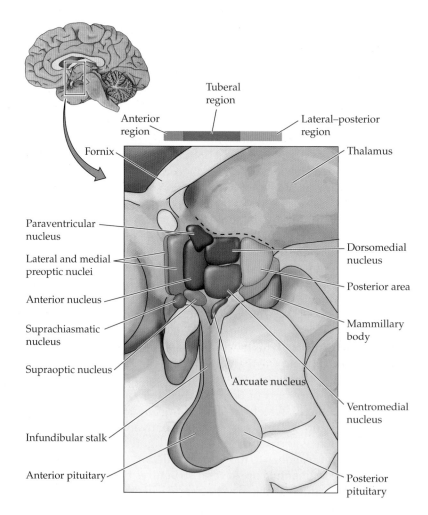

FIGURE 2.23 **Hypothalamus** The hypothalamus is a cluster of nuclei at the base of the forebrain that is often subdivided into three groups based on region: anterior, tuberal, and lateral–posterior. Each of the nuclei has its own complex pattern of neural connections and regulates one or several components of homeostatic function and motivated behavior.

BOX 2.5 ■ OF SPECIAL INTEREST

Neuroendocrine Response to Stress

The principal neuroendocrine response to stress is often referred to as the HPA axis because it depends on the interaction of the hypothalamus (H), the pituitary (P) gland, and the adrenal (A) gland. HPA axis activation is one part of complex emotional responses orchestrated by the amygdala. In essence, stress causes the secretion of corticotropin-releasing factor (CRF) by the paraventricular nucleus of the hypothalamus into the blood vessels ending in the anterior pituitary (see **FIGURE**). The binding of CRF in that gland causes the release of adrenocorticotropic hormone (ACTH) into the general blood circulation. ACTH subsequently binds to the adrenal cortex to increase the secretion of cortisol and other glucocorticoids, all of which contribute to the mobilization of energy to cope with stress or exertion. Under optimal conditions, cortisol feeds back to the hypothalamus (and hippocampus) to shut down HPA activation and return cortisol levels to normal. It also acts on the anterior pituitary (not shown) to reduce the production of ACTH.

Although HPA activity is critical for survival and adaptation to the environment, overuse of this adaptive mechanism leads to damaging changes to the brain and body. Damaging effects of prolonged cortisol response include such events as lower inflammatory response causing slower wound healing and immune system suppression. Stress has also been linked to an exacerbation of autoimmune diseases such as multiple sclerosis (MS), gastric problems, diabetes, elevated blood pressure, premature aging, and many other disorders. In addition, stress affects neuron structure and brain function.

Several later chapters in this text will describe the relationship between stress and alcohol use disorder, the damaging effect of stress on cells in the hippocampus and its relationship to clinical depression, and the impact of early life traumas that alter the set point of the HPA axis, making it overly responsive to stressors later in life. The differential activation of stress response circuitry in men and women will also

be addressed in the chapter on anxiety disorders. In Chapter 19, you will learn how stress-induced epigenetic events may alter the expression of a gene that is linked to the cognitive deficits characteristic of schizophrenia. All of these issues point to the critical need to evaluate more thoroughly the significant interaction between psychiatric and systemic medical disorders with the hope for potential new approaches to prevent and treat disabling conditions.

The **limbic system** is a complex neural network that is involved in integrating emotional responses and regulating motivated behavior and learning. The limbic system includes the limbic cortex, which is located on the medial and interior surface of the cerebral hemispheres and is transitional between allocortex (phylogenetically older cortex) and neocortex (the more recently evolved six-layer cortex). A significant portion of the limbic cortex is the cingulate. Chapter 11 describes the importance of the anterior portion of the cingulate in mediating the emotional component of pain. Some of the significant subcortical limbic structures are the amygdala, nucleus accumbens, and hippocampus, which is connected to the mammillary bodies and the septal nuclei by the fornix, the major tract of the limbic system (**FIGURE 2.24**). The **hippocampus** is most closely associated with the establishment of new long-term memories, spatial memory, and contextual memory and has been the focus of research into Alzheimer's disease and its treatment, as you will read in Chapter 7.

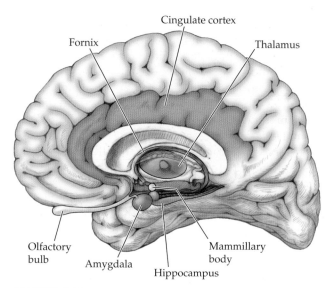

FIGURE 2.24 Limbic system Multiple subcortical structures interconnect to form the limbic system, which is critical for learning, memory, emotional responses, and motivation. Rich connections of limbic areas with association areas of the cortex contribute to decision making and planning.

Additionally, the vulnerability of the hippocampus to high levels of stress hormones suggests its involvement in clinical depression and antidepressant drug treatment (see Chapter 18). The **amygdala** plays a central role in coordinating the various components of emotional responses through its profuse connections with the olfactory system, hypothalamus (which is sometimes included in the limbic system, even though it is a diencephalic structure), thalamus, hippocampus, striatum, and brainstem nuclei, as well as portions of the neocortex, such as the orbitofrontal cortex. The amygdala and associated limbic areas play a prominent role in our discussions of antidepressants, alcohol, and antianxiety drugs. Chapters that describe the reinforcing value of abused substances also focus on limbic structures, notably the **nucleus accumbens**.

The cerebral cortex is divided into four lobes, each having primary, secondary, and tertiary areas

The cerebral cortex is a layer of tissue that covers the cerebral hemispheres. In humans, the cortex (or "bark") is heavily convoluted and has deep grooves called **fissures**, smaller grooves called **sulci**, and bulges of tissue between called **gyri**. Thus the bulge of tissues immediately posterior to the central sulcus is the post-central gyrus. The convolutions of the cortex greatly enlarge its surface area, to approximately 2.5 square feet. Only about one-third of the surface of the cortex is visible externally; the remaining two-thirds is hidden in the sulci and fissures. **FIGURE 2.25** shows some of the external features of the cerebral cortex. There may be as many as 100 billion cells in the cortex, arranged in six layers horizontal to the surface. Since these layers have large numbers of cell bodies, they appear gray; hence they are the gray matter of the cerebral cortex. Each layer can be identified by cell type, size, density, and arrangement. Beneath the six layers, the white matter of the cortex consists of millions of axons that connect one part of the cortex with another or connect cortical cells to other brain structures. One of the largest of these pathways is the **corpus callosum** (see Figure 2.21B). It connects corresponding areas in the two hemispheres, which are separated by a deep groove, the medial longitudinal fissure. In addition to the horizontal layers, the cortex has a vertical arrangement of cells that form slender vertical columns running through the entire thickness of the cortex. These vertically oriented cells and their synaptic connections apparently provide functional units for integration of information between various cortical regions.

The central sulcus and the lateral fissure (see Figure 2.25) visually divide the cortex into four distinct lobes

FIGURE 2.25 Lateral view of the exterior cerebral cortex The four lobes of the cerebral cortex are shown with distinct colors. Within each lobe is a primary area (darker in color) and secondary and tertiary association cortices. The caudal-most three lobes carry out sensory functions: vision (occipital), auditory (temporal), and somatosensory (parietal). The frontal lobe serves as the executive mechanism that plans and organizes behavior and initiates the appropriate sequence of actions.

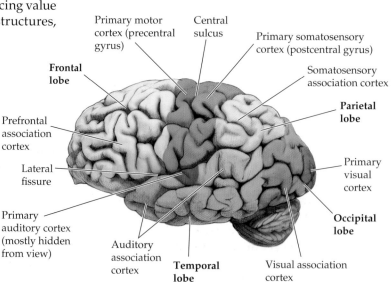

in each hemisphere: the **parietal lobe**, **occipital lobe**, and **temporal lobe**, all of which are sensory in function, and the **frontal lobe**, which is responsible for movement and executive planning. Within each lobe is a small primary area, adjacent secondary cortex, and tertiary areas called *association cortex*. Within the occipital lobe is the primary visual cortex, which receives visual information from the thalamus that originates in the retina of the eye. The primary auditory cortex receives auditory information and is located in the temporal lobe; the primary somatosensory cortex, which receives information about body senses such as touch, temperature, and pain, is found in the parietal lobe just posterior to the central sulcus. Neither the gustatory cortex, which involves taste sensations, nor the primary olfactory area, which receives information regarding the sense of smell, is visible on the surface, but both lie within the folds of the cortex. The **primary cortex** of each lobe provides conscious awareness of sensory experience and the initial cortical processing of sensory qualities. Except for olfaction, all sensory information arrives in the appropriate primary cortex via projection neurons from the thalamus. In addition, except for olfaction, sensory information from the left side of the body goes to the right cerebral hemisphere first, and information from the right side goes to the left hemisphere. Visual information is somewhat different in that the left half of the visual field of each eye goes to the right occipital lobe and the right half of the visual field of each eye goes to the left occipital lobe.

Adjacent to each primary area is **secondary cortex**, which consists of neuronal circuits responsible for analyzing information transmitted from the primary area and providing recognition (or perception) of the stimulus. These areas are also the regions where memories are stored. Farther from the primary areas are association areas that lay down more-complex memories that involve multiple sensory systems such that our memories are not confined to a single sensory system but integrate multiple characteristics of the event. For example, many of us remember pieces of music from the past that automatically evoke visual memories of the person we shared it with, or the time in our lives when it was popular. These **tertiary association areas** are often called the parietal–temporal–occipital association cortex because they represent the interface of the three sensory lobes and provide the higher-order perceptual functions needed for purposeful action.

Within the frontal lobe, the primary motor cortex mediates voluntary movements of the muscles of the limbs and trunk. Neurons originating in primary motor cortex directly, or in several steps, project to the spinal cord to act on spinal motor neurons that end on muscle fibers. As was true for the sensory systems, the motor neurons beginning in the frontal cortex are crossed, meaning that areas of the right primary motor cortex control movements of limbs on the left side of the body, and vice versa. Adjacent to the primary motor cortex is the secondary motor cortex, where memories for well-learned motor sequences are stored. Neurons in this area connect directly to the primary motor cortex to direct movement. The rest of the frontal lobe comprises the prefrontal cortex, which receives sensory information from the other cortices via the large bundles of white matter running below the gray matter. Emotional and motivational input is contributed to the prefrontal cortex by limbic and other subcortical structures. The prefrontal cortex is critical for making decisions, planning actions, and evaluating optional strategies. Impaired prefrontal function is characteristic of several psychiatric disorders, including borderline personality disorder, memory loss after traumatic brain injury, attention-deficit/hyperactivity disorder, and others. The significance of this brain region for the symptoms and treatment of schizophrenia is discussed in Chapter 19.

Rat and human brains have many similarities and some differences

Since the rat is one of the most commonly used animals in neuroscience and psychopharmacological research, it may be helpful to compare the neuroanatomy of the rat brain with that of the human brain. Overall, there has been great conservation of brain structures during the evolution of mammals. Despite differences in absolute and relative sizes of the whole brain, all mammalian brains have the same major subdivisions, which are topographically organized in relatively the same locations with similar neural connections among structures. **FIGURE 2.26** shows the striking correspondence of brain structures in the brains of rats and humans. Extensive similarities can also be found for individual nuclei, fiber tracts, and types of cells, although human neurons are much larger than rat neurons and have more elaborate dendritic trees.

Despite the many similarities, there are also notable differences. What differs among mammals is the relative size of the brain regions, which likely reflects the environmental conditions encountered by each species and the importance of the functions of specific brain regions for adaptation of the species. For example, rats have relatively larger olfactory bulbs than humans, presumably because a very sensitive sense of smell provided evolutionary advantages for survival for these nocturnal rodents. More striking is the difference in cerebral cortex. The paired cerebral hemispheres occupy a much greater proportion of the brain in the human than in the rat. The six-layered nature of the neocortex (the outermost layers of the cerebral hemispheres) is characteristic of all mammals, and it is the

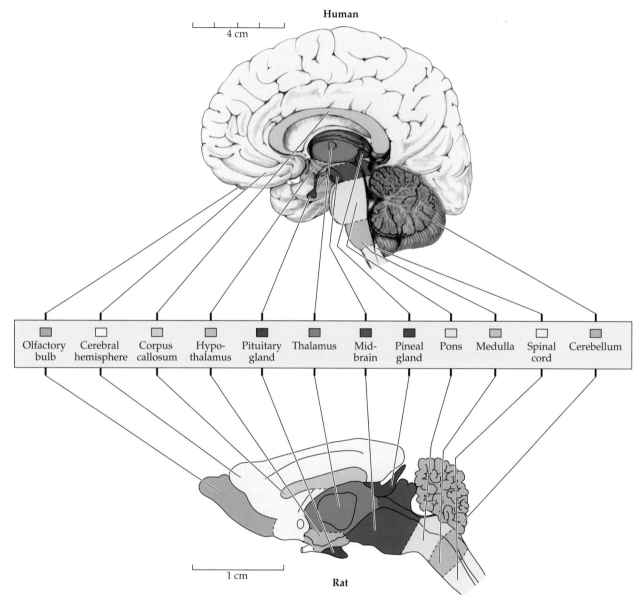

FIGURE 2.26 **Comparison of human and rat brains** Midsagittal views of the right hemispheres of human and rat brains show extensive similarities in brain structures and their relative topographic location. The brains differ in that the cerebral hemispheres are relatively much larger in the human brain, while the rat has a relatively larger midbrain and olfactory bulb. The rat brain has been enlarged about six times in linear dimensions relative to the human brain. (From S. M. Breedlove et al. 2010. *Biological Psychology*, 6th ed., Oxford University Press/Sinauer Associates: Sunderland, MA)

newest part of the cerebral cortex to evolve. In humans, the surface area of the neocortex is approximately 2322 cm^2 (2.5 ft^2), which explains why the surface must bend and fold to fit within the skull, producing the extensively convoluted surface. As much as two-thirds of the neocortex is not visible on the surface but is buried in the grooves. In contrast, the surface of the rat cerebral cortex is smooth and has no gyri or fissures (**FIGURE 2.27**). It is also clear from Figure 2.27 that the expanded surface area of the human cortex does not involve the primary sensory areas (pink, green, and orange), which are the first cortical areas to receive input from ascending sensory pathways, nor does it involve the primary motor cortex (blue). Instead, one can see enlargement of the secondary and tertiary association areas responsible for the complex sensory, perceptual, and cognitive functions (e.g., speech, abstract thinking) of which humans are capable.

FIGURE 2.27   Lateral view of the left hemisphere of human and rat brains Note that the expanded human cortex does not involve the primary sensory or motor cortex (colored areas). Human cortical expansion involves the secondary and tertiary association areas that are responsible for higher-order perception and cognition. (After M. F. Bear et al. 2007. *Neuroscience*, 3rd ed. Lippincott Williams & Wilkins: New York. © 2007 Lippincott Williams & Wilkins.)

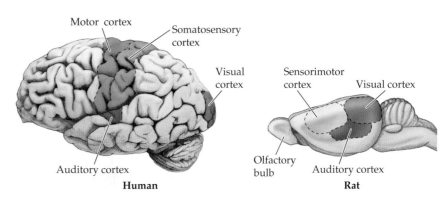

Motor cortex — Somatosensory cortex — Visual cortex — Auditory cortex

Human

Sensorimotor cortex — Visual cortex — Olfactory bulb — Auditory cortex

Rat

SECTION SUMMARY

- The central nervous system (CNS) includes the brain and the spinal cord. The remaining nerves of the body constitute the peripheral nervous system (PNS).

- The PNS is divided into the somatic nervous system, which includes spinal nerves that transmit sensory and motor information for skeletal muscles, and the autonomic nervous system (ANS), which serves smooth muscles, glands, and visceral organs.

- The ANS has two divisions: the sympathetic, which serves to mobilize energy for times of "fight or flight"; and the parasympathetic, which reduces energy usage and stores reserves.

- The CNS is protected by a bony covering, three layers of meninges (dura, arachnoid, and pia), and cerebrospinal fluid.

- Neurotrophic factors are neuronal growth factors that guide the development of neurons, regulate dendritic growth and retraction, and aid in survival of neurons.

- The CNS can be divided into six regions containing multiple nuclei and their associated axons, which form interconnecting neural circuits: spinal cord, myelencephalon, metencephalon, mesencephalon, diencephalon, and telencephalon.

- The gray matter of the spinal cord constitutes cell bodies that receive sensory information and cell bodies of motor neurons that serve muscles. The white matter consists of tracts of myelinated axons that carry signals in the ascending direction, to the brain, and the descending direction, for cortical control of the spinal cord.

- Continuous with the spinal cord is the myelencephalon, or medulla, which contains nuclei that serve vital functions for survival, such as respiration, heart rate, and vomiting.

- The metencephalon includes two major structures. The cerebellum functions to maintain posture and balance and provides fine motor control and coordination. The pons contains several nuclei that represent the origins of most of the tracts utilizing the neurotransmitters norepinephrine (the locus coeruleus) and serotonin (the raphe nuclei).

- Beginning in the medulla, running through the pons, and extending into the midbrain is the reticular formation—a network of interconnected nuclei that control arousal, attention, and survival functions.

- The mesencephalon, or midbrain, contains nuclei that control sensory reflexes such as pupillary constriction. Other nuclei (substantia nigra and ventral tegmental area) are the cell bodies of neurons that form three major dopaminergic tracts. The periaqueductal gray organizes behaviors such as defensive rage and predation and serves as an important pain-modulating center.

- The diencephalon contains the thalamus, which relays information to the cerebral cortex, and the hypothalamus, which is important for maintaining homeostasis of physiological functions and for modulating motivated behaviors. The nuclei of the hypothalamus control both the autonomic nervous system and the endocrine system.

- The telencephalon includes both the cerebral cortex and multiple subcortical structures, including the basal ganglia and the limbic system. The basal ganglia modulate movement.

- The limbic system is made up of several interconnected brain structures that modulate emotion, motivation, and learning. Prominent limbic structures include the amygdala, hippocampus, nucleus accumbens, and limbic cortex.

- The six-layered cerebral cortex is organized into four lobes: the occipital, temporal, and parietal, which are the sensory lobes involved in perception and memories, and the frontal, which regulates motor movements and gives rise to higher-order cognitive functions.

- Although there are differences in absolute and relative size, rat and human brains have the same major subdivisions, which are topographically organized in similar locations. Rat brains have relatively larger olfactory bulbs and midbrains. Human brains have expanded secondary and tertiary association areas of the cerebral cortex that serve higher-order sensory perception and cognitive functions.

STUDY QUESTIONS

1. What are embryonic stem cells? Describe several potential benefits from stem cell research.

2. Name the three major external features of neurons and their basic functions.

3. What is myelin and why is it important to neuron function?

4. Briefly describe the two stages of protein synthesis as well as epigenetic modification of gene expression.

5. Describe the role of the cytoskeleton in normal axoplasmic transport and its contribution to Alzheimer's disease.

6. Compare and contrast ligand-gated and voltage-gated ion channels.

7. Name the four types of glial cells and describe their basic functions.

8. What is the resting membrane potential, and how is it established and maintained? Be sure to include the equilibrium potential for potassium in your description

9. How are local potentials generated? Why is summation or integration so important to neuronal signaling?

10. What happens at the axon hillock to generate an action potential? Describe the movement of ions during an action potential. What is responsible for the absolute refractory period and the relative refractory period?

11. Why is saltatory conduction so much more rapid and energy efficient than conduction on non-myelinated axons?

12. Compare the characteristics of local potentials and action potentials.

13. Provide an example of a drug that interferes with action potential conduction and describe its mechanism of action.

14. Describe the somatic nervous system and its functions. Discuss the autonomic nervous system and compare the sympathetic and parasympathetic divisions.

15. Describe the four protective features of the CNS: skull, meninges, cerebrospinal fluid, and blood–brain barrier.

16. What are the principal functions of neurotrophic factors?

17. Describe the basic functions and cell groups in the spinal cord, medulla, pons, and cerebellum.

18. What are the important functions of the peri-aqueductal gray, substantia nigra, and ventral tegmental area? How do the latter two nuclei control dopamine function?

19. What is the role of the hypothalamus in survival? Be sure to describe autonomic nervous system regulation as well as control of both anterior and posterior pituitary. How does it help us cope with stress?

20. What is the limbic system? What roles do the hippocampus and amygdala play in behavior?

21. How is the cerebral cortex organized? What is the distinction between primary, secondary, and tertiary cortical regions?

22. What are the most significant differences between rat and human brains? What are the important similarities?

Chemical Signaling by Neurotransmitters and Hormones

3

IF YOU ARE READING THIS TEXTBOOK, you have probably taken one or more courses in psychology, biology, or neuroscience, in which you learned that the nerve cell (neuron) is the basic functional unit of the nervous system and that information is usually transmitted from one nerve cell to another by the release of a chemical substance called a **neurotransmitter**. Of course, these basic facts seem so obvious to us now, but they were not always obvious and had to be acquired over years of painstaking observation and experimentation, along with some good old-fashioned luck. Indeed, the discovery of chemical neurotransmission is marked by two great controversies involving some of the greatest pioneers in the relatively young history of neuroscience. The first controversy centered around two different views of nervous system structure: (1) the neuron doctrine, which proposed that the nervous system is composed of individual cells that are not physically connected and that information flow is unidirectional from one cell to another and (2) the reticulum theory, which proposed instead that the nervous system consists of a series of vast continuous networks, in which all network elements are physically interconnected, and information can flow in any direction among these elements.

The most distinguished proponents of these theories were two extraordinary late-19th-century histologists—a reserved and humble Spaniard named Santiago Ramón y Cajal (sometimes considered the "father" of modern neuroscience), who strongly favored the neuron doctrine, and an outspoken and arrogant Italian named Camillo Golgi (discoverer of the remarkable silver staining method that bears his name), who was a fierce advocate of the reticulum theory and a bitter rival of Cajal. Despite working with what we now consider primitive tools, sometimes in a makeshift kitchen laboratory and often in obscurity (particularly in the early stages of Cajal's career), the two scientists ultimately made such great contributions that they shared the 1906 Nobel Prize in Physiology or Medicine "in

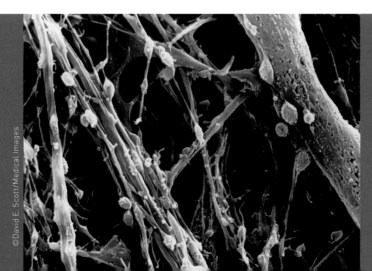

Scanning electron micrograph showing sites of axoaxonic and axodendritic synaptic contacts (in blue) within the hypothalamus.

recognition of their work on the structure of the nervous system."*

By 1906, the neuron doctrine controversy was already resolved in the minds of most researchers, with Golgi still a notable exception. Yet a second great controversy was starting to brew concerning the mechanism by which these separate nerve cells communicate with each other. Some researchers, particularly neurophysiologists like John Eccles, argued that communication between axon terminals and dendrites occurred by means of electrical currents that cross the gap between sending and receiving cells. In contrast, the work of various pharmacologists suggested that information might instead be transmitted by release of a chemical substance. Confirmation of chemical transmission was first obtained in the autonomic nervous system, which was much more amenable than the brain to this type of research. One of the defining studies was a brilliant experiment performed by the German pharmacologist Otto Loewi in 1920. Loewi stimulated the vagus (parasympathetic) nerve of a frog heart, causing slowing of the heartbeat. He then immediately transferred the fluid that had been bathing the first heart to a second heart, from which the vagus nerve had been removed. Remarkably, the second heart slowed down as well, proving that a chemical substance had been released into the fluid due to the vagal stimulation. Loewi and the British pharmacologist Henry Dale, who had been investigating both the autonomic and neuromuscular systems, were co-recipients of the 1936 Nobel Prize in Physiology or Medicine for their respective contributions to the discovery of chemical neurotransmission. Still, it wasn't until the 1960s and later that researchers generally accepted this process as the primary basis for intercellular communication in the brain, not just in the peripheral nervous system.**

This historical summary has introduced you to one of the body's great systems of cellular communication—the system of synaptic transmission. Throughout the rest of this chapter, you will learn more about synapses, neurotransmitters, and the mechanisms of neurotransmitter action. The final section is devoted to another important communication system, the endocrine system, which is responsible for the secretion of hormones into the bloodstream. ■

---

*https://www.nobelprize.org/nobel_prizes/medicine/laureates/1906/

**Students interested in learning more about these controversies and discoveries are referred to three excellent sources: *Nerve Endings: The Discovery of the Synapse*, by Richard Rapport, which recounts the stories of Cajal and Golgi; *The War of the Soups and the Sparks: The Discovery of Neurotransmitters and the Dispute Over How Nerves Communicate*, by Eliot Valenstein, which gives the history of the discovery of chemical neurotransmission; and Loewi's 1960 autobiographical sketch published in *Perspectives in Biology and Medicine*, in which he reminisces about his famous frog heart experiment and the nighttime dream that prompted it.

3.1 Chemical Signaling in the Nervous System

Basic concepts

The word **synapse** was coined in 1897 by the British physiologist Charles Sherrington. He derived the term from the Greek word *synapto*, which means "to clasp." Using only a light microscope, Sherrington could not see the actual point of communication between neurons, but physiological experiments had shown that transmission occurs in only one direction (from what we now call the **presynaptic cell** to the **postsynaptic cell**). The synapse was considered to be the specialized mechanism underlying this neuronal communication. Sherrington correctly inferred that sending (presynaptic) and receiving (postsynaptic) cells do not actually touch each other, as discussed above. Of course, the concept of chemical transmitter substances had barely been conceived, much less confirmed experimentally.

Our current knowledge of synaptic structure comes, in part, from the electron microscope. This and other modern imaging tools give us much greater magnification than the standard light microscope. The most common synapses in the brain are **axodendritic synapses**. In these synapses, an axon terminal from the presynaptic neuron communicates with a dendrite of the postsynaptic cell. An electron micrograph displaying this kind of synapse is shown in **FIGURE 3.1A** (see also **FIGURE 3.2A**). The dendrites of some neurons have short spines along their length, which are reminiscent of thorns growing out from a rosebush. **FIGURE 3.1B** shows a small segment of a dendrite from a **pyramidal neuron***** in the human cingulate cortex containing a high density of long-necked spines. This type of spiny dendrite is often found in human pyramidal neurons. When dendritic spines are present, they are important locations for synapses to form. You can see this directly in the electron micrograph shown in Figure 3.1A; although the staining method used for Figure 3.1B does not permit the visualization of presynaptic nerve terminals, we can be certain that synapses were present on those spines as well.

There is an exceedingly small (about 20 nm, which is 20×10^{-9} m) gap between presynaptic and postsynaptic cells that must be traversed by neurotransmitter molecules after their release. This gap is called the **synaptic cleft**. Although the use of the term "cleft" might seem to imply an empty space, in fact the synaptic cleft contains numerous proteins that help organize and maintain the structure of the synapse. On the postsynaptic side, the area of the dendritic membrane facing

---

***Pyramidal neurons are pyramid-shaped cells that function as the principal output neurons of the cerebral cortex.

(A)

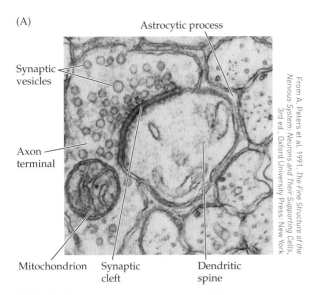

Astrocytic process

Synaptic vesicles

Axon terminal

Mitochondrion   Synaptic cleft   Dendritic spine

From A. Peters. et al. 1991. The Fine Structure of the Nervous System: Neurons and Their Supporting Cells, 3rd ed., Oxford University Press: New York

(B)

From R. Yuste. 2010. Dendritic Spines. MIT Press: Cambridge, MA

2 µm

FIGURE 3.1 **Structure of synapses** (A) An electron micrograph of an axodendritic synapse illustrating the major features of a typical connection between an axon terminal of the presynaptic cell and a dendritic spine of the postsynaptic cell. (B) Microscopic view of dendritic spines on a pyramidal neuron from human cerebral cortex. The dendrite and spines were visualized by means of a fluorescent dye and a confocal microscope.

the synaptic cleft appears dark and somewhat fuzzy looking. This structure, called the **postsynaptic density**, is rich in neurotransmitter receptors along with other proteins that help anchor the receptors in place. In the axon terminal, we can see many small saclike objects, termed **synaptic vesicles**, each of which is filled with several thousand molecules of a neurotransmitter. As discussed later, these vesicles are the main source of transmitter release.

Figure 3.1A shows additional features of a typical synapse, including the profile of a mitochondrion in the axon terminal. Mitochondria are the cellular organelles responsible for energy (adenosine triphosphate, or ATP) production. They are needed in large quantities in the terminals for various functions such as ion pumping and transmitter release. Finally, we see that the synapse is surrounded by processes (fibers) from astrocytes. In Chapter 8, we'll discuss an important role for these glial cells in regulating transmission by amino acid transmitters.

Other types of synapses are also present in the brain. For example, **axosomatic synapses** are synapses between a nerve terminal and a nerve cell body (**FIGURE 3.2B**). They function in a manner similar to axodendritic synapses. **Axoaxonic synapses** involve one axon synapsing on the terminal of another axon (**FIGURE 3.2C**). This unusual arrangement permits the presynaptic cell to alter neurotransmitter release from the postsynaptic cell directly at the terminals. For example, activity at

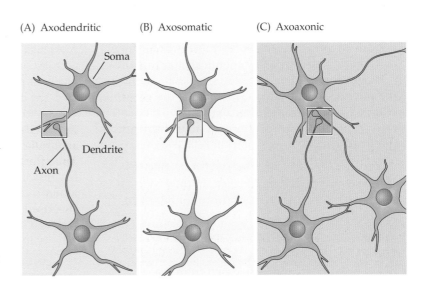

(A) Axodendritic   (B) Axosomatic   (C) Axoaxonic

Soma

Dendrite

Axon

FIGURE 3.2 The three types of synaptic connections between neurons

an axoaxonic synapse may reduce transmitter release from the terminal. This is called **presynaptic inhibition** of release. Enhanced release of transmitter, on the other hand, is called **presynaptic facilitation**.

In neuronal communication, the receiving cell may be another neuron, or it may be a muscle cell or a cell specialized to release a hormone or other secretory product. The connection point between a neuron and a muscle is called a **neuromuscular junction** instead of a synapse. A neuromuscular junction has many structural and functional similarities to a conventional synapse, and much has been learned about synaptic transmission by studying neuromuscular junctions.

Before concluding this section, we need to mention that the proponents of electrical transmission in the nervous system, as discussed in the chapter opener, were not entirely wrong. **Electrical synapses** occur in many parts of the brain. In this kind of synapse, two adjacent neurons are connected by means of specialized proteins that permit the flow of electric current from one cell to the other (Connors and Long, 2004). Consequently, if one of the cells fires an action potential, the connected cell is also stimulated. Researchers have additionally discovered **mixed synapses** at which both chemical transmission and electrical transmission occur between neurons (Pereda, 2014). Despite the existence of electrical synapses, we will focus on chemical transmission because psychoactive drugs almost always act on that type of neuronal communication.

Neurotransmitter synthesis, release, and inactivation

The nervous system of any organism contains thousands of different chemical substances, which raises the important question of how neuroscientists determine which of these substances might function in a neurotransmitter capacity. Over time, criteria have been proposed by which this determination can be made.

Several criteria must be met for a chemical substance to be considered a neurotransmitter. Scientists first thought that only a few chemicals were involved in neurotransmission, but well over 100 chemicals have now been identified. This makes the determination of a neurotransmitter extremely important. Verifying a chemical's status as a neurotransmitter can be a difficult process, but here are some of the important criteria:

- The presynaptic cell should contain the proposed substance along with a mechanism for manufacturing it.
- A mechanism for inactivating the substance should also be present.
- The substance should be released from the axon terminal upon stimulation of the neuron.

- Receptors for the proposed substance should be present on the postsynaptic cell. (Receptors are discussed in greater detail later in the chapter.)
- Direct application of the proposed substance or of an agonist drug that acts on its receptors should have the same effect on the postsynaptic cell as stimulating the presynaptic neuron (which presumably would release the substance from the axon terminals).
- Applying an antagonist drug that blocks the receptors should inhibit both the action of the applied substance and the effect of stimulating the presynaptic neuron.

Note that researchers do not require that all of these criteria be met for a substance to be considered a neurotransmitter. We can argue that the most important criteria are that the substance is synthesized in a group of nerve cells, that the substance can be released by those cells, and that receptors for the substance have also been identified and have been shown to mediate a response by the receiving (postsynaptic) cells.

Neurotransmitters encompass several different kinds of chemical substances

Despite the great numbers of neurotransmitters, most of them conveniently fall into several chemical classes. The major types of transmitters and examples of each are shown in **TABLE 3.1**. A few neurotransmitters are categorized as **amino acids**.* Amino acids serve numerous functions: they are the individual building blocks of proteins, and they play other metabolic roles besides their role as neurotransmitters. In Chapter 8, we'll cover the two most important amino acid neurotransmitters, glutamate and γ-aminobutyric acid (GABA). Several other transmitters are **monoamines**, which are grouped together because each possesses a single (hence "mono") amine group. Monoamine transmitters are derived from amino acids through a series of biochemical reactions that include removal of the acidic part (–COOH) of the molecule. Consequently, we say that the original amino acid is a **precursor** because it precedes the amine in the biochemical pathway. In Chapters 5 and 6, we will discuss the best-characterized monoamine transmitters: dopamine (DA), norepinephrine (NE), and serotonin (5-HT). One important neurotransmitter that is neither an amino acid nor a monoamine is acetylcholine (ACh). This transmitter, which is covered in Chapter 7, serves key functions at the neuromuscular junction, in the autonomic nervous system, and in the brain. You may be surprised to learn that the purine-containing molecules ATP and its precursor adenosine have neurotransmitter activity in addition to their roles in energy metabolism.

---

*Amino acids are so named because they contain both an amino group (–NH$_2$) and a carboxyl group (–COOH), the latter of which releases a hydrogen ion (H$^+$) and thus acts as an acid.

TABLE 3.1 Major Categories of Neurotransmitters

Classical neurotransmitters	Nonclassical neurotransmitters

Amino acids
  Glutamate
  γ-aminobutyric acid (GABA)
  Glycine
Monoamines
  Dopamine (DA)
  Norepinephrine (NE)
  Serotonin (5-HT)
  Histamine (HA)
Acetylcholine (ACh)
Purines
  Adenosine triphosphate (ATP)
  Adenosine
	Neuropeptides
	  Endorphins and enkephalins
	  Corticotropin-releasing factor (CRF or CRH)
	  Orexin
	  Brain-derived neurotrophic factor (BDNF)
	  Vasopressin
	  Oxytocin
	  Many others
	Lipids
	  Anandamide
	  2-Arachidonoylglycerol
	Gases
	  Nitric oxide (NO)
	  Carbon monoxide (CO)
	  Hydrogen sulfide (H_2S)

Note: This is only a small sample of more than 100 substances known or suspected to be neurotransmitters in the brain and/or peripheral nervous system.

Like ACh, ATP is a transmitter both in the brain and in the autonomic nervous system (Kennedy, 2015; Burnstock, 2020), where it helps regulate cardiovascular (Burnstock, 2017), gastrointestinal (Burnstock, 2016), and bladder (Takezawa et al., 2017) function. Adenosine signaling is discussed in Chapter 13 in conjunction with caffeine, a substance that blocks certain adenosine receptors. Acetylcholine, the amino acid and monoamine neurotransmitters, and to a lesser extent the purine neurotransmitters are sometimes called "classical" transmitters because they were generally discovered before the other categories and they follow certain principles of transmission that are discussed later in the chapter.

Besides the classical transmitters, there are several other types of neurotransmitters. The largest group of "nonclassical" neurotransmitters are the **neuropeptides**, whose name simply means "peptides found in the nervous system." Peptides are small proteins, typically made up of three to 40 amino acids instead of the 100-plus amino acids found in most proteins. Neuropharmacologists are very interested in the family of neuropeptides called *endorphins* and *enkephalins*, which stimulate the same opioid receptors that are activated by heroin and other abused opioid drugs (see Chapter 11). Other neuropeptides relevant to neuropsychiatric illness and drug treatment include the following:

- Corticotropin-releasing factor (CRF), which plays a role in anxiety, depression, and drug addiction (see Chapters 9, 17, and 18)
- Brain-derived neurotrophic factor (BDNF), which has also been implicated in depression (see Chapter 18)
- Orexin (sometimes also called hypocretin), which plays major roles in feeding behavior and energy

homeostasis (Arrigoni et al., 2019; Milbank and López, 2019), reward-seeking behaviors and addiction (Haghparast et al., 2017; Hopf, 2020), and arousal and sleep (Tyree et al., 2018; Arrigoni et al., 2019). Indeed, the sleep disorder **narcolepsy** has been linked to dysfunction of the orexin system located in the lateral hypothalamus (Bassetti et al., 2019; Mahoney et al., 2019). **WEB BOX 3.1** presents more information about the relationship between orexin and narcolepsy.

Two other closely related neuropeptides, vasopressin and oxytocin, function both as hormones (secreted from the pituitary gland into the bloodstream) and as neurotransmitters (released from nerve endings in many areas of the brain). Because of these dual roles, we will be discussing vasopressin and oxytocin in greater detail later in the book when we take up the organization and functioning of the endocrine system.

A few other neurotransmitters are classified either as **lipids** or **gases**. The word "lipid" is the scientific term for a fatty substance. For example, in Chapter 14, we discuss two lipid transmitters that act on the brain like marijuana (or, more specifically, Δ^9-tetrahydrocannabinol [THC], which is the major active ingredient in marijuana). The most recently discovered and intriguing group of neurotransmitters are the **gaseous transmitters** (sometimes shortened to **gasotransmitters**; Wang, 2014; Hendriks et al., 2019), which include nitric oxide (Garthwaite, 2016; Picón-Pagès et al., 2019), carbon monoxide (Levitt and Levitt, 2015), and hydrogen sulfide (Paul and Snyder, 2018). Later in this chapter, we will further discuss the lipid and gaseous transmitters and see that they break some of the rules followed by classical transmitter molecules.

When scientists discovered the existence of neurotransmitters, it was natural to assume that each neuron made and released only one transmitter substance,* suggesting a simple chemical coding of cells in the nervous system. However, much research over the past several decades has shattered that initial assumption. We now know that many neurons make and release two, three, and occasionally even more different transmitters. In some cases, multiple small-molecule neurotransmitters are released from the same neuron. In Chapter 8 we will touch on an unusual example of cells that co-release the excitatory transmitter glutamate and the inhibitory transmitter GABA at the same synapses. Other instances of transmitter coexistence within the same cell involve one or more neuropeptides, along with a classical transmitter (Cropper et al., 2018; Hökfelt et al., 2018). In such cases, the neuron has two different types of synaptic vesicles: small vesicles, which contain only the classical transmitter, and large vesicles, which contain the neuropeptide along with the classical transmitter (**FIGURE 3.3**).

---

*This notion has sometimes been called "Dale's law," although what Henry Dale actually proposed is subtly different: that if one branch of a cell's axon were found to release a particular chemical substance when stimulated, then all axonal branches of that cell would also release that substance (notice that this statement does not preclude the cell from releasing multiple substances from its various branches).

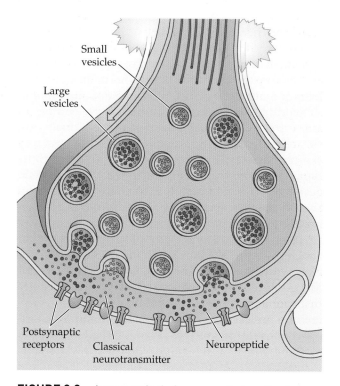

FIGURE 3.3 Axon terminal of a neuron that synthesizes both a classical neurotransmitter and a neuropeptide   The small vesicles contain only the classical transmitter, whereas the large vesicles contain the neuropeptide and the classical neurotransmitter, which are stored and released together.

Neuropeptides are synthesized by a different mechanism than other transmitters

How and where in the nerve cell are neurotransmitters manufactured? Except for the neuropeptides, transmitters are synthesized by enzymatic reactions that can occur anywhere in the cell. Typically, the enzymes required for producing a neurotransmitter are shipped out in large quantities to the axon terminals, so the terminals are an important site of transmitter synthesis. The neuropeptides are different, however. Their precursors are protein molecules, within which the peptides are embedded. The protein precursor for each type of peptide must be made in the cell body, which is the site of most protein synthesis in the neuron. The protein is then packaged into large vesicles, along with enzymes that will break down the precursor and liberate the neuropeptide (**FIGURE 3.4**). These vesicles are transported to the axon terminals, so release occurs from the terminals, as with the classical transmitters. On the other hand, new neuropeptide molecules can be generated only in the cell body, not in the terminals. An important consequence of this difference is that replenishment of neuropeptides is slower than for small-molecule transmitters. When neurotransmitters are depleted by high levels of neuronal activity, small molecules can be resynthesized rapidly within the axon terminal. In contrast, neuropeptides cannot be replenished until large vesicles containing the peptide have been transported to the terminal from their site of origin within the cell body.

Neuromodulators are chemicals that do not act like typical neurotransmitters

Some investigators use the term **neuromodulators** to describe substances that do not act exactly like typical neurotransmitters. For example, a neuromodulator might not have a direct effect itself on the postsynaptic cell. Instead, it might alter the action of a standard neurotransmitter by enhancing, reducing, or prolonging the transmitter's effectiveness. Such effects may be seen when monoamine transmitters such as DA, NE, or 5-HT modulate the excitatory influence of another transmitter (e.g., glutamate) on the postsynaptic cell. Peptides that are co-released with a classical transmitter may also function as neuromodulators. Yet another common property of neuromodulators is diffusion away from the site of release to influence cells more distant from the releasing cell than is the case at a standard synapse. This phenomenon has been termed **volume transmission** to distinguish it from the tight cell-to-cell synaptic interactions that constitute **wiring transmission** (Fuxe et al., 2013; Fuxe and Borroto-Escuela, 2016). No matter which criteria you use, though, the dividing line between neurotransmitters and neuromodulators is vague. For example, a particular chemical like serotonin may sometimes act

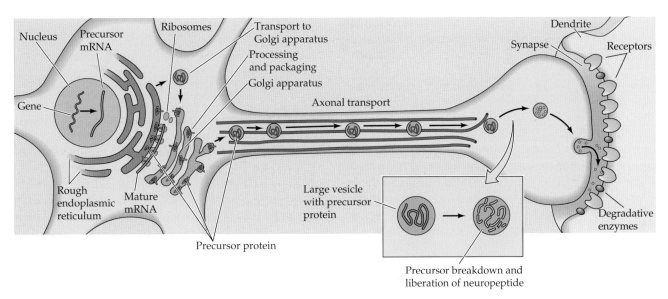

FIGURE 3.4 **Features of neurotransmission using neuro-peptides** Neuropeptides are synthesized from larger precursor proteins, which are packaged into large vesicles by the Golgi apparatus. During transport from the cell body to the axon terminal, enzymes that have been packaged within the vesicles break down the precursor protein to liberate the neuropeptide. After it is released at the synapse and stimulates postsynaptic receptors, the neuropeptide is inactivated by degradative enzymes.

within the synapse, but in other circumstances, it may act at a distance from its site of release. Therefore, we will refrain from talking about neuromodulators and instead will use the term *neurotransmitter* throughout the remainder of the book.

Classical transmitter release involves exocytosis and recycling of synaptic vesicles

As shown in **FIGURE 3.5**, synaptic transmission involves a number of processes that occur within the axon terminal and the postsynaptic cell. We will begin our discussion of these processes with a consideration of neurotransmitter release from the terminal. When a neuron fires an action potential, the depolarizing current sweeps down the length of the axon and enters all of the axon terminals. This wave of depolarization has a very important effect within the terminals: it opens voltage-sensitive calcium (Ca^{2+}) channels in the membrane, causing a rapid influx of Ca^{2+} ions into the terminals. The resulting increase in Ca^{2+} concentration within the terminals is the direct trigger for neurotransmitter release. One of the many features of synaptic complexity is that synapses in different parts of the brain express Ca^{2+} channels with different properties. A consequence of this diversity is that for some synapses, opening of a vesicle that's ready for release only requires activation of a single Ca^{2+} channel, whereas in other synapses vesicle opening may require activation of three of more channels (Dolphin and Lee, 2020).

EXOCYTOSIS You already know that for most neurotransmitters, the transmitter molecules destined to

be released are stored within synaptic vesicles, yet these molecules must somehow make their way past the membrane of the axon terminal and into the synaptic cleft. This occurs through a remarkable process known as **exocytosis**. Exocytosis is a fusion of the vesicle membrane with the membrane of the axon terminal, which exposes the inside of the vesicle to the outside of the cell. In this way, the vesicle is opened, and its transmitter molecules are allowed to diffuse into the synaptic cleft. If you look back at the synapse shown in Figure 3.1A, you can see that some vesicles are very close to the terminal membrane, whereas others are farther away. In fact, transmitter release occurs not just anywhere along the terminal, but only at specialized regions near the postsynaptic cell, which stain darkly on the electron micrograph. These release sites are called **active zones**. Only the vesicles located at an active zone are capable of immediate neurotransmitter release. These constitute the **readily releasable pool** of vesicles, whereas the remainder that are located farther away within the nerve terminal make up a **reserve pool** that can be called upon for release when the neuron is firing for a prolonged period of time.

For a vesicle to become part of the readily releasable pool, it must be transported to an active zone by a mechanism that is not yet fully understood. There, the vesicle "docks" at the active zone, much like a boat docking at a pier. This docking step is carried out by a cluster of proteins—some located in the vesicle membrane and others residing in the membrane of the axon terminal. Docking is followed by a step called priming, which readies the vesicle for exocytosis once it receives

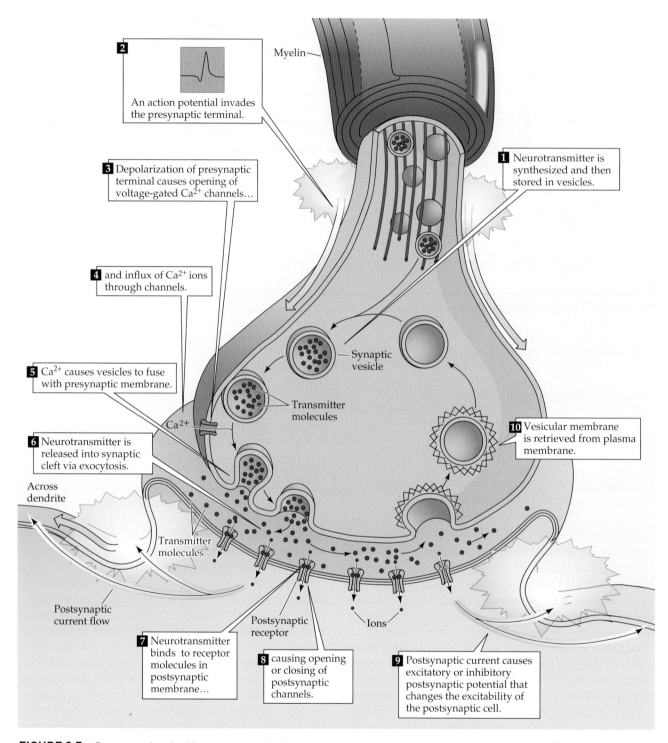

FIGURE 3.5 Processes involved in neurotransmission at a typical synapse using a classical neurotransmitter

the Ca^{2+} signal. Indeed, Ca^{2+} channels that open in response to membrane depolarization are concentrated in active zones near the sites of vesicle docking, so the protein machinery is exposed to particularly high concentrations of Ca^{2+} when the channels open. A Ca^{2+}-sensitive protein in the synaptic vesicle membrane called **synaptotagmin-1** rapidly responds to this Ca^{2+} influx by

permitting the vesicle and terminal membranes to fuse (Park and Ryu, 2018). This process allows the vesicle to open and the transmitter to be released (**FIGURE 3.6**).

In addition to the vesicle membrane proteins required for exocytosis, other proteins are required for other processes: some are required for pumping neurotransmitter molecules from the cytoplasm of the nerve terminal into

FIGURE 3.6 **The life cycle of the synaptic vesicle** Small vesicles containing classical neurotransmitters are constantly being recycled in the axon terminal. Vesicles are filled with neurotransmitter molecules, after which they are transported to the vicinity of release sites in the terminal and undergo processes of docking and priming. Ca^{2+}-dependent fusion with the axon terminal membrane, called exocytosis, permits release of the contents of the vesicle into the synaptic cleft. The vesicle membrane is retrieved by a process of invagination (budding) from the terminal membrane, endocytosis, and transmitter refilling, thus completing the cycle.

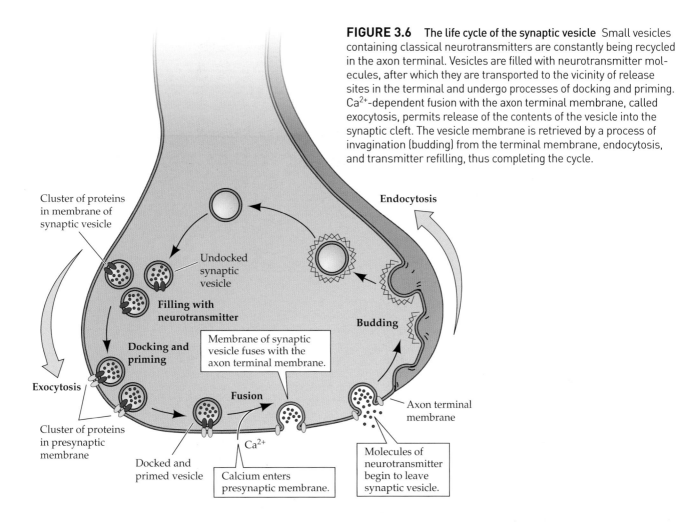

the interior of the vesicle, whereas others are required for vesicle recycling, discussed in the next section. **FIGURE 3.7** shows a cutaway model of a typical synaptic vesicle that highlights the variety of proteins present in the vesicle membrane. One of these is **synaptobrevin**, another protein besides synaptotagmin-1 that plays a key role in helping the vesicle fuse with the axon terminal membrane to cause exocytosis. A detailed discussion of these proteins is beyond the scope of this book, but it is nevertheless important to note that some of them are targets for various drugs or naturally occurring toxins. For example, botulism poisoning results from a bacterial toxin (botulinum toxin) that blocks transmitter release at neuromuscular junctions, thus causing paralysis. Researchers have found that this blockade of release is due to enzymes within the toxin that attack some of the proteins required for the exocytosis process. This topic is covered in greater detail in Chapter 7, where we will also see how botulinum toxin has come to be used therapeutically in a wide range of neuromuscular disorders. Various studies have also shown that either acute or chronic exposure to ethanol can affect neurotransmitter release by acting on presynaptic proteins involved in the exocytosis process

(Lovinger, 2018). Indeed, these actions may contribute to both the intoxicating effects of ethanol and the development of ethanol dependence (i.e., alcoholism).

VESICLE RECYCLING When a synaptic vesicle fuses with the axon terminal to release its transmitter contents, the vesicle membrane is temporarily added to the membrane of the terminal. Using glutamate synapses as a model system, Lou (2018) estimated that fusion of a single synaptic vesicle increases the surface area of the active zone by approximately 16%. This may not seem like much, but if the exocytotic process was not reversed, the terminal membrane would keep growing larger and larger as more vesicle membrane was added to it. In fact, we know that synaptic vesicles undergo a process of **vesicle recycling** that serves several key functions: (1) preventing an accumulation of vesicle membrane within the membrane of the nerve terminal, (2) recovering components of the vesicle membrane (especially vesicle proteins) for reuse, and (3) preventing depletion of synaptic vesicles, especially when the neuron is firing rapidly and many vesicles are releasing their contents into the synaptic cleft.

(A)

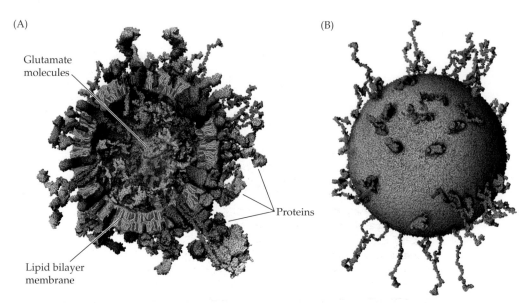

Glutamate molecules

Proteins

Lipid bilayer membrane

(B)

FIGURE 3.7 **Molecular model of a glutamate synaptic vesicle** This model depicts a synaptic vesicle used to store and release the neurotransmitter glutamate from nerve terminals. The model can be considered representative of all classical transmitter vesicles. (A) A cutaway view of the vesicle shows the lipid bilayer membrane in yellow along with many different proteins (drawn with different shapes and colors) inserted into or passing completely through the vesicle membrane. The small particles in the interior of the vesicle depict molecules of glutamate, several thousand of which are packed tightly within that space. (B) A simplified view of the exterior of the vesicle only shows a protein called synaptobrevin. This protein is the most abundant one found in synaptic vesicles. It helps vesicles to fuse with the axon terminal membrane during exocytosis. (From S. Takamori et al. 2006. *Cell* 127: 831–846. Reprinted with permission from Elsevier.)

Research into the details and mechanisms of vesicle recycling has led to much controversy over the years because of conflicting experimental findings. Fortunately, it seems that a consensus is finally developing based on the idea that several different recycling mechanisms can occur, depending on the type of synapse and the rate of cell firing (Chanaday and Kavalali, 2017; Gan and Watanabe, 2018; Lou, 2018). Three of the currently proposed models are depicted in **FIGURE 3.8**. The first two models, shown in Figure 3.8A and B, involve a full fusion of the vesicle membrane with the nerve terminal followed (after neurotransmitter release) by a flattening of the vesicle membrane. The semicircular figures illustrate a vesicle in the process of flattening. The model shown in Figure 3.8A is the most widely accepted model of vesicle recycling and is the one depicted previously in Figures 3.5 and 3.6. In this model, a protein called **clathrin** forms a coating on the membrane that is needed for membrane invagination and vesicle retrieval. For this reason, the mechanism is called **clathrin-mediated endocytosis**. Note that in this model, endocytosis is a relatively slow process that occurs in an area of the nerve terminal away from the release site. This slow time scale is a challenge for neurons during periods of rapid firing and potential vesicle depletion. Another challenge is that of identifying the vesicle membrane proteins so that they can be selectively retrieved during endocytosis and used to reconstitute new vesicles.

Figure 3.8B illustrates a more recently proposed model called **ultrafast endocytosis** in which vesicle retrieval occurs extremely quickly in an area close to the release site. The retrieved vesicles are thought to join with intracellular organelles called **endosomes** (membranous compartments inside the nerve terminal), after which the recycling process is completed when new synaptic vesicles bud off from the endosomes using a clathrin-dependent mechanism. The third model, which is still somewhat controversial, is called **kiss-and-run** (Figure 3.8C). This model proposes that the vesicle fuses with the nerve terminal membrane merely for an extremely brief period of time to allow the neurotransmitter molecules to escape from the vesicle interior. The temporary pore formed during fusion then closes, and the original vesicle remains intact for refilling with neurotransmitter molecules and subsequent participation in synaptic transmission. Clathrin protein is not required for any of the steps involved in the kiss-and-run mechanism. Watanabe (2015) likens kiss-and-run versus the two endocytosis models to the recycling of glass bottles: kiss-and-run would be like refilling the same bottle, whereas recycling via endocytosis would be like combining each bottle with many others at a recycling plant before remolding a new bottle from the mixture.

Two additional points need to be added about vesicle recycling. First, the three mechanisms just described occur under typical conditions of low to moderate neuronal activity. However, when neurons are stimulated

(A) Clathrin-mediated endocytosis

(B) Ultrafast endocytosis and and endosomal budding

(C) Kiss-and-run

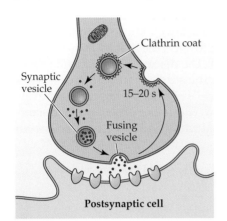
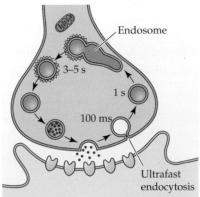
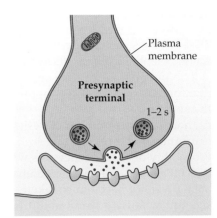

FIGURE 3.8 Models of synaptic vesicle recycling (A) In the well-established clathrin-mediated endocytosis model, the vesicle fully collapses after fusing with the plasma membrane. The vesicle membrane is subsequently retrieved at a point distant from the release site, using a process that requires the protein clathrin. (B) In the more recently proposed model called ultrafast endocytosis and endosomal budding, the vesicle membrane is retrieved extremely rapidly at a point near the release site. Clathrin is not required for membrane retrieval according to this model. The vesicle membrane fuses with an endosome, after which new vesicles bud off from the endosome in a clathrin-dependent mechanism. (C) In the kiss-and-run model, the vesicle membrane briefly fuses with the plasma membrane of the nerve terminal without collapsing. After the vesicle has released its contents into the synaptic cleft, it reforms and detaches from the plasma membrane. Neither clathrin nor endosomes play a role in this model. (After S. Watanabe. 2015. *Science* 350: 46–47. Reprinted with permission from AAAS.)

very strongly, yet another mechanism, **bulk endocytosis**, is used to retrieve the large amounts of vesicle membrane that have fused with the nerve terminal membrane. This process, which is not shown, has a mixture of properties shared with the other mechanisms. Like clathrin-mediated endocytosis, bulk endocytosis is slow and takes place at a distance from the release site. But like ultrafast endocytosis, bulk endocytosis makes use of endosomes and only requires clathrin for budding of new vesicles off of the endosome. The second point is that these recycling mechanisms only occur with the small vesicles containing classical transmitters, not with the larger neuropeptide-containing vesicles. You will recall that neuropeptide precursor proteins must be packaged into the large vesicles in the cell body; therefore, recycling of such vesicles cannot occur at the axon terminal.

DIVERSITY OF NERVE TERMINAL CHARACTERISTICS

The photomicrograph shown in Figure 3.1A is only one example of a synapse and, therefore, cannot provide a sense of the diversity of synapses within the central and peripheral nervous systems. Such diversity brings with it a number of interesting questions about neurotransmitter release at a particular type of synapse; for example:

- How many vesicles does a nerve terminal contain?
- How many of these are in the readily releasable pool?
- How many active zones available for vesicle fusion are present in the terminal membrane?

Researchers have discovered a wide range of nerve terminal characteristics that together have an enormous influence on the number of exocytotic events and the amount of neurotransmitter release that occurs when an action potential invades the terminal (Gan and Watanabe, 2018).

The frog neuromuscular junction represents a model system at the high end of the spectrum. This should not surprise us, because when the frog needs to contract a muscle (for example, when extending its tongue to catch an insect or using its legs to jump away from a predator), there must be a lot of neurotransmitter release to ensure an immediate and powerful response by the muscle being called to action (because ACh is the transmitter used at vertebrate neuromuscular junctions, we will discuss this topic in greater detail in Chapter 7). Thus, each frog neuromuscular nerve terminal contains roughly 200,000 to 500,000 synaptic vesicles, of which over 4000 are docked and presumably belong to the readily releasable pool. The terminal membrane contains 50 to 250 active zones, with 30 to 40 vesicles docked at each active zone.

Rodent (rat or mouse) hippocampal synapses represent a model system at the other end of the spectrum. Most of the nerve terminals at these synapses are quite small compared to those at the neuromuscular junction; thus, only a small amount of neurotransmitter (glutamate in this case; see Chapter 8) can be released at each synapse when the neuron fires. Each nerve terminal usually contains about 270 vesicles, although the terminals at a particular type of hippocampal synapse may contain over 1000 vesicles. In the terminals with the smaller number of vesicles, about 10 are in the readily releasable pool. Moreover, the release probability at these synapses is much less than 1, meaning that a single action potential often results in no vesicle fusion at all!

The purpose of this discussion is to emphasize that there is no universally applicable description of the synapse. As we have seen, synapses vary widely in their size, the number of vesicles participating in neurotransmitter release, and even the probability of vesicle exocytosis when the cell generates an action potential. Such diversity needs to be taken into account when we think about how neural circuits with different synaptic properties respond to environmental stimuli, drugs, or other kinds of challenges.

Lipid and gaseous transmitters are not released from synaptic vesicles

We mentioned earlier that lipid and gaseous transmitters break some of the normal rules of neurotransmission. One of the reasons is that these substances readily pass through membranes. Consequently, these substances cannot be stored in synaptic vesicles like classical and peptide transmitters, so nerve cells must make these substances "on demand" when needed. Moreover, as lipid and gaseous transmitters are not present in vesicles, they are not released by exocytosis but simply diffuse out of the nerve cell through the cell membrane. Once the transmitter molecules reach the extracellular fluid, they may not be confined to the synapse but may travel far enough to reach other cells in the vicinity of the release point. This is particularly true for the gaseous transmitters. Finally, lipid and gaseous transmitters typically are released by the postsynaptic rather than the presynaptic cell in the synapse. Molecules such as these that signal information from the postsynaptic to the presynaptic cell are called **retrograde messengers** (Suvarna et al., 2016). In Chapter 14 we describe an example of retrograde signaling by endogenous cannabinoids. **FIGURE 3.9** illustrates how signaling by gaseous and lipid transmitters differs from classical neurotransmitter signaling.

As with many different neurotransmitters, lipids and gases have signaling functions outside of the central nervous system (CNS). A well-known example of this pertains to nitric oxide (NO), the first gaseous transmitter to be discovered. The discovery of NO came about unexpectedly from the study of smooth muscle cells that surround the walls of arteries, regulating the rate of arterial blood flow. A number of chemical substances, including the neurotransmitter ACh, were known

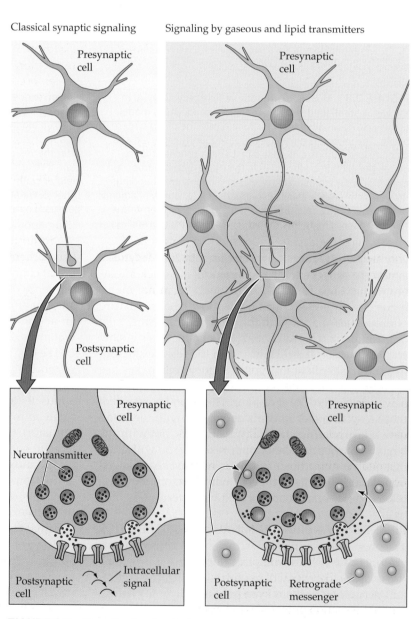

FIGURE 3.9   Signaling by classical versus gaseous and lipid transmitters In contrast to signaling by classical neurotransmitters (left), gaseous and lipid transmitters (right) are not released from synaptic vesicles. Gases and lipids cannot be stored within vesicles and therefore must be synthesized enzymatically when needed. Synthesis of gaseous and lipid transmitters usually occurs in the postsynaptic cell following release of a classical transmitter from the presynaptic cell and postsynaptic receptor activation. The newly formed gas or lipid subsequently diffuses across the membrane and acts as a retrograde messenger on the presynaptic cell as well as other neurons close enough to receive the signal.

to relax these smooth muscle cells, thus causing vaso-dilation (widening of the blood vessels) and increased blood flow. However, the mechanism by which this occurred was unclear until the early 1980s, when researchers showed that endothelial cells were necessary for the relaxant effects of ACh on the muscle. In addition, they showed that ACh stimulated the endothelial cells to produce a chemical factor that traveled to nearby muscle cells and caused them to relax. This chemical factor was subsequently shown to be NO. The discovery of NO and of its role in regulating cardiovascular function was recognized by the awarding of the 1998 Nobel Prize in Physiology or Medicine to the three key pioneers in these discoveries: Robert Furchgott, Louis Ignarro, and Ferid Murad.

Several mechanisms control the rate of neurotransmitter release by nerve cells

Neurotransmitter release is regulated by several different mechanisms. The most obvious is the rate of cell firing. When a neuron is rapidly firing action potentials, it will release much more transmitter than when it is firing at a slow rate. A second factor is the probability of transmitter release from the terminal. It might seem odd that an action potential could enter a terminal and open Ca^{2+} channels without releasing any transmitter. Yet many studies have shown that synapses in different parts of the brain vary widely in the probability that even a single vesicle will undergo exocytosis in response to an action potential. Estimated probabilities range from less than 0.1 (10%) to 0.9 (90%) or greater for different populations of synapses (Branco and Staras, 2009). This discovery raises the obvious question of why a population of synapses should ever have a low release probability. Although the full answer must be complicated, one reasonable hypothesis is that synaptic populations that have evolved with low release probabilities are located within neural circuits where transmission at those specific synapses is not appropriate *unless* the presynaptic cells are firing at a high rate (which would significantly increase the likelihood of neurotransmitter release even if the release probability for a single action potential was low). Circuits of this kind could, for example, play a role in learning and the formation of new memories.

A third factor in the rate of transmitter release is the presence of **autoreceptors** on axon terminals or cell bodies and dendrites (**FIGURE 3.10**). An autoreceptor on a particular neuron is a receptor for the same neurotransmitter released by that neuron (*auto* in this case means "self"). Neurons may possess two different types of autoreceptors: **terminal autoreceptors** and **somatodendritic autoreceptors**. Terminal autoreceptors are so named because they are located on axon terminals. When they are activated by the neurotransmitter, their main function is to inhibit further transmitter release. This function is particularly important when the cell is firing rapidly and high levels of neurotransmitter are present in the synaptic cleft. Think of the thermostat ("autoreceptor") in your house, which shuts off the furnace ("release mechanism") when the level of heat ("neurotransmitter") gets too high. Somatodendritic autoreceptors are also descriptively named, in that they are autoreceptors found on the cell body (soma) or on dendrites. When these autoreceptors are activated, they slow the rate of cell firing, which ultimately causes less neurotransmitter release because fewer action potentials reach the axon terminals to stimulate exocytosis.

Researchers can use drugs to stimulate or block specific autoreceptors, thereby influencing the release of a particular neurotransmitter for experimental purposes. For example, administration of a low dose of the drug apomorphine to rats or mice selectively activates the terminal autoreceptors for DA. This causes lessened DA release, an overall reduction in dopaminergic

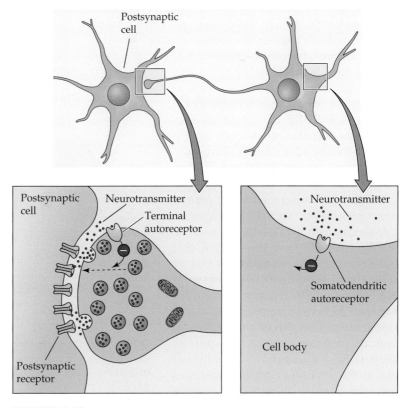

FIGURE 3.10 **Terminal and somatodendritic autoreceptors** Many neurons possess autoreceptors on their axon terminals and/or on their cell bodies and dendrites. Terminal autoreceptors inhibit neurotransmitter release, whereas somatodendritic autoreceptors reduce the rate of cell firing.

transmission, and reduced locomotor activity among animals. A different drug, whose name is abbreviated 8-OH-DPAT, activates the somatodendritic autoreceptors for 5-HT and powerfully inhibits the firing of serotonergic neurons. The behavioral effects of administration of 8-OH-DPAT include increased appetite and altered responses on several tasks used to assess anxiety.

Finally, you will recall from our earlier discussion that in addition to autoreceptors, axon terminals may have receptors for other transmitters released at axoaxonic synapses. Such receptors have come to be known as **heteroreceptors** to distinguish them from autoreceptors. Heteroreceptors also differ from autoreceptors in that they may either enhance or reduce the amount of transmitter being released from the axon terminal. Although heteroreceptors have not been studied as extensively as autoreceptors, many examples of heteroreceptors have been discovered that are capable of playing a significant role in the local regulation of neurotransmitter release (Langer, 2015).

Mechanisms of neurotransmitter inactivation

Any mechanical or biological process that can be turned on must have a mechanism for termination (imagine the problem you would have with a car in which the ignition could not be turned off once the car had been started). Thus, it is necessary to terminate the synaptic signal produced by each instance of transmitter release, so the postsynaptic cell is free to respond to the next release. This termination is accomplished by removing neurotransmitter molecules from the synaptic cleft. How is this done?

Several different processes responsible for neurotransmitter removal are shown in **FIGURE 3.11**. One mechanism is enzymatic breakdown within or near the synaptic cleft. This mechanism is very important for the classical neurotransmitter ACh, for the lipid and gaseous transmitters, and also for the neuropeptide transmitters. An alternative mechanism involves removal of the neurotransmitter from the synaptic cleft by a transport process that makes use of specialized proteins called **transporters** located on the cell membrane. This mechanism is important for amino acid transmitters like glutamate and GABA and also for monoamine transmitters such as DA, NE, and 5-HT. Transport out of the synaptic cleft is sometimes accomplished by the same cell that released the transmitter, in which case it is called **reuptake**. In other cases, the transmitter may be taken up either by the postsynaptic cell or by nearby glial cells

(specifically astrocytes). Some important psychoactive drugs work by blocking neurotransmitter transporters. Cocaine, for example, blocks the transporters for DA, 5-HT, and NE. Many antidepressant drugs block the 5-HT transporter, the NE transporter, or both. Since these transporters are so important for clearing the neurotransmitter from the synaptic cleft, it follows that when the transporters are blocked, neurotransmitter molecules remain in the synaptic cleft for a longer time, and neurotransmission is enhanced at those synapses.

When neurotransmitter transporters are active, some transmitter molecules removed from the synaptic cleft are reused by being packaged into recycled vesicles. However, other transmitter molecules are broken down by enzymes present within the cell. Thus, uptake and metabolic breakdown are not mutually exclusive processes. Many transmitter systems use both mechanisms. Finally, it is important to keep in mind the distinction between autoreceptors and transporters. Even though both may be present on axon terminals, they serve different functions. Terminal autoreceptors modulate transmitter release, but they do not transport the neurotransmitter. Transporters take up the transmitter from the synaptic cleft, but they are not autoreceptors.

Subsequent chapters will describe more details about the uptake mechanisms for specific neurotransmitters; however, two general principles can be mentioned here. First, in some cases (for example, 5-HT), the transporters are present along the length of the axon and not concentrated in the area of the synaptic cleft. Together with other findings, this suggests that

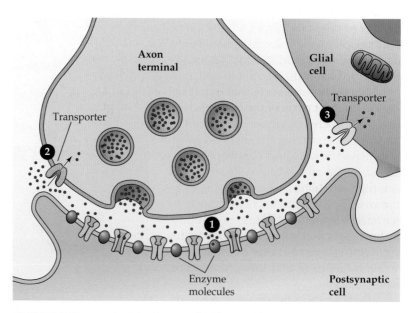

FIGURE 3.11 **Neurotransmitter inactivation** Neurotransmitter molecules can be inactivated by (1) enzymatic breakdown, (2) reuptake by the axon terminal, or (3) uptake by nearby glial cells. Cellular uptake is mediated by specific membrane transporters for each neurotransmitter.

significant amounts of 5-HT escape the cleft and enter the surrounding extracellular fluid. Second, even for neurotransmitters in which transporter localization is more confined to the area of the synapse, the uptake process may not be sufficiently efficient to avoid spillover of transmitter molecules outside of the synaptic cleft. In both cases, we can see the possibility of volume transmission (i.e., chemical transmission at a distance from the point of transmitter release) occurring.

Neurotransmitters outside of the CNS

This chapter focuses mainly on features of neurotransmission within the CNS. However, many of the same transmitters are found outside of the CNS, and the same principles of transmitter release, receptor signaling, and so forth apply in most instances. For example, ACh plays a key role as the neurotransmitter at vertebrate neuromuscular junctions that stimulate contraction of the skeletal muscles (discussed in Chapter 7). ACh, DA, and NE are neurotransmitters at specific synapses within the autonomic (sympathetic and parasympathetic) nervous system (Chapters 5 and 7). In Chapter 6, you will learn about the enteric nervous system, a large system of ganglia that controls gut function. 5-HT and various neuropeptides including enkephalins are important signaling molecules within the enteric nervous system.

Especially intriguing is the growing knowledge that some neurotransmitters are synthesized by bacteria in our gut and that drugs (including psychoactive drugs) alter the population of gut bacteria in ways that can influence our health. This new knowledge falls under the general topic of the **human microbiome**. The term "microbiome" refers to the sum total of microbial cells (i.e., bacteria, viruses, yeast, and fungi) that colonize the human body both in health and in disease. Just taking bacteria into account, current research estimates that there are more bacterial cells colonizing a healthy body than the body's own cells put together (Gilbert et al., 2018). Different parts of the body such as the skin, gut, and vagina are colonized by different species of microbiota. Considering the diversity of bacterial species within just the gut microbiome, researchers have estimated that these bacterial populations together express roughly 2,000,000 different genes, which is 100 times the 20,000 genes estimated to make up the human genome (Gilbert et al., 2018).

Recent studies, particularly those using animal models, have provided strong evidence that the gut microbiome interacts bidirectionally with the nervous system, influences neurotransmitter synthesis and metabolism, and exerts significant effects on behavior. This research has given rise to the term **gut–brain axis**, which refers to signaling back and forth between the gut (including the gut microbiome) and the brain. Human studies similarly support a role for the gut–brain axis in behavioral regulation and have begun to implicate dysfunction of this system in various psychiatric and neurological disorders. This topic is discussed in greater detail in **WEB BOX 3.2**.

SECTION SUMMARY

- Synapses are the sites of communication between neurons. Most synapses in the vertebrate nervous system are chemical, although electrical synapses and mixed (both chemical and electrical) synapses have also been identified.

- At a synapse, the sending neuron is called the presynaptic cell and the receiving neuron is called the postsynaptic cell. Synapses may occur on the dendrite (axodendritic), cell body (axosomatic), or axon (axoaxonic) of the postsynaptic cell.

- Key structural components of the synapse include the synaptic vesicles, synaptic cleft, and postsynaptic density.

- The following criteria must be met for a substance to be considered a neurotransmitter: (1) mechanisms for synthesis, release, and inactivation of the substance and (2) responsiveness of cells to application of the substance.

- Most neurotransmitters fall into one of the following categories (with acetylcholine as a notable exception): amino acid transmitters, monoamine transmitters, lipid transmitters, neuropeptide transmitters, and gaseous transmitters.

- Classical neurotransmitters (amino acids, monoamines, and acetylcholine) are mainly synthesized in the nerve terminal and then are transported into synaptic vesicles; neuropeptides are synthesized from a protein precursor and are packaged into vesicles in the cell body.

- The sleep disorder narcolepsy can be attributed to loss of neurons synthesizing the neuropeptide orexin in the lateral hypothalamus. These cells play an important role in regulating the wake–sleep cycle.

- In some instances, a neurotransmitter signals not only to its immediate postsynaptic cell (wiring transmission) but also to cells that are more distant from the site of release (volume transmission).

- Neurotransmitters are released from nerve terminals at active zones by a Ca^{2+}-dependent process called exocytosis.

- There are two pools of synaptic vesicles: the readily releasable pool consists of vesicles at the active zones that can rapidly undergo exocytosis upon presynaptic cell stimulation, whereas the reserve pool contains vesicles farther away from the active zones that can undergo exocytosis later if the presynaptic cell is persistently stimulated.

- Synaptic vesicles are replenished by recycling processes. Three models have been proposed to explain vesicle recycling at low to moderate rates of neuronal activity: clathrin-mediated endocytosis, ultrafast endocytosis, and kiss-and-run. At very high rates of activity, a fourth process, bulk endocytosis, comes into play to retrieve and recycle large amounts of vesicle membrane that has fused with the nerve terminal membrane.

- Synapses (including neuromuscular junctions) vary widely in their size, the number of vesicles contained within the axon terminals, the number of active zones, and the probability of releasing at least one vesicle in response to a single action potential. These disparities reflect differences in the characteristics of information transmission when we compare one population of synapses with another.

- Lipid and gaseous transmitters are synthesized upon demand, are not stored in synaptic vesicles, and often function as retrograde messengers by signaling from the postsynaptic to the presynaptic cell.

- The rate of neurotransmitter release is regulated by many factors, including rate of cell firing, probability of vesicle exocytosis, activation of terminal and somato-dendritic autoreceptors, and activation of heteroreceptors on nerve terminals.

- Termination of neurotransmitter action is accomplished by the processes of uptake (including reuptake by the presynaptic cell) and/or enzymatic breakdown.

- Enzymatic breakdown is particularly important for ACh, lipid and gaseous transmitters, and neuropeptides, whereas uptake/reuptake plays the most important role for the amino acid and monoamine transmitters.

- Many psychoactive drugs act by inhibiting the reuptake process, thereby enhancing transmission by increasing neurotransmitter concentrations within the synaptic cleft.

- The uptake process is often relatively inefficient, raising the possibility of volume transmission by neurotransmitter molecules that have diffused some distance away from the sites of release.

- Neurotransmitters with important roles outside of the brain include ACh (neuromuscular junction and autonomic nervous system), DA and NE (autonomic nervous system), 5-HT (enteric nervous system), and several peptides, including enkephalins (enteric nervous system).

- The gut–brain axis refers to pathways of bidirectional communication between the gut (including the gut microbiome) and the brain. Neural (vagus nerve), immune (cytokines), endocrine (cortisol and gut hormones), and metabolic (neurotransmitters, transmitter metabolites, and short-chain fatty acids) pathways mediate communication within the gut–brain axis.

- Researchers are beginning to investigate the role of the gut–brain axis in many neuropsychiatric and neurological disorders. Other studies are looking for bacterial products that could have a therapeutic benefit in these same disorders (psychobiotics). Lastly, some of the standard drugs used in clinical practice appear to alter the composition of the gut microbiome, raising questions about whether such alterations play some role in either the therapeutic effects or the side effects of these medications.

3.2 Neurotransmitter Receptors, Signaling Mechanisms, and Synaptic Plasticity

Chemical signaling by neurotransmitters requires the presence of molecules on the membrane of the postsynaptic cell called **receptors** that are sensitive to the neurotransmitter signal. Moreover, receptors must have a way to alter the activity of the postsynaptic cell, thereby passing along information from the presynaptic cell. Several different mechanisms have evolved to accomplish this function, some of which involve complex biochemical pathways known as **second-messenger systems**. Signaling molecules such as neurotransmitters or hormones are considered "first messengers" because they represent the initial link in the chain of information transfer from one cell to another. In this terminology, a "second messenger" is an intracellular molecule regulated by the first messenger (i.e., levels of the second messenger are either increased or decreased through the action of the first messenger on its receptor) in order to transmit the information carried by that first messenger.

Neurotransmitter receptor families

In Chapter 1, you were introduced to the concept of a drug receptor. Many of the receptors for psychoactive drugs are actually receptors for various neurotransmitters. For this reason, it is very important to understand the characteristics of neurotransmitter receptors and how they function.

Virtually all neurotransmitter receptors are proteins, and in most cases, these proteins are located on the plasma membrane of the cell. As we saw earlier, the cell possessing the receptor may be a neuron, a muscle cell, or a secretory cell. The neurotransmitter molecule binds to a specific site on the receptor molecule, which activates the receptor and produces a biochemical alteration in the receiving cell that may affect its excitability. For example, postsynaptic receptors on neurons usually influence the likelihood that the cell will generate an action potential. The effect of receptor activation may be either excitatory (increasing the probability of an action potential) or inhibitory (decreasing the probability of an action potential), depending on what the receptor does to the cell (see following sections). Recall that if a particular drug mimics the action of the neurotransmitter in activating the receptor, we say that the drug is an *agonist* at that receptor (see Chapter 1). If a drug blocks or inhibits the ability of the neurotransmitter to activate the receptor, then the drug is called an *antagonist*.

Three key concepts are necessary for understanding neurotransmitter receptors. First, receptors *do not* act like the neurotransmitter transporters described above.

Their role is to pass a signal (i.e., presence of released neurotransmitter molecules) from the presynaptic to the postsynaptic cell. Unlike transporters, receptors do not carry neurotransmitter molecules across the cell membrane. Instead, after a neurotransmitter molecule binds briefly to a receptor to activate it, the neurotransmitter physically disengages and is now available to activate another receptor, be taken up by a transporter, or become inactivated by a neurotransmitter metabolizing enzyme.

Second, almost all neurotransmitters discovered so far have more than one kind of receptor. Different varieties of receptors for the same transmitter are called **receptor subtypes** for that transmitter. The existence of subtypes adds complexity to the study of receptors, making the task of pharmacologists (as well as students!) more difficult. But this complexity has a positive aspect: if you can design a drug that stimulates or blocks just the subtype that you're interested in, you may be able to treat a disease more effectively and with fewer side effects. This is one of the central ideas underlying modern drug design and the continuing search for new pharmaceutical agents.

The third key concept is that most neurotransmitter receptors fall into two broad categories: **ionotropic receptors** and **metabotropic receptors**. A particular transmitter may use only receptors that fit one or the other of these general categories, or its receptor subtypes may fall into both categories. As shown in **TABLE 3.2**, ionotropic and metabotropic receptors differ in both structure and function, so we will discuss them separately.

Ionotropic receptors consist of multiple subunits that together form an ion channel

Ionotropic receptors work very rapidly, so they play a critical role in fast neurotransmission within the nervous system. Each ionotropic receptor is made up of several proteins called **subunits**, which are assembled to form the complete receptor before insertion into the cell membrane. Four or five subunits are needed, depending on the overall structure of the receptor (**FIGURE 3.12A**). At the center of every ionotropic receptor is a channel or pore through which ions can flow. The receptor also possesses one or more binding sites for the neurotransmitter. In the resting state with no neurotransmitter present, the receptor channel is closed, and no ions are moving. When the neurotransmitter binds to the receptor and activates it, the channel immediately opens and ions flow across the cell membrane (**FIGURE 3.12B**). When the neurotransmitter molecule leaves (dissociates from) the receptor, the channel quickly closes. Because of these features, a common alternative name for ionotropic receptors is **ligand-gated channel receptors**.* Another feature of ionotropic receptors is that they can undergo a phenomenon called **desensitization**, in which the channel remains closed even though there may be ligand molecules bound to the receptor (the details of this process are beyond the scope of the chapter). Once this occurs, the channel must resensitize before it can be activated once again.

Some ionotropic receptor channels allow sodium (Na^+) ions to flow into the cell from the extracellular fluid. Because these ions are positively charged, the cell membrane is depolarized, thereby producing an excitatory response of the postsynaptic cell. One of the best-known examples of this kind of excitatory ionotropic receptor is the nicotinic receptor for ACh, which we will discuss further in Chapter 7. A second type of ionotropic receptor channel permits the flow of Ca^{2+} as well as Na^+ ions across the cell membrane. As we will see shortly, Ca^{2+} can act as a **second messenger** to trigger many biochemical processes in the postsynaptic cell. One important ionotropic receptor that functions in this way is the N-methyl-D-aspartate (NMDA) receptor for the neurotransmitter glutamate (see Chapter 8). Finally, a third type of receptor channel is selective for chloride (Cl^-) ions to flow into the cell. These ions are negatively charged, thus leading to hyperpolarization of the membrane and an inhibitory response of the postsynaptic cell. A good example of this kind of inhibitory ionotropic receptor is the $GABA_A$ receptor (see Chapter 8). From this discussion, you can see that

---

*This terminology distinguishes such channels from voltage-gated channels, which are controlled by voltage across the cell membrane rather than by binding of a ligand such as a neurotransmitter or a drug.

TABLE 3.2   Comparison of Ionotropic and Metabotropic Receptors

Characteristics	Ionotropic receptors	Metabotropic receptors
Structure	4 or 5 subunits that are assembled and then inserted into the cell membrane	1 subunit
Mechanism of action	Contain an intrinsic ion channel that opens in response to neurotransmitter or drug binding	Activate G proteins in response to neurotransmitter or drug binding
Coupled to second messengers?	No	Yes
Speed of action	Fast	Slower

(A)

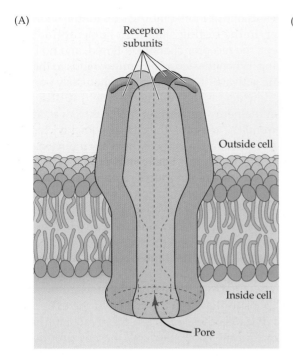

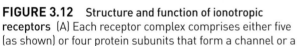

(B)

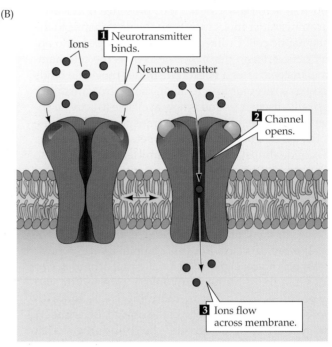

FIGURE 3.12 **Structure and function of ionotropic receptors** (A) Each receptor complex comprises either five (as shown) or four protein subunits that form a channel or a pore in the cell membrane. (B) Binding of the neurotransmitter to the receptor triggers channel opening and the flow of ions across the membrane.

the characteristics of the ion channel controlled by an ionotropic receptor are the key factor in determining whether that receptor excites the postsynaptic cell, inhibits the cell, or activates a second-messenger system.

Metabotropic receptors consist of a single subunit that works by activating G proteins

Metabotropic receptors act more slowly than ionotropic receptors. It takes longer for the postsynaptic cell to respond, but its response can be much more long-lasting than in the case of ionotropic receptors. Representative excitatory postsynaptic responses (EPSPs) for ionotropic and metabotropic receptors are depicted in **FIGURE 3.13**. Metabotropic receptors are composed

of only a single protein subunit, which winds its way back and forth through the cell membrane seven times. Using the terminology of cell biology, we say that these receptors have seven transmembrane domains; in fact, they are sometimes abbreviated 7-TM receptors (**FIGURE 3.14**). It is important to note that metabotropic receptors do not possess a channel or pore. How, then, do these receptors work?

Metabotropic receptors work by activating other proteins in the cell membrane called **G proteins** (students interested in learning more about the structure and functioning of G proteins are referred to **WEB BOX 3.3**). Consequently, another name for this receptor family is **G protein–coupled receptors**. Many different kinds of G proteins have been identified, and how a metabotropic receptor influences the postsynaptic cell depends on which G protein(s) the receptor activates. However, all G proteins operate by two major mechanisms. One is by stimulating or inhibiting the opening of ion channels in

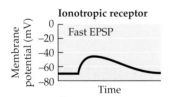

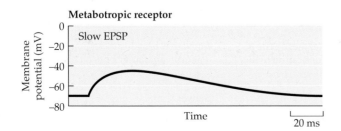

FIGURE 3.13 **Fast and slow excitatory postsynaptic potentials (EPSPs) elicited by ionotropic versus metabotropic receptors** As shown in this representative figure, activation of metabotropic receptors elicits responses that are slower to develop but last much longer than ionotropic receptor–mediated responses. Note the time scale on the lower right measured in milliseconds (ms). (After J. H. Byrne. 2014. In *From Molecules to Networks, An Introduction to Cellular and Molecular Neuroscience*, 3rd ed., J. H. Byrne et al. [Eds.], pp. 489–507. Academic Press: San Diego. © 2014. Reprinted with permission from Elsevier.)

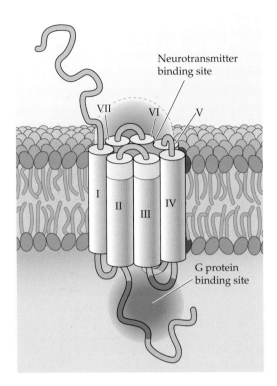

FIGURE 3.14 **Structure of metabotropic receptors** Each receptor comprises a single protein subunit with seven transmembrane domains (labeled here by Roman numerals).

(A)

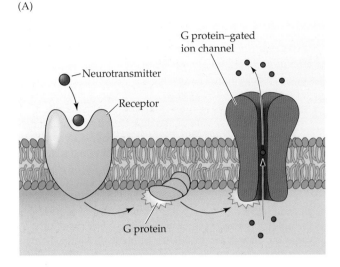

(B)

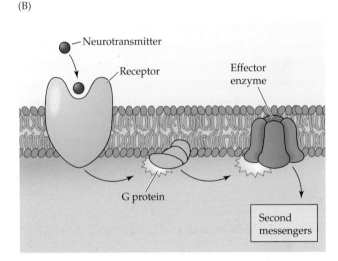

FIGURE 3.15 **Functions of metabotropic receptors** Metabotropic receptors activate G proteins in the membrane, which may either (A) alter the opening of a G protein–gated ion channel or (B) stimulate or inhibit an effector enzyme that either synthesizes or breaks down a second messenger.

the cell membrane (**FIGURE 3.15A**). Potassium (K^+) channels, for example, are stimulated by specific G proteins at many synapses. When these channels open, K^+ ions flow out of the cell, the membrane is hyperpolarized, and consequently the cell's firing is suppressed. This is a common mechanism of synaptic inhibition used by various receptors for ACh, DA, NE, 5-HT, and GABA and some neuropeptides like the endorphins. Note that the K^+ channels controlled by G proteins are not the same as the voltage-gated K^+ channels that work together with voltage-gated Na^+ channels to produce action potentials.

The second mechanism by which metabotropic receptors and G proteins operate is by stimulating or inhibiting certain enzymes in the cell membrane (**FIGURE 3.15B**). These enzymes are sometimes called **effector enzymes** because they produce biochemical and physiological effects in the postsynaptic cell. Most of the effector enzymes controlled by G proteins are involved in either the synthesis or the breakdown of small molecules called *second messengers*. Second messengers were discovered in the 1960s and later found to play an important role in the chemical communication processes of both neurotransmitters and hormones. As mentioned above, this terminology arose because the neurotransmitter or hormone was considered to be the first messenger, while the second messenger within the receiving cell (the postsynaptic cell, in the case of a neurotransmitter) carried out the biochemical change

signaled by the first messenger. When everything is put together, this mechanism of metabotropic receptor function involves (1) activation of a G protein, followed by (2) stimulation or inhibition of an effector enzyme in the membrane of the postsynaptic cell, followed by (3) increased synthesis or breakdown of a second messenger, followed by (4) biochemical or physiological changes in the postsynaptic cell due to the altered levels of the second messenger (see Figure 3.15B). This sequence of events is an example of a biochemical "cascade."

Medicinal pharmacologists have traditionally focused on developing new receptor agonists and antagonists for treating disease. In recent years, however, much of this focus has shifted toward the development of a different class of compounds, known as **allosteric modulators**. This topic is discussed in **BOX 3.1**.

BOX 3.1 ■ THE CUTTING EDGE

Allosteric Modulation of Neurotransmitter Receptors

Researchers investigating the pharmacology of both ionotropic and metabotropic receptors have discovered that most (perhaps all) such receptors possess functional binding sites besides the site(s) recognized by a typical agonist or antagonist (Changeux and Christopoulos, 2016; Felder, 2019). These binding sites are called **allosteric sites**, and molecules such as drugs that bind to such sites and alter the functioning of the receptor are called **allosteric modulators**.

The figure illustrates the concept of allosteric modulation using a metabotropic receptor as an example. You can see that allosteric modulators can have either a positive or a negative effect on receptor signaling. Also shown is the important fact that allosteric modulators only modify the effects of an agonist; they have no effects when given alone. That key difference, along with the fact that the allosteric binding site differs from the agonist binding site, is why allosteric modulators are not simply receptor agonists or antagonists. The discovery of allosteric binding sites is actually not surprising, since the complex three-dimensional structures of metabotropic and ionotropic receptors are quite likely to contain binding pockets for small molecules (i.e., drugs) that, when occupied, can modulate how the receptor protein changes its conformation upon agonist activation.

Allosteric modulators, particularly modulators of metabotropic receptors, are becoming increasingly important in the search for better drugs to treat psychiatric and neurological disorders. Among the many

disorders being targeted are schizophrenia, depression, anxiety disorders, addiction, autism spectrum disorders, Alzheimer's disease, and Parkinson's disease (Nickols and Conn, 2014). Compared with traditional agonists or antagonists, allosteric modulators often possess greater receptor subtype selectivity, which would decrease the likelihood of adverse side effects when the drug is given to a patient. Moreover, when an allosteric modulator is used to alter the effect of a neurotransmitter agonist on its receptor, the modulator may "fine-tune" signaling by that neurotransmitter (either amplifying or diminishing such signaling) in a more controllable manner than would administering a direct agonist or antagonist for the receptor. For example, because the DA system is known to be dysregulated in patients with schizophrenia, the standard medications for treating this disorder are DA D2 receptor antagonists (see Chapter 18). Unfortunately, these drugs have a number of serious side effects that can lead patients to stop taking their medication. On the other hand, DA receptors can be modulated allosterically, and other receptor systems such as the cholinergic and glutamatergic systems have also been implicated in schizophrenia and/or the mechanism of action of antipsychotic medications. Thus, allosteric modulators of dopaminergic, muscarinic cholinergic, and metabotropic glutamate receptors are being tested in animal models to determine whether such compounds could have value in the treatment of schizophrenia (Foster and Conn, 2017).

Allosteric modulation of neurotransmitter receptor signaling Using metabotropic receptors as an example, the figure shows how allosteric modulators can either positively or negatively influence receptor signaling. In the absence of an agonist, including the neurotransmitter itself, the allosteric modulator produces no receptor signaling. (After D. Wootten et al. 2013. *Nat Rev Drug Discov* 12: 630–644.)

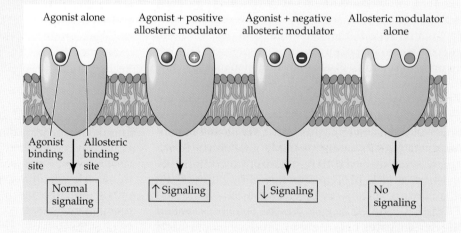

Second-messenger systems

Second-messenger systems are too complex to be completely covered in this text. We will therefore highlight several of the most important systems and how they alter cellular function. One of the key ways in which second messengers work is by activating enzymes called **protein kinases** (**FIGURE 3.16**). Kinases are enzymes that **phosphorylate** another molecule—that is, they catalyze the addition of one or more phosphate

groups ($-PO_4^{2-}$) to the molecule. As the name suggests, a protein kinase phosphorylates a protein. The substrate protein might be an ion channel, an enzyme involved in neurotransmitter synthesis, a neurotransmitter receptor or transporter, a structural protein, or almost any other kind of protein. The phosphate groups added by the kinase then alter functioning of the protein in some way. For example, an ion channel might open, a neurotransmitter-synthesizing enzyme might

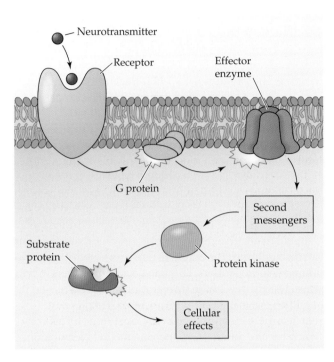

FIGURE 3.16 The mechanism of action of second messengers Second messengers work by activating protein kinases to cause phosphorylation of substrate proteins within the postsynaptic cell.

be activated, a receptor might become more sensitive to the neurotransmitter, and so forth. Furthermore, kinases can phosphorylate proteins in the cell nucleus that turn on or turn off specific genes in that cell. You can see that protein kinases activated by second messengers are capable of producing widespread and profound changes in the postsynaptic cell, even including long-lasting changes in gene expression.

Now let us consider several specific second messengers and their protein kinases. The first second messenger to be discovered was **cyclic adenosine monophosphate** (**cAMP**). Levels of cAMP are controlled by receptors for several different neurotransmitters, including DA, NE, 5-HT, and endorphins. Cyclic AMP stimulates a protein kinase called **protein kinase A** (**PKA**). A related second messenger is **cyclic guanosine monophosphate** (**cGMP**). One of the key regulators of cGMP is the gaseous messenger nitric oxide, which activates the enzyme that synthesizes this second messenger. Cyclic GMP has its own kinase known as **protein kinase G** (**PKG**). A third second-messenger system is sometimes termed the **phosphoinositide second-messenger system**. This complex system, which works by breaking down a phospholipid in the cell membrane, actually liberates two second messengers: **diacylglycerol** (**DAG**) and **inositol trisphosphate** (**IP3**). Working together, these messengers cause an elevation of the level of Ca^{2+} ions within the postsynaptic cell and activation of **protein kinase C** (**PKC**). The phosphoinositide system

is controlled by receptors for several neurotransmitters, including ACh, NE, and 5-HT. Finally, Ca^{2+} itself is a second messenger. Calcium levels in the cell can be increased by various mechanisms, including the phosphoinositide second-messenger system, voltage-sensitive Ca^{2+} channels, and, as mentioned earlier, certain ionotropic receptors like the NMDA receptor. The nervous system contains a family of protein kinases activated by Ca^{2+} that require the participation of an additional protein known as *calmodulin*. At the synapse, the most important of these kinases is **calcium/calmodulin kinase II** (**CaMKII**). Finally, another function of Ca^{2+} in second-messenger signaling is to help activate PKC. **TABLE 3.3** summarizes these second-messenger systems and their associated protein kinases.

The second messengers cAMP and cGMP are inactivated by enzymes called phosphodiesterases (PDEs). Eleven different PDE families have been discovered, some of which are specific for cAMP (PDEs 4, 7, and 8), others of which are specific for cGMP (PDEs 5, 6, and 9), and the remainder of which break down both cAMP and cGMP (PDEs 1, 2, 3, 10, 11) (Francis et al., 2011). Although this plethora of PDEs may seem like "overkill," it's important to realize that a given tissue or organ may express only one or a few of the forms of this enzyme. Of relevance for pharmacology is that various compounds have been developed that selectively target particular forms of PDE. The best-known examples of this concern PDE5 inhibitors like sildenafil (Viagra), tadalafil (Cialis), and vardenafil (Levitra), which are used to treat erectile dysfunction. Cyclic GMP causes relaxation of smooth muscles surrounding the penile blood vessels, thereby leading to dilation of the vessels and production of an erection. Inhibitors of PDE5 facilitate this process by increasing the levels and prolonging the action of cGMP in the penile smooth muscles. PDE inhibitors are also currently being used to treat cardiac failure (PDE3), chronic obstructive pulmonary disease (PDE4), and pulmonary hypertension (PDE5 again) (Francis et al., 2011). Most relevant for psychopharmacologists, researchers are actively working to assess the potential usefulness of PDE inhibitors for treating age-related memory loss and neurodegenerative disorders such as Alzheimer's disease (Hansen and Zhang, 2017; Wennogle et al., 2017;

TABLE 3.3 Second-Messenger Systems and Protein Kinases

Second-messenger system	Associated protein kinase
Cyclic AMP (cAMP)	Protein kinase A (PKA)
Cyclic GMP (cGMP)	Protein kinase G (PKG)
Phosphoinositide	Protein kinase C (PKC)
Calcium (Ca^{2+})	Calcium/calmodulin kinase II (CaMKII)

Liu et al., 2019), depression (Bolger, 2017; Duarte-Silva et al., 2020), stroke (Wang et al., 2018), and obesity and diabetes (Clapcote, 2017). These studies are primarily targeting PDEs 1, 4, and 5, which is understandable given the high expression of these PDEs in the brain and their presence in key neural circuits involved in cognition and mood (Heckman et al., 2018).

Tyrosine kinase receptors

There is one more family of receptors that you need to learn about: the **tyrosine kinase receptors**. These receptors mediate the action of **neurotrophic factors**, proteins that stimulate the survival and growth of neurons during early development and that are also involved in neuronal signaling. Nerve growth factor (NGF) was the first neurotrophic factor to be discovered, but many others are now known, including BDNF, which was mentioned earlier, neurotrophin-3 (NT-3), and NT-4.

Three specific tyrosine kinase receptors are used by these neurotrophic factors: trkA (pronounced "track A") for NGF, trkB for BDNF and NT-4, and trkC for NT-3. The trk receptors are activated through the following mechanism. After the neurotrophic factor binds to its receptor, two of the resulting complexes come together in the cell membrane, which is a process that is necessary for receptor activation When the two trk receptors are activated, they phosphorylate each other on tyrosine residues* (hence the "tyrosine kinase receptor") located within the cytoplasmic region of each receptor. This process then triggers a complex sequence involving additional protein kinases, including some that differ from those described in the previous section. Tyrosine kinase receptors and the neurotrophic factors they serve generally participate more in regulation of long-term changes in gene expression and neuronal functioning than in rapid synaptic events that determine the rate of cell firing.

Pharmacology of synaptic transmission

Drugs can either enhance or interfere with virtually all aspects of synaptic transmission. Synaptic effects form the basis of almost all of the actions of psychoactive drugs, including drugs of abuse, as well as those prescribed for the treatment of serious mental disorders such as depression and schizophrenia. **FIGURE 3.17** illustrates the major ways in which such drugs can alter the neurotransmission process.

Drugs may either increase or decrease the rate of transmitter synthesis. If the drug is a chemical precursor

---

*Proteins are long chains of amino acids. When amino acids are strung together in the synthesis of a protein, each adjacent pair of amino acids loses a water molecule (an H from one amino acid and an OH from the other). What remain are called "amino acid residues." Each residue is named for the specific amino acid from which it was derived (tyrosine in this case). Tyrosine kinases are differentiated from the kinases mentioned earlier (e.g., PKA), because those kinases phosphorylate proteins on residues of the amino acids serine and threonine instead of tyrosine. This difference, in turn, is important because it influences how phosphorylation affects the functioning of the target protein.

to the transmitter, then the rate of transmitter formation may be increased. Two examples of this approach involve L-dihydroxyphenylalanine (L-DOPA), which is the precursor to DA, and 5-hydroxytryptophan (5-HTP), which is the precursor to 5-HT. Because patients with Parkinson's disease are deficient in DA, the primary treatment for this neurological disorder is L-DOPA (see Chapter 5 for more information). Alternatively, a drug can decrease levels of a neurotransmitter by inhibiting a key enzyme needed for transmitter synthesis. Alpha-methyl-*para*-tyrosine inhibits the enzyme tyrosine hydroxylase, which helps manufacture both DA and NE, and *para*-chlorophenylalanine inhibits the 5-HT–synthesizing enzyme tryptophan hydroxylase.

Besides administering a precursor substance, you can also enhance the action of a neurotransmitter by reducing its inactivation. This can be accomplished in two ways. First, levels of the transmitter can be increased by blocking the enzyme involved in its breakdown. Physostigmine blocks the enzyme acetylcholinesterase, which breaks down ACh, and phenelzine blocks monoamine oxidase (MAO), an enzyme that is important in the breakdown of DA, NE, and 5-HT. As we will see in Chapter 18, phenelzine and other MAO-inhibiting drugs are sometimes used to treat patients with depression. For neurotransmitters that use transporters for reuptake out of the synaptic cleft, a second way to reduce neurotransmitter inactivation is to block those transporters. This increases the amount and prolongs the presence of the transmitter in the synaptic cleft, thereby enhancing its effects on the postsynaptic cell. As described previously, cocaine blocks the transporters for DA, NE, and 5-HT, and drugs that more selectively prevent reuptake of 5-HT are commonly used as antidepressant medications (see Chapters 12 and 18).

Other drugs affect neurotransmitter storage or release. For example, reserpine blocks the storage of DA, NE, and 5-HT in synaptic vesicles. Reserpine treatment initially causes a burst of neurotransmitter release as the vesicles empty out, but this is followed by a period of extremely low transmitter levels because storage in vesicles is necessary to prevent breakdown of transmitter molecules by enzymes present in the axon terminal. Amphetamine stimulates the release of DA and NE from the cytoplasm of the axon terminal, and a related substance called fenfluramine produces the same effect on 5-HT. These releasing agents work by reversing the effects of the neurotransmitter transporters. That is, instead of the transporters taking up transmitter molecules into the neuron from the synaptic cleft, they work in the reverse direction to carry the transmitter out of the neuron and into the synaptic cleft. As we saw earlier, some drugs alter neurotransmitter release in a different way, by stimulating or inhibiting autoreceptors that control the release process. Clonidine and 8-OH-DPAT stimulate autoreceptors for NE and 5-HT, respectively. In both cases, such stimulation reduces release of

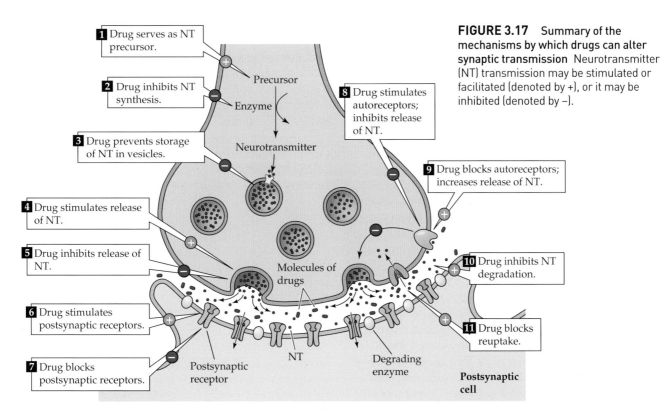

1 Drug serves as NT precursor.

2 Drug inhibits NT synthesis.

3 Drug prevents storage of NT in vesicles.

4 Drug stimulates release of NT.

5 Drug inhibits release of NT.

6 Drug stimulates postsynaptic receptors.

7 Drug blocks postsynaptic receptors.

8 Drug stimulates autoreceptors; inhibits release of NT.

9 Drug blocks autoreceptors; increases release of NT.

10 Drug inhibits NT degradation.

11 Drug blocks reuptake.

Precursor

Enzyme

Neurotransmitter

Molecules of drugs

Postsynaptic receptor

NT

Degrading enzyme

Postsynaptic cell

FIGURE 3.17 Summary of the mechanisms by which drugs can alter synaptic transmission Neurotransmitter (NT) transmission may be stimulated or facilitated (denoted by +), or it may be inhibited (denoted by –).

the related transmitter. Autoreceptor inhibition can be produced by yohimbine in the case of NE and pindolol in the case of 5-HT. Not surprisingly, administration of these compounds increases transmitter release.

One final mechanism of action can be seen in drugs that act on postsynaptic receptors for a specific neurotransmitter. If the drug is an agonist for a particular receptor subtype, it will mimic the effect of the neurotransmitter on that receptor. If the drug is a receptor antagonist, it will inhibit the effect of the transmitter on the receptor. Many psychoactive drugs, both therapeutic and recreational, are receptor agonists. Examples include benzodiazepines, which are agonists at benzodiazepine receptors and are used clinically as sedative and antianxiety drugs (see Chapter 17); opioids like heroin and morphine, which are agonists at opioid receptors (see Chapter 11); nicotine, which is an agonist at the nicotinic receptor subtype for ACh (see Chapter 7); and THC, which is an agonist at cannabinoid receptors (see Chapter 14). Receptor antagonists are likewise important in pharmacology. As mentioned earlier, most drugs used to treat patients with schizophrenia are antagonists at the D_2 receptor subtype for DA (see Chapter 19), and the widely ingested substance caffeine is an antagonist at receptors for the neurotransmitter adenosine (see Chapter 13).

Synaptic plasticity

The human neocortex is estimated to contain roughly 150 trillion synapses, a truly astonishing number (Tang et al., 2001). These communication structures connect an intricate network of 20 to 25 billion neocortical neurons (Pakkenberg and Gundersen, 1997). Dividing the

total synapse number by the total number of neurons tells us that the average human neocortical neuron is estimated to receive 6000 to 7500 synaptic connections. Of course, those are average figures, meaning that some neurons receive fewer and others receive even more synaptic connections.

For many years after the first visualization of synapses in the 1950s using the electron microscope, most researchers believed that these structures were stable once they were formed. Since it was also thought (erroneously) that no new neurons could be generated in the mature brain, there was no obvious need for new synapses, because existing ones presumably could be strengthened or weakened as needed. Subsequent research has, indeed, confirmed that various kinds of experiences (e.g., learning) can alter the strength of synaptic connections activated by those experiences (see discussion of long-term potentiation and long-term depression in Chapter 8). But there is also abundant evidence that even in adulthood, axons can grow new terminals, dendrites can expand or contract their branches and/or gain or lose spines, and synapses can be created or lost (Holtmaat and Svoboda, 2009). The term **synaptic plasticity** was coined to reflect the whole variety of synaptic changes, ranging from functional changes in the strength of existing synapses to structural changes involving the growth of new synapses or the loss of previously existing ones.

Synaptic plasticity can be studied at several levels, including molecular (changes in neurotransmitter receptors and/or their signaling pathways), electrophysiological (changes in the strength of postsynaptic responses to synaptic input), and structural (growth or loss of nerve terminals, changes in dendritic branching, and increases or decreases in dendritic spine density). Of course, these levels are not mutually exclusive. Synaptic plasticity in a population of neurons could encompass many different changes together, such as increased dendritic branching, more spines per unit length of a dendritic branch, increased density of neurotransmitter receptors on the spines, *and* elevated postsynaptic responses to presynaptic stimulation.

Studies of structural plasticity usually focus on dendritic length, branching patterns, and dendritic spines, since dendrites (and particularly dendritic spines) are the principal sites of synaptic input. Neurons can rapidly change the size and shape of their dendritic spines, grow new spines, and/or lose existing ones. The most profound changes in the number of dendritic spines occur during development of the brain, when most spines are formed. Spines and synapses are normally "pruned" during adolescence, a period when excess neuronal connections are eliminated. Dendritic abnormalities occurring during the time of brain growth have been implicated in a number of neurodevelopmental disorders (Nishiyama, 2019). One example of this is a genetic disorder called fragile X syndrome, which is discussed in Chapter 8. Synaptic plasticity is relevant for neuropharmacologists because many abused drugs such as cocaine, opioids, and alcohol can produce changes in dendritic length, dendritic branching, and/or the density of spines along the dendrites in various brain areas (Collo et al., 2014; Spiga et al., 2014). Because the brain must be sliced, stained, and examined microscopically to visualize and quantify dendritic and spine characteristics, studies of drug effects on structural plasticity are almost always conducted using experimental animals. Nevertheless, there is good reason to believe that the findings are relevant for human drug exposure.

SECTION SUMMARY

- Neurotransmitter receptors serve the purpose of signaling information from the presynaptic to the postsynaptic cell. Unlike transporters, they do not carry neurotransmitter molecules across the cell membrane.

- Most neurotransmitters make use of multiple receptor subtypes. Neurotransmitter receptors fall into two categories: ionotropic and metabotropic.

- Ionotropic receptors are composed of multiple subunits and form an intrinsic ion channel that is permeable either to cations such as Na^+ (and sometimes also Ca^{2+}) or to anions such as Cl^-. These receptors respectively mediate fast excitatory or fast inhibitory transmission.

- Metabotropic receptors are coupled to G proteins in the cell membrane and mediate slower transmission involving ion channel opening (e.g., inhibitory K^+ channels) or second-messenger synthesis or breakdown. Second messengers are intracellular molecules that mediate the transfer of information carried by the first messenger (neurotransmitter or hormone).

- Second messengers work by activating protein kinases that phosphorylate target proteins in the postsynaptic cell.

- Some important second-messenger systems and their respective kinases are the cAMP (protein kinase A), cGMP (protein kinase G), Ca^{2+} (calcium/calmodulin kinase II), and phosphoinositide (protein kinase C) systems. The second messengers cAMP and cGMP are inactivated by enzymes called phosphodiesterases (PDEs). Inhibitors of specific PDEs are being tested for their potential efficacy in treating various CNS disorders.

- Neurotrophic factors like NGF and BDNF work by activating tyrosine kinase receptors.

- Allosteric modulators are molecules that have no receptor activity alone, but together with a receptor agonist the allosteric modulator either increases or decreases the response to the agonist (positive or negative allosteric modulator). Allosteric modulators work by binding to sites on the receptor protein separate from the agonist binding site. One potential advantage of using an allosteric modulator instead of a direct receptor agonist or antagonist is if the modulator induces biased signaling of a metabotropic receptor.

- Psychoactive drugs usually exert their subjective and behavioral effects by modifying synaptic transmission. Neurotransmitter precursors increase the rate of transmitter synthesis, whereas drugs that block an enzyme in the synthesis pathway cause a decrease in transmitter synthesis rate.

- Neurotransmitter action can be enhanced by blocking transmitter breakdown or by inhibiting transmitter reuptake. Drugs may also cause increased neurotransmitter release by blocking vesicle storage or by reversing the action of membrane transmitter transporters.

- Autoreceptor agonists reduce transmitter release, whereas autoreceptor antagonists enhance release.

- Neurotransmitter effects on postsynaptic receptors may be mimicked by a receptor agonist or blocked by a receptor antagonist.

- Synaptic plasticity refers to functional and structural changes in synaptic connectivity. Structurally, synaptic plasticity is often manifested by changes in dendritic length and branching and in the dendritic spine density. Dendrites and dendritic spines reach a peak during development, after which they are pruned during the period of adolescence.

- A number of neurodevelopmental disorders are characterized by abnormal development of dendrites and dendritic spines.

- Animal studies have demonstrated that repeated exposure to various abused drugs can cause changes in dendritic structure in certain parts of the brain. Such changes likely contribute to increases in drug-seeking behavior.

3.3 The Endocrine System

As we have seen, neurotransmitters normally travel only a tiny distance before reaching their target at the other side of the synaptic cleft, or sometimes a little farther away. Another method of cellular communication, however, involves the release of chemical substances called **hormones** into the bloodstream. Hormones are secreted by specialized organs called **endocrine glands**. Upon reaching the circulation, hormones can travel long distances before reaching target cells anywhere in the body. To respond to a given hormone, a target cell must possess specific receptors for that hormone, just as a postsynaptic cell must respond to a neurotransmitter. Moreover, sometimes the same substances (e.g., norepinephrine, epinephrine, vasopressin, and oxytocin) are used both as neurotransmitters within the brain and as hormones within the endocrine system. Thus, synaptic and endocrine communications are similar in many respects, although they differ in terms of the proximity of the cells involved and the anatomic features of the synapses described earlier (**FIGURE 3.18**).

Endocrine glands and their respective hormones

As shown in **FIGURE 3.19**, numerous endocrine glands are located throughout the body. Some of these glands secrete more than one type of hormone. We will now briefly describe each gland and its associated hormone(s), including the chemical classification and functions of that hormone.

The **adrenal glands** lie over the kidneys. An adrenal gland is actually two separate glands that have come together during embryonic development (**FIGURE 3.20**). The inner part of the gland, which is called the **adrenal medulla**, is derived from nervous system tissue. Like a sympathetic ganglion, it receives input from the preganglionic fibers of the sympathetic nervous system (see Chapter 2). Cells of the adrenal medulla,

which are called **chromaffin cells**, secrete the hormones **epinephrine** (**EPI**) and **norepinephrine** (**NE**), both of which are monoamines. Physical or psychological stressors stimulate the release of EPI and NE as part of the classic "fight-or-flight" response. Once in the bloodstream, these hormones mobilize glucose (sugar) from the liver to provide immediate energy, and they also divert blood from the internal organs (e.g., the organs of digestion) to the muscles, in case physical action is needed. Some of their effects contribute to the physical sensations that we experience when we're highly aroused or stressed, such as a racing heart and cold, clammy hands.

The outer part of the adrenal gland, the **adrenal cortex**, secretes hormones called **glucocorticoids**. Which glucocorticoid is present depends on the species: humans, nonhuman primates, and most other large mammals make **cortisol** (sometimes called *hydrocortisone*), whereas most rodents (including rats and mice) and birds make **corticosterone**. Glucocorticoids belong to a class of molecules known as **steroids**, all of which are derived from the precursor cholesterol. Among the functions of glucocorticoids are (1) to maintain normal blood glucose levels while helping to store excess glucose for future use (hence the term glucocorticoids), (2) to regulate activity of the immune system, and (3) to interact with neurotransmitter systems in the brain to modulate cognitive and emotional processing. Glucocorticoids are well known to be secreted in increased amounts during stress, thereby helping us cope with stressful experiences. However, there is substantial evidence that chronic stress may lead to serious health consequences, even including damage to certain parts of the brain, if high glucocorticoid levels persist for long periods of time (McEwen et al., 2015; Lupien et al., 2018).

Other glands that secrete steroid hormones are the **gonads**: the **ovaries** in females and the **testes** in males. The ovaries secrete female sex hormones called **estrogens** (such as **estradiol**) and **progestins** (mainly **progesterone**), whereas the testes secrete male sex hormones called **androgens** (such as **testosterone**). These gonadal hormones determine some of the physical differences between males and females (the so-called secondary sex characteristics) that occur after puberty. Testosterone also has two other important roles. During early development, this hormone acts within the brain to produce neural changes important for determining later gender-based differences in behavior. Later on, it plays a significant role in stimulating sexual motivation in males and even in females (both genders possess some quantity of each other's sex hormones).

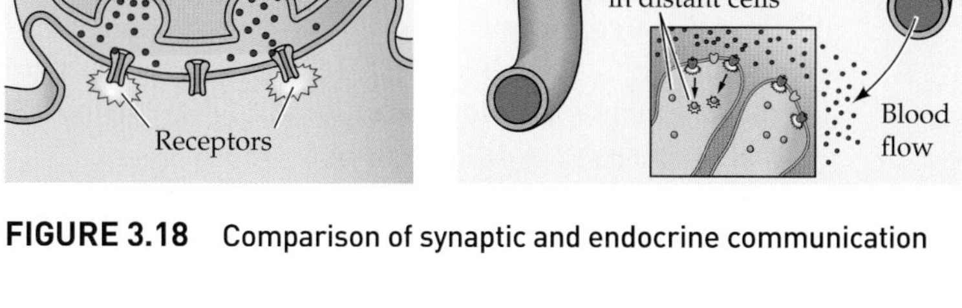

Synaptic   Endocrine

FIGURE 3.18   Comparison of synaptic and endocrine communication

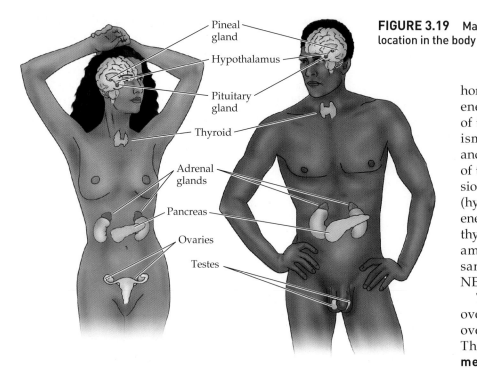

Within the pancreas is an endocrine gland known as the **islets of Langerhans**. Cells within this tissue secrete two hormones: **insulin** and **glucagon**. These are peptide hormones, similar to the neuropeptides discussed earlier but somewhat larger in size. Insulin release is stimulated by food intake, and together with glucagon, it plays an important role in regulating glucose and other sources of metabolic energy. Type 1 diabetes is caused by a total or near-total lack of insulin production by the pancreas. In type 2 diabetes, insulin production is present but either the amount produced is insufficient or the person's body does not respond adequately to the insulin (insulin resistance). Being chronically overweight is a risk factor for developing type 2 diabetes, which, unfortunately, is on the rise in many parts of the world

Residing in the throat is the **thyroid gland**, which secretes **thyroxine (T4)** and **triiodothyronine (T3)**. These

hormones are important for normal energy metabolism. Underactivity of the thyroid gland (hypothyroidism) causes feelings of weakness and lethargy (even mimicking some of the symptoms of clinical depression), whereas thyroid overactivity (hyperthyroidism) leads to excessive energy and nervousness. These two thyroid hormones are made from the amino acid tyrosine, which is the same precursor used to make DA, NE, and EPI (see Chapter 5).

The **pineal gland** is situated just over the brainstem and is covered over by the cerebral hemispheres. This gland secretes the hormone **melatonin**, which is synthesized using the neurotransmitter 5-HT as a precursor. Melatonin has been implicated in the control of various rhythmic functions, which differ depending on the species. In humans and in many other vertebrates, most melatonin secretion occurs during the night, which suggests a possible role in controlling sleep rhythms. Tablets that contain small amounts of melatonin can be purchased over the counter in drugstores and supermarkets, and for some people, these tablets induce drowsiness and faster sleep onset.

The **pituitary gland** is sometimes called the "master gland" because it secretes several hormones that control other glands. The pituitary is found just under the hypothalamus and is connected to that brain structure by a thin stalk. Like the adrenals, the pituitary actually comprises two separate glands with different hormones that serve distinct functions. The **anterior pituitary** secretes **thyroid-stimulating hormone (TSH;** also known as thyrotropin), **adrenocorticotropic hormone (ACTH)**, **follicle-stimulating hormone (FSH)**, **luteinizing hormone (LH)**, **growth hormone (GH)**, and **prolactin (PRL)**. TSH stimulates the thyroid gland, and ACTH promotes the synthesis and release of glucocorticoids from the adrenal cortex. FSH and LH together control the growth and functioning of the gonads. LH stimulates estrogen and androgen secretion by the ovaries and testes, respectively. GH stimulates the production of insulin-like growth factor I (IGF-I) from peripheral organs such as the liver; IGF-I is critical for skeletal growth during development. Finally, PRL promotes milk production by the mammary glands.

The pituitary stalk connecting the hypothalamus with the pituitary gland contains blood vessels that carry special **hypothalamic releasing hormones**

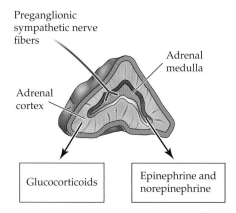

FIGURE 3.20 Structure of the adrenal gland, showing the outer cortex and the inner medulla

(**FIGURE 3.21**). These hormones are mainly neuropeptides manufactured by various groups of neurons in the hypothalamus. Instead of forming normal synapses, these neurons release peptides into blood capillaries in a region called the **median eminence**. Blood vessels then carry releasing hormones to the hormone-secreting cells of the anterior pituitary. For example, **thyrotropin-releasing hormone (TRH)** is a hypothalamic peptide that stimulates the release of TSH, **corticotropin-releasing hormone (CRH)** (alternatively called *corticotropin-releasing factor*, or CRF) stimulates ACTH release (corticotropin is another name for ACTH),

and **gonadotropin-releasing hormone (GnRH)** stimulates both FSH and LH. We can see that the endocrine system sometimes functions through the interactions of several glands, with one gland controlling another until the final hormone is secreted. For example, stress does not directly cause increased glucocorticoid secretion from the adrenal cortex. Instead, stress leads to enhanced CRH release from the hypothalamus, which provokes ACTH release from the anterior pituitary; ACTH travels through the bloodstream to the adrenal glands, where it stimulates the secretion of glucocorticoids. Because of this complicated control system, it often takes a few

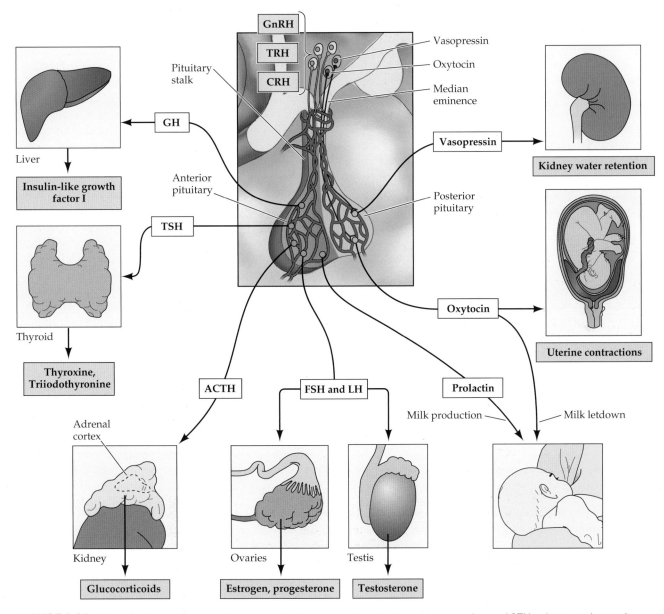

FIGURE 3.21 **Organization of the hypothalamic–pituitary axis** Note that the axon terminals of the hypothalamic releasing hormone neurons are located near blood capillaries in the median eminence, whereas oxytocin and vasopressin neurons send their axons all the way into the posterior lobe of the pituitary gland. For the purpose of simplicity, not all hypothalamic releasing hormones are shown. ACTH, adrenocorticotropic hormone; CRH, corticotropin-releasing hormone; FSH, follicle-stimulating hormone; GH, growth hormone; GnRH, gonadotropin-releasing hormone; LH, luteinizing hormone; TRH, thyrotropin-releasing hormone; TSH, thyroid-stimulating hormone.

minutes before the level of glucocorticoids in our blood is significantly increased. Thus the endocrine system works much more slowly than chemical communication by neurotransmitters.

Hormonal and neurotransmitter functions of oxytocin and vasopressin

In addition to blood vessels that connect the hypothalamus to the anterior pituitary, the pituitary stalk contains the axons of specialized secretory neurons located within the **paraventricular** and **supraoptic** nuclei of the hypothalamus. These neurosecretory cells, which are called **magnocellular neurons** because of their unusually large size, synthesize either **vasopressin** (**VP**) or **oxytocin** (**OT**) for release into the bloodstream. The axons of the magnocellular neurons reach the **posterior pituitary**, where, like the other hypothalamic neurons mentioned earlier, they form endings on blood vessels instead of other cells. Circulating VP (also called *antidiuretic hormone*) released from the posterior pituitary acts on the kidneys to increase water retention (i.e., make the urine more concentrated). Alcohol inhibits VP secretion, which is one of the reasons why people urinate so frequently when they drink (it's not just the increased fluid consumption). Oxytocin, in contrast, exerts two important physiological functions in female mammals: stimulation of uterine contractions during childbirth, and triggering of milk letdown from the breasts during lactation.

The paraventricular nucleus possesses not only magnocellular VP and OT neurons but also smaller cells called **parvocellular neurons**. The parvocellular neurons send VP- and OT-containing axons to a variety of different brain regions where these neuropeptides are released like neurotransmitters onto other nerve cells (**FIGURE 3.22**). The figure additionally depicts a

VP pathway emanating from neurons within the bed nucleus of the stria terminalis. Importantly, the brain areas that receive VP and/or OT projections are part of or interact with an extensive circuit called the **social behavioral neural network**. This network regulates a variety of social behavioral processes such as social recognition memory (memory for a familiar species member), pair bonding (formation of a social bond between males and females for reproductive purposes), mother–offspring social bonds, and other interactions among conspecifics (members of the same species), including both affiliative and competitive/aggressive interactions (Caldwell, 2017; Walum and Young, 2018). Because many of these social behaviors differ between males and females, it is not surprising that some VP and OT pathways are sexually dimorphic (i.e., different in male and female species members). Moreover, the same behaviors are influenced by male and female gonadal steroids (i.e., testosterone and estradiol), and indeed VP and OT work together with these steroids to carry out their behavioral effects. The variety of social behaviors observed not only in nonhuman species but also in humans depend on **social cognition**, which refers to the processing of social cues (including attention, emotion and motivation, learning, and memory) to determine the appropriate behavioral responses to these cues.

Many studies have investigated whether OT (and to a lesser extent VP) can influence human social behaviors. Most such studies have used intranasal delivery by means of a nasal spray (Quintana et al., 2018). This route of administration is necessary because of poor passage of OT (and peptides in general) across the blood–brain barrier, thereby limiting the usefulness of more traditional methods such as oral administration or intravenous injection. Researchers have identified several potential

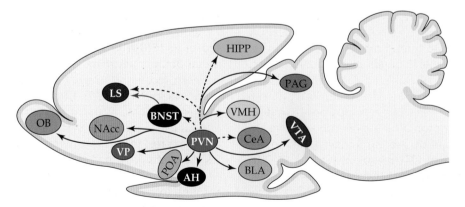

FIGURE 3.22 Central pathways of vasopressin (VP) and oxytocin (OT) fibers The cell bodies of centrally projecting VP and OT neurons are located in the paraventricular nucleus and, in the case of VP only, the bed nucleus of the stria terminalis. Solid black lines indicate OT-only fibers, dashed black lines indicate both VP and OT fibers, and the solid red line indicates a VP-only pathway. All of the brain areas receiving VP and/or OT input are either part of or interact with the social

behavioral neural network. AH, anterior hypothalamus; BLA, basolateral amygdala; BNST, bed nucleus of the stria terminalis; CeA, central amygdala; HIPP, hippocampus; LS, lateral septum; NAcc, nucleus accumbens; OB, olfactory bulb; PAG, periaqueductal gray; POA, preoptic area; PVN, paraventricular nucleus; VMH, ventromedial hypothalamus; VP, ventral pallidum; VTA, ventral tegmental area. (After H. K. Caldwell. 2017. *Neuroscientist* 23: 517–528. © 2017. SAGE Publications.)

routes by which substances could reach the CNS from the nasal cavity (see Lochhead and Thorne, 2012), and there is direct experimental evidence for elevated OT levels in the cerebrospinal fluid following intranasal OT administration (Striepens et al., 2013). Various findings suggest that OT administered exogenously to healthy human participants can influence a variety of social behaviors, including empathy, altruism, trust, preference for and cooperation with in-group members, and social memory (De Dreu, 2012; Kendrick et al., 2018). To account for these findings, some researchers have hypothesized that OT may regulate the salience of social cues (i.e., the ability of social cues to garner attention in different contexts) (Shamay-Tsoory and Abu-Akel, 2016).

The prosocial effects of OT in healthy individuals raise the possibility that this substance might be useful for treating autism spectrum disorder (ASD) (See Web Box 1.2). ASD is a pervasive developmental disorder characterized by two major kinds of behavioral symptoms: deficits in social communication and interaction, and a significant occurrence of restricted, repetitive behavior patterns (Hodges et al., 2020). A number of associated neurological and physical symptoms are often present in children with ASD (**FIGURE 3.23**). The spectrum subsumes several previous diagnostic categories, including autism and Asperger's disorder. Symptoms of ASD usually begin to manifest in infancy but a formal diagnosis may not be made until childhood. Drugs are sometimes prescribed to treat behavioral symptoms that may be comorbid with ASD such as irritability and aggressiveness (risperidone [trade name Risperdal]; aripiprazole [trade name Abilify]), hyperactivity (methylphenidate [trade name Ritalin]), or depression (selective serotonin reuptake inhibitors such as fluoxetine [trade name Prozac]) (LeClerc and Easley, 2015; Mason and Burns, 2019). In contrast, the core social communication deficits associated with ASD must be treated with behavioral interventions, since no standard medications are available for those symptoms.

Could OT play a role in ameliorating the social deficits in ASD patients? A number of controlled clinical trials have now been conducted to test this hypothesis. Although a few of these trials reported positive effects of OT on ASD symptomatology, overall reviews and statistical analyses of this research have failed to find consistent benefits of OT treatment (Ooi et al., 2017; Keech et al., 2018). In light of these findings, researchers are pursuing novel approaches such as developing synthetic OT agonists that cross the blood–brain barrier and therefore do not need to be administered intranasally (Gulliver et al., 2019).

Mechanisms of hormone action

As mentioned in Chapter 1, two broad types of receptors are used in cellular communication: extracellular (membrane) receptors and intracellular receptors.

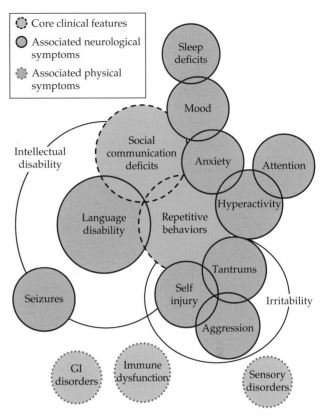

FIGURE 3.23   **Clinical symptoms of autism spectrum disorder** ASD patients exhibit core social deficits and repetitive behaviors. Other associated neurological and physical symptoms may also be present to varying degrees, depending on the individual and the severity of the disorder. (After M. J. Kas et al. 2014. *Psychopharm* 231: 1125–1146. doi.org/10.1007/s00213-013-3268-5.)

Earlier in this chapter, we observed that most neurotransmitter receptors are located on the cell membrane. In contrast, hormones use various types of receptors, both extracellular and intracellular.

Peptide hormones function by means of membrane receptors (**FIGURE 3.24A**). Some of these are just like metabotropic neurotransmitter receptors, working through second-messenger systems. For example, the receptors for VP and OT stimulate the phosphoinositide second-messenger system, thereby activating protein kinase C. However, some hormones, such as insulin, use tyrosine kinase receptors that are similar to the trk receptors described earlier.

Steroid and thyroid hormones operate mostly through intracellular receptors (**FIGURE 3.24B**). These receptors are proteins just like the membrane receptors for neurotransmitters or peptide hormones, but they are generally located within the cell nucleus, where they function as **transcription factors** to either turn on or turn off the expression of specific genes within the cell. Since gene expression determines which proteins are made by the cell, the ultimate effects of steroid and thyroid hormones are seen in the altered synthesis of

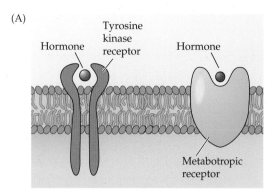

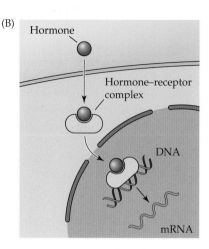

FIGURE 3.24 **Hormonal signaling** A variety of extracellular (A) and intracellular (B) receptors mediate hormone signaling.

particular proteins. This process takes much longer (many minutes to a few hours or longer) than the rapid effects typically produced by membrane receptors. On the other hand, changes in gene expression and protein synthesis are also longer-lasting, thus allowing an animal or person to keep responding to a hormone long after it is released. In addition to this classical, relatively slow action of steroid hormones, some effects, such as stimulation of neuronal firing, occur very rapidly (Roepke et al., 2011; Joëls et al., 2013). Such effects are far too quick to be mediated by altered gene expression but could be produced by receptors in the cell membrane. Indeed, researchers have made progress in identifying membrane receptors for glucocorticoids (Johnstone 3rd et al., 2019), estrogens (Vajaria and Vasudevan, 2018; Vail and Roepke, 2019), and androgens (Thomas, 2019).

The endocrine system is important to pharmacologists

Our discussion about OT and ASD provides an example of why pharmacologists might be interested in the endocrine system. However, the OT system targeted in those studies was released centrally and did not involve peripheral secretion from the pituitary gland. Nevertheless, there are a number of good reasons why pharmacologists are interested in the classical endocrine system and hormones released into the bloodstream. Four of these reasons are as follows:

1. Both therapeutic and abused drugs can alter the secretion of many hormones, causing physiological abnormalities. For example, chronic alcoholism can lead to reduced testosterone levels, testicular atrophy, and impotence in men. Alcoholic women may have menstrual disorders and at least temporarily may become infertile (see Chapter 10).

2. Hormones may alter subjective and behavioral responses to drugs (Terner and de Wit, 2006). This is illustrated by the important role of female sex hormones in modulating sensitivity to drugs of abuse such as cocaine and nicotine (**WEB BOX 3.4**).

3. Hormones themselves sometimes have psychoactive properties like those of certain drugs. We

mentioned earlier that melatonin has a sedative effect on many people. In addition, thyroid hormones are occasionally prescribed along with an antidepressant drug to enhance the therapeutic response.

4. The secretion of pituitary hormones and other hormones dependent on the pituitary is controlled by neurotransmitter systems in the brain. This fact sometimes enables us to use the endocrine system as a "window to the brain" that tells us whether a particular neurotransmitter system has been altered by disease (such as a psychiatric or neurological disorder), injury, or the effect of a psychoactive drug.

Most fundamentally, the classification of some substances as neurotransmitters and other as hormones is based merely on where they are released (i.e., into a synapse in one case and into the bloodstream in the other). Indeed, there are numerous examples of the same molecule being used for both purposes, such as NE and EPI (as we will see in Chapter 5), VP, OT, and many other peptides. Studying the mechanisms of hormone release, receptor structure, and signaling pathways has given researchers much information that is equally applicable to neurotransmitter systems.

SECTION SUMMARY

■ Hormones are released into the bloodstream, where they may travel long distances before reaching target cells in the body. Despite important differences between synaptic and endocrine communications, the same substance is sometimes used as both a neurotransmitter and a hormone.

■ The adrenal gland is composed of the inner medulla and the outer cortex, both of which are activated by stress. The chromaffin cells of the adrenal medulla secrete the hormones EPI and NE, whereas the adrenal cortex secretes glucocorticoid steroids such as cortisol and corticosterone.

■ Other steroid hormones that are synthesized and released by the gonads include estrogens and progesterone from the ovaries in females, and androgens such as testosterone from the testes in males. These gonadal steroids are responsible for many of the secondary sex characteristics that appear after puberty; testosterone is additionally involved in sexual differentiation of the brain during early development, as well as in stimulation of sexual motivation later in life.

- The islets of Langerhans and the thyroid gland secrete hormones important in energy metabolism. Insulin and glucagon are released from separate populations of cells within the islets of Langerhans, and together these two peptide hormones regulate the disposition of glucose and other sources of metabolic energy.

- The pineal gland, which is situated just over the brainstem, synthesizes the hormone melatonin using 5-HT as a precursor. Melatonin has been implicated in the regulation of various types of rhythmic activity, including sleep.

- The pituitary gland is found just under the hypothalamus and is connected to it. The pituitary is divided into two separate glands, the anterior and posterior pituitary glands, which serve different functions.

- The anterior pituitary secretes TSH, ACTH, FSH, LH, GH, and PRL. TSH and ACTH stimulate the thyroid and adrenal glands (cortex), respectively, whereas FSH and LH together control the growth and functioning of the gonads. GH stimulates skeletal growth during development, and PRL plays an important role in promoting milk production during lactation.

- The hypothalamic releasing hormones TRH, CRH, and GnRH are neuropeptides synthesized within the hypothalamus that trigger the release of TSH, ACTH, and the gonadotropins FSH and LH. Because of this organizational structure, in which several glands must stimulate each other until the final hormone product is secreted, the endocrine system works much more slowly than chemical communication by neurotransmitters.

- Magnocellular neurons in the paraventricular and supraoptic nuclei of the hypothalamus send their axons to the posterior pituitary gland where they secrete two small peptide hormones, VP and OT, into the bloodstream. VP enhances water retention by the kidneys, whereas OT stimulates uterine contractions during childbirth and also triggers milk letdown from the breasts during lactation.

- The paraventricular nucleus also contains parvocellular VP and OT neurons that project to brain areas that are part of the social behavioral neural network, which helps regulate many different social behavioral processes, including social cognition. These pathways are sexually dimorphic and are influenced by gonadal steroids such as estradiol and testosterone.

- Peptide hormones exert their actions through membrane metabotropic receptors. In contrast, steroid and thyroid hormones act primarily through intracellular receptors that function as transcription factors controlling gene expression.

- The endocrine system is important to pharmacologists for several reasons. These include the fact that (1) drugs can adversely alter endocrine function, (2) hormones may alter behavioral responses to drugs, (3) hormones themselves sometimes have psychoactive properties, and (4) the endocrine system can be used as a window to the brain to help us determine the functioning of a specific neurotransmitter system by measuring changes in hormone secretion under appropriate conditions.

- Autism spectrum disorder is a developmental neuropsychiatric disorder characterized by core deficits in social communication as well as restricted, repetitive behavior patterns. Because of the positive effects of intranasal OT administration on a variety of different social cognitive functions in healthy people, researchers have tested whether this substance could be beneficial in treating ASD. Although no consistent benefits have yet been demonstrated, this area of research is ongoing.

STUDY QUESTIONS

1. Describe the structure of a typical axodendritic synapse, including both presynaptic and postsynaptic elements. How do axosomatic synapses, axoaxonic synapses, and neuromuscular junctions differ from axodendritic synapses?

2. Excitatory synapses can work either by increasing the electrical excitability of the postsynaptic cell or by increasing neurotransmitter release from that cell without affecting its overall excitability. Comparing axodendritic and axoaxonic synapses, which of these works by the first mechanism and which works by the second mechanism? Explain your answer.

3. List the criteria required for a substance to be verified as a neurotransmitter. If you discovered a novel chemical in the brain, what would be the first step you would take in trying to determine whether your newly discovered chemical was a neurotransmitter? Why would that be your first step?

4. Neurotransmitters can be classified based on the chemical category to which they belong. Name these categories and give at least one example of a member of each category.

5. Describe how the synthesis of neuropeptides differs from that of other types of neurotransmitters. How does this difference impact the ability of neuropeptide release to be maintained under conditions of continuous neuronal firing?

6. _____ is a sleep disorder characterized by excessive daytime sleepiness and attacks of cataplexy. What neuropeptide has been linked to this disorder?

(Continued)

STUDY QUESTIONS (continued)

7. What is exocytosis and what is its role in neurotransmitter release? What components of the nerve terminal are needed for exocytosis to occur?

8. When a neuron is only firing occasionally, neurotransmitter release will be confined to vesicles within the _____ pool; however, when the cell is firing continuously for a prolonged period of time, then vesicles within the _____ pool will be recruited to participate in the release process.

9. Describe the process of vesicle recycling and the various models that have been proposed to explain the recycling process. How do these models differ with respect to factors such as speed of recycling, area of the nerve terminal where vesicle membrane retrieval occurs, and the involvement of the protein clathrin and of endosomes?

10. Why are lipid and gaseous transmitters better suited to be retrograde messengers than classical transmitters?

11. Inhibitory autoreceptors that work by reducing the rate of cell firing are called _____ autoreceptors, whereas inhibitory autoreceptors that work by reducing neurotransmitter release without affecting cell firing are called _____ autoreceptors.

12. Some inhibitory autoreceptors are coupled to K^+ channels, whereas others are coupled to Ca^{2+} channels. In each case, will activation of the autoreceptor cause an increase or a decrease in channel opening, and why?

13. Compare the functions of neurotransmitter transporters with those of neurotransmitter autoreceptors.

14. Volume transmission by neurotransmitters is made possible, in part, by the inefficiency of neurotransmitter reuptake. Is this statement true or false? Explain your answer.

15. Why is a knowledge of receptor subtypes important when developing a new pharmaceutical medication?

16. Describe the structural and functional differences between ionotropic and metabotropic receptors. Which of these is better suited for fast signaling and why?

17. Discuss the concept of allosteric receptor modulation. How is the influence of a positive or negative allosteric modulator different from the influence of a direct agonist or antagonist on a particular receptor's functioning? When an allosteric modulator influences one receptor signaling pathway but has little or no effect on other signaling pathways, this is called _____.

18. What is a second messenger, and how do "second" messengers differ from "first" messengers? List the main second-messenger systems described in this chapter. What is the role of protein kinases in second-messenger signaling?

19. Enzymes that catalyze the removal of phosphate groups from phosphorylated proteins are called _____. A drug that blocks dephosphorylation of proteins that are phosphorylated in response to receptor activation will _____ (prolong or terminate?) the effects of that receptor on the postsynaptic cell.

20. Discuss the hypothesis that microbes in our gut may affect our mood and behavior. What is the term used to describe the system of communication between the gut and the brain, and what are the pathways that mediate this communication?

21. What is meant by the term *synaptic plasticity*? Many abused drugs can produce signs of structural synaptic plasticity. Almost all evidence for this type of effect comes from animal studies. Why?

22. List the major steroid hormones and the name of the endocrine gland responsible for synthesizing each hormone.

23. Discuss the relationships among the hypothalamic releasing hormones, the anterior pituitary gland, and the hormones secreted by the anterior pituitary. What is the anatomical relationship between the hypothalamus and the pituitary gland that contributes to the ability of hypothalamic releasing hormones to regulate anterior pituitary secretory activity?

24. Vasopressin and oxytocin that are released from the posterior pituitary gland are synthesized by _____ neurons in the hypothalamus. In contrast, hypothalamic neurons that make vasopressin and oxytocin and that form pathways within the brain to regulate social behavior are called _____ neurons.

25. What are the differences between the peripheral effects of vasopressin and oxytocin (that is, produced by circulating hormone molecules released from the posterior pituitary) and the central effects of these same substances (that is, after release from pathways within the brain)?

26. What are the core symptoms of ASD? What is the rationale for studying oxytocin as a potential treatment for this disorder?

27. Describe the difference in the main signaling mechanisms between steroid and peptide hormones. Are there any alternative mechanisms that can permit steroid hormones to signal other cells as rapidly as peptide hormones?

28. Why are studies of the endocrine system valuable to pharmacologists?

Methods of Research in Psychopharmacology

THE BRAIN, THE MOST AMAZING ORGAN OF THE BODY, composed of tens of billions of neurons, perhaps 100 trillion synapses, and 100,000 miles of axons, is what allows us to think, comprehend speech, remember events, experience a wide variety of emotions, perceive complex sensory experiences, and guide our appropriate responses. Trying to decipher the functioning of this complex organ is an incredible undertaking. For much of history, philosophers and scientists believed our thoughts and emotions were due to "vapors" that swirled through our bodies and brains. By the 17th century, anatomical features of the brain began to be considered, and Luigi Galvani (an Italian physiologist) showed that if you electrically stimulated a nerve attached to a muscle, it could cause contraction of the muscle. But it was not until the Spaniards Golgi and Ramón y Cajal began to stain neurons to evaluate their structure microscopically (see Chapter 2) that they began to appreciate the complexity of the nervous system in its infinite detail. Now the sophisticated imaging techniques described in this chapter and other techniques yet to be developed have begun to piece together the intricate puzzle that is the human brain. Thanks to the National Institutes of Health (NIH) and public funding and the work of thousands of researchers, progress has been made toward mapping all the axonal pathways in the human brain. These researchers along with the entire scientific community have free access to the data. This initiative is called the Human Connectome Project (see www.humanconnectome.org), and in conjunction with the Human Genome Project that mapped the entire human gene sequence, neuroscience is leaping forward at an amazing pace, a true voyage of discovery that will explain what makes us human, yet different from one another. It may soon be able to change the lives of individuals with a variety of brain disorders. The opening figure provides an idea of the beauty and complexity of the neural networks that are being mapped. ■

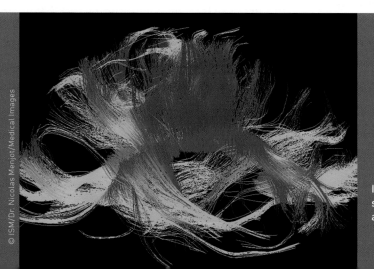

© ISM/Dr. Nicolas Menjot/Medical Images

Images such as this diffusion tensor image (DTI) show some of the approximately 100,000 miles of axons connecting the many regions of the brain.

The discovery of chemical transmission of information between nerve cells paved the way for the birth of neuropsychopharmacology. Since then, an explosion of research has been directed toward understanding the nature of brain function and the biology of what makes us human. With the variety and power of new analytic tools and techniques, we can look inside the brain to find answers to questions that touch individual lives. Even non-scientists can appreciate the advances in neuroscience research that bring us ever closer to understanding the essence of human behavior, as well as some of the most troubling problems of mankind: dementia, depression, autism, and neurodegenerative disorders.

The new tools provide the means to explore the brain to answer our questions, but it takes disciplined and creative scientific minds and teamwork to pose the right questions and to optimally use available tools. The scientific method, utilizing rigorous hypothesis testing under controlled conditions, is the only real method that we have to investigate how molecules responsible for nerve cell activity relate to complex human behaviors and thinking. Analysis spans the entire range from molecular genetics to cell function to integrated systems of neuronal networks, and finally to observable behavior. To understand the brain requires a convergence of efforts from multiple disciplines, which together form the basis of neuroscience: psychology, biochemistry, neuropharmacology, neuroanatomy, endocrinology, bioinformatics, neuropsychology, and molecular biology. Ultimately, we acquire knowledge by integrating information derived by a wide variety of research techniques from all of these fields.

As you might expect, the list of techniques is very long and grows longer every day. This chapter focuses on a few of the more common methods and helps you to understand the purpose of each method, as well as some of its potential weaknesses. Perhaps the most important goal of this chapter is to encourage you, when you read scientific papers, to critically evaluate the methods and controls used, because the conclusions we draw from experiments are only as good as the methodology used to collect the data.

In the first part of this chapter, we focus on behavioral pharmacology. Behavior, mood, and cognitive function represent the focus of neuropsychopharmacology, so it is of tremendous importance to understand and critically evaluate the techniques used to quantify behavioral changes. The second part of the chapter emphasizes techniques that look at the locations and functions of neurotransmitters and neurotransmitter receptors. The methods described are both **in vivo**, meaning observed in the living organism, and **in vitro**, which refers to measurements performed outside the living body (traditionally in a test tube). We also look at a variety of rather remarkable imaging techniques that

permit us to visualize the activity of the living human brain. Because genetic engineering is an increasingly powerful tool, we will describe its use in psychopharmacology. Both the biochemical and behavioral techniques selected will be used in subsequent chapters. Although this chapter is artificially divided into sections, keep in mind that much of the most informative research in psychopharmacology utilizes techniques of neuroscience in combination with behavioral analysis. Feel free to return to this chapter to review a method when you encounter it later.

4.1 Techniques in Behavioral Pharmacology

Evaluating animal behavior

The techniques of behavioral pharmacology allow scientists to evaluate the relationship between an experimental manipulation, such as a lesion or drug administration, and changes in behavior. In a well-designed experiment, it is necessary to compare the behavior of the experimental treatment group with that of placebo control subjects. Neurobiological techniques such as selective lesioning and intracerebral drug administration, described in the second section of this chapter, tell us very little unless we have an objective measure of the behavioral consequences. Behavioral measures are crucial for (1) understanding the neurochemical basis of behavior, as well as drug-induced changes in that behavior; (2) developing animal models of psychiatric disorders; and (3) screening the large number of newly designed and synthesized drug molecules in preclinical pharmaceutical settings in an effort to determine therapeutic usefulness.

Animal testing needs to be valid and reliable to produce useful information

Animal studies clearly provide several advantages over studies using human participants. The most obvious advantage is the use of rigorous controls. The living conditions (e.g., diet, exercise, room temperature, exposure to stress, day–night cycle) of animal subjects can be regulated far more precisely than those of humans. In addition, the histories of animal subjects are well known, and the genetic backgrounds of a group of animals are very similar and well characterized. Finally, animals are the most appropriate subjects for the study of mechanisms of drug action, because an understanding of the electrophysiological and neurochemical bases of drug effects often requires invasive techniques that are obviously unethical with human participants. Consider, for example, the valuable information gained from genetically manipulated animals. In addition, drugs can be administered to animal subjects in ways not generally appropriate for humans, for example over long periods of time to determine toxic effects or the potential for addiction. Finally, the brains and behaviors of non-human mammals and humans are similar enough to allow generalization across species. For instance, lesions of the central nucleus of the amygdala of rats produce profound changes in the conditioned emotional response of these animals. Likewise, tumors, strokes, and surgical procedures that damage the human amygdaloid complex produce profound changes in fearfulness, anxiety, and emotional memory.

The impact of animal testing in biomedical research on the quality of human life (**FIGURE 4.1**) is discussed in a thought-provoking manner by Hollinger (2008), as are its alternatives. The need for animal experimentation is best seen under conditions when research using human participants is impossible, as when testing the effects of alcohol on fetal development. Ethical constraints prohibit researchers from administering varying doses of alcohol to groups of pregnant women to evaluate the effects on their newborns. Instead, data collected on alcohol consumption during pregnancy and the occurrence of fetal alcohol syndrome (FAS) suggest a relationship that tells us that the more alcohol a pregnant female consumes, the more likely it is that

FIGURE 4.1   Poster used to counter the claims of animal rights activists   Scientists hope to increase public awareness about the benefits of animal research.

her infant will show signs of FAS. Although we know that infants of mothers who consume alcohol are more likely to show fetal abnormalities, the type of study described shows only a **correlational relationship**; we cannot conclude that alcohol *causes* FAS, because other factors may be responsible for both. For example, poverty, poor diet, or other drug use may lead to increased alcohol consumption *and* cause developmental defects in the fetus. Therefore, to learn more about how alcohol affects fetal development, we need to perform animal studies. Since animal testing remains an important part of new drug development and evaluation, strict animal care guidelines have been developed to ensure proper treatment of subjects. The animal-testing stage provides an important step between basic science and the treatment of human conditions.

The Health Research Extension Act of 1985 provided strict guidelines for the care of animals used in biomedical and behavioral research. The goals of that legislation include humane animal maintenance and experimentation that limits both the use of animals and animal distress. Each research institution must have an animal care committee that reviews each scientific protocol with three considerations in mind:

1. The research should be relevant to human or animal health, advancement of knowledge, or the good of society.

2. Alternative methods such as computer simulations that do not require animal subjects must be considered.

3. Procedures must avoid or minimize discomfort, distress, and pain.

Periodic inspection of living conditions ensures that they are appropriate for the species and contribute to health and comfort; cage size, temperature, lighting, cleanliness, access to food and water, sanitation, and medical care are ensured. Animal care and use committees have the authority to veto any studies that they feel do not meet all predetermined criteria.

Some animal tests used to evaluate drug effects on physiological measures such as blood pressure or body temperature closely resemble tests used for humans. These tests have high **face validity**. However, for many psychiatric disorders, the symptoms are described in typically human terms, such as feelings of guilt, delusions, altered mood, or disordered thinking. In these cases, a correlated, quantifiable measure in an animal is substituted for a more cognitive human behavior for testing purposes. When the correlation is strong, a drug that modifies animal behavior in a specific way can be expected to predictably alter a particular human behavior, even though the two behaviors may seem unrelated. For instance, if a new drug were to reduce apomorphine-induced hyperactivity in rats, tests on humans might show it to be effective in treating schizophrenia (see Chapter 19). Tests such as these have low face validity. However, if the drug effects observed in the laboratory test closely parallel or predict the clinical effect, the tests may be said to demonstrate **predictive validity**. **Construct validity** refers to the extent to which the animal measurement tool actually measures the characteristic being investigated. A test with high construct validity optimally would create the disease in the animal or would mimic the neural and behavioral features of the disorder.

The validity of animal tests that measure the behavioral effects of drugs depends on the degree to which extraneous and confounding variables are controlled. As described in Chapter 1, when an experiment is well controlled, researchers can more easily reject alternative explanations of results, allowing for more meaningful conclusions about how a test drug may affect behavior. In animal studies, the placebo condition frequently consists of an injection of the solution that the drug is dissolved in, typically referred to as the **vehicle solution**, which is often physiological saline or some other biocompatible solvent. Injection of vehicle solution is sometimes referred to as a **negative control** because the drug agent is absent from the treatment and the effect on behavior is thus expected to be minimal. In contrast, many studies are designed to include a **positive control**, in which a drug that produces well-characterized effects on a given behavioral test is tested in addition to the compound of interest. Including a positive control allows researchers to determine that the behavior test was conducted properly and is appropriately sensitive to pharmacological manipulation.

Unfortunately, the underlying neurobiology of most brain disorders is not clear, and our understanding of the underlying causes changes over time with enhancements in technology. For this reason, it is critical to avoid the temptation to assume that high degrees of either face or predictive validity necessarily mean that a given test has a correspondingly high degree of construct validity. Decades of research in Alzheimer's disease (see Chapter 20) have yielded considerable knowledge and led to the development of numerous genetically modified mouse models that exhibit high face validity, faithfully recapitulating both behavioral and neurobiological aspects of the human disease, including cognitive impairment and the formation of amyloid plaques. Nevertheless, investigational drugs that have shown efficacy in improving cognition and reducing disease markers, such as amyloid plaques, in mouse models have failed to yield therapeutic benefits in human trials. For a discussion of the factors that likely contribute to the failure of novel Alzheimer's treatments in clinical trials, see Mullane and Williams (2019). In contrast, behavioral tests that have traditionally been used to screen drugs for the treatment of schizophrenia typically reveal the extent to which these drugs suppress motor behavior. As mentioned

above, while tests like this might possess predictive validity for detecting conventional antipsychotic drugs, these tests rely on measuring the capacity of drugs to produce motor side effects that are correlated with their therapeutic effects. In this example, tests that depend on detecting the motor side effects of antipsychotic drugs therefore lack utility in the discovery of new classes of antipsychotic drugs that strive to avoid these side effects.

To be optimal, an animal behavioral test, in addition to being well validated, should also do the following:

1. It should be specific for the class of drug being screened. For example, if antidepressants produce a consistent response in a behavioral test, we probably would not want to see analgesic drugs producing the same effect.

2. It should be sensitive so that the doses used reflect a normal therapeutic range and show a dose–response relationship.

3. It should demonstrate the same rank order of potency (i.e., ranking drugs according to the dose that is effective) as the order of potency of the therapeutic action of the drugs.

In addition, good behavioral measures have high **reliability**, meaning that the same results will be recorded each time the test is used (Treit, 1985).

Valid and reliable animal tests are important for studying the neurobiological basis for complex disorders of the central nervous system (CNS) and testing the potential of new therapeutic approaches. Although animal testing and disease modeling are crucial to the development of psychoactive drugs, many of the current approaches are very limited and are poor predictors of drug efficacy in humans (see the section on translational research). Unfortunately, many of the diagnostic symptoms, such as thoughts of suicide or feelings of guilt, cannot be easily translated to animal behavior. Also, since most psychiatric disorders are highly complex in symptomatology, most animal testing is forced to evaluate only one or a few behavioral symptoms. Further, it is rare to have individuals with the same diagnosis demonstrate the same cluster of symptoms, so there are multiple animal models for the same disorder with little in common. In addition, there is insufficient information on the genetic or molecular basis of most disorders of the CNS. Nevertheless, neuroscientists are hopeful that better testing will be gradually achievable through genetic techniques, manipulations of environmental factors that have been associated with onset of the disorder, selective brain lesioning, or activation of specific brain cells using techniques such as optogenetics. The second part of this chapter will describe some of these neuropharmacological techniques. For an excellent review of animal models of CNS disorders as well as their utility and limitations, see McGonigle (2014).

A wide variety of behaviors are evaluated by psychopharmacologists

There are many behavioral tests used by psychopharmacologists, and they vary considerably in complexity, time needed to be carried out, and cost, as well as validity and reliability. In this next section, we will describe just a few of the available procedures, many of which will be referred to in subsequent chapters.

SIMPLE BEHAVIORAL OBSERVATION Many simple observations of untrained behaviors require little or no instrumentation. Among the observations made are measures of tremors, ptosis (drooping eyelids), salivation, defecation, catalepsy, reflexes, response to tail pinch, and changes in eating or drinking. Animals demonstrating catalepsy are still and immobile and sometimes will remain in an unusual posture if positioned by the experimenter. The time it takes for the animal to return to normal posture gives an indication of the extent of catalepsy. The use of catalepsy as a test to identify antipsychotic drugs that produce motor side effects demonstrates the usefulness of screening tests that are not clearly related to human behavior.

MEASURES OF MOTOR ACTIVITY These measures identify drugs that produce sleep, sedation, or motor impairment and, in contrast, drugs that stimulate activity. Spontaneous activity can be measured in a variety of ways. One popular method counts the number of times infrared light beams (invisible to rodents) directed across a designated space are broken. Automated video tracking with computerized analysis is a second method (see also section on automated quantification of behavior). A third, less automated technique (**open field test**) involves placing the animal in a prescribed area that is divided into squares so the investigator can record the number of squares traversed in a unit of time. It is also possible to count the number of fecal droppings and to observe the amount of time an animal spends along the walls of the chamber rather than venturing toward the open space. High fecal counts and low activity seen primarily at the perimeter of the cage are common indicators of anxiety-like behavior.

OPERANT CONDITIONING Operant conditioning has also made contributions to the study of the effects of drugs on behavior. It is a highly sensitive method that can be used to evaluate a wide variety of behaviors, including analgesia, anxiety, addiction potential, and drug discrimination, as well as learning and memory. The underlying principle of operant conditioning is that consequences control behavior; animals learn to respond to obtain reinforcers and avoid punishment.

Although it is possible to teach many types of operant responses, depending on the species of animal used, experiments are typically carried out in an operant chamber (Skinner box). An operant chamber is a soundproof box with a grid floor that can be electrified for shock delivery, a food or water dispenser for rewards, lights or a loudspeaker for stimulus cue presentation, and levers that the animal can press (**FIGURE 4.2**). A modern variation of the traditional operant chamber uses an interactive touchscreen for both visual stimulus presentation and recording of responses. Computerized stimulus presentation and data collection provide the opportunity to measure the total number of responses per unit of time, providing a stable and sensitive measure of continuous behavior.

In a brief training session, the animal learns to press a lever to receive a food reinforcer. Once the behavior is established, the requirements for reinforcement can be altered according to a predetermined schedule (**schedule of reinforcement**). The rate and pattern of the animal's behavior are controlled by the schedule; this allows us to examine the effect of a drug on the pattern of behavior. For instance, on a fixed-ratio (FR) schedule, reinforcement is delivered after a fixed number of responses. Thus, an FR-3 schedule means that the animal must press the lever three times to receive one food pellet. Changing the fixed ratio from 3 to 20 or 45 will tell us how hard the animal is willing to work for the reinforcement. Interval schedules also are commonly used and are characterized by the availability of reinforcement after a certain amount of time has elapsed

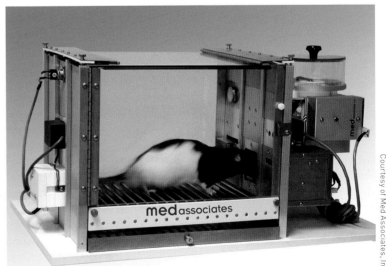

Courtesy of Med Associates, Inc.

FIGURE 4.2   Rat in an operant chamber The rat can be trained to press the lever (response) to activate a food delivery mechanism (reinforcement). An animal can also learn to press the lever to terminate or postpone shocks that can be delivered through the grid floor.

(rather than a particular number of bar presses). Thus, on an FI-2 schedule (fixed interval of 2 minutes), reinforcement follows the first response an animal makes after 2 minutes have passed since the last reinforcement. Responses made during the 2-minute interval are "wasted"—that is, elicit no reinforcement. This schedule produces a pattern of responding that includes a pause after each reinforcement and a gradual increase in the rate of responding as the interval ends. For a description of other variations in schedules and their use in drug testing, see Carlton (1983).

MEASURES OF ANALGESIA   Analgesia is the reduction of perceived pain without loss of consciousness. Analgesia testing with human participants is difficult because the response to experimentally induced pain is quite different from that to chronic or pathological pain, in which anxiety and anticipation of more pain influence the individual's response. Of course, we cannot know whether an animal "feels pain" in the same way that a human does, but we can measure the animal's avoidance of a noxious stimulus. One simple test is the **tail-flick test**, in which heat produced by a beam of light (the intensity of which is controlled by a rheostat) is focused on a portion of a rat's tail (**FIGURE 4.3**). The latency between onset of the stimulus and the animal's removal of its tail from the beam of light is assumed to be correlated with pain intensity. Another method of measuring analgesic drug action using thermal stimuli is the **hot plate test**. The animal to be tested is placed in a cylinder on a metal plate maintained at a constant temperature, which can be varied between 55°C and 70°C. Drug evaluation is based on observation of the latency between an increase in temperature of the plate and when the rat starts licking paws or kicking with the hind paws, vocalizing, or attempting to escape the cylinder. The sensitivity of this test is approximately equal to that of the tail-flick test. It seems to produce reliable and fairly stable pain thresholds with which to measure analgesic activity.

A variation of the operant FR schedule utilizes negative reinforcement, which increases the probability of a response that terminates an aversive condition. This technique can be easily applied to **operant analgesia testing**. First, the animal is trained to turn off an unpleasant foot shock by pressing the lever. In the test phase, the researcher administers increasing amounts of foot shock up to the point at which the animal responds by pressing the lever. The lowest shock intensity at which the animal first presses is considered the aversive threshold. Analgesic drugs would be expected to raise the threshold of electric shock. The method is very sensitive even to mild analgesics such as aspirin. However, an independent measure of sedation is necessary to distinguish between failure to respond due to analgesia and failure to respond due to behavioral sedation.

TESTS OF LEARNING AND MEMORY   Objective measures of learning and memory, accompanied by careful interpretation of the results, are important whether you are using animal subjects or human participants. Keep in mind that these tests very often do not determine whether altered responses are due to drug-induced changes in attention or motivation, consolidation or retrieval of the memory, or other factors contributing to overall performance. Unless these other factors are considered, tests of learning are open to misinterpretation. Despite the challenges posed, finding new ways to manipulate the brain processes involved in these functions will be central to developing drugs that are useful in treating memory deficits due to normal aging or neurological injuries or diseases such as Alzheimer's and other dementias. A wide variety of tests are available that depend on the presentation of information (training stage) followed by a delay and then the opportunity for performance (test stage). Higher cognitive processes can be evaluated by creating situations in which reorganization of the information presented is necessary before the appropriate response can be made.

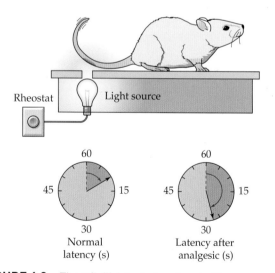

FIGURE 4.3   **The tail-flick test of analgesia**   The response of the animal to a thermal stimulus is measured with this test. The quantitative measure made is the time between onset of the light beam, which provides heat, and movement of the tail. The clockfaces show that the response to the noxious stimulus is delayed after treatment with an analgesic that is known to reduce pain in humans. (After L. W. Hamilton and C. R. Timmons. 1990. *Principles of Behavioral Pharmacology: A Biopsychological Perspective.* Prentice Hall: Englewood Cliffs, NJ.)

MAZES   Although the size and complexity of mazes can vary dramatically, what they have in common is a start box at the beginning of an alley with one (**T-maze**) or more (**multiple T-maze**) choice points that lead to the final goal box, which contains a small piece of food or another reinforcer. A hungry rat is initially given an opportunity to explore the maze and find the food

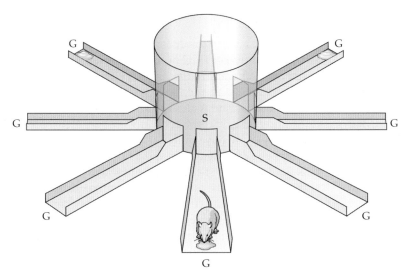

FIGURE 4.4   The radial arm maze A central start box (S) has a number of arms or alleys radiating from it. Goal areas (G) containing food are at the ends of the arms.

been entered and move down only those that still contain food. For a typical rat, the task is not complex because it mimics the foraging behavior of animals in the wild, where they must remember where food has been found. But animals with selective lesions in the hippocampus (and other areas), as well as those injected with a cholinergic-blocking drug, show significant impairment. Low doses of alcohol also interfere with spatial memory. Because the arms are identical, the animals must use cues in the environment to orient themselves in the maze, hence the need for spatial memory. The task is similar to our daily activity of driving home from work. Not only do we need to recognize landmarks along our route, but we must learn the relative locations of these objects with respect to each other. As we move along our route, our perceptions of the objects and their relative locations to us tell us where we are and where we should be going. Failure in this complex cognitive process is characteristic of patients with Alzheimer's disease who wander away and fail to find their way home.

A second test of spatial learning, the **Morris water maze**, uses a large, circular pool of water that has been made opaque by the addition of milk or a dye. Animals placed in the pool must swim until they find the escape platform that is hidden from view just below the surface of the water (**FIGURE 4.5**). The subject demonstrates

goal. On subsequent trials, learning is evaluated on the basis of the number of errors at choice points and/or the time taken to reach the goal box. Careful evaluation of results is needed because drug-induced changes in behavior may be due to a change in either learning or motivation (e.g., Does the drug make the animal more or less hungry? Sedated? Disoriented?). This task can also be used to evaluate working memory if the goal is alternated from side to side at each trial.

Spatial learning tasks help us investigate the role of specific brain areas and neurotransmitters, such as acetylcholine, in forming memories for the relative locations of objects in the environment. One special type of maze, the **radial arm maze**, is made up of multiple arms radiating away from a central choice point (**FIGURE 4.4**) with a small piece of food at the end of each arm. With very little experience, typical rats learn to forage efficiently by visiting each arm only once on a given day, indicating effective spatial memory for that particular episode. The task can be made more complex by blocking some arms on an initial trial. After the initial trial the animal is returned to the central choice point for a second trial. The animal is expected to remember which arms have already

FIGURE 4.5   The Morris water maze A circular pool is filled with opaque water. The escape platform is approximately 1 cm below the water level. The rat's task is to locate the submerged, hidden platform by using visuospatial cues available in the room. A video camera is mounted above the pool and is connected to the video recorder and the computer link to trace the individual swim path. (After B. Kolb and I. Q. Whishaw. 1989. *Prog Neurobiol* 32: 242. © 1989. Reprinted with permission from Elsevier.)

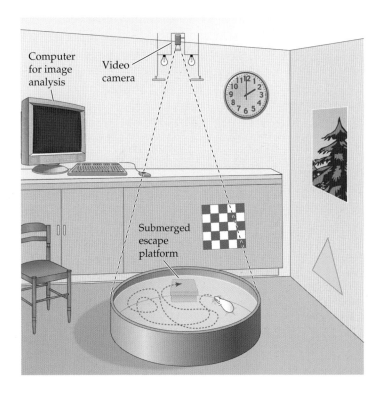

that it has learned the spatial location of the submerged platform by navigating from different starting positions to the platform. Since there are no local cues to direct the escape behavior, successful escape requires that the subject learn the spatial position of the platform relative to landmarks outside the pool. When curtains surrounding the pool are drawn to block external visual cues, performance falls to chance levels, demonstrating the importance of visuospatial cues. As a laboratory technique, the water maze has several advantages. No extensive pretraining is required, and testing can be carried out over short periods of time. Escape from water motivates without the use of food or water deprivation or electric shock; this makes interpretation of drug studies easier, in that drug-induced changes in motivation are less likely. One disadvantage, however, is that water immersion may cause endocrine or other stress effects that can interact with cognitive performance as well as the drugs administered. A video demonstration can be found on YouTube (Nunez, 2014).

DELAYED-RESPONSE TEST   This design assesses the type of memory often impaired by damage to the prefrontal cortex in humans. It is similar to tasks included in the Wechsler Memory Scale, which is used to evaluate working memory deficits in humans. In this task (**FIGURE 4.6**), an animal watches the experimenter put a piece of food into one of the food boxes in front of it. The boxes are then closed, and a sliding screen is placed between the monkey and the boxes for a few seconds or minutes (the delay). At the end of the delay, the screen is removed and the animal has the opportunity to recall under which of the covers food is available. To receive its reward, the animal must hold in working memory the location of the food.

Visual short-term memory can be tested by slightly modifying the procedure. At the beginning of the trial, an object or other stimulus is presented as the sample. After a short delay, during which the sample stimulus is removed, the animal is given a choice between two or more visual stimuli, one of which is the same as the sample. If the animal chooses the pattern that matches the sample, it is given a food reward; an incorrect response yields no reward. This match-to-sample task can of course be modified to make a non-match-to-sample task, in which case the animal must choose the visual stimulus that is different from the original sample. This task is a good example of the use of operant conditioning. To make the correct choice after the interval, the animal must "remember" the initial stimulus.

MEASURES OF ANXIETY-LIKE BEHAVIOR   There are many biobehavioral measures available for identifying novel antianxiety compounds and for evaluating the neurochemical basis of anxiety. Cryan and Sweeney (2011) have reviewed the animal models and discuss their importance for drug discovery. Most anxiety models use induced fearfulness as an analogy to human anxiety. Some use unconditioned animal reactions such as a tendency to avoid brightly lit places or heights; others depend on traditional learning designs. The **light–dark crossing task** involves a two-compartment box with one side brightly lit (normally avoided by rodents) and the other side dark. Measures include the number of crossings between the bright and dark sections and the amount of time spent on each side, as well as total motor activity. Anxiety-reducing drugs produce a dose-dependent increase in the number of crossings and in overall activity while also increasing the amount of time spent in the light. Similar to the light–dark crossing task is the open field test. In this test, the animal is allowed to freely explore the test chamber, which is a novel and unprotected environment that is usually brightly lit. Both the number and pattern of the animal's movements

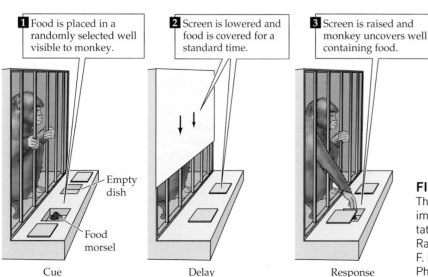

1 Food is placed in a randomly selected well visible to monkey.

2 Screen is lowered and food is covered for a standard time.

3 Screen is raised and monkey uncovers well containing food.

Empty dish

Food morsel

Cue   Delay   Response

FIGURE 4.6   The delayed-response task This test evaluates working memory by imposing a delay between stimulus presentation and testing. (After P. S. Goldman-Rakic. 1987. In *Handbook of Physiology*, F. Plum [Ed.], pp. 373–417. American Physiological Society: Bethesda, MD.)

Methods of Research in Psychopharmacology 115

are monitored either manually or with an automated system. Rodents typically explore the periphery of the chamber while staying in contact with the walls. Anti-anxiety drugs increase the amount of time spent in the exposed center of the box. The **elevated plus-maze** is a cross-shaped maze raised 50 cm off the floor that has two open arms (normally avoided because of aversion to heights and open spaces) and two arms with enclosed sides (**FIGURE 4.7**). This quick and simple test shows a selective increase in open-arm exploration following treatment with antianxiety drugs and a reduction after treatment with caffeine or amphetamine—drugs considered to increase anxiety. Very similar to the elevated plus-maze, the **zero maze** is a donut-shaped elevated platform that has two enclosed sections and two open sections. The circular construction lacks the ambiguous central square area in the plus-maze that sometimes makes scoring difficult. All of these naturalistic tests are easy to perform, relatively quick, and based on the assumption that the animals are in conflict between their natural desire to explore and the drive to avoid an aversive stimulus. Although the elevated mazes are among the most popular laboratory measures of anxiety, the construct validity of the tasks has been questioned (Ennaceur, 2014).

In another naturalistic task, the **one-chamber social interaction test** designed by File measures the amount of sniffing, following, walking over, crawling under, and mutual grooming behaviors that occur between two male rats when they are placed in an area where neither has established territory. In the original design it was found that these normal behaviors were reduced

in an unfamiliar test chamber and when illumination was increased, conditions that may evoke anxiety in rodents. As the normal interactions decreased, traditional indicators of emotionality (defecation and freezing) increased, as did plasma levels of the rodent stress hormone, corticosterone. A review of 25 years of research using this test has shown that a variety of anxiolytics (drugs that reduce anxiety) increase the social interaction under the aversive conditions, while anxiogenic drugs, which increase anxiety, further reduce the social interaction (see File and Seth, 2003). A modification of this model has been created to test for sociability, social memory, and novelty (**WEB BOX 4.1**).

In the **novelty suppressed feeding paradigm**, animals are presented their usual food in a new, potentially threatening environment, or conversely, they are provided novel food in their usual environment. In either case, the novelty prolongs the latency to begin eating. In very young animals, anxiety-like behavior can be evaluated by recording and quantifying the **ultrasonic vocalizations** of rat pups when they are separated from their mothers. These distress calls, which are inaudible to most predators and humans, reflect anxiety in the young and represent a call to their mothers to retrieve them. These vocalizations are very sensitive to a variety of antianxiety drugs from several drug classes.

The **water-lick suppression test** (**Vogel test**) is a **conflict procedure** that reliably screens anxiety-reducing drugs while requiring little training of the animals. Rats deprived of water quickly learn to lick the tip of a metal drinking spout for liquid. During testing, animals are given the opportunity to drink from the spout for a 3-minute session. However, after every 20 licks, the rats receive a mild tongue shock, which causes them to suppress responding. The conflict between the urge to lick the spout and the desire to avoid the shock is a classic paradigm for anxiety. Pretreatment with classic anxiety-reducing drugs such as the benzodiazepines increases water consumption; however, the test is insensitive to some newer anxiolytics.

Researchers have taken advantage of the natural tendency of rodents to dig in their bedding and bury foreign objects using the **defensive burying** and **marble burying tasks**. In the defensive burying task (see De Boer and Koolhas, 2003, for review), an electrified probe is inserted through a hole in the side of the cage, just above the level of the bedding material. Incidental contact with the probe results in the animal receiving a shock. Following the initial shock, both rats and mice will vigorously bury the probe with their bedding material, while treatment with anxiolytics will reliably reduce the time spent burying, demonstrating good predictive validity. In the marble burying task, rats and mice will bury glass marbles that are placed on the surface of their cage bedding, although this is thought to reflect a different psychological process, since unlike an electric

FIGURE 4.7 **The elevated plus-maze** This maze is used to test anxiety and is based on rodents' natural aversion to heights and open space and their predisposition for enclosed places.

shock probe, marbles do not possess any inherently aversive properties. While drugs that reduce anxiety in humans do suppress marble burying behavior, this task is also thought to model the compulsive component of obsessive-compulsive disorder (OCD; de Brouwer et al, 2019; Dixit et al., 2020), which was formerly categorized as an anxiety disorder in the 4th edition of the Diagnostic and Statistical Manual of Mental Disorders (DSM-IV) but is classified separately in the DSM-5.

MEASURES OF FEAR   Several common measures of fear involve classical conditioning. The **conditioned emotional response** (often called emotional memory in humans) depends on presentation of a signal (a light or tone) followed by an unavoidable electric shock to form a classically conditioned association. When the warning signal is presented during ongoing behavior, the behavior is suppressed (i.e., "freezing" occurs). Although this method has not always produced consistent results when used to screen antianxiety drugs, it has become an important tool in understanding the role of the amygdala and its neurochemistry in the conditioned fear response.

A second method is **fear-potentiated startle**, which refers to enhancement of the basic startle response when the stimulus is preceded by the presentation of a conditioned fear stimulus. For example, if a light has been previously paired with a foot shock, the presentation of that light normally increases the magnitude of the startle response to a novel stimulus, such as a loud clap.

MEASURES OF DEPRESSIVE-LIKE BEHAVIOR   Animal models are used to study the neurobiology of depression and to evaluate the mechanism of antidepressant drugs, as well as to screen new drugs for effectiveness. There is no available model that mimics all the symptoms of depression; instead, each model is associated with a specific aspect of the disorder, such as reductions in psychomotor activity, neuroendocrine responses, cognitive changes, or such functions as eating, sleeping, and deriving pleasure from everyday activities. Therefore, the usefulness of any single model in evaluating the complex etiology of depression is limited, and the ability of models to predict which new drugs will be effective for the clinical population is challenging.

A commonly used measure that permits rapid behavioral screening of novel antidepressants, called the **behavioral despair** or **forced swim test**, requires rats or mice to swim in a cylinder from which there is no escape. After early attempts to escape are unsuccessful, the animals assume an immobile posture except for the minimal movements needed to keep their heads above water (**FIGURE 4.8**). In a closely related test, the **tail suspension test**, mice are suspended by the tail from a lever, and the duration of movements (a period of agitation followed by immobility) is recorded. These models

are based on the anthropomorphic idea that the immobility reflects a lowered mood in which the animals are resigned to their fate and have given up hope. Acute administration of effective antidepressants reduces the time spent in this phase of immobility relative to untreated control animals. This test has similarities to the **learned helplessness** test, in which subjects are initially exposed to aversive events such as *unescapable* foot shock for several hours or for periods over several days. When the subjects are placed in a new situation in which a response could alter an aversive event, they fail to make the appropriate response. The animal behavior is thought to resemble clinical depression in that depressed humans frequently fail to respond to environmental changes and express feelings of hopelessness and the belief that nothing they do has an effect. Although these three antidepressant screening tests are frequently used, all three have been criticized because the stress is only short-lived, the animals tested are not genetically vulnerable to depression, and the antidepressants reduce behavioral despair after acute drug treatment rather than after the chronic antidepressant

Courtesy of Porsolt & Partners Pharmacology

FIGURE 4.8   **Forced swim test**   After its initial attempts to escape, the rat in the water-filled cylinder is shown in a posture reflecting a sense of futility. Antidepressant drugs reduce the amount of time spent in the immobile posture.

administration that is needed to reverse symptoms in humans. In other words, while these behavioral tests exhibit satisfactory predictive validity for the discovery of novel antidepressants, they lack robust construct validity and as such are not well suited to assessing a depressive phenotype in animals (Commons et al., 2017; Molendijk and de Kloet, 2019).

Several chronic stress procedures are more difficult to perform but are considered to have greater construct validity because stress is a risk factor for depression (Nestler and Hyman, 2010). The **chronic mild unpredictable stress** model exposes rodents to a series of physically stressful events such as cold temperatures, wet bedding, restraint, and sudden loud noises for several weeks. Following the stress, these animals show several behaviors that parallel those of depressed individuals, including multiple cognitive impairments, increased anxiety-like behaviors, social withdrawal, and a reduced preference for sucrose that models human anhedonia (i.e., failure to derive pleasure from normally pleasant events), all of which give the model face validity. Of significance is that chronic rather than acute antidepressant treatment is required to reverse the behaviors, so construct validity is good. As is true for many of the most validated models, the downside of this model is that it is labor-intensive, requires significant laboratory space, and takes a long time. Also, because the procedure is complex, replication of studies across laboratories can be a challenge (Abelaira et al., 2013). **Chronic social defeat stress** uses the resident–intruder paradigm to create intense stress. The animal is placed in another conspecific's territorial cage, and this generates nonlethal aggression. Exposure to the conflict is repeated over several days, and between exposures the animal may be housed in a cage adjacent to the dominant animal to expose it further to visual and olfactory cues. Animals stressed in this manner show multiple depression-like behaviors including reductions in motor activity, exploration, sucrose preference, and copulatory behaviors, as well as social withdrawal and a metabolic syndrome (e.g., weight gain and insulin resistance) characteristic of depressed humans. Chronic, but not acute, antidepressant administration reverses these behaviors. Hence this model also has construct, face, and predictive validity, as does the model using maternal separation, discussed next.

To evaluate the importance of early life stress as a vulnerability factor in the development of depression, **maternal separation** can be used. Stress is induced by separating young animals (usually rats) from their mothers for brief periods daily during the first few weeks of life. Early stress provides the opportunity to evaluate long-term behavioral and neuroendocrine abnormalities in the animals as adults. Nemeroff (1998) originally used this model to evaluate the hypothesis that abuse or neglect early in life activates the stress response at the

time but also produces long-term changes in the function of corticotropin-releasing factor (CRF) that may predispose the individual to clinical depression later in life. The relationship of early life stress to clinical depression is discussed further in Chapter 18.

The **sucrose preference test** is a measure of anhedonia. In the test, the animals are provided with two drinking tubes, one of which contains water, the second a solution sweetened with sucrose or saccharin. The animals have free access to the tubes over several days. Each day the volume of water and sucrose is measured, and the positioning of the bottles is reversed to prevent a bias toward one side of the enclosure. The typical animal will show a strong preference for the sweetened solution. Animals failing to show that preference demonstrate anhedonia, a common symptom of clinical depression. A variety of stressors can reduce sucrose preference. As described earlier, those animals exposed to chronic mild unpredictable stress tend to experience anhedonia in this test, and their behavior can be returned to normal with chronic, but not acute, antidepressant treatment. Evidence for stress-induced anhedonia provides incentive to examine the neurobiology of the reward circuitry as a component of major clinical depression.

METHODS OF ASSESSING DRUG REWARD AND REINFORCEMENT The simple operant FR schedule has been used very effectively in identifying drugs that have abuse potential—that is, drugs that are capable of inducing dependence. We assume that if an animal will press a lever to receive an injection of drug into the blood or into the brain, the drug must have reinforcing properties. The drug **self-administration method** (**FIGURE 4.9**) used with rodents is a very accurate indicator of abuse potential in humans. For instance,

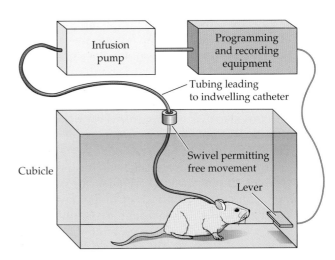

FIGURE 4.9   The drug self-administration method Pressing the lever according to a predetermined schedule of reinforcement triggers drug delivery into a vein or into discrete brain areas. This method predicts abuse liability of psychoactive drugs.

TABLE 4.1 Drugs That Act as Reinforcers in the Rhesus Monkey

Category	Specific Drug
Central stimulants	Cocaine Amphetamine Methylphenidate (Ritalin) Nicotine Caffeine
Opioids	Morphine Methadone Codeine
CNS depressants	Pentobarbital Amobarbital Chlordiazepoxide (Librium) Ethyl alcohol

animals will readily self-administer morphine, cocaine, and amphetamine—drugs that we know are readily abused by humans. In contrast, drugs like aspirin, antidepressants, and antipsychotic drugs are neither self-administered by animals nor abused by humans. **TABLE 4.1** lists some of the drugs that are reinforcing in the rhesus monkey. Compare this list with what you know about substances abused by humans. Drug self-administration is considered the most valid model of drug seeking in humans.

Furthermore, we can ask the animal which of several drugs it prefers by placing two levers in the operant chamber and training the animal to press lever A for one drug and lever B for the alternative. If given free access to the levers, the animal's choice will be readily apparent. An additional question we can pose involves how much the animal really "wants" a particular drug. By using a progressively increasing ratio schedule of reinforcement, we can tell how reinforcing the drug is by how hard the animal works for the injection. The point at which the effort required exceeds the reinforcing value is called the **breakpoint**, which is thought to reflect the degree to which a drug is reinforcing.

A modification of the drug self-administration method allows the animal to self-administer a weak electrical current to discrete brain areas via an indwelling electrode. The underlying assumption of **electrical self-stimulation** is that certain brain circuits are necessarily for the reinforcement of behavior. It is assumed that when the animal works to stimulate a particular cluster of neurons, the electrical activation causes the release of neurotransmitters from nerve terminals in the region, which, in turn, mediate a reinforcing effect. The fact that pretreatment with certain drugs, such as morphine or heroin, increases responding for even low levels of electrical stimulation indicates that the drugs enhance the brain reinforcement mechanism (Esposito et al., 1989). In combination with mapping techniques,

this method provides an excellent understanding of the neural mechanisms of reinforcement and the effects of psychoactive drugs on those pathways.

Although several popular measures used to evaluate the reinforcing effects of drugs are operant techniques, a method called **conditioned place preference** relies on a classically conditioned association between drug effect and environment (**FIGURE 4.10**). During conditioning trials over several days, the animal is injected with either drug or saline and is consistently placed in one compartment or the other so that it associates the environment with the drug state. The rewarding or aversive effect of the drug is determined in a test session in which the animal is given access to both compartments and the amount of time spent in each is monitored. If the drug is rewarding, the animal spends much more time in the compartment associated with the drug. If the drug is aversive, the animal prefers the compartment associated with saline injection. Additionally, researchers may study the biological basis for the rewarding effects by pretreating animals with selected receptor antagonists or neurotoxins to modify the place preference. For reviews of the many behavioral principles and methods related to drug reward and reinforcement, see O'Brien and Gardner (2005) as well as Green and Bardo (2020).

DRUGS AS DISCRIMINATIVE STIMULI A discriminative stimulus is any stimulus that signals reinforcement for a subject in an operant task. For example, "light on" in the chamber may signal that reinforcement is available following pressing one of two available levers, while "light out" may signal that reinforcement is available only after pressing the other lever. An animal that learns to

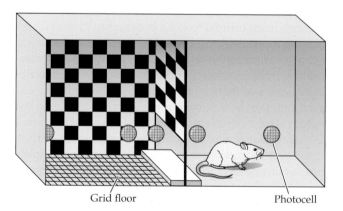

Grid floor   Photocell

FIGURE 4.10 **Place-conditioning apparatus** The apparatus consists of two distinctly different compartments that vary in the pattern and texture of the floor and walls. Photocells monitor the animal's movement. Each compartment is repeatedly paired with either drug or saline injection. On the test day, the animal is allowed free access to both compartments, and the amount of time spent in each tells us whether the drug effect was rewarding or aversive. (After I. Stolerman. 1992. *Trends Pharmacol Sci* 13: 170–176. © 1992. Reprinted with permission from Elsevier.)

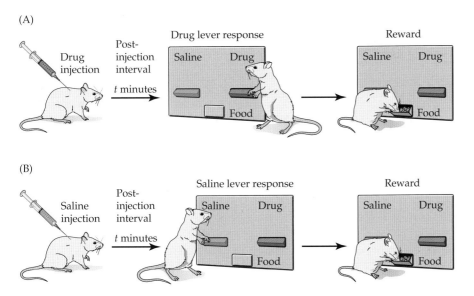

FIGURE 4.11 Drug discrimination testing (A) A rat is injected with a drug before being placed in an operant chamber. If it presses the right lever ("drug"), it receives a food reward. If it presses the left (saline) lever, no reinforcement occurs. (B) On days that the rat receives a saline injection before it is placed in the operant chamber, it receives food reinforcement if it presses the saline lever, and no reinforcement if it presses the drug lever. Discrimination of internal drug cues determines the animal's response.

press one lever when the light is on and the opposite lever when the light is out can discriminate between the two conditions. Although discriminative stimuli are usually changes in the physical environment, internal cues after drug administration can also be discriminative (**FIGURE 4.11**). Thus, an animal can learn that on days when it receives an injection of a particular drug and experiences the internal cues associated with that drug state (like the "light on"), it can press one lever for reinforcement, and on days when it receives a saline injection and experiences different internal cues, it can press the alternative lever for reinforcement, as in the "light off" condition. The animal's response depends on its discriminating among internal cues produced by the drug.

By using this technique, we can find out how the animal experiences a drug cue. For example, if an animal has been trained to lever press on the left after receiving morphine, and on the right on days when it has been pretreated with saline, other opioids can be substituted for the internal cue and signal to the animal that reinforcement can be obtained by pressing the "morphine" lever. In this way, it has been shown that the opioid drugs heroin and methadone are experienced in a way that is similar to that for morphine (i.e., they show generalization to morphine). In contrast, drugs like amphetamine or marijuana, which apparently produce subjective effects very different from those of morphine, do not lead to pressing the "morphine" lever. In this way, novel drugs can be characterized according to how similar their internal cues are to those of the known drug. This can be useful in screening new therapeutic drugs by determining whether animals respond as they did when trained on a known effective agent. The same technique can be used to identify the neurochemical basis for a given drug cue. The drug cue can be challenged with increasing doses of a suspected neurotransmitter antagonist until the cue has

lost its effect. Likewise, neurotransmitter agonists can be substituted to find which more closely resembles the trained drug cue. Drug discrimination testing is relatively easy to do and requires no surgical procedures. However, it is time-consuming because of the extensive training time and the limitation of generalization testing to only once or twice a week (with continued retraining on the remaining days). The technique has high predictive validity, meaning that results from animal tests are usually quite similar to those from human testing in analogous experimental designs. Solinas and colleagues (2006) provide an excellent description of the basic methodology of drug discrimination, as well as an assessment of advantages and disadvantages. For an example of the utility of drug discrimination testing, read **WEB BOX 4.2**.

AUTOMATED QUANTIFICATION OF BEHAVIOR As computing hardware becomes increasingly powerful, new technologies are being developed to harness this previously unattainable level of computational muscle. **Computer vision** is a rapidly evolving technology that can be used in psychopharmacological research to discern an incredibly wide array of behaviors. Sophisticated artificial intelligence algorithms can be applied to analyze video recordings of animals in a habitat-based test environment, by comparing the position and posture of the animal in sequential video frames (**FIGURE 4.12**). Although computationally intensive, with enough video data, these algorithms can detect vast numbers of unique behavioral features with a high level of detail. In combination with advanced statistical techniques, this largely automated, "deep phenotyping" approach to the measurement of spontaneous animal behavior enables scientists to quantify and systematically analyze patterns in behavior that may otherwise go undetected, revealing subtle behavioral signatures of

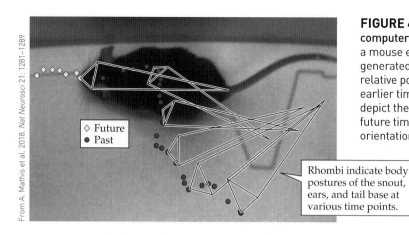

FIGURE 4.12 Automated analysis of behavior with computer vision An example video frame capture showing a mouse engaged in locomotor behavior. The polygons are generated by highly specialized software and represent the relative position and orientation of the mouse at various earlier time points, while the red circles and yellow diamonds depict the snout position of the mouse at both earlier and future time points, respectively. By encoding the position, orientation, and posture of the mouse over time, on a frame-by-frame basis, complex algorithms can be applied to detect behavioral patterns that reflect both phenotype and subtle drug treatment effects.

◇ Future
● Past

Rhombi indicate body postures of the snout, ears, and tail base at various time points.

brain circuits and their responses to drug effects and genetic mutations (see Pereira, Shaevitz, and Murthy, 2020; Wiltschko et al., 2020, for reviews). In parallel, advanced technological tools are being used to collect and analyze vast amounts of behavioral data from humans, using commonly available wearable sensor technology. Subtle patterns in activity levels, sleep duration, as well as other behavioral and physiological measures can be similarly detected and analyzed to provide novel insights into disease progression and treatment efficacy (Rohani et al., 2018).

TRANSLATIONAL RESEARCH Neuroscience research has seen rapid gains in recent years and as a result our understanding of the nervous system has increased considerably. Somewhat frustratingly, our understanding of the brain has far outpaced our ability to develop effective new therapies for neuropsychiatric disorders, due in part to the fact that animal models do not always exhibit adequate construct validity for the disorders they are intended to model. Despite the difficulties associated with developing animal models of human psychiatric conditions, it is an extremely important step in translational research. Translational research represents an effort to transform discoveries from basic neuroscience research into clinical applications for treating mental and neurological disorders—an important goal of psychopharmacology. Translational research is not a new concept, and a good deal of early research in psychopharmacology was directed toward the ultimate goal of developing more effective medications. However, more recently, there has been greater emphasis on improving the predictability of therapeutic effects based on animal research, because running lengthy and expensive human clinical trials (**BOX 4.1**) on drugs that prove ineffective makes new drug development both slow and costly. This, in turn, makes medication more expensive and delays the opportunity for effective treatment. It also takes valuable research time and money away from the pursuit of potentially more successful drug development. Because

there have been so many failures in translation of animal models to clinical effectiveness, many pharmaceutical companies are no longer eager to pursue therapeutics for disorders such as depression and anxiety (see McGonigle and Ruggeri, 2014; Bale et al., 2019). Since pharmaceutical companies have been criticized for emphasizing research and development of highly profitable drugs rather than those that are most innovative and/or those that address unmet medical needs, the research contribution of biotechnology companies and universities has become increasingly important. In response to the need for additional cutting-edge therapeutics for significant psychiatric disorders, the NIH has begun a consortium of academic health centers to nurture *interdisciplinary* research teams, whose goal is to develop inventive research tools to stimulate the development of drugs for clinical use. Yu (2011) describes some of the advances that have been made in the development of translational tools with the collaboration of preclinical and clinical scientists. It is estimated that up to 60 such research teams comprising molecular and psychopharmacological researchers, clinical investigators, and representatives of the pharmaceutical industry will be established in the very near future. Open-access websites and journals will further enhance communication among researchers and will encourage information sharing.

As is true for methods in neuropharmacology and molecular biology, animal testing and behavior analysis must continue to undergo improvement and refinement. Animal modeling will improve with advances in understanding disease causality and development of objective measures for clinical diagnosis. For a review of some of the challenges in developing translational animal models, see McGonigle and Ruggeri (2014).

It has long been wondered whether the translation of animal data into useful human drug treatments was hindered because drug effects were frequently tested on an adaptive animal response to a specific challenge, which may produce effects quite different from the response in humans with existing pathology.

BOX 4.1 ■ CLINICAL APPLICATIONS

Drug Testing for FDA Approval

All new drugs produced and sold in the United States by pharmaceutical companies must be approved by the Food and Drug Administration (FDA). For approval, they must be demonstrated to be both effective and safe. Design and testing of new drugs is a long, complex, and expensive procedure involving extensive evaluation in both laboratory and clinical settings. The approval process utilizes many of the methods we have discussed so far, in addition to extensive testing in humans (Zivin, 2000).

The **FIGURE** shows a timeline of typical drug development beginning with preclinical trials, which include in vitro neuropharmacological methods, such as receptor binding, autoradiography, and so forth. In vivo animal studies provide important information about pharmacokinetics (absorption, distribution, and metabolism), effective dose range, and toxic and lethal doses. In addition, animal behavioral models and animal models of neurological and psychiatric disorders provide a means to screen and evaluate potentially useful drugs.

After preclinical testing, a drug that is considered safe is tested with humans in three distinct phases. In *phase 1*, the drug is evaluated for toxicity and pharmacokinetic data in a small group of healthy human volunteers. Although serious injuries during phase 1 testing are rare, they are particularly disturbing because the subjects are typically young and healthy individuals who may join the study for the monetary compensation because they are poor and unemployed. One recent example involves the testing of a new drug to relieve mood, anxiety, and motor problems that often accompany neurodegenerative diseases. Of the 90 study participants, six were hospitalized. One of these was brain dead, and three were likely to have irreversible brain damage (Chan, 2016). The examples of harm, though limited, point to the inherent dangers in clinical drug trials.

In *phase 2*, limited clinical testing is conducted to evaluate the effectiveness of the drug in treating a

particular disease. It has been argued that genomic screening should be a part of the FDA approval process (Urban and Goldstein, 2014; see Chapter 1). Such routine screening would provide a database of genetic information that predicts effective clinical outcomes and potential side effects, which is a necessary step in personalized medicine (i.e., drug treatment assigned to patients based on their genetic profile). An advantage for pharmaceutical developers would be that the screening and treatment outcome would give them an indication of the potential market for the new drug and might reduce their costs by including patients in phase 3 that have genetic indications of potential efficacy.

Finally, the drug is tested again in large clinical trials (*phase 3*) involving thousands of patients at multiple testing sites around the country.

After the third phase has been completed, the FDA can evaluate the data collected on both effectiveness and safety. If the drug receives FDA approval, it can be marketed and sold. Once in general use, the drug may still be evaluated periodically and new warnings may be issued to maximize safety by monitoring adverse reactions, dangerous drug interactions, and product defects.

Although arguments that new drugs are excessively expensive for the consumer are valid, it is important to understand that as few as 20% of new drugs that are tested reach final approval. This means that the remaining 80% are eliminated only after testing that is both time-consuming and expensive. If we look at the total cost in today's dollars for research and development of the average drug approved by the FDA, we see a startling increase over time. In 1975, the average cost was $100 million; 12 years later costs increased to $300 million. By 2005 the cost of the average drug was over four times greater at $1.3 billion, and in 2011 the figure rose further to an amazing $5.8 billion (Roy, 2012). This enormous increase in the cost of

(Continued)

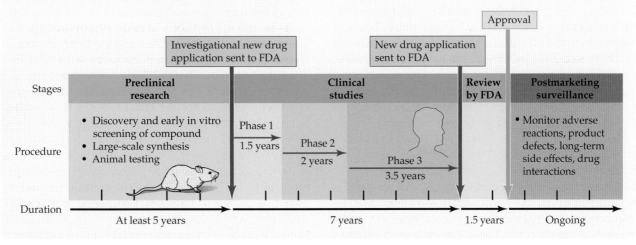

BOX 4.1 ■ CLINICAL APPLICATIONS (*continued*)

developing new drugs has been primarily driven by the expenses associated with phase 3 trials, which have gotten larger, more complex, and longer in duration. For these reasons, improvements in translational research that transfers results from animal testing and basic neuroscience to predictable clinical outcomes for patients are critical (see the text). If more drugs moved successfully through the three phases, the average development costs for drugs ultimately approved by the FDA would go down.

To protect its investment, a pharmaceutical company patents its drug so that no other company can sell it for a period of 20 years. The company develops a trade name (also called a proprietary name) and

has exclusive rights to market that product. After 20 years, the drug becomes "generic," and other companies can manufacture and sell their own formulations of the drug after proving to the FDA that they are equivalent to the original, with similar bioavailability. Once the patent has expired, the drug may acquire a variety of trade names, each developed by the individual manufacturer. For example, the newly patented antidepressant drug vilazodone is called Viibryd by its manufacturer. In contrast, because the patent on chlordiazepoxide has expired, the original manufacturer is still marketing Librium, but other pharmaceutical companies now produce chlordiazepoxide under the trade names Reposans, Sereen, and Mitran.

For instance, is it likely that drugs that suppress the normal aggression of a resident rodent on an intruder in its territory will also be effective in reducing pathological aggression in humans? Such questions have led researchers to suggest that the best models for translation to human treatment are those that depend on creating abnormal behaviors or neurobiological changes that closely resemble some of the focal symptoms of the disorder (Miczek and de Wit, 2008), while others have emphasized the need for animals models to be continuously updated and refined based on clinical findings in humans (Markou et al., 2009). Certainly, as molecular research continues to identify genetic differences associated with psychiatric disorders, additional animal models utilizing genetic mutations will be developed. For example, in one mouse model of OCD, selective deletion of genes produces animals that as adults show OCD-like behaviors such as excessive grooming with severe hair loss analogous to the compulsive washing seen in some individuals with OCD, self-injurious behavior, and increased anxiety. Furthermore, these behaviors respond to treatment with the same serotonergic agonists that are effective for individuals treated for OCD. Additionally, the mice show abnormal corticostriatal connectivity—again, similar to human neuropathology (OCD will be described further in Chapter 17). These similarities suggest the value of this genetic model in studying the etiology of OCD and in screening potential therapeutic agents (Yang and Lu, 2011). Be sure to refer to the section on genetic engineering for a discussion of the limitations of gene mutations.

Selective brain lesioning can also be used to induce a pattern of behavior and neurochemical change that mimics significant components of psychiatric syndromes. In one model of schizophrenia developed in the early 1990s, neonatal mice are subjected to ventral hippocampal lesioning, which alters the developmental trajectory of the animals. Although their behaviors are normal early in

life, at rodent pubescence, behaviors and physiological changes emerge that resemble multiple clinical signs of schizophrenia. This model is appealing because schizophrenia is considered a neurodevelopmental disorder whose diagnostic symptoms most often begin in adolescence and early adulthood. Similar to patients with schizophrenia, these lesioned rats show limbic dopamine dysregulation, hyperresponsiveness to stress and amphetamine injection, impaired functional development of the prefrontal cortex, and other abnormalities. This model is providing a template to study the impact of genetic, environmental, and neurobiological factors contributing to the pathophysiology of schizophrenia. The model was reviewed in detail and evaluated by Tseng and colleagues (2009) and is discussed in Web Box 19.4.

Another approach to improving translational research is to make the results from animal studies better predictors of therapeutic efficacy by developing parallel methodologies. To this end, the National Institute of Mental Health (NIMH) has funded a series of conferences for interdisciplinary researchers focused on cognitive processes, because cognitive dysfunction, including deficits in attention, memory, and behavioral regulation, is central to many psychiatric disorders. Researchers first worked to identify the most important cognitive processes that should be tested, and then they developed testing methods for human participants in parallel with animal models (Barch et al., 2009). Among the tasks that evaluate cognitive function that have been adapted for use with humans, non-human primates, and rodents is the **stop-signal task**. This is a commonly employed procedure used to measure impulsivity. Impulsivity or failure of behavioral inhibition is a significant component of disorders such as attention-deficit/hyperactivity disorder (ADHD), OCD, and substance abuse, among others. Impulsivity represents failure of an important cortical control mechanism that suppresses the execution of responses that are inappropriate in a changing environment, hence decreasing flexible behaviors. The stop-signal task requires the subject (human or otherwise) to rapidly press one button or lever when a square is displayed, and the other button or lever when any other shape appears. Periodically, a tone, which is the "stop" signal, is sounded following the visual presentation. The tone indicates that the subject should withhold responding. This paradigm can be used to integrate neurochemical contributions to the task performance derived from rodent pharmacological studies with imaging results in humans performing the same tasks. It is anticipated that the synthesis of discoveries will translate into more effective treatments for enhancing behavioral inhibition. For a more complete discussion, refer to the paper by Eagle and colleagues (2008). The translational technique called prepulse inhibition of startle is another example of a task that is performed in the same manner across species and has been used to examine the sensory processing of schizophrenic individuals (see Chapter 19 and Web Box 19.3).

SECTION SUMMARY

- Techniques in behavioral pharmacology provide a means of quantifying animal behavior for drug testing, developing models for psychiatric disorders, and evaluating the neurochemical basis of behavior. Creating animal models of complex psychiatric disorders with uniquely human symptoms poses numerous hurtles.

- Advantages of animal testing include having a subject population with similar genetic background and history, maintaining highly controlled living environments, and being able to use invasive neurobiological techniques.

- Animal testing includes a wide range of measures that vary not only in validity and reliability, but also in complexity, time needed for completion, and cost.

- Some measures use simple quantitative observation of behaviors such as motor activity, response to noxious stimuli, and time spent in social interaction.

- Operant behaviors controlled by various schedules of reinforcement provide a sensitive measure of drug effects on patterns of behavior. Operant behaviors are also used in tests of addiction potential, anxiety, and analgesia.

- Other methods assess more complex behaviors such as learning and memory, using a variety of techniques such as the classic T-maze, as well as mazes modified to target spatial learning: the radial arm maze and Morris water maze. The delayed-response task assesses working memory.

- Many measures of anxiety use unconditioned animal reactions such as the tendency to avoid brightly lit places (light–dark crossing task, open field test), heights (elevated plus-maze, zero maze), electric shock (Vogel test, defensive burying), and novelty (novelty suppressed feeding, marble burying test).

- To assess fear memory, a classically conditioned response is established by presenting a light or tone followed by an unavoidable foot shock. The light or tone becomes a cue associated with shock, and when presented alone, it produces physiological and behavioral responses of fearfulness. When the conditioned fear stimulus precedes a startle-producing stimulus, the startle is much greater.

- Common behavioral tests to screen for novel antidepressant drugs, such as the forced swim test, tail suspension test, and learned helplessness, utilize acute stress to create a sense of helplessness and have demonstrated predictive validity, but have also been criticized for responding to acute rather than chronic antidepressant treatment. Other models of depression use more prolonged stress (chronic mild unpredictable stress, chronic social defeat stress), which more closely resembles the human experience. These stress-induced depressive behaviors respond to chronic but not acute drug treatment. Early maternal separation models the impact of stress early in life on later biobehavioral outcomes.

- The sucrose preference test is a measure of anhedonia (i.e., loss of interest in normally reinforcing stimuli).

- The operant self-administration technique, in which animals lever press for drugs rather than food reward, is an accurate predictor of abuse potential in humans. Varying the schedule of reinforcement indicates how reinforcing a given drug is, because when the effort of lever pressing exceeds the reinforcement value, the animals fail to press further (the "breakpoint").

- In conditioned place preference, animals learn to associate a drug injection with one of two distinct compartments, and saline with the other. On test day, if the drug is rewarding, the animal spends more time in the environment associated with the drug. If aversive, the animal stays in the saline-associated environment.

- Drug effects act as discriminative stimuli in operant tasks, which means that the lever-pressing response of an animal depends on its recognizing internal cues produced by the drug. Novel drugs can be characterized by how similar their internal cues are to those of the known drug.

- Advances in computing technology have allowed for automation of naturalistic behavioral observation. In combination with statistical techniques, researchers can quantify subtle patterns in behavior that are characteristic of different drug classes.

- Translational research is the interdisciplinary approach to improving the transfer of discoveries from molecular neuroscience, animal behavioral analysis, and clinical trials, with the goal of more quickly and inexpensively developing useful therapeutic drugs.

- To make animal research more predictive of therapeutic benefits in humans, animal models that create abnormal behaviors or neurobiological changes that closely resemble the pathophysiology and focal symptoms of the disorder are needed. Genetic manipulations and brain lesions are two approaches for achieving this goal.

- Developing parallel tasks for humans, non-human primates, and rodents will allow integration of neurochemical data from rodent studies with findings of imaging studies in humans performing the same task.

4.2 Techniques in Neuropharmacology

Multiple neurobiological techniques for assessing the CNS

Answering questions in psychopharmacology requires expertise not only in the techniques of behavioral analysis, but also in methods that allow us to examine the anatomy, physiology, and neurochemistry of the brain. The most productive research will utilize multiple approaches to the same problem.

Stereotaxic surgery is needed for accurate in vivo measures of brain function

The classic techniques of physiological psychology (lesioning, microinjection, and electrical recording) are equally important in understanding the actions of

psychoactive drugs. Stereotaxic surgery is an essential technique in neuroscience that permits a researcher to implant one of several devices into the brain of an anesthetized animal with significant precision. The stereotaxic device itself (**FIGURE 4.13A**) essentially serves as a means of stabilizing the animal's head in a fixed orientation so that the carrier portion can be moved precisely in three dimensions for placement of the tip of an electrode or a drug delivery tube in a predetermined brain site. Brain site coordinates are calculated using a brain atlas, which is a collection of frontal sections of brain of appropriate species, in which distances are measured from skull surface features (**FIGURE 4.13B**). Accuracy of placement is determined histologically after the experiment is complete. The halo bracket (**FIGURE 4.13C**) is the equivalent apparatus used in human neurosurgery; the target site is identified with the use of a computerized imaging

(A)

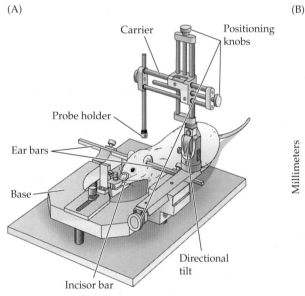

(B)

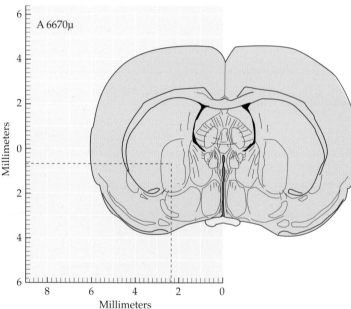

(C)

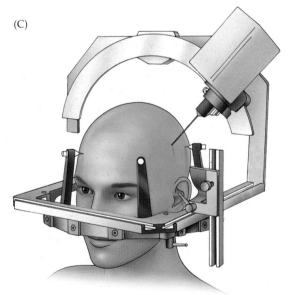

FIGURE 4.13   Stereotaxic surgery (A) A stereotaxic device used for precise placement of electrodes during brain surgery on animals. The base holds the anesthetized animal's head and neck in a stationary position. The carrier portion places the electrode or the cannula in a precise location based on the coordinates of the target area identified with the brain atlas (B). The precise target within the brain is defined by the intersection of three planes. The measurement (A 6670μ) in the upper left corner indicates the anterior–posterior position of the brain slice. The lateral and dorsal–ventral dimensions can be read directly from the axes provided. (C) A similar apparatus is used for human brain surgery. The location of the procedure is determined by CT or MRI.

technique such as magnetic resonance imaging (MRI) or computerized tomography (CT) (see the section on imaging techniques later in this chapter).

LESIONING AND MICROINJECTION Experimental ablation, or **lesioning**, uses a stereotaxic device to position a delicate electrode, insulated along its length except for the exposed tip, deep within the brain. The tissue at the tip is destroyed when a very-high-frequency radio current is passed through the electrode to heat the cells. The rationale of the experiment is that a comparison of the animal's behavior before and after the lesion will tell us something about the function of that brain area. Electrolytic lesion studies in animals can be used by cognitive neuroscientists to model human functions altered by injury to specific brain areas.

Electrolytic lesions destroy all tissue at the tip of the electrode, including cell bodies, dendrites, and axons. Alternatively, a **neurotoxin** (a chemical that is damaging to nerve cells) can be injected via a cannula (a hollow tube inserted like an electrode) to destroy cells. Of course, the same type of cannula can be used to administer drugs or neurotransmitters that stimulate cells in the CNS before behavior is evaluated (see the discussion of intracerebroventricular administration in Chapter 1). Chemical lesions have the advantage of being significantly more specific because neurotoxic

chemicals, such as kainic acid or ibotenic acid, kill cell bodies in the vicinity of the cannula tip but spare the axons passing through the same area. In either case, this procedure can be used to identify the brain area responsible for a drug-induced change in behavior.

Because neuropharmacologists are interested in neurochemical regulation of behavior, the lesioning techniques used are often specific for different neural pathways that use particular neurotransmitters. These **specific neurotoxins** most often are injected directly into the brain, where they are taken up by the normal reuptake mechanism of neurons. Once inside the cell, the toxin destroys the cell terminal. In this way, behavioral measures obtained before and after a neurotoxic lesion tell us about the role of the neurotransmitter in a particular behavior. For example, we might test our understanding of the role of the nucleus accumbens in reinforcement by selectively destroying the large number of dopamine cell terminals in that area, using the neurotoxin 6-OHDA, before evaluating the drug-taking behavior in the self-administration paradigm.

MICRODIALYSIS A different technique that uses stereotaxic surgery is **microdialysis**, which allows researchers to measure neurotransmitters released in a specific brain region while the subject is actively engaged in behavior (**FIGURE 4.14A**).

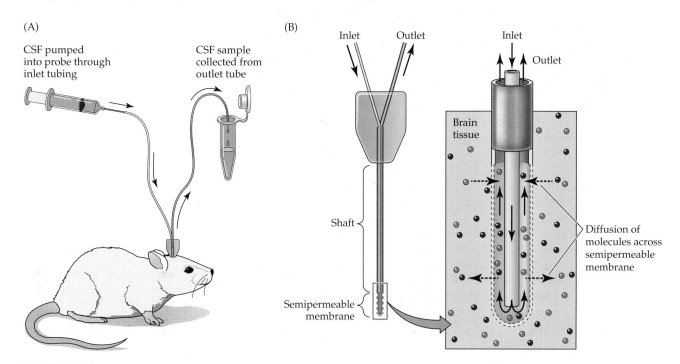

FIGURE 4.14 **Sampling of extracellular fluid with microdialysis** (A) Microdialysis allows the collection of samples from deep within the brain in unanesthetized and freely moving animals under relatively normal conditions. The collected samples are identified and are measured by one of several analytic techniques, such as high-performance liquid chromatography (HPLC; not shown). (B) Typical microdialysis probe, which uses flexible tubing that is sealed except at the tip, where it is semipermeable. It is held in place by dental plastic on the animal's skull. CSF, cerebrospinal fluid. (After L. Penicaud et al. 2013. In *Animal Models for the Study of Human Disease*, P. M. Conn [Ed.], pp. 569–593. Academic Press: San Diego. © 2013. Reprinted with permission from Elsevier.)

The technique requires a specialized cannula made of a fine, cylindrical semipermeable membrane that is implanted stereotaxically (**FIGURE 4.14B**). The membrane surface is sealed along its length except at the tip, allowing investigators to sample material in the extracellular space at precise sites, even deep within the brain. Artificial cerebrospinal fluid (CSF) is continuously pumped through the microdialysis cannula. The CSF in the cannula and in the extracellular fluid are identical except for the material to be collected. On the basis of the difference in concentration, chemicals in the extracellular space, including neurotransmitters, diffuse across the membrane from the synaptic space into the cannula. The CSF is pumped out of the cannula through an outlet tube where it is collected for subsequent analysis by high-performance liquid chromatography (HPLC) or another method. HPLC, like other types of chromatography, serves two purposes. First, chromatography separates the sample into component parts depending on characteristics of the sample, such as molecular size or ionic charge. Second, the concentration of the molecules of interest can be determined (**FIGURE 4.15**).

Microdialysis is important to neuropsychopharmacology because it can be used in several types of experiments that combine biochemical and behavioral analyses. For example, we might evaluate the released neurochemicals during ongoing behaviors, such as sleep and waking, feeding, or operant tasks, to obtain a window into the functioning CNS. We might also investigate the effects of drugs on extracellular concentrations of neurotransmitters in selected brain areas. Since multiple samples can be collected from freely moving animals over time, correlated changes in behavior can be monitored simultaneously. Finally, we

might sample extracellular materials at nerve terminals following discrete electrical or chemical stimulation of neural pathways.

A second method used to measure neurotransmitter release is **in vivo voltammetry**. Whereas microdialysis collects samples of extracellular fluid for subsequent analysis, in vivo voltammetry uses stereotaxically implanted microelectrodes to measure neurochemicals in the extracellular fluid of freely moving animals. In voltammetry, a very fine electrode is implanted, and a small electrical potential is applied. Changes in the flow of current at the electrode tip reflect changes in the concentration of electroactive substances such as neurotransmitters or their metabolites. A major advantage of this method is that because measurements are made continuously and require as little as 15 ms to complete, researchers can evaluate neurotransmitter release as it is occurring in real time. For an historical overview of the techniques used for monitoring extracellular neurotransmitter concentrations, see Kehr and Yoshitake (2013).

ELECTROPHYSIOLOGICAL STIMULATION AND RECORDING   In a similar fashion, implanted **macroelectrodes** (**FIGURE 4.16A**) can be used to activate cells at the tip while the change in animal behavior during stimulation is evaluated. The minute amount of electrical current applied changes the membrane potential of those cells and generates action potentials. The action potentials in turn cause the release of neurotransmitter at the cell terminals to mimic normal synaptic transmission. Hence the electrical stimulation should produce biobehavioral effects that are similar to those seen upon injection of the natural neurotransmitter or neurotransmitter agonists into the brain. In addition,

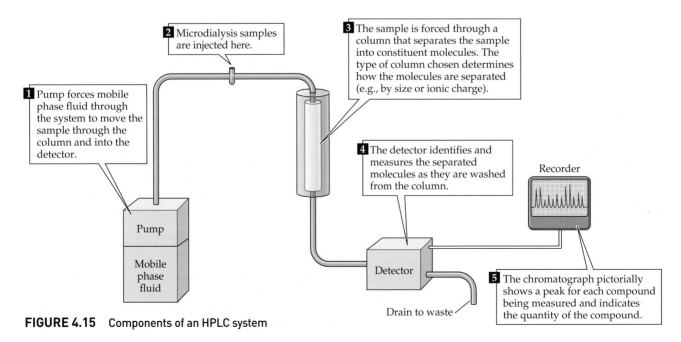

1 Pump forces mobile phase fluid through the system to move the sample through the column and into the detector.

2 Microdialysis samples are injected here.

3 The sample is forced through a column that separates the sample into constituent molecules. The type of column chosen determines how the molecules are separated (e.g., by size or ionic charge).

4 The detector identifies and measures the separated molecules as they are washed from the column.

Recorder

5 The chromatograph pictorially shows a peak for each compound being measured and indicates the quantity of the compound.

Pump

Mobile phase fluid

Detector

Drain to waste

FIGURE 4.15   Components of an HPLC system

(A)

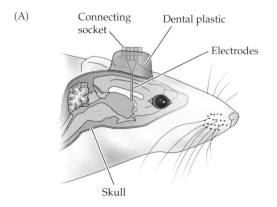

FIGURE 4.16 **Electrical brain stimulation and recording** (A) Stereo-taxically implanted electrodes are held in place on the skull with dental plastic. After recovery, the animal can be plugged into a device that can electrically stimulate cells at the tip or monitor and record changes in electrical activity. (B) Diagram of a system used for tremor control, consisting of an insulated wire electrode surgically implanted deep in the brain. The electrode is connected to a pulse generator implanted under the skin near the collarbone. The generator is programmed to deliver the amount of electrical current needed to reduce the tremor on the opposite side of the body. Patients also can have individual control by passing a handheld magnet over the skin above the pulse generator.

(B)

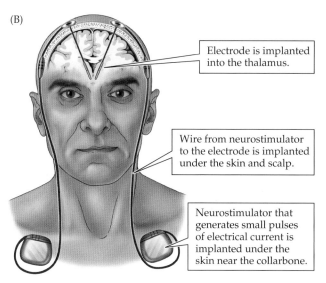

Electrode is implanted into the thalamus.

Wire from neurostimulator to the electrode is implanted under the skin and scalp.

Neurostimulator that generates small pulses of electrical current is implanted under the skin near the collarbone.

one would expect that stimulation of a given cell group would produce effects opposite those caused by a lesion at the same site. Macroelectrodes can also be used to record the summated electrical response of thousands of neurons in a specific brain region following drug treatment or other experimental manipulation in a freely moving animal. If we had found, for example, that lesioning the periaqueductal gray (PAG) in the midbrain prevented the pain-reducing effects of morphine, we might want to find out what effect activating those PAG neurons has. What we would find is that if electrodes implanted in the PAG are activated, the animal fails to respond to painful stimuli. Likewise, if pain-killing opioids like morphine or codeine are microinjected into that brain area via an indwelling cannula, the animal also demonstrates profound analgesia.

Many years of animal research into stereotaxic implantation of electrodes into the brain have translated into clinical benefits. **FIGURE 4.16B** shows the adaptation of the technique to humans being treated for Parkinson's disease. Small pulses of electrical current applied to the subthalamic nucleus cause the cells to fire and release neurotransmitter, which reduces the tremor on the opposite side of the body.

An alternative to macroelectrode recording, which is a summation of electrical activity in a brain region, is single-unit recording, which uses **microelectrodes**. Stereotaxically implanting a fine-tipped electrode either into a single cell (**intracellular recording**) or into the extracellular fluid near a single cell (**extracellular recording**) allows the response of individual cells under various conditions to be monitored. Intracellular recording must involve an anesthetized animal, because the electrode must remain in a precise position to record the membrane potential of the cell. An advantage of extracellular single-cell recording is that it can be done in a mobile animal (**FIGURE 4.17**). The downside to extracellular recording is that the electrode records only the occurrence of action potentials in the nearby neuron and cannot monitor the change in the cell's membrane potential. Returning to our earlier example of morphine action, we find that the drug produces strong selective inhibition of neurons in the spinal cord, and this prevents the projection of pain information to higher brain centers, thereby contributing to the analgesic effect.

In addition to measuring membrane potentials of groups of cells and single cells, thanks to the Nobel Prize–winning research of Neher and Sakmann conducted in the 1970s, neuroscientists can study the function of *individual* ion channels, which collectively are responsible for the membrane potential. This technique, known as **patch clamp electrophysiology**, works best with individual cells in culture but can also be used on exposed cells in slices of brain. The method involves attaching a recording micropipette to a piece of cell membrane by suction. When the pipette is pulled away, a small membrane patch containing one or more ion channels remains attached. The subsequent electrical recording through the pipette represents in real time the channel opening, the flow of ions (electrical current) during the brief period when it is open, and the channel closing.

Neurotransmitters, receptors, and other proteins can be quantified and visually located in the CNS

To both quantify and locate neurotransmitters and receptors in the CNS, several methods are required. To count or measure a particular molecule, a "soup" method is often used, in which a tissue sample is precisely

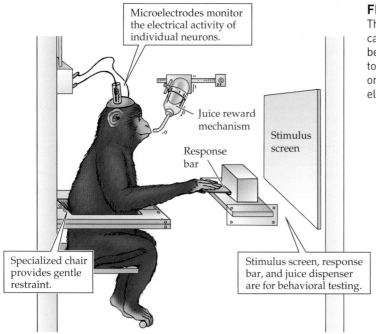

Microelectrodes monitor the electrical activity of individual neurons.

Juice reward mechanism

Stimulus screen

Response bar

Specialized chair provides gentle restraint.

Stimulus screen, response bar, and juice dispenser are for behavioral testing.

FIGURE 4.17 **Extracellular microelectrode recording** This electrophysiological technique records the electrical activity from single neurons in the brain of an awake, behaving animal. This experimental setup might be used to evaluate the effects of a previously administered drug on the animal's response to visual stimuli and on the electrical activity of a single cell.

dissected out and ground up, creating a homogenate before it is evaluated. Homogenates are used in many possible neurochemical analyses, which are referred to as *assays*. In contrast, for localization, the landmarks of the tissue and the relationships of structures must be preserved, so the visualization method is done on an intact piece or slice of tissue. Hence, when we want to measure the number of receptors in a particular brain area, we are likely to use a radioligand binding assay in a tissue homogenate, but if we want to see where in the brain particular receptors are located (and measure them), we are more likely to use a slice preparation with autoradiography. **TABLE 4.2** summarizes the "soup" and "slice" techniques described in the following section of the chapter.

RADIOLIGAND BINDING   To study the number of receptors in a given brain region and their affinity for drugs, the **radioligand binding** method was developed. Once the brain region we are interested in is dissected out, it is ground up to make a homogenate. A ligand (usually a drug or chemical) that is radioactively labeled (now called the *radioligand*) is incubated with the tissue

under conditions that optimize its binding. After a brief time, any radioligand that has not bound is removed, often by washing and filtering. The amount of radioligand bound to the tissue is then measured with a scintillation (or gamma) counter and reflects the number of receptors in the tissue.

Although the binding procedure is quite simple, interpretation of the results is more complex. How can we be sure that the radioligand is actually binding to the specific biological receptors of interest, rather than to other sites that represent artifacts of the procedure? Several criteria that must be met include (1) specificity, (2) saturability, (3) reversibility and high affinity, and (4) biological relevance. Specificity means that the ligand is binding only to the receptor we are concerned with in this tissue, and to nothing else. Of course, drugs often bind to several receptor subtypes, but they may also attach to other cell components that produce no biological effects. To measure the amount of a ligand that binds to the site that we are concerned with, we add very high concentrations of a nonradioactive competing ligand to some tubes to show that most of the radioactive binding is displaced. That which remains is likely to be nonspecifically bound to sites such as assay additives (e.g., albumin) or cellular sites (e.g., enzymes), which we are less interested in at the moment. Nonspecific binding is subtracted when the data are calculated for specific binding. When binding to specific subtypes of receptors is necessary, ligands must be designed to distinguish between receptor proteins.

Saturability means that there is a finite number of receptors in a given amount of tissue. By adding increasing amounts of radioligand to a fixed amount of tissue, one would expect to see gradual increases in binding until all sites are filled (**FIGURE 4.18A**). The point at which the

TABLE 4.2	Methods Used to Quantify and Visualize Target Molecules in the Nervous System	
Target Molecule	**Tissue Extract Assay to Quantify**	**Brain Slice Preparation to Visualize**
Receptor site	Radioligand binding	Receptor autoradiography
Receptors and other proteins	Radioimmunoassay (RIA); Western blot; ELISA	Immunocytochemistry (ICC)
mRNA	Dot blot or Northern blot	In situ hybridization (ISH)

(A)

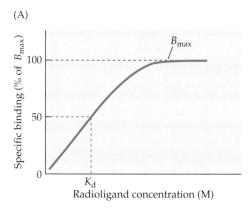

FIGURE 4.18 **Radioligand binding to receptors** (A) A hypothetical saturation curve shows that as radioligand concentration increases, specific binding to the receptor also increases until all sites are filled (B_{max}). The K_d is defined as the ligand concentration at which 50% of the receptors are occupied; it is an indication of receptor affinity and is called the dissociation constant. (B) Hypothetical association and dissociation curves. The dotted red line represents the association of a radioligand with its receptors over time. The rate of association (k_1) is estimated by calculating the slope of the straight line that best fits the curvilinear data. After maximum binding has occurred (association and dissociation are in equilibrium), excess unlabeled ligand is added. The solid blue line represents the dissociation of the radioligand from its receptors in the presence of large amounts of unlabeled ligand. The slope of the straight line that best fits that portion of the curve provides an estimate of the rate of dissociation (k_{-1}).

(B)

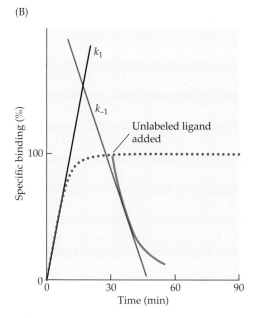

drugs in reducing the symptoms of schizophrenia (see Chapter 19). Unfortunately, in vitro binding data do not always transfer to in vivo results, because in vitro receptors are not in their natural environment. Also, drug effects in the intact organism are dependent on many factors in addition to drug–receptor interaction, for example absorption, distribution, and metabolism. The use of in vivo receptor binding (see the section below) can help to account for absorption, distribution, and metabolism of the drug.

RECEPTOR AUTORADIOGRAPHY   Receptor binding is a classic tool in neuropharmacology that tells us about receptor number and affinity for a particular drug in a specific piece of brain tissue. When we want to visualize the distribution of receptors within the brain, we may use receptor autoradiography. The process begins with standard radioligand binding as described previously, except that slide-mounted tissue slices rather than ground-up tissue are used. After the unbound radioactively labeled drug is washed away, the slices are processed by **autoradiography**. The slides are put into cassettes, a specialized autoradiographic film is placed on top of the slides so that it is in physical contact with the tissue sections, and the cassettes are stored in the dark to allow the radioactive material that is bound to receptors to act on the film. The particles that are constantly emitted from the radioactive material in the tissue expose the film and show not only the amount of radioligand bound but also its location. This method is especially good for studying the effects of brain lesions on receptor binding because each lesioned animal can be evaluated independently by comparing the lesioned and nonlesioned sides of the brain. This method might give us clues about how various psychoactive drugs produce their behavioral effects. For instance, mapping of the binding of cocaine in monkey brain shows a distinct pattern of localization and density in selected brain areas (**FIGURE 4.19**). With a clear understanding of anatomical distribution, we can begin to test specific hypotheses regarding the behavioral consequences of activating these receptors, using microinjections of receptor-selective agonists and antagonists.

binding curve plateaus represents maximum binding, or B_{max}. Binding within the assay must also be reversible because a neurotransmitter in vivo will bind and release many times to initiate repeated activation of the cellular action. This reversibility is demonstrated in binding assays because the radioactive ligand can be displaced by the same drug that is not radiolabeled (**FIGURE 4.18B**). If you compare the rate of dissociation with the rate of binding, you get an estimate of receptor affinity called the dissociation constant, or K_d. Clearly those ligands that bind readily and dissociate slowly have the highest affinity for the receptor. The unbinding (dissociation) of the ligand from the receptor must also be consistent with the reversal of physiological effects of the ligand.

Ideally, binding of chemically similar drugs should correlate with some measurable biochemical or behavioral effect to show the biological relevance of the receptor. For example, the classic antipsychotic drugs all bind to a particular subtype of receptor (D_2) for the neurotransmitter dopamine. Not only do the drugs in this class bind to the D_2 receptor, but their affinity for the receptor correlates with the effectiveness of the

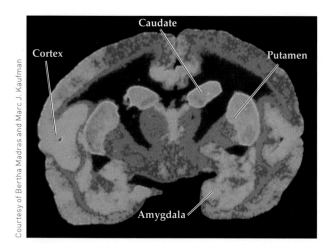

Courtesy of Bertha Madras and Marc J. Kaufman

FIGURE 4.19 Autoradiogram of the distribution of cocaine binding in monkey brain The highest levels of cocaine binding are in areas colored yellow and orange.

IN VIVO RECEPTOR BINDING The same autoradiographic processing can be done on brain slices of an animal that had previously been injected in vivo with a radiolabeled drug. The drug enters the general circulation, diffuses into the brain, and binds to receptors. Then the animal is killed, and the brain is sliced and processed by autoradiography. This technique shows the researcher where a particular drug or neurotransmitter binds in an intact animal.

ASSAYS OF ENZYME ACTIVITY Enzymes are proteins that act as biological catalysts to speed up reaction rates but are not used up in the process. We find many different enzymes in every cell, and each has a role in a relatively specific reaction. The enzymes that are particularly interesting to neuropharmacologists are those involved in the synthesis or metabolism of neurotransmitters, neuromodulators, and second messengers. In addition, neuropharmacologists are interested in identifying the conditions that regulate the rate of activity of the enzyme. For example, acute morphine treatment inhibits adenylyl cyclase activity. Adenylyl cyclase is the enzyme that synthesizes the second messenger cyclic adenosine monophosphate (cAMP). However, long-term exposure to morphine produces gradual but dramatic up-regulation of the cAMP system, suggesting that the second-messenger system acts to compensate for the acute effect of opioid inhibition. It is perhaps one of the best-studied biochemical models of opioid tolerance and is discussed further in Chapter 11.

Sometimes the mere presence of an enzyme within a cell cluster is important because it can be used to identify those cells that manufacture a specific neurotransmitter. The next section describes the use of antibodies and immunocytochemistry to locate enzymes and other proteins in the brain.

ANTIBODY PRODUCTION Some of the newest methods for identifying and measuring receptors and other proteins are far more specific and sensitive than ever before because they use an antibody. An **antibody** is a protein produced by the white blood cells of the immune system to recognize, attack, and destroy a specific foreign substance (the antigen). Researchers use this immune response to create supplies of antibodies that bind to specific proteins (e.g., receptors, neuropeptides, or enzymes) that they want to locate in the brain (**FIGURE 4.20A**). The

(A)

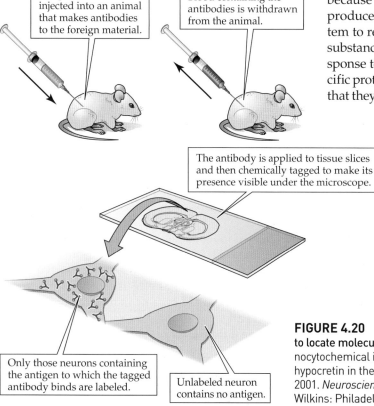

The protein is first injected into an animal that makes antibodies to the foreign material.

Blood containing the antibodies is withdrawn from the animal.

The antibody is applied to tissue slices and then chemically tagged to make its presence visible under the microscope.

Only those neurons containing the antigen to which the tagged antibody binds are labeled.

Unlabeled neuron contains no antigen.

(B)

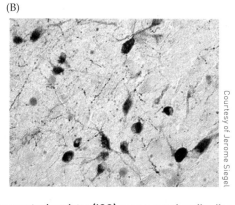

Courtesy of Jerome Siegel

FIGURE 4.20 Immunocytochemistry (ICC) uses tagged antibodies to locate molecules within cells (A) Steps in ICC localization. (B) Immunocytochemical identification of cells containing the neuropeptide hypocretin in the human lateral hypothalamus. (A after M. F. Bear et al. 2001. *Neuroscience: Exploring the Brain*, 2nd ed., Lippincott, Williams & Wilkins: Philadelphia. © 2001 Lippincott Williams & Wilkins.)

first step is to create an antibody by injecting the antigen (e.g., the neuropeptide hypocretin) into a host animal and at various times taking blood samples to collect antibodies. With the antibody prepared, we are ready to look for the peptide in tissue slices using immunocytochemistry. Antibodies can also be used to quantify very small amounts of material using radioimmunoassays (see later in this chapter).

IMMUNOCYTOCHEMISTRY   For **immunocytochemistry (ICC)**, the brain is first fixed (hardened) using a preservative such as formaldehyde. Tissue slices are then cut and incubated with the antibody in solution. The antibody attaches to the antigen wherever cells that contain that antigen are present. In the final step, the antibody is tagged so that the antigen-containing cells can be visualized (see Figure 4.19A). This is usually accomplished by means of a chemical reaction that creates a colored precipitate within the cells or with the use of a fluorescent dye that glows when exposed to light of a particular wavelength. The researcher can then examine the tissue slices under a microscope to see which brain areas or neurons contain the antigen. This technique is limited only by the ability to raise antibodies, so it is suitable for a wider range of proteins than autoradiography. **FIGURE 4.20B** shows the visualization of cells that contain the neuropeptide hypocretin in the lateral hypothalamus of a healthy human. In patients with the sleep disorder narcolepsy, the number of hypocretin neurons is reduced by about 90% (Thannicakal et al., 2000). These results, along with animal experiments using neurotoxin lesioning and genetic modification, suggest that hypocretin in the hypothalamus may regulate the onset of sleep stages. ICC is similar to autoradiography in principle, but it is far more selective because the antibody (which recognizes only a very specific protein) is used, and it is much quicker because it does not require the development time of autoradiographic film. A related technique called **Western blot** uses antibodies to detect specific proteins in a tissue rather than a slice. The proteins in the homogenate are separated out based on size, using a method called gel electrophoresis, and placed onto a blotting membrane. As is true for ICC, the membrane is incubated with the antibody of the protein of interest. Because the antibody–antigen interaction is so specific, the method can identify the target protein even in a complex mixture of proteins. After brief rinsing to remove unbound antibody, a second antibody is applied that binds to the first antibody and provides a chemical reaction to create a detectable product, either an insoluble colored dye that stains the membrane or a luminescence. These reaction products are formed in proportion to the amount of bound antibody and provide an accurate quantification of the protein of interest in the sample.

RADIOIMMUNOASSAY   Antibodies are useful in quantifying physiologically important molecules in body fluids such as blood, saliva, or CSF, as well as in tissue extracts. **Radioimmunoassay (RIA)** is based on competitive binding of an antibody to its antigen (the molecule being measured). The use of antibodies makes the procedure highly specific for the molecule of interest and very sensitive (**FIGURE 4.21**).

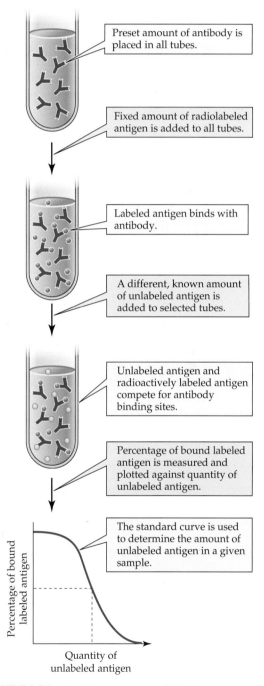

Preset amount of antibody is placed in all tubes.

Fixed amount of radiolabeled antigen is added to all tubes.

Labeled antigen binds with antibody.

A different, known amount of unlabeled antigen is added to selected tubes.

Unlabeled antigen and radioactively labeled antigen compete for antibody binding sites.

Percentage of bound labeled antigen is measured and plotted against quantity of unlabeled antigen.

The standard curve is used to determine the amount of unlabeled antigen in a given sample.

Percentage of bound labeled antigen

Quantity of unlabeled antigen

FIGURE 4.21   Radioimmunoassay (RIA)   The steps in the RIA procedure that produce a typical standard curve. The curve in turn is used to calculate the amount of unknown antigen in a given sample.

RIA involves preparing a standard curve of known antigen concentrations against which unknown samples can be compared. The standard curve is created by first combining a preset amount of antibody with a known concentration of radioactively labeled antigen in all the assay tubes. At this point, all the tubes are identical—that is, all of the antibody would be reversibly attached to radioactive antigen. However, the experimenter then adds different, known concentrations of unlabeled antigen, which compete with the radioactively labeled antigen. The higher the concentration of unlabeled competitor antigen added, the lower the amount of bound radioactive antigen there will be after the mixture has been incubated. Values are plotted as a standard curve and analyzed using appropriate computer software.

To determine how much of the antigen is present in any experimental sample, other test tubes are prepared in just the same way, except that samples containing unknown amounts of antigen are added instead of the known antigen used to create the standard curve. By measuring the amount of radioactive antigen bound in the sample tubes compared with the standard curve, the amount of antigen in the sample can be calculated.

Although the RIA was an extremely popular analytic technique following its development in 1960, there were several problems that made it costly and hazardous. Many laboratories felt compelled to build special facilities to protect investigators from the hazardous radioactivity (powerful beta and gamma radiation) needed to label the antigen. A second significant expense was the purchase of costly radioactivity-counting equipment. Finally, consideration of how to dispose of the radioactive waste became an increasing problem. Even though the radioisotopes typically used now in RIAs are much less dangerous than those used before, some of the disadvantages of this technique are still present. Because of the need to develop safer and more convenient alternatives to RIA, the **enzyme-linked immunosorbent assay** (**ELISA**) was developed in Sweden and the enzyme immunoassay (EIA) was developed in the Netherlands by two independent groups of researchers. Like the RIA both are immunoassays, but instead of using radioactivity for detection, they rely on an enzyme that acts on a substrate (i.e., starting material) to form a colored product. There are many modified protocols, but one of the most commonly found in commercial kits is the competition ELISA. Rather than using individual tubes or cuvettes as are used in the RIA, ELISA uses a plate with typically 96 wells (**FIGURE 4.22**) that immobilizes the reactants. For example, to measure the amount of a given substance (called the antigen, as in RIA) in a biological sample, the wells are first coated with a thin film of the antibody against the antigen. Standards (known quantities) of antigen (protein of interest) or test samples containing unknown amounts of antigen are then added to various wells, followed by antigen that has been linked to a reporting enzyme. The unlabeled antigen from samples or the known concentrations constituting the standard curve compete with the enzyme-linked antigen molecules for the limited number of antibodies in each well. After the unbound antigen is rinsed away, a colorless chemical substrate is added. The enzyme on any labeled antigen will turn the colorless substrate into a colored product. The product is measured in a microplate reader, and samples are compared with the color change in the known standards. In this assay, the amount of colored product at the end of the assay reaction is inversely related to the amount of the substance of interest (standard or unknown). Hence, the more substance is in the sample, the less color change will occur. Enzyme-linked immunoassays are quick and simple to perform, because they are designed to process a large number of samples in parallel. They are very popular methods to measure a wide variety of proteins, peptides, antibodies, and hormones.

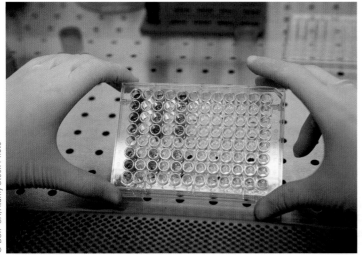

FIGURE 4.22 A sample 96-well ELISA plate A colored reaction product can be seen in some of the wells of the plate. Commercially available ELISA or EIA kits are available in a few different configurations. The most common type of ELISA is the competitive ELISA, in which the greater the amount of antigen present in a given well, the less colored product is produced. However, other formats exist in which there is a positive instead of an inverse relationship between antigen concentration and colored product formation. In either case, after the enzymatic reaction has been terminated, the optical density in each well (an index of light absorbance by the colored reaction product in the wells) is measured by a microplate reader, and the concentrations of antigen in the experimental samples are determined by means of a standard curve using known amounts of antigen provided by the manufacturer.

IN SITU HYBRIDIZATION **In situ hybridization (ISH)** makes it possible to locate cells in tissue slices that are *manufacturing* a particular protein or peptide, in much the same manner that ICC identifies cells *containing* a particular protein. ISH is particularly useful in neuropharmacology for detecting the specific messenger RNA (mRNA) molecules responsible for directing the manufacture of the wide variety of proteins essential to neuron function, such as enzymes, structural proteins, receptors, ion channels, and peptides. For example, **FIGURE 4.23A** shows the location of the mRNA for enkephalin, one of several opioid peptides in the adult rat brain (see Chapter 11). Because the method detects cells with a precise RNA sequence, it is exceptionally specific and extremely sensitive. Besides locating cells that contain specific mRNA, ISH is used to study changes in regional mRNA levels after experimental manipulations. The amount of mRNA provides an estimate of the rate of synthesis of the particular protein. This means that if chronic drug treatment caused a decrease in enkephalin mRNA, we could conclude that the protein the mRNA codes for had been down-regulated—that is, less of that protein was being synthesized.

As you may recall from Chapter 2, the double strands of DNA and the corresponding mRNA (**FIGURE 4.23B,C**) have a unique base-pair sequence responsible for directing the synthesis of each particular protein with its unique amino acid sequence. ISH depends on the ability to create probes by labeling single-stranded fragments of RNA made up of base-pair sequences complementary to those of the mRNA of interest (**FIGURE 4.23D**). After the single strands have been prepared, they are labeled radioactively or with dyes. When the tissue slices or cells are exposed to the labeled probe, the probe attaches (binds, or hybridizes) to the complementary base-pair sequences. After incubation, the tissue is washed and dehydrated before it is placed in contact with X-ray film or processed in other ways for visualization of cells containing the specific mRNA. This technique is extremely sensitive and can detect a very small number of cells that express a particular gene. If the researcher is interested only in measuring the amount of mRNA rather than visualizing its location, hybridization can be done using a tissue homogenate rather than a tissue slice. Two available methods of ISH that use homogenates are called Northern blot and dot blot.

DNA MICROARRAYS Microarrays, also called DNA chips or gene chips, allow scientists to measure the expression of thousands of genes at the same time. Because the nervous system exhibits the greatest complexity of gene expression of all tissues, being able to examine thousands of genes simultaneously can tell researchers which genes switch on and off together in

response to a disease state, drug treatment, or environmental condition. One would assume that genes that increase or decrease their expression under the same condition probably work together to induce a cellular

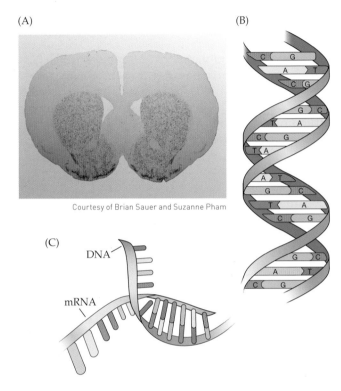

(A)

Courtesy of Brian Sauer and Suzanne Pham

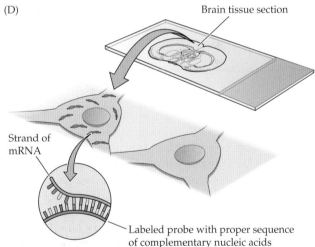

FIGURE 4.23 **In situ hybridization (ISH)** (A) Localization of enkephalin mRNA in a slice from rat brain. (B) Structure of a DNA molecule. The nucleotide bases always bind in a complementary fashion: thymine to adenine, and guanine to cytosine. (C) A strand of mRNA has copied the code from a partially unraveled DNA molecule in the nucleus and will carry the genetic code to ribosomes in the cytoplasm, where the protein will be created. (D) In ISH, a labeled probe has been created with the correct sequence of complementary bases. When the strand of mRNA in the cell and the labeled probe hybridize, or bond to one another, the product will label the cell that contains the genetic code for the protein of interest.

response. In addition, measuring the number of various RNAs in a sample tells us both the types and quantities of proteins present. A study by Mirnics and colleagues (2000) demonstrated the technical elegance of microarray by identifying multiple presynaptic proteins that are underexpressed in the frontal lobes of individuals with schizophrenia. Their results provide a predictive and testable model of the disorder.

The method is similar to that described for ISH, but rather than measuring a single mRNA, microarrays consist of between 1000 and 20,000 distinct complementary DNA sequences (spots) on a single chip (a structural support) of approximately thumbnail size. Each spot is only about 50 to 150 µm in diameter. This makes it possible to screen the expression of the entire genome of an organism in a single experiment on just a few chips. The tissue to be evaluated (e.g., the frontal lobe from an individual with schizophrenia compared with a frontal lobe from a healthy individual) is dissected, and the mRNAs are isolated and labeled, then hybridized to the large number of immobilized DNA molecules on the chip. A scanner automatically evaluates the extent of hybridization of each of the thousands of spots on the chip, and computer analysis is used to identify the patterns of gene activity. Several excellent reviews of the microarray procedure and its application in areas such as aging, neuropharmacology, and psychiatric disorders are available (Luo and Geschwind, 2001; Marcotte et al., 2001).

A modification of the standard microarray technology spurred the development of **genome-wide association studies** (**GWAS**). This technique utilizes gene chips consisting of large sets of single-nucleotide polymorphisms (SNPs) (i.e., gene alleles that differ in only one nucleotide). DNA samples from people with a disorder and matched controls are assayed on the chips. If a particular allele is found more often in people with the disease, it is "associated" with the disorder. The method is data driven rather than hypothesis driven, meaning that researchers do not need to know anything about the function of the gene, although sometimes this makes the results difficult to interpret. Although originally limited to detecting common SNPs (i.e., those found in more than 5% of the population), it is now possible to identify rare SNPs, as well as more of the copy number variants (CNVs). CNVs are chromosomal abnormalities in which portions of a chromosome are duplicated, deleted, inverted, or translocated. The technology is highly accurate, relatively inexpensive, and very fast, and it uses powerful statistical methods that reduce the risk of finding false-positive associations between genotype and phenotype. For details on the history, rationale, and application of GWAS, see a paper by the Psychiatric GWAS Consortium Coordinating Committee (2009).

A more recent, related technology is RNA sequencing (RNA-seq), which, like DNA microarrays, allows researchers to assess expression levels of thousands of genes. RNA-seq offers several advantages over DNA microarrays. First, RNA-seq measures the cellular transcriptome, which reflects the actual protein expression at a given time. Second, RNA-seq sequences the entire transcriptome and is therefore unbiased because it is not limited to quantifying a predetermined selection of genes. Moreover, RNA-seq can detect novel transcripts that would otherwise be impossible to detect with microarray technology. For a discussion of the advantages and disadvantages of DNA microarrays and RNA-seq, see Rao and colleagues (2019). As was described in Chapter 1, a potential application of tools to evaluate gene transcription levels is the emerging field of **pharmacogenetics**. Knowledge of the genetic factors that may predict therapeutic or adverse responses to drug effects has enormous potential to enhance treatment of psychiatric and neurological diseases.

New tools are used for imaging the structure and function of the brain

Most conventional neurobiological techniques are designed to quantify or to localize significant substances in the nervous system. One of the greatest challenges in psychopharmacology has been to evaluate the functioning of the brain under various conditions, particularly in the living human being. Advances in technology not only make visualization of the CNS far more precise, but also provide the opportunity to visualize the functioning brain.

AUTORADIOGRAPHY OF DYNAMIC CELL PROCESSES

You are already familiar with the technique of autoradiography for mapping cell components such as neurotransmitter receptors that have been radioactively labeled. A second application of autoradiography is the tracing of active processes in the brain such as cerebral blood flow, oxygen consumption, local glucose utilization, or local rates of cerebral protein synthesis that indicate neural activity.

The technique called **2-deoxyglucose autoradiography** is based on the assumption that when nerve cell firing increases, the metabolic rate (i.e., the utilization of glucose and oxygen) also increases. By identifying cells that take up more glucose, we can tell which brain regions are most active. A modified form of the glucose molecule, 2-deoxyglucose (2-DG), is taken up by active nerve cells but is not processed in the same manner as glucose and remains trapped in the cell. If the 2-DG has been labeled in some way, the most active cells can be identified. A similar (but nonlethal) technique can be performed with human participants using PET, as described in the next section.

A second way of identifying which brain cells are active is to locate cells that show increases in nuclear proteins involved in protein synthesis. The assumption is that when cells are activated, selected proteins called transcription factors (such as **c-fos**) dramatically increase in concentration over 30 to 60 minutes. The c-fos protein subsequently activates the expression of other genes that regulate protein synthesis. In order to visualize which neurons are active, ICC is used to stain the cells that have increased levels of the fos protein.

IMAGING TECHNIQUES   Since our ultimate goal is to understand how drugs affect the human brain and behavior, the most exciting advance in recent years has been the ability to visualize the living human brain. Although we can learn a lot by studying individuals with brain damage, until recently we could only guess at where the damage was located, because the brain was not accessible until the individual died, often many years later. It was virtually impossible to know which specific brain area was responsible for the lost function. The human brain remained a bit of a "black box," and our understanding of the neural processes responsible for human thinking and behavior was advanced primarily through animal experiments. Because of recent advances in X-ray and computer technology, neuroscience can now not only safely visualize the detailed anatomy of the human brain, but also identify the neural processes responsible for a particular mental activity. CT and MRI are techniques that create pictures of the human nervous system that show far greater detail than was previously possible with standard X-rays. Other techniques are designed to see functional activity in the human brain. These include PET, functional MRI, and computer-assisted electrical recording (see the electroencephalography [EEG] section).

When standard X-rays are passed through the body, they are differentially absorbed depending on the density of the various tissues. Rays that are not absorbed strike a photographic plate, forming light and dark images. Unfortunately, the brain is made up of many overlapping parts that do not differ dramatically in their ability to absorb X-rays, so it is very difficult to distinguish the individual shapes of brain structures. **Computerized tomography** (**CT**) not only increases the resolution (sharpness of detail) of the image but also provides an image in three dimensions.

The individual undergoing a CT scan (sometimes called CAT scan, for computerized axial tomography) lies with his head placed in a cylindrical X-ray tube (**FIGURE 4.24A**). A series of narrow, parallel beams of radiation are aimed through the tissue and toward the X-ray detectors. The X-ray source is rotated around the head while the detectors move on the opposite side in parallel. At each point of rotation, the source and detectors also move linearly. In this manner, they make a series of radiation transmission readings, which is calculated by a computer and visually displayed as a "slice" through the brain (**FIGURE 4.24B**). The slices can be reconstructed by the computer into three-dimensional images for a better understanding of brain structure.

Magnetic resonance imaging (**MRI**) further refines the ability to view the living brain by using computerized measurements of the distinct waves that different atoms emit when placed in a strong magnetic field and activated by radiofrequency waves. This method distinguishes different body tissues on the basis of their individual chemical composition. Because tissues contain different amounts of water, they can be distinguished by scanning the magnetically induced resonance of hydrogen. The image provides exquisite detail and, as is true for CT, sequential slices can be reconstructed to provide three-dimensional images (**FIGURE 4.25**).

(A)

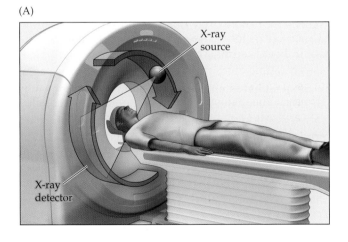

(B)

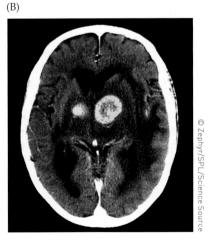

© Zephyr/SPL/Science Source

FIGURE 4.24   Computerized tomography (CT)   (A) The cylindrical CT scanner rotates around the head, sending parallel X-ray beams through the tissue to be detected on the opposite side. A computerized image in the form of a brain slice is constructed from the data. (B) Horizontal CT scan showing a tumor (orange) at the level of the basal ganglia. Anterior is toward the top of the scan.

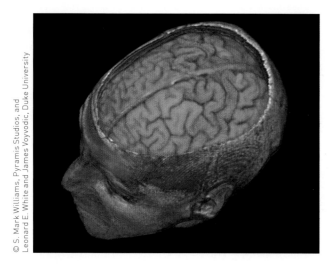

FIGURE 4.25 A three-dimensional image formed with MRI
Computer technology provides the opportunity to create
three-dimensional representations of the brain from
sequential slices.

Magnetic resonance spectroscopy (MRS) comple-
ments MRI because it can use the MRI-generated data
to calculate the concentration of brain chemicals as well
as evaluating metabolic changes in individuals with Alzheimer's disease, Parkinson's disease, depression, epilepsy, and other conditions. Although MRI shows only
structure, MRS is an important new tool for researchers
and physicians to measure levels of specific molecules
such as glutamate, choline, and neurotransmitter metabolites in discrete brain regions in living individuals. Although only a few molecules can be measured at
present, the future expansion of the field is likely.

A further modification of MRI technology called **diffusion tensor imaging (DTI)** depends on the ability to scan
the microscopic three-dimensional movement of water in
neural tissue. While water molecules normally disperse
in every direction, in axon bundles that are generally
myelinated with fatty sheaths, movement is restricted
and the water can diffuse only along the length of the
myelinated axons. Scanning the water movement provides the data needed to visualize the axonal pathways
and provides a structural view of connectivity among
brain structures. The data collected tell not only the total
amount of water molecule diffusion, but also the direc-
tionality of diffusion, called anisotropy. The higher the
anisotropy, the more tightly bundled the axons; higher
diffusion levels indicate poorly myelinated or damaged
axon connectivity. This technology is the basis for the
Human Connectome Project, introduced in the chapter
opener, that aims to map all the neural connections in
the human brain. The chapter opening photo is an image
from a DTI scan. The significance of connectivity to mental function will be described in subsequent chapters (see
Chapters 18, 19, and 20). What is becoming clear is that
any single brain structure may not be functionally important to a brain disorder, but the *connections* between
regions may be the critical consideration.

It did not take long for scientists to realize the power
of their new tools, and they proceeded to use the computerized scanning techniques to view the localization
of radioactively labeled materials injected into a living
human. **Positron emission tomography (PET)** does not
create images of the brain but maps the distribution of
a radioactively labeled substance that has been injected
into an individual. To do this safely, we must use radioisotopes that decay quickly rather than accumulate.
Although radioactive isotopes used in many laboratory
experiments have relatively long half-lives, on the order
of 1200 years for ^{3}H or 5700 years for ^{14}C, those used
for PET have half-lives of 2 minutes (^{15}O), 20 minutes
(^{11}C), or 110 minutes (^{18}F). Isotopes that decay and lose
their radioactivity quickly (i.e., have short half-lives)
emit positrons, which are like electrons except that they
have a positive charge. When a positron expelled from
the nucleus collides with an electron, both particles
are annihilated and emit two gamma photons traveling in opposite directions. In a PET scanning device
(**FIGURE 4.26A**), detectors surround the head to track
these gamma photons and locate their origin. The information is analyzed by computer and visualized as
an image on the monitor.

PET is useful in neuropharmacology in several ways
(Farde, 1996). First, a radioactively labeled drug or ligand can be administered, and the location of binding in brain tissue can be seen. The technique has been
used successfully to localize neurotransmitter receptors and identify where drugs bind. Perhaps even more
exciting is the use of PET to determine which parts of
the brain are active during the performance of particular tasks or cognitive problem solving (**FIGURE 4.26B**).
PET allows us to visualize brain activity, which is reflected in increases in glucose utilization, oxygen use,
and blood flow, depending on which reagent has been
labeled. Very much like autoradiography in living humans, PET can be used along with 2-DG to map brain
areas that utilize increased glucose or demonstrate
increased blood flow—both indicative of heightened
neural activity.

**Single-photon emission computerized tomography
(SPECT)** is very similar to PET imaging, but it is much
simpler and less expensive because the radiolabeled
probes do not have to be synthesized but are commercially available. When scanned, the radioactive compounds, either inhaled or injected, show the changes in
regional blood flow. Although resolution is less accurate than with PET, SPECT data can be combined with
CT or MRI scans to localize active areas more precisely
than with SPECT alone.

While MRI visualizes brain structure, **functional
MRI (fMRI)** has become the newest and perhaps the
most powerful tool in the neuroscientist's arsenal
for visualizing brain activity. To meet the increased
metabolic demand of active neurons, the flow of blood
carrying oxygen to these cells increases. Functional

(A)

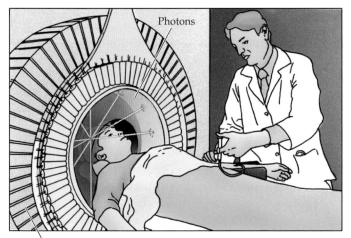

Photons

Photon
detectors

(B)

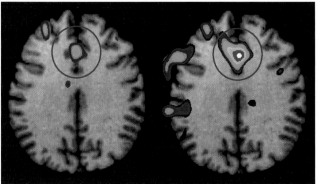

From P. Rainville, 2002. *Curr Opin Neurobiol* 12: 195–204.; courtesy of Pierre Rainville

FIGURE 4.26 Positron emission tomography (PET) (A) A typical scanning device for PET. Notice the photo-detectors that surround the head to track the gamma photons produced when a positron expelled from the nucleus collides with an electron. (B) PET scan image showing active brain areas by measuring regional cerebral blood flow under two conditions. The person on the left, who was told to expect only mild discomfort from putting a hand into 47°C (116.6°F) water, showed less neuronal activity (correlated with less blood flow) in the anterior cingulate cortex than the person on the right, who expected more pain. Highly active areas are colored orange, red, and white. Additional experiments might assess how certain drugs change the pattern of activation.

MRI can detect the increases in blood oxygenation caused by cell firing (called BOLD, for blood-oxygen-level-dependent, brain activity) because oxygenated hemoglobin (the molecule that carries oxygen in the blood and provides the red color) has a different magnetic resonance signal than oxygen-depleted hemoglobin. Functional MRI offers several advantages over PET. First, fMRI provides both anatomical and functional information for each individual, and the detail of the image is far superior. Second, because the individual does not have to be injected with radioactive material, the measures can be made repeatedly to show changes over time. For the same reason, the procedure is essentially risk-free, except for the occasional case of claustrophobia caused by the scanner. Third, the process is so rapid that brain activity can be monitored in real time (i.e., as it is occurring). In combination with recording of electrical activity with EEG (see the next section), fMRI can produce three-dimensional images that show neural activity in interconnecting networks of brain centers. Temporal sequencing of information processing becomes possible, so one can see the changing locations of brain activity during tasks and cognitive processes.

Resting-state fMRI (rs-fMRI) is a relatively new modification and powerful tool to investigate connectivity among brain regions when the individual is awake but not actively engaged in a task that requires attention. Examining BOLD brain activity at rest allows researchers to find highly reliable patterns of correlated spontaneous neural activity. Such data can be used to compare connectivity in healthy individuals with that in individuals with neurological or psychiatric diseases. For example, a large number of studies have compared healthy individuals and those with major depressive disorder (reviewed by Dutta et al., 2014). There have been multiple distinct networks identified in the resting state that are associated with particular symptoms of depression and that are different in depressed individuals than in controls. One such network, called the default mode network (DMN), includes the posterior cingulate cortex, medial prefrontal cortex, ventral anterior cingulate cortex, and portions of parietal cortex. The DMN is more active in depressed individuals than in controls, and this hyperactivity is greatest when the individual is not actively involved in any activity that requires attention or performance of an explicit task. That fact has led to the idea that DMN hyperactivity is the basis for self-referential processing, which refers to the negative inwardly directed ruminations of depressed individuals. Perhaps of greatest interest to psychopharmacologists and clinicians is that resting-state connectivity is differentially altered by various antidepressant treatments. Additionally, there is indication that the extent of connectivity may help identify which individuals will respond or not respond to a given treatment. Such ability to predict responders and nonresponders has the potential to greatly improve the treatment of major depressive disorder (reviewed by Dichter et al., 2015). For an older but excellent introduction to brain imaging and its relationship to cognitive processes, refer to Posner and Raichle (1994).

Pharmacological MRI (phMRI), a spinoff of fMRI, has developed into an important technique in drug development. It images the mechanism of drug action by analyzing changes in brain function following drug administration and identifies the location of drug action within the CNS. It aids early clinical studies that evaluate relationships between drug dose, drug plasma levels, brain receptor occupancy (using PET), and changes in brain function. Further, visualizing the time course of drug action can provide pharmacokinetic data. Most important, it has the potential to predict treatment response, avoiding weeks of treatment that often is needed to ultimately see a measurable clinical response. It could do this by screening patients' brain function profiles in response to the drug to determine whether they will ultimately respond to that particular treatment. This use of phMRI would be an important tool in personalized medicine (see Chapter 1) by matching a given treatment to those individuals most likely to show beneficial results, and avoiding expensive and time-consuming treatment of a patient who will not have a good treatment outcome. This would be particularly important for high-risk, high-cost treatments or those taking months to show clinical effectiveness.

ELECTROENCEPHALOGRAPHY (EEG) In addition to improved visualization techniques and methods of mapping metabolic function in the human brain, a third noninvasive method of investigating human brain activity is now used in neuropharmacology: electrical recording with **electroencephalography (EEG)**. As is true for other imaging techniques, the EEG has become more sophisticated with the assistance of computer analysis. Electrodes are taped to the scalp in multiple locations (**FIGURE 4.27A**) according to the international 10–20 system that describes the location of the scalp electrodes (**FIGURE 4.27B**) based on the underlying area of the cerebral cortex. This type of mapping is important for standardization of placement and permits comparison and reproducibility from person to person and in the same individual over time. The electrical activity that is recorded reflects the sum of electrical events of populations of neurons. Multiple electrodes are used because a comparison of the signals from various locations can identify the origin of some waves. **Quantitative EEG (qEEG)** uses computerized analysis to evaluate the large amount of complex data collected with an EEG, which is frequently converted into colored maps of the changes taking place in the brain during cognitive processing tasks. While useful to clinicians to evaluate brain functions associated with things such as traumatic brain injury or epilepsy, application of qEEG in psychopharmacology includes evaluating the effects of medications on neural function. Additionally, it can be used to predict individual response to particular treatments to enhance personalized medicine. Hence qEEG can be used to determine whether a given individual will be helped by medication and

which of the classes of medications will be most beneficial (see Arns and Olbrich, 2014).

Because EEG can detect electrical events in real time, one of the most useful applications of EEG data is recording electrical changes that occur in response to momentary sensory stimulation; these changes are called **event-related potentials** (**ERPs**). ERPs allow researchers to visualize the processing of the cognitive response to a given stimulus as it occurs. Because ERPs are quite small, the raw EEG response must be computer averaged over many (perhaps several hundred) stimulus presentations to reduce the appearance of random brain activity (**FIGURE 4.27C**) while the significant electrical wave form is retained (the ERP). Evaluation of electrical responses in various clinical populations has led to improved understanding of attention deficits and processing differences in individuals with schizophrenia, Huntington's disease, ADHD, and many other disorders. It has been suggested that these differences in processing may help to identify subtypes of clinical disorders that might be used for selecting appropriate treatment. Other brain scans may be used in combination with qEEG because while PET and fMRI can show which areas of the brain are active during a task, ERPs help to understand the time course of the activation.

Genetic engineering helps neuroscientists to ask and answer new questions

The excitement surrounding completion of the Human Genome Project, in which all human genetic material has been mapped, has permeated both the scientific and the popular press. Although the term *genetic engineering* evokes both excitement and some trepidation in most people, the technology has at the very least provided amazing opportunities for neuroscience. Genetic engineering involves procedures in which the DNA of the organism is altered (knockouts or knock-ins) or a foreign gene is added to the genetic material of the organism (transgenic). These procedures provide the opportunity to produce highly specific mutations in the mouse genome to study subsequent changes in brain function and behavior. **FIGURE 4.28** shows the essential steps in genetic engineering. Genes of interest are extracted or extracted and modified and then are injected into fertilized mouse eggs taken from a pregnant mouse. After the injection procedure, the eggs are implanted in the uterus of a surrogate mother. Offspring are assessed for evidence of the mutation. Chimeric mice (i.e., those in which the transgene is expressed in some cells and not in others) are subsequently mated with wild-type mice. The offspring from these matings produce some heterozygous mice (i.e., those having one transgene and one wild-type gene) that in turn will be mated to other heterozygous mice to ultimately produce some mice

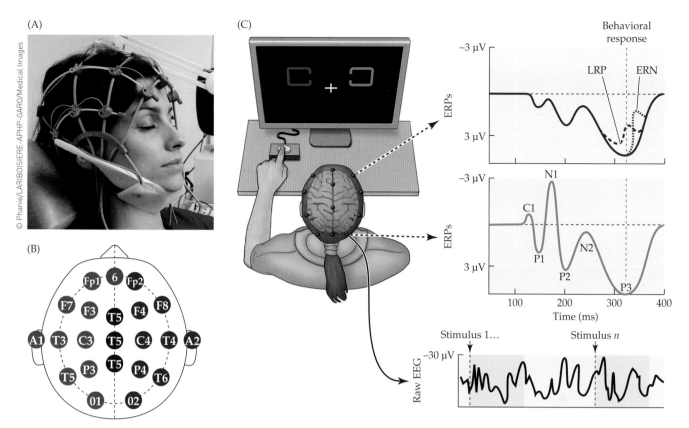

FIGURE 4.27 **Electroencephalography (EEG)** (A) In humans, changes in electrical activity of the brain are detected by recording electrodes that are attached to the surface of the individual's scalp. The electrodes record the activity of thousands of cells simultaneously. (B) The standardized international 10–20 system for electrode placement, with the view of the skull from above, nose indicating frontal, ears to each side. The electrodes are marked as the ground (G), frontal pole (Fp), frontal (F), central (C), parietal (P), occipital (O), and temporal (T). The midline electrodes are marked as FZ, CZ, and PZ, with the Z standing for zero. Odd numbers are used for points over the left hemisphere, and even numbers over the right. The ear lobes are indicated with (A). (C) Event-related potential (ERP) patterns of voltage change in response to a visual stimulus in a discrimination task. On the left is a model of a human head with the placement of a subset of electrodes from the 10–20 system. The right side of the figure shows how the ERPs are extracted from the raw EEG record while the subject performs the visual discrimination task. The lower ERP (blue) shows the wave forms at occipito-temporal lobe electrode sites during the visual task. The upper ERP (purple) shows the wave forms while the finger response occurs. Processes associated with voltage fluctuations of the ERP are labeled: C1, primary visual cortex; P1 and N1, information moves through the visual system; P2, not well understood; N2, categorizing the stimulus; P3 (often called P300 because it occurs 300 ms after the stimulus onset), working memory encoding; LRP, preparation for the motor response; ERN, evaluation of performance after the response. (C after G. F. Woodman. 2010. *Atten Percept Psychophys* 72: 2031–2046. doi.org/10.3758/BF03196680)

homozygous for the transgene. Because the combined gestation time of mice is approximately 3 weeks and mice are reproductively mature at 4 to 7 weeks of age, the entire procedure takes about 9 to 12 months.

Creating genetically modified mice may represent the most sophisticated of all techniques yet described. With the ability to identify which piece of chromosomal DNA (i.e., the gene) is responsible for directing the synthesis of a particular protein, neuroscience has the opportunity to alter that gene, causing a change in expression of the protein, thus creating **knockout mice**. Comparing the behavior and the drug response

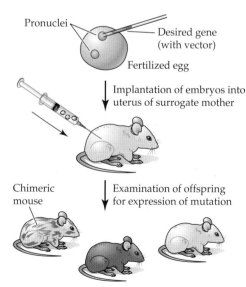

FIGURE 4.28 **Illustration of genetic engineering** Genetic material is extracted from cells, injected into fertilized eggs, and implanted in the uterus of a surrogate mother. Offspring that are chimeric are mated with wild-type mice. Any of their offspring that are heterozygous for the genetic trait of interest are subsequently mated to produce some homozygous mice of interest.

FIGURE 4.29 Jennifer Doudna (left) and Emmanuelle Charpentier (right), recipients of the 2020 Nobel Prize in Chemistry for their contributions to CRISPR gene-editing technology. Photographed in 2016.

can examine epigenetic modifications of gene expression and chemical- or light-induced control of Cas9 (see Ledford, 2016, for more detail). Many variations of the technique have been developed by multiple research labs. See **BOX 4.2** for a discussion of the ethical implications of using CRISPR technology in humans.

In contrast to the knockout technique, to create **knockin mice**, the inserted gene is modified so that it produces a slightly different protein from that found in wild-type mice. Often the protein manufactured is different from that of wild-type mice by only a single amino acid residue, allowing investigation of the relationship between protein structure and function. For neuropharmacologists, the protein of interest is often a receptor subtype or an enzyme that controls an important synthesizing or metabolizing process.

A second strategy involves the substitution of one gene for another, producing **transgenic mice**. As we learn more about the pathological genes responsible for neuropsychiatric diseases such as Huntington's and Alzheimer's diseases, it is possible to isolate the human genes and insert them into mice to produce animal models of the disorders. For an example, see the work by Carter and coworkers (1999), which measures motor deficits in mice transgenic for the gene mutation that causes Huntington's disease (**BOX 4.3**). With authentic animal models, neuroscience will be able to identify the cellular processes responsible for a disorder and develop appropriate treatments.

As is true for any revolutionary new technique, caution in interpreting the results is warranted. First, because behaviors are regulated not by single genes but by multiple interacting genes, changing or eliminating only one alters only a small part of the overall behavioral trait. Second, compensation by other genes for the missing or overexpressed gene may mask the functional effect of the mutation. Third, since the altered gene function occurs in all tissues at all stages of development, it is possible that changes in other organs or in other brain areas are responsible for the behavioral changes. Finally, because these animals are developing organisms, environmental factors also have a significant effect on the ultimate gene expression. Several articles provide greater detail on the potential pitfalls of gene-targeting studies (Crawley, 1996; Gerlai, 1996; Lathe, 1996).

In addition to its use in creating "mutant" animals, genetic material can be inserted into cells (maintained in cell culture) that do not normally have a particular protein (e.g., receptor). The normal cell division process produces large numbers of identically altered

of altered mice with those of unaltered animals will tell us about the function of the protein that has been deleted. We can also use these animals to identify the importance of that protein in specific drug effects. The knockout technology has led to exciting new discoveries in neuroscience and the development of animal models of human diseases, leading to more effective therapeutics..

What is needed is a faster and less expensive method to create genetically modified organisms. In 2020, Emmanuelle Charpentier and Jennifer Doudna (**FIGURE 4.29**) were awarded the Nobel Prize in Chemistry for their contributions to inventing **CRISPR (clustered regularly interspaced short palindromic repeat)** technology. CRISPR uses "guide RNA" to identify a specific genomic sequence to be modified. Along with the "guide," a nuclease (Cas9) is also introduced, and it cuts out the specified section of DNA. A new section of DNA is then inserted. In the future, CRISPR may make it possible to correct genetic mutations at specific locations for the treatment of human diseases. The new technique is highly specific, avoids the prolonged process of traditional gene-targeting methods used in animal research (see Figure 4.28), and is therefore less expensive. Additionally, modifications of the method can damage the Cas9 enzyme, which still allows it to identify the specified DNA sequence, but rather than cutting it out, it prevents gene expression. Gene expression can also be stimulated by attaching an activating protein to the damaged Cas9 enzyme, which means that genes can be turned on or off using this technique. Other alternatives in the procedure

BOX 4.2 ■ CASE STUDIES

CRISPR Babies: The case of Lulu and Nana

Genetic engineering, in particular gene-editing technology, has already begun to live up to its promise to revolutionize research, not only in neuropharmacology, but in other biomedical disciplines as well. With the ability to know the transcription level of any gene in nearly any cell in the body, coupled with the ability to edit genes in a time-efficient and cost-effective manner, scientists are rapidly making breakthrough discoveries that reveal how the genetic code determines biological function. While the case for genetic engineering in research is quite convincing, there is also great interest in how these tools might be directly applied as novel therapeutic strategies in humans. Applied genetic engineering is not a new concept and it has been in use for many years to make food crops that are resistant to things like drought and disease. However, you already be familiar with the notion that applied genetic engineering is controversial, with many countries and localities around the world requiring labeling of food produced with genetic engineering technology.

The use of genetic engineering technology for so-called gene therapy offers the potential to unlock novel treatments for a broad range of human diseases. In 2018, to the shock of the world, it was revealed that Chinese scientist He Jianku had conducted a secret experiment that used CRISPR technology to edit the genome of human embryos. The purpose of the experiment was to introduce a mutation to the CCR5 gene, a manipulation of the genome that was hoped to confer resistance to HIV, for which the father of the embryos was a carrier. The story of the experiment, and the resulting birth of twin girls, known in the media as Lulu and Nana, was first reported in the MIT Technology Review (Regalado, 2018) and was followed by the release of a series of YouTube videos in which He described both the procedure and the birth of two healthy baby girls. A manuscript describing the experimental gene editing was submitted for publication in a peer-reviewed journal, although it was ultimately rejected on ethical grounds and was thus never published.

Once the story of Lulu and Nana broke, it sparked immense controversy and debate. While the birth of the world's first genetically modified babies represents an astonishing medical breakthrough, the secrecy of He's work reflects the fact that it was conducted in violation of numerous ethical norms and regulations. Scientists and bioethicists have warned against potential unintended consequences of both **somatic genetic engineering**, which only affects somatic cells of the treated individual, as well as **human germline engineering**, whereby the genome is edited in such a way that the modification also affects gametes and is thus heritable, as with Lulu and Nana. In both cases, there is a pressing need to understand the risks associated with off-target genome edits, which may result in adverse health consequences (Ledford, 2019). In the particular case of germline engineering, the concerns are all the more compelling, since such genetic modifications have the potential to be transmitted to all future generations, including modifications that could be subsequently prove harmful. Once introduced, such harmful modifications could be difficult to remove. Additionally, valid concerns have been raised about the possibility of using genetic engineering technology in humans for non-therapeutic purposes: to enhance offspring by introducing desirable traits and eliminating undesirable traits. In addition to reducing genetic diversity, non-therapeutic application of genetic engineering has significant potential to give rise to new forms of genetic discrimination and worsen existing societal inequities. For a discussion of the safety and ethical concerns associated with CRISPR technology, see Baltimore and coworkers (2015) and Doudna (2019).

Nonetheless, with the genetic tools described in this chapter and referenced elsewhere in this book, scientists are poised to make significant breakthroughs in understanding the etiology of, and developing treatments for, psychiatric and neurological diseases. As gene-editing technology continues to advance, there is much need for further research to understand the risks associated with off-target edits, as well as how to avoid the associated unintended consequences. The biological and societal implications of genetic engineering need to be fully examined in order to develop a well-informed regulatory framework that allows gene-editing technology to be ethically used for its potential life-changing and life-saving benefits, while avoiding its potential for harm and abuse.

---

cells, which we call **cloning**. These cells can then be used to screen new drugs, using conventional pharmacological techniques for identifying agonists and antagonists.

Optogenetics is an exciting field of biology that uses light (hence *opto*) to exert temporally and spatially precise control over the functioning of genetically specified cells (hence *genetics*). This approach has particular utility in neurobiology by enabling researchers either to excite or to inhibit selected populations of nerve cells almost instantaneously (reviewed by Deisseroth, 2015; Guru et al., 2015). Optogenetic control of neuronal firing is accomplished using microbial opsins, light-sensitive proteins synthesized by several

BOX 4.3 ■ PHARMACOLOGY IN ACTION

Transgenic Model of Huntington's Disease

(A)

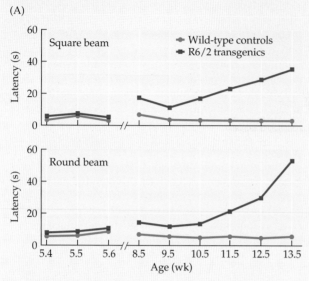
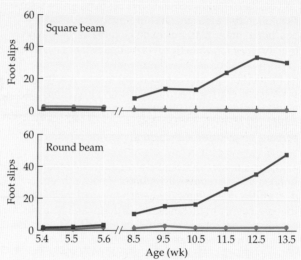

Beam walking Mice were taught to walk across square or round elevated beams to reach an enclosed safety platform. The time to cross and the number of foot slips were recorded. Each data point represents the mean time to cross. (After R. J. Carter et al. 1999. *J Neurosci* 19: 3248–3257. © 1999 Society for Neuroscience.)

Huntington's disease (HD) is characterized by progressive impairment in movement, such as slow, uncoordinated actions; involuntary jerking; and impaired gait, posture, and balance. Additionally, individuals develop cognitive dysfunction, which includes difficulty in planning, lack of flexibility in thinking, poor impulse control, inability to focus attention, learning deficits, and others. Furthermore, there are marked mood and personality changes accompanied by a variety of psychiatric disorders. Further details of the symptoms of this disease, its progression, and approaches to treatment can be found in Chapter 20. This genetically transmitted disease strikes individuals when they are in their 30s and 40s and progresses over time. Individuals typically live 15 to 20 years after onset of symptoms, which means that their life span is significantly shortened. At present, although some symptoms can be treated initially, no treatment is available to modify the course of the disease. What is needed is a translational animal model of the disease that would lead to improved drug development.

Using a host of behavioral measures, Carter and colleagues (1999) characterized the progressive neurological symptoms in a model created by inserting the human HD gene into mice (R6/2 mice). Because patients with HD show a variety of gradually worsening motor deficits and progressive hypoactivity, a battery of tests measuring the motor function of the transgenic mice was started at 5 to 6 weeks of age and administered weekly for 10 weeks. Functioning of the transgenic mice was compared with that of wild-type control mice. To evaluate fine motor coordination and balance, the investigators used **beam walking**, in which the raised beam resembles a human gymnastic balance beam. They found no difference in performance between R6/2 transgenic mice and wild-type control mice at 5 to 6 weeks of age on either the square or the round beam, although R6/2 mice were somewhat slower in performing the task (**FIGURE A**). However, by 8 to 9 weeks of age, the R6/2 mice took 12 times as long and had many more foot slips. At 13 to 14 weeks, many of the transgenic mice fell off the beam repeatedly. Motor coordination and balance were further evaluated on a **rotarod**—a horizontally oriented cylinder that is mechanically rotated at set speeds (**FIGURE B**). The researchers timed how long the mice remained on the rod (i.e., latency to fall). As you can see in **FIGURE C**, control mice readily maintained their balance and coordination for the maximum trial length at all speeds tested. In contrast, transgenic mice had difficulty at the highest speeds at 5 to 6 weeks, and by 13 to 14 weeks, they failed to maintain their coordination at any speed. When their **swimming performance** was examined at 5 to 6 weeks, R6/2 mice showed overall slowness, a tendency to float temporarily without making efforts to swim, and significant incoordination in swim movements that progressively worsened over time. Additionally, rather than the fluid, coordinated **gait** shown by healthy mice, transgenic mice

BOX 4.3 ■ PHARMACOLOGY IN ACTION (*continued*)

showed staggering and weaving with uneven short strides, reminiscent of the typical patient with HD. In a final task, researchers examined the startle reflex to an intensely loud sound. Transgenic mice showed a decline in response only at the final time point. More important, the acoustic startle response is normally reduced when the intense stimulus is preceded by a small prepulse stimulus. Patients with HD characteristically show a deficit in that **prepulse inhibition of startle**. Likewise, by 8 weeks, the transgenic mice showed significant deficits.

A variety of behavioral measures that reflect the symptoms of HD show clearly that R6/2 mice represent a valid model of the motor deficits that gradually appear in patients with HD. Subsequent studies have shown other analogous characteristics, including the development of diabetes, deficits in spatial learning, shortened life span, and a host of pathological changes in the brain. You might be interested in reading more about these animals and some of the newer drugs tested on them that target progressive brain pathology and gene transcription (Li et al., 2005). It is hoped that these drugs may become effective agents in preventing the progression of this devastating disease.

(B)

Courtesy of Susan Urmy, Vanderbilt University

Rotarod

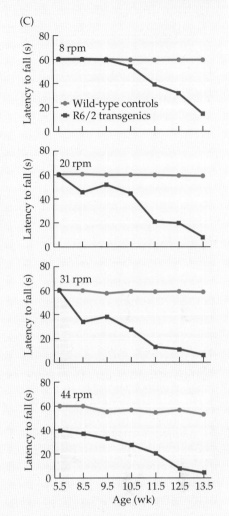

(C)

Rotarod performance Data points represent the mean latency to fall from the rotarod (maximum trial length = 60 seconds) at various speeds of rotation. rpm, revolutions per minute. (After R. J. Carter et al. 1999. *J Neurosci* 19: 3248–3257. © 1999 Society for Neuroscience.)

---

different types of microorganisms.* **FIGURE 4.30A** illustrates three kinds of opsins currently being used in optogenetic research. ChR2 (channelrhodopsin-2) forms a nonspecific cation channel permeable to sodium (Na^+), potassium (K^+), and calcium (Ca^{2+}) ions, so light-activated channel opening depolarizes the cell membrane and rapidly stimulates cell firing primarily due to Na^+ influx. A genetically modified form of channelrhodopsin called iC1C2 forms an inhibitory chloride (Cl^-) channel. NpHR (halorhodopsin) is a

Cl^- pump instead of a channel, thus enabling it to inhibit neuronal firing as iC1C2 does but with a slower onset of action. Each of these opsin proteins is sensitive to a particular wavelength of light, which is used to selectively activate the ion channel or pump. This can be seen in **FIGURE 4.30B**, which shows electrophysiological recording from a single neuron in vitro that was made to express both ChR2 and NpHR. Note that each short pulse of blue light, which activates ChR2, led to the firing of an action potential (left and right sides of the trace); however, this ChR2-mediated effect was completely blocked by NpHR activation using simultaneous application of a yellow light (middle of the trace).

---

*Of course, the prototypical opsin is rhodopsin, the light-sensitive retinal pigment found in rod photoreceptors.

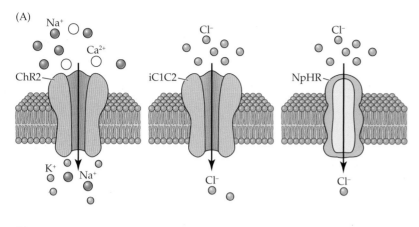

(A)

(B)

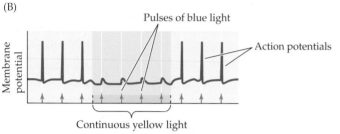

FIGURE 4.30 Light-sensitive proteins used in optogenetic studies (A) The figure depicts three of the major opsins currently used in optogenetic research, each embedded in a neuronal membrane along with the ions it causes to pass through the membrane. ChR2 and iC1C2 are ion channels, whereas NpHR is an ion pump. (B) This electrical tracing was taken from a neuron in vitro that was engineered to express both ChR2 and NpHR. Vertical blue arrows represent brief flashes of blue laser light; the horizontal yellow line represents continued application of yellow light from a different laser. Large upward deflections of the red line are action potentials elicited by ChR2 stimulation. (A after A. Guru et al. 2015. *Int J Neuropsychopharmacol* 18: pyv079/CC BY 4.0; B after F. Zhang et al. 2007. *Nature* 446: 633–639. doi.org/10.1038/nature05744)

The power of optogenetics stems from the ability of researchers to express the gene for ChR2, iC1C2, NpHR, or any other opsin in a specific population of neurons (e.g., dopamine or serotonin neurons) using viral vectors to target the cells of interest in a particular brain area (**FIGURE 4.31A**). The viruses used in optogenetics and related methods deliver genetic material to neurons but are otherwise harmless to the cells. Once the gene-bearing virus has infected the target cells and the opsin transgene has been expressed by those cells, the animal is surgically implanted with a fiber-optic probe aimed at the area containing the target. After the animal has recovered from the surgery, a laser connected to the probe by a fiber-optic cable can deliver light of the appropriate wavelength to the target area while the animal is freely behaving in an apparatus such as an open field or an operant chamber (**FIGURE 4.31B**). Using this setup, researchers can determine the behavioral effects of either activating or silencing the specific neurons engineered to express the light-sensitive protein.

Since the introduction of optogenetics to neuroscience less than 20 years ago, there has been an enormous upsurge in research using this technology. It's easy to see why. For most of the history of neuroscience, one of the few ways to determine the effects of stimulating a group of nerve cells was to use the electrophysiological stimulation approach described earlier in the chapter. Unfortunately, electrical stimulation affects all neurons within range of the electrode, not just the ones of interest to the experimenter. Therefore,

you could never be sure that the behavioral effects of the stimulation were due to the specific neurons you were studying and not to adjacent cells with a different neurochemistry (e.g., GABA neurons intermingled with dopamine neurons). Furthermore, the only techniques that were previously available for temporarily silencing neurons were very crude and also nonspecific. These limitations have all been overcome by the advent of optogenetics. As with other areas of neuroscience research, the long-term goal of optogenetic studies is not just to identify the basic behavioral and physiological functions of specific neuronal populations, but also to learn more about the causes of neuropsychiatric disorders and to help develop more effective treatments (Huang et al., 2013).

An alternative to optogenetics is the technique called **chemogenetics**, sometimes referred to as **DREADD** (designer receptor exclusively activated by a designer drug). As its name suggests, a genetically engineered receptor is stereotaxically targeted to specific brain cells, usually with viral vectors, and then is either activated or suppressed by administering a ligand that has been created to very specifically bind to the inserted receptor and nothing else. The ligand can be injected or given orally in the animal's drinking water, so the technique is easier to implement and is less invasive than optogenetics. Because these designer drugs bind to altered G protein–coupled receptors, their actions take longer to be initiated and are more prolonged (over minutes to hours) compared with the neuronal excitation and inhibition produced optogenetically. Hence, while optogenetics is optimal for controlling changes over milliseconds, providing the finest level of temporal control over the behavior investigated, chemogenetics may be chosen for studying behavioral effects of longer duration, such as anxiety or feeding, because the designer ligands last longer than pulses of light. The longer duration and the fact that designer ligands can be administered orally suggest the potential for translation to therapeutic applications such as treatment of obesity, epilepsy, and addiction disorders. For further details of the method and discussion of therapeutic potential, refer to Urban and Roth (2015).

Behavioral and neuropharmacological methods complement one another

Bear in mind that under normal circumstances, several of these techniques are used in tandem to approach a problem in neuroscience from several directions (see **WEB BOX 4.3**). The power of these experimental tools is that when they are used together, a more reasonable picture emerges, and conflicting results can be incorporated into the larger picture. Only in this way can we uncover the neurobiological substrates of cognitive function and dysfunction. In every case, interpretation of these sophisticated approaches is subject to the same scrutiny required by the earliest lesion experiments. Remember, healthy skepticism is central to the scientific method.

SECTION SUMMARY

■ Using a stereotaxic device, lesioning destroys brain cells in selected areas with high-frequency radio current. More selective lesions are made by injecting an excitatory neurotoxin that destroys cell bodies in the region without damaging axons passing through, or by injecting a neurotoxin selective for a given neurotransmitter.

■ Using a specialized cannula, microdialysis allows researchers to collect material from extracellular fluid from deep within the brain in a freely moving animal, so corresponding changes in behavior can be monitored simultaneously. The material is analyzed and quantified by high-pressure liquid chromatography. In vivo voltammetry is a second way to measure the neurotransmitter released into the synapse.

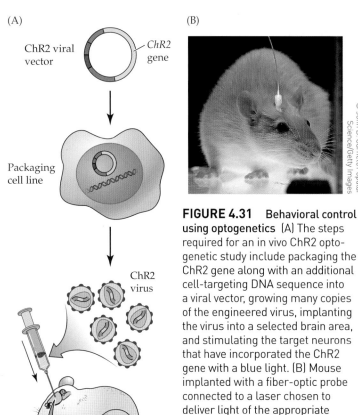

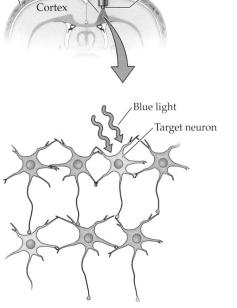

FIGURE 4.31 **Behavioral control using optogenetics** (A) The steps required for an in vivo ChR2 optogenetic study include packaging the ChR2 gene along with an additional cell-targeting DNA sequence into a viral vector, growing many copies of the engineered virus, implanting the virus into a selected brain area, and stimulating the target neurons that have incorporated the ChR2 gene with a blue light. (B) Mouse implanted with a fiber-optic probe connected to a laser chosen to deliver light of the appropriate wavelength. (A from K. Deisseroth. 2015. *Nat Neurosci* 18: 1213–1225. doi.org/10.1038/nn.4091)

■ Macroelectrodes that are stereotaxically implanted are used to electrically stimulate deep brain regions while monitoring behavioral changes. They can also record electrical response following drug treatment or other experimental manipulation. Microelectrodes can record electrical activity from either inside a cell (intracellular) or near a single cell (extracellular).

■ The function of individual ion channels is monitored with patch clamp electrophysiology.

■ The radioligand binding method evaluates the number and affinity of specific receptor molecules in tissue homogenates. Verification of binding requires proof of selectivity, saturability, reversibility, high affinity, and biological relevance.

■ To visualize the location of receptors in the brain, receptor autoradiography, both in vitro and in vivo, is used.

■ The ability to make antibodies to proteins allows more precise cellular localization of receptors or other protein cell components such as enzymes with ICC. Antibodies are also used to very sensitively measure proteins in tissue homogenates with Western blot. Radioimmunoassays and ELISA measure important molecules in body fluids or tissue extracts with competitive binding of an antibody to its antigen.

■ ICC identifies cells that *contain* a given protein; the complementary technique ISH is used to locate cells in a tissue slice that are *manufacturing* a particular protein by detecting the corresponding mRNA. It can also determine changes in mRNA levels, which provide an estimate of the rate of synthesis of that protein. Although ISH measures a single mRNA, microarrays (or gene chips) screen up to 20,000 genes on a single support (chip). The entire genome can be screened in one experiment with the use of just a few chips.

■ Although they use two distinct scanning technologies, CT and MRI both create extremely detailed "slices" through the brains of living individuals that can also be displayed as three-dimensional images. Their excellent detail of brain structure depends on computer analysis. MRS uses MRI-generated data to calculate brain chemical concentration. Diffusion tensor imaging is one of several methods available to show structural connectivity among brain structures.

■ PET maps the distribution of a radioactively labeled substance that has been injected into an individual.

A labeled drug or ligand is administered to identify where drugs bind and to localize neurotransmitter receptors. It can also allow visualization of regional brain activity during task performance, which is reflected in increased glucose utilization, oxygen use, and blood flow, depending on the reagent labeled. SPECT depends on similar technology at a lower cost but with less resolution.

■ Functional MRI (fMRI) provides both anatomical and functional imaging of the human brain by allowing visualization of changes in regional blood oxygenation caused by cell firing. It monitors brain activity as it is occurring and, unlike PET, requires no radioactivity. Resting-state fMRI shows correlated patterns of brain activity when the individual is not engaged in a task. Pharmacological MRI utilizes fMRI to image brain function following drug administration, provides information on the location of drug action and pharmacokinetic data, and potentially can predict patient treatment response.

■ EEG utilizes electrodes placed on the scalp of humans to measure the electrical activity of populations of neurons. Quantitative EEG requires computer analysis of the data to produce color-coded maps of brain activity. EEG recording of event-related potentials (ERPs) shows the processing of the cognitive response to momentary sensory stimulation in real time.

■ Deleting a specific gene in mice produces an animal model that lacks a particular protein (knockout) in order to evaluate post-lesion behavior and drug effects. Knockin mice have a gene inserted, so they produce a slightly different protein than is produced by wild-type mice. Transgenic mice are mice in which genetic material from another species is introduced into the genome.

■ Optogenetics provides the opportunity to temporally and spatially excite or inhibit genetically specific cells while evaluating the animal's behavior. Chemogenetics (DREADD) uses orally or systemically administered chemicals to stimulate implanted genetically engineered receptors in specific brain cells to alter animal behavior. Chemogenetics is slower, but longer lasting, than optogenetic effects.

■ CRISPR is a technique that provides a more rapid and less costly way to genetically engineer mice. CRISPR technology has potential for therapeutic applications in humans, although gene editing in humans is controversial.

STUDY QUESTIONS

1. Discuss the advantages of using laboratory animals in neuroscience research and the safeguards in place to ensure humane treatment.

2. Compare face validity, predictive validity, and construct validity. What is the difference between validity of an animal model and reliability?

3. What are the differences between negative and positive experimental controls? Provide examples of how each might be used in experimental psychopharmacology.

4. Animal behavioral tests that closely mimic aspects of the human disease have relatively high degrees of _____ validity.

5. Provide examples of how over-reliance on face validity and predictive validity can result in the development of drugs that lack therapeutic effect in humans.

6. Describe the three common measures of analgesia.

7. Why are tests of learning and memory challenging to interpret? Describe simple mazes as well as tests for spatial memory and working memory.

8. What are the anxiety-inducing situations that are central to the naturalistic tests of anxiety in rodents? Provide several examples. Why do you think some of these anxiety-inducing situations are evolutionarily important for survival?

9. Compare the acute versus chronic stress models of depressive-like behaviors. What are the advantages and disadvantages? Do these models afford good face validity? Predictive validity?

10. Describe the three most important animal tests to evaluate drug reinforcement and potential dependence in humans.

11. Why are internal drug-induced cues important in the operant task evaluating discriminative stimuli? Given an example of how this test can be used.

12. What is translational research, and why is it so important? Describe three potential ways that translational research can be improved.

13. Describe stereotaxic surgery, and give examples of techniques that depend on its use.

14. Compare electrolytic lesioning with neurotoxin and specific neurotoxin lesioning.

15. What is microdialysis? In vivo voltammetry? How are they similar, and how are they different?

16. Why is electrophysiological stimulation and recording important to psychopharmacology?

17. What factors must be considered when interpreting radioligand binding data?

18. How is autoradiography performed when mapping receptor binding? In vivo receptor binding?

19. What is one significant difference between ICC and Western blot? How are antibodies used in these procedures?

20. Describe two important ways that RIAs differ from ELISAs.

21. What do ISH, microarrays, and RNA-seq measure? In what ways are they similar? Different?

22. Compare the use of 2-deoxyglucose in autoradiography and PET.

23. What information is provided by MRI? What two complementary techniques depend on MRI technology, and what do they determine?

24. How is PET used in neuropharmacology?

25. What are the advantages of fMRI compared with PET? Briefly describe the importance of two techniques that depend on fMRI.

26. What is the EEG? Quantitative EEG? Event-related potential (ERP)? What are the advantages and disadvantages of EEG relative to imaging techniques?

27. Compare knockout mice, knockin mice, and transgenic mice. What role do they all play in psychopharmacology?

28. What are the advantages of CRISPR technology over other gene-editing technologies?

29. What are the goals of optogenetics? In a general way, tell how they are achieved. Compare the advantages and disadvantages of optogenetics and chemogenetics (DREADD) and give examples of how these techniques can inform psychopharmacology research.

5

Catecholamines

THE PREGNANT LABORATORY MOUSE gives birth to her litter of six pups, all of which appear normal. If you performed a CT scan or MRI on the head of each pup, the brain would look to be of normal size and shape. Other bodily organs and tissues, including the skeletal muscles, also seem to be fine. During the first week of postnatal life, the pups are nursing and are gaining weight at a rate that you expected. As a new student who recently joined the lab to obtain research experience, you're happy that things are going so well. But soon thereafter something seems to be going very wrong. First, the pups have stopped gaining weight. Moreover, they have developed a hunched posture, they move very sluggishly, and their fur doesn't look well groomed. As the pups gradually wean from their mother to a state of independence in which they must feed themselves, they surprisingly fail to eat at all despite having continuous access to the standard food that normal lab mice eagerly consume. In fact, all six pups die before they reach 1 month of age.

Remarkably, if you were to perform a post-mortem analysis of all of the thousands of chemicals that constitute a mouse brain and compare the results from these unfortunate animals with those obtained from normal healthy mice, you would find that the pups that had died lacked only a single chemical in their brains, namely the neurotransmitter **dopamine** (**DA**). Mice that lacked DA from embryonic development onward were first generated in the 1990s in the laboratory of Richard Palmiter at the University of Washington. In this chapter, we will learn much more about the neurobiology, pharmacology, and functions of this intriguing substance, including more details about Palmiter's DA-deficient mice. We will similarly cover a well-known sister transmitter to DA, namely **norepinephrine** (**NE**).

DA, NE, and the related substance **epinephrine** (**EPI**) make up a small but important group of neurotransmitters and hormones called **catecholamines**. The term *catecholamine* is derived from the fact that the members of this group all share two chemical similarities: a core structure of catechol and a nitrogen-containing group called an amine (**FIGURE 5.1**). ■

Mutant mice produced by genetic engineering (e.g., gene "knockout mice") may show phenotypic changes that emerge during development of the pups.

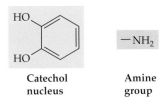

FIGURE 5.1 Structural features of catecholamines
A catechol nucleus and an amine group are found in all catecholamines.

The catecholamines, in turn, belong to a wider group of transmitters called either **monoamines** (transmitters that possess one amine group) or **biogenic amines** (*biogenic* refers to compounds made by living organisms). EPI and NE are sometimes called adrenaline and noradrenaline, respectively. It is important to note that the adjective forms for these substances are **adrenergic** and **noradrenergic**, although the term *adrenergic* is sometimes used broadly to refer to NE- as well as EPI-related features. The adjective form for DA is **dopaminergic**. Varying amounts of these substances are found within the central nervous system, the peripheral nervous system, and the inner part of the adrenal glands (adrenal medulla). The adrenal medulla secretes EPI and NE into the bloodstream, where they act as hormones. You will recall from Chapter 3 that stimulation of catecholamine secretion from the adrenal glands is a vital part of the physiological response to stress.

The main emphasis in this chapter is on DA and NE, as the neurotransmitter function of EPI is relatively minor. We begin by considering the basic neurochemistry of the catecholamines, including their synthesis, release, and inactivation. This will be followed by a discussion of the neural systems for DA and NE, including the anatomy of these systems, the receptors for DA and NE, some of the drugs that act on these receptors, and several behavioral functions in which catecholamine transmitters are key participants.

5.1 Catecholamine Synthesis, Release, and Inactivation

The overall level of catecholamine neurotransmission depends on a complex interplay between neurotransmitter synthesis, release, and inactivation. This section will consider the factors that regulate the first two of these, namely catecholamine synthesis and release.

Catecholamines are synthesized by a multistep pathway in which tyrosine hydroxylase catalyzes the rate-limiting step

Classical transmitters (see Chapter 3) like the catecholamines are manufactured in one or more biochemical steps. These synthetic pathways offer neurons a

mechanism for regulating the amount of transmitter available for release. At the same time, they offer us the opportunity to intervene with drugs that alter transmitter synthesis in specific ways. For example, we may administer a precursor that will be converted biochemically into a particular neurotransmitter. One application of this approach is seen in neurological disorders in which the neurons that make a certain transmitter have been damaged. Precursor therapy represents an attempt to boost transmitter synthesis and release in the remaining undamaged cells. Alternatively, we may give subjects a drug that blocks a step in the biochemical pathway, thereby causing a depletion of the transmitter synthesized by that pathway. Neurotransmitter depletion is not as widely used clinically, but nevertheless, it can be valuable in certain experimental settings.

The synthesis of catecholamine neurotransmitters occurs in several steps, as shown in **FIGURE 5.2**. The biochemical pathway begins with the amino acid **tyrosine**. Like other amino acids, tyrosine is obtained from dietary protein and is transported from the blood into the brain. Each of the steps in catecholamine formation depends on a specific enzyme that acts as a catalyst (an agent that increases the rate of a chemical reaction) for that step. Neurons that use DA as their transmitter contain only the first two enzymes, **tyrosine hydroxylase** (**TH**) and **aromatic amino acid decarboxylase** (**AADC**), and thus the biochemical pathway stops at DA. In contrast, neurons that need to synthesize NE also possess the third enzyme, which is called **dopamine β-hydroxylase** (**DBH**).[*]

The conversion of tyrosine to dihydroxyphenylalanine (DOPA) by TH occurs at a slower rate than subsequent reactions in the biochemical pathway. Consequently, TH is the **rate-limiting enzyme** in the pathway because it determines the overall rate of DA or NE formation. The activity of TH is regulated by a variety of factors, including how much DA or NE is present within the nerve terminal. High catecholamine levels tend to inhibit TH, thus serving as a negative feedback mechanism. Another important factor is the rate of cell firing, because neuronal activity has a stimulatory effect on TH. The mechanism by which cell firing stimulates TH activity is through phosphorylation of the enzyme. TH can be phosphorylated by all of the second-messenger-associated protein kinases mentioned in Chapter 3, namely protein kinase A (PKA), protein kinase G (PKG), protein kinase C (PKC), and calcium/calmodulin kinase II (CaMKII) (Tekin et al., 2014). Although the exact effect of phosphorylation depends on the particular kinase and on the location within the TH protein where the phosphate group is added, the general result is an increase

---

[*] It is worth noting some of the basics of how enzymes are named. Hydroxylases like TH and DBH add a hydroxyl group (–OH) to the molecule they're acting on. A decarboxylase like AADC removes a carboxyl group (–COOH) from the molecule. These reactions can be seen by following the biochemical pathway shown in Figure 5.2.

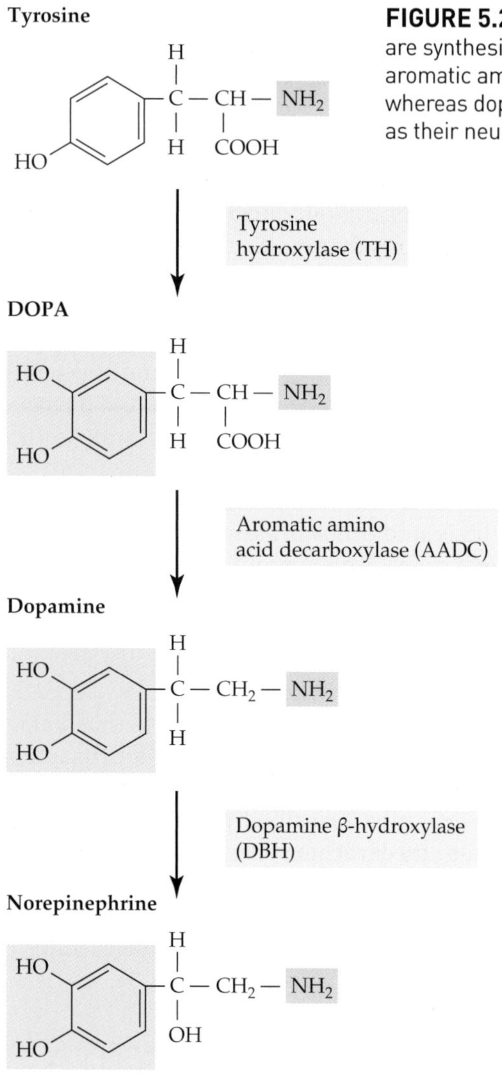

Tyrosine

FIGURE 5.2 **Multistep pathway of catecholamine synthesis** Catecholamines are synthesized from the precursor amino acid tyrosine. Tyrosine hydroxylase and aromatic amino acid decarboxylase are found in all catecholaminergic neurons, whereas dopamine β-hydroxylase is present only in cells that use norepinephrine as their neurotransmitter.

Tyrosine hydroxylase (TH)

DOPA

Aromatic amino acid decarboxylase (AADC)

Dopamine

Dopamine β-hydroxylase (DBH)

Norepinephrine

in enzyme activity and, therefore, catecholamine synthesis. Some catecholamine systems are activated by stress, resulting in enhanced cell firing, a stimulation of catecholamine release, and increased TH phosphorylation (Dunkley and Dickson, 2019).

These elegant mechanisms of phosphorylation activation and catecholamine feedback inhibition enable dopaminergic and noradrenergic neurons to carefully control their rate of neurotransmitter formation. When the levels are too high, TH is inhibited and catecholamine synthesis is slowed. But when the neurons are activated and firing at a high rate, such as during stress, TH is stimulated and catecholamine synthesis accelerates to keep up with the increased demand. Although the enzymes involved in synthesizing catecholamines (as well as other classical transmitters like acetylcholine and serotonin) can be found throughout the neurons using those transmitters, the rate of synthesis is greatest at the nerve endings near the sites of transmitter release. As mentioned in Chapter 3, this is important for the refilling of recycling vesicles.

As would be expected from our earlier discussion, catecholamine formation can be increased by the administration of biochemical precursors such as tyrosine and L-DOPA. For many years, this idea has been exploited clinically by giving L-DOPA to patients with Parkinson's disease, a disorder involving loss of midbrain dopaminergic neurons and their projections to the dorsal striatum (see Chapter 20). But even in people without a neurodegenerative disorder, catecholamine precursor administration can have detectable effects. This has been demonstrated in studies where acute tyrosine administration modestly but measurably enhanced cognitive functions such as working memory under conditions of high cognitive demand or stress (Hase et al., 2015; Jongkees et al., 2015). Such enhancement is thought to occur because dopaminergic and noradrenergic neurons are activated under the aforementioned conditions, and therefore tyrosine supplementation provides the necessary substrate to keep up with the demand for increased neurotransmitter synthesis. If the tyrosine dose is too high, however, cognitive functioning can be negatively affected instead (van de Rest et al., 2017). Since most people are not supplementing their diet with extra tyrosine, we may ask whether normal dietary tyrosine intake has any influence on cognition. A recent study addressed this question and found a significant positive relationship between dietary tyrosine consumption and performance on tests of working memory, fluid intelligence, and, to a lesser extent, episodic memory (Kühn et al., 2019). Keep in mind, however, that this effect was subtle and could only be observed when various other factors influencing cognition were controlled for statistically.

Drugs that reduce catecholamine synthesis by inhibiting one of the synthetic enzymes are not as clinically important, but they have had widespread use in both animal and human research. The best example is a drug known as **α-methyl-para-tyrosine** (**AMPT**). This compound blocks TH, thereby preventing overall catecholamine synthesis and causing a general depletion of these neurotransmitters. In a group of psychiatric studies reviewed by Booij and colleagues (2003), AMPT treatment caused a return of depressive symptoms in many patients who had been successfully treated with antidepressant medication. Subsequently, Hasler and coworkers (2008) replicated this finding but with the addition of brain imaging to localize the effects of AMPT administration on neural metabolism. The results implicated a neural circuit involving parts of the neocortex, striatum, and thalamus in the symptom relapse provoked by the drug. Together, these findings suggest that at least for some depressed patients who recover following antidepressant treatment, continued recovery depends on maintaining adequate catecholamine levels in the brain.

Catecholamine storage and release are regulated by vesicular uptake, autoreceptor activity, and cell firing rate

Once catecholamines have been synthesized, they are transported into synaptic vesicles for later release (**FIGURE 5.3**). Vesicular packaging is important not only because it provides a means of releasing a predetermined amount of neurotransmitter (usually several thousand molecules per vesicle), but also because it protects the neurotransmitter from degradation by enzymes within the nerve terminal (see the next section). A specific protein in the vesicle membrane is responsible for vesicular catecholamine uptake. This protein recognizes several different monoamine transmitters and therefore is called the **vesicular monoamine transporter** (**VMAT**). There are actually two related VMATs: VMAT1 is found in the adrenal medulla, whereas VMAT2 is present in the brain. Both of these vesicular transporters are blocked by an interesting drug called **reserpine**, which comes from the roots of the plant *Rauwolfia serpentina* (snake root). Blocking the vesicular transporter means that DA and NE are no longer

protected from breakdown within the nerve terminal. As a result, both transmitters temporarily drop to very low levels in the brain. The behavioral consequence of this neurochemical effect is sedation in animals and depressive symptoms in humans. Many years ago, a study by the eminent Swedish pharmacologist Arvid Carlsson and his colleagues (Carlsson et al., 1957) showed that the sedative effects of reserpine could be reversed by restoration of catecholamines with DOPA, the immediate biochemical precursor of DA (**FIGURE 5.4**). Carlsson's work, which played a key role in the development of the catecholamine theory of depression (see Chapter 18), resulted in his being a co-recipient of the 2000 Nobel Prize in Physiology or Medicine.

Reserpine is an irreversible inhibitor of both VMAT1 and VMAT2, which accounts for its powerful sedating action. As the name implies, an **irreversible inhibitor** of a protein (whether a transporter, receptor, or enzyme) does not permit any action of that protein until the cell synthesizes new protein molecules that have not been subjected to the inhibitory drug. In contrast, a **reversible inhibitor** may allow some action of the target protein and, thus, exert less profound physiological or behavioral effects. This difference has led to the development of selective reversible VMAT2 inhibitors that have therapeutic applications in several neurological syndromes. We shall see shortly that DA plays a critically important role in the control of movement. Several neurological syndromes are characterized by excessive and/or uncontrolled movements, including Huntington's disease, Tourette syndrome, and tardive dyskinesia (caused by chronic exposure to dopamine receptor–blocking drugs used in the treatment of schizophrenia). The reversible VMAT2 inhibitors **tetrabenazine** (trade name **Xenazine**), **deutetrabenazine** (**Austedo**), and **valbenazine** (**Ingrezza**), all of which cause a *partial* depletion of presynaptic DA, are currently among the treatments of choice for the reducing uncontrolled movements associated with Huntington's disease and tardive dyskinesia (Heo and Scott, 2017; Niemann and Jankovic, 2018). The ability of these drugs to reduce unwanted movements (i.e., tics) in patients with Tourette syndrome is not yet as well established.

Release of catecholamines normally occurs when a nerve impulse enters the terminal and triggers one or more vesicles to release their contents into the synaptic cleft through the process of exocytosis (see Chapter 3). Each mouse dopaminergic vesicle is estimated to contain about 30,000 DA molecules under normal conditions.

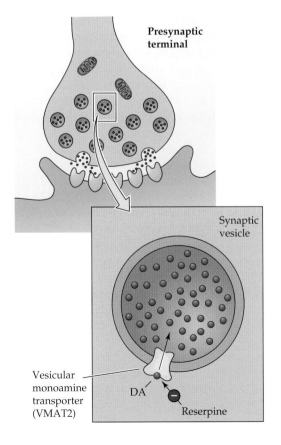

FIGURE 5.3 **Catecholaminergic neurons use a vesicular monoamine transporter protein** That protein, VMAT2, transports neurotransmitter molecules from the cytoplasm of the cell to the interior of the synaptic vesicles. This transport system is blocked by reserpine, which causes a marked depletion of catecholamine levels resulting from a lack of protection of the transmitter from metabolizing enzymes located outside of the vesicles.

(A)

(B)

FIGURE 5.4 **Role of catecholamine depletion in the behavioral depressant effects of reserpine** Rabbits injected with reserpine (5 mg/kg IV) showed extreme behavioral sedation (A) that was reversed (B) by subsequent treatment with DOPA (200 mg/kg IV).

However, when mice are given a high dose of the DA precursor DOPA, the vesicular transmitter content can increase by more than 2-fold (Sulzer et al., 2016). At the same time, vesicles grow in size to accommodate the extra DA molecules! These findings introduce us to a rule that pertains to classical neurotransmitters in general, not just DA. The rule is that vesicular content and quantal size (an index of the amount of transmitter released by a single synaptic vesicle) are not fixed but can vary depending on circumstances such as the amount of neurotransmitter available within the nerve terminal or varicosity for vesicle loading.

Several drugs can bypass the requirement for cellular excitation and cause a release of catecholamines independently of nerve cell firing. The most important of these compounds are the psychostimulants **amphetamine** and **methamphetamine**. In contrast to the behavioral sedation associated with reserpine-induced catecholamine depletion, catecholamine release leads to behavioral activation. In laboratory animals such as rats and mice, this activation may be shown by increased locomotor activity. At high doses, locomotor activation is replaced by **stereotyped behaviors**

FIGURE 5.5 **A typical dopaminergic neuron** The membrane of its terminals possesses autoreceptors. When these receptors are stimulated, they inhibit subsequent DA release by the cell.

consisting of intense sniffing, repetitive head and limb movements, and licking and biting. Researchers believe that locomotion and stereotyped behaviors represent a continuum of behavioral activation that stems from increasing stimulation of DA receptors in the nucleus accumbens and striatum. In humans, amphetamine and methamphetamine produce increased alertness, heightened energy, euphoria, insomnia, and other behavioral effects (see Chapter 12).

Catecholamine release is inhibited by autoreceptors located on the cell bodies, terminals, and dendrites of dopaminergic and noradrenergic neurons. Terminal autoreceptors and other features of a typical dopaminergic neuron are illustrated in **FIGURE 5.5**. Current evidence indicates that at least in the case of DA, these autoreceptors inhibit neurotransmitter release through two combined mechanisms: (1) by inhibiting the action of voltage-gated Ca^{2+} channels in the nerve terminal membrane and (2) by enhancing the opening of a specific type of voltage-gated K^+ channel in the terminal (Ford, 2014). The first mechanism would reduce DA release by directly reducing the amount of activity-mediated Ca^{2+} influx needed for vesicular exocytosis, whereas the second mechanism could indirectly reduce Ca^{2+} influx by shortening the duration of action potentials entering the terminal. Consequently, if a dopaminergic cell fires several action

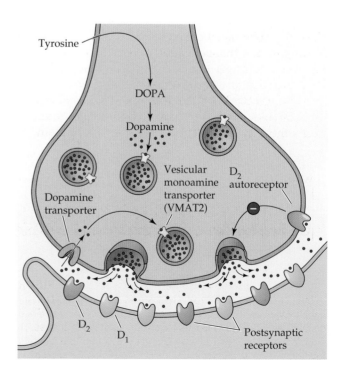

potentials in a row, we can imagine that DA released by the first few impulses stimulates the terminal autoreceptors and reduces the amount of DA released by the later action potentials. On the other hand, the somatodendritic autoreceptors exert a somewhat different effect on DA and NE neurons. As mentioned in Chapter 3, these autoreceptors inhibit release indirectly by reducing the rate of firing of the cell.

The firing pattern of the neuron is yet another factor that influences catecholamine release. This has been studied extensively in midbrain dopaminergic neurons, which fire in two different patterns. In **single-spiking mode**, the cell generates action potentials ("spikes") that appear at irregular intervals but with a typical average frequency of 4 to 5 Hz (4 or 5 spikes per second). Excitatory input to the cell can switch it from single-spiking mode to **burst mode**, which is characterized by trains of 2 to 20 spikes at a frequency of approximately 20 Hz. The difference between these firing modes can be seen in **FIGURE 5.6**, which shows representative firing patterns of dopaminergic neurons within the ventral tegmental area (VTA; see section below entitled Organization and Function of the Dopaminergic System for more information on this brain area) in a rat under conditions of quiet wakefulness, slow-wave sleep, rapid-eye-movement (REM) sleep, and feeding. Burst firing can be seen during REM sleep and feeding, which is the result of greater dopaminergic neuronal activation. DA released when the cell is in single-spiking mode is often called **tonic release**, whereas DA released in burst mode is called **phasic release**. Importantly, the extracellular level of DA in areas of release following a burst of spikes is greater than would be expected from the number of spikes in the burst, mainly because release of neurotransmitter is occurring faster than it can be cleared and/or metabolized (Chergui et al., 1994). This finding means that activation of burst firing in dopaminergic neurons is especially important for producing large increases in DA transmission in the brain.

Although the DA nerve terminal illustrated in Figure 5.5 looks like a typical axon bouton, DA and NE axons more typically form *en passant* ("in passing")

synapses in which the fibers exhibit repeated swellings (termed **varicosities**) along their lengths (imagine beads on a string) that are filled with synaptic vesicles and that represent the sites of neurotransmitter release. **FIGURE 5.7** shows a cartoon depicting a single varicosity located along the axon of a dopaminergic neuron (panel A) as well as a photomicrograph showing many actual varicosities among axons of rat dopaminergic neurons living in cell culture (panel B). The cartoon of the dopaminergic varicosity depicts a release site with a structure similar to the active zones described in Chapter 3. However, detailed studies have found that only about 30% of the varicosities possess these release sites (Liu and Kaeser, 2019). Different studies have found that only about 30% of dopaminergic varicosities are located near a postsynaptic element such as a dendrite or dendritic spine. These results raise several important but as yet unanswered questions:

1. Are the varicosities containing active zone-like release sites the same ones that are near postsynaptic elements?

2. Are varicosities that lack the release sites "silent," meaning that they do not release DA even if invaded by an action potential?

3. Are varicosities that lack observable release sites still capable of DA release by some other mechanism?

4. Can silent varicosities (if they exist) be converted to active ones, and vice versa?

We shall await further research to address these important issues.

Catecholamines are recycled after release by a process of reuptake

Inactivation of catecholamines depends on the two different kinds of processes first mentioned in Chapter 3. The first process is removal from the extracellular fluid by uptake mechanisms. Uptake can occur by the releasing cell, in which case it is called **reuptake**, or it can occur into the postsynaptic neuron

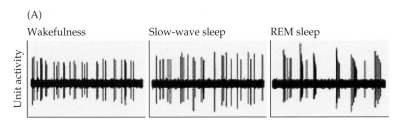

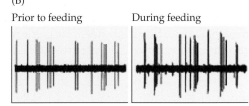

FIGURE 5.6 **Spike firing patterns of dopaminergic neurons in the rat VTA under different behavioral states** Unit activity (i.e., firing of an individual nerve cell) was recorded from VTA dopaminergic neurons in rats (A) during quiet wakefulness, slow-wave sleep, and REM sleep and (B) before and during feeding of a palatable food. The electrophysiological traces show short bursts of action potentials (burst mode) during REM sleep and feeding, which contrast with single action potentials (single-spiking mode) during the other behavioral states. (From L. Dahan et al. 2007. *Neuropsychopharmacology* 32: 1232–1241. doi.org/10.1038/sj.npp.1301251)

(A)

Dopamine
vesicles

Active zone-like
release site

(B)

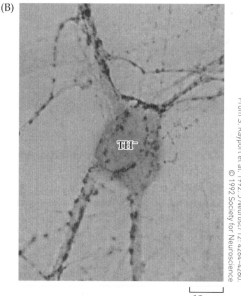

TH⁻

From S. Rayport et al. 1992. *J Neurosci* 12: 4264–4280.
© 1992 Society for Neuroscience

10 µm

FIGURE 5.7   Varicosities along the lengths of dopaminergic fibers (A) As depicted in this cartoon, dopaminergic fibers possess intermittent swellings that are filled with synaptic vesicles and that serve as the sites of DA release. (B) This photomicrograph obtained from cultured rat midbrain tissue depicts dopaminergic fibers and their associated varicosities in close proximity to the dendrites and cell body of a non-dopaminergic cell. To obtain the image, tissue from the midbrain of a young rat was removed and the cells were allowed to grow in a Petri dish. Some of the neurons in this brain area synthesize DA, whereas others use a different neurotransmitter. After 21 days in culture, the cells were stained using an antibody to TH, causing any structure containing this enzyme to appear dark in the photomicrograph. Note the large gray cell in the center of the image, which is labeled TH⁻. This means that the cell lacked the TH stain and, therefore, was not a dopaminergic neuron. The relatively thick fibers emanating from the cell body are its dendrites, which are studded with many small dark oblong structures that are TH⁺ (i.e., dopaminergic) varicosities that appear to be making connections with the non-DA neuron's dendrites. Even axons such as the one in the mid-left region of the photomicrograph that don't come into proximity with a dendrite still possess varicosities along their length. Finally, note the presence of the 10-µm scale bar at the lower right. This is a common method of showing the size of the cellular structures visible in the image. (A after L. Changliang and P. S. Kaeser. 2019. *Curr Opin Neurobiol* 57: 46–53.)

or neighboring glial cells. DA and NE reuptake occur by means of transporter proteins in the dopaminergic or noradrenergic neuronal cell membrane. The transporter protein found in dopaminergic neurons is called the **DA transporter** (see Figure 5.5), whereas the analogous protein in noradrenergic neurons is called the **NE transporter**. After the neurotransmitter molecules are returned to the terminal, some of them are repackaged into vesicles for rerelease, and the remainder are broken down and eliminated. It is important to keep in mind that neurotransmitter transporters differ from the autoreceptors discussed earlier in terms of both structure and function.

Interestingly, neither the DA transporter nor the NE transporter is selective for its particular neurotransmitter. That is, the DA transporter can take up NE, and the NE transporter can take up DA. This feature has functional relevance in a few brain areas, notably the prefrontal cortex (PFC) and hippocampus, where the dopaminergic varicosities express low levels of the DA transporter. In those areas, the NE transporter in nearby noradrenergic varicosities plays a more important role in clearing DA from the extracellular fluid than does the DA transporter (Morón et al., 2002; Borgkvist et al., 2012). In contrast, DA transporter expression is abundant in the striatum, where it mediates DA reuptake and recycling in the dopaminergic varicosities.

The importance of uptake for catecholamine functioning can be seen when the DA or NE transporter is missing. For example, mutant mice lacking a functional gene for the DA transporter do not show the typical behavioral activation in response to psychostimulants like cocaine or amphetamine, whereas genetic deletion of the NE transporter gene causes increased sensitivity to these same drugs (F. Xu et al., 2000). These results suggest that the behavioral activating effects of psychostimulants are mainly caused by their dopaminergic effects, whereas NE reuptake blockade by those drugs may in some way interfere with the stimulating effects of DA. A role for the NE transporter in cardiovascular function was demonstrated by a case study of identical twins carrying a mutation of the NE transporter gene (Shannon et al., 2000). These patients exhibited abnormally high NE levels in the bloodstream, along with heart rate and blood pressure abnormalities. Animal studies have similarly shown that transporter-mediated uptake plays a vital role in the normal regulation of catecholamine activity.

Since the transporters are necessary for rapid clearance of released catecholamines from the extracellular fluid, transporter-blocking drugs enhance DA or NE transmission by increasing the amount of neurotransmitter available to activate the receptors for these transmitters. This can be demonstrated using microdialysis, a technique that permits us to extract and measure chemicals present in the extracellular fluid of a living animal's brain (see Chapter 4). **FIGURE 5.8** illustrates the effect of a selective DA transporter inhibitor on extracellular DA levels in the nucleus accumbens, a brain area rich in dopaminergic terminals. The increased extracellular DA shown in this experiment would have activated postsynaptic DA receptors for a long period of time until the drug effect had worn off.

Catecholamine transporter inhibition is an important mechanism of action of several kinds of psychoactive drugs. Some of these compounds block both DA and NE reuptake, including **methylphenidate (Ritalin)** and **amphetamine (Adderall)**, both of which are standard treatments for attention-deficit/hyperactivity disorder (ADHD). Amphetamine not only inhibits catecholamine reuptake but also releases the neurotransmitters from their nerve terminals (see Chapter 12). A few compounds in clinical use more selectively block the NE transporter. These include **atomoxetine (Strattera)**, a newer ADHD medication, and **reboxetine (Edronax)**, a newer-generation antidepressant drug. Lastly, there are compounds that block combinations of catecholamine and serotonin (5-HT) reuptake. Examples of these are the classical **tricyclic antidepressants**, which block the NE and 5-HT transporters (see Chapter 18), and **cocaine**, which inhibits the reuptake of all three major monoamine transmitters: DA, NE, and 5-HT. As we will see in Chapter 12, the addictive properties of cocaine are largely attributable to its DA reuptake-blocking effect.

Catecholamine levels are regulated by metabolizing enzymes

Although reuptake can quickly terminate the synaptic actions of catecholamines, there must also be processes of metabolic inactivation to prevent excessive neurotransmitter accumulation. The initial breakdown of catecholamines involves two enzymes: **monoamine oxidase (MAO)** and **catechol-O-methyltransferase (COMT)**. Both enzymes are found *inside* of the cells where they are expressed. This is important because it means that metabolic breakdown does not contribute to the immediate termination of catecholamine signaling.

Two distinct types of MAO have been identified: MAO-A and MAO-B. MAO-A is expressed by the catecholamine neurons, whereas MAO-B is primarily found in other types of neurons as well as glial cells (astrocytes) (Finberg, 2019). We mentioned above that some catecholamine uptake occurs into postsynaptic neurons and glial cells. This uptake, which is mediated by nonselective transport proteins (not the DA or NE transporters), allows for some catecholamine metabolism by MAO-B.

Nonselective MAO inhibitors (i.e., they block both MAO-A and MAO-B) such as **phenelzine (Nardil)** or **tranylcypromine (Parnate)** have long been used in the treatment of clinical depression (see Chapter 18). Although these drugs have largely fallen from favor due to potentially dangerous side effects, they may still have application for some patients who have proven resistant to other medications (Menkes et al., 2016). On the other hand, several drugs have been developed that are relatively selective inhibitors (Finberg, 2014), which means that the drug blocks a particular MAO subtype at low to moderate doses but affects both subtypes at high doses. For example, **moclobemide** is relatively selective for MAO-A inhibition and has been approved

FIGURE 5.8 Extracellular DA levels are strongly elevated by treatment with a DA reuptake inhibitor Microdialysis probes were surgically implanted in the nucleus accumbens of mice. Two days later, mice were injected intraperitoneally with either 10 mg/kg of the selective DA reuptake inhibitor GBR 12909 or saline vehicle. Samples of extracellular fluid were collected at 20-minute intervals and analyzed for DA. In genetically intact control mice with two copies of the transporter gene (designated +/+), the inhibitor caused extracellular DA levels to rise to more than 200% of baseline for at least 3 hours. Saline treatment of the control mice showed no change in DA. When mice that had been genetically engineered to eliminate the DA transporter (i.e., DA transporter knockout mice, designated –/–) were given either GBR 12909 or saline, there was no change in extracellular DA levels. This demonstrated that the enhancing effect of GBR 12909 was mediated by its effects on the DA transporter. Note that all DA levels are expressed as percent of the baseline at time 0. This obscures the fact that baseline extracellular DA is markedly increased in the transporter knockout mice because they cannot efficiently remove DA from the extracellular fluid. (From E. Carboni et al. 2001. *J Neurosci* 21: RC141. © 2001 Society for Neuroscience.)

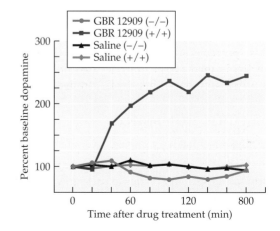

in several countries outside of the United States for the treatment of depression and social anxiety. **Selegiline (Eldepryl)** and **rasagiline (Azilect)** are relatively selective inhibitors of MAO-B that are used clinically to elevate brain DA levels in the early stages of Parkinson's disease (Finberg, 2019). The fact that MAO-B inhibitors are effective in this context suggests that as the dopaminergic nerve terminals containing MAO-A begin to degenerate, a significant amount of DA metabolism is mediated by MAO-B after uptake into non-DA cells (particularly glial cells, based on existing evidence).

COMT is a widely expressed enzyme. Within the brain it is found in neurons and glial cells, and it is also present peripherally in many other organs throughout the body. COMT acts on a variety of compounds containing the basic catechol structure. Indeed, in patients with Parkinson's disease, peripheral COMT metabolizes a significant proportion of the administered L-DOPA before it reaches the brain. Consequently, many patients are additionally given a COMT inhibitor to enhance L-DOPA availability (Finberg, 2019). Currently licensed drugs of this type are **entacapone (Comtan)**, **opicapone (Ongentys)**, and **tolcapone (Tasmar)**, although tolcapone is the least preferred of these medications because of its undesirable side effects.

The action of MAO and COMT, either individually or together, gives rise to several catecholamine **metabolites** (breakdown products). We mention only the most important ones here. In humans, DA has only one major metabolite, which is called **homovanillic acid (HVA)**. In contrast, NE breakdown gives rise to several important compounds, including **3-methoxy-4-hydroxy-phenylglycol (MHPG)** and **vanillylmandelic acid (VMA)**. Metabolism of NE within the brain primarily leads to MHPG, whereas VMA is the more common metabolite in the peripheral nervous system. The brain metabolites HVA and MHPG make their way into the cerebrospinal fluid for subsequent clearance from the brain into the bloodstream and, along with VMA, are eventually excreted in the urine. Levels of these substances in the various fluid compartments (i.e., blood and urine for all three metabolites, and cerebrospinal fluid for HVA and MHPG) provide a rough indication of catecholaminergic activity in the nervous system. Such measurements have sometimes been used to help discern the possible involvement of these neurotransmitters in neuropsychiatric disorders such as depression and schizophrenia (see Chapters 18 and 19).

SECTION SUMMARY

- The major catecholamine transmitters in the brain are DA and NE. These transmitters are synthesized in several steps from the amino acid tyrosine. The biochemical steps are catalyzed in turn by TH (the rate-limiting enzyme), AADC, and (in the case of NE) DBH.

- Catecholamine synthesis can be enhanced by administration of biochemical precursors such as tyrosine and L-DOPA, the latter of which is the main therapeutic agent used in the treatment of Parkinson's disease.

- Once they have been synthesized, catecholamines are loaded into synaptic vesicles by the neuronal transporter VMAT2. VMAT2 can be inhibited irreversibly by reserpine, which causes profound sedation due to extreme catecholamine depletion. Reversible VMAT2 inhibition by several other drugs causes only partial depletion, as a result of which such drugs are used clinically to treat disorders like Huntington's disease or tardive dyskinesia that involve DA-related excessive and uncontrollable movements.

- Although catecholamine release is normally dependent on cell firing, this process is bypassed by certain drugs, notably amphetamine and methamphetamine, that produce activity-independent catecholamine release. Administration of these substances causes strong behavioral activation, the characteristics of which depend on the dose and the species.

- The process of catecholamine release is controlled by inhibitory autoreceptors located on the cell body, dendrites, and terminals of catecholamine neurons. Terminal autoreceptors function by inhibiting voltage-gated Ca^{2+} channels and enhancing voltage-gated K^+ channels in the terminal membrane.

- Another factor regulating catecholamine release is the rate of cell firing. For example, dopaminergic neurons can fire either in single-spike or burst mode, leading to tonic or phasic release of DA. Burst firing causes especially large amounts of DA to be available to post-synaptic cells, primarily because the rate of DA release is greater than the rate at which the neurotransmitter can be cleared and/or metabolized.

- The structures from which catecholamines are released are called varicosities, which refer to intermittent swellings along the length of the axon. Research on dopaminergic varicosities, which have been studied more intensively than those for NE, have raised questions about whether the transmitter can be released from all varicosities along a particular axon or only a fraction of them.

- The immediate termination of catecholamine signaling is mediated by transmitter uptake from the extracellular fluid. Most of this uptake is reuptake into the presynaptic cell, which is mediated by DA and NE transporter proteins expressed by the dopaminergic and noradrenergic neurons respectively. Pharmacological blockade of reuptake causes a prolonged increase in extracellular transmitter levels.

- Neither the DA nor the NE transporter protein is selective for its transmitter. That is, the NE transporter can take up DA, and vice versa. This lack of selectivity is important in brain areas like the prefrontal cortex and hippocampus where the dopaminergic varicosities express low levels of the DA transporter. In those areas, the NE transporter plays the major role in DA uptake after its release.

- A number of reuptake inhibitors are used clinically: methylphenidate and amphetamine (both DA and NE) for ADHD, atomoxetine (NE) for ADHD, reboxetine (NE) for depression, and tricyclic antidepressants (NE and 5-HT) for depression.
- Catecholamine breakdown is catalyzed by MAO (mainly MAO-A) and COMT. Both enzymes are located intracellularly, which means that they are not positioned to metabolize catecholamine molecules in the extracellular fluid.
- The nonselective MAO inhibitors (inhibit both MAO-A and MAO-B) phenelzine and tranylcypromine have a long history of use as antidepressants but have mostly been replaced by safer medications.
- Selective MAO inhibitors used clinically are moclobemide (MAO-A) for depression and selegiline and rasagiline (MAO-B) for Parkinson's disease.
- The COMT inhibitors entacapone, opicapone, and tolcapone are also prescribed for the treatment of Parkinson's disease.
- The major catecholamine metabolites are HVA for DA, and MHPG (mostly central metabolism) and VMA (mostly peripheral metabolism) for NE.

5.2 Organization and Function of the Dopaminergic System

The dopaminergic system originates in several cell groups located primarily in the midbrain. Ascending fibers from these cells innervate a number of forebrain areas, where they regulate several important behavioral functions.

Two important dopaminergic cell groups are found in the midbrain

In the early 1960s, Swedish researchers first began to map the location of DA- and NE-containing nerve cells and fibers in the brain using a fluorescence method (Dahlström and Fuxe, 1964). They developed a classification system in which the catecholamine cell groups (clusters of neurons that stained for either DA or NE) were designated with the letter *A* plus a number from 1 to 16. According to this system, cell groups A1 to A7 are noradrenergic, whereas groups A8 to A16 are dopaminergic. In this book, we will focus on only a few catecholaminergic cell groups that are of particular interest to psychopharmacologists. To identify the various systems arising from these cells, we will use both the Swedish classification system and standard anatomical names.

Several dense clusters of dopaminergic neuronal cell bodies are located near the base of the mesencephalon (midbrain). Particularly important is the A9 cell group, which is associated with a structure called the substantia nigra,* and the A10 group, which is found in a nearby area called the **ventral tegmental area (VTA)**. Axons of dopaminergic neurons in the substantia nigra ascend to a forebrain structure known as the caudate–putamen or dorsal striatum. Note that the caudate and putamen are separate, though closely related, structures in humans and non-human primates, whereas the two structures are fused in rodents (hence "caudate–putamen"). Nerve tracts in the central nervous system are often named by combining the site of origin of the fibers with their termination site. Hence, the pathway from the substantia nigra to the dorsal striatum is called the **nigrostriatal tract (FIGURE 5.9A)**.

Two other important ascending dopaminergic systems arise from cells of the VTA. Some of the axons from these neurons travel to various structures of the limbic system, including the nucleus accumbens (the major component of the ventral striatum), septum, amygdala, and hippocampus. These diverse projections constitute the **mesolimbic dopamine pathway** (*meso* represents mesencephalon, which is the site of origin of the fibers; *limbic* stands for the termination of fibers in structures of the limbic system) (**FIGURE 5.9B**). Other DA-containing fibers from the VTA go to the cerebral cortex, particularly the PFC. This group of fibers is termed the **mesocortical dopamine pathway** (**FIGURE 5.9C**). Together, the mesolimbic and mesocortical pathways are very important to psychopharmacologists because they have been implicated in the neural mechanisms underlying drug abuse (see Chapter 9) and also schizophrenia (see Chapter 19).

A few other sites of dopaminergic neurons can be mentioned briefly. For example, a small group of cells in the hypothalamus gives rise to the **tuberohypophyseal dopamine pathway**. This pathway is important in controlling the secretion of the hormone prolactin by the pituitary gland. There are also DA-containing neurons within sensory structures such as the olfactory bulbs and the retina.

Ascending dopamine pathways have been implicated in several important behavioral functions

One of the key functions of DA innervation of the dorsal striatum via the nigrostriatal tract is to facilitate voluntary movement. Loss of this function is illustrated dramatically in the case of Parkinson's disease, which involves a massive loss of DA neurons in the substantia nigra and consequent DA denervation of the dorsal striatum. Parkinson's disease is characterized by progressive motor dysfunction, typically beginning

---

*The term "substantia nigra" means "black substance." It is so named because the dopaminergic neurons contain the dark pigment neuromelanin, which is related to the melanin pigment found in skin and hair.

(A)

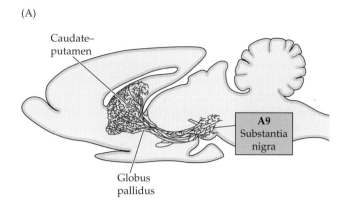

Caudate–putamen

Globus pallidus

A9
Substantia nigra

(B)

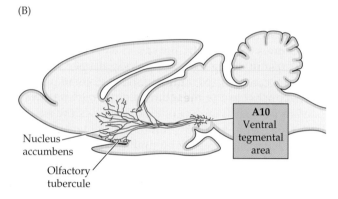

Nucleus accumbens

Olfactory tubercle

A10
Ventral tegmental area

(C)

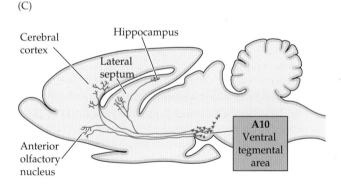

Cerebral cortex

Hippocampus

Lateral septum

Anterior olfactory nucleus

A10
Ventral tegmental area

FIGURE 5.9 **The ascending DA system can be divided into three pathways** The nigrostriatal pathway (A) originates in the substantia nigra (A9 cell cluster) and innervates the caudate–putamen (dorsal striatum). The mesolimbic pathway (B and C) originates in the VTA (A10 cell cluster) and innervates various limbic system structures such as the nucleus accumbens, hippocampus, lateral septum, and amygdala (not shown here). The mesocortical pathway (C) also originates in the VTA and innervates the cerebral cortex. The pathways have been depicted in a sagittal view of a rodent (e.g., rat or mouse) brain for ease in identification.

with tremors and advancing to postural disturbances, **akinesia** (lack of movement), and rigidity (see Chapter 20 for a more extensive discussion of this disorder). Information about the motor functions of DA in humans has also been derived from individuals with certain rare **inborn errors of metabolism** caused by genetic mutations that interfere with DA synthesis. The mutated genes in these cases are those coding for TH, AADC, and also enzymes that regulate the production and metabolism of **tetrahydrobiopterin**, a co-factor needed for TH to perform its function. The exact behavioral manifestations of such mutations vary depending on the particular enzyme and how much enzymatic activity is produced by the mutant protein. In general, symptoms include **hypotonia** (reduced muscle tone), **dystonia** (repetitive involuntary movements and muscle spasms), dysfunction of the autonomic nervous system, and delayed development (Brennenstuhl et al., 2019; Jung-Klawitter and Hübschmann, 2019). An example of the severe symptoms associated with a point mutation in the TH gene is presented as a case study in **WEB BOX 5.1**.

In experimental animals, a range of symptoms, including those seen in Parkinson's disease, can be produced by administering **neurotoxins** that damage or destroy midbrain DA neurons and lesion their ascending pathways. Two such compounds are **6-hydroxydopamine (6-OHDA)** and **1-methyl-4-phenyl-1,2,3,6-tetrahydropyridine (MPTP)**. Although the two substances produce similar damage to the dopaminergic system with similar functional consequences, here we focus on the effects produced by 6-OHDA administration. The use of MPTP as a DA neurotoxin will be covered later in Chapter 20. To lesion the central dopaminergic system with 6-OHDA, one must inject the drug directly into the brain since it does not readily cross the blood–brain barrier. The toxin is taken up mainly by the catecholaminergic neurons (thus sparing neurons that use other neurotransmitters) because of its close structural similarity to DA. Once the toxin is inside the neuron, the nerve terminals are severely damaged, and sometimes the entire cell dies. Animals with bilateral 6-OHDA lesions of the ascending dopaminergic pathways show severe behavioral dysfunction. They exhibit sensory neglect (they pay little attention to stimuli in the environment), motivational deficits (they show little interest in eating food or drinking water), and motor impairment (like patients with Parkinson's disease, they have difficulty initiating voluntary movements). It is also possible to damage the nigrostriatal DA pathway on only one side of the brain, as illustrated in **FIGURE 5.10**. In this case, the lesioned animals display a postural asymmetry characterized by leaning and turning toward the damaged side of the brain because of the dominance of the untreated side. The severe abnormalities seen following either bilateral or unilateral lesions of the DA system indicate how important this neurotransmitter is for many behavioral functions, not just for initiation and control of movement.

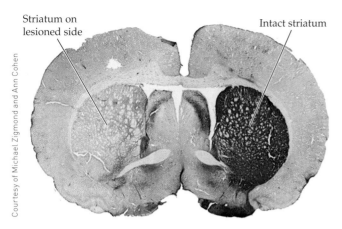

Striatum on lesioned side

Intact striatum

Courtesy of Michael Zigmond and Ann Cohen

FIGURE 5.10 Unilateral damage to the nigrostriatal pathway Shown here is a photomicrograph of a tissue section from the brain of a rat that had received a unilateral 6-OHDA lesion of the medial forebrain bundle, which contains the axons of the nigrostriatal pathway. The section, which was stained using an antibody against tyrosine hydroxylase, depicts the loss of dopaminergic fibers and terminals in the striatum on the side of the lesion.

At the beginning of this chapter we mentioned some of the characteristics of mice genetically engineered to lack DA. These mice constitute another model that illustrates many of the same functions of the dopaminergic system learned from bilateral 6-OHDA–lesioned animals. Two studies from different laboratories published over 20 years ago showed that if the gene for TH is disrupted embryonically in mice (*Th*-knockout mice), the animals die either in utero or shortly after they're born (Kobayashi et al., 1995; Zhou et al., 1995). Although disruption of the TH gene prevents the synthesis of all catecholamines, researchers noted that a similar early lethality occurred when the DBH gene, which is necessary for NE but not for DA synthesis, was knocked out instead of the TH gene (Thomas et al., 1995).* This finding raised the possibility that lack of NE, not DA, was responsible for the early mortality of *Th*-knockout mice. This is relevant to the case study in **WEB BOX 5.1**, since the patient described in that study *did* show a low level of NE synthesis and may have survived for that reason. To determine more selectively the possible role of DA in behavioral and physiological development, Palmiter's lab created the so-called **dopamine-deficient (DD) mouse**. This was done very cleverly by genetically knocking out *Th* but restoring the gene in *Dbh*-expressing (i.e., noradrenergic) cells. In this manner, the ability to synthesize catecholamines was lacking only in the dopaminergic cells. There is some similarity between DD mice and genetically normal animals that have been given 6-OHDA, although two important differences should be mentioned. First, the dopaminergic neurons are physically

*Examination of the *Dbh*-knockout mice showed defects in the heart, suggesting that the death of the animals was caused, at least in part, by a failure of normal heart development.

undamaged in the DD mice; they just can't synthesize DA. Second, in contrast to animals given a 6-OHDA lesion in adulthood, DD mice lack DA throughout development because the genetic manipulations are performed at an early embryonic stage.

As described in the chapter opener, DD mice appear normal from birth through the first week of postnatal life. Afterward, however, they stop gaining weight and exhibit severe **aphagia** (lack of feeding behavior), **adipsia** (lack of drinking), and hypoactivity (Zhou and Palmiter, 1995). Remarkably, all of these behaviors can be restored within minutes by an injection of L-DOPA, which, as we noted, circumvents the TH-mediated step and is converted directly to DA in the dopaminergic neurons (see Figure 5.2). But once the effects of the L-DOPA wear off within a few hours, the mice show a tremendous reduction in movement and seem to have no interest in eating food or drinking despite the fact that they can physically grasp food and swallow liquids that are placed into their mouths. Space limitations prevent us from fully describing all of the subsequent research that has been performed with DD mice; however, one key finding worth noting is that many of the behavioral deficits observed in these mutant animals can be rescued by selectively restoring DA synthesis just in the caudate–putamen (dorsal striatum). Among the rescued behaviors are locomotor activity, eating and drinking behavior, nest building, and performance in many kinds of learning and memory tasks (Palmiter, 2008; Darvas and Palmiter, 2009). In summary, the findings obtained from DD mice taken together with evidence from nigrostriatal DA lesion studies point to a critical role for the dorsal striatum in many of the activational, motivational, and cognitive functions of DA.

The mesolimbic dopaminergic pathway, particularly the part of the system that innervates the nucleus accumbens, has several well-described roles in behavioral regulation. One such role is to activate behavioral arousal and locomotor behavior. Accordingly, microinjection of DA into specific parts of the nucleus accumbens produces locomotor hyperactivity (Campbell et al., 1997). A second key function of the mesolimbic pathway involves the mediation of natural rewards such as food and sex, and also artificial rewards such as those produced by addictive drugs and (for some people) gambling. The role of DA in reward is described in detail in Chapter 9. Until recently, it was unclear whether the same or different VTA dopaminergic neurons participate in locomotor activation versus reward. Based on studies by Howe and Dombeck (2016), it now appears that different cells underlie these two functions.

Yet another line of research has shown that some VTA dopaminergic neurons are activated by stressful or aversive (i.e., unpleasant) stimuli. How can these results be reconciled with DA's role in reward? Once again, it appears that rewarding and aversive stimuli activate different subsets of VTA neurons (Chandler et al., 2014; Verharen et al., 2020). Moreover, these subsets are also differentiated by both their inputs and outputs. As illustrated in **FIGURE 5.11**, the VTA dopaminergic neurons involved in reward receive input from the laterodorsal tegmentum (LDT) in the dorsal midbrain and project to the nucleus accumbens (NAc) as part of the mesolimbic pathway, whereas the neurons that respond to aversive stimuli receive input from the lateral habenula (LHb) and project to the medial PFC (mPFC) as part of the mesocortical pathway. Of course, both subsets of cells receive other inputs that provide additional information about whether a particular stimulus is rewarding or aversive.

Lastly, the mesocortical input to the PFC helps regulate various cognitive functions such as attention and working memory (reviewed in Clark and Noudoost, 2014; Ranganath and Jacob, 2016). Indeed, DA hypoactivity in the PFC is thought to underlie some of the cognitive deficits in patients with schizophrenia (see Chapter 19). A substantial body of research has additionally implicated genetic variation in the COMT gene in the modulating role of DA in PFC-dependent cognitive tasks. More than MAO, COMT has the major responsibility for DA degradation in the PFC. Consequently, dopaminergic signaling in this brain area is influenced by the rate of COMT-related DA breakdown. The functional significance of COMT activity in the PFC first began to emerge when Lachman and coworkers (1996) discovered the presence of two forms of the human COMT gene that code for slightly different proteins. One form of the COMT protein contains the amino acid valine (Val) at position 158 in the molecule, while the other form contains the amino acid methionine (Met) at this same position. This single amino acid substitution (Val → Met) produces a COMT molecule that is three to four times *less* active; that is, DA in the PFC

is degraded much more slowly in people with the Met form of COMT than in people with the Val form of the enzyme. Of course, everyone possesses two copies of the COMT gene, one on each chromosome, so it is possible to have two Val forms (homozygous Val/Val), two Met forms (homozygous Met/Met), or one Val and one Met form of COMT (heterozygous Val/Met). A number of studies (though not all) have found that carriers of the Met form of COMT show better DA-related cognitive function than Val carriers (Witte and Flöel, 2012). This difference, which is usually clearest when comparing homozygous Met-Met carriers with homozygous Val-Val carriers, supports the hypothesis that PFC levels of DA in people with the Val form of COMT are too low for optimal cognitive functioning. A recent developmental study by Dumontheil and colleagues (2020) found that the influence of COMT genotype on working memory was present in adults but not in a combined group of children and adolescents. DA levels in the PFC are known to increase during adolescence and then decline in the transition from adolescence to adulthood (Wahlstrom et al., 2010). Accordingly, it is only after this developmental decline in DA levels has occurred that the more rapid DA metabolism in Val carriers manifests itself in poorer working memory performance.

There are five main subtypes of dopamine receptors organized into D₁- and D₂-like families

In the previous chapter, we discussed the concept of receptor subtypes. The neurotransmitter DA uses five main subtypes, designated D_1 to D_5, all of which are metabotropic receptors. That is, they interact with G proteins and they function, in part, through second messengers. Various studies have shown that the D_1 and D_5 receptors are similar to each other in structure

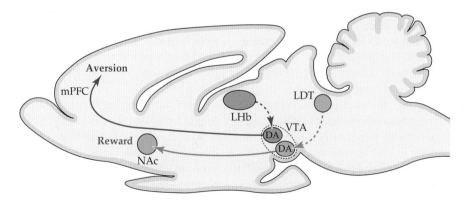

FIGURE 5.11   Different subsets of VTA dopaminergic neurons mediate the effects of rewarding versus aversive stimuli   The diagram depicts a sagittal section through a rodent brain illustrating the features of VTA dopaminergic neurons that help encode rewarding versus aversive stimuli. The reward-mediating pathway (green) includes input to the VTA from the laterodorsal tegmentum (LDT) and dopaminergic output from the VTA to the nucleus accumbens (NAc). The aversion-mediating pathway (red) includes input to the VTA from the lateral habenula (LHb) and dopaminergic output from the VTA to the medial prefrontal cortex (mPFC). (From D. J. Chandler et al. 2014. *Front Neural Circuits* 8: 53. doi: 10.3389/fncir.2014.00053; CC BY 3.0, https://creativecommons.org/licenses/by/3.0/us/)

and in their pharmacological properties, whereas the D_2, D_3, and D_4 receptors represent a separate family.

The D_1 and D_2 receptors were discovered first, and they are the most common subtypes in the brain. Both receptor subtypes are found in large numbers in the dorsal striatum and the nucleus accumbens, major termination sites of the nigrostriatal and mesolimbic DA pathways, respectively. D_1 and to a lesser extent D_2 receptors are also expressed in the PFC, though at lower levels than in the striatum. The modulating effects of prefrontal DA on cognition described above are mediated by the D_1 receptor subtype. Interestingly, D_2 receptors are additionally found on cells in the pituitary gland that make the hormone prolactin. Activation of D_2 receptors by DA from the hypothalamus leads to inhibition of prolactin secretion, whereas the blockade of these receptors stimulates prolactin release. We will see in Chapter 19 that nearly all current antischizophrenic drugs are D_2 receptor antagonists—a characteristic that is believed to play a key role in the therapeutic efficacy of these compounds.

D_3 receptors are expressed within areas of the limbic system where they help regulate emotional and motivational processes. Additionally, there is a descending dopaminergic pathway from the hypothalamus to the spinal cord that terminates on spinal D_3 receptors. The localization of these receptors in the spinal cord is consistent with an involvement in processing of ascending sensory information from the spinal cord to the brain. D_4 receptors show the lowest expression of any of the five subtypes in the human brain; however, these receptors have been found in the frontal cortex, hippocampus, amygdala, and a few other brain areas. Lastly, the D_5 receptor has a wide distribution in the brain, with expression in the same regions as the D_4 receptor but with additional areas as well, including the striatum. D_5 receptors also have a much higher affinity for DA than D_1 receptors, which means that they can respond to much lower levels of DA in the extracellular fluid.

In the early stages of research on DA receptors, investigators discovered that the D_1 and D_2 subtypes have opposite effects on the second-messenger substance cyclic adenosine monophosphate (cAMP) (Kebabian and Calne, 1979). More specifically, D_1 receptors stimulate the enzyme adenylyl cyclase, which is responsible for synthesizing cAMP (see Chapter 3). Consequently, the rate of cAMP formation is increased by stimulation of D_1 receptors. In contrast, D_2 receptor activation inhibits adenylyl cyclase, thereby decreasing the rate of cAMP synthesis (**FIGURE 5.12**). These opposing effects can occur because the receptors activate two different G proteins: G_s in the case of D_1 receptors, and G_i in the case of D_2 receptors. Resulting changes in the level of cAMP within the postsynaptic cell alter the excitability of the cell (i.e., how readily it will fire nerve impulses) in complex ways that are beyond the scope of this discussion. A second important mechanism of D_2 receptor function involves the regulation of membrane ion channels for potassium (K^+). In some cells, D_2 receptor stimulation activates a G protein that subsequently enhances K^+ channel opening. As we saw in Chapter 3, opening of such channels causes hyperpolarization of the cell membrane, thus decreasing the excitability and rate of firing of the cell. In general, the other members of the D_1 and D_2 receptor families use the same signaling mechanisms as described for the D_1 and D_2 subtypes.

D_1 and D_2 receptors differ not only with respect to their signaling mechanisms but also in their affinity for DA. D_2 receptors have a significantly higher affinity for DA than D_1 receptors (Marcellino et al., 2012). This means that less DA is required to occupy a given percentage (for example, 50%) of D_2 compared to D_1 receptors. This difference has led to the hypothesis that tonic DA release primarily activates the higher-affinity D_2 receptors, whereas the large increase in synaptic DA levels produced by phasic release additionally activates the lower-affinity D_1 receptors (Grace et al., 2007). Note that although the D_5 receptor subtype belongs to the D_1 family, D_5 receptors are similar to D_2 receptors in having a high affinity for DA and thus being sensitive to low levels of the neurotransmitter.

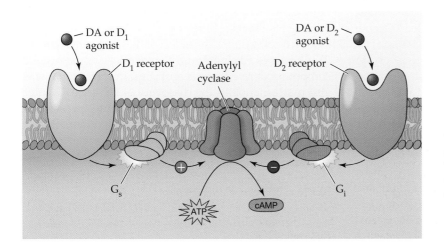

FIGURE 5.12 Signaling mechanisms of D_1 and D_2 receptors Activation of D_1 receptors stimulates the enzyme adenylyl cyclase and enhances DA synthesis, whereas activation of D_2 receptors inhibits adenylyl cyclase and decreases DA synthesis. These effects are produced by the activation of different G proteins in the postsynaptic cell membrane, namely G_s for the D_1 receptor and G_i for the D_2 receptor.

D_2 receptors are not only found postsynaptically but are also expressed by the dopaminergic neurons, where they function as autoreceptors. Terminal D_2 autoreceptors reduce DA release, whereas somatodendritic D_2 autoreceptors inhibit dopaminergic cell firing (Ford, 2014). For technical reasons, it was extremely difficult for many years to determine how important these autoreceptors are for the normal functioning of catecholamine neurons and how those receptors might influence the cellular and behavioral responses to various pharmacological agents. However, Bello and colleagues (2011) developed a powerful genetic method for deleting the D_2 receptor gene *just* from the DA neurons in mice, thus eliminating the DA autoreceptors but allowing normal expression of postsynaptic D_2 receptors (i.e., D_2 receptors in non-DA neurons). Results showed that the DA neurons from the mutant mice released more DA, that the mutant mice were more spontaneously active than controls (in the next section we discuss the key role of DA in regulating locomotor activity), and that the animals were more sensitive to the behavioral effects of cocaine, a drug that exerts many of its effects through the DA system (see Chapter 12 for more details). These findings confirm that D_2 autoreceptors are, indeed, functionally active under normal circumstances and that they influence behavioral responses to dopaminergic agents.

Dopamine receptor agonists and antagonists affect locomotor activity, motor control, and other behavioral functions

Many studies of DA pharmacology have used compounds that directly stimulate or block DA receptors. **Apomorphine** is a widely used agonist that stimulates both D_1 and D_2 receptors. At appropriate doses, apomorphine treatment causes behavioral activation similar to that seen with classical stimulants like amphetamine and cocaine. There is also a relatively new use for apomorphine—treating erectile dysfunction in men (trade name **Uprima**). At present, the best-known remedy for this disorder is, of course, Viagra. You will recall that the mechanism of action of Viagra, which involves inhibiting the breakdown of cyclic guanosine monophosphate (cGMP) in the penis, was discussed in Chapter 3. In contrast, apomorphine seems to increase penile blood flow, which is necessary for an erection, by acting through DA receptors in the brain. This effect of apomorphine has actually been known for some time, but clinical application for this purpose was previously thwarted by undesirable side effects, particularly nausea, as well as poor bioavailability when the drug is taken orally. These problems have been overcome to some extent through the development of a lozenge that is taken sublingually (under the tongue), thereby bypassing the digestive system and delivering the drug directly into the bloodstream.

Psychopharmacologists also make use of drugs that are more selective for members of the D_1 or D_2 receptor family. Receptor-selective agonists and antagonists are extremely important in helping us understand which behaviors are under the control of a particular receptor subtype. One commonly used agonist for D_1 receptors is a compound known as **SKF 38393**.* Administration of this compound to rats or mice dose-dependently elicits locomotor activity and self-grooming behavior. Unfortunately, standard D_1 agonists such as SKF 38393 have not proven to be useful clinically due to adverse side effects and development of **tachyphylaxis** (a form of rapid tolerance involving diminished responses following repeated drug dosing). These problems have led to a search for positive allosteric modulators of the D_1 receptor that might have a better clinical profile. One promising drug in this category is called **DETQ**. Preclinical testing of this compound has been conducted using a model of transgenic mice engineered to express the human D_1 receptor. In this model, DETQ has broad stimulating effects manifested by increased locomotor activity, a reversal of reserpine-induced sedation, decreased immobility in the forced-swim test (a test of depressive-like behavior; see Chapter 4), and enhanced performance in the novel object recognition test of memory (Svensson et al., 2017; Bruns et al., 2018; Svensson et al., 2019). **FIGURE 5.13** shows the locomotor stimulating effects of DETQ and the lack of tolerance with repeated administration compared to the tolerance observed with a D_1 receptor agonist. These findings suggest that DETQ could be developed therapeutically to help treat symptoms of hypoactivity, depressed behavior, and cognitive impairment associated with various neuropsychiatric disorders.

Researchers have had considerable difficulty developing agonists that are highly selective for the D_2 receptor. However, many compounds have been discovered that activate both D_2 and D_3 receptors. Researchers have often used a combined D_2/D_3 agonist called **quinpirole** to investigate the behavioral effects of these receptors in rodents. Administration of this compound generally increases locomotion and sniffing behavior. These responses are reminiscent of the effects of amphetamine or apomorphine, although quinpirole is not as powerful a stimulant as the former compounds.

Several other combined D_2/D_3 receptor agonists have clinical applications. The oldest of these is **bromocriptine** (trade names **Parlodel** and **Cycloset**), a semisynthetic compound derived from ergot (a grain fungus that was also instrumental in the discovery of LSD; see Chapter 15). Bromocriptine (Parlodel) is sometimes prescribed as an adjunct to L-DOPA treatment to help ameliorate the symptoms of Parkinson's disease. A second use of

---

*Many drugs used in research never receive common names like cocaine or reserpine. In such instances, the drug is designated with an abbreviation for the pharmaceutical company at which it was developed, along with an identifying number. In the present instance, *SKF* stands for Smith Kline & French, which is now part of GlaxoSmithKline.

(A) DETQ (30 mg/kg, p.o.)

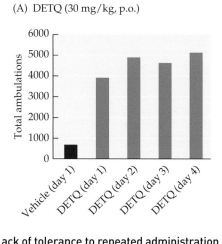

(B) A-77636 (10 mg/kg, s.c.)

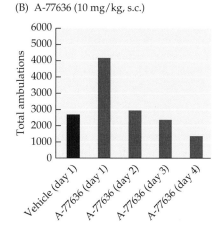

FIGURE 5.13   Lack of tolerance to repeated administration of the D_1 receptor positive allosteric modulator DETQ Genetically engineered mice expressing the human D_1 receptor were tested for their locomotor activity (ambulations) in a photocell-equipped activity monitor. Some mice were administered 30 mg/kg DETQ orally (p.o.) daily for 4 days (A), whereas others were given 10 mg/kg of the D_1 agonist A-77636 subcutaneously (s.c.) for the same time period (B). Compared to vehicle treatment, both drugs significantly stimulated locomotor activity on the first treatment day, with a particularly large increase in activity in the DETQ-treated animals. By the second day of treatment, there was no longer a locomotor response to A-77636, whereas no such tolerance occurred with DETQ even after 4 consecutive days of drug administration. (From K. A. Svensson et al. 2017. *J Pharmacol Exp Ther* 360: 117–128. Republished with permission of American Society for Pharmacology and Experimental Therapeutics; permission conveyed through Copyright Clearance Center, Inc.)

Parlodel is to reduce pituitary prolactin secretion in cases of hyperprolactinemia (excessive prolactin blood levels). This effect is mediated by activation of D_2 receptors in the prolactin-secreting cells themselves. Third, a quick-release formulation of bromocriptine (Cycloset) is sometimes prescribed for patients with type 2 diabetes to help regulate blood insulin and glucose levels. The mechanism of action in this case is thought to involve an inhibition of sympathetic nervous system activity, resulting in less glucose production by the liver. Three other clinically used D_2/D_3 agonists are **pramipexole (Mirapex)**, **ropinirole (Requip)**, and **rotigotine (Neupro)**. Neupro is a transdermal patch that delivers a steady dose of rotigotine continuously over a 24-hour period. These compounds are not only prescribed like bromocriptine for patients with Parkinson's disease but are also administered to people with **restless legs syndrome**. The classic symptom of this disorder is an irresistible urge to move one's legs, usually occurring at night or at other occasions when the legs have not moved for a long period of time. However, many patients report additional disturbing feelings in their legs, including tingling, itching, burning, cramping, pain, and numbness. The etiology of restless legs syndrome is unknown, although one factor is believed to be abnormal functioning of the dopaminergic system. Current evidence suggests that activation of D_3 rather than D_2 receptors by pramipexole, ropinirole, or rotigotine is primarily responsible for their therapeutic benefit in this syndrome (Casoni et al., 2019).

The typical effect of administering a DA receptor antagonist is suppression of spontaneous exploratory and locomotor behavior. At higher doses, such drugs elicit a state known as **catalepsy**. Catalepsy refers to a lack of spontaneous movement, which is usually demonstrated experimentally by showing that the subject does not change position when placed in an awkward, presumably uncomfortable posture. Nevertheless, the subject is neither paralyzed nor asleep, and in fact it can be aroused to move by strong sensory stimuli such as being picked up by the experimenter. Catalepsy is usually associated with D_2 receptor blockers such as **haloperidol**, but it can also be elicited by giving a D_1 blocker such as **SCH 23390**. Given the important role of the nigrostriatal DA pathway in movement, it is not surprising that catalepsy is particularly related to the inhibition of DA receptors in the striatum. We mentioned earlier that D_2 receptor antagonists are used in the treatment of schizophrenia. The therapeutic benefit of these drugs is thought to derive from their blocking of DA receptors mainly in the limbic system. It should be clear from the present discussion, however, that the same drugs are also likely to produce inhibition of movement and other troublesome motor side effects because of simultaneous interference with dopaminergic transmission in the striatum.

The various effects of DA receptor agonists and antagonists have given researchers a lot of useful information about the behavioral functions of DA. A somewhat newer approach is to manipulate the genes for individual components of the dopaminergic system, determine the behavioral consequences of such manipulations, and ascertain whether the genetic engineering approach provides information similar to or different from that obtained from traditional pharmacological studies. Results from this approach are discussed in **BOX 5.1**.

BOX 5.1 ■ THE CUTTING EDGE

Using Molecular Genetics to Study the Dopaminergic System

Many researchers use techniques from molecular biology to investigate how neurotransmitter systems function, how they control various behaviors, and the mechanisms of psychoactive drug action. One of the most powerful tools in this field of molecular pharmacology is the production of genetically engineered animals, which means animals in which one or more genes have been altered experimentally (rather than animals with genetic changes like mutations that can occur spontaneously in nature; see Chapter 4). Until fairly recently, almost all genetically engineered animal strains were mice; however, the relevant techniques are constantly improving, so other species, including rats and monkeys, can now also be genetically modified. Several different kinds of mutations can be created, depending on the aim of the experiment. To briefly review the information presented in Chapter 4, genetically engineered mutant animal lines include (1) gene knockout animals, in which the target gene is modified so that it no longer yields a functional protein product; (2) gene "knockin" animals, which are usually produced by making a point mutation in the gene that alters the identity of one particular amino acid in the protein product; (3) gene "overexpressing" animals, engineered by inserting one or more additional copies of the target gene into the recipient's genome; and (4) transgenic animals, in which one or more genes from a different species have been inserted into the recipient's genome. An example of that last approach is the insertion of a mutant form of a human gene that causes disease (e.g., rare mutations that cause inherited forms of Alzheimer's or Parkinson's disease) into mice to provide an animal model for testing potential new treatments for that disease. Note that we are using the traditional definition of the term *transgenic*, although sometimes the word is used more loosely to describe any genetically modified strain of organism.

When genetic modifications such as gene knockouts were first created, they could only be implemented during embryonic development and affected the gene being manipulated throughout the brain and body. Researchers soon realized the limitations of this approach, including the fact that loss of a gene during embryogenesis can alter developmental expression of other genes to influence the resulting phenotype. Because of subsequent technical improvements, researchers can now create "conditional" knockouts or knockins that permit the deletion or addition of a gene in adulthood (instead of embryonically) and, in some cases, within a specific population of cells.

Genetic engineering studies manipulating the dopaminergic system have focused on three areas: (1) investigating how this system regulates behavioral functions, (2) dissecting the molecular actions of dopaminergic drugs, and (3) providing novel animal models for several neuropsychiatric disorders, particularly attention-deficit/hyperactivity disorder (ADHD) and schizophrenia. One example was shown by our earlier discussion of DD mice, whereas other strains of mutant mice have been generated that lack either the DA transporter or one of the DA receptors. Each gene knockout was found to produce a unique behavioral phenotype, which refers to the behavior of the mutant strain compared with that of wild-type animals (animals carrying the form of the gene found in nature). Here we will focus on manipulations of the DA transporter and the D_1 and D_2 receptor genes, which are the most heavily studied components of the dopaminergic system.

Deletion of the DA transporter in either mice or rats causes numerous biochemical and behavioral effects (Giros et al., 1996; Leo et al., 2018). Extracellular DA concentrations are extremely elevated because of the inability of the dopaminergic neurons to take up the neurotransmitter after release. At the same time, striatal DA content is dramatically reduced, probably reflecting a combination of autoreceptor activation by extracellular DA and an unavailability of DA for vesicular repackaging that would normally occur following reuptake. Behaviorally, the DA transporter knockout animals are extremely hyperactive because of the persistent activation of postsynaptic DA receptors (**FIGURE A**). These animals also show cognitive deficits and impulsivity, traits that are often seen in children suffering from ADHD. Moreover, hyperactivity in these animals is reduced by administration of amphetamine or methylphenidate, medications commonly prescribed for ADHD patients (see Chapter 12). Based on these findings, some researchers have proposed DA transporter knockout mice and rats to be animal models of ADHD (Leo and Gainetdinov, 2013; Leo et al., 2018).

The behavioral phenotype of DA receptor knockout mice has also been investigated (Holmes et al., 2004).

(A)

Dopamine transporter (DAT) knockout mice show increased locomotor activity Mutant mice lacking a functional DAT (homozygous DAT–/–) were compared with wild-type mice (DAT+/+) and with heterozygous mice (DAT+/–) that carry one functional copy of the DAT gene. Mice were tested in a photocell apparatus, and the number of photobeam breaks was recorded every 20 minutes for a total of 3 hours. All groups showed a gradual habituation to the apparatus, as indicated by decreasing beam breaks over time, but the activity of the DAT knockout mice (DAT–/–) was consistently higher than that of the other two groups. (After B. Giros et al. 1996. *Nature* 379: 606–612. doi.org/10.1038/379606a0)

BOX 5.1 ■ THE CUTTING EDGE (continued)

D_1 receptor knockout mice are similar to DA-deficient (DD) mice in that they appear normal at birth. However, by the age of weaning, they begin to show reduced growth and may even die if their normally dry food isn't moistened to make it more palatable. In adulthood, these animals show complex behavioral abnormalities, including increased locomotor activity and reduced habituation in an open field, deficits in motor coordination in the rotarod test, and reduced self-grooming behavior (recall that D_1 receptor agonists given to wild-type rodents stimulate grooming behavior). Not surprisingly, D_1 receptor knockout mice also exhibit deficits in several kinds of cognitive tasks (Holmes et al., 2004). Okubo and colleagues (2018) recently examined the effect of silencing the D_1 receptor gene in adulthood rather than during early embryonic development. Compared to wild-type mice, these animals exhibited deficient motor coordination like D_1 knockouts; however, they also showed *reduced* locomotor activity, which is the opposite effect to that seen in D_1 knockout mice. Thus, silencing this receptor during adulthood instead of early development is consistent with the behavioral activation produced by D_1 agonist drugs. Genetic and biochemical adaptations during development may have overcompensated for the loss of D_1 receptor gene activity in the traditional knockout animals, leading to the unexpected phenotype of hyperactivity.

Initial studies on D_2 receptor knockout mice revealed impairments in spontaneous movement, coordination, and postural control; however, the degree of impairment seemed to depend on which genetic strain of mouse was used to create the mutation (Holmes et al., 2004; Nakamura et al., 2014). The issue of background strain (i.e., which alleles are present in the remaining genes that have *not* been altered) is important not just in this specific instance but in all studies of genetically engineered animals. Fortunately, some of the controversy around the phenotypic effects of D_2 receptor deletion has been resolved by the development again of a mouse model in which the receptor is deleted in adulthood (Bello et al., 2017). The genetically engineered animals show severe impairment of motor function, manifested by reduced locomotor activity, poor motor coordination, and spontaneous episodes of catatonia. These symptoms resemble those seen in animals given a high dose of a D_2 receptor antagonist, thus providing validation of the genetic model and supporting a key role for D_2 receptors in motor control.

Pharmacologists have naturally taken advantage of these mutant strains of mice to study how disruptions in various DA system genes affect reactions to different psychoactive drugs. Several studies have looked at behavioral responses to psychostimulant drugs such as cocaine, amphetamine, and methamphetamine because DA is already known to play an important role in the effects of these compounds. DA transporter knockout mice and mice lacking either the D_1 or D_2 receptor show reduced or, in some cases, no increase in locomotion after psychostimulant treatment (M. Xu et al., 2000; Holmes et al., 2004) (**FIGURE B**). D_2 receptor knockout mice also exhibit reduced behavioral sensitization to repeated administration of either cocaine or amphetamine (Solis et al., 2019). On the other hand, mutant mice that overexpress the DA transporter exhibit an exaggerated locomotor response to amphetamine (Salahpour et al., 2008). Taken together, these findings demonstrate that both the DA transporter on the presynaptic side and both D_1 and D_2 receptors on the postsynaptic side play pivotal roles in the behavior-stimulating effects of cocaine and amphetamine (see Chapter 12).

The findings discussed in this box show that genetically engineered strains of animals can be a powerful tool to help clarify and expand upon the behavioral functions of a neurotransmitter such as DA that previously could only be studied pharmacologically. On the other hand, we also identified some of the limitations of genetic manipulations. That is, results can vary depending on the background strain of the animals and on whether the gene has been deleted during early embryonic development or in adulthood. Despite these limitations, genetically engineered animals will continue to be heavily used in our search for the neuromolecular mechanisms underlying various behaviors and the behavioral responses to psychoactive drugs.

D1 receptor knockout mice show decreased reaction to a psychostimulant drug Mutant mice lacking D_1 receptors (D_1–/–) are insensitive to the locomotor-stimulating effects of cocaine. Wild-type (D_1+/+) and homozygous mutant mice were injected twice daily for 7 consecutive days with either cocaine (20 mg/kg intraperitoneally) or a saline control solution. The animals were tested in a photocell apparatus for 30 minutes after each injection to record their locomotor activity. Cocaine greatly increased locomotor activity in the wild-type but not the mutant mice on all test days. (After M. Xu et al. 2000. *Brain Res* 852: 198–207. © 2000. Reprinted with permission from Elsevier.)

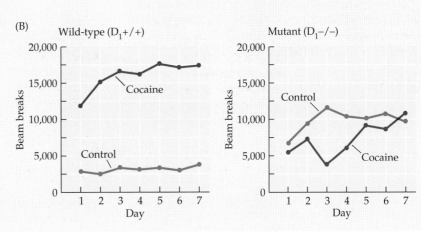

We conclude this section by considering the consequences of administering a D_2 receptor antagonist repeatedly rather than just once or twice. When drugs like haloperidol are given on a long-term basis to rats, the animals develop a syndrome called **behavioral supersensitivity**. This means that if the haloperidol treatment is stopped to unblock the D_2 receptors and then subjects are given a DA agonist like apomorphine, they respond more strongly than controls not pretreated with haloperidol. Since the experimental and control animals both received the same dose of apomorphine, this finding suggests that somehow the DA receptors in the experimental group are more sensitive to the same pharmacological stimulation. A similar effect occurs after DA depletion by 6-OHDA. The similarity between the effects of haloperidol and 6-OHDA is because both treatments persistently reduce DA stimulation of D_2 receptors. Haloperidol accomplishes this by blocking the receptors, whereas 6-OHDA achieves the same result by causing a long-lasting depletion of DA. Various studies suggest that the supersensitivity associated with haloperidol or 6-OHDA treatment is related, at least in part, to an increase in the density of D_2 receptors on postsynaptic cells in the striatum. This phenomenon, which is called **receptor up-regulation**, is considered to be an adaptive response whereby the lack of normal neurotransmitter (in this case DA) input causes the neurons to increase their sensitivity by making more receptors. However, at least in the case of chronic D_2 receptor blockade, changes in other neurotransmitter systems may also contribute to the development of behavioral supersensitivity (Servonnet and Samaha, 2020).

Patients with schizophrenia who are treated with haloperidol or other classical antipsychotic medications are also thought to develop DA supersensitivity based on a reduction in treatment effectiveness as well as other symptoms. Later generations of antipsychotic medications are less likely to exhibit this phenomenon but are still not ideal (see Chapter 19). Based on a combination of animal and human clinical studies, there is evidence that intermittent drug dosing that permits periods of reduced striatal D_2 receptor occupancy may help reduce the development of supersensitivity both in animal models and in patients (Servonnet and Samaha, 2020).

SECTION SUMMARY

- The dopaminergic neurons of greatest interest to neuropsychopharmacologists are found near the base of the midbrain in the substantia nigra (A9 cell group) and the VTA (A10 cell group). Neurons in the substantia nigra send their axons to the dorsal striatum, thus forming the nigrostriatal tract. The dorsal striatum is composed of two separate structures, called the caudate and putamen, in humans and non-human primates, whereas these structures are fused in rodents.

- The nigrostriatal pathway plays an important role in the control of movement and is severely damaged in Parkinson's disease. This disorder is characterized by symptoms of tremors, postural disturbances, akinesia, and rigidity.

- Rare genetic mutations (inborn errors of metabolism) are known that interfere with DA synthesis. Individuals carrying such mutations typically show hypotonia, dystonia, autonomic nervous system dysfunction, and delayed development.

- Two different animal models have not only confirmed the involvement of nigrostriatal DA in the initiation of voluntary motor activity (e.g., locomotion) but also implicated this pathway in the regulation of motivation (e.g., motivation to eat and drink) and in cognitive function. These animal models involve either biochemical lesioning of the nigrostriatal tract (e.g., using the neurotoxin 6-OHDA) or the genetic engineering of DD mice.

- Dopaminergic neurons in the VTA form two major dopaminergic systems: the mesolimbic system, which has terminations in several limbic system structures (e.g., nucleus accumbens, septum, amygdala, hippocampus), and the mesocortical system, which terminates in the cerebral cortex (particularly the PFC). The nucleus accumbens is a major constituent of the ventral striatum.

- The mesolimbic and mesocortical DA systems have been implicated in mechanisms of drug abuse, as well as in schizophrenia. A specific subset of VTA dopaminergic neurons activated by rewarding stimuli receive input from the laterodorsal tegmentum and project to the nucleus accumbens, whereas a separate subset that is activated by aversive stimuli receive input from the lateral habenula and project to the medial PFC.

- Dopamine input to the PFC helps regulate cognitive functions such as attention and working memory. COMT in the PFC is largely responsible for DA metabolism and, therefore, modulates the influence of DA on cognition.

- Two genetic forms of COMT exist, one with the amino acid Val in position 158 and the other with Met in this position. The Met form of COMT is less active, thereby leading to increased DA levels in the PFC. In several studies people carrying the Met form have demonstrated better cognitive function (e.g., in working memory tasks) than people carrying the Val form.

- Researchers have identified five main DA receptor subtypes, designated D_1 to D_5, all of which are metabotropic receptors. These subtypes fall into two families, the first consisting of D_1 and D_5 and the second consisting of D_2, D_3, and D_4.

- D_1 and D_2, the most common receptor subtypes, are found in large numbers in the striatum and the nucleus accumbens. D_1 receptors in the PFC are important for modulating cognitive function, whereas D_2 receptors in the pituitary gland mediate the inhibitory effect of DA on prolactin secretion.

- D_3 receptors are expressed within areas of the limbic system, where they help regulate emotional and motivational processes. Additional expression in the spinal cord regulates ascending sensory information. D_4 receptors have been found in several brain areas but at low levels of expression. In contrast, D_5 receptors are widely distributed in many regions of the brain.

■ D_1 and D_2 receptor subtypes can be differentiated partly on the basis that D_1 receptors stimulate adenylyl cyclase, thus increasing the rate of cAMP synthesis, whereas D_2 receptors decrease the rate of cAMP synthesis by inhibiting adenylyl cyclase. Activation of D_2 receptors can also enhance the opening of K^+ channels in the cell membrane, which hyperpolarizes the membrane and therefore reduces cell excitability. In addition, D_2 receptors have a greater affinity for DA than D_1 receptors, thereby leading to the hypothesis that tonic DA release primarily activates D_2 receptors, whereas significant activation of D_1 receptors requires the additional amount of DA released by phasic activity of the dopaminergic neurons.

■ D_2 receptors are expressed by dopaminergic neurons, where they function as autoreceptors. Terminal D_2 autoreceptors reduce DA release, whereas somatodendritic D_2 autoreceptors inhibit dopaminergic neuronal firing.

■ Some of the drugs that affect the dopaminergic system and their primary use (clinical, recreational, or experimental) are presented in **TABLE 5.1**. In general, enhancement of dopaminergic function has an activating effect on behavior, whereas interference with DA causes suppression of normal behaviors, ranging from temporary sedation and catalepsy to the profound deficits observed after treatment with a DA neurotoxin such as 6-OHDA.

TABLE 5.1   Drugs That Affect the Dopaminergic System

Drug	Mechanism of action	Clinical, recreational, or experimental use
Dihydroxyphenylalanine (L-DOPA)	Dopamine (DA) precursor	Treatment for Parkinson's disease
Carbidopa	Peripheral aromatic amino acid decarboxylase (AADC) inhibitor	Adjunct treatment for Parkinson's disease
Phenelzine and tranylcypromine	Nonselective monoamine oxidase (MAO) inhibitors	Antidepressant medications
Moclobemide	Selective MAO-A inhibitor	Antidepressant medication
Selegiline and rasagiline	Selective MAO-B inhibitor	Treatments for early-stage Parkinson's disease
Entacapone, opicapone, and tolcapone	Catechol-O-methyltransferase (COMT) inhibitors	Adjunct treatments for Parkinson's disease
α-Methyl-*para*-tyrosine (AMPT)	Tyrosine hydroxylase inhibitor	Experimental use
Reserpine	Irreversible VMAT inhibitor	Experimental use
Tetrabenazine, deutetrabenazine, and valbenazine	Reversible VMAT inhibitors	Treatments for Huntington's disease and tardive dyskinesia
6-Hydroxydopamine (6-OHDA) and MPTP	DA neurotoxins	Experimental use
Amphetamine*	Catecholamine releaser and reuptake blocker	Treatment for ADHD and recreational use
Cocaine*	Catecholamine reuptake blocker	Recreational use and occasional medical use as a local anesthetic
Methylphenidate*	Catecholamine reuptake blocker	Treatment for ADHD and recreational use
Apomorphine	Nonselective D_1 and D_2 receptor agonist	Treatment for erectile dysfunction
SKF 38393	D_1 receptor agonist	Experimental use
DETQ	D_1 receptor positive allosteric modulator	Under development for clinical use
Quinpirole	D_2/D_3 receptor agonist	Experimental use
Bromocriptine, pramipexole, ropinirole, and rotigotine	D_2/D_3 receptor agonists	Adjunct treatments for Parkinson's disease and primary treatments for restless legs syndrome
SCH 23390	D_1 receptor antagonist	Experimental use
Haloperidol	D_2 receptor antagonist	Antipsychotic medication

The table shows instances in which multiple drugs have similar mechanisms of action but only some are used clinically or clinical uses vary between drugs. Compounds with a similar primary mechanism can differ in several ways that influence their clinical applications, including (1) side effects and patient tolerability, (2) pharmacokinetics (i.e., rates of drug absorption and/or metabolism), (3) suitability for the desired route of administration, (4) additional mechanisms of action not shown in the table, and (5) potential for abuse.

* These drugs are not selective for catecholamines, as they also affect serotonin release or reuptake.

- Dopaminergic drugs with clinical applications include L-DOPA and several D_2/D_3 receptor agonists for treating Parkinson's disease, D_2/D_3 agonists for restless legs syndrome, and D_2 receptor antagonists for the treatment of schizophrenia.

- When D_2 receptor transmission is persistently impaired either by chronic antagonist administration or by denervation (e.g., 6-OHDA lesions), animals become supersensitive to treatment with a D_2 agonist. This response is mediated at least in part by up-regulation of D_2 receptors by postsynaptic neurons in areas such as the striatum. Supersensitivity may also occur in patients following continuous administration of a D_2 receptor antagonist.

5.3 Organization and Function of the Noradrenergic System

The noradrenergic system has both a central and peripheral component. The cell bodies of the central noradrenergic system are found in the brainstem, and their ascending fibers innervate a wide range of forebrain structures. Peripheral noradrenergic neurons are an important component of the sympathetic nervous system. NE released from these cells acts on adrenergic receptors located either in the central nervous system or in peripheral target organs.

Norepinephrine is an important transmitter in both the central and peripheral nervous systems

The NE-containing neurons within the brain are located in the parts of the brainstem called the *pons* and the *medulla*. Of particular interest is a structure known as the **locus coeruleus (LC)**,* a small area of the pons that contains a dense collection of noradrenergic neurons corresponding roughly to the A6 cell group (according to the numbering system described previously). At first glance, the LC might not seem to be a very impressive structure; the rat LC contains a few more than 3000 nerve cells out of the millions of neurons present in the entire rat brain. Of course, more LC cells are found in the larger brains of primates, but even the human brain only contains approximately 50,000 noradrenergic neurons in the LC (Sharma et al., 2010). Location and size of the LC in the human brain are shown in the histological sections and magnetic resonance image (MRI) of **FIGURE 5.14**. Virtually all neurons within the LC express the enzyme DBH and, thus, synthesize NE as their primary neurotransmitter. However, it should be noted that many different neuropeptides are also present in LC neurons, providing

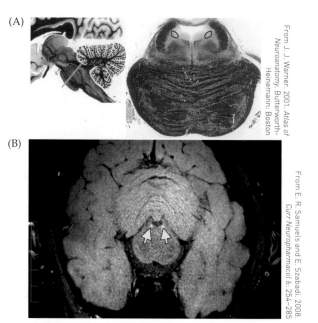

(A)

(B)

From J. J. Warner. 2001. *Atlas of Neuroanatomy*. Butterworth-Heinemann: Boston

From E. R. Samuels and E. Szabadi. 2008. *Curr Neuropharmacol* 6: 254–285

FIGURE 5.14 Location of the locus coeruleus (LC) in the human brain (A) Histological section from a human brain at the level of the pons. The image at the left shows the plane of section of the brain, whereas the image at the right shows the resulting section with the LC on each side of the brain outlined in red. The tissue was treated with a myelin stain, which accounts for why cell-rich, myelin-poor areas like the LC are so lightly stained. (B) Structural magnetic resonance image (MRI) in which the LC is marked by the yellow arrows. The plane of the MRI is oriented with the front of the head toward the top, thus producing an image with a different plane than the histological section shown above it.

the opportunity for these co-transmitters to modulate postsynaptic noradrenergic responses (Aston-Jones and Waterhouse, 2016).

Despite its small size, the LC sends fibers to almost all areas of the forebrain, thereby providing nearly all of the NE in the cortex, limbic system, thalamus, and hypothalamus (**FIGURE 5.15**). The LC also provides noradrenergic input to the cerebellum and the spinal cord. Many fibers originating in the LC terminate in cortical or subcortical brain regions involved in sensory information processing. This projection pattern is consistent with evidence that one of the many functions of LC noradrenergic neurons is to help control goal-directed behaviors by selectively modulating sensory input (Waterhouse and Navarra, 2019).

Norepinephrine additionally plays an important role in the peripheral nervous system. Many neurons that have their cell bodies in the ganglia of the sympathetic branch of the autonomic nervous system (see Chapter 2) use NE as their transmitter. These cells, which send out their fibers to various target organs throughout the body, are responsible for the autonomic actions of NE. We mentioned earlier in the chapter that NE (as well as EPI) functions as a hormone secreted by the

---

*The name of this structure comes from the Latin "locus coeruleus," meaning "blue place." In unstained human brain tissue, this brain area has a bluish appearance because of the neuromelanin content of the noradrenergic neurons.

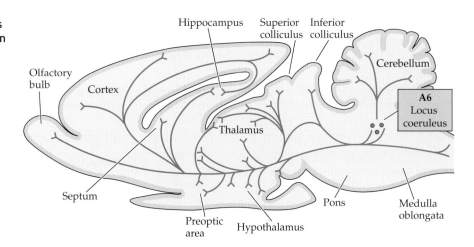

FIGURE 5.15 The locus coeruleus (LC) sends fibers to much of the brain The LC contains a dense cluster of noradrenergic neurons designated the A6 cell group. These cells send their fibers to almost all regions of the forebrain, as well as to the cerebellum and spinal cord.

adrenal glands directly into the bloodstream. In this way, NE can reach an organ such as the heart through two routes: it can be released from sympathetic noradrenergic neurons at axonal varicosities that come into close proximity with cardiac cells, and it can be released from the adrenal glands and travel to the heart through the circulatory system. On the other hand, bloodborne NE does not reach the brain, because it is effectively excluded by the blood–brain barrier.

Bloodborne NE and EPI work together with NE released as a transmitter from sympathetic nerve endings to mediate most of the physiological changes that make up the "fight-or-flight" response described roughly 100 years ago by the great physiologist Walter Cannon (1922). These changes include alterations in blood vessel constriction that prepare the organism for rapid action (i.e., dilation of vessels in skeletal muscle, heart, and brain, but constriction of blood vessels in other organs), elevated blood pressure, increased heart rate and contractile force of heart muscle, increased oxygen intake caused by dilation of the airways and elevated respiration rate, reduced digestive activity caused by relaxation of intestinal smooth muscle, pupil dilation to let more light into the eyes, increased liberation of metabolic fuels from the liver and adipose tissue (sugar and fats, respectively), and decreased secretion of gastric juices and saliva (reviewed by Tank and Wong, 2015). Below we describe the adrenergic receptor subtypes responsible for these effects and the use of drugs targeting these receptors for the treatment of various medical conditions.

Norepinephrine and epinephrine act through α- and β-adrenergic receptors

Receptors for NE and EPI are called *adrenergic receptors* (an alternate term is **adrenoceptors**). Like DA receptors, adrenergic receptors all belong to the general family of metabotropic receptors. However, they serve a broader role by having to mediate both neurotransmitter (mainly NE) and hormonal (mainly EPI) actions of the catecholamines.

Early studies by Ahlquist (1948; 1979) and other investigators suggested the existence of two adrenoceptor subtypes, which were designated alpha (α) and beta (β). Since the time of Ahlquist's pioneering research, many experiments have shown that the α- and β-adrenoceptors actually represent two families, each composed of several receptor subtypes. For present purposes, we will distinguish between α_1- and α_2-receptors, and also between β_1 and β_2. Postsynaptic adrenoceptors are found at high densities in many brain areas, including the cerebral cortex, thalamus, hypothalamus, and cerebellum, and in various limbic system structures such as the hippocampus and amygdala. In addition, α_2-autoreceptors are located on noradrenergic nerve terminals and on the cell bodies of noradrenergic neurons in the LC and elsewhere. These autoreceptors cause an inhibition of noradrenergic cell firing and a reduction in NE release from the terminals.

Like dopamine D_1 receptors, both β_1- and β_2-adrenoceptors stimulate adenylyl cyclase and enhance the formation of cAMP. In contrast, α_2-receptors operate in a manner similar to that of D_2 receptors. That is, α_2-receptors reduce the rate of cAMP synthesis by inhibiting adenylyl cyclase, and they can also cause hyperpolarization of the cell membrane by increasing K^+ channel opening. Yet another kind of mechanism is used by receptors of the α_1 subtype. These receptors operate through the phosphoinositide second-messenger system, which, as we saw in Chapter 3, leads to an increased concentration of free calcium (Ca^{2+}) ions within the postsynaptic cell. The α_2-receptor subtype has a higher affinity for NE than the α_1-receptor subtype, the functional significance of which is discussed in the following section.

Drugs that stimulate autoreceptors, like the neurotransmitter itself, inhibit catecholamine release. In contrast, autoreceptor antagonists tend to enhance the rate of release by preventing the normal inhibitory effect of the autoreceptors. We can see these effects illustrated dramatically in the case of the noradrenergic α_2-autoreceptor system. Withdrawal from opioid drugs such as heroin and morphine activates the noradrenergic system, which is one of the factors leading to withdrawal symptoms such as increased heart rate, elevated blood pressure, and diarrhea. For this reason, α_2-agonists such as **clonidine (Catapres)** and more recently **lofexidine (Lucemyra)** are sometimes used to treat the symptoms of opioid withdrawal because of their ability to stimulate the autoreceptors and inhibit noradrenergic cell firing. In contrast, experimental administration of the α_2-antagonist **yohimbine**, which blocks the autoreceptors and thus increases noradrenergic cell firing and NE release, was found to provoke withdrawal symptoms and drug craving in opioid-dependent patients (Stine et al., 2002). Norepinephrine may also be involved in producing feelings of anxiety, especially in patients suffering from a mental illness called *panic disorder* (see Chapter 17). But even in healthy individuals, pharmacological manipulation of the noradrenergic system has predicted effects on anxiety-related responses. This was documented in a study by Biedermann and coworkers (2017), who tested people in a humanized version of the elevated plus-maze test of anxiety (see Chapter 4) using a mixed reality procedure (a combination of real-world and virtual elements) (**FIGURE 5.16A**). This testing caused increases in subjective feelings of anxiety, autonomic nervous system activity (i.e., heart rate, respiration rate, and skin conductance), and release of the stress hormone cortisol. Importantly for the present discussion, the amount of time spent on the open arms (an inverse measure of anxious behavior) was significantly reduced by yohimbine but increased by the antianxiety GABAergic drug lorazepam compared to placebo administration (**FIGURE 5.16B**).

The central noradrenergic system plays a significant role in arousal, cognition, and the consolidation of emotional memories

Neurochemical, pharmacological, and electrophysiological studies in experimental animals indicate that the central noradrenergic system is involved in a large number of behavioral functions, only some of which can be discussed here because of space limitations. We have already presented some evidence for an involvement of the noradrenergic system in anxiety. In this section, we focus on the role of NE in arousal, cognition, and the consolidation of memories of emotional experiences. Later chapters will present evidence for noradrenergic dysregulation in various psychiatric disorders, particularly mood and anxiety disorders.

A large body of literature has demonstrated that the firing of LC noradrenergic neurons and the activation of adrenergic receptors in the forebrain are important for both behavioral and electrophysiological (i.e., EEG)

(A)

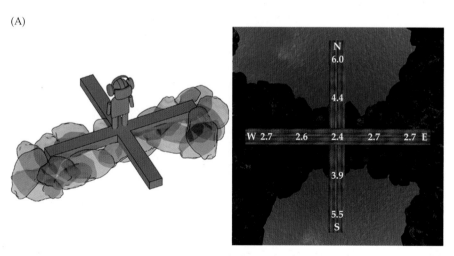

(B)

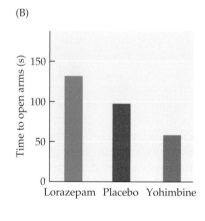

FIGURE 5.16 Effects of pro- and anti-anxiety drugs on open-arm time in the humanized elevated plus-maze Healthy men and women (age 18–50 years) were tested for the amount of time spent in the open arms of a humanized version of the elevated plus-maze test of anxiety-like behavior. (A) The maze consisted of a wooden platform with arm dimensions of 30 cm width, 175 cm length, and 20 cm height, placed on the floor of the laboratory (left). During testing, the participants found themselves in a virtual reality consisting of a mountainous environment in which the "closed" arms (oriented E–W) appeared to be surrounded by rocks, whereas the "open" arms (oriented N–S) appeared to reach out over water that was placed visually about 55 m below (right). Note that the rocks depicted on the left-hand diagram were only visible in the virtual environment. Participants were permitted to physically explore the simulated environment and spend time in the open or closed arms for a total of 300 s. The numbers shown on the arms are the mean reported anxiety levels (on a 0–9 scale with 9 representing very strong anxiety) at each position on the maze. (B) Administration of the α_2-adrenoceptor antagonist yohimbine significantly reduced the amount of time spent in the open arms compared to placebo (indicating increased anxious behavior), whereas the antianxiety GABAergic drug lorazepam significantly increased the amount of time spent in the open arms. (From S. V. Biedermann et al. 2017. *BMC Biol* 15: 125/ CC BY 4.0, https://creativecommons.org/licenses/by/4.0/)

arousal* (España et al., 2016). One of the earliest indications of this relationship comes from studies in the 1970s and 1980s showing that LC neurons fire more rapidly during waking than during sleep and that changes in the firing of these cells come *before* the transition between these behavioral states. The ability of LC noradrenergic neurons to trigger arousal was further supported by the demonstration that selective stimulation of these cells at the right frequency caused sleeping mice to awaken, whereas inhibition of the cells reduced wakefulness in the animals (Carter et al., 2010). Projections from the LC to the medial septal, medial preoptic, and lateral hypothalamic areas have been implicated in the wakefulness-promoting effects of NE (España et al., 2016). In one experiment, for example, researchers microinjected the α_1-receptor agonist **phenylephrine** and/ or the general β-receptor agonist **isoproterenol** directly into the lateral hypothalamic area of rats (Schmeichel and Berridge, 2013). The animals were then monitored to determine the amount of time they spent awake or asleep. As illustrated in **FIGURE 5.17A**, phenylephrine infusion dose-dependently increased the amount of time spent awake. The infusion also reduced the amount of time spent in both slow-wave and REM sleep (data not shown). Isoproterenol caused a much weaker response, with a modest increase in waking and a reduction in REM but not slow-wave sleep

---

*During states of drowsiness and slow-wave sleep, EEG measurements taken from the cortex show a predominant pattern of slow, high-voltage, synchronized wave forms. During a state of aroused wakefulness, the cortical EEG instead shows a predominance of fast, low-voltage, desynchronized waves.

(**FIGURE 5.17B**). Interestingly, combined treatment with low doses of the two compounds produced an additive effect on waking (**FIGURE 5.17C**). These results show that in the lateral hypothalamic area, α_1-receptors play the most important role in NE-mediated arousal and wakefulness, although β-receptor activation can add to the effects of moderate α_1-receptor stimulation.

In Chapter 3, we described the presence of orexin neurons in the lateral hypothalamic area that represent another cluster of cells that can exert a powerful arousing effect. This raises the possibility that the mutual arousing properties of orexin and noradrenergic neurons could involve an interaction between these cell groups. Based on the fact that noradrenergic agonists infused into the lateral hypothalamic area cause rapid arousal, it seems logical that NE might produce its effects by activating the orexin cells. However, not only is this *not* the case (Schmeichel and Berridge, 2013), but the functionally important connection is also in the opposite direction. Carter and coworkers (2013) reviewed evidence that orexin works, at least in part, by activating LC noradrenergic neurons. The key finding in that research is that inhibition of the LC prevented the wakefulness-promoting effects of stimulating the orexin neurons. In summary, the combined findings from these studies on NE and orexin have revealed part of an intricate circuit that is critically important for transitioning from sleep to wakefulness and for the maintenance of an appropriate state of arousal when interacting with the environment.

Another brain area to which the LC projects is the PFC, which expresses α_1-, α_2-, and β-adrenoceptors. We

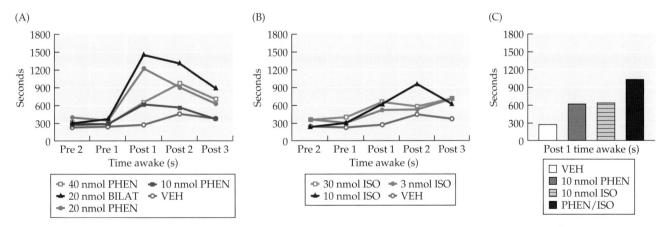

FIGURE 5.17 **Wakefulness-promoting effects of adrenergic agonists infused into the lateral hypothalamic area** Rats were given infusions of varying doses of the α_1-agonist phenylephrine (PHEN) and/or the β-agonist isoproterenol (ISO) directly into the lateral hypothalamic area. Control injections were of the vehicle (VEH) used to dissolve the active drugs. Behavioral state (awake or asleep) was determined for two 30-minute intervals prior to drug administration (Pre 1 and Pre 2) as well as three 30-minute postdrug intervals (Post 1, Post 2, and Post 3). All animals received unilateral infusions except for one group denoted as BILAT. (A) Infusions of PHEN alone markedly increased the amount of time spent awake, with the largest effect seen in the 20-nanomole (20 nmol) BILAT group. (B) Infusions of ISO alone exerted a modest effect on time spent awake, with a significant increase only seen in the 30 nmol ISO group. (C) Infusions of 10 nmol PHEN or ISO individually produced nonsignificant increases in time spent awake; however, infusion of both drugs together at the same doses produced a larger, statistically significant increase in waking time. (From B. E. Schmeichel and C. W. Berridge. 2013. *Eur J Neurosci* 37: 891–900.)

mentioned earlier that the mesocortical dopaminergic projection to the PFC is important for attention and working memory, and the same is true for the noradrenergic input to this region (Chamberlain and Robbins, 2013; Clark and Noudoost, 2014). The relationship between NE release in the PFC and cognitive function can be described as an inverted U-shaped function in which the optimal amount of release is neither too low nor too high. Abnormally low release that is caused, for example, by damage to the LC noradrenergic neurons or administration of drugs that suppress LC neuronal firing leads to behavioral sedation (loss of NE-mediated arousal) and poor cognitive function. Cognition is also impaired by excessive noradrenergic activity that can be caused by stress or by high doses of adrenergic agonist drugs.

The facilitatory effects on PFC-related cognitive processes are mediated primarily by activation of α_2-receptors. Thus, administration of a selective α_2-receptor agonist such as clonidine or **guanfacine** has been shown to enhance working memory under a variety of conditions, including animals with NE depletion, aged animals that suffer from a natural reduction in catecholamine levels, and animals tested under particularly demanding task conditions (Ramos and Arnsten, 2007; Arnsten, 2011). **FIGURE 5.18** presents an example of the facilitating effects of guanfacine (GFC) in a study of working memory in aged monkeys. The study used a two-choice spatial delayed response task in which monkeys observed the experimenter placing a food treat into one of two food wells, after which the wells were covered and a screen was imposed between the wells and the animal for a variable length of time (i.e., a delay). After the delay, the monkeys were permitted access to the wells but had to remember which well contained the treat in order to make the correct response and receive the reward. The animals typically perform quite well when the delay is very short (under

10 seconds), but their performance declines at longer delays. Just like humans, aged monkeys perform more poorly on this task than young monkeys; that is, older monkeys are more severely affected by increasing delay length. Moreover, task difficulty can be increased further by imposing "distracter" stimuli during the delay period on some trials. The figure illustrates the decline in task performance produced by the distracters and the ability of guanfacine to enhance working memory, thereby restoring performance on the task. These and other findings have led to the clinical use of guanfacine (trade name **Intuniv**) to treat ADHD, a disorder thought to involve abnormal PFC functioning (Arnsten and Jin, 2012; Connor et al., 2014).

In contrast to the facilitative effects of α_2-receptors, pharmacological activation of α_1-receptors in the PFC has a deleterious effect on cognitive functions mediated by this brain area (Berridge and Spencer, 2016). These differing effects raise the question of how an organism's own NE might regulate PFC functioning. The answer lies in the previously mentioned difference in NE affinity between α_2- and α_1-receptors. Several researchers have proposed that NE facilitates PFC functioning and PFC-dependent cognitive tasks under normal (i.e., nonstressful) conditions mainly by activating the high-affinity α_2-adrenoceptors in this brain area (Ramos and Arnsten, 2007; Berridge and Spencer, 2016). On the other hand, the heightened release of NE associated with stress would increase the amount of α_1-adrenoceptor activation, which presumably overrides the beneficial effects of the α_2-receptors and leads to cognitive impairment. **FIGURE 5.19** illustrates this hypothesis, which predicts that cognitive functions such as working memory function are optimized at intermediate levels of PFC noradrenergic activity.

Earlier in this chapter we noted that psychostimulants like amphetamine and methylphenidate enhance

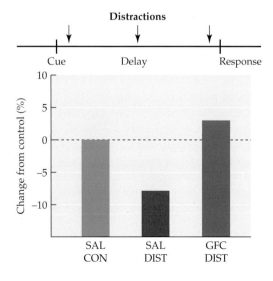

FIGURE 5.18 Guanfacine facilitation of working memory in aged monkeys Working memory was tested in aged rhesus monkeys using a two-choice spatial delayed response task. This task requires that the animals remember the location of a food treat with a delay period interposed between presentation of the treat and the opportunity to make a response. Distracting stimuli can be presented during the delay period to determine their influence on response accuracy. The first two bars demonstrate that in monkeys given saline vehicle (SAL), distracters impaired working memory performance (SAL/DIST) compared to the no-distracter control condition (SAL/CON). The third bar shows that guanfacine administration abolished the deleterious effect of the distracters (GFC/DIST) and returned performance to the control condition or slightly better. (From A. F. T. Arnsten and L. E. Jin. 2012. *Yale J Biol Med* 85: 45–58.)

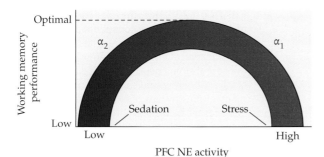

FIGURE 5.19 Modulation of arousal and working memory by adrenergic receptor subtypes in the prefrontal cortex
The figure depicts an inverted U-shaped curve relating arousal and working memory function to noradrenergic activity in the prefrontal cortex (PFC). Activation of high-affinity α_2-adrenoceptors increases arousal and facilitates working memory, whereas activation of lower-affinity α_1-receptors has the opposite effect. Consequently, abnormally low levels of noradrenergic activity in the PFC, which can be caused by certain drugs or by locus coeruleus lesions, result in behavioral sedation and impaired working memory. These effects are due to understimulation of α_2-adrenoceptors, since they can be reversed by selective activation of this receptor subtype. On the other hand, abnormally high levels of noradrenergic activity in the PFC, which can be caused by stress, activate the α_1-receptors and result in memory impairment. Optimal working memory is, therefore, predicted to occur at intermediate levels of PFC noradrenergic activity. (After C. W. Berridge and R. C. Spencer. 2016. *Brain Res* 1641: 189–196. © 2015. Reprinted with permission from Elsevier, and C. Berridge et al. 2012. In *Translational Neuroscience: Applications in Psychiatry, Neurology and Neurodevelopmental Disorders*, J. E. Barrett, J. T. Coyle, and M. Williams [Eds.] pp. 303–320. Cambridge University Press: Cambridge, UK.)

catecholaminergic activity. At appropriate doses, these compounds also increase performance on certain cognitive tasks (see Chapter 12). Although the pro-cognitive effects of psychostimulants are most commonly attributed to their dopaminergic actions in the PFC, some researchers have suggested that facilitation of noradrenergic activity in the PFC as well as in sensory processing areas additionally contributes to psychostimulant-induced cognitive enhancement (Spencer et al., 2015; Navarra and Waterhouse, 2019).

In a recent review of emotional memory recollection, Clewitt and Murty (2019) state, "Emotional events are resistant to forgetting and are vividly remembered … This privileged status of emotional experiences in memory is highly adaptive, because it promotes future behaviors that help us avoid threat and maximize well-being" (p. 1). Is there something special about how emotional events are stored in memory that makes them so long-lasting? Studies conducted mainly with laboratory animals suggest that this may, indeed, be the case. Such studies, which take advantage of arousal-inducing learning tasks, have yielded

strong evidence for an involvement of NE, EPI, and glucocorticoid hormones in the consolidation of emotional memories. One type of task often used to study the mechanisms of emotional memory consolidation is the one-trial **passive avoidance learning** paradigm (sometimes also called *inhibitory avoidance learning*). This paradigm uses a two-chamber apparatus with one side brightly lit and the other side dark. The two sides are separated by a partition with an opening in it to allow passage of the animal. For the training (learning) trial, a rat or a mouse is first placed in the brightly lit side, which is naturally aversive to the animal. However, when the subject spontaneously moves from the lit to the dark side, it receives a foot shock on the dark side. This single experience is sufficient to produce long-lasting avoidance of the dark side, which is typically measured on a test trial one or more days after the learning. The memory of the event is quantified by measuring the increased length of time (latency) that it takes for a trained animal to move from the lit to the dark side compared to unshocked controls. A major advantage of such a one-trial learning paradigm is that memory consolidation (i.e., transfer of information from short-term to long-term memory) for the task occurs entirely during the single period of time after the learning trial. Another feature of this paradigm is that the foot shock induces a certain amount of fear and stress in the animals and thus can be considered a paradigm for emotional learning.

The stress associated with one-trial passive avoidance learning is well known to produce increased EPI and glucocorticoid secretion from the adrenal glands (see Chapter 3), as well as activation of central LC noradrenergic neurons and increased release of NE. Circulating EPI doesn't readily cross the blood–brain barrier; therefore, it must initially act peripherally to alter central nervous system functioning. Current evidence suggests that bloodborne EPI stimulates the vagus nerve, which subsequently activates LC noradrenergic neurons through a multi-synaptic brainstem pathway (LaLumiere et al., 2017). At the same time, glucocorticoids like corticosterone in rodents or cortisol in humans readily cross the blood–brain barrier and passively diffuse into all parts of the brain.

The proposed neural circuit underlying consolidation of emotional memories is depicted in **FIGURE 5.20**. A key brain structure where information about the arousing task is modulated by EPI, NE (through the action of EPI), and glucocorticoids is the basolateral amygdala (BLA). BLA neurons have extensive projections to several other key subcortical structures, notably the hippocampus, caudate nucleus, and nucleus accumbens, as well as projections directly to cortical regions where memories are ultimately stored. Note also that glucocorticoids can additionally modulate

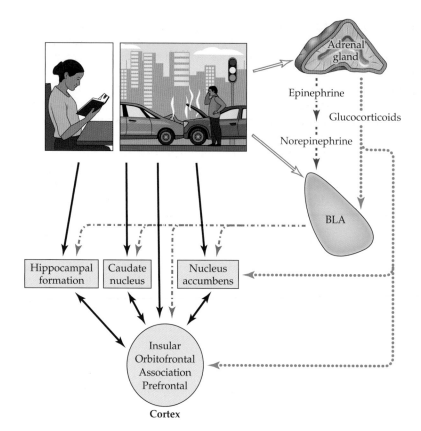

FIGURE 5.20 **Hypothesized mechanism of emotional memory consolidation** Studies primarily using laboratory animals suggest that consolidation of emotional memories involves the neural circuit depicted in the diagram. The black solid arrows indicate that learned information from any type of event (arousing or not) is processed by various parts of the circuit, depending on the kind of learning involved. If, however, the event is emotionally arousing, it additionally elicits activation of the basolateral amygdala (BLA) and increased release of epinephrine and glucocorticoids (corticosterone in rodents, cortisol in humans) from the adrenal glands (blue open arrows). Epinephrine acts at a peripheral site to signal release of NE by LC noradrenergic fibers terminating in the BLA (red dashed arrows). Glucocorticoids freely enter the brain to coordinate with NE in the BLA and to additionally modulate information processing in other brain areas shown in the diagram (green dotted arrows). Lastly, projections from the BLA to the memory-processing system (purple dash-dotted arrows) strengthen the consolidation process, resulting in longer-lasting and more vivid recall of the emotional event. (After R. T. LaLumiere et al. 2017. *Pharmacol Rev* 69: 236–255. © 2017 by The American Society for Pharmacology and Experimental Therapeutics.)

memory processing in some other parts of the circuit due to the presence of glucocorticoid receptors in these brain areas. The BLA and other parts of the amygdala play an important role not only in the learning of passive avoidance tasks but also in other types of fear conditioning. This raises the important question of whether the emotional memory circuit depicted in the figure only pertains to situations that elicit the high level of arousal produced by foot shock or equivalent kinds of fear/anxiety-evoking stimuli. Some findings indicate that the BLA circuit may participate in memory consolidation of tasks eliciting somewhat lower levels of arousal (LaLumiere et al., 2017). Nevertheless, we do not yet know whether this circuit plays a role in memory consolidation under very low arousal conditions.

Several medications work by stimulating or inhibiting peripheral adrenergic receptors

Adrenergic agonists or antagonists are frequently used in the treatment of nonpsychiatric medical conditions because of the widespread distribution and important functional role of adrenergic receptors in various peripheral organs (**TABLE 5.2**). For example, general adrenergic agonists that activate both α- and β-receptors have sometimes been used in the treatment of bronchial asthma. Stimulating the α-receptors causes constriction of the blood

vessels in the bronchial lining, thus reducing congestion and edema (tissue swelling) by restricting blood flow to the tissue. On the other hand, β-receptor stimulation leads to relaxation of the bronchial muscles, thereby providing a wider airway. Although general adrenergic agonists can be effective antiasthma medications, they

TABLE 5.2 **Location and Physiological Actions of Peripheral α- and β-Adrenergic Receptors**

Location	Action	Receptor subtype
Heart	Increased rate and force of contraction	β
Blood vessels	Constriction Dilation	α β
Smooth muscle of the trachea and bronchi	Relaxation	β
Uterine smooth muscle	Contraction	α
Bladder	Contraction Relaxation	α β
Spleen	Contraction Relaxation	α β
Iris	Pupil dilation	α
Adipose (fat) tissue	Increased fat breakdown and release	β

also cause several adverse side effects. For this reason, asthma and chronic obstructive pulmonary disease (COPD) are more commonly treated with a selective β_2-adrenoceptor agonist. Several such medications are available by prescription, including **albuterol (Ventolin)** and **levalbuterol (Xopenex)**. These drugs are packaged in an inhaler that delivers the compound directly to the respiratory system. The β-receptors found in the airways are of the β_2 subtype, in contrast to the heart, which contains mainly β_1-receptors. Consequently, albuterol and levalbuterol are effective in alleviating bronchial congestion of patients with asthma and COPD without producing adverse cardiovascular effects. However, these particular drugs are short-acting and, therefore, only recommended for acute symptom relief. Longer-acting compounds are required for alleviation of chronic asthma and COPD symptoms.

Even over-the-counter cold medications are based on the properties of peripheral adrenergic receptors.

Thus, the α_1-receptor agonist phenylephrine is the key ingredient in several decongestant medications available in most pharmacies. This compound, which may be taken either in tablet form or in a nasal spray, constricts the blood vessels and reduces inflamed and swollen nasal membranes resulting from colds and allergies. In the form of eye drops, it is also used to stimulate α-receptors of the iris to dilate the pupil during eye examinations or before surgery of the eyes.

Alpha$_2$-receptor agonists such as clonidine are commonly used in the treatment of hypertension (high blood pressure). The therapeutic benefit of these drugs is a result of their ability to inhibit activity of the sympathetic nervous system while stimulating the parasympathetic system. The consequence of these actions is to reduce the patient's heart rate and blood pressure. Unfortunately, sedation and feelings of sleepiness are common side effects of clonidine treatment. On the other hand, these effects and others have

TABLE 5.3   Drugs That Affect the Noradrenergic System

Drug	Mechanism of action	Clinical, recreational, or experimental use
Phenelzine and tranylcypromine	Nonselective MAO inhibitors	Antidepressant medications
Moclobemide	Selective MAO-A inhibitor	Antidepressant medication
α-Methyl-*para*-tyrosine (AMPT)	Tyrosine hydroxylase inhibitor	Experimental use
Reserpine	Irreversible VMAT inhibitor	Experimental use
Amphetamine*	Catecholamine releaser and reuptake blocker	Treatment for ADHD and recreational use
Cocaine*	Catecholamine reuptake blocker	Recreational use and occasional medical use as a local anesthetic
Methylphenidate*	Catecholamine reuptake blocker	Treatment for ADHD and recreational use
Atomoxetine	Selective norepinephrine (NE) reuptake blocker	Treatment for ADHD
Reboxetine	Selective NE reuptake blocker	Antidepressant medication
Phenylephrine	α_1-Receptor agonist	Decongestant medication
Midodrine and metaraminol	α_1-Receptor agonists	Treatments for hypotension
Clonidine and lofexidine	α_2-Receptor agonists	Treatments for opioid withdrawal
Guanfacine	α_2-Receptor agonist	Treatment for ADHD
Dexmedetomidine	α_2-Receptor agonist	Combined sedative, anxiolytic, and analgesic medication
Isoproterenol	Nonselective β-receptor agonist	Treatment for bradycardia
Albuterol and levalbuterol	Selective β_2-receptor agonists	Treatments for asthma and COPD
Prazosin	α1-Receptor antagonist	Treatment for hypertension
Yohimbine	α2-Receptor antagonist	Treatment for male impotence
Propranolol	Nonselective β-receptor antagonist	Treatment for hypertension
Metoprolol	Selective β1-receptor antagonist	Treatment for hypertension

The table shows instances in which multiple drugs have similar mechanisms of action but only some are used clinically or clinical uses vary between drugs. Compounds with a similar primary mechanism can differ in several ways that influence their clinical applications, including (1) side effects and patient tolerability, (2) pharmacokinetics (i.e., rates of drug absorption and/or metabolism), (3) suitability for the desired route of administration, (4) additional mechanisms of action not shown in the table, and (5) potential for abuse.

* These drugs are not selective for catecholamines, as they also affect serotonin release or reuptake.

been exploited therapeutically with the development of **dexmedetomidine (Precedex)**, an α_2-agonist with combined sedative, anxiolytic (antianxiety), and analgesic (pain-reducing) effects that is particularly useful for surgical patients in the intensive care unit. The sedative and anxiolytic effects of dexmedetomidine are believed to be mediated by α_2-autoreceptors in the LC, whereas the analgesic effect probably occurs at the level of the spinal cord.

Adrenergic receptor antagonists likewise have varied clinical uses. For example, the general β-receptor agonist isoproterenol (**Isuprel**) is sometimes used to treat conditions involving bradycardia (abnormally slow heart rate). In contrast, the α_2-antagonist yohimbine (**Yocon**) helps in the treatment of certain types of male sexual impotence. This compound increases parasympathetic and decreases sympathetic activity, which is thought to stimulate penile blood inflow and/or to inhibit blood outflow.

The α_1-antagonist **prazosin (Minipress)** and the general β-adrenoceptor antagonist **propranolol (Inderal)** are both used clinically in the treatment of hypertension. Prazosin causes dilation of blood vessels by blocking the α_1-receptors responsible for constricting these vessels. In contrast, the main function of propranolol is to block the β-receptors in the heart, thereby reducing the heart's contractile force. The discovery that β_1 is the major adrenoceptor subtype in the heart has led to the introduction of β_1-selective antagonists such as **metoprolol (Lopressor)**. These compounds exhibit fewer side effects than the more general β-antagonist propranolol. Beta-receptor antagonists like propranolol and metoprolol are also useful in the treatment of cardiac arrhythmia (irregular heartbeat) and angina pectoris (feelings of pain and constriction around the heart caused by deficient blood flow and oxygen delivery to the heart). In situations where hypotension (low blood pressure) instead of hypertension is a problem, an α_1-agonist may be used to increase vascular constriction. For example, **midodrine (ProAmatine)** is prescribed for patients with orthostatic hypotension (a potentially dangerous drop in blood pressure when standing up after being in a sitting or supine position), whereas **metaraminol (Aramine)** is used to treat hypotension caused by spinal anesthesia.

Finally, it should be mentioned that propranolol and other β-antagonists have also been applied to the treatment of generalized anxiety disorder, which is one of the most common types of anxiety disorder (see Chapter 17). Many patients with generalized anxiety disorder suffer from physical symptoms such as palpitations, flushing, and tachycardia (racing heart). Beta-blockers do not alleviate anxiety per se, but instead they may help the patient feel better by reducing some of these distressing physical symptoms of the

disorder. **TABLE 5.3** presents a list of drugs that affect the noradrenergic system and their primary use clinically, recreationally, or experimentally.

SECTION SUMMARY

- The most important cluster of noradrenergic neurons is the A6 cell group, which is located in a region known as the locus coeruleus. These neurons innervate almost all areas of the forebrain as well as the cerebellum and spinal cord.

- NE and EPI released into the bloodstream as hormones work together with NE released from sympathetic neurons to mediate the physiological reactions that make up the "fight-or-flight" response. These reactions include (1) vascular changes that direct more blood flow to skeletal muscles, heart, and brain; (2) increases in blood pressure, heart rate, and cardiac muscle contractile force; (3) respiratory changes that produce increased oxygen intake; (4) reduced digestive activity; (5) pupil dilation; (6) increased availability of metabolic fuels due to liberation of sugar from the liver and fats from adipose tissue; and (7) decreased secretion of gastric juices and saliva.

- NE and EPI activate a group of metabotropic receptors called adrenoceptors. They are divided into two broad families, α and β, which are further subdivided into α_1, α_2, β_1, and β_2. Both β-receptor subtypes enhance the synthesis of cAMP, whereas α_2-receptors inhibit cAMP formation.

- Another mechanism of action of α_2-receptors involves hyperpolarization of the cell membrane by stimulating K^+ channel opening. In contrast, α_1-receptors increase the intracellular concentration of Ca^{2+} ions by means of the phosphoinositide second-messenger system.

- The effects of drugs acting on inhibitory α_2-autoreceptors reveal a significant role for NE in drug withdrawal and anxiety. Autoreceptor activation by an α_2-agonist (which reduces noradrenergic cell firing) can help reduce withdrawal symptoms in physically dependent drug users, whereas an α_2-antagonist (which stimulates firing of these cells) can provoke withdrawal symptoms and can also increase anxiety in healthy nondependent individuals.

- The noradrenergic system is involved in many behavioral functions, including arousal, cognition, and the consolidation of emotional memories (e.g., related to fear-inducing situations).

- The arousal- and wakefulness-promoting effects of NE are primarily mediated by pathways from the LC to the medial septal, medial preoptic, and lateral hypothalamic areas. Both α_1- and β-receptors are involved in these effects. LC neurons constitute one of the components of an arousal circuit that also includes orexin cells of the lateral hypothalamic area.

- The cognitive-enhancing effects of NE (e.g., on attention and working memory) are mediated by activation of high-affinity α_2-adrenoceptors in the PFC. Activation of lower-affinity α_1-receptors has the opposite effect, namely a decrease in cognitive function. Consequently, the relationship between NE release in the PFC and cognition can be described as an inverted U-shaped function: optimal cognitive function occurs at moderate amounts of NE release, whereas either too little or too much release can cause cognitive impairment.

- The facilitatory effects of α_2-adrenoceptors on cognition has led to the use of the α_2-agonist guanfacine for the treatment of ADHD.

- The vivid recall of emotional events is believed to depend on the arousal-mediated release of EPI and glucocorticoids from the adrenal glands. Because EPI does not cross the blood–brain barrier, its role in emotional memory consolidation involves stimulation of NE release in the BLA, which is also a key site of glucocorticoid action. Output of the BLA to components of the memory consolidation circuitry would then be responsible for the added strength and longevity of the memories of emotionally evocative events.

- Adrenergic agonists are used therapeutically for a variety of physiological and psychological disorders. These include β_2-agonists for producing bronchodilation in patients with asthma and COPD; the α_1-agonist phenylephrine for relief of nasal congestion; other α_1-agonists for the treatment of hypotensive conditions; and several compounds for relief of hypertension, including the α_2-agonist clonidine, the α_1-antagonist prazosin, and the β_1-antagonist metoprolol. Each of these latter medications reduces blood pressure through a different site of action.

STUDY QUESTIONS

1. Which neurotransmitters make up the category called catecholamines? What are the distinguishing chemical features of this category?

2. Describe the steps involved in the biosynthesis of dopamine and norepinephrine. Name the enzyme that catalyzes each biochemical reaction, and indicate which reaction is the rate-limiting step in catecholamine synthesis.

3. (a) How is the rate of catecholamine regulated? (b) Why is precursor administration more effective in enhancing catecholamine functionality under conditions of high neurotransmitter demand?

4. List the names of the proteins that transport catecholamines into synaptic vesicles. Which of these proteins is expressed in the brain, and which is expressed in the adrenal medulla?

5. Reversible inhibitors of catecholamine vesicular uptake have therapeutic applications, whereas irreversible inhibitors do not. Explain why this is the case.

6. How do amphetamine and methamphetamine affect catecholamine release, and what are the behavioral effects of these drugs in laboratory rats and mice?

7. Describe how catecholamine release is regulated by autoreceptors, including differences in the location and mechanism of action of terminal versus somatodendritic autoreceptors.

8. What is meant by single-spiking versus burst firing mode as applied to the firing patterns of midbrain dopaminergic neurons? Single-spiking mode leads to _____ DA release, whereas _____ DA release occurs when the neurons are firing in burst mode.

9. Define the term "varicosities" as applied to catecholaminergic axons.

10. What are the two basic mechanisms by which catecholamine transmission is terminated?

11. Describe the effect of blocking DA or NE reuptake on signaling by that transmitter.

12. What is the functional significance of the fact that the DA and NE transporter proteins are not selective for their respective neurotransmitters?

13. Monoamine oxidase (MAO), which is important for catecholamine metabolism, has two forms, designated _____ and _____. The form of the enzyme expressed by catecholamine neurons is _____, whereas the form expressed by non-catecholamine neurons and glial cells is _____.

14. Homovanillic acid (HVA) is the major metabolite of _____; 3-methoxy-4-hydroxy-phenylglycol (MHPG) and vanillylmandelic acid (VMA) are major metabolites of _____.

15. Name and discuss the clinical uses of drugs that alter either catecholamine reuptake or catecholamine metabolism.

16. Describe the three major dopaminergic pathways that originate in the midbrain and project to forebrain structures. Include in your answer the derivation of each one.

17. The midbrain dopaminergic cell groups have been shown to play important roles in motor function, motivation, and cognition. Much of this information has been obtained using either neurotoxins to damage/kill the cells or genetic engineering methods to produce a biochemical DA deficiency (i.e., DD mice). Compare and contrast these methodological approaches, and then discuss the behavioral characteristics of laboratory animals that have been generated using one or the other technique.

18. In humans, researchers can investigate the behavioral functions of DA by studying patients born with genetic mutations that interfere with DA synthesis. What are the typical symptoms observed in such patients, and how are these symptoms similar to or different from those observed in animal models of DA deficiency?

19. Dopaminergic neurons in the VTA play a role in responding to both reward and aversive stimuli. What features of these neurons make this dual function possible?

20. The dopaminergic input to the PFC helps regulate cognitive functions such as attention and working memory. How is this regulation influenced by genetic variation in the COMT gene?

21. How many different subtypes of DA receptors exist, and how are these subtypes grouped into families?

22. Comparing D1 to D2 receptors: (a) Which subtype stimulates and which inhibits cAMP synthesis? (b) Which subtype also signals by increasing K+ channel opening? (c) Which subtype has the higher affinity for DA, and what is the functional significance of this affinity difference?

23. Describe the behavioral effects of DA receptor agonists and antagonists and, where relevant, their clinical applications.

24. (a) Define behavioral supersensitivity. (b) In the case of D2 receptor supersensitivity, how is this phenomenon produced pharmacologically, and what is the hypothesized mechanism?

25. (a) Discuss the major sources of NE in the forebrain and in the peripheral nervous system. (b) What is the "fight-or-flight" response, and how do EPI and NE mediate this response?

26. List the adrenergic receptor subtypes and their respective signaling mechanisms.

27. What is the evidence for an involvement of the central noradrenergic system in arousal?

28. (a) Current evidence suggests that the relationship between noradrenergic activity in the PFC and cognitive function can be represented by an "inverted U-shaped relationship." What does this mean? (b) How does this inverted U-shaped relationship depend on the affinity for NE of different adrenergic receptor subtypes in the PFC?

29. Highly emotional events that we experience in our lives tend to be remembered more vividly and more persistently than non-emotional events. The difference in these memories is believed to depend on the increased arousal produced by emotional events. Describe the hypothesized mechanism underlying the enhanced consolidation of emotional memories, including the relevant neural circuitry and biochemical processes.

30. Peripheral adrenergic receptors are targeted by many different medications, a number of which help regulate the function of either the respiratory (e.g., asthma or COPD) or cardiovascular (hypertension or hypotension) system. For each of these systems, (a) list one or more medications used for treating abnormalities in that system, (b) identify the adrenergic receptor targeted by that medication and whether the medication is an agonist or antagonist, and (c) indicate the mechanism whereby activation or inhibition of that receptor helps normalize the functioning of the system in question.

Serotonin

THE PATIENT WAS A 29-YEAR-OLD MAN who was brought to the hospital's emergency department (ED) by friends after he had developed generalized tonic-clonic seizures 30 minutes earlier. This is the most serious kind of seizure, involving loss of conscious awareness, falling to the ground in a state of whole-body rigidity, and then repeated convulsing of the limbs. Examination of the patient revealed the following symptoms: extreme fever (43°C [109.4°F]), elevated heart rate (160 bpm), mottled skin, labored breathing, whole-body rigidity, and lack of responsiveness to stimulation (i.e., in a coma). The physicians administered sedative and paralytic medication so that they could intubate and ventilate the patient. They also began immediate actions to cool the patient by administering cold saline intravenous solution and applying ice packs all over his body. Further testing revealed additional problems, including acute kidney failure, which required dialysis treatment for an entire month. The patient was finally discharged from the hospital once his kidney function had normalized.

This real case report was published in 1999 by E. Connolly and G. O'Callaghan, two Australian physicians. What caused this nearly fatal set of symptoms? Friends who had accompanied the patient to the hospital revealed that he had consumed two ecstasy tablets along with alcohol approximately 12 hours before arriving at the ED, and had taken a third ecstasy tablet about 7 hours later. Although we cannot determine how the alcohol consumption may have contributed to the person's reaction, the symptoms described above are all characteristic of ecstasy toxicity. Such extreme toxic reactions to ecstasy are rare, but the case report illustrates the potential severity of such reactions, and not surprisingly, in some instances the ultimate outcome has been death.

This chapter opener is focused on ecstasy because this street drug is usually composed mainly of the compound **3,4-methylenedioxymethamphetamine (MDMA)**, which powerfully affects the neurotransmitter **serotonin** (more technically known as **5-hydroxytryptamine, or 5-HT**). Over the course of the chapter, we will explore the biochemistry of 5-HT, the anatomy and physiology of **serotonergic neurons** (neurons that use 5-HT as their transmitter), the projections of these neurons, the surprising variety

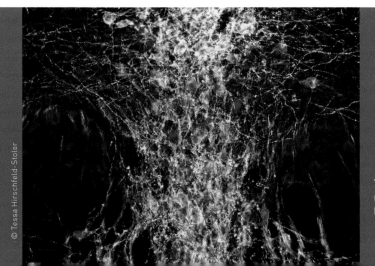

© Tessa Hirschfeld-Stoler

The serotonergic neurons of the dorsal raphe nucleus (shown here in pink) are located in the midbrain and send their axons to many forebrain areas.

of serotonergic receptors, and of course the mechanisms of action not only of MDMA but of other serotonergic drugs as well. We also consider several of the key behavioral and physiological functions of this important neurotransmitter. ■

6.1 Serotonin Synthesis, Release, and Inactivation

The level of serotonergic transmission depends on the relative contributions of synthesis, release, and inactivation of the transmitter.

Serotonin synthesis is regulated by enzymatic activity and precursor availability

Serotonin was discovered and first isolated not from the brain, but rather from its presence in the bloodstream and its ability to cause vasoconstriction (see Whitaker-Azmitia, 1999, and Göthert, 2013, for the history of serotonin's discovery). Indeed, the name *serotonin* is a combination of *sero*, referring to serum (the liquid that remains after blood has been allowed to clot), and *tonin*, referring to the substance's effect on vascular tone (contraction of smooth muscles that constrict blood vessels). Later in this chapter you will learn about the cells in the gut that are the source of bloodborne 5-HT.

Serotonin is synthesized from the amino acid **tryptophan**, which comes from protein in our diet. As shown in **FIGURE 6.1**, the biochemical pathway comprises two steps. The first step is catalyzed by the enzyme **tryptophan hydroxylase** (**TPH**), which converts tryptophan to **5-hydroxytryptophan** (**5-HTP**). 5-HTP is then acted upon by **aromatic amino acid decarboxylase** (**AADC**) to form 5-HT. In 2003, researchers discovered that there are two forms of the TPH gene, designated *TPH1* and *TPH2*. *TPH2* is expressed by serotonergic neurons, whereas *TPH1* is expressed by certain types of non-neuronal cells, including 5-HT–secreting enterochromaffin cells located in the gut and melatonin-secreting cells in the pineal gland.

Many features of the 5-HT synthesis pathway are similar to those of the pathway described in Chapter 5 involving the formation of dopamine (DA) from the amino acid tyrosine. Just as the initial step in the synthesis of DA (i.e., tyrosine to DOPA) is the rate-limiting step, the conversion of tryptophan to 5-HTP is rate limiting in the 5-HT pathway. Furthermore, just as tyrosine hydroxylase is found only in neurons that synthesize catecholamines, TPH in the brain is a specific marker for the serotonergic neurons. Another important point is that the second enzyme in the pathway, AADC, is the same for both catecholamines and 5-HT.

Throughout the remainder of this chapter, we will primarily be discussing TPH2 because of its localization

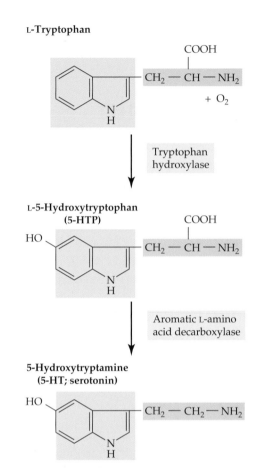

FIGURE 6.1 Synthesis of serotonin Serotonin (5-HT) is synthesized from the amino acid tryptophan in two steps, catalyzed by the enzymes tryptophan hydroxylase and aromatic amino acid decarboxylase.

in serotonergic neurons. However, before continuing, we will delve briefly into a clinical syndrome involving TPH1 and the recent development of a medication to treat that syndrome. Certain kinds of neuroendocrine tumors arise in the gut and metastasize to various internal organs. Such tumors secrete a variety of different signaling molecules and hormones, including 5-HT synthesized by TPH1. The clinical effects of these secretory products, called the **carcinoid syndrome**, include severe diarrhea and abdominal pain, weight loss, skin flushing, sweating, and wheezing (Matthes and Bader, 2018; Rendell, 2019). The patient is additionally at risk for developing abnormalities of the cardiac valves. Many of these symptoms, including valvular heart disease, can be linked directly to elevated blood levels of 5-HT produced by the tumor. The search for medications to treat carcinoid syndrome led to the development and licensing of **telotristat** (trade name **Xermelo**). Telotristat inhibits both TPH1 and TPH2, but unlike previously studied TPH inhibitors, *it does not cross the blood–brain barrier*, therefore depleting only peripheral 5-HT derived from TPH1.

TRYPTOPHAN METABOLIC PATHWAYS AND THEIR FUNCTIONAL CONSEQUENCES Tryptophan is among the nine essential amino acids for human beings. This means that because we lack the biochemical machinery needed to synthesize tryptophan, we must obtain it from our diet. Fortunately, people who are consuming adequate amounts of protein in their diet are probably ingesting more tryptophan than they actually need. When psychopharmacologists study the disposition of dietary tryptophan, they are usually interested in the conversion of this amino acid to 5-HT as described above. However, over 95% of ingested tryptophan is actually metabolized through a pathway that leads to a substance called **kynurenine** instead of 5-HT (Savitz, 2020). Because of the focus of the present chapter, we will first discuss the 5-HT–related biochemical and functional consequences of manipulating tryptophan availability. At the end of this section we will return to the kynurenine pathway of tryptophan metabolism.

Synthesis of 5-HT in the brains of animals can be stimulated by giving them large doses of tryptophan, but administration of 5-HTP is even more effective because it is converted rapidly and efficiently to 5-HT. There is also an interesting link between food intake and 5-HT synthesis that was first discovered many years ago by John Fernstrom and Richard Wurtman (1972). Imagine a group of rats that have been fasted overnight and then fed a protein-rich meal. The level of tryptophan in their blood goes up, and thus you probably would expect brain 5-HT levels to rise as well, since an injection of pure tryptophan produces such an effect. Surprisingly, however, Fernstrom and Wurtman found that consumption of a protein-rich meal did not cause increases in either tryptophan or 5-HT in the brain, even though tryptophan levels in the bloodstream were elevated. The researchers explained this result by showing that tryptophan competes with a group of other amino acids (called large neutral amino acids; LNAA) for transport from the blood to the brain across the blood–brain barrier (**FIGURE 6.2**). Consequently, it's the *ratio* between the amount of tryptophan in the blood and the overall amount of its competitors that counts. Most proteins contain larger amounts of these competitor amino acids than tryptophan; thus, when these proteins are consumed, the critical ratio either stays the same or even goes down.

Even more surprising was an additional finding by Fernstrom and Wurtman. When these researchers fed previously fasted rats a meal low in protein but high in carbohydrates, that experimental treatment led to increases in brain tryptophan and 5-HT levels. How can we explain this result? You might already know that eating carbohydrates (starches and sugars) triggers release of the hormone **insulin** from the pancreas. One important function of this insulin response is to

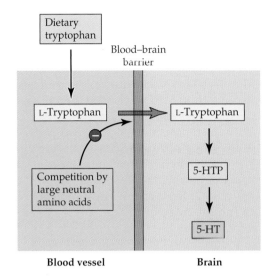

FIGURE 6.2 **Tryptophan entry into the brain and 5-HT synthesis** Transport and synthesis are regulated by the relative availability of tryptophan versus large neutral amino acids that compete with it for transport across the blood–brain barrier. In rats, a high-protein, low-carbohydrate meal does not increase brain tryptophan levels or 5-HT synthesis rate, because of this competitive process. However, the ratio of circulating tryptophan to large neutral amino acids is elevated after a high-carbohydrate, low-protein meal, thereby enhancing entry of tryptophan into the brain and stimulating 5-HT synthesis.

stimulate the uptake of glucose from the bloodstream into various tissues, where it can be metabolized for energy. But glucose is not the only substance acted upon by insulin. This hormone also stimulates the uptake of most amino acids from the bloodstream; tryptophan, however, is relatively unaffected. Because of this difference, a low-protein, high-carbohydrate meal will increase the tryptophan-to-LNAA ratio, allowing more tryptophan to cross the blood–brain barrier and more 5-HT to be made in the brain. Yet another nutrient-based method for increasing this ratio is to have subjects consume a diet enriched with high-tryptophan proteins such as the milk protein α-lactalbumin (Markus et al., 2000).

Pharmacological depletion of 5-HT has been widely used to assess the role of this neurotransmitter in various behavioral functions. One method often used in rodent studies consists of administering the drug *para*-**chlorophenylalanine** (**PCPA**), which selectively blocks 5-HT synthesis by irreversibly inhibiting TPH. One or two high doses of PCPA can reduce brain 5-HT levels in rats by 80% to 90% for as long as 2 weeks, until the serotonergic neurons make new TPH molecules that haven't been exposed to the inhibitor. Because PCPA can cause adverse side effects in humans, researchers have developed an alternative method for decreasing brain 5-HT in human studies. Based in part on the rat studies of Fernstrom and Wurtman, this method (termed **acute tryptophan depletion**, or **ATD**) involves the administration of an amino acid "cocktail" containing a large quantity of amino acids except for tryptophan. Ingestion of this cocktail causes large reductions in both plasma and cerebrospinal fluid (CSF) levels of tryptophan over a period of roughly 6 to 12 hours (reviewed by Hulsken et al., 2013). Tryptophan depletion occurs for two reasons: (1) the surge of amino acids in the bloodstream stimulates protein synthesis by the liver, which reduces the level of plasma tryptophan to below its starting point; and (2) the large neutral amino acids in the cocktail inhibit entry of the remaining tryptophan into the brain. Brain 5-HT synthesis and metabolism are also reduced by ATD, but at this time there is no consistent evidence for a corresponding reduction in 5-HT release. Indeed, some researchers have raised questions about the standard interpretation (i.e., reduced serotonergic transmission) of ATD-related findings, while others have defended this methodology. Interested readers are referred to the critical review by van Donkelaar and colleagues (2011) and the reply by Crockett and colleagues (2012).

Manipulation of tryptophan availability (and therefore brain 5-HT) has been used to assess the role of 5-HT in cognition, mood, and sleep. First we will discuss the results of increasing tryptophan availability by administration of pure tryptophan (sometimes called **tryptophan loading**), consumption of a diet supplemented with α-lactalbumin or other high-tryptophan proteins, or consumption of a diet rich in carbohydrates but low in protein. Overall, the findings are inconsistent across studies, which is probably related at least partly to differences in the method used to increase tryptophan and other elements of the experimental design. Nevertheless, elevating tryptophan availability has been shown to enhance cognitive functions such as memory or attention in a number of studies (Hulsken et al., 2013). Recent reviews conclude that dietary tryptophan supplementation can also lead to elevated mood (Layman et al., 2018; Kikuchi et al., 2020) and improved sleep (Layman et al., 2018; Binks et al., 2020). Later in the chapter we will discuss in greater detail the involvement of 5-HT in the sleep–wake cycle.

Quite a few studies have investigated the effects of reducing brain 5-HT using the ATD method. This procedure seems to impair memory consolidation of verbal information but has little or no influence on working memory or attention (Mendelsohn et al., 2009). Other studies found that ATD can induce a negative cognitive bias (Cools et al., 2007). This means that the individuals display increased sensitivity to threat- or punishment-related stimuli. Cools and colleagues (2007) further hypothesized that this effect is mediated by reducing serotonergic activity in an anxiety/fear-related circuit that includes the amygdala and medial frontal cortex. The role of 5-HT in anxiety is further discussed later in the chapter. Finally, examination of sleep parameters in people subjected to ATD found reduced sleep duration and quality (Binks et al., 2020). Taken together with the negative cognitive bias results, these findings complement those showing elevated mood and improved sleep after increased tryptophan consumption.

A different use of ATD has been to investigate its effects on patients diagnosed with major clinical depression. Two reviews found that patients with clinical depression who were taking an antidepressant that acts on the serotonergic system at the time of tryptophan depletion experienced a relapse in their symptoms (Ruhé et al., 2007; Hulsken et al., 2013). This effect was not seen in patients being treated with antidepressants that work on the noradrenergic instead of the serotonergic system (see Chapter 18 for a detailed discussion of the hypothesized roles of 5-HT and norepinephrine in the etiology of depression). A subsequent study compared the mood-altering effects of either 5-HT depletion (using the ATD method) or catecholamine depletion (using the tyrosine hydroxylase inhibitor α-methyl-*para*-tyrosine) in previously depressed patients who were in remission at the time of the study and not taking any antidepressant medication (Homan et al., 2015). The results were quite striking: on most measures of depressed mood, the effects of 5-HT depletion were much greater than those of catecholamine depletion, whereas the opposite was true for measures of anxiety. These findings suggest that abnormalities in the serotonergic versus the catecholaminergic systems may underlie different symptoms in patients with mood or anxiety disorders.

We close this section by returning briefly to the biochemical pathway by which tryptophan is metabolized to kynurenine rather than 5-HT. As illustrated in **FIGURE 6.3**, this reaction can be catalyzed by two different enzymes: indoleamine 2,3-dioxygenase (IDO), which is active in the brain and in cells of the immune system, or tryptophan dioxygenase (TDO), which is active in the liver. Once formed, kynurenine is metabolized further into a host of other substances that are the primary mediators of the kynurenine pathway. Of particular relevance clinically is that stress and inflammation both stimulate IDO activity, thereby increasing tryptophan processing through this pathway (O'Farrell and Harkin, 2017). Indeed, metabolites produced by the kynurenine pathway have been implicated in several psychiatric disorders (e.g., major depression and schizophrenia) and neurodegenerative diseases (e.g., Alzheimer's disease and Parkinson's disease). Readers interested in learning more about this area of research are referred to several excellent reviews (O'Farrell and Harkin, 2017; Arnone et al., 2018; Savitz, 2020).

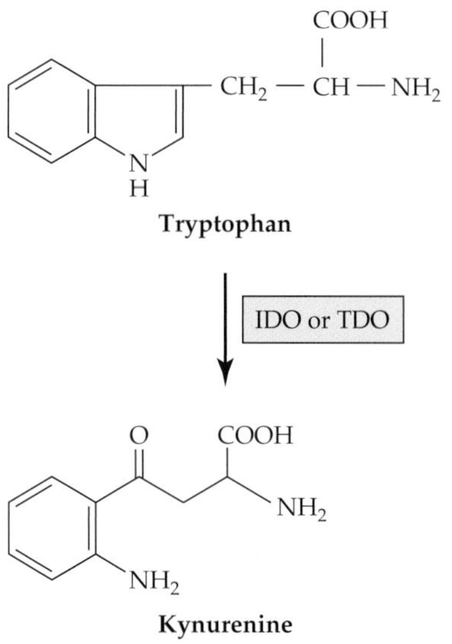

FIGURE 6.3 Conversion of tryptophan to kynurenine is catalyzed either by IDO (indoleamine 2,3-dioxygenase) or by TDO (tryptophan dioxygenase). (After M. S. Hamdy et al. 2012. *Catal Lett* 142: 338–344. doi.org/10.1007/s10562-012-0775-7. © The Authors 2012. CC BY 2.0, creativecommons.org/licenses/by/2.0/)

Similar processes regulate storage, release, and inactivation of serotonin and the catecholamines

The main features of a serotonergic neuron are depicted in **FIGURE 6.4**. Serotonin (5-HT) is transported into synaptic vesicles using vesicular monoamine transporter 2 (VMAT2), which is the same vesicular transporter found in dopaminergic and noradrenergic neurons. As with the catecholamines, storage of 5-HT in the vesicles plays a critical role in protecting the transmitter from enzymatic breakdown in the nerve terminal. Consequently, the VMAT blocker reserpine depletes serotonergic neurons of 5-HT, just as it depletes catecholamines in dopaminergic and noradrenergic cells.

Serotonergic autoreceptors control release of 5-HT in the same way as the DA and NE autoreceptors discussed in Chapter 5. Terminal autoreceptors directly inhibit 5-HT release, whereas other autoreceptors on the cell body and dendrites of the serotonergic neurons (somatodendritic autoreceptors) indirectly inhibit release by slowing the rate of firing of the neurons. Somatodendritic autoreceptors are of the 5-HT_{1A} subtype, whereas the terminal autoreceptors are of either the 5-HT_{1B} or 5-HT_{1D} subtype, depending on the species (see later discussion of 5-HT receptors). Although most serotonergic neurons express these somatodendritic autoreceptors, there is a small percentage that do not (Kiyasova et al., 2013). Furthermore, the autoreceptor-lacking neurons fire more rapidly than those with autoreceptors when stimulated electrically, perhaps due to the absence of the inhibitory effect conferred by somatodendritic autoreceptor activation.

Release of 5-HT can be directly stimulated by a family of drugs based on the structure of amphetamine. These compounds include *para*-**chloroamphetamine**, which can exert toxic effects on the serotonergic system at higher doses; **fenfluramine**, which at one time was prescribed for appetite suppression in obese patients but was later removed from clinical use; and MDMA, which was the topic of the chapter opener. **BOX 6.1** describes the discovery of MDMA, its emergence as a recreational drug, evidence for toxic effects on the serotonergic system, and lastly recent studies promoting its potential clinical uses.

When we examine the processes responsible for inactivation of 5-HT after its release, many similarities to the catecholamine systems become apparent. After 5-HT is released, it is removed from the extracellular fluid by a reuptake process. As with DA and NE, this mechanism involves a protein on the nerve

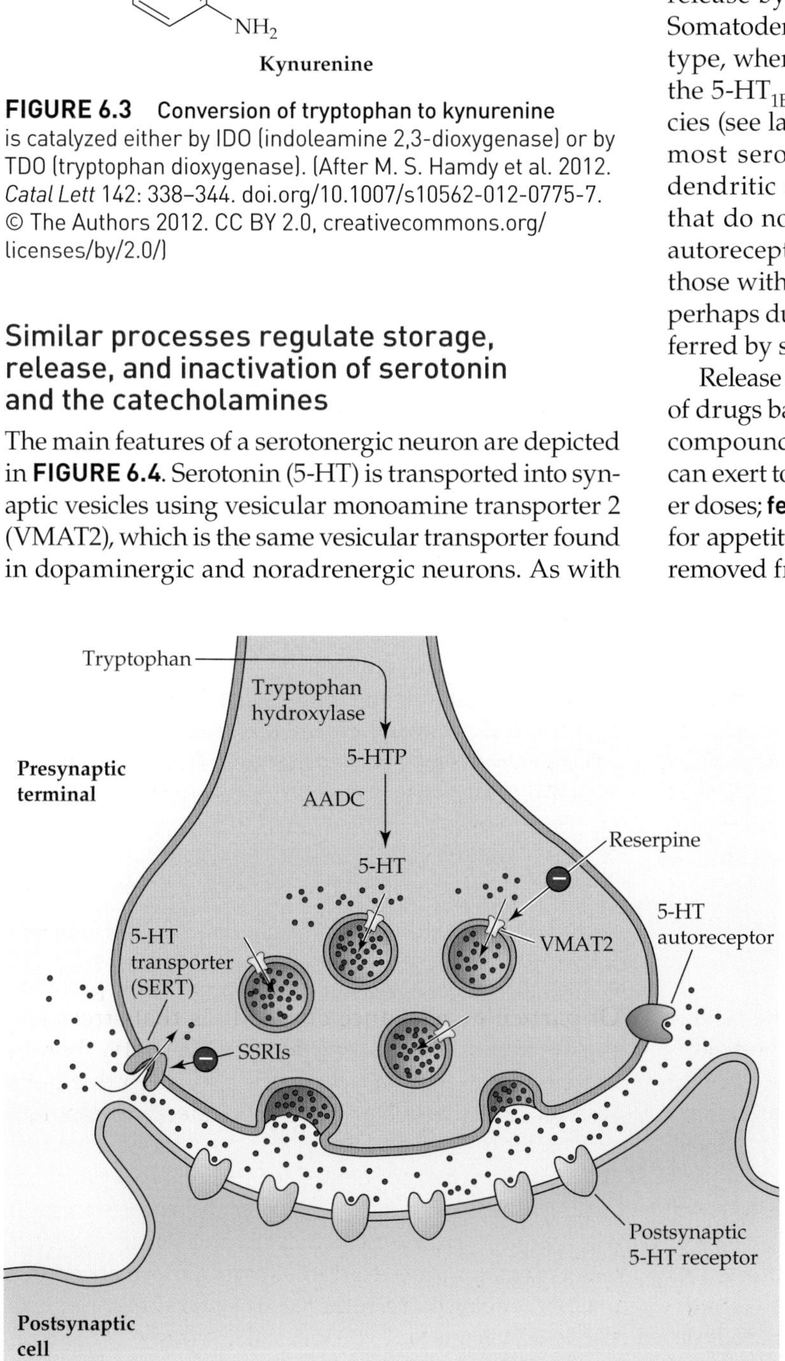

FIGURE 6.4 Features of a serotonergic neuron Serotonergic neurons express the enzymes tryptophan hydroxylase and aromatic L-amino acid decarboxylase (AADC), the vesicular monoamine transporter VMAT2, the 5-HT transporter (SERT), and 5-HT_{1B} or 5-HT_{1D} autoreceptors in their terminals. 5-HTP, 5-hydroxytryptophan; SSRIs, selective serotonin reuptake inhibitors.

BOX 6.1 ■ OF SPECIAL INTEREST

"Ecstasy"—Harmless Feel-Good Drug, Dangerous Neurotoxin, or Miracle Medication?

Over the years, pharmaceutical companies have synthesized many thousands of new compounds in the search for drugs that might be useful in the treatment of one or another medical disorder. Unfortunately, a vast majority of these compounds are discarded, either because they do not produce a useful biological effect or because they fail somewhere along the rigorous process of safety and efficacy testing (see Box 4.1). Of course, occasionally a drug is discovered that does produce an interesting set of biological actions that are ultimately exploited for therapeutic benefit, illicit recreational use, or sometimes both. The present discussion deals with one such compound—3,4-methylenedioxymethamphetamine (MDMA), which is known on the street by a variety of names, including "ecstasy," "E," "X," "Adam," "love drug," and most recently "Molly." When someone purchases a pill that the seller says is ecstasy, it may or may not actually contain MDMA. For this reason, we will use the term **MDMA** when we are referring to the pure chemical compound (e.g., as might be used in a controlled animal study or a controlled clinical study); however, we will use the term **ecstasy** when we are referring to the literature pertaining to recreational use, because of the uncertainty associated with the purchase and consumption of street drugs that contain variable and unknown amounts of MDMA.

The early history of the discovery of MDMA and the route by which it became a recreational drug have been thoroughly reviewed by Pentney (2001), Rosenbaum (2002) and Freudenmann and colleagues (2006). Chemically, MDMA is a close relative of amphetamine and methamphetamine (**FIGURE A**), and it shares some but not all of their biological and behavioral characteristics. In particular, all three compounds acutely release catecholamines and 5-HT from their respective nerve terminals, although MDMA has a more potent effect on 5-HT release than is seen with amphetamine or methamphetamine. MDMA was first synthesized by the Merck pharmaceutical company in Germany in 1912. Although many textbooks and other sources claim that MDMA was produced as part of a project to find new anorectic (appetite-suppressing) compounds, original documents demonstrate that Merck was, in fact, seeking new hemostatic agents (drugs that would help stop bleeding) (Freudenmann et al., 2006). Merck went so far as to patent MDMA in 1914 and did perform some later unpublished studies on the drug; however, the company never marketed it for any therapeutic use.

Harold Hardman and his colleagues reported the first study on the effects of MDMA on experimental animals in 1973. This work had actually been conducted 20 years earlier under a classified contract from the U.S. Army to investigate the mechanisms of action of mescaline and other potential hallucinogenic compounds with a similar chemical structure. Later declassification of the results allowed them to finally be published, and we now know that the Army research on MDMA and related compounds was part of a program to develop so-called truth drugs that could aid in subject interrogation (Passie and Benzenhöfer, 2018). The first published information regarding the influence of MDMA on humans was authored by Alexander Shulgin and David Nichols in 1978. Shulgin was an American chemist who, while working for the Dow Chemical Company, had become interested in developing and characterizing new mind-altering drugs.

(A)

Chemical structures of MDMA and the related compounds MDA and MDE
These three compounds share some similarity with the structures of amphetamine and methamphetamine. MDA, 3,4-methylenedioxyamphetamine; MDE, 3,4-methylenedioxyethamphetamine; MDMA, 3,4-methylenedioxymethamphetamine.

BOX 6.1 ■ OF SPECIAL INTEREST (continued)

He began the practice of taking the drugs himself and/or offering them to close colleagues and friends (Benzenhöfer and Passie, 2010). After leaving Dow in 1966, Shulgin continued this work as a private researcher and consultant. In the Shulgin and Nichols 1978 article, which included a report on the effects of taking MDMA (75 to 150 mg orally, which is a common recreational dose even now), the authors stated that "the drug appears to evoke an easily controlled altered state of consciousness with emotional and sensual overtones. It can be compared in its effects to marijuana, to psilocybin devoid of the hallucinatory component, or to low levels of MDA" [p. 77]). It is noteworthy that the authors mention MDA (3,4-methylenedioxyamphetamine), which, although studied before MDMA, was later discovered to be a biologically active metabolite of the latter compound.

Following this "rediscovery" of MDMA, events started to move rapidly in several different directions. MDA, which produces psychological effects similar to those elicited by MDMA, had already been proposed as a potential adjunct to psychotherapy because of its purported ability to increase empathy between therapist and client (Naranjo et al., 1967). After experiencing the effects of MDMA himself, Shulgin apparently decided that this drug would be even better therapeutically than MDA. Consequently, in the 1970s, he began to distribute MDMA to many psychotherapists for use during their therapy sessions (Pentney, 2001). Note that both the distribution and use of MDMA were performed quietly because of the uncertain legal status of the compound at that time. During this same period, MDMA was (perhaps inevitably) gradually beginning to make its way onto the street. By the early 1980s, "Adam" or "ecstasy," depending on where one lived, was growing in popularity. Use was particularly heavy in Dallas, Austin, and other parts of Texas. Therefore, it was no surprise when MDMA began to attract the attention of the Drug Enforcement Administration (DEA), an arm of the U.S. Justice Department that determines the legal status of drugs and prosecutes users of illegal substances. Several research laboratories had already been studying the short- and long-term effects of MDMA in laboratory animals such as rats and monkeys and had found alarming evidence for large depletions of 5-HT in the forebrains of animals given high doses of this compound. Moreover, if brain slices were stained with an anti–5-HT antibody to allow visualization of serotonergic axons in the forebrain, most of the staining disappeared within a week after high-dose MDMA exposure. In a particularly striking study by Hatzidimitriou and coworkers (1999) using squirrel monkeys, some of the animals exhibited a marked reduction in staining even 7 years after receiving drug treatment. These and other experimental animal findings were taken as evidence for

a drug-induced degeneration of forebrain serotonergic fibers. The DEA held hearings concerning the status of MDMA in 1985, and largely because of the testimony of the animal researchers, the agency assigned the drug Schedule I status. As discussed in Chapter 9, Schedule I is the most restrictive schedule and is reserved for substances that have no recognized medical use and high abuse potential (e.g., heroin).

Of course the scheduling of MDMA did not prevent the continued use of ecstasy each year by thousands of young people, often at "raves" and other dances. As with all recreational drugs, we must consider the positive effects of ecstasy that motivate its use as well as the potential risks of such use. Heightened arousal, euphoria, enhanced perceptual awareness, and prosocial effects (e.g., feelings of empathy and closeness with others) are among the positive effects reported by users (Meyer, 2013). Indeed, MDMA and related drugs are sometimes considered to form a special class of drugs, called **entactogens**. This term refers to compounds that promote empathy and closeness to others in the absence of hallucinogenic effects (Nichols, 1986). Users of typical recreational doses of ecstasy sometimes also experience relatively minor adverse reactions such as nausea, headache, tachycardia (increased heart rate), bruxism (teeth grinding), and trismus (tightening of the jaw muscles). Of much greater concern, however, are the potentially toxic effects of chronic and/or high-dose use. Excessive release of 5-HT, including both central and peripheral sources of the transmitter, can give rise to a spectrum of symptoms that make up the **serotonin syndrome**. In its most severe, life-threatening form, symptoms of the serotonin syndrome include extreme hyperthermia, unstable blood pressure and pulse rate, respiratory distress, muscle rigidity, seizure activity, and a state of delirium (Davies et al., 2018). This syndrome can be caused not only by high doses of a single 5-HT–releasing agent like MDMA but also by more moderate doses of serotonergic drugs taken together (e.g., MDMA plus an SSRI, or an SSRI combined with an MAO inhibitor).

Even if an individual doesn't overdose on ecstasy, the experimental animal studies that found long-lasting reductions in brain 5-HT levels or staining raised concerns about possible 5-HT depletion or other serotonergic abnormalities in chronic users. Since there have been few opportunities to examine the brains of regular ecstasy users post-mortem, the theory of serotonergic toxicity in humans has primarily been tested using brain imaging methods and/or assessments of cognitive functions believed to rely, in part, on normal serotonergic activity. Cognitive deficits or altered brain activity during task performance have been observed in many studies of regular

(Continued)

BOX 6.1 ■ OF SPECIAL INTEREST *(continued)*

ecstasy users compared to control groups (Roberts et al., 2018; Aguilar et al., 2020); however, in almost all cases it is impossible to know whether deficient cognitive function *preceded* rather than *was caused by* repeated ecstasy use. In the brain imaging studies, the most important outcome measure is the amount of SERT binding, since this protein is a marker of serotonergic fibers in forebrain projection areas. A recent meta-analysis concluded that compared to controls, regular ecstasy users showed significant reductions in SERT binding in several cortical areas along with the thalamus and hippocampus (Müller et al., 2019). However, most of the studies included in the analysis involved very heavy users (defined as >100 lifetime episodes of ecstasy use). Indeed, an earlier review by the same research group of neuroimaging results from moderate ecstasy users concluded that in this population, there were no conclusive changes in SERT binding (Müller et al., 2016). In very heavy ecstasy users, therefore, it is possible that some degeneration of the forebrain serotonergic innervation has occurred. Nonetheless, two important caveats must be mentioned. First, almost all ecstasy users are polydrug users, which means that they also consume other recreational drugs such as marijuana, tobacco, alcohol, or even cocaine or heroin. The possibility of drug interactions influencing the integrity of the serotonergic system cannot be excluded. Second, animal studies have raised the possibility that MDMA-related changes in the serotonergic system may result from long-lasting reductions in gene expression rather than degeneration of the serotonergic axons (Biezonski and Meyer, 2011; Meyer, 2013). While such reductions could very well compromise serotonergic function for some period of time, they are more likely to permit recovery than if the axons were physically damaged.

Perhaps the most fascinating part of the MDMA/ecstasy story is that the drug is again being considered for therapeutic use. We mentioned earlier that beginning in the 1970s, MDMA was being administered in an unregulated way by many psychotherapists to their clients to assist in the therapeutic process. This practice mostly stopped once MDMA was given a Schedule I classification in 1985. However, around the year 2000, a private organization called the Multidisciplinary Association for Psychedelic Studies (MAPS) began to initiate the process of organizing, obtaining regulatory permissions, and raising funding for controlled studies into the use of low-dose MDMA treatment as an adjunct to psychotherapeutic treatment of patients with several different disorders, particularly chronic post-traumatic stress disorder (PTSD). Treatment sessions are conducted under carefully controlled conditions with therapists trained in the use of the medication. A total of six phase 2 clinical

trials have now been completed, and the results clearly show significant PTSD symptom reduction following MDMA-assisted psychotherapy (Feduccia et al., 2019; Mithoefer et al., 2019; Sessa et al., 2019) (**FIGURE B**). Moreover, follow-up studies 12 months or longer after MDMA-assisted psychotherapy revealed continued benefits from the treatment (Jerome et al., 2020). Consequently, phase 3 clinical trials are now under way with the aim of eventually submitting this therapeutic approach for FDA approval. The mechanism by which MDMA assists the psychotherapeutic process is unclear, but Feduccia and Mithoefer (2018) have hypothesized that trauma recall, fear extinction, and memory reconsolidation may play a role. MDMA-assisted psychotherapy is also being considered for other psychiatric disorders, including alcohol use disorder (Sessa, 2018; Sessa et al., 2019). If MDMA-assisted psychotherapy is eventually approved by the FDA, we will have come full circle with this compound: from a possible therapeutic agent to potential neurotoxin and then back again to a legitimate medical application.

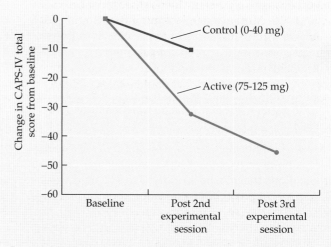

Pooled data from six blinded placebo-controlled clinical trials testing the effectiveness of MDMA-assisted psychotherapy for treating chronic PTSD All participants were initially given two or three 90-minute psychotherapy sessions. The "Active" group subsequently underwent two or three 8-hour psychotherapy sessions, 3 to 5 weeks apart, during which 75 to 125 mg of MDMA was administered. Members of the "Control" group instead received either placebo or a dose of MDMA considered to be therapeutically inactive (up to 40 mg). At baseline and again 1 to 2 months after the second and third drug (Experimental) sessions, each participant was assessed for PTSD symptomatology using the CAPS-IV (Clinician-Administered PTSD Scale for DSM-IV). The Active group showed significantly greater symptom reduction than the Control group after the second Experimental session, and the symptoms continued to decline further after the third session. (From C. Mithoefer et al. 2019. *Psychopharm* 236: 2735–2745. CC BY 4.0. doi.org/10.1007/s00213-019-05249-5.)

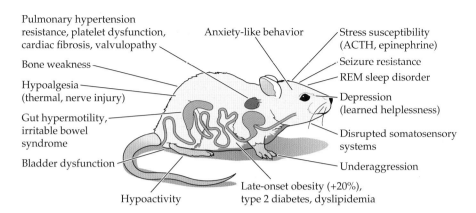

FIGURE 6.5 **Behavioral and physiological phenotypes of SERT knockout mice** Widespread SERT expression both in the brain (by serotonergic neurons and their axons and terminals) and in various peripheral tissues leads to dysfunction in many behavioral and physiological systems when normal 5-HT uptake is impaired by loss of this transporter. ACTH, adrenocorticotropic hormone; REM, rapid-eye-movement. (After D. L. Murphy and K.-P. Lesch. 2008. *Nat Rev Neurosci* 9: 85–96.)

terminal known as the **5-HT transporter**, also known as **SERT** (see Figure 6.4). This protein turns out to be a key target of drug action. For example, the introduction of **fluoxetine**, better known as **Prozac**, in late 1987 spawned a whole new class of antidepressant drugs based on the idea of inhibiting 5-HT reuptake. These compounds are, therefore, called **selective serotonin reuptake inhibitors** (**SSRIs**) (see Chapter 18). Certain abused drugs such as cocaine and MDMA likewise interact with SERT, but they are not selective in their effects because they also influence the transporters for DA and NE. Mutant mice lacking a functional SERT exhibit an astonishing array of behavioral and physiological abnormalities that presumably arise as the result of chronic enhancement of serotonergic activity (since the neurotransmitter cannot be taken up after it is released) during the animal's lifetime (Murphy and Lesch, 2008; Murphy et al., 2008) (**FIGURE 6.5**). Subsequent production of SERT knockout rats revealed many of the same abnormalities but also some species differences compared to mice (Kalueff et al., 2010). Some of the functions that can be ascribed to 5-HT on the basis of the phenotype of SERT knockout mice and rats are discussed in the last part of this chapter.

You will recall that DA and NE are metabolized by two different enzymes—monoamine oxidase (MAO) and catechol-O-methyltransferase (COMT). Because 5-HT is not a catecholamine, it is not affected by COMT. However, its breakdown is catalyzed by MAO-A to yield the metabolite **5-hydroxyindoleacetic acid** (**5-HIAA**). The level of 5-HIAA in the brains of animals or in the CSF of humans or animals is often used as a measure of the activity of serotonergic neurons. This practice is based on research showing that when these neurons fire more rapidly, they make more 5-HT, and a corresponding increase in the formation of 5-HIAA occurs.

SECTION SUMMARY

■ The neurotransmitter 5-HT is synthesized from the amino acid tryptophan in two biochemical reactions. The first and rate-limiting reaction is catalyzed by the enzyme TPH. Two forms of TPH exist: TPH1, which is expressed by non-neuronal cells, and TPH2, which is expressed only by serotonergic neurons.

■ Peripheral neuroendocrine tumors that express TPH1 cause a spectrum of symptoms known as the carcinoid syndrome. Symptoms of the carcinoid syndrome can be treated with telotristat, a nonselective TPH inhibitor that does not cross the blood–brain barrier and, therefore, only blocks peripherally expressed TPH1.

■ Brain 5-HT synthesis is controlled, in part, by tryptophan availability. Tryptophan entry into the brain from the bloodstream is determined by the plasma ratio of tryptophan to other large neutral amino acids (LNAA) that compete for transport across the blood–brain barrier.

■ 5-HT synthesis is increased by several methods, including direct tryptophan administration (tryptophan loading), consumption of proteins with very high tryptophan content, or consumption of a high-carbohydrate, low-protein meal. 5-HT synthesis is reduced by administration of an amino acid mixture lacking tryptophan, which causes acute tryptophan depletion (ATD).

■ In healthy participants, at least some studies in which tryptophan availability was increased found enhanced cognitive function (e.g., memory or attention), elevated mood, and improved sleep. Conversely, ATD was reported to impair verbal memory consolidation, induce a negative cognitive bias, and reduce sleep duration and quality.

■ The majority of dietary tryptophan is converted to kynurenine by the enzymes IDO and TDO, after which the kynurenine is further metabolized to a variety of different bioactive compounds. Conditions of stress and inflammation activate IDO and kynurenine pathway activity, which may be important in certain psychiatric and neurodegenerative disorders.

■ VMAT2 is responsible for loading 5-HT into synaptic vesicles for subsequent release.

■ Serotonin release is inhibited by autoreceptors located on the cell body, dendrites, and terminals of serotonergic neurons. The terminal autoreceptors are of either the 5-HT$_{1B}$ or 5-HT$_{1D}$ subtype, depending on the species, whereas the somatodendritic autoreceptors are of the 5-HT$_{1A}$ subtype.

■ Serotonergic transmission is terminated by reuptake of 5-HT from the extracellular fluid. This process is mediated by the 5-HT transporter (SERT), which is an important target of several antidepressant drugs.

- Serotonin is ultimately metabolized by MAO-A to form the major breakdown product 5-HIAA.

- Several compounds have been identified that stimulate 5-HT release, one of which is MDMA. Ecstasy, which is a common term for recreationally used MDMA, exerts a number of positive effects on users, including feelings of empathy and closeness to others. For this reason, MDMA and related drugs are considered to form a novel class of compounds called entactogens.

- Ecstasy overdose causes a severe, potentially life-threatening toxic reaction. High MDMA doses result in 5-HT depletion in experimental animals, and heavy ecstasy use by humans also seems to cause serotonergic deficits determined by neuroimaging. However, low controlled doses of MDMA have been shown to be highly beneficial as an adjunct to psychotherapy in people with chronic PTSD.

6.2 Basic Features of the Serotonergic System: Anatomical Organization, Cell Firing, and Receptor Families

This section will describe the anatomical organization of the serotonergic system, the properties of serotonergic cell firing, and the various families of serotonergic receptor subtypes.

The serotonergic system originates in the brainstem and projects to all forebrain areas

The Swedish researchers who first mapped the catecholamine systems in the 1960s (see Chapter 5) used the same experimental techniques to study the distribution of neurons and pathways using 5-HT. But in this case, they designated the 5-HT–containing cell groups with the letter *B* instead of *A*, which they had used for the dopaminergic and noradrenergic cell groups. It turns out that almost all of the serotonergic neurons in the CNS are found along the midline of the brainstem (medulla, pons, and midbrain), loosely associated with a network of cell clusters called the **raphe nuclei**.* Of greatest interest to neuropharmacologists are the **dorsal raphe nucleus** (**DRN**) and the **median raphe nucleus** (**MRN**) located in the area of the caudal midbrain and rostral pons. Together, these nuclei give rise to most of the serotonergic fibers in the forebrain. Virtually all forebrain regions receive serotonergic innervation, including the neocortex, striatum and nucleus accumbens, thalamus and hypothalamus, and limbic system structures such as the hippocampus, amygdala, and septal area (Tork, 1990) (**FIGURE 6.6**).

As with other neurotransmitters, the serotonergic fibers innervating a particular brain area are not uniformly distributed. **FIGURE 6.7** illustrates this principle using a photomicrograph of serotonergic fibers in the mouse neocortex and hippocampus (Donovan et al., 2002). Note that in the cortex, the fibers are particularly dense at the cortical surface (layer 1), which is a layer that has very few nerve cells but has a high density of dendrites and synaptic connections. In contrast, there are very few serotonergic fibers within the white matter separating the hippocampus from the cortex above and also very few fibers in the two major cell layers of the hippocampus, the pyramidal cell layer and the dentate gyrus granule cell layer. The paucity of serotonergic fibers within these cell layers tells us that the serotonergic inputs to the cells in these layers are not

*The term *raphe* is Greek for "seam" or "suture." In biology, the term is applied to structures that look as if they are joined together in a line. This is applicable to the raphe nuclei, which are aligned with each other along the rostral-caudal axis of the brainstem.

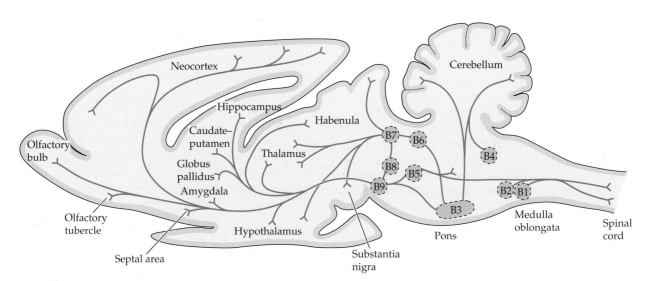

FIGURE 6.6 Anatomy of the serotonergic system The B7 cell group corresponds to the dorsal raphe, and the B8 cell group corresponds to the median raphe.

FIGURE 6.7 Photomicrograph of serotonergic fibers in the mouse neocortex and hippocampus
The photomicrograph shows a parasagittal section from a young mouse brain that was stained using an antibody against the 5-HT transporter. This method permits visualization of serotonergic fibers (axons) because the transporter protein is present throughout the length of the axonal membrane. The photomicrograph was taken using dark-field microscopy, which reverses light and dark structures. Consequently, the stained axons appear brightly colored, whereas the cell bodies of the hippocampal pyramidal cell layer and dentate gyrus granule cell layer appear dark. Note that in some areas, such as the deep layers of the hippocampus and layer 1 of the cortex, the serotonergic axons are so numerous that individual fibers cannot be resolved at the present magnification.

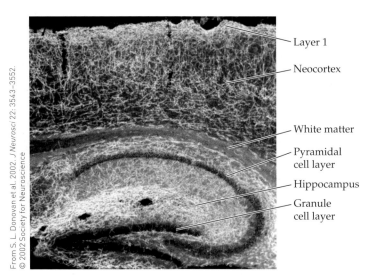

From S. L. Donovan et al. 2002. *J Neurosci* 22: 3543–3552.
© 2002 Society for Neuroscience

Layer 1
Neocortex
White matter
Pyramidal cell layer
Hippocampus
Granule cell layer

targeting the cell bodies but instead are targeting dendrites that have branched out away from the cells.

The firing of dorsal raphe serotonergic neurons varies with behavioral states

Firing patterns of the DRN neurons have been well characterized, particularly in cats. When a cat is awake, each cell fires at a relatively slow but very regular rate (tonic firing), almost like a ticking clock (**FIGURE 6.8**). When the cat enters slow-wave sleep (also called non-REM sleep), which is the stage of sleep in which large-amplitude, slow electroencephalographic (EEG) waves can be recorded in the cortex, the serotonergic neurons slow down and become more irregular in their firing. Most

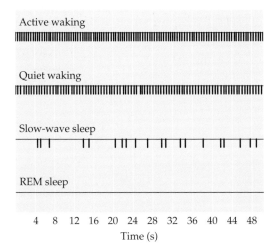

Active waking

Quiet waking

Slow-wave sleep

REM sleep

4   8   12   16   20   24   28   32   36   40   44   48
Time (s)

FIGURE 6.8 The firing rate of serotonergic neurons in the cat dorsal raphe is related to the animal's behavioral state During quiet waking, the cells fire at a steady rate of approximately 2 spikes (action potentials) per second. The firing rate is slightly increased during behavioral activity, but greatly diminished during slow-wave sleep. Dorsal raphe firing is essentially abolished during REM sleep. (After B. L. Jacobs and C. A. Fornal. 1993. *Trends Neurosci* 16: 346–352.)

intriguingly, the cells are almost completely shut down when the cat is in rapid-eye-movement (REM) sleep, a stage of sleep characterized by side-to-side eye movements and low-amplitude, fast EEG waves in the cortex (reviewed by Jacobs and Fornal, 1999).

This classical research in cats (chosen because of their frequent passages between waking and sleep) established a *correlation* between different behavioral states and DRN cell firing, but do these neurons have a role in *causing* behavioral state changes? For this research, mice have been the main experimental subjects because of the relative ease of performing genetic manipulations in these animals. Based on recent studies by investigators using a combination of genetically controlled deletion of DRN and MRN serotonergic neurons and optogenetic activation of DRN serotonergic neurons, we may hypothesize that slow, tonic firing of DRN neurons promotes sleep (specifically non-REM sleep), whereas burst firing of the same cells favors a state of wakefulness (Moriya et al., 2017; Oikonomou et al., 2019). Subsystems of serotonergic neurons within the DRN have been discovered that differ in their neurochemical characteristics and their neuronal inputs and outputs (Ren et al., 2018; Huang et al., 2019). As discussed by Oikonomou and colleagues, it is possible that separate DRN subsystems mediate the differential effects of tonic versus burst firing of the serotonergic neurons within this anatomical area.

There is a large family of serotonin receptors, most of which are metabotropic

One of the remarkable properties of 5-HT is the number of receptors that have evolved for this transmitter. At the present time, pharmacologists have identified at least 14 5-HT receptor subtypes. Among these is a group of five different $5\text{-}HT_1$ receptors (designated $5\text{-}HT_{1A}$, $5\text{-}HT_{1B}$, $5\text{-}HT_{1D}$, $5\text{-}HT_{1E}$, and $5\text{-}HT_{1F}$), along with a smaller group of three $5\text{-}HT_2$ receptors ($5\text{-}HT_{2A}$, $5\text{-}HT_{2B}$, and $5\text{-}HT_{2C}$) and additional receptors designated 5-HT$_3$, 5-HT$_4$, 5-HT$_{5A}$, 5-HT$_{5B}$ (not expressed in humans), 5-HT$_6$, and 5-HT$_7$. All of these receptors are metabotropic, except for the 5-HT$_3$ receptor, which is an excitatory ionotropic receptor. The attentive reader will have noticed that there is no 5-HT$_{1C}$ subtype listed. One of the serotonergic receptors initially had that designation, but it was later determined to belong to the 5-HT$_2$ family by structural and functional criteria, and therefore it was renamed 5-HT$_{2C}$. The following discussion will focus largely on 5-HT$_{1A}$ and 5-HT$_{2A}$ receptors, which are the best-known receptor subtypes in terms of their cellular and behavioral effects. We will subsequently touch on three other subtypes that have successfully been targeted for therapeutic purposes.

5-HT$_{1A}$ RECEPTORS   5-HT$_{1A}$ receptors are found in many brain areas, but they are particularly concentrated in the hippocampus, the septal area, parts of the amygdala, and the DRN. In the forebrain, these receptors are located postsynaptic to 5-HT–containing nerve terminals. As mentioned earlier, 5-HT$_{1A}$ receptors additionally function as somatodendritic autoreceptors in the DRN and MRN. 5-HT$_{1A}$ receptors work through two major mechanisms. First, the receptors reduce cAMP synthesis by inhibiting adenylyl cyclase (**FIGURE 6.9A**). The second mechanism involves increased opening of K$^+$ channels and membrane hyperpolarization, which we have seen is a property shared by D$_2$ dopamine receptors and α$_2$-adrenergic receptors. You will recall from Chapter 2 that this hyperpolarization leads to a decrease in firing of either the postsynaptic cell (in the case of 5-HT$_{1A}$ receptors located postsynaptically) or the serotonergic neuron itself (in the case of the 5-HT$_{1A}$ autoreceptors).

Several drugs act as either full or partial agonists at 5-HT$_{1A}$ receptors, including **buspirone**, **ipsapirone**, and

8-hydroxy-2-(di-n-propylamino) tetralin (8-OH-DPAT). Some of the behavioral effects produced by administering a 5-HT$_{1A}$ agonist are described in the last part of this chapter. The most widely used 5-HT$_{1A}$ receptor antagonist is the experimental drug **WAY-100635**, which was originally developed by the Wyeth-Ayerst pharmaceutical company (hence the "WAY" designation). One limitation of administering this compound systemically is that both postsynaptic 5-HT$_{1A}$ receptors and 5-HT$_{1A}$ autoreceptors are antagonized, thereby complicating interpretation of the results.

5-HT$_{2A}$ RECEPTORS   Large numbers of 5-HT$_{2A}$ receptors are present in the cerebral cortex. This receptor subtype is also found in the striatum, in the nucleus accumbens, and in a variety of other brain areas. Similar to α$_1$-adrenergic receptors, 5-HT$_{2A}$ receptors function mainly by activating the phosphoinositide second-messenger system (**FIGURE 6.9B**). In Chapter 3 you learned that this system increases Ca^{2+} levels within the postsynaptic cell and also activates protein kinase C (PKC). Thus, our discussion of different neurotransmitters and their receptor subtypes has included common mechanisms of transmitter action that occur over and over again. These mechanisms may involve a second messenger such as cAMP or Ca^{2+}, or some type of ion channels such as K$^+$ channels, which are opened by a wide variety of receptors. **1-(2,5-dimethoxy-4-iodophenyl)-2-aminopropane (DOI)** is a 5-HT$_{2A}$ agonist that is widely used experimentally, whereas **ketanserin** and **ritanserin** are typical 5-HT$_{2A}$ antagonists.

Giving DOI or another 5-HT$_{2A}$ agonist to rats or mice leads to a characteristic "head-twitch" response (periodic, brief twitches of the head), which is a useful measure of 5-HT$_{2A}$ receptor stimulation in these species.

(A)

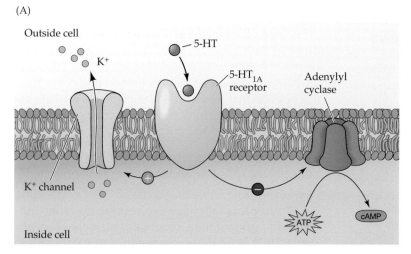

(B)

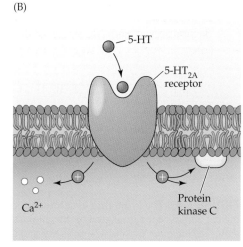

FIGURE 6.9   5-HT$_{1A}$ and 5-HT$_{2A}$ receptors operate through different signaling mechanisms 5-HT$_{1A}$ receptors inhibit cAMP production and activate K$^+$ channel opening (A), whereas 5-HT$_{2A}$ receptors increase intracellular Ca^{2+} levels and stimulate protein kinase C via the phosphoinositide second-messenger system (B). For purposes of simplification, the G proteins required for coupling the receptors to their signaling pathways are not shown.

More interesting is the fact that DOI and related drugs are **hallucinogenic** (hallucination producing) in humans. Indeed, the hallucinogenic effects of **lysergic acid diethylamide (LSD)** are believed to stem from its ability to stimulate 5-HT$_{2A}$ receptors. LSD and other hallucinogens are discussed in greater detail in Chapter 15.

In recent years, the possible role of 5-HT$_{2A}$ receptors has become a major topic of discussion and research with respect to the treatment of schizophrenia. In particular, so-called atypical antipsychotics have significantly reduced motor side effects compared with earlier-generation drugs, which has been attributed to their actions as inverse agonists* at 5-HT$_{2A}$ and/or 5-HT$_{2C}$ receptors (Sullivan et al., 2015). This topic is discussed in more detail in Chapter 19.

OTHER RECEPTOR SUBTYPES Widespread expression of other serotonergic receptor subtypes, both within the nervous system and in non-neural tissues, has led to the development of various medications that target these receptors. Two well-known examples pertain to the 5-HT$_{1B/1D}$, 5-HT$_{1F}$, and 5-HT$_3$ subtypes. Abnormal dilation of blood vessels within the brain is thought to be one of the key factors contributing to migraine headaches. A class of 5-HT$_{1B/1D}$ agonists known as triptans (**sumatriptan [Imitrex or Zecuity], zolmitriptan [Zomig], frovatriptan [Frova], naratriptan [Amerge]**) causes constriction of the vessels, thereby providing relief from migraine symptoms. However, because these drugs also lead to some constriction of the coronary arteries, they are contraindicated in patients at risk for cardiovascular disease. Interestingly, 5-HT$_{1F}$ receptor stimulation is also effective in treating migraine headaches, although in this case the mechanism appears to be reducing activity within the pain pathway instead of provoking vasoconstriction (Clemow et al., 2020). This discovery led to the development of the novel 5-HT$_{1F}$ agonist **lasmiditan (Reyvow)**, which was recently approved by the FDA. Because one of the side effects of this medication is drowsiness, it may be best suited for treating migraines that occur in the evening before and during bedtime.

The 5-HT$_3$ receptors are located on peripheral terminals of the vagus nerve. One function of the vagus is to transmit sensory information from the viscera, including the gastrointestinal (GI) tract, to the brain. Cancer chemotherapy drugs and radiation treatment have both been found to stimulate the release of 5-HT in the gut, which subsequently stimulates the vagal 5-HT$_3$ receptors and induces activation of the vomiting center in the brainstem (Babic and Browning, 2014). Consequently, 5-HT$_3$ antagonists such as **ondansetron (Zofran), granisetron (Kytril)**, and **palonosetron (Aloxi)** are prescribed to counteract the nausea and vomiting associated with cancer treatments. More information on the role of gut 5-HT and the potential therapeutic benefits of drugs that target it can be found at the end of the chapter.

SECTION SUMMARY

- Most of the serotonergic neurons in the CNS are associated with the raphe nuclei of the brainstem. Together, the cells of the DRN and MRN send 5-HT–containing fibers to virtually all forebrain areas.

- DRN neuronal firing correlates with the behavioral state of the organism. Tonic firing is slow and regular in the awake state, becomes even slower in slow-wave (non-REM) sleep, and completely ceases during REM sleep. Additional studies established a causal relationship between raphe cell firing and sleep/waking. Slow, tonic cell firing promoted non-REM sleep, while burst firing led to increased time awake.

- At least 14 different 5-HT receptor subtypes have been identified. Some of these fall within groups, such as the 5-HT$_1$ family (5-HT$_{1A}$, 5-HT$_{1B}$, 5-HT$_{1D}$, 5-HT$_{1E}$, and 5-HT$_{1F}$) and a smaller group of three 5-HT$_2$ receptors (5-HT$_{2A}$, 5-HT$_{2B}$, and 5-HT$_{2C}$). The remaining 5-HT receptors are designated 5-HT$_3$, 5-HT$_4$, 5-HT$_{5A}$, 5-HT$_{5B}$, 5-HT$_6$, and 5-HT$_7$. All of the 5-HT receptors are metabotropic, except for the 5-HT$_3$ receptor, which is an excitatory ionotropic receptor.

- Two of the best-characterized 5-HT receptor subtypes are the 5-HT$_{1A}$ and 5-HT$_{2A}$ receptors. High levels of 5-HT$_{1A}$ receptors have been found in the hippocampus, the septum, parts of the amygdala, and the dorsal raphe nucleus. In the raphe nuclei, including the DRN, these receptors are mainly somatodendritic autoreceptors on the serotonergic neurons themselves. In other brain areas, 5-HT$_{1A}$ receptors are found on postsynaptic neurons that receive serotonergic input. 5-HT$_{1A}$ receptors inhibit neuronal excitability by inhibiting cAMP formation and by enhancing the opening of K$^+$ channels within the cell membrane. Among a variety of compounds that act on the 5-HT$_{1A}$ receptor subtype are the agonist 8-OH-DPAT, buspirone, and ipsapirone, as well as the antagonist WAY-100635.

- There are 5-HT$_{2A}$ receptors in the neocortex, striatum, and nucleus accumbens, as well as in other brain regions. This receptor subtype activates the phosphoinositide second-messenger system, which increases the amount of free Ca^{2+} within the cell and stimulates protein kinase C. When given to rodents, 5-HT$_{2A}$ receptor agonists such as DOI trigger a head-twitch response. In humans, such drugs (which include LSD) produce hallucinations. Several drugs used in the treatment of schizophrenia act as inverse agonists at 5-HT$_{2A}$ and/or 5-HT$_{2C}$ receptors, and some researchers hypothesize that this serotonergic receptor activity may reduce the motoric side effects often associated with antischizophrenic medications.

- Other 5-HT receptor subtypes are currently targeted for specific medical conditions. Thus, migraine headaches may be treated using a class of 5-HT$_{1B/1D}$ agonists

*Recall from Chapter 1 that inverse agonists don't merely block a receptor, they exert the opposite effect that an agonist would produce on cell signaling by that receptor.

known as triptans, which stimulate cerebral vaso-constriction, or the 5-HT$_{1F}$ agonist lasmiditan, which reduces activity within the pain pathway. In addition, 5-HT$_3$ antagonists such as ondansetron, granisetron, and palonosetron offer relief from the nausea and vomiting that can be produced by cancer chemotherapy and radiation treatments.

6.3 Behavioral and Physiological Functions of Serotonin

Serotonin helps regulate numerous behavioral and physiological functions, several of which have been selected for discussion below.

Multiple approaches have identified several behavioral and physiological functions of serotonin

It is clear from numerous genetic, neurochemical, and pharmacological studies in both animals and humans that the serotonergic system helps regulate many behavioral and physiological functions. In human clinical research, serotonergic function has been investigated using several different methodological approaches, including the following:

- Determining the association between levels of CSF 5-HIAA or postmortem regional brain 5-HT and 5-HIAA concentrations and behavioral traits or, in some cases, the occurrence of neuropsychiatric disorders

- Assessing behavioral, subjective, and physiological responses to pharmacological challenges with SSRIs or with receptor agonists or antagonists

- Identifying associations between psychiatric disorders and polymorphisms in the genes for SERT or for various serotonergic receptors

Some findings relating SERT polymorphisms with risk for major depression will be presented later, in the chapter on affective disorders (Chapter 18). With respect to CSF and brain concentrations of 5-HIAA and 5-HT, various findings have related the serotonergic system to aggressive behavior, particularly impulsive aggression. These and other results linking 5-HT to aggression are discussed below. Preclinical (animal model) studies of serotonergic function have relied on pharmacological approaches, direct neurochemical assessment of 5-HT and/or 5-HIAA concentrations in specific brain regions, optogenetic or chemogenetic manipulation of serotonergic cell firing, and genetically engineered elimination of 5-HT in the brain or periphery.

Numerous pharmacological tools are available for probing the serotonergic system, ranging from serotonergic neurotoxins to drug challenges with selective receptor agonists and antagonists, as done in human

research studies (**TABLE 6.1**). Serotonergic neurotoxins include the previously mentioned compounds *para*-chloroamphetamine and MDMA. Two other compounds, **5,6-dihydroxytryptamine (5,6-DHT)** and **5,7-dihydroxytryptamine (5,7-DHT)**, have also been widely used to produce serotonergic lesions in experimental animals, although one limitation of using these drugs is that they must be given directly into the brain because they don't cross the blood–brain barrier. 5,6-DHT and 5,7-DHT cause massive damage to serotonergic axons and nerve terminals in the forebrain, yet cell bodies in the raphe nuclei are usually spared. Due to space limitations, we cannot review all of the behavioral effects produced by lesioning the serotonergic system; however, various studies have reported changes in hunger and eating behavior, anxiety, pain sensitivity, and learning and memory (reviewed in Paterak and Stefański, 2014). Indeed, the involvement of 5-HT in a multitude of behavioral and physiological functions has led to the development of serotonergic receptor agonist and antagonist compounds for the treatment of many clinical disorders. Some of these disorders, the putative role of 5-HT, and the identities of either currently licensed or investigational compounds targeting the relevant serotonergic receptors are discussed in the subsections below. But first we will describe the profound behavioral and physiological consequences of genetically manipulating animals so that they lack brain 5-HT throughout life, from embryonic development onward.

LIFE WITHOUT SEROTONIN*   Much important information has been obtained about serotonergic system function by pharmacologically manipulating 5-HT levels, activating or blocking specific serotonergic receptors with agonists and antagonists, and using SSRIs to prevent 5-HT reuptake following release. However, there are several common limitations to these pharmacological approaches: drug effects are temporary; the targeted receptor, transporter, or enzyme may only be partially affected by the drug (e.g., incomplete receptor blockade, residual 5-HT synthesis following attempted depletion); and the chosen drug may not be fully selective for its intended target at the administered dose. Are there any alternatives that avoid these limitations? The answer leads us to genetic engineering approaches, specifically mice engineered to lack 5-HT from embryonic development onward. There are two distinct ways to achieve this goal: knocking out the gene for TPH, which leaves the serotonergic cells intact but doesn't permit them to synthesize 5-HT, or preventing the normal differentiation of cells that were destined to become serotonergic neurons. Because the first method involving TPH knockout mice has

---

*The title of this section is adapted from a review by Mosienko and colleagues (2015) entitled "Life without brain serotonin: Reevaluation of serotonin function with mice deficient in brain serotonin synthesis."

TABLE 6.1   Drugs That Affect the Serotonergic System

Drug	Mechanism of Action	Clinical, Recreational, or Experimental Use
para-Chlorophenylalanine (PCPA)	General tryptophan hydroxylase inhibitor	Experimental use
Telotristat	Peripheral tryptophan hydroxylase inhibitor	Treatment for carcinoid syndrome
Reserpine	Irreversible VMAT inhibitor	Experimental use
para-Chloroamphetamine and fenfluramine	5-HT releaser	Experimental use
MDMA	5-HT releaser	Recreational use and proposed treatment for severe PTSD
Fluoxetine and others	5-HT reuptake inhibitors (SSRIs)	Antidepressant medications
Buspirone	5-HT$_{1A}$ partial agonist	Antianxiety and antidepressant medication
Ipsapirone	5-HT$_{1A}$ partial agonist	Experimental use
Vilazodone	Combined SSRI and 5-HT$_{1A}$ partial agonist	Antianxiety medication
8-OH-DPAT	5-HT$_{1A}$ full agonist	Experimental use
WAY-100635	5-HT$_{1A}$ antagonist	Experimental use
DOI	5-HT$_{2A}$ agonist	Experimental use
LSD	5-HT$_{2A}$ agonist	Recreational use
Ketanserin and ritanserin	5-HT$_{2A}$ antagonists	Experimental use
Triptans	5-HT$_{1B/1D}$ agonists	Treatments for migraine headaches
Lasmiditan	5-HT$_{1F}$ agonist	Treatment for migraine headaches
Ondansetron, granisetron, and palonosetron	5-HT$_3$ antagonists	Treatments for cancer chemotherapy–related nausea
5,7-DHT	5-HT neurotoxin	Experimental use
Lorcaserin	5-HT$_{2C}$ agonist	Treatment for obesity
Alosetron	5-HT$_3$ antagonist	Treatment for IBS-D
Prucalopride and tegaserod	5-HT$_4$ agonists	Treatments for IBS-C

been used much more widely by researchers, we will primarily discuss the results of those studies.

Most TPH knockout studies specifically eliminate TPH2, the form of the enzyme expressed by serotonergic neurons, without influencing TPH1, since the latter is coded for by a different gene. Knockout of the TPH2 gene causes a virtually complete loss of 5-HT in brain (**FIGURE 6.10**) but a preservation of 5-HT levels in the bloodstream (where it's stored in blood platelets) and in peripheral organs like the intestines, liver, spleen, and pineal gland (Mosienko et al., 2015). This finding confirms the independent expression of *TPH2* and *TPH1* in neuronal compared to non-neuronal tissues.

Brain 5-HT in *TPH2*-knockout mice can be restored in a dose-dependent manner by injecting the animals with 5-HTP (see Figure 6.10). This method works because 5-HTP is the *product* of the reaction catalyzed by TPH and, therefore, bypasses the missing step in the biosynthetic pathway (refer back to see Figure 6.1). However, recovery of 5-HT levels is only temporary because the newly synthesized transmitter is gradually metabolized by MAO-A and cannot be replenished in the mutant mice. Also worth noting is the fact that AADC, the enzyme that converts 5-HTP to 5-HT, is additionally present in catecholamine neurons (see Chapter 5). Thus, animals given 5-HTP make 5-HT not only within the serotonergic neurons, where the transmitter is normally

FIGURE 6.10   TPH2-knockout mice show a near-complete loss of brain 5-HT Whole-brain 5-HT concentrations were determined in wild-type mice (*TPH2*+/+) and knockout mice with a homozygous loss of *TPH2* gene expression (*TPH2*–/–) (left two bars). Partial restoration of 5-HT concentration could be produced either by intraperitoneal (IP) injection of 5-HTP (measured 1 hour after the indicated dose) or by 5 days of oral 5-HTP administration at a dose of 300 mg/kg/day (right four bars). (After V. Mosienko et al. 2015. *Behav Brain Res* 277: 78–88. © 2014. Reprinted with permission from Elsevier.)

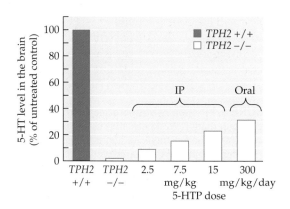

present, but also within dopaminergic and noradrenergic neurons, where 5-HT should *not* be present.

In Chapter 5, you learned that mice with a complete deletion of tyrosine hydroxylase from embryonic development onward died either in utero or soon after birth. The same is not true for TPH2, indicating that 5-HT is not required for the animal to survive gestation or the immediate postnatal period. However, over time *TPH2*-knockout mice do show reduced body mass and fat stores, and they also have an increased rate of mortality (Mosienko et al., 2015). The severity of postnatal growth deficits and increased mortality depends on which genetic strain of mouse and which genetic methods are used to create the knockout animals.

Extensive behavioral studies have been conducted on *TPH2*-knockout mice (reviewed in Fernandez and Gaspar, 2012; Lesch et al., 2012; Aragi and Lesch, 2013; Mosienko et al., 2015). The most consistently observed effect of eliminating brain 5-HT is a large increase in aggressive behavior, which is typically studied in male mice but also occurs in females (Kästner et al., 2019). Aggression in male mice is usually measured by the **resident–intruder test**. In this procedure, an adult male mouse (the "resident") is housed alone in a plastic tub for several weeks. In essence, the tub becomes the male's territory, which he will aggressively defend against intruding males. To test this aggressiveness, an unfamiliar male is introduced into the tub and the behavioral interactions between the resident and intruder are observed for the next several minutes. The level of aggressiveness by the resident is measured by the latency to attack the intruder (shorter latencies reflect greater aggressiveness) and the total number of attacks during the testing period. **FIGURE 6.11A** illustrates the heightened aggressiveness of male *TPH2*-knockout mice compared with wild-type males (Angoa-Pérez et al., 2012). In this particular study, even female *TPH2*-knockout mice were more aggressive than wild-type females (data not shown). Additional experiments demonstrated that injection of 5-HTP along

with a drug called **carbidopa**, which is an AADC inhibitor that doesn't cross the blood–brain barrier, reverses the high level of aggressive behavior in *TPH2*-knockout males (**FIGURE 6.11B**). Because there is substantial AADC activity in some peripheral tissues (e.g., kidneys), carbidopa was given to block peripheral conversion of 5-HTP to 5-HT. This method permits more 5-HTP to be available to the brain and also prevents adverse consequences of elevated peripheral 5-HT levels such as GI distress and diarrhea. Further discussion of the role of 5-HT in aggressive behavior is continued later in this section.

Genetic deletion of TPH2 leads to additional changes in behavioral control, mood-related and motivated behaviors, and social communication. Compared with wild-type animals, *TPH2*-knockout mice are reported to be more impulsive (Aragi and Lesch, 2013), more compulsive (Angoa-Pérez et al., 2012; Kane et al., 2012), and less anxious, at least in some tests of anxiety-like behavior (Mosienko et al., 2015). These animals also show poor social communication and social behaviors, including deficient maternal behavior severe enough to cause increased offspring mortality (Kane et al., 2012; Angoa-Pérez et al., 2014; Beis et al., 2015). The lack of normal social communication in *TPH2*-knockout mice is consistent with the hypothesis that abnormal development of the serotonergic system may underlie some cases of autism spectrum disorder (Muller et al., 2016).

TPH2-knockout mice not only are abnormal behaviorally, but also suffer from several physiological deficits. Two such deficits are (1) poor thermoregulation leading to inadequate maintenance of core body temperature when mice are placed into a cold environment, and (2) abnormal respiration (Alenina et al., 2009). These same deficits have been observed in a different kind of transgenic mouse engineered so that the animals actually develop without most of their brain serotonergic neurons (Hodges and Richerson, 2010). Respiratory problems in these mice are particularly severe in the early postnatal period, during which time pups exhibit frequent,

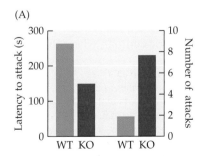
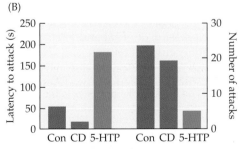

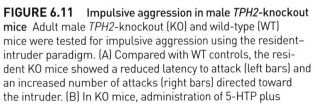

FIGURE 6.11 Impulsive aggression in male *TPH2*-knockout mice Adult male *TPH2*-knockout (KO) and wild-type (WT) mice were tested for impulsive aggression using the resident–intruder paradigm. (A) Compared with WT controls, the resident KO mice showed a reduced latency to attack (left bars) and an increased number of attacks (right bars) directed toward the intruder. (B) In KO mice, administration of 5-HTP plus carbidopa (5-HTP group) but not carbidopa alone (CD group) increased the latency to attack and reduced the number of attacks, compared with the control group given drug vehicle alone (Con). (After M. Angoa-Pérez et al. 2012. *J Neurochem* 121: 974–984. © 2012 The Authors. Journal of Neurochemistry © 2012 International Society for Neurochemistry.)

long-lasting episodes of **apnea** (cessation of breathing). Indeed, evidence from both animal and human studies has led to the hypothesis that abnormalities in the serotonergic system may play a critical role in some cases of **sudden infant death syndrome** (**SIDS**) (see **WEB BOX 6.1**).

ANXIETY A large body of research has established a key role for 5-HT in the regulation of anxiety. As we shall see in Chapter 17, SSRIs are among the drugs used most commonly in the treatment of several kinds of anxiety disorders. One of the key receptor subtypes thought to be involved in the anxiolytic (antianxiety) effects of these compounds is the 5-HT$_{1A}$ receptor, and indeed the 5-HT$_{1A}$ partial agonist **buspirone** (**BuSpar**) is licensed as an antianxiety medication. **Vilazodone** (**Viibryd**) is a newer compound that is both an SSRI and a 5-HT$_{1A}$ partial agonist (Sahli et al., 2016). Although vilazodone was developed mainly for the treatment of major depression, it additionally has anxiolytic efficacy and may be particularly useful in patients who suffer from depression-related anxiety (Thase et al., 2014). This compound is also being tested as a treatment for generalized anxiety disorder, although at the time of this writing it has not yet been formally licensed for this purpose.

The role of the 5-HT$_{1A}$ receptor subtype in anxiety regulation has been studied extensively in experimental animals. Both partial and full 5-HT$_{1A}$ receptor agonists exert anxiolytic effects, whereas 5-HT$_{1A}$-knockout mice show increased anxiety-like behavior in standard tests, including the elevated plus-maze (Żmudzka et al., 2018; Olivier and Olivier, 2020). However, in the absence of additional information, it's not clear whether the anxiety-regulating 5-HT$_{1A}$ receptors are *postsynaptic* or *presynaptic* (i.e., autoreceptors on the serotonergic neurons). To address this question, Garcia-Garcia and colleagues (2018) optogenetically excited or inhibited serotonergic terminals innervating the dorsal part of the bed nucleus of the stria terminalis (BNST) from the raphe nuclei in mice. **FIGURE 6.12** shows that excitation of the serotonergic nerve terminals (which increases 5-HT release) exerted an anxiolytic effect, as shown by increased open-arm time in the elevated plus-maze, whereas inhibition of the terminals (which reduces 5-HT release) was anxiogenic, as shown by decreased open-arm time. Other experiments not shown here demonstrated that the anxiolytic effect of exciting the BNST serotonergic terminals was dependent on 5-HT$_{1A}$ receptor activation. The experiments not only confirm earlier pharmacological studies with 5-HT$_{1A}$ receptor agonists

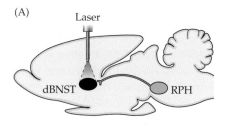

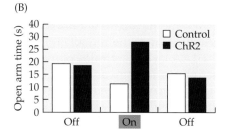

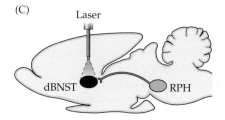

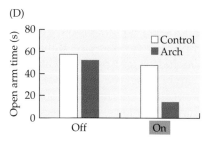

FIGURE 6.12 Effects of optogenetic excitation or inhibition of serotonergic nerve terminals in the dorsal bed nucleus of the stria terminalis (dBNST) on anxiety-like behavior in the elevated plus-maze Mice were genetically manipulated to express either the excitatory blue-light sensitive protein channelrhodopsin-2 (ChR2) or the inhibitory green-light sensitive protein archaerhodopsin (Arch) in raphe (RPH) serotonergic neurons. The animals were then implanted with fiber-optic probes in the dBNST to permit delivery of blue or green light to this area by a laser. Control mice received all the same procedures except for ChR2 or Arch gene expression. Delivery of blue light to excite the serotonergic nerve terminals was anxiolytic in the ChR2 mice but not the controls as shown by increased time spent in the open arms of the maze (A and B). This increase only occurred when the light was ON. In contrast, delivery of green light to inhibit the serotonergic nerve terminals was anxiogenic in the Arch mice but not the controls as shown by reduced time spent in the open arms (C and D). Note the difference in open-arm time under control conditions between the two experiments. To allow the genetic manipulations to have clear effects, the researchers altered the baseline experimental parameters to be more anxiety-provoking (i.e., less open-arm time in the controls) when they expected to produce an anxiolytic effect of the laser light but less anxiety-provoking (i.e., more open-arm time in the controls) when they expected to produce an anxiogenic effect of the laser light. (From A. L. Garcia-Garcia et al. 2018. *Mol Psychiatry* 23: 1990–1997. Reprinted by permission from Springer Nature. doi.org/10.1038/mp.2017.165)

but also indicate the importance of *postsynaptic* 5-HT$_{1A}$ receptors in reducing anxiety since there are no serotonergic cell bodies and therefore no somatodendritic autoreceptors in the area of excitation or inhibition. The results additionally show that the BNST is an important site of serotonergic modulation of anxiety-like behaviors. Although the amygdala has received the most attention as a brain region that mediates negative emotions such as fear and anxiety, human imaging studies have begun to show a role for the BNST in threat processing during anxiety-producing situations (Knight and Depue, 2019).

AGGRESSIVE BEHAVIOR　What is aggression, and how do we define and conceptualize aggressive behaviors? In the case of human aggression, the intent of the actor is important. Thus, a common definition of aggression in human studies is "behavior that is intended to cause physical or psychological harm or pain to the victim." A few different categorical systems have been used to classify human aggression. One such system is to classify aggressive acts as either reactive or proactive (Rosell and Siever, 2015). Reactive aggression is a response to provocation, threat, or frustration; is accompanied by strong negative emotions of anger or rage; and functions to allay those emotions. In contrast, proactive aggression is planned rather than provoked; is not typically accompanied by a negative emotional state; and functions to achieve some tangible benefit, such as monetary gain, social status, and so forth. The following discussion will focus on reactive aggression, since we know much more about the neurobiology of reactive compared to proactive aggression.

Whereas studies of human aggression can benefit from self-reports of intentionality and emotional state, animal studies must operationalize the concept of aggression. This difference in approach has led to the development of several formal typologies of aggressive behavior. For example, the typology of Nelson and Chiavegatto (2001) includes eight different categories of aggression that can be observed in animals under naturalistic and/or specific experimental conditions: predatory, antipredator, dominance, sex-related, maternal, territorial, defensive, and irritable aggression.

The neural circuit underlying reactive aggression in humans has been elucidated using a combination of approaches, including brain imaging studies and examination of behavioral changes in patients with lesions of various brain areas (produced by stroke, tumor, head trauma, or other forms of brain injury). These approaches have implicated an extensive circuit that includes several cortical areas, the striatum, amygdala, BNST, hippocampus, hypothalamus, and the periaqueductal gray in the brainstem (Siever, 2008; Rosell and Siever, 2015). Because of their involvement in processing threatening stimuli, the amygdala and BNST have a central role in this circuit. Relevant inputs to the amygdala, its

projection to the BNST, and the outputs of these brain areas are illustrated in **FIGURE 6.13**. We saw in the previous section that the amygdala and BNST have been strongly associated with fear and anxiety; however, this circuitry has also been linked to the emotion of anger (Blair, 2012). Thus, it appears that when an individual is faced with a provocative or threatening situation, the situation is evaluated in light of the current context and past experiences to determine whether the response is defensive (elicitation of anxiety or fear along with defensive behaviors) or aggressive (elicitation of anger along with aggressive behaviors).

Historically, the first studies linking 5-HT to aggression appeared in the 1970s and 1980s (reviewed in Rosell and Siever, 2015). Particularly noteworthy were reports that levels of 5-HIAA in the CSF, used as an indicator of brain serotonergic activity, were inversely related to aggressiveness in people with personality disorders such as borderline personality disorder. Combined with other findings, these results gave rise to the **serotonin deficiency hypothesis of aggression**, which proposes that low CNS serotonergic activity is associated with hyperaggressiveness (Umukoro et al., 2013). Animal studies designed to test this hypothesis generally support the notion that relatively high serotonergic levels/activity are associated with reduced aggressive behavior, whereas relatively low serotonergic levels/activity are associated with increased aggressive behavior (Ferrari et al., 2005; Siever, 2008; Carrillo et al., 2009; Lesch et al., 2012; Mosienko et al., 2015; Kästner et al., 2019; Liu et al., 2019).

Studies on the link between 5-HT and aggression in humans have used three major approaches: (a) correlating CSF 5-HIAA levels with aggressive mood or behavior, (b) determining the effects of reducing central 5-HT levels by means of the ATD procedure, and (c) manipulating the serotonergic system pharmacologically and assessing the resulting effects on aggressiveness. The results showed no reliable relationship between CSF 5-HIAA levels (an index of overall brain serotonergic activity) and aggressiveness, a small but statistically significant effect of ATD on aggressive mood or behavior, and a moderately strong relationship between 5-HT and aggression based on pharmacological challenge studies (reviewed in Duke et al., 2013). Consistent with the last point, several studies have found that administration of the SSRI sertraline can reduce anger and irritability in a variety of different psychiatric disorders (reviewed in Romero-Martinez et al., 2019). On the other hand, the weak findings using other methodological approaches suggest that the relationship between 5-HT and aggression in humans may be more complex than implied by the serotonin deficiency hypothesis.

In summary, although the serotonin deficiency hypothesis appears to be too simplistic, there is still substantial evidence for a significant role of 5-HT in aggressive mood and behavior both in animals and in

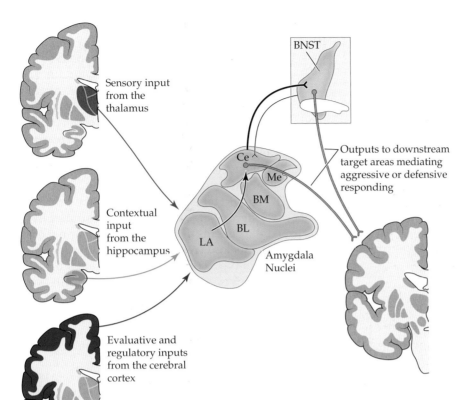

FIGURE 6.13   The amygdala–
BNST circuit involved in threat
processing The amygdala receives
sensory input from the thalamus,
contextual input from the hippocampus, and evaluative/regulatory inputs
from the cerebral cortex. These
inputs are received primarily by the
lateral (LA) nucleus of the amygdala.
Information processing within the
amygdala involves connections from
the lateral nucleus to the basolateral
(BL) and basomedial (BM) nuclei,
and from those areas to the central
nucleus (Ce). The central nucleus
provides input to the bed nucleus of
the stria terminalis (BNST), and both
the central nucleus and BNST project
to downstream target areas that mediate either defensive or aggressive
behavioral and physiological responses to the threat. Me, medial nucleus.
(After A. J. Shackman and A. S. Fox.
2016. *J Neurosci* 36: 8050–8063.)

humans. Furthermore, serotonergic medications such
as SSRIs may be clinically useful in treating symptoms
of excessive aggressiveness.

HUNGER AND EATING BEHAVIOR   Serotonin has long
been known to influence hunger and eating behavior.
Early pharmacological studies found that enhancing
serotonergic activity reduced food intake and body
weight, whereas 5-HT depletion had the opposite effects. As a result, in the early 1990s some physicians
began prescribing the 5-HT–releasing drugs fenfluramine and dexfenfluramine to obese patients for weight
loss. Although the drugs proved modestly successful in
helping patients lose weight, they also led to a significantly elevated risk for two potentially fatal disorders:
heart valve abnormalities and pulmonary hypertension (elevated blood pressure in the arteries between
the heart and lungs). Consequently, both compounds
were withdrawn from clinical use in 1997. Subsequent
research showed that the cardiac side effects of fenfluramine and dexfenfluramine were caused by activation
of 5-HT$_{2B}$ receptors in the heart valve tissue, indicating
that more selective serotonergic agents would have to
be developed to avoid this complication.

Extensive research over the past 30 years or so has
revealed that hunger, satiety, and eating behavior
are controlled by an enormously complex signaling
system involving many different neurotransmitters
and peptide hormones. As such, 5-HT plays only a
small part in this system, yet it is an important one
that has been exploited for the development of safer
anti-obesity medications. **FIGURE 6.14** depicts the main
neural circuit by which central 5-HT influences the motivation to eat (Wyler et al., 2017). Within this circuit
are two kinds of neurons within the **arcuate nucleus**
that synthesize neuropeptides. One type synthesizes
pro-opiomelanocortin (POMC), which is a large peptide that is broken down in the cell into the smaller
bioactive molecule **α-melanocyte stimulating hormone
(α-MSH)**. The second type of arcuate nucleus neuron
co-expresses two different peptides: **neuropeptide Y
(NPY)** and **agouti-related peptide (AgRP)**. As depicted
in the diagram, both types of cells project to the nearby **paraventricular nucleus (PVN)** of the hypothalamus
and synapse on **melanocortin receptor neurons**, so
named because they express MC$_3$ and MC$_4$ melanocortin receptors (designated MC$_{3/4}$R in the diagram).
α-MSH is an agonist at the MC$_{3/4}$ receptors, whereas
the AgRP peptide from the other type of neuron is an
antagonist that blocks the effect of α-MSH. Activation
of the MC$_{3/4}$ receptors by α-MSH is **anorexigenic** (i.e.,
appetite-suppressing), whereas inhibition of these receptors by AgRP is **orexigenic** (appetite-promoting). An
additional and important orexigenic signal is the action
of NPY on the PVN neurons; however, for simplicity,
the NPY receptors are not shown in the diagram.

A careful consideration of the information presented
above along with the figure should make it clear that the
relative balance of activity of the anorexigenic POMC

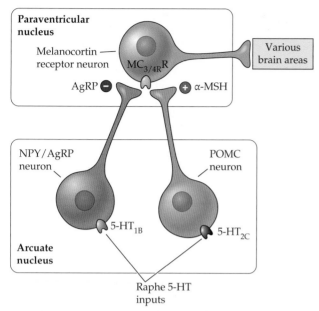

FIGURE 6.14 **Neural circuit through which 5-HT suppresses appetite** Appetite (motivation to eat) is controlled by a circuit of neurons within the arcuate and paraventricular nuclei of the hypothalamus. Arcuate neurons that co-express NPY and AgRP send orexigenic signals to melanocortin receptor neurons in the paraventricular nucleus, while POMC neurons send a contrasting anorexigenic signal instead. The anorexigenic signal is mediated by α-MSH activation of MC$_{3/4}$ receptors, whereas the orexigenic signal is mediated by a combination of AgRP blocking of the MC$_{3/4}$ receptors and NPY activation of its own receptors on the melanocortin neurons (not shown). 5-HT released from DRN and MRN projections to the arcuate nucleus exerts an anorexigenic effect by dual mechanisms: stimulation of the POMC neurons through excitatory 5-HT$_{2C}$ receptors and suppression of the NPY/AgRP neurons through inhibitory 5-HT$_{1B}$ receptors. The balance of orexigenic and anorexigenic signals is integrated by the melanocortin receptor neurons to determine the organism's appetitive state, which is then transmitted to other brain areas responsible for food seeking and eating behaviors as well as the physiological systems that are coordinated with food intake. Note that the figure omits many other neurotransmitters and bloodborne hormones that influence this circuit. AgRP, agouti-related peptide; α-MSH, α-melanocyte stimulating hormone; MC$_{3/4}$R, melanocortin 3 and melanocortin 4 receptors; NPY, neuropeptide Y; POMC, pro-opiomelanocortin. (After S. C. Wyler et al. 2017. *Front Cell Neurosci* 11: 277. doi.org/10.3389/fncel.2017.00277. © 2017 Wyler, Lord, Lee, Elmquist and Liu. CC BY 4.0, creativecommons.org/licenses/by/4.0/)

versus the orexigenic NPY/AgRP neurons determines the relative strength of the organism's motivation to seek out food and eat. Now we can add in how 5-HT is able to influence the circuit. The figure shows that ascending serotonergic fibers from the raphe nuclei (both DRN and MRN) synapse on both types of peptide neurons within the arcuate nucleus. However, the receptors in the POMC cells are of the excitatory 5-HT$_{2C}$ subtype, whereas the receptors in the NPY/AgRP cells are of the inhibitory 5-HT$_{1B}$ subtype. Therefore, global increases in

5-HT release would stimulate the anorexigenic POMC neurons while inhibiting the orexigenic NPY/AgRP neurons, resulting in an overall reduction in appetite.

Even before this appetite-regulating circuit was fully understood, pharmacological studies had already found that 5-HT$_{1B}$ or 5-HT$_{2C}$ receptor agonists reduce food intake and promote weight loss in rodent models of obesity (Voigt and Fink, 2015). For various reasons, pharmacologists chose to focus on the 5-HT$_{2C}$ receptor subtype in the search for anti-obesity medications. This work led to the development and licensing of the selective 5-HT$_{2C}$ agonist **lorcaserin** (**Belviq**) for the treatment of obesity (Nigro et al., 2013). Follow-up studies have confirmed the benefits of this medication for not only helping patients lose weight but also improving their risk profiles for type 2 diabetes, cardiovascular disease, and chronic kidney disease (Tchang et al., 2020). Nevertheless, lorcaserin is not a "magic bullet" for fighting obesity. As with other weight loss medications, patients must increase their physical exercise and modify their diet appropriately in order to achieve maximum benefit.

SEROTONIN IN THE GUT It may surprise you to learn that 90% to 95% of the total bodily 5-HT content is located in the gut, not the brain (McLean et al., 2006). Some of this 5-HT can be found in neurons of the **enteric nervous system**, a large system of ganglia situated within the muscle walls of the intestines. Activity of the enteric nervous system is stimulated by entry of food into the GI tract; this stimulation leads to increased peristalsis (contractions that are necessary for moving food through the GI tract) and release of fluid and hormones by secretory cells of the gut. Even more gut 5-HT, however, is synthesized by **enterochromaffin cells** using the enzyme TPH1, the non-neuronal form of TPH. Enterochromaffin 5-HT is released onto sensory nerve endings within the wall of the gut (**FIGURE 6.15**), after which it is cleared from the extracellular space by SERT. 5-HT taken up by SERT in the membrane of enterocytes (epithelial cells lining the wall of the intestines) is simply metabolized and excreted, whereas other 5-HT molecules reach the bloodstream and are taken up and stored by blood platelets for later release.*

When ingested food reaches the intestines, the combined effect of nutrient signaling and intestinal contractions leads to enhanced release of 5-HT from both the serotonergic neurons of the enteric nervous system and the enterochromaffin cells. The resulting increase in 5-HT levels promotes intestinal secretory activity and increases the rate of peristaltic contractions (Jones et al., 2020). Because of the high concentration of 5-HT in the enterochromaffin cells, many researchers thought that those cells played the most important role

---

*Stored 5-HT is released locally by platelets during blood clotting at the site of an injury. This 5-HT facilitates the clotting process, though it is not required for clotting to occur.

At rest	Stimulation	Recovery
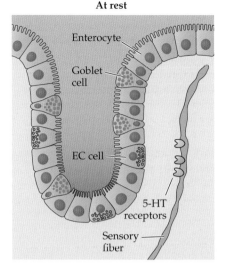	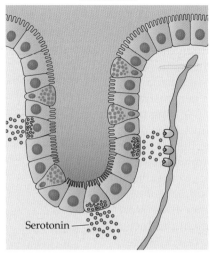	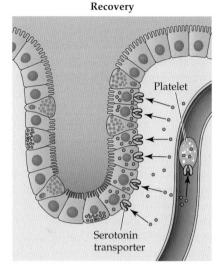

FIGURE 6.15 Release and uptake of 5-HT in the intestine Serotonin is synthesized by specialized secretory cells in the intestinal wall called enterochromaffin (EC) cells. The other cell types depicted in the figure are enterocytes, which are epithelial cells that mediate absorption of nutrients from the gut, and goblet cells, which secrete a layer of protective mucus that lines the intestinal wall. From left to right, the figure first depicts a resting state characterized by minimal 5-HT release, a stimulated state during which 5-HT released by EC cells activates serotonergic receptors on intestinal sensory fibers, and a recovery state in which the released 5-HT is cleared by uptake either into cells of the intestinal wall or into blood platelets in the case of 5-HT molecules that have diffused into the bloodstream. Such uptake is mediated by the serotonin transporter, which is expressed by the EC cells, enterocytes, and platelets. (From G. M. Mawe and J. M. Hoffman. 2013. *Nat Rev Gastroenterol Hepatol* 10: 473–486. Reprinted by permission from Springer Nature. doi.org/10.1038/nrgastro.2013.105)

in mediating the serotonergic effects on gut function. Surprisingly, however, those effects were eliminated in *TPH2*- but not *TPH1*-knockout mice, demonstrating that 5-HT modulation of gut resides primarily in the serotonergic neurons of the enteric nervous system (Amireault et al., 2013; Gershon, 2013).

Understanding the functional role 5-HT in the GI tract has significant clinical ramifications. About 10% to 20% of adults suffer from a distressing disorder known as **irritable bowel syndrome** (**IBS**), the symptoms of which include abdominal pain, gas and bloating, frequent abnormal bowel movements (diarrhea, constipation, or an alternation between the two), and mucus in the stool. IBS is more frequent in women than in men for reasons that are not yet known. There are two subtypes of IBS: diarrhea-predominant (IBS-D) and constipation-predominant (IBS-C). Altered serotonergic activity within the gut may be one of the factors contributing to IBS, which has led to interest in treating IBS symptoms with serotonergic agents (Stasi et al., 2014).

The serotonergic receptor subtype studied most extensively with respect to IBS treatment is the 5-HT$_3$ receptor. 5-HT$_3$ antagonists have been shown to reduce the rate of food transit through the gut and also relieve abdominal pain in patients with IBS-D (Moore et al., 2013). In fact, the only gut-acting serotonergic medication currently approved for IBS is the 5-HT$_3$ antagonist **alosetron** (**Lotronex**), which specifically targets IBS-D (Brenner and Sayuk, 2020). Importantly, alosetron has been linked to rare but potentially dangerous side effects, as a result of which the medication can only be prescribed for women with severe IBS-D that has not responded to other kinds of treatment. Alosetron is a full antagonist at the 5-HT$_3$ receptor, and thus its effects on gut motility are quite strong. However, it might be possible to more subtly influence GI activity using a relatively weak partial agonist at the receptor. As discussed in Chapter 1, partial agonists at a receptor exert lower peak cellular responses than full agonists, but at the same time they block the ability of the full agonist (the neurotransmitter itself) from exerting its peak response. If we hypothesize that IBS-D is due to serotonergic hyperactivity and that IBS-C is due to serotonergic hypoactivity, then a 5-HT$_3$ partial agonist might be successful in treating the symptoms of both disorders (Moore et al., 2013).

Two other receptor subtypes targeted in the development of IBS medications are the 5-HT$_4$ and the 5-HT$_7$ receptors. 5-HT$_4$ agonists accelerate the movement of food through the GI tract, which makes such compounds useful for reducing constipation in patients with IBS-C (Stasi et al., 2014). Two 5-HT$_4$ agonists are currently licensed for treating IBS-C: **prucalopride** (**Motegrity**) and **tegaserod** (**Zelnorm**) (Binienda et al., 2018). Finally, activation of 5-HT$_7$ receptors causes relaxation of intestinal muscles and, therefore, slows peristaltic activity and transit of food through the gut. Compounds acting on this receptor subtype are being considered for the treatment of not only IBS but also other GI tract disorders such as inflammatory bowel disease (Kim and Khan, 2014).

Lastly, the ability of gut 5-HT to signal the brain has become an intriguing topic of study among researchers interested in neuropsychiatric disorders such as depression. We first discussed this area of research in Web Box 3.2, in which we introduced the gut–brain axis and the existence of bidirectional communication between the gut and the brain by way of the vagus nerve. Using a mouse model of depressive-like behavior, Neufeld and coworkers (2019) recently demonstrated that the firing rate of vagal afferents emanating from the gut was increased by chronic administration of either of two SSRIs, fluoxetine or sertraline, but not by the catecholamine reuptake inhibitor bupropion. A separate group of antidepressant-treated mice were subjected to the tail-suspension test, which is similar conceptually to the forced swim test (see Chapter 4). In intact mice, both SSRI and bupropion treatment produced an antidepressant-like response in the test; however, this effect was eliminated by cutting the vagus nerve in the SSRI-treated but *not* the bupropion-treated mice. Taken together, these findings show that chronically elevating serotonergic activity by blocking reuptake (i.e., administering an SSRI) enhances vagal transmission to the brain, and this enhancement contributes to (and may even be necessary for) antidepressant efficacy in this animal model. Moreover, this effect was specific to 5-HT, since the same results were not obtained using a catecholaminergic antidepressant drug. We note that the study does have a significant limitation, namely that only a single behavioral test of antidepressant action was used. The results would have been even more powerful if multiple tests had yielded similar results. Nevertheless, the findings open up the possibility that the gut–brain axis could play a role in the therapeutic benefits of SSRIs in people with mood disorders.

SECTION SUMMARY

■ Mutant mice in which the TPH2 gene has been knocked out lack the capacity to synthesize 5-HT in the nervous system. Such mice suffer postnatal growth retardation and increased mortality. They exhibit heightened aggressiveness, impulsive and compulsive behaviors, and impaired social communication, but less anxiety (at least under some conditions) than wild-type mice. Physiologically, *TH2*-knockout mice suffer from poor thermoregulation and abnormal respiration, manifested in part by episodes of apnea during early postnatal development. Serotonergic neurons are believed to be important in the brain's response to hypercapnia, which has led to the hypothesis that abnormalities in the serotonergic system may be involved in some cases of SIDS.

■ The anxiolytic actions of 5-HT$_{1A}$ receptor agonists demonstrate an important role for this receptor subtype in regulating anxiety and anxiety-related behaviors. Animal studies showed that anxious behavior can be reduced by selective activation of postsynaptic 5-HT$_{1A}$ receptors in the dorsal BNST.

■ Aggressive behaviors in humans can be categorized as reactive or proactive. Reactive aggression is provoked and is accompanied by anger or rage, whereas proactive aggression is planned and usually is devoid of strong emotion. Reactive aggression is mediated by a widespread neural circuit in which the amygdala and BNST have a central role. Several lines of research both in humans and animals have given rise to the serotonin deficiency hypothesis of aggression. While this hypothesis has some experimental support, the involvement of 5-HT in anger and aggressive behavior is undoubtedly more complex than the simple deficiency hypothesis that was first proposed.

■ The motivation to eat has been linked to a hypothalamic circuit that consists of neuropeptide-releasing neurons within the arcuate nucleus that project to melanocortin receptor neurons in the paraventricular nucleus. Arcuate POMC neurons release the anorexigenic peptide α-MSH, while other arcuate neurons co-release the orexigenic peptides NPY and AgRP. Serotonergic fibers from the DRN and MRN synapse on both types of arcuate neurons, but with different cellular effects: the POMC cells are excited by 5-HT$_{2C}$ receptors, whereas the NPY/AgRP cells are inhibited by 5-HT$_{1B}$ receptors. Thus, the overall effect of 5-HT acting on these cellular populations is anorexigenic (suppression of hunger), which prompted the development of the 5-HT$_{2C}$ agonist lorcaserin as a treatment for obesity.

■ Most of the body's 5-HT is located in the gut, where it is synthesized by intestinal enterochromaffin cells and by a subset of neurons within the enteric nervous system. Entrance of food in the gut stimulates local 5-HT release, which, in turn, promotes intestinal secretion of metabolic hormones and increases peristaltic activity. Because of the ability of 5-HT to regulate intestinal motility, several serotonergic medications have been developed to treat irritable bowel syndrome (IBS). Current medication of this type are the 5-HT$_3$ antagonist alosetron for IBS-D and the 5-HT$_4$ agonists prucalopride and tegaserod for IBS-C.

STUDY QUESTIONS

1. (a) List the steps involved in 5-HT synthesis, including the name of the enzyme catalyzing each step. (b) Which is the rate-limiting step in the synthetic pathway? (c) How is the synthesis of 5-HT similar to that of dopamine?

2. Why does a meal rich in carbohydrates but low in protein increase tryptophan entry into the brain? Why doesn't a high-protein, low-carbohydrate meal have a similar effect?

3. (a) The most common procedure used to deplete brain 5-HT in humans is called _____. (b) Describe how this procedure is done.

4. Summarize the effects in humans of either increasing or decreasing brain 5-HT on mood, cognition, and sleep.

5. Like other neurotransmitters, the levels of 5-HT and the activity of serotonergic neurons are maintained in a careful balance. Discuss the mechanisms by which this balance is maintained, including the consequences of 5-HT imbalance (either excessively high or excessively low).

6. Various drugs can be used to manipulate 5-HT synthesis, storage, or reuptake. (a) These drugs include _____, which inhibits tryptophan hydroxylase; _____, which blocks 5-HT vesicular storage; and _____, which blocks 5-HT reuptake. (b) In each case, indicate the effect of the drug on serotonergic transmission.

7. Discuss the pharmacology of MDMA. Include in your answer the history of its discovery and its use as both a recreational drug and as an adjunct to psychotherapy for treatment-resistant PTSD. What is the current status of research concerning MDMA's putative neurotoxic effects on the serotonergic system?

8. What is the name given to the group of cells that synthesize 5-HT in the brain? Name the two specific cell groups that are responsible for most of the serotonergic projections to the forebrain, and list the major forebrain areas that receive these projections.

9. The chapter discusses research on cats showing how the firing of dorsal raphe serotonergic neurons varies according to the stages of sleep and waking. This is followed by experiments on mice that also illustrate relationships between raphe cell firing and sleep or waking. Which of these sets of studies are correlative and which demonstrate causal relationships? Explain your answer.

10. List the names of all the serotonergic receptor subtypes. Which of these receptors are metabotropic, and which are ionotropic?

11. Activation of 5-HT_{1A} receptors _____ (select either "increases" or "decreases") the opening of _____ (select among Na^+, K^+, or Ca^{2+}) channels, which has an _____ (select either "excitatory" or "inhibitory") effect on the postsynaptic cell.

12. Activation of 5-HT_{2A} receptors is mediated by the phosphoinositide second-messenger system. By what biochemical mechanisms does this system affect the postsynaptic cell?

13. For the following list of drugs, identify the specific serotonergic receptor targeted by that drug and indicate whether the drug is an agonist or antagonist at the receptor: (a) DOI, (b) WAY-100635, (c) ketanserin, and (d) 8-OH-DPAT.

14. Which serotonergic receptor subtype can cause hallucinations in humans when activated?

15. What are triptans, what is their clinical use, and how do they work to achieve their therapeutic benefit?

16. What serotonergic receptor antagonists are administered to treat nausea and vomiting associated with cancer chemotherapy? Which receptor subtype do they block?

17. (a) Briefly describe the methodological approaches used to investigate the role of 5-HT in mood and behavior in humans. (b) What are the limitations of such approaches that can be overcome in experimental animal studies?

18. Some of the important functions mediated by brain 5-HT have been studied using *Tph2*-knockout mice along with mice that have developed without central serotonergic neurons. Discuss the various ways in which these mice differ from normal mice behaviorally and physiologically.

19. (a) What are the features of sudden infant death syndrome (SIDS)? (b) Experimental animal studies and post-mortem studies of infants who were believed to have died from SIDS suggest that abnormalities in the serotonergic system are present in <u>some</u> cases of SIDS. What kind of evidence would be necessary to conclude that 5-HT was involved in <u>all</u> instances of death by SIDS?

20. Several medications used clinically to treat anxiety disorders exert their primary actions on the serotonergic system. Which serotonergic receptor subtype has been most strongly implicated in the control of anxiety and anxiety-related behaviors? Provide relevant findings (both human and animal) to support your answer.

21. Situations that involve provocation or threat can elicit several different emotions, including

(Continued)

anxiety or fear on one hand and anger or rage on the other hand. Likewise, different behavioral responses accompany these diverse emotions. Yet, neural circuitry centered around the amygdala and BNST has been implicated in both kinds of emotional states and related behavioral responses. How can this be explained?

22. What is meant by the "serotonin deficiency" hypothesis of aggression? Discuss experimental evidence that either supports or contradicts this hypothesis. Which kind of aggressive behavior in humans is thought to be most clearly related to the serotonergic system?

23. (a) Describe the roles of α-MSH, AgRP, NPY, and melanocortin receptors in the arcuate–PVN circuit within the hypothalamus that regulates the motivation to eat. (b) Serotonergic inputs from the raphe nuclei to the arcuate nucleus stimulate the activity of one type of arcuate neuron and inhibit the activity of a second type of neuron, yet both actions result in an anorexigenic (appetite-suppressing) effect on behavior. Please explain.

24. What are the sources of 5-HT in the GI tract, and why are pharmacologists interested in 5-HT from these sources? Include in your answer a discussion of the clinical relevance of gut 5-HT, including serotonergic medications that have been developed to treat irritable bowel syndrome.

Acetylcholine

IF YOU WERE A SCIENTIFIC RESEARCHER, how much discomfort would you be willing to endure as a participant in your own experiments? For example, would you be willing to take a drug that would cause complete paralysis, thus preventing you from breathing, while you might still be fully conscious and aware of the sensations of asphyxia? Remarkably, that is exactly what was done independently by two research- ers, Frederick Prescott and Scott Smith, in the mid-1940s (Prescott et al., 1946; Smith et al., 1947). Both were experimenting with curare, a toxin found in the bark of several South American plants that was discovered centuries ago by native tribes, who used the substance to tip their poison arrows for hunting and fighting. According to Mann (2000), some tribes calibrated the potency of their curare-containing plant extracts based on the effects of the material on prey animals. For example, a highly potent preparation was called "one-tree" curare, because a monkey hit with an arrow containing this preparation only had time to leap to one nearby tree in its attempts to escape before it became paralyzed and died.

Accounts of the effects of curare were first brought back to Europe by Sir Walter Raleigh at the end of the sixteenth century, but as late as the 1940s some pharmacologists were still unsure whether curare caused unconsciousness and/or analgesia, in addition to paralysis. This was important information since curare was still occasionally being administered during medical (including surgical) procedures with- out the accompaniment of a known anesthetic agent. Answering this question was the primary rationale offered by Smith and colleagues when they published the account of his experience under curare alone. Prescott and coworkers focused instead on deter- mining the optimal dose and method of administration as an adjunct (i.e., additional medication) to a regular anesthetic, but their paper also provides a graphic account of Prescott's reactions to receiving curare by itself. On the basis of self-reports given by both Prescott and Smith after recovery from the drug, the results were conclusive— curare does *not* cause anesthesia. Indeed, both men were fully awake as their growing paralysis prevented them from breathing, and they began to become asphyxiated. Both

© Jim Clare/Minden Pictures

Curare, a toxin that blocks acetylcholine receptors at the neuromuscular junction, has long been used as an arrow poison by various South American tribesmen.

teams provided artificial respiration to their "subjects" during the experiments; however, the method used by Prescott's group was less effective, which resulted in a subjective experience described in the paper as "terrifying."*

How does curare work to induce muscular paralysis? And why doesn't it alter conscious experience when given to an individual? As we shall see in this chapter, the toxic agent in curare blocks a particular kind of receptor for the neurotransmitter **acetylcholine (ACh**; adjective form, **cholinergic**). Acetylcholine is a particularly fascinating transmitter—a molecule that is life sustaining in its function but that is also the target of some of the most deadly known toxins, both naturally occurring and synthetic. ■

7.1 Acetylcholine Synthesis, Release, and Inactivation

Acetylcholine is a key neurotransmitter at many synapses in the peripheral nervous system (PNS), including the type of synapse that is between motor neurons and muscles (called the **neuromuscular junction**) and specific synapses within the sympathetic and parasympathetic divisions of the autonomic nervous system. In contrast, this transmitter is synthesized by only a small number of neurons in the brain; yet, those neurons play an important role in several important behavioral functions. The following sections examine the processes through which this vital transmitter is produced, released, and inactivated. Since both too much and too little ACh are dangerous or even deadly, we also take a look at the various agents that act to either increase or limit the level of ACh in the body.

Acetylcholine synthesis is catalyzed by the enzyme choline acetyltransferase

In contrast to the multiple steps required to synthesize the catecholamine transmitters, ACh is formed in a single step from two precursors: **choline** and **acetyl coenzyme A (acetyl CoA)** (**FIGURE 7.1**). The choline comes mainly from fat in our diet (choline-containing lipids), although it is also produced in the liver. Acetyl CoA is generated within all cells by the metabolism of

*Readers interested in learning more about the history of curare, including how Prescott and Smith came to perform their bold experiments, are referred to an excellent account by Anderson (2010).

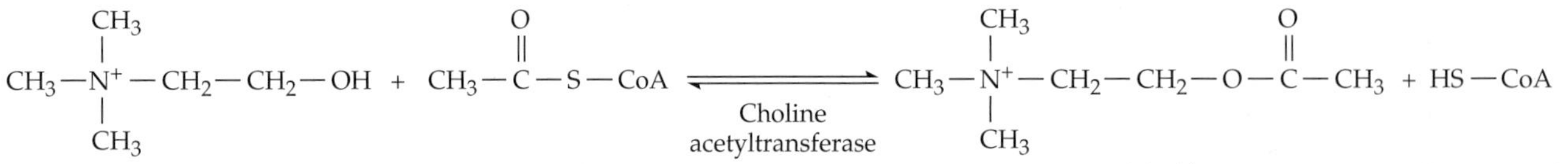

sugars and fats. The synthesis of ACh is catalyzed by the enzyme **choline acetyltransferase (ChAT)**, which does just what its name implies: it transfers the acetyl group (–$COCH_3$) from acetyl CoA to choline to form ACh. Choline acetyltransferase is present in the cytoplasm of the cell, and this enzyme is found only in neurons that use ACh as their transmitter. This specificity allows us to identify cholinergic neurons by staining for ChAT.

The rate of ACh synthesis is controlled by several factors, including the availability of its precursors inside the cell, as well as the rate of cell firing. Thus, cholinergic neurons make more ACh when more choline and/or acetyl CoA is available and when the neurons are stimulated to fire at a higher rate. Although knowledge of these regulatory processes has helped researchers understand how the cholinergic system functions, it has not yet led to the development of useful pharmacological agents. For example, it has been difficult to find highly selective inhibitors of ChAT, and even if such drugs are eventually isolated, it is not clear that inhibiting ACh synthesis will have any obvious clinical usefulness. At one time, it was thought that boosting brain ACh levels by administering large doses of choline might be beneficial for patients with Alzheimer's disease, since damage to the cholinergic system is one of the factors contributing to the cognitive deficits seen in that disorder. However, not only did choline treatment fail to produce symptom improvement, peripheral metabolism of this compound unfortunately caused the patients to give off a strong fishy odor!

Many different drugs and toxins can alter acetylcholine storage and release

The axon terminals of cholinergic neurons contain many small synaptic vesicles that store ACh for release when the nerve cell is active. It is estimated that a few thousand molecules of transmitter are present in each vesicle. Vesicles are loaded with ACh by a transport protein in the vesicle membrane called, appropriately, the **vesicular ACh transporter (VAChT)** (**FIGURE 7.2**). This protein can be blocked by a drug called **vesamicol**. What effect would you expect vesamicol to have on cholinergic neurons? Would you predict any drug-induced change in the distribution of ACh between the cytoplasm and the synaptic vesicles within the cholinergic nerve terminals? Furthermore, if redistribution of ACh occurred, what effect

FIGURE 7.1   Synthesis of acetylcholine (ACh) by choline acetyltransferase

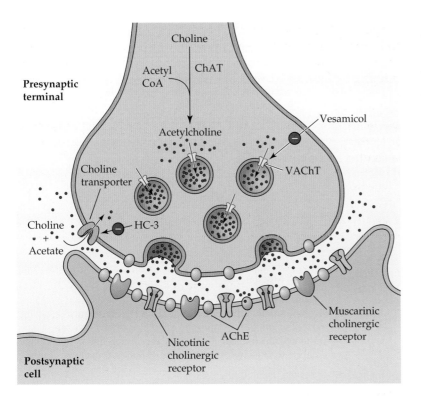

FIGURE 7.2 A cholinergic synapse
The processes of ACh synthesis and metabolism, presynaptic choline uptake, and vesicular ACh uptake and release occur at the synapse. Postsynaptic nicotinic and muscarinic ACh receptors are also shown. AChE, acetylcholinesterase; ChAT, choline acetyltransferase; HC-3, the drug hemicholinium-3; VAChT, vesicular ACh transporter.

Latrodectus mactans, leads to a massive release of ACh at synapses in the PNS. Overactivity of the cholinergic system causes numerous symptoms, including muscle pain in the abdomen or chest, tremors, nausea and vomiting, salivation, and copious sweating. Ounce for ounce, black widow spider venom is 15 times more toxic than prairie rattlesnake venom, but a single spider bite is rarely fatal in healthy young adults because of the small amount of venom injected into the victim. In contrast to the effects of black widow spider venom, toxins that cause botulism poisoning potently inhibit ACh release, which can have deadly consequences due to muscular paralysis. On the other hand, careful localized administration of the same toxin has several medical and cosmetic applications (**BOX 7.1**).

Acetylcholinesterase is responsible for acetylcholine breakdown

Levels of ACh are carefully controlled by an enzyme called **acetylcholinesterase** (**AChE**), which breaks down the transmitter into choline and acetic acid (**FIGURE 7.3**). Within cholinergic neurons as well as postsynaptic neurons that receive a cholinergic innervation, the AChE molecule is initially synthesized as a single globular molecule (an AChE subunit). Four of these subunits subsequently combine to form a tetramer (a structure with four parts) that is denoted G4 ("G" for globular, and "4" designating the four subunits). A certain percentage of the G4 tetramer remains free within the cell and is thus designated "soluble"; however, the majority of the G4 tetramers are linked to an anchor that tethers them to the cell membrane in an excellent location to rapidly break down ACh after its release (**FIGURE 7.4**). Finally, a unique

would this have on ACh release by the cells? If you predicted that vesamicol treatment would decrease vesicular ACh but increase the level of ACh in the cytoplasm, you were correct. This is because vesamicol doesn't affect the rate of ACh synthesis; therefore, ACh molecules that normally would have been transported into the vesicles remain in the cytoplasm of the terminal. Moreover, because synaptic vesicles are the main source of ACh release when the cholinergic neurons fire, such release is reduced in the presence of vesamicol. Studies by Parsons and colleagues (1999) demonstrated that after vesamicol treatment, empty synaptic vesicles continue to undergo exocytosis and recycling when the cholinergic neurons are activated. It's rather remarkable that considering all the feedback and regulatory mechanisms that have evolved within the nervous system and other physiological systems, there is no feedback mechanism to prevent neurons from continuing to release and recycle vesicles that contain little or no neurotransmitter!

The release of ACh is dramatically affected by various animal and bacterial toxins. For example, a toxin found in the venom of the black widow spider,

$$CH_3-\underset{\underset{CH_3}{|}}{\overset{\overset{CH_3}{|}}{N^+}}-CH_2-CH_2-O-\overset{\overset{O}{||}}{C}-CH_3 + H_2O \xrightarrow{\text{Acetylcholinesterase}} CH_3-\underset{\underset{CH_3}{|}}{\overset{\overset{CH_3}{|}}{N^+}}-CH_2-CH_2-OH + HO-\overset{\overset{O}{||}}{C}-CH_3$$

Acetylcholine   **Choline**   **Acetic acid**

FIGURE 7.3 Breakdown of ACh by acetylcholinesterase

BOX 7.1 ■ PHARMACOLOGY IN ACTION

Botulinum Toxin—Deadly Poison, Therapeutic Remedy, and Cosmetic Aid

The bacterium **Clostridium botulinum**, which is responsible for botulism poisoning, produces what is perhaps the most potent toxin known to pharmacologists. The estimated lethal dose of botulinum toxin in humans is 0.3 micrograms; in other words, 1 gram (equivalent to the weight of three aspirin tablets) is enough to kill more than 3 million individuals. *Clostridium botulinum* does not grow in the presence of oxygen; however, it can thrive in an anaerobic (oxygen-free) environment such as a sealed food jar or can that has not been properly heated to kill the bacteria.

Botulinum toxin actually consists of a mixture of seven related proteins known as botulinum toxins A through G. These proteins are taken up selectively by peripheral cholinergic nerve terminals, including those located at the neuromuscular junction, autonomic ganglia, and postganglionic parasympathetic fibers (e.g., cholinergic fibers innervating smooth muscle and secretory glands). The toxin molecules interfere with the process of ACh release at the terminals, thereby blocking neurotransmission (see **FIGURE**). When cholinergic motor neurons have been affected by botulinum toxin, the result is muscle weakness and possible paralysis. Other symptoms of botulism poisoning include blurred vision, difficulty speaking and swallowing, and gastrointestinal distress. Most victims recover, although a small percentage die as the result of severe muscle paralysis and eventual asphyxiation.

Once the mechanism of action of botulinum toxin became known, researchers began to consider that this substance, if used carefully and at very low doses, might be helpful in treating clinical disorders characterized by involuntary muscle contractions (Ting and Freiman, 2004). After appropriate testing, in 1989 the U.S. Food and Drug Administration approved the use of purified botulinum toxin A for the treatment of strabismus (crossed eyes), blepharospasm (spasm of the eyelid), and hemifacial spasm (muscle spasms on just one side of the face). Since that time, this substance has been administered for a variety of other disorders, including spastic cerebral palsy, stroke-related spasticity, dystonias (prolonged muscle contractions, sometimes seen as repeated jerking movements), axillary hyperhidrosis (extreme underarm sweating), sialorrhea (excessive salivation leading to drooling), overactive bladder, achalasia (failure of sphincter muscles to relax when appropriate), and bruxism (habitual teeth grinding) (Alster and Harrison, 2020; Dressler, 2021). You should be able to discern that some of these treatments are aimed at relaxation of specific skeletal muscles, whereas others are aimed at reduction of smooth muscle or secretory activity. It's also worth mentioning that some of these are "off-label" uses, meaning that the drug is being administered for medical conditions that have not received prior FDA approval. This practice is not illegal and is, in fact, not uncommon in the medical

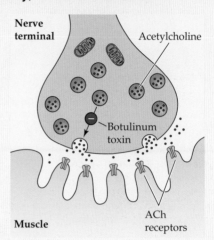

Mechanism of action of botulinum toxin at the neuromuscular junction Botulinum toxin blocks ACh release at the neuromuscular junction by preventing fusion of synaptic vesicles with the nerve terminal membrane.

profession. Off-label drug use is frequently the topic of research studies as investigators explore the wider clinical potential of a particular medication. However, care must be used, as adverse side effects can occur (for botulinum toxin, adverse reactions were recently reviewed by Witmanowski and Blochowiak, 2020).

Interestingly, in addition to its action as a long-acting muscle relaxant, botulinum toxin A also exerts analgesic effects in certain kinds of chronic pain disorders. This has led to its use as a treatment for migraine headaches, trigeminal neuralgia (severe chronic pain of the fifth cranial nerve), and chronic pelvic pain syndrome. The mechanisms underlying pain relief from botulinum toxin A have been investigated but are not yet fully understood (Matak et al., 2019).

Even if you're not familiar with the abovementioned medical applications of botulinum toxin, you may have heard of its use (under the trade name Botox) by dermatologists for cosmetic purposes in patients with excessive frown lines, worry lines, or crow's-feet around the eyes. Such "dynamic wrinkles," as they are called, result from chronic contraction of specific facial muscles. When injected locally into a particular muscle or surrounding area, Botox causes paralysis of that muscle as the result of blockade of ACh release from incoming motor nerve fibers. This leads to a reduction in the offending lines or wrinkles, although each treatment remains effective for only a few months, after which it must be repeated. Despite this limitation, many dermatologists and their patients have chosen Botox treatment over plastic surgery for improving facial appearance (Satriyasa, 2019). It seems safe to say that both the medical and cosmetic uses of botulinum toxin will continue to grow in the coming years.

Soluble G4

Individual
AChE subunit

Membrane-bound G4

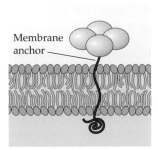

Membrane
anchor

A12 neuromuscular junction

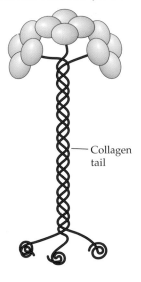

Collagen
tail

FIGURE 7.4 **Forms of acetylcholinesterase in the nervous system** Three main forms of AChE occur within the brain and peripheral nervous system. Cholinergic neurons and postsynaptic neurons that receive ACh input synthesize the G4 forms of the enzyme. Most of the G4 AChE is bound to the cell membrane by a tail, as shown. At the neuromuscular junction, muscle cells synthesize the A12 form of AChE that possesses a collagen tail. This form is secreted into the neuromuscular junction, where the collagen tail anchors it to the extracellular matrix. (After R. L. Rotundo. 2020. *Neurosci Lett* 735: 135157. © 2020. Reprinted with permission from Elsevier.)

type of AChE is found at neuromuscular junctions, the specialized synapses between neurons and muscle cells where ACh is released by motor neurons to stimulate muscular contraction. Within the muscle cells, 12 AChE subunits are combined, given a long tail containing three molecules of the protein collagen wound into a helical structure, secreted into the neuromuscular junction space, and finally anchored to the extracellular matrix* by means of the collagen tail. This form of AChE is designated A12, meaning "asymmetric" AChE containing 12 subunits. The unique localization of A12 AChE helps the transmission process function very precisely at neuromuscular junctions. Immediately after a squirt of ACh causes a particular muscle to contract, the transmitter is metabolized extremely rapidly, and the muscle can relax until the next command arrives to squirt out some more ACh and contract that muscle once again. On the other hand, if a sustained contraction is required, the motor neurons can fire at rates up to 100 Hz (Dunant and Gisiger, 2017). In this case, rapid ACh breakdown between individual release events (which occur at intervals of 10 milliseconds for a 100-Hz burst of nerve impulses) prevents the muscle receptors from becoming desensitized to the neurotransmitter. We discuss the phenomenon of desensitization in greater detail in a later section.

---

*The extracellular matrix is a network of large molecules including structural proteins and enzymes that is s present in all tissues and organs of the body but is situated outside of the individual cells (hence "extracellular"). Components of the extracellular matrix interact with cell membranes as well as substances secreted by cells, thereby helping to maintain the structural and functional integrity of each tissue.

Once ACh has been broken down within the synaptic cleft or neuromuscular junction, a significant portion of the liberated choline is taken back up into the cholinergic nerve terminal by a **choline transporter** in the membrane of the terminal (see Figure 7.2). If the choline transporter is blocked by means of the drug **hemicholinium-3** (**HC-3**), the rate of ACh production declines. Furthermore, mutant mice in which the choline transporter has been knocked out die within about 1 hour after birth (Ferguson et al., 2004). The cause of death in these animals is lack of normal breathing due to failure to sustain ACh synthesis and release at the neuromuscular junction. These findings tell us that utilization of recycled choline plays a critical role in maintaining ongoing ACh synthesis.

Drugs that block AChE prevent inactivation of ACh, thereby increasing the postsynaptic effects of the transmitter. Several AChE inhibitors occur naturally, but many others are synthetic compounds. Inhibition of ACh breakdown can be beneficial for neurological disorders in which cholinergic transmission is deficient, but such inhibition can also be highly toxic, even fatal (reviewed by Čolović et al., 2013). Besides the obvious factor of drug dose, whether a particular compound is likely to be used as a medicine or as a poison depends on whether it crosses the blood–brain barrier and whether it blocks AChE reversibly or irreversibly.

The most widespread use of AChE inhibitors is for the treatment of age-related **dementia**, which refers to a broad reduction of cognitive functions (e.g., memory, language, and problem solving) that is severe enough to interfere significantly with daily functioning. There are several different types of dementia that differ in their etiology. Examples include frontotemporal dementia (caused by progressive loss of neurons in the frontal and temporal lobes), vascular dementia (caused by damage to the cerebral blood vessels, such as from a stroke), dementia associated with Parkinson's disease, and especially dementia associated with Alzheimer's disease. Currently licensed drugs used to treat age-related dementias are **donepezil** (**Aricept**), **rivastigmine** (**Exelon**), and **galantamine** (**Reminyl**), all of which are synthetic compounds that enter the brain and inhibit AChE activity. The rationale for the use of AChE inhibitors in patients with Alzheimer's disease is the significant loss of forebrain cholinergic neurons in this disorder and the evidence that such loss contributes to the profound cognitive deficits suffered by these patients. Thus, increasing the availability of the remaining ACh offers some cognitive benefit, although the effects are modest, last only 1 to 3 years, and do not prevent progression of the disease (Ferreira-Vieira et al., 2016; Stanciu et al., 2020). Much more information about Alzheimer's disease, including symptoms, neuropathology, and current treatments, is provided in Chapter 20. Of the other age-related dementias described above, some benefit from AChE inhibitor treatment but others do not (Knight et al., 2018). This variability is likely related to the relative degree of involvement of cholinergic dysfunction in producing the cognitive deficit in different forms of dementia and from one patient to another.

One of the best-characterized natural AChE inhibitors is **physostigmine**, also known as **eserine**, which is a compound isolated from Calabar beans (the seeds of a woody plant found in the Calabar region of Nigeria). When applied directly to the eyes, physostigmine can help treat glaucoma because of its ability to increase drainage of the excess fluid. But when given systemically, the drug can cause serious symptoms both peripherally and centrally because of its ability to cross the blood–brain barrier. Symptoms of physostigmine poisoning include slurred speech, mental confusion, hallucinations, loss of reflexes, convulsions, and even coma and death. Nineteenth-century missionaries to West Africa discovered societies that used extracts of the Calabar bean to determine the guilt of accused prisoners (Davis, 1985). The defendant was considered innocent if they were fortunate enough to regurgitate the poison or, alternatively, if they could manage to walk 10 feet under the influence of the toxin (in which case vomiting was induced). Needless to say, however, most prisoners did neither and were consequently judged guilty and were permitted to die a horrible death.

Physostigmine as well as the drugs used to treat Alzheimer's disease are reversible AChE inhibitors. This means that drug molecules bind temporarily to the enzyme protein to inhibit its action, after which the drug dissociates from the enzyme and ACh breakdown is restored. However, certain other chemicals, which are called **organophosphorus compounds** due to their chemical structure, produce a nearly irreversible inhibition of AChE activity. This can occur either because dissociation of the compound from the enzyme is extremely slow or because the compound actually forms a covalent chemical bond with the enzyme. Weaker versions of these irreversible inhibitors are widely used as insecticides, since preventing ACh breakdown is just as harmful to ants and wasps as it is to humans. On the other hand, it's important to be aware that acute organophosphate poisoning is a significant health problem in developing countries as well as in agricultural workers in the developed world (Chowdhary et al., 2014; Suratman et al., 2015; Muñoz-Quezada et al., 2016). In addition to cases of accidental poisoning, some developing countries are plagued by intentional

consumption of the poison for suicidal purposes. Finally, long-term exposure to organophosphorus compounds in the environment poses a worldwide health risk both to humans and to other organisms, with a special emphasis on the adverse consequences of developmental exposures (Jokanović, 2018; Eddleston, 2019; Pascale and Laborde, 2020).

Tragically, even more-toxic varieties of irreversible AChE inhibitors have been developed as "nerve gases" for use in chemical warfare. These agents go by names such as **sarin** and **soman**. **FIGURE 7.5** shows the chemical structure of sarin. Sarin and soman are designed to be dispersed as a vapor cloud or spray, which allows their entry into the body through skin contact or by inhalation. In either case, the drug quickly penetrates into the bloodstream and is distributed to all organs, including the brain. Symptoms of nerve gas poisoning, which include profuse sweating and salivation, vomiting, loss of bladder and bowel control, and convulsions, are due to rapid ACh accumulation and overstimulation of cholinergic synapses throughout both the CNS and the PNS. Death occurs through asphyxiation due to paralysis of the muscles of the diaphragm. Sarin and other chemical warfare agents were reportedly used by Iraqi forces during the Iran–Iraq war of the 1980s (Haines and Fox, 2014). More recently the Syrian government has been accused of sarin gas attacks in 2013 and 2017 during the course of that country's civil war (Sellström et al., 2013; Brooks et al., 2018).

When an enemy possesses a stockpile of nerve agents and has demonstrated a willingness to use them, the opponent must take measures to counteract the threat. During the Persian Gulf War of 1990–1991, as well as the later conquest of Iraq, Allied forces were very concerned about possible use of sarin by the Iraqi army. Consequently, tablets of the reversible AChE inhibitor **pyridostigmine** were widely distributed to Allied troops for use as a nerve gas antidote. How can a reversible AChE inhibitor be an antidote against sarin or soman? It appears that the temporary interaction of pyridostigmine with the enzyme protects AChE from permanent inactivation by the nerve gas. This protective effect, however, requires that the antidote be administered ahead of time—before exposure to the toxic agent. Therefore, soldiers were instructed to take three pyridostigmine pills daily at times when they were thought to be at risk for nerve gas attack. However, some soldiers took the drug much more frequently,

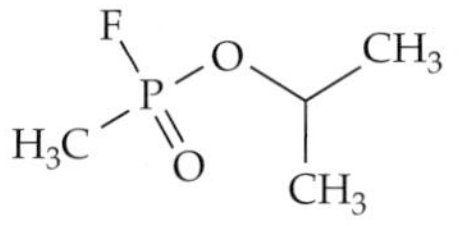

Sarin

FIGURE 7.5 Chemical structure of sarin

thus leading to heavy exposure. Review of scientific findings by the Research Advisory Committee on Gulf War Veterans' Illnesses (2008; 2014) led the committee to conclude that such exposure may have contributed significantly to the development of "Gulf War illness," a complex multisymptom disorder currently thought to afflict at least 25% of U.S. veterans who served in that combat theater. Other contributors to Gulf War illness may be exposure to the nerve gases themselves, such as during demolition of storage sites for munitions containing these chemicals. Michalovicz and colleagues (2020) recently proposed that exposure to AChE inhibitors, combined with the stress of combat, may have initiated a chronic neuroimmune disorder that is responsible for Gulf War illness symptoms. While speculative, this theory may help the medical community better understand Gulf War illness and find better treatments for veterans suffering from that condition.

Several neuromuscular disorders are associated with abnormal cholinergic functioning at the neuromuscular junction

Proper control of our skeletal muscles requires precise regulation of ACh release, breakdown, and activation of cholinergic receptors on the muscle cells. We have already seen that prevention of ACh release at the neuromuscular junction due to botulism poisoning causes a potentially fatal muscle paralysis. Abnormal functioning of the neuromuscular junction cholinergic system is also the cause of several rare clinical disorders that manifest as severe muscle weakness and fatigue. The best known of these is **myasthenia gravis** (which literally means "grave muscle weakness"). Myasthenia gravis is an example of an **autoimmune disorder**, a condition in which a part of the body is attacked by one's own immune system. In most cases of this disorder, antibodies are formed against the skeletal muscle cholinergic receptors, first blocking the receptors, and eventually causing them to be broken down by the muscle cells (**FIGURE 7.6**). Loss of receptor function causes the patient's muscles to be less sensitive to ACh, which, in turn, leads to a variety of neuromuscular symptoms including generalized weakness, persistent fatigue, dysarthria (speech difficulties), dyspnea (labored breathing), and ptosis (drooping of the upper eyelid) (Souto et al., 2019). The symptoms of myasthenia gravis are shared with many other neuromuscular disorders, which can lead to initial difficulty in diagnosing the disorder (see **WEB BOX 7.1**). However, once the proper diagnosis has been made, patients are

administered an AChE inhibitor to enhance the effectiveness of the remaining cholinergic receptors. Two drugs used for this purpose are the previously mentioned pyridostigmine (**Mestinon**) as well as **neostigmine (Prostigmin)**, both of which are synthetic analogs of physostigmine that do not cross the blood–brain barrier. This property prevents the adverse side effects of inhibiting central AChE. Unfortunately, treatment with pyridostigmine or neostigmine does not prevent progression of the disease. Yet, if the disorder is well controlled and the person is highly motivated, it is possible engage in strenuous physical activities, even up to running in a marathon race (Birnbaum et al., 2018).

People are not born with myasthenia gravis. Rather, the disorder begins to manifest some time in young adulthood or later. On the other hand, there are congenital neuromuscular disorders called **myasthenic syndromes** that result from mutations in the genes that encode either ChAT or AChE (Arican et al., 2018; Legay, 2018). If a mutation causes ChAT activity to be abnormally low, then insufficient amounts of ACh are released at the neuromuscular junction, leading to neuromuscular symptoms. Paradoxically, somewhat similar effects are caused by deficient AChE activity. In this case, the persistently elevated levels of ACh at the neuromuscular junction lead to desensitization of the receptors and reduced cholinergic transmission. Symptoms of myasthenic syndromes begin to appear during infancy, and they may include muscle weakness, respiratory distress, episodes of apnea, and ptosis. In cases where the disorder is caused by inadequate ChAT activity, it should not be surprising that the standard

Normal neuromuscular junction

Neuromuscular junction in myasthenia gravis

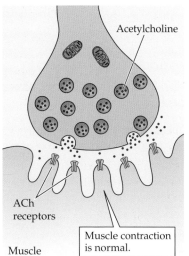
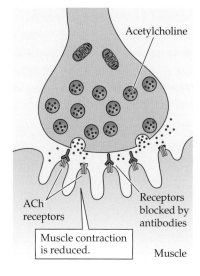

Acetylcholine

Acetylcholine

ACh receptors

Muscle contraction is normal.

Muscle

ACh receptors

Muscle contraction is reduced.

Receptors blocked by antibodies

Muscle

FIGURE 7.6 **Myasthenia gravis, an autoimmune disorder** In myasthenia gravis, antibodies interfere with cholinergic transmission at the neuromuscular junction by binding to and blocking the muscle ACh receptors.

treatment is pyridostigmine, just like the treatment of myasthenia gravis. In contrast, you can see that when AChE is already deficient or absent, administration of a drug that blocks this enzyme would be ineffective at best or even increase the symptoms at worst. Indeed, there are currently no good remedies for myasthenic syndromes caused by AChE gene mutations.

SECTION SUMMARY

- ACh is not only found in the brain but is also a key transmitter at the neuromuscular junction and at specific synapses within the sympathetic and parasympathetic branches of the autonomic nervous system.

- ACh is synthesized from choline and acetyl CoA in a single reaction catalyzed by the enzyme choline acetyltransferase. The rate of ACh synthesis is controlled by precursor availability and is increased by cell firing.

- ACh is loaded into synaptic vesicles by the specific vesicular transporter VAChT, which can be blocked by vesamicol.

- A variety of animal and bacterial toxins influence the cholinergic system either by stimulating or inhibiting ACh release. Local administration of the paralytic toxin botulinum toxin A has both medical and cosmetic uses due to its ability to prevent ACh release from cholinergic nerve terminals.

- Following its release into the synapse or neuromuscular junction, ACh is rapidly degraded by the enzyme AChE. Within the brain, most of the AChE is consists of tetramers of the globular form of the enzyme (designated G4) that are tethered to the cell membrane. The neuromuscular junction contains a specialized asymmetric form of AChE (A12) that is secreted by muscle cells and anchored to extracellular matrix.

- Much of the choline liberated from ACh breakdown is taken back up into the cholinergic nerve terminal by a choline transporter that plays a critical role in maintaining ongoing ACh synthesis. This transporter can be blocked by HC-3.

- Drugs that block AChE cause prolongation of ACh action at postsynaptic or muscular cholinergic receptors.

- Several reversible AChE antagonists that enter the brain are currently used to treat mild to moderate Alzheimer's disease.

- Organophosphorus compounds that block AChE irreversibly are the active ingredients of some insecticides, and similar but more potent inhibitors are the main components of dreaded nerve gases.

- Cholinergic abnormalities at the neuromuscular junction give rise to several different neuromuscular disorders such as myasthenia gravis that are characterized by weakness, fatigue, and related symptoms. This is an autoimmune disorder usually caused by the development of antibodies against the muscle acetylcholine receptors. Neuromuscular function can be at least partially restored by treatment with reversible AChE inhibitors that do not cross the blood–brain barrier.

- Muscle weakness and other symptoms can also be caused by rare congenital myasthenic syndromes related to a deficiency in either ChAT or AChE activity at the neuromuscular junction.

7.2 Organization and Function of the Cholinergic System

We have already noted the presence of ACh as a transmitter at the neuromuscular junction and within the autonomic nervous system. Indeed, this substance was first identified as a neurotransmitter in the PNS. In the following sections we will describe the location of cholinergic cell bodies and synapses in both the PNS and CNS, the receptor subtypes for ACh, and some of the key behavioral and physiological functions of this neurotransmitter.

Cholinergic neurons play a key role in the functioning of both the peripheral and central nervous systems

Before we examine the function of cholinergic neurons, let's briefly review the organization of the autonomic nervous system. Both the sympathetic and parasympathetic branches consist of preganglionic neurons, which are cells located within the CNS that send their axons to the autonomic ganglia, as well as ganglionic neurons located within the ganglia that innervate various target organs throughout the body. The preganglionic neurons of both branches are cholinergic, as are the ganglionic neurons of the parasympathetic system (we saw in Chapter 5 that norepinephrine is the transmitter of the sympathetic ganglionic neurons). **FIGURE 7.7** illustrates the chemical coding of these cells and the synapses they make. Widespread involvement of ACh in both the neuromuscular

Parasympathetic branch

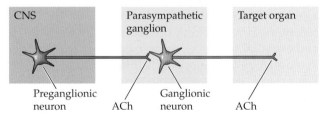

Sympathetic branch

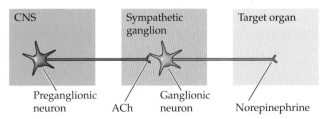

FIGURE 7.7 Cholinergic synapses in the parasympathetic and sympathetic branches of the autonomic nervous system

and autonomic systems explains why drugs that interfere with this transmitter exert such powerful physiological effects and sometimes are highly toxic.

Within the brain, the cell bodies of cholinergic neurons are clustered within just a few areas (**FIGURE 7.8**). Some of these nerve cells, such as the ones found within the striatum, are interneurons. Cholinergic interneurons make up only 1% to 2% of total striatal neurons; however, each of these cells contains an average of 500,000 synaptic varicosities along the length of its axon (reviewed by Ztau and Amalric, 2019). By virtue of this extensive communication with the striatal output neurons, ACh plays an important role in striatal functioning in both health and disease. In Chapter 5, we learned that the dopaminergic input to the striatum is critical for the normal regulation of movement. However, this input does not work in isolation but rather interacts with the cholinergic interneurons to determine striatal output (Tanimura et al., 2018; Ztau and Amalric, 2019). Indeed, the loss of this interaction when the striatal dopaminergic fibers degenerate in Parkinson's disease is believed to contribute to the motor disturbances produced by this disorder. One long-standing hypothesis has been that Parkinsonian symptoms are related, in part, to hyperactivity of the cholinergic interneurons after release from D$_2$ receptor-mediated dopaminergic inhibition. In support of this hypothesis, Maurice and coworkers (2015) used the 6-hydroxydopamine lesion model of Parkinson's disease (see Chapter 5) to demonstrate that the

motor deficits produced by the lesion could be reversed by inhibiting cholinergic interneuron firing.

The involvement of ACh in Parkinson's disease has been exploited clinically by the use of anticholinergic drugs such as **orphenadrine** (**Norflex**), **benztropine mesylate** (**Cogentin**), **trihexyphenidyl** (**Artane**), **procyclidine** (**Kemadrin**), and **biperiden** (**Akineton**) as treatment options (DeMaagd and Philip, 2015). Anticholinergic medications may be prescribed instead of L-DOPA in the early stages of Parkinson's disease or they may be used later in conjunction with L-DOPA therapy. Because of the potential side effects of blocking the cholinergic receptors (see below), caution should be used when prescribing these medications. Such caution is particularly warranted in older patients, which is almost exclusively the population at risk for Parkinson's disease (López-Álvarez et al., 2019).

Other cholinergic neurons send their axons longer distances to innervate many different brain areas. For example, a diffuse collection of cholinergic nerve cells called the **basal forebrain cholinergic system** (**BFCS**) comprises neurons interspersed among several anatomical areas, including the nucleus basalis/substantia innominata, medial septal nucleus, and diagonal band nuclei. The BFCS is the origin of a dense cholinergic innervation of the cerebral cortex, as well as the hippocampus and other limbic system structures. **BOX 7.2** discusses a few of the well-established roles of the BFCS in cognitive function.

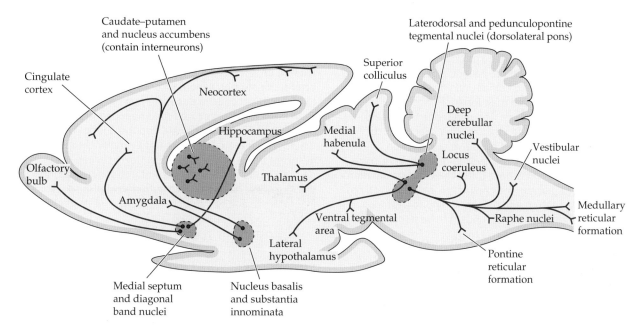

FIGURE 7.8 **Anatomy of cholinergic pathways in the brain** The cell bodies of cholinergic neurons are located primarily in the caudate–putamen, nucleus accumbens, nucleus basalis/substantia innominata, medial septum, diagonal band nuclei, pedunculopontine tegmental nucleus, and dorsolateral tegmental nucleus. Note that the basal forebrain cholinergic cell groups send fibers to all areas of the cortex, as well as to limbic system structures such as the hippocampus and amygdala. Cell groups of the pedunculopontine tegmental and dorsolateral tegmental nuclei primarily innervate subcortical structures except for those that (a) receive input from the basal forebrain system, and (b) contain cholinergic interneurons (i.e., caudate–putamen, and nucleus accumbens).

BOX 7.2 ■ THE CUTTING EDGE

Acetylcholine and Cognitive Function

Cognition is an amazingly complex process that requires attending to external and internal sensory stimuli; processing this stimulus information and relating it to past experience; forging connections between multiple stimuli, between stimuli and responses, and between responses and rewards (i.e., "learning"); encoding newly learned information into short-term memory; consolidating short-term memories into long-term memory stores; and finally recalling the learned information when needed. Research over many years has led to the view that ACh plays an important role in several features of cognitive functioning. Indeed, as we have already seen, AChE inhibitors, which boost synaptic availability of ACh, are among the first-line treatments for Alzheimer's disease–related cognitive deficits.

The earliest evidence for involvement of ACh in cognition came from observations that the anticholinergic agents atropine and scopolamine can produce amnesic effects in humans. The memory loss produced by these drugs mimics, to some extent, the memory deficits observed in people with Alzheimer's disease (Ebert and Kirch, 1998). During the first half of the twentieth century, it was common for obstetricians to administer morphine and scopolamine to pregnant women in labor. The resulting state, often called "twilight sleep," enabled patients to avoid both the pain and the memory of labor; however, the procedure unfortunately had adverse effects on the newborn infants and, therefore, is rarely used in modern obstetrics. Behavioral pharmacologists later began to administer scopolamine or occasionally atropine to experimental animals, particularly rats and mice, and found that these compounds produced deficits in the acquisition and maintenance of many different kinds of learning tasks. The challenge of subsequent research has been to pin down the exact nature of anticholinergic-related cognitive dysfunction.

Researchers have discovered that different components of the BFCS have different roles in cognition. We will first discuss the cholinergic projections from the medial septum and diagonal band to the hippocampus. The hippocampus is thought to be necessary for the encoding of declarative memories (memories of facts and events that can be consciously recalled) but not implicit memories (memories of skills or procedures like riding a bicycle) (Bird and Burgess, 2008). Anticholinergic drug administration or damage to the septohippocampal cholinergic pathway produces selective deficits in declarative but not procedural memory (Haam and Yakel, 2017). In experimental animal research, declarative-type memories are often studied using spatial navigation tasks like the Morris water maze (see Chapter 4). Many studies have shown that the acquisition of such tasks is indeed impaired by

disrupting cholinergic transmission. Thus, Hasselmo (1999; 2006) has proposed that ACh is important for the memory encoding of hippocampal-dependent learning.

Other cell bodies of the BFCS that are located in the nucleus basalis/substantia innominata are the main source of cholinergic innervation of the cerebral cortex. One of the key functions of cortical ACh, particularly in the prefrontal cortex, is to enhance performance of tasks requiring sustained attention. Research on sustained attention in rats and mice is often conducted using the 5-choice serial reaction time task. In this task, the animals must detect a brief flash of light randomly presented in one of five apertures in the test chamber and then quickly respond with a nose poke into the aperture in which the light had appeared. Detection of the light stimulus and responding in the correct aperture leads to a food reward. Early studies showed that selective lesions of the nucleus basalis cholinergic neurons in rats caused the animals to perform poorly in the 5-choice serial reaction time task (McGaughy et al., 2002). Later work by Sarter and colleagues built upon these initial findings. First, the researchers demonstrated phasic ACh release in the prefrontal cortex of rats and mice when the animals detect a light stimulus (i.e., cue) during performance of another type of sustained-attention task (reviewed in Sarter et al., 2016; Sarter and Lustig, 2020). Because such results are only correlative in nature, a subsequent study used optogenetics to test whether these brief pulses of ACh are *causally* related to the ability of animals to detect and respond accurately to a cue (Gritton et al., 2016). In this study, mice were first trained on a task requiring them to detect whether a brief flash of light, ranging from 25 milliseconds (ms) to 500 milliseconds in duration, had been presented. Both cued (light presented) and noncued (no light presented) trials were given, and the animal reported whether it detected a cue or not by making one of two different nose-poke responses. Correct responses on both kinds of trials were reinforced. In reporting the results of the study, the authors referred to trials in which the subject detected the cue and responded with the correct nose poke "hits."

To experimentally control activity of the BFCS neurons, the researchers transfected some mice with channelrhodopsin-2 (ChR2), a light-sensitive protein that excites neurons when activated by a laser, whereas other mice were transfected with halorhodopsin (NpHR), which inhibits neuronal activity when activated by laser light of a different wavelength. Key results of the study are shown in the figures. **FIGURE A** depicts the effects on hit rate of strongly stimulating ChR2 in the BFCS neurons under conditions of long and short cue duration. With a long-duration cue, which is easy for the mice to

BOX 7.2 ■ THE CUTTING EDGE (continued)

detect, the mean control hit rate (left) was approximately 85%, and this rate was unaffected by BFCS neuronal stimulation (right). On the other hand, with a short-duration cue, which is much more difficult for the mice to detect, the mean control hit rate was much lower (just over 55%) but the hit rate was increased to that of the long-duration cue when the cholinergic neurons were stimulated. In contrast, **FIGURE B** shows that the hit rate with the long-duration cue was reduced to the hit rate of the short-duration cue when firing of the BFCS neurons was inhibited using NpHR. Together, these results strongly support the hypothesis that bursts of ACh release from BFCS neurons play a key role in detecting and responding to learned sensory cues. Current evidence summarized in Sparks and colleagues (2018) suggests that the ACh-mediated increase in sensory attention depends on excitation of prefrontal layer VI pyramidal cells that project to the thalamus (corticothalamic tract), whereas the transition from attention to action (e.g., making the nose-poke response) is enhanced by cholinergic excitation of layer V pyramidal cells that project to the pons (corticopontine pathway).

Roughly 40 years ago, Raymond Bartus and colleagues proposed that the cognitive decline that often occurs with aging is due, at least in part, to dysfunction of the BFCS (Bartus et al., 1982). This spurred tremendous interest in the BFCS, not only with respect to normal aging but also regarding a possible role in the age-related disorder Alzheimer's disease (Ballinger et al., 2016). Indeed, the cholinergic hypothesis of Alzheimer's dementia subsequently led to the development of AChE inhibitors for treating this disorder (see above and Chapter 20). Although damage to the BFCS almost certainly contributes to the cognitive deficits seen in patients with Alzheimer's, it is only part of the problem, because widespread loss of other cells and synaptic connections throughout the cerebral cortex and hippocampus also occurs. Nevertheless, there is continued interest in developing novel cholinergic agents targeting either muscarinic or nicotinic receptors for treating not only Alzheimer's dementia but also the cognitive deficits associated with schizophrenia and

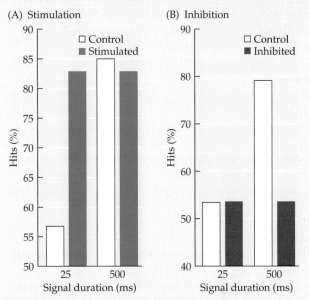

(A) Stimulation

(B) Inhibition

Effects of optogenetic stimulation or inhibition of BFCS cholinergic neurons on visual cue detection (A) Mice exposed to a short-duration (25 ms) or long-duration (500 ms) visual cue (light flash) reported whether they detected the cue by performing a nose-poke response. The open bars show control performance that consisted of a low hit rate associated with the short cue and a high hit rate associated with the long cue. The solid blue bars show that optogenetic stimulation of the BFCS cholinergic neurons increased the hit rate to the short cue but had no effect on the hit rate to the long cue. (B) The open bars show results from the same control conditions as in (A). The solid red bars show performance associated with optogenetic inhibition of the cholinergic neurons. In this case, inhibition of the cells diminished the hit rate to the long cue but had no effect on the hit rate to the short cue. (A, B after H. J. Gritton et al. 2016. *Proc Natl Acad Sci USA* 113: E1089–E1097.)

certain other neuropsychiatric disorders (Bock et al., 2018; Hoskin et al., 2019; Moran et al., 2019). Allosteric receptor modulators are of particular interest in this regard because of their potential for tuning receptor activation more subtly and with fewer adverse side effects than standard receptor agonists.

A third group of behaviorally important cholinergic neurons is located in the dorsolateral pons within the **laterodorsal** and **pedunculopontine tegmental nuclei** (abbreviated **LDTg** and **PPTg**, respectively). These cells give rise to extensive projections, some of which ascend to the basal ganglia and thalamus and others that descend to the lower brainstem and spinal cord. Among the ascending projections are fibers that synapse with midbrain dopaminergic neurons in the ventral tegmental area and substantia nigra. ACh released from this

pathway exerts a powerful excitatory influence on dopamine neuron firing, which is mediated, in part, by activation of postsynaptic nicotinic cholinergic receptors (Mena-Segovia and Bolam, 2017). Indeed, experiments with laboratory animals indicate that the excitation of midbrain dopamine neurons by the pontine cholinergic cells is important for the rewarding and reinforcing effects of several addictive drugs, including nicotine (Xiao et al., 2020), cocaine (Kaneda, 2019), and opioids (Steidl et al., 2017). In contrast, the main role of the descending cholinergic fibers is to help promote rapid-eye-movement (REM) sleep. Although the pontine cholinergic cells are not *necessary* for REM sleep to occur, when they are activated the transition from non-REM sleep to REM sleep is facilitated (Fraigne et al., 2015; Grace and Horner, 2015).

Like the catecholaminergic and serotonergic systems described in previous chapters, many cholinergic varicosities throughout the brain do not have a postsynaptic element (dendritic branch, dendritic spine, or cell soma) in close proximity (Disney and Higley, 2020). Thus, a certain portion of ACh signaling likely occurs by volume transmission (i.e., receptor activation following neurotransmitter diffusion away from the sites of release).

There are two acetylcholine receptor subtypes: nicotinic and muscarinic

Like dopamine and norepinephrine, ACh has many different kinds of receptors. The story can be simplified a little by recognizing that the various cholinergic receptors belong to one of two families: **nicotinic receptors** and **muscarinic receptors**. Nicotinic receptors

were so named because they respond selectively to the agonist nicotine, a toxic alkaloid found in the leaves of the tobacco plant.* The pharmacology of nicotine is discussed in Chapter 13. Muscarinic receptors are selectively stimulated by muscarine, another alkaloid toxin, which was first isolated in 1869 from the fly agaric mushroom, *Amanita muscaria*. **TABLE 7.1** presents some of the drugs that affect the cholinergic system, including nicotinic and muscarinic receptor agonists and antagonists. A discussion of these receptors and the mechanisms of action of the drugs listed in the table is presented in the sections below.

NICOTINIC RECEPTORS   Nicotinic acetylcholine receptors (nAChRs) are highly concentrated on muscle cells at neuromuscular junctions, on ganglionic neurons of both the sympathetic and parasympathetic systems, and on certain neurons within the brain. They

---

*Alkaloids are nitrogen-containing compounds, usually bitter tasting, that are often found in plants. These compounds are usually toxic and are synthesized by plants for defensive purposes against being eaten by insects and other predators.

TABLE 7.1   Drugs and Toxins That Affect the Cholinergic System

Drug/Toxin	Mechanism of Action	Clinical, Recreational, or Experimental Use; Toxin
Vesamicol	VAChT inhibitor	Experimental use
Black widow spider venom	Stimulates ACh release	Experimental use; toxin
Botulinum toxin	ACh release inhibitor	Treatment for muscle spasms, secretory disorders, and others; toxin
Hemicholinium-3	Choline uptake inhibitor	Experimental use
Donepezil, rivastigmine, and galantamine	Reversible central and peripheral AChE inhibitors	Treatments for Alzheimer's disease
Physostigmine	Reversible central and peripheral AChE inhibitor	Experimental use; toxin
Sarin and soman	Irreversible central and peripheral AChE inhibitors	Toxins (nerve gases)
Pyridostigmine and neostigmine	Reversible peripheral AChE inhibitors	Treatments for myasthenia gravis
Orphenadrine and others	Cholinergic receptor (muscarinic) antagonists	Adjunct treatments for Parkinson's disease
Nicotine	General nicotinic receptor agonist with selectivity for neuronal receptors	Recreational use; toxic at high doses
Succinylcholine	Muscle nicotinic receptor agonist that produces depolarization block	Muscle relaxant/paralytic
Mecamylamine	Neuronal nicotinic receptor antagonist	Experimental use
D-Tubocurarine	Muscle nicotinic receptor antagonist	Experimental use; toxin
Imidacloprid and others (neonicotinoids)	Insect nicotinic receptor agonists	Toxins (insecticides)
Muscarine, pilocarpine, and arecoline	Muscarinic receptor agonists (parasympathomimetic)	Experimental use; toxins
Atropine and scopolamine	Muscarinic receptor antagonists (parasympatholytic)	Atropine is used surgically to reduce secretory activity and in ophthalmology for pupillary dilation; toxins

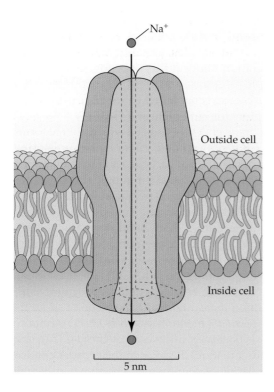

Na⁺

Outside cell

Inside cell

5 nm

FIGURE 7.9 Structure of the nicotinic ACh receptor The receptor comprises five protein subunits that are arranged to form a central pore or channel that allows Na⁺ (and to some extent Ca²⁺) ions to flow into the cell when the receptor is activated.

chapter, interested readers can find more information in Chen et al. (2019) and Mucchietto et al. (2016).

The nAChR was the first neurotransmitter receptor to be biochemically isolated, purified, and then characterized. Much of the key work in this discovery process was carried out in the 1960s and 1970s by a team led by Jean-Pierre Changeux (see Changeux, 2020, for a historical account of this research). Importantly, the structure of the nAChR determined biochemically was subsequently verified using molecular biological approaches. Together, this research showed that each nAChR is a complex that contains five **subunits**, which are proteins that are assembled and then inserted into the cell membrane. These subunits are identified by the Greek letters α, β, γ, δ, and ε. However, their complexity is increased by the existence of 10 different kinds of α subunits (designated α1 through α10) and four different kinds of β subunits (designated β1 through β4). All nAChRs contain α subunits, since the interaction of these subunits either with one another or with a β subunit forms the ACh binding site.

nAChR subunit composition differs between muscle cells and neurons. Specifically, each muscle receptor contains two α1 subunits, one β1, one γ, and either a δ or an ε subunit (**FIGURE 7.10**). Because of the presence of two α subunits, two ACh binding sites are present and both must be occupied for the receptor channel to open. In contrast, neuronal nAChRs have no γ, δ, or ε subunits but instead come in three main forms with the

are ionotropic receptors, which, you will recall from Chapter 3, means that they possess an ion channel as an integral part of the receptor complex (**FIGURE 7.9**). When ACh binds to a nAChR, the channel opens very rapidly, and sodium (Na⁺) and calcium (Ca²⁺) ions enter the neuron or muscle cell. This flow of ions causes depolarization of the cell membrane, thereby increasing the excitability of the cell. If the responding cell is a neuron and the receptor is located on the cell soma or a dendrite, then the cell's likelihood of firing is increased. If it is a muscle cell, it responds by contracting. In this manner, nAChRs mediate fast excitatory responses in the autonomic nervous system and at the neuromuscular junction. Surprisingly, however, the large majority of nAChRs within the *brain* are located presynaptically on nerve terminals (Brown, 2019). Activation of these presynaptic receptors has no effect on firing of the receiving cell but instead enhances neurotransmitter release from the nerve terminal by depolarizing the terminal.

Researchers have discovered that nAChRs are expressed by many nonneuronal cells both within and outside of the brain (Zoli et al., 2018). Perhaps most strikingly, nAChRs are often found in tumor cells (for example, breast or lung cancer tumors) and contribute to tumor growth when activated. While this topic is outside of the scope of the present

Muscle nicotinic receptor

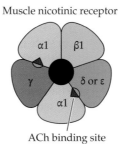

ACh binding site

Neuronal α4β2 receptor

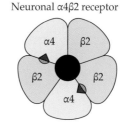

Neuronal α7 receptor

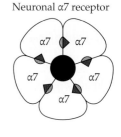

FIGURE 7.10 Three common types of nicotinic ACh receptors The muscle nicotinic receptor shown on the left is designated as (α1)₂(β1)(γ)(δ/ε), which means that each receptor complex contains two α1 subunits, one β1 subunit, one γ subunit, and one δ or ε subunit. The γ, δ, and ε subunits each have only one form, which is why no numbering is needed in those cases. Nicotinic receptors in neurons are more complex because of the variety of α and β subunit combinations that have been detected in these cells. For simplicity, we are depicting here just two important kinds of neuronal nicotinic receptors found in the brain: (α4)₂(β2)₃ and (α7)₅. Note that the muscle and the (α4)₂(β2)₃ receptors have two ACh binding sites, whereas the (α7)₅ receptor has five ACh binding sites. Whether two or five such sites are present, all must be occupied by ACh or another agonist such as nicotine for the receptor channel to open.

following subunits: (1) two α and three β subunits [designated $(\alpha)_2(\beta)_3$], (2) three α and two β subunits [designated $(\alpha)_3(\beta)_2$], or (3) five α subunits [designated $(\alpha)_5$]. Figure 7.10 illustrates two particularly important types of neuronal nAChRs—$(\alpha4)_2(\beta2)_3$ and $(\alpha7)_5$—both of which have been implicated in the cognitive effects of ACh and are current targets of medications under development (see Box 7.2). Receptors with other subunit compositions have also been identified, and their distribution varies with brain area (Zoli et al., 2015; 2018; **FIGURE 7.11**). To understand the nAChR numbering system, keep in mind that the number *within* the parentheses shown after the Greek letter represents which member of a family of subunits (e.g., 1–10 in the case of the α subunit) is present, whereas the subscript number shown just *after* the parentheses represents how many of that subunit (e.g., two, three, or five αs) help make up the receptor complex.

At this point in our discussion, the reader may be wondering why so much attention is paid to nAChR subunit composition. The answer is that key features of the receptor such as (1) affinity of the receptor binding sites for ACh and for pharmacological agonists and antagonists, (2) ionic selectivity of the channel (the degree to which the channel is selective in permitting flux of Na^+ and Ca^{2+} ions while excluding other cations), (3) ionic permeabilities of the channel (rates of Na^+ and Ca^{2+} flux through the open channel pore), (4) channel

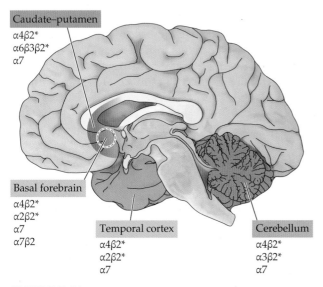

FIGURE 7.11 **Composition of nicotinic receptor subtypes identified in selected areas of the human brain** Multiple receptor subtypes are found in each of the brain regions shown in the figure. All of the receptors shown with an asterisk (*) contain two α and two β subunits [e.g., $(\alpha4)_2(\beta2)_2$ in the caudate–putamen] that form the two agonist binding sites. The fifth subunit is either an α or a β that does not participate in agonist binding. The α7β2 receptor shown in the basal forebrain is a rare subtype that is thought to be expressed only in this brain area. (After M. Zoli et al. 2015. *Neuropharmacology* 96: 302–311. © 2014. Reprinted with permission from Elsevier.)

opening and closing kinetics (rates of channel opening and closing), and (5) presence and characteristics of allosteric binding sites, are all dependent on subunit composition. Indeed, this dependence is true for *all* ionotropic receptors, and we shall encounter other examples in the next chapter when we discuss the ionotropic receptors for glutamate and GABA.

The functional effects associated with different forms of the nAChR can be studied either by administering drugs that are selective for particular subunit-containing forms or by using molecular biological techniques to inactivate the gene for a specific subunit (i.e., creating a knockout of that gene). Note that in the latter approach, all receptors that would normally contain the knocked-out subunit are eliminated in the mutant animals. Both of these approaches have been used to investigate the composition of nAChRs involved in the cholinergic enhancement of cognition, particularly sustained attention measured using the 5-choice serial reaction time task first mentioned in Box 7.2. Performance on this task is positively influenced by the $(\alpha4)_2(\beta2)_3$ and $(\alpha7)_5$ nAChRs mentioned earlier in the broader context of ACh regulation of cognitive functioning (Guillem et al., 2011; Kolisnyk et al., 2015). nAChRs containing the unusual composition $(\alpha4)_2(\alpha5)(\beta2)_2$ also seem to play a role in attentional performance, particularly under highly demanding conditions (Proulx et al., 2014). These receptors are found in many of the layer VI pyramidal neurons of the medial prefrontal cortex, which are the same neurons discussed in Box 7.2 that are excited by BFCS cholinergic input and that project to the thalamus.

Ionotropic receptors, indeed all ion channels, can exist in three different states: **closed**, **open**, and **desensitized**. In the "closed" state of an ionotropic receptor, the neurotransmitter (in this case ACh) is not bound to the receptor and the channel pore is closed. When a "closed" nAChR is activated by the binding of an agonist such as ACh or nicotine, the receptor converts to the "open" state in which the pore opens and ions can flow across the membrane. The third state, "desensitized," is unlike either of the other two states in that the pore is closed and *cannot* be opened while the receptor remains in the desensitized state. nAChRs and other ionotropic receptors can spontaneously convert from one state to the other, depending, in part, on agonist association or dissociation from the ligand binding site (**FIGURE 7.12**). But it is important to note that *prolonged* exposure to an agonist enhances the rate of conversion to the desensitized state. Only after a desensitized nAChR spontaneously undergoes **resensitization** is it capable of responding to an agonist. In Chapter 13 we will discuss the relevance of this phenomenon for nicotine addiction. Even if cells are continuously exposed to nicotinic stimulation, not all of the receptors are desensitized. Those that remain active produce a persistent depolarization of the cell membrane. If this continues for very long, a process

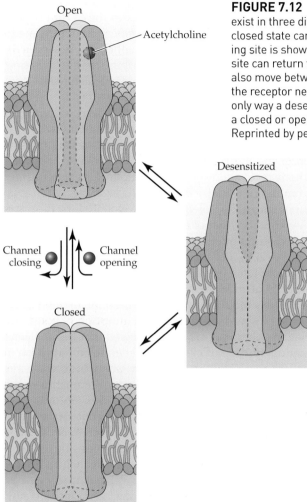

Open

Acetylcholine

Channel closing

Channel opening

Closed

Desensitized

FIGURE 7.12 **Functional states of the nicotinic ACh receptor** The receptor can exist in three different states: open, closed, and desensitized. A channel in the closed state can be opened by agonist binding (note that only a single agonist binding site is shown for the sake of simplicity). Dissociation of agonist from its binding site can return the receptor to the closed state. However, receptor complexes can also move between open or closed states to a state of desensitization, in which the receptor neither permits ion flow nor can be activated by agonist binding. The only way a desensitized receptor can be activated is to be resensitized into either a closed or open state. (After Z. S. Wu et al. 2015. *Acta Pharmacol Sin* 36: 895–907. Reprinted by permission of Springer Nature. doi.org/10.1038/aps.2015.66)

effect of mecamylamine led to its development many years ago as an antihypertensive agent, although in modern medicine it has been largely supplanted by other medications with fewer side effects. A structurally different compound, **D-tubocurarine**, is a well-known antagonist of muscle nAChRs. This substance is the main active ingredient of curare, the paralytic agent discussed in the chapter opener. D-Tubocurarine has relatively little effect on central cholinergic transmission, not only because of its selectivity for muscle nAChRs but also because it exhibits low penetrance across the blood–brain barrier.

Neonicotinoids such as imidacloprid, acetamiprid, and thiacloprid make up an unusual class of receptor agonists that are relatively selective for insect nAChRs (Simon-Delso et al., 2015). Since their discovery in the 1980s, these compounds have become the most widely used insecticides in the world, particularly for crop protection. Following application, neonicotinoids are absorbed and distributed throughout the treated plants, to be consumed subsequently by any insect pests feeding on those plants. Once inside the insects, toxicity is believed to result from continuous excitation of neuronal nAChRs. The relative lack of activity of neonicotinoids on vertebrate nAChRs is related mainly to receptor subunit differences between insects and vertebrates. Because of their effectiveness in protecting crops from insect damage, the introduction and widespread adoption of neonicotinoids for pest control has undoubtedly been a boon to agriculture worldwide (Jeschke and Nauen, 2008). On the other hand, there is growing concern that these substances are harmful not only to insect pests but also to beneficial pollinating insects like honeybees and bumblebees (Grünewald and Siefert, 2019). Neonicotinoids may even exert subtle adverse effects on vertebrate species (Gibbons et al., 2015). Primarily because of demonstrated effects on bee populations, several neonicotinoid-containing insecticides have been banned in the United States and/or Europe, yet others remain on the market. As with any industrial or agricultural chemical, government regulators must make difficult decisions based on risk-versus-benefit calculations.

called **depolarization block** occurs, in which the resting potential of the membrane is lost, and the cell cannot be excited until the agonist is removed and the membrane repolarized.

A chemical relative of ACh called **succinylcholine** (also called **suxamethonium**) is a powerful muscle relaxant that is used medically to induce brief paralysis for insertion of a breathing tube (e.g., in a hospital emergency room) or sometimes for maintaining a longer period of paralysis in surgical procedures for which anesthesia alone may not provide sufficient relaxation. Unlike ACh, succinylcholine is resistant to breakdown by AChE; thus it continuously stimulates the nAChRs and induces a depolarization block of the muscle cells. It is important to note that one of the paralyzed muscles is the diaphragm, which is the large muscle responsible for inflating and deflating the lungs. Consequently, the patient must be maintained on a ventilator until the effect wears off as succinylcholine is metabolized by nonspecific cholinesterases present in the blood.

Mecamylamine (Inversine) is an antagonist at neuronal nAChRs that blocks these receptors both centrally and in autonomic ganglia. The ganglionic blocking

MUSCARINIC RECEPTORS As mentioned earlier, muscarinic receptors represent the other family of ACh receptors. Like the receptors for dopamine and norepinephrine, muscarinic receptors are all metabotropic. Five different types of muscarinic receptors (designated M_1 through M_5) have been identified, each with specific pharmacological characteristics and coded for by a different gene. Muscarinic receptors operate through several different second-messenger systems. The odd-numbered muscarinic receptor subtypes (i.e., M_1, M_3, and M_5) function by activating the phosphoinositide second-messenger system. In contrast, the M_2 and M_4 subtypes have three primary modes of action: (1) inhibition of cyclic adenosine monophosphate (cAMP) synthesis, (2) stimulation of potassium (K^+) channel opening, and (3) inhibition of nerve terminal calcium (Ca^{2+}) channel opening (Brown, 2019). Because of these different signaling mechanisms, activation of M_1, M_3, or M_5 receptors typically leads to excitation of the postsynaptic cell, where activation of M_2 or M_4 receptors typically leads to postsynaptic inhibition. The latter effect may be related either to hyperpolarization of the cell membrane (caused by increased K^+ channel opening) when the receptor is located on the cell soma or dendrite, or inhibition of neurotransmitter release (caused by decreased Ca^{2+} channel opening) when the receptor is located on a nerve terminal. Some M_2 and/or M_4 receptors are located on cholinergic nerve terminals where they function as autoreceptors.

Muscarinic receptors are widely distributed in the brain. Some areas containing high levels of muscarinic receptors are the neocortex, hippocampus, thalamus, striatum, and basal forebrain. Receptors in the neocortex and hippocampus play an important role in the cognitive effects of ACh, whereas those in the striatum are involved in motor function. As in the case of nAChR subunits, researchers have investigated muscarinic receptor functions using a combination of selective agonists and antagonists, as well as knockout mice for each receptor subtype. Allosteric muscarinic receptor modulators have become increasingly important targets of drug development for treating various neuropsychiatric and neurological disorders, including schizophrenia, Alzheimer's disease, and substance use disorders (Moran et al., 2019; Walker and Lawrence, 2020). Among the interesting findings are those pertaining to the M_5 muscarinic receptor, which is expressed in the brain primarily in the hippocampus, hypothalamus, and midbrain DA areas (i.e., the substantia nigra pars compacta and the ventral tegmental area, or VTA). Indeed, M_5 is the only muscarinic receptor subtype expressed in those midbrain dopaminergic neurons. We mentioned

earlier that cholinergic neurons in the LDTg exert an excitatory effect on VTA dopaminergic neurons mediated by nAChRs on the postsynaptic cells. However, M_5 muscarinic receptors also contribute to this excitation, and the muscarinic effects are more prolonged because the receptors are metabotropic in contrast to the ionotropic nAChRs (Foster et al., 2014). Indeed, a number of studies have demonstrated a role for M_5 receptors in the reinforcing effects of electrical self-stimulation of the brain and in drug reinforcement (Yeomans et al., 2001; Thomsen et al., 2018). One example of the latter comes from recent work by Berizzi and coworkers (2018), who investigated the potential involvement of M_5 receptors in voluntary ethanol consumption by a genetically selected strain of ethanol-preferring (iP) rats (see Ciccocioppo, 2013, for a review of this and other strains of ethanol-preferring rats). **FIGURE 7.13** shows that administration of an M_5 receptor negative allosteric modulator selectively reduced ethanol consumption in the subjects while having no effect on consumption of a sucrose (sugar) solution. This result showed that the allosteric modulator did not produce a generalized reduction in reward motivation in the animals, and it illustrates the potential value of this or similar drugs for treating abuse of alcohol or other substances.

Outside of the brain, muscarinic receptors are found at high densities in cardiac muscle, in the smooth muscle associated with many organs (e.g., bronchioles, stomach, intestines, bladder, urogenital organs), and in secretory glands, including salivary glands, sweat glands, and the β-cells of the pancreas that are responsible for

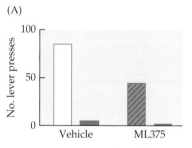
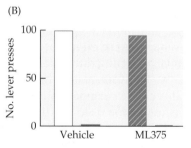

FIGURE 7.13 Administration of an M_5 muscarinic receptor negative allosteric modulator reduces voluntary ethanol consumption in iP rats Male iP rats (a strain of animals genetically selected to consume ethanol voluntarily) were trained to press a lever for a 10% ethanol/water solution reinforcer. A second lever in the chamber delivered a water-only solution instead. A separate set of learning trials was conducted using a sucrose (sugar) solution as the reinforcer. After the animals had been trained on these tasks, they were given test trials with either ethanol or sucrose reinforcement after being given either the M_5 receptor negative allosteric modulator ML375 (30 mg/kg, injected IP three times at 27, 11, and 3 hours before testing) or the drug vehicle. (A) In the ethanol test, ML375 pretreatment significantly reduced the number of responses on the ethanol lever (open vs. striped bars) but had no effect on the small number of responses on the lever that delivered water (solid bars). (B) In contrast to the ethanol results, ML375 had no effect on responding for sucrose reinforcement. (From A. E. Berizzi et al. 2018. *Neuropsychopharmacology* 43: 1510–1517. doi.org/10.1038/s41386-017-0007-3. CC BY 4.0, creativecommons.org/licenses/by/4.0/)

insulin secretion. These peripheral muscarinic receptors are activated by ACh released from postganglionic fibers of the parasympathetic nervous system. Stimulation of the parasympathetic system has two effects on the heart: a slowing of heart rate and a decrease in the strength of contraction, both of which are mediated by M_2 muscarinic receptors in cardiac muscle. In contrast, smooth muscle cells and secretory glands express M_3 receptors and are typically excited by receptor activation, thus causing muscle contraction and increased secretory activity. Unfortunately, many of the drugs used to treat depression, schizophrenia, and other major psychiatric disorders produce serious side effects because of their blockade of peripheral muscarinic receptors, especially the receptors associated with secretory glands. Consequently, patients taking such medications often complain about the so-called **dry mouth effect** (technically referred to as xerostomia), which reflects the reduced production of saliva that results from muscarinic receptor blockade. For some, the dry mouth effect is severe enough to cause the patient to stop taking their medication. If the medication is continued, the chronic lack of salivation can lead to mouth sores, tooth decay, and difficulty in chewing and swallowing food. Later in the book, we will see that pharmaceutical companies have worked to develop newer medications that react less with muscarinic receptors and therefore do not produce the dry mouth effect.

Several muscarinic receptor agonists occur in nature, including muscarine, from *Amanita muscaria*; **pilocarpine**, from the leaves of the South American shrub *Pilocarpus jaborandi*; and **arecoline**, which is found in the seeds of the betel nut palm *Areca catechu*. These substances are sometimes referred to as **parasympathomimetic agents** because their ingestion mimics many of the effects of parasympathetic activation. Thus, poisoning due to accidental ingestion of *Amanita* or the two plants mentioned leads to exaggerated parasympathetic responses, including lacrimation (tearing), salivation, sweating, pinpoint pupils related to constriction of the iris, severe abdominal pain, strong contractions of the smooth muscles of the viscera, and painful diarrhea. High doses can even cause cardiovascular collapse, convulsions, coma, and death.

Given the autonomic effects of muscarinic agonists, it is understandable that antagonists of these receptors would inhibit the actions of the parasympathetic system. Such compounds, therefore, are called **parasympatholytic agents**. The major naturally occurring muscarinic antagonists are **atropine** (also sometimes called hyoscyamine) and the closely related drug **scopolamine** (hyoscine). These alkaloids are found in a group of plants that includes henbane (*Hyoscyamus niger*) and deadly nightshade (*Atropa belladonna*) (**FIGURE 7.14**). Extracts of these plants are toxic when taken systemically—a fact that was exploited during the Middle Ages, when deadly

FIGURE 7.14 Deadly nightshade *Atropa belladonna* is a natural source of the muscarinic antagonist atropine.

nightshade was used as a lethal agent to settle many political and family intrigues. On the other hand, a cosmetic use of the plant also evolved, in which women instilled the juice of the berries into their eyes to cause pupillary dilation by blocking the muscarinic receptors on the constrictor muscles of the iris. The effect was considered to make the user more attractive to men. Indeed, the name *Atropa belladonna* reflects these two facets of the plant, since *bella donna* means "beautiful woman" in Italian, whereas Atropos was a character in Greek mythology whose duty it was to cut the thread of life at the appropriate time.

Muscarinic antagonists have several current medical applications. Modern ophthalmologists use atropine just as women of the Middle Ages did, except in this case they are dilating the patient's pupils to obtain a better view of the interior of the eye. Another use is in human and veterinary surgery, where the drug reduces secretions that could clog the patient's airways. Atropine is also occasionally needed to counteract the effects of poisoning with a cholinergic agonist. Scopolamine in therapeutic doses produces drowsiness, euphoria, amnesia, fatigue, and dreamless sleep. As mentioned in Box 7.2, this drug was historically used along with narcotics as a preanesthetic medication before surgery, or alone prior to childbirth to produce "twilight sleep," a condition characterized by drowsiness and amnesia for events that occur during the duration of drug use.

Despite their therapeutic uses, muscarinic antagonists can themselves be toxic when taken systemically at high doses. CNS effects of atropine poisoning include restlessness, irritability, disorientation, hallucinations, and delirium. Even higher doses can lead to CNS depression, coma, and eventually death by respiratory paralysis. As in the case of nicotinic drugs, these toxic effects point to the delicate balance of cholinergic activity in both the CNS and the PNS that is necessary for normal physiological functioning.

SECTION SUMMARY

- Acetylcholine is an important neurotransmitter in the PNS, where it is released by motor neurons innervating skeletal muscles, by preganglionic neurons of both the parasympathetic and sympathetic branches of the autonomic nervous system, and by ganglionic parasympathetic neurons.

- In the brain, cholinergic neurons include a group of interneurons within the striatum, a diffuse system of projection neurons that constitute the basal forebrain cholinergic system (BFCS), and a group of brainstem neurons in the laterodorsal and pedunculopontine tegmental (LDTg and PPTg) nuclei.

- Imbalance between the activity of striatal cholinergic interneurons and the dopaminergic input to the striatum is hypothesized to contribute to the motor symptoms of Parkinson's disease.

- The BFCS plays an important role in cognitive functioning. Cholinergic projections from the medial septum and diagonal band to the hippocampus are involved in the encoding of declarative memories, whereas other projections from the nucleus basalis/substantia innominata to the prefrontal cortex are important for maintaining sustained attention.

- Cholinergic neurons located in the LDTg and the PPTg exert multiple roles, including stimulation of midbrain dopamine neurons (important for drug reward and reinforcement) and initiation of rapid-eye-movement sleep.

- Cholinergic receptors are divided into two major families: nicotinic and muscarinic receptors.

- Nicotinic receptors are ionotropic receptors comprising five subunits. When the receptor channel opens, it produces a fast excitatory response resulting from an influx of Na^+ and Ca^{2+} ions across the cell membrane. In the brain, the majority of these receptors are located presynaptically, where they enhance neurotransmitter release from nerve terminals.

- Nicotinic receptors in neurons and muscles possess somewhat different subunits, and this leads to significant pharmacological differences between the two types of receptors. Some of the cognitive functions of ACh have been ascribed to activation of $(\alpha 4)_2(\beta 2)_3$, $(\alpha 4)_2(\alpha 5)(\beta 2)_2$ or $(\alpha 7)_5$ nicotinic receptors.

- Ionotropic receptors, including nicotinic receptors, can exist in a closed, open, or desensitized state. Prolonged exposure to a nicotinic receptor agonist such as nicotine itself promotes conversion of the receptor to a desensitized state in which the channel will not open despite the presence of the agonist. In such a case, the receptor must be resensitized before it can be activated again. Nicotinic receptors can also cause a process of depolarization block involving temporary loss of the cell's resting potential and an inability of the cell to generate action potentials. This is the basis for certain muscle relaxants used in medicine.

- There are five kinds of muscarinic receptors, designated M_1 through M_5, all of which are metabotropic receptors. Activation of M_2 or M_4 receptors has an inhibitory effect mediated by inhibition of cAMP synthesis and stimulation of K^+ channel opening. Activation of the other muscarinic receptor subtypes is generally excitatory, which is mediated by the phosphoinositide second-messenger system,

- Muscarinic receptors are widely distributed in the brain, with particularly high densities in various forebrain structures. M_5 receptors in the VTA contribute to drug reward and dependence.

- Outside of the brain, muscarinic receptors are found in targets of the parasympathetic system, including the heart, secretory glands, and smooth muscle found in many internal organs. Consequently, general muscarinic agonists are called parasympathomimetic agents, whereas antagonists are considered parasympatholytic in their actions.

- M_2 receptors mediate the effects of the parasympathetic system on the heart, whereas M_3 receptors stimulate secretory responses of the sweat and salivary glands and also the insulin-secreting β-cells of the pancreas. Blockade of muscarinic receptors in the salivary glands leads to the dry mouth effect, which is a serious side effect of many drugs used to treat various psychiatric disorders.

STUDY QUESTIONS

1. What are the chemical reactions involved in ACh synthesis and breakdown? Include the names of the enzymes catalyzing each reaction. Why is the enzyme that catalyzes ACh synthesis the appropriate marker for cholinergic neurons rather than the enzyme that catalyzes ACh breakdown?

2. How does AChE at the neuromuscular junction differ from AChE in the brain?

3. Among the various AChE inhibitors, some block the enzyme both centrally and peripherally, whereas others are preferential inhibitors at the neuromuscular junction. Another differentiating feature is that some AChE inhibitors are reversible whereas others are irreversible. List the chemicals discussed in the chapter that have these various characteristics, and then describe whether each specific chemical is characterized as a toxin or as a medicinal compound. Explain the underlying reasons for this categorization.

4. _____ is the name of a drug that blocks vesicular uptake of ACh. True or false: When this drug has been applied, the lack of ACh in the vesicles prevents the cholinergic neuron from undergoing exocytosis when it generates an action potential.

5. List and discuss the effects of toxins that either stimulate or inhibit ACh release. Include in your answer the therapeutic applications of toxins that inhibit the release of this neurotransmitter.

6. Unlike the monoamine transmitters discussed in previous chapters, there is no reuptake system for ACh itself. Describe the alternative mechanism that has evolved to help cholinergic neurons recycle/reutilize the transmitter. How do we know that this recycling process plays an important role in normal functioning of the nervous system?

7. Name and describe the causes of disorders of cholinergic transmission at the neuromuscular junction that lead to weakness, fatigue, and other motor symptoms.

8. A cluster of cholinergic neurons called the _____ gives rise to ascending projections to the cortex and hippocampus that help regulate cognitive function. The cell bodies of these neurons are located in _____ (list several brain regions).

9. What is meant by "sustained attention"? How is sustained attention studied experimentally in laboratory animals such as rats and mice? Discuss experimental findings that support a role for ACh in facilitating sustained attention.

10. Nicotinic cholinergic receptors belong to the family of _____ (ionotropic or metabotropic) receptors. Each receptor is composed of _____ subunits. Which of these subunits is required for a nicotinic receptor to be formed, and why? Which nicotinic receptor subunit structures have been implicated in cognitive function?

11. A nicotinic receptor complex can be in one of three different states: open, closed, and desensitized. Describe the properties of each state, including whether agonist is bound or not as well as the state of the receptor channel.

12. The text discusses three different drugs that act on nicotinic receptors: succinylcholine, mecamylamine, and D-tubocurarine. For each compound, indicate whether it is an agonist or an antagonist, and briefly discuss the effects of administering the drug (including any current medical use).

13. How many subtypes of muscarinic receptors have been identified? Based on their signaling mechanisms and postsynaptic effects (i.e., excitatory or inhibitory), the receptors can be divided into two families. Identify the members of each family, their signaling mechanisms, and whether that family of receptors is excitatory or inhibitory.

14. Discuss the role of M_5 muscarinic receptors in the control of dopaminergic cell firing and the rewarding and reinforcing effects of abused drugs. Include relevant experimental findings in your answer.

15. Describe the locations and functional roles of muscarinic receptors expressed by peripheral organs and glands. What is the "dry mouth effect," and what is its cause?

16. Explain the underlying rationale for the idea of using nicotinic or muscarinic allosteric modulators in the treatment of Alzheimer's disease or other neuropsychiatric disorders involving deficits in cognitive functioning.

17. What is meant by the terms *parasympathomimetic* and *parasympatholytic*? List examples of drugs belonging to these categories along with their physiological effects and medicinal or other uses.

Glutamate and GABA

THE IDEA OF A "SMART PILL" THAT WOULD ENHANCE YOUR INTELLIGENCE
without requiring effort on your part is appealing to many. Indeed, an informal survey
conducted by Marilyn vos Savant (author of the "Ask Marilyn" column in the popular
Sunday newspaper magazine *Parade*) found that if given a choice, a large majority of
respondents would prefer raising their intelligence to improving their physical appearance. Pills that turn ordinary people into astounding geniuses have been a topic of
science fiction novels and movies, one example being the 2011 movie *Limitless*, which
spawned a 2015–2016 TV series of the same name that featured an average guy (played
in the movie by Bradley Cooper) who could temporarily achieve super intelligence by
consuming a pill called NZT.

No genius pills are yet in sight, despite claims by internet purveyors of the miracu-
lous effects of substances they are selling. Nevertheless, researchers have been hard at
work to find drugs that improve cognitive function. Most of this effort is directed toward
ameliorating the cognitive deficits associated with Alzheimer's disease, schizophrenia,
and various other neuropsychiatric disorders. However, research has shown that cognition can be enhanced above baseline in healthy individuals, a prospect that raises not
only practical but also ethical and health issues (Lynch et al., 2014; Frati et al., 2015;
Whetstine, 2015; Urban and Gao, 2017). Apparently, significant numbers of people are
so highly motivated to enhance their neurocognitive function that they consume substances that have never even been tested in human clinical trials. One such example
is given by Fulvio Gualtieri (2016), who recounts the story of two unique drugs synthesized in the late 1990s by his research team at the University of Florence and shown to
enhance memory in several tests using laboratory rats and mice. Gualtieri later discovered that despite a complete lack of human testing to determine potential toxicity, not to
mention efficacy in human memory tasks, these drugs are being sold over the internet
as nutritional supplements with claims to boost memory and provide other mental benefits. Although this practice is legal under U.S. law, we must question the ethics of

Some day we may be able to purchase "smart pills"
that will enable us to generate "pearls of wisdom"
much more easily than we do now.

companies that offer substances for consumption whose safety has not been established either for short-term or long-term exposure.

Some cognitive-enhancing compounds, which are called **nootropics**,* act on the cholinergic system (see Chapters 7 and 13). Others, such as amphetamine and methylphenidate, work primarily through catecholaminergic activation (Chapters 5 and 12). Still others influence the amino acid neurotransmitter glutamate, which is the subject of the first part of the present chapter. You will learn about the basic neurochemistry of glutamate, its role in learning and memory, and the development of novel glutamate-related drugs that show promise in treating cognitive impairment. The second part of the chapter covers γ-**aminobutyric acid** (**GABA**), another important amino acid neurotransmitter that has a very different role in brain and behavioral functioning. ∎

Glutamate is the term we use for the ionized (i.e., electrically charged) form of the amino acid glutamic acid. Since most of the glutamic acid in our bodies is in this ionized state, we will refer to it as glutamate throughout the text. Like other common amino acids, glutamate is used by all of our cells to help make new proteins. But glutamate also has numerous other biochemical functions (e.g., in energy metabolism); this is reflected in the fact that it is the most abundant amino acid in the brain. Glutamate and **aspartate** (the name for the ionized form of aspartic acid) are the two principal members of a small family of **excitatory amino acid neurotransmitters**. These transmitters are so named because they cause a powerful excitatory response when applied to most neurons in the brain or spinal cord. We will focus on glutamate, which is the principal excitatory transmitter in the brain.

8.1 Glutamate Synthesis, Release, and Inactivation

When a nerve cell synthesizes a molecule of dopamine (DA), acetylcholine (ACh), or serotonin (5-HT), it is almost always done for the purpose of neurotransmission. Moreover, in the brain, these substances are localized specifically within the cells that use them as transmitters. However, we must recognize that the situation is different for glutamate because of its roles in protein synthesis and general cellular metabolism. First, all neurons and glial cells contain significant amounts of glutamate, although neurons that use glutamate as a transmitter (called **glutamatergic neurons**) possess even greater concentrations than other cells in the brain. Second, glutamatergic neurons are thought to segregate the

pool of glutamate that they use for transmission from the pool of glutamate used for other cellular functions. These facts complicate both our ability to determine which nerve cells actually are glutamatergic and our understanding of how these cells synthesize, release, and dispose of the transmitter-related glutamate. Nevertheless, researchers have accumulated considerable information, which we summarize in this section.

Neurons generate glutamate from the precursor glutamine

Glutamate can be synthesized by several different chemical reactions. Most molecules of glutamate are derived ultimately from the normal metabolic breakdown of the sugar glucose. The more immediate precursor for much of the transmitter-related glutamate is a related substance known as **glutamine**. Neurons can transform glutamine into glutamate using an enzyme called **glutaminase** (**FIGURE 8.1**). We will see in the next section that the role of glutamine in glutamate synthesis involves a fascinating metabolic partnership between glutamatergic neurons and nearby glial cells, specifically astrocytes.

Glutamate packaging into vesicles and uptake after release are mediated by multiple transport systems

GLUTAMATE PACKAGING AND RELEASE Like the other transmitters already discussed, glutamate is packaged in and released from synaptic vesicles. It is

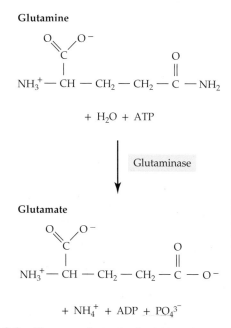

FIGURE 8.1   Glutamate is synthesized from glutamine This reaction, catalyzed by the enzyme glutaminase, requires energy provided by the breakdown of adenosine triphosphate (ATP) into adenosine diphosphate (ADP) and phosphate (PO_4^{3-}).

---

*The term *nootropic* comes from two Greek words: *noos*, which means "mind," and *tropein*, which means "toward."

technically challenging to measure exactly how many glutamate molecules are present in a single vesicle, but recent research yielded an estimate of approximately 8000 (Wang et al., 2019). Researchers assumed that a system must exist to transport glutamate from the cell cytoplasm into the vesicles, but this system eluded discovery for a long time. Then between the years 2000 and 2002, researchers discovered *three* distinct proteins that package glutamate into vesicles: **VGLUT1**, **VGLUT2**, and **VGLUT3** (**VGLUT** standing for **vesicular glutamate transporter**). These proteins serve as good markers for glutamatergic neurons because unlike glutamate itself, they are found only in cells that use glutamate as a neurotransmitter. Furthermore, when glutamatergic neurons are undergoing sustained firing, vesicle refilling by VGLUTs plays an important role in maintaining the required rate of neurotransmitter release (Nakakubo et al., 2020).

Most glutamatergic neurons possess either VGLUT1 or VGLUT2 (but usually not both), with VGLUT3 being much less abundant than the other two transporters. *VGLUT1* gene expression occurs primarily in the cortex and hippocampus, whereas *VGLUT2* gene expression is found mostly in subcortical structures (El Mestikawy et al., 2011; Vigneault et al., 2015). VGLUT2 knockout mice die immediately after birth, signifying the critical importance of glutamate signaling by VGLUT2-expressing neurons for life-sustaining functions (Wallén-Mackenzie et al., 2010). In contrast, VGLUT1 knockout mice survive birth but eventually begin to die during the third week of life. Interestingly, mice lacking VGLUT3 are viable but are completely deaf (Seal et al., 2008). The reason for this unusual defect is that the inner hair cells of the cochlea use glutamate as their neurotransmitter, and the only vesicular transporter they express is VGLUT3. Consequently, when the inner hair cells from VGLUT3 knockout mice are stimulated by sound waves striking the eardrum, they have no glutamate in their vesicles to transmit the stimulus to the auditory nerve.

VGLUT3 and to a lesser extent VGLUT1 and VGLUT2 mRNA and protein are sometimes co-expressed with markers of other classical neurotransmitters. This implies that in neurons with such co-expression, glutamate is also stored and released as a co-transmitter. After the discovery of numerous examples of vesicular transporter co-expression, investigators began to ask important questions such as whether a VGLUT and another transporter (e.g., VMAT2) are present on the same vesicles in the nerve terminal, or whether neurons exhibiting this kind of transporter co-expression segregate their vesicles into two different types (i.e., one type of vesicle that takes up and releases glutamate and a second type of vesicle that takes up and releases the other transmitter synthesized by that neuron). Evidence suggests that both types of situations can exist (El Mestikawy et al., 2011). Moreover, the possibility exists that some neurons not only segregate their vesicle populations but also segregate their axon terminals so that the two different neurotransmitters are released at separate kinds of terminals. The DA–glutamate co-expressing neurons of the ventral tegmental area may represent an example of this phenomenon. These cells are believed to release DA alone from varicosities that do not have a classical synaptic morphology and to release glutamate alone from terminals that make classical synaptic contacts with postsynaptic elements (Trudeau and Gutiérrez, 2007; Trudeau et al., 2014). Another example comes from the serotonergic system, where most of the raphe axon varicosities express *either* a serotonergic marker like 5-HT or the membrane 5-HT transporter (i.e., for 5-HT reuptake) *or* VGLUT3, but not both (Voisin et al., 2016). Additional research is needed to identify the mechanism involved in neurotransmitter segregation when it occurs and, more importantly, to determine the functional significance of glutamate as a co-transmitter with other classical transmitters such as DA, 5-HT, ACh, GABA, and glycine.

GLUTAMATE UPTAKE AFTER RELEASE   After glutamate molecules are released into the extracellular space, they are rapidly removed by glutamate transporters located on cell membranes. Always keep in mind that the plasma membrane transporters that remove neurotransmitters from the extracellular space, including the synaptic cleft, are distinct from the transporters on the vesicle membranes that are responsible for loading the vesicles in preparation for transmitter release. In the case of glutamate, five different plasma membrane transporters have been identified with different cellular localizations (Rose et al., 2018; Malik and Willnow, 2019). Because these transporters take up aspartate as well as glutamate, they are considered to represent a class of **excitatory amino acid transporters** (**EAATs**). There are five members of this class, designated **EAAT1** to **EAAT5**. Interestingly, astrocytes rather than neurons play the most important role in taking up glutamate after its release. This is particularly true for EAAT2, which is expressed by astrocytes throughout the brain. Some studies have estimated that EAAT2 accounts for about 90% of total glutamate uptake in the brain (Divito and Underhill, 2014). As we will see later, prolonged high levels of glutamate in the extracellular fluid are very dangerous, producing excessive neuronal excitation and even cell death. The importance of EAAT2 in glutamate clearance was shown in an early study by Tanaka and coworkers (1997), who found that knockout mice lacking EAAT2 (termed GLT-1 in their paper, which used different terminology) developed spontaneous epileptic seizures, were more susceptible than wild-type mice to experimentally induced seizures and brain injury, and had a greatly shortened life span (**FIGURE 8.2**). EAAT1, another transporter found in astrocytes, has a particularly high expression in

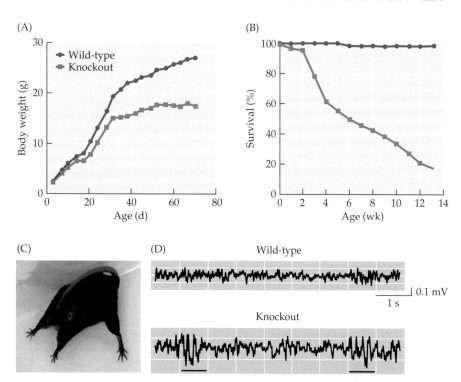

FIGURE 8.2 Phenotypic characteristics of mutant mice lacking EAAT2 (A) EAAT2 knockout mice exhibited a reduction in weight gain compared with genetically normal wild-type mice, particularly once they reached 30 days of age. (B) The knockout mice showed increased mortality beginning at 3 weeks of age. (C) and (D) Mice lacking EAAT2 had increased brain excitability that manifested as spontaneous behavioral seizures (note the abnormal posture in C, which is caused by epileptic activity in the brain) and seizure-like EEG changes (underlined traces in D) when given a subthreshold dose of the convulsant agent pentylene-tetrazole. Note that at this drug dose, the wild-type mice showed no such EEG changes. (From K. Tanaka et al., 1997. *Science* 276: 1699–1702.)

specialized astrocytes of the cerebellum, where it plays an important role in cerebellar function. The major neuronal glutamate transporter is EAAT3, which has a *postsynaptic* rather than a *presynaptic* localization (Malik and Willnow, 2019). Finally, EAAT4 is expressed primarily by Purkinje cells in the cerebellum, whereas EAAT5 is present in bipolar cells within the retina.

Besides playing a key role in removing excess glutamate from the extracellular space, astrocyte transporters are also intimately involved in the metabolic partnership between neurons and astrocytes. After astrocytes have taken up glutamate by means of EAAT1 or EAAT2, they convert a major portion of it to glutamine by means of an enzyme called **glutamine synthetase**. Glutamine is then transported out of the astrocytes and picked up by neurons, where it can be converted back into glutamate by glutaminase, as described earlier. This interplay between glutamatergic neurons and nearby

astrocytes is illustrated in **FIGURE 8.3**. We might wonder why such a complex system has evolved: why don't the neurons themselves have the primary responsibility for glutamate reuptake, as we have seen previously for the catecholamine neurotransmitters and for serotonin? Although we aren't certain about the answer to this question, it's worth noting that glutamine does not produce neuronal excitation and therefore is not potentially dangerous, as is glutamate. Hence, glial cell production of glutamine may be the brain's way of storing glutamate in a form that is "safe" but still available for use

FIGURE 8.3 Cycling of glutamate and glutamine between glutamatergic neurons and astrocytes After neurons release glutamate, it can be transported into nearby astrocytes by EAAT1 or EAAT2, or less commonly it can be transported into the postsynaptic cell by EAAT3. Inside the astrocyte, glutamate is converted into glutamine by the enzyme glutamine synthetase. The glutamine can be later released by the astrocytes, taken up by neurons, and converted back into glutamate by the enzyme glutaminase.

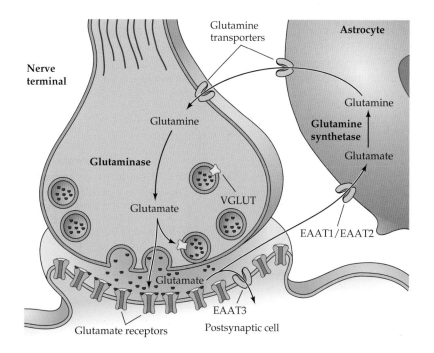

once the glutamine has been transferred to the neurons and reconverted to glutamate.

In addition to inactivation of glutamate, a second function of glutamine synthetase is to help in the metabolism and removal of ammonia that is either generated metabolically in the brain or taken up from the bloodstream (Zhou et al., 2020). The adverse effects of eliminating glutamine synthetase can be seen in mice with a knockout of the glutamine synthetase gene and in rare human mutations that result in significantly reduced activity of the enzyme. The knockout mice die before birth, and humans with congenitally reduced glutamine synthetase activity suffer from brain deformities, seizures, and a short life span (Rose et al., 2013). These consequences likely result from abnormalities both in glutamate metabolism (i.e., reduced or absent ability to inactivate glutamate by conversion to glutamine) and in ammonia clearance.

SECTION SUMMARY

- Glutamate and aspartate are amino acid neurotransmitters that have potent excitatory effects on neurons throughout the brain and spinal cord. Although glutamate is contained within all cells because of its multiple biochemical functions, glutamatergic neurons are thought to possess higher glutamate concentrations than other cells and to segregate their neurotransmitter pool of this amino acid.

- Many of the glutamate molecules that are released synaptically are synthesized from glutamine in a chemical reaction catalyzed by the enzyme glutaminase.

- Glutamate is packaged into vesicles by the vesicular transporters VGLUT1, VGLUT2, and VGLUT3. In some neurons, these transporters are expressed with markers for other neurotransmitters such as 5-HT, DA, ACh, and GABA, indicating that glutamate is a cotransmitter in these cells. Some evidence suggests that the DA–glutamate co-expressing neurons of the ventral tegmental area release the two transmitters from separate vesicles at different kinds of axon terminals.

- After they are released, glutamate molecules are removed from the extracellular fluid by five different excitatory amino acid transporters, designated EAAT1 to EAAT5. Uptake of glutamate into astrocytes by EAAT2 is especially important for glutamate clearance, as can be seen by the fact that mutant mice lacking this transporter exhibit seizures, neuronal cell death, and a shortened life span. The major neuronal glutamate transporter is EAAT3, which is thought to be located postsynaptically rather than presynaptically.

- Glutamate taken up by astrocytes is converted to glutamine by the enzyme glutamine synthetase.

- This glutamine subsequently can be transported from the astrocytes to the glutamatergic neurons, where it is transformed back into glutamate by the enzyme glutaminase and then reutilized. This constitutes an important metabolic interplay between glutamatergic nerve cells and their nearby glial cells.

8.2 Organization and Function of the Glutamatergic System

Glutamate is the workhorse transmitter for fast excitatory signaling in the nervous system. Not only is it used in many excitatory neuronal pathways, but the most important receptors for glutamate are ionotropic receptors that produce fast postsynaptic responses (see the next section). We will not discuss a large number of glutamatergic pathways here but will simply mention several that have been extensively studied. We will also consider a few important functions of the glutamatergic system in health and in disease.

Glutamate is the neurotransmitter used in many excitatory pathways in the brain

In the cerebral cortex, glutamate is the main neurotransmitter used by the pyramidal neurons. These cells, which are named on the basis of their pyramid-like shape, are the major output neurons of the cortex. Their axons project to numerous subcortical structures, including the striatum, the thalamus, various limbic system structures, and regions of the brainstem. Glutamate is also used by the numerous parallel fibers of the cerebellar cortex and by several excitatory pathways within the hippocampus.

Because glutamate is found throughout the brain, it is more difficult to assign specific functional roles to this neurotransmitter than it is for some of the other transmitters covered previously. Glutamate is undoubtedly involved in many different behavioral and physiological functions under both normal and abnormal conditions. Among the most important are synaptic plasticity (i.e., changes in the strength of synaptic connections), learning and memory, cell death in some neurological disorders, and possibly also the development of various psychopathological disorders, including drug addiction and schizophrenia. Later in this chapter we will consider the role of glutamate in synaptic plasticity, learning and memory, and neuronal cell death. Current findings regarding the possible involvement of glutamate in drug addiction, schizophrenia, and other types of psychopathology will mainly be taken up in other chapters of this book (with the exception of a few examples presented in the section on metabotropic glutamate receptors).

Both ionotropic and metabotropic receptors mediate the synaptic effects of glutamate

Glutamate receptors are divided into two broad families: a group of ionotropic receptors for fast signaling and a group of slower metabotropic receptors that function by means of second-messenger systems. We will focus first on the ionotropic receptors, since they are most important for understanding the mechanisms of glutamate action in the brain. Note that glutamate receptors are also used by aspartate and possibly by other excitatory amino acid transmitters that may exist. Hence, these receptors are sometimes called excitatory amino acid receptors rather than simply glutamate receptors.

IONOTROPIC GLUTAMATE RECEPTORS Three subtypes of ionotropic glutamate receptors have been identified. Each is named for a relatively selective agonist for that receptor subtype. First is the **AMPA receptor**, which is named for the selective agonist AMPA (α-amino-3-hydroxy-5-methyl-4-isoxazole propionic acid), a synthetic (not naturally occurring) amino acid analog. Most fast excitatory responses to glutamate are mediated by stimulation of AMPA receptors. The second ionotropic receptor subtype is the **kainate receptor**, which is named for the selective agonist kainic acid. Even though kainic acid powerfully stimulates kainate receptors in the mammalian brain, this substance actually comes from a type of seaweed called *Digenea simplex*. The third ionotropic glutamate receptor is the **NMDA receptor**, the agonist of which is obviously NMDA (*N*-methyl-D-aspartate). Like AMPA, NMDA is a synthetic amino acid. Thus, we see that pharmacologists have had to take advantage of several unusual compounds (either synthetic or plant derived) to distinguish between the different ionotropic receptor subtypes, since glutamate itself obviously activates all of these receptors.

Like the nicotinic receptors discussed in Chapter 7, ionotropic glutamate receptors depolarize the membrane of the postsynaptic cell, which leads to an excitatory response. For the AMPA and kainate receptors, this depolarizing effect is produced mainly by the flow of sodium (Na^+) ions into the cell through the receptor channel. In the case of NMDA receptors, the channel conducts not only Na^+ but also significant amounts of calcium (Ca^{2+}). Because Ca^{2+} can function as a second messenger within the postsynaptic cell (see Chapter 3), this is an interesting case in which an ionotropic receptor (the NMDA receptor) directly activates a second-messenger system (**FIGURE 8.4**).

Going back to the nicotinic receptor (see Figure 7.9), recall that the complete receptor contains five separate proteins (subunits) that come together to form the receptor channel. Ionotropic glutamate receptors are similarly formed from multiple subunits, but in this case, there are four subunits making up each receptor complex. Each receptor subtype (AMPA, kainate, and NMDA) is composed of a different set of subunits, which explains why the three subtypes differ in their pharmacology (**TABLE 8.1**). AMPA receptors are composed of two pairs of subunits: two GluA2 (present in most AMPA receptors) plus two GluA1, two GluA3, or two GluA4 subunits. NMDA receptors are similarly composed of subunit pairs: two GluN1 (present in all NMDA receptors) plus two GluN2A, two GluN2B, two GluN2C, or two GluN2D. The GluN3 subunits listed

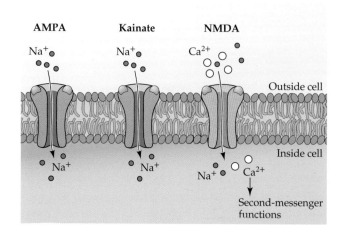

FIGURE 8.4 **Ion permeabilities of ionotropic glutamate receptor channels** All three ionotropic glutamate receptor channels conduct Na^+ ions into the cell. NMDA receptor channels additionally conduct Ca^{2+} ions, which can activate several important second-messenger functions.

in the table are only expressed in a small percentage of NMDA receptor complexes. Lastly, subunit composition of kainate receptors is more variable, although these receptors most commonly contain GluK1, GluK2, and/or GluK3 subunits.

Researchers have developed antagonists with varying degrees of selectivity toward the ionotropic glutamate receptors. One widely used antagonist called **NBQX** [6-nitro7-sulfamoyl-benzo(f)quinoxaline-2,3-dione] can block both AMPA and kainate receptors, although it is somewhat more effective against the former subtype. This compound has no effect on NMDA receptors. Rats and mice treated with high doses of NBQX exhibit sedation, reduced locomotor activity and ataxia (impaired coordination in movement; an example in humans is staggering), poor performance in the rotarod task (another test of coordination), and protection against electrically or chemically induced seizures. These findings indicate a broad role for AMPA (and possibly also kainate)

TABLE 8.1 Subunits Making Up the Ionotropic Glutamate Receptors

AMPA	NMDA	Kainate
GluA1	GluN1	GluK1
GluA2	GluN2A	GluK2
GluA3	GluN2B	GluK3
GluA4	GluN2C	GluK4
	GluN2D	GluK5
	GluN3A	
	GluN3B	

Note: Subunit designations pertain to each specific ionotropic receptor subtype: A for AMPA, N for NMDA, and K for kainate.

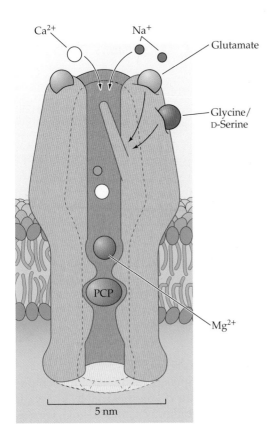

FIGURE 8.5 **NMDA receptor properties** The NMDA receptor is activated by simultaneous binding of glutamate and a co-agonist, either glycine or D-serine. Note that the locations of the glutamate and glycine binding sites are highly stylized and are not meant to accurately depict the locations of the actual sites shown in Figure 8.6. The diagram further illustrates that the receptor channel can be blocked by Mg²⁺ ions under resting conditions and also by the presence of the abused drug phencyclidine (PCP).

Another amino acid, **D-serine**, also binds to and activates the glycine binding site on the NMDA receptor. This unusual substance (amino acids normally exist in the L-conformation) is not a typical constituent of cells and, therefore, must be synthesized enzymatically. Current evidence suggests that D-serine formation primarily occurs in neurons (Billard, 2018). Because the NMDA receptor channel cannot open unless both the glutamate and glycine binding sites are occupied at the same time, glycine and D-serine are considered to be **co-agonists** with glutamate at the NMDA receptor.

There are two additional binding sites on the NMDA receptor that affect its function. One is a site within the receptor channel that binds magnesium (Mg^{2+}) ions. When the cell membrane is at the resting potential (typically −60 or −70 mV), Mg^{2+} ions are bound to this site relatively tightly. This causes the receptor channel to be blocked, even if glutamate and either glycine or D-serine are present to activate the receptor. However, if the membrane becomes depolarized, then the Mg^{2+} ions dissociate from the receptor and permit the channel to open if glutamate and a co-agonist are present. Consider the implications of this property of NMDA receptors. How does the membrane become depolarized? The answer, of course, is that some other source of excitation (other than NMDA receptors) must have already activated the cell. This other source of excitation could have been glutamate, acting through AMPA or kainate receptors, or a different transmitter such as ACh, acting through nicotinic receptors. The point is that an NMDA receptor is a kind of biological "coincidence detector." That is, the channel only opens when two events occur close together in time: (1) glutamate is released onto the NMDA receptor (assuming that a co-agonist is also bound to its site on the receptor complex), and (2) the cell membrane is depolarized by stimulation of a different excitatory receptor.

The second site, which is also located within the receptor channel, recognizes several different NMDA receptor antagonists that block the channel and thus prevent ion flow. These channel blockers are called **uncompetitive antagonists*** because they require the receptor to be activated by an agonist (thereby producing channel

receptors in locomotor activity, coordination, and brain excitability (as shown by the seizure results).

NMDA receptors possess a number of characteristics not found in the other glutamate ionotropic receptors (**FIGURE 8.5**). First, as we've already mentioned, unlike AMPA and kainate receptor channels, the channels for NMDA receptors allow Ca^{2+} ions to flow into the postsynaptic cell, thus triggering Ca^{2+}-dependent second-messenger activities. Second, NMDA receptors are very unusual in that two different neurotransmitters are required to stimulate the receptor and open its ion channel. The first neurotransmitter, of course, is glutamate. But in addition to the binding sites for glutamate on the NMDA receptor complex, there are binding sites that recognize the amino acid **glycine**. Glycine binding sites are located within the GluN1 subunits, whereas glutamate binding sites are located within the GluN2 subunits. **FIGURE 8.6** shows a three-dimensional model of the predicted structure of a typical NMDA receptor in the cell membrane (Zhu and Paoletti, 2015). Note how most of the receptor complex sticks out from the membrane into the extracellular space. The right-hand part of the figure presents a cutaway view that shows the locations of the ion channel pore within the cell membrane, one of the glutamate binding sites on a GluN2 subunit, and one of the glycine binding sites on a GluN1 subunit. Because the receptor complex contains two of each type of subunit, we can see that there is a total of four binding sites on the receptor.

---

*Uncompetitive antagonists are similar to noncompetitive antagonists in that neither prevents an agonist from binding to its binding site on the receptor. The difference between the two is the requirement for prior receptor activation in the case of an uncompetitive antagonist.

(A)

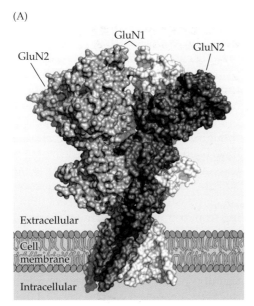

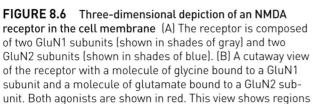

(B)

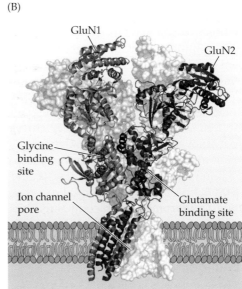

FIGURE 8.6   **Three-dimensional depiction of an NMDA receptor in the cell membrane** (A) The receptor is composed of two GluN1 subunits (shown in shades of gray) and two GluN2 subunits (shown in shades of blue). (B) A cutaway view of the receptor with a molecule of glycine bound to a GluN1 subunit and a molecule of glutamate bound to a GluN2 subunit. Both agonists are shown in red. This view shows regions of the two subunits that are predicted to have a ribbon structure (wavy lines) and other regions that are predicted to have a helical structure (lines in a corkscrew configuration). Note that the ion channel pore is shown in the closed state. (From S. Zhu and P. Paoletti. 2015. *Curr Opin Pharmacol* 20: 14–23. © 2014. Reprinted with permission from Elsevier.)

opening) before they can take effect. One of these compounds, called **MK-801** or **dizocilpine,** is mainly used for research purposes. Other members of this group are the abused drugs **phencyclidine** (**PCP**) and **ketamine**, as well as the drug **memantine** (**Namenda**), which is used to treat mild to moderate Alzheimer's disease. Memantine and ketamine are believed to bind in a very similar location within the NMDA receptor channel pore (Johnson et al., 2015). Indeed, it may seem remarkable that compounds that share this common mode of NMDA channel blockade are used for such different purposes and have such different effects on cognitive function (PCP and ketamine disrupt normal cognition, whereas memantine is a cognitive enhancer in patients with Alzheimer's disease). However, there are several key differences between PCP/ketamine and memantine that help account for this apparent paradox (Folch et al., 2018). First, memantine has a lower affinity for the NMDA receptor than PCP or ketamine, which allows it to dissociate much more rapidly from its binding site and avoid longer-term receptor blockade. Second, memantine only acts on the receptor channel under conditions of excessive glutamate levels, as is thought to be the case in Alzheimer's disease. Third, memantine primarily targets extrasynaptic NMDA receptors (receptors located on dendritic branches outside of the synaptic areas), which have a different subunit composition than the synaptic receptors and are only activated by high levels of glutamate. Lastly, memantine appears to interact with other neurotransmitter systems besides glutamate, which may contribute to its

therapeutic efficacy (Johnson et al., 2015). Chapter 15 describes in more detail the behavioral and psychological effects of PCP and ketamine, whereas Chapter 20 presents more information on the use of memantine in Alzheimer's disease pharmacotherapy.

METABOTROPIC GLUTAMATE RECEPTORS   Besides the three ionotropic receptors, there are also eight different metabotropic glutamate receptors, designated **mGluR1** to **mGluR8**. The metabotropic glutamate receptors can be divided into three groups based on their amino acid sequences, subcellular localization, and signaling pathways (Golubeva et al., 2015). Group I receptors, which include mGluR1 and mGluR5, are located postsynaptically and mediate excitatory responses by activating the phosphoinositide second-messenger system. Group II receptors, consisting of mGluR2 and mGluR3, and group III receptors, consisting of mGluR4, mGluR6, mGluR7, and mGluR8, signal by inhibiting cyclic adenosine monophosphate (cAMP) formation. Many of these group II and group III receptors are located presynaptically, where they function as auto- or heteroreceptors to inhibit release of glutamate (autoreceptors) or other neurotransmitters (heteroreceptors). The novel amino acid **L-AP4** (**L-2-amino-4-phosphonobutyrate**) is a selective agonist at group III glutamate autoreceptors, thereby suppressing glutamatergic synaptic transmission.

Metabotropic glutamate receptors are widely distributed throughout the brain, and they participate in many normal functions, including locomotor activity, motor coordination, cognition, mood, and pain perception. Recognition of this involvement has led to increasing interest in the development of mGluR-targeting drugs for the treatment of numerous neuropsychiatric disorders and other clinical conditions, including depression (Chaki et al., 2019), anxiety disorders (Ferraguti, 2018), schizophrenia (Maksymetz et al., 2017), chronic pain (Pereira and Goudet, 2019), epilepsy (Celli et al., 2019), drug addiction (Mihov and Hasler, 2016), Alzheimer's disease (Caraci et al., 2018), and amyotrophic lateral sclerosis (ALS; Lou Gehrig's disease) (Battaglia and Bruno, 2018). **BOX 8.1** describes a congenital disorder known as **fragile X syndrome** for which mGluR5 has been investigated as a potential therapeutic target.

AMPA and NMDA receptors play a key role in learning and memory

Earlier, we mentioned that AMPA and NMDA receptors are two glutamate receptor subtypes that have been strongly implicated in the mechanisms underlying learning and memory. Many neuropsychiatric disorders are associated with cognitive impairment, and dysregulation of glutamate receptors has been found in at least some of these disorders, including intellectual disability (previously called mental retardation), autism spectrum disorders, and schizophrenia (Volk et al., 2015). Consequently, a search has been under way to identify new glutamatergic compounds that could help patients suffering from cognitive impairment.

COGNITIVE ENHANCEMENT BY AMPA RECEPTOR MODULATORS   Several types of proposed cognitive enhancers are positive allosteric modulators of AMPA receptors (Chang et al., 2012; Partin, 2015). In Chapter 7 we mentioned the use of positive allosteric modulators of muscarinic or nicotinic cholinergic receptors as potential cognitive enhancers. Because AMPA receptors are likewise important for various aspects of learning and memory (see below and **WEB BOX 8.1**), drugs that positively modulate these receptors are also under development for possible clinical use. These compounds enhance the action of glutamate at the AMPA receptor but do not directly activate the receptor themselves. The principal mechanism of action of most positive AMPA receptor modulators is to reduce the rate of receptor deactivation (i.e., transition from an active to an inactive

state) and/or the rate of receptor desensitization (i.e., transition to a desensitized state; see Chapters 3 and 7 for a discussion of ionotropic receptor desensitization) (Arai and Kessler, 2007). Both mechanisms increase the time during which the AMPA receptor channel remains open, thereby permitting glutamate to exert a more prolonged excitatory effect on the postsynaptic cell. Although AMPA receptor positive allosteric modulators have been shown to enhance learning and memory in tests of experimental animals (for example, see Bretin et al., 2017), clinical trials using this class of drugs have not yet demonstrated therapeutic benefit in patients suffering from cognitive impairment (Partin, 2015).

NMDA RECEPTORS IN LEARNING AND MEMORY   The NMDA receptor is the other ionotropic glutamate receptor subtype believed to play a key role in learning and memory. It has been well established that release of glutamate from a nerve terminal coupled with strong activation of NMDA receptors in the postsynaptic cell receiving that glutamate input can lead to a strengthening of that synapse. The mechanism underlying this phenomenon, which is called long-term potentiation (LTP), is described in the next section. But first, we will simply point out that one aspect of this mechanism involves the coincidence detector feature of the NMDA receptor mentioned earlier (i.e., the fact that the postsynaptic cell membrane must be depolarized simultaneously with occupation of agonist binding sites on the receptor). A possible link between this coincidence detection feature and learning can most readily be seen in the case of associative learning, which involves the pairing of two events, such as two different stimuli or a stimulus and a response. All psychology students are exposed to a simple kind of associative learning called classical (Pavlovian) conditioning, as exemplified by Pavlov's original experiment with dogs. Like the opening of an NMDA receptor channel, classical conditioning is based on the close timing of two events: the pairing of a conditioned stimulus (the bell in Pavlov's experiment) with an unconditioned stimulus (the meat powder). **FIGURE 8.7** depicts what is thought to be occurring at the synaptic level in this kind of simple associative learning. Neurons that receive input from the unconditioned stimulus (US) start out with strong connections to their postsynaptic partners, while neurons that receive input from the conditioned

FIGURE 8.7   A hypothesized role for NMDA receptors in associative learning CS, conditioned stimulus; US, unconditioned stimulus (After J. W. Rudy. 2008. *The Neurobiology of Learning and Memory*. Sinauer/Oxford University Press: Sunderland, MA.)

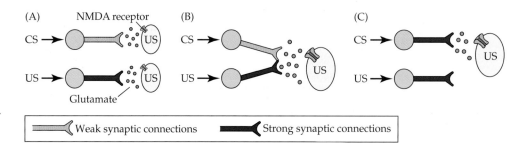

BOX 8.1 ■ CLINICAL APPLICATIONS

Fragile X Syndrome and Metabotropic Glutamate Receptor Antagonists: A Contemporary Saga of Translational Medicine

This box presents an example of **translational medicine** as applied to neuropharmacology. In this type of translational medicine, researchers determine the mechanisms underlying a disease or disorder, develop animal models of the disorder, use information derived from the model systems to test potential therapeutic approaches (including drugs) for the disorder, and finally conduct clinical trials, which, if successful, will result in new and effective treatments. The National Institutes of Health (NIH) even has a research program called "Bench-to-Bedside and Back" that funds "research teams seeking to translate basic scientific findings into therapeutic interventions for patients" (National Institutes of Health, 2020).

The specific disorder discussed here is fragile X syndrome (FXS), a congenital disorder that is the leading cause of inherited intellectual disability and autistic symptoms that can be attributed to a single gene (Razak et al., 2020). The core symptoms of FXS include cognitive deficits of varying severity, impaired social behavior (including avoidance of eye contact), repetitive stereotyped behaviors, abnormal speech, and anxiety (Bagni and Zukin, 2019). These symptoms overlap considerably with the core symptoms of autism spectrum disorders (ASD), often leading to a co-diagnosis of FXS and ASD. Severely affected individuals with this co-diagnosis may additionally exhibit aggressive behaviors and/or self-injury.

Brain structure and function associated with FXS have been investigated using magnetic resonance imaging (MRI) and post-mortem studies. Post-mortem studies of brain tissue from fragile X patients has revealed the presence of many long and thin, immature-looking dendritic spines in the cerebral cortex, and also a higher spine density than in healthy control brains (Irwin et al., 2000). Additional evidence suggests an abnormal balance of excitatory compared to inhibitory brain activity because of deficits in the GABAergic system (Bagni and Zukin, 2019). Structural brain MRI studies have suggested several abnormalities in patients, the most common of which are white matter abnormalities and increased brain volume, especially volume of the caudate nucleus (Razak et al., 2020). The latter has been implicated in perseverative responding and lack of cognitive flexibility in patients with FXS (Schmitt et al., 2019).

Fragile X syndrome is caused by mutations in the **fragile X mental retardation 1 gene (FMR1)**, which (as its name implies) is located on the X chromosome,* where it codes for the **fragile X mental retardation protein (FMRP)**. Certain mutations in the *FMR1* gene can cause the gene to be underexpressed during embryonic development, and in the most severe cases, the gene is completely silenced and no FMRP is produced at all because of epigenetic hypermethylation of the *FMR1* gene promoter region (see Chapter 2 for a discussion of epigenetic mechanisms of gene regulation). To understand the cellular consequences of losing FMRP expression, we need to review some basic information about the sites of protein synthesis in neurons. According to classical cell biology, mRNA is translated into protein within the body of a cell. In neurons, however, some mRNAs are translocated out of the soma into axons and dendrites, where those mRNAs are translated in a process of local protein synthesis. In turn, local protein synthesis at postsynaptic sites plays an important role in synaptic plasticity and long-term memory consolidation. The major function of FMRP is to bind to many of these mRNAs, thereby not only affecting mRNA transport out of the cell body but also inhibiting local mRNA translation to protein (Fernández et al., 2013). Consequently, loss of FMRP in FXS leads to dysregulated local protein synthesis in many parts of the brain, causing abnormal brain development and persistent aberrant synaptic functioning.

Researchers have knocked out the *FMR1* gene in mice, rats, and *Drosophila* in order to reproduce the silencing of this gene in FXS patients (Razak et al., 2020). Of these mutant strains, by far the largest amount of research has been conducted using the *FMR1* knockout mouse. The phenotypic characteristics of *FMR1* knockout mice were first reported in 1994, and one of the most consistent findings from various laboratories has been dendritic spine abnormalities similar to those observed in patients with FXS; however, behavioral studies have yielded considerably more variable results as to whether the knockout mice exhibited significant autism-like cognitive and social deficits (Kazdoba et al., 2014; Razak et al., 2020). This variability seems to be one of the limitations of the *FMR1* knockout mouse model.

One of the key synaptic functions of FMRP is to regulate a form of plasticity in the hippocampus called **long-term depression (LTD)**. Normal learning and memory require that synapses can be strengthened at certain times but weakened at others. Long-lasting synaptic strengthening is called **long-term potentiation (LTP)**, which we discuss in detail below and in **WEB BOX 8.1**. In contrast, LTD is a mechanism for weakening neurotransmission at the affected synapses. Relevant to FXS is a specific type of LTD that is activated by the group I metabotropic glutamate receptors, mGluR1 and mGluR5 (Gladding et al., 2009). Research with *FMR1* knockout mice found that *too much* LTD was occurring at the group I metabotropic glutamate synapses, because FMRP restricts the LTD process when the protein is present in genetically normal mice (and presumably also in healthy people not suffering from

---

*Fragile X syndrome was so named because the location of the *FMR1* gene on the X chromosome is susceptible to breakage (hence "fragile") under certain conditions.

(Continued)

BOX 8.1 ■ CLINICAL APPLICATIONS *(continued)*

FXS) (Sidorov et al., 2013). Together, these findings led Bear and colleagues (2004) to propose a **metabotropic glutamate receptor theory** of FXS. This theory hypothesizes that loss of FMRP causes exaggerated group I mGluR-related functions, including dendritic spine abnormalities and elevated LTD, which together lead to the phenotypic characteristics of FXS.

A logical extension of the metabotropic glutamate receptor theory is that group I mGluR antagonists might alleviate at least some of the symptoms of FXS. Consequently, pharmaceutical companies began drug development programs to test this idea. The primary focus of these programs was mGluR5 rather than mGluR1, because the former has a regional expression pattern in the brain that implicates it more strongly in FXS symptoms. Leading the race was pharmaceutical giant Novartis, based in Switzerland, which developed a selective mGluR5 antagonist designated AFQ056 during experimental testing and then later renamed **mavoglurant** for clinical use (Gomez-Mancilla et al., 2014). Theoretically, chronic treatment with mavoglurant should help normalize synaptic function, including dendritic structure and rates of LTD, by blocking glutamate activation of mGluR5 (see **FIGURE**). In fact, either mavoglurant or other mGluR5 antagonists worked as predicted when administered to *FMR1* knockout mice (Gomez-Mancilla et al., 2014).

The promising findings using the mouse model prompted Novartis, at great effort and cost, to sponsor two double-blind, placebo-controlled clinical trials with FXS patients, one involving adults and the other involving adolescents. To the great disappointment of the company, the trial participants and their families, and the psychiatric community at large, both trials showed little measurable improvement in the treated cohorts (Bailey Jr. et al., 2016; Berry-Kravis et al. 2016). As a result, the mavoglurant development program at Novartis was canceled. A later clinical trial tested the effectiveness of basimglurant, an mGluR5 negative allosteric modulator developed by the Roche pharmaceutical company (Youssef et al., 2018). This trial similarly yielded no clinical benefit to the patients. Finally, an alternative approach has been to restore the balance of excitatory and inhibitory neural activity by boosting GABAergic function; however, clinical trials using this approach have also been negative thus far (Lee et al., 2018).

All of the compounds tested in these clinical trials showed beneficial effects when tested using the *FMR1* knockout mouse model. Why, then, did all of the clinical trials based on these preclinical results fail? Unfortunately, this situation is not unique to FXS. In a review by Lee and colleagues (2018) that offers a pharmaceutical industry perspective, the authors state, "The failure of animal models to predict the efficacy of potential therapies in psychiatric diseases and neurologic disorders, including FXS, is a central problem in drug development" (p. 8). While there are many possible reasons to account for the present translational research failure, because of space consideration we will focus on just three. First, the mouse behavioral phenotypes that were improved by the drug treatments may not correspond well to the abnormal behaviors in FXS patients. Second, the

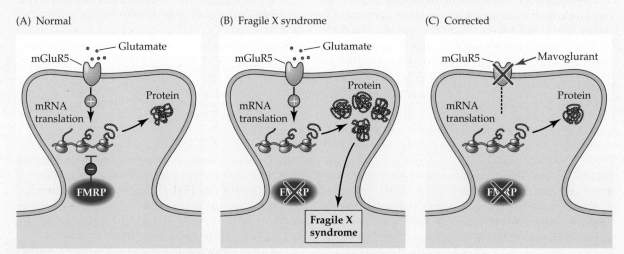

(A) Normal (B) Fragile X syndrome (C) Corrected

mGluR5, FMRP, and synaptic plasticity in health and in fragile X syndrome (A) In a normal healthy brain, the presence of FMRP regulates postsynaptic mRNA translation and synaptic plasticity in response to activation of mGluR5 and other neurotransmitter receptors. (B) Loss of FMRP in fragile X syndrome causes excessive mRNA translation, increased long-term depression, and abnormal dendritic structure. (C) Blockade of mGluR5 by mavoglurant is hypothesized to at least partially reverse the effects of FMRP loss, potentially leading to normalization of synaptic structure and plasticity. (After G. Dölen and M. Bear. 2009. *J Neurodev Disord* 1: 133–140, doi.org/10.1007/s11689-009-9015-x. CC BY 4.0, creativecommons.org/licenses/by/4.0/)

BOX 8.1 ■ CLINICAL APPLICATIONS (continued)

pharmacological interventions may have been administered too late to overcome the earlier adverse effects of the *FMR1* gene silencing on brain development. Finally, because of the diverse functions of the *FMR1* gene, it is probably naïve to think that FXS symptomatology can be ameliorated by targeting just a single neurochemical mechanism (whether mGluR5 or GABA). One suggested alternative approach is to target simultaneously the mGluR5 and GABAergic systems (Zeidler et al., 2017). Even better, theoretically, would be to reactivate the silenced *FMR1* gene (Kumari et al., 2019; Shitik et al., 2020).

We hope that this story illustrates how difficult it is to develop new medications for neuropsychiatric disorders and why the pace of progress has been so slow despite the remarkable recent advances in our understanding of the nervous system at a molecular genetic level. Although the story shows some of the limitations of animal models of human disorders, we emphasize that such models continue to be crucial in our search for new treatments. Indeed, in the absence of animal research, pharmacologists would have no clues about what drugs to even test, since they wouldn't have the underlying knowledge of metabotropic glutamate receptor signaling pathways, mechanisms of LTD, the balance of excitatory versus inhibitory neural activity, and the detailed molecular effects of FMRP and the consequences of its absence.

---

stimulus (CS) initially have weak connections with the US postsynaptic cells (Figure 8.7A). However, repeated pairings of the CS and the US (Figure 8.7B) theoretically strengthen the synaptic connections between the CS input neurons and the postsynaptic cells, because those latter cells (which express NMDA receptors) are being depolarized at the same time that the nerve terminals of the CS neurons are releasing glutamate. Finally, presentation of the CS alone elicits a strong response in the US postsynaptic cells (Figure 8.7C), which then can trigger the conditioned response.

MECHANISMS OF LTP The discovery of LTP was reported by Bliss and Lømo (1973) almost 50 years ago, and this discovery had such a powerful impact on neuroscience that it has given rise to thousands of subsequent experiments aimed at elucidating its underlying mechanisms and behavioral functions. When researchers refer to LTP, they generally mean a persistent (at least 1 hour) increase in synaptic strength produced by a burst of activity in the presynaptic neuron. This burst of firing can be produced experimentally by a single brief train of electrical stimuli (e.g., 100 stimuli over a period of 1 second) called a **tetanic stimulus** (or simply a **tetanus**).* The synaptic enhancement produced by the tetanus is measured by changes in the excitatory postsynaptic potential (EPSP) recorded in the postsynaptic cell. Several different forms of LTP can be elicited, depending on the stimulation parameters and the brain area where the process is being studied. Varieties of LTP may differ in the time period of potentiation (i.e., how long it lasts), whether the potentiation is pre- or postsynaptic, whether the synapses undergo structural in addition to biochemical modification, and the underlying cellular mechanisms (e.g., which neurotransmitter receptors are involved and which signaling pathways are activated by those receptors).

Although LTP occurs in many brain areas, it was first discovered in the hippocampus and has been studied most extensively in that structure. A focus on hippocampal synaptic plasticity was prompted, at least in part, by the report of profound anterograde amnesia (inability to form new memories) in patient H.M., whose medial temporal lobe (including the hippocampus) had been surgically removed to treat persistent epileptic seizures (Scoville and Milner, 1957). In this section we will primarily discuss LTP in the hippocampal CA1 region, which is mediated postsynaptically and requires activation of NMDA receptors (Nicoll, 2017).** A very different kind of LTP occurs at hippocampal mossy fiber-CA3 synapses (see below for a description of the relevant hippocampal anatomy), involves presynaptic changes in neurotransmitter release, and is independent of NMDA receptors (Nicoll and Schmitt, 2005).

CA1 hippocampal LTP can be divided into two distinct phases. The first phase is relatively short-lived, meaning a few hours at most. This phase has been termed **early LTP** (**E-LTP**) and is usually studied in a brain slice. In contrast, **late LTP** (**L-LTP**) can last for days or even months when produced in an animal instead of a slice. We will initially consider the properties of E-LTP, which was discovered first and provides the conditions required for L-LTP. Later we will mention some of the additional conditions needed to produce L-LTP.

---

*This kind of stimulus is called a "tetanus" because eliciting the same type of repetitive, high-frequency firing in motor neurons causes prolonged contraction of the affected muscle, similar to the persistent muscle contractions and stiffness associated with the bacterial infection tetanus (i.e., "lockjaw").

**This highly recommended review recounts the history of NMDA receptor-dependent LTP that covers the key experiments needed to resolve various controversies that arose regarding the mechanisms of this phenomenon.

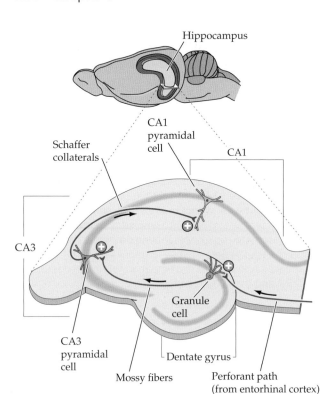

FIGURE 8.8 **Long-term potentiation of synaptic transmission** LTP can be studied in vitro using the hippocampal slice preparation.

To investigate E-LTP, researchers typically cut slices about 200 μm (0.2 mm) thick from the hippocampus of a rat or a mouse. These slices are then placed in a dish where the neurons can be maintained in a healthy state for many hours while the investigator stimulates them and records their electrophysiological responses. The key cellular anatomy of a hippocampal slice is illustrated in **FIGURE 8.8**. It is important to know that all of the pathways shown in the diagram use glutamate as their transmitter and that LTP occurs at all of the synaptic connections depicted. The postsynaptic LTP to be discussed here occurs at the pyramidal neurons of the hippocampal CA1 region, which receive excitatory

glutamatergic inputs from CA3 neurons via the Schaffer collaterals. As is depicted in the next several figures, the glutamatergic nerve terminals synapse mainly on dendritic spines on the pyramidal neurons.

FIGURE 8.9 depicts what happens to a typical spine synapse on a CA1 pyramidal neuron before, during, and after the tetanic stimulus. A test pulse (single electrical stimulus) of the presynaptic cell is used to assess the strength of the synaptic connection. The test pulse elicits the release of a small amount of glutamate from the presynaptic nerve endings. As shown in the left panel, this glutamate binds to both AMPA and NMDA receptors in the postsynaptic membrane. A small EPSP is produced mainly by activation of the AMPA receptors. However, the NMDA receptor channels fail to open because the membrane is not depolarized sufficiently to release the Mg^{2+} block of those channels. As long as test pulses are separated in time, you can give many of these pulses and not see any enhancement of the EPSP. But look at what happens in response to a tetanic stimulus (middle panel). Much more glutamate is released, and this causes prolonged activation of the AMPA receptors and greater postsynaptic depolarization. This permits Mg^{2+} ions to dissociate from the NMDA receptor channels and Ca^{2+} ions to enter the cell through these channels. Acting as a second messenger, these Ca^{2+} ions alter the functioning of the postsynaptic cell so that the same test pulse as given before now produces an enhanced EPSP (right panel).

E-LTP can be divided into two phases: an **induction phase**, which takes place during and immediately after the tetanic stimulation, and a later **expression phase**, during which the resulting increase in synaptic strength can be measured. NMDA receptors play a critical role in the induction phase but not in the expression phase. We know this because application of an NMDA receptor antagonist to the hippocampal slice during the tetanus blocks induction, but the same drug applied during the test pulse does not prevent the enhanced EPSP. In contrast, AMPA receptors are necessary for LTP expression,

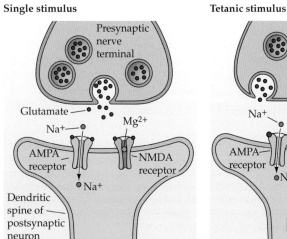

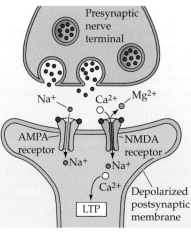

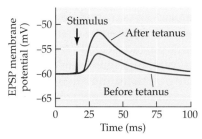

FIGURE 8.9 **Induction of long-term potentiation** LTP is induced by a tetanic stimulation of the presynaptic input.

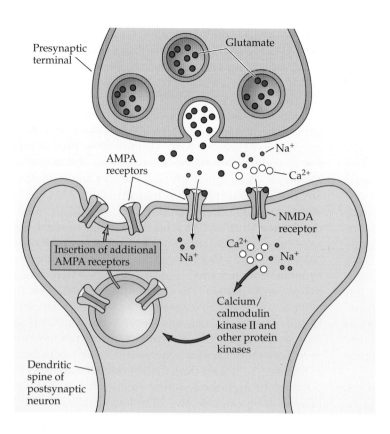

FIGURE 8.10

FIGURE 8.10   The underlying mechanism LTP involves modification of AMPA receptors in the postsynaptic cell.

since it is an AMPA receptor–mediated EPSP that is facilitated in LTP.

The principal biochemical mechanisms thought to underlie E-LTP are illustrated in **FIGURE 8.10**. The influx of Ca^{2+} ions through the NMDA receptor channels activates several protein kinases, including one type of calcium/calmodulin protein kinase called CaMKII (see Chapter 3). CaMKII is an unusual enzyme in that it can remain activated well after the level of intracellular Ca^{2+} has returned to baseline (Zalcman et al., 2018). Two key consequences of postsynaptic Ca^{2+} influx and CaMKII activation are rapid expansion of the dendritic spine and insertion of additional AMPA receptors into the spine membrane (Nicoll, 2017). Although not shown in Figure 8.10, the tetanic stimulus additionally provokes the release of brain-derived neurotrophic factor (BDNF), which participates in the process of E-LTP (Leal et al., 2017). AMPA receptor insertion is actually a modulation of the normal process that we call **receptor trafficking**, in which neurotransmitter receptors (in this case, AMPA receptors) are continuously moved into and out of the cell membrane (**FIGURE 8.11**, middle). In LTP, the rate of receptor insertion is increased (Figure 8.11, right), thereby enhancing sensitivity of the cell to glutamate. In contrast, some forms of LTD involve withdrawal of AMPA receptors from the membrane (Figure

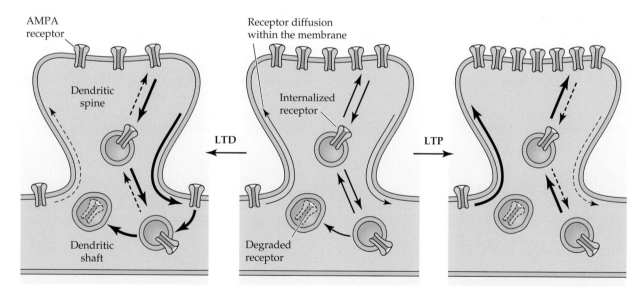

FIGURE 8.11   **AMPA receptor trafficking** Movement of AMPA receptors in dendritic spines can be altered under conditions of synaptic plasticity. The middle spine depicts normal receptor trafficking, which is maintained by an equilibrium of receptor movement into and out of the membrane and a low rate of receptor degradation. LTP (right spine) favors increased receptor insertion into the spine membrane and reduced degradation, whereas LTD (left spine) favors increased receptor removal from the membrane and degradation. Compared to normal trafficking, thicker arrows indicate greater rates of receptor movement whereas dashed arrows indicate reduced rates. Additional arrows running along the spine membrane depict movement of receptors into and out of the spine from the membrane of the dendritic shaft. (After L. Volk et al. 2015. *Annu Rev Neurosci* 38: 127–149.)

8.11, left), thereby reducing the cell's sensitivity (Volk et al., 2015). As the figure illustrates, the AMPA receptors are transported by vesicle-like structures, and indeed, receptor insertion into the membrane uses a process of exocytosis similar to the exocytosis of synaptic vesicles at nerve terminals (Jurado, 2014).

An additional key feature of E-LTP is the conversion of so-called silent synapses into functional synapses (Kerchner and Nicoll, 2008). Researchers found that nonfunctional dendritic spine synapses (later termed "silent synapses") were interspersed with functional spine synapses along the same dendritic branch. These synapses were nonfunctional in the sense that firing of the presynaptic cell failed to induce a postsynaptic response within the dendritic spine. Subsequent studies revealed that the spines were unresponsive because of a lack of AMPA receptors within the spine membrane. Importantly, when nearby functional spines were subjected to LTP, AMPA receptors contained within the interior of the silent spine were trafficked into the spine membrane, thereby rendering it functional (**FIGURE 8.12**).

Thus far, our discussion has covered the mechanisms underlying E-LTP, which is a key form of short-term synaptic strengthening in the nervous system. However, we have not yet explained L-LTP, nor have we touched on how LTP may be related to learning and memory. These topics are taken up in **WEB BOX 8.1**.

High levels of glutamate can be toxic to nerve cells

Despite the vital role of glutamate in normal neural and behavioral functioning, this neurotransmitter system also has a dark side. More than 60 years ago, two researchers published a report showing retinal damage in mice following subcutaneous injection of the sodium salt of glutamic acid—monosodium glutamate (MSG) (Lucas and Newhouse, 1957). Furthermore, this toxic effect of glutamate was more severe in infant than in adult mice. Twelve years later, Olney (1969) presented the first evidence that MSG also produces brain damage in young mice. Subsequent research showed that glutamate could lesion any brain area of adult animals when injected directly into that structure. This effect was shared by other excitatory amino acids, including kainate and NMDA, and the damage was shown to occur at postsynaptic sites but not at nerve terminals. These and other findings led to the **excitotoxicity hypothesis**, which proposed that the effects produced by excessive exposure to glutamate and related excitatory amino acids are caused by a prolonged depolarization of receptive neurons that in some way leads to their eventual damage or death. Administration of an excitatory amino acid kills nerve cells but spares fibers of passage (i.e., axons from distant cells that are merely passing through the lesioned area). Thus **excitotoxic lesions** are more selective than lesions produced by passing electrical current through the targeted area (called electrolytic lesions), since the latter method damages both cells and fibers of passage. For this reason, excitotoxic lesions have replaced electrolytic lesions in many research applications.

MECHANISMS OF EXCITOTOXICITY The mechanisms underlying amino acid excitotoxicity have been studied primarily using cultured nerve cells. In such

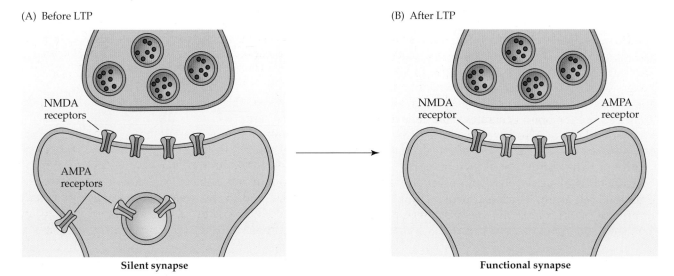

(A) Before LTP

(B) After LTP

Silent synapse

Functional synapse

FIGURE 8.12 **Conversion of a silent to a functional synapse by LTP** Some dendritic spines possess NMDA receptors in the membrane but lack AMPA receptors (left). The absence of AMPA receptors renders the spine unresponsive to normal low levels of glutamate release (i.e., the synapse is "silent").

However, LTP applied to nearby spine synapses causes trafficking of internal AMPA receptors into the membrane of the silent synapse, thereby rendering it functional (right). (After X. Huang. 2019. *Pharmacol Res* 141: 586–590.)

tissue culture models, neuronal cell death is most readily triggered by strong activation of NMDA receptors. Nevertheless, non-NMDA receptors (AMPA and/or kainate receptors) may contribute to the excitotoxic effects of glutamate, and under certain conditions, these receptors can even mediate cell death themselves without NMDA receptor involvement. When both NMDA and non-NMDA receptors are subjected to prolonged stimulation by a high concentration of glutamate, a large percentage of the cells die within a few hours. The mode of cell death in this case is called **necrosis**, which is characterized by **lysis** (bursting) of the cell due to osmotic swelling and other injurious consequences of prolonged glutamate receptor activation. But a different pattern occurs if either the neurotransmitter concentration or the time of exposure is significantly reduced. In this case, the osmotic swelling is temporary, and the cells appear to return to a normal state. However, there may be a delayed response that emerges over succeeding hours and that is characterized by a gradual disintegration of the cells and their eventual death. This delayed excitotoxic reaction is highly dependent on NMDA receptor activation, since it can be elicited by the selective application of NMDA or blocked by the presence of an NMDA receptor antagonist such as MK-801.

In contrast to the necrotic reaction, which occurs relatively quickly, the later-appearing type of cell death is known as **programmed cell death**. To add to the complexity, there are two types of programmed cell death. The first type, which is seen in vitro using cultured cells and in vivo when the subjects are young animals, is called **apoptosis**. Apoptosis involves a complex cascade of biochemical events that lead to disruption of the cell's nucleus, DNA breakup, and ultimately cell death. One of the differences between necrosis and apoptosis is that apoptotic cells do not lyse and spill their contents into the extracellular space. Instead, they are cleared away by other cells through a process called phagocytosis (**FIGURE 8.13**). A significant amount of apoptosis occurs normally during fetal brain development because the brain generates more cells than will be needed later on. However, excitotoxic treatment of young animals can also activate the apoptotic cell death program, thereby leading to inappropriate and excessive loss of nerve cells. The second type of programmed cell death, which is provoked by excitotoxic treatment of adult animals, has been termed either **programmed necrosis** or **necroptosis** (Fayaz et al., 2014) because the appearance of the dying neurons is different from the appearance of neurons undergoing apoptosis. Apoptosis and programmed necrosis also differ significantly in the biochemical mechanisms by which the cell is killed.

Fujikawa (2015) has summarized evidence that excitotoxicity in the adult brain is typically mediated by

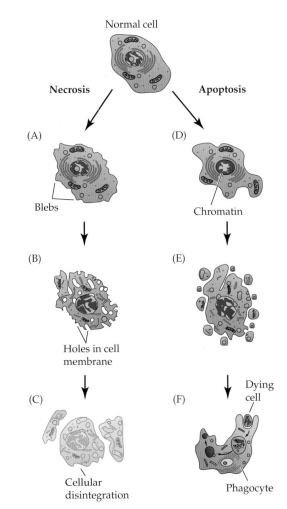

FIGURE 8.13 Cell death by necrosis versus apoptosis
During the initial stages of necrosis (A), the cell swells and the membrane forms protrusions called blebs. In the next stage (B), the membrane begins to break up and release the contents of the cell cytoplasm. Finally, the cell disintegrates completely (C). In apoptotic cell death, the cell also blebs (D), but instead of swelling, it shrinks. At the same time, the chromatin (genetic material) condenses within the cell nucleus. The cell then breaks up into smaller pieces (E) that are subsequently engulfed and digested by phagocytes (F).

programmed necrosis rather than apoptosis. Furthermore, glutamate triggering of this cell death program depends on NMDA receptors with a specific subunit composition and cellular localization. NMDA receptors localized to the area of the synapse primarily contain GluN2A subunits. These receptors mediate NMDA-dependent LTP, and they also participate in a signaling pathway that promotes neuronal survival. In contrast, the extrasynaptic NMDA receptors mentioned earlier primarily contain GluN2B subunits. These receptors can be activated during times of abnormally high glutamate levels in the extracellular space, due to excessive glutamate release and/or inadequate uptake by EAATs. Although both synaptic and extrasynaptic

NMDA receptors permit Ca^{2+} influx when activated, the Ca^{2+}-dependent signaling pathway linked to extrasynaptic NMDA receptors is the one responsible for triggering excitotoxic cell death (Lai et al., 2014; Li and Wang, 2016).

Glutamate is present in some prepared foods in the form of the flavor enhancer **monosodium glutamate (MSG)**. As the name indicates, MSG is just the sodium salt of glutamate. Based on the existence of glutamate excitotoxicity as well as potential adverse effects on other organs and tissues, researchers have conducted many preclinical and clinical studies to ascertain the possible health risks from dietary glutamate consumption. As the reader may be aware, there are numerous anecdotal claims of unpleasant acute reactions to MSG-containing foods, including headache, sweating, skin flushing, tightening of the facial muscles, numbness, and rash. Although it is possible that some individuals are sensitive, perhaps allergic, to MSG, reliable evidence for this syndrome has been difficult to obtain (Zanfirescu et al., 2019). Experimental animal (mostly rodent) studies have reported a number of adverse effects on the brain and behavior following chronic administration of extremely high MSG doses (Onaolapo and Onaolapo, 2020). However, the clinical relevance of this research has been questioned because of the high doses and poor study design (Zanfirescu et al., 2019). Moreover, other studies have shown that dietary MSG does not raise brain glutamate levels because of the inability of circulating glutamate to penetrate the blood–brain barrier (Fernstrom, 2018). Thus, most researchers have concluded that MSG is generally safe for use as a food additive (Henry-Unaeze, 2017; Fernstrom, 2018). On the other hand, individuals who have identified a personal sensitivity to this chemical should obviously avoid consuming foods in which it is present.

EXCITOTOXIC CELL DEATH IN CLINICAL MEDICINE

Mechanisms of excitotoxicity have been studied most extensively in cell culture and in experimental animals. But this phenomenon also occurs in humans, with significant clinical implications. Indeed, excitotoxic brain damage has been implicated as a factor in Alzheimer's disease, Parkinson's disease, traumatic brain injury, several psychiatric disorders, and even Gulf War illness (Khatri et al., 2018; Olloquequi et al., 2018; Armada-Moreira et al., 2020; Joyce and Holton, 2020). Rather than attempting to cover the potential involvement of excitotoxicity in all of these conditions, we have chosen to limit our discussion to three major topics: (1) excitotoxicity from consumption of domoic acid, (2) contribution of excitotoxicity to stroke-related brain damage, and (3) evidence for excitotoxicity in the neurodegenerative disorder amyotrophic lateral sclerosis. This discussion may be found in **WEB BOX 8.2**.

SECTION SUMMARY

- Glutamate is the workhorse for fast excitatory signaling in the nervous system. There are numerous glutamatergic pathways in the brain, including the projections of the pyramidal neurons of the cerebral cortex, the parallel fibers of the cerebellar cortex, and several excitatory pathways within the hippocampus.

- AMPA, kainate, and NMDA receptors constitute the three subtypes of ionotropic glutamate receptors. Each is named for an agonist that is relatively selective for that subtype. All of these receptors permit Na^+ ions to cross the cell membrane, thereby producing membrane depolarization and an excitatory postsynaptic response. NMDA receptors also conduct Ca^{2+} ions and can trigger Ca^{2+}-dependent second-messenger actions within the postsynaptic cell.

- Each ionotropic receptor subtype is composed of four subunits, which differ among the three subtypes. Variation in subunit composition is responsible for differences in receptor ionic conductances, electrophysiological properties, and pharmacology.

- AMPA receptors are formed from GluA1–GluA4 subunits; kainate receptors are formed from GluK1–GluK5 subunits; most NMDA receptors are composed of two GluN1 and two GluN2 subunits.

- Behavioral functions of AMPA receptors have been revealed through the use of the antagonist NBQX. Administration of high doses of this compound to rodents leads to sedation, ataxia, deficient rotarod performance, and protection against seizures, indicating involvement of this receptor subtype in locomotor activity, coordination, and brain excitability.

- NMDA receptors are distinct from the AMPA and kainate receptor subtypes in several ways, in addition to the difference in ionic conductances. First, the opening of NMDA receptor channels requires a co-agonist in addition to glutamate. This co-agonist may be either glycine or D-serine. Second, NMDA receptors possess a binding site for Mg^{2+} ions within the receptor channel. When the cell membrane is at the resting potential, this site is occupied and the channel is blocked even if the receptor has been activated by agonists. However, depolarization of the membrane reduces Mg^{2+} binding, thus allowing the channel to open. Consequently, for the NMDA receptor to function, some other synaptic input must excite the cell at the same time that glutamate and either glycine or D-serine bind to the receptor. Third, NMDA receptors also possess a channel binding site that recognizes PCP, ketamine, memantine, and MK-801. These compounds act as uncompetitive antagonists of the NMDA receptor.

- There are also eight different metabotropic receptors for glutamate, designated mGluR1 to mGluR8. Group I metabotropic glutamate receptors, consisting of mGluR1 and mGluR5, are located postsynaptically and mediate excitatory responses by stimulating the phosphoinositide second-messenger system. Group II receptors, consisting of mGluR2 and mGluR3, and group

III receptors, consisting of mGluR4 and mGluR6–8, are typically located presynaptically, where they reduce transmitter release by inhibiting cAMP formation.

■ Compounds acting at various mGluRs are being tested for their possible usefulness in treating a variety of neuropsychiatric disorders, including schizophrenia. One potential application is in fragile X syndrome, a leading genetic cause of intellectual disability and autistic symptoms. This syndrome is caused by mutations in the *fragile X mental retardation 1* gene, which codes for the fragile X mental retardation protein (FMRP). Researchers proposed a metabotropic glutamate receptor theory of fragile X syndrome, in which loss of FMRP causes exaggerated group I mGluR–related functions, leading to dendritic spine abnormalities and elevated rates of LTD. However, clinical trials with mavoglurant, an mGluR5 antagonist, failed to produce significant symptom improvement in patients with fragile X syndrome.

■ NMDA and AMPA receptors are believed to play an important role in learning and memory. NMDA receptor antagonists impair the acquisition of various learning tasks. Activation of this receptor is necessary for the *induction* of hippocampal LTP, a mechanism of synaptic strengthening. The Ca^{2+}-activated enzyme CaMKII has an obligatory role in LTP induction. LTP *expression*, which is independent of NMDA receptors, involves increased trafficking of AMPA receptors into the postsynaptic membrane. LTP can be divided into two phases: E-LTP, which has just been described and only persists for a few hours, and the longer-lasting L-LTP, which involves protein synthesis, release of the neuropeptide BDNF, activation of atypical PKCs, and dendritic spine growth. LTP may occur in the human brain, particularly a form of LTP induced by theta burst stimulation.

■ Excessive exposure to glutamate and other excitatory amino acids can damage or even kill nerve cells through a process of depolarization-induced excitotoxicity. This process is usually mediated primarily by NMDA receptors, with some contribution from AMPA and/or kainate receptors. One type of excitotoxic cell death occurs via rapid necrosis, which involves cellular swelling and eventual lysis. Additionally, there are slower programmed forms of cell death that either have some of the features of necrosis or are mediated by apoptosis, which involves disruption of the cell nucleus and breakdown of DNA.

■ In humans, excitotoxic cell death can be caused by ingestion of food contaminated with the algal toxin domoic acid. Excitotoxicity is also thought to be a major contributory factor to the brain damage that occurs in the penumbra of a focal ischemic event (e.g., stroke) and in some kinds of traumatic brain injury. This type of excitotoxic cell death is mediated by Ca^{2+} entry through extrasynaptic NMDA receptors containing GluN2B subunits. A slower form of excitotoxicity may be a contributing factor in the loss of motor neurons in ALS. Therapeutic approaches to reduce excitotoxic cell death include blockade of glutamate receptors, inhibition of glutamate release, and enhancement of glutamate uptake (e.g., by EAAT2 up-regulation).

8.3 GABA Synthesis, Release, and Inactivation

Earlier in this chapter we saw that glutamate plays a dominant role in fast excitatory transmission in the central nervous system (CNS). Inhibitory transmission is equally important in behavioral control mechanisms. The significance of neural inhibition is evident from the fact that blocking the action of either of the two major inhibitory amino acid transmitters leads to convulsions and even death. These two transmitters are **GABA (γ-aminobutyric acid)** and glycine. The remainder of this chapter focuses primarily on GABA, which is the more important of the two transmitters in the brain.

Whereas the amino acid glutamate participates widely in cellular metabolism, including protein synthesis, the only function of GABA is to serve as a neurotransmitter. Hence, it is manufactured only by GABAergic neurons. This section of the chapter will discuss the synthesis, release, and inactivation of GABA.

GABA is synthesized by the enzyme glutamic acid decarboxylase

GABA is synthesized from glutamate in a single biochemical step, which is catalyzed by the enzyme **glutamic acid decarboxylase (GAD)** (**FIGURE 8.14**). It is interesting to note that GABA, the principal inhibitory neurotransmitter in the brain, is made from glutamate, the principal excitatory transmitter. GAD is localized specifically to GABAergic neurons; therefore, researchers can identify such neurons by staining for GAD.

Several drugs, including **allylglycine**, **thiosemicarbazide**, and **3-mercaptopropionic acid**, are known to block GABA synthesis. Because of the critical role of GABA in regulating brain excitability, a significant reduction in the synthesis of this neurotransmitter leads to convulsions. For this reason, GAD inhibitors are

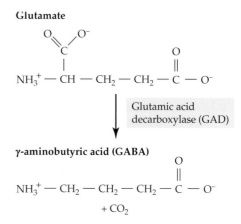

FIGURE 8.14   GABA is synthesized from glutamate The synthesis is catalyzed by the enzyme glutamic acid decarboxylase (GAD).

normally used to study GABAergic transmission only in vitro, not in vivo.

GABA packaging into vesicles and uptake after release are mediated by specific transporter proteins

Like the vesicular transporters that take up glutamate into synaptic vesicles, the **vesicular GABA transporter** (**VGAT**) was discovered later than some of the other vesicular transporters. Subsequent studies revealed an interesting and unexpected feature of this protein, namely that it is also found in neurons that release **glycine**, another inhibitory neurotransmitter. Thus the same transporter is used to load GABA or glycine into synaptic vesicles. For this reason, this transporter is sometimes referred to as **VIAAT** (**vesicular inhibitory amino acid transporter**) instead of VGAT. This situation of transport of multiple neurotransmitters by the same protein is similar to the previously discussed example of VMAT, the vesicular monoamine transporter, which is responsible for vesicle filling of three different neurotransmitters: dopamine (DA), norepinephrine (NE), and serotonin (5-HT).

Following the synaptic release of GABA, it is removed from the extracellular space by three different transporters on the membranes of nerve cells and glia, designated **GAT-1**, **GAT-2**, and **GAT-3**. GAT-1 and GAT-2 appear to be expressed in both neurons and astrocytes, whereas GAT-3 is found in astrocytes only. GAT-1 has received particular attention for two reasons. First, this transporter has been found at the nerve terminals of GABAergic neurons; therefore, it is likely to be important for GABA reuptake by these cells. Second, in contrast to GAT-2 and GAT-3, a selective inhibitor of GAT-1 is available for pharmacological study. Administration of this compound, **tiagabine**, elevates extracellular GABA levels and enhances GABAergic transmission in several brain areas, including the cortex and the hippocampus. Given the fact that depleting GABA (e.g., by blocking GAD activity) causes seizures, we might predict that tiagabine protects against seizure onset.

Indeed, tiagabine was licensed in 1997 under the trade name **Gabitril** for use as an adjunctive therapy (an additional treatment given along with more-standard antiepileptic drugs) in treatment-resistant patients with focal (also called partial) seizures (seizures involving only part of the brain). Although tiagabine is effective in reducing seizure frequency, patients report some adverse side effects that need to be accounted for in risk/benefit calculations for this medication (Bresnahan et al., 2019).

Whereas the immediate inactivation of GABA in the synapse occurs through a combination of neuronal and astroglial uptake, there is also a cellular mechanism for metabolizing and recycling this neurotransmitter. GABA breakdown occurs through several steps, beginning with the enzyme **GABA aminotransferase** (**GABA-T**) and leading eventually to the final product, succinate. It is worth noting that a byproduct of this metabolic pathway is the formation of one molecule of glutamate for every molecule of GABA that is broken down. GABA-T is found in both GABAergic neurons and astrocytes. Hence, within GABAergic neurons, some of the glutamate regenerated by the action of GABA-T could be used to synthesize more GABA. Moreover, some of the glutamate produced by GABA-T in astrocytes could be converted to glutamine by astrocytic glutamine synthetase, and the glutamine could subsequently be transported to the GABAergic neurons to be converted back to glutamate by the enzyme glutaminase (**FIGURE 8.15**). This shows that the metabolic

FIGURE 8.15 Cycling of GABA between GABAergic neurons and astrocytes After neurons release GABA, it can be transported back into the nerve terminal by GAT-1 or transported into nearby astrocytes by GAT-2 or GAT-3. Inside the cell, GABA is metabolized to glutamate and succinate by GABA aminotransferase (GABA-T). In the case of astrocytes, the glutamate is converted into glutamine by the enzyme glutamine synthetase. The glutamine can later be released by the astrocytes, taken up by neurons, converted back into glutamate by the enzyme glutaminase, and finally used to resynthesize GABA.

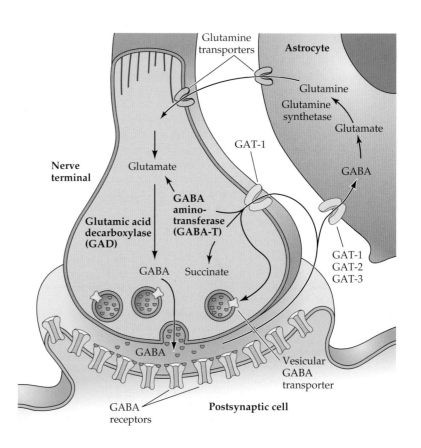

interplay between neurons and glial cells discussed earlier for glutamate is equally important for GABA.

Vigabatrin is an irreversible inhibitor of GABA-T. By preventing GABA metabolism, administration of this drug leads to a buildup of GABA levels within the brain. By now, you should be able to predict correctly that vigabatrin has anticonvulsant effects in animals and humans. Like tiagabine, vigabatrin (trade name, **Sabril**) is used clinically as either an adjunctive treatment or the primary therapeutic agent for certain types of epilepsy, particularly infantile spasms (repeated generalized seizures in young infants) (Chiron, 2016; Bresnahan et al., 2020). Concerns about potential retinal toxicity from vigabatrin use arose after reports of visual field constriction in both adults and children treated with this medication. However, newer studies have found that most such patients have pre-existing visual deficits, perhaps as a result of their seizure disorder (Foroozan, 2018; Jastrzembski et al., 2020). Consequently, it seems that the prevalence of this side effect of vigabatrin has been significantly overestimated.

GABA is co-released with several other classical neurotransmitters

Researchers have increasingly become aware that GABA is synthesized and co-released by many neurons that were previously characterized as using a different classical transmitter. Such co-expression and co-release of GABA has been demonstrated for certain neurons that also use glycine, ACh, DA, or glutamate as neurotransmitters (Tritsch et al., 2016; Granger et al., 2017). A neurotransmitter role for glycine mainly occurs in the brainstem and spinal cord, and current evidence

suggests that inhibitory neurons in these areas of the CNS may release GABA only, glycine only, or a combination of both (Aubrey, 2016). Because VGAT/VIAAT can fill vesicles with either transmitter, it is easy to imagine how a given neuron co-expressing both transmitters could regulate the relative availability of one substance or another for the purpose of vesicle filling and release. Yet another pattern is seen in neurons within the ventrolateral medulla that help regulate breathing. Developmental studies in mice found many GABA–glycine co-expressing neurons in this area during embryonic development. However, during the early postnatal period, most of these cells differentiated into GABAergic-only or glycinergic-only inhibitory neurons (Hirrlinger et al., 2019).

More complicated are the situations in which GABA is co-released with a neurotransmitter other than glycine. One example is that of the basal forebrain cholinergic neurons, which release both ACh and GABA (Saunders et al., 2015). Recent studies found that in the hippocampus, the terminals formed by these basal forebrain neurons possess separate populations of vesicles filled with either ACh or GABA using VAChT or VGAT respectively (Takács et al., 2018) (**FIGURE 8.16A**). When released at the same time, the two transmitters interact to influence activity of the postsynaptic hippocampal neurons. A second example is the co-release of DA and GABA from midbrain (substantia nigra and ventral tegmental area) dopaminergic neurons. These neurons lack GAD expression; rather, it is believed that they either take up GABA from the extracellular fluid by means of GAT-1 or synthesize the transmitter using an unusual GAD-independent pathway. Moreover,

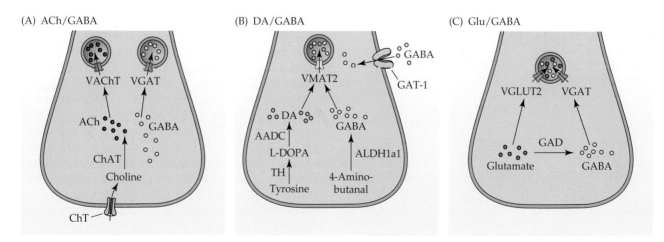

FIGURE 8.16 **Examples of co-transmission of GABA with other neurotransmitters** (A) Basal forebrain cholinergic neurons additionally synthesize GABA. In the projections of these cells to the hippocampus, ACh and GABA are taken up and stored in separate vesicle populations. (B) Midbrain dopaminergic neurons can accumulate GABA either through GAT-1-mediated uptake or from 4-amino-butanal by an usual biosynthetic pathway. DA and GABA are taken up into the same synaptic vesicles by VMAT2. (C) Neurons of the entopeduncular nucleus that project to the lateral habenula synthesize both glutamate and GABA, and the two transmitters are taken up into the same synaptic vesicles by their respective vesicular transporters, VGLUT2 and VGAT. (After A. J. Granger et al. 2017. *Curr Opin Neurobiol* 45: 85–91.)

since there is no expression of VGAT for GABA vesicular packaging, such packaging is thought to be mediated by the vesicular monoamine transporter 2 (VMAT2) (Granger et al., 2017) (**FIGURE 8.16B**). In this case, therefore, both DA and GABA are stored and released from the same vesicles. The last example involves instances in which the same neurons express both VGAT for GABA and VGLUT1 or VGLUT2 for filling vesicles with glutamate (Münster-Wandowski et al., 2016; Tritsch et al., 2016). It is not known in all of these cases whether separate GABAergic and glutamatergic vesicle populations are present (like ACh and GABA) or whether the same vesicles contain both transmitters (like DA and GABA). One situation where this has been investigated involves the neural pathway from the entopeduncular nucleus to the lateral habenula, a pathway that helps mediate the behavioral responses to negative emotional/motivational stimuli (Li et al., 2019). The entopeduncular cells express GAD, so they are able to synthesize both glutamate and GABA. The most recent information indicates that the nerve terminals in the lateral habenula contain two separate types of vesicles, one with VGLUT2 to take up glutamate and the other with VGAT to take up GABA (Root et al., 2018) (**FIGURE 8.16C**). Interestingly, these distinct vesicle populations are segregated within the terminals, and each type localizes to distinct active zones where transmitter release presumably occurs. Thus, the postsynaptic cells may receive both excitatory and inhibitory inputs from the same nerve terminals. It may seem paradoxical for a neuron to release both an excitatory and an inhibitory transmitter at the same time, but such a situation allows for a fine-tuning of the postsynaptic response that would be difficult to achieve using a single neurotransmitter (Tritsch et al., 2016; Granger et al., 2017).

SECTION SUMMARY

- GABA is the major inhibitory amino acid neurotransmitter in the brain. This transmitter is synthesized from glutamate in a single biochemical reaction catalyzed by GAD, an enzyme found only in GABAergic neurons.

- Because of the widespread inhibitory effects of GABA on neuronal excitability, treatment with drugs that inhibit GABA synthesis by blocking GAD leads to seizures.

- GABA is taken up into synaptic vesicles by the vesicular transporter VGAT (also known as VIAAT because the same vesicular transporter is used by glycine).

- After release into the synaptic cleft, GABA is removed from the cleft by three different transporters designated GAT-1, GAT-2, and GAT-3. Astrocytes express all three of these transporters and therefore must play a significant role in GABA uptake. GAT-1 is also found in GABAergic neurons, and the GAT-1 inhibitor tiagabine (Gabitril) is used clinically in the treatment of some patients with epilepsy.

- In addition to uptake, the other process that regulates GABAergic transmission is GABA metabolism. The key enzyme in GABA breakdown is GABA-T, which is present in both GABAergic neurons and astrocytes. A byproduct of the reaction catalyzed by GABA-T is glutamate, which is the precursor of GABA. Hence, GABA breakdown in neurons or in glial cells may involve a recycling process that assists in the formation of new GABA molecules.

- Vigabatrin (Sabril) is an irreversible inhibitor of GABA-T and thereby elevates GABA levels in the brain. Like tiagabine, vigabatrin has been licensed for the treatment of certain types of epilepsy. Although there are reports of visual system abnormalities in patients treated with vigabatrin, current evidence suggests that these abnormalities are most likely the result of the seizure activity rather than the drug treatment.

- GABA is co-expressed and co-released with several other classical neurotransmitters, including glycine, acetylcholine, dopamine, and glutamate. This is accomplished, in some cases, by co-expression of the vesicular transporters for multiple transmitters in the same neuron. Co-release of glutamate is of particular interest, as it involves a combination of inhibitory and excitatory neurotransmitter signaling.

8.4 Organization and Function of the GABAergic System

Like glutamate, GABA is used by many populations of neurons in the brain. Here we discuss some features of the anatomy of the GABAergic system, subtypes of GABA receptors, and a few basic functions of GABAergic transmission.

Some GABAergic neurons are interneurons, while others are projection neurons

Fonnum (1987) estimated that as many as 10% to 40% of the nerve terminals in the cerebral cortex, hippocampus, and substantia nigra use GABA as their neurotransmitter. A subsequent study of biopsy samples from the human frontal cortex found that approximately 20% of all neurons were positively stained using an antibody against GABA (Hornung and De Tribolet, 1994). These cortical GABAergic cells are all inhibitory interneurons of many different shapes and molecular phenotypes (Lim et al., 2018). Other cortical interneurons use various neuropeptides such as somatostatin, neuropeptide Y, cholecystokinin, and vasoactive intestinal peptide as their signaling agent (Markram et al., 2004).

In addition to the cortex, hippocampus, and substantia nigra, significant amounts of GABA are also found in the cerebellum, striatum, globus pallidus, and olfactory bulbs. The hippocampus is similar to the cortex in that its GABAergic cells are all interneurons. However, there are also GABAergic projection neurons that carry inhibitory information longer distances within the brain. For example, GABAergic neurons of the striatum project to the globus pallidus and the substantia nigra. When DA input to the striatum is damaged in Parkinson's disease, the result is abnormal firing of the striatal GABAergic neurons, which causes the motor abnormalities seen in this neurological disorder (see Chapter 20). GABA is also the transmitter used by Purkinje cells of the cerebellar cortex. These neurons, which project to the deep cerebellar nuclei and to the brainstem, have an important function in fine muscle control and coordination. This is illustrated in a group of disorders collectively known as **spinocerebellar ataxias** (Robinson et al., 2020). Patients with these disorders carry rare genetic mutations that cause degeneration and death of the Purkinje cells. The resulting symptoms include not only ataxia, but also impaired balance and poor motor coordination. Some patients additionally exhibit visual dysfunction and cognitive deficits.

The actions of GABA are primarily mediated by ionotropic GABA$_A$ receptors

Like glutamate, GABA makes use of both ionotropic and metabotropic receptors. However, only one type of each is used: the **GABA$_A$ receptor**, which is ionotropic, and the **GABA$_B$ receptor,** which is metabotropic. Our discussion will concentrate on the GABA$_A$ receptor because of its prominent role in GABAergic transmission and because it is a crucial target of many important psychoactive drugs.

STRUCTURE AND FUNCTION OF THE GABA$_A$ RECEPTOR

GABA$_A$ receptors are ion channels that permit Cl$^-$ ions to move across the cell membrane from outside to inside. This causes inhibition of the postsynaptic cell as the result of membrane hyperpolarization. More Cl$^-$ ions flow through open GABA$_A$ receptor channels when the membrane has previously been depolarized by excitatory synaptic inputs. In such cases, these receptors function to blunt depolarization and prevent the cell from firing an action potential. Although we normally think about the GABA$_A$ receptor mediating Cl$^-$ influx and, consequently, membrane hyperpolarization, there are circumstances under which the opposite occurs, namely Cl$^-$ outflow that leads to membrane depolarization and cellular excitation instead of inhibition. One such circumstance may be seizure-prone areas of the brain in patients with epilepsy. Later in the chapter we discuss the potential roles of GABA and GABA$_A$ receptors in the genesis of seizure activity and in pharmacotherapy for epilepsy.

Structurally, each GABA$_A$ receptor contains five subunits. Three or four different *kinds* of subunits may be found within a particular GABA$_A$ receptor complex.

These different kinds of subunits are designated by the Greek letters α, β, γ, and δ.* Most GABA$_A$ receptors are thought to contain two α subunits, two β subunits, and one γ subunit (**FIGURE 8.17**). There are multiple isoforms of all of these subunits, consisting of six different αs (designated α1–α6), three different βs (β1–β3), and three different γs (γ1–γ3). According to Jembrek and Vlainić (2015), approximately 60% of GABA$_A$ receptors in the brain have a subunit composition of $(α1)_2(β2)_2(γ2)$ (this means two α1 subunits, two β2 subunits, and one γ2 subunit). At 15% to 20%, the next most common receptor composition is $(α2)_2(β3)_2(γ2)$, followed by receptors that contain two α3 subunits, two β subunits of some kind, and one γ2 subunit (10%–15%). The GABA$_A$ receptors just described are generally localized to the synaptic area where they mediate phasic neuronal inhibition (i.e., brief inhibition in response to GABA release

*There are additional kinds of subunits designated with other Greek letters, but these subunits are found in relatively few GABA$_A$ receptors in the brain and, therefore, are not discussed here.

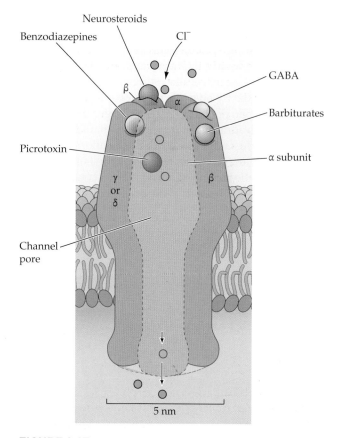

FIGURE 8.17   The GABA$_A$ receptor The receptor consists of five subunits that form a Cl$^-$-conducting channel. In addition to the GABA binding site on the receptor complex, there are additional modulatory sites for benzodiazepines, barbiturates, neurosteroids, and picrotoxin. Note that the locations of the various binding sites are depicted arbitrarily and are not meant to imply the actual locations of these sites on the receptor.

from the presynaptic nerve terminal). However, there exist extrasynaptic receptors that respond to low levels of GABA that have avoided immediate uptake following release and have escaped from the synaptic cleft. Their role is to exert a mild tonic (continuous) hyperpolarizing and thus inhibitory effect on the cells that express those receptors. These extrasynaptic receptors contain two α4, α5, or α6 subunits, two β subunits, and either the typical γ2 subunit or a δ subunit in place of γ2 (Belelli et al., 2009; Chua and Chebib, 2017).

The classic agonist for the GABA$_A$ receptor is a drug called **muscimol**. This compound is found in the mushroom *Amanita muscaria* (**FIGURE 8.18**), which was mentioned in Chapter 7 as the original source of the cholinergic agonist muscarine. In earlier times, this mushroom apparently would be chopped up and placed in a dish with milk to attract flies. Ingestion of muscimol and the related compound ibotenic acid would make the flies stuporous and easy to catch. The common name for *A. muscaria* is therefore "fly agaric" (*agaric* is an old term meaning "mushroom"). Rudgley (1999) discusses the custom of eating fly agaric, as practiced by various Siberian peoples for hundreds of years. The mushroom was prized for its stimulatory and hallucinogenic qualities—effects that can also be obtained by drinking urine from an intoxicated individual (not a very appealing idea to most Westerners!).* One of the interesting hallucinatory effects produced by the fly agaric is macroscopia, which refers to the perception of objects as being larger than they really are. When administered to humans at relatively high doses, pure muscimol causes an intoxication characterized by hyperthermia (elevated body temperature), pupil dilation, elevation of mood, difficulties in concentration,

---

*Fly agaric intoxication was apparently enjoyed not only by Siberians but by their reindeer as well. Animals were observed to eat the mushrooms of their own accord and were also sometimes given urine to drink from a person who had previously partaken.

© Arie v.d. Wolde/Shutterstock.com

FIGURE 8.18 The fly agaric mushroom, *Amanita muscaria*

anorexia (loss of appetite), ataxia, catalepsy, and hallucinations. Many of these effects are similar to those associated with more traditional hallucinogenic drugs such as lysergic acid diethylamide (LSD; see Chapter 15).

Bicuculline is the best-known competitive antagonist for the GABA$_A$ receptor. It blocks the binding of GABA to the GABA$_A$ receptor, and when taken systemically, it has a potent convulsant effect. **Pentylenetetrazol (Metrazol)** and **picrotoxin** are two other convulsant drugs that inhibit GABA$_A$ receptor function by acting at sites distinct from the binding site of GABA itself. Pentylenetetrazol is a synthetic compound that once was used as convulsant therapy for major depression. Although it is no longer used for that purpose, it still has value for the induction of experimental seizures in laboratory animals. Picrotoxin is obtained from the seeds of the East Indian shrub *Anamirta cocculus*. Because neither pentylenetetrazol nor picrotoxin prevents GABA from interacting with the GABA$_A$ receptor, these agents are noncompetitive rather than competitive receptor antagonists.

ALLOSTERIC MODULATORS OF THE GABA$_A$ RECEPTOR

For psychopharmacologists, the most remarkable property of the GABA$_A$ receptor is its sensitivity to certain CNS-depressant drugs that display an anxiolytic (antianxiety), sedative–hypnotic (sedating and sleep-inducing), anticonvulsant, and muscle relaxant profile. Among such drugs are the **benzodiazepines (BDZs)** and the **barbiturates**. There is overwhelming evidence that the principal mechanism of action of BDZs and barbiturates is positive allosteric modulation of the GABA$_A$ receptor, thereby potentiating GABA-mediated synaptic inhibition. **Ethanol** is another CNS-depressant drug that has many of the same properties as BDZs and barbiturates. Although the actions of ethanol are complex, one of its major effects is likewise to enhance GABA$_A$ receptor activity (Förstera et al., 2016). Chronic administration of any of these GABA$_A$ receptor positive modulators can lead to the development of tolerance, dependence, and withdrawal symptoms if drug treatment is suddenly terminated (Calixto, 2016; Gravielle, 2018). Various studies have shown that these phenomena are mediated, at least in part, by changes in GABA$_A$ receptor expression and function. Interactions of GABA$_A$ receptors with sedative–hypnotic and anxiolytic drugs and with ethanol are discussed in later chapters that cover these compounds. Below we discuss two other groups of positive modulators: anesthetics such as **propofol (Diprivan)**, an intravenously administered drug frequently used for surgical anesthesia and also the drug responsible for the overdose death of Michael Jackson, and **neuroactive steroids** (also called **neurosteroids**), which consist of steroid hormones synthesized in the brain that act locally on the GABA$_A$ receptor.

How do BDZs, barbiturates, ethanol, anesthetics, and neurosteroids exert their influence on the GABA$_A$

receptor? All of these substances interact with sites on the receptor complex that are distinct from the GABA binding site. This concept is illustrated in Figure 8.17, which depicts binding sites for BDZs and barbiturates, as well as a negative modulatory site for picrotoxin and related convulsant drugs. Ethanol, anesthetics, and neurosteroids are not shown in the figure, as these compounds are thought to interact with multiple binding sites on the receptor (Sieghart, 2015). There are also important differences among these compounds in their ability to affect $GABA_A$ receptor activity. BDZs and ethanol can only modulate receptor activity, regardless of the administered dose. In contrast, sufficiently high doses of barbiturates, anesthetics, and neurosteroids can open the receptor channel even in the absence of GABA (Sieghart, 2015).

BENZODIAZEPINE INTERACTIONS WITH THE $GABA_A$ RECEPTOR

Although the pharmacology of BDZs is covered extensively in Chapter 17, it is worth noting here some of the key features of the interactions of BDZs with the $GABA_A$ receptor. When a BDZ such as **diazepam (Valium)** binds to its binding site on the receptor, the potency of GABA to activate the receptor is increased. If we examine this interaction by measuring the amount of inward current flow carried by Cl^- ions across the cell membrane, we can see that the current flow produced by a given concentration of GABA is greatly enhanced by the simultaneous application of diazepam (**FIGURE 8.19A**; Sigel and Ernst, 2018). Note that application of diazepam alone has no effect, confirming that BDZs are positive allosteric modulators of the $GABA_A$ receptor and not receptor agonists. Another way of visualizing the interaction of GABA with BDZs is to hold the concentration of diazepam constant while varying the GABA concentration. In this case, we see that the BDZ shifts the concentration–response curve to the left (**FIGURE 8.19B**).

It is important to recognize that not all $GABA_A$ receptors are sensitive to BDZs. Genetic engineering studies in mice have shown that BDZ binding and functional sensitivity to BDZs require the presence of a γ subunit (usually γ2), along with α1, α2, α3, or α5 subunits and any β subunit (Sieghart and Sperk, 2002). Such studies have additionally allowed researchers to determine the relative contributions of particular α subunits to the various behavioral and physiological effects of BDZs (Cheng et al., 2018). Based on this work, researchers have concluded that $GABA_A$ receptors containing α1 subunits are almost completely responsible for the sedating effects of BDZs, with receptors containing α2, α3, or α5 subunits having little or no effect on this behavioral action. The anxiolytic actions of BDZs have been attributed largely to receptors containing α2 and α3 subunits; however, it is difficult to rule out a potential contribution of α1 subunit–containing receptors, which are expressed significantly within

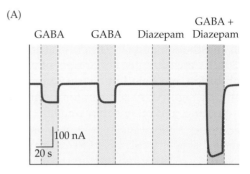

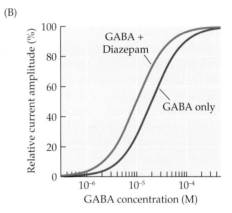

FIGURE 8.19 **Positive allosteric modulation of the $GABA_A$ receptor by diazepam** (A) Downward traces depict inward current flow across the membrane of a $GABA_A$ receptor–expressing cell. Currents are elicited by application of a low concentration of GABA (left two traces). Application of diazepam (1 μM) by itself has no effect (third trace), but diazepam applied together with GABA elicits a large increase in current amplitude (rightmost trace). (B) The graph illustrates a concentration–response curve in the absence (red line) and presence (blue line) of a fixed concentration of diazepam. Note that the curve is shifted to the left in the presence of diazepam, indicating an enhancement of current amplitude in response to low to moderate concentrations of GABA. However, the maximum current amplitude elicited by a high concentration of GABA is unaffected by diazepam. (After E. Sigel and M. E. Steinmann. 2012. *J Biol Chem* 287: 40224–40231. doi.org/10.1074/jbc.R112.386664. © 2012 ASBMB. Currently published by Elsevier Inc; originally published by American Society for Biochemistry and Molecular Biology. CC BY 4.0, creativecommons.org/licenses/by/4.0/.)

several cell populations in the amygdala (a brain area known to play a key role in mediating anxiety and anxiety-related behaviors; Engin et al., 2018). With respect to other BDZ-mediated behaviors, genetic studies have particularly implicated α1 subunit–containing $GABA_A$ receptors in the anticonvulsant and addictive properties of these drugs, whereas receptors containing α2 subunits are most important to BDZ-related muscle relaxation (Cheng et al., 2018).

Most $GABA_A$ receptors in the brain have the requisite composition for BDZ sensitivity, but there are exceptions. For example, the extrasynaptic receptors that contain α4 or α6 subunits are not affected by administration of a BDZ. On the other hand, these extrasynaptic receptors are an important target for ethanol, anesthetics, and neurosteroids (Brickley and Mody, 2012). Consequently, enhancement of tonic cellular inhibition, mediated by extrasynaptic GABA$_A$ receptors, is a significant contributor to the sedating, sleep-promoting, and other behavioral effects of many non-BDZ positive allosteric modulators.

Whereas diazepam and related BDZs are positive allosteric GABA$_A$ receptor modulators, researchers have discovered certain compounds that act at the same binding site but negatively modulate the receptor. Such compounds have a pharmacological profile opposite to that of BDZs. That is, they are anxiogenic (anxiety producing), arousing, and proconvulsant (seizure promoting) instead of anxiolytic, sedating, and anticonvulsant (see Chapter 17 for further discussion). Drugs that interact with the allosteric BDZ binding site but exert effects opposite to those of BDZs are sometimes termed **inverse agonists** at that site. Lastly, in almost all cases in which pharmacologists have discovered allosteric binding sites that modulate (either positively or negatively) neurotransmitter receptor function, the substances that act on these sites are synthetic. Of course, this is the case for the BDZs. However, over a period of years, researchers have discovered and characterized several endogenous neuropeptides (termed **endozepines**, meaning endogenous BDZs) that allosterically modulate the GABA$_A$ receptor by acting at the same site as BDZs. This interesting topic is discussed further in **WEB BOX 8.3** (Farzampour et al., 2015; Masmoudi-Kouki et al., 2018; Tonon et al., 2020).

ANESTHETIC AND NEUROSTEROID INTERACTIONS WITH THE GABA$_A$ RECEPTOR

Anesthetics are drugs that not only induce a state of unconsciousness, but also block sensory awareness. Lack of pain sensitivity is what enables patients to undergo surgery without discomfort and without waking up. Anesthetics act on a complex array of molecular targets, including both voltage-gated ion channels (Covarrubias et al., 2015) and ligand-gated channels (Antkowiak and Rudolph, 2016; Weir et al.,

2017). **FIGURE 8.20** illustrates the effects of several structurally distinct IV anesthetics on ligand-gated channel receptors. While several anesthetics exert mostly small or moderate inhibitory effects on excitatory receptor channels, they all strongly enhance GABA$_A$ receptor activity. This effect typically manifests as an allosteric modulation of channel opening, though at high concentrations, some anesthetics can open the channel even in the absence of GABA. As with BDZs and other modulatory compounds, anesthetics differentially affect receptors with a particular subunit composition. An interesting example of this concerns a sparsely expressed family of GABA$_A$ receptors that contain an α5 subunit. This subunit is most heavily expressed in the hippocampus and the olfactory bulbs (Engin et al., 2018). Hippocampal expression is noteworthy because of this brain area being a key site for LTP and memory encoding. If you have ever undergone a medical procedure (e.g., major surgery) that required general anesthesia, you may have experienced a loss of memory of events that occurred just *before* administration of the anesthetic agent. A combination of human and animal research strongly suggests that anesthetic potentiation of extrasynaptic hippocampal α5 receptor activity plays an important role in this kind of amnesia (Perouansky and Pearce, 2011; Rudolph and Möhler, 2014). Conversely, negative allosteric modulators targeting α5 subunit–containing GABA$_A$ receptors have potential therapeutic value for cognitive enhancement (Möhler and Rudolph, 2017).

As mentioned earlier, GABA$_A$ receptors are additionally modulated by neurosteroids. These substances are made from cholesterol and possess a steroid structure like that of the glucocorticoids and gonadal steroids (see Chapter 3). Although they can be made by the endocrine glands, their role as *neurosteroids* pertains to the fact that they are also synthesized in the brain by neurons and glial cells, and they act as local signaling molecules rather than as hormones that circulate throughout the body by means of the bloodstream. More information on the structure, function, and pharmacology of neurosteroids is presented in **BOX 8.2**.

FIGURE 8.20 Modulation of ligand-gated ion channel activity by IV anesthetics Depicted are the effects of four structurally disparate IV anesthetics on the activity of inhibitory and excitatory ligand-gated ion channels. Upward arrows denote enhancement of channel activity, whereas downward arrows denote channel inhibition. The number of arrows corresponds to the magnitude of the effect. (After C. J. Weir et al. 2017. *Br J Anaesth* 119: i167–i175. © 2017. Reprinted with permission from Elsevier.)

	Inhibitory		Excitatory			
	GABA$_A$	Glycine	AMPA/ Kainate	NMDA (+ glycine)	α4β2 nicotinic	5-HT$_3$
Etomidate	↑↑↑	—	—	—	—	—
Propofol	↑↑↑	↑	—	—	↓↓	↓
Alphaxalone	↑↑↑	—	—	—	↓↓	—
Pentobarbital	↑↑↑	—	↓↓	↓	↓↓↓	↓

BOX 8.2 ■ THE CUTTING EDGE

GABA$_A$ Receptor Modulation by Neurosteroids

Neurosteroids are a class of steroid molecules that are synthesized within the nervous system, where they act locally as signaling agents. Like the endozepines mentioned earlier, these substances are endogenous molecules that target allosteric binding sites on the GABA$_A$ receptor. There are two classes of neurosteroids based on their modulatory actions and behavioral/physiological effects. Allopregnanolone (ALLO), allotetrahydrodeoxycorticosterone (THDOC), and androstanediol (AS) are GABA$_A$ receptor positive allosteric modulators that exert sedating, anxiolytic, and anticonvulsant effects. In contrast, pregnenolone sulfate (PS) and dehydroepiandrosterone sulfate (DHEAS) negatively modulate GABA$_A$ receptors, but they also positively modulate NMDA receptors (Belilli and Lambert, 2005; Tuem and Atey, 2017). As would be expected, these two neurosteroids are anxiogenic and proconvulsant. Interestingly, however, PS and DHEAS also exert beneficial effects by enhancing cognitive function in humans as well as in experimental animals (Ratner et al., 2019). Although ALLO and the other positive allosteric GABA$_A$ receptor modulators have functional profile similar to that of the BDZs, there is an important difference regarding the nature of their modulation. Whereas BDZs enhance phasic neuronal inhibition by modulating synaptic γ2 subunit–containing receptors, the positive modulating neurosteroids enhance tonic inhibition by interacting with the BDZ-insensitive extrasynaptic δ subunit–containing receptors.

Neuropharmacologists are interested in neurosteroids because of their potential roles in the etiology of certain pathological conditions or their use as therapeutic agents (Reddy and Estes, 2016; Blanco et al., 2018). We have chosen here to focus on two conditions in which neurosteroids have been extensively studied: catamenial epilepsy and postpartum depression.

Researchers have estimated that roughly 40% to 60% of women suffering from epilepsy have a specific type of disorder called catamenial epilepsy (Reddy, 2007). The term *catamenial* comes from the Greek word *katamenios*, which means monthly. Indeed, in catamenial epilepsy, seizures are most likely to occur at specific stages of the monthly menstrual cycle. Two main patterns of seizure timing have been identified: type I periovulatory (around the time of ovulation) and type II perimenstrual (around the time of menstruation). Although the precise cause of catamenial epilepsy is not yet known, one major theory is that seizure susceptibility is related to menstrual cycle changes in the levels of circulating estrogens and progesterone (**FIGURE**). Estrogens are known to have proconvulsant properties, where progesterone is anticonvulsant because of its conversion to the neurosteroid ALLO. According to this theory, therefore, type I catamenial

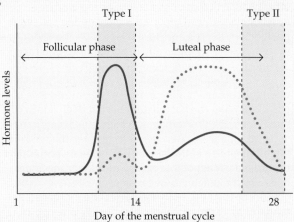

Increased seizure frequency is related to menstrual cycle phase in catamenial epilepsy The figure depicts the times of increased seizure frequency in relation to menstrual phase and circulating hormone levels. The solid red line depicts levels of estrogens (mainly estradiol), whereas the dotted blue line depicts levels of progesterone. Increased seizure frequency occurs either around the time of ovulation (type I), when the ratio of estrogen to progesterone is high, or around the time of menstruation (type II), when the levels of progesterone are declining. (From S. Joshi and J. Kapur. 2019. *Brain Res* 1703: 31–40. © 2018. Reprinted with permission from Elsevier.)

epilepsy is related to the high estrogen/progesterone ratio during the periovulatory period, whereas type II is related to withdrawal from progesterone/ALLO during the perimenstrual period (Reddy, 2016; Joshi and Kapur, 2019). Studies using animal models of type II catamenial epilepsy support the hormone withdrawal theory and additionally show that during the withdrawal period, there is a decrease in BDZ anticonvulsant efficacy but an increase in the anticonvulsant action of neurosteroids, possibly due to an upregulation of δ subunit–containing extrasynaptic GABA$_A$ receptors (Reddy, 2016). Based on these findings, neurosteroids such as ALLO could prove to be beneficial in treating some women with catamenial epilepsy. However, other factors yet to be discovered are undoubtedly involved in the etiology of this seizure disorder, and further research is needed to identify these factors.

Postpartum depression is a form of major depressive disorder in which symptoms begin either during pregnancy or within 4 weeks following parturition (Kroska and Stowe, 2020). Prevalence of postpartum depression is estimated at roughly 17% of women who have given birth. It is important to distinguish postpartum depression from "postpartum blues," which is a more common, brief reduction in mood

(Continued)

BOX 8.2 ■ THE CUTTING EDGE *(continued)*

after childbirth that does not impair the woman's functioning. Several theories regarding the causes of postpartum depression have focused on the endocrine system, primarily either the hypothalamic-pituitary-adrenocortical stress response system (see Chapter 3) or the reproductive hormone system, the latter of which undergoes major changers over the course of pregnancy and the postpartum period (Meltzer-Brody and Kanes, 2020). Women experience a large increase in circulating progesterone (even greater than during the luteal phase of the menstrual cycle) as pregnancy progresses. Most of this excess progesterone is produced by the placenta. Because progesterone is the precursor to ALLO, both hormones are increased in tandem. As term approaches, progesterone and ALLO levels begin to decline, which is followed by precipitous declines in both hormones after parturition. Parallels between the time course of these changes and the onset of postpartum depression led to the theory that in susceptible women, postpartum depression is attributable to GABAergic dysregulation related to withdrawal of ALLO (Meltzer-Brody and Kanes, 2020). Initial clinical studies using progesterone supplementation failed to achieve consistent therapeutic benefits in women with postpartum depression. Later studies, however, tried ALLO itself instead of progesterone, and those studies did show the treatment to be effective in helping many patients. These results led to the 2019 FDA approval of brexanolone (trade name Zulresso), a synthetic form of ALLO, for treating postpartum depression. Women with postpartum depression were previously treated with standard antidepressant medications like selective serotonin reuptake inhibitors (SSRIs) or other therapeutic modalities for major depressive disorder. Thus, brexanolone is the first medication specifically approved for this particular form of depression (Dacarett-Galeano and Diao, 2019; Powell et al., 2020). Moreover, the drug provides more rapid symptom relief than SSRIs, which is beneficial both for mothers and their babies.

This discussion has highlighted the importance of neurosteroids in regulating such basic functions as brain excitability and affective state. Many other functions not reviewed here have also been investigated. The licensing of brexanolone illustrates that neurosteroids possess therapeutic potential, and we anticipate additional clinical applications for these substances in the coming years.

GABA$_A$ RECEPTORS AND EPILEPSY The term *epilepsy* refers to a class of neurological disorders characterized by recurrent convulsive and nonconvulsive seizures. An estimated 3.4 million Americans currently suffer from epilepsy, with 150,000 new cases occurring every year (Epilepsy Foundation). The seriousness of this disorder can be seen in the fact that post-mortem studies of patients with epilepsy, especially temporal lobe epilepsy, have shown brain cell loss in the hippocampus (termed **hippocampal sclerosis**) and that an excitotoxic, NMDA receptor–mediated process may be involved in such loss (Thom, 2014). In Box 8.2, we discussed a potential role for GABA$_A$ receptors in one specific type of epilepsy. Here we present evidence for a more general involvement of GABA and GABA$_A$ receptors in the etiology and maintenance of seizure disorders.

Some of the evidence for GABA involvement in epilepsy comes from studies of epileptic tissue obtained surgically from patients who failed to respond to standard drug treatments. Surgical intervention occurs most commonly in cases of treatment-resistant temporal lobe epilepsy. Although surgical removal of brain tissue is obviously of serious concern to the patient, researchers have utilized this opportunity to study living human epileptic brain tissue to help determine how it may be malfunctioning. These studies found that application of GABA to the tissue paradoxically led to excitatory instead of inhibitory postsynaptic responses (Auer et al., 2020). Additional experiments demonstrated that the shift in GABA$_A$-mediated responses from inhibitory to excitatory was due to the fact that opening of the receptor channel resulted in Cl⁻ *efflux* from the cell instead of the normal Cl⁻ *influx*, thus causing membrane depolarization instead of hyperpolarization. Interestingly, it turns out that GABA$_A$ receptors behave this way during early brain development because the ratio of Cl⁻ ions inside versus outside the cells differs from that ratio in the mature brain (i.e., during development, the Cl⁻ ion concentration inside these neurons is much greater than it is later on; Ben-Ari et al., 2012; Kaila et al., 2014). These findings suggest that one factor in this form of severe temporal lobe epilepsy may be the return of at least some hippocampal GABA$_A$ receptor–expressing neurons to an earlier developmental state, at least with respect to their regulation of Cl⁻ ion distribution.

A loss of GABA-mediated inhibition is particularly significant in the development of **status epilepticus**, a highly dangerous condition characterized either by a continuous seizure lasting longer than 30 minutes or by episodes of repeated seizures that recur so quickly that the patient has insufficient time to recover from one seizure before another one begins. Diazepam and other BDZs are usually effective in suppressing seizures in patients with epilepsy. However, these compounds are much less effective in patients with a history of status epilepticus. Such resistance to BDZs has been linked to seizure-induced internalization (i.e., endocytosis) of BDZ-sensitive GABA$_A$ receptors from the cell surface (Goodkin and Kapur, 2009; Deeb et al., 2012). For this reason, drugs targeting BDZ-insensitive extrasynaptic GABA$_A$ receptors that mediate tonic neuronal inhibition may represent the best treatments for patients suffering from status epilepticus (Schipper et al., 2015; Chuang and Reddy, 2018).

Most cases of epilepsy have no known genetic cause; however, in some instances mutations have been discovered either in the GABAergic system or in other systems (e.g., voltage-gated ion channels) that can be causally linked to the seizure disorder. Epilepsy-related mutations have been discovered in the genes coding for the α1, α2, α5, α6, β1, β2, β3, γ2, and δ subunits of the GABA$_A$ receptor (Hernandez and Macdonald, 2019). Because such mutations are congenital, the associated epileptic disorders all begin during infancy or childhood. These disorders exhibit a range of different physical manifestations, and many of them are characterized by additional adverse health outcomes such as developmental delay or disability, and shortened life span. Finally, the nature of the seizure activity depends on whether the affected receptors are synaptic (mediating phasic neuronal inhibition) or extrasynaptic (mediating tonic inhibition) (Gataullina et al., 2019).

GABA also signals using metabotropic GABA$_B$ receptors

STRUCTURE AND FUNCTION OF THE GABA$_B$ RECEPTOR

As mentioned earlier, the other GABA receptor subtype is a metabotropic receptor termed GABA$_B$. Interestingly, unlike virtually all other known metabotropic receptors, the GABA$_B$ receptor requires two different subunits in order to assemble in the membrane and work properly (Fritzius and Bettler, 2020). GABA$_B$ receptors are located both postsynaptically and presynaptically. The postsynaptic receptors inhibit neuronal firing through stimulation of K$^+$ channel opening (Heaney and Kinney, 2016). Presynaptic GABA$_B$ receptors are found on axon terminals of GABAergic neurons (autoreceptors) and on some terminals of cells using a different neurotransmitter such as glutamate (heteroreceptors). These presynaptic receptors reduce neurotransmitter release from the nerve terminal by inhibiting Ca^{2+} channel opening. Both post- and presynaptic GABA$_B$ receptors also inhibit adenylyl cyclase, thereby reducing the rate of cAMP formation.

Behavioral functions of GABA$_B$ receptors have been studied using pharmacological and genetic engineering approaches. The classical agonist at the GABA$_B$ receptor is **baclofen** (**Lioresal**), which has been used for many years as a muscle relaxant and an antispastic agent (Kent et al., 2020). **Saclofen** and **2-hydroxysaclofen**, which are chemical analogs of baclofen, are competitive

antagonists at the GABA$_B$ receptor. Studies of knock-out mice lacking one of the GABA$_B$ receptor subunits or animals given a GABA$_B$ agonist or antagonist have demonstrated a role for this receptor in a wide variety of behavioral functions, including learning and memory, anxiety, and depression-like behaviors, and responses to drugs of abuse. Of particular interest to neuropharmacologists is that in animal studies, direct GABA$_B$ receptor agonists like baclofen or GABA$_B$ positive allosteric modulators inhibit behavioral responses to various abused drugs (Phillips and Reed, 2014; Chiamulera et al., 2017). These findings have led to suggestions that drugs targeting the GABA$_B$ receptor might help in the treatment of substance use disorders, particularly alcohol use disorder. Thus, a recent review reported on the results of 15 randomized controlled trials testing the potential benefit of baclofen in patients with alcohol use disorder (de Beaurepaire et al., 2019). Although the results of these trials have been inconsistent, the authors conclude that baclofen can be a valuable medication for the treatment of moderate to severe alcohol use disorder. However, use of baclofen for this purpose is currently popular mainly in Europe and Australia, whereas such use is infrequent in the United States, where the drug is not yet approved by the FDA for substance use disorder treatment.

SECTION SUMMARY

■ Many brain areas, including the cerebral cortex, hippocampus, substantia nigra, cerebellum, striatum, globus pallidus, and olfactory bulbs, are rich in GABA. GABAergic neurons may function as interneurons, as in the cortex and hippocampus, or they may function as projection neurons, as in pathways originating in the striatum and in the cerebellar Purkinje cells.

■ There are two general GABA receptor subtypes: ionotropic GABA$_A$ receptors and metabotropic GABA$_B$ receptors.

■ GABA$_A$ receptors conduct Cl$^-$ ions into the postsynaptic cell, causing membrane hyperpolarization and an inhibitory effect on cell excitability. Each receptor is composed of five subunits, usually including two α subunits, two βs, and one γ. A small number of GABA$_A$ receptors contain a δ subunit instead of γ.

■ The most common synaptic GABA$_A$ receptor composition is (α1)$_2$(β2)$_2$(γ2). There are also extrasynaptic receptors containing two α4 or two α6 subunits, along with two β subunits and a δ subunit. Such receptors are sensitive to low GABA concentrations and mediate a mild tonic inhibitory effect on cell firing.

■ Muscimol is a GABA$_A$ receptor agonist derived from the mushroom *Amanita muscaria* (fly agaric). Ingestion of this mushroom or of pure muscimol causes hallucinations (including macroscopia) and other behavioral and physiological effects similar to those associated with LSD.

■ GABA$_A$ receptor antagonists include the competitive antagonist bicuculline and the noncompetitive inhibitors pentylenetetrazol (Metrazol) and picrotoxin, all of which are seizure inducing.

■ BDZs, barbiturates, ethanol, anesthetics, and neurosteroids all act as positive allosteric modulators of the GABA$_A$ receptor, which means that they enhance the action of GABA on the receptor. At high doses, barbiturates, anesthetics, and neurosteroids can open the receptor channel in the absence of GABA. Functionally, all of these compounds exert a CNS depressant effect that is manifested behaviorally as anxiolytic, sedative–hypnotic, and anticonvulsant properties. Inverse agonists at the BDZ receptor also require the presence of GABA, but such compounds reduce instead of enhance the effectiveness of GABA in activating the GABA$_A$ receptor. BDZ inverse agonists produce behavioral effects opposite to those produced by BDZ agonists, namely anxiety, arousal, and increased susceptibility to seizures.

■ BDZ sensitivity requires the presence of a γ subunit (usually γ2), any β subunits, and an α1, α2, α3, or α5 subunit. Genetic studies in mice have identified relationships between the behavioral effects of BDZs and specific α subunits as follows: α1 for sedation, α2 or α3 for anxiety reduction, α1 or α2 for anticonvulsant activity, and α1 for BDZ addiction. Additionally, hippocampal α5 subunits play a key role in anesthetic-mediated amnesia.

■ Two distinct groups of neurosteroids have been discovered. One class, which includes ALLO, THDOC, and AS, exerts sedating, anxiolytic, and anticonvulsant actions by positively modulating GABA$_A$ receptors. The second group, which includes PS and DHEAS, negatively modulates GABA$_A$ receptors, which results in the opposite spectrum of behavioral and physiological effects. PS and DHEAS also positively modulate NMDA receptors and enhance cognitive function.

■ Studies have implicated neurosteroids, particularly ALLO, in catamenial epilepsy (characterized by heightened seizure susceptibility during the periovulatory or perimenstrual periods) and in postpartum depression. The research on postpartum depression led to the licensing of a synthetic form of ALLO as a new treatment for this disorder.

■ The metabotropic GABA$_B$ receptor is composed of two different subunits and is located both post- and presynaptically. Postsynaptic GABA$_B$ receptors inhibit neuronal firing by stimulating K$^+$ channel opening, whereas presynaptic GABA$_B$ receptors (acting as either autoreceptors or heteroreceptors) inhibit neurotransmitter release by inhibiting Ca^{2+} channel opening. The receptors additionally inhibit cAMP formation.

■ GABA$_B$ receptors contribute to many behavioral functions, including learning and memory, anxiety- and depression-like behaviors, and responses to drugs of abuse. This information has been obtained from studies of knockout mice lacking one of the receptor subunits and from pharmacological studies involving the selective agonist baclofen (Lioresal), which is used clinically as a muscle relaxant and an antispastic agent, or the competitive antagonists saclofen or 2-hydroxysaclofen. There is additional evidence that baclofen may be of helpful in treating alcohol use disorder.

STUDY QUESTIONS

1. Show the reactions for glutamate interconversion with glutamine, including the name of the enzyme catalyzing each reaction. What is the hypothesized reason why glutamate is stored in the form of glutamine?

2. Experimentally, how would you go about determining whether a particular group of anatomically defined neurons used glutamate as their neurotransmitter?

3. _____ and _____ are the most widely distributed vesicular glutamate transporters in the brain.

4. What can we conclude when a group of neurons is found to express both a VGLUT and the vesicular transporter for a different neurotransmitter or group of transmitters?

5. Discuss (a) the function and cellular expression of excitatory amino acid transporters and (b) the interplay between neurons and glial cells in the regulation of glutamate metabolism and signaling.

6. The text states, "Glutamate is the workhorse transmitter for fast excitatory signaling in the nervous system." What is the evidence for this statement?

7. Describe the three subtypes of ionotropic glutamate receptors, including how they were named, their subunit structure, and their ion conductances.

8. What is the functional significance of the fact that NMDA receptor channels are permeable to Ca^{2+} ions?

9. Describe the properties of the NMDA receptor, including its binding sites both outside of and within the ion channel. What conditions are necessary for the receptor channel to open, and how are these conditions related to the idea that the NMDA receptor is a "coincidence detector"?

10. List the ionotropic glutamate receptor antagonists mentioned in the chapter, including their channel selectivity and use, either as an abused drug or as a therapeutic agent.

11. Several NMDA receptor antagonists are characterized as _____ antagonists because they require the receptor to be activated by an agonist (thereby producing channel opening) before they can take effect.

STUDY QUESTIONS *(continued)*

12. Describe the family of metabotropic glutamate receptors, including their signaling mechanisms.

13. What is the rationale for testing the effectiveness of AMPA receptor positive allosteric modulators as cognitive enhancers? What are the possible reasons why such compounds have not proven beneficial in clinical trials despite their efficacy in animal models of learning and memory?

14. Discuss the phenomenon of long-term potentiation (LTP) in the hippocampal CA1 area. Include in your answer the specific roles of NMDA and AMPA receptors in LTP, changes in AMPA receptor trafficking, and differences between early and late LTP in their characteristics and underlying mechanisms.

15. Is there any evidence that LTP occurs in the human brain? If so, what kind of memory is thought to be encoded by this mechanism?

16. What meant by the term "excitotoxicity"? What are the types of excitotoxic cell death and the mechanisms underlying this phenomenon (including the role of ionotropic glutamate receptors)? Discuss the clinical conditions in which excitotoxic cell death is thought to occur.

17. What are the features of fragile X syndrome? What is the genetic basis of this disorder? Discuss the metabotropic glutamate receptor theory of fragile X syndrome, and the current status of medications that have been developed on the basis of this theory.

18. What is the biochemical pathway by which GABA is synthesized? Pharmacological inhibition of GABA synthesis _____ (increases or decreases?) brain excitability and susceptibility to seizure activity.

19. The vesicular GABA transporter, VGAT, is sometimes called VIAAT instead because this transporter can take up the neurotransmitter _____ in addition to GABA.

20. Of the three cell membrane GABA transporters, which ones are expressed by both neurons and astrocytes?

21. The GABAergic drugs tiagabine and vigabatrin both have clinical applications. Tiagabine blocks _____ and is used for the treatment of _____, whereas vigabatrin blocks _____ and is used for the treatment of _____.

22. (a) Discuss the phenomenon of GABA co-expression and co-release with other classical transmitters. Provide relevant examples, including whether the vesicular transporters in each case are present on the same or different synaptic vesicles. (b) What is the potential benefit of two or more neurotransmitters being co-expressed and co-released by the same neurons?

23. Where in the brain are GABA projection neurons and/or GABA interneurons found?

24. Describe the basic subunit composition of GABA$_A$ receptors.

25. Muscimol, bicuculline, pentyltetrazole, and picrotoxin are all drugs that interact with the GABA$_A$ receptor. Which of these are agonists, and which are antagonists? For the antagonists, indicate whether the compound is a competitive or noncompetitive (i.e., acting at a site distinct from the agonist binding site) antagonist.

26. Contrast the subunit composition of synaptic versus extrasynaptic GABA$_A$ receptors. Which of these mediates phasic neuronal inhibition, and which mediates tonic inhibition?

27. By what mechanism do benzodiazepines (BDZs) enhance GABA$_A$ receptor function? Are all GABA$_A$ receptors sensitive to BDZs? If not, what aspect of the receptor determines its sensitivity to this class of drugs?

28. What is meant by an "inverse agonist" at the BDZ binding site on the GABA$_A$ receptor? What is the behavioral profile of such compounds?

29. Endozepines are hypothesized to be endogenous substances acting at the _____ binding site of the _____ receptor.

30. Anesthetic-related amnesia is mediated by _____ subunit–containing GABA$_A$ receptors located in the _____.

31. What are neurosteroids? List the neurosteroids that are either positive or negative allosteric modulators of the GABA$_A$ receptor.

32. _____ is a type of epilepsy in which seizure activity most often occurs either in the periovulatory or perimenstrual period. Reduced levels of the neurosteroid _____ may be an important factor in perimenstrual seizures. This same substance has been developed as a new treatment for the mood disorder _____.

33. Discuss the evidence for an involvement of GABA in certain types of epileptic disorders other than the one mentioned in the previous question.

34. (a) Describe the properties of the GABA$_B$ receptor, including its signaling mechanisms. (b) The GABA$_B$ receptor agonist baclofen is used clinically for the treatment of _____.

9 Drug Misuse and Addiction

"**CHRIS THRALL LEFT THE ROYAL MARINES** [a unit of the Royal Navy of the United Kingdom] to find fortune in Hong Kong but a year later was suffering from drug-induced psychosis resulting from his crystal meth addiction. He became homeless, lost his sanity and almost his life after becoming addicted to the deadly drug, also known as 'ice.' Chris, from Plymouth, joined the Marines at 18 and served 7 years. He got an opportunity to get involved in a new business venture, left the Forces and moved to Hong Kong. Unfortunately, the venture failed; he was in debt and jobless. He found a job in marketing for a Hong Kong firm. A few months after starting he walked in on a colleague in the toilets smoking meth. Chris accepted the offer to try some, the next day he wanted more . . . His life went out of control and in an attempt to get straight, he went from a day job to working as a nightclub doorman with the intention that if he worked at night he wouldn't be able to take drugs. But his addiction was life consuming; he was on it constantly, hallucinating, and became psychotic. He got sacked and several other jobs followed. He was living on the streets and believed he was part of a global underground conspiracy. He put his life at risk deciding to climb a huge construction crane 'for a laugh.' Thirteen months after arriving in Hong Kong Chris booked a return flight to the UK paid for by his worried family. He was ravaged, 4 stone [56 pounds] lighter, wild-eyed and gaunt. He returned to Plymouth and even though he was ashamed of the addiction he continued to score the drug and carried on using for another 18 months. Crystal meth wasn't hard to find. One day [he] looked in the mirror and didn't know himself anymore; after a long battle and several attempts, he slowly started his recovery. He has now been clean for over 10 years." ■

— From Love PR London Ltd.

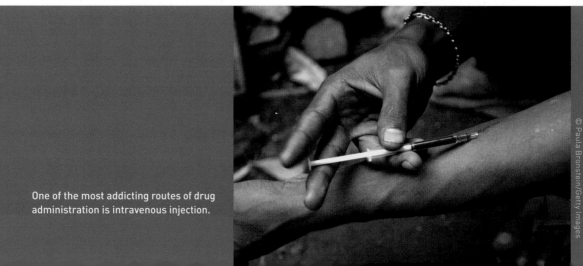

One of the most addicting routes of drug administration is intravenous injection.

© Paula Bronstein/Getty Images

The above is the true story of a young Englishman whose life unraveled after he became addicted to methamphetamine. In 2011, Thrall published an account of his ordeal entitled *Eating Smoke: One Man's Descent into Drug Psychosis in Hong Kong's Triad Heartland*. His story dramatically illustrates what we might call the "paradox" of addiction. That is, how can a person develop and maintain a pattern of behavior (in this case, repeated methamphetamine use) that is so obviously destructive to the individual's life? No one has a complete explanation for this paradox, but a variety of theories have been proposed. The aim of this chapter is to introduce you to several facets of this intriguing problem, including various psychosocial, genetic, and neurobiological factors thought to underlie the development and maintenance of an addicted state. We will describe the history and current prevalence of drug use in the United States, as well as the laws that determine which substances are legal and which are not. Finally, we will consider the important issue of whether drug addiction should be considered a disease, and how this issue bears on the kinds of treatments used to combat this disorder.

9.1 Introduction to Drug Misuse and Addiction

The first part of this chapter considers the prevalence of psychoactive drug use in our society, the discovery and use of such drugs in earlier times, and the history of drug laws in the United States.

Recreational drugs are widely consumed in our society

A recreational drug may be defined as a psychoactive substance that (1) is consumed voluntarily because the substance affects mood or behavior in a manner that is desirable to the user and (2) has the potential to be used in a problematic way that leads to adverse consequences (termed drug or substance *misuse*). Each year,

the Substance Abuse and Mental Health Services Administration conducts a National Survey on Drug Use and Health (NSDUH), which estimates the prevalence and incidence of drug use among civilians 12 years of age and older. Information is obtained about the use of both legal (e.g., alcohol and tobacco) and illegal drugs, and for each drug or drug class, survey participants are asked about "past month" use (which is considered an index of current use at the time of the survey) and "past year" use. According to the 2019 survey, approximately 57.2 million Americans had engaged in illegal drug use during the previous year (Substance Abuse and Mental Health Services Administration, 2020). That number constituted 20.8% of the population, which was substantially higher than the corresponding 17.8% of the population recorded in the 2015 survey.* **FIGURE 9.1** shows that the greatest amount of illegal drug use involved marijuana.** Also illustrated in the figure is the misuse of legal medications in the categories of pain relievers (opioid drugs), tranquilizers or sedatives (barbiturates and benzodiazepines), and stimulants (amphetamine and methylphenidate). The large number of people misusing prescription pain relievers such as oxycodone

---

*20.8 minus 17.8 = 3.0, and 3.0 divided by 17.8 = 0.1685, thereby showing an *increase* of illegal drug use of greater than 16%.

**As discussed in detail in Chapter 14, marijuana and other forms of cannabis are still illegal at the federal level even though medical and (in some cases) recreational marijuana use is legal in many states. Because the NSDUH is conducted by a federal agency, all marijuana use is categorized as illegal for survey purposes.

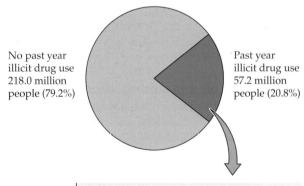

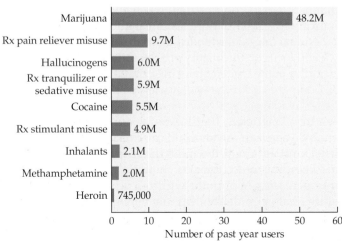

FIGURE 9.1 Data on illegal drug use in the United States Results from the 2019 National Survey on Drug Use and Health include the overall numbers and percentages of surveyed people age 12 or older who engaged in illegal drug use at least once during the prior year. Note that the estimated numbers of users of different drugs are not mutually exclusive, since many users consume multiple substances within a given time period (polydrug use). Rx refers to prescription medications. (After Substance Abuse and Mental Health Services Administration. 2020. *Key substance use and mental health indicators in the United States:* Results from the 2019 National Survey on Drug Use and Health [HHS Publication No. PEP20-07-01-001, NSDUH Series H-55]. Center for Behavioral Health Statistics and Quality, Substance Abuse and Mental Health Services Administration, Rockville, MD. Retrieved from https://www.samhsa.gov/data/)

(e.g., Oxycontin), hydrocodone (e.g., Vicodin), and fentanyl reflects the ongoing epidemic of opioid addiction that is plaguing the country (see Chapter 11).

We have long known that illegal drug use occurs most prominently in young adults. Consistent with this age distribution, the greatest percentage of illegal drug users based on the 2019 NSDUH was in the age range of 18 to 25 years old. Within that age bracket, 39.1% of those surveyed endorsed illegal drug use, compared to 17.2% in the 12- to 17-year-old age bracket and 18.3% in the 26-years-or-older bracket. Indeed, other findings show that illegal drug use continues to decline with age until the percentage is quite low among the elderly.

It is no surprise that legal drugs such as tobacco and alcohol are consumed even more widely than illegal substances. The 2019 survey estimated that more than 58 million Americans were current tobacco users (mostly cigarette smokers), 139 million drank alcohol, and, of the latter, approximately 16 million were heavy drinkers (defined as consuming five or more drinks at one time on 5 or more days within a single month). How did we reach a state where psychoactive drug use and misuse are so prevalent?

Drug use in our society has increased and has become more heavily regulated over time

Psychoactive drugs have been a part of human culture since antiquity. However, the substances available to drug users and the prevalence of use have varied in different periods.

HISTORICAL TRENDS   Many psychoactive substances such as nicotine, caffeine, morphine, cocaine, and tetrahydrocannabinol are made by plants and were available to ancient peoples in their native forms. Likewise, alcohol is a naturally occurring product of sugar fermentation by yeast. In his 1989 book *Intoxication: Life in Pursuit of Artificial Paradise*, Ronald Siegel presents many anecdotal accounts of wild animals becoming intoxicated after eating drug-containing plants. He goes on to suggest that early societies may have come to identify the pharmacological properties of such plants after first observing the behaviors of these intoxicated animals. More historical information on individual drugs is provided in later chapters. Here, we will focus on the history of drug use and cultural attitudes in the United States over the past 200 years.

Compared with the wide variety of psychoactive drugs available (legally or illegally) to twenty-first-century Americans, the situation was quite different 200 years ago. Alcohol and caffeine were widely used, and although the modern cigarette had not yet been invented, tobacco chewing was becoming increasingly popular within a large segment of the male population. Opium, either alone or in the form of laudanum (opium extract in alcohol),

was available for the purpose of pain relief. On the other hand, there was no cocaine, heroin, marijuana, 3,4-methylenedioxymethamphetamine (MDMA, or "ecstasy"), methamphetamine, barbiturates, lysergic acid diethylamide (LSD), or phencyclidine (PCP). There were also few drug control laws, especially none at the federal level.

As time went on, however, a number of events and cultural trends set us on the path to where we are today. First, the alcohol temperance movement started to gain strength. The founding of this movement, which promoted abstention from hard liquor in favor of moderate beer or wine consumption, is generally credited to a highly regarded Philadelphia physician named Benjamin Rush. Rush not only identified a number of adverse physiological consequences of excessive drinking but also argued that such consumption impaired the drinker's moral faculty, leading to irresponsible and even criminal acts. Although the temperance movement reached its height in the failed twentieth-century attempt at complete alcohol prohibition (except for "medicinal" use), its aftermath still colors the attitudes of many people toward alcohol- and drug-related problems. In particular, the equating of drug use with criminal behavior can be seen in the "War on Drugs" that has pervaded our society for so many years.

Second, advances in chemistry during the nineteenth century made it possible to purify the primary active ingredient of opium, namely morphine, and then later the active ingredient of coca, which of course is cocaine. This allowed the drugs to be taken in much more concentrated form, increasing their addictive potential. But since the route of administration is also important, an equally significant event was the development of the hypodermic syringe in 1858 (**FIGURE 9.2**), which permitted the purified substances to be injected directly into the bloodstream. One consequence of this marriage of purified drug and improved delivery vehicle was the widespread use of morphine to treat wounded and ill soldiers during the Civil War. Many developed an opiate addiction, which was called "soldier's disease" in the common parlance.

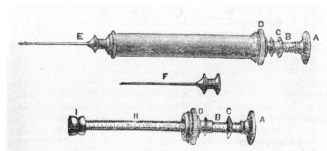

FIGURE 9.2   An early hypodermic syringe and needle used in the 1870s

From H. W. Morgan, 1981. *Drugs in America: A Social History, 1800–1980.* Syracuse University Press: Syracuse; original photograph from H. H. Kane, 1880. *The Hypodermic Injection of Morphia,* p. 21

Third, the increasing availability of purified drugs combined with the lack of drug control laws led to growing use of these substances in many different forms. Cocaine was the major ingredient in a variety of tonics and patent medicines sold over the counter. The most notorious of these was *Vin Mariani*, which was made by the French chemist Angelo Mariani by soaking coca leaves in wine along with spices and other flavorings. Heroin was synthesized by Bayer Laboratories in 1874 and was first marketed 14 years later as a non-addicting (!) substitute for codeine. If you've ever had a severe cough, the doctor probably prescribed a codeine-containing cough syrup. At the turn of the twentieth century, you could purchase heroin-containing cough syrup at any neighborhood pharmacy without a prescription (**FIGURE 9.3**). It does not surprise us now that the ready availability of these substances led many people to become dependent on them.

The last factor that we wish to mention here is the medicalization of drug addiction that occurred primarily in the second half of the twentieth century. The medicalization of addiction had two components: that addiction was now thought of as a disease, and that drug addicts should be treated by the medical establishment. We can trace the origin of these views to the American Association for the Cure of Inebriates, an organization founded in 1870, which stated that inebriety (excessive drinking) was a disease and proposed that inebriates (alcoholics) be admitted to hospitals and sanitaria for help. However, this medical approach to alcoholism and drug addiction later faded and was not seriously revived until the early 1950s, when alcoholism was declared a disease first by the World Health Organization and subsequently by the American Medical Association. Alcoholics Anonymous (AA), which embraces many aspects of the disease model of alcoholism, was gaining prominence during this period. The disease model of drug addiction continues to be strongly promoted by the treatment community, by self-help groups such as AA and Narcotics Anonymous, and by much of the research establishment, including the National Institute on Drug Abuse, an agency of the National Institutes of Health. It is also the view most widely accepted by the lay public. On the other hand, this model has also been the subject of some criticism, an issue that we will take up at the end of the chapter.

DRUGS AND THE LAW   Since 1980, the United States has witnessed the introduction of "crack" cocaine, the increased potency of heroin and marijuana sold on the street, an upsurge in methamphetamine use, and the rise of so-called club drugs such as MDMA and γ-hydroxybutyrate (GHB). More recently, we have seen a veritable epidemic of opioid drug use (both heroin and prescription opioids), the appearance of novel compounds like synthetic marijuana ("spice") and cathinone-based stimulants ("bath salts," "flakka," and others), and a resurgence in the use of psychedelic drugs like psilocybin and LSD. Although these developments led to the establishment and continuation of our government's "War on Drugs," illicit drug use continues on a massive scale despite the best efforts of the drug warriors. At the federal level, the political climate remains strongly against any consideration of legalization or even decriminalization of any currently illegal drugs, including marijuana. In contrast, many states have moved toward decriminalization or even legalization of marijuana, sometimes restricted to medical use but in other cases extending all the way to recreational use of the drug.

Given the recent history of drug politics in the United States, it is easy to forget that things were not always this way. As discussed earlier, by the beginning of the twentieth century, there was widespread use of cocaine, opium, and heroin in over-the-counter or patent medicines. In the absence of any federal regulations governing the marketing, distribution, or purchase of these preparations, sales increased from $3.5 million in 1859 to $74 million in 1904 (Hollinger, 1995). Over time, however, the federal government became increasingly involved in controlling the commercialization of drugs (**TABLE 9.1**). This involvement began

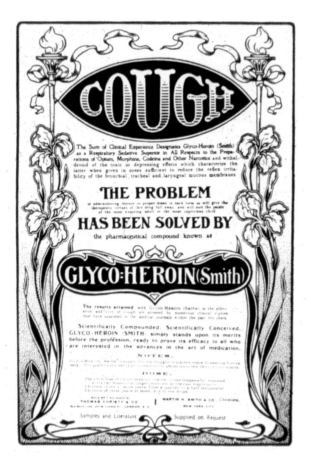

FIGURE 9.3   An early ad for heroin-containing cough syrup

TABLE 9.1 History of Federal Drug Legislation in the United States

Name of law	Year enacted	Purpose
Pure Food and Drug Act	1906	Regulated labeling of patent medicines and created the FDA
Harrison Act	1914	Regulated dispensing and use of opioid drugs and cocaine
Eighteenth Constitutional Amendment (Prohibition)	1920	Banned alcohol sales except for medicinal use (repealed in 1933)
Marijuana Tax Act	1937	Banned nonmedical use of cannabis (overturned by U.S. Supreme Court in 1969)
Controlled Substances Act	1970	Established the schedule of controlled substances and created the DEA

with an initial concern about the quality and purity of both medications and food, which led to the passage in 1906 of the Pure Food and Drug Act. The new law mandated the accurate labeling of patent medicines so that the consumer would be aware of the presence of alcohol, cocaine, opiates, or marijuana in such products. It also created the Food and Drug Administration (FDA), which is charged with assessing the potential hazards and benefits of new medications and with licensing their use. The Pure Food and Drug Act was clearly an educational approach to the drug problem, since the law did not make any of the abovementioned substances illegal to sell or use.

Around the same time that drug labeling and purity were under discussion, concern over the burgeoning problem of drug misuse and addiction was growing. For example, importation of opium grew rapidly between 1870 and 1900. Rightly or wrongly, opium smoking had become associated with Chinese laborers who had immigrated to the United States following the Civil War to work on the railroads. Meanwhile, China itself began a vigorous campaign against opium, viewing it as a symbol of Western imperialism.* These events culminated in the convening of the first International Opium Conference in 1911, where each participating country agreed to enact its own legislation restricting narcotic drug use except for legitimate medical purposes.

It took the United States several more years to pass its antinarcotic law, the Harrison Act of 1914. A major reason for the delay was lobbying by drug and patent medicine manufacturers who objected to the initial wording of the bill. The Harrison Act was designed to regulate the dispensing and use of opiates (opium and its derivatives such as morphine) and cocaine by prohibiting use of opiates and cocaine for nonmedical

purposes, taxing the sales of these substances, and enforcing these provisions by requiring pharmacists and physicians to register with the Treasury Department. Patent medicines containing small amounts of opiates or cocaine remained legal for retail sale. The principal aims of the Harrison Act were to control rather than abolish the use of opiates and cocaine and to link their use with government revenue through taxation (it's worth noting that during the Prohibition era, the federal government finally managed to convict the notorious gangster Al Capone not on alcohol trafficking or murder, but rather on tax evasion!).

Many physicians had previously been providing maintenance doses of opiates or cocaine to patients who were addicted to these substances. However, because addiction was not considered a disease by government authorities at that time, one immediate effect of the Harrison Act was to cut addicts off from this source of drugs. The consequences are easily predicted: addicts were forced to turn to street dealers, and prices skyrocketed. According to Hollinger (1995), the cost of heroin increased from $6.50 per ounce to roughly $100 (a huge sum in the early 1900s). People who could not afford to pay these prices were forced into abstinence and withdrawal. One result of these events was the establishment of many municipal clinics to treat drug addicts. The clinic in New York City registered approximately 7700 patients between April 1919 and March 1920 (Morgan, 1981). Unfortunately, these clinics failed to solve the problem; most addicts went back to using street drugs soon after their treatment, and illegal drug sales continued to flourish.

The Harrison Act did not regulate the use of alcohol, which had nevertheless been a major social problem in the United States for many years. As a consequence of increasing support for the alcohol temperance movement mentioned previously, the Eighteenth Amendment to the Constitution went into effect in 1920. The new Prohibition law banned the dispensing of any beverage with alcohol content greater than 0.5% (1/10 the typical alcohol content of regular beer) except by

*In the eighteenth and nineteenth centuries, England profited enormously from Chinese purchase of opium obtained through the British colony in India. The Opium Wars of the mid-1800s at least partially revolved around the desire of Western powers to maintain this lucrative drug trade against China's wishes. Although the United States was not a participant in the wars, it benefited from favorable trade agreements negotiated after the conclusion of hostilities.

physicians for medicinal purposes. Once again, the consequences were disastrous. Speakeasies (establishments where alcohol was sold illegally) sprang up everywhere, and the organized crime movement really took off during this period. The experiment in Prohibition finally ended in 1933.

Cannabis was another substance disregarded by the Harrison Act. The practice of marijuana smoking was initially associated with Mexican immigrants who entered the United States in the early 1900s. After World War I, public opposition to marijuana grew, and eventually numerous state laws were passed against its possession or sale. The federal government subsequently entered the picture with passage of the Marijuana Tax Act of 1937. This law was similar to the Harrison Act in banning nonmedical use of cannabis and levying a tax on importers, sellers, and dispensers of marijuana.

The Marijuana Tax Act was declared unconstitutional and was overturned by the U.S. Supreme Court in 1969. But in the very next year, the federal government passed a much broader law meant to apply to all potentially addictive substances. This was the Comprehensive Drug Abuse Prevention and Control Act (also called the Controlled Substances Act [CSA]) of 1970. The CSA replaced or updated virtually all previous federal legislation concerning narcotic drugs and other substances thought to have addiction potential. Among other provisions, the CSA established five schedules of controlled substances, which are discussed later in this chapter. It also created the Drug Enforcement Administration (DEA), which was charged with enforcement of the CSA. Although this law has been revised several times since its inception, it remains the cornerstone of federal drug control legislation. Moreover, many states have adopted the Uniform Controlled Substances Act, a model drug control law patterned after the CSA.

Several conclusions can be drawn from this brief survey of the history of federal drug laws. The first is that each time the federal government became more involved in drug regulation, the action resulted from increases in drug use and/or perceived societal dangers posed by such use. Those who wish to make drug laws more lenient must start by changing such antidrug perceptions. The second conclusion is that existing laws are not entirely consistent with available medical and scientific evidence. For example, we will see later that nicotine (obtained via tobacco or tobacco-derived products) is more addictive than marijuana by all established criteria, yet tobacco smoking and nicotine vaping are legal, whereas marijuana smoking is still not legal according to federal law. A final conclusion is that legal mechanisms have only limited effectiveness in preventing drug use. This is most obvious in the events that occurred during Prohibition, as well as in the current widespread use of marijuana even in states where it's still illegal. We acknowledge that cocaine and heroin use would almost certainly be greater than it is now if those substances were legal. But large numbers of people have little trouble obtaining cocaine, heroin, or any other illicit drug they desire. Many would argue that a more important restraint on drug use is the individual's own concerns that a particular substance might harm their health, jeopardize other important goals or values, or put them at risk for becoming addicted to that substance.

SECTION SUMMARY

- Recreational psychoactive drugs are consumed at high levels in our society. Not surprisingly, legal drugs such as alcohol and tobacco products are consumed the most. Among illicit (at the federal level) drugs, by far the greatest consumption is of cannabis.

- Use of illicit drugs is age-related. The highest percentage of illicit drug users are in the age range of 18 to 25 years. Only a small percentage of elderly people use illicit drugs.

- In the early history of the United States, very few of the currently available recreational drugs had yet been discovered or invented, and there were no federal laws governing the drugs that were available at that time.

- Advances in chemistry during the nineteenth century made possible the purification of addictive drugs like cocaine and morphine from the plants that synthesize these substances. Another important event was the development of the hypodermic syringe, which allowed drugs to be injected directly into the bloodstream.

- Not until the second half of the twentieth century did addiction come to be considered a disease and to warrant medical treatment.

- At the beginning of the twentieth century, sale of over-the-counter products containing cocaine, opium, and heroin was largely unregulated. This soon led to the first federal legislation that had relevance for such products, namely the Pure Food and Drug Act. This legislation additionally created the Food and Drug Administration (FDA), which is charged with assessing the risks and benefits of proposed new medications and licensing those medications that the agency has approved.

- Later passage of the Harrison Act regulated sales and use of opiate drugs and cocaine but disregarded other substances that had become problematic, such as alcohol and cannabis. Problems related to those substances led to the period of alcohol criminalization (Prohibition) and then later the Marijuana Tax Act.

- Drug use is currently regulated by the Comprehensive Drug Abuse Prevention and Control Act (also called the Controlled Substances Act, or CSA), which was passed in 1970. The CSA classifies potentially addictive drugs into five categories, or schedules, based on their degree of potential misuse and medicinal value. Because alcohol and tobacco are not listed on the schedule, they can be purchased for recreational use without a prescription.

■ This historical information shows that (1) passage of new laws that increased regulation over recreational drug use has been prompted by increases in such use, perceived societal dangers from drug use, and/or a desire to obtain revenues by taxing a particular drug; (2) existing drug laws are not entirely consistent with scientific evidence regarding the dangers of various drugs; and (3) governmental attempts to prevent or at least minimize illicit drug use (i.e., the War on Drugs) have largely been ineffective.

9.2 Features of Drug Misuse and Addiction

Before proceeding further, try writing down your definition of drug addiction in one or two sentences. Were you easily able to come up with a satisfactory definition? If not, don't be concerned, because addiction is not a simple concept. This problem was highlighted by Burglass and Shaffer (1984) in the following (not entirely frivolous) description of addiction: "Certain individuals use certain substances in certain ways thought at certain times to be unacceptable by certain other individuals for reasons both certain and uncertain." The medical establishment has attempted to develop a broadly acceptable definition, yet many experts continue to disagree about exactly what it means to be addicted to a drug (Walters and Gilbert, 2000).

Drug addiction is considered to be a chronic, relapsing behavioral disorder

Early views of drug addiction emphasized the importance of physical dependence. As you learned in Chapter 1, this means that abstinence from the drug leads to highly unpleasant withdrawal symptoms that motivate individuals to reinstate their drug use. It is true that some recreational drugs, such as alcohol and opioid drugs, can create strong physical dependence and severe withdrawal symptoms in dependent individuals. Certain other substances, however, produce relatively minor physical dependence. It may surprise you to learn that cocaine is one such substance, and that there was a time when cocaine was not considered to be addictive because of this lack of an opioid-like withdrawal syndrome.

Modern conceptions of addiction have focused more on other features of this phenomenon. First, there is an emphasis on behavior, specifically the compulsive nature of drug seeking and drug use in the addict. The addict is often driven by a strong urge to take the drug, which is called drug **craving**. Second, addiction is thought of as a chronic, relapsing disorder. This means that individuals remain addicted for long periods of time and that drug-free periods (**remissions**) are often followed by **relapses** in which drug use recurs despite negative consequences. This is the paradox of addiction mentioned earlier in the chapter. The current scientific

view of addiction is encompassed by the following definition: "Drug addiction can be defined as a chronically relapsing disorder, characterised by compulsion to seek and take the drug, loss of control in limiting intake, and emergence of a negative emotional state (e.g., dysphoria, anxiety, irritability) when access to the drug is prevented" (Koob and Volkow, 2016, p. 760). This definition will serve as a framework for most of the discussion that follows in later sections of the chapter.

The term *addiction* has strong negative emotional associations for most of us. Despite the fact that drug addicts live in all parts of the country and come from all walks of life, we usually think of them as urban and poor. Although some drug addicts fit this description, many others do not. For this reason, and because of conflicting definitions of addiction, the American Psychiatric Association (APA) stopped using the terms *addiction* and *addict* in its professional writings. This can be seen in the fifth edition of the APA's *Diagnostic and Statistical Manual of Mental Disorders*, known as *DSM-5®* (American Psychiatric Association, 2013). The *DSM* represents an attempt to classify the entire range of psychiatric disorders, with objective criteria provided for the diagnosis of each disorder. Instead of using the term *drug addiction*, the *DSM-5* specifies a group of **substance-related disorders** that cover 10 designated classes of drugs: (1) alcohol, (2) caffeine, (3) cannabis, (4) hallucinogens, (5) inhalants, (6) opioids, (7) sedative–hypnotic and anxiolytic drugs, (8) stimulants, (9) tobacco, and (10) other substances (note that all nine named drug classes are discussed in depth in this textbook). The *DSM-5* posits that all of these substances share the ability to activate the neural circuitry that mediates "reward," an issue that we will elaborate on in a subsequent section of the chapter. It is this ability, which is commonly experienced as a drug-induced "high," that confers upon these substances a risk for misuse and, in some cases, the development of an addictive pattern of behavior.

Substance-related disorders are further broken down in the *DSM-5* into **substance use disorders** and **substance-induced disorders**. A substance use disorder is characterized by "a cluster of cognitive, behavioral, and physiological symptoms indicating that the individual continues using the substance despite significant substance-related problems" (APA, 2013, p. 483). A substance-induced disorder is characterized by "the development of a reversible substance-specific syndrome due to recent ingestion of a substance" (APA, 2013, p. 485). The substance-induced syndromes mentioned in the *DSM-5* consist of "intoxication, withdrawal, and other substance/medication-induced mental disorders (e.g., substance-induced psychotic disorder, substance-induced depressive disorder)" (APA, 2013, p. 485).

The *DSM-5* provides a specific set of criteria to diagnose a substance use disorder for eight of the nine drug classes listed above. Caffeine is excluded in this case because it is considered to produce only substance-induced disorders, namely caffeine intoxication (i.e., symptoms produced by excessive caffeine consumption) and caffeine withdrawal (i.e., symptoms produced by acute abstinence in a regular caffeine user). As the criteria for the remaining eight are very similar, we have chosen to illustrate the basic diagnostic approach by listing the specific criteria for alcohol use disorder in **TABLE 9.2**. A few key points need to be made about these criteria. First, the *DSM-5* states that for an alcohol use disorder to be diagnosed, the pattern of use must be "problematic" and it must lead to "clinically significant impairment or distress." This may seem fairly obvious when considering a legal drug like alcohol that is used regularly by millions of people without adverse consequences. But the same ideas pertain to dangerous illegal drugs like cocaine or heroin. Thus, mere use of either cocaine or heroin does not constitute a psychiatric disorder as long as the use does not lead to significant impairment or distress (although it is always possible that the current use pattern could evolve into a more problematic pattern that *does* meet *DSM-5* criteria for a substance use disorder). Second, you can see from the table that there is no single criterion for determining the presence of an alcohol use disorder; this is true for any substance use disorder. This reflects the fact that problematic drug use may result in many different adverse consequences, depending on which drug is being taken and on the amount and pattern of drug taking. Of course, someone with a longstanding, severe case of substance use disorder may meet virtually all of the listed criteria, not just a few. To reflect this fact, the *DSM-5* adds an important severity component to the diagnosis. Specifically, individuals who meet only two or three of the specified criteria are considered to have a "mild" substance use disorder, individuals who meet four or five criteria are considered to have a "moderate" disorder, and individuals who meet six or more criteria are considered to have a "severe" disorder.

The substance-related disorders in *DSM-5* fall within a larger classification called "substance-related and addictive disorders." The reason for this is the continually growing discussion over whether the concept of addiction should be applied to other uncontrolled or compulsive behaviors such as binge eating, sexual preoccupation, compulsive gambling, excessive internet use, and so forth. These uncontrolled behaviors are sometimes called **behavioral addictions**. After considerable deliberation, the authors of the *DSM-5* decided to add a category called "non-substance-related disorders;" gambling disorder is its sole current entry. In **BOX 9.1**, we

---

TABLE 9.2 *DSM-5* Diagnostic Criteria for Alcohol Use Disorder

A problematic pattern of alcohol use leading to clinically significant impairment or distress, as manifested by at least two of the following, occurring within a 12-month period:

1. Alcohol is often taken in larger amounts or over a longer period than was intended.

2. There is a persistent desire or unsuccessful efforts to cut down or control alcohol use.

3. A great deal of time is spent in activities necessary to obtain alcohol, use alcohol, or recover from its effects.

4. Craving, or a strong desire or urge to use alcohol.

5. Recurrent alcohol use resulting in a failure to fulfill major role obligations at work, school, or home.

6. Continued alcohol use despite having persistent or recurrent social or interpersonal problems caused or exacerbated by the effects of alcohol.

7. Important social, occupational, or recreational activities are given up or reduced because of alcohol use.

8. Recurrent alcohol use in situations in which it is physically hazardous.

9. Alcohol use is continued despite knowledge of having a persistent or recurrent physical or psychological problem that is likely to have been caused or exacerbated by alcohol.

10. Tolerance, as defined by either of the following:
    a. A need for markedly increased amounts of alcohol to achieve intoxication or desired effect.
    b. A markedly diminished effect with continued use of the same amount of alcohol.

11. Withdrawal, as manifested by either of the following:
    a. The characteristic withdrawal syndrome for alcohol [listed elsewhere in *DSM-5* as an alcohol-induced disorder].
    b. Alcohol (or a closely related substance, such as a benzodiazepine) is taken to relieve or avoid withdrawal symptoms.

BOX 9.1 ■ OF SPECIAL INTEREST

Should the Term *Addiction* Be Applied to Compulsive Behavioral Disorders That Don't Involve Substance Use?

The term *addiction* has traditionally been associated with harmful use of substances such as alcohol, cocaine, and heroin. But articles in the mainstream media now commonly use the same term when referring to behavioral problems that don't involve chemical substances. Examples include *gambling addiction*, *sex addiction*, *food addiction*, *internet addiction*, and so forth. On what basis can we determine whether this is a legitimate use of *addiction* or whether we should restrict the term to its original usage?

In a search of the addiction literature, the first use of the term *behavioral addictions* we could find was in the title of a 1990 editorial in the *British Journal of Addiction* by Isaac Marks (Marks, 1990). Marks argued that behavioral addictions shared important similarities with drug addictions, which is generally consistent with current theories; however, his classification of behavioral addictions included obsessive-compulsive disorder, Tourette syndrome, and trichotillomania (compulsive hair pulling), none of which are currently thought of as addictive disorders. Nevertheless, the editorial by Marks set the stage for a great deal of research and discussion about behavioral addictions. Indeed, a commentary by Holden (2001) published just 11 years later summarized the growing acceptance of the concept of behavioral addictions, with a particular focus on pathological gambling, eating disorders, compulsive sexual behavior, compulsive shopping, and excessive internet use.

Indeed, the list of behavioral disorders either accepted or being considered for inclusion as a behavioral addiction continues to grow. This list currently includes gambling disorder (Barrera-Algarín and Vázquez-Fernández, 2021; Gori et al., 2021), internet gaming disorder (King and Delfabbro, 2014; Paulus et al., 2018), compulsive sexual behavior (Andreassen et al., 2018; Grubbs et al., 2020), compulsive online pornography use (de Alarcón et al., 2019; Grubbs et al., 2019), uncontrolled eating behavior (Adams et al., 2019; Gearhardt and Hebebrand, 2021), buying-shopping disorder (Müller et al., 2019; 2021), compulsive cell phone use (Gutiérrez et al., 2016; Sahu et al., 2019), compulsive need to exercise (Granziol et al., 2021; Trott et al., 2021), and compulsive need to work (Urbán et al., 2019; Kun et al., 2021). This list of proposed behavioral addictions is already long, but papers have appeared in the literature that would add even more candidates to the list, such as "dance addiction" (Maraz et al., 2015), "tango addiction" (presumably a variety of dance addiction) (Targhetta et al., 2013), "tanning addiction" (Kourosh et al., 2010), and "fortune-telling addiction" (Grall-Bronnec et al., 2015). The proliferation of proposed behavioral addictions raises the obvious question of whether, as suggested

by Billieux and colleagues (2015), we are "overpathologizing everyday life." Mihordin (2012) raised similar concerns that strong enthusiasts of pastimes such as model railroading exhibit some of the features characteristic of a behavioral addiction. Does that mean that we need to consider a category called "model railroading addiction"? A young person who has a passion to become a world-class gymnast, dancer, or solo violinist may similarly feel compelled to practice their skill to the exclusion of almost any other activity. Such individuals may additionally feel irritable or depressed if prevented from practicing, say due to sickness or injury. Are these feelings pathological?

One important way to help us determine which behavior patterns might qualify as *addictive* is to examine the types of behavioral addictions included in major diagnostic classifications. When the *DSM-5* was published in 2013, it placed gambling disorder within the broad category of "substance-related and addictive disorders" but did not formally include any other behavioral addictions within that category. The major criteria for a diagnosis of gambling disorder are presented in the **TABLE**. These criteria have several similarities to the diagnostic criteria for alcohol use disorder (see Table 9.2), including the presence of tolerance (item 1), withdrawal (items 2 and 3), and craving (items 4 and 5). Understandably, there are additional criteria that are specific to gambling. The decision to include gambling disorder within the same category as substance-related disorders stemmed not only from similarities in phenomenology but also from research demonstrating neurobiological and cognitive dysfunctions in compulsive gamblers that overlap with the neurobiological and cognitive features of drug addiction. Subsequent studies have provided even more detailed information that shows similarities but also some differences between gambling disorder and substance use disorders with respect to cognition, emotion regulation, and neurobiology (Rash et al., 2016; van Timmeren et al., 2018; Clark et al., 2019; Velotti et al., 2021).

Researchers continue to investigate areas of overlap between drug addiction and behavioral addictions, including evidence for an abstinence syndrome (i.e., withdrawal symptoms) during periods of discontinuation of the activity. This feature of behavioral addictions has not been studied as extensively as one might imagine; however, at least in the case of "exercise addiction," significant psychological (mood disturbances) and somatic (fatigue) symptoms have been documented during abstinence (Fernandez et al., 2020). Other proposed behavioral addictions are being studied with respect to their underlying biological mechanisms. For example, biological factors involved

BOX 9.1 ■ OF SPECIAL INTEREST *(continued)*

in "food addiction" have been a topic of recent reviews (Leigh and Morris, 2018; Katherine et al., 2021), and studies have provided evidence of how the rewarding effects of sugar may contribute to addictive-like food consumption (Olszewski et al., 2019).

To summarize, researchers continue to debate whether excessively performed behaviors should be labeled as addictions (Potenza, 2015; Grant and Chamberlain, 2016; Petry et al., 2018). For any given proposed disorder and for people deemed to be suffering from that disorder, at least two questions must be resolved:

1. First and most important, how problematic is the behavior—that is, does it reach the threshold for consideration as a psychopathology?

2. Second, even if the answer to the first question is "yes," do the behavioral and biological features of the proposed disorder align with the *DSM-5* category of substance-related and addictive disorders, or should the disorder be included in the category of impulse control disorders?

This distinction may not mean a lot to the patient, but it may help guide the practitioner in determining what kind of therapeutic intervention is most likely to help that patient.

DSM-5 Diagnostic Criteria for Gambling Disorder

Persistent and recurrent problematic gambling behavior leading to clinically significant impairment or distress, as indicated by the individual exhibiting four (or more) of the following in a 12-month period:

1. Needs to gamble with increasing amounts of money in order to achieve the desired excitement.

2. Is restless or irritable when attempting to cut down or stop gambling.

3. Has made repeated unsuccessful efforts to control, cut back, or stop gambling.

4. Is often preoccupied with gambling (e.g., having persistent thoughts of reliving past gambling experiences, handicapping or planning the next venture, thinking of ways to get money with which to gamble).

5. Often gambles when feeling distressed (e.g., helpless, guilty, anxious, depressed).

6. After losing money gambling, often returns another day to get even ("chasing" one's losses).

7. Lies to conceal the extent of involvement with gambling.

8. Has jeopardized or lost a significant relationship, job, or educational or career opportunity because of gambling.

9. Relies on others to provide money to relieve desperate financial situations caused by gambling.

Source: Reprinted with permission from American Psychiatric Association. 2013. *Diagnostic and Statistical Manual of Mental Disorders*, Fifth Edition. American Psychiatric Association: Arlington, VA. © 2013. American Psychiatric Association. All rights reserved.

---

discuss the rationale for specifying gambling disorder as a non-substance-related disorder in *DSM-5,* the current status of behavioral addictions more generally, and the extent to which these behavior patterns show similarities to classical substance-based addictions.

Before we conclude this section, a brief consideration of terminology is in order. The *DSM-5* not only substituted the term *substance use disorder* for *addiction* but also eliminated the previously used term *substance abuse* from its lexicon of psychiatric disorders. Nevertheless, that terminology can be seen in the older published literature, and the notions of drug abuse and addiction continue to be present in popular parlance and in the lay press. For the present edition of this textbook, we have chosen to replace mentions of *drug abuse* or *substance abuse* with *drug misuse* or *substance misuse* to conform to the terminology used in most of the current scientific literature. It should be understood by the reader that when the terms *drug misuse* and *substance misuse* are used, we are generally referring to a kind

of problematic drug use that might, for example, meet the *DSM-5* criteria for a mild or (at most) moderate substance use disorder. We will use *substance use disorder* when the broad range of problematic substance use is under discussion. On the other hand, we will continue to use the term *drug addiction* either when an earlier study specifically used that term or when we want to make clear that we are referring to instances of problematic drug use that likely meet the *DSM-5* criteria for a severe substance use disorder.

There are two types of progression in drug use

Drug use can involve two different kinds of progression. In one type of progression characteristic of many young people, the individual starts out taking a legal substance such as alcohol or tobacco, later progresses to marijuana, and in a small percentage of cases moves on to cocaine, heroin, other illicit substances, or illegally obtained prescription drugs. One of the theories that attempts to account for this type of progression, namely the **gateway theory**, is discussed in **WEB BOX 9.1**.

The second kind of progression pertains to changes in the amount, pattern, and consequences of drug use as they affect the user's health and functioning. After first experimenting with a recreational drug, an individual may or may not progress to regular, non-problematic use or beyond. Despite the popular view that drugs like cocaine and heroin are instantly and automatically addictive, this is not the case. Indeed, one of the central unresolved questions in the addiction field is why some drug-using individuals eventually develop a pattern of compulsive drug use, whereas many others do not (Swendsen and Le Moal, 2011; George and Koob, 2017). Once a regular pattern of non-problematic use has been established, a percentage of users progress further to escalated drug use and then to compulsive and/or problematic use. People who have been using a substance compulsively (i.e., having a persistent urge to use the substance that is difficult to resist) may attempt to abstain, but in such cases abstinence is often unsuccessful and leads to relapse (e.g., the person who smokes two packs of cigarettes a day and tries to quit "cold turkey"). Once an individual reaches the stage of compulsive substance use, undergoes repeated attempts at abstinence, and repeatedly relapses back into their former use pattern, they likely meet the criteria for addiction (**FIGURE 9.4**). However, even at this point in the drug use cycle, extended periods of reduced use or even abstinence may occur during an individual's attempts to overcome their drug-using habit.

For many people, the use of both alcohol and illicit drugs such as marijuana naturally declines once they reach adulthood and begin to take on the responsibilities associated with earning a living and having a family. This pattern is consistent with data from longitudinal studies documenting a reduction in drug use beyond the period of adolescence (Chen and Kandel, 1995). Some writers have called this process "maturing out" of a drug-using lifestyle, and studies have associated recovery from alcohol dependence with a variety of transitional life events (Dawson et al., 2006). Of course, not all individuals stop or reduce their substance use in this way; recovery from addiction is a complex process that cannot be accounted for by any single factor (Waldorf, 1983).

Which drugs are the most addictive?

Just as we all have mental images of drug addicts, we also have ideas about which drugs are the most addictive. Drugs thought to have high addictive potential are sometimes called "hard drugs." Aside from popular opinion, however, there are legal standards meant to classify drugs according to their addictive potential. The Controlled Substances Act of 1970 established a system by which most substances that have the potential to be used recreationally are classified into one of five different schedules within a **Schedule of Controlled Substances**. These schedules, along with representative drugs, are shown in **TABLE 9.3**. Schedule I substances are considered to have no medicinal value and thus can be obtained only for research use by registered investigators.* Keep in mind that the schedule is based on federal law, which explains why marijuana and its active ingredient THC (Δ^9-tetrahydrocannabinol) are listed in Schedule I despite their medical and/or recreational use in many states. Items listed under Schedules II to V are available for medicinal purposes with a prescription from a medical professional such as a physician, dentist, or veterinarian. They can also be obtained for research use. Note that the Schedule of Controlled Substances specifically excludes alcohol and tobacco, thus permitting those substances to be purchased and used legally without registration or prescription. The Schedule of Controlled Substances was formulated over 50 years ago and was based not only on the scientific knowledge of that time but also partly on political considerations. Although it has been updated periodically since its inception, we may still ask whether this classification system accurately reflects our current

*For all controlled substances, but particularly for Schedule I and II items, there are strict federal requirements for investigator registration, ordering, and recordkeeping. The substances must be maintained securely, as in a locked safe, with careful control over who has access to the drug supply

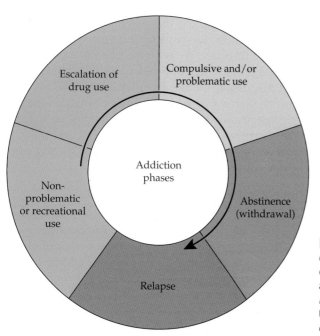

FIGURE 9.4 Progression of drug use from non-problematic or recreational use to an addictive pattern of use involving compulsive and/or problematic use and repeated attempts at abstinence followed by relapse (After M. Venniro, et al. 2020. *Nat Rev Neurosci* 21: 625–643. doi.org/10.1038/s41583-020-0378-z, based on data from *The Diagnostic and Statistical Manual of Mental Disorders*, Fourth Edition.)

TABLE 9.3   Schedule of Controlled Substances

Schedule	Description	Representative substances
I	Substances that have no accepted medical use in the United States and have a high abuse potential	Heroin, LSD, mescaline, marijuana, THC, MDMA
II	Substances that have a high abuse potential with severe psychic or physical dependence liability	Opium, morphine, codeine, meperidine (Demerol), cocaine, amphetamine, methylphenidate (Ritalin), pentobarbital, phencyclidine (PCP)
III	Substances that have an abuse potential less than those in Schedules I and II, including compounds containing limited quantities of certain narcotics and nonnarcotic drugs	Paregoric, barbiturates other than those listed in another schedule
IV	Substances that have an abuse potential less than those in Schedule III	Phenobarbital, chloral hydrate, diazepam (Valium), alprazolam (Xanax)
V	Substances that have an abuse potential less than those in Schedule IV, consisting of preparations containing limited amounts of certain narcotic drugs generally for antitussive (cough suppressant) and antidiarrheal purposes	

understanding of various recreational substances, or whether it continues to be too politicized. This issue is discussed in **WEB BOX 9.2**.

SECTION SUMMARY

■ Although early ideas about addiction emphasized the role of physical dependence, more recent conceptions have focused on the compulsive features of drug seeking and use (despite potentially harmful consequences) and on the concept of drug addiction as a chronic, relapsing disorder characterized by repeated periods of remission followed by relapses.

■ In the *DSM-5*, problematic patterns of drug use are categorized by a disorder called "substance use disorder." Mere use of a substance does not qualify as a disorder. Such use must be "problematic" and lead to "clinically significant impairment or distress."

■ A substance use disorder may qualify as mild, moderate, or severe, depending on how many of the *DSM-5* diagnostic criteria are met by the patient. In its severe form, substance use disorder has characteristics that correspond closely to those usually associated with addiction.

■ The *DSM-5* also contains a diagnostic category called gambling disorder. This disorder falls within a group of compulsive non-substance-related behaviors sometimes called behavioral addictions.

■ A number of other pathological behaviors, some of which have already been classified as psychiatric disorders, may qualify as behavioral addictions based on their similarities to drug addiction.

■ Young people often progress from legal substances like alcohol or tobacco to marijuana, and a small percentage go on to try cocaine, heroin, or illegally obtained prescription drugs. The gateway theory attempts to account for this progression, although other explanations have been offered to explain the same findings.

■ A second kind of progression consists of changes over time in the amount, pattern, and negative consequences of drug use. Individuals who have progressed to a pattern of compulsive use find it difficult to maintain long-term abstinence, thus leading to repeated cycles of drug use, abstinence, and relapse. However, illicit drug use during adolescence may stop later on as the individual reaches adulthood and takes on the associated responsibilities (termed "maturing out" of a drug-using lifestyle).

■ The Schedule of Controlled Substances classifies potentially addictive drugs into five categories, or schedules, on the basis of their degree of potential misuse and medicinal value. Alcohol and tobacco are not listed on the schedule, so they can be purchased for recreational use without a prescription.

■ Debate has arisen about whether the Schedule of Controlled Substances is a reasonable classification system based on current scientific knowledge, or whether it has been driven too much by socio-political considerations.

9.3 Factors That Influence the Development and Maintenance of Drug Misuse and Addiction

Over the years, researchers have discovered a variety of different factors that contribute to the development and maintenance of drug misuse and addiction. In this section, we will discuss the most important of these factors, including how they are studied in animal models of addiction. Such models are critical for our ability to investigate the neurobiological underpinnings of addiction and to screen new pharmacological agents that might have therapeutic value in treating drug addicts. Later in the chapter, we will consider how different contributory factors are brought together in current theories of addiction.

The addictive potential of a substance is influenced by its route of administration

In Chapter 1, you learned about the various routes by which drugs can enter a person's body. Routes of administration such as oral or transdermal result in relatively slow absorption of the drug and, therefore, equally slow drug availability to the brain. In contrast, intravenous (IV) injection or inhalation* yields rapid drug entry into the brain and a fast onset of drug action. Conversely, a fast onset is associated with a shorter duration of action. Researchers and addiction treatment providers have known for many years that the addiction potential of a substance is related to the route of administration, with routes that cause a fast onset of drug action having the greatest addiction potential (Allain et al., 2015). **FIGURE 9.5** illustrates this principle for opiate drugs, cocaine, and nicotine. Although we don't fully understand why IV injection and inhalation are associated with the greatest vulnerability to addiction, we do know that those routes produce (1) the strongest euphoric effects for a given drug dose, and (2) the shortest latency between the act of consuming the drug (i.e., pushing the syringe plunger or puffing on the cigarette or vape pen) and experiencing the euphoric effect because of rapid drug delivery to the brain. According to learning theory, shorter latencies between response and reinforcement should lead to stronger and faster drug conditioning, thereby contributing to an increased motivation to use the drug. It is also possible that repeated exposure of the brain to rapid drug delivery facilitates production of the long-term neurobiological changes thought to underlie the development of addiction. A later section of this chapter discusses our current understanding of addiction neurobiology.

Most recreational drugs exert rewarding and reinforcing effects

Most drugs that are used recreationally act as **positive reinforcers**. This means that consuming the drug

---

*As used here, inhalation refers to both smoking/vaping a drug (e.g., tobacco, cannabis, or crack cocaine) and inhaling a drug that exists as a gas (e.g., nitrous oxide) or as fumes given off by a liquid (e.g., gasoline fumes).

strengthens whatever preceding behavior was performed by the organism. **Drug reward** is a different but related concept that refers to the positive subjective experience associated with the drug. Examples include the euphoric feeling or "high" induced by a variety of drugs; the feeling of relaxation induced by alcohol, marijuana, opioids, and sedative drugs such as barbiturates; and the altered state of consciousness associated with psychedelic drugs. Obviously, the rewarding effects of a substance are likely to play an important role in its reinforcing properties, but other factors (e.g., increased alertness produced by stimulant drugs) may also play a role.

DRUG SELF-ADMINISTRATION Drug reinforcement is most often studied operationally by investigating an organism's propensity to self-administer the substance using procedures introduced in Chapter 4. As you will recall, an experimental animal such as a rat, mouse, or monkey is typically fitted with an IV catheter attached to a drug-filled syringe. When the animal performs an operant response such as pressing a lever or poking its nose into a hole in the wall of the apparatus, a pump is briefly activated that slightly depresses the plunger of the syringe and infuses a small dose of the drug directly into the animal's bloodstream. This is directly analogous to drug addicts giving themselves an IV drug injection. The ability of animals to learn and maintain the lever-pressing/nose-poking response or of addicts to learn and maintain drug-seeking and drug-using behaviors means that the drug is acting as a reinforcer, just as food is a reinforcer for those who are hungry. Substances that are strong reinforcers in the IV self-administration paradigm virtually always have great addiction liability in humans, particularly when taken intravenously or by inhalation. Classic examples of this kind are cocaine, heroin, and amphetamine or methamphetamine. In contrast, drugs that are not readily self-administered by animals, such as antidepressant or antipsychotic medications, are generally not addictive in humans.

One of the many factors that can be manipulated in the IV self-administration paradigm is the amount of drug (dose) given in each infusion. Studies on a

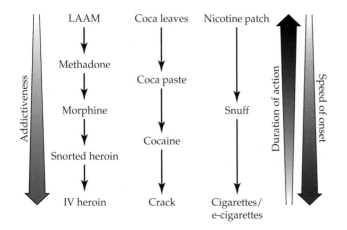

FIGURE 9.5 Relationship between route of administration and addiction potential of opiates, cocaine, and nicotine Opiates: LAAM (levo-alpha-acetyl-methadol) and methadone are orally administered treatments for opiate addiction; morphine taken orally has a more rapid onset and a shorter duration than methadone; and heroin may be taken by snorting, IV injection, or smoking (not shown) (see Chapter 11). Cocaine: Coca leaves are chewed, coca paste is a crude extract of the leaves, powdered cocaine is often snorted, and crack cocaine is smoked (see Chapter 12). Nicotine: The nicotine patch is a transdermal delivery system used for smoking cessation, snuff is powdered tobacco leaves that are snorted, and cigarettes and e-cigarettes are smoked and vaped respectively (see Chapter 13). (After J. K. Melichar et al. 2001. *Curr Opin Pharmacol* 1: 84–90. ©2001. Reprinted with permission from Elsevier.)

variety of drugs have shown that when the drug is delivered using a simple schedule of reinforcement such as a fixed-ratio (FR) schedule (see Chapter 4), the typical dose–response function is an inverted U-shaped curve (**FIGURE 9.6A**). The ascending part of the curve is thought to reflect increasing reinforcing effectiveness of the drug over that range of doses. On the other hand, the descending limb is potentially attributable to multiple factors, including satiation to the drug, aversive reactions, or behaviorally disruptive side effects (e.g., extreme hyperactivity in the case of stimulant drugs, or sedation in the case of sedative–hypnotic agents). Because of the complications introduced by these factors, simple dose–response functions are not very useful for determining the reinforcing strength of one substance versus another. A better measure of the relative strength of drug reinforcement makes use of a **progressive-ratio procedure**. In this procedure, animals are initially trained to lever press on a continuous-reinforcement (CR) schedule, which means that each press is followed by drug delivery. In the second phase, the animals are switched to a low FR schedule, such as an FR-5 (one drug delivery for every five responses). Finally, the FR schedule is progressively increased until the animals stop responding, presumably because the dose being delivered is not sufficiently reinforcing to support the amount of effort required. The response ratio at which responding ceases is called the **breakpoint**.

Breakpoints vary across drugs and also across doses. What do you think is the relationship between dose and breakpoint? If you guessed that breakpoint generally increases with higher doses, you were correct. This is illustrated in a study conducted by Negus and Mello (2003) in which they compared the average breakpoints for a range of cocaine doses in rhesus monkeys. The researchers showed that the breakpoints for cocaine were directly related to the unit dose, with higher doses yielding higher breakpoints than lower doses (**FIGURE 9.6B**). This result indicates that within the dose range tested, the higher doses were more motivating to the animals than the lower doses. Keep in mind, however, that if the dose of the drug being tested becomes too high, determination of the breakpoint may be compromised by some of the same factors that can interfere with dose–response analyses.

Just as mere drug use by humans does not constitute a psychiatric disorder, self-administration of a drug by a rat, mouse, or monkey is not a model of addiction per se even though it demonstrates that the substance has positive reinforcing properties. To produce a more convincing model of addiction, researchers must implement procedures that result in additional features such as escalating self-administration, relapse to renewed drug-seeking behavior after a period of abstinence, and preference of drug taking over alternative reinforcers available to the animal (Vanderschuren and Ahmed, 2013; Bank and Negus, 2016; Kuhn et al., 2019; Venniro et al., 2020). Chapter 12 provides examples of procedures that lead to escalating cocaine self-administration by rats. Relapse is typically modeled in self-administration

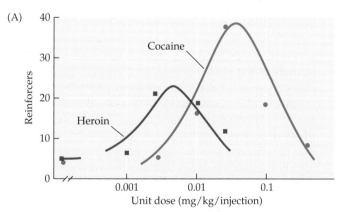

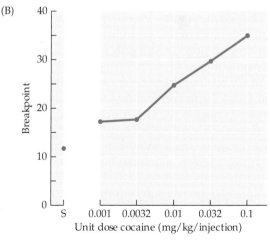

FIGURE 9.6 Features of intravenous drug self-administration by laboratory animals (A) Representative data for cocaine and heroin illustrate the typical inverted U-shaped curve relating dose per infusion to number of reinforcers (drug deliveries) obtained during a self-administration session. (B) Breakpoint on a progressive-ratio (PR) schedule is an index of the reinforcing effectiveness of different doses of a drug. In this experiment, rhesus monkeys were trained to self-administer cocaine and stabilized on a fixed-ratio schedule requiring 20 responses (FR-20) to obtain an IV infusion of cocaine at a dose of 0.032 mg/kg. After the breakpoint was established using the 0.032-mg/kg maintenance dose, the monkeys were subsequently tested for their breakpoints on a PR schedule using two lower and one higher dose of cocaine. The value shown for "S" represents the breakpoint measured when saline vehicle was substituted for cocaine during the test session. Taken together, the results show that the lowest unit doses of cocaine were more reinforcing than saline, and the reinforcing value of the cocaine infusions continued to increase as the unit dose rose above 0.0032 mg/kg. (A after J. Bergman and C. A. Paronis. 2006. *Mol Interv* 6: 273–283; B from S. S. Negus and N. K. Mello. 2002. *Psychopharm* 167: 324–332. doi.org/10.1007/s00213-003-1409-y)

studies by stopping drug delivery (thus producing a forced abstinence that results in extinction of the operant response) and then exposing the animals to stimuli that are known to provoke renewed responding in an attempt to obtain the drug again. Such renewed responding is termed **reinstatement of drug-seeking behavior**. Three main types of stimuli are effective in reinstating drug-related responding: (1) the experimenter delivering a small dose of the drug to the animal, known as **drug priming**; (2) subjecting the animal to stress; and (3) exposing the animal to environmental cues that were previously paired with drug delivery (prior to extinction). The general paradigm used in this type of research is illustrated in **FIGURE 9.7**.

The scientific literature on drug self-administration consists almost entirely of studies on experimental animals, yet this procedure is also applicable to humans (Jones and Comer, 2013). It is important to note that for ethical reasons, study participants are often individuals who are already experienced users of the substance being investigated. Human self-administration procedures are used for several purposes, including testing the addictive potential of a substance based on its value as a reinforcer, or assessing the effectiveness of current or prospective medications for individuals addicted to a particular drug. A study by Kirkpatrick and co-workers (2012) provides an example of using self-administration to assess the strength of a drug reinforcer. The study showed that amphetamine or methamphetamine users will sometimes choose a monetary reward over a dose of the drug depending on the relative magnitudes of the two reinforcers.

The positive reinforcing effects of drugs undoubtedly play a significant role in addiction. But we also know that drug addiction commonly leads to numerous negative consequences that can include such extreme effects as family breakup, loss of one's job and financial destitution, engaging in criminal activity to support drug purchases, damage to one's health, contracting needle-borne diseases such as AIDS or hepatitis, and even fatal overdose for some drugs. Why don't these negative consequences effectively counteract the positive reinforcement so that the individual stops using and remains abstinent? One possible answer concerns the temporal relationship between drug consumption and the positive or negative effects. Drug-induced euphoria occurs very quickly after consumption, particularly in the case of IV injection or inhalation. In contrast, the negative consequences occur later in time and, in most cases, are linked to a long period of use rather than to a specific occasion of drug consumption. According to well-established principles of reinforcement, an event (euphoria) that occurs very soon after a response (drug consumption) exerts much greater control over that response than events (negative consequences) that occur later in time. Even for humans, who have the ability to plan and to foresee the consequences

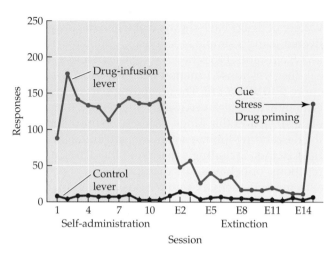

FIGURE 9.7 Representative data showing extinction and reinstatement of drug self-administration by drug-related cues, stress, or drug priming The graph depicts typical data from rats that were first stabilized on IV drug (e.g., cocaine) self-administration using an FR schedule of reinforcement. The red data points show the number of responses per session on a lever that is linked to drug delivery. Each drug infusion is accompanied by presentation of a cue, which is typically a light or a tone. The purple data points show the number of responses per session on a control lever that has no consequences when pressed. After 12 days of self-administration in this particular paradigm, the animals are switched to a 14-day extinction (E) phase in which pressing the drug lever no longer elicits either drug delivery or cue presentation. Note the rapid falloff of responding during this phase. However, if the drug-paired cue is presented, if the animals are subjected to stress (e.g., foot shock), or if a priming dose of the drug is administered by the experimenter, the animals resume a high rate of responding on the drug lever despite the fact that the drug is still withheld (E14). This phenomenon, which is termed reinstatement, is considered to be an animal model of relapse to drug use after abstinence in drug addicts. (After P. W. Kalivas et al. 2006. *Mol Interv* 6: 339–344.)

of their actions in ways that most animals cannot, this property of reinforcers has considerable influence over many behaviors, not just drug use. On the other hand, many individuals who take drugs once or even a few times stop their drug use before they develop a compulsive pattern and become addicted. This is true even for highly reinforcing drugs like cocaine and heroin. Thus, additional factors must contribute to the development of addiction in some drug users, but not in others. Such factors likely include the individual's personality traits and mental health status, childhood experiences, current lifestyle and living environment, and the presence of major life stressors.

PROCEDURES USED TO STUDY DRUG REWARD Two different procedures are commonly used to study the rewarding properties of drugs (see Chapter 4). The first is a classical conditioning procedure called place conditioning (Tzschentke, 2007). Animals (typically rats and mice) are trained in a two- or three-compartment apparatus in which one of the compartments is paired with the presence of a drug over several conditioning sessions. A test session is then conducted under drug-free conditions. If the drug produced a rewarding effect during training, the animal will spend more time in the drug-paired compartment than in a compartment that had been paired with a placebo. The second procedure makes use of electrical self-stimulation of the brain—a method in which the performance of an operant response causes the delivery of an electrical stimulus to a part of the brain's reward circuit (see later section for a discussion of this circuit). Numerous studies have shown that the threshold for rewarding brain stimulation is reduced when animals have been treated acutely with various recreational drugs (Negus and Miller, 2014). Because a lower threshold indicates a more sensitive system, such results indicate that the underlying neural circuitry for drug reward overlaps with the circuitry for brain stimulation reward. On the other hand, withdrawal of animals from chronic treatment with these same substances causes an increased threshold for electrical self-stimulation. A similar phenomenon occurring in a drug-dependent addict might contribute to the negative mood state and inability to experience pleasure (anhedonia) that are often reported during drug withdrawal.

RECREATIONAL DRUGS CAN BE AVERSIVE RATHER THAN REWARDING Interestingly, drugs that are taken recreationally sometimes can be shown to exert aversive effects on animals or humans (Varendeev and Riley, 2013). For example, even though rats will self-administer nicotine under some conditions, they will also learn to press a lever to prevent experimenter-controlled infusions of the same drug. Considerable evidence suggests that a number of substances are reinforcing when under the animal's control but either are not as reinforcing or are even aversive when administered by the experimenter. For humans as well, drugs may produce aversive psychological or behavioral effects in addition to their rewarding effects. One example is the ability of cocaine to bring about feelings of anxiety that follow soon after the initial period of drug-induced euphoria. However, even though such aversive effects presumably inhibit the tendency toward future drug seeking and drug use, they may not be sufficient to outweigh the many factors promoting these behaviors.

Drug dependence leads to withdrawal symptoms when abstinence is attempted

Certain drugs or drug classes, including alcohol, sedative–hypnotic, and anti-anxiety medications and opioid drugs, can lead to physical dependence when taken repeatedly (Lerner and Klein, 2019). Some researchers have proposed that this process plays a key role in the establishment and maintenance of drug addiction. According to this idea, once an individual has become physically dependent as the result of repeated drug use, attempts at abstinence lead to highly unpleasant withdrawal symptoms (also called an **abstinence syndrome**). This motivates the user to take the drug again (relapse) to alleviate the symptoms. In the language of learning theory, relief of withdrawal symptoms promotes drug-taking behavior through a process of negative reinforcement, thus leading ultimately to a continuous behavioral loop consisting of repeated abstinence attempts followed by relapses.*

Negus and Banks (2018) reviewed a series of studies with rhesus monkeys aimed at assessing the role of negative reinforcement in addiction. In one of these studies, monkeys were first given an extended opportunity to self-administer heroin, a procedure that renders them dependent on the drug. Animal were then given a choice between varying doses of IV heroin or food under either the standard testing condition or after 1 day of abstinence to produce a state of drug withdrawal. As shown in **FIGURE 9.8**, the dose–response function for choosing heroin over

---

*Recall that negative reinforcement refers to the concept of reinforcement by removal of an undesirable stimulus (in this case, painful or distressing withdrawal symptoms).

FIGURE 9.8 Heroin choice dose–response functions in heroin-dependent monkeys Rhesus monkeys were given extended self-administered access to IV heroin until they had become dependent on the drug. The animals were then given a series of tests in which they could choose either an available dose of heroin or food (banana-flavored pellets) over a number of trials. Testing was performed under both the standard experimental condition or after 1 day of abstinence in order to provoke drug withdrawal. Under the withdrawal condition, the dose–response function for choosing heroin over food was markedly shifted to the left. For example, at the lowest heroin dose (0.0032 mg/kg per injection), the monkeys always selected the food reward when they were not abstinent, but under the withdrawal condition, they chose the heroin injection about 75% of the time. (After S. S. Negus and M. L. Banks. 2018. *Pharmacol Biochem Behav* 164: 32–39. © 2017. Reprinted with permission from Elsevier; data adapted from S. S. Negus 2006. *J Pharmacol Exp Ther* 317: 711–723, S. S. Negus and K. C. Rice. 2009. *Neuropsychopharm* 34: 899–911.)

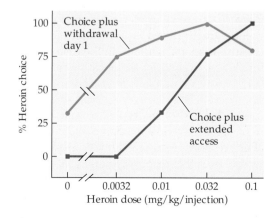

food was markedly shifted to the left in the abstinent compared to the non-abstinent monkeys. This finding is consistent with the hypothesis that in the case of heroin and presumably other opioid drugs, withdrawal elicits a strong motivation to obtain the drug compared to the non-abstinent state. Results such as these support the use of agonist replacement therapy (e.g., methadone or buprenorphine) in the treatment of opioid-dependent individuals, since the replacement drug prevents withdrawal symptoms from occurring. Interestingly, a similar study conducted using cocaine instead of heroin showed absolutely no shift in the dose–response function, suggesting that agonist replacement (e.g., with another stimulant such as amphetamine) might not be as beneficial for people dependent on cocaine.

Koob and Le Moal (2005) proposed that in the development of addiction, drug-taking behavior progresses from an "impulsive" stage, in which the primary motivation for drug use is the substance's positive reinforcing effects, to a "compulsive" stage, in which the primary motivation is the negative reinforcement obtained by relief from drug withdrawal. This progression is illustrated in **FIGURE 9.9** using alcohol addiction as an example (Heilig and Koob, 2007). The instigation of an aversive state (negative affect) of withdrawal that underlies such negative reinforcement was termed the "dark side" of addiction by Koob and Le Moal, and they further proposed that this process is due to the gradual recruitment of an "antireward" system in the brain (depicted as a "neuroadapted state" in the figure). We will discuss this theory later in the section on addiction neurobiology.

One of the early proponents of an important role for physical dependence was Abraham Wikler, who studied and treated heroin addicts over a period of several decades. Because of lack of money or other factors, addicts do not have constant access to heroin. Over time, therefore, they are likely to undergo many episodes of withdrawal. Wikler argued that if these withdrawal reactions repeatedly occur in specific environments, such as the places where the addict either "hustles" for or takes the drug, the responses will become classically conditioned to the stimuli associated with those environments (Wikler, 1980). Consequently, even if an addict has been drug-free for some length of time and is therefore no longer experiencing an acute abstinence syndrome, withdrawal symptoms can be triggered by exposure to the conditioned stimuli.

For drugs that produce significant physical and/or psychological dependence, such dependence undoubtedly is an important contributor to the maintenance of addiction because unpleasant withdrawal symptoms provide motivation to obtain and take the drug again. Nevertheless, the relative importance of this factor varies among different drugs. As mentioned earlier, some major recreational drugs, including cocaine, do not produce strong physical dependence, although psychological dependence does occur in some users. In addition, drug-seeking behavior to obtain relief from withdrawal symptoms fails to explain relapse of addicts after they have gone through **drug detoxification** (elimination of the drug from one's system and passage through the abstinence syndrome). After the withdrawal symptoms have gone away, what still motivates an addict to take heroin again, for example? Research on addicts' self-reported reasons for returning to drug use as well as animal model studies such as those depicted in Figure 9.7 suggest that many factors can contribute to relapse, including exposure to drug-related stimuli, stress, boredom, lack of other reinforcers, or simply a desire to "get high" again.

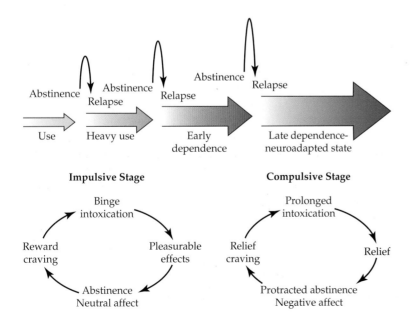

FIGURE 9.9 Transition from the impulsive to the compulsive phase of alcohol addiction In the *impulsive* stage, an episode of binge drinking results in a pleasant state of intoxication. Since dependence has not yet occurred in this stage, the individual's mood (i.e., affect) is neutral during abstinence. However, because of repeated pairing of intoxication with environmental stimuli, a conditioning process causes those stimuli to trigger a renewed craving for the alcohol reward, thus leading to more bingeing and intoxication. Once the *compulsive* stage has been reached, individuals undergo periods of prolonged intoxication that bring relief from their depressed baseline mood state. Because they are also now alcohol-dependent, abstinence leads to withdrawal symptoms that include even greater negative affect. Alcohol craving in this stage is related to relief from the state of withdrawal. (After M. Heilig and G. F. Koob. 2007. *Trends Neurosci* 30: 399–406. ©2007. Reprinted with permission from Elsevier.)

Discriminative stimulus effects contribute to drug-seeking behavior

Psychoactive drugs, including those used recreationally, can produce powerful discriminative stimulus effects both in animals and in people (McMahon, 2015; Bolin et al., 2016; Porter et al., 2018). As summarized in Chapter 4, this means that drugs can produce internal states that can serve as cues controlling the organism's behavior in a learning task. In typical animal studies, the drug discrimination paradigm can be used in a few different ways. For example, not only can researchers determine whether an animal can reliably discriminate a drug from a drug vehicle such as saline, but they can also test for stimulus generalization. In a stimulus generalization task, animals are first trained to discriminate a drug from the vehicle. Following the training, the subjects are administered varying doses of a test compound. If any doses of the test compound produce an internal state (i.e., stimulus cue) similar to that produced by the training drug, then the subjects will make the drug-correct response. An example of stimulus generalization was shown in an experiment using rhesus monkeys initially trained to discriminate cocaine from saline by pressing a different key under each condition. When later tested with various doses of amphetamine, 3,4-methylenedioxymethamphetamine (MDMA), or 3,4-methylenedioxyamphetamine (MDA), the animals showed full generalization to a high dose of amphetamine but only partial generalization (i.e., only a percentage of responses on the cocaine-correct key) to MDMA or MDA (Smith et al., 2017). These findings are in accord with the biochemical mechanisms of action of these drugs, with cocaine, amphetamine, and methamphetamine primarily activating the catecholamine systems (Chapter 12) but MDMA and MDA primarily acting on the serotonergic system (Chapter 6). The discriminative stimulus effects of drugs in animals are considered to be analogous to the subjective effects that people experience when they take the same substances. Experienced users come to expect these subjective effects, and such expectations are thought to contribute to the persistence of drug-seeking and drug-using behaviors.

Genetic factors contribute to the risk for addiction

The contribution of genetics to the risk for addiction or more broadly substance use disorder has been assessed using family, adoption, and twin studies (e.g., comparing concordance rates for monozygotic versus dizygotic twins). From these studies, researchers have estimated that the overall **heritability** of substance use disorders is in the range of 40% to 60%, with some substances, like cocaine, showing greater heritability and others, such as psychedelic drugs, showing lower heritability (Lopez-Leon et al., 2021). In the field of genetics, *heritability* is a mathematical term representing the estimated

contribution of genetic variation within a population to the total population variation for a particular trait (in this case, the trait is the presence or absence of addiction or a substance use disorder). Because the maximum heritability value is 100%, it is clear that the remaining variability is due to environmental influences and gene-by-environment interactions.* Now that we've shown that genetics is clearly involved in the risk for substance misuse, we discuss the methods used to study this involvement, the hypotheses put forward to explain the relationship between genetics and substance use disorders, and the current status of the field in **WEB BOX 9.3**.

Psychosocial variables also contribute to addiction risk

It is important to consider individual differences in susceptibility to drug addiction, not only at a biological level but also with respect to psychosocial factors (Kalant, 2009; Swendsen and Le Moal, 2011). Much of the research in this area has focused on how psychosocial factors influence substance use during adolescence, the time when such use typically begins (Whitesell et al., 2013; Trucco, 2020). As discussed below, psychosocial factors can either increase the risk for substance use and possible progression to addiction, or they can decrease these risks, thereby exerting a protective effect.

RISK FACTORS   Many modulating factors can influence either the likelihood of someone becoming a drug addict or the probability that they will relapse after a period of abstinence. For example, one survey relating sociodemographic variables to later development of a substance use disorder found increased risk to be associated with younger age, less education, non-white racial background, and lack of employment (Swendsen et al., 2009). Individuals who exhibit conduct problems during childhood are also at increased risk for later substance misuse.

Stress is another important factor that can influence initiation of substance use, progression to a substance use disorder, and vulnerability to relapse after abstinence (even after undergoing treatment). Consideration should be given to the frequency and severity of stressful life events as well as the individual's ability to cope with such events. The life histories of drug addicts often show instances in which stressful events either promoted increased drug use or precipitated relapse from a previous period of abstinence. Numerous animal studies have confirmed that stress can increase drug self-administration and can trigger renewed

---

*A gene-by-environment interaction occurs when a genetic contribution to a trait is only manifested in individuals who also experience a specific type of life event. For example, there might be evidence that a particular gene contributes to vulnerability for developing a substance use disorder in people who experience major stressful events in their life but not in people who don't have such experiences

drug-taking behavior in models of relapse (Sinha, 2008; Ruisoto and Contador, 2019). For this reason, many treatment providers teach their clients new coping skills to help them deal with life stresses without relapsing.

People with severe substance use disorders (i.e., addiction) are often diagnosed with an anxiety, mood, or personality disorder in addition to their drug problem (Swendsen and Le Moal, 2011; National Institute on Drug Abuse, 2020). Such co-occurrences are called **comorbidity** in the medical literature. Some investigators have proposed that comorbid psychiatric disorders are causally related to addiction. For example, stressful life events could trigger anxiety and mood disorders such as depression, which in turn could lead to substance use in an attempt at self-medication. This idea, which has been called the **self-medication hypothesis**, predicts that individuals suffering from elevated anxiety should prefer alcohol and other sedative–anxiolytic drugs (**FIGURE 9.10**), whereas depressed individuals should seek out stimulant drugs such as cocaine or amphetamine. Also possible is a reverse direction of causality in which a substance use disorder gives rise to symptoms of anxiety and/or depressed mood. An alternative to these causal models is the hypothesis of **shared etiology**, which proposes that certain factors (genetic and/or environmental) contribute to an elevated risk of *both* addiction and other psychiatric disorders. Current evidence does not rule out any of these competing hypotheses.

Finally, familial and sociocultural influences can also influence the risk of developing a pattern of misusing alcohol or other drugs (Whitesell et al., 2013; Trucco, 2020). Chartier and colleagues (2010) reviewed evidence implicating childhood maltreatment, presence of violence within the family, and being subjected to less parental monitoring as risk factors for developing problematic alcohol use during adolescence. Other

research has found that adult children of alcoholics are at increased risk for having alcohol or other substance use problems (Windle and Davies, 1999). In the case of alcohol, this may be related in part to modeling (imitation) of the parent's drinking behavior or to a heightened expectancy that drinking will lead to positive mood changes. Sociocultural studies have identified at least four different functions served by substance misuse (Thombs, 1999). These are (1) social facilitation (enhancement of social bonds between participants using the substance together in the same setting); (2) removing the user from the burdens of normal social roles and responsibilities; (3) promoting group solidarity within a particular ethnic group (e.g., the association of Irish culture with heavy alcohol use and a high rate of alcoholism; and (4) formation of a "drug subculture" that embraces social rituals surrounding a particular subculture and rejects conventional social norms and lifestyles. Sociological studies have identified distinct subcultures for many different substances, including heroin, cocaine, alcohol, marijuana, methamphetamine, and PCP. This is not to say that all users of a particular substance participate in the rituals of a subculture, or that users necessarily limit themselves to just one substance. Nevertheless, one can find groups of individuals who share their common experiences with a specific recreational drug and who have a similar disdain for the "straight" lifestyle.

PROTECTIVE FACTORS We can think about protective factors in drug addiction in two different ways. First, an absence of the various risk factors described in the previous section should be relatively protective with respect to drug misuse or addiction. Put another way, individuals who do not suffer from a preexisting personality or mood disorder, who do not exhibit the trait clusters mentioned earlier, who come from stable families with no substance-related problems, who do not belong to ethnic groups that promote substance use, and who do not become involved in the social rituals surrounding drug use are at reduced risk for acquiring a substance use disorder. Protective factors for initiation of adolescent substance use include family cohesion along with specific aspects of parental behavior, including parental warmth, monitoring of the adolescent's behavior, and parental control, which means appropriate supervision and the setting of clear rules for acceptable behavior by the adolescent (Trucco, 2020).

The second way that protective factors can operate is to help maintain a stable state of abstinence or of non-problematic substance use in people attempting to recover from substance misuse. Individuals with a substance use disorder who seek treatment tend to be the most heavily dependent and seriously affected. Protective factors like having a support network of family and friends, maintaining a stable lifestyle,

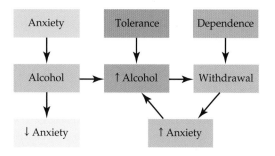

FIGURE 9.10 **Self-medication hypothesis applied to the development of alcohol dependence** Some people drink alcohol to alleviate anxiety. If anxiety is persistent and alcohol use continues, the onset of tolerance leads to increased alcohol consumption and potentially to the development of alcohol dependence. Attempts at abstinence then lead to withdrawal symptoms that include heightened anxiety, thereby provoking relapse to drinking. (After A. Lingford-Hughes et al. 2002. *Psychiatric Treat* 8: 107–116. Reproduced with permission.)

having sources of reinforcement outside of drugs, and acquiring mechanisms to cope with stress can all contribute to long-term recovery from substance misuse and even addiction.

Sex differences in substance use, misuse, and addiction

Biological sex (i.e., male or female based on the person's sex chromosomes and glands) influences a number of different features of substance use, misuse, and addiction (reviewed in Quigley et al., 2021). One of these concerns the initiation of substance use. Men often report that their initial substance use was in a social context (examples might include groups of adolescent boys drinking, smoking, or vaping together), whereas the beginning of substance use by women is often related to a negative life event and/or the onset of feelings of depression or anxiety. Among individuals who have developed a drug addiction problem, women more commonly than men report that their substance use rapidly escalated. This phenomenon has been termed "telescoping." Other sex differences are related to attempts at abstinence among drug-addicted men and women. During periods of abstinence (which usually end with a relapse to drug use), women are more sensitive than men to drug-related environmental cues, and they generally experience more severe drug craving. Based on a combination of human clinical and experimental animal studies, many of these sex differences have been linked to female reproductive hormones and to differences in stress responding between men and women (Quigley et al., 2021).

Natural recovery from substance misuse and addiction

It may be surprising to learn that many people with significant problems related to alcohol and other drugs can transition either to long-term abstinence or, in some cases, to non-problematic substance use with little or no treatment (Klingemann et al., 2009; Humphreys, 2015; Fan et al., 2019). A relatively recent example of this comes from a study comparing people with cannabis use disorder who recovered (defined here either as abstinence or non-problematic use) with or without the assistance of treatment (Hodgins and Stea, 2018). Of the 119 participants, 55% recovered without treatment compared to 45% whose recovery was treatment-assisted. The authors provided additional information from the participants regarding the factors that led to their cannabis use problem as well as the factors that contributed to their recovery.

Transitioning from substance misuse/addiction to either non-problematic use or nonuse (abstinence) without the need for an intervention has been termed **natural recovery** or spontaneous recovery. Before discussing that process, we need to know more about how often

such transitions occur. Information about transitioning from one category of substance use to another category can be obtained from the National Epidemiologic Survey on Alcohol and Related Conditions (NESARC), a longitudinal study of substance use among U.S. adults 18 years and older that began in 2001–2002 (Hasin and Grant, 2015). The initial participants, who constituted Wave 1 of the survey, totaled 43,093. A Wave 2 survey conducted 3 years later consisted of 34,653 of the original participants. The NESARC surveys covered past-year use of alcohol, tobacco products, and all 10 categories of illicit substances included in the *DSM-IV* diagnostic criteria for drug abuse and dependence.* Some analyses of the resulting data focused on alcohol and/or tobacco use. In contrast, a study by Compton and coworkers (2013) focused on the prevalence of illicit substance use and transitions in use from Wave 1 to Wave 2 based on three substance use categories: nonuse, asymptomatic use (use without any of the drug abuse or dependence symptoms defined in the *DSM-IV*), and problem use (experiencing at least one of the *DSM-IV* symptoms of abuse or dependence). The possible transitions among these states are illustrated in **FIGURE 9.11**.

TABLE 9.4 presents the numbers and percentages of participants within each substance use category at Wave 1 and the percentages of *those* participants who were in each category at Wave 2. A few points will help the reader understand the table. First, the "Wave 1 Prevalence" lists the percentages out of all participants who belonged to each substance use category at the first wave (e.g., 93.9% of the total 34,653 participants reported no past-year illicit substance use at Wave 1). Second, regardless of the percentages shown in the "Wave 1 Prevalence" column, if all participants within a particular category remained within that category at Wave 2, that category listed under "Distribution by Wave 2 Drug Status" would list 100% and the remaining two categories would show 0%. Differences from

*Note that the *DSM-5* had not yet been developed at the time of NESARC Waves 1 and 2.

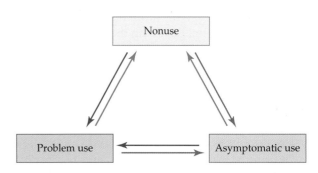

FIGURE 9.11   Possible transitions among substance use categories used in the analysis of NESARC Wave 1 and Wave 2 findings (From W. M. Compton et al. 2013. *Am J Psychiatry* 170: 660–670.)

TABLE 9.4 Percentage of Individuals in Each Substance Use Category in NESARC Wave 1 Versus Wave 2

Wave 1 Drug Status	N	Wave 1 Prevalence (%)	Distribution by Wave 2 Drug Status		
			Nonuse (%)	Asymptomatic Use (%)	Problem Use (%)
Nonuse	32,675	93.9	95.4	2.1	2.5
Asymptomatic Use	861	2.6	66.6	14.3	19.1
Problem Use	1,117	3.5	49.0	10.9	40.1

Source: W. M. Compton et al. 2013. *Am J Psychiatry* 170: 660–670. Reprinted with permission from the American Journal of Psychiatry, (© 2013). American Psychiatric Association. All Rights Reserved.

100% indicate that some participants within the initial Wave 1 substance use category transitioned to another category when they were surveyed again at Wave 2. Of significance to the present discussion, 66.6% of the participants who reported asymptomatic use of at least one illicit substance at Wave 1 transitioned to Nonuse, 19.1% transitioned to Problem Use, and only 14.3% remained in the Asymptomatic Use category 3 years later. Even more striking, 49.0% of the participants who reported problem use of at least one illicit substance at Wave 1 transitioned to Nonuse, 10.9% transitioned to Asymptomatic Use, and 40.1% remained in the Problem Use category. These results show that while problem use of illicit recreational drugs can persist over years, many individuals are capable of changing from problem use to non-problem (asymptomatic) use or, more commonly, abstinence.

People who recovered from severe substance use disorders recount many different tales of how they made and kept the decision to quit using drugs. It appears that in some cases, addicts must hit "rock bottom" or go through an "existential crisis" before they'll be sufficiently motivated to stop using. One such example was recounted several years ago by Luana Ferreira, a business reporter for the BBC (Ferreira, 2017). Her article described the story of Khalil Rafati, a homeless heroin and crack addict weighing only 109 lbs and with severely ulcerated skin when he was found unconscious by Los Angeles paramedics in 2003. At the age of 33, Rafati had just suffered his ninth heroin overdose, one that nearly killed him. Realizing that if he didn't overcome his addiction he would die, Rafati spent 4 months in a rehab facility and has remained "clean" since then. Indeed, he went from being a homeless drug addict to being the multimillionaire owner of SunLife Organics, a successful chain of juice and smoothie bars located in the West and Southwest.

Some individuals with significant drug problems find the means to abstain without reaching such a crisis situation. Spontaneous recovery from drug misuse may be triggered by a variety of major life changes, including transitional events like getting married, becoming pregnant, or obtaining a good job. Another kind of positive change would be having a spiritual/religious experience. Other motivations for voluntarily stopping drug use stem from the negative consequences of such use, including health problems, financial problems, loss of one's job, social pressures, fear of imprisonment, or death of a drug-using friend.

Once the decision has been made, the risk of relapse is reduced by such actions as moving to a new area, developing new social relationships with nonusers, obtaining employment, and engaging in substitute activities like physical exercise or meditation. Some of these changes involve avoidance of drug-associated cues (e.g., moving to a new location and shunning drug-using acquaintances), whereas other changes serve to provide substitutes for the former substance use, new sources of reinforcement, a new social support network, financial stability, and general structure to the individual's life. Note that the relative importance of these factors varies somewhat with different recreational drugs. For example, health concerns are particularly important in motivating tobacco smokers to stop smoking, and, much more than other drug users, smokers cite simple willpower as a critical factor in maintaining abstinence (Walters, 2000).

The factors contributing to substance misuse and addiction can be combined into a biopsychosocial model

FIGURE 9.12 summarizes the effects of the factors discussed in this section that can contribute to substance misuse and the progression to compulsive use (i.e., addiction). You can see that some of these factors promote the likelihood that substance misuse and addiction may occur, whereas others reduce this likelihood. A model that includes the full range of pharmacological, biological, and psychological/sociocultural factors that influence addiction risk can be called a **biopsychosocial model** of addiction (e.g., see Skewes and Gonzalez, 2013). Although it is beyond the scope of this text to propose our own model of addiction, we believe that consideration of all such factors, crossing multiple levels of analysis, is necessary for achieving an adequate understanding of the addiction process.

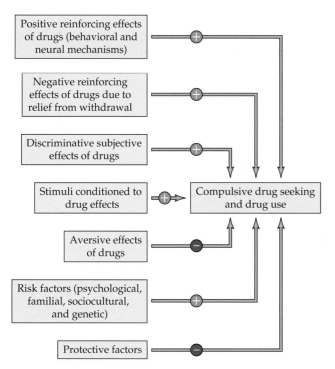

FIGURE 9.12   **A biopsychosocial model of drug addiction**
(After I. Stolerman. 1992. *Trends Pharmacol Sci* 13: 170–176.
©1992. Reprinted with permission from Elsevier.)

SECTION SUMMARY

- Route of administration influences the addictive potential of a substance. Addictive potential is greatest with IV injection and inhalation because those routes provide the most rapid delivery of the drug to the brain.

- Most addictive drugs are reinforcing in experimental animals, as shown by IV self-administration. The reinforcing efficacy of a drug can be investigated by means of a dose–response function (which typically yields an inverted U-shaped curve) or preferably by means of breakpoint determination using a progressive-ratio schedule.

- In experimental paradigms involving acquisition of stable drug self-administration followed by extinction, renewed operant responding can be provoked by administering a priming dose of the drug, presenting a stimulus cue that was previously paired with drug delivery, or stressing the animal. This procedure, called reinstatement of drug-seeking behavior, provides an animal model of relapse in drug users attempting to maintain abstinence.

- The rewarding effects of drugs are studied using place-conditioning and electrical self-stimulation of the brain. Most addictive drugs cause an acute reduction in the self-stimulation threshold, whereas withdrawal from drug exposure in dependent animals leads to an increased threshold.

- Drugs also sometimes produce aversive effects, although these may not be sufficiently strong to outweigh other factors that promote compulsive drug use.

- Repeated use of some drugs, such as opioids, leads to physical dependence and highly unpleasant withdrawal symptoms (abstinence syndrome) when drug use is stopped. Koob and Le Moal proposed that in the development of addiction, drug-taking behavior progresses from an impulsive stage (primary motivation for drug use is the positive reinforcing effect) to a compulsive stage (primary motivation is negative reinforcement from alleviation of these unpleasant withdrawal symptoms). This shift is hypothesized to involve the recruitment of an antireward system in the brain.

- Through conditioning, environmental stimuli previously associated with drug use can elicit withdrawal symptoms such as drug craving in an abstinent individual.

- Psychoactive drugs, including addictive drugs, can produce discriminative stimulus effects in animals that are thought to correspond to the subjective effects produced by these same compounds in human users. Experienced users come to expect these subjective effects, which may contribute to the persistence of drug use.

- Addiction is a heritable disorder, but there is no addiction gene per se. Rather, specific alleles of many different genes are believed to each contribute a small increase in the risk for developing addiction (i.e., addiction is a polygenic disorder). Psychosocial variables may either increase addiction risk or have a protective effect. Risk factors include experiencing stressful life events and having a preexisting psychiatric disorder. The self-medication hypothesis proposes that addicts use drugs to treat the symptoms of an anxiety or mood disorder. Alternative hypotheses such as shared etiology could also explain the high comorbidity of such disorders with addiction.

- The risk of drug misuse or addiction is also affected by familial and sociocultural influences. For example, childhood maltreatment, violence within the family, and inadequate parental monitoring are all risk factors for problematic alcohol use during adolescence. More generally, drug use (and misuse) may promote social facilitation, remove the user from normal social roles and responsibilities, promote solidarity within a particular ethnic group, or lead to association with a specific drug subculture.

- Protective factors can reduce the likelihood of an individual's becoming addicted or can help prevent relapse during periods of abstinence. These factors include family cohesion and various aspects of parental behavior, having a social support network, maintaining a stable lifestyle, having non-drug sources of reinforcement, and developing mechanisms to cope with stress.

- Biological sex influences a number of features of substance use, misuse, and addiction. Men often begin their substance use in a social context, whereas women may begin such use in response to a negative life event and/or after the onset of depression or anxiety. Women more often than men rapidly escalate their substance use (called "telescoping"). Many sex differences in substance use or addiction have been linked to female reproductive hormones or to differences in stress responding.

■ The NESARC survey showed that many individuals who at one time had a substance use disorder were able to achieve remission over time. Natural recovery from substance use (i.e., recovery without assistance) may be facilitated by transitional life events and/or by the negative consequences of continuing drug use. Maintaining abstinence is helped by avoiding drug-associated cues, obtaining non-drug sources of reinforcement and a new social support network, and achieving financial stability and a general structure to the individual's life.

■ Combining the full range of pharmacological, biological, and psychological/sociocultural factors that influence addiction risk can be called a biopsychosocial model of addiction.

9.4 The Neurobiology of Drug Addiction

Over the past few decades researchers have made tremendous progress in elucidating the neurobiological mechanisms that underlie the development of addiction. Much of this progress has been driven by technological advances in areas such as molecular pharmacology and neuroimaging. Although there is still much to learn, researchers are coming ever closer to understanding how recreational drugs acutely alter brain function and, more importantly, how repeated exposure to these same substances can produce long-lasting changes in the brain that may lead to compulsive drug use, even in the presence of adverse consequences to the user.

The development of addiction has been conceptualized by some researchers as a repeating sequence of three stages associated with substance use: (1) preoccupation with and anticipation of obtaining and using the substance, (2) escalating use, which for some substances results in drug "binges" and intoxication from the substance, and (3) withdrawal and the associated negative affect (i.e., mood state) when coming down from the drug "high" (**FIGURE 9.13**; Koob and Le Moal, 2008). In this model, the negative affect that occurs in the third stage is the primary motivating factor responsible for maintaining the cycle. The three-stage framework has been helpful for understand the neurobiology of addiction, including the neural circuits and neurotransmitters implicated most directly in each stage (Koob and Volkow, 2016). Accordingly, we will first discuss addiction neurobiology within this framework. Next, we will consider the role of molecular and synaptic adaptations in addiction. Last, we will address the important question of whether addiction should be considered a brain disease.

Drug reward and incentive salience drive the binge/intoxication stage of drug use

DRUG REWARD Studies conducted using laboratory rats, mice, and occasionally non-human primates have allowed researchers to construct a **reward circuit** that mediates the acute rewarding and reinforcing effects (defined operationally as described previously) of most recreational drugs. **FIGURE 9.14** depicts this circuit superimposed on a sagittal section of a rodent brain. Anatomical pathways contained within this circuit include the mesolimbic and mesocortical DA pathways (shown in red) that originate in the ventral tegmental area (VTA) of the midbrain and terminate in the nucleus accumbens (NAcc), amygdala (AMG), and frontal cortex (FC). Other important connections are those within the extended amygdala system (shown in blue)—a collection of anatomically and functionally linked structures that includes the central nucleus of the amygdala, the shell of the NAcc, and the bed nucleus of the stria terminalis (BNST). Two additional pathways within the reward circuit that are not shown in the figure are (1) the medial forebrain bundle, a collection of ascending

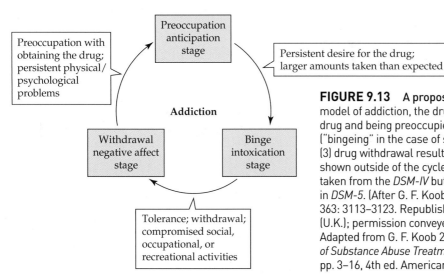

FIGURE 9.13 **A proposed three-stage addiction cycle** In this model of addiction, the drug user cycles between (1) anticipating the drug and being preoccupied with obtaining it, (2) escalating drug use ("bingeing" in the case of some drugs) and frequent intoxication, and (3) drug withdrawal resulting in a negative affect (mood). The features shown outside of the cycle represent criteria for drug dependence taken from the *DSM-IV* but also relevant for substance use disorders in *DSM-5*. (After G. F. Koob and M. Le Moal. 2008. *Phil Trans R Soc B* 363: 3113–3123. Republished with permission of The Royal Society (U.K.); permission conveyed through Copyright Clearance Center, Inc., Adapted from G. F. Koob 2008. Neurobiology of addiction. In *Textbook of Substance Abuse Treatment* M. Galanter and H. D. Kleber [Eds.], pp. 3–16, 4th ed. American Psychiatric Press: Washington, DC.)

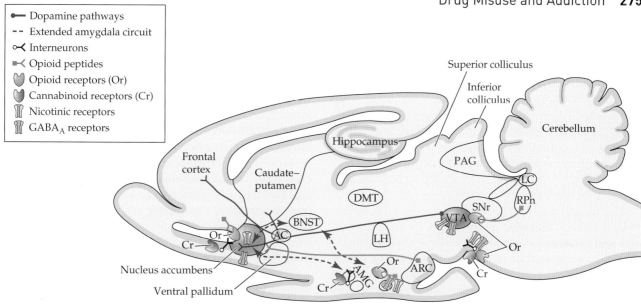

FIGURE 9.14 **The neural circuit responsible for the acute rewarding and reinforcing effects of recreational drugs** Also shown are additional brain areas that provide points of reference for anatomical orientation. AC, anterior commissure; AMG, amygdala; ARC, arcuate nucleus of the hypothalamus; BNST, bed nucleus of the stria terminalis; DMT, dorsomedial nucleus of the thalamus; LC, locus coeruleus; LH, lateral hypothalamus; PAG, periaqueductal gray; RPn, reticular pontine nucleus; SNr, substantia nigra pars reticulata; VTA, ventral tegmental area. (After G. F. Koob. 2005. *Clin Neurosci Res* 5: 89–101. © 2005. Reprinted with permission from Association for Research in Nervous and Mental Disease, via Elsevier.)

and descending fibers that connects the VTA with areas of the ventral forebrain including the NAcc, septal area, and olfactory tubercle, and (2) an output pathway from the NAcc to the ventral pallidum. Neuroimaging studies have confirmed that the human brain possesses a reward circuit similar to that identified in animals and that this circuit is activated by both drug and non-drug rewards (Haber and Knutson, 2010) (**FIGURE 9.15**).

The reward circuit can also be characterized neurochemically by considering the locations within the circuit that contain the specific molecular targets for each type of addictive drug. For example, psychostimulants such as cocaine and amphetamine exert their rewarding effects by directly releasing DA from dopaminergic terminals in the NAcc and/or by blocking DA reuptake after its release (see Chapter 12). Opioid drugs (e.g., morphine and heroin) and endogenous opioid peptides (endorphins and enkephalins) activate the reward circuit by stimulating opioid receptors in the VTA, NAcc, and AMG (see Chapter 11). Opioid reward is mediated by a combination of DA-dependent (through increased DA release) and DA-independent mechanisms. Alcohol enhances the action of γ-aminobutyric acid (GABA) on GABA$_A$ receptors, and this causes increased DA release in the

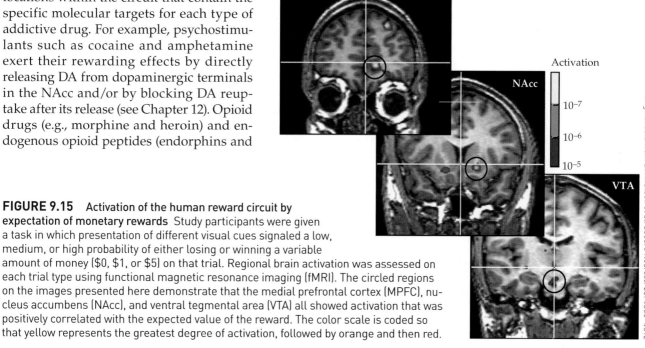

FIGURE 9.15 **Activation of the human reward circuit by expectation of monetary rewards** Study participants were given a task in which presentation of different visual cues signaled a low, medium, or high probability of either losing or winning a variable amount of money ($0, $1, or $5) on that trial. Regional brain activation was assessed on each trial type using functional magnetic resonance imaging (fMRI). The circled regions on the images presented here demonstrate that the medial prefrontal cortex (MPFC), nucleus accumbens (NAcc), and ventral tegmental area (VTA) all showed activation that was positively correlated with the expected value of the reward. The color scale is coded so that yellow represents the greatest degree of activation, followed by orange and then red.

From S. N. Haber and B. Knutson. 2010. *Neuropsychopharm* 35: 4–26; original data from B. Knutson et al. 2005. *J Neurosci* 25: 4806–4812

NAcc and opioid peptide release in the VTA, NAcc, and AMG (see Chapter 10). Nicotine derived from tobacco activates the reward circuit by stimulating nicotinic cholinergic receptors in the VTA, NAcc, and AMG (see Chapter 13), whereas endogenous cannabinoids and THC derived from marijuana are rewarding because of stimulation of cannabinoid receptors in the same brain areas (see Chapter 14). Nicotine and THC enhance DA release in the NAcc by acting both locally and within the VTA.

The mesolimbic DA pathway from the VTA to the NAcc has been accorded a central role in drug reward and reinforcement. Animal studies have shown that almost all recreational drugs activate this pathway either by enhancing VTA cell firing or by increasing extracellular DA levels in the NAcc, as in the case of psychostimulants. In Chapter 5, we saw that burst firing of midbrain dopaminergic neurons causes much greater DA release than single-spiking firing mode. In essence, we can think of recreational drugs as producing a similar DA surge. We also noted that D_1 DA receptors have a lower affinity than D_2 receptors for the transmitter, as a result of which elevated DA levels are required for significant D_1 receptor activation. Indeed, the D_1 receptor subtype is more important than D_2 for drug reward, although activation of both subtypes seems to be necessary to achieve a maximum effect (Volkow and Morales, 2015).

INCENTIVE SALIENCE As individuals progress repeatedly through the cycle depicted in Figure 9.4, drug reward often declines because of tolerance. Consequently, other factors become increasingly important in motivating continued substance use. One such factor is **incentive salience**, which is a key component of the **incentive sensitization theory** of addiction first proposed by Robinson and Berridge in 1993 and updated in subsequent reviews (e.g., Robinson and Berridge, 2008; Berridge and Robinson, 2016). A central feature of this theory is the distinction between *liking* versus *wanting* a reward, including rewards from recreational drugs. *Liking* refers to the hedonic (pleasurable) aspects of a reward, which in the case of drug reward may be the drug "high," drug-induced stimulation or relaxation, or simply an altered state of consciousness produced by the drug. *Wanting*, on the other hand, refers to the motivational aspect of a reward along with any environmental cues that have been linked to that reward through learned associations. This *wanting* aspect causes us to seek out and obtain the reward (i.e., the reward is an "incentive") and, in the case of a reward that can be consumed like food or a drug, to complete the process by engaging in such consumption. The powerful craving for a drug experienced during withdrawal by someone who is addicted to that drug is an extreme example of *wanting*. Some kinds of rewards, including but not limited to recreational drugs, are particularly effective in attracting our attention once we have experienced that reward. In the terminology of perceptual psychology, this feature is called "salience." Putting these concepts together, the incentive sensitization theory proposes that over the course of developing a drug addiction, the user experiences a marked increase in "wanting" the drug even though there is no change or even a decrease in drug "liking" (**FIGURE 9.16**).

The proposed changes in drug "wanting" but not drug "liking" can occur because different brain mechanisms are responsible for these two components of drug use motivation, and repeated drug use is hypothesized to cause sensitization of the "wanting" system but no sensitization or even tolerance in the "liking" system. Olney and colleagues (2018) reviewed the brain areas and circuits associated with hedonic versus motivational responses to rewards based on experimental criteria used by the Berridge laboratory. The "liking" system is composed of specific "hedonic hot spots" in the brain where local stimulation enhances the pleasurable effect of an administered reward. Such hot spots have been identified in the NAcc shell, ventral pallidum, insula, parabrachial nucleus, and orbitofrontal cortex. Several of these hot spots are represented in the reward circuit shown in Figure 9.14; however, even those that are not (i.e., insula and parabrachial nucleus) possess neural connections to the reward circuit and could potentially be incorporated as additional circuit components. Considering the neurotransmitters that operate within each system, we find that the hedonic (*liking*) system includes endogenous opioid peptides, endocannabinoids, and orexins but *not* DA. In contrast, the *wanting* system revolves around the widespread dopaminergic projections from the VTA, including but not limited to the mesolimbic and mesocortical DA pathways. An association of DA with the *wanting* but not the *liking* system is supported not only by animal studies but also by research with humans (Leyton et al., 2005; Liggins et al., 2012).

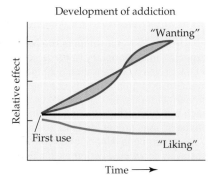

Development of addiction

FIGURE 9.16 Sensitization of drug "wanting" but not drug "liking" Incentive sensitization is proposed to contribute to the development of addiction. The horizontal line represents the initial relative levels of liking and wanting during first use of the drug. (After K. C. Berridge et al. 2009. *Curr Opin Pharmacol* 9: 65–73. ©2008. Reprinted with permission from Elsevier.)

UNDERSTANDING THE ROLE OF DA IN REWARD AND MOTIVATION   The previous two sections showed that the dopaminergic system is an important component of the reward circuit and additionally suggested, based on the work of Berridge and colleagues, that the function of this system is to mediate the *wanting* of rewarding stimuli instead of encoding the hedonic (pleasurable) aspects of such stimuli. It is not clear that all evidence is consistent with this hypothesis. For example, various studies have found that optogenetic stimulation of VTA dopaminergic neurons is reinforcing to animals, which could be construed as supporting a hedonic role for the mesolimbic DA pathway, although other interpretations are also possible. It's particularly important to recognize that based on animal studies, the dopaminergic system is *necessary* for the rewarding effects of only a limited number of substances, mainly psychostimulants like cocaine or amphetamine. For many other substances, including alcohol and heroin, dopaminergic signaling *contributes* to drug reward but is *not required* (Koob and Volkow, 2010; Badiani et al., 2011). Consistent with the animal research, human brain imaging studies indicate that certain drugs such as opiates or THC provoke very little DA release in the NAcc (Nutt et al., 2015). Such results suggest that neurotransmitter systems besides DA must also be involved in drug reward. Two such systems are the endogenous opioid and cannabinoid systems, based on findings that drug reward often can be blunted or even blocked by interfering with either of those systems pharmacologically or genetically (Solinas et al., 2008; Trigo et al., 2010; Volkow et al., 2019). Indeed, components of those systems can be seen in the diagram of the reward circuit shown in Figure 9.14.

Wolfram Shultz (2010) has proposed yet another important hypothesis regarding the role of DA in drug reward. Based on the firing patterns of midbrain neurons (substantia nigra and VTA) of monkeys engaged in a learning paradigm, Schultz proposed that a key function of DA neuronal firing is to signal the difference between prediction of receiving a reward and actual occurrence of the reward (i.e., it encodes **reward-prediction error**). This hypothesis and the relevant experimental findings are discussed in **WEB BOX 9.4**.

The withdrawal/negative affect stage is characterized by stress and by the recruitment of an antireward system

During the withdrawal/negative affect stage of repeated drug use, the user experiences stress and a dysphoric mood, often characterized by irritability, anxiety, and depression. Drug reward is reduced, as mentioned above with respect to the incentive sensitization theory of addiction. We can conceptualize this process as a type of tolerance such that the user experiences less and less pleasure from each episode of drug use. Indeed, addicts often report that they need to take

drugs just to feel "normal" instead of feeling "high," as they did before becoming addicted. Moreover, as mentioned earlier, laboratory animals withdrawing from chronic drug administration exhibit elevated thresholds for rewarding electrical stimulation of the brain. Those findings are consistent with a general impairment of the reward circuit during the withdrawal/negative affect stage.

Koob (2021) has applied the term **hyperkatifeia** (derived from the Greek word *katifeia*, which refers to a negative emotional state or a state of dejection) to denote the highly distressing emotional and motivational state evoked by drug withdrawal. This characterization of hyperkatifeia as a psychological construct is important because it distinguishes hyperkatifeia from the physical symptoms of drug withdrawal (e.g., withdrawal from alcohol or from opioid drugs) that have often been the focal point of the abstinence syndrome. Kwako and coworkers (2016) proposed a framework for assessing drug addiction that includes a negative emotional state as one of the core features of addictive disorders. This framework was supported by the results of a subsequent factor analysis performed on a large number of psychological and behavioral measures obtained from over 400 people with alcohol use disorder (Kwako et al., 2019). The importance of negative emotionality increases over the course of escalating drug use. As shown in **FIGURE 9.17**, in the early stages of drug use, drug seeking and consumption is motivated primarily by the positive reinforcing effects of the drug. With repeated drug exposure, this positive reinforcement wanes and is gradually replaced by relief from the abstinence-related negative emotional state as the prime motivator for continued use. Because this model does not depend on *physical* withdrawal symptoms, it can be applied to a wider range of drugs (including psychostimulants like cocaine and amphetamine) that do not elicit the kind of physical abstinence syndrome seen with alcohol, sedative drugs, and opioids.

The transition from positive to negative reinforcement proposed to underlie the progression to addiction is mediated by **neuroadaptations** in multiple neural circuits. The term *neuroadaptation* pertains to persistent neurobiological changes that can encompass neurotransmitter activity, gene expression, cellular structure (e.g., altered dendritic branching), and neural circuitry (e.g., synaptic plasticity). Koob and Le Moal have argued that the progression to addiction involves two different kinds of neuroadaptations (see Koob and Le Moal, 2008; Koob, 2015, 2021). The progressive down-regulation of the reward circuit is considered to be a *within-system* neuroadaptation, because it is a direct attempt by the brain to counteract the repeated drug-induced activation of that circuit. In contrast, a key *between-systems* neuroadaptation is the gradual recruitment of a neural circuit that Koob

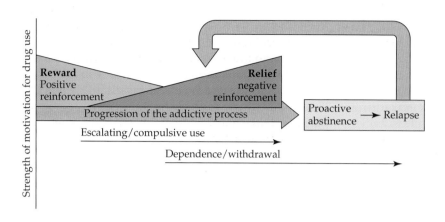

FIGURE 9.17 The primary motivation for drug use is hypothesized to switch from positive to negative reinforcement over the progression from initial drug use to addiction Drug seeking and consumption are initially motivated by the positive reinforcing effects of the drug. As a consequence of repeated drug exposure, the positive reinforcing effects are reduced, while the user progressively experience a negative emotional state during periods of abstinence. Relief from this negative emotionality (negative reinforcement) is now the primary motivating factor underlying continued drug use. (After G. F. Koob 2021. *Pharmacol Rev* 73: 163–201. Republished with permission of American Society for Pharmacology and Experimental Therapeutics; based on an original diagram by L. Parsons.)

and Le Moal call the **antireward system**. The neuro-anatomical substrate of the antireward system is the previously mentioned extended amygdala, which includes the bed nucleus of the stria terminalis, the central nucleus of the amygdala, and part of the NAcc. However, the neurotransmitters involved in this system are very different from those that mediate reward. Instead, activation of the antireward system leads to increased release of norepinephrine (NE) and two neuropeptides, corticotropin-releasing factor (CRF) and dynorphin. This system has two major functions: it puts a limit or brake on reward (imagine a situation in which the hedonic effects of natural rewards like food and sex were unlimited), and it mediates some of the aversive effects of stress such as increased anxiety.

In a drug-dependent person or experimental animal, the antireward system is activated during drug withdrawal and plays a major role in the aversive effects of withdrawal and the negative reinforcement produced by renewed drug taking. **FIGURE 9.18** illustrates some of the key neurochemical components involved in drug reward before dependence (addiction) has occurred (i.e., dominance of positive reinforcement mediated by the reward system) compared with the components involved after dependence has taken place (i.e., dominance of negative reinforcement mediated by the antireward system). This model is relevant for the negative

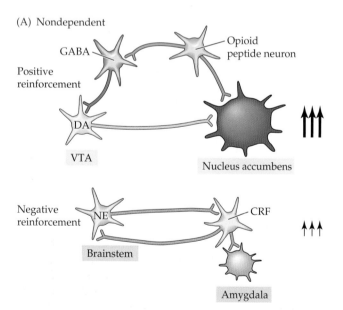

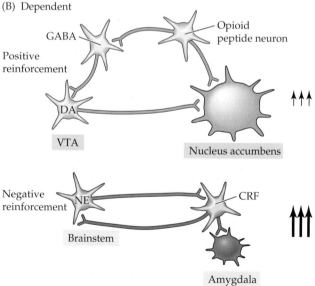

FIGURE 9.18 Neurochemical changes underlying the transition from positive to negative reinforcement in addiction (A) In a nondependent individual, the positively reinforcing effects of drug use are mediated by the reward system (large arrows) where there is relatively little involvement of the antireward system (small arrows). The part of the reward system involving DA and opioid peptides in the NAcc is illustrated. (B) In a dependent individual, the reward system has been down-regulated and the antireward system has been recruited. As a result, drug use is now supported mainly by negative reinforcement (alleviation of withdrawal symptoms). The part of the antireward system involving norepinephrine (NE) and corticotropin-releasing factor (CRF) acting in the central amygdala is illustrated. VTA, ventral tegmental area. (After G. F. Koob and M. Le Moal. 2008. *Ann Rev Psychol* 59: 29–53. Republished with permission of Annual Reviews, Inc.)

reinforcement produced by relief from both the psychological (i.e., negative emotionality) and physical symptoms of abstinence.

The preoccupation/anticipation stage involves dysregulation of prefrontal cortical function and corticostriatal circuitry

Brain imaging studies comparing addicted subjects with healthy controls have revealed both structural and functional abnormalities in the prefrontal cortex (PFC) in the addict group (Goldstein and Volkow, 2011; Volkow et al., 2012, 2019). To understand the relevance of the PFC for addiction, it is useful first to summarize some of the major behavioral functions of the PFC and the major subregions that are believed to mediate these functions. The PFC is best known for its role in **executive function**, which consists of higher-order cognitive abilities, including planning, organization, problem solving, mental flexibility, and valuation of incentives. Damage either to the PFC or to certain parts of the circuitry that connects the PFC with the rest of the brain can cause major impairments in executive function. Note, however, that the PFC contributes not only to executive function, but also to the regulation of emotional and motivational processes. All three of these aspects of PFC functioning could be important for understanding the core features of drug addiction. The PFC has massive excitatory (glutamatergic) projections to various subcortical areas that can be organized into three main circuits: (1) a dorsolateral circuit that projects from the dorsolateral PFC (DLPFC) to the dorsolateral caudate nucleus and is particularly important for executive function, (2) a ventromedial circuit that connects the anterior cingulate cortex (ACC) with the NAcc and is involved in drive and motivation, and (3) an orbitofrontal circuit that projects from the orbitofrontal cortex (OFC) to the ventromedial caudate and has been associated with behavioral inhibition and impulse control (Alvarez and Emory, 2006).

Dysfunction within the PFC and its associated circuitry is hypothesized to play a key role in the preoccupation/anticipation stage of the addiction cycle. This stage is characterized by intrusive thinking, drug craving, and lack of impulse control. Intrusive thinking, in this case, consists of persistent, uncontrollable rumination on obtaining and using the drug again. Craving provides a strong motivation to act on the intrusive thoughts. And finally, failure of impulse control means that the individual has difficulty resisting the impulse to use the drug, despite the potential adverse consequences. Researchers have identified the neural circuitry underlying each of these processes. First, intrusive thinking, whether associated with addiction or with certain other disorders such as obsessive-compulsive disorder, has been linked to abnormal activity within pathways from the PFC, hippocampus, and amygdala to the ventral striatum (Kalivas and Kalivas, 2016). Second, cue-induced craving has been found to correlate with activation of the DLPFC, OFC, ACC, dorsal and ventral striata, and the insula (Jasinska et al., 2014). The insula is a deep cortical area implicated in motivational regulation, including drug craving and control over drug use (Naqvi et al., 2014). For example, cigarette smokers with damage to the insula had reduced tobacco craving and found it much easier to quit than smokers with non-insula brain damage (Naqvi et al., 2007). The thalamus relays drug-induced interoceptive stimuli (i.e., internal cues produced by drug taking) to the insula, which then mediates the conscious awareness of these stimuli (Naqvi and Bechara, 2010). Projections of the insula to the ventromedial prefrontal cortex (VMPFC) and amygdala, modulated by DA from the VTA, transform the interoceptive information into feelings of pleasure and desire for the drug (**FIGURE 9.19**).

Finally, the transition to uncontrolled drug use is a complex process involving several brain areas and their associated circuits. One part of this process is a shift of behavioral control from striatal areas that are associated with goal-directed behavior to other areas associated with habitual behavior (Everitt and Robbins, 2013; Lüscher et al., 2020). This shift helps change drug taking from a reward-motivated behavior to a behavior that is automatic and habitual. A second component results from a blunting of striatal DA transmission, which has been linked to increased impulsivity. This decrease in DA neurotransmission, which has been found in both human and animal studies, consists of reduced striatal DA release and lower D_2 receptor binding (Trifilieff and Martinez, 2014; Trifilieff et al., 2017). Changes in the dopaminergic system observed in substance-dependent subjects could precede drug use and act as a vulnerability factor for addiction, or such changes could be a consequence of repeated drug exposure. Current evidence favors a combination of both.

The information presented above can be conceptualized as representing two opposing behavioral control systems: a "go" system that motivates and activates learned responses, and a "stop" system that pulls back on the reins (Koob, 2015). In this scheme, the pathway from initial drug use to addiction invokes an enhancement of the "go" system, as seen in the process of incentive sensitization and the transition of drug use from a goal-directed behavior to a behavioral habit. Simultaneously there is a progressive dysfunction of the "stop" system, which includes the PFC and components of the corticostriatal circuitry. This dysfunction leads to intrusive thinking, drug craving, and loss of impulse control. Involvement of the PFC in substance use disorders suggests that this brain area could be an important therapeutic target in future treatment of people with such disorders.

FIGURE 9.19 Hypothesized role of the insula in deriving conscious pleasure from drug-induced interoceptive cues According to this model, the insula mediates conscious awareness of drug-induced interoceptive stimuli upon receiving such stimuli through a pathway from the thalamus. Projections of the insula to the ventromedial prefrontal cortex (VMPFC) and amygdala, modulated by input from VTA dopaminergic neurons, transform the interoceptive information into feelings of pleasure and desire for the drug. (After N. H. Naqvi and A. Bechara. 2010. *Brain Struct Funct* 214: 435–450. doi.org/10.1007/s00429-010-0268-7)

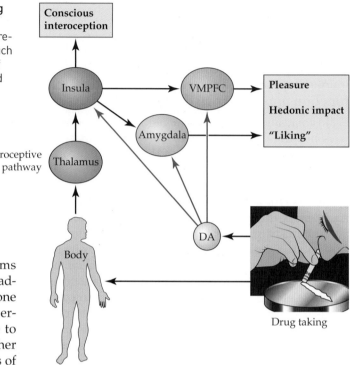

The persistence of addiction has been studied at both the molecular and synaptic levels

In the previous sections, we discussed some key elements of the neurobiological mechanisms underlying the transition from initial drug use to addiction. However, this discussion did not address one of the cardinal features of addiction, namely its persistence. Even though some individuals are able to recover from their maladaptive substance use (either naturally or with the aid of treatment) over periods of months to a few years, others persist in such use for very long periods of time, with periods of abstinence interspersed with episodes of relapse and a return to drug use. This pattern is why addiction is characterized as a chronic, relapsing disorder. Even individuals who have recovered from addiction may still experience a desire to use drugs from time to time. There must be long-lasting changes in the brain driven by repeated drug exposure that underlie the persistence of drug craving and relapse. These changes can be studied at multiple levels of analysis, two of which we will discuss: (1) long-lasting molecular changes in the form of altered gene expression, and (2) synaptic plasticity, referring to the formation of new synapses and/or changes in synaptic strength within the reward or antireward circuits. Both kinds of long-lasting neural changes are discussed in **BOX 9.2**.

Is addiction a brain disease?

Investigating the neurobiology of addiction is vitally important for helping us understand the etiology of this disorder and for generating new biologically-based treatments. Yet, acquiring this information does not, in itself, provide a simple answer to an important question: *Is addiction a disease?* The most widely accepted model of addiction in our society is the **disease model**. Not only has this view been popularized in the mass media, but addicts themselves and their treatment providers commonly ascribe to this model. The disease model of addiction arose from early work with alcoholics and was only later applied to cocaine and opioid addiction (Meyer, 1996). Benjamin Rush, the Philadelphia physician who founded the alcohol temperance

movement, was the first to consider alcoholism a disease. This view was later expanded and promoted by E. M. Jellinek in his influential book, *The Disease Concept of Alcoholism* (Jellinek, 1960). For many years, alcoholism has been formally considered a disease by medical organizations such as the World Health Organization and the American Medical Association. Indeed, the disease model is sometimes called a **medical model**. It is the leading model used both in the professional treatment of alcoholics and other drug addicts (e.g., in 12-step programs) and in self-help groups such as Alcoholics Anonymous (AA) and Narcotics Anonymous. Note that the disease model is not an alternative to the various neurobiological models or even the more inclusive biopsychosocial model presented earlier. Rather, it is a way of thinking about the fundamental nature of addiction and the best approach to treating it.

The current disease model of addiction is based largely on evidence for dysregulation of brain function in addiction which, at least partly, is caused by repeated drug exposure (i.e., the neuroadaptations described above). This notion was presented forcefully in an article entitled "Addiction Is a Brain Disease, and It Matters" by Alan Leshner, former director of the National Institute on Drug Abuse (NIDA). Leshner said, "That addiction is tied to changes in brain structure and function is what makes it, fundamentally, a brain disease. A metaphorical switch in the brain seems to be thrown as a result of prolonged drug use. Initially, drug use is a voluntary behavior, but when the switch is thrown, the individual moves into the state

BOX 9.2 ■ THE CUTTING EDGE

Epigenetic Processes and Synaptic Plasticity as Mechanisms for the Development and Persistence of Drug Addiction

Epigenetic changes in gene expression can be very long-lasting, which raises the possibility that such changes could contribute to the persistence of drug craving and drug use in people who have acquired a drug addiction problem. The concept and mechanisms of epigenetics were presented in Chapter 2 of this text, but to refresh the reader's memory, the term "epigenetics" refers to a group of processes that can produce relatively stable changes in gene expression ("relatively stable" means more long-lasting than the transient changes in expression associated with transcription factors). As described in that chapter, the most widely studied epigenetic processes are DNA methylation and histone modifications such as histone acetylation, phosphorylation, or methylation. DNA methylation usually results in condensation of the chromatin and repression of the affected gene, whereas histone acetylation or phosphorylation leads to chromatin opening and enhanced gene expression. Histone methylation has more complex effects, but it is most often associated with repression of gene expression. **FIGURE A** depicts the potential effects of chronic exposure to an addictive drug on two different genes, one of which undergoes histone acetylation and phosphorylation and the other of which undergoes both DNA and histone methylation. The first gene becomes "primed" for expression, as a result of which the gene responds to subsequent exposure to that drug (drug challenge) with a robust transcriptional activation. In contrast, the second gene becomes "desensitized" by chromatin condensation, and as a result, the drug challenge is met with repression of that gene (Nestler, 2014). A third kind of epigenetic mechanism involves gene regulation by several types of non-coding RNAs. These are RNA molecules that, unlike mRNAs, do not transcribe gene sequences for directing protein synthesis.

Before continuing this discussion, it is important for the reader to understand that our knowledge about the role of epigenetic mechanisms in drug addiction is derived almost entirely from laboratory animal studies using brain tissue obtained after euthanasia of the subjects. Until fairly recently, there has been no way to investigate epigenetic changes in the *human* brain without similarly using postmortem brain tissue. However, researchers have begun to develop exciting new imaging techniques that can circumvent this problem and should, in the future, provide new information on drug-induced epigenetic changes in the living human brain. The literature on epigenetic mechanisms associated with addiction has grown too large to cover in the limited space available. Therefore, we will provide just a few representative examples. Because the most extensive work has been conducted on histone modifications, especially histone acetylation, that will be our focus. To begin, repeated exposure to cocaine, either

(Continued)

(A)

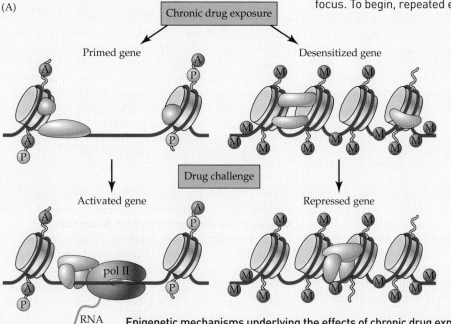

Epigenetic mechanisms underlying the effects of chronic drug exposure on gene expression Chronic drug exposure can result in either an epigenetically primed or a desensitized target gene, thereby causing activated or repressed transcription of that gene when the organism is subsequently challenged with the same drug. M, methyl groups attached to DNA and histone proteins that tend to repress gene transcription by compacting the chromatin structure; A and P, acetyl and phosphate groups, respectively, that are attached to histone proteins and that tend to activate gene transcription by opening up the chromatin structure; pol II, RNA polymerase II, which is responsible for transcribing DNA to RNA. (After A. J. Robison and E. J. Nestler. 2011. *Nat Rev Neurosci* 12: 623–637. doi.org/10.1038/nrn3111)

BOX 9.2 ■ THE CUTTING EDGE (continued)

experimenter-administered or self-administered, for up to 3 to 4 weeks, produced hyperacetylation of H3 or H4 histone proteins associated with several different genes in the dorsal striatum or NAcc (Cadet et al., 2016). Similar results have been obtained using alcohol, nicotine, or opioid drugs (Hamilton and Nestler, 2019). Hyperacetylation (addition of excess acetyl groups to the protein) is driven by activation of histone acetyltransferase enzymes (HATs) that catalyze the acetylation reaction, whereas acetyl groups can be removed by a family of histone deacetylases (HDACs). Thus, the acetylation status of any particular histone is determined by the balance of HAT versus HDAC activity. This balance can be disrupted pharmacologically by administering drugs that block the deacetylation reaction (i.e., HDAC inhibitors), thereby globally enhancing histone acetylation. Several studies have used either systemic or intracerebral administration of an HDAC inhibitor to examine the effects of enhancing histone acetylation on the rewarding effects of morphine or heroin using place-conditioning procedures. In almost all cases, HDAC inhibition promoted formation of the conditioned place preference, suggesting an increase in opioid reward (Browne et al., 2019). Results such as those support the idea that not only do addictive drugs influence epigenetic processes such as histone acetylation or deacetylation, but these effects likely contribute to the *behavioral* changes observed in the drug user over time.

Animal studies have also played a central role in establishing how addictive drugs can produce long-lasting changes in synaptic activity. Drug-induced synaptic plasticity occurs in several brain areas, involves both excitatory (glutamatergic) and inhibitory (GABAergic) synapses, can occur both postsynaptically (altering the responsiveness of postsynaptic cells) or presynaptically (altering neurotransmitter release), and varies according to whether the synaptic changes are transient or more long-lasting. Here we will describe examples of postsynaptic plasticity of glutamatergic signaling in the VTA and NAcc produced by a variety of addictive drugs. Just as the neural plasticity represented by long-term potentiation (LTP) discussed in Chapter 8 is a possible neurobiological basis for memory formation, synaptic changes produced by drug exposure may mediate the memory-like features of addiction (Carmack et al., 2017).

The first demonstration of drug-induced plasticity was the ability of a single injection of cocaine in mice to enhance the responsiveness of synapses between incoming glutamatergic fibers and postsynaptic neurons in the VTA. This enhanced responsiveness was evident within 3 hours after drug administration and was still present at 5 days but not 10 days later (reviewed by Anderson and Hearing, 2019). A similar phenomenon was produced by amphetamine, nicotine, and alcohol, showing that this kind of synaptic plasticity in the VTA was not unique to cocaine. However, because of the

transient nature of the synaptic changes, such changes could not be a mechanism for the long-term subjective and behavioral effects of addictive drug exposure.

More persistent kinds of drug-induced synaptic plasticity have been shown to occur in the NAcc. One well-studied example of this concerns the mechanisms underlying animal models of incubation of drug craving. Incubation of drug craving occurs when someone addicted to a particular substance is going through a period of prolonged abstinence. As time passes since the last drug exposure, the ability of an environmental cue previously associated with drug use (e.g., an abstinent alcohol-dependent person seeing a bottle of whiskey) to elicit craving for the drug progressively increases, thereby elevating the risk for relapse to drug use (Li et al., 2015). Incubation of drug craving can be modeled in laboratory animals, usually rats or mice, in the following way. Animals are first trained to self-administer the drug intravenously and then switched to a regimen in which they have access to the drug daily for multiple hours per day. This regimen is continued for a number of days (e.g., 6 hours of access per day for at least 10 days) to establish dependence on the drug. During this period, each drug infusion is paired with a cue such as illumination of a light and/or presentation of a tone inside the testing chamber. Once dependence has occurred, drug exposure stops and the animals are kept in their home cages, where they remain abstinent for variable lengths of time (days to weeks) before being returned to the self-administration chamber for testing. During the test, performance of the operant response that previously elicited a drug infusion results in the cue presentation, but no drug is delivered. The number of responses made by the animal during the test period is taken to be a measure of drug "craving," and increases in responding as abstinence progresses reflect the "incubation" of this craving.

The laboratory of Marina Wolf has extensively investigated the mechanisms of incubation of craving for cocaine and methamphetamine. The left panel of **FIGURE B** presents the results from a study of cue-induced cocaine craving, illustrating that responding for the cocaine-associated cue began to increase after 1 week of withdrawal and continued to increase for up to 60 days. Wolf and colleagues have identified a form of delayed-onset synaptic plasticity in the NAcc that plays a key role in the craving incubation process and that, like the short-term plasticity in the VTA, also involves glutamate signaling (Murray et al., 2014). In earlier chapters, we learned that the pharmacological properties of ionotropic receptors are determined by their subunit composition. Yet another important subunit-dependent property is the ionic permeability of the receptor. Although most glutamate AMPA receptors are impermeable to Ca^{2+} ions, a specific change in one of the receptor's

BOX 9.2 ■ THE CUTTING EDGE *(continued)*

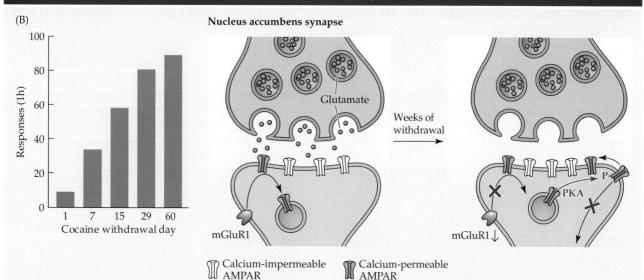

(B)

Nucleus accumbens synapse

Responses (1h) / Cocaine withdrawal day

Glutamate

Weeks of withdrawal

PKA / P / mGluR1↓

mGluR1

⊞ Calcium-impermeable AMPAR   ⊞ Calcium-permeable AMPAR

Incubation of craving for cocaine in a rat model The graph presents craving incubation data from rats that had become cocaine-dependent over 10 days of extended access to drug self-administration for 6 hours per day. During this period, each drug infusion was paired with a compound tone/light cue. Following the number of days of withdrawal shown, the animals were returned to the training chamber and allowed to respond (lever press) as before for a period of 1 hour. Responding during this test period was accompanied by presentation of the tone/light cue, but no cocaine was delivered. The illustration presents a model of delayed synaptic plasticity in the NAcc that is responsible for cocaine craving incubation. Over 3 to 4 weeks of withdrawal, glutamatergic synapses within this area undergo an accumulation of

Ca^{2+}-permeable AMPA receptors (CP-AMPARs) in the postsynaptic membrane that strengthens connectivity between the presynaptic and postsynaptic cells. This accumulation results from a combination of two mechanisms: (1) PKA-mediated AMPA receptor phosphorylation, which promotes membrane insertion and reduces membrane removal of CP-AMPARs, and (2) down-regulation of membrane mGluR1s, which alleviates the removal of CP-AMPARs from the membrane that is normally driven by this metabotropic glutamate receptor. ([Left] From J. A. Loweth et al. 2014. *Neuropsychopharm* 76: 287–300. © 2013. Reprinted with permission from Elsevier, data from J. W. Grimm et al. 2001. *Nature* 412: 141-142. [Right] From J. A. Loweth et al. 2014. *Neuropsychopharm* 76: 287–300.)

subunits renders the receptors permeable to Ca^{2+}. In animals not previously exposed to addictive drugs, most of the AMPA receptors in NAcc neurons show the usual absence of Ca^{2+} permeability. Remarkably, however, when animals are given the craving incubation procedure described in the previous paragraph, the expression of Ca^{2+}-permeable AMPA receptors (CP-AMPARs) begins to increase, resulting in an accumulation of those receptors on the cell surface within 3 to 4 weeks of withdrawal. The significance of this change in receptor composition is that it confers enhanced responsiveness of the postsynaptic cell, thereby strengthening the synaptic connection between that cell and its presynaptic counterpart. Various studies have not only confirmed that CP-AMPARs are necessary for the incubation of craving but have also identified two mechanisms that drive this type of synaptic plasticity (Figure B, right panel). One mechanism involves increased AMPA receptor phosphorylation by protein kinase A (PKA), which has the effect of promoting insertion of CP-AMPARs into the cell membrane and reducing their removal from the membrane. The second mechanism involves reduced surface expression of the mGluR1 metabotropic

glutamate receptor subtype. Normal activation of that receptor seems to promote removal of CP-AMPARs from the membrane; therefore, decreased mGluR1 signaling allows CP-AMPAR accumulation to occur. The process of synaptic strengthening by CP-AMPAR accumulation has some similarity to the mechanism of long-term potentiation (LTP) discussed in Chapter 8, since both involve changes in AMPA receptor trafficking. CP-AMPAR accumulation in the NAcc also underlies craving incubation for methamphetamine, although some of the mechanisms that drive this accumulation differ from those described for cocaine (Scheyer et al., 2016; Murray et al., 2019). Note that the strengthening of glutamatergic inputs to the NAcc mediated by CP-AMPARs may not be the only outcome of this receptor change. It's possible that the Ca^{2+} ions that enter the cell through CP-AMPAR channels participate in various Ca^{2+}-dependent second-messenger functions, thereby altering postsynaptic cell functioning in additional ways. Further studies are needed to elucidate all of the synaptic changes that occur in this model and to understand how those changes lead to the elevated drug-seeking behavior shown in animals that undergo the craving incubation procedure.

of addiction, characterized by compulsive drug seeking and use" (Leshner, 1997, p. 46). Almost all neurobiologists who study addiction advocate some version of the brain disease model, most notably Nora Volkow, current director of NIDA, and George Koob, current director of the National Institute on Alcohol Abuse and Alcoholism (Volkow and Koob, 2015; Volkow and Morales, 2015; Koob and Volkow, 2016; Volkow et al., 2016, 2019). Heilig and colleagues (2021) have also recently published a defense of the brain disease model along with their rebuttal of some of the criticisms of that model (see below).

The disease model has had a tremendously valuable impact on society's reaction toward drug use and addiction. For a long time, excessive drug use and addiction were seen primarily as signs of personal and moral weakness (Nathan et al., 2016). Indeed, this earlier view has sometimes been termed a **moral model** of addiction. Adoption of the disease model was thought to remove the social stigma of addiction (after all, no one *blames* you for coming down with a disease) and to involve the medical profession in helping addicts deal with their problem through treatment programs. Yet, our society is still ambivalent about disease versus moral conceptions of drug use. Although you can obtain treatment for alcohol- or tobacco-related problems without fear of prosecution, because those substances are legal, problematic use of heroin, cocaine, or (in some states) marijuana often leads to a jail sentence instead of medical help.

Despite its wide acceptance, however, the disease model of addiction has been criticized by a number of writers, some of whom have experience working with drug-addicted patients. Books that offer alternative theories of addiction include *Addiction Is a Choice*, by Jeffrey Schaler; *Addiction: A Disorder of Choice*, by Gene Heyman; and most recently, *The Biology of Desire: Why Addiction Is Not a Disease*, by Marc Lewis. Other critiques may be found in articles such as "The brain disease model of addiction: Is it supported by the evidence and has it delivered on its promises?" (W. Hall et al., 2015), "Addiction and the brain-disease fallacy" (Satel and Lillienfeld, 2014), "Addiction is not a brain disease (and it matters)" (Levy, 2013), "Addiction: choice or compulsion" (Henden et al., 2013), "How individuals make choices explains addiction's distinctive non-eliminable features" (Heyman, 2021), "Brain change in addiction as learning, not disease" (Lewis, 2018), "Q: Is addiction a brain disease or a moral failing? A: Neither" (Heather, 2017), "How to recover from a brain disease: Is addiction a disease, or is there a disease-like stage in addiction?" (Snoek, 2017), "The purpose in chronic addiction" (Pickard, 2012), and "People control their addictions: No matter how much the 'chronic' brain disease model of addiction indicates otherwise, we know that people can quit

addictions—with special reference to harm reduction and mindfulness" (Peele, 2016).

Space limitations preclude our discussing all of the issues raised in the abovementioned sources; however, several key points are worth noting. First, most critiques of the disease model acknowledge the wealth of research demonstrating that repeated exposure to addictive drugs alters the brain in significant ways. However, this alone does not prove that addiction is a disease. After all, *every* set of experiences we encounter, whether learning to ride a bike, memorizing molecular formulas in a chemistry class, or falling in love, affects the structure and functioning of our brain, often permanently. The proposition that the brain changes observed in addicted people are *pathological*, and therefore constitute a disease state, is a matter of debate, since some of these same changes may occur under other conditions.

Second, there are disorders of the brain that unequivocally constitute disease but that differ importantly from addiction. A few clear-cut examples include Alzheimer's and Parkinson's diseases, multiple sclerosis, ALS (Lou Gehrig's disease), epilepsy, and brain cancers such as neuroblastomas. All of these disorders can be diagnosed conclusively by specific laboratory tests either in the living patient or using postmortem brain tissue. In contrast, there is not a single diagnostic test to confirm that someone has a substance use disorder according to the *DSM-5*. Instead, such a diagnosis must be made entirely on the basis of behavioral symptomatology. Moreover, none of the abovementioned brain diseases can be cured by changes in the person's behavior. Yet, that is exactly what occurs when people recover from addiction, either of their own accord or with the assistance of medication, a therapist, or a self-help group.

Third, the disease conception of addiction as a chronic (often implying life-long) disorder characterized by loss of control over drug use is contradicted by a substantial amount of empirical evidence. In an earlier section we presented data from NESARC showing the extent to which people are able to recover from addiction, often without treatment. Addiction researchers also know that of the many American soldiers who used, and even became addicted to, heroin during the Vietnam War, only a small percentage maintained their addiction upon returning to the United States (Hall and Weier, 2017). Laboratory studies have even shown that regular drug users can cognitively control their cravings and the associated regional brain activations when instructed to do so in an experimental setting (Kober et al., 2010; Volkow et al., 2010). Taken together, these findings raise serious questions about whether heavy drug use is inevitably outside the control of the user.

Fourth, non-disease theories of addiction typically argue that addicts choose to use drugs because such use serves a purpose such as alleviating emotional pain, because other positive reinforcers are lacking in their lives, and/or because the available reinforcers fail to provide sufficient motivation to be chosen over the drug. Such a framework suggests that treatments for addiction should aim for a reallocation of behavior away from using drugs for reinforcement toward healthier reinforcers (**FIGURE 9.20**; Banks and Negus, 2017). Such reallocation can be aided by an existing type of program called **contingency management**. Contingency management is a behavioral intervention in which the user is regularly subjected to urine testing and receives reinforcement for each negative test, typically in the form of vouchers redeemable for retail goods or services (Dallery et al., 2015; Petry et al., 2017; McPherson et al., 2018). Even the lowly lab rat adjusts its drug-taking behavior based on the availability of alternative reinforcers. This was shown many years ago in the "Rat Park" studies of Bruce Alexander (Alexander, 2010). During the 1970s, Alexander and colleagues at Simon Fraser University set out to test whether drugs are, as he put it, "irresistibly addictive." The reason for their skepticism stemmed from the realization that in a typical drug addiction experiment, the rats, which in the wild are highly social, are housed by themselves in small cages with few or no sources of stimulation outside of the drug being tested. Consequently, the researchers set up a large enclosure

containing objects to interact with, running wheels, and many animals living together, including both males and females that were allowed to breed (photos of Rat Park are available at Alexander, 2010). When given the opportunity to voluntarily consume a morphine-laced solution, the Rat Park animals consumed much less than the animals housed in the usual barren and socially isolated environment.* More recent studies described in Web Box 12.1 have shown that many rats choose to consume a sweetened water solution over receiving an IV injection of cocaine, even after considerable experience with the drug. However, some rats prefer the cocaine, which arguably are the ones that most closely model humans who prefer drugs even when other reinforcers are available.

Finally, researchers and clinicians who question the disease model of addiction argue that a brain-centric view of this problem pays too little attention to the whole *person* in whose head the brain resides. This is not to deny the vital role that neuroscience has played and will

---

*It is worth noting that since the 1970s, increasing concern for the welfare of laboratory animals, including rodents, has led to improved living conditions; however, even now the requirements of some experimental procedures make it necessary to house animals individually, and they are rarely allowed to breed unless it is specifically required for the study.

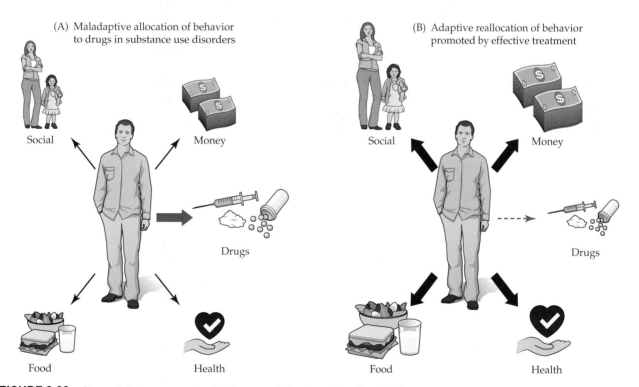

FIGURE 9.20   Drug addiction conceptualized as a maladaptive allocation of behavior
(A) People suffering from a substance use disorder (addiction) maladaptively allocate their behavior toward procuring and using addictive drugs, to the detriment of other choices. (B) For maximum effectiveness, treatments for substance use disorders should aim not only to reduce drug-related behaviors, but also to promote behavioral allocation to more adaptive, healthier reinforcers. (After M. L. Banks and S. S. Negus. 2017. *Trends Pharmacol Sci* 38: 181–194. ©2017. Reprinted with permission from Elsevier.)

continue to play in helping us unravel the problem of addiction. But it's also true that despite many years of research and millions of dollars spent in the pursuit of new medications to combat addiction, very few have yet emerged. Taken together with the lessons from Rat Park, heroin-using Vietnam War veterans, and the many drug users who have achieved a natural recovery, the relative lack of progress from research based on the brain disease model suggests that we need to pay more attention to the psychosocial roots of addiction and allow that addictive behaviors may fall within a wide range of compulsivity versus controllability.

Whether society conceptualizes addiction as a disease or not has important implications besides the obvious ones regarding addiction research and treatment. First, it has an effect on the addicts themselves. Some addicts and therapists contend that the disease model helps reduce the sense of guilt associated with the problems caused by the person's prior drug use. If such problems are viewed as stemming from a disease, then the therapeutic process may benefit. As one alcoholic put it, "Calling [alcoholism] a disease allows us to put the guilt aside so that we can do the work that we need to do" (Thombs, 1999). Believing that one has a disease may also help the individual deal with relapses, since these returns to drug use could otherwise be construed as resulting from a moral failing. But there is an alternative view expressed by Marc Lewis, author of *The Biology of Desire: Why Addiction Is Not a Disease*, who is both a neuroscientist and a former addict himself. Based not only on his own experience but also his interactions with many other present and former drug addicts, Lewis states:

> While shame and guilt may be softened by the disease definition, many addicts simply don't see themselves as ill, and being coerced into an admission that they have a disease can undermine other—sometimes highly valuable—elements of their self-image and self-esteem. Many recovering addicts find it better not to see themselves as helpless victims of a disease, and objective accounts of recovery and relapse suggest that they may be right. Treatment experts and addiction counselors often identify empowerment or self-efficacy as a necessary resource for lasting recovery. (Lewis, 2015, pp. 9–10)

Before concluding this section, it is necessary to acknowledge the role of the disease model in justifying health insurance coverage for addiction treatment (McLellan et al., 2000). Medically based treatment programs have undoubtedly helped many people overcome their drug use problems, and access to such programs is often out of reach without insurance coverage. While health insurers are willing to pay for medically based treatment programs, very few will cover the cost of a contingency management program despite the documented successes of such programs.

In summary, the brain disease model of addiction is the principal model held by major health organizations, neuroscience researchers who study addiction, many (most?) addiction treatment providers, and many (though not all) addicts themselves. This model is also widely accepted in society, which accounts for health insurance coverage for treating substance use disorders. However, some strong evidence-based arguments have been made against the central tenets of the disease model. Whether or not the reader is convinced by these arguments, we hope to have made clear that people diagnosed with a substance use disorder vary tremendously, not only in how they came to that stage in their lives, but also in how they perceive their substance use, the extent to which they are motivated to stop using (or not), and their future trajectory, including an eventual recovery that may or may not require outside help.

SECTION SUMMARY

- The development of addiction has been conceptualized as a repeating cycle of three stages: (1) preoccupation/anticipation, (2) binge/intoxication, and (3) withdrawal/negative affect. Each stage is associated with several features related to the diagnostic criteria of drug dependence (*DSM-IV*) or substance use disorder (*DSM-5*).

- The binge/intoxication stage is motivated by drug reward and incentive salience. A key component of the reward circuit, which mediates the acute rewarding and reinforcing effects of most addictive drugs, is the DA pathway from the VTA to the NAcc. Addictive drugs elevate extracellular DA levels in the NAcc either by enhancing VTA cell firing or by acting locally to release DA from the dopaminergic nerve terminals and/or blocking DA reuptake. Drug-induced elevations in DA mimic the effect of burst firing of the dopaminergic neurons and cause activation of low-affinity D_1 receptors.

- Over repeated drug exposures, rewarding effects often decline because of drug tolerance. However, the incentive properties of the drug and its related cues become sensitized, thus leading to an increasingly important role for incentive salience as a motivator of continued drug use. The concepts of drug reward versus incentive salience are captured in the difference between drug *liking* and drug *wanting* as described in the incentive sensitization theory of addiction.

- In addition to the proposed involvement of DA in reward and incentive salience, midbrain dopaminergic neuronal firing appears to encode novel stimulus (physical) salience and reward-prediction error. These two components of cell responding are temporally distinct, with salience responses occurring prior to reward-prediction error responses.

- During the withdrawal/negative affect stage of repeated drug use, the user experiences a dysphoric and distressing mood state that Koob has termed hyperkatifeia. Because hyperkatifeia is distinct from the physical symptoms of withdrawal associated with alcohol and opioid drugs, it is applicable to substances that do not produce a significant physical abstinence syndrome. The positive reinforcing effects of drugs are hypothesized to be the initial driver of drug seeking and consumption, but with repeated drug exposure over time, this motivating force is largely replaced by the negative reinforcement of alleviating the dysphoric mood state (along with physical withdrawal if applicable) present during withdrawal.

■ The transition from positive to negative reinforcement is mediated by within-system and between-systems neuroadaptations. Progressive down-regulation of the reward system is an important within-system neuroadaptation, whereas a key between-systems neuroadaptation is the recruitment of an antireward circuit that mediates the withdrawal/negative affect stage of addiction.

■ The antireward system, which is centered around the extended amygdala, is activated during stress and drug withdrawal. Activation of this system results in increased release of NE and the neuropeptides CRF and dynorphin.

■ The preoccupation/anticipation stage is characterized by intrusive thinking, drug craving, and lack of impulse control. Chronic drug misuse and addiction are additionally associated with impaired executive function. Together, these abnormalities have been related to dysregulation of the PFC and its descending glutamatergic projections to the striatum and other subcortical structures. Cue-induced craving activates several brain regions, notably a deep cortical area known as the insula. Loss of control over drug use is associated with a shift of behavioral control from the ventral striatum (especially the NAcc) to the dorsal striatum, a brain area important for stimulus–response habit learning. Increased impulsivity has been linked to blunted striatal DA transmission, consisting of reduced DA release and lower D_2 receptor binding.

■ Epigenetic processes such as DNA methylation, histone modifications, and non-coding RNAs are important contributors to the development and maintenance of drug addiction. One example involves hyperacetylation of histones H3 and H4 in the dorsal striatum or NAcc produced by several different addictive drugs. Other studies using HDAC inhibitors have shown that histone acetylation is involved in the rewarding effects of opioid drugs.

■ Drug-induced plasticity at either excitatory (glutamatergic) or inhibitory (GABAergic) synapses is another key mechanism of drug addiction. Synaptic changes can be relatively short-term (several days) or much longer-lasting. Plasticity of NAcc glutamatergic synapses mediated by altered AMPA receptor subunit composition has been shown to be a key component of an animal model of drug craving incubation.

■ The most influential model of addiction in our society is the disease, or medical, model, which is based on brain dysfunction brought about by repeated drug exposure. Despite its wide acceptance, the disease model has criticized by a number of writers. Alternative models of addiction focus on the ability of drug users to choose what behaviors they perform and on the psychosocial factors that led to and now maintain excessive drug use. Such models generally advocate for behavioral interventions that focus the person's behavior toward healthier kinds of reinforcers.

STUDY QUESTIONS

1. How did the availability and use of psychoactive drugs in the United States differ 200 years ago compared with the present time?

2. Trace the history of federal drug laws from 1900 to the present. Which of these laws was responsible for instituting the Schedule of Controlled Substances and the Drug Enforcement Agency (DEA)?

3. How does the modern conception of addiction differ from the earlier idea that addiction is determined primarily by the development of physical dependence?

4. Define the terms *relapse* and *remission*.

5. In the fifth edition of the *Diagnostic and Statistical Manual of Mental Disorders* (*DSM-5*), what are the meanings of the terms *substance use disorder* and *substance-induced disorder*? Include in your answer a listing of the criteria used to diagnose an alcohol use disorder, which has been provided in the text as an example that reflects the criteria applied to most addictive substances.

6. If someone was diagnosed with a "mild" form of cocaine use disorder according to *DSM-5* criteria, would you be likely to consider that person addicted to cocaine? Explain your answer.

7. (a) What are behavioral addictions? Which behavioral addiction has its own diagnostic classification in the *DSM-5*? (b) You happen to know someone who spends nearly all of their time playing and practicing the guitar. They spend a lot of money on guitar lessons and seem to get very irritable if a day goes by in which they are prevented from playing the guitar. Should your acquaintance be diagnosed with "guitar playing addiction"? Why or why not? If you are not sure about your answer, what kinds of additional information would you want to know, not only about this individual but also about others who have been shown to behave in a similar manner?

8. Drug use for some young people begins with legal drugs like alcohol and tobacco, then progresses to marijuana, and (in a small percentage of cases) may progress further to drugs like cocaine or opioids. One theory to account for such a progression is the "gateway theory." What is the basic idea behind this theory? What alternative explanation of drug progressions has been proposed by critics of the gateway theory?

(Continued)

9. What is meant by the phrase "maturing out" of a drug-using lifestyle?

10. List the five drug classifications in the Schedule of Controlled Substances and describe each class. Provide at least one example of a drug belonging to classes I through IV. What is the status of alcohol and tobacco in the schedule?

11. Discuss how the route of administration influences the addiction potential of recreational drugs. Provide at least one example of this influence.

12. (a) Animals can be trained to self-administer cocaine by intravenous injection, but they will not self-administer the antipsychotic drug haloperidol even if given the same training as for cocaine. What does this finding tell us about the two different drugs? (b) Design a set of experiments to determine whether dopamine transmission in the nucleus accumbens is necessary for cocaine self-administration by laboratory rats.

13. Why is the measurement of breakpoint for self-administration of a drug a better measure of that drug's reinforcing properties than measuring the number of drug infusions obtained per hour under a continuous-reinforcement schedule?

14. What does the phrase "reinstatement of drug-seeking behavior" mean, and how is it modeled in laboratory animal studies?

15. The text mentions experiments in which animals find a drug to be reinforcing when they are allowed to self-administer the drug, but they will also perform an operant response to prevent the drug from being administered by the experimenter. How can this be explained?

16. Define the term *abstinence syndrome*. What is the role of drug craving, either unconditioned or conditioned, in drug abstinence?

17. How are the discriminative stimulus effects of a drug studied experimentally? Consider an experiment in which an animal is trained to discriminate drug A from vehicle and then is tested for its response to administration of a new drug (drug B) to which it has never been exposed previously. If the animal makes the "drug-correct response" when given drug B, what information have we learned about the relationship of drug B to drug A?

18. Define the common disease–common variant and common disease–rare variant hypotheses of neuropsychiatric disorders.

19. Describe the three main approaches used to study the genetics of neuropsychiatric disorders, including addiction. What is the "streetlight effect," and which genetic approach suffers from this effect?

20. What are single-nucleotide polymorphisms (SNPs), and how do they differ from gene mutations?

21. (a) If you were a drug addiction counselor meeting with a client for the first time, what kinds of information would you gather to help you understand the psychosocial risk or protective factors operating in your client's life? (b) Would it be important to determine whether your client has been diagnosed with any other psychiatric disorder such as a mood, anxiety, or personality disorder? Explain your answer.

22. The features of drug use and addiction are very similar between men and women. True or false? Explain your answer.

23. What evidence do we have that environmental context influences drug choice?

24. What is meant by the term *natural recovery* as applied to addiction? What is the evidence for this phenomenon?

25. Describe the three stages associated with substance use that can lead to the development of compulsive drug use and addiction.

26. Describe the components of the reward circuit with respect to both anatomy and neurochemistry.

27. Define the terms *incentive salience* and *incentive sensitization*, and discuss the hypothesized role of these factors in the development of a substance use disorder.

28. Much attention has been paid to the role of dopamine in drug reward. (a) What are the two primary mechanisms by which addictive drugs can elicit increased dopaminergic transmission in the nucleus accumbens? (b) Is such an increase in dopaminergic transmission equally important for all addictive drugs? Explain your answer.

29. What is *reward-prediction error*, and how is it encoded by the firing of midbrain dopamine neurons?

30. The concept of *hyperkatifeia* as used by Koob refers to the distressing physical symptoms associated with withdrawal from certain drugs such as alcohol and opioids. True or false? Explain your answer.

31. Define the term *neuroadaptation*, and discuss the hypothesized role of neuroadaptive recruitment of an antireward system in the development of a substance use disorder. What are the neuroanatomical and neurochemical features of that system?

32. Discuss the evidence for dysregulation of prefrontal cortical function in the preoccupation/anticipation stage of the addiction cycle.

33. (a) What are the three main kinds of epigenetic mechanisms involved in regulating gene expression? (b) What is the rationale behind administering an HDAC inhibitor to animals as a way of showing that epigenetics can influence the behavioral responses to addictive drugs?

34. (a) What is "incubation of drug craving," and how is this phenomenon studied in laboratory animals? (b) Describe the role of Ca^{2+}-permeable AMPA receptors in incubation of craving for cocaine.

35. Discuss evidence for and against the idea that addiction is a brain disease. If you find either side of the argument to be significantly stronger than the other, give the reasons why.

Alreohol

THE HEART OF BRITAIN WAS BROKEN the day Diana, Princess of Wales, died, August 31, 1997. Many are still asking how it could have happened, how a beautiful young life could be snuffed out in an instant when her chauffeured limousine slammed into a concrete tunnel. The events immediately preceding the disaster included a high-speed chase as the princess was trying to avoid the harassment of a herd of tabloid photographers who were chasing her in their cars and on motorcycles. Was her professional driver, Henri Paul, to blame? Or was the accident caused by the vicious persistence of the paparazzi?

On face value, the chauffeur's blood level of 0.175% was clearly beyond legal intoxication, so the cause seems clear. Yet those who spoke to Henri Paul before the fateful trip claimed he seemed fine, walked normally, held normal conversations, and showed no external signs of intoxication. That would seem impossible, yet the occurrence may be explained by behavioral tolerance. Since the chauffeur was a chronic heavy drinker, he had had many opportunities to practice walking and talking under the influence of alcohol. He had considerable motivation to learn these behaviors, since his job would be jeopardized by signs of intoxication. Could he also have learned to maneuver his car while intoxicated? We cannot know for sure. But driving is a complex task involving timing, reflexes, coordination, alertness, memory, and judgment. Tolerance does not affect all skills equally. Perhaps simple operation of the vehicle was possible, but when the task became more complex because of the chase and rapidly changing conditions where judgement was critical, the effects of alcohol became tragically fatal. ■

The tragic outcome of a high-speed chase that took the life of Diana, Princess of Wales.

10.1 Psychopharmacology of Alcohol

Alcohol, after caffeine, is the most commonly used psychoactive drug in America and is certainly the drug that is most misused. Despite the fact that alcohol has dramatic effects on mood, behavior, and thinking, and that its chronic use is damaging to the individual, the individual's family, and society, most people accept its use. In fact, many people do not consider alcohol to be a drug. How many people do you know who shun taking over-the-counter (OTC) or prescription medicines because they don't want to take "drugs" but will have a beer at a party or a cocktail before dinner? How many books and magazine articles have been titled "Drugs and Alcohol," as though alcohol was not included in the drug category? The popularity of alcohol use means that almost everyone has an idea about its effects. Some of these ideas are based on fact, but frequently people's beliefs about alcohol are misconceptions based on myth and "common" wisdom. Our job is to present the empirical evidence that describes not only the acute effects of the drug and its mechanism of action in the brain but also some of its long-term effects on other organ systems.

Alcohol has a long history of use

Alcohol use in America began with the very first immigrants, but its history is really very much longer than that. Perhaps as early as 8000 BCE, mead was brewed from fermented honey, producing the first alcoholic beverage. Archeological evidence shows that about 3700 BCE, the Egyptians prepared the first very hearty beer, called *hek*, which might have been thick enough to stand up a spoon in, and wine may have first come from Babylonia in 1700 BCE. Later still, the popularity of alcohol may have contributed to the decline of the Roman Empire. Certainly, many historians believe that the civilization was doomed by the corruption of society, alcohol intemperance, and moral decay, but the mental instability of the Roman nobility is an additional factor. Some members of the noble class exhibited signs of confusion and dementia, which may have been due to lead poisoning caused by alcohol prepared with a flavor enhancer that had a high lead content. *Aqua vitae* (meaning "the water of life" in Latin) represents the first distilled conversion of wine into brandy during the Middle Ages in Italy. Production of gin by the Dutch in the early seventeenth century is frequently credited with the start of serious alcohol misuse in Europe. Not only was gin far more potent than wine and very inexpensive to buy, but it was introduced during a time of social upheaval. Gin turned out to be a common method of dealing with the poor living

conditions and social instability caused by the newly created urban societies following the feudal period. Gin consumption became associated with the lower class, while the more respectable middle class drank beer (**FIGURE 10.1**).

Colonial Americans brought their habit of heavy drinking from Europe, and alcohol had a large part in their daily lives. The American tavern was not just a place for food and drink and overnight accommodation but was also the focal point in each town for conducting business and local politics and for mail delivery. The Continental Army supplied each soldier with a daily ration of rum, and employers and farmers supplied their workers with liquor on the job. Students, then as now, had reputations for hard drinking, and Harvard University operated its own brewery. At some point, the celebrations at Harvard's graduation ceremonies became so wild and unrestrained that the administration developed strict rules of behavior. American drinking of alcohol remained at a high level until the 1830s, when the temperance movement began a campaign to educate society about the dangers of long-term alcohol consumption. Although their initial goal was to reduce rather than prevent alcohol consumption, later

FIGURE 10.1 **Engraving of Gin Lane** The artist William Hogarth (1697–1764) depicted the popular opinion that the "lower classes" drank gin and got drunk.

offshoots of the group used social and religious arguments to convince Americans that alcohol itself was the source of evil in the world and was directly responsible for broken families, poverty, social disorder, and crime. Some of these same arguments are currently being used to regulate the use of other drugs in our society, such as marijuana, heroin, and cocaine.

In 1917, Congress passed a law that in 1920 became the Eighteenth Amendment to the United States Constitution; it prohibited the "manufacture, sale, transportation, and importation" of liquor. Despite its intent, the period of Prohibition increased illegal manufacturing that often produced highly toxic forms of alcohol, increased consumption of distilled spirits rather than beer because they were easier to hide and store, and made drinking in illegal speakeasies a fad. Medicinal "tonics" containing up to 75% alcohol became increasingly popular. Worst of all, Prohibition increased the activity of organized crime mobs that were heavily involved in the sale and distribution of alcohol. By 1933, most Americans realized that the experiment was a failure, and the Eighteenth Amendment was repealed by Congress during the presidency of Franklin D. Roosevelt. (For a brief history of alcohol use in America, see Goode, 1993.) Presumably as a reflection of this realization, at the onset of the COVID-19 pandemic in the United States, many local and state governments ordered non-essential retail businesses to shut down in an effort to slow disease transmission. Notably, liquor stores in most jurisdictions were recognized as essential businesses and were allowed to operate in order to prevent alcohol-dependent individuals from experiencing dangerous withdrawal symptoms or obtaining alcohol from unsafe sources. Today, the use of alcohol is restricted by age and circumstance (e.g., prohibited when operating a motor vehicle) and is regulated to some extent by an increased tax on the cost of consumption (the "sin tax"). Such liquor laws vary by state. Phillip Cook's book *Paying the Tab: The Costs and Benefits of Alcohol Control* (2007) provides a history of the attempts to "legislate morality" and discusses the potential to control alcohol use with supply-side economics.

What is an alcohol and where does it come from?

Alcohols come in many forms, and although they have similarities in structure, they have very different uses. Ethyl alcohol is the alcohol with which we are most familiar because it is used as a beverage. An ethyl alcohol molecule has only two carbon atoms, a complement of hydrogens, plus the –OH (hydroxyl group) characteristic of all alcohols (**FIGURE 10.2**). Methyl alcohol, or wood alcohol, has an even simpler chemical structure but is highly toxic if consumed, because the liver metabolites of methyl alcohol include formic acid and formaldehyde. Drinking wood alcohol causes

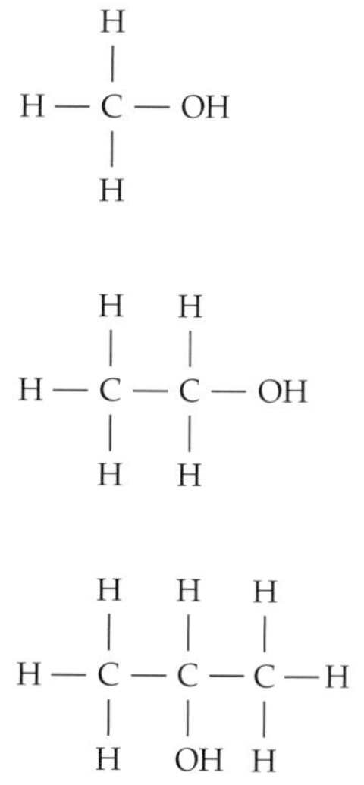

FIGURE 10.2 Chemical structures of three commonly used forms of alcohol

blindness, coma, and death. Denatured alcohol is typically a mixture of ethanol and other organic solvents, including methanol and acetone, as well as bittering agents to make a toxic and unpalatable solution to discourage drinking. Denatured ethanol and methanol are commonly used as fuel, antifreeze, and industrial solvents. Isopropyl alcohol has a small molecular side chain that changes its characteristics and makes it most useful as rubbing alcohol or as a disinfectant. It is also dangerous to consume.

Ethyl alcohol (or ethanol) is the form we focus on in this chapter. It is produced by fermentation—a process that occurs naturally whenever microscopic yeast cells in the air fall on a product containing sugar, such as honey, fruit, sugar cane, or grains like rye, corn, and others. The material that provides the sugar determines the type of alcoholic beverage, for example grapes (wine), rice (sake), or grains (beer). Yeast converts each sugar molecule into two molecules of alcohol and two molecules of carbon dioxide. This fermentation process is entirely natural and explains why alcohol has been discovered in cultures all over the world. The fermentation process continues until the concentration of alcohol is about 15%, beyond which the yeast is unable to survive. Most wines have alcohol content in this range. While commercially scaled fermentation processes are well controlled and use purified yeast cultures, contamination with microbes, including other yeast strains, bacteria, and mold, can result in the formation of other volatile organic compounds, including methanol, in addition to ethanol. As discussed in the section below on ethanol metabolism, low concentrations of methanol present in ethanol-containing beverages are generally tolerated; however, poorly controlled distillation to achieve higher alcohol concentrations can result in dangerously high methanol content. Distillation requires heating the fermented mixture to the point where the alcohol boils off in steam (since it has a lower boiling point than water), leaving some of the water behind. The alcohol vapor passes through a series of cooling tubes (called a still) and condenses to be collected as "hard liquor," or distilled spirits, such as whiskey, brandy, rum, tequila, and so forth. The alcohol concentration of these beverages varies from 40% to 50%. A second way to increase alcohol concentrations to above 15% is to add additional alcohol; this procedure is used to make fortified wines such as sherry. Flavoring and sugar may also be added to produce liqueurs such as crème de menthe (mint), amaretto (almond), and ouzo (anise). Lastly, alcohol concentration can be increased through the process of fractional freezing, whereby the fermented mixture is cooled until partially frozen, and the ice crystals are removed, resulting in the removal of water while the unfrozen alcohol remains in the mixture. This process is used to make ice beer, and less commonly to make applejack. Unlike distillation, which allows for the selective concentration of ethanol, because fractional freezing relies on the removal of only water, this process results in higher concentrations of ethanol along with any impurities, such as methanol, that are present in the fermented mixture. Regardless of the form, alcohol is high in calories, which means that it provides heat or energy when it is metabolized. However, no nutritional value is associated with those calories, because alcohol provides no proteins, vitamins, or minerals that are necessary components of a normal diet. For this reason, individuals who chronically consume large quantities of alcohol in lieu of food frequently suffer from inadequate nutrition, leading to health problems and brain damage.

Although it would make the most sense to describe alcohol content as a percentage, if you look at a bottle of distilled spirits, you are more likely to see alcohol content described according to "proof." This convention is based on an old British army custom of testing an alcoholic product by pouring it on gunpowder and attempting to light it. If the alcohol content is 50%, the gunpowder burns, but if the alcohol is less concentrated, the remaining water content prevents the burning. Hence, the burning of the sample was 100% proof that it was at least 50% alcohol. The proof number now corresponds to twice the percent of alcohol concentration.

The pharmacokinetics of alcohol determines its bioavailability

To evaluate the effects of alcohol in the central nervous system (CNS), we need to know how much alcohol is freely available to enter the brain from the blood (i.e., its bioavailability). Ethyl alcohol is a unique drug in several respects. Although alcohol is a small, simple molecule that cannot be ionized, it nevertheless readily mixes with water and is not high in lipid solubility. Despite these characteristics, it is easily absorbed from the GI tract and diffuses throughout the body, readily entering most tissues, including the brain. The rates of absorption, distribution, and clearance of alcohol are modified by many factors, all of which contribute to the highly variable blood levels that occur after ingestion of a fixed amount of the drug. For this reason, behavioral effects are described on the basis of **blood-alcohol concentration** (**BAC**) rather than the amount ingested. In general, it takes a BAC of 0.02% (i.e., 20 mg of alcohol per 100 ml of blood) to produce measurable behavioral effects. Keep in mind that one "drink" may take the form of one 12-ounce can of beer, one 5-ounce glass of wine, a cocktail with 1.5 ounces of spirits, or a 12-ounce wine cooler, but each will raise blood levels by the equivalent amount (**FIGURE 10.3**).

ABSORPTION AND DISTRIBUTION Since oral administration is about the only way the drug is used recreationally (although see the case study in Box 1.2 in Chapter 1), absorption will necessarily occur from the GI tract: about 10% from the stomach and 90% from the small intestine. The small molecules move across membrane barriers by passive diffusion from the higher concentration on one side (the GI tract) to the lower concentration on the other (blood). Of course, this means that the more alcohol you drink in a short period of time or the more alcohol you drink in an undiluted form (i.e., more concentrated), the more rapid will be the movement from

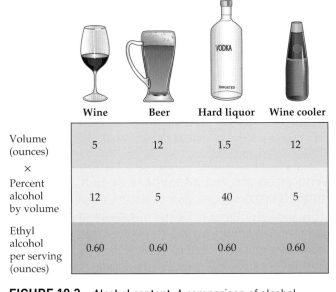

	Wine	Beer	Hard liquor	Wine cooler
Volume (ounces)	5	12	1.5	12
× Percent alcohol by volume	12	5	40	5
Ethyl alcohol per serving (ounces)	0.60	0.60	0.60	0.60

FIGURE 10.3 Alcohol content A comparison of alcohol content of various beverages shows an equivalent amount despite differences in volume. To calculate the amount of alcohol in a given beverage, multiply the number of ounces in the container by the percent alcohol content by volume. Note that the alcohol content of beer varies from 3% to well over 10% for some microbrews.

stomach and intestine to blood, producing a higher blood level (**FIGURE 10.4A**). The presence of food in the stomach slows absorption because it delays movement into the small intestine through the pyloric sphincter, a muscle that regulates the movement of material from stomach to intestine (**FIGURE 10.4B**). The delayed absorption means alcohol dehydrogenase has more opportunity to metabolize alcohol in the stomach (see the next section on metabolism). Milk seems to be particularly effective in delaying absorption. In contrast, carbonated alcoholic beverages such as champagne are absorbed more rapidly because carbonation speeds the movement of materials from the stomach into the intestine.

Sex differences also exist in the absorption of alcohol from the stomach, because certain enzymes (particularly alcohol dehydrogenase) that are present in gastric fluid are about 60% more active in men than in women, leaving a higher concentration of alcohol that will be absorbed more rapidly in women (Freeza et al., 1990). Further, taking aspirin generally inhibits gastric alcohol dehydrogenase, but to a greater extent in women than in men. Because women have lower levels of alcohol dehydrogenase to begin with, aspirin use before drinking may essentially eliminate any gastric metabolism of alcohol in women (Roine et al., 1990). Ulcer medications (such as Tagamet or Zantac) also impair gastric metabolism, increasing alcohol concentrations and hence increasing absorption.

Once alcohol is in the blood, it circulates throughout the body. It readily moves, by passive diffusion, from the higher concentration in the blood to all tissues and fluid compartments. Body size and sex play a part in the distribution of alcohol and in the magnitude of its effect. The same amount of alcohol, say one beer, is much more concentrated in the average woman than in the average man, because her fluid volume is much smaller as a result of her size and because women have a higher fat-to-water ratio.

METABOLISM Of the alcohol that reaches the general circulation, approximately 95% is metabolized by the liver before it is excreted as carbon dioxide and water in the urine. The remaining 5% is excreted by the lungs and can be measured in one's breath by using a Breathalyzer, which provides law enforcement officials a means to calculate alcohol levels. Alcohol metabolism is different from that of most other drugs in that alcohol follows zero-order kinetics (see Chapter 1), whereby the rate of oxidation is constant over time and does not occur more quickly when the drug is more concentrated in the blood. The rate of metabolism is quite variable from one person to another, but the average rate is approximately 1 to 1.5 ounces or 12 to 18 ml of 80-proof alcohol per hour. Because the metabolic rate is relatively constant for an individual, if the rate of consumption is faster than the rate of metabolism, alcohol accumulates in the body, and the individual becomes intoxicated.

Several enzyme systems in the liver are capable of oxidizing alcohol. The most important is **alcohol dehydrogenase**, which we already know is also found in the stomach and reduces the amount of available alcohol for absorption—a good example of the first-pass effect (see Chapter 1). Alcohol dehydrogenase converts alcohol to acetaldehyde, a potentially toxic intermediate, which normally is rapidly modified further by **aldehyde dehydrogenase** (**ALDH**) to form acetic acid. Further oxidation yields carbon dioxide, water, and energy (**FIGURE 10.5A**). As mentioned above, alcohol dehydrogenase and ALDH can also convert methanol to formaldehyde and formic acid, respectively. While methanol itself, like ethanol, can be acutely toxic in high doses due to CNS depressant effects, the production of formic acid interferes with mitochondrial function, resulting in severe metabolic disturbances.

Because methanol toxicity relies on the conversion of methanol by the same enzymes that metabolize ethanol, the antidote for methanol poisoning includes treatment with the alcohol dehydrogenase inhibitor, fomepizole. Interestingly, if fomepizole is unavailable, ethanol can be administered as an antidote, because

(A) Different oral doses

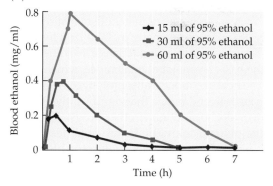

(B) Full or empty stomach

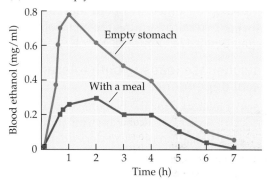

FIGURE 10.4   Blood levels of alcohol after oral administration
(A) Larger oral doses of alcohol produce higher concentrations in the stomach, and this causes faster absorption and higher peak blood levels. (B) The presence of food in the stomach slows absorption of alcohol and prevents the sharp peak in blood level.

(A)

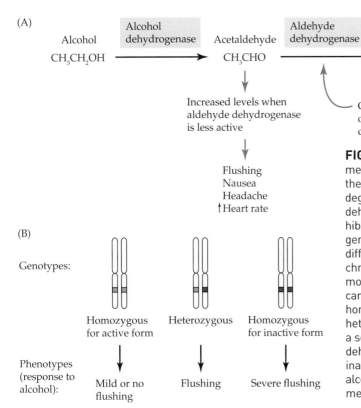

Alcohol
CH_3CH_2OH → [Alcohol dehydrogenase] → Acetaldehyde CH_3CHO → [Aldehyde dehydrogenase] → Acetic acid CH_3COOH → [Oxidation reaction] → Carbon dioxide $CO_2 + H_2O$ + Energy

Increased levels when aldehyde dehydrogenase is less active

Flushing
Nausea
Headache
↑Heart rate

Genetic differences in enzyme activity
or
drug inhibition (e.g., Disulfiram)

(B)

Genotypes:

Homozygous for active form   Heterozygous   Homozygous for inactive form

Phenotypes (response to alcohol):

Mild or no flushing   Flushing   Severe flushing

FIGURE 10.5 **Metabolism of alcohol** (A) The principal metabolic pathway for alcohol involves the formation of the toxic metabolite acetaldehyde, which must be further degraded to acetic acid. Genetic differences in aldehyde dehydrogenase (ALDH) and the use of certain drugs can inhibit enzyme activity, causing toxic effects. (B) Three possible genetic variations of ALDH are responsible for large individual differences in response to alcohol. Each person has a pair of chromosomes with the *ALDH* gene—one contributed by the mother and the second by the father. The two chromosomes can have either the same form (allele), making the individual homozygous, or two different alleles, making the individual heterozygous. Individuals with two inactive alleles experience a severe reaction if they consume alcohol, because acetaldehyde levels remain high. Those with one active and one inactive allele show some flushing response following alcohol ingestion. Two active alleles produce normal metabolism of acetaldehyde.

like fomepizole, ethanol competes with methanol for alcohol dehydrogenase, slowing the formation of toxic methanol metabolites and thereby allowing methanol to be excreted by the kidneys. For this reason, low methanol concentrations that may naturally occur in some fermented drinks generally do not meet the threshold for toxicity provided the ethanol concentration is sufficiently high.

ALDH exists in several genetically determined forms with varying activities. About 10% of Asian individuals (e.g., Japanese, Korean, Chinese) have genes that code only for an inactive form of the enzyme (**FIGURE 10.5B**). For these individuals, drinking even small amounts of alcohol produces very high levels of acetaldehyde, causing intense flushing, nausea and vomiting, tachycardia, headache, sweating, dizziness, and confusion. Because these individuals almost always totally abstain from using alcohol, they are at no risk for alcohol use disorder (AUD). Another 40% of the Asian population has genes that code for both the active and inactive enzyme. These heterozygous individuals exhibit a more intense response to alcohol but not necessarily an unpleasant one. They are partially protected from alcohol dependence and have less vulnerability, making the *ALDH* gene a marker for low risk of AUD.

The second class of liver enzymes that convert alcohol to acetaldehyde are those that belong to the **cytochrome P450** family. The enzyme of importance within this family is CYP2E1, which is sometimes called the **microsomal ethanol oxidizing system** (**MEOS**). These enzymes metabolize many drugs in addition to alcohol. When alcohol is

consumed along with these other drugs, they must compete for the same enzyme molecules; therefore, alcohol consumption may lead to high and potentially dangerous levels of the other drugs. If you drink alcohol, be sure to look for warnings on both prescription and OTC medications before consuming alcohol with any other drug. In contrast to the acute effect, when alcohol is consumed on a regular basis, these liver enzymes *increase* in number, which increases the rate of metabolism of alcohol as well as any other drugs normally metabolized by these enzymes. The process, called **induction** of liver enzymes, serves as the basis for metabolic tolerance, which is described in the next section. Finally, prolonged heavy use of alcohol causes liver damage that significantly impairs metabolism of alcohol and many other drugs.

Given the pharmacokinetic factors just described, you know that the amount of alcohol in the blood depends on how much an individual has consumed and on rates of absorption and metabolism. **TABLE 10.1** provides a rough estimate of BAC that is based on the number of drinks consumed in 1 hour and the body weight of the individual, assuming the metabolism of approximately 1 ounce per hour.

Chronic alcohol use leads to both tolerance and physical dependence

Several types of tolerance for the biobehavioral effects of alcohol occur with repeated consumption. Prolonged use can also lead to physical dependence and cross-dependence with other sedative–hypnotic drugs such as the benzodiazepines.

TABLE 10.1   Estimated BAC and Impairment for Men and Women According to Body Weight

	Approximate Blood-Alcohol Concentration (Men)							
	Body weight (pounds)							
Drinks	100	120	140	160	180	200	220	240
0	0.00	0.00	0.00	0.00	0.00	0.00	0.00	0.00
1	0.04	0.03	0.03	0.02	0.02	0.02	0.02	0.02
2	0.08	0.06	0.05	0.05	0.04	0.04	0.03	0.03
3	0.11	0.09	0.08	0.07	0.06	0.06	0.05	0.05
4	0.15	0.12	0.11	0.09	0.08	0.08	0.07	0.06
5	0.19	0.16	0.13	0.12	0.11	0.09	0.09	0.08
6	0.23	0.19	0.16	0.14	0.13	0.11	0.10	0.09
7	0.26	0.22	0.19	0.16	0.15	0.13	0.12	0.11
8	0.30	0.25	0.21	0.19	0.17	0.15	0.14	0.13
9	0.34	0.28	0.24	0.21	0.19	0.17	0.15	0.14
10	0.38	0.31	0.27	0.23	0.21	0.19	0.17	0.16

	Approximate Blood-Alcohol Concentration (Women)							
	Body weight (pounds)							
Drinks	90	100	120	140	160	180	200	220
0	0.00	0.00	0.00	0.00	0.00	0.00	0.00	0.00
1	0.05	0.05	0.04	0.03	0.03	0.03	0.02	0.02
2	0.10	0.09	0.08	0.07	0.06	0.05	0.05	0.04
3	0.15	0.14	0.11	0.10	0.09	0.08	0.07	0.06
4	0.20	0.18	0.15	0.13	0.11	0.10	0.09	0.08
5	0.25	0.23	0.19	0.16	0.14	0.13	0.11	0.10
6	0.30	0.27	0.23	0.19	0.17	0.15	0.14	0.12
7	0.35	0.32	0.27	0.23	0.20	0.18	0.16	0.14
8	0.40	0.36	0.30	0.26	0.23	0.20	0.18	0.17
9	0.45	0.41	0.34	0.29	0.26	0.23	0.20	0.19
10	0.51	0.45	0.38	0.32	0.28	0.25	0.23	0.21

Source: After L. J. Roberts and B. S. McCrady. 2003. *Alcohol Problems in Intimate Relationships: Identification and Intervention, A Guide for Marriage and Family Therapists.* National Institute on Alcohol Abuse and Alcoholism (NIAAA): Washington, D.C.; adapted from BAC Charts produced by the National Clearinghouse of Alcohol and Drug Information.

TOLERANCE   The effects of alcohol are significantly reduced when the drug is administered repeatedly; hence, **tolerance** occurs. There is also **cross-tolerance** with a variety of other drugs in the sedative–hypnotic class, including the barbiturates and the benzodiazepines. Each of the four mechanisms that we described in Chapter 1 contributes to alcohol tolerance.

1. **Acute tolerance** occurs within a single exposure to alcohol. Several of the subjective and behavioral drug effects are greater while the blood level of alcohol is increasing and are less while the blood level is falling even if the BAC is the same at both times (**FIGURE 10.6A**). LeBlanc and colleagues (1975) found that alcohol-induced

incoordination in rats was 50% less while blood levels were falling, as measured by the amount of time off a mini-treadmill during a single exposure to alcohol. More problematic is the finding that interoceptive cues that determine the subjective evaluation of intoxication undergo acute tolerance, particularly in binge drinkers,* although in some studies, social drinkers also reported feeling less intoxicated by alcohol on the declining limb of the blood-alcohol curve than on the ascending limb. Failure to accurately predict their blood-alcohol levels and the amount of

---

*Binge drinking is generally defined as five or more drinks for men and four or more drinks for women in a single 2-hour session.

impairment they will experience leads individuals to risk driving while legally intoxicated. Unfortunately, although binge drinkers perceived that they were less intoxicated on the descending limb of the blood-alcohol curve and were more willing to drive an automobile at that time, their driving performance as measured on a simulated driving test was significantly worse than on the ascending limb. Deterioration of driving skills may have been due to fatigue or to the fact that these individuals failed to compensate for their intoxication, which they failed to recognize (Marczinski and Fillmore, 2009). This differential development of acute tolerance for various effects of alcohol may explain why binge drinkers are responsible for about 80% of the alcohol-impaired driving incidents each year. Why acute tolerance occurs is not entirely clear, but some rapid adaptation of neuronal membranes is one possibility.

2. Chronic alcohol use significantly increases the P450 liver microsomal enzymes that metabolize the drug. More rapid metabolism means that blood levels of the drug will be reduced (**FIGURE 10.6B**), producing diminished effects. This is **metabolic tolerance**.

3. Neurons also adapt to the continued presence of alcohol by making compensatory changes in cell function. The mechanism of this **pharmacodynamic tolerance** is described in later sections of this chapter dealing with specific neurotransmitters.

4. Finally, there is also clear evidence of **behavioral tolerance**. Rats, like humans, seem to be able to learn to adjust their behaviors when allowed to practice while under the influence of alcohol (Wenger et al., 1981). Although initially unsuccessful, rats readily learned to run on a treadmill by trial and error despite administration of alcohol. Other rats given the same amount of drug each day *after* their treadmill session showed only minimal improvement when tested on the treadmill under the influence of alcohol. This small amount of improvement may have been due to metabolic tolerance.

Classical conditioning may also contribute to behavioral tolerance. In animal experiments, alcohol initially reduces body temperature, but when the drug is administered repeatedly in the same environment, a compensatory increase in body temperature occurs, and this reduces the initial hypothermia (low body temperature). If these animals are given saline instead of alcohol in this environment, they show *only* the compensatory mechanism and their body temperature rises (hyperthermia). The importance of environment

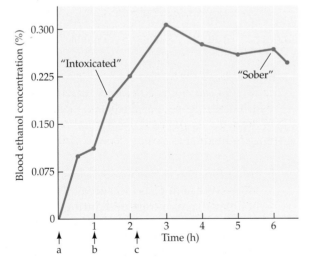

(A) Acute tolerance

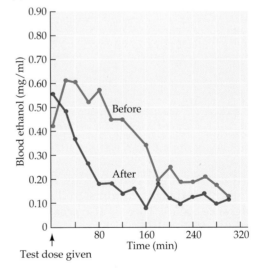

(B) Metabolic tolerance

FIGURE 10.6 Tolerance to alcohol (A) In a trial using a human participant given three doses of alcohol (a,b,c), signs of intoxication (such as incoordination in the balance beam test) appeared during the rising phase of blood-alcohol levels at about 0.20%. However, as blood alcohol was declining, the person became "sober" at a higher concentration (about 0.265%), showing that acute tolerance had occurred. In this case *sober* does not mean unimpaired in skills other than the balance beam test. Note that the high blood levels for intoxication reflect the fact that the participant was a chronically heavy user of alcohol. (B) Blood-alcohol levels were calculated at 20-minute intervals after a test dose was given at time zero. The blue line represents blood levels before a 7-day period of drinking; the red line shows blood levels in the same person after 7 days of drinking (3.2 grams of ethanol per kilogram of body weight per day in individual doses). Tolerance after repeated alcohol consumption is shown by the more rapid decrease in blood alcohol. (A after I. E. Mirsky et al. 1941. *Q J Studies Alcohol* 2: 35–45; B after J. H. Mendelson et al. 1965. *Metabolism* 14: 1255–1266.)

is further demonstrated by evidence that in a novel environment, tolerance is significantly less, because no conditioned hyperthermia is present (Le et al., 1979).

PHYSICAL DEPENDENCE We know that prolonged use of alcohol produces **physical dependence**, because a significant withdrawal syndrome occurs when drinking is terminated. As you already know, the intensity and duration of withdrawal (i.e., abstinence) signs are dependent on the amount and duration of drug taking (**FIGURE 10.7**). In addition, alcohol shows **cross-dependence** with other drugs in the sedative–hypnotic class, including barbiturates and benzodiazepines. A quick review of Chapter 1 will remind you that withdrawal signs can be eliminated by taking the drug again or by taking any drug in the same class that shows cross-dependence.

Some investigators suggest that the **hangover** that occurs after even a single bout of heavy drinking may in fact be evidence of withdrawal, although others consider it a sign of acute toxicity. Possible explanations for hangover symptoms include residual acetaldehyde in the body; alcohol-induced gastric irritation; rebound drop in blood sugar; excess fluid loss the previous night; sleep deprivation; and perhaps toxic effects from congeners, which are small quantities of by-products from fermentation and distillation, including acetone and other alcohols, such as methanol (Rohsenow and Howland, 2010). The classic symptoms of hangover are recognized by many social drinkers who on occasion consume an excess of alcohol.

Among the usual signs are nausea and perhaps vomiting, headache, dehydration, increased light sensitivity, fatigue, and general malaise. Psychological symptoms can include mild cognitive dysfunction as well as feelings of depression, anxiety, and irritability.

Withdrawal from repeated heavy drinking over months or years produces an intense abstinence syndrome that develops within a few hours after drinking stops and may continue over 2 to 4 days, depending on the dose previously consumed. Generally, symptoms include tremor (the "shakes") and intense anxiety, high blood pressure and rapid heart rate, excessive sweating, rapid breathing, and nausea and vomiting. A small percentage of alcohol-dependent individuals undergoing withdrawal demonstrate more-severe effects called **delirium tremens**, or **DTs**. Signs of DTs include irritability, headaches, agitation, and confusion. In addition, convulsions; vivid and frightening hallucinations that include snakes, rats, or insects crawling on their bodies; total disorientation; and delirium may occur. Withdrawal signs such as unstable blood pressure, depression and anxiety including panic attacks, and sleep disturbances may last for several weeks. Because the most extreme symptoms are potentially life threatening, detoxification of an individual with AUD (see the section on AUD later in the chapter) should always be done under medical supervision. The signs of withdrawal are characteristically a "rebound" phenomenon and represent a hyperexcitable state of the nervous system after the prolonged depressant effects of alcohol. The neuroadaptive mechanisms responsible are described more completely later in this chapter.

Alcohol affects many organ systems

Alcohol, like all drugs, produces dose-dependent effects that are also dependent on the duration of drug taking. Because it is so readily absorbed and widely distributed, alcohol has effects on most organ systems of the body. As you read this section, keep in mind that most individuals who use alcohol drink in ways that do not increase their risk for alcohol use problems, and at low doses alcohol may even have some minor beneficial effects. However, the transition from moderate to heavy drinking that leads to the chronic intoxication associated with AUD is a part of the same dose–response curve, and the precise point at which alcohol becomes damaging is not clear for a particular individual.

A second thing to keep in mind is that the environment and expectations have a great influence on many of the behavioral effects of alcohol. A host of well-controlled studies clearly show that an individual's *belief* that alcohol will produce relaxation, sexual desire, or aggression may have a far greater effect on the individual's behavior than the pharmacological effects of the drug, at least at low to moderate doses. Pronounced behavioral effects occur under placebo

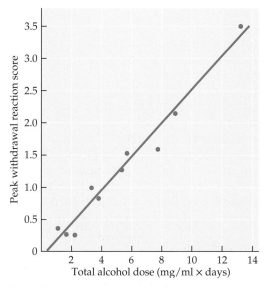

FIGURE 10.7 **Relationship between alcohol dose and withdrawal severity** A linear relationship exists between the total alcohol dose (amount of alcohol consumed multiplied by number of days of alcohol exposure) and the maximum withdrawal response at abstinence in mice. Withdrawal response was calculated on the basis of standard physiological and behavioral measures. (After D. B. Goldstein. 1972. *J Pharmacol Exp Ther* 180: 203–210.)

conditions when the individual believes that alcohol has been ingested (**WEB BOX 10.1**). As you might expect, the environment plays less of a role in the effects of alcohol as the dose increases.

CNS EFFECT   As is true for all drugs in the sedative–hypnotic class, at the lowest doses individuals feel relaxed and less anxious. In a quiet setting they may feel somewhat sleepy, but in a social setting where sensory stimulation is increased, the relaxed state is demonstrated by reduced social inhibition, which may make individuals more gregarious, talkative, and friendly or inappropriately outspoken. Self-perception and judgment are somewhat impaired, and one may feel more confident than reality proves true. Reduced judgment and overconfidence may increase risk-taking behaviors and may make sexual encounters more likely. In a large representative sample of 12,069 young men and women, a significant relationship between alcohol use and sexual risk taking was found even after controls were applied for age, education, and family income (Parker et al., 1994). Because the relationship between alcohol use and unsafe sex is correlational, no clear cause-and-effect relationship can be assumed, and other factors such as rebellion against societal expectations may be responsible for both.

Of additional concern is the effect of alcohol-induced loss of judgment on the initiation of unsafe sex practices that may lead to increased risk for AIDS and other sexually transmitted diseases. Using a natural quasi-experimental design including cross-state comparisons, Staras and colleagues (2016) investigated the relationship between alcohol taxes, which have been shown to inversely impact consumption, and the incidence of sexually transmitted infections as quantified by the National Notifiable Disease Surveillance System. When compared with states with no change in the alcohol tax, they found that after the 50% increase in the tax in Maryland in 2011, gonorrhea rates decreased 24% over the 1.5-year study period. The researchers argue that the practical application of their results should provide incentive to change tax rates for the public health benefits.

Acute effects of alcohol on memory vary with dose and task difficulty (Jung, 2001). At low doses, memory deficits are based more on expectation than on the quantity of alcohol actually consumed. Further, under high-stress conditions, alcohol may enhance performance by minimizing the damaging effects of anxiety. However, high doses of alcohol rapidly consumed may produce total amnesia for events that occur during intoxication, despite the fact that the individual is behaving quite normally. This amnesia is called a **blackout**, and it is a common occurrence for individuals with AUD but also occurs in about 25% of social drinkers (Campbell and Hodgins, 1993).

Reduced coordination leads to slurred speech, impaired fine motor skills, and delayed reaction time. Impaired reaction times for multiple stimuli, along with reductions in attention, increased sedation and drowsiness, and impaired judgment and emotional control, contribute to the increased probability of being involved in automobile accidents. In 2018, nearly one-third of all traffic-related fatalities in the United States involved alcohol-impaired drivers (NHTSA, 2019). **FIGURE 10.8A** shows the distinct temporal pattern of high-risk alcohol-related deaths. In addition, a clear statistical relationship between BAC and the relative risk for an accident has been reported. At a BAC lower than 0.05%, the chances of having an accident are about the same as for nondrinking drivers, but between 0.05% and 0.10%, the curve rises steeply to seven times the nondrinking rate. It is this large increase that has prompted all states to change their blood level for legal intoxication from 0.10% to 0.08%, while most European and Asian countries consider driving with a BAC of 0.02% to 0.05% as driving under the influence. Beyond 0.10%, risk increases dramatically by 20 to 50 times. However, the relationship is complex, and BAC interacts with both age and driving experience (**FIGURE 10.8B**). Crash risk is higher for young people than for older people at all levels of BAC. See Table 10.1 for estimates of the amounts of alcohol that must be consumed in 1 hour to reach the BAC that increases risk.

In addition to involvement in automobile fatalities, alcohol use is associated with homicide, rape, and other violent activities, although the role of the direct pharmacological effect of alcohol is less clear. **WEB BOX 10.2** looks at this relationship. Aggression and many of the other effects of alcohol on behavior are highly dependent on the environment, the user's mental set, and one's expectations.

With increasing doses, mild sedation deepens and produces sleep. Alcohol suppresses rapid-eye-movement (REM) episodes (periods when the most dreaming occurs), and withdrawal after repeated use produces a rebound in REM sleep that may interfere with normal sleep patterns and produce nightmares. Higher doses produce unconsciousness and death. The blood-alcohol level that is lethal in 50% of the population is in the range of 0.45%, which is only about five or six times the blood level (0.08%) that produces intoxication. Fortunately, most people do not reach a lethal blood level because at about 0.15%, vomiting may occur, and a BAC of 0.35% usually causes unconsciousness, thereby preventing further drinking. However, if alcohol is consumed very rapidly, as might occur in binge drinking, it is possible that a lethal dose can be consumed before the individual passes out.

The usual symptoms of **alcohol poisoning** include unconsciousness; vomiting; slow and irregular breathing; and skin that is cold, clammy, and pale bluish in

(A)

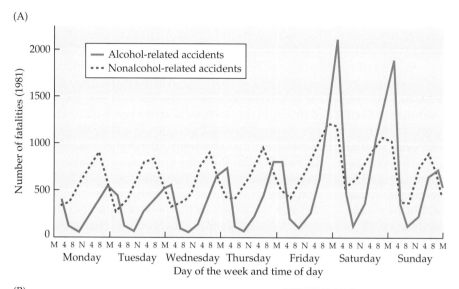

(B)

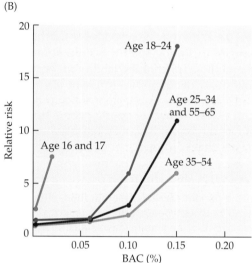

FIGURE 10.8 Relationship between alcohol use and traffic accidents (A) The number of fatal auto accidents varies by day of the week, time of day, and alcohol involvement. Note that alcohol-related fatalities peak on Friday and Saturday nights after midnight and that on other days, accidents involving alcohol also occur most frequently late at night. Non-alcohol-related fatalities appear to be greatest during rush hours on weekdays and just before midnight on weekends. (B) The relationship between BAC and relative risk for auto accidents is affected by several factors, including age of the driver and years of driving experience. Note that, in general, alcohol has a less detrimental effect on driving as drivers get older, but the 55- to 65-year age group is similar to the 25- to 34-year age group, which may indicate an interaction with age-related decreases in reaction time. The rapid rise in the number of accidents at BAC over 0.10% has prompted all states to reduce the definition of legal intoxication from 0.10% to 0.08%. M, midnight; N, noon. (A after National Institute on Alcoholism and Alcohol Abuse [NIAAA]. 1983. *Fifth Special Report to the U.S. Congress on Alcohol and Health*. Government Printing Office: Washington, DC; B after OECD. 1978. *Road research: New research on the role of alcohol and drugs in road accidents. A report prepared by an Organization for Economic Co-operation and Development [OECD] Road Research Group*.)

color. Death from acute alcohol ingestion is caused by depression of the respiratory control center in the brainstem. Once the respiratory mechanism is depressed, the drinker can survive for about 5 minutes, although brain damage may result from oxygen deprivation. The CDC (2019) reported an average annual death rate of 2288 from alcohol poisoning between 2011 and 2015. The occurrence was the highest among men, accounting for 76% of the total overdose deaths. Some of the dose-dependent effects of alcohol are summarized in **TABLE 10.2**.

BRAIN DAMAGE Brain damage that occurs after many years of heavy alcohol consumption is caused by the interaction of several factors, including high levels of alcohol, elevated acetaldehyde, liver deficiency, and inadequate nutrition. In particular, heavy alcohol use produces a serious deficiency in vitamin B_1 (thiamine) as the result of both a poor diet and failure to absorb that vitamin, as well as

TABLE 10.2 Blood-Alcohol Concentration and Effects on Behavior

BAC (%)	Effects on behavior
0.00–0.05%	Minimal effects on speech, memory coordination; slight relaxation, mild mood elevation
0.06–0.15%	Increased relaxation; impaired memory, attention and coordination; driving ability significantly impaired; increased risk of injury to self and others.
0.16–0.30%	Significant impairment in judgement and decision-making, as well as memory and attention; coordination and balance significantly impaired; signs of alcohol overdose, such as vomiting and loss of consciousness are evident.
0.31–0.45%	Significant risk of coma and/or death due to suppression of vital functions.

Source: National Institute on Alcohol Abuse and Alcoholism, 2021.

other nutrients, during digestion. Because thiamine is critical for brain glucose metabolism, its deficit causes cell death. Lack of vitamin B_1 may lead to Wernicke's encephalopathy (WE). WE is characterized by confusion and disorientation, as well as poor coordination, tremors, weakness, and ataxia (see **BOX 10.1**). Often there is some form of oculomotor dysfunction such as abnormal eye movements or double vision. WE results from lesions in the periaqueductal gray, medial thalamus, and mammillary bodies of the hypothalamus. When treated early, the symptoms are readily reversible with massive vitamin supplementation that reverses the biochemical damage. Without treatment the brain damage is permanent and leads to death in approximately 20% of cases. WE is associated with excessive alcohol use but can be caused by malnutrition, weight loss surgery, HIV/AIDS, anorexia nervosa, and other conditions that may cause vitamin B_1 deficiency. A high proportion of patients who survive WE develop Korsakoff syndrome (in combination, called Wernicke–Korsakoff syndrome), which is characterized by potentially irreversible memory loss, anterograde amnesia (inability to form new memories), decreased

spontaneity, confabulation (creating false memories), hallucinations, and personality changes. Korsakoff syndrome is a result of permanent damage to thalamic nuclei and brain regions involved with memory subsequent to lack of thiamine. Although nutritional deficits are not the sole cause of the disorder, the importance of thiamine to the degenerative process is evident in animal studies. Feeding animals a thiamine-deficient diet or treating them with a thiamine antagonist produces lesions in the same brain areas and also impairs learning and memory (Langlais and Savage, 1995).

Although thiamine deficiency causes the selective damage described in the previous paragraph, other brain areas frequently show cell loss that seems to be unrelated to diet. The enlarged ventricles in the brains of individuals with AUD attest to the extensive shrinkage of brain tissue (**FIGURE 10.9A**). Exterior views of brains from alcohol misusers compared with controls show smaller brain mass (**FIGURE 10.9B**). Frontal lobes are most affected, and this may be responsible for the personality changes, including apathy, disinhibition, and diminished executive functioning (ability to formulate strategies and make decisions) seen. Tissue shrinkage

BOX 10.1 ■ CASE STUDIES

The Case of a Neurodegenerative Disease Disguised by Alcohol Use Disorder

Fragile X syndrome (FXS) is a genetic disorder that causes intellectual disability (see Chapter 8, Box 8.1). Mutation of the *FMR1* gene on the X chromosome is characterized by a CGG triplet repeat expansion, whereby the syndrome occurs in individuals who carry the full mutation, with more than 200 repeats, while the unaffected gene normally contains between 5 and 40 repeats. Individuals who carry an *FMR1* gene with between 55 and 200 repeats are considered to be carriers of a premutation, which confers risk for a related syndrome known as fragile X–associated tremor/ataxia syndrome (FXTAS). Onset of FXTAS typically occurs after the age of 50, although not all carriers of the premutation develop the syndrome. Unlike full-blown FXS, FXTAS does not result in intellectual disability; however, an array of neurological signs can occur that resemble signs of Parkinson's or Alzheimer's disease, including ataxia (balance problems), tremor, dysarthria (slowed or slurred speech), irritability, and peripheral neuropathy (tingling or burning sensation in extremities), along with a range of cognitive deficits, including memory loss and difficulty learning new things.

Grigioni and colleagues (2020) present the case of a 48-year-old man who experienced gait abnormalities and difficulty walking, along with tremor, dysarthria, and peripheral neuropathy, all signs that can be present in Wernicke's encephalopathy (WE) and thus attributed to alcohol abuse. Previous genetic testing

revealed that the patient carried a premutation in the *FMR1* gene, with 87 CGG repeats, although on prior occasions his case had been dismissed as alcohol related because of his history of alcohol abuse, coupled with the fact that all of the patient's first-degree relatives were healthy. In the present report, structural MRI indicated that the patient had mild fronto-parietal atrophy, as well as diffuse cerebellar atrophy, although signs of WE, including lesions to brainstem, thalamic, and hypothalamic structures were absent.

The authors noted that differentiating between FXTAS and alcohol-related clinical signs can be challenging, drawing attention to studies showing that alcohol abuse can potentially accelerate the progression of FXTAS signs (Seritan et al., 2013; Muzar et al., 2014). Importantly, if WE is suspected, it should be treated as a medical emergency and prompt treatment with thiamine should be initiated.

In light of these challenges, Grigioni and colleagues recognized that the neurological signs, in combination with the presence of the premutation and brain imaging results, met the diagnostic criteria for FXTAS. Initiation of appropriate therapy for FXTAS begins with a diagnosis. While there is no treatment that can cure FXTAS or stop its progression, a combination of medication, physical and occupational therapy, and psychological and genetic counseling can help improve quality of life for individuals and their families.

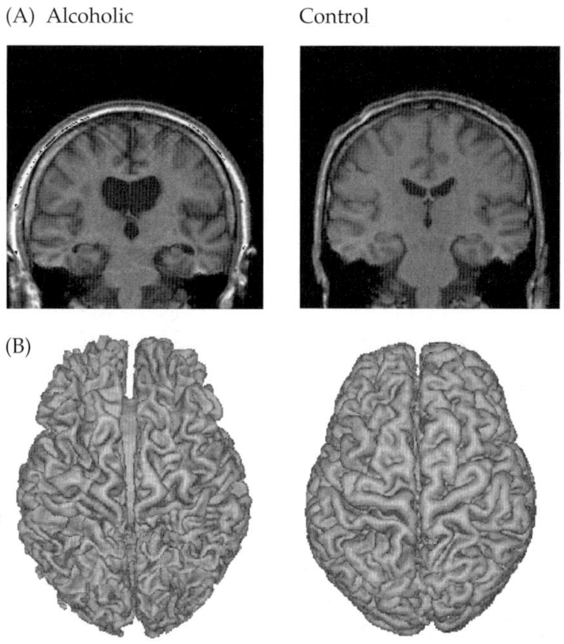

From A. Pfefferbaum and E. V. Sullivan 2004. In *Physiological Magnetic Resonance in Clinical Neuroscience*, J. Gillard et al. [Eds.], Cambridge University Press: Cambridge

(A) Alcoholic   Control

(B)

From E. V. Sullivan. 2000. *NIAAA Res Monogr 34: 477–508*

FIGURE 10.9 Alcohol-induced brain damage (A) Brain images of a man with alcohol use disorder and a healthy male control. Note the extreme difference in ventricle size, indicating tissue shrinkage in the brain of the heavy user of alcohol. (B) Exterior views of the brains above. In the alcohol abuser, the gyri are more narrow, and the sulci and fissure between the hemispheres are very enlarged, showing significant loss of tissue volume.

that occurs in medial temporal lobe structures, including the hippocampus and cholinergic cells in the basal forebrain, contributes to memory disturbances. Symptoms that implicate the hippocampus and the basal forebrain include failure to remember recent events and failure to form new memories. Cerebellar cell loss is correlated with ataxia and incoordination, particularly of the lower limbs. These brain changes are probably caused by multiple mechanisms, but glutamate-induced hyperexcitability of neurons during abstinence (see the section on neurotransmitters later in the chapter) may play a central role (Becker and Mulholland, 2014).

EFFECTS ON OTHER ORGAN SYSTEMS Alcohol has many effects on the body outside the CNS, including the following:

- Cardiovascular system
- Renal–urinary system
- Reproductive system
- Gastrointestinal system
- Liver

One well-known cardiovascular effect of alcohol is the dilation of peripheral blood vessels, which brings them closer to the surface of the skin and makes an

individual look flushed and feel warm. Of course, superficial vasodilation means that heat is actually being lost from the body rather than being retained. Although the myth of the Saint Bernard dog rescuing stranded skiers with a keg of brandy around his neck is widespread, in reality, drinking alcohol when you are truly cold produces an even more serious drop in body temperature. Heavy drinkers who fall asleep outside in cold climates risk death from hypothermia. Within the brain, vasodilation may improve cognitive function in older adults. Several studies have found that older adults who consumed low to moderate quantities of alcohol were significantly less likely to develop dementia. While many researchers have linked this beneficial effect of moderate alcohol consumption on brain health to enhanced vascular function, there is some evidence that moderate alcohol consumption can exert protective effects through anti-inflammatory mechanisms (see Collins et al., 2009 for a review).

In addition to aiding circulation, a low to moderate daily dose of alcohol may reduce the risk of heart disease, because it increases the amount of "good" cholesterol in the blood while reducing the "bad" (Gaziano and Hennekens, 1995), and seems to reduce the incidence of blood clots and stroke. In contrast, a recent study found that a relatively modest median daily dose of 1.2 drinks per day was associated with significantly increased risk of developing atrial fibrillation, a condition that can lead to elevated risk of stroke or heart failure (Csengeri et al., 2021). According to the Dietary Guidelines for Americans, moderate alcohol consumption is defined as having up to one drink per day for women and up to two drinks per day for men (U.S. Department of Health and Human Services, 2015). Importantly, these beneficial effects are counteracted when consumption is greater. AUD is associated with a higher-than-expected incidence of high blood pressure, stroke, and inflammation and enlargement of the heart muscle, which may be alcohol induced or due to malnutrition and vitamin deficiency.

It is also worth noting that the research literature on whether moderate alcohol consumption is beneficial or harmful is challenging to interpret because many studies appear to contradict one another. It is possible that narrow focus on a particular health outcome or a specific population fails to account for the bigger picture. A large-scale global study examined the degree to which alcohol may contribute to a comprehensive range of health outcomes, whether beneficial or harmful, and found that in total, all causes of mortality, particularly cancer, increase with any amount of alcohol consumption (Griswold et al., 2018).

The action of alcohol on the renal–urinary system produces larger volumes of urine that is far more dilute than normal. The loss of fluids is caused by reduced secretion of antidiuretic hormone. Although this is not normally a matter of concern, alcohol consumption should be avoided by individuals involved in strenuous athletic activities for which fluids need to be maintained. Further, athletes should not try to rehydrate with any beverage that contains alcohol.

The effect of alcohol on reproductive function is complex. Alcohol is widely believed to enhance sexual arousal and lower inhibitions. However, as Web Box 10.1 shows, expectation plays a large part in the effects of alcohol on sexual response. Furthermore, we need to distinguish between psychological arousal and physiological response. In one study, male college students consumed alcohol to achieve a BAC of 0%, 0.025%,

0.050%, or 0.075% while watching an erotic film (George and Norris, 1991). A plethysmograph was attached around the penis to measure degree of erection (both rate of tumescence and maximum achieved) during the film viewing. **FIGURE 10.10A** shows that low doses of alcohol enhanced arousal to a small extent, but higher blood levels reduced the male sexual response. Parallel studies with college women measured sexual arousal by assessing vaginal blood pressure or orgasmic latency. Physiological measures of sexual arousal decreased with increasing alcohol levels (**FIGURE 10.10B**); however, reported subjective arousal was increased. Although laboratory evaluations of sexual response are necessarily artificial, and ethical restraint prohibits testing higher levels of alcohol, research in general supports the inverse nature of physiological and subjective arousal with low to moderate alcohol use.

When alcohol use is heavy and chronic, males may become impotent and may show atrophy of the testicles, reduced sperm production, and shrinkage of the prostate and seminal vesicles. Women misusing alcohol often experience disrupted ovarian function and show a higher-than-normal incidence of menstrual disorders.

Alcohol alters GI tract function in several ways. It increases salivation and secretion of gastric juices, which may explain its ability to increase appetite and aid digestion, although higher concentrations irritate the stomach lining, and chronic use produces inflammation of the stomach (gastritis), as well as of the esophagus. Heavy alcohol use causes diarrhea, inhibits utilization of proteins, and reduces absorption and metabolism of vitamins and minerals.

One of the most damaging effects of heavy chronic alcohol consumption is liver dysfunction. Three distinct disorders may develop. The first is **fatty liver**, which involves the accumulation of triglycerides inside liver cells. The liver normally takes up and metabolizes fatty acids as part of the digestive process; however, when alcohol is present, it is metabolized first, leaving the fat for storage. Alcohol also affects adipose tissue. Adipose tissue stores energy in the form of fat. It also secretes a wide variety of hormones and inflammatory peptides called cytokines. For example, alcohol intake enhances cortisol secretion, which changes the way fat is distributed in the body, leading to greater abdominal and liver accumulation.

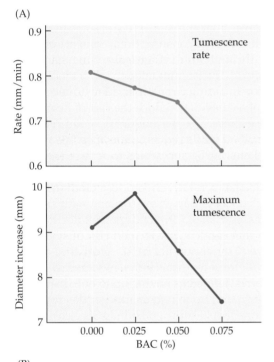

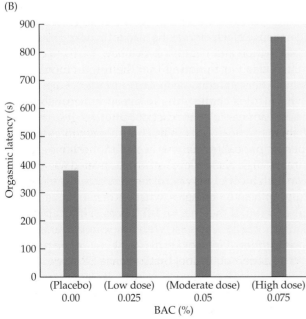

FIGURE 10.10 Effects of alcohol on sexual response
(A) Changes in male sexual response occur after varying amounts of alcohol. With increasing concentrations of blood alcohol, both the rate of penile tumescence and the maximum size achieved decreased. (B) In women, increasing blood-alcohol levels were directly proportional to orgasmic latency. (A from G. Farkas and R. C. Rosen 1976. *J Stud Alcohol* 37: 265–272 . Reproduced with permission of the Alcohol Research Documentation, Inc.; B from S. Blume. 1991. *Alcohol Health Res World* 15: 139–145.)

Alcohol also causes inflammation of the tissue along with increased breakdown of fat into fatty acids. These changes in adipose tissue release fatty acids into the blood, which contributes to the increased deposit of triglycerides by liver cells (Kema et al., 2015). The condition produces no warning symptoms but is reversible, so if drinking stops, the liver begins to use the stored fat and returns to normal. However, some individuals who have misused alcohol for many years develop a serious and potentially lethal condition called **alcohol-induced hepatitis**, which leads to the death of liver cells.

Heavy drinkers may progress from fatty liver to alcohol-induced hepatitis and then to cirrhosis. Clinical signs of alcohol-induced hepatitis include inflammation of the liver, fever, yellowing of the skin (jaundice), and pain. The death of liver cells stimulates the formation of scar tissue, which is characteristic of **alcohol-induced cirrhosis**. As scar tissue develops, blood vessels carrying oxygen are cut off, leading to further cell death. **FIGURE 10.11** compares pieces of normal liver, fatty liver, and cirrhotic liver from an individual with AUD. Cirrhotic livers are usually firm or hard to the touch and develop nodules of tissue that give them a pebbly appearance. As cirrhosis continues, liver function decreases proportionately. Consumption of large quantities of alcohol over a prolonged period is necessary for the development of cirrhosis, and even among heavy drinkers, only 10% to 15% are likely to develop the disease. Cirrhosis is most common in men between 40 and 60 years of age. However, although more men develop cirrhosis, probably because men typically drink more than women, at any given level of alcohol consumption, women have a greater chance of developing the disease than men. Cirrhosis mortality has been gradually declining since the peak following World War II, perhaps because of increased utilization of treatment programs that reduce drinking behavior. In addition, during that time alcohol consumption, particularly of spirits, has fallen. Although the liver damage is irreversible, cessation of drinking slows the rate of damage. People with cirrhosis who stop drinking have a 90% 5-year survival rate, while for those who continue to consume alcohol, the rate drops to 70%. However, for those in the late stages of the disease, survival rates drop significantly (Mann et al., 2004). For severe liver damage, the most effective treatment is liver transplant surgery. Although the damaging effects of alcohol are found in both men and women, there are significant gender differences, detailed in **WEB BOX 10.3**.

The precise cause of liver cell damage is not known, but there are promising leads. There is an abundance of endoplasmic reticulum (ER) in hepatocytes (liver cells), and abnormal ER function may be a major contributor to the liver cell damage following heavy and prolonged alcohol consumption. Alcohol metabolism is one of the many roles of the ER in the liver. The alcohol metabolizing enzyme CYP2E1 located on the smooth ER (see Chapter 1) is induced by chronic alcohol use. Subsequently, the enhanced metabolism causes the release of free radicals (i.e., especially reactive molecules that can damage cells, proteins, and DNA by changing their chemical structure), producing oxidative stress (i.e., physiological stress on the body caused by free radical–induced damage) that induces cellular injury.

A second significant function of the ER involves the processing and maturation of newly synthesized proteins. Normally there is an equilibrium between the input of new proteins that need processing and the capacity of the ER to do the work. If changing conditions increase protein synthesis, a series of intracellular events is initiated to help the cells to adapt and survive. If the adaptive mechanism is insufficient to handle the increased processing demands (called ER stress), the cell undergoes a pathological response that includes increased fat formation, inflammation, and cell death, all signs of liver injury. Laboratory animals that have been fed chronic high doses of alcohol showed significant increases in multiple intracellular markers that indicate high levels of ER stress response, which may explain why they develop signs of liver disease. Alcohol ingestion for as short a time as 2 weeks has been shown to induce ER stress in healthy humans as well. In addition, abnormally high plasma levels of homocysteine were found in both individuals with alcohol-induced liver disease and the mouse intragastric alcohol feeding model. This amino acid interferes with ER processing of proteins and hence increases the ER stress response leading to cell toxicity. Homocysteine is just one of the possible alcohol-related factors that increase ER stress. Other possibilities include acetaldehyde, oxidative stress, epigenetic modifications, insulin resistance, and others (reviewed by Ji, 2014).

© Arthur Glauberman/Science Source

FIGURE 10.11 **The effects of chronic alcohol use on the liver** Portions of a healthy liver (left), a fatty liver (center), and a cirrhotic liver (right).

Of special concern is the circular nature of the interaction between the ER stress response and the events that promote it and the resulting outcome. Apparently, not only does the ER stress response initiate fat accumulation, inflammation, and cell injury, but those same outcomes further increase the ER stress response. Drugs targeting this vicious cycle may be beneficial in reducing further liver cell damage.

EFFECTS ON FETAL DEVELOPMENT Because alcohol readily passes through the placental barrier, the alcohol that a pregnant female consumes is delivered almost immediately to her fetus, who reaches the same BAC. The damaging developmental effects of prenatal alcohol exposure lead to **fetal alcohol spectrum disorders (FASD)** or the more severe **fetal alcohol syndrome (FAS)**. One of the greatest tragedies of FAS is that it occurs at all. Fetal alcohol exposure is the most common preventable cause of intellectual disability in the United States. Although the damaging effects of alcohol on an adult generally take decades of heavy drinking, the developing embryo is far more susceptible. The major and minor birth defects that constitute FASD and FAS present a challenge to families, social services, law enforcement, and the educational system. The cost for serving those individuals with only the most severe symptoms was estimated at more than $4 billion a year in the United States, and billions more might be spent on special care for the less impaired (CDC, 2021).

Diagnostic signs and symptoms include the following:

- *Intellectual disability and other developmental delays.* The average IQ for an individual with FAS is 68. Such an individual generally attains an average reading level of a fourth grader and average second-grade math skills. The development of typical motor milestones is delayed, and evidence of poor coordination, slow response times, and language disabilities is common.

- *Low birthweight (below the 10th percentile).* In addition, infants fail to thrive, exhibiting poor catch-up growth.

- *Neurological problems.* Some infants are born with high alcohol levels and experience withdrawal from the drug, which includes tremors and seizures starting within 6 to 12 hours of birth and lasting as long as a week. Abnormal electroencephalogram recordings persist, and the infant shows a high degree of irritability and hypersensitivity to sound. These infants show poor sucking reflexes, hyperactivity, attentional deficits, and poor sleep patterns.

- *Distinctive craniofacial malformations.* These include a small head, small wide-set eyes with drooping eyelids, a short upturned nose, a thin upper lip, and flattening of the vertical groove between the nose and upper lip (**FIGURE 10.12A**). The infants may also show low-set and nonparallel ears, malformations of the ear that produce hearing deficits, cleft palate, and reduced growth of the lower jaw.

- *Other physical abnormalities.* Cardiac defects such as a hole between the chambers or deformed blood vessels in the heart, failure of kidney development, undescended testes, and skeletal abnormalities in fingers and toes are common.

Although the estimates of the prevalence of FAS vary considerably depending on criteria used, the range is from 0.2 to 2.0 cases per 1000 live births. In addition,

(A)

© Rick's Photography/Shutterstock.com

(B) Normal

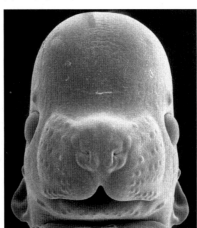

Exposed to alcohol

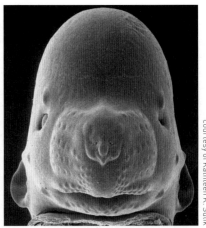

From K. K. Sulik et al. 1981. *Science* 214: 936–938, courtesy of Kathleen K. Sulik

FIGURE 10.12 Fetal alcohol syndrome (A) Distinctive craniofacial malformations in a child with FAS. (B) Fetal abnormalities in mice exposed to alcohol in utero.

it has become clear that prenatal alcohol can have effects that are distinct from FAS. Fetal alcohol spectrum disorders are a cluster of disorders characterized by neurological abnormalities leading to attention deficits, hyperactivity, poor coordination, poor impulse control, delayed speech, deficits in memory, and learning disabilities. Other individuals show defects in skeletal and major organ systems. The incidence rate for FASD may be as high as 10 in 1000. Because the symptoms are so varied, diagnosis is difficult. However, although there is no cure for FASD, diagnosis before age 6 can improve the child's development by implementing such things as behavior therapy, medication for specific symptoms, and parent training in structuring the environment to optimize the child's functioning and coping with particular disabilities (CDC, 2020).

How sure are we that alcohol itself is teratogenic (i.e., causes birth defects)? After all, women who use high doses of alcohol during pregnancy often have poor nutrition, smoke cigarettes or use other drugs, have poor health overall, and receive poor prenatal care. These issues have been well controlled in animal research that can regulate the amount of alcohol, the pattern of consumption, the timing of alcohol use during the pregnancy, and the diet of the mother. Early conclusions and subsequent research agree that prenatal alcohol does induce both physical defects and behavioral deficits in animals that closely resemble those seen in humans. Single large doses of alcohol given to pregnant mice produced abnormalities in the developing fetuses (**FIGURE 10.12B**), including eye damage, smaller brains, and facial deformities similar to those seen in human babies with FAS (see Almeida et al., 2020, for a review).

Blood-alcohol level is important in estimating the risk and severity of teratogenic effects, but the pattern of alcohol use that contributes to the peak maternal blood-alcohol level is equally important. In one rodent study, 12 equally spaced doses of alcohol that produced maternal blood levels up to 0.12% did not affect fetal brain growth. In contrast, the same total amount of alcohol given in condensed fashion raised maternal blood levels to a range between 0.20% and 0.35% and caused a significant decrease in brain weight (Randall et al., 1990). Although this blood level is quite high, it is consistent with blood levels seen after binge drinking in humans.

Animal research is well supported by many studies with humans showing that heavy maternal drinking, particularly of the binge type, is associated with significant behavioral and emotional problems, as well as cognitive deficits, in offspring. However, the effects of low to moderate alcohol consumption on fetal development are somewhat less clear. Although multiple studies have shown deficits in attention, aggressive behavior, and learning difficulties after moderate prenatal alcohol exposure, others have reported no measurable adverse outcomes following low to moderate amounts.

The discrepancies among studies are troubling because evidence suggesting that low levels of alcohol are relatively safe could encourage women to drink during pregnancy and if erroneous could lead to less optimal fetal outcomes. On the other hand, if small amounts of alcohol are safe to consume, women who drank lightly early in their pregnancy (when many are unaware of their status) would experience less guilt, anxiety, and stress over unintentionally harming their children. Unfortunately, correlational epidemiological studies such as these are plagued with methodological difficulties because in this retrospective research, women may inaccurately recall the quantity, timing, frequency, and pattern of alcohol use, all of which are critical factors determining fetal outcome. Some may underreport their consumption because of social pressure against drinking during pregnancy. In addition, many other variables such as the psychological health of the mother, maternal medical issues and other drugs being used, socioeconomic differences, level of stress experienced, adequacy of maternal nutrition, genetics, and parenting styles are likely to modulate the effects of prenatal alcohol and behavioral outcomes in the child. Others have suggested that the differences among studies may reflect the particular cognitive test used and its sensitivity or the manner in which behavioral outcomes were evaluated. Additionally, sociocultural differences, including the type of liquor consumed and whether it is part of a meal, may make results less generalizable across cultures (Todorow et al., 2010). Although controversy is likely to continue in the future, given that the threshold for adverse effects is unknown and how the threshold might vary from individual to individual is equally unclear, the *safest option at this time is abstinence* during pregnancy. In fact, both the Surgeon General and the American Academy of Pediatrics have stated that drinking *any* alcohol at *any* stage of pregnancy can cause some disability in the child (American Academy of Pediatrics, 2018). In addition, the CDC recommends that women who are considering becoming pregnant should stop using alcohol because they will be unaware of their status during the early weeks of pregnancy.

In addition to the amount and pattern of alcohol ingestion, the developmental stage of the fetus when exposed to alcohol is critical in determining the specific effects. Organ systems are most vulnerable to damage during the period of most rapid development. Alcohol ingestion at the time of conception significantly increases the risk of teratogenic effects, and within the first 3 weeks, the fetus may not survive. Alcohol use during the fourth to ninth weeks—a time when many women are unaware of their pregnancy—produces the most severe formative damage and severe mental retardation. Alcohol use later in pregnancy causes slowed growth. Since the brain is one of the first organ systems to begin to develop but is the last to be complete, alcohol use at any point in the pregnancy can have damaging effects on the CNS. Obviously, if drinking is constant throughout fetal development, the effects will be much greater than if drinking is stopped midpregnancy.

Although the damaging effects of fetal alcohol exposure are clear, its precise mechanism is less certain. It has been suggested that acetaldehyde may be the toxic agent; other possible mechanisms include decreased blood flow in the uterine artery, reduced oxygen availability, and placental dysfunction, which reduces the transport of vital amino acids, glucose, folate, and zinc. Hormone-like substances called prostaglandins are suspected of mediating teratogenic effects because inhibitors of prostaglandins, such as aspirin, reduce alcohol-induced birth defects in animals. Additional research showed that ethanol acting on both glutamate and γ-aminobutyric acid (GABA) neurons may trigger significant cell death (apoptosis) in the developing brain (Ikonomidou et al., 2000).

An additional potential mechanism responsible for alcohol-induced fetal brain damage is the occurrence of epigenetic events. The transcription of multiple genes involved in cell maturation and neurodevelopment is epigenetically altered by exposure to alcohol. Laufer and colleagues (2013) showed that fetal alcohol exposure following voluntary maternal alcohol consumption in mice produced widespread disruption in DNA methylation (see Chapter 2) that persisted into adulthood. The altered gene transcription involved genes previously implicated in several other neurodevelopmental disorders. One of the many genes epigenetically modified (*Akt*) regulates multiple processes of neuronal development, including dendritic development, synapse formation, and synaptic plasticity, all processes found altered in FASD. A second gene (*Nmnat1*), whose function was down-regulated, normally protects against neurodegeneration by inhibiting cell death. Loss of function leaves many brain regions, such as the hippocampus, vulnerable to damaging events. An additional down-regulated gene (*Otx2*) is associated with mood disorders. Hence epigenetically altered gene expression may contribute to the neurobiological and behavioral characteristics associated with FASD.

SECTION SUMMARY

- The small non-ionized ethanol molecule is absorbed from the GI tract by passive diffusion—a process slowed by food in the stomach. Absorption in women is faster because reduced gastric metabolism and smaller body size increase the concentration.

- About 95% of ingested alcohol is metabolized by the liver at a constant rate of 1 to 1.5 ounces per hour; about 5% is excreted by the lungs.

- Alcohol dehydrogenase converts alcohol to the toxic product acetaldehyde. Further metabolism by aldehyde dehydrogenase (ALDH) converts acetaldehyde to acetic acid, which is ultimately converted into carbon dioxide, water, and energy.

- Methanol toxicity occurs when methanol is converted by alcohol dehydrogenase and ALDH into formaldehyde and formic acid, respectively. Ethanol and methanol compete for alcohol dehydrogenase.

- The cytochrome P450 enzyme CYP2E1 metabolizes alcohol, as well as other drugs. Consuming them together may lead to dangerous blood levels because they compete for the limited amount of enzyme.

- Acute tolerance occurs within a single drinking episode and may lead to dangerous driving when binge drinkers perceive that they are less intoxicated on the descending limb of the blood-alcohol curve.

- Chronic alcohol use increases cytochrome P450 enzymes (enzyme induction), so metabolism is more rapid, causing metabolic tolerance to the effects of alcohol and cross-tolerance to other drugs metabolized by the same enzyme.

- Continued presence of alcohol produces compensatory changes in neuron function (pharmacodynamic tolerance).

- Practicing an operant task under the influence of alcohol leads to improved performance (behavioral tolerance of the operant type). Repeated alcohol administration in the same environment leads to the development of a compensatory response that occurs only in that environment (behavioral tolerance of the classical conditioning type).

- Alcohol produces physical dependence and cross-dependence with other sedative–hypnotic drugs.

- Withdrawal after chronic heavy use lasts for days and includes tremor, anxiety, high blood pressure and heart rate, sweating, rapid breathing, and nausea and vomiting. Severe withdrawal effects called delirium tremens include hallucinations, convulsions, disorientation, and intense anxiety.

- Behavioral effects of alcohol are directly related to BAC, but at low doses, the environment and expectations of effects also have significant effects.

- Dose-dependent effects on the CNS include relaxation, reduced anxiety, intoxication, impaired judgment, impaired memory, and sleep. Higher doses produce coma and death as the result of respiratory depression.

- Heavy long-term alcohol use causes a vitamin B_1 deficiency leading to cell death in the periaqueductal gray, medial thalamus, and mammillary bodies, causing Wernicke's encephalopathy: tremors, weakness, ataxia, confusion, and disorientation. Multiple brain regions may be damaged by glutamate-induced excitotoxicity. Korsakoff syndrome is caused by permanent damage to thalamic nuclei and brain regions involved in memory subsequent to vitamin B_1 deficiency. Symptoms of Korsakoff syndrome include potentially permanent memory loss, personality changes, and hallucinations.

- Beneficial alcohol-induced cardiovascular effects include vasodilation, elevation of good cholesterol, and lowering of bad cholesterol, although these benefits are thought to be offset by other harmful effects. AUD increases the risk of high blood pressure, stroke, and heart enlargement.

- Alcohol has a diuretic effect, increases sexual arousal while decreasing performance, increases appetite, and aids digestion by increasing gastric secretions.

- Liver damage associated with AUD includes fatty liver, alcohol-induced hepatitis, and cirrhosis.

- Prenatal exposure to alcohol may produce FAS, which is characterized by intellectual disability and other developmental delays, low birthweight, neurological problems, head and facial malformations, and other physical abnormalities. A larger number of infants are affected by a cluster of FAS-related disorders (fetal alcohol spectrum disorders) having highly varied symptom presentation, which makes them harder to diagnose and treat.

- Effects of prenatal exposure are dependent on blood-alcohol level, pattern of alcohol use, fetal developmental stage at time of exposure, maternal nutrition, genetics, and comorbid drug use. Multiple possible mechanisms for alcohol-induced FASD have been identified, including maternal alcohol-induced epigenetic effects that alter various stages of neuronal development.

10.2 Neurochemical Effects of Alcohol

The neurochemical effects of alcohol have proved more difficult to examine than those of some other drugs. One important reason is the chemical nature of the alcohol molecule, which not only provides the means for easy penetration into the brain but, more importantly, influences the phospholipid bilayer of neurons. The latter action has a widespread impact on many normal cell functions and also modifies the actions of many neurotransmitter systems. In addition, the initial effects of alcohol must be separated from the neuronal changes that occur after long-term drug use. For these and other reasons, research using animal experimentation is particularly important.

Animal models are vital for alcohol research

Animal models are particularly important in alcohol studies for several reasons. First, because research animals are maintained in controlled and healthful environments, some of the common human correlates of heavy alcohol use are eliminated: poor nutrition, liver damage, associated psychiatric disorders, and use of multiple drugs. Second, animal models allow us to use methods that are not appropriate for humans. For example, studies using controlled chronic alcohol consumption can tell us about the long-term damaging effects on body functions and behavior and can model the effects of alcohol withdrawal. The effects of prenatal alcohol can be evaluated independently of issues such as maternal nutrition and substance misuse. Also, invasive procedures, including genetic engineering, can be used to manipulate and measure the neurobiological correlates of intoxication, reinforcement, and behavioral effects of alcohol. Third, animal models serve as screening tools for evaluating treatment strategies.

When evaluating animal models, it is important to remember that alcohol addiction is not a unitary concept, but rather one that develops through several stages, beginning with the early pleasurable positive reinforcing effects or the elimination of a noxious state, for example stress (early acquisition stage). These reinforcing events establish the repeated drug-taking behavior (maintenance stage), but it is not until neuroadaptive mechanisms develop in response to chronic use that the development of dependence and compulsive drug taking occurs. Animal models need to reflect these stages of drug misuse as well as the occurrence of binge-type drinking, withdrawal signs, and relapse behaviors (alcohol-seeking behavior) following prolonged abstinence. Since animals do not naturally develop AUD, no direct animal model of the complex human condition with its drinking pattern and quantity of consumption, development of compulsion to drink, and escalation of drinking despite aversive events is possible. The best efforts can model only specific components of AUD (i.e., biomarkers that contribute to the disorder).

The operant self-administration model used to evaluate the reinforcing effects of various drugs is described in Chapter 4. It differs from the two-bottle free-choice technique in which animals are free to choose between a low concentration of alcohol or water, because in the operant technique the animals must make an effort (usually pressing a lever) to earn access to the alcohol. Although the paradigm is an important way to evaluate positive reinforcement and potential substance misuse, self-administration procedures are more difficult with alcohol than with other drugs of abuse because most animals will not spontaneously consume enough alcohol to produce intoxication. However, one of several initiation procedures can be used to get animals to self-administer alcohol. One such method is the sucrose substitution procedure (Samson, 1986). In this technique animals that have access to both food and water readily learn to bar press in an operant chamber for a 20% sucrose solution. Over a series of sessions, the sucrose concentration is gradually reduced while ethanol is gradually added. After about 25 of these sessions, the animals will bar press for the ethanol without sucrose and, when given a choice between water or ethanol, will choose the ethanol solution.

Manipulation of the access to alcohol has been used to model relapse behavior characterized by excessive and uncontrolled drinking following abstinence. In either operant self-administration or free-choice drinking, animals that consume alcohol for at least 6 to 8 weeks and then are deprived of access to the drug for several days, weeks, or months will show a two- to threefold increase in consumption over baseline when provided the opportunity. Since not all strains of rat will show this behavior, differences in genetic background play a significant role. When the drinking and deprivation stages are repeated multiple times, the animals show the compulsive drinking behavior that resembles the human condition, including selecting high-concentration alcohol solutions to rapidly elevate blood levels, choosing alcohol even if adulterated with bitter-tasting quinine, and choosing the bitter drink over the normally preferable sucrose solution. These behaviors resemble those of AUD: the classic loss of control over drinking despite negative consequences, as well as failure to choose a normally reinforcing alternative. This model, described by Vengeliene and colleagues (2014), provides the opportunity to test drugs that would potentially remediate the most challenging aspect of human AUD—relapse. Additionally, repeated episodes of withdrawal lead to impaired fear conditioning and poor cognitive processing. Similar impairments were noted in individuals with AUD who had experienced repeated episodes of detoxification. These cognitive impairments were further found to be associated with withdrawal-induced loss of gray matter in the ventromedial prefrontal cortex. These types of models represent efforts to improve translational research and to move discoveries from animal research more quickly into clinical applications (see Chapter 4). Several excellent reviews of animal models of various components of AUD, including adolescent onset, motivation, abstinence, and relapse, are available for further study (Ripley and Stephens, 2011; Goltseker et al., 2019).

Another approach to animal models involves genetic manipulations (reviewed by Crabbe et al., 2010). Although most laboratory animals drink very little of an ethanol solution, when large numbers of animals (usually mice or rats) are screened, a few will be found to voluntarily drink large quantities of alcohol rather than water. Two populations of animals can be developed by selectively breeding the heaviest drinkers and the abstainers over several generations (**FIGURE 10.13**). Numerous strains of alcohol-preferring (AP) and high-alcohol-drinking (HAD) rodents have been developed. These animals, given 24-hour access to alcohol, will freely choose a 10% ethanol solution over water that elevates their blood alcohol to pharmacologically relevant and intoxicating levels, even in the presence of food or highly palatable sweet solutions. When tested with an operant progressive ratio task, these rats exhibit high breaking points (see Chapter 4) for alcohol, suggesting that the animals are willing to work for access to the drug and that it has high reinforcement value for them. AP rats also demonstrate

other characteristics typical of individuals with AUD. The animals show not only metabolic tolerance but also behavioral tolerance in tasks such as balancing on a swinging platform. They ingest enough alcohol during free-access sessions to produce physical dependence and withdrawal signs at abstinence. Following prolonged abstinence, the rats exhibit alcohol-seeking behavior (that is, choosing alcohol over water) when returned to the initial alcohol self-administration environment. These animals model human alcohol consumption and misuse and can be used to study behavioral, biochemical, and genetic differences (reviewed by McBride et al., 2014). Animals can also be bred for numerous alcohol-related characteristics such as sensitivity to alcohol, intensity of withdrawal, and so forth.

Using these inbred strains, Bell and colleagues (2014) have modeled human adolescent binge-like drinking, the typical form of early onset alcohol use. Their procedure uses scheduled access to alcohol, such as three or four 1-hour sessions a day during the dark cycle, which is the rodents' active period. Under these conditions the rats, in either the home cage or operant chamber, consume enough alcohol to reach binge-like blood levels (greater than 0.08%) on a daily basis, even when provided a highly palatable sweet alternative. Furthermore, they demonstrate intoxicated behaviors in tasks involving balance and coordination. It is of interest that the drinking pattern resembles human consumption. For instance, *adolescent* AP rats drink more during the limited-access sessions than when given continuous 24-hour access. In contrast, *adult* AP rats consume greater quantities when given continuous access than during scheduled binge-like sessions. Further, if the AP rats are provided with a selection of alcohol concentrations during the restricted access, they choose to drink the higher concentrations of alcohol, while control animals are apparently more sensitive to the aversive effects. Under those conditions blood levels two or three times higher are

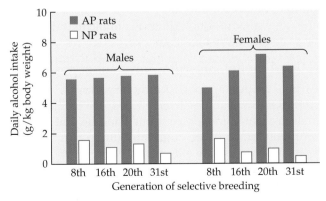

FIGURE 10.13 **Average daily alcohol consumption for selected generations of rats** These rats were bred for alcohol-preferring (AP) and non-preferring (NP) behavior. Males and females show similar alcohol consumption. (From R. B. Stewart and T.-K. Li. 1997. *Alcohol Health Res World* 21: 169–176.)

achieved, indicating loss-of-control drinking. The adolescent binge-type drinking in these rodents provides a means to study neural mechanisms contributing to early onset drinking, a frequent precursor to AUD in adults.

In addition to selective breeding, a second type of study uses genetically altered animals that fail to express a particular protein. These knockout animals are used to evaluate the role of one particular protein (for example, a specific receptor) in the effects of ethanol. The AP and HAD rat strains have been useful in identifying genes that influence alcohol consumption. Comparing the genomic sequencing of the AP and non-preferring (NP) rats, researchers identified several regions linked to alcohol preference (Zhou et al., 2013). Further, they found a variant in the gene (*Grm2*) that encodes the metabotropic glutamate receptor 2 (mGluR2) in AP but not NP rats that impaired the expression of the receptor. Electrophysiological measures showed that application of an mGluR2 agonist in brain slices from the hippocampus and striatum produced a 40% to 60% reduction in excitation in NP rats, but less than 10% depression in AP rats, which reflects their loss of mGluR2 function. Using normal Wistar rats, chosen because they are the parental strain of both AP and NP rats, the investigators found that those animals that were administered an mGluR2 antagonist, compared with controls administered vehicle, showed a significant increase in self-administration of alcohol. Those results further indicate a role for the glutamate receptor in alcohol reinforcement. To further demonstrate the significance of mGluR2 in alcohol consumption, the researchers utilized *Grm2*-knockout mice. Homozygous knockout mice lacking mGluR2 escalated their alcohol consumption in a two-bottle free-choice design in which alcohol concentration was gradually increased from 3% to 17% over 80 days. This increase was significantly greater than that found in wild-type mice (**FIGURE 10.14A**). Furthermore, in control mice the percent preference for alcohol was reduced at the highest concentrations of alcohol, which is a typical response to the aversive taste, while the knockout mice continued to prefer consistently high levels of alcohol (**FIGURE 10.14B**). Overall, mGluR2-knockout mice resemble AP inbred mice in their alcohol self-administration. Although similar gene variants have been identified in human populations, they are rare and usually contribute only a small amount to the risk factor for excessive alcohol use. Nevertheless, this type of research with animal models may help to identify potential drug targets for alcohol misuse treatment.

Alcohol acts on multiple neurotransmitters

Because alcohol is such a simple molecule, it readily crosses cell membranes, including the blood–brain barrier, and can be detected in the brain within minutes after consumption. Alcohol has both specific and nonspecific actions. *Nonspecific actions* depend on its ability

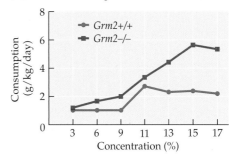

(A) Alcohol consumption

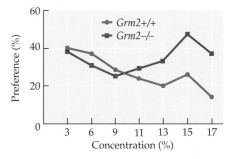

(B) Alcohol preference

FIGURE 10.14 **Grm2-knockout mice show increased alcohol consumption and preference** (A) Homozygous knockout mice (*Grm2–/–*) drink increasing amounts of alcohol as the alcohol concentration increases from 3% to 17%. Wild-type controls (*Grm2+/+*) consume significantly less than the knockout mice at the higher concentrations. (B) *Grm2–/–* mice showed a consistent percent preference for alcohol over water in a two-bottle free-choice situation, even at high alcohol concentrations, while control mice reduced their preference for alcohol at high concentrations. (From Z. Zhou et al. 2013. *Proc Natl Acad Sci USA* 110: 16963–16968.)

to move into membranes, changing the fluid character of the lipids that make up membranes (**FIGURE 10.15**). As you might expect, the protein molecules that are embedded in membranes are likely to function differently when their "environment" changes so dramatically and becomes less rigid. In contrast, at low to moderate doses, alcohol seems to interact with specific sites on particular proteins, and these *specific actions* are probably responsible for most of the acute effects of ethanol at intoxicating doses. Alcohol not only influences several ligand-gated channels but also directly alters second-messenger systems. For example, ethanol stimulates the G protein (G_s) that activates the cyclic adenosine monophosphate (cAMP) second-messenger system (see Figure 10.15, step 7). The ability to identify specific sites of ethanol action ultimately will lead to discovery of new drugs that will compete with ethanol to prevent particular undesirable effects.

Although alcohol affects virtually all neurotransmitter systems, this section describes the acute effects of alcohol on a limited number of neurotransmitters, suggesting possible connections between the transmitter

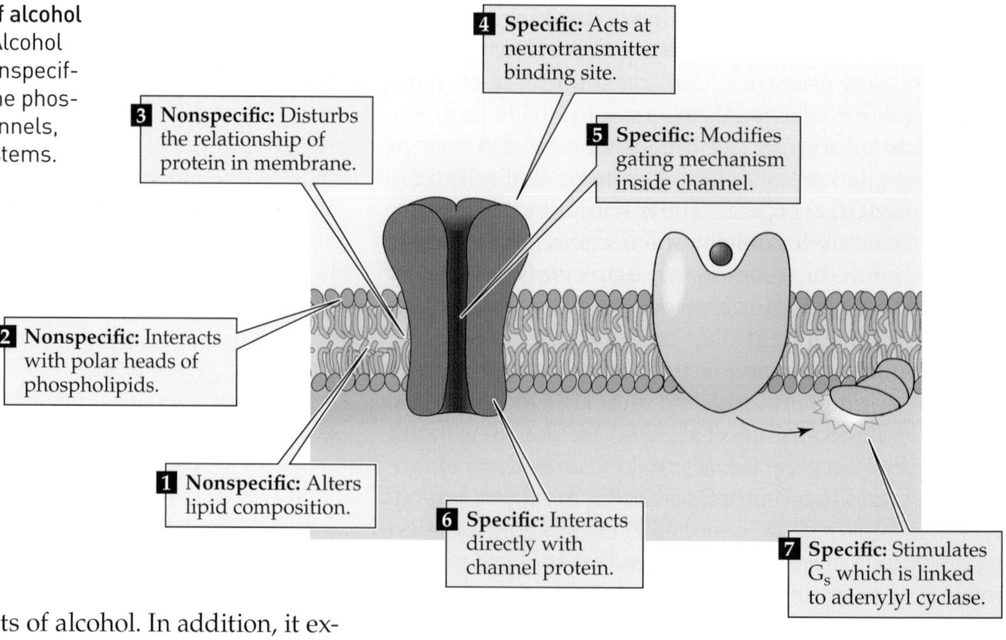

FIGURE 10.15 Effects of alcohol on neuronal membranes Alcohol acts at both specific and nonspecific sites, including membrane phospholipids, ligand-gated channels, and second-messenger systems.

4 **Specific:** Acts at neurotransmitter binding site.

5 **Specific:** Modifies gating mechanism inside channel.

3 **Nonspecific:** Disturbs the relationship of protein in membrane.

2 **Nonspecific:** Interacts with polar heads of phospholipids.

1 **Nonspecific:** Alters lipid composition.

6 **Specific:** Interacts directly with channel protein.

7 **Specific:** Stimulates G_s which is linked to adenylyl cyclase.

action and specific effects of alcohol. In addition, it examines the neuroadaptations that occur with repeated alcohol use as they link to pharmacodynamic tolerance and dependence. Throughout this discussion, keep in mind that no neurotransmitter system works in isolation; changes in each one certainly modify other neurotransmitters in an interdependent fashion.

GLUTAMATE As you may recall from Chapter 8, glutamate is a major excitatory neurotransmitter in the nervous system and has receptors on many cells in the CNS. All glutamate receptors are inhibited by acute alcohol exposure, but some are only affected by high concentrations. Of the several subtypes of glutamate receptor, alcohol has its greatest effect on the *N*-methyl-D-aspartate (NMDA) receptor, which is a ligand-gated channel that allows positively charged ions (Ca^{2+} and Na^+) to enter and cause localized depolarization. Glutamate action at NMDA receptors mediates associative learning (see Chapter 8) and also has a role in the damaging effects of excessive glutamate activity (excitotoxicity), as in the case of prolonged seizures or after stroke. Let's look at the role of NMDA receptors in several effects of alcohol: (1) memory loss associated with intoxication, (2) rebound hyperexcitability associated with the abstinence syndrome after long-term use, and (3) NMDA-mediated excitotoxicity associated with alcohol-induced brain damage.

Alcohol acutely inhibits glutamate neurotransmission by reducing the effectiveness of glutamate at the NMDA receptor. These effects occur at concentrations as low as 0.03%, blood levels normally achieved by social drinkers. Alcohol, like other glutamate antagonists, impairs learning and memory, as has been shown in studies of long-term potentiation and conditioning (Fadda and Rossetti, 1998). In addition, alcohol significantly reduces glutamate release in many brain areas,

including the hippocampus, as measured by microdialysis. Reduced glutamate release in the hippocampus is correlated with deficits in spatial memory. The combination of temporary inhibition of NMDA receptors by alcohol and reduced glutamate release may produce the amnesia that occurs for events that take place during intoxication (i.e., the blackouts so typical of heavy drinking; Diamond and Gordon, 1997).

In the adult brain, repeated use of alcohol leads to a neuroadaptive *increase* in the number of NMDA receptors (up-regulation) as a compensatory response to reduced glutamate activity. The number of NMDA receptors in both the cerebral cortex and hippocampus is elevated in human alcohol misusers, as well as in animal models of chronic alcohol exposure. In addition, in dependent rats, glutamate release, normally inhibited by alcohol, is dramatically increased at about 10 hours after withdrawal of alcohol. This combination of increased NMDA receptor expression and increased glutamate release during withdrawal contributes to pronounced hyperexcitability in the CNS. The time course (**FIGURE 10.16**) of this CNS hyperexcitability and the seizures that are typical of the alcohol abstinence syndrome matches the pattern of increased glutamate release during withdrawal. Further, there is a strong positive correlation between the magnitude of glutamate output during withdrawal and the intensity of abstinence signs. This means that the increased glutamate acting on up-regulated NMDA receptors may be one neurochemical correlate of alcohol withdrawal. Additionally, the elevated glutamate activity during withdrawal causes excessive calcium influx, which contributes to cell death. Frequently experienced withdrawal may be responsible for some of the irreversible brain damage described earlier.

Additionally, studies with rats show that maternal BACs as low as 0.04% during the last trimester of pregnancy can impair NMDA receptors and decrease glutamate release in the newborn. Unlike in the mature brain, inhibition of glutamate systems in the fetus may disrupt normal brain development, resulting in *reduced* NMDA receptors in the adult. It is reasonable to suspect that a reduction in NMDA receptors is related to subtle impairments in learning and memory in children born to mothers with AUD, but further investigation is required.

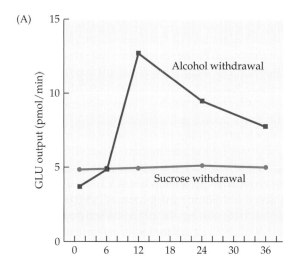

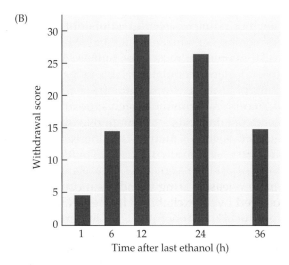

FIGURE 10.16   Relationship between alcohol withdrawal and glutamate release Withdrawal from chronic alcohol in dependent rats increases glutamate (GLU) release in the striatum (A) and behavioral rebound withdrawal hyperexcitability (B). The time course of the two withdrawal-related events is very similar. Experimental animals received intragastric delivery of ethanol at intoxicating concentrations (2–5 g/kg) every 6 hours for 6 consecutive days. Control animals received an equally caloric sucrose solution. On day 7, ethanol administration was terminated, and behavioral testing of abstinence signs and simultaneous microdialysis collection began. (From Z. L. Rossetti and S. Carboni 1995. *Eur J Pharmacol* 283: 177–183.)

GABA   GABA (γ-aminobutyric acid) is a major inhibitory amino acid neurotransmitter described in Chapter 8. It binds to the $GABA_A$ receptor complex and opens the chloride (Cl^-) channel, allowing Cl^- to enter the cell to hyperpolarize the membrane. Many classic sedative–hypnotic drugs (see Chapter 17), such as the benzodiazepines (e.g., Valium) and the barbiturates (e.g., phenobarbital), are known to enhance the effects of GABA at the $GABA_A$ receptor by binding to their modulatory sites on the receptor complex. Since the drugs in this class and alcohol produce many of the same actions and show both cross-tolerance and cross-dependence, it is not surprising to find that alcohol also modulates GABA function, both directly via $GABA_A$ receptors and indirectly by stimulating GABA release.

What kind of biochemical and electrophysiological evidence suggests that alcohol increases GABA-induced Cl^- flux and hyperpolarization? First, picrotoxin (which blocks the Cl^- channel) and bicuculline (which competes with GABA for its receptor) antagonize both the hyperpolarization and some of the behavioral effects of alcohol. This suggests that both Cl^- conductance and GABA binding to the receptor are necessary for the effects of alcohol to occur. Second, manipulations that increase GABA (e.g., inhibiting its degradation) also increase alcohol-induced behavioral effects. Likewise, reducing GABA function with antagonists reduces signs of ethanol intoxication and its antianxiety effects (Grobin et al., 1998). Third, lines of mice bred for their sensitivity to some of the behavioral effects of alcohol show a relationship between the ability of ethanol to increase GABA-induced Cl^- entry and the intensity of their response to alcohol. Greater incoordination and loss of righting reflex in vivo corresponded to greater alcohol-induced Cl^- influx into the animals' brain preparations in vitro (Mihic and Harris, 1997).

Just as benzodiazepines modulate some $GABA_A$ receptors and not others, depending on the isoform of subunits of the receptor that are present (see Chapter 8), so too alcohol acts on some $GABA_A$ receptors and not others. For instance, male knockout mice lacking $GABA_A$ receptors that have an α1 or β2 subunit show less loss of the righting reflex after alcohol administration, indicating that those receptors mediate the sedative–hypnotic effects of alcohol. Furthermore, some receptors respond to the low doses of alcohol achieved by social drinking, and others modulate GABA function only at the high concentrations associated with greater intoxication. $GABA_A$ receptors that are highly sensitive to alcohol contain a δ subunit (instead of the more usual γ), along with α4 or α6 subunits, and are located *extrasynaptically*. Although most $GABA_A$ receptors located synaptically respond transiently to GABA released into the synapse, extrasynaptic receptors respond in a more persistent fashion to GABA that remains in the extracellular space to produce tonic inhibition. Because they are more sensitive to the effects of alcohol, these extrasynaptic receptors are more likely to have a role in the behavioral and subjective effects produced by low or moderate amounts of drinking.

Additionally, evidence from several studies suggests that extrasynaptic GABA receptors have a role in the reinforcing effects of oral ethanol and, in that way, may contribute to the development of alcohol misuse (Nie et al., 2011; Rewal et al., 2012). Using a gene-silencing technique in adult rodents, researchers produced rats that had fewer δ- and α4-subunit-containing $GABA_A$ receptors. These animals showed a lower preference for alcohol, consumed less alcohol, and bar pressed less for access to oral alcohol. Furthermore, this effect was specific for alcohol and did not alter the animals' response to other reinforcers (sucrose solution), nor did it interfere with bar-pressing motor performance. It is significant that reducing receptors specifically in the shell of the nucleus accumbens (NAcc) but not in the core region altered alcohol intake, because the shell has long been associated with self-administration not only of alcohol but of other drugs of abuse (see the section below on dopamine). Additional evidence from knockout, knockin, and pharmacological studies is needed to clarify which receptor subtypes in which cellular and anatomical locations respond to high and low concentrations of alcohol to produce various ethanol-related responses.

In contrast to the acute GABA-enhancing effects of alcohol, repeated exposure to ethanol *reduces* $GABA_A$-mediated Cl^- flux. Also, chronic alcohol makes animals more sensitive to seizure-inducing doses of the GABA antagonist bicuculline. We might expect this result, since it should take less of the antagonist to reduce GABA function, because it has already been down-regulated by chronic alcohol. This neuroadaptive mechanism apparently compensates for the initial GABA-enhancing effect of alcohol and may contribute to the appearance of tolerance and some of the signs of withdrawal, such as hyperexcitability, seizures, and tremors because of reduced GABA-mediated inhibition. Benzodiazepines also lose their GABA-enhancing effects at the receptor in mice treated chronically with ethanol, and this may serve as a mechanism for cross-tolerance with other sedative–hypnotic drugs.

$GABA_B$ RECEPTORS In addition to altering $GABA_A$ receptor function, ethanol also impacts both pre- and postsynaptic metabotropic $GABA_B$ receptors. As you learned in Chapter 8, postsynaptic $GABA_B$ receptors inhibit cell firing by opening K^+ channels and additionally inhibit synthesis of the second messenger cAMP. Also, $GABA_B$ receptors may be presynaptic autoreceptors or axoaxonic heteroreceptors and reduce neurotransmitter release by reducing voltage-gated Ca^{2+} channel opening. $GABA_B$ receptors have a role in

a variety of behaviors, including modulation of alcohol consumption (reviewed by Agabio and Colombo, 2014). The classic $GABA_B$ agonist baclofen prevented the selection of alcohol over water in a two-bottle choice design in AP rats until baclofen administration was terminated, at which time alcohol consumption increased. Not only did the drug prevent the initial acquisition of alcohol drinking in the rats, but it also reduced alcohol consumption once acquisition was established (that is, in the "maintenance" phase of alcohol use), as well as in mouse models of binge drinking. Relapse alcohol consumption in response to an alcohol-associated cue after withdrawal was also reduced by acute administration, raising the possibility that baclofen may be an effective treatment for loss of control and relapse in human alcohol misusers. However, despite the strong preclinical results, there have been an insufficient number of large-scale, randomized, placebo-controlled clinical trials to draw a conclusion. Those studies completed thus far have produced conflicting results regarding the efficacy of baclofen in reducing consumption and craving or achieving abstinence. The multiple actions of baclofen on alcohol use may be due to its inhibitory effects on ventral tegmental area (VTA) cell firing and subsequent reduction of dopamine (DA) release in the NAcc. Unfortunately, the reduced reinforcing value found for alcohol in animal studies was also demonstrated for other substances, including sucrose solutions and regular food pellets.

Just as benzodiazepines enhance $GABA_A$ receptor function by binding to specific modulatory sites on the receptor complex, modulatory sites for $GABA_B$ function also exist. Agonists at those sites, called $GABA_B$ PAMS (positive allosteric modulators), have no agonist effect alone but enhance the effectiveness of GABA binding at $GABA_B$ receptors. Since these agents have effects similar to baclofen on alcohol consumption with fewer adverse effects such as sedation and motor incoordination, they represent an alternative therapeutic approach to treating AUD (Maccioni and Colombo, 2019).

It seems appropriate to once again mention that neuronal excitability is caused by a balance between excitation and inhibition. Since GABAergic neurons frequently have glutamate receptors and GABA frequently modulates glutamate release, the compensatory changes in each of the neurotransmitter systems may reflect an interaction of the two (Fadda and Rossetti, 1998).

DOPAMINE Evidence from biochemical, electrophysiological, and behavioral studies suggests that the dopaminergic mesolimbic system plays a significant role in the reinforcement and motivational mechanisms underlying behaviors that are vital to survival (see Chapter 5). The pathway begins in the VTA of the midbrain and courses rostrally to innervate various limbic

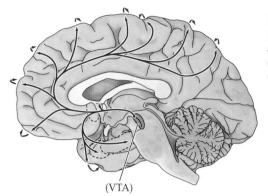

FIGURE 10.17   Dopaminergic mesolimbic and mesocortical pathways
Midsagittal view of dopaminergic neurons involved in alcohol reinforcement and withdrawal-induced dysphoria. The ventral tegmental area (VTA) is the origin of neurons that innervate the nucleus accumbens, amygdala, hippocampus (mesolimbic), and the cortex (mesocortical).

(VTA)

structures, including the NAcc and the central nucleus of the amygdala (**FIGURE 10.17**). The NAcc is particularly important because part of it (the shell) belongs to a network of structures called the extended amygdala, which is involved in integrating emotion with hormonal responses and sympathetic nervous system activity. The core of the NAcc is associated with the striatum, which modulates movement and establishes habitual behavior. Afferents to and efferents from the NAcc provide a means for combining motivational status, emotional content, and motor responses (DiChiara, 1997). The role of the NAcc in substance misuse seems to consist of supplying the primary reinforcing qualities that lead to repeated drug use and the incentive or motivation for the drug, which helps to explain why alcohol is so addictive for some people.

Increased dopaminergic transmission in the mesolimbic pathway occurs in response to administration of most drugs of abuse, including alcohol. In rats, alcohol consumption at intoxicating concentrations increases the firing rate of dopaminergic neurons in the VTA and subsequently elevates the amount of DA released in the NAcc, as measured by microdialysis, although the release is greater in genetically selected AP rats than in NP animals. Rats in operant chambers self-administer ethanol directly into the VTA, which presumably activates those neurons (probably by inhibiting inhibitory cells). Microinjection of dopamine receptor antagonists into the NAcc reduces (but does not abolish) the self-administration of ethanol in rats, as you would expect because alcohol-induced DA release is ineffective when postsynaptic receptors are blocked.

Because alcohol consumption clearly increases mesolimbic cell firing, we might ask how alcohol withdrawal affects the same pathway. In contrast to the acute effects, when animals have been allowed to consume alcohol in a chronic fashion, withdrawal of the drug dramatically reduces the firing rate of mesolimbic neurons and decreases DA release in the NAcc (Diana et al., 1993). **FIGURE 10.18** shows the decrease in synaptic DA in the NAcc, as well as the reduction in the DA metabolites 3,4-dihydroxyphenylacetic acid

(DOPAC) and homovanillic acid (HVA), as measured by microdialysis at various times after the last injection of ethanol. This decrease began at approximately 5 hours after the last alcohol administration and reached a maximum at around 10 to 12 hours. The same animals showed behavioral signs of withdrawal that began at 8 to 10 hours and continued throughout the testing period. The behavioral signs, reduced DA outflow, and reduced mesolimbic cell firing were all reversed by a single administration of alcohol. The reduction in mesolimbic DA is also reflected in a rebound depression of reinforcement mechanisms, as is shown by elevation of the threshold for intracranial stimulation. Elevated thresholds mean that more electrical current is needed to activate the reinforcing pathway (i.e., reinforcement is less rewarding than it was during the initial alcohol use). **FIGURE 10.19** shows that elevation of thresholds reached a maximum 6 to 8 hours after abrupt withdrawal and disappeared by 72 hours.

Although release of DA within the NAcc is clearly instrumental in ethanol-induced reinforcement, VTA cell firing during previously established, compulsive alcohol self-administration may have very different behavioral effects depending on the frequency of cell firing. This was elegantly demonstrated by Bass and colleagues (2013) using optogenetic technology. Using viral-mediated gene delivery to selectively express channelrhodopsin-2 (ChR2) on dopaminergic cells in the VTA (see Chapter 4 for a description of optogenetics), they stimulated the VTA neurons with pulses of blue light during binge-type alcohol drinking periods. Optical stimulation of the VTA produced corresponding time-locked release of DA in the NAcc as measured with voltammetry. When stimulation was of high frequency (50 Hz) and delivered in a phasic fashion, there was a large spike of DA released at the terminal regions that was short-lived. This stimulation had no effect on the rats' compulsive drinking. In contrast, more prolonged tonic stimulation at lower frequency (5 Hz) produced less DA efflux that was more prolonged. This tonic VTA activation produced a significant decrease in the number of licks on the alcohol drinking tube and amount of alcohol consumed, without having an effect on water consumption. It is well known that different populations of VTA neurons have low-frequency tonic and high-frequency phasic firing properties that serve different functions and modulate behavior in distinct ways. While phasic firing is associated with motivating goal-directed behaviors, the tonic firing that produces more prolonged synaptic DA may

(A)

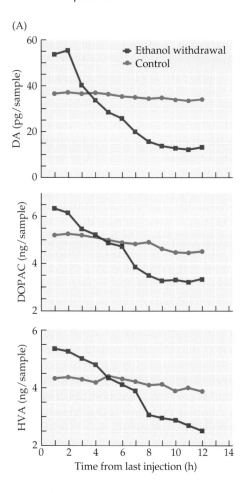

(B)

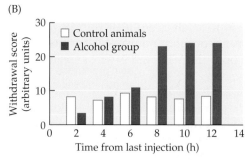

FIGURE 10.18 **Dopamine turnover and alcohol withdrawal** (A) Microdialysis collection of DA and its major metabolites, DOPAC and HVA, in the NAcc of rats at varying times after ethanol withdrawal shows significant reduction in DA turnover compared with control. (B) Development of abstinence signs in the same animals. Note the similarity in time course of biochemical measures and the occurrence of behavioral signs. The alcohol group received intoxicating doses of alcohol every 6 hours for 6 days before withdrawal. Control animals received sucrose of caloric value equal to the alcohol. The microdialysis collection of extracellular fluid and the behavioral measures of abstinence occurred at various times over the 12-hour period following ethanol withdrawal. Withdrawal scores were a composite of separate measures of tremor, vocalization on handling, bracing posture, rigidity, and others. (From M. Diana et al. 1993. *Proc Natl Acad Sci USA* 90: 7966–7969. © 1993 National Academy of Sciences, U.S.A.)

reduce phasic DA release by acting on presynaptic autoreceptors. The researchers conclude that such a negative feedback mechanism would reduce the salience of the contextual cues associated with the drinking chamber and reduce the binge-drinking behavior.

Dopamine is clearly important in the reinforcing effects of alcohol, but alcohol may increase mesolimbic firing indirectly secondary to its modulation of other neurotransmitter actions in the VTA, such as those produced by GABA, acetylcholine, serotonin, or endorphins. Despite the apparent importance of the dopaminergic neurons, almost total destruction of the mesolimbic terminals with 6-hydroxydopamine (6-OHDA) does not abolish self-administration of alcohol, suggesting that other dopamine-independent mechanisms contribute to ethanol reinforcement. One such mechanism may be the opioid peptide transmitters.

FIGURE 10.19 **Rebound depression of reinforcement during withdrawal** After alcohol withdrawal from dependent rats, a time-dependent increase in the current thresholds for electrical brain stimulation occurs, with maximum effect at 6 to 8 hours. The increase in threshold indicates that the animals need more stimulation to achieve reinforcement. Note that the *x*-axis is not a linear scale. (From G. Schulteis et al. 1995. *Proc Natl Acad Sci USA* 92: 5880–5884. © 1995 National Academy of Sciences, U.S.A.)

OPIOID SYSTEMS A family of neuropeptides (called endorphins) that have opiate-like effects modulate pain, mood, feeding, reinforcement, and response to stress, among other things (see Chapter 11). Opioids also contribute to the reinforcing effects of alcohol. Support for this statement comes from three types of studies (Froehlich, 1997). First, alcohol enhances endogenous opioid activity in both rodents and humans. Acute administration of alcohol increases endogenous opioid (endorphin and enkephalin) release from brain slices and the pituitary gland in vitro and also increases blood levels of opioids in humans in vivo. Opioids are released into the blood from the pituitary gland. Acute alcohol administration also increases gene expression of both endorphin and enkephalin in selected brain areas of rats, which would increase the amount of peptides available. In contrast, chronic alcohol administration reduces gene expression, making less of the peptides available for release. In humans, chronic

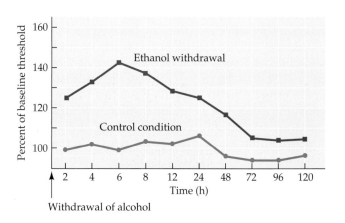

alcohol use leads to reduced brain levels of endorphin. Since the release of DA in mesolimbic neurons is regulated by opioid cells in both the VTA and NAcc, alcohol-induced opioid release may produce reinforcement by modulating DA (Herz, 1997). Reduced opioid levels may contribute to the dysphoria that accompanies chronic alcohol use and withdrawal.

Second, if alcohol-induced enhancement of opioid systems is at least partially responsible for reinforcement, then blocking opioid receptors should reduce alcohol consumption. Opioid receptor antagonists like naloxone and naltrexone, which compete for the endogenous opioid receptors, do significantly reduce alcohol self-administration in animals. Antagonists that act on specific subtypes (μ and δ) of opioid receptors (see Chapter 11) also reduce operant self-administration. Several clinical trials of opioid antagonists in patients with AUD found reduced alcohol consumption, relapse, and craving, as well as a reported decrease in the subjective "high." (Further discussion can be found in the section on treatment of alcohol use disorder later in this chapter.) Finally, μ-opioid receptor knockout mice fail to self-administer ethanol and in some experimental conditions show an aversion to the drug (Roberts et al., 2000).

Third, if opioids have a role in reinforcement, then perhaps we should expect to see a difference in the opioid systems of genetic strains of animals that show greater or lesser preference for alcohol. In rat strains that have been genetically bred for alcohol preference, endogenous opioid systems are generally more responsive to the effects of alcohol. For example, AP rats, when compared with NP rats, released significantly more β-endorphin from the hypothalamus when infused with alcohol in vitro and showed enhanced β-endorphin gene expression in the pituitary. Additionally, AP rats have higher baseline levels of μ-opioid receptors in selected limbic areas, including the shell of the NAcc and the amygdala.

In addition to having a role in reinforcement, evidence suggests that opioids play a part in alcohol craving. In individuals with AUD, positron emission tomography (PET) imaging was used to determine the number of μ-opioid receptors in the NAcc and in other brain areas associated with reinforcement and craving following several weeks of abstinence. Abstinence increased the μ-opioid receptors found in these individuals, and the number of receptors was positively correlated with scores on the Obsessive-Compulsive Drinking Scale developed by Raymond F. Anton, indicating that as μ-opioid receptor numbers increased, craving scores also increased (Heinz et al., 2005). A similar correlation of receptor number in the frontal cortex with craving scores suggested to researchers that activation of opioid receptors may impair executive control, leading to an increased probability of relapse. These results may explain individual differences among alcohol misusers in their ability to abstain from alcohol use.

OTHER NEUROTRANSMITTERS **TABLE 10.3** summarizes some of the cellular effects of alcohol and their

TABLE 10.3 Role of Selected Neurotransmitters in Cellular and Behavioral Effects of Alcohol

Neurotransmitter	Acute cellular effects	Chronic cellular effects	Behavioral effects
Glutamate	Receptor antagonism and reduced glutamate release	——	Memory loss
	——	Up-regulation of receptors and rebound increase in glutamate release	Rebound hyperexcitability of the abstinence syndrome
	——	Extreme hyperexcitability and massive Ca^{2+} influx (rebound)	Brain damage
GABA	Increase in GABA-induced Cl⁻ influx to hyperpolarize	——	Sedative effects: anxiety reduction, sedation, incoordination, memory impairment
	——	Neuroadaptive decrease in GABA function without change in receptor number	Tolerance and signs of hyperexcitability during withdrawal (seizures, tremors)
Dopamine	Increase in dopamine transmission in mesolimbic tract	——	Reinforcement
	——	Reduced firing rate, release, metabolism	Negative affect as a sign of withdrawal
Opioids	Increase in endogenous opioid synthesis and release	——	Reinforcement
	——	Neuroadaptive decrease in endorphin levels	Dysphoria

contributions to behavior. Both laboratory animal and human studies implicate many more interacting neurotransmitter systems in the action of alcohol than we have had the space to discuss. The effects of acute and chronic alcohol administration on these receptors are responsible for the changes in cell signaling, both rapid ionotropic and slower metabotropic actions such as those regulated by second messengers. Second messengers such as cAMP and their cascade of effects within the cell that ultimately lead to phosphorylation of the transcription factor CREB (pCREB) may be responsible for more long-term changes in cell function, including altered gene expression. Those changes may represent the transition from casual drinking to dependence to compulsive alcohol use. Among the target genes for CREB are those for neuropeptide Y and brain-derived neurotrophic factor (BDNF), both implicated in long-term memory, neuroplasticity associated with alcohol drinking, and anxiety-like behaviors. The effects of alcohol on adenylyl cyclase–cAMP–PKA activity depend upon the nature of alcohol status (acute, chronic, withdrawal) as well as the brain region (prefrontal cortex [PFC], hippocampus, amygdala) investigated. In the cortex and hippocampus, acute alcohol enhances adenylyl cyclase–cAMP–PKA activity, while more prolonged exposure to alcohol reduces it, possibly by inducing the expression of a protein kinase inhibitory factor. A weakened control of the amygdala by PFC has been suggested as a preliminary step in the neuroadaptation underlying alcohol dependence and may be responsible in part for the enhanced anxiety at acute alcohol withdrawal. In the central and medial nuclei of the amygdala, acute alcohol withdrawal reduces pCREB and subsequent gene expression. In AP rats this reduction is associated with heightened anxiety and excessive alcohol consumption. These types of studies suggest that drugs that enhance the cAMP cascade, such as rolipram, a drug that inhibits the breakdown of cAMP, may be therapeutically useful in treating AUD. An excellent discussion of the role of this intracellular signaling pathway in alcohol drinking can be found in Mons and Beracochea (2016). Further discussion of the neurochemical effects of alcohol is beyond the scope of this chapter, but details can be found in several reviews (Sprow and Thiele, 2012; Most et al., 2014).

SECTION SUMMARY

- Ethanol has specific actions on multiple neurotransmitter systems but also has nonspecific actions that change the fluid nature of membrane phospholipids.

- The use of animal models in alcohol research does the following: (1) It controls for poor nutrition, liver damage, comorbid drug use, and psychiatric disorders associated with human alcohol misusers; (2) It permits the use of techniques inappropriate in humans; (3) It allows genetic manipulations; and (4) It allows researchers to evaluate novel treatment strategies.

- Rodent models exist for acquisition and maintenance of drinking, physical dependence, relapse (alcohol seeking), compulsive drinking, and binge-type drinking.

- Inbred strains of AP and HAD rats provide the means to evaluate behavior, neural mechanisms, and genetics of AUD.

- Alcohol acutely inhibits glutamate neurotransmission by reducing the effects of glutamate at the NMDA receptor and reducing glutamate release.

- Modulation of glutamate by alcohol has a role in ethanol-induced memory impairment, rebound hyperexcitability during withdrawal, NMDA-mediated excitotoxicity causing brain damage, and the intellectual disability associated with FAS.

- Chronic ethanol up-regulates NMDA receptors in humans and animal models and increases glutamate release, providing an explanation for the hyperexcitability and seizures seen at abrupt withdrawal.

- Alcohol enhances GABA-induced chloride entry and hyperpolarization by modulating $GABA_A$ receptors and stimulating GABA release.

- The effect of alcohol on synaptic $GABA_A$ receptors requires high concentrations that are associated with high levels of intoxication. Extrasynaptic $GABA_A$ receptors having δ and $\alpha 4$ or $\alpha 6$ subunits are extremely sensitive to the low concentrations of GABA that remain in the extracellular space, making them more likely to be mediators of low to moderate amounts of drinking.

- Extrasynaptic $GABA_A$ receptors in the shell region of the NAcc seem to mediate some of the reinforcing effects of alcohol.

- Chronic ethanol leads to down-regulation of $GABA_A$ receptors, making the organism more sensitive to seizure-inducing agents.

- Alcohol acts on both pre- and postsynaptic metabotropic $GABA_B$ receptors and modulates alcohol consumption.

- Ethanol activates dopaminergic cells in the VTA, causing the release of DA in the NAcc, which is involved in the positive reinforcement processes that lead to repeated drug taking.

- In physically dependent rodents, withdrawal of alcohol reduces the firing rate of mesolimbic neurons, decreases DA release in the NAcc, and causes rebound depression of reinforcement mechanisms as shown by an elevation in the threshold for intracranial self-stimulation.

- Low-frequency tonic stimulation of VTA cells, in contrast to high-frequency phasic stimulation, has produced prolonged low DA efflux and has inhibited compulsive drinking in rats.

- Acute alcohol use increases opioid release and increases gene expression of opioid peptides. Chronic alcohol use reduces gene expression and lowers levels of peptides.

- Blocking opioid receptors with naloxone reduces alcohol self-administration. μ-opioid receptor knockout mice fail to self-administer ethanol. High levels of μ-opioid receptors correlate with scores on craving.

- AP rats release more opioids in response to ethanol and show enhanced opioid peptide gene expression.

- Ethanol modulates the function of many additional neurotransmitters to alter ionotropic and metabotropic signaling.

10.3 Alcohol Use Disorder (AUD)

AUD is a serious and complex phenomenon that consists of psychological, neurobiological, genetic, and sociocultural factors, making it difficult to define and treat. According to the latest *Diagnostic and Statistical Manual of Mental Disorders* (DSM-5) the term *alcoholism* has been replaced with *alcohol use disorder*. You can find the specific criteria for AUD according to the DSM-5 in Chapter 9. Regardless of the specific definition, AUD damages the health and well-being of sufferers and those around them. Financial costs of the disorder are huge and include medical treatment of alcohol-induced disease, loss associated with accidents on the road and at work, lost productivity, criminal justice costs, and financial disruption that accompanies the breakdown of families (**TABLE 10.4**). Many volumes have been written about alcohol use and AUD from various points of view—some emotionally evocative, others based on theoretical models or empirical research. The final section of this chapter presents a brief synopsis of some of the research findings.

Defining AUD and estimating its incidence have proved difficult

Chapter 9 describes substance use disorder and identifies some of the criteria used by professionals to diagnose the condition. In addition, the chapter provides multiple theoretical models of substance misuse and

TABLE 10.4 Estimated Costs of Excessive Drinking by Type of Cost[a]	
Cost category	**Total cost**
Specialty care for alcohol abuse treatment	$10,668
Hospitalization attributed to alcohol-related illness	$5,156
Medical care for fetal alcohol syndrome	$2,538
Special education for fetal alcohol syndrome	$369
Decreased productivity at work	$74,102
Lost productivity due to absenteeism	$4,237
Lost productivity due to incarceration	$6,329
Lost productivity due to premature death	$65,062
Motor vehicle crashes	$13,718

Source: After E. E. Bouchery et al. 2011. *Am J Prev Med* 41: 516–524.
[a]Costs are in millions of dollars for the year 2006 in the United States.

provides a critique of each. In this section, we look specifically at **alcohol use disorder**, a form of substance misuse that has been historically difficult to define because the drug is legal and is used by most individuals in a way that does not harm themselves or others. For the layperson, someone with an "alcohol problem" may be anyone who drinks more than he or she does. It is important to realize that not everyone who drinks alcohol consumes excessive amounts, and not all heavy drinkers develop dependence. However, it is difficult to objectively define inappropriate amounts of alcohol because the frequency and pattern of use are as significant as the total amount consumed. For example, consuming five alcoholic drinks over 1 week's time does not have the same physical and social consequences as consuming five drinks in a row for men, or four for women, which is the usual definition of **binge drinking**. Individuals with AUD do not necessarily have to start each day with a drink, nor do they necessarily drink all day long, but they may drink very heavily periodically. Instead of emphasizing quantity, the diagnosis of AUD depends on identifying a cluster of behavioral, cognitive, and physical characteristics. For the clinician, the essential features of AUD are compulsive alcohol seeking and use despite damaging health and social consequences. Unfortunately, because other groups and government agencies use different criteria, there is still a great deal of variability in how professionals use the terms *addiction*, *misuse*, *abuse*, *dependency*, and *problem drinking*.

Part of the difficulty in defining AUD is the tremendous heterogeneity among those individuals misusing alcohol. A clear classification scheme of alcohol-misusing individuals is needed for studying neurobiological etiology and genetic analysis, predicting the course of the disorder and optimal treatment approach, and developing prevention strategies. The interest in identifying subtypes of alcohol misusers was initiated by Cloninger (1987), who proposed a popular categorization of alcohol misusers into type I and type II alcoholics. These categories were based on differences in alcohol-induced defining characteristics, such as inability to control drinking and age of onset; personality characteristics such as behavioral inhibition and novelty seeking; and etiology, including family history of AUD and environmental influence. Type I alcoholics generally begin drinking later in life and experience guilt and fear about their AUD. These individuals rarely have trouble with the law or display antisocial activities. Many drink to escape stress or unpleasant situations in their environment. Most females with AUD are type I, although many men also fit this description. Type II alcoholics are almost always male and display thrill-seeking, antisocial, and perhaps criminal activities. They have lower cerebrospinal fluid levels of the serotonin (5-HT) metabolite 5-hydroxyindoleacetic acid (5-HIAA)—a result that matches the human and animal

TABLE 10.5 Babor's Type A/B AUD

Characteristics	Type A	Type B
Age of onset	Late	Early
Childhood risk factors	Fewer	More
Severity of dependence	Less	Greater
Alcohol-related physical consequences	Fewer	More
Alcohol-related social consequences	Fewer	More
Previous treatment history for alcohol problems	Fewer	More
Psychopathological dysfunction	Less	Greater
Life stress	Less	More
Polydrug use	Less	More
Distress in work and family	Less	More

Source: After T. F. Babor et al., 1992. *Arch Gen Psychiatry* 49: 599–608.

literature regarding impulsivity, aggression, and suicide. Type II drinkers have greater genetic vulnerability and begin drinking at an early age.

Since Cloninger's early attempt at categorization, a variety of multidimensional typologies have been developed that include larger sample sizes and improved sample selection methods, though they have many similarities to the original. Babor and coworkers (1992) used a biopsychosocial approach because the variability among those with AUD is likely due to an interaction of those multiple factors. Their clustering technique looked for a pattern of naturally occurring common features (derived from 17 severity-related dimensions) to increase homogeneity within the types. Using that technique, they identified two types, A and B. The characteristics for types A and B are shown in **TABLE 10.5**. There have been a number of subsequent efforts at typology, with some researchers identifying as many as five types with a large number of defining characteristics. These more complex and specific categorizations are important for neurobiological and genetic research but may prove unwieldy in the clinic because of the increased time needed for assessment of patients. Also, the individuals within the types are rarely followed up longitudinally, so clinicians do not have data regarding the expected course of illness or response to treatment. Finally, most previous typologies used individuals from treatment-seeking samples, and they are likely to be quite different from individuals with AUD in the general population.

Disparities in the definition of AUD have led to equally large differences in estimated incidence.

Although you may think of an individual with AUD as a poor, aging, homeless individual living on the street, in reality there is no such thing as typical (**FIGURE 10.20**). Although many homeless individuals do suffer from a variety of psychiatric disorders and misuse both illicit drugs and alcohol at high rates, only 5% of alcohol-dependent individuals fit that category. Based on the U.S. government's annual survey of drug use, the rates of alcohol use in the United States have remained relatively steady for the last 10 years, although other major public health surveys suggest a steady increase in both alcohol use and misuse. The most commonly accepted statistic is that approximately 10% of Americans have some problem with alcohol use, and as many as 15 million adults are dependent on alcohol (Substance Abuse and Mental Health Services Administration, 2016). Significant gender differences are seen in alcohol use and misuse for all age groups. The 2019 National Survey on Drug Use and Health found that among drinkers age 18 and older, more men (88.4%) than women (83.0%) consumed alcohol to some extent over their lifetimes. Heavy drinking, defined as five or more drinks on the same occasion on each of 5 days in the past month, was reported in 8.3% of males and 4.5% of females. Binge alcohol use

The typical alcoholic American

There's no such thing as typical. We have all kinds.

FIGURE 10.20 **A wide variety of individuals suffer from alcohol use disorder** About 15.7 million Americans have AUD, making it our largest drug problem.

during the past month was also higher in men (31.1%) than women (22.2%). (Substance Abuse and Mental Health Services Administration, 2019). While alcohol misuse drops significantly in the elderly, problems associated with drinking can be more serious because of drug interactions and medical complications.

A closer focus on the drinking patterns of college students might be appropriate, since there has been a great deal of public concern regarding student accidents and fatalities where alcohol was involved. Several large-scale studies are available to guide you in further research (Hingson and Zha, 2009; Hingson et al., 2009; White et al., 2013). A variety of U.S. government surveys have estimated that 44.7% of 18- to 24-year-old college students engaged in binge drinking at least once in the last month. That behavior has led to a variety of serious outcomes for many. An estimated 15% of full-time 4-year college students suffered alcohol-related injury, and 12% were assaulted by other drinking students. Furthermore, alcohol overdose deaths remain a significant problem: each year more than 5000 deaths in that age group have been attributed to alcohol use. Although this group reported a significant number of alcohol-related problems (**TABLE 10.6**), only 1% believed that they had a drinking problem.

Underage drinking has become the focus of a major initiative by the National Institute on Alcohol Abuse and Alcoholism (NIAAA) and several other governmental agencies aimed at developing effective prevention and intervention programs. The focus is on this age group because according to the CDC, 16% of all the alcohol consumed in the United States is consumed by individuals between 12 and 20 years of age, much of it (90%) during binge drinking. Numerous analyses of national surveys show that the younger the individuals are when they begin to drink (less than 13 years old), the greater is the probability that they will develop AUD later in life. This association occurs even for low levels of alcohol consumption but is exaggerated by binge drinking. Additionally, early drinking predicts other risky behaviors, including driving after drinking, riding with drinking drivers, becoming involved in physical fights, carrying weapons, and unintentionally injuring another person (Research Society on Alcoholism, 2015). Impulse-control problems such as compulsive gambling and antisocial behaviors are also predicted by early adolescent drinking. Additionally, adolescents are more vulnerable to alcohol-induced neurological deficits because neurodevelopmental events occurring at that time of life include synaptic pruning, changes in receptor number and sensitivity, and the refinement of neural circuits. A disruption of neurodevelopment is suggested by animal research showing that immature neuronal function and behavior *persist* in the adult animals that were exposed to alcohol as adolescents. Among the altered behaviors is an increase in social anxiety in the adults, as demonstrated by a reduction in social investigation and play with a novel partner. Fear conditioning and spatial learning that are dependent on the hippocampus are also impaired in adulthood by adolescent, but not adult, administration of alcohol. This deficit has been associated with impairments in neurogenesis in the hippocampus (Spear, 2014) as well as changes in hippocampal dendritic morphology. These morphological changes include an increase in immature dendritic spines and corresponding decrease in mature spines, reduction in postsynaptic proteins that are associated with neurodevelopmental disorders, and alterations in memory-related synaptic plasticity (Risher et al., 2015). Such neurodevelopmental pathology may be responsible for promoting the retention of adolescent-like phenotypes such as impulsivity, cognitive deficits, and reduced sensitivity to alcohol, leading to increased drinking.

The causes of AUD are multimodal

No specific cause of AUD has been identified, but a variety of factors contribute to the vulnerability of any given individual. It

---

TABLE 10.6 Percentage of Non binge, Infrequent and Frequent Binge Drinkers Reporting Alcohol-Related Problems[a]

Alcohol-related problem	Percentage		
	Non binge	Infrequent	Frequent
General disorientation Do something you later regret	14%	37%	63%
Sexual activity Engage in unplanned or unprotected sex	12%	30%	63%
Violent or aggressive behavior Argue with friends or damage property	10%	30%	64%
Disciplinary action Have contact with law enforcement	1%	4%	11%
Personal injury Get injured	2%	9%	23%
School performance Miss a class	8%	30%	61%

Source: After H. Wechsler et al. 1994. *JAMA* 272: 1672–1677.

[a] Binge drinkers reported having at least four (women) or five (men) drinks in a row at least once during the 2 weeks prior to completing the survey. Infrequent binge drinkers binged one or two times in the prior two weeks, while frequent binge drinkers binged three or more times in the prior two weeks. Non binge drinkers reported consuming alcohol in the last year but did not binge.

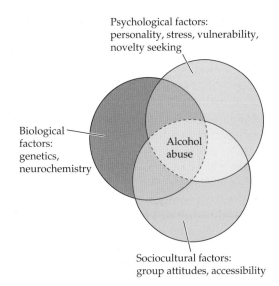

Psychological factors:
personality, stress, vulnerability,
novelty seeking

Biological
factors:
genetics,
neurochemistry

Alcohol
abuse

Sociocultural factors:
group attitudes, accessibility

FIGURE 10.21 **Three-factor vulnerability model**
Biological, psychological, and sociocultural influences
contribute to the development of alcohol abuse.

is quite clear that multiple factors stem from three essential areas: (1) psychological, (2) neurobiological, and (3) sociocultural (**FIGURE 10.21**). Although we are forced to discuss them in a linear fashion, keep in mind that complex interactions exist among the areas. Because the literature is extensive, this section will provide an overview and suggest methods for future research.

PSYCHOLOGICAL FACTORS Although no alcoholic personality has ever been defined, one vulnerability factor for AUD is the response to stress. Both animal and human studies show an interaction between both acute and chronic stress and initiation of alcohol use, maintenance of drug consumption, and relapse after withdrawal (Brady and Sonne, 1999). Some have used the term *symptomatic* drinking to describe the reinforcing effects of alcohol when stress and tension are relieved. The individual who no longer drinks on a social occasion but drinks each day after work to relieve tension represents an example of symptomatic drinking. However, although alcohol has been found to reduce anxiety in some cases, the relationship between stress and alcohol use is complex and depends on multiple variables, including the nature and timing of the stressor. Animal studies show that the effects of stress on voluntary alcohol consumption depend on the nature of the stressor applied (e.g., restraint, forced swimming, social isolation), whether it is acute or chronic, and whether the animal can predict the onset of the stress and/or control the stressful event. Furthermore, a circular association is seen because although alcohol can be shown to relieve stress under some conditions, alcohol also increases the function of brain and endocrine stress systems, making alcohol itself an additional stressor that may lead to further alcohol use

(see Box 2.5 for an introduction to the neuroendocrine stress response of the hypothalamic–pituitary–adrenal [HPA] axis). Numerous rodent studies have shown that acute alcohol administration elevates levels of the stress hormones corticotropin-releasing factor (CRF), adrenocorticotropic hormone (ACTH), and glucocorticoids (e.g., cortisol). Furthermore, withdrawal of alcohol after several weeks of chronic administration produces more anxiety-like behavior in rodents in the elevated plus-maze following restraint stress compared with controls. The fact that the anxiety-like behavior could be reduced by blocking CRF receptors demonstrates that CRF mediates the anxiety. Additionally, during withdrawal, CRF expression was greater in brain areas regulating anxiety, including the bed nucleus of the stria terminalis and the central nucleus of the amygdala (see Chapter 17 for a discussion of the neural substrates of anxiety), and the behavioral stress response was enhanced. Likewise, in humans, alcohol withdrawal increases anxiety as well as alcohol consumption. More important, it appears that although post-withdrawal anxiety subsides within a few weeks, sensitization to stressors and increased reactivity persists for long periods. This increased sensitivity is responsible for stress-induced craving and relapse. The fact that stressors frequently lead to further alcohol consumption suggests the potential usefulness of CRF receptor antagonists in preventing relapse.

The significance of stress to alcohol misuse is also demonstrated by the epidemiological evidence of high comorbidity of anxiety disorders and AUD. The central nucleus of the amygdala is the brain region responsible for orchestrating the various components of an emotional response to fearful or anxiety-provoking stimuli. As such, it activates the sympathetic nervous system and HPA axis and increases vigilance, among other things. Hence it should come as no surprise that the amygdala is overactive in many anxiety disorders, including post-traumatic stress disorder (PTSD), social phobia, panic disorder, and generalized anxiety disorder (see Chapter 17). Animal models of alcohol dependence and withdrawal have also shown neuroadaptations in the central nucleus of the amygdala that have been considered the basis for a stress "kindling" process—that is, an enhanced sensitivity to environmental stressors. This increased sensitivity intensifies the magnitude of the stress response to aversive environmental stimuli, as is well documented in humans attempting to abstain from alcohol use (see Gilpin et al., 2015).

Another significant risk factor for AUD is family history, which is associated with greater cortisol response following psychosocial stress compared with individuals without a family history of AUD. Furthermore, alcohol has a greater suppressing effect on the stress responses in those with a family history. Since HPA reactivity to stressors shows significant heritability, researchers are working to identify gene polymorphisms that are involved in the differences, with the hope of developing targeted drug treatment plans for selected individuals. Alcohol misuse has long been known to be associated with high levels of lifetime anxiety. Consistent with the findings of rodent studies, stress early in life is a significant environmental risk factor for alcohol misuse in the adult, just as it predicts adult depression (see Chapter 18) and anxiety disorders (see Chapter 17). However, in agreement with several other studies, Schmid and colleagues (2010) found that the number of early stressful life events could predict early onset of drinking and higher levels of alcohol consumption at age 19, but only for those individuals with a particular polymorphism of the *corticotropin-releasing factor receptor 1* (*CRF$_1$*) gene, clearly indicating a gene × stress × alcohol interaction. The fact that gene polymorphisms of *CRF$_1$* are associated with risky drinking behavior suggests a potential screening method for identifying future problem behaviors and perhaps indicates the optimal treatment approach for these individuals should such behaviors develop. Differences in individuals' stress response systems and in their perception and appraisal of stress may help to explain some of the differential vulnerability to alcohol misuse. These and other pivotal studies are summarized in two excellent reviews (Clarke and Schumann, 2009; Spanagel et al., 2014).

In an earlier section, we mentioned that alcohol increases DA transmission in the mesolimbic tract, thereby mediating reinforcement. It is significant that cortisol seems to sensitize this circuitry, which means that alcohol-induced increases in the HPA axis function and subsequent elevations in cortisol may contribute to its reinforcing properties. It is intriguing to find that corticosterone (the rodent version of cortisol) itself is self-administered by laboratory animals, apparently because its binding to glucocorticoid receptors in NAcc activates a feedback loop to VTA that enhances mesolimbic cell firing. This idea is supported by rodent studies showing that glucocorticoids enhance mesolimbic DA and increase drug-seeking behaviors. A striking relationship exists: even among individuals without substance misuse problems, those who secreted more cortisol in response to stress also released more mesolimbic DA and experienced greater subjective effects of psychostimulants. It is suspected that this relationship may cause some individuals to increase consumption beyond casual use. In contrast, as was mentioned in the section on DA, withdrawal reduces the mesolimbic neuron firing rate and is associated with a negative affective state that acts as an internal stressor. Hence, although mild stress enhances mesolimbic function, chronic stress further reduces the function of this pathway and increases craving—a state that would make relapse to alcohol consumption more likely (Uhart and Wand, 2009; Spangel et al., 2014).

Novelty seeking by individuals may also increase the risk for using alcohol and other drugs of abuse because exposure to novel events activates the dopaminergic mesolimbic pathway in a manner similar to that seen with most misused substances (Bardo, 1996). Individual differences in the need for novelty and drug-seeking behavior are under genetic control and may explain why some individuals experiment with drugs initially and why some more readily become compulsive users. Differences in the need for stimulation have been applied to drug and alcohol prevention programs that use fast-paced, physiologically arousing, and unconventional message delivery to appeal to the target audience.

In replicating and expanding on earlier studies, Nees and colleagues (2012) found that behavior (risk taking and aversion for delayed reward), neural response in the brain reward circuitry in response to large versus small rewards, and personality (extraversion, impulsivity, sensation seeking, and novelty seeking) interacted and were predictive of early alcohol use and subsequent alcohol addiction. Personality traits represented the strongest predictor. Since genetics contributes to these phenotypic characteristics, future research may be directed toward evaluating genetic factors in early adolescent drinking models.

NEUROBIOLOGICAL FACTORS One significant neurobiological factor in AUD is genetic vulnerability. Close relatives of alcohol-dependent individuals have a three to seven times greater risk for AUD than the general population. Both twin and adoption studies show that genetics is correlated with vulnerability, particularly for the more severe type of AUD. In adoption studies, the risk of AUD is higher in children of alcohol-dependent parents even when they are adopted into nonalcoholic families. AUD concordance rates are higher in monozygotic (54%) than in dizygotic (28%) twins, demonstrating the influence of genes but leaving significant variability to be explained by other factors. Overall, genetics explains 50% to 60% of the variance of risk for dependence in both men and women, although the percentage may be higher for some types of AUD than others. The heritability of alcohol misuse is less, at about 38%.

Although the importance of heritability is clear, identifying specific genes is much more difficult because of the complexity of the disorder. To help with genetic analysis, researchers utilize subgroups of people with AUD on the basis of various characteristics such as severity, craving, occurrence of withdrawal, gender, and so forth. Many genes have been identified as potential vulnerability factors, but each of them contribute only a small amount to the risk of developing AUD.

To find genetic patterns in humans with AUD, several methods may be used. Rietschel and Treutlein

(2013) summarize recent findings using each of the methods. One method, called **linkage studies**, examines the inheritance pattern of genes that increase disease susceptibility using DNA analysis and the occurrence of AUD in many members of a large number of families. Researchers look for easily identified genetic markers and determine which are most closely related to alcohol-associated behaviors. Affected family members would be expected to have more of those markers than their unaffected relatives. The most consistently identified region that is related to several traits of AUD and that has been found in multiple ethnic groups is on chromosome 4. Within a broad region of the chromosome (4q22–4q32) is a group of seven genes for the enzyme alcohol dehydrogenase that metabolizes alcohol (discussed further below). A region of chromosome 2 (2q35) has been linked to the alcohol-dependence phenotype and to low sensitivity to alcohol, which is a risk factor for AUD (see Rietschel and Treutlein, 2013). Individuals with AUD frequently report that early in their drinking, they experienced very little effect of alcohol unless they consumed large quantities. Schuckit (2000) measured subjective intoxication, "sway score" when balanced on a straight line, and hormonal response to alcohol in young sons of alcohol-dependent parents compared with controls. The men who later developed AUD showed a reduced response to moderate levels of alcohol for each of the measures (**FIGURE 10.22**). More important, Schuckit found that the low response rate increased the risk for AUD fourfold *regardless of family history* when the men were evaluated 8 years later.

The **case–control method**, a type of **association analysis**, compares the genes of unrelated affected and unaffected individuals to see whether more members of the affected population have a particular form (allele) of a gene. The gene does not necessarily have to be directly associated with the disorder but may be a marker associated with a characteristic that increases the risk of developing AUD. For example, meta-analyses of case–control studies show the strongest association for genes responsible for the manufacture of alcohol dehydrogenase (in agreement with linkage analysis) and aldehyde dehydrogenase. As you know, both enzymes are involved in alcohol metabolism (see Figure 10.5). Alcohol dehydrogenase converts alcohol to the toxic metabolite acetaldehyde that is subsequently metabolized to acetic acid by aldehyde dehydrogenase. Increased levels of acetaldehyde cause flushing, nausea, headache, and increased heart rate. Since individuals with the gene for the inactive form of the aldehyde dehydrogenase experience these unpleasant effects when drinking alcohol, they have essentially no risk for AUD. Alternatively, acetaldehyde concentration may be elevated by greater alcohol dehydrogenase activity, producing the same unpleasant effects when alcohol is consumed. Hence, individuals with the gene for the more active form of alcohol dehydrogenase have low probability of AUD. Rodents carrying a particular human allele have a 90% increase in enzyme activity, which produces a 3.5- to 5.0-fold elevation in blood acetaldehyde and reduces alcohol consumption by 50% (Rietschel and Treutlein, 2013), making that allele a protective factor against AUD. Readers interested in learning more about the genetic basis of AUD are encouraged to read a recent review by Sanchez-Roige and colleagues (2021).

Other case–control studies have looked for variants in genes involved in neurotransmitter function, such as receptor subtypes, synthesizing enzymes, and reuptake transporters. For example, a genetic variant of the 5-HT transporter is associated with anxiety and with low sensitivity to alcohol, and this makes affected individuals more vulnerable to developing AUD.

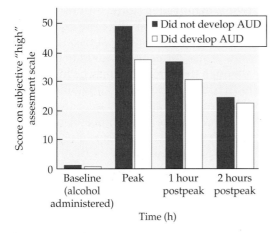
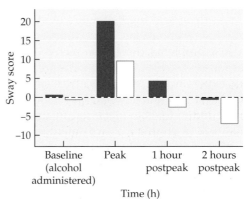

FIGURE 10.22 Low sensitivity to alcohol is a risk factor for AUD Subjective assessment of "high" and sway scores following a moderate dose (0.75 ml/kg) of alcohol in men who later developed alcohol dependence and in those who did not. Those vulnerable to alcohol dependence showed significantly less response to the same dose at peak blood level (1 hour) and 1 and 2 hours after the peak. (After M. A. Schuckit. 1994. *Am J Psychiatry* 151: 184–189.)

As described in Chapter 4, **genome-wide association studies** (**GWAS**) analyze hundreds of thousands of genomic markers to detect differences in the frequency of alleles across the entire genome. Describing the many research projects conducted that compare cases of AUD phenotype and controls is beyond the scope of this chapter, but Rietschel and Treutlein (2013) provide in-depth details for those interested. However, suffice it to say that specific markers located in the alcohol dehydrogenase gene cluster achieved genome-wide significance in multiple reports, which is in agreement with the most consistent linkage analyses and association studies.

Rodent models, as described in an earlier section, are extremely important in evaluating the genetic contribution to isolated drinking behaviors. Researchers use selectively bred lines of animals that differ with respect to alcohol-related traits, such as withdrawal sensitivity, level of alcohol consumption, or alcohol-induced hypothermia, to search for clusters of genes linked to the particular trait. A second technique uses gene knockout animals, in which a particular gene is selectively deleted, before evaluating animal alcohol-associated behaviors.

SOCIOCULTURAL FACTORS Social and cultural factors mold changing attitudes about drinking, as well as the definition of problem drinking. Group attitudes also determine how much alcohol is available in a particular environment—for example, by controlling hours of sale, public consumption, and advertising. The examination of cultural influences on drinking was pioneered by Bales (1946), who suggested that cultures of those who abstain from alcohol use or who restrict it for religious purposes have the lowest rates of alcohol misuse. In contrast, societies that engage in social drinking in public settings and in which drinking is condoned for personal reasons, such as tension reduction, have higher rates of alcohol misuse. The importance of cultural influence is well demonstrated by the low rate of AUD among Muslims and Mormons, two groups with religious prohibitions on alcohol use. A low rate of AUD is also seen in Jewish populations, who use alcohol in a religious ceremonial way among family and do not condone intoxication. Further discussion of cultural influences on vulnerability to alcohol dependence can be found in several sources, including McNeece and DiNitto (1998). An excellent pictorial article by Boyd Gibbons (1992) in *National Geographic* describes many cultural differences in alcohol use and misuse.

The most obvious conclusion that can be drawn from our discussion of etiology is that multiple factors contribute to AUD. The neurochemical effects of alcohol and genetic predisposition to heavy drinking; the personality, cognitive structure, and expectations of the individual; and social, cultural, and economic variables all affect the use of alcohol and vulnerability to alcohol dependence.

Multiple treatment options provide hope for rehabilitation

An increasing number of treatment programs for AUD have been developed over the past few years, with the goal of promoting abstinence or reduced drinking, reducing the number and severity of relapses, and improving function in daily living. Multiple approaches give alcohol misusers increased hope for recovery.

The first step in treatment is **detoxification** because withdrawal symptoms (if present) are strong motivators and can be physiologically dangerous. Under medical care, detoxification involves substituting a benzodiazepine such as chlordiazepoxide (Librium) or diazepam (Valium). These drugs prevent alcohol withdrawal, including seizures and DTs. The long-acting nature of the drugs stabilizes the individual, and as the dose is gradually reduced, withdrawal symptoms are minimized. It should be mentioned that some symptoms of withdrawal increase in magnitude with successive withdrawals. This is true for seizure activity, and repeated episodes of withdrawal-induced seizures may be responsible for some of the long-term deficits in cognitive processing and emotional regulation that in turn may lead to less control over drinking.

PSYCHOSOCIAL REHABILITATION After detoxification, **psychosocial rehabilitation** programs help the alcohol misuser to prevent relapse through abstinence or to reduce the amount of alcohol consumed if relapse occurs (Fuller and Hiller-Sturmhofel, 1999). Many programs are available, but we provide here only a cursory survey of a few of them. For a more thorough discussion, see Jhanjee (2014). The three basic types are (1) individual and group therapy to provide emotional support and address psychological and social problems associated with dependence, (2) residential alcohol-free treatment settings, and (3) self-help groups such as Alcoholics Anonymous (AA). All of these methods reduce alcohol use among patients, although as is true for other chronic diseases, the relapse rate is high. Approximately 40% resume drinking within 3 years, and estimates of long-term relapse rates vary between 20% and 70% (Moos and Moos, 2006). However, rather than being considered a failure of treatment, relapse should be the signal for initiating a new treatment plan. Following multiple episodes of treatment and self-help, approximately 60% eventually reach a state of sustained abstinence.

AA is perhaps the best known of the self-help treatment programs and is the most frequently recommended. It is an organization in which all members suffer from AUD because an underlying assumption is that only a peer group is able to understand alcohol-dependent individuals and help them accept their disorder and admit their powerlessness over it. The emphasis of the group is a spiritual one in which individual rely on a "higher power" to help them remain sober. The self-help group provides peer support, role modeling, practical problem-solving advice, and a social support network. **WEB BOX 10.4** provides the 12 steps in the program and describes some of the benefits and drawbacks of AA.

The community reinforcement approach (CRA) is one of several counseling approaches available that is more effective than standard care in reducing the number of drinking days (Roozen et al., 2004). CRA assumes that environmental contingencies (rewards and punishers) are powerful in encouraging drinking behavior but that they can be modified to become powerful reinforcers of nondrinking as well. If a nondrinking lifestyle is more appealing than a drinking one, the alcohol misuser will no longer turn to the drug. CRA focuses on problems (e.g., job loss, marital issues, family stress) as perceived *by individuals with AUD* and helps them set their own goals, enhances their motivation to achieve these goals, and teaches the skills needed to create the positive lifestyle they desire.

In a similar manner, cognitive behavior therapy is based on the belief that alcohol misuse is a maladaptive behavior pattern that has been learned. In therapy, the individual learns to identify problematic behaviors that have led to alcohol use and develop effective coping strategies. For example, by recognizing the cues for craving and at-risk situations, the alcohol misuser can learn a variety of methods to control the craving and avoid high-risk situations. Cognitive behavior therapy is frequently combined with pharmacotherapeutic treatment for maximum effectiveness.

PHARMACOTHERAPEUTIC APPROACHES   There is no wonder drug available that will magically eliminate the overwhelming urges to drink in an individual with AUD, but combined with psychosocial rehabilitation, pharmacotherapy can significantly reduce craving and heavy-drinking days. At present there are three drugs approved by the FDA to treat AUD: disulfiram (Antabuse), naltrexone (Revia), and acamprosate (Campral). **Pharmacotherapeutic treatment** for AUD includes two basic strategies: making alcohol ingestion unpleasant and reducing its reinforcing qualities (Garbutt et al., 1999; Swift, 1999). The drug **disulfiram** (**Antabuse**) inhibits ALDH, the enzyme that converts acetaldehyde to acetic acid in the normal metabolism of alcohol. An individual who drinks as little as a quarter of an ounce of alcohol within a week of taking disulfiram experiences a sharp rise in blood acetaldehyde accompanied by facial flushing, tachycardia, pounding in the chest, drop in blood pressure, nausea, vomiting, and other symptoms. This method is clearly aimed at making ingestion of alcohol unpleasant. Patients must be cautious about unknowingly consuming alcohol in beverages, foods, over-the-counter medications like cough syrup, or mouthwash. Because disulfiram can cause hepatitis,

frequent liver function tests must be done. For obvious reasons, compliance with the drug-taking regimen is quite low, with sometimes as many as half of the participants dropping out of the study. Unfortunately, rigorous double-blind studies show little difference in rates of abstinence between men on disulfiram and controls, although some studies show an increase in the duration of abstinence before relapse (see Jonas et al., 2014). To address the issue of low compliance, some practitioners have implanted long-acting disulfiram pellets subdermally (e.g., Sezgin et al., 2014), although the efficacy of this route of administration is not well characterized. While disulfiram clearly does not treat AUD or reduce craving, in some cases it may act as a powerful deterrent for those who are determined to avoid alcohol.

Preclinical animal studies described earlier (in the section on opioid systems) showed that μ-opioid agonists increase alcohol consumption and μ-antagonists decrease self-administration, presumably because they compete for the endogenous opioid receptors. In individuals with AUD, **naltrexone**, which is an opioid receptor antagonist, reduces alcohol consumption and craving and improves abstinence rates, according to several double-blind studies (**FIGURE 10.23**), although it seems to be less promising in longer studies. It is assumed that naltrexone reduces the positive feelings and the subjective "high" of alcohol by blocking the effects of alcohol-induced endorphin release. Social drinkers report more negative effects and greater sedation from a moderate amount of alcohol when taking naltrexone. Increased abstinence rates in humans during naltrexone treatment show parallels with rodent studies in which naltrexone reduced the reinstatement of alcohol consumption triggered by priming injections of ethanol or ethanol-associated cues. Although clinical studies show significant effects, the effect size is small because only a fraction of individuals show meaningful benefit. Some of the variability in response may be due to genetics, since evidence demonstrates that people with a family history of AUD respond better to naltrexone treatment than people with no family history. Furthermore, a μ-receptor polymorphism that leads to reduced receptor expression predicts greater success for alcohol relapse rates with naltrexone therapy (see the meta-analysis by Chamorro et al., 2012). It is possible that naltrexone is more effective for those with a gene variant because they have a different type of AUD and may, for example, differ in their reinforcement mechanisms (see Ripley and Stephens, 2011). Hence targeting the opioid receptor seems to produce substantial benefit for some individuals and limited benefit for others, which indicates the potential value of pharmacogenetic screening for individualizing treatment approaches (see Hartwell and Kranzler, 2019). As is often the case in AUD rehabilitation, the effectiveness of naltrexone is most pronounced when

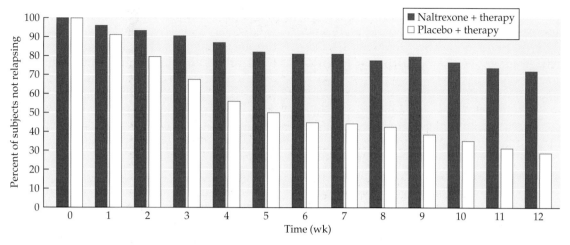

FIGURE 10.23 **Effectiveness of naltrexone in treatment of AUD** Naltrexone along with coping skills therapy is more effective in preventing relapse than placebo and therapy over a 12-week period. At 12 weeks, relapse rates were approximately 70% for the placebo group compared with 30% for the naltrexone treatment group. (After J. R. Volpicelli et al. 1992. *Arch Gen Psych* 49: 876–880.)

accompanied by counseling aimed at enhancing individual coping skills and relapse prevention. Naltrexone is now available as a once-a-month injectable (Vivitrol), which increases the ease of compliance.

Several laboratory studies demonstrated the potential use of κ-opioid receptor antagonists in AUD treatment by demonstrating effects of selective opioid receptor subtype antagonism. In one such study, following a month of alcohol exposure, dependent animals and their nondependent controls were allowed to self-administer alcohol 6 hours after their last alcohol exposure (considered acute withdrawal). As expected, alcohol-dependent rodents self-administered more alcohol than did nondependent animals. Both the μ-receptor antagonist naltrexone and the dual κ- and μ-opioid receptor modulator **nalmefene** were effective in reducing lever pressing for alcohol in a dose-dependent manner in both dependent and nondependent animals. However, nalmefene, because of its action at κ-opioid receptors as well as μ-receptors, was more effective than naltrexone in reducing consumption among dependent animals. The third drug tested, nor-binaltorphimine (nor-BNI), which is a selective κ-opioid antagonist, reduced self-administration only in dependent animals. These results suggest that the μ-opioid receptor mediates acute reinforcing effects, as shown by the ability to reduce alcohol self-administration with μ-antagonists. The fact that antagonists at κ-receptors reduced the withdrawal-induced increase in consumption of only *dependent* animals suggests that κ-receptors have a role in the development of alcohol dependence and withdrawal-induced alcohol consumption. This conclusion is supported by evidence that shows κ-receptor up-regulation during chronic alcohol administration. It is suggested that this up-regulation may be responsible for an anhedonic state (i.e., the inability to experience

pleasure) that develops during the formation of physical dependence and leads to dysphoria when drug cessation occurs. This dysphoria produces a withdrawal-induced increase in alcohol consumption (Walker and Koob, 2008; Nealey et al., 2011). Studies such as these imply that blocking both μ-receptor-induced reinforcement and κ-receptor-mediated anhedonia may improve abstinence rates in those with AUD.

Nalmefene has been approved for use in treatment of heavy alcohol use in Europe but has not yet been FDA approved. Clinical evidence suggests that compared with placebo, nalmefene along with psychosocial support reduces the number of heavy-drinking days and total amount of alcohol consumed. It has been suggested that it can be used on an as-needed basis (that is, patients can choose to take the drug on days when they feel heavy drinking is likely) rather than taking it chronically. The clinical benefit seen is that patients could maintain moderate drinking over time and reduce the most damaging effects of heavy alcohol consumption. When abstinence is not required, more heavy-drinking individuals enter treatment, which leads to better health outcomes and may be an interim step toward abstinence (Mann et al., 2016). As you might expect, this as-needed approach has met with some criticism, and active debate is likely to continue.

Acamprosate (Campral) is a somewhat newer agent available for the treatment of AUD. Several large, well-controlled studies have shown that acamprosate increases nondrinking days by 30% to 50% and approximately doubles the rate of abstinence, even though most patients ultimately return to drinking. The drug seems to reduce the insomnia, anxiety, restlessness, and unpleasant mood changes experienced by heavy drinkers when they abstain. Eliminating those symptoms may help to prevent relapse. In head-to-head comparisons, acamprosate and naltrexone are essentially equivalent in effectiveness and their side-effect profiles are similar, including dizziness, nausea and vomiting, diarrhea, and anxiety. Acamprosate acts as a partial antagonist at the glutamate NMDA receptor and significantly blocks the glutamate increase that occurs during alcohol withdrawal in rats (**FIGURE 10.24**), which may explain its therapeutic effects. Acamprosate has a chemical structure similar to that of GABA and returns basal GABA levels to normal in alcohol-dependent rats. Its ability to modify the functions of both GABA and glutamate in the NAcc may serve as the ultimate basis for its efficacy in preventing relapse.

Other available drugs have been tested in fewer well-controlled trials, but they have generally shown disappointing results despite encouraging findings with animal testing. Serotonergic agents such as the antidepressant fluoxetine, whose effectiveness is predicted by animal studies, have not consistently been effective in humans, except in cases when dependence is accompanied by depression or anxiety disorders. The dopamine antagonist tiapride, sold only in Europe, reduces the symptoms of alcohol withdrawal and increases abstinence. However, in at least one clinical trial, compliance was an issue, and only about half of the participants completed 1 month of treatment (Shaw et al., 1994). Likewise, although cannabinoid receptor antagonists reduce alcohol self-administration in numerous animal models, double-blind, placebo-controlled clinical trials report little efficacy in reducing alcohol consumption or relapse rates among alcohol-dependent

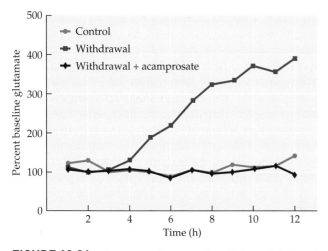

FIGURE 10.24 Acamprosate prevents withdrawal-induced glutamate release The red squares plot line shows the rebound release of glutamate (measured by microdialysis) that occurs in the nucleus accumbens when alcohol is withdrawn from dependent rats. Alcohol-dependent animals no longer receiving alcohol but receiving acamprosate (purple diamond plot line) are no different in glutamate release from non-alcohol-treated controls. (After A. Dahchour and P. DeWitte. 2000. *Prog Neurobiol* 60: 343–362.)

individuals. Such failures of basic research to translate to effective clinical treatment may be due to several factors, including poor clinical research designs, inability to identify subpopulations of individuals who may benefit from treatment, and animal models that poorly predict efficacy in humans (see Ripley and Stephens, 2011). It is hoped that collaborative efforts in translational research, as described in Chapter 4, will produce more effective therapies in the future.

PROMISING NEW DIRECTIONS IN TREATMENT In an earlier section, we described the complex reciprocal interaction between stress and alcohol consumption and the importance of stress in leading to relapse in the abstinent individual with AUD. Since both animal and human studies show that repeated episodes of intoxication and withdrawal lead to increased CRF_1 receptors in the amygdala, sensitization of the reactivity to stressors, and significantly elevated rates of alcohol consumption, it is reasonable to consider pharmacological interventions to minimize this stress response. One approach is to block the CRF_1 receptors that mediate both the hypothalamic-regulated neuroendocrine response and the extrahypothalamic CRF_1 receptors that modulate the behavioral response to stress. Several animal studies have shown that either systemic or intracerebral injections of **CRF_1 antagonists** into the central nucleus of the amygdala reduced the post-withdrawal escalation of alcohol self-administration to baseline consumption levels. Additionally, although the antagonist had no effect on basal alcohol self-administration in animals that had no history of dependence, it did reduce excessive binge-like consumption in nondependent animals. Importantly, the CRF_1 antagonists prevented stress-induced relapse-type behavior. Unfortunately, there have been few efforts to test CRF_1 antagonists on the alcohol-misusing population, because medicinal chemists have had difficulty in creating agents that penetrate the blood–brain barrier and achieve the high receptor occupancy needed for efficacy as determined by animal research.

Taking a different approach to understanding the importance of the stress response in AUD, Vendruscolo and colleagues (2015) tested the hypothesis that glucocorticoid receptor (GR) signaling has a role in compulsive alcohol consumption. Glucocorticoids released by the adrenal cortex in response to stress bind to GRs located in many brain regions, but they are especially dense in the PFC, hippocampus, and amygdala, which explains the sensitivity of those regions to stress. The initial findings demonstrated that increased phosphorylation of GR occurred during acute withdrawal in alcohol-dependent compared with nondependent rodents. Systemic treatment with a GR antagonist reduced alcohol self-administration in dependent rats without altering consumption of water or saccharin, demonstrating that response to nondrug reinforcers is not altered. The importance of the central nucleus of the amygdala was demonstrated by bilateral intracerebral injection that reduced self-administration of alcohol in dependent rats. In a proof-of-concept study to translate these results to humans, the GR antagonist was tested on the craving response to alcohol-related cues and self-reported drinking in a small number ($n = 56$) of human alcohol-dependent participants. After 1 week of treatment, craving was significantly reduced compared with placebo, as was the number of drinks per drinking day during the treatment week and 1 week after treatment (**FIGURE 10.25**). Because the participants reported no adverse effects, further investigation of GR antagonists as treatment for AUD is warranted.

An intriguing series of studies have examined the potential for ketamine in the treatment of AUD. Similar to acamprosate, ketamine is an antagonist of NMDA glutamate receptors. It was originally developed as an anesthetic but later developed a reputation as a drug of abuse. Most recently, ketamine was approved by the FDA for the treatment of otherwise treatment-resistant depression (see Chapter 18). There is substantial evidence for the high degree of comorbidity between stress-related disorders such as depression, anxiety, and PTSD, and AUD. Given the efficacy of ketamine in treating stress-related disorders, it is thought that its ability to alleviate these negative affective states could also interfere with the withdrawal-related dysphoria that promotes ongoing alcohol use. Mechanistically, because the hyperexcitable state observed during withdrawal from chronic alcohol use is mediated in part by increased NMDA receptor expression and increased extracellular glutamate, it is logical that an

NMDA receptor antagonist such as ketamine could reverse this hyperexcitable state. The therapeutic effect of ketamine on AUD may also be mediated by its effects on other neurochemicals, including GABA, DA, and opioid neurotransmitter systems. Because ketamine is already approved by the FDA for the treatment of depression, it is certainly plausible that it could also be used for the treatment of AUD. For a current review of the potential for ketamine to treat AUD and other substance use disorders, interested readers are directed to a recent article by Worrell and Gould (2021).

COMBINED PHARMACOTHERAPY AND TALK THERAPY

The National Institute of Alcohol Abuse and Alcoholism (NIAAA) initiated a multisite, controlled clinical trial of treatments for alcohol dependence utilizing almost 1400 alcohol-dependent study participants (Anton et al., 2006). The focus of this research was to evaluate the efficacy of pharmacotherapy, behavioral treatment, and a combination on a number of alcohol use parameters. The research, called Combining Medications and Behavioral Interventions (COMBINE), aimed to enhance treatment outcomes. Investigators used four treatments singly and in combination: naltrexone, acamprosate, medical management, and combined behavioral intervention (CBI). Medical management was designed to be used in a normal medical setting by medical doctors and nurses to increase medication adherence and provide support for abstinence, while CBI was used in specialized alcohol treatment programs and provided more intense individual psychotherapy. A wide variety of physiological and behavioral outcomes were evaluated at multiple time points during the 16-week active phase of treatment, as well as during the post-treatment phase, but the principal measures included percent days of abstinence and time to the first heavy drinking. Results showed that the most effective treatments were medical management with either naltrexone or CBI, which led to 79% days of abstinence. The interaction of naltrexone and the behavioral intervention was particularly important because naltrexone with medical management also prolonged the time to the first heavy drinking. Oddly, in contrast to the findings of earlier studies,

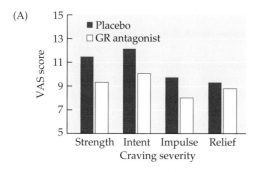

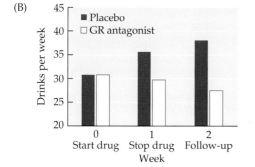

FIGURE 10.25 Glucocorticoid receptor (GR) antagonism reduced alcohol-cued craving and drinking in dependent individuals (A) Visual analog scale (VAS) scores on four VAS measures of craving severity following presentation of alcohol-related cues. Strength: How strong is your craving to drink alcohol? Intent: If I could drink alcohol now, I would drink it. Impulse: It would be hard to turn down a drink right now. Relief: Having a drink would make things just perfect. Higher scores indicate greater craving. Significant differences were reported for strength, intent, and impulse. (B) Total number of alcoholic drinks consumed per week for individuals treated with the GR antagonist or placebo at baseline, following treatment, and at 2-week follow-up. (After L. Vendruscolo et al. 2015. *J Clin Invest* 125: 3193–3197.)

acamprosate had no effect either alone or in combination with either naltrexone or behavioral intervention. The authors suggest that the difference may be due to the fact that participants in earlier successful acamprosate trials were inpatients who had a significantly longer period of abstinence before the trial began. The importance of these findings for treatment options is that pharmacotherapy with naltrexone and medical management can be provided by family doctors in readily available health care settings, and treatment does not depend on specialized treatment programs that are not always accessible to the alcohol-dependent population. It was interesting to see that during longer follow-up, CBI began to show significant benefit over medical management that was not evident in the initial clinical trial, although all treatments showed a diminishing outcome over time. It is likely that alcohol dependence should be treated much like other chronic conditions such as diabetes and hypertension, with regular monitoring over time and rapid intervention with follow-up treatments as needed. Such monitoring and follow-up treatment should reduce the amount of health care needed to treat alcohol-related disease and associated costs in the long run.

SECTION SUMMARY

- AUD involves compulsive alcohol seeking and use despite damaging health and social consequences. Frequency and pattern of drinking are as important as the quantity consumed.

- Approximately 10% of Americans have an alcohol use problem. There are significant gender differences in alcohol use, binge drinking, and heavy drinking.

- Defining subtypes of individuals with AUD is important for neurobiological and genetic research, predicting the course of the disorder, and identifying the most effective treatment approach. Babor's type A and type B have been validated in the general population and are defined by such characteristics as age of onset, childhood risk factors, presence of psychopathology, social impact of alcohol, and so forth.

- Underage drinking disrupts neurodevelopmental events, causing long-lasting change in neurological function and behavior.

- Neurobiological, psychological, and sociocultural factors contribute to the vulnerability of a given individual to AUD.

- Stress reduces or increases alcohol consumption under different conditions. Alcohol increases the activity of the brain stress systems and neuroendocrine stress systems that may lead to further alcohol use. Sensitization to stressors persists long after withdrawal.

- Early life stress is a risk factor for adult alcohol misuse. Family history is a risk factor and is associated with a greater stress response and greater alcohol-induced suppression of the response.

- Cortisol sensitizes the DA mesolimbic pathway, which makes drug reinforcement more rewarding.

- Early (before age 13) drinking, impulse-control problems, high novelty seeking, low harm avoidance, and aversion to delayed gratification predict future substance misuse.

- Genetics explains 50% to 60% of the variance of risk for alcohol dependence. Twin and adoption studies, linkage analysis, association studies, and GWAS provide evidence for a genetic risk for AUD.

- Genes for the inactive form of aldehyde dehydrogenase, the enzyme that converts the toxic metabolite acetaldehyde, predict low risk for AUD because alcohol has unpleasant effects.

- Gene polymorphisms for the 5-HT reuptake transporter, associated with anxiety and low sensitivity to alcohol, increase vulnerability to alcohol misuse.

- Social and cultural factors determine attitudes about drinking and how much alcohol is available. Cultures that restrict use of alcohol have lower rates of AUD.

- Detoxification under medical supervision is the first step in treatment and is followed by benzodiazepine substitution to prevent withdrawal, and gradual dose reduction.

- Psychosocial rehabilitation includes individual and group therapies, residential treatment settings, and self-help groups.

- FDA-approved pharmacotherapies for AUD include disulfiram, naltrexone, and acamprosate. Disulfiram inhibits the enzyme that converts acetaldehyde to acetic acid so that alcohol consumption causes very unpleasant effects such as nausea and vomiting, which discourages drinking.

- Naltrexone is an opioid receptor antagonist that reduces consumption and craving in some individuals with AUD, perhaps by reducing the positive feeling caused by alcohol. Those with a family history of AUD and those with a μ-receptor polymorphism associated with reduced receptor expression respond better to this treatment.

- Targeting the opioid κ-receptor with an antagonist reduced self-administration only in dependent animals, suggesting that the κ-receptor may have a role in the anhedonic states associated with physical dependence. Blocking μ- and κ-receptors with a dual antagonist like nalmefene may improve abstinence rates in humans.

- Acamprosate reduces the relapse rate. It reduces the glutamate increase that occurs at withdrawal and returns basal GABA levels to normal in the nucleus accumbens.

■ Promising rodent studies targeting the stress response with CRF$_1$ antagonists suggest that they may be effective in reducing withdrawal-induced increase in consumption, as well as stress-induced relapse behavior.

■ A glucocorticoid receptor antagonist reduced self-administration of alcohol in rodents without altering water or saccharin consumption. The same antagonist reduced craving in response to alcohol cues in humans and reduced drinking.

■ The NMDA glutamate receptor antagonist ketamine, which has recently been approved for the treatment of depression, holds promise as a potential therapy for AUD.

■ The COMBINE study showed the most effective treatment for alcohol dependence is medical management along with either naltrexone or combined behavioral intervention. Since medical management with naltrexone can be provided by family doctors without special training, it provides accessible health care.

STUDY QUESTIONS

1. How is alcohol produced?
2. Describe the pharmacokinetics of alcohol absorption and distribution. What are the variables that determine absorption? Why are blood levels higher for women than men given the same amount of alcohol?
3. Summarize the two ways alcohol is metabolized.
4. Name the four types of tolerance, and briefly describe their mechanisms. What roles do operant and classical conditioning have in behavioral tolerance?
5. List several signs of withdrawal from chronic alcohol use. Why is medically supervised detoxification recommended for heavy alcohol misusers?
6. Describe the CNS effects of alcohol, including those on judgment, memory, motor skills, and CNS depression.
7. What are the signs of alcohol poisoning?
8. Discuss the nature of brain damage caused by heavy alcohol use and its functional outcome.
9. Describe the effects of alcohol on the cardiovascular, renal–urinary, reproductive, and gastrointestinal systems.
10. Describe the progression in liver damage from fatty liver to alcohol-induced hepatitis to alcohol-induced cirrhosis. Where possible, describe one potential cause.
11. What are fetal alcohol syndrome and the less severe fetal alcohol spectrum disorders? Provide evidence from animal studies for a role of alcohol use in the disorders. Why are correlational epidemiological studies with humans much more difficult to conduct?
12. Why are animal models especially important in alcohol research? Compare the self-administration model and the two-bottle free-choice procedure. How does the manipulation of access to alcohol model relapse behavior? Compulsive drinking?
13. Provide evidence for the validity of inbred alcohol-preferring (AP) and high-alcohol-drinking (HAD) rat strains in modeling characteristics of AUD.

14. Describe the most important effects of alcohol on the glutamate NMDA receptor and associated biobehavioral effects. Do the same for the GABA$_A$ receptor, mesolimbic dopamine pathway, opioid systems, and second-messenger signaling leading to phosphorylation of CREB.
15. What are some of the significant characteristics of Babor's type A and type B alcoholics?
16. Summarize the hazardous effects of college student and underage drinking. Explain why adolescents are more likely to develop long-lasting neurological and behavioral deficits.
17. Discuss the role of stress in the vulnerability to AUD.
18. Tell how stress interacts with mesolimbic DA to increase vulnerability to AUD.
19. What are the personality factors that predict early alcohol use and addiction?
20. How important is genetic vulnerability to AUD? Provide one piece of evidence each from linkage, case–control, and genome-wide association studies. Why are gene polymorphisms for alcohol dehydrogenase and aldehyde dehydrogenase of particular significance?
21. How do social and cultural factors influence alcohol use?
22. Distinguish among the psychosocial rehabilitation approaches: Alcoholics Anonymous (AA), the community reinforcement approach (CRA), and cognitive behavior therapy.
23. What are the pros and cons of the three FDA-approved pharmacotherapies (disulfiram, naltrexone, and acamprosate)?
24. Provide evidence for the effectiveness of nalmefene, a κ-opioid receptor antagonist, in AUD treatment programs.
25. Why are CRF$_1$ antagonists a focus of pharmacotherapeutic research? Glucocorticoid receptor antagonists? Substance P and its neurokinin receptor?
26. Why was the NIAAA-initiated trial of combined pharmacotherapy and talk therapy important?

11 The Opioids

IN 2019, ON AVERAGE OVER 136 PEOPLE DIED EVERY DAY IN THE UNITED STATES FROM OPIOID OVERDOSES, with the majority of those deaths attributable to fentanyl. Fentanyl is an entirely synthetic opioid that is approximately 80 to 100 times more potent than morphine, and correspondingly about 50 times more potent than heroin. Like most opioids, fentanyl has high abuse liability on its own, but it is particularly dangerous when it is added to other drugs. Illicit drug manufacturers have found that it is more cost effective to add fentanyl to low-purity heroin or to counterfeit pills resembling prescription opioids. In many cases, people are unaware that the drug contains fentanyl, and because dose is not well controlled in the illicit manufacture of drugs, these individuals are exposed to a high risk of a fatal overdose. As you will read later in the chapter, opioid overdose deaths involving fentanyl have risen dramatically in the United States since 2013. Given this alarming trend, municipalities across the nation have implemented an array of harm reduction strategies, including warning people who use opioids about the dangers of fentanyl-tainted batches of drug circulating on the streets. Social media has also played a role in harm reduction, with the emergence of online communities dedicated to providing information on strategies for reducing harm. In addition to providing warnings on locality-specific fentanyl overdoses, these online communities list information on how reduce risk associated with opioid use, including how to obtain fentanyl test strips as well as naloxone (an opioid receptor antagonist), which is used as an emergency treatment for reversing an overdose. Alongside education and regulation, harm-reduction strategies such as these are part of a multifaceted approach to reducing the immense human toll of the opioid epidemic. ■

Flyers distributed by the New York City Department of Health in neighborhoods with high rates of opioid overdose deaths warn residents of the dangers of fentanyl.

11.1 Narcotic Analgesics

The opioid drugs all belong to the class known as **narcotic analgesics**. These drugs reduce pain without producing unconsciousness but do produce a sense of relaxation and sleep and, at high doses, coma and death. As a class, they are the very best painkillers known. In addition to inducing analgesia, opioids have a variety of side effects and also produce a sense of well-being and euphoria that may lead to increased use of the drugs. Continued use leads to tolerance and sometimes physical dependence. In contrast to analgesics, **anesthetics** reduce all sensations by depressing the central nervous system (CNS) and produce unconsciousness.

The opium poppy has a long history of use

Opium is an extract of the poppy plant and is the source of a family of drugs known as the *opiates* or sometimes *opioids*.* Opium is prepared by drying and powdering the milky juice (latex) taken from the seed capsules of the opium poppy, *Papaver somniferum* (meaning "the poppy that causes sleep"), just before ripening (**FIGURE 11.1**). When the capsules are sliced open, the latex leaks out and thickens into a reddish-brown syrupy material. Cultivation of the opium poppy has been successful in the temperate zones as far north as England and Denmark, but the majority of the world's supply historically came from Southeast Asia, India, China, Iran, Turkey, and southeastern Europe. At present, Afghanistan accounts for approximately 84% of the global opium production over the last 5 years (U.N. World Drug Report, 2020). The plant grows to about 3 or 4 feet in height and has large flowers in white, pink, red, or purple. This variety is the only poppy that has significant psychoactive effects.

The opiates have been used both as medicine and for recreational purposes for several thousand years. As early as 1500 BCE, the Egyptians described opiates' preparation and medicinal value. Archeological evidence from Cyprus dated as early as 1200 BCE includes ceramic opium pipes and vases with poppy capsules for decoration. By the second century CE, the famous Greek physician Galen prescribed opium for a wide variety of medical problems, including headache, deafness, asthma, coughs, shortness of breath, colic, and leprosy, among others. But the Greek author Homer, in *The Odyssey*, refers to the drug's recreational properties when he describes the plant as eliciting a feeling of warmth and well-being followed by sleep. More modern use began in Europe, when news of the "miracle cure" was brought back by the religious crusaders from the Near East. Eating or smoking opium was accepted in Islamic countries such as Arabia, Turkey, and Iran, where it replaced the consumption of alcohol, which was prohibited. By 1680, an opium-based medicinal

FIGURE 11.1 **Preparing opium** The immature opium poppy capsule has been scored and the latex, which is collected and dried to produce opium, is dripping from the incision.

drink was introduced by the father of clinical medicine, the English physician Thomas Sydenham. His recipe for the drink called *laudanum* (meaning "something to be praised") included "2 ounces of strained opium, 1 ounce of saffron, and a dram of cinnamon and cloves dissolved in 1 pint of Canary wine." Drinking laudanum-laced wine was the accepted form of opium use in both Victorian England and America, especially among women, who considered it far more respectable than "common" alcohol use. A number of notable literary figures of that period were addicted to laudanum and opium, including William Taylor Coleridge, Charles Dickens, and Elizabeth Barrett Browning. Laudanum was also a common ingredient of many popular remedies for a wide variety of problems, including teething pain and restlessness in infants, muscle aches and pains, and alcoholism.

Right up to the turn of the twentieth century, opium-containing products with names such as "A Pennyworth of Peace," "Mrs. Winslow's Soothing Syrup," and "White Star Secret Liquor Cure" could be ordered through the Sears, Roebuck and Co. catalog for about $4 a pint (**FIGURE 11.2**). In nineteenth-century America, neither the federal government nor individual states chose to control the availability and advertising of drugs such as opium and cocaine. There was clearly no significant concern about safety, long-term health issues, or dependence. Finally, in 1914, the Harrison Narcotics Tax Act was passed, which required physicians to report their prescriptions for opioids. Only in the

---

Opiate refers specifically to substances derived directly from the opium poppy. *Opioid* is a broader term that includes opiates, synthetic substances, and endogenous peptides that bind to opioid receptors.

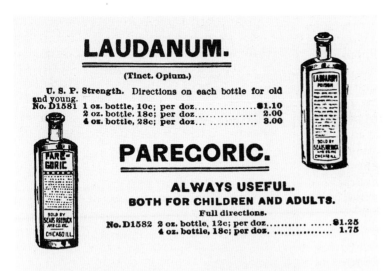

FIGURE 11.2 Mail-order source for opium preparations Laudanum was used to treat pain and cough, and paregoric was used to treat diarrhea. The advertisement is from the 1897 Sears, Roebuck and Co. catalog.

1920s did the Supreme Court broadly interpret the law to mean that prescriptions should be limited to *medical* use, making it illegal to provide opioids for addicted individuals or recreational use.

Minor differences in molecular structure determine behavioral effects

The principal active ingredient in opium was called *morphine* after the Roman god of dreams, Morpheus, and it was first isolated in the early 1800s by a German chemist, Friedrich Wilhelm Sertürner. His extraction of morphine crystals from the latex of the poppy seed capsules is considered a milestone in the history of pharmacology because it was the first time the active ingredient of any medicinal plant was isolated. Having the extract enabled physicians to prescribe the painkiller in known dosages. In addition to morphine, opium contains other active ingredients, including codeine, thebaine, narcotine, and others. Although morphine was isolated from opium in the early 1800s, the structure of morphine was not identified until 1925 (**FIGURE 11.3**). The naturally occurring opiate codeine is identical in structure to morphine except for the substitution of a methoxy (–OCH$_3$) for a hydroxyl (–OH) group. Perhaps unsurprisingly, codeine acts as a prodrug by virtue of its metabolism by a number of liver enzymes, including the cytochrome P450 enzyme CYP2D6, which converts a relatively low proportion of codeine to morphine. It was exciting for pharmacologists to discover

that simple modifications of the morphine molecule produce great variations in potency, duration of action, and oral effectiveness. In many cases, these differences are due to differences in pharmacokinetics rather than to intrinsic activity. For example, heroin was manufactured by adding two acetyl groups onto the morphine molecule. This drug was developed by the Bayer Company to be more effective in relieving pain without the danger of developing opioid use disorder (**FIGURE 11.4**). Today we know that the pharmacological effects of morphine and heroin are essentially identical because heroin is converted to morphine in the brain. Heroin is, however, approximately twice as potent when injected and is faster acting because the change in the molecule makes the drug more lipid soluble and allows it to get into the brain much more quickly to act on receptors there. When taken orally, morphine and heroin are approximately equal in potency. The very rapid action of heroin is apparently also responsible for the dramatic euphoric effects achieved with that drug. Like heroin, methadone is a full agonist at opioid receptors; however, its slow onset after oral administration and its long half-life make it useful in treating opioid dependence (see the last section of this chapter).

Some of the modifications to morphine's molecular structure produce **partial agonists**, which are drugs that bind readily to (i.e., have a high affinity for) the receptors but produce less biological effect (i.e., low efficacy). Therefore, when administered alone, they produce partial opioid effects, but when given along with an opioid that has higher effectiveness, they compete for the receptor and subsequently reduce the action of

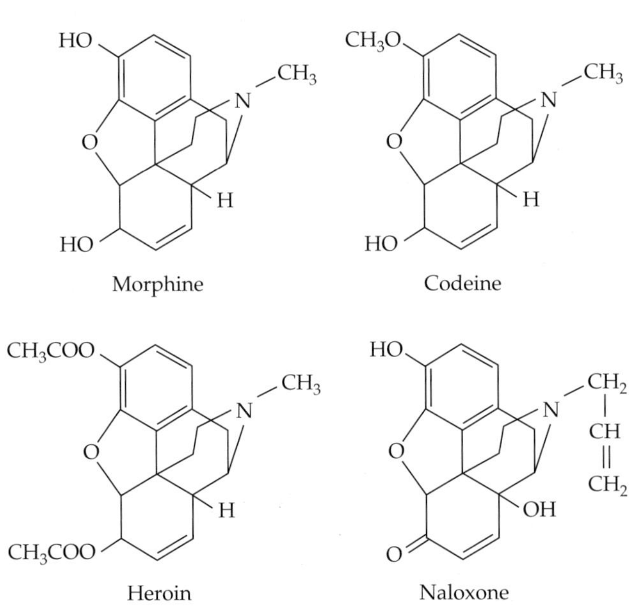

FIGURE 11.3 Molecular structure of morphine, codeine, heroin, and naloxone It is easy to see the similarities in structure. The minor differences contribute to effectiveness and side effects.

Morphine

Codeine

Heroin

Naloxone

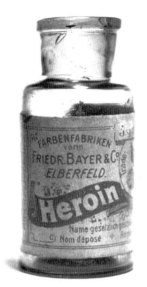

FIGURE 11.4 Heroin was commercialized by Bayer pharmaceutical products Marketed as a non-addictive morphine substitute, heroin was legally sold in the United States until it was outlawed in 1924.

opioid overdose. Specific receptor antagonists are also important for understanding the mechanism of action of opioid analgesics. As you will learn a bit later, the four principal types of opioid receptors (μ, δ, κ, and NOP-R) mediate different opioid actions.

While some narcotic drugs are natural derivatives, others are considered semisynthetic because they require chemical modifications of the natural opiates. For instance, hydromorphone (Dilaudid) and heroin are modifications of the morphine molecule; others are entirely synthetic and may have quite distinct structures (e.g., propoxyphene [Darvon], meperidine [Demerol]). Thebain, another constituent of opium, is chemically converted into several opioid compounds, including oxycodone, oxymorphone, buprenorphine, and etorphine. The relationship of the major opiates and some of their derivatives, as well as some of the synthetic opioids, is shown in **FIGURE 11.5**.

the more effective drug. The prototypic partial agonist is pentazocine (Talwin), but others in this category are nalbuphine (Nubain) and buprenorphine (Buprenex). Although as analgesics they are much less potent than morphine, they do not cause significant respiratory depression or constipation, and they have a reduced risk for dependence.

Other chemical modifications of the morphine molecule produce **neutral antagonists** such as naloxone and nalorphine. These are drugs that have structures similar to those of the opiates but produce no pharmacological activity of their own (i.e., no efficacy). The receptor antagonists can prevent or reverse the effect of administered opioids because of their ability to occupy opioid receptor sites. **WEB BOX 11.1** describes how intravenously administered naloxone can revive an unconscious individual in a matter of seconds and reverse all of the opioid effects and how it can be used to save the lives of those brought to the emergency room after

Bioavailability predicts both physiological and behavioral effects

When morphine is administered for medical purposes, it is usually given orally, by intravenous injection, or by epidural and intrathecal routes of administration. Recreational users often smoke opium for its rapid absorption from the lungs, although "snorting" heroin also leads to rapid absorption through the nasal mucosa. In addition, subcutaneous administration ("skin popping") may precede the more dangerous "mainlining" (intravenous injection).

Although morphine has pronounced psychoactive effects, only a small fraction of the drug crosses the blood–brain barrier to act on opioid receptors in the brain. Opioid distribution is fairly uniform in the rest of the body, and the drugs easily pass the placental barrier, exposing the unborn child to high levels. The newborn of an opioid-dependent mother suffers withdrawal symptoms within several hours after birth,

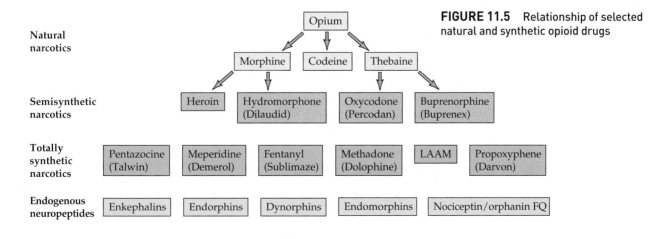

FIGURE 11.5 Relationship of selected natural and synthetic opioid drugs

which may have severe consequences for the infant, especially if the child is weak from inadequate prenatal nutrition. However, infants are readily stabilized with low doses of opioids to prevent withdrawal signs, and the dose is gradually reduced. Following metabolism in the liver, most of the opioid metabolites are excreted in the urine within 24 hours.

Opioids have their most important effects on the CNS and on the gastrointestinal tract

The multiple effects of morphine and other opioids on the CNS are dose related and are also related to the rate of absorption. At low to moderate doses, pain is relieved, respiration is somewhat depressed, and pupils are constricted. The principal subjective effects are drowsiness, decreased sensitivity to the environment, and impaired ability to concentrate, followed by a dreamy sleep. Because opioids have actions in the limbic system, some researchers suggest that the drugs relieve "psychological pain," including anxiety, feelings of inadequacy, and hostility, which may lead to increased drug use. In a longitudinal survey with over 37,000 participants, Martins and colleagues (2012) found that presence of any mood disorder at time 1 predicted nonmedical opioid use at time 2 (3 years later), supporting the self-medication model of drug abuse—that is, drug use is initiated to reduce the individual's symptoms (see Chapter 9). However, there was also evidence that nonmedical opioid use or dependence at time 1 was associated with psychopathology at time 2, indicating that the relationship between opioid use and mood disorders is complex and bidirectional. Morphine also suppresses the cough reflex in a dose-dependent manner and has actions on the hypothalamus that lead to decreased appetite, drop in body temperature, reduced sex drive, and a variety of hormonal changes. Each of these effects can be associated with opioid receptors in particular areas of the CNS.

At slightly higher doses, particularly if the drug is administered intravenously or inhaled, the individual experiences a state of elation or euphoria. To achieve the maximum euphoria, rapid penetration into the brain is needed. Although it is experienced as intense pleasure, the "rush" is not the principal basis for abuse but acts as a powerful reinforcer that encourages repeated drug use.

It is also important to know that the euphoric effect does not always accompany intravenous (IV) administration. For many individuals being medically treated, the drug may produce dysphoria, consisting of restlessness and anxiety. In addition, the nausea and vomiting that may accompany low doses of morphine are increased with higher doses. They are directly related to morphine's effect on the chemical trigger zone (the area postrema) in the brainstem that elicits vomiting. Although clearly unpleasant for most individuals, for the individual with opioid use disorder, the nausea may become a "good sick" because it is closely associated with the drug-induced euphoria by classical conditioning.

At the highest doses of opioids, the sedative effects become more pronounced and may lead to unconsciousness. Body temperature and blood pressure fall, while pupils become constricted and represent a clinical sign of opioid overdose in a comatose patient. Respiration is dangerously impaired because of morphine's action on the brainstem's respiratory center, which normally responds to high blood CO_2 levels by triggering increased respiration. Respiratory failure is the ultimate cause of death in overdose.

Apart from the CNS, the effects of morphine are greatest on the gastrointestinal tract. Opium was used for relief from diarrhea and dysentery even before it was used for analgesia. It remains one of the most important lifesaving drugs because of its ability to slow gastrointestinal motility and thus stop the life-threatening dehydration associated with diarrhea that accompanies many bacterial and parasitic illnesses especially prevalent in developing countries. Unfortunately, when opioids are used for pain management, constipation is a common and disturbing side effect that does not diminish even after prolonged use.

More modern treatment for diarrhea utilizes modified opioid molecules such as loperamide, which was designed so that it cannot cross the blood–brain barrier. The major advantage is that it effectively slows gastrointestinal function but does not have any effect on the CNS at recommended doses. At very high doses loperamide can penetrate the blood–brain barrier to enter the CNS and produce mild euphoria. Opioid-dependent individuals have discovered that by taking 200 to 400 mg of loperamide rather than the antidiarrheal dose of 4 mg, they can achieve a euphoric effect. Others use the drug to reduce withdrawal symptoms such as vomiting and muscle pains when the preferred opioid, such as morphine or heroin, is not available (Lee et al., 2019). Such high doses are associated with extreme constipation as well as cardiovascular toxicity, including irregular heartbeats and abnormal electrical conduction through the heart, leading to fatalities (Saint Louis, 2016). At present these over-the-counter antidiarrhea drugs are inexpensive and can be purchased in drugstores and supermarkets in large quantities. However, emergency medicine physicians and toxicologists are encouraging the U.S. Food and Drug Administration (FDA) to limit the amount of the medication that can be purchased at one time, just as purchase of the decongestant pseudoephedrine was limited to reduce the clandestine manufacture of methamphetamine.

Opioid receptors and endogenous neuropeptides

The opioid drugs produce biobehavioral effects by binding to and activating specific neuronal receptors.

Since minor modifications of the morphine molecule produce significant changes in effect, analyses of the molecular structure of the drugs provide sufficient information to hypothesize definite structural features of opioid receptors. Further, naloxone's blocking effects can be overcome by increasing concentrations of morphine, which demonstrates competition for the receptor (see Martin, 1967, for a detailed historical perspective on this discovery process). Not long after opioid receptors were identified, the natural neuropeptide ligands that act at the receptors were characterized.

Receptor binding studies identified and localized opioid receptors

Although the existence of opioid receptors was evident, the initial attempts to label and locate these receptors in brain tissue using standard radioligand binding methods (see Chapter 4) proved to be a difficult task. Ultimately, the first opioid receptor was labeled (Pert and Snyder, 1973) by making several technical refinements in the assay and separation procedure, as well as by having access to newer radioactive ligands that had a greater amount of radioactivity per drug molecule. The receptors that they identified met the criteria described in Chapter 4. First, **FIGURE 11.6A** shows the classic binding curve, demonstrating that as the amount of radioactive opioid (in this case, the antagonist naloxone) is increased, binding also increases and gradually tapers off until the receptors are fully occupied. The leveling off of the binding curve at B_{max} shows that a finite number of receptors exist in a given amount of tissue. This saturation would not occur if the radioligand happened to be "sticky" and attached randomly to many cellular materials. Second, looking at the concentrations used in the assay makes it clear that the binding sites have a high affinity for the opioids. Third, the binding was shown to be reversible, with a time course that matches the loss of physiological effectiveness. Fourth, the concentrations needed in the binding assay are meaningfully related to the concentration of agonist needed to elicit a biological response.

But how do we know that these sites are responsible for the opioids' pharmacological activity? Snyder (1977) calculated binding affinity by measuring the ability of a number of nonradioactive opioids to compete with radioactive naloxone for the receptors. They found that the relative potency of various opioids in the competition experiments closely paralleled their relative potencies in pharmacological effects on the intestine (**FIGURE 11.6B**). In this case, the pharmacological effect measured is the ability of opioids to inhibit electrically induced contraction of the ileum (the lowest portion of the small intestine). This inhibition occurs because opioids inhibit the release of neurotransmitter from stimulated nerves. Although many more-sophisticated methods are possible, opioid action on the ileum is considered a classic bioassay and is described in **WEB BOX 11.2**.

(A)

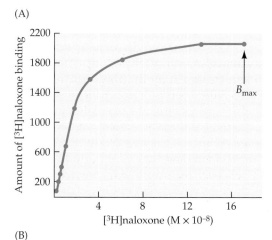

(B)

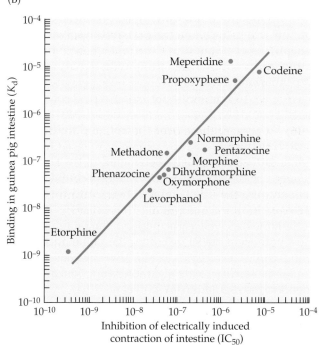

FIGURE 11.6 Opioid receptor binding (A) Binding of [³H] naloxone to rat brain shows the saturation of opioid receptors. As the concentration of the opioid ligand (naloxone) increases, binding to the receptors increases steadily until the receptors are filled at B_{max}. (B) There is a strong positive correlation between the concentration of opioid drugs needed to inhibit electrically induced contraction of the intestine (IC_{50}) and the concentration needed to bind to opioid receptors in the same tissue. The results show clearly that drugs that bind readily at low concentrations of ligand (e.g., etorphine) also are effective in inhibiting the intestinal contraction at low doses. Drugs that bind less well (e.g., codeine) also require higher concentrations to inhibit the contraction. (A after C. B. Pert and S. H. Snyder. 1973. *Proc Natl Acad Sci USA* 70: 2243–2247; B after S. H. Snyder. 1977. *Sci Am* 236: 44–56. Reproduced with permission. © 1977 SCIENTIFIC AMERICAN, Inc. All rights reserved.)

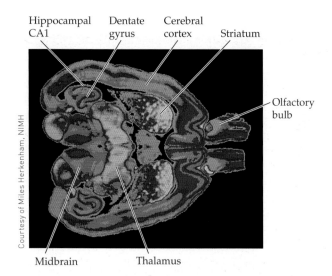

Hippocampal CA1 — Dentate gyrus — Cerebral cortex — Striatum — Olfactory bulb — Midbrain — Thalamus

Courtesy of Miles Herkenham, NIMH

FIGURE 11.7 The distribution of opioid receptors in rat brain In this autoradiogram higher densities, seen as warmer colors, occur in the striatum, medial thalamus, locus coeruleus, periaqueductal gray, and raphe nuclei.

Once the receptors were labeled and characterized, autoradiography could be used to locate the receptors in the brain. **FIGURE 11.7** shows a color-enhanced distribution of opioid receptors in rat brain.

Four opioid receptor subtypes exist

Although the classic dose–response curves used by Martin and colleagues (1976) suggested that several subtypes of opioid receptors exist, researchers needed to develop highly *selective* radioactive ligands to directly label the subtypes. Selectivity means that a given molecule readily binds to one receptor subtype and has relatively low binding affinity for the others (Simon, 1991). The three classical subtypes have been called μ (mu), δ (delta), and κ (kappa). A more recent addition to the opioid receptor family is the nociceptin/orphanin FQ receptor (NOP-R). Based on genetic criteria, the NOP-R and classical opioid receptors belong to the same family. The same is true for the opioid peptides and the ligand for the NOP-R, nociceptin/orphanin FQ (see the following section). However, despite their familial relationship, opioids do not bind to NOP-R, nor does nociceptin/orphanin FQ bind to classical opioid receptors. The four opioid receptor subtypes have distinct distributions in the brain and spinal cord, which suggests that they mediate a wide variety of effects.

The **μ-receptor** is the receptor that has a high affinity for morphine and related opioid drugs. The location of the μ-receptors has been mapped by autoradiography in several species (Mansour and Watson, 1993), including human brain postmortem (Quirion and Pilapil, 1991). Other researchers have performed

in vivo mapping using positron emission tomography (PET) imaging (Mayberg and Frost, 1990). The results consistently show a wide distribution of μ-receptors in both the brain and the spinal cord. The brain areas rich in μ-receptors (e.g., the medial thalamus, periaqueductal gray, median raphe, and clusters within the spinal cord) support their role in morphine-induced analgesia. Other high-density areas suggest a role in feeding and positive reinforcement (nucleus accumbens [NAcc]), cardiovascular and respiratory depression, cough control, nausea and vomiting (brainstem), and sensorimotor integration (thalamus, striatum) (Mansour and Watson, 1993; Carvey, 1998). **FIGURE 11.8A** is an autoradiogram of μ-receptor binding in the rat CNS.

The **δ-receptors** have a distribution similar to that of μ-receptors (**FIGURE 11.8B**) but are more restricted. They are predominantly found in forebrain structures such as the neocortex, striatum, olfactory areas, substantia nigra, and NAcc. Many of these sites are consistent with a possible role for δ-receptors in modulating olfaction, motor integration, reinforcement, and cognitive function. δ-receptors in areas overlapping μ-receptors suggest modulation of both spinal and supraspinal analgesia. δ-receptor knockout mice and animals treated with δ-receptor antagonists show increased anxiety and depressive-like behavior in rodent tests while agonists reduce the emotional behaviors. However, human clinical trials with δ-receptor agonists showed minimal effects and suggest significant species differences (see Chu Sin Chung and Kieffer [2013] for a review of δ-opioid receptor function).

The **κ-receptors** (**FIGURE 11.8C**) have a very distinct distribution compared with the μ- and δ-receptors. The κ-receptor was initially identified by high-affinity binding to ketocyclazocine, which is an opioid analog that produces hallucinations and dysphoria. This receptor is also found in the striatum and amygdala but additionally has a unique distribution in the hypothalamus and pituitary. These receptors may participate in the regulation of pain perception, gut motility, and dysphoria but also modulate water balance, feeding, temperature control, and neuroendocrine function.

The **NOP-R** are widely distributed in the CNS and the peripheral nervous system. They are found in high concentration in the cerebral cortex and the limbic areas, including the amygdala, hippocampus, and hypothalamus, as well as the periaqueductal gray, thalamus, brainstem nuclei including the raphe nuclei, and spinal cord. The receptor localization suggests a role in analgesia, feeding, learning, motor function, and neuroendocrine regulation (Witkin et al., 2014).

Almost 20 years after the initial successful receptor binding studies, the genetic material for each of the

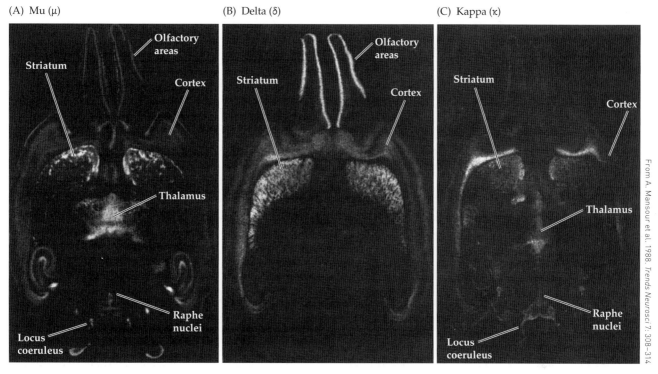

(A) Mu (μ)   (B) Delta (δ)   (C) Kappa (κ)

From A. Mansour et al. 1988. *Trends Neurosci* 7: 308–314

FIGURE 11.8 Autoradiograms of opioid receptor subtype binding in rat brain
Notice the distinct locations of (A) μ-, (B) δ-, and (C) κ-receptors.

four receptor types was isolated. Then it was inserted into cells (a process called **transfection**) maintained in culture to produce large numbers of identical cells (cloning). The **receptor cloning** and molecular sequencing of the opioid receptor subtypes provided several key pieces of information:

1. For each of the receptors, we now know the specific nucleic acid sequence making up the DNA that directs the synthesis of each receptor protein.

2. Using the nucleic acid sequence, the amino acids of the protein can be identified and compared with other families of receptor proteins.

3. The transfected cells can be used to study the intracellular changes induced by receptor agonists.

4. By radioactively labeling the genetic material, in situ hybridization makes it possible to visualize those cells in the brain that synthesize the receptor protein and more precisely localize the receptors themselves. (See Chapter 4 for a review of the techniques of molecular biology.)

Although the first opioid receptor to be successfully cloned was the δ-receptor (Evans et al., 1992; Kieffer et al., 1992), cloning of the others was soon to follow. Each of the four receptors has between 370 and 400 amino acids, and they bind with the ligands specific to each. All four of the protein receptors have a structure similar to the family of receptors that are linked to G proteins, which suggests that they mediate metabotropic (rather than ionotropic) responses. The structure of the δ-receptor, with the classic seven transmembrane portions, is shown in **FIGURE 11.9**.

A great diversity in opioid signaling exists because interactions occur among the receptor subtypes forming heteromeric complexes. Such heteromeric associations exist for κ–δ, μ–nociceptin, μ–κ, and μ–δ interactions (recently reviewed by Costantino and colleagues [2012]). These associations of two different receptor subtypes alter opioid binding and intracellular events. What this means is that the interaction of the two receptors could enhance or diminish opioid drug effects. For example, low subanalgesic doses of a δ-receptor ligand enhanced morphine-induced analgesia (acting on the μ-receptor) in the tail-flick test. Of further significance is the finding that both in vivo and in vitro exposure to chronic (but not acute) morphine increases the co-localization of μ–δ-receptor heteromers in the cell membrane of neurons in brain areas important to pain signaling. This enhanced receptor interaction is apparently a homeostatic process related to the development of tolerance. In fact, interfering with the μ–δ heteromer-mediated functions prevented the development of tolerance to chronic morphine. Understanding the function and pharmacology of this heteromer has the potential to improve opioid therapies by producing

FIGURE 11.9 Proposed structure of the δ-opioid receptor Each circle represents an identified amino acid. The seven regions spanning the cell membrane are typical for receptors that are coupled to G proteins.

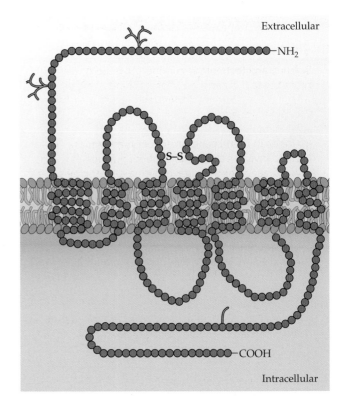

analgesia with a minimum of tolerance. **BOX 11.1** will tell you more about further developments in the fascinating story of opioid pharmacology.

Several families of naturally occurring opioid peptides bind to these receptors

It was not long after the receptors were initially identified that researchers were quick to ask why the nervous system would have receptors for the derivatives of the opium poppy. It seemed more reasonable to hypothesize that an endogenous neurochemical must exist to act on opioid receptors.

DISCOVERY In 1974 two different laboratories identified a peptide in brain extracts and other tissues that mimicked opioid activity (electrophysiologically and in a mouse vas deferens bioassay) and could also bind to opioid receptors (Terenius and Wahlstrom, 1974; Hughes, 1975). They named the first peptide *enkephalin*, meaning "in the brain." Soon a number of peptides were found to have these properties and were called endogenous opioids, or **endorphins** (from *endo*, signifying "endogenous," and *orphin*, from *morphine*). The great similarity in structure among the peptides led researchers to conclude that there were several larger peptides, called propeptides (or precursor peptides), that are broken into smaller active opioids. Any confusion was resolved when molecular biologists found that there are four large propeptides and each is coded for by a separate gene. These large propeptides are called **prodynorphin** (254 amino acids), **pro-opiomelanocortin** or **POMC** (267 amino acids), **proenkephalin** (267 amino acids), and **pronociceptin/ orphanin FQ** (180 amino acids). Each of the large propeptides manufactured in the soma must be processed by enzymes

(called proteases) that are packaged in the Golgi apparatus along with them. These enzymes are responsible for chopping or cleaving the propeptides into individual peptide products that are stored in vesicles and are further processed as they are transported down the axon to be released at the synapse. Each of the large propeptides produces a number of biologically active opioid and non-opioid peptides (**FIGURE 11.10**). Some years

FIGURE 11.10 The four opioid propeptides and some of their possible products POMC is cleaved into β-endorphin (β-END) and a number of other peptides, including γ- and α-melanocyte-stimulating hormone (MSH), β-MSH, adrenocorticotropic hormone (ACTH), and several forms of lipotropin (LPH). Proenkephalin cleavage produces several copies of met- and leu-enkephalin (ENK). Prodynorphin contains α- and β-neoendorphin, as well as dynorphin (DYN) A and B. Pronociceptin/ orphanin FQ cleavage produces one copy each of orphanin FQ, orphanin-2, and nocistatin. Tiny enkephalin peptides are also frequently found within the larger peptide fragments.

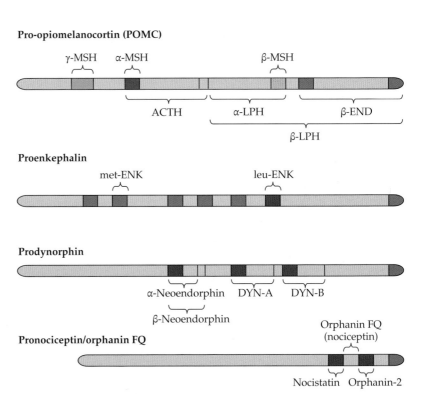

BOX 11.1 ■ THE CUTTING EDGE

Science in Action

Science and technology continue to build on past research to further the understanding of opioid transmission. In addition to labeling and localizing the receptors and cloning them to determine amino acid sequence, researchers now are using the latest methods in membrane protein crystallization. This method involves the solubilization, purification, and crystallization of receptor proteins to determine their three-dimensional structure with ultra-high resolution, down to individual atoms. Although images of the crystal structure of proteins had been achieved as early as the 1950s, the proteins crystallized were all water soluble. However, proteins such as the signaling receptors coupled to G proteins (including the opioid receptors) are embedded in the phospholipid membrane and are poorly soluble in either water or oil. Crystallization was also made more difficult because G protein–coupled receptors move within the membrane when activated by the appropriate ligand (i.e., ligand binding causes a conformational change or movement in the receptor, which activates the G protein; see Chapter 3). Additional technical problems exist, but in 2011 Kobilka and his team (Rasmussen et al., 2011) developed a modified membrane protein crystallization technique to image the β_2-adrenergic receptor at just the precise instant when it was activated by a hormone and transferred the signal to the G protein. This extraordinary technological achievement and decades of earlier research to characterize the receptor led to the 2012 Nobel Prize in Chemistry for Brian Kobilka and Robert Lefkowitz (his mentor). To read more about the decades of research leading to this prize, read "The Nobel Prize in Chemistry 2012: Popular Information" on the Nobelprize.org website (Nobelprize.org, 2014).

Based on their work, modification of the crystallization technique was applied to the imaging of the opioid receptors. Since 2012, the crystal structures of all four opioid receptors have been determined. Despite the extensive chemical manipulation required, these engineered receptors, when expressed in cells in culture, still showed their ligand selectivity and affinity and were able to initiate appropriate intracellular functions. The four receptors have similar deep binding "pockets" located in the center that are open to the extracellular

fluid. Details of ligand–receptor binding are discovered by creating mutations in selective amino acid residues. For example, mutating the charged amino acid asparagine (Asp) to a noncharged alternative amino acid prevents opioid activity. That suggests that the negatively charged Asp residue forms an ionic interaction with a positively charged group in the opioid ligands. The crystallized receptors, although similar, also have distinct molecular features, which are likely responsible for their selectivity for particular opioid agonists. Describing the molecular interactions of these receptors is beyond the scope of this chapter, but Cox (2013) and Shang and Filizola (2015) provide greater detail for those who are interested. Suffice it to say that with insight into the crystal structures of the receptors and detail of the mechanism of signal transduction, it is hoped that structure-based drug design may develop new painkilling medications. These medications would interact with amino acid residues in a precise fashion to produce distinct, predictable clinical benefits with fewer troublesome side effects.

Although it has taken a few years and the collaboration of a large number of international researchers specializing in different disciplines, one new custom-engineered drug ligand that acts at Kobilka's three-dimensional atomic structure of the μ-opioid receptor has been identified (Manglik et al., 2016). Using computer modeling techniques developed in the 1980s, the researchers evaluated ligand–receptor interactions for large libraries of over 3 million different molecules. They then used techniques in medicinal chemistry to enhance specificity and affinity of the new molecule to the μ-opioid receptor. The new ligand with the best fit, PZM21, was then preclinically tested in animal behavioral models (see Chapter 4). Dose-dependent PZM21 analgesia in the mouse hotplate test reached a maximal response of 87%, comparable to morphine's maximal effect of 92% (**FIGURE A**). The analgesic effects of the new molecule were absent in μ-opioid receptor knockout

(Continued)

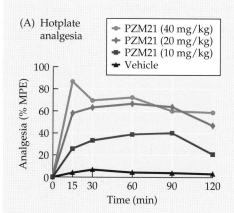
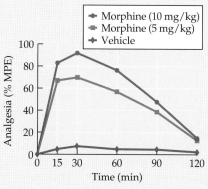

PZM21 is an effective analgesic with reduced side effects
(A) Dose–response curves for PZM21-induced analgesia (left) and morphine-induced analgesia (right). Latency to withdraw from a heated surface in the hotplate test is expressed as a percentage of the maximal possible effect (% MPE). The x-axis represents the time after subcutaneous administration of drug or saline (vehicle). The analgesic effect of 40 mg/kg of PZM21 was comparable to the effect of 10 mg/kg of morphine. (After A. Manglik et al. 2016. *Nature* 537: 185–190.)

BOX 11.1 ■ THE CUTTING EDGE (continued)

mice, demonstrating that PZM21 analgesia depends upon that receptor. The analgesic effects of PZM21 lasted longer than those of morphine, which would make it easier to administer clinically. Also, PZM21 had fewer significant side effects normally produced by morphine, specifically constipation and respiratory depression. **FIGURE B** shows that although PZM21 reduced defecation compared with controls, it had less of a constipating effect than morphine. Furthermore, while morphine greatly depressed the respiration rate, PZM21 was no different than vehicle in reducing

respiration frequency (**FIGURE C**). The finding that PZM21 did not activate the dopaminergic reward pathway nor induce a conditioned place preference (**FIGURE D**) indicates that the molecule is unlikely to cause the typical opioid reinforcement and abuse.

Although it would be premature to applaud the development of a new wonder drug, the science behind this discovery may mean that the structure-based approach used by these neuroscientists will ultimately help to develop a less hazardous pain control medication for those who are suffering.

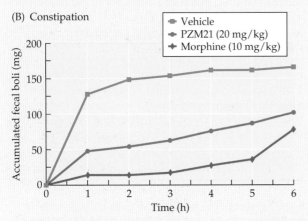

(B) Constipation

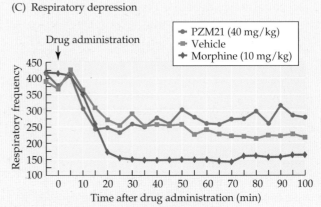

(C) Respiratory depression

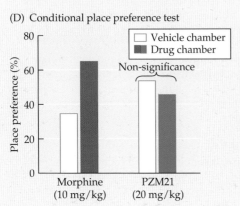

(D) Conditional place preference test

PZM21 is an effective analgesic with reduced side effects (B) Defecation (mg of fecal boli) was less after PZM21 administration than with saline, indicating constipation, but not as severe as with morphine. (C) About 20 minutes after administration, respiration frequency was significantly lower in subjects treated with morphine than in those receiving saline, while an equally analgesic dose of PZM21 did not impair respiration frequency. (D) Animals conditioned to associate a particular chamber with morphine rather than saline administration showed a preference for that chamber. Animals trained with PZM21 and saline failed to show such a place preference. (After A. Manglik et al. 2016. *Nature* 537: 185–190. doi.org/10.1038/nature19112.)

later, Zadina and colleagues (1999) described a group of peptides with a distinct structure and distribution in the CNS. These peptides, called **endomorphins**, bind quite selectively to the μ-receptor and are as potent as morphine in relieving pain. Thus far, their propeptide has not been identified.

LOCALIZATION   Mapping of the pathways utilizing the endogenous opioids was achieved by in situ hybridization to visualize propeptide mRNA, and immunohistochemistry was used to localize the propeptide itself (see Chapter 4). These propeptides are found in the brain, spinal cord, and peripheral autonomic nervous

system, where their opioid products act as neurotransmitters and neuromodulators at specific synapses. The propeptides are concentrated in areas related to pain modulation and mood. In addition, POMC is found in particularly high concentration in the pituitary gland, which releases a variety of hormones in response to hypothalamic releasing factors. The hypothalamus releases corticotropin-releasing factor (CRF) in response to stress, which in turn increases adrenocorticotropic hormone (ACTH) release from the pituitary and ultimately glucocorticoids from the adrenal cortex (**FIGURE 11.11**). CRF also causes a rapid increase in POMC mRNA and subsequent increases in release of β-endorphin from

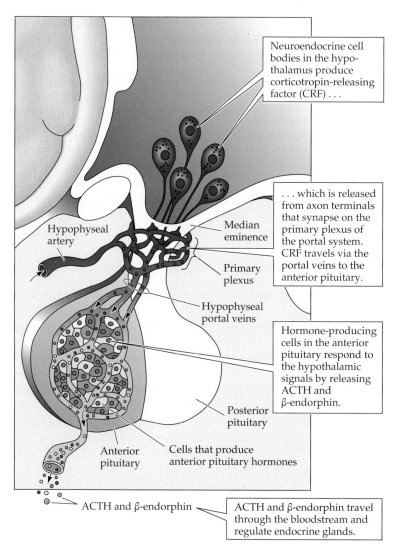

Neuroendocrine cell bodies in the hypothalamus produce corticotropin-releasing factor (CRF) . . .

... which is released from axon terminals that synapse on the primary plexus of the portal system. CRF travels via the portal veins to the anterior pituitary.

Hypophyseal artery

Median eminence

Primary plexus

Hypophyseal portal veins

Hormone-producing cells in the anterior pituitary respond to the hypothalamic signals by releasing ACTH and β-endorphin.

Posterior pituitary

Anterior pituitary

Cells that produce anterior pituitary hormones

ACTH and β-endorphin

ACTH and β-endorphin travel through the bloodstream and regulate endocrine glands.

FIGURE 11.11 **Hypothalamic control of ACTH and β-endorphin release** The hypothalamus releases CRF, which causes the anterior pituitary to secrete ACTH, which in turn acts on the adrenal gland to prepare the individual to deal with stress. CRF also influences β-endorphin synthesis and release from the pituitary in response to stress. Notice in Figure 11.10 that ACTH and β-endorphin come from the same propeptide, POMC.

neurotransmitters, they are likely to have a neuromodulatory role; that is, they modify the function of the neurotransmitter or produce changes in ion conductance and membrane potential.

Although we have four peptide families plus the endomorphins and three principal receptor subtypes, the peptides are not selective for a receptor type but show only a relative preference. The natural ligands for the δ-receptors are thought to be those derived from proenkephalin (enkephalins), and products from prodynorphin (dynorphin) are likely the natural κ-receptor agonists. The endomorphins bind preferentially to the μ-receptors, while POMC peptides (endorphins) bind readily to both μ- and δ-receptors. Since opioids do not bind to NOP-R, the receptor remained an "orphan" with no neuropeptide until two groups of researchers isolated a distinct peptide that one group called nociceptin because, in contrast to opioids, it *lowers* pain threshold. Since the other group called the same peptide orphanin FQ, it is now called nociceptin/orphanin FQ (N/OFQ). Pronociceptin/orphanin FQ and its peptides deserve a bit more discussion because although they are similar to the opioids, there are significant differences. The prohormone is widely distributed throughout the brain and spinal cord, with especially high concentrations in limbic regions. Although distribution of its peptides is different from that of the classical opioid peptides, in other instances they are found to be co-localized with the opioids. Significant evidence suggests that there is *reciprocal* modulation of N/OFQ neurons and the classical opioids. Additionally, although N/OFQ and the opioid peptides in some cases have similar effects, in other cases N/OFQ may cause effects opposite to those caused by the opioids. For example, although it is an analgesic at the spinal cord level, in supraspinal regions it is pronociceptive and has anti-opioid properties, including suppressing opioid-mediated analgesia. However, the complex action on analgesia is dependent on species, dose, assays, and pain modalities. For instance, it produces only analgesia in both spinal and supraspinal sites in non-human

the pituitary. A variety of stressors, such as painful foot shock, restraint, and swim stress, increase both CRF mRNA and POMC mRNA and induce analgesia that can be partially blocked by naloxone. Hence, that stress-induced analgesia must be mediated in part by the release of endogenous opioids. The intimate relationship of these neuropeptides provides a physiological link between pain and stress regulation (Young, 1993). Overall, the widespread locations of the peptides strongly implicate them in many functions, including pain suppression, reward, motor coordination, endocrine function, feeding, body temperature and water regulation, and response to stress. **WEB BOX 11.3** describes some of the effects of opioids on feeding.

While some of the neurons containing the opioid propeptides have long projections, many more are small cells that form local circuits. Many of the peptides are co-localized with other neurotransmitters in the same neuron, including acetylcholine, GABA (γ-aminobutyric acid), serotonin, catecholamines, and other peptides. When peptides coexist with other

TABLE 11.1	Locations, Functions, and Endogenous Ligands for Opioid Receptor Subtypes		
Receptor subtype	Endogenous ligands (prohormone sources)	Locations (most dense)	Functions
μ	Endomorphins (unknown), endorphins (POMC)	Thalamus, periaqueductal gray, raphe nuclei, spinal cord, striatum, brainstem, nucleus accumbens, amygdala, hippocampus	Analgesia, reinforcement, feeding, cardiovascular and respiratory depression, antitussive, vomiting, sensorimotor integration
δ	Enkephalin (proenkephalin), endorphins (POMC)	Neocortex, striatum, substantia nigra, nucleus accumbens, spinal cord, hippocampus, amygdala, hypothalamus	Analgesia, reinforcement, cognitive function, olfaction, motor integration
κ	Dynorphins (prodynorphin)	Pituitary, hypothalamus, amygdala, striatum, nucleus accumbens	Neuroendocrine function, water balance, feeding, temperature control, dysphoria, analgesia
NOP-R	Nociceptin/orphanin FQ (pronociceptin/orphanin FQ)	Cortex, amygdala, hypothalamus, hippocampus, periaqueductal gray, thalamus, substantia nigra, brainstem, spinal cord	Spinal analgesia, supraspinal pronociception, feeding, learning, motor function, neuroendocrine function

primates (reviewed by Kiguchi et al., 2016). Other effects include impairing motor performance, suppressing spatial learning, inducing feeding, and regulating stress-induced release of pituitary hormones. The peptide has many other functions and some that remain undiscovered (for a review of the NOP receptor system, see Toll et al., 2021). **TABLE 11.1** summarizes receptor subtype locations, functions, and preferences for endogenous opioids. For further detail, you may turn to the forty-second annual review of the behavioral effects of molecular, pharmacological, and genetic manipulations of the endogenous opioid system (Bodnar, 2021).

Opioid receptor–mediated cellular changes are inhibitory

You are already aware that each of the four opioid receptor types is linked to G proteins. You may recall from Chapter 3 that there are multiple forms of G proteins that have two principal actions. Some G proteins directly stimulate or inhibit the opening of ion channels (see Figure 3.14A), and others stimulate or inhibit enzymes to alter second-messenger production (see Figure 3.14B). Opioids and N/OFQ work by both of those mechanisms to open potassium (K$^+$) channels, close calcium (Ca^{2+}) channels, and inhibit adenylyl cyclase activity. The overall effects of the neuropeptides on nerve cell function include the reduction of membrane excitability and subsequent slowing of cell firing and inhibition of neurotransmitter release.

The neuropeptides reduce synaptic transmission in three principal ways: (1) by postsynaptic inhibition, (2) through axoaxonic inhibition, and (3) via presynaptic autoreceptors. First, opioid- and N/OFQ receptor–G protein opens K$^+$ channels, which increases K$^+$ conductance. Potassium exits the cell, forced by its concentration gradient, causing hyperpolarization. When the receptors are on the soma or dendrites of neurons,

the hyperpolarization decreases the cell's firing rate (**FIGURE 11.12A**).

Second, opioids and N/OFQ also produce an inhibitory effect by closing voltage-gated Ca^{2+} channels. In this case (**FIGURE 11.12B**), receptors on the presynaptic terminal activate G proteins, which in turn close the Ca^{2+} channels. Reducing the amount of Ca^{2+} entering during an action potential proportionately decreases the amount of neurotransmitter released. For example, opioid-induced inhibition of norepinephrine and dopamine release has been found in many brain areas. As expected, this effect is prevented by the receptor antagonist naloxone. Note that naloxone does not antagonize N/OFQ because N/OFQ does not bind to classical opioid receptors. Likewise, NOP-R antagonists, such as SB-612,111, would not be expected to prevent opioid-mediated effects on Ca^{2+} channels. The inhibition of glutamate and substance P release in the spinal cord is of particular significance because those neurotransmitters are released from the afferent sensory neurons that transmit pain signals from the periphery into the CNS (see the section on opioids and pain).

Third, opioid autoreceptors also produce inhibitory effects. Somatodendritic autoreceptors hyperpolarize cells in the locus coeruleus by enhancing K$^+$ conductance and subsequently reducing cell firing (not shown in figure). Elsewhere, presynaptic autoreceptors reduce the release of co-localized neurotransmitters (**FIGURE 11.12C**). In summary, neuropeptide effects on both K$^+$ and Ca^{2+} channels produce inhibitory effects and reduce neurotransmitter release. These actions in the appropriate circuitry are ultimately responsible for the analgesic effects (DiChiara and North, 1992).

All four types of opioid receptor are also coupled to inhibitory G proteins (called G$_i$) that inhibit adenylyl cyclase, which normally synthesizes the second messenger cyclic adenosine monophosphate (cAMP).

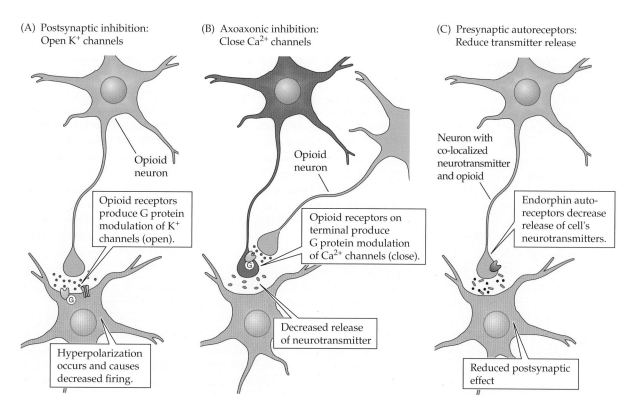

FIGURE 11.12 Inhibitory actions of endogenous opioids
Opioids inhibit nerve activity in several ways. (A) Opioids bind to receptors that activate a G protein that opens K^+ channels to hyperpolarize the postsynaptic cells, thereby reducing the rate of firing. (B) Opioid receptors on nerve terminals (axoaxonic) activate G proteins that close Ca^{2+} channels, reducing the release of the neurotransmitter. (C) Presynaptic autoreceptors activate G proteins and reduce the release of a co-localized neurotransmitter. The mechanism may involve closing Ca^{2+} channels or opening K^+ channels that hyperpolarize the presynaptic cell.

The reduced cAMP and subsequent decreased function of cAMP-dependent protein kinase may in part be responsible for opioid-induced ion channel changes; however, the immediate effects of the inhibition on cell function are not entirely clear. Nevertheless, the cAMP cascade has been implicated in chronic effects of opioids, including drug tolerance, dependence, and withdrawal. These topics are discussed in later sections.

SECTION SUMMARY

- Opiates are natural narcotics derived from the opium poppy. Other narcotics are semisynthetic or totally synthetic.

- Minor differences in molecular structure give rise to differences in potency and determine whether the drugs are full agonists, partial agonists, or neutral antagonists.

- Opioids relieve pain and produce drowsiness and sleep. Euphoria or dysphoria may occur. Opioids cause pinpoint pupils, vomiting, suppression of the cough reflex, drop in body temperature, reduced appetite, constipation, and a variety of hormonal effects. Respiratory and cardiac depression may also occur at higher doses.

- Repeated use produces tolerance to many but not all of the drugs' effects, as well as physical dependence.

- There are four opioid receptors (μ, δ, κ, and NOP-R), which are widely and unevenly distributed in the central and peripheral nervous systems. Opioids and opioid neuropeptides bind to the three classical receptors but not to NOP-R. Nociceptin/orphanin FQ is the neuropeptide that binds to NOP-R but not to the three classical receptors. Each of the receptors has been isolated and cloned and examined with membrane protein crystallization to visualize in ultra-high resolution their three-dimensional structures. All four are coupled to G proteins that induce metabotropic effects. The principal cellular activities include actions on ion channels (open K^+, close Ca^{2+}), which are responsible for cell hyperpolarization and inhibition of neurotransmitter release, and inhibition of adenylyl cyclase.

- Endogenous ligands for the opioid receptors are small peptides that are cleaved from larger propeptides manufactured in the soma. Molecular biology has shown four distinct propeptides (prodynorphin, POMC, proenkephalin, and pronociceptin/orphanin FQ), which produce a variety of opioid and non-opioid fragments. The propeptide for a fifth endogenous peptide, endomorphin, is not known.

- Endogenous opioids inhibit synaptic transmission by postsynaptic inhibition, by axoaxonic inhibition, and via presynaptic autoreceptors.

■ The locations of these peptides in the brain, spinal cord, and pituitary implicate them in regulating pain, reward, stress response, water balance, feeding, body temperature, and endocrine function. Nociceptin/orphanin FQ acts at cellular and molecular levels much the same way as opioids but often produces different and opposing effects. See Table 11.1 for locations, functions, and endogenous ligands for opioid receptor subtypes.

11.2   Opioids and Pain

Pain is distinct from other sensory systems in that it can be caused by a variety of stimuli detected by several types of nociceptors (detectors of noxious stimuli). The nociceptors are networks of free nerve endings that are sensitive to intense pressure, extreme temperature including heat and cold, electrical impulses, cuts, chemical irritants, and inflammation. Pain varies not only in intensity but also in quality and may be described as "pricking," "stabbing," "burning," "aching," and so forth. Its perception is also highly subjective, and no single stimulus will be described as painful by all individuals nor perhaps even by the same individual under different circumstances. Pain is modified by a number of factors, including strong emotion, environmental stimuli like stress, hypnosis, acupuncture, and opioid drugs.

Although we can get subjective reports of pain, quantification is difficult, particularly when analgesic drugs are tested. In the laboratory, when methods such as the application of sudden pressure, pinpricks, or stabs are used to induce pain, most analgesic drugs show ineffective or inconsistent analgesic effects. The failure of these drugs to show a significant reduction in pain is probably a result of the low emotional impact of those types of pain. More consistent results are obtained with the analgesics through the use of techniques that produce slowly developing or sustained pain. One technique used with humans is to stop blood flow to an exercising muscle with a tourniquet. With this method, the pain is slow in onset and is directly related to amount of exercise. Cutaneous pain in humans can be produced by the intradermal injection of various chemicals. A reliable method to test this kind of pain uses cantharidin to induce a blister, from which the outer layer of epidermis is removed to expose the blister base, on which small quantities of various agents can be applied for testing. Techniques that have been designed to produce more intense or more persistent pain are infrequently used because finding willing participants is difficult. Animal testing is overall more reliable, yielding conditions that are comparable to pathological pain in humans. This may be because the human participant in the experimental setting realizes that the pain stimulus poses no real threat, whereas for the animal subject, all pain is potentially serious. Animal tests are described in Chapter 4.

The two components of pain have distinct features

Pain is often described as having several components. "First," or early, pain represents the immediate sensory component and signals the onset of a noxious stimulus and its precise location to cause immediate withdrawal and escape from the damaging stimulus. "Second," or late, pain has a strong emotional component—that is, the unpleasantness of the sensation. Adaptation occurs more slowly to the secondary component, so it attracts our attention in prolonged fashion to motivate behaviors that limit further damage and aid recovery. Late pain is less localized and is often accompanied by autonomic responses such as sweating, fall in blood pressure, or nausea. The separation of these two components can be clearly seen in the patient who, after receiving morphine for persistent pain, describes the pain as just as intense as before treatment but much less aversive.

These distinct components of pain are in part explained by the types of neuron that carry the signals. Fibers called Aδ are larger in diameter and are myelinated, so they conduct action potentials more rapidly than the thin and unmyelinated C fibers. The difference in speed explains why when you smash your finger in the car door, you first experience a sharp pain that is well localized but brief, followed by a dull aching that is a prolonged reminder of the damage your body has experienced. These neurons have their cell bodies in the dorsal root ganglia and terminate in the gray matter of the dorsal horn of the spinal cord, ending on projection neurons that transmit pain signals to higher brain centers (**FIGURE 11.13**).

A second distinction between the two components of pain is their route and final destination in the brain. Early pain is transmitted from the spinal cord via the spinothalamic tract to the posteroventrolateral (PVL) nucleus of the thalamus before going directly to the primary and then secondary somatosensory cortex. The primary somatosensory cortex provides sensory discrimination of pain, while the secondary cortex is involved in the recognition of pain and memory of past pain. Late pain also goes to the thalamus, but in addition it gives off collaterals to a variety of limbic structures such as the hypothalamus and amygdala, as well as the anterior cingulate cortex. The anterior cingulate has a role in pain affect, attention, and motor responses (Rainville, 2002).

Researchers have demonstrated both the temporal and spatial relationships between pain-evoked cortical activation and reported pain in humans. Ploner and colleagues (2002) subjected individuals to brief painful laser stimuli and continuously monitored their subjective pain ratings while simultaneously recording faint magnetic fields on the surface of the skull using magnetoencephalography (MEG), which is excellent for showing the neural changes over very small units of time (from one millisecond to another). In this way,

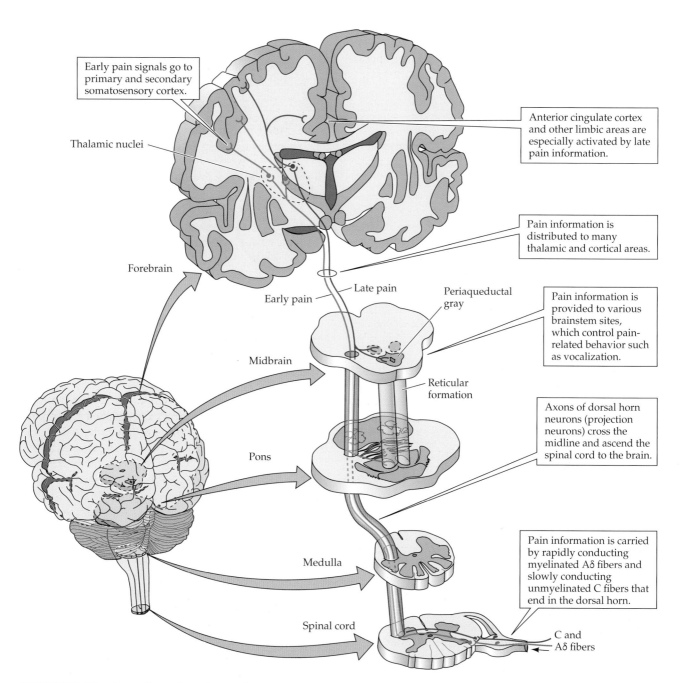

Early pain signals go to primary and secondary somatosensory cortex.

Anterior cingulate cortex and other limbic areas are especially activated by late pain information.

Thalamic nuclei

Forebrain

Pain information is distributed to many thalamic and cortical areas.

Early pain

Late pain

Periaqueductal gray

Pain information is provided to various brainstem sites, which control pain-related behavior such as vocalization.

Midbrain

Reticular formation

Axons of dorsal horn neurons (projection neurons) cross the midline and ascend the spinal cord to the brain.

Pons

Medulla

Pain information is carried by rapidly conducting myelinated Aδ fibers and slowly conducting unmyelinated C fibers that end in the dorsal horn.

Spinal cord

C and Aδ fibers

FIGURE 11.13 Ascending pain pathways Sensory neurons (Aδ and C fibers) activated by noxious stimuli enter the dorsal horn of the spinal cord. Dorsal horn neurons travel up the spinal cord on the contralateral side and ultimately reach various nuclei in the thalamus. Neurons transmitting "early" (first) pain end first in the primary somatosensory cortex for well-localized sensory discrimination, before the information is transferred to the secondary somatosensory cortex, where pain recognition occurs. The slower-conducting neurons transmit information (second pain) to a variety of limbic areas, including the anterior cingulate cortex, which is important for the emotional or suffering aspect of pain.

researchers could trace a wave of brain activity from its origin to sequential brain areas during processing (**FIGURE 11.14A**). When the cortical activation was superimposed on magnetic resonance images (**FIGURE 11.14B**), they showed that first pain (pain recognition), identified by participants' ratings, was temporally related to activation of the primary somatosensory cortex, whereas second pain (identified by participants' ratings

of unpleasantness) was strongly associated with anterior cingulate activation. Both types of pain were associated with neural activity in the secondary somatosensory cortex. Building on this work, Omori and colleagues (2013) used MEG with higher spatial resolution to show that pain is not only temporally related to activation of somatosensory cortex but is also somatotopically organized. As shown in **FIGURE 11.14C**, painful

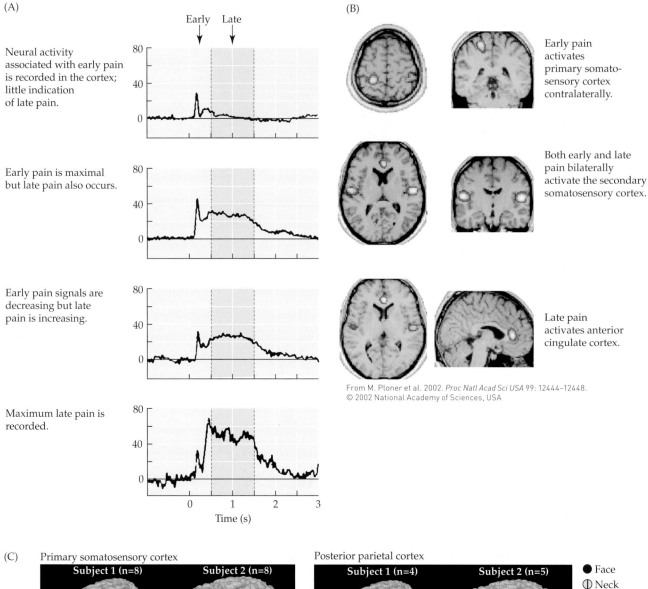

(A)

Neural activity associated with early pain is recorded in the cortex; little indication of late pain.

Early pain is maximal but late pain also occurs.

Early pain signals are decreasing but late pain is increasing.

Maximum late pain is recorded.

Time (s)

(B)

Early pain activates primary somatosensory cortex contralaterally.

Both early and late pain bilaterally activate the secondary somatosensory cortex.

Late pain activates anterior cingulate cortex.

From M. Ploner et al. 2002. *Proc Natl Acad Sci USA* 99: 12444–12448.
© 2002 National Academy of Sciences, USA

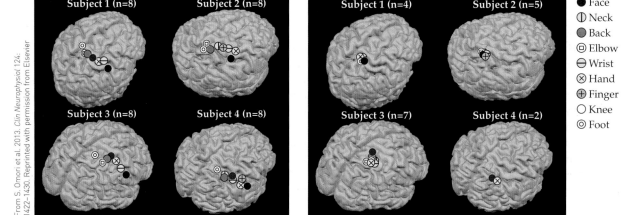

(C)   Primary somatosensory cortex   Posterior parietal cortex

Subject 1 (n=8)   Subject 2 (n=8)   Subject 1 (n=4)   Subject 2 (n=5)

Subject 3 (n=8)   Subject 4 (n=8)   Subject 3 (n=7)   Subject 4 (n=2)

● Face
Ⓘ Neck
◕ Back
⊡ Elbow
⊖ Wrist
⊗ Hand
⊕ Finger
○ Knee
◎ Foot

From S. Omori et al. 2013. *Clin Neurophysiol* 124: 1422–1430. Reprinted with permission from Elsevier

FIGURE 11.14 Location and time course of pain-evoked neural activity in humans (A) Sequential MEG tracings of the changes in cortical magnetic fields over 3 seconds following the initiation of the painful stimulus. (B) Brain areas that are active at corresponding points in time are shown as light-shaded areas that have been superimposed on magnetic resonance images. (C) Adjacent areas of primary somatosensory cortex are responsive to application of correspondingly adjacent painful stimuli on the body. (A from M. Ploner et al. 2002. *Proc Natl Acad Sci USA* 99: 12444–12448. © 2002 National Academy of Sciences, U.S.A.)

stimuli applied to adjacent parts of the body roughly correspond to activation of adjacent regions on somatosensory cortex, although this somatotopic organization was not evident in secondary somatosensory cortex.

Opioids inhibit pain transmission at spinal and supraspinal levels

By binding to opioid receptors, morphine and other opioid drugs mimic the inhibitory action of the endogenous opioids at many stages of pain transmission within the spinal cord and brain. To simplify, we can say that opioids regulate pain in three ways:

1. Within the spinal cord by small inhibitory interneurons
2. By two significant descending pathways originating in the periaqueductal gray (PAG)
3. At many higher brain sites, which explains opioid effects on emotional and hormonal aspects of the pain response.

As you know, information about pain, from either the surface or deep within the body cavity, is carried by neurons from the periphery into the spinal cord. Some of these primary afferent neurons end directly on projection neurons that transmit pain signals to higher brain centers (e.g., first to the thalamus and then to the somatosensory cortex) (**FIGURE 11.15A**). Others end on small excitatory interneurons (i.e., short neurons within the spinal cord) that in turn synapse onto the projection neurons (**FIGURE 11.15B**).

Opioids reduce the transmission of pain signals at the spinal cord in two ways. First, small inhibitory **spinal interneurons** release endorphins that inhibit the activation of the spinal projection neurons (**FIGURE 11.15C**). Morphine can act directly on the same opioid receptors on the spinal projection neurons to inhibit the transmission of the pain signal to higher brain centers that normally allow us to become aware of the sensory experience. Second, endorphins regulate several modulatory pathways that descend from the brain to inhibit spinal cord pain transmission, either by directly inhibiting the projection neuron (Figure 11.14A) or the excitatory interneuron (Figure 11.14B), or by exciting the inhibitory opioid neuron (Figure 11.14C). These **descending modulatory pathways** (**FIGURE 11.16**) begin in the midbrain and modify the pain information carried by spinal cord neurons.

The most important descending pathways begin in the PAG. The PAG is a brain area rich in endogenous opioid peptides and high concentrations of opioid receptors, particularly μ and κ. Local electrical stimulation of the PAG produces analgesia but no change in the ability to detect temperature, touch, or pressure. Treatment of chronic pain in human patients by electrical stimulation of the PAG is frequently successful,

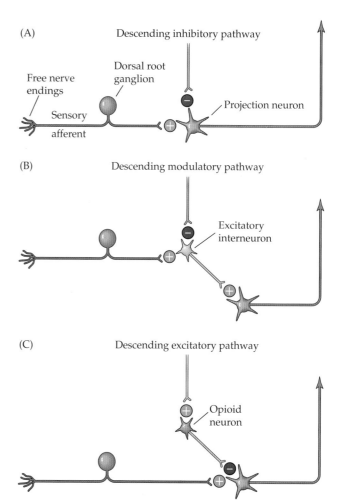

FIGURE 11.15 **Pain transmission in the spinal cord** Descending modulatory neurons modify transmission via (A) inhibition of the projection neuron, (B) inhibition of an excitatory interneuron, and (C) excitation of an inhibitory opioid interneuron. Opioid drugs can influence the activity of the descending pathways and can act directly on opioid receptors in the spinal cord.

although tolerance occurs with repeated use, and cross-tolerance (see Chapter 1) with injected morphine also occurs. This phenomenon suggests that electrical stimulation releases a morphine-like substance onto the same postsynaptic receptor sites occupied by exogenous morphine. Partial blockade of stimulation-induced analgesia with the specific opioid antagonist naloxone further supports that idea.

The neurons beginning in the PAG end on cells in the medulla, including the serotonergic cell bodies of the nucleus of the raphe. Microinjection of opioids into the raphe produces significant analgesia. The serotonergic neurons descend into the spinal cord to inhibit cell firing there and in that way reduce pain transmission. Similarly, other cells originating in the PAG terminate in the brainstem in an area close to the locus coeruleus, an important cluster of noradrenergic cell bodies that also send axons to the spinal cord to

FIGURE 11.16 Descending pain modulation pathways
Neurons from the periaqueductal gray descend to the
brainstem nucleus of the raphe (serotonergic neurons) and
the locus coeruleus (adrenergic neurons). The neurons in
both pathways descend to the spinal cord to modulate the
transmission of the pain signal at that level.

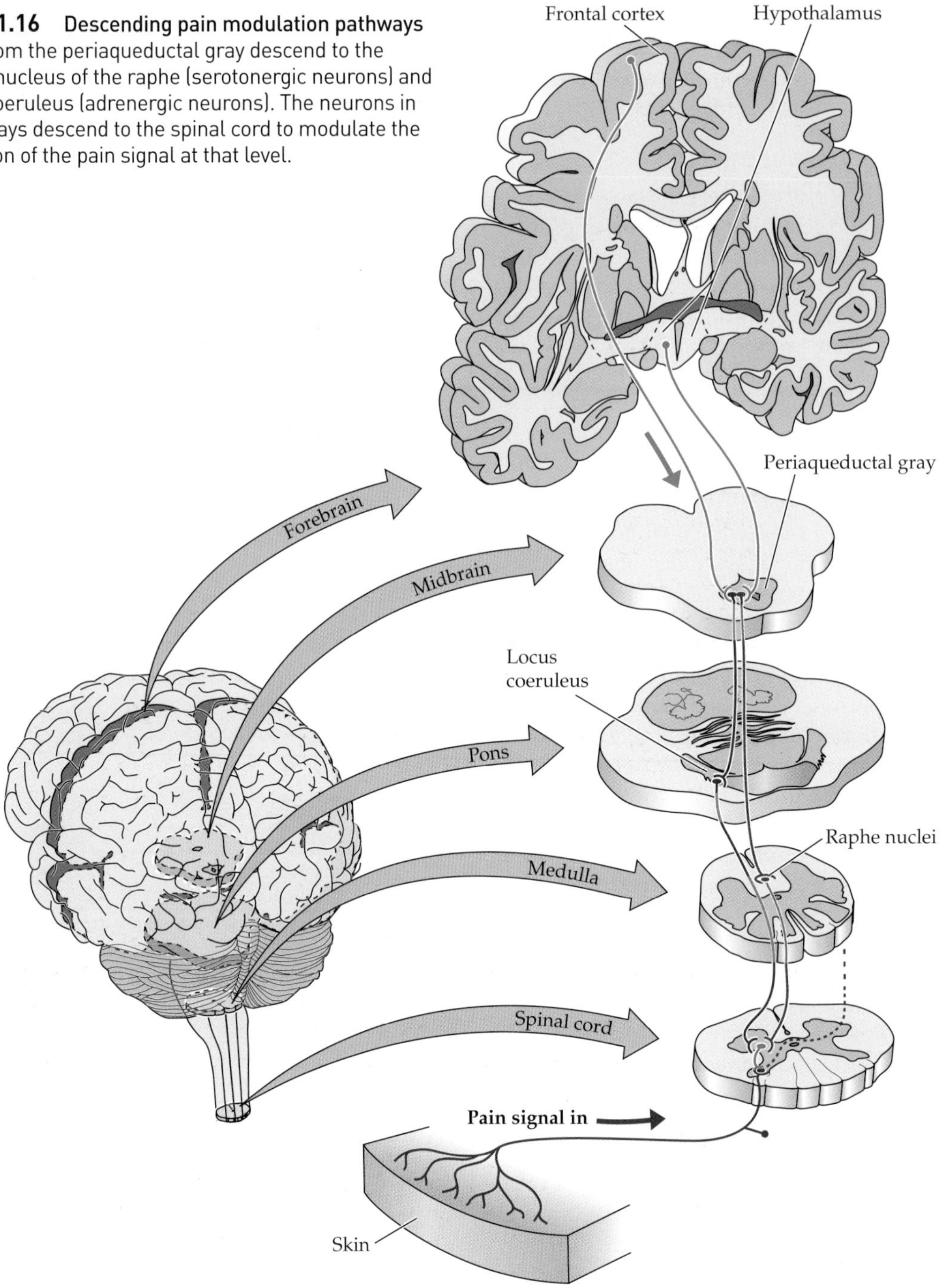

modulate pain conduction. In both cases, these descending pathways are activated when opioids inhibit
an inhibitory GABA "brake." Furthermore, neurotoxic
lesions of the descending serotonergic and noradrenergic cells prevent systemic morphine-induced analgesia.
Therefore, there are at least two major pathways that
descend to the spinal cord to inhibit the projection of
pain information to higher brain centers. However, the
inhibitory action is direct in some cases, while at other
times the inhibition occurs by action on small spinal
interneurons (as seen in Figure 11.16).

In summary, opioids modulate pain directly in the
spinal cord and by regulating the descending pain inhibitory pathways ending in the spinal cord. In addition,
significant opioid action occurs in other **supraspinal**
(above the spinal cord) locations, including higher sensory areas and limbic structures, as well as the hypothalamus and the medial thalamus. A high concentration of endogenous opioids and the presence of opioid
receptors suggest that these areas may be responsible
for the emotional component of pain, as well as for autonomic and neuroendocrine responses. In one PET study,

the endogenous activation of the μ-opioid system was evaluated during sustained pain induced by injection of hypertonic saline into the masseter muscle, which was compared with reaction to placebo injection in the same study participants. Zubieta and colleagues (2001) found a significant negative correlation between μ-opioid activity (measured as displacement of [¹¹C]carfentanil from μ-receptors) in the NAcc, amygdala, and thalamus and reported *sensory* pain scores (**FIGURE 11.17**). That is, the greater the μ-opioid activation, the lower was the individual's sensory pain score. The PAG also showed increased μ-receptor displacement, although it was not significant. When the scores on the *affective* component of pain were evaluated, increased μ-opioid activity was found in the bilateral anterior cingulate cortex, thalamus, and NAcc. These results indicate that endogenous μ-opioids modulate both the sensory and emotional components of pain and that morphine and other opioids likewise act at these sites. The existence of multiple circuits carrying pain information demonstrates the redundancy and diffuse nature of pain transmission, which reflects its tremendous evolutionary significance for survival. Stein (2016) reviews receptor subtypes, opioid receptor ligands, and central and peripheral mechanisms of opioid analgesia. Other forms of pain control depend on opioids.

ACUPUNCTURE The discovery of the endogenous opioids led to a dramatic increase in research into the mechanisms of the ancient Chinese method for pain relief called *acupuncture*. Acupuncture involves inserting a metallic needle into the skin to reach deep structures, such as muscles and tendons. Rhythmic movement of the needle or application of mild electrical current reduces pain perception. Beginning in the late 1950s, scientific studies using modern technology were initiated in China to determine the physiological basis of acupuncture-induced analgesia. Although naloxone was shown to reduce acupuncture-induced analgesia in human dentally evoked pain, it became clear that its antagonistic effect depended on the characteristics of the acupuncture treatment, which may be mediated by distinct opioid peptides. For instance, a look at electrically induced analgesia shows that the κ-receptor antagonist MR 2266 blocked the analgesia induced by 100-Hz electroacupuncture but not that induced by 2 Hz. In contrast the δ-opioid antagonist ICI 174864 blocked electroacupuncture-induced analgesia from 2 Hz, but not that induced by 100 Hz. Further support for the selectivity comes from the finding that 2-Hz acupuncture develops cross-tolerance with δ- but not κ-agonists, while 100-Hz acupuncture shows cross-tolerance to κ-agonists but not δ-agonists.

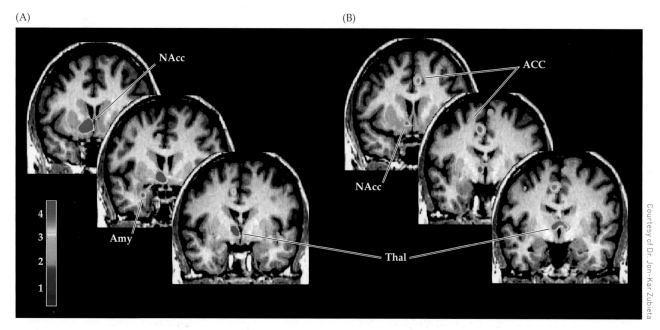

FIGURE 11.17 PET scans showing endogenous opioid activation during sustained pain In study participants injected with [¹¹C]carfentanil, endogenous opioid action is shown by the ability of the endogenous opioid to displace the radiolabeled μ-receptor ligand from the receptors. Pain was induced by continuous infusion of hypertonic saline in the masseter muscle and was compared with a control condition of isotonic saline infusion. (A) Activation of the μ-opioid system in the nucleus accumbens (NAcc), amygdala (Amy), and anterior thalamus (Thal) after the participants were exposed to the prolonged noxious stimulus. The warmer colors indicate greater activation. These increases were negatively correlated with the participants' *sensory* scores of pain. (B) μ-Opioid activity in the bilateral anterior cingulate cortex (ACC) and anterior thalamus and unilaterally in the NAcc. These increases were negatively correlated with pain *affect* scores. Therefore, the greater the μ-opioid activation in these areas, the lower was the emotional component of pain. Areas in red indicate greatest activity.

More direct measurements demonstrated that 2-Hz electroacupuncture caused significant elevations in the proenkephalin peptide, whose cleavage products would be expected to act at δ-receptors, and 100 Hz raised CSF levels of dynorphin, which acts most robustly on κ-receptors (Han, 2004).

Notably, most of the findings that show a beneficial analgesic effect of acupuncture utilize electroacupuncture, which would be expected to result in more pronounced physiological effects. However, when traditional acupuncture is compared to "sham" acupuncture, which uses non-penetrating needles or targets non-acupuncture points, sham acupuncture was as effective as true acupuncture in nearly all such studies, suggesting that it is either very difficult to properly control for acupuncture effects, or acupuncture produces clinically useful placebo effects (Musial, 2019).

DUAL INHIBITION OF PEPTIDASES   A different physiological approach to achieving antinociception involves enhancing the effects of endogenous enkephalin by inhibiting the two peptidase enzymes that degrade it (Noble and Roques, 2007). Microdialysis studies in rats showed that the dual inhibitors such as RB-101, RB-120, RB-3007, and others increase the extracellular levels of enkephalin in vivo in numerous brain regions. These drugs are good examples of prodrugs (see Chapter 1) because their lipophilic nature allows rapid passage across the blood–brain barrier into the brain, where a bond between the two inhibitors is biologically broken, making them active. Although inhibiting either one of the two peptidases produces only weak analgesic effects, inhibiting both produces far more robust dose-dependent effects in the hotplate, tail flick, and other animal tests of analgesia. The relatively long-lasting antinociceptive effects following intraperitoneal (IP), IV, or oral (PO) administration are blocked by naloxone. The importance of enkephalin to the pharmacological action of the dual inhibitors is further demonstrated by the lack of analgesic effect in mutant mice lacking proenkephalin. Which opioid receptor is involved is somewhat unclear because the analgesic effect is mediated by μ-receptors or both μ- and δ-receptors, depending on the nature of the pain (thermal, chemical, mechanical, or inflammatory) used in animal testing. The mechanism of action has clinical significance because it may explain a synergistic effect of a dual inhibitor and morphine. Research shows that a subanalgesic dose of RB-101 significantly potentiates a subanalgesic dose of morphine. Being able to use low doses of the two drugs for pain control would prevent the unwanted side effects caused by high doses of either one. One possible explanation for the synergism is that low doses of morphine increase the release of enkephalins that is further enhanced by the peptidase inhibition.

Of further importance is that because completely inhibiting the peptidases with high doses of dual inhibitors never achieves the maximum analgesic effect of morphine, it is assumed that endogenous enkephalin does not saturate opioid receptors and overstimulate them. This may be part of the reason that the dual inhibitors avoid some of the major disadvantages of morphine treatment. At doses that produce significant analgesia, the dual inhibitors do not depress either the rate or volume of respiration and induce only a partial tolerance to the analgesic effect. Furthermore, following chronic administration, naloxone administration fails to induce a morphine-like withdrawal syndrome, so the risk of physical dependence is minimal. Low abuse potential is suggested by studies showing that animals rarely develop conditioned place preference or altered intracranial electrical self-stimulation behavior (see Chapter 4). Additionally, animals do not distinguish the dual inhibitors from saline in drug discrimination tests; nor do morphine-trained animals generalize to the dual inhibitors, which indicates that their interoceptive cues are different. These characteristics make the dual inhibitors tempting targets for future clinical trials once toxicology and safety studies have been completed.

GENE THERAPY   On the basis of strong preclinical evidence using a variety of rodent models of pain, a small clinical trial of gene therapy in patients with intractable pain from terminal cancer was undertaken (Fink et al., 2011). This study used the cold sore–causing herpes simplex virus to act as the gene transfer vector because this virus is taken up from the skin by sensory nerve endings and transported along their axons to the nuclei in the cell bodies located in the corresponding dorsal root ganglia. The virus was modified so it could not replicate and was engineered to contain the gene coding for human proenkephalin. The newly synthesized proenkephalin would be expected to be packaged in vesicles, spliced into multiple enkephalin peptides, and ultimately released by the sensory nerve terminals in the dorsal horn of the spinal cord to inhibit pain signal conduction (see Figures 11.13 and 11.15). Earlier studies of the technique using laboratory animals showed significant analgesic effects that were blocked by pretreatment with naloxone, demonstrating the importance of opioid receptors. Additionally, the analgesic effect was additive with morphine and shifted the dose–response curve for morphine to the left, which indicates that less morphine was needed to achieve the same level of analgesia. Of potential importance is that the vector-mediated analgesia occurred in animals that were tolerant to the effects of morphine, quite possibly because the analgesic effect was mediated by δ-opioid receptors, while the morphine-induced analgesia depends primarily on μ-opioid receptors.

This clinical trial included only 10 patients, all of whom had moderate to severe pain that was not eliminated by at least 200 mg of morphine. After receiving 10 injections in a single session into the skin where pain was localized, they were evaluated seven times over a 28-day follow-up and monthly thereafter for 4 months. Although there were reports of mild and transient side effects such as elevation of body temperature, no serious adverse effects were reported throughout the period of evaluation. Despite the small number of patients and the lack of a placebo group, the researchers found an apparent dose response. The lowest dose produced no pain relief, while the higher doses reduced pain to 50% of pretreatment levels initially and continued to reduce pain to 20% over several weeks. These encouraging results are being expanded into a larger phase II randomized, double-blind, placebo-controlled trial using similar patient populations.

DUAL μ-RECEPTOR/NOP-R AGONISTS

An exciting new approach has produced an agent that is highly effective in reducing pain without many of the common narcotic side effects. The focus has been on the NOP-R because agonists for the receptor produce analgesia but are not reinforcing and can reduce the reinforcing effects of μ-receptor agonists. Medicinal chemists have identified ligands that bind to both μ-receptors and NOP-R and produced analgesia in rodent models. One of particular interest is BU08028. Ding and colleagues (2016) performed extensive experiments on BU08028 in 12 rhesus monkeys because, like humans, these animals display opioid-induced abuse liability and respiratory depression. For that reason, their findings with the monkeys, compared with rodent studies, are more likely to translate to humans. The rationale for using the dual μ-receptor/NOP-R agonist is that the NOP-R stimulation will reduce some of the pain so less μ-receptor stimulation will be needed and side effects will be correspondingly reduced. Ding's group measured analgesia by placing the monkeys' shaved tails in hot (120°F) water and measuring latency to withdraw. They found dose-dependent analgesia that at 0.01 mg/kg produced the maximum possible effect. Further, a single injection lasted up to 30 hours, which is an extremely long duration of action. The fact that both the opioid receptor antagonist naltrexone and the NOP-R antagonist J-113397 shifted the dose–response curve to the right to the same extent indicates that the two receptors were equally responsible for the analgesia. After 3 days of morphine treatment alone, naltrexone precipitated measurable withdrawal signs. In contrast, when naltrexone and J-113397 were administered to animals following 3 days of BU08028, no withdrawal was evident, suggesting lack of physical dependence. In the drug self-administration breaking point test, both the opioids remifentanil and buprenorphine were readily self-administered, with remifentanil being significantly more reinforcing

than buprenorphine. In contrast, self-administration of BU08028 was not significantly different from saline self-administration, indicating little reinforcement and no abuse potential. In evaluation of multiple respiratory functions, BU08028 at maximum analgesic dose and doses 10 times higher did not decrease any of the measures, nor did it alter cardiovascular function (e.g., bradycardia, hypotension, or electrocardiogram parameters). In sum, this study provides evidence that the dual μ-receptor/NOP-R agonist BU08028 is highly effective as an analgesic in non-human primates and has a wider therapeutic window than morphine because it produces less respiratory depression and fewer cardiovascular effects. Furthermore, physical dependence and abuse potential are minimal. Further testing in non-human primates is needed at higher doses and for longer periods of time to pave the way toward clinical trials with human patients. This pharmacological approach and the structure-based drug development described in Box 11.1 are promising advances in the search for safer painkillers (briefly summarized by Perlman, 2017).

BIASED OPIOID AGONISTS

A relatively recent approach to opioid analgesic development has taken advantage of the fact that the μ-opioid receptor exists in multiple constitutive states, which gives rise to its involvement in different signaling pathways. For instance, depending on constitutive state, a μ-opioid receptor may be coupled to a G protein, or may interact with a signaling pathway through proteins called beta arrestins. A biased agonist is designed to selectively target the μ-opioid receptor in only one such state. Studies in beta arrestin knockout mice showed that morphine more effectively induced analgesia but produced fewer peripheral side effects, such as constipation or respiratory depression, when compared to wild-type control mice, suggesting that opioid receptors mediate these side effects through beta arrestin, but not G-protein-mediated signaling. Follow-up studies in humans using the G-protein-biased μ-opioid receptor agonist oliceridine revealed similar findings: oliceridine produced analgesia that was superior to morphine with side effects that were similar or less severe (see Machelska and Celik, 2018, for a review of biased agonists and other related advances in opioid analgesic development). In a similar vein, biased antagonists are also being explored for their therapeutic potential, particularly for their ability to interfere with pathways that are critical for the develop of opioid abuse and dependence (Sadee et al., 2020). Lastly, other drugs under development are aimed at targeting peripheral opioid receptors in order to induce analgesia in peripheral tissues while avoiding altogether the side effects that are mediated by the CNS, such as respiratory depression and dependence (Seth et al., 2021).

SECTION SUMMARY

- Nociceptors are free nerve endings that are sensitive to a variety of pain stimuli.

- Pain has two components. First pain is the immediate sensory component carried by myelinated Aδ neurons and transmitted via the spinothalamic tract to the PVL nucleus of the thalamus before projecting to primary, then secondary, somatosensory cortex. Second pain is the emotional component carried by C fibers and transmitted to the thalamus with collaterals to limbic areas, including the anterior cingulate.

- Opioids (both endogenous and exogenous) act at spinal and supraspinal levels to relieve pain. Endorphin neurons in the spinal cord decrease the conduction of pain signals from the spinal cord to higher brain centers. Descending neurons from the periaqueductal gray activate pathways from the locus coeruleus (noradrenergic) and nucleus of the raphe (serotonergic) that impede pain signals in the spinal cord. Opioid receptors in the neocortex and limbic regions modulate the emotional component of pain to relieve the sense of suffering.

- Analgesic effects of electroacupuncture depend on opioids. Acupuncture induced by 100 Hz is blocked by κ-receptor antagonists, shows cross-tolerance to κ-agonists, and increases CSF levels of dynorphin. Acupuncture induced by 2 Hz is antagonized by δ-receptor blockers, shows cross-tolerance to δ-agonists, and elevates proenkephalin.

- Analgesia can be produced by drugs that inhibit both of the enkephalin-degrading enzymes. Elevating endogenous enkephalin has fewer side effects than morphine: less respiratory depression, partial tolerance, and low abuse potential.

- A gene therapy clinical trial showed that the gene coding for proenkephalin carried by a herpes simplex viral vector reduced pain in patients with cancer with minimal side effects.

- Dual μ-receptor/NOP-R agonists produce analgesia without respiratory depression, cardiovascular effects, physical dependence, or abuse liability.

- New opioid receptor drugs selectively target opioid receptors in different constitutive states or in peripheral tissue in order to induce analgesia without producing side effects mediated by the CNS.

11.3 Opioid Reinforcement, Tolerance, and Dependence

Although the opioids are the best pain-reducing drugs currently available, their use continues to be problematic because of the potential for abuse. The drugs in this class are highly reinforcing, and despite strict legal controls, they sometimes wind up in the hands of individuals who abuse them. Furthermore, chronic use leads to tolerance and ultimately to physical dependence, with some reports suggesting that prescription opioid misuse occurs in approximately 25% of patients (Martell et al., 2007).

In order to learn more about how medical patients become chronic drug users, multiple studies have been done recently looking at both acute pain and emergency room visits as well as chronic pain conditions. Barnett and colleagues (2017) examined the records of almost 400,000 older individuals on Medicare over several years who had visited emergency rooms (ERs) in multiple hospitals with similar types of injury/pain. Opioids are frequently prescribed by ER physicians because they are highly effective and act rapidly for treatment of pain from broken bones and other severe acute pain. What the researchers found was that those patients who were treated by "high-intensity" opioid-prescribing physicians (those with a high prescription rate) were significantly more likely to develop long-term opioid use (180 days or more in the next year) than those patients who were treated by "low-intensity" opioid prescribers. Since clear guidelines do not exist, ER physicians base their decisions on past experience, which varies between physicians, so there are examples of both excessive treatment and insufficient treatment within the same hospital. This study was of particular interest because it involved just a short-term exposure to opioid use, so most of the long-term use must also have involved securing subsequent prescriptions from primary care physicians outside the hospital setting. Of course, the dangers, especially for older individuals, are the side effects of constipation, sleepiness or confusion, impaired balance leading to falls, and opioid use disorder.

Unfortunately, at this point there is no quantitative measure to help physicians identify individuals who will experience adequate analgesia but few side effects and will have low potential abuse liability (Bruehl et al., 2013), although there are multiple risk-assessment tools available (see Jamison and Mao, 2015). **TABLE 11.2** provides some of the identified risk factors for opioid misuse. Perhaps in the future, pharmacogenetic testing will provide information regarding the probability of opioid misuse in a given individual as well as predicting effective pain relief (Crist et al., 2018). Obvious candidate genes for predicting abuse potential involve the receptors and propeptides for opioid transmission, and they have been most extensively studied. Researchers look for gene variants that associate with the disorder of interest. Among the most replicated findings involves a single-nucleotide polymorphism (SNP) of the gene coding for the μ-receptor. Altering just a single nucleotide changes the identity of one of the amino acids in the protein coded by the gene and modifies function of the protein. In the case of opioid function, the SNP identified reduces mRNA expression, leading to reduced μ-receptor levels and also altered β-endorphin binding affinity. It also alters the hypothalamic–pituitary–adrenal axis stress response. Multiple

TABLE 11.2 Risk Factors for Opioid Misuse

Family history of substance abuse

Personal history of substance abuse

Young age

History of criminal activity and/or legal problems including DUIs[a]

Regular contact with high-risk people or high-risk environments

Problems with past employers, family members, and friends

Risk-taking or thrill-seeking behavior

Heavy tobacco use

History of severe depression or anxiety

Psychosocial stressors

Prior drug and/or alcohol rehabilitation

Source: After R. N. Jamison and J. Mao. 2015. *Mayo Clin Proc* 90: 957–68.
doi: 10.1016/j.mayocp.2015.04.010. © 2015 Mayo Foundation for Medical
Education and Research. Reprinted with permission from Elsevier.
[a] DUI, driving under the influence.

studies report an association of that SNP with significantly increased vulnerability to heroin addiction and also overdose severity. These findings are encouraging, but since opioids modify both dopamine (DA) in the reward pathway and serotonin (5-HT) function that alters mood, components of those transmitter systems, including receptors, transporters, and synthesizing enzymes, are also being investigated. Discussing the genetic contribution to addiction potential is beyond the scope of this chapter, but Reed and colleagues (2014) describe the genetics of addiction, considering not only opioid, DA, and 5-HT function, but also GABA, norepinephrine, glutamate, and neuromodulators.

A second focus of research into the precursor to chronic drug use has been on patients with chronic pain conditions. About 25% of the U.S. general population suffers from some chronic pain condition, including arthritis, back pain, inflammatory pain, diabetic neuropathy, and residual effects following accidents. It is clear that many people require opioids for severe, acute pain or pain associated with cancer, but a recent meta-analysis suggests that opioids are much less effective for chronic non-cancer pain and that some non-pharmacological methods, such as physical therapy and cognitive therapy, may be equally useful for some patients (Reinecke et al., 2015). The analysis compared non-opioid analgesics, weak opioids, strong opioids, physical therapy, and cognitive therapy against placebo. To be optimal the treatment must not just relieve pain, but also increase physical functioning, quality of sleep, and quality of life with minimal side effects. In the study, statistical averages showed not much difference among treatments regarding pain control. Opioids improved sleep quality but not quality of life; also, opioids showed the greatest number of adverse effects. Physical therapy and cognitive therapy produced no significant effects on quality of life, sleep quality, or physical function. Although averaging the data showed little difference, each patient responded differently, so individual treatment strategies using a combination of approaches is recommended.

The first nonbinding federal guidelines from the U.S. Centers for Disease Control and Prevention (CDC) for pain regulation are aimed at reducing the increase in opioid misuse and deaths that often begin with prescription drugs. The CDC recommendation is that physicians suggest the use of ibuprofen and aspirin for their patients rather than prescribing opioids unless necessary, and with opioids they should limit the duration of treatment. Of course, the over-the-counter drugs have their own sets of side effects, which prohibit their use for some patients, and they may or may not provide the extent of pain relief needed. Physicians are trained to relieve their patients' pain and suffering, so some are uncomfortable monitoring their patients' drug use. Additionally, many resent following a formula for treatment when each patient is different and many are in severe and constant pain. Intense chronic pain conditions severely limit normal daily activities and the ability to work and are responsible for both stress and depression. Nevertheless, some state medical boards are trying to limit the number of opioid doses per month for any given individual. Some of these limits are especially hard on the older population, who are more likely to suffer from the chronic pain of arthritis, diabetes and shingles neuropathy, cancer, and multiple surgeries, and yet are typically less likely to misuse or abuse opioids than the younger population. However, it must be said that because of their slower metabolism, they are more likely to suffer from side effects. A second issue to be addressed is that of cost. Although treatments other than the opioids are available, including acupuncture, hypnosis, chiropractic manipulation, physical therapy, therapeutic massage, yoga, cognitive behavioral therapy, and mindfulness meditation, and each can be effective for a given individual, these alternative treatments can be quite expensive and are rarely covered by insurance, including Medicare. Hence, if government officials want physicians to reduce opioid prescribing, they may have to expand insurance coverage for alternative approaches to treating pain.

Animal testing shows significant reinforcing properties

Experimental techniques used to demonstrate the reinforcement value of opioids are described in Chapter 4. Intracerebral electrical self-stimulation allows subjects to press a lever to self-administer a weak electrical current to certain brain areas that constitute central reward pathways. When the animal presses the lever, electrical activation causes release of neurotransmitters from the nerve terminals in the region, which in turn mediate a rewarding effect. The fact that morphine and other opioids lower the electrical current threshold for self-stimulation indicates that the drugs enhance the brain reward mechanism.

When the drug self-administration technique is used, one striking finding is that the reinforcement value and the pattern of opioid use in animals are quite similar to those seen in humans. Self-injection gradually increases over time until the animals self-administer a stable and apparently optimal amount of drug. The ability of animals to maintain a stable blood level is demonstrated by pretreatment with morphine, codeine, or meperidine, which subsequently reduces IV self-administration of morphine. In contrast, when some receptors are blocked with naloxone, the self-administration rate increases and matches that seen during morphine abstinence. It is evident from these studies that the animals learn to regulate with some accuracy the amount of morphine that they require. Dose–response curves can be used to compare the relative potencies of opioid drug reinforcement (Woods et al., 1993).

The endogenous opioid β-endorphin is also self-administered, which strongly suggests that it mediates opioid reinforcement. β-endorphin self-administration is blocked by either μ- or δ-receptor antagonists. Thus, both types of receptor are involved in reward processes. In contrast, κ-agonists fail to produce self-injection and may induce aversive states, leading to avoidance behavior (Shippenberg, 1993).

Dopaminergic and nondopaminergic components contribute to opioid reinforcement

Two important methods are used to identify the neurobiology of opioid reinforcement. In one, self-administration of opioid ligands microinjected into discrete brain areas is evaluated. In the second, selective lesions are used to identify the brain areas and neurotransmitter pathways that eliminate opioid-induced reinforcement.

Microinjection studies from many laboratories demonstrate the contribution of the dopaminergic mesolimbic pathway to opioid reinforcement. This pathway originates in the ventral tegmental area (VTA) of the midbrain and projects to limbic areas, including the NAcc. Return to Figure 5.9 to review the important DA pathways in the brain. Self-administration of morphine or endogenous peptides occurs when the microcannula is implanted near the DA cell bodies within the VTA. Intra-VTA microinjection of morphine or selective μ-agonists also produces conditioned place preference and reduces the threshold for intracranial electrical self-stimulation. Each of these results argues for a direct action of opioids on central reward mechanisms served by the mesolimbic pathway.

But what exactly happens to the cells in the VTA in the presence of opioids? Both systemic opioids and opioids microinjected into the VTA increase dopaminergic cell firing, which subsequently increases DA release within the NAcc. Intraventricular β-endorphin produces similar enhancements of neuronal firing. In contrast, κ-agonists produce the opposite effects on mesolimbic neurons and reduce dopaminergic neuronal activity and subsequent DA turnover (release and metabolism). Since microinjected κ-agonists produce conditioned place *aversions*, it seems possible that the mesolimbic DA system may mediate aversive effects of opioids, as well as their reinforcing properties (Shippenberg et al., 1991).

A model of the opposing effects of opioid neurons on mesolimbic dopaminergic cells is shown in **FIGURE 11.18**. β-endorphin and opioid drugs seem to increase VTA cell firing by inhibiting the inhibitory GABA cells found in the VTA. They can decrease the release of GABA by opening K^+ channels or reducing Ca^{2+} influx on GABA terminals. This inhibition of inhibitory neurons leads to increased firing and greater DA release in the NAcc. The endogenous peptide dynorphin, which acts on κ-receptors on the terminals of the DA neurons, can reduce the release of DA by similar mechanisms, causing dysphoria.

How sure are we that mesolimbic DA is really important? DA receptor antagonists are seen to block the reinforcing effects of opioids when evaluated by each of the three standard behavioral measures. However, inducing lesions of dopaminergic neurons with the neurotoxin 6-hydroxydopamine (6-OHDA) reduces (but does *not* abolish) the reinforcement value. The

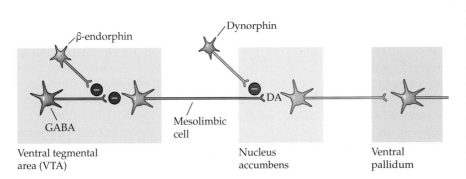

FIGURE 11.18 Model of the effects of opioids on mesolimbic dopaminergic cells The β-endorphin cell has an inhibitory effect on the normally inhibitory GABAergic cell, allowing the firing rate of the mesolimbic dopaminergic cells to increase and the cells to release more dopamine (DA) in the nucleus accumbens. In contrast, the axoaxonic dynorphin cell inhibits the release of dopamine from the mesolimbic cell by preventing calcium entry.

fact that heroin self-administration is only *partially* reduced rather than eliminated by the lesion certainly suggests that other brain areas and other neurotransmitters in addition to DA are also involved. Although these studies clearly support earlier results showing that increased mesolimbic firing is a common link in the actions of many self-administered drugs, including ethanol, nicotine, and psychostimulants (see Chapter 9), opioids do not have to release mesolimbic DA to be reinforcing (Gerrits and Vanree, 1996).

Further, the mesolimbic pathway may be more specifically involved in the salience (or significance) of events to an individual. What we mean is that the dopaminergic cell firing may tell an organism when some event is important or meaningful, regardless of whether it is appetitive (positive) or aversive (negative). We would therefore have incentive (or motivation) to approach (in the case of a reinforcer) or avoid (in the case of a noxious event) a particular significant stimulus. This idea has been developed in the "incentive sensitization" hypothesis of addiction as described in Box 9.2 (see the next section).

Long-term opioid use produces tolerance, sensitization, and dependence

You have just read about the acutely rewarding effects of opioids, which increase the likelihood that the drug will be used again. Chronic use subsequently leads to neuroadaptive changes in the nervous system, which are responsible for tolerance, sensitization, and dependence.

Tolerance (see Chapter 1) refers to the diminishing effects of a drug with repeated use, and it occurs for all of the opioids, including the endorphins. Although tolerance to the opioids develops quite rapidly, tolerance does not occur for all of the pharmacological effects to the same extent or at the same rate. For example, tolerance to the analgesic effect occurs relatively rapidly, but the constipating effects and the pinpoint pupils persist even after prolonged opioid use.

Cross-tolerance among the opioids also exists. For this reason, when tolerance develops to one opioid drug, other chemically related drugs also show a reduced effectiveness. For instance, following chronic heroin use, treatment with codeine will elicit a smaller-than-normal response even if the individual has never used codeine before. Since we now know that at least four types of opioid receptors exist, we might wonder whether the receptor subtype plays a role in cross-tolerance. Indeed, it seems that selective agonists for the μ-receptor reduce the effectiveness of other μ-receptor agonists, but they only minimally reduce κ-agonist activity. Likewise, repeated exposure to κ-agonists diminishes the effects of other κ-agonists but not μ-agonists.

As is true for many drugs, several mechanisms are responsible for the development of tolerance to the opioids. An increased rate of metabolism with repeated use (metabolic tolerance) is responsible for some small portion of opioid tolerance. Classical conditioning processes also contribute to this phenomenon. However, most tolerance is based on changes in nerve cells that compensate for the presence of chronic opioids (pharmacodynamic tolerance). The cell mechanisms are discussed in more detail in the section on neurobiological adaptation and rebound.

Under some circumstances, repeated exposure to opioids produces **sensitization**. Sensitization refers to the increase in drug effects that occurs with repeated administration. In their incentive sensitization hypothesis Robinson and Berridge (2001) propose that in the case of substance abuse, the motivation (incentive) to approach, better called *craving* or desire for the drug, undergoes sensitization. Meanwhile, the neural mechanism responsible for the high, or liking of the drug, remains unchanged or decreases as tolerance develops over repeated administration. Both the decrease in liking and the increase in craving lead to further drug taking and may explain the intense compulsion to use a drug that no longer produces pleasurable effects.

The third consequence of chronic opioid use is the occurrence of **physical dependence** (see Chapter 9), which is a neuroadaptive state that occurs in response to the long-term occupation of opioid receptors. Because the adaptive mechanism produces effects that oppose those of the opioid, when the drug is no longer present, cell function not only returns to normal but also overshoots basal levels. The effects of drug withdrawal are *rebound* in nature and are demonstrated by the occurrence of a pattern of physical disturbances called the **withdrawal** or **abstinence syndrome**. Since opioids in general depress CNS function, we consider opioid withdrawal to be rebound hyperactivity (**TABLE 11.3**). You already

TABLE 11.3 Acute Effects of Opioids and Rebound Withdrawal Symptoms

Acute action	Withdrawal sign
Analgesia	Pain and irritability
Respiratory depression	Panting and yawning
Euphoria	Dysphoria and depression
Relaxation and sleep	Restlessness and insomnia
Tranquilization	Fearfulness and hostility
Decreased blood pressure	Increased blood pressure
Constipation	Diarrhea
Pupil constriction	Pupil dilation
Hypothermia	Hyperthermia
Drying of secretions	Tearing, runny nose
Reduced sex drive	Spontaneous ejaculation
Flushed and warm skin	Chilliness and "gooseflesh"

know that opioid effects are due to drug action at various receptors in a variety of locations in the CNS and elsewhere in the body, so it should not be a surprise to learn that the abstinence signs reflect a loss of inhibitory opioid action at all of those same receptors as blood levels of the drug gradually decline. Withdrawal can also be produced by administering an opioid antagonist that competes with the drug molecules for the receptors and thus functionally mimics the termination of drug use. Note, however, that the withdrawal following antagonist administration is far more severe than that following drug cessation, because the opioid receptors are more rapidly deprived of opioid.

Opioid withdrawal is not considered life threatening, but the symptoms are extremely unpleasant and include pain and dysphoria, restlessness, and fearfulness, as well as several symptoms that are flu-like in nature. How severe the symptoms are and how long they last depend on a number of factors: the particular drug used, as well as the dose, frequency, and duration of drug use and the health and personality of the opioid-dependent individual. To give an example, morphine withdrawal symptoms generally peak 36 to 48 hours after the last administration and disappear within 7 to 10 days. In contrast, methadone, which has a more gradual onset of action and is longer lasting, has a withdrawal syndrome that does not abruptly peak but increases to a gradual maximum after several days and decreases gradually over several weeks. Abstinence for the very-long-acting opioid buprenorphine is even more prolonged, but as is true for all of the longer-lasting opioids, the withdrawal signs are milder (**FIGURE 11.19**). From this, you should conclude that the longer the duration of action of the opioid, the more prolonged is the abstinence syndrome but the lower is the intensity of the syndrome. At the point when abstinence signs end, the user is considered to be **detoxified**.

Readministering the opioid any time during withdrawal will dramatically eliminate all the symptoms. In addition, administering any other opioid drug will stop or reduce the withdrawal symptoms because these agents show **cross-dependence**. This characteristic plays an important part in drug abuse treatment and is discussed further later in the chapter.

It may be surprising to learn that although physical dependence commonly occurs following chronic opioid use, it does not necessarily lead to abuse or opioid use disorder. Patients treated with opioids for protracted pain (e.g., postsurgical or cancer-related pain) show both tolerance and physical dependence, although withdrawal signs can be minimized by gradually reducing the dose when pain relief is no longer needed. However, most patients treated with opioids do not show addictive behaviors, such as craving and

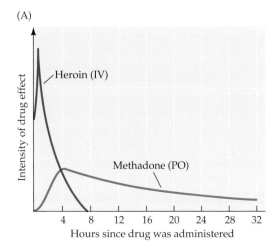

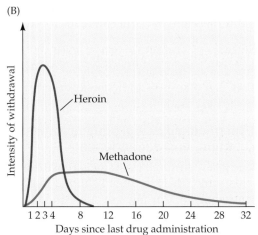

FIGURE 11.19 Relationship between acute effects and withdrawal (A) Time course showing the intensity and duration of the acute effects of IV heroin and oral (PO) methadone, and (B) the corresponding intensity and duration of withdrawal after chronic drug treatment.

compulsive drug seeking. Nevertheless, as discussed earlier, there is a great deal of concern regarding opioid prescribing because of the sudden rash of overdose deaths, especially among young people. Unfortunately, current fears of drug diversion, opioid use disorder, and overdose deaths may prevent many individuals from receiving the relief from severe pain that they require. Failure to use adequate painkilling treatment produces much more suffering and subsequently much slower healing than is warranted. Transdermal patches and patient-controlled drug delivery systems in the hospital setting are drug administration techniques that provide more humane control of pain and more effective recovery.

Although effective relief from pain is vital to patients to enhance the quality of life, when opioids are diverted to illicit use, serious societal problems occur. **BOX 11.2** describes the recent epidemic of abuse of oxycodone, fentanyl, and other opioids.

BOX 11.2 ■ OF SPECIAL INTEREST

The Opioid Epidemic

The startling increase in opioid-related overdose deaths has prompted a reexamination of our approach to treating chronic pain. A large proportion of opioid-addicted individuals initiated their abuse by taking prescription painkillers following surgery, recovery from a broken bone, or dental surgery. One of the most common prescription painkillers is oxycodone, a semisynthetic opioid that works in a manner similar to morphine. The short-acting formulation Percodan is used to treat acute pain, while the long-acting time-release version OxyContin is used for cancer or musculoskeletal pain that is chronic and moderate to severe. These drugs have never been found to be better than morphine, which remains the gold standard for pain relief. Nor are they free from morphine-like side effects and the danger of abuse or fatal respiratory depression, especially when combined with CNS depressants such as alcohol. Oxycodone is classified by the DEA as a Schedule II drug because although it is used medically, it also has high abuse potential.

One of the most significant factors contributing to the onset of the first wave of the opioid epidemic in the late 1990s was the misleading and aggressive marketing of OxyContin to prescribing physicians and consumers. The maker of OxyContin, Purdue Pharma, claimed that the extended-release formulation allowed for less frequent dosing, thereby reducing the abuse liability of the drug. In reality, pharmacokinetic data indicated that the ideal dosing regimen was likely *more* frequent, and patients would frequently take subsequent doses early to avoid withdrawal symptoms, thus misusing their prescribed drug and falling into a maladaptive pattern of drug taking (Kibaly et al., 2021). Another aspect of the aggressive marketing of OxyContin was to host physicians at all-expenses-paid speaker training conferences at resorts in attractive destinations, which promoted the more liberal use of opioids in treating pain. Additionally, marketing efforts were directed at physicians who were already high prescribers of opioids, with sales representatives distributing a range of promotional items, including branded fishing hats, plush toys, and music compact discs (Van Zee, 2009). As a result of these efforts, sales of OxyContin increased by an astounding 866% between 1997 and 2007 (Kibaly et al., 2021).

The dramatic increase in the number of patients receiving prescription opioids undoubtedly contributed to increased rates of diversion and abuse. In the late 1990s and early 2000s, geographic areas that were associated with higher rates of OxyContin prescriptions were also among the first to be affected by increases in diversion and abuse. OxyContin became a popular street drug around this time because it produces a heroin-like euphoria when crushed to circumvent the time-release mechanism. It is then snorted, ingested, or dissolved and injected. The fact that OxyContin readily dissolves in water encourages the injection of the drug, which increases not only the subjective effects but also the dangers of overdose and medical problems associated with needle use.

In addition to legitimate prescriptions, OxyContin was also relatively easy to access with fake or tampered prescriptions, with theft from pharmacies or family members, or via the internet from other countries. Unfortunately, the high markup of street value prices compared with legal prices provided financial incentive to divert drugs into the black market. On occasion, unconscionable physicians and pharmacists were found running OxyContin "pill mills" that increased the availability of the drug to those without medical need. "Doctor shopping" (visiting multiple doctors with complaints of pain) became highly visible when the radio commentator Rush Limbaugh acknowledged his addiction to the drug.

The initial warning of the increase in OxyContin abuse came from Maine, but abuse rapidly expanded down the East Coast, hitting rural Appalachia and the Ohio Valley particularly hard. The spread of OxyContin use was paralleled by a dramatic increase in arrests for theft in those areas as well as overdose fatalities. As OxyContin abuse spread further, some officials called it a national epidemic, and that prompted efforts by state and federal government agencies, physicians' groups, and manufacturers to formulate a solution to the problem.

Unfortunately, more recent epidemics of opioid abuse have developed and spread across the country, the most recent being the surge in opioids, including heroin and counterfeit pills, being adulterated with illicitly manufactured fentanyl. Fentanyl is also a synthetic opioid and is 50 times more potent than heroin and 100 times more potent than morphine (**FIGURE A**). For the individual with opioid use disorder, it provides "higher highs" at lower costs because it can

(Continued)

(A)

Courtesy NH State Police Forensic Lab

Comparison of the doses of heroin and fentanyl that are fatal to an average-sized adult male

BOX 11.2 ■ OF SPECIAL INTEREST *(continued)*

(B)

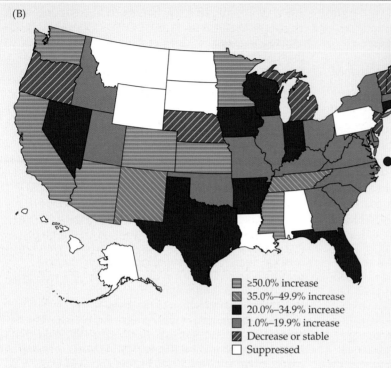

The increase in synthetic opioid-related deaths from 2018 to 2019 was highest in the Western United States (From C. L. Mattson et al. 2021. *MMWR Morb Mortal Wkly Rep* 70: 202–207. doi: http://dx.doi.org/10.15585/mmwr.mm7006a4)

- ≥50.0% increase
- 35.0%–49.9% increase
- 20.0%–34.9% increase
- 1.0%–19.9% increase
- Decrease or stable
- Suppressed

be manufactured more cheaply than heroin. Since it works very rapidly, the opportunity to treat overdoses with naloxone is reduced (see Web Box 11.1), and because of its potency, multiple applications of naloxone are frequently required.

In fact, over 70% of drug overdose deaths in 2019 involved opioids. Since 1999, overdose deaths involving opioids have increased by more than six times, with the majority of the increase attributable to fentanyl-related deaths, which saw a nearly 12-fold increase between 2013 and 2019 (CDC, 2020; see figure in Box 11.1). Most recently, synthetic opioid–related

deaths increased at an especially high rate in western U.S. states (**FIGURE B**). Since past misuse of prescription pain relievers is the strongest risk factor for heroin use and abuse, more rigorous controls over prescription practices have been called for (discussed previously in the text). In addition to professional education, the creation of a national pharmacy database to identify abusers, and tamper-resistant prescription pads, manufacturers have attempted to develop several opioid formulations to discourage abuse. One such formulation uses oxycodone and naloxone in a combined pill (e.g., Targiniq ER). This works on the principle that while oxycodone has relatively high oral bioavailability, naloxone does not, thus allowing oxycodone to function as intended when taken orally. However, when the combined drug is crushed and taken either intranasally or by injection, naloxone has much higher bioavailability by these routes of administration, thus antagonizing the oxycodone dose and defeating the attempted abuse.

Several brain areas contribute to the opioid abstinence syndrome

The signs of withdrawal represent the rebound hyperactivity in many different systems, including the gastrointestinal tract, the autonomic nervous system, and many sites within the brain and spinal cord. To identify which of the many brain areas are involved in the appearance of the particular signs of abstinence, an animal model is used. Pellets of opioid drugs are implanted under the skin so that the subcutaneous administration produces significant blood levels of drug over a week or longer. After the animals have become physically dependent, selective intracerebral injection of an opioid antagonist produces distinctive and easily quantifiable signs of withdrawal. Withdrawal signs in rodents include jumping, rearing, "wet dog" shakes, and increased locomotor

behavior. Intracerebral injection of opioid antagonists into specific brain areas can help to identify which sites produce particular signs of abstinence. On the basis of these measures, no single brain area has been found to precipitate the entire withdrawal syndrome, but the locus coeruleus and the PAG are particularly sensitive to the antagonist in terms of precipitating withdrawal. As you will see in the next section, the locus coeruleus has become a neurochemical model for dependence.

In Chapter 9, you learned that the NAcc is a limbic structure that is particularly important for the reinforcement value of many abused substances. For this reason, it is somewhat surprising that microinjection of opioid antagonists into this area is not very effective in eliciting bodily signs of withdrawal in a dependent animal. However, Koob and coworkers (1992) have suggested that the NAcc may be important in the aversive stimulus effects or motivational aspect of opioid withdrawal. This conclusion was based on a series of experiments in which opioid-dependent rats experienced naloxone-precipitated withdrawal in a novel environment. Under such conditions, the animals develop a place aversion for the novel location and remain in an adjacent compartment (see Figure 4.10). Koob and colleagues were interested in finding out which brain area, when microinjected with antagonist, is responsible for the place aversion. They found that the areas most sensitive to low doses of antagonist are the NAcc, followed by the amygdala and the PAG. In conclusion, the brain areas implicated in the physiological response to opioid withdrawal are the PAG and the locus coeruleus, which may also mediate withdrawal-induced anxiety, while the NAcc is likely responsible for the aversive qualities of withdrawal, as well as some of the positive-reinforcing values of opioid use.

Neurobiological adaptation and rebound constitute tolerance and withdrawal

The classic hypothesis of opioid tolerance and dependence was first developed by Himmelsbach (1943) and is shown in **FIGURE 11.20A**. He suggested that acute administration of morphine disrupts the organism's homeostasis but that repeated administration of the drug initiates an adaptive mechanism that compensates for the original effects and returns the organism to the normal homeostasis. At this point, tolerance to the drug has occurred, since the same dose of morphine no longer produces the original disturbance. When morphine administration is abruptly stopped, the drug's effects on the body are terminated, but the adaptive mechanism remains active and overcompensates. The subsequent disruption of homeostasis is the withdrawal syndrome.

Although the Himmelsbach model was entirely theoretical, in the mid-1970s a physiological correlate was described by Sharma and coworkers (1975). They used cells with opioid receptors and maintained them in cell culture. They found that the acute administration of morphine caused an inhibition of adenylyl cyclase, the enzyme that manufactures cAMP (**FIGURE 11.20B**). Himmelsbach would call this stage "disturbed homeostasis." However, when the cells were kept in the morphine solution for 2 days, they showed tolerance to the drug's inhibitory effect. That is, after 2 days, they had levels of cAMP equal to control cells that had not been exposed to morphine. Apparently, the adaptive mechanism proposed by Himmelsbach became effective. When the opioid was abruptly removed from the cell culture solution or naloxone was added, the concentration of cAMP rose significantly above control levels because the adaptive mechanism was still operating, although the drug's inhibitory effect was gone. This rebound in cAMP levels corresponds with the withdrawal phenomenon and clearly represents disturbed homeostasis again. Other parts of the cAMP system, such as cAMP-dependent protein kinase A (PKA) and phosphorylated neuronal proteins, are also up-regulated by the chronic use of opioids.

The relationship of cAMP to neural activity and the withdrawal syndrome is suggested by the parallel time course of changes in those three factors. Nestler

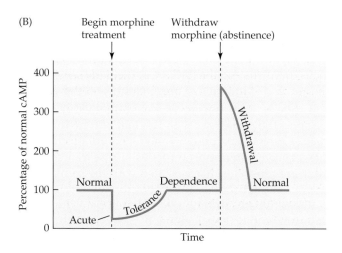

FIGURE 11.20 Model of tolerance and withdrawal (A) Himmelsbach's theoretical model suggests that the nervous system adapts to the disturbing presence of a drug, so tolerance develops, but if the drug is suddenly withdrawn, the adaptive mechanism continues to function, causing a rebound in physiological effects (withdrawal). (B) Morphine acutely inhibits the synthesis of cAMP, but the effect becomes less as tolerance develops and neural adaptation occurs. If morphine is suddenly withdrawn, a far larger than normal amount of cAMP is produced, suggesting that the adaptive mechanism is still operating. With time, the cells once again adapt, now to the absence of the drug.

and coworkers (1994) examined the electrophysiological effects of morphine on cells in the locus coeruleus. The acute effect of opioids acting at μ-receptors consists of hyperpolarization and reduced rate of firing. Repeated exposure to opioids produced a gradual increase in firing rates of locus coeruleus cells as tolerance developed. Administration of an opioid antagonist after chronic opioid treatment induced a significant rise in firing rate to levels well above pretreatment levels, reflecting a rebound withdrawal that gradually returned to normal. A similar time course occurred for the overshoot of cAMP synthesis, the up-regulation of PKA and protein phosphorylation, and their return to control levels. Behavioral manifestations of abstinence also declined over the same 72-hour period. It is of interest that in subsequent research, Punch and colleagues (1997) showed that intra–locus coeruleus infusion of a PKA inhibitor attenuated several prominent behavioral signs of morphine withdrawal in dependent animals. Conversely, activating PKA produced quasi-withdrawal symptoms in nondependent drug-naive animals.

Despite the evidence for the importance of cAMP signaling to tolerance and withdrawal, many research strategies, including animal models, cell culture, or pharmacological manipulations to disrupt tolerance development, have found a variety of cellular mechanisms potentially responsible in addition to cAMP. In fact, it is likely that multiple mechanisms are responsible for tolerance (reviewed by Williams, 2013). It has been suggested that the very rapid process of desensitization, as shown in vitro with just a few minutes of exposure to agonists, is likely due to uncoupling between the opioid receptor and G protein signaling. However, development of tolerance over longer periods of drug administration may be due to loss of receptors. Such down-regulation of receptors has been shown in some brain regions, but not others. Additionally, down-regulation occurs for some opioids, such as etorphine, but chronic morphine does not alter receptor number in most brain regions. Hence down-regulation is not a likely explanation for morphine tolerance. Another possibility is that receptors are internalized—that is, their location is altered, moving from the plasma membrane to other internal cellular compartments. Finally, a role for learning in tolerance development is another potential factor (see next section).

Environmental cues have a role in tolerance, drug abuse, and relapse

We have already alluded to the idea that environmental factors can be classically conditioned to parts of the drug experience (see the section on behavioral tolerance in Chapter 1). Conditioning theory has also been applied to the development of tolerance to opioids. Siegel and Ramos (2002) and Tiffany and colleagues (1992) propose that narcotic tolerance is in part the result of the learning

of an association between the effects of the drug and the environmental cues that reliably precede the drug effects. Several experiments have shown that after repeated drug administration in a particular environment, the animal begins to show anticipatory physiological responses when it is in that same situation. Thus, it is argued that tolerance to the analgesic effects of morphine results because environmental cues regularly paired with drug administration begin to elicit the compensatory response of hyperalgesia, which diminishes the analgesic effect of the drug. Some have suggested this mechanism as the basis for some of the drug overdose fatalities among people with opioid use disorder. One would have to assume that individuals who have developed significant tolerance to their drug of choice in their standard environment might find that their tolerance is much less if they use the drug in a novel situation. Their usual dose may then be enough to produce overdose.

Environmental factors can also clearly have a role in portions of the drug experience. For example, if euphoria is associated with certain stimuli such as the camaraderie of the drug-using subculture, drug acquisition activities, or drug injection rituals, those aspects of the environment will act as secondary reinforcers, strengthening the drug-taking behavior. What this means is that many components of drug-taking behavior become so closely associated with the drug-induced euphoria and sense of well-being that they are in themselves reinforcing. This association can be used to explain the unusual behavior of the "needle freak" who can inject any substance and achieve some measure of the "high" associated with drug taking. Childress and coworkers (1999) reported changes in limbic system neural activity as measured by PET scans of increased cerebral blood flow in drug users who were merely exposed to drug cues that increase their craving. The brain areas activated were similar to those activated by the drug (in this case cocaine). Increased metabolic activity in the amygdala and the anterior cingulate (**FIGURE 11.21**) during cue-induced craving suggests the importance of emotional memory (amygdala) and emotional expectation (anterior cingulate) to the conditioning. Since these regions are both connected to the NAcc and are activated during drug exposure, it is reasonable to suggest that they help the individual learn the signals that are linked to rewarding events. When these cues, acting as secondary reinforcers, are present, they may act as **triggers** that promote drug taking because they remind the individual of how the drug feels. Cue-induced craving and its neural mechanism have become an important focus of research because they are most closely associated with the compulsive drug-seeking behavior that characterizes drug abuse.

Objective (respiration rate, skin temperature, heart rate) and subjective elements of narcotic withdrawal symptoms can be experimentally conditioned to

FIGURE 11.21 PET scans of cerebral blood flow Blood flow in a cocaine-dependent individual differed during exposure to a non–drug-related video (nature video) and exposure to a cocaine-related video containing many cues. Areas with the greatest activity are shown in red. Activity in the amygdala and anterior cingulate is significantly increased during the cocaine video.

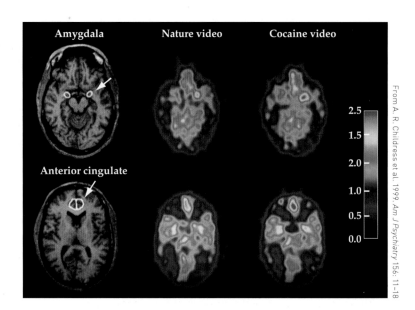

From A. R. Childress et al. 1999 Am J Psychiatry 156: 11–18

environmental stimuli in humans as well (Childress et al., 1986). The high rate of relapse among detoxified people may be due to the conditioned abstinence syndrome in the old environment. O'Brien (1993) and others have presented reports of individuals who describe withdrawal symptoms when they visit areas of prior drug use even years after the withdrawal syndrome has ended. These findings have convinced many researchers that learning is a critical factor in opioid use disorder (**WEB BOX 11.4**). Under what circumstance individuals develop drug-enhancing associations or drug-opposing responses is not clear, but the mesolimbic DA pathway may be involved in both (Self and Nestler, 1995).

Treatment programs for opioid use disorder

Treating opioid use disorder requires understanding the multiple contributors to the problem. Treatment clearly depends on more than eliminating the drug from the body (detoxification), since the relapse rate for detoxified people is very high. Ultimately, a host of behavioral and social factors must be identified and altered for a successful outcome.

Most drug treatment programs utilize a biopsychosocial model as the basis for therapy. Models in this category take into account the multidimensional nature of chronic drug use:

- The physiological effects of the drug on nervous system functioning, as when the opioids activate the mesolimbic reward pathway
- The psychological status of the individual and the individual's unique neurochemical makeup and history of drug use
- The environmental factors that provide salient cues for drug taking and powerful secondary reinforcement.

Detoxification is the first step in the therapeutic process

Detoxification, or the elimination of the abused drug from the body, can be assisted or unassisted. Unassisted detoxification is often referred to as going "cold turkey," and many opioid abusers experience withdrawal symptoms on a fairly regular basis because they have difficulty securing more drug. Alternatively, detoxification may be assisted by the administration of a long-acting opioid drug, such as **methadone**, that reduces the symptoms to a tolerable level. The dose of methadone is gradually reduced over a period of 5 to 7 days until it can be terminated with only mild symptoms. Sometimes the α_2-adrenergic agonist **clonidine** is used in this stage. Clonidine acts on noradrenergic autoreceptors to reduce norepinephrine activity. Since the noradrenergic neurons in the locus coeruleus are inhibited by opioids and the cells increase firing during withdrawal (see Nestler et al., 1994, described earlier), clonidine-induced inhibition of firing reverses this hyperexcitable state. The drug seems to relieve the chills, tearing, yawning, stomach cramps, sweating, and muscle aches that are associated with the activity of the locus coeruleus but does not reduce the remaining withdrawal symptoms nor the subjective discomfort and craving (Gold, 1989; O'Brien, 1993). Unfortunately, clonidine itself has side effects, including insomnia, dry mouth, sedation, joint pain, and dizziness. For these reasons, it is not very popular with opioid-dependent individuals, who much prefer detoxification with an opioid.

An ultrarapid detoxification that is completed in a few hours or over several days requires that withdrawal be initiated with opioid antagonists while the patient is treated with clonidine, a benzodiazepine, or general anesthesia. This method is considered by many to be ineffective because it does not produce improved abstinence rates and is associated with potentially life-threatening events.

Rather than pharmacological intervention to prevent withdrawal, it is possible to use electroacupuncture (EA) instead. Using morphine-dependent rats, G. B. Wang and colleagues (2011) showed that 30 minutes of 100-Hz EA delivered 12 hours after the last morphine administration significantly reduced the classic signs of rodent withdrawal. They found an apparent "dose-dependent" effect in that a single EA treatment had a small effect, two sessions 11 hours apart had a significant effect, and four administrations had still greater effects on four out of five withdrawal signs measured. Perhaps even more interesting was the finding that EA restored the low levels of prodynorphin mRNA to normal in the spinal cord, hypothalamus, and PAG, which suggests that withdrawal is suppressed by increasing dynorphin synthesis. EA has been used in China to treat both opioid withdrawal and relapse for a number of years, but more recently, more controlled studies with animals and humans have been conducted. Cui and colleagues (2008) review that evidence.

Treatment goals and programs rely on pharmacological support and counseling

Treatment for heroin use disorder offers several options and may be selected on the basis of availability in a given location, cost, or personal preference. A description and evaluation of treatment options is provided by Connery (2015). Most programs begin with detoxification before starting intensive treatment on either an inpatient or an outpatient basis. Prolonged periods of follow-up care and supplementary services are advantageous in preventing relapse.

METHADONE MAINTENANCE   The most commonly used treatment method for heroin use disorder is the **methadone maintenance program**. Originally developed by Dole and Nyswander (1965), the program involves long-term pharmacotherapy in which methadone relieves the withdrawal syndrome and cravings associated with opioid use disorder. The rationale for the program is that by having their cravings relieved, people are able to redirect their energy away from the activities needed to secure the drug toward more productive behaviors such as education or job training.

A large number of studies over many years have shown that when compared with any other treatment method, methadone maintenance has been the most effective in reducing heroin and other illicit drug use and has at least doubled the rate of abstinence compared with psychosocial treatment. The percentage of patients who remained abstinent has been reported to be as high as 90% among those who continued in the program for the recommended duration, while among those who dropped out, the abstinence rate fell to 12% (California Society of Addiction Medicine, 2011). In addition, those people involved in the program showed significantly lower rates of criminal activity, HIV infection, and mortality, while showing greater involvement in becoming self-supporting (Bertschy, 1995). For these reasons, it has been estimated that methadone treatment programs save taxpayers $12 for every $1 spent

(California Society of Addiction Medicine, 2011). Prolonged involvement with the program is expected, and in many cases methadone is used in a chronic fashion, just as one would treat a diabetic with insulin. Alternatively, the individual may be gradually weaned from the drug support, but in these cases relapse rates are higher.

Among the hazards of methadone maintenance is the significant risk for accidental overdosing of the patient at the start of the treatment. Overdosing is a common event because it is difficult to determine the precise level of the individual's tolerance, making it difficult to choose the appropriate starting dose. There is also a large variation in required effective dose among individuals. Because methadone has such a long half-life, blood levels gradually increase for up to 5 days at the same dose (see steady-state plasma levels in Chapter 1). Hence a dose that was initially ineffective can become toxic. Careful monitoring of the patient and dose adjustments must occur daily during the first 2 weeks and less frequently thereafter. In the future, pharmacogenetics may make it easier to determine the appropriate daily maintenance dose. For example, particular gene variants of the metabolizing cytochrome P450 enzyme (CYP2B6) are associated with lower methadone dose requirements because individuals with those gene variants metabolize the drug more slowly, so their blood levels are higher for a given dose. Other gene variants of the transporter protein that is responsible for moving methadone across the blood–brain barrier have also been identified. Clearly differences in how much drug reaches the brain can help to explain the significant variability among individuals in their treatment needs. For more detail, see Reed and associates (2014).

Methadone was chosen for use in opioid drug treatment programs for several reasons. First, cross-dependence with morphine or heroin means that it can prevent the more severe withdrawal associated with the abused drug. Second, the cross-tolerance that develops to repeated methadone use means that the normal euphoric effects of heroin are reduced or prevented. If an opioid-dependent person uses the illicit drug but gets little or no "rush," continued drug use should be less likely. Unfortunately, the tolerance can be overcome by high (and expensive) doses of heroin. In addition, methadone itself can produce a "rush" of euphoria if it is injected intravenously, which can lead to illegal diversion and trafficking of the drug. For this reason, most programs require *supervised* daily administration of *oral* methadone. The oral administration of methadone is a third important factor in the popularity of methadone maintenance because although little or no euphoria occurs with oral administration, the drug is fully effective in relieving craving for opioids. Craving is believed to be an important motive for relapse. In addition, oral administration reduces the use of needles and the rituals surrounding their use. It also eliminates the danger of disease due to unsterile injection techniques. The spread of infectious diseases such as hepatitis and HIV is also reduced by eliminating the need to share contaminated needles.

Fourth, methadone is relatively long-acting, which produces a more constant blood level of drug such that the individual experiences fewer extremes of drug effect. A more even blood level produces a more stable daily experience and also normalizes body functions such as hormone secretion. Methadone is needed only once a day to prevent methadone withdrawal for 24 to 36 hours. The time course of drug action means daily contact and interaction with clinical staff who can provide behavioral therapy, group and family counseling, and support in education or job training. In addition, medical care can be provided. Of particular significance are the prenatal care for pregnant women with opioid use disorder and treatment of diseases, such as HIV, hepatitis, and syphilis, that are common among opioid-dependent pregnant women. Additionally, nutritional status is much improved, which leads to increased birthweight of infants born to mothers enrolled in the methadone program. However, since methadone passes the placental barrier like other opioids, the infant at delivery will sometimes show withdrawal signs, including tremors, twitching, seizures, vomiting, diarrhea, and poor feeding. These symptoms are treated by low doses of opioids, which are then tapered down until no drug is needed.

Fifth, methadone is considered medically safe even with long-term use and does not interfere with daily activities. Unfortunately, some side effects do not diminish with repeated use, so constipation, excessive sweating, reduced sex drive, and sexual dysfunction may persist during treatment for some individuals. It is noteworthy that long-term use of any opioid drug has few damaging effects on organ systems. The greatest dangers stem from poor living conditions, including inadequate diet, lack of medical care, and homelessness; dangerous and unlawful behaviors required to secure the drugs; and potentially fatal side effects of using contaminated needles or impure sources of drug.

BUPRENORPHINE MAINTENANCE   Another opioid, **buprenorphine** (**Buprenex**), is an opioid partial agonist and is used in the same manner as methadone. Because it has a high affinity but low efficacy at the μ-opioid receptor, as well as antagonist activity at the κ-receptor, it has weaker opioid effects and is less likely to result in overdose or respiratory depression. It produces similar treatment results but has a longer duration of action and so produces more stable physiological effects and an extremely mild withdrawal syndrome.

The longer duration of action also means less frequent administration (one to three times a week), which significantly reduces the costs of the program and gives an extra measure of freedom compared to the opioid abuser who needs daily clinic visits for methadone. Fewer clinic visits also tends to improve the relationship with members of the surrounding community, who often object to high rates of drug user visits to their neighborhood. Buprenorphine is the only opioid substitute that can be prescribed in a physician's office that is not part of a federally regulated opioid treatment program. It is hoped that greater use of this drug will reduce costs and make more treatment facilities available. In fact, the U.S. Department of Health and Human Services (2016) is trying to expand access to agonist-assisted treatment by enabling nurse practitioners and physician assistants to take the 24-hour training session required in order to prescribe buprenorphine. Although initially they can prescribe for a limit of 30 patients, after 1 year they can prescribe for up to 100 people. The increase in access to medication-assisted treatment is part of the government's efforts to stem the opioid addiction crisis, along with changing opioid prescription practices and increasing availability of naloxone to reverse opioid overdoses.

In addition, because buprenorphine does not produce more than a mild euphoria when taken as directed, the drug abuser can get a supply of the drug rather than just a single dose. To further reduce its potential for IV use, buprenorphine is available in a sublingual formulation (Suboxone) that also contains the antagonist naloxone. When taken sublingually, the buprenorphine is absorbed but the naloxone is not. If the tablet is crushed and injected intravenously in an effort to experience the euphoria, the naloxone blocks buprenorphine's effects. However, Suboxone can still be abused if crushed and snorted. Unfortunately, there has been an increase in law enforcement seizures of the drug that has been diverted to individuals without a prescription, and ER visits related to nonmedical use of buprenorphine rose almost fivefold from 2006 to 2011 (Crane, 2015) (**FIGURE 11.22**). Although buprenorphine is less likely to lead to overdose than methadone, in combination with CNS depressants, it can lead to respiratory depression and death. The newest approach to buprenorphine treatment involves administering a long-acting drug depot, either in the form of an implant (e.g., Probuphine) or a liquid depot injection (Sublocade) that forms a gel upon contact with subcutaneous fluid, which slowly releases buprenorphine over the course of a month. The depot administration enhances compliance with the drug treatment regimen because the individual does not have to remember to take a pill every day. It also means the pills cannot be lost or stolen. Finally, the depot administration prevents diversion of drug and its abuse and protects against accidental ingestion by children. An additional advantage is that the sustained delivery avoids the peaks and troughs in blood level that occur with oral medications, so there is less risk of sudden craving.

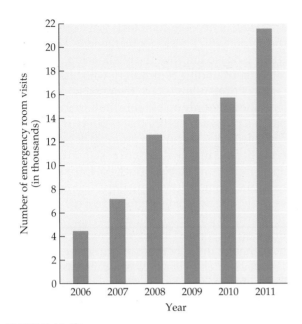

FIGURE 11.22 **U.S. emergency department visits related to nonmedical use of buprenorphine** The number of visits, including those in which buprenorphine was the direct cause or a contributing factor, rose from 2006 to 2011. (After E. H. Crane. 2015. *The CBHSQ Report: Emergency Department Visits Involving Narcotic Pain Relievers*. Rockville, MD: Substance Abuse and Mental Health Services Administration, Center for Behavioral Health Statistics and Quality.)

Although during pregnancy complete abstinence of opioid use would be ideal, abrupt withdrawal could be hazardous to the fetus (see **BOX 11.3**). Since relapse is common after withdrawal, a pattern of repeated intoxication and withdrawal causes significant fetal distress that can cause miscarriage, impaired fetal growth, low birthweight that is a risk factor for later developmental delay, or premature birth. Maintenance treatment with methadone or buprenorphine is preferable to heroin use, and when combined with prenatal care, it produces better outcomes. When compared in a meta-analysis, researchers found that buprenorphine compared with methadone maintenance was associated with lower risk of preterm birth, higher birthweight, and larger head circumference. There did not seem to be any difference in congenital abnormalities, although most studies did not do follow-up evaluating through the first year of life (Zedler et al., 2016).

Research comparing the two drug maintenance approaches shows that the neonatal abstinence syndrome is also milder than that after methadone maintenance and that buprenorphine-exposed infants require significantly less morphine to treat the withdrawal. Because the withdrawal is less stressful, recovery is more rapid and the infants spend about half as much time in the hospital as methadone-exposed infants. Although there were no lasting differences (over the first 30 days) between the two groups of infants, the methadone-exposed infants

were initially more stressed and excitable, were unable to self-regulate or manage sleep and wakeful periods, and showed difficulty with handling. These kinds of neurobehavioral differences may pose greater challenges as the infant transitions home, which may be an at-risk environment (Coyle et al., 2012).

Although buprenorphine maintenance seems to have advantages for pregnant women, the developmental consequences of prenatal buprenorphine have not been fully determined in humans. In rats, pre- and postnatal exposure to buprenorphine produced dose-dependent effects on several proteins needed for myelin formation, smaller-diameter myelinated axons, and reduced thickness of the myelin in the corpus callosum (Sanchez et al., 2008). More recently Hung and colleagues (2013) administered buprenorphine to pregnant rats starting at 7 days' gestation for 14 days and studied the weanlings at 21 days of age. The animals were tested in the open field test, Morris water maze, forced swim test, and tail suspension test (see Chapter 4) and also were subjected to neurochemical analyses. Those young animals exposed to high doses of buprenorphine (but not their mothers) showed behavioral signs of depression in the forced swim test and tail suspension test that could be reversed with the antidepressant drug imipramine. Anatomically, both brain mass and body mass were reduced. Neurochemically, there were reductions in plasma 5-HT and the neurotrophic factor BDNF. In addition, in cortical tissues there was reduced activation of the transcription factor CREB, which is important for expression of BDNF. These signaling molecules have long been associated with clinical depression (see Chapter 18). Further studies should be conducted to determine which opioid receptor is involved and whether these changes persist over the long term.

In summary, compared with psychological treatments alone or managed tapering off of opiate use, long-term maintenance with opioid agonists produces better treatment outcomes as measured by days of illicit opiate use. Also, those individuals on the opioid agonists were more persistent in follow-up medication and psychological therapies. Meta-analyses suggest that there is no difference in efficacy associated with methadone compared with buprenorphine (Nielsen et al., 2017). Maintenance therapy is more problematic during pregnancy.

USE OF NARCOTIC ANTAGONISTS We have already described the utility of naloxone in reversing the effects of opioid toxicity. Antagonists also represent a component of some drug abuse treatment programs. After detoxification, antagonist treatment will block the effects of any self-administered opioid. Naltrexone (Trexan) is the most commonly used because it has a longer duration of action than naloxone and is effective when taken orally. It also has fewer side effects than cyclazocine, which may produce irritability, delusions,

BOX 11.3 ■ CASE STUDIES

A Case of Neonatal Abstinence Syndrome Following Maternal Kratom Use

Neonatal abstinence syndrome (NAS), or more specifically neonatal opioid withdrawal syndrome (NOWS), is observed in newborn infants who were chronically exposed to opioids in utero. At the time of birth, this opioid exposure suddenly ceases, and clinical signs of opioid withdrawal are generally observed within the first several hours of life. While any opioid taken by the mother during pregnancy can potentially cause NOWS, this syndrome is typically characterized by either illicit opioid use or misuse of prescription opioids. At the same time, the clinical presentation of NOWS is highly variable. These factors combined make it difficult to fully understand the precise relationship between opioid use during pregnancy and the severity of NAS signs in newborns. Women who used opioids during pregnancy may not always accurately report their opioid use for a variety of reasons. Moreover, it is relatively common for people who abuse opioids to also take other drugs of abuse, whether intentionally or unknowingly, adding to the complexity of the problem (Jansson et al., 2009).

The clinical signs of NOWS typically emerge within 20 to 72 hours after birth, with much of the variation attributable to the recency of the last drug exposure and whether the infant was last exposed to a drug with a short half-life, such as heroin, or a drug with a longer half-life, such as methadone or buprenorphine (Patrick et al., 2020). Clinical signs include sleep disturbance; altered muscle tone and tremors; autonomic dysfunction, including sweating, sneezing, fever, and frequent yawning; and hyperarousal, including excessive irritability and crying. The clinical signs of NOWS are typically evaluated using a scoring system to evaluate severity and optimize treatment.

In an initially perplexing case, Eldridge and colleagues (2018) describe an infant born to a mother who had a prior history of oxycodone abuse but had been abstinent for the 2 years preceding delivery. Urinary drug screens of both the mother and infant were found to be negative for all commonly tested drugs of abuse. Nonetheless, the infant began exhibiting clinical signs consistent with opioid withdrawal at about 33 hours of age, including sneezing, jitteriness, tremor, irritability, excessive crying, and hypertonia. As this presentation was consistent with NOWS, treatment with morphine commenced, which resulted in a significant improvement in his clinical signs. However, the infant displayed concerning levels of sedation and bradycardia (slow heart rate), so morphine treatment was discontinued, which led to the return of NOWS signs. Additional treatment included the α_2 adrenergic receptor agonist clonidine, which also improved NOWS signs but again was associated with bradycardia. Clonidine treatment was also discontinued. Fortunately, by this point the NOWS signs began to improve without treatment.

In a follow-up interview, the mother further denied the use of prescription or illicit opioids during pregnancy, although the father ultimately disclosed that the mother had been using kratom tea on the daily basis throughout the pregnancy. Kratom is a plant that is native to Southeast Asia, and its leaves are commonly dried and ground and consumed in a tea-like infusion. While not classified as an opioid, kratom contains mitragynine, an indole alkaloid that has affinity for and acts as an agonist at μ-opioid receptors. Although the pharmacology of kratom is not fully understood, it is commonly consumed for its mild opioid-like effects, and to self-medicate for opioid dependence. Another action of mitragynine is to stimulate α_2 adrenergic receptors, which commonly act as autoreceptors for noradrenergic neurons; therefore, α_2 receptor agonists have the net effect of suppressing norepinephrine release. This mechanism of mitragynine may explain why clonidine was effective in improving the baby's NOWS signs, although it is worth noting that there is evidence that clonidine may be effective in treating NOWS even when maternal kratom use is not suspected (Streetz et al., 2016). Wright and colleagues (2021) review other published reports of prenatal kratom exposure, indicating that pharmacological treatment of NOWS is frequently necessary in such cases.

As of 2021, kratom is not scheduled as a drug of abuse by U.S. Drug Enforcement Agency, although its use remains controversial, and the FDA has issued statements indicating that it is unsafe for any medical or recreational use (e.g., FDA, 2018). Moreover, several states have passed laws banning the sale of kratom. In contrast, proponents of kratom use cite findings that it does not fit the profile of typical drugs of abuse in animal studies (Hemby et al., 2019; Harun et al., 2020). The consensus in the scientific community is that more research, including controlled clinical trials, needs to be conducted to properly evaluate its health risks (Prozialeck et al., 2019).

hallucinations, and motor incoordination. Nalmefene (Revex) is a newer pure opioid antagonist and is similar to naltrexone but more potent and longer lasting.

This method is effective for individuals who are highly motivated, have strong family support, and are involved in careers (e.g., addicted medical personnel).

Reliable patients have taken naltrexone for 5 to 10 years without relapse to drug-taking behavior and with minimal adverse effects on appetite, sexual behavior, or endocrine function (O'Brien, 1993). Unfortunately, this method appeals to only about 10% of the addicted population, because a great deal of motivation is needed to voluntarily substitute an antagonist for a drug with highly reinforcing properties. Since craving for the drug is not eliminated, most less-motivated individuals stop antagonist treatment and return to drug use. Only about 27% of people with opioid use disorder in these treatment programs complete a 12-week preliminary session (Osborn et al., 1986).

VACCINES FOR ADDICTION TREATMENT   The rationale for using vaccines for the treatment of opiate abuse is that abused substances must enter the brain to exert their behavioral effects. A vaccine would produce antibodies in the individual that would bind to the drug molecules in the blood circulation and prevent entry into the brain. The interest in vaccines to treat opioid use disorder or prevent overdose is longstanding, with early studies demonstrating the concept of vaccinating against fentanyl effects in animals over 40 years ago (Torten et al., 1975). Although it is not feasible to vaccinate the general population against every abused drug, vaccines might be useful in treating existing abuse of specific drugs. One such vaccine for opioids recognizes heroin and its active metabolites, 6-acetylmorphine and morphine (Stowe et al., 2011). This vaccine prevents the self-administration and analgesic effects of heroin in rats. Clinical trials with humans still need to be conducted.

COUNSELING SERVICES   Most often, people with opioid use disorder benefit from a **medication-assisted treatment** that includes a combination of detoxification, pharmacological support, and group or individual counseling. Counseling frequently is used to help patients identify the environmental cues that trigger relapse for them. Having identified their "triggers," individuals with opioid use disorder must then design a behavioral response to those cues to prevent relapse. Furthermore, job training, educational counseling, and family therapy may be useful. Based on a model program for alcohol abuse treatment, Narcotics Anonymous is another option for motivated drug abusers to achieve drug abstinence.

SECTION SUMMARY

- Predicting which patients receiving opioids for pain will become chronic drug users is difficult. Physicians struggle with the dilemma of needing to treat serious pain and yet follow new CDC guidelines intended to limit opioid prescriptions because of the rising number of opioid fatalities.

- Animal studies show that opioids have reinforcing effects in self-administration paradigms, in conditioned place preference, and in reducing the threshold for electrical self-stimulation of the brain.

- Opioid drugs inhibit inhibitory GABA cells, increasing mesolimbic cell firing and DA release in the NAcc. Both dopaminergic and nondopaminergic mechanisms are necessary for the reinforcing effects.

- Opioid drugs demonstrate tolerance to many of the drug effects and cross-tolerance with other drugs in the same class, as well as with endogenous opioids.

- Prolonged use produces physical dependence, which is characterized by a classic rebound withdrawal syndrome that includes many flu-like symptoms, insomnia, depression, and irritability. Cross-dependence means that any drug in the opioid family can abruptly stop withdrawal symptoms.

- A model of the physiological mechanism for tolerance and dependence is the compensatory response of cells in the locus coeruleus to the acute inhibition of adenylyl cyclase. Tolerance may also be due to uncoupling of the receptor from G protein, down-regulation of receptors, or receptor internalization.

- Classical conditioning of environmental cues associated with components of drug use is important in the development of tolerance and in maintaining the drug habit. Conditioned craving is significant in producing relapse in the detoxified individual.

- Detoxification is the first step in drug abuse treatment.

- Opioid abuse treatment programs include pharmacotherapy with a long-acting opioid such as methadone or buprenorphine. These drugs, when given orally, produce no euphoria but eliminate craving for heroin and reduce exposure to HIV and hepatitis. The long-acting opioids stabilize the physiological effects and encourage contact with support staff. Methadone produces a mild withdrawal. There are few damaging effects on organs with prolonged use.

- Compared with methadone, buprenorphine is longer acting, has a milder withdrawal and neonatal withdrawal, and can be prescribed in a physician's office. When combined with naloxone, abuse potential is reduced. An implantable device to administer buprenorphine has multiple advantages over the pill form of the drug.

- Maintenance treatment with methadone or buprenorphine is preferable to heroin use in pregnant women with opioid use disorder. Buprenorphine and methadone are equally effective in reducing heroin use, but buprenorphine may have advantages in fetal outcome.

- Opioid antagonists are effective in blocking the opioid receptors so that self-administered narcotics have no effect.

- In rats, a heroin vaccine produces antibodies which bind to drug molecules, preventing entry to the CNS and reducing self-administration of opioids.

- The most successful treatment approaches are multidimensional ones.

STUDY QUESTIONS

1. How do differences in molecular structure determine opioid effects?

2. Describe opioid effects on the CNS and gut.

3. Briefly discuss the localization and function of the four opioid receptor subtypes.

4. What are the classic neuropeptides that bind to opioid receptors. Describe how they are synthesized. How is nociceptin/orphanin FQ different?

5. Describe the cellular mechanisms responsible for opioid-induced inhibition.

6. Compare early and late pain.

7. Describe the three ways that opioids inhibit pain transmission in the spinal cord. How does opioid action in higher brain centers modulate pain transmission?

8. What is the mechanism of action of acupuncture? Dual inhibition of peptidases? Gene therapy? Dual receptor agonists?

9. Describe the research on ER patients and patients with chronic pain that helps to explain how medical patients become chronic drug users. Why do physicians find that treating pain is so difficult?

10. Provide evidence for opioid reinforcement, and describe the neurochemical basis.

11. Define tolerance, cross-tolerance, sensitization, physical dependence, and cross-dependence. Be sure to tell how they apply to opioid use.

12. Which brain areas are responsible for opioid withdrawal signs? What is the role of the NAcc?

13. Describe the Himmelsbach model of tolerance and withdrawal. Provide several experimental findings in support of the model.

14. How do environmental cues influence tolerance? Drug abuse? Relapse?

15. Describe several ways that detoxification can be achieved.

16. What are the advantages of using methadone maintenance treatment for opioid use disorder?

17. Compare methadone and buprenorphine maintenance. What are the potential disadvantages of these methods?

18. Beyond opioid maintenance treatment, what other options are available to the opioid abuser?

12 Psychomotor Stimulants: Cocaine, Amphetamine, and Related Drugs

WE'VE ALL HEARD ABOUT A HIGHLY ADDICTIVE FORM OF COCAINE called "crack cocaine." What is this drug, and when did it first appear in the United States? As discussed in the first part of this chapter, "crack" refers to a smokable form of cocaine typically packaged as inexpensive single-dose units in vials or baggies. The development of crack cocaine was spurred by a surge in cocaine powder smuggling into the United States in the late 1970s, causing a large price drop and concomitant decrease in profits to the drug cartels, importers, and dealers. Crack was less expensive than cocaine powder; however, users experienced a highly unpleasant "crash" when coming down from the drug. This withdrawal reaction motivated a strong desire to obtain the next dose. As early as 1980, reports of crack use were appearing in Los Angeles, San Diego, and Houston. Crack then spread until it was reportedly available in 46 states plus the District of Columbia by 1987 (Foundation for a Drug-Free World). Now, of course, crack cocaine can obtained anywhere in the country if you seek it out.

Cocaine, the subject of this chapter opener, is a member of a powerful class of drugs called **psychomotor stimulants**. Other members of this class include **amphetamine**, methamphetamine, **methylphenidate**, **modafinil**, and a group of compounds known as **synthetic cathinones**. The name for this drug class stems from the marked sensorimotor activation that occurs in response to drug administration. Indeed, psychomotor stimulants are characterized by their ability to increase alertness, heighten arousal, and cause behavioral excitement. Beginning with cocaine, this chapter will consider the behavioral and physiological effects of these stimulants, their mechanisms of action, and their potential for producing escalating use and dependence. Chapter 13 covers nicotine and caffeine, two less potent but more widely used stimulants. ■

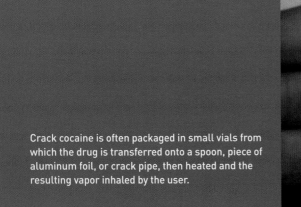

Crack cocaine is often packaged in small vials from which the drug is transferred onto a spoon, piece of aluminum foil, or crack pipe, then heated and the resulting vapor inhaled by the user.

12.1 Background, Pharmacology, and Mechanisms of Action of Cocaine

Background

Cocaine is an alkaloid found in the leaves of the shrub *Erythroxylon coca*. The coca shrub is native to South America and is primarily cultivated in the northern and central Andes Mountains extending from Colombia into Peru and Bolivia (**FIGURE 12.1**). Consistent with the figure, about 90% of the cocaine entering the United States is estimated to come from Colombia (Drug Enforcement Administration, 2019). The inhabitants of these coca-growing regions consume cocaine by chewing the leaves—a practice thought to have begun at least 2000 and perhaps as many as 5000 years ago, according to archaeological evidence. The chewing of coca leaves and the consumption of coca tea continue to be cultural practices in the Andes, and consumption of coca has sometimes been recommended to travelers journeying to mountainous destinations to combat altitude sickness (Bauer, 2019). Because cocaine is a weak base, chewers also include some mineral lime or ash* to make the pH of the saliva more alkaline. This decreases ionization of the cocaine and promotes absorption across the mucous membranes of the oral cavity.

The history of cocaine and its pharmacology are reviewed by Drake and Scott (2018). Coca chewing was an important feature of ceremonial or religious occasions in the Incan civilization, and use of the drug was ordinarily restricted to the ruling classes up to the time of the Spanish conquest. After the fall of the Incan empire, coca chewing became more widespread and commonplace, and there are even reports that coca was used as a medium of exchange. Over time, many Spanish missionaries and churchmen argued that coca chewing was idolatrous and interfered with conversion of the Incas to Catholicism. The practice was consequently discouraged and even banned in some areas. The Spaniards soon discovered, however, that without the stimulating and hunger-reducing effects of coca, Incan workers lacked the endurance necessary to work long hours in the mines and fields at high altitudes and with little food. Thus coca cultivation and chewing were restored with the blessing of the Spanish rulers and the church.

Although coca leaves were brought back to Europe, coca chewing never caught on, possibly owing to degradation of the active ingredient during the long sea voyage. But travelers to the New World had occasion to sample the leaf, and several came back with glowing reports of its beneficial effects. By the late 1850s, German chemists had isolated pure cocaine and had characterized it chemically. Over the next 30 years, cocaine became tremendously popular as many scientists and physicians of the time lauded its properties. A chemist named Angelo Mariani concocted an infamous mixture of cocaine and wine called *Vin Mariani*, which was awarded a Vatican gold medal by Pope Leo XIII and was consumed by many other notables, including Queen Victoria of England, Thomas Edison, and Ulysses S. Grant (Wielenga and Gilchrist, 2013).

*Both mineral lime (the type of lime used in agriculture and gardening) and wood ash contain calcium compounds, such as calcium carbonate, which confer an alkaline property.

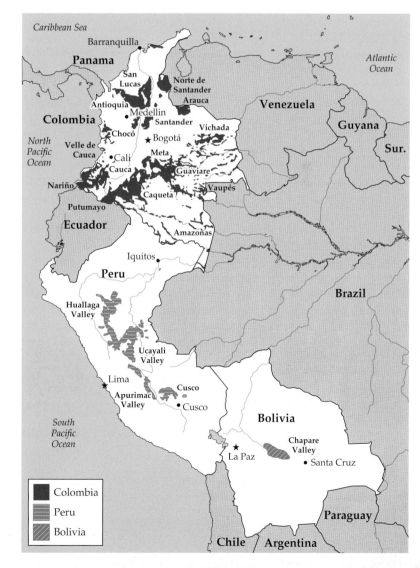

FIGURE 12.1 Map of 19 identified coca-growing regions in South America (From J. Mallette et al. 2016. *Sci Rep* 6: 23520. doi.org/10.1038/srep23520; CC-BY 4.0.)

Another famous cocaine user was Sigmund Freud. In 1885, Freud published the monograph *Über Coca* ("On Coca"), which extolled the drug's virtues and recommended its use in the treatment of alcoholism, morphine addiction, depression, digestive disorders, and a variety of other ailments. Freud also performed the first recorded psychopharmacological experiments on cocaine and published the results in a paper entitled "Contribution to the Knowledge of the Effect of Cocaine." In his last written comments about cocaine in 1887, Freud acknowledged its dangers when used to treat morphine addiction, although he continued to maintain that the drug was nonaddictive under other circumstances.* Others, however, were more perceptive. The harshest critic was the German psychiatrist A. Erlenmeyer, who labeled cocaine the "third scourge of the human race," after alcohol and opium.

Despite the warning signs emanating from Europe, cocaine's popularity grew in the United States during the late nineteenth and early twentieth centuries. By 1885, Parke, Davis & Co., an early pharmaceutical firm, was manufacturing 15 different forms of cocaine and coca, including cigarettes, cheroots (a type of cigar), and inhalants. One year later, a pharmacist from Georgia named John Pemberton introduced a new beverage, "Coca-Cola," which contained cocaine from coca leaves and caffeine from cola nuts.** Coca-Cola and similar concoctions were marketed as suitable alternatives to alcoholic drinks because of the growing strength of the alcohol temperance movement at that time. Cocaine-containing tooth drops were even given to infants to relieve the discomfort of teething (the local anesthetic effects of cocaine are discussed further in the section on mechanisms of action). Not surprisingly, widespread cocaine misuse began to spread across the United States until President Taft declared cocaine to be "public enemy number one" in 1910. Congress then passed the 1914 Harrison Narcotic Act prohibiting the inclusion of cocaine (as well as opium) in over-the-counter medicines and specifying other restrictions on its import and sale (see Chapter 9). Subsequent state and federal laws, of course, placed even tighter regulations on cocaine distribution and use.

From the 1920s to the 1960s, cocaine use continued primarily among a relatively small group of avant-garde artists, musicians, and other performers. Beginning in the 1970s, however, two successive waves of increasing cocaine use were seen in the United States. The first involved an escalation of cocaine

---

*In fairness to Freud, it should be noted that he normally took cocaine orally—a route of administration with less addictive potential than IV injection, smoking, or even snorting.

**Although cocaine itself was removed from the product in 1903, Coca-Cola continues to contain a non-narcotic extract from the coca leaf that is regularly prepared by a chemical company in the United States (Goldstein et al., 2009).

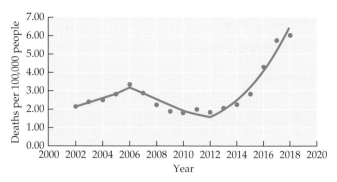

FIGURE 12.2   Age-adjusted cocaine overdose mortality rate over time   2002–2018 data from two different national surveys were compiled to produce the figure. The line represents the best fit to the data points determined by regression analysis. (From M. Cano et al. 2020. *Drug Alcohol Depend* 214: 108148. © 2020. Reprinted with permission from Elsevier.)

use by snorting or intravenous (IV) injection, whereas a later surge was and continues to be driven by the smoking of "crack" cocaine.

According to estimates derived from the 2019 National Survey on Drug Use and Health, approximately 2 million people age 12 or older (0.7% of the U.S. population) were current users of cocaine at the time of the survey (Center for Behavioral Health Statistics and Quality, 2020). By "current user," we mean that the individual had used cocaine at least once during the previous month. Of these current users, roughly half were considered to have developed **cocaine use disorder** (the *DSM-5* diagnostic category for misuse of cocaine that causes significant distress and/or impairment; see later section for more information). The numbers of Americans using cocaine and having cocaine use disorder have been stable for several years. On the other hand, the rate of drug overdose deaths involving cocaine increased roughly threefold from 2014 to 2018 (Cano et al., 2020; Hedegaard et al., 2020; **FIGURE 12.2**). Such deaths occur disproportionately among non-Hispanic Blacks, which is thought to be related to various socioeconomic and other factors discussed by Cano and colleagues (2020). The recent *increase* in mortality rates may be linked, at least in part, to an upsurge in co-use of opioids with cocaine. We also need to be aware of the many different substances that are used to "cut" (i.e., adulterate) cocaine for sale on the street (Kudlacek et al., 2017). Some of these compounds pose health risks in their own right, which could also contribute to cocaine-related mortality.

Basic pharmacology

FIGURE 12.3 presents the chemical structure of alkaloidal cocaine, which is its naturally occurring form. The molecule contains two rings: the six-carbon phenyl ring shown on the right and the unusual nitrogen (N)-containing ring shown on the left. Both are necessary for the drug's biological activity. Other features of the

FIGURE 12.3   Chemical structures of cocaine, WIN 35,428, and RTI-55

Cocaine   WIN 35,428 (CFT)   RTI-55 (β-CIT)

molecule have been manipulated with interesting results. For example, Figure 12.3 also depicts the structures of two synthetic cocaine-like drugs: WIN 35,428 (also known as CFT) and RTI-55 (also called β-CIT). Notice that both compounds lack the ester (–O–CO–) linkage between the rings, and both possess a halogen (fluorine [F] or iodine [I]) atom on the phenyl ring. WIN 35,428 and RTI-55 are more potent than cocaine, and if available on the street, they presumably would be highly addictive. Fortunately, they are used only experimentally, primarily for in vitro studies with brain tissue.

Coca leaves contain between 0.6% and 1.8% cocaine. Initial extraction of the leaves results in a coca paste containing about 80% cocaine. The alkaloid is then converted to a hydrochloride (HCl) salt and is crystalized. Cocaine HCl is readily water soluble and thus can be taken orally (as in *Vin Mariani*), intranasally (snorting), or by IV injection. One disadvantage of cocaine HCl is its vulnerability to heat-induced breakdown, thereby preventing it from being smoked. However, the hydrochloride salt can be transformed back into cocaine freebase by two different methods. The method developed first was to dissolve cocaine HCl in water, add an alkaline solution such as ammonia, and then extract the resulting cocaine base with an organic solvent, typically ether. The term **freebasing** refers to smoking cocaine that was obtained in this manner. However, this preparation method is dangerous because of ether's high flammability and vulnerability to explosion. Even freebasing itself can be risky, since an ether residue may still be present if one is not careful. In the early 1980s, drug dealers discovered that cocaine base could be made more safely by mixing dissolved cocaine HCl with baking soda, heating the mixture, and then drying it. Chunks of the dried, hardened mixture are known on the street as **crack** (so named because of the popping sounds produced when the chunks are heated), or "rock" cocaine. Such chunks are generally sold inexpensively in small amounts sufficient for only one or two doses. **FIGURE 12.4** shows the difference in appearance of crack cocaine versus powdered cocaine HCl taken by snorting. The cocaine that ends up in a user's bloodstream is the same substance regardless of whether its initial form was the hydrochloride salt or the free base. However, the heat involved in smoking crack produces unique chemical products that can be

(A)

(B)

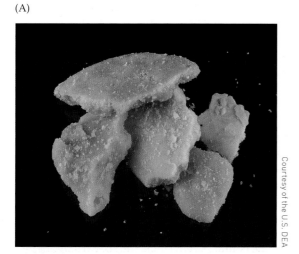

Courtesy of the U.S. DEA

© Valerii_Dex/Shutterstock.com

FIGURE 12.4   **Comparison of crack cocaine with powdered cocaine HCl** (A) Crystals of crack cocaine are consumed by heating and then smoking the resulting vapor.

(B) Powdered cocaine HCl is typically placed on a flat surface for consumption by insufflation (snorting) using a hollow tube.

detected in the urine and used by forensic chemists to verify crack use (Dinis-Oliveira, 2015).

Different routes of consumption yield somewhat different patterns and levels of plasma cocaine. Extremely rapid absorption occurs with both IV injection and smoking. Hence, typical single doses taken by these routes yield rather high concentrations of circulating cocaine, and even higher values can be attained with multiple doses that mimic the pattern of a cocaine "binge" (see later section on cocaine misuse). Absorption is somewhat slower following oral administration or snorting; consequently, these routes yield lower cocaine levels. **FIGURE 12.5** compares the time course of plasma cocaine concentrations as a function of route of administration. It is interesting to note that a few hours of coca leaf chewing delivers enough drug to mimic the plasma concentrations produced by a modest dose taken either orally or intranasally.

Although researchers normally measure blood levels of drugs in a peripheral vein such as the antecubital vein located in the arm, even more important for a psychoactive drug is the level present in the brain. Cocaine is sufficiently lipophilic (fat soluble) that it passes readily through the blood–brain barrier (see Chapter 1). This property particularly comes into play when cocaine is smoked, because it results in exposure of the brain to a very large surge in drug levels not reflected in peripheral venous concentrations. Rapid entry into the brain is believed to be an important factor in the strong addictive properties of crack cocaine.

Once absorbed into the circulation, cocaine is rapidly broken down by enzymes found in the bloodstream and the liver. It is also rapidly eliminated, with a half-life ranging from about 0.5 to 1.5 hours. For this reason, the subjective high produced by a single IV or smoked dose of cocaine may last only about 30 minutes. However, the breakdown products of cocaine persist in the body for a longer period of time. For

example, in a heavy cocaine user, the major metabolite **benzoylecgonine** can be detected in the urine for several days following the last dose.

Alcohol or other depressant drugs are sometimes taken along with cocaine to "take the edge off" the extreme arousal produced by cocaine alone. By studying the combined effects of cocaine and alcohol, researchers have discovered an unexpected and potentially important interaction between these two compounds. When taken together, cocaine and alcohol (ethanol) produce a unique metabolite called **cocaethylene**. This substance not only has biological activity similar to that of cocaine itself, but it also has a longer half-life. As we shall see later, cocaine can exert toxic effects on the heart and other organs. Such toxicity may be exacerbated in individuals consuming large amounts of cocaine and alcohol together (Dinis-Oliveira, 2015).

Mechanisms of action

Cocaine is a complex drug because it interacts with several neurotransmitter systems. Most of the behavioral and physiological actions of cocaine can be explained by its ability to block the reuptake of three monoamine neurotransmitters: the two catecholamines dopamine (DA) and norepinephrine (NE), and also serotonin (5-HT). In earlier chapters, we learned that these transmitters are cleared from the synaptic cleft by membrane proteins called *transporters*. Cocaine binds to these transporters and inhibits their function, thereby leading to increased neurotransmitter levels in the synaptic cleft and a corresponding increase in transmission at the affected synapses. Cocaine does not affect all monoamine transporters equally. In vitro binding studies have shown that cocaine has higher affinity for both the 5-HT transporter (SERT) and the NE transporter (NET) than for the DA transporter (DAT). Nevertheless, blockade of DA reuptake is considered to be most important for cocaine's stimulating, reinforcing,

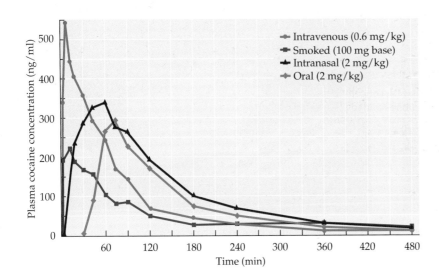

FIGURE 12.5 **Time course of plasma cocaine concentrations following different routes of administration** Each curve shows the mean for 10 human participants. For cocaine freebase smoking, participants were allowed only one to three puffs of the vapor from 100 mg of drug heated in a flask. The peak plasma concentrations produced under these conditions probably underestimate the levels occurring from recreational use. (After R. T. Jones. 1990. *NIDA Res Monogr* 99: 30–41.)

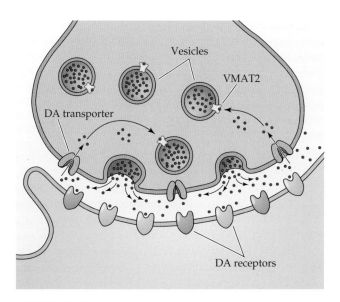

FIGURE 12.6 **Mechanisms of cocaine action** Cocaine increases synaptic DA levels by binding to the plasma membrane DA transporter and blocking reuptake of the neurotransmitter. A similar process occurs at serotonergic and noradrenergic synapses because of cocaine's inhibition of 5-HT and NE reuptake. VMAT2, vesicular monoamine transporter 2.

and addictive properties. Indeed, many drugs used in the treatment of depression block SERT and/or NET (see Chapter 18). Yet these agents do not have the strong arousing effect produced by cocaine in nondepressed individuals, nor do they have any addictive potential. Nevertheless, 5-HT and NE must also be taken into account, as alterations in the DA system do not explain all of cocaine's effects.

Cocaine causes an increase in extracellular DA levels by two different mechanisms. The first and more important is inhibition of DA reuptake following cocaine binding to DAT. This mechanism of cocaine action is depicted in **FIGURE 12.6**. Depending on the route of administration, inhibition of DA reuptake can occur very rapidly. Indeed, Yorgason and associates (2011) reported that cocaine administered IV to rats begins to block DA reuptake within 5 seconds, with peak inhibition occurring approximately 30 seconds after injection. The second mechanism, which is not as well studied, involves increases in the firing of ventral tegmental area (VTA) dopaminergic cells and the frequency of transient (brief) DA release events (Stuber et al., 2005; Covey et al., 2014).

Microdialysis studies in which extracellular concentrations of both cocaine and DA are measured illustrate the close relationship between the time course of brain cocaine levels and changes in DA overflow (DA molecules that escaped the reuptake mechanism and, therefore, can be detected in the extracellular fluid). One example can be seen in **FIGURE 12.7**, which displays the results of a study in rats given a rapid (5-second) IV infusion of cocaine. Changes in extracellular DA in the dorsal striatum followed the rise and fall in striatal cocaine concentrations over a 14-minute period after the drug infusion (Minogianis et al., 2018). The study additionally showed that when the same dose of cocaine was delivered over 45 or 90 seconds, the rises in both cocaine and DA were delayed by several minutes and the resulting locomotor activation was not as great. These findings show that the neurochemical and behavioral responses to cocaine depend not only on the dose and the route of administration but also on the

FIGURE 12.7 **Time course of striatal cocaine and DA concentrations following rapid IV cocaine infusion** Microdialysis probes aimed at the dorsal striatum collected samples for measurement of cocaine and DA concentrations at 2-minute intervals following a 5-second infusion of 2 mg/kg cocaine. The close relationship between these variables is consistent with cocaine causing rapid increases in extracellular DA in this brain region. Note that the DA concentrations measured in the extracellular fluid were much lower than the respective cocaine concentrations; however, because microdialysis assesses neurotransmitter *overflow* (i.e., transmitter molecules that have eluded uptake mechanisms), the *synaptic* DA levels were likely much greater than those shown here. (After E.-A. Minogianis et al. 2019. *Eur J Neurosci* 50: 2054–2064. © 2018 Federation of European Neuroscience Societies and John Wiley & Sons Ltd.)

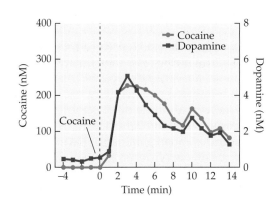

rate of drug delivery. Studies investigating the effects of mutating DAT structure further confirm a key role for this transporter in cocaine reinforcement. A key example comes from Thomsen and colleagues (2009), who produced mice carrying a mutant DAT that was still functional for DA (i.e., was able to take up DA from the extracellular fluid) but was insensitive to cocaine. Unlike wild-type mice, homozygous mutants failed to self-administer cocaine, thereby showing a loss of the drug's reinforcing properties.

A number of years ago, Carboni and coworkers (2001) surprisingly reported that cocaine and amphetamine could increase extracellular DA in the nucleus accumbens (NAcc) in knockout mice lacking the DA transporter. How could this occur when there was no DA transporter for these drugs to block? The mechanism seems to involve the noradrenergic system and activation of excitatory α_1-adrenoceptors in the VTA, prefrontal cortex (PFC), and NAcc. First, VTA dopaminergic neurons receive a direct noradrenergic input and are stimulated by NE acting on postsynaptic α_1-adrenoceptors (Goertz et al., 2015). Second, glutamatergic pyramidal neurons in the PFC are also stimulated by NE, and these cells provide an additional excitatory input to the VTA (dela Peña et al., 2015). Third, *presynaptic* α_1-adrenoceptors on NAcc dopaminergic and glutamatergic nerve terminals enhance release of the respective transmitters from those terminals (Mitrano et al., 2012). Thus, VTA dopaminergic cell firing and local DA release in the NAcc are both regulated by the noradrenergic system and contribute to cocaine-related dopaminergic activation and subsequent behavioral responses.

Another neurotransmitter strongly implicated in cocaine-mediated behaviors is acetylcholine (ACh). We learned in Chapter 7 that cholinergic interneurons in the dorsal striatum (caudate-putamen) interact with the dopaminergic input from the substantia nigra such that cholinergic neuronal hyperactivity following degeneration of the nigral dopaminergic neurons plays a significant role in Parkinson's disease motor symptoms. Two recent studies strongly implicate this same reciprocal relationship in controlling the behavioral responses to cocaine, including cocaine reward and reinforcement (Lee et al., 2020; Lewis et al., 2020). First, the results confirmed that the activity of striatal cholinergic interneurons and ACh release are inhibited by DA, acting mainly through D_2 receptors. Second, ACh from these interneurons was shown to exert a blunting effect on several cocaine-associated responses, including cocaine-induced hyperactivity, cocaine sensitization, cocaine reward in the place conditioning procedure, and cocaine-seeking behavior in the progressive ratio self-administration paradigm. This means that the ability of cocaine to elicit the above-mentioned responses depends on the relative balance of dopaminergic versus cholinergic activity in the striatum.

Because cocaine is an effective SERT inhibitor, we must consider 5-HT as a third neurotransmitter that helps mediate the neural and behavioral effects of cocaine. Understanding the role of SERT blockade in cocaine's actions has been aided by the creation of a mutant mouse in which SERT functions normally with respect to 5-HT reuptake but is insensitive to behaviorally active doses of cocaine (Simmler and Blakely, 2019). Insensitivity of the mutated SERT was demonstrated by the failure of cocaine administration to elevate extracellular 5-HT levels at a dose that produced a strong elevation in wild-type mice. Behaviorally, the mutant mice responded similarly to wild-type animals with respect to locomotor activation following acute cocaine administration as well as locomotor sensitization to repeated cocaine dosing. However, mice carrying the cocaine-insensitive SERT showed *increases* in the strength of cocaine place conditioning and in voluntary consumption of a cocaine-containing solution. These findings suggest that cocaine's serotonergic actions tend to blunt the rewarding and reinforcing effects of the drug that are mediated by DA and NE reuptake inhibition (Simmler and Blakely, 2019). Such information is significant not only for gaining a better understanding of cocaine's mechanisms of action but also for developing therapeutic agents to treat cocaine addiction.

Many different compounds block DA reuptake, yet only some of them produce arousing, euphoric, and behaviorally activating effects similar to those of cocaine. For example, the stimulant methylphenidate exerts a similar behavioral profile to cocaine (see later in the chapter for more information on this compound), but the DAT blockers mazindol, nomifensine, bupropion, vanoxerine (also known as GBR 12909), and GBR 12935 do not produce euphoria and lack cocaine's addictive potential. This discrepancy has plagued researchers for many years, and although a number of explanations have been proposed, no consensus has yet been reached. Numerous studies have shown that DA uptake inhibitors interact in different ways with the transporter protein, and one possibility is that these interactions may help explain why so-called atypical (i.e., non-cocaine-like) DA uptake inhibitors have different behavioral effects than cocaine (Schmitt et al., 2013; Reith et al., 2015). We shall see later in the chapter that amphetamine, methamphetamine, and related drugs operate by a somewhat different mechanism of action: those drugs are both transporter blockers and *substrates* for the transporter, which means that they are carried across the membrane into the cell. None of the previously mentioned uptake inhibitors, whether cocaine, methylphenidate, or the atypical inhibitors, is a DAT substrate. Because of this dual action, amphetamine-type compounds elevate extracellular DA concentrations to a much greater extent than cocaine.

Finally, relatively high concentrations of cocaine cause an inhibition of voltage-gated sodium (Na^+) channels in nerve cell axons. As these channels are necessary for neurons to generate action potentials, this action of cocaine causes a block of nerve conduction. Thus, when cocaine is applied locally to a tissue, it acts as a local anesthetic by preventing transmission of nerve signals along sensory nerves. Indeed, two synthetic local anesthetics that are widely used in medical and dental practice, procaine (Novocaine) and lidocaine (Xylocaine), were developed from the structure of cocaine.

SECTION SUMMARY

- Cocaine is an alkaloid derived from the leaves of the shrub *Erythroxylon coca*, which is indigenous to the northern and central Andes Mountains of South America.

- Although the peoples of that region have been chewing coca leaves for perhaps 5000 years, cocaine use did not become popular in Western cultures until after the pure compound was isolated in the late 1850s. Freud was one of many notable cocaine users in nineteenth-century Europe.

- In the United States, cocaine was a constituent of numerous popular beverages and over-the-counter pharmaceutical products in the late nineteenth and early twentieth centuries until its nonprescription use was banned by the Harrison Narcotic Act in 1914. Cocaine then went "underground" until the 1970s, at which time the first of two waves of increased cocaine use began in this country.

- Recent household survey data indicate that about 2 million people in the United States are current users of cocaine, with roughly half meeting criteria for cocaine use disorder.

- Cocaine HCl is water soluble and therefore can be taken orally, intranasally, or by IV injection. On the other hand, cocaine base (including crack cocaine) is the chemical form most suitable for smoking.

- The most rapid absorption and distribution of cocaine occur following IV injection and smoking, which may account for the highly addictive properties of these routes of consumption.

- One of the main cocaine metabolites is benzoylecgonine, whereas a compound called cocaethylene is also formed when alcohol is ingested along with cocaine.

- At typical doses, cocaine acts mainly to block synaptic uptake of DA, 5-HT, and NE by binding to their respective membrane transporters. This enhances transmission at monoaminergic synapses by increasing the synaptic concentrations of each transmitter. However, inhibition of DA uptake is most important for cocaine's behavioral effects and addictive potential.

- A second mechanism by which cocaine enhances dopaminergic transmission is an increased frequency of transient DA release events. This effect may be mediated by cocaine's inhibition of NE uptake in the PFC, causing an α_1-adrenoceptor–mediated stimulation of glutamatergic pyramidal neurons that project to the VTA.

- Because of how the activity of striatal cholinergic interneurons and ACh release are regulated by DA, these interneurons exert a blunting effect on several cocaine-associated responses, including cocaine-induced hyperactivity, cocaine sensitization, cocaine reward, and cocaine-seeking behavior.

- Studies with mutant mice bearing a cocaine-insensitive SERT have additionally shown that activation of serotonergic signaling specifically counteracts cocaine-related reward and reinforcement.

- Not all DA uptake inhibitors share cocaine's euphoric effects and addictive potential. Such atypical uptake inhibitors seem to interact with the transporter protein in a different manner than cocaine.

- At higher concentrations, cocaine also blocks voltage-gated Na^+ channels, which leads to a local anesthetic effect.

12.2 Acute Behavioral and Physiological Effects of Cocaine

Cocaine is used and misused for the "high" and the "rush" it produces. The pleasurable feelings associated with the "high" serve as a reinforcer, causing many users to use the drug repeatedly. In this section, we will discuss the behavioral and physiological effects of cocaine and the neurochemical mechanisms underlying them.

Cocaine stimulates mood and behavior

Typical aspects of the cocaine "high" are feelings of exhilaration and euphoria, a sense of well-being, enhanced alertness, heightened energy and diminished fatigue, and great self-confidence. Taken by IV injection or by smoking, cocaine also produces a brief "rush," described by some users as involving a sense of great pleasure and power and by others as being like an intense orgasm. At low and moderate doses, cocaine often increases sociability and talkativeness. There are also reports of heightened sexual interest and performance under cocaine's influence, although the drug's legendary ability to enhance sexual prowess is highly exaggerated. Cocaine can apparently also increase aggressive behavior, which suggests that some of the street violence associated with cocaine might be attributable to a direct effect of the drug.

The major behavioral and subjective effects of cocaine and other psychostimulants are summarized in **TABLE 12.1**. Effects listed in the "mild to moderate" category are generally produced by single, low to moderate doses of cocaine either in naive individuals or in users who have not yet progressed to heavy, chronic patterns of drug intake. "Severe" effects are most likely to be seen with high-dose use, particularly in individuals with longstanding patterns of chronic intake. It is

TABLE 12.1   Mild to Moderate versus Severe Behavioral and Subjective Effects of Cocaine and Other Psychostimulants in Humans*

Mild to moderate effects	Severe effects
Mood amplification; both euphoria and dysphoria	Irritability, hostility, anxiety, fear, withdrawal
Heightened energy	Extreme energy or exhaustion
Sleep disturbance, insomnia	Total insomnia
Motor excitement, restlessness	Compulsive motor stereotypies
Talkativeness, pressure of speech	Rambling, incoherent speech
Hyperactive ideation	Disjointed flight of ideas
Increased sexual interest	Decreased sexual interest
Anger, verbal aggression	Possible extreme violence
Mild to moderate anorexia	Total anorexia
Inflated self-esteem	Delusions of grandiosity

Source: From R. M. Post and N. R. Contel. 1983. In *Stimulants: Neurochemical, Behavioral, and Clinical Perspectives*, I. Creese [Ed.], pp. 169–203. Raven: New York. © Raven Press Books, Ltd.

* The actual effects observed show individual variability and depend on the dose, route of administration, pattern and duration of use, and environmental context.

easy to see that many of the positive characteristics of cocaine that may contribute to its powerful reinforcing properties become negative or aversive with escalation of dose and duration. Some of these aversive effects (e.g., irritability) are present in most high-dose users, whereas others mainly occur in cases of cocaine-induced psychosis (e.g., incoherence or delusions; see the discussion on health consequences later in the chapter).

Cocaine and other psychomotor stimulants also cause profound behavioral activation in rats, mice, and other animals used in psychopharmacological studies. At low doses, such activation takes the form of increased locomotion, rearing, and mild sniffing behavior. As the dose is increased, these behaviors are replaced by **focused stereotypies** (repetitive, seemingly aimless behaviors performed in a relatively invariant manner) confined to a small area of the cage floor. Psychostimulant stereotypies vary according to species and other factors. In rats and mice, one observes intense sniffing, continuous head and limb movements, and licking and biting. Humans using large amounts of cocaine occasionally also exhibit motor stereotypies such as repetitive picking and scratching.

All species tested thus far readily learn to self-administer cocaine IV. Marilyn Carroll and colleagues (1990) were also able to train monkeys to smoke cocaine freebase, a procedure that has led to a number of follow-up studies on the mechanisms underlying self-administration via this route (e.g., Campbell et al., 1999). Furthermore, unlimited access to cocaine can lead to heavy self-administration, gradual debilitation of the animals, and a high rate of mortality. These findings underscore the drug's powerful reinforcing properties in animals and its high potential for misuse by humans.

On the other hand, it is important to recognize that such compulsivity is not observed under all circumstances. When cocaine is pitted against an alternative reinforcer under controlled laboratory conditions, preference for the drug in both humans and other species depends on the relative magnitude of each reinforcer and other experimental conditions (**WEB BOX 12.1**).

Animals can also learn to discriminate cocaine from vehicle treatment. Subjects initially trained on cocaine readily generalize to amphetamine, indicating a fundamental similarity in the cue properties of these two drugs. In contrast, there is much less generalization to caffeine, a weaker stimulant that exerts its behavioral effects by a different mechanism than cocaine or amphetamine (see Chapter 13).

Cocaine's physiological effects are mediated by the sympathetic nervous system

Cocaine is considered a **sympathomimetic** drug, which means that it produces symptoms of sympathetic nervous system activation. The physiological consequences of acute cocaine administration include tachycardia (increased heart rate), vasoconstriction (narrowing of blood vessels), hypertension (increased blood pressure), and hyperthermia (elevated body temperature). At low doses, these physiological changes are usually not immediately harmful to the individual, although chronic use may contribute to coronary atherosclerosis in vulnerable individuals (Kim and Park, 2019). On the other hand, very high doses of cocaine can be toxic or even fatal. Cocaine intoxication syndrome produced by an overdose of the drug is characterized by extreme tachycardia and hypertension, tachypnea (rapid breathing), hyperthermia, diaphoresis (excessive sweating), and various psychological/behavioral symptoms that can include agitation, mania, paranoia, and a state of delirium (Zimmerman, 2012; Plush et al., 2015). Heart failure, stroke, seizures, and intracranial hemorrhage are other potential consequences of high-dose cocaine use (Treadwell and Robinson, 2007; Havakuk et al., 2017).

Dopaminergic pathways from the midbrain to the striatum are critical for the behavioral effects of cocaine and other psychostimulants

Several neurotransmitters, including 5-HT (Müller and Huston, 2006) and NE (Sofuoglu and Sewell, 2009; Schmidt and Weinshenker, 2014), contribute to the behavioral responses of animals to cocaine, amphetamine, and related psychostimulant drugs. However, as mentioned earlier, there is overwhelming evidence that DA plays the most important role in mediating these responses (Zhu and Reith, 2008). Of special relevance are the dopaminergic projections from the midbrain (substantia nigra and VTA) to the dorsal striatum and NAcc, which were first described in Chapter 5.

Early studies used microinjection and lesion methods to investigate the involvement of these DA systems in the behavioral effects of psychostimulants. The results of these studies are summarized in **TABLE 12.2**. For example, psychostimulants elicit a locomotor response when microinjected directly into the NAcc. Injection into the dorsal striatum instead leads to a pattern of stereotyped behavior. Another approach has been to lesion DA nerve terminals in either the accumbens or the striatum using the catecholamine neurotoxin 6-hydroxydopamine (6-OHDA). Such lesions cause a profound reduction of both DA and its transporter in the affected area, thereby preventing activation of dopaminergic transmission by psychostimulants. 6-OHDA lesions of the NAcc blunt psychostimulant-induced locomotion, whereas similar lesions of the striatum antagonize the stereotypies associated with higher drug doses.

The mesolimbic DA pathway to the NAcc also plays a key role in the reinforcing effects of cocaine and amphetamine in animals. However, here it is important to consider that the NAcc contains two subareas that vary in their behavioral functions. These subareas, termed the NAcc **shell** and **core**, are depicted in **FIGURE 12.8**. Researchers have found differences in the innervation of each subarea, their projections, and their behavioral functions. For our purposes, the most important difference is that the NAcc shell is most closely associated with psychostimulant-related reward and reinforcement, whereas the NAcc core is more closely related to psychostimulant-induced hyperlocomotion. For example, rats will self-administer cocaine into the NAcc shell but not the core (Rodd-Henricks et al., 2002). Moreover, when 6-OHDA lesions were performed selectively in the NAcc shell or core, the loss of DA innervation of the shell was correlated with a reduction in amphetamine reward (measured using conditioned place preference) whereas the loss of DA innervation of the core was correlated with a reduction in amphetamine-induced locomotor stimulation (Sellings and Clarke, 2003).

NAcc DA has also been implicated in cocaine reward by using paradigms that test for **drug-seeking behavior** as a model of relapse in previously abstinent individuals. Such paradigms typically train animals to self-administer cocaine IV and then extinguish the operant response (e.g., pressing a lever) by substituting saline for cocaine over a number of trials. Many studies have shown that following extinction, one can provoke a reinstatement of responding (i.e., drug seeking) by administering a single priming dose of cocaine to the animals through the IV catheter, despite the fact that the resumption of responding continues to result in the delivery of the saline vehicle instead of the drug. More relevant to the present discussion, two separate studies demonstrated that a reinstatement of cocaine-seeking behavior in previously extinguished rats could be stimulated by microinjection of either a D_1 or a D_2 DA receptor agonist

---

TABLE 12.2 Dopaminergic Projections to the Dorsal Striatum and Nucleus Accumbens: Role in Psychostimulant-Induced Behaviors in Animals

Experimental manipulation	Brain area	Behavioral effect
Psychostimulant microinjection	Nucleus accumbens	Increased locomotor behavior
Psychostimulant microinjection	Dorsal striatum	Increased stereotyped behaviors
6-Hydroxydopamine (6-OHDA) lesion	Nucleus accumbens	Decreased locomotor response following systemic administration of a low-dose psychostimulant
6-OHDA lesion	Dorsal striatum	Decreased stereotyped behaviors following systemic administration of a high-dose psychostimulant
6-OHDA lesion	Nucleus accumbens	Decreased reinforcing effectiveness of systemically administered psychostimulants
Psychostimulant microinjection	Nucleus accumbens*	Reinforcing to the animal

*Psychostimulant reinforcement is mainly associated with the shell region of the nucleus accumbens.

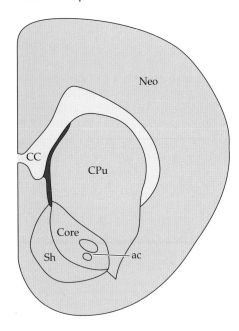

FIGURE 12.8 **Anatomy of the nucleus accumbens shell and core** This diagram depicts a coronal section through a rat brain at the striatal level to illustrate the anatomy of the NAcc shell (Sh) and core (Core). Other structures shown are the caudate–putamen (CPu, also called the dorsal striatum), the neocortex (Neo), two white matter tracts (corpus callosum [CC] and anterior commissure [ac]), and one of the lateral cerebral ventricles (the darkened brown area between the CPu and CC). (After D. A. Hamilton and B. Kolb. 2005. *Behav Neurosci* 119: 355–365. © 2005 by American Psychological Association., adapted from K. Zilles. 1985. In *The Cortex of the Rat — A Stereotaxic Atlas*, p. 17. Springer-Verlag: Berlin, Germany. © Springer-Verlag Berlin Heidelberg 1985.)

directly into the NAcc shell (Bachtell et al., 2005; Schmidt et al., 2006). If these findings can be applied to human cocaine users, they suggest that DA acting within the shell of the NAcc may play an important role in the urge to take cocaine in dependent users who are attempting to maintain abstinence from their drug use.

Brain imaging has revealed the neural mechanisms of psychostimulant action in humans

Given the critical role of DA in the activating, rewarding, and reinforcing effects of psychostimulants, are the mood-altering properties of these compounds in human users dependent on the same neurochemical system? This question has been addressed using brain imaging techniques such as positron emission tomography (PET) (see Chapter 4). For example, a research team headed by Nora Volkow, the current director of the National Institute on Drug Abuse, used PET imaging to estimate DAT occupancy by behaviorally active doses of either cocaine or methylphenidate. Methylphenidate, a stimulant that is commonly used to treat attention-deficit/hyperactivity disorder (ADHD), also binds to DAT and blocks DA reuptake (ADHD is discussed further in Box 12.2, later in this chapter). This compound is preferred over cocaine for some studies because as a medication, it can be administered ethically to study participants who are not already using psychostimulants recreationally, whereas cocaine cannot.

The studies of Volkow and colleagues (1999a) indicate that once a certain minimum level of DAT occupancy (about 40% to 60%) is attained following either cocaine or methylphenidate administration, the individual *may* experience a drug-induced high. However, the intensity of the high and even the likelihood that a high will occur depend not only on the amount of DAT occupancy but also on at least two other factors. One

factor is the rate at which transporter occupancy occurs after the drug has been taken. Thus, routes of administration like smoking or IV injection that lead to quick drug entry into the brain and rapid DAT occupancy are more likely to produce an intense high than oral or intranasal administration, which are associated with delayed drug entry into the brain and slower DAT occupancy (Volkow et al., 1998; 2000). Although we don't yet know how the rate of DA reuptake blockade influences the subjective effects of psychostimulants, this information does help us understand why smoking and IV injection of psychostimulants have greater addiction potential than other routes of administration.

A second factor influencing the psychostimulant high is believed to be the baseline level of DA activity in the mesolimbic pathway. Volkow's group found that even with IV administration of cocaine or methylphenidate, some individuals failed to experience a high, even with 60% or greater DAT occupancy, as indicated by PET imaging (Volkow et al., 1997; 1999b). However, when a different imaging procedure was used to assess the effects of IV methylphenidate on the occupancy of D_2 receptors by DA (not by the drug), there was a high correlation between this measure and the subjective high (Volkow et al., 1999c). What does this result mean? Imagine two people, A and B. Because of individual differences in dopaminergic system activity, person A starts with a relatively low level of baseline DA release, whereas person B starts with a relatively high level of release. Both people are now given sufficient methylphenidate or cocaine to produce 60% DAT occupancy. Even with equivalent amounts of reuptake blockade, the effect of this blockade on stimulating postsynaptic DA receptors will be greater in person B than in person A because of the higher initial concentration of DA molecules in the synaptic cleft. These findings suggest that variation in sensitivity to psychostimulant drugs can be produced by at least two different mechanisms: (1) differing DA transporter levels or (2) differing levels of baseline DA release.

Several DA receptor subtypes mediate the functional effects of psychostimulants

Given that the functional effects of psychostimulants are dependent primarily on inhibition of DA uptake and the resulting increase in synaptic DA levels, it is necessary to consider which postsynaptic DA receptor subtypes mediate these effects. You will recall from

Chapter 5 that there are five DA receptor subtypes: D_1 to D_5. D_1 and D_5 constitute the D_1-like family, whereas the D_2-like family is composed of the D_2, D_3, and D_4 receptors. Numerous pharmacological studies have shown that relatively non-selective antagonists at either the D_1-like or the D_2-like family of receptors can reduce both the behaviorally activating and the reinforcing effects of psychostimulants (Gold et al., 1989; Bergman et al., 1990; Fibiger et al., 1992; Self et al., 1996). The obvious limitation of these studies is their inability to distinguish which members of each receptor family are critical for the response being measured. Fortunately, progress is being made in developing antagonists that are more selective for specific DA receptor subtypes. This is illustrated in a recent study comparing the effects of the selective D_2 antagonist L-741,626 with the D_3 antagonist PG01037 on acute cocaine-induced locomotor stimulation in mice (Manvich et al., 2019). L-741,626 pretreatment dose-dependently attenuated cocaine's locomotor stimulating effect, whereas PG01037 pretreatment actually enhanced this effect (**FIGURE 12.9**). D_3 receptors are of particular interest with respect to the activating and reinforcing effects of psychostimulants because of the receptors' relatively high expression in the NAcc. Indeed, Manvich and coworkers (2019) found that PG01037 also enhanced cocaine-induced locomotor stimulation when infused directly into the NAcc. In contrast to these findings, however, D_3 antagonists have been shown to reduce the motivation for cocaine in IV self-administration paradigms by causing increased breakpoints in high fixed-ratio schedules and reducing reinstatement of cocaine responding in previously extinguished animals exposed to a drug-conditioned cue (Heidbreder and Newman, 2010). The reason for this discrepancy is not fully understood, but it could be related to differential roles of the D_3 receptor in the NAcc core versus the shell.

Other studies have investigated the behavioral functions of DA receptor subtypes by testing genetic knockouts lacking a particular receptor. With respect to the locomotor-stimulating effects of cocaine, these gene knockout studies have shown that D_1 receptors are required for such effects (Xu et al., 1994), whereas neither D_2 nor D_3 receptors are needed (Chausmer et al., 2002; Karasinska et al., 2005).* Likewise, mutant mice lacking

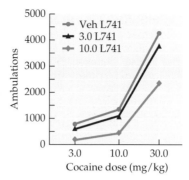
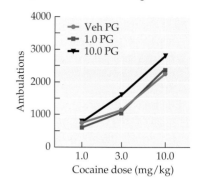

FIGURE 12.9 Cocaine stimulation of locomotor activity is reduced by pretreatment with a D_2 receptor antagonist but enhanced by pretreatment with a D_3 antagonist Mice were injected IP with varying doses of cocaine and then tested for their locomotor activity (measured as ambulations) over a 30-minute period. (A) In one experiment, the mice were pretreated with two different doses of the selective D_2 antagonist L-741,626 (L741) or the drug vehicle (Veh L741). Mice given 10.0 mg/kg of L-741,626 showed fewer ambulations than the respective vehicle controls at all cocaine doses. (B) In a second experiment, the mice were pretreated with two different doses of the selective D_3 antagonist PG01037 (PG) or the drug vehicle (Veh PG). Mice given 10.0 mg/kg of PG01037 showed small but statistically significant increases in number of ambulations compared to the vehicle controls at the 3.0 and 10.0 mg/kg doses of cocaine. Not shown is that neither antagonist significantly affected locomotor activity when administered by itself at the doses used in this study. (After D. F. Manvich et al. 2019. *Neuropsychopharmacology* 44: 1445–1455. doi.org/10.1038/s41386-019-0371-2)

D_2 or D_3 receptors were reported to self-administer cocaine, although with differences in dose–response function compared with wild-type mice suggesting some contribution of these subtypes to cocaine reinforcement (Caine et al., 2002; 2012). In contrast, D_1 receptor knockout mice do not self-administer cocaine, which suggests a critical role for this receptor subtype in the drug's reinforcing effects (Caine et al., 2007). Together, these findings indicate that the D_1 receptor plays a central role in the behavioral effects of cocaine in rodent models, but that other subtypes, particularly D_2 and D_3, contribute to these effects as well.

SECTION SUMMARY

- Cocaine exerts powerful effects on mood and behavior. The cocaine "high" is characterized by feelings of exhilaration, euphoria, well-being, heightened energy, and enhanced self-confidence. Smoked or intravenously injected cocaine also causes a "rush" in the user.

- At high doses and/or with prolonged use, cocaine can give rise to a number of negative effects such as irritability, anxiety, exhaustion, total insomnia, and even psychotic symptomatology.

- In animal studies, cocaine elicits locomotor stimulation and, at higher doses, stereotyped behaviors.

- Cocaine can function as a discriminative stimulus, and it exhibits powerful reinforcing effects in standard self-administration paradigms.

- Physiologically, cocaine produces sympathomimetic effects such as increased heart rate, vasoconstriction,

---

*Note the important difference between antagonist and gene knockout approaches in studying cocaine-induced locomotor stimulation. The antagonist results show that D_2 receptors *contribute* to such stimulation, whereas the knockout results indicate that this contribution is not *required* for the response to occur.

hypertension, and hyperthermia. High doses can be toxic or even fatal as the result of seizures, heart failure, stroke, or intracranial hemorrhage.

■ Microinjection, lesion, and gene knockout studies have demonstrated that most of the behavioral effects of cocaine and other psychostimulants are attributable to enhanced dopaminergic transmission (blockade of DA reuptake by cocaine, DA release and reuptake inhibition by amphetamines).

■ DA in the dorsal striatum mediates psychostimulant-induced stereotyped behaviors, whereas DA in the NAcc mediates psychostimulant-induced locomotion. DA specifically in the shell of the NAcc plays a critical role in psychostimulant reward and reinforcement.

■ Brain imaging studies in humans have found that the subjective effects (e.g., the "high") of psychostimulants are related to the amount of DAT occupancy, the rate at which occupancy occurs, and baseline DA activity.

■ Of the various DA receptor subtypes, the D_1 receptor plays the most important role in mediating cocaine's locomotor activating and reinforcing effects in animals; however, these effects are additionally modulated by D_2 and D_3 receptors.

12.3 Cocaine Use and the Effects of Chronic Cocaine Exposure

Most individuals who try cocaine do not progress to misuse of the drug. Those who eventually develop cocaine use disorder typically experience tolerance and/or sensitization and many adverse health effects, including brain abnormalities and cognitive deficits. Treatments for cocaine use disorder have yielded mixed results, with pharmacotherapies being especially disappointing thus far.

Experimental cocaine use may escalate over time to the development of a cocaine use disorder

Cocaine users give many different reasons for their initial decision to use the drug. Some of these reasons are to satisfy their curiosity; to facilitate social interactions; to relieve feelings of depression, anxiety, or guilt; to have fun and celebrate; or simply to get "high." Cocaine users typically describe early experimentation with both legal (e.g., alcohol) and illegal drugs, often beginning by 13 or 14 years of age. Early use of other substances may therefore be an important risk factor for the initiation of cocaine use.

People usually begin taking cocaine via the intranasal route—that is, by snorting it. As mentioned above, initial cocaine use most frequently does not lead to subsequent misuse or dependence. There are various reasons why the majority of people who try cocaine either do not continue their use or, if they do continue for some time, they do not subsequently undergo a transition to cocaine misuse or dependence. Some individuals report a strong anxiety response as their initial reaction to cocaine and are thereby dissuaded from further experimentation. Other factors may likewise mitigate against the development of a long-term pattern of use, including unavailability of the drug, the cost of maintaining a steady supply, the social and legal consequences of illicit drug use, and the very real fear of losing control over one's drug-taking behavior. These factors often lead to a termination of cocaine use, although some intranasal users maintain long-term periodic and controlled cocaine consumption.

The current edition of the *Diagnostic and Statistical Manual of Mental Disorders* (*DSM-5*; American Psychiatric Association, 2013) avoids using terms like *cocaine abuse* or *cocaine dependence*. Instead, this version of the *DSM* introduced a new category, "stimulant use disorder," that covers maladaptive use of any stimulant drug. Severity can be rated as mild, moderate, or severe depending on the number of diagnostic criteria (i.e., symptoms) that apply to the individual. Moreover, a particular drug type may be specified, as in "cocaine use disorder." In the current chapter, we will refer to this newer terminology where applicable, but we will also have occasion to use terminology such as cocaine (or other psychostimulant) abuse or dependence when describing earlier research that uses such wording.

A recent study utilized data from the 2012–2013 National Epidemiologic Survey on Alcohol and Related Conditions-III (NESARC-III) to identify various patterns of cocaine use (Liu et al., 2021). From the survey, 3543 individuals reported at least some use of cocaine during their lifetime; of those, 3117 provided sufficient data for analysis. Participants were asked how much cocaine they used per day, how many days per week they used, and the route of cocaine consumption *during their period of heaviest use*. The survey additionally obtained data that enabled the researchers to identify which participants met criteria for cocaine use disorder. Four classes of cocaine use patterns were identified: class 1 (low use; 72.6% of the sample), class 2 (moderate use; 8.2%), class 3 (daily use; 17.9%), and class 4 (daily use of a very high quantity; 1.3%). Although space considerations do not permit a detailed description of every class, we offer some key results from the study. Members of class 1 (low use) used cocaine infrequently and in small amounts, and the large majority only took the drug by snorting. Although some members of this class met criteria for cocaine use disorder, the severity of the disorder was generally mild. In contrast, members of class 3 (daily use) not only took cocaine almost every day during their period of heaviest use but also consumed a larger amount of the drug per day, often smoked or injected the drug, had a high likelihood of using other illicit drugs such as opioids, and were likely to meet criteria for a moderate to severe form of cocaine use disorder. Lastly, the small number of individuals in class 4 were fairly similar to class 3 except for the extraordinarily high cocaine doses taken daily (estimated at approximately 19 g/day vs/ about 2.5 g/day for class 3).

The results from Liu and coworkers (2021) suggest that many, perhaps most, people who use cocaine at some time during their life never move past the class 1 category. But for those individuals who progress from occasional to moderate or even daily use, two factors are particularly important. First, the amount of cocaine use escalates as the individual discovers that higher doses produce a more powerful euphoric effect. Second and equally important, the user may switch from intranasal administration to crack smoking, freebasing, or IV injection. For many, this is a significant event in their drug history because of the greater addictive potential of these latter routes of administration. Indeed, Chandra and Anthony (2020) recently published statistics showing that only 5% of individuals who restrict their use to cocaine HCl powder (taken mainly intranasally) develop cocaine dependence (*DSM-IV* criteria) within 1 to 12 months after first use, whereas about 22% of those who start with powder cocaine but transition to crack cocaine smoking develop cocaine dependence.

Individuals who engage in frequent cocaine use, especially by smoking or injection, are also in danger of developing a pattern of **cocaine binges**. These binges are episodic bouts of repeated use lasting from hours to days with little or no sleep. During these periods, nothing is important to the user except maintaining the "high," and all available supplies of cocaine are consumed in this pursuit. A 3-day freebasing binge may involve consuming as much as 150 g of cocaine—an enormous amount. More than 30 years ago, Gawin and Kleber (1986; 1988) reported the presence of an abstinence syndrome that they observed following a cocaine binge. They proposed that this abstinence syndrome occurred in three phases: *crash*, *withdrawal*, and *extinction*. During the crash, the user feels exhausted and experiences intense dysphoria, anhedonia (inability to experience normal pleasures), insomnia, and other psychological symptoms (Koob and Le Moal, 2006; **TABLE 12.3**). During the subsequent withdrawal phase, the anhedonia continues and is accompanied by

anergia (decreased energy), disinterest in the environment, and a growing craving for cocaine that increases the risk of relapse. Although most symptoms subside during the extinction phase, occasional episodes of cocaine craving, either spontaneous or cue induced, may trigger relapse.

Other factors also contribute to the transition from occasional cocaine use to more frequent use, to the development of a cocaine use disorder, and/or to relapse in individuals who are attempting to achieve abstinence from the drug. As described in Chapter 9 for drug addiction generally, such factors may include comorbidity with other psychiatric disorders, such as depression, anxiety disorders, or personality disorders (Quello et al., 2005), stress (Mantsch et al., 2014), exposure to environmental stimuli previously associated with cocaine use (Crombag et al., 2008), or cocaine priming (i.e., exposure to a small amount of the drug that elicits craving for more) (Mahoney et al., 2007). Interestingly, animal studies indicate that cocaine craving and relapse to cocaine use actually increase over time (although not permanently) following withdrawal from drug use (Lu et al., 2004; Wolf, 2016). This phenomenon, which has been termed **incubation** of cocaine craving, is consistent with the high rate of relapse in cocaine-dependent individuals, even those enrolled in treatment programs (see later in this chapter). Moreover, incubation of craving is not unique to cocaine but has been observed with other drugs as well (Pickens et al., 2011; Li et al., 2015). In Chapter 9, we presented evidence from laboratory animal studies regarding the mechanisms underlying incubation of cocaine craving.

The neurobiology of cocaine craving has been investigated using PET imaging studies of people with cocaine dependence as well as neurochemical studies involving relevant animal models of cocaine-directed motivation. PET imaging studies have found that DA release is increased in the dorsal and ventral striatum, amygdala, hippocampus, and PFC when cocaine users (diagnosed as having cocaine dependence, in most of the cited studies) are presented with cocaine-related stimuli such as videotapes of people smoking cocaine (Volkow et al., 2006; Wong et al., 2006; Fotros et al., 2013; Milella et al., 2016). These studies make use of

TABLE 12.3 Phases of the Abstinence Syndrome Following a Cocaine Binge

Phase	Phase 1: Crash	Phase 2: Withdrawal	Phase 3: Extinction
Length of phase	9 hours to 4 days	1 to 4 weeks	Indefinite (until next relapse)
Symptoms	Intense dysphoria (distressed mood) and anhedonia (lack of pleasure) Insomnia Irritability Anxiety	Anhedonia Anergia (lack of energy) Decreased interest in the environment Increasing craving	Brief episodes of spontaneous craving Cue-induced craving

Source: Adapted from F. H. Gawin and H. D. Kleber. 1986. *Arch Gen Psychiatry* 43: 107–113. © 1986 American Medical Association.

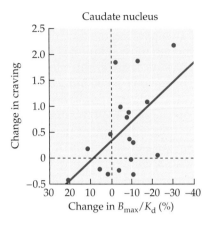

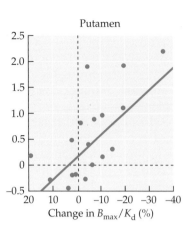

FIGURE 12.10 Relationship between striatal DA release and craving elicited by exposure to cocaine-related visual stimuli Cocaine-addicted individuals were exposed to a video of cocaine-related cues including purchase, preparation, and smoking of the drug while undergoing PET scanning of striatal DA release measured by DA displacement of radiolabeled raclopride from D_2 receptors. The y-axis of the graph plots changes in subjective cocaine craving from before to the end of the video. The x-axis plots changes in DA release measured by alterations in raclopride binding. Significant positive correlations were found for both the caudate nucleus and the putamen, indicating that cue-induced cocaine craving is associated with heightened striatal DA release. (After N. D. Volkow et al. 2006. *J Neurosci* 26: 6583–6588. © 2006 Society for Neuroscience.)

radiolabeled D_2 receptor ligands that can be displaced from the receptor by DA released from the dopaminergic nerve terminals. Consequently, reductions in drug binding as measured by PET imaging are interpreted as increased local DA release. An example of this approach using radiolabeled raclopride is shown in **FIGURE 12.10**. The data illustrate a significant correlation between the craving elicited by the cocaine cues and the neuroimaging-derived index of DA release in the dorsal striatum (caudate and putamen) (Volkow et al., 2006). A more recent study further reported cue-induced DA release in the dorsal striatum in recreational cocaine users studied *before* they had developed cocaine dependence (Cox et al., 2017). DA release in the NAcc (ventral striatum) has also been implicated in cocaine "craving" using an experimental rat model (Saunders et al., 2013). Other rat models have been developed to reproduce the features of escalating cocaine use and to discover its underlying neurobiological mechanisms. Several of these models are described in **WEB BOX 12.2**.

Finally, we should mention that research using functional magnetic resonance imaging (fMRI), which measures regional neural activity independently of specific neurotransmitters, has implicated many of the same brain areas mentioned above in the process of cocaine craving (e.g., Risinger et al., 2005; Hanlon et al., 2018). In addition, Zhang and colleagues have demonstrated activation of the hypothalamus, a brain area strongly implicated in motivation, following presentation of cocaine-related cues to individuals with cocaine dependence (Zhang et al., 2019; 2020). Together with the PET imaging results, these findings have identified a neural circuit in cocaine users (particularly those who meet criteria for cocaine dependence/cocaine use disorder) consisting of the PFC, striatum (dorsal and ventral), limbic system, and hypothalamus that responds to cocaine-related cues with neural activation (fMRI studies) and/or DA release (PET studies) and that likely plays an important role in the cue-induced craving for the drug.

Chronic cocaine exposure leads to significant neurobiological and behavioral changes

ALTERATIONS IN DOPAMINERGIC FUNCTION Since the dopaminergic system plays such a central role in the acute effects of cocaine and other psychostimulants, it is important to understand whether chronic use of these drugs alters the basic functioning of this system. This question has been addressed by brain imaging studies that compare psychostimulant users with a control group with respect to markers of pre- and postsynaptic DA activity in the striatum. In all cases except for DA synthesis, markers of interest (i.e., DAT, D_2/D_3 receptors, and VMAT2) were labelled with a radioactively tagged drug that binds selectively to that marker. DA release was assessed by measuring D_2/D_3 receptor availability after a challenge dose of methylphenidate or amphetamine. In all studies, the drug users had been abstinent for varying periods of time (typically between 5 days and 3 weeks) before being studied to avoid confounding the results by residual drug levels. **FIGURE 12.11** depicts a summary of the findings based on a systematic review and meta-analysis of this research (Ashok et al., 2017). Virtually every feature of striatal dopaminergic activity was found to be reduced in the drug-using group. The only exception were the levels of VMAT2, which varied depending on the relative length of drug abstinence prior to imaging. A recent study extended the previous research on the striatum by showing reduced D_2/D_3 receptor availability and amphetamine-stimulated DA release in cocaine-dependent individuals (compared to healthy controls) in neocortical areas (Narendran et al., 2020).

These findings powerfully demonstrate a downregulation of dopaminergic activity with chronic use of cocaine and other psychostimulants. Moreover, they support the "dopamine depletion hypothesis" of

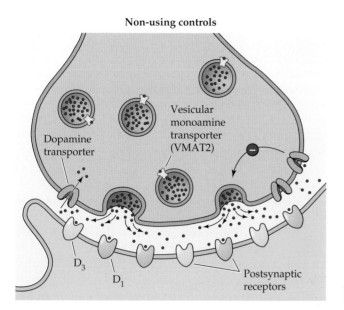

Non-using controls

Psychostimulant Users

FIGURE 12.11 **Summary of altered striatal dopaminergic markers in chronic psychostimulant users compared to non-using controls** Brain imaging methods such as PET were used to quantify several markers of striatal dopaminergic activity including DA synthesis, DA release, VMAT2 binding, DAT binding, and D_2/D_3 receptor binding. Relative levels of each marker are shown for non-using controls (A) versus chronic psychostimulant (cocaine, amphetamine, or methamphetamine) users (B). The figure illustrates that the psychostimulant users showed decreased DA synthesis (illustrated by fewer DA molecules per synaptic vesicle and fewer vesicles), decreased DA release (illustrated by fewer DA molecules in the synaptic cleft), less DAT binding, and less D_2/D_3 receptor binding. Note that because the drug used to label the DA receptors did not differentiate between D_2 and D_3 receptors, this uncertainty is reflected in a decrease in both receptor subtypes. Not shown are the VMAT2 binding results, which varied depending on the period of abstinence from psychostimulant use. Elevated VMAT2 binding was observed in users who were recently abstinent at the time of the study, whereas decreased binding was found after prolonged drug abstinence. (Adapted from A. H. Ashok et al. 2017. *JAMA Psychiatry* 74: 511–519. doi:10.1001/jamapsychiatry.2017.0135.)

cocaine addiction proposed many years ago by Dackis and Gold (1985). Down-regulation of dopamine synthesis, DA release, and DA transporter and receptor levels may result from repeated psychostimulant-induced increases in extracellular DA levels. Such down-regulation would be expected to result in a tolerance to subsequent psychostimulant use, a topic taken up in the next section.

TOLERANCE AND SENSITIZATION As is the case with many potentially addictive drugs, chronic exposure to cocaine or other psychostimulants causes either **tolerance** (reduced drug responsiveness) or **sensitization** (increased responsiveness), sometimes called **reverse tolerance**. One of the amazing aspects of sensitization is that just a few exposures to cocaine or amphetamine can produce an increased responsiveness that lasts for weeks, months, or even longer (Paulson et al., 1991). Although this kind of long-lasting sensitization has usually been studied in experimental animals, a laboratory study by Boileau and colleagues (2006) demonstrated sensitized behavioral and neurochemical responses to amphetamine at 1 year after a mere four doses of the drug given orally to human participants over a 2-week period.

How can psychostimulants produce both tolerance and sensitization? Various studies have shown that the

kind of change one observes depends on the pattern of drug exposure, the response that's being measured, and the time interval that has elapsed since the last dose. For example, continuous cocaine infusion into rats causes tolerance to the drug's locomotor-stimulating effect (Inada et al., 1992), whereas once-daily cocaine injections lead to behavioral sensitization, as shown by enhanced stereotyped behaviors (Post and Contel, 1983). Several studies have examined tolerance or sensitization to self-administered cocaine rather than cocaine given by the experimenter. Once again, different results were obtained depending on the pattern of drug exposure. Cocaine self-administered daily by IV injection for 6 hours per day (long-access model; see Web Box 12.1 for details) caused a reduction in the stimulatory effects (both locomotor activity and stereotypies) of a 5 mg/kg intraperitoneal (IP) cocaine challenge given on the day after the last self-administration session (Calipari et al., 2014a). In contrast, intermittent access to self-administered cocaine led to a sensitization of the drug's behavioral effects (Calipari et al., 2014b; 2015). Earlier studies of psychostimulant sensitization showed that this phenomenon can be divided into two phases: **induction** (the process by which sensitization is established) and **expression** (the process by which the sensitized response is manifested). Between these two phases (i.e., after the last drug dose has been administered), sensitization can actually increase in strength as a result of ongoing neurochemical changes in the brain.

In humans using cocaine on a regular basis, evidence for both tolerance and sensitization has been observed, depending on the specific outcome measure (Narendran and Martinez, 2008; Small et al., 2009). Researchers have generally reported that cocaine's euphoric effects tend to show tolerance over time, which could contribute to increased drug-taking behavior in an attempt to recapture the level of pleasure experienced during earlier episodes of use. Interestingly, not only does tolerance occur following chronic cocaine exposure, but a form of rapid tolerance to both the subjective and cardiovascular effects of cocaine has also been demonstrated (Ambre et al., 1988; Foltin and Haney, 2004). This means that users who take repeated cocaine doses *within a drug-using session* will experience diminished responses after the initial dose.

The neurochemical mechanisms underlying both psychostimulant tolerance and sensitization have been studied extensively in animal models and to a lesser extent in humans, using brain imaging methods. These studies have strongly implicated changes in the dopaminergic system in the development of both response patterns (see **BOX 12.1**).

OTHER FACTORS THAT MAY CONTRIBUTE TO COCAINE DEPENDENCE Individuals diagnosed as being cocaine-dependent have lost control over their drug-seeking and drug-using behaviors. Numerous studies have demonstrated an association between cocaine abuse or dependence (using *DSM-IV* criteria) and deficits in various cognitive domains. The most severely affected cognitive functions are reported to be sustained attention, impulse control, working memory, verbal learning and memory, performance on psychomotor tasks, and decision making in reward-based learning tasks (Spronk et al., 2013; Potvin et al., 2014; note, however, that the claims of cognitive impairment in cocaine users are disputed in a review by Frazer et al., 2018). Structural and functional brain imaging studies have found numerous differences between cocaine-using participants and non-users in the PFC (including medial PFC, dorsolateral PFC, and orbitofrontal cortex), anterior cingulate cortex, insula, dorsal striatum, amygdala, and thalamus (Crunelle et al., 2012; Hanlon and Canterberry, 2012; Taylor, S. B., et al., 2013). Depending on the brain area, reported abnormalities include reduced gray matter volume or cortical thickness, increased volume (caudate nucleus), reduced functional connectivity within a neural circuit, impaired integrity of white matter tracts, and/or altered functional activation during cognitive task performance. Reduced gray matter volume in areas of the PFC has been correlated with measures of impulsivity, raising the possibility

that this change could contribute to the loss of inhibitory control in cocaine-dependent individuals and their inability to monitor and evaluate the consequences of their behavior (Ersche et al., 2011; Meade et al., 2020). An intriguing report by Ersche and colleagues (2013) compared age-related gray matter volume (both cortical and subcortical) in cocaine-dependent individuals and healthy controls. Although both groups showed less gray matter with increasing age, the decline was much steeper in the cocaine-dependent group. This finding indicates that chronic cocaine use may accelerate the rate of brain aging. Potential causes of gray matter loss include cell death, retraction of dendritic processes, and synapse elimination (Rasakham et al., 2014; Guha et al., 2016).

Is it possible that the cognitive deficits and neurobiological abnormalities observed in people diagnosed with a cocaine-related disorder *precede* rather than follow from their repeated drug exposure? This possibility arises from the hypothesis that differences in brain structure/function and the resulting cognitive deficits are produced by genetic and/or environmental factors apart from substance use; once in place, however, these deficits increase the predisposition to substance use and misuse (including use and misuse of cocaine). Although there may be neurobiological and behavioral differences between cocaine users compared to non-users that precede the onset of drug use, several studies indicate that (1) chronic exposure to cocaine has deleterious effects on brain structure and cognition regardless of any preexisting differences, and (2) prolonged abstinence may, at least partially, reverse these effects (Hanlon et al., 2011; Connolly et al., 2013; Parvaz et al., 2017; Jedema et al., 2021). Whether full recovery can occur over a very long time period is not yet known.

Repeated or high-dose cocaine use can produce serious health consequences

The previous section summarized the effects of long-term cocaine use at typical recreational doses on brain structure and function. Higher doses taken over a long period or acute overdosing on cocaine can exert other adverse physiological and behavioral consequences. Such consequences can include a stroke or seizure, as mentioned earlier (Siniscalchi et al., 2015). Behaviorally, high-dose cocaine use can lead to panic attacks or the development of a temporary paranoid psychosis with delusions and hallucinations (Roncero et al., 2014; Tang et al., 2014). Risk factors for cocaine-induced psychotic disorder include being male, using cocaine in relatively large amounts and for long durations, and taking the drug by the IV route of administration. One particularly frightening type of hallucination is called "cocaine bugs," which refers to the sensation of tiny creatures crawling under or over the user's skin. More than 100 years ago, some of Freud's colleagues were already

BOX 12.1 ■ THE CUTTING EDGE

Neurochemical Mechanisms of Cocaine Tolerance and Sensitization

Several molecular adaptations occur in NAcc dopaminergic nerve terminals in rats that have been made cocaine tolerant using the long-access self-administration paradigm. These adaptations are illustrated in **FIGURE A** and can be summarized as follows: (1) reduced intracellular DA levels and reduced DA release, (2) reduced baseline rate of DA uptake, (3) reduced ability of cocaine to block DAT and to inhibit DA reuptake, and (4) reduced sensitivity of terminal D_2 DA autoreceptors (Calipari et al., 2014a; Siciliano et al., 2015). Thus, repeated prolonged exposure to cocaine in this model strikingly reduced not only responses to a subsequent cocaine challenge but also the basic functioning of the dopaminergic system in the absence of a drug challenge. Given this profound tolerance of that system, it is not surprising that long-access self-administering rats also exhibit behavioral tolerance to cocaine.

We mentioned in the text that *intermittent* access to self-administered cocaine causes behavioral sensitization instead of tolerance. Indeed, researchers have shown that this procedure also leads to *increased* rather than *decreased* potency of cocaine to inhibit DA uptake (Siciliano et al., 2015). It is likely that the production of tolerance versus sensitization depends on differences in the pattern of cocaine concentrations in the brain. The intermittent access procedure has been estimated to produce repeated spikes in brain cocaine, as opposed to the high and relatively constant brain cocaine concentration produced by long-access self-administration. These differing patterns of neural exposure to cocaine are believed to play a critical role in producing the different dopaminergic changes seen in the tolerant compared with the sensitized animals.

Although most research on psychostimulant sensitization has focused on repeated drug exposure, there is also strong evidence for rapid sensitization of the mesolimbic DA pathway produced by a single drug exposure. This sensitization occurs at the level of both the VTA dopaminergic cell bodies and the nerve terminals in the NAcc. Thus, Argilli and colleagues (2008) found that a single dose of cocaine given to rats enhanced the excitatory responses of VTA dopaminergic neurons to glutamate receptor stimulation measured as early as 3 hours later. This enhanced responsiveness is mediated by a type of long-term potentiation (see Chapter 8) in the VTA neurons. A later study by Singer and associates (2017) demonstrated increased DA overflow in the NAcc shell in rats administered cocaine IV after a prior cocaine injection given 2 hours earlier (**FIGURE B**).

The clinical relevance of the animal studies on tolerance and sensitization has been tested using brain imaging to assess DA displacement of radiolabeled drug binding to D_2 receptors, as described earlier in Figure 12.11. One important difference, however, is the addition of a challenge with a psychostimulant such as amphetamine or methylphenidate. Increased sensitivity to the drug challenge would result in greater reuptake blockade and, therefore, greater displacement of the radiolabel by endogenous DA. On the

(Continued)

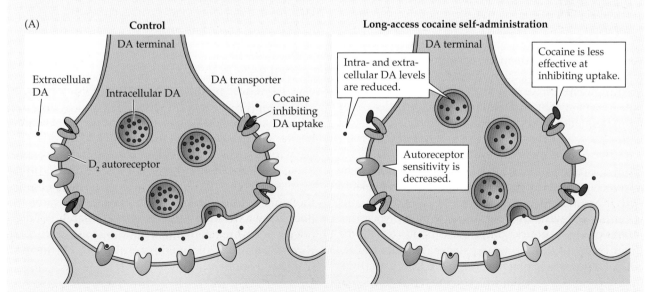

(A) **Control** — **Long-access cocaine self-administration**

DA terminal

Extracellular DA

Intracellular DA

DA transporter

Cocaine inhibiting DA uptake

D_2 autoreceptor

Intra- and extra-cellular DA levels are reduced.

Cocaine is less effective at inhibiting uptake.

Autoreceptor sensitivity is decreased.

Molecular adaptations in the nucleus accumbens underlying tolerance due to long-access cocaine self-administration (After C. A. Siciliano et al. 2015. *Chem Neurosci* 6: 27–36. http://pubs.acs.org/doi/10.1021/cn5002705. Further permissions related to the material excerpted should be directed to the ACS.)

BOX 12.1 ■ THE CUTTING EDGE *(continued)*

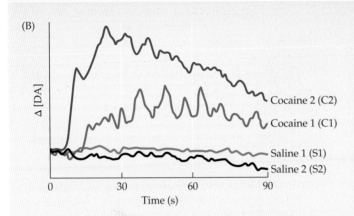

(B)

DA overflow in the NAcc shell following the first (S1 or C1) or second (S2 or C2) administration of saline or cocaine Rats were first implanted surgically with carbon fiber electrodes to measure rapid changes in DA overflow using in vivo voltammetry (see Chapter 4). After recovery, the animals were given sequential injections of saline vehicle (S) and 1.0 mg/kg cocaine (C) IV. S1 was given first to determine baseline DA overflow, followed by C1. C2 was administered 2 hours after C1, and S2 was given 1 hour after C2 to ensure that the cocaine injections had not altered the DA response to saline. The figure shows that the mean change in DA concentration (Δ [DA]) to cocaine (C2) was substantially increased by the prior cocaine exposure 2 hours earlier. Note the much more rapid time course of measurement compared to microdialysis as shown, for example, in Figure 12.7. (From B. F. Singer et al. 2017. *Behav Brain Res* 324: 66–70. © 2017. Reprinted with permission from Elsevier.)

other hand, decreased sensitivity would result in less reuptake blockade and, therefore, less displacement of the radiolabel. The results of these studies vary depending on whether the participants are current psychostimulant users or not. As mentioned in the text, healthy non-psychostimulant users showed a long-lasting sensitization of striatal DA release after several low doses of amphetamine (Boileau et al., 2006). On the other hand, different results were obtained in challenge studies performed with individuals who had a history of cocaine use and, in some cases, dependence. In this case, methylphenidate (which increases extracellular DA by blocking reuptake) produced less raclopride displacement in the chronic cocaine users than in healthy controls in all three major forebrain DA target areas: dorsal striatum (caudate and putamen), ventral striatum (including NAcc), and PFC (Volkow et al., 1997; 2014). This finding is consistent with a functional dopaminergic tolerance in the cocaine users (Narendran and Martinez, 2008).

To summarize both the clinical and preclinical (i.e., animal) studies, the first dose (or first few doses) of a psychostimulant such as cocaine or amphetamine elicits a sensitization of the mesolimbic DA system to subsequent drug exposure. This phenomenon may play a significant role in a later escalation of psychostimulant use and the development of dependence. In rodent studies, patterns of intermittent drug administration can increase the strength of both neurochemical and behavioral sensitization. On the other hand, patterns involving more continuous psychostimulant exposure in rodents or repeated drug use in humans are likely to result in neurochemical and behavioral tolerance. For this reason, once individuals are using the drug on a regular basis, they need to seek higher doses in order to obtain the desired subjective effects.

seeing patients with this kind of psychotic reaction. Episodes of cocaine-induced psychotic disorder occur more frequently with repeated use, which is consistent with a growing sensitization to this effect of the drug.

Other organs or organ systems such as the heart, lungs, gastrointestinal system, and kidneys can also be adversely affected by cocaine. Complications associated with the cardiovascular system range from chest pains to cardiac arrhythmias (irregular heart rate), myocardial infarction (heart attack), aortic dissection (a tear in the inner lining of the aorta), and stroke (Havakuk et al., 2017). Frequent snorting of cocaine can lead to perforation of the nasal septum, which is the tissue that separates the two sides of the nose. Survey data indicate that heavy cocaine users may die from many different causes, including acute toxicity from overdose, traumatic deaths (e.g., homicide, motor vehicle accidents, falls, and fires), heart or liver disease, and pneumonia (Degenhardt et

al., 2011). Those who take the drug by IV injection are also at high risk for contracting HIV and dying from AIDS. Finally, ingestion of cocaine by a pregnant woman has variable effects on the unborn child. Many offspring seem to escape without obvious harm; others may show behavioral problems, attention deficits, and/or other cognitive abnormalities; and in a small number of cases, the fetus is killed prior to birth. (Space constraints do not permit a detailed account of this research, so interested readers are referred to reviews by Cain et al. [2013], Richardson et al. [2015], Gkioka et al. [2016], Martin et al. [2016], and Smith and Santos [2016].)

Pharmacological, behavioral, and psychosocial methods are used to treat cocaine use disorder

High rates of cocaine misuse and dependence in our society have spurred a great deal of interest in developing effective therapies for cocaine users. We will first describe existing pharmacotherapeutic approaches, the idea of a cocaine vaccine, and programs that rely on behavioral and psychosocial methods. We will conclude this section with a brief discussion of novel treatment approaches that are under consideration.

PHARMACOTHERAPIES   A large variety of compounds targeting several different neurotransmitter systems have been tested as potential medications to help cocaine users stop their current use and then to help maintain abstinence. Indeed, a review published several years ago identified over 100 blinded placebo-controlled clinical trials that had already been conducted to determine the efficacy of various medications for treating cocaine dependence/cocaine use disorder (Czoty et al., 2016). More recent reviews describe the wide range of medications tested thus far and their molecular targets (Chan et al., 2019; Kampman, 2019; Brandt et al., 2021). Yet despite this enormous effort, at present not a single medication has been approved by the U.S. Food and Drug Administration (FDA) for the treatment of cocaine use disorder. There are numerous reasons for this lack of success, including the surprising observation that many medications have been tested without the benefit of prior laboratory studies to at least suggest possible therapeutic efficacy (Czoty et al., 2016). Nevertheless, even in cases where therapeutic efficacy seemed plausible based on preclinical animal studies of cocaine-seeking behavior and/or cocaine relapse, outcomes of clinical trials have been discouraging (Humphreys, 2021). Clinical trial failure is generally attributed to lack of therapeutic benefit, participant dropout, and/or noncompliance with trial protocols.

Many medications for substance use disorders, either approved or proposed, fall into the category of "agonists" or "antagonists" with respect to the mechanism of action of the substance being misused. Examples of agonist therapies are methadone and buprenorphine maintenance for opioid addiction (Chapter 11) and nicotine replacement medications for nicotine addiction (Chapter 13). In contrast, naltrexone and nalmefene are antagonist medications used to treat opioid addiction. For treatment of cocaine use disorder, antagonist therapies would include DA receptor blockers or, potentially, novel compounds that would prevent cocaine access to the DAT while still permitting DA reuptake. Agonist medications would include full or partial DA receptor agonists and prescription psychostimulants (DA-releasing and/or reuptake-blocking compounds) such as amphetamine, methylphenidate, or modafinil. Current evidence clearly favors the agonist approach, particularly high-dose amphetamine treatment (Tardelli et al., 2020). By increasing dopaminergic transmission, psychostimulants have the potential to serve as "replacement" drugs for cocaine, much like the opioid and nicotine medications mentioned above.

Several roadblocks must be overcome before any psychostimulant replacement therapy could be approved by the FDA for the treatment of cocaine use disorder (Negus and Henningfield, 2015). One key issue is the potential for misuse of these compounds themselves, although it's worth noting that the three drugs being tested are already approved for treating other psychiatric disorders (see later sections of the chapter). Therefore, continued research on psychostimulant replacement therapy seems to be warranted.

COCAINE VACCINE   Some researchers have taken a much different approach by attempting to develop a vaccine against cocaine. Vaccine-induced antibodies may simply bind cocaine molecules, or alternatively, they may be engineered to have catalytic activity that actually breaks down cocaine in the bloodstream. Both methods cause less cocaine to get into the brain, and both have been shown to reduce (or even completely block) cocaine self-administration and reinstatement in animals. Cocaine-binding antibodies have been tested in several clinical trials. Thus far, the results are mixed, as some people who developed relatively high antibody titers (high concentrations of cocaine-targeted antibodies) in their bloodstream did show reduced cocaine use, but many other people showed a poorer response to the vaccination and continued a high level of cocaine use (Kosten et al., 2014; Orson et al., 2014). Newer approaches have been developed to improve vaccine efficacy (Tang et al., 2019; St. John et al., 2020). Nonetheless, one important limitation of cocaine-binding antibodies is that their effectiveness can be overcome by taking larger doses of cocaine. Antibody therapy might, therefore, work best when coupled with behavioral approaches to reduce the patient's motivation to seek out and use the drug. A second issue is that successfully vaccinated individuals who can no longer respond to cocaine remain free to switch to other psychostimulants such as amphetamine or methamphetamine. For this reason, it is not clear that an anti-cocaine vaccine is the best long-term approach to treating cocaine use disorder.

BEHAVIORAL AND PSYCHOSOCIAL THERAPIES   As with other psychiatric disorders, approaches to treating cocaine use disorder include various behavioral and psychosocial therapies. Even in those cases where pharmacotherapy may aid in patient stabilization (e.g., by reducing craving or other abstinence symptoms), equally important are counseling and support structures that enable the patient to learn new coping responses, avoid triggers for relapse, and function effectively in a drug-free lifestyle. Indeed, psychosocial factors such as feelings of self-efficacy, demonstrating a strong commitment to abstinence, and having good social support predict an increased likelihood of recovery from cocaine dependence (McKay et al., 2013).

A variety of different treatment programs are available for cocaine-dependent individuals (Penberthy et al., 2010; Minozzi et al., 2016). Many are conducted on an outpatient basis, although the most severe cases usually receive the greatest benefit from hospitalization and either short- or long-term inpatient treatment. **Psychosocial treatment programs** involve individual, group, or family counseling designed to educate the user, promote behavioral change, and alleviate some of the problems caused by use of the drug. **Cognitive behavioral therapy (CBT)** is aimed at restructuring cognitive (thought) processes and training the user either to avoid high-risk situations that might cause relapse or to employ appropriate coping mechanisms to manage such situations when they occur. This approach is sometimes called **relapse prevention therapy**. Also available are 12-step programs such as Narcotics Anonymous or Cocaine Anonymous. The general approach of all 12-step programs is based on that of Alcoholics Anonymous, which is described in Chapter 10.

One of the most interesting approaches to treating cocaine users was developed by Stephen Higgins and coworkers at the University of Vermont (Higgins et al., 1991). This **contingency management program** is a behavioral treatment approach based on the premise that drug taking is an operant response that persists mainly as a result of the reinforcing properties of the drug. Hence, altering reinforcement contingencies to reduce drug-associated reinforcement and to increase the availability of nondrug reinforcers should help promote abstinence and the adoption of a drug-free lifestyle. As part of this program, each negative urine test of the client is reinforced with a voucher. These vouchers cannot be redeemed for money per se, to avoid patients accumulating funds for drug purchases; however, they can be exchanged for retail items available locally. Contingency management can be paired with a community reinforcement approach (Hunt and Azrin, 1973), which is designed to enhance the patient's social (including family) relationships, recreational activities, and job opportunities. The combination of contingency management plus community reinforcement appears to be one of the most effective approaches for treating cocaine or amphetamine addiction and should be considered a front-line treatment option when available (De Crescenzo et al., 2018).

BRAIN STIMULATION Beyond the conventional pharmacological and psychosocial treatment methods, investigators have begun to consider new approaches to address cocaine and other psychostimulant use disorders. One such approach is to use brain stimulation to alter the brain circuitry underlying drug craving, impulsive drug seeking, and other factors contributing to substance misuse (Saling and Martinez, 2016; Wang et al., 2018; Ma et al., 2019). Three different kinds of brain stimulation methods have been developed for therapeutic purposes: **repetitive transcranial magnetic stimulation (rTMS)**, **transcranial direct current stimulation (tDCS)**, and **deep brain stimulation (DBS)** (Coles et al., 2018; **FIGURE 12.12**). In rTMS (sometimes just called TMS), an electromagnetic coil is placed on a selected area of the scalp and repeated electrical pulses are passed through it. The effect of this procedure is to generate magnetic pulses that, in turn, induce electrical responses within the underlying brain tissue. TMS was approved by the FDA over 10 years ago for treating major depression, but it is also being tested for efficacy in other neuropsychiatric

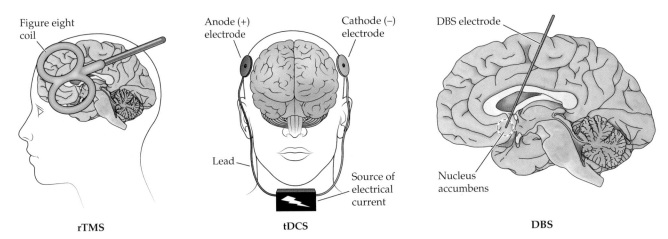

FIGURE 12.12 Brain stimulation methods being tested for the treatment of substance use disorders The brain stimulation methods illustrated are being tested for the treatment of substance use disorders, including cocaine use disorder. The methods are repetitive transcranial magnetic stimulation (rTMS), transcranial direct current stimulation (tDCS), and deep brain stimulation (DBS). (After A. S. Coles et al. 2018. *Am J Addict* 27: 71–91. © 2018 American Academy of Addiction Psychiatry.)

disorders, including substance use disorders. In tDCS, two or more electrodes are placed on the scalp and used to pass a constant direct current at low intensity. Although tDCS is not yet FDA approved for any specific therapeutic application, like TMS this method of brain stimulation is being tested for possible benefit in several different disorders, including those involving substance misuse. Lastly, DBS is a significantly more invasive approach since it requires the surgical implantation of electrodes into deep brain structures. DBS is currently FDA approved for the treatment of Parkinson's disease and several other movement disorders. As shown in the figure, the NAcc is usually the brain area targeted in experimental tests of DBS efficacy in substance use disorders. Because of its invasiveness, DBS seems less likely than TMS or tDCS to be a major candidate for treating substance use disorders except for seriously impaired individuals who have proved resistant to other treatment modalities.

SECTION SUMMARY

■ Early use of other substances seems to be an important risk factor for the initiation of cocaine use.

■ Some users quickly stop taking cocaine for various reasons, some maintain controlled use for long periods, and still others progress to a pattern of uncontrolled use (i.e., misuse). Such a progression may come about through dose escalation and/or switching from intranasal use to smoking or IV injection—routes of administration with greater potential for developing uncontrolled use.

■ Maladaptive use of psychostimulants generally is categorized as stimulant use disorder in the *DSM-5*. Maladaptive cocaine use can be categorized more specifically as cocaine use disorder.

■ Maladaptive cocaine use (i.e., cocaine misuse) may be manifested by daily or near-daily use or by a pattern of bingeing. Many individuals who misuse cocaine also suffer from other psychiatric disorders.

■ Cocaine craving and relapse to cocaine use increase over time following withdrawal; this has been called incubation of cocaine craving.

■ Brain imaging studies have identified a neural circuit consisting of the PFC, striatum, limbic system, and hypothalamus, which is (a) activated by cocaine-related cues and (b) in the case of the striatum shows DA release in response to such cues.

■ Other neuroimaging studies have found that regular users of cocaine or other psychostimulants show significant down-regulation of striatal dopaminergic functioning, consisting of reductions in DA synthesis, DA release, DAT binding, and D_2/D_3 receptor binding.

■ Animal models of cocaine dependence include such features as escalation of drug intake, relapse to cocaine seeking after a period of abstinence, cocaine-seeking behavior despite aversive consequences, and increased motivation to take cocaine, as shown by an elevated breakpoint on a progressive-ratio schedule. These models support the hypothesis that both sensation seeking and impulsivity are traits that contribute to the development of compulsive cocaine use.

■ Chronic exposure to cocaine or other psychostimulants can lead to tolerance and/or sensitization. Changes in drug responsiveness depend on the pattern of drug exposure, the outcome measure, and the time since the last dose.

■ Animal studies have implicated increased dopaminergic activity in the VTA and increased NAcc DA release as being important for locomotor sensitization to psychostimulants.

■ In humans, the subjective effects (including euphoria) and cardiovascular activation to cocaine show chronic tolerance with repeated use as well as rapid tolerance within a drug-taking session.

■ Individuals suffering from cocaine use disorders show deficits in many cognitive domains, including sustained attention, impulse control, working memory, verbal learning and memory, performance on psychomotor tasks, and decision making in reward-based learning tasks. These deficits are additionally associated with structural and functional differences in several cortical and subcortical brain areas. Evidence from both human and experimental animal studies suggests that at least some of these cognitive and neurobiological differences are *caused* by repeated cocaine exposure.

■ The adverse effects of repeated or high-dose cocaine use include stroke or seizure, abnormalities in both gray and white matter in the cortex, cardiovascular problems including heart attack, damage to other organ systems, and possible abnormalities in the development of offspring exposed prenatally to cocaine. High-dose cocaine use can also lead to panic attacks or the onset of a paranoid psychotic reaction.

■ Much effort in the area of treating cocaine use disorders has been focused on the development of medications that might reduce craving and promote abstinence among users. Some of these medications act on the dopaminergic system (e.g., DA receptors or the DA transporter), whereas others that have been tested target other neurotransmitter systems. The psychostimulants amphetamine, methylphenidate, and modafinil have been investigated as potential replacement drugs for cocaine. Despite these efforts, there is currently no FDA-approved medication to treat cocaine dependence.

■ Yet another approach still under consideration is to use an anti-cocaine vaccine that either traps the drug in the bloodstream or breaks it down enzymatically.

■ Current behavioral and psychosocial treatments include various types of counseling, cognitive behavioral therapies aimed at relapse prevention, 12-step programs like Narcotics Anonymous and Cocaine Anonymous, and contingency management programs based on a combination of vouchers and a community reinforcement approach. Contingency management programs seem to have the greatest success rates in treating cocaine dependence; however, they are labor intensive and costly compared to other approaches, and this has limited their application.

■ Brain stimulation procedures such as rTMS, tDCS, and DBS are also under consideration as potential treatments for individuals with psychostimulant (including cocaine) use disorders.

12.4 Background, History, and Basic Pharmacology of the Amphetamines

Background and history

Amphetamine is the parent compound of a family of synthetic psychostimulants. It is available in two chemical forms, L-amphetamine (trade name Benzedrine) and D-amphetamine (also called dextroamphetamine; trade name Dexedrine). Another key member of this family is **methamphetamine**. Two naturally occurring plant compounds have structures similar to those of amphetamine and methamphetamine, namely **cathinone** and **ephedrine**. As can be seen in **FIGURE 12.13**, all of these compounds are structurally related to the neurotransmitter DA.

Cathinone is the primary active ingredient in khat (alternately spelled qat) (*Catha edulis*), an evergreen shrub native to the Horn of Africa and the Arabian Peninsula. Cathinone is typically consumed by chewing the fresh leaves of the plant, a practice that dates back at least to the 13th century (El-Menyar et al., 2015). An estimated 20 million people worldwide use khat regularly for its stimulant properties, with greatest use occurring in Ethiopia, Somalia, and Yemen. There are health risks associated with repeated khat use, and one particular

area of concern is the growing practice of khat chewing among young people. More information about khat and its effects can be found in **WEB BOX 12.3**.

A closely related plant-derived stimulant is ephedrine, a constituent of the herb *Ephedra vulgaris*. Chinese physicians have used *Ephedra* (known to them as ma huang) for more than 5000 years as an herbal remedy. Like other amphetamine-like substances, ephedrine reduces appetite, and it also provides a subjective feeling of heightened energy. For these reasons, a number of companies began to market ephedra-containing dietary supplements as weight loss products sold in health food stores. These supplements became so popular that in 1999, the General Accounting Office estimated that Americans were consuming about 2 billion doses of ephedra-containing products each year! Unfortunately, ephedrine sharply elevates blood pressure and exerts other sympathomimetic effects as well. These effects can increase the risk of heart attack or stroke, particularly with large drug doses or in vulnerable individuals. Because of the many reports of adverse reactions (including several deaths) associated with the use of ephedra, the FDA became increasingly concerned about this substance and eventually banned the sale of ephedra-containing dietary supplements in 2004.

Interestingly, ephedra played a key role in the development of amphetamine. In the 1920s, purified ephedrine was found to be a valuable anti-asthmatic agent because of its powerful bronchodilator (widening of the airways) action.* However, the medical profession soon became concerned that demand for ephedrine might exceed its supply and therefore began to search for an appropriate synthetic substitute. That substitute turned out to be amphetamine, which had first been synthesized in 1887 by the Romanian chemist Lazar Edeleanu. Because Edeleanu was not interested in amphetamine's pharmacological properties, the drug remained "under the radar" until its rediscovery by an American chemist named Gordon Alles. In 1929, Alles injected himself with 50 mg of amphetamine and reported the following physiological and psychological effects: "Nose cleared-dry," "Feeling of well-being—palpitation," and later "Rather sleepless night. Mind seemed to run from one subject to another" (Rasmussen, 2015; p. 12). The Smith, Kline & French pharmaceutical company had begun studying amphetamine's bronchodilator effects around the same time, leading to the introduction of an

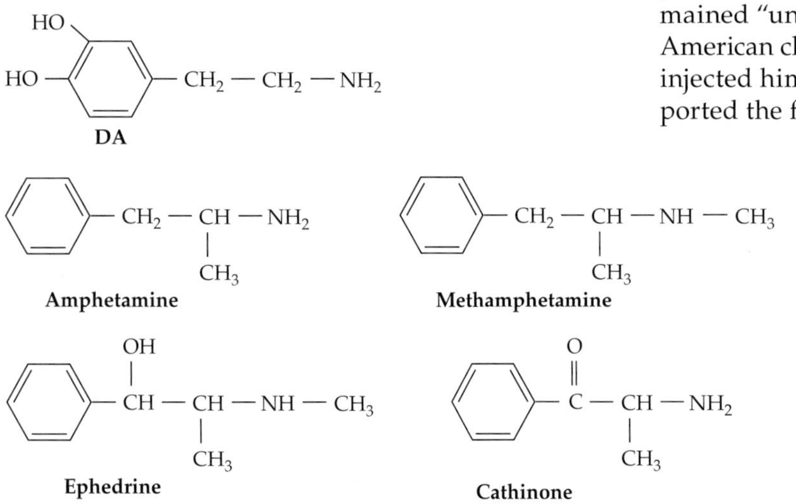

FIGURE 12.13 **Amphetamine and related psychostimulants resemble the neurotransmitter DA in their chemical structure** This accounts for their potent effects on the dopaminergic system.

---

*Some decongestants still contain pseudoephedrine as their active ingredient, but availability of these drugs (i.e., only from the pharmacist rather than the open shelves) is closely regulated because pseudoephedrine is used illegally to synthesize methamphetamine for street use.

amphetamine-containing inhaler in 1933. The inhaler, which contained 325 mg of Benzedrine (later reduced to 250 mg) in a cotton plug, proved to be effective in temporarily relieving nasal or bronchial congestion. Unfortunately, however, some individuals began to overuse these inhalers, particularly since many varieties could be purchased without a prescription. Other people learned to open the container, remove the amphetamine-containing plug, and chew the cotton, swallow it, or extract the drug for the purpose of injection. Amphetamine in tablet form was first marketed in the 1930s as a treatment for narcolepsy, depression, and a form of Parkinsonism that can after a bout of encephalitis. By the 1940s, amphetamine had become so widely embraced by the medical profession that one author documented 39 supposed clinical uses for the drug. In addition, during World War II many American military personnel were given amphetamine to forestall sleep and maintain a heightened level of alertness during prolonged periods on duty (Rasmussen, 2015).

After the war, the United States experienced a surge in amphetamine consumption. The drug was prescribed widely for weight loss and for treating depression and other major or minor mental health problems (Rasmussen, 2008). Not surprisingly, many individuals became dependent on amphetamine or methamphetamine, which had also been introduced in prescription form for weight loss. Heavy use of amphetamine continued until the 1970s, when it began to be supplanted by cocaine as the major psychostimulant used recreationally. Moreover, growing availability of illicit methamphetamine led to a rise in the misuse of that compound. In the following discussion, amphetamine and methamphetamine are presented together because of their similar neurochemical and behavioral effects.

Basic pharmacology

Amphetamine is typically taken either orally or by IV or subcutaneous injection (the latter is sometimes called "skin popping"). Street names for amphetamine include "uppers," "bennies," "dexies," "black beauties," and "diet pills." Because absorption from the gastrointestinal tract is relatively slow, it may take up to 30 minutes for behavioral effects to be experienced after a typical oral dose of 5 to 15 mg. In contrast, IV injection provides a much more rapid and intense "high" than oral consumption and has much greater addictive potential.

Methamphetamine is more potent than amphetamine in its effects on the central nervous system and is therefore favored by recreational users when it is available. Typical street names for methamphetamine are "meth," "speed," "crank," "zip," and "go." The drug can be taken orally, snorted, injected intravenously, or smoked. Methamphetamine can be smoked either by using a glass pipe or by heating the compound on a piece of aluminum foil (sometimes called "chasing the dragon"). Smoking is a very effective route of methamphetamine consumption because the drug vaporizes at a low temperature and is not readily broken down by heat. In the late 1970s, methamphetamine for recreational use was primarily being manufactured by various motorcycle gangs on the West Coast, and the practice of hiding the drug in motorcycle crankcases is what led to the street name "crank." Subsequently, methamphetamine hydrochloride in a crystalline form particularly suitable for smoking (called "ice" or "crystal" on the street) began showing up in Hawaii in the 1980s. It soon spread to other parts of the United States, particularly the West, South, and Midwest. Because "ice" is inexpensive to make and is highly addictive, it poses a serious risk for society's attempts to control and reduce the incidence of stimulant misuse (Maxwell and Rutkowski, 2008; Gonzales et al., 2010). Methamphetamine is usually synthesized from pseudoephedrine, which accounts for the government's tight control over this precursor. If you have ever needed to obtain pseudoephedrine from a pharmacy, you know that only small quantities of pills are sold at one time even though no prescription is needed from a physician.

Some amphetamine or methamphetamine users (called "speed freaks") go on binges, or "runs," of repeated IV injections to experience recurrent highs. During a run, the drug is typically injected approximately every 2 hours for as long as 3 to 6 days or more. Little sleep or eating occurs during a run. The user finally becomes exhausted, ends the run, and sleeps for many hours. Barbiturates or other depressant drugs are sometimes used either to "take the edge off" during a run or to assist in sleeping following the run. Yet another approach is to moderate the extreme stimulatory effect of IV amphetamine or methamphetamine by combining it with heroin to yield a so-called "speedball."

Amphetamine and methamphetamine are metabolized by the liver, although at a slow rate. Metabolites, as well as some unmetabolized drug molecules, are mainly excreted in the urine. The elimination half-life of amphetamine ranges from 7 to more than 30 hours depending on the pH of the urine. Methamphetamine has a similar half-life of approximately 10 hours. Because of these long half-lives, users obtain a much longer-lasting high from a single dose of amphetamine or methamphetamine than they can get from a dose of cocaine.

SECTION SUMMARY

- Amphetamine and methamphetamine are synthetic psychomotor stimulants that are closely related structurally to two similarly acting plant compounds, cathinone and ephedrine.

- Amphetamine was introduced in the United States in 1933 in the form of a nasal inhaler. People soon realized that they could achieve powerful stimulatory and euphoric effects by consuming the drug orally or by injecting it. The incidence of amphetamine use and misuse peaked in the 1970s. Since then, the drug has been largely supplanted by cocaine, except for a recent upsurge in methamphetamine use in certain parts of the country.

■ Amphetamine is typically taken orally or by IV or sub-cutaneous injection. Crystalline methamphetamine, which is more potent than amphetamine, can also be taken by snorting or smoking. Some amphetamine or methamphetamine users take the drug repeatedly in binges called speed runs. Both drugs are metabolized slowly by the liver, thus causing a longer duration of action than cocaine.

12.5 Mechanisms of Action and Neurobehavioral Effects of Amphetamines

Mechanisms of amphetamine and methamphetamine action

Amphetamine and methamphetamine are indirect agonists of the catecholaminergic systems. Unlike cocaine, which only blocks catecholamine reuptake, amphetamine and methamphetamine also release catecholamines from nerve terminals. At very high doses, these compounds can even inhibit catecholamine metabolism by monoamine oxidase.

Studies on the mechanism of catecholamine release by amphetamine have particularly focused on DA. The results of this research suggest that two related drug actions are involved. One action is to cause DA molecules to be released from inside the vesicles into the cytoplasm of the nerve terminal. These DA molecules are subsequently transported outside of the terminal by a reversal of the DAT (**FIGURE 12.14A**). The result is a massive increase in synaptic DA concentrations and an associated stimulation of dopaminergic transmission. Amphetamine-mediated reversal of DAT function is facilitated by an activation of protein kinase C and calcium/calmodulin kinase II, resulting in phosphorylation of the transporter (Karam and Javitch, 2018) (**FIGURE 12.14B**). Importantly, the dopaminergic nerve terminals cannot resynthesize and store DA quickly enough to keep up with the massive release provoked by amphetamine. Hence, the acute release of DA is followed by a period of reduced DA concentrations until neuronal stores can be replenished.

Amphetamine- or methamphetamine-stimulated DA release has been demonstrated in rodents by using techniques such as in vivo microdialysis. Brain imaging studies have likewise provided evidence for DA release in humans (Slifstein et al., 2010; Schrantee et al., 2015) and non-human primates (Gallezot et al., 2014; Ota et al., 2015) following amphetamine administration either orally or by IV injection. It is important to recognize that the NE-releasing effects of amphetamines occur not only in the brain but also in the sympathetic nervous system. Consequently, these compounds exert potent sympathomimetic actions similar to those seen with cocaine.

Neurobehavioral effects of amphetamines

Like cocaine, amphetamine causes heightened alertness, increased confidence, feelings of exhilaration, reduced fatigue, and a generalized sense of well-being in human users. A number of other effects have also been

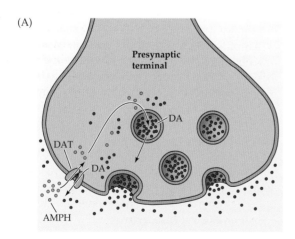

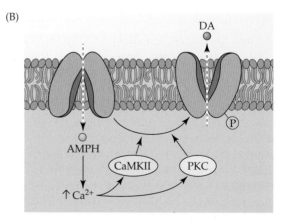

FIGURE 12.14 **Mechanisms of amphetamine-stimulated DA release** (A) Amphetamine (AMPH) molecules enter DA nerve terminals in part through uptake by the dopamine transporter (DAT). Once inside the terminal, the drug provokes DA release from the synaptic vesicles into the cytoplasm. (B) Amphetamine additionally alters DAT function so that the transporter acts in a reverse direction to release DA from the cytoplasm into the extracellular fluid. Reversal of DA transport is mediated by DAT phosphorylation by the protein kinases calcium/calmodulin kinase II (CaMKII) and protein kinase C (PKC). Acting together, the processes of vesicular DA release and DAT reversal result in a massive increase in synaptic DA levels. (B after C. S. Karam and J. A. Javitch. 2018. In *Advances in Pharmacology*. G. W. Pasternak and J. T. Coyle [Eds.], 82: 205–234. Academic Press: San Diego.)

observed, including improved performance on simple, repetitive psychomotor tasks; a delay in sleep onset; and a reduction in sleep time, particularly with respect to REM (rapid-eye-movement) sleep. Indeed, amphetamine permits sustained physical effort without rest or sleep, which accounts for its distribution to military personnel during World War II, as well as its occasional use by truck drivers and other workers who want to stay awake for extended periods. The drug can also enhance athletic performance and is therefore one of the many banned substances in athletic competitions. In rodents and other animals, amphetamine elicits behavioral activation (locomotor stimulation and stereotypy) similar to that seen with cocaine. It is also highly reinforcing, as shown by numerous studies involving drug self-administration or place conditioning.

Amphetamine and methamphetamine have therapeutic uses

As mentioned earlier, one medical use for amphetamine is in the treatment of narcolepsy; however, many patients are prescribed modafinil instead of amphetamine because of amphetamine's greater addictive potential. Amphetamine and particularly methylphenidate are even more widely used in treating children with ADHD. The pharmacology and therapeutic applications of modafinil and methylphenidate are discussed in a later section. Earlier in the chapter, Table 12.1 mentioned that cocaine has an anorexic effect (i.e., produces weight loss). Suppression of appetite and weight reduction are common to all psychostimulants, including not only cocaine but also amphetamine and methamphetamine. For many years, methamphetamine tablets (trade name Desoxyn) have been available as an anti-obesity treatment. One of the mechanisms thought to underlie the appetite-suppressing effect of psychostimulants is the induction of an interesting neuropeptide called CART (cocaine- and amphetamine-regulated transcript) (Lau and Herzog, 2014). Needless to say, because of methamphetamine's high addictive potential, this treatment is now only rarely used to treat obese patients who have failed to respond to more conventional therapeutic approaches.

Narcolepsy typically involves recurring and irresistible attacks of sleepiness during the daytime hours, often along with other symptoms such as cataplexy (sudden and transient loss of muscle tone that can be severe enough to cause bodily collapse, often brought about by strong emotional stimuli), hypnagogic hallucinations (vivid sensations that occur at the onset of sleep, upon awakening, or sometimes during a cataplectic attack), and sleep paralysis (muscle paralysis that persists after waking from a REM sleep episode). Narcolepsy is caused by loss (perhaps autoimmune related) of hypothalamic neurons that secrete the neuropeptide hypocretin (also called orexin). Refer back to Box 3.1 for more information on this disorder.

High doses or chronic use of amphetamines can cause a variety of adverse effects

Illicit use of amphetamines, especially methamphetamine, is a growing problem worldwide. The highest rates of use are found in the United States, Mexico, Japan, China, and areas of South Asia and the Middle East (Chomchai and Chomchai, 2015). According to the 2020 World Drug Report of the United Nations Office on Drugs and Crime, global seizures of amphetamine-type stimulants rose fourfold between 2009 and 2018 (United Nations Office on Drugs and Crime, 2020). Most of this rise is due to increased seizure of methamphetamine.

Because recreational use of methamphetamine in the United States is currently greater than that of amphetamine, this section of the chapter will focus primarily on the adverse behavioral, physiological, and neurobiological effects of chronic methamphetamine use. Nevertheless, it is important to note that at least some of these same effects can occur in cases of heavy amphetamine rather than methamphetamine use.

DEPENDENCE, WITHDRAWAL, AND COGNITIVE FUNCTION   Chronic methamphetamine use commonly leads to dependence on the drug and a withdrawal syndrome when the individual undergoes abstinence (Cruickshank and Dyer, 2009). Principal symptoms of methamphetamine withdrawal include depressed mood, increased anxiety, sleep disturbances, cognitive deficits, and craving for the drug. Users may also experience agitated behavior, reduced energy, and increased appetite. Interestingly, a survey of methamphetamine-dependent individuals found that the strongest reason both for continued methamphetamine use and for relapse was the drug's positive reinforcing effects (Newton et al., 2009). This result contrasts with the model of addiction presented in Chapter 9 in which negative reinforcement (including alleviation of drug-induced withdrawal) is hypothesized to be increasingly important in the trajectory to drug dependence. The methamphetamine abstinence syndrome is less severe than the syndromes associated with opioid or alcohol dependence, which may account for the reduced role of negative reinforcement in methamphetamine users.

Compared to healthy controls, individuals with methamphetamine use disorder show impairments in multiple cognitive domains. The strongest differences have been found in impulse control, verbal learning, working memory, and social cognition (Potvin et al., 2018). Because these findings are based on cross-sectional studies, they cannot readily distinguish between cognitive differences that preceded the onset of drug use and differences *caused* by the drug. Some longitudinal studies have investigated whether cognitive deficits in methamphetamine users are reversible after prolonged abstinence (Proebstl et al., 2018). The results of this research are inconclusive, possibly due to differences in degree of initial impairment as well as length of abstinence.

Investigators have identified several important sex differences in methamphetamine use and the consequences of such use. First, women are more likely than men to become dependent on the drug (Dluzen and Liu, 2008). Second, certain female populations are particularly vulnerable to developing methamphetamine dependence, including sex workers, homeless women, and women with comorbid psychiatric disorders (Kittirattanapaiboon et al., 2017). Third, methamphetamine use in women has been linked with risky sexual practices, contracting HIV/AIDS, and antisocial and violent behaviors (Venios and Kelly, 2010). Lastly, a structural MRI study focusing on sex differences among people diagnosed with stimulant dependence (over 80% of whom were dependent on methamphetamine or other amphetamines) found widespread reductions in gray matter volume in the women that were not observed in the men (Regner et al., 2015). It is unclear whether this difference stems from the use of more stimulants in the women or a greater vulnerability to drug-induced gray matter loss in women.

PSYCHOTIC REACTIONS   Beginning in the 1930s and continuing over the next few decades, cases were reported of amphetamine (e.g., Benzedrine) overuse resulting in a psychotic reaction consisting of visual and/or auditory hallucinations, behavioral disorganization, and the development of a paranoid state with delusions of persecution (reviewed by McKetin, 2018). Some users experienced the same hallucination of a parasitic skin infestation described earlier for cocaine. These reactions to amphetamine usually did not occur upon first exposure to the drug, but only after a pattern of high-dose use had developed.

As methamphetamine use has increased, the incidence of psychotic reactions to this substance has also grown. Risk factors for the development of methamphetamine-induced psychosis include a long history of use, use of high doses, becoming dependent on the drug, and (not surprisingly) having a preexisting history of psychotic symptoms (Darke et al., 2008). Roughly 30% to 40% of individuals who develop methamphetamine use disorder experience a psychotic reaction at least once (Chiang et al., 2018). Indeed, psychotic symptoms are often present in methamphetamine users who present at hospital emergency departments (Jones et al., 2018). Of particular concern is that continued methamphetamine use can cause a transition to a psychotic state that persists long after abstinence from the drug and has a symptomatology that is difficult to distinguish from paranoid schizophrenia (Wearne and Cornish, 2018). Current evidence suggests that some individuals may have an underlying schizophrenic disorder that is unmasked by methamphetamine use, whereas in other cases the psychosis is directly caused

by drug exposure. Regardless of which situation pertains, methamphetamine users who present with psychotic symptoms are typically administered the same kinds of antipsychotic medications that are given to patients with schizophrenia.

NEUROTOXICITY   There is a special danger to methamphetamine users that is due to its neurotoxic properties. Investigators have known for many years that administration of multiple doses of methamphetamine to animals causes long-lasting reductions in the levels of DA, tyrosine hydroxylase (the key enzyme in DA synthesis), and DAT in the dorsal striatum (Moratalla et al., 2017). These changes are indicative of damage to DA axons and terminals, which has been confirmed by histological experiments showing the presence of degenerating fibers. Additional studies have demonstrated significant death of dopaminergic neurons in the substantia nigra, the source of the nigrostriatal DA system. For reasons that aren't completely understood, the mesolimbic DA system is relatively spared in methamphetamine-treated animals. This difference can be seen in **FIGURE 12.15**, which presents tissue sections from a methamphetamine-treated mouse compared with a saline vehicle–treated mouse in which the sections were stained for tyrosine hydroxylase immunoreactivity. Note the striking reduction in staining in the dorsal striatum (caudate–putamen, or CPu) compared with the more ventral NAcc subregions (AcbC and AcbSh) and nearby areas. A number of factors contribute to methamphetamine-induced neurotoxicity. Binge-treated animals experience severe hyperthermia, and blocking this effect has a substantial ameliorative effect on the drug's toxic effects. Activation of both D_1 and D_2 receptors also appears to play an important role. At a molecular level, damage to the dopaminergic system has been linked to multiple processes, including oxidative stress (cellular stress due to increased production of oxygen-containing free radicals), excitotoxicity, neuroinflammation, and mitochondrial dysfunction (Moratalla et al., 2017; Yang et al., 2018).

These experimental animal studies raise a critical health question of whether repeated methamphetamine exposure causes damage to the dopaminergic system in humans. There is ample evidence that this system is, at the very least, highly dysfunctional in chronic methamphetamine users. Brain imaging studies combined with one biochemical study of post-mortem brain tissues have shown reduced striatal DA levels, reduced DAT binding, and reduced binding to D_2/D_3 receptors in the drug users compared with nonusers (Volkow et al., 2015; Kish et al., 2017). Yet, the available evidence is not consistent with loss of substantia nigra dopaminergic neurons, suggesting that the dopaminergic dysfunction may be a neurochemical response to the recurring drug

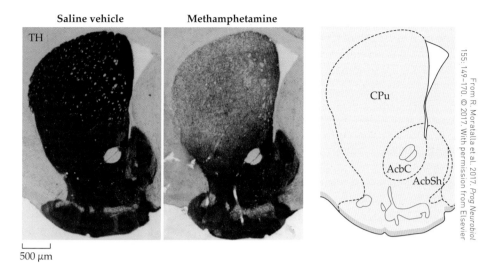

Saline vehicle   Methamphetamine

500 μm

From R. Moratalla et al. 2017. *Prog Neurobiol* 155: 149–170. © 2017. With permission from Elsevier

FIGURE 12.15 **Methamphetamine-induced loss of tyrosine hydroxylase immunoreactivity in the nigrostriatal compared with the mesolimbic DA pathways in mice** Female mice were given IP injections of either 4 mg/kg methamphetamine or saline vehicle, three times on a single day, with a 3-hour interdose interval. The animals were killed 7 days later, and coronal brain sections through the caudate–putamen (CPu) and nucleus accumbens core and shell (AcbC and AcbSh) were stained using an antibody against tyrosine hydroxylase (TH) as a marker of dopaminergic fibers and nerve terminals. The two photomicrographs on the left show that methamphetamine-induced DA neurotoxicity was more pronounced in the nigrostriatal pathway (CPu) than in the mesolimbic pathway (AcbC and AcbSh). The figure on the right is a plate from a mouse brain atlas used to identify the key anatomical areas shown in the photomicrographs.

insult rather than physical damage to the system. This may seem to be relatively good news to hard-core methamphetamine users; however, epidemiological studies show an elevated risk for developing Parkinson's disease and/or an earlier disease onset in the methamphetamine-using population (Kish et al., 2017; Lappin et al., 2018). Factors such as amount and duration of methamphetamine use, age at cessation of use, and individual vulnerability factors may determine the user's risk of developing Parkinson's disease.

GENERAL PHYSICAL HEALTH In addition to the neurotoxic and cognitive effects mentioned above, heavy methamphetamine use has been associated with a variety of adverse health outcomes. Among these are cardiovascular problems such as elevated heart and blood pressure, atherosclerosis, myocardial infarction, and increased incidence of stroke (Lappin et al., 2017; Schwarzbach et al., 2020). Some authors have even argued for the existence of a novel form of heart disease associated with heavy amphetamine/methamphetamine use that has been termed "amphetamine type stimulants associated cardiomyopathy" (Giv, 2017). Other health problems related to methamphetamine use include gastrointestinal distress, increased susceptibility to infection, male sexual dysfunction, and oral diseases such as "meth mouth" (Chou et al., 2015; De-Carolis et al., 2015; Prakash et al., 2017). Considering the severity of some of these health outcomes, it is not surprising that chronic methamphetamine users have an increased mortality rate (Panenka et al., 2013). There is also anecdotal evidence

for premature aging among chronic methamphetamine users. This can be seen from a website called Faces of Meth (https://facesofmeth.us), which posts photos of the same people taken at different times during the course of their drug use. The Faces of Meth website was initially developed by the Sheriff's Office of Multnomah County in Oregon, which posted "mug shots" of drug offenders from early and later arrests. Two photos from the original website are shown in **FIGURE 12.16**, which illustrates the physical toll inflicted on heavy methamphetamine users over the course of just a few years. It is hoped that the message of these pictures will deter at least some people from becoming trapped in the scourge of methamphetamine use.

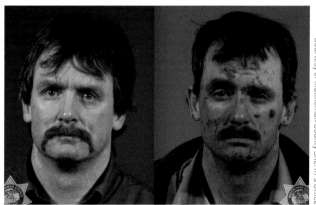

Courtesy of Multnomah County Sheriff's Office

FIGURE 12.16 An example of the physical deterioration produced by chronic methamphetamine use

SECTION SUMMARY

- Amphetamine and methamphetamine are indirect catecholamine agonists. They stimulate release of DA and NE from nerve terminals and block the reuptake of these neurotransmitters. At high doses, there is also an inhibition of the catecholamine-degrading enzyme monoamine oxidase.

- Amphetamine-stimulated DA release is mediated by a reversal of DAT function. This release may be followed by a period of DA depletion because the dopaminergic nerve terminals cannot resynthesize the transmitter quickly enough.

- Amphetamine and methamphetamine also have sympathomimetic effects due to their effects on NE in the sympathetic nervous system.

- Acute administration of amphetamine to humans leads to a well-known constellation of behavioral reactions, including increased arousal, reduced fatigue, and feelings of exhilaration. Sleep is delayed, and performance of simple, repetitive tasks is improved.

- Amphetamine is one of the medications prescribed for children with ADHD and can also be used to alleviate the daytime sleepiness that occurs in patients with narcolepsy.

- Heavy use of amphetamine or particularly methamphetamine can result in the development of dependence and in deficits in cognitive function. Women are more likely than men to develop methamphetamine dependence and are at greater risk for reductions in gray matter volume.

- High-dose amphetamine or methamphetamine users are additionally at risk for psychotic reactions that closely resemble paranoid schizophrenia, DA neurotoxicity, early development of Parkinson's disease, and numerous adverse health consequences.

12.6 Methylphenidate and Modafinil

Methylphenidate

Methylphenidate (trade name **Ritalin**) has been mentioned a number of times previously in this chapter. Its chemical structure is distinct from that of either cocaine or amphetamine-type drugs (**FIGURE 12.17**). Methylphenidate was first synthesized in 1944 by the chemist Leandro Panizzon of the Ciba-Geigy pharmaceutical company. To assess the drug's effects, Panizzon offered it to his wife, Marguerite, an avid tennis player. Marguerite reported that methylphenidate did, indeed, improve her tennis game, and to acknowledge her participation in the testing of this compound, the company named the drug "Ritalin" based on her nickname, Rita (Lange et al., 2010; Wenthur, 2016). By the late 1950s and early 1960s, Ritalin was being marketed clinically for several disorders, including "hyperkinetic syndrome" (now expanded and reconceptualized as

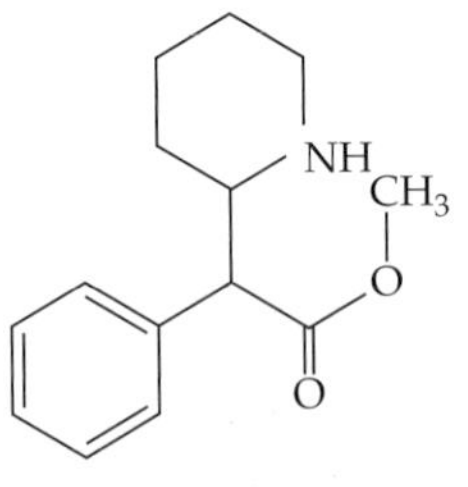

FIGURE 12.17 Chemical structure of methylphenidate

ADHD), narcolepsy, depression, and extreme sedation/coma due to overdose with drugs such as barbiturates (Challman and Lipsky, 2000; CESAR, 2013). As discussed below, by far the major continued medical use of methylphenidate is in the treatment of ADHD.

The neurochemical actions of methylphenidate are well established. Once inside the brain, the drug binds to DAT on the membrane of dopaminergic neurons and to the norepinephrine transporter (NET) on the membrane of the noradrenergic cells. The effect of this binding is to block reuptake of both DA and NE in their respective target areas, thereby elevating extracellular levels of both transmitters and stimulating overall catecholaminergic neurotransmission (Wenthur, 2016). Initial studies of methylphenidate binding to catecholamine transporters were performed using experimental animals; however, in vivo occupancy of both DAT and NET has been demonstrated in the human brain using PET imaging. This research has revealed that when administered orally at a therapeutic dose, methylphenidate blocks 60% to 70% of DATs in the striatum and 70% to 80% of NETs in the frontal cortex (Zimmer, 2017).

Taken orally, methylphenidate has the subjective and behavioral profile of a typical psychostimulant. Laboratory studies of healthy, non-ADHD participants found dose-dependent increases in subjective arousal and alertness, perceived ability to concentrate, positive mood/drug liking, and (at higher doses) anxiety (Chait, 1994; Kollins et al., 2009). Two recent reviews examined the results of studies that specifically focused on whether methylphenidate is an effective cognitive enhancer in healthy participants (Kapur, 2020; Roberts et al., 2020). Positive effects were found on several cognitive domains, notably free recall, sustained attention, and inhibitory control. However, only small to medium effect sizes were observed, which raised questions about the extent to which methylphenidate is likely to influence cognitive functioning under real-world conditions. Interestingly, this question was addressed in a randomized, double-blind, placebo-controlled study on the ability of methylphenidate or modafinil to improve competitive performance by highly skilled chess players (Franke et al., 2017). Both compounds enhanced chess performance compared with placebo treatment. A subsequent commentary in the *Journal of the American Medical Association* cited evidence for use of such cognitive enhancers by several types of professionals, including physicians, business executives, and academicians (Lyon, 2017).

Probably the most widespread diversion of prescription stimulants for nonmedical use is by young people. One longitudinal survey of students enrolled at a large public university in the mid-Atlantic region found that over 60% of respondents had been offered a prescription stimulant at least once over a 4-year period (Garnier-Dykstra et al., 2012). Over 30% had used a prescription stimulant for nonmedical purposes. A more recent study surveyed students enrolled in three different northeastern pharmacy schools about their nonmedical use of prescription stimulants during their time as undergraduates (Yuan et al., 2019). The two main reasons offered were overall cognitive enhancement and promoting wakefulness (**FIGURE 12.18**). Although most of the available data have been obtained from college students, prescription stimulant use is not restricted to this group. A large national survey of high school seniors found that almost 10% reported having used prescription stimulants for nonmedical purposes at least once (McCabe and West, 2013). College (and presumably high school) students who misuse prescription stimulants commonly believe that these drugs can improve their academic performance (Arria et al., 2018). However, the existing data indicate that this belief is fallacious. For example, Arria and colleagues (2017) found no significant influence of nonmedical prescription stimulant use on grade point average (GPA). Another study that sampled students enrolled at six different public universities focused on individuals who had relatively poor academic performance related to low executive functioning. Even within this group, which might be expected to benefit most from stimulant use, no beneficial effect on GPA was observed (Munro et al., 2017). These findings do not support a conclusion that prescription stimulants like methylphenidate can help students improve their academic performance.

Methylphenidate has clear potential for misuse due to its pharmacological profile of elevating brain dopaminergic transmission; however, the degree of risk depends greatly on the route of administration. There is little risk of this happening when the drug is taken orally at recommended doses. On the other hand, methylphenidate tablets that are formulated for immediate release can be crushed and taken either by intranasal insufflation (i.e., "snorting") or by IV injection. As we have seen previously for other compounds, these routes of administration produce much more rapid drug entry into the brain (especially IV injection), thereby causing a methylphenidate "high" similar to that produced by cocaine or amphetamine (Kollins et al., 2001; Bogle and Smith, 2009). When taken repeatedly by these methods, methylphenidate use can lead to dependence, just like other psychostimulants. Nevertheless, the drug's liability for misuse and addiction appears to be lower than that of cocaine, amphetamine, or methamphetamine.

Finally, it is important to discuss the therapeutic applications of methylphenidate. The main features of ADHD and its treatment by methylphenidate and amphetamine are discussed in **BOX 12.2**. We also mentioned that methylphenidate is sometimes prescribed for patients with the sleep disorder narcolepsy; however, narcolepsy is more commonly treated with a different stimulant, modafinil, which is discussed in the next part of the chapter. Yet another possible therapeutic application of methylphenidate is to accelerate emergence from general anesthesia. Animal studies have demonstrated that emergence from anesthesia occurs more quickly after IV administration of methylphenidate (Solt et al., 2011; Chemali et al., 2012). Subsequent research found that this effect depends on an arousal-promoting effect of DA, since similar results were obtained by selective optogenetic activation of VTA dopaminergic neurons (N. E. Taylor et al., 2016) or by administration of a D_1 receptor agonist (N. E. Taylor et al., 2013). At the time of this writing, patients are being tested to determine whether IV methylphenidate can help them recover more rapidly from propofol sedation.

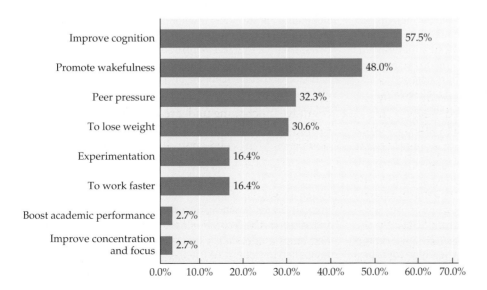

FIGURE 12.18 Motivations reported by students for their nonmedical use of prescription stimulants The participants were students enrolled in three different schools of pharmacy in the northeastern United States who had used prescription stimulant drugs for nonmedical purposes during their undergraduate careers. The graph illustrates the percentage of students endorsing a particular reason for such use. The percentages add up to more than 100% since each participant was permitted to offer more than one reason. (After B. W. Yuan et al. 2019. *J Am Coll Clin Pharm* 2: 525–530. © 2019 The Authors.)

BOX 12.2 ■ CLINICAL APPLICATIONS

Psychostimulants and ADHD

The most important clinical use for psychostimulants is in the treatment of a developmental disorder known as attention-deficit/hyperactivity disorder (ADHD). Children with ADHD exhibit extreme degrees of inattentiveness, impulsivity, and hyperkinesis (excessive motor activity). They have a very short attention span and impulsively turn their attention to almost anything in the environment. The *DSM-5* identifies three different subtypes of ADHD: a predominantly inattentive subtype, a predominantly hyperactive–impulsive subtype, and a combined subtype. In severe cases of the hyperactive–impulsive or combined subtype, there may be destructiveness, stealing, lying, fire setting, and sexual "acting out." The child is frequently unruly in the classroom and disruptive of family interactions within the home.

ADHD occurs in roughly 5% to 7% of school-age children around the world (Leung and Hon, 2016). The disorder is more prevalent in males than in females, but with differences in manifestation. Boys are more likely to exhibit hyperactivity and impulsivity, whereas girls are more likely to exhibit inattention. Although ADHD most often resolves with age, approximately 40% of children with this disorder will still be affected in adulthood. In general, adults with ADHD show signs of distractibility, impulsivity, restlessness, hyperemotionality, and problems both at work and in interpersonal relationships. Moreover, such individuals are at heightened risk for developing conduct disorder, antisocial personality disorder, and/or substance use problems.

The relevance of psychostimulants for the treatment of ADHD is that low doses of these drugs benefit about 75% to 80% of affected children. Most strikingly, psychostimulant administration has a seemingly paradoxical calming effect in hyperactive children. This phenomenon was first reported by Bradley in 1937 (Lange et al., 2010) and has since been observed in many other studies. A number of stimulant medications are now available for the treatment of ADHD that differ not only in the active ingredient but also in the length of action (i.e., short acting, intermediate acting, or long acting). The active ingredient in most of these medications is D-amphetamine (e.g., Dexedrine), mixed amphetamine salts (e.g., Adderall), lisdexamfetamine (Vyvanse, which is a prodrug for D-amphetamine), or methylphenidate (Ritalin and other trade names) (Briars and Todd, 2016; Wenthur, 2016). The most important benefit of intermediate- and long-acting preparations is that a single dose given in the early morning (or the night before, as in the case of the recently approved methylphenidate formulation Jornay PM) will continue to benefit the child throughout the day without the need for additional dosing. However, a secondary benefit is that the delayed-release aspect of intermediate- and long-acting ADHD drugs makes them unsuitable for snorting or IV injection of crushed tablets. A methylphenidate-containing skin patch (Daytrana) serves the same function as the long-acting oral medications and is particularly useful for children who find it difficult or may be unwilling to swallow pills.

A major advance in ADHD treatment occurred in 2002 with the introduction of atomoxetine (Strattera), the first nonstimulant medication for ADHD. Atomoxetine is a selective norepinephrine transporter inhibitor that is thought to work, at least in part, by enhancing the action of NE on α_{2A}-adrenergic receptors in the PFC (see below). Extended-release formulations of the α_{2A}-receptor agonists clonidine (Kapvay) and guanfacine (Intuniv) have also been approved for the treatment of ADHD. These latter drugs may be used alone or in combination with a stimulant to achieve maximum reduction in symptomatology. It is important to note that although many children are treated with drugs alone, concomitant psychotherapy and parental counseling are often required for best results. Moreover, there is evidence supporting the efficacy of cognitive behavioral therapy, either with or without medication, in treating adults with ADHD (Knouse and Safren, 2010).

Certain safety concerns have been raised regarding the long-term use of stimulants to treat ADHD. One of the first concerns is the possibility that these compounds may result in reduced growth. A recent meta-analysis examining the effects of long-term methylphenidate exposure on weight and height found statistically significant reductions in both parameters (Carucci et al., 2021). However, the effect sizes were small and the growth deficits generally lessened with age. Although long-term methylphenidate use appears to have minimal adverse effects on growth, the authors caution that treated children's growth rate should be monitored regularly, particularly when dosing is begun during the preschool years. Second, because of their sympathomimetic effects, stimulants cause small but measurable increases in heart rate and blood pressure. These compounds should, therefore, be avoided by any children or adults who have preexisting cardiovascular disease or are at increased risk of developing cardiovascular problems. Similarly, there is some concern (although not without controversy) that stimulants may exacerbate the occurrence of tics in patients with tic disorders. Clinicians concerned about this possibility have the option of prescribing the nonstimulant noradrenergic drugs (e.g., atomoxetine) for those patients. Third, because stimulants are being administered during periods that are important for brain development (i.e., childhood and adolescence), it is possible that such development is adversely influenced by these drugs. This concern is based largely on animal studies, since the few clinical studies performed to date do not support the notion that stimulant treatment is somehow "neurotoxic" (Loureiro-Vieira et al., 2017). Nevertheless, subtle adverse effects on brain development cannot be ruled out, given that truly long-term clinical studies are still lacking. Finally, as discussed in the text, there exists the potential for psychostimulants to be misused. Parents of medicated ADHD children need to be vigilant for signs of either excessive use by the child or distribution of the medication to siblings or friends for recreational use (Clemow, 2017).

BOX 12.2 ■ CLINICAL APPLICATIONS (continued)

Understanding the symptomatology of ADHD and the mechanisms by which psychostimulants and noradrenergic agents can reduce this symptomatology requires a brief review of the neurobiology of ADHD. A large number of neuroimaging studies have identified multiple neural circuits that appear to be dysfunctional in patients with ADHD. Among these are (1) frontoparietal intracortical circuits important for attention and orienting responses; (2) dorsal frontostriatal circuits encompassing the dorsolateral PFC, cingulate cortex, dorsal striatum, and thalamus, which play a key role in inhibitory control; and (3) mesocorticolimbic circuits containing the orbitofrontal cortex, ventral striatum (including NAcc), and anterior hippocampus, which help mediate reward anticipation and motivation (Gallo and Posner, 2016; Faraone, 2018). Given that all of these areas receive dopaminergic and/or noradrenergic innervation, the drugs used to treat ADHD undoubtedly have manifold effects across these circuits. Nevertheless, many researchers have focused on the PFC as potentially playing a critical role in ADHD pharmacotherapy. The pyramidal (i.e., output) neurons of the PFC are innervated by both the noradrenergic and dopaminergic systems. The key receptors involved are α_{2A} in the case of NE and D_1 in the case of DA. Experimental animal studies have suggested that NE activation of α_{2A} receptors enhances the strength of relevant sensory input to the PFC (i.e., increases the "signal"), whereas DA activation of D_1 receptors weakens irrelevant sensory input (i.e., decreases the "noise") (Berridge and Arnsten, 2015). These effects work together to increase the signal-to-noise ratio of sensory input to the PFC, thus helping the individual attend to the appropriate stimuli. Bringing this information to bear on the issue of ADHD, Arnsten and colleagues have argued that (1) PFC functioning is an inverted U-shaped function of the activity of both catecholaminergic systems, (2) individuals with ADHD may have deficient catecholaminergic activity within the PFC, and (3) a critical mode of action of compounds used to treat ADHD is to restore optimal catecholaminergic activity within this brain area (Berridge and Arnsten, 2013; 2015) (**FIGURE**). This hypothesis accounts for the therapeutic efficacy of catecholamine-releasing agents like amphetamine as well as dual DA and NE uptake inhibitors such as methylphenidate. Furthermore, α_{2A} adrenoceptor agonists like guanfacine enhance cognitive function by

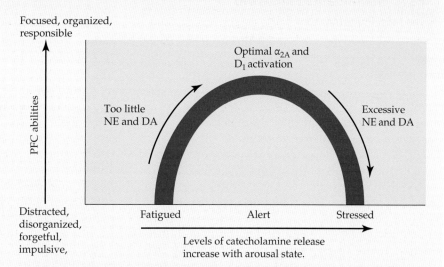

Hypothesized role of prefrontal cortical α_{2A} and D_1 receptors in cognitive performance and the treatment of ADHD Activation of α_{2A} and D_1 receptors in the PFC is thought to depend on the organism's state of arousal. A moderate level of arousal leads to intermediate levels of receptor activation that are optimal for PFC functioning, whereas either too little or too much activation has detrimental effects on PFC functioning and cognitive performance. (After A. F. T. Arnsten. 2009. *CNS Drugs* 23 (Suppl. 1): 33–41; and C. Berridge et al. 2012. In *Translational Neuroscience: Applications in Psychiatry, Neurology and Neurodevelopmental Disorders*, J. E. Barrett et al. [Eds], pp. 303–320. Cambridge University Press: Cambridge, UK.)

strengthening excitatory glutamatergic inputs to the PFC pyramidal neurons, thereby increasing the firing of those cells (Arnsten, 2020). Atomoxetine has a similar effect because blocking NE reuptake increases activation of the postsynaptic α_{2A} receptors. But there is an additional mechanism that may contribute to this compound's therapeutic benefit in patients with ADHD. Unlike the dopaminergic fibers innervating the striatum, those innervating the PFC express very low levels of DAT (Sesack, 2014). In contrast, the noradrenergic fibers innervating the PFC express ample levels of NET. Because DA is a very effective substrate for NET, it turns out that NET, not DAT, is the major source of DA uptake and clearance in the PFC. Thus, a selective NE uptake inhibitor like atomoxetine acts like methylphenidate in the PFC by increasing extracellular levels of *both* NE and DA in this brain area.

In summary, ADHD is characterized by several kinds of deficits in cognition and executive function, particularly an inability to concentrate, lack of impulse control, and hyperkinesis. These deficits are thought to be related to dysfunction in several complex neural circuits, especially circuits that include the PFC. Most patients with ADHD respond positively to psychostimulants (amphetamine and methylphenidate formulations) or to other agents that enhance catecholaminergic activity (atomoxetine, guanfacine, and clonidine). The therapeutic efficacy of these compounds is hypothesized to rely on activation of α_{2A} and D_1 receptors in the PFC, thereby alleviating a state of suboptimal catecholaminergic activity in this brain area.

Modafinil

Modafinil (trade name **Provigil**) is an unusual stimulant, with respect to both its history and its mechanism of action. Like many of the compounds that were first developed to treat depression, anxiety, or psychotic disorders, modafinil was discovered serendipitously in the course of pharmaceutical development for other purposes (Rambert et al., 2006). In the 1970s, a small French pharmaceutical company named Laboratoire Louis Lafon was searching for novel nonsteroidal anti-inflammatory drugs. While screening a group of newly synthesized test compounds, one of the company's experimenters noticed that mice treated with one of these compounds became hyperactive. This compound, which was given the name adrafinil, not only caused increased locomotor activity but also antagonized barbiturate-induced sedation. Interestingly, despite its stimulant-like characteristics in some behavioral and physiological tests, adrafinil had a unique pharmacological profile that differed substantially from amphetamine (a classic psychostimulant) in many other such tests. The lead compound adrafinil was subsequently modified chemically to produce modafinil, which was more potent and longer acting than the parent drug.

The structure of modafinil is shown in **FIGURE 12.19**. Some similarity can be seen to the structure of methylphenidate, but with several key differences, including a change in one of the two rings, a sulfur atom in the side chain, and a terminal amino group. The mechanisms underlying modafinil's stimulant activity seem to be more complex than the mechanisms underlying the effects of cocaine, amphetamine, or methylphenidate. In vitro studies have shown that modafinil binds to DAT with relatively low affinity and acts as a weak DA uptake inhibitor (Loland et al., 2012). Brain imaging studies have further confirmed modafinil occupancy of DAT in the human brain and an ability of the drug to elevate extracellular DA (Volkow et al., 2009). Consistent with those findings, administration of modafinil to mice led to a dose-dependent increase in DA overflow in the NAcc (Mereu et al., 2017). This effect may have been caused not only by inhibition of DA reuptake but also by increased phasic DA release in the striatum (Bobak et al., 2016). Moreover, modafinil's stimulant properties are blocked in mice genetically engineered to lack DAT and in wild-type mice pretreated with either a D_1 or D_2 receptor antagonist (reviewed in Wisor, 2013), confirming the importance of DA for modafinil action. Yet, even though DAT may be one of the direct molecular targets of modafinil, other effects of this compound are at least as important. Specifically, modafinil administration stimulates release of NE and orexin (Salerno et al., 2019), both of which are integral components of the brain's arousal system (see Chapters 3 and 4), and it additionally inhibits GABA release (Ishizuka et al., 2012). The combined effects on orexin and GABA lead to increased release of histamine, another component of the waking/arousal neural circuitry (Chapter 3). Together, these actions of modafinil are hypothesized to cause increased wakefulness as well as enhanced alertness and vigilance.

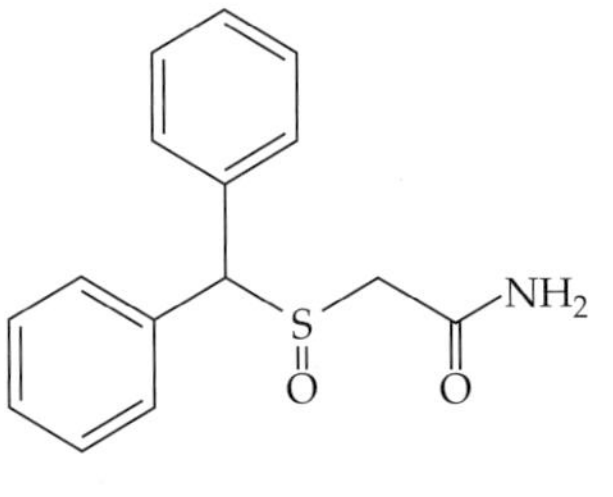

Because of its ability to increase wakefulness, modafinil is currently approved by the FDA for the treatment of excessive daytime sleepiness in patients with narcolepsy (see Box 3.1), people with obstructive sleep apnea,* and individuals with disordered sleep due to shift work (Murillo-Rodríguez et al., 2018). In off-label use, modafinil has also been reported to reduce sleepiness and/or fatigue in cancer patients, people with depression, and operating military personnel. Like other psychostimulants, modafinil can also enhance cognitive function; however, in individuals who are not sleep deprived the effects are generally small (Kredlow et al., 2019; Roberts et al., 2020). Regardless of these experimental findings, some students perceive a benefit to using modafinil (without a prescription) for the same purposes as methylphenidate and amphetamine (Teodorini et al., 2020).

Because of its dopaminergic activity, concerns have been raised about the possibility of modafinil addiction (Murillo-Rodríguez et al., 2018). Some animal studies indicate rewarding/reinforcing effects of modafinil (e.g., Gold and Balster, 1996; Wuo-Silva et al., 2011), but others do not (Deroche-Gamonet et al., 2002). Importantly, a recent study in healthy human participants found no positive subjective effects of oral modafinil despite administering an even higher dose than is used clinically (Dolder et al., 2018). These findings along with the fact that reports of modafinil misuse are infrequent suggest that unlike most other psychostimulants, modafinil has low addictive potential. For this reason, some researchers have suggested that modafinil or related compounds could be developed as medications for psychostimulant use disorders (Tanda et al., 2021).

FIGURE 12.19 Chemical structure of modafinil

---

*Obstructive sleep apnea is a condition in which the airway closes partially or fully upon going to sleep. This causes the person to wake up, often without realizing it. In severe cases, several hundred brief awakenings may occur in the course of the night, thereby leading to sleep deprivation and extreme sleepiness during the daytime hours.

SECTION SUMMARY

- Methylphenidate is a prescription psychostimulant that activates catecholamine transmission by blocking DAT and NET, thereby increasing extracellular levels of DA and NE.

- Methylphenidate has typical psychostimulant subjective and behavioral effects, including increased arousal and alertness, perceived ability to concentrate, elevated mood, and (at higher doses) anxiety. Low to medium doses of methylphenidate exert a positive influence on various cognitive functions such as working memory, cognitive processing speed, verbal learning and memory, and vigilance and attention.

- Methylphenidate is frequently diverted for nonprescription use, particularly by students. Although users feel more alert and less fatigued, current evidence does not indicate that use of this drug enhances academic performance.

- Recreational use of methylphenidate can lead to misuse and dependence, particularly when the drug is taken by snorting or by IV injection.

- The primary clinical application of methylphenidate is for the treatment of ADHD, a disorder characterized by extreme inattentiveness, impulsivity, and hyperkinesis. Other pharmacological treatments for ADHD include various amphetamine formulations, the NE reuptake inhibitor atomoxetine, and two different α_{2A}-receptor agonists.

- Individuals with ADHD are thought to have deficient catecholaminergic activity in multiple neural circuits that subserve cognitive functioning. One of the principal sites of action of ADHD medications may be the PFC, which is a key brain area participating in several of these circuits. In this brain area, DA is taken up primarily by NET instead of DAT, which helps explain why catecholamine releasing agents (i.e., amphetamines), catecholamine reuptake inhibitors (methylphenidate), and a selective NE reuptake inhibitor (atomoxetine) can all reduce ADHD symptomatology.

- Modafinil is an unusual psychostimulant that is often prescribed to treat daytime sleepiness associated with the sleep disorder narcolepsy, obstructive sleep apnea, and shift work.

- Modafinil is a weak DA reuptake inhibitor, which helps account for its stimulant properties. However, there are several downstream effects of the drug that are also thought to be important, including increased release of NE, orexin, and histamine, and inhibition of GABA release.

12.7 Synthetic Cathinones

At the beginning of the section on amphetamines, we briefly mentioned and showed the structure of cathinone, a naturally occurring psychostimulant found in the khat plant of eastern Africa and Arabia. Over the past 15 years or so, there has been a surge in Europe, the United States, and Asia in availability and recreational use of synthetic cathinone derivatives. Well over 100 distinct synthetic cathinones have been identified (Schifano et al., 2019); however, a much smaller number of these compounds have been significantly investigated. Here we will focus on the four drugs that have received the most attention in the popular media and have been studied most extensively by researchers: **mephedrone** (4-methylmethcathinone), **methylone** (3,4-methylenedioxy-*N*-methylcathinone), **MDPV** (3,4-methylenedioxypyrovalerone), and **α-PVP** (α-pyrrolidinovalerophenone) (**FIGURE 12.20**). Mephedrone and methylone were the first synthetic cathinones to be sold widely for recreational use (Valente et al., 2014; Karila et al., 2015). Mephedrone came to the attention of European authorities in 2007, after which its dissemination and use grew rapidly. Common street names for mephedrone include "meow meow," "M-Cat," "Meph," "bounce," and "bubbles." Mephedrone was also sold in Israel under the name "Neodove." Methylone originated in the mid-2000s in the Netherlands and Japan under the name "Explosion." Other methylone-containing products include "Neocor" and "Room Odorizer." MDPV began to appear in 2009 under various product names

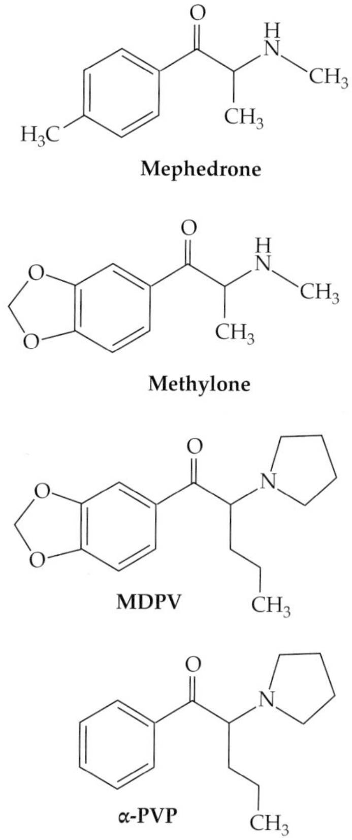

FIGURE 12.20 Chemical structures of some recreationally used synthetic cathinones

such as "Vanilla Sky," "Ivory Wave," and "Energy-1." Most recently, use of α-PVP has surged in Europe and the United States, particularly in southern Florida (Katselou et al., 2016). Common street names for this compound are "flakka" (derived from "la flaca," a slang Spanish term meaning "beautiful woman" [Kolesnikova et al., 2019]) and "gravel" (because α-PVP crystals resemble aquarium gravel) (**FIGURE 12.21**).

Besides the brand or street names associated with individual synthetic cathinones, the general terms "bath salts," "plant food," "pond water cleaner," and "legal highs" have been used to sell this group of compounds in head shops and over the internet. As an additional protective measure, websites typically state that the materials for sale are "not for human consumption." Of course, neither buyers nor government authorities are fooled by these tactics. Interestingly, when synthetic cathinones first began to be taken recreationally, they *were* legal. But this changed rather quickly once the addiction liability of these compounds was recognized. Accordingly, mephedrone and related compounds were banned by the U.S. Drug Enforcement Administration (DEA) in 2011, and they were banned even earlier by Britain, where the "legal high" problem has been particularly severe. In the remainder of this section, we will discuss the pharmacology and toxicology of the four major synthetic cathinones, while keeping in mind that new compounds continue to be synthesized in an ongoing race between underground chemists and the DEA.

Synthetic cathinones are taken by several routes of administration, the most common of which are nasal insufflation (snorting) and oral ingestion. Snorting within the synthetic cathinone user community is often done by "keying," which involves using a key that has been dipped into the powdered drug. Oral ingestion may involve consuming capsules of the drug or "bombing" (wrapping drug powder or crystals inside a

cigarette wrapper and then swallowing the wrapper). These drugs can also be taken by IV injection or by sublingual or rectal administration. Synthetic cathinone users are most commonly young men between the ages of 18 and 35 (Pieprzyca et al., 2020), although use by a small percentage of younger students has also been documented (Debnam et al., 2018).

Acute subjective and physiological effects of synthetic cathinones are similar to those of other psychostimulants discussed earlier. The subjective effects consist of euphoria, increased energy, alertness, disinhibition/impulsivity, talkativeness, and sexual stimulation (Dybdal-Hargreaves et al., 2013; Karila et al., 2016). Acute physiological effects include tachycardia, hypertension, hyperthermia, and sweating. Adverse psychological/subjective reactions have also been reported and most commonly include insomnia, feelings of tension, numbness/tingling, and muscle twitching (Ashrafioun et al., 2016; Zimmerman et al., 2019). High doses of synthetic cathinones can lead to severe somatic toxic reactions including liver failure, kidney damage, rhabdomyolysis (skeletal muscle breakdown), and abnormal blood clotting within the systemic vasculature (German et al., 2014; Karila et al., 2015). Indeed, a number of fatalities have been reported involving synthetic cathinone overdose, most occurring in men within the typical age distribution (Kraemer et al., 2019). Furthermore, cathinone-related death is often associated with high-dose use in combination with one or more other substances such as methamphetamine, cocaine, opioids, benzodiazepines, or alcohol (deRoux and Dunn, 2017; Zaami et al., 2018). Lastly, adverse psychiatric reactions range from acute anxiety to a state of excited delirium, with the most extreme cases involving psychotic reactions characterized by delusions, hallucinations, violent aggression, and self-injury in some cases. Mephedrone, MDPV, and α-PVP are more likely to produce severe psychiatric reactions than methylone.

In terms of their neurochemical mechanisms of action, synthetic cathinones fall into two categories that parallel the mechanisms of amphetamine and methamphetamine versus cocaine and methylphenidate (Baumann et al., 2018). Mephedrone and methylone are substrates for DAT, NET, and SERT. Consequently, these drugs act like amphetamine in their ability to release DA, NE, and 5-HT from their respective nerve terminals and to block the reuptake of these neurotransmitters. In contrast, MDPV and α-PVP are more like cocaine and methylphenidate in that they block monoamine transporters without leading to release. But unlike cocaine, MDPV and α-PVP are selective for DAT and NET and have relatively little influence on SERT. Moreover, these compounds are much more potent than cocaine, which contributes to the risk of toxic overdose. To summarize, all four synthetic cathinones elevate extracellular levels of DA and NE, with mephedrone and methylone

© iStock.com/bert_phantana

FIGURE 12.21   Crystals of "flakka"

additionally stimulating 5-HT release. The ability of these compounds to enhance dopaminergic activity and to produce a euphoric state points to a risk for dependence. Not surprisingly, experimental animal studies examining various synthetic cathinones in tests of drug self-administration, place conditioning, and effects on brain electrical self-stimulation have demonstrated potent rewarding and reinforcing properties of this drug class (King and Riley, 2017; Watterson and Olive, 2017; **FIGURE 12.22**). In accordance with these results, synthetic cathinone users report experiencing symptoms of dependence and withdrawal; however, empirical studies of cathinone dependence are still in their infancy.

High doses of methamphetamine or MDMA, especially when administered in a binge-like dosing regimen, can cause long-lasting reductions in biochemical markers for DA (methamphetamine; see earlier in this chapter) or 5-HT (MDMA; see Chapter 6) in rodents. Due to the structural similarities of synthetic cathinones with one or the other of these other compounds, researchers have begun to investigate whether mephedrone, methylone, and MDPV exert similar toxic actions on the dopaminergic or serotonergic systems

(thus far, little research has been performed to determine α-PVP's neurotoxicity). Overall, this research has yielded mixed results: some studies have found little effect of these compounds on markers of dopaminergic or serotonergic nerve terminals, others have found small and transient reductions, while still others using repeated high-dose administration have observed significant and longer-lasting evidence for deficits in these biochemical markers (reviewed in Angoa-Pérez et al. 2017; Simmons et al., 2018). In vitro studies have additionally shown an ability of methylone and MDPV at very high concentrations to provoke apoptotic cell death in cultured cells differentiated to have a dopaminergic phenotype (Valente et al., 2017). Finally, rats self-administering MDPV in a binge-like paradigm showed subsequent signs of neurodegeneration in the perirhinal and entorhinal cortical areas (Sewalia et al., 2018). No evidence for cellular degeneration was observed in any other brain region, including striatum, hippocampus, or other cortical areas. Taken together, these findings raise the possibility that high-dose use of mephedrone, methylone, or MDPV could produce neurotoxic effects in users. Much more research in this area is clearly warranted, particularly as more and more young people become exposed to these substances over time.

SECTION SUMMARY

■ In recent years, a variety of synthetic cathinone derivatives have become available for recreational use under names such as "bath salts," "plant food," "meow meow," and "flakka." Four such compounds are mephedrone, methylone, MDPV, and α-PVP.

■ Synthetic cathinones are most commonly taken by snorting or oral ingestion, although other routes of administration such as IV injection have been reported.

■ Acute subjective and physiological effects of low to moderate doses are like those of other psychostimulants. However, higher doses can produce severe adverse reactions all the way up to organ failure, psychotic episodes, and death.

■ Mechanistically, mephedrone and methylone are similar to amphetamine in that they are substrates for DAT, NET, and SERT, thereby causing acute release of DA, NE, and 5-HT. In contrast, MDPV and α-PVP are selective reuptake inhibitors of DA and NE, which is similar to the neurochemical action of methylphenidate.

■ Animal studies have shown that synthetic cathinones are highly rewarding and reinforcing, which suggests that these compounds have the potential to produce dependence in regular users.

■ These compounds may also produce neurotoxic deficits at very high doses. More research is needed to define the conditions for such neurotoxic effects in animal and in cell culture models and to determine whether these effects may be occurring in human cathinone users.

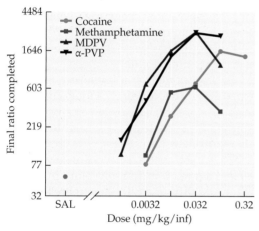

FIGURE 12.22 **Dose-dependent IV self-administration of MDPV, α-PVP, cocaine, and methamphetamine in rhesus monkeys** Four monkeys were trained to self-administer the listed drugs intravenously and were then tested on a progressive ratio (PR) schedule to determine the reinforcing effectiveness (E_{max}) of each compound based on the highest completed response ratio, similar to the breakpoint discussed earlier in the chapter. The graph illustrates the mean number of completed ratios for each drug at the indicated dose (dose = mg/kg per infusion). At low to moderate doses, both synthetic cathinones yielded a higher E_{max} than either cocaine or methamphetamine, indicative of greater reinforcing value at those doses. The highest drug doses showed either a flattening or a downward inflection of the dose–response function, which may be related to the onset of aversive drug effects at those doses (see King and Riley, 2017). SAL shows the mean number of responses for saline vehicle instead of drug. (After G. T. Collins et al. 2019. *Psychopharmacology* 236: 3677–3685. doi.org/10.1007/s00213-019-05339-4)

STUDY QUESTIONS

1. Why are drugs like cocaine, amphetamine, and other compounds that produce similar psychological and behavioral effects called "psychostimulants"?

2. In what part of the world is the coca shrub cultivated? How did coca and cocaine make their way to Europe and then to the United States?

3. What are the different routes of administration by which people take cocaine? How are the two forms of cocaine, namely cocaine HCl and cocaine base, related to these different routes?

4. Studies performed many years ago showed that in vitro, cocaine binds to the plasma membrane transporters for DA, NE, and 5-HT. What are the consequences of such binding when an animal is administered cocaine or when a person consumes the drug?

5. Acute administration of cocaine causes an increased frequency of transient DA release events. Describe the hypothesized mechanism for this effect.

6. Although DA plays the most important role in mediating the behavioral effects of cocaine, ACh and 5-HT additionally modulate these effects. Provide experimental findings that support this statement.

7. What is the mechanism of action of cocaine-based local anesthetic drugs such as Novocaine?

8. Compare and contrast the effects of cocaine on mood and behavior when taken occasionally at low to moderate doses versus when taken chronically and/or at high doses.

9. The acute physiological effects of cocaine (e.g., on heart rate and blood pressure) can be antagonized by administering adrenergic receptor blockers. Explain this finding.

10. Discuss the varying lines of evidence from animal studies that indicate a role of DA, especially in the nucleus accumbens (shell and core) and dorsal striatum, in the behaviorally activating and rewarding/reinforcing effects of cocaine and other psychostimulants such as amphetamine.

11. The text states that based on PET imaging studies, "once a certain minimum level of DAT occupancy (about 40% to 60%) is attained following either cocaine or methylphenidate administration, the individual *may* experience a drug-induced high." Note the use of the word "may." What are the two factors that are believed to determine whether or not a high is likely to occur?

12. The _____ DA receptor subtype is *necessary* for cocaine's behavioral effects to occur. What experimental evidence supports the critical role of this subtype? What other DA receptor subtypes contribute to these effects and in what way?

13. Describe (a) the observed patterns of cocaine use that most commonly lead to a progression from occasional use to development of cocaine dependence/cocaine use disorder, and (b) the phenomenon of a cocaine binge and the phases of the abstinence syndrome that have been observed following a typical binge.

14. What is the role of craving in the development of cocaine dependence, and what is known about the neurobiology of cocaine craving?

15. Brain imaging studies in regular cocaine users have shown that several markers of striatal dopaminergic function are _____ (increased, decreased, or unaffected) compared to controls who are not cocaineusers. These changes are _____ (consistent or inconsistent) with the dopamine depletion hypothesis of cocaine addiction.

16. How is it possible that repeated cocaine use can lead to tolerance in some cases but sensitization in others? What are the patterns of cocaine use that lead to one or the other change in drug sensitivity, and what is known about the underlying mechanisms of these changes?

17. Discuss the evidence for cognitive deficits and brain abnormalities in regular users of cocaine. Are these deficits and abnormalities present *before* drug use begins, or are they a *consequence* of such use? Explain your answer.

18. What are the major health consequences (other than neurobiological) of chronic or high-dose cocaine use?

19. The following true/false questions pertain to current treatment approaches for cocaine use disorder. (a) Several different drugs have been approved by the FDA to treat cocaine use disorder. True or false? (b) Maintenance therapy with other psychostimulants such as amphetamine, methylphenidate, or modafinil is being tested as a possible treatment approach. True or false? (c) If an effective cocaine vaccine could be developed, it would protect people against addiction to a wide range of different psychostimulants. True or false? (d) One of the most effective currently available treatments for addiction to cocaine or amphetamine is a combination of contingency management plus community reinforcement. True or false?

20. Amphetamine, methamphetamine, cathinone, and ephedrine are related structurally to the neurotransmitter _____.

21. Describe the key historical events in the discovery of amphetamine and its subsequent progression to recreational use.

22. What are the typical routes of administration of amphetamine and methamphetamine? What are the features of binge use (i.e., a "speed run") of these drugs?

STUDY QUESTIONS *(continued)*

23. With respect to their mechanism of action, amphetamine and methamphetamine differ from cocaine because the former drugs cause a massive release of DA due to reversal of _____.

24. (a) Discuss the adverse consequences of chronic and/or high-dose use of amphetamines, including dependence and withdrawal, effects on cognitive function, psychotic reactions, potential neurotoxic effects, and consequences for general physical health. (b) In what ways do women differ from men in their methamphetamine use and the consequences of such use?

25. The mechanism of action of methylphenidate is similar to that amphetamine. True or false? Explain your answer.

26. Amphetamine and methylphenidate are front-line medications used to treat ADHD. (a) What the primary symptoms of this disorder, including the recognized ADHD subtypes? (b) What is the proposed mechanism of action of psychostimulants in alleviating ADHD symptomatology? (c) What other medications are approved for treating ADHD, and how do these medications differ in their mechanisms of action compared to amphetamine or methylphenidate?

27. (a) What is modafinil and what are its approved therapeutic applications? (b) What are the hypothesized mechanisms by which this compound increases wakefulness?

28. (a) List the names of the four synthetic recreationally used cathinones mentioned in the text. (b) Discuss how these four compounds can be placed into two different categories based on their neurochemical mechanisms of action. (c) Synthetic cathinones have been shown to be neurotoxic, even at low doses. True or false? Explain your answer.

13

Nicotine and Caffeine

ONE MORNING IN 2002, AN OBSCURE CHINESE CHEMIST NAMED HON LIK AWOKE AFTER A NIGHT FILLED WITH NIGHTMARES. Hon, a two-packs-a-day smoker, had been trying to quit using the nicotine patch. But on this particular night, he had forgotten to remove the patch before going to bed and he believed that this had led to his bad dreams. Hon additionally reflected on the realization that the steady delivery of nicotine from the patch did not produce the same satisfying "rush" he felt when inhaling tobacco smoke from a cigarette. Hon's father was also a smoker who would soon be diagnosed with lung cancer and die in 2004. Knowing that nicotine was the main rewarding element in tobacco smoke but that other constituents of the smoke (i.e., "tar") produced the most harm, Hon wondered whether he could produce a device that permitted vaporized nicotine to be inhaled without actually burning tobacco leaves. Employed at the time by the Liaoning Provincial Institute of Chinese Medicine, he worked on his idea and by 2003, he filed a patent on what is considered to be the first modern commercial e-cigarette (Geller, 2015; Ridley, 2015).

Use of e-cigarettes has skyrocketed since their introduction into the marketplace. At the same time, a huge controversy has arisen among both researchers and public health officials about whether e-cigarette use should be encouraged as a safer alternative to cigarette smoking (and even a novel approach to smoking cessation) or discouraged because of its potential as a path to nicotine addiction and other harms in young people.

Nicotine, the psychoactive ingredient in tobacco, e-cigarettes, and other electronic nicotine delivery systems (ENDS) such as vape pens and e-hookahs, is the third most widely consumed recreational drug in the world after caffeine and alcohol. Every day, millions of men and women around the world consume this drug, usually by smoking tobacco in cigarettes, cigars, or hookahs or by inhaling nicotine through various ENDS. What is the lure of nicotine? Why do so many people smoke, despite the known dangers of lung cancer and other respiratory diseases? The first several parts of this chapter will address these and other questions about nicotine and smoking or vaping. We will discuss the controversy over the benefits versus the harms of e-cigarette use. The second

Vape shops specialize in offering a variety of e-cigarette brands and flavored nicotine-containing solutions.

part of the chapter is concerned with the properties and mechanisms of action of caffeine, the other widely used and legal stimulant drug. ■

13.1 Background, History, and Basic Pharmacology of Nicotine

Background and history

Nicotine is an alkaloid found in tobacco leaves (**FIGURE 13.1**). There are two major species of tobacco plant: a large-leaf form and a small-leaf form. The large-leaf variety (*Nicotiana tabacum*), which is the principal source of present-day tobacco, originated in South America, where it was domesticated by native peoples more than 5000 years ago (**FIGURE 13.2**). The small-leaf variety (*Nicotiana rustica*) is native to eastern North America and the islands of the West Indies. Tobacco and nicotine were unknown to Europeans until Columbus's expedition to the New World in 1492. There his sailors discovered tobacco smoking by the native peoples and brought samples of *N. rustica* back on their return voyage (Burns, 2007). An early proponent of tobacco was Jean Nicot de Villemain, the French ambassador to Portugal, who was instrumental in introducing the plant to his native country from Portugal. Indeed, the botanical name of the more popular tobacco plant, *N. tabacum*, is derived from both Nicot's surname and *tabaco*, the term for "tobacco" in both Spanish and Portuguese.

In Britain, tobacco was initially scarce and thus costly. Early pipes, called "fairy pipes" in England and "elfin pipes" in Scotland, were extremely small to conserve the dried leaves. But the popularity of smoking grew so rapidly that based on historical records, by the early 1600s there were perhaps thousands of shops in London alone where tobacco could be purchased. At first, most tobacco use took place through pipe smoking, cigar smoking, and chewing, but this was later supplanted to a large extent by the snorting of finely powdered tobacco leaves called snuff.

In 1610, England attempted to commercialize tobacco growing in the Virginia colony using the native *N. rustica*. However, this venture failed because the *N. rustica* species had a disagreeable flavor to Europeans compared with *N. tabacum*, which had been a Spanish monopoly up to that time. Luckily for the British, John Rolfe, the local leader of this effort, managed to obtain some *N. tabacum*, which grew just as well in Virginia as it had for thousands of years in South America. Thus was the American tobacco industry born.

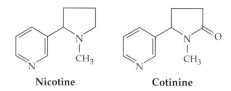

FIGURE 13.1 Chemical structure of nicotine and the principal metabolite cotinine

Cigarettes began to be used in Europe in the mid-nineteenth century, and their popularity in the United States exploded over the next 30 years. This change was fostered by two separate developments: new methods of curing tobacco leaves that improved their flavor, and the invention of the cigarette machine. When cigarettes were rolled manually, a skilled worker could make about 2500 to 3000 cigarettes per day, which may seem like a large number. In 1884, however, a cigarette machine was built that could make 120,000 cigarettes in one day, and modern machines can produce 4000 to 8000 per minute!

In the case of e-cigarettes, the device heats and vaporizes a solution of nicotine, thereby resulting in an aerosol that is inhaled by the user. This vaporization step, which is common to all ENDS, is the source of the street term "vaping." From its start as a tiny industry, the e-cigarette has grown enormously in popularity, with global sales estimated to have exceeded $18 billion in 2020 (www.statista.com/outlook/cmo/tobacco-products/e-cigarettes/worldwide). According to the 2019 National Youth Tobacco Survey, an estimated 31.2% (corresponding to 4.7 million individuals) of U.S. high school students were users of some kind of

FIGURE 13.2 Leaves of the *Nicotiana tabacum* plant from which tobacco is derived

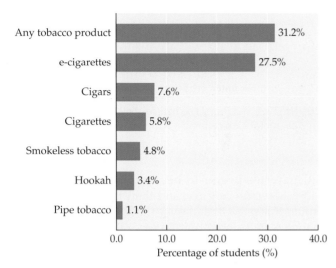

FIGURE 13.3 Percentage of U.S. high school students who were current users of tobacco products in 2019 Current usage is defined as one or more uses within the past 30 days. Data are from the National Youth Tobacco Survey. (Centers for Disease Control and Prevention, 2019.)

tobacco product, the bulk of which were e-cigarettes (**FIGURE 13.3**; Centers for Disease Control and Prevention, 2019). Early e-cigarettes delivered relatively small amounts of nicotine, but this changed with the advent of later designs that allow much greater drug delivery. In response to the growing use of e-cigarettes, the U.S. Food and Drug Administration (FDA) in 2016 extended its regulatory authority over tobacco products to include e-cigarettes and other ENDS (U.S. Food and Drug Administration, 2016). This was followed in 2020 by an FDA guidance document in which the agency warned manufacturers that it would prioritize enforcement of restrictions against unauthorized flavored e-cigarette products (e.g., containing fruit or mint flavors) that are particularly appealing to children. Beginning in 2021, new legislation prohibits the delivery of e-cigarettes to consumers by the U.S. Postal Service. These recent regulations were prompted by a growing body of research demonstrating harms from repeated vaping (see later section on health risks from tobacco smoking and vaping).

Nicotine pharmacokinetics related to tobacco smoking

When nicotine was first isolated in 1828 by Wilhelm Posselt and Karl Reimann, it was found to constitute about 5% of the weight of dry tobacco leaves. However, this relatively minor fraction imbues tobacco with many physiological and psychological effects when the leaves are smoked, chewed, or snorted and the nicotine is absorbed into the human bloodstream. Without nicotine, it is quite likely that tobacco would be regarded as a useless weed.

The typical tobacco cigarette contains between 6 and 11 mg of nicotine, although no more than 1 to 3 mg actually reaches the bloodstream of the smoker.

The amount of available nicotine depends mainly on features of the smoker's behavior such as the number of puffs and the length of each puff. Nicotine in the tobacco is vaporized by the 800°C temperature at the burning tip of the cigarette. It enters the smoker's lungs mainly on tiny particles called **tar**, a complex mixture of hydrocarbons of which some are known to be carcinogenic. Tar is an important contributor to the taste and smell of cigarette smoke, and along with nicotine, these sensory qualities contribute significantly to the reinforcing effects of smoking. Once the smoke has been inhaled, the nicotine is rapidly absorbed by the lungs through roughly 500 million air sacs known as alveoli. These alveoli, which are responsible for gas exchange between the air and the person's bloodstream, possess an estimated total surface area of 70 to 130 square meters (equivalent to 750 to 1400 square feet). When tobacco is chewed or snorted as snuff, nicotine is absorbed through the membranes of the mouth and nostrils, although this process is considerably less efficient than absorption from tobacco smoking.

A smoker usually takes about 10 to 15 total puffs on a cigarette at intervals of approximately 30 to 60 seconds. Researchers have shown that each puff delivers nicotine to the brain beginning within about 7 seconds, which is roughly twice as fast as when the drug is administered intravenously. Thus smoking a cigarette is the quickest and most efficient method of delivering nicotine to the brain, where the drug produces its reinforcing effects (see the section on behavioral and physiological effects later in the chapter). For many years, the accepted lore was that each individual puff produced a large "spike" of nicotine in the brain; however, brain imaging using positron emission tomography (PET) suggests that nicotine rapidly accumulates in the brain starting with the first puff (Rose et al., 2010). Hence, each subsequent puff causes just a small increase in brain nicotine levels that is superimposed on the previously existing level.

Nicotine pharmacokinetics related to e-cigarette vaping

Recent studies have determined the amount of nicotine available in various e-cigarette brands, the parameters of vaping* behavior in e-cigarette users, and the levels of circulating nicotine produced in these users. This research enables us to compare and contrast vaping e-cigarettes versus smoking conventional tobacco cigarettes.

FIGURE 13.4 presents photos of the various types of ENDS most commonly sold in the marketplace. Although the size and shape of these devices vary considerably, they have in common a container (either disposable or refillable, as in a cartridge, tank, or pod)

---

*We will use the term *vaping* instead of *smoking* when referring to inhalation of vapor from e-cigarettes or other ENDS.

FIGURE 13.4 Various types of electronic nicotine delivery systems (ENDS) (From U.S. Department of Health and Human Services, 2016.)

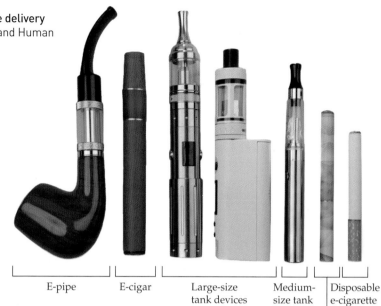

E-pipe   E-cigar   Large-size tank devices   Medium-size tank device   Disposable e-cigarette

Rechargeable e-cigarette

containing a solution of nicotine dissolved in propylene glycol or glycerin (e-liquid, also colloquially called "e-juice" or "vape juice"), a battery-powered heating element/atomizer that vaporizes the nicotine so it can be inhaled, and sometimes a controller that permits the user to regulate the voltage or wattage put out by the unit's battery. A survey of e-cigarette websites performed in July 2016 recorded a total of 433 different brands (Hsu et al., 2018). However, many more distinct varieties were available because of added flavorings. These flavorings fell into many categories such as tobacco flavors, menthol flavors, fruit flavors, dessert flavors, coffee flavors, and other beverage flavors. Note, however, that most of these novel flavors are now heavily regulated if not banned because of their attractiveness to children. Nicotine content varied across a wide range. Indeed, you can even vape an e-cigarette with no nicotine just for the purpose of experiencing the taste and other sensory qualities of using the device.

Before we discuss the delivery of nicotine from e-cigarettes, we need to review the history of e-cigarette design. Thus far, four generations of e-cigarettes have been identified that differ significantly in their design features and amount of nicotine delivery (Williams and Talbot, 2019). The first generation, called "cig-a-likes," were designed to look and feel like tobacco cigarettes. Some of these devices provided poor nicotine delivery, but more efficient designs (e.g., V2 Cig) are still available for purchase. A major class of second generation e-cigarettes is termed "clearomizers." These devices have larger batteries than cig-a-likes and also possess clear refillable reservoirs (tanks) containing the e-liquid. Aspire, Innokin, and Kanger are among the popular brands of clearomizers. Alternatively, there are similar second-generation devices called "cartomizers" in which the tank is not refillable. "Mods" are the third generation of e-cigarettes. Mods have large, higher-voltage batteries with large tanks that yield a high vapor delivery. Sample mod brands are Geek Vape, Vaporesso, and SMOK. Finally, the fourth generation of e-cigarettes are the "pods." In contrast to clearomizers and mods, e-cigarette pods are small, sleek devices with either disposable or refillable liquid containers. By far the most popular brand of e-cigarette pod is JUUL, which has the appearance of a portable flash drive, can be recharged using a computer's USB port, and is sufficiently stealthy that students often boast of "Juuling" at school (Huang et al., 2019; Kavuluru et al., 2019) (**FIGURE 13.5**).

Nicotine concentrations in e-liquids vary as a function of (1) whether the dissolved nicotine is in the free base form or in the form of a nicotine salt, (2) the type of device and its rate of vapor production, and (3) the user's preference for a higher or lower concentration. For example, pod-type e-cigarettes are typically listed as containing 12 to 24 mg/ml of free base nicotine or 30 to 60 mg/ml of nicotine salt (the higher concentration is necessary because addition of the atoms making up the salt adds to the mass of each molecule). For example, the manufacturer states that a 5% JUUL pod contains 59 mg/ml of nicotine salt. We note, however, that laboratory measurements performed on some early e-cigarette brands found that the actual nicotine

FIGURE 13.5 A JUUL e-cigarette

content was frequently lower than the content stated by the manufacturer (Goniewicz et al., 2013; Lisko et al., 2015). More recently, a survey of the measured nicotine content of refillable e-liquids found that many deviated by more than 10% (either lower or higher) from the stated content (Miller et al., 2021).

When studying recreational drug use, pharmacologists always need to investigate the drug's pharmacokinetics, including the peak plasma drug levels produced in the user, the latency to attain this peak from the time of onset of drug consumption, and the rate of drug clearance from the bloodstream. In the case of tobacco cigarette-derived nicotine, such information has been known for many years; however, only in the past several years have comparable data become available on nicotine pharmacokinetics when delivered by e-cigarettes. Importantly, the rapidity of e-cigarette nicotine delivery through the lungs is similar to that from tobacco cigarettes, thereby providing the same opportunity for rapid nicotine-mediated reinforcement (St. Helen et al., 2016). On the other hand, the levels of plasma nicotine produced in users have been shown to vary widely across different types and brands of e-cigarettes, with newer types (i.e., tank and mod systems) yielding greater nicotine levels than earlier types (Hajek et al., 2017; Fearon et al., 2018). Of particular interest is a recent study focusing on JUUL e-cigarettes that measured plasma nicotine levels in participants who regularly used e-cigarettes and also occasionally smoked tobacco cigarettes (Hajek et al., 2020). In the first experiment, users smoked a JUUL on one occasion and then their own chosen cigarette brand on a different day. **FIGURE 13.6A** shows that the average time course and peak plasma nicotine levels were very similar when comparing JUULs with tobacco cigarettes. JUULs were subsequently compared to eight other e-cigarette products by obtaining data from a subset of the initial participants. This experiment revealed that JUULs delivered much more nicotine than the comparison brands (**FIGURE 13.6B**). Furthermore, in the first experiment JUULs were reported to be comparable to users' own tobacco cigarettes with respect to subjective nicotine delivery, taste, pleasantness, and ability to relieve the urge to smoke. These findings have significant relevance to several aspects of JUUL use. On the positive side, JUULs might be more helpful than other brands in assisting tobacco smokers to quit smoking (see later discussion of e-cigarettes and smoking cessation). But on the negative side, JUULs compared to other brands that deliver less nicotine might be more addictive and/or might have greater propensity for users to transition from e-cigarette vaping to tobacco cigarette smoking.

Nicotine metabolism

The elimination half-life of nicotine is typically about 2 hours, although this value can vary with individual differences in metabolism rate. The first step in nicotine elimination is conversion to its principal metabolite, **cotinine** (see Figure 13.1). About 70% to 80% of nicotine

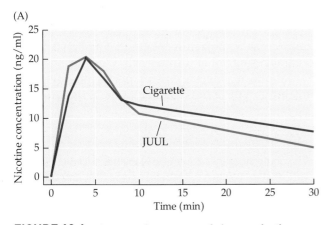

(A)

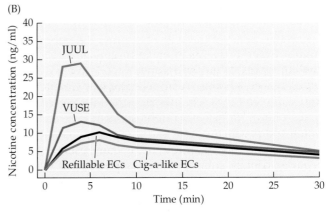

(B)

FIGURE 13.6 Average time course of plasma nicotine concentrations after smoking tobacco cigarettes or vaping JUULs or other brands of e-cigarettes (A) Twenty users of regular e-cigarettes (not specifically JUULs) who also occasionally smoked tobacco cigarettes were examined for their plasma nicotine concentrations after smoking their own brand of tobacco cigarette or, on a different day, vaping with a JUUL. Note the similarities in plasma nicotine rise, peak level, and rate of decline after the peak. (B) A subset of eight participants from the first experiment were further tested by vaping, on separate days, a JUUL, two different refillable e-cigarettes (ECs), and six different cig-a-like e-cigarettes, including VUSE. Manufacturer's stated e-liquid nicotine concentrations were

59 mg/ml for JUUL, 48 mg/ml for VUSE, 20 mg/ml for the refillable brands, and 16 to 24 mg/ml for the cig-a-like brands. Peak plasma nicotine concentrations were clearly related to the nicotine concentration of the e-liquid, except that the refillable brands were a bit higher than the cig-a-likes since the former had the capability of adjusting the battery voltage to yield a greater amount of vapor. The difference in average JUUL peak plasma nicotine in panel B compared to panel A is likely related to the fact that only a subset of participants from the first experiment were included in the second. (From P. Hajek et al. 2020. *Addiction* 115: 1141–1148. © 2020 The Authors. doi.org/10.1111/add.14936. CC BY 4.0, creativecommons. org/licenses/by/4.0/.)

in the body is converted to cotinine, catalyzed primarily by the liver enzyme **cytochrome P450 2A6 (CYP2A6)**. Cotinine and other nicotine metabolites are excreted mainly in the urine. Expression and activity of CYP2A6 is regulated by hormones, menthol (sometimes used as a flavorant in tobacco cigarettes or e-cigarettes), and genetic variation (i.e., differing gene alleles) (reviewed in Tanner and Tyndale, 2017). Thus, CYP2A6 expression is increased by estrogens, resulting in generally faster nicotine metabolism in women than in men. In contrast, menthol appears to inhibit CYP2A6 activity, as shown by slower nicotine conversion to cotinine when smoking mentholated compared to non-mentholated cigarettes. Finally, variation in the CYP2A6 gene causes some individuals to have low activity of the enzyme and thus reduced rates of nicotine metabolism. Studies on CYP2A6 genetics among different ethnic and racial groups have found that slow nicotine metabolism is more prevalent in Asian and in African American populations than in Whites.

CYP2A6 genetic variation and nicotine breakdown rate have been linked to smoking behavior and nicotine addiction. Smokers carrying low functioning CYP2A6 alleles smoke fewer cigarettes per day than smokers carrying wild-type alleles (Tanner and Tyndale, 2017). These slow nicotine metabolizers are also less likely to become dependent on smoking, and have greater success quitting smoking than people with moderate or high rates of nicotine metabolism (Zdanowicz and Adams, 2014; Tanner et al., 2015). Thus, a slow rate of nicotine breakdown exerts somewhat of a protective effect against cigarette smoking.

Mechanisms of nicotine action

Nicotine works mainly by activating **nicotinic acetylcholine receptors (nAChRs)**, one of the two basic subtypes of acetylcholine (ACh) receptor (see Chapter 7). You will recall that nAChRs are ionotropic receptors that conduct Na^+ and Ca^{2+} ions across the cell membrane and produce a rapid excitatory response by the postsynaptic cell. Each nAChR is composed of five separate protein subunits, the composition of which differs between neurons and muscle cells and also varies across different brain areas. One of the functional consequences of this receptor diversity is differential sensitivity to receptor agonists and antagonists. For example, neuronal receptors containing two α4 or α3 subunits along with three β subunits (typically β2) are much more sensitive to nicotine than those composed of five α7 subunits because of their higher affinity for the compound (Wittenberg et al., 2020). These high-affinity nAChRs are found in many parts of the brain, including the cerebral cortex, thalamus, striatum, hippocampus, and monoamine-containing nuclei such as the substantia nigra, ventral tegmental area (VTA), locus coeruleus, and raphe nuclei. Peripherally, such

receptors are found in the ganglia of the autonomic (parasympathetic and sympathetic) nervous system. Some nAChRs, particularly those containing α7 subunits, are located presynaptically on nerve terminals where they enhance neurotransmitter release. Thus, a secondary consequence of nicotine exposure is glutamate-mediated neuronal excitation due to increased release from glutamatergic neurons. This topic will be covered in greater detail later when we discuss nicotine addiction and the role of nicotinic receptor activation of the mesolimbic dopaminergic system.

High-affinity nAChRs rapidly desensitize in response to agonist exposure. Because of this effect, nicotine can paradoxically decrease the effectiveness of normal cholinergic transmission (Dani, 2015). Very high doses of nicotine lead to a persistent activation of nAChRs and a continuous depolarization of the postsynaptic cell. As we saw in Chapter 7, this causes a depolarization block, and the cell cannot fire again until the nicotine is removed. In this way, a high dose of nicotine exerts a biphasic effect that begins with stimulation of nicotinic cholinergic functions but then turns to a nicotinic receptor blockade. This biphasic action accounts for the features of nicotine poisoning discussed later.

SECTION SUMMARY

- Nicotine is an alkaloid found in tobacco leaves. Tobacco plants are native to North and South America, and these plants were domesticated several thousand years ago by Native Americans.

- When tobacco was first brought back to Europe from the New World, use of this substance was primarily by means of pipe smoking, cigar smoking, and chewing. Snorting finely powdered tobacco leaves (snuff) later became popular.

- Tobacco cigarettes were introduced in the mid-nineteenth century, and cigarette smoking subsequently increased as the result of improved methods of curing the tobacco leaves, as well as the advent of modern cigarette manufacturing machines.

- The contemporary e-cigarette was introduced in 2003 by the Chinese chemist Hon Lik. Since that time, e-cigarettes and other electronic nicotine delivery systems (ENDS) have greatly increased in popularity.

- A typical tobacco cigarette contains 6 to 11 mg of nicotine, of which only about 1 to 3 mg actually reaches the smoker's bloodstream. Nicotine is vaporized by the high temperature at the tip of the burning cigarette and enters the smoker's lungs on tiny particles called tar.

- Once in the lungs, the nicotine is readily absorbed into the blood and quickly reaches the brain. The rapid delivery of nicotine to the brain is believed to be a powerful reinforcer of smoking behavior.

- Many different e-cigarette designs have been introduced to the marketplace, most of which fall within one of the following types: cig-a-likes, clearomizers, cartomizers, mods, and pods. The most popular mod device is the JUUL brand. All e-cigarettes have in common a container filled with a solution of nicotine in propylene glycol or glycerin (e-liquid), and a battery-powered heating device to vaporize the nicotine. Nicotine is present in the form of either the free base or a salt, and the concentrations of nicotine vary substantially across e-cigarette type and brand. Flavorings are often added to the nicotine solution to enhance its taste. The rapidity of nicotine delivery from an e-cigarette is similar to that from tobacco cigarettes.

■ Nicotine is metabolized primarily to cotinine by the liver enzyme CYP2A6, with an elimination half-life of about 2 hours. The cotinine and other nicotine metabolites are then excreted mainly in the urine. People who metabolize nicotine inefficiently because of genetically determined low CYP2A6 activity smoke less than efficient metabolizers and are less likely to become nicotine dependent.

■ The principal mechanism of nicotine action is to stimulate nAChRs in the brain and the autonomic nervous system. In particular, there are high-affinity nAChRs that most commonly are composed of two α4 or α3 subunits, along with three β2 subunits. Some nicotinic receptors, typically composed of α7 subunits, are located presynaptically on nerve terminals where they function to enhance the release of neurotransmitters such as glutamate.

■ The opening of nAChR channels permits Na^+ and Ca^{2+} ions to flow across the cell membrane, thereby causing membrane depolarization and a fast excitatory response. High-affinity nAChRs desensitize rapidly in the presence of nicotine, thereby leading to reduced transmission by ACh. Very high doses of nicotine can cause persistent activation of nAChRs, leading to a temporary depolarization block of the postsynaptic cell.

13.2 Behavioral and Physiological Effects of Nicotine

If one wishes to determine the pharmacological effects of nicotine itself, separated from the complex behavioral aspects of smoking or vaping, it is necessary to give study participants the pure drug. This is routinely accomplished through the use of nicotine injections, nicotine patches, or nicotine-containing gum. Nevertheless, many early studies suffer from a significant methodological problem due to the use of current smokers, who are required to refrain from smoking for a specified period of time, typically ranging from 8 to 24 hours. Because nicotine abstinence produces withdrawal symptoms in dependent individuals, it is often difficult to determine whether nicotine-induced changes represent true differences from "normal," or simply reversal of withdrawal symptoms. Fortunately, researchers subsequently began to study participants who had never smoked, thereby permitting us to compare the findings of those studies with the results from abstinent smokers.

Smoking-related mood changes are related to both pharmacological (nicotine) and non-pharmacological factors

With respect to mood states, nicotine is usually found to increase calmness and relaxation in recently abstinent smokers. This fits well with numerous self-reports of smokers indicating that smoking a cigarette has a relaxing, tension-reducing effect. However, it seems likely that these mood changes are related at least partly to relief from nicotine withdrawal symptoms, because nicotine administration to nonsmokers tends to elicit feelings of heightened tension or arousal, along with lightheadedness, dizziness, and even nausea (Kalman, 2002). If you either smoke now or have ever smoked in the past, you may recall having experienced some of these same effects when you tried your first cigarette.

As is the case with other psychoactive drugs, expectations significantly influence the subjective effects of smoking-derived nicotine intake (reviewed by Schlagintweit et al., 2020). In one example of this phenomenon, Gu and coworkers (2016) deprived chronic smokers of nicotine overnight before testing them in the laboratory. Participants were tested under four conditions using a within-subjects design: (1) smoking a standard nicotine cigarette while correctly told that the cigarette contained nicotine, (2) smoking the same nicotine cigarette while incorrectly told that the cigarette contained no nicotine, (3) smoking a denicotinized cigarette while correctly told that the cigarette had no nicotine,* and (4) smoking a denicotinized cigarette while incorrectly told that the cigarette contained nicotine. Among the key outcome measures were changes in nicotine craving from before to after smoking the cigarette, and activation of the insula, a cortical area that has been strongly implicated in drug craving and addiction (see Chapter 9). The researchers found that nicotine craving and insula activation were significantly reduced only in the group that smoked the nicotine-containing cigarette *and* was informed that the cigarette contained active drug (**FIGURE 13.7**).

Nicotine enhances cognitive function

We saw in Chapter 7 that ACh plays an important role in certain aspects of cognitive functioning, including memory and attention. In this section we focus on the specific involvement of nicotinic receptors in cognition and research demonstrating an ability of nicotine to enhance cognitive performance.

Early studies on the effects of nicotine on cognition were often conducted using regular smokers instructed to refrain from smoking for some period of time

---

*The denicotinized cigarettes used in this and many other studies actually contain small amounts of nicotine; however, the levels are so low that they produce little or no pharmacological activity. Therefore, these kinds of denicotinized cigarettes can be considered placebos for the purpose of testing nicotine expectancies.

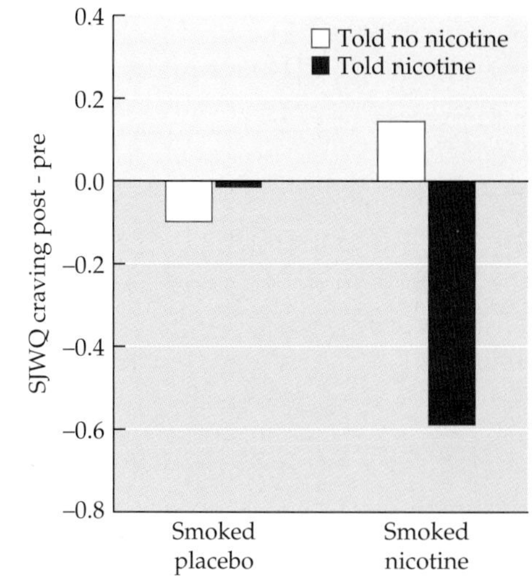

FIGURE 13.7 **Interaction of nicotine exposure with drug expectation in affecting nicotine craving in deprived smokers** The study participants were regular adult smokers (mean of 15 cigarettes smoked per day) tested under four separate conditions, each after overnight nicotine deprivation: (1) smoking a standard nicotine cigarette and told that they were receiving nicotine, (2) smoking the same cigarette but told that they were receiving no nicotine, (3) smoking a denicotinized (placebo) cigarette but told that they were receiving nicotine, and (4) smoking the same placebo cigarette but told that they were receiving no nicotine. Changes in nicotine craving from before to after the cigarette smoking were measured using the Shiffman-Jarvik Withdrawal Questionnaire (SJWQ). The graph shows that craving was significantly reduced only under the condition of smoking a nicotine cigarette and being told that the participant would be receiving the active drug. (After X. Gu et al. 2016. *Front Psychiatry* 7: 126. © 2016 Gu, Lohrenz, Salas, Baldwin, Soltani, Kirk, Cinciripini and Montague. doi.org/10.3389/fpsyt.2016.00126. CC BY 4.0, https://creativecommons.org/licenses/by/4.0/.)

(typically overnight) before the experiment. The problem with this approach was that the forced abstinence led to cognitive deficits in comparison to a nonsmoking control group, making it unclear whether nicotine was simply reversing such deficits. Later studies examining cognitive function following administration of pure nicotine (administered by means of injection, skin patch, inhaler, or nasal spray) either in nonsmokers or nonabstinent smokers confirmed that nicotine has a positive influence on cognition, particularly short-term episodic and working memory, attention, and fine motor performance (Valentine and Sofluoglu, 2018).

Because tobacco smoking is common in people with cognitive disorders such as attention-deficit/hyperactivity disorder (ADHD) (McClernon and Kollins, 2008) and schizophrenia (D'Souza and Markou, 2012), some researchers have hypothesized that patients may be attempting to medicate their cognitive impairment with nicotine (Valentine and Sofluoglu, 2018). Furthermore, we might expect that nicotine would have a greater influence on attention in people with poor baseline levels of attention than in people with higher baseline attentional performance. This idea was tested by Poltavski and Petros (2006), who prescreened nonsmoking college students for baseline levels of attention and then divided them into low-attention and high-attention groups. Both groups were then subjected to the Conners' Continuous Performance Test (CPT), a well-known test of sustained attention that is sometimes used to diagnose ADHD. The test required that participants press a specific key on a computer keyboard in response to brief presentation of the letter *X* but to withhold their

response when any other letter was displayed. Nicotine administered before CPT testing by means of a transdermal nicotine patch produced no change in the high-attention group but increased the d' score (a measure of stimulus detectability) in the low-attention group to the same level as the high-attention group given either nicotine or a placebo patch (**FIGURE 13.8**).

To determine which nAChR subunit combinations mediate nicotine-induced cognitive enhancement using animal models, some studies have examined the ability of subunit-selective antagonists like **dihydro-beta-erythroidine (DhβE)** (antagonist of α4 and β2 subunit-containing high-affinity nAChRs) or **methyllycaconitine (MLA)** (antagonist of α7 subunit-containing low-affinity nAChRs). A different approach has been to use genetic engineering to knock out or otherwise mutate specific receptor subunits. Taken together, the pharmacological and genetic studies generally suggest that high-affinity nAChRs play a more important (though not exclusive) role than low-affinity nAChRs in mediating nicotine's enhancement of hippocampal-dependent tasks (Kutlu and Gould, 2015).

Finally, it's important to recognize that nicotine affects cognition by acting through a neural circuit that includes not only ACh but also other neurotransmitters and their receptors (Valentine and Sofluoglu, 2018). These include norepinephrine and β-adrenergic receptors (Hahn and

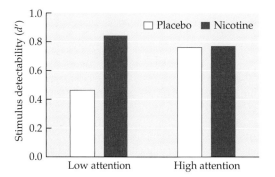

FIGURE 13.8 **Nicotine enhancement of stimulus detectability in low-attention study participants** After screening for baseline attentional performance, participants were tested for their ability to detect and correctly identify a brief visual stimulus displayed on a computer monitor. Those who received a transdermal nicotine patch (7 mg) prior to testing showed enhanced stimulus detectability if they were in the low-baseline-attention group but not in the high-baseline-attention group. (After D. V. Poltavski and T. Petros. 2006. *Physiol Behav* 87: 614–624.)

Stolerman, 2005), glutamate activation and *N*-methyl-D-aspartate (NMDA) receptors (Hahn, 2015), and DA and D_1 receptors, specifically within the prefrontal cortex (PFC) (Jasinska et al., 2014; Valentine and Sofuoglu, 2018; also see Chapters 5 and 12).

Nicotine exerts both reinforcing and aversive effects

Nicotine can exert either reinforcing or aversive actions. This section discusses both of these effects, along with their underlying neurobiological mechanisms.

NICOTINE REINFORCEMENT Under the right experimental conditions, experienced cigarette smokers as well as laboratory animals will self-administer pure nicotine by intravenous (IV) injection (Caille et al., 2012; Goodwin et al., 2015; Henningfield et al., 2016). This shows that nicotine by itself can be reinforcing even in the absence of the behavioral components of cigarette smoking. On the other hand, it is clear that the reinforcement provided by smoking is much more complex than simply the delivery of nicotine to the individual. In a later section, we will discuss the relative contributions of nicotine versus other aspects of smoking in the reinforcing properties of this behavior.

Nicotine reinforcement can be influenced by a number of factors, including sex and age. For example, numerous studies have shown that female rats show greater nicotine reinforcement than males based on IV self-administration (Flores et al., 2019). These preclinical findings are consistent with human studies demonstrating that compared to men, women are more sensitive to nicotine reward/reinforcement, report greater positive mood effects of smoking, and have a more difficult

time quitting smoking (O'Dell and Torres, 2014). Rodent studies have additionally found that in comparison to adults, adolescents show greater nicotine reward and reinforcement, as well as less aversion to high nicotine doses (see next section on aversive effects of nicotine) (Leslie, 2020). Such age differences are hypothesized to stem from the incomplete maturation of key neuronal pathways underlying nicotine reward and aversion. Of course, we have known for many years that tobacco use almost always begins at a young age, well before adult brain development has been attained.

Animal studies have played a key role in assessing the mechanisms underlying nicotine reinforcement. As in the case of cocaine and amphetamine, the mesolimbic dopamine (DA) pathway from the VTA to the nucleus accumbens (NAcc) plays a key role in nicotine's reinforcing effects. Nicotine administered to rats or mice activates high-affinity nicotinic receptors located in the VTA, thereby stimulating burst firing of the dopaminergic neurons and increasing DA release in the NAcc (Subramaniyan and Dani, 2015; see **FIGURE 13.9**). The importance of accumbens DA for nicotine reinforcement was demonstrated by Corrigall and coworkers (1992), who showed that lesioning the dopaminergic innervation of this area with 6-hydroxydopamine (6-OHDA) significantly attenuated nicotine self-administration.

Both animal and human studies have investigated the involvement of specific nAChR subunits in nicotine reinforcement and, in the case of humans, smoking behavior. Research with gene knockout mice has shown that nicotine-mediated dopaminergic neuronal activation and nicotine self-administration and/or conditioned place preference require the presence of β2, α4, and α6

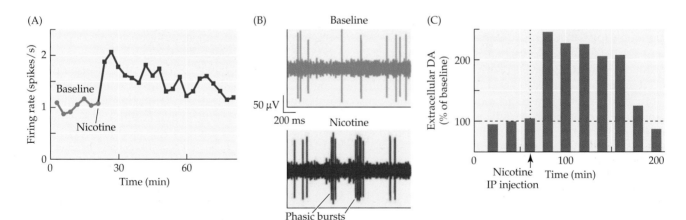

FIGURE 13.9 Nicotine stimulation of VTA dopaminergic neuron firing and DA release in the NAcc (A) Nicotine administration (0.4 to 0.5 mg/kg given intraperitoneally [IP]) to awake, freely moving rats caused a doubling of the average firing rate of VTA dopaminergic neurons compared with the baseline control condition. (B) This effect was mediated by increased burst firing by the cells. (C) Microdialysis performed in the shell of the NAcc of a separate group of rats showed a large increase in DA release following nicotine administration (0.6 mg/kg IP). (After M. Subramaniyan and J. A. Dani. 2015. *Ann NY Acad Sci* 1349: 46–63. © 2015 The Authors; and T. Zhang et al. 2009. *J Neurosci* 29: 4035–4043. © 2009 Society for Neuroscience; original data in panel C from V. I. Pidoplichko et al. 2004. *Learn Mem* 11: 60–69.)

subunits, all of which are common to high-affinity nAChRs. These findings are consistent with human genetic studies showing that polymorphisms (variations in DNA sequence) in the genes for the α4, α6, and β2 subunits are linked to the subjective effects of smoking, smoking rates, and the risk for developing nicotine dependence (Brunzell et al., 2015). Brain imaging studies of smokers have additionally investigated nicotine occupancy of high-affinity α4β2 subunit–containing nAChRs. In one study, tobacco-dependent smokers underwent an initial period of abstinence to clear the brain of nicotine. Participants were then subjected to PET imaging under one of three conditions: no smoking, smoking a denicotinized cigarette (containing 0.05 mg nicotine), or smoking a low-nicotine cigarette (containing 0.6 mg nicotine). The images shown in **FIGURE 13.10** reveal that nicotine

from the low-nicotine cigarette was sufficient to cause substantial occupancy (mean of 79%) of high-affinity nAChRs in all of the brain areas examined (Brody et al., 2009). Even smoking denicotinized cigarettes, which simulate the sensory and motoric experiences of smoking in the relative absence of nicotine consumption, produced a noticeable effect on high-affinity nAChRs. An earlier PET imaging study showed that even a single puff on a standard cigarette led to measurable occupancy of high-affinity nAChRs measured 3 hours later! As would be predicted, receptor occupancy was dose-dependent, with greater occupancy following three puffs and nearly complete receptor saturation following the smoking of three entire cigarettes (Brody et al., 2006). These findings emphasize that neurons expressing high-affinity nAChRs are exquisitely sensitive to nicotine.

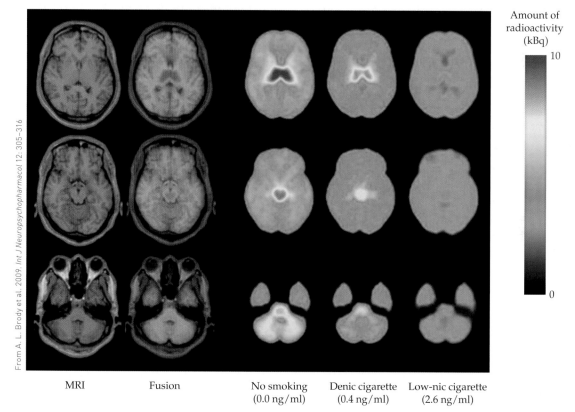

| MRI | Fusion | No smoking (0.0 ng/ml) | Denic cigarette (0.4 ng/ml) | Low-nic cigarette (2.6 ng/ml) |

Amount of radioactivity (kBq)

FIGURE 13.10 **Dose-dependent occupancy of brain α4β2 subunit–containing nAChRs by cigarette-derived nicotine** Tobacco-dependent cigarette smokers were subjected to PET imaging using a radiolabeled drug that binds selectively to high-affinity α4β2 subunit–containing nAChRs in the brain. Following 43 hours of abstinence from smoking, participants were imaged under control (no smoking) conditions or after smoking a denicotinized (Denic) cigarette or a low-nicotine (Low-nic) cigarette. The images in column 1 (far left) show magnetic resonance imaging (MRI) scans obtained for the purpose of anatomical localization of drug binding. Columns 3 to 5 show PET scans obtained under the various smoking conditions. The second column (Fusion) shows the MRI images laid over the PET images. The three rows represent different planes of imaging that capture receptor binding in three brain areas of interest. The top row shows binding at the level of the thalamus; the middle row shows binding at the level of the brain stem; and the bottom row shows binding at the level of the cerebellum. The highest amount of receptor binding is depicted in red, followed in descending order by yellow, green, and blue. The concentration values beneath the labels under columns 3, 4, and 5 are the mean plasma levels of nicotine produced by each experimental condition. The reductions in radiolabeled drug binding (i.e., displacement of the radiolabel by nicotine) show that even low levels of nicotine cause significant occupancy of high-affinity nAChRs in multiple brain areas.

AVERSIVE EFFECTS OF NICOTINE Depending on the dose and other circumstances, nicotine can produce aversive instead of reinforcing effects. In an early study of nonsmokers, subcutaneous injection of a high dose of nicotine elicited various unpleasant reactions, including nausea, dizziness, sweating, headache, palpitations, stomach ache, and clammy hands (Foulds et al., 1997). This reaction did not occur in smokers, which demonstrates the presence of chronic nicotine tolerance in smokers (see section below on nicotine tolerance and dependence). The results suggest that tolerance to these aversive effects may need to occur before individuals can fully experience nicotine reinforcement.

Laboratory animal studies have shown that nicotine aversion is dependent on nAChRs containing the α5 subunit, which commonly assembles with α3 and β4 subunits. Activation of these α5-, α3-, and β4-containing receptors enhances nicotine's aversive properties, thereby reducing the propensity to consume or self-administer the drug (Fowler and Kenny, 2014; Antolin-Fontes et al., 2015). On the other hand, reducing receptor expression by selectively knocking out the α5 subunit enhances nicotine self-administration at high doses where the aversive effects usually limit the animal's consumption (Fowler et al., 2011; **FIGURE 13.11**). The α5-containing nAChRs that help mediate nicotine aversion are heavily expressed in the interpeduncular nucleus, where they are activated by cholinergic input from the medial habenula (Antolin-Fontes et al., 2015).

Relevant to the above findings, the human chromosome 15 contains a region that regulates nicotine aversion, smoking behavior, and nicotine intake (Lassi et al., 2016). This chromosomal region, which is called *CHRNA5-CHRNA3-CHRNB4*, encodes the genes for the nAChR α5, α3, and β4 subunits, respectively. Moreover, researchers discovered a mutation in the *CHRNA5* gene that causes a single amino acid substitution in the receptor subunit protein. This mutant allele and the resulting change in the subunit protein results in a receptor that has lower responsiveness to nicotine, and cigarette smokers carrying the allele show less of an aversive response when administered pure nicotine (although their pleasure ratings are unchanged) and smoke more heavily than smokers carrying the wild-type allele (Jensen et al., 2015; Lassi et al., 2016). This effect accounts for a major portion (though not all) of the link between the *CHRNA5-CHRNA3-CHRNB4* chromosomal region and smoking behavior.

Nicotine produces a wide range of physiological effects

We mentioned earlier that nAChRs are abundantly expressed in autonomic ganglia. Consequently, nicotine can activate elements of both the sympathetic and parasympathetic systems to cause a wide spectrum of physiological manifestations. For example, smoking a cigarette stimulates the adrenal glands to release epinephrine (adrenaline) and norepinephrine (noradrenaline). These hormones, along with direct nicotine-induced activation of sympathetic ganglia, lead to symptoms of physiological arousal such as tachycardia (increased heart rate) and elevated blood pressure. This mild physiological arousal is thought to contribute to the reinforcing features of smoking. On the other hand, repeated exposure to nicotine and other components of cigarette smoke alters the balance of autonomic nervous system activity, resulting in chronically elevated sympathetic activity (Middlekauff et al., 2014). This effect helps explain why smoking increases the risk for cardiovascular disease and cerebrovascular accidents (strokes), particularly if the smoker has high blood pressure to begin with.

The action of nicotine on parasympathetic ganglia increases hydrochloric acid secretion in the stomach, which exacerbates or contributes to the formation of stomach ulcers. There is also increased muscle contraction in the bowel, which sometimes leads to chronic diarrhea that is especially harmful to individuals vulnerable to colitis, a condition of chronic irritability of the colon. Together, these autonomic nervous system effects contribute to the deleterious consequences of heavy and prolonged use of tobacco products (see the section on smoking-related illness).

One consequence that many cigarette smokers find desirable is the constraining effect of nicotine on body weight. Adult cigarette smokers weigh an average of 8 to 11 pounds less than gender- and age-matched non-smokers, and quitting smoking usually results in weight

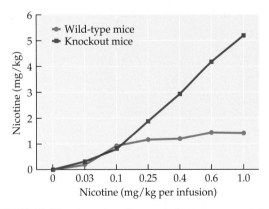

FIGURE 13.11 **Aversive effects of nicotine are mediated by a specific neural circuit that includes activation of α5 subunit–containing nAChRs** Results of dose-dependent changes in nicotine self-administration in α5 subunit knockout mice compared with wild-type mice. The *y*-axis shows total nicotine intake at each dose. The knockout mice administer successively greater amounts of nicotine as the dose per infusion increases, whereas the wild-type mice plateau at a relatively low level of intake because of the aversive effects of nicotine at higher doses. (After C. D. Fowler et al. 2011. *Nature* 471: 597–601. doi.org/10.1038/nature09797.)

gain (Audrain-McGovern and Benowitz, 2011). This effect of nicotine has been attributed to appetite suppression coupled with an increase in metabolic rate. The mechanisms underlying these effects are not yet fully understood; however, current evidence suggests that appetite suppression involves activation of nAChRs located mainly within the hypothalamic hunger/feeding circuit described previously in Chapter 6 (Calarco and Picciotto, 2020), whereas altered metabolic rate is governed by effects of nicotine on various peripheral organs involved in energy metabolism (Seoane-Collazo et al., 2021).

Nicotine is a toxic substance that can cause severe distress or even death at high doses

Nicotine can exert toxic effects, primarily because of its actions on the autonomic nervous system. Many textbooks cite a lethal adult human dose to be as little as 60 mg, which corresponds roughly to the amount of nicotine contained within a couple of 5% JUUL pods or the nicotine extracted from 5 to 10 typical tobacco cigarettes. However, measurement of plasma nicotine concentrations in fatal compared to nonfatal overdose cases has shown that this value may be far too low (i.e., that it takes much more oral nicotine consumption than 60 mg to cause a fatal reaction; Mayer, 2014; Maessen et al., 2020). Moreover, tobacco and e-cigarettes are only smoked/vaped one at a time, and much of the nicotine content is not taken in for two reasons: the high heat required to burn the tobacco or vaporize the e-liquid, and (2) the loss of sidestream smoke/vapor (smoke/vapor not inhaled by the user). Nevertheless, toxic effects of nicotine can result from exposure to pure nicotine used in certain insecticides or from absorption of nicotine through the skin (or possibly also by breathing airborne nicotine) by field workers harvesting wet tobacco leaves. Symptoms of nicotine exposure in field workers has been termed **green tobacco illness**. These symptoms include nausea, vomiting, dizziness, weakness, abdominal pain, and excessive sweating and salivation (Alkam and Nabeshima, 2019; McMahon, 2019). An estimated 8 million people worldwide, which includes women and children in developing countries, are suffering from green tobacco illness, even though the risk of developing the disorder can be reduced by wearing appropriate personal protective equipment.

Nicotine is toxic not only to people (and other vertebrates) but also to insects. Indeed, the evolution of nicotine synthesis by the tobacco plant is believed to have been driven by the protection it affords against insect predation, a topic discussed in **WEB BOX 13.1**.

The most dangerous cases of acute nicotine poisoning primarily occur through the swallowing of tobacco or of nicotine-containing products such as nicotine gum, patches, or the liquid contained in e-cigarette refill cartridges. In this case the symptoms include those mentioned above for green tobacco illness but in a more severe form. Victims may also experience mental confusion and disturbed hearing and vision. The initial symptoms are quickly followed by fainting and prostration, falling blood pressure, difficulty breathing, weakening of the pulse (which becomes rapid and irregular), and finally collapse. Left untreated, an extremely high nicotine overdose may end with convulsions followed shortly by fatal respiratory failure due to depolarization block of the muscles of breathing. The treatment of acute nicotine poisoning involves inducing vomiting if the poison has been swallowed, placing adsorptive charcoal in the stomach, giving artificial respiration, and treating for shock. When they do occur, fatal nicotine overdoses are mostly categorized as accidental exposures in young children or intentional exposures in suicidal adolescents or adults (Maessen et al., 2020; Scarpino et al., 2021). Intentional poisoning by e-liquids is occasionally performed by injection rather than oral consumption. Regardless of the route of exposure, it possible in such cases that e-liquid constituents besides nicotine, notably the typical propylene glycol solvent, contribute to the toxic effects of such exposure.

Chronic exposure to nicotine induces tolerance and dependence

NICOTINE TOLERANCE Repeated exposure to nicotine leads to a complex pattern of tolerance and, in some instances, sensitization. It is useful to distinguish between acute and chronic nicotine tolerance. For example, acute tolerance can be studied by pretreating subjects (e.g., by injection or nasal spray) with either nicotine or vehicle and then testing their responses to a subsequent nicotine challenge. In both smokers and nonsmokers, many behavioral and physiological responses are attenuated by nicotine pretreatment, indicating the occurrence of tolerance. In much the same way, cigarette smokers undergo a significant degree of nicotine tolerance during the course of the day. Acute tolerance is short-lived; after an overnight period of abstinence, smokers awaken the next morning more sensitive to nicotine than at the end of the previous day. This neurobiological mechanism helps explain why smokers often report that the first cigarette of the day is the most pleasurable one.

Acute tolerance is related to a desensitization (i.e., temporary inactivation) of central nAChRs, including those that mediate nicotine reinforcement. The nicotine from even a single cigarette is able to induce some degree of receptor desensitization. However, the properties of desensitization, including the concentration of nicotine required for desensitization, latencies to desensitize and to recover, and the proportion of receptors that are inactivated, vary significantly with subunit composition. As discussed previously, receptors composed of both α and β subunits (e.g., α4β2) are desensitized at lower nicotine concentrations than α7-containing receptors, because the former have a higher affinity for nicotine (Picciotto et al., 2008). On the other hand, α4β2 nicotinic receptors recover more rapidly than α7 receptors, which may permit the high-affinity receptors to at least partially regain their sensitivity by the time the next cigarette is smoked. For this reason, some investigators theorize that individuals who smoke frequently over the course of a day undergo numerous cycles of nicotinic receptor activation, desensitization, and resensitization.

Long-term exposure to nicotine causes chronic tolerance. This chronic tolerance is superimposed on the acute within-a-day tolerance, and of course it is present only in smokers and others who use tobacco frequently. An early clue to the existence of chronic nicotine tolerance was the observation that green tobacco sickness was found to occur much more frequently among tobacco harvesters who didn't smoke than among those who were smokers (Gehlbach et al., 1974). The subjective effects of nicotine, both positive (rewarding) and negative (aversive), are most susceptible to chronic tolerance in regular smokers (Perkins, 2002). There is also some tolerance to the cardiovascular effects of the drug. Chronic tolerance to at least some of these effects is surprisingly slow to dissipate, even after prolonged abstinence from smoking. Nicotinic receptor desensitization is generally thought to be the primary mechanism underlying chronic, as well as acute, tolerance, although other factors are probably also involved. Interestingly, chronic exposure to nicotine elicits a compensatory response manifested by an up-regulation of high-affinity nAChR expression in many parts of the brain (Melroy-Greif et al., 2016). In humans, this effect has been demonstrated using both neuroimaging and post-mortem binding studies. For example, **FIGURE 13.12** shows a large increase in high-affinity nicotinic receptor binding in layer 6 of the prefrontal cortex of a smoker compared with a nonsmoker (Perry et al., 1999). Such receptor up-regulation may play a significant role in the development of nicotine dependence and withdrawal (see next section).

NICOTINE DEPENDENCE AND WITHDRAWAL   Nicotine is a highly addictive drug. Indeed, the National Epidemiologic Survey on Alcohol and Related Conditions, a survey conducted between 2001 and 2005, found that over 67% of nicotine users eventually became dependent, whereas the percentages for alcohol, cocaine, and cannabis were only 22.7%, 20.9%, and 8.9%, respectively (Lopez-Quintero et al., 2011). The *Diagnostic and Statistical Manual of Mental Disorders*, fifth edition (*DSM-5*), lists "tobacco use disorder" as a subcategory within the broader category of substance use disorders (American Psychiatric Association, 2013). To be diagnosed with tobacco use disorder, a person must have used tobacco (i.e., nicotine-containing) products for over 1 year and

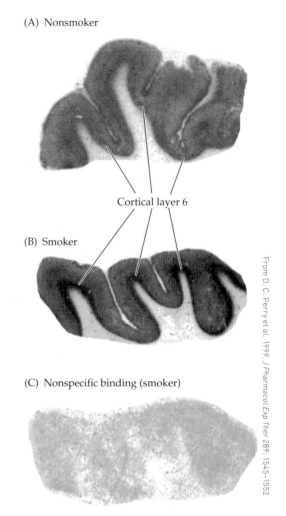

(A) Nonsmoker

Cortical layer 6

(B) Smoker

(C) Nonspecific binding (smoker)

From D. C. Perry et al. 1999, *J Pharmacol Exp Ther* 289: 1545–1552

FIGURE 13.12   **Up-regulation of nicotinic receptor binding in the prefrontal cortex of smokers**   Post-mortem slices of prefrontal cortex were incubated with radiolabeled epibatidine, a compound that binds to high-affinity nicotinic binding sites. (A and B) Total binding in a nonsmoker and a smoker, respectively, illustrating the particularly large amount of receptor up-regulation in cortical layer 6. (C) Nonspecific epibatidine binding (i.e., binding to tissue elements other than nicotinic receptors), which was very low.

have met at least two of the following three criteria: (1) use of more tobacco products for a longer time than planned, (2) signs of nicotine tolerance, and (3) appearance of withdrawal symptoms when the person stops using tobacco. For habitual smokers who meet these criteria, even a brief abstinence of a few hours leads to a growing urge to smoke. These feelings correlate with a drop in nicotine levels in the individual's bloodstream. A series of case histories of adolescent-to-young-adult smokers performed by DiFranza and colleagues (2010) led the investigators to propose three temporal stages of compulsion to use tobacco—"wanting," "craving," and "needing"—with each successive stage being more powerful than the one before. These stages are more fully characterized as follows: "Wanting is mild, short-lived and easily ignored. Craving is a desire to smoke that is more intense and compelling than wanting. Wanting will go away if ignored, but craving is more persistent. Smokers say they are needing to smoke when withdrawal symptoms are so troublesome that they cannot function normally" (DiFranza, 2015, p. 44).

The much longer withdrawal that occurs when people try to quit smoking leads to a more complex abstinence syndrome characterized by three kinds of symptoms: affective (mood related), somatic, and cognitive (McLaughlin et al., 2015). Affective symptoms include anxiety, anger/irritability, depressed mood, anhedonia (decreased ability to experience pleasure), insomnia, restlessness, hyperalgesia (abnormal sensitivity to pain), and of course a powerful desire to smoke. Somatic symptoms consist of tremors, bradycardia (slowed heart rate), nausea and gastrointestinal distress, and hunger and weight gain. Finally, the cognitive features of nicotine withdrawal include difficulty concentrating (i.e., deficient attention) and memory impairment (McClernon et al., 2015). A recent review of withdrawal symptoms over the first 24 hours after smoking cessation found that anxiety was the strongest affective symptom, with anger/irritability being the second strongest (Conti et al., 2020). These symptoms can begin as quickly at 3 hours after cessation of smoking and continue to increase over the 24-hour period. Depressed mood seems to occur later during the period of abstinence. Withdrawal symptoms reach a peak around 1 week post-cessation and then gradually diminish over the next several weeks (Wittenberg et al., 2020). An early study by Hughes and colleagues (1991) found that use of nicotine gum prevented almost all of the withdrawal symptoms, supporting the conclusion that these symptoms are largely due to nicotine dependence. It is important to note, however, that even with amelioration of withdrawal symptoms by nicotine replacement, more than two-thirds of the individuals were back smoking at a 6-month follow-up test. These and other experimental results indicate that the nicotine abstinence syndrome is not the only reason that most regular smokers find it so difficult to quit their habit.

Animal models of nicotine dependence have been critical for studying the neurochemical mechanisms underlying this phenomenon and for testing potential pharmacotherapies for smoking cessation (Falcone et al., 2016). Nicotine dependence can be induced in laboratory animals by giving them continuous exposure to the drug, often by surgically implanting a small device known as an **osmotic minipump** under the skin of the animal. The minipump is filled with a nicotine solution and slowly infuses the solution subcutaneously at a constant rate for a predetermined period such as 1 or 2 weeks. Some withdrawal symptoms can be observed when the nicotine clears the animal's system after the pump either runs out of solution or is removed by the experimenter. However, a stronger reaction can be triggered by administering a nicotinic receptor antagonist such as **mecamylamine**, thereby blocking the action of any residual nicotine still present in the animal. In rats, typical nicotine withdrawal symptoms include gasps, shakes or tremors, teeth chatter, ptosis (drooping eyelids), reduced locomotor activity, and increased startle reactivity (Helton et al., 1993; Hildebrand et al., 1997). Brain reward function measured by the threshold for intracranial electrical self-stimulation is also significantly impaired during nicotine withdrawal (Epping-Jordan et al., 1998)—an effect seen during withdrawal from other addictive drugs as well (see Chapter 9). Decreased functioning of the brain reward system is a sign of anhedonia, which is present during tobacco withdrawal in smokers and might contribute to the well-known difficulty in stopping smoking.

Animal studies have also contributed key information on the neurobiological mechanisms underlying the nicotine abstinence syndrome. This syndrome is mediated, in part, by resensitization of the desensitized and up-regulated nAChRs, reduced activity of the mesolimbic dopaminergic pathway, and increased activity of the central corticotropin-releasing factor (CRF) system, a system that has been broadly implicated in drug dependence and withdrawal (see Chapter 9) (McLaughlin et al., 2015). In addition, activation of the previously described nicotine aversion circuit that includes the medial habenula and interpeduncular nucleus plays a key role in withdrawal-related anxiety (Molas et al., 2017). Lastly, as first mentioned in an earlier section, neuroimaging findings have shown that activation of the insula is important for cigarette craving during nicotine abstinence (Regner et al., 2019).

SECTION SUMMARY

- The mood-altering effects of nicotine depend on whether the individual is an abstinent smoker or a nonsmoker. In temporarily abstinent smokers, administration of pure nicotine usually increases calmness and relaxation. This effect is due, in part, to relief from nicotine withdrawal symptoms, because nicotine given to nonsmokers more often elicits feelings of tension, arousal, lightheadedness or dizziness, and sometimes nausea.

- The mood-altering effects of nicotine interact with the expectation of receiving the drug, since a reduction in nicotine craving by abstinent smokers only occurred when participants were given a nicotine-containing cigarette and were correctly informed that the cigarette contained nicotine but not when incorrectly informed that the cigarette was denicotinized.

- Administration of nicotine to abstinent smokers also leads to enhanced performance on many different kinds of cognitive tasks. In this case, however, nicotine-related functional enhancement has also been reported for nonsmokers on tests of short-term episodic and working memory, attention, and fine motor performance. Some research has found that nicotine enhancement of attention task performance is most clearly evident in people with a low baseline level of attention.

- Animal studies have found that nicotine improves performance on tasks requiring sustained attention and working memory. Certain hippocampal-dependent tasks, such as contextual fear conditioning and spatial learning, are also sensitive to nicotine. Research with nAChR subunit knockout mice as well as the antagonists DhβE (selective for α4β2-containing high-affinity nAChRs) and MLA (selective for α7-containing low-affinity nAChRs) revealed that high-affinity nAChRs play a greater role in the nicotine enhancement of hippocampal-dependent tasks. Other neurotransmitters involved in cognitive enhancement by nicotine include norepinephrine (mediated by β-adrenergic receptors), glutamate (mediated by NMDA receptors), and DA (mediated by the mesocortical dopaminergic pathway).

- Within a certain dose range, pure nicotine is reinforcing to both humans and experimental animals, as shown by IV self-administration. Females are more sensitive than males to nicotine reward/reinforcement in both humans and rodents. Rodent studies have additionally found greater nicotine reward/reinforcement in adolescent than in adult animals.

- The reinforcing properties of nicotine involve activation of high-affinity nAChRs located in the VTA, which stimulates burst firing of the dopaminergic neurons and increases DA release in the NAcc. This hypothesis is supported by the finding that β2, α4, and α6 nAChR subunits must all be present in the VTA for nicotine self-administration to occur. In humans, high-affinity nAChRs composed of these subunits are occupied by very low levels of nicotine, indicating the pronounced sensitivity of the receptors for the drug. Polymorphisms in the genes coding for these subunits alter the degree of nicotine binding and have been associated with the subjective effects of smoking, smoking rates, and the risk for developing nicotine dependence.

- Nicotine can also exert aversive effects, although such effects are susceptible to chronic tolerance with continued nicotine exposure. Nonsmokers injected with a high dose of nicotine experienced a number of symptoms such as nausea, dizziness, sweating, headache, palpitations, and stomach ache. Nicotine aversion in both humans and experimental animals involves the stimulation of nAChRs containing α5, α3, and β4 subunits. These receptors are expressed at high levels in the medial habenula–interpeduncular nucleus pathway, and the genes for the subunits are clustered together on human chromosome 15, where they form the *CHRNA5-CHRNA3-CHRNB4* chromosomal region. Researchers have identified a mutation in the *CHRNA5* gene (which codes for the α5 subunit) that leads to receptors with reduced responsiveness to nicotine, resulting in less aversion to nicotine and heavier smoking behavior.

- Nicotine additionally produces a variety of peripheral physiological effects. These include release of epinephrine and norepinephrine from the adrenal glands, tachycardia, and elevated blood pressure, all of which contribute to the arousing effects of the drug. Nicotine also increases hydrochloric acid secretion in the stomach and muscle contraction in the bowel, both of which can adversely affect the gastrointestinal tract. Finally, nicotine modestly increases metabolic rate and suppresses appetite, which is why smokers typically gain weight after quitting.

- Nicotine is a toxic substance that, at high doses, can cause potentially dangerous symptoms including nausea, vomiting, dizziness, weakness, abdominal pain, and excessive sweating and salivation. These symptoms can occur from accidental exposure to a nicotine-containing insecticide or from exposure to wet tobacco leaves during harvesting (i.e., green tobacco illness). If a sufficient dose has been ingested, death may occur from respiratory failure. Fatal nicotine overdoses may result from accidental poisoning of young children or from intentional exposure in suicidal adolescents or adults.

- Repeated exposure to nicotine can lead to tolerance or, in some cases, sensitization. Single doses of nicotine cause a rapid but transient form of acute tolerance that depends on desensitization of nicotinic receptors. Long-term nicotine exposure is associated with chronic tolerance, as a consequence of which smokers do not exhibit the adverse reactions to high doses of nicotine that are observed in nonsmokers. Smokers show an up-regulation of nAChR levels in many brain areas, seemingly as a compensatory response to the chronic receptor desensitization associated with repeated nicotine exposure.

- Chronic nicotine can also cause dependence, thereby leading to withdrawal symptoms upon abstinence. The *DSM-5* contains the category tobacco use disorder, which is diagnosed by meeting at least two of the three listed criteria. Compulsive cigarette use is characterized by successive stages of wanting, craving, and finally needing a cigarette. Prolonged abstinence in nicotine-dependent people evokes a complex syndrome of affective, somatic, and cognitive symptoms. Within the first 24 hours after smoking cessation, anxiety and anger/irritability are the most powerful affective symptoms. Depressed mood occurs later during the period of abstinence. Initial studies suggest that e-cigarette users are generally less dependent than tobacco cigarette users, but additional research is needed to confirm this finding.

- Animal models of nicotine dependence are important for studying the mechanisms of dependence and for testing new drug treatments. When rats are made dependent on nicotine by giving them continuous exposure to the drug (e.g., with osmotic minipumps), withdrawal symptoms can be observed if the dependent animals are administered a nicotinic receptor antagonist such as mecamylamine. This withdrawal syndrome has been related to resensitization of desensitized and up-regulated nAChRs, reduced activity of the mesolimbic dopaminergic pathway, increased CRF signaling in the central nucleus of the amygdala, and activation of the nicotine aversion pathway involving the medial habenula and interpeduncular nucleus. Nicotine craving has additionally been linked to activation of the insula.

13.3 Cigarette Smoking and Vaping

Useful information about the causes and consequences of smoking has been obtained by documenting changes in the prevalence of smoking over time and by identifying the characteristics of smokers and the pattern of progression from occasional to regular smoking. This information has been combined with knowledge about the mechanisms of nicotine action and data on the serious health consequences of smoking to develop smoking cessation programs. Although fewer data are available on vaping and how it compares to smoking, research continues to be performed and some of the results obtained thus far are presented below.

What percentage of the population are current users of tobacco and/or e-cigarettes?

The amount of cigarette smoking in the United States has varied tremendously over the past 120-plus years. As illustrated in **FIGURE 13.13**, yearly per capita cigarette consumption was quite low at the beginning of the twentieth century but then rose steeply until the mid-1950s. A significant cultural influence promoting cigarette smoking was the depiction of this behavior in films, which was

quite common from the 1930s through the 1960s and was even used by advertisers to promote specific brands of cigarettes (Castaldelli-Maia et al., 2016). There was a brief dip in cigarette consumption following publication of the first studies linking smoking with lung cancer, but consumption rose again with the marketing of filtered cigarettes. The decline in cigarette consumption since the 1960s coincides with the Surgeon General's reports on the health consequences of smoking, the appearance of antismoking ads, large increases in cigarette taxes, and general disapproval of smoking in many parts of society.

More recent data on the use of nicotine-containing products can be obtained from the national survey results reported in Cornelius and coworkers (2020). While tobacco cigarette smoking has continued to decline, much of this reduction has been replaced by the rise in e-cigarette vaping. In 2019, an estimated 50.6 million Americans (roughly 1/5 of the adult population) were current users (defined as use at least once during the previous 30 days at the time of the survey) of any tobacco (i.e., nicotine-containing) product. Of those, 67.4% were tobacco cigarette smokers, 21.5% used e-cigarettes, and the remainder were cigar or pipe smokers or users of smokeless tobacco. Interestingly, an age breakdown

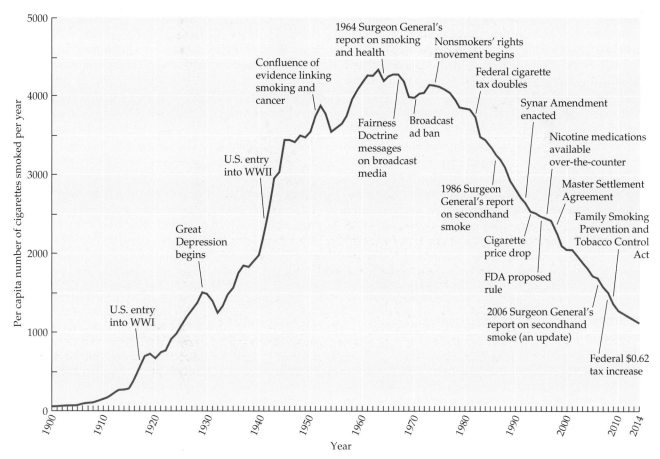

FIGURE 13.13   Yearly per capita cigarette consumption in the United States from 1900 to 2014 Data are for individuals 18 years of age or older. (After U.S. Department of Health and Human Services, 2014; modified from K. E. Warner, 1977, 1981, 1985.)

of tobacco product users revealed that e-cigarettes were most popular among people 18 to 44 years of age, whereas tobacco cigarettes were most popular among people 45 years of age or older. Moreover, among all surveyed e-cigarette users, 36.9% were also current tobacco cigarette smokers (i.e., dual tobacco product users), 39.5% were former tobacco cigarette smokers, and 23.6% had never smoked tobacco cigarettes. Finally, for the youngest surveyed group of e-cigarette users, namely those who were 18 to 24 years of age, over 50% indicated that they had never smoked tobacco cigarettes (Cornelius et al., 2020). Taken together, these findings depict an overall trend of e-cigarettes gradually replacing tobacco cigarettes as the nicotine vehicle of choice.

Nicotine users progress through a series of stages in their pattern and frequency of use

INITIATION AND SUBSEQUENT TRAJECTORY OF TOBACCO CIGARETTE SMOKING Most smokers pick up the habit during adolescence. Looked at another way, early smoking greatly increases the chances that one will smoke as an adult. For this reason, smoking and, more recently, vaping by teenagers have received a lot of attention from researchers as well as from policy makers whose goal is to reduce the use of tobacco products in our society. There are many theories about why teenagers take up smoking. Some of the hypothesized reasons include establishing feelings of independence and maturity (by defying parental wishes or societal norms), improving self-image and enhancing social acceptance (assuming that one's friends are already smokers), counteracting stress and/or boredom, and simple curiosity. Moreover, young people tend to emphasize the positive elements of smoking and vaping while disregarding or denying the negative aspects, including the health consequences. Longitudinal surveys have gone beyond self-reported reasons for smoking to examine empirically the various factors that predict smoking onset. A review of this research found that poor academic performance, rebelliousness, sensation seeking, receptivity to cigarette advertising/marketing, and smoking by family and/or friends were all significant predictors of smoking onset (Wellman et al., 2016).

Early adolescent experimentation with cigarettes can lead to a variety of outcomes. Some individuals, called **intermittent smokers**, develop a stable habit of non-daily smoking. In one study, for example, the intermittent smoking group smoked a mean of 4.45 cigarettes per smoking day, with smoking days averaging 4.5 per week (Shiffman et al., 2014). This group had been smoking an average of 19.25 years, indicating that their intermittent smoking pattern was not a temporary phenomenon on the way to greater cigarette consumption. A comparison group that smoked daily averaged 15.0 cigarettes per day. Not surprisingly, daily smokers

had much higher scores than intermittent smokers on a standard test of nicotine dependence. As a result, daily smokers exhibit a more compulsive smoking habit that is accompanied by strong cravings for tobacco and is difficult to stop. Why intermittent smokers fail to develop strong nicotine dependence despite years of exposure is not yet well understood.

A group of Canadian researchers determined the rate of progression through predetermined "milestones" from the first cigarette to clinically defined nicotine dependence by following over 1000 students prospectively for 5 years beginning at the seventh grade (Gervais et al., 2006). The researchers found that the first signs of craving, tolerance, and withdrawal symptoms often occurred before the smoker had smoked a total of 100 cigarettes (just five packs!) in their life. These results are consistent with other findings suggesting an early onset of nicotine dependence (DiFranza et al., 2011, 2015). On the other hand, the researchers also found that the time from first puff to the milestone of daily smoking ranged from 20 months to almost 40 months for the study participants who reached that milestone (Gervais et al., 2006). Therefore, the progression of smoking frequency can be fairly slow despite earlier signs of nicotine tolerance and dependence.

INITIATION AND SUBSEQUENT TRAJECTORY OF E-CIGARETTE USE We have previously noted that more adolescents now use e-cigarettes than tobacco cigarettes. This raises three important questions. First, what are the self-reported reasons for initiating vaping and the risk factors that are associated with e-cigarette use compared to non-use? Second, what are the factors that lead young people to choose e-cigarettes over tobacco cigarettes for their initial exposure to tobacco products? Finally, does e-cigarette use by adolescents increase the likelihood of a later onset of tobacco cigarette smoking?

In self-report studies, young people typically cite curiosity, taste (flavor), relief from boredom, having a good time with friends, and alleviation of tension as major reasons for beginning to vape (e.g., see Patrick et al., 2016). Furthermore, e-cigarette users compared to non-users were found to have less parental support and monitoring, more parental conflict, less academic involvement, and poorer behavioral and emotional self-control and regulation (Wills et al., 2015). The users were characterized as being more rebellious and sensation-seeking, and they were greater users of alcohol and marijuana. These findings are hardly unique to e-cigarettes, since many of the same risk factors have previously been reported for adolescent users of other substances. Additional risk factors for e-cigarette use include having friends or family members who smoke tobacco cigarettes (Wang et al., 2018) and having internalizing and/or externalizing problems (Buu et al., 2020). Once e-cigarette use has begun, many users increase their frequency of use and amount of nicotine exposure over time, resulting in an elevated risk of becoming nicotine-dependent (Vogel et al., 2019). In this regard, e-cigarette use is not obviously "safer" than smoking tobacco cigarettes.

Several hypotheses have been proposed to explain the initial choice of e-cigarettes over tobacco cigarettes by adolescents. These hypotheses include (1) the "flavor hypothesis," which argues that e-cigarettes are preferred because of the availability of many different e-cigarette flavors (although as mentioned earlier, this factor will likely become less important as strict flavorant regulations come into play); (2) the "health hypothesis," which proposes that adolescents choose e-cigarettes because they are perceived to be a healthier option than tobacco cigarettes; (3) the "price hypothesis," which is based on the fact that in some locales, e-cigarettes are less expensive than tobacco cigarettes; (4) the "role model hypothesis," which posits that adolescent e-cigarette use is prompted by peer users who are perceived as role models; (5) the "concealment hypothesis," which is based on the idea that e-cigarette vaping is easier to hide than tobacco cigarette smoking; and (6) the "acceptance hypothesis," which proposes that e-cigarettes are more readily accepted socially than tobacco cigarettes among adolescents (reviewed by Schneider and Diehl, 2016). It is important to recognize that these hypotheses are not mutually exclusive. That is, any number of these reasons could play a role in adolescents' choice to begin their tobacco product use by selecting e-cigarettes.

E-cigarette use often precedes the initiation and continuation of tobacco cigarette smoking, either by itself as a replacement for e-cigarettes or as an additional source of nicotine (i.e., dual e-cigarette and tobacco cigarette use) (Soneji et al., 2017; Barrington-Trimis et al., 2018; Chaffee et al., 2018; Owotomo et al., 2020). This is true even for adolescents who had no prior intention to begin smoking. Schneider and Diehl (2016) reviewed three potential explanations for the transition from e-cigarettes to tobacco cigarettes: (1) the "addiction hypothesis," which is based on the idea that nicotine addiction produced by chronic e-cigarette use leads to the adoption of other nicotine-containing products, notably tobacco cigarettes, especially if the individual has been using a type of e-cigarette that yields less nicotine than a standard tobacco cigarette; (2) the "accessibility hypothesis," which proposes that retail vendors of e-cigarettes often sell tobacco cigarettes as well, thereby increasing customer exposure to tobacco cigarettes and making it easy to purchase them; and (3) the "experience hypothesis," which suggests that the experience of handling cigarette-like ENDS, inhaling the vapor produced by these devices, and using e-cigarettes in a social context eases the transition to smoking tobacco cigarettes in addition to or instead of e-cigarettes. **FIGURE 13.14** illustrates the various pathways from no tobacco consumption to either e-cigarette or tobacco cigarette use, as well as the transition from e-cigarettes to tobacco cigarettes. The figure includes the hypothetical mechanisms just

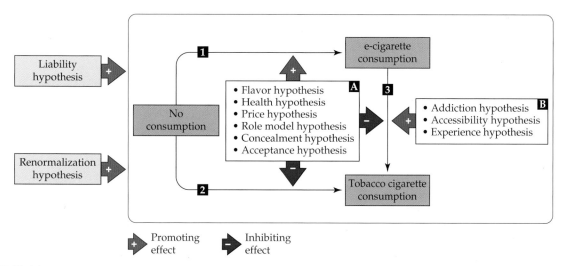

FIGURE 13.14   **Model illustrating transitions of adolescent nicotine product use and hypotheses proposed to influence each transition**   Current non-consumers of tobacco products may transition initially to e-cigarette consumption (pathway 1) or to tobacco cigarette consumption (pathway 2). Once e-cigarette use has begun, some users later transition to tobacco cigarette consumption (pathway 3). Box A contains hypotheses about why adolescents are more likely to initially select e-cigarettes (+ arrow) than tobacco cigarettes (– arrow). These same factors presumably also inhibit the transition to tobacco cigarette consumption (– arrow directed toward pathway 3). Box B contains hypotheses about factors that may promote the transition from e-cigarette to tobacco cigarette consumption (+ arrow directed toward pathway 3). Two additional hypotheses shown on the far left involve factors thought to promote the initiation of tobacco product use, whether e-cigarettes or tobacco cigarettes (+ arrows). (After S. Schneider and K. Diehl. 2016. *Nicotine Tob Res* 18: 647–653.)

discussed that are thought to modulate each pathway, as well as two additional hypotheses proposed to explain the initial decision to try either e-cigarettes or tobacco cigarettes. These are (1) the "liability hypothesis," which posits that some adolescents, by virtue of their genetics, personality, and/or environment (e.g., e-cigarette use or cigarette smoking by family members or friends), are predisposed to begin use of a tobacco product; and (2) the "renormalization hypothesis," which is based on the idea that increased use of e-cigarettes within the population has made both e-cigarettes and tobacco cigarettes more socially acceptable than was the case before the introduction of e-cigarettes (Schneider and Diehl, 2016).

The finding that many e-cigarette users undergo a transition to tobacco cigarette smoking has led to the hypothesis that the former may serve as a "gateway" to the latter (Chatterjee et al., 2016; Chapman et al., 2019). Unlike the model shown in Figure 13.14, the gateway hypothesis is mainly concerned with how one kind of substance exposure (e.g., e-cigarette use) may prime an individual to be more vulnerable to take up a riskier or more dangerous kind of exposure (e.g., tobacco cigarette smoking). As previously discussed in Web Box 9.1, the gateway hypothesis was originally developed to account for other types of substance use trajectories and is not unique to e-cigarettes.

Why do smokers smoke and vapers vape?

Researchers have identified multiple factors that contribute to the development and maintenance of a smoking or vaping habit. As discussed below, these include not only nicotine but also other pharmacological and psychological factors.

THE ROLE OF NICOTINE IN SMOKING AND VAPING
Delivery of nicotine is obviously one of the key factors in smoking. As mentioned earlier, nicotine is intravenously self-administered by animals as well as by humans under some conditions. Over a 24-hour period, a regular smoker undergoes repeated elevations and drops in plasma nicotine, as shown in **FIGURE 13.15**. However, whereas cigarettes early in the day (beginning particularly with the first cigarette, which is smoked after the overnight period of abstinence) may elevate mood above the baseline level, later in the day even the peaks in plasma nicotine may not be sufficient to do more than merely maintain a neutral mood (by preventing withdrawal symptoms), because of the nicotinic receptor desensitization discussed previously (Benowitz, 2010). Overnight abstinence permits the receptors to resensitize and the cycle to begin again the following day. Although comparable research has not yet been performed with regular users of e-cigarettes, it's reasonable to conclude that the same patterns are present for those individuals because the same route

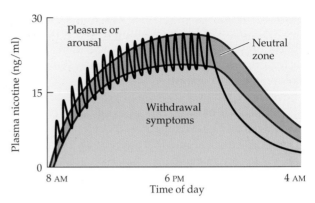

FIGURE 13.15 The daily smoking cycle and nicotine-induced mood changes Plasma nicotine levels are low in the morning as a result of overnight abstinence from smoking. Each cigarette over the course of the day leads to a spike followed by a decline in nicotine levels. The purple area depicts the zone of neutral affect (mood) between the pleasure and arousal produced by elevated nicotine levels (i.e., levels above the neutral zone) and the withdrawal symptoms produced by declining levels in a dependent smoker (i.e., levels below the neutral zone). Note that nicotine-induced positive effects diminish with repeated smoking episodes as a result of rapid tolerance to the drug's action, whereas withdrawal symptoms may become more pronounced. The nicotinic receptors resensitize significantly during overnight abstinence, allowing the cycle to repeat itself each day. (After N. L. Benowitz. 1992. *Med Clin North Am* 72: 415-437.)

of drug administration (inhalation) applies to both nicotine-containing vehicles.

We earlier discussed the involvement of tolerance and dependence in the maintenance of smoking behavior. Although both processes contribute to smoking, we note that they are distinct from each other. In fact, intermittent smokers develop tolerance to nicotine despite their limited exposure to the drug compared to daily smokers (Perkins, 2002). The finding that nicotine dependence and tolerance can be at least partly separated from each together suggests that they are produced by different physiological processes. As mentioned earlier, we don't yet know why some individuals can maintain low levels of smoking and a minimal degree of dependence. Also unknown is whether over the long term, e-cigarettes (especially those with a high nicotine content like JUUL) have the same propensity as tobacco cigarettes to engender a pattern of heavy daily use.

ENVIRONMENTAL CUES CONDITIONED TO SMOKING
For many smokers, nicotine plays the most important role in their behavior; however, other factors can also be quite important, as discussed in this and the next few sections (Garcia-Rivas and Deroche-Gamonet, 2019). One such factor is the presence of sensory and environmental cues associated with the act of smoking that have become conditioned to the reinforcing effects of nicotine and are thus able to function as secondary

reinforcers themselves. Such cues include the sensory components of tobacco smoking (i.e., the sight, smell, and touch of cigarettes), seeing other people smoking, and being in a place where smoking has habitually occurred. Indeed, formerly secret internal documents obtained from major cigarette manufacturers reveal that these companies know about the importance of the sensory qualities of tobacco smoke and manipulate these qualities to enhance smoker satisfaction (Carpenter et al., 2007). Moreover, sensory cues previously paired with smoking as well as smoking-associated behavioral rituals (e.g., rolling a cigarette) can provoke a desire to smoke by eliciting nicotine craving.

MOOD, STRESS, AND COGNITION Stress and negative affective states, especially anxiety, also play significant roles in smoking (F. S. Hall et al., 2015; Holliday and Gould, 2016). Smokers routinely report that smoking causes relaxation and alleviation of stress. Yet another reported reason for smoking is an increased ability to concentrate. Consequently, some researchers have hypothesized that smoking (presumably through the delivery of nicotine) provides two specific advantages to the smoker: greater mood control (specifically with respect to stress reduction) and enhancement of concentration. This has been termed the **nicotine resource model**. A hypothesized dual motivation for nicotine consumption that incorporates the nicotine resource model is presented in **FIGURE 13.16**. According to this hypothesis, smoking and vaping are driven by actions of nicotine on the brain that lead to a combination of both direct reward/reinforcement and enhanced cognitive function. These effects are mediated by nicotine activation of VTA dopaminergic neurons in conjunction with stimulation of nAChRs in relevant subcortical and cortical target areas. An alternative model, sometimes called the **deprivation reversal model**, suggests that the positive effects of smoking actually represent the alleviation of irritability, stress, and poor concentration experienced by smokers between cigarettes. This model, therefore, proposes that having a smoking habit increases overall stress, which then must be countered by repeated smoking.

There is ample evidence for both of these models. Clearly, nicotine withdrawal causes a dysphoric mood

and impaired attention, both of which are alleviated by nicotine consumption. Nevertheless, other evidence indicates that nicotine and other unconditioned or conditioned aspects of smoking behavior exert positive effects on these outcome measures. Advocates of the nicotine resource model can also point to the high rates of cigarette smoking among people with major depression, anxiety disorders, and schizophrenia (Featherstone and Siegel, 2015; Kutlu et al., 2015; Fluharty et al., 2017; Weinberger et al., 2017). It is possible that at least some of these individuals are engaged in self-medication to treat their negative affect and/or cognitive deficits.

We mentioned earlier that women overall are more susceptible to smoking than men. Furthermore, women are more likely than men to smoke in order to alleviate negative mood states, especially anxiety. Based on these and other findings, Torres and O'Dell (2016) proposed a model emphasizing that anxiety is a more important factor in smoking initiation and relapse in women than in men. Ovarian hormones, particularly estrogens, are believed to play a key role in the increased vulnerability of women to tobacco use and addiction (Park et al., 2016; Torres and O'Dell, 2016).

CHEMICAL CONSTITUENTS OF TOBACCO SMOKE AND E-LIQUID VAPOR The great majority of studies on tobacco dependence focus on nicotine because of its known reinforcing properties. However, cigarette smoke contains over 8000 other chemical constituents (Rodgman and Perfetti, 2013), and many chemicals are added to tobacco cigarettes and e-cigarette nicotine solutions as flavorings or for other purposes. Significantly, researchers have

FIGURE 13.16 Dual motivation for nicotine consumption involving both direct reward/reinforcement and cognitive enhancement Nicotine consumption from either tobacco cigarettes or e-cigarettes has rewarding/reinforcing effects mediated by activation of the mesolimbic DA pathway and by stimulation of nAChRs in the VST/NAcc and amygdala. A second source of nicotine motivation comes from cognitive enhancement mediated by activation of the mesocortical DA pathway and by stimulation of nAChRs in the PFC and ACC. ACC, anterior cingulate cortex; DARs, dopamine receptors; NAcc, nucleus accumbens; nAChRs, nicotinic acetylcholine receptors; PFC, prefrontal cortex; VST, ventral striatum; VTA, ventral tegmental area. (After A. J. Jasinska et al. 2014. *Neuropharmacology* 84: 111–122. © 2014. Reprinted with permission from Elsevier.)

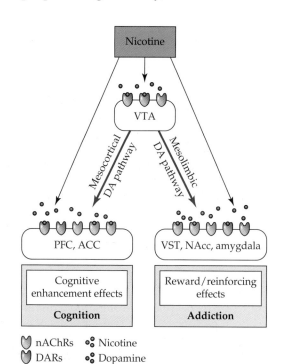

found evidence that some of these endogenous or added chemicals either have their own reinforcing properties or alter nicotine uptake, bioavailability, or neurophysiological effects (Brennan et al., 2014; van de Nobelen et al., 2016). Below we discuss two major lines of research: (1) inhibition of monoamine oxidase (MAO) enzymes by cigarette smoke and e-cigarette vapor and (2) the influence of flavor additives on smoking and vaping.

Researchers discovered some years ago that smokers have substantially lower levels of MAO-A and MAO-B activity in the brain as well as in several peripheral organs that express one or both of these enzymes. **FIGURE 13.17** shows PET scans demonstrating MAO-B inhibition in various organs of a smoker compared with a nonsmoker. MAO inhibition in smokers has been attributed to non-nicotine constituents of cigarette smoke, although it's not yet clear which of these substances is most important for this effect (Hogg, 2016). Because MAO is important in the breakdown of DA, it is plausible that MAO inhibition might contribute to the reinforcing effects of smoking. This hypothesis is supported by experiments demonstrating that pharmacological inhibition of MAO-A, the MAO subtype important for DA metabolism, enhances IV self-administration of low nicotine doses (Smith et al., 2016). The interaction between MAO and nicotine reinforcement indicates that inhibition of the enzyme is probably only important for people smoking low-nicotine cigarettes. E-cigarette vaping does not seem to contain the MAO-inhibiting substance(s) found in cigarette smoke. However, recent research found that certain flavored e-liquid brands, including several containing vanilla flavor, also possess varying degrees of MAO inhibitory activity (Truman et al., 2019).

A second line of research has focused on flavorings, which have been associated with tobacco products as early as the seventeenth century (Klus et al., 2012). One of the most widely used flavorings in both tobacco cigarettes and e-cigarettes is menthol, a chemical extracted from the mint plant (*Mentha arvensis*). Most cigarettes contain at least some menthol, although only certain brands contain high enough levels to be marketed as mentholated cigarettes. Such brands represent about 25% of cigarette sales overall but are especially appealing to adolescents and to new smokers generally. Menthol is used in cigarettes to provide a pleasant sensory experience that combats the harsh, irritating qualities of tobacco smoke. This effect is mediated by menthol-induced activation of TRPM8 receptors, a class of ion channels expressed by sensory neurons, that elicits a sensation of cooling (Wickham, 2015). Menthol has also been found to be a negative allosteric modulator of both high- and low-affinity nAChRs in vitro, which results in reduced nicotine-mediated activation of these receptors (Kabbani, 2013; Wickham, 2015). This interaction might require the user to smoke or vape more frequently or more intensively (in terms of puff rate and/or volume) in order to experience the same effects of the nicotine. Flavorings are particularly important for e-cigarette use (Zare et al., 2018; Patten and De Biasi, 2020). The availability of different flavors, especially sweet or fruity ones, is an important factor in the initiation of e-cigarette use by adolescents. The same flavors are often perceived as being less harmful than tobacco flavor, even though there is no evidence to support this assumption. Moreover, the addition of sweet or fruity flavorings enhanced the subjective rewarding effects of e-cigarettes when the nicotine content was relatively low but not in the case of e-cigarettes containing more nicotine (Patten and De Biasi, 2020). These findings indicate that beyond the delivery of nicotine, flavor additives play a key role in the initiation and maintenance of e-cigarette use.

Smoking is a major health hazard and a cause of premature death

The World Health Organization (WHO) collects global information on the prevalence of tobacco use and the consequent health effects. According to estimates provided by WHO, over 7 million people worldwide die each year from the direct consequences of tobacco use, and an additional 1.2 million nonsmokers are killed because of exposure to second-hand smoke (World Health Organization, 2020). In 1964, the Surgeon General of the United States released the first federally authorized report on the health consequences of tobacco smoking.

From J. S. Fowler et al. 2003. *Proc Natl Acad Sci USA* 100: 11600–11605.
© 2003 National Academy of Sciences

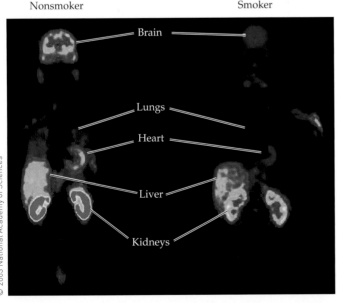

FIGURE 13.17 Whole-body PET scans illustrating reduced MAO-B activity The organs of a smoker are compared with those of a nonsmoker. Warmer colors indicate higher MAO-B activity.

There have been periodic updates of the Surgeon General's report, with the most recent one focusing on the methods and consequences of smoking cessation (U.S. Department of Health and Human Services, 2020). This report concludes that smoking cessation reduces the risk of many different cancers (not just lung cancer) along with cardiovascular disease (e.g., atherosclerosis), coronary heart disease (narrowing or blocking of the coronary arteries), and stroke. In general, the reduction in risk increases with time since quitting smoking. In the discussion that follows, we will cover the health consequences of tobacco cigarette smoking in adults, the effects of e-cigarettes on health and whether use of these devices is less dangerous than cigarette smoking, and finally the consequences of developmental exposure to tobacco smoke and/or nicotine.

ADVERSE HEALTH EFFECTS OF SMOKING OR VAPING

Cigarette smoking increases the long-term risk for many life-threatening illnesses, including several kinds of cancer, cardiovascular disease, and respiratory disease (Price and Martinez, 2020). The organs known to be adversely affected by direct exposure to tobacco smoke and the resulting cancers and chronic diseases are depicted in **FIGURE 13.18**. The deleterious effects of smoking stem from a combination of factors, including

tar, carbon monoxide gas produced by the burning of tobacco, and nicotine. Tar contains a number of toxic substances, such as nitrosamines, that have been implicated in smoking-related carcinogenesis and other disease mechanisms (Yalcin and de la Monte, 2016). Besides the well-known strong association between cigarette smoking and lung cancer, smoking can also lead to other respiratory diseases such as emphysema and chronic bronchitis. The latter two conditions are sometimes combined into a single disorder called chronic obstructive pulmonary disease (COPD).

Although there is less public recognition of the relationship between smoking and cardiovascular disease, this relationship is actually quite strong. Smokers are at increased risk for heart attack, stroke, and atherosclerosis. Other disorders linked to long-term smoking are diabetes, rheumatoid arthritis, macular degeneration (deterioration of the central region of the retina), reduced immune system function, an acceleration of cognitive decline with aging, and erectile dysfunction and impaired sperm motility in men (U.S. Department of Health and Human Services, 2014; Corona et al., 2020; Heldt et al., 2021). Some of the mechanisms by which cigarette smoking predisposes people to later development of these diseases are well defined, while others are not. Important information on this issue comes from a

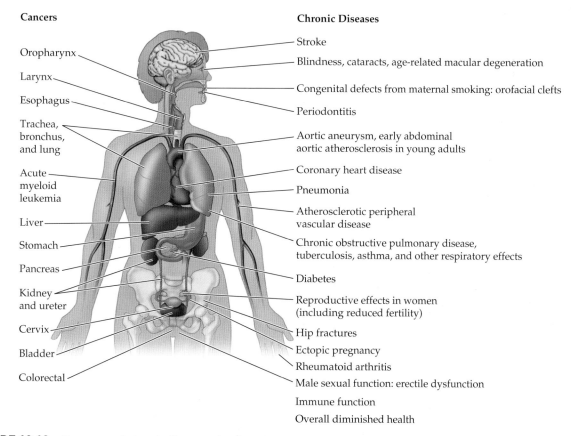

Cancers
- Oropharynx
- Larynx
- Esophagus
- Trachea, bronchus, and lung
- Acute myeloid leukemia
- Liver
- Stomach
- Pancreas
- Kidney and ureter
- Cervix
- Bladder
- Colorectal

Chronic Diseases
- Stroke
- Blindness, cataracts, age-related macular degeneration
- Congenital defects from maternal smoking: orofacial clefts
- Periodontitis
- Aortic aneurysm, early abdominal aortic atherosclerosis in young adults
- Coronary heart disease
- Pneumonia
- Atherosclerotic peripheral vascular disease
- Chronic obstructive pulmonary disease, tuberculosis, asthma, and other respiratory effects
- Diabetes
- Reproductive effects in women (including reduced fertility)
- Hip fractures
- Ectopic pregnancy
- Rheumatoid arthritis
- Male sexual function: erectile dysfunction
- Immune function
- Overall diminished health

FIGURE 13.18 Cancers and chronic diseases that have been causally related to tobacco smoke exposure (After U.S. Department of Health and Human Services, 2014.)

large-scale study of current smokers, former smokers, and people who never smoked showing that smoking produces epigenetic effects, expressed as changes in DNA methylation, on over 1000 genes (Joehanes et al., 2016). Such epigenetic effects, which can powerfully alter gene expression for long periods of time, may be a key mechanism linking smoking with disease risk later in life even in people who have stopped smoking.

The potential health risks of vaping have not been studied nearly as extensively as the risks associated with tobacco smoking. When e-cigarettes were introduced, they were advertised as being a safer alternative to tobacco smoking because of the absence of tar. Nevertheless, recent research has begun to show that e-cigarette use also poses significant dangers to health (**BOX 13.1**).

Most of the writing of this textbook, including the present chapter, was done at a time when the world was in the grip of the COVID-19 pandemic. For several reasons, smoking and vaping are believed to have had a significant influence both on the risk for contracting this disease and on the severity of illness in stricken individuals. First, the physical act of smoking or vaping increased the opportunities for one's hands to touch one's face, potentially causing SARS-CoV-2 viral transfer from the hands to the mucous membranes of the eyes, nose, or mouth. Second, having a preexisting respiratory condition from long-term smoking or vaping likely led to a more serious outcome if the smoker became infected with the virus. Lastly, chronic nicotine exposure up-regulates angiotensin-converting enzyme 2 (ACE2), the membrane protein used by the SARS-CoV-2 virus to enter and infect its cellular targets. This up-regulation, which appears to be mediated by nicotine activation of $\alpha 7$ nAChRs, may make users of tobacco products (including e-cigarettes) more susceptible to contracting COVID-19 (Russo et al., 2020; Sifat et al., 2020).

DEVELOPMENTAL CONSEQUENCES OF SMOKE OR NICOTINE EXPOSURE Researchers concerned with the developmental consequences of smoke or nicotine exposure have focused on two periods of exposure, namely fetal exposure and adolescent exposure. Fetal exposure occurs when a woman smokes during her pregnancy. When this happens, nicotine and many other chemicals present in cigarette smoke pass through the placenta to reach all organs of the developing fetus, including the brain. Other impacts can occur by disrupting the mother's endocrine system and placenta (Marom-Haham and Shulman, 2016). To ascertain the developmental effects of nicotine in isolation from other chemicals present in tobacco smoke or e-cigarette aerosols, researchers have exposed rats or mice to pure nicotine either during the fetal period (i.e., dosing of pregnant animals for the purpose of studying their offspring) or during the early postnatal period (a model of third-trimester human exposure). Taken together, these studies have found that nicotine exposure early in life results in abnormal brain development, hyperactivity, cognitive deficits, and increased anxiety (Jamshed et al., 2020; McGrath-Morrow et al., 2020). Other adverse consequences of early nicotine exposure manifest later in life, including diminished lung function, hypertension, increased risk for obesity, and increased risk of developing childhood cancers (Jamshed et al., 2020). As is the case for all developmental toxicants, the specific effects produced by developmental nicotine administration depend on the dose and period of exposure.

Based on human clinical studies, maternal cigarette smoking is associated with an increased incidence of several adverse pregnancy outcomes, including stillbirth, sudden infant death syndrome, and intrauterine growth restriction (IUGR) (England et al., 2017). IUGR means that fetal growth is hampered, resulting in babies born underweight (commonly defined as below the tenth percentile for gestational age) (Reeves and Bernstein, 2008). This outcome is significant because it puts the infant at a greatly elevated risk for perinatal mortality. Affected infants who survive to adulthood may still be susceptible later to developing cardiovascular disease, type 2 diabetes, or stroke. These long-term consequences of maternal smoking on the offspring are consistent with the **developmental origins of health and disease** hypothesis. This hypothesis, which originated from the work of David Barker and colleagues, postulates that characteristics of the intrauterine environment, such as nutrient availability and the presence of drugs, environmental toxins, or infectious agents, "program" the fetus in a way that determines subsequent vulnerability for developing chronic diseases (Wadhwa et al., 2009). Such diseases may be either somatic or neuropsychiatric, and there is growing evidence that the programming depends on epigenetic mechanisms within the fetus and, in some cases, the placenta (reviewed in Mochizuki et al., 2017; Conradt et al., 2018; Goyal et al., 2019; Shallie and Naicker, 2019). For these reasons, pregnant smokers are urged to quit smoking or, at the very least, to reduce their cigarette consumption. Because nicotine alone can exert adverse effects on the fetus, vapers as well as women using the nicotine patch or other kinds of nicotine replacement therapy for smoking cessation should likewise attempt to stop their exposure to the drug.

The influence of nicotine exposure on the adolescent brain has also been a significant area of concern. Adolescence is a vulnerable period because the brain is still developing during this time. Although most of the adult complement of neurons are formed by the beginning of adolescence, synaptic connections are changing rapidly (some synapses are strengthened significantly while others are pruned away), myelination of the cerebral cortex is not yet completed, and neurotransmitter systems are still maturing during adolescence.

BOX 13.1 ■ THE CUTTING EDGE

How Safe Are E-cigarettes?

The global debate over e-cigarettes and other ENDS revolves mainly around two contrary points of view. One of the arguments *against* e-cigarettes is their potential for inducing nicotine dependence in young people (leading, in many cases, to a transition to tobacco cigarette smoking) who might otherwise not have ever used any tobacco product. A major argument *for* e-cigarettes is based on the notion that they are much safer than tobacco cigarettes, and therefore they are a healthier substitute for the latter and could even be used as a tool for smoking cessation. So what *is* the available evidence regarding the overall safety of e-cigarettes and their relative safety compared to tobacco cigarettes?

One of the primary means of comparing the health risks of e-cigarette use to tobacco cigarette smoking is to assess the potential toxicity of the chemicals contained in e-liquids and e-cigarette vapor compared to tobacco smoke. In part because of the chemical simplicity of e-liquids compared to the complexity of tobacco leaves, there are fewer toxic chemicals and lower levels of these chemicals in e-cigarette aerosols (i.e., vapor) than in cigarette smoke. Furthermore, analyses of urine samples obtained from smokers and vapers show that the latter experience less exposure to various toxicants than smokers (St. Helen et al., 2020). Nevertheless, vaping is by no means completely safe from a health perspective. Chemical analyses of the e-liquids and/or e-liquid aerosols have revealed the presence of many toxic and potentially carcinogenic organic chemicals (e.g., aldehydes like formaldehyde, acetaldehyde, and acrolein) and metals (Goniewicz et al., 2014; Wilson and Gartner, 2016; Strongin, 2019; Zhao et al., 2020). Much of the toxic organic chemical content of e-cigarette aerosols is generated by pyrolysis (heat-induced breakdown) of e-liquid constituents such as glycerin. The metal content of e-liquids and corresponding aerosols appears to originate mainly from exposure of the liquid to wires, heating coils, and soldered joints within the e-cigarette. It should be noted that the concentrations of these substances vary significantly across brands (Ward et al., 2020). This is illustrated in a recent study of the aerosol composition from JUUL pods that showed much lower levels of toxic aldehydes than measured either in other e-cigarette brand aerosols or in tobacco cigarette smoke (Talih et al., 2019).

Over the past several years, researchers have used several different approaches to assess the potential adverse health consequences of e-cigarette use (reviewed in Miyashita and Foley, 2020; Tsai et al., 2020). Studies examining very short-term effects have shown that inhalation of e-cigarette aerosols for just 5 to 30 minutes leads to cellular reactivity and flow resistance in the airways. Longer-term studies have been based on examination of regular e-cigarette users, chronic administration of e-cigarette aerosols to animals, or in vitro exposure of cultured cells to aerosol components. This research has revealed a variety of effects of chronic exposure to e-cigarette aerosols, including airway obstruction, inflammation, impaired respiratory immune defense, and other signs of respiratory damage/disease. Epidemiological studies have additionally revealed a significant association of e-cigarette use with COPD, chronic bronchitis, and asthma, which shows that cumulative airway damage eventually results in respiratory disease (Xie et al., 2020; Wills et al., 2021). Cardiovascular effects of e-cigarettes are similar to those produced by tobacco cigarette smoking, including short-term increases in heart rate and blood pressure and long-term development of atherosclerosis and aortic stiffness (stiffening of the aortic wall that is a risk factor for later heart failure or heart attack). These short- and long-term effects of e-cigarette aerosols on the pulmonary and cardiovascular systems are depicted in the **FIGURE**.

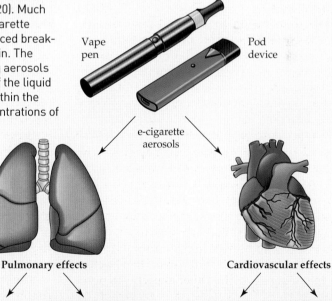

Short- and long-term effects of exposure to e-cigarette aerosols on pulmonary and cardiovascular function. (After M. Tsai et al. 2020. *J Physiol* 598: 5039–5062. © 2020 The Physiological Society.)

Pulmonary effects

Short term	Long term
• Increased flow resistance • Increased airflow reactivity	• Higher airway resistance • Airway obstruction • Airway inflammation • COPD • Chronic bronchitis • Asthma

Cardiovascular effects

Short term	Long term
• Increased heart rate • Increased blood pressure • Increased aortic stiffness	• Increased atherosclerosis • Increased aortic stiffness

BOX 13.1 ■ THE CUTTING EDGE (continued)

Beyond the adverse health consequences described above, health providers have documented a novel disorder termed **e-cigarette, or vaping, product-associated lung injury (EVALI)**, sometimes shortened to simply **vaping-associated lung injury (VALI)** (Layden et al., 2020; McAlinden et al., 2020). EVALI first came to the attention of public health officials based on reports coming out of Illinois and Wisconsin during the summer of 2019. Most patients within this cohort had recently been vaping e-cigarettes containing Δ^9-tetrahydrocannabinol (THC), although a small number had been vaping only nicotine-containing e-cigarettes. The patients presented at hospitals with a syndrome characterized by dyspnea (shortness of breath), nonproductive cough, chest pain, nausea and vomiting, abdominal pain and diarrhea, and fever. Imaging of the lungs revealed significant pathology, in most cases including "ground-glass opacities" (a diffuse pattern of hazy white flecks seen in CT scans). Of the initial 98 patients reported in Illinois and Wisconsin, almost 80% were male and the median age was 21 years. Ninety-five percent of the patients required hospitalization, 26% had to be mechanically ventilated, and two eventually succumbed to their illness. The causes of EVALI are still being investigated; however, for those patients who had vaped THC, the culprit is

thought to be vitamin E acetate, a substance often used as a thickening agent in e-liquids containing that drug.

We can now return to our original question: Are e-cigarettes safer than tobacco cigarettes? In some respects, they are safer because e-cigarette aerosols contain lower amounts of the many injurious and carcinogenic chemicals found in tobacco smoke. Initial studies of tobacco cigarette smokers who switched to e-cigarettes found a reduced incidence of respiratory illnesses, although no change in the risk for adverse cardiovascular outcomes was reported (Goniewicz et al., 2020). It is also possible that regular e-cigarette users will develop fewer cancers than regular smokers over time. The more important point, however, is that e-cigarettes are not *safe* per se. We have described ample evidence for pulmonary and cardiovascular diseases related to e-cigarette use, including the recently discovered EVALI. Accordingly, health providers and public health officials are unanimous in advising youth NOT to take up vaping, or to stop if they are already engaged in that practice. If, on the other hand, a tobacco cigarette smoker finds it impossible to quit their nicotine addiction (including use of the approaches discussed in the later section on smoking cessation), then it might be reasonable to switch to e-cigarettes despite the continued health risks.

Because of the dynamic processes taking place during adolescence, it shouldn't be surprising that nicotine can perturb the ongoing developmental trajectory. Specifically, a combination of experimental animal research and human clinical studies has shown that nicotine exposure during adolescence leads to long-term changes in neurotransmission, altered dendritic branching in many brain areas, deficits on various behavioral tasks, and increased risk for developing neuropsychiatric disorders, including depression, anxiety disorders, and addiction (Lydon et al., 2014; R. F. Smith et al., 2015; Leslie, 2020; Laviolette, 2021). These findings show that even though e-cigarette vapor doesn't contain most of the harmful chemicals found in tobacco cigarette smoke, use of vaping products by young people may pose a hazard to their neurobehavioral development.

Behavioral and pharmacological strategies are used to treat tobacco dependence

Once a regular cigarette smoking habit has taken hold, it is very difficult to quit. Most attempts at quitting are performed without the use of medication or psychological counselling; smokers who try to quit on their own often believe that quitting is their personal responsibility and that going it alone is the best approach for them (A. L. Smith et al., 2015). However,

addiction to nicotine is so powerful that the success rate is quite low, even with medication. This is borne out by the available statistics on smoking cessation. Over their lifetime, more than 90% of smokers try to quit, with most making multiple quit attempts. Of smokers who are able to quit for a day, 60% have relapsed within a week. Despite having significant motivation to quit, only about half of smokers are able to eventually reach long-term abstinence (Prochaska and Benowitz, 2019). In the sections below we discuss the potential value of self-help programs as well as medical, behavioral, and pharmacological interventions for treating tobacco dependence.

SELF-HELP MATERIALS Beginning many years ago, various self-help programs published in books or manuals have been available to assist smokers in quitting. The efficacy of print-based materials for smoking cessation was recently reviewed by Livingstone-Banks and colleagues (2019). The authors concluded that such materials are more beneficial than having no help or guidance at all; however, even greater benefit is obtained from face-to-face interventions or pharmacological treatments (see following sections). In general, we may conclude that the use of printed self-help materials has largely been supplanted by better approaches to smoking cessation.

BRIEF CESSATION ADVICE The first line of intervention for smoking cessation involves administering the "5As" brief intervention by physicians and other health care providers like physician assistants, nurse practitioners, nurses, dentists, and periodontists. In routine visits with patients, providers are instructed to (1) ask whether the patient is a smoker or user of any other tobacco product, (2) advise any user to quit, (3) assess the individual's readiness to make the attempt to quit, (4) assist the individual with respect to potential treatments (counseling, medications, etc.), including referrals to specialists if appropriate, and (5) arrange follow-up contacts to keep track of the individual's progress (Quinn et al., 2009). An alternative to the 5As that requires less time and effort by the health provider is the so-called Ask-Advise-Refer (AAR) model. In this case, the provider asks if the patient is a smoker, advises the patient to quit, and then refers the individual to a publicly funded cessation program (Schroeder, 2005). Smokers currently have available a variety of web-based cessation programs such as Smokefree.gov, the daily texting program SmokefreeTXT, and the free smoking cessation app quit-START. Another government-sponsored cessation tool is a toll-free telephone quitline at 1-800-QUIT-NOW. The phone line is staffed by experienced counselors who help smokers develop individualized quit plans based on their personal history.

INTENSIVE INDIVIDUAL OR GROUP COUNSELING Smokers seeking to quit may benefit from intensive counseling delivered either individually or within a group setting. The framework underlying smoking cessation counseling is most typically cognitive behavioral or motivational in nature; however, other approaches such as mindfulness are also used (Spears et al., 2017). Overall, intensive counseling programs are more successful than either self-help materials or brief cessation advice in helping smokers quit (Prochaska and Benowitz, 2019). Moreover, some smokers respond best to a combination of counseling with one of the medications described in the following section.

MEDICATIONS The development of medications for smoking cessation has followed three main paths: (1) nicotine replacement therapy, (2) non-nicotine drugs aimed at reducing tobacco craving and withdrawal symptoms, and (3) anti-nicotine vaccines. We will discuss each of these in turn, considering their current status and efficacy.

One of the most common interventions for smoking cessation is **nicotine replacement therapy** (**NRT**). This approach is based on the following premises: that the difficulty associated with smoking cessation is significantly related to nicotine withdrawal symptoms; that blocking (or at least reducing) these symptoms by maintaining a certain circulating level of nicotine can assist in terminating smoking; that maintaining some nicotine in the smoker's system can blunt the reinforcing effectiveness of nicotine derived from smoking a cigarette; and that there are safer ways for individuals to obtain nicotine than by smoking. This last point is embodied by Russell's (1976) comment that "people smoke for nicotine but they die from tar." NRT was first made available after the formulation of a special nicotine-containing chewing gum (nicotine polacrilex), which has the advantage that nicotine can be absorbed more readily through the buccal mucosa (mucous membranes lining the mouth) than the gastrointestinal tract, where absorption is minimal and there is substantial first-pass metabolism by the liver. Nicotine gum was approved as a therapeutic aid for treating cigarette dependence in 1984 under the trade name Nicorette. This was later followed by the transdermal nicotine patch (Nicoderm, Habitrol, Nicotrol), nicotine nasal spray (Nicotrol NS), nicotine inhaler (Nicotrol Inhaler), and nicotine lozenge (Commit). Of these many nicotine-containing products, only the nasal spray and inhaler require a doctor's prescription. Making at least some over-the-counter (OTC) nicotine medications available was a significant advance in the battle against smoking, because some smokers are reluctant or unable financially to enter a formal treatment program yet may still be willing to try something they can obtain at a drugstore without a prescription. **TABLE 13.1** lists some of the advantages and disadvantages of each nicotine delivery vehicle. A recent review of the extensive literature in this area concluded that on average, use of NRT (regardless of vehicle) increases the likelihood of quitting smoking by 50% to 60% compared to controls given either a placebo or no intervention (Hartmann-Boyce et al., 2018). To improve the efficacy of NRT even further, some researchers advocate that the smoker first switch from their preferred brand to a low-nicotine cigarette, thereby theoretically reducing their nicotine dependence before giving up cigarettes entirely (Piper et al., 2019).

Earlier in the chapter we discussed the negative aspects of e-cigarettes because of the health risks they pose for youth who might otherwise not begin using tobacco products. But for current smokers, it is possible that e-cigarettes and other ENDS could serve as a new kind of NRT. Recent reviews comparing e-cigarettes to either standard NRT vehicles, counseling, or no intervention found evidence that e-cigarettes may prove to be a beneficial addition to the currently available smoking cessation approaches (Patil et al., 2020; Rigotti, 2020; Ibrahim et al., 2021). It is clear, however, that more research needs to be conducted, particularly assessing the long-term outcome of using e-cigarettes for this purpose.

Although NRT continues to be an important tool for smoking cessation, two other pharmacological

TABLE 13.1 Advantages and Disadvantages of Different Kinds of Nicotine Replacement Therapy

Treatment	Advantages	Disadvantages
Nicotine polacrilex (gum)	Ease of use; flexible dosing; OTC availability; rapid nicotine delivery	Need for frequent dosing; bad taste; side effects such as throat irritation, mouth soreness, and jaw pain
Nicotine lozenge	Ease of use; flexible dosing; OTC availability; rapid nicotine delivery	Need for frequent dosing; side effects such as heartburn or indigestion with rapid lozenge consumption
Transdermal nicotine patch	Ease of use; OTC availability; reduced morning craving with overnight use	Slower delivery of nicotine than with other treatments; possible insomnia with overnight use; side effects such as skin irritation, dizziness, and headache
Nicotine nasal spray	Flexible dosing; fastest nicotine delivery and reduction of cravings	Need for frequent dosing; initial side effects such as nasal irritation, sneezing, and watery eyes
Nicotine inhaler	Flexible dosing; similarity to hand-to-mouth feature of smoking	Need for frequent dosing; initial side effects such as coughing and irritation of the nose, mouth, and/or throat

approaches have proven valuable in helping people quit smoking. The first is **bupropion**, a compound that was initially developed as an antidepressant and then later reformulated as a sustained-release preparation (trade name **Zyban**) for treating tobacco dependence. The efficacy of bupropion as a smoking cessation medication was discovered serendipitously when researchers noticed that depressed patients who were smokers and were given this compound for their depression reported reduced cigarette cravings and were able to quit smoking without additional therapeutic intervention. The antismoking properties of bupropion are thought to be related to its pharmacological profile as a reuptake inhibitor of DA and NE and as a weak nAChR antagonist. The second non-NRT medication is **varenicline** (**Chantix**), which acts as a partial agonist at high-affinity α4β2 nAChRs that are expressed in the VTA as well as in other brain areas. This partial agonism elicits a moderate amount of receptor activation, in contrast to the full receptor agonism produced by cigarette-derived nicotine. The resulting effect is a reduction of nicotine cravings and of adverse withdrawal reactions in the abstinent smoker (Prochaska and Benowitz, 2019).

You may recall that in Chapter 12 we discussed efforts by researchers to develop a vaccine against cocaine. Similar work targeting nicotine has led to the development of vaccines that, in animal studies, reduce nicotine availability to the brain and block reinstatement of nicotine-seeking behavior (Zalewska-Kaxzubska, 2015). One of the first-generation vaccines, NicVax, even reached phase III clinical trials. Unfortunately, neither this vaccine nor any subsequent ones was successful in generating a strong anti-nicotine antibody response in people (Ozgen and Blume, 2019). Nevertheless, there is continued interest in using new methods to produce better nicotine vaccines for clinical testing (Heekin et al., 2017).

SECTION SUMMARY

■ In 2019, an estimated 50.6 million Americans were current users of a tobacco product. Most of these individuals were users of tobacco cigarettes and/or, to a lesser extent, e-cigarette users. Whereas tobacco cigarettes were most popular among people 45 years of age or older, e-cigarettes were preferred by people 18 to 44 years of age. Many e-cigarette users currently or formerly also smoked tobacco cigarettes.

■ Smokers typically begin during adolescence, and many different reasons have been given for teenage smoking. Longitudinal surveys found that poor academic performance, rebelliousness, sensation seeking, receptivity to cigarette advertising/marketing, and smoking by family and/or friends are significant predictors of smoking onset.

■ Although first exposure to a cigarette is aversive in many cases, other individuals experience relaxation at their first smoking experience. This response could be an early contributor to the development of a smoking habit.

■ Individuals go through several successive stages on the way from nonsmoking through occasional smoking and then eventually to established smoking. These stages can be characterized as "wanting," "craving," and finally "needing" a cigarette. Once nicotine dependence has developed, cigarettes become compulsory (i.e., smoked in order to alleviate withdrawal symptoms) instead of elective.

■ Although most established cigarette smokers have become strongly nicotine-dependent and smoke daily, others develop less dependence and have an intermittent (non-daily) smoking habit.

■ Young people typically cite curiosity, taste (flavor), relief from boredom, having a good time, and alleviation of tension as reasons for beginning to vape e-cigarettes. Similar to the pattern of tobacco cigarette smoking, many e-cigarette users increase their frequency of use, amount of nicotine exposure, and risk of becoming nicotine-dependent over time.

- Several hypotheses have been offered to explain why young people are more attracted to e-cigarettes than tobacco cigarettes. These hypotheses are related to flavor, health, price, concealment, role models, and acceptance of e-cigarettes compared to tobacco cigarettes. Recent studies have shown that e-cigarette use often precedes the initiation and continuation of tobacco cigarette smoking, either as a replacement for e-cigarettes or in combination with the latter. Some researchers have hypothesized that e-cigarettes function as a "gateway" to tobacco cigarette use. Alternate hypotheses to explain this transition are centered around the ideas of "addiction," "accessibility," and "experience." Additional "liability" and "renormalization" hypotheses have been raised to account for the initial decision of adolescents to try either e-cigarettes or tobacco cigarettes.

- Several factors contribute to the development and maintenance of a smoking habit. These factors include nicotine reward, environmental cues conditioned to smoking, enhancement of mood and cognition, and stress reduction. The nicotine resource model hypothesizes that nicotine has direct beneficial effects of increasing mood control (in relation to stress reduction) and enhancing concentration, whereas the deprivation reversal model argues that the positive effects experienced during smoking actually constitute the alleviation of withdrawal effects such as irritability, anxiety, and poor concentration. Both models are supported by certain evidence, with mood regulation (i.e., alleviation of anxiety) possibly being more important in female than male smokers.

- Other constituents of cigarette smoke or e-cigarette vapor may also influence smoking or vaping behavior. Certain non-nicotine constituents of tobacco inhibit MAO-A, an enzyme important for DA metabolism. Researchers have hypothesized that this effect is likely to be most important for enhancing the reinforcement of low-nicotine cigarettes. Menthol, a well-known flavorant used in both tobacco cigarettes and e-cigarettes, acts as a negative allosteric modulator of nAChRs. The net effects of this interaction may be to increase the frequency and/or intensity of smoking or vaping by the user.

- Chronic use of tobacco results in many adverse health consequences, including cancer, cardiovascular disease, and COPD. The deleterious effects of inhaling cigarette smoke have been related not only to nicotine but also to tar and carbon monoxide gas that is produced by the burning of tobacco.

- Use of e-cigarettes may be somewhat safer for health than smoking tobacco cigarettes because of the absence of various toxic and carcinogenic substances present in cigarette smoke. However, e-cigarette aerosols contain their own toxic and carcinogenic substances, and regular vaping has been associated with COPD and other respiratory disorders. Cannabis vaping has recently been associated with EVALI, which is believed to be caused by vitamin E acetate, a frequent constituent of cannabis e-liquids.

- Smoking by a pregnant woman has adverse consequences for her fetus due to a combination of nicotine exposure, exposure to other components of cigarette smoke, and disruption of the woman's endocrine system. Maternal cigarette smoking has been associated with increased risk of stillbirth, sudden infant death syndrome, and intrauterine growth restriction. Infants born to smokers have increased susceptibility for later developing cardiovascular disease, type 2 diabetes, or stroke. The long-term consequences of smoking during pregnancy are consistent with the developmental origins of health and disease hypothesis.

- The brain is still developing during adolescence, and animal studies have found that exposure of the adolescent brain to nicotine can have deleterious effects on dendritic branching and on neurotransmitter development. Adolescent smokers are more likely to develop neuropsychiatric disorders such as depression, anxiety disorders, and addiction later in life.

- Cognitive, behavioral, and psychosocial strategies to assist smokers in quitting include self-help materials, brief cessation advice, and individual or group counseling. Medical/pharmacological interventions take three forms: nicotine replacement therapy (NRT), non-nicotine drugs aimed at reducing craving and withdrawal symptoms, and anti-nicotine vaccines. Nicotine replacement can be accomplished by means of nicotine gum, lozenges, patches, nasal spray, or an inhaler. For some, e-cigarettes may represent yet another potential kind of NRT. Currently available non-nicotine drugs for smoking cessation are bupropion (Zyban), which is a mixed DA and NE reuptake inhibitor and weak nAChR antagonist, and varenicline (Chantix), which is a partial agonist at high-affinity $\alpha4\beta2$ nAChRs. Both NRT and these alternative pharmacological approaches are more effective when paired with some type of behavioral or psychosocial intervention. Finally, a nicotine vaccine that reduces nicotine availability to the brain has been under development for a number of years; however, clinical testing has not yet demonstrated significant therapeutic efficacy of this approach. Because breaking the smoking habit is almost always a difficult proposition, it is much better never to become dependent in the first place.

13.4 Caffeine

If you are like most people living in Western societies, you probably had at least one cup of coffee (or perhaps tea) this morning, possibly followed by additional cups as the day progressed. Whether you like the taste of coffee (which is bitter when taken black) or not, you are probably consuming it at least partly for its pharmacological properties as a stimulant. This, of course, brings us to the subject of **caffeine**, the principal psychoactive ingredient in coffee. The major source of caffeine is coffee beans, which are the seeds of the plant *Coffea arabica* (**FIGURE 13.19**). Tea leaves contain significant amounts of both caffeine and a related compound called **theophylline** (which is Greek for "divine

FIGURE 13.19 The coffee plant, *Coffea arabica*

leaf") (**FIGURE 13.20**). Caffeine and theophylline are members of a wider group of plant-derived chemicals called **methylxanthines**. Minor sources of dietary caffeine include cocoa beans, kola nuts, yerba mate (tea made from a type of holly), and guarana berries.

Coffee is believed to have been discovered in Ethiopia around 850 CE, and indeed the names of the plant genus *Coffea* and the beverage made from its seeds are derived from the Arabic word *quahweh* (Gonzalez de Mejia and Ramirez-Mares, 2014). Coffee was brought to Europe by Venetian merchants in 1615, after which its consumption spread rapidly. The stimulating effects of coffee have been known for hundreds of years. For example, the nineteenth-century French author Honoré de Balzac, who reportedly consumed immense amounts of the beverage, wrote an article in 1830 entitled "Pleasures and Pains of Coffee" in which he stated, "Coffee slips into the stomach and you immediately feel a general commotion. Ideas begin to move like the battalions of the Grand Army on the field of battle and the battle takes place. Memories come at a gallop, carried by the wind" (cited in Cappeletti et al., 2015).

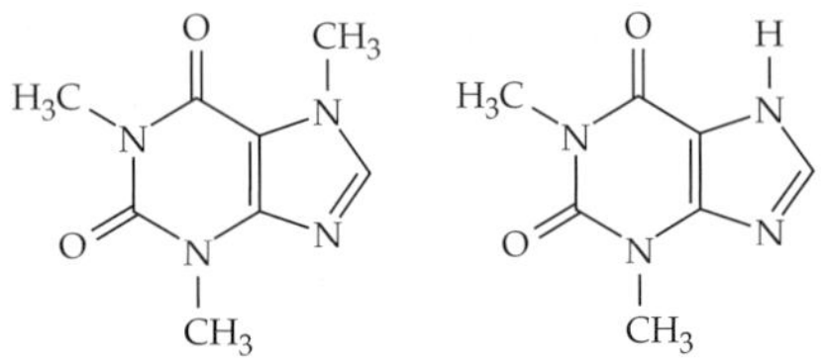

Caffeine is currently one of the most widely used drugs in the world. In the United States, for example, a large survey found that about 85% of the population (excluding children younger than 2 years of age) consume at least one caffeinated beverage per day (Mitchell et al., 2014). The same survey estimated the mean daily caffeine consumption to be 165 mg across all age groups. The typical caffeine content of various beverages, foods, and OTC drugs is shown in **TABLE 13.2**. Not surprisingly, coffee is the largest contributor to overall caffeine intake, with tea, caffeinated soft drinks, and energy drinks being the other significant sources of dietary caffeine. Information about the history and current status of caffeine-containing energy drinks is provided in **BOX 13.2**.

Basic pharmacology of caffeine

Caffeine is normally consumed orally through the beverages in which it is present. Under this condition, it is virtually completely absorbed from the gastrointestinal tract within 30 to 60 minutes. Caffeine absorption begins in the stomach but takes place mainly within the small intestine. The plasma half-life of caffeine varies substantially from one person to another, but the average value is about 4 hours. Consequently, people who drink coffee repeatedly over the course of a day experience gradually rising plasma caffeine concentrations. Most of this caffeine is then cleared from the circulation during sleep. The rate of plasma clearance is stimulated by smoking and is reduced when smoking is terminated (Doepker et al., 2016). The resulting increase in plasma caffeine levels could contribute to cigarette withdrawal symptoms in heavy coffee drinkers, particularly since caffeine is anxiogenic (anxiety provoking) at high doses (see the next section). In contrast, pregnant women metabolize caffeine more slowly and, therefore, they should at least moderate their caffeine intake accordingly and possibly stop their consumption altogether (see later section on health risks of caffeine).

Caffeine is converted to a variety of metabolites by the liver. Importantly, most ingested caffeine is initially converted to a substance called **paraxanthine**, which is a CNS stimulant just like caffeine (Nehlig, 2018). For this reason, the effects of caffeine may persist for some time even after circulating levels of the parent drug are low. Further breakdown of paraxanthine and other initial metabolites leads to a variety of secondary compounds that are targeted for excretion. In humans, approximately 95% of caffeine metabolites are eliminated through the urine, 2% to 5% through the feces, and the remainder through other bodily fluids such as saliva.

Behavioral and physiological effects of caffeine

Caffeine is best known for its ability to increase arousal; however, it can also enhance cognitive function

FIGURE 13.20 Chemical structures of caffeine and theophylline

Caffeine

Theophylline

TABLE 13.2 Caffeine Content of Selected Beverages, Foods, and Drugs

Source	Serving size	Caffeine content (mg)*
Coffee		
Regular brewed coffee	8 oz	95–330
Brewed decaffeinated coffee	8 oz	3–12
Instant coffee	8 oz	30–70
Espresso	1 oz	50–150
Tea		
Black, brewed or tea bag	8 oz	40–74
Black, decaffeinated	8 oz	2–5
Green, brewed or tea bag	8 oz	25–50
Oolong, brewed or tea bag	8 oz	21–64
White, brewed or tea bag	8 oz	15
Instant tea	8 oz	33–64
Yerba mate, brewed or tea bag	8 oz	65–130
Iced tea	12 oz	27–42
Other beverages		
Carbonated beverages with caffeine	12 oz	22–69
Alcoholic beverages with caffeine	1 oz	3–9
Energy drinks with caffeine	8.2–23.5 oz	33–400
Water with caffeine	16.9–20.0 oz	42–125
Foods		
Chocolates	8 oz	0–6
Sweets	Various	1–122
Snacks	1 oz or 1 bar	3–41
Gums and mints	Various	20–400
Fast foods	Various	1–49
Drugs		
NoDoz or Vivarin	1 tablet	200
Extra Strength Excedrin	2 tablets	130

Sources: Data for beverages and foods from E. Gonzalez de Mejia and M. V. Ramirez-Mares. 2014. *Trends Endocrinol Metab* 10: 489–92; for drugs from L. M. Burke. 2008. *Appl Physiol Nutr Metab* 33: 1319–1334.

*Typical range in milligrams per serving.

and athletic performance when taken at appropriate doses. Regular use of caffeine can produce tolerance and dependence, and excessive ingestion poses significant health risks. Nevertheless, caffeine also has a few therapeutic uses that are mentioned below.

ACUTE SUBJECTIVE AND BEHAVIORAL EFFECTS OF CAFFEINE DEPEND ON DOSE AND PRIOR EXPOSURE

In laboratory animals such as rats and mice, caffeine has biphasic effects related to dose. At low doses, it has stimulant effects, as shown by increased locomotor activity. At high doses, this effect is reversed and animals

actually show reduced activity. Later in the chapter we will learn that the underlying mechanism for locomotor stimulation with low to moderate doses of caffeine has been elucidated, but not the locomotor depressant effect of high doses.

People ingest caffeine mostly for its ability to stimulate arousal, increase concentration, and reduce fatigue. According to a survey of college students, caffeine-containing beverages or foods are also consumed for reasons of taste, social factors, mood enhancement, and stress reduction (Doepker et al., 2016). The arousing effects of caffeine can disrupt sleep, particularly in older adults and when the drug is consumed shortly before going to bed (Clark et al., 2017). Consuming 400 mg of caffeine (roughly equivalent to two 12-oz. cups of coffee) as much as 6 hours before bedtime still caused sleep disturbance (Drake et al., 2013; Doty and Collen, 2020). On the other hand, these same effects can be helpful to people under conditions in which alertness has been compromised, such as working late in the day or into the night, trying to function after a period of sleep deprivation, or feeling fatigued while operating a motor vehicle (Irwin et al., 2020). Caffeine and even stronger stimulants are also used by military personnel when they must remain alert during a long, sustained operation (Crawford et al., 2017). As with any drug, there are significant individual differences in sensitivity to caffeine. But in general, doses that exceed 400 mg cause feelings of tension, jitteriness, and anxiety (Nehlig, 2016). Interestingly, patients suffering from panic disorder appear to be hypersensitive to caffeine's anxiogenic effects and may even suffer panic attacks in response to caffeine administration (Vilarim et al., 2011).

Caffeine does more than just increase our arousal. In controlled laboratory studies, humans receiving low or intermediate doses of caffeine report a variety of positive subjective effects, including feelings of well-being, enhanced energy or vigor, increased alertness and ability to concentrate, self-confidence, increased work motivation, and enhanced sociability (Glade, 2010). Caffeine is particularly effective in improving concentration in fatigued individuals and in the elderly (Nehlig, 2010). Tests of specific cognitive domains indicate that low or intermediate caffeine doses exert positive effects on reaction time and performance on simple and complex attention tasks (Einöther and Giesbrecht, 2013; McClellan et al., 2016). Other cognitive domains such as memory and decision making are not as clearly impacted by caffeine.

Because chronic caffeine consumption can lead to dependence and abstinence-related withdrawal symptoms (see later in this chapter), some investigators have raised concerns that cognitive enhancement may be due to alleviation of withdrawal symptoms rather than improvement over baseline levels (James, 2014; O'Callaghan et

BOX 13.2 ■ OF SPECIAL INTEREST

Energy Drinks: Caffeine and More

Beverages containing sugar for energy and caffeine for mental stimulation have been around for a long time. Of course, regular (i.e., not diet) caffeinated sodas fit this description, with some varieties containing as much added caffeine as a typical cup of coffee. But the term *energy drink* typically refers to "beverages that contain high levels of caffeine plus specialty ingredients not commonly found in sodas and juices" (Harris and Munsell, 2015, p. 248). Current interest in energy drinks and their smaller cousins, energy shots, can be traced to the introduction of Red Bull in 1987. Sales of these beverages began to rise slowly and then more rapidly over time, coinciding with the creation of many competitor brands such as Monster Energy and Rockstar. Global sales of energy drinks reached $53 billion in 2018 and are predicted to reach $86 billion by 2026 (Allied Market Research, 2019).

Energy drinks are claimed to boost energy and alertness, alleviate fatigue, assist recovery from lack of sleep, and improve athletic endurance and performance (Reissig et al., 2009). These drinks contain caffeine in varying amounts (listed either as caffeine itself or as guarana, a caffeine-containing plant extract), sugar (except for "diet" drinks), and often other ingredients such as the amino acid taurine, L-theanine (a naturally occurring glutamate analog), ginseng, sodium, and vitamins. Caffeine content of energy drinks varies widely, from 80 mg (similar to a standard cup of brewed coffee) in Red Bull to 400 mg (equivalent to five cups of coffee) in a single 5-ml serving of Fixx energy shot. A recent review of energy drink studies found that the most common reasons for consuming these products were to increase energy and reduce fatigue, to stay awake (including use to counteract the effects of sleep deprivation), and (among students) to help with concentration during studying (Nadeem et al., 2020).

Do energy drinks work as advertised? Controlled studies either with a commercially available drink such as Red Bull or with prepared mixtures that duplicate typical energy drink constituents have confirmed that these beverages can improve performance on measures of subjective alertness, concentration, memory, reaction time, and physical endurance (Alford et al., 2001; Scholey and Kennedy, 2004; Smit et al., 2004). Although some investigators have argued that the positive effects of energy drinks are simply due to reversal of caffeine deprivation (Smit et al.,

2004), research described elsewhere in this chapter on the performance-enhancing effects of pure caffeine administration suggests that the caffeine content of energy drinks may be capable of significantly improving performance beyond that of mere deprivation reversal. In some instances, multiple constituents of energy drinks may work together to promote the desired effects. This has been demonstrated experimentally for the enhancement of cognitive function by caffeine plus glucose or caffeine plus L-theanine (Childs, 2014), and for the improvement of motor skills in athletes by caffeine and carbohydrates such as glucose (Baker et al., 2014).

Despite these positive findings, several concerns have been raised about the regular use of energy drinks. The first concern is centered around the ability of heavy caffeine consumption to cause sleep disturbance (Wesensten, 2014). This can occur at any age but is particularly problematic in children and adolescents. A 2014 survey conducted on U.S. adolescents age 13 to 17 years found that 41% of respondents had consumed at least one caffeinated energy drink during the past 3 months (Miller et al., 2018). Second, consumers should be aware that overconsumption of energy drinks can lead to adverse health consequences, some of which are quite serious. The most commonly reported adverse reactions to energy drinks are elevated heart rate and/or heart palpitations, jitteriness, headache, gastrointestinal upset and abdominal pain, insomnia, and mood changes (e.g., depressed mood, feeling stressed) (Nadeem et al., 2020). Cardiovascular abnormalities associated with energy drink consumption are of particular concern (Somers and Svatikova, 2020). Between 2005 and 2011, the number of reported visits to U.S. hospital emergency departments that were related to energy drink consumption rose from 1494 to 20,783 (Substance Abuse and Mental Health Services Administration, 2013). Some of these cases involved consumption of an energy drink in combination with other substances, including alcohol, CNS stimulants, or marijuana. A small number of fatalities have also been reported, typically as the result of cardiac arrest (e.g., Cannon et al., 2001; Rottlaender et al., 2012).

Yet another concern has been raised around the combination of alcohol with energy drinks. A few energy drinks already contain alcohol, whereas in other cases, people consume energy drinks with alcohol-containing

al., 2018). However, there are experimental findings that argue against this interpretation (Nehlig, 2010; Einöther and Giesbrecht, 2013). For example, **TABLE 13.3** presents some of the results from a study examining the influence of a single 2-mg/kg dose of caffeine on a variety of

cognitive measures in both chronic caffeine consumers (tested after overnight abstinence) and non-consumers (Smith et al., 2006). Note that in terms of performance on a vigilance (i.e., sustained attention) task, there was no difference between caffeine consumers and

BOX 13.2 ■ OF SPECIAL INTEREST (*continued*)

beverages at social events (see **FIGURE**). The aim of such a combination may be to use the stimulant properties of the energy drink to counteract the debilitating effects of alcohol intoxication. In fact, consumption of caffeine does increase alertness and counteract alcohol-related feelings of fatigue, even though users recognize that they are still alcohol intoxicated (Benson et al., 2014). Importantly, however, there is still alcohol-related impairment of complex psychomotor tasks (e.g., driving) despite caffeine consumption (Verster et al., 2012; McKetin et al., 2015). An additional problem is the increased tendency of young people to engage in risky behaviors, including risky driving, when combining alcohol with energy drinks (Striley and Khan, 2014).

In conclusion, the increasing growth of energy drink sales has caught the attention of researchers and policy makers alike. The studies reviewed above indicate that overconsumption of these beverages as well as use with alcohol can pose significant health risks. Children and adolescents are at particular risk for adverse reactions to energy drinks. This has led to calls for more education about such risks and greater government regulation of these products (Crawford and Gosliner, 2017; Talpos, 2019).

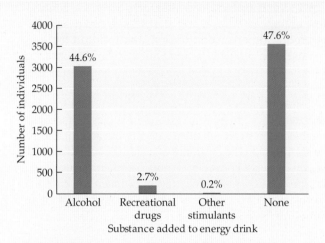

Percent of energy drink users consuming substances in addition to the energy drink "Recreational drugs" refers to non-alcohol and non-stimulant substances such as marijuana. "Other stimulants" refers to drugs such as methylphenidate, amphetamines, or cocaine. Data are from 6976 surveyed energy drink users. (From I. M. Nadeem. et al. 2021. *Sports Health* 13: 265–277.)

non-consumers when administered a placebo instead of caffeine, suggesting a lack of performance decrement due to caffeine withdrawal. On the other hand, both groups benefited significantly from the caffeine treatment, indicating that an appropriate dose of caffeine can increase attentiveness over baseline levels.

CAFFEINE CONSUMPTION CAN ENHANCE SPORTS PERFORMANCE The influence of caffeine on athletic performance has been a topic of research for many years. Most studies have examined the acute effects of low to moderate doses of caffeine (typically 3 to 6 mg/kg, which corresponds to about 200 to 400 mg for a 70-kg person) administered before and sometimes also during performance of the sport. Caffeine may be delivered through coffee, through a preweighed amount of caffeine powder dissolved in a caffeine-free liquid, or through caffeine-containing gum. This research has generally demonstrated modest but statistically significant benefits of caffeine for muscle strength and power, and for resistance exercise (Grgic et al., 2018, 2019, 2020). These benefits further extend to enhanced performance in endurance sports such as

distance running, cycling, swimming, rowing, and triathlon (Southward et al., 2018); however, whether caffeine supplementation also benefits performance in short-term high-intensity activities like sprint running or sprint swimming is not as clear cut (Astorino and Roberson, 2010; Brown et al., 2013). Even though research findings show that some individuals do not benefit much from caffeine, many athletes hope to enhance their performance by consuming the drug (either by ingesting a caffeine supplement or by drinking a caffeinated beverage) before exercising and/or competing (Diel, 2020; Pickering and Grgic, 2020).

TABLE 13.3　Effects of Caffeine on Attention

Placebo		Caffeine	
Consumer	**NonConsumer**	**Consumer**	**NonConsumer**
27.02	27.15	29.28	30.47

Source: After A. P. Smith et al. 2006. *Nutr Neurosci* 7: 127–139.

Caffeine (2 mg/kg) or a placebo was administered to two groups of participants: regular caffeine consumers who had undergone overnight withdrawal and nonconsumers of caffeine. The same individuals were tested under both drug conditions on separate days. The table shows performance on a vigilance task of sustained attention measured as the mean number of correct detections of a digit signal on a computer screen. Caffeine administration compared to placebo produced a modest but statistically significant improvement in performance in both treatment groups.

The mechanisms underlying the ergogenic (performance-enhancing) effects of caffeine are complex and may include increased force of muscle contraction, enhanced arousal and alertness as discussed earlier, reduced perceived exertion, and reduced feelings of muscle pain (Doherty and Smith, 2005; Tarnopolsky, 2008; Gonglach et al., 2016). Spriet (2014) has argued that the ergogenic properties of caffeine depend more on CNS-related cognitive and mood enhancement than on peripheral (i.e., muscular) effects of the drug (see section below on the mechanisms of caffeine action). Lastly, we should note the existence of a significant placebo effect on exercise/sport performance and neuromuscular fatigue. That is, mere expectation of receiving caffeine exerts some of the same effects as actual caffeine consumption (Shabir et al., 2018; Elhaj et al., 2021).

REGULAR CAFFEINE USE LEADS TO TOLERANCE AND DEPENDENCE What happens when people are chronically exposed to caffeine through regular coffee, tea, or soda consumption? For many years, it was believed that tolerance to the stimulating action of caffeine did not occur. However, several studies have shown that tolerance does develop to at least some of caffeine's subjective effects as well as its ability to disrupt sleep (Griffiths and Mumford, 1995). This may, for example, enable a heavy coffee drinker to consume caffeine shortly before bedtime and still fall asleep, whereas a late-night cup of coffee is likely to cause insomnia in someone who normally consumes little caffeine. Chronic caffeine use also produces tolerance to the cardiovascular and respiratory effects of the drug (see next section).

Some of you who are regular caffeine users may have occasionally been forced to miss your morning cup of coffee or tea. It is likely that you experienced at least a few psychological and/or physical symptoms, including headache and lethargy or fatigue. If so, then you are dependent on caffeine. Don't worry, though, as this is a very common type of drug dependence and is harmless except in a small percentage of individuals who engage in extremely high levels of caffeine intake. Controlled studies have demonstrated a range of caffeine withdrawal symptoms, including headache, drowsiness, fatigue, impaired concentration and psychomotor performance, and, in some cases, mild anxiety or depression. An intense craving for coffee may also be experienced. Symptoms of caffeine withdrawal can occur in individuals who are consuming as little as 100 mg/day, which is the equivalent of one 6-ounce cup of regular coffee or three cans of a caffeinated soft drink (Juliano and Griffiths, 2004). If caffeine is withheld for a prolonged period of time, the abstinence syndrome lasts for a few days but then dissipates (**FIGURE 13.21**).

Researchers believe that relief from withdrawal is a major factor in chronic coffee drinking, particularly with regard to the first cup in the morning.

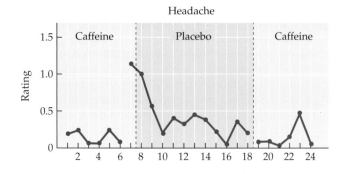

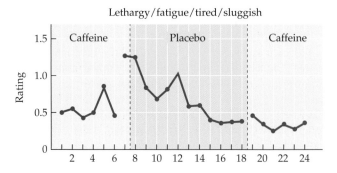

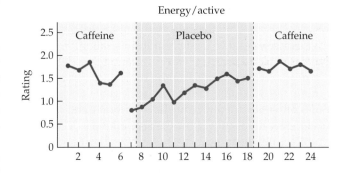

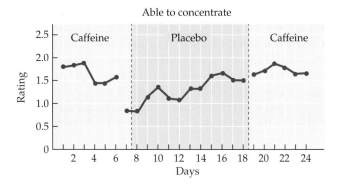

FIGURE 13.21 **Time course of caffeine withdrawal in regular users** During the first phase of the study (left panel in each graph), participants were maintained on 100 mg of caffeine daily in capsule form while abstaining from all dietary sources of caffeine. During the second phase (middle panel), placebo capsules were substituted for caffeine without the knowledge of the participants. In the third phase (right panel), caffeine administration was reinstated. Caffeine withdrawal symptoms rapidly appeared during abstinence; however, the symptoms gradually disappeared over the course of several days. (After R. R. Griffiths et al. 1990. *J Pharmacol Exp Ther* 255: 1123–1132.)

This hypothesis is supported by controlled studies showing that physical dependence plays an important role in the reinforcing effects of caffeine and the choice to consume caffeinated beverages (Garrett and Griffiths, 1998). Caffeine withdrawal symptoms can be severe enough to cause occupational and/or social dysfunction in heavy users who have severe physical dependence on the drug. There is even evidence that some schoolchildren become dependent on caffeine as the result of heavy intake of cola and other caffeine-containing beverages or food. Indeed, frequent headaches have been reported in children and adolescents who were consuming at least 1.5 liters of cola drinks (containing about 200 mg of caffeine) per day (Hering-Hanit and Gadoth, 2003). In almost all cases, the headaches completely disappeared following gradual cessation of caffeine consumption.

CAFFEINE AND CAFFEINE-CONTAINING BEVERAGES CAN CONFER BOTH BENEFITS AND RISKS TO HEALTH

Daily caffeine consumption up to 400 mg (equivalent to three to five standard cups of coffee) is generally considered to pose little or no risk to healthy, nonpregnant, adults (Nehlig, 2016). Individuals who are not regular caffeine consumers experience several physiological responses to acute caffeine administration, including increased blood pressure and respiration rate, enhanced water excretion (diuresis), and stimulation of catecholamine release from the adrenal medulla (van Dam et al., 2020). However, these effects show considerable tolerance under conditions of chronic caffeine intake.

Although moderate caffeine consumption is regarded as safe, problems can occur at higher caffeine doses. Clinicians and researchers have identified two disorders related to excessive caffeine use: (1) **caffeine intoxication** and (2) **caffeine dependence syndrome** or **caffeine use disorder**. Caffeine intoxication (previously called "caffeinism") is associated with high-dose caffeine use (typically 1 to 1.5 g daily) and is characterized by symptoms of restlessness, nervousness, insomnia, and physiological disturbances including tachycardia (increased heart rate), muscle twitching,

and gastrointestinal upset. This disorder is recognized both by the *DSM-5* of the American Psychiatric Association and by the *International Classification of Diseases*, tenth edition (ICD-10), of the World Health Organization (Meredith et al., 2013). A case study of this disorder is presented in **WEB BOX 13.2**. Extremely high doses of caffeine (3 to 5 g or more) can produce severe toxicity and even death due to ventricular fibrillation or other fatal reactions (Cappelletti et al., 2018; Willson, 2018). Caffeine-related fatalities, whether accidental or intentional (i.e., suicidal), almost always result from ingestion of pure caffeine tablets or other caffeine-containing dietary supplements, since it is nearly impossible to drink the volume of coffee required to ingest a lethal dose.

The idea of caffeine dependence (meaning something like caffeine "addiction," unlike the common mild form of dependence described in the previous section) has been somewhat more controversial, even though evidence for such a disorder has been available for some time (Striley et al, 2011). The *DSM-5* contains a category called caffeine use disorder that is designated for additional research before (potentially) being included as a recognized diagnostic category. The following three specific criteria must be met for the proposed syndrome to be present: (1) difficulty in reducing caffeine use, (2) continued caffeine use despite knowledge of adverse physical and/or psychological effects associated with such use, and (3) withdrawal symptoms upon abstinence from caffeine. Using these criteria, a recent online survey of over 1000 caffeine-consuming adults found that 8% of respondents met the diagnosis for caffeine use disorder (Sweeney et al. 2020). This result tentatively supports the notion that caffeine use disorder is a real phenomenon that occurs among some regular caffeine consumers.

In addition to the potential for caffeine intoxication or dependence, caffeine may also carry specific risks when consumed by pregnant women. Multiple studies have found associations between the amount of caffeine consumed during pregnancy and the likelihood of miscarriage, stillbirth, or low birthweight (Qian et al., 2020; James, 2021). **FIGURE 13.22** illustrates the

FIGURE 13.22   Dose-dependent increase in risk of stillbirth in pregnant women consuming caffeine A meta-analysis performed on the results of 53 different studies examined the relationship between amount of caffeine consumption during pregnancy and several adverse pregnancy outcomes. This analysis showed that every additional 100 mg of caffeine consumed daily was associated with a 19% increase in the relative risk of stillbirth compared to the baseline risk associated with no caffeine consumption. Thus, women consuming approximately 100 mg of caffeine daily had an increased risk of 19%, women consuming 200 mg of caffeine had an increased risk of 38%, and so on. It's important to emphasize that the data show changes in relative risk. The baseline risk of stillbirth in a healthy pregnancy ranges from roughly 4 to 10 per 1000 pregnancies depending on the woman's racial or ethnic group. Thus, the percentages shown in the figure relate to the difference in risk from the baseline rate. (After D. C. Greenwood et al. 2014. *Eur J Epidemiol* 29: 725–734.)

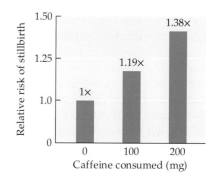

results of a meta-analysis on the dose-related increase in risk of stillbirth in pregnant women consuming caffeine. Furthermore, caffeine crosses the placenta and enters the fetus, where it may exert adverse developmental effects. One such effect that has been observed later in life is an increased risk for childhood obesity (Frayer and Kim, 2020; Jin and Qiao, 2021). As mentioned with respect to stillbirth risk, the adverse effects of caffeine consumption during pregnancy are dose-dependent. Some experts argue that the current guideline of less than 200 mg caffeine per day is reasonably safe (Baptiste-Roberts and Leviton, 2020), while others argue that pregnant women should abstain from caffeine completely if possible (Frayer and Kim, 2020; James, 2021).

Caffeine is not usually regarded as a medicinal agent; however, it does have a few therapeutic uses. First, it has mild analgesic effects, and it can also potentiate the analgesic properties of aspirin and acetaminophen (Shapiro, 2008). For this reason, caffeine is a constituent of several OTC analgesic agents, including Anacin and Excedrin. Second, an even more important clinical use of caffeine is in the treatment of newborn infants suffering from apneic episodes (periodic cessation of breathing). Premature infants whose respiratory systems have not yet matured are particularly vulnerable to this disorder, and caffeine can be lifesaving for these babies by regularizing their breathing (Moschino et al., 2020). In addition, pediatric patients suffering from asthma or persistent cough may benefit from treatment with two other methylxanthines, theophylline and theobromine, respectively (Oñatibia-Astibia et al., 2016). Lastly, Liu and colleagues (2021) recently reported that caffeine administration can benefit patients who have developed COVID-19. Of course more research is needed to confirm these preliminary findings.

Although people primarily consume coffee for its caffeine content, for its flavor, and/or for other reasons mentioned earlier, you may have come across claims in the popular media that moderate coffee consumption has health benefits. The type of research needed to test such claims involves large-scale epidemiological studies in which the prevalence of a disease in regular coffee drinkers is compared with the prevalence in people who don't drink coffee and are matched as closely as possible to the first group. Such research entails certain pitfalls, notably the difficulty of matching all potentially relevant lifestyle variables in the two groups being compared. Despite this problem, a consensus is emerging that regular consumption of three to five cups of coffee per day exerts some protective effect against the development of obesity, type 2 diabetes, cirrhosis of the liver, and several kinds of cancer (Grosso et al., 2017; Gökcen and Şanlier, 2019; van Dam et al., 2020). These effects have been attributed mainly to various antioxidant and anti-inflammatory constituents of coffee, including chlorogenic acid, caffeic acid, cafestol, and kahweol (although caffeine may also provide some benefit as well).* Substantial research has also been performed to determine whether coffee consumption exerts either harmful or beneficial effects on the development of cardiovascular diseases such as atherosclerosis, coronary heart disease, congestive heart failure, and stroke. Evidence accumulated to date suggests that coffee may reduce risk for some cardiovascular diseases but increase risk for others, especially in people who are slow caffeine metabolizers (Whayne, 2015; Zulli et al., 2016). Finally, there is growing evidence that moderate caffeine consumption through coffee or green tea reduces the risk of developing Parkinson's disease as well as age-related dementia (Hussain et al., 2018; Chen et al., 2020; Hong et al., 2020). Even in people already suffering from these disorders, continued caffeine consumption has been associated with a slower rate of symptom progression. These findings provide further support for the notion that moderate consumption of coffee can be part of a healthy diet throughout life.

Mechanisms of caffeine action

Although the mechanism by which caffeine exerts its stimulant effects is not yet completely understood, substantial progress has been made through intensive research efforts. It is clear that caffeine does not directly influence catecholamine systems in the manner of the psychomotor stimulants amphetamine and cocaine. How else might it work? Researchers have identified several cellular actions of caffeine that contribute to its physiological and behavioral effects. These include inhibition of cAMP phosphodiesterase, blockade of $GABA_A$ receptors, stimulation of Ca^{2+} release within cells, and blockade of A_1 and A_{2A} receptors for a substance called **adenosine**. **FIGURE 13.23** illustrates idealized concentration–response functions for the various cellular effects of caffeine. We can see that at the levels of caffeine associated with one or a few cups of coffee, only the adenosine receptor blockade would come into play. The other effects require much higher doses, even into the toxic range associated with caffeine intoxication. Indeed, biochemical effects of caffeine that come into play at high doses are responsible for the irritability, anxiety, and other symptoms of caffeine intoxication (Fredholm et al., 2017).

There is now overwhelming evidence that blockade of adenosine receptors, particularly the A_{2A} subtype, underlies caffeine-induced behavioral stimulation (Huang et al., 2005). These same receptors are thought

---

*Brewed coffee contains over 1000 identifiable chemicals of varying concentrations. This complex chemical mixture is responsible for the distinctive tastes and aromas associated with different blends of coffee and different methods of coffee roasting, grinding, and brewing.

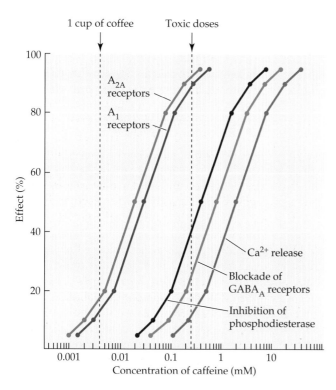

FIGURE 13.23 Concentration–response curves for caffeine's effects on various neurochemical processes Partial blockade of adenosine A_1 and A_{2A} receptors occurs at caffeine concentrations produced by doses like those typically consumed in one or a few cups of coffee. In contrast, other effects of caffeine require concentrations in the toxic range. (After J. W. Daly and B. B. Fredholm. 1998. *Drug Alcohol Depend* 51: 199–206. © 1998 Elsevier Science Ireland Ltd. Reprinted with permission from Elsevier.)

to mediate the neuroprotective action of caffeine in Parkinson's disease and the neural component of caffeine's ergogenic effects in exercise and sports (Arguiar Jr. et al., 2020; Chen and Schwarzschild, 2020). Researchers have known for many years that adenosine not only is a constituent of the vital energy-containing compound adenosine triphosphate (ATP) and one of the nucleosides in RNA but also serves a neurotransmitter-like function within the brain. In this case, adenosine is produced outside of the cell by the breakdown of extracellular ATP. This extracellular localization enables the adenosine molecules to activate receptors present in the neuronal cell membrane.

Four different adenosine receptor subtypes have been identified: A_1, A_{2A}, A_{2B}, and A_3. Of these subtypes, the A_1 and A_{2A} receptors are responsible for mediating most of adenosine's effects in the brain and therefore are the major adenosine receptor targets of caffeine (Ribeiro and Sebastião, 2010). The A_1 receptor is the predominant subtype in the cerebral cortex, hippocampus, and cerebellum, whereas the A_{2A} subtype is enriched in the striatum and olfactory bulb (Ribeiro et al., 2003). Importantly, one of the primary locations of the A_{2A} receptor is the GABAergic output neurons of the dorsal striatum (caudate–putamen) and ventral striatum (NAcc), cells that are also rich in DA receptors. Researchers have demonstrated that striatal A_{2A} receptors form heteromers (complexes containing more than one type of molecule) with D_2 receptors (Ferré et al., 2007; Casadó-Anguera et al., 2016). Current evidence suggests that the structure is a heterotetramer consisting of two A_{2A} and two D_2 receptors. Furthermore, the interaction between these different

receptors helps account for caffeine's stimulatory effects in the following way. Occupancy of the A_{2A} receptor by adenosine exerts an allosteric influence on the D_2 receptor, reducing its affinity for DA and, therefore, decreasing the arousing and behaviorally activating effects of DA (Ferré, 2016). Consequently, under conditions when extracellular adenosine levels are low, D_2 receptor signaling is unimpeded and the organism is alert and aroused (**FIGURE 13.24**, left). When adenosine levels are higher, however, adenosine inhibition of D_2-mediated signaling leads to lower levels of arousal and psychomotor activation (Figure 13.24, right). Consumption of caffeine releases this inhibition by blocking the adenosine receptors and enhancing D_2 signaling, thus leading to mild arousal and psychomotor activation. Note that the degree of activation is much less pronounced than the activation produced by cocaine- or amphetamine-mediated increases in extracellular DA levels, which are sufficient to overcome the negative allosteric influence of adenosine (see Chapter 12). Finally, researchers have established adenosine as a key neurotransmitter/neuromodulator in the production of sleep, although the neural circuit through which adenosine exerts this function is not yet fully understood (Lazarus et al., 2019). Nevertheless, the sleep-promoting effect of adenosine makes clear why caffeine blockade of adenosine receptors is especially beneficial for enhancing wakefulness in drowsy individuals.

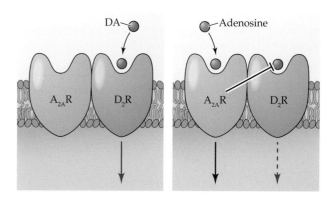

FIGURE 13.24 Activation of A_{2A} receptors allosterically inhibits D_2 receptor signaling $A_{2A}R$, A_{2A} receptor; D_2R, D_2 receptor. (After S. Ferré et al. 2007. *Trends Neurosci* 30: 440–446.)

SECTION SUMMARY

- Caffeine and theophylline are members of a class of plant-derived substances called methylxanthines. Caffeine, especially, is contained in a number of foods such as coffee and tea. When consumed orally, it is readily absorbed from the gastrointestinal tract and is gradually metabolized and excreted with a typical half-life of approximately 4 hours. Paraxanthine, an important first-level caffeine metabolite, has similar stimulant activity to the parent compound.

- Caffeine and other ingredients (e.g., sugar, amino acids, and sometimes alcohol) are constituents of so-called energy drinks. These beverages are consumed for the same stimulating effects as other caffeine-containing foods and beverages. While energy drinks can serve a useful function by combating fatigue and inattention, they can also contribute to excessive caffeine consumption and may be dangerous when the caffeine is combined with significant amounts of alcohol in an effort to counteract alcohol's intoxicating effects.

- In rodents, caffeine has locomotor stimulant effects at low doses but actually reduces activity at high doses.

- Humans generally experience heightened attention and arousal, reduced fatigue, and reduced sleep in response to normal amounts of caffeine. Higher doses, typically greater than 400 mg, can lead to feelings of tension and anxiety.

- Laboratory studies have demonstrated enhanced mood, improved psychomotor performance, and increased memory consolidation following caffeine administration. Caffeine enhances muscle strength and power, and it facilitates athletic performance, particularly in endurance sports.

- Regular caffeine use leads to tolerance and physical dependence. Symptoms of caffeine withdrawal include headache, drowsiness, fatigue, impaired concentration, and reduced psychomotor performance.

- In non-users, caffeine acutely produces various physiological effects, such as increased blood pressure and respiration rate, diuresis, and increased catecholamine release. However, these effects show substantial tolerance in regular caffeine users.

- Daily caffeine use up to 400 mg is generally considered to be safe, except in pregnant women. Consumption of high doses, however, has been associated with two psychiatric disorders: caffeine intoxication, and caffeine dependence syndrome or caffeine use disorder. Caffeine intoxication, caused by recent excessive caffeine consumption, is characterized by symptoms of restlessness, nervousness, insomnia, and physiological disturbances such as tachycardia, muscle twitching, and gastrointestinal upset. Caffeine dependence syndrome is a syndrome of substance dependence (see Chapter 9) associated with chronic, maladaptive caffeine use. This syndrome is currently accepted by the ICD-10 but needs further confirmation according to the *DSM-5*.

- Caffeine use during pregnancy dose-dependently increases the risk of miscarriage, stillbirth, and low birthweight. Prenatal exposure to caffeine may additionally have adverse effects on offspring development. For these reasons, it is advisable for pregnant women to reduce their caffeine consumption or, ideally, to abstain from caffeine entirely.

- Caffeine has several clinical uses, including pain relief and the treatment of newborn infants with apnea.

- Epidemiological studies indicate that regular coffee consumption of three to five cups per day reduces vulnerability to obesity, type 2 diabetes, liver cirrhosis, and several kinds of cancer. These protective effects have been attributed mainly to the presence in coffee of antioxidant and anti-inflammatory substances such as chlorogenic acid, caffeic acid, cafestol, and kahweol. Additional research suggests that moderate caffeine consumption reduces the risk of developing Parkinson's disease and age-related dementia.

- Although caffeine has a number of biochemical effects on the brain, its psychological and behavioral properties are mediated primarily by its ability to block A_1 and A_{2A} receptors for the neurotransmitter/neuromodulator adenosine. Extracellular adenosine is derived largely from the breakdown of ATP that has been released into the extracellular space. The behavioral stimulant properties of caffeine have been linked especially to antagonism of A_{2A} receptors, which form heteromeric complexes with DA D_2 receptors in the striatum. Under drug-free conditions, adenosine activation of striatal A_{2A} receptors exerts a negative allosteric effect on the D_2 receptors, thereby weakening cellular signaling through those receptors. Caffeine blockade of the adenosine receptors releases the D_2 receptors from this negative effect, thereby enhancing dopaminergic transmission in the striatum.

STUDY QUESTIONS

1. What do we know about delivery of nicotine to the brain when smoking a tobacco cigarette? How rapid is such delivery, and is there any accumulation of brain nicotine over the course of the day as a result of repeated smoking?

2. Since the invention of the original e-cigarette, there have been several changes in the design of these devices. List the main categories of e-cigarettes, including differences in design features and relative differences in the amount of nicotine typically provided by each category. Which type of e-cigarette most closely mimics standard tobacco cigarettes with respect to nicotine delivery?

3. Most nicotine is metabolized by the liver enzyme _____, and the principal nicotine metabolite is _____. How do differences in the rate of nicotine metabolism influence smoking behavior and the risk for nicotine dependence? Explain how the processes of nicotine aversion versus nicotine reward help account for the relationship between nicotine metabolism and smoking behavior.

4. Nicotine's behavioral and physiological effects are mediated by its agonist activity at the _____ receptor. How do differences in the subunit composition of these receptors affect their affinity for nicotine and their susceptibility to desensitization when persistently exposed to nicotine?

5. What was the major methodological problem associated with early research investigating nicotine's effects on mood and cognition using cigarette smokers as the participants? How was this problem ameliorated in later studies, and what were the findings from that research? Which receptor subtypes (in terms of subunit composition and nicotine affinity) are most responsible for nicotine's effects on cognition?

6. Cigarette smoke contains many chemicals besides nicotine. How do we know that among these chemicals, nicotine is the primary one that has reinforcing properties? Laboratory animal studies have found that females are more sensitive than males to nicotine's reinforcing effects, and that adolescent animals are more sensitive than adults. What is the relevance of these findings for human smoking behavior?

7. Describe the neural circuit that mediates nicotine's rewarding and reinforcing actions, including the anatomical sites of nicotine action on its target receptors. Your answer should contain a description of the several mechanisms by which nicotine can increase DA release within the NAcc.

8. The fact that millions of people in the United States regularly use tobacco products is consistent with the idea that nicotine has rewarding/reinforcing effects but seems inconsistent with the idea that nicotine can be aversive. How do we reconcile this apparent paradox? What is the evidence for nicotine aversion and what is known about the underlying neurobiological and genetic mechanisms both in laboratory animals and in humans?

9. Describe the effects of nicotine on physiological processes such as heart rate, blood pressure, epinephrine secretion, stomach acid secretion, and body weight regulation. Which of these effects are mediated by the sympathetic nervous system, the parasympathetic system, or the hypothalamus?

10. If you suspected someone of having acute nicotine poisoning, what symptoms would you look for? What are the most likely ways that someone could be exposed to a massive overdose of nicotine? A milder but still dangerous form of nicotine toxicity can occur in field workers harvesting wet tobacco leaves. This syndrome is called _____.

11. Compare the neural mechanisms underlying acute nicotine tolerance versus chronic tolerance. Under what circumstances does each kind of tolerance occur?

12. List the three criteria (at least two of which must be met) used by the *DSM-5* to diagnose tobacco use disorder. Are the criteria for tobacco use disorder similar to the criteria for other substance use disorders in *DSM-5* (based on your other readings in the textbook)?

13. Imagine a heavy smoker who wakes up one morning and decides to quit smoking right then and there. How long do you think it will take before they begin to experience withdrawal? Would it make any difference in the latency to begin withdrawing if the same person smoked their regular number of cigarettes in the morning but then decided to quit at noon? Explain your answer.

14. The previous question was related to the nicotine abstinence syndrome. Describe the symptoms of nicotine withdrawal on affect (mood-related symptoms), one's body (somatic symptoms), and cognition (cognitive symptoms).

15. What is an osmotic minipump, and how has this device been used in the creation and study of animal models of nicotine dependence? What procedure do researchers use to precipitate rapid withdrawal in animals that have been made nicotine dependent by continuous exposure to the drug?

16. Compare and contrast the reasons given for adolescents taking up tobacco cigarette smoking versus e-cigarette vaping. Perform the same comparison for risk factors/predictors of early smoking or vaping.

STUDY QUESTIONS (continued)

17. List and discuss six hypotheses proposed to account for why adolescents are more likely to select e-cigarettes over tobacco cigarettes for their initial use of a nicotine-containing product. Is it uncommon for e-cigarette users to transition to tobacco cigarettes? What hypotheses have been proposed to explain this transition?

18. Many smokers and vapers probably think that their desire for nicotine is the only factor that maintains their smoking habit. Is this correct? If not, what are other important factors that underlie the maintenance of tobacco cigarette and e-cigarette use? How do the nicotine resource and deprivation reversal models attempt to explain the results of studies using abstinent smokers to account for the effects of nicotine on mood, stress, and cognition?

19. Chemicals besides nicotine that are present within tobacco smoke and e-cigarette vapor can influence use of their respective products. Explain this statement, including relevant mechanisms (neurochemical and/or psychological).

20. Here are three statements for consideration: (1) tobacco cigarette smoking is hazardous to your health; (2) e-cigarette vaping is safe; (3) e-cigarette vaping is safer than tobacco cigarette smoking. Evaluate each statement, providing specific information to justify your answer.

21. If you knew a woman who was a regular smoker or vaper who had just become pregnant, what scientific information would you provide to try to convince her to stop her tobacco cigarette or e-cigarette use?

22. List the various nonmedical approaches available to help smokers stop smoking. What is known about the effectiveness of these approaches?

23. Several medical approaches are also available to smokers trying to quit. Nicotine gum, patch, lozenge, nasal spray, or inhaler are all examples of _____. Alternatively, the smoker may be prescribed _____, which was first developed as an antidepressant medication, or _____, which reduces nicotine craving and withdrawal reactions by acting as a _____ agonist at _____ (high-affinity or low-affinity) nAChRs.

24. Clinical trials have shown highly promising results with nicotine vaccines. True or false?

25. Caffeine and theophylline are members of a group of plant-derived chemicals known as _____.

26. Why do the stimulatory effects of caffeine persist even after it has been converted to its metabolite paraxanthine?

27. Caffeine consumption can exert a range of mood and behavioral effects. Describe these effects and their relationship to the amount of caffeine consumed.

28. Some athletes consume caffeine to improve their performance. Is this justified by experimental findings? Which kinds of sports are best known to benefit from caffeine?

29. What is the evidence for caffeine tolerance and dependence, and what are the symptoms of caffeine withdrawal? Can an individual who consumes only one cup of caffeinated coffee per day become caffeine-dependent?

30. Two disorders related to excessive caffeine use are _____ and _____. Describe the symptoms associated with toxic amounts of caffeine consumption. What is the position of the *DSM-5* with respect to caffeine having the potential to be an addictive-like substance?

31. Some researchers now recommend that pregnant women abstain from consuming any caffeine-containing beverages. Why?

32. List the ingredients found in a typical energy drink. Why have researchers and policy makers raised concerns over the increasing consumption of energy drinks, especially among children and adolescents?

33. What are the demonstrated therapeutic/health benefits of caffeine and/or coffee consumption?

34. Discuss the mechanism of action underlying caffeine's effects on behavior. Include in your answer a description of the adenosine signaling system, including the source of neurotransmitter-related adenosine, the principal receptors for this substance, and interactions between adenosine and dopamine signaling.

Marijuana and the Cannabinoids

A MAN COMES INTO THE EMERGENCY ROOM in Jackson, Mississippi. Six-foot-four, 240 lbs. "Solid, brick muscle," recalls Dr. Robert Galli, a professor of emergency medicine and toxicology at the University of Mississippi medical center (UMMC) in Jackson. "This big guy was fumbling around in the street, he was rolling around in the grass, he had no shirt on, his pants and underwear were down to his shoes, and he's flopping around in the rain with about 15 people taking videos of him." Someone called 911. First the fire department arrived, followed by police, then paramedics, who ascertained from the surrounding crowd that the man smoked "Spice."

— Glenza, 2016

This account, published in May 2016 in the British newspaper *The Guardian*, is just one of many recent stories warning of the dangers of "synthetic marijuana" (also known as Spice, K2, and many other street names). Typical headlines are "Why synthetic marijuana is more dangerous than ever" (Kroll, 2016b), "Spotlighting the effects and dangers of K2, or synthetic marijuana" (Arps, 2018), and "Why synthetic marijuana is so risky" (White, 2018). These headlines raise many important questions: just what *is* synthetic marijuana, where does it come from, how does it act on the body, and is it as dangerous as portrayed in the popular media?

The present chapter deals with cannabis, an ancient drug that continues to be the center of much controversy. You will first learn about the history of cannabis, from early times through the anti-marijuana campaign of the 1930s and into the current era in which medical marijuana and recreational marijuana legalization have been implemented in many states. This will be followed by the pharmacology and mechanism of action of cannabinoids, including both the biologically active compounds present in the cannabis plant and the so-called endocannabinoids, which are cannabinoid substances made by one's own body. The psychological and behavioral effects of cannabis use will be covered, including current information about excessive use and misuse of this drug. Finally, you will learn about the current status of marijuana and cannabinoids

Spencer Platt/Getty Images

"Spice," which is a street term for potent synthetic marijuana, can cause severe adverse reactions in users.

as therapeutic agents, and importantly, some answers to the questions raised in the chapter opening will be offered. ■

14.1 Background, History, and Basic Pharmacology of Cannabis and Marijuana

Forms of cannabis and their chemical constituents

Marijuana (alternately spelled "marihuana") is produced from the flowering hemp, a weed-like plant given the botanical name *Cannabis sativa* by Linnaeus in 1753 (**FIGURE 14.1**). Historically, hemp has served an important function in many cultures as a major source of fiber for making fishing nets, rope, cloth, and even paper (Bonini et al., 2018). At times, its seeds have been used for their oil content and as bird feed. More important for neuropharmacologists is that cannabis plants contain over 120 unique compounds that are collectively known as **phytocannabinoids** (meaning compounds with a cannabinoid structure that are found in the cannabis plant), as well as more than 400 other identified compounds (Andre et al., 2016; Morales et al., 2017). The psychoactive properties of some of these compounds, particularly a substance called **Δ⁹-tetrahydrocannabinol** (**THC**), are primarily responsible for the use of cannabis as a drug. **Cannabidiol** (**CBD**) is another important phytocannabinoid that we will be discussing. Although cannabinoids can be found to some extent in all parts of the plant, they are concentrated in a sticky yellowish resin that is secreted in particularly large amounts by the flowering tops of female plants.

Cannabis can be obtained in a number of different forms for the purpose of consumption. The most familiar to us is **marijuana**, which is derived from the Mexican word *maraguanquo*, meaning "an intoxicating plant." *Marijuana* refers to a crude mixture of dried and crumbled leaves, small stems, and flowering tops. Traditionally, marijuana has usually been smoked in rolled cigarettes known as "joints" or in various kinds of pipes and bongs. Users desiring to combine marijuana and tobacco created "blunts," which are hollowed-out cigars filled with marijuana, or "spliffs" or "mulled cigarettes," which are joints containing a mixture of marijuana and tobacco (Schauer et al., 2017). However, with the legalization of recreational cannabis in many states as well as the increasing use of e-cigarettes by young people (see Chapter 13), new methods of cannabis consumption have emerged. These include oral consumption of cannabis edibles and cannabis vaping using vape pens or other kinds of vaporizers (Struble et al., 2019). Vaporizers are available for use with either THC-containing liquids or dry plant material.

FIGURE 14.1 Cannabis plants

Marijuana potency measured by its THC content varies widely, depending on the genetic strain of the plant and its growing conditions. For example, potency can be significantly increased by preventing pollination and, therefore, seed production by the female plants. Marijuana produced by this method is called sinsemilla (meaning "without seeds"). Analyses of collected cannabis samples show a marked rise in THC content worldwide over the past 40 to 50 years. Whereas cannabis THC content in the 1970s was typically in the range of 1% to 4%, current samples often contain 10% or more THC (Freeman et al., 2020). Recent data on the THC content of illicit cannabis samples seized by the U.S. Drug Enforcement Administration (DEA) from 2009 to 2019 are shown in **FIGURE 14.2** (ElSohly et al., 2021). The increase in cannabis potency over time has been attributed to a shift of marijuana production from "regular" marijuana to sinsemilla. Also popular among some users are strains of high-potency cannabis called "skunk," named after the pungent aroma emanating from the herbal material.

Cannabis can also be processed using methods that concentrate its psychoactive ingredients. One example

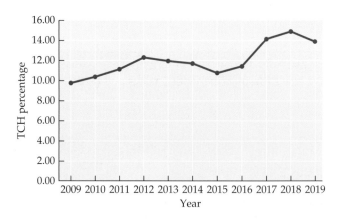

FIGURE 14.2 Yearly mean THC content of marijuana samples seized by the DEA from 2009 to 2019 (From M. A. ElSohly et al. 2021. *Cogn Neurosci Neuroimaging* 6: 603–606.)

Courtesy of the U.S. DEA

FIGURE 14.3 The potent form of cannabis called hashish

of this is a cannabis extract called **hashish**. Like marijuana, hashish may be smoked or eaten (**FIGURE 14.3**). The potency of hashish greatly depends on how it has been prepared. In the Middle and Far East, for example, hashish generally refers to a relatively pure resin preparation with a very high cannabinoid content. Whereas hashish has a long history, a new form of high-potency cannabis consumption has been developed called **dabbing** (Loflin and Earleywine, 2014; Miller et al., 2016). This practice typically involves extraction of cannabis with butane followed by evaporation of the solvent. The result is a waxy residue that, like hashish, contains an extremely high concentration of THC. Some common street names for this material are "dabs," "earwax," "butter," "shatter," "honey oil," and "butane hash oil." A "dab" refers to a single dose of the extract that is heated with a blowtorch or an e-cigarette/vape pen in order to vaporize and inhale the THC (Giroud et al., 2015). Informal interviews with young users revealed that dabbing is preferable to smoking marijuana because it's easier to do surreptitiously and it produces a much stronger "high" (Nirmay, 2016).

History of cannabis

Cannabis is believed to have originated in central Asia, probably in China. There is archeological evidence for the use of hemp fibers 8000 years ago (**FIGURE 14.4**).

Medical and religious use of cannabis can be traced back to ancient China, India, and the Middle East (Ligresti et al., 2016; Bonini et al., 2018). Recently published findings from the Pamir region of central Asia suggest that ritualized cannabis smoking was taking place as early as 500 BCE, roughly 2500 years ago (Ren et al., 2019). From its origins in Asia, cannabis spread to the Arab world, where the consumption of hashish became commonplace. Indeed, hashish is frequently mentioned in the Arabian folk stories that constitute *The Thousand and One Nights*. However, Western interest in this substance did not begin until the early to mid-nineteenth century, when some of Napoleon's soldiers reportedly brought hashish from Egypt back with them to France. Around the same time, a French physician named Jacques-Joseph Moreau encountered the intoxicating effects of hashish in the course of several trips to the Middle East. After returning to Paris, Moreau helped found a notorious association of French writers and artists known as *Le Club des Haschischins* ("club of the hashish eaters"), which included such notables as Victor Hugo, Alexandre Dumas, Théophile Gautier, and Charles Baudelaire.

The history of cannabis in the United States dates back to the colonial era, when hemp was an important agricultural commodity. No less than George Washington himself was a hemp farmer, which is ironic in view of the patriotic fervor associated with the contemporary "war on drugs." Yet domestic hemp growers of the seventeenth and eighteenth centuries apparently had little awareness of the plant's intoxicating properties.* Rather, historians believe that the social practice of consuming cannabis (mainly marijuana smoking) was brought into the United States in the early 1900s by Mexican immigrants crossing the Mexican–American border, and by Caribbean seamen and West Indian immigrants entering the country by way of New Orleans and other ports on the Gulf of Mexico.

Marijuana use rapidly spread outward from these points of origin, resulting in its coming to the attention

---

*To be fair, the strains of hemp that are used for fiber and other non-recreational purposes have very low, non-intoxicating levels of THC. This helps explain why Washington and other hemp farmers of that period were ignorant of the psychoactive effects associated with high-THC strains of the plant.

FIGURE 14.4 An 8000-year timeline of cannabis use around the world (After S. R. Childers and C. S. Breivogel. 1998. *Drug Alcohol Depend* 51: 173–187. © 1998 Elsevier Science Ireland Ltd. Reprinted with permission from Elsevier.)

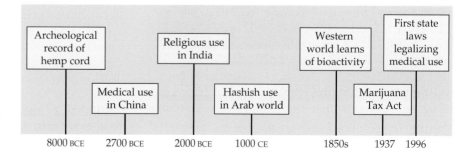

of the federal government. In the 1930s, Harry Anslinger spearheaded a public relations campaign to portray marijuana as a social menace capable of destroying the youth of America. Anslinger had been appointed in 1930 to be the first commissioner of narcotics in the Bureau of Narcotics of the U.S. Treasury Department. In congressional hearings, Anslinger testified as follows: "Those who are habitually accustomed to use of the drug [marijuana] are said to develop a delirious rage after its administration, during which they are temporarily, at least, irresponsible and liable to commit violent crimes. The prolonged use of this narcotic is said to produce mental deterioration. It apparently releases inhibitions of an antisocial nature which dwell within the individual" (Schaffer Library of Drug Policy). At the same time, Anslinger's Bureau of Narcotics was feeding information to the popular media about the evils of marijuana use. This stream of propaganda resulted in magazine articles with titles such as "Marihuana: Assassin of Youth" (*American Magazine*) and "Sex Crazing Drug Menace" (*Physical Culture*), as well as anti-marijuana movies such as *Reefer Madness* (**FIGURE 14.5**) that are now regarded as cult classics.

FIGURE 14.5 Poster advertising the 1936 film *Reefer Madness*

As a consequence of Anslinger's anti-marijuana campaign, the federal government in 1937 passed its first legislation designed to control marijuana sales, called the Marijuana Tax Act. This legislation instituted a national registration and taxation system aimed at discouraging all use of cannabis for commercial, recreational, and medical purposes. Although the Marijuana Tax Act was overturned as unconstitutional by the U.S. Supreme Court in 1969, marijuana and other forms of cannabis remain regulated by state laws and by the federal Controlled Substances Act of 1970.

Basic pharmacology of marijuana

THC Modern cannabinoid pharmacology began in 1964, when two Israeli researchers, Yehiel Gaoni and Raphael Mechoulam, identified THC as the major active ingredient of *C. sativa* (**FIGURE 14.6**). A typical hand-rolled marijuana cigarette ("joint") consists of about 0.5 to 1 g of cannabis. If the THC content is 10%, then a 1-g joint contains 100 mg of active ingredient that is available to the smoker. As in the case of nicotine in tobacco leaves (see Chapter 13), burning of the marijuana causes the THC to vaporize and to enter the smoker's lungs in small particles. But because of a variety of factors, only about 20% to 30% of the original THC content is absorbed in the lungs. In practice, the amount of THC absorbed is affected not only by the initial amount of plant material used and the potency of this material but also by the pattern of smoking. The effective dose and latency to onset of effects of smoked marijuana are influenced by puff volume, puff frequency, inhalation depth, and breath-hold duration (Gorelick and Heishman, 2006).

Smoked THC is quickly absorbed through the lungs, resulting in rapidly rising levels in the blood plasma of the smoker (**FIGURE 14.7**). After peak levels are reached, plasma THC concentrations begin to decline as a result of a combination of metabolism in the liver and accumulation of the drug in the body's fat stores. In contrast, oral consumption of marijuana leads to prolonged but poor absorption of THC, thus resulting in low and variable plasma concentrations. The reduced bioavailability of THC following oral consumption compared with smoking probably results from both degradation in the stomach and first-pass hepatic metabolism; that is, once orally ingested THC has been absorbed from the gastrointestinal tract, it must pass through the liver, where much of it is metabolized before it can enter the general circulation. THC metabolism is quite complicated, with over 80 metabolites having been identified (Dinis-Oliveira, 2016). Two of the major metabolites are 11-hydroxy-THC and 11-nor-9-carboxy-THC (THC-COOH). These substances as well as various minor metabolites are

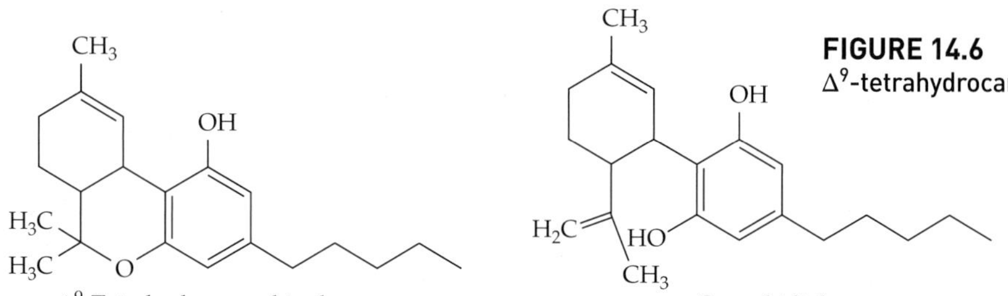

FIGURE 14.6 Chemical structures of Δ^9-tetrahydrocannabinol (THC) and cannabidiol (CBD)

Δ^9-Tetrahydrocannabinol

Cannabidiol

excreted primarily in the feces (about two-thirds of the administered dose) and the urine (about one-third of the administered dose). Even though THC levels in the bloodstream decline fairly rapidly after one smokes marijuana, complete elimination from the body is much slower because of persistence of the drug in fat tissue. Consequently, the elimination half-life ($t_{1/2}$) of THC is generally estimated at about 20 to 30 hours. Furthermore, the gradual movement of THC and fat-soluble metabolites back out of fat stores means that sensitive urine screening tests for THC-COOH can detect the presence of this metabolite more than 2 weeks after a single marijuana use.

CANNABIDIOL Recent advances in cannabinoid research have shown that other phytocannabinoids besides THC have biological activity despite their low affinity for the neuronal cannabinoid receptor. The best studied of these compounds is CBD, which is similar in structure to THC (see Figure 14.6). CBD lacks the intoxicating and dependence-producing effects of THC. Consequently, this substance is available legally in most states, and CBD-containing oils, edibles, ointments, and so forth are readily available for purchase in most parts of the United States. Moreover, researchers have developed great interest in the therapeutic potential of CBD for a variety of disorders. This topic, along with the proposed mechanisms of CBD action, are taken up in later sections of the chapter.

SECTION SUMMARY

- *Cannabis sativa*, the flowering hemp plant, exudes a resin containing a number of unique compounds known as phytocannabinoids. The most important psychoactive phytocannabinoid is Δ^9-tetrahydrocannabinol (THC). The potency (percentage THC content) of cannabis has risen significantly since the 1970s, which is related to the production of sinsemilla marijuana and high-potency strains sometimes called "skunk" marijuana.

- A non-psychoactive constituent, cannabidiol (CBD), is also of interest because of its emerging potential for treating a variety of medical conditions.

- Cannabis can be obtained in several different types of preparations, including marijuana and hashish, both of which may be smoked or taken orally. Dabbing refers to inhalation of the heated vapors of a newer kind of cannabis extract. Hashish and dabs are preferred by some users because of their greater potency compared with marijuana and the resulting increase in subjective "high."

- The consumption of cannabis for its intoxicating effects is thought to date back thousands of years in Eastern cultures. The practice of marijuana smoking was introduced into the United States in the early 1900s by Mexican and West Indian immigrants.

- An anti-marijuana campaign instituted in the 1930s led to the first federal legislation controlling this substance, the Marijuana Tax Act. This law was later overturned.

- Inhaled THC is rapidly absorbed from the lungs into the circulation, where it is almost completely bound to plasma proteins. Oral THC consumption yields slower absorption and a lower plasma peak than occurs following smoking.

- THC is extensively metabolized in the liver, and the metabolites are excreted mainly in the feces and urine. Following a single dose of THC, total clearance of the drug and its metabolites may take days because of sequestration of these compounds in fat tissue.

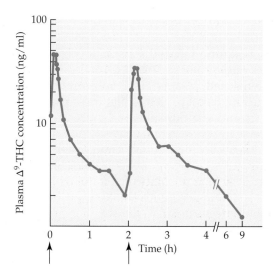

FIGURE 14.7 Mean time course of plasma THC concentrations Data were obtained from individuals who smoked a marijuana cigarette containing approximately 9 mg of THC at the two time points indicated by the arrows. (After S. Agurell et al. 1986. *Pharmacol Rev* 38: 21–43; and G. Barnet et al. 1982. *J Pharmacokinet Biopharm* 10: 495–506.)

14.2 Mechanisms of Cannabinoid Action

For many years, researchers interested in how THC and other cannabinoids work in the brain were hampered by the lack of an identified cellular receptor for these compounds. Subsequent discovery of cannabinoid receptors permitted the synthesis of selective cannabinoid agonists and antagonists, as well as elucidation of the endogenous cannabinoid system.

Cannabinoid effects are primarily mediated by cannabinoid receptors

Pharmacological characterization of a central nervous system (CNS) **cannabinoid receptor** was announced in 1988 by a group of researchers that included William Devane and Allyn Howlett, at St. Louis University, and Lawrence Melvin and M. Ross Johnson, at the Pfizer pharmaceutical company (Devane et al., 1988).* This initial characterization was quickly followed by other studies showing significant expression of cannabinoid receptors in many brain areas such as the basal ganglia (including the caudate nucleus, putamen, globus pallidus, entopeduncular nucleus, and substantia nigra pars reticularis), cerebellum, hippocampus, and cerebral cortex. Areas of the human brain expressing high and medium cannabinoid receptor levels are shown in **FIGURE 14.8**. As discussed later, high expression of

*Readers interested in more information on the history of the discovery and characterization of cannabinoid receptors are referred to the excellent review by Mackie (2007).

cannabinoid receptors in the basal ganglia, cerebellum, and hippocampus is consistent with the well-known behavioral effects of cannabinoids on locomotor activity, coordination, and memory.

Around the same time that the St. Louis University and Pfizer researchers were first characterizing the cannabinoid receptor pharmacologically, another group of scientists at the National Institute of Mental Health (NIMH), including Lisa Matsuda and Tom Bonner, cloned a novel gene from rat cerebral cortex that coded for a membrane protein with the characteristics of a G protein–coupled (metabotropic) receptor. Further studies revealed that these investigators, who were working on an unrelated problem, had actually cloned the gene for the rat brain cannabinoid receptor (Matsuda et al., 1990). This is a good example of an approach that is sometimes called *reverse pharmacology*—namely, the cloning of a novel receptor gene, the identity of which must then be determined by more classical pharmacological methods. The CNS cannabinoid receptor is designated CB_1.

The cellular and subcellular localization of CB_1 receptors within the CNS has been studied extensively using a variety of experimental approaches (reviewed by Hu and Mackie, 2015). Most of these receptors are expressed by various neuronal populations, with expression being higher in GABAergic than in glutamatergic neurons. However, low but meaningful CB_1 receptor expression has also been found in astrocytes (Metna-Laurent and Marsicano, 2015). Within neurons, CB_1 receptors are primarily found in presynaptic structures, specifically nerve terminals and axon segments

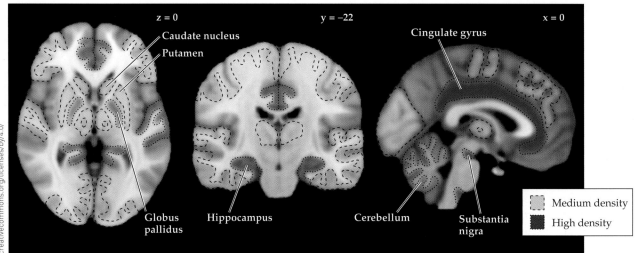

From M. A. P. Bloomfield et al. 2019. *Pharmacol Ther* 195: 132–161. doi.org/10.1016/j.pharmthera.2018.10.006. CC BY 4.0. https://creativecommons.org/licenses/by/4.0/

FIGURE 14.8 Areas of high and medium cannabinoid (CB$_1$) receptor levels in the human brain CB$_1$ receptor levels determined by quantitative autoradiography were characterized as high or medium based on the relative amount of radioligand binding. Color-coded representations of these categories were then superimposed on axial/horizontal (left), coronal (middle), and sagittal (right) MRI images of the human brain. The coordinate shown above each image refers to the position of the MRI "slice" in a standard human brain atlas. Labels point to several brain areas expressing high or medium receptor levels that are known to play important roles in cannabinoid behavioral effects. Within the neocortex, the cingulate gyrus had a high level of receptor expression whereas other cortical areas had medium receptor levels. Not shown on any of the images is the amygdala, which had a high level of receptor expression.

near the terminals. On the other hand, some neurons possess somatodendritic CB_1 receptors that mediate self-inhibition by these cells (Lu and Mackie, 2020). Despite the fact that CB_1 receptors are typically characterized as the CNS cannabinoid receptor, these receptors are additionally expressed at low levels by many other organ systems, including the endocrine system, immune system, heart, and liver (Howlett and Abood, 2017). This widespread expression indicates that the endocannabinoid system probably regulates a variety of physiological functions and that exogenous cannabinoids like THC or CBD are capable of altering those same functions.

A second cannabinoid receptor, CB_2, was discovered after the identification of the CB_1 subtype. CB_2 receptors were initially found in the immune system (Malfitano et al., 2014) and then later in other tissues such as bone, adipose (fat) cells, lung, testes, and the gastrointestinal tract (Atwood and Mackie, 2010; Howlett and Abood, 2017). CB_2 receptors are also expressed by microglia, the brain's immune cells, and by astrocytes, especially when those cells have been activated by inflammatory or degenerative processes occurring within the brain (e.g., in Alzheimer's disease or multiple sclerosis). Finally, CB_2 receptors are expressed by neurons in some areas of the brain, though at lower levels than the CB_1 receptor (Lu and Mackie, 2016). Studies of CB_2 knockout mice revealed that these receptors play a significant role in several behavioral functions. For example, the mutant mice showed increased locomotor activity, greater depressive-like behavior in the forced-swim and tail-suspension tests, less anxiety-like behavior in the elevated plus-maze and light–dark box tests, and reduced reinforcing effects of alcohol compared to wild-type controls (Liu et al., 2017). Among the neuronal populations expressing CB_2 receptors are the dopaminergic neurons of the ventral tegmental area (VTA) (Zhang et al., 2014), and many of the phenotypic characteristics of the CB_2 knockout mice may be related to the loss of CB_2 receptors in these dopaminergic cells.

Cannabinoid receptors belong to the large family of metabotropic receptors. The cellular effects of the CB_1 receptor are mediated primarily through coupling to the G proteins G_i and G_o, which leads to inhibition of cyclic adenosine monophosphate (cAMP) formation, inhibition of voltage-sensitive Ca^{2+} channels, and activation of K^+ channel opening (Howlett, 2005; Ronan et al., 2016). For presynaptic CB_1 receptors located on nerve terminals, these signaling events combine to exert a powerful inhibitory effect on neurotransmitter release. Indeed, cannabinoids can inhibit the release of many different neurotransmitters, including acetylcholine, dopamine, norepinephrine, serotonin, GABA (γ-aminobutyric acid), and glutamate (Iversen, 2003). An additional effect of cannabinoid receptors

is to modulate gene expression by several different mechanisms. One such mechanism is activation of the MAP kinase system, which plays an important role in synaptic plasticity, learning, and memory. Additional mechanisms involve epigenetic changes such as DNA methylation that may contribute to the long-term consequences of cannabis use (Szutorisz and Hurd, 2016).

Pharmacological and genetic studies reveal the functional roles of cannabinoid receptors

THC has similar binding affinity for CB_1 and CB_2 receptors (Pertwee, 2008), so it is not useful for investigating the functional effects of one receptor subtype versus the other. Rather, selectivity of action has been accomplished using various synthetic cannabinoid agonists and antagonists that were developed initially for research use and are now being investigated for potential therapeutic applications. Two of the earliest-developed compounds are CP-55,940 and WIN 55,212–2, which are full agonists at both CB_1 and CB_2 receptors (Svíženská et al., 2008). Interestingly, THC is known to be a partial rather than a full CB_1 and CB_2 receptor agonist, since it produces lower peak receptor-mediated effects than the above-mentioned synthetic agonists. The first selective CB_1 antagonist was **SR 141716A**, also known as **rimonabant**, which was developed by the French pharmaceutical firm Sanofi Recherche. Other compounds, such as the structurally related CB_1 antagonist **AM251**, were developed later. Both rimonabant and AM251 exert inverse-agonist activity at the CB_1 receptor; however, they remain most useful for their antagonist properties when administered in conjunction with THC or a selective CB_1 receptor agonist.

Administration of THC to mice leads to a classical "tetrad" of effects consisting of (1) reduced locomotor activity, (2) hypothermia (a decrease in core body temperature), (3) catalepsy, as indicated by immobility in the ring test (a test that measures the animal's activity after being placed on a horizontal wire ring), and (4) hypoalgesia (reduced pain sensitivity) measured using the hot plate or tail-flick test. These effects are mediated primarily by CB_1 receptors, because they can be blocked by a CB_1 antagonist, they can be duplicated by administration of a selective CB_1 agonist, and they are largely absent in CB_1 knockout mice given THC (Valverde et al., 2005; Pertwee, 2008). The receptors that mediate the tetrad of cannabinoid effects are located mainly in the principal output neurons of the neocortex (glutamatergic pyramidal neurons) and the striatum (GABAergic medium spiny neurons) (Monory et al., 2007).

Activation of CB_1 receptors additionally affects several other behaviors in laboratory animals, including responses on tests of anxiety-like behavior (Sharpe et al., 2020). Such responses are biphasic, with anxiolysis (reduced anxiety) observed at low agonist doses but anxiogenesis (increased anxiety) at high doses. This dose–response function has linked to a greater sensitivity of CB_1 receptors on cortical glutamatergic nerve terminals compared to the receptors on forebrain GABAergic nerve terminals. Activation of CB_1 receptors on the glutamatergic terminals (thereby inhibiting glutamate release) leads to an anxiolytic effect, whereas activation of CB_1 receptors on the GABAergic terminals (which inhibits GABA release) causes increased anxiety (Rey et al., 2012). Other CB_1 receptors are located in the central reward circuit, which accounts for the reinforcing actions of CB_1 receptor agonists in both animals and humans (see later section on recreational cannabis use).

Cannabis use can adversely affect human cognitive function, which has led to many studies on the effects of these compounds on learning and memory in laboratory animals. This work has shown that cannabinoids disrupt memory in several different kinds of learning tasks, including the radial arm maze, the Morris water maze, and the delayed non-match-to-position task (Riedel and Davies, 2005). Furthermore, such effects rely on activation of CB_1 receptors in the hippocampus. This was demonstrated by showing that microinjection of THC or CP-55,940 directly into the dorsal hippocampus produced significant memory deficits in the radial arm maze, an effect that was completely blocked by intrahippocampal infusion of rimonabant (Wise et al., 2009; **FIGURE 14.9**). Cannabinoids' interference with memory for spatial tasks involves inhibition of long-term potentiation (LTP) in the hippocampal CA1 area (Puighermanal et al., 2012). Such interference may additionally depend on a reduction in oscillatory (i.e., rhythmic) electrical activity within the hippocampal circuitry (Holderith et al., 2011). Electroencephalographic (EEG) studies in humans along with studies on LTP in hippocampal slices have shown that gamma and theta oscillations play an important role in memory encoding and retrieval (Nyhus and Curran, 2010).

The function of CB_2 receptors in immune function is shown by the ability of CB_2 receptor agonists to inhibit the release of cytokines, which are immune cell signaling molecules such as interleukins and interferons. Among the effects of CB_2 agonist-mediated cytokine suppression are alterations in migration of immune cells toward the site of an inflammatory reaction (Miller and Stella, 2008). Space limitations preclude a more extensive discussion of the CB_2 receptor subtype in immune system regulation. However, these receptors are involved in other functions discussed below, and they are also potential therapeutic targets of cannabinoid-type drugs.

Cannabidiol is not a cannabinoid receptor agonist

Unravelling the mechanisms of CBD action has proved challenging. Quoting Adel and Alexander (2021), "In contrast to THC, our knowledge of the neuromolecular mechanisms of cannabidiol is limited, which is a frustration" (p. 20). CBD is neither a cannabinoid receptor agonist nor does it reproduce either the intoxicating effects of THC in humans or THC-related behavioral changes in laboratory animals. Nevertheless, researchers are gradually making progress in this area. For example, recent studies suggest that CBD can act as a negative allosteric modulator of the CB_1 receptor, meaning that it binds to an allosteric site on the receptor where it functions to antagonize the positive effects of agonist (e.g., THC) receptor activation (Tham et al., 2019). This antagonistic action has been observed in several functional studies; however, results are inconsistent and it appears, therefore, that the effects of combined THC and CBD administration depend on the dose of each compound and the relative ratio of one to the other (Niesenk and van Laar, 2013; Boggs et al., 2018). Some evidence suggests that CBD may also be a negative allosteric modulator of CB_2 receptors (Morales et al., 2018), but the findings are not yet conclusive.

The molecular mechanisms of CBD action are not limited to its negative allosteric modulation of cannabinoid receptors (Adel and Alexander, 2021). CBD appears to inhibit the breakdown of endogenous cannabinoids (see next section), thereby enhancing activity of the endocannabinoid system. Other evidence points to activation of serotonergic $5\text{-}HT_{1A}$ receptors, which may contribute to CBD's anxiolytic effects, allosteric enhancement of glycine receptor activity, and inhibition of adenosine uptake, thereby increasing adenosine signaling. How these and other actions of CBD are related to functional outcomes remains a key topic of future

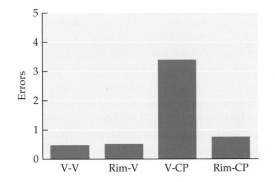

FIGURE 14.9 Hippocampal CB_1 receptors are responsible for cannabinoid-induced memory impairment Rats were trained to a high degree of performance on an eight-arm radial arm maze (see Chapter 4). After training was completed, intraperitoneal injection of the cannabinoid agonist CP-55,940 (0.05 mg/kg) along with a vehicle microinjection into the hippocampus (V-CP) produced a significant number of errors on the task compared with the control group (V-V), indicating an impairment in working memory. This effect was completely blocked by microinjection of rimonabant (0.06 µg) into the dorsal hippocampus (Rim-CP), whereas rimonabant by itself had no effect on maze performance (Rim-V). (After L. E. Wise et al. 2009. *Neuropsychopharmacology* 34: 2072–2080.)

research. It will be particularly important to establish the dose-relatedness of various molecular mechanisms and their related outcomes, since CBD effects are dose-dependent, just like those associated with THC.

Neuroimaging studies have begun to compare the effects of THC and CBD on the human brain. The available findings suggest that in a number of brain areas, including the striatum, amygdala, parahippocampal gyrus, and anterior cingulate/medial prefrontal cortex, the two drugs have opposing actions in which THC tends to promote regional brain activation and enhanced local blood flow, whereas CBD tends to decrease these processes (Gunasekera et al., 2020). CBD also differs from THC in its effects on functional connectivity between various brain regions either under resting conditions or when individuals were challenged by some type of cognitive task (Batalia et al., 2021). While these results are still preliminary, they are important in demonstrating that CBD produces measurable effects on brain activity, that the influence of this cannabinoid is significantly different than the influence of THC, and that in some functional paradigms CBD seems to oppose the actions of THC. Later in the chapter we discuss some of the potential therapeutic applications that are specific to CBD rather than THC.

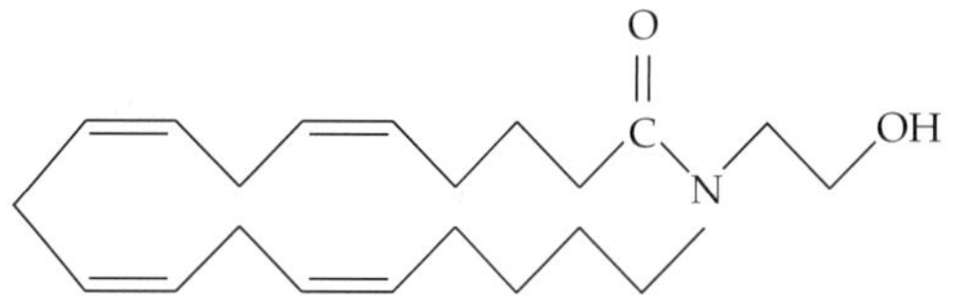

Endocannabinoids are cannabinoid receptor agonists synthesized by the body

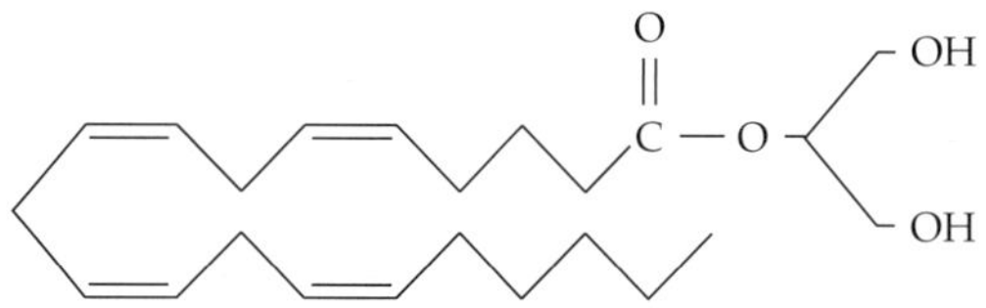

ENDOCANNABINOID BIOCHEMISTRY AND PHARMACOLOGY The discovery and characterization of cannabinoid receptors finally enabled pharmacologists to study the cellular mechanisms by which marijuana produces its behavioral effects. Yet why should our brain possess receptors for substances made by a plant? This situation is reminiscent of the quandary faced by opiate researchers when opioid receptors were first identified as mediating the actions of morphine, which comes from a poppy plant (see Chapter 11). Accordingly, the same assumption was made that there must be an endogenous neurotransmitter-like substance that acts on the newly discovered receptors. Within a few years, a group headed by Raphael Mechoulam, the same Israeli scientist involved in the discovery of THC almost 30 years earlier, announced that they had isolated a substance from pig brain that exerted cannabinoid-like activity (Devane et al., 1992). Chemical analysis revealed the substance to be a lipid with a structure related to that of arachidonic acid. The formal chemical name of this substance is **arachidonoyl ethanolamide (AEA)**, but the researchers gave it the additional name **anandamide**, from the Indian Sanskrit word *ananda*, meaning "bringer of inner bliss and tranquility" (Felder and Glass, 1998, p. 186). Later studies demonstrated the existence of other arachidonic acid derivatives, such as **2-arachidonoylglycerol (2-AG)**, that

Anandamide

2-Arachidonoylglycerol (2-AG)

FIGURE 14.10 Chemical structures of the endocannabinoids anandamide (AEA) and 2-arachidonoylglycerol (2-AG)

also bind to and activate CB_1 receptors (**FIGURE 14.10**). Together, these substances came to be known as **endocannabinoids**, meaning endogenous cannabinoids.

The endocannabinoids are generated from inositol phospholipids in the membrane that contain the fatty acid arachidonic acid within their structure. Unlike the classical neurotransmitters, however, endocannabinoids are too lipid soluble to be stored in vesicles, since they would just pass right through the vesicle membrane. Consequently, these substances are synthesized and released when needed. Endocannabinoid synthesis and release are usually triggered by a rise in intracellular Ca^{2+} levels, which follows from the fact that some of the enzymes involved in the generation of these compounds are Ca^{2+} sensitive. This rise can be caused by the opening of voltage-gated Ca^{2+} channels or NMDA receptor channels in the membrane or by release of Ca^{2+} from intracellular storage sites due to the action of a second-messenger system such as the phosphoinositide system.

After being released, endocannabinoids are thought to be removed from the extracellular fluid by an uptake mechanism (Hu and Mackie, 2020). This mechanism presumably involves a membrane protein carrier that has been termed the **endocannabinoid membrane transporter**. However, this transporter had proved to be quite elusive, since the relevant protein has not yet been isolated nor has its gene been cloned.

Once inside the cell, the endocannabinoids can be metabolized by several different enzymes. For anandamide, this is accomplished primarily by **fatty acid amide hydrolase (FAAH)**. In contrast, 2-AG is broken down largely by a different enzyme known as **monoacyl-glycerol lipase (MAGL)** (Kilaru and Chapman, 2020). Interestingly, both endocannabinoids can also be metabolized by **cyclooxygenase-2 (COX-2)**, an enzyme that plays an important role in the process of inflammation. Thus, even though interaction with COX-2 is a minor pathway for endocannabinoid metabolism, it is possible that repeated use of COX-2 inhibitors (commonly known as **nonsteroidal anti-inflammatory drugs**, or **NSAIDs**; e.g., ibuprofen) for pain relief could alter endocannabinoid activity in the brain and elsewhere.

Despite the discovery of anandamide before 2-AG, the latter substance is present in the brain at much higher levels than anandamide and is considered to be the more important synaptic signaling molecule. Furthermore, pharmacological studies have shown that 2-AG is a full agonist at both CB_1 and CB_2 receptors, whereas anandamide is only a partial agonist at CB_1 and has relatively little efficacy at CB_2. Differences in synthesis, metabolism, localization, and receptor activity of 2-AG and anandamide are consistent with the view that these two endocannabinoids are independently regulated and have different functional roles (Di Marzo and De Petrocellis, 2012).

ENDOCANNABINOID SIGNALING Like other transmitters discussed in previous chapters, endocannabinoid signaling can be either tonic (continuous) or phasic (briefly on or off). In brain regions where this has been investigated, anandamide seems to be the main candidate for tonic signaling and 2-AG the main candidate for phasic signaling (Augustin and Lovinger, 2018). Endocannabinoid signaling can also vary in other ways, as depicted in **FIGURE 14.11** (Castillo et al., 2012). In the three mechanisms shown in the figure, the endocannabinoid is synthesized in a postsynaptic element such as a dendritic spine; however, the location of the receptor and the effects of receptor activation vary in each case. The most common endocannabinoid signaling mechanism is

retrograde signaling (Figure 14.11A), in which the endocannabinoid activates CB_1 receptors on nearby nerve terminals. This signaling mechanism, which is usually mediated by 2-AG, inhibits Ca^{2+}-mediated neurotransmitter release from the terminal (Lovinger, 2008). We learned in Chapter 3's discussion of nitric oxide that retrograde signaling is so named because it involves a signaling molecule carrying information in the opposite direction from normal (i.e., postsynaptic to presynaptic). There is overwhelming evidence that endocannabinoids are retrograde messengers at synapses in a number of brain regions, including the hippocampus, striatum, and cerebellum (Lu and Mackie, 2016; Augustin and Lovinger, 2018). The second type of endocannabinoid signaling, which is usually mediated by anandamide, is shown in Figure 14.11B. In this case, the endocannabinoid remains within the postsynaptic cell and activates either a cannabinoid receptor or a different type of receptor called **TRPV1**. TRPV1 receptors are nonspecific cation channels that were first discovered in sensory neurons, where they play a key role in the heat and pain sensations produced by capsaicin, the "hot" ingredient in chili peppers. TRPV1 receptors are also expressed in many areas of the brain, where they regulate numerous functions when activated either by anandamide or by non-cannabinoid agonists (Tóth et al., 2009). Interestingly, low doses of anandamide that selectively activate CB_1 receptors are anticonvulsant, whereas higher doses that additionally activate TRPV1 receptors (anandamide has a higher affinity for CB_1 than for TRPV1 receptors) have a proconvulsant effect (Manna and Umathe, 2012). This finding emphasizes that

(A) Retrograde signaling

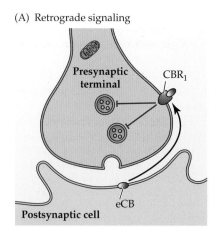

(B) Non-retrograde signaling

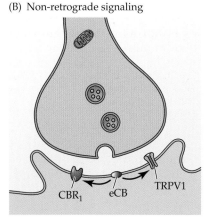

(C) Neuron–astrocyte signaling

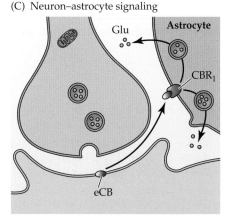

FIGURE 14.11 **Mechanisms of endocannabinoid signaling** (A) The most common and well-understood mechanism of endocannabinoid action is retrograde signaling. This mechanism involves release of the endocannabinoid (eCB), typically 2-AG, which diffuses from its site of synthesis in a dendritic spine to a presynaptic element where it activates CB_1 receptors (CBR_1). Such activation inhibits Ca^{2+}-mediated vesicular neurotransmitter release. (B) In the second mechanism, an endocannabinoid such as anandamide remains within the dendritic spine to activate either postsynaptic CB_1 receptors or TRPV1 cation channels. (C) The third mechanism involves endocannabinoid activation of astrocyte CB_1 receptors, which has been shown to provoke glutamate (Glu) release from the cells. (After P. E. Castillo et al. 2012. *Neuron* 76: 70–81.)

endocannabinoids, particularly anandamide, target more than one type of receptor. Finally, Figure 14.11C illustrates an unusual mode of signaling in which endocannabinoids activate cannabinoid receptors in the membranes of nearby astrocytes, which results in release of glutamate from the glial cells.

The retrograde signaling described above often causes a type of short-term synaptic plasticity in the presynaptic neuron in which neurotransmitter release is suppressed for several seconds up to a minute (Augustin and Lovinger, 2018). When the presynaptic cell is excitatory (e.g., glutamatergic), the effect is termed **depolarization-induced suppression of excitation (DSE)**, since the endocannabinoid (2-AG) release that starts the process is triggered by depolarization of the postsynaptic cell. When the presynaptic cell is inhibitory (e.g., GABAergic), then the effect is called **depolarization-induced suppression of inhibition (DSI)**. DSE and DSI are produced by brief postsynaptic depolarization. In contrast, longer-lasting postsynaptic stimulation can give rise either to LTP or long-term synaptic depression (LTD). This is one of the mechanisms by which endocannabinoids participate in the processes of learning and memory (Kruk-Slomka et al., 2017). This topic is discussed further in the next section.

FUNCTIONAL EFFECTS OF THE ENDOCANNABINOID SYSTEM **FIGURE 14.12** provides an overview of the major behavioral processes regulated by the endocannabinoid system and the relevant brain areas involved in such regulation. We briefly discuss several of these processes.

As previously mentioned, it is well established that exogenous cannabinoids such as THC disrupt short- and long-term memory of hippocampal-dependent tasks. Surprisingly, the role of the endogenous cannabinoid system in memory processes is not as

clear (reviewed in Marsicano and Lafenêtre, 2009; Kruk-Slomka et al., 2017). Using several different experimental approaches, researchers have found that in the Morris water maze spatial navigation task, the clearest role for the endocannabinoid system is to facilitate extinction of the original platform location when the animals are required to learn a new location (Varvel and Lichtman, 2002; Varvel et al., 2005, 2007).

When people consume cannabis at typical recreational doses, they commonly experience feelings of relaxation, reduced anxiety, elevated mood, and stress relief (see the section on acute behavioral and physiological effects of cannabinoids below). This pattern of subjective responses led to the hypothesis that the endocannabinoid system helps regulate mood states, anxiety and fear, and reactions to stress. Indeed, this hypothesis has been confirmed in a large number of rodent studies (reviewed in McLaughlin and Gobbi, 2012; Yin et al., 2019). For example, tests of depressive-like behaviors such as the forced-swim and tail-suspension tests have shown that elevated endocannabinoid activity exerts an antidepressant effect, whereas reduced endocannabinoid activity or deletion of the *CB1* gene is associated with a depression-like phenotype (McLaughlin and Gobbi, 2012; Soriano et al., 2021). Other research found that enhancement of endocannabinoid signaling by inhibiting endocannabinoid metabolism or uptake has anxiolytic effects in the elevated plus-maze, elevated zero-maze, light–dark test, and social interaction test. In contrast, *CB1*-knockout mice that lack most CNS endocannabinoid signaling show increased anxiety-like behaviors (McLaughlin and Gobbi, 2012; Soriano et al., 2021). A different approach was taken by Guggenhuber and colleagues (2016), who used genetic methods to enhance 2-AG breakdown selectively in hippocampal glutamatergic neurons. The result was

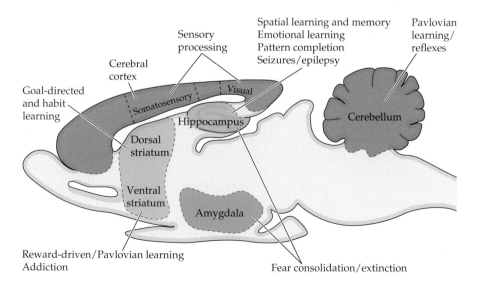

FIGURE 14.12 Brain regions associated with behavioral regulation by the endocannabinoid system Research on the neural mechanisms of endocannabinoid action has largely been performed using laboratory mice and rats. Based on this research, the brain regions where endocannabinoid activity helps regulate particular behaviors are depicted on a sagittal section of a rodent brain. (Adapted with permission from S. M. Augustin and D. M. Lovinger. 2018. *ACS Chem Neurosci* 9: 2146–2161. © 2018 American Chemical Society.)

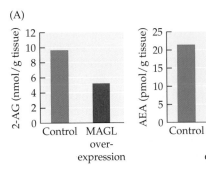

(A)

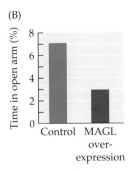

(B)

FIGURE 14.13 Biochemical, neurophysiological, and behavioral effects of enhancing 2-AG breakdown in hippocampal glutamatergic neurons The investigators used genetic methods to selectively enhance expression of MAGL (the main enzyme for 2-AG metabolism) in hippocampal glutamatergic neurons of mice. This led to a significant decrease in hippocampal 2-AG concentrations but no change in AEA (anandamide) (A). Note the thousand-fold greater unit of measure for 2-AG concentrations (nmol/g, or 10^{-9} moles per g) compared to AEA (pmol/g, or 10^{-12} moles per g). The MAGL-overexpressing mice additionally showed a deficit in hippocampal DSE but no significant change in DSI (data not shown). When the animals were tested in the elevated plus-maze, overexpression of MAGL in the hippocampus led to increased anxiety-like behavior shown by less time spent in the open arms of the maze (B). (From S. Guggenhuber et al. 2016. *Int J Neuropsychopharmacol* 19: 2. doi: 10.1093/ijnp/pyv091. By permission of Oxford University Press.)

lower hippocampal 2-AG levels, impaired hippocampal DSE, and increased anxiety-like behavior in the elevated plus-maze (**FIGURE 14.13**). These findings implicate the hippocampal endocannabinoid system as an important mediator of anxiety responses.

In addition to their fundamental role in the acquisition and expression of anxiety- and fear-related behaviors, endocannabinoids seem to be particularly important in facilitating extinction of learned fear. Such a function may be important in preventing fear responses from becoming too pervasive (Riebe et al., 2012; Lutz et al., 2015). Some researchers have even hypothesized that deficient activity of the endocannabinoid system may be a risk factor for posttraumatic stress disorder (PTSD), and that administration of cannabinoid agonist drugs or compounds that raise endocannabinoid levels (i.e., by blocking metabolism or uptake) could be developed as novel treatments for PTSD (Hill et al., 2018; Gunduz-Cinar, 2021).

Hunger, eating behavior, and energy metabolism represent yet another behavioral and physiological system regulated by endocannabinoids. CB_1 receptor antagonists reliably reduce food consumption in both animals and people, and more detailed studies suggest that endocannabinoid activity within the hypothalamus, the mesolimbic dopamine (DA) pathway, and the olfactory system combine to enhance the motivation to eat, the hedonic properties of food (especially highly palatable food), and food-mediated reward (Cristino et al., 2014; Soria-Gomez et al., 2014; Lau et al., 2017). Also important is endocannabinoid signaling in the gut and in adipose tissues, where such signaling contributes to the regulation of dietary fat consumption and fat storage (DiPatrizio, 2016; Jung et al., 2021). Because of the early success of

CB_1 antagonism in reducing food intake, rimonabant (under the trade name Accomplia) was approved and released by Sanofi-Aventis in the European Union in June 2006 as an anti-obesity agent. Unfortunately, reports of adverse psychiatric side effects such as depressive symptomatology in some users resulted in voluntary suspension of Accomplia marketing by the company in December 2008, followed shortly by withdrawal of approval of the medication by the European Medicines Agency. Nevertheless, targeting the cannabinoid system for the treatment of obesity has continued to be of interest to researchers and pharmaceutical companies, particularly since endocannabinoids are believed to contribute to development of the so-called metabolic syndrome, which precedes outright obesity and is characterized by elevated blood sugar and lipids, high blood pressure, and excess body fat (Quarta et al., 2011; Mazier et al., 2015).

The last functional role of endocannabinoids to be discussed here is pain regulation. Wild-type animals given rimonabant, as well as CB_1 and CB_2 knockout mice, exhibit **hyperalgesia** (increased pain sensitivity) to several different types of pain stimuli. These findings clearly demonstrate a role for endocannabinoids acting on both cannabinoid receptor subtypes in the modulation of pain perception (Valverde et al., 2005; Buckley, 2008; Wolf et al., 2020). **FIGURE 14.14** illustrates the location of CB_1 and CB_2 receptors in the forebrain, brainstem, spinal cord, and periphery that participate in regulating both pain perception and the cognitive–affective responses to pain. Of particular importance is the potential role of endocannabinoids in chronic pain syndromes such as **neuropathic pain**. Neuropathic pain refers to a type of pain produced within the nervous system itself, not in direct response

FIGURE 14.14 Location of CB$_1$ and CB$_2$ receptors involved in the modulation of pain perception Both cannabinoid receptor subtypes (CBR$_1$ and CBR$_2$) participate in pain stimulus processing and perception at multiple levels of the nervous system. Activation of these receptors inhibits ascending pain information originating from peripheral nociceptive fibers, enhances descending pain-inhibitory pathways, and modulates the emotional and cognitive components of perceived pain. The presence of pain-modulating CB$_2$ receptors in the forebrain is currently uncertain, which accounts for the "?" in that part of the figure. DRG, dorsal root ganglia. (After R. Maldonado et al. 2016. *Pain* 157 [Suppl. 1]: S23–S32. © 2016 International Association for the Study of Pain. doi.org/10.1097/j.pain.0000000000000428.)

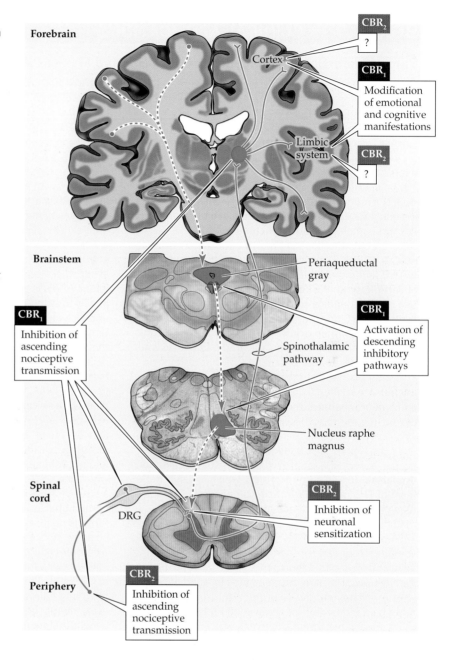

to a nociceptive (pain-inducing) stimulus like a stab wound or burn. Opioid drugs are relatively ineffective in alleviating neuropathic pain compared to nociceptive pain, which accounts for the search for alternative medications that might be more efficacious. Laboratory animal studies have found an up-regulation of cannabinoid receptors in models of neuropathic pain, pointing to the endocannabinoid system as a prime target for new therapeutic approaches to this problem (Maldonado et al., 2016). Analgesic effects of cannabinoid agonists may prove valuable even for types of pain that are responsive to opioid drugs. Cannabinoids potentiate opioid-induced analgesia and decrease opioid-related tolerance, thereby permitting the use of lower opioid doses and reducing the risk of opioid addiction (Ozdemir, 2020).

Involvement of endocannabinoids in so many different systems suggests an immense potential for therapeutic interventions. Pure preparations of THC, CBD, or THC plus CBD, are already used medically for several different disorders. Furthermore, prescription of marijuana itself (i.e., "medical marijuana") has become legal in an increasing number of states. **BOX 14.1** discusses the current therapeutic applications of cannabinoid-containing drugs as well as medically prescribed cannabis.

BOX 14.1 ■ CLINICAL APPLICATIONS

Cannabinoid-Based Medications: THC, CBD, and Medical Marijuana

Medicinal use of cannabis in various cultures can be traced back for many hundreds, perhaps thousands, of years (Pisanti and Bifulco, 2019). During the late nineteenth and early twentieth centuries, crude cannabis extracts were accepted pharmaceuticals in Europe and the United States. Indeed, six different types of cannabis preparations were listed in an early edition of *The Merck Index* (1896) of pharmaceutical compounds. However, the medicinal use of cannabis gradually declined, in part because the available preparations tended to be unstable and had inconsistent potency.

Interest in the possible therapeutic benefits of cannabinoids was later revived following the discovery of THC and the subsequent manufacture and testing of various synthetic compounds. Current therapeutic use of cannabinoids takes four major forms: (1) pure synthetic THC or other cannabinoid agonists that are typically consumed orally; (2) extracts from the cannabis plant that contain specific amounts of THC and CBD; (3) medications containing CBD but little or no THC; and (4) medical marijuana, in which marijuana itself is prescribed by a physician and then usually smoked or inhaled through some other method. After discussing the first three forms of medicinal cannabis, we will take up the issue of medical marijuana.

In the United States, adult patients currently have access to two FDA-approved cannabinoid medications: **dronabinol** (trade name **Marinol**), which is a synthetic form of THC, and the synthetic cannabinoid **nabilone** (**Cesamet**). Dronabinol and nabilone are both oral medications approved to treat appetite and weight loss in patients with HIV/AIDS and to suppress nausea and vomiting from cancer chemotherapy in patients who haven't responded adequately to first-line anti-nausea medications. Both medications also have off-label uses for management of chronic pain and various other conditions. A third medication that should be mentioned is **nabiximols** (**Sativex**), which is a cannabis extract containing a mixture of THC and CBD that is administered as an oral spray. Nabiximols is currently licensed in a number of countries for the treatment of neuropathic pain and spasticity in patients with multiple sclerosis (Überall, 2020). Several phase 3 clinical trials for nabiximols were initiated in the United States in 2020, with the hope that positive results would lead to future FDA approval of this medication.

In 2018, the FDA approved the first specific CBD-based cannabinoid medication, trade name **Epidiolex**. This is an oil-based formulation containing 99% CBD extracted from low-THC hemp plants and administered orally. Epidiolex is currently licensed for the treatment of seizures in infants or children who suffer from any of three rare genetic disorders: Dravet syndrome, Lennox-Gastaut syndrome, or tuberous sclerosis. The ability of cannabis to suppress epileptic seizures has been known for hundreds, if not thousands, of years (Friedman and Devinsky, 2015). For this reason, significant numbers of patients with epilepsy self-medicate with marijuana, either illegally or legally under applicable medical marijuana laws. However, cannabis is not suitable for young children who have drug-resistant forms of epilepsy. The story of Epidiolex began with a girl named Charlotte Figi, who was born in 2006 and seemed like a healthy baby until she experienced her first seizure at 3 months of age. Over the next few years, Charlotte's symptoms progressively worsened until she was having 300 grand mal seizures a week. She was finally diagnosed with Dravet syndrome, also known as severe myoclonic epilepsy in infancy. This is a severe seizure disorder that responds poorly to standard antiepileptic medications and, if left unchecked, may cause significant neurological problems and developmental delays. Once it became clear that Charlotte's life was in danger from her illness, her parents began to consider nontraditional avenues for treatment, including cannabis. Finally, a breakthrough occurred when Charlotte began to receive daily oral doses of a hemp oil extract that was high in CBD but with very low levels of THC. CBD was known to have anticonvulsant activity from animal studies (Jones et al., 2012; see **FIGURE A**), but human clinical testing had not yet been performed. The strain of hemp from which the CBD-rich oil was derived was supplied by a small company in Colorado and was subsequently named Charlotte's Web in recognition of its most famous patient. Widespread publicity about Charlotte's success story (see, for example, Young, 2013) led to the treatment of other children suffering from intractable epilepsy with the same or similar formulations high in CBD and ultimately to the development and clinical testing of Epidiolex. Despite continuing research, however, the mechanism of CBD's antiseizure activity is not yet understood (Franco et al., 2021).

In addition to the medications just discussed, medical marijuana has become increasingly available for large numbers of patients. At the time of this writing, 36 states had enacted legislation legalizing marijuana or cannabis-based products (e.g., edibles or cannabis extracts for vaping) for medical use.

The arguments for and against medical marijuana are well known and are brought up every time the issue comes up for debate (Russo, 2016; also see Web Box 14.1, which discusses the issues around cannabis legalization). One common argument favoring medical marijuana is a presumption of greater efficacy compared to synthetic THC. Aside from a few clinical studies on this topic, the efficacy argument is based mainly on anecdotal testimony by patients who have compared the degree of symptom relief from smoked marijuana with that provided by dronabinol. Even if

BOX 14.1 ■ CLINICAL APPLICATIONS *(continued)*

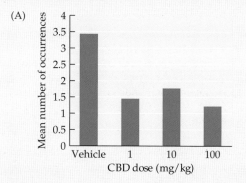

(A)

Dose-dependent anticonvulsant effects of CBD in rats
Temporal lobe seizures were induced in rats by intraperitoneal (IP) administration of 380 mg/kg of pilocarpine. Animals were additionally pretreated either with 1, 10, or 100 mg/kg of CBD IP or drug vehicle, and the number of occurrences of tonic-clonic seizures (the most severe kind of seizure activity) in each group was determined. CBD significantly reduced seizure occurrence at all doses, with the highest dose producing a slightly greater effect than the two lower doses. (After N. A. Jones et al. 2012. *Seizure* 21: 344–352. © 2012. Reprinted with permission from British Epilepsy Association, via Elsevier.)

we discount such testimony, however, the efficacy argument is plausible based on at least two considerations. First, as we saw earlier in the chapter, THC is subject to extensive first-pass hepatic metabolism when taken orally, thereby limiting its bioavailability. This problem is avoided when cannabis is smoked or inhaled in vapor form (i.e., "cannavaping"; see Varlet et al., 2016). The second consideration arises from the observation that other molecules besides THC that are produced by cannabis plants may interact with THC and/or have their own biological activity that contributes to therapeutic benefit. The molecules in question range from other phytocannabinoids such as CBD to entirely different classes of substances called terpenes and flavonoids (Lowe et al., 2021). Some authors have used the term "entourage effect" to denote the synergistic interactions among different cannabis components that produce greater effects than individual chemicals alone (Ferber et al., 2020; Koltai and Namdar, 2020; but also see Cogan, 2020, for a more skeptical view). Beyond the question of efficacy, an additional argument favoring medical marijuana concerns price, as marijuana is inexpensive to produce and, therefore, may be more cost-effective than many alternative prescription medications.

Arguments *against* medical marijuana are many, including the difficulty of standardizing dosage in an herbal preparation, health concerns that are particularly relevant for patients who use marijuana regularly for a long period of time, the possibility of developing cannabis dependence, and not least, the fact that cannabis possession is still illegal at the federal level because of its designation as a Schedule I substance by the DEA.

Now that medical cannabis is available in the majority of states, we can inquire about the illnesses or conditions for which cannabis is being prescribed. Thus far, only a few studies have been conducted addressing this question. One such study obtained 2016 survey data from 15 states that maintained cannabis registries documenting the medical condition for which the patient sought treatment (Boehnke et al., 2019). States that imposed stricter regulations on cannabis prescribing were termed "medicalized states" by the researchers, whereas states with looser regulations were termed "nonmedicalized states." **FIGURE B** shows that there were significant differences in cannabis prescribing between the two types of states. Nevertheless, in both cases, the greatest percentage of patients sought relief from chronic pain followed by treatment for muscular spasticity caused by multiple sclerosis. Interestingly, a somewhat different picture recently emerged from a different survey using patient data from a large group of privately managed cannabis clinics. In that survey, chronic pain was still the number-one reason for seeking medical cannabis treatment; however, the next two conditions were anxiety and post-traumatic stress disorder (Mahabir et al., 2020). Taken together, these findings suggest that somewhat different patient populations may make use of private versus state-managed medical cannabis facilities.

A review of the health effects of cannabis and cannabinoids by the National Academies of Sciences, Engineering, and Medicine (2017) concluded that cannabis or cannabinoid-based medications are at least moderately effective in treating chemotherapy-related nausea and vomiting, conditions involving chronic pain, and muscle spasticity in patients with multiple sclerosis. For other conditions, there were insufficient data to conclusively demonstrate therapeutic efficacy.* Patients contemplating use of any cannabinoid drugs should be aware that they can produce various side effects such as sedation, dizziness, confusion, dry mouth, and mild euphoria. Alternatively, dysphoria may occur in people unfamiliar with the effects of smoked marijuana. Fortunately, such side effects tend to be greatest when the drug is first taken and generally diminish within a few days or weeks.

Because of the side effects of both marijuana and some of the currently available cannabis-based medications, novel approaches are being studied that have a different mode of action. Such approaches include selectively targeting CB_2 instead of CB_1 receptors,

---

*It seems remarkable that cannabis is being prescribed for so many different disorders despite the lack of clinically proven efficacy!

(Continued)

BOX 14.1 ■ CLINICAL APPLICATIONS (*continued*)

(B)

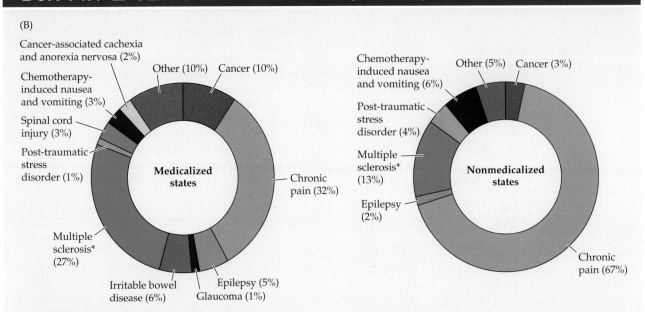

FIGURE B Percentage of qualifying conditions reported by patients seeking medical cannabis treatment Data shown are from 2016 medical cannabis registries combined from 15 states. Note the percentage differences in qualifying conditions between medicalized and nonmedicalized states. * denotes that cannabis use in patients with multiple sclerosis is to relieve muscular spasticity produced by the disorder. (After K. F. Boehnke et al. 2019. *Health Affairs* 38: 295–302.)

developing allosteric CB_1 and CB_2 receptor modulators, identifying compounds that have poor blood–brain barrier penetrance and thus only affect peripheral cannabinoid receptors, and elevating endocannabinoid levels by blocking either endocannabinoid metabolism or uptake (Toczek and Malinowska, 2018; Gado et al., 2019; Ren et al., 2020). Although none of these approaches has yet led to any new FDA-approved medications, it seems likely that at least some of them will prove fruitful as research continues.

Lastly, there is current excitement among both medical researchers and the lay public concerning the therapeutic potential of CBD besides the treatment of pediatric epilepsies. The legality of CBD at the present time is complicated: if derived from cannabis, it is considered Schedule I by the DEA but is legal for medical use in states with medical cannabis laws. On the other hand, CBD derived from hemp is legal even at the federal level. The more relaxed classification of CBD compared to THC or marijuana has led to an explosion of over-the-counter (OTC) CBD-containing remedies for many different health problems and a common belief that CBD is an effective remedy for such problems. The popularity of this belief is revealed by activity on the online Reddit CBD forum r/CBD, a venue for people to discuss their reactions to using CBD. Leas and colleagues (2020) surveyed data from this forum and calculated the number of monthly posts from January 1, 2014, through August 31, 2019. At the time of the survey, the forum had 104,917 registered members. The results showed a large increase in monthly posts

beginning in the latter part of 2016 and continuing into 2019. A random sample of posts containing testimonials regarding the health benefits of consuming CBD revealed that people were using the drug primarily to treat neuropsychiatric conditions (e.g., depression, anxiety, or autism), arthritis or other painful conditions, insomnia, and stress (Leas et al., 2020). Unfortunately, there is little rigorous scientific evidence supporting these testimonials (Scholler et al., 2020). In the absence of controlled clinical trials, we cannot rule out the possibility that self-reported benefits of OTC CBD formulations represent, in large part, a placebo effect. Moreover, researchers have identified several problems common to such formulations, including (1) CBD doses are typically much lower than the doses present in FDA-approved CBD medications known to be therapeutically efficacious, (2) CBD has poor bioavailability when taken orally (the route of administration of many of these formulations), which exacerbates the problem of inadequate dosing, (3) CBD content of an OTC product may vary substantially from the stated content, and (4) the purity of CBD formulations is not guaranteed, and some have even been found to contain unacceptable levels of THC (Chesney et al., 2020; Nelson et al., 2020). Indeed, some reported adverse effects of CBD products may be related to THC contamination (Lachenmeier et al., 2020). Keep in mind that this discussion pertains specifically to OTC CBD-containing products. Research is ongoing to identify potential new therapeutic applications for CBD beyond the proven benefits of drugs like nabiximols and Epidiolex (Britch et al., 2021).

SECTION SUMMARY

- Two cannabinoid receptors, CB_1 and CB_2, have been identified and their genes cloned.

- The CB_1 receptor is the principal cannabinoid receptor in the brain, where it is expressed at a high density in the basal ganglia, cerebellum, hippocampus, and cerebral cortex.

- The CB_2 receptor was first identified in the immune system, but it is also found in a number of other tissues, including the brain. CB_2 receptors within the brain are expressed most heavily by microglial cells; however, there are also neuronal CB_2 receptors (for example, on VTA dopaminergic neurons) that have important behavioral functions.

- Cannabinoid receptors belong to the G protein–coupled receptor superfamily. Receptor activation can inhibit cAMP formation, inhibit voltage-sensitive Ca^{2+} channels, and activate K^+ channels.

- CB_1 receptors are primarily located on axon terminals, where they act to inhibit the release of many different neurotransmitters. Some neurons also possess somatodendritic CB_1 receptors that mediate self-inhibition.

- Agonists at the CB_1 receptor include the synthetic full agonists CP-55,940 and WIN 55,212-2 and the partial agonist THC. The first selective CB_1 antagonist was SR 141716A, also known as rimonabant.

- THC administration to mice causes a classical tetrad of CB_1 receptor–mediated effects that consist of reduced locomotor activity, hypothermia, catalepsy, and hypoalgesia.

- CB_1 receptor activation has biphasic effects on anxiety consisting of anxiolytic effects at low agonist doses but anxiogenesis at high doses. This dose–response function has been attributed to a differential influence of CB_1 receptors on glutamate release (relatively selective inhibition at low agonist doses causing anxiolysis) versus GABA release (additional inhibition at higher agonist doses causing anxiogenesis).

- CB_1 agonists also impair learning and memory consolidation in several different kinds of tasks. Interference with memory of hippocampal-dependent spatial tasks has been linked to inhibition of LTP in the hippocampal CA1 area and a reduction in oscillatory activity within the hippocampal circuitry.

- CB_2 receptor activation in the immune system causes cytokine release and changes in immune cell migration toward an inflammatory site.

- In contrast to THC, CBD does not act as a cannabinoid receptor agonist. Rather, CBD seems to be a negative allosteric modulator of the CB_1 receptor. Additional proposed mechanisms of action include inhibition of endocannabinoid breakdown, activation of serotonergic 5-HT_{1A} receptors, enhancement of glycine receptor activity, and inhibition of adenosine uptake. Compared to THC, CBD has opposing effects on neural activity in a number of different brain areas, including the striatum, amygdala, parahippocampal gyrus, and anterior cingulate/medial prefrontal cortex.

- The brain synthesizes several substances, called endocannabinoids, that are neurotransmitter-like agonists at cannabinoid receptors. Anandamide was the first endocannabinoid to be discovered; however, another endocannabinoid called 2-AG is present in the brain at much higher levels than anandamide.

- The two major endocannabinoids differ in several other important ways. 2-AG is a full agonist at both CB_1 and CB_2 receptors, whereas anandamide is just a partial agonist at CB_1. 2-AG and anandamide also differ in their synthesis, metabolism, localization within the brain, and functional roles.

- Endocannabinoids are generated on demand from arachidonic acid–containing membrane lipids by a Ca^{2+}-dependent mechanism and are released from the cell by a process that does not involve synaptic vesicles. They are believed to be removed from the extracellular space by a carrier protein called the endocannabinoid membrane transporter.

- Anandamide and 2-AG are degraded primarily by FAAH and MAGL, respectively. Both endocannabinoids can also be metabolized by COX-2, raising the possibility that COX-2 inhibitors, which are widely prescribed because of their anti-inflammatory activity, could alter the endocannabinoid system.

- Endocannabinoids usually function as retrograde messengers that are synthesized and released from postsynaptic cells to activate CB_1 receptors on nearby nerve terminals. This process leads to an inhibition of voltage-gated Ca^{2+} channel opening and a consequent reduction in neurotransmitter release from the terminals. However, two other modes of endocannabinoid signaling have been discovered. First, in some cases the endocannabinoid (usually anandamide) remains within the postsynaptic cell where it activates either a cannabinoid receptor or an excitatory ion channel called TRPV1. Second, endocannabinoids can activate cannabinoid receptors on astrocytes, thus causing release of glutamate from those glial cells.

- Two well-characterized examples of 2-AG retrograde signaling involve inhibition of presynaptic excitatory glutamate release (termed depolarization-induced suppression of excitation; DSE) or inhibition of presynaptic inhibitory GABA release (termed depolarization-induced suppression of inhibition; DSI). Both of these phenomena are produced by brief postsynaptic depolarization of 2-AG-synthesizing neurons. Longer-lasting postsynaptic stimulation can give rise to processes of synaptic plasticity such as LTP or LTD.

- The endocannabinoid system plays a complex role in learning and memory of hippocampal-dependent tasks, including facilitation of extinction of an already learned spatial task.

- Enhancing endocannabinoid signaling has anxiolytic effects as well as an antidepressant profile in standard rodent tests of depressive-like behavior. In contrast, reduced endocannabinoid levels or inactivation of the *CB1* gene are associated with increased anxiety- and depressive-like behaviors. Other findings indicate that endocannabinoids play an important role in responding to fear-inducing and stressful situations, including facilitating extinction of learned fear. Researchers have hypothesized that deficient endocannabinoid activity may be a risk factor for developing PTSD following exposure to a traumatic event.

- The endocannabinoid system plays an important role in the regulation of hunger and energy storage. The motivation to eat and the processes of energy metabolism (e.g., fat storage) are partly controlled by endocannabinoids within the hypothalamus, gut, and adipose tissue, and endocannabinoid dysregulation may contribute to development of the metabolic syndrome.

- Endocannabinoids have been shown to inhibit the perception of certain kinds of pain (especially neuropathic pain) by acting on both cannabinoid receptor subtypes localized within the forebrain, brainstem, spinal cord, and periphery. Therefore, cannabinoid agonists are being studied for their clinical use as analgesic agents.

- Cannabinoids for medicinal use are available in four different forms: (1) synthetic THC or other cannabinoid agonists (dronabinol or nabilone) taken orally to enhance appetite or combat nausea under certain medical conditions; (2) cannabis extracts containing both THC and CBD (nabiximols) administered as a mouth spray to treat neuropathic pain and muscle spasticity in MS patients; (3) CBD-containing oil (Epidiolex) prescribed to reduce seizure activity in several kinds of severe pediatric epilepsies; and (4) cannabis or cannabis-derived formulations ("medical marijuana") prescribed for a variety of health conditions. CBD-containing preparations are additionally available over the counter for self-medication, although the clinical benefits from such preparations have yet to be determined.

14.3 Acute Behavioral and Physiological Effects of Cannabinoids

Cannabinoid use produces a range of behavioral and physiological effects that vary depending on the dose, the frequency of use, the characteristics of the user, and the setting in which use occurs.

Cannabis consumption produces a dose-dependent state of intoxication

The earliest recorded clinical studies on the intoxicating properties of cannabis were performed by Moreau, the French physician mentioned earlier who introduced hashish to nineteenth-century Parisian literary society. Moreau, who is sometimes called the "father of psychopharmacology," became interested in the possible relationship between hashish intoxication and the characteristics of mental illness. Consequently, he and his students meticulously recorded their subjective experiences after consuming varying amounts of hashish. Because of the potency of their preparation, these individuals reported profound personality changes and perceptual distortions, even frank hallucinations.* Hallucinogenic responses have also been reported either following a high dose of pure THC administered to volunteers in a research setting, or as an occasional side effect of ingesting a synthetic cannabinoid for medicinal purposes (Koukkou and Lehmann, 1976; Timpone et al., 1997).

The lower cannabis doses associated with smoking one or two marijuana cigarettes produce a somewhat more modest reaction, although many of the same *kinds* of effects are found across the dose–response curve. The subjective and behavioral effects of marijuana have been studied using approaches ranging from the distribution of questionnaires to experienced marijuana users (Tart, 1970) to controlled laboratory studies involving administration of oral THC to infrequent users (e.g., Curran et al., 2002). According to Iversen (2000), these effects can be separated into four stages: the "buzz," the "high," the stage of being "stoned," and finally the "come-down." The "buzz" is a brief period of initial responding during which the user may feel lightheaded or even slightly dizzy. Tingling sensations in the extremities and other parts of the body are commonly experienced. The marijuana "high" is characterized by feelings of euphoria and exhilaration, as well as a sense of disinhibition often manifested as increased laughter. A sufficiently large dose of marijuana leads to the next stage of intoxication, that of being "stoned." In this stage, the user usually feels calm, relaxed, perhaps even in a dreamlike state. Indeed, relaxation is the most common effect reported by cannabis users in self-report studies involving open-ended questions (Green et al., 2003). The "stoned" user can experience floating sensations, enhanced visual and auditory perception, visual illusions, and a tremendous slowing of time passage. Changes in sociability are variable, in that the user may experience either an increased desire to be with others or a desire to be alone. The final "come-down" stage is the gradual cessation of these effects, which varies in length depending on the THC dose and the individual's rate of THC metabolism.

Marijuana and other forms of cannabis also produce several physiological responses. Heart rate and blood pressure are increased, probably as a result of sympathetic nervous system activation (Latif and Garg, 2020). In addition, marijuana increases hunger (the infamous "munchies"), which is consistent with the earlier discussion of endocannabinoid regulation of eating behavior. Cannabis stimulation of food intake has been documented in controlled laboratory studies of both humans (Foltin et al., 1988) and rats (Williams et al.,

---

*Moreau's work culminated in a book entitled *Du Hachich et de l'aliénation mentale* (*Hashish and Mental Alienation*), major excerpts of which can be found in Nahas (1975).

1998; also see Kirkham, 2009), and appetite stimulation is one of the recognized therapeutic uses for cannabinoids (see Box 14.1).

Not surprisingly, the marijuana "high" and its other subjective and physiological effects are dose-dependent, in that the concentration of THC in a smoked marijuana cigarette has a direct relationship to the intensity of these effects (Cooper and Haney, 2008). Moreover, these effects are at least partially mediated by CB_1 receptors. Huestis and colleagues (2001, 2007) found that according to self-reported ratings, intoxication following the smoking of a single marijuana cigarette was significantly although not completely inhibited by prior treatment with rimonabant (**FIGURE 14.15**). Similar results were found for the heart rate–elevating effects of the drug. Either a higher dose of the antagonist is needed to fully block the effects of marijuana or some other mechanism in addition to CB_1 receptor activation (e.g., activation of central CB_2 receptors) is involved in producing these effects.

As with most psychoactive drugs, the psychological effects of marijuana vary greatly as a function not only of dose but also of the setting, the individual's past exposure to the drug, and the user's mental set, which refers to the expectation of what effects the drug will produce. The influence of expectancy was demonstrated by Kirk and coworkers (1998), who gave volunteers capsules containing either THC or a placebo. The volunteers were separated into an "informed" and an "uninformed" group. All were instructed beforehand that the capsules would contain placebo or one of several types of psychoactive compounds, but only for the informed group were cannabinoids included in the list of possible drugs. When asked to rate their responses to the substance they had consumed, the informed group gave higher ratings than the uninformed group in the categories of "like drug" and "want more drug." The expectation of consuming cannabinoids not only enhanced the pleasurable effects of actual cannabinoid administration, it also elicited a more positive reaction when the volunteers were given placebo instead.

Plasma THC levels peak much more rapidly following intravenous (IV) THC injection or marijuana smoking than after oral ingestion. Consequently, users reach the peak "high" sooner with the first two routes of administration. Nevertheless, users who are smoking marijuana do not reach this peak until some time after the cigarette

has been finished. This delay means that the maximum level of intoxication occurs when plasma THC concentrations are already declining, suggesting that the brain and plasma THC concentrations are not yet equilibrated at the time when the plasma level is peaking. Another possible factor is the contribution of active THC metabolites (whose peak does not coincide with that of THC itself) to the psychoactive properties of marijuana.

Several kinds of acute adverse reactions to cannabis have been documented. For example, high cannabis doses can elicit feelings of increased anxiety instead of the reduced anxiety commonly associated with lower doses (Andrade et al., 2019). Even more striking is the elicitation of transient psychotic symptoms such as depersonalization (feeling separated from the self), derealization (feeling that the external world is unreal), agitation, and occasionally paranoia and violent behavior (Sewell et al., 2009; Miller et al., 2020). Such symptoms are most likely to occur in first-time users, although regular users may also experience these effects if they consume an unusually high dose. Indeed, a recent study from the United Kingdom found that paranoia, anxiety, and sleep disturbance were more likely to occur in adolescent users of high-potency skunk than low-potency cannabis (Mackie et al., 2021). Flashbacks, which are well known to occur in LSD users, have occasionally been reported for marijuana as well (Iversen, 2000). Lastly, consuming extremely large amounts of cannabis, either through inhalation (smoking or vaping) or ingestion of edibles, can lead to an acute toxic reaction manifested as CNS excitation or depression, tachycardia, and gastrointestinal symptoms (Noble et al., 2019). Accidental exposure to excessive amounts of cannabis most commonly occurs in children; however, this may also occur intentionally in the case of adolescents or adults. Fortunately, cases of cannabis toxicity are rarely life-threatening, and most require no more than palliative care of the patient.

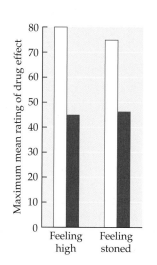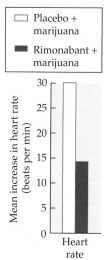

FIGURE 14.15 **Reduction in the subjective and physiological effects of smoked marijuana by rimonabant pretreatment** Study participants received either 90 mg of the CB_1 cannabinoid receptor antagonist rimonabant or a placebo orally, after which they smoked either an active (2.64% THC content) or a placebo marijuana cigarette. Self-reported subjective effects and heart rate were measured over the next 65 minutes. The data shown represent the maximum mean effects of the active marijuana cigarette in the presence or absence of the receptor antagonist. (After M. A. Huestis et al. 2001. *Arch Gen Psychiatry* 58: 322–328.)

Marijuana use can lead to deficits in memory and other cognitive processes

Clinical accounts of marijuana intoxication have often noted deficits in thought processes and in verbal behavior. These may include illogical or disordered thinking, fragmented speech, and difficulty in remaining focused on a given topic of conversation. The early descriptive work later gave rise to quantitative experimental assessments of marijuana's effects on a variety of cognitive functions, including learning, memory, attention, impulse control, and decision making. Among these different processes, learning and memory (e.g., immediate recall in episodic memory tasks) have most consistently shown impairment as a result of acute cannabis exposure (Broyd et al., 2016; Kroon et al., 2021). Other effects include deficits in the individual's ability to orient their attention to task-relevant stimuli, and difficulty withholding ongoing responses in certain kinds of psychomotor tasks. Interestingly, pretreatment with CBD has been reported to protect against THC-induced deficits in verbal learning and memory. Moreover, amount of prior marijuana use has been shown to influence the results on some cognitive tests, with heavier use reducing the adverse effects of acute cannabinoid exposure. This finding has led to the hypothesis that behavioral ("cognitive") tolerance develops in heavy marijuana smokers (Hart et al., 2001).

The neurobiological mechanisms underlying cannabis-induced cognitive deficits have been investigated using both laboratory animal and human neuroimaging studies. The neuroimaging work, which is reviewed by Bloomberg and colleagues (2019), has yielded complex findings that indicate altered neuronal activation in brain areas with significant CB_1 receptor expression. The laboratory animal studies are also important to consider for two major reasons: they avoid the many confounding variables associated with research on human cannabis users (e.g., variation in prior cannabis exposure, polysubstance use, and so forth), and they permit much more detailed examination of cannabinoid-induced neurochemical changes. Many of the studies determining the neurochemical mechanisms of cannabinoid-related cognitive impairment have focused on the hippocampus because of the susceptibility of hippocampal-mediated learning/memory tasks to cannabinoid disruption and the high expression of CB_1 receptors in this brain area. Several of these studies found that administering an NMDA receptor antagonist can block THC-induced memory deficits, suggesting that a key factor in the memory impairment is excessive glutamate release leading to NMDA receptor overactivation (Prini et al., 2020).

In addition to its adverse effects on learning, memory, and attention, marijuana use acutely impairs performance on complex psychomotor tasks. Reaction time, ability to perform divided-attention tasks, and critical tracking are among the processes affected by "being under the influence" of cannabis. Not surprisingly, therefore, acute cannabis exposure has been demonstrated to produce deficits in driving ability, using both driving simulators and tests of on-road performance (Bondallaz et al., 2016). Even more pronounced effects can occur when marijuana is combined with alcohol. These findings are not just of academic interest, as cannabis intoxication has been shown to increase the risk of being in a motor vehicle crash (Rogeberg and Elvik, 2016). Based on an Australian study in which blood THC concentrations were measured in drivers involved in fatal motor vehicle accidents, Grotenhermen and colleagues (2007) computed the mathematical relationship between blood THC and accident risk (**FIGURE 14.16**). When this graph is compared to Figure 14.7, which shows the time course of plasma THC after smoking a single marijuana cigarette, it is clear that increased accident risk persists for at least 30 minutes. Smoking multiple joints or a single high-potency joint, or vaping a high-THC–containing pod, would lead to an even longer period of impairment. Although the mathematical function shown in the figure is specific to one study and may not be identical to the results from other studies, it is prudent for individuals who have just smoked marijuana or vaped THC to avoid driving for a substantial period to allow the intoxicating effects to dissipate.

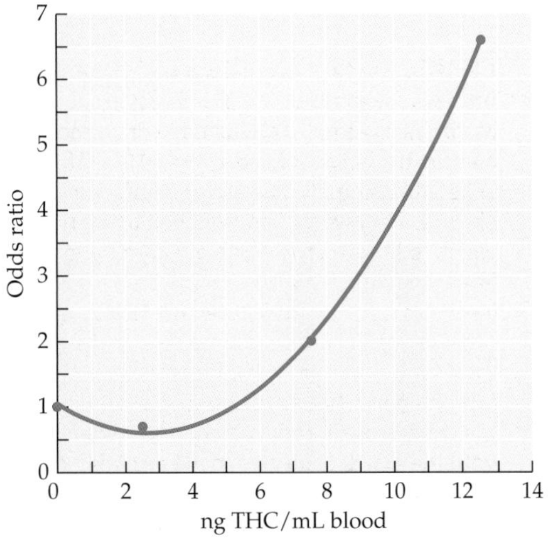

FIGURE 14.16 Estimated relationship between the driver's blood THC concentration and the odds ratio of being in a motor vehicle accident Based on an Australian study of fatal motor vehicle accidents, the risk of being in such an accident (calculated as an odds ratio; OR) was mathematically related to whether THC could be measured in the driver's blood post-mortem, and if so, the concentration level. The figure shows that for this study cohort, the OR was doubled by the time the concentration reached 8 ng/ml and continued to rise dramatically with increasing THC levels. Note that the small dip in the graphical function between 0 (no detectable THC) and the lowest THC level was produced by the curve-fitting function and probably has no real-world consequences. (After F. Grotenhermen et al. 2007. *Addiction* 102: 1910–1917, data from O. H. Drummer et al. 2004. *Accid Anal Prev* 36: 239–248.)

Rewarding and reinforcing effects of cannabinoids have been studied in both humans and animals

Not only are cannabinoid reward and reinforcement evident from self-report data, but these phenomena have also been studied under controlled laboratory conditions. For example, Chait and Zacny (1992) found that regular marijuana users could discriminate THC-containing marijuana cigarettes from placebo cigarettes with no THC, and that all their study participants preferred the THC-containing marijuana when given a choice. In the same study, pure THC taken orally in capsule form was also preferred over a placebo. Chait and Burke (1994) subsequently related marijuana preference to THC content, as users reliably selected marijuana with a 1.95% THC content over marijuana containing only 0.63% THC.

In contrast to psychostimulants (e.g., cocaine or methamphetamine) or opiates (e.g., heroin or morphine), THC administration does not have robust rewarding and reinforcing properties in standard laboratory animal tests (Vlachou and Panagis, 2014; Tanda, 2016). One exception to this general observation comes from several studies demonstrating reliable self-administration of THC by squirrel monkeys (reviewed by Panlilio et al., 2010). A key factor in these experiments was the use of low drug doses that are within the range of estimated human THC intake from a single puff on a typical marijuana cigarette (**FIGURE 14.17**). Lever pressing for THC was completely blocked by pretreatment with rimonabant, indicating that the reinforcing effect was dependent on CB_1 receptor activation. These same investigators showed that THC can induce drug-seeking behavior (a model of relapse in human drug users) in monkeys (Justinová et al., 2008) and that the endocannabinoid 2-AG is also self-administered (and thus reinforcing) in the squirrel monkey model (Justinová et al., 2011).

One potentially important factor in the relatively weak reinforcing effectiveness of THC is that the drug is only a partial agonist at the CB_1 receptor. This hypothesis is supported by numerous findings that WIN 55,212–2, a synthetic cannabinoid that is a full agonist at the CB_1 receptor, is self-administered by both rats and mice (Vlachou and Panagis, 2014; Tanda, 2016). Administration of WIN 55,212-2 additionally can produce both a conditioned place preference and a reduced threshold for electrical self-stimulation of the brain.

The ability of WIN 55,212-2 to enhance electrical self-stimulation suggests an involvement of CB_1 receptors in the brain's reward system. This has been confirmed in studies demonstrating (1) reductions in the rewarding effects of natural substances such as food or sweetened solutions in animals that lack normal endocannabinoid activity, and (2) enhanced reward created by pharmacological manipulations that increase endocannabinoid signaling (Vlachou and Panagis, 2014). Interestingly, there is substantial evidence for interactions between the endocannabinoid and endogenous opioid systems within both the VTA and nucleus accumbens (NAcc) (Wenzel and Cheer, 2018). As a result of these interactions, the rewarding and reinforcing effects of opiates are reduced or eliminated in CB_1 knockout mice, whereas these same effects of cannabinoids are similarly blunted in mice with a null mutation of the μ-opioid receptor (Befort, 2015). Additional evidence has implicated CB_1 receptor activation either by endocannabinoids or by exogenous agonists (e.g., THC) in the processes of reinforcement, dependence, and/or relapse (i.e., reinstatement of previously extinguished drug-seeking behavior) for a number of other drugs, including ethanol, heroin, nicotine, and cocaine (Covey et al., 2015; Peters et al., 2021).

Similar to other recreational substances, a key factor in cannabinoid reinforcement is activation of the mesolimbic DA system, as both exogenous cannabinoids and endocannabinoids have been found to stimulate both tonic and phasic (burst) firing of dopaminergic neurons in the VTA and to enhance DA release in the NAcc of laboratory animals (De Luca et al., 2014; Peters et al.,

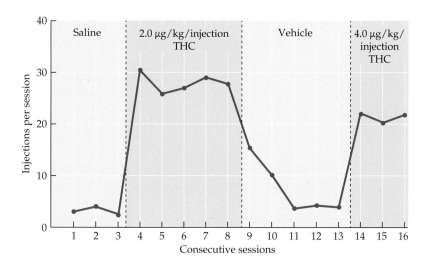

FIGURE 14.17 Acquisition of THC self-administration by squirrel monkeys Monkeys were initially trained in drug self-administration on a fixed-ratio-10 (FR-10) schedule using cocaine as the reinforcer (not shown). They were then switched to saline, which led to a nearly complete elimination of lever-pressing behavior. When THC (2.0 μg/kg/injection) was substituted for saline, lever pressing immediately increased to an amount sufficient to deliver approximately 30 drug injections per 1-hour session. Substitution with the vehicle again reduced operant responding until the active drug was made available once again. (After G. Tanda et al. 2000. *Nat Neurosci* 3: 1073–1074. doi.org/10.1038/80577.)

2021). Stimulation of dopaminergic cell firing has been attributed at least partly to inhibition of GABA release onto the VTA neurons by presynaptic CB_1 receptors on the GABAergic nerve terminals (Bloomfield et al., 2016). On the other hand, the previously mentioned CB_2 receptors on the dopaminergic neurons themselves exert an inhibitory effect on those cells (Zhang et al., 2014). Consequently, cannabinoids modulate activity in the mesolimbic DA pathway by multiple mechanisms involving both cannabinoid receptor subtypes.

SECTION SUMMARY

■ The subjective characteristics of cannabis intoxication include feelings of euphoria, disinhibition, relaxation, altered sensations, and increased appetite. The pleasurable effects produced by smoking marijuana are mediated at least partly by CB_1 receptor activation, but they additionally reflect the individual's expectation of experiencing such effects.

■ Sympathetic nervous system activation by cannabis leads to increased heart rate and blood pressure. Cannabis also acutely increases hunger.

■ Adverse reactions to cannabis can occur such as feelings of anxiety and paranoia. Such reactions are more likely to occur with high-potency cannabis and/or in first-time users.

■ Cannabis acutely causes impairment in episodic verbal memory, attention, impulse control, decision making, and psychomotor performance. Animal studies suggest that impairment of hippocampal-dependent task performance is related to cannabinoid effects on the glutamatergic system within this brain area.

■ Endocannabinoids are involved in the brain's reward circuit, where they interact closely with the endogenous opioid system.

■ Although THC is not as strongly reinforcing as many other addictive substances, it can support IV self-administration under appropriate experimental conditions. Synthetic cannabinoids are more strongly reinforcing because of their property as full rather than partial agonists at the CB_1 receptor.

■ Cannabinoid reinforcement is dependent on CB_1 receptor-mediated activation of VTA dopaminergic cell firing and DA release within the NAcc. This is mediated at least partly by presynaptic CB_1 receptors on GABAergic nerve terminals that synapse on the VTA neurons, thereby suppressing GABA-mediated inhibition of cell firing.

14.4 Cannabis Use, Misuse, and the Effects of Chronic Cannabis Exposure

This section will begin with a discussion of global cannabis/marijuana use, the factors influencing early initiation of marijuana use, and the adverse consequences

of persistent marijuana use throughout the lifetime. We will then discuss the features of cannabis use disorder and the negative health effects of chronic exposure to cannabis.

Global cannabis/marijuana use, initiation of use, and subsequent age-related changes in use are well documented

The United Nations (UN) regularly reports on trends of drug use around the world. Their findings indicate that among illicit substances such as cocaine, amphetamines, or heroin, cannabis is the most widely used globally. The 2020 UN World Drug Report estimated that among people aged 15 to 64 years worldwide, approximately 192 million (3.9%) used cannabis during 2018 (United Nations Office on Drugs and Crime, 2020). When the data were broken down by region, the greatest percentage of cannabis users were in North America (14.6%), followed by Australia and New Zealand (10.6%) and then West and Central Africa (9.3%). As in the case of global use, cannabis (mainly in the form of marijuana) is the most widely used illicit drug in the United States. According to the 2019 National Survey on Drug Use and Health, almost 30 million Americans age 18 or older were current marijuana users at the time of the survey (Center for Behavioral Health Statistics and Quality, 2020). Moreover, the survey estimated there were an additional 1.8 million users between 12 and 17 years of age. Both of these numbers are higher than those cited in the previous edition of this textbook.

First use of marijuana typically occurs in adolescence and use peaks during young adulthood. Individuals who have not yet tried marijuana by their mid-20s are unlikely to begin at a later age. This is shown in **FIGURE 14.18**, which is derived from a longitudinal study of 976 people drawn from upstate New York. In this cohort, the peak age for initiating marijuana use was 17, although a few children began as early 10 or 11 years of age. The prevalence of marijuana use follows a similar trajectory, with a peak during young adulthood and a decline thereafter. In the 2019 National Survey, 13.2% of responders between 12 and 17 years of age had used marijuana during the past year. The figure rose to 35.4% among responders from 18 to 25 years of age, and then declined to 15.2% in those 26 years of age or older.

Initiation of adolescent marijuana use has been linked to a number of personality, behavioral, and environmental factors (Schreier and Griffin, 2021). Early marijuana users have traditionally been characterized as sensation seeking and impulsive, with poor behavioral control. Additional features of early marijuana use reportedly include a high degree of autonomy, rebelliousness against authority and conventional norms, and low academic motivation. A study by Falls and colleagues (2011) found a significant association between early conduct problems and early initiation of marijuana use (i.e., before 15 years

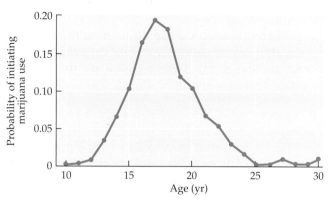

FIGURE 14.18 Probability of initiating marijuana use as a function of age (After J. S. Brook et al. 1999. *Dev Psychopathol* 11(2): 901–914. Reproduced with permission.)

of age) in a large sample of college students. In addition, many adolescents have prior experience with alcohol and/or cigarettes before trying marijuana. For this reason, alcohol and tobacco have been hypothesized as "gateway" drugs to marijuana use, although not all findings are consistent with this hypothesis. Indeed, there is evidence for a "reverse gateway" in which marijuana is a precursor to tobacco use (Lemyre et al., 2019). Other researchers have proposed that marijuana could be a gateway to so-called hard drugs or misuse of prescribed psychoactive drugs such as sedatives (Mayet et al., 2012). However, it is difficult to determine whether marijuana actually facilitates the progression to more dangerously perceived substances like cocaine or heroin or whether certain users are already predisposed to seek out these substances because of some combination of personality traits, life circumstances, and other factors independent of their exposure to marijuana (see Web Box 9.1).

An estimated 5% to 10% of individuals who initiate marijuana use become persistent users throughout their life. Compared to casual marijuana users or non-users, these persistent users tend to experience a

number of adverse outcomes, including more stress and less life satisfaction, more interpersonal problems, a greater incidence of mood and anxiety disorders, and an increased likelihood of developing a substance use disorder (Schreier and Griffin, 2021). Yet it is important to recognize that with our current information, it is impossible to determine the extent to which chronic marijuana use is a *causal* agent in these outcomes or is itself a *consequence* of other underlying problems in the individual's life.

Chronic use of cannabis can lead to the development of a cannabis use disorder

As in the case of other recreationally used substances, cannabis use and the risks associated with such use cover a wide range beginning with low-risk experimental or occasional use, to regular use at levels that pose known risks to physical and/or mental health, and finally to even greater levels of use that meet diagnostic criteria for a clinical disorder (Connor et al., 2021; **FIGURE 14.19**). Two points should be noted here. First, there is no defined cutoff for hazardous use, since reaching that condition depends on many factors, including frequency and pattern of use, dose, method of consumption (e.g., marijuana smoking, vaping THC-containing oils, hashish consumption), and individual factors influencing vulnerability to the adverse effects of cannabis use. The second point, which is illustrated in the figure, is that several different classification systems have been used, either historically or currently, to categorize disorders of cannabis use. Versions 10 and 11 of the International Classification of Diseases (ICD) include a category of harmful cannabis use and a higher (in severity) category defined as cannabis dependence. The fourth edition of the *Diagnostic and Statistical Manual of Mental Disorders* (*DSM-IV*) specified categories of cannabis abuse and cannabis dependence that corresponded closely to the respective ICD categories. However, when *DSM-IV* was replaced by the current *DSM-5*, this newer edition combined the two categories in *DSM-IV* and collectively termed them cannabis use disorder (CUD; American Psychiatric Association, 2013). In the discussion that follows, we will use the *DSM-5* terminology unless otherwise indicated.

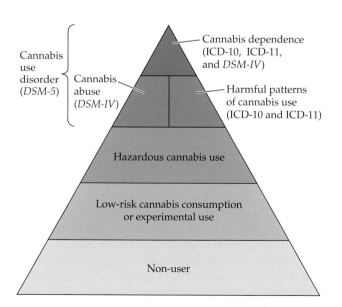

Cannabis use disorder (*DSM-5*)

Cannabis abuse (*DSM-IV*)

Cannabis dependence (ICD-10, ICD-11, and *DSM-IV*)

Harmful patterns of cannabis use (ICD-10 and ICD-11)

Hazardous cannabis use

Low-risk cannabis consumption or experimental use

Non-user

FIGURE 14.19 Classification systems of cannabis use and misuse As depicted in the figure, most people do not use cannabis. Experimental or occasional use is thought to pose relatively little risk to health. Increased levels of use have been associated with demonstrable risks to physical and/or mental health. Finally, high levels of use pose the greatest health risks and may cause the individual to meet diagnostic criteria for clinical disorders of cannabis use according to the *DSM* and ICD. (After J. P. Connor et al. 2021. *Nat Rev Dis Primers* 7: 16, hierarchy based on J. B. Saunders et al. [Eds.] 2016. *Addiction Medicine*. 2nd ed. Oxford University Press: Oxford.)

CANNABIS USE DISORDER To define CUD, *DSM-5* applies the overall list of criteria for a substance use disorder to cannabis users. These criteria entail significant impairment and/or distress across several functional areas, including problematic behaviors resulting from persistent cannabis use; failed attempts to control or decrease cannabis use; excessive amount of time spent procuring the drug; adverse impact of cannabis use on performance at work, at school, or in social roles; persistent use of cannabis in potentially hazardous situations; the development of tolerance; and the experience of withdrawal symptoms upon cessation of use (Panlilio et al., 2015; Simpson and Magid, 2016). Severity of a CUD may be rated as mild, moderate, or severe depending on how many criteria are met. Besides a clinical interview, problematic cannabis use can be assessed using any of several questionnaires such as the Cannabis Problems Questionnaire, Cannabis Abuse Screening Test, Cannabis Use Disorder Identification Test, Marijuana Screening Inventory, and Marijuana Problem Scale (López-Pelayo et al., 2015). A recent meta-analysis of research published between 2009 and early 2019 suggests that roughly 20% to 25% of cannabis users meet criteria for CUD, with about half of those showing mild to moderate CUD symptoms and the remaining half showing moderate to severe symptoms (Leung et al., 2020).

FACTORS CONTRIBUTING TO THE DEVELOPMENT OF CANNABIS USE DISORDER A number of factors influence the risk of developing CUD, the rate of progression from non-hazardous use to CUD, and the relationship between CUD and other disorders (Connor et al., 2021). Two key factors are the age of initiation of cannabis use and the frequency of use. First, starting to use cannabis before the age of 16 increases both the overall risk of developing CUD and the rate of progression from initial use to CUD. Second, frequency of use has similar effects on both outcomes. Over the span of a year, adults with CUD were found to use cannabis an average of 6.2 out of every 10 days. A third factor is co-use of tobacco, which has been associated with an increased risk for CUD, more withdrawal symptoms upon cessation of cannabis use, and greater difficulty maintaining abstinence compared to cannabis users who do not also use tobacco products (Connor et al., 2021). Lastly, there are important sex/gender differences in cannabis use and CUD (Greaves and Hemsing, 2020). While the prevalence of CUD is reportedly greater in men than in women, women appear to suffer more severe symptoms of the disorder and to progress more rapidly from initial use to CUD onset. This latter phenomenon has been termed "telescoping." These differences highlight the importance of studying cannabis use patterns and vulnerability to CUD in both women and men.

CUD risk is additionally influenced by biological and psychosocial variables, and by the legal status of cannabis availability. Twin studies using the *DSM-IV* criteria for cannabis abuse or dependence estimated the heritability of these disorders to be 50% to 60% (Connor et al., 2021). Several genes that may contribute to this heritability have been identified through either candidate gene studies or genome-wide association studies (GWAS); however, caution should be applied until the genes in question have been confirmed by further research (Thorpe et al., 2021). Psychosocial factors associated with risk for cannabis dependence or CUD include experiencing highly positive reactions to cannabis during adolescence, use of cannabis to cope with negative emotions, living alone, experiencing major life stressors, and having a comorbid mood, anxiety, or personality disorder (Ferland and Hurd, 2020; **FIGURE 14.20**). As shown in Figure 14.20, people with CUD are also likely to suffer from at least one additional substance use disorder. Lastly, the prevalence of CUD is potentially affected by the legality of cannabis production, sales, and use. Some of the key issues surrounding cannabis legalization and its consequences are discussed in **WEB BOX 14.1**.

TOLERANCE Repeated exposure to THC produces tolerance to the behavioral effects of the drug in laboratory rats and mice (Nguyen et al., 2018; Parks et al., 2020). Whether tolerance also occurs in people who use cannabis regularly is important for at least two major reasons: first, the development of tolerance could lead to escalation of use (frequency and/or dose), thereby increasing the risk of developing CUD; and second, the presence of tolerance might mitigate some of the adverse acute effects of cannabis, such as cognitive impairment. A recent review of the relevant literature concluded that compared to non-regular users, regular cannabis users showed tolerance to (1) the acute intoxicating effects of cannabis, including the drug's euphoric effects, (2) cannabis-induced impairment of cognitive function, (3) feelings of anxiety induced by higher doses of cannabis or pure THC, and (4) cannabis-induced physiological changes such as tachycardia (Colizzi and Bhattacharya, 2018).

Cannabinoid tolerance appears to be largely pharmacodynamic in nature, involving a combination of desensitization and down-regulation of CB_1 receptors (reviewed in Ramaekers et al., 2020). For example, Breivogel and coworkers (1999) found that rats given daily THC injections (10 mg/kg) over a 3-week period showed gradual reductions both in regional CB_1 receptor density and in cannabinoid agonist-mediated receptor activation. In some brain areas, the cannabinoid receptors were almost entirely desensitized following 3 weeks of THC exposure. Cannabinoid receptor desensitization was shown to result from internalization of receptors

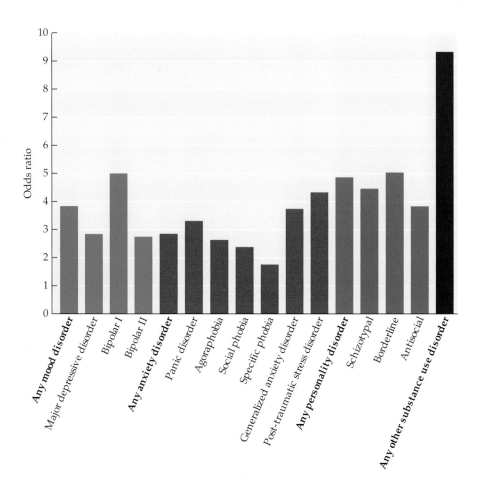

FIGURE 14.20 Odds ratio of having a comorbid psychiatric condition for individuals with CUD These odds ratios show the difference in risk of having the indicated condition when individuals with and without CUD are compared. (Data from D. S. Hasin et al. 2016. *Am J Psychiatry* 173: 588–599.)

off the cell membrane, thereby dissociating them from their normal signaling mechanisms (Dudok et al., 2015).

PET imaging studies have demonstrated widespread decreases in brain CB_1 receptor binding in regular marijuana smokers (Ceccarini et al., 2015; D'Souza et al., 2016). These findings are consistent with the above-mentioned animal studies showing CB_1 receptor down-regulation in animals treated chronically with THC. The imaging studies further showed that receptor binding recovered following abstinence from cannabis, with data indicating partial recovery within a period as short as 2 days when measurements were obtained from heavy users diagnosed as being dependent on cannabis (D'Souza et al., 2016). Furthermore, in those individuals there was a significant negative correlation between the intensity of withdrawal symptoms after 2 days of abstinence and the magnitude of overall CB_1 receptor binding; that is, individuals who showed the strongest withdrawal symptoms soon after stopping marijuana use also had the lowest levels of receptor binding measured at the same time point. This correlation suggests that changes in brain CB_1 receptors due to heavy marijuana use are related to the development of cannabis dependence.

FIGURE 14.21 shows that the development of CUD and associated cannabis tolerance are accompanied by additional neurochemical changes besides CB_1 receptor

down-regulation. For example, reduced levels of glutamate were observed in the anterior cingulate cortex and dorsal striatum (Ferland and Hurd, 2020). These changes may be related to the cognitive deficits observed in people with CUD. Similar to other substance use disorders, alterations in the dopaminergic system have been of particular interest in CUD. Two PET studies found reduced striatal DA synthesis in regular cannabis users compared with non-users (Bloomfield et al., 2014a, 2014b). DA synthesis capacity in the cannabis group was correlated with scores on a self-rated apathy scale (i.e., lower DA synthesis was related to greater apathy), amount of cannabis use (i.e., lower DA synthesis was related to greater use), and age of onset of use (i.e., lower DA synthesis was related to earlier onset of use). Two other PET studies examined striatal responses to amphetamine, which releases DA, or methylphenidate, which blocks DA reuptake. Individuals who met criteria for marijuana abuse or dependence exhibited decreased striatal DA responses to these drugs. Moreover, the dopaminergic deficits in the amphetamine study were correlated with poorer attention, poorer working memory, and negative symptoms (van de Giessen et al., 2016), whereas the deficits in the other study were related to blunted subjective and physiological responses to methylphenidate, negative emotionality, severity of cannabis dependence, and craving (Volkow et al., 2014b). Together, these PET imaging studies provide

FIGURE 14.21 **Neurochemical changes related to acute cannabis use, chronic use and the development of CUD, and abstinence from use** Brain imaging studies have demonstrated that in occasional cannabis users or non-users, acute cannabis exposure causes increased striatal DA synthesis and release, and increased glutamate levels in the dorsal striatum and anterior cingulate cortex. With chronic cannabis use leading to CUD, these acute effects are reversed, resulting in below-normal DA synthesis and release and reduced glutamate levels. CB_1 receptors throughout the brain are also down-regulated, contributing to cannabis tolerance. During abstinence, the reduction in CB_1 receptors rapidly normalizes but not the DA- or glutamate-related changes. Striatal D_2/D_3 receptors do not seem to be affected in CUD. (After J.-M. N. Ferland and Y. L. Hurd. 2020. *Nat Neurosci* 23: 600–610.)

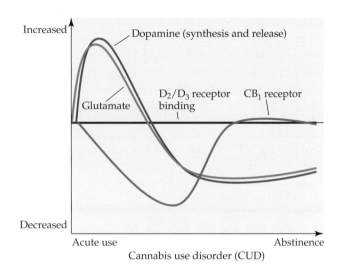

compelling evidence that chronic use of cannabis, including use patterns that result in CUD, is associated with (and may have caused) substantially impaired dopaminergic function in the striatum. Such impairment likely plays a role in long-term disturbances in mood, motivation, and cognition observed in chronic cannabis users.

WITHDRAWAL Cannabinoid withdrawal symptoms were first reported in laboratory studies in the 1970s. Later research began to recognize the existence of cannabis dependence, craving, and withdrawal in some marijuana users. The abstinence syndrome in long-term heavy marijuana users consists of irritability, increased anxiety, depressed mood, sleep disturbances, heightened aggressiveness, and decreased appetite (Cooper and Haney, 2008, 2009). These withdrawal symptoms resemble those seen with several other drugs of abuse, most notably nicotine. Overall symptomatology is greatest during the first 1 to 2 weeks of withdrawal (**FIGURE 14.22**), but some symptoms may persist for a month or longer. The *DSM-5* defines a diagnostic category of cannabis withdrawal that includes all of the above-mentioned symptoms but also adds physical symptoms such as abdominal pain, tremors, sweating, fever, chills, and headache (Panlilio et al., 2015; Simpson and Magid, 2016). Cannabis users in withdrawal often experience craving for the substance, and

a similar kind of craving can additionally be elicited by presentation of cannabis-related cues (Norberg et al., 2016). In a nationwide survey conducted by Hasin and colleagues (2016), 60.5% of survey participants with CUD reported cannabis craving, 32.5% reported cannabis withdrawal symptoms, and 23.1% reported both craving and withdrawal. Cannabinoid withdrawal can be alleviated by providing either smoked marijuana or oral THC, demonstrating a key role for this compound in both the development of dependence and the manifestation of withdrawal symptoms.

Early experimental studies in which animals were administered THC chronically and then examined after the treatment was stopped found few if any signs of withdrawal. Although these results may seem to be at odds with reports of an abstinence syndrome in humans, researchers recognized that the absence of withdrawal symptoms might have been due to the long elimination half-life of THC, which causes the cannabinoid receptors to remain partially occupied for a significant time even after termination of drug treatment. The CB_1 receptor antagonist rimonabant was used to test this hypothesis, since administration of the drug would abruptly block the receptors despite the continued presence of THC in the animal. This approach, which is called **precipitated withdrawal**, revealed an abstinence syndrome characterized by tremors, wet-dog shakes, increased grooming behaviors (facial rubbing, licking, and scratching),

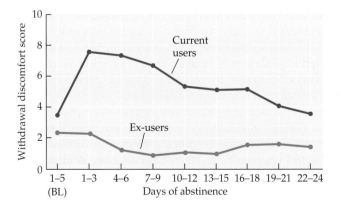

FIGURE 14.22 **Time course of overall withdrawal discomfort in heavy marijuana users undergoing abstinence** Current marijuana users were compared with ex-users on a battery of 15 possible self-reported withdrawal symptoms over a 5-day baseline period (BL) during which marijuana use was permitted and then during a 45-day period of abstinence. Data shown represent the mean composite withdrawal scores (up to a possible maximum of 36) during baseline and the first 24 days of abstinence. (After A. J. Budney et al. 2003. *J Abnorm Psychol* 112: 393–402. © 2003 by American Psychological Association. Reproduced with permission.)

ataxia, and hunched posture (González et al., 2005; Panagis et al., 2008). As expected, no withdrawal symptoms were observed in CB_1 knockout mice given chronic THC and then challenged with rimonabant.

The neurochemical mechanisms underlying the marijuana abstinence syndrome are not yet fully understood. Some of the important findings based on the precipitated withdrawal paradigm include decreased DA cell firing in the VTA and reduced DA release in the NAcc, increased corticotropin-releasing factor (CRF) release in the central nucleus of the amygdala, increased secretion of stress hormones such as corticosterone, and various changes in the endocannabinoid system (González et al., 2005; Panagis et al., 2008). Together, these alterations could contribute to the mood reduction, irritability, and stress experienced by dependent cannabis users during periods of abstinence. Moreover, at least some of the same responses have been reported to occur during withdrawal from cocaine, alcohol, and opiates, thereby linking cannabinoids with substances generally considered to have greater addictive potential.

TREATMENT OF CANNABIS USE DISORDER

Although most cannabis users do not develop CUD and do not seek treatment, those who do become dependent on the drug report not only craving and withdrawal symptoms but also many other problems that adversely influence their daily functioning. Such problems may include deteriorating social relationships, financial difficulties, and poor general satisfaction with life (Budney et al., 2007; Copeland and Swift, 2009). Some, although not all, dependent individuals eventually seek professional treatment for their problems.

Marijuana users seeking treatment are typically entered into an outpatient program that may involve cognitive behavioral therapy, relapse prevention training, and/or motivational enhancement therapy (Lévesque and Le Foll, 2018). These approaches can also be combined with a contingency management program in which participants who submit cannabinoid-negative urine samples earn vouchers redeemable for various goods and services. Although these different treatment programs have all met with some success, patients are highly vulnerable to relapse even after an initial period of abstinence. Thus, marijuana appears to be similar to other recreational drugs with regard to the difficulty in achieving long-term treatment success in dependent individuals.

At the time of this writing, the FDA has not approved any medications for treatment of CUD. However, the idea of pharmacotherapy for this disorder is certainly being investigated. Medications tested to date include various antidepressants, anxiolytic and antipsychotic drugs, methylphenidate (treatment for attention-deficit/hyperactivity disorder), lithium (treatment for bipolar disorder), gabapentin (anticonvulsant medication), naltrexone (an opioid receptor antagonist), and *N*-acetylcysteine,

which is hypothesized to normalize substance-induced dysregulation of the glutamatergic system (Winters et al., 2020). Although some of these medications seem to reduce cannabis withdrawal-related symptoms, overall none has proven to reliably improve long-term abstinence rates. An alternative approach is to treat patients with a cannabinoid agonist, which follows the same agonist substitution approach as seen in the use of nicotine-based medications for cigarette smokers or methadone for opiate addicts. Medications tested for this purpose include dronabinol, nabilone, and nabiximols (Werneck et al., 2018). Current evidence suggests that these drugs can be useful for reducing cannabis withdrawal symptoms and, therefore, may eventually be approved as adjunct medications for use either with psychosocial therapy or with other medications later found to be efficacious in treating CUD.

Chronic cannabis use can lead to adverse behavioral, neurobiological, and health effects

Given that dedicated cannabis users may consume the drug on a regular, even daily, basis for many years, concern has arisen over whether such lengthy periods of chronic drug exposure might lead to adverse psychological, neuropsychiatric, or physiological effects. Evidence for such effects is discussed in this final section of the chapter.

COGNITIVE EFFECTS In the earlier section on acute effects of cannabis use, we saw that memory and other cognitive functions are impaired shortly after smoking marijuana. However, most people do not engage in this behavior while they're at work or in class or at other times when a high level of functioning is required. If marijuana is used only during recreational times (e.g., evenings and weekends), and if drug-related cognitive deficits do not outlast the period of use, then one could argue that such deficits are harmless. On the other hand, it is possible that heavy recreational use over a long period of time somehow compromises brain function such that cognitive problems persist even after drug use is stopped. The question of residual cognitive deficits from marijuana use has been controversial, but some reasonably consistent findings have emerged. There is substantial evidence that long-term cannabis use leads to impairment in many cognitive domains when assessed following 2 weeks of abstinence, a time period sufficient for withdrawal symptoms to subside (Crean et al., 2011; Broyd et al., 2016; Ganzer et al., 2016). The affected functions include attention, the ability to concentrate, executive functions, verbal learning and memory, and psychomotor performance. **TABLE 14.1** compares the effects of acute versus chronic cannabinoid exposure on cognitive function, noting that acute effects are more reliably observed. Of additional importance is the question of whether partial or full

TABLE 14.1 Summary of Acute and Chronic Effects of Cannabinoid Exposure on Cognitive Processes

Acute effects

Impaired verbal learning and memory

Impaired working memory

Impaired attention (task- and dose-dependent)

Impaired inhibitory control and (to a lesser extent) other executive functions

Impaired psychomotor function

Chronic effects

Impaired verbal learning and memory

Impaired attention; attentional bias

Possibly impaired psychomotor function

Possibly impaired executive function (depending on frequency of use and age of onset)

Recovery of function with abstinence

Likely persistent effects on attention and psychomotor function

Possibly persistent effects on verbal learning and memory (insufficient and mixed evidence)

Source: After S. J. Broyd et al. 2016. *Biol Psychiatry* 79: 557–567.

Note: Some acute cannabinoid effects are dependent on the specific task and dose, whereas some chronic effects depend on frequency of use and age of onset of cannabis use. Lesser reliability of findings is denoted by terms such as *possibly* and *likely*.

recovery of function occurs following longer periods of abstinence from the drug. As shown in Table 14.1, some kinds of cognitive deficits may be persistent, although the data are not entirely consistent and more research is needed (Crean et al., 2011; Schreiner and Dunn, 2012; Broyd et al., 2016). Indeed, persistent deficits are most likely to occur in individuals who begin regular, heavy cannabis use early in adolescence.

EDUCATIONAL AND OCCUPATIONAL OUTCOMES OF EARLY USE Since the onset of cannabis use typically occurs during adolescence, researchers have been concerned about whether cognitive impairment is already evident during the school years and if so, whether it might be linked to poor educational attainment and later occupational outcomes (Cyrus et al., 2021). Although an early review of longitudinal studies on cannabis use and psychosocial outcomes reported an association between cannabis use and lower educational attainment (Macleod et al., 2004), a later review of this literature concluded that the confidence in this association was limited by several problems, including co-use of tobacco products as a confounding variable (National Academies of Sciences, Engineering, and Medicine, 2017). A similar conclusion was reached with respect

to cannabis use and negative work-related outcomes such as lower occupational prestige, lower income, and an increased likelihood of being unemployed. Yet, longitudinal studies continue to be reported that find a significant relationship between early cannabis use and later educational and/or occupational achievements, even after controlling for potential confounders such as tobacco and alcohol use. One example is a large prospective study of Canadian youth from 15 to 28 years of age that found that participants who either were chronic cannabis users throughout the study or showed a trajectory of increased use over time reported lower educational attainment and lower occupational prestige and income than participants who either did not use cannabis or decreased their use over time (Thompson et al., 2019).

At the present time, we do not know whether there is a causal relationship between amount of cannabis use and educational or occupational achievement. Even if there is, the direction of causation would still need to be established. Does early cannabis use cause a lack of success in school, or does a lack of success early in one's academic career cause an increase in cannabis use? One hypothesis is that the cognitive deficits associated with heavy cannabis use lead to poor school performance (Jacobus et al., 2009). Alternatively, some researchers have argued that the social context surrounding heavy cannabis use at a relatively early age promotes the rejection of mainstream social values such as educational achievement in favor of a more unconventional lifestyle (Fergusson et al., 2003a; Lynskey et al., 2003).

Another possibility involves drug-related motivational changes that would have a negative impact on performance in the classroom. Indeed, research going back more than 50 years found evidence for apathy, aimlessness, loss of achievement motivation, lack of long-range planning, and decreased productivity in chronic marijuana users. For example, a 1968 review by McGlothlin and West states, "Clinical observations indicate that regular marihuana use may contribute to the development of more passive, inward-turning, amotivational personality characteristics. For numerous middle-class students, the subtly progressive change from conforming, achievement-oriented behavior to a state of relaxed and careless drifting has followed their use of significant amounts of marihuana" (p. 372). This so-called **amotivational syndrome** has continued to be discussed in the cannabis literature (e.g., see Lac and Luk, 2018). We cannot rule out the possibility that some users experience a loss of drive and achievement motivation as a result of chronic, heavy exposure to cannabis. However, one could argue just as plausibly that such personality characteristics are a cause, rather than a consequence, of adopting a marijuana-centered lifestyle. For example, the Victorian Adolescent Health Cohort Study found evidence that disengagement with school, culminating in some cases with completely dropping out, was concomitant with or even preceded the onset of daily cannabis use (Coffey and Patton, 2016). Thus, it seems that current evidence is still insufficient to determine the potential direction of causality with respect to marijuana use, motivation, and educational achievement.

CHANGES IN BRAIN STRUCTURE AND FUNCTION

Neuroimaging techniques such as structural and functional magnetic resonance imaging (MRI) have identified potential neural correlates of the impaired cognitive function and motivation associated with long-term cannabis use. Even though the results of this research have been somewhat inconsistent, several findings have been sufficiently consistent to warrant discussion. Structural MRI studies have shown that the regularity and/or duration of cannabis use, as well as the severity of CUD where relevant, are related to lower gray matter volumes of the orbitofrontal cortex (OFC), temporal lobe, hippocampus, and amygdala (reviewed in Ferland and Hurd, 2020). Interestingly, for reasons that are not yet clear, imaging of the cerebellum has shown increased rather than decreased gray matter volume in CUD.

Neuroimaging methods alone are incapable of determining the cellular changes responsible for decreased or increased gray matter volume; however, assuming that there is no change in the number of cells within the affected area, we can hypothesize that altered volume might reflect changes in dendritic arborization and/or

synaptic connectivity. For example, cannabis-related gray matter reductions could be a result of withdrawal of dendritic arbors and an accompanying decrease in the number of synapses in the affected areas. Hypotheses such as this one obviously require experimental confirmation.

Researchers have used functional MRI (fMRI) and EEG to compare regional task-related brain activation patterns in regular cannabis users (including individuals with CUD in some studies) with those seen in healthy controls (Sagar and Gruber, 2019; Ferland and Hurd, 2020). Cannabis users were abstinent at the time of testing to avoid interference from acute cannabis effects on brain activation. **FIGURE 14.23** presents a summary of brain areas that are differentially activated in the two groups depending on the kind of task used to challenge the participants. First, note that several of the highlighted areas, such as the OFC, hippocampus, amygdala, and cerebellum, are the same mentioned above that show altered gray matter volume in cannabis users. Second, while reduced task-related neural activation (right panel) generally coincides with poorer task performance, cases of increased neural activation (left panel) have two possible interpretations depending on the associated behavior. For example, compared to non-users, chronic cannabis users and people with CUD show heightened responsiveness to cannabis cues and to negative emotional stimuli, both of which have been associated with increased neuronal activation in relevant brain areas and networks. In those cases, subjective and

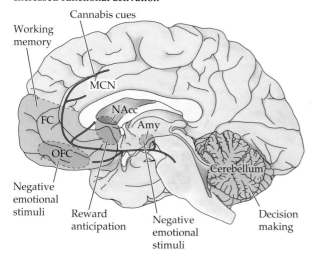

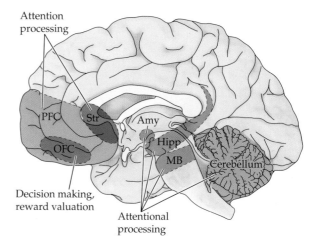

FIGURE 14.23 **Altered task-dependent functional brain activity in CUD compared to controls** Studies compared regional brain activation in chronic cannabis users with controls during performance of specific cognitive or emotional tasks. Task-dependent activation patterns were measured using fMRI or EEG. The figure depicts summary results in which the indicated brain area showed either increased task-dependent activation in the cannabis-using group (left) or decreased activation in that group (right). Amy, amygdala; FC, frontal cortex; Hipp, hippocampus; MB, midbrain; MCN, mesocortico-limbic network (corresponding to the combined mesolimbic and mesocortical dopaminergic pathways); NAcc, nucleus accumbens; OFC, orbitofrontal cortex; PFC, prefrontal cortex; Str, striatum. (After J.-M. N. Ferland and Y. L. Hurd. 2020. *Nat Neurosci* 23: 600–610. doi.org/10.1038/s41593-020-0611-0.)

behavioral responses go hand in hand with the underlying neural substrates. On the other hand, chronic cannabis users typically show deficits in working memory. In that case, therefore, frontal cortical hyperactivation during working memory tasks, rather than mediating the deficits, is thought to represent an "overcompensation of neural networks…to achieve apparent normal executive function when cognitive demand is required" (Ferland and Hurd, p. 603).

Rodent studies, particularly when conducted during the adolescent period of development, have played a significant role in modeling the neurochemical and behavioral effects of chronic cannabinoid exposure (Hurd et al., 2019). Overall, this research has shown that chronic dosing of adolescent rats or mice either with THC or with synthetic cannabinoids such as WIN 55,212-2 or CP-55,940 results in numerous changes in the glutamatergic, GABAergic, and dopaminergic systems (reviewed in Renard et al., 2016a; Rubino and Parolaro, 2016; Molla and Tseng, 2020). These neurochemical changes are accompanied by altered synaptic plasticity (i.e., LTP and LTD), dysregulated emotional (i.e., anxiety-like and depressive-like) and social behaviors, and impaired cognitive function. Structural studies of the PFC, hippocampus, and nucleus accumbens additionally found evidence for cannabinoid-induced developmental abnormalities of dendritic arbors and spines, both of which are critical for synapse formation and synaptic function. One such example involves a study in which adolescent rats received daily doses of CP-55,940 from postnatal day 29 through day 50 (Renard et al., 2016b). Drug doses

were increased at the beginning of the second and third weeks of treatment to model escalation of use and to account for potential cannabinoid-induced tolerance. No additional drug treatments were given after day 50. Some of the cannabinoid-exposed and vehicle-treated rats were killed in adulthood at 92 days of age for examination of dendritic arborization in pyramidal neurons within the PFC. Other animals were tested at about the same age for LTP in the pathway from the hippocampal CA1 area to the PFC. The results from these measurements are presented in **FIGURE 14.24**. The average total dendritic length was significantly reduced in the cannabinoid-treated animals, and this effect was almost entirely due to a difference in the basal dendrites, which are dendrites that emanate from the base of the cell (Figure 14.24A). The cannabinoid-treated rats also exhibited a deficiency in LTP induced at the synaptic pathway from the hippocampus to the PFC (Figure 14.24B). Thus, an animal model of daily cannabis use during adolescence demonstrated deficits in prefrontal pyramidal cell dendritic development and a concomitant impairment of synaptic plasticity in the hippocampal–PFC circuitry. Although not proven by the existing data, it is reasonable to speculate that these structural and functional changes contribute to the well-known cognitive deficits associated with chronic adolescent cannabis exposure.

HEALTH EFFECTS Earlier in the chapter we discussed some of the consequences of long-term cannabis use, including the development of tolerance, dependence (withdrawal symptoms), and possibility

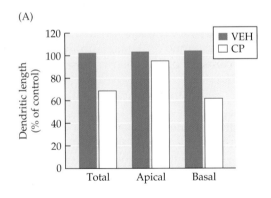

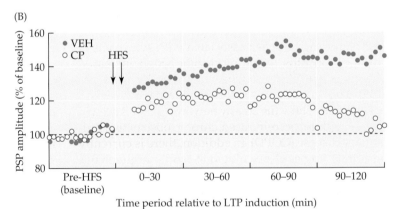

FIGURE 14.24 **Chronic treatment of adolescent rats with CP-55,940 reduced PFC dendritic length and impaired LTP at hippocampal–PFC synapses** Male rats were given daily IP injections of CP-55,940 (CP) or drug vehicle (VEH) from postnatal day 29 through day 50. Doses were 0.15 mg/kg for the first 7 days, 0.20 mg/kg for the next 7 days, and 0.30 mg/kg for the last 7 days. No further treatments were given after day 50. (A) On postnatal day 92, some of the CP-55,940–treated and control rats were killed and their brains were stained to visualize dendritic arbors using a modification of the Golgi technique

(see Chapter 2). Measurement of dendritic length of cortical layer 2/3 pyramidal neurons in the PFC revealed a significant reduction in basal dendrites and in total dendritic length (basal + apical). (B) Separate groups of rats at day 92 or later were anesthetized for electrophysiological analysis of long-term potentiation (LTP) at hippocampal–PFC synapses that was induced by high-frequency stimulation (HFS). LTP in the drug-treated rats (measured as postsynaptic potential [PSP] amplitude) was impaired when compared with vehicle-treated animals. (After J. Renard et al. 2016. *Eur Neuropsychopharmacol* 26: 55–64.)

of developing CUD. However, there are many more health risks that encompass various domains, ranging from vulnerability to psychiatric disorders to adverse effects on the respiratory, cardiovascular, gastrointestinal, reproductive, and immune systems (for an overall review, see Campeny et al., 2020). This section will, therefore, review some of the major health consequences of chronic cannabis use, especially beginning during adolescence. As with other drugs, the severity of adverse effects from repeated cannabis use depend on the frequency of use, the dose (i.e., primarily related to THC content), and the typical route of administration. For example, cannabis vaping may pose somewhat less risk to the lungs and airways when a cannabis extract is vaped instead of raw plant material; however, if the THC content of the extract is high, then there is an increased risk of adverse psychological reactions such as anxiety and paranoia (Chadi et al., 2020).

When cannabis is consumed by smoking, the possibility of injury to the respiratory system is one obvious area of concern. In this regard, there is both "bad" and "good" news for marijuana smokers. The "bad" news starts with the fact that the smoke from marijuana joints and tobacco cigarettes contains the same kinds of irritants and carcinogens. Tar from cannabis smoke actually contains higher concentrations of the carcinogens benzanthracenes and benzpyrenes. Moreover, Wu and coworkers (1988) reported that the amounts of tar and carbon monoxide taken in *per cigarette* are much greater for marijuana joints than for tobacco cigarettes. To some extent, this is balanced by the typically lower daily frequency of marijuana smoking compared to daily smoking of tobacco cigarettes by people who are addicted to nicotine. Nevertheless, regular marijuana smoking has been associated with symptoms of chronic bronchitis, including chronic cough, increased phlegm production, and wheezing (Tashkin and Roth, 2019). The "good" news is that marijuana smokers do not generally show the airway narrowing that is seen in people with tobacco-induced chronic obstructive pulmonary disease (COPD). In addition, there is currently no compelling evidence that long-term marijuana use increases the risk for lung cancer, although more research needs to be done in this area. Tashkin and Roth (2019) cite evidence that in both of these cases in which marijuana smoking seems to be less hazardous to the respiratory system than tobacco smoking, the presence in marijuana smoke of THC may be a key factor. THC has bronchodilator effects that may help prevent the development of COPD, and it also has anti-tumor effects that may help counteract the carcinogenic substances mentioned earlier.

Marijuana smoking can also adversely affect the cardiovascular and cerebrovascular systems. Marijuana use has been associated with increased risk for atrial fibrillation, ventricular arrhythmias, myocardial infarction (heart attack), and sudden cardiac death (Rezkalla and Kloner, 2019; Latif and Garg, 2020). Increased risk for these cardiovascular disorders may be related, in part, to the previously mentioned cannabis-induced elevations in heart rate and blood pressure. Additional evidence links marijuana smoking with an increased risk for ischemic stroke related to cerebral vasoconstriction and blood clot formation (Archie and Cucullo, 2019). Note that the cardiovascular and cerebrovascular events associated with marijuana are not limited to older users who may already have developed atherosclerosis or coronary artery disease but have also been documented in users who are in their 20s or 30s.

Because the endocannabinoid system plays an important role in both the male and female reproductive systems (du Plessis et al., 2015; Brents, 2016), marijuana smoking could have an adverse influence on reproduction. In support of this possibility, animal studies have consistently shown that THC suppresses the release of hypothalamic gonadotropin-releasing hormone (GnRH) in both males and females. In turn, this reduction in GnRH leads to decreased secretion of luteinizing hormone (LH) from the pituitary gland (Maccarone and Wenger, 2005). Some human clinical studies have additionally reported reproductive abnormalities such as reduced sperm counts in men and irregular menstrual cycles in women. Nevertheless, there is currently no conclusive evidence for deleterious effects of marijuana use on fertility (Maccarrone et al., 2021).

Since the discovery of CB_2 receptor expression in cells of the immune system, this system has been closely associated with endocannabinoid modulation. Both CB_1 and particularly CB_2 receptors are expressed by various immune cells, and administration of THC or other cannabinoid receptor agonists generally suppresses immune function (Tanasescu and Constantinescu, 2010). This immunosuppressive action is mediated, in part, by activation of CB_2 receptors on T lymphocytes. Interestingly, however, this same effect could potentially be exploited therapeutically by administering a selective CB_2 receptor agonist to patients with autoimmune disorders or those who have received tissue grafts (Eisenstein and Messler, 2015). In both instances, benefit is obtained from dampening native immune responses. In laboratory animals under controlled experimental conditions, THC has been found to impair an organism's resistance to bacterial and viral infections (Eisenstein and Meissler, 2015). Despite these results, the review by the National Academies of Sciences, Engineering, and Medicine (2017) on the health effects of chronic cannabis use failed to find clear evidence that such use leads to compromised immune function.

TABLE 14.2   Odds Ratios of Developing Depression, Anxiety, or Suicidality after Early Cannabis Use (before 18 years of age)

Disorder	Number of studies	Odds ratio (OR)	95% Confidence interval (CI)
Depression in young adulthood	7	1.37*	1.16–1.62
Anxiety in young adulthood	3	1.18	0.84–1.67
Suicidal ideation in adolescence or young adulthood	3	1.50*	1.11–2.03
Suicide attempts in adolescence or young adulthood	3	3.46*	1.53–7.84

Source: Adapted from L. G. Gobbi et al. 2019. *JAMA Psychiatry* 76: 426–434.

* OR is significantly different from 0. Note that statistical significance for ORs is determined by the 95% CI. If this interval is entirely above 0, then the OR is significantly >1; if the interval is entirely below 0, then the OR is significantly <1.

In the earlier section on CUD, we discussed the finding of frequent comorbidity of this disorder with other psychiatric disorders such as major depression, anxiety disorders, and psychoses. Those findings are based on cross-sectional data that can't discriminate whether the disorders came on at roughly the same time or whether one preceded the other. Are there any findings that *prior* cannabis use, especially during early adolescence, predisposes individuals to developing another psychiatric disorder later in life? Gobbi and colleagues (2019) recently performed a systematic review and meta-analysis of prospective studies in which adolescent cannabis use (before 18 years of age) was associated with the later onset of major depression, an anxiety disorder, suicidal ideation, or suicide attempts. Despite the small number of studies available for inclusion in the meta-analysis, the results showed that early cannabis use significantly predicted later onset of major depression, suicidal ideation, and suicide attempts (**TABLE 14.2**). A trend in the same direction was observed for anxiety disorders, but the result did not reach statistical significance. In a subsequent review, Patten (2021) points out that even though the findings of Gobbi and associates (2019) suggest a causal relationship between early cannabis use and later depression and suicidality, such a relationship remains unproven because depressive symptomatology may already have been present during adolescence that contributed to the use of cannabis (i.e., individuals may have been self-medicating with cannabis).

A related area of research involves large studies that have linked adolescent cannabis use with an increased risk of later developing a psychotic disorder. Earlier in the chapter we saw that heavy marijuana smoking causes short-term cognitive deficits, but any effects that persist after stopping seem to be modest. Similarly, immediate psychotic-like responses to cannabis are usually transient in nature. But what if young people knew that heavy marijuana use significantly increased their risk for developing a psychotic disorder such as schizophrenia later in life? This topic is discussed in **WEB BOX 14.2**.

A different health concern is related to cannabis use by pregnant or lactating women. Indeed, marijuana is the most frequently used illicit drug by pregnant women, the majority of these women consider the drug to be safe for their offspring, and marijuana has even been touted as a remedy for pregnancy-related nausea (Volkow et al., 2017). Does the use of cannabis during and/or after pregnancy pose risks to the offspring? We know that because of its lipophilic nature, THC readily passes from the maternal circulation into the fetus (by way of the placenta) or the nursing infant (by way of breast milk). Cannabinoid receptors are present in the placenta, and the fetal brain expresses these receptors beginning at 14 weeks of gestation (beginning of the second trimester). Thus, perturbation of the endocannabinoid system in both the fetal brain and placenta by THC or other exogenous cannabinoids could have profound effects on placental function and fetal brain development. The possible risks to offspring from maternal cannabis use are discussed in **WEB BOX 14.3**. Although the discussion focuses on use during pregnancy, the possibility exists that cannabis use by nursing mothers could also have an adverse impact on their infant's subsequent neurobehavioral development (Ordean and Kim, 2020).

The final topic of this chapter brings us back to the chapter opener, which gave a published account of a man severely intoxicated from using a potent synthetic cannabinoid. Use of these substances has increased in recent years because of their easy access and the powerful "high" they produce. However, synthetic cannabinoids pose even greater health risks than cannabis. The history, mechanism of action, and toxicity of synthetic cannabinoids are discussed in **BOX 14.2**.

BOX 14.2 ■ OF SPECIAL INTEREST

Beyond Cannabis: The Rise of Synthetic Cannabinoids

Several synthetic compounds with cannabinoid activity, such as CP-55,940 and WIN 55,212-2, have been widely used in research for several decades. However, recreational use of synthetic cannabinoids was unknown until 2004, when advertisements began to appear on the internet for new herbal preparations containing synthetic designer cannabinoids that were legal at the time (Debruyne and Le Boisselier, 2015; Karila et al., 2016a). Synthetic cannabinoid preparations were initially sold under the names K2 or Spice. Although these names are still in use, many additional names have since been added to the street lexicon (see www.drugfreeworld.org/drugfacts/synthetic/synthetic-marijuana.html). The first synthetic cannabinoid constituent of Spice was identified as JWH-018* in 2008 by a German forensic laboratory. Since then, more and more distinct drugs have become available as illicit laboratories that synthesize these compounds attempt to stay ahead of the legal system. Indeed, testing of herbal mixtures has identified over 250 different synthetic cannabinoids that could potentially

be obtained for recreational use (Worob and Wenthur, 2020). A timeline showing introduction of some of the major synthetic cannabinoids is shown in **FIGURE A**. The reason for the continued introduction of new compounds is presumably to escape detection, since forensic drug laboratories are constantly trying to "catch up" with illicit drug labs in their need to identify these compounds once they have appeared in the marketplace.

Synthetic cannabinoids are produced in a powdered form that can be solubilized and then sprayed onto herbs or other plant materials. The resulting material is then sold with labels like "herbal incense," often with the disclaimer "not for human use." The spiked herbs can be rolled into a joint or mixed with tobacco or regular marijuana. Alternatively, the drugs are vaporized and inhaled using a bong or an e-cigarette cartridge. Users of synthetic cannabinoids are typically adolescents and young adults, including high school and college students (Hu et al., 2011; Johnston et al., 2016). Some individuals prefer synthetic cannabinoids over marijuana because of differences in their respective subjective effects (Tebo et al., 2020). Other reasons offered for this choice include perceived or actual legality, avoidance of detection in drug screens, easy availability through the internet or other sources,

(Continued)

---

*Compounds with the designation "JWH" belong to a class of cannabinoids first synthesized and characterized by the organic chemist John W. Huffman. Although Huffman's work was intended for potential therapeutic applications, publication of the chemical structures and synthetic pathways has enabled others to use the information to synthesize and sell many of these same cannabinoids for recreational purposes. A different group of synthetic cannabinoids is designated "AM," which stands for Alexander Makriyannis, another pioneer in the discovery and characterization of synthetic cannabinoid drugs.

(A)

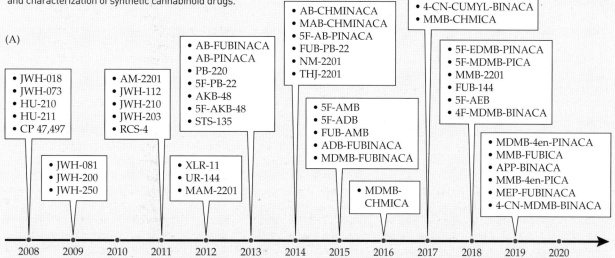

Timeline of introduction of new synthetic cannabinoids in the United States from 2008 through 2019 At present, there is no systematic nomenclature system for synthetic cannabinoids, which is the reason for the confusing variety of names shown in the figure. To some extent, however, drug name similarities can be seen that indicate particular families of compounds in which modifications have been made to

the basic structure of the drug while retaining cannabinoid agonist activity (e.g., JWH series, FUB series, MDMB series). The information presented was provided by the U.S. Drug Enforcement Administration (DEA). (After A. J. Krotulski et al. 2021. *Drug Test Anal* 13: 427–438. © 2020 John Wiley & Sons Ltd.)

BOX 14.2 ■ OF SPECIAL INTEREST (*continued*)

or simple curiosity. Synthetic cannabinoids may also be preferred because their peak effects occur more rapidly, but these effects also dissipate more quickly. Nevertheless, several surveys found that the majority of users reported a preference for natural cannabis over synthetic cannabinoids (Winstock and Barratt, 2013; Cooper, 2016), which helps account for why the synthetic compounds continue to lag behind natural cannabis in prevalence of use.

Synthetic cannabinoids that are used recreationally are similar to THC in that they typically activate both CB_1 and CB_2 receptors. However, they are more potent on a per-dose basis, are typically full rather than partial agonists at the receptors, are metabolized by different biochemical pathways, and are far more likely to result in toxic reactions (Worob and Wenthur, 2019). An example of potency difference for the compound AM-2201 is illustrated in **FIGURE B**. Like JWH-018, AM-2201 has been used and abused recreationally. Järbe and Raghav (2016) provided the following description of the powerful effects of AM-2201 intoxication: "My heart starts pounding so fast and hard and doesn't feel real. As of that moment, I no longer know who I am, where I am and what is real" (p. 265). As noted by Järbe and Raghav, such a description is similar to the accounts of Parisian hashish users almost 200 years earlier!

The acute psychological and behavioral effects of synthetic cannabinoids, particularly JWH-018, have recently been studied using controlled laboratory experiments. Inhalation of a moderate dose of JWH-018 (75 µg/kg) by cannabis users caused impaired memory, attention, and psychomotor coordination in addition to the expected drug "high" (Theunissen et al., 2021a). In a related study, inhaled JWH-018 at the same or higher doses produced various psychedelic (altered perceptions) and dissociative (derealization and depersonalization) effects that are more typically associated with hallucinogenic drugs and dissociative anesthetics such as phencyclidine (PCP) and ketamine (see Chapter 15) (Theunissen et al., 2021b). Additional information on synthetic cannabinoid intoxication comes from published case reports summarized by Castaneto and colleagues (2014). Reported psychological symptoms include agitation or restlessness, anxiety, confusion, and memory loss. Intoxicated users also exhibited somatic symptoms such as elevated heart rate and blood pressure, nausea and vomiting, chest pain, breathlessness, sweating, twitching, and dilated pupils.

Even more serious toxic reactions have been linked with synthetic cannabinoids, including myocardial infarction, respiratory failure, kidney injury, rhabdomyolysis (muscle tissue breakdown), fever, coma, and seizures (Armstrong et al., 2019; Gounder et al., 2020; Kouroni et al., 2020). Cannabinoid-induced

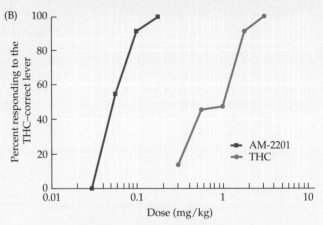

(B)

Potency of AM-2201 compared with THC in a rat drug discrimination paradigm Rats were trained on a two-lever drug discrimination paradigm (Chapter 4) to discriminate THC (3 mg/kg IP) from vehicle. When different doses of THC were administered to previously trained rats (circles), the resulting dose–response curve yielded an ED_{50} of 0.76 mg/kg (ED_{50} in this task is defined as the dose resulting in 50% of responses on the drug-correct lever). When AM-2201 was substituted for THC and a similar dose–response function was determined (squares), the curve was shifted far to the left and the calculated ED_{50} was 0.06 mg/kg. The leftward shift and lower ED_{50} indicate greater potency of the synthetic cannabinoid. (After T. U. C. Järbe and J. G. Raghav. 2016. *Curr Topics Behav Neurosci* 32: 263–281; and T. U. C. Järbe et al. 2016. *Behav Pharmacol* 27: 211–214. © 2016 Wolters Kluwer Health, Inc. All rights reserved.)

seizure activity is unexpected, since cannabis itself generally has the opposite effect. A number of cases of first-onset psychotic reactions have also occurred (Fattore, 2016; Skryabin and Vinnikova, 2019). Some researchers have hypothesized that CBD may serve a protective role against acute psychotic reactions to the THC constituent of cannabis and that the lack of CBD in synthetic cannabinoid preparations increases the risk of experiencing such a reaction (also see Web Box 14.2). Synthetic cannabinoid toxicity may be related not only to the greater potency and efficacy of these compounds but also to a phenomenon called "super-concentrations" or "hot spots" (Papanti et al., 2014). These terms refer to instances in which the synthetic cannabinoid is not mixed uniformly with the herbal material, thereby allowing the user to consume excessive amounts of the drug. Finally, there are documented reports of fatal reactions to synthetic cannabinoids (Trecki et al., 2015), which contrasts with natural cannabis, for which fatalities are exceedingly rare. Some of these cases seem to involve cannabinoid overdose alone, whereas others may involve reactions to polydrug use involving synthetic cannabinoids taken together with other substances.

BOX 14.2 ■ OF SPECIAL INTEREST (continued)

The longer-term effects of synthetic cannabinoid use are also being explored. Clinicians have identified a synthetic cannabinoid use disorder with features similar to CUD but also possibly including signs of cardiovascular, renal, neurological, or psychiatric toxicity (Grigg et al., 2019). Another common symptom of synthetic cannabinoid use disorder is the development of dependency and the appearance of withdrawal symptoms upon cessation of use (Macfarlane and Christie, 2015; Grigg et al., 2019). As with CUD, people with synthetic cannabinoid use disorder also exhibit cognitive impairment; however, in this case the deficits may be even more severe than in CUD (Cengel et al., 2018).

In summary, a large variety of different synthetic cannabinoids have appeared on the street. Unlike natural cannabis material that contains known cannabinoid compounds, K2, Spice, and similar products contain unknown mixtures of synthetic drugs. Use of these substances can produce highly toxic reactions due to their potency, their ability to function as full agonists at cannabinoid receptors, and the possibility of super-concentrations or hot spots in an herbal preparation. Prospective users of synthetic cannabinoids should be aware of the risks to their health when considering such products.

SECTION SUMMARY

- Cannabis (mainly in the form of marijuana) is the most heavily used illicit drug both globally and within the United States.

- Marijuana use typically begins in adolescence and peaks during young adulthood. An increased likelihood of early marijuana use has been associated with sensation seeking and impulsivity, early conduct problems, rebelliousness, and low academic motivation.

- Adolescent marijuana use often occurs after the individual has already had experience with alcohol and/or cigarettes. Some investigators have hypothesized that alcohol and tobacco are "gateway" drugs to marijuana, which then serves as a potential gateway to other illicit drugs. However, it is difficult to determine whether marijuana actually facilitates the progression to these more dangerous substances.

- Other factors such as family issues, poor school performance, and a strong positive response to early marijuana experience are risk factors for the transition to regular use and possibly misuse.

- DSM-5 contains diagnostic criteria for cannabis intoxication, withdrawal, and use disorder. Criteria for cannabis use disorder (CUD) are the same DSM-5 criteria for any substance use disorder but applied specifically to cannabis. Severity may be mild, moderate, or severe depending on the number of criteria met by the patient. Current data indicate that roughly 22% of users develop CUD, and perhaps half of those experience moderate to severe symptoms.

- Many factors contribute to the risk of developing CUD, including early onset of use, progressing to daily use, experiencing highly positive reactions to cannabis, use of cannabis to cope with negative emotions, concurrent use of tobacco, living alone, experiencing major life stressors, having a comorbid psychiatric disorder, and being male. However, women tend to suffer more severe CUD symptoms and to progress more rapidly from initial cannabis use to CUD (a phenomenon termed "telescoping").

- Controlled laboratory studies have demonstrated tolerance to repeated THC exposure in both humans and experimental animals. Such tolerance is related to a desensitization and down-regulation of central CB_1 receptors in many areas of the brain.

- Additional neurochemical changes occur in people who are regular cannabis users, especially if they have developed CUD. Such changes include reduced glutamate levels in the anterior cingulate cortex and striatum and impaired striatal dopaminergic functioning. These changes may at least partly underlie the cognitive deficits and abnormal mood and motivation observed in CUD.

- Heavy (e.g., daily) marijuana users are at significant risk for developing dependence on the drug and for undergoing withdrawal symptoms upon becoming abstinent. Withdrawal symptoms include heightened irritability, anxiety, aggressiveness, depressed mood state, sleep disturbances, reduced appetite, craving for marijuana, and a cluster of physical symptoms consisting of abdominal pain, tremors, sweating, fever, chills, and headache.

- Chronic THC exposure in laboratory rodents also causes the development of dependence that can be demonstrated using the procedure of precipitated withdrawal with rimonabant. Neurochemical studies of cannabinoid-dependent animals undergoing withdrawal have found reduced DA cell firing, increased CRF release, and endocannabinoid system changes that could contribute to some of the symptoms of cannabis withdrawal in human users.

- Individuals suffering from CUD who seek professional help are typically entered into an outpatient treatment program involving cognitive behavioral therapy, relapse prevention training, and/or motivational enhancement therapy. Additional improvement in outcome may be achieved by adding a voucher-based incentive program (contingency management). Nevertheless, most dependent individuals find it difficult to maintain long-term abstinence.

- Pharmacotherapeutic approaches to the treatment of cannabis dependence are now being investigated. Approaches using cannabinoid agonists such as nabiximols spray are also being tested. Although such treatments can reduce withdrawal symptoms in cannabis-dependent patients, they have not yet demonstrated efficacy in improving long-term recovery from the disorder.

■ Concerns have been raised over possible adverse consequences of chronic cannabis consumption. Testing of long-term cannabis users after withdrawal symptoms have subsided has revealed deficits in several cognitive domains, including attention, ability to concentrate, executive functions, verbal learning and memory, and psychomotor performance. Some, though not all, of these deficits may persist over a long time period following abstinence.

■ Some studies have found a negative association between the early and heavy cannabis use by young people and later educational and occupational outcomes, although other findings do not support such a relationship. Even if future research solidifies an association between this kind of cannabis use pattern use and later adverse educational and occupational outcomes, we will still not know whether the association is causal. It is possible that early and heavy cannabis use can produce persistent cognitive deficits and/or an amotivational syndrome characterized by apathy, loss of achievement motivation, and decreased productivity. Alternatively, such use may be linked to the adoption of an unconventional lifestyle that devalues educational striving and achievement.

■ Neuroimaging studies of regular cannabis users (including some with CUD) have reported structural and biochemical changes in certain brain regions, including reduced gray matter volumes of the OFC, temporal lobe, hippocampus, and amygdala. In contrast, gray matter volume of the cerebellum seems to be increased. Functional studies have additionally identified many brain areas that are differentially activated in cannabis users compared to non-using controls, either under resting conditions or during various cognitive challenges. Chronic use has also been associated with decreased striatal DA synthesis and decreased dopaminergic responses to challenge with psychostimulant drugs. These neurochemical differences were correlated with some of the psychological (cognitive and mood) differences between users and non-users.

■ Rodent studies have investigated the neurobiological and behavioral consequences of repeated cannabinoid exposure during adolescence. This research has shown cannabinoid-mediated changes in several neurotransmitter systems, altered synaptic plasticity, dysregulated emotional and social behaviors, and impaired cognitive function. In addition, abnormal growth of dendritic arbors and spines has been observed in the PFC, hippocampus, and nucleus accumbens.

■ Health consequences of heavy marijuana smoking include respiratory problems such as bronchitis, increased risk of serious cardiovascular and cerebrovascular disorders (including atrial fibrillation, ventricular arrhythmias, myocardial infarction, sudden cardiac death, and ischemic stroke), and possible adverse effects on reproduction and immune function (although the evidence is currently inconclusive in both cases).

■ Increased risk for developing depression, an anxiety disorder, or psychosis (e.g., schizophrenia) has also been linked to early and heavy cannabis use.

■ Pregnant and lactating women should avoid using cannabis, since the offspring is exposed to maternal THC via the placenta or breast milk, and such exposure can have deleterious effects on subsequent neurodevelopment.

■ Numerous arguments have been raised in favor of or against the legalization of cannabis for medicinal use (i.e., "medical marijuana") or for recreational use. Despite the opposing arguments, increasing numbers of states have implemented medical marijuana programs or even legalized sales of cannabis for recreational purposes, usually under strict regulations. Some of the predicted adverse consequences of cannabis legalization have come to pass, including increased cannabis use, increased prevalence of CUD among adults, and greater numbers of adverse cannabis reactions requiring a hospital visit or hospital admission. Over time, more information will become available to provide a broader picture of the socioeconomic and health impacts of cannabis legalization.

■ Synthetic designer cannabinoids, sometimes called "K2" or "Spice," began to be sold over the internet in 2004 and now number over 250 distinct compounds. The designer drug may be sprayed onto cannabis plant material, after which the resulting mixture is marketed as "herbal incense." Synthetic cannabinoids act as highly potent full agonists at both CB_1 and CB_2 receptors. Because of their potency and efficacy, these substances can produce a severe state of intoxication characterized not only by the typical cannabinoid euphoria and cognitive impairments but also by altered perceptions, dissociative effects, agitation, anxiety, confusion, and various somatic symptoms.

■ Synthetic cannabinoid consumption has additionally been linked to a range of adverse health effects and even a small number of fatalities. These consequences indicate the unusually high degree of toxicity of synthetic cannabinoids and they highlight the danger of using these substances.

STUDY QUESTIONS

1. What is the difference between phytocannabinoids and endocannabinoids? List two examples from each category.

2. What was the name of the first federal legislation aimed at regulating the sale of marijuana? Is that law still in effect now?

3. (a) Describe the principal routes of cannabis administration. Which of these routes provides the greatest cannabinoid bioavailability? (b) Name two major metabolites of THC.

4. (a) Discuss the main characteristics of cannabinoid receptors, including receptor subtypes, receptor distribution within and outside of the brain, and whether the receptors are metabotropic or ionotropic. (b) Why did the discovery of cannabinoid receptors prompt a search for endocannabinoids?

5. (a) For a typical neuron expressing CB_1 receptors, what part of the neuron would be most likely to contain these receptors? What is the functional implication of this subcellular localization? (b) CB_1 receptor stimulation _____ (activates or inhibits) Ca^{2+} channel opening and _____ (activates or inhibits) K^+ channel opening.

6. Describe the features of cannabinoid receptor pharmacology presented in the text. Your answer should include a description of receptor agonists (natural versus synthetic, full versus partial agonism) and antagonists.

7. What is the current hypothesis offered to explain the biphasic effects of CB_1 receptor activation on anxiety (anxiolytic at low doses but anxiogenic at high doses)?

8. Explain how experimental animal studies have helped us understand the mechanism by which THC impairs memory in hippocampal-dependent learning tasks.

9. Describe the differences between CBD and THC with respect to mechanisms of cellular action and effects on regional neural activity within the human brain.

10. (a) The two major endocannabinoids are called _____ and _____. (b) True or false? These two chemicals are similar to each other in how they are synthesized, the enzymes that metabolize them, their activity at the CB_1 and CB_2 receptor subtypes, and their regional distribution within the brain.

11. True or false? Endocannabinoids are generated on demand and released from cells by a process that does not involve synaptic vesicles.

12. (a) Describe the retrograde signaling mechanism used by endocannabinoids, particularly 2-AG. How does this kind of signaling produce DSE or DSI, and what are the presynaptic neurotransmitters associated with those two processes? (b) A different mechanism sometimes used by anandamide involves signaling within the same cell and subsequent activation of an excitatory ion channel called _____.

13. Describe the experimental evidence that has led some researchers to hypothesize that deficient endocannabinoid activity could be a risk factor for developing PTSD after a traumatic experience.

14. Activation of the endocannabinoid system can regulate hunger and energy metabolism. What are the locations within the body (both inside and outside of the brain) where such regulation occurs?

15. Cannabinoid agonists are used therapeutically for relief from certain kinds of pain, and researchers are exploring additional applications for cannabinoid-mediated analgesia. Explain the basis for these applications (i.e., how the endocannabinoid system modulates pain perception).

16. (a) Another approved medicinal use of cannabinoids is for the treatment of appetite loss and nausea associated with HIV/AIDS or cancer chemotherapy. Name the two medications used for these purposes, and for each one, indicate whether it is chemically in the form of THC or a different cannabinoid receptor agonist. (b) What group of clinical disorders is being treated with a formulation of CBD extracted from hemp oil?

17. A close friend of yours is contemplating purchase of CBD-containing gummies from an internet provider to help them reduce their stress and sleep better. The friend asks your advice about whether these gummies are safe to consume and will provide the needed relief. What should you tell them, and why?

18. What are the most important reasons why consuming cannabis (e.g., smoking marijuana prescribed for medical use) might be more effective therapeutically than pure THC?

19. Describe the features of cannabis intoxication in humans, including the four stages characterized by Iversen and discussed in the section on acute behavioral and physiological effects of cannabinoids.

20. Summarize the reported acute adverse reactions to cannabis use. Under what conditions are such reactions most likely to occur?

21. (a) What cognitive functions are acutely impaired by cannabis? (b) What is the mechanism thought to mediate the deleterious effects of cannabinoids on hippocampal-dependent learning and memory tasks?

22. Describe the evidence for cannabinoid-mediated reward and reinforcement. How does the strength of cannabinoid reinforcement compare with the reinforcing effects of, for example, psychostimulants or opioid drugs?

(Continued)

STUDY QUESTIONS (*continued*)

23. How do glutamatergic and GABAergic cells modulate the firing of VTA dopaminergic neurons and NAcc DA release? How do cannabinoids act within this system to produce their reinforcing/rewarding effects?

24. What do we know about the initiation of marijuana use, including the typical developmental period of initiation and the risk factors for early marijuana use?

25. The _____ theory hypothesizes that early alcohol and/or tobacco use predisposes individuals to begin using marijuana, and that early marijuana use additionally predisposes individuals to use more dangerous illicit drugs like cocaine.

26. Summarize the risk factors for transitioning from experimental/infrequent marijuana use to regular use or even misuse.

27. As a diagnostic category, "cannabis use disorder" in the *DSM-5* has similar features to the category called _____ in the ICD-10 or ICD-11.

28. Do most recreational cannabis users ultimately develop cannabis use disorder? What factors contribute to the development of this disorder?

29. Cannabinoid tolerance has been related to _____ and _____ of CB_1 receptors within the brain.

30. (a) Describe the symptoms of withdrawal from chronic cannabis use. (b) How is cannabis withdrawal studied in experimental animal models?

31. Similar to the use of methadone for treating opioid use disorder, cannabinoid drugs are being tested for possible use in treating cannabis use disorder. Based on the similarity to this approach, the kinds of cannabinoid drugs being tested are _____ (agonists or antagonists) at the CB_1 receptor.

32. Chronic cannabis use, especially early and heavy use, has been associated with a variety of adverse effects. Summarize these effects in the realms of (a) educational performance and IQ, (b) cognitive effects, (c) neuropsychiatric effects, and (d) overall health effects.

33. Neuroimaging studies have found a number of differences between regular cannabis users (including some with CUD) and non-users with respect to regional gray matter volumes and neural activation either at rest or in response to various cognitive tasks. Can we conclude that cannabis use caused these differences in brain structure and function? Why or why not? Explain your answer.

34. In light of our current knowledge, present the arguments both in favor of and against the legalization of marijuana either for medical or recreational use.

35. (a) What is meant by the street names "Spice" and "K2"? (b) How do these substances differ from THC, and how are they typically consumed recreationally? (c) What are the main adverse effects that can occur from consuming these substances?

Psychedelic and Hallucinogenic Drugs, PCP, and Ketamine

15

"I PUT MY LIGHTER TO THE BOWL AND INHALED.... After about twenty seconds I started to feel extremely light headed kind of like after I stand up suddenly after reclining for extended periods of time. With my eyes still closed I exhaled. It's hard to describe how I arrived at my destination. All I can remember is that the reality that I had previously known had ceased to exist. I was face to face with what looked like an entity composed of hundreds of my faces. They were all leering at me in the sort of way that made me feel like they were happy in the knowledge I had finally gone insane. I immediately winced in my mind and tried to tell myself everything was going to be all right but at the same time I was terrified and had no idea why I was seeing what I saw. As if my subconscious was answering my fears, a voice said from behind me 'This is a bad trip (my name). You are going to have to deal with it.' I tried screaming 'how' but as the monster made up of all my faces moved closer, my body seemed to crumble into multiple interlocking puzzle pieces which made it impossible to run or defend myself. Eventually these puzzle pieces became so distorted and strung out, I could no longer identify them as my body. I could vaguely remember something called 'salvia' but I made no connection from the drug to where I was. All my hope of ever returning to reality was beginning to fade."

The above is a segment from a self-reported account of a user's first experience with the hallucinogenic plant *Salvia divinorum*.* As we will see in the first section of this chapter, substances like *Salvia*, LSD, psilocybin, and others have powerful effects on perceptual and conscious processes. Where do these substances come from, and how do they produce their effects? We will also cover phencyclidine (PCP), ketamine, and related compounds. These drugs are also known for their mind-altering properties, but they act through a different neurochemical mechanism than typical psychedelic drugs. ■

---

*This passage was taken from "The End of All Existence: An Experience with *Salvia divinorum*" on the Erowid.org website.

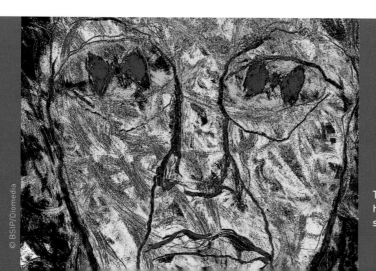

The surreal visual experiences produced by hallucinogenic drugs are reflected in works such as this of "psychedelic art."

15.1 Psychedelic Drugs

Background

For the recreational user, some substances are valued primarily for the unusual perceptual and cognitive distortions they produce. Users may find such distortions novel, stimulating, or even spiritually uplifting. Among the substances categorized in this way are **lysergic acid diethylamide (LSD)**, **mescaline**, **psilocybin**, **bufotenine, dimethyltryptamine (DMT), 5-methoxy-dimethyltryptamine (5-MeO-DMT)**, **salvinorin A** (the main psychoactive ingredient of *Salvia*), and **ibogaine**. Over the years, many different names have been given to this drug class, including **psychotomimetic** (psychosis-mimicking), **psychedelic** (mind-manifesting or mind-opening),* and **hallucinogenic** (hallucination-producing). The term *psychotomimetic* is now rarely used in this context, because most researchers no longer consider these compounds to be useful models of psychosis. Of the two remaining alternatives, the term *psychedelic* is often preferred by recreational users and by those who take such drugs in a quest for spiritual or mystical experiences. Until fairly recently, the modern pharmacological literature strongly favored the term *hallucinogenic*, and that was the term used in previous editions of this textbook. However, the newer published literature increasingly shows a preference for *psychedelic* over *hallucinogenic*. This change is particularly apt in light of the growing interest in applying psychedelic drugs to a therapeutic setting in which the primary aim is to render the individual's mind open to confronting their sources of trauma. Any hallucinogenic experiences that occur within this context are meant to further the therapeutic aim. Accordingly, the remainder of the chapter will primarily use the term *psychedelic* except when we are specifically discussing the hallucinogenic properties of a substance or the hallucinatory experiences resulting from its ingestion.

Many different definitions of this class of substances have been offered over the years. A reasonable definition of the term "psychedelic drug" is a psychoactive substance that causes perceptual changes, visual hallucinations, altered awareness of the mind and body, and cognitive distortions without producing a state of toxic delirium. The latter caveat in the definition is important to distinguish psychedelics from drugs that, at toxic doses, can produce a delirious state with some of the features of the psychedelic drug experience.

MESCALINE Many psychedelic drugs either are synthesized by plants or are based on plant-derived compounds. Mescaline, for example, is found in several species of cactus, such as the **peyote cactus** (*Lophophora williamsii*) (**FIGURE 15.1**). When the crown

FIGURE 15.1 Peyote cactus

Courtesy of Gerhard Köhres

(top part) of this small spineless cactus is cut off and dried, it is known as a **mescal button** or **peyote button**. These buttons can be chewed raw or cooked and then eaten to obtain their psychoactive effects. Alternatively, the mescaline can be extracted from the cactus and consumed as a relatively pure powder. The peyote cactus is native to the southwestern United States and northern parts of Mexico, and archeological evidence suggests that inhabitants of these regions were using peyote over 5000 years ago (Dinis-Oliveira et al., 2019). Peyote was used by Native Americans for religious and healing rituals, and such rituals continue to take place under the auspices of the Native American Church of North America, which was founded in 1918 and has chapters in many states as well as in Canada and Mexico.

Pure mescaline was first isolated from peyote in 1898 by Arthur Heffter and was synthesized in 1919 by Ernst Späth. However, the drug did not enter mainstream American culture until the famous novelist Aldous Huxley tried mescaline in 1953 and subsequently described his experience in a book entitled *The Doors of Perception*. This book and its sequel, *Heaven and Hell*, were among the seminal events that spawned a major rise in psychedelic drug use in the United States in the 1960s. Pure mescaline is not widely used at present because of the relatively high cost of doses needed to achieve the desired psychoactive effects. However, it is possible to legally purchase the peyote cactus and harvest one's own peyote buttons for consumption.

PSILOCYBIN Numerous species of mushrooms manufacture alkaloids with psychedelic properties. These fungi, which are sometimes called "magic mushrooms" or simply "shrooms," include members of the genera *Conocybe*, *Copelandia*, *Panaeolus*, *Psilocybe*, and *Stropharia*, which are found in many places around the world (**FIGURE 15.2**). Depending on the

---

*Origination of the word *psychedelic* in pharmacology is attributed to Humphry Osmond, a British psychiatrist who began using drugs of this class therapeutically in the 1950s.

FIGURE 15.2 *Psilocybe* mushrooms

species, users take 1 to 5 g of dried mushrooms to obtain the desired effects. The dried material may be eaten raw, boiled in water to make tea, or cooked with other foods to mask its bitter flavor. The major ingredients of these mushrooms are psilocybin and the related compound **psilocin**. After ingestion, the psilocybin is enzymatically converted to psilocin, which is the actual psychoactive agent. A different species of mushroom, *Amanita muscaria* (fly agaric; see Figure 8.18), produces a state of delirium that also includes vivid sensory experiences, but its primary active agents are muscimol and ibotenic acid.

The use of psychedelic mushrooms probably goes back historically at least as far as peyote use. There are two spectacular rock cave paintings in Algeria, dated at least to 3500 BCE, depicting people holding mushrooms in their hands and dancing. The more famous of the two paintings shows a single man (possibly a shaman*) with a beelike head and mushrooms sprouting from his entire body. In Mexico and Central America, the Aztec, Mayan, Mazatec, and other peoples developed religious rituals around the eating of psilocybin-containing mushrooms (Carod-Artal, 2015).

After defeating the Aztecs, the Spaniards soon learned of their use of psychedelic mushrooms, which they called *teonanácatl*, meaning "flesh of the gods." The conquerors brutally suppressed mushroom eating along with other features of the Aztec religion, but they were unable to completely wipe it out. Nevertheless, the existence of psychedelic mushrooms in the New World was largely ignored until 1938, when Richard Schultes of the Harvard Botanical Museum traveled to Oaxaca, Mexico, and collected specimens

of several different types of mushrooms being used in sacred rituals by the Mazatec people of that region. The publication of Schultes's findings ultimately led Gordon Wasson, a wealthy investment banker and amateur mycologist (someone who studies fungi), to visit Oaxaca in 1953 and again in 1955. During the second visit, Wasson and a photographer friend became the first known Westerners to participate in a Native American mushroom-eating ritual, which was led by a Mazatec *curandera*, or shaman, named María Sabina (**FIGURE 15.3**). In a 1957 *Life* magazine article entitled "Seeking the Magic Mushroom,"** Wasson described his reaction as follows:

> We lay down on the mat that had been spread for us, but no one had any wish to sleep except the children, to whom mushrooms are not served. We were never more wide awake, and the visions came whether our eyes were opened or closed. They emerged from the center of the field of vision, opening up as they came, now rushing, now slowly, at the pace that our will chose. They were in vivid color, always harmonious. They began with art motifs…. Then they evolved into palaces with courts, arcades, gardens… Then I saw a mythological beast drawing a regal chariot. Later it was as though the walls of our house had dissolved, and my spirit had flown forth, and I was suspended in mid-air viewing landscapes of mountains, with camel caravans advancing slowly across the slopes, the mountains rising tier above tier to the very heavens…. For the first time the word ecstasy took on real meaning. For the first time it did not mean someone else's state of mind.

Wasson, 1957, pp. 102, 103, 109

Among those who read Wasson's account was Timothy Leary, a young clinical psychologist pursuing a mainstream academic career. But after gaining a lectureship at Harvard in late 1959, Leary began to have reservations about his chosen career path. Then while vacationing in Mexico the following summer, Leary ate a handful of "magic mushrooms" and underwent the same kind of transformative experience reported by Huxley several years earlier with mescaline. Leary returned to work, where he founded the Harvard Psilocybin Project. In his own words, the purpose of this project was "to teach individuals how to self-administer psychoactive drugs in order to free their psyches without reliance upon doctors or institutions" (Leary, 1984, p. 35). Over the next few years, Leary and his colleague Richard Alpert (later known as Ram Dass) gave psilocybin to many graduate students and faculty members, as well as to notable artists, writers, and musicians. He also began experimenting with LSD, having taken the drug for the first time in 1962. Leary and Alpert's work

---

*In ancient cultures, shamans were people thought to possess special abilities to contact the spirit world.

**The title of this article is generally considered to be the first use of the term "magic mushroom."

The Tina & R. Gordon Wasson Ethnomycological Collection Archives, Harvard University

FIGURE 15.3 María Sabina engaged in the mushroom-eating ritual

became increasingly controversial, and they were dismissed from Harvard in 1963, but they continued their activities privately and went on to become leaders of the psychedelic movement.

DIMETHYLTRYPTAMINE AND RELATED TRYPTAMINES
DMT and the related tryptamines 5-MeO-DMT and bufotenine are found in a number of plants that are indigenous to South America. Native tribes in Brazil, Colombia, Peru, and Venezuela make hallucinogenic snuffs from plants containing these compounds (Araújo et al., 2015). Bufotenine and 5-MeO-DMT are additionally present in toxic secretions of an American desert toad, *Bufo alvarius*, which accounts for the origin of the name "bufotenine." Of these three substances, DMT is most often used recreationally. DMT lacks bioactivity when ingested orally because of liver metabolism (i.e., first-pass metabolism) by monoamine oxidase (MAO); however, when smoked or taken by insufflation (snorting), it can produce a brief but intense hallucinatory experience lasting about 30 minutes.

Several orally active synthetic DMT analogs, such as α-methyltryptamine (AMT) and 5-methoxy-diisopropyltryptamine, have become popular in recent years. The latter compound is known on the street as "Foxy Methoxy," or simply "Foxy." Foxy is typically taken orally in tablet form, although the pills can also be crushed and then either snorted or smoked.

Finally, it is important to mention **ayahuasca**, which is a Quechua Indian word meaning "vine of the soul." Ayahuasca is a strong reddish-brown tisane (herbal tea) originally created by peoples of the Amazonian rain forest. This potent brew requires at least two different kinds of plants, typically stalks from the *Banisteriopsis caapi* vine as well as leaves from *Psychotria viridis* and/or *Diplopteris cabrerena*. *Psychotria* and *Diplopteris* provide DMT, whereas the vines contribute several alkaloids called β-carbolines, which are known to inhibit MAO activity. The β-carbolines block DMT breakdown by liver MAO, thereby permitting the substance to reach the brain and exert its psychedelic effects. Because of the drug's oral route of administration, the onset of these effects is delayed for up to an hour after ingestion, but the effects persist for about 4 hours (Araújo et al., 2015).

Use of ayahuasca by native South American peoples dates back to the pre-Columbian era, the period before European influence on the indigenous peoples. Like peyote and *Psilocybe* mushrooms, ayahuasca was used in spiritual/religious ceremonies in order to "enter into contact with the unseen side of reality" (Luna, 2011, p. 9). It continues to be used in the same manner not only in South America but elsewhere in the world by practitioners of religions such as *Santo Daime*, *União do Vegetal*, and *Barquinha* that merge elements of Catholicism, shamanism, and various folk traditions (dos Santos et al., 2016a). Possession and use of ayahuasca is illegal in the United States except in sacred ceremonies by members of these religions. Whether or not the user formally belongs to one of these groups, ayahuasca is most often consumed for the purpose of enhancing one's personal or spiritual growth (Harris and Gurel, 2012).

LSD Unlike mescaline, psilocybin, and DMT, LSD is a synthetic compound, although its structure is derived from a family of fungal alkaloids. The famous story about the synthesis of LSD and the discovery of its astonishing psychoactive potency is presented in **BOX 15.1**. LSD was made available to psychiatrists and medical researchers in the late 1940s and early 1950s, which was followed by a period of intensive study. Indeed, more than 1000 LSD-related articles appeared in the scientific literature between 1951 and 1962 (U.S. Department of Health, Education, and Welfare, 1968). During the same period, researchers were beginning to appreciate that nerve cells in the brain communicate with each other chemically by means of neurotransmitters like serotonin (5-HT). When LSD was reported to alter serotonergic activity (see the later section on the basic pharmacology of psychedelic drugs), the finding generated tremendous excitement about the possibility of understanding human mental activity and behavior at a chemical and physiological level.

BOX 15.1 ■ HISTORY OF PHARMACOLOGY

The Discovery of LSD

LSD was first synthesized in 1938 by Albert Hofmann, a chemist working for the Sandoz pharmaceutical company in Switzerland. Sandoz was interested in alkaloids obtained from **ergot**, a substance produced by the parasitic fungus *Claviceps purpurea*, which can infest rye and wheat (see **FIGURE**). Ergot is an extremely toxic material, and consumption of ergot-contaminated grain can cause a serious illness known as **ergotism**.

Although no outbreak of ergotism has occurred in recent years, the disease was quite common in the Middle Ages and is thought to have caused the death of as many as 40,000 people in the year 944. Nevertheless, ergot came to have medicinal value because it produces powerful contractions of the uterus that can help trigger labor and reduce postbirth uterine hemorrhage.

Hofmann began to combine **lysergic acid**, which is the core structure in all ergot alkaloids, with other compounds to see what would emerge. The 25th different substance synthesized in the course of this research was D-lysergic acid diethylamide, which Hofmann abbreviated LSD-25 (from the German name *LysergSäure-Diäthylamid*). Hofmann's purpose in making this compound was to generate a new circulatory and respiratory stimulant (such drugs are sometimes called **analeptics**). This expectation was based on the structural similarity of LSD to nicotinic acid diethylamide, a known analeptic drug. However, LSD failed to show any analeptic activity, so the compound was temporarily abandoned.

Five years later, Hofmann decided to reexamine LSD, thinking that it might have useful pharmacological properties not recognized during initial testing. In the final stages of synthesizing a new batch of the compound, he was overcome by a series of strange sensations that prevented him from continuing in the lab. The following famous passage is taken from Hofmann's report to Sandoz, which describes the world's first LSD "trip":

> Last Friday, April 16, 1943, I was forced to interrupt my work in the laboratory in the middle of the afternoon and proceed home, being affected by a remarkable restlessness, combined with a slight dizziness. At home I lay down and sank into a not unpleasant intoxicated-like condition, characterized by an extremely stimulated imagination. In a dreamlike

© Manfred Ruckszio/Alamy Stock Photo

> state, with eyes closed (I found the daylight to be unpleasantly glaring), I perceived an uninterrupted stream of fantastic pictures, extraordinary shapes with intense, kaleidoscopic play of colors. After some two hours this condition faded away.
>
> Hofmann, 1979, p. 58

Hofmann suspected that this amazing experience had come from accidentally ingesting a small amount of the newly synthesized LSD. Therefore, the following Monday, he carefully measured out a minute amount of the drug, 250 µg (1/4000 of a gram), dissolved it in a small volume of water, and drank it. Hofmann soon underwent an even more intense experience than before. He somehow managed to ride his bicycle home with the help of a lab assistant (that day came to be known as "Bicycle Day"), and his hallucinations took a threatening form that later passed, leaving him the next day with a profound sense of well-being and a temporarily heightened perceptual awareness.

Hofmann's colleagues at Sandoz initially did not believe that LSD could be as potent as he claimed, but when they took minute quantities themselves, they were able to confirm Hofmann's result. Sandoz first marketed LSD in 1947 under the name Delysid for the purpose of helping patients with neuroses to uncover repressed thoughts and feelings. The company also suggested that psychiatrists self-administer the drug in order to better understand the perceptual distortions and hallucinations suffered by patients with schizophrenia.

Albert Hofmann continued to write and lecture about the positive effects of LSD and other psychedelic drugs, even after retiring from Sandoz in 1971. He passed away in 2008 at the age of 102.

Some researchers approached LSD as a psychotomimetic drug that would help reveal the biochemical underpinnings of schizophrenia. However, the LSD model proved to be inadequate in a number of ways, and it subsequently gave way to a PCP/ketamine model that is discussed later in this chapter. Others believed that LSD could be a valuable tool in psychotherapy or psychoanalysis. Practitioners in continental Europe mainly used **psycholytic therapy**, which was based on the concept of drug-induced "psycholysis" (i.e., psychic loosening or opening). This approach involved giving LSD in low but gradually increasing doses to promote the release of repressed memories and to enhance communication with the analyst. British, Canadian, and American psychiatrists, on the other hand, tended to prefer **psychedelic therapy**, in which patients were typically given a single high dose of LSD with the hope of gaining insight into their problems through a drug-induced spiritual experience. During the 1950s and 1960s, a number of studies were performed using this technique to treat patients who were alcoholics (Dyck, 2005). Unfortunately, almost all of these studies were marred by poor experimental control and inconsistent findings, which compromises our ability to draw sound conclusions from the published findings.

While LSD was being investigated as a possible psychotherapeutic aid, this and other psychedelic agents were also being considered by the U.S. government as potential weapons. During the post-WWII period of the U.S. "cold war" with the Soviet Union and Communist China, our government seemed willing to consider any strategy that might give us an advantage over those countries and their allies. The idea of weaponizing psychedelic drugs sprang from a 1949 report entitled "Psychochemical Warfare: A New Concept of War," written by L. Wilson Green, technical director of the Edgewood Arsenal Chemical and Radiological Laboratories (Kinzer, 2019). According to Green's theory, after exposure of the enemy population to LSD, mescaline, or another mind-altering drug, "Their will to resist would be weakened greatly, if not entirely destroyed, by the mass hysteria and panic which would ensue" (quoted in Kinzer, 2019, p. 36). For many years, the U.S. Army conducted secret experiments at the Edgewood Arsenal during which it exposed thousands of military volunteers to numerous compounds, including LSD and other powerful psychoactive drugs (Ketchum, 2006; Smith et al., 2014). One of the goals of these experiments was to find a chemical agent that could be dispersed in the battlefield, sparing enemy property and weapons, and (unlike nerve gases) incapacitating enemy soldiers without killing them. Another top-secret program, called MK-ULTRA, was instituted in the early 1950s by the Central Intelligence Agency (CIA). To test the effects of LSD on the behavioral reactions of unsuspecting participants, the CIA funded research in which hundreds of students from Harvard, MIT, and Emerson College were paid a small sum of money to drink a liquid that, according to the experimenter, might produce an altered state of consciousness. For the experimental group, the liquid contained a dose of LSD. This research led to ridiculous schemes in which LSD would be used to "attack" foreign leaders such as Fidel Castro and then Egyptian president Gamal Abdel Nasser. For Castro, the CIA proposed that an LSD-containing aerosol be sprayed into a radio studio from which he made regular broadcasts to the Cuban people (Kinzer, 2019). In theory, Castro's resulting disorientation and bizarre behavior would cause him to lose popular support. Ultimately, both the Army and CIA programs were disbanded as ineffective, and it appears that no psychochemical attacks were actually carried out.

Within the larger society, LSD's popularity exploded with the hippie culture of the 1960s. As part of their nonconformist, anti-Establishment attitudes, hippies openly sought mind expansion through the use of psychedelic drugs, especially LSD. However, the inevitable backlash soon occurred amid growing anecdotal accounts along with scientific reports of adverse reactions to the drug. A 1965 federal law greatly restricted new research on LSD, and soon thereafter Sandoz stopped distributing LSD for research purposes and recalled all of the existing drug that had previously been supplied to investigators. After a long period of inactivity, however, clinical research on LSD has begun to make a slow comeback. An organization called MAPS (Multidisciplinary Association for Psychedelic Studies) has been promoting new research on the potential psychotherapeutic applications of psychedelics (see the MAPS website at www.maps.org). Nevertheless, considering the general cultural and governmental attitudes toward LSD and other psychedelic drugs, more evidence must be obtained regarding the safety and efficacy of these compounds before they are widely accepted within mainstream psychiatric practice.

FIGURE 15.4 illustrates the timeline of notable events in the history of the "classic" psychedelic drugs, namely mescaline, LSD, and psilocybin, from the pre-scientific era up to 2017.

Recreational use of LSD was banned nationwide in 1967. Of course, LSD didn't disappear; it merely went underground. Indeed, in recent years, psychedelic drug use has increased as a new generation of young people has discovered these substances. According to the 2019 National Survey on Drug Use and Health, approximately 580,000 people aged 12 years or older were current (i.e., past month) users of LSD (Center for Behavioral Health Statistics and Quality, 2020). This figure is up by more than 25% compared to the previous year's results. LSD is active orally, and that is the standard mode of administration. The drug is so potent that a single dose in crystalline form is barely visible to the naked eye (see Box 15.1). Consequently, larger amounts of LSD representing many doses are usually dissolved in water, and then droplets containing single-dose units are applied to a sheet of paper (a "blotter") and dried. The paper is subsequently divided into individual squares, often decorated with fanciful designs, and sold as single-dose "tabs" to be swallowed by the user.

NBOMes A new class of synthetic psychedelics, the **N-benzylphenethylamines** (abbreviated **NBOMes**), appeared on the scene in 2010 (Halberstadt, 2017).

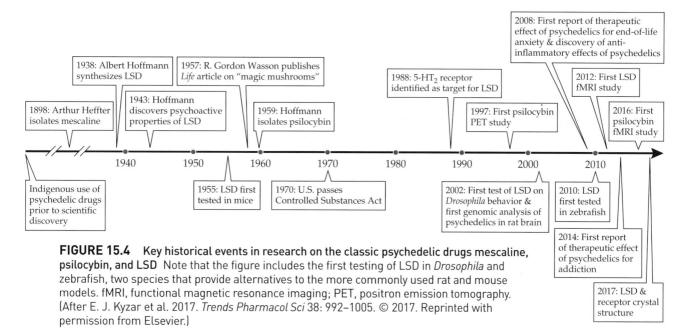

FIGURE 15.4 **Key historical events in research on the classic psychedelic drugs mescaline, psilocybin, and LSD** Note that the figure includes the first testing of LSD in *Drosophila* and zebrafish, two species that provide alternatives to the more commonly used rat and mouse models. fMRI, functional magnetic resonance imaging; PET, positron emission tomography. (After E. J. Kyzar et al. 2017. *Trends Pharmacol Sci* 38: 992–1005. © 2017. Reprinted with permission from Elsevier.)

The first member of the class, *N*-(2-methoxybenzyl)-2,5-dimethoxy-4-iodophenethylamine (**25I-NBOMe**), continues to be widely distributed. The *iodo* in the chemical name and the corresponding *I* in 25I-NBOMe refer to the presence of an iodine atom on the phenyl ring. Other NBOMes include 25B-NBOMe, which contains a bromine atom in place of the iodine, and 25C-NBOMe, which contains a chlorine atom. Like LSD, NBOMes may be distributed as single doses on blotter paper, or alternatively larger amounts can be obtained in powdered form. Because NBOMes are subject to first-pass metabolism when consumed orally, they are usually taken by the sublingual or buccal routes of administration by placing a piece of drug-infused blotter paper under the tongue or on the surface of the gum until the drug has been absorbed through the tissue membranes. Powdered drug can be taken by insufflation. NBOMes are very potent, which makes it easy for the user to overdose. Numerous cases of NBOMe toxicity have been reported, often with severe, even fatal, consequences. Toxic reactions to NBOMes are described later in the chapter.

SALVINORIN A *Salvia divinorum* is a member of the mint family native to Oaxaca, the same region of Mexico mentioned earlier with respect to psychedelic mushrooms (**FIGURE 15.5**). Indeed, the plant's psychoactive properties were first reported by Albert Hofmann, the discoverer of LSD, and Gordon Wasson, of "magic mushroom" fame (Casselman et al., 2014). Like psilocybin-containing mushrooms, *Salvia* was historically used in religious rituals by Mazatec shamans and then later attained the status of a recreational substance in Western countries such as the United States. Despite knowledge of *Salvia*'s properties and its recreational use, the Drug Enforcement Agency (DEA) has surprisingly not listed the herb in its Schedule of Controlled Substances. However, it is worth noting that sale or possession of *Salvia* is illegal in the majority of states.

An unusual compound called salvinorin A is the principal psychoactive ingredient in *Salvia* (Hernández-Alvarado et al., 2020). Recreational users may chew fresh *Salvia* leaves, smoke dried and crushed leaves, or consume a concentrated salvinorin A-containing extract either through sublingual and buccal absorption of a liquid preparation or by smoking a dried extract. Chewing *Salvia* leaves or placing a liquid extract under the tongue or into the cheek permits absorption of the compound through the oral mucosa. Few, if any, psychoactive effects are produced by swallowing *Salvia*, because the salvinorin A is inactivated in the gastrointestinal tract. On the other hand, the drug is quickly and effectively absorbed through the lungs when smoked, thereby yielding the most rapid and intense perceptual experience. As with

FIGURE 15.5 *Salvia divinorum*

DMT, the effects of smoking *Salvia* dissipate rapidly, typically within 15 minutes.

Consumption of *Salvia* typically produces vivid hallucinations, out-of-body experiences, and other feelings resembling but not identical to those produced by other psychedelic agents (see the chapter opener). Self-reported responses from an early study by Siebert (1994) including becoming a foreign object (e.g., a drawer, a pant leg, or a Ferris wheel); seeing some kind of two-dimensional surface, film, or membrane; experiencing various sensations of motion, pulling, or twisting; laughing uncontrollably; visiting places from the past, especially childhood; losing one's body and/or identity; and feeling that one is in several locations at once. Subsequent studies have reported that the subjective effects of *Salvia* overlap with, but are not identical to, those produced by LSD (González et al., 2006), DMT and psilocybin (Johnson et al., 2011), marijuana (Albertson and Grubbs, 2009), or the dissociative anesthetic ketamine (Dalgarno, 2007) (see the PCP and Ketamine section below). This diversity has led to the view that *Salvia* has a unique psychoactive profile (MacLean et al., 2013).

IBOGAINE   Yet another plant with psychedelic properties is the West African iboga shrub, *Tabernanthe iboga* (**FIGURE 15.6**). African users of iboga typically dry the roots and bark of the shrub and then either chew thin strips of the material or grind it into a powder for consumption. Low doses primarily act as a psychostimulant, increasing energy, reducing hunger, and producing a euphoric feeling. In contrast, high doses elicit a profound psychedelic effect characterized by a dream-like or trance-like state, with visual and auditory hallucinations, altered time perception, and ataxia (Alper, 2001; Underwood et al., 2021). The psychedelic properties of iboga play an important role in ceremonies of the African Bwiti and Mbiri religions, where ingestion of the plant is used to create a near-death experience.

Iboga was introduced to Europe in the mid-19th century when specimens of the plant were brought back to France. Numerous alkaloidal compounds are present within iboga, with ibogaine being the principal psychoactive ingredient. Pure ibogaine was first isolated in 1901, which allowed the later development of this drug as a medication. Indeed, between 1939 and 1970 ibogaine was marketed in France as a stimulant and antidepressant medication under the trade name Lamberène (Alper, 2001). Although ibogaine is sometimes used recreationally for its psychedelic properties, it is better known as a potential therapeutic agent for treating drug addiction. This property of the drug was discovered serendipitously by Howard Lotsof in 1962. Then 19 years old and already a heroin addict, Lotsof was given a dose of the drug by a friend who thought he would find the experience interesting. After a long "trip" complete with vivid hallucinations and insights into his life, Lotsof seemed to emerge without any heroin withdrawal symptoms despite having gone through more than a day without a "fix." He further reported an absence of subsequent heroin craving, suggesting that his addiction had somehow been abruptly terminated by his ibogaine experience (Wasko et al., 2018). Lotsof became a lifelong advocate for ibogaine therapy to treat drug addiction. As part of his work, he founded the Global Ibogaine Therapy Alliance, a not-for-profit organization "dedicated to supporting the sacramental and therapeutic uses of iboga" (www.ibogainealliance.org).

Notwithstanding the efforts of Lotsof (who died in 2010) and other ibogaine advocates, the drug is not currently an FDA-approved medication, nor is it legal for recreational use since it was given a Schedule I designation by the DEA in 1970. Nevertheless, sufficient research has been conducted to suggest that careful administration of ibogaine under controlled conditions can have beneficial effects in counteracting opioid withdrawal symptoms and drug craving, and the drug

FIGURE 15.6   Iboga shrub

may additionally help promote abstinence in other substance use disorders (Alper and Lotsof, 2007; Schenberg et al., 2014; Corkery, 2018; Mash et al., 2018). Ibogaine must be used cautiously because of toxic reactions that have led to a number of fatal reactions (Corkery, 2018). For this reason, some researchers are seeking to develop non-hallucinogenic, non-toxic analogs of ibogaine that retain the parent compound's therapeutic potential (see, for example, Cameron et al., 2021).

Basic pharmacology of psychedelic drugs

The chemical structures of psychedelic drugs, their potency and time course of action, and the psychological and physiological responses they produce are well characterized. Researchers have also obtained considerable information about the mechanisms of action of psychedelic agents, although the story is not yet complete.

COMPARISONS OF DRUG POTENCY AND TIME COURSE

One way of comparing the potency of various psychedelic drugs is to consider the typical doses taken by recreational users. Common dose ranges for LSD, 25I-NBOMe, psilocybin, mescaline, DMT, salvinorin A, and ibogaine are presented in **TABLE 15.1**. You can see that these compounds vary widely in their potency, with LSD as the most potent and ibogaine and mescaline as the least potent. All of the drugs that are taken orally have a fairly similar time course of action. Depending on the dose and when the user last ate, the psychedelic effects of these substances generally begin within 30 to 90 minutes following ingestion. An LSD or mescaline "trip" typically lasts for 6 to 12 hours or even longer, whereas the effects of psilocybin-containing mushrooms may dissipate a bit sooner. The effects of NBOMes persist for 3 to 10 hours, depending on the dose and route of administration. Ibogaine ingestion produces an initial dream-like hallucinatory state that lasts 4 to 8 hours, followed by a more contemplative experience that may continue for another 8 to 20 hours. In contrast to these long time periods, the effects of smoked DMT and *Salvia*

are felt within seconds, reach a peak over the next few minutes, and are over within an hour or less.

PSYCHOLOGICAL AND PHYSIOLOGICAL RESPONSES

Having already given a description of some of the subjective experiences produced by psychedelic mushrooms and *Salvia*, here we will focus on the psychological and physiological responses associated with the prototypical psychedelic agents LSD and psilocybin. The core effects of these substances are similar across most psychedelic drugs even though some responses may be drug-specific.

The state of intoxication produced by LSD and other psychedelics is usually called a "trip," presumably because users are taking a mental journey to a place different from their normal conscious awareness. The LSD trip can be divided into four phases: (1) onset, (2) plateau, (3) peak, and (4) "comedown." Trip onset occurs about 30 minutes to an hour after ingestion. Visual effects begin to occur, with intensification of colors and the appearance of geometric patterns or strange objects that can be seen even with closed eyes. The next 2 hours of the trip represent the plateau phase, during which the subjective sense of time begins to slow and the visual effects become more intense. The peak phase generally begins after about 3 hours and lasts for another 2 or 3 hours. During this phase, users feel as if they're in another world in which time has been suspended. They see a continuous stream of bizarre, distorted images that may be either beautiful or menacing. Users may experience **synesthesia**, a crossing-over of sensations in which, for example, colors are "heard" and sounds are "felt." The peak is followed by the comedown, a phase lasting 2 hours or longer, depending on the dose. Most of the drug effects are gone by the end of the comedown, although the user may still not feel completely normal until the following day. In addition to the sensory–perceptual effects just described, psychedelic drugs produce a wide variety of other psychological changes, including feelings of depersonalization, emotional shifts to a euphoric or to an anxious and fearful state, and disruption of logical thought.

A psychedelic trip as a whole may be experienced either as mystical and spiritually enlightening (a "good trip") or as disturbing and frightening (a "bad trip"). Whether the user has a good or a bad trip depends in part on the dose; the individual's personality, expectations, and previous drug experiences; and the physical and social setting (Preller and Vollenweider, 2016). But even in the best of circumstances, it is impossible to predict the outcome of an LSD trip.

Scientific studies investigating the influence of psychedelics on mental state often rely on psychometric instruments developed to quantify the effects of these compounds. Two prominent

---

TABLE 15.1   Route of Administration and Potency of Various Psychedelic Drugs

Drug	Usual route of administration	Typical dose range
Mescaline	Oral	200–500 mg
Psilocybin	Oral	10–20 mg
LSD	Oral	50–100 µg (0.05–0.10 mg)
DMT	Smoking	20–50 mg
25I-NBOMe	Sublingual/buccal	250–800 µg (0.25–0.80 mg)
Salvinorin A	Smoking	200–1,000 µg (0.2–1.0 mg)
Ibogaine	Oral	500–800 mg

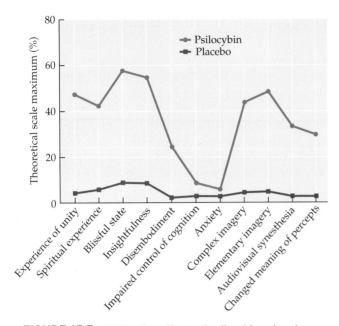

FIGURE 15.7 Subjective effects of psilocybin using the 11 subdimensions of the five-dimension Altered States of Consciousness (ASC) rating scale The graph shows that psilocybin (0.2 mg/kg) exerted significant subjective effects on all subdimensions of this psychological instrument except for "impaired control of cognition" and "anxiety." (After A. L. Halberstadt. 2015. *Behav Brain Res* 277: 99–120. © 2014. Reprinted with permission from Elsevier.)

examples are the **Altered States of Consciousness (ASC) rating scale**, which was introduced by Dittrich (1998), and Strassman's **Hallucinogen Rating Scale** (Strassman et al., 1994). The following five primary dimensions make up the ASC scale: oceanic boundlessness, ego-disintegration anxiety, visionary restructuralization, reduced vigilance, and auditory alterations (Dittrich, 1998; Vollenweider and Kometer, 2010). *Oceanic boundlessness* refers to derealization and loss of ego boundaries (i.e., feeling one

with the world), which corresponds closely to the positive mystical experiences often reported by psychedelic drug users. In contrast, the ego-disintegration anxiety dimension includes drug-induced thought disorder as well as negative emotional responses to the loss of ego boundaries. Dittrich (1998) likened this dimension to the experience of a "bad trip" on the part of the user. *Visionary restructuralization* refers to distortions of visual perception, including visual illusions, hallucinations, and visual synesthesias. The last two dimensions, reduced vigilance and auditory alterations (including auditory hallucinations), do not occur with all psychedelic drugs and are considered less important items in the ASC scale.

The five primary dimensions of the ASC rating scale can be further divided into subdimensions to provide more detailed information on drug-induced reactions. **FIGURE 15.7** shows the subjective responses to a moderate dose of psilocybin compared with placebo, measured using 11 subdimensions of the five-dimension ASC (Halberstadt, 2015). At this dose, the drug produced particularly strong effects on the categories "blissful state" and "insightfulness" but little or no effect on "impaired control of cognition" or "anxiety."

Besides their psychological effects, psychedelics also give rise to various physiological responses. For LSD, these responses consist of pupil dilation and small increases in heart rate, blood pressure, and body temperature, all of which reflect activation of the sympathetic nervous system. LSD use can also lead to dizziness, nausea, and vomiting, although such reactions are more likely to occur after consumption of peyote or psilocybin-containing mushrooms.

CHEMICAL STRUCTURES Most psychedelic drugs have either a serotonin-like or a catecholamine-like structure. The serotonin-like, or indoleamine, psychedelics include LSD, psilocybin, psilocin, DMT, 5-MeO-DMT, ibogaine, and the synthetic tryptamines mentioned earlier. When the 5-HT molecule is oriented in the proper manner, it is easy to see how its basic structure is incorporated into the structures of these psychedelic compounds (**FIGURE 15.8**). Studies in the early 1950s by

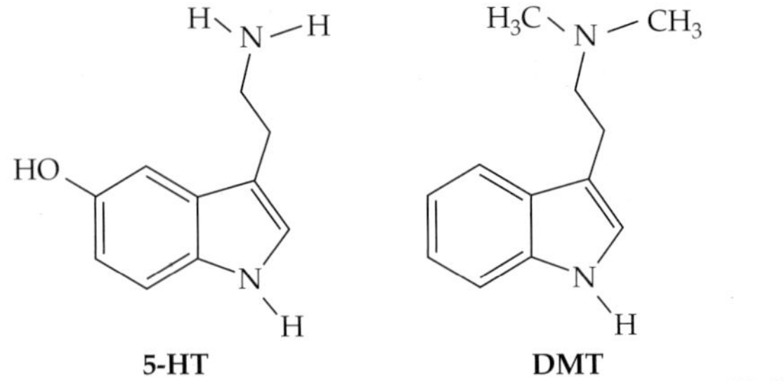

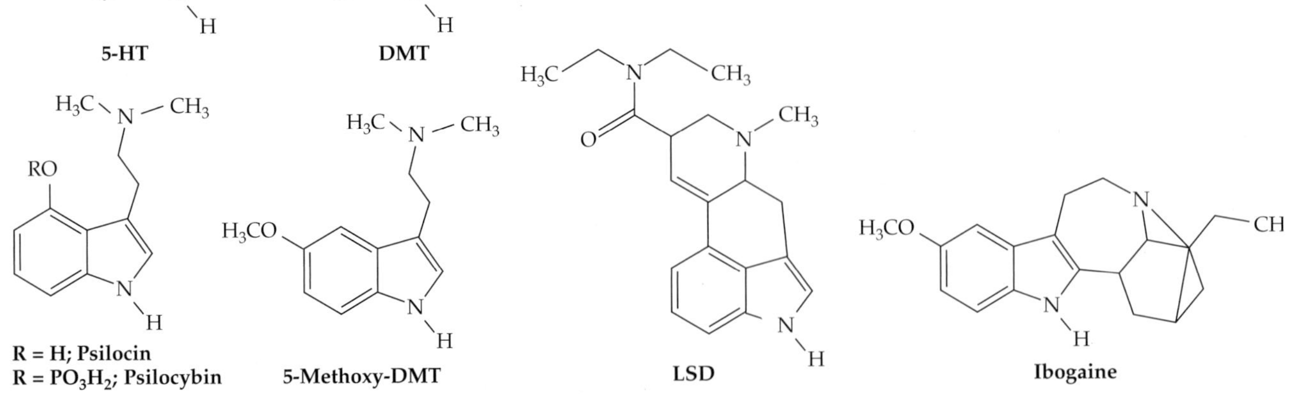

FIGURE 15.8 Structures of 5-HT and the indoleamine psychedelics

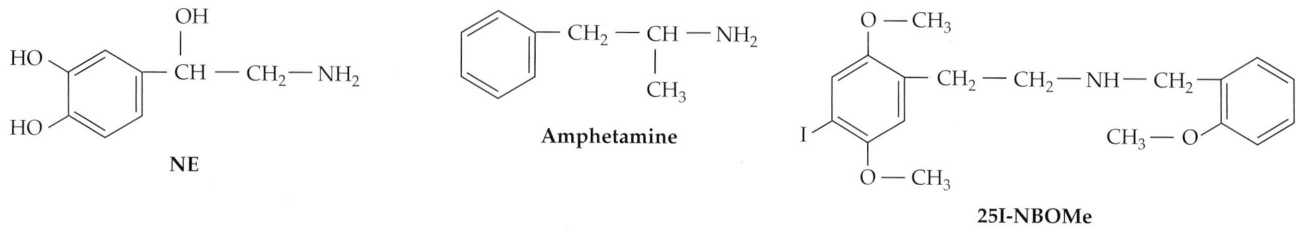

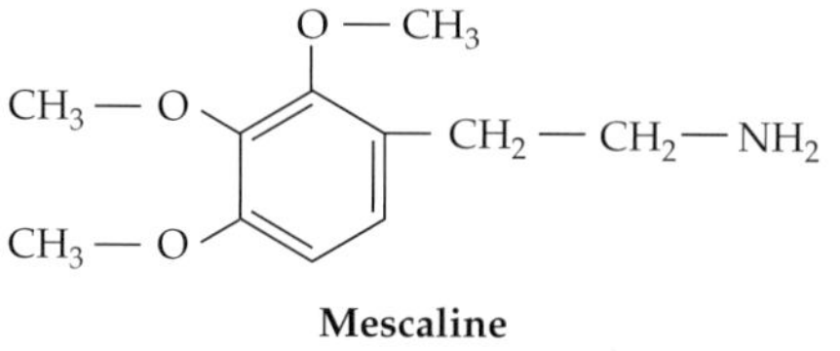

FIGURE 15.9 Structures of NE and the phenethylamine psychedelics

John Gaddum in Scotland and by Edward Wooley and David Shaw in the United States led to the conclusion that LSD works by antagonizing the action of 5-HT in the brain. We shall see in the next section that LSD can be understood more as an agonist than as an antagonist of the serotonergic system. Nevertheless, the linking of 5-HT with such a powerful psychoactive drug as LSD brought this recently discovered neurotransmitter into the forefront of behavioral and psychiatric research—a place that it continues to hold to the present day.

Of the psychedelics covered in this chapter, only mescaline and the NBOMes have a catecholamine-like structure. As shown in **FIGURE 15.9**, mescaline and 25I-NBOMe are structurally related to the neurotransmitter norepinephrine (NE) and also to the psychostimulant amphetamine. Indeed, amphetamine can produce hallucinations with prolonged administration of high doses, and several amphetamine analogs such as 2,5-dimethoxy-4-methylamphetamine (DOM, also known as "STP") and 3,4,5-trimethoxyamphetamine (TMA) possess even greater hallucinogenic properties. Mescaline, the NBOMes, DOM, and TMA are known as **phenethylamine** psychedelics.

The most unusual psychedelic compound both structurally and functionally is salvinorin A, which chemically is known as a neoclerodane diterpene (**FIGURE 15.10**). Also shown is a related drug called ketocyclazocine, which has a similar mechanism of action as salvinorin A and can also induce powerful perceptual effects.* The shared mechanism of action of these compounds is discussed in a later section.

---

*Although ketocyclazocine has psychedelic properties, it also produces extreme dysphoria when ingested and, therefore, is not used recreationally.

NEUROCHEMICAL ACTIONS OF INDOLEAMINE AND PHENETHYLAMINE PSYCHEDELICS The neurochemical mechanisms through which psychedelic drugs produce their dramatic perceptual and cognitive effects have been investigated using in vitro molecular and biochemical approaches (e.g., receptor binding and second-messenger signaling studies), genetic approaches (e.g., testing of gene knockout mice), pharmacological approaches (e.g., receptor antagonist studies) in humans given psychedelic drugs, and animal model studies. Regarding the latter, psychedelic-like drug effects are studied in rodents primarily using either the head-twitch response (a behavior induced in mice by almost all known psychedelic drugs; see **FIGURE 15.11A**) or drug discrimination tests in which rats or mice are first trained on a classical psychedelic like LSD and then challenged with varying doses of a test compound to determine whether generalization to the LSD interoceptive cue occurs at any of the administered doses (Kyzar et al., 2017; also see Chapter 4 for more information on the drug discrimination paradigm). **FIGURE 15.11B** depicts a dose–response function for 25I-NBOMe to elicit the head-twitch response. Note that a dose of 0.3 mg/kg elicited nearly a peak response, thus demonstrating the high potency of this compound.

Receptor binding studies in the 1960s were among the first to suggest an involvement of the serotonergic system in the actions of both the indoleamine (except for ibogaine) and phenethylamine psychedelics. This

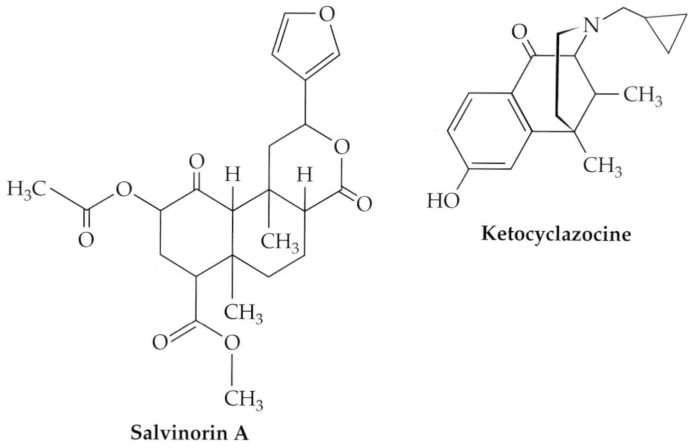

FIGURE 15.10 Structures of salvinorin A and ketocyclazocine

FIGURE 15.11   Dose-dependent stimulation of the head-twitch response in mice (A) The head-twitch response consists of rapid side-to-side movement of the animal's head. (B) Male C57BL/6J mice were injected subcutaneously with varying doses of 25I-NBOMe or saline (0 dose). The total number of head-twitch responses (HTR) was recorded over a 30-minute period. (A after A. L. Halberstadt and M. A. Geyer. 2014. *Neuropharmacology* 77: 200–207; B after A. L. Halberstadt. 2017. *Curr Topics Behav Neurosci* 32: 283–311; A. L. Halberstadt and M. A. Geyer. 2014. *Neuropharmacology* 77: 200–207.)

(A) Head-twitch response

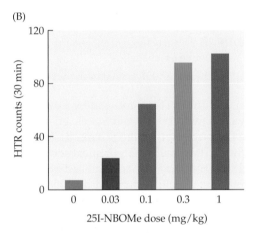

discovery was extremely important at the time, since psychedelics were then being explored as models for understanding the biochemical events underlying psychotic disorders. However, the receptor binding results were complicated, particularly in the case of LSD. This compound was found to bind with relatively high affinity to eight different serotonergic receptor subtypes: 5-HT_{1A}, 5-HT_{1B}, 5-HT_{1D}, 5-HT_{2A}, $5\text{-HT}_{2}C$, 5-HT_{5A}, 5-HT_{6}, and 5-HT_{7} (Nichols, 2004). Other classical indoleamine psychedelic drugs such as psilocybin (psilocin) and DMT similarly possess a relatively nonselective serotonergic receptor binding profile. On the other hand, the phenethylamine compounds, including mescaline, DOM, and the NBOMes, only bind with high affinity to the class of 5-HT_2 receptors. Finally, the key 5-HT receptor subtype was identified as the 5-HT_{2A} receptor based on abolition of psychedelic-like behaviors in 5-HT_{2A} knockout mice and loss of subjective effects in humans given the 5-HT_{2A} receptor antagonist ketanserin prior to LSD, psilocybin, or DMT administration (Nichols, 2016; Vollenweider and Preller, 2020). A recent brain imaging study provided additional support for this view by showing a strong relationship between neocortical 5-HT_{2A} receptor occupancy and subjective psychedelic intensity rating in people given psilocybin (Madsen et al., 2019) (**FIGURE 15.12**).

Since its discovery, researchers have been puzzled about why LSD is so potent and why an LSD "trip" lasts so long. Drug molecules typically bind rather loosely to their receptors, thereby requiring more drug molecules to produce a biological effect and curtailing the length of time during which the effect is manifested. This mystery was finally solved by researchers at the University of North Carolina who, in a heroic series of experiments, were able to visualize the structure of LSD bound to the human 5-HT_{2A} receptor. What the researchers discovered is that when the drug binds to its target, a kind of "lid" formed by part of the receptor protein closes over the binding pocket, thus temporarily trapping the drug in place (Wacker et al., 2017; also see commentary by Chen and Tesmer, 2017). This type of discovery attests to the power of contemporary pharmacological methods for understanding the mechanisms of drug action on the brain.

Despite the evidence for 5-HT_{2A} receptor activation being necessary for psychedelic activity, a significant problem had to be overcome. The problem is that certain

drugs such as the LSD-like compound lisuride also activate 5-HT_{2A} receptors but *do not* have psychedelic properties. How can this be? Researchers hypothesize that distinct signaling pathways may underlie this difference. This can occur, for example, if the receptor forms multi-protein complexes either with itself (homomeric complexes) or with a different kind of receptor (heteromeric complexes as discussed in Chapter 13 with respect to adenosine A_{2A} and dopamine D_2 receptor interactions). In the present case, it appears that (1) the 5-HT_{2A} receptor can complex with the metabotropic glutamate receptor mGluR2, (2) formation of this complex alters the receptor's second-messenger signaling pathways, and (3) these events are necessary for psychedelic activity of 5-HT_{2A} agonists (González-Maeso et al., 2007, 2008; Moreno et al., 2011). Other features of 5-HT_{2A} receptor signaling may also be involved in the production of psychedelic drug effects, but those are beyond the scope of this chapter (López-Giménez and González-Maeso, 2018).

The emphasis on 5-HT_{2A} receptor activation does not preclude the involvement of other molecular targets of psychedelic drug action, even for the above-mentioned compounds. Zamberlan and co-workers (2018) related the binding properties of 18 different compounds, including mescaline, psilocin, LSD, DMT, 25I-NBOMe, and ibogaine, to the reported subjective effects of each drug. While the importance of 5-HT_{2A} receptor affinity was confirmed in most

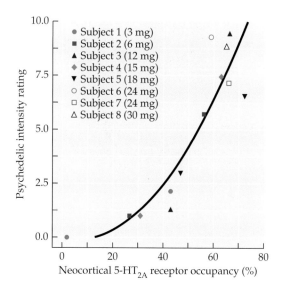

FIGURE 15.12   Relationship between the intensity of subjective psychedelic effects and neocortical 5-HT$_{2A}$ receptor occupancy in subjects given psilocybin   Subjects were administered a single oral dose of psilocybin ranging from 3 to 30 mg. Approximately 1 hour later, the subjects underwent an initial 2-hour positron emission tomography (PET) scan using the radioligand [^{11}C]Cimbi-36. Subjects 1 through 5 were scanned a second time later in the day (thereby contributing two data points to the figure), whereas subjects 6 through 8 had only the first PET scan (thereby contributing only a single data point). Each subject's subjective rating of psychedelic intensity was assessed during the scans, with intensity scores ranging from 0 to 10. The figure plots the relationship between psychedelic intensity rating and peak neocortical 5-HT$_{2A}$ receptor occupancy using the individual data points as well as the statistically generated best-fit curve. (After M. K. Madsen et al. 2019. *Neuropsychopharmacology* 44: 1328–1334.)

cases (though not for ibogaine), the results suggested that activity at other target sites likely contributes to psychoactivity of many indoleamine and phenethylamine psychedelic agents. Indeed, an earlier study by Marona-Lewicka and colleagues (2005) demonstrated dual discriminative stimulus properties of LSD, with one stimulus component produced by the expected activation of 5-HT$_{2A}$ receptors but a second component produced by D$_2$ receptor activation.

NEUROCHEMICAL ACTIONS OF SALIVORIN A AND IBOGAINE   As mentioned earlier, the mechanism of action of salvinorin A differs significantly from that of the indoleamine and phenethylamine psychedelic agents. Salvinorin A has little effect on 5-HT$_{2A}$ or any other 5-HT receptors. Instead, this compound, along with the previously mentioned ketocyclazocine, is a potent agonist at the κ-opioid receptor (Cunningham et al., 2011). Positron emission tomographic (PET) imaging of rats given salvinorin A confirmed significant occupancy by that drug of brain κ-opioid receptors (Placzek et al., 2015). Moreover, in humans the subjective and physiological effects produced by inhalation of vaporized salvinorin A were blocked by the general opioid receptor antagonist naltrexone but not by the 5-HT$_{2A}$ antagonist ketanserin (Maqueda et al., 2016). These results confirm that the responses to salvinorin A are mediated by κ-opioid receptor activation, and they further account for the dissimilarities in the drug's subjective properties compared to those associated with the indoleamine and phenethylamine psychedelics. The sites in the brain responsible for salvinorin A's perceptual effects are not known; however, Maqueda and colleagues (2015) have proposed involvement of the thalamus, temporal cortex, parietal cortex, and claustrum (a thin sheet of neurons beneath the cortex), all of which express high levels of κ-opioid receptors.

Based on their receptor binding properties, ibogaine and its bioactive metabolite noribogaine also have an unusual mechanism of action. Both compounds have very low affinity for the 5-HT$_{2A}$ receptor, but like salvinorin A, they bind to κ-opioid receptors where they exert partial agonist activity. Other potential contributors to ibogaine's psychoactive effects are partial agonist activity at the μ-opioid receptor, NMDA receptor antagonism, and inhibition of 5-HT and DA reuptake (Wasko et al., 2018).

Neurobiology of psychedelic drugs: neural circuitry, therapeutic applications, and adverse reactions

NEURAL CIRCUITRY   We have discussed that 5-HT$_{2A}$ receptor activation is necessary for the psychedelic effects of indoleamine and phenethylamine compounds; however, this information alone does not tell us *where* the critical receptors are located or *how* activation of these receptors produces the sensory and cognitive distortions experienced during a "trip." The key 5-HT$_{2A}$ receptor-expressing neurons have been termed a "trigger population" whose excitation begins a cascade of cellular events that culminate in the psychedelic experience (Kyzar et al., 2017). This trigger population is thought to consist of pyramidal neurons located in layer 5 of the prefrontal cortex (PFC) and other cortical areas that are dually excited by 5-HT$_{2A}$ receptor activation and by AMPA and NMDA receptor activation elicited by glutamate release from other pyramidal neurons located in the deep cortical layers (**FIGURE 15.13**). Excitation of these layer 5 pyramidal neurons in the PFC along with other 5-HT$_{2A}$ receptor-expressing cells not shown in the figure disrupts the functioning of a cortico-striatal-thalamo-cortical loop necessary for the gating of sensory and cognitive input from subcortical to cortical areas, thereby resulting in the subjective and cognitive distortions associated with a "trip" (Calvey and Howells, 2018; Vollenweider and Preller, 2020).

Recent functional magnetic resonance imaging (fMRI) and electroencephalography (EEG) studies have yielded additional information about how regional brain

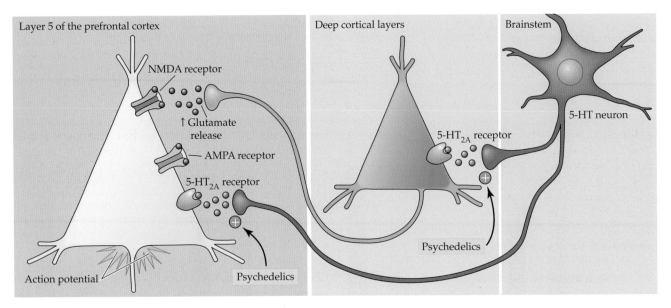

FIGURE 15.13 Simplified model of the cellular mechanism of action of indoleamine and phenethylamine psychedelics Activation of 5-HT$_{2A}$ receptors is necessary for the subjective effects of indoleamine and phenethylamine psychedelic agents. The key ("trigger") neurons are believed to be pyramidal cells in cortical layer 5 of the PFC that are directly stimulated by activation of 5-HT$_{2A}$ receptors on the cells themselves and are secondarily stimulated by glutamate released from other 5-HT$_{2A}$ receptor–bearing pyramidal cells in the deep cortical layers that project to layer 5. (After F. X. Vollenweider and M. Kometer. 2010. *Nat Rev Neurosci* 11: 642–651. doi.org/10.1038/nrn2884)

activity is altered during the psychedelic drug experience (reviewed in Calvey and Howells, 2018; Müller and Borgwardt, 2019; Vollenweider and Preller, 2020). The results of this research have been analyzed using two different approaches. One approach has been to determine how psychedelics alter activity *within* different neural circuits or networks. The most consistent finding from this approach is reduced activity within the default mode network (DMN), a neural network that is active when subjects are in a resting state (i.e., not performing a cognitive task) and engaged in mental wandering or self-related thinking. LSD (Müller et al., 2018), psilocybin (Carhart-Harris et al., 2012), and ayahuasca (Palhano-Fontes et al., 2015) have all been reported to reduce DMN activity, suggesting that this is a common feature of psychedelic agents that act through 5-HT$_{2A}$ receptor stimulation. Activity within the DMN is also decreased during meditation (Brewer et al., 2011), indicating a feature in common with the psychedelic experience.

The second approach to investigating the influence of psychedelic drugs on regional brain activity has been to determine changes *between* brain regions or networks, particularly with respect to the functional connectivity* of these regions or networks. Based on this approach, Vollenweider and Preller (2020) proposed a working model in which psychedelic agents cause increased connectivity among sensory cortical areas and between those areas and other brain regions (especially the thalamus), increased connectivity between the thalamus and the ventral striatum and posterior cingulate cortex (PCC), and decreased connectivity between association cortices and thalamus. Together, these changes are hypothesized to cause enhanced processing of sensory inputs, less integrative cortical information processing, and reduced gating (filtering) of sensory inputs by the thalamus, as mentioned in the previous paragraph. Note that because the studies on which the model is based were performed using LSD or psilocybin as the psychedelic drug, it is possible that non-classical psychedelics like salvinorin A or ibogaine produce somewhat different results because of the differences in their neurochemical mechanisms of action.

THERAPEUTIC APPLICATIONS   The earliest mentions in the medical literature of potential therapeutic benefits of psychedelic drugs begin with mescaline in the late nineteenth and early twentieth centuries (reviewed in Rucker et al., 2018). However, by the mid-20th century, attention turned away from mescaline and toward the new "wonder drug" LSD, which was being supplied by Sandoz free of charge to psychiatrists around the world. In their 1979 book *Psychedelic Drugs Reconsidered*, Grinspoon and Bakalar state that over 1000 clinical articles were published between 1950 and the mid-1960s discussing the treatment of roughly 40,000 patients with psychedelic drug therapy. Early

*"Functional" connectivity is determined by measuring the activity of multiple brain regions simultaneously (e.g., by fMRI or EEG) and then correlating those measurements between regions. Stated another way, functional connectivity is an index of the degree of synchronization of activity between brain regions. High functional connectivity between two areas is often taken to imply that the areas directly communicate with each other (e.g., synaptically), but because the data are correlational in nature, this conclusion remains speculative until there is confirmation of the suspected anatomical link.

claims touted the efficacy of LSD in treating alcohol dependence, along with many other disorders (Grinspoon and Bakalar, 1979). Interestingly, Bill Wilson, the founder of Alcoholics Anonymous, tried LSD himself and subsequently became a proponent of taking LSD to help overcome alcoholism (Nutt, 2019). Although most of the early information on LSD and alcoholism was based on uncontrolled/poorly controlled clinical trials or anecdotal reports like Wilson's, six randomized controlled trials involving a single dose of LSD in conjunction with individual or group psychotherapy were performed and the results published between 1966 and 1970. Krebs and Johansen (2012) subsequently performed a meta-analysis of these six trials and reported that the single LSD exposure was associated with a significant reduction in alcohol misuse for up to 6 months after the treatment. This effect is at least comparable, if not superior, to the results typically obtained with FDA-approved medications such as naltrexone, acamprosate, or disulfiram (see Chapter 10).

Therapeutic use of psychedelic drugs was quickly abandoned when LSD and other psychedelics were given a Schedule I designation in the 1970 Schedule of Controlled Substances (see Chapter 9). However, a renewed interest in exploring the potential benefits of these substances began to emerge in the 1990s, both in the United States and abroad. David Nutt, a British pharmacologist and psychedelic researcher, attributes this change to two major factors: (1) the application of modern neuroscience tools such as fMRI to investigate the neural mechanisms of psychedelic drug action, and (2) new findings showing long-lasting psychological benefits of a single psychedelic drug exposure in healthy participants (Nutt, 2019). For example, Griffiths and colleagues at Johns Hopkins University studied a group of adults who had not had previous psychedelic drug exposure but had routinely engaged in activities of a spiritual or religious nature. The study used a randomized, double-blind, crossover design in which the participants were given two 8-hour experimental sessions, separated by a 2-month interval, in which either psilocybin or methylphenidate was administered in a psychotherapeutic setting. Half the participants received psilocybin (30 mg/70 kg given orally) during the first session and methylphenidate (40 mg/70 kg given orally) during the second session as an active, non-psychedelic drug control. The other half received the same drugs but in the reverse order. Follow-up reactions to psilocybin or methylphenidate were tested at 2 months after the initial drug session and before the second session had been conducted. After unblinding about the identity of the psilocybin and methylphenidate sessions, all but one participant reported that psilocybin had produced "the most pronounced changes in [their] ordinary mental processes." At 14 months after psilocybin administration, those participants were retested on the same measures as the initial 2-month tests. **FIGURE 15.14** shows that experiencing a single moderate dose of psilocybin was personally and spiritually meaningful to more than half of the participants, and that participants additionally attributed increased personal well-being and positive behavior change to their psilocybin experience (Griffiths et al., 2008). Furthermore, participant ratings of long-term personal or spiritual meaningfulness of the psilocybin session were positively correlated with their responses on the Hood Mysticism Scale (Hood, 1975), which was administered near the end of the session. This scale was originally devised to quantify mystical religious experiences but has since also been used in psychedelic drug research. Other studies have confirmed that exposure to a psychedelic drug under controlled

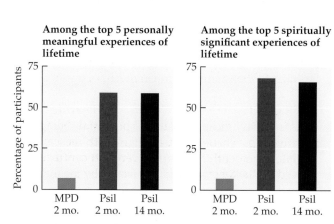
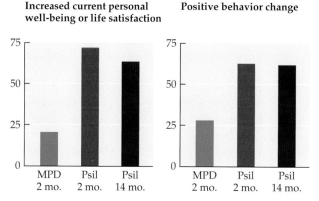

FIGURE 15.14 **Two- and 14-month responses of participants to their experience with a single dose of psilocybin (Psil) or methylphenidate (MPD)** Two months after a single session with one or the other drug, more than half of the participants reported that their Psil session was among the top five personally or spiritually meaningful experiences of their life. A much smaller percentage reported this reaction to their session with MPD. Psil was also associated with increased personal well-being and positive behavior change, both at 2 months and again at 14-month follow-up. See text for experimental details. (After R. R. Griffiths et al. 2008. *J Psychopharmacol* 22: 621–632.)

conditions can lead to positive long-term changes in mood, personality, well-being, mindfulness, and spirituality (Ada et al., 2020).

Contemporary research investigating the therapeutic use of psychedelic drugs is performed with careful attention to patient selection and the therapeutic setting (Tupper et al., 2015). Sessions are conducted in quiet treatment facilities designed to have a pleasant and relaxing ambience. At least one, if not two, therapists are present at all times during the period of drug action. However, instead of interacting with the therapist(s) as in a typical psychotherapy session, patients are asked to turn their attention inward during the session. These measures are designed to maximize the likelihood of therapeutic benefit while minimizing the possibility of an adverse reaction to the treatment.

The theoretical underpinnings of psychedelic drug therapy can be related to the time course of the drug's subjective effects (**FIGURE 15.15**). The first important component of the therapeutic process is the **peak experience**, which is the desired subjective state during the period of drug action. Pahnke and coworkers (1970) describe six elements of the peak psychedelic experience: "(1) sense of unity or oneness…, (2) transcendence of time and space, (3) deeply felt positive mood (joy, peace, and love), (4) sense of awesomeness, reverence, and wonder, (5) meaningfulness of psychological or philosophical insight or both; and (6) ineffability (sense of difficulty in communicating the experience by verbal description)" (p. 1857). The goal of the therapist(s) is to assist the patient in reaching and maintaining a peak experience. If this is accomplished, then the session may be followed by an **afterglow** lasting days to weeks. The features of this second therapeutic component are described as follows: "Mood is elevated and energetic; there is a relative freedom from concerns of the past and from guilt and anxiety, and the disposition and capacity to enter into close relationships is enhanced" (Pahnke et al., 1970, p. 1858).

Psychedelic drug therapy is currently being explored for treating a variety of conditions, including major depression (especially for patients who have not responded to standard antidepressant medications), anxiety disorders, obsessive-compulsive disorder (OCD), post-traumatic stress disorder (PTSD), substance use disorders, and the stress of dealing with a life-threatening illness such as cancer. Recent meta-analyses have demonstrated beneficial effects of psychedelic-assisted therapy (mostly using the classical serotonergic psychedelics psilocybin, LSD, or ayahuasca) on depression and anxiety in patients with a mood disorder or with a cancer diagnosis (Goldberg et al., 2020; Luoma et al., 2020; Vargas et al., 2020; Galvão-Coelho et al., 2021). **WEB BOX 15.1** presents four published case studies recounting the experiences of cancer patients who benefited from psilocybin-assisted psychotherapy. Researchers have additionally reported therapeutic benefits of psychedelic agents in other disorders such as OCD and substance use disorders (Nutt, 2019). While PTSD has not been extensively investigated with the drugs covered in this chapter, severe cases of this disorder have been successfully treated with the serotonergic compound 3,4-methylenedioxymethamphetamine (MDMA), a topic that is discussed in Chapter 6.

Interestingly, outside of the above-mentioned controlled clinical studies of psychedelic-assisted therapy, some people regularly consume very low doses of a psychedelic drug (e.g., 5% to 10% of the standard dose), most often LSD or psilocybin, in a practice called "microdosing." Stated motivations for microdosing include self-medication for mental or physical health problems (similar to cannabinoid self-medication), cognitive enhancement, personal/spiritual growth, or simply experiencing a pleasurable reaction (Lea et al., 2020). Some research has already been conducted to assess the potential benefits as well as risks of psychedelic microdosing, but many questions remain (Kuypers et al., 2019; Kuypers, 2020). In particular, we don't yet know whether repeated psychedelic drug exposure is safe, even at very low doses.

To advance the field of psychedelic-assisted therapy, investigators need to determine both the factors that

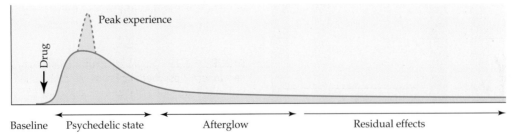

FIGURE 15.15 Hypothesized time course of the therapeutic effects elicited by psychedelic drugs According to Majić and coworkers, the potential therapeutic actions of psychedelic drugs encompass several different stages of subjective experience, beginning with an acute "psychedelic state" that lasts from minutes to hours, followed by an "afterglow" that lasts from days to weeks, and, if successful, a long-term stage of "residual effects" on the patient's mood and cognitive set. The greatest likelihood of success is thought to be associated with elicitation of an intense "peak experience" during the acute stage. (After T. Majić et al. 2015. *J Psychopharmacol* 29: 241–253.)

predict a strong therapeutic response and the mechanisms underlying that response. A recent review by Romeo and colleagues (2021) concluded that the best predictor of a good therapeutic outcome was the intensity of the psychedelic experience, regardless of whether the patient was being treated for a mood disorder or a substance use disorder. The patient's experience can be influenced by many variables, including the dose of the drug, competence of the therapist, quality of the therapeutic environment, personality traits of the patient (e.g., mindfulness, spirituality, or openness to new experiences), and the patient's expectancies. Mechanistically, there is an emerging hypothesis that the antidepressant actions of classical serotonergic psychedelic agents are mediated, at least in part, by a rapid process of glutamate-dependent neural plasticity (recall the psychedelic drug–related cortical glutamate release described earlier) resulting in increased dendritic complexity, dendritic spine outgrowth, and synapse formation (Ly et al., 2018; **FIGURE 15.16**). Psychedelics and other psychoactive drugs that cause rapid structural and functional changes in the brain have come to be called "psychoplastogens" (Ly et al., 2018; Benko and Vranková, 2020).

In summary, a growing number of studies suggest that psychedelic-assisted therapy may have significant benefits for patients suffering from depressive or anxiety symptoms. However, it will likely be some time before this becomes a "mainstream" approach within the fields of psychiatry and psychotherapy (see Saniotis, 2020). First, practitioners within these fields must be convinced that the addition of psychedelic agents to their treatment regimens provides the necessary benefit-to-risk ratio for the patient. Second, routine therapeutic use of these agents will require significant changes in health care policy on the part of both government agencies and health care insurers (dos Santos et al., 2021).

ADVERSE REACTIONS Classical psychedelic drugs such as LSD and psilocybin produce rapid tolerance with repeated use, which has been linked to 5-HT_{2A} receptor down-regulation (Halberstadt, 2015). However, these compounds rarely give rise to the compulsive use patterns seen with most other recreational drugs such as opioids, psychostimulants, cannabis, alcohol, and nicotine (Johnson et al., 2018; Bates and Trujillo, 2021). This lack of addictive potential is additionally supported by evidence that psychedelics are not effective reinforcers in animal tests such as the self-administration paradigm. Nevertheless, a small percentage of psychedelic drug users persist in their use despite significant adverse consequences. For such cases, the *Diagnostic and Statistical Manual of Mental Disorders*, 5th edition (*DSM-5*), contains a category called **other hallucinogen use disorder**, which covers the classical psychedelic drugs plus MDMA but not PCP, which has its own diagnostic categories (Hardaway et al., 2016).

Despite the relative lack of addictive potential, psychedelics can still cause harm for some users. As mentioned earlier, users may have a "bad trip" in which they experience an acute anxiety or panic reaction in response to the drug's effects. Such reactions are probably related to an interaction between the drug, the individual's emotional state going into the trip, and the external environment. In most cases, friends talk the person through the ordeal. Other potential complications from psychedelics are the occurrence of occasional **flashbacks** and a more serious problem called **hallucinogen persisting perception disorder** (HPPD) (Martinotti et al., 2018; Orsolini et al., 2019). Flashbacks are transient, usually innocuous, re-experiences of some of the visual distortions that occurred during previous episodes of psychedelic drug consumption.

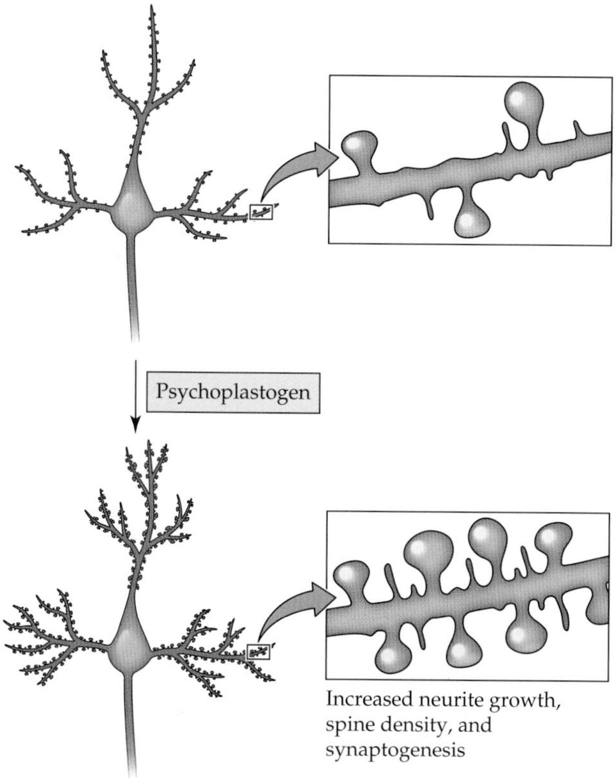

Psychoplastogen

Increased neurite growth, spine density, and synaptogenesis

FIGURE 15.16 **Rapid structural changes produced by serotonergic psychedelic drugs** A combination of in vitro and in vivo studies found that administration of LSD, DMT, or DOI (a 5-HT_{2A} receptor-stimulating psychedelic more typically associated with animal research than with human use) produces rapid increases in dendritic complexity, density of dendritic spines (number of spines per unit length of dendrite), and synapse number. The insets illustrate the structures and densities of different types of dendritic spines. The changes shown here are hypothesized to contribute to the rapid antidepressant effects of this class of psychedelic agents. (After C. Ly et al. 2018. *Cell Rep* 23: 3170–3182. © 2018 The Author(s).)

Users typically do not consider occasional flashbacks to be distressing, and some users even refer to them as "free trips." In contrast, HPPD is a more serious disturbance in which severe perceptual symptoms persist for a long period of time following drug use and are experienced sufficiently frequently to cause significant distress or impairment to the individual. Recent studies have identified cases of HPPD in some users of the 5-HT–releasing drug MDMA (see Chapter 6), which suggests that the serotonergic system may play a role in the development of this disorder (Litjens et al., 2014).

The most severe adverse reactions to psychedelic drug use are toxic reactions that can involve psychiatric and/or somatic symptoms, depending on the drug and dose. For example, psychotic episodes have occurred following use of LSD or tryptamines (e.g., DMT) in vulnerable individuals either suffering from a current psychiatric disorder or possessing a preexisting risk for developing psychosis (Araújo et al., 2015; De Gregorio et al., 2016). Acute psychotic symptoms have additionally been seen in some *Salvia* and *Psilocybe* mushroom users (Zawilski and Wojcieszak, 2013; Vallersnes et al., 2016). Overdosing on LSD or a related drug can produce an array of symptoms including florid hallucinations, agitation, paranoia, hypertension, tachycardia, hyperthermia, and vomiting (Williams and Erickson, 2000). The most severe cases require a visit to a hospital emergency department for treatment. The recent increase in psychedelic drug use among adolescents has led to a rise in the number of psychedelic-related telephone calls to U.S. poison control centers from 2007 to 2017 (Ng et al., 2019). Moreover, NBOMes are even more dangerous than LSD or other psychedelic agents. Numerous reports have appeared in the literature of NBOMe users suffering from delusions, severe agitation and aggressive behavior, seizures, tachycardia, hypertension, extreme hyperthermia, rhabdomyolysis (muscle breakdown), and kidney damage (Kyriakou et al., 2015; Nikolaou et al., 2015; Suzuki et al., 2015). Severe NBOMe toxicity can lead to hospitalization in an intensive care unit and even death. Based on these findings, it's clear that people seeking a psychedelic experience should avoid using NBOMes because of the risk of serious adverse reactions.

SECTION SUMMARY

■ Psychedelic drugs are substances that cause perceptual changes, visual hallucinations, altered awareness of the mind and body, and cognitive distortions without producing a state of toxic delirium. Some psychedelics, such as mescaline, psilocybin, DMT, 5-MeO-DMT, salvinorin A, and ibogaine are plant compounds that were used historically in spiritual or religious ceremonies before their discovery by Western culture. Other psychedelic drugs such as LSD and NBOMes are synthetic compounds.

■ Recognition of the powerful mind-altering properties of psychedelic drugs led to clinical, experimental, and recreational use beginning in the late 1950s. Psychiatrists gave patients LSD in the course of psycholytic or psychedelic therapy, whereas secret government programs tested the feasibility of weaponizing LSD and other potent psychedelics. LSD became readily available on the street despite a federal ban on recreational use in 1967.

■ Many psychedelic drugs are orally active, with a slow onset of action and a long time course of action. Two exceptions are DMT and *Salvia*, which are usually smoked, thereby leading to rapid drug effects and a much shorter duration of action. NBOMes are most typically administered by the sublingual or buccal routes. Among the commonly used psychedelics, LSD is the most potent and ibogaine is the least potent, based on the range of doses taken by users.

■ An LSD "trip" consists of four phases: onset, plateau, peak, and comedown. During the trip, the user experiences vivid visual hallucinations, a slowing of the subjective sense of time, feelings of depersonalization, strong emotional reactions, and a disruption of logical thought. Research on psychedelics has made use of the Altered States of Consciousness rating scale, which consists of the following five primary dimensions: oceanic boundlessness, ego-disintegration anxiety, visionary restructuralization, reduced vigilance, and auditory alterations. These primary dimensions can be divided into subdimensions to provide more detailed information on drug-induced reactions.

■ Most psychedelic drugs are classified chemically as either indoleamines or phenethylamines. The indoleamines are related structurally to 5-HT, whereas the phenethylamines instead share a common structure with NE. Of the psychedelics discussed in this chapter, only mescaline and the NBOMes belong to the phenethylamine class. Both the indoleamine and phenethylamine hallucinogens are 5-HT$_{2A}$ receptor agonists. The extended length of an LSD trip occurs because binding of the drug to the receptor causes it to be trapped temporarily within the binding pocket by a lid-like structure.

■ Salvinorin A and ibogaine differ in their neurochemical mechanisms from other psychedelic drugs. Salvinorin A does not interact with the 5-HT$_{2A}$ receptor but instead is a κ-opioid receptor agonist. This difference accounts for why the subjective effects produced by salvinorin A are somewhat different from the effects associated with compounds that act through the serotonergic system. Ibogaine is a partial agonist at κ-opioid and μ-opioid receptors, an NMDA receptor antagonist, and an inhibitor of 5-HT and DA reuptake.

■ Researchers have identified some of the neural circuits responsible for the actions of classical (i.e., 5-HT$_{2A}$ receptor agonist) psychedelic drugs. A key component of this neural circuitry is a "trigger population" of glutamatergic pyramidal neurons in layer 5 of the PFC that is activated by stimulation of 5-HT$_{2A}$, AMPA, and NMDA receptors. Excitation of these neurons disrupts the functioning of a cortico-striatal-thalamo-cortical loop, leading to decreased gating of sensory and cognitive input from subcortical to cortical areas.

- Classical psychedelic drugs additionally alter network activity and functional connectivity within the brain. These alterations include reduced activity within the default mode network, increased functional connectivity among sensory cortical areas, increased connectivity between the thalamus and the ventral striatum and posterior cingulate cortex, and decreased connectivity between the thalamus and association cortices. Functional connectivity changes are hypothesized to reduce thalamic sensory gating, increase cortical sensory processing, and decrease integrative cortical information processing.

- Use of psychedelic drugs as adjuncts to psychotherapy has increased in recent years. Furthermore, several early randomized controlled trials found that LSD may have efficacy in treating alcoholism. Other studies suggest that ibogaine administration may also provide benefit for treating substance use disorders, particularly in counteracting opioid craving and other withdrawal symptoms.

- Most current studies of psychedelic-assisted psychotherapy involve the use of psilocybin. These studies are much more carefully and safely conducted than in the early days of LSD-based therapy. Psychedelic drug therapy is theoretically based on the ability of the drug to produce a peak experience in the patient, followed over succeeding days or weeks by an afterglow period characterized by elevated mood, reduced guilt and anxiety, and an enhanced ability to form close social relationships. Psilocybin-assisted psychotherapy has been found to reduce symptoms of depression and anxiety in patients with a mood disorder or with a diagnosis of a life-threatening illness such as cancer. The best predictor of a good therapeutic response appears to be the intensity of the psychedelic experience. Researchers have hypothesized that the antidepressant actions of classical psychedelics require a process of glutamate-dependent neural plasticity.

- Psychedelics are not dependence forming or addictive for most users; however, a small percentage of users meet the *DSM-5* diagnostic criteria for other hallucinogen use disorder. Most of the 5-HT–acting psychedelic drugs produce a rapid tolerance with repeated use that has been linked to 5-HT_{2A} receptor down-regulation.

- Use of psychedelics can lead to adverse effects such as "bad trips" and flashbacks. People who suffer from severe, recurring flashbacks long after discontinuing hallucinogenic drug use are diagnosed as having hallucinogen persisting perception disorder. Ingesting high doses of a psychedelic agent can cause dangerous toxic reactions involving psychiatric and/or somatic symptoms. Psychiatric symptoms resemble those seen in acutely psychotic patients and are most likely to occur in users who either are suffering from a current psychiatric disorder or possess a preexisting vulnerability for developing psychosis. NBOMes are responsible for the most severe reactions, which consist of delusions, severe agitation and aggressive behavior, and physiological reactions that can even be fatal.

15.2 PCP and Ketamine

Background and history

This section of the chapter deals with two closely related compounds: **phencyclidine** and **ketamine**. Phencyclidine is usually abbreviated **PCP**, which comes from the drug's full chemical name, 1-(1-*p*henylcyclohexyl) *pi*peridine (**FIGURE 15.17**). PCP (trade name Sernyl) was synthesized accidentally by a chemist at Parke-Davis and Company (the chemist was actually attempting to synthesize a different compound) in 1956 as part of an ongoing project to develop new anesthetic agents (Bertron et al., 2018). PCP was quickly found to have unusual properties when first tested. Although individuals given PCP showed no responsiveness to nociceptive (painful) stimuli, they were not in the typical state of relaxed unconsciousness seen with traditional anesthetics like barbiturates. Instead, they exhibited a trance-like or catatonic-like state characterized by a vacant facial expression, fixed and staring eyes, and maintenance of muscle tone. Indeed, it was not unusual for individuals to develop either rigidity or waxy flexibility—motor symptoms often observed in catatonic patients with schizophrenia (Li and Vlisides, 2016).

PCP was initially thought to be clinically promising because it did not produce the respiratory depression associated with barbiturate anesthesia and, therefore, possessed a high therapeutic index (see Chapter 1). However, early enthusiasm was soon tempered by reports of problematic reactions in many patients. In a few cases, this took the form of marked agitation rather than quieting during the drug-induced state. Other patients experienced postoperative reactions ranging from blurred vision, dizziness, and mild disorientation to much more serious reactions involving hallucinations, severe agitation, and even violence. These problems caused the clinical use of PCP to be terminated in 1965.

Of course, the abandonment of PCP as a medication did not prevent it from coming into illicit use. By 1967, PCP had found its way onto the streets of several cities, including San Francisco, where it was dubbed the "PeaCe Pill" by the drug culture protesting the Vietnam War. Over the next several years, recreational PCP use under new street names such as "angel dust" and "hog" became much more widespread across the

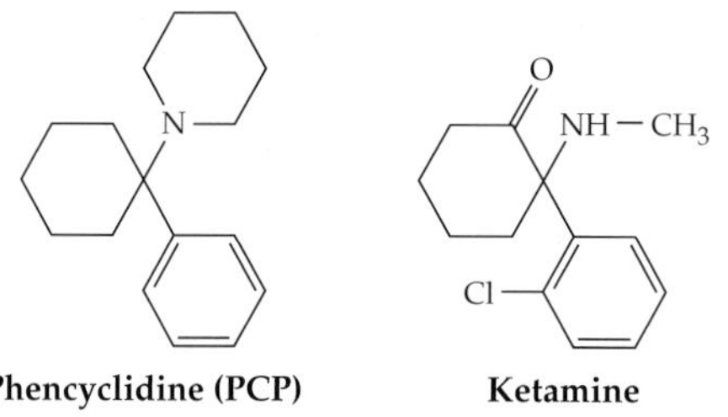

FIGURE 15.17 Chemical structures of PCP and ketamine

Phencyclidine (PCP)   Ketamine

country. Lurid stories about crazed behavior under the influence of PCP (e.g., "Person High on PCP Gouges Out His Own Eyes") began to appear widely in the national media, despite the fact that most of the stories were exaggerated, misrepresented, or never proven to be PCP-related (Morgan and Kagan, 1980). Yet the popularity of this drug never rivaled that of marijuana or even cocaine or heroin, and the incidence of PCP use subsequently declined to a relatively low level compared to these other substances.

Ketamine came into being as a safer alternative to PCP. Even before PCP was withdrawn, Parke-Davis had begun to screen related compounds in the hope of finding one with less behavioral toxicity. One such compound, designated CI-581, was synthesized in 1962 and was first tested in humans 2 years later. CI-581, later renamed ketamine, was less potent and shorter acting than PCP. Ketamine was soon found to be a valuable anesthetic for certain medical procedures, particularly in children, and it is also widely used by veterinarians as a general sedating and immobilizing agent. It is currently marketed legally as a prescription medication under the trade names Ketalar, Ketaset, and Vetalar. Despite its lower potency, ketamine can still cause adverse emergence reactions in human patients similar to those seen with PCP. Fortunately, the frequency of such reactions is low in infants and children—the groups for which ketamine is most commonly used. Ketamine also surpassed PCP for recreational use, not only because of its more tolerable behavioral profile but also because of its availability as a medical- or veterinary-grade drug that has been stolen or diverted from a hospital or veterinary clinic.

Pharmacology of PCP and ketamine

Although PCP and ketamine can be considered anesthetic agents, the subjective experience produced by these compounds is unlike that produced by more typical anesthetic drugs. In this section we discuss the characteristics of PCP- and ketamine-induced dissociation, the mechanism of action of these compounds, their addictive potential, and the current and possible future therapeutic applications of ketamine.

BASIC PHARMACOLOGY PCP is generally obtained in powdered or pill form, and the drug can be ingested by virtually any common route. It can be taken orally, administered intranasally (i.e., snorted), or injected intravenously or intramuscularly. Many PCP users apply the drug to tobacco, marijuana, or parsley cigarettes for purposes of smoking. Ketamine for medical or veterinary use comes as an injectable liquid, but street sellers commonly evaporate the liquid to yield a powder that is either snorted directly, compressed into pill form, or redissolved in liquid for the purpose of injection (**FIGURE 15.18**). It is sold on the street under such

FIGURE 15.18 Ketamine crystals

names as "K," "special K," or "cat Valium." Users who don't wish to become too intoxicated often snort small lines or piles of ketamine called "bumps." However, this practice can escalate over time to intramuscular or intravenous (IV) injection of the liquid solution as the user develops tolerance to the drug or seeks a more powerful effect.

DISSOCIATIVE EFFECTS The first studies on the subjective effects of PCP were conducted in the late 1950s and early 1960s. After being given a subanesthetic dose of PCP, study participants reported feeling detached from their bodies, sensations of vertigo or of floating, numbness, and sometimes a dream-like state. They also experienced a variety of affective reactions including drowsiness and apathy, loneliness, negativism or hostility toward the experimenters, or, alternatively, feelings of euphoria and inebriation. Finally, all of the treated individuals exhibited a marked cognitive disorganization manifested by difficulty in maintaining concentration or focus, deficiencies in abstract thinking, and halting speech. These effects of PCP, which have been compared to the symptoms of schizophrenia, may have contributed to the waning of the drug's popularity. In fact, Edward Domino and Elliott Luby, two of the early researchers studying the influence of PCP on humans, noted, "It was astounding to us that phencyclidine [initially] became a major street drug of abuse .... Few of our volunteer subjects were ever willing to take the drug a second time" (Domino and Luby, 2012, p. 916).

Domino and colleagues at the University of Michigan also published the first study on the pharmacological effects of ketamine in 1965. Intermediate doses of ketamine yielded reactions similar to those mentioned above for subanesthetic doses of PCP. However, when study participants received doses in the anesthetic range (at least 1 mg/kg IV), a remarkable effect was observed: the individuals appeared to lose all mental contact with their environment for up to 10 minutes or longer, despite the fact that their eyes remained open and they retained significant muscle tone. When Domino described to his wife how the ketamine-treated individuals seemed to be disconnected from their environment, she proposed the term **dissociative anesthesia** to describe this unique state of detachment (E. F. Domino, personal communication). This term was subsequently applied to both ketamine and PCP.

Subsequent studies have documented the subjective experiences reported by ketamine users while in the dissociated state (**TABLE 15.2**). As noted in the table, individuals may feel separated from their body, perhaps floating above and looking down at themselves (Jansen, 2000, 2001; Newcombe, 2008). Some have described this as a "near-death" experience, even though the person is not actually dying. This state of being, which is called the "K-hole," can be either spiritually uplifting or terrifying. As one user put it, "A K-hole can be anything from going to hell and meeting Satan to going to heaven and meeting God" (quote from *Time Out*, 2000, p. 20, cited in Kelly, 2001).

MOLECULAR MECHANISMS The principal molecular target for both PCP and ketamine is the NMDA (*N*-methyl-D-aspartate) receptor. To review briefly, the NMDA receptor is an important ionotropic receptor for the excitatory amino acid neurotransmitter glutamate. PCP and ketamine are both NMDA receptor uncompetitive antagonists that bind to a site within the receptor's ion channel, thereby blocking ion flow through the channel (see Figure 8.5). Because of the location of this binding site, the channel must be open for binding to occur; that is, the drugs are "open channel" blockers. Additional studies have shown that PCP, ketamine, and structurally related compounds are "trapping blockers," which means that the drug molecule remains trapped within the channel even after the agonist (glutamate) dissociates from its binding site and the channel closes (Zorumski et al., 2016). Once the receptor is reactivated, the trapped blocker must detach from the interior of the channel to permit ion flow. This accounts for the longer-lasting receptor blockade produced by PCP and ketamine compared to other NMDA receptor antagonists (although it should be noted that ketamine dissociates faster than PCP, which probably contributes to differences in the effects of the two drugs).

Several additional mechanisms may contribute to the subjective and behavioral effects of PCP and ketamine (Sleigh et al., 2014; McMillan and Muthukumaraswamy, 2020). One of these is a secondary consequence of PCP/ketamine-mediated NMDA receptor blockade, namely increased glutamate release from cortical pyramidal neurons that leads to overactive glutamate

TABLE 15.2 Subjective Experiences Reported by Ketamine Users

Sensations of light coming through the body and/or of colorful visions
Complete loss of time sense
Bizarre distortions of body shape or size
Altered perception of body consistency (e.g., feeling as though one is made of a strange material such as rubber, plastic, or wood)
Sensations of floating or hovering weightlessly in space
Feelings of leaving one's body
Sudden insights into the mysteries of existence or of the self
Experiences of being "at one" with the universe
Visions of spiritual or supernatural beings

Source: From P. J. Dalgarno and D. Shewan 1996. *J Psychoactive Drugs* 28: 191–199.

transmission via non-NDMA receptors (Deakin et al., 2008; Gunduz-Bruce, 2009). This effect was confirmed in a human study using a type of brain imaging technique known as proton magnetic resonance spectroscopy,* which showed a significant increase in glutamate levels in the anterior cingulate cortex after a single IV infusion of ketamine (Stone et al., 2012). This increase was significantly correlated with the positive psychotic symptoms induced by the drug treatment. Enhancement of cortical glutamate release by PCP or ketamine may depend on preferential blockade of NMDA receptors located on GABAergic interneurons innervating the pyramidal cells. As depicted in **FIGURE 15.19**, this receptor blockade leads to reduced GABA release, increased firing of the pyramidal cells because of the loss of GABAergic inhibition, glutamate AMPA receptor-mediated excitation of the postsynaptic targets of those cells, and enhanced Ca^{2+} signaling produced by the opening of voltage-dependent Ca^{2+} channels (McMillan and Muthukumaraswamy, 2020).

PCP/KETAMINE MODELS OF SCHIZOPHRENIA Following discovery of the hallucinogenic and cognition-impairing features of acute LSD administration, researchers argued that these symptoms were similar to those observed in patients with schizophrenia. This is why LSD and other psychedelics are sometimes called psychotomimetic agents, as mentioned in the chapter introduction. However, there are important differences between the features of LSD intoxication and the symptoms of schizophrenia. For example, psychedelic drugs produce mainly visual distortions,

---

*Magnetic resonance spectroscopy (MRS) is an imaging method that uses equipment similar to that used for magnetic resonance imaging (MRI), but instead of yielding information on brain structure or regional activation, it measures the levels of various brain chemicals.

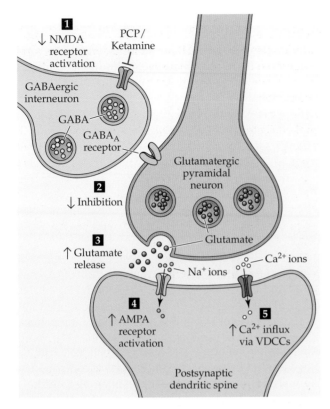

FIGURE 15.19 Proposed mechanism of PCP- or ketamine-induced enhancement of cortical glutamate release (1) Blockade of NMDA receptors on cortical GABAergic interneurons by PCP or ketamine results in less GABA release, (2) a reduction in tonic GABAergic inhibition of the glutamatergic pyramidal neurons, (3) enhanced glutamate release from the pyramidal cells, (4) increased activation of postsynaptic non-NMDA (mostly AMPA) receptors, and (5) membrane depolarization resulting in opening of voltage-dependent Ca^{2+} channels (VDCCs) and stimulation of Ca^{2+}-mediated signaling pathways. (After R. McMillan and S. D. Muthukumaraswamy. 2020. *Rev Neurosci* 31: 457–503. Republished with permission of Walter de Gruyter and Co.)

of their symptoms following ketamine administration. These findings led to a glutamate hypothesis of schizophrenia, which proposed that hypoactivity of the glutamatergic system, particularly with respect to NMDA receptor signaling, is a key factor in the pathogenesis of the disorder (Cohen et al., 2015; Uno and Coyle, 2019). This hypothesis is supported not only by the symptomatology associated with NMDA receptor blockade but also by the finding of reduced NMDA receptor subunit expression in post-mortem brain tissues from patients with schizophrenia.

Several rodent models of schizophrenia have been developed using PCP or ketamine administration to reproduce schizophrenia-like symptoms. Rats or mice may be treated acutely with the drug or more typically are given a sub-chronic dosing regimen consisting of daily dosing for 3 to 14 days. Examples of relevant behavioral responses used in these studies include hyperlocomotion, stereotypic behaviors, and ataxia to model the positive symptoms; decreased social interactions to model the negative symptoms; and impaired learning and reduced sensorimotor gating to model the cognitive symptoms of schizophrenia (Lee and Zhou, 2019) (see Chapter 19 for a discussion of the categories of schizophrenia symptoms). The degree to which these behavioral responses parallel those of patients with schizophrenia can be debated; however, as is the case for all neuropsychiatric disorders, animal models play an important role as test platforms in the development of new medications.

Recreational use, adverse effects, and therapeutic applications

Rodents and non-human primates will self-administer both PCP and ketamine, thereby demonstrating the reinforcing properties of these compounds. Indeed, both compounds are subject to misuse and dependence, although the prevalence of harmful ketamine use is currently much greater than that of PCP.

REINFORCING EFFECTS Rhesus monkeys have served as subjects for a number of PCP and ketamine self-administration studies. Interestingly, early studies on monkeys that self-administered high doses of PCP found that the animals took in sufficient quantities of the drug to be intoxicated almost continuously (Balster and Woolverton, 1980, 1981). Under the influence of PCP, the animals could not support themselves on four legs, but instead were typically found near the response lever either in an awkward sitting position or lying on the cage floor. The ability to elicit self-intoxication in animals is not unique to PCP; it has also been observed with cocaine, amphetamine, opioids, and alcohol.

PCP and ketamine activate midbrain DA cell firing and stimulate DA release in the dorsal striatum, nucleus accumbens, and PFC (Hertel et al., 1995; Kokkinou et al., 2018). Enhanced dopaminergic neurotransmission

whereas hallucinations in patients with schizophrenia are typically auditory, such as hearing voices that aren't real. Furthermore, psychedelic drugs fail to reproduce the so-called negative symptoms of schizophrenia, which include reduced speech, flat affect, and social withdrawal (see Chapter 19).

The LSD model of schizophrenia was later replaced by a model involving the subjective and behavioral effects of PCP or ketamine (Steeds et al., 2015; Ham et al., 2017). Healthy people given a high dose of either of these drugs display a variety of symptoms consisting of disordered thought, delusions, and motor disturbances ranging from extreme agitation to catatonia. Some negative symptoms may also be observed. Indeed, admission to a hospital emergency department while suffering from severe PCP or ketamine intoxication may lead to a misdiagnosis of acute schizophrenia until a toxicological screen has been performed. We also know that patients with schizophrenia show an exacerbation

is likely an important factor in the reinforcing effects of both compounds. A recent study using mice additionally found a significant role for the endocannabinoid system in ketamine's stimulant and reinforcing properties (Xu wet al., 2020). The pleasurable effects of IV ketamine were investigated in healthy volunteers without prior exposure to this compound (Morgan et al., 2004). The investigators found dose-dependent increases in drug liking and in the desire for more drug (**FIGURE 15.20**), confirming that ketamine is rewarding not only in laboratory animals but also in humans.

RECREATIONAL USE AND MISUSE As mentioned earlier, PCP is not widely used compared with many other recreational drugs. The 2018 National Survey on Drug Use and Health estimated that only about 30,000 people age 12 or older were current users of PCP, and the 2019 survey did not even provide an estimate, indicating that the data from that year were "low precision" (Center for Behavioral Health Statistics and Quality, 2020). Despite the low prevalence of PCP use, the *DSM-5* lists diagnostic categories of phencyclidine use disorder and phencyclidine intoxication. The latter category is important for differentiating some of the symptoms of PCP intoxication, such as analgesia, ataxia, and muscle rigidity, from the symptoms associated with intoxication produced by psychedelics such as LSD or psilocybin. Individuals who use PCP have found some novel (and dangerous) drug combinations, including a combination variously referred to as "fry," "wet," or "illy," in which tobacco or marijuana cigarettes are dipped in a liquid containing PCP and embalming fluid (!) and then smoked (Peters Jr. et al., 2008). Moreover, because PCP is inexpensive to manufacture, suppliers of illicit street drugs sometimes add PCP to another drug to "boost" its effects or substitute PCP completely for the drug that users think they are purchasing (e.g., PCP in place of MDMA in tablets sold as "Ecstasy"). This practice has led to the existence of PCP "users" who are not even aware of what they are ingesting.

In contrast to PCP, the use of ketamine has grown because of the drug's popularity within the dance scene (Wolff and Winstock, 2006). Although widespread recreational use of ketamine is a relatively recent phenomenon, illicit use of this substance actually dates back many years. Some users were, and continue to be, medical or veterinary practitioners who have easy access to ketamine in the course of their work. Ketamine was also favored by some intellectuals as a mind-expanding drug in the tradition of LSD. Two famous ketamine users were Marcia Moore, a well-known astrologer and author in the 1970s, and Dr. John Lilly, a physician and researcher known for his ground-breaking studies on communication with dolphins and on the psychological effects of sensory isolation. Both Moore and Lilly became heavily dependent on ketamine, and both developed psychotic reactions as a result.*

Development of ketamine tolerance and dependence can be seen not only in the extreme cases of Marcia Moore and John Lilly but also in the self-reports of other heavy users. Accounts of dose escalation and compulsive use are presented by Karl Jansen, a British psychiatrist who investigated ketamine use for many years (Jansen, 2001; Jansen and Darracot-Cankovic, 2001). Interestingly, many of the ketamine-dependent individuals studied by Jansen are described as being highly intelligent, even PhD students. One straight-A PhD candidate said that

---

*In Moore's case, the consequences were especially tragic when she left her home on a cold wintry night in 1979, climbed a tree, gave herself a ketamine injection, and froze to death while in a state of drug intoxication.

(A) Desire for drug

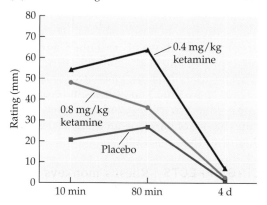

(B) Drug liking

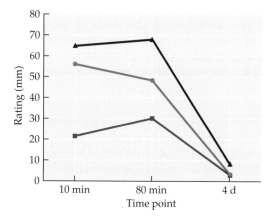

FIGURE 15.20 IV ketamine administration produces dose-dependent rewarding effects in humans Study volunteers who had never used ketamine before were given an IV infusion of placebo or 0.4 or 0.8 mg/kg ketamine over a period of 80 minutes. At the 10- and 80-minute time points, as well as 4 days later (follow-up), the volunteers were tested for their subjective responses to the drug, using a visual analog scale (see Web Box 12.1, Figure 3 caption, for a description of this method). Both doses produced increased desire for the drug (A) and increased drug liking (B) compared with placebo. (After C. J. A. Morgan et al. 2004. *Psychopharmacology* 172: 298–308. doi: 10.1007/s00213-003-1656-y)

overcoming his ketamine problem was "harder than heroin" (Jansen, 2001, p. 167). Case reports and studies by other investigators indicate that frequent ketamine users may increase their dose over time and upon cessation of use, may show withdrawal symptoms such as drug craving, depression, and anxiety (Morgan et al., 2012; Chen et al., 2020). In the *DSM-5*, ketamine misuse that meets the relevant diagnostic criteria would fall under the same category as LSD and psilocybin, namely "other hallucinogen use disorder."

Recreational ketamine use typically occurs outside the home at parties, raves, or clubs (De Luca et al., 2012). For that reason, ketamine is sometimes included in the category of "club drugs," along with MDMA, the benzodiazepine flunitrazepam (Rohypnol), and gamma-hydroxybutyrate (GHB; see Chapter 16). At the lowest psychoactive dose range, ketamine produces a state of relaxation sometimes referred to as "going to K-land." Somewhat higher doses give rise to an altered state of consciousness that has similar properties to the state produced by classical psychedelic drugs like LSD or psilocybin (Bowdle et al., 1998; Vlisides et al., 2018). When British clubbers were asked about their motivation for using ketamine, the responses focused on two main features. First, control of the dose was much easier than with other psychedelic agents. Users commonly took a dose that provided a low to intermediate level of intoxication, which they reported as both pleasurable and consistent with maintaining good sociability at the event (Moore and Measham, 2008). Most users sought to avoid too intense a level of intoxication; that is, they wanted to avoid going into a K-hole. The second positive feature was that the effects of ketamine are relatively short-lived compared to an LSD or psilocybin trip, which, along with dose titration, contributed to the perceived control the users had over their drug experience.

Several other uncompetitive NMDA receptor antagonists are also used recreationally for their psychoactive properties (Morris and Wallach, 2014). One of these is **dextromethorphan**, a common ingredient in over-the-counter cough and cold medications. This compound is discussed in **BOX 15.2**. Another important compound in this category is methoxetamine, a potent analog of ketamine. Methoxetamine (street names "Mexxy," "MXE," or "special M") first appeared in 2010 and continues to be sold on the internet even though an increasing number of countries have declared the drug to be illegal for non-research use. Methoxetamine can be taken orally, by insufflation, and by intramuscular injection. It produces a dissociative reaction like that of ketamine, but the effect is much longer lasting (Botanas et al., 2019). As with ketamine, methoxetamine users report a variety of experiences that may be euphoric, spiritual, or terrifying (Kjellgren and Jonsson, 2013).

The most recent development with regard to street use of NMDA receptor antagonists is the advent of PCP or ketamine analogs that have been synthesized in an attempt to avoid a positive test in a drug screen and/or to maintain legality until authorities have placed the drug into the category of controlled substances. Examples of such compounds include 4-F-PCP, 4-keto-PCP, 4-methoxy-PCP, 3-methoxy-PCP, and 2-oxo-PCE. These drugs should be avoided, as a growing number of reports indicate substantial toxic effects and even fatalities linked to their use (e.g., Johansson et al., 2017; Mitchell-Mata et al., 2017; Tang et al., 2018; Berar et al., 2019). Severe toxic reactions have also been reported for methoxetamine (Zawilska, 2014; Chiappini et al., 2015; Zanda et al., 2016), and thus the same warning about avoiding PCP analogs pertains to this compound as well.

ADVERSE EFFECTS OF CHRONIC USE   Chronic use of ketamine or PCP can produce many different negative effects on physical health, behavior, and brain structure and function. With respect to physical health, some ketamine users develop distressing urological symptoms including cystitis (bladder inflammation), painful urination, and incontinence (Myers Jr. et al., 2016). Severe cases may even involve damage to the kidneys. Ketamine users may also develop gastrointestinal disturbances such as upper abdominal pain, gallbladder problems, and signs of liver toxicity (Bokor and Anderson, 2014).

Studies of long-term, high-dose ketamine users have shown that some individuals develop a persisting psychosis with psychopathology and cognitive impairments similar to those of patients diagnosed with schizophrenia (Cheng et al., 2018). This finding is reminiscent of the previously described experiences of Marcia Moore and John Lilly. Even chronic recreational use of ketamine that doesn't cause such severe symptomatology has been associated with memory deficits and other cognitive dysfunction involving the frontal and medial temporal lobes (Morgan and Curran, 2006; Chan et al., 2013). Some of these deficits seem to persist even following a significant reduction in drug consumption. Ketamine users have also exhibited much greater delusional thinking than non-users (Morgan et al., 2009), although it is impossible to know from this study whether such abnormal ideation was caused by or preceded ketamine exposure. The neurobiological mechanisms underlying these psychological effects are not yet known, although brain imaging studies of chronic ketamine users have found evidence for gray and white matter abnormalities as well as altered functional connectivity between certain brain areas (Liao et al., 2010, 2011, 2016; Hung et al., 2020). There is also a report of increased D_1 dopamine receptor binding in the prefrontal cortex of ketamine users, which may be a result of decreased presynaptic dopaminergic transmission in this brain area (Narendran et al., 2005).

BOX 15.2 ■ PHARMACOLOGY IN ACTION

Getting High on Cough Syrup

One of the most annoying features of a bad cold is the persistent cough that it may bring on. That is why **antitussives**, medications that suppress the cough reflex, are big sellers in pharmacies across the country. The main ingredient in most of these over-the-counter products is an opioid-like compound called dextromethorphan. For example, dextromethorphan is the antitussive agent in Robitussin DM cough syrup, Coricidin HBP cough and cold tablets, and many other nonprescription medications sold to alleviate cold symptoms.

Cough medications based on dextromethorphan have been on the market for many years. The first one was Romilar, a dextromethorphan-containing tablet that was introduced in the 1960s. Romilar was meant to be a replacement for codeine-containing medications, since the latter were already being abused. However, it did not take long before users discovered the psychoactive properties of Romilar and began abusing it as well. The drug was eventually withdrawn from the market and was later replaced with a codeine-containing, prescription-only version. Pharmaceutical companies subsequently decided to put dextromethorphan into a cough syrup, presumably to discourage recreational use by requiring the ingestion of large amounts of the syrup to obtain a psychoactive effect.

Following ingestion, dextromethorphan is metabolized to the active substance **dextrorphan**, which is thought to be responsible for most of the psychoactive effects produced by high doses of dextromethorphan-containing cough medicines. Based on the results from in vitro binding studies involving neurotransmitter receptors and transporters, dextromethorphan had the highest affinity for the serotonin transporter whereas dextrorphan had the highest affinity for NMDA receptors (C. P. Taylor et al., 2016). Dextromethorphan showed additional weak binding to α-adrenergic receptors and 5-HT$_{1B/D}$ receptors. Like PCP and ketamine, dextromethorphan and its metabolite can produce a dissociative reaction through uncompetitive antagonism of NMDA receptors.

When used recreationally, dextromethorphan is typically taken orally in the form of cough syrup or tablet. On the street, it goes by names like "Red Devils," "Triple C's," "Skittles," or "Robo." Consuming high doses of dextromethorphan-containing products to become intoxicated is commonly referred to as "Robotripping" (Stanciu et al., 2016). The standard dose of dextromethorphan for cough suppression is 20 mg (found in 0.33 ounces of cough syrup), but recreational users take single doses that are eight to 50 times higher (Banken and Foster, 2008). This requires drinking anywhere from a quarter of a typical 8-ounce bottle of cough syrup to as much as two whole bottles. There are even reports of heavy users ingesting three or four bottles in one day. Drinking this much cough

syrup usually causes nausea and vomiting from the effects of guaifenesin, an expectorant (agent that facilitates expulsion of phlegm from the throat or airways) found in most cough syrups. Some users have tried to avoid this unpleasant side effect by taking large amounts of dextromethorphan-containing Coricidin tablets. However, this is a very dangerous, even potentially fatal, practice because of the presence of chlorpheniramine in these tablets. Chorpheniramine is an antihistamine/anticholinergic agent that not only produces serious reactions by itself at high doses but also intensifies the effects of dextromethorphan by inhibiting its metabolism by the liver.

Given the limitations associated with dextromethorphan use via standard cough medications, enterprising users have discovered methods for extracting the substance from cough syrup (Hendrickson and Cloutier, 2007). As a result, dextromethorphan has become available on the street or via the internet in repackaged pills or capsules for oral administration, and even in powdered form for intranasal use. Indeed, tablets sold as "ecstasy" occasionally contain dextromethorphan instead of the expected MDMA.

Users report that the subjective effects of dextromethorphan occur as a series of four dose-related "plateaus" (Romanelli and Smith, 2009; Burns and Boyer, 2013). Low doses (100 to 200 mg dextromethorphan) produce the first plateau, during which users feel a mild euphoria and intoxication and may also experience slight perceptual effects. This stage is said to be similar to the effects of MDMA consumption. The second plateau is the most commonly sought after and requires a dose of 200 to 400 mg dextromethorphan. At this stage, users suffer from impaired balance, experience visual hallucinations when they close their eyes, and are significantly more intoxicated than at the first plateau. The third plateau occurs at doses ranging from 300 to 600 mg and yields more intense hallucinations, cognitive impairment, and partial dissociation. At the fourth plateau, produced by more than 600 mg dextromethorphan, users become severely ataxic, experience complete personality dissociation, and may become delusional.

The subjective effects of dextromethorphan have also been studied under controlled laboratory conditions. At the appropriate doses, such effects resemble those produced by classical psychedelic drugs. For example, Ressig et al. (2012) investigated the reactions to dextromethorphan using a standard hallucinogen rating scale as well as a mysticism scale to assess the intensity of drug-induced mystical experiences. The **FIGURE** illustrates two drug-induced psychedelic effects—namely, increases in perceptual distortions

(Continued)

BOX 15.2 ■ PHARMACOLOGY IN ACTION (*continued*)

(A) Hallucinogen rating scale

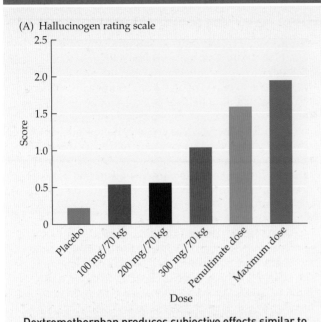

(B) Mysticism scale

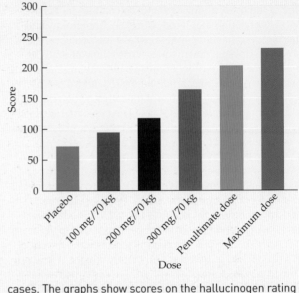

Dextromethorphan produces subjective effects similar to those observed with classical psychedelics Individuals who were experienced users of psychedelic drugs (including dextromethorphan in some cases) were given varying oral doses of dextromethorphan or placebo under relaxing conditions that facilitated the possibility of experiencing psychedelic drug–like effects. The highest possible drug dose was 800 mg/70 kg body weight, but not all individuals achieved that dose because of adverse effects in some cases. The graphs show scores on the hallucinogen rating scale (perception scale), which reflects hallucinations, illusions, and synesthesias (A), and on a mysticism scale that has been used to assess both natural and drug-induced mystical experiences (B). The maximum and penultimate doses are the highest and next-to-highest doses tolerated by each individual. (After C. J. Reissig et al. 2012. *Psychopharmacology* 223: 1–15. doi: 10.1007/s00213-012-2680-6.)

(illusions and hallucinations) and increases in overall mystical experience. A later double-blind study compared the subjective effects of dextromethorphan and psilocybin (Carbonaro et al., 2018). Whereas three different psilocybin doses were administered (10, 20, and 30 mg/70 kg), only a single dose of dextromethorphan (400 mg/70 kg) was used, presumably as a precaution due to the adverse effects of higher doses. Compared to dextromethorphan, psilocybin at the high dose produced more vivid visual hallucinations and experiences that were rated as more mystical and more psychologically insightful. In contrast, the dextromethorphan dose was associated with more feelings of disembodiment, more lightheadedness, and more nausea and vomiting. These differences may contribute to the significantly greater recreational use of psilocybin compared to dextromethorphan (Carbonaro et al., 2020).

Repeated use of dextromethorphan can lead to dose escalation, dependence, and, in some cases, toxic responses. Although dextromethorphan tolerance has not yet been systematically studied, published case reports suggest the existence of this phenomenon, thereby accounting for increasing consumption over time (Miller, 2005; Olives et al., 2019). A preliminary study of people being treated for dextromethorphan dependence (or, to use *DSM-5* language,

severe dextromethorphan use disorder) found significant withdrawal symptoms, including depression and anxiety, and additionally showed a high rate of relapse over the succeeding year (Xu et al., 2021). Acute toxicity to dextromethorphan can occur not only from consumption of extremely high doses but also because of a genetic deficiency in metabolism of the drug (Schwartz, 2005). Extreme dextromethorphan intoxication has been linked to psychotic reactions, violent behavior, and even death (Miller, 2005; Logan et al., 2009; Amaladoss and O'Brien, 2011; Logan et al., 2012). The behavioral symptoms of high-dose dextromethorphan intoxication are illustrated in the case report of a 40-year-old woman with a long history of misusing this drug (Martinak et al., 2017). She had commonly consumed doses exceeding 1000 mg (in the form of cough-and-cold tablets) and even reported binging 3000 to 4000 mg on a few occasions! After sleeping in a stranger's house and assaulting a police officer, she was finally brought to the hospital for examination and treatment and was admitted to a hospital psychiatric unit in a psychotic state.

Although the present discussion has centered mainly around dextromethorphan abuse, it's worth noting that this drug has a few interesting therapeutic applications beyond its common use as an antitussive

BOX 15.2 ■ PHARMACOLOGY IN ACTION (*continued*)

agent. Thus far, the one FDA-approved application is for the treatment of a rare neurological condition called **pseudobulbar affect**. This condition, which is seen in a small percentage of patients with brain injury or disease, is characterized by frequent, uncontrollable episodes of laughing or crying that are incongruent with the person's emotional state. Pseudobulbar affect is treated with a formulation (trade name **Nuedexta**) containing 20 mg of dextromethorphan along with 10 mg of quinidine sulfate, which prolongs dextromethorphan's bioavailability by inhibiting its metabolism (C. P. Taylor et al., 2016). Researchers do not yet understand how dextromethorphan works to reduce the symptoms of pseudobulbar affect, although the mechanism likely involves some combination of the drug's actions on its various molecular targets. More recently, a combination of dextromethorphan and bupropion has been undergoing clinical trials for treating major depression, including depression associated with bipolar disorder (Majeed et al., 2021). The addition of bupropion has a dual function: first, the drug has well-known antidepressant and antianxiety activity, and second, it acts like quinidine in Nuedexta to inhibit dextromethorphan's

metabolism. Similar to ketamine, dextromethorphan relieves depression symptoms rapidly, and the therapeutic effectiveness of dextromethorphan in combination with bupropion is thought to involve multiple molecular mechanisms, including NMDA receptor antagonism (thereby stimulating glutamate release) and inhibition of serotonin, norepinephrine, and dopamine reuptake (Stahl, 2019).

In summary, dextromethorphan is a powerful substance that, at high doses, exhibits psychoactive properties similar to those of the other drugs discussed in this chapter. It has significant abuse potential and can produce severe adverse reactions in users who are poor metabolizers of the compound and/or who take extremely large amounts of the drug. Dextromethorphan is not currently included in the Schedule of Controlled Substances, which explains why over-the-counter medications containing the drug can be sold without a prescription. At lower doses, dextromethorphan in combination with quinidine has approved therapeutic use for treating pseudobulbar affect, and emerging clinical data indicate that dextromethorphan plus bupropion is effective in treating multiple forms of depression.

The above-described research on human ketamine users has been complemented by studies on rodents and non-human primates that have demonstrated a variety of effects of repeated PCP or ketamine exposure on the brain. These include reduced tyrosine hydroxylase immunoreactivity (a marker of DA axons and terminals) in the prefrontal cortex (Yu et al., 2012), altered NMDA receptor levels (Newell et al., 2007; Xu and Lipsky, 2015), and a reduced number of asymmetrical spine synapses (usually considered to be excitatory glutamatergic synapses) in the prefrontal cortex (Elsworth et al., 2011a, 2011b). In a recent study by Sun and coworkers (2019), ketamine was administered to young adult rhesus monkeys several days per week on an escalating dosing regimen for 10 weeks. Compared to vehicle-treated controls, the ketamine-treated monkeys showed histological signs of neuronal damage in the PFC along with reduced expression of both the plasma membrane DA transporter and DA D_2 receptors. Lastly, there is evidence from experimental animal studies of PCP/ketamine-related toxicity to the developing brain, which has relevance for ketamine use in pediatric medicine. This research is discussed further in **WEB BOX 15.2**.

THERAPEUTIC APPLICATIONS We have seen that ketamine is an approved anesthetic for veterinary use as well as for some procedures in human infants and children. Considerable research has shown that this

drug has additional therapeutic applications in the treatment of major depression and in pain relief. Practitioners have known for many years that selective serotonin reuptake inhibitors (SSRIs), the first-line drugs prescribed for patients with major depression, require several weeks of administration before significant therapeutic benefit occurs (see Chapter 19). This so-called therapeutic lag is of significant concern not only because of the continued suffering of patients, but also because depressed patients who are suicidal could take their life before their mood improves. In contrast, administration of ketamine was found to produce a rapid reduction in depressive symptoms. After the necessary clinical testing, a nasal spray formulation of esketamine (one of two molecular forms of ketamine) under the trade name Spravato was approved by the FDA in 2019 for patients who have not responded to standard treatment methods (Kohtala, 2021; Sanders and Brula, 2021). The drug is an adjunct medication prescribed along with an oral antidepressant drug like an SSRI, and it must be taken by the patient in the doctor's office to ensure proper administration and prevent diversion for recreational use. More information about ketamine's antidepressant action is presented in Chapter 19.

A second potential therapeutic application of ketamine is its use as a non-opioid analgesic agent for various acute and chronic pain conditions and for peri- and postoperative analgesia (Crumb et al., 2018; Balzer et al., 2021; Culp et al., 2021). Because tolerance to repeated opiate drug treatment is partially mediated by the NMDA receptor, an additional benefit of ketamine administration is the ability to reverse opioid tolerance. Based on the available clinical evidence, it seems likely that ketamine will be approved for analgesic use in the coming years. Finally, ketamine is being tested for possible therapeutic efficacy in a few other disorders, including addiction and PTSD (Ezquerra-Romano et al., 2018; Feder et al., 2020). It remains to be seen whether the drug is effective for these conditions and meets the necessary criteria of benefit versus risk.

SECTION SUMMARY

- PCP and ketamine belong to the class of drugs known as dissociative anesthetics.

- PCP was withdrawn from clinical use because of its prominent adverse side effects, but ketamine, which is less potent than PCP, has significant applications in both human and veterinary medicine.

- The acute effects of PCP and ketamine include sensory distortions and altered body image, cognitive disorganization, and various affective changes. Low recreational doses of ketamine cause a state of relaxation sometime termed "going to K-land." Moderate doses can produce reactions similar to those obtained from classical psychedelic drugs; however, high doses of ketamine give rise to a state called the "K-hole," in which users feel separated from their body, perhaps in the manner of a near-death experience.

- PCP and ketamine bind to a site within the NMDA receptor channel, thereby acting as uncompetitive receptor antagonists. These and related compounds require the channel to be open for binding to occur, after which they are trapped within the channel until the receptor is reactivated. A secondary consequence of NMDA receptor antagonism is increased presynaptic glutamate release, which is thought to result from preferential blockade of receptors on inhibitory GABAergic interneurons that innervate the cortical pyramidal neurons. This glutamate surge likely contributes to the subjective and behavioral effects of PCP and ketamine.

- Models of schizophrenia in both humans and experimental animals have been developed based on the hallucinogenic and cognition-impairing effects of PCP and ketamine.

- Both PCP and ketamine are reinforcing to animals, as indicated by drug self-administration. These reinforcing effects are mediated, at least in part, by activation of midbrain dopaminergic neuronal firing and enhanced DA release in the dorsal striatum, nucleus accumbens, and PFC. Ketamine reinforcement in animals is paralleled by the drug's rewarding properties shown in controlled laboratory experiments.

- Although illicit use of ketamine has occurred for many years, the popularity of this compound is on the rise. Heavy ketamine users show dose escalation and compulsive use, which indicate the development of tolerance and dependence on the drug.

- Abuse potential has been shown for a few other uncompetitive NMDA receptor antagonists. These include dextromethorphan, an opioid-like compound found in cough medications, the potent ketamine analog methoxetamine, and other recently synthesized analogs of either PCP or ketamine. These compounds produce dissociative subjective effects and, in the case of dextromethorphan, other effects like those of the classical psychedelics.

- Chronic ketamine or PCP exposure leads to a variety of adverse effects including urological symptoms, gastrointestinal disturbances, cognitive deficits, and gray and white matter abnormalities. Animal studies have additionally revealed reduced dopaminergic function and other neuronal abnormalities.

- Repeated high ketamine doses also cause apoptotic cell death in the developing brains of laboratory animals, which has raised concerns about the use of this compound as a pediatric anesthetic agent. The general consensus based on the existing human research literature is that the medical use of ketamine for infants and children appears to be safe, despite the experimental animal findings. However, because we cannot exclude the possibility of subtle, later-appearing effects of early life ketamine exposure, such exposure should be minimized to whatever extent possible.

- A nasal spray containing esketamine, a form of the ketamine molecule, was approved a few years ago for treatment of treatment-resistant depression. This drug alleviates depressive symptoms without the lengthy therapeutic lag seen with conventional antidepressant drugs such as SSRIs. Ketamine is also being tested for other therapeutic applications, especially involving pain relief.

STUDY QUESTIONS

1. The substances discussed in the first section of this chapter have variously been termed "hallucinogenic," "psychedelic," and "psychotomimetic." (a) What do each of these terms mean? (b) Why have the authors chosen to use the term "psychedelic" in most of the chapter? (c) What is the definition of a psychedelic drug?

2. Mescaline and psilocybin are two plant-derived psychedelic compounds. (a) In what plants are these substances found? (b) How were the effects of psilocybin discovered by Westerners?

3. Why does the preparation of ayahuasca require the use of two different plants? What is the purpose of each plant in producing ayahuasca's psychedelic effects?

4. Describe the circumstances around the discovery of LSD, its subsequent use in psycholytic and psychedelic therapy, its testing (along with other psychedelic agents) by the U.S. government as a secret pharmacological weapon, and the features of its recreational use.

5. What are NBOMEs, and how are they administered by recreational users?

6. The key psychedelic compound found in *Salvia divinorum* is called _____.

7. Based on his personal experience and later testimonials by others, Howard Lotsof claimed that ibogaine was helpful in treating _____.

8. Psychedelic drugs vary greatly in (a) their potency and (b) the time course (i.e., length) of the effects produced by their consumption. Using your basic knowledge of pharmacology, how can you explain (a) differences in potency based on receptor affinity and (b) differences in the time course of drug action based on route of administration and pharmacokinetic considerations?

9. (a) Describe the four phases of a typical LSD trip and the typical user's experiences in each phase. (b) Define synesthesia, a phenomenon that is sometimes experienced by LSD users.

10. (a) Why has it been important for researchers studying psychedelic drug effects to use psychometric instruments like the Altered States of Consciousness (ASC) rating scale and Strassman's Hallucinogen Rating Scale? (b) Name and describe the five primary dimensions of the ASC scale.

11. What is the difference between indoleamine and phenethylamine psychedelics? What members of each group are discussed in this chapter?

12. (a) What experimental evidence supports the contention that 5-HT_{2A} receptor activation plays a key role in the subjective and behavioral effects of the classical (i.e., indoleamine and phenethylamine) psychedelic drugs? (b) Lisuride has a structure similar to that of LSD and, like LSD, it binds to the 5-HT_{2A} receptor. Yet, lisuride does not produce psychedelic effects when administered. What is the presumed mechanism underlying this difference between LSD and lisuride? (c) What behavioral test procedures are used to screen for psychedelic-like effects in laboratory animals?

13. How do the mechanisms of action of salvinorin A and ibogaine differ from those of the classical psychedelic drugs?

14. (a) The "trigger population" of neurons hypothesized to elicit the cascade of cellular events that culminate in the psychedelic experience is composed of _____ neurons located in layer _____ of the _____. (b) By what mechanism is this trigger population activated when a psychedelic drug is consumed?

15. (a) Explain the meaning of the term "default mode network (DMN)." (b) Under what conditions is the DMN most active? (c) Describe the effect of classical psychedelic drugs on activity within the DMN, and discuss the significance of this effect.

16. You are conversing with a friend about psychedelic drugs like psilocybin. They tell you they've heard that some people with symptoms of depression are being treated using psilocybin-assisted psychotherapy, and they ask your opinion about whether this kind of treatment is safe and whether it is effective. What is your response, and what information do you cite to support your argument?

17. Classical psychedelic drugs have significant potential for producing addiction. True or false? Explain your answer.

18. _____ is a disorder occasionally seen in psychedelic drug users in which severe perceptual symptoms persist for a long period of time following drug use that cause significant distress or impairment to the individual.

19. Among LSD, psilocybin, salvinorin A, and NBOMEs, which drug (or class of drugs) presents the greatest risk of producing a severe and dangerous toxic reaction?

20. Describe the discovery and development of PCP and ketamine for medical use as anesthetic agents. How does the anesthetic state produced by these compounds differ from the state produced by more traditional anesthetics such as barbiturates?

21. PCP and ketamine have been described both as "open channel blockers" and "trapping blockers" of the NMDA receptor. What do these terms mean? Logically, can a drug be a "trapping blocker" if it is not an "open channel blocker" of a ligand-gated channel?

(Continued)

22. Researchers have hypothesized that PCP and ketamine preferentially block NMDA receptors on GABAergic interneurons innervating cortical pyramidal cells. What is the consequence of this action?

23. (a) Why is administration of PCP or ketamine usually considered to be a better model of schizophrenia than administration of LSD? (b) How has the mechanism of action of these drugs been related theoretically to the neurochemical basis of schizophrenia?

24. (a) At the present time, which is more widely consumed recreationally, PCP or ketamine? What are the reasons for this preference? (b) If someone wants to experience a relaxing effect from taking ketamine, should they take a relatively low dose or a relatively high dose? Explain your answer.

25. Describe the adverse consequences of heavy PCP or ketamine use on the brain and on peripheral organ systems.

26. You are the parent of an infant who needs to undergo a surgical procedure, and the doctor tells you that they are going to administer ketamine anesthetic to your baby in order to perform the surgery. Should you be worried about this? Explain your answer, including any conversation you may wish to have with the doctor prior to the procedure.

27. In addition to its recreational use and its use as a pediatric anesthetic, ketamine has additional therapeutic applications. What are these applications, and which are currently FDA-approved and which are still undergoing clinical studies?

28. Discuss the pharmacology and recreational use of dextromethorphan.

Inhalants, GHB, and Anabolic–Androgenic Steroids

16

AIR CONDITIONING IS ONE OF THE MARVELS OF MODERN CIVILIZATION, especially for those living in areas with hot and humid summer weather. We usually think of air conditioners as safe appliances; however, intentional exposure to the refrigerant inside the air conditioner by inhalation can be very dangerous. Why would someone purposely inhale air conditioning refrigerant? The answer, as you may already know, is because the fumes produce a brief "high" in the user. The same can be said for numerous other volatile liquids and gases, including glues, aerosol propellants, cigarette lighter fluids, and so-called "laughing gas."

These and related chemicals all belong to a broad class of misused substances known as **inhalants**. Most inhalants are perfectly legal, can easily be purchased at retail stores by people of any age, and are readily accessible in the home by anyone who can reach into a medicine cabinet or a kitchen drawer, or who can walk down the stairs to the basement or open the door to the garage. Moreover, in recent years these substances have been responsible for the abrupt death of a number of children and teenagers in many countries, including the United States. Indeed, the parents of children who have died from using inhalants invariably say that they never knew how dangerous these substances could be.

The first part of this chapter, section 16.1, discusses where inhalants come from, how they affect behavioral and neural functioning, and what health risks they pose. Sections 16.2 and 16.3 cover cover γ-hydroxybutyrate (GHB) and anabolic–androgenic steroids respectively. Although inhalants, GHB, and steroids differ in their mechanisms of action, they share the fact that they are all relative newcomers to the recreational drug scene compared with many other substances, such as alcohol, cannabis, tobacco, opioids, and the plant-derived hallucinogens. ■

Young people are particularly attracted to inhalants because of their low cost and easy availability and the rapid "high" they produce.

16.1 Inhalants

Inhalants represent a novel and diverse group of misused substances. They are also unusual in that users are typically children and adolescents.

Inhalants comprise a range of substances including volatile solvents, fuels, halogenated hydrocarbons, anesthetics, and nitrites

Abused inhalants often come from everyday household items. These substances have the following characteristics:

- They are either volatile (easily vaporized) liquids or gases at room temperature.

- They are used by inhaling fumes from a rag saturated with the substance ("huffing"),* sniffing fumes from a container of the substance ("sniffing" or "snorting"), inhaling fumes of the substance inside a plastic or paper bag ("bagging"), inhaling the substance from a balloon (a common method of nitrous oxide inhalation), or spraying an aerosol of the substance directly into one's nose or mouth (e.g., "glading" from a can of air freshener or "dusting" from a dust removal spray can).

- They do not belong to another defined class of misused substances that can be inhaled through smoking, which includes nicotine, Δ^9-tetrahydrocannabinol (THC), and cocaine.

Inhalants that are susceptible to recreational use mostly come from four categories: volatile solvents, fuels, halogenated hydrocarbons, and anesthetics (**TABLE 16.1**). **Volatile solvents** are chemicals that are liquid at room temperature but give off fumes that can be inhaled. Solvents are found in numerous household and industrial products, including adhesives, the ink used in felt-tip marking pens, spray paints, paint thinners and removers, nail polish remover, air fresheners, moth balls, and industrial degreasing agents. Yet a different group of products that contain a volatile solvent are cooling sprays that are applied topically to reduce muscle pain. The solvent in this case is ethyl chloride, which was a popular recreational inhalant in the 1980s, later disappeared from the scene, but has reappeared in this new guise. **Fuels** are volatile liquids or gases that serve many purposes, including automobile fuel, fuels for lamps and heating appliances, lighter fluids, and propellants used in many kinds of spray cans. The third category, **halogenated hydrocarbons**, is defined by the chemical structures of its members. These substances are all hydrocarbon molecules possessing one or more chlorine or fluorine atoms. Halogenated hydrocarbons

have numerous commercial uses as refrigerants, solvents, degreasers, and adhesives. They are also present as propellants in some compressed air dusters for computers and other devices and as the solvent in bottled typewriter or ink correction fluids. A small category of **anesthetics** includes nitrous oxide (also known as laughing gas), which is used in dentistry and in whipped cream dispensers, and two liquids (chloroform and ether) that were formerly used as small-animal anesthetic agents in veterinary medicine and laboratory research. Although these two compounds have been phased out as anesthetics in the United States, they are still produced and sold for specific chemical applications.

The fifth group of inhalants, called **nitrites**, is often placed in a separate category apart from other inhaled substances. Whereas most inhalants are taken to obtain a euphoric effect, or "high," nitrites are typically used to heighten sexual arousal and pleasure. Furthermore, unlike other inhalants, which are thought to act directly on nerve cells, nitrites produce their subjective effects primarily by dilating blood vessels and causing muscle relaxation. The most common members of this group are amyl nitrite ("poppers") and butyl nitrite. In the remainder of this section, we will focus on the first four classes of inhalants.

Inhalants are rapidly absorbed and readily enter the brain

We saw in previous chapters that drugs taken by vaporization and smoking, for example nicotine, crack cocaine, or THC, are rapidly absorbed through the lining of the lungs. The same is true for inhalant drugs. Once absorbed into the bloodstream, inhaled compounds rapidly reach the brain and readily cross the blood–brain barrier. For this reason, the acute effects of inhalants occur very quickly and may dissipate just as quickly once brain concentrations decline to low levels after a single use.

Most of us are occasionally exposed to low concentrations of abused inhalants because of their presence in glues, household cleaners, spray cans, paints and paint removers, and gasoline. One example is toluene, which not only has several common uses (see Table 16.1) but has also been studied extensively as a representative inhalant. Unlike other drugs discussed in previous chapters, inhalant doses are calculated with respect to the amount of the chemical in the air. The typical units used are **parts per million (ppm)**, which correspond to the number of molecules of inhalant (e.g., toluene) per million molecules of other gases in the air, which are mostly nitrogen and oxygen.

Because of the toxic nature of inhalants and the fact that workers in certain industries like the construction and chemical industries are at risk for higher exposures than the general public, regulatory agencies in the United States and other countries have adopted exposure

*Although the term huffing has the specific meaning given here, it is often used more generally to denote the breathing in of an inhalant.

TABLE 16.1	Some Commonly Abused Inhalants
Compound	**Principal uses**
Volatile solvents	
Acetone	Adhesives, nail polish remover, paint thinner
Ethyl chloride	Muscle spray (topical anesthetic)
n-Hexane	Adhesives, degreasers
Methanol	Paint remover, degreasers
Methylene chloride	Paint remover
Methyl butyl ketone	Denaturant, adhesive thinner, degreasers
Naphtha	Spray paint, adhesives, marker pens, lighter fluid
Naphthalene	Moth balls, toilet fresheners
Paradichlorobenzene	Moth balls, toilet fresheners
Toluene	Spray paint, adhesives, paint remover
Xylene	Spray paint, adhesives
Fuels	
Butane	Cigarette lighter refill, propellant
Gasoline (petrol)	Portable containers
Kerosene	Lighter fluid, lamp oil
Naphtha	Lighter fluid, propellant
Propane	Portable heating appliances
Halogenated hydrocarbons	
1,1-Difluoroethane (R-152a)	Compressed gas computer duster, propellant
Tetrachloroethane (R-130 and R-130a)	Refrigerant
Tetrafluoroethane (R-134a)	Refrigerant, computer duster
Tetrachloromethane (CCl_4)	Solvent, refrigerant
Trichloromethane	Adhesives, degreaser, spot remover
Trichloroethane	Adhesives, degreaser, spot remover, typewriter or ink correction fluid
Tetrachloroethylene ("PERC")	Dry cleaning solvent
Trichloroethylene	Degreaser
Anesthetics	
Chloroform	Laboratory anesthetic
Ether	Laboratory anesthetic
Nitrous oxide	Dental anesthetic, whipped cream dispensers
Nitrites	
Amyl nitrite	"Poppers"
Butyl nitrite	Video head cleaner, poppers

Source: Adapted from J. B. Ford et al. 2014. *Clinic Rev Allerg Immunol* 46: 19–33. doi.org/10.1007/s12016-013-8371-1

limits that cannot be exceeded legally. For example, the Permissible Exposure Limit for general industry specified by the Occupational Safety and Health Administration is 200 ppm averaged over time (i.e., an 8-hour work shift), with peak exposure not to exceed 500 ppm for a 10-minute period (United States Environmental Protection Agency, 2012). On the other hand, the National Institute for Occupational Safety and Health has adopted a Recommended Exposure Limit of 100 ppm based on the finding of "changes in muscle coordination, reaction time, and production of mental confusion and irritation of mucous membranes" at 200 ppm but not 100 ppm (United States Environmental Protection Agency, 2012; pp. 2–3). Even more stringent is the time-weighted average exposure of 20 ppm for toluene recommended by the American Conference of Governmental Industrial Hygienists, based on evidence that higher levels may increase the risk for spontaneous abortion in pregnant women. These differing values illustrate the complexity involved in ascertaining "safe" exposure to chemicals in the environment. Needless to say, people who are purposely inhaling toluene for recreational purposes are exposing themselves to much higher levels than those allowed legally or recommended to be safe.

These substances are particularly favored by children and adolescents

Statistics from the 2019 National Survey on Drug Use and Health indicate that an estimated 807,000 Americans 12 years of age or older were current users of inhalants at the time of the survey (Center for Behavioral Health Statistics and Quality, 2020). This figure shows an increase of over 31% from the estimated number of users in 2018. Even accounting for this increase, inhalant use is much less common than use of the other drug categories covered in previous chapters. What is troubling, however, is that inhalants are most commonly used by children and adolescents, with first use typically occurring between the ages of 12 and 16 (Nonnemaker et al., 2011). Indeed, it is not uncommon for inhalants to be the first substances tried by children, used even earlier than alcohol, tobacco, or marijuana. Solvents and aerosols in particular can be obtained legally and inexpensively. In fact, there are almost certainly plenty of them at home already in the kitchen, basement, or garage, and it may be difficult for parents and teachers to detect the use of inhalants if the child is careful. This is not to say that adults don't use inhalants, because obviously some do. Nevertheless, this class of substances is unusual in its special attractiveness to young people.

Researchers have investigated both the factors that contribute to inhalant use and the consequences of such use. For example, U.S. adolescents who have been maltreated and have come to the attention of the child welfare system are at higher risk for inhalant use than those who have not had those experiences. Increased inhalant use by child welfare–involved adolescents has been related to a high frequency of delinquent behaviors, affiliation with deviant peers (other adolescents who engage in serious problem behaviors like stealing, cheating, substance use, and aggression), and symptoms of depression (Merritt and Snyder, 2019). Not surprisingly, inhalant use by young people is a global problem and has been investigated in many countries outside of the United States. A study from Australia suggested that inhalant use (particularly gasoline sniffing in this particular study) might be a "gateway" to the subsequent use of other substances such as tobacco, alcohol, and marijuana (Crossin et al., 2017; see Section 9.1 for a discussion of the "gateway theory" of progression of substance use). Moreover, because inhalants are so easy to obtain and relatively inexpensive, they are widely used by "street children" in many low-income countries (Embleton et al., 2013). A study of street children in the city of Butwal, Nepal, found that 88% of the children surveyed engaged in glue sniffing, and of those, 40% were 9 to 12 years of age (Sah et al., 2020). Munaway and colleagues (2020) recently conducted a review and meta-analysis of inhalant use, particularly glue sniffing, among street children in India, Pakistan, Nepal, and Bangladesh. Glue was the preferred inhalant because of its availability, low cost, and lack of restrictions on purchasing. Across the various studies reviewed, reasons offered for glue sniffing included curiosity, peer pressure, an unhappy family environment, and simply seeking pleasure in the absence of other sources of pleasure in the children's lives. Some

children, both boys and girls, reported engaging in prostitution to earn money for their glue-sniffing habit.

Nitrous oxide tends to be used by a somewhat older population, ranging in age from late teens to young adults. This drug, which is commonly referred to as "hippy crack" by recreational users, can be obtained from small bulbs used to charge whipped cream dispensers or from larger commercial tanks. Taking nitrous oxide, called "nagging," can be done by inhaling directly from a whipped cream bulb, but more commonly, bulbs or large tanks are used to fill balloons, which then serve as the source of the gas. Unlike the inhalants discussed above, nitrous oxide is commonly used at music clubs and raves to enhance the social experience, similar to other "club drugs" like ecstasy (van Amsterdam et al., 2015).

The sections below will discuss the subjective effects of inhalants, their mechanism of action, and their propensity for abuse and dependence.

Many inhalant effects are similar to alcohol intoxication

The acute effects of volatile and gaseous inhalants are often compared to those seen with alcohol intoxication. The user initially experiences euphoria, stimulation, and disinhibition, which are followed by drowsiness and lightheadedness (Duncan and Lawrence, 2013). Heavier exposure causes stronger depressant effects, characterized by slurred speech, poor coordination, ataxia, and lethargy. Sensory distortions, even hallucinations, may occur. Accordingly, most common symptoms of inhalant intoxication reported by urban adolescent users in India were euphoria, hallucinations, lightheadedness, and drowsiness (Dhoble and Bibra, 2013). Moreover, a study of Mexican teenagers found that some users took inhalants specifically for the resulting illusions and hallucinations (Cruz and Domínguez, 2011). Very high doses can lead to anesthesia, loss of consciousness, and coma.

The pattern of inhalant effects varies not only with dose but also with frequency of use. Garland and Howard (2010) found that low-frequency inhalant users mainly reported positive effects of use (e.g., euphoria), whereas high-frequency users reported a mixture of positive and aversive effects (e.g., depressed mood, irritability, or suicidal thoughts). Some inhalant users experience delusional ideas, including the delusion that one can fly. In an early study by Evans and Raistrick (1987), users who thought they could fly actually jumped out of windows or trees, leading to at least one broken bone and various minor injuries, but fortunately no fatalities.

Chronic inhalant use can lead to tolerance and dependence

Although some individuals who try inhalants discontinue their use relatively quickly, others escalate their usage and subsequently develop tolerance and dependence on these substances (Perron et al., 2009a; Dhawan et al., 2015). Similar to users of other recreational substances, tolerant inhalant users need to take higher doses to obtain the expected euphoric effect. There is also evidence for an inhalant withdrawal syndrome, with symptoms such as nausea, fatigue, irritability, anxiety, sleep disturbances, and intense craving (Perron et al., 2009b; 2011). Not surprisingly, withdrawal symptoms are most commonly experienced by users who meet the criteria for inhalant dependence. **BOX 16.1** presents a case study of an adolescent inhalant user who developed severe dependence and withdrawal symptoms associated with his drug use.

Knowledge about how best to treat inhalant misuse and addiction has lagged that of other recreational substances; however, the situation has begun to improve. Inhalant users suffering from symptoms of acute intoxication are monitored closely and given supportive care until the symptoms subside. For longer-term treatment of individuals seeking to recover from chronic inhalant use, treatment providers have typically employed standard approaches used with other abused substances, such as 12-step programs, cognitive behavioral therapy, motivational enhancement, and family therapy (Nguyen et al., 2016). A few reports on more

targeted therapeutic approaches have also appeared in the literature. For example, Dell and coworkers (2005) reported on a holistic treatment program for inhalant users among First Nations* youth in Canada. A different approach was taken by researchers at Arizona State University in Phoenix, who developed a synchronized youth/parent intervention program aimed at *preventing* inhalant use in adolescent Latinos (Marsiglia et al., 2019). There is a continued need for more research on how to both prevent and treat the use of this category of recreational substances.

Rewarding and reinforcing effects have been demonstrated in animals

There are relatively few studies of inhalant reward and reinforcement using animal models, partly because of the difficulty of controlling airborne delivery of these substances by investigators who wish to model the typical route of human exposure. Some years back, procedures were developed that demonstrated the ability of toluene vapors to support place conditioning in laboratory rats and mice (Funada et al., 2002; Lee et al., 2006). Recently, a major advance in inhalant pharmacology

---

*"First Nations" refers to aboriginal peoples of Canada, comprising over 600 groups, and excluding the Inuit and Métis peoples who have separate ethnic origins.

BOX 16.1 ■ CASE STUDIES

Dependence and Withdrawal in an Adolescent Inhalant User

This case study is of a 14-year-old boy (C.) who was admitted to an inpatient adolescent unit of a major hospital in Charleston, SC, suffering from problems related to chronic inhalant use (Keriotis and Upadhyaya, 2000). According to the patient, he had begun using inhalants 3 years earlier, with the first episode occurring in his school bathroom. Over that period of time, C. had used a wide variety of inhalants, including glue, air fresheners, typewriter correction fluid, paint, and paint thinner. At school, he sniffed hidden marking pens during class as well as other substances that he had concealed in the bathroom for use during excused bathroom breaks. At home, he regularly "huffed" gasoline in the family garage, including multiple times at night when he would awaken with strong cravings. C. reported to his doctors that an episode of inhalant use would bring about a 3- to 5-minute period of intoxication, during which he experienced feelings of euphoria, striking visual hallucinations, and a racing heart.

Because C. was not permitted to use inhalants while in the hospital, he began to exhibit severe withdrawal symptoms. After the first day of abstinence, he reported feeling intense craving along with growing irritability and an inability to concentrate. The next day was characterized by increasing tension, anxiety, and

restlessness, accompanied by several somatic symptoms such as sweating, diarrhea, and tremors. C.'s mood became dysphoric, and he reported thoughts of suicide. After a week in the hospital, his physical symptoms had waned, though he continued to experience strong cravings. Feeling guilty about his inhalant use and being concerned about the risk of relapse, upon release from the hospital C. asked to be transferred to another facility where he could be monitored to ensure continued abstinence.

Several themes emerge from this case study. First is the ready availability of a wide range of products that emit chemical fumes with psychoactive properties. Second is that users like C. will readily avail themselves of whatever products are both handy and can be used discreetly without detection. Third is the powerful dependence that regular inhalant use can produce and the severe abstinence syndrome that can occur in the heavy user. The report by Keriotis and Upadhyaya does not provide any follow-up information, so we do not know what became of C. after his release from the hospital. Neither do we know whether his chronic use of inhalants over a 3-year period led to any lasting adverse effects on his health, a topic that we discuss later in this part of the chapter.

was made by the development of a method to train rats to self-administer toluene vapor (Braunscheidel et al., 2020). Briefly, adolescent rats were initially habituated to the odor of toluene vapor in the air (up to 500 ppm) over a period of 10 days. The animals were then trained in a vapor chamber with air inlets and outlets to perform a nose-poke response that resulted in a 15-second-long delivery into the chamber of either toluene vapor or air as a control. Data from a representative subject obtained during a 1-hour toluene testing session are shown in **FIGURE 16.1**. Toluene concentrations in ppm within the vapor chamber were measured every 15 seconds and are shown by the circles. Red circles indicate a nose-poke response that resulted in toluene delivery. As expected, each delivery of the vapor led to an increase in toluene concentration in the chamber. Furthermore, it appears that after 1200 seconds (20 minutes) of testing had elapsed, the subject had adjusted its response rate to obtain relatively consistent peak toluene concentrations of around 500 ppm. Dose titration of this kind is routinely seen with other recreational drugs. During the last week of testing, rats obtained an average of 11 toluene deliveries over each 1-hour session (data not shown here). These findings show that toluene, a representative member of the class of inhalant drugs, can serve as a reinforcer in the drug self-administration paradigm.

Researchers are slowly coming to understand the neural mechanisms underlying inhalant reward and reinforcement. In previous chapters, we saw that dopamine (DA) plays a role in the reinforcing properties of many abused drugs. Both in vivo and in vitro studies have shown that toluene can directly stimulate the firing of a subpopulation of dopaminergic neurons in the ventral tegmental area (VTA) (Riegel et al., 2007; Woodward and Beckley, 2014). This effect may result from an interaction of the compound with ion channels in the membrane of the VTA neurons. In accordance with its electrophysiological effects, toluene also increases extracellular DA levels in forebrain dopaminergic projection areas such as the dorsal striatum, nucleus

accumbens (NAcc), and prefrontal cortex (Woodward and Beckley, 2014). Furthermore, repeated exposure to high levels of toluene vapor for 7 days led to a reduction in electrically stimulated DA release in the NAcc (Apawu et al., 2020). This effect may contribute to inhalant tolerance in chronic users. Although the stimulatory actions of toluene on VTA cell firing and NAcc DA release suggest that DA may be involved in inhalant reward and reinforcement, at the time of this writing we are not aware of any direct tests of this hypothesis.

Inhalants have complex effects on central nervous system (CNS) function and behavioral activity

As mentioned earlier, inhalants are rapidly absorbed from the lungs into the bloodstream, and they quickly enter the brain because of their high lipid solubility. Madina Gerasimov and colleagues at the Brookhaven National Laboratory used positron emission tomography (PET) to investigate the localization of [^{11}C]toluene that had been administered to baboons (Gerasimov et al., 2002). The radiolabeled toluene reached all parts of the brain, but its distribution was not uniform (**FIGURE 16.2**). Quantitative measurements of the striatum, frontal cortex, thalamus, cerebellum, and white matter showed particularly high uptake in the striatum, thalamus, and deep cerebellar nuclei. These findings indicate that localization of inhalants within the brain needs to be taken into account by researchers who are trying to understand how these substances affect brain function and behavior.

Rodent studies have examined the influence of toluene on locomotor activity as well as the compound's interoceptive properties, using the drug discrimination paradigm. The effects of toluene on locomotor activity are biphasic: concentrations up to 1000 ppm produce locomotor activation, whereas higher concentrations produce increasing degrees of sedation (Beckley and Woodward, 2013). This inverted U-shaped dose–response curve is seen with ethanol and many other

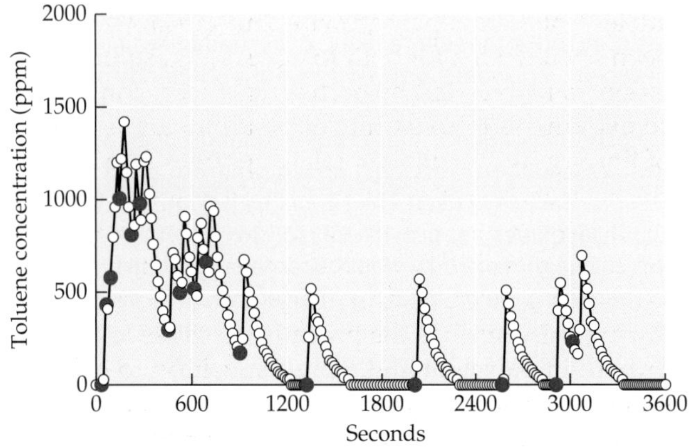

FIGURE 16.1 **Self-administration of toluene vapor** Following 10 days of habituation to the odor of toluene in the air, adolescent rats were trained on a nose-poke task to obtain a 15-second delivery of toluene vapor into the testing chamber during 1-hour (3600 seconds) testing sessions. The graph illustrates the results from one such session with a representative subject. Toluene concentrations within the chamber were measured every 15 seconds and are shown as circles on the graph. Red-filled circles represent nose-poke responses that resulted in delivery of the toluene vapor. Because the air within the chamber was constantly being replaced, toluene concentrations can be seen to decline to 0 if sufficient time had elapsed since the last vapor delivery. (After K. M. Braunscheidel et al. 2020. *Front Neurosci* 14: 880. © 2020 Braunscheidel, Wayman, Okas and Woodward. doi: 10.3389/fnins.2020.00880.)

(A)

(B)

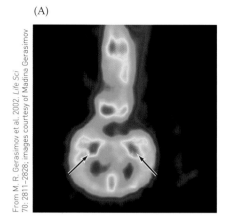
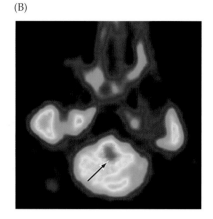

From M. R. Gerasimov et al. 2002. *Life Sci* 70: 2811–2828; images courtesy of Madina Gerasimov

Toluene concentration

High   Low

FIGURE 16.2 PET images of brain uptake and distribution of radiolabeled toluene in a baboon The animal was injected intravenously with [^{11}C]toluene and then was imaged 2 minutes later. The arrows show toluene being concentrated in the striatum (A) and in the deep cerebellar nuclei (B).

sedative drugs, and it also fits well with the initial euphoric and disinhibitory effects of toluene intoxication in humans that are later followed by sedation as brain inhalant concentrations continue to increase. Toluene-induced hyperactivity in rats can be attenuated by 6-hydroxydopamine lesions of the NAcc or by pretreating the animals with a D_1, D_2, or D_3 receptor antagonist (Riegel et al., 2003; Lo et al., 2009). Drug discrimination studies have shown that volatile solvents such as toluene exert stimulus effects similar to the barbiturates and benzodiazepines, two classes of sedating and anxiolytic drugs (see Chapter 17). In contrast, nitrous oxide has a profile more similar to that of uncompetitive NMDA receptor antagonists like phencyclidine and ketamine (Shelton, 2018).

The CNS-depressant actions characteristic of most inhalants at high doses can be explained, at least in part, by their effects on various ionotropic receptors. For example, toluene acutely enhances the function of inhibitory $GABA_A$ and glycine receptors, whereas it inhibits the activity of excitatory *N*-methyl-D-aspartate (NMDA) glutamate and nicotinic cholinergic receptors (Beckley and Woodward, 2013). Several voltage-gated ion channels are also influenced by inhalants. A similar profile of ionotropic receptor and voltage-gated ion channel effects has been demonstrated for other depressant drugs, including ethanol and various anesthetic compounds. Combining these data with the behavioral findings discussed above, we may hypothesize that the sedating and discriminative properties of inhalants involve brain mechanisms that are shared with many other CNS depressant agents.

It is important to note that prolonged exposure to toluene and other inhalants affects ion channels in a very different manner than acute exposure. Indeed, prolonged exposure seems to evoke a counter-regulatory response in which the function and expression of $GABA_A$ receptors is reduced and the function and expression of NMDA receptors is enhanced (Beckley and Woodward, 2013). Such changes would tend to promote increased rather than decreased brain excitability, and they may also help account for the locomotor sensitization that occurs as a result of repeated toluene exposure.

Health Risks Associated with Inhalant Use

The health risks of inhalant use are significant. Even a single use can be fatal through several possible mechanisms such as cardiac arrhythmia (loss of normal heart rhythm). This outcome, which was identified over 50 years ago (Bass, 1970), is termed **sudden sniffing death syndrome** (Bowen, 2011; Phatak and Walterscheid, 2012). Some cases of fatal cardiac arrhythmia have occurred following inhalation of refrigerant gases such as used in air conditioning units; however, other reported cases have involved toluene, butane, and propane.

Even though sudden sniffing death syndrome is rare, regular inhalant use can lead to many other serious adverse health consequences. These include damage to the heart, liver, kidneys, respiratory tract, and bone marrow (Ford et al., 2014; **FIGURE 16.3**). Bone marrow toxicity is responsible for the severe anemia observed in some chronic inhalant users. Of additional concern is that over time, chronic inhalant use by juveniles or adolescents can impair growth. This effect, which has been documented for both toluene and gasoline inhalation, is manifested by both weight loss (sometimes so extreme as to constitute emaciation) and stunting of linear growth. Inhalant-related growth impairment results from a combination of mechanisms involving disordered eating and metabolic abnormalities (Crossin et al., 2019a; 2019b). Because adolescence is normally a period of accelerated growth, chronic use of inhalants during this time has the potential to cause long-term growth impairment and a predisposition to develop metabolic disorders like type 2 diabetes later in life. Crossin and colleagues (2020) additionally discussed

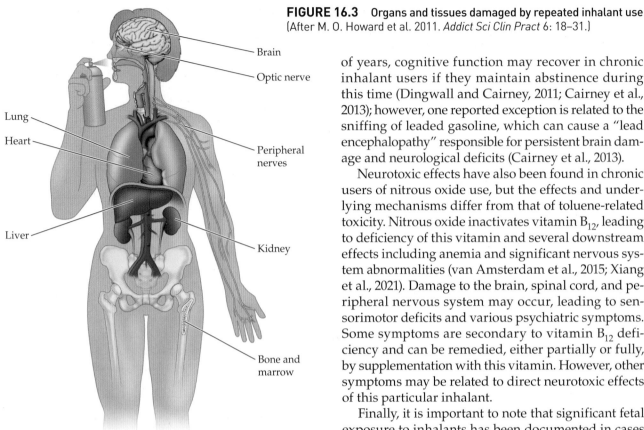

FIGURE 16.3 Organs and tissues damaged by repeated inhalant use (After M. O. Howard et al. 2011. *Addict Sci Clin Pract* 6: 18–31.)

of years, cognitive function may recover in chronic inhalant users if they maintain abstinence during this time (Dingwall and Cairney, 2011; Cairney et al., 2013); however, one reported exception is related to the sniffing of leaded gasoline, which can cause a "lead encephalopathy" responsible for persistent brain damage and neurological deficits (Cairney et al., 2013).

Neurotoxic effects have also been found in chronic users of nitrous oxide use, but the effects and underlying mechanisms differ from that of toluene-related toxicity. Nitrous oxide inactivates vitamin B_{12}, leading to deficiency of this vitamin and several downstream effects including anemia and significant nervous system abnormalities (van Amsterdam et al., 2015; Xiang et al., 2021). Damage to the brain, spinal cord, and peripheral nervous system may occur, leading to sensorimotor deficits and various psychiatric symptoms. Some symptoms are secondary to vitamin B_{12} deficiency and can be remedied, either partially or fully, by supplementation with this vitamin. However, other symptoms may be related to direct neurotoxic effects of this particular inhalant.

Finally, it is important to note that significant fetal exposure to inhalants has been documented in cases where the mother either was an inhalant abuser or was exposed to inhalants occupationally. Offspring of these women are often born prematurely and with reduced birth weight. In the most extreme cases, the infants exhibit physical malformations of the head and face that are similar to the abnormalities seen in newborn offspring of some alcoholic women (see Chapter 10). In parallel with the concept of a fetal alcohol syndrome, investigators in the inhalant field have coined the term **fetal solvent syndrome** to describe the craniofacial anomalies seen in the affected infants (Hannigan and Bowen, 2010; Bowen, 2011). It is well established that infants suffering from fetal alcohol syndrome show significant cognitive deficits, including severe mental retardation in the most

the possibility that repeated inhalant exposure by females could lead to reproductive abnormalities. However, the existing evidence is largely from women exposed to toluene in occupational settings. Future studies are needed that test this hypothesis in adolescent females who are misusing inhalants.

Of special concern to neuropharmacologists is the brain's vulnerability to inhalant toxicity. The brain tends to concentrate inhalants because of its high lipid content (especially myelin-rich white matter) and the tendency of these substances to readily dissolve in lipids. Consequently, chronic use of inhalants such as toluene can cause a syndrome called **toxic leukoencephalopathy**, which refers to generalized white matter damage caused by exposure to a toxic agent (Filley, 2013; Filley et al., 2017). The signs of toxic leukoencephalopathy include myelin degeneration, cerebellar dysfunction, damage to both the cranial and peripheral nerves, and dementia. Loss of myelin subsequently leads to pathological changes in axons and even loss of axons that had previously been covered by myelin sheaths (Licata and Renshaw, 2010). The brain damage caused by chronic abuse of inhalants, particularly toluene, has been studied extensively using magnetic resonance imaging (MRI), and the observed damage has been associated with cognitive and motivational impairment (**TABLE 16.2**) (Filley, 2013). Over a period

TABLE 16.2 Neurological Symptoms and Associated MRI Findings in Chronic Toluene Abusers

Neurological symptoms	MRI findings
Apathy and inattention	Cerebral, cerebellar, and brainstem atrophy
Memory impairment	Lateral, third, and fourth ventricle enlargement
Visuospatial dysfunction	Loss of gray–white matter differentiation

Source: After C. M. Filley 2013. *Psychiatr Clin N Am* 36: 293–302. © 2013. Reprinted with permission from Elsevier.

extreme cases. Some research indicating developmental delays and cognitive impairment in inhalant-exposed offspring has been published, but long-term outcome studies are still lacking at the time of this writing. Indeed, despite the occasional preclinical study examining the effects of prenatal toluene exposure in rodents, it seems that very little human clinical work of this kind is currently under way.

SECTION SUMMARY

■ Inhalants are misused substances that are often obtained from everyday household items. These substances are volatile liquids or gases at room temperature; are used by sniffing, inhaling, or spraying the substance; and do not belong to another defined class of misused drugs.

■ Inhalants comprise five categories of substances: volatile solvents, fuels, halogenated hydrocarbons, anesthetics, and nitrites. They are rapidly absorbed from the lungs and readily enter the brain because of their high lipid solubility. In contrast to most other misused substances, inhalant doses are calculated in parts per million (ppm).

■ Inhalants are most commonly used by children and adolescents, and they are often the first recreational substance tried by a child. A variety of adverse experiences during childhood and adolescence increase the risk for inhalant use. Contrary to other inhalants, nitrous oxide tends to be used by a somewhat older population.

■ Low doses of volatile and gaseous inhalants produce effects resembling those seen with alcohol intoxication. Users exposed to greater amounts of these substances show stronger depressant effects, including slurred speech, poor coordination, ataxia, sleepiness, and at very high doses, loss of consciousness and even coma. Sensory distortions, including hallucinations, may also occur.

■ Repeated inhalant use can lead to tolerance, dependence, and an abstinence syndrome when drug use is stopped. Withdrawal symptoms include nausea, fatigue, irritability, anxiety, sleep disturbances, and craving.

■ Inhalants are reinforcing to humans because of their euphoric effects, and laboratory animal studies have also established the rewarding and reinforcing properties of these substances by means of self-administration, place conditioning, and electrical stimulation of the brain. Studies using toluene as a representative inhalant have found that this compound activates ascending dopaminergic systems, causing increased firing of VTA dopaminergic neurons and enhanced DA release in forebrain projection areas. Activation of the mesolimbic dopaminergic system may play an important role in toluene's reinforcing and rewarding properties.

■ Toluene exerts biphasic effects on locomotor activity in rodents—that is, locomotor activation at low concentrations and locomotor inhibition/sedation at higher concentrations. In drug discrimination studies, toluene and related volatile solvents fully substitute for ethanol and pentobarbital, indicating that these substances

produce interoceptive cues like those of other sedative–hypnotic drugs.

■ The depressant effects of acute exposure to high concentrations of inhalants such as toluene can generally be attributed to a combination of enhanced activity of inhibitory $GABA_A$ and glycine receptors and inhibited activity of excitatory NMDA and nicotinic receptors. In contrast, prolonged inhalant exposure induces a counter-regulatory response characterized by increased $GABA_A$ receptor expression and function and decreased function and expression of NMDA receptors. These changes favor greater brain excitability and may also contribute to locomotor sensitization produced by repeated toluene exposure.

■ Inhalants present serious health risks, including damage to the liver, kidneys, respiratory tract, and bone marrow. Severe anemia in chronic inhalant users can result from bone marrow toxicity or, in the case of nitrous oxide, as a secondary consequence of vitamin B_{12} deficiency. Myelin-rich white matter in the brain is particularly vulnerable to repeated inhalant exposure, thereby resulting in a syndrome of toxic leukoencephalopathy. Symptoms of this syndrome include myelin degeneration, cerebellar dysfunction, nerve damage, and dementia. Some evidence exists for neurological recovery in most users following long-term abstinence.

■ Inhalant use can additionally lead to a rare disorder called sudden sniffing death syndrome, which in some cases results from an inhalant-induced cardiac arrhythmia. Moreover, some offspring exposed to inhalants in utero reportedly suffer from fetal solvent syndrome, which involves craniofacial abnormalities and possibly also cognitive deficits. These effects resemble those seen in individuals diagnosed with fetal alcohol syndrome.

16.2 Gamma-Hydroxybutyrate

Background

The second part of this chapter concerns **γ-hydroxybutyrate** (**GHB**), a simple chemical with a complicated history. As can be seen in **FIGURE 16.4A**, GHB is closely related structurally to the important inhibitory neurotransmitter GABA. In fact, GHB is actually produced in the brain as a by-product of GABA metabolism (**FIGURE 16.4B**) and is thought to function as a novel neurotransmitter/neuromodulator (Maitre et al., 2016; Trombley et al., 2020). GHB is one of only two recreational drugs (the other is the psychedelic drug dimethyltryptamine) known to be produced in the brain since all others are either plant-derived or are "man-made."

The localization and disposition of GHB in the brain have been well characterized. In the human brain, the highest levels of endogenous GBH are found in the striatum and the lowest levels are found in the cerebellum. A rare genetic disorder leads to overproduction

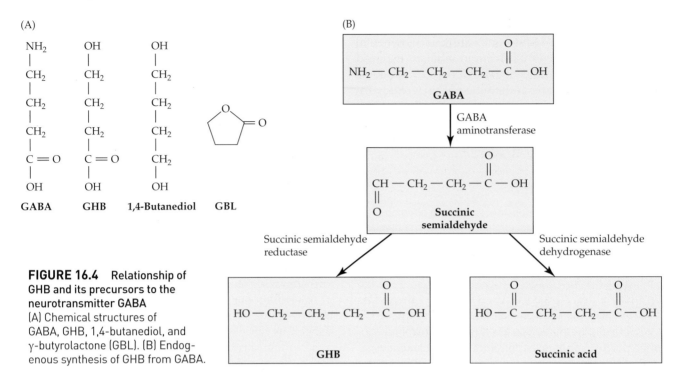

FIGURE 16.4 Relationship of GHB and its precursors to the neurotransmitter GABA (A) Chemical structures of GABA, GHB, 1,4-butanediol, and γ-butyrolactone (GBL). (B) Endogenous synthesis of GHB from GABA.

of GHB and a characteristic cluster of symptoms that may be related to excess levels of this substance (see **WEB BOX 16.1**). GHB can be taken up into GABAergic vesicles by the vesicular inhibitory amino acid transporter (VIAAT; see Chapter 8), which has led to the idea that some GHB may be co-released with GABA when the neuron fires and vesicular exocytosis occurs at the nerve terminal. GHB is a substrate for several forms of monocarboxylate transporters, membrane proteins that transport a wide range of monocarboxylates such as the intermediary metabolites lactate and pyruvate. These proteins are believed to be responsible for (1) transporting exogenous GHB (i.e., GHB taken as a drug) across the blood–brain barrier into the brain, and (2) mediating the uptake of extracellular GHB into neurons and astrocytes (Felmlee et al., 2021).

The first recorded synthesis of GHB was by the Russian chemist Alexander Zaytsev in 1874. However, the pharmacologic properties of this compound were not recognized until a 1960 report by a French team headed by Henri Laborit, the same scientist who discovered the antipsychotic drug chlorpromazine (Trombley et al., 2020). Laborit was looking for a GABA analog that would cross the blood–brain barrier more efficiently than GABA and thus might have therapeutic potential as a CNS depressant. Although early studies did confirm the ability of GHB to produce sedation and even anesthesia in laboratory animals and humans, it later fell into disfavor as an anesthetic and is currently used for other therapeutic purposes (see Section 16.2).

In the United States, little attention was paid to GHB until the 1980s, when it began to be marketed by health food stores as a nutritional supplement for bodybuilders. Despite a lack of supporting evidence, manufacturers claimed that GHB could reduce body fat and enhance muscle mass through its ability to stimulate growth hormone secretion by the pituitary gland. As time went on, the Food and Drug Administration (FDA) began to receive a number of reports of GHB-related illness, and in 1990 the FDA declared the drug to be unsafe and banned over-the-counter sales.

Despite the FDA ban, GHB use continued to grow, largely as the result of an upsurge in recreational use under various street names such as "liquid X," "liquid E," "Georgia home boy," "grievous bodily harm," "Heaven," "cherry meth," "organic Quaalude," and "nature's Quaalude." Some stores as well as internet sites began to sell GHB-containing formulations, and even now it's easy to find internet sellers who offer this product to customers. The GHB precursors γ-butyrolactone (GBL) and 1,4-butanediol (1,4-BD; see Figure 16.4A) are also available for purchase either for the purpose of synthesizing GHB at home or for direct consumption. Indeed, many users have begun to consume GBL directly instead of GHB because this precursor is rapidly converted to GHB within the body.

Recreational users typically report that they take GHB or its precursors for relaxation, euphoria, and/or sexual arousal (Bosch and Seifritz, 2016). Additionally, GHB is still thought by some users to help build muscle mass. In accordance with these real or perceived benefits, current evidence suggests that GHB is most likely to be consumed by three different subgroups of users: (1) attendees at nightclubs and dances or "raves," (2) bodybuilders, and (3) men who have sex with men (MSM) (Brennan and Van Hout, 2014). Use of GHB or its precursor GBL by MSM is most likely to occur in the context of chemsex or slamsex sessions (Busardò et al., 2018; Drevin et al., 2021). "Chemsex" is a term introduced to describe the use of enhancing substances during sexual encounters, and "slamsex" refers to a variety of chemsex in which the substance(s) is/are injected instead of consumed orally (Giorgetti et al., 2017; Scheibein et al., 2020). GHB and GBL are just two of the many substances used for chemsex; some of the others include methamphetamine, ketamine, mephedrone, synthetic cathinones, sildenafil (Viagra), and alkyl nitrites ("poppers").

Because of its availability and consumption at nightclubs and dances, GHB has sometimes been called a **club drug**.* Unfortunately, GHB has also been used as a "date rape" drug because of its intoxicating and heavily sedating effects at high doses (see **WEB BOX 16.2**). Increasing concerns over the problems associated with illicit GHB use led to its designation as a Schedule I controlled substance in 2000, thus making possession of the drug illegal except for medicinal use with a prescription.

The sections below will discuss the subjective and behavioral effects of GHB and its proposed mechanisms of action.

GHB produces behavioral sedation, intoxication, and learning deficits

Pure GHB is a solid powdery material; however, it is usually sold as a solution in water. GHB-containing solutions are clear, odorless, and almost tasteless. Such solutions are often packaged in small bottles similar to those used to package shampoo in hotel rooms. Typical recreational doses range from 1 to 3 g (approximately 14 to 42 mg/kg for a 70-kg adult), although some regular users may take as much as 4 or 5 g (about 57 to 71 mg/kg) at a time.

*Two other substances considered to be club drugs are 3,4-methylenedioxymethamphetamine (MDMA; see Chapter 6) and ketamine (see Chapter 15).

When a GHB-containing solution is drunk, the drug is rapidly absorbed from the gastrointestinal tract, enters the bloodstream, and crosses the blood–brain barrier without difficulty. The ensuing psychological and physiological effects are strongly dose related. Low doses of GHB produce an alcohol-like experience. Users report mild euphoria, relaxation, and increased sociality following drug ingestion (Abanades et al., 2006; Bosch et al., 2015). Indeed, these are among the experiences sought by typical recreational users of GHB, GBL, or 1,4-BD, although some users have also mentioned enhanced sexual arousal (Bosch and Seifritz, 2016). Sexual enhancement explains the use of GHB in chemsex and slamsex settings. Higher doses of GHB can cause lethargy, ataxia, slurring of speech, dizziness, nausea, and vomiting. Memory impairment has also been reported following a high dose of GHB (Carter et al., 2006). Finally, overdosing on this compound is very dangerous, since respiration is depressed and the user may become unconscious or even comatose (Dyer, 1991; Brennan and Van Hout, 2014). Alternatively, the individual may exhibit signs of seizure activity. Overdosing can readily occur if the user takes multiple doses over a short period of time, if there is a greater-than-expected concentration of GHB in the bottle, or if the drug is taken in combination with alcohol or another sedative–hypnotic drug.

In laboratory animals, acute GHB administration causes sedation, reduced locomotor activity, and decreased anxiety in certain tests such as the elevated plus-maze. At higher doses, animals show signs of catalepsy. Some of these behavioral effects, particularly hypolocomotion and catalepsy, are thought to be due to GHB-induced inhibition of DA release. Other studies found impaired spatial learning in young rats repeatedly given moderate doses of GHB (Pedraza et al., 2009; Sircar et al., 2010) (**FIGURE 16.5**). Such impairment may be related to neurotoxic effects of the drug treatment on the hippocampus, including reduced NMDA receptor expression and neuronal cell loss (Pedraza et al., 2009; Sircar et al., 2011).

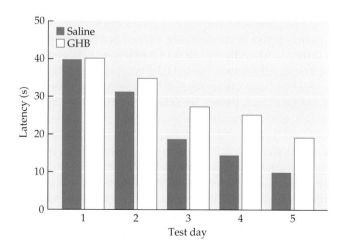

FIGURE 16.5 GHB impairs spatial navigation learning in adolescent female rats Female rats were trained in the Morris water maze for 5 days beginning at 30 days of age. The graph shows the latency to find the hidden platform by animals given either GHB (100 mg/kg IP) or saline vehicle 30 minutes before training each day. Beginning on day 3, the drug-treated group took significantly longer than the controls to find the platform. This impairment was not observed in adult rats treated in the same way, indicating greater vulnerability to GHB-induced learning impairment during adolescence. (After R. Sircar et al. 2010. *Pharmacol Biochem Behav* 96: 187–193. © 2010. Reprinted with permission from Elsevier.)

Electroencephalographic (EEG) recordings have revealed the presence of a paradoxical CNS excitation at high doses of GHB that some investigators have likened to absence (petit mal) seizures in humans and that may be related to the occasional reports of seizure activity in human overdose cases (Binienda et al., 2011). Absence seizures involve a temporary loss of consciousness and cessation of activity without the whole-body convulsions seen in a grand mal seizure. Researchers have investigated the possibility of developing an animal model of absence seizures based on GHB or GBL administration. Of the various species tested thus far, it appears that laboratory rats are the best choice for such a model (Venzi et al., 2015).

GHB and its precursors have reinforcing properties

We mentioned above that recreational users report a mild euphoria upon consumption of a low dose of GHB. This phenomenon was studied experimentally by Johnson and Griffiths (2013), who assessed the subjective effects of a range of GHB doses, compared with the effects elicited by alcohol. The participants consisted of a small group of regular users of sedative–hypnotic drugs, including ethanol but not necessarily GHB. Using several different questionnaires, the investigators showed dose-dependent positive effects of GHB that were similar to the effects of alcohol.

Consistent with these findings in humans, GHB also exerts rewarding and reinforcing effects in laboratory animals when tested at appropriate doses and under the right experimental conditions. Such effects were first shown in studies with rats and mice using standard place conditioning and self-administration methods (Nicholson and Balster, 2001; Itzhak and Ali, 2002). GHB was additionally found to induce a conditioned place preference when microinjected directly into the VTA (Watson et al., 2010). Subsequent research demonstrated intravenous (IV) self-administration of GHB, GBL, and 1,4-BD by baboons (Goodwin et al., 2011; 2013). However, the experiment required that the subjects initially be trained to lever press for infusions of cocaine, after which GHB or one of its precursors was substituted for cocaine as the infusion drug. Not all of the baboons responded reliably for GHB, and even in those baboons for which GHB served as an effective reinforcer, daily numbers of lever presses for GHB were often lower than the numbers of presses elicited by cocaine (**FIGURE 16.6**). Moreover, for some of the baboons switched to one of the substitute drugs, lever pressing dropped to the low response rates elicited by vehicle infusions (data not shown). From these findings we can conclude that while GHB, GBL, and 1,4-BD show some ability to serve as reinforcers in animal models, the effects seen with this class of drugs are not nearly as robust as those seen with many other major drugs of abuse such as cocaine, opioids, and alcohol.

Effects of GHB are mediated by multiple mechanisms

Historically there has been much confusion regarding the mechanism of action of GHB. Fortunately, recent findings have begun to clarify the situation, although some uncertainties remain. It's important that we first differentiate between potential sites of action of endogenous versus exogenous GHB. If GHB does function as a signaling agent in the brain, the receptors that mediate such signaling must have a high affinity for GHB because of the relatively low endogenous levels of this compound. Radioligand binding studies have, indeed, revealed the existence of sites in the rat brain that bind both GHB and the selective GHB antagonist NCS-382 with high affinity (Bay et al., 2014; Maitre et al., 2016); however, the nature of these sites continues to be controversial. A proposed GHB-specific receptor was initially cloned from rat brain; this was followed several years later by the isolation of two clones from human brain tissue that were proposed to code for GHB receptor isoforms. However, it appears that most other researchers within the field have not accepted these binding sites as authentic GHB receptors. It seems plausible that the putative specific, high-affinity GHB receptor might have excitatory effects on neuronal activity, since low GHB doses administered to rats increased cell firing in the prefrontal cortex (Godbout et al., 1995). This increase was blocked by NCS-382, and higher GHB doses caused an inhibition instead of an enhancement of cell firing, suggesting mediation by different receptors.

A different line of research found that GHB can act as a high-affinity partial agonist at $GABA_A$ receptor subtypes containing α4, β (particularly β1), and δ subunits. It is interesting to note that $GABA_A$ receptors containing α4, β, and δ subunits are located at extrasynaptic sites and exert a tonic inhibition of the neurons in which they're expressed (see Chapter 8). Thus, it is possible that the inhibitory effect mediated by these extrasynaptic $GABA_A$ receptors is produced not only by GABA but also by co-released GHB.

Exogenous administration of GHB, as occurs in human recreational or therapeutic use and in experimental animal studies, considerably elevates brain GHB concentrations. This increase permits an additional mechanism to come into play, namely the activation of $GABA_B$ receptors (Maitre et al., 2016; Felmlee et al., 2021). GHB is a weak agonist at $GABA_B$ receptors, and therefore at high tissue concentrations it could activate these receptors directly. The importance of $GABA_B$ receptor activation in the effects of exogenously administered GHB was shown by the fact that mutant mice lacking functional $GABA_B$ receptors retain high-affinity GHB binding sites but lack the behavioral and physiological responses to GHB treatment (e.g., reduced locomotor activity, hypothermia, and induction

Baboon 1

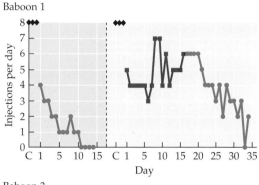

Baboon 2

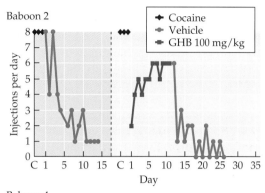

Baboon 3

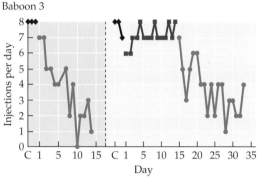

Baboon 4

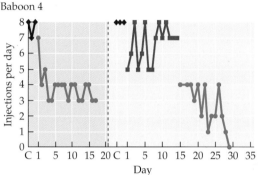

Baboon 5

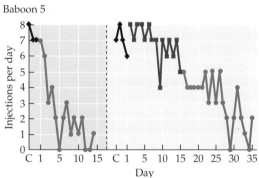

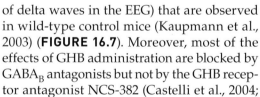

FIGURE 16.6 **Intravenous self-administration of GHB by baboons**
Nine adult male baboons were implanted with intravenous catheters and subsequently trained to respond on a pull-and-release lever for IV injections of cocaine (0.32 mg/kg). Researchers gradually increased the task demands until the subjects were reliably responding on a fixed-ratio-160 (FR-160) schedule of reinforcement (i.e., 160 responses were required to obtain each cocaine infusion). Five of the nine subjects trained to self-administer cocaine exhibited strong evidence for GHB reinforcement when given the opportunity to inject the latter drug, and the panels of the figure depict the individual response patterns measured in injections per day for these animals. The first set of data points in each panel (diamonds) shows that animal's injection rate for the last 3 days of cocaine (C) self-administration, which served as a baseline response measure. The subsequent blue circles show the expected falloff of responding when the drug vehicle was substituted for cocaine for 15 days (extinction). Cocaine availability was then restored for 3 to 4 days (data points immediately after the vertical dashed line) to induce a restoration of lever responding. Finally, GHB (100 mg/kg; squares) was substituted for cocaine for up to about 15 days, followed by vehicle again. The data show that GHB supported a response rate greater than that for vehicle (demonstrating a reinforcing effect) but generally lower than that for cocaine. (After A. K. Goodwin et al. 2011. *Drug Alcohol Depend* 114: 217–224. © 2010 Elsevier Ireland Ltd. Reprinted with permission from Elsevier.)

of delta waves in the EEG) that are observed in wild-type control mice (Kaupmann et al., 2003) (**FIGURE 16.7**). Moreover, most of the effects of GHB administration are blocked by $GABA_B$ antagonists but not by the GHB receptor antagonist NCS-382 (Castelli et al., 2004; Carter et al., 2009a). However, experimental animals can be trained to discriminate GHB from the $GABA_B$ agonist baclofen, which is consistent with the notion that non-$GABA_B$ receptors like those discussed above may contribute to some of the effects of GHB.

To summarize, GHB effects are thought to be mediated by three different kinds of receptors: (1) proposed high-affinity GHB-specific receptors, which may mediate the excitatory (neuronal) and stimulatory (behavioral) effects of low GHB doses; (2) a class of inhibitory extrasynaptic $GABA_A$ receptors; and (3)

$GABA_B$ receptors. The first two kinds of receptors are activated at relatively low GHB concentrations, whereas only high concentrations of GHB are able to activate $GABA_B$ receptors. Keep in mind, however, that GHB can also be metabolized to GABA. The GABA produced from this metabolic pathway is capable of activating any GABA receptors that are accessible to the transmitter.

Although GHB is discussed in the popular press primarily with regard to its recreational use and misuse, this compound also has recognized medical uses.

(A)

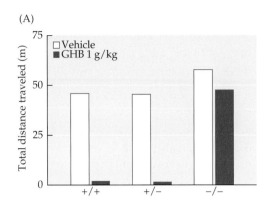

(B)

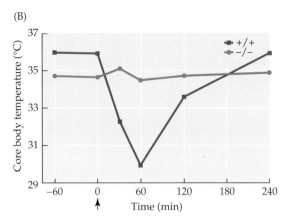

FIGURE 16.7 Loss of responses to exogenous GHB in mutant mice lacking functional GABA$_B$ receptors GHB (1 g/kg) was administered orally to wild-type mice (+/+), to mice that were homozygous for a null mutation of the GABA$_{B1}$ receptor subunit that is necessary for the formation of functional GABA$_B$ receptors (–/–) (see Chapter 8), and in one experiment, to heterozygous GABA$_{B1}$ knockouts (+/–). The wild-type mice but not the homozygous mutants showed (A) a strong sedative effect of GHB as indicated by distance traveled in a locomotor activity cage, and (B) a transient reduction in core body temperature after dosing (shown by the arrow at time 0). (After K. Kaupmann et al. 2003. *Eur J Neurosci* 18: 2722–2730.)

GHB is used therapeutically for the treatment of narcolepsy and alcoholism

Early clinical studies of GHB in the 1960s and 1970s showed that bedtime administration of this compound promoted normal sleep. These findings led to the first trials of GHB assessing its potential usefulness for treating narcolepsy, a sleep disorder previously discussed in Web Box 3.1. GHB was administered in the form of a sodium salt under the alternate name **sodium oxybate** (trade name **Xyrem**). The clinical trials showed that over time, sodium oxybate not only improved nighttime sleep, but also reduced daytime sleepiness and attacks of cataplexy. Unfortunately, the rise in recreational GHB use and misuse, evidence implicating GHB in some cases of sexual assault (see Web Box 16.2), and the subsequent scheduling of GHB as a controlled substance in 1990 all contributed to a delay in the clinical development and FDA approval of sodium oxybate for the treatment of narcolepsy. Despite these hurdles, FDA approval was granted in 2002, and the introduction of this pharmacotherapy has led to significant symptom reduction in patients with narcolepsy (Robinson and Keating, 2007; Boscolo-Berto et al., 2012). A recent meta-analysis of clinical trials involving administration of sodium oxybate to patients with narcolepsy found that compared to placebo, GHB treatment led to significant reductions in number of cataplexy attacks, amount of daytime sleepiness, and incidence of hypnagogic hallucinations (vivid, dream-like sensory experiences that can occur during the transition from waking to sleep) (Xu et al., 2019). Treated patients also reported an improvement in their overall quality of life. Unfortunately, therapeutically effective doses of GHB also caused several adverse side effects, including nausea, vomiting, dizziness, and enuresis (loss of bladder control), which led some patients to withdraw from the trial and stop taking the medication.

Sodium oxybate is approved for other medical applications in several European countries. In France and Germany, sodium oxybate is used as an IV anesthetic, which is understandable in light of the drug's sedating properties at high doses. This compound has also been administered for many years in Italy and Austria as a pharmacotherapeutic agent for treating alcohol use disorder (Keating, 2014; Caputo et al., 2016). Clinical studies have indicated that the drug is particularly useful in dealing with alcohol withdrawal symptoms and in helping to prevent relapse by reducing craving. Some of these studies suggest that sodium oxybate compares favorably in therapeutic efficacy with the pharmacotherapies currently licensed in the United States, namely disulfiram, naltrexone, and acamprosate (see Chapter 10 for more information on these medications). On the other hand, some investigators have argued that there is greater risk of misuse of sodium oxybate by patients with alcohol use disorder than by individuals with narcolepsy (Sewell and Petrakis, 2011). Thus, if this compound is eventually accepted for the treatment of alcoholism in this country, it will probably be used under carefully controlled conditions (e.g., in inpatient settings).

GHB has significant dependence potential when used recreationally

Miotto and coworkers (2001) surveyed 42 regular GHB users in the Los Angeles area about their experiences while under the influence of GHB and the effects that occurred after drug use. As shown in **TABLE 16.3**, GHB users reported the expected feelings of euphoria and well-being, heightened sexuality and sensory perception, and feelings of relaxation and disinhibition during the period of drug intoxication. Loss of consciousness, which is a sign of GHB overdose, sometimes also occurred. In contrast to the (mostly) subjectively positive

TABLE 16.3 Commonly Reported Experiences during and after Recreational GHB Use

During GHB use	After GHB use
Euphoria	Sluggishness and exhaustion
Enhanced sexual experience	Amnesia
Increased feelings of well-being	Confusion
Feelings of relaxation and tranquility	Anxiety
Heightened sensory perception	Insomnia
Disinhibition	Weakness
Loss of consciousness	Agitation

Source: From K. Miotto et al. 2001. *Am J Addict* 10: 232–241.

aspects of GHB intoxication, the period of drug "comedown" seemed to be rather unpleasant. Users commonly reported sluggishness, mental confusion and amnesia, weakness, and increased arousal, as indicated by feelings of anxiety and agitation and difficulty sleeping during the period following GHB consumption.

Numerous risks have been associated with recreational GHB use. The intoxicated state produced by this compound is similar to alcohol intoxication (i.e., drunkenness), and indeed GHB consumption has been linked to real-world cases of risky driving because of drug-induced psychomotor deficits (Centola et al., 2018). Even the lower dose of GHB used to treat narcolepsy was found to produce significant impairment in a laboratory study of simulated driving (Liakoni et al., 2018). This impairment was observed at 1 hour but not 3 hours after dosing, indicating that patients taking GHB can safely drive as long as they wait a sufficient length of time after taking the medication.

Excessive consumption (overdose) of GHB can cause an acute toxic reaction that includes unconsciousness or even coma, respiratory depression, bradycardia (slowed heart rate), and hypotension (Drasbek et al., 2006; Wood et al., 2011). Concurrent use of alcohol results in an additive response that is extremely dangerous and can lead to hospitalization (Galicia et al., 2019). Most people who experience a GHB overdose recover without obvious adverse consequences (Munir et al., 2008); however, fatalities have been reported, mostly as the result of cardiorespiratory arrest (Zvosec et al., 2011).

Repeated GHB exposure can lead to the development of tolerance and dependence. For example, daily treatment of mice with 200 mg/kg GHB produced tolerance to the activity-suppressing effects of the drug (Itzhak and Ali, 2002) (**FIGURE 16.8**). Chronic GHB use by humans can elicit not only tolerance but also a syndrome of dependence and withdrawal when abstinence is attempted. Indeed, some dependent users engage in binges characterized by GHB consumption every 2 to 4 hours around the clock. Symptoms of GHB withdrawal include anxiety, agitation, tremor, tachycardia (increased heart rate), insomnia, confusion, and, in extreme cases, hallucinations and a state of delirium (Brunt et al., 2014; Busardò and Jones, 2015). Withdrawal starts to occur within a few hours of the last dose and, in severe cases, can last up to a few weeks. Clinicians typically treat the symptoms of GHB withdrawal with high doses of a benzodiazepine such as diazepam, but such treatment is not always effective. Consequently, the Netherlands instituted a different protocol for detoxifying GHB-dependent patients by administering Xyrem at a high starting dose and then tapering the medication until the individual is symptom-free. This treatment program proved effective in the short-term management of GHB dependence, but unfortunately the majority of treated patients relapsed to either occasional or frequent GHB use within 3 months (Brunt et al., 2014). More recently, researchers have presented preliminary evidence that the $GABA_B$ receptor agonist baclofen may be beneficial in mitigating GHB withdrawal symptoms (Floyd et al., 2018) and in reducing the risk of relapse in detoxified GHB users (Beurmanjer et al., 2018; Habibian et al., 2019). However, properly controlled and more extensive clinical trials need to be performed before any firm conclusions can be drawn with respect to baclofen's efficacy for these purposes.

Although we know relatively little about the long-term effects of heavy GHB use, concerns have been raised with regard to users who have overdosed and gone into a drug-induced coma, particularly if this has occurred multiple times. Patients who are admitted to the hospital following a GHB overdose often present with symptoms of bradycardia (low heart rate), hypothermia, and coma (Liechti et al., 2006). A research group in the Netherlands reported that regular GHB

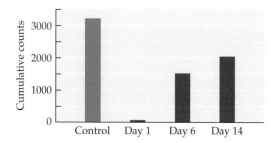

FIGURE 16.8 Tolerance to the locomotor suppressant effects of GHB in mice Mice were given 200 mg/kg GHB IP for 14 days. Locomotor activity in a photobeam apparatus was measured for 2 hours following drug administration on days 1, 6, and 14 of treatment. The figure illustrates the number of beam breaks recorded from 30 to 60 minutes post-treatment on each of these days. Compared with control mice administered saline, the GHB-treated animals showed a nearly complete cessation of locomotor activity on day 1, whereas a partial return of activity was observed on subsequent test days. (After Y. Itzhak and S. F. Ali. 2002. *Ann NY Acad Sci* 965: 451–460.)

users who had experienced four or more comas showed memory deficits compared to non-coma GHB users or users of recreational substances other than GHB (Pereira et al., 2018a; 2018b). These findings do not prove that the GHB-induced comas *caused* the deficient memory performance; however, they raise sufficient concern that users should be aware of the potential risk to their cognitive functioning if they repeatedly overdose to the point of becoming comatose.

SECTION SUMMARY

- GHB is an analog of the inhibitory neurotransmitter GABA. It is synthesized in the brain in small amounts and is thought to function as a neurotransmitter/neuromodulator that may be co-released with GABA at some synapses.

- GHB was developed pharmacologically as a CNS depressant, but it was later marketed in the United States as a bodybuilding supplement and for recreational use.

- Over-the-counter sales of GHB were banned in 1990, and the drug was designated as a Schedule I controlled substance in 2000. Nevertheless, GHB and its precursors GBL and 1,4-BD continue to be available for sale over the internet. GHB is most likely to be consumed by three different subgroups of users: attendees at dances and raves, bodybuilders, and men who have sex with men. Men who have sex with men are most likely to consume GBH during chemsex sessions.

- GHB is sometimes placed within the category of "club drugs." Whether in a club or in a different kind of social context, GBH is one of a number of different compounds, most of which have sedative properties, that have been used in drug-facilitated sexual assaults.

- GHB is usually taken orally in the form of an aqueous solution. Low doses produce alcohol-like effects including mild euphoria, relaxation, and social disinhibition. These effects, along with enhancement of sexual arousal, are the experiences sought by typical recreational users of GHB, GBL, or 1,4-BD. Higher doses of these compounds are associated with stronger sedating effects, as well as dizziness, nausea, vomiting, and memory impairment. Severe overdosing with GHB causes severe respiratory depression, unconsciousness, and even coma.

- Animals treated with GHB exhibit sedation, reduced locomotor activity, decreased anxiety behavior, and catalepsy at high doses. Impaired spatial learning has also been reported, which may be related to neurotoxic effects on the hippocampus.

- High doses of GHB can lead to EEG excitation resembling absence (petit mal) seizures in humans. A rat model of absence seizures has been developed based on administration of the appropriate doses of GHB or GBL.

- In regular users of sedative–hypnotic drugs, GHB ingestion produced positive subjective effects similar to those produced by ethanol. In laboratory animals, GHB and its precursors exert rewarding and reinforcing effects when tested under the appropriate dose and experimental conditions. However, these effects are not as robust as those seen with many other major drugs of abuse.

- The functional effects of GHB are mediated by multiple mechanisms. The low levels of endogenous GHB are believed to act on putative high-affinity GBH-specific receptors and on extrasynaptic $GABA_A$ receptors containing $\alpha4$, β, and δ subunits. High levels of exogenously administered GHB are additionally capable of activating $GABA_B$ receptors, which mediate many of the behavioral and physiological effects observed in GHB-treated animals.

- The sodium salt of GHB (also called sodium oxybate; trade name Xyrem) is approved in the United States for the treatment of the sleep disorder narcolepsy. This treatment improves nighttime sleep and reduces the incidence of daytime sleepiness and attacks of catalepsy. In several European countries, sodium oxybate is approved for use as an IV anesthetic or for the treatment of alcoholism. In the latter application, the drug has been shown to ameliorate alcohol withdrawal symptoms and to reduce craving during abstinence from alcohol.

- Recreational GHB users reportedly experience euphoria, heightened sexuality, and feelings of relaxation during drug intoxication. In several respects, GHB intoxication resembles the state of alcohol intoxication, including impairment of psychomotor function and even loss of consciousness with overdose. The "comedown" following GHB use is characterized by sluggishness, mental confusion and amnesia, weakness, and increased arousal.

- Repeated GHB use can lead to tolerance, dependence, and withdrawal. Consumption patterns may escalate to dosing every 2 to 4 hours around the clock. In heavy GHB users, withdrawal symptoms can start within a few hours after the last dose and can persist for up to a few weeks. Typical withdrawal symptoms include insomnia, anxiety, and tremors, although use of extremely high doses can apparently cause a psychotic reaction involving hallucinations, delirium, and extreme agitation.

- Researchers have reported memory deficits in regular GHB users who have experienced multiple comas from overdosing on the drug.

- Patients diagnosed with GHB dependence are typically treated with high doses of a benzodiazepine such as diazepam to help them get through the withdrawal period. Alternative medications that have been tested include Xyrem itself, starting with a high dose and then gradually tapering the medication until the patient is symptom free, and more recently the $GABA_B$ receptor agonist baclofen.

16.3 Anabolic–Androgenic Steroids

Going back a number of years, the popular press has revealed numerous instances of formerly revered sports heroes being found guilty of taking various performance-enhancing substances (sometimes also called **doping agents**). Use of specific foods or drugs to enhance performance dates back at least to the ancient Greek and Roman athletes, who consumed a variety of natural substances thought to provide increased energy, strength, and endurance (Conti, 2010). Although many doping agents are currently available, especially to a world-class athlete, one particularly important category of performance enhancers is a group of compounds called **anabolic–androgenic steroids (AAS)**. These are defined as steroid hormones that increase muscle mass (the "anabolic" part) and also have masculinizing, or testosterone-like, properties (the "androgenic" part).* On the street, these substances are usually just called anabolic steroids, but there are no members of the group that aren't also androgenic.

Why are AAS being discussed in a chapter on recreational substances? Compared with other misused substances, AAS have a unique structure and mechanism of action. However, they share the ability to cause dependence when used regularly in large amounts. There is significant evidence that these hormones are misused by many individuals, and there is evidence that AAS can produce an addiction-like pattern of compulsive use. Before we discuss these ideas, however, we will present basic information on these substances and how they entered the realm of bodybuilding and athletic competition.

AAS are structurally related to testosterone

The chemical and trade names of some common AAS are presented in **TABLE 16.4**. These compounds are taken by several different routes. Steroids being used for muscle building and performance enhancement are most often taken orally or by intramuscular injection. AAS prescribed for medicinal purposes are sometimes formulated for buccal or transdermal absorption from a topical gel or skin patch. Intramuscularly administered steroids are formulated for depot injection and maintain their potency for periods ranging from several days to 3 weeks, depending on the steroid. As shown in **FIGURE 16.9**, these compounds are all structurally related to testosterone, the principal androgen synthesized by the testes. However, because it is the anabolic rather than androgenic effects that are desired by most users, the chemical modifications that differentiate various synthetic steroids from testosterone are aimed at selectively enhancing their anabolic potency. Because the oral steroids are potentially vulnerable to first-pass metabolism in the liver, these compounds are chemically designed to minimize this problem and thus retain adequate bioavailability.

AAS were developed to help build muscle mass and enhance athletic performance

The chemical structure of testosterone was elucidated in 1935, followed soon by the development of methods to synthesize this hormone. It also did not take too long for the strength-enhancing properties of testosterone to be recognized. For example, a 1945 book by Paul de Kruif entitled *The Male Hormone* states on the cover that this hormone "boosts muscle power." According to Kanayama and Pope (2018), rumors existed that bodybuilders on the West Coast had already begun to use AAS by the late 1940s and early 1950s. Nevertheless, most American athletes knew little about these compounds before the 1954 World Weight-lifting Championships held in Vienna, Austria. Until 1953, American weightlifters had routinely beaten teams from what was then the Soviet Union (USSR), but the Soviets outscored the Americans in that year and again in 1954.

TABLE 16.4	Some Common Anabolic–Androgenic Steroids	
Generic name	**Trade name**	**Route of administration**
Methandrostenolone	Dianabol	Oral
Testosterone undecanoate	Andriol	Oral
Oxandrolone	Oxandrin	Oral
Oxymetholone	Anadrol	Oral
Stanozolol	Winstrol	Oral or injection
Tetrahydrogestrinone	"The Clear" (street name)	Oral or injection
Testosterone cypionate	Depot-Testosterone	Injection
Testosterone enanthate	Primoteston	Injection
Testosterone propionate	Testoprop	Injection
Nandrolone phenylpropionate	Durabolin	Injection
Nandrolone decanoate	Deca-Durabolin	Injection
Methenolone acetate	Primobolan	Injection
Methenolone enanthate	Primobolan Depot	Injection
Trenbolone enanthate	None	Injection
Testosterone	Striant	Buccal
Testosterone	AndroGel	Topical gel
Testosterone	"The Cream" (street name)	Topical gel
Testosterone	Androderm	Transdermal (skin patch)

*One of the first recorded uses of anabolic steroids was that of the sixth-century BCE Olympian wrestler Milo of Croton, who ate a diet that included bull testicles in order to maintain his award-winning performance (Conti, 2010).

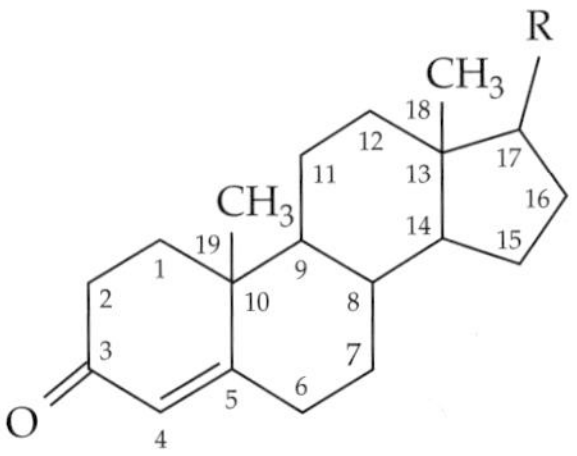

Core structure of
testosterone-related steroids

Compound	R
Testosterone	— OH
Testosterone enanthate	— O — CO(CH$_2$)$_5$CH$_3$
Testosterone undecanoate	— O — CO(CH$_2$)$_9$CH$_3$
Testosterone cypionate	— O — COCH$_2$CH$_2$ — (cyclopentyl) 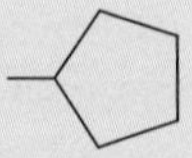
Nandrolone decanoate	— O — CO(CH$_2$)$_8$CH$_3$ (no methyl group at position 19)
Nandrolone phenylproprionate	— O — CO(CH$_2$)$_2$ 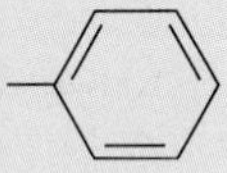 — (phenyl) (no methyl group at position 19)

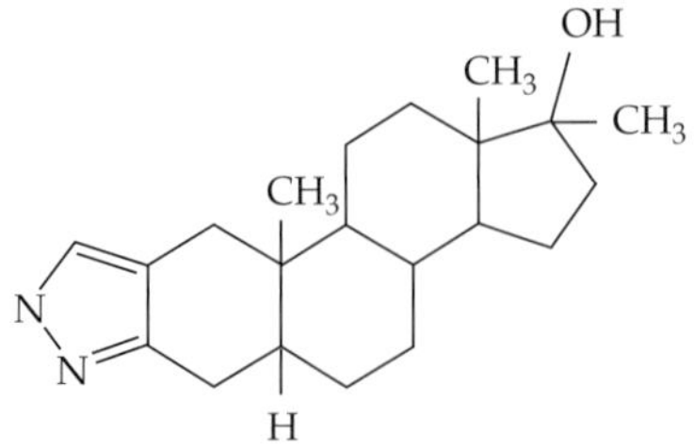

Stanozolol

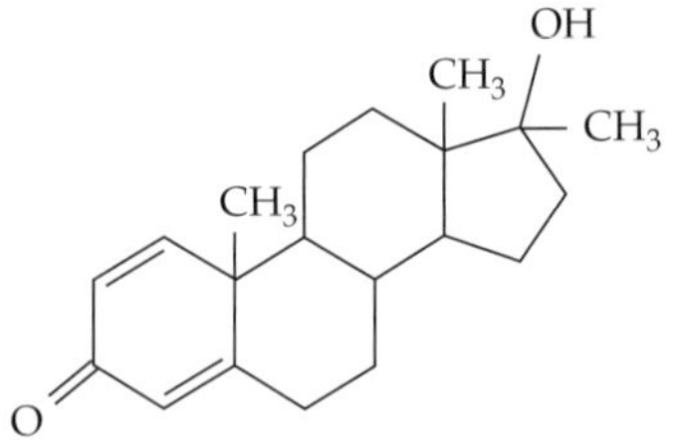

Methandrostenolone

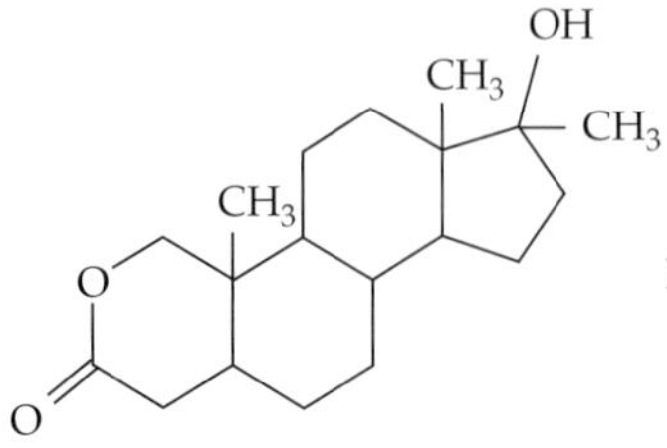

Oxandrolone

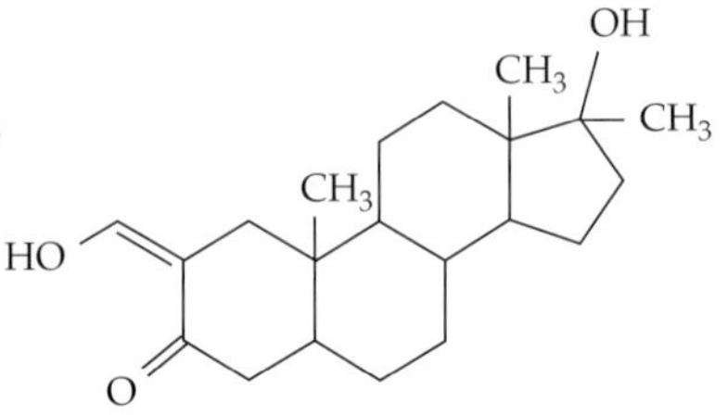

Oxymetholone

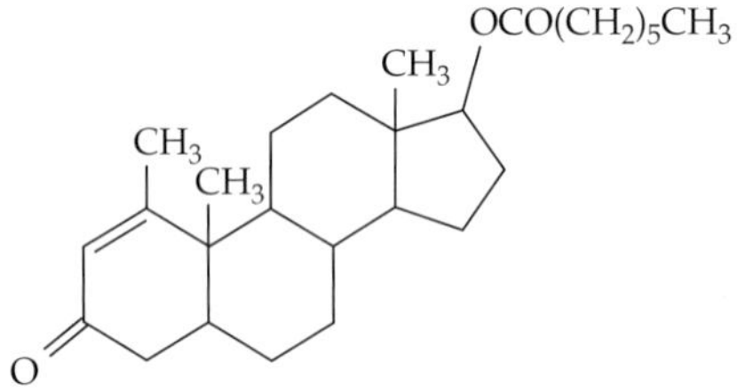

Methenolone enanthate

FIGURE 16.9 Chemical structures of some commonly abused anabolic–androgenic steroids

During the Vienna competition, the U.S. and Soviet team physicians reportedly went out in the evening for entertainment, and after a few drinks, the physician for the Soviet Union squad confided that some of his men were using testosterone. Dr. John Ziegler, who was the American physician, went back home and began to experiment with testosterone, but he didn't like the strong androgenic side effects. Ziegler expressed to the giant pharmaceutical company Ciba the need for a more anabolic, less androgenic compound. Within a few years, Ciba introduced Dianabol, an orally active compound with enhanced anabolic properties. When Dianabol was administered to elite weightlifters at the famous York Barbell Club in Pennsylvania, the drug produced spectacular results. Once the news got out, many similar compounds quickly followed, and strength athletes began to view steroids as the only way to reach the highest level of achievement. According to a 1969 article in the magazine *Track and Field News* entitled "Steroids: Breakfast of Champions," these substances were readily available to athletes either from physicians who were willing to write the necessary prescription or even from some pharmacists who dispensed steroids without requiring a prescription (Hendershott, 1969).

Furthermore, for many years AAS were viewed within the user community as being safe to use. Daniel Duchaine, a former bodybuilder and promoter of AAS use, offered the following statement in his 1989 *Underground Steroid Handbook II*: "The more you take, the more you will grow … there is no such thing as taking too much steroid … and the risk has been virtually non-existent in healthy athletes" (quoted in Basaria, 2018, p. 2). As we will see, Duchaine was wrong, since there are numerous adverse side effects of repeated AAS use. Indeed, Dr. Ziegler later recognized the monster that he had helped create, and by the time of his death in 1984, he profoundly regretted that part of his life.

Besides the Soviet Union, the German Democratic Republic (GDR, or East Germany) began secretly giving AAS to its elite athletes in the 1960s, and this doping program continued until the fall of communist rule in the GDR in 1989. Overall, approximately 10,000 athletes (!) were administered steroids in order to enhance their performance at national and international competitions (Franke and Beredonk, 1997; Huang and Basaria, 2018). The most commonly used compound in the GDR was chlordehydromethyltestosterone, known as Oral Turinabol. The East Germans had especially

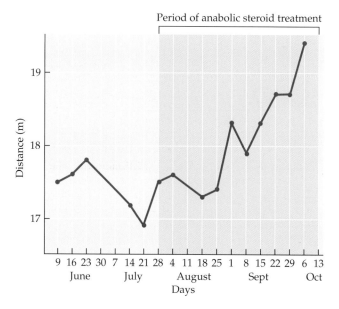

Period of anabolic steroid treatment

FIGURE 16.10 Performance enhancement of a female shot-putter in former East Germany Shot-put distance increased markedly over the 11-week period during which the athlete was chronically treated with an anabolic–androgenic steroid. (After K-H. Bauersfeld et al. 1973. *Scientific Report. German Athletic Association (DVfL) of the GDR.* Science Center of the DVfL: 41pp.; and W. W. Franke and B. Berendonk. 1997. *Clin Chem* 43: 1262–1279. By permission of American Association of Clinical Chemistry.)

great success with their female athletes, who won many Olympic and world championships with the aid of AAS. **FIGURE 16.10** illustrates the improved performance of a female shot-putter over an 11-week period of Oral Turinabol treatment. Unfortunately, these competitors paid a high price for their achievements, in part because of the powerful side effects of AAS in women. As we will discuss later, one of these side effects is the development of male secondary sex characteristics such as facial hair and an Adam's apple. Indeed, the masculine appearance of many female athletes from the GDR and other Soviet bloc countries during this time led to speculation that these competitors either were hermaphrodites (individuals possessing both sets of sex organs) or were men disguising themselves as women. As a result, officials for the 1967 European Championship soccer tournament required testing to verify the chromosomal sex of the participants (Bird et al., 2016).

Widespread public awareness of AAS use by elite athletes can be traced to the revelation that Ben Johnson, a Canadian sprinter and world record setter in the 100-meter dash at the 1988 Seoul Olympic Games, had been taking the banned steroid stanozolol during his training. Johnson was stripped of his Olympic gold medal and was suspended from athletic competition. Later, a San Francisco–area enterprise called the Bay Area Laboratory Cooperative (BALCO) was reported to have provided AAS to a number of famous athletes, most notably Barry Bonds, who is the Major League Baseball career leader in home runs per season and total home runs. Among the steroids provided by BALCO were preparations that came to be called "the Cream" and "the Clear" by athletes seeking to enhance their performance with these substances (see Table 16.4). Members of the public and sports journalists have voiced their concerns over allegations of steroid use, which has been reflected in recent balloting for the Baseball Hall of Fame. Thus

far, no former player who is strongly suspected of steroid use, including Bonds and the all-time great pitcher Roger Clemens, has been elected to the Hall.

By the mid-1980s, there were increasing reports of rampant AAS use not only in professional sports but also reaching down into colleges and even high schools. This progression was aided by the publication of practical guides to steroid use, such as Duchaine's *Underground Steroid Handbook I* and *II*, and Phillips's *Anabolic Reference Guide* (Kanayama and Pope, 2018). In response, the U.S. Congress held a series of hearings between 1988 and 1990 that culminated in the Anabolic Steroids Control Act of 1990. This legislation classified 27 specific AAS preparations as Schedule III controlled substances, thus making their use illegal without a medical prescription. In addition, these substances are banned by many amateur and professional sports organizations, including the National Collegiate Athletic Association, the International Olympic Committee, the National Football League, the National Basketball Association, and Major League Baseball.

It should be noted that AAS represent only one class of substances used to enhance performance in competitive sports. **FIGURE 16.11** shows the range of different doping substances, the sports in which each is typically used, and whether the substance is taken in or out of competition (i.e., during the sporting event or during pre-competition training or post-competition recovery) (Handelsman, 2020). For example, so-called "skill" sports do not require athletes to bulk up with extra muscle or to increase their stamina using blood-doping methods. Rather, competitors in those sports may choose to use beta-blockers (β-adrenergic receptor antagonists) to reduce anxiety and fine muscle tremors. Alternatively, other competitors may use stimulants like amphetamine to enhance focus during the event. Erythropoietin is a kidney hormone that increases the formation of red blood cells, thereby increasing blood oxygen-carrying capacity. Growth hormone (GH) and other growth-promoting substances are particularly valued for their ability to accelerate recovery from injury or from intense training.

AAS are currently taken by many adolescent and adult men

Despite legal restrictions governing the availability of AAS for nonmedical purposes, these compounds continue to be misused because of their availability from

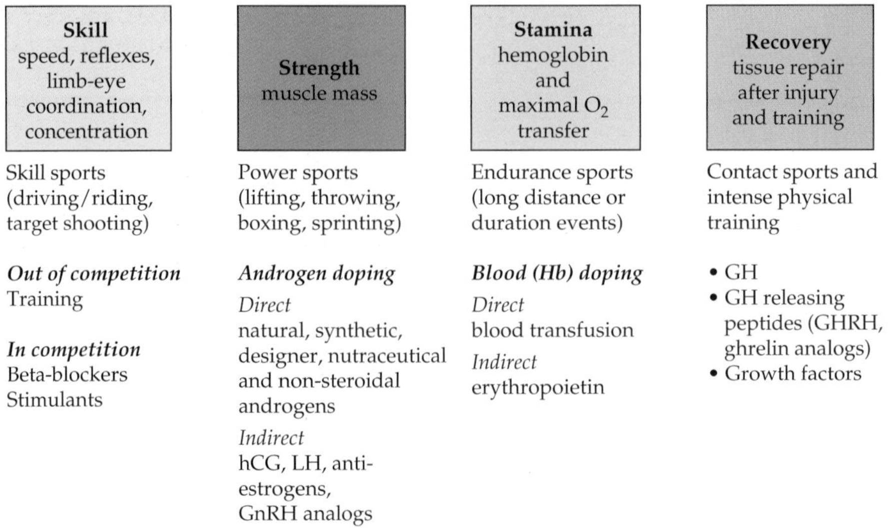

FIGURE 16.11 Substances that enhance sports performance
A variety of substances are used by competitors to enhance performance in their particular sport. Abbreviations: GH, growth hormone; GHRH, growth hormone releasing hormone; GnRH, gonadotropin releasing hormone; Hb, hemoglobin; hCG, human chorionic gonadotropin; LH, luteinizing hormone. (After D. J. Handelsman et al. 2020. In *Endotext* K. R. Feingold et al. [Eds.], MDText.com Inc. 2000–. PMID: 26247087)

Skill speed, reflexes, limb-eye coordination, concentration	**Strength** muscle mass	**Stamina** hemoglobin and maximal O$_2$ transfer	**Recovery** tissue repair after injury and training
Skill sports (driving/riding, target shooting)	Power sports (lifting, throwing, boxing, sprinting)	Endurance sports (long distance or duration events)	Contact sports and intense physical training
Out of competition Training	*Androgen doping* *Direct* natural, synthetic, designer, nutraceutical and non-steroidal androgens	*Blood (Hb) doping* *Direct* blood transfusion	• GH • GH releasing peptides (GHRH, ghrelin analogs) • Growth factors
In competition Beta-blockers Stimulants	*Indirect* hCG, LH, anti-estrogens, GnRH analogs	*Indirect* erythropoietin	

several different sources. A survey of AAS users found that the majority obtained the drugs through the internet (Fink et al., 2019). AAS may also be procured from other users whom the individual has met at a gym or health club, through a prescription written by a physician, or even by traveling overseas to a country where procurement may be easier than in the United States.

For a number of years, the popular media have promoted an image of muscularity as one of the defining characteristics of masculinity, and this image has contributed to the expansion of AAS use beyond the traditional groups of strength athletes and bodybuilders. Indeed, surveys of male AAS users have found that 70% to 80% of responders reported that the primary motivation for use was improving their physical appearance (Kanayama and Pope, 2018). A study of the prevalence of AAS use estimated that roughly 3 to 4 million Americans between the ages of 13 and 50 had taken one or more of these substances at some time in their lives (Pope et al., 2014a). The ratio of male to female users in this study was approximately 50:1, confirming that AAS use by the general public is largely a male phenomenon. Another important feature of AAS is that initiation of use generally occurs later than for many other misused substances such as tobacco, alcohol, and cannabis. Nevertheless, in some cases AAS use begins while the individual is in high school or even earlier (Nicholls et al., 2017). For this reason, a program entitled "Adolescents Training and Learning to Avoid Steroids" (ATLAS) was developed to educate young people (mostly male athletes) about the dangers of steroids and to deter their use (Goldberg et al., 1996). A related program, "Athletes Targeting Healthy Exercise and Nutrition Alternatives" (ATHENA), was subsequently introduced to promote healthy behaviors, including good eating habits and avoidance of steroids and other performance-enhancing substances, among young female athletes (Elliot et al., 2004).

AAS are taken in specific patterns and combinations

AAS are taken in a variety of doses, patterns, and combinations (Mottram and George, 2000). Endurance athletes (e.g., marathon runners) and sprinters tend to take relatively low doses of steroids, whereas bodybuilders and strength athletes such as weightlifters may take up to 100 times the therapeutic doses of these hormones. AAS are often used in patterns called **cycling**. Cycles are typically 6 to 12 weeks in duration, with periods of abstinence between successive cycles. Athletes use cycling for the following reasons:

- To minimize the development of tolerance to the drug
- To reduce the occurrence of adverse side effects
- To maximize performance at an athletic competition
- To avoid detection of a banned substance

Cycling is sometimes combined with **pyramiding**, in which the steroid dose is gradually increased until the midpoint of the cycle and then is gradually decreased as the cycle is completed. Pyramiding is thought to reduce possible withdrawal effects resulting from sudden termination of steroid use. Another common feature of steroid use is **stacking**, which refers to the simultaneous use of two or more AAS. Stacking is often done by combining a short-acting oral steroid with a long-acting injectable preparation. **FIGURE 16.12** illustrates some typical patterns of concomitant steroid use that demonstrate the phenomena of cycling, pyramiding, and stacking. Users who prefer to cycle without abstaining from use may engage in **bridging** (also called "blast and cruise"), a process in which a low dose (the "cruise") is used to bridge between each high dose of the steroid (the "blast"). It is important to note that many of the reasons offered for using

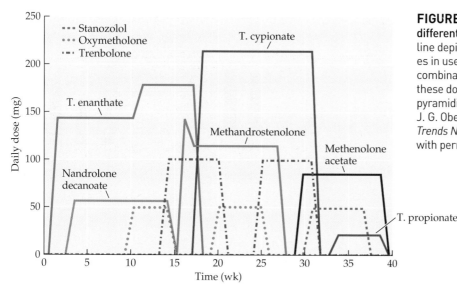

FIGURE 16.12 Typical dosing patterns of different anabolic–androgenic steroids Each line depicts time-related increases and decreases in use of a particular steroid, sometimes in combination with another steroid. Together, these dosing regimens are illustrative of cycling, pyramiding, and stacking. T, testosterone. (After J. G. Oberlander and L. P. Henderson. 2012. *Trends Neurosci* 35: 382–392. © 2012. Reprinted with permission from Elsevier.)

AAS in these various patterns are based on anecdotal information rather than on controlled scientific studies.

Finally, AAS users frequently engage in **polypharmacy**, in which additional substances are taken to augment the performance-enhancing properties of the steroids, to attempt to mask their presence in the individual's system, and/or to minimize some of the undesirable side effects that will be discussed below. Several different masking strategies are discussed in Alquraini and Auchus (2018). One relatively simple approach is to take high doses of a diuretic, which is a drug that increases urine production. This may permit the user to pass a urine test because the concentration of the banned steroid has been diluted to a level below the limit of detection of the assay being performed by the testing lab. Other masking strategies involve biochemical approaches that are beyond the scope of this book. The World Anti-Doping Agency maintains a record of positive doping results from accredited testing laboratories around the world. Their findings confirm that doping by elite athletes involves the use of a variety of other banned drugs in addition to AAS.

AAS are unlike other misused substances discussed in this book because of their powerful action on muscle. However, they are similar to other substances in their ability to produce adverse health effects and dependence in some users.

AAS enhance performance through multiple mechanisms of action

For many years, most researchers were unconvinced about the ability of AAS to increase muscle mass and strength despite the seemingly obvious evidence of such effects shown by actual users. Partly for that reason, AAS users have traditionally been scornful of the medical establishment (Kanayama and Pope, 2018). The reason for skepticism among researchers was that initial studies testing the hypothesis of increased muscle

mass and strength all yielded negative results. Not recognized for some time was that the studies themselves were deeply flawed, often because the AAS doses administered to participants were much lower than those actually used by athletes and bodybuilders. Finally, a key series of studies by Bhasin and colleagues showed that giving high doses of testosterone to healthy young men led to muscle fiber hypertrophy (increased size), increased muscle mass, and enhanced strength (Bhasin et al., 1996, 2001; Sinha-Hikim et al., 2002). Some of the results from one of these studies are presented in **FIGURE 16.13** (Bhasin et al., 2001). The men were given weekly injections of testosterone enanthate at different doses for a period of 20 weeks. They also received another drug at the same time to suppress endogenous testosterone secretion so that their testosterone levels would depend solely on the exogenous treatment. The lowest doses (25 and 50 mg per week) produced subnormal circulating testosterone concentrations, the 125-mg dose produced concentrations in the normal range, and the 600-mg dose produced testosterone levels that were at least four times the average pretreatment concentration. As shown in Figure 16.13A–C, AAS administration caused dose-dependent increases in muscle volume and strength. In contrast, sexual function was unchanged (Figure 16.13D), indicating that this aspect of androgen action is not influenced by testosterone level within the dose range used and over the time period of testing.

The findings of Bhasin's group are important because they were obtained under carefully controlled conditions. On the other hand, laboratory studies do not tell us how much benefit is gained by the typical AAS user. To address that question, Andrews and coworkers (2018) conducted a systematic review and meta-analysis of published studies on AAS use by healthy exercising adults. Among the study's main findings was that AAS users gained an average of 52% more muscle strength

FIGURE 16.13 Increased muscle strength and volume in men following chronic testosterone administration The study participants were healthy men, 18 to 35 years of age, who had prior weightlifting experience but who had not previously taken AAS. All participants were given monthly treatments with a long-acting drug to suppress their endogenous testosterone synthesis. Matched groups were also administered weekly intramuscular injections of testosterone enanthate for 20 weeks at doses ranging from 25 to 600 mg per injection. A comparison of circulating testosterone levels at the beginning of the study (baseline) with levels present at the 16-week time point showed that the 25- and 50-mg doses produced testosterone concentrations significantly below baseline, the 125-mg dose produced concentrations similar to baseline, and the 300- and 600-mg doses produced testosterone levels that were approximately two to four times baseline, respectively (data not shown). Leg press strength (A), thigh muscle volume (B), quadriceps muscle volume (C), and sexual function as determined by sexual activity and desire (D) were assessed at baseline and at the end of the 20-week dosing period. Muscle strength and volume were enhanced by increasing doses of testosterone, whereas sexual function remained relatively constant regardless of dose. (After S. Bhasin et al. 2001. *Am J Physiol Endocrinol Metab* 281: E1172–E1181.)

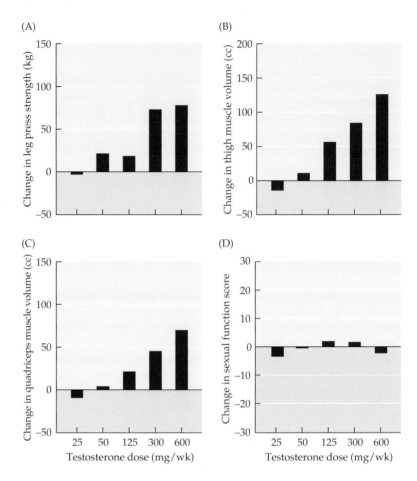

than placebo controls who exercised without taking steroids. These real-life results support the contention by users that AAS provide a measurable benefit beyond those obtained by exercise alone.

Researchers have extensively studied the mechanisms by which AAS exert their **ergogenic effects** (effects that result in enhancement of physical performance). These substances all have androgenic action, which means that they are agonists at the **androgen receptor**. Androgen receptors are present in many different tissues, including skeletal muscle. In the inactive state, androgen receptors are located in the cytoplasm of the cell (**FIGURE 16.14**). Androgen molecules diffuse across the cell membrane and bind to the receptor, thereby activating it. The activated hormone–receptor complex then translocates into the cell nucleus, where it regulates the transcription of specific genes, depending on the cell type (Matsumoto et al., 2013). The result in this case is to increase overall muscle protein synthesis with a particular influence on proteins needed for muscle growth. This boost in protein synthesis manifests in two ways: formation of new muscle fibers and hypertrophy of existing fibers.

FIGURE 16.14 Mechanism of action of androgens in altering gene transcription Androgens enter target cells by diffusing across the cell membrane. After the hormone binds to androgen receptors in the cell cytoplasm, the hormone–receptor complex translocates to the cell nucleus, where it alters the transcription of specific genes.

Several additional factors may contribute to the ergogenic effects of AAS (Cheung and Grossmann, 2018). Androgens have been found to stimulate release of the growth factors GH and insulin-like growth factor I (IGF-1), both of which may facilitate AAS-related muscle growth. Androgens additionally enhance the formation of red blood cells, thereby increasing the AAS user's blood oxygen-carrying capacity. Lastly, it is possible that AAS use could exert psychological effects that are beneficial in the competitive arena. This hypothesis is based on evidence that endogenous testosterone levels rise during

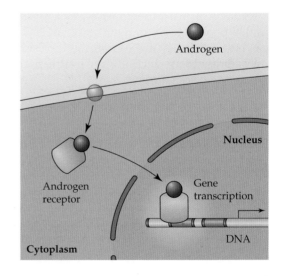

anticipation of participating in a competitive event, and that androgenic effects on the brain may confer a benefit on competitors by augmenting their mood and motivation (Wood and Stanton, 2012). Nevertheless, we must remain skeptical that the same benefit is derived from the extremely supraphysiological androgen levels produced by typical AAS use, since other findings suggest that such levels have deleterious rather than advantageous effects on brain function and mood.

This chapter is focused on AAS use by males, since they account for the majority of users both within the general population and within the much smaller group of competitive athletes and bodybuilders. However, earlier we mentioned AAS doping by female East German athletes and provided an example of the performance enhancement in one woman who competed during that era. It's important to add that more systematic research has been performed to ascertain the potential benefits of androgens for female athletes competing in sporting events that rely on muscle strength and/or stamina. This research has shown that women who have very high androgen levels, whether from their own androgen production or from AAS use, have an estimated 2% to 5% advantage over women with lower androgen levels (Bermon, 2017). For an elite athlete, even that small of a performance boost may well make the difference between winning or not.

Many adverse side effects are associated with AAS use

Determining the adverse effects of AAS use has been complicated by two major factors. First, as mentioned earlier, steroid users often take other substances, both legal and illegal. This practice may confound our ability to attribute any observed health problem to a specific effect of the steroid. Second, the doses taken by athletes and bodybuilders are usually many times greater than the doses of testosterone prescribed medicinally (see the section below on the use of anabolic steroids to treat hypogonadism). Since controlled studies involving supraphysiological steroid doses are not ethically permissible, data must be obtained by documenting the occurrence of adverse health outcomes in steroid users without the benefit of matched controls. With these caveats in mind, researchers have accumulated sufficient evidence to show a number of side effects of AAS, which are described in Albano et al. (2021) and listed in **TABLE 16.5**. Indeed, emerging evidence for adverse health effects of AAS led the Endocrine Society, the leading international society of physicians and

TABLE 16.5	Potential Health Consequences of Anabolic–Androgenic Steroid Use
Category	**Effects**
Cardiovascular effects	Left ventricular hypertrophy Abnormal cardiac structure and electrical activity Hypertension (high blood pressure) Decreased HDL cholesterol (the "good" kind of cholesterol)
Effects on the liver (not all anabolic steroids)	Jaundice Peliosis hepatis (blood-filled cysts in the liver) Tumors
Effects on the kidneys	Elevated serum creatinine and blood urea nitrogen (BUN) levels Impaired renal function
Effects on the skin and hair	Oily skin and scalp Severe acne Male-pattern baldness
Growth effects	Growth stunting in adolescents due to premature epiphyseal closure
Behavioral effects	Increased libido (sex drive) Mood changes (depression and mania) Increased anxiety, irritability, and aggressiveness Muscle dysmorphia Dependence
Specific effects on men	Testicular shrinkage Reduced sperm counts and possible infertility Prostate enlargement Gynecomastia (breast development)
Specific effects on women	Menstrual abnormalities Growth of an Adam's apple and deepening of the voice Excessive hair growth, especially on the face Enlargement of the clitoris Decreased breast size

researchers concerned with hormonal function and disease, to issue a policy statement in 2008 identifying the dangers of using these substances (Endocrine Society, 2008). We will first discuss side effects that involve the user's physical condition, after which we will consider neurobehavioral and psychological effects.

PHYSICAL HEALTH Abnormalities in heart structure and function, high blood pressure, and reduced high-density lipoprotein (HDL) cholesterol (the "good" type of cholesterol, thought to be protective against cardiovascular disease) have been reported in some AAS users (Nieschlag and Vorona, 2015a). Torrisi and colleagues (2020) recently reviewed evidence that the cardiotoxic effects of AAS may contribute to dangerous heart arrhythmias that, in the most serious cases, lead to sudden cardiac death. Liver toxicity can occur with chronic use of a particular chemical class of AAS, members of which include the oral steroids methandrostenolone, oxandrolone, oxymetholone, and stanozolol (Solimini et al., 2017). Liver toxicity ranges from mild effects such as elevated liver enzymes in the bloodstream to more serious but rarer complications including peliosis hepatis (a vascular disease of the liver) and liver tumors. The kidneys play an important role in the clearance of AAS metabolites. As with liver toxicity, steroid-associated renal toxicity typically manifests in a mild, unsymptomatic form characterized by elevations in creatinine and blood urea nitrogen (BUN) levels in the bloodstream. On the other hand, excessive steroid use has been linked to severe impairment in renal function (Davani-Davari et al., 2019). Skin and hair problems are common in AAS users, with a particularly high risk of outbreaks of acne (Melnik et al., 2007) (**FIGURE 16.15A**). The effects of steroid use on reproductive function has been studied extensively (Nieschlag and Vorona, 2015b; Christou et al., 2017). Chronic use of AAS leads to a persistently suppressed release of the gonadotrophins luteinizing hormone (LH) and follicle-stimulating hormone (FSH) from the pituitary gland (see Chapter 3). This occurs because the androgenic actions of these steroids engage the negative feedback system that controls normal androgen and estrogen secretion in men and women. In men, the consequences of suppressed LH and FSH release can include testicular shrinkage, low testosterone levels, and reduced sperm counts (which, in turn, can cause infertility). Furthermore, there is evidence that testicular function remains impaired for at least a few years after stopping AAS use (Kanayama et al., 2015; Rasmussen et al., 2021). Yet another effect of these substances concerns their influence on secondary sex characteristics in both men and women. For example, **FIGURE 16.15B** illustrates the masculinizing effects of these compounds in women, which are irreversible. Young people who are still growing also need to be

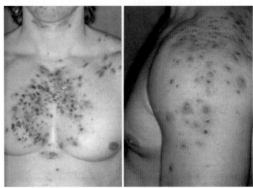

(A)

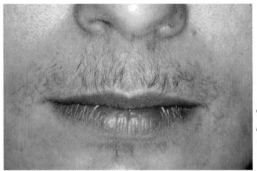

(B)

From B. Melnik et al. 2007. J Dtsch Dermatol Ges 5: 110–117

From D. Kopera. 2012. In *Handbook of Hair in Health and Disease. Human Health Handbooks No. 1, Vol 1.*, V. R. Preedy (Ed.), Wageningen Academic Publishers: Wageningen, Holland

FIGURE 16.15 Examples of acne and facial hair growth in anabolic–androgenic steroid users Anabolic steroids can cause severe acne in users (A) and can also stimulate the growth of facial hair in women (B).

concerned about the possible stunting effects of AAS produced by premature closure of the epiphyses.*

Of the many side effects mentioned here, a number of factors will determine which ones occur and how severe they may be. These factors include the age and sex of the user, the type of steroid used (especially oral versus injectable), the dose, and the pattern and duration of use. The description provided above of the potential adverse health effects of AAS, some of which can be quite serious, should prompt serious reservations on the part of anyone who is contemplating the use of these substances.

NEUROBEHAVIORAL AND PSYCHOLOGICAL EFFECTS Chronic use of AAS has also been associated with a variety of adverse psychological and behavioral effects. Recent studies have additionally found deleterious effects on brain function. We will begin this section focusing on abnormalities in mood (ranging from mania to depression), body image, and anxiety/irritability and aggressiveness.

The relationship between AAS and psychological and behavioral variables has been investigated using

---

*These are the end regions of long bones, which retain the capacity to further lengthen the bone. Once the epiphyses are "closed," the individual stops growing.

prospective studies (controlled administration of steroids or placebo to volunteers), naturalistic studies (investigation of steroid users compared with controls), and individual case reports. Naturalistic studies and case reports suffer from the limitation that differences observed between steroid users and nonusers may have preceded the onset of use. Keeping this limitation in mind, current findings from the AAS literature suggest that a relatively small subset of vulnerable individuals does experience psychological and behavioral abnormalities following repeated exposure to high doses of these compounds. In such vulnerable individuals, heavy steroid use can lead to extreme mood changes typically consisting of mania (abnormally elevated or irritable mood, racing thoughts, grandiosity, and sometimes psychotic delusions) or hypomania (less intense manic symptoms with no psychosis) during periods of active use that contrast with depressive episodes during steroid withdrawal (Kanayama et al., 2008; Piacentino et al., 2015). In severe cases, depressed mood has included suicidal ideation and behavior. Almost all of the human studies regarding the mood-altering effects of AAS have been conducted with males. Future studies need to take into account potential effects on women, given that experimental animal studies have revealed significant sex differences in the affective responses to steroid administration (Onakomaiya and Henderson, 2016).

Mood changes in heavy users of AAS are not confined to feelings of anxiety or depression. Another reported effect is the development of increased anxiety/irritability and aggressiveness. This may lead, in the most extreme cases, to violent outbursts known on the street as "roid rage." The relationship between steroids and aggressiveness is discussed in **BOX 16.2**.

An unusual body image disorder that has been diagnosed in some AAS users is **muscle dysmorphia**, also known as "reverse anorexia" (Rohman, 2009; Tod et al. 2016). In the fifth edition of the *Diagnostic and Statistical Manual of Mental Disorders* (*DSM-5*), muscle dysmorphia is listed as belonging to a more general diagnostic category called body dysmorphic disorder. The *DSM-5* describes this disorder as follows: "Muscle dysmorphia … consists of preoccupation with the idea that one's body is too small or insufficiently lean or muscular. Individuals with this form of [body dysmorphic disorder] actually have a normal-looking body or are even very muscular. They may also be preoccupied with other body areas, such as skin or hair. A majority (but not all) diet, exercise, and/or lift weights excessively, sometimes causing bodily damage"* (American Psychiatric Association, 2013, p. 243). Although muscle dysmorphia is almost always diagnosed in men, occasional cases in women have been reported. In addition, the symptoms of muscle

dysmorphia are more prevalent in bodybuilders than in non-bodybuilder resistance trainers (Mitchell et al., 2017). The *DSM-5* classification of muscle dysmorphia places it within the context of obsessive-compulsive and related disorders; however, some researchers have proposed that muscle dysmorphia might be better classified as an addiction to body image, thus placing it within the broader category of behavioral addictions (Foster et al., 2015) (see Section 9.2).

Turning to the effects of AAS use on the brain, this is an area that researchers have recently begun to investigate using modern neuroimaging and neuropsychological approaches. Of particular relevance is a group of studies conducted by the laboratory of Astrid Bjørnebekk at the Oslo University Hospital in Norway. Comparing AAS users to non-using controls, this research group has reported deficits in executive function (Hauger et al., 2020), abnormalities in functional brain connectivity (Westlye et al., 2017), reductions in cerebral cortical thickness and gray matter volume (Bjørnebekk et al., 2016), and most recently, accelerated brain aging in long-term users (Bjørnebekk et al., 2021). Given that these differences are correlational in nature, they do not prove causation by AAS use. In addition, we cannot rule out the possibility of neurobiological abnormalities that preceded (and perhaps even contributed to) AAS use. Nevertheless, it is tempting to speculate that chronic AAS use has deleterious effects on brain structure and function that become more and more severe as time goes on.

Regular AAS use causes dependence in some individuals

By the late 1980s and early 1990s, reports began to appear suggesting that some AAS users met *DSM* criteria for dependence on these substances. Case studies and self-reports by bodybuilders and athletes provide some insight into the nature of steroid dependence. One such case is that of Lyle Alzado, a three-time All-Pro NFL defensive end who played for 15 seasons with the Denver Broncos, Cleveland Browns, and Los Angeles Raiders before coming down with brain cancer and dying in 1992 at the age of 43. In a 1991 guest article for *Sports Illustrated*, Alzado admitted taking AAS beginning in his college days and continuing throughout his NFL career and beyond. At the height of his steroid use, he would cycle 10 to 12 weeks on steroids and then go off the drugs for only 2 to 3 weeks before starting again. In his own words, "It was addicting, mentally addicting. I just didn't feel strong unless I was taking something." Alzado also described the aggressiveness produced by his steroid use. "I became very violent on the field. Off it, too. I did things only crazy people do. Once in 1979 in Denver, a guy side-swiped my car, and I chased him up and down hills through the neighborhoods. I did that a lot. I'd chase a guy, pull him out of his car, beat the hell out of him" (Alzado, 1991).

*Reprinted with permission from the *Diagnostic and Statistical Manual of Mental Disorders*, Fifth Edition, © 2013. American Psychiatric Association. All rights reserved.

BOX 16.2 ■ OF SPECIAL INTEREST

Anabolic–Androgenic Steroids and "Roid Rage"

You may have heard the term "roid rage" used to describe a sudden eruption of intense anger or violent behavior by someone taking AAS. Case reports have documented instances in which violent outbursts appear to be linked to heavy steroid use. But before we discuss such extreme examples of violent behavior, it's important to consider information about the general relationship between AAS and irritability and aggression. One source of information is a study conducted in Australia that included personal interviews with 60 male users of performance- and image-enhancing drugs (PIEDs), including but not restricted to AAS (Larance et al., 2005). When questioned about events that had occurred during the 6-month period prior to their interview, 37% of these PIED users reported episodes of "roid rage," typically associated with domestic or automobile-related conflicts. Study participants described these episodes as "requiring a specific trigger, a sudden rush of anger or arousal, and possible escalation to verbal or physical aggression" (Larance et al., 2005, p. 94). Indeed, 23% of the participants had been in a situation that evoked aggressive behavior or violence. Other studies by Pagonis and coworkers support a specific association between AAS use and aggressiveness. One of these studies found large increases in hostility, phobic anxiety, paranoid ideation, and psychoticism (measured by means of the Symptom Checklist-90 [SCL-90]) following a cycle of steroid use, compared with pre-cycle levels, in a group of amateur and recreational athletes and bodybuilders (Pagonis et al., 2006a). These changes were most marked in a subgroup characterized as heavy users, thereby demonstrating a dose dependency of the mood-altering effects of AAS. A second study reported on two pairs of male monozygotic twins, of which one member of each pair was a steroid user. The SCL-90 again revealed noteworthy differences between users and non-users, with consistently higher hostility and paranoid ideation scores in the users (Pagonis et al., 2006b). In addition, a recent study of male Norwegian weightlifters found that self-reported aggressiveness was significantly higher in AAS users than in non-users, and that the highest level of aggressiveness was in users who additionally met criteria for AAS dependence (Hauger et al., 2021). Finally, a review of randomized controlled trials of AAS use found an overall increase in self-reported aggression, although the effect size was small (Chegeni et al., 2021).

The ability of AAS to increase hostility and aggressive tendencies is accompanied by a greater propensity for violent behavior, at least in some users (Pope et al., 2021). Importantly, this behavioral change can begin as early as adolescence. For example, data from over 6000 survey respondents from the National Longitudinal Study of Adolescent Health showed a statistically significant association between steroid use and violent behaviors such as physical fighting (Beaver et al., 2008). Elkins and coworkers (2017) subsequently reported a significant relationship between AAS use and school violence and violent victimization. Moreover, a survey of 2080 high school–aged males found an increased likelihood of engaging in dating-related violence in participants who had used AAS at least once in their lifetime (Ganson and Cadet, 2019).

Although most AAS users show either no or relatively modest increases in violent behavior, there are rare cases of extreme violence and criminality. Two such cases were recently reviewed by Pope and colleagues (2021), one of which we describe here:

Mr. A., a 58-year-old man, had been bullied and sexually abused as a child. He later began playing soccer and his athletic success in high school helped boost his self-esteem. He began using AAS at the age of 15 and continued over the years. His drug use was accompanied by weightlifting to maintain a good physical appearance. This was important since in his 20s, he had embarked upon a career as a male exotic dancer. Although initially successful in this business, his work opportunities declined by his 40s, causing him to endure significant financial difficulties and even forcing him to live in his van for a while. At the age of 56, Mr. A. was hired as a bouncer at a men's club, which prompted him to increase his AAS use to "bulk up" since in his words, "in gentlemen's clubs, size and image is everything."* The high-dose regimen of AAS he was consuming not only substantially enhanced his strength, but also began to have a psychological impact. On one hand, he began to behave irritably; but at the same time, the drugs made him feel "invincible," stating that "nothing could harm me, and I did not need to bow to anyone." Politically, he supported then-President Trump, and he became infuriated with anti-Trump rhetoric on the part of the media and numerous figures within the social, political, and entertainment spheres. In an attempt to frighten or even deter these individuals, which included Barack Obama, Hilary Clinton, George Soros, and Robert de Niro, Mr. A. purchased fireworks, constructed crude (inoperable) devices that resembled pipe bombs, and mailed them to the perceived offenders. Mr. A. was quite pleased with his actions until he saw a federal official on TV announcing the FBI's hunt for the "mail bomber," as he had become known in the popular media. He was suddenly shocked to realize that he was the object of a nationwide manhunt. Not having

---

*All quotes from H. G. Pope, Jr. et al. (2021). *Am J Addict* 30: 423–432.

BOX 16.2 ■ OF SPECIAL INTEREST (continued)

covered his tracks very carefully, Mr. A. was quickly caught by authorities, tried, and sentenced to 20 years in prison. Since he was forced to discontinue using AAS during his incarceration and trial, he lost his feeling of invincibility and could scarcely believe how he had acted. In Mr. A.'s previous history, he had committed only a few petty crimes such as shoplifting; nothing in his past would have predicted the serious criminal acts he committed while taking high doses of AAS. Indeed, one of the authors of the paper (HGP) testified at Mr. A.'s trial about the mitigating circumstances surrounding his crimes, which likely caused the judge to hand down a somewhat more lenient sentence than otherwise would have been applied.

The mechanisms by which AAS may increase irritability and aggression in humans are not yet understood. Therefore, researchers have turned to experimental animal models to investigate such mechanisms. Early studies using electrical stimulation and lesion methods began to identify neural circuits that underlie several different kinds of aggressive behaviors (e.g., predatory and defensive aggression) in rats, mice, and cats (Haller, 2013). This work has recently been extended using contemporary methods such as optogenetics and pharmacogenetics (Yamaguchi, 2021). With respect to AAS-induced aggressive and anxiety-related behaviors, some studies have used laboratory rats and mice as experimental subjects (Cunningham et al., 2013; Bertozzi et al., 2017). However, the most well-characterized model is one developed by Richard Melloni and colleagues that involves chronic administration of AAS to adolescent Syrian hamsters, followed by assessment of aggressive behaviors using the resident–intruder paradigm, which was described in Chapter 6 (Melloni and Ricci, 2010; Ricci et al., 2012). In a typical study, individually housed male hamsters are injected daily for 30 days with an AAS mixture containing several steroids that are commonly taken by human AAS users. Control

Effects of repeated AAS administration on attack and biting behaviors in Syrian hamsters Individually housed male hamsters received daily SC injections of either an AAS mixture (2 mg/kg testosterone cypionate, 2 mg/kg nandrolone decanoate, and 1 mg/kg boldenone undecylenate) or sesame oil vehicle. Injections were given from postnatal day 27 to postnatal day 56. On day 57, all animals were subjected to a resident–intruder test of aggressive behavior during which number of attack behaviors (aggressive upright postures plus lateral attacks), number of bites, and latencies to attack and to bite were recorded over a 10-minute period. AAS administration increased the mean numbers of attacks and bites and also reduced the mean latencies to the first attack and the first bite. (After T. R. Morrison et al. 2016. *Neuroscience* 315: 1–17. © 2015. Reprinted with permission from IBRO, via Elsevier.)

subjects are injected daily with vehicle only. On the day after the last injection, each one of the experimental and control hamsters (the "residents") is challenged by the introduction of an unfamiliar, similar-sized male hamster (the "intruder") into the animal's cage. As is typical of the resident–intruder paradigm, the resident animal behaves aggressively toward the intruder and almost always dominates the encounter. Among the agonistic behaviors recorded during the encounter are upright postures that signify aggressive intent, lateral attacks (attacks directed to the intruder's flank or rump), and flank/rump bites by the resident. **FIGURE A** shows the results of a typical experiment demonstrating the aggression-inducing effects of repeated AAS exposure in the hamster model (Morrison et al., 2016). Not only are the numbers of attacks and bites substantially increased by AAS treatment, but the latencies to first attack and first bite are reduced. These shorter latencies are suggestive of greater impulsivity in the treated resident hamsters compared with the control residents.

The hamster model has additionally provided the most detailed information on the neurobiological underpinnings of AAS-induced aggression and anxiety. Researchers have identified the anterior hypothalamus

(Continued)

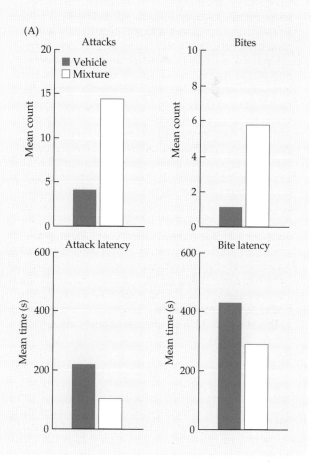

BOX 16.2 ■ OF SPECIAL INTEREST (continued)

as the key component of a complex neural circuit that helps regulate these two behavioral functions (**FIGURE B**; Ricci et al., 2012). Overlap between the aggression-mediating and anxiety-mediating brain areas may help explain why AAS users can experience both symptoms. Current findings additionally indicate that chronic AAS administration to hamsters alters the activity of several neurotransmitter systems known to modulate this circuit, including the dopaminergic, serotonergic, and vasopressin systems (reviewed in Morrison et al., 2016). Most recently, GABA acting through $GABA_A$ receptors was found to be another important regulator of AAS-induced aggression in adolescent hamsters (Lee et al., 2021).

Symptoms of anxiety in human AAS users are particularly prominent during withdrawal. Therefore, Melloni's group modeled this phenomenon by giving adolescent hamsters the standard 30 days of AAS administration, removing the drugs for the next 21 days, and then testing the animals for anxiety-like behaviors. Studies using this model demonstrated not only that AAS withdrawal leads to increases in such behaviors, but also that serotonin activation of $5\text{-}HT_3$ receptors in the lateral anterior hypothalamus plays a key role in the transition from aggressive to anxiety-like behaviors (Ricci et al., 2012; Morrison et al., 2020). Whether the neuroanatomical and neurochemical mechanisms of AAS-induced aggression and anxiety in humans are similar to those of hamsters remains to be determined.

To summarize, repeated exposure to AAS at the high doses taken by human users has been linked with elevated levels of irritability and/or aggressiveness in some individuals. To the extent that this may be a causal relationship, it is important to determine why some users are affected this way whereas others are not. We can speculate that this difference may be related to parameters of steroid dosing along with individual susceptibility and/or preexisting tendencies toward aggressive behaviors. In fact, there is evidence that adolescents who score high on self-reported aggressiveness report greater likelihood of initiating AAS use than those with low aggressiveness scores (Sagoe et al., 2016). This raises the important question of whether the increased aggressive behavior of AAS users versus non-users observed in some cross-sectional studies came *after* (and perhaps was caused by) initiation of AAS use or came *before* such use was started (Dunn, 2015). An evaluation of this literature should also take into consideration a

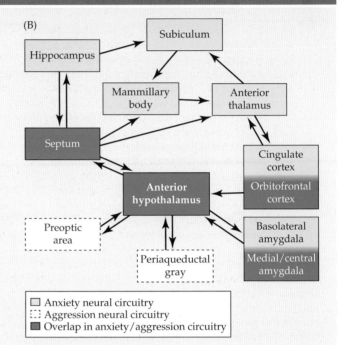

Model of the neural circuit subserving offensive aggression and anxiety in hamsters The anterior hypothalamus has been identified as a key area within a larger circuit involved in regulating both aggression and anxiety. As shown in the figure, some of the structures within this circuit participate only in aggressive behavior, others participate only in anxiety, and still others participate in both. (After L. A. Ricci et al. 2012. *Horm Behav* 62: 569–576. © 2012. Reprinted with permission from Elsevier.)

few potential confounding factors. The first such factor is the use of other substances (i.e., polysubstance use) (Lundholm et al., 2015). Some recreational drugs may interact with AAS to increase irritability and the potential for aggressive behavior. Second, Börjesson and colleagues (2020) reported that aggressiveness and criminality in AAS users are frequently associated with a comorbid personality disorder. In support of that finding, Hauger and coworkers (2021) additionally reported that AAS-dependent weightlifters who showed high levels of aggression and interpersonal violence also exhibited antisocial personality traits. Taken together, these results provide another indication that for many or even most users, AAS alone may not be responsible for observed occurrence of aggressive and criminal behaviors. Additional research is needed to resolve these and other questions around the issue of "roid rage."

Kanayama and coworkers (2009) summarized the results of five field studies that assessed the prevalence of *DSM-IV* dependence criteria in 426 AAS users. When these studies were taken together, the percentages of users exhibiting specific criteria were as follows: tolerance, 20.7%; withdrawal, 44.6%; taking the substance in larger amounts than intended, 27.9%; inability to cut down or control use of the substance, 12.0%; significant amount of time spent on substance-related activity, 28.6%; other activities reduced in favor of substance use, 17.8%; and continued substance use despite recognition of use-related problems, 24.9%. Most important, 33.8% of the users studied met three or more of the above criteria, indicating that they were classified as being dependent on AAS. A later analysis of 10 pooled studies again estimated that over 30% of AAS users developed dependence over the course of their steroid use (Pope et al., 2014).

When comparing AAS dependence to the dependence seen with most recreational drugs, one important similarity is the occurrence of withdrawal symptoms when substance use is discontinued. According to Mędraś and colleagues (2018), the AAS abstinence syndrome in dependent users occurs in two phases. The first, acute, phase is characterized by anxiety, tremors, nausea, headaches, and increased heart rate and blood pressure. This phase, which is caused in large part by sympathetic nervous system activation, begins within 1 to 2 days of withdrawal and lasts for about a week. Symptoms can be treated with the α_2-adrenergic receptor agonist clonidine. The second phase of AAS withdrawal takes several days to emerge and typically consists of depression, insomnia, muscle pain and weakness, decreased libido, dissatisfaction with body image, and a desire for more steroids.

Differences between AAS dependence and dependence produced by other substances include the lack of an immediate steroid-induced euphoria or other intoxicating effect, relatively little impairment in the performance of daily activities, and less frequent occurrence of tolerance (Kanayama et al., 2009). Moreover, even heavy steroid users rarely seek treatment for their problem, and specific treatment protocols for steroid dependence have yet to be developed and tested empirically (Bates et al., 2019). At the present time, the typical medical approach when dealing with long-term AAS users is to provide symptomatic relief during withdrawal, assess the degree of gonadal (testicular, in the case of men) hypofunction present in the patient, and prescribe medications that can help the patient regain normal gonadal function during their recovery (Anawalt, 2019).

The potential for AAS to produce dependence has been extensively studied using experimental animal models. These animal studies have shown that acute or chronic AAS administration can produce various neurotransmitter changes in the brain's reward circuitry (Mhillaj et al., 2015). More importantly, the reinforcing and rewarding properties of these compounds have been demonstrated by self-administration and place-conditioning studies in rats, mice, and hamsters (Wood, 2008; Grönbladh et al., 2016). For example, hamsters will self-administer testosterone or various

synthetic AAS directly into the cerebral ventricles (Wood et al., 2004; Ballard and Wood, 2005). The demonstration of AAS reinforcement by the intracerebroventricular route is important in showing that this effect is mediated by mechanisms within the brain, not by peripheral anabolic activity. On the other hand, the data also indicate that AAS are not as strongly reinforcing as highly addictive drugs like cocaine, methamphetamine, or heroin, which is consistent with the lack of a rapid euphoric effect experienced by human AAS users.

Until recently, little was known about the mechanisms underlying AAS reward and reinforcement. However, a recent series of experiments by Bontempi and Bonci (2020) using male mice have uncovered an interesting potential mechanism. These experiments indicate that acute administration of either testosterone or the testosterone derivative nandrolone (a popular AAS used by bodybuilders) led to increased levels of β-endorphin, a μ-opioid receptor agonist, both in the bloodstream and in the VTA. Importantly, intra-VTA injection of the irreversible μ-opioid receptor antagonist β-funaltrexamine (β-FNA) blocked the rewarding effects of both testosterone and nandrolone in the conditioned place preference test (**FIGURE 16.16**). Other experiments not shown here resulted in two additional findings: AAS activated VTA dopaminergic neurons, and the rewarding effects of these steroids are *not* mediated by androgen receptors. Taken together, the results indicate that the rewarding properties of AAS are likely mediated by VTA dopaminergic neurons (similar to other misused substances), that this activation may result from stimulation of β-endorphin release and subsequent activation of μ-opioid receptors, and that AAS reward is independent of the hormones' androgenic actions.

Testosterone has an important role in treating hypogonadism

As we have discussed in previous chapters, substances that are misused recreationally may, nevertheless, have legitimate therapeutic applications. The same is true for AAS, especially testosterone. The principal medical use of testosterone is for hormone replacement in cases of **male hypogonadism** (Basaria, 2014). **FIGURE 16.17A** shows that in a healthy man, the hypothalamus stimulates the pituitary gland to secrete LH and FSH, which together act on the testes to promote testosterone synthesis and secretion along with spermatogenesis. Damage to the testes, certain rare genetic mutations, or several diseases can render the testes unresponsive to LH and FSH. This condition is called **primary hypogonadism** (**FIGURE 16.17B**). Notice that a lack of the normal negative feedback of testosterone on the hypothalamus and pituitary gland leads to hypersecretion of LH and

(A)

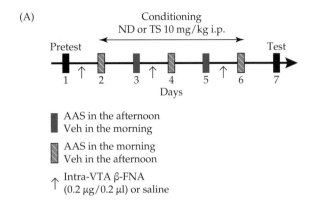

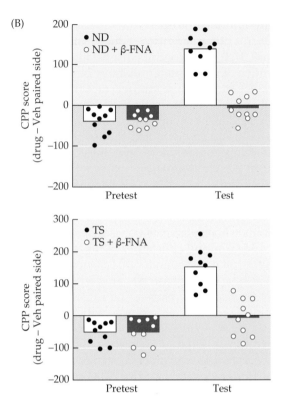

FIGURE 16.16 Effect of blocking μ-opioid receptors in the VTA on anabolic–androgenic steroid conditioned place preference in male mice (A) Mice were trained on a conditioned place preference (CPP) task using a three-compartment apparatus (including outer black and white compartments) and the experimental design shown here. On day 1, each mouse received a pretest in which it was allowed free access to the apparatus during which the amount of time spent in the black and white compartments was measured. The less preferred compartment was then designated to be paired with the hormone treatment to determine if this preference could be reversed. On days 2 through 6, each mouse received two conditioning trials per day, one in the morning and the other in the afternoon. For each trial, the mouse was injected either with 10 mg/kg of the designated AAS or with the drug vehicle (Veh). Separate experiments were performed with testosterone (TS) or with nandrolone (ND). During a hormone trial, the mouse was confined to its initial non-preferred compartment; during a Veh trial, the mouse was confined to its initial preferred compartment. The effect of chronic VTA μ-opioid receptor blockade was tested by giving some mice an intra-VTA injection of either the irreversible antagonist β-flunaltrexamine (β-FNA; 0.2 μg in saline) or saline control on day 1 after the pretest and again after the days 3 and 5 conditioning sessions (arrows). On day 7, the mice were tested for the development of CPP by again being given free access to all compartments. (B) CPP score was determined by subtracting the time spent in the Veh-paired compartment from the time spent in the drug-paired compartment. Group means are shown by the bars; open circles denote the data from each individual mouse. Pretest: Because of the experimental design in which hormone during the conditioning trials was always paired with the non-preferred compartment, each mouse showed a negative score. Test: Mean CPP scores were significantly increased following AAS treatment, as each mouse spent more time in the initially non-preferred compartment during post-treatment testing. Furthermore, the results from the β-FNA group showed that the antagonist completely blocked the rewarding effects of TS or ND based on the mean CPP scores. (After L. Bontempi and A. Bonci. 2020. *Sci Signal* 13: eaba1169. Reprinted with permission from AAAS.)

FSH, despite the inability of these hormones to stimulate testicular activity. Alternatively, a condition called **secondary hypogonadism** can occur in which pituitary damage, trauma to the hypothalamus, or other mutations or diseases can cause a severe reduction in LH and FSH secretion from the pituitary (**FIGURE 16.17C**). Although the testes remain functional in such cases, the loss of stimulation again leads to reduced testosterone levels and deficient spermatogenesis.

The consequences of either kind of hypogonadism can be deduced from the biological actions of testosterone on multiple organs throughout the body (**FIGURE 16.18**).

Thus, hypogonadal men may exhibit poor libido (sex drive), erectile dysfunction, and sterility. They additionally may show loss of muscle mass and bone density, and they may suffer from adverse effects on the kidneys and skin. For these reasons, testosterone replacement therapy is routinely administered to hypogonadal men. The hormone may be given in an injectable form, in a tablet or pill, as a pellet that is surgically implanted under the skin, as a transdermal patch or gel, or as a solution that is applied to the underarms (Basaria, 2014).

Testosterone is sometimes also prescribed for patients suffering from **sarcopenia** (skeletal muscle loss related to aging or to certain diseases) or **cachexia** (extreme body wasting, including loss of muscle, resulting from diseases such as cancer, HIV AIDS, etc.). Elderly men commonly experience a moderate form of hypogonadism that causes lower levels of circulating testosterone (Christie and Meier, 2015). If the reduction in testosterone is great enough to cause symptoms, then the individual may seek medical attention. Not only can the effects of aging-related hypogonadism be psychologically distressing to men who wish to continue having active sexual relations, reduced strength (due to loss of muscle mass) and bone density lead to an increased risk of dangerous falls. Consequently, testosterone replacement may be prescribed for aged men who show these symptoms and who have been

(A) Normal physiology

(B) Primary hypogonadism

(C) Secondary hypogonadism

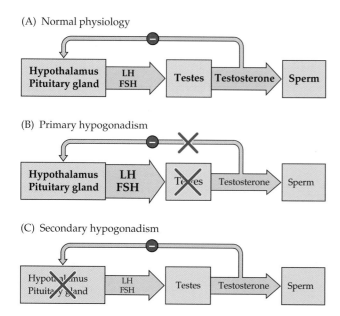

FIGURE 16.17 Functioning of the male hypothalamic–pituitary–gonadal axis in health and in primary and secondary hypogonadism (A) In men with normal physiology, the hypothalamus stimulates the pituitary gland to secrete luteinizing hormone (LH) and follicle-stimulating hormone (FSH), which together stimulate the testes to secrete testosterone and to produce sperm. Through a negative feedback loop (–), testosterone acts back on the hypothalamus and pituitary gland to prevent excessive LH and FSH release. (B) In primary hypogonadism, the testes are unresponsive to LH and FSH, which leads to reduced testosterone levels and sperm counts and to increased LH and FSH secretion due to loss of the negative feedback signal. (C) In secondary hypogonadism, an abnormality in either the hypothalamus or the pituitary gland causes reduced LH and FSH secretion, which leads to effects on testosterone and sperm production like those in primary hypogonadism. (After N. Christie and C. A. Meier. 2015. *Swiss Med Wkly* 145: w14216. doi: 10.4414/smw.2015.14216.)

diagnosed with hypogonadism based on clinical testing. Testosterone treatment is also helpful in partially restoring muscle mass in patients with cachexia. A systematic review and meta-analysis on AAS (testosterone or another AAS) treatment for sarcopenia or cachexia revealed that hormone treatment alone significantly increased lean body (i.e., muscle) mass and muscle strength (Falqueto et al., 2021). However, even greater benefits were obtained when patients were able to combine AAS treatment with exercise.

Because testosterone is thought of as the "male" sex hormone, its therapeutic use has been restricted almost entirely to men. Yet women also possess significant amounts of testosterone in their bloodstream, and some studies have associated testosterone with sexual function in women as well as men (Davis et al., 2016). Furthermore, women undergo a sharp decline in levels of gonadal hormones after menopause. Because many of the actions of testosterone are similar in men and women (see Figure 16.18 legend), researchers have begun to consider the potential benefits of testosterone administration for improving both sexual function and musculoskeletal health in postmenopausal women (Davis and Wahlin-Jacobsen, 2015).

SECTION SUMMARY

- Anabolic–androgenic steroids (AAS) are hormones that increase muscle mass and strength and also produce masculinizing effects in the user. These substances either contain the naturally occurring male sex hormone testosterone or are similar to testosterone in their chemical structure. Some AAS are taken orally, others by intramuscular injection.

- AAS were initially developed for their muscle-building and performance-enhancing effects. However, many current users are adolescent and adult men who take these substances mainly to attain a more muscular physical appearance.

- The Soviet Union was the first country in which steroids were administered to athletic competitors; however, the practice quickly spread to other countries. When the use and abuse of these substances became more widespread and numerous adverse side effects began

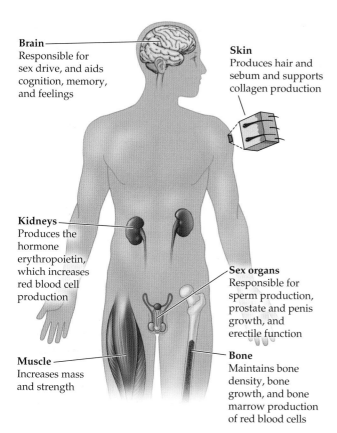

FIGURE 16.18 Multiple effects of testosterone on the body Testosterone acts on many organs of the body. These actions occur in both men and women except for those that are specific to the male sex organs. (After R. A. Kloner et al. 2016. *J Am Coll Cardiol* 67: 545–557.)

to emerge, steroids were classified as Schedule III controlled substances in the United States. They were also banned by a variety of national and international athletic organizations.

- AAS are usually taken in specific patterns and combinations. In the case of cycling, the steroid is taken in alternating on and off periods. Cycling can be combined with pyramiding, in which the dose is increased during the early part of the cycle and then is gradually decreased after the peak dose is reached at the midpoint of the cycle. Bridging is a pattern that avoids periods of abstinence, since the user continues to take a low steroid dose in between the high doses of one cycle and the next. Some users also engage in stacking, which refers to combining two or more steroids (often one that is injected and another that is taken orally). Steroid users frequently practice polypharmacy, in which additional substances (e.g., stimulants or masking agents like diuretics) are taken along with the steroid.

- Controlled studies have confirmed that AAS such as testosterone dose-dependently enhance muscle fiber size, muscle mass, and strength. These effects are mediated by intracellular androgen receptors and involve increased protein synthesis, ultimately leading to formation of new muscle fibers and hypertrophy of existing fibers. Other factors that may contribute to the ergogenic effects of AAS include increased release of the growth factors GH and IGF-1, enhanced formation of red blood cells, and possibly psychological benefits in the competitive arena. Of these factors, the last is mainly speculative, given the evidence for high-dose AAS causing adverse effects on the user's mood.

- There are a number of adverse side effects of AAS. Chronic steroid users may exhibit cardiovascular problems such as abnormalities in heart structure and function, high blood pressure, and reduced circulating HDL. Other physiological side effects may include renal toxicity, skin and hair problems (e.g., severe acne), liver toxicity (particularly with the use of certain oral steroids), and risk of stunted growth in young users. Women are vulnerable to significant masculinizing effects of AAS use.

- Reproductive function can be disrupted by AAS use. Men show suppressed release of LH and FSH from the pituitary gland because the androgenic properties of AAS activate the negative feedback system that controls gonadotropin release. Chronically reduced LH and FSH causes testicular shrinkage, low circulating testosterone, and low sperm counts, which can lead to infertility.

- AAS have also been associated with a variety of psychological side effects. Mood shifts may range from depression to mania. Some individuals suffer from an unusual male body image disorder known as muscle dysmorphia. Case reports as well as controlled and naturalistic studies have also linked AAS with heightened irritability and aggressiveness in a significant percentage of users. In rare cases, a heavy AAS user may exhibit severe aggressive outbursts colloquially known as "roid rage."

- Research with experimental animals has yielded important information regarding the neurobiological mechanisms of AAS-related aggression. A particularly well-studied model involves daily administration of an AAS mixture to adolescent male Syrian hamsters, after which the animals are tested in the resident–intruder paradigm. The treated animals show substantially elevated amounts of aggressive behaviors compared with controls, and they additionally show increased anxiety-like behaviors. Researchers have identified a complex neural circuit mediating these behaviors, with the anterior hypothalamus serving as a point of convergence of both aggression- and anxiety-related neural pathways.

- A certain percentage of steroid users develop a characteristic pattern of dependence and withdrawal related to these substances. Feelings of anxiety are frequently experienced either at the end of a cycle of AAS use or after a period of prolonged abstinence and withdrawal. Self-administration of steroids via IV and intracerebroventricular routes has been demonstrated in laboratory animals, although steroids are not as strongly reinforcing as classical addictive drugs like cocaine or heroin. The mechanisms underlying steroid reinforcement are not yet well understood; however, a recent study indicates that AAS reward may be mediated by β-endorphin–mediated activation of VTA dopaminergic neurons. This effect does not require AAS stimulation of androgen receptors.

- Testosterone has an important therapeutic role in the treatment of male hypogonadism. Primary hypogonadism occurs when the testes are unresponsive to LH and FSH. Secondary hypogonadism occurs when an abnormal condition causes reduced secretion of LH and FSH. Both types of hypogonadism result in low testosterone levels, which in turn can cause poor libido, erectile dysfunction, sterility, and loss of muscle mass and bone density. Fortunately, these symptoms are usually responsive to testosterone replacement therapy. Besides the severe hypogonadism that may develop at a relatively young age, a more moderate reduction in circulating testosterone typically occurs in elderly men, who may seek medical attention if the symptoms are sufficiently distressing. In addition, testosterone may be prescribed to counteract muscle wasting in cases of cachexia. Lastly, researchers have begun to consider the potential benefits of testosterone administration for improving sexual function and musculoskeletal health in postmenopausal women.

STUDY QUESTIONS

1. Name the five classes of substances that make up the category of inhalants.
2. What are the characteristics common to all types of inhalants?
3. How are inhalant doses calculated, and how do these substances enter the brain?
4. Inhalants are often the first substances used recreationally by children and adolescents. Why is this the case?
5. Which inhalant is used by a somewhat older population, mainly at music clubs and raves?
6. How are the acute psychological effects of inhalants influenced by the time since exposure and the amount of exposure?
7. A young sister of yours has been sniffing glue almost every day. Your parents recently discovered this activity, as a result of which they are going to enroll your sister in a residential addiction treatment program in which recreational substance use is prevented by careful monitoring of the patients. Do you expect your sister to have any reaction to her withdrawal from inhalant use? If so, what symptoms might you, your parents, and the treatment staff observe?
8. How do we know that inhalants are rewarding/reinforcing based on experimental animal studies? Does the mesolimbic dopaminergic pathway play a role in inhalant reward/reinforcement? If so, what is the evidence?
9. (a) Describe the acute effects of inhalants such as toluene on locomotor activity in animals. (b) How can these effects be explained by the action of these substances on ionotropic receptors and voltage-gated ion channels? (c) How do the effects of prolonged inhalant exposure on ion channels differ from the effects of acute exposure?
10. (a) What is meant by the term "toxic leukoencephalopathy," and how does this disorder relate to inhalant use? (b) Besides the brain, what other organs or organ systems are adversely affected by repeated inhalant exposure?
11. The term _____ refers to an event in which someone dies unexpectedly after a single inhalant exposure.
12. What is the evidence that endogenously synthesized GHB may act like a neurotransmitter within the brain?
13. For what purposes and by what user groups is GHB consumed recreationally?
14. (a) Describe the dose–response characteristics of acute GHB consumption on mood and behavior in people. (b) Why is it dangerous to combine GHB with alcohol?
15. Using the results from experimental animal studies, compare and contrast the rewarding and reinforcing effects of GHB with those of cocaine or opioids such as morphine or heroin.
16. Discuss the various mechanisms thought to underlie GHB's behavioral actions, making sure to differentiate between mechanisms requiring high exogenous GHB doses and those that may mediate the effects of the low levels of GHB that are produced endogenously. How can these different mechanisms be explained by the relative affinities of different receptors for GHB?
17. In the United States, GHB is used therapeutically for the treatment of _____. An additional therapeutic application in several European countries involves the treatment of _____.
18. Describe the features of recreational use of GHB and evidence for GHB tolerance and dependence.
19. Overdosing on GHB can lead to loss of consciousness (coma) due to the drug's sedating effects. If you were conducting research on the long-term effects of repeated overdoses and coma in chronic high-dose GHB users, which of the following functional domains should you choose to study (based on previous findings), and why? Choices: (a) mood, (b) impulsivity, (c) aggressive behavior, or (d) memory.
20. What are anabolic–androgenic steroids (AAS), and why are these substances given that general name?
21. List the major routes of administration of AAS.
22. (a) For what purposes were AAS developed historically? (b) Who are the primary users of AAS at the current time?
23. The modern pentathlon is an Olympic event that combines the following five competitions: (a) fencing, (b) swimming, (c) equestrian jumping, and (d) a combined shooting and running competition. If you were a pentathlon competitor (illegally) using AAS to improve your performance, in which event do you think your AAS use would benefit you the most, and why?
24. Among the terms used to describe various patterns and combinations of AAS use are "cycling," "pyramiding," "stacking," and "bridging." What does each term mean?
25. What are the mechanisms by which AAS increase muscle mass and physical strength?
26. Describe the adverse effects of chronic AAS use on the cardiovascular system, liver, and kidneys.
27. Chronic AAS use by men can result in loss of fertility. What is the explanation for this effect?
28. What is muscle dysmorphia? Is this disorder associated with the motivation to use AAS or to abstain from such use?

(Continued)

STUDY QUESTIONS (continued)

29. A friend of yours tells you about a recent report in the media of an athlete who was suspected of using AAS regularly who severely assaulted a sportswriter who had publicly criticized the athlete's recent performance. Your friend contends that this episode is an example of "roid rage." Based on our current understanding of the relationship between AAS use and aggressive behavior, how would you respond to your friend? How would your response be different if the suspected AAS use was still unproven, or if there was solid evidence for such use (e.g., if the athlete had failed a drug test for the presence of AAS).

30. What have we learned about the neural mechanisms of AAS-mediated aggression and anxiety using the hamster model?

31. What are the symptoms of AAS dependence and withdrawal?

32. A recent study concluded that AAS reward in the conditioned place preference test depends on the release of _____ in the _____, thereby stimulating _____ receptors and causing increased firing of _____ neurons.

33. (a) What is hypogonadism in males, what are the symptoms of this disorder, and what is the usual treatment? Include in your answer a discussion of the physiology of primary versus secondary hypogonadism. (b) For what other condition is testosterone sometimes prescribed?

Disorders of Anxiety and Impulsivity and the Drugs Used to Treat Them

17

A NUMBER OF YEARS AGO, a psychologist was asked to make a house call to a woman having panic disorder with agoraphobia. Mrs. M. was 67 years old and lived in a lower-middle-class section of the city. Her adult daughter was one of her few remaining contacts with the world and had requested the evaluation. Mrs. M. was friendly and was glad to see the clinician. He was the first person she had seen in 3 weeks. Mrs. M. had not set foot out of that apartment in 20 years, and she had suffered from panic disorder with agoraphobia for over 30 years.

As her story was told, she provided vivid images of the tragedy of a wasted life. Early in her very stressful marriage to a man who abused alcohol and her, Mrs. M. had her first panic attack and had gradually withdrawn from the world. Even areas of her apartment signaled the potential for terrifying panic attacks. She did not answer the door herself, because she had not looked out in her hallway for the past 15 years. She reported that she could enter her kitchen and go into the areas containing her stove and refrigerator but that she had not been to the back of her kitchen overlooking the backyard for the past 10 years. Thus, her life for the past decade had revolved around her bedroom, her living room, and the front half of her kitchen. She relied on her daughter to bring in groceries and visit once a week. Her only remaining contact with the outside world was through the television and the radio. As long as she stayed within her apartment, she was relatively free of panic. In her mind, there were few reasons left in her life to venture out, and she declined treatment (adapted from Barlow and Durand, 1995). ■

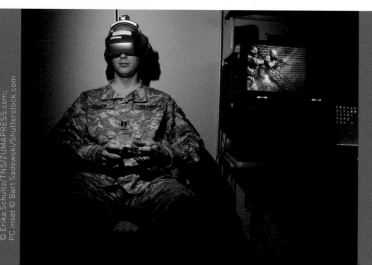

Virtual reality can be effective in treating PTSD and phobias.

17.1 Neurobiology of Anxiety

We turn now to a class of maladaptive behaviors that produce an enormous amount of suffering, contribute to low productivity, and generate a poor quality of life for a large number of individuals. The fifth edition of the *Diagnostic and Statistical Manual of Mental Disorders* (*DSM-5*) has reclassified the anxiety disorders into three major categories: anxiety disorders; obsessive–compulsive disorder (OCD) and related disorders; and trauma-related disorders, including post-traumatic stress disorder (PTSD). Although specific symptoms vary, all three of the major categories have anxiety or more severe stress response as a major component. Furthermore, as you will see, there are a number of common neurobiological features, so we will continue to include OCD and PTSD in this chapter. Although the incidence of each syndrome varies, it has been estimated that 10% to 30% of Americans will suffer from debilitating anxiety at some point in their lives. The ways in which that anxiety is expressed vary greatly and include episodes of panic, phobic avoidance of anxiety-eliciting stimuli, intrusive thoughts or compulsive behaviors, and damaging negative thinking patterns. In addition, anxiety is a factor commonly associated with other psychopathology, particularly clinical depression. The link between anxiety and depression is well documented: according to the National Comorbidity Survey, 58% of patients with major depression also show signs of anxiety disorder (Ninan, 1999). Furthermore, both neurobiological and pharmacological evidence support the idea of a common link between the two. Before considering some specific psychiatric disorders in the "Characteristics of Anxiety Disorders" section, let's look a little closer at the neurobiology of anxiety itself. The final section of this chapter will discuss the drugs that can be used to treat anxiety disorders—barbiturates, benzodiazepines, and second-generation anxiolytics*—as well as some of the potential new approaches to treatment.

What is anxiety?

Most anxiety manifests as a subjectively unsettling feeling of concern or worry that is displayed by behaviors such as having a worried facial expression, as well as by bodily responses such as increased muscle tension, restlessness, impaired concentration, sleep disturbances, and irritability. In addition, activation of the sympathetic branch of the autonomic nervous system (ANS) produces increased heart rate, sweating, shortness of breath, and other signs of the "fight-or-flight" response (see Chapter 2). Anxiety can vary in intensity from feelings of vague discomfort to intense sensations of terror.

Evolutionarily, anxiety is important to survival since it warns us of danger and activates the fight-or-flight

response, enabling us to cope with impending emergency. Unfortunately, many of the dangers we face in the modern world do not involve fighting off or running from predators like the saber-toothed tiger, when increased heart rate and blood pressure, elevated blood glucose, and surges of adrenaline would be beneficial. Most of the anxiety-provoking situations that we face demand instead that we restrain our aggressive impulses (wanting to attack our hostile boss), think clearly (during a difficult exam), and remain in the anxiety-producing situation (giving a speech to a large group) until a resolution occurs. In these circumstances, the fight-or-flight response is not helpful and may impair our ability to perform at our best.

Nevertheless, despite its unpleasantness, anxiety in small doses is clearly a necessary stimulus for optimal performance in many everyday situations. If it is contextually appropriate, anxiety is a highly adaptive response to threat. Anxiety before an exam encourages more study; anxiety before public speaking forces us to practice our presentation one more time; anxiety before a first date prompts us to recheck our plans for the evening. Regardless of whether we are students, factory workers, or business people, anxiety boosts our energy level and pushes us to work harder and longer. But sometimes we experience too much of a good thing. When anxiety increases beyond a certain level, performance deteriorates noticeably, particularly on complex tasks. What begins as increasing alertness and focus becomes preoccupation with our own agitation that distracts us from our task. The ANS prepares our bodies for emergency; our muscles are tense, and we may suffer from digestive problems, sleep disturbances leading to fatigue, and psychosomatic illness. Overanxious students often cannot focus on an important exam, because they are too preoccupied with thoughts of how awful it would be to fail. Worst of all, because high anxiety has damaged our performance, our failures provide more reason to be anxious, creating an escalating circular pattern (**FIGURE 17.1**). Once we begin to have negative feelings about ourselves and our lack of productivity, depression may develop or the initial stages of substance abuse may begin.

Brief episodes of anxiety, even when rather intense, are not likely to be harmful and may be quite rational in many situations. Acute anxiety occurs in response to real-life stressors, and symptoms occur only in response to these events. Pharmacological treatment is very effective in providing relief from the anxiety associated with major life changes such as death of a loved one, divorce, or permanent disability or with sudden stressors like major surgery that trigger intense anxiety. The anxiolytics in the benzodiazepine class are extremely effective for relieving this type of anxiety.

Although anxiety is related to the negative emotion fear, it is also somewhat different. Anxiety is

---

*An anxiolytic is a drug that reduces anxiety.

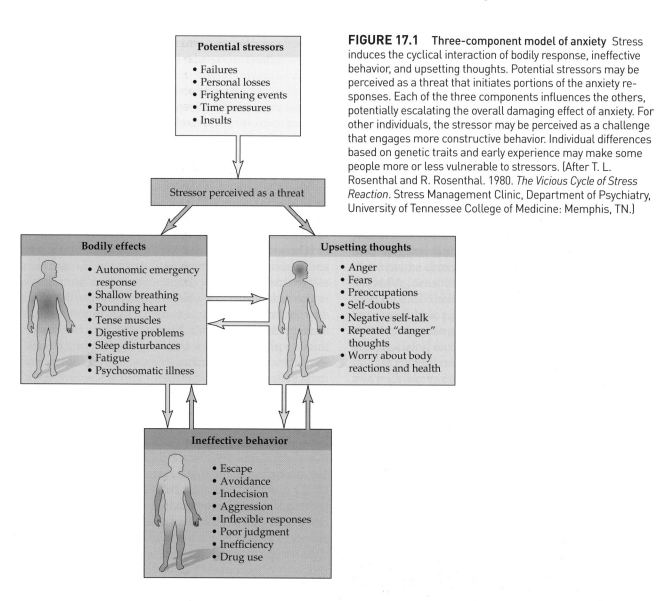

FIGURE 17.1 **Three-component model of anxiety** Stress induces the cyclical interaction of bodily response, ineffective behavior, and upsetting thoughts. Potential stressors may be perceived as a threat that initiates portions of the anxiety responses. Each of the three components influences the others, potentially escalating the overall damaging effect of anxiety. For other individuals, the stressor may be perceived as a challenge that engages more constructive behavior. Individual differences based on genetic traits and early experience may make some people more or less vulnerable to stressors. (After T. L. Rosenthal and R. Rosenthal. 1980. *The Vicious Cycle of Stress Reaction*. Stress Management Clinic, Department of Psychiatry, University of Tennessee College of Medicine: Memphis, TN.)

apprehension about possible future events or misfortune and concern about the ability to predict or deal with these events. In contrast, fear is an emotional response to clear and current danger, as occurs when you are confronted by a threatening bear. It is characterized by a strong urge to escape, and it elicits a strong activation of the ANS to mobilize the energy for fight or flight. These two emotions differ not only in their temporal nature, but also in terms of psychological and neurobiological consequences.

The amygdala is important to emotion-processing circuits

The amygdaloid complex, a structure deep within the temporal lobes, is a major component of several emotion-processing circuits. These circuits have many components in addition to the amygdala and include structures of the limbic cortex (insula and anterior cingulate cortex [ACC]), hypothalamus, and hippocampus. The circuits evaluate environmental stimuli,

contextual cues, and cognitions that have emotional relevance and initiate appropriate responses via the amygdala. To activate these emotional responses, the amygdala receives highly processed sensory and cognitive information about the environment from the sensory thalamus, sensory and association cortices, and hippocampal formation. These brain areas project to the lateral nucleus of the amygdala (**FIGURE 17.2**). After processing, the information is sent from the lateral nucleus to the central nucleus by direct connections, and by indirect connections via the basolateral nucleus. Negative emotional stimuli activate the amygdala in healthy humans, as visualized with positron emission tomography (PET) scanning and functional magnetic resonance imaging (fMRI). This activation is significantly greater in individuals with anxiety disorders. In laboratory animals, electrical stimulation of the amygdala produces signs of anxiety and fear, while bilateral lesions produce deficits in fearful responses.

FIGURE 17.2 **Flow diagram of connections of the amygdala** This much-simplified diagram shows how anxiety-related information processed by several brain areas inputs first to the lateral nucleus of the amygdala. From the lateral nucleus, it goes to the central nucleus (directly and indirectly) and the bed nucleus of the stria terminalis (BNST), which innervate widespread brain regions to orchestrate the components of emotion.

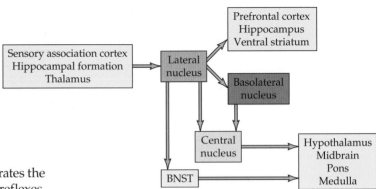

The central nucleus of the amygdala orchestrates the components of fear: ANS activation, enhanced reflexes, increased vigilance, activation of the hypothalamic–pituitary–adrenal (HPA) axis, and other responses (LeDoux, 1996). Stimulation of the central nucleus has such widespread effects because of its multiple connections with brain areas that are responsible for how emotion is expressed. For example, projections to the lateral hypothalamus activate the sympathetic nervous system, those to the periaqueductal gray cause freezing, others that activate the locus coeruleus (LC) initiate arousal and vigilance, and so forth (**FIGURE 17.3**). Damaging selected brain areas that receive projection neurons from the central nucleus can eliminate specific components of the anxiety response, and damaging the central nucleus itself reduces or eliminates most emotional behaviors and physiological responses. Furthermore, intracerebral injection of various drugs into the amygdala reduces anxiety in a number of animal tests.

Although the amygdala plays a central role, it may be the plasticity of the connections among regions in the emotion-processing circuits that is responsible for the development of various psychopathologies. Using resting state fMRI (rs-fMRI; see Chapter 4), van Marle and colleagues (2010) evaluated regional brain connectivity in healthy human volunteers immediately after (not during) experiencing a stressful, violent video. They found that the stressed volunteers, compared with controls who saw non-arousing movie clips, showed enhanced connectivity between the amygdala and LC, as well as other structures in emotion-processing circuits, including the insula and ACC. Although their results showed normal responses to stress, the authors suggest that such studies may provide insight into the early stages of stress-related psychopathologies because after intense stress, prolonged activation of the stress circuit may lead to an extended pathological response to trauma, including overconsolidated fear memories and hypervigilance. It also may help to explain why individuals exposed to stress are more vulnerable to various anxiety disorders.

Although the central nucleus is vital for fear responses, evidence suggests that the physiology of anxiety may be somewhat different from that of fear (Miles and Maren, 2019). While amygdaloid processing still plays a central role in the emotional circuit, the behavioral

responses in anxiety may be initiated by a brain area referred to as the "extended amygdala," the bed nucleus of the stria terminalis (BNST). It is possible that each of these areas may be involved in different types of anxiety disorders. The BNST is similar to the central nucleus in anatomy, cytoarchitecture, and neurochemistry. It projects to the same brain regions as the central nucleus (see Figure 17.2) but functions somewhat differently. The central nucleus plays a role in the fear response when threatening stimuli are distinct cues that appear suddenly and predict an aversive event, which also ends abruptly. This is modeled by conditioned fear-potentiated startle paradigm in rats (see Chapter 4). In contrast to the rapid response system mediated by the central nucleus, the BNST initiates components of the emotional response when the stimuli are less precise predictors of a potentially dangerous situation. It produces a state of sustained preparedness for an unclear danger and a prolonged period of anticipation that something unpleasant might occur. In addition, this response persists long after the initial stimulus is ended and resembles the state of anxiety.

Anxiety in several animal tests (see Chapter 4) is modulated by manipulations of the BNST. One such manipulation is optogenetic control of that brain region. Activation of the BNST in mice expressing the light-sensitive protein channelrhodopsin-2 reduced exploration in the open field test and the open arms in the elevated plus-maze. In contrast, optogenetic-induced inhibition reduced the anxiety-like behaviors in those tests. The researchers further investigated the microcircuitry, using a combination of optogenetics and electrical recording. They found that subregions of BNST with distinct projections have opposite effects in modulating anxiety. Those multiple projections may explain how the various features of the anxious behavioral state are selected and coordinated for a given situation (Kim et al., 2013). It is especially interesting to note that chronic restraint stress or chronic unpredictable stress increases dendritic length and branching, as well as volume of the BNST. This stress-induced plasticity was accompanied by increased anxiety in the elevated plus-maze.

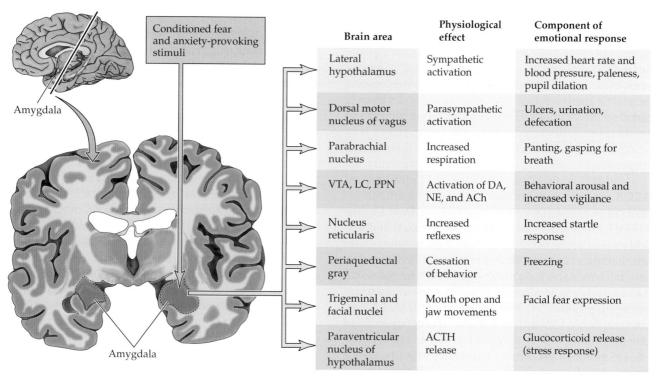

Brain area	Physiological effect	Component of emotional response
Lateral hypothalamus	Sympathetic activation	Increased heart rate and blood pressure, paleness, pupil dilation
Dorsal motor nucleus of vagus	Parasympathetic activation	Ulcers, urination, defecation
Parabrachial nucleus	Increased respiration	Panting, gasping for breath
VTA, LC, PPN	Activation of DA, NE, and ACh	Behavioral arousal and increased vigilance
Nucleus reticularis	Increased reflexes	Increased startle response
Periaqueductal gray	Cessation of behavior	Freezing
Trigeminal and facial nuclei	Mouth open and jaw movements	Facial fear expression
Paraventricular nucleus of hypothalamus	ACTH release	Glucocorticoid release (stress response)

FIGURE 17.3   **The amygdala coordinates components of emotion** The amygdala has neuronal connections with all of these brain areas that produce individual pieces of emotional expression. ACh, acetylcholine; ACTH, adrenocorticotropic hormone; DA, dopamine; LC, locus coeruleus; NE, norepinephrine; PPN, pedunculopontine nucleus; VTA, ventral tegmental area.

It is tempting to speculate that similar stress-induced plasticity may increase vulnerability to anxiety disorders. Additionally, the increased vulnerability is significant because BNST-dependent anxiety is modulated by sex hormones and may explain gender differences in anxiety disorders. Gender differences in stress response are discussed more fully later in this section.

In addition to identifying the emotional significance of events, the amygdala aids in the formation of emotional memories, sometimes called conditioned fear or conditioned emotional response (CER). An emotional memory, or CER, involves making an association between an environmental stimulus and an aversive stimulus, for example the sound of a tone preceding the onset of a brief electrical shock. After only a few pairings, hearing the tone will lead to elevated heart rate, rapid breathing, secretion of stress hormones, and other signs of anxiety. Emotional memories are established quickly and are long lasting. Formation of the classically conditioned CER is significant for survival because it allows an animal to anticipate danger and to be prepared physiologically and behaviorally to cope with the situation. The association is formed in the lateral amygdala, which activates the central nucleus that in turn activates those brain areas responsible for individual components of the response. Although this emotional memory is important for survival, it is clear that if the emotional response generalizes to many similar stimuli, a chronic state of anxiety could result characteristic of generalized anxiety disorder. Of special significance is the fact that emotional memories can be learned vicariously; that is, we do not have to have personal experience with every aversive event but can learn to fear by watching another person experience fear or harmful consequences. Although vicarious conditioning is generally highly beneficial, can you think of times when it is harmful?

The amygdala also contributes to the enhancement of memory consolidation through its connections with the hippocampus (shown in Figure 17.2). Memories of events and their contexts are established in the hippocampus, and memory consolidation is significantly improved for events with strong emotional relevance. In addition to memory consolidation, the hippocampus may have a role in some anxiety disorders because reciprocal connections with the amygdala modulate emotional responses on the basis of context. The anxious behaviors of people suffering from the disorders described in this chapter are not abnormal in character, but they are expressed in contextually inappropriate situations (Davidson et al., 2000). Recent research has also uncovered that different anatomical locations within the hippocampus contribute to context-dependent fear learning. Using optogenetics to either stimulate or suppress the activity of neurons along the dentate gyrus (DG) in mice, it has been discovered that more dorsal portions of the hippocampal DG play a role in memory encoding, while more ventral DG neurons govern memory retrieval (Kheirbek et al., 2013). Indeed, the authors showed that suppressing ventral DG neural activity eliminated context-dependent fear in these animals, illuminating one potential target for therapeutic development.

Although activation of the amygdala elicits emotional responses, the prefrontal cortex (PFC), particularly the orbitofrontal and medial prefrontal, and the subgenual ACC exert inhibitory control over the more primitive responses of the subcortical regions. Without control by the PFC, which is responsible for planning, decision making, and evaluating consequences of behavior, the anxiety response produces more limited patterns of behavior that may not be suitable for coping with modern stressors that are not resolved by fighting or running away. Furthermore, the medial PFC (mPFC) is important for fear extinction; that is, for learning that a cue that once predicted danger no longer does so. The disorders in this chapter are frequently considered to arise from an imbalance between emotion-generating centers and higher cortical control (see the section that describes the characteristics of anxiety below). Neuroimaging has become increasingly important in generating neurocircuitry models of the disorders (see Martin et al., 2010; Farb and Ratner, 2014, for reviews of this important topic).

Multiple neurotransmitters mediate anxiety

Neurobiological hypotheses of anxiety disorders have been tested in animal studies and in clinical evaluation. The anatomical complexity of emotion and its importance to survival makes it highly likely that many neurotransmitters modulate the anxiety response.

ROLE OF CORTICOTROPIN-RELEASING FACTOR IN ANXIETY Corticotropin-releasing factor (CRF; sometimes called corticotropin-releasing hormone, or CRH) is a small neuropeptide that controls the neuroendocrine (HPA axis), autonomic, and behavioral responses to stress. As you know from Chapter 2, the HPA axis is activated by the release of CRF from the paraventricular nucleus of the hypothalamus in response to stress. CRF is responsible for inducing the anterior pituitary to release the stress hormone adrenocorticotropic hormone (ACTH) into the blood, which in turn increases the release of glucocorticoids such as cortisol from the adrenal cortex. These hormones induce a variety of physiological changes that provide the means to adapt to environmental challenges. In addition, the elevated cortisol initiates a negative feedback loop by binding to glucocorticoid receptors in the hippocampus, hypothalamus, and pituitary, which inhibits HPA axis function and brings cortisol levels back to normal. In addition to its role in stress hormone regulation and body

physiology, CRF acts as a neurotransmitter in neural circuits involved in the stress response, including the amygdala (**FIGURE 17.4**). Therefore, the release of this tiny peptide may help coordinate the distinct behavioral strategies needed to adapt to stressful events and hence may contribute to disorders with prominent signs of anxiety (see McEwen and Akil, 2020).

Intraventricular administration of CRF stimulates the sympathetic nervous system and causes increases in plasma adrenaline and increased heart rate and blood pressure. These effects are not due to HPA axis activation, because removing the adrenal gland does not change this response to cerebral CRF. Therefore, the effects must be mediated by extrahypothalamic neural control such as excitation of the LC (see the following section on the role of norepinephrine). The dual role for CRF means that the endocrine response to stress via the HPA axis is well coordinated with the autonomic and adaptive cognitive portion of the stress response. CRF also has wide-ranging effects on feeding, gastrointestinal activity, and energy balance that are consistent with

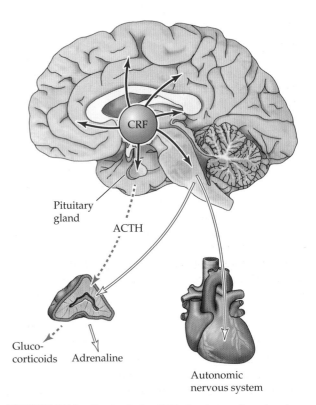

FIGURE 17.4 Dual role for CRF Corticotropin-releasing factor (CRF) is released by the hypothalamus to act on the pituitary gland to control the release of glucocorticoids from the adrenal cortex (HPA axis) in response to stress (dashed arrow pathway). CRF also acts as a neurotransmitter in multiple brain areas associated with anxiety (solid arrow pathway) and is released following threatening stimuli. Intracerebral CRF causes behavioral signs of anxiety as well as altered autonomic nervous system function (open arrow pathways). ACTH, adrenocorticotropic hormone.

preparation for dealing with environmental stressors. CRF causes increased anxiety, as seen in conflict tests, social interaction, exploration in novel open fields, and the elevated plus-maze (these and other tests of anxiety are described in Chapter 4). Direct neuronal application of CRF produces strong excitatory effects in many brain areas that contain significant numbers of CRF receptors, including the hippocampus, amygdala, LC, cortex, and hypothalamus, all of which are parts of the neural circuit for anxiety. Of particular significance are the large numbers of CRF nerve endings and CRF receptors found in the amygdala. Further, individual differences in anxiety level may be due to differences in the amount of CRF in the amygdala (Shekhar et al., 2005). For example, rats that show greater "freezing" responses to stress and show enhanced physiological signs also have higher levels of CRF mRNA in the central nucleus of the amygdala compared with less anxious rat strains. Clinical studies show that CRF levels are higher in the cerebrospinal fluid of combat veterans with PTSD than in veterans without the anxiety disorder.

Stressful stimuli such as physical restraint cause a release of CRF in the amygdala, particularly the basolateral amygdala, as measured by microdialysis. The major source of this release appears to be the central amygdala and the BNST, both of which are rich in CRF-containing cell bodies projecting to the amygdala (particularly the basolateral nucleus), with the remainder of CRF afferents originating from sparse sources in the cortex (VanPett et al., 2000). The increased extracellular CRF is accompanied by a variety of signs of anxiety. Many of these effects can be prevented by pretreatment with the CRF antagonist α-helical CRF9-41. However, not all measures of anxiety are attenuated by intra-amygdaloid infusion of the CRF antagonist, which suggests that other areas within the central nervous system (CNS) such as the LC must also mediate aspects of anxiety.

CRF neurons originating in the central nucleus of the amygdala project to the LC and activate the adrenergic component of the stress response (reviewed in Valentino and Van Bockstaele, 2008). Intracranial injection of CRF increases the firing rate of cells in the LC and increases the turnover of norepinephrine (NE), as determined by the increase in the NE metabolite MHPG in the amygdala (via reciprocal connections), hypothalamus, hippocampus, and PFC. It should be no surprise that infusion of CRF into the LC produces anxiety, as measured by time spent in the novel open field. For all these reasons, the neuroendocrine and CNS effects of CRF are generating a great deal of research in neuroscience, and the neuropeptide is a target for new drug development. **WEB BOX 17.1** describes CRF antagonists and several other novel approaches to treating anxiety, including neuropeptide Y agonists and glutamate antagonists.

ROLE OF NOREPINEPHRINE IN ANXIETY Reciprocal connections between the amygdala and the LC provide a mechanism for generating arousal, orienting, and responding to fear-evoking stimuli. The LC is a major cluster of noradrenergic cell bodies in the dorsal pons that has a widely distributed network of axons to many brain areas involved in emotional processing, vigilance, and attention to physiologically relevant stimuli. The LC consists of several histologically differentiated neurons having distinct electrophysiological properties. One type fires at a low tonic (i.e., continuous) rate (1–2 Hz) that corresponds to general wakefulness, while other neurons show phasic bursts of activity (i.e., responding strongly, but briefly, followed by a longer period of inhibition) in response to non-noxious environmental stimuli, such as a brief tone, a flash of light, or a light touch. A third type of cell responds to stressors and stress-induced CRF release with high rates (3–8 Hz) of tonic activity. McCall and colleagues (2015) evaluated the importance of neurons showing high tonic activity during stress and identified the neural mechanism responsible. They performed a series of experiments using several of the genetic (optogenetic and chemogenetic) and behavioral (open field test and elevated zero maze) techniques described in Chapter 4. Their research showed that restraint stress increased tonic activity of a discrete population of adrenergic cells in the LC. The cell firing was responsible for causing stress-induced anxiety behaviors that were prevented by chemogenetically inhibiting the LC neurons. Further, the increased LC activity was generated by photostimulation of CRF terminals of neurons originating in the central nucleus of the amygdala, demonstrating a role for CRF in stress-induced anxiety.

Of particular interest is that the magnitude of phasic firing depends on the level of tonic activity. Hence if tonic firing changes from a moderate level to either low or high firing, phasic bursting in response to an environmental stimulus is reduced. This differential responding may reflect a role for the LC in establishing the appropriate level of arousal and sensory processing needed to produce optimal behavioral adjustments under changing conditions. For instance, during a stressful episode, visual scanning of the environment may be more beneficial than responding to a discrete sensory stimulus that would normally cause a phasic burst.

The CRF-induced high tonic firing of LC neurons is of further interest because male rats with a history of stress show sensitization to low doses of CRF. That means that lower levels of CRF, not normally significant, are able to activate the LC that in turn enhances NE release in LC target regions of the brain. That sensitization may help to explain why previous exposure to stress increases the vulnerability to anxiety disorders. Such a mechanism may also contribute to the hypervigilance seen in PTSD. However, although female rats show greater LC activation to CRF at all stages of their estrous cycle compared with male rats, they do not develop the same stress-related sensitization to CRF. It would appear that gender differences need to be considered both in diagnosis and treatment of anxiety disorders. (Refer to Valentino and Van Bockstaele, 2008, for further discussion of the regulation of stress-induced LC activity by CRF, endogenous opioids, and glutamate.)

Several other lines of evidence demonstrate the importance of NE in anxiety. Numerous studies over many years have indicated the significant role of the LC as a mediator of stress-induced anxiety. Researchers used optogenetics and various tracing methods to demonstrate that stimulation of LC-NE fibers in the basolateral amygdala robustly induces anxiety-like behavior in mice (McCall et al., 2017) (see **BOX 17.1** for details). Moreover, it was shown that this effect could be blocked by pharmacological pretreatment with a β-adrenergic receptor antagonist, implicating a role of this receptor in anxiety. These findings complement other studies showing that animals that are exposed to novel stimuli that signal threat or that are subjected to various forms of acute stressors show increased electrical activity and enhanced expression of the immediate

early gene product c-fos, another indicator of neuronal activation in the LC. Electrical stimulation of the LC or administration of the α_2-autoreceptor antagonist yohimbine (which increases NE release) induces a wide range of alerting and fear responses accompanied by pupil dilation, piloerection, and increased heart rate in primates. Yohimbine likewise produces panic attacks in patients with panic disorder, but not in healthy individuals (Kaplan et al., 2012). A wide variety of stressors also increase release of NE in LC target regions of the brain as shown by microdialysis.

Second, clinical studies of patients with a variety of anxiety disorders suggest that abnormal ANS response is a common key feature. NE is the neurotransmitter released at the target visceral organs, including the heart, during sympathetic activation. Additionally, the catecholamine adrenaline (epinephrine), released from the adrenal medulla, produces widespread effects that prepare the individual to respond to danger. Individuals with panic disorder and PTSD have especially dramatic body responses to anxiety-provoking stimuli. Furthermore, war veterans with PTSD have higher-than-normal levels of circulating NE.

BOX 17.1 ■ THE CUTTING EDGE

Toward Unraveling the Cellular and Molecular Mechanisms Underlying LC-NE Modulation of Anxiety

In 2015, McCall and colleagues published a landmark paper showing that induction of anxiety in mice through restraint stress led to a tonic elevation in neural activity within LC-NE cell bodies. Moreover, they showed that chemogenetically (i.e., using the DREADD system) blocking this rise in activity before restraint stress was sufficient to prevent anxiogenesis. Although this study provided strong evidence for the involvement of the LC-NE system in modulating anxiety, it did not address the critical question of which downstream projection targets and receptors are involved in this process. In a follow-up study, McCall and colleagues (2017) performed an elegant variety of experiments combining neural tracing, optogenetics, cyclic voltammetry, pharmacology, and behavior in order to comprehensively understand how the LC-NE system impacts the limbic system to modulate anxiety. In particular, the authors focused on the putative connections from LC-NE neurons onto the basolateral amygdala (BLA), a nucleus of the amygdala known for its role in mediating both anxiety (through its connections with the central amygdala [ceA] and ventral hippocampus [vHPC]) and aspects of reward (through its connections with the nucleus accumbens [NAc]). First, it was established through several dye- and genetics-based tracing experiments that LC-NE neurons indeed send efferents that innervate the BLA (**FIGURE A**). Next, a

virus was introduced into the LC that drove the expression of channelrhodopsin-2 (ChR2) only in neurons expressing the catecholamine synthesis enzyme tyrosine hydroxylase (TH), which in the LC occurs exclusively in NE cells. The researchers then placed a light-emitting electrode into the BLA in order to activate ChR2 within innervating NE fibers while simultaneously capturing changes in voltage within this region. Importantly, this strategy allowed the authors to only activate LC-NE neurons that innervate the BLA, rather than all terminals across the brain as would occur if the fiber-optic probe was placed in the LC to activate NE cell bodies. They discovered that stimulating NE fibers within the BLA caused a change in local perisynaptic voltage characteristic of NE release (**FIGURE B**). Next, a similar experiment was performed but this time using a light-emitting electrode that could capture firing activity of cell bodies within the BLA. Upon ChR2 activation, the authors found that the resulting stimulation of NE terminals in the BLA caused a change in the firing of a subset of cells within this region (**FIGURE C**), with some increasing and others decreasing in activity (**FIGURE D**). The authors next tested which targets of these BLA neurons might be preferentially impacted by NE modulation from the LC. Using a combination of optogenetic stimulation of ChR2-positive NE fibers in the BLA, c-fos immunohistochemistry as a marker of

BOX 17.1 ■ THE CUTTING EDGE *(continued)*

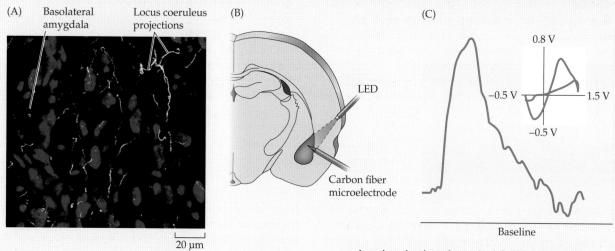

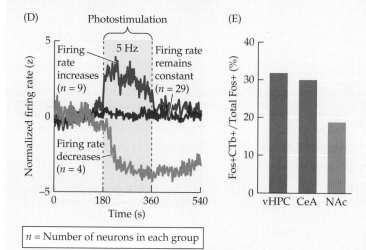

(A) Basolateral amygdala
Locus coeruleus projections

20 μm

(D) Photostimulation

Firing rate increases (*n* = 9)

5 Hz

Firing rate remains constant (*n* = 29)

Firing rate decreases (*n* = 4)

Normalized firing rate (z)

Time (s)

n = Number of neurons in each group

(B) LED

Carbon fiber microelectrode

(C) 0.8 V

−0.5 V · · 1.5 V

−0.5 V

Baseline

(E)

Fos+CTb+/Total Fos+ (%)

vHPC CeA NAc

Local projections from the LC-NE activate BLA neurons involved in anxiogenesis (A) The LC of mice was injected with a virus coding for enhanced yellow fluorescent protein (eYFP) that was engineered to only express in LC neurons. Image shows an immunohistochemically stained BLA section with Nissl-stained cell bodies in blue and eYFP-positive NE fibers from the LC in yellow, demonstrating that LC-NE fibers directly innervate the BLA. (B) A virus was used to express ChR2 exclusively in LC-NE neurons, and a light-emitting diode (LED) cyclic voltammetry electrode was embedded in the BLA as depicted in the schematic. (C) Upon light stimulation, the electrode detected a voltage signature consistent with NE release. Representative cyclic voltammograms are shown in the inset. (D) This experiment was repeated as in (B), but this time embedding an LED electrophysiology electrode. Light stimulation of LC-NE terminals in the BLA resulted in a mix of neurons with increased (red), decreased (light blue), or unchanged (dark blue) activity, with "*n*" denoting the relative numbers of neurons that were measured in each category. This demonstrated that LC-NE activation in the BLA was sufficient to alter neuronal firing within the BLA. (E) Mice were optogenetically stimulated to release LC-NE in the BLA as before to pinpoint activated neurons via c-fos staining, after which one group of mice was injected with a retrograde tracer (CTb) in the vHPC, one in the CeA, and one in the NAc. Graph shows relative percentages of neurons stained for both markers, demonstrating that LC-NE-activated BLA neurons preferentially project to the vHPC and CeA rather than the NAc, the former two projections involved in anxiogenesis, and the latter in reduction of anxiety. (After J. G. McCall et al. 2017. *Elife* 6: e18247. doi: 10.7554/eLife.18247. CC BY 4.0, creativecommons.org/licenses/by/4.0/.)

resulting neural activity within the BLA, and Cholera toxin subunit B (CTb) retrograde tracing from either the ceA, vHIPP, or NAc (see above), the authors found that BLA neurons co-expressed both c-fos and the tracer more preferentially when projecting to the CeA and vHIPP than the NAc (**FIGURE E**). This suggested that LC-NE projections to the BLA modulate neurons that then drive the genesis of anxiety.

To test this behavioral hypothesis more directly, the researchers examined whether activating LC-NE terminals in the BLA could cause anxiety-like behavior as measured by a conditioned place preference test. Here, mice were placed in one of two distinct chambers within a box, after which optogenetic stimulation of LC-NE terminals in the BLA was paired with that chamber for 2 days. Control animals lacking the ChR2 protein but where the fiber-optic probe was implanted and activated in the BLA underwent the same paradigm. On the third day, each mouse was allowed to run freely between the two chambers

(Continued)

without any additional stimulation, and the amount of time spent in each chamber was recorded. Compared with control animals, the authors found that the test mice showed an aversion to the chamber where LC-BLA stimulation was previously paired with that particular chamber, as reflected by relatively less time spent in that chamber (**FIGURE F**). This finding suggested that the NE projections from LC to the BLA can cause animals to learn negative associations leading to a conditioned aversion, a fundamental underpinning of many anxiety disorders. Finally, the authors asked whether this effect could be modulated by a particular noradrenergic receptor within the BLA, specifically the beta noradrenergic receptor known for its role in anxiogenesis. To address this, the authors performed another behavioral experiment but this time using an open field test, which measures acute anxiety-like behaviors on the basis of time spent in the center (risk) versus periphery (safety) of a box. Presumably, more relative time spent in the periphery is consistent with a higher state of anxiety about the risk associated with exploring the center of the box, which from an ethological standpoint may reflect a mouse balancing the need to forage versus risking predation. Here, the authors photostimulated ChR2 on LC-NE terminals within the BLA while each mouse explored the box ad libitum, and found that this activation was sufficient to induce acute anxiety-like behavior as inferred by more relative time spent in the periphery than the center of the box. Remarkably, when this experiment was repeated but with the infusion of a local β-adrenergic receptor blocker, propranolol, in the BLA, the effects on anxiety resulting from LC-NE fiber stimulation in the BLA were abolished (**FIGURE G**). The results of this experiment strongly suggest that NE release from LC-NE neurons in the BLA impacts anxiety-like behaviors through activation of β-receptors on BLA neurons. Together, this elegant study provided the next critical step in understanding how the LC-NE system, and in particular its tonic activity observed after stress, interacts with BLA neurons and the greater limbic system to modulate anxiety. This moves the field forward in terms of delineating anxiety circuitry and generating promising targets for therapeutic intervention.

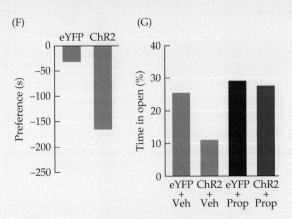

Activation of LC-NE projections in the BLA causes anxiety-like behavior that is blocked by local infusion of a β-receptor antagonist (F) The LC of mice was injected with a virus coding for ChR2, and fiber-optics were implanted in the BLA to stimulate ChR2-positive LC-NE fibers. During conditioning, stimulation was paired with one of two distinct chambers for 2 days. On day 3, animals were given free access to the chamber without further stimulation. Mice showed a conditioned aversion to the chamber previously paired with LC-NE stimulation in the BLA, as reflected by a significantly less time (s) spent in the paired than the non-conditioned chamber (green) relative to controls not expressing the ChR2 protein (blue). This suggests that the LC-NE-BLA connection is sufficient to induce anxiety-like behavior. (G) As in (F), mice were implanted with a fiber-optic cable to stimulate ChR2 on LC-NE neurons in the BLA, but this time acutely while measuring patterns of locomotion within an open-field box. Compared with eYFP controls (light blue), ChR2-positive animals (light green) showed a significant, immediate aversion to the center of the box, consistent with anxiety-like behavior. Remarkably, when this experiment was repeated but with local infusion of propranolol (Prop) into the BLA right before optogenetic activation, the effect of ChR2 activation on anxiety was abolished (control, dark blue; ChR2, dark green). This experiment suggested that LC-NE neurons activate the BLA through β-adrenergic receptors to modulate at least some aspects of anxiolysis. (After J. G. McCall et al. 2017. *Elife* 6: e18247. doi: 10.7554/eLife.18247. CC BY 4.0, creativecommons.org/licenses/by/4.0/.)

Third, both NE and epinephrine have a significant role in the formation of emotional memories that may contribute to disorders in which memories of past trauma or stress can influence future behavior (as in agoraphobia seen in the chapter opener, panic, and PTSD). The normal enhancement of memory by the catecholamines in basolateral amygdala may be a way to help us remember what is emotionally significant and therefore important for future use. Fortunately, modifying NE function with drugs may represent a useful treatment for PTSD. Animal studies have shown that β-adrenergic agonists injected into the amygdala improve the consolidation of memory into long-term storage, and β-adrenergic antagonists impair the formation of emotional memories and associated physiological changes. This means that in humans, it may be possible to interfere with the formation of traumatic memories by blocking β-adrenergic receptors right after a severe trauma. It may also be possible to modify existing traumatic memories, because in addition to helping consolidate new memories, β-adrenergic agonists may have a role in reconsolidation processes. It is believed that recalling or retrieving a memory makes it temporarily unstable and susceptible to interference that would prevent the reconsolidation needed to maintain the memory. On this basis, it was suggested that the use of β-adrenergic antagonists may disrupt the already consolidated traumatic memories and associated physiological responses of those suffering from PTSD. Although clinical findings are not entirely consistent, a number of reports show that the β-adrenergic antagonist propranolol reduces the initial consolidation of emotional memories. In one study, survivors of auto accidents who received propranolol in the emergency room and for the next 6 days developed fewer cases of PTSD, and those who developed PTSD had fewer symptoms compared with those individuals who declined the propranolol treatment (Vaiva et al., 2003). Propranolol treatment also was effective in disrupting emotional memories that had been previously consolidated and retrieved in response to a learned fear cue or personalized trauma scripts (i.e., specific reminders of the individual's traumatic experience). The β-blocker given before retrieval of the emotional memory does not seem to impair the declarative memory of the association of the conditioned and unconditioned stimuli, but it does seem to significantly diminish the emotional effects. This means that the individual would still remember the traumatic event but would not respond emotionally to associated cues (Shad et al., 2011).

In addition to the enhancement of memory following rapid activation of the basolateral nucleus by NE from LC neurons, Joels and colleagues (2011) propose that cortisol following HPA axis activation acts on G protein–coupled receptors on that nucleus (albeit some minutes later) and reinforces the establishment of emotional memories. The reviewers provide neurophysiological, behavioral, and brain imaging evidence to support the synergistic interaction. For example, corticosterone (the rodent equivalent of cortisol) administered to rodents after an emotionally arousing training session enhanced the 24-hour memory of the event. However, corticosterone had no such effect in animals that did not show arousal-induced adrenergic activation because they had been previously habituated to the experimental event. Furthermore, the corticosterone-induced memory enhancement could be prevented by β-adrenergic antagonist administration into the basolateral amygdala, indicating that NE is necessary for the memory formation but the glucocorticoid enhances its action.

One intriguing aspect of their proposal is that the slower and more prolonged genomic effects of cortisol (see Chapter 3) several hours later gradually normalize the NE-induced activity of the basolateral nucleus.

Furthermore, these slower effects make the basolateral cells less responsive to further stress, possibly by allowing greater mPFC control to develop gradually. Conceivably that means that pretreatment with a cortisol-like drug administered hours before a trauma could reduce the effects of the NE surge and prevent the formation of traumatic memories. It also could mean that low levels of cortisol, as seen in individuals with PTSD, are unable to reduce the sensitivity of the basolateral nucleus of the amygdala to further stress, allowing intense adrenergic response during the re-experiencing of their traumatic event (see the section on PTSD below). The memories become intrusive and these individuals re-experience the extreme anxiety associated with their trauma over and over, both during the day as flashbacks and at night as nightmares. The proposed model may also explain the somewhat curious finding that individuals with PTSD typically have low levels of cortisol, but high levels of circulating catecholamines.

Fourth, some of the therapeutic effects of anxiolytic drugs can be explained by modulation of LC firing (Sullivan et al., 1999). Noradrenergic cells in the LC are excited by CRF synaptic input and are inhibited by γ-aminobutyric acid (GABA) and serotonin (5-HT), as well as by stimulation of α_2-adrenergic somatodendritic autoreceptors (**FIGURE 17.5**). Since benzodiazepines enhance the inhibitory function of GABA, reduced LC firing may be responsible for at least some of the anxiolytic effects of these drugs. Serotonin reuptake blockade by selective serotonin reuptake inhibitors (SSRIs) and subsequent enhancement of serotonergic function would likewise reduce LC firing and explain some of their antianxiety effects. Tricyclic antidepressants such as desipramine and monoamine oxidase inhibitors (MAOIs) that are used to treat selective anxiety disorders enhance NE function, which inhibits firing of LC neurons by acting on the α_2-autoreceptors (see Figure 17.5). In support of the therapeutic evidence, clinical studies have found abnormal autoreceptor response in individuals with **generalized anxiety disorder** (**GAD**) and social phobia (Sullivan et al., 1999).

ROLE OF GABA IN ANXIETY The inhibitory amino acid neurotransmitter GABA has a major role in modulating anxiety. GABA-induced inhibition is important for controlling the excitability of local circuits, and it regulates the activation of the central nucleus of the amygdala. Further, glutamatergic neurons from the PFC stimulate these GABA neurons in the amygdala to provide top-down control of amygdaloid activity. Hence an impaired GABA function could both lead to overactive bottom-up signaling from the amygdala, which indicates a menacing or aversive event, and hinder the top-down control by the PFC, which would fail to control the emotional impact of the stimuli. As you recall from Chapter 8, GABA is the principal inhibitory

FIGURE 17.5 **Drug effects on locus coeruleus (LC) cell firing** Some of the anxiolytic effects of the benzodiazepines (BDZs), tricyclic antidepressants (TCAs), monoamine oxidase inhibitors (MAOIs), and selective serotonin reuptake inhibitors (SSRIs) may be explained by their inhibitory effect on LC neurons. On the other hand, corticotropin-releasing factor (CRF) increases anxiety and has excitatory effects on the LC. CRF antagonists may be effective in reducing anxiety. 5-HT, serotonin.

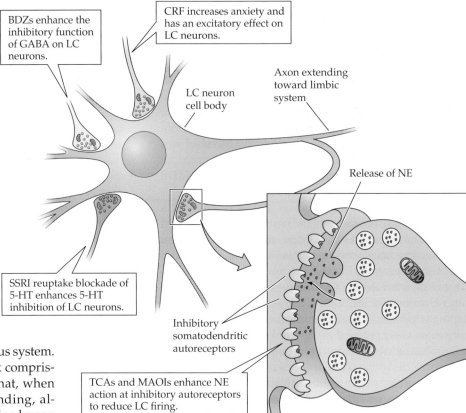

BDZs enhance the inhibitory function of GABA on LC neurons.

CRF increases anxiety and has an excitatory effect on LC neurons.

LC neuron cell body

Axon extending toward limbic system

Release of NE

SSRI reuptake blockade of 5-HT enhances 5-HT inhibition of LC neurons.

Inhibitory somatodendritic autoreceptors

TCAs and MAOIs enhance NE action at inhibitory autoreceptors to reduce LC firing.

neurotransmitter in the nervous system. The GABA$_A$ receptor complex comprises a chloride (Cl$^-$) channel that, when opened following GABA binding, allows Cl$^-$ to enter the cell, causing hyperpolarization. Several sedative–hypnotics enhance the function of GABA, causing sedation, reduced anxiety, and anticonvulsant effects. Benzodiazepines and barbiturates produce these effects by binding to distinct modulatory sites different from the GABA binding site on the receptor complex (further discussion of these drugs is found in the final section of this chapter). Ethyl alcohol also enhances GABA function, although its precise mechanism remains unclear (see Chapter 10). Naturally occurring neurosteroids such as allopregnanalone additionally act as positive modulators at distinct sites on the receptor complex and also produce sedative–hypnotic and anxiolytic effects. The reader is directed to Figure 8.17 for a schematic diagram of the GABA receptor complex and to an excellent, readable summary in Nuss (2015).

THE BENZODIAZEPINE BINDING SITE A great deal is known about the mechanism of action of the benzodiazepines (BDZs) because they are clinically useful GABA modulators, and their neuropharmacology has told us a great deal about the neurochemistry of anxiety. The BDZ binding sites were identified in 1977. When their location was mapped in the rat brain using autoradiography, it became clear that benzodiazepine modulatory sites are widely distributed and are found on many, but not all, GABA receptor complexes. A PET scan of BDZ modulatory sites in the human brain shows their wide distribution (**FIGURE 17.6**). Their high concentration in the amygdala and in other parts

of the limbic system that regulate fear/anxiety responses, and in the cerebral cortex (particularly the frontal lobe), which exerts control over limbic structures, provides the first clue to their function.

To clarify the role of the BDZ binding sites in neuropharmacological and behavioral experiments, a specific receptor antagonist, flumazenil, was developed. Flumazenil prevents the effects of BDZ binding but

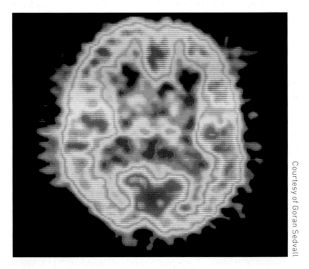

FIGURE 17.6 **PET scan of BDZ receptors in the human brain** The highest concentrations are shown in orange and red.

FIGURE 17.7   Modulation of GABA-induced chloride (Cl⁻) flux
The anxiolytic BDZs are agonists (blue bars) and enhance the
effects of GABA. The competitive antagonist flumazenil binds to
the BDZ receptor but has no action of its own. However, it prevents either the BDZs or the inverse agonists from acting. The
anxiety-producing β-carbolines (red bars) are inverse agonists
at the BDZ receptor. They not only prevent the effect of GABA
on Cl⁻ flux but also produce the opposite effect, which leads
to cell excitation. β-CCE, β-carboline-3-carboxylic acid ethyl
ester; β-CCM, methyl β-carboline-3-carboxylate; DMCM, methyl
6,7-dimethoxy-4-ethyl-β-carboline-3-carboxylate. (After J. G.
Richards et al. 1991. In *5-HT₁ₐ Agonists, 5-HT3 Antagonists and
Benzodiazepines: Their Comparative Behavioral Pharmacology*,
R. J. Rogers and S. J. Cooper [Eds.], pp. 1–30. Wiley: New York.)

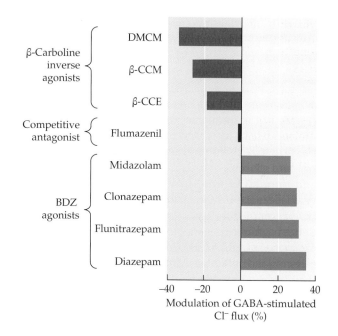

has no effect on the GABA receptor. A second group
of substances have been found to bind to the BDZ sites
and act as inverse agonists. They produce the opposite
actions of the BDZ drugs, namely increased anxiety,
arousal, and seizures. One class of inverse agonists is
the **β-carboline** family, which, when administered to
humans, produce extreme anxiety and an overwhelming sense of panic. β-Carbolines have been very useful
tools in the study of the neurobiology of anxiety. These
inverse agonists are presumed to uncouple the GABA
receptors from the Cl⁻ channels so that GABA is less
effective in causing entry of Cl⁻ into the cells (**FIGURE
17.7**), leading to increased membrane excitability.

The importance of GABA is directly shown by the
reduction in anxiety produced by local administration of GABA or the GABA agonist muscimol into the
amygdala. Intracranial administration of BDZs into the
amygdala also has anxiolytic effects in several animal
tests, including the light–dark crossing test, freezing response, elevated plus-maze, and operant conflict tests.
The anticonflict effects indicative of reduced anxiety
can be reversed by the benzodiazepine binding site
antagonist flumazenil and also by coadministration of
the GABA antagonist bicuculline into the amygdala.
Furthermore, Sanders and Shekhar (1995) found that
intra-amygdaloid injection of flumazenil or bicuculline
also blocks *systemic* antianxiety effects of the benzodiazepine chlordiazepoxide in the social interaction
test. The bicuculline effect demonstrates the necessity
for GABA activity in the anxiolytic effects of BDZs.

FIGURE 17.8   PET scans of a control individual (left) and
a patient with panic disorder (right)   The scans made in the
horizontal plane with the frontal cortex at the top show decreased density of BDZ binding sites in the patient with panic
disorder, particularly in the frontal cortex (Fr), anterior cingulate (A Cin), and insula (Ins), areas important in anxiety modulation. Other brain areas also show reduced numbers of BDZ
binding sites. Warm colors indicate the most receptors; cool
colors indicate fewer. Receptors were labeled with [¹¹C]fluma-
zenil. CN, caudate nucleus; OC, occipital cortex; Th, thalamus;
TL, temporal lobe.

The amygdala, particularly the basolateral nucleus,
is clearly an important site mediating the antianxiety
effects of BDZs. However, since BDZs can still have
anxiety-reducing effects following destruction of the
amygdala, multiple redundant brain areas must be involved in the response to anxiety (see Davis, 2006, for
an excellent summary).

Malizia and coworkers (1998) and others have shown
with PET scans that patients with panic disorder show
less benzodiazepine binding in the CNS, particularly
in portions of the frontal lobes including the orbitofrontal cortex, medial prefrontal, and insula, as well
as limbic structures involved in the anxiety neurocircuitry (**FIGURE 17.8**). These patients, compared with
healthy individuals, are also less sensitive to BDZs
on several psychophysiological measures such as eye
movement to targets, and clinical evidence confirms
that these patients require higher doses to reduce
anxiety. Reductions in BDZ binding have also been

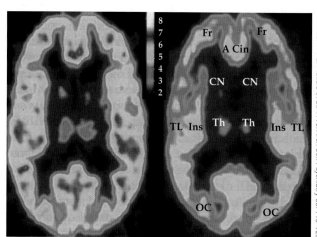

From A. L. Malizia et al. 1998. *Arch Gen Psychiatry* 55: 715–720

found in selected brain areas of individuals with GAD and PTSD. Reduced [^{11}C]flumazenil binding in cortical areas, hippocampus, and thalamus was found in veterans with PTSD compared with veterans who did not have PTSD but had experienced similar traumatic events. From that one might conclude that trauma per se was not responsible for the reduced binding. Furthermore, care was taken to match the individuals in the two groups for age as well as the year and country of deployment, ensuring similar experiences. In addition, both groups were tested approximately 10 years after the trauma (Geuze et al., 2008). The reduced BDZ receptor binding in frontal cortex may reflect the deficits in working memory that are associated with abnormal GABA neurotransmission in that brain region. Reduced BDZ–GABA$_A$ function in hippocampus may impair hippocampal modulation of the stress response and prevent adequate evaluation of the context in which an emotional response is expressed. Nevertheless, it is not clear whether the differences reflect a predisposing characteristic in these individuals or are adaptive changes to trauma-induced stress. It seems reasonable that reduced BDZ binding sites may result in failure of GABA inhibition leading to uncontrolled panic attacks, phobias, generalized anxiety, and the hyperarousal of PTSD. Refer to a review by Liberzon and colleagues (2003) for more detail on the relationship between GABA and anxiety disorders based on animal studies, molecular pharmacology, and brain imaging.

ROLE OF NEUROSTEROID MODULATION OF GABA IN ANXIETY Substantial evidence indicates that neuroactive steroids provide an additional modulatory role in anxiety. A family of neurosteroids, including pregnenolone, allopregnanolone, tetrahydrodeoxycorticosterone, and dehydroepiandrosterone (DHEA), are synthesized from cholesterol in both the central and peripheral nervous systems. They are elevated by physiological stressors such as forced swim and foot shock stress and have anxiolytic effects in animal models, including the light–dark, open field, and water-lick suppression tests and the elevated plus-maze. Additionally, they have potent anticonvulsant effects. The anxiolytic effects occur following both systemic and intraventricular administration. The importance of amygdala mediation of these effects was shown by direct infusion into the central nucleus. Inhibiting the synthesis of allopregnanolone leads to increased emotional reactivity, impaired social interaction, and enhanced fear conditioning. Neuroactive steroids bind to a site on the GABA$_A$ receptor that is different from those sites described thus far and potentiate the effect of GABA by increasing the duration of GABA-induced chloride channel opening.

Surprisingly, baseline levels of neurosteroids are elevated in individuals with panic disorder compared with controls. However, some have suggested that the higher levels may represent a natural self-defense mechanism that protects against spontaneous panic attacks. When a panic attack was induced in these patients, the levels dropped; this signals reduced GABA control of the anxiety. Since there was no change in control individuals even when they experienced similar levels of panic anxiety, it suggests that the reduction in neurosteroid is not caused by anxiety itself but may represent the underlying pathophysiology of the disorder. In contrast, neurosteroid levels tend to be lower in individuals treated for GAD and generalized social phobia. Hence neurosteroid levels may represent a distinguishing biomarker among the individual anxiety disorders. Nuss (2015) and Schule and colleagues (2014) provide thorough discussions of the relationship of several neurosteroids to both anxiety disorders and depression. Evidence suggests that neurosteroids may be a potential target for new drug development. Unfortunately administering neurosteroids themselves does not seem feasible because they are rapidly metabolized and therefore have low bioavailability. Also, they have the potential to cause undesirable endocrine side effects. However, other potential strategies include creating synthetic neurosteroid-like agonists or manipulating neurosteroid synthesis or degradation. One such approach will be described briefly in Section 17.3

ROLE OF SEROTONIN IN ANXIETY There is a rich literature on the serotonergic link with mood, suicide, violence, and impulsivity (Lowry et al., 2008). Likewise, 5-HT plays a large role in anxiety modulation, although the precise role has been difficult to delineate, because of the large number of receptor subtypes and 5-HT's widespread innervation of the brain structures in the complex neurocircuitry regulating anxiety. Results from animal studies show that 5-HT modulates anxiety in a complex fashion and depends on manipulations of the particular receptor subtype, the behavioral measure of anxiety, the brain regions and neural circuits underlying the procedures, and genetic contributions (e.g., see Bauer, 2015). Among the many receptor subtypes, the 5-HT$_{1A}$ has received the most attention. Knockout mice lacking the 5-HT$_{1A}$ receptor represent a genetic model of anxiety, demonstrated by increased anxious behaviors in the light–dark, open field, elevated plus-maze, and novel object tests. In most cases 5-HT$_{1A}$ agonists have anxiolytic effects in these measures of anxiety while antagonists are anxiogenic. The reduced anxious behavior after administration of 5-HT$_{1A}$ agonists and partial agonists is correlated with the inhibition of 5-HT cell firing and reduced 5-HT release onto postsynaptic heteroreceptors in target brain regions. Studies using intracerebral injections of 5-HT$_{1A}$ agonists indicate that the site of injection determines the behavioral outcome. In general, direct injection of 5-HT$_{1A}$ agonists into the hippocampus or amygdala where 5-HT$_{1A}$ receptors are located postsynaptically increases anxious behaviors. In contrast, local injection of 5-HT$_{1A}$ agonists into the raphe nuclei, where 5-HT$_{1A}$ receptors are somatodendritic autoreceptors that inhibit firing rate of the serotonergic neurons and reduce 5-HT release in target regions, has an anxiolytic effect. Hence it would appear that the autoreceptors and the postsynaptic receptors have opposing roles in modulating anxious behavior (see Akimova et al., 2009; Garcia-Garcia et al., 2014).

It has long been known that inability to control a stressor, such as foot shock in animal studies, leads to amplification of a variety of anxious behaviors including greater fearfulness, less social interaction, avoidance of novel stimuli, and more submissive behaviors. In addition, the animals that have been exposed to uncontrollable stress fail to learn escape responses even when given the option. Those maladaptive behaviors do not occur in animals that are given the opportunity to control the shock (see learned helplessness in Section 4.1). The behavioral changes following uncontrollable shock are prevented by lesioning the dorsal raphe nucleus, indicating a role for serotonergic function. Other evidence shows that the inability to control the stressor increases the expression of the transcription factor c-fos in the dorsal raphe nucleus, indicating enhanced activation. That activation causes increased levels of extracellular 5-HT in the dorsal raphe nuclei as well as in projection regions. The intense activation makes the cells more sensitive, so the 5-HT neurons respond more vigorously and will under future challenge release more 5-HT in projection regions, causing exaggerated anxious behaviors (see Maier and Watkins, 2010). To further clarify the mechanism responsible for the increased sensitivity, researchers used extracellular single-unit recording of 5-HT neuronal activity in brain slices from the dorsal raphe nucleus that were prepared from brains of animals exposed to uncontrollable stress 24 hours before. They found desensitization of 5-HT$_{1A}$ inhibitory somatodendritic autoreceptors in the raphe nuclei, demonstrated by the reduced effectiveness of the autoreceptor agonist ipsapirone in inhibiting cell firing (**FIGURE 17.9A**). The reduced inhibition was responsible for the increased neurotransmitter release. One intriguing possibility suggested by their research is that failure to control life stressors and the subsequent sensitizing of 5-HT neurons may make some individuals prone to developing anxiety disorders. Equally significant was the demonstration that giving the rats control over the shock (called behavioral immunization) by use of a running wheel not only prevented the exaggerated anxiety during subsequent uncontrollable stress events, but also prevented the desensitization of 5-HT$_{1A}$ autoreceptors (**FIGURE 17.9B**; Rozeske et al., 2011). Clinical relevance of this research is supported by neuroimaging studies of individuals with panic disorder or social anxiety disorder

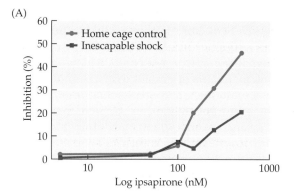

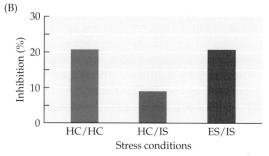

FIGURE 17.9 **Autoreceptor-induced inhibition of dorsal raphe cell firing** (A) Twenty-four hours after exposure to inescapable shock, rats showed less inhibition of dorsal raphe nucleus cell firing in response to the 5-HT$_{1A}$ agonist ipsapirone compared with home cage control animals. Significant differences between the groups occurred at 150 and 250 nM doses of ipsapirone. (B) Behavioral immunization prevents desensitization of inhibitory 5-HT$_{1A}$ autoreceptors caused by inescapable stress. Ipsapirone-induced inhibition (at 150 nM) of dorsal raphe cells was significantly reduced in rats that experienced home cage treatment followed by inescapable stress (HC/IS) compared with control rats that never experienced stress (HC/HC). Rats in the HC/IS condition also showed impaired ipsapirone-induced inhibition compared with rats provided with behavioral immunization (ES/IS)—that is, those that were given control of the stressor in trials preceding an uncontrollable stress event. (After R. R. Rozeske et al. 2011. *J Neurosci* 31: 14107–14115.)

who showed reduced 5-HT$_{1A}$ receptor binding in the raphe nuclei, which would increase 5-HT function in limbic regions as well as in cortical circuits that regulate limbic-induced anxiety (see Akimova et al., 2009).

Another approach to understanding the role of 5-HT in anxiety is to examine the effectiveness of drug treatments. The first line of treatment for anxiety includes several SSRIs, drugs that acutely block the reuptake of 5-HT from the synapse, prolonging the neurotransmitter's effects. This initial increase in 5-HT function paradoxically increases anxiety in the early phase of treatment for some individuals treated with SSRIs and also increases anxious behaviors in several animal tests, including the noise-induced startle response and freezing. Of further interest was the finding that those animals that demonstrated high baseline anxiety were more likely to show robust anxiety responses to acute

SSRI administration than the more laid-back rodents (Pettersson et al., 2015). Those results predict the clinical experience of patients with anxiety disorders such as panic disorder, who demonstrate increased anxiety in the early treatment phase (Grillon et al., 2007). Since the anxiolytic effects of the SSRIs require several weeks of chronic administration, it is apparent that long-term neuronal adaptations beyond the acute increase in 5-HT function are required for their clinical effectiveness (SSRI antidepressants will be discussed in Chapter 18).

In addition to the effects of 5-HT in the adult, 5-HT has a neurotrophic effect during fetal development and is critical for normal development of the anxiety circuitry. This means that appropriate regulation of both pre- and postnatal serotonergic function is needed to prevent anatomical, functional, and behavioral abnormalities. The amygdala and the PFC are two brain areas that show serotonin-dependent developmental differences in morphology and activity. It is of interest that infants and adults having a certain polymorphism within the promoter region of the serotonin reuptake transporter (SERT) gene show increased emotionality and anxiety. This polymorphism comes in two flavors: either a "short" or a "long" allele. During early development (but not adulthood), the short allele results in lower SERT expression than the long allele, which causes relatively less 5-HT reuptake and therefore higher baseline 5-HT activity in the brain. People with one or two short alleles showed a significantly smaller volume of the amygdala and the subgenual ACC compared to those with the long allele. In addition, neuronal connectivity between the two regions was weaker. Similar reductions in white matter connections between the amygdala and several regions of the PFC were reported by others. It seems reasonable to assume that such differences may also be responsible for variations in processing of emotional events. In fact, when anticipating public speaking, individuals with social phobia having one or two short alleles reported higher symptom severity and increased anxiety and showed greater neural activity in the amygdala than phobic individuals with two long alleles (Furmark et al., 2004).

Although elevated 5-HT following chronic treatment with SSRIs in the adult is associated with enhanced mood and reduced symptoms of depression, animal studies have shown that administration of SSRIs to animals prenatally increases anxiety and depression in the adult animal. It would seem that elevated 5-HT has distinctly different effects on anxiety circuitry depending on the maturity of the animal. It is likely that individuals with the short polymorphism and the resulting elevation in synaptic 5-HT experience altered development of circuits underlying anxiety and mood. Animal studies support this conclusion since similar increases in anxiety occur in knockout mice lacking SERT or 5-HT$_{1A}$ receptors, suggesting that the 5-HT$_{1A}$ receptor

mediates the neurodevelopmental effect. In addition, reducing 5-HT reuptake during the first 2 weeks of life in rodents increases anxious behaviors in those animals as adults, indicating that the developmental effect of elevated 5-HT may extend to early postnatal periods as well. Since environmental events influence 5-HT function, it is possible that stress-induced alterations in 5-HT during prenatal or early postnatal development may in part explain why early life stress predisposes some individuals to anxiety disorders and depression later in life (more detail is provided in the section on gene–environment interactions below). For further information, the reader may refer to excellent reviews by Gingrich and colleagues (2017), Gross and Hen (2004), and Nordquist and Oreland (2010).

ROLE OF DOPAMINE IN ANXIETY A modulatory role for dopamine (DA) is suggested by the significant DA projections (mesocortical tract) from the ventral tegmental area (VTA) to the mPFC as well as the mesolimbic tract that connects the VTA and limbic regions including the amygdala. Stress such as forced swimming or administration of the anxiety-producing β-carboline FG7142 increases firing of mesocortical dopaminergic neurons and increases DA turnover in the prefrontal cortex. Further, the vicarious stress of observing another rat receiving foot shocks also increases DA turnover in the prefrontal neurons and elevates adrenal glucocorticoids. Enhancement of GABA function by the benzodiazepine diazepam blocks the anxiety responses to the stressors and to β-carboline treatment and also prevents the DA turnover (Kaneyuki et al., 1991).

Dopaminergic projections to the amygdala from the VTA apparently inhibit the normal descending inhibition from the mPFC and permit expression of adaptive anxiety responses. These mesolimbic DA cells are activated by stressful or threatening environmental stimuli. The released DA acting on D$_1$ and D$_2$ receptors in the amygdala reduces the inhibitory control of local GABA interneurons that are activated by the PFC. Decreasing inhibitory control increases amygdaloid activation. In support of this hypothesis, a variety of stressors increase release and turnover of DA in the central and basolateral nuclei of the amygdala, where D$_2$ and D$_1$ receptors, respectively, are most densely located. As would be expected, reducing dopaminergic transmission with neurotoxic lesions of the VTA–amygdala pathway reduces conditioned fear and fear-potentiated startle and impairs acquisition of avoidance behavior. Furthermore, intra-amygdaloid injection of D$_1$ receptor agonists increases anxiety responses in a variety of rodent models, and antagonists at the D$_1$ receptor produce anxiolytic effects. The effects of D$_2$ agonists and antagonists are more difficult to interpret, since their effects vary depending on the type of fear/anxiety paradigm utilized, which may reflect the distinct role played by D$_1$ and D$_2$

receptors in fear and anxiety. De la Mora and colleagues (2010) provide an in-depth discussion of the structure and function of DA mechanisms in fear and anxiety.

Just as we saw for the LC, discrete populations of neurons in the VTA have distinctive firing patterns. Cells in the VTA have low-frequency tonic and high-frequency phasic firing properties. The phasic burst firing is increased by stress, including restraint, fear, and chronic social defeat stress, and is correlated with enhanced release of DA lasting several seconds, most notably in the nucleus accumbens (NAcc). Although the DA release may aid the animal by enhancing the salience of the environmental threat, chronic activation persisting when the threat is no longer present may predict vulnerability to dysfunctional responses in social interaction. Razzoli and colleagues (2011) exposed mice to 10 days of social defeat stress by aggressive resident mice and found the expected increase in phasic burst firing. Of special significance is that it lasted at least 3 weeks after the termination of the social defeat stress. Furthermore, the stressed animals at that time point still showed avoidance behaviors in the social interaction test as well as hyperphagia (i.e., abnormally increased feeding). This chronic activation of VTA neurons is associated with neuroadaptive changes that may be responsible for enduring maladaptive responses to social cues. Of particular interest is that individual differences in stress responsiveness and coping behaviors exist among animals in various rodent strains. It is tempting to speculate that those animals that demonstrate the increased phasic firing and subsequent neuroadaptive modification of VTA neurons may be those most vulnerable to dysfunctional behavior, while those that do not show the prolonged changes may represent animals more resilient to stress.

Chaudhury and coworkers (2013) provided a more precise demonstration that increased phasic burst firing (but not tonic activity) is responsible for the dysfunctional behaviors occurring after social defeat stress. The researchers optogenetically activated the VTA neurons projecting to the NAcc and in real time evaluated social interaction and sucrose preference in animals previously exposed to subthreshold (i.e., a mild form that does not usually elicit abnormal behaviors) social defeat stress. Not only could they induce impaired social behaviors and reduced preference for sucrose in those animals, but mice that were initially resilient to the mild stress and showed normal VTA firing and behavior could be made to demonstrate the abnormal behaviors as much as 12 hours after optogenetic stimulation. As you might predict, optogenetic inhibition of the VTA cells projecting to NAcc could enhance the resilience of the mice.

Genes and environment interact to modulate anxiety

Now that you have an appreciation for the complexities of the anatomy and neurochemistry of anxiety, we are left with the questions of why some individuals are more anxious than others, and why some develop anxiety disorders while others are resilient. Differences in neurosteroid levels, BDZ receptors, SERT polymorphisms, and 5-HT$_{1A}$ receptors are several possible explanations described earlier. It is quite clear that there are large individual differences in the levels of trait anxiety (the enduring characteristic to experience anxiety in a variety of situations) among individuals and that this characteristic is reasonably consistent over one's lifetime. For example, evidence suggests that behavioral inhibition in young children is associated with a CRF gene polymorphism, and these individuals are more likely than average to develop social phobia and panic disorder as adolescents. Rodents also can vary in innate anxiety level, and inbred strains of rodents can be used to study the neurobiology and treatment of anxiety. Several rodent lines have been bred for anxiety as well as abnormal regulation of the HPA axis. These differences in trait anxiety levels and hormone responses indicate genetically determined brain differences, and these differences may predispose some individuals to anxiety disorders.

Another approach used to predict stress vulnerability and stress resilience among healthy individuals is the evaluation of HPA axis function by measuring both basal cortisol levels and stress-induced cortisol responses. Henckens and colleagues (2016) found in their research using healthy males that those individuals with the highest basal levels of cortisol were those most resilient to stress, as measured with a psychological trait questionnaire. In contrast, those individuals also demonstrated less stress-induced increase in amygdala activity, which the researchers contend reflects a protective function of basal cortisol that acts by reducing the hyperactivity of neural stress circuits. A neuroimaging study by the same research team had previously found that cortisol administration does indeed suppress hyperactivity in the amygdala. In contrast, individuals with the most robust cortisol response following stress had the strongest activation of the amygdala and showed high stress sensitivity in a psychological trait questionnaire. The proposed explanation for these findings is that stress-sensitive people (with lower basal cortisol levels) are more likely to demonstrate a hyperactive amygdala during stress and so need the greater cortisol response to help them recover. Further discussion of the potentially protective effect of cortisol and a meta-analysis of research showing an inverse relationship between cortisol levels and the negative emotional arousal following acute stress is provided by Het et al. (2012).

As you will see, many of the anxiety disorders are more prevalent among individuals in the same family. Nevertheless, family and twin studies estimate heritability across the disorders at a midrange of 30% to 60%, which demonstrates that life experiences must interact with a genetic vulnerability in shaping the anxious individual (Purves et al., 2019). A large volume of evidence has shown that aversive childhood experiences have multiple damaging effects on the adult body and brain and predispose the individual to health problems, such as cardiovascular disease, as well as to psychiatric disorders including depression, anxiety, schizophrenia, and others. Although the brain shows plasticity throughout the life span, animal studies suggest that adverse events occurring prenatally or during early development have the most profound effects because of maximal brain plasticity during those times.

Both animal and human studies have shown that early exposure to stress and neglect alters the developing brain and can produce a lifelong tendency to respond to stimuli with enhanced anxiety. Both pre- and postnatal stressors have been shown to produce behaviors resembling anxiety, such as enhanced freezing, increased fear-potentiated startle, hyperarousal, reduced feeding and increased defecation under stress, and avoidance of novel stimuli. In addition, early stress alters the programming of the HPA axis, causing a hyperactive hormonal response to challenge that persists throughout adulthood. The stability of these changes suggests epigenetic factors at work. Evidence exists for changes in DNA methylation of promoter elements that control the expression of genes within the stress circuits (see Chapter 2 for a discussion on epigenetic effects). For example, Mueller and Bale (2008) studied male offspring of mice who had been exposed to chronic, variable stressors during early fetal development (days 1 through 7 of gestation). As adults these mice not only showed heightened HPA axis responsivity to stress compared with controls (**FIGURE 17.10A**), but also showed long-term increases in the expression of CRF in the central nucleus of the amygdala (**FIGURE 17.10B,C**), indicating an enhancement of stress neurocircuitry. These adult male mice also showed decreased expression of glucocorticoid receptors in several regions of the hippocampus that are normally responsible for restoring HPA activation to normal via the negative feedback mechanism (**FIGURE 17.10D,E**). Epigenetic effects were associated with these changes, including reduced methylation of the CRF promoter region in the hypothalamus and central nucleus of the amygdala and increased methylation of the glucocorticoid receptor promoter region. These may be expected to contribute to stress circuit programming during fetal

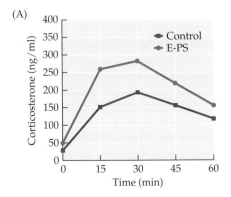

(A)

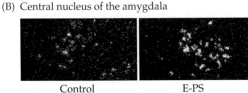

(B) Central nucleus of the amygdala

(D) Hippocampus

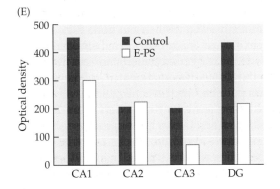

(E)

(C)

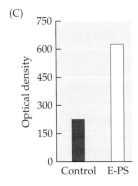

FIGURE 17.10 Stress pathway dysregulation following early prenatal stress (A) Adult male mice exposed to early prenatal stress (E-PS) during the first 7 days of gestation showed elevated blood levels of corticosterone (the principal glucocorticoid in rodents) after 15 minutes of restraint stress compared with controls, indicating an increased HPA axis function. (B,C) In situ hybridization showed significantly increased CRF expression in the central nucleus of the amygdala in adult male E-PS mice compared with controls, indicating an enhancement of stress neurocircuitry. (D,E) In situ hybridization showed glucocorticoid receptors were significantly less expressed in the CA3 and dentate gyrus (DG) regions of the hippocampus in E-PS adult male mice compared with controls, indicating a reduction in HPA axis negative feedback. Glucocorticoid receptor expression was less, but not significantly, in the CA1 region, and there was no difference in CA2. (From B. R. Mueller and T. L. Bale. 2008. *J Neurosci* 28: 9055–9065. © 2008 Society for Neuroscience.)

development. As you will see later, postnatal stress also is capable of programming the stress responsivity, and this effect is gender specific. **WEB BOX 17.2** highlights the impact of early maternal neglect in determining the emotional response and hormonal reactivity of offspring to stressful events.

We are now left with the question of how epigenetic changes in the stress response might increase the probability of developing anxiety disorders. The activation of the HPA axis is critical to the survival of an animal, and destruction of the adrenal gland ultimately leads to death. However, excessive HPA activation leads to damaging effects on the body, including changes in brain structure and synaptic transmission. Prolonged stress and the subsequent elevation in glucocorticoids impair the function of the hippocampus by reducing neurogenesis, failing to protect cells against cell death (apoptosis), and preventing the normal dendritic growth and elaboration that enhance synaptic connectivity. Loss of such hippocampal plasticity is reflected in a reduction in cognitive processing and memory consolidation. Glucocorticoids also influence other brain regions that do not support neurogenesis, by preventing synaptic restructuring including dendritic elaboration and an increase in dendritic spines. Most significant to our discussion of anxiety are the changes to limbic structures that comprise the emotion-regulating circuits, including the hippocampus, amygdala, and PFC. Of interest is the finding that prolonged stress apparently produces opposite effects on the hippocampus, where synaptic structures atrophy, and on the amygdala, where

dendritic growth, increased arborization, and increased spine connectivity are seen (McEwen, 2010; McEwen et al., 2016) (**FIGURE 17.11**). These differences are reflected in behavioral effects: impaired hippocampus-mediated contextual learning, which helps an individual to distinguish between context-appropriate and context-inappropriate emotional responding, and enhanced amygdala-mediated fear conditioning. Furthermore, the medial prefrontal area that is responsible for extinguishing conditioned emotional responses shows a decrease in dendritic connections. The molecular mechanism of these effects is less well studied than in the hippocampus, but as you will see in the next section, abnormal neural activity in these brain regions is characteristic of several clinical disorders.

The effects of early stress are dependent on timing

Not only does stress affect various brain regions in a distinct fashion, but several other variables also help to determine the nature of the effects of early stress. As is true for any other teratogenic agent, an important factor is the timing of the exposure. It is apparent that periods of greatest brain development are the most sensitive to insult, but how the trajectory of brain development will be altered depends on the particular developmental stage. Nervous system development continues throughout gestation, and most structures continue to elaborate after birth. In fact, the PFC is not fully mature until late adolescence and hence is highly vulnerable throughout this period.

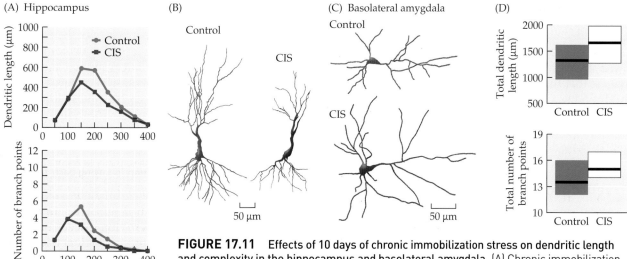

FIGURE 17.11   Effects of 10 days of chronic immobilization stress on dendritic length and complexity in the hippocampus and basolateral amygdala   (A) Chronic immobilization stress (CIS) rats compared with controls showed decreased length (top) and number of branch points (bottom) of hippocampal apical dendrites. (B) Drawings of neurons processed with Golgi staining for computerized image analysis show clearly the shrinkage and reduced dendritic complexity in hippocampal neurons of stressed rats compared with controls. (C) Similar drawings of neurons from the basolateral amygdala show the increased length and branching in animals exposed to CIS compared with controls. (D) Plots of median values and ranges for the length (top) and number of branch points (bottom) of basolateral amygdala neurons from control and CIS rats. (After A. Vyas et al. 2002. *J Neurosci* 22: 6810–6818.)

Although most prenatal stress research has been done using rodents, several researchers in a series of studies have provided important data using non-human primates because their stages of gestation and early brain development are more similar to those of humans (see Schneider et al., 2002). In rhesus monkeys, repeated random noise blasts several times a day during pregnancy produced offspring that were lighter in weight at birth and showed impaired motor coordination. In addition to having various motor deficits, when exposed to new stressors, the offspring showed a hyperresponsive HPA axis in the form of elevated ACTH and cortisol, heightened signs of anxiety during social separation, reduced exploration of their environment, limited play behavior, and more clinging to their peers than control monkeys. Additionally, the prenatally stressed animals showed deficits in learning a non-match-to-sample task that requires both working memory and attention shifting as the animals select the object that is different from the one previously presented, to get a food reward. Furthermore, at adolescence, the stressed monkeys demonstrated an increasing preference for ethyl alcohol compared with controls. Both physiological and behavioral effects were most pronounced when the stressor occurred during the most intense period of neuronal migration early in gestation. Since these effects also occurred in the offspring of mothers who were administered ACTH, the elevation of stress hormones, including glucocorticoids, was the likely cause of the altered fetal development. Since such experiments cannot be performed on humans, alternative approaches must be used.

One retrospective study was performed using volumetric magnetic resonance imaging (MRI) of individuals who had been sexually abused during discrete stages of development. The preliminary results showed that several brain regions had unique periods sensitive to the damaging effects of early stress. The findings suggest that hippocampal volume was reduced when childhood sexual abuse occurred during the ages of 3 to 5 and 11 to 15. The corpus callosum was reduced in women abused at 9 to 10 years of age, and the vulnerable period of the slowly developing PFC occurred between 14 and 16 years of age (Andersen et al., 2008).

The effects of early stress vary with gender

A second significant variable that determines the effects of stress on the brain is gender. Animal studies have shown that the behavioral and hormonal effects of prenatal stress depend on the sex of the offspring. Although it has been frequently assumed that male and female brains are identical, over the past 15 years, brain imaging has shown significant differences not only in structure but also in neurotransmitter systems and function. Many studies have shown gender differences in hormonal, physiological, and behavioral responses to stress, although the results are frequently contradictory

because of the types of stressors used, timing of stress, brain regions examined, hormonal changes during stages of the estrous cycle, and methodological differences. Some have suggested that on the basis of the evolutionary roles of the sexes, it is reasonable to expect differences in the ways that males and females respond to stress. While the males of many species actively respond to acute danger in the environment by fighting or running, females frequently respond by engaging in social interaction such as organizing the herd and protecting the young. These differences are important to study because they may help to explain some of the differences in the incidence and symptomology of psychiatric disorders in men and women. Important to our discussion are the epidemiological studies showing that the male-to-female ratio of lifetime prevalence rates of having any anxiety disorder is 1:1.7. Women have higher rates for each of the disorders, although the literature is not always consistent regarding social anxiety disorder. Also, there are variations in comorbidity and in the overall burden of illness (McLean et al., 2011). Although some of the differences may be explained by sociocultural influences experienced by girls, such as the greater acceptance of women expressing fearfulness, it is apparent that several brain areas in the circuitry modulating emotion respond to stress in different ways. Using fMRI, Goldstein and colleagues (2010) found that brain activity in the stress response circuitry was dissimilar in men and women when they were exposed to negative affect/high arousal pictures, but that difference was highly dependent on the phase of the women's menstrual cycle. This evidence suggests that women have a hormonal regulation of the stress response that is not found in men. Others have shown that glucocorticoid levels fluctuate in synchrony with changes in hormone levels over the menstrual cycle, demonstrating the impact of female hormones on HPA axis function. Both laboratory animal and human studies have found that when estrogen levels are elevated, sensitivity to stress is greater and glucocorticoid release is increased.

MORPHOLOGICAL DIFFERENCES IN RESPONSE TO STRESS In a series of studies, morphological and behavioral differences between the sexes were found in animal tests using chronic restraint stress, chronic foot shock stress, or glucocorticoid administration (reviewed in McLaughlin et al., 2009). Such stressors cause the previously described reduction in hippocampal neurogenesis, shrinking of the dendritic arbor, and loss of giant dendritic spines in the CA3 region in male rodents. These neurobiological changes are accompanied by spatial memory deficits in the radial arm maze and the Morris water maze. In contrast, similar treatment of females produced neither dendritic atrophy nor memory impairment unless they had had their ovaries removed, in which case dramatic shrinkage occurred. The relative resistance of the female hippocampal cells to stress-induced damage suggests a neuroprotective effect of female hormones. Of particular interest is that in rodents, synaptic complexity in the CA1 region of the hippocampus changes over the 5-day estrous cycle in such a way that synaptic complexity gradually increases over the days when estrogen is elevated and drops when progesterone levels rise. This type of change shows very rapid effects of female hormones on hippocampal plasticity.

Chronic stress also causes shrinking and simplification of dendritic arbors as well as loss of dendritic spines in the PFC of male rats. These changes are associated with the expected deficits in extinction of fear conditioning. In contrast, in females, similar stress causes estrogen-dependent enhancement of dendritic trees of neurons in the PFC that project to the amygdala.

Finally, dendritic arborization in the amygdala of chronically stressed males is enhanced, and this is associated with enhanced conditioned fear acquisition. In humans, this enhanced fear conditioning is correlated with glucocorticoid levels in men but not in women. Although chronic stress impairs fear conditioning in women, the neural basis is not yet clear. In sum, it is quite clear that males and females respond to prenatal and postnatal stress in different ways, and those disparities may help to explain the differences in incidence and characteristics of a variety of clinical disorders, including autism, ADHD, depression, and anxiety. However, it is somewhat puzzling to find that women apparently have a diminished neurobiological response to stress yet show an increased incidence of anxiety and mood disorders. One possible resolution to this paradox is to consider male responsiveness as an adaptive mechanism that protects against some psychiatric disorders (Altemus, 2006). For example, stress-induced impairment of hippocampal memory consolidation may serve to limit memories of a trauma and associated stimuli, thereby enhancing recovery. Alternatively, it is perhaps significant that although males have a greater neurobiological response to stress, their receptor affinity for glucocorticoids in the hippocampus is almost twice as great as in females, suggesting that the negative feedback that returns stress hormone levels to normal is more effective. Perhaps the robust response followed by rapid recovery is key to males' relative resilience to some disorders. Finally, one needs to consider that women face many significant reproductive hormonal changes over their lifetimes, including during the prenatal period, puberty, the estrous cycle, pregnancy and lactation, and menopause, each of which may alter neural circuits of emotion regulation. Because of space limitations, we cannot review all the behavioral effects of gonadal hormones that might contribute to vulnerability and resilience to anxiety disorders, but we suggest three review articles for consideration: Altemus (2006, 2014) and Maeng and Milad (2015).

SECTION SUMMARY

■ Anxiety is a disturbing feeling of concern accompanied by bodily changes including activation of the "fight-or-flight" response that prepares an animal to cope with impending danger.

■ Fear and anxiety differ in duration, psychological consequences, and neurobiology.

■ Many brain regions (including the insula, cingulate cortex, hypothalamus, and hippocampus) are involved in emotion processing, but the amygdala plays a central role.

■ The central nucleus of the amygdala and the BNST project widely and orchestrate the components of the emotional response. The central nucleus organizes the fear response when threatening stimuli appear suddenly and end abruptly. The BNST orchestrates components of emotion to produce sustained preparedness for unclear danger, a state resembling anxiety.

■ The amygdala forms emotional memories and enhances semantic memory consolidation by the hippocampus.

■ Regions of the prefrontal and cingulate cortices exert inhibitory control over the amygdala and mediate fear extinction.

■ Anxiety disorders may arise from an imbalance between emotion-generating brain regions and higher cortical control.

■ CRF regulates stress hormone secretion and activates neuronal circuits of emotion that produce anxious behaviors in animal models.

■ Noradrenergic neurons in the LC are activated by threatening stimuli and produce hypervigilance and fearfulness. Stress-induced CRF release by the amygdala causes LC neurons to fire at a high tonic rate. Other LC cells respond to non-noxious stimuli with phasic bursts of activity.

■ NE, aided by adrenal cortisol, mediates the formation and reconsolidation of traumatic memories. Elevated adrenergic function is found in some anxiety disorders. Several therapeutic drugs modulate LC firing by several different mechanisms.

■ Drugs that enhance GABA function (particularly in the amygdala) indirectly via modulatory sites on the GABA receptor for barbiturates, BDZs, and neuroactive steroids reduce anxiety and seizures and produce sedation. Manipulation of neurosteroid synthesis and manipulation of degradation represent potential new drug targets.

■ Low levels of BDZ modulatory sites are associated with elevated anxiety in rodents and with panic disorder, PTSD, and GAD in human patients.

■ Anxiety is modulated by 5-HT in a complex fashion. 5-HT_{1A} agonists binding to somatodendritic receptors in the raphe nucleus inhibit firing and release of 5-HT at projection sites causing anxiolysis. Local injection of 5-HT_{1A} agonists into the amygdala acting at postsynaptic receptors increases anxiety. Individuals with panic disorder or social anxiety disorder show reduced 5-HT_{1A} binding in the raphe.

- Exposure to uncontrollable (compared with controllable) stress leads to increased anxious behavior that can be prevented by lesioning the raphe nucleus. A high extracellular level of 5-HT during uncontrollable stress desensitizes the somatodendritic autoreceptors in the raphe nucleus and subsequently increases the firing of projection neurons and release of 5-HT in limbic regions.

- The anxiolytic drugs that block 5-HT reuptake (SSRIs) acutely increase synaptic 5-HT and may initially increase anxiety. Chronic administration over several weeks produces neuronal adaptations that are required for clinical effectiveness.

- The neurotrophic effect of 5-HT during fetal development is needed for normal development of the anxiety circuitry. People with a polymorphism within the promoter of the 5-HT transporter gene who have higher prenatal 5-HT levels show increased emotionality. They also have reduced volume of the amygdala and ACC and weaker connections between these structures as adults.

- Dopaminergic projections to the amygdala that are activated by threatening stimuli reduce the inhibitory control from the mPFC and increase emotional responses.

- Stress increases phasic burst firing of select cells in VTA, causing increased release of DA, particularly in the NAcc. The acute increase in DA enhances the salience of the threat, but chronic activation in the absence of threat is associated with dysfunctional behavior.

- The tendency to express anxiety is determined by both genes and environmental events. Prenatal and early postnatal exposure to stress cause epigenetic changes that alter the stress circuitry and increase the behavioral and hormonal response to stressors in the adult. Stress-induced glucocorticoids damage the hippocampus and the PFC but increase synaptic connectivity in the amygdala.

- Stress-induced brain abnormalities depend on the timing and the developmental period. Significant gender differences in stress response are found in neural activity of the anxiety circuit, in HPA response, and in morphological differences after chronic stress.

17.2 Characteristics of Anxiety Disorders

Among the disorders that are recognized as anxiety syndromes by the American Psychiatric Association, this chapter will consider the principal categories: GAD disorder, panic disorder, and several types of phobias. PTSD and OCD, now recognized as separate categories by the *DSM-5*, are included here because of similarities in neurobiology and the significance of stress in their presentation. These disorders vary significantly in the constellation of symptoms, the precipitating stimulus, and the time course, but all include high levels of anxiety that significantly impair the quality of life for those suffering with the disorder. The maladaptive emotional responses that characterize these disorders may be a function of inadequate regulation of a hyperactive amygdala by attenuated top-down control by the PFC. Because of space limitations, this discussion will include only an introduction to each of the disorders. Students are directed to Martin and coworkers (2010) for an excellent review of neuroimaging, associated neurotransmitter signaling, and genetic contributions to each disorder.

Generalized anxiety disorder

Although acute anxiety may at times need to be treated, it generally is not long lasting and is not considered a clinical disorder. In contrast, for some people the symptoms of anxiety have no real focus, and they can be present for much of the day and can persist for months or years. These individuals suffer from **generalized anxiety disorder** (**GAD**). Individuals with GAD show signs of constant worry and continuously predict, anticipate, or imagine dreadful events. For them, life is generally stressful, and even minor events provoke worry. Being late for an appointment, not completing a task, and making a minor mistake are all causes of worry. The most common physical symptoms include muscle tension and agitation that lead to fatigue, poor concentration, irritability, and sleep difficulties. As you might expect, the chronic anxiety reduces the performance of these individuals on many tasks and decreases the pleasure derived from their efforts. GAD is one of the more common anxiety disorders, with an estimated lifetime prevalence rate of 3.7% worldwide (Ruscio et al., 2017). Most cases begin gradually, usually in the teens or early adulthood, and persist throughout life.

Although some genetic contribution is suggested by the fact that GAD tends to run in families, twin studies are not consistent in supporting the role of heritability. It is perhaps not surprising that patients with GAD demonstrate an increased volume of the amygdala, which resembles the hypertrophy of that structure in laboratory animals exposed to repeated stressors. In addition, during PET scans, exposure to stimuli evoking negative emotions increases amygdala and insula activity to a greater extent in individuals with GAD than in healthy individuals. It is not entirely clear whether amygdala hyperactivity is secondary to too little inhibitory control by the prefrontal cortex, but the significant reduction in temporal cortical $GABA_A$ receptors demonstrated in imaging studies would suggest that this is the case. Furthermore, other imaging studies showed reduced functional connectivity between the amygdala and PFC, and the extent of connectivity was inversely related to anxiety ratings. The weaker connectivity in combination with elevated PFC activation found in most studies may reflect enhanced attempts to cope but in a less efficient manner (reviewed by Hilbert et al.,

2014). Furthermore, symptoms of GAD are reduced by drugs that enhance GABA function, such as the BDZs.

Panic attacks and panic disorder with anticipatory anxiety

In contrast to anxiety, which is the anticipation of potential danger, fear is the physiological reaction to immediate danger that prepares us to fight or run away. When an individual experiences all the effects of a fear reaction without a threatening stimulus, they are having a **panic attack**. The sudden intense fearfulness is accompanied by strong arousal of the sympathetic ANS. The symptoms associated with panic include heart pounding or chest pain, sweating, shortness of breath, faintness, choking, and fear of losing control or dying. These symptoms, which last minutes or even hours, may occur (1) in response to a particular environmental cue (producing a phobia); (2) totally without warning in unexpected fashion; or (3) in a situation where an attack occurred previously, thus making it more likely to occur again. The latter two cases are the basis for **panic disorder**. Panic disorder usually begins in the late 20s and may last for many years, with attacks occurring at different frequencies and intensities over that time. Individuals with panic disorder experience both panic (in the form of individual attacks) and anxiety (called **anticipatory anxiety**) over the possibility that they may have an attack in a place that is not safe (for example, in the middle of a movie theater or during a church service), where it would be embarrassing or perhaps impossible to escape. The anxiety associated with being in an "unsafe" place leads to **agoraphobia**, a fear of public places, and subsequent avoidance of many common situations (**TABLE 17.1**). Individuals with agoraphobia often lead very limited lives because they never leave the safety of their own homes. You were introduced to such an individual in the chapter opener.

TABLE 17.1	Typical Agoraphobia Situations
Driving	Unfamiliar areas
Traveling by subway, bus, or taxi	Hairdressing salon or barbershop
Flying	Long walks
Waiting in lines	Wide, open spaces
Crowds	Closed-in spaces (e.g., basements)
Stores	Boats
Restaurants	Being at home alone
Theaters	Auditioriums
Long distances from home	Elevators, escalators

Source: M. G. Craske and D. H. Barlow. 2007. *Mastery of Your Anxiety and Panic*, 4th ed., pp. 5–6. Oxford University Press: New York.

Unlike some of the other anxiety disorders, a genetic predisposition for panic is well documented. The concordance rate is significantly higher in monozygotic than in dizygotic twins. Furthermore, a significant number of patients with panic disorder have parents with the same diagnosis.

It has been suggested that panic attacks represent a normal physiological response that is not regulated by appropriate feedback. It is also possible that the anxiety response is triggered too easily and may be initiated by environmental events that are not consciously processed. It is not entirely clear whether people with panic disorder have a more reactive ANS, but panic attacks can be triggered in individuals with the disorder by a variety of stimuli that activate the ANS. These include injected lactic acid (a product of muscle exertion), caffeine, or yohimbine (an α_2-adrenergic autoreceptor antagonist) and increased amounts of carbon dioxide in the air they breathe. Because these same techniques do not elicit panic in individuals without panic disorder, they have been useful in studying the disorder in the laboratory (see Nutt et al., 1998). The ability of these agents to induce ANS arousal suggests that dysregulation of noradrenergic function may occur in the disorder. During a panic attack, blood and urine levels of both NE and epinephrine are elevated. Additionally, not only does increasing the release of NE with the α_2-adrenergic autoreceptor antagonist yohimbine induce panic in these individuals, but reducing NE release with the α_2-adrenergic autoreceptor agonist clonidine produces an anxiolytic effect. Preliminary research also suggests that genetic variation in the norepinephrine transporter gene may increase susceptibility to panic disorder. Adrenergic dysfunction in the neurons originating in the LC would produce widespread effects, including arousal and vigilance.

Anatomically, the most consistent findings suggest that individuals suffering from panic disorder have abnormalities such as small white matter lesions in the temporal lobes and enlargement of the lateral ventricles, which suggests tissue reduction. The temporal lobes are overall smaller in a significant number of patients with panic disorder, which may be accounted for by a reduction in amygdala volume and in some cases reduced hippocampal volume. As is frequently true in anxiety disorders, despite the reduced volume of the amygdala, it shows increased activity under challenge conditions. For example, during an induced panic attack, patients showed a significantly greater increase in activity of the amygdala, cingulate cortex, and insula compared with controls. Projections from the amygdala would contribute to the many bodily signs of panic, and the insula may make the individual more aware of the bodily sensations. In these panicked individuals, widespread areas of cerebral cortex, including the PFC, showed reduced function, indicating a lack of top-down control and failure of appropriate cognitive evaluation of the situation.

Phobias

Phobias involve fears that the individual recognizes as irrational. Fears may focus on specific objects or situations such as high places, closed-in spaces, water, mice, or snakes, or they may relate to social or interpersonal situations such as speaking in public (see the social anxiety disorder section below). Phobias can affect the individual's daily existence and can reduce their quality of life. Although many of us have irrational fears of things like spiders, usually we can avoid those things with little modification of lifestyle. However, for some people, an irrational fear significantly alters their daily activities. One example of such an individual is John Madden, the well-known American sports announcer and former football coach. He suffers from claustrophobia and is overwhelmed with anxiety when traveling within the confined space of an airplane. Although he maintains a busy schedule of cross-country appearances for television, he travels only by train or on a bus designed for his use.

Although there is an almost infinite list of items that can elicit phobic anxiety (**TABLE 17.2**), what people fear is at least partially determined by culture. For instance, in the Chinese culture, *pa-leng* is a morbid fear of the cold and loss of body heat. This fear is based on the Chinese belief that yin represents the cold, dark, and energy-draining parts of life, which optimally should be balanced with yang, the warm, light, and sustaining

elements. People with *pa-leng* often wear several layers of clothing even on extremely hot days.

Fortunately, phobias can usually be effectively treated with behavior therapy that involves presenting the fear-inducing stimulus in gradual increments, allowing the individual to maintain a relaxed state while confronting the source of their fear. This technique, called **behavioral desensitization**, or exposure therapy, is a common modern treatment method but may reflect an ancient Chinese proverb: "Go straight to the heart of danger, for there you will find safety." A more contemporary version utilizes exposure therapy in a virtual reality setting, which is easier than reproducing real-world situations and is more realistic than having the patient imagine the danger (see chapter opener photo). Medication for phobias is rarely needed. Regardless of the method, effective treatment reduces the hyperactivity of the amygdala, bed nucleus of the stria terminalis, ACC, and insula.

Social anxiety disorder

Social anxiety disorder (SAD), or social phobia, is among the most common anxiety disorders, with an estimated lifetime prevalence of approximately 12%. It is characterized by extreme fear of being evaluated or criticized by others. Other symptoms are provided in **TABLE 17.3**. Those with SAD tend to avoid most interpersonal situations or suffer extreme anxiety when these situations are unavoidable. The extreme anxiety may take the form of a panic attack. The disorder restricts many activities, such as public speaking, attending parties, meeting new people, dating, using a public restroom, going to work or school, and even eating in public places. Onset is typically at a young age, with almost half of affected individuals developing symptoms by age 11. The disorder is slightly more common in women and in those individuals with low self-esteem and high levels of self-criticism. Evidence suggests that cognitive therapy that modifies negative thoughts, such as the likelihood of looking foolish, plus social skills training is frequently highly beneficial. SSRIs may be prescribed along with cognitive behavior therapy for persistent symptoms. BDZs and β-adrenergic blockers that reduce ANS arousal can be effective for controlling symptoms for a particular situation, such as giving a speech, but they are not used as an overall treatment strategy.

The amygdala is once again central to this anxiety disorder, and numerous studies have shown that the level of activation of the amygdala in response to pictures of emotional faces correlates with the severity of symptoms. There is also a significantly greater elevation in blood flow in the amygdala during public speaking compared with controls, which is normalized after successful treatment. The neurobiology of social anxiety disorder is highly reminiscent of other anxiety

TABLE 17.2 Some Common and Less Common Phobias	
Phobia	**Fear of**
Acrophobia*	Heights
Aichmophobia	Sharp, pointed objects; knives
Ailurophobia	Cats
Algophobia	Pain
Astraphobia*	Storms, thunder, lightning
Claustrophobia*	Tight enclosures
Hematophobia*	Blood
Monophobia*	Being alone
Nyctophobia	Darkness, night
Ochlophobia	Crowds
Pyrophobia	Fire
Thanatophobia*	Death
Xenophobia*	Strangers

*Common

TABLE 17.3 Emotional and Behavioral Symptoms of Social Anxiety Disorder

Fear of situations in which you may be judged

Worrying about embarrassing yourself

Concern that you'll offend someone

Intense fear of talking with strangers

Worry that others will notice that you look anxious

Fear that sweating, trembling, or having a shaky voice may cause you embarrassment

Fearing events where you might be the center of attention

Being anxious anticipating a feared activity

Spending time after a social situation finding flaws in your performance

disorders that show increased activity not only in the amygdala, but also in other limbic areas such as the insula and hippocampus, which in this case would lead to the anticipatory anxiety and autonomic response.

Post-traumatic stress disorder

Severe and chronic emotional disorders can occur after traumatic events such as war, natural disasters like hurricanes or earthquakes, terrorist attacks such as 9/11, physical assault, or auto accidents. In each case, the individual involved feels not only fear but also a sense of helplessness and horror. As many as 10,000 individuals who witnessed the terrorist attack on the World Trade Center in New York City have developed **post-traumatic stress disorder** (**PTSD**), and the soldiers returning from the wars in Iraq and Afghanistan show a particularly high rate of PTSD. Individuals with PTSD frequently experience nightmares and memories that may occur as sudden flashbacks of the traumatic event. In addition, they show increased physiological reactivity to reminders of the trauma, sleep disturbances, avoidance of stimuli associated with the trauma, and a numbing of emotional responses for many years after the original event. Many exhibit sudden outbursts of irritability that can emotionally injure family and friends who are making an effort to be supportive. The individuals often feel detached from others and fail to experience the full range of emotions, which leads to diminished interest in life activities. In addition, the probability of attempting suicide is significantly greater in these individuals, as is the incidence of substance abuse and of marital problems, depression, and feelings of guilt and anger. Children also develop PTSD following trauma, although their symptoms are somewhat different.

Although statistics tell us that lifetime prevalence of PTSD ranges from 1% to 10% in the United States, the occurrence varies widely depending on the trauma. For example, approximately 3% of people who have experienced a personal attack, 4% to 16% surviving a

natural disaster, 30% of war veterans, as many as 50% of those who have experienced rape, and 50% to 75% of prisoners of war who were torture victims develop PTSD (Yehuda et al., 1998). Given the frequent occurrence of war, starvation, forced immigration, terrorist activities, and ethnic and religious conflict occurring globally, it is painful to think of the number of cases of PTSD around the world.

Although PTSD is clearly related to the intensity of the traumatic event, some individuals seem far more susceptible than others. Clearly, not all war veterans or those in active combat develop PTSD, nor do all women who experience rape. Family studies of individuals who develop PTSD after trauma show that as many as 74% had a family history of psychopathology (PTSD, anxiety, depression, or antisocial behavior). The significantly higher concordance among monozygotic twins than dizygotic twins further supports the genetic vulnerability model. The interaction of family history and the magnitude of trauma is suggested by the fact that under conditions of high stress, people with a family history of PTSD may be only slightly more vulnerable to PTSD. However, when the magnitude of trauma is less intense, biologically vulnerable individuals are significantly more likely to show signs of the disorder. One possibility is that vulnerable individuals may perceive events as more traumatic than other individuals.

Gender also increases vulnerability, because women show an increased incidence of PTSD compared with men. An additional factor that increases the risk of not only PTSD but also anxiety disorders and associated depression is a history of chronic stress, abuse, or trauma.

Because of the central role of trauma in the etiology of PTSD, early research investigated the function of the major neuroendocrine stress pathway: the HPA axis. Daskalakis and colleagues (2015) provide a recent review of the endocrine aspects of PTSD. Many, but not all, studies found that patients with PTSD had a lower-than-normal level of blood cortisol that was associated with increases in CRF and NE. The fact that the magnitude of the cortisol response to a stressor can predict the development of PTSD in the future suggests that low cortisol levels represent a vulnerability factor. For instance, the victims of serious automobile accidents who had low levels of cortisol after the accident were more likely to develop PTSD during the next 6 months. Unfortunately the data did not reach significance, because cortisol levels fluctuate with a circadian rhythm, and the time of the accident and subsequent blood sampling could not be controlled. Galatzer-Levy and coworkers (2014) measured the acute cortisol response of a group of police officer recruits immediately following the viewing of a video of police officers exposed to real-life trauma. This measure of cortisol was made during the officers' academic training. The researchers followed this group over their subsequent 4 years of active duty in an urban setting where they would routinely be exposed to multiple stressors and potentially highly traumatic events. The study results showed that a weak cortisol response to the trauma video predicted those individuals who would subsequently develop more chronic, nonremitting distress responses over the 4 years while those with stronger cortisol responses were resilient and demonstrated healthy adaptations to subsequent stress. The practical application of these results is that blunted cortisol response may represent a risk factor for poor adaptation to stress and may help to predict the likely outcome for individuals who may be exposed to work-related trauma, such as police, firefighters, first responders, and soldiers.

Although on the surface it seems paradoxical to have low stress hormones associated with a stress disorder, in individuals with PTSD the normal feedback mechanism that turns off cortisol and ACTH secretion is hypersensitive. The increased sensitivity is related to the higher density of glucocorticoid receptors, as was found in both combat veterans and civilians with PTSD compared with combat veterans and civilians without PTSD. The premature attenuation of the cortisol response apparently enhances the sympathetic nervous system activation, which is responsible for the high circulating levels of NE found in individuals with PTSD. As described earlier in the chapter (see Joels et al., 2011), in normal individuals, the slow effects of cortisol on gene regulation through the glucocorticoid receptor not only return the adrenergic activity within the basolateral amygdala to normal, but also make that brain region less sensitive to further stress. When the cortisol response to stress is blunted as in PTSD, the individual has no control over the intense anxiety that occurs during the re-experiencing of the trauma.

Children who have parents with PTSD have an increased risk for PTSD and also tend to have lower-than-normal blood cortisol levels. Yehuda and colleagues (2000) showed that in the high-risk population of Holocaust survivor offspring, those who both developed PTSD themselves and had a parent with PTSD had the lowest levels of cortisol (**TABLE 17.4**). Those whose parents had PTSD but who did not themselves show PTSD had intermediate levels, and those who neither had a family history of PTSD nor had symptoms themselves had cortisol levels equal to controls (non-Holocaust survivors). More recent work by this group (Lehrner et al., 2014) showed that not only was the cortisol response reduced intergenerationally, but the offspring also showed enhanced glucocorticoid receptor sensitivity resulting in enhanced cortisol suppression. These differences were associated with maternal PTSD, rather than paternal PTSD, in which case reduced receptor sensitivity has been found in offspring. These gender-based opposing outcomes argue against a genetic explanation for the transmission.

TABLE 17.4 Average Blood Cortisol Levels in the Children of Holocaust Survivors

	Blood cortisol level
Controls	65 µg/day
Children of Holocaust survivors	
No parental PTSD; no resulting PTSD	65 µg/day
Parental PTSD; no resulting PTSD	45 µg/day
Parental PTSD; PTSD present	32 µg/day

Source: After R. Yehuda et al. 2000. *Am J Psychiatry* 157: 1252–1259.

The intergenerational transmission of stress response could be explained by parental modeling of behaviors or exposure of the offspring to vicarious parental trauma. However, another possible explanation for these results is that epigenetic programming may be involved in the transgenerational transmission of the trauma-related effects, even when the stress occurred years before conception. Nevertheless, these potential epigenetic modifications of glucocorticoid receptor functioning and HPA axis activity could be due to several factors. First, parenting behavior modified by symptoms of PTSD would impact the offspring's environment significantly, producing epigenetic markers. Earlier we described the role of early maternal neglect in rodents in determining the emotional response and hormonal reactivity of offspring to stressful events (see Web Box 17.2). Second, the maternal transmission of altered stress responsivity could also have occurred in utero if the mother exposed the fetus to high levels of glucocorticoids due to postwar symptoms. (The effects of early prenatal exposure to stress are demonstrated in Figure 17.10.) Finally, the intergenerational transmission of glucocorticoid receptor functioning could have occurred from preconception maternal stress-induced epigenetic methylation of the glucocorticoid receptor gene and been passed on via gametes (eggs, or in the case of paternal transmission, the sperm or seminal fluid). The reader may want to return to the section on transgenerational epigenetic transmission in Section 2.1 for further discussion.

The abnormal glucocorticoid functioning found in individuals with PTSD apparently has clinical significance because several of the biomarkers that predicted symptom improvement after 12 weeks of exposure therapy included higher bedtime salivary cortisol level, lower 24-hour urinary cortisol excretion, and a particular polymorphism of the glucocorticoid receptor gene. Exposure therapy is a cognitive behavior therapy characterized by gradually approaching trauma-related memories and feelings. Furthermore, for those individuals whose symptoms improved, glucocorticoid sensitivity decreased. There was a significant correlation between the pre- and post-treatment glucocorticoid sensitivity and the pre- and post-treatment symptom scores (Yehuda et al., 2014).

Many neuroimaging studies have used patients with PTSD as participants. The most consistent finding is a reduction in the volume of the hippocampus, although differences regarding laterality of the reduction have been reported. A smaller hippocampus might explain some of the cognitive symptoms of PTSD, including deficits in short-term memory, flashbacks, and amnesia for the traumatic events in those individuals with dissociative PTSD. Since the hippocampus plays a part in contextual learning, dysfunction might also explain why individuals with PTSD respond physiologically to cues that are not directly related to trauma. Situations resembling the trauma stimuli activate the amygdala and elicit emotional responses. Normally, the hippocampus would assist in determining whether the present context is safe or resembles the original dangerous context and would inhibit the emotional response of the amygdala in the safe context. Since reduced hippocampal volume is found so frequently and is associated with more severe symptoms, it is tempting to assume that it is a component of PTSD. However, several pieces of evidence suggest otherwise. First, reduced hippocampal volume has been reported in traumatized burn victims who do not have PTSD, suggesting that the brain change may be a consequence of trauma, not PTSD. Second, researchers have found that individuals with PTSD have lower-than-average hippocampal volume very soon after traumatic events, which may mean that the smaller hippocampus was present before the trauma. A more direct evaluation utilized monozygotic twins, only one of whom suffered combat trauma and developed PTSD. The twin with PTSD had a smaller hippocampus than other traumatized GIs with no PTSD, but the identical twin with no trauma-induced PTSD also had a hippocampus with reduced volume, suggesting that the abnormality represents a vulnerability factor for PTSD (Gilbertson et al., 2002).

Since the symptoms of PTSD resemble an unregulated activation of emotional memories, the increased neural activity of the amygdala to trauma cues would be expected along with reduced inhibitory control by the PFC. In fact, both structural imaging studies and functional studies show smaller, less active anterior cingulate cortices and medial prefrontal cortices, which normally inhibit the amygdala and establish extinction of conditioned emotional responses.

Obsessive–compulsive disorder

Have you ever tried to forget some peculiar, sexual, or aggressive thought and found the thought recurring over and over? Have you ever checked your alarm clock before you got ready for bed and then felt compelled to check it again and again before you climbed into the sack even though you know you set it correctly? Having experienced those normal events will help you begin to understand **obsessive–compulsive disorder** (**OCD**). However, while these examples are trivial ones, OCD is anything but trivial. It is a severe, chronic psychiatric problem that may require hospitalization, or in the most extreme cases psychosurgery, to control the symptoms. The disorder is characterized by recurring, persistent, intrusive, and troublesome thoughts of contamination, violence, sex, or religion (**obsessions**) that the individual tries to resist but that cause a great deal of anxiety, guilt, and shame. **Compulsions** are repetitive rituals considered attempts to relieve the tremendous anxiety generated by the obsessive thoughts, although they may be directly related or totally unrelated to the obsessive ideas. In the first instance, affected individuals may wash their hands hundreds of times a day until the skin is raw and bleeding because of an obsession about contracting a fatal disease. Other compulsions are unrelated to obsessions; they may involve meaningless repetitive acts like counting each crack in the sidewalk, jumping through doorways, or chewing each bite of food 100 times because of the belief that a family member may otherwise become fatally ill. Regardless of the compulsion, the individuals are convinced that unless their compulsive rituals are completed, disastrous consequences will occur, and they experience extreme anxiety unless they perform their compulsive behaviors. These activities are recognized by sufferers as inappropriate or irrational and consume most of their waking hours, yet they feel forced to do them against their will. The disorder causes intense emotional distress but is often left untreated because the individuals are so ashamed of the symptoms that they recognize as irrational or bizarre. Only when the symptoms become extreme do they seek help. Although OCD was once considered rare, its lifetime prevalence is now estimated at 2% to 3%. A YouTube video from Johnson & Johnson interviews one young boy with OCD and discusses his cognitive behavior therapy (Johnson & Johnson, 2011).

The caudate nucleus (part of the striatum) is believed to have a central role in the neurobiology responsible for the characteristic repetitive and ritualistic thoughts and actions of OCD. Although there are disparities among studies examining the volume of the caudate nucleus in OCD, functional imaging more consistently shows increased metabolic activity in response to provocative stimuli. More significantly, imaging shows coordinated activity of the caudate with several cortical regions. These results led to the formulation of the cortico-striatal-thalamic-cortical loop (see Vaghi et al., 2017) as central to OCD symptomology. However, expanded circuitry models have been developed to explain some of the secondary cognitive symptoms such as selective deficits in attention and nonverbal memory. In addition, symptoms associated with subtypes of OCD (e.g., checking rituals, washing rituals, or hoarding disorder) call for dimensional models of the disorder. Nakao and coworkers (2014) review recent neuropsychological and neuroimaging studies of OCD that provide the basis for several of those neural models. **WEB BOX 17.3** explains more about the neurobiology of OCD.

In addition to research with humans, an increasing number of animal models are being developed to further refine our understanding of the neural circuits responsible for compulsive behavior with the hope of defining potential therapeutic drug targets (reviewed in Szechtman et al., 2017). A variety of animals apparently spontaneously engage in repetitious and meaningless behaviors such as repeated hair biting, paw licking that produces wounds, and repeated pacing of caged zoo animals, all of which model compulsive behaviors. Perhaps the best-studied naturalistic model for OCD is the compulsive behavior demonstrated by a fraction of deer mice in a given population. These animals spontaneously develop purposeless, stereotyped behaviors, including running in fixed patterns, backward somersaulting, and repetitive jumping. Since the stereotypic behaviors are not induced by pharmacological or genetic manipulations, it is likely that there is a genetic basis for their development. Hence this naturally occurring compulsive behavior provides the opportunity to study the genetics of OCD as well as the neurochemical basis of the behavior. One example of the model's usefulness in directing future research is the discovery by researchers, using in vivo microdialysis, that glutamate release increased in the striatum just before the compulsive behaviors were initiated. That finding suggests that glutamate dysfunction may be a component of OCD pathophysiology.

In addition to naturalistic models, several transgenic models have been developed. Of particular interest are SAPAP3 knockout mice that lack a postsynaptic protein normally heavily concentrated in corticostriatal synapses. These mice not only show intense, repetitive grooming activity that leads to bloody facial wounds, but also show increased anxiety in the elevated plus-maze. Electrophysiological evidence further suggests that both of these behaviors are linked to abnormal glutamate NMDA receptor function in corticostriatal, but not thalamostriatal, synapses. Transgenic models are important to drug discovery because a large number of animals with predictable abnormalities can be produced quickly and easily.

Animal models can also be used in conjunction with optogenetic and electrophysiology techniques to clarify the underlying pathophysiology of OCD-like symptoms. Researchers studied neural connectivity in a mouse model of OCD-like behavior. With the use of optogenetics to stimulate orbitofrontal and M2 motor cortical fibers in the striatum, slice electrophysiology revealed an important contribution of M2 synapses to hyperfunction of striatal medium spiny neurons considered central to OCD pathophysiology. This finding was intriguing in light of the role of the M2 in not only motor output but also the behavioral planning of motor actions that goes awry in compulsive behaviors. These data are in line with human findings where abnormal activity of a homologous M2 region (called the preSMA/SMA) was detected in human patients by fMRI, and highlight a potential brain target for therapeutic development (Corbit et al., 2019).

Perhaps most significant to the development of effective treatment strategies in humans is the use of animal models that directly mimic performance abnormalities in patients with OCD. For instance, patients with OCD show deficits in the delayed alternation task in which they are required to change their strategy immediately after making a correct response. The nature of the behavioral task can easily be translated to animal testing in order to trace the neural networks involved and evaluate the neurochemical basis, which ultimately may lead to potential treatment that can translate to humans. The animal models described here and many more are discussed more fully and evaluated by Ahmari (2016).

SECTION SUMMARY

- Anxiety disorders vary in symptoms, incidence, and time course, but all include high levels of anxiety.

- The chronic anxiety experienced in GAD is associated with enlargement and hyperactivity of the amygdala and too little inhibitory control by the PFC. Increasing inhibition with GABA agonists reduces symptoms.

- There is a genetic predisposition to sudden episodes of panic disorder. Dysregulation of adrenergic neurons in the ANS and LC may be involved. A genetic polymorphism of the NE transporter gene is associated with increased vulnerability to panic.

- In panic disorder, the volumes of the amygdala and the hippocampus are reduced. During a panic attack, neural activity is increased in the amygdala, cingulate cortex, and insula and is reduced in the PFC.

- The individual with panic disorder experiences intense fearfulness with autonomic activation as well as anticipatory anxiety over the concern of being observed having an attack in a public place.

- Phobias involve irrational fears of objects or situations and are best treated with behavioral desensitization.

- SAD involves extreme fear of being evaluated in public and is associated with increased blood flow in the amygdala during challenge that normalizes after treatment.

- Not all trauma victims develop PTSD. Genetic vulnerability factors increase the probability that PTSD will occur following a less intense traumatic event. Other vulnerability factors include female gender, lack of social support after the trauma, and a history of chronic stress or abuse.

- Low blood cortisol is a marker of vulnerability for PTSD and may be due to a hypersensitive negative feedback mechanism.

- Neuroimaging shows a reduction in hippocampal volume in patients with PTSD. It may be a consequence of trauma itself rather than of PTSD. Other researchers have found that the reduction preceded the trauma-induced PTSD, making it a vulnerability factor.

- In PTSD the amygdala shows increased neural activity, and the ACC and the mPFC are less active and fail to inhibit the limbic structures.

- OCD is a severe, chronic psychiatric problem characterized by recurring, persistent, intrusive thoughts and repetitive rituals. The irrational acts of OCD must be performed to prevent extreme anxiety.

- The caudate nucleus has a central role in the pathophysiology of OCD and is one component in the dysfunctional cortico-striatal-thalamic-cortical loop.

- Animal models of OCD can be naturalistic or produced by genetic manipulations. Optogenetics and chemogenetics provide the opportunity to dissect the neural circuits more precisely than previously. Well-designed behavioral tasks using laboratory animals are needed to ensure that therapeutic drug testing in the lab can translate to clinical application in humans.

17.3 Drugs for Treating Anxiety, OCD, and PTSD

Drugs that are used to relieve anxiety are called **anxiolytics**. Many belong to the class of **sedative–hypnotics**, which is part of a still larger category, the **CNS depressants**. CNS depressants include the barbiturates, the BDZs, and alcohol, and all of these drugs reduce neuron excitability. As you may know, the oldest known anxiety-reducing drug is ethyl alcohol, and it is still popular as an over-the-counter remedy for stress (see Chapter 10). However, because it is difficult to administer in accurate doses and has a very poor therapeutic index, alcohol has no medical use.

To be considered an anxiolytic, a drug should relieve the feelings of tension and worry and signs of stress that are typical of the anxious individual with minimal side effects such as sedation. As we saw in animal models described in Chapter 4, drugs in this class increase behaviors that are normally suppressed by anxiety or punishment. **FIGURE 17.12** shows the strong correlation between the effectiveness of anxiolytic drugs from several classes in a conflict procedure and the potency of these drugs in clinical trials with human patients.

Drugs that relieve anxiety often also produce a calm and relaxed state, with drowsiness and mental clouding, incoordination, and prolonged reaction time. At higher doses, these drugs also induce sleep, and they are therefore sometimes called hypnotics. At the highest doses, CNS depressants induce coma and death, although even

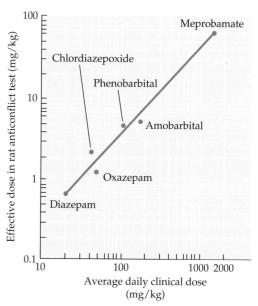

FIGURE 17.12 **Correlation of drug potency in rat anticonflict test with clinical potency** Drugs that increase punished behaviors in the conflict procedure test at low doses are also clinically useful for treating anxiety in patients at low doses. Less potent anticonflict drugs also require higher doses to be effective for human anxiety. The drugs tested include benzodiazepines (diazepam, oxazepam, chlordiazepoxide), barbiturates (phenobarbital, amobarbital), and a barbiturate-like anxiolytic (meprobamate). (After L. Cook, and J. Sepinwall. 1975. In *Mechanism of Action of Benzodiazepines*, E. Costa and P. Greengard [Eds.], pp. 1–28. Raven Press: New York.)

at therapeutic doses they can be fatal if combined with other drugs (**FIGURE 17.13**). Selected sedative–hypnotics also reduce seizures and may be used to treat epilepsy. Others produce muscle relaxation as needed to treat muscle spasms, for example following an auto accident.

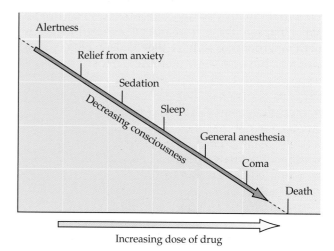

FIGURE 17.13 **Dose-dependent effects of CNS depressants on levels of consciousness** With increasing doses, the level of awareness and arousability gradually decreases along a continuum until death occurs.

Although the classic sedative–hypnotic drugs affect the functioning of many types of neurons in the CNS, their primary mechanism of action involves enhancing GABA transmission. Since GABA is the major inhibitory neurotransmitter in the nervous system, it has receptors on most cells in the CNS to exert widespread inhibitory effects. You may recall that the $GABA_A$ receptor complex regulates a Cl^- channel that increases Cl^- current into the cell to move the membrane potential farther away from the threshold for firing. Therefore, GABA agonists produce a local hyperpolarization, or inhibitory postsynaptic potential, and inhibit cell firing. As you learned earlier, both barbiturates and BDZs have binding sites as part of the $GABA_A$ receptor complex and enhance the inhibitory effects of GABA. **FIGURE 17.14A** shows the hyperpolarization caused by GABA and its enhancement by diazepam.

When BDZs bind to their modulatory sites on the $GABA_A$ complex, they enhance the effect of GABA by increasing the number of times the channel opens. However, in the absence of GABA, the BDZs have no effect on Cl^- channel opening. Apparently the presence of a BDZ alters the physical state of the receptors, increasing the receptor affinity for GABA so that GABA opens the channels more easily, shifting the dose–response curve to the left. As you would expect, the addition of the competitive antagonist flumazenil prevents the BDZ-induced enhancement of GABA action but does not affect GABA-induced hyperpolarization (**FIGURE 17.14B**). In contrast, the addition of a GABA antagonist prevents GABA from opening the channel, and the presence of a BDZ has no further effect. It is generally assumed that the fact that BDZs do not enhance the maximum response to GABA is responsible for their high therapeutic index (i.e., clinical safety).

Competition experiments that measured the effectiveness of various BDZs in displacing [³H]diazepam showed a positive correlation between the ability to displace the radioligand and the clinically effective dose for relieving anxiety (**FIGURE 17.15**). This means that the drugs that bind most readily to the BDZ receptor (i.e., require low concentrations to displace [³H]diazepam) are also clinically effective at low doses. Likewise, BDZs that bind less easily need higher doses to be effective.

BDZs also increase the affinity of the $GABA_A$ receptor for GABA; however, they increase the duration of the opening of GABA-activated Cl^- channels rather than the number of openings. In addition to enhancing GABA's action at the receptor, barbiturates directly open the Cl^- channel without GABA. This additional action may explain why barbiturates can be lethal but benzodiazepines are not.

Barbiturates are the oldest sedative–hypnotics

Sodium amytal was the first barbiturate, but as many as 50 others with different profiles of bioavailability were developed. The pharmacokinetic factors of absorption, distribution, and metabolism described in Chapter 1 determine each drug's onset of effect and duration of action, and it is on this basis that the drugs are classified into three groups: ultrashort-acting, short/intermediate-acting, and long-acting. Because the barbiturates have essentially been replaced by the BDZs in the treatment of anxiety disorders, our discussion of these drugs will be brief.

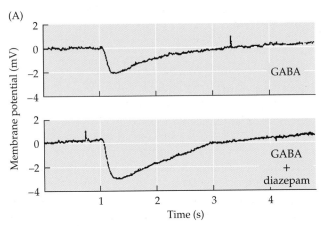

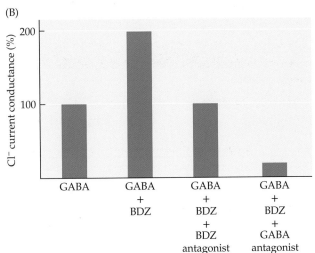

FIGURE 17.14 Effects of GABA and diazepam on membrane potentials and chloride (Cl^-) flux (A) Electrical recording of the hyperpolarizing effect of GABA and the enhanced hyperpolarization caused by the addition of diazepam to a mouse spinal cord neuron. Diazepam alone would produce little or no hyperpolarization. (B) GABA alone increases the conductance of Cl^- through its channel. Adding a BDZ enhances the amount of Cl^- movement into the cell. Blocking the BDZ binding site prevents the drug's enhancement of GABA but not the effect of GABA itself. A GABA antagonist prevents GABA from opening the Cl^- channel, and the presence of BDZ has no effect. (After E. R. Kandel. 2000. In *Principles of Neural Science* (4th ed.), E. R. Kandel, et al. [Eds.], pp. 1209–1226. McGraw-Hill: New York. © McGraw-Hill)

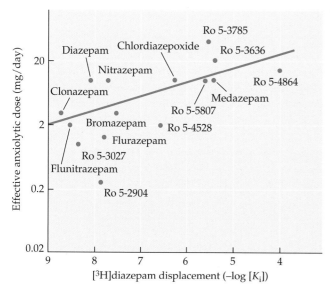

FIGURE 17.15 Correlation of BDZ binding and antianxiety effect The ability of the BDZs (including several experimental compounds having the "Ro" designation) to displace [³H]diazepam from the BDZ binding site is correlated with the doses required for anxiolytic action. The negative log scale on the x-axis reflects increasing concentrations from left to right. Therefore, the benzodiazepines that displace labeled diazepam at low concentrations (e.g., clonazepam and flunitrazepam) also tend to be those that require lower doses to reduce anxiety. Those that are less effective at binding (needing higher concentrations) to the diazepam site (e.g., Ro 5-4864) also need higher doses for antianxiety effects. (After C. Braestrup and R. F. Squires. 1978. *Eur J Pharmacol* 48: 263–270. © 1978. Reprinted with permission from Elsevier.)

PHARMACOKINETICS All of the barbiturates have a similar basic ring structure but vary in the length and complexity of the side chain attached to the ring. These molecular differences are responsible for their differences in lipid solubility and determine rate of onset and duration of action. These pharmacokinetic factors determine their clinical uses. **TABLE 17.5** summarizes these characteristics and provides examples.

SIDE EFFECTS First, although barbiturates readily induce sleep, it is not a normal, restful sleep. The drugs alter sleep architecture by reducing the amount of REM (rapid-eye-movement) sleep and causing a rebound in REM after withdrawal.

Second, the anxiolytic effects of these drugs are accompanied by pronounced cognitive side effects, including mental clouding, loss of judgment, and slowed reflexes, making driving particularly dangerous. High doses also lead to gross intoxication, staggering, jumbled speech, and impaired thinking. Coma and death due to respiratory depression occur at 10 to 20 times the normal therapeutic dose. These drugs are extremely dangerous when combined with alcohol.

Third, when used repeatedly, barbiturates increase the number of liver microsomal enzymes. This increase enhances drug metabolism, producing lower blood levels (metabolic tolerance) and reduced effectiveness. Since the same liver enzymes metabolize many other drugs, cross-tolerance diminishes the effectiveness of other drugs as well. Further, pharmacodynamic tolerance occurs when CNS neurons adapt to the presence of the drug and become less responsive with chronic drug use. Mood changes and sedation seem to show the greatest and most rapid tolerance, but the lethal respiratory depressant action of the drug does not show tolerance at all. Therefore, as one gradually increases the dose of the drug needed to achieve a desired effect, the margin of safety (therapeutic index) becomes less (**FIGURE 17.16**).

Fourth, barbiturates produce significant physical dependence and potential for abuse. Terminating drug use after extended treatment produces a potentially fatal rebound hyperexcitability withdrawal syndrome similar to that for alcohol. The potent reinforcing effect of barbiturates is demonstrated by the high rate of self-administration found in rats and monkeys in an operant chamber, which predicts significant abuse potential in humans. It was the concern about abuse potential among patients, as well as the diversion of the prescription medications to street use and the high incidence of side effects, potential lethality, and rapid tolerance of barbiturates, that prompted the search

TABLE 17.5 Duration of Action and Uses of Major Barbiturates				
Duration of action	**Lipid solubility**	**Onset**	**Duration**	**Use**
Ultrashort Thiopental (Pentothal) Methohexital (Brevital)	High	10–20 s	20–30 min	IV anesthesia
Short/intermediate Amobarbital (Amytal) Secobarbital (Seconal) Pentobarbital (Nembutal)	Moderate	20–40 min	5–8 h	Surgical anesthesia and sleep induction
Long Phenobarbital (Luminal) Mephobarbital (Mebaral)	Low	Over 1 h	10–12 h	Prolonged sedation and seizure control

FIGURE 17.16 **Margin of safety** Dose–response curves for the barbiturate-induced desired effect (mood change or sedation) and lethal respiratory depression. The top panel shows that with early drug use (nontolerant), the individual experiences mood effects without significant respiratory depression. However, as tolerance develops with repeated use (bottom panel), larger amounts of drug are needed to experience the sedation (the curve shifts to the right), but no change in the dose causing depression of respiration occurs. The margin of safety shrinks dramatically in the tolerant individual.

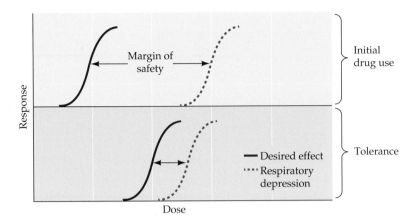

for a novel anxiolytic drug without these undesirable characteristics. The BDZs were introduced in 1960 and in general have replaced the prescription of barbiturates. The decline in prescriptions for barbiturates over the years has made these drugs less available and has caused a parallel decline in abuse.

BDZs are highly effective for anxiety reduction

The first BDZ to be introduced was chlordiazepoxide (Librium). It represented the first true anxiolytic that targeted anxiety without producing excessive sedation. It has a low incidence of metabolic tolerance, a less severe withdrawal syndrome than barbiturates, and a

very safe therapeutic index. Within a few years, diazepam (Valium), oxazepam (Serax), flurazepam (Dalmane), and at least a dozen other chemically related drugs were developed.

PHARMACOKINETICS All BDZs have a common molecular ring structure but vary in the complexity of the side chains (**FIGURE 17.17**). Additionally, they all have a similar mechanism of action. The choice of a particular BDZ for a given therapeutic situation depends primarily on the speed of onset and the duration of drug action. The onset of action is determined by the drug's lipid solubility; the most soluble are quickest to be absorbed and moved through the blood–brain barrier to initiate the drug effect, but they also readily move out of the brain and redistribute to other body tissues, producing a short duration of action. Those with moderate lipid solubility take longer to reach significant brain levels. Termination depends more on liver metabolism than on redistribution. The long-acting BDZs undergo several metabolic steps to produce multiple active metabolites that may have half-lives of 60 hours or longer (**FIGURE 17.18**). These can be problematic for elderly individuals, who may rapidly accumulate drug in the body because of their reduced metabolic capacity, increasing the probability of side effects. The short-acting BDZs, such as temazepam (Restoril) and lorazepam (Ativan), are metabolized in one step into inactive metabolites by conjugation with glucuronide. Redistribution to other body

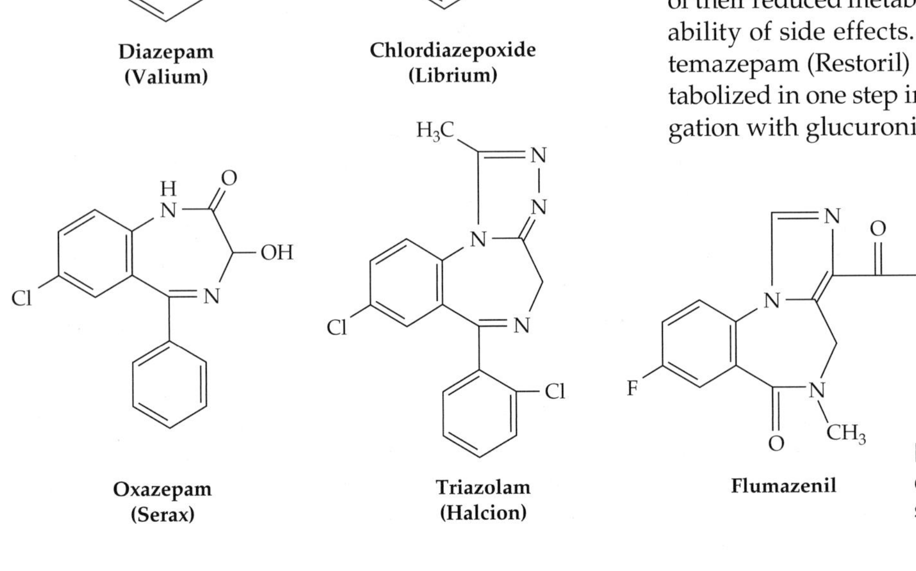

Diazepam
(Valium)

Chlordiazepoxide
(Librium)

Oxazepam
(Serax)

Triazolam
(Halcion)

Flumazenil

FIGURE 17.17 Molecular structure of several BDZs and the BDZ binding site antagonist flumazenil

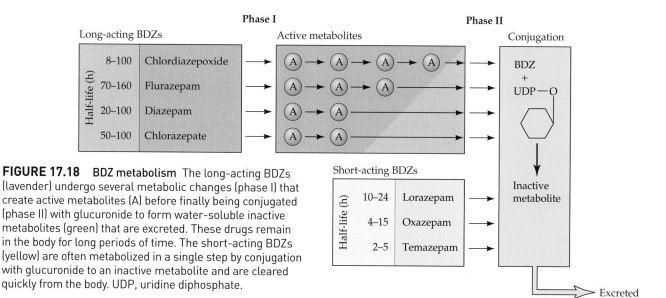

FIGURE 17.18   BDZ metabolism The long-acting BDZs (lavender) undergo several metabolic changes (phase I) that create active metabolites (A) before finally being conjugated (phase II) with glucuronide to form water-soluble inactive metabolites (green) that are excreted. These drugs remain in the body for long periods of time. The short-acting BDZs (yellow) are often metabolized in a single step by conjugation with glucuronide to an inactive metabolite and are cleared quickly from the body. UDP, uridine diphosphate.

tissues reduces CNS levels of drug and also contributes to the short duration of action. The slow release from inert depots back into circulation is responsible for any drug hangover effects that might occur.

THERAPEUTIC EFFECTS   Unlike barbiturates, the BDZs cannot be used for deep anesthesia, but they are useful as **presurgical anesthetics**, during which patients are conscious but less aware of their surroundings and quite relaxed. They are also commonly used before major dental work as well as for a wide range of stressful diagnostic procedures. One of the newer BDZs is midazolam (Versed), used for rapid onset of relaxation and deep sleep during brief surgical procedures done with local anesthetics. Because it has a short half-life, recovery takes only a few hours without hangover. It also induces an anterograde amnesia that creates an illusion of anesthesia in some patients, which is considered a beneficial drug effect.

In other cases, however, the drug-induced amnesia is highly undesirable. Since the 1990s a BDZ that is marketed outside the United States as a sleep aid has been illegally imported and used as a "date rape" drug. Flunitrazepam (Rohypnol) is quite potent and, when combined with alcohol, impairs judgment and causes amnesia along with significant sedation. There have been a limited number of reports of women who were sexually assaulted and then found themselves in unfamiliar locations with no memory of the events surrounding the attack. Although such situations produced serious concern on college campuses and at social establishments serving alcohol, the number of documented cases is quite small and the risk is low. However, because of the illicit use, the U.S. Drug Enforcement Administration (DEA) has classified flunitrazepam as a Schedule I drug (i.e., a drug with high potential for abuse and no medical use).

The most popular use for BDZs is as an anxiolytic. They relieve the sense of worry and fearfulness, as well as the physical symptoms associated with anxiety, with less mental clouding, loss of judgment, and motor incoordination than is typical of other sedative–hypnotics. Empirical evidence shows BDZ efficacy in treating the somatic symptoms associated with GAD, panic disorder, OCD, and SAD. The mild sedation that accompanies use of some of the BDZs decreases with repeated use over a week to 10 days, but little or no tolerance occurs for the antianxiety effects. Nevertheless, in older individuals with slower drug metabolism, excessive confusion and reduced cognitive function may be quite serious and may resemble senile dementia.

Several of the longer-acting BDZs are useful **hypnotics**. BDZs shorten the time needed to fall asleep and increase the duration of sleep time, as well as reduce the number of nighttime awakenings. Despite their relative safety, all sleep medications pose potential problems, such as causing reduced alertness the next day and rebound withdrawal insomnia after prolonged use (see **WEB BOX 17.4**). Some BDZs are useful **muscle relaxants**, and others are **anticonvulsants** for the management of particular forms of epilepsy. Intravenous diazepam is the treatment of choice for status epilepticus, a period of severe and persistent seizures that can be life threatening. BDZs are also the drugs of choice in preventing acute **alcohol** or **barbiturate withdrawal** symptoms, including seizures. Alcohol, barbiturates, and BDZs are cross-dependent, so withdrawal from any one of them can be terminated by administration of any of the others. Since withdrawal from heavy alcohol or barbiturate use can produce a life-threatening situation, the treatment of choice is to substitute a long-acting BDZ (usually Valium) to stop the abstinence syndrome and then to gradually lower the dose of the BDZ over several weeks to minimize the withdrawal.

ADVANTAGES OVER OTHER SEDATIVE–HYPNOTICS

BDZs were originally developed to be safer and more effective than the drugs available at the time, such as chloral hydrate, meprobamate, glutethimide, methaqualone, and the barbiturates. BDZs have several clear advantages over the older drugs. Overall they are more effective, but the most notable advantage is their high therapeutic index. Extremely high doses produce disorientation, cognitive impairment, and amnesia and, in some cases, a paradoxical increase in aggressiveness, irritability, and anxiety (Hobbs et al., 1996). However, since they have almost no effect on the respiratory center in the medulla, lethal overdose is extremely rare unless the drugs are taken in combination with other CNS depressants such as alcohol. Unfortunately, recreational use of BDZs is often combined with alcohol, opioids such as methadone, or other CNS depressants, which can produce highly toxic interactions. Although no specific antagonist is available for alcohol or barbiturate overdose, flumazenil (Romazicon) is a competitive antagonist for the BDZ receptor. Individuals brought to the emergency room unconscious can be treated with flumazenil, which quickly reverses the effects of the BDZ while the non-BDZ depressant is gradually eliminated from the body through normal metabolic processes.

BDZs are also safer because they do not increase the number of liver microsomal enzymes that normally metabolize the drugs. The lack of enzyme induction means there is reduced metabolic tolerance during repeated drug administration and also fewer drug interactions.

PHYSICAL DEPENDENCE AND ABUSE

BDZs have a reputation for lower probability of physical dependence and abuse when taken as prescribed. Nevertheless, chronic use (as recreational use or patients' misuse) and physical dependence do occur. The abstinence syndrome, which is milder than that of the barbiturates and is not life threatening, develops gradually over several weeks, especially for those drugs with very long half-lives. Symptoms may include insomnia, restlessness, headache, anxiety, mild depression, subtle perceptual distortions, muscle pain, and muscle twitches (Carvey, 1998). The most severe symptoms, which resemble those of other CNS depressants, include panic, delirium, and seizures. These occur in individuals who are abusing the drugs at high doses for prolonged periods, often in combination with other drugs, although prolonged use (defined as daily use for at least 3 months) at therapeutic doses also can produce dependence in some vulnerable individuals. Withdrawal is more severe for those long-term users if the drug is withdrawn abruptly or if the dose is rapidly reduced rather than tapered off gradually. Withdrawal can occur even after low therapeutic doses if it is abruptly precipitated by administration of flumazenil.

While physical dependence is manifested by the development of the abstinence syndrome, potential abuse is best predicted by the magnitude of reinforcing properties, which have been evaluated by drug self-administration experiments (see Chapter 4). Abuse of BDZs is not new. In the 1960s and 1970s prescriptions of BDZs to manage stress were extremely popular and the drugs were freely utilized by many, from businessmen to housewives. In fact, middle-class women were the heaviest users. For years, Valium was the number-one prescription drug sold in the United States, and it was the first to reach $1 billion in sales (Cooper, 2013). Ultimately the DEA categorized several of the BDZs as Schedule IV drugs (i.e., drugs having a medical use and a real but low potential for abuse or dependence), limited the number of refills, and imposed sanctions for illegal sales. Congressional hearings were held to deal with the BDZ "epidemic," and there was increased media attention following the death of Elvis Presley in 1977 due to massive quantities of Valium combined with other drugs. The next year First Lady Betty Ford openly discussed her addiction to Valium and alcohol. In response to government involvement and high-profile exposure, Valium prescriptions dropped 50% from 1975 to 1980 (Cooper, 2013). Although concern about the abuse potential of these drugs has led to fewer prescriptions, their misuse seems to be increasing, based on data from drug-related emergency department visits, especially among recreational polydrug users and individuals abusing alcohol. Additionally, the number of sedative-related admissions to treatment programs suggests the problem is serious. Sources for recreational use of BDZs include "doctor shopping," forged prescriptions, diversion of drugs from the legal supply by unethical doctors and pharmacists, and unregulated purchases via the internet.

In initial research, laboratory animals did not readily self-administer BZDs in an operant chamber, suggesting that the drugs have little reinforcement value and low abuse potential in humans. However, BDZs with more rapid onset were more likely to be self-administered by animals compared with placebo. Although animals will self-administer BDZs, in breaking point experiments (see Chapter 4) BDZs were weaker reinforcers than other drugs of abuse. In these experiments, the schedule of reinforcement is progressively increased, requiring more lever presses for each reinforcement. The point at which the effort required exceeds the reinforcing value is the "breaking point." The breaking point for the BDZ midazolam was seen to be significantly lower than for an opioid or cocaine, indicating lower reinforcement value and hence less abuse potential in humans (reviewed in Licata and Rowlett, 2008). It is of interest that in animals that are first trained to self-administer a barbiturate, the reinforcing effects of BDZs are more apparent. This animal behavior models that of humans, for whom the reinforcing effects of BDZs are relatively low in general but are higher in individuals who have previously self-administered other sedative drugs or alcohol. In drug discrimination tests (see Chapter 4) in which rats are taught to discriminate between barbiturates and saline by pressing a lever for reinforcement, BDZs will substitute for barbiturates. However, rats can also be trained to discriminate chlordiazepoxide from barbiturates and alcohol. These results indicate that the subjective drug-induced states of the three drugs must be similar if they substitute for each other in the discrimination test yet have some qualitative differences that can be distinguished. Overall, animal studies suggest that the reinforcement value of BDZs is much less than that of barbiturates and other drugs of abuse (Griffiths et al., 1991; Griffiths and Weerts, 1997; Licata and Rowlett, 2008).

Studies with humans show that nonanxious volunteers prefer to take a placebo over diazepam and that anxious individuals also choose the placebo unless they are seeking treatment for anxiety. In laboratory studies BDZs are not consistently reinforcing in humans except in those with a history of drug or alcohol abuse or who suffer from anxiety or sleep disorders. However, individuals who are experiencing withdrawal after termination of use of chronic diazepam or other sedative–hypnotics do tend to self-administer a BDZ rather than placebo. These results suggest that BDZs have a relatively low risk of abuse but that physical dependence and withdrawal may encourage continued use. The probability of abuse is almost always associated with polydrug use; that is, individuals who have a history of drug or alcohol abuse are those who most likely will abuse BZDs (Woods et al., 1995; Licata and Rowlett, 2008). Nevertheless, because of the risk of abuse, most clinical guidelines suggest restricting BDZ use to short-term treatment. As you might expect, there is some disagreement among clinicians and researchers. Some clinicians suggest that guidelines should be reassessed for the use of BDZs as first-line, long-term pharmacological treatment for panic disorder, GAD, and SAD (Starcevic, 2014). Evidence to support the reconsideration includes clinical trials showing that the BDZs are equal or superior to the current first-line treatment, the SSRIs. In addition, BDZs act immediately, making them ideal for quick symptomatic relief and use on an as-needed basis. They are also useful in combination with SSRIs during the early course of treatment when the SSRIs may actually increase anxiety and during the time lapse before antidepressant-induced anxiety relief occurs. The BDZs are superior to the antidepressants when there are symptoms of autonomic hyperarousal, prominent muscle tension, and sleep disturbance. They are also generally tolerated better than the antidepressants. Despite these arguments, most clinicians continue to prescribe the safer antidepressants.

SUBUNIT-SELECTIVE DRUG DEVELOPMENT Studies using knockout mice suggest that drugs may be developed to act selectively on $GABA_A$ receptors with distinct α subunit isoforms (see Chapter 8 and Figure 8.17 for a review of GABA receptor subunits and isoforms).

Such selectivity would permit targeting of a specific GABA-associated symptom with minimal side effects. The first clinically useful subunit-selective $GABA_A$ receptor modulators are zolpidem (Ambien) and zaleplon (Sonesta), which bind preferentially to $GABA_A$ receptors with the α_1 subunit (also called α_1 $GABA_A$ receptors). These drugs are useful in treating insomnia while having little anxiolytic, muscle relaxant, or anticonvulsant effects except at high doses.

Ever since the discovery of the subunit-selective modulators of $GABA_A$ function, researchers have made valiant attempts to screen drugs that have the potential to be nonsedating anxiolytics (reviewed by Rudolph and Knoflach, 2011; Farb and Ratner, 2014). More than a dozen agents showing preference for the α_2 $GABA_A$ receptor and perhaps the α_3 have been identified (e.g., TPA023, ocinaplon, alpidem) and shown to have anxiolytic effects in animal tests such as the elevated plus-maze and various conflict procedures without impairing motor function or producing sedation or memory impairment. These results demonstrate that it is possible to develop a nonsedating anxiolytic. Unfortunately, in many instances in human clinical trials the drugs were not anxioselective and produced concomitant fatigue, drowsiness, and muscle incoordination. The failure to show selectivity has caused some to question whether sedation is associated with subunits other than the α_1, at least in humans (Skolnick, 2012). In addition, in most cases the clinical trials of these agents have been terminated because of a variety of dangerous developments, including liver toxicity, prolonged elevated liver enzyme levels that did not resolve after drug termination, severe hepatitis, cataract development, and poor pharmacokinetic properties.

Another goal of research has been to develop BDZ-like drugs without the potential for abuse. To do that it is necessary to understand which $GABA_A$ receptor subtype is responsible for the reinforcing effects of the drug, the precursor of substance abuse. Immunohistochemical analysis has shown $GABA_A$ receptors with the α_1 subunit are located on interneurons that inhibit mesolimbic DA neurons, cells responsible for reinforcement. Hence BDZ-induced inhibition of an inhibitory neuron activates the DA cells, which subsequently increases synaptic DA in the NAcc, an event common to all abused drugs. Genetically modified mice with their α_1 subunits made insensitive failed to self-administer midazolam, while wild-type mice and those with altered α_3 subunits readily consumed the BDZ, suggesting that α_1 subunits are necessary for reinforcement. In breaking point experiments, drugs that modulate α_1 receptors, such as midazolam and zolpidem, had higher breaking points (meaning the animals were more willing to work for reinforcement) than the experimental compound L-838,417. This compound is a partial agonist at $GABA_A$ receptors with α_2, α_3, or α_5 subunits, but is an antagonist at receptors with the

α_1 subunit. However, animals that were first trained to self-administer a short-acting barbiturate readily self-administered L-838,417, although its breaking point was lower than that of the nonselective BDZs midazolam and diazepam. The nonselective BDZs in turn had lower breaking points than the α_1 GABA$_A$ receptor modulator zolpidem. Based on these results, one would have to conclude that α_1 subunit modulation may be important for reinforcement but is not necessary.

More recent work using a different approach also suggests that the α_1 GABA$_A$ receptor is responsible for the BDZ potential for abuse (Fischer et al., 2016). After a dose–response curve for self-administration of triazolam was established, a variety of selective GABA$_A$ subunit antagonists were administered. The nonselective BDZ site antagonist flumazenil shifted the dose–response curve to the right in a dose-dependent fashion. That shift indicates that higher doses of triazolam were needed to achieve the same level of self-administration because it needed to compete with the antagonist. In a similar fashion, the α_1 subunit–preferring antagonists βCCT and 3-PCB caused a right shift in the triazolam dose–response curve, demonstrating the importance of the α_1 subunit for drug self-administration, while the α_5 subunit antagonist had no effect. Unfortunately, there are no α_2 or α_3 receptor antagonists currently available. These results demonstrate the importance of the α_1 subunit in the reinforcing effects of triazolam. However, when the researchers compared the binding of the antagonists to receptors with the α_1 subunit, they found that the rank order for binding to the receptor did not match the rank order of potencies for blocking triazolam self-administration. Their conclusion was that while the α_1 GABA$_A$ receptors have a significant modulatory effect on BDZ reinforcement, they do not have the sole role in self-administration. These results all indicate that a designed BDZ that acts effectively at the α_2 GABA$_A$ receptor with minimal activity at the α_1 GABA$_A$ receptor could be anxiolytic with reduced abuse potential.

MODULATION OF NEUROSTEROIDS   Another way to enhance GABA$_A$ receptor function is to act at the neurosteroid modulatory site, described previously. The use of allopregnanolone itself is limited by its poor bioavailability and the fact that it is metabolized to active hormonal steroids that act at peripheral receptors to cause endocrine side effects. Alternatively, synthetic allopregnanolone-like agents could be designed to reduce their metabolism to other active steroids and lengthen their half-lives. Additionally, these agents could be made to cross the blood–brain barrier more readily. Another option for drug development includes drugs that increase synthesis of allopregnanolone. The synthesis of neurosteroids occurs in both neurons and glial cells in the CNS and is regulated by the mitochondrial translocator protein (TSPO). TSPO transports the precursor cholesterol into mitochondria, where neurosteroid

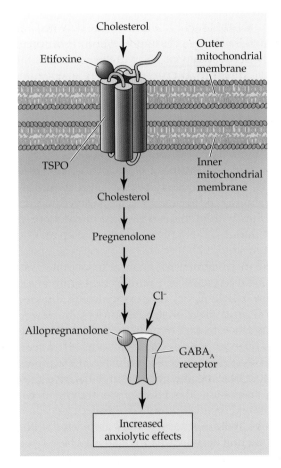

FIGURE 17.19   Neurosteroid synthesis TSPO is a translocator protein that is located on the outer mitochondrial membrane and transports cholesterol through the inner mitochondrial membrane. The conversion of cholesterol to pregnenolone is the rate-limiting step in neurosteroid synthesis. Pregnenolone is further modified in several steps to allopregnanolone, which binds to the GABA$_A$ receptor modulatory site to enhance GABA-induced chloride influx, producing anxiolytic effects. Etifoxine is one drug that targets TSPO to increase neurosteroids and reduces anxiety. (After R. Rupprecht et al. 2010. *Nat Rev Drug Discov* 9: 971–988; and C. Schule et al. 2014. *Prog Neurobiol* 113: 79–87.)

synthesis occurs (**FIGURE 17.19**). Because the transport is the rate-limiting step in synthesis, TSPO is an important therapeutic target for enhancing GABA$_A$ inhibition (see Nothdurfter et al., 2012a, or Schule et al., 2014).

Drugs that target TSPO and induce a significant increase in neurosteroids include etifoxine as well as many experimental compounds such as XBD-173 (emapunil) and FGIN-127. These compounds bind to TSPO and significantly increase brain levels of allopregnanolone and other neurosteroids and also produce anxiolytic effects in a variety of animal tests. The reduction in anxiety can be attenuated by finasteride, an inhibitor of neurosteroid synthesis. Etifoxine is used clinically in some parts of the world but has not received FDA approval in the United States. Etifoxine is a non-BDZ drug that reduces seizures and anxiety as effectively as the BDZ lorazepam, and reduces neuropathic pain without some of the adverse effects of BDZs such as sedation, memory impairment, and withdrawal upon cessation. It does, however, potentiate the action of other CNS depressants, including ethyl alcohol. In addition to stimulating allopregnanolone synthesis, it has modulatory effects on $GABA_A$ receptors, but it does not act at either the neurosteroid or BDZ modulatory sites. What seems clear is that the β subunit of the $GABA_A$ receptor complex is necessary for the etifoxine-enhanced Cl^- influx produced by GABA binding. In particular, the binding to $GABA_A$ receptors with the $β_2$ or $β_3$ subunits produces the greatest enhancement of the chloride-induced hyperpolarization and provides selectivity for those brain regions high in those subunits. Hence the anxiolytic effects of etifoxine are likely due to direct modulation of the $GABA_A$ receptors, as well as the enhanced synthesis of neurosteroids (see Choi and Kim, 2015; Nuss, 2015). Etifoxine and other enhancers of neurosteroid function hold promise for the development of anxiolytics that have fewer side effects than BDZs and work more quickly than the antidepressants, which take 4 to 6 weeks to be effective. However, a report that acute hepatitis occurred in some patients after several weeks of treatment needs further evaluation. An in-depth review of the multiple approaches for targeting neurosteroid synthesis and the potential utility of these drugs in treating not only anxiety but also alcohol use disorders and degenerative diseases such as Alzheimer's disease is provided by Porcu and colleagues (2016).

Second-generation anxiolytics produce distinctive clinical effects

The drugs in this group were developed to provide anxiety reduction without some of the side effects of the benzodiazepines. The best known is **buspirone (BuSpar)**, which has a novel structure and mechanism of action (a partial agonist at $5\text{-}HT_{1A}$ receptors) compared with the sedative–hypnotics (GABA receptor modulators). It is also unusual in that it does not necessarily increase punished behaviors, as in the water-lick suppression test. Furthermore, in drug discrimination tests, it does not substitute for either barbiturates or BDZs. Clearly, buspirone has distinctive subjective

effects as well as a distinctive mechanism of action from classical anxiolytics.

In clinical tests, buspirone has measurable anxiolytic actions, although it is much less effective in reducing the physical symptoms of anxiety than the cognitive aspects of worry and poor concentration. It has been shown to be effective in treating GAD, but effectiveness for other anxiety disorders and OCD is less clear. Some suggest that it may be best used in combination with other pharmacotherapies, such as the SSRIs, or along with cognitive behavior therapy (Harvey and Balon, 1995).

Buspirone has several advantages over the BDZs, including its usefulness in treating the depression that often accompanies anxiety. In addition, its anxiety reduction is not accompanied by sedation, confusion, or mental clouding. Buspirone does not enhance the CNS-depressing effects of alcohol or other CNS depressants, so it is still safer than the BDZs. It also has a minimum of severe side effects, and fatalities have not been reported. Further, it has little or no potential for recreational use or dependence. In fact, some patients report a dysphoric effect, described as a feeling of restlessness and malaise. Finally, no rebound withdrawal syndrome has been reported for buspirone. **FIGURE 17.20** compares the effects of buspirone and diazepam in the light–dark exploration test. Mice treated for 14 days with either drug spent more time in the lighted box than saline-treated controls, demonstrating antianxiety effects. When the drugs were abruptly stopped, the mice that had been treated with buspirone showed a slow gradual return of anxiety (the time in the white box decreased) to control values, with no rebound in anxiety. In contrast, mice treated with diazepam showed an abstinence-induced rebound to less than control levels of exploration (suggesting increased anxiety) followed by a slow recovery.

One downside of buspirone use is that its onset of effectiveness in humans is quite long and its effectiveness in relieving anxiety is less than that of BDZs. In general, several weeks of daily use are required for significant anxiolytic effects to be seen. This characteristic makes it less desirable for individuals who are accustomed to the immediate relief induced by BDZs. Also, its delayed action makes it less useful for patients who take the

FIGURE 17.20 **Abstinence effect after chronic diazepam use but not buspirone** Mice treated with buspirone (circles) or diazepam (squares) for 14 consecutive days and placed in the light–dark test on days 3, 7, and 14 showed reduced anxiety by exploring the bright box for a longer time than control mice. Neither drug produced tolerance over the 14 days. When the test was repeated at various times after drug withdrawal, the buspirone-treated mice showed a gradual return of anxiety. In contrast, mice treated with diazepam showed an abstinence-induced rebound in anxiety. This effect is shown by levels of exploration significantly less than control levels, followed by a slow recovery. (After B. Costall and R. J. Naylor. 1991. In *5-HT₁A Agonists, 5-HT3 Antagonists and Benzodiazepines: Their Comparative Behavioral Pharmacology*, R. J. Rodgers and S. J. Cooper [Eds.], pp. 133–157. Wiley: New York.)

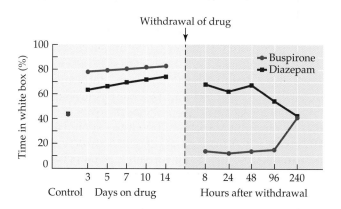

drug only when needed for situational anxiety. Second, buspirone has a rather short half-life, so dosing must occur twice daily. Third, buspirone, as well as other structurally related drugs (gepirone and ipsapirone), does not show cross-tolerance or cross-dependence with BDZs or sedative–hypnotics. This feature makes it inappropriate for use as a substitution in cases of alcohol or barbiturate withdrawal. Finally, it lacks the hypnotic effects necessary to treat insomnia, has no muscle relaxant effects, and does not control seizures.

Buspirone has unusual characteristics because, unlike the sedative–hypnotics, it does not enhance GABA function but instead acts as a partial agonist at serotonergic 5-HT$_{1A}$ receptors. These receptors are in heavy concentration in the limbic system, raphe nucleus, and frontal and entorhinal cortices. Although some of these receptors are located postsynaptically, autoradiographic and immunohistochemical studies also show 5-HT$_{1A}$ somatodendritic autoreceptors in the nucleus of the raphe. The neurochemical basis of the anxiolytic action of buspirone is not fully understood, but its partial agonist action at 5-HT$_{1A}$ receptors is the likely mediator of its effectiveness. Its delayed onset of action would lead one to believe synaptic plasticity is necessary.

Antidepressants relieve anxiety and depression

Several of the disorders described in earlier sections are effectively treated with antidepressant drugs. In fact because of fear of abuse of BDZs, the SSRIs are considered the first line of treatment. In all cases it is worth noting that individual drug treatment response is quite variable among patients with anxiety and stress disorders, and symptoms are lessened but not eliminated for many individuals. Furthermore, in contrast to the immediate effectiveness of the BDZs, the antidepressants take 4 to 6 weeks to become effective. In some cases, the optimal treatment is cognitive behavior therapy with or without adjunctive pharmacotherapy (e.g., see Ivarsson et al., 2015). The antidepressants are important because anxiety and depression very often occur in the same individual and a single drug can be used to treat both conditions. However, several antidepressants have beneficial effects in treating anxiety apart from their antidepressant action. For example, in OCD, the SSRIs clomipramine (Anafranil), fluoxetine (Prozac), fluvoxamine (Luvox), and sertraline (Zoloft) have been found somewhat effective in reducing some symptoms, and the benefits are apparently unrelated to the antidepressant action of the SSRIs. Keep in mind that although the antidepressants initially enhance monoamine function by blocking reuptake from the synapse, the prolonged treatment needed for clinical effectiveness may be causing neuronal adaptations that reverse the stress-induced atrophy of cells in brain regions such as the hippocampus and PFC and enhance synaptic restructuring and dendritic elaboration. Further discussion of the neurotrophic effects of the

antidepressants will be found in the chapter on affective disorders (see Chapter 18).

Tricyclic antidepressants such as imipramine (Tofranil) and MAOIs (e.g., phenelzine [Nardil] and tranylcypromine [Parnate]) are also often effective in treating some anxiety disorders, including panic, phobic disorders, and GAD, although side effects are often troublesome (see Chapter 18). Since the side effects of SSRIs are sometimes less disturbing to patients and they have a more favorable therapeutic index, the serotonergic drugs are more often prescribed as a first choice than the other antidepressants. However, as you would expect, the SSRIs are not without side effects, including increased anxiety, restlessness, movement disorders, muscle rigidity, nausea, headache, insomnia, and sexual dysfunction. Also, when taken in combination with other 5-HT agonists, a potentially fatal event called the serotonin syndrome can occur. Because abuse potential of the SSRIs is low, they may be used on occasions when BZD dependence is a concern. Although there is low abuse potential, the SSRIs cause physical dependence, and as many as 60% of patients show signs of withdrawal on terminating the drug. More detail on the SSRIs and other classes of antidepressants is provided in Chapter 18.

Because buspirone is frequently used as an adjunctive therapy with SSRIs when the latter fail to produce adequate relief from symptoms, a relatively new drug (approved by the FDA in 2011) has been developed that combines 5-HT reuptake inhibition with potent partial agonist activity at 5-HT$_{1A}$ receptors. In rodent experiments vilazodone reduced anxiety, including predator-induced stress and ultrasonic vocalizations of rat pups separated from their mothers. The drug also showed antidepressant action in the forced swim test (see Chapter 4). These results translated to positive clinical outcomes in several double-blind, placebo-controlled trials in patients with GAD and also in patients with anxious depression. Side effects over 8 weeks were generally mild, and vilazodone did not impair sexual functioning, as is common with SSRIs. Long-term safety evaluation is still necessary, but vilazodone looks promising at this point (Sahli et al., 2016). It represents one more potential tool in the pharmacological arsenal to optimize treatment for a given individual. **TABLE 17.6** summarizes a variety of treatment options for anxiety disorders. Keep in mind that behavioral therapy is the principal way of treating simple phobias and, along with cognitive therapy, is a significant approach in treating GAD, social phobia, OCD, and PTSD.

Many novel approaches to treating anxiety are being developed

Over the years, GABA and 5-HT have been the primary focus of drug development in the treatment of anxiety. However, the field has dramatically slowed the progression of novel drug development (Miller, 2010), creating a need for innovative approaches to treatment.

TABLE 17.6 Drugs Used to Treat Various Anxiety Disorders

Drug class	Trade name	Anxiety disorders
BZDs	Valium, Xanax	GAD, panic disorder, OCD, social phobia, alcohol withdrawal, acute situational anxiety
Tricyclic antidepressants	Tofranil, Aventil	Panic disorder, GAD, OCD, PTSD
MAOIs	Nardil, Parnate	Social phobia, panic disorder
SSRIs	Prozac, Zoloft, Paxil	Social phobia, panic disorder, OCD, PTSD
Buspirone	BuSpar	GAD, panic disorder

In this regard, several efforts over the past two decades have begun to address the question of whether more exotic substances might augment the efficacy of traditional psychotherapy (reviewed in Schenberg, 2018; Nutt, 2019). For example, the dissociative anesthetic ketamine has been successfully used in several clinical studies to mitigate symptoms associated with OCD as well as PTSD. Similarly, the psychedelics LSD and psilocybin have shown long-term efficacy in treating depression and anxiety when combined with psychotherapy, with improvement maintained at 6- and 8-month follow-ups. Finally, the entactogen 3,4-methylenedioxidemethamphatemine (MDMA, or "ecstasy") has been extensively studied in the context of terminally ill cancer patients, where it has been found to dramatically reduce existential anxiety associated with death from the disease. However, much more work is needed to address long-term effects of treatment, efficacious dosing regimens, and the best integrative therapy to achieve optimal results.

When combined with psychotherapy, it is thought that the dissociative, mystic, and empathogenic effects of these substances in patients allows them to more safely identify and face the underlying trauma than with therapy alone, leading to a greater recession of associated symptoms of anxiety and depression. While ketamine acts by blocking NMDA receptors in the brain to cause cognitive and emotional dissociation, drugs such as LSD, psilocybin, and MDMA work through the serotonergic system to exert their effects. However, although the use of LSD and psilocybin is relatively safe, some evidence suggests that prolonged use of MDMA may alter the function of the serotonergic system. Thus, more research is needed to understand the neural basis of its empathogenic effects, such that novel and safer therapies can be developed to combat these disorders.

SECTION SUMMARY

- Anxiolytics are sedative–hypnotics that belong to the larger class of CNS depressants.
- Dose-dependent effects of sedative–hypnotics begin with reduction in anxiety and progress through stages of increasing sedation, incoordination, sleep, coma, and death.
- Sedative–hypnotics increase GABA-induced Cl⁻ current into the cell, causing enhanced hyperpolarization and inhibition of many cells.

- BDZs enhance GABA inhibition but have no effect of their own on chloride conductance. Flumazenil is a BDZ receptor competitive antagonist that reduces BDZ effects but has no effect on GABA-induced hyperpolarization. Since BDZs shift the GABA dose–response curve to the left but do not increase the maximum GABA response, they are safer than barbiturates and other sedative–hypnotics.
- Barbiturates increase GABA-induced Cl⁻ conductance and directly open the Cl⁻ channel without GABA.
- The barbiturates are ultrashort-acting, short/intermediate-acting, and long-acting drugs, depending on their lipid solubility, which determines the rate of penetration into the brain and the extent of redistribution to drug depots and liver metabolism. Duration of action determines their clinical uses.
- Side effects of barbiturates include altered sleep architecture, mental clouding and cognitive impairment, low therapeutic index, rapid tolerance and cross-tolerance, physical dependence, and dangerous withdrawal.
- BDZs are prescribed on the basis of onset and duration. Lipid solubility determines onset. Redistribution to depots and metabolism determine duration. Many BDZs have active metabolites, making them long acting.
- Therapeutic uses of BDZs include presurgical anesthesia, anxiolysis, sleep induction, muscle relaxation, seizure control, and termination of alcohol withdrawal.
- Advantages of BDZs compared with other sedative–hypnotics include high therapeutic index, availability of a competitive antagonist to reverse overdose, reduced tolerance and drug interactions, less physical dependence and milder withdrawal, less reinforcement value, and lower abuse potential. Fatalities do not occur unless a BDZ is combined with another sedative–hypnotic.
- Because of the risk of abuse, most clinical guidelines recommend BDZ use only for short-term treatment.
- Multiple forms of the GABA$_A$ receptor subunits provide targets in drug development aimed at increasing therapeutic selectivity and reducing side effects. Drugs selective for the α_2 GABA$_A$ receptor show anxiolysis without sedation in animal studies, but not in clinical trials. The α_1 GABA$_A$ receptor is likely to play a significant role in sedation, as well as BDZ reinforcement, predicting abuse potential. New drugs targeting the α_2 GABA$_A$ receptor with minimal activity at α_1 GABA$_A$ receptors may be anxiolytic with less risk of abuse.
- Allopregnanolone and other similar neurosteroids bind to the neurosteroid modulatory site on GABA$_A$ receptors and enhance the function of GABA, causing

antianxiety effects. Synthetic allopregnanolone analogs reduce anxiety without sedation. Drugs that increase the synthesis of allopregnanolone by targeting the rate-limiting step (i.e., the transport of cholesterol into mitochondria) have anxiolytic properties without some of the usual adverse effects of anxiolytics, such as sedation, memory impairment, and signs of withdrawal.

■ Buspirone is an anxiolytic that does not enhance GABA action but is a partial agonist at 5-HT$_{1A}$ receptors. Its advantages over BDZs are that it reduces both anxiety and depression without sedation or mental clouding, it does not enhance other sedative–hypnotics, and it has no withdrawal syndrome or abuse potential.

■ The disadvantages of buspirone are its slow onset of anxiolytic effects; its ineffectiveness for relieving alcohol or barbiturate withdrawal, insomnia, or seizures; and its lack of muscle relaxant effects.

■ Antidepressants, including tricyclic antidepressants, MAOIs, and SSRIs, may be used to reduce the anxiety accompanying depression. Some antidepressants relieve symptoms of specific anxiety disorders.

■ SSRIs are a drug class of first choice for anxiety because they have a high therapeutic index and low abuse potential. However, SSRIs take 4 to 6 weeks to show effectiveness following neural adaptations to chronic use. Side effects that are problematic include increased anxiety and insomnia and sexual dysfunction. Withdrawal symptoms are common following drug cessation.

■ Given the paucity of novel drug development in the past decade, some research has turned to more exotic compounds to test their therapeutic value in treating anxiety disorders. While much work remains, several clinical studies and trials are showing positive results of using ketamine, the psychedelics LSD and psilocybin, and MDMA in treatment of a variety of anxiety disorders as well as depression. More studies are needed to understand how to optimally combine specific dosing regimens with the variety of available psychotherapeutic interventions.

STUDY QUESTIONS

1. Identify the most important brain regions in the emotion-processing circuits.
2. Describe the important role of the central nucleus of the amygdala in orchestrating emotion. How does that compare with the role of the bed nucleus of the stria terminalis?
3. How does the amygdala form emotional memories? Explain why that is important.
4. Describe the HPA axis.
5. Provide several pieces of evidence that demonstrate the role of CRF in extrahypothalamic neural circuits involved in anxiety and the response to stress.
6. Distinguish among the three types of neurons found in the locus coeruleus.
7. Describe four lines of evidence showing that NE has an important role in anxiety.
8. Compare the effects of a BDZ, flumazenil, and β-carboline on the BDZ modulatory site on GABA$_A$ receptors.
9. What are the behavioral effects of neurosteroid modulation of GABA function? Which brain area is important for these effects?
10. Describe the complex effects of 5-HT$_{1A}$ agonists on anxiety.
11. In what ways does uncontrollable stress alter serotonergic function?
12. Describe the neurotrophic effect of 5-HT during fetal development.
13. Discuss the effects of stress on mesocortical and mesolimbic pathways as well as on the VTA.
14. How does early exposure to aversive childhood experiences predispose the adult to medical and psychiatric disorders? Include a discussion of glucocorticoid-induced neural plasticity in the hippocampus, amygdala, and mPFC.
15. Compare the effects of stress on males and females.
16. Briefly summarize the symptoms of GAD, panic disorder, phobias, SAD, PTSD, and OCD. Provide at least one neurobiological correlate for each.
17. Describe the GABA$_A$ receptor and its function. How do BDZs and barbiturates modify the receptor function?
18. What are the significant side effects of barbiturates that prompted the development of new sedative–hypnotics?
19. How do pharmacokinetic factors determine the duration of BDZ action?
20. What are the principal therapeutic uses of BDZs?
21. What are the advantages of BDZs compared with other sedative–hypnotics? What are the drugs' side effects?
22. How do GABA$_A$ receptor subunit–selective drugs target specific symptoms such as insomnia? Anxiety? Reinforcement?
23. Describe two ways that neurosteroids can be used to enhance GABA$_A$ receptor function. How is neurosteroid synthesis enhanced by drugs that act at TSPO? What is the mechanism of action of etifoxine, and what are its clinical effects?
24. Describe the advantages and disadvantages of buspirone.
25. Discuss the advantages and disadvantages of SSRIs, including potential side effects.
26. Describe how ketamine, psychedelics, and MDMA are being used clinically to mitigate a variety of anxiety disorders.

Affective Disorders: Antidepressants and Mood Stabilizers

CLINICAL DEPRESSION CAN BE TOTALLY DEBILITATING, leaving the individual in absolute despair and feeling empty and worthless, unable to function, and preoccupied with their own death. But sometimes during breaks in their depression, people can accomplish important things. Consider Abraham Lincoln. Biographers have described him as the classic image of gloom. He often wept in public and cited maudlin poetry. He told jokes at odd times—he needed laughs, he said, for his survival. As a young man, he talked of suicide, and as he grew older, he said he saw the world as hard and grim. His law partner once said about Lincoln, "His melancholy dripped from him as he walked." There were times when the depression overwhelmed him and he remained in bed. On his wedding day, suffering from a severe depressive episode, he never showed up and left his bride and wedding party waiting for him at the ceremony. To quote Lincoln, "I am now the most miserable man living." Nevertheless, his lifelong illness shaped his character and helped him avoid the pitfalls of inappropriate optimism, making him a realist with vision. His troubles gave him wisdom and deeper humanity and prepared him for the painful tasks of his presidency. He possessed insight, fortitude, and moral will. His depression made him stronger, graced him with dignity, and gave him the courage and confidence to take the risks that made him one of our greatest and most beloved presidents. (For more on Lincoln's story, readers can go to *Lincoln's Melancholy*, by Joshua Wolf Shenk, 2005.) ∎

Abraham Byers, 1858

Our revered 16th president struggled with clinical depression at various times throughout his life.

18.1 Characteristics of Affective Disorders

The *Diagnostic and Statistical Manual of Mental Disorders*, fifth edition (*DSM-5*), describes two principal types of affective disorder: **major depression** and **bipolar disorder**. Both of these are characterized by extreme and inappropriate exaggeration of mood (or affect). Major depression, also called unipolar depression, is characterized by recurring episodes of dysphoria and negative thinking that are also reflected in behavior. Bipolar disorder (also called bipolar depression) is also cyclical, but moods swing from depression to mania over time. The thinking and behavior of individuals with affective disorders reflect these exaggerated moods, which do not reflect a realistic appraisal of the environment. Mood disorders are among the most common forms of mental illness today and were described as early as 400 BCE by Hippocrates. The Greeks called depression *melancholia*, meaning "black bile," and recognized that it was associated with anxiety and heavy alcohol use. However, only in the past 150 years has it been recognized as a disorder of brain function.

Major depression damages the quality of life

We are all familiar with the essential feelings associated with depression: feeling down and blue, feeling listless, and lacking energy to do even the fun things we normally enjoy. The state of sadness that occurs in response to situations such as the loss of a loved one, failure to achieve goals, or disappointment in love is called **reactive depression** and does not constitute mental illness unless symptoms are disproportionate to the event or are significantly prolonged. The fact that we all have experienced depression does not make the clinical condition any easier to understand. In clinical depression, the mood disorder is so severe that the individual withdraws from life and from all social interactions. The intense pain and loneliness may make suicide seem like the only option. Pathological depression resembles the emotional state that we have all experienced but differs significantly in both intensity and duration.

The dysphoric mood is characterized by a loss of interest in almost everything and an inability to experience pleasure in anything (anhedonia). Most depressed patients express feelings of hopelessness, worthlessness, sadness, guilt, and desperation. Frequently, patients exhibit loss of appetite, insomnia (characterized particularly by early morning awakening), crying, diminished sexual desire, loss of ambition, fatigue, and either motor retardation or agitation. Self-devaluation and loss of self-esteem are very common and are combined with a complete sense of hopelessness about the future. Individuals may stop eating or caring for themselves physically, sometimes remaining in bed for prolonged periods. Other physical symptoms may include localized pain, severe digestive disturbances, and difficulty breathing. Thoughts of suicide are common; one estimate of suicide rates suggests that 7% to 15% of depressed individuals commit suicide, in contrast to a rate of 1% to 1.5% of the overall population. **TABLE 18.1** summarizes the *DSM-5* criteria for manic episodes and major depression.

Although there are some common features of clinical depression, symptom clusters do vary with the individual. Furthermore, particular patterns of symptoms suggest that there are depression subtypes that may be associated with distinct pathophysiologies and distinct causes. What has been well recognized since the time of Hippocrates (around 400 BCE) is that there is an extensive overlap of depression with anxiety and alcohol dependence (see Chapter 10). Confirmation of this relationship has been shown by many epidemiological surveys that estimate comorbidity (i.e., when two or more disorders occur in the same individual) at almost 60%. When the disorders are comorbid, it is usually the anxiety disorder, particularly generalized anxiety disorder or social anxiety disorder (see Chapter 17), that precedes the onset of depression. Comorbidity of the disorders predicts more *severe* symptoms, causing impaired daily function in work or while attending school or social events. Comorbidity also predicts more *persistent* symptoms that are more difficult to treat. Further discussion of the relationship between anxiety and depression follows in the sections on the roles of heredity and stress in depression etiology. Belzer and Schneier (2004) provide more information on diagnosis and treatment and theoretical explanatory models for the comorbidity of anxiety and depression.

If left untreated, most episodes of unipolar depression improve in about 6 to 9 months. However, the episodes usually recur throughout life, often increasing in frequency and intensity in later years. Although stress often precedes the first episodes of depression, later episodes are more likely to occur without the influence of psychosocial stress. Estimates of the incidence of depression vary significantly, but it is generally believed that 15% to 20% of the population experience depressive symptoms at any given time. The lifetime risk for a first episode of unipolar depression is between 3% and 4% for men and from 5% to 9% for women. The gender difference in the risk for depression is a topic of considerable interest and debate. The mean age of onset for depression is 27 years. This figure has decreased in recent years: **FIGURE 18.1** shows that among Americans born before 1905, only 1% developed depression by age 75, whereas among those born since 1955, 6% had become depressed by age 24.

TABLE 18.1	Symptoms of Manic Episodes and Major Depression
Diagnosis	**Symptom**
Manic episode	A. A distinct period of abnormally and persistently elevated, expansive, or irritable mood and abnormally and persistently increased goal-directed activity or energy, lasting at least 1 week and present most of the day, nearly every day (or any duration if hospitalization is necessary).
	B. During the period of mood disturbance and increased energy or activity, three (or more) of the following symptoms (four if the mood is only irritable) are present to a significant degree and represent a noticeable change from usual behavior:
	1. Inflated self-esteem or grandiosity
	2. Decreased need for sleep (e.g., feels rested after only 3 hours of sleep)
	3. More talkative than usual or pressure to keep talking
	4. Flight of ideas or subjective experience that thoughts are racing
	5. Distractibility (i.e., attention too easily drawn to unimportant or irrelevant external stimuli), as reported or observed
	6. Increase in goal-directed activity (either socially, at work or school, or sexually) or psychomotor agitation (i.e., purposeless non-goal-directed activity)
	7. Excessive involvement in activities that have a high potential for painful consequences (e.g., engaging in unrestrained buying sprees, sexual indiscretions, or foolish business investments)
	C. The mood disturbance is sufficiently severe to cause marked impairment in social or occupational functioning or to necessitate hospitalization to prevent harm to self or others, or there are psychotic features.
	D. The episode is not attributable to the physiological effects of a substance (e.g., a drug of abuse, a medication, other treatment) or to another medical condition.
Major depressive episode	A. Five (or more) of the following symptoms have been present during the same 2-week period and represent a change from previous functioning; at least one of the symptoms is either (1) depressed mood or (2) loss of interest or pleasure.
	1. Depressed mood most of the day, nearly every day, as indicated by either subjective report (e.g., feels sad, empty, hopeless) or observation made by others (e.g., appears tearful). (**Note:** In children and adolescents, can be irritable mood.)
	2. Markedly diminished interest or pleasure in all, or almost all, activities most of the day, nearly every day (as indicated by either subjective account or observation)
	3. Significant weight loss when not dieting or weight gain (e.g., a change of more than 5% of body weight in a month), or decrease or increase in appetite nearly every day. (**Note:** In children, consider failure to make expected weight gain.)
	4. Insomnia or hypersomnia nearly every day
	5. Psychomotor agitation or retardation nearly every day (observable by others; not merely subjective feelings of restlessness or being slowed down)
	6. Fatigue or loss of energy nearly every day
	7. Feelings of worthlessness or excessive or inappropriate guilt (which may be delusional) nearly every day (not merely self-reproach or guilt about being sick)
	8. Diminished ability to think or concentrate, or indecisiveness, nearly every day (either by subjective account or as observed by others)
	9. Recurrent thoughts of death (not just fear of dying), recurrent suicidal ideation without a specific plan, or a suicide attempt or a specific plan for committing suicide
	B. The symptoms cause clinically significant distress or impairment in social, occupational, or other important areas of functioning.
	C. The episode is not attributable to the physiological effects of a substance or another medical condition.

Source: Reprinted with permission from the *Diagnostic and Statistical Manual of Mental Disorders*, 5th ed., © 2013. American Psychiatric Association. All rights reserved.

In bipolar disorder moods alternate between mania and depression

The second type of exaggerated mood is mania. Mania rarely occurs alone but rather alternates with periods of depression to form bipolar disorder. The primary symptom of mania is elation. Manic individuals feel faultless, full of fun, and bursting with energy. Their need for sleep is significantly reduced. They tend to be more talkative

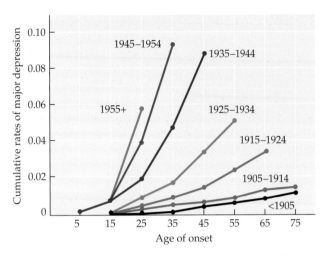

FIGURE 18.1   **Age of onset of major depression** Americans are developing major depression at higher rates and younger ages than previously, according to this analysis of data. The study evaluated 18,244 people at five sites, grouped in cohorts on the basis of year of birth. Cross-cultural surveys indicate a similar phenomenon worldwide. (After D. H. Barlow and V. M. Durand. 1995. *Abnormal Psychology: An Integrative Approach.* Brooks/Cole: New York.)

than usual and experience racing thoughts and ideas. In some individuals, the predominant mood is characterized by irritability, belligerence, and impatience because the rest of us are just too slow. They tend to make impulsive decisions of the grandiose sort and have unlimited confidence in themselves. The manic individual becomes involved in activities that have a high potential for negative consequences that often go unrecognized by the individual, such as foolish business investments, reckless driving, buying sprees, or sexual indiscretions. You may be interested in watching a short video from the University of Nottingham in which a manic patient is being interviewed by his psychiatrist (University of Nottingham, 2012). Despite the potential danger, some individuals during a manic phase are capable of highly productive efforts when channeled appropriately. A high proportion of creative individuals in the arts and sciences have experienced bipolar disorder and find that during the manic periods, their thought processes quicken and they feel both creative and productive. Is creativity linked to mental illness? **WEB BOX 18.1** considers that possibility.

The incidence of bipolar disorder is the same in men and women: it occurs in approximately 1% of the population. The time of onset for bipolar illness is typically between 20 and 30 years of age, and episodes continue throughout the life span.

Risk factors for mood disorders are biological and environmental

Most scientists agree that psychiatric disorders develop in a given individual because of the interaction of genes and environmental events. Individuals with particular clusters of genes inherit the tendency to express certain traits or behaviors that increase their vulnerability to specific disorders. Having those genes does not mean that you will develop the disorder, but exposure to particular environmental events is more likely to trigger the disorder in the vulnerable individual. Heredity, environmental stress, and altered biological rhythms are risk factors for affective disorders.

ROLE OF HEREDITY   Evidence for a genetic contribution to affective disorders comes from several sources. **Adoption studies** help to clarify the roles of genetics and family environment. In these studies, individuals with a firm diagnosis who were adopted at an early age are the focus of the research. If a heritable component exists, one would expect to see that compared with controls, the individual with an affective disorder would have a greater number of biological relatives with the same disorder, despite being raised in a different environment. Although many adoption studies have found such a relationship and suggest a role for genetics, the results have not always been consistent.

The best evidence for a heritable component of affective illness comes from **twin studies**, which show a significant difference between monozygotic (identical) and dizygotic (fraternal) twins in the rate of concordance for the disorders. The data in **FIGURE 18.2** show that if one twin has a mood disorder, the concordance rate (i.e., the likelihood of the other twin sharing the

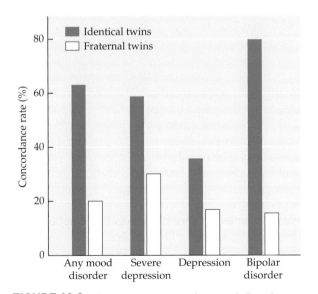

FIGURE 18.2   **Concordance rates for mood disorders among identical and fraternal twins** Identical twins are far more likely to share mood disorders than are fraternal twins, especially in the case of bipolar disorder. Concordance for clinical depression depends to some extent on severity. In this case, severe depression is defined as three or more episodes of depression. Data were derived from 110 pairs of twins. (After A. Bertelsen et al. 1977. *Br J Psychiatry* 130: 330–351.)

trait) for a monozygotic twin is approximately 65%. This means that if one of the pair of identical twins (having the same genes) experiences affective illness, the probability that the other twin will also experience some affective disorder is 65%. In contrast, the concordance rate for dizygotic twins (who are genetically no more similar than other siblings) is 20%. The difference in these two rates suggests the extent to which genetics contributes to the disorder (estimated at between 40% and 50%) and that a family history of clinical depression is the strongest predictor of vulnerability to the disorder. Keep in mind that if genetics were the only determining factor, the concordance rate in identical twins would be 100%. The genetics of an individual can certainly make them more vulnerable, but whether or not they actually develop the disorder must also depend on other psychosocial or pathophysiological factors.

If you look again at Figure 18.2, you will see that the concordance rate is also dependent on the severity of clinical depression: more severe mood disorders may have a stronger genetic contribution than less severe disorders. Of additional interest is the finding that there are shared genetic risk factors for clinical depression and anxiety disorders, although the magnitude depends on the particular anxiety disorder. For instance, major depressive disorder is most closely related genetically to generalized anxiety disorder. Figure 18.2 also shows that the genetic contribution to bipolar disorder is significantly greater than that to major depression. Eighty percent concordance in monozygotic twins compared with 16% in dizygotic twins indicates a very strong role for heredity in bipolar disorder.

Despite **linkage studies**, which look for similarities in gene location on chromosomes in families with affected members, and other more sophisticated methods of molecular biology that examine DNA fragments, no single dominant gene for affective disorders is known. We may well find that the genes involved confer a general vulnerability to a host of mood and anxiety disorders. For example, linkage studies for major depressive disorder and associated personality traits like neuroticism have been attempted because high scores on neuroticism are a strong predictor of future depressive disorder and other psychiatric ailments. Individuals who score high on neuroticism experience more negative emotions, including anxiety, anger, guilt, and depressed mood, and are more bothered by psychosocial stress. The particular disorder that is expressed in such an individual may ultimately be determined by developmental or psychosocial factors. Discussion of several candidate genes associated with clinical depression will be found in the section on serotonin dysfunction and in the discussion of brain-derived neurotrophic factor (BDNF). It is important to keep in mind that in any complex psychiatric disorder, there are many vulnerability genes, each of which contributes only a very modest amount.

ROLE OF STRESS   Both neurobiological studies and family studies indicate that anxiety and depression are closely related. First, anxiety along with its associated physiological symptoms is a frequent accompaniment to depression. Second, intense environmental stress and anxiety often precede episodes of depression, particularly early on in the course of the disorder. Further, altered patterns of stress hormone levels are frequently found in depressed patients. Chapter 17 has already introduced the relationship between anxiety and depression. Despite the importance of environmental stress, keep in mind that identical life stresses may be perceived very differently by individuals. Many people seem resilient and capable of coping despite extraordinary stresses, while others seem to succumb to relatively minor problems. It is likely that genetics plays a role in determining how one responds physically and behaviorally to daily traumas and stress. The dual importance of nature (genetics) and nurture (environment) can never be ignored. This has led to the emergence of the *diathesis–stress model* of depression and other psychiatric disorders. This model posits that patients with a certain inherent predisposition, or diathesis, to a particular disorder may not manifest the associated symptoms until experiencing a threshold level of stress or stresses that overwhelm any genetic or psychological buffers existing to keep the underlying vulnerability at bay.

The importance of stress to the etiology of depression and its mediation by the hypothalamic–pituitary–adrenal (HPA) axis is a significant focus in neuroscience. In response to stress, multiple neurotransmitters (including norepinephrine [NE], acetylcholine [ACh], and γ-aminobutyric acid [GABA]) regulate the secretion of corticotropin-releasing factor (CRF) from hypothalamic cells. CRF controls the release of adrenocorticotropic hormone (ACTH) from the pituitary into the blood. ACTH in turn acts on the adrenal gland to increase secretion of cortisol and other glucocorticoids, all of which play a role in the mobilization of energy to deal with stress (see Box 2.5 for a diagram of the HPA axis). Normally, cortisol feeds back to shut down HPA activation, resulting in transient activity of the system and brief surges in cortisol.

Among the most consistent neuroendocrine abnormalities in depressed individuals is abnormal secretion of cortisol, which is demonstrated in several ways. First, many depressed patients have elevated levels of cortisol (**FIGURE 18.3A**) in response to a greater-than-normal release of ACTH. Although both the pituitary and adrenal glands are enlarged as a result of hypersecretion, evidence from several sources suggests that the abnormality is not in the glands but in the brain. The hypersecretion is most likely due to abnormal regulation of CRF by the hypothalamus. Numerous studies have found higher-than-normal levels of CRF in the cerebrospinal

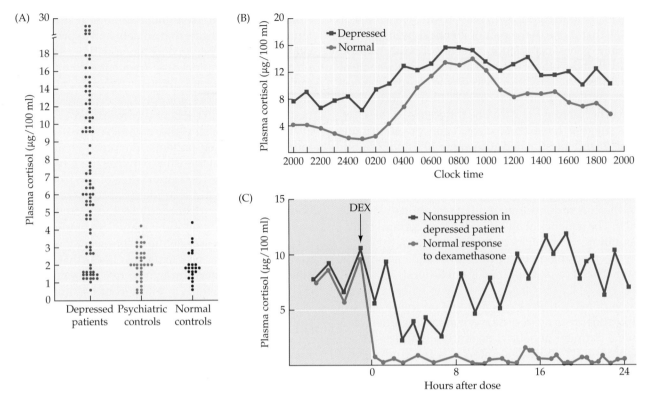

FIGURE 18.3 **Abnormalities in glucocorticoids** (A) Many (but not all) depressed patients have elevated cortisol levels compared with controls. Each dot represents a single individual. (B) Differences exist in circadian changes in blood cortisol levels between depressed patients and healthy controls. The measures were made each hour over a 1-day period. The decline in cortisol that normally occurs in the early morning and evening occurs to a lesser extent in depressed patients.

(C) Depressed individuals fail to respond with reduced cortisol levels after injection with 1 mg dexamethasone (DEX). The injected glucocorticoid also normally reduces both CRF release from the hypothalamus and pituitary release of ACTH. (B after E. R. Kandel. 2000. In *Principles of Neural Science* (4th ed.), E. R. Kandel et al. [Eds.], pp. 1209–1226, McGraw-Hill: New York © McGraw-Hill. C after S. B. Klein. 2000. *Biological Psychology*, Prentice-Hall: Upper Saddle River, NJ.)

fluid (CSF) of depressed patients and increased numbers of CRF-producing cells in the hypothalamus in post-mortem brain tissue. This exaggerated HPA axis function may be explained in part by the impact of early life traumas on the vulnerable individual. Early life stress apparently alters the set point of the HPA axis, making it permanently overly responsive and increasing the risk for later depression as well as anxiety disorders and alcohol abuse (**WEB BOX 18.2**). It is important to note that antidepressant drug treatment and electroconvulsive therapy reduce CRF levels in depressed patients.

Second, the high level of cortisol found in depressed patients is characterized by an abnormal circadian rhythm in cortisol secretion. The elevated and relatively flat pattern (depicted in **FIGURE 18.3B**) may reflect a more general abnormality in the biological clock, since altered rhythmicity also occurs for body temperature changes and sleep patterns (see later in this chapter). Third, since many depressed individuals have elevated cortisol, it is not surprising that some fail to respond to dexamethasone challenge. **Dexamethasone** is a synthetic glucocorticoid that should act as a negative feedback stimulus to suppress hypothalamic release of CRF and

pituitary release of ACTH, resulting in decreased cortisol levels (**FIGURE 18.3C**). Several studies have suggested that patients who remain non-responders to dexamethasone (i.e., fail to have cortisol release suppressed) after successful antidepressant treatment have a higher probability of relapse than those who show normal response.

Although usually adrenal glucocorticoids (including cortisol) are helpful in preparing an organism for stress, when the levels are persistently elevated, several systems begin to show pathological changes. Besides having damaging effects on immune system and organ function, glucocorticoids are associated with neuronal atrophy in the hippocampus, leading to cognitive impairment, imbalances in the serotonin (5-HT) system correlated with anxiety, and hormonal changes associated with depression (McEwen, 2008). The section on the neurobiological models of depression in Section 18.2 will provide more detail on the role of glucocorticoids in depression.

ALTERED BIOLOGICAL RHYTHMS Cortisol secretion is not the only biological rhythm that is disturbed in major depression. Altered sleep rhythms are among the

(A) Sleep pattern of a patient with depression

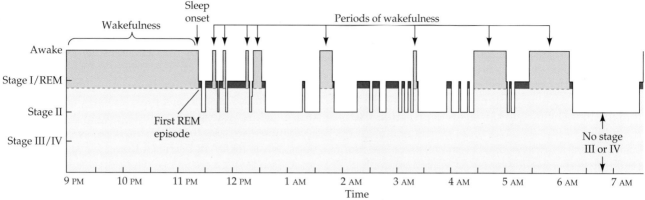

(B)

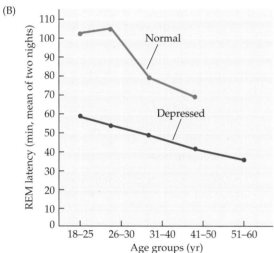

FIGURE 18.4 Altered sleep architecture in depression (A) In depressed patients, the onset of sleep is delayed and REM periods (colored red) get shorter as the night goes on rather than longer, which is typical in healthy adults. Also, notice the many awakenings that occur during the night because of failure to reach deep sleep (stages III and IV). (B) REM episodes begin sooner after the onset of sleep in depressed than in nondepressed individuals at every age.

most common and persistent symptoms of depression. Circadian rhythm controls the onset, pattern, and termination of sleep. The typical healthy sleep cycle is quite regular, having four stages of non-rapid-eye-movement (REM) sleep (stages I to IV) lasting a total of 70 to 100 minutes, followed by a 10- to 15-minute period of REM sleep, during which time dreaming occurs. This cycle is repeated four or five times a night. Depressed individuals show several distinct abnormalities in their sleep rhythm (**FIGURE 18.4A**). First, there is a long period before sleep onset. Second, there is a significant decrease in the time spent in slow-wave sleep, or deep sleep (stages III and IV), which leads to repeated awakenings during the night. Third, the onset of REM sleep occurs much earlier after the onset of sleep. Although REM latency decreases with age, individuals who are depressed show a shorter latency at all ages (**FIGURE 18.4B**). In extreme cases, the individual may enter REM sleep almost immediately after falling asleep. Fourth, REM sleep is significantly increased during the first third of the night in depressed individuals, but nondepressed individuals have proportionately more REM sleep in the final third of sleep. Also, although normal REM periods tend to increase in duration during the night, depressed patients

do not show such a pattern. Finally, when ocular movement is measured, depressed individuals show more frequent and vigorous eye movements during REM sleep, which suggests more intense dreaming.

Although we don't know what the altered rhythms mean, the irregularities in sleep patterns found in depressed individuals resemble the sleep patterns of nondepressed individuals who must alter their time of sleep by 12 hours. Since other indicators of biological rhythms, such as body temperature fluctuation and hormonal secretion (e.g., cortisol), are often also altered, one might consider the possibility that the biological clocks of people with depression are "phase shifted." In some individuals, the three rhythms are out of harmony (called desynchronization) or are mismatched. Since it is well documented that neurotransmitters involved in emotion regulation, such as 5-HT and NE, show circadian rhythms in function, the importance of evaluating altered rhythms in mood disorders is clear. The implications of these irregularities in sleep cycles have led to several novel treatment strategies, including the use of melatonin agonists, described in **WEB BOX 18.3**, and sleep deprivation therapy, discussed in **WEB BOX 18.4**.

It is probably no surprise that patients with bipolar disorder also show altered sleep rhythms (Geoffroy et al., 2013). Although their sleep during depressive episodes resembles that of unipolar depression with its shortened REM latency onset, one of the hallmark diagnostic symptoms of mania is the severely reduced need (sometimes almost absence) of sleep with no loss of energy. It is particularly interesting that in the asymptomatic bipolar individual, sleep deprivation that is intentional or is associated with environmental events such as experiencing jet lag, bereavement, or late-night studying can actually trigger an episode of mania. It is not clear whether the lack of sleep causes the onset of mania or represents an early occurring symptom. However, when manic patients are treated with a sleep-inducing benzodiazepine, the manic symptoms subside. Such sedatives are used as a common additive treatment along with a mood stabilizer such as lithium (see the last section of this chapter).

The sleep–wake cycle is not the only disturbed circadian rhythm found in patients with bipolar disorder. In addition, feeding, activity patterns, body temperature, blood pressure, plasma cortisol, thyroid-stimulating hormone, and melatonin rhythms are irregular. All of these are controlled by the molecular biological clock in the suprachiasmatic nucleus of the hypothalamus. Further, as was described for clinical depression, circadian rhythms, determined by the molecular clock, also control NE, 5-HT, and dopamine (DA) synthesis, degradation, levels, release, and some of their receptors. Abnormalities in these systems may be the basis for mood dysfunction, so the genes that are responsible for the molecular clock proteins are being extensively investigated. One such circadian gene is the *CLOCK* gene. A particular single-nucleotide polymorphism of the gene has been associated with several bipolar symptoms, such as the extent of insomnia during the depressive stage, evening activity, and measures of neuropsychological performance as well as violent suicide attempts (Dallaspezia and Benedetti, 2015; Logan and McClung, 2016). Why different genes involved with modulating circadian rhythms are associated with quite different psychiatric outcomes is not clear at this point, but Landgraf and colleagues (2014b) propose that because the circadian biological clock and the HPA axis stress response are so closely interconnected, the circadian rhythm abnormalities may affect the individual's response to environmental stressors. That in turn would alter the expression of genetic vulnerability to distinct psychiatric disorders. Given the role of psychosocial stress on numerous psychiatric disorders, modulation by circadian rhythms should be investigated more fully.

ALTERED GUT–BRAIN AXIS One emerging area of research has focused on what is termed the gut–brain axis, which reflects a known interaction of the CNS with the enteric nervous system of the gut, a "second brain" that contains millions of neurons, including 5-HT neurons. Bacterial flora within the gut, which aid in various digestive processes, have been shown to directly and indirectly impact CNS function, typically though interaction with the vagus cranial nerve that innervates the gut, heart, and throat muscles. Fascinating data from the past decade have shown that germ-free mice lacking intestinal bacteria exhibit a heightened response to stress through sensitization of the HPA axis, while different bacterial flora profiles have been associated with a variety of psychiatric symptoms, including anxiety and depression. While research into how the enteric nervous system interacts with the CNS to impact psychiatric disorders is still in its infancy, it is worth noting that treatment with certain probiotics in rodents can lower the stress response and depressive symptoms, postulated to result from bacterial interactions with the vagus nerve (**FIGURE 18.5**). Another striking study found that transplantation of fecal microbiota from depressed patients to germ-free rodents was sufficient to yield symptoms of anxiety and depression in these animals, possibly as a result of altered tryptophan metabolism, highlighting the potential role of gut microbiota composition in the emergence of psychopathology (Kelly et al., 2016). While the majority of these studies have been performed in rodent models of anxiety and depression, some limited studies in humans are showing similar results, although larger clinical trials are needed. For two excellent reviews on this topic, please see Foster and McVey Neufeld (2013) and Kim and Shin (2018).

Animal models of affective disorders

Although the affective symptoms of depression, such as feelings of worthlessness and guilt, can really be described only in human terms, animal models are critically needed as important tools for understanding the neurobiology of affective disorders, and evaluating the efficacy of novel treatments. In Chapter 4 you read that if a screening test predicts clinical effectiveness of a drug, its face validity is less important because it has predictive validity. Unfortunately even many of the available tests that predict effective antidepressant treatment in rodents do not translate to the human condition. More important for neurobiological studies of mental illness is construct validity, in which the tool or model actually reflects and measures the neural and behavioral features of the disorder. Modeling poses a particular challenge in such a complex disorder, since the neurobiology underlying depression is not clear and there is no neurochemical or neuroendocrine abnormality in depression that is sufficiently consistent to use as a diagnostic tool or to validate an animal model. For example, although several models are based on altering the HPA axis

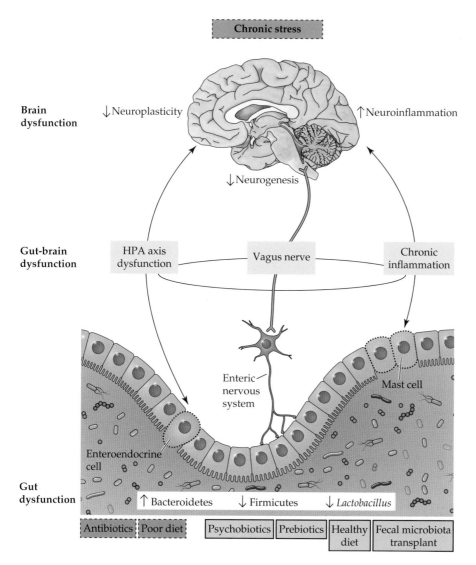

Brain dysfunction

↓Neuroplasticity   ↑Neuroinflammation

↓Neurogenesis

Gut-brain dysfunction

HPA axis dysfunction   Vagus nerve   Chronic inflammation

Enteric nervous system   Mast cell

Enteroendocrine cell

Gut dysfunction

↑ Bacteroidetes   ↓ Firmicutes   ↓ *Lactobacillus*

Antibiotics   Poor diet   Psychobiotics   Prebiotics   Healthy diet   Fecal microbiota transplant

FIGURE 18.5 **The potential involvement of the gut–brain axis in the pathophysiology of depression** Schematic shows how chronic stress, antibiotics, and poor diet (dashed outlines) may impact the enteric nervous system (ENS) and its interactions with the brain through the HPA axis, the vagus nerve, and chronic inflammation. This can lead to brain dysfunctions such as decreased neuroplasticity, neurogenesis, and neuroinflammation as seen in animal models of depression as well as in patients. Therapies such as treatment with pre/probiotics, fecal transplants from healthy donors, and healthy diet (heavy solid outlines) have the potential to mitigate these dysfunctions and improve the symptoms of depression in patients. (After S. Liang et al. 2018. *Int J Mol Sci* 19: 1592. doi.org/10.3390/ijms19061592. CC BY 4.0, creativecommons.org/licenses/by/4.0/)

function, such dysfunction is found in only a subset of depressed individuals, so construct and face validity may be questioned. Additionally, in depressed individuals many genetic variants have been identified that contribute only a small amount to the depression phenotype, which limits genetic modeling. The variable and complex symptom presentation in depression means that most often models reflect only one or a few behavioral symptoms. However, there is no reason to expect a model to reflect all the symptoms of depression, since patients vary in which symptoms they experience. Because there is a tremendous effort to both understand the neurobiology of depression and identify medications that translate to human efficacy, many models continue to be developed. Although there are too many to evaluate here, several reviews can be found that describe and provide guidelines to evaluate those models, as does Chapter 4 (Krishnan and Nestler, 2011; Abelaira et al., 2013; Logan and McClung, 2016).

Models of bipolar disorder

In general, researchers rely on the tests for screening antidepressants to model the depression phase of bipolar disorder and have focused more recently on developing models for mania. Attempts to develop models eliciting spontaneously cycling episodes of mania and depression are even more limited. Several models are based on the significance of the altered circadian rhythms observed in bipolar individuals and the fact that circadian rhythm disruption and sleep disturbances can trigger manic episodes. In one environmentally induced model, the animals are exposed to **sleep deprivation** for an extended period. At the end of the deprivation period, the animal does not immediately fall asleep but instead remains awake for about 30 minutes and demonstrates multiple manic-like symptoms, including insomnia, hyperactivity, irritability, aggressiveness, hypersexuality, and stereotypical behaviors. This sleep deprivation–induced mania resembles that observed in individuals with bipolar disorder. If lithium (a drug commonly used to treat bipolar disorder) is added to the animal's food during the sleep deprivation, some but not all of the manic behaviors are reduced. Although it has face validity, this test is time-consuming and provides only a 30-minute window of opportunity for investigation.

A second approach utilizes **mutant mice** and targets genes of the circadian clock. Altered diurnal patterns of the biological clock genes have been found in patients with bipolar disorder. Even more interesting is that the clinical state (mania or depression) seems to alter the molecular clock gene transcription. The best-studied gene is the *CLOCK* gene. In patients with bipolar disorder, a polymorphism of *CLOCK* has been associated with more frequent manic episodes, insomnia, early morning waking, and reduced need for sleep (see Logan and McClung, 2016). Mice lacking the Clock protein show manic-like behaviors such as less depression-like behavior in the forced swim test, reduced anxiety, hyperactivity, disrupted circadian rhythms, decreased sleep, and increased risk taking. Logan and McClung (2016) describe a translational behavioral task to evaluate activity and goal-directed behavior that can be used with both human participants and rodent subjects. *Clock* mutant mice show sensorimotor deficits and hyperactivity similar to those seen in manic individuals. However, the amount, pattern, and organization of activity as measured in the behavioral pattern monitor (BPM) are different from those of human patients evaluated in a similar manner. The BPM is an open field containing novel and familiar objects available to explore and interact with. Manic patients, in addition to showing high levels of activity, spend large amounts of time exploring the objects and showing linear, purposeful, goal-directed behavior. The rodents, in contrast, show more short, repetitive movements, and their patterns of activity are distinctly different. Further research may identify the neurobiological mechanisms of the similarities and differences in this translational paradigm.

One further similarity between acute manic patients and *Clock* mutant mice is their heightened sensitivity to reward. Their enhanced reward seeking has been demonstrated in multiple behavioral tasks. For instance, the animals show high levels of cocaine self-administration, greater sucrose preference, and higher consumption of alcohol than control animals in a two-bottle choice design, and they have lower reward thresholds during intracranial self-stimulation (i.e., lower amounts of electrical current are reinforcing). These behaviors are reminiscent of individuals with bipolar disorder, who frequently develop substance abuse disorders. Chronic lithium treatment, a common therapeutic approach in patients, restores most manic-like behaviors in the mice to control levels. *Clock* mutant mice provide an enticing model of bipolar disorder, and more investigation into these behaviors and into pharmacological treatments that are effective and ineffective in altering manic-like behaviors will be forthcoming.

At least some of these manic behaviors in the knockout mice have been linked to increased dopaminergic cell firing and bursting, which supports the substantial evidence of a link between the mesolimbic DA pathway and mania. In addition there are increases in DA levels, greater sensitivity to DA shown by higher firing rates, and increased numbers of DA receptors in the striatum. One elegant study demonstrated that a viral-mediated *Clock* gene transferred into the ventral tegmental area (VTA) of *Clock* mutant mice restored locomotor activity and anxiety levels to the levels of wild-type mice. Additionally, knockout of *VTA-specific Clock* gene transcription produced multiple manic-type behaviors. Furthermore, chronic lithium is known to reduce VTA function. Hence at least some manic-like behaviors are a result of *Clock* function loss in the VTA. *Clock* expression in other brain areas is likely to modulate other aspects of bipolar symptoms, so there is a need to manipulate gene expression in specific mood-regulating brain areas (Roybal et al., 2007; Landgraf et al., 2014a).

A second genetic model of bipolar disorder, also associated with circadian cycling, is transgenic mice overexpressing the enzyme glycogen synthase kinase-3 (GSK-3). The gene in individuals with bipolar disorder is associated with impulsivity and suicide risk, age of onset of the disorder, and response to treatment. In animals, the genetic manipulation produces multiple mania-like behaviors, including hyperactivity, impulsivity, and enhanced reward seeking. Perhaps most significant is that lithium inhibits GSK-3 and that its action alters circadian rhythms, which may be responsible for its mood-stabilizing effects (for further discussion see the section below on drugs for treating bipolar disorder). However, there are also distinct differences between the mice and patients with bipolar disorder. Those differences include an increased startle response and a normal, rather than blunted, corticosterone response to acute stress. For the interested reader, Logan and McClung (2016) and Young and colleagues (2011) provide reviews and assessment of pharmacological, environmental, and genetic models of bipolar disorder.

SECTION SUMMARY

■ Affective disorders, including major depression and bipolar disorder, are chronic disorders that recur in episodes over the life span. Symptoms are listed in Table 18.1.

■ The incidence of depression is approximately 15% to 20% of the population at any one time. Depression is twice as common in women and is highly comorbid with anxiety and alcohol abuse.

■ Bipolar disorder constitutes episodes of depression alternating with mania and occurs in about 1% of the population.

■ On the basis of twin studies and adoption studies, genetic contribution to the occurrence of major depression is estimated at 45%, and family history is the strongest predictor of vulnerability. Genetic contribution to bipolar disorder is significantly greater than that for depression. The diathesis–stress model of depression and other psychiatric disorders states that such genetic vulnerabilities may not manifest in the affected individual until unmasked by the experience of severe or repeated life stresses.

■ Depression is associated with abnormalities of HPA axis function: high plasma ACTH and cortisol, hypersecretion of CRF, flat circadian rhythm of cortisol, and failure of dexamethasone-induced negative feedback.

■ In depression, altered sleep architecture is seen in the following conditions: onset insomnia, reduced slow-wave sleep, early onset of REM sleep, more frequent and longer REM episodes early in the night, and more vigorous eye movement during REM.

■ Individuals with mania sleep very little without loss of energy. In symptom-free patients, sleep deprivation initiates a manic episode. Because many rhythms are irregular, research into the *CLOCK* gene has increased.

■ Emerging studies are beginning to show a relationship between altered functioning of the gut–brain axis and the manifestations of psychiatric disorders such as depression and anxiety. As this field evolves, more large-scale clinical trials are needed to determine causal links, mechanisms of action, and possibilities for therapeutic intervention.

■ Modeling complex psychiatric disorders poses multiple challenges, and each model focuses on one or a few symptoms. Each varies in face, predictive, and construct validity.

■ Exposing rodents to sleep deprivation and creating mutant mice with genes that affect the biological clock and circadian cycling are two means used to produce models of mania in rodents.

18.2 Neurochemical Basis of Affective Disorders

The earliest attempt to develop a cohesive theory of the neurochemical basis of affective disorders was the **monoamine hypothesis**. The monoamine hypothesis originated with the observation that reserpine, a drug effective in reducing high blood pressure, induces depression as a side effect in a significant number of patients. The drug prevents the packaging of neurotransmitters into vesicles, leaving the molecules in the cytoplasm, where monoamine oxidase (MAO) degrades them. In this way, reserpine treatment produces empty vesicles and reduces the levels of DA, NE, and 5-HT (all monoamines). Early researchers wondered if it could be that the reduced level of monoamines in the central nervous system (CNS) is responsible for the depressed mood. This possibility seemed increasingly likely when the

mechanism of action of two types of antidepressants, monoamine oxidase inhibitors (MAOIs) and tricyclic antidepressants (TCAs), was considered. Despite their varied synaptic action, the antidepressant drugs acutely increase the function of NE or 5-HT or both. In addition, drugs in both classes reverse reserpine-induced reduction in motor activity—a popular animal model at the time for screening antidepressant agents. The drug studies were combined with early data showing reduced levels of the NE metabolite 3-methoxy-4-hydroxy-phenylglycol (MHPG), suggesting lowered NE synaptic activity, and reduced levels of 5-hydroxyindoleacetic acid (5-HIAA), suggesting lowered 5-HT synaptic activity, in the CSF, plasma, or urine of some depressed patients. These measures suggest low utilization of the monoamines; however, these differences were not consistently found. Nevertheless, this type of evidence formed the basis of the early monoamine hypothesis of affective disorders (Schildkraut, 1965).

Although many new questions have challenged the original hypothesis, when it was first proposed, the best evidence supported the idea that depression is associated with low levels of monoamines, whereas mania coincides with excess monoamine activity. Because reserpine acts on all monoamines and the early antidepressants also were nonselective in increasing NE and 5-HT, it really was not clear which of the neurotransmitters was most important in the etiology of depression. Unfortunately, we have not yet resolved this issue, and more and more researchers are coming to the conclusion that both of these amines, as well as DA, are likely to play some role in clinical depression, and other neurotransmitters may also contribute to the complex pattern of symptoms. Increasing evidence suggests that there is anatomical and functional interaction between noradrenergic neurons in the locus coeruleus (LC) and serotonergic neurons originating in the midbrain raphe. Each of the two transmitter systems seems to be capable of modulating the other. In the meantime, it is important to remember that neurotransmitter systems should be considered not in isolation but instead as a part of a complex network of interacting neurons.

Although we now know that the monoamine hypothesis is overly simple, it provided an important theoretical model that was the focus of enormous amounts of research over many years. It provided the basis for new drug development, for the creation and testing of new animal models, and for the formulation of new questions that could not be answered within the old theory. Keep in mind that although our thinking about depression and antidepressant drugs has evolved since 1965, the most commonly used classical antidepressants still target 5-HT and NE. As is always the case in good science, new and often conflicting evidence must be accounted for, and old theories modified, as more sensitive biochemical and imaging techniques are developed.

The monoamine hypothesis as originally stated was based heavily on acute antidepressant drug effects. It is too simplistic to account for the complex syndrome of affective disorders, and it fails to resolve several discrepancies. The most important of these is the discrepancy in time between the rapid neurochemical actions of antidepressants and the slow onset of clinical effects over several weeks. This disparity in time course clearly demonstrates that the acute enhancement of monoamine function is *not* the neurochemical basis for therapeutic activity and that downstream effects such as changes in synaptic plasticity and synapse remodeling are more central to antidepressant effects (Duman and Duman, 2015). Despite the vast improvements in technology, newer testable models of the neurobiological basis of affective disorders still use three basic approaches: (1) developing animal models including gene manipulation, (2) evaluating the mechanism of action of effective drug treatment, and (3) examining neurobiological and genetic differences in patient populations. It has been and remains a long and difficult process. Nevertheless, clarifying the neurobiological mechanisms of major depression will ultimately pave the way for the discovery of new and more effective treatments (Belmaker and Agam, 2008).

Serotonin dysfunction contributes to mood disorders

Serotonin continues to be a focus of research because it has a significant influence on sensitivity to pain, emotionality, and response to negative consequences as well as to reward. The effects of 5-HT on sleep, eating, and thermoregulation are likewise well documented and intuitively seem to contribute to depressive symptoms. There is no solid evidence of abnormal 5-HT function in depressed patients, but one indication of function is the measurement of the principal synaptic metabolite of serotonin, 5-HIAA. It is generally assumed that high 5-HIAA reflects increased function of serotonergic neurons, and low 5-HIAA the converse. Lower 5-HIAA levels have been found in post-mortem brains of depressed individuals, most consistently in the brains of suicide victims. Several studies have also reported lower 5-HIAA levels in the CSF of depressed individuals.

The newest techniques to modify serotonin function include creating knockout mice that lack tryptophan hydroxylase, the rate-limiting enzyme involved in 5-HT synthesis, which depletes stores of 5-HT. Other manipulations include knocking out specific 5-HT receptor subtypes. Among the behavioral outcomes are irritability and aggression, increased sensitivity to pain, modified anxiety-like behavior, and altered patterns of eating and satiety. Details of these 5-HT manipulations are provided in Chapter 6 as well as in a review by Mosienko and colleagues (2015). Parallels in humans suffering from major affective disorders can be easily seen.

MEASURING 5-HT IN HUMANS Unfortunately there has never been solid evidence of abnormal 5-HT function in depressed patients because, as mentioned previously, there are often inconsistent results due to patient variables in symptoms, duration of illness, history of drug use, and other lifestyle issues. One of the most intriguing ways to investigate the role of serotonin in depressive disorders is the **tryptophan depletion challenge**, in which individuals consume a tryptophan-deficient amino acid cocktail that transiently reduces 5-HT levels in the brain by 70% to 80% because tryptophan is necessary for 5-HT synthesis. It should be pointed out that although brain synthesis and metabolism are reduced, it is not yet clear whether the procedure alters 5-HT release and synaptic signaling. Tryptophan depletion of unmedicated patients in remission causes a relapse of depression symptoms. The same depletion leads to a depressed mood in healthy individuals who have a family history of depression, but not in healthy people without such a family history. These findings together indicate that merely having low levels of brain serotonin does not cause depression, except in vulnerable individuals. Hence sensitivity to reduced brain serotonin represents a *vulnerability (or risk) factor* and may be considered a trait abnormality in depression. In addition, those patients who were medicated with certain classes of antidepressant drugs also showed a relapse following tryptophan depletion, demonstrating that at least some antidepressant drug effects rely on 5-HT availability.

The identification of a relatively common gene variation, a polymorphism within the **serotonin reuptake transporter** (**SERT**) gene, has generated a good deal of interest, particularly because it is a key target of many commonly used antidepressants such as the selective serotonin reuptake inhibitors (SSRIs) like fluoxetine (Prozac). The SERT polymorphism produces two versions (or, alleles) of the SERT gene: the long (*l*) and short (*s*) allele. Studies have shown that that the short allele, whether present on one chromosome (*s/l*) or both chromosomes (*s/s*), is associated with significantly reduced level and function of the transporter in early development, but not adulthood. It is thought that this may lead to altered neurodevelopment within 5-HT circuits that could set the stage for the development of depression later in life. Although the short allele has been found by some researchers to be associated with depressive disorder, the relationship occurs only in association with increased stressful life events. In one prominent and highly acclaimed early study by Caspi and colleagues (2003), the researchers evaluated almost 850 people over a period of 20 years. They found that the likelihood of both depression and suicide attempts increased with the number of significant stressful life events. However, in both cases the effects of stressful events were moderated, or buffered, in those individuals with two long alleles. Those with two short alleles were most likely to develop symptoms, while heterozygous (*s/l*) individuals were intermediate. The stress–gene interaction may help to explain why not all people experiencing stressful events ultimately develop depression. It also would explain why not all people with the short allele develop depression. Additionally, patients with two long alleles have shown better and longer-lasting treatment outcomes with antidepressant medication than patients with a single or two short alleles. Despite the seemingly convincing evidence for the significance of the SERT genotype in depressive behaviors, at least one meta-analysis that examined 31 data sets found no evidence for an association of the SERT genotype–stress interaction with elevated risk for depression (Culverhouse et al., 2017). Outcomes such as these teach us that despite their difficulty, replication studies are critical to good science. However, despite the failure to replicate the earlier findings, the overall approach of evaluating the interaction of genotype with environmental events to predict mental illness has been embraced because of frustration with earlier lack of progress in gene identification for mental illness.

Receptor binding studies in post-mortem brain samples from unmedicated individuals with mood disorders have usually found *increased* density of postsynaptic 5-HT$_2$ receptors, which may be considered a compensatory response to low serotonergic activity. In accord with this finding, animal studies show that chronic antidepressant treatment with a variety of compounds leads to a fairly consistent decrease (down-regulation) in 5-HT$_2$ receptors. Only the clinically effective use of chronic electroconvulsive therapy (ECT) fails to reduce these receptors. Further discussion of the role of receptor subtypes and variations based on brain region is beyond the scope of this chapter.

ANTIDEPRESSANT EFFECTS ON 5-HT IN ANIMALS

In addition to evaluating depressed patients, we can look at the long-term effects of antidepressant drugs on 5-HT by using animals. Because SSRIs are the most commonly prescribed drugs, research into their cellular and molecular mechanism of action has become a focal point. Much of the research stems from the fact that although they are most often prescribed, not only do they take weeks of chronic treatment to be effective, but 60% to 70% of patients fail to achieve complete remission and 30% to 40% show no significant response. Animal studies have shown that most antidepressants increase 5-HT by blocking reuptake through SERT or inhibiting MAO. When administered acutely, the increased synaptic 5-HT has postsynaptic action but also acts on 5-HT$_{1A}$ autoreceptors to slow the firing rate of cells and to reduce 5-HT synthesis as well as release. Therefore, initially the two effects tend to cancel one another out. Overall, lower neuronal activity reduces metabolism of 5-HT to 5-HIAA, indicating reduced

turnover (**FIGURE 18.6**). However, chronic treatment results in tolerance and reduces the action of the autoreceptor through down-regulation that results in gradual increases in the amount of 5-HT in the synapse. SERT blockade is still effective, so at this point the two actions both produce an increase in 5-HT. Since the full therapeutic effects of antidepressants take several weeks to develop, the delay in autoreceptor desensitization and subsequent enhanced 5-HT activity may be in part responsible for the delayed therapeutic onset or explain the limited efficacy (Blier et al., 1990). Several pieces of evidence suggest the importance of 5-HT$_{1A}$ autoreceptors in depression. For instance, genetic and imaging studies show that individuals with a higher density of presynaptic 5-HT$_{1A}$ receptors are more vulnerable to depression and suicide and tend to show less response to antidepressant drugs. Further evidence for a role of presynaptic 5-HT$_{1A}$ comes from several studies suggesting that reducing the expression of the presynaptic autoreceptors in mice, which would be analogous to drug-induced down-regulation (see Celada et al., 2013), elicits antidepressant-like behavioral effects. Additionally, acute 5-HT$_{1A}$ autoreceptor knockdown (an RNA interference technique that silences the activity of specific genes without totally abolishing the gene in adult mice) did not change *basal* extracellular 5-HT in the medial prefrontal cortex (mPFC) as measured by microdialysis. However, when animals were exposed to a forced swim test, they showed robust antidepressant behaviors that were accompanied by elevations of prefrontal 5-HT and enhanced 5-HT release, possibly resulting from stress-induced activation of the apparently sensitized 5-HT neurons. Other studies have similarly shown that silencing the 5-HT$_{1A}$ autoreceptor produces 5-HT–mediated antidepressant effects (Ferres-Coy et al., 2013).

A more recent study suggests that the autoreceptor down-regulation hypothesis of SSRI action may be more complex than originally believed. In their meta-analysis of 42 in vivo microdialysis studies of chronic SSRIs, Fritze and colleagues (2017) found that the time course of enhanced 5-HT release varied with brain region. In support of the 2- to 3-week time course of down-regulation of autoreceptors, they found that in frontal cortex, after an initial reduction in extracellular 5-HT during week 1 of treatment, the levels steadily increased over the subsequent 2 weeks. In contrast, in hippocampus, prefrontal cortex (PFC), VTA, and nucleus accumbens (NAcc), the extracellular 5-HT increased within 3 days, long before autoreceptor desensitization would have occurred. Clearly multiple adaptive mechanisms are needed to explain the slow onset of SSRI clinical effectiveness (see the neurotrophic hypothesis in the section on neurobiological models of depression).

Arguing against the importance of the autoreceptor down-regulation, Richardson-Jones and colleagues

FIGURE 18.6 Effects of anti-depressants on serotonergic cells (A) The initial effects of reuptake blockade include increased 5-HT in the synapse and activity at both post-synaptic receptors and autoreceptors. Autoreceptor activation reduces the rate of firing of the cell as well as the rate of synthesis and release of 5-HT and subsequently also reduces the rate of formation of 5-HIAA. (B) With repeated administration, the autore-ceptors become less sensitive, and their inhibition of serotonergic neurons decreases, which leads to an increase in 5-HT function and 5-HIAA. However, the increase in 5-HT is perhaps just the initial step, and subsequent changes downstream, postsynaptically, are re-quired, including hippocampal neuro-genesis and functional remodeling of corticolimbic circuits.

(A) Acute effects of antidepressants

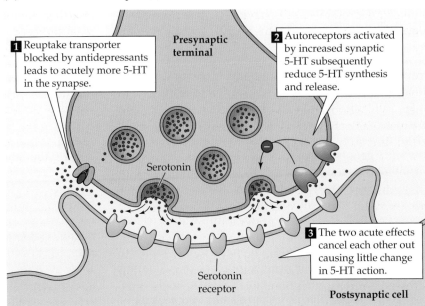

1 Reuptake transporter blocked by antidepressants leads to acutely more 5-HT in the synapse.

Presynaptic terminal

2 Autoreceptors activated by increased synaptic 5-HT subsequently reduce 5-HT synthesis and release.

Serotonin

3 The two acute effects cancel each other out causing little change in 5-HT action.

Serotonin receptor

Postsynaptic cell

(B) Chronic effects of antidepressants

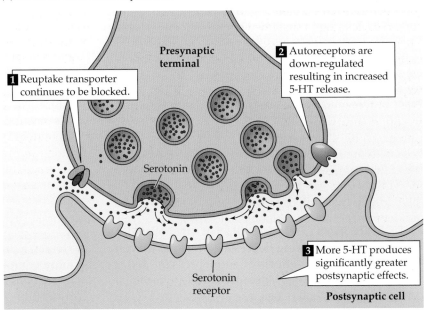

Presynaptic terminal

1 Reuptake transporter continues to be blocked.

2 Autoreceptors are down-regulated resulting in increased 5-HT release.

Serotonin

Serotonin receptor

3 More 5-HT produces significantly greater postsynaptic effects.

Postsynaptic cell

(2010), using novel manipulations in adult mice, were able to suppress 5-HT$_{1A}$ presynaptic receptors selec-tively but leave intact 5-HT$_{1A}$ postsynaptic receptors. Their study comprised two groups of mice: those with normal levels of the autoreceptor, and those where the levels were low. During chronic administration of fluoxetine, the low-autoreceptor mice showed faster increases (8 days) in raphe firing rate and subsequent increases in 5-HT function in the hippocampus and PFC, as would be expected since there were many fewer inhibitory autoreceptors. They also showed an antidepressant response in tests of behavioral de-spair (see Chapter 4). However, the mice with normal

autoreceptor densities ultimately reached the same level of serotonin function after 26 days when the auto-receptors were desensitized, but they still did not show a behavioral antidepressant response. The authors con-clude that 5-HT$_{1A}$ autoreceptor desensitization cannot be the explanation for fluoxetine's antidepressant ef-fect. Instead they suggest that serotonergic function existing before treatment begins may be the critical factor and that individuals who have a higher baseline functioning of the serotonin system are most likely to benefit from antidepressant treatment.

One recently tested hypothesis is that the outcome of elevating 5-HT with antidepressants is highly dependent on the environment in which it occurs. The researchers induced depression-like behavior in mice through 14 days of stress exposure. For the next 21 days the animals received fluoxetine or vehicle while being maintained in either an enriched environment or a stressful one. There were a number of significant differences among fluoxetine-treated animals, depending on the environment. While fluoxetine treatment in the enriched environment had antidepressant effects, the same treatment administered to animals living in a stressful situation showed a worsening of depression-like behaviors. BDNF levels and several proteins (e.g., p11) implicated in modulating depression were enhanced in the hippocampus of those mice in the enriched environment but remained unchanged under stress. Oddly, fluoxetine did not enhance BDNF-induced neurogenesis in the enriched conditions as would be expected; however, the drug treatment *reduced* proliferation of cells in the stressed animals. Additionally, fluoxetine apparently enhanced glucocorticoid feedback on the HPA axis, leading to reduced stress hormones in the enriched environment. In contrast, the animals in the stressed condition showed blunted negative feedback by glucocorticoids, leading to sustained stress hormone release. These and other differences reported by the authors demonstrate that the effects of fluoxetine vary depending on the living conditions of the subjects. They interpret their findings by saying that the SSRI-induced 5-HT enhancement leads to plasticity that provides the opportunity for either improvement or deterioration based on the environment. Practically speaking, human living environments are not easy to change, but the authors suggest that cognitive therapy could teach individuals to reduce the impact of a stressful environment and in that way improve the effectiveness of the antidepressant therapy (Alboni et al., 2017).

Norepinephrine activity is altered by antidepressants

Norepinephrine also continues to be a focus of research because it has a known role in neuroendocrine function, reward mechanisms, attention and arousal, and response to stress, each of which may contribute to the symptoms of the affective disorders. Regrettably, results of studies with depressed patients are difficult to interpret. Levels of the principal noradrenergic metabolite MHPG in the body fluids of depressed patients have been found to be higher, lower, or no different from those of controls. In general, MHPG is usually found to be elevated in patients undergoing treatment, suggesting an increase in turnover with antidepressant use. Animal studies show that chronic antidepressant treatment leads to down-regulation of both β-receptors and α_2-autoreceptors. Unfortunately, when both α_2- and β-receptors are down-regulated, they have opposite effects on adrenergic synapses. Since α_2-autoreceptors

acutely reduce noradrenergic cell function by decreasing the rate of firing and reducing NE release, α_2-autoreceptor down-regulation increases both of these cell functions. With the use of α_2-challenge measures, the majority of experiments show that chronic, but not acute, antidepressant treatment produces a reduction in autoreceptor responsiveness that coincides with the increase in turnover described earlier.

One of the most consistent findings regarding catecholamine response to chronic antidepressant treatment is the down-regulation of β-receptors, which requires 7 to 21 days of treatment—a lag that parallels that seen in the onset of therapeutic response in depressed patients. Similar results occur with many of the antidepressant drugs tested, including TCAs, MAOIs, SSRIs, and second-generation antidepressants. ECT, lithium (used to treat bipolar disorder) under some conditions, and even REM sleep deprivation that has antidepressant action seem to reduce β-receptors. However, not all antidepressants reduce β-receptors, and yohimbine, an α_2-autoreceptor antagonist that enhances the antidepressant-induced down-regulation of β-receptors, does not enhance the antidepressant effects as would be expected.

To help clarify these discrepant findings by using human brain tissue, Rivero and colleagues (2014), using post-mortem PFC of depressed nonmedicated individuals, showed elevations in both α_2- and β_1-adrenergic receptors, and in agreement with earlier studies, they found significant down-regulation of β_1-receptors in those individuals who had been treated with antidepressant medication. However, contrary to earlier reports, they found that people who had been treated with antidepressant drugs showed little down-regulation of α_2-autoreceptors. Interpretation of their findings is complicated by the fact that the post-mortem tissue was from suicide victims who were clinically depressed and that they had been treated with a variety of antidepressant drugs over their lifetimes. Nevertheless, among the most consistent differences in noradrenergic receptor binding is that untreated depressed individuals and those with bipolar disorder had increased density of α_2-autoreceptors.

The importance of NE to the actions of antidepressant drugs can be demonstrated in patients treated with adrenergic antidepressants (i.e., NE reuptake inhibitors), who show relapse of symptoms if NE synthesis is prevented by depletion of the NE precursor tyrosine. Clearly NE is necessary for those drugs to be effective. A similar NE synthesis inhibition does not cause relapse in patients treated with the serotonergic reuptake inhibitors.

Norepinephrine and serotonin modulate one another

Because the most consistent chronic effects of antidepressants are down-regulation of β-receptors and 5-HT$_2$

receptors and an enhanced physiological response to 5-HT, Sulser (1989) proposed a "serotonin–norepineph-rine" hypothesis of depression. Both anatomical and functional interactions exist between the noradrenergic neurons originating in the LC and the serotonergic neurons in the raphe nuclei (**FIGURE 18.7**), and each system is capable of modulating the other. Destroying 5-HT terminals with the neurotoxin 5,6-dihydroxytryptamine prevents the down-regulation of β-receptors that follows chronic antidepressant treatment. Others have shown that 5-HT agonists can indirectly stimulate the noradrenergic system, causing β-receptor down-regulation, and that increased noradrenergic function may also increase electrophysiological activity in the raphe nuclei. Sulser

(A) Norepinephrine

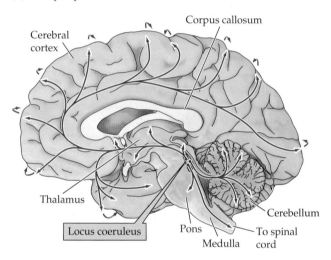

(B) Serotonin

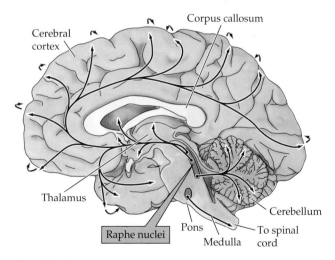

FIGURE 18.7 **Two monoamine pathways in the human brain** This schematic diagram shows noradrenergic pathways originating in the locus coeruleus (A) and serotonergic pathways originating in the raphe nuclei (B). The overlapping nature and interaction of the two neurotransmitter systems are very apparent.

suggests that NE function involves multiple feedback loops that use a variety of neurotransmitters, including 5-HT, ACh, DA, GABA, and opioid peptides. For more information on the contribution of these neurotransmitters to the symptoms of depression, refer to several excellent reviews (Ordway et al., 2002; Maletic and Raison, 2009).

Neurobiological models of depression

In addition to the consideration of neurotransmitter function in depression, other hypotheses pose alternative neurobiological models that are now being tested. For years it has been known that there are multiple structural and functional abnormalities in the brains of clinically depressed individuals (reviewed by aan het Rot et al., 2009). Neuroimaging studies have focused particularly on reduced hippocampal volume because it has been the most consistent finding, but other brain regions also show reductions, including the amygdala, ventral striatum, anterior cingulate cortex, orbitofrontal cortex, and PFC. Some of these regions show decreased metabolic activity as well, but others show increased function, based on PET or fMRI scans. For example, blood flow changes in the brains of patients with depression, compared with normal blood flow in controls, show increased activity in part of the medial orbitofrontal cortex and in the amygdala, brain areas important in emotion regulation (**FIGURE 18.8**). Increased metabolic activity in the amygdala is correlated with the severity of depression and returns to normal after antidepressant drug treatment. Increased activity of the orbitofrontal cortex may reflect the individual's effort to control unpleasant thoughts and emotions (Drevets, 2001).

Increasing evidence suggests that visualizing isolated brain structures may not be as important as evaluating the connectivity among the regions of what might be called depression circuits. In fact, a common finding has been the lack of cortical control over limbic structures that leaves the individual more vulnerable to stress, impulsivity, cognitive dysfunction, anhedonia, and emotional dysregulation. Also, resting-state fMRI (see Chapter 4) has shown that successful treatment is associated with increased connectivity between PFC and limbic areas and with restoring the cortical inhibitory control (Dichter et al., 2015). Other research using resting-state fMRI techniques has demonstrated that depressed individuals show more highly coupled connectivity between nodes in the brain termed the default-mode network (DMN). The DMN has been shown to function in psychological rumination, or deep, repeated thoughts or musings on more trivial aspects of life such as daily decisions, to more profound existential questions about one's place in the world. The DMN is functionally anticorrelated with the salience network, which when activated silences the DMN and acts to promote awareness and goal-directed behavior. Thus, more robust DMN connectivity in depressed

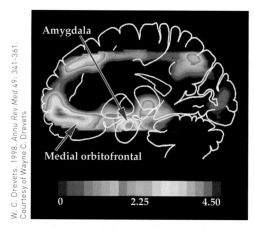

W. C. Drevets. 1998. *Annu Rev Med 49*: 341-361. Courtesy of Wayne C. Drevets

FIGURE 18.8 PET scan of blood flow in the brain of a patient with unipolar depression Increased metabolic activity occurs in the amygdala and the medial orbitofrontal cortex. Activation is shown in red and orange.

individuals may underlie their regression to a state of constant worry, negative thinking, and low motivation to perform daily tasks. Critically, it has been shown that antidepressant treatments normalize DMN function. This is illustrated in **FIGURE 18.9**, which shows an fMRI image of the DMN comparing connectivity strength between patients with mild, persistent depression (dysthymic disorder) and healthy control individuals, and how increased DMN connectivity in patients is normalized to control levels following antidepressant treatment (Posner et al., 2013). However, more work is needed to determine whether DMN connectivity can be used as a biomarker for depression in patients.

Altered connectivity in depression does of course depend on axonal integrity, but of much greater significance are the identified synaptic abnormalities such as altered dendritic complexity and density of dendritic spines. Of importance is the role of stress in producing dendritic atrophy and dendritic spine loss in multiple brain areas that show significant plasticity in response to environmental events. These areas include the hippocampus and PFC. However, other brain regions, such

as the orbitofrontal cortex and amygdala, show *enhanced* dendritic arborization. A more detailed discussion of stress-induced synaptic remodeling was presented in Chapter 17. For more details on the role of dendritic arborization in both the onset and treatment of depression, as well as the importance of sex hormones in that plasticity, refer to Duman and Duman (2015) or McEwen (2010). The importance of stress to these brain changes has led to the formulation of the glucocorticoid hypothesis and a related BDNF or neurotrophic hypothesis.

The **glucocorticoid hypothesis** focuses on the stress-related neuroendocrine abnormalities that are frequently found in depressed individuals (see the section on biological rhythms earlier in the chapter). McEwen and coworkers (2016) provides an excellent discussion of how stress hormones and lifestyle behaviors interact to promote pathophysiology of the brain and the rest of the body. In the depressed individual, the abnormal secretion of CRF from the hypothalamus is apparently responsible for the hypersecretion of ACTH from the pituitary and cortisol from the adrenal cortex. The hypothalamic CRF neurons are normally controlled by other areas of the CNS: the amygdala, which is central to emotional responses, normally stimulates the CRF circuit, and the hippocampus has inhibitory control (see Box 2.5). The hippocampus has glucocorticoid receptors that when activated by high levels of glucocorticoids (such as cortisol) help to inhibit CRF release from the hypothalamus, and is therefore central to the glucocorticoid feedback loop that returns glucocorticoid levels to normal. However, when stress is intense and/or prolonged, glucocorticoid levels remain high, and as shown in animal studies, hippocampal neurons become damaged and no longer respond. The principal damage includes decreases in dendritic branches and loss of dendritic spines, both of which occur in the PFC as well as in the hippocampus. Additionally, the elevated cortisol reduces the formation of new hippocampal cells (neurogenesis).

Hippocampal cell loss seen in depression means reduced response to circulating cortisol and loss of inhibition of the HPA axis, inducing further

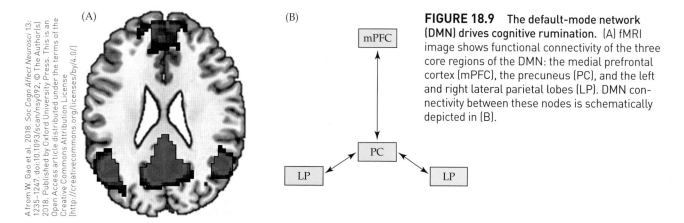

FIGURE 18.9 The default-mode network (DMN) drives cognitive rumination. [A] fMRI image shows functional connectivity of the three core regions of the DMN: the medial prefrontal cortex (mPFC), the precuneus (PC), and the left and right lateral parietal lobes (LP). DMN connectivity between these nodes is schematically depicted in (B).

glucocorticoid-mediated hippocampal cell loss in a perpetual cycle that is thought to underlie the gradual worsening of symptoms and resistance to therapy in patients with lifelong depression. This hypothesis is supported by studies showing small reductions in hippocampal volume are found in MRI scans of depressed patients. Further, antidepressant drugs and ECT reduce CRF levels in depressed patients. In animals, several types of antidepressant drugs also reverse the loss of dendrites in the hippocampus and other brain areas and increase neurogenesis in the hippocampus. Finally, intracerebroventricular administration of CRF elicits stress-related behavioral and physiological responses in animals, including the expected enhancement of cortisol levels and sympathetic nervous system activity. CRF also elicits behaviors in animals that are closely correlated with symptoms of clinical depression in humans: arousal, insomnia, decreased eating, reduced sexual activity, and anxiety. The glucocorticoid hypothesis of affective disorders is the basis for the clinical tests of CRF receptor antagonists, which showed early promise as antidepressants in small pilot studies (Holsboer and Ising, 2008). Further development of these compounds and large-scale clinical trials are still ongoing to determine their antidepressant efficacy and side-effect profiles.

A second, closely related neurobiological model looks at potential mechanisms underlying the hippocampal cell loss following stress-induced glucocorticoid elevation: deficits in neurotrophic factors such as **BDNF** (**brain-derived neurotrophic factor**). Neurotrophic factors are important proteins that are needed during brain development, but they also regulate changes in synapses and cell survival in adult brains. The **neurotrophic hypothesis** suggests that low BDNF may be responsible for the loss of dendritic branches and spines in the hippocampus and PFC and for reduced neurogenesis in the hippocampus. Furthermore, antidepressants may protect vulnerable cells by preventing the decrease in BDNF. Evidence in support can be summarized as follows: (1) chronic stress reduces BDNF in the hippocampus in rats, (2) chronic but not acute antidepressant treatment increases BDNF in both animals and humans, and (3) antidepressants prevent stress-induced reductions in BDNF and neuronal atrophy (**FIGURE 18.10**). Thus, it seems that treatment with antidepressants reverts depressed individuals to a state of plasticity seen in juveniles, which facilitates alterations in neural circuits underlying symptom improvement (Castrén and Hen, 2013).

A *causal* connection between BDNF-enhanced neurogenesis and antidepressant effects is more difficult to determine. However, direct demonstration that enhanced neurogenesis is necessary for antidepressant action was initially provided by Santarelli and colleagues (2003) using mice and several animal models of depression. The 90% reduction in hippocampal cell

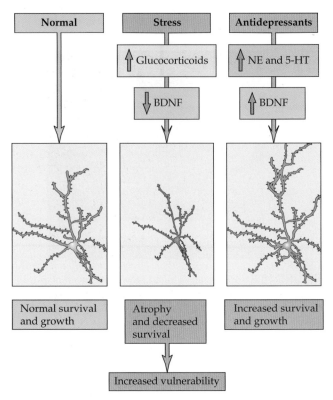

FIGURE 18.10 **Effect of stress and antidepressant treatment on BDNF in hippocampal cells** The box on the left shows a typical hippocampal cell in the CA3 area. Chronic stress (center) elevates glucocorticoids and decreases BDNF, which may be responsible for the loss of dendritic trees and may make the cells more vulnerable to a variety of detrimental factors. Chronic antidepressant treatment (right) not only alters monoamine transmission but also increases BDNF. BDNF may protect the cells from further damage and may help repair those already damaged. (After R. S. Duman et al. 1999. *Biol Psychiatry* 46: 1181–1191.)

proliferation following focused irradiation prevented both fluoxetine- and imipramine-induced neurogenesis as well as their antidepressant action in the chronic unpredictable stress model of depression. Although this finding is a critical component of the neurogenesis hypothesis, cautious interpretation is needed because irradiation does not act selectively to interfere with the production of neurons, and other damaging effects occur. Nevertheless, more recent studies supported the earlier work and indicated that antidepressants may impact neurons in several ways: by enhancing proliferation of new cells, by protecting them from apoptosis and atrophy, and by strengthening neuropil development by increasing the number and length of dendrites. Each of these changes is influenced by neurotrophins; however, how the cellular changes contribute to function at the circuit level and how that translates into changes in affect in depressed individuals remain unclear (Balu and Lucki, 2009). If neuroprotective effects are central to antidepressant action, an additional treatment approach might be to use modulation of epigenetic events (**BOX 18.1**). As you learned earlier, environmental events, including the stress of early abuse or neglect, can cause

BOX 18.1 ■ THE CUTTING EDGE

Epigenetic Modifications in Psychopathology and Treatment

You learned in Chapter 17 that genes and environment interact to determine the tendency to express anxiety. Environmental stress, including parental abuse or neglect, causes long-lasting epigenetic changes to the genes of several components of the stress circuit, leading to enhanced CRF expression in the amygdala and hypothalamus and decreased glucocorticoid receptors in the hippocampus. These and other changes contribute to stress circuit programming during development, making it more sensitive, and increasing the vulnerability to both anxiety disorders and depression in the adult. Given the close relationship between stress and depression, this outcome is not surprising.

Other genes of significance are also modified by stress-induced chromatin remodeling. Chromatin remodeling or rearrangement occurs when the small proteins known as histones, which are complexed with DNA, are altered by any one of several chemical changes brought about by enzymes. These chemical changes, including methylation, acetylation, phosphorylation, and others less well studied, occur on the amino acid tails of the histone molecules. These changes either make the chromatin more tightly packed, which limits gene expression by physically limiting the access of transcription factors, or loosen the chromatin structure, enhancing transcription. A delicate balance of epigenetic factors maintains normal cell function. Dysregulation in the form of either too much expression of a gene or too little may be the basis of pathological conditions. Initial evidence for the role of epigenetics in psychiatric disorders was based on findings that treatment of chronically stressed mice—which models depressive symptoms (Chapter 4)—with a histone deacetylase (HDAC) inhibitor provided antidepressant relief to

the animals. Further, local infusion of these inhibitors into the hippocampus, nucleus accumbens, amygdala, or prefrontal cortex yielded similar antidepressant outcomes, highlighting regional specificity of these effects to circuits known to be impacted in depression. These findings prompted further research on how early life stressors modify chromatin structure to affect gene expression changes that underlie psychiatric disorders such as depression, and whether antidepressants reverse these changes as a mechanism of their therapeutic action (reviewed in Nestler et al., 2016).

Among many other gene expression changes, chronic social defeat stress (Chapter 4) causes a long-lasting reduction in BDNF expression that represents one of the hallmark alterations in depression as discussed in this chapter. Later studies found that this likely occurs as a result of epigenetic modification of the BDNF gene by increasing histone methylation more than fourfold. The methylation of histone induces a more "closed" chromatin state that reduces transcription of the gene for BDNF (see **FIGURE**). Chronic, but not acute, antidepressant treatment with imipramine reverses the stress-induced depression-like symptoms but, somewhat surprisingly, does not

(Continued)

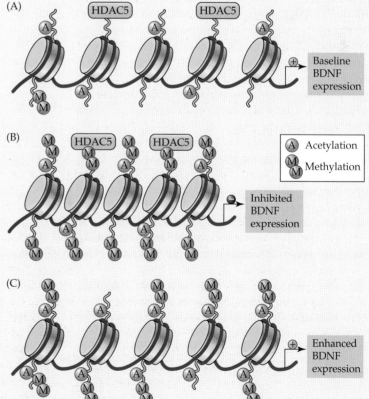

Chromatin remodeling (A) Under nonstress conditions, the chromatin of the BDNF gene has low levels of acetylation and virtually no methylation, providing a basal BDNF expression. (B) The histone methylation following prolonged episodes of defeat stress induces a tighter envelope of chromatin proteins and blocks BDNF gene expression. (C) Chronic antidepressant use increases acetylation without altering the chronic stress–induced methylation, which produces a "relaxation" of the repressed chromatin, encouraging transcription of the BDNF gene, which may be necessary for the antidepressant effects. HDAC5, histone deacetylase 5. (After N. Tsankova et al. 2007. *Nat Rev Neurosci* 8: 355–367. doi.org/10.1038/nrn2132)

reverse the stress-induced methylation of histone. Instead, it apparently reverses the suppression of BDNF expression by increasing the level of histone acetylation through the action of histone acetylase. The acetylation of histone induces a more "open" chromatin state, resulting in an imipramine-induced increase in BDNF that correlates with symptom improvement.

The importance of down-regulation of HDAC to antidepressant action has been investigated further as a potential approach to treating mood disorders (see Misztak et al., 2018). If HDAC inhibitors could reverse dysfunctional epigenetic changes, neurotrophic proteins could be elevated and could enhance

the neural connectivity that is necessary for behavioral adaptation. Several preclinical studies have now demonstrated antidepressant effects in rodents after intracerebral injection of several different HDAC inhibitors. Further, the HDAC inhibitors have been shown to reverse oxidative stress–induced neuronal injury in vitro. Oxidative stress is characteristic of individuals with bipolar disorder, who often find lithium and valproate, drugs that reduce oxidative stress, to be therapeutic. Clearly this early research has promise, and the role of epigenetic acetylation in both pathophysiology of mood disorders and therapeutics deserves further study.

---

long-lasting epigenetic changes that alter brain development and increase vulnerability to a variety of disorders. Hence early intervention to reverse the epigenetic effects of stress may enhance resilience.

Since the production of BDNF is dependent on the cyclic adenosine monophosphate (cAMP) second-messenger system, it is significant that *chronic* antidepressant drug treatment up-regulates several components of the system in the hippocampus and frontal cortex. This up-regulation occurs despite the down-regulation of the β-adrenergic receptors and 5-HT receptors that are coupled to the cAMP cascade (**FIGURE 18.11**). Upregulation occurs in several stages of the cascade, including enhanced coupling between stimulatory G_s protein and adenylyl cyclase, an increase in activated cAMP-dependent protein kinase A (PKA), and an increase in phosphorylation of cAMP response element binding protein (CREB), which is a transcription factor that induces protein synthesis of BDNF and other proteins.

Although at present there is no way to directly inject BDNF into humans as a test for antidepressant activity, intracerebral injection of BDNF or CREB into the hippocampus in rodents produced antidepressant effects in the forced swim and learned helplessness tests (Shirayama et al., 2002). Brain levels of CREB are low in depressed patients and are increased by most antidepressant drugs after several weeks. It is tempting to try

to develop therapeutic methods that might rapidly enhance CREB and the neurotrophic factors. One might consider that enhancing any portion of the cAMP cascade could ultimately enhance BDNF production and relieve depression. One approach involves inhibiting **phosphodiesterase (PDE)**, the enzyme that normally degrades cAMP to 5'-AMP. Inhibition of PDE would

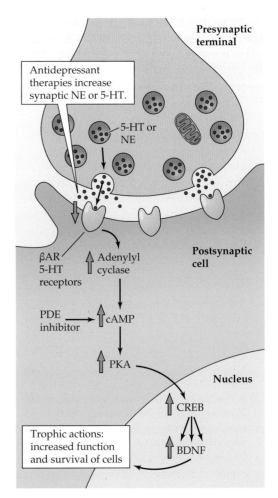

FIGURE 18.11   Up-regulation of second-messenger pathway by chronic antidepressant treatment   The increase in NE and 5-HT caused by acute antidepressant treatment produces down-regulation of their receptors when treatment is chronic. In response to the reduction in receptors, the cAMP pathway is up-regulated, producing increases in adenylyl cyclase activity, cAMP, protein kinase A (PKA), and the transcription factor within the nucleus, CREB. CREB increases the synthesis of several proteins, including BDNF. βAR, β-adrenergic receptor; PDE, phosphodiesterase. (After R. S. Duman et al. 1997. *Arch Gen Psychiatry* 54: 597–606.)

up-regulate the cAMP cascade in a prolonged fashion. One PDE inhibitor, rolipram, reduced symptoms in a small trial of depressed patients, but side effects prohibit its regular use. More selective inhibitors may prove effective with reduced side effects. Although the possibilities are exciting, application to human therapeutics is clearly a long way off.

Although there is fairly convincing evidence that increased neurogenesis is needed for antidepressant effects, a causal role for neurogenesis in the etiology of depression remains more difficult to demonstrate. The reduction in hippocampal volume and the morphological changes found in depressed patients that are reversed by antidepressant treatment could be related to the reduced levels of BDNF found in the hippocampus and the PFC post-mortem, although these findings are not consistent and are best documented in depressed suicides. Also, a common polymorphism of the gene that codes for BDNF (*val66met*) has sometimes been associated with mood disorders, although it is not specific to depression as it also occurs with higher frequency in patients with Alzheimer's disease, obsessive–compulsive disorder, and others. More convincing are the results of studies finding that *temporary* reduction of BDNF gene expression in *specific* regions of the forebrain produces depression-like behaviors in mice, particularly in females. However, others have found that heterozygous BDNF knockout mice display increased aggressiveness, hyperphagia, deficits in spatial learning, and subtle alterations in sensory systems, but rarely depressive-like behaviors. Whether the differences can be explained by the permanence of the BDNF loss in the knockout studies or the lack of brain specificity is not clear. Further research in this area is ongoing.

These two neurobiological hypotheses, along with a third that considers the impairment of brain reward pathways, are discussed in detail in an excellent review by Krishnan and Nestler (2010). They provide both an overview and supporting evidence as well as a discussion of future directions for research.

SECTION SUMMARY

- The monoamine hypothesis was based on pharmacological evidence showing that depression is associated with low levels of monoamines, whereas mania coincides with excess monoamine activity.

- Modifications of the hypothesis were needed to explain the discrepancy in time between the rapid increase in monoamines by antidepressant drugs and the slow onset of clinical effects over several weeks.

- A role for 5-HT in depression is suggested by the following: (1) lower 5-HIAA occurs in depressed individuals, (2) knockout mice show some behaviors analogous to human depression, (3) depletion of tryptophan causes depressed mood in patients in remission,

(4) a polymorphism of the SERT gene is associated with depression, and (5) increased postsynaptic 5-HT$_2$ receptors are found in patients post-mortem.

- Chronic antidepressant treatment causes the down-regulation of 5-HT autoreceptors, which increases synaptic 5-HT and subsequent intracellular changes leading to neurogenesis and synaptic remodeling. The effects of fluoxetine on autoreceptor down-regulation and depression may depend on several factors, including pretreatment 5-HT function and the nature of the environment. The electrophysiological response to 5-HT is enhanced by chronic antidepressant treatment.

- In depressed patients, chronic antidepressants increase NE turnover, which leads to down-regulation of β-adrenergic receptors and α$_2$-autoreceptors.

- Inhibiting the synthesis of 5-HT causes relapse in patients treated with serotonin reuptake inhibitors, but not in those treated with adrenergic antidepressants. Likewise, inhibiting NE synthesis produces relapse in patients treated with NE reuptake inhibitors, but not in those treated with serotonergic agents.

- Emerging research has found that individuals with depression show a higher connectivity within the default-mode network (DMN), which underlies rumination, or introspective thinking. It has also been shown that antidepressant treatment normalizes DMN dysfunction. More research is needed to determine whether DMN connectivity could be used as a biomarker of depression in patients.

- Prolonged hypersecretion of CRF, ACTH, and glucocorticoids damages dendritic branching and spines in the hippocampus and PFC. It also reduces neurogenesis in the hippocampus, which further diminishes the negative feedback on HPA axis function. Chronic antidepressants reverse these effects.

- Intracerebroventricular administration of CRF elicits stress-related behavior and hormone response and signs of depression in rodents. A small clinical trial of a CRF antagonist improved depression and anxiety scores in patients, although larger studies are needed.

- The neurotrophic hypothesis suggests that stress hormones that reduce BDNF may cause neuronal damage, and antidepressants may prevent it by elevating BDNF. Intrahippocampal BDNF has antidepressant action.

- Preventing hippocampal cell proliferation prevents antidepressant-induced neurogenesis and behavioral effects.

- Chronic antidepressants up-regulate the cAMP cascade, leading to increased phosphorylated CREB and subsequent expression of BDNF. Enhancing the cAMP cascade by inhibiting PDE produced antidepressant effects in some patients.

- Evidence for BDNF in the etiology of depression includes the following: (1) BDNF is low in the hippocampus and the PFC of depressed patients post-mortem, (2) a BDNF gene polymorphism may be associated with mood disorders, and (3) modifying BDNF gene expression in mice leads to depressive behaviors.

18.3 Therapies for Affective Disorders

Three major classes of antidepressants have proved effective in reducing symptoms of affective disorders (**TABLE 18.2**): the MAOIs, the TCAs, and the second-generation antidepressants, which include the SSRIs. In addition, there are several atypical antidepressants as well as several nondrug therapies, including sleep deprivation (see Web Box 18.4), ECT, transcranial magnetic stimulation, vagal nerve stimulation, and deep brain stimulation. These brain-stimulation treatments are discussed in **WEB BOX 18.5**. Drugs for treating the manic episodes of bipolar disorder will be considered separately.

The availability of a variety of antidepressant drugs means that many clinically depressed individuals can find significant relief. However, double-blind, placebo-controlled trials of antidepressants show that no one specific drug or drug type is more effective than any other, and there is no way to predict which patient will respond to a particular drug. Each drug is effective in reducing, but not necessarily eliminating, symptoms for about two-thirds of the cases of clinical depression. The different pharmacological characteristics of the agents mean that they will reduce different symptoms and will produce distinct but characteristic side effects. Each patient must usually undergo trials to find an antidepressant that optimally balances effectiveness and side effects. Frequently, outcomes are enhanced by the addition of a second drug to the treatment regimen. Every one of the treatment methods currently available requires chronic administration, suggesting that although we understand how each works acutely at the synapse, the clinical effect must depend on compensatory changes in neural function that require time to develop. Although significant changes in symptoms can occur during the first 1 to 3 weeks of drug treatment, maximal effectiveness may not be achieved until after 4 to 6 weeks of therapy. This time lag is especially worrisome in patients who are severely depressed and suicidal. Some symptoms, including irregularities in sleep and appetite, are the first signs that show improvement, followed over the next few weeks by mood enhancement. Several long-term studies from the National Institute of Mental Health suggest a period of maintenance drug treatment of at least 6 to 8 months after symptoms are reduced. Because maintenance therapy significantly reduces the probability of relapse, treatment is extended indefinitely for some individuals.

Although we are treating antidepressant drugs and drugs used for anxiety (see Chapter 17) as separate entities, we would like to make it clear that the distinction is often more semantic than real. As we noted earlier, stress and anxiety are components of affective disorders, and the trend in drug treatment further blurs the distinction. Antidepressant drugs reduce the anxiety that accompanies depression, and they are increasingly being used to treat anxiety disorders unrelated to depression.

MAOIs are the oldest antidepressant drugs

The first true antidepressant action was discovered quite by accident as the result of a lucky clinical observation. The drug iproniazid was used in the early 1950s to treat tuberculosis but had significant mood-elevating effects unrelated to its effects on the disease. Following that observation, iproniazid was found to inhibit MAO. Although they were met with enthusiasm following their early introduction as antidepressants, the **MAO inhibitors** (**MAOIs**) fell into disfavor because of their reputation for having severe and dangerous side effects (see the section on side effects below). However, over the years it has become apparent that, with appropriate dietary restrictions, MAOIs can be used safely

TABLE 18.2	Major Classes of Antidepressants and Their Most Notable Side Effects	
Class	**Antidepressants**	**Side effects**
MAOIs	Phenelzine (Nardil) Tranylcypromine (Parnate) Isocarboxazid (Marplan)	Insomnia, weight gain, hypertension, drug interactions, tyramine effect
Classic TCAs	Imipramine (Tofranil) Amitriptyline (Vanatrip) Desipramine (Norpramine)	Sedation, anticholinergic effects, cardiovascular toxicity
SSRIs	Fluoxetine (Prozac) Sertraline (Zoloft) Paroxetine (Paxil)	Insomnia, gastrointestinal disturbances, sexual dysfunction, serotonin syndrome
Atypical antidepressants	Maprotiline (Ludiomil) Bupropion (Wellbutrin) Mirtazapine (Remeron)	Varies with individual mechanism of action
Electroconvulsive shock and transcranial magnetic stimulation		Memory impairment, confusion, amnesia

and often work well for patients who are resistant to treatment (do not respond to other drugs) and who reject the idea of ECT. In addition to their use in affective disorders, MAOIs are used in the treatment of several anxiety states and have positive effects on the eating behavior and mood of patients with bulimia and anorexia nervosa. The currently available MAOIs include phenelzine (Nardil), tranylcypromine (Parnate), and isocarboxazid (Marplan).

MECHANISM OF ACTION   You will recall from Chapter 5 that MAO is an enzyme found inside the cells of many tissues, including neurons. The normal function of the enzyme is to metabolize the monoamine neurotransmitters in the presynaptic terminals that are not contained in protective synaptic vesicles. The inhibition of MAO increases the amount of neurotransmitter available for release. A single dose of an MAOI increases NE, DA, and 5-HT and thus increases the action of the transmitters at their receptors. It was initially assumed that enhanced neurotransmitter function was responsible for the antidepressant action; however, those biochemical changes occur within hours, but the antidepressant effects require weeks of chronic treatment. It is now apparent that neuron adaptation involving change in receptor density or second-messenger function must play an important part in these drug effects (**FIGURE 18.12**).

SIDE EFFECTS   The more common side effects of MAOIs include changes in blood pressure, sleep disturbances including insomnia, and overeating, especially of carbohydrates, which may lead to excessive weight gain. In addition to these side effects, three other types of side effects are significantly more dangerous. First, because inhibition of MAO elevates NE levels in peripheral nerves of the sympathetic branch of the autonomic nervous system as well as in the CNS, any prescription or over-the-counter drug that enhances NE function will have a much greater effect than normal. For example, nasal sprays, cold medications, antiasthma drugs, amphetamine, and cocaine will all have greater-than-expected effects and will produce elevated blood pressure, sweating, and increased body temperature. Second, some serious side effects are due to the inhibition of MAO in the liver as well as in the brain. The MAO in the liver is responsible for deaminating tyramine, which is a naturally occurring amine formed as a by-product of fermentation in many foods, including cheeses, certain meats, and pickled products. These foods must be avoided by individuals using MAOIs. Elevated tyramine levels release the higher-than-normal stores of NE at nerve endings, causing a dramatic increase in blood pressure. Blood pressure may reach critical levels, and this is accompanied by headache, sweating, nausea, vomiting, and sometimes stroke. Third, MAOIs also inhibit other

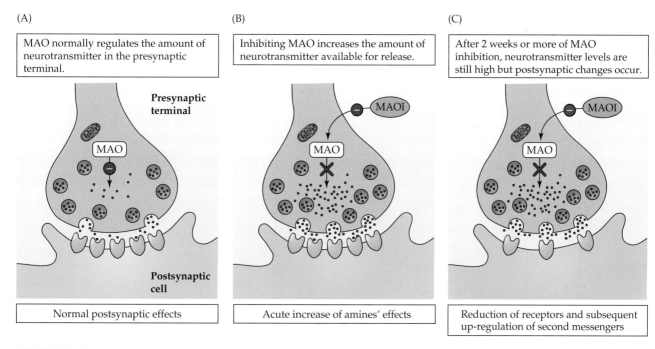

FIGURE 18.12   Acute and long-term effects of MAOIs on synaptic function (A) Presynaptic MAO degrades neurotransmitter molecules that are not in vesicles, to keep amines at "normal" levels. (B) MAOIs inhibit the enzyme, causing an elevation in available neurotransmitter for release, resulting in increased action at receptors. (C) After 10 days to 2 weeks of antidepressant treatment, the amount of neurotransmitter in the synapse is still elevated over control conditions, but neural adaptation has occurred: down-regulation of amine receptors and up-regulation of the cyclic adenosine monophosphate (cAMP) second-messenger system. Other antidepressant drugs produce similar adaptive changes in neurons.

liver enzymes such as the cytochrome P450 enzymes (see Chapter 1), which normally degrade such drugs as barbiturates, alcohol, opioids, aspirin, and many others. The effects of these drugs are prolonged and intensified in the presence of MAOIs.

TCAs block the reuptake of NE and serotonin

This class of antidepressant is named for its characteristic three-ring structure (**FIGURE 18.13**), which is closely related to that of the antipsychotic drugs in the phenothiazine class (see Chapter 19). Although the prototypical **tricyclic antidepressant (TCA)** imipramine (Tofranil) failed its original test for antipsychotic effects, it did appear to have mood-elevating actions. Many other TCAs were subsequently developed.

MECHANISM OF ACTION The drugs in this class act by binding to the presynaptic transporter proteins and inhibiting reuptake of neurotransmitters into the presynaptic terminal. Inhibition of reuptake prolongs the duration of transmitter action at the synapse, ultimately producing changes in both pre- and postsynaptic receptors. Although many of the drugs in this class are equally effective in inhibiting the reuptake of NE and 5-HT, some are more effective on one transmitter than the other. Although this difference does not change their antidepressant action, it does determine the side effects of the drugs. **TABLE 18.3** provides a comparison of the relative NE and 5-HT reuptake-blocking potencies of several TCAs and some second-generation antidepressants as well. You may notice that just as

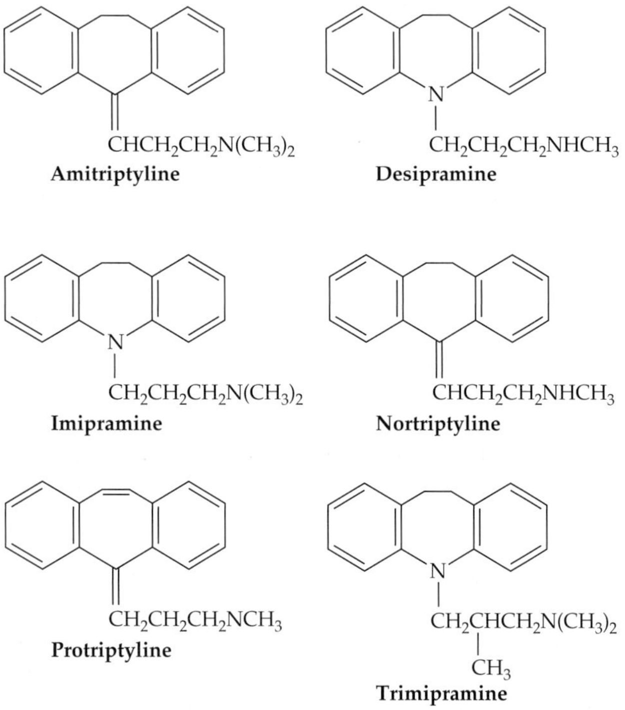

selective reuptake inhibitors for serotonin were developed, so too are there selective norepinephrine reuptake inhibitors. As was true for the MAOIs, the immediate increase in NE and 5-HT function is not correlated with clinical effectiveness, which takes several weeks. Clearly, an acute increase in synaptic activity is only the first step in antidepressant action; neuronal adaptation, occurring over a period of time, also plays an important role. In addition to reuptake blockade, most of the TCAs block ACh, histamine, and α-adrenergic receptors, and this contributes to their side effects.

SIDE EFFECTS While the therapeutic effects of TCAs are likely due to enhancement of monoamine activity followed by compensatory changes in the transmitter systems, their receptor-blocking activity contributes to side effects. Histamine receptor blockade is responsible for the sedation and fatigue that are frequent side effects that limit the drugs' usefulness in individuals who must remain alert. On the other hand, for patients who experience agitation, the sedative effects may be welcome. Anticholinergic side effects are troublesome for others and include dry mouth, constipation, urinary retention, dizziness, confusion, impaired memory, and blurred vision. The α_1-blockade in combination with the NE reuptake-blocking effects leads to several potentially dangerous cardiovascular side effects, including orthostatic hypotension, tachycardia, and arrhythmias. This particular set of side effects makes it especially difficult to treat depression in elderly patients with known cardiac disorders.

In addition, toxicity following overdose causes cardiovascular depression, delirium, convulsions, respiratory depression, and coma. Heart arrhythmias may produce cardiac arrest and fatalities. Since the fatalities associated with TCA treatment occur at approximately 10 times the normal dose, these drugs have a relatively low therapeutic index (TD_{50}/ED_{50}), particularly when used by patients demonstrating suicidal tendencies.

Second-generation antidepressants have different side effects

In an attempt to offer drugs with fewer side effects and more rapid onset of action, a host of new antidepressants have been developed. In general, they are designed to be more selective in their action with the hope of eliminating the anticholinergic and cardiovascular effects produced by the older drugs while still elevating levels of NE and/or 5-HT to provide antidepressant action. None are more effective, however, nor do they have a more rapid onset. The most significant difference is seen in the nature of their side effects, which are related to their neurochemical mechanisms of action. Many are considered safer than the older drugs if taken as an overdose.

CHCH$_2$CH$_2$N(CH$_3$)$_2$
Amitriptyline

CH$_2$CH$_2$CH$_2$NHCH$_3$
Desipramine

CH$_2$CH$_2$CH$_2$N(CH$_3$)$_2$
Imipramine

CHCH$_2$CH$_2$NHCH$_3$
Nortriptyline

CH$_2$CH$_2$CH$_2$NCH$_3$
Protriptyline

CH$_2$CHCH$_2$N(CH$_3$)$_2$
|
CH$_3$
Trimipramine

FIGURE 18.13 Characteristic three-ring structure of TCAs

TABLE 18.3 Relative Specificity of Antidepressant Drugs That Block Monoamine Reuptake

Drug name	Extent of reuptake inhibition*	
	Norepinephrine	Serotonin
TCAs		
Desipramine (Norpramine)	+++	+
Protriptyline (Vivactil)	+++	+
Amitriptyline (Vanatrip)	++	++
Imipramine (Tofranil)	++	++
Clomipramine (Anafranil)	++	++++
SSRIs		
Fluoxetine (Prozac)	0	++++
Sertraline (Zoloft)	0	++++
Paroxetine (Paxil)	+	++++
SNRIs		
Reboxetine (Edronax)	++++	0
Atomoxetine (Strattera)	++++	0

*0, no effect; +, mild effect; ++, moderate effect; +++, strong effect; ++++, maximal effect.

The **selective serotonin reuptake inhibitors (SSRIs)** deserve special mention because they are often the first choice among antidepressants because of their greater relative safety. In addition to major depression, these drugs are also used to treat several distinct disorders: panic and anxiety disorders, obsessive–compulsive disorder, obesity, and alcohol use disorder.

MECHANISM OF ACTION Drugs in this class, which include fluoxetine (Prozac), sertraline (Zoloft), and paroxetine (Paxil), are more selective than TCAs in enhancing serotonin function because they block the presynaptic reuptake transporter for 5-HT to a greater extent than the noradrenergic transporter. As is true for all of the antidepressants discussed, we assume that the antidepressant action requires compensatory changes in neurons that occur over several weeks, as shown in Figure 18.11.

SIDE EFFECTS The side effects of the SSRIs are different from those of the TCAs because the drugs do not alter NE, histamine, or ACh. Hence the frequent TCA-induced side effects of sedation, cardiovascular toxicity, and anticholinergic effects are absent. Nevertheless, SSRIs produce a different pattern of side effects because they enhance 5-HT function at all serotonergic receptors. Although the antidepressant action may be related to increased 5-HT function at some serotonergic receptors, increased 5-HT activity at other receptors causes side effects: anxiety, restlessness, movement disorders, muscle rigidity, nausea, headache, insomnia, and sexual dysfunction. The sexual dysfunction, which occurs in 40% to 70% of patients, is a frequent reason for terminating therapy, particularly among young male patients. However, many individuals experience a regression of at least some of these side effects after several months of therapy.

Although the SSRIs are generally safer than the older drugs, they have potentially life-threatening effects when combined with other serotonergic agonists or with drugs that interfere with the normal metabolism of the SSRIs. For example, this is known to occur when combining MAOIs with SSRIs. These effects, referred to as the **serotonin syndrome**, are characterized by severe agitation, disorientation and confusion, ataxia, muscle spasms, and exaggerated autonomic nervous system functions, including fever, shivering, chills, diarrhea, elevated blood pressure, and increased heart rate, and may even lead to death (Lane and Baldwin, 1997).

One other distinctive characteristic of the SSRIs compared with the older antidepressants is their ability to cause physical dependence. As many as 60% of patients suffer withdrawal effects following drug termination, particularly with the short-acting SSRIs, unless the dose is tapered off gradually (Zajecka et al., 1997). These withdrawal symptoms, which can last for several weeks, include dizziness and ataxia, nausea, vomiting and diarrhea, fatigue, chills, sensory disturbances, insomnia, vivid dreams and increased anxiety, agitation, and irritability. Although the SSRIs avoid many of the dangerous side effects of the older drugs, caution in their use is still warranted.

Although the SSRIs are second-generation antidepressants, some of the newer antidepressants are once again **dual NE/5-HT modulators** termed **SNRIs** (serotonin and norepinephrine reuptake inhibitors). This reflects current thinking that suggests that enhancing both NE and 5-HT function may be more beneficial than acting on a single monoamine. The reuptake blocker duloxetine (Cymbalta) and mirtazapine (Remeron) are two such drugs. Mirtazapine is an antidepressant with a unique mechanism of action. It blocks α_2-autoreceptors, which increases synaptic NE and α_2-heteroreceptors on serotonergic cells, which increases 5-HT release. Additionally, to reduce side effects, the drug specifically blocks selected 5-HT receptors. Early mirtazapine trials showed clear clinical benefit in a broad range of patients when compared with placebo, and equal effectiveness compared with the TCA amitriptyline, but it had somewhat fewer (65%) adverse side effects compared with placebo (70%) or amitriptyline (87%).

Third-generation antidepressants have distinctive mechanisms of action

Third-generation antidepressants are currently in the development and testing stages. The goals for the newest drugs will be to continue to minimize side effects and toxicity as well as speed up the onset of effectiveness. Despite our best attempts, it is evident that the neuropharmacology is still unclear with respect to the cellular changes that produce effective antidepressant action, but it is clear that a series of molecular changes underlie the therapies. The two newest approaches—CRF receptor antagonism and enhancement of the cAMP intracellular second-messenger system and subsequent synaptic plasticity—were discussed earlier in the chapter, in the section on neurobiological models of depression. In addition to these approaches, regulation of circadian dysfunctions by agomelatine (as discussed in Web Box 18.3) holds great promise. It has passed both phase 2 and phase 3 clinical trials and is already approved for use in Europe. Several others that also attack depression symptoms from a novel direction include intravenous ketamine and galanin agonists.

INTRAVENOUS KETAMINE Among the more troublesome problems in depression therapy is finding a way to reduce symptoms in the large number of treatment-resistant patients (i.e., those who do not respond to available medications or cannot tolerate the side effects). One new approach has been the use of the N-methyl-D-aspartate (NMDA) receptor antagonist ketamine, a dissociative anesthetic (reviewed by Park et al., 2019). This glutamate receptor subtype has received new attention because there is evidence of abnormal NMDA receptor binding in suicidal patients. Also, chronic stress alters NMDA receptor binding in animal studies, and NMDA receptor antagonists have shown antidepressant properties in a wide variety of animal models (see Chapter 4), including learned helplessness, forced swim test, sucrose preference tests, chronic mild stress, and others (reviewed by Alshammari, 2020).

When administered intravenously at subanesthetic doses, ketamine has been shown in multiple small clinical trials to produce a rapid (generally within an hour) reduction in depression symptoms for 65% to 70% of *treatment-resistant* patients. In some cases it has led to total remission of all symptoms. Although the antidepressant effect has a rapid onset, the duration of action varies widely. A recent meta-analysis of 20 studies showed antidepressant effects lasted a week for most patients, with a small subset experiencing alleviation of symptoms for up to 2 weeks (Coyle and Laws, 2015; Kryst et al., 2020). However, for patients with bipolar disorder the antidepressant effects last on average only a few days. A limited number of follow-up studies have evaluated the efficacy and safety of *multiple* ketamine infusions in treatment-resistant patients; however, the majority of patients relapsed in an average of 2 to 3 weeks after the last administration. Interestingly a very few individuals showed more prolonged effects, lasting up to 3 months. It could be important to identify characteristics of those individuals that differed from the majority of patients, to identify a subtype of responders. Based on the data, it would seem that multiple administrations show only modest benefits for a given individual beyond a single infusion.

In 2019, the U.S. Food and Drug Administration (FDA) approved an internasal esketamine spray (Spravato™) for treatment-resistant major depressive disorder. As with all chemical compounds, ketamine is a racemic mixture of R-ketamine and S-ketamine, the latter also termed esketamine. Esketamine has certain advantages over racemic ketamine, in that it is two to four times more potent at the NMDA receptor than R-ketamine, has moderate to high bioavailability (48%) that obviates the need for intravenous administration at a clinic (thereby facilitating access to therapy), and is well tolerated by patients without any significant dissociative effects as seen with intravenous ketamine. Dosing is recommended twice weekly for 4 weeks followed by a once-a-week administration for maintenance. It is noteworthy that recent small-scale trials are also investigating the utility of R-ketamine, which shows even fewer side effects than both racemic ketamine and esketamine while retaining antidepressant properties (reviewed in Salahudeen et al., 2020).

With its rapid onset of effectiveness, the therapeutic actions of ketamine and its racemates are clearly distinct from that of the classical antidepressant drugs, which take weeks to be effective. Additionally, ketamine seems to be effective in patients who are not helped by the usual antidepressants. The fact that it does not act on the monoamines provides new hope for developing a novel class of antidepressant drugs that act on the glutamate receptor. Because other NMDA receptor antagonists have antidepressant effects in a wide variety of animal models, the pressure to translate these findings to clinical use is significant. Unfortunately, as we have seen before, results from animal experiments do not necessarily transfer to human clinical benefits. For example, the NMDA antagonist memantine, which shows antidepressant effects in rodent tests, did not consistently show antidepressant effects in clinically depressed patients (Sanacora and Schatzberg, 2015). We have to ask what is different about ketamine than other NMDA antagonists.

The next question is how to explain the prolonged effect of a single infusion of ketamine, which lasts far longer than the drug's short half-life. One potential explanation is that ketamine may initiate intracellular mechanisms that have an extended duration of effects. The concept of antidepressant enhancement of BDNF-stimulated neurogenesis and elaboration of dendritic spine growth and development has taken center stage because BDNF is the common factor involved with both conventional antidepressant effects and the rapid-acting ketamine. Additionally, ketamine has no antidepressant effects in BDNF knockout mice or in mice without the BDNF receptor trkB (see Monteggia and Zarate, 2015). However, the question of how it can work so quickly remains, while conventional antidepressant drugs take weeks to enhance BDNF and its neurotrophic functions. Among the possible mechanisms is the rapid activation of the mTOR signaling cascade that is important in the synthesis of proteins that support the development, maturation, and function of new dendritic synapses promoting synaptic plasticity (Alshammari, 2020). Through a series of events,

blocking the NMDA receptor with ketamine subsequently enhances glutamate function at AMPA receptors on GABA interneurons and initiates multiple signal transduction cascades to ultimately activate the protein kinase mTOR that produces changes in synaptic plasticity (**FIGURE 18.14A**). Enhanced spine density was visualized on dendrites of pyramidal neurons in the mPFC 24 hours after ketamine infusion (**FIGURE 18.14B**). Coinciding with those changes, animals show antidepressant effects in the forced swim and learned helplessness tests. The inhibition of mTOR by rapamycin prevents the ketamine-induced synaptic changes and the antidepressant effects. The ketamine-enhanced synaptic strengthening shown by increased electrophysiological responses to 5-HT was also reduced by rapamycin (Li et al., 2010; **FIGURE 18.14C**). mTOR and other downstream modulators, including BDNF, that are activated by ketamine provide other opportunities to identify drugs that have the rapid antidepressant action of ketamine without some of its liabilities, such as causing transient

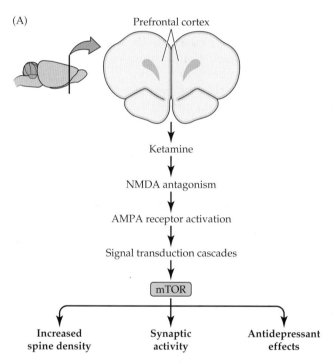

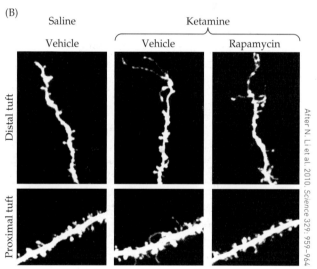

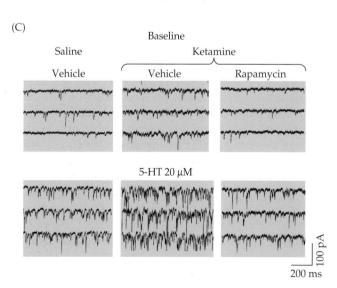

FIGURE 18.14 Ketamine's rapid activation of mTOR
(A) The cascade of events beginning with intravenous injection of ketamine inhibits NMDA receptor function but additionally enhances glutamate activation of AMPA receptors. Multiple signal transduction cascades mediate the activation of the protein kinase mTOR. The action of mTOR in turn increases dendritic spine density, enhances synaptic activity by modifying synaptic proteins, and produces rapid antidepressant effects. A reciprocal relationship between mTOR and BDNF forms a positive feedback loop (not shown). (B) Two-photon microscopy shows increased spine density on both distal and proximal segments of dendrites in medial prefrontal cortex (mPFC) pyramidal neurons 24 hours after ketamine administration, compared with control animals. There was an increase in large-diameter, more mature (mushroom) spines. The increase was prevented by the mTOR antagonist rapamycin. (C) Whole-cell voltage-clamp recordings show ketamine enhanced the 5-HT–induced excitatory postsynaptic currents in pyramidal cells of mPFC, 24 hours after ketamine injection. (A after J. F. Cryan and O. F. O'Leary. 2010. *Science* 329: 913–914. C after N. Li et al. 2010. *Science* 329: 959–964.)

psychosis-like symptoms that last up to 2 hours, and dissociative symptoms. An additional incentive to find an alternative to ketamine is that although ketamine does not produce physical dependence, it is an abused substance (considered a "party drug"), which further limits its usefulness in treatment programs.

One of the newest explanations for the failure of other NMDA antagonists to be effective is that the antidepressant effects of ketamine may depend not so much on the molecule itself, but on one of its specific metabolites that, rather than blocking NMDA receptors, activates AMPA receptors. Its importance was shown by administration of AMPA receptor antagonists, which prevented the antidepressant effects of ketamine. The metabolite, which was three times higher in the brains of female mice than in males, reversed depression-like behaviors more effectively in females than males. When the researchers prevented the formation of the metabolite, ketamine lost its effectiveness, so apparently the metabolite is necessary for the behavioral effect. Of special significance is that when the metabolite itself was administered, it did not cause the psychosis-like or anesthetic effects seen with ketamine. This approach provides one more avenue for research into a more effective, faster-acting drug to treat clinical depression (Zanos and Gould, 2018).

Because ketamine reduces NMDA receptor function but potentiates glutamate action at the AMPA receptor, it makes AMPA receptor *agonists* potentially useful targets. AMPA agonist action may explain the increased neural activity in the anterior cingulate cortex that predicts antidepressant response to ketamine as well as other antidepressant drugs. The synaptic resculpturing that is seen may again be related to the rapid activation of mTOR. It is especially interesting that the rapid (overnight) antidepressant effect of sleep deprivation (see Web Box 18.4) also enhances AMPA-induced synaptic plasticity.

Other potential explanations for these rapid synaptic changes exist. Ketamine has been shown to bind to μ-opioid receptors, initiate multiple second-messenger cascades, and increase BDNF, as well as altering the expression of several genes central to the operation of the molecular biological clock. Its ability to alter circadian rhythms as well as increase BDNF may be due to the drug's ability to inhibit the signaling properties of the protein kinase GSK-3 (see the section on the mechanism of action of lithium below), but more preclinical research is needed and there are many potential pathways to investigate. Sial and colleagues (2020) provide an excellent summary of some of the possible mechanisms responsible for ketamine's unusual properties. Although much more research is needed before these approaches are adapted into clinical use, at this point ketamine has utility as a short-term solution in acute crisis situations, such as when emergency room physicians deal with suicidal depressed patients.

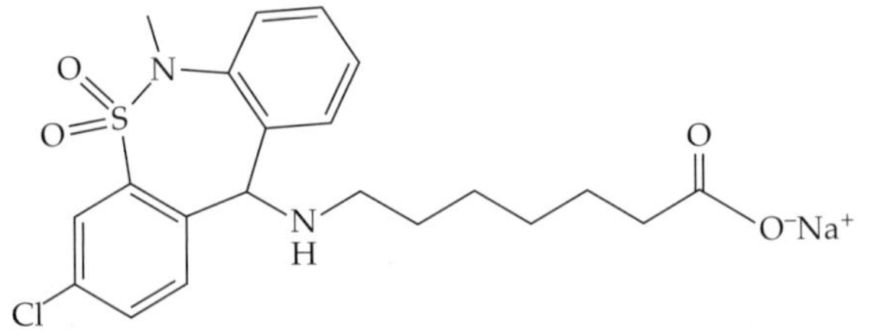

FIGURE 18.15 Chemical structure of tianeptine Note the three-ring structure. While tianeptine is similar in structure to the TCAs, it has very different pharmacological properties.

Another effective antidepressant that modulates glutamate function is **tianeptine**, a TCA in structure but with different and complex pharmacological actions (**FIGURE 18.15**). Its unique neurobiological properties may explain its effectiveness in reducing symptoms of depression and comorbid anxiety with only mild side effects and little sedation or cognitive impairment. The drug increases phosphorylation of glutamate receptor subtypes in selective brain areas. Given the current interest in ketamine's potentiation of AMPA receptor function, it is interesting to note that the phosphorylation of glutamate receptor GluR1 by tianeptine potentiates AMPA receptor function. Its ability to enhance phosphorylation by intracellular kinases such as calcium/calmodulin-dependent protein kinase may further contribute to the synaptic plasticity characteristic of antidepressant drugs. Additionally, in animal studies, tianeptine prevents stress-induced changes in glutamate transmission (perhaps by adjusting the NMDA–AMPA balance) in hippocampus and amygdala, which contributes to its neuroprotective action. McEwen and colleagues (2010) provide a thorough description of the neurobiological effects of tianeptine.

GALANIN Galanin is a 30–amino acid neuropeptide implicated in mood disorders as well as in regulating feeding, cognitive performance, sleep, sexual activity, and stress responses. It is widely distributed in the brain and is co-localized with 5-HT in the raphe nuclei and with NE in the LC. It acts as an inhibitory modulator of the two monoamines by hyperpolarizing the cells and reducing neurotransmitter release at their projection areas in the limbic system and cerebral cortex. Contradictory evidence regarding whether intracerebral injections of galanin produce depressive or antidepressant effects may be explained by the existence of three distinct galanin G protein–coupled receptors that are differentially distributed in the brain and are coupled to distinct intracellular signaling mechanisms. Agonists at GalR1 and GalR3 cause depression-like behaviors in rodents, while agonists of GalR2 have antidepressant effects in the same rodent models (Hökfelt et al., 2018). Hence galanin may have a role in the pathophysiology of depression and represents a potential target for novel antidepressant medications. Of particular interest is the finding that 14 days of treatment with the SSRI fluoxetine up-regulated galanin mRNA expression by 100% and GalR2 (but not GalR1) expression by 50% in the dorsal raphe (Lu et al., 2005). Electroconvulsive shock also increased galanin mRNA in the nucleus of the raphe, but sleep deprivation increased it in the LC. These researchers also found that intraventricular injection of a nonselective galanin antagonist could prevent the antidepressant effects of fluoxetine in the forced swim test, indicating that galanin may mediate the drug's clinical effectiveness. Furthermore, galnon, a nonspecific, nonpeptide galanin receptor agonist, produced a dose-dependent reduction in immobilization in the forced swim test. These results suggest that GalR2 agonists might augment standard antidepressant treatment. Additionally, on the basis of preclinical studies, antagonists at GalR1 or GalR3 would be expected to have clinically significant antidepressant effects, and several GalR3 antagonists have recently been developed for testing. One final fascinating aspect is that evidence suggests that galanin has neuroprotective effects. Ligands binding specifically to GalR1 or GalR1/2 significantly reduced the excitotoxic cell death in hippocampal neurons following intracerebroventricular injection of kainic acid (Webling et al., 2016). Furthermore, galanin increases hippocampal neurogenesis, providing further support for the neurotrophic hypothesis described earlier.

NONDRUG THERAPY   A less conventional but apparently effective antidepressant treatment is physical exercise. Yau and colleagues (2011) have shown in a series of studies that administration of corticosterone (the rodent equivalent of the human stress hormone cortisol) at low (30 mg/kg), moderate (40 mg/kg), or high (50 mg/kg) doses for 14 days produces a dose-dependent increase in depression-like behaviors seen in the forced swim and sucrose preference tests as well as impaired spatial learning in the Morris water maze. Voluntary running reversed these behavioral effects except at the highest corticosterone levels, and the positive behavioral effects were associated with increased hippocampal neurogenesis, dendritic length, and spine density. Preventing the increase in neurogenesis diminished the positive effect of running. A follow-up study examined the failure of exercise to reverse the high-stress–induced (50 mg/kg corticosterone) depressive behaviors and impairments in cognitive function. Their results provide motivation for all of us to exercise regularly because they found that exercise could reverse the damaging effects of high stress if the animals were allowed to exercise both before and during the corticosterone administration. Under these conditions, not only were the behaviors restored to normal but neurogenesis and levels of synaptic proteins were

also normalized. Hence it would appear that exercise makes us resilient to future stress (Yau et al., 2014). Recently, it has been shown that the mediator between exercise and its effects on neurogenesis may be the hormone adiponectin, which is released mainly by fat cells in the body, but also the muscle and the brain. Critically, mice in whom this hormone is globally genetically deleted fail to show antidepressant effects of exercise compared to wild-type mice, including a lack of exercise-induced hippocampal neurogenesis (Wang et al., 2020). By contrast, infusion of this hormone into the hippocampus of wild-type mice mimics the antidepressant effects of exercise while increasing hippocampal neurogenesis.

Drugs for treating bipolar disorder stabilize the highs and the lows

For the majority of patients with bipolar disorder, **lithium carbonate** (Carbolith, Eskalith) is the most effective medication and is the usual drug of choice. Although lithium has no effect on mood or behavior in healthy individuals, J. Cade in 1949 discovered that it had powerful effects on patients with mania. After 1 to 2 weeks of lithium use, symptoms are eliminated or reduced in approximately 60% to 80% of manic episodes without causing depression or producing sedation. The drug is somewhat less effective in terminating episodes of depression, so it is often administered along with a TCA or other antidepressant drug. Most important is that it is useful for reducing the occurrence of future episodes of mania and depression. Additionally, it is particularly effective in reducing suicide in bipolar individuals. Patients who continue with lithium treatment have an average hospital stay of less than 2 weeks per year, but without lithium therapy patients spend an average of 8 to 13 weeks per year in the hospital. Based on an 18-month, placebo-controlled trial, Calabrese and associates (2003) found that typical time to recurrence of any mood episode was on average 93 days in the placebo group and 170 days in the lithium group, demonstrating the superiority of lithium therapy in preventing relapse during long-term maintenance (for an excellent review, see Curran and Ravindran, 2014).

Treatment of bipolar disorder with a mood stabilizer is a lifelong necessity for most patients. Either abrupt termination or gradual withdrawal of lithium results in recurring periods of mania and heightened suicide risk. Despite the risks, many patients stop taking the drug. In some cases, side effects are a significant problem for the patient, especially if they involve impaired memory and confusion. In other cases, patients stop taking the drug because they fail to experience normal mood changes, and this diminishes the richness of life. Finally, others object to the loss of the manic phase of bipolar disorder because this time is perceived as a period of heightened creativity and productiveness.

MECHANISM OF ACTION It is probably not surprising to find that lithium enhances 5-HT actions: it elevates brain tryptophan, 5-HT, and 5-HIAA (the principal 5-HT metabolite) and increases 5-HT release, which ultimately alters receptor response in several brain areas. Lithium reduces catecholamine activity by enhancing reuptake and reducing release. Despite these neurochemical changes, it is unlikely that lithium acts on individual neurotransmitters to normalize mood swings of both mania and depression. Given that the drug flattens the extremes of emotion in both directions, it is more likely that it directly modifies synaptic transmission at points beyond the neurotransmitter receptors, for instance in second-messenger function. Lithium has pronounced effects on adenylyl cyclase, phosphoinositide cycling, G protein coupling, brain neurotrophic factors, and multiple other intracellular cascades. One such signaling cascade involves the enzyme glycogen synthase kinase-3 (GSK-3). GSK-3 has numerous cell functions, but of particular importance for bipolar disorder is that the biological clock regulates GSK-3, which in turn feeds back to modulate circadian rhythms. Since lithium inhibits GSK-3 in mouse brain and in blood cells of patients with bipolar disorder, it is possible that the mood-stabilizing effects of lithium are in part due to the inhibition of GSK-3 regulation of circadian rhythms. Lithium's ability to slow down the typical abnormally fast circadian rhythms in patients with bipolar disorder is associated with a stabilization of mood, while those patients with excessively slow circadian rhythms do not show symptom improvement (Moreira and Geoffroy, 2016). Further evidence for this hypothesis comes from rodent models of mania that can be attenuated by synthetic inhibitors of GSK-3, opening the inquiry into potentially new treatment strategies (see Logan and McClung, 2016). Additionally, polymorphisms of GSK-3 predict lithium's effects on circadian rhythms and are associated with several symptoms of the disorder. As you might expect, GSK-3 exerts other physiological effects, including the modulation of other intracellular signaling pathways. One effect of lithium-induced inhibition of GSK-3 in turn enhances the plasticity of neurons by altering dendritic spine stability and density, which is associated with reduced depression-like behavior and reduced amphetamine-induced hyperactivity and sensitization in rodents. Given the potential role of GSK-3 in lithium's effectiveness, continuing research is investigating the use of GSK-3–overexpressing mice as a rodent model (reviewed by Logan and McClung, 2016). Its ability to alter intracellular actions regardless of the triggering neurotransmitter may explain its effects in both mania and depression.

SIDE EFFECTS Lithium is not metabolized but is excreted by the kidney in its intact form. Sodium depletion due to extreme sweating, diarrhea, vomiting, dehydration, use of diuretic medication, or severely salt-restricted diets may lead to toxic levels of lithium because lithium is reabsorbed from kidney tubules instead of sodium. The effective therapeutic range of lithium concentration in the blood is 0.4 to 1.0 mM. Since toxic effects begin to occur at blood levels of 2.0 mM, the therapeutic index is very low, and a patient's blood level of lithium must be monitored on a regular basis. Side effects are generally quite mild at therapeutic doses but may include increased thirst and urination, impaired concentration and memory, fatigue, tremor, and weight gain. Toxic effects are more severe and include cramps, vomiting, diarrhea, kidney dysfunction, coarse tremor, confusion, and irritability. Levels of lithium above 3.0 mM may lead to seizures, coma, and death (Haussmann et al., 2015).

OTHER THERAPIES FOR BIPOLAR DISORDER Because only about 50% to 60% of patients show a good response to lithium, and because it has a significant potential for toxicity, alternative therapies have been developed. Of the alternatives, the anticonvulsant drugs carbamazepine (Tegretol) and valproate (Depakene) are the most common and will be described briefly. However, several drugs that have classically been used as antipsychotics, such as aripiprazole and olanzapine, are similarly effective when compared with lithium and have a different side-effect profile. Further discussion of these drugs is beyond the scope of this text and is left to others (Grandjean and Aubry, 2009; Curran and Ravindran, 2014).

Valproate (Depakote), also known as valproic acid, is a simple branched-chain fatty acid, and the first anticonvulsant approved by the FDA for treatment of acute mania. Although valproate is readily absorbed after oral administration, it is low in potency, so high doses are administered. It is highly bound to plasma proteins, and because of the high dosage requirements, the depots may become saturated. Toxicity can occur with continued administration after saturation of the depots or after consumption of other free fatty acids that displace valproate from the depots, raising the level of free drug in the blood. Valproate is also capable of displacing other drugs bound to plasma protein, causing drug interactions. Valproate's metabolism creates a number of active metabolites that contribute to its action. Although its effectiveness is similar to that of lithium, one advantage of valproate is that it has a different side-effect profile. Common side effects include drowsiness, lethargy, hand tremor, hair loss, weight gain, and gastrointestinal distress. Some evidence indicates that the drug can cause liver toxicity and pancreatitis, but the probability is low. However, overdose is potentially life threatening. Since valproate is teratogenic and is associated with neural tube defects and with increased risk of polycystic ovary syndrome, its use in women of childbearing age is limited. For a review of its use in psychiatry, see Haddad and coworkers (2009).

Valproate has a complex mechanism of action. Valproate increases GABA levels by stimulating glutamic acid decarboxylase, which enhances synthesis, and inhibiting GABA transaminase, which decreases GABA degradation. Additionally, it has multiple actions on DA and glutamate neurotransmission. However, it also may have a common mechanism of action with other mood stabilizers on intracellular signaling, including the inhibition of the circadian modulatory enzyme GSK-3 (see the section on lithium above) and regulation of several cell survival pathways involving neurotrophic factors.

Carbamazepine (Tegretol) is a structurally atypical anticonvulsant because it resembles TCAs, and this similarity allows it to inhibit NE reuptake. It also acutely blocks adenosine receptors and up-regulates them with chronic use. Its actions on intracellular signaling are similar to those of valproate and lithium. The time course and extent of effectiveness are similar to those of lithium, but its side effects differ. The most common side effects, which usually diminish over time, include sedation, dizziness, somnolence, incoordination, nausea, and vomiting. More severe potential side effects include liver toxicity, severe skin rashes, and various blood conditions and diseases such as reduced white cell count, agranulocytosis, and aplastic anemia. The induction of several liver metabolizing enzymes in the cytochrome P450 family, including CYP3A4, CYP1A2, and CYP2C19, is also therapeutically significant because by increasing the amount of liver enzyme, carbamazepine accelerates its own rate of metabolism and that of many other drugs (enzyme induction is discussed in Chapter 1). The more effective metabolism leads to reduced blood levels and the need to monitor and increase drug dosages to optimize treatment response and prevent drug interactions.

SECTION SUMMARY

- Antidepressants of all classes reduce symptoms in about two-thirds of individuals after 4 to 6 weeks of treatment. Total remission of symptoms occurs less often. Continued treatment prevents relapse.

- MAOIs elevate brain levels of monoamines by preventing their destruction in the presynaptic terminal by MAO and subsequently altering receptor number and intracellular signaling.

- The most common side effects of MAOIs include changes in blood pressure, sleep disturbances, and weight gain. More serious side effects are associated with enhanced response to sympathomimetics, hypertensive crisis following elevation of tyramine levels, and drug interactions due to liver enzyme inhibition.

- TCAs block reuptake of NE or 5-HT or both, and this increases synaptic levels and produces subsequent compensatory changes in receptors and intracellular signaling.

- Side effects of TCAs include sedation, anticholinergic effects, and potentially dangerous cardiovascular effects.

- Second-generation antidepressants, including the SSRIs, are not more effective or more rapid in onset but are safer.

- Side effects of SSRIs are due to enhanced 5-HT function at multiple 5-HT receptors and include sexual dysfunction. Potentially fatal serotonin syndrome occurs when SSRIs are combined with other serotonergic drugs. Physical dependence occurs in 60% of cases.

- Mirtazapine enhances NE and 5-HT function by blocking α_2-autoreceptors and heteroreceptors on 5-HT cells. It also blocks selective 5-HT receptors to reduce side effects.

- Third-generation agents comprise CRF receptor antagonists, enhancers of the cAMP intracellular cascade, agomelatine, ketamine, galanin agonists, tianeptine, and AMPA agonists. Multiple potential mechanisms may explain ketamine's rapid onset of antidepressant effects.

- The ability of physical exercise to relieve depression may depend on its ability to increase neurogenesis and dendritic resculpturing. Emerging evidence suggests a role for the hormone adiponectin in this process.

- Lithium carbonate reduces manic episodes without causing depression and reduces bipolar cycling. It is more effective than alternatives in reducing suicide rates.

- Side effects of lithium are relatively mild, but toxic effects at the highest doses lead to seizures, coma, and death. The therapeutic index is very small, so frequent monitoring of blood levels is needed.

- Lithium and other antimanic drugs modulate several intracellular signaling pathways, including the GSK-3 pathway, and neurotrophic factors.

- The anticonvulsant valproate is as effective as lithium and has different side effects but is teratogenic, so its use in women of childbearing age is limited.

- Carbamazepine has a time course and effectiveness similar to those of lithium with different side effects, some of which are liver toxicity and blood diseases. Induction of several cytochrome enzymes causes significant drug interactions.

STUDY QUESTIONS

1. Summarize the central characteristics of major depressive disorder and bipolar disorder.

2. Provide evidence for a genetic contribution to affective disorders.

3. Describe the diathesis–stress model of psychiatric disorders.

4. Describe the HPA axis, including its negative feedback mechanism. What are the three most consistent neuroendocrine abnormalities found in clinically depressed patients?

5. Discuss the significance of an altered sleep–wake cycle in depression and bipolar disorder.

6. Describe the emerging role of the gut–brain axis in the etiology of neuropsychiatric disorders, including depression and anxiety.

7. What are the three types of validity that ideally should be met by animal models of psychiatric disorders? Describe several models for bipolar disorder.

8. What is the monoamine hypothesis, and why has it been modified?

9. Provide evidence for the importance of 5-HT dysfunction in major depression.

10. What is the default-mode network, and what role does it play in the pathophysiology of depression?

11. What role does NE play in antidepressant action? What is the role of NE/5-HT interaction?

12. How do the structural and functional abnormalities in the brains of depressed individuals prompt the formulation of the glucocorticoid hypothesis? The neurotrophic hypothesis?

13. Describe the mechanism of action of MAOIs. How does their mechanism of action explain the occurrence of their major side effects?

14. What is the mechanism of action of the TCAs? Why have their side effects prompted the development of the SSRIs?

15. Describe the mechanism of action of the SSRIs. What are their significant side effects, and why are they different from the TCAs? Although considered safer than the older drugs, what potential serious outcomes are associated with the SSRIs?

16. Why is the mechanism of action of ketamine generating so much research attention? Describe several of the potential mechanisms of action. What is esketamine, what is its recommended dosage regimen, and how does it differ in side effects relative to racemic ketamine?

17. How can galanin cause depression and also have antidepressant effects? What is its relationship to other antidepressant agents?

18. Provide evidence to suggest that exercise has antidepressant effects, and describe the emerging role of adiponectin in this process.

19. Describe the effectiveness of lithium for bipolar disorder, as well as its side effects. Describe one signaling cascade that may be responsible for the drug's ability to modify both the highs and the lows of mood.

20. Compare lithium, valproate, and carbamazepine in terms of efficacy and side effects. If you needed to be treated with one of these, which would you choose? Why?

Schizophrenia: Antipsychotic Drugs

ARTHUR WAS 22 YEARS OLD WHEN HE WAS BROUGHT TO THE CLINIC
because his parents were upset by his unusual behavior. He was an average student
taking classes at a local junior college. He had taken a series of temporary jobs until
he was laid off from the most recent one. It was then that he started talking about
his blueprints to save all the starving children in the world. He said he had a secret
plan that he would reveal only at the right time to the right person. His family became
more distressed when he said he was going to the German embassy because they
were the only ones who would listen to him. He said he would climb the fence at night
and present his plan to the German ambassador. After several visits to the clinic the
psychiatrist finally saw the plan, which consisted of random thoughts (e.g., "The poor,
starving souls" and "The moon is the only place") and drawings of rocket ships that
would go to the moon, where Arthur would create a community for the poor children.
As time went on, Arthur began to show dramatic changes in emotion, often crying
and acting apprehensive. He stopped wearing socks and underwear and, despite the
extremely cold weather, would not wear a jacket outdoors. He had moved into his
mother's apartment, but he wouldn't sleep much at night and kept the family up until
early morning. For his mother, it was a living nightmare because she felt so unable to
help her son (Barlow and Durand, 1995).

This chapter describes the characteristics of the devastating mental disorder
known as schizophrenia and the drug therapies that are currently available to treat it.
It also describes several models that attempt to explain the neuropathology that leads
to its hallmark abnormal behavior and multiple symptoms. ■

© iStock/PointImages

The symptoms of schizophrenia frequently
lead to personal isolation and failure to
achieve a meaningful and productive lifestyle.

19.1 Characteristics of Schizophrenia

Major mental disorders called psychoses are characterized by severe distortions of reality and disturbances in perception, intellectual functioning, affect (emotional expression), motivation, social relationships, and motor behavior. Schizophrenia is one relatively common form of the psychiatric diseases known as schizophrenia spectrum and other psychotic disorders. Other conditions in this category are schizophreniform disorder, brief psychotic disorder, schizoaffective disorder, delusional disorder, schizotypal (personality) disorder, and catatonia. Subtypes of schizophrenia that were classified in the *DSM-IV* (i.e., paranoid, disorganized, catatonic, undifferentiated, and residual types) have been eliminated from the *DSM-5* due to the inherent heterogeneity of the disorder and their relatively undifferentiated response to treatment. Individuals with schizophrenia demonstrate many different symptoms, including hearing voices that are not there, holding unrealistic ideas and beliefs, and communicating in a way that is difficult to understand. They may be so incapacitated that voluntary or involuntary hospitalization is required at various times in their lives.

Although drug use or environmental toxins may cause brief episodes of psychosis, schizophrenia is generally a chronic condition. Furthermore, while its symptoms can usually be controlled to some extent, schizophrenia cannot at this time be cured or prevented. Despite therapy, approximately 30% of people with schizophrenia spend a significant portion of their lives in psychiatric hospitals, accounting for a majority of the total hospital beds in these facilities. Approximately 1% to 1.5% of the world's population will suffer from schizophrenia during their lifetimes. Another 2% to 3% will suffer from less severe schizophrenic-like symptoms but will not meet diagnostic criteria.

Symptoms of schizophrenia most often begin during the late teenage years and early 20s, although the disorder may first occur in childhood. The early onset of the disorder means that the episodes recurring throughout life disrupt the individual's most productive years. Although epidemiological studies have indicated that schizophrenia affects men and women equally, a clear sex difference in the age of onset and the course of this disorder exists. **FIGURE 19.1** shows that among 9006 men and 7142 women, in one study the age of onset of schizophrenia spectrum disorders was highest in early adulthood for both sexes. However, for men the chances of experiencing a first episode of schizophrenia decreased rapidly with age. The age of first diagnosis for women is lower than for men until age 36. At that time, more women than men demonstrate a first episode, and this difference continues into old age (Sommer et al., 2020). Earlier age of onset is associated with more severe symptoms, particularly more frequent and intense negative symptoms and more severe loss of cognitive

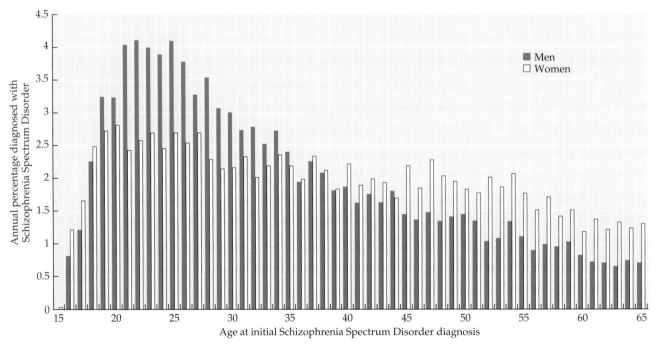

FIGURE 19.1 **Sex differences in age at onset of schizophrenia** Although both sexes show peak onset of symptoms between 16 and 25 years of age, this sample of 470 patients shows that more women than men experience their first episode after age 36, a difference that continues in every age bracket through old age. (After I. E. Sommer et al. 2020. *npj Schizophr* 6: 1–7. doi.org/10.1038/s41537-020-0102-z.; CC BY 4.0, creativecommons.org/licenses/by/4.0/)

function, both of which are not well managed by the current antipsychotic drugs (see the section on diagnosis below). In addition, episodes of symptom relapse are more frequent in individuals with earlier age of onset, so males tend to experience an overall poorer prognosis. The implication of the sex difference for age of onset is not clear, but it may suggest the existence of two qualitatively distinct subtypes of the disorder. Recent studies suggest a gene × sex interaction, which supports the preclinical rodent findings of an impact of sex steroids on the function of dopamine (DA), a neurotransmitter that has a central role in the pathophysiology of psychosis. Female estrogen levels may explain their higher rate of symptom onset (compared with males) with increasing age (see Figure 19.1) as estrogen hormone levels gradually decline. Further, the age of onset in females is inversely related to puberty onset, indicating a possible neuroprotective effect of the female hormone on neurodevelopment leading up to the onset of symptoms (see Godar and Bartoloto, 2014).

Schizophrenia can destroy lives and also cause a great deal of emotional pain and suffering, not only for afflicted individuals but also for their families as they attempt to cope emotionally and financially with the disorder. On this basis, the direct (e.g., hospitalization and medication) and indirect (e.g., loss of productive employment, participation in society, and family stress) costs of schizophrenia have been estimated to be between $134 billion and $174 billion a year in the United States for 2013 (Cloutier et al., 2016), reflecting an average annual cost of over $44,000 for each person with schizophrenia.

Schizophrenia is a heterogeneous disorder

According to the *DSM-5* (American Psychiatric Association, 2013), schizophrenia is formally defined by the presence of delusions, hallucinations, or disorganized thought. Additionally, grossly disorganized or abnormal motor behavior and negative symptoms are frequently apparent; however, the specific symptoms show a great deal of individual variation. Delusions are false beliefs that are firmly held, even when the person is presented with evidence to the contrary. Delusions may be classified as bizarre if they are clearly implausible, such as beliefs about alien abduction. In contrast, delusions may be classified as non-bizarre if they are at least plausible (for instance, the belief that one is under constant government surveillance). Particularly prevalent are delusions of persecution involving the individual's belief that others are spying on or planning to harm them. Also quite common is the delusion that one's thoughts are broadcast from one's head to the world, or that thoughts and feelings are not one's own but are imposed by an outside source, such as from outer space. Disturbances in perception (hallucinations) occur without external stimuli and are a frequent occurrence in schizophrenia. These hallucinations are most often auditory and generally consist of voices that are insulting or commanding, and perceived as separate from the thoughts of the afflicted individual. For a closer look at auditory hallucinations, see **WEB BOX 19.1**. Language, particularly speech, is often disorganized or incoherent, with individuals frequently switching to unrelated topics or giving unrelated answers to questions. Speech that is so illogical that it substantially interferes with communication is thus thought to reflect disorganized thinking.

Grossly disorganized or abnormal motor behavior is characterized by reduced motor activity, as well as inappropriate and bizarre postures, rigidity that resists efforts to be moved, or purposeless and stereotyped movements, for example rocking or pacing. At times, people with schizophrenia can be agitated and violent (Krakowski and Czobor, 1997). Negative symptoms frequently manifest as reduced emotional expression and lack of volition. Many individuals with schizophrenia show no expression, speak in a monotone, and report a lack of feeling. Sudden and unpredictable changes of emotion are also common. People with schizophrenia are frequently socially withdrawn and display extreme apathy and an inability to initiate activities (avolition). These negative symptoms contribute significantly to the disability associated with schizophrenia, whereby the individual has no interest in performing everyday activities, including maintaining personal hygiene, which further isolates the individual from mainstream society. Additionally, a variety of cognitive deficits impair the individual's ability to function at home, school, and the workplace.

Diagnosing schizophrenia can be challenging

Although the symptoms described here seem to be easily recognizable, making the diagnosis of schizophrenia is not so simple. One reason is that no two individuals show the identical pattern of symptoms, nor is there a single symptom that occurs in every patient with schizophrenia. Furthermore, symptoms increase and decrease over time, and the predominant symptoms or symptom clusters often change over the years in the same individual, which may lead to a change in diagnosis. The question of whether schizophrenia is a single disorder or a collection of disorders has never been fully resolved.

One useful classification scheme, stemming from the work of Crow (1980) and modified more recently by Andreasen (1990), is that of **positive**, **negative**, and **cognitive symptoms**. The positive symptoms of schizophrenia include the more dramatic symptoms of the disorder, such as delusions and hallucinations, disorganized speech and thinking, and bizarre behavior. Patients who demonstrate predominantly positive symptoms tend to be older when they experience a sudden onset of symptoms. These patients respond well to conventional antipsychotic medications that block dopamine receptors (D_2), and their symptoms are made worse by drugs that enhance DA function. Current thinking suggests that neurochemical abnormalities are significant in this disorder (see Section 19.3 on abnormal DA function).

Negative symptoms are characterized by a decline in normal function and include reduced speech (alogia), deficits in emotional responsiveness (flattened affect), loss of initiative and motivation (avolition), social withdrawal, and inability to derive pleasure from normally pleasurable activities (anhedonia). These symptoms are harder to recognize and may be mistaken for other conditions such as major depression. The cognitive symptoms characteristic of schizophrenia include impaired working memory, executive functioning, and attention. Together, negative symptoms and cognitive deficits are responsible for poorer functioning in the community and greater isolation. Unfortunately, the negative and cognitive symptoms are among the most resistant to antipsychotic drugs and make it difficult for the individual to perform tasks of daily living or to lead a routine life, even when medication reduces the positive symptoms. Unlike patients with prominent positive symptoms, patients with dominant negative and cognitive symptoms tend to show early onset of some symptoms and a long course of progressive deterioration, perhaps reflecting long-term neurodegeneration or developmental errors. Although the film *A Beautiful Mind* does not reflect the medical realities of mental illness, it does provide an excellent insight into the experiences of a brilliant individual (John Nash, as portrayed by Russell Crowe) as he copes with the onset of schizophrenia.

SECTION SUMMARY

- Schizophrenia is a chronic psychosis that occurs in 1% to 1.5% of the population worldwide. Symptoms begin during late adolescence and early adulthood. Men have an earlier onset than women and a poorer prognosis.

- Schizophrenia is characterized by illogical thinking, lack of reasoning, and failure to recognize reality. Specific symptoms show large variation among individuals, making diagnosis difficult.

- Positive symptoms are dramatic and lead to diagnosis. They include hallucinations, delusions, disorganized speech, and abnormal behavior. These symptoms respond to antipsychotic drug treatment.

- Negative symptoms are the absence of normal functions and include reduced speech, flat affect, loss of motivation, social withdrawal, apathy, and anhedonia.

- Cognitive deficits include impaired working memory, executive function, and attention. Negative symptoms and cognitive deficits are resistant to current treatments.

19.2 Etiology of Schizophrenia

Scientists from several disciplines use a variety of strategies to uncover the causes of schizophrenia. The goal is to develop an integrated approach to psychopathology that considers anatomical, neurochemical, and functional factors. Schizophrenia is best understood as a disorder having a genetic component that makes the individual more vulnerable than the average person to particular environmental factors.

Abnormalities of brain structure and function occur in individuals with schizophrenia

Until recently, no differences could be detected in the brains of individuals with schizophrenia compared with controls. However, with the development of new techniques in neuroscience, differences of several kinds have been found, including structural differences, functional abnormalities, and abnormalities in immune function.

STRUCTURAL ABNORMALITIES   Brain imaging techniques such as computerized tomography (CT) and magnetic resonance imaging (MRI) continue to produce evidence of structural abnormalities in the brains of people with schizophrenia. Many studies show cerebral atrophy (shrinking or wasting away) and corresponding enlargement of fluid-filled ventricles following cell shrinkage (**FIGURE 19.2**). Among the brain areas showing reduced volume are the basal ganglia, the temporal and frontal cortices, and several limbic regions such as the hippocampus, as well as white matter tracts connecting these regions. Differences in the temporal lobe and hippocampus in people with chronic schizophrenia compared with controls are some of the most consistent MRI findings (DeLisi et al., 1991). Structural differences in these areas also occur in monozygotic twins when only one has the disorder.

28-year-old male identical twins

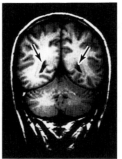
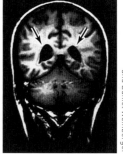

Healthy   Affected

Courtesy of Drs. E. Fuller Torrey and Daniel Weinberger

FIGURE 19.2   Brain images of twins not concordant for schizophrenia The arrows in the figure point to the ventricles filled with cerebrospinal fluid. The healthy twin has normal-sized ventricles, and his schizophrenic twin has ventricles that are much enlarged.

Using post-mortem brains, researchers found that the reduced volume of various brain regions was not due to a diminished number of cells, but rather to neurons having smaller somas, reduced dendritic trees and dendritic spine density, and increased cell packing. Numerous studies show that hippocampal cells of patients with schizophrenia are more disorganized (**FIGURE 19.3A**) than those of healthy people (**FIGURE 19.3B**) and that selected cortical layers in the brains of patients with schizophrenia are atrophied. Additionally, many brain areas showing shrinking of dendritic trees were associated with failures of connectivity among neurons and abnormal neuronal processing. With the use of new technologies such as diffusion tensor imaging (DTI) and resting-state fMRI (rs-fMRI; see Chapter 4 for a description of these techniques), the strength and integrity of myelinated white matter tracts can be more readily assessed. Studies using these techniques show altered patterns and inefficiency of networks of neurons that would impair the integration of signals among brain areas needed for sensory and cognitive processing as well as the organization of behavioral responses. In particular, a diminished amount of structural connectivity is especially apparent in white matter projections that link the frontal, temporal, and parietal regions. Both the extent of myelination and organization of the tracts are impaired in patients with schizophrenia, suggesting these fiber bundles play an important role in the pathophysiology of schizophrenia. Abnormalities in neural connections have been associated with lower IQ and performance on a variety of tests of cognitive function in healthy adults. In schizophrenia the severity of multiple connectivity deficits is correlated with the severity of positive and negative symptoms as well as cognitive function (van den Heuvel and Fornito, 2014). Indeed, specific symptom clusters (e.g., positive symptoms in first-episode patients) have been linked to distinct abnormalities in functional connections between brain regions, such as between caudate and dorsolateral prefrontal cortex (DLPFC). Recent analyses using advanced machine learning techniques have suggested that there may be neuroanatomical subtypes of schizophrenia that account for much of the variance in brain morphology (Chand et al., 2020). Occurrence of some of the more subtle brain differences in healthy family members, in early-onset patients, and even neonatal offspring of patients argues for a genetic predisposition to developmentally abnormal connectivity, which increases vulnerability to psychosis (see van den Heuvel and Fornito, 2014; Tamnes and Agartz, 2019). Ideally these findings may ultimately provide a diagnostic tool to identify those individuals who are at most risk for developing schizophrenia so that prevention or treatment intervention may be utilized.

Investigators are always concerned that some brain changes may be due to progressive deterioration during the course of illness, rather than being the cause of the illness, or may be due to the effects of antipsychotic medication used chronically over many years. A meta-analysis of MRI studies demonstrated reduced whole brain and hippocampal volume in patients experiencing their first psychotic episode, indicating that changes in brain morphology are present early in the

(A) Patient with schizophrenia

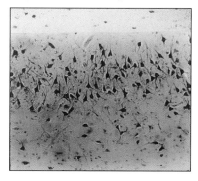

(B) Healthy control

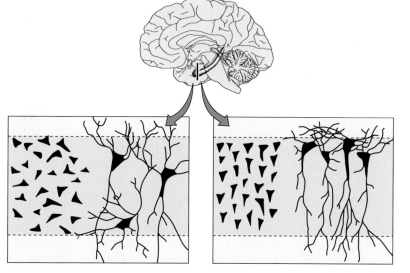

FIGURE 19.3 **Disorganization of cells in the hippocampus** Histological cross-sections of hippocampus showing the disorganized cells in the brain of a patient with schizophrenia (A) compared with the brain of a healthy control (B). Corresponding schematic diagrams show the haphazard arrangement of pyramidal cells in the hippocampus of patients with schizophrenia and the normal parallel organization in controls. (After J. A. Kovelman and A. B. Scheibel. 1984. *Bio Psychiatry* 19: 1601–1621.)

disease, and leaving open the possibility of neurodevelopmental abnormalities that may precede symptom onset by many years (Steen et al., 2006). A subsequent meta-analysis examining published data from over 9000 patients indicated that in addition to reduced brain volume, intracranial volume is also reduced, providing further evidence for a relatively early abnormality in development, since the cranium reaches 90% of adult size by the age of 5 years, and reaches adult size by 16 or 17 years of age. Thus, reduced cranial volume would necessarily reflect the occurrence of an abnormality relatively early in development. Moreover, researchers found that gray matter reductions were correlated with progression of the disease and dose of antipsychotic pharmacotherapy (Haijma et al., 2013). On the basis of these results, researchers have concluded that ventricular enlargement is not due to progressive loss of brain cells but may represent abnormalities of brain development preceding the onset of symptoms. Additional evidence for this idea is the discovery that more subtle cellular abnormalities are rarely accompanied by gliosis (proliferation of astrocytes and microglia). Since gliosis is a response to neuronal damage that occurs in the mature brain, but not in the immature brain, it is likely that the cell abnormalities occurred during development (Weinberger, 1995). Lastly, although many individuals diagnosed with schizophrenia have a relatively poor long-term prognosis, symptom severity, including that of cognitive deficits, does not typically worsen over time, as would expected with most brain diseases that arise due to degenerative processes. Prenatal inflammation represents one potential explanation for the abnormalities in brain structure (see Immune System Dysfunctions section).

FUNCTIONAL ABNORMALITIES In addition to structural abnormalities in the brains of individuals with schizophrenia, regional brain function differs from that in controls. Measures of brain function include rate of cell metabolism, blood flow, electrical activity, and chemical changes. The most consistent difference is reduced function of the prefrontal cortex (PFC), called hypofrontality (Buchsbaum, 1990). Positron emission tomography (PET) and single-photon emission computerized tomography (SPECT) studies show less of an increase in cerebral blood flow in the frontal cortex of patients with schizophrenia than in healthy individuals while performing PFC-dependent cognitive tasks. These tasks include executive functioning, working memory, response inhibition, and problem solving that require planning, strategy, and attentional set shifting, such as the Wisconsin Card Sorting Test (WCST; **FIGURE 19.4A**). Reduced blood flow is associated with less glucose use, which in turn indicates how active the brain cells are. **FIGURE 19.4B** shows that the frontal cortex is less active in a patient with

schizophrenia compared with a non-schizophrenic twin, both at rest and during the WCST. Nevertheless, further research indicates that the picture is not quite so simple. When performing several different executive tasks, healthy individuals and those with schizophrenia activated the same brain regions, including the DLPFC, ventrolateral prefrontal cortex (VLPFC), anterior cingulate cortex (ACC), and thalamus. However, patients with schizophrenia showed much less activation in the left DLPFC, ACC, and left thalamus and in areas in the inferior and posterior cortex during selective tasks, which is consistent with their impairment in cognitive control. Somewhat surprising is the finding that individuals with schizophrenia showed *greater* activation than controls in several brain structures such as the VLPFC, amygdala, and insula. It is not clear whether the enhanced neural activity reflects a compensatory use of other brain areas to handle the cognitive tasks, or whether shifting of the network of activity represents a disease-specific pattern (Minzenberg et al., 2009). Hypofrontality in schizophrenia is especially interesting because the negative and cognitive symptoms of schizophrenia resemble the deficits seen following surgical disconnection of the frontal lobes (prefrontal lobotomy). Included in these deficits are poor social functioning, loss of motivation, defective attention, emotional blunting, and inability to shift strategies during problem solving (Gur, 1995).

IMMUNE SYSTEM DYSFUNCTIONS Almost 100 years ago inflammation was considered a potential etiological factor in the development of psychosis. It was observed that individuals with schizophrenia frequently have dysfunctional immune systems and that this dysfunction could be at least in part responsible for the observed neuropathology. A confluence of evidence supports the association between immune dysfunction and schizophrenia. According to multiple meta-analyses, blood levels of pro-inflammatory cytokines (a variety of small proteins released by immune cells) are elevated and anti-inflammatory cytokines are reduced in first-episode schizophrenic patients who have never taken antipsychotic drugs. Those cytokine levels return to normal after successful antipsychotic drug treatment. Further, levels in the cerebrospinal fluid (CSF) of the pro-inflammatory cytokine interferon-β were significantly elevated in patients with schizophrenia, suggesting a potential role for the action of pro-inflammatory cytokines in the central nervous system (CNS) (Hidese et al., 2021). Whether the cytokines are causing the symptoms or are released in response to the disease is not clear, although animal studies suggest a causative role.

Epidemiological research has shown that maternal levels of cytokines that are elevated due to exposure to any one of a variety of infectious diseases (e.g.,

(A)

(B)

At rest

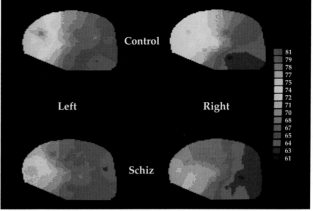

During card-sorting task

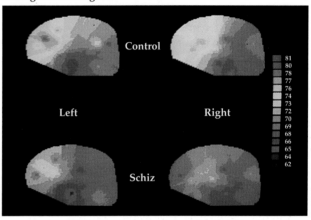

Courtesy of Karen Berman

FIGURE 19.4 **Hypofrontality in schizophrenia** (A) The Wisconsin Card Sorting Test is used to evaluate the ability of an individual to shift response strategies on the basis of feedback from the tester. The person is presented with stimulus cards having simple designs that differ in color, shape, and number of elements. The individual is asked to sort the remaining cards into piles. With each attempt, the person is told whether the choice is correct or incorrect. Over the test period, the sorting principle may first be color and then may covertly shift to form or number. Patients with schizophrenia and those with frontal lobe lesions fail to adjust strategies and may continue to sort on the basis of the original stimulus (e.g., color) despite being told that color sorting is no longer correct. (B) PET scans comparing frontal lobe activity of a patient with schizophrenia and a non-schizophrenic twin. The sibling with schizophrenia has less frontal lobe activity at rest (top) as well as during a frontal lobe challenge with the Wisconsin Card Sorting Test (bottom).

influenza, rubella, pneumonia, sinusitis) predict increased risk of schizophrenia in the offspring (see the section on developmental errors below). Additionally, individuals with immune disorders, such as type 1 diabetes, rheumatoid arthritis, and Crohn's disease, have an increased genetic risk of developing schizophrenia compared with the general population. It is of interest that individuals with schizophrenia experienced more infections as children, and the more infections they experienced, the greater the likelihood of developing schizophrenia. Adults with schizophrenia also suffer from more infections, and it has been suggested that their sensitivity to environmental agents (e.g., viruses, food antigens) is due to early (perhaps prenatal) abnormal cytokine production. This early cytokine

production sensitizes neural substrates that alter the set point of the immune system and subsequently more readily trigger neuroinflammation and progressive brain pathology (see Meyer, 2013). It has been suggested that their immune responses to these environmental agents may be related to the onset of symptom relapse. It is of further interest that genome-wide association studies (GWAS) show a strong relationship between a region on chromosome 6 that is responsible for proteins involved in multiple immune functions and schizophrenia (see Sperner-Unterweger and Fuchs, 2015, for further discussion of genetic links).

Maternal peripheral cytokines elevated by infection can bypass the placenta and fetal blood–brain barrier in several ways to influence brain function. They also activate microglia (glial cells with immune function in the brain; see Chapter 2), producing an inflammatory assault and potential structural brain changes such as modification of neuronal synapses. Microglia normally detect infectious microorganisms and waste materials before becoming activated. Activation involves swelling up into an amoeboid shape and moving toward the pathogen to initiate processes for phagocytosis of the debris and production of cytokines, which initiates pro-inflammatory cascades. The extent of inflammation is normally under homeostatic control that ensures that the pathogens are destroyed and healing progresses, but the inflammation is then counteracted to protect uninfected, healthy tissue. Given that there must be a delicate balance between neuroprotection and neurotoxic functions for the brain to recover after injury, abnormal microglial action could have damaging outcomes regarding brain function in the developing individual.

Although accumulated evidence points to the significance of immune functioning in the etiology of schizophrenia, there has been limited research into the precise mechanism by which prenatal inflammation causes abnormal neurodevelopment that increases the risk for schizophrenia. Unfortunately, studies measuring microglia number or density in the brains of individuals with schizophrenia post-mortem have not produced consistent results. Although in some studies microglia were increased, others showed no difference from control brains. Certainly there may be several technical reasons for the disparity; however, there is evidence that patients showing *active* psychosis represent a subgroup with enhanced microglia number, so variation in the study population selection may explain the differences among studies. When *activated* microglia and increased cytokine gene expression have been assessed in post-mortem brains, much more consistent increases have been reported in selected brain regions such as frontal cortex, superior temporal gyrus, and subcortical regions—which are all brain areas with gray and white matter abnormalities in schizophrenia. Once again, activation of microglia seems greatest during acute illness relapses (see Laskaris et al., 2016). However, Bloomfield and coworkers (2015) found that elevated microglia activity *precedes* the onset of symptoms by using ultra-high-risk individuals, as assessed with the Comprehensive Assessment of At-Risk Mental States. These individuals did not have active psychosis and were medication-free. Using PET binding of the translocator protein TSPO, which is expressed on microglia, Bloomfield and associates found greater microglial activity in temporal lobe, frontal lobe, and total gray matter that was correlated to their risk assessment score.

Genetic, environmental, and developmental factors interact

Although schizophrenia is an ancient disorder described as early as 1000 BCE, its causes remain unknown. Schizophrenia is increasingly regarded as a neurodevelopmental disorder with a strong genetic component; however, psychological, biological, and sociological factors combine in a unique manner to contribute to its psychopathology, course, and outcome.

HEREDITY The importance of heredity has been demonstrated by numerous family, twin, and adoption studies, showing that relatives of individuals with schizophrenia are afflicted with the disorder at an elevated rate. In fact, the closer the genetic relationship, the greater is the probability of schizophrenia in the relative. In a classic study, Gottesman (1991) summarized a large number of family and twin studies of individuals with schizophrenia that had been completed between 1920 and 1987 (**FIGURE 19.5**). These data demonstrate that the risk of having schizophrenia varies according to how many genes one shares with someone who has the disorder. Compared with the lifetime risk in the general population of about 1%, first-degree relatives such as parents, children, and siblings have an average lifetime risk 12 times greater (ranging from 6% to 17%), but more distant (second-degree) relatives, including uncles and aunts, nephews and nieces, grandchildren, and half-siblings, have an average risk of 4% (ranging from 2% to 6%). Dizygotic twins, who have the genetic similarity of siblings but who share the prenatal environment, show a concordance of 17%, which means that if one twin of the pair develops schizophrenia, the probability of the second twin developing the disorder is 17%. In comparison, monozygotic (identical) twins, who have identical genes, have a concordance of 48% or higher. This concordance exists even when the twins are reared apart in different environments, which further demonstrates the heritability of schizophrenia. However, although the concordance is striking, it is important to point out that other factors must be involved in the occurrence of the disorder, because if genetic abnormalities were totally responsible, concordance for identical twins would be 100%. Hence individuals having a gene that predisposes them to schizophrenia do not necessarily develop the disorder.

Molecular genetic research is working to identify the specific genes that predict vulnerability to schizophrenia, which could allow early intervention to prevent disease and identify molecular pathways involved in its etiology (Muglia, 2011). The task is difficult because multiple genes located at different **loci** (sites on our chromosomes) are involved. Multiple gene abnormalities would explain why the risk of having schizophrenia increases with the number of affected relatives in the family. It also might explain why the symptom clusters vary in nature and intensity from individual to individual. Developments in technology such as **DNA microarray** and GWAS provide the means for rapid screening of large quantities of genomic data. These methods, described in Chapter 4, can identify complex gene expression patterns. For example, Maycox and colleagues (2009) reported multiple defects in the gene groups related to presynaptic function in the PFC of individuals with schizophrenia compared with healthy controls. In particular, they found the greatest and most consistent

FIGURE 19.5 Lifetime risks of developing schizophrenia among relatives of an affected individual Data are summarized from about 40 family and twin studies conducted between 1920 and 1987. Compared with a 1% risk of developing schizophrenia in the general population, second-degree relatives have an average risk of 4%, first-degree relatives have a 6% to 17% risk, monozygotic twins have a 48% risk, and children having two parents with schizophrenia have an average 47% risk. (After I. I. Gottesman 1991. *Schizophrenia Genesis*. W. H. Freeman: New York.)

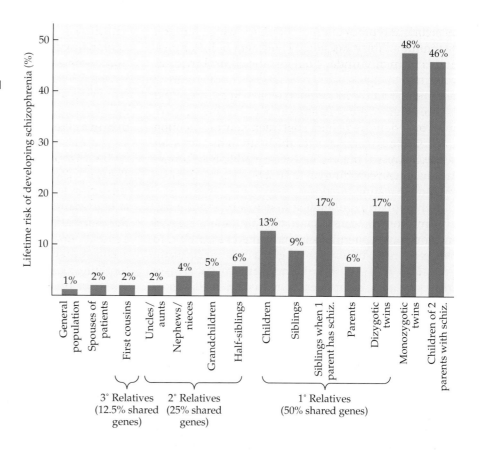

defects in proteins needed for synaptic vesicle recycling, neurotransmitter release, and cytoskeleton organization and function. At present, 145 loci have been identified as likely sites for genes that increase the risk for developing schizophrenia (Pardiñas et al., 2018).

The new technology has produced a huge number of studies and identified hundreds of genetic risk variants in an attempt to predict vulnerability to schizophrenia. The work has generated an enormous amount of enthusiasm among researchers because it holds such tremendous promise for understanding the neural basis for the disorder, developing better animal models for drug testing, and improving treatment options. The excitement is in part due to refined statistical approaches capable of handling very large amounts of data, along with the establishment of the Schizophrenia Working Group of the Psychiatric Genomics Consortium. The consortium provides the opportunity to pool data from multiple large research projects to enhance the statistical power of analysis (Devor at al., 2017). Nevertheless, others are more pessimistic because despite the great effort and cost, success has been quite modest. Certainly one reason is that there is little precision in diagnosis of schizophrenia (as is true for other psychiatric disorders) because there is no objective measure (as there is for diabetes or cancer), and researchers cannot know whether their sampling population is homogeneous or whether it contains multiple subsets of patients. Also,

compared with other, more common diseases such as diabetes, the size of the population sampled has been much smaller for schizophrenia. It is also possible that the genetic variants identified are associated not with the complex disorder of schizophrenia, but with specific symptom clusters. Indeed, recent GWAS evidence suggests a large genetic overlap for schizophrenia, autism, and bipolar disorder, as well as cardiovascular risk factors and multiple sclerosis.

Recent research reported that examination of a vast array of independent GWAS using a powerful statistical approach showed that many genes associated with schizophrenia involve the disruption of communication between large numbers of ionotropic and metabotropic families of receptors, as well as voltage-gated calcium channels (Devor et al., 2017; Pardiñas et al., 2018). The failure of information processing based on abnormal synaptic regulation supports our earlier discussion of schizophrenia as a disorder of connectivity, since the integration of synaptic signaling is critical for all neurotransmitter systems and intracellular functions. Devor and coworkers found genetic variations in a large array of ionotropic and metabotropic receptors, including those for DA, glutamate, GABA, acetylcholine (ACh), opioids, and serotonin (5-HT), all of which impact symptoms of schizophrenia.

It is clear that a single gene that makes a large contribution to the susceptibility to such a complex disorder as schizophrenia will not be found. Instead it seems that large numbers of genetic variants will be found and that each will contribute only a small amount, conferring what is often referred to as polygenic inheritance. It has been estimated that combining all the identified polymorphisms together explains approximately 45% of the variability in disease risk (Sullivan et al., 2018); however, the Psychiatric Genomics Consortium stresses that indices of polygenic risk thus far lack adequate sensitivity and specificity to be used for predictive testing purposes (Ripke et al., 2014). In addition to inherited polymorphisms, it is possible that environmental factors causing epigenetic changes modify developmental mechanisms not by altering the gene itself, but by altering the expression of the gene (**BOX 19.1**). Another alternative is that some of the missing genetic component may be explained by rare chromosomal abnormalities in candidate genes such as *disrupted in schizophrenia 1* (*DISC1*).

Chubb and colleagues (2008) summarize the evidence suggesting that mutations of the **DISC1 gene** (as many as 15 variants of the gene exist) increase the probability of developing schizophrenia and other mental disorders. The initial finding showed that a chromosomal abnormality, specifically a translocation of pieces of DNA on chromosomes 1 and 11, was strongly linked to schizophrenia in a large Scottish family (St. Clair et al., 1990). One gene that was disrupted by the translocation is *DISC1*, which codes for proteins essential for neuronal functions such as embryonic neurogenesis and neuronal migration, intracellular transport functions, and axon elongation. Each of these could contribute to the morphological abnormalities seen in the schizophrenic brain. Since DISC1 protein is found in cell bodies, axon terminals, the postsynaptic density, and dendritic spines, it is likely to have multiple roles in synaptic function, in addition to its known role in regulating mitochondrial function. Subsequently, *DISC1* was implicated in several psychiatric disorders, including bipolar disorder, depression, and autism.

DEVELOPMENTAL ERRORS   Many investigators now believe that genetic vulnerability increases the probability that events during perinatal (including prenatal and postnatal) brain development will contribute to the occurrence of schizophrenia (Lewis and Levitt, 2002). The abnormal pattern of cortical connections and other brain structure irregularities that exist in the brains of individuals with schizophrenia are likely to be due to disruptions in the normal processes of cell multiplication and cell loss that continue into adolescence.

Exposure to viral infection (e.g., pneumonia, influenza, measles, or polio), especially during the second trimester of pregnancy, significantly increases the risk of schizophrenia in the child. The damaging effects of maternal infection are not likely due to the direct viral effects on the developing fetus, but rather to maternal and/or fetal inflammatory responses. Animal studies suggest that cytokines can have neurodevelopmental effects by affecting cell neurogenesis, proliferation, migration, and survival (see Meyer, 2013). Infectious pathogens of many types are known to increase microglial activation and cytokine release and have been suspected to cause neurodevelopmental brain abnormalities and increase the risk for schizophrenia (see previous discussion of immune system dysfunctions). However, multiple studies have shown that in addition to exposure to an infectious pathogen, many other prenatal assaults cause inflammation that predicts schizophrenia. Hence dysfunctions of the immune system may be the common denominator that explains increased risk of schizophrenia from a broad range of prenatal insults including various obstetric complications, starvation, exposure to war conditions, maternal gestational diabetes, maternal depression, and others (see Miller et al., 2013). Although none of these stresses or immune dysfunction alone explain the occurrence of the illness, the assault may increase the probability of schizophrenia in the individual who is genetically at risk. The finding that the elevated risk of schizophrenia associated with prenatal infection is much higher in offspring with a family history of psychotic disorders supports the idea of genetic predisposition. You have already seen in Chapter 17, Box 18.1 and Box 19.1 how environmental events that cause epigenetic modification of gene transcription may increase the risk for psychiatric disorders, which may include schizophrenia.

Further evidence for early developmental errors potentially predicting later schizophrenia is provided by the observation of several behavioral characteristics of early infancy, particularly if the infant has other risk factors. The infant behaviors identified were passivity and apathy, reduced responsiveness to verbal commands, more difficult temperament, and poor sensorimotor performance. In later childhood, deficits in attentional and information-processing tasks, along with impairments in fine motor coordination, were the best predictors of psychiatric disorders.

Although evidence suggests that observers could identify subtle differences in the behavior of children who later developed schizophrenia, such as more negative facial expression, increased social withdrawal, and unusual motor movements, the more flamboyant symptoms that lead to diagnosis do not appear until adolescence, which is also a period of significant brain development. Keshavan and colleagues (1994) found significant abnormalities in synaptic pruning that normally occurs during puberty. Excessive synaptic pruning in the PFC (associated with negative symptoms) and failure of pruning in certain subcortical structures (associated with positive symptoms)

BOX 19.1 ■ THE CUTTING EDGE

Epigenetic Modifications and Risk for Schizophrenia

Schizophrenia is likely due to the interaction of numerous susceptibility genes, each contributing a small amount to overall risk, in combination with environmentally induced epigenetic modifications. As discussed in the text, complications of labor and delivery, prenatal exposure to viral infection, malnutrition, and many other such events occur to a greater extent in people who develop schizophrenia. Although no single event will be predictive, all of these things as well as trauma later in life may be considered environmental stressors. Early life stress produces epigenetic modifications that alter neurodevelopment. In earlier chapters (see Chapters 17 and 18), you learned that exposure to stress and neglect early in life alters the development of the brain and endocrine stress circuits, leading to subsequent hyperarousal to stressors and an increased probability of psychopathology. Environmental stressors can also alter the expression of genes, such as the one for reelin (*RELN*).

Since abnormal neural connectivity characterizes schizophrenia, the discovery of epigenetic modification of the *RELN* gene has received a great deal of attention. Reelin is an extracellular glycoprotein secreted by neurons, and among its many functions is its role in guiding neuron positioning during fetal brain development. A reduction in reelin in the developing nervous system could explain the cell disorganization and morphological abnormalities typically seen in post-mortem neuroanatomical studies of patients with schizophrenia. In adulthood, reelin seems to play a role in learning and memory by enhancing dendritic spine growth and synaptic plasticity. Consequently, low levels in the adult may reduce synaptic plasticity in the hippocampus and PFC, leading to cognitive deficits typical of schizophrenia. In fact, several studies have found up to 50% less reelin and its mRNA in the brains of patients with schizophrenia post-mortem, compared with controls, particularly in the PFC, but also in the hippocampus, cerebellum, and basal ganglia.

At least some of the reduced reelin expression is due to epigenetic modulation, which has prompted some researchers to consider it a critical factor in psychosis (Guidotti and Grayson, 2011). Several post-mortem studies have shown greater *RELN* hypermethylation (an epigenetic change described in Chapter 2) in several corticolimbic brain areas in patients with schizophrenia compared with controls. The added methyl groups would cause a more "closed" chromatin state and reduce transcription of the gene so that less reelin would be produced. The down-regulation of reelin may be due, at least in part, to an observed up-regulation of a methyltransferase enzyme responsible for the transfer of the methyl groups. Further evidence to support a role for epigenetic modification of *RELN* was noted when the amino acid methionine, which increases methylation, was given to patients with schizophrenia. It dramatically worsened symptoms for more than 60% of the patients. Of special significance is the finding that there are differences in DNA methylation between monozygotic twins discordant for schizophrenia, which may explain how the differences in experientially induced epigenetic processes increase one individual's vulnerability despite the presence of identical genes.

These findings have several important ramifications. First, they suggest ways to create animal models that mimic the cognitive deficits of schizophrenia by prenatal administration of methionine, stress, or viral infection. In one such study, Palacios-Garcia and colleagues (2015) used 2 hours of restraint stress of pregnant dams during embryonic days 11 to 20, times corresponding to early and late cortical development in the fetus. Using immunohistochemistry on gestation day 20, they found a significant decrease in reelin-positive neurons that was not due to loss of cells but suggested a deficit in reelin gene expression in the stressed animals (**FIGURE A**). Of the cortical areas analyzed, the decrease in reelin immunoreactivity was greatest in PFC (79%) and dorsolateral parietal cortex (58%). Parallel changes in the reelin

(*Continued*)

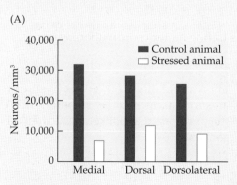

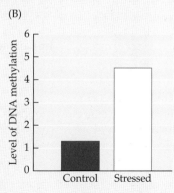

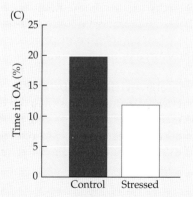

Reactions to prenatal stress (A) Prenatal stress reduces reelin-expressing neurons in the prenatal (E20) rat frontal cortex (medial, dorsal, and dorsolateral regions). (B) Level of DNA methylation at the reelin gene promoter region in samples of cerebral cortex from stressed and control rats.

(C) Prenatally stressed animals spent less time in the open arms (OA) of the elevated plus-maze. (After I. Palacios-Garcia et al. 2015. *PLOS ONE* 10: e0117680. doi: 10.1371/journal.pone.0117680; CC-BY 4.0. creativecommons.org/licenses/by/4.0/)

BOX 19.1 ■ THE CUTTING EDGE *(continued)*

signaling pathway were also found. DNA methylation was significantly elevated in the cerebral cortex of stressed pups compared with controls, which would explain the reduced transcription of the reelin gene (**FIGURE B**). Behavioral measures were taken when the remaining pups reached young adulthood at 2 months. The researchers found that the prenatally stressed animals showed increased locomotor activity and spontaneous rearing and spent significantly less time in the open arms of the elevated plus-maze, indicating increased anxiety-like behavior (**FIGURE C**). In addition they showed deficits in emotional memory of an aversive situation, which may be related to deficits in synaptic plasticity in the amygdala–PFC circuit. This and other similar models that evaluate the association of early stress, reelin DNA methylation and subsequent decrease in gene expression, and behavioral changes in the adult provide a platform to evaluate the etiology of schizophrenia. Additionally, these models can be used to identify drugs to reverse the cognitive symptoms that currently are not effectively treated.

A second ramification of the above-mentioned findings is that unlike genetic impairments, epigenetic programming can be reversed, creating new treatment options. As you learned earlier (see Box 18.1), down-regulation of gene expression due to hyper-methylation can be reversed by enhancing histone acetylation, either by activating histone acetylase or by inhibiting histone deacetylase. It is interesting that the mood stabilizer valproate, which is used to treat bipolar disorder (see Section 18.3), inhibits histone deacetylase and increases reelin expression in animals with suppressed reelin following methionine administration. Notably, epigenetic modifications of numerous other genes involved in neurotransmission and neurodevelopment have been identified, including genes for COMT, glutamate decarboxylase (GAD), and brain-derived neurotrophic factor (BDNF). In addition to histone deacetylase inhibitors, histone demethylase inhibitors and DNA methyltransferase inhibitors are being explored as novel "epidrugs" to target epigenetic modifications (Smigielski et al., 2020).

---

occur more often in the brains of individuals with schizophrenia than in healthy individuals. Using different technology, Thompson and coworkers (2001) imaged the brains of early-onset patients over several years with high-resolution MRI and compared them with age-matched controls. Although relatively rare, early-onset patients provide a unique opportunity to evaluate the timing and pattern of cortical gray matter changes to see how the disease emerges. What investigators found was that over the 5 years of the study, the patients lost twice as much cortical gray matter as the healthy controls. The excessive loss started in the parietal lobes and progressed anteriorly to the temporal lobes, to the DLPFC, and ultimately to the frontal eye fields (**FIGURE 19.6**). Of particular interest was that the extent of gray matter loss was correlated with the nature and severity of symptoms. Alterations in these

normal developmental processes could be caused by genetic programming errors, early brain insults, and environmental factors. The nature and extent of interaction of these factors remain unclear.

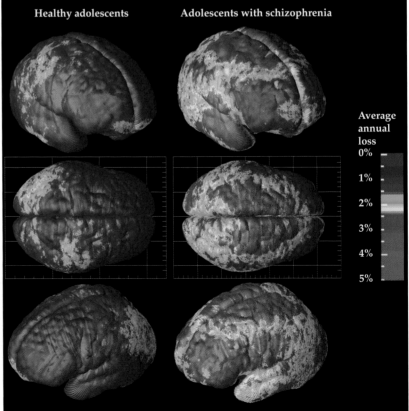

From P. M. Thompson et al. 2001. *Proc Natl Acad Sci* 98: 11650–11655. © 2001. National Academy of Sciences, U.S.A.; courtesy of Paul Thompson

FIGURE 19.6 Cortical gray matter loss Three-dimensional maps of brain changes show the average annual rate of loss of cortical gray matter in healthy adolescents (left) and in adolescents with schizophrenia (right).

BIOPSYCHOSOCIAL INTERACTION It is easy to imagine an interactive basis for schizophrenia that depends on genetic predisposition, structural brain-wiring errors, and subsequent biochemical abnormalities. Environmental or social factors that challenge susceptible individuals beyond their ability to deal with the stress further contribute to the development of the disorder. **WEB BOX 19.2** provides a fascinating case study demonstrating the interaction of genetic and environmental factors in a set of quadruplets with schizophrenia. **FIGURE 19.7** summarizes the stages in the development of schizophrenia on the basis of material presented in the text. This complex etiology and time course of the disorder is often referred to as the "two-hit" model. The perinatal events in the genetically vulnerable individual that cause altered brain development represent the first "hit." The second "hit" occurs at adolescence when neurodevelopmental errors in combination with environmental events produce the diagnosable symptoms of schizophrenia.

Preclinical models of schizophrenia

Developing animal models for schizophrenia is especially difficult because the primary symptoms involve perceptual and thought disturbances involving language that rely on higher-order cortical processes that researchers are unable to assess in lower animals. No single animal model can mimic the complex symptomatology of schizophrenia, so each one tends to focus on one aspect of the disorder and experimentally induce homologous (similar) changes in animal behavior. It is assumed that subsequent attempts to manipulate the experimental response both neurochemically and neuroanatomically should provide evidence for the neurobiological and genetic bases of human behavior.

Animal models are also used to screen new therapeutic drugs for effectiveness. These models may not resemble the psychiatric condition in any way and may instead depend on neurochemically induced behaviors that are known to respond to currently useful drugs. Many of these behavioral screens have relied on inducing the motor side effects caused by conventional antipsychotics, such as suppression of locomotion or catalepsy. These motor side effects are easy to observe in non-human animals and tend to be correlated with antipsychotic efficacy. However, the disadvantage of this approach is that such screening tools often fail to identify drugs with novel mechanisms of action, or drugs that avoid such motor side effects, which are of greatest interest to researchers.

There are multiple approaches to creating these models, including pharmacological, developmental, and environmental manipulations as well as gene modification. In all cases, the models must be evaluated for face validity, construct validity, and predictive validity, as discussed in Chapter 4. This section of the chapter will highlight just a few of the many techniques used.

The response to high doses of CNS stimulants is an early model that is still used because it is quick and easy to perform before further evaluation with other tests. It was found quite accidentally when clinicians realized that people who abuse CNS stimulants (amphetamine and cocaine) frequently show signs of psychosis, including paranoid delusions; various stereotyped, compulsive behaviors; and either visual or auditory hallucinations that are indistinguishable from those of schizophrenia.

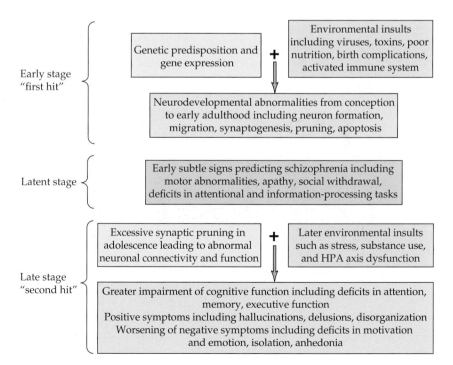

FIGURE 19.7 Etiology of schizophrenia This schematic diagram shows the importance of the interaction of genes and environmental factors in the development of schizophrenia, based on material presented in the text. Genes and environment interact to cause abnormal development of the nervous system. The neurodevelopmental abnormalities, such as errors in connectivity, make the individual susceptible to later environmental events at adolescence, which exacerbates the cognitive deficits and negative symptoms and elicits the positive symptoms leading to diagnosis.

Also, when amphetamine is administered to patients with schizophrenia, the patients report that their existing symptoms get worse, not that new symptoms are produced. Finally, amphetamine-induced psychosis can be treated with the same drugs that are most effective in treating schizophrenia.

In animals, high doses of amphetamine produce a characteristic stereotyped sniffing, licking, and gnawing. Because stereotyped behavior also occurs in response to high doses of amphetamine in humans and is similar to the compulsive repetitions of meaningless behavior seen in schizophrenia, **amphetamine-induced stereotypy** is used in the laboratory as an animal model for schizophrenia. For many years, it has been a classic screening device to identify effective antipsychotic drugs that block D_2 receptors. Because high doses of amphetamine release DA, the abnormal behaviors produced by the drug support the DA hypothesis of schizophrenia (this hypothesis is described later in the chapter). The downside to this model is that it presumably mimics only the positive symptoms, and since it depends on DA-regulated behavior, it is unlikely to identify drugs with novel mechanisms of action.

A second pharmacological model, the **hypoglutamate model**, relies on the acute reduction of glutamate neurotransmission, which reflects the hypoglutamatergic activity seen in patients with schizophrenia (see the following section on neurochemical models). The administration of the N-methyl-D-aspartate (NMDA) receptor antagonists phencyclidine (PCP) and ketamine produce rodent behaviors reminiscent of positive (e.g., deficits in prepulse inhibition of startle [PPI] and PCP-induced hyperactivity), negative (e.g., decreased social interaction and increased anxiety-like behaviors), and cognitive (e.g., deficits in working memory, novel object recognition, and attention) symptoms of schizophrenia. The drugs also produce positive, negative, and cognitive symptoms in healthy humans, which formed the basis for the hypoglutamate hypothesis of schizophrenia. The classic antipsychotics, such as haloperidol, are effective in reducing PCP- and ketamine-induced positive, but not negative or cognitive, symptoms. In contrast, the atypical antipsychotic clozapine can restore normal behavior. In the last section of this chapter you will see that these rodent results reflect human clinical experience. As was true for the high-dose amphetamine model, the hypoglutamate model is relatively easy and quick to use, but neither of them addresses the issue of neurodevelopmental abnormalities, which are believed to have a significant role in the etiology of schizophrenia. However, some evidence suggests that *chronic* NMDA antagonism causes inflammation and activation of microglia along with increased cytokines in specific brain regions. The fact that the cognitive deficits caused by chronic PCP administration can be reduced by anti-inflammatory drug treatment further supports the role of immune function in PCP-induced schizophrenia-like behavioral effects.

Mattei and colleagues (2015) provide an excellent review of the pharmacological models as well as many others. The disruption of immune function with chronic PCP administration links this model to the neurodevelopmental model of prenatal inflammation described below.

A technique used to evaluate the motor side effects of antipsychotic drugs is the **vacuous chewing movements test**. In this test, mouth and facial dyskinesias (i.e., involuntary mouth opening not directed to physical material) that occur after chronic (between 4 and 36 weeks) administration of antipsychotic medication are counted. Since these movements persist even after withdrawal of the drug, they are thought to resemble the tardive dyskinesia that occurs in some patients (see a later section on drug side effects). Clinical evidence and rodent testing both show that the movements are exacerbated by stress and that there is a higher incidence in older individuals.

Recently, cognitive symptoms have been an important focus for modeling because these symptoms are highly disruptive to individuals and their ability to function in the community. Also, the currently available antipsychotics are relatively ineffective in reversing the deficits. Some commonly used tasks that reflect deficits in schizophrenia were described in Chapter 4 and include tests of working memory, attention, and sensory processing. Of special interest is the development of the **attentional set-shifting task**, the rodent version of the WCST (see Figure 19.4A). In the animal task developed by Birrell and Brown (2000), rodents are presented with pairs of bowls to dig into. Only one has a food reward. Unlike the human version, which requires sorting cards by color, shape, or number, the animals must choose the bowl on the basis of either odor or surface texture. More recently an automated visual discrimination analog of the WCST has been developed to be used with monkeys. Because of their similarity to the WCST, if these tasks are fully validated, their results are expected to have good translation to human behavior. Interested readers are directed to a review by Brown and Tait (2016) that addresses the applicability of set-shifting tasks across species.

One very different type of model is based on evidence that schizophrenic individuals fail to "gate," or filter, much of the sensory stimuli they experience. Such a defect may lead to sensory overload and fragmented thinking because schizophrenic individuals are overwhelmed by sights, sounds, and odors in the environment that they cannot filter out. The acoustic startle response, used in the technique called **prepulse inhibition of startle** (**PPI**), is one of the most reliable and generalizable models used to study sensory-filtering deficits. The procedure is almost identical when used with human participants and laboratory animals, so the translation of findings is excellent. Reversal of induced sensory-filtering deficits predicts antipsychotic effects. Furthermore, when deficits are induced by administration of glutamate antagonists like PCP, it is a screening device that distinguishes between classical and atypical antipsychotics. The interested reader can find an update and review in Swerdlow and colleagues (2016). **WEB BOX 19.3** describes the technique and demonstrates the elegance of this model.

Since schizophrenia is a developmental disorder, models based on interfering with normal prenatal brain development have been developed. Many of the neurodevelopmental models are based on the epidemiological findings discussed earlier. That means that investigators subject pregnant rodents to inadequate diets, viral infections, elevated pro-inflammatory cytokines, or stressors that elevate glucocorticoids, or they create complications during delivery such as hypoxia. Each of these methods alters development of brain circuitry, produces neurochemical aberrations, and causes behavioral deficits that mimic some of the pathophysiology of schizophrenia. Since several methods produce a developmental delay in the onset of abnormalities, they may be particularly important for understanding the etiology of the disorder. One such model, the **neonatal ventral hippocampal lesion model** (**NVHL**), is described in **WEB BOX 19.4**.

There are many rodent models of **prenatal inflammation** based on the human epidemiological evidence

and animal data suggesting that prenatal exposure to cytokine-induced inflammation and microglial activation increases the risk of neurodevelopmental abnormalities associated with schizophrenia. These are considered excellent examples of the neurodevelopmental hypothesis of schizophrenia because they do not require lesioning, genetic, or pharmacological manipulations. In each case the animals show a natural development of aberrations as they approach adolescence and adulthood. These models involve administration of pro-inflammatory agents, such as human influenza virus; polyiosinic–polytidylic acid (polyI:C), a synthetic agent used to simulate viral infections; one of the many cytokines (e.g., interleukin-6, or IL-6); or bacterial lipopolysaccharide, to pregnant rodents at various embryonic time points. The offspring are then evaluated for long-term brain and behavioral effects, compared with offspring of vehicle-treated mothers. The timing of the infection is important because the developmental outcome varies with gestational age of the fetus. **BOX 19.2** provides greater detail on the use of prenatal infections and their neurobiological and behavioral outcomes as they relate to schizophrenia.

BOX 19.2 ■ PHARMACOLOGY IN ACTION

The Prenatal Inflammation Model of Schizophrenia

One early model of maternal immune activation in mice utilized infection with human influenza virus and was investigated in an extensive series of papers by Fatemi and coworkers (reviewed by Kneeland and Fatemi, 2012). When the researchers examined the offspring, they found significant differences in gene expression in multiple brain areas, including frontal cortex, hippocampus, and cerebellum. For example, after viral exposure at embryonic day 16 (E16, considered the middle of the murine second trimester), 1463 genes were up-regulated and 797 genes were down-regulated. Many of these genes are involved in inflammation, cell structure, neuronal function, and myelination. As you might expect, protein levels also varied with brain region and timing of the infection. It is of importance that some of the significant proteins that had higher levels, such as nitric oxide synthase that manufactures nitric oxide, are responsible for fetal brain injury. In contrast, other protein levels were reduced—for instance, reelin, which is important in migration and maturation of cells during brain development. Another protein with a reduced level was SNAP25, which is involved in axonal development, release of neurotransmitters, and apoptosis of infected cells. Structural brain and neurotransmitter abnormalities were reported in studies of both rodents and rhesus monkeys, along with behavioral differences, such as prepulse inhibition of startle (PPI) deficits, reduced spatial exploration, and social interaction, that

were reversible with antipsychotic drug treatment. The testing with rhesus monkeys is particularly important because cortical development is more advanced in primates than rodents, so it validates this model and suggests that results translate to humans. Once again, all of the findings were highly dependent on the timing of the prenatal infection. Hence this model shows that exposure to viral infection during narrow windows of gestational development leads to elements of a schizophrenia-like phenotype in the maturing animal.

Two of the best-established rodent models using maternal immune activation are those utilizing polyI:C as the inflammatory agent, mimicking the acute response to viral infection, or lipopolysaccharide, a bacterial endotoxin. Levels of pro-inflammatory cytokines are elevated by these agents, not only in the fetal brain, but also in the placenta and amniotic fluid, indicating widespread neuroinflammation during fetal development. As we saw for human influenza infections, these inflammatory agents also produce brain structural, neurochemical, cognitive, and behavioral outcomes that resemble components of schizophrenia in the adult offspring of treated mothers. An especially appealing characteristic of this model is that the adult offspring show behavioral correlates of positive, negative, and cognitive symptoms of schizophrenia. For psychopharmacologists, it is especially exciting to find that both

(Continued)

BOX 19.2 ■ PHARMACOLOGY IN ACTION *(continued)*

classical and second-generation antipsychotics reverse some of the disease-like behavioral effects. More important is that the anti-inflammatory antibiotic and antioxidant minocycline also reverses some behavioral abnormalities (see the last section of this chapter on renewed efforts to treat cognitive symptoms).

Many of the neuroanatomical effects of in utero exposure to inflammatory agents may begin early and persist postnatally. For example, maternal polyI:C challenge reduces hippocampal neurogenesis, and the condition persists into the offspring's adulthood. Also, the trajectory of postnatal brain development is altered by maternal exposure to polyI:C on gestational day 15. The volume of the hippocampus generally increases between adolescence and adulthood,

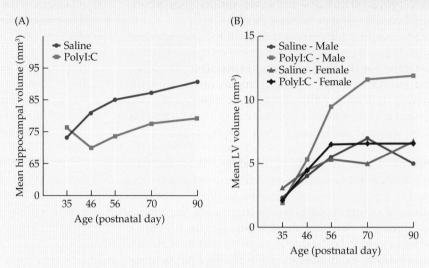

Brain volume differences in animals treated prenatally with polyI:C (A) Postnatal hippocampal volume differences in animals treated with polyI:C prenatally were compared to controls at five time points. (B) Mean lateral ventricle (LV) volume of male and female saline- or polyI:C-treated offspring at five post-adolescent time points. (After Y. Piontkewitz et al. 2011. *Biol Psychiat* 70: 842–851. © 2011. Reprinted with permission from Society of Biological Psychiatry, via Elsevier.)

but it is much reduced in polyI:C offspring (**FIGURE A**). During that developmental period, the lateral ventricles increase in size, but they increased to a much greater extent in the animals experiencing embryonic inflammation. Interestingly the difference occurred only in male, but not female, offspring (**FIGURE B**; Piontkewitz et al., 2011). Other research suggests that the same maternal immune response increases DA neurons in the fetal midbrain and produces DA hyperactivity that can be seen in striatal slices from adult brains. This finding is appealing because of its link to the DA hypothesis of positive symptoms of schizophrenia and suggests that the abnormalities in DA mesolimbic function in the adolescent and adult may be due to prenatal developmental events (Meyer, 2013). Of course, other neurotransmitter systems are also altered by prenatal inflammation, including GABA, glutamate, and 5-HT levels as well as receptors and receptor subunit expression. Additionally, cell cytoarchitecture, such as reduced density and complexity of dendritic spines, a feature of schizophrenia, also occurs. Further, polyI:C causes altered white matter connectivity, especially in frontostriatal–limbic tracts, which may be responsible for altered communication between the PFC and hippocampus, leading to deficits in PPI and cognitive dysfunction (Mattei et al., 2015). Once again, in each case the differences reported depend on the timing of the maternal infection (see Mattei et al., 2015).

Keep in mind that the events of pre- and perinatal development are progressive, and their effects may not be apparent in behavior, brain morphology, and

neurochemistry until early adulthood. In effect, the persistent effects of early events related to immune function set the stage for later psychopathology when environmental stimuli (e.g., stress, drug use) in combination with abnormal adolescent neurodevelopment in myelination, synaptic pruning, and synaptic remodeling lead to the symptom-based diagnosis of schizophrenia. This is frequently referred to as the "two-hit" hypothesis, and it is summarized in Figure 19.7. One empirical test of the two-hit hypothesis found a *synergistic* interaction between prenatal exposure to inflammation, induced in the maternal mice with polyI:C on gestational day 9, and exposure to unpredictable stress of the offspring at peripuberty. That means the effect of significant increases in activated microglia and pro-inflammatory cytokines in the hippocampus and prefrontal cortex, indicative of neuroinflammatory processes in utero, plus the neurobiological effect of adolescent stress was greater than the sum of their individual effects. These synergistic effects were seen for PPI disruptions, behavioral hypersensitivity to amphetamine and an NMDA antagonist, and activation of microglia in the hippocampus and PFC. Interestingly, just as the time of exposure to inflammation in utero determines the outcome, these researchers found that the timing of adolescent stress is critical. These synergistic effects occurred only when stress was initiated at peripubertal age but not later in adolescence. Hence, the latent neuropathological consequences of prenatal immune activation ("first hit") were unmasked by stress during puberty ("second hit") (Giovanoli et al., 2013).

As you probably suspect, there is a good deal of interest in creating **genetic models** with the hope that by modifying a schizophrenia susceptibility gene, abnormal behavior that is relevant to schizophrenia will be produced. This may entail creating knockout, knockin, or transgenic mice (see Chapter 4). For instance, when the gene for the DA reuptake transporter is deleted, the animals show hyperactivity in novel environments, deficits in PPI, stereotyped movements, and spatial learning impairments, behaviors analogous to schizophrenic behavior. Based on our earlier discussion, it should be clear that genetic factors can contribute only a portion of the vulnerability to schizophrenia. Hence newer animal models rely on integrating genetic and environmental factors. Thus, in addition to a genetic manipulation, environmental factors are manipulated. Some of these include enriched versus sensory-deprived housing, exposure to prenatal inflammation, postnatal stress, vitamin D deficiency, and exposure to drugs of abuse. For example, pre- or neonatal treatment with polyI:C in transgenic mice expressing mutant *DISC1* (a candidate gene described earlier) may demonstrate synergistic gene × environment effects that would more closely resemble human psychosis than either manipulation alone. A discussion of the development of such gene × environment models is provided by Kannan and coworkers (2013).

SECTION SUMMARY

■ Imaging shows cerebral atrophy, enlargement of ventricles, and smaller basal ganglia, temporal lobe, and hippocampus in patients with schizophrenia. Hippocampal cells are disorganized. Lack of gliosis coupled with reduced intracranial volume indicates developmental error rather than degeneration.

■ Abnormal myelination and organization of white matter tracts is responsible for reduced connectivity between brain regions, which prevents integration of signals for cognitive processing.

■ Brain function deficits include hypofrontality during tasks of working memory, executive function, response inhibition, and planning and strategy.

■ Elevated cytokines and microglia activation are associated with higher risk for schizophrenia. The immune responses are localized to brain regions with gray and white matter abnormalities. Microglia activation is greatest during acute illness relapses.

■ Family studies show that relatives of individuals with schizophrenia have increased risk for the disorder. The closer the genetic relationship, the greater is the risk.

■ Concordance for schizophrenia is much higher in monozygotic than dizygotic twins, indicating significant genetic contribution.

■ Linkage studies and genome-wide association studies have identified numerous gene variants that may each contribute a small amount to the increased risk for schizophrenia.

■ Mutations of the *DISC1* gene increase the probability of developing schizophrenia. This gene codes for proteins necessary for embryonic brain development.

■ Gene variants are associated with electroencephalographic (EEG) abnormalities, impaired cognitive function, and brain volume reductions.

■ Perinatal events such as stress during pregnancy and delivery, exposure to viral infection, and malnutrition may alter the trajectory of brain development and predispose the individual to schizophrenia. Activation of the immune response by the perinatal events may be the common factor explaining altered brain development.

■ Behavioral abnormalities that are apparent in young children who later develop schizophrenia suggest early developmental errors. Other developmental errors during adolescence cause twice the cell loss in cortical areas compared with that seen in healthy teens.

■ Animal models of schizophrenia created by pharmacological or environmental manipulations generally focus on one aspect of the disorder and induce similar changes in animal behavior. Neurodevelopmental models and genetic mutations are also used.

19.3 Neurochemical Models of Schizophrenia

To identify the neurochemical basis for any mental disorder, three general approaches can be taken. First, neurochemical correlates of animal and human models of the disorder can be studied. Second, the neuronal mechanisms of effective drug treatment are considered, keeping in mind that it is dangerous to assume that because the neurochemical effects of a drug reverse the symptoms, the drug is acting on the neurochemical mechanism that gives rise to the disorder. Third, the functioning of neurotransmitter systems in patient populations is assessed by measuring neurochemicals in blood, CSF, or urine or in post-mortem brain tissue. Brain imaging techniques provide the newest way of evaluating CNS function in patient populations. Based on these three approaches, evidence strongly suggests that although several neurotransmitters probably play a role in schizophrenic symptoms, malfunction of dopaminergic transmission is almost certainly involved.

Abnormal DA function contributes to schizophrenic symptoms

The finding that amphetamine can produce a psychotic reaction in healthy individuals that can be reversed by DA antagonists initially suggested the **dopamine hypothesis of schizophrenia**. Also, patients with schizophrenia who have been given amphetamine and cocaine say that the drugs make their symptoms worse but do not produce different symptoms. In addition, stereotyped behavior in rats can be elicited by intracerebral injection of amphetamine into forebrain DA areas and can be blocked by administration of DA receptor blockers, such as haloperidol.

As you will see in the following section, there is a strong correlation between D_2 receptor blockade and effectiveness in reducing schizophrenic symptoms. Finally, the finding that antipsychotic treatment induces changes in DA turnover, as determined by plasma levels of the DA metabolite homovanillic acid (HVA), further supports the DA hypothesis of schizophrenia, which suggests that excess DA function is related to the manifestation of the positive symptoms.

Of the approaches used to understand the neurochemistry of schizophrenia, evaluation of DA functioning in patient populations has been the least consistent. To substantiate the DA hypothesis, we would expect to see an increase in DA neurotransmission either through increased turnover (synthesis, release, metabolism) or by altered receptor number. Significant increases in DA synthesis have been found not only in patients with schizophrenia, but also in very early prodromal stages of the disorder—that is, a time when initial symptoms occur, preceding full development of the disorder. Early abnormal DA synthesis predicts progression to psychosis. With the onset of psychosis, synthesis capacity increases further. Although the change in the DA metabolite HVA in response to antipsychotic treatment (i.e., an initial increase followed by a significant decrease over several weeks) predicts treatment outcome, under baseline (nondrug) conditions neither plasma nor CSF levels of HVA are consistently different in patients with schizophrenia compared with controls. Nor are HVA levels correlated with symptom type or severity (Friedhoff and Silva, 1995). However, high-risk individuals and those with schizophrenia show significantly greater HVA response to stress, indicating a more robust impact of stress on DA synaptic function.

In addition, Laruelle and colleagues (1999) and subsequent replicated studies found that in patients with schizophrenia, a challenge dose of amphetamine elicited a significantly greater release of DA than was seen in controls. Baseline levels of DA are also elevated, indicating higher resting levels of DA. This effect was found at the onset of illness and in patients who had never taken antipsychotic drugs. Hence the hyperdopaminergic state is not due to prolonged illness, hospitalization, or chronic drug treatment. Further, a correlation was found between the exaggerated DA response and worsening of the positive symptoms. Other evidence for DA involvement comes from several studies that found increased D_2 receptors in the basal ganglia, nucleus accumbens, and substantia nigra of post-mortem schizophrenic brains. PET scan quantification of DA receptors also suggests increased D_2 receptors in drug-free patients with

schizophrenia, particularly in patients with positive symptoms as well as in those who are more acutely ill (Kahn and Davis, 1995). Recent genetic research suggests genes encoding the D_2 receptor and regulation of DA synthesis are associated with increased risk for schizophrenia. Evidence summarized by Howes and colleagues (2017) indicates that increased presynaptic synthesis and release represent the major DA dysfunction in schizophrenia, appear early in the prodromal stage, and cause the occurrence of psychosis. Acute stress releases DA and triggers psychotic symptoms. In addition, it is of particular interest that many stress-inducing environmental factors such as neurodevelopmental assaults, inflammation, childhood adversity, cannabis use, urban living, and others increase risk for developing schizophrenia. Therefore, early stress-inducing release of DA may make those individuals less tolerant to later stress and hence more vulnerable to psychosis.

Much of the evidence has been synthesized into a **DA imbalance hypothesis**, as described by Davis and colleagues (1991). They suggest that schizophrenic symptoms are due to reduced DA function in mesocortical neurons along with excess DA function in mesolimbic dopaminergic neurons. The negative symptoms and impaired thinking may be explained by impaired PFC function (low mesocortical activity). In contrast, positive symptoms seem to be improved by reducing DA function in mesolimbic neurons.

The neurodevelopmental model integrates anatomical and neurochemical evidence

Weinberger (1995) has developed a **neurodevelopmental model** that combines evidence of altered dopaminergic function with the loss of specific nerve cells (as described earlier in the section on etiology) and symptom clusters. The first part of the model is supported by several pieces of evidence that associate negative symptoms (flat affect, social withdrawal, lack of motivation, poor insight, and intellectual impairment) and cognitive symptoms (poor executive function, lack of attention, hypofrontality, and so forth) with reduced frontal lobe function. First, the negative symptoms of schizophrenia resemble the characteristics of patients with lesions of the frontal lobe (e.g., following frontal lobotomy). Also, the severity of the negative symptoms is correlated with reduced prefrontal cell metabolism, as evaluated by PET scan. In addition, neuropsychological testing in humans shows a relationship between poor performance on tasks requiring frontal lobe function, reduced cerebral blood flow in the PFC, and decreased DA function, as determined by lowered HVA levels in CSF. Further, in animal experiments, prefrontal lesions produce deficits in behaviors that require insight and strategy. Intracerebral injection of D_1 receptor antagonists impairs delayed-response performance and produces impulsivity and deficits in responding for delayed reward. Conversely, D_1 agonists improve cognitive deficits caused by injection of a DA neurotoxin into the PFC. These experiments indicate an important role for DA acting at the D_1 receptor in PFC in cognitive processes.

Animal studies also implicate mesocortical cells in normal response to stress. Mesocortical cells originate in the ventral tegmental area (VTA) and innervate the frontal cortex and other cortical areas. These cells respond with increased DA turnover not only to acute stress but also to learned stress, for instance when an animal is returned to a previously stressful environment. In summary, these results suggest that the onset of negative symptoms of schizophrenia is due to the occurrence of early mesocortical dysfunction. However, although this dysfunction occurs relatively early in life, the abnormal behavior may not appear until the system would normally reach functional maturity (i.e., after puberty, when development, myelination, and synaptic pruning are complete). Thus complex cognitive functions, including insightful behavior and the ability to respond to the social stresses commonly occurring at adolescence, would be expected to be compromised.

The second part of the model attempts to explain positive symptoms of schizophrenia with evidence of hyperactive subcortical cells. In animal studies, lesioning of prefrontal dopaminergic neurons produces chronic subcortical DA hyperactivity, manifested by increased DA turnover (Kahn and Davis, 1995). In addition, when DA receptor agonists such as apomorphine are injected into the PFC, DA metabolites are reduced in the striatum. Thus when the inhibitory cortical feedback is lost, mesolimbic cells increase their activity. Furthermore, studies of epileptic patients suggest that psychotic experiences, hallucinations, perceptual distortions, and irrational fears are associated with electrical discharge in limbic regions. Thus Weinberger (1995) suggests that excessive mesolimbic DA activity following mesocortical cell loss could explain the more dramatic positive symptoms of schizophrenia. Those are the same symptoms that are most readily reversed by antipsychotic-induced DA receptor blockade.

The neurodevelopmental model makes no attempt to identify the cause of the proposed early mesocortical cell loss. The defect could be due to one of many factors, including genetically programmed errors, perinatal complications, viral infection, and other possibilities discussed earlier in the chapter. Weinberger argues that such a lesion produces few symptoms early in life but reveals itself later, at a time when social stresses demand maximum prefrontal cognitive function. Loss of the DA input prevents the individual from making appropriate responses and instead leads to confused thinking, perseveration of inappropriate behavior, and social withdrawal. The loss of inhibitory cortical feedback onto subcortical neurons plus the stress-induced increase in mesolimbic cell function leads to agitation, fearfulness, and hallucinations. The appeal of this model of schizophrenia is in its ability to incorporate many distinct pieces of the puzzle (neurochemical, anatomical, and developmental pieces, and social stress). It also provides several testable hypotheses on which future research can be designed.

Glutamate and other neurotransmitters contribute to symptoms

Since glutamate is known to have an important role in learning and memory as well as synaptic plasticity (see Chapter 8), glutamate hypofunction may explain the negative symptoms, abnormal cognitive function, and impaired neural connectivity seen in schizophrenia. Moreover, because there is a great deal of similarity in the cognitive deficits caused by either D_1 or NMDA receptor blockade, it is clear that both receptors contribute to working memory processes. Inadequate glutamate function at the NMDA receptor may be a precursor to the DA dysfunction and may explain the apparent *increase* in mesolimbic DA and *decrease* in PFC function. **FIGURE 19.8A** shows the relationship of the brain structures involved and how descending glutamatergic neurons influence both DA pathways. **FIGURE 19.8B** is a schematic diagram that shows the details of the glutamate–dopamine interaction. Descending excitatory glutamatergic cells projecting from the PFC activate NMDA receptors on mesocortical DA cells in the VTA. These mesocortical DA cells reciprocally project back to the cortex. If glutamate levels are insufficient to activate mesocortical cells, low cortical DA neurotransmission and subsequent low D_1 receptor activation will lead to deficits in working memory, hypofrontality, and negative symptoms. In contrast, other PFC glutamatergic neurons acting on NMDA receptors have indirect *inhibitory* control of midbrain mesolimbic DA neurons that project to limbic regions. This happens because the glutamate neurons excite midbrain GABA cells (not shown in part A) that have an inhibitory effect on mesolimbic DA neurons. In this case, low levels of glutamate signaling would fail to inhibit mesolimbic neurons and would produce excessive DA release and associated positive symptoms, which can be relieved with DA receptor–blocking antipsychotic drugs. Evidence in support of this relationship was demonstrated in rats by blocking NMDA receptors in VTA, which resulted in an increase in DA release in the nucleus accumbens and reduced release of DA in the PFC. Hence the PFC provides tonic inhibition of mesolimbic neurons and tonic excitatory regulation of mesocortical cells. A more detailed discussion of glutamate–dopamine interaction is provided by Winterer and Weinberger (2004).

Evidence for the importance of NMDA receptors in schizophrenia comes from multiple sources. Challenge studies consistently show that blocking the glutamatergic NMDA receptor with PCP or ketamine produces a psychotic syndrome that closely resembles

(A)

(B)

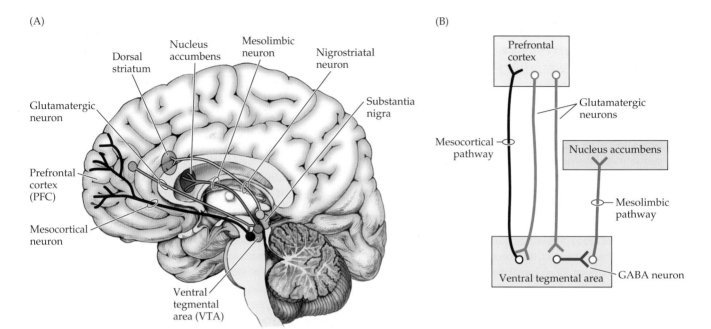

FIGURE 19.8 **Hypoglutamate hypothesis of schizophrenia** (A) Midsagittal view showing nigrostriatal (yellow), mesolimbic (blue), and mesocortical (black) dopaminergic neurons as well as a descending glutamatergic neuron (green) originating in the prefrontal cortex (PFC). (B) Since descending glutamatergic neurons (green) excite mesocortical DA neurons (black), poor glutamate signaling would produce low DA release in PFC, exacerbating negative and cognitive symptoms. Other glutamatergic neurons (green) excite inhibitory GABA neurons (red) that subsequently inhibit the dopaminergic mesolimbic pathway. (These tiny neurons within the VTA could not be depicted in part A.) In this case, low glutamate signaling would fail to inhibit mesolimbic firing, leading to excess DA release in the nucleus accumbens and positive symptoms. (B after G. Winterer and D. R. Weinberger. 2004. *Trends Neurosci* 27: 683–690.)

schizophrenia in healthy individuals and exacerbates symptoms in patients with schizophrenia. Of special significance is the fact that PCP and ketamine produce the positive, negative, and disorganized symptoms of schizophrenia. NMDA receptor blockade also produces cognitive deficits indicative of schizophrenia, including poor performance on the WCST, impairments in verbal memory, and reduced spatial and verbal learning. Loss of such functions indicates hippocampal and frontal lobe dysfunctions (see Lin et al., 2012). Rodent studies showed that even brief treatment with an NMDA receptor antagonist impaired cognitive flexibility and working memory in young animals. Additionally, changes in glutamate receptor subunit composition in several brain areas of individuals with schizophrenia have been described, and these may affect the quality of glutamate signaling (Ulas and Cotman, 1993). For instance, reduced mRNA and protein levels of the NR1 and NR2 subunits of the NMDA receptor were found in the DLPFC of patients with schizophrenia. Additional genetic evidence also implicates the NMDA receptor. A very large GWAS identified 128 significant associations, many of which involved glutamatergic function. (See Balu and Coyle, 2015, for more details.)

There is accumulating evidence that the glutamatergic signaling deficit associated with schizophrenia is due to hypofunction of the NMDA receptors rather than levels of the amino acid. Nevertheless, some direct evidence for low CSF glutamate levels in patients with schizophrenia compared with controls has been found, although the differences are not consistent. More consistently, in post-mortem studies, decreased levels are reported for both glutamate and aspartate in PFC and hippocampus, compared with controls, as well as reduced NMDA function. Additionally, some studies have found that lower levels of the amino acid are correlated with greater brain atrophy and cognitive impairment. However, there have been multiple reports of *increased* glutamate levels in many brain areas, as determined by magnetic resonance spectroscopy. Coyle and Konopaske (2016) and Poels and colleagues (2014) provide some potential explanations for the difficulties in interpreting the data in an effort to resolve the discrepancies.

Of particular interest is that the antipsychotic drug clozapine interacts with the glutamate receptor and increases glutamate levels in the PFC of rats, which may explain the drug's unique ability to reduce negative and cognitive symptoms in patients (see the section on atypical antipsychotics below). This characteristic of clozapine suggests that glutamate may be a new target for the development of antipsychotic drugs (see the final section of this chapter). For a more detailed discussion of the interaction of glutamate and DA in the production of schizophrenic symptoms and its potential therapeutic benefits, see Yang and Chen (2005).

Because the circuitry of the limbic structures and of the frontal cortex is complex, it is not surprising that many other neurotransmitters modulate or interact with DA transmission. ACh, GABA, norepinephrine, serotonin, and endorphins each may play a part in the presentation of individual symptoms of the disorder.

SECTION SUMMARY

- The dopamine hypothesis suggests that positive symptoms are caused by excessive mesolimbic DA activity. Evidence includes the following: (1) amphetamine produces positive symptoms in healthy individuals and makes symptoms worse in patients with schizophrenia; (2) a strong correlation exists between D_2 receptor blockade and antipsychotic efficacy; (3) schizophrenic individuals show exaggerated DA release after amphetamine challenge as well as in basal conditions; and (4) there is some evidence for increased D_2 receptors in schizophrenia.

- Evidence that the negative and cognitive symptoms are due to reduced frontal lobe function includes the following: (1) the negative/cognitive symptoms resemble characteristics after frontal lobotomy; (2) the severity of negative symptoms is negatively correlated with prefrontal brain activity and decreased DA function; and (3) prefrontal brain lesions or D_1 receptor antagonists injected into PFC impair cognitive performance.

- The neurodevelopmental model suggests that early mesocortical deficits due to genetics or environmental events that alter brain development are followed by loss of inhibitory control of mesolimbic cells and the onset of positive symptoms.

- Poor glutamate signaling due to hypofunction of NMDA receptors may be responsible for positive, negative, and cognitive symptoms and corresponding changes in DA activity.

- Descending glutamate neurons from PFC activate mesocortical neurons. Low glutamate signaling at NMDA receptors (or NMDA receptor antagonist administration) reduces mesocortical function, causing negative/cognitive symptoms.

- Descending glutamate neurons from PFC activate midbrain inhibitory GABA cells that reduce mesolimbic DA cell firing. Low glutamate signaling at NMDA receptors (or NMDA receptor antagonist administration) prevents the inhibition, leading to excessive mesolimbic firing and positive symptoms.

- Accumulating evidence from challenge studies, rodent studies, receptor subunit studies, and genetics suggests that NMDA hypofunction is central to schizophrenia.

- Low levels of glutamate are found in hippocampus and PFC of patients with schizophrenia post-mortem, and low levels are correlated with greater brain atrophy. Glutamate release is lower in patients with schizophrenia than in controls, and glutamate receptor subunits are different.

19.4 Classic Neuroleptics and Atypical Antipsychotics

Drugs useful in treating schizophrenia are called antipsychotic drugs or **neuroleptics**, an older term that refers to their ability to selectively reduce emotionality and psychomotor activity. A large number of drugs are included in this category, and they are commonly divided into two classes: classic neuroleptics and the newer second-generation (often called "atypical") antipsychotics. Although none of the drugs is consistently more effective than the others, a particular individual may respond better to one drug than to another. Therefore, treatment may require testing several antipsychotic drugs to find the one that is most effective for a given patient. The classic antipsychotic drugs are the phenothiazines, such as chlorpromazine (Thorazine), and the butyrophenones, such as haloperidol (Haldol). The second-generation antipsychotics, such as clozapine (Clozaril), risperidone (Risperdal), and aripiprazole (Abilify), are noteworthy because they appear to produce fewer side effects involving abnormal movements (e.g., tremors, rigidity). A review of classic and atypical antipsychotics is provided by Li and colleagues (2016).

Phenothiazines and butyrophenones are classic neuroleptics

Chlorpromazine was the first phenothiazine used in psychiatry, but many small changes in the shape of the drug molecule produced a family of related compounds that differ in potency, clinical effectiveness, and side effects. **FIGURE 19.9** shows the three-ring phenothiazine nucleus and the structural relationships of several other drugs in this class. By changing the chemical groups at the R_1 and R_2 positions, many new compounds can be created that vary in their effects. For example, chlorpromazine (which has a chlorine at R_2) is much more potent than promazine (which has hydrogen at the R_2 position). By substituting at R_1, an antipsychotic (thioridazine [Mellaril]) with fewer motor side effects is created. Further changes at R_1 and R_2 produce drugs (trifluoperazine [Stelazine], fluphenazine [Prolixene]) that further vary in potency and side effects. This structure–activity relationship provides clear evidence that molecular modifications alter the ability of the drugs to bind to specific receptor recognition sites in the cell membranes.

EFFECTIVENESS The introduction of antipsychotic drugs during the 1950s dramatically improved the treatment of patients with schizophrenia. The effectiveness of these drugs has been demonstrated hundreds of times in double-blind, placebo-controlled trials. After only a few doses, the hyperactive and manic symptoms usually disappear, whereas the positive symptoms of schizophrenia typically improve over several weeks. Delusions, hallucinations, and disordered thinking

FIGURE 19.9 Phenothiazine nucleus and related compounds
Minor molecular modifications determine the three major subgroups of phenothiazines and change drug potency, pharmacological activity, and side effects.

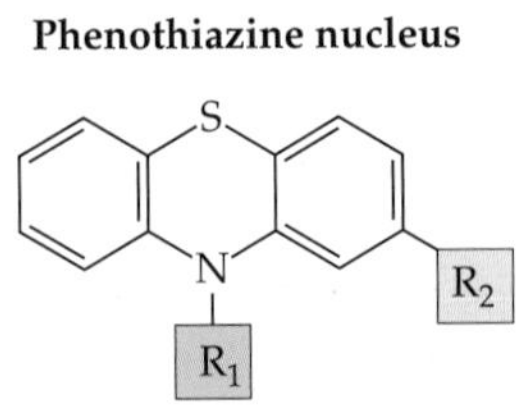

Phenothiazine nucleus

	R_1	R_2
	Aliphatic group	
Promazine (Prazine)	$-CH_2-CH_2-CH_2-N(CH_3)_2$	$-H$
Chlorpromazine (Thorazine)	$-CH_2-CH_2-CH_2-N(CH_3)_2$	$-Cl$
Trifluopromazine (Psyquil)	$-CH_2-CH_2-CH_2-N(CH_3)_2$	$-CF_3$
	Piperidine group	
Thioridazine (Mellaril)	$-CH_2-CH_2-$ (piperidine ring, $N-CH_3$)	$-SCH_3$
Mesoridazine (Serentil)	$-CH_2-CH_2-$ (piperidine ring, $N-CH_3$)	$-\overset{O}{\underset{\parallel}{S}}-CH_3$
	Piperazine group	
Trifluoperazine (Stelazine)	$-CH_2-CH_2-CH_2-N$ (piperazine ring) $N-CH_3$	$-CF_3$
Perphenazine (Trilafon)	$-CH_2-CH_2-CH_2-N$ (piperazine ring) $N-CH_2-CH_2-OH$	$-Cl$
Fluphenazine (Prolixene)	$-CH_2-CH_2-CH_2-N$ (piperazine ring) $N-CH_2-CH_2-OH$	$-CF_3$

are reduced, and improvements in insight, judgment, and self-care are seen. More resistant to treatment are the negative and cognitive symptoms of schizophrenia.

Although estimates of effectiveness vary, psychiatrists often refer to the law of thirds. One-third of the patients treated with antipsychotics show excellent symptom reduction in response to the drugs and may not experience subsequent hospitalizations even when they discontinue medication. These individuals show few residual signs of the disorder. They are employed outside the institution, may marry, and maintain a relatively normal social life. The second third show significant improvement in symptoms but may experience relapses that require hospitalization from time to time. These individuals may be employed, although usually at a reduced occupational level, and they may remain socially isolated. Some require significant help in day-to-day living, for example in maintaining personal hygiene, preparing meals, or keeping scheduled appointments. The final third show a lesser degree of recovery and may spend a significant amount of time each year in a psychiatric institution. These patients need much more help in dealing with the stresses of everyday living. Since many of the behavioral abnormalities remain, these individuals are often unemployed, have few social relationships, and exist on the margins of society. Some portion of this final third fail to adequately respond to any drug treatment and remain institutionalized. Estimates suggest that more than 30% of the adult homeless population in the United States may suffer from unmedicated or inadequately medicated psychosis.

Following a patient's initial recovery, antipsychotic drugs are prescribed as maintenance therapy to prevent relapse. Recovered patients maintained on antipsychotics have about a 55% chance of remaining in the community for 2 years after leaving the hospital, compared with a 20% chance for those on placebo. Thus drug maintenance more than doubles an individual's chances of avoiding significant relapse. Unfortunately, because the side effects of these drugs (discussed later in this section) are often debilitating and extremely unpleasant, many patients fail to continue treatment, which leads to a high relapse rate.

Although psychotherapy and group therapy are not considered substitutes for pharmacotherapy, social skills training and family therapy are important additions to drug treatment. Psychoeducation involves enhancing social competence and family problem solving, teaching vocational skills, minimizing stress, and enhancing cooperation with medication schedules (Goldstein, 1995; see the description of a multimodal approach called NAVIGATE at the end of this section).

Dopamine receptor antagonism is responsible for antipsychotic action

Antipsychotic drugs modify several neurotransmitter systems; however, their clinical effectiveness is best correlated with their ability to antagonize DA transmission by competitively blocking D_2 DA receptors or by inhibiting DA release. Evidence comes from several sources, including receptor binding studies, changes in DA turnover, second-messenger function, and neuroendocrine effects.

RECEPTOR BINDING   First- and second-generation antipsychotics block D_2 receptors. Drugs that readily bind to the DA receptor at low concentration because of their high affinity also reduce symptoms at low doses (**FIGURE 19.10A**). Likewise, antipsychotics that require higher concentrations to bind to D_2 receptors require higher doses to be clinically effective. Indeed, doses of D_2 receptor antagonists that occupy 65% to 80% of D_2 receptors produce maximum antipsychotic effects (Pani et al., 2007). Although antipsychotic drugs bind to other neurotransmitter receptors in addition to D_2 receptors, there is no clear relationship between clinical effectiveness and binding to serotonin (**FIGURE 19.10B**),

α-adrenergic, or histamine receptors. Nor is there a correlation for D_1 receptor binding; in fact doses, of D_1 receptor antagonists that occupy over 80% of D_1 receptors fail to produce antipsychotic effects (Karlsson et al., 1995). Therefore, the correlation with D_2 receptor binding establishes quite clearly the mechanism of antipsychotic drug action.

Antipsychotics have a particularly high affinity for D_2 receptors, which serve as both normal postsynaptic receptors and autoreceptors and are located in the basal ganglia, nucleus accumbens, amygdala, hippocampus, and cerebral cortex. **FIGURE 19.11** shows a series of PET images in which D_2 receptors in the basal ganglia were labeled with [^{11}C]raclopride. The bright areas show the binding of the labeled drug to D_2 receptors. The control is a scan of a healthy man injected only with the [^{11}C] raclopride to show maximum binding. The remaining scans are from patients with schizophrenia given [^{11}C] raclopride in addition to one of the antipsychotic drugs. Reduction of radioactive ligand binding indicates competition for the sites. Striatal D_2 receptors were almost completely blocked by haloperidol and risperidone, but clozapine had less affinity. Although a drug's ability to bind to the D_2 receptor is closely correlated with its

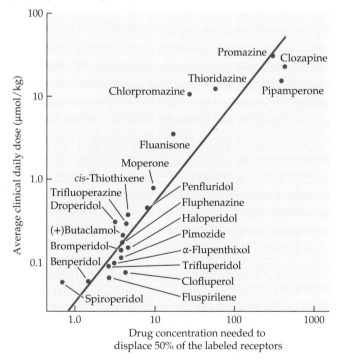

(A) Dopamine receptors

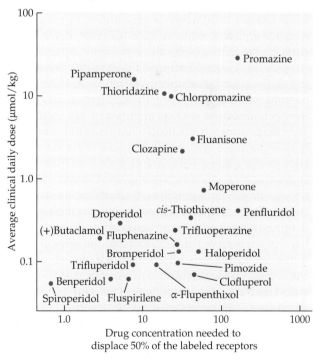

(B) Serotonin receptors

FIGURE 19.10   Correlation between antipsychotic drug binding to neurotransmitter receptors and clinical effectiveness   The receptor binding studies were accomplished by first labeling the receptors with an appropriate radioactive ligand for each neurotransmitter. The antipsychotic drug was added in increasing concentrations until it competed successfully for half of the labeled sites. That value (K_i) is plotted along the x-axis, and the corresponding average clinical

daily dose for that drug is plotted on the y-axis. A clear positive correlation is found for dopamine receptor binding (A), but serotonin receptor binding shows no apparent correlation with effectiveness (B). Further experiments found no correlation between clinical effects and binding to either α-adrenergic or histamine receptors. (After S. H. Snyder. 1996. *Drugs and the Brain*, p. 80. Scientific American Library: New York.)

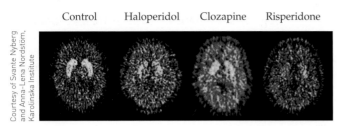

Control   Haloperidol   Clozapine   Risperidone

Courtesy of Svante Nyberg and Anna-Lena Nordström, Karolinska Institute

FIGURE 19.11 D$_2$ receptor occupancy by antipsychotic drugs PET scans of a healthy, untreated male (control) and three patients with schizophrenia treated with the classic neuroleptic haloperidol or with an atypical antipsychotic drug (clozapine or risperidone). In all individuals, striatal D$_2$ receptors were labeled with [^{11}C]raclopride. The scans show that the radioactive label of striatal D$_2$ receptors was displaced almost completely by haloperidol and risperidone binding but less effectively by clozapine. These and other differences in receptor antagonism are thought to be responsible for the ability of the clozapine-like neuroleptics to reduce symptoms without producing serious motor side effects.

effectiveness in reducing psychotic symptoms, some of the atypical antipsychotics, such as clozapine, may produce their unique effects by acting on a combination of receptor types.

DOPAMINE TURNOVER Clinical response to antipsychotic treatment is associated with an initial increase in DA metabolism, which is determined by measuring the concentration of the principal DA metabolite, HVA. An increase in metabolism is assumed to reflect an increase in neurotransmitter release. Notably, in addition to reducing dopaminergic neurotransmission by blocking postsynaptic D$_2$ receptors, antipsychotics also readily block presynaptic D$_2$ autoreceptors. The inhibitory autoreceptors are responsible for controlling the rate of firing of the cell as well as the rate of synthesis and release of neurotransmitter. Applying a DA receptor agonist, such as apomorphine, to the DA cell bodies in the substantia nigra (origin of nigrostriatal cells) or ventral tegmentum (origin of mesolimbic and mesocortical neurons) stimulates the autoreceptors, thereby decreasing the rate of firing of the dopaminergic neurons. This inhibition is antagonized by administration of an effective antipsychotic drug such as chlorpromazine. The increase in firing rate after antipsychotic administration is accompanied by increased turnover (synthesis, release, and metabolism) of DA. Importantly, because postsynaptic DA receptors are also blocked, this initial increase in DA release does not worsen symptoms. The initial increase in HVA is followed by a gradual decrease with chronic treatment, because the chronic blockade with antipsychotics leads to supersensitivity (up-regulation) of the autoreceptors. The up-regulation once again allows them to respond appropriately to DA by reducing DA synthesis, release, and metabolism. An alternative explanation for the gradual decrease in turnover,

originally posed by Grace (1992), suggests that after the initial neuroleptic-induced increase in DA turnover, dopaminergic cells have the ability to temporarily inactivate themselves. This temporary inactivation, called depolarization block, would reduce the release of DA and its subsequent metabolism. The time-dependent change in receptors and the depolarization block are among the homeostatic changes that occur over time, leading to improvement and helping to explain the gradual onset of effectiveness of antipsychotic drugs.

PROLACTIN RELEASE An additional consequence of DA receptor blockade is evident from neuroendocrine measures of prolactin. Under normal conditions, DA inhibits prolactin release, and in the context of neuroendocrinology, DA is sometimes referred to as prolactin release-inhibiting hormone. Thus, by blocking D$_2$ receptors in the pituitary gland, antipsychotics stimulate the secretion of prolactin, which leads to lactation and breast enlargement, even in males, disturbing side effects of antipsychotic drug use (Fitzgerald and Dinan, 2008). Measuring serum prolactin levels in patients provides an easy measure of D$_2$ receptor function in the CNS.

Side effects are directly related to neurochemical action

Unfortunately, both traditional and atypical antipsychotic drugs frequently produce a large number of side effects, some of which are so disturbing that non-hospitalized patients stop taking the drug and suffer a relapse of psychiatric symptoms. Each drug may have different potential side effects based on the neurotransmitter receptors it binds to. Because patient compliance is a large problem, clinicians most often choose the antipsychotic to prescribe in order to optimize compliance by minimizing the side effects for a given patient. **TABLE 19.1** summarizes some of the benefits and side effects associated with the blockade of various receptors.

Antipsychotic-induced DA receptor antagonism occurs in each of the DA pathways described in Chapter 5 and is responsible not only for the clinical effectiveness of antipsychotics but also for many of their side effects. There are four dopamine pathways in the brain that are important for understanding antipsychotic drug action (three are illustrated in Figure 19.8A):

1. The mesolimbic pathway projects from the VTA to the nucleus accumbens and other limbic areas. It is involved in many behaviors, including reinforcement processes and the delusions and hallucinations of schizophrenia. It is reasonable to consider the mesolimbic pathway as the site for the drug-induced reduction of positive symptoms.

TABLE 19.1 Clinical Implications of the Blockade of Various Receptors by Antipsychotics

Receptor	Possible benefits	Possible side effects
Dopamine D_2	Reduced positive symptoms	Extrapyramidal side effects (EPS) including parkinsonism, akathisia, tardive dyskinesia; endocrine effects such as prolactin secretion, menstrual changes, sexual dysfunction
Serotonin $5\text{-}HT_{2A}$	Reduced EPS?	Sexual dysfunction
Serotonin $5\text{-}HT_{2C}$	Unknown	Weight gain
Histamine H_1	Sedation	Sedation, increased appetite, weight gain, hypotension
Muscarinic cholinergic	Reduced EPS	Autonomic side effects such as blurred vision, dry mouth, constipation, urinary retention, tachycardia; memory dysfunction
α_1-adrenergic	Unknown	Orthostatic hypotension, dizziness, reflex tachycardia
α_2-adrenergic	Unknown	Drug interactions

legs and an inability to sit still), and loss of facial expression. We know that Parkinson's disease is caused by a loss of cell bodies in the substantia nigra (see Figure 19.8A). The lack of inhibitory DA function in the striatum (a subcortical brain area that modulates movement) via D_2 receptors causes increased activity of the indirect basal ganglia pathway, thus inhibiting motor output, as well as excess activity of cholinergic striatal interneurons (**FIGURE 19.12**). Knowing that the classic antipsychotic drugs block D_2 dopamine receptors, we assume that drug-induced parkinsonism is due to D_2 receptor blockade in that area of the brain. To verify this hypothesis, experiments using PET showed that neuroleptic-treated patients with parkinsonian symptoms had *more* dopamine receptors of the D_2 type in the striatum than did those without those side effects (Farde et

2. The mesocortical pathway also projects from the VTA but sends axons to the prefrontal and limbic cortex, where it may have a role in the cognitive effects and negative symptoms of schizophrenia.

3. The nigrostriatal pathway originates in the substantia nigra and projects to the striatum, where it contributes to the modulation of movement. Parkinsonian symptoms are caused by insufficient DA binding to receptors in the striatum. Therefore, neuroleptic effects on nigrostriatal DA are likely to be responsible for parkinsonian tremors and other motor side effects.

4. Projecting from the hypothalamus to the pituitary gland are the short neurons that constitute the tuberohypophyseal pathway, which regulates pituitary hormone secretion. Blockade of DA receptors in this pathway is the likely source of the neuroendocrine side effects.

PARKINSONISM The most serious and troublesome side effects of classic antipsychotics are the movement disorders that resemble the symptoms of Parkinson's disease (see Chapter 20) and involve the extrapyramidal motor system, collectively called extrapyramidal side effects (EPS). **Parkinsonian symptoms** include tremors, bradykinesia or akinesia (slowing or loss of voluntary movement), muscle rigidity, akathisia (a strong feeling of discomfort in the

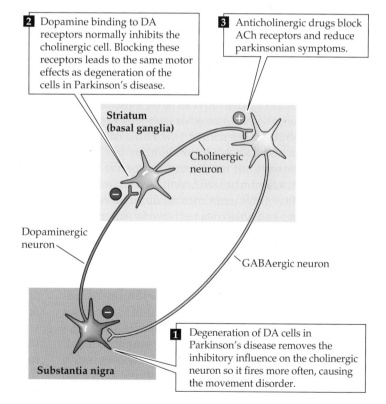

2 Dopamine binding to DA receptors normally inhibits the cholinergic cell. Blocking these receptors leads to the same motor effects as degeneration of the cells in Parkinson's disease.

3 Anticholinergic drugs block ACh receptors and reduce parkinsonian symptoms.

Striatum (basal ganglia)

Cholinergic neuron

Dopaminergic neuron

GABAergic neuron

1 Degeneration of DA cells in Parkinson's disease removes the inhibitory influence on the cholinergic neuron so it fires more often, causing the movement disorder.

Substantia nigra

FIGURE 19.12 Schematic diagram showing the neurotransmitters involved in parkinsonian symptoms Parkinson's disease is caused by degeneration of the nigrostriatal dopaminergic neurons, which originate in the substantia nigra. The reduced dopaminergic cell function causes a loss of inhibitory control of the cholinergic cells in the striatum, so the cholinergic cells fire at higher rates. Drug-induced parkinsonian symptoms follow DA receptor blockade in the striatum and subsequent excess acetylcholine activity, which is functionally similar to the loss of dopaminergic cells in Parkinson's disease. Anticholinergic drugs reduce the symptoms of Parkinson's disease and the side effects of antipsychotic drug treatment.

al., 1992). Such compensatory receptor up-regulation is likely to occur after reduced DA transmission. Therefore, it is assumed that the antipsychotic-induced tremors are due to the blockade of D_2 receptors in the striatum, the terminal field of the nigrostriatal dopaminergic neurons. Since one way to treat the symptoms of Parkinson's disease is to reduce excess ACh activity, one approach involves combining antipsychotic drug treatment with a muscarinic ACh receptor antagonist such as benztropine (Cogentin), although anticholinergics are known to worsen cognition in patients with schizophrenia (Ogino et al., 2014). In addition, several of the atypical antipsychotics, such as clozapine and risperidone, produce a lower-than-normal incidence of EPS (see the section on atypical antipsychotics below).

TARDIVE DYSKINESIA   A second type of motor side effect associated with prolonged use of antipsychotic drugs is **tardive dyskinesia (TD)**. TD is characterized by stereotyped involuntary movements, particularly of the face and jaw, such as sucking and lip smacking, lateral jaw movements, and "fly-catching" movements of the tongue. There may also be purposeless, quick, and uncontrolled movements of the arms and legs or slow squirming movements of the trunk, limbs, and neck. Estimates suggest that TD appears in about 10% to 20% of patients treated with neuroleptics overall. Although TD may appear in any age group, the incidence increases to 50% in patients older than 60 years and may exceed 70% in geriatric patients. Moreover, women exhibit a higher risk for developing TD. It is generally assumed that the dose of antipsychotic and the treatment duration are related to the occurrence of TD, although it is worth noting that duration of treatment covaries with age. Although the symptoms are considered to be irreversible in some patients, for many individuals improvement does gradually occur. However, in many cases, the symptoms are much worse when the drug is first terminated and persist for long periods after the withdrawal of antipsychotics. Treatment for TD has historically been challenging since withdrawal from antipsychotic treatment is not always feasible. Switching from a first-generation antipsychotic to a second-generation antipsychotic with lower D_2 receptor affinity may be beneficial when possible, but many second-generation antipsychotics are also associated with TD, albeit at lower rates (Correl and Schenk, 2008). Recently, the vesicular monoamine transporter, subtype 2 (VMAT2) inhibitors valbenazine and deutetrabenazine have been approved by the U.S. Food and Drug Administration (FDA) for the treatment of TD. Drugs that inhibit VMAT2 selectively interfere with the ability of dopamine neurons to package dopamine into vesicles, thereby reducing the amount of DA that can be released into the synapse. While the exact cause of TD is not known, one possibility is that chronic treatment

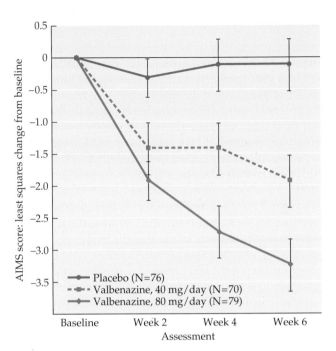

FIGURE 19.13   **Effect of VMAT2 inhibition on tardive dyskinesia**   Results from a Phase 3 clinical trial showed that ongoing treatment with the VMAT2 inhibitor valbenazine significantly decreased abnormal movements associated with TD, as measured by the Abnormal Involuntary Movement Scale (AIMS). This effect was dose-dependent, with the 80-mg dose showing the largest effect. (After R. A. Hauser et al. 2017. *Am J Psychiatry* 174: 476-484. © 2017. American Psychiatric Association. All Rights Reserved.)

with D_2 receptor antagonists leads to a compensatory hypersensitivity, or upregulation of D_2 receptors, which contributes to the etiology of TD. It is thought that decreasing extracellular DA mitigates the effect of this D_2 receptor hypersensitivity, thus reducing the symptoms of TD. As shown in **FIGURE 19.13**, in a Phase 3 clinical trial, treatment of patients with TD using valbenazine substantially reduced the clinical signs of TD when compared to placebo, as measured by the standardized Abnormal Involuntary Movement Scale (AIMS) (Hauser et al., 2017).

NEUROENDOCRINE EFFECTS   Blockade of receptors in the DA pathway that regulates pituitary function produces a variety of neuroendocrine effects, such as breast enlargement and tenderness, decreased sex drive, lack of menstruation, increased release of prolactin (frequently producing lactation), and inhibition of growth hormone release. Reduced growth hormone release represents a significant therapeutic issue when children and adolescents are medicated. In addition, significant weight gain and the inability to regulate body temperature can be disturbing side effects.

NEUROLEPTIC MALIGNANT SYNDROME   Of the possible side effects, **neuroleptic malignant syndrome (NMS)** is the most serious and life threatening. NMS is characterized by fever, rigidity, altered consciousness, and autonomic nervous system instability (including rapid heart rate and fluctuations in blood pressure). NMS is potentially lethal, but rapid diagnosis and immediate action have significantly reduced the mortality risk.

ADDITIONAL SIDE EFFECTS Many of the older and newer antipsychotic drugs have not only DA-blocking effects but also anticholinergic and antiadrenergic actions. These complex interactions produce widespread effects on the autonomic nervous system. For example, blocking cholinergic synapses produces effects such as dry mouth, blurred vision, constipation, difficulty in urination, and decreased gastric secretion and motility. You may notice that although anticholinergic effects in the autonomic nervous system are problematic, anticholinergic effects in the striatum reduce parkinsonian side effects. Orthostatic hypotension (low blood pressure when an individual stands upright) from the antiadrenergic action of antipsychotics leads to dizziness, faintness, or blacking out. Many of these drugs produce significant sedation, which may be very troublesome for some patients but useful for those who suffer from agitation and restlessness.

In general, the particular drug chosen for a patient depends on its side effects. For example, chlorpromazine may be used because it tends to minimize EPS, although the sedative effects may be undesirable and the probability of autonomic side effects is relatively high. Haloperidol, in contrast, tends to produce less sedation and fewer autonomic side effects but is associated with a greater probability of movement disorders. Many of the newer antipsychotic drugs have been developed to provide professionals with more options for matching a particular patient and the side effects that they can tolerate. **TABLE 19.2** compares a number of traditional and atypical antipsychotic drugs and rates the incidence of specific side effects for each drug.

PHARMACOGENETIC FACTORS There is significant interest in identifying genetic risk factors that may predispose certain individuals to the side effects of antipsychotics. Notable progress has been made in identifying gene variations that predict both therapeutic and adverse responses. Relatively consistent findings have shown that polymorphisms in the gene that encodes the CYP2D6 enzyme likely account for some of the variability in the therapeutic response to a number of antipsychotics, including aripiprazole, risperidone and haloperidol (Milosavljevic et al., 2021). At the same time, variants of the *CYP2D6* gene that encode

TABLE 19.2 Relative Benefits and Risks of Atypical and Conventional Antipsychotic Drugs[a]

Property	Atypical antipsychotic agents						Conventional antipsychotic agents by potency[b]		
	Aripip-razole	Cloza-pine	Olan-zapine	Que-tiapine	Risper-idone	Zipra-sidone	High	Moderate	Low
Efficacy in terms of:									
Positive symptoms	++	++++	+++	++	+++	+++	+++	+++	+++
Negative symptoms	+	++	+	+	+	+	+	+	+
Relapse[c]	++	++++	+++	?	+++	+	++	++	++
Adverse effects:									
Anticholinergic	0	+++	+	0	0	0	0	++	+++
Hypotension	+	+++	++	++	+++	+	+	++	+++
Hyperprolactinemia	0	0	+	0	++	+	++	++	++
Diabetes mellitus	+	++	++	+	+	+	+	+	+
Sexual dysfunction	+	++	++	+	++	+	++	++	+++
Weight gain	0	+++	+++	++	+	0	0	+	++
Extrapyramidal symptoms	+	0	+	0	++	+	++++	+++	++
Neuroleptic malignant syndrome	?	+	+	+	+	+	+++	++	+

Source: From D. M. Gardner et al. 2005. *CMAJ* 172: 1703–1711. © 2005 CMA Media Inc. or its licensors. www.cmaj.ca
[a] Benefit or risk: ++++, very high; +++, high; ++, moderate; +, low; 0, negligible; ?, not defined.
[b] High-potency agents are flupenthixol, fluphenazine, haloperidol, and trifluoperazine; moderate-potency agents are clozapine and zuclopenthixol; low-potency are chlorpromazine, methotrimeprazine, and thioridazine.
[c] Relapse was compared with placebo after 1 year.

for both poor metabolizer and ultra-rapid metabolizer phenotypes have been associated with increased incidence of TD. Interestingly, the *SLC18A2* gene, which encodes VMAT2, has also been implicated in TD, which is consistent with the finding that VMAT2 inhibitors have therapeutic efficacy in treating TD (see Figure 19.13). Genetic susceptibilities to antipsychotic-induced weight gain and clozapine-induced agranulocytosis both appear to be highly polygenic in nature, making it challenging to develop adequate pharmacogenomic screens, although it is possible that with additional research, algorithms may be developed that help clinicians predict these outcomes and select appropriate therapeutic strategies that minimize these adverse drug effects. For a current review of pharmacogenomic strategies for antipsychotic treatments, readers are directed to recent papers by Islam and colleagues (2021) and Lisoway and associates (2021).

Atypical antipsychotics are distinctive in several ways

At present, the designation of "atypical" or "second generation" is reserved for antipsychotics that reduce positive symptoms of schizophrenia as well as the classical drugs do, but without causing significant EPS. In addition, some of the newer agents fail to increase serum prolactin and have a low incidence of TD. Three general approaches have been taken to develop these second-generation drugs: selective D_2 receptor antagonists, DA receptor partial agonists, and broad-spectrum antipsychotics.

SELECTIVE D_2 RECEPTOR ANTAGONISTS Since effective antipsychotic drugs block D_2 receptors, the first attempts to develop new drugs with fewer side effects evaluated **selective D_2 receptor antagonists**. Examples of such drugs include sulpiride and amisulpride. These drugs bind specifically to D_2 receptors and have a slight affinity for D_3 receptors (**TABLE 19.3**), which may explain why their behavioral effects differ to some extent from those of traditional neuroleptics. Their selectivity for DA receptors also means that effects on the autonomic nervous system and the cardiovascular system are minimal and sedation is mild. However, hormonal side effects tend to be common, and the risk of fatal blood disorders reduces the utility of the drugs.

DOPAMINE RECEPTOR PARTIAL AGONISTS Among the newer of the atypical antipsychotics are DA receptor partial agonists, sometimes referred to as DA system stabilizers. The prototypical drug aripiprazole (Abilify) and its successor, brexpiprazole (Rexulti), are DA partial agonists, which means that these drugs readily bind to DA receptors but produce less of an effect than DA itself (Kikuchi et al., 2021). Hence aripiprazole competes with DA for DA receptors in overactive synapses,

TABLE 19.3 Relative Neurotransmitter Receptor Affinities for Selected Antipsychotics at Therapeutic Dose[a]

| Receptor[b] | Broad spectrum | | | | | | Selective D_2 | | Partial agonist | Classical |
	Clo-zapine	Risperi-done	Olan-zapine	Que-tiapine	Zipra-sidone	Sertin-dole	Sul-piride	Amis-ulpride	Aripiprazole	Halo-peridol
D_1	+	+	++	−	+	++	−	−	−	+
D_2	+	+++	++	+	+++	+++	++++	++++	++++	++++
D_3	+	++	+	−	++	++	++	++	++	+++
D_4	++	−	++	−	++	+	−	−	+	+++
5-HT$_{1A}$	−	−	−	−	+++	ND	ND	ND	++	−
5-HT$_{1D}$	−	+	−	−	+++	ND	ND	ND	+	−
5-HT$_{2A}$	+++	++++	+++	++	++++	++++	−	−	+++	+
5-HT$_{2C}$	++	++	++	−	++++	++	−	−	+	−
5-HT$_6$	++	−	++	−	+	ND	ND	ND	+	−
5-HT$_7$	++	+++	−	−	++	ND	ND	ND	++	−
α_1	+++	+++	++	+++	++	++	−	−	+	+++
α_2	+	++	+	−	−	+	−	−	+	+
H_1	+++	−	+++	++	−	+	−	−	+	−
m_1	++++	−	+++	++	−	−	−	−	−	−

Source: S. Miyamoto et al. 2005. *Mol Psychiatry* 10: 79–104. doi.org/10.1038/sj.mp.4001556

[a] −, minimal to none; +, low; ++, moderate; +++, high; ++++, very high; ND, no data.

[b] D, dopamine; 5-HT, serotonin; α, adrenergic; H, histamine; m, muscarinic cholinergic.

reducing the effect of DA for as long as the drug is bound. When excessive DA activity is reduced, the positive symptoms are reduced. In contrast, the same drug stimulates DA receptors (but to a lesser extent than DA) in brain areas where there may be too little DA, thus in principle reducing negative symptoms and motor side effects. In clinical trials, aripiprazole had a relatively low incidence of side effects (see Table 19.2). There was little evidence of cardiotoxicity, weight gain, or motor side effects. Reported adverse effects such as headache, agitation, insomnia, and nervousness were minor. Aripiprazole and related compounds may represent a new class of antipsychotics that is more readily accepted because of fewer unpleasant side effects.

BROAD-SPECTRUM ANTIPSYCHOTICS   A second trend in neuropharmacology is to evaluate **broad-spectrum antipsychotics** that block other receptor types in addition to D_2 receptors. The rationale for this work is the clinical effectiveness of clozapine, a drug that has relatively weak affinities for D_1 and D_2 and substantial serotonergic, muscarinic, and histaminergic affinities, as well a high affinity for the D_4 receptor (see Table 19.3). Clozapine is the best-known atypical antipsychotic. Although clozapine is no more effective than standard neuroleptics in treating the positive symptoms of schizophrenia, it is often effective in patients who are treatment resistant. Clozapine produces significant improvement in 60% of patients who do not respond to typical neuroleptics. Clozapine is also the first antipsychotic that can reduce some of the negative and cognitive symptoms as well as reduce anxiety and tension. While the improved effectiveness of clozapine in otherwise treatment-resistant individuals, coupled with its ability to improve cognitive and negative symptoms, may be due in part to its broad mechanistic profile, this property may also contribute to its relatively wide range of side effects. Clozapine reduces the seizure threshold, making seizures more likely in the vulnerable individual. It can also produce hypersalivation, weight gain, and cardiovascular problems. A more dangerous side effect is the occurrence of agranulocytosis, a serious blood abnormality that can be detected only with frequent (i.e., weekly or biweekly) blood screening tests. The increased expense of testing and the seriousness of side effects restrict the use of clozapine to selected patients.

The initial discovery of the effectiveness of clozapine led to a great deal of excitement and efforts to design a new class of antipsychotics with similar efficacy but without dangerous side effects. These atypical drugs, which include risperidone, olanzapine, quetiapine, ziprasidone, and sertindole, bind with varying affinities for multiple neurotransmitter receptor subtypes. Table 19.3 allows you to compare binding affinities of these agents with those of the selective D_2 antagonists, the DA receptor partial agonist aripiprazole, and the classic drug haloperidol. Keep in mind that these atypical drugs are a heterogeneous group neurochemically and in clinical profiles, making it difficult to allow broad generalizations about the class, but you can predict side effects on the basis of receptor affinity (refer to Table 19.1). You can compare clinical benefits and risks of these drugs by examining Table 19.2. Although they all reduce positive symptoms better than placebo, there is little evidence to suggest *superiority* of the atypical drugs over conventional drugs. Keep in mind that clinical studies are difficult to perform and that variability in results may be explained by differences in sampling of patient populations, durations of treatment, high dropout rates, inappropriate dose comparisons, and small outcome measures that may be statistically significant but not significant to the patient (Gardner et al., 2005). Superiority of the newer agents in treating negative symptoms is even more difficult to demonstrate, because evaluating behavior such as social and emotional withdrawal and lack of motivation is problematic with the usual measuring devices. Although a number of clinical studies and meta-analyses suggest that cognitive deficits such as verbal memory, attention, psychomotor processing, and verbal fluency frequently show improvement with some atypical drugs such as risperidone compared with haloperidol, other studies and meta-analyses report no difference.

Most significant for atypical status is the lower incidence of motor side effects (EPS) described earlier. Clozapine does not appear to cause EPS even at high doses, and reports of TD are uncommon. Although all of the newer drugs are generally considered less likely to cause EPS, keep in mind that the occurrence of motor side effects varies significantly among the atypical agents (see Table 19.2). Furthermore, the occurrence of EPS is frequently dose-dependent, meaning that motor side effects may emerge with higher doses of atypical drugs. A prominent endocrine side effect with the classical antipsychotics is hyperprolactinemia and associated sexual dysfunction. Several of the newer agents, including quetiapine and the DA receptor partial agonist aripiprazole, lack this effect entirely, although some of the newer drugs such as risperidone elevate prolactin to the same moderate level as the older agents. Finally, some NMS cases have been reported for the atypical drugs.

Metabolic side effects including weight gain, hyperglycemia, and elevated plasma cholesterol are troublesome characteristics of at least some of the atypical antipsychotics, although these side effects also occur with some of the older drugs. Significant weight gain is common with atypical antipsychotics and with some classical agents and is most robustly correlated with the extent of histamine H_1 receptor binding, although 5-HT_{2C} receptor antagonism may also contribute to this effect. Adolescents tend to gain even more weight than adults.

Clozapine and olanzapine seem to cause the most weight gain and the most prolonged weight gain over time, probably through suppression of the satiety response. Clozapine-induced weight gain was also most persistent despite efforts to behaviorally reverse the gain with diet and exercise. Some of the atypical antipsychotics cause sometimes severe elevations in blood sugar and insulin resistance, leading to type 2 diabetes. The risk of developing diabetes is 9% to 14% greater in patients taking atypical antipsychotics than in those taking the first-generation drugs. The elevated plasma lipid levels caused by some of the drugs increase risk for high blood pressure and heart disease. Metabolic syndrome side effects are reviewed by Yogaratnam and colleagues (2013).

Several traditional and second-generation drugs cause alterations in the electrical activity of the heart in some individuals. If severe enough, these arrhythmias can cause sudden death. Several antipsychotics, including thioridazine, have been removed from the market because of this side effect. Because of these cardiac changes, off-label use (i.e., for a condition not approved by the FDA) for the treatment of behavioral disorders in the elderly with dementia has been evaluated. The FDA reported a two-fold increase in sudden death in this population caused by cerebral ischemia, stroke, cerebrovascular events, or infection. Subsequent evaluation suggests as much as a 10-fold increased risk for sudden death in elderly patients taking the drug for 1 week, which gradually decreases to control levels after 3 months. Nevertheless, the FDA (2008) has recommended a boxed warning on drug labels describing the potential risks. As is always the case, the potential risks and benefits along with the costs must be weighed for each patient.

Although there is general agreement that D_2 receptors are important in antipsychotic effects for all antipsychotics, we have to wonder what is different about clozapine that explains its efficacy for reducing negative symptoms and its low potential for EPS. Some laboratories hypothesize that typical and atypical neuroleptics can be differentiated by their ratio of antagonism for various receptors. For instance, a high degree of binding to D_4 receptors, found in high concentration in the mesolimbic system and the frontal cortex, may enhance the therapeutic effect but minimize the nigrostriatal motor symptoms associated with D_2 occupation. Other evidence suggests the importance of antagonism of the 5-HT$_2$ receptor in combination with D_2 blockade. **FIGURE 19.14** shows that the atypical antipsychotics clozapine and risperidone readily bind to 5-HT$_2$ receptors, but haloperidol does not. In contrast, haloperidol almost completely blocks D_2 receptors (see Figure 19.11), but clozapine shows only a partial effect on D_2. Because 5-HT$_2$ receptors modulate DA release, it has been suggested that this difference in receptor

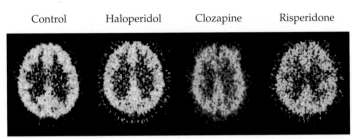

Courtesy of Svante Nyberg and Anna-Lena Nordström, Karolinska Institute

FIGURE 19.14 5-HT$_2$ receptor binding by atypical antipsychotics PET scans of a healthy, untreated male (control) and three patients with schizophrenia treated with the traditional neuroleptic haloperidol or with an atypical antipsychotic drug (clozapine or risperidone). In all individuals, neocortical 5-HT$_2$ receptors were labeled with [^{11}C] N-methylspiperone ([^{11}C]NMSP). The scans show that both atypical antipsychotics but not haloperidol reduced 5-HT$_2$ binding. These and other differences in receptor antagonism are thought to be responsible for the ability of clozapine to reduce schizophrenic symptoms (negative and positive) with a minimum of motor side effects.

antagonism is responsible for increasing DA efflux in cortex and hippocampus, potentially improving cognitive symptoms while producing less DA release in striatum, which would be expected to reduce EPS. For this reason, extensive research is being conducted into the potential enhancement of cognitive function by modulating 5-HT$_{2A}$ and several other 5-HT receptor subtypes (Meltzer and Massey, 2011). In contrast, other researchers believe that atypicality can be explained solely by low D_2 receptor binding affinity, regardless of any other receptor type function (Seeman, 2002). Receptor affinity (K_d) is the ratio of how readily the drug moves off the receptor compared with how readily it binds (see Chapter 4 for radioligand binding). Hence, a drug with low affinity could be one that binds slowly or that after binding moves off the receptor rapidly. Most antipsychotic drugs bind at similar rates, but there are large differences in how quickly they unbind. For example, clozapine binds to and unbinds from the D_2 receptor 100 times faster than haloperidol. Low affinity means that the drug is not constantly bound to the receptor, and when it is not bound, normal DA transmission can occur. This characteristic might prevent EPS, maintain prolactin levels, and protect cognitive function.

Practical clinical trials help clinicians make decisions about drugs

Since their inception, the second-generation antipsychotics have been the first line of treatment and have been prescribed in about 90% of cases, despite no conclusive evidence that they are superior to the first-generation drugs. In many instances, the clinical effects seen in the "real-world" applications have been less robust than the results from randomized, placebo-controlled trials performed as part of drug development. There can be several reasons for this disparity, such as differences in the duration of drug treatment. Others have suggested that the drug development trials are biased toward the atypical agents because they use as the comparator a high-potency classical drug like haloperidol, which is known to have significant EPS. Bias would also occur when first-generation drugs are used at higher-than-necessary doses, which increases the potential for side effects. Often an older drug is used to compare outcomes without the usual coadministration of an anticholinergic agent that would reduce the appearance of EPS. At other times, the outcome measures, although statistically significant, are insufficient to make the patient feel better. Finally, well-controlled trials, by necessity, exclude patients with comorbid medical or psychiatric conditions, although these excluded individuals are more typical of the usual schizophrenic patient in the real world. For these reasons, drug-trial results comparing antipsychotic drugs may not be generalizable to the larger population. Because the newer drugs generally cost about 10 times what older generic agents cost, cost–benefit considerations are important in clinical decisions.

For all these reasons, the National Institute of Mental Health (NIMH) between January 2001 and December 2004 initiated the Clinical Antipsychotic Trials of Intervention Effectiveness (CATIE), a blinded and controlled study, to compare effectiveness, tolerability, and cost-effectiveness of treatments. These variables were determined by measuring the duration of use before discontinuation of treatment by a patient (Lieberman et al., 2005). Discontinuation of treatment (i.e., switching to another drug) was chosen as a critical measure because it combined several factors, including *both* the patients' and the clinicians' judgments of effectiveness, safety, and side effects, into an overall measure of effectiveness that balances benefits and undesirable effects. Secondary measures of outcome included the specific reasons for discontinuation of treatment and scores on two symptom scales. Additional secondary measures of safety and tolerability were made every 3 months for 18 months. These measures included the incidence of serious adverse effects, the incidence of serious neurological effects, and changes in body weight, electrocardiographic findings, and lab blood analyses. At 57 sites in a variety of treatment settings in the United States, almost 1500 patients were recruited and randomly assigned to receive the classic antipsychotic perphenazine or one of the atypical agents, olanzapine, quetiapine, risperidone, or ziprasidone. The goal of the study was to replicate the "real-world" prescription of these drugs to patients who are more representative of the typical outpatient population, without the normally extensive exclusion criteria required in clinical studies. Hence the results of this practical clinical trial are intended to serve as a guide for clinical practice and to allow patients to make more informed decisions.

The biggest surprise of the study results, counter to the hypothesis, was that the newer drugs were no more effective than the first-generation drug perphenazine.

Overall rates of discontinuation (74%) were high, which means that the majority of patients had to switch to another drug either because of lack of effectiveness or because they could not tolerate the side effects. Among all the drugs, olanzapine had the longest duration before discontinuation and produced the greatest improvement initially, although this advantage decreased over the 18 months. Also, olanzapine showed the highest discontinuation rate as the result of adverse side effects, particularly weight gain and metabolic effects. To the researchers' surprise, there were no differences among the drugs in terms of effectiveness for reducing negative symptoms or cognitive deficits. Further, the incidence of EPS was the same for all agents, and this may be attributed to the low but effective dose of perphenazine used. This study was important because it showed that drug effectiveness is quite different under conditions similar to routine clinical practice compared with tightly controlled trials. The database has been used in subsequent studies looking at other factors, including cost-effectiveness, quality of life, and patient characteristics that predict response (see Lieberman and Stroup, 2011, for a list of references). Subsequent naturalistic research, such as the Cost Utility of the Latest Antipsychotic Drugs in Schizophrenia Study (CUtLASS) performed in the United Kingdom, supported the findings from CATIE and found no difference among the first- and second-generation drugs, except that clozapine was superior (see Lewis and Lieberman, 2008, for a brief review). It would seem that only clozapine is truly "atypical." These findings should encourage the use of older first-generation drugs, which are effective at a significantly lower cost. For the patient, this means more treatment options are available to optimize benefits and side effects for the individual.

There are renewed efforts to treat the cognitive symptoms

It is quite clear that the cognitive symptoms along with the negative symptoms represent aspects of the disorder that are the most damaging to the quality of life of the schizophrenic individual. These symptoms prevent integration into the community and reduce the probability of functioning in a productive manner. Since neither the first- nor second-generation antipsychotics improve the cognitive impairments of schizophrenia, several new pharmacological approaches are being considered (Buchanan et al., 2007).

ACETYLCHOLINE Because ACh has a role in attention, sensory processing, and several aspects of memory, enhancing ACh is one reasonable approach to treating cognitive symptoms. In addition, the fact that the rate of cigarette smoking is extremely high among individuals with schizophrenia (58% to 88% compared with about 17% in the general population) has led some to suggest that nicotine use may be a form of self-medication

(Boggs et al., 2014). Nicotine binds to and activates nicotinic cholinergic receptors and has been found to enhance performance in cognitive tests (see Chapter 13). Furthermore, ACh is an appropriate target because post-mortem and imaging studies have shown cholinergic deficits in patients with schizophrenia. For example, reduced numbers of ACh receptors have been reported in the DLPFC and hippocampus, brain areas critical to cognitive function. It is interesting that clozapine, the only antipsychotic drug currently available that enhances cognitive deficits, increases the release of ACh in the hippocampus and DA in the PFC. Acute administration of nicotine or subtype-selective nicotinic agonists for the α7 nicotinic acetylcholine receptors (α7 nAChRs; see Chapter 7 for a description of ACh receptors and their subtypes) produces some limited cognitive improvement, particularly enhancing selective attention. Several subtype-specific nicotinic partial agonists were found to normalize auditory gating deficits in rodents, as well as in early trials with patients with schizophrenia. At least part of the problem in developing drugs for enhancing cholinergic function is that the receptors undergo desensitization (see Chapter 7). One way around that problem is to develop drugs that bind to sites on the receptor other than the ACh binding site and enhance agonist function in that way. These types of drugs are called positive allosteric modulators (PAMs). One recent preclinical study of interest tested several PAMs of the α7 nAChRs on ketamine-induced cognitive deficits (Nikiforuk et al., 2016). The study found that the drugs reversed ketamine-induced cognitive inflexibility in the attentional set-shifting task, and in fact, the animals performed somewhat better than controls. The PAMs also enhanced performance in the novel object recognition task, in which the animals demonstrated that they could remember, after treatment with either of two PAMs, which object was familiar and which was novel (**FIGURE 19.15**). Interestingly, earlier these same researchers had shown that the two PAMs could also improve *natural* (not drug-induced) forgetting, an effect

that was dependent on the α7 nAChR. Finally, they also found that the social withdrawal induced by ketamine was reversed by the PAMs. Hence these PAMs improved cognitive and social behaviors in the ketamine model of schizophrenia and suggest further study as a potential therapeutic approach.

DOPAMINE In an earlier section, you saw that negative symptoms and cognitive deficits including hypofrontality are associated with reduced DA function in PFC, particularly at D_1 receptors, which are the most common receptor subtype in that region. It is well known that increasing synaptic DA with amphetamine improves cognitive deficits in patients with schizophrenia; however, since the positive symptoms are due to excessive DA release from mesolimbic neurons, those symptoms worsen. The goal then is to selectively enhance D_1 receptor signaling in PFC with D_1 agonists. The first agent, dihydrexidine, was found to reverse cognitive performance deficits in aged primates and in other animals after neurotoxin-induced lesions of DA cells. In a small number of patients with schizophrenia, the drug increased blood flow in prefrontal regions but unfortunately failed to improve task performance in delayed recall or working memory. Recent research showed that very high plasma concentrations are needed to reach detectable D_1 receptor occupancy of the brain. Because of poor bioavailability of the drug, insufficient dosage may in part explain the failure to improve cognitive function (see Arnsten et al., 2017).

A second approach to enhancing PFC DA function is to inhibit the enzyme catechol-*O*-methyltransferase (COMT), which degrades DA in the synapse, ending its signaling. Inhibition of the enzyme with a drug such as tolcapone causes a relatively selective increase of DA in PFC because there are few DA transporters in PFC relative to striatal dopamine terminal fields; hence, metabolism via COMT accounts for a relatively higher proportion of DA inactivation in the PFC compared to the striatum and nucleus accumbens (Käenmäki et al., 2010).

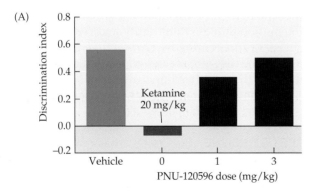
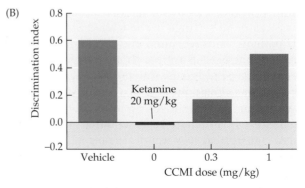

FIGURE 19.15 Effects of PAMs on novel object recognition The discrimination index represents the animals' ability to remember an object that was presented on day 1 and to spend more time investigating a novel object when both the old object and the new object are presented on day 2. Both bar graphs show that 20 mg/kg of ketamine dramatically reduced the cognitive function in the absence of either PAM. As PAM (PNU-120596 and CCMI) dosages increased, the ability to discriminate increased to approximately control levels. (After A. Nikiforuk et al. 2016. *Neuropharmacol* 101: 389–400.)

Accordingly, in COMT knockout mice, DA levels are increased in PFC but not in striatum, and performance on memory tasks is improved. In patients with advanced Parkinson's disease, tolcapone improved performance on attentional tasks, verbal short-term memory, and visuospatial recall. Others found tolcapone-induced improvement in executive function and verbal episodic memory in healthy volunteers that was accompanied by improvement in information processing in PFC, as visualized with functional MRI (fMRI). Given that COMT polymorphisms influence frontal lobe function and performance on tasks of working memory, the genetic variation may represent a predictive marker for effective pharmacotherapy. Unfortunately, tolcapone can produce serious liver dysfunction, which requires frequent liver enzyme testing; it has already been withdrawn from the market in Canada and Europe. Gupta and colleagues (2011) provide a review of COMT function and its significance as a therapeutic target for cognitive disorders. Alternative strategies to treat cognitive symptoms via selective PFC dopamine enhancement have been considered, namely using the norepinephrine transporter (NET) inhibitor atomoxetine to selectively increase extracellular levels of dopamine in PFC. Following similar logic to the COMT inhibition strategy described above, NET inhibitors such as atomoxetine are thought to selectively prevent PFC dopamine inactivation, because like COMT, norepinephrine transporters account for a substantial proportion of DA inactivation in PFC, but not in striatum. Atomoxetine (Strattera) is probably best known as a non-stimulant drug to treat attention-deficit/hyperactivity disorder (ADHD), precisely due to its selective ability to increase extracellular DA in PFC, but not basal ganglia. Interested readers are encouraged to read the elegant study by Bymaster and colleagues (2002) that used microdialysis to examine the anatomically selective effects of a range of different catecholamine transporter inhibitors, including atomoxetine, on extracellular catecholamine concentrations. Initial studies of atomoxetine on the cognitive and negative symptoms of schizophrenia were modestly positive, or equivocal at best (Solmi et al., 2019).

GLUTAMATE   In a previous section, you learned that glutamate antagonists such as PCP and ketamine produce behaviors that resemble the positive, negative, and cognitive symptoms of schizophrenia. Figure 19.8 showed that low glutamate signaling could explain the decrease in mesocortical activity that is believed to cause negative and cognitive symptoms. On the basis of this notion, enhancing glutamate activity at NMDA receptors might reverse these symptoms. Although administering an NMDA receptor agonist seems reasonable, it is not possible because these drugs produce neuronal hyperexcitability and seizures. Instead, glycine site agonists can be used to enhance NMDA signaling because glycine is an obligatory co-agonist at

this receptor and in addition to glutamate, is necessary for receptor activation (see Chapter 8). The glycine receptor agonists glycine, D-cycloserine, and D-serine, when combined with antipsychotics, reduced negative and cognitive symptoms in some but not all clinical trials. Despite inconsistent results, there are many potential methodological explanations to explore. For instance, studies vary in drug dosage, duration of trials, outcome measures, differences in which classic or second-generation antipsychotics are used adjunctively, and even whether those studied were outpatient or inpatients (in the latter, compliance with the drug regimen is ensured). Despite the difficulties, a meta-analysis of double-blind, placebo-controlled studies looked at the efficacy of the NMDA enhancers on multiple symptom domains, dose–response relationships, the effects of concomitant antipsychotics (both conventional and second-generation), and side effects in patients with schizophrenia. Using 800 patients from 26 studies, the meta-analysis found that these glycine modulatory site agonists were effective in most symptom domains, including depressive, negative, cognitive, positive, and general psychopathology. Glycine and D-serine were overall more effective than D-cycloserine, which may be explained because glycine and D-serine are full agonists at the glycine modulatory site while D-cycloserine is a partial agonist that would not maximally activate the receptor. Since no trials reported significant side effects, these agents appear to be safe and effective.

An alternative way to increase synaptic glycine is to administer an inhibitor of the glycine transporter that moves synaptic glycine from the synapse to neurons and glial cells. A clinical trial administering the glycine transporter inhibitor sarcosine, along with atypical antipsychotics, shows that sarcosine has greater efficacy than the glycine agonist D-serine in overall symptom reduction, reduction of negative symptoms, and improvement in quality-of-life ratings of social activity, sense of purpose, motivation, anhedonia, capacity for empathy, aimless inactivity, and emotional interaction (Lane et al., 2010). Meanwhile, other approaches for enhancing NMDA function are being studied, including enhancement of D-serine synthesis and inhibition of its inactivation. Only with time will we know whether NMDA enhancement lives up to its promise.

ANTI-INFLAMMATORY DRUGS   Earlier we discussed the potential role that perinatal inflammation may play in the neurodevelopmental pathogenesis of schizophrenia. If brain inflammation leads to schizophrenic symptoms, then it is possible that anti-inflammatory drugs may be a useful therapeutic approach. A wide variety of anti-inflammatory drugs have been tested to varying extents, including aspirin, celecoxib, polyunsaturated fatty acids, minocycline, and others. One of the more interesting is minocycline, an antibiotic that reduces inflammation and also reduces microglia activation, so fewer pro-inflammatory cytokines are released. It also has neurotrophic, antioxidant, and antiapoptotic properties. Animal studies have shown that minocycline provides neuroprotection following ischemic stroke or glutamate-induced excitotoxicity and in animal models of neurodegenerative diseases such as Huntington's disease and Parkinson's disease, as well as in animal models of schizophrenia. In one study Monte and colleagues (2013) found that minocycline both *prevented* and reversed ketamine-induced impairment of PPI and hyperlocomotion (models of positive symptoms) as effectively as the antipsychotic risperidone. The anti-inflammatory agent also prevented and reversed ketamine-induced social withdrawal (negative symptom) and impaired Y-maze performance (cognitive symptom), neither one of which was improved by risperidone. Their results encouraged the further study of minocycline as a novel approach to schizophrenia therapy, although these trials have produced mixed results. Multiple reports suggest that minocycline, along with antipsychotic drugs, improves negative symptoms and general outcome along with executive functioning and working memory. Others found it to be ineffective. There is some indication that anti-inflammatory drugs may be helpful for early-phase schizophrenia or for patients with high levels of CRP, a protein that increases in the blood during inflammation. Perhaps more subgroups of patients who respond to anti-inflammatories will be identified. As is always the case, risk–benefit ratios must be considered since many of the anti-inflammatory drugs have the potential for serious consequences. In the case of minocycline, because of potential damaging effects it is not likely to be the first choice for adjunctive use (Fond et al., 2014). Moreover, many anti-inflammatory drugs have additional mechanisms of action beyond suppression of inflammation, making it difficult to discern precisely how these drugs improve schizophrenia. For a review of minocycline and other anti-inflammatory drugs for their potential in the treatment of schizophrenia, see Jeppesen and colleagues (2020).

NAVIGATE COMBINED TREATMENT APPROACH

Thus far our emphasis has been on pharmacotherapies for schizophrenia, but a new initiative based on earlier European designs has refocused care for first-episode patients on a comprehensive multimodal, multidisciplinary, team-based approach. The program, called NAVIGATE, involves several components: education of the family to increase their understanding of the disease and relapse prevention; supported employment and education to help patients decide on appropriate classes or job opportunities that are most suitable for them based on their symptoms; individual resiliency training provided by one-on-one talk therapy intended to help the patients reduce substance use, build social

relationships, and cope with symptoms such as suicidal thoughts as well as positive symptoms; and individualized low-dose medication treatment to minimize side effects and enhance compliance. Every effort is made to include the family and the patient in the decision-making processes and help them navigate through the complexities of the mental health care system. Details are beyond the scope of this chapter, but Mueser and colleagues (2015) summarize the program, team staffing, and conceptual foundations. Large controlled studies have compared outcomes of patients getting standard drug-focused community care with those in NAVIGATE. After 2 years patients in the comprehensive program showed enhanced quality-of-life scores, motivation, social interactions, sense of purpose, and engagement in regular activities. Improvements were greatest for those treated earliest after the onset of psychosis. In most cases drug dosages were 20% to 50% lower than standard, leading to fewer side effects. Because of lower drug costs with generic drugs and, in some cases, reduced relapse and hospitalization and increased productivity and quality of life, NAVIGATE can be considered a cost-effective treatment approach.

SECTION SUMMARY

- All antipsychotics show efficacy in reducing positive symptoms and decreasing length of hospitalization.
- The law of thirds says one-third of patients treated with antipsychotics improve dramatically and return to normal lives. A second third show some improvement but experience relapses and need help with day-to-day living. The final third show little improvement and have significant periods of hospitalization.
- Prolonged maintenance therapy doubles the odds of avoiding relapse.
- There is a strong positive correlation between antipsychotic binding to D_2 receptors and clinical effectiveness.
- Antipsychotic blocking of D_2 autoreceptors causes an initial increase in DA neuron firing and increased turnover of DA, followed by a gradual decrease as the autoreceptors up-regulate. Depolarization block may contribute to the decrease in turnover. These adaptive changes may explain the gradual onset of effectiveness.
- Parkinsonian symptoms are the most troubling side effects with traditional antipsychotic treatment. Combining the drugs with anticholinergic agents reduces risk. Second-generation drugs have a lower incidence of motor side effects.
- Tardive dyskinesia involves involuntary movement of face, jaw, tongue, neck, or extremities, which may be irreversible in some patients. VMAT2 inhibitors represent a new treatment strategy that may work by reducing extracellular DA levels.
- Neuroendocrine side effects are caused by DA receptor blockade of tuberohypophyseal neurons that project to the pituitary.

■ Neuroleptic malignant syndrome is a potentially life-threatening effect of antipsychotics.

■ Anticholinergic effects of antipsychotics produce widespread effects on autonomic nervous system function.

■ Atypical antipsychotics may be selective D_2 antagonists, DA partial agonists (DA system stabilizers), or broad-spectrum antipsychotics.

■ The atypical antipsychotics are heterogeneous neurochemically and clinically but overall cause fewer motor side effects than the older drugs.

■ Several of the atypical antipsychotics are especially problematic in causing weight gain, hyperglycemia, cardiotoxicity, elevated cholesterol, and increased risk for diabetes.

■ Only clozapine improves negative and cognitive symptoms without motor side effects, and it is often effective for treatment-resistant patients. Serious side effects limit its use.

■ The neurochemical property that makes clozapine unique is not known. It may be high affinity for D_4 receptors, antagonism of 5-HT_2 receptors, or low D_2 affinity.

■ A practical clinical trial (CATIE) using 1500 patients under "real-world" conditions showed that the atypical antipsychotics were no more effective than the traditional agents in reducing positive, negative, or cognitive symptoms. Occurrence of EPS was the same for both. Only clozapine is superior.

■ Nicotinic partial agonists, D_1 agonists, COMT inhibitors, glycine agonists, glycine transporter inhibitors, anti-inflammatories, and combined drug treatment and behavioral intervention programs are being investigated as methods to improve cognitive processing and negative symptoms.

STUDY QUESTIONS

1. Describe the symptoms of schizophrenia. What makes it difficult to diagnose? What are the positive, negative, and cognitive symptoms?

2. What are some of the brain structure abnormalities found in patients with schizophrenia? Functional abnormalities? Immune system dysfunctions?

3. Provide evidence for the hereditary nature of schizophrenia. Why do researchers believe the candidate gene *DISC1* contributes to the risk for developing schizophrenia?

4. What evidence exists to suggest there are developmental errors early in the life of a patient? At adolescence? How is that evidence incorporated into the "two-hit" model?

5. Describe each of the following animal models: amphetamine-induced stereotypy, hypoglutamate model, vacuous chewing movements test, attentional set shifting, prepulse inhibition of startle, prenatal inflammation, and genetic models.

6. Summarize the dopamine hypothesis of schizophrenia and provide several pieces of evidence.

7. How does the neurodevelopmental model attempt to explain the positive and negative symptoms?

8. How does glutamate regulate mesocortical and mesolimbic neurons? What seems to be responsible for the hypoglutamate function?

9. Discuss the importance of D_2 receptor antagonism in antipsychotic drug action.

10. Describe the four DA pathways, and tell how each is responsible for the effectiveness and side effects of antipsychotics.

11. What are parkinsonian side effects? How are they treated?

12. What is tardive dyskinesia? Why is this side effect especially troubling?

13. List side effects of antipsychotics and their neurochemical basis.

14. All the antipsychotics block D_2 receptors except aripiprazole and similar compounds. Describe the mechanism of action of aripiprazole

15. What is the principal benefit of the "atypical" antipsychotics? Describe the three general approaches used to develop those drugs.

16. What are the benefits and risks of the broad-spectrum antipsychotic clozapine?

17. Discuss the metabolic side effects and cardiac arrhythmias caused by some of the broad-spectrum antipsychotics.

18. What are the possible neurochemical explanations for the atypical effects of clozapine?

19. Why are "real-world" clinical trials important, and how do they differ from the usual well-controlled drug development trials? What did the CATIE study demonstrate?

20. In what three ways have researchers attempted to enhance cholinergic function to treat cognitive symptoms of schizophrenia?

21. Describe two approaches for enhancing PFC DA function.

22. Why are glycine modulatory site agonists, glycine transporter inhibitors, and serine racemase enhancers considered potential therapeutic adjuncts to antipsychotic drugs? How do they work?

23. Describe the therapeutic potential of anti-inflammatory drugs.

24. What is the treatment approach called NAVIGATE, and what are its benefits?

20 Neurodegenerative Diseases

WHEN HER HUSBAND STARTED TO SMELL DIFFERENT, AND UNPLEASANT, TO HER, Joy Milne insisted repeatedly that he shower. The musty, yeasty smell didn't go away with any amount of washing, and in fact, grew worse and worse over time. No one else noticed the smell, and her husband grew annoyed at her nagging. Ten years after that first change in smell, Joy's husband was diagnosed with Parkinson's disease (PD). But it would still be another 20 years, after they joined a support group for people with PD, that Joy realized that what she had been smelling all those years WAS his PD! Every PD patient in the room smelled the same to her, with varying degrees of intensity. Though she was at first dismissed by the PD scientist they approached with their suspicions that PD had a distinct smell, he eventually put her olfactory sensitivity to the test. PD and control subjects wore T-shirts for several days and she had to determine whether each shirt had been worn by someone with or without PD. She was remarkably accurate in distinguishing the smells of those with PD from those without it— and at distinguishing how far along they were in their disease process. In fact, the one "mistake" she made, a control subject that she labeled as having PD, was diagnosed a year later! As with her husband, she was able to detect this change in smell before clinical symptoms presented and a diagnosis was reached. Since the discovery of her unique ability, further study has been done on what is causing the smell and investigating whether tests might be developed to identify PD, or other disorders, well before clinical signs drive someone to seek medical attention. If we can identify the presence of the disease before enough damage has been done to bring about symptoms, we may be able to develop and administer therapies to prevent disease progression. Learn more about what it is that she is sensing in Box 20.1. ■

Joy Milne (pictured) is one of the very few people who can detect the distinct odor emitted by patients with Parkinson's disease.

20.1 Parkinson's Disease

Parkinson's disease (**PD**), is a chronic, progressive, neurodegenerative disorder (Davie, 2008). The symptoms of the disorder are irreversible and worsen as the degeneration of neurons progresses. Although there are genetic and environmental risk factors, a definitive cause of the disorder has not yet been discovered. Treatments are symptomatic in nature; no treatments are known to affect disease progression. Generally, age is the most significant risk factor for development of PD, and the incidence of the disorder increases with age. There is also an early-onset variant of the disease in which symptoms begin before the age of 40. Perhaps the most famous case of early-onset PD is that of Michael J. Fox (**FIGURE 20.1**), who disclosed his diagnosis the day before it was to be reported in a tabloid newspaper. He has since become a vocal and dedicated advocate for research on PD and care for those with the disorder with the Michael J. Fox Foundation (michaeljfox.com).

The clinical features of PD are primarily motor related

Often the most visible outward sign of PD is a 4- to 6-hertz **resting tremor**, which occurs in about 70% of patients with PD. It generally starts in the hand (where it is called a "pill-rolling" tremor for its characteristic motion) or foot on one side of the body, although it can also happen in the jaw or face. The tremor is present when the limb is relaxed and generally disappears with intentional movement. It can be exacerbated by stress or excitement and can spread to the other side of the body with disease progression (although the initially affected limb generally shows a more severe tremor throughout the disease process).

Parkinson's disease is characterized by both **akinesia** (difficulty in initiating movement) and slowing of movement in general. This slowing, called **bradykinesia** (from the Greek *bradys*, "slow," and *kinesis*, "motion"), leads to several seemingly unrelated symptoms. Many patients with PD are described as "stone-faced" because their facial muscles do not move as much and therefore don't allow the range of facial expression that was previously achievable. Perhaps less obvious as consequences of slowed/reduced movement are the micrographia (smaller handwriting), hypophonia (decreased volume of speaking), and monotonous speech (decreased prosody in the voice) that accompany PD.

Rigidity, or stiffness and inflexibility in the joints, is another common symptom of PD. This difficulty in joint movement often manifests (together with bradykinesia) as lack of arm swing when walking. This contributes to the "Parkinson's shuffle" often seen in patients. The two particular types of rigidity that may be seen with PD are described as "lead-pipe" rigidity (joint inflexibility that is maintained consistently through a range of passive movement) and "cog-wheel" rigidity (ratchet-like interruptions in muscle tone). Cog-wheel rigidity is likely the result of a tremor superimposed over the rigidity.

Postural instability (impaired balance and coordination) causes patients to lean forward or backward when standing upright. This leads to **retropulsion** in some patients: when bumped from the front or when starting to walk, patients with a backward lean tend to step backward. Postural instability can also cause patients to have **anteropulsion**, a stooped posture in which the head is bowed and the shoulders are drooped. Both anteropulsion and retropulsion can manifest as counterintuitive symptoms of **festination** (uncontrollable acceleration of gait). Unwanted acceleration of movement can also happen in a patient's speech, a condition called tachyphemia.

Another early sign of motor dysfunction is evident in eye movement, primarily as difficulty in tracking moving objects. This occurs in both medicated and nonmedicated patients with PD and may be useful in the differential diagnosis of PD. Other, less consistently seen, motor symptoms include **dystonia** (persistent involuntary muscle contractions), impaired gross and fine motor control, **akathisia** (a constant urge to move certain body parts), speech problems, difficulty swallowing, sexual dysfunction, cramping, and drooling.

Although the symptoms of PD are primarily motor related, other difficulties accompany the disorder. Early signs include anosmia (loss of the sense of smell), constipation, REM (rapid-eye-movement) sleep behavior disorder (lack of normal loss of muscle tone during REM sleep), mood disorders, and orthostatic hypotension (also known as postural hypotension—a sudden drop in blood pressure upon standing, resulting in dizziness or fainting). As the disease progresses,

MediaPunch Inc./Alamy Stock Photo

FIGURE 20.1   Among the most public faces of Parkinson's disease have been Muhammad Ali, who passed away in 2016, and Michael J. Fox   In addition to educating the public and federal leaders, Fox (shown here testifying before the U.S. Senate health committee) created and advocates for the Michael J. Fox Foundation for Parkinson's Research.

patients may also experience sleep disturbances; bladder problems; weight loss or gain; vision problems; dental issues; fatigue or loss of energy; skin problems, including seborrheic dermatitis (overproduction of sebum, resulting in oily skin); and medication side effects.

Several other disorders can mimic the effects of PD. PD symptoms in the absence of the hallmark pathology of PD are referred to as parkinsonism. Some disorders that may bring about parkinsonian symptoms are strokes, encephalitis, and repeated brain trauma. Additionally, medications, including many antipsychotic drugs (e.g., haloperidol), some drugs used to treat high blood pressure (e.g., reserpine), and some mood stabilizers (e.g., valproate and lithium), can cause parkinsonian symptoms as side effects.

Patients with Parkinson's may also develop dementia

Parkinson's disease dementia (**PDD**) is diagnosed when one or more cognitive functions are impaired to the point of interfering with the patient's ability to navigate everyday life. Prevalence estimates vary, but it is likely between 15% and 40% and increases to near 70% after 15 years of disease progression. The tricky part of the diagnosis of PDD is differentiating it from comorbid Alzheimer's disease (AD) or **Lewy body dementia**. Generally, AD and PDD share symptoms, but they tend to occur in a different order. Early PDD may be characterized

by **bradyphrenia** (slowed answers), although patients may still be able to give correct answers if allowed adequate time. They may also show mental inflexibility and changes in visuospatial function. Hallucinations are fairly common in PDD early in the dementia process, but they don't show up in AD until very late in the disease progression. Patients may show improvement on cognitive tests of dementia severity, such as the **Mini-Mental State Examination** (**MMSE**), if they take cholinesterase inhibitors, particularly rivastigmine (Exelon) (Emre et al., 2004), a medication also used to treat AD symptoms.

The primary pathology of PD is a loss of dopaminergic neurons in the substantia nigra

The **substantia nigra** is generally considered part of the **basal ganglia**, a group of structures that are instrumental in translating motivation into action (see Chapter 2). A common model uses the concepts of an accelerator and a brake for voluntary movements. These neurons are key, but are not the start of the pathology in PD. In 2003, Braak and coworkers described stages (now called Braak stages) of pathological changes that happen in PD. The degeneration starts in the dorsal motor nucleus of the vagus and the anterior olfactory structures. This loss of olfactory processing accounts for the **anosmia** experienced by many of those with PD. The degeneration then moves to two sets of brainstem nuclei: the raphe nucleus and the locus coeruleus (**FIGURE 20.2**).

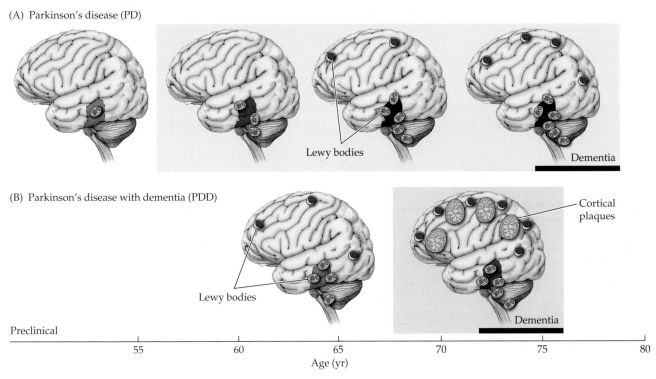

(A) Parkinson's disease (PD)

Lewy bodies

Dementia

(B) Parkinson's disease with dementia (PDD)

Lewy bodies

Cortical plaques

Dementia

Preclinical

55   60   65   70   75   80

Age (yr)

FIGURE 20.2   Disease progression in early- and late-onset Parkinson's disease   Cellular degeneration (represented by progressively darker red shading in the midbrain) and the accumulation of Lewy bodies spread at different rates through the brainstem nuclei and midbrain depending on the age of onset. Compared with those with earlier-onset PD (A), more pronounced pathology earlier in disease progression is seen in those with later-onset PD (B). Latency to dementia onset from disease onset is also faster in later-onset cases. (After J. A. Obeso et al. 2010. *Nat Med* 16: 653–661. doi.org/10.1038/nm.2165)

Parkinson's   Without Parkinson's

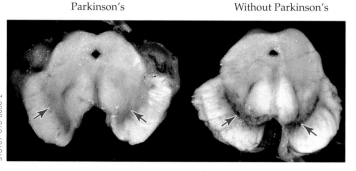

FIGURE 20.3 Selective loss of pigmented dopaminergic cells occurs in the substantia nigra The brain of a person with Parkinson's disease is compared with that of a healthy control. The substantia nigra is marked with red arrows.

Only in the third stage do we start to see degeneration of the substantia nigra (**FIGURE 20.3**), along with the amygdala and the nucleus basalis of Meynert. It is in this third stage that clinical diagnosis generally occurs with the onset of motor symptoms. Degeneration of the temporal lobe mesocortex (an area of cortex where layers 3, 4, and 5 are fused into one; e.g., the parahippocampal cortex) follows in stage 4, followed by degeneration of the neocortex in the temporal lobe along with neocortex sensory association and premotor areas in stage 5. Finally, the neocortex areas of primary sensory function and motor areas show degeneration in stage 6.

Motor symptoms, other than the resting tremor, are generally explained by the loss of dopaminergic substantia nigra cells. Loss of these cells results in less dopaminergic input to the striatum (the putamen and the caudate nucleus) of the basal ganglia. This loss increases excitation to the subthalamic nucleus and the internal globus pallidus through the direct and indirect pathways of the basal ganglia. Excitation of inhibitory neurons leads to inhibition of the thalamus and

subsequent inhibition of motor structures in the cortex (**FIGURE 20.4**). This results in the akinesia and bradykinesia of PD.

In most cases, the onset of PD is a sporadic event. Estimates of the percentage of cases resulting from familial inheritance generally are only around 10%. Age is the most significant risk factor for PD; the incidence increases as the population ages. Environmental contributors are also suspected in the development of PD (a result of the observation of heroin addicts who had mistakenly taken MPTP [a neurotoxin that destroys DA neurons], as discussed in Chapter 5). Although research has not identified any one specific cause, it has supported the idea that pesticides and other toxins may contribute to PD onset (Tanner et al., 2011).

Regardless of the cause of PD, several processes contribute to the degeneration of neurons, including mitochondrial dysfunction, oxidative stress, inflammation, excitotoxicity, protein misfolding, and proteosomal dysfunction (Davie, 2008). These mechanisms then lead to **Lewy body** formation (see later in this section), other protein accumulation, and ultimately apoptosis of the cells (see Chapter 8 for a discussion of apoptosis).

Supporting evidence for these mechanisms comes from many different places. Mitochondrial dysfunction is indicated from the process by which **MPTP** (1-methyl-4-phenyl-1,2,3,6-tetrahydropyridine) destroys cells. Actually, it is not the MPTP itself that damages the cells, but the oxidation product MPP^+. MPP^+ is formed by the activity of monoamine oxidase B (MAO-B) in astrocytes and serotonergic neurons and is transported by the dopamine (DA) transporter into substantia nigra cells. Once inside the cells, MPP^+ accumulates in mitochondria, blocking mitochondrial respiration (i.e., oxygen-dependent energy production). Mutations in genes supporting mitochondrial function have been

FIGURE 20.4 The effects of Parkinson's disease on motor control pathways With the degeneration of the substantia nigra, the balance of signals in the direct and indirect pathways is changed such that there is less inhibition from the caudate and putamen into the globus pallidus. This keeps the thalamus inhibited by the globus pallidus, thus decreasing activation of the motor cortex by the thalamus. VA, ventral anterior nucleus; VL, ventral lateral nucleus. (From D. Purves et al. 2018.; after DeLong, 1990. *Neuroscience*, 6th ed., Sinauer: Sunderland, MA; after M. R. DeLong. 1990. *Trends Neurosci* 13: 281–285.)

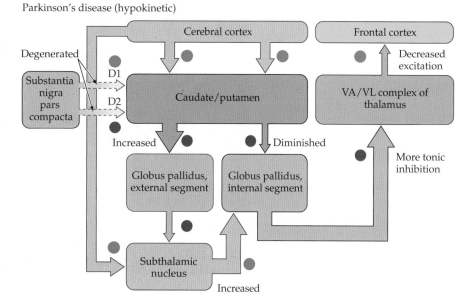

identified in familial forms of PD. The "MitoPark" mouse model was designed to test the hypothesis that mitochondrial dysfunction is particularly important in the pathogenesis of PD. In this mouse, mitochondrial transcription factor A (TFAM) was inactivated in substantia nigra dopaminergic neurons. The results of this inactivation are depletion of mitochondrial DNA (mtDNA), loss of gene transcripts, and deficiency in the respiratory chain, the end result of which is cell death (Sorensen et al., 2001). The behavioral outcomes in these mice were similar in manner and scope to PD and were reversed by L-DOPA treatment, one of the most common therapies for PD (discussed in detail later in this chapter). Both support for the theory of loss of dopaminergic neurons and a powerful new diagnostic tool are provided by fluorodopa F18 PET scanning. This technique has been used to study the pathology of PD and other parkinsonian syndromes. In 2019, the U.S. Food and Drug Administration (FDA) approved the compound for diagnosis of PD. This imaging technology allows for DA terminal visualization by binding to DA transporters (Seibyl et al., 2012; Stoessl, 2012) (**FIGURE 20.5**).

Oxidative stress is indicated as a contributor to the pathology of PD by post-mortem analysis of patient brain tissue, which shows oxidative damage, accumulation of iron, glutathione depletion (Martin and Teismann, 2009), and a decrease in glutathione peroxidase (Kish et al., 1985). Additionally, in an experimental model, the use of **6-hydroxydopamine (6-OHDA)** destroys dopaminergic neurons by producing reactive oxygen species (see Chapter 5 for discussion of DA neurotoxins). This destruction produces symptoms of parkinsonism. A caveat is required when discussing

oxidative stress, because antioxidants such as tocopherol, more commonly known as vitamin E (Parkinson Study Group, 1993), and coenzyme Q (Shults et al., 2002; Storch et al., 2007) have not been shown to be consistently effective against the degeneration and symptomatology of PD.

The roles of inflammation and excitotoxicity in the pathology of PD are primarily supported by the fact that the therapeutic effects of agents block them in some animal models and in some clinical trials. In particular, some evidence suggests a protective effect of nonsteroidal anti-inflammatory drugs like ibuprofen (Gagne and Power, 2010). Glutamate excitotoxicity can also be blocked with some therapeutic benefit in both animal models and patients. N-methyl-D-aspartate (NMDA) receptor modulators and antagonists can be beneficial because of their glutamatergic connections to the DA-containing neurons of the substantia nigra (Koutsilieri and Riederer, 2007).

One of the key components of PD degeneration, though, is protein aggregation, which makes PD similar in pathology to AD. In particular, Lewy bodies are formed in the cells that are affected by PD (**FIGURE 20.6**). Lewy bodies are primarily composed of the **α-synuclein** protein, along with associated proteins such as ubiquitin, neurofilament protein, and alphaB-crystallin. The purported role of α-synuclein in healthy cells involves interactions with membranes, particularly those of vesicles. In these interactions, the protein mediates vesicle movement at the axon terminal (the name *synuclein* comes from its role at the *syn*apse). For a comprehensive review of α-synuclein function and dysfunction, see Auluck and colleagues (2010). There can also be tau

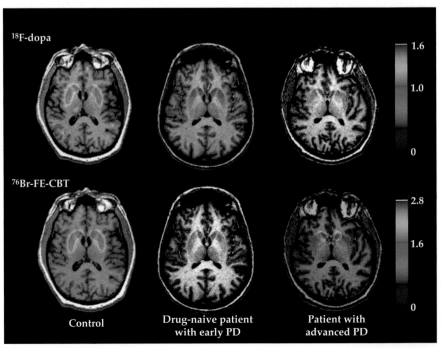

FIGURE 20.5 PET scan visualization of fluorodopa F18 and [76]Br-FE-CBT uptake The scans are at the level of the striatum in a control subject, a drug-naive patient with early Parkinson's disease (PD), and a patient with advanced PD. Uptake of both tracers is asymmetrically decreased in patients with PD and is less in the posterior than in the anterior striatum, indicating decreased dopaminergic cells. The decrease is more severe in more advanced disease.

From M-J. Ribeiro et al. 2002. *Arch Neurol* 59: 580–586

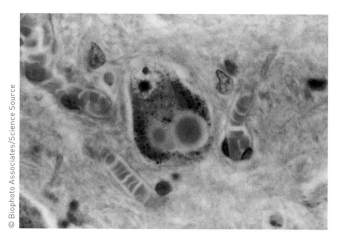

FIGURE 20.6 Lewy bodies are formed by abnormal accumulations of proteins They are composed mostly of α-synuclein but also contain ubiquitin, tau, and other proteins.

proteins and surrounding neurofibrillary tangles that are more often associated with AD. These Lewy body protein accumulations result from a combination of pathological processes, including protein misfolding and proteosomal dysfunction. Proteins require a precise three-dimensional conformation to function correctly. Those that are misfolded should be destroyed by proteosomes in the cells, but this process does not happen effectively, resulting in aggregation of these proteins and the formation of Lewy bodies. These protein aggregations interrupt normal cellular functions and trigger apoptotic cell death. In fact, the Braak stages discussed earlier are based on the accumulation of α-synuclein in the cells of the listed brain areas, not on neuronal death. Selective vulnerability has been noted in low-speed, long, nonmyelinated neurons in the brain.

Animal models of PD have strengths and limitations

We have already mentioned a couple of useful animal models: the use of MPTP (in mice or non-human primates) or 6-OHDA to make lesions, and the genetic model of the MitoPark mouse. These represent two classes of animal models: toxins and genetic manipulations. Another substance that falls into the category of toxin administration is rotenone. Rotenone is a compound obtained from the roots, seeds, and stems of several plants and is used as a pesticide, both as an insecticide and as a piscicide (fish poison). When administered to a mammal, this compound produces a pattern of pathology that is very similar to PD in humans. It triggers the accumulation and aggregation of α-synuclein and ubiquitin and causes oxidative damage and apoptosis (Li et al., 2003). It is thought that it produces this effect by blocking complex I in the mitochondrial respiratory chain. Blocking mitochondrial respiration results in the production of reactive oxygen species (particularly

superoxide and hydrogen peroxide), which cause membrane lipid peroxidation and cell death (Lin and Beal, 2006). This provides further evidence for mitochondrial dysfunction as a mechanism in PD.

A pharmacological model uses the drug reserpine, an antihypertensive drug that depletes stores of three key neurotransmitters (DA, norepinephrine and serotonin [5-HT]), to mimic the lack of DA release and effects on norepinephrine neurons in PD, including cell death in the locus coeruleus. Lesion models include intentional damage to the nigrostriatal tract (cutting the dopaminergic axons as they run from the substantia nigra to the striatum), usually at the level of the medial forebrain bundle (a collection of ascending fiber tracts that include the nigrostriatal tract). Generally, these are good models of the motor dysfunction that occurs with PD, but there are certainly some limitations. Some of the models have problems with specificity. It is impossible to target only the DA neurons in the substantia nigra with 6-OHDA or reserpine. Many of these models are not degenerative in a progressive way as PD is, particularly the drug and lesion models. Most of the animal models are limited in the scope of the PD phenotype they exhibit and may not mimic the specific cellular changes seen in PD (e.g., Lewy bodies, α-synuclein accumulation, apoptosis).

Pharmacological treatments for PD are primarily symptomatic, not disease altering

There are several categories of drugs for PD:

1. Drugs that are symptomatic monotherapies (i.e., given alone for treatment of a particular symptom)
2. Drugs that are given as adjunct treatments to L-DOPA therapy
3. Drugs that prevent motor complications
4. Drugs that treat motor complications

We will address primarily those that are symptomatic treatments given alone or in conjunction with the most common pharmacological treatment, L-DOPA.

LEVODOPA Levodopa (**L-DOPA**), a metabolite of the amino acid tyrosine, immediately precedes the production of DA in its metabolic pathway (see Chapter 5). Because the pathway continues on to form NE and epinephrine (EPI), it is also a precursor to those neurotransmitters. The reason L-DOPA is given as a treatment, rather than DA itself, is that L-DOPA can cross the blood–brain barrier but DA cannot. Once L-DOPA has reached the brain, it can be converted to DA by cells that contain the enzyme **aromatic amino acid decarboxylase**. Because aromatic amino acid decarboxylase is also present in the periphery, L-DOPA is often administered with a peripheral inhibitor of this enzyme such as **carbidopa**, which allows more of the compound to reach the brain. Some drugs on the market are a combination of these two compounds.

L-DOPA is very effective, even compared with other DA agonist drugs (**FIGURE 20.7**), but this treatment is prone to several side effects. In the short term, L-DOPA therapy can result in nausea, hypotension, and neuropsychiatric side effects (e.g., hallucinations, confusion, and anxiety). The long term can bring motor fluctuations (e.g., "off periods," where motor function is slowed or stopped, fluctuating with "on periods") and **dyskinesias**. Dyskinesias are generally unwanted movements like severe tics or choreic movements. You have heard this term before in the context of side effects of antipsychotics that result in tardive (delayed) dyskinesias (see Chapter 19).

Several options exist to combat or minimize the off periods of L-DOPA/carbidopa therapy. One option is Duodopa, a gel suspension of the two drugs administered directly into the intestines through a surgically inserted tube. The gel is administered in a morning bolus dose, then a steady infusion for 16 hours per day. Another administration route that can alleviate off periods is inhaled levodopa (Inbrija). Four drugs are approved for adjunct therapy to carbidopa/levodopa to minimize off periods. Safinamide (Xadago) is a monoamine oxidase inhibitor (MAOI); istradefylline (Nourianz) is an adenosine receptor antagonist; apomorphine HCl (Kynmobi) is a dopamine agonist; and opicapone (Ongentys) is a catechol-*O*-methyl-transferase (COMT) inhibitor, a class of drugs discussed more in the next section.

MONOAMINE OXIDASE INHIBITORS, COMT INHIBITORS, AND DA AGONISTS

Other treatments are also aimed at increasing DA signaling in the brain. Three classes of drugs used for this purpose are the **monoamine oxidase inhibitors** (**MAOIs**), the **catechol-*O*-methyltransferase** (**COMT**) inhibitors, and DA agonists.

The two most common MAOIs used for this purpose are selegiline (Eldepryl) and rasagiline (Azilect). These can be given as monotherapies or as adjuncts to L-DOPA treatment. As in their use in depression, MAOIs prevent the breakdown of DA, NE, and EPI before their repackaging into vesicles, allowing these neurotransmitters to be released in greater quantities with cell stimulation, which increases the opportunity to connect with postsynaptic receptors and bring about signaling between neurons. Because PD is often comorbid with depression, it is important to watch for interactions between MAOIs and other antidepressants, such as **selective serotonin reuptake inhibitors** (**SSRIs**) or **tricyclic antidepressants** (**TCAs**), and to adhere to the strict dietary restrictions that come with MAOIs to avoid side effects such as severe hypertension (see Chapter 18).

COMT inhibitors also prevent the breakdown of DA in the synapse but are given only as adjuncts to L-DOPA. The most common COMT inhibitor used is a drug called entacapone. There is a single-drug treatment (Stalevo) that combines carbidopa, levodopa, and entacapone into one pill for ease of dosing. Several side effects are associated with entacapone, including dyskinesia, dizziness, nausea, diarrhea, and urine discoloration.

DA receptor agonists may also be used to treat PD. The three most popular options are pramipexole (Mirapex), ropinirole (Requip), and rotigotine (Neupro). These drugs all have longer half-lives than L-DOPA (5 to 8 hours versus 0.75 to 1.5 hours for L-DOPA; however, with carbidopa coadministration, the half-life is on the longer end of the range). These drugs also carry lower risks for dyskinesias and off periods. However, the usefulness of these medications is decreased by several side effects, including nausea, sedation, insomnia, orthostatic hypertension, hallucinations, leg edema, and impulse-control disorders.

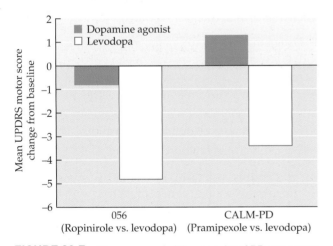

FIGURE 20.7 One measure of the severity of PD symptoms is the Unified Parkinson's Disease Rating Scale (UPDRS) Two large-scale studies—the Comparison of Agonist Pramipexole versus Levodopa on Motor Complications in Parkinson's Disease (CALM-PD) and the 056 study—compared long-term UPDRS scores (a higher rating on this scale denotes more severe disability) in patients receiving levodopa or the dopamine agonists pramipexole (CALM-PD) and ropinirole (056). Levodopa was more effective over time than either ropinirole or pramipexole. (Adapted from W. Poewe et al. 2010. *Clinical Interventions in Aging* 2010: 5 229–238. Copyright © 2010 Poewe et al, publisher and licensee Dove Medical Press Ltd. Originally published by and used with permission from Dove Medical Press Ltd.)

AMANTADINE Another approach to pharmacological treatment involves the drug amantadine (Symmetrel, Gocovri) as monotherapy or to decrease dyskinesias related to L-DOPA use. Amantadine was originally approved and used to treat and prevent infection caused by influenza A virus. The mechanism of the drug is anticholinergic and antiglutamatergic (an NMDA receptor antagonist). These actions lead to an increase in DA release in the nigrostriatal pathway and in other areas of the brain.

BOX 20.1 ■ PHARMACOLOGY IN ACTION

Can We Smell Parkinson's Disease?

At the beginning of the chapter, you were introduced to Joy Milne, who realized that she could actually smell her husband's PD. After testing Mrs. Milne's ability to distinguish between those who had PD and those who didn't based solely on smell, scientists went to work determining what compounds might account for the distinct odor (Trivedi et al., 2019; Sinclair et al., 2021). Sebum is the oily substance produced by sebaceous glands that lubricates skin and hair and has long been evaluated for volatile compounds to find indicators of skin disease (Gallagher et al., 2008). It is overproduced in up to 60% of those with PD and can be collected noninvasively. Sebum samples were taken from PD subjects, some who were taking medications and others who were not, and from matched control subjects (Trivedi et al., 2019). Findings were validated by Joy for having the odor that she associates with PD. From this analysis of sebum samples, four volatile metabolites were found to be distinguishably different between PD and control samples: perillic aldehyde, hippuric acid, eicosane, and octadecanal. No differences were found between those PD subjects who were medicated and those that were not, indicating that the metabolites were likely due to disease processes, not metabolism of L-DOPA or other medications. Because sebum is a mix of triglycerides, wax esters, squalene, and free fatty acids, it is likely that these metabolomic changes are due to differences in lipid metabolism, and a second study showed 10 volatile compounds related to these changes in PD (Sinclair et al., 2021). Again, there were no differences between medicated and non-medicated PD subjects, only between PD subjects and controls. As these metabolites are being discovered, information about the pathways that produce them may give further insight into not only the diagnosis of PD, but also the disease process. These could potentially lead to earlier and more effective interventions for PD.

It's also interesting to note, that upon further testing, Joy Milne's "super smeller" capabilities also allow her to detect odors from cancer, tuberculosis, Alzheimer's disease, and diabetes. Perhaps, with her help, new insights will be found for those disorders as well.

STATIN DRUGS Evidence has shown that taking statin drugs to lower cholesterol levels may reduce the risk of developing PD. This protection is likely provided by a decrease in cholesterol that subsequently improves heart health and increases anti-inflammatory effects. Additionally, evidence suggests that DA receptors are up-regulated by statin therapy (Q. Wang et al., 2011).

ANTIPSYCHOTIC MEDICATION As you read in Chapter 19, typical (and many atypical) antipsychotics have a mechanism of action that decreases DA signaling. That can exacerbate PD symptoms. But as many as 50% of patients with PD experience hallucinations and/or delusions that can be caused by medications that increase DA, Parkinson's dementia, or delirium. In 2016, pimavanserin (Nuplazid) was approved by the FDA, specifically for the treatment of hallucinations and delusions in PD. A selective serotonin inverse agonist, it reduces psychosis without directly affecting DA levels and therefore does not increase motor symptoms.

There are several unmet needs in PD diagnosis and treatment

As of June 2020, there were 145 registered pharmaceutical clinical trials for treatment of PD. Of those, 51 were phase 1, 66 phase 2, and 28 phase 3 (McFarthing et al., 2020). The majority (61%) of the trials were focused on symptomatic therapies, two thirds of those on motor symptoms. The remaining trials were focused on long-term disease modification. Although researchers have made great strides in understanding the etiology of PD and in developing new treatments, more research and knowledge is needed in several areas. Although symptomatic treatments are available, none have yet convincingly showed slowing of the disease process. A treatment that could interrupt this process would be most useful. Treatment options for gait freezing to help patients avoid falls and for nonmotor symptoms of PD, particularly the cognitive and behavioral changes, should be explored. Finally, treatment options that promote regeneration and restoration of structure and function should also be actively pursued. While there are several drugs that work on the primary motor symptoms of bradykinesia and tremor, there is a dearth of therapies that provide relief for the postural instability and resulting gait problems. And while recent advances in imaging like fluorodopa F18 allow for detection of the disease once DA neurons are already damaged, an earlier diagnostic test may allow for earlier intervention. That is the hope for the work being done with Joy Milne, whom you met in the chapter opener. Might she be smelling biomarkers that could allow for earlier detection and intervention? Find out more in **BOX 20.1**.

SECTION SUMMARY

■ Parkinson's disease is a chronic, progressive neurodegenerative disorder.

■ The primary symptoms of PD are motor disturbances that result in a visible resting tremor and slowing of movement (bradykinesia). Other motor symptoms include rigidity and postural instability.

- Nonmotor effects of the disorder start with loss of the sense of smell and include REM behavior disorder and mood disorders.

- Cognitive disturbance can be a result of PD and is called Parkinson's disease dementia (PDD). The slowing of thought and verbal responses (bradyphrenia) is a cardinal symptom.

- These motor and cognitive symptoms are traced to loss of dopaminergic neurons in the substantia nigra, a major input pathway to the basal ganglia.

- Onset of PD is most commonly a sporadic event, although about 10% of cases have an inherited genetic cause.

- Pathology in PD is likely due to mitochondrial dysfunction and resulting oxidative stress. Additionally, protein aggregation in cells causes the formation of Lewy bodies, which trigger apoptotic cell death.

- Several animal models of PD allow investigation of various aspects of PD pathology, including the MPTP model, 6-OHDA lesions, and administration of the pesticide rotenone or the drug reserpine.

- The primary therapies in PD aim to increase DA signaling and include L-DOPA, a DA precursor, MAOIs, COMT inhibitors, and DA agonists such as pramipexole, ropinirole, and rotigotine.

20.2 Alzheimer's Disease

Alzheimer's disease (AD) is a chronic, progressive dementia disorder that is much more widespread than PD. Among the 46.8 million patients worldwide who suffer from dementia, 50% to 70% are afflicted with AD. The disorder affects approximately 4.4% of people over the age of 65 and 9.7% of those over 70 and is said to roughly double in prevalence for each 5 years over age 65 (Qui et al., 2009). It is currently the sixth leading cause of death in the United States. With the aging of the population, the incidence of AD will continue to grow (**FIGURE 20.8**). Although the typical course of the disease includes an increase in risk as one ages, there is an early-onset form of the disease that begins before age 60, progresses more quickly, and has a genetic basis. AD is diagnosed as mild or major neurocognitive disorder (NCD) with possible or probable AD. Mild NCD is marked by a decline in cognitive functioning from previous levels of performance in one or more domains such as complex attention, executive function, learning and memory, language, perceptual, motor, or social cognition. The difficulties must be noticed by the person experiencing them, a close

observer, or a clinician, and they are often confirmed using standardized neuropsychological or clinical assessment. These difficulties, though, do not interfere with a person's ability to function independently.

As mild NCD progresses to major NCD, the deficits interfere with independent self-care and other tasks. The neuropsychological and clinical tests indicate substantial impairment in one or more of the cognitive domains mentioned above. To attribute mild or major NCD to AD, the onset must be insidious and symptoms must progress gradually. Possible AD is indicated if there is no evidence of contributing genetic mutation, while probable AD is diagnosed if deterministic gene variants are confirmed. Patients and caregivers may notice that tasks that used to be relatively easy are now more difficult, particularly more complex cognitive tasks. Anhedonia (loss of enjoyment of previously pleasurable things) is also common. Some anomia or anomic aphasia may be experienced, in which the ability to name familiar objects or people is impaired. Additionally, problems with misplacing or not finding items or getting lost on familiar routes occur with increasing frequency. For a comprehensive discussion of the symptoms of AD, see the Alzheimer's Association website (www.alz.org).

As the disease progresses, these issues worsen and other behavioral and cognitive changes occur. Changes in physiological processes, such as disrupted sleep, incontinence, and difficulty swallowing, are seen. Psychiatric symptoms such as delusions, hallucinations, depressed mood, and agitation (including violent outbursts) may occur. Tasks that allow for basic self-sufficiency may suffer, including the ability to prepare food, to choose appropriate clothing, and, particularly, to drive. Additionally, the person's ability to recognize danger and to accurately and appropriately judge a situation is diminished. Reading and writing become more difficult, and strategies such as using lists and notes as memory cues may become less effective. Verbal communication also suffers as the disease progresses, and language becomes confused, with incorrect word usage and mispronunciation of words. Much of our sense of "self" comes from our memory and cognitive function, and this commonly

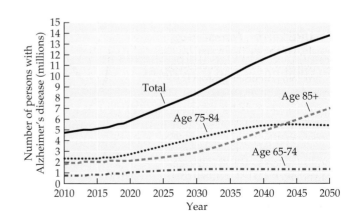

FIGURE 20.8 **Past and projected rates of Alzheimer's disease (AD)** With the aging population, about a fivefold increase in cases of AD is expected over the next 90 years. (After L. E. Hebert et al. 2013. *Neurology* 80: 1778–1783; and U.S. Census Bureau.)

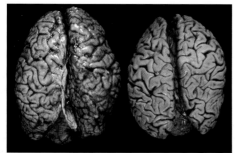

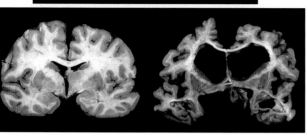

Healthy   AD

FIGURE 20.9 Pathological changes in the brain with advanced Alzheimer's disease (AD) The brain of an individual with AD is compared with a healthy brain from an age-matched individual. The brain of the individual with AD shows significant atrophy, narrowing of the gyri, widening of the sulci, and enlargement of the ventricles.

AMYLOID PLAQUES The accumulation of the **beta-amyloid protein** (**β-amyloid**, or **A-beta [Aβ]**) between neurons in the brain results in the formation of amyloid plaques. Aβ is a protein fragment normally produced by the brain by enzymatic cleavage of **amyloid precursor protein** (**APP**). APP is first cleaved by a β-secretase, most commonly BACE1, although BACE2 may also play a role in AD pathology. The cleavage product, APP-CTFβ, is then further cleaved by γ-secretase to generate either the 40-amino-acid (Aβ40) or the 42-amino-acid (Aβ42) form of Aβ (Goedert and Spillantini, 2006; Zhang et al., 2011) (**FIGURE 20.10**). In healthy brains, there are several proposed functions of the fragments of APP (including soluble APPα, which is formed by APP cleaving by α-secretase), including kinase activation, facilitation of gene transcription, cholesterol transport regulation, and pro-inflammatory actions and antimicrobial activities.

is lost in those with advancing AD. The loss of personal episodic memories contributes to this. With loss of these functions comes withdrawal from social contact with family and friends. AD will eventually take away completely the ability to use language, interact with or even recognize family or friends, and live independently.

AD is defined by several pathological cellular disturbances

The cardinal cellular pathologies in AD are amyloid plaques and neurofibrillary tangles. These changes, described in detail in the following sections, result in degeneration of cells throughout the cortex but primarily in the frontotemporal association cortex (Perl, 2010), as seen in **FIGURE 20.9**. Additionally, a significant loss of synapses (up to 45%) may be the basis for the significant cognitive deficits seen in AD.

FIGURE 20.10 Formation of amyloid plaques β-amyloid (Aβ) is formed by the sequential cleavage of amyloid precursor protein (APP) by β-secretase and γ-secretase. The accumulation of Aβ results in several different pathological changes, which, in turn, result in neural degeneration and cognitive and behavioral symptoms. APP-CTFβ, cleavage product; sAPPβ, soluble APPβ. (After J. L. Cummings. 2004. *N Engl J Med* 351: 56–67.)

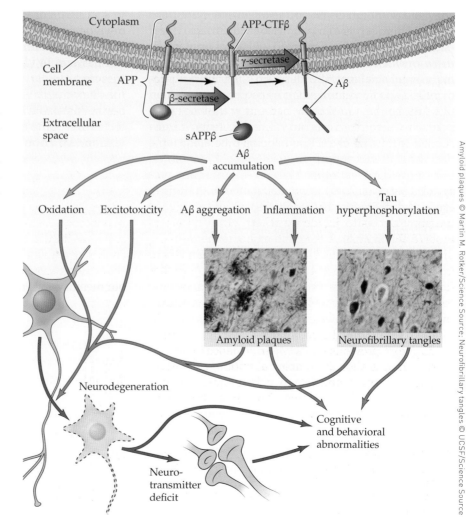

After use, these fragments are degraded and cause no harm. In the brains of those with AD, these protein fragments, particularly Aβ42, accumulate to form plaques. Several different subtypes of plaques exist, and they include the senile or neuritic plaque, which has a core of the amyloid protein surrounded by abnormal neurites (dendrites or axons). Often, microglial cells or reactive astrocytes are found in the periphery of these plaques. A second form of the plaque has focal diffuse deposits of amyloid with no neurites surrounding the core. The third form has a dense core of amyloid without neurites. These are generally considered the long-term outcome of neuritic plaques, after the neurites have died off.

NEUROFIBRILLARY TANGLES **Neurofibrillary tangles** (**NFTs**) are fibrous inclusions that are abnormally located in the cytoplasm of neurons. The neurons particularly susceptible to NFTs are pyramidal neurons—those with a pyramid-shaped cell body. The primary component of these tangles is the protein **tau**, which is a protein associated with microtubules (long filaments that help maintain cellular structure and also participate in axonal transport; see Chapter 2). As a component of these tangles, the tau is abnormally phosphorylated. Other proteins, including ubiquitin, are also found in NFTs. The accumulation of these tangles follows a relatively typical pattern of trans-synaptic spread. In early stages of the disease (Braak and Braak, 1995), these tangles are found in the entorhinal cortex, with progression to the hippocampus and neocortex as the disease process continues (**FIGURE 20.11**). Additionally, neurons in the basal forebrain cholinergic and monoaminergic systems are susceptible to damage by AD pathological processes.

There are several behavioral, health, and genetic risk factors for AD

Several risk factors for dementia in general, and for AD specifically, are known. The most basic of these risk factors are advancing age and a family history of dementia or AD. Several of these risks are similar to those for the development of heart disease (e.g., diabetes, obesity, untreated hypertension, high cholesterol, stress, and a sedentary lifestyle). In addition, a history of head trauma or hypoxic brain injury, depression, bipolar disorder, or post-traumatic stress disorder (PTSD) can increase the risk for dementia.

Genetic contributors to AD consist of risk genes and deterministic genes (Zetzsche et al., 2010). Deterministic genes are those that can directly cause disease. Three genes are known to directly cause AD: the genes for APP, found on chromosome 21; for **presenilin-1** (**PS-1**), on chromosome 14; and for **presenilin-2** (**PS-2**), on chromosome 1. Mutations of these genes result in **autosomal dominant Alzheimer's disease** (**ADAD**). In this familial version of the disease, symptom onset is likely to occur before age 60 (it can occur as early as the 30s). Although ADAD is of concern, only about 5% of AD cases are familial.

The risk gene with the greatest influence on disease development is the gene for **apolipoprotein E** (**ApoE**). ApoE is normally a component of very-low-density lipoproteins (VLDLs). These lipoproteins remove excess cholesterol from the blood and carry it to the liver for degradation. The presence of the gene for the E4 form of this (*APOEε4*) increases risk; inheritance of this form from both parents increases risk further and may lead to earlier onset of the disease. Other risk genes

(A) Neurofibrillary tangle

(B)

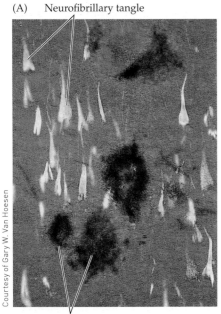

Amyloid plaque

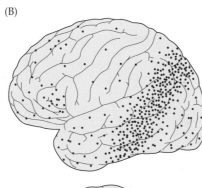

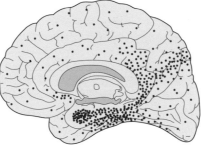

FIGURE 20.11 Cellular pathology in Alzheimer's disease Amyloid plaques and neurofibrillary tangles (A) accumulate in the brain (B). Dot density here indicates degree of pathology. (B after H. Blumenfeld. 2002. *Neuroanatomy through Clinical Cases*. Sinauer: Sunderland, MA. Based on illustration by Arne Brun, Lund University Hospital, Lund, Sweden, in M. N. Rossor. 1991. In *Neurology in Clinical Practice*, 1st ed., W. G. Bradley et al., [Eds.], p. 1414. Butterworth-Heinemann: Woburn, MA.)

produce protein products that normally interact with the proteins listed previously, or with their products. The protease produced by the alpha-2 macroglobulin gene (*A2M*) would normally contribute to the degradation and clearance of the Aβ protein produced by APP. *UBQLN1*, the gene that codes for the protein ubiquitin 1, is associated with AD because ubiquitin 1 promotes the accumulation of uncleaved PS-1 and PS-2 proteins, which are part of the structure of γ-secretase. SORL1 (sortilin-related receptor 1) is the neuronal receptor for ApoE. In the brains of those with AD, there can be a marked reduction of this receptor. In addition, this receptor is associated with the activity of APP such that decreased SORL1 production is correlated with higher Aβ load in the brain (**FIGURE 20.12**).

Perhaps surprisingly, AD is also closely linked to trisomy 21, the genetic variant that causes Down syndrome. By the age of 30 to 40, most patients with Down syndrome will develop the plaques and tangles associated with AD. These changes are nearly universal among patients with Down syndrome who reach this age, and although the severity of plaque and tangle accumulation mimics that found in AD, not all such individuals will develop AD. One of the possibilities for the connection is that patients have three copies of the *APP* gene, which is located on chromosome 21.

AD cannot be definitively diagnosed until post-mortem analysis

AD is defined by changes that happen in the brain during degenerative processes, as in the plaques and tangles described previously. These processes generally are not visible without direct examination of the brain, so AD is a diagnosis of elimination rather than confirmation. There is no definitive test to rule *in* AD, but there are several tests that will rule *out* other sources of dementia. By performing physical and neurological exams, taking a thorough medical history, and doing a mental state exam (generally the MMSE, 2nd edition, or the Alzheimer's Disease Assessment Scale [ADAS], which has both cognitive [ADAS-Cog] and non-cognitive subscales [ADAS-Noncog]) along with other tests, doctors can rule out anemia, brain tumor, chronic infection, medication intoxication, severe depression, stroke, thyroid disease, and vitamin deficiency. Only when other causes of dementia have been ruled out can a differential diagnosis of AD be given to a living patient. Several technologies allow visualization of the plaques formed around deposits of Aβ protein. One, called florbetapir (Amyvid), is a ^{18}F-tagged small molecule that binds β-amyloid; it was developed by Eli Lilly and is used with a positron emission tomography (PET) scanner to examine those who already show signs of cognitive decline. It is a tool of elimination rather than confirmation for AD, because amyloid plaques can be present without AD. Another imaging technique with a similar mechanism, also used with a PET scanner, uses florbetaben. This technique has a small but significant false-positive rate. The risk of a false-positive result ("You might have Alzheimer's") when a person does not have the disease is the reason why it is used exclusively in those in whom cognitive decline has already

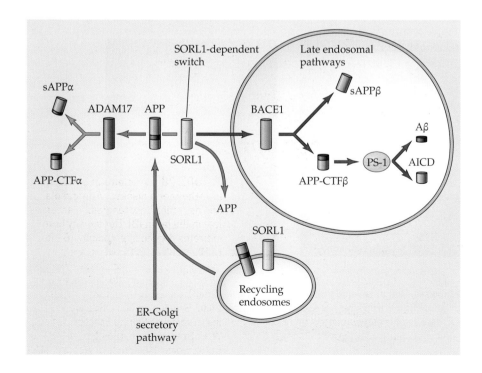

FIGURE 20.12 The amyloid precursor protein (APP) processing pathway Sortilin-related receptor 1 (SORL1) plays an important role as a switch in this process. After synthesis in the endoplasmic reticulum (ER), APP can be cleaved by ADAM17 (an α-secretase) to form soluble APPα (sAPPα) and a cytoplasmic fragment (APP-CTFα). Alternatively, SORL1 can bind APP and sort it into a recycling pathway. If SORL1 is absent, the APP is directed into β-secretase processing (e.g., by BACE1). BACE1 cleavage forms an N-terminal fragment (sAPPβ) and APP-CTFβ, which is cleaved again by presenilin-dependent γ-secretase (PS-1) to form Aβ and amyloid intracellular domain (AICD). A similar effect can be produced by inhibition of APP recycling from endosomes within the cell. (After E. Rogaeva et al. 2007. *Nat Genet* 39: 168–177.)

occurred. A third technique, based on work by Wolk and associates (2009), uses [¹⁸F]flutemetamol (Pittsburgh compound B [PiB]), which accumulates in the amyloid plaques (**FIGURE 20.13**). More recently, the FDA approved the use of fluortaucipir F18 (Tauvid) as a PET tracer to visualize tau protein aggregates.

Despite these advances, definitive diagnosis still requires post-mortem analysis to look for the trademark neuronal changes of AD. Post-mortem analysis of brain tissue is performed to look for the presence of two key indicators: NFTs and amyloid plaques. If these two pathologies are present, a diagnosis of AD is made; if these plaques are not detected, another explanation is put forth for the cognitive deficits that were seen in the patient. While post-mortem diagnosis can confirm AD in the deceased, it is not useful in developing treatment strategies in those who are still alive.

Several different animal models contribute to our understanding of AD

As with other disorders, the primary goal of AD animal models is to closely approximate one or more aspects of the human condition of AD. Several transgenic mouse models aim to produce the progressive neuropathology seen with AD. Two common models (the APP/PSδE9 and APPswe/PS1δE9 models) involve mutations on the *APP* gene. Each of these mutations results in memory deficits, high levels of Aβ42 in the brain, and amyloid deposits. The APPswe/PSδE9 model also shows the formation of neuritic plaques. The senescence-accelerated prone (SAMP8) mouse shows early learning and memory deficits along with the accumulation of Aβ protein, oxidative damage, and tau phosphorylation. Even *Drosophila* can be used to model some of these issues. These transgenic flies produce Aβ42 in their neurons. They show age-dependent short-term memory impairment and neurodegeneration. For further discussion of the models in this section, as well as others, see *Handbook of Animal Models in Alzheimer's Disease* (2011), edited by Casadesus.

A more natural (non-transgenic) model may be found in the beagle. Aged beagles can develop learning and memory deficits, as well as problems with executive function. This naturally occurring pathology shows similarity to the human condition in terms of cortical atrophy, neuron loss, lack of neurogenesis, β-amyloid plaques, and other damage. The pathological changes correlate with the deficits in function. The progressive nature of the disorder in these animals is beneficial for longitudinal study.

Sometimes, models of other pathological processes can inadvertently bring about neuropathology. Originally used as models of coronary artery disease, cholesterol-fed rabbits also developed Aβ deposits, NFTs, and cognitive deficits at rates higher than those seen in rabbits that ate a normal diet. If the cholesterol feeding was paired with the administration of copper, outcomes were even worse. This is likely a result of copper interfering with clearance of Aβ from the brain by LDL receptor–related protein 1 (LRP1). Like humans with AD, these rabbits are deficient in eyeblink conditioning and show neuronal loss in the frontal cortex, hippocampus, and cerebellum.

From D. A. Wolk et al. 2009. *Ann Neurol* 65: 557–568; courtesy of the University of Pittsburgh Amyloid Imaging Group

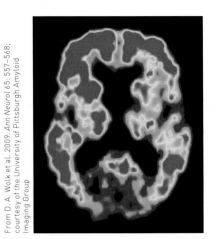
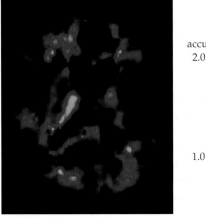

PiB accumulation
2.0
1.0

Alzheimer's disease   Cognitive impairment   Control

FIGURE 20.13 **Visualization of amyloid plaques** One of several new methods for visualizing amyloid plaques in living brains, Pittsburgh compound B (PiB) dye accumulates in the plaques and can be visualized using PET scanning. Presence of these plaques is more common in individuals with Alzheimer's disease or significant cognitive impairment.

Symptomatic treatments are available, and several others are under study for slowing disease progression

Current treatments fall into two categories: **cholinesterase inhibitors** and an **N-methyl-D-aspartate (NMDA)** glutamate receptor antagonist. AD seems to target cholinergic cells involved in cognition, and the cholinesterase inhibitors improve cognition by increasing the presence of acetylcholine in the synapse by decreasing its breakdown. The first cholinesterase inhibitor approved for use in AD was tacrine (Cognex) for the treatment of mild to moderate AD. Soon after (in 1996) came donepezil (Aricept). Like Cognex and the cholinesterase inhibitors that followed, it was initially prescribed for mild to moderate AD, but newer evidence suggests that staying on the drug through the moderate stage (when previously the drug would have been stopped) may slow memory decline. After donepezil (in 2000) came rivastigmine (Exelon), which can be given in pill or transdermal patch form, and (in 2001) galantamine (Razadyne). The drugs in this class share several side effects, including nausea, vomiting, loss of appetite, muscle cramps, and increased frequency of bowel movements.

After it was observed that damaged neurons release significant amounts of glutamate, the drug **memantine (Namenda)** was introduced to prevent further excitotoxic neuron damage. Approved in 2003, memantine works by blocking current flow through the NMDA subtype of glutamate receptor. This prevents the drastic increase in cell firing that leads to excitotoxicity, without producing significant side effects. As a result of binding to two sites on the receptor, modulation of the receptor is less severe than with other NMDA receptor antagonists such as MK-801 and ketamine (Johnson and Kotermanski, 2006). Memantine and donepezil were combined into a single drug with the FDA approval of Namzaric in 2014. Namenda and Namzaric are the only two drugs approved for treatment of moderate to severe AD. Their side effects include headaches, constipation, confusion, and dizziness.

Because of the devastating effects of AD, its increase in incidence and prevalence among those over age 65, and the increasing age of the population (at least in the United States), there is an urgent need for more effective AD therapies. Several recent studies have indicated promise for new types of therapies (see **BOX 20.2** for a technology-based treatment in clinical trials for AD), but also the challenges of translating therapies from preclinical models to patients. Three antibodies have recently been the focus of clinical trials in humans. The first antibody, bapineuzumab, decreases levels of phosphorylated tau protein in the brains of mice, although its target is β-amyloid (which it does

not decrease). The phase 3 trials for this antibody were terminated after clinical efficacy was not seen. For the second antibody, crenezumab, early indications from preclinical work and from early-stage clinical trials were that it may be useful in preventing the onset of familial AD (Adolfsson et al., 2012), but two large phase 3 trials were terminated in January 2019 when an interim analysis showed that they were unlikely to meet their primary endpoints.

The latest antibody therapy to go to clinical trials is aducanumab. Two phase 3, double-blind, placebo-controlled, randomized clinical trials were done for this antibody, the ENGAGE and EMERGE trials. Those trials were terminated when they met predetermined "futility" criteria at an interim analysis point. This means that the analysis indicated that the trials would not meet their primary endpoints. What happened next was unusual: the data added after the futility determination in the EMERGE study indicated that there was a statistically significant difference between high-dose aducanumab and the placebo on the primary endpoint, the Clinical Dementia Rating—Sum of Boxes (CDR-SB) score. But in addition to this small improvement, subjects in both studies who received aducanumab were much more likely to show amyloid-related imaging abnormalities and had a higher incidence of consequences like confusion, gait issues, falls, and other issues. The FDA advisory panel charged with evaluating these trials voted against approving the drug. Despite these concerns, the FDA approved aducanumab as Aduhelm in June 2021 (Alexander et al., 2021).

A potential therapy that is in an earlier stage of development consists of a class of compounds called spin-labeled fluorene compounds. These compounds reduce amyloid plaque formation in cultured neurons and can cross the blood–brain barrier (Petrlova et al., 2012; Hilt et al., 2018). The next step is to test these compounds in animal models of AD. Another area of research involves the use of antibiotics as a potential treatment for AD. This is tied to the relationship between the gut microbiome and neuroinflammation.

As with the other disorders discussed in this chapter, AD symptoms are often treated with other drug classes to increase daily functioning and improve quality of life. For low mood and irritability, antidepressants are often prescribed, primarily from the SSRI class. For anxiety, restlessness, resistance, and disruptive behavior, anxiolytic drugs can be helpful. Extreme caution needs to be used when treating AD patients with antipsychotic medications for hallucinations, delusions, aggression, agitation, hostility, or lack of cooperation. These drugs carry a black box warning for use in these patients because of an increased risk of death or stroke.

BOX 20.2 ■ THE CUTTING EDGE

Can Focused Ultrasound Help Treat Alzheimer's Disease?

When most of us think of ultrasound, we likely think of the tool used to visualize fetuses in utero or tumors in abdominal organs. But ultrasound can actually be a powerful tool in the treatment of neurodegenerative and movement disorders. The Exablate Neuro, an MRI-guided focused ultrasound (MRgFUS) tool (insightec.com), uses directed beams of ultrasound energy, focused on a particular target, to have an effect on the brain. The frequency of those ultrasound beams as well as the effect on the targeted tissues varies by the disorder and intended outcomes. With high-frequency focused ultrasound (HiFu), areas of the brain can be lesioned without invasive surgery. This type of FUS procedure is done for cases of essential tremor or Parkinson's disease. A current clinical trial is investigating whether bilateral treatment with HiFu for essential tremor can provide additional benefit over unilateral treatment (clinicaltrials.gov #NCT04112381). Temporary neuromodulation is

one possible effect of low-intensity focused ultrasound (LiFu), which is currently in a clinical trial for evaluation of safety in reducing craving in addiction (clinicaltrials.gov #NCT04197921). But what may be the most impactful use of MRgFUS is as a mechanism to open the blood–brain barrier (BBB) and as a potential treatment, or treatment catalyst, in AD. In a multicenter clinical trial (clinicaltrials.gov #NCT03671889), Insightec is sponsoring a phase 2 study of the safety and feasibility of LiFu with microbubbles as a treatment for AD. The focused ultrasound, which is delivered with 1024 individual FUS transducers in the Insightec Exablate helmet, causes acoustic cavitation energy, which vibrates the microbubbles introduced by an intravenous infusion or bolus that mechanically opens the tight junctions in brain capillaries only in the area targeted by the MRgFUS.

Preclinical data (Burgess et al., 2014) and a phase 1 trial (Lipsman et al. 2018) showed that it is possible to

(A)

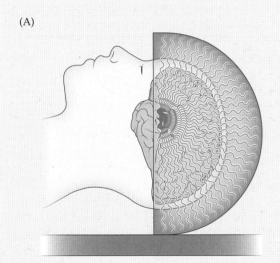

(B)

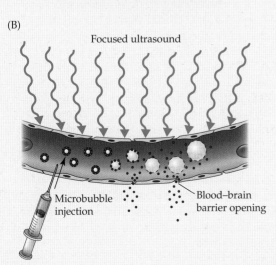

Focused ultrasound

Microbubble injection

Blood–brain barrier opening

(C)

Targets

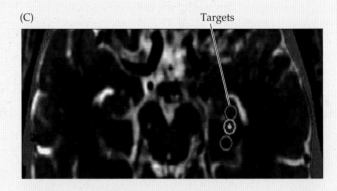

(D)

Targeting volumes

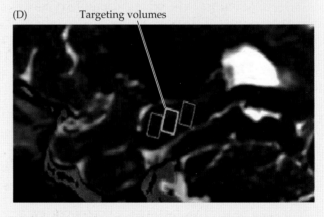

(A) The INSIGHTEC ultrasound system uses 1024 ultrasound transducers to target specific brain areas. (B) The ultrasound beams travel transcranially and interact with intravenously administered microbubbles. Movement of the bubbles then causes short-lived opening of the blood–brain barrier. (C) and (D) show three targets in the hippocampus and the volume of treated tissue. (From A. R. Rezai et al. 2020. *Proc Natl Acad Sci* 117: 9180–9182.)

BOX 20.2 ■ THE CUTTING EDGE *(continued)*

open the BBB in animal models and AD patients and have the BBB reclose using this method. This may allow the major limiting factor of drug delivery to the brain to be bypassed. Data from the first six patients in the study show that the BBB of the hippocampus and entorhinal cortex can be safely, reliably, noninvasively, focally, and reproducibly opened and that it closes again, generally within 24 hours after treatment (Rezai et al., 2020), without serious adverse events.

And while the study is focused on safety and feasibility, secondary outcomes include effects on cognitive measures and impact on the deposition of beta-amyloid. D'Haese and colleagues (2020) showed that in those same patients, beta-amyloid plaques were reduced in the hippocampus following the LiFu treatment protocol. The beta-amyloid load was measured in this study before and after treatment using the ^{18}F-Florbataben imaging discussed earlier in the chapter. A closer look at the opening of the BBB in these subjects (Mehta et al., 2021) indicates that there is permeability gained in the meningeal veins following the MRgFUS treatment, which is likely a sign of immunological response and downstream healing mechanisms. While these are early results from the ongoing trial, they are remarkably encouraging given the lack of approved treatments for AD in the last roughly 20 years. The beneficial effects seen in these studies are exciting on their own, but perhaps even more so is the possibility that the opening of the BBB may allow for introduction of therapeutic agents to the brain that normally would not be able to gain entry. Limitations on size and other characteristics will impact the utility of this method to allow drugs to enter the brain, but it certainly creates a new opportunity.

(E)

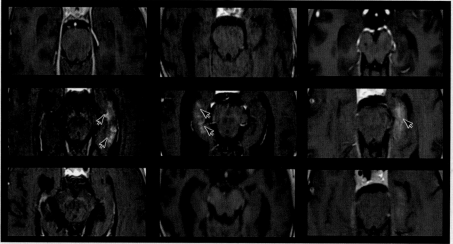

Baseline

Post-FUS

24 hr

From A. R. Rezai et al. 2020. *Proc Natl Acad Sci* 117: 9180–9182

MRI images obtained at baseline, immediately after FUS, and 24 hours after FUS show contrast enhancement at targeted sites (arrows), indicating BBB opening immediately after FUS and closure by 24 hours.

SECTION SUMMARY

- AD is a dementia disorder that affects increasing numbers of people in the United States.

- The onset of AD is preceded by neurocognitive disorder (NCD), but not all cases of NCD develop into AD.

- Early symptoms of AD include forgetfulness and impairment in other cognitive functions, including language, thinking, and judgment. Physiological changes include difficulty swallowing and disrupted sleep. Psychiatric difficulties come in the form of delusions, hallucinations, depression, and agitation. As the disease progresses, communication becomes increasingly difficult because of reading, writing, and verbal communication problems.

- Two pathological findings are the hallmark of disease progression in AD: amyloid plaques and neurofibrillary tangles (NFTs). Amyloid plaques are formed by accumulation of Aβ (primarily Aβ42) after production by secretase cutting of the amyloid precursor protein (APP). NFTs are composed primarily of abnormally phosphorylated tau, a microtubule-associated protein, and other proteins like ubiquitin. Accumulation of NFTs results in disruption of cellular processes and eventually apoptotic cell death.

- Risk factors for development of AD include advancing age and poor cardiovascular health. Previous head injury or psychopathology can also increase risk.

- Several genes are associated with the development of autosomal dominant Alzheimer's disease (ADAD) and include the genes for APP, presenilin-1, and presenilin-2.

- Several other genes impart increased risk for AD, including the APOEε4 allele, A2M, UBQLN1, and SORL1.

- Because of the location of risk genes on chromosome 21, AD has a strong association with Down syndrome (trisomy 21).

- AD generally is not diagnosed until after death, although newer imaging technologies may allow earlier diagnosis in the future.

- Animal models for AD include transgenic mice with alterations in the genes listed above, a natural aged-beagle model, and a cholesterol-fed rabbit model.

- Current treatments for AD are primarily cholinesterase inhibitors and an NMDA receptor modulator.

- Research indicates that Aβ antibodies, chemotherapy drugs, and perhaps even antibiotics may be effective treatments that will become available in the future.

20.3 Huntington's Disease, Amyotrophic Lateral Sclerosis, and Multiple Sclerosis

Huntington's disease

Mr. R. was working for a large international bank in England—his dream job. When he forgot his password to the company banking system, he feared the worst. While most of us would attribute that slip to a rough day, he suspected that it was the beginning of a long, painful process that he had seen in his mother and grandmother. Anger and time management issues followed the memory lapses. These eventually led to loss of his job and the need to move back to the United States. He started a roofing business, but soon physical symptoms such as loss of balance prevented him from doing the job, and cognitive and psychiatric symptoms interfered with his ability to run the business. A genetic test for a clinical trial confirmed Mr. R.'s fears that he had inherited the **Huntington's disease** (HD) gene from his mother. His focus became raising awareness of issues surrounding HD, receiving treatment for his increasing symptoms, and recognizing his fear for the future of his children, who have a 50% chance of developing the disorder, just as he and his siblings had. Mr. R. now faces progressive loss of cognitive and physical abilities and ongoing psychiatric problems. This will end with his death from HD.

HD is one of the few neurodegenerative disorders with a clear, single genetic cause. A **trinucleotide repeat** (a CAG sequence) results in a gain-of-function mutation in the *huntingtin* gene (HTT). *Huntingtin* is a highly penetrant mutation (meaning that if the gene is a certain form, the chance of developing the disease is very high or is guaranteed) and is noted differently than the normal version by the designation mHTT. In this case, the likelihood of developing HD depends on the number of CAG repeats in the gene. There is essentially complete **penetrance** at 40 repeats, but there is lesser penetrance at smaller numbers of repeats, and no development of the disease at fewer than 35 copies. There is 90% penetrance at 39 copies, meaning that 90% of those with 39 copies of the CAG repeat will develop the disease and 10% will not. There is 75% penetrance at 38 copies, 50% at 37, and 25% at 36 (Myers, 2011, personal communication). Those with 27 to 35 copies do not develop the disease themselves, but because of the instability of the gene, men can pass on a longer version of the gene to their offspring and increase the risk that they will develop the disorder. The number of repeats generally correlates with the age of onset, such that a larger number of repeats results in earlier disease development. Age of onset can range from 4 to 65 years of age but generally comes in middle age. The "normal" version of the gene has about 20 CAG repeats at this location. The extra repeats in the gene cause a toxic gain of function resulting in protein aggregation and cell death.

SYMPTOMS OF HD HD tends to be grouped with motor disorders when it is classified, but significant cognitive and psychiatric symptoms have been noted as well (Novak and Tabrizi, 2011). The motor symptoms result from degenerative effects on the basal ganglia (**FIGURE 20.14**) and reduced ability to suppress unwanted movement. Originally named **Huntington's chorea**, these involuntary movements are jerky or writhing, "dance-like" movements of the limbs. In addition to these gross motor function changes, fine movement is significantly impaired in speed and coordination. Other issues in motor function include rigidity, dystonia, problems with speech and swallowing, and gait problems. Generally, the cause of death in HD is associated with these changes in motor function. Many with HD die from pneumonia and other complications of the inability to swallow or of injuries related to falls.

Motor symptoms, however, are not the only consequences of the significant degeneration in this disorder. Cognitively, patients with HD often find that they have difficulty with higher-order functions like planning and organizing. There are perseveration issues, where thoughts or behaviors are repeated over and over. There are issues with learning and memory, attention, and language usage. While this may seem unrelated to a movement disorder, these cognitive issues also result from damage to basal ganglia circuits. In addition to circuits initiating movement, the basal ganglia initiate cognitive and emotional processes through connections to the dorsolateral prefrontal cortex, the orbitofrontal cortex, and the cingulate cortex (Middleton and Strick, 2000). One of the more confounding symptoms of this disorder is the patient's unawareness or denial of the symptoms, which are obvious to others. This lack of awareness, called

(A)

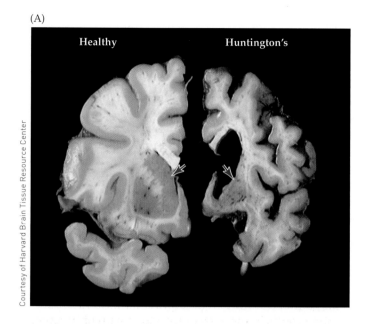

Courtesy of Harvard Brain Tissue Resource Center

(B)

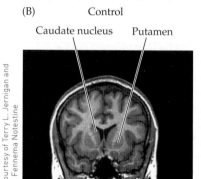
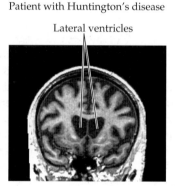

FIGURE 20.14 **Neuropathology in Huntington's disease** (A) Significant degeneration is seen in the brain of a patient with Huntington's disease compared with a healthy control. In particular, the size of the striatum (the caudate and putamen) is decreased by neurodegeneration of cells found there. (B) On MRI, the degeneration of the caudate and putamen can be seen in the enlargement of the lateral ventricles in patients with HD (right) compared with those of a healthy control (left).

Courtesy of Terry L. Jernigan and C. Fennema Notestine

anosognosia, increases the difficulties of both patients and caregivers (Sitek et al., 2014; Wibawa et al., 2020).

HD is also comorbid with several psychiatric symptoms and disorders. These comorbidities include obsessive–compulsive disorder (OCD), bipolar disorder, and mania. Several symptoms of depression, including changes in sleep patterns and energy, sadness, and thoughts of death, are also common in those with HD. Personality characteristics may change in HD, bringing about irritability, impulsivity, and anxiety.

TREATMENTS FOR HD No treatments yet tested can alter the course of HD; all of the treatments are symptomatic in nature. Tetrabenazine (Xenazine) was the first drug specifically approved by the FDA for HD. This drug is useful in decreasing the excessive movement found in the disorder. The mechanism of this decrease in motor function is a decrease in monoamine vesicle packaging. Tetrabenazine is a reversible antagonist of the type 2 vesicular monoamine transporter (VMAT2; see Chapter 5). The half-life of tetrabenazine is 4 to 8 hours, and the duration of effect of a dose is approximately 5.5 hours.

Because of the depletion of monoamines, the drug may increase psychiatric symptoms, particularly those associated with depression. Other side effects include parkinsonism and sedation.

A similar compound, deutetrabenazine (Austedo), was approved for use to treat both HD and tardive dyskinesia. The side effects are similar to those for tetrabenazine and are particularly problematic for those with depression. It can also cause irregular heartbeat, neuroleptic malignant syndrome, restlessness, and parkinsonism in those with HD. Interestingly, while sedation is one of the most common side effects in those with HD treated with deutetrabenazine, those with tardive dyskinesia report high levels of insomnia while using this drug.

DA antagonist drugs, such as those usually used to treat schizophrenia, are also used to suppress the unwanted movements. Anticonvulsants and anxiolytic drugs are often used to combat both the choreic movements and the dystonia or rigidity that may accompany HD. To combat the psychiatric symptoms of the disorder, antidepressants, particularly the SSRIs, are used, as are the typical antipsychotics and mood stabilizers. More information about the mechanisms of these drugs is available in Chapters 18, 17, and 19, respectively.

Because HD is caused by a single gene coding for a single protein, there may be greater potential than the other diseases discussed here for treatment with therapies that interrupt gene expression or protein production. A recent phase 3 trial of tominersen (GENERATION HD1), an anti-sense therapy that reduces production mutant forms of the huntingtin protein, was the biggest trial ever of an HD drug. The drug was administered intrathecally (directly into the spinal canal) to allow for distribution throughout the cerebrospinal fluid. A phase 1/2 trial had indicated a reduction in mutant HTT in patients with early HD and drove the phase 3 study. A planned data analysis point in this phase 3 trial indicated that there was an unacceptable value in the risk/benefit ratio that caused the sponsor (Roche) to discontinue dosing subjects. Further analysis will be completed, but this was a disappointing setback in a disease with no disease-altering treatments.

Nondrug treatments that may be included in a treatment plan for someone with HD include physical and occupational therapy to combat changes in fine motor control, speech therapy, and psychotherapy.

Amyotrophic lateral sclerosis

Certainly the most famous patient with amyotrophic lateral sclerosis (ALS) was Lou Gehrig, a New York Yankee who, in 1939, retired from baseball after he was diagnosed with the disorder. Today, the disorder often bears his name. ALS is another degenerative disorder with principally motor symptoms. The degeneration of upper and lower motor neurons results in a progressive loss of fine and then gross motor function (Hardiman et al., 2011). The disorder leads to death from respiratory failure, generally within 5 years.

The incidence of ALS is about 1 to 3 cases per 100,000 people. Most patients are between 40 and 70 years old; the average age at diagnosis is 55. Both familial (about 10% of cases) and nonfamilial cases (90%) have been reported. Nonfamilial cases are more likely to occur in men than women (by about 20%). Risk factors may include exposure to some chemicals (such as insecticides and pesticides, which may also contribute to the development of PD). Those who smoke are at higher risk, as are those who have served in the military.

SYMPTOMS AND DISEASE PROGRESSION IN ALS

ALS is diagnosed using the El Escorial World Federation of Neurology criteria. In the early stages of ALS, with degeneration of spinal motor neurons, focal muscle weakness may manifest as tripping, clumsiness (particularly dropping things), and abnormal fatigue in the arms or legs. As the muscles are denervated, fasciculations (muscle twitches) and cramping may be noted. If the motor neurons most affected early on are those that give rise to the corticobulbar tract (the tract that runs from the cortex to the brainstem to control cranial nerve functions), the disease may start with difficulty chewing and swallowing and general facial weakness. The swallowing difficulties often lead to sialorrhea, excessive salivation and drooling. Strangely, this degeneration may also be associated with an involuntary exaggeration of emotional reflexes, including uncontrolled laughing or crying, called pseudobulbar affect (PBA). PBA happens secondary to ALS and other neurological disorders and injury and is measured with the Center for Neurologic Study—Lability Scale (CNS-LS). In addition to being exaggerated, the emotional expression is also often mood incongruent, meaning that patients may laugh in response to sad events or cry when others would laugh. Other

manifestations of loss of these cells include slurred speech and difficulty projecting the voice.

Despite the start of symptoms in focal, distinct areas, eventually nearly all of the motor neurons are affected. For diagnosis, both lower and upper motor neuron degeneration must be present. This will lead to difficulty in breathing, which eventually will require ventilatory support for survival. Motor neurons are spared in only a couple of systems: eye movements are not compromised, nor is bladder and bowel function.

LOSS OF MOTOR NEURONS IN ALS   The neurons lost in ALS are particularly motor neurons. Within these neurons there is disruption of the cytoskeleton and aggregation of the component neurofilaments with other proteins to form "spheroids." This pathology leads to the activation and proliferation of astrocytes and microglia, resulting in neuroinflammation. The term *lateral sclerosis* comes from the scarred appearance of the spinal cord caused by the loss of the lateral corticospinal tract neurons (**FIGURE 20.15**).

How and why these cells die is a subject of much research. Several mechanisms seem to contribute to this loss (Joyce et al., 2011). Excitotoxicity from excessive glutamate signaling is one component of the damage. Other mechanisms include aggregation of proteins, breakdown of axonal transport with loss of neurofilament structure, reduced production of adenosine triphosphate neuroinflammation, and triggering of cell death pathways. Indications suggest that some RNA binding proteins are mutated in some ALS cases. How problems in these proteins might lead to the death of motor neurons is not clear.

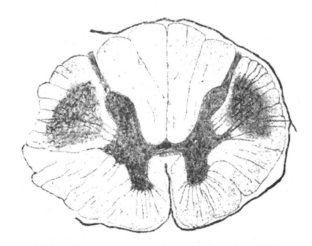

FIGURE 20.15   Amyotrophic lateral sclerosis ALS is characterized by scarring of the spinal cord (dark pink areas) that is caused by the loss of lateral corticospinal tract neurons. (From B. Bramwell. 1886. *Diseases of the Spinal Cord.* Young J. Pentland: Edinburgh.)

ALS TREATMENT For years, the only treatment approved by the FDA specifically for the treatment of ALS was riluzole (Rilutek). Riluzole has a modest disease-modifying effect: it extends the average survival time by 2 to 3 months. The drug acts as a presynaptic inhibitor of glutamate release. Because excitotoxic damage to neurons occurs in the pathological processes of ALS, this drug is thought to provide benefit by blocking this glutamate-mediated excitotoxicity (**FIGURE 20.16**). Some small benefit is associated with riluzole therapy in terms of symptom severity (including bulbar and limb function), but no benefit has been noted for muscle strength. Other indications suggest that the drug may delay the need for intubation and ventilatory support.

Following a grassroots fundraising effort called the Ice Bucket Challenge, a new drug was approved in 2017 for the treatment of ALS. In July and August 2014, an online challenge started by Pete Frates and Pat Quinn (ALS patients) and Frates's friend Corey Griffin asked those challenged to either dump a bucket of ice water on their heads or donate to an ALS charity. The challenge resulted in more than $100 million in donations to the ALS Association and millions more to ALS charities in other countries. That funding led directly to new drug development. Edaravone (Radicava) is a free-radical scavenger that is thought to be neuroprotective by preventing oxidative stress damage to neurons. It is administered in an intravenous infusion daily for 14 days, with a break of 2 weeks that is followed by 10 days of infusion. The drug slows physical decline in patients on the infusion, as measured by the Revised ALS Functional Rating Scale (ALSFRS-R). The most common side effects of the infusion are bruising, gait (walking) disturbance, and headache. While the drug is still new to the market, longer-term effects on disease progression and survival are being studied, with two trials indicating continued benefits from the drug. The benefits were seen both in patients who started on placebo and then were switched to edaravone (Shefner et al., 2019) and in a retrospective study of patients who were treated with edaravone (Okada et al., 2018). The cost, however, is steep, with a year-long, undiscounted cost of over $145,000.

Few symptomatic pharmacotherapeutic treatments exist for ALS. Several clinical trials indicate that Botulinum toxin types A and B can be used effectively to minimize the sialorrhea that results from swallowing difficulties (though care should be used since Botulinum toxin misapplied could also lead to further reductions in swallowing ability). For the PBA that manifests in emotional reactions that are out of scope and type, dextromethorphan HBR and quinidine sulfate (Nuedexta) provides symptom relief, but side effects include diarrhea, dizziness, coughing, vomiting, weakness, and swelling of lower limbs. Nuedexta may also be used for other neurological disorders or injuries that cause PBA, including multiple sclerosis.

Other treatments for ALS are also symptomatic and are not pharmacological. These might include splinting of affected limbs and, after working with a respiratory therapist, measures to augment breathing function. Patients often engage in physical and/or occupational therapy. When swallowing function is lost, patients might be fed through a gastrostomy tube. Augmented or alternative communication methods (speech-generating devices, eye-tracking devices, symbol/picture boards, or sign language) may be used with the assistance of a speech therapist.

Multiple sclerosis

Multiple sclerosis (**MS**) is perhaps the least predictable of the disorders discussed in this chapter. Thought to be primarily an autoimmune disorder, MS is the result of a chronic attack on the brain, spinal cord, and optic nerves. In particular, the autoimmune target is the protein in the myelin produced by **oligodendrocytes**, as opposed to that produced by **Schwann cells** in the peripheral nervous system (see Chapter 2). MS might take one of four courses: (1) relapsing–remitting MS (RRMS), (2) primary progressive MS (PPMS), (3) secondary progressive MS (SPMS),

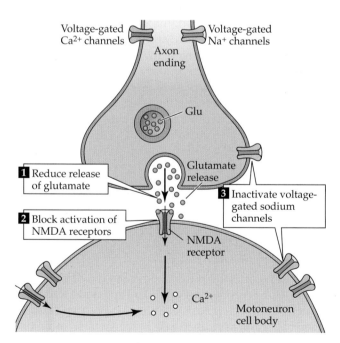

FIGURE 20.16 Riluzole is effective in preventing glutamate transmission by three mechanisms It can (1) reduce release of glutamate (Glu), (2) block activation of NMDA receptors, and (3) inactivate voltage-gated sodium channels, thereby preventing the transmission of action potentials. (After A. Doble. 1996. *Neurology* 47: 233S–241S.)

TABLE 20.1 MS Can Take One of Four Courses

Type	Incidence	Course
Relapsing–remitting (RRMS)	85%	Clearly defined attacks of neurological deficits, which are followed by times of partial or complete recovery. During the remissions, disease progression is halted.
Primary progressive (PPMS)	10%	Neurological deficits are experienced slowly but progressively worsen over time. The rate of progression varies across cases and even for a given patient such that there can be plateaus or brief periods of minor improvement.
Secondary progressive (SPMS)	Approximately 50% of those with RRMS developed this before disease-modifying medications were available. Long-term data are not yet available on whether this number has declined.	After first presenting with RRMS, these patients start a period of steady decline. There may still be periods of relapse and minor improvement (remissions) or plateaus in progression.
Progressive–relapsing (PRMS)	5%	The worst of the possibilities, this course includes steady decline from disease onset, along with clear attacks of worsening function. While there may be some recovery from these attacks, there are no periods of remission from disease symptoms.

or (4) progressive–relapsing MS (PRMS) (**TABLE 20.1**). Disease progression is evaluated in several ways:

- Lesions in the central nervous system (CNS) can be visualized on magnetic resonance imaging (MRI); doctors will look for scarred lesions and gadolinium-enhanced new lesions (when given during an MRI, gadolinium is a contrast material that indicates areas of active inflammation).

- Sensory-evoked potentials can indicate deficits in signaling through sensory pathways.

- Neurological and functional exams can be used to assess physical and cognitive function.

For more information about the various aspects of MS, the National MS Society website is an excellent resource (www.nationalmssociety.org).

SYMPTOMS OF MS   The symptoms experienced by any one person with MS vary widely across the disease course and vary to an even greater extent across patients. The more common symptoms include **fatigue**, numbness/tingling, walking/balance/coordination problems, bladder and/or bowel dysfunction, vision problems, dizziness and vertigo, sexual dysfunction, pain and itching, cognitive dysfunction, emotional changes, vision problems, and **spasticity**. Other, less common symptoms include speech disorders, swallowing problems, persistent headache, hearing loss, seizures, tremor, and breathing problems.

These symptoms can lead to secondary and tertiary symptoms of the disease. People with MS who are experiencing bladder dysfunction may be at significant risk for repeated urinary tract infections (UTIs). Other examples of secondary symptoms include muscle weakness, pressure sores, poor posture, and decreased bone density caused by prolonged periods of inactivity due to motor symptoms. Tertiary symptoms are those that are a result of the disease's impact on the person's life (e.g., job loss or limitations, stress, failure of relationships, and social isolation).

Depression is more common in those with MS than in the general population; the lifetime risk is approximately 50% in people with MS versus about 12% to 15% in those without MS (Siegert and Abernethy, 2005). This condition can be either a primary symptom or a tertiary symptom of MS. Studies of lesion location and symptom severity reveal variation in the association of depression with lesion location, although there may be a relationship between some frontal and temporal region lesions and depression. Rates of suicidal ideation in those with MS, along with the impact of depression, in general, on quality of life and on participation in therapeutic interventions raise significant concerns. **TABLE 20.2** summarizes the symptoms of MS and the other neurodegenerative diseases discussed in this chapter.

DIAGNOSIS OF MS   The diagnosis of MS is an inexact science and often takes some time, but the criteria have recently undergone a revision. The updated McDonald Criteria for the Diagnosis of Multiple Sclerosis (Thompson et al., 2018) are aimed at achieving faster and more accurate diagnosis of MS. A key challenge in diagnosis is that MS symptoms can result from several disorders. To receive a diagnosis of MS, one must have lesions in at least two distinct areas of the CNS (or optic nerves) OR several possible combinations of lesions, symptom attacks, CSF oligoclonal bands, or progression of disease. When two lesions are present, evaluation must

TABLE 20.2 Neurodegenerative Disorders Can Have a Variety of Symptoms

Disorder	Symptoms			
	Motor	Sensory	Cognitive	Psychiatric
Parkinson's disease (PD)	Resting tremor, akinesia, bradykinesia, rigidity, postural instability, retropulsion, anteropulsion, festination, dystonia, akathisia	Loss of smell	PD dementia, bradyphrenia, mental inflexibility, visuospatial deficits	PD dementia, hallucinations
Alzheimer's disease (AD)	Inability to perform self-care activities such as bathing, cooking, and driving	—	Forgetfulness, progressive memory loss, verbal communication deficits, anomia, poor judgment, slowed thinking	Altered emotional processing, personality changes, anhedonia, sleep disturbance, agitation, delusions, hallucinations
Huntington's disease (HD)	Choreic movements, rigidity, dystonia, swallowing and speech difficulties, gait problems	—	Planning and organization difficulties, perseveration, attention deficits, memory difficulties, language use issues	Obsessive–compulsive disorder, bipolar disorder, mania, depression, irritability, impulsivity, anxiety, other personality changes
Amyotrophic lateral sclerosis (ALS)	Focal and progressive muscle weakness; tripping; clumsiness; abnormal fatigue; muscle fasciculation; slurred speech; difficulty with voice projection, breathing, and chewing and swallowing	—	—	Exaggerated emotional responses such as uncontrolled laughing or crying
Multiple sclerosis (MS)	Fatigue; problems with coordination and gait; sexual, bladder, and bowel dysfunction; spasticity; difficulty swallowing	Vision loss, dizziness/vertigo, persistent headache, pain	Memory and attention deficits	Emotional changes

indicate that these lesions happened at least 1 month apart. Perhaps most important, other causes of the symptoms (such as viral infections, exposure to toxic chemicals, vitamin B_{12} deficiency, and Guillain–Barré syndrome) must be ruled out.

Lesions are visualized using T2 MRI scanning. To differentiate between older and more current lesions, gadolinium can be used as a contrast agent to reveal active inflammation. This can help with the timing of lesions for diagnosis. However, about 5% of those who have MS do not have lesions visible on MRI in the early stages of symptoms. Another test that can be done to support a diagnosis of MS is measurement of responses to visual evoked potentials. These potentials measure the speed at which information passes through the visual system to reach the appropriate processing area of the brain. Brief visual stimuli are presented, and electrodes on the scalp overlying the visual cortex in the occipital lobe measure resulting brain

activity. Another indicator of MS, but unfortunately also of other immune-activating issues in the brain, is the presence of **oligoclonal bands** in the CSF but not in the blood. These bands, visualized with protein electrophoresis methods, are actually immunoglobulins that indicate inflammatory processes within the CNS. When combined with MRI and visual evoked potential data, they strengthen confidence in a diagnosis of MS.

CAUSES OF MS The causes of MS are still unknown, but researchers have identified several factors that may contribute to the development of the disease: immunological, environmental, infectious, and genetic.

MS is generally thought of as an *autoimmune* disease because of the presence of autoreactive **T cells**, which recognize oligodendrocyte myelin-specific antigens. Although the exact antigens have yet to be definitively identified, it is known that T cells cross the blood–brain barrier and secrete molecules that are damaging to neurons and release pro-inflammatory cytokines. While the brain is generally considered immunoprivileged (meaning that there is normally little interaction with the immune system), some immune cells enter the brain to surveil the environment. If they do not find a target, they die in the unwelcoming brain environment. If they do find their target, they recruit more cells to the area.

Some of the evidence for an *environmental* contributor to the development of MS is the interesting trend toward a geographical risk map (Simpson et al., 2011). Generally, the risk for MS is very much greater in those who live above 40° latitude in the Northern Hemisphere (**FIGURE 20.17**). The risk for development of MS seems to be determined by the location of residence up to about age 15. Those who move to a temperate climate from a tropical one before the age of 15 take on the increased risk of a temperate climate. Those who make this move after age 15 keep the risk level from the tropical climate. There are several risk factors for MS that might also be linked to this geographical anomaly. One is that vitamin D may be protective: those who live in more tropical climates tend to spend more time in the sun and therefore produce more vitamin D.

Interestingly, the warmer months in both the United States and Italy tend to increase relapses of MS in diagnosed patients. The risk in the United States, particularly in Massachusetts, was found to be highest between May and August (Meier et al., 2010). In the study conducted in Italy, the highest risk was between May and June, with a smaller peak in November and December. Although these studies are small, they do indicate an interesting seasonal pattern that may invite further study.

As with PD and ALS, there may be a role for environmental toxins and metals in disease onset. There are clusters, or areas, where the rate of MS is higher than would normally be expected that are currently being investigated for the presence of a toxin or toxins that may influence the development of the disease.

Infectious processes can also increase the likelihood of developing MS. Infection with measles, human herpesvirus 6, Epstein–Barr (EB) virus, and *Chlamydia pneumoniae* may increase one's risk (about 90% of all those with MS have also had an EB virus infection such as mononucleosis). These infections are more likely (and spread more easily) in colder climates, where residents are likely to spend more time inside.

Finally, MS is not a strictly hereditary disease. There has been no identified "MS gene," as there is for HD. But indications suggest that some *genes* may increase a person's risk for developing this disorder. This conclusion comes from the fact that first-degree relatives of those with MS are at greater risk for developing MS than are those in the general population. It is likely that there are gene variants that make some people more likely to react to certain environmental or immune triggers with the development of autoimmunity.

TREATMENTS FOR MS Treatments for MS may be either (1) disease modifying or (2) intended to treat an acute exacerbation. Others may be used to treat specific symptoms. In contrast to many of the other disorders discussed in this chapter, in MS there are several drugs that can reduce the frequency and severity of relapses and the accumulation of lesions and that appear to slow the accumulation of disability.

Injectable medications The first class of drugs approved for use in MS was the interferons. **Interferon beta-1a** and **-1b** likely work in MS by increasing the function of **suppressor T cells**. These T cells modulate the immune system and maintain tolerance to self-antigens in contrast or opposition to the myelin-reactive T cells described previously. Thus, they decrease the self-attack in MS. Four interferon drugs are Avonex and Rebif (interferon beta-1a) and Betaseron and Extavia (interferon beta-1b). Each is

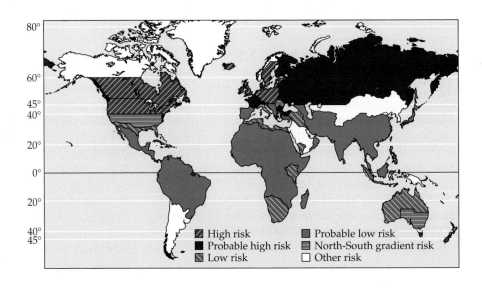

FIGURE 20.17 Geographical patterns to the distribution of multiple sclerosis (MS) cases In general, colder climates bring increased risk for the development of MS. (After J. W. Rose et al. 1996, updated 2000. *Multiple Sclerosis.* Accessed December 29, 2012 from library.med.utah.edu/kw/ms/mml/ms_worldmap.html ; and D. McAlpine 1965. *Multiple Sclerosis: A Reappraisal by Douglas McAlpine.* Livingstone: Edinburgh.)

administered by injection—Avonex once per week by intramuscular injection, the rest every other day or three times per week by subcutaneous injection. The side effects of these drugs are flu-like symptoms and injection-site reactions. Evidence suggests the possibility of a relationship between therapy with these drugs and depression, but it remains unclear whether this represents an increased risk for depression above the effect of MS itself. Peginterferon beta-1a (Plegridy) is one the most recent interferon drugs available for relapsing MS. It was originally approved in 2014 as a subcutaneous injection but was approved as an intramuscular injection in early 2021.

Glatiramer acetate (Copaxone, glatopa) is a synthetic protein that simulates myelin basic protein, a component of myelin that may be one of the antigenic targets of autoimmunity. It is thought to work by blocking myelin-damaging T cells, but it is unclear how it achieves this effect. Side effects of Copaxone generally resolve on their own and include injection-site reactions, runny nose, tremor, unusual tiredness or weakness, and weight gain. About 13% of patients taking the drug have a one-time (although not necessarily a first-time) reaction, which includes very short-lived (about 15 minutes) flushing, chest tightness, palpitations, anxiety, and difficulty breathing. Glatopa is the generic version of Copaxone.

Approved in 2020, ofatumumab (Kesimpta) is an injectable treatment that comes contained in a self-injecting pen. The *mab* at the end of the generic drug name indicates that the drug is a monoclonal antibody, a biological treatment. Doses are given on the start date, then 1 week and 2 weeks later; following that, the drug is given monthly starting at week 4. Kesimpta's target is the CD20 molecule on B cells, which results in a decrease in circulating B cells.

Infusion medications   Mitoxantrone (Novantrone) is the only MS drug currently available as a generic drug. It is an antineoplastic agent, and before its use for MS, it had been used only to treat cancers. Novantrone works in MS because it suppresses several components of the immune system, including T cells, B cells, and macrophages. Unlike most of the MS drugs, this drug is approved for subtypes of MS other than RRMS. It is approved for use in worsening RRMS, SPMS, and PRMS, but not in PPMS. Four infusions are administered across a year (once every 3 months). Risks are similar to those of other chemotherapy drugs and include cardiotoxicity and secondary acute myelogenous leukemia.

Following its original approval, natalizumab (Tysabri) was briefly removed from the market by the FDA because of an increased incidence of progressive multifocal leukoencephalopathy (PML). An intravenous infusion administered four times per year, Tysabri is a monoclonal antibody that hampers movement of damaging immune cells from the bloodstream across the blood–brain barrier. Further study revealed that the risk for PML is increased in those who have been exposed to **John Cunningham (JC) virus** and have JC virus antibodies. JC virus causes PML in those with suppressed immune systems (e.g., individuals with acquired immunodeficiency syndrome [AIDS] or those receiving treatment with immunosuppressants). After this discovery, Tysabri was reapproved but contraindicated for those at particular risk for development of PML.

Alemtuzumab (Lemtrada) was approved by the FDA in 2014. The target of alemtuzumab is the CD52 protein on B cells. This depletes the circulating B cells in the body, resulting in lower immune activation and reduction of the autoimmune mechanisms of MS. In fact, alemtuzumab was originally approved under the trade name Campath for treatment of B-cell chronic lymphocytic leukemia. It is given in two rounds. Round 1 involves one infusion per day for 5 days; round 2, given a year later, involves one infusion per day for 3 days. Additional rounds can be given (one infusion per day for 3 days) as needed, but no sooner than a year after round 2. About half of patients end up receiving at least one additional round of treatment.

Prior to 2017, all of the MS therapies on the market were focused on RRMS, not because of lack of interest in the progressive forms but because of a lack of efficacious therapies. That changed with the approval of ocrelizumab (Ocrevus) for PPMS. The antibody targets CD20-positive B cells, which contribute to the autoimmune activity that results in MS symptoms. Ocrevus is administered as an infusion—initially two infusions are given 2 weeks apart and then one infusion is given every 6 months. As with all MS drugs that affect the immune system, infections are a possible side effect, including reactivation of hepatitis B and potentially PML (though no PML infections were seen in clinical trials). Ocrevus may also increase a patient's risk for cancer, particularly breast cancer. Ocrevus reduces relapses in RRMS and slows progression in about a quarter of patients with PPMS. It costs approximately $67,000 per year, which is less than the cost of many other MS treatments.

Oral medications   The goal in the field of MS therapy research had long been to develop a disease-modifying medication that can be administered orally. Recent advances have led to a large number of such medications. Fingolimod (Gilenya) is a sphingosine 1-phosphate receptor modulator. This therapy causes retention of lymphocytes in lymph nodes, thereby preventing their entry to the CNS through the blood–brain barrier. This, in turn, prevents inflammatory damage to neurons. The side effects are relatively mild and include headache, flu, diarrhea, back pain, and cough. The side effect of abnormal liver test results is a little more serious.

Two other drugs have the same outcome of lymphocyte retention: siponimod (Mayzent), a once-daily tablet, and ozanimod (Zeposia), a once-daily capsule. Mayzent was approved by the FDA in 2019, Zeposia in 2020.

Teriflunomide (Aubagio) is a pyrimidine synthesis inhibitor that inhibits the function of specific immune cells. It is closely related to a therapy for another autoimmune disorder, rheumatoid arthritis. Aubagio reduces the proliferation of both T and B cells. It also reduces T-cell cytokine release. The side effects are similar to those seen with Gilenya and include diarrhea, nausea, flu, alopecia (thinning/loss of the hair), and abnormal liver tests.

Three drugs are related by their active substance. Dimethyl fumarate (Tecfidera) is the first of the oral drugs to be available as a generic. The active compound for this drug is actually a metabolite, monomethyl fumarate. Diroximel fumarate (Vumerity) has the same active metabolite. Monomethyl fumarate can be taken directly as the drug Bafiertam. These drugs are thought to decrease relapses and slow disease progression by triggering antioxidative responses in neurons.

Cladribine (Mavenclad) is only recommended for those for whom other drugs do not work. The primary risks are malignancies and teratogenicity. Mavenclad is a pro-drug that is activated by kinases. When activated, it accumulates in B and T cells and decreases their numbers. Unlike several of the other oral therapies, it is not a daily therapy. Two treatment courses are given about a year apart. During the first cycle, one or two tablets are given once daily for 4 or 5 consecutive days; the second cycle starts 23 to 27 days later. Then, 1 year later, the cycles are repeated using the same schedule. The patient must be monitored closely (e.g., bloodwork, infection screening, cancer screening, pregnancy and breastfeeding, liver injury, drug interactions, and lymphocyte counts) after these cycles.

TREATING EXACERBATIONS The most common mechanism for treating acute exacerbations that are affecting the patient's ability to perform at home or at work is the administration of corticosteroids. Three are commonly used on a short-term basis, generally for 3 to 5 days, to treat a relapse: prednisone (administered orally), methylprednisolone (Solu-Medrol, given intravenously), and dexamethasone (also administered intravenously). Methylprednisolone is also used for acute optic neuritis. These drugs have powerful anti-inflammatory effects. However, their side effects prohibit their long-term use in the management of MS and include stomach irritation, elevated blood sugar levels, water retention, restlessness, insomnia, and mood swings. Other options for treating acute exacerbations include repository corticotropin injection (HP Acthar gel), which is effective for the exacerbations but has no overall effect on disease course. A second-line treatment is plasmapheresis, in which the plasma is separated from the blood and replaced with donor plasma.

MANAGING SYMPTOMS Many medications are used to minimize MS symptoms, in addition to the disease-modifying and exacerbation-treating medications. Antidepressants, pain medications, and drugs for bladder and bowel dysfunction are common, as are therapeutics for vertigo, PBA, fatigue, pain, sexual dysfunction, spasticity, and tremors. Dalfampridine (Ampyra) has been approved for the treatment of walking dysfunction in those with MS. A potassium channel blocker, Ampyra, allows transmission through demyelinated fibers in motor pathways. This medication has several side effects, including urinary tract infections, difficulty sleeping, dizziness, headache, nausea, weakness, back pain, problems with balance, MS relapse, burning, tingling/itching of the skin, irritation of the nose and throat, constipation, indigestion, and throat pain. Recently, the FDA added a notice to the prescribing information for Ampyra indicating that there is a risk for seizures associated with this medication in patients with reduced kidney function.

Several nonmedication treatments are also used to manage MS symptoms. These include physical or occupational therapy, visits to a speech/language pathologist, cognitive rehabilitation, and assistive devices used inside and outside the home.

In addition to the therapies currently used to try to prevent damage, much research is being focused on repairing damage, particularly through remyelination of affected neurons.

SECTION SUMMARY

- Huntington's disease (HD) is an inherited, single-gene, neurodegenerative disorder that leads to significant motor, cognitive, and psychiatric symptoms.

- The *huntingtin* gene contains a CAG trinucleotide repeat, and HD is tied to an abnormal number of repeats (generally 40 repeats) yielding mHTT.

- Motor function deficits in HD are characterized by choreic movements, which are jerky, writhing movements that are present during waking hours. Additionally, speech, swallowing, and gait problems are noted in patients. Psychiatric symptoms associated with HD include OCD, bipolar disorder, depression, and mania.

- No disease-modifying treatments are available for HD, but two drugs, tetrabenazine and deutetrabenazine, are approved for treatment of the excessive movement found in HD. They work by decreasing monoamine vesicle packaging, thereby reducing DA signaling. The decreased DA signaling, however, can bring about depressive and parkinsonian side effects.

- Amyotrophic lateral sclerosis (ALS) is a degenerative disorder that affects motor function but spares most other cognitive and mood function.

- In ALS, degeneration of upper and lower motor neurons results in a progressive loss of motor function that generally starts with the far extremities and moves "inward" until muscles of breathing are finally affected. Some motor groups are spared, including bladder and bowel function and eye movements. A strange side effect of this degeneration is an exaggeration of emotional behavioral responses, including laughing and crying.

- The mechanism of degeneration of the motor neurons in ALS is still poorly understood but seems to involve protein aggregation in the cells and inflammation. These processes cause the triggering of apoptotic cell death pathways.

- Two FDA-approved therapies are available for ALS. Riluzole has modest disease-modifying effects, generally increasing life expectancy by about 2 to 3 months, and may delay reliance on mechanical breathing support. Radicava is a disease-modifying drug that slows progression of motor symptoms.

- Multiple sclerosis (MS) is widely believed to be the result of an autoimmune attack on CNS myelin.

- Four subtypes of MS are defined by their course: relapsing–remitting, primary progressive, secondary progressive, and progressive–relapsing.

- Symptoms of MS vary widely and are largely unpredictable. Depending on the location of the immune attack, symptoms may include motor, sensory, gait, emotional, cognitive, or vision problems. Depression is often comorbid with MS, at rates that are not explained entirely by the stress of having a neurological disorder.

- MS is diagnosed by MRI, neurological exam, and evidence of neuroinflammation.

- Immunological, environmental, infectious, and genetic contributors may play a role in the development of MS, but no clear-cut cause has been identified.

- MS treatments fall into disease-modifying and symptomatic categories.

- Disease-modifying treatments for MS include several injectable drugs, several drugs that are administered via infusion, and also a number of oral medications. Recently, Ocrevus was approved for treatment of both RRMS and PPMS; it is the first available therapy for the progressive form of the disease.

- Symptomatic MS treatments include corticosteroids for treating acute exacerbations, antidepressants, drugs for bowel and bladder function, Nuedexta for PBA, and Ampyra for treating gait and walking dysfunction.

STUDY QUESTIONS

1. What are the major motor symptoms of Parkinson's disease? What other types of symptoms are common in the disorder?

2. What neurotransmitter system is most-often targeted in PD therapeutics? How does this treatment relate to the pathological processes of the disease?

3. Create a research question/experimental design to answer one of the unmet needs of Parkinson's treatment or diagnosis.

4. Explain the presence and consequences of amyloid plaques and neurofibrillary tangles in Alzheimer's disease.

5. Explain the impact of risk and deterministic genes for Alzheimer's disease on likelihood of developing disease and age of onset.

6. What treatments are available for Alzheimer's and how to they affect the symptoms of the disease?

7. How is the genetic risk of developing Huntington's disease different from the genetic contributions to the other disorders discussed in this chapter?

8. What treatments are available for the different symptoms of Huntington's disease? Are there disease-modifying treatments available for this disease?

9. Explain the pathological processes that happen in amyotrophic lateral sclerosis. How does this manifest in the symptoms of the disorder?

10. What treatments are available for ALS? How do they affect disease course and symptomology?

11. Describe the general nature of the different subtypes of multiple sclerosis. What about the disease process makes this disorder particularly unpredictable? How does that impact those who have the disease?

12. Explain the general mechanism of the different treatment types for MS. Compare the disease-modifying, exacerbation abatement, and symptom-targeting approaches.

Glossary

Numbers in brackets refer to the chapter(s) in which the item is a key term.

A

AADC   See aromatic amino acid decarboxylase. [5, 6, 20]

AAS   See anabolic–androgenic steroids. [16]

absolute refractory period   Short period of time after an action potential when Na$^+$ channels close and are refractory until repolarization to resting potential occurs. [2]

absorption   Movement of a drug from the site of administration to the circulatory system. [1]

abstinence syndrome   Condition characterized by unpleasant symptoms when an individual tries to cease drug use. [9, 11]

acamprosate (Campral)   Partial antagonist at NMDA receptors used for the treatment of alcoholism. [10]

acetyl coenzyme A (acetyl CoA)   Precursor necessary for ACh synthesis. [7]

acetylcholine (ACh)   Neurotransmitter involved with the central and peripheral nervous system and synthesized by the cholinergic neurons. It is the target of many of the deadliest neurotoxins. [7]

acetylcholinesterase (AChE)   Enzyme that controls levels of ACh by breaking it down into choline and acetic acid. [7]

ACh   See *acetylcholine*. [7]

AChE   See acetylcholinesterase. [7]

ACTH   See adrenocorticotropic hormone. [3]

action potential   Major depolarization generated in the axon hillock that is transmitted down the axon. [2]

active zones   Areas along the axon terminal membrane, near the postsynaptic cell, that are specialized for neurotransmitter release. [3]

acute tolerance   Rapid tolerance formed during a single administration of a drug, as is the case with alcohol. [1, 10]

acute tryptophan depletion (ATD)   A procedure for depleting brain tryptophan (and reducing brain serotonin synthesis) that involves administering an amino acid cocktail containing a large quantity of amino acids except for tryptophan. [6]

AD   See *Alzheimer's disease*. [20]

ADAD   See *autosomal dominant Alzheimer's disease*. [20]

Adderall   See *amphetamine*. [5]

additive effects   Drug interactions characterized by the collective sum of the two individual drug effects. [1]

adenosine   Blockade of receptors for this substance is responsible for caffeine's stimulant effects. [13]

adipsia   Loss of thirst. [5]

adoption studies   Studies used to understand how heredity contributes to a disorder by comparing the incidence of the disorder in the biological and adoptive parents of people adopted at an early age who have the disorder. A higher incidence of the disorder among biological parents than adoptive parents suggests a hereditary influence. [18]

adrenal cortex   Outer portion of the adrenal gland that secretes glucocorticoids. [3]

adrenal glands   Endocrine glands that are located above the kidney and secrete EPI, NE, and glucocorticoids. An adrenal gland is composed of the adrenal medulla and the adrenal cortex. [3]

adrenal medulla   Inner portion of the adrenal gland that secretes the catecholamines EPI and NE. [3]

adrenergic   Adjectival form of adrenaline, also called epinephrine (EPI). May be used broadly to include both NE- and EPI-related features. [5]

adrenoceptors   Receptors to which NE and EPI bind; part of the metabotropic receptor family. Also known as adrenergic receptors. [5]

adrenocorticotropic hormone (ACTH)   Hormone secreted by the anterior pituitary that stimulates glucocorticoid synthesis and release from the adrenal cortex. [3]

AEA   See *arachidonoyl ethanolamide*. [14]

affinity   Ability of a molecule to bind to a receptor, which then determines potency. [1]

afterglow   Desired subjective state that may follow the peak experience produced during a hallucinogenic drug-assisted therapeutic session. [15]

2-AG   See *2-arachidonoylglycerol*. [14]

agoraphobia   Fear of public places. [17]

agouti-related peptide (AgRP)   Neuropeptide synthesized by neurons in the arcuate nucleus that stimulates hunger and eating behavior when released onto postsynaptic cells in the paraventricular nucleus. [6]

AgRP   See agouti-related peptide. [6]

akathisia   Constant urge to move certain body parts. [20]

akinesia   Difficulty in initiating movement. [5, 20]

Akineton   See *biperiden*. [7]

albuterol (Ventolin)   Selective β_2-adrenoceptor agonist administered as an inhaler to treat the symptoms of asthma. [5]

alcohol dehydrogenase   Enzyme in the liver and stomach that oxidizes alcohol into acetaldehyde. [10]

alcohol or barbiturate withdrawal Symptoms associated with the termination of alcohol, barbiturate, or benzodiazepine use. The three drugs are cross dependent; administration of one alleviates withdrawal symptoms of the other. [17]

alcohol poisoning Toxic effects associated with the ingestion of excess alcohol, characterized by unconsciousness, vomiting, irregular breathing, and cold, clammy skin. [10]

alcohol use disorder A form of substance misuse characterized by compulsive alcohol seeking and use despite damaging social and health effects. Formerly called *alcoholism.* [10]

alcohol-induced cirrhosis Condition seen in chronic alcohol users caused by scar tissue formation that promotes cell death as scar tissue cuts off blood supplies. [10]

alcohol-induced hepatitis Condition seen in chronic alcohol users caused by death of liver cells and characterized by inflammation of the liver, fever, jaundice, and pain. [10]

aldehyde dehydrogenase (ALDH) Enzyme in the liver that metabolizes the acetaldehyde intermediate formed by alcohol oxidation into acetic acid. [10]

ALDH See *aldehyde dehydrogenase.* [10]

allosteric modulators Compounds that bind to a receptor site distinct from the main agonist binding site, may or may not have an effect on the receptor when administered alone, and either enhance (in the case of a positive allosteric modulator) or reduce (in the case of a negative allosteric modulator) the effectiveness of an agonist on the receptor. They have potential therapeutic use because of their ability to tune receptor activity more subtly than either a receptor agonist or an antagonist. [3]

allosteric sites Binding sites on a receptor protein that modulate the receptor's response, either positively or negatively, to a receptor agonist. [3]

allylglycine Drug that blocks GABA synthesis, inducing convulsions. [8]

alosetron (Lotronex) Drug that inhibits 5-HT$_3$ receptors. It is used to treat the diarrhea-predominant form of irritable bowel syndrome. [6]

α-methyl-para-tyrosine (AMPT) Drug that inhibits TH activity, thereby reducing catecholamine synthesis. [5]

α-MSH See *α-melanocyte stimulating hormone.* [6]

α-PVP Potent cathinone derivative (α-pyrrolidinovalerophenone) that is a misused stimulant drug. Common street names for this compound are "flakka" and "gravel." [12]

α-synuclein A protein that is found primarily in neurons and accumulates to form Lewy bodies in people affected with Parkinson's disease and some forms of dementia. [20]

Aloxi See *palonosetron.* [6]

altered states of consciousness (ASC) rating scale Psychometric scale developed to quantify the subjective effects of psychedelic agents. [15]

Alzheimer's disease Neurodegenerative disorder, almost always occurring in the elderly, which is characterized behaviorally by progressive loss of cognitive function and histologically by the presence of extracellular plaques containing beta-amyloid protein and intracellular neurofibrillary tangles containing hyperphosphorylated tau protein. It is the most common cause of dementia. [20]

AM251 Cannabinoid CB1 receptor antagonist/inverse agonist. [14]

Amerge See *naratriptan.* [6]

Amines Organic molecules containing at least one nitrogen atom with three or four substituents bound to it. [5]

amino acids Essential building blocks of proteins, some of which also act as neurotransmitters. [3]

amotivational syndrome Symptoms of cannabis use that relate to poor educational achievement and motivation. [14]

AMPA receptor An ionotropic glutamate receptor selective for the synthetic amino acid agonist AMPA. [8]

amphetamine-induced stereotypy Model for schizophrenia induced by giving animals high doses of amphetamine to produce repetitive, stereotyped behavior. [19]

amphetamine Psychostimulant that acts by increasing neurotransmitter release from catecholaminergic neurons. [5, 12]

AMPT See *α-methyl-para-tyrosine.* [5]

amygdala Part of the limbic system that helps to modulate emotional behavior and coordinates the various components of emotion. [2]

amyloid precursor protein (APP) Transmembrane protein. Cleavage by secretases forms Aβ. [20]

anabolic–androgenic steroids (AAS) Group of performance enhancers characterized by their ability to increase muscle mass and produce or enhance masculine qualities. The name may be shortened to anabolic steroids. [16]

analeptics Drugs that act as circulatory, respiratory, or general CNS stimulants. [15]

anandamide Common chemical name of the arachidonic acid derivative that functions as an endogenous ligand for cannabinoid receptors in the brain. [14]

androgen receptor Target site of testosterone and other androgens, located within the cytoplasm of the cell and present in many tissues. [16]

androgens Male sex hormones either secreted by the testes like testosterone or synthesized to produce testosterone-like effects. [3]

anesthetics General anesthetics are substances that depress the CNS, decreasing all sensations in the body and causing unconsciousness. Local anesthetics do not cause unconsciousness but prevent pain signals by blocking Na$^+$ channels. Some anesthetics such as nitrous oxide (also known as laughing gas), chloroform, and ether comprise a class of misused inhalant substances. [11, 16]

anorexigenic Substance that reduces appetite. [6]

anosmia Inability to perceive odors. [20]

Antabuse See *disulfiram.* [10]

anterior Located near the front or head end of an organism. [2]

anterior pituitary Portion of the pituitary gland that secretes the hormones TSH, ACTH, FSH, LH, GH, and PRL. [3]

anteropulsion Feeling of being pushed forward. [20]

antibody Protein produced by the immune system for the purpose of recognizing, attacking, and destroying a specific foreign substance (i.e., an antigen). [4]

anticipatory anxiety Feeling of extreme worry over the possibility that a certain unpleasant event will occur in a particular, often public, situation. [17]

anticonvulsants Drugs, such as benzodiazepines, that prevent or control seizures. They are used to treat epilepsy. [17]

antireward system   System within the brain that is recruited during the withdrawal/negative affect stage of the addiction spiral and plays an important role in the transition from controlled to compulsive drug use. Key components include the central amygdala and the neurotransmitters NE and CRF. [9]

antitussives   Drugs that suppress the coughing reflex. [15]

anxiolytics   Drugs that alleviate feelings of anxiety in humans and that reduce anxiety-related behaviors in animals. [17]

apnea   Cessation of breathing. [6]

apolipoprotein E (ApoE)   Protein that helps break down amyloid. Individuals carrying the E4 allele of the gene encoding this protein develop AD. [20]

apomorphine (Uprima)   Drug that is a D_1 and D_2 receptor agonist and causes behavioral activation. It is also used to treat erectile dysfunction by acting through DA receptors in the brain to increase penile blood flow. [5]

apoptosis   Cell death resulting from a programmed series of biochemical events designed to eliminate unnecessary cells. It may also be called programmed cell death. [8]

APP   See *amyloid precursor protein*. [20]

arachidonoyl ethanolamide (AEA)   Formal chemical name of *anandamide*. [14]

2-arachidonoylglycerol (2-AG)   An arachidonic acid derivative that functions as an endogenous ligand for brain cannabinoid receptors. [14]

arachnoid   Membrane consisting of a weblike sublayer that covers the brain and spinal cord and contains CSF. One of the three meninges. [2]

Aramine   See *metaraminol*. [5]

arcuate nucleus   Nucleus located at the base of the hypothalamus that contains NPY/AgRP and POMC neurons involved in the regulation of hunger and eating behavior. [6]

area postrema   Area in the medulla of the brain stem that is not isolated from chemicals in the blood. It is responsible for inducing a vomiting response when a toxic substance is present in the blood. [2]

arecoline   Chemical from the seeds of the betel nut palm *Areca catechu* that stimulates muscarinic receptors. [7]

Aricept   See *donepezil*. [7]

aromatic amino acid decarboxylase (AADC)   Enzyme that catalyzes the removal of a carboxyl group from certain amino acids. It is responsible for the conversion of DOPA to DA in catecholaminergic neurons and the conversion of 5-HTP to 5-HT in serotonergic neurons. [5, 6, 20]

Artane   See *trihexyphenidyl*. [7]

ASC   See *Altered States of Consciousness rating scale*. [15]

aspartate   Ionized form of aspartic acid. It is an excitatory amino acid neurotransmitter of the CNS. [8]

association analysis   Determination of whether a particular genetic polymorphism is associated with a particular disease or trait. [10]

astrocytes   Star-shaped glial cells that have numerous extensions and that modulate the chemical environment around neurons, metabolically assist neurons, and provide phagocytosis for cellular debris. [1, 2]

astroglia   The collective terms for astrocytes. [1]

ATD   See *acute tryptophan depletion*. [6]

atomoxetine (Strattera)   Selective norepinephrine uptake inhibitor used in the treatment of ADHD. [5]

atropine   Drug found in nightshade, *Atropa belladonna*, and henbane, *Hyoscyamus niger*, that blocks muscarinic receptors. [7]

attentional set-shifting task   Rodent version of the WCST in which the animals must choose the bowl with the food reward based on either odor or surface texture. [19]

Austedo   See *deutetrabenazine*. [5]

autoimmune disorder   Condition in which the immune system attacks part of one's own body. [7]

autoradiography   Process used to detect the amount and location of bound radioligand by using a specialized film to create an image of where the radioligand is located within a tissue slice. [4]

autoreceptors   Neuronal receptors in a cell that are specific for the same neurotransmitter released by that cell. They typically inhibit further neurotransmitter release. [3]

autosomal dominant Alzheimer's disease (ADAD)   Familial version of AD caused by mutations in the genes for presenelin-1, presenilin-2, and amyloid precursor protein. [20]

axoaxonic synapses   Junctions used for communication between the axon terminals of two neurons, permitting the presynaptic cell to control neurotransmitter release from the postsynaptic cell at the terminals. [3]

axodendritic synapses   Junction used for communication between the axon terminal of a presynaptic neuron and a dendrite of a postsynaptic neuron. [3]

axon   Long tubular extention from the soma of the nerve cell that conducts electrical signals away from the cell body and toward the axon terminals. [2]

axon collaterals   Branches formed when an axon splits, giving the neuron the ability to signal more cells. [2]

axon hillock   The segment of axon adjacent to the soma where the action potential is first generated. [2]

axoplasmic transport   Method of transporting proteins along the microtubules of the cytoskeleton to designations throughout a neuron. Anterograde transport moves newly synthesized proteins from the soma. Retrograde transport moves waste back to the soma from the terminals. [2]

axosomatic synapses   Junctions used for communication between a nerve terminal and a nerve cell body. [3]

ayahuasca   Hallucinogenic mixture originating in the Amazon rain forest. It typically contains stalks from the *Banisteriopsis caapi* vine and leaves from *Psychotria viridis* and/or *Diplopterys cabrerana*. Together, these plants provide the hallucinogenic tryptamine DMT along with β-carbolines that inhibit MAO and permit the DMT to reach the brain when the ayahuasca is consumed orally. [15]

Azilect   See *rasagiline*. [5]

B

BAC   See *blood alcohol concentration*. [10]

baclofen (Lioresal)   Drug that is a selective agonist for the $GABA_B$ receptors. It is used as a muscle relaxant and an antispastic agent. [8]

barbiturates   Drugs that act as a CNS depressant, in part by enhancing $GABA_A$ receptor activity. [8]

barbiturate withdrawal   A set of psychological and physiological symptoms that may occur following rapid cessation from prolonged barbiturate use. These may include, but are not limited to, anxiety, restlessness, nausea, and agitation. [17]

basal forebrain cholinergic system (BFCS)   Collection of cholinergic nerve cells that innervates the cerebral cortex and limbic system structures. Damage to this system contributes to the symptoms of Alzheimer's disease. [7]

basal ganglia   Nuclei of the telencephalon that includes the caudate, putamen, and globus pallidus. The structures help regulate motor control. [2, 20]

BDNF   See *brain-derived neurotrophic factor*. [18]

BDZs   See *benzodiazepine*. [8]

beam walking   Device resembling a human gymnastics balance beam used to evaluate rodent fine motor coordination and balance. [4]

behavioral addictions   Uncontrolled behaviors not involving substance use but that have characteristics similar to those seen in substance-related disorders. [9]

behavioral desensitization   Technique used to treat phobias by introducing the fear-inducing stimulus in increments, allowing the patient to maintain a relaxed feeling in its presence. [17]

behavioral despair test   Technique used to measure depression in animals by placing them in a cylinder of water from which they cannot escape and recording the time it takes for them to abandon attempts to escape. Also called forced swim test. [4]

behavioral supersensitivity   Increased response to a drug treatment as a direct result of previous drug history or drug intake. [5]

behavioral tolerance   The reduced effectiveness of a drug administered chronically that involves learning: either instumental or classical conditioning. [1, 10]

Belviq   See *lorcaserin*. [6]

benzodiazepines (BDZs)   Drugs that act as $GABA_A$ receptor positive allosteric modulators, thereby depressing CNS activity. [8]

benzoylecgonine   Major metabolite of cocaine. [12]

benztropine mesylate (Cogentin)   Anticholinergic drug used to treat early symptoms of Parkinson's disease. [7]

beta-amyloid protein (β-amyloid or A-beta [Aβ])   Protein fragment derived from enzymatic cleavage of amyloid precursor protein. Primary component of the plaques characteristic of Alzheimer's disease. Also called A-beta and Aβ. [20]

β-carboline   Inverse agonist at the BDZ modulatory site on $GABA_A$ receptors that makes GABA less effective in producing hyperpolarization. It is anxiogenic and is a useful tool in studying the neurobiology of anxiety. [17]

BFCS   See *basal forebrain cholinergic system*. [7]

bicuculline   Drug that blocks the binding of GABA to the $GABA_A$ receptor and acts as a convulsant. [8]

binge drinking   Consumption of five or more alcoholic drinks within a 2-hour period. [10]

bioactivation   A metabolic process that converts an inactive drug into an active one. [1]

bioavailability   Concentration of drug present in the blood that is free to bind to specific target sites. [1]

biogenic amine   A transmitter that is made by a living organism and contains at least one amine group. [5]

biomarker   Quantifiable biological process that can be used to determine the presence of disease, as well as therapeutic or toxic effects of a drug [1]

biopsychosocial model   Model of addiction that attempts to give a full account of addiction by incorporating biological, psychological, and sociological factors. [9]

biotransformation   Inactivation of a drug through a chemical change, usually by metabolic processes catalyzed by enzymes in the liver. [1]

biperiden (Akineton)   Anticholinergic drug used in the treatment of Parkinson's disease. [7]

bipolar disorder   Type of affective disorder characterized by extreme mood swings between depression and mania. [18]

blackout   Amnesia directly associated with heavy alcohol consumption. [10]

blood alcohol concentration (BAC)   The amount of alcohol in a given unit of blood, usually given as a percent representing milligrams of alcohol per 100 milliliters of blood. [10]

bradykinesia   General slowing of movement that is characteristic of Parkinson's disease. Examples include slowed movement of facial muscles leading to "stone-faced" expression and reduced hand movement resulting in micrographia (smaller handwriting). [20]

bradyphrenia   Slowed response to questioning. [20]

brain-derived neurotrophic factor (BDNF)   Protein of the CNS that stimulates cell proliferation, aids in cell survival and synaptic restructuring. It is also implicated in the neurotrophic hypothesis of depression. [18]

brainstem   Portion of the brain, consisting of the medulla, pons, and midbrain. [2]

breakpoint   The point at which an animal will no longer expend the effort required to receive the reward (e.g., in a drug self-administration paradigm). [4, 9]

bridging   Pattern of anabolic–androgenic steroid use in which a low dose is used to bridge between each high dose of the steroid (also called "blast and cruise"). [16]

broad-spectrum antipsychotics   Class of drugs used to treat schizophrenia by blocking a wide range of receptors in addition to the D_2 receptor. [19]

bromocriptine (Parlodel, Cycloset) D_2/D_3 receptor agonist sometimes prescribed as an adjunct to L-DOPA in the treatment of Parkinson's disease. [5]

bufotenine   Tryptamine hallucinogen present in the toxic secretions of an American desert toad, *Bufo alvarius*. [15]

bulk endocytosis   Mechanism for retrieval of large amounts of synaptic vesicle membrane after very strong or prolonged neuronal firing. [3]

Buprenex   See *buprenorphine*. [11]

buprenorphine (Buprenex)   An opioid agonist–antagonist used in opioid treatment programs that may be substituted for methadone and yields similar treatment results. [11]

bupropion (Zyban)   Drug that inhibits DA and NE uptake and is also a weak *nAChR* antagonist. It is used in the treatment of tobacco dependence. [13]

burst mode   Mode of neuronal cell firing characterized by the production of bursts of action potentials. [5]

buspirone (BuSpar)   Drug that is a partial agonist at $5-HT_{1A}$ receptors. Symptoms include increased appetite, reduced anxiety, reduced alcohol cravings, and a lower body temperature. It is prescribed as an antianxiety medication that lacks sedation, mental clouding, potential for misuse, or physiological dependence. [6, 17]

C

c-fos Transcription factor that rises rapidly within cells during increased neural activity. [4]

cachexia Syndrome involving extreme loss of muscle mass and body weight. [16]

caffeine Stimulant drug found naturally in coffee and tea. It is also consumed in tablet form and in various beverages such as such drinks and energy drinks. [13]

caffeine dependence syndrome Disorder produced by chronic high-dose caffeine use and characterized by caffeine craving, difficulty controlling caffeine consumption, caffeine tolerance, and withdrawal symptoms that occur following abstinence. It is a recognized disorder within ICD-10 but not within *DSM-5*. [13]

caffeine intoxication Disorder produced by recent high-dose caffeine use and characterized by symptoms of restlessness, nervousness, insomnia, and physiological disturbances including tachycardia (increased heart rate), muscle twitching, and gastrointestinal upset. [13]

caffeine use disorder *DSM-5* category with features similar to those of caffeine dependence syndrome. It is not a recognized disorder but has been designated for additional research. [13]

calcium/calmodulin kinase II (CaMKII) Enzyme stimulated by calcium and calmodulin that phosphorylates specific proteins in a signaling pathway. [3]

cAMP See *cyclic adenosine monophosphate*. [3]

Campral See *acamprosate*. [10]

cannabidiol (CBD) Phytocannabinoid that lacks the intoxicating and dependence-producing effects of THC. [14]

cannabinoid receptor Class of metabotropic receptors responsive to both endocannabinoids like anandamide and phytocannabinoids such as THC. In the CNS, they are concentrated in the basal ganglia, cerebellum, hippocampus, and cerebral cortex. [14]

Carbamazepine (Tegretol) An anticonvulsant drug used to treat bipolar disorder. [18]

carbidopa A decarboxylase inhibitor that cannot cross the blood–brain barrier. Increases the availability of L-DOPA to the brain. [6, 20]

carcinoid syndrome Cluster of symptoms produced by the secretory products (including serotonin) of carcinoid tumors. [6]

case–control method Technique used to identify genes associated with a disorder by comparing the genes of unrelated affected and unaffected people to determine if those who are affected are more likely to possess a particular allele. [10]

catalepsy State characterized by a lack of spontaneous movement. It is usually associated with D_2 receptor blockers (a DA receptor subtype), but can also be induced with a D_1 blocker. [5]

Catapres See *clonidine*. [5]

catechol-O-methyltransferase (COMT) One of the enzymes responsible for metabolic breakdown of catecholamines. [5, 20]

catecholamines Group of neurotransmitters and hormones characterized by two chemical similarities: a core structure of catechol and a nitrogen-containing amine. They belong to a wider group of transmitters called monoamines or biogenic amines. [5]

cathinone Psychostimulant that is the primary active ingredient in khat. [12]

caudal The tail end of the nervous system is caudal or posterior. [2]

CBD See *cannabidiol*. [14]

CBT See *cognitive behavioral therapy*. [12]

central Of, or relating to, the central nervous system (brain and spinal cord). [1]

central canal Channel within the center of the spinal cord filled with CSF. [2]

cerebellar peduncles Large bundles of axons that connect the cerebellum to the pons. [2]

cerebellum Large structure of the metencephalon that is located on the dorsal surface of the brain and that is connected to the pons by the cerebellar peduncles. It is an important sensorimotor control center of the brain. [2]

cerebral ventricles Cavities within the brain filled with CSF. [2]

cerebrospinal fluid (CSF) Fluid that surrounds the brain and spinal cord, providing cushioning that protects against trauma. It also fills the cerebral ventricles and the central canal of the spinal cord. [1]

Cesamet See *nabilone*. [14]

cGMP See *cyclic guanosine monophosphate*. [3]

Chantix See *varenicline*. [13]

ChAT See *choline acetyltransferase*. [7]

chemogenetics The activation or suppression of a genetically engineered receptor with a designer ligand in order to study behavioral effects of longer duration compared to optogenetic manipulation. Sometimes referred to as DREADD. [4]

choline Precursor necessary for ACh synthesis. [7]

choline acetyltransferase (ChAT) Enzyme that catalyzes the synthesis of ACh from acetyl CoA and choline. [7]

choline transporter Protein in the membrane of the cholinergic nerve terminal responsible for the uptake of choline from the synaptic cleft. [7]

cholinergic Adjectival form of ACh. [7]

cholinesterase inhibitors Drugs that improve cognitive symptoms by increasing the presence of acetylcholine in the synapse by lessening breakdown of ACh. One of two categories of treatment for AD. [20]

chromaffin cells The cells of the adrenal medulla. [3]

chromatin remodeling One type of environmentally induced epigenetic modification that increases or decreases gene transcription.[2]

chromosomes Double helical strands of DNA that carry genes. [2]

chronic mild unpredictable stress Rodent model of depression created by exposing animals to a series of stressful events in an unpredictable fashion. [4]

chronic social defeat stress Rodent model of depression created by the intense stress of being repeatedly placed as an intruder in a cage with a resident animal. [4]

classical conditioning Repeated pairing of a neutral stimulus with an unconditioned stimulus. Eventually the neutral stimulus becomes a conditioned stimulus and elicits a (conditioned) response that is similar to the original unconditioned response. This type of learning has a role in drug use and tolerance. [1]

clathrin Protein that participates in synaptic vesicle recycling, either in the endocytotic step of retrieving vesicle membrane from the axon terminal membrane or in the budding of new vesicles from endosomes in the axon terminal. [3]

clathrin-mediated endocytosis Process of synaptic vesicle membrane recovery that relies on the protein clathrin. [3]

clonidine (Catapres) Selective α_2-adrenergic receptor agonist that stimulates autoreceptors and inhibits noradrenergic cell firing. It is used to reduce symptoms of opioid withdrawal. [5]

cloning Method used to produce large numbers of genetically identical cells. [4]

closed State of a receptor channel in which the channel pore is closed, thereby preventing ion flow across the cell membrane. [7]

clostridium botulinum Species of bacteria responsible for synthesizing botulinum toxins and producing botulism poisoning. [7]

club drug Street name for a group of drugs that includes GHB, MDMA, flunitrazepam, and ketamine. The term was coined as a result of the drugs' popularity at raves and dance clubs. [16]

CNS depressants Large category of drugs that inhibit nerve cell firing within the central nervous system. They include sedative–hypnotics and are used to induce sleep and to treat symptoms of anxiety. [17]

co-agonists Substances needed simultaneously to activate a specific receptor. [8]

cocaethylene Metabolite formed from the interaction of cocaine and alcohol. It produces biological effects similar to those of cocaine. [12]

cocaine Stimulant drug derived from the coca shrub that blocks reuptake of DA, NE, and 5-HT by neurons, thereby increasing their concentration in the synaptic cleft. [5, 12]

cocaine binges Periods of cocaine use lasting hours or days with little or no sleep. [12]

cocaine use disorder *DSM-5* diagnostic category referring to maladaptive use of cocaine. [12]

coding region Portion of the gene that codes for the amino acid sequence of a protein. [2]

Cogentin See *benztropine mesylate*. [7]

cognitive behavioral therapy (CBT) Type of psychotherapy that can be used to treat drug addiction by restructuring the drug user's cognitive (thought) processes and training the user either to avoid high-risk situations that might cause relapse or to employ appropriate coping mechanisms to manage such situations when they occur. [12]

cognitive symptoms A category of symptoms of schizophrenia that includes impaired working memory, poor executive function, and attention deficits. [19]

comorbidity Diagnosis of simultaneous but distinct disease processes in an individual, such as the propensity for recreational drug users to be diagnosed with other psychiatric problems. [9]

competitive antagonist Drug that binds to a receptor but has little or no efficacy. When it competes with an agonist for receptor sites, it reduces the effect of the agonist. [1]

compulsions Repetitive tasks that an individual feels obligated to complete in an effort to quell the anxiety caused by obsessive thoughts. [17]

computer vision Technology in which artificial intelligence algorithms are employed to analyze images or video for patterns that indicate behavioral features of interest. [4]

computerized tomography (CT) X-ray based technique that provides computer-generated "slices" through the brain or body part that can be computer reconstructed into 3-dimensional images. [4]

COMT See *catechol-O-methyltransferase*. [5, 20]

Comtan See *entacapone*. [5]

concentration gradient Difference in the amount or concentration of a substance on each side of a biological barrier, such as the cell membrane. [1]

conditioned emotional response Learned response to a neutral stimulus presented just prior to a negative stimulus (e.g., an electric shock) in an effort to create a fear association to the neutral stimulus. [4]

conditioned place preference Method used to determine the rewarding effects of a drug by allowing an animal to associate the drug with a specific environment and measuring its subsequent preference for that environment. [4]

conflict procedure Method that creates a dilemma for an animal by giving it the choice of selecting a reward that is accompanied by a negative stimulus. Conflict procedures screen drugs for antianxiety effects. [4]

constitutive activity The baseline state of a protein, such as a neurotransmitter receptor, in the absence of a ligand. [1]

construct validity Term that represents the extent to which the animal measurement tool actually measures the human characteristic of interest. [4]

contingency management Type of addiction treatment program in which the client's drug taking is monitored by regular urine testing and abstinence is reinforced with vouchers redeemable locally for consumer products or services. [9, 12]

convergence Process by which neurons receive and integrate the numerous signals from other cells. [2]

core Following an ischemic stroke, this is the inner region of damage within which the dying neurons cannot be rescued. [12]

coronal Sections cut parallel to the face. [2]

corpus callosum Large pathway connecting corresponding areas of the two brain hemispheres, allowing communication between each half of the brain. [2]

correlational relationship Connection between two events that appear related but cannot be assumed to be cause and effect. [4]

corticosterone Glucocorticoid secreted by the adrenal cortex of rats and mice. [3]

corticotropin-releasing hormone (CRH) Hormone synthesized by neurons of the hypothalamus that stimulates ACTH release. Also known as corticotrophin-releasing factor (CRF). [3]

cortisol Specific glucocorticoid secreted by the adrenal cortex of primates. [3]

cotinine Principal product of nicotine metabolism by the liver. [13]

COX-2 See *cyclooxygenase-2*. [14]

crack Form of cocaine made by adding baking soda to a solution of cocaine HCl, heating the mixture, and drying the solid. [12]

craving Strong urge addicts feel, compelling them to take a drug. [9]

CRF1 antagonists Drugs that bind to CRF$_1$ receptors and produce little or no conformational change. In the presence of a CRF agonist, the agonist effect is reduced. [10]

CRH See *corticotropin-releasing hormone*. [3]

CRISPR (clustered regularly interspaced short palindromic repeat) Acronym for *c*lustered *r*egularly *i*nterspaced *s*hort *p*alindromic *r*epeats. A faster and less expensive way to create genetically engineered mice. The technique uses a "guide RNA" to locate a specific gene sequence that is then cut out or replaced. [4]

cross dependence Withdrawal signs occurring in a dependent individual can be terminated by administering drugs in the same class. [10, 11]

cross-tolerance Tolerance to a specific drug can reduce the effectiveness of another drug in the same class. [1, 10, 11]

CSF See *cerebrospinal fluid*. [1]

CT See *computerized tomography*. [4]

cyclic adenosine monophosphate (cAMP) Second messenger that is produced by the enzyme adenylyl cyclase and that functions by activating PKA. In many cells, cAMP is regulated by receptors for DA, NE, 5-HT, or endorphins. [3]

cyclic guanosine monophosphate (cGMP) Second messenger that is produced by the enzyme guanylyl cyclase and that functions by activating PKG. cGMP synthesis is regulated in part by NO. [3]

cycling Pattern of steroid use characterized by 6 to 12 weeks of drug use, followed by a period of abstinence before repeating the drug use pattern. [16]

Cycloset See *bromocriptine*. [5]

cyclooxygenase-2 (COX-2) Enzyme that can metabolize endocannabinoids and that plays an important role in the process of inflammation. [14]

CYP450 See *cytochrome P450*. [1, 10]

CYP4502AS See *cytochrome P450 2AS*. [13]

cytochrome P450 (CYP450) Class of liver enzymes, in the microsomal enzyme group, responsible for both phase 1 and phase 2 biotransformation of psychoactive drugs. [1, 10]

cytochrome P450 2A6 (CYP2A6) Specific type of cytochrome P450 that metabolizes nicotine into cotinine. [13]

cytoplasm Salty gelatinous fluid of the cell, outside of the nucleus and bounded by the cell membrane. [2]

cytoskeleton Structural matrix of a cell that is composed of tubular materials such as microtubules and neurofilaments. [2]

D

D-serine Amino acid that is a co-agonist with glutamate for the NMDA receptor. [8]

D-tubocurarine Active ingredient in curare, a potentially fatal toxin that blocks cholinergic transmission at muscle nicotinic receptors. [7]

DA See *dopamine*. [5]

DA imbalance hypothesis Theory that excessive DA function of mesolimbic neurons produces positive symptoms and insufficient DA function of mesocortical neurons produces negative and cognitive symptoms of schizophrenia. [19]

DA transporter Protein in the membrane of dopaminergic neurons that is responsible for DA uptake from the extracellular fluid. [5]

dabbing Form of high-potency cannabis consumption. It typically involves extraction of cannabis with butane, evaporation of the solvent, and then smoking the resulting waxy residue. [14]

DAG See *diacylglycerol*. [3]

DBH See *dopamine β-hydroxylase*. [5]

DBS See *deep brain stimulation*. [12]

deep brain stimulation (DBS) Method of selectively stimulating structures deep within the brain using surgically implanted electrodes. [12]

defensive burying Rodent behavioral task designed to detect anxiolytic drug effects whereby rodents naturally bury foreign objects, such as marbles, with bedding material. [4]

delirium tremens (DTs) Severe effects of alcohol withdrawal characterized by irritability, headaches, agitation, hallucinations, and confusion. [10]

δ-receptors A type of opioid receptor primarily in the forebrain that may help regulate olfaction, motor integration, reinforcement, and cognitive function. [11]

Δ^9-tetrahydrocannabinol (THC) Psychoactive chemical found in cannabis plants; a cannabinoid. [14]

dementia Broad reduction of cognitive functions (e.g., memory, language, and problem solving) that is severe enough to interfere significantly with daily functioning. [7]

dendrites Projections from the soma that receive signals and information from other cells. [2]

dendritic spines Projections from dendrites that increase the receiving surface area. [2]

2-deoxyglucose autoradiography A research tool that visually identifies neurons that are active by measuring glucose uptake. [4]

Depakote See *valproate*. [18]

depolarization Change in membrane potential making the inside of the cell more positive, increasing the likelihood that the cell will have an action potential. [2]

depolarization block Process in which the resting potential across the cell membrane is lost. The neuron cannot be excited until the membrane is repolarized. [7]

depolarization-induced suppression of excitation (DSE) Type of short-term synaptic plasticity in an excitatory presynaptic neuron, produced by a brief postsynaptic depolarization, that involves suppression of neurotransmitter release for several seconds up to a minute. [14]

depolarization-induced suppression of inhibition (DSI) Type of short-term synaptic plasticity in an inhibitory presynaptic neuron, produced by a brief postsynaptic depolarization, that involves suppression of neurotransmitter release for several seconds up to a minute. [14]

depot binding Type of drug interaction involving binding to an inactive site, such as to proteins in the plasma, to bone, or to fat. [1]

deprivation reversal model Theory that smoking is maintained by mood enhancement and increased concentration that occur when nicotine withdrawal symptoms are alleviated. [13]

descending modulatory pathways Bundles of nerve fibers originating at higher brain regions that influence lower brain or spinal cord function. One arises from the PAG in the midbrain and influences pain signals carried by the spinal cord neurons. [11]

desensitization Process by which an ionotropic channel receptor remains closed despite the presence of an agonist bound to the receptor. The receptor cannot respond again until it leaves the desensitized state. [3]

desensitized Altered receptor state characterized by a lack of response to an agonist. [7]

detoxification Procedure used to treat addicted individuals in which the drug is stopped and withdrawal symptoms are treated until the abstinence syndrome has ended. [10]

detoxified A drug user undergoing detoxification is considered to be detoxified when signs of the abstinence syndrome end. [11]

deutetrabenazine (Austedo) Reversible VMAT2 inhibitor used to reduce uncontrolled movements associated with Huntington's disease and tardive dyskinesia. [5]

developmental origins of health and disease Hypothesis that postulates that characteristics of the intrauterine environment, such as nutrient availability and the presence of drugs, environmental toxins, or infectious agents, "program" the fetus in a way that determines the vulnerability for developing chronic diseases in adulthood. [13]

dexamethasone A synthetic corticosteroid used to test the function of the negative feedback mechanism regulating the HPA axis. [18]

dexmedetomidine (Precedex) Drug that stimulates α_2-receptors, characterized by its sedative, anxiolytic, and analgesic effects. It is used to treat surgical patients in intensive care. [5]

dextromethorphan Opioid-like drug that is the major antitussive agent in most over-the-counter cough medicine. [15]

dextrorphan Biologically active metabolite of dextromethorphan. [15]

DhβE See *dihydro-beta-erythroidine*. [13]

5,6-DHT See *5,6-dihydroxytryptamine*. [6]

5,7-DHT See *5,7-dihydroxytryptamine*. [6]

diacylglycerol (DAG) Second messenger generated by the phosphoinositide second messenger system; stimulates protein kinase C (PKC). [3]

diazepam (Valium) A BDZ that binds to the BDZ receptor, increasing the effectiveness of GABA to open the GABA$_A$ receptor channel. [8]

diffusion tensor imaging (DTI) An imaging technique that allows visualization of axonal connections and evaluates the integrity of the neuronal pathway. [4]

dihydro-beta-erythroidine (DhβE) Blocks high-affinity nAChRs (i.e., receptors containing α4 and β2 subunits). [13]

5,6-dihydroxytryptamine (5,6-DHT) Neurotoxin that selectively damages serotonergic neurons. [6]

5,7-dihydroxytryptamine (5,7-DHT) Neurotoxin that selectively damages serotonergic neurons. [6]

1-(2,5-Dimethoxy-4-iodophenyl)-2-aminopropane (DOI) Drug that stimulates 5-HT$_{2A}$ receptors, producing "head-twitch" in rodents and hallucinations in humans. [6]

dimethyltryptamine (DMT) Hallucinogenic drug found in several South American plants. [15]

Diprivan See *propofol*. [8]

DISC1 gene *DISC1* variants may increase the probability of developing schizophrenia. [19]

disease model Model of addiction that treats addiction as a distinct medical disorder or disease. Sometimes called a medical model. [9]

dissociative anesthesia An unusual type of anesthetic state characterized by environmental detachment. It is produced by certain noncompetitive NMDA receptor antagonists such as ketamine and PCP. [15]

disulfiram (Antabuse) A drug used to treat alcoholism by causing the buildup of toxic metabolites producing illness after alcohol ingestion. [10]

divergence Process by which neurons transmit their integrated signals back out to many neurons. [2]

dizocilpine See *MK-801*. [8]

DMT See *dimethyltryptamine*. [15]

DNA methylation Environmentally-induced epigenetic covalent attachment of methyl groups to a gene decreases its expression. [2]

DNA microarray Method used to screen tissue or cell extracts for changes in the expression of many genes at the same time. [19]

DOI See *1-(2,5-dimethoxy-4-iodophenyl)-2-aminopropane*. [6]

donepezil (Aricept) Drug that blocks AChE activity. It is used in the treatment of Alzheimer's disease. [7]

dopamine (DA) Neurotransmitter, related to NE and EPI, that belongs to a group called catecholamines. [5]

dopamine hypothesis of schizophrenia Theory that altered DA function leads to the symptoms observed in individuals with schizophrenia. [19]

dopamine β-hydroxylase (DBH) Enzyme that catalyzes the third step of NE synthesis in neurons, the conversion of DA to NE. [5]

dopamine-deficient (DD) mouse Mutant strain of mouse lacking dopamine from embryonic development onward. It is produced by genetically knocking out the tyrosine hydroxylase gene but restoring the gene in dopamine β-hydroxylase-expressing (i.e., noradrenergic) cells. [5]

dopaminergic Adjectival form of dopamine. [5]

doping agents Substances such as anabolic steroids that are used to enhance athletic performance despite being banned by sports organizations. [16]

dorsal Located toward the top of the brain and back of the body in humans. [2]

dorsa raphe nuclei (sing. nucleus) (DRN) Structure located in the area of the caudal midbrain and rostral pons that contains a large number of serotonergic neurons. In conjunction with the median raphe nucleus, it is responsible for most of the serotonergic fibers in the forebrain. Together they regulate sleep, aggression, impulsiveness, emotions, and other psychological/behavioral functions. [2, 6]

dose–response curve Graph used to display the amount of biological change in relation to a given drug dose. [1]

double-blind experiment Type of experiment in which neither the patient nor the observer knows the treatment received by the patient. [1]

down-regulation Decrease in the number of receptors, which may be a consequence of chronic agonist treatment. [1]

DREADD See *chemogenetics*. [4]

dronabinol (Marinol) Synthetic form of THC used to treat appetite and weight loss in patients with HIV/AIDS and to suppress nausea and vomiting in cancer patients receiving chemotherapy. [14]

drug action Molecular changes associated with a drug binding to a particular target site or receptor. [1]

drug competition A factor that modifies biotransformation capacity. When two drugs share a metabolic system and compete for the same metabolic enzymes bioavailability of one or both increases. [1]

drug depots Inactive sites where drugs accumulate. There is no biological effect from drugs binding at these sites, nor can they be metabolized. [1]

drug detoxification Process whereby an individual eliminates a drug from the body and goes through an abstinence syndrome. [9]

drug disposition tolerance See *metabolic tolerance*. [1]

drug effects Alterations in physiological or psychological functions associated with a specific drug. [1]

drug priming Delivery of a small dose of a drug by the experimenter for the purpose of eliciting drug-seeking behavior, typically in an animal whose drug self-administration responding was previously extinguished. See *reinstatement of drug-seeking behavior*. [9]

drug redistribution Transfer of drug molecules from organs of high drug concentration to those of low concentration until equilibrium is reached in all tissues. [1]

drug reward A positively-motivating subjective response to a drug, often experienced by humans as a euphoric feeling or "high." [9]

drug-seeking behavior Performance of an operant response such as a lever-press or a nose-poke with the expectation of receiving delivery of a drug dose. [12]

dry mouth effect Lack of salivation that is a side effect of drugs with muscarinic receptor blocking activity. [7]

DSE See *depolarization-induced suppression of excitation*. [14]

DSI See *depolarization-induced suppression of inhibition*. [14]

DTI See *diffusion tensor imaging*. [4]

DTs See *delirium tremens*. [10]

dual NE/5-HT modulators (SNRIs) Antidepressants that enhance both NE and 5-HT function. [18]

dura mater The outer layer of the meninges. It is the strongest of the three meninges layers. [2]

dyskinesias Abnormal or impaired movement such as severe tics or choreic movements. [20]

dystonia Persistent involuntary muscle contractions. [5, 20]

E

EAATs See *excitatory amino acid transporters*. [8]

early LTP (E-LTP) Type of long-term potentiation that lasts no longer than a few hours. [8]

e-cigarette, or vaping, product-associated lung injury (EVALI) Syndrome that can be produced by vaping and that has the following features: dyspnea, nonproductive cough, chest pain, nausea and vomiting, abdominal pain, diarrhea, fever, and an unusual lung pathology shown by the appearance of "ground-glass opacities" in CT scans. [13]

ecstasy Common street name for a drug that usually contains MDMA. [6]

Edronax See *reboxetine*. [5]

EEG See *electroencephalography*. [4]

effector enzymes Enzymes of the cell membrane that may be regulated by G proteins and that cause biochemical and physiological effects in postsynaptic cells (e.g., by means of second messengers). [3]

efficacy The extent to which a ligand-receptor binding initiates a biological action (e.g., the ability of an agonist to activate its receptor). [1]

Eldepryl See *selegiline*. [5]

electrical self-stimulation A procedure whereby an animal self-administers a weak electrical shock to a specific brain area due to the reinforcing properties of the stimulation. [4]

electrical synapses Physical connection between adjacent neurons that permits electrical current to flow from one cell to the other. [3]

electroencephalography (EEG) Technique used to measure brain activity by using electrodes taped on the scalp to obtain electrical recordings in humans. [4]

electrostatic pressure Force drawing an ion to either side of the cell membrane in an attempt to balance or neutralize ionic charges. [2]

elevated plus-maze Maze type that involves a cross-shaped maze that has two open arms, two enclosed arms, and has been raised off the floor. It is used to test a rodent's level of anxiety. [4]

ELISA See *enzyme-linked immunosorbent assay*. [4]

endocannabinoid membrane transporter Hypothesized membrane carrier protein that binds anandamide and transports it into the cell. [14]

endocannabinoids Lipid-like substances produced from arachidonic acid that activate CB receptors. [14]

endocrine glands Specialized organs that secrete hormones into the bloodstream. [3]

endomorphins Group of endogenous opioid peptides in the CNS that selectively bind to the opioid receptor and eliminate pain. [11]

endorphins Group of endogeneous peptides in the brain that stimulate mu and delta opioid receptors, reducing pain and enhancing one's general mood. [11]

endosomes Membranous structures present in axon terminals that play a role in one type of vesicle recycling. [3]

endozepines Endogenously synthesized neuropeptides that exert BDZ-like effects by positively modulating $GABA_A$ receptor function. [8]

entacapone (Comtan) COMT inhibitor used in conjunction with L-DOPA to treat Parkinson's disease. [5]

entactogens Compounds that promote empathy and closeness to others in the absence of hallucinogenic effects. [6]

enteral Drug administration by oral or rectal routes. [1]

enteric nervous system Large system of ganglia located in the muscle walls of the intestines. Some of the neurons within this system use 5-HT as a neurotransmitter. [6]

enterochromaffin cells Specialized secretory cells within the walls of the intestines that synthesize and secrete 5-HT. [6]

enzyme induction Increase in liver drug-metabolizing enzymes associated with repeated drug use, which leads to drug tolerance. [1]

enzyme inhibition In drug metabolism, reduction in liver enzyme activity associated with a specific drug may cause more intense or prolonged effects of other drugs taken at the same time. [1]

enzyme-linked immunosorbent assay (ELISA) An immunoassay, designed to quantify a specific molecule such as a protein or hormone, that does not rely on radioactivity for detection but instead uses a colored or fluorescent reaction product. [4]

ephedrine   Psychostimulant that is a constituent of the herb *Ephedra vulgaris*. [12]

EPI   See *epinephrine*. [3, 5]

Epidiolex   Oil-based formulation containing 99% CBD extracted from low-THC hemp plants and used for treating several rare seizure disorders in infants or children. [14]

epidural   Method that involves administration of a drug into the cerebrospinal fluid surrounding the spinal cord. [1]

epigenetic   Modifications to a gene arising from environmental or behavioral factors that can influence gene function. [1]

epinephrine (EPI)   Hormone related to NE that belongs to a group called catecholamines. It is secreted by the chromaffin cells of the adrenal medulla, and it produces the "fight-or-flight" response by regulating the diversion of energy and blood to muscles. Also known as adrenaline. [3, 5]

EPSPs   See *excitatory postsynaptic potentials*. [2]

equilibrium potential for potassium   Point at which the electrostatic pressure and the concentration gradient for potassium are balanced. [2]

ergogenic effects   Effects that produce enhancement of physical performance. Often applied to the performance-enhancing effects of AAS. [16]

ergot   Fungus, *Claviceps purpurea*, that infects certain grains and that contains several important alkaloids from which the structure of LSD was derived. [15]

ergotism   Disorder caused by ergot-contaminated grains that can lead to death. [15]

ERPs   See *event-related potentials*. [4]

eserine   See *physostigmine*. [7]

estradiol   Specific estrogen and a powerful female sex hormone. [3]

estrogens   Female sex hormones either secreted by the ovaries or synthesized to produce the same effects. [3]

ethanol   Proper chemical name for the type of alcohol consumed by humans. Similar to BDZs, it acts as a CNS-depressant in part by enhancing $GABA_A$ receptor activity. [8, 10]

EVALI   See *e-cigarette, or vaping, product-associated lung injury*. [13]

event-related potentials (ERPs)   Electrical changes in neuron activity in response to a sensory stimulus. [4]

excitatory amino acid neurotransmitters   Transmitters, including glutamate, aspartate, and some other amino acids, that cause an excitatory response in most neurons of the brain or spinal cord. [8]

excitatory amino acid transporters (EAATs)   Proteins that transport glutamate and aspartate across the plasma membrane. There are five such transporters, designated EAAT1 to EAAT5. [8]

excitatory postsynaptic potentials (EPSPs)   Small localized membrane depolarizations of a postsynaptic neuron that result from neurotransmitters binding to specific receptors that open ion channels. EPSPs move the membrane potential closer to the threshold for firing. [2]

excitotoxic lesions   Selective lesions of cell bodies in a specific brain area produced by local infusion of an excitotoxic amino acid. [8]

excitotoxicity hypothesis   Theory that excessive glutamate or other excitatory amino acid exposure results in prolonged depolarization of receptive neurons, leading to their damage or death. [8]

executive function   Collection of higher-order cognitive abilities including planning, organization, problem solving, mental flexibility, and valuation of incentives. The prefrontal cortex plays an important role in executive function. [9]

Exelon   See *rivastigmine*. [7]

exocytosis   Method by which vesicles release substances and neurotransmitters, characterized by fusion of the vesicle and the cell membrane, specifically the axon terminal membrane in the case of neurotransmitters. The vesicle opens toward the synaptic cleft allowing neurotransmitter molecules to diffuse out. [3]

expression   Process that leads to manifestation of a sensitized response and that requires enhanced reactivity of DA nerve terminals in the nucleus accumbens. [12]

expression phase   The period of time after a tetanic stimulation is administered, characterized by enhanced synaptic strength (i.e., LTP). [8]

extracellular fluid   Salty fluid surrounding nerve cells that provides oxygen, nutrients, and chemical signals, and that removes secreted cell waste. [2]

extracellular recording   Method of taking measurements of cell firing by inserting a fine-tipped electrode into the extracellular fluid surrounding the cell. [4]

F

FAAH   See *fatty acid amide hydrolase*. [14]

face validity   Term used to describe the relationship between a testing procedure done on animals and its direct correlation to human test results or behavior. [4]

FAS   See *fetal alcohol syndrome*. [10]

FASD   See *fetal alcohol spectrum disorder*. [10]

fatigue   State of weariness that diminishes an individual's energy and mental capacity. [20]

fatty acid amide hydrolase (FAAH)   Enzyme that metabolizes endocannabinoids, especially anandamide. [14]

fatty liver   Damaging effect of alcohol characterized by the accumulation of triglycerides inside liver cells. [10]

fear-potentiated startle   Enhancement of a startle response when the stimulus is preceded by the presentation of a conditioned fear stimulus. [4]

fenestrations   Large pores in endothelial cells allowing rapid exchange of materials between blood vessels and tissue. [1]

fenfluramine   Drug similar in structure to amphetamine that stimulates 5-HT release. It is an appetite suppressor formerly used as a treatment for obesity. [6]

festination   Uncontrollable acceleration of gait. [20]

fetal alcohol spectrum disorders (FASD)   A cluster of disorders due to developmental abnormalities caused by prenatal exposure to alcohol. Features vary but may include learning disabilities, poor impulse control, and attention deficits. [10]

fetal alcohol syndrome (FAS)   The damaging developmental effects of prenatal alcohol exposure. [10]

fetal solvent syndrome   Cluster of symptoms, typically including cognitive deficits and craniofacial (i.e., head and face) abnormalities, seen in some newborn infants of inhalant-abusing women. [16]

first-order kinetics   Term used to describe exponential elimination of drugs from the bloodstream. [1]

first-pass metabolism   Phenomenon in which the liver metabolizes some of a drug before it can circulate through the body, particularly when the drug has been taken orally. [1]

fissures   Deep grooves of the cerebral cortex. [2]

flashbacks   Reexperience of the perceptual effects of a previously consumed psychedelic compound in the absence of taking the drug again. [15]

fluoxetine (Prozac)   A member of the class of selective serotonin reuptake inhibitors. It is used as an antidepressant. [6]

fMRI   See *functional MRI*. [4]

FMR1   See *fragile X mental retardation gene*. [8]

FMRP   See fragile X mental retardation protein. [8]

focused stereotypies   Behaviors produced by high doses of psychostimulants (e.g., cocaine and amphetamine) and characterized by repetitive and aimless movement. [12]

follicle-stimulating hormone (FSH)   Hormone secreted by the anterior pituitary that helps stimulate gonadal growth and function. [3]

forced swim test   See *behavioral despair test*. [4]

fragile X mental retardation 1 gene (FMR1)   Gene that codes for the fragile X mental retardation protein (FMRP). [8]

fragile X mental retardation protein (FMRP)   Protein encoded by the *FMR1* gene that regulates local protein synthesis at postsynaptic sites. Deficiency of FMRP due to *FMR1* mutations is the cause of fragile X syndrome. [8]

fragile X syndrome   Congenital disorder that is a leading cause of intellectual disability and autistic symptoms. It is caused by a mutation in the *fragile X mental retardation 1* gene (*FMR1*). [8]

freebasing   Smoking the freebase form of cocaine obtained by dissolving cocaine HCl in water, adding an alkaline solution, and then extracting with an organic solvent. [12]

frontal   Tissue sections cut parallel to the face. [2]

frontal lobe   One of four lobes of the cerebral cortex. It is responsible for movement and executive planning. [2]

frovatriptan (Frova) $5\text{-HT}_{1B/1D}$ receptor agonist that causes constriction of cerebral blood vessels. It is used to treat migraine headaches. [6]

Frova   See *frovatriptan*. [6]

FSH   See *follicle-stimulating hormone*. [3]

fuels   Class of inhalants composed of volatile liquids or gases that serve many purposes, including automobile fuel, fuels for lamps and heating appliances, lighter fluids, and propellants used in many kinds of spray cans. [16]

functional MRI (fMRI)   Technique used to regionally visualize brain activity by detecting the increase in blood oxygen levels through magnetic resonance measurements of oxygenated and oxygen-depleted hemoglobin. [4]

G

G protein–coupled receptor   Slow-acting receptor type composed of a single large protein in the cell membrane that activates G proteins. It may also be called a metabotropic receptor. [3]

G proteins   Group of membrane proteins that are necessary for neurotransmitter signaling by metabotropic receptors. They operate by regulating ion channels or effector enzymes involved in the synthesis or breakdown of second messengers, ultimately causing biochemical or physiological changes in the postsynaptic cell. [3]

GABA   See *γ-aminobutyric acid*. [8]

GABA aminotransferase (GABA-T)   Enzyme that breaks down GABA in GABAergic neurons and astrocytes. [8]

GABA_A receptor   Ionotropic receptor for GABA that allows Cl⁻ ions to enter the cell, thereby inhibiting cell firing. [8]

GABA_B receptor   Metabotropic receptor for GABA. [8]

Gabitril   See *tiagabine*. [8]

GAD   See *generalized anxiety disorder or glutamic acid decarboxylase*. [8, 17]

gait   Pattern of limb movement during locomotion over a solid surface. [4]

galantamine (Reminyl)   Drug that blocks AChE activity. It is used in the treatment of Alzheimer's disease. [7]

γ-aminobutyric acid (GABA)   Amino acid that is the principal inhibitory neurotransmitter in the CNS. [8]

γ-hydroxybutyrate (GHB)   Chemical similar in structure to GABA that produces sedative and anesthetic effects in users and that is used medicinally as well as recreationally. [16]

ganglia   A cluster of cell bodies outside the CNS. [2]

gaseous transmitters   Substances in the gas phase that acts as neurotransmitters in the body. Sometimes referred to as gasotransmitters. [3]

gases   See *gaseous transmitters*. [3]

GAT-1   Member of the plasma membrane GABA transporter family, expressed in neurons and astrocytes. [8]

GAT-2   Member of the plasma membrane GABA transporter family, expressed in neurons and astrocytes. [8]

GAT-3   Member of the family of plasma membrane GABA transporters that is expressed only in astrocytes. [8]

gated channels   Ion channels that are normally in a closed configuration that can be opened momentarily by specific stimuli. [2]

gateway theory   Theory proposing that use of certain recreational drugs, particularly during childhood or adolescence, increases the risk of progressing to other substances. For example, tobacco or alcohol have been proposed as gateways to marijuana use, and in turn marijuana has been proposed as a gateway to so-called "hard drugs" like cocaine or heroin. [9]

gene therapy   Application of DNA that encodes a specific protein to increase or block expression of the gene product to correct a clinical condition. [1]

generalized anxiety disorder (GAD)   An anxiety disorder characterized by excessive worrying that does not have a specific cause. [17]

genes   Portions of a chromosome that code for particular proteins. [2]

genetic models   Creation of knockout, knockin, or transgenic mice to produce a phenotype analagous to the human clinical disorder of interest. [19]

genetic polymorphisms   Genetic variations in a population resulting in multiple forms of a particular protein. [1]

genome-wide association studies (GWAS) A modification of microarray technology used to compare the incidence of single-nucleotide polymorphisms and copy number variants in DNA samples from people with a given disorder and matched controls. [4, 10]

GH See *growth hormone*. [3]

GHB See *γ-hydroxybutyrate*. [16]

glial cells Supporting cells of the nervous system that insulate, protect, and metabolically support neurons. [2]

glucagon Hormone secreted by the islets of Langerhans that, along with insulin, regulates metabolic energy sources in the body. [3]

glucocorticoid hypothesis Theory that stress-induced elevation of glucocorticoid levels accelerates brain cell damage, including decreased dendritic branching, loss of dendritic spines, apoptosis in multiple brain regions, and failure of neurogenesis in the hippocampus, thereby leading to the symptoms of depression. [18]

glucocorticoids Hormones such as cortisol that belong to the steroid family and are secreted by the adrenal cortex at increased amounts in response to an acute stressor. They exert several biological functions, including suppression of immune function, regulation of glucose and other metabolic fuels, and modulation of mood and consolidation of emotional memories. [3]

glutamate The ionized form of glutamic acid. It is an excitatory amino acid neurotransmitter of the CNS. [8]

glutamatergic neurons Neurons that use glutamate as a transmitter. [8]

glutamic acid decarboxylase (GAD) Enzyme that transforms glutamate into GABA. [8]

glutaminase Enzyme that transforms glutamine into glutamate. [8]

glutamine Precursor of the transmitter-related glutamate. [8]

glutamine synthetase Enzyme in astrocytes that converts glutamate into glutamine. [8]

glycine Amino acid characterized by the lack of a functional group. It is a co-agonist with glutamate for the NMDA receptor. [8]

GnRH See *gonadotropin-releasing hormone*. [3]

gonadotropin-releasing hormone (GnRH) Hormone that stimulates FSH and LH release. It is synthesized by neurons of the hypothalamus. [3]

gonads Glands that secrete sex-specific steroid hormones. [3]

granisetron (Kytril) Drug that blocks 5-HT$_3$ receptors. It is used to treat the nausea and vomiting side effects of cancer chemotherapy. [6]

green tobacco illness Cluster of symptoms produced by exposure to nicotine in workers harvesting tobacco plants. [13]

growth hormone (GH) Hormone secreted by the anterior pituitary that increases production of IGF-I in peripheral organs. [3]

guanfacine (Intuniv) α_{2A}-adrenergic agonist prescribed for the treatment of ADHD. Guanfacine is believed to improve attention and memory by stimulating α_{2A}-adrenergic receptors in the prefrontal cortex. [5]

gut–brain axis Bidirectional system of communication between the brain and the gastrointestinal tract. [3]

GWAS See *genome-wide association studies*. [4, 10]

gyri (sing. gyrus) Bulges of tissue between the grooves in the cerebral cortex. [2]

H

half-life Time required to remove half of the drug from the blood. It is referred to as $t_{1/2}$. [1]

hallucinogen persisting perception disorder (HPPD) Disorder of psychedelic/hallucinogenic drug use characterized by severe perceptual symptoms (i.e., flashbacks) that persist for a long period of time following drug use and are experienced sufficiently frequently to cause significant distress or impairment to the individual. [15]

hallucinogen rating scale Psychometric scale developed to quantify the subjective effects of psychedelic/hallucinogenic agents. [15]

hallucinogenic Adjectival form of hallucinogen. [6, 15]

halogenated hydrocarbons Class of inhalants composed of hydrocarbon molecules possessing one or more chlorine or fluorine atoms. [16]

haloperidol D$_2$ receptor blocker that can induce catalepsy in animals when administered in high doses. It is used clinically as an antipsychotic agent. [5]

hangover Effect of heavy alcohol consumption that may be a sign of withdrawal, acute toxicity, or other negative effects on body regulation. [10]

hashish Type of potent cannabis derivative that is smoked or eaten. [14]

HD See *Huntington's disease*. [20]

hemicholinium-3 (HC-3) Drug that blocks the choline transporter in cholinergic nerve terminals. [7]

heritability The relative contribution of genetics to the variability of a trait within a population. [9]

heteroreceptors Axon receptors that are specific for neurotransmitters released by other cells at axoaxonic synapses. They may either decrease or increase further neurotransmitter release. [3]

5-HIAA See *5-hydroxyindoleacetic acid*. [6]

hippocampal sclerosis Brain cell loss in the hippocampus that occurs in some patients with temporal lobe epilepsy. [8]

hippocampus Subcortical structure of the limbic system that helps to establish long-term, contextual, and spatial memories. The hippocampus is where LTP was first discovered and is also one of the brain areas damaged in Alzheimer's disease. [2]

homovanillic acid (HVA) Major metabolite of DA. [5]

horizontal Brain sections cut parallel to the horizon. [2]

hormones Chemical substances secreted by endocrine glands into the bloodstream, where they travel to target locations in the body. [3]

hot plate test Method used to evaluate analgesia by subjecting an animal to a heated metal plate and measuring the time it takes to make an avoidance response. [4]

HPPD See *hallucinogen persisting perception disorder*. [15]

5-HT See *serotonin*. [6]

5-HT transporter (SERT) Membrane protein that is responsible for 5-HT reuptake from the extracellular fluid. [6]

5-HTP See *5-hydroxytryptophan*. [6]

HTT See *huntingtin gene*. [20]

human germline engineering Application of genetic engineering whereby the human genome is edited in such a way that the modification affects gametes and is heritable. [4]

human microbiome Totality of microbial cells that colonize various parts of the human body. [3]

huntingtin gene (HTT) Gene containing a CAG trinucleotide repeat. A mutation resulting in more than 40 repeats of the CAG sequence results in Huntington's disease. [20]

Huntington's chorea Involuntary jerky, writhing movements of the limbs. [20]

Huntington's disease (HD) An inherited disorder caused by a genetic defect on chromosome 4. The defect results in the abnormal repetition of a CAG sequence. The disorder causes progressive degeneration of nerve cells in the brain resulting in movement, cognitive, and psychiatric symptoms. [20]

HVA See *homovanillic acid*. [5]

5-hydroxyindoleacetic acid (5-HIAA) Major metabolite of 5-HT that is produced by the action of MAO. [6]

6-hydroxydopamine (6-OHDA) Neurotoxin similar in structure to DA that damages catecholaminergic nerve terminals and is used to study catecholamine pathways. [5, 20]

2-hydroxysaclofen Chemical analog of baclofen that is a competitive antagonist at the $GABA_B$ receptor. [8]

5-hydroxytryptamine (5-HT) See *serotonin*. [6]

5-hydroxytryptophan (5-HTP) Substance produced from tryptophan by the enzyme tryptophan hydroxylase. It is the immediate precursor of 5-HT. [6]

8-hydroxy-2-(di-n-propylamino) tetralin (8-OH-DPAT) Drug that stimulates $5-HT_{1A}$ receptors. Effects include increased appetite, reduced anxiety, reduced alcohol cravings, and a lower body temperature. [6]

hyperalgesia Condition characterized by an increased sensitivity to pain. [14]

hypercapnia Elevated blood CO_2 levels. [6]

hyperkatifeia Highly distressing emotional and motivational state that can occur during withdrawal from chronic recreational drug use. [9]

hyperpolarization Change in membrane potential making the inside of a cell more negative relative to the resting potential, reducing the likelihood that the cell will fire an action potential. [2]

hypnagogic hallucinations Vivid dreamlike sensations that occur during the daytime in some patients with narcolepsy. [3]

hypnotics Drugs, such as barbiturates and benzodiazepines, that help a person fall asleep and stay asleep. [17]

hypoglutamate model NMDA antagonists produce rodent behaviors analogous to the positive, negative, and cognitive symptoms of schizophrenia. [19]

hypothalamic releasing hormones Neuropeptide hormones synthesized by neurons of the hypothalamus and carried by blood vessels to the anterior pituitary, where they control the release of many of the pituitary hormones. [3]

hypothalamus Structure of the diencephalon located at the base of the brain, ventral to the thalamus. It provides many functions important for survival, including the maintenance of body temperature and salt balance, regulation of hunger and thirst, control of the ANS and pituitary gland, and modulation of emotional responses. [2]

hypotonia Abnormally low muscle tone. [5]

I

ibogaine Psychoactive substance derived from the iboga shrub. It is used recreationally for its psychedelic properties, and it may also be helpful in treating people with a substance use disorder. [15]

IBS See *irritable bowel syndrome*. [6]

IM See *intramuscular*. [1]

immunocytochemistry (ICC) Technique that uses antibodies to determine the brain areas or neurons that contain a specific antigen such as a protein, neuropeptide, or neurotransmitter. [4]

in situ hybridization (ISH) Technique used to locate cells that manufacture a specific protein or peptide by detecting the specific mRNA sequence coding for that substance. It can also be used to study changes in regional mRNA levels (i.e., gene expression). [4]

in vitro Refers to measurements performed outside the living body (traditionally in a test tube). [4]

in vivo Refers to measurements observed in the living organism. [4]

in vivo voltammetry Technique used to measure neurotransmitter release in the brain of an awake, freely moving animal by using a microelectrode to measure electrochemical responses to an applied electrical signal. [4]

25I-NBOMe Member of the NBOMe class of hallucinogens containing an iodine atom attached to the phenyl ring. [15]

inborn errors of metabolism Rare genetic disorders that affect key metabolic pathways, often leading to clinically significant symptoms. [5]

incentive salience Psychological process by which drug-related stimuli gain increased prominence and attractiveness. It is an important component of the incentive-sensitization model of addiction. [9]

incentive sensitization theory Model of addiction based on the theory that repeated drug use leads to an increase in "wanting" the drug (i.e., craving) but no increase in drug "liking" (reward or euphoria) because only the neural system underlying drug "wanting" becomes sensitized. [9]

incubation Time-dependent increase in drug craving and drug seeking behavior during abstinence. [12]

Inderal See *propranolol*. [5]

induction 1. Increase in liver enzymes specific for drug metabolism in response to repeated drug use. 2. Process that establishes psychostimulant sensitization by activating glutamate NMDA receptors and, in some cases, D_1 receptors. [10, 12]

induction phase Phase of LTP, occurring during and shortly after administration of a tetanic stimulus, which requires activation of NMDA receptors. [8]

inferior Located toward the underside of the brain in humans. [2]

infusion pump Drug delivery via an implanted pump (e.g., subcutaneous) that delivers regular, constant doses to the body or into the cerebral ventricles. [1]

Ingrezza See *valbenazine*. [5]

inhalants Group of volatile substances, such as glue, that may be misused as a drug by inhaling the fumes. [16]

inhalation Route of drug administration involving intake through the lungs. [1]

inhibitory postsynaptic potentials (IPSPs) Hyperpolarizing responses of a postsynaptic cell typically resulting from neurotransmitter-mediated ion channel opening. [2]

inositol trisphosphate (IP_3) Second messenger generated by the phosphoinositide second messenger system; stimulates release of calcium from intracellular stores. [3]

insulin Polypeptide hormone that is secreted by the islets of Langerhans and, along with glucagon, regulates glucose and metabolic energy sources in the body. It stimulates uptake of glucose and various amino acids from the bloodstream into tissues. [3, 6]

integration Process at the axon hillock whereby several small depolarizations or hyperpolarizations will summate to create a larger change in membrane potential. Because of the same additive effects, simultaneous depolarizations and hyperpolarizations tend to cancel each other out. [2]

intercellular clefts Small gaps between adjacent cells. These gaps between endothelial cells of typical blood vessels permit the passage of molecules to and from the blood. [1]

Interferon beta 1a Drug used in the treatment of relapsing forms of MS. [20]

Interferon beta 1b Drug used in the treatment of relapsing forms of MS. [20]

intermittent smokers Individuals who maintain a stable habit of non-daily cigarette smoking. [13]

interneurons Nerve cells in the CNS and spinal cord that form complex neural circuits providing sensorimotor integration. [2]

intracellular recording Method of measuring neuronal activity by inserting a fine-tipped electrode into the cell. [4]

intracerebroventricular Route of drug administration involving delivery of the compound into the cerebrospinal fluid of the ventricles. [1]

intracranial Route of drug administration involving delivery of the compound into the brain tissue. [1]

intramuscular (IM) Route of drug administration involving injection of the compound into a muscle. [1]

intranasal administration Route of drug administration involving delivery of the compound to the nasal mucosa. [1]

intraperitoneal (IP) Route of drug administration involving injection of the compound through the abdominal wall into the peritoneal cavity—the space that surrounds the abdominal organs. It is a common route of administration for small laboratory animals. [1]

intrathecal Route of administration in which a drug is infused into the subarachnoid space of the central nervous system. [1]

intravenous (IV) Route of drug administration involving delivery of the compound directly into the bloodstream by means of injection into a vein. [1]

Intuniv See *guanfacine*. [5]

inverse agonists Substances that activate a receptor but produce the opposite effect of typical agonists at that receptor. [1, 8]

Inversine See *mecamylamine*. [7]

ionization Process involving the dissociation of an electrically neutral molecule into charged particles (ions). [1]

ionotropic receptor Fast-acting receptor type comprised of several subunits that come together in the cell membrane. The receptor has an ion channel at its center, which is regulated by neurotransmitters binding to specific sites on the receptor causing the channel to open. It may also be called a ligand-gated channel receptor. [3]

IP See *intraperitoneal*. [1]

ipsapirone Drug that stimulates 5-HT$_{1A}$ receptors. Some of its effects include increased appetite, reduced anxiety, reduced alcohol cravings, and a lower body temperature. [6]

IPSPs See *inhibitory postsynaptic potentials*. [2]

irreversible inhibitor Inhibitor (e.g., of an enzyme, receptor, or transporter) for which the blocking effect does not wear off until new molecules of the inhibited protein have been synthesized. [5]

irritable bowel syndrome (IBS) Gastrointestinal disorder characterized by abdominal pain, gas and bloating, frequent abnormal bowel movements (diarrhea, constipation, or an alternation between the two), and mucus in the stool. [6]

ISH See *in situ hybridization*. [4]

islets of Langerhans Endocrine gland in the pancreas that secretes insulin and glucagon. [3]

isoproterenol (Isuprel) β-adrenergic receptor agonist. It is sometimes used to treat bradycardia. [5]

IV See *intravenous*. [1]

J

John Cunningham (JC) virus Common virus that is present in more than 50% of the population. Most people acquire it sometime during childhood. It lives in a latent harmless state in the kidneys and the gastrointestinal tract in individuals with healthy immune systems but becomes life-threatening in those whose immune systems are compromised. The virus causes progressive multifocal leukoencephalopathy (PML), a rare, but frequently deadly condition that destroys myelin, a protective covering of nerve cells in the brain. [20]

K

kainate receptor An ionotropic glutamate receptor selective for the agonist kainic acid. [8]

κ-receptors An opioid receptor located in the striatum, amygdala, hypothalamus, and pituitary gland that may help regulate pain, perception, gut motility, dysphoria, water balance, hunger, temperature, and neuroendocrine function. [11]

Kemadrin See *procyclidine*. [7]

ketamine Uncompetitive antagonist of the NMDA receptor that binds to a site within the receptor channel. It is a dissociative anesthetic used in both human and veterinary medicine, and it is also used recreationally. [8, 15]

ketanserin Drug that blocks 5-HT$_{2A}$ receptors. [6]

kiss-and-run Hypothesized type of exocytosis in which the synaptic vesicle does not collapse during the neurotransmitter release process, thus eliminating the need for an endocytotic mechanism to retrieve vesicle membrane components from the membrane of the axon terminal. [3]

knockin mice Mice that have been genetically modified either by inserting a novel gene into the animals' DNA or by modifying one or more nucleotides at an existing genetic locus. Both cases result in the production of a protein not found in wild-type mice. They are used experimentally for the same purposes as knockout mice. [4]

knockout mice Mice that are homozygous for the targeted deletion of a specific gene. They are used to study the normal function of that gene as well as the involvement of the gene in behavioral and physiological responses to various psychoactive drugs. [4]

kynurenine Metabolite of tryptophan synthesized by either the brain and immune system enzyme indoleamine 2,3-dioxygenase or by the liver enzyme tryptophan dioxygenase. [6]

Kytril See *granisetron*. [6]

L

L-2-amino-4-phosphonobutyrate (L-AP4) Synthetic amino acid that is an agonist selective for metabotropic glutamate autoreceptors. [8]

L-DOPA Precursor necessary for the synthesis of DA. L-DOPA is formed by the addition of a hydroxyl group to tyrosine by the enzyme TH. It is used to treat Parkinson's disease by increasing striatal DA formation. [5, 20]

lasmiditan (Reyvow) 5-HT$_{1F}$ receptor agonist used to treat migraine headaches. [6]

late LTP (L-LTP) Form of LTP that is dependent on protein synthesis and that can last for much longer periods of time than early LTP. [8]

lateral Located to either side of the body or brain. [2]

laterodorsal tegmental nuclei (LDTg) Structure within the dorsal lateral pons containing cholinergic neurons that project to the ventral tegmental area (important for stimulating VTA dopamine neurons) and others that project to the brainstem and thalamus (important for behavioral arousal, sensory processing, and initiation of rapid-eye-movement sleep). [7]

LBD See *Lewy body dementia*. [20]

LC See *locus coeruleus*. [2, 5]

LDTg See *laterodorsal tegmental nucleus*. [7]

learned helplessness A classic screening device for antidepressant drugs. After being subjected to periods of unescapable foot shock, rodents fail to respond when given the opportunity to avoid or escape an aversive event. Antidepressant drugs increase appropriate responding. [4]

lesioning Process whereby brain cells are destroyed either by using an electrode to administer a high radio frequency current or by injecting a neurotoxin that kills the cells. [4]

leukoencephalopathy General term for disorders involving damage to the brain's white matter. [16]

levalbuterol (Xopenex) Selective β$_2$-adrenoceptor agonist administered as an inhaler to treat the symptoms of asthma. [5]

Levodopa See *L-DOPA*. [20]

Lewy body Abnormal aggregate of protein that develops inside neurons in Parkinson's disease and Lewy body dementia. [20]

Lewy body dementia (LBD) Progressive form of dementia that is similar in symptomology to Parkinson's disease and Alzheimer's disease. Characterized by abnormal accumulations of proteins (Lewy bodies) in the nuclei of neurons in the brain that control memory and movement. [20]

LH See *luteinizing hormone*. [3]

ligand Molecule that selectively binds to a receptor. [1]

ligand-gated channel receptors See *ionotropic receptor*. [3]

ligand-gated channels Group of ion channels that are regulated by a ligand binding to a receptor site associated with that channel. [2]

light–dark crossing task Test used to determine a rodent's level of anxiety by placing it in a two-compartment box, one side lit and the other side dark. Fewer crossings and less time spent in the lighted side indicate greater anxiety. [4]

limbic system Neural network that integrates emotional responses and regulates motivated behavior, reinforcement, and learning. Some major structures include the limbic cortex, amygdala, nucleus accumbens, and hippocampus. [2]

linkage studies Methods used to locate genes responsible for a disorder, such as alcohol use disorder or schizophrenia, by comparing similarities in the genetic loci of families with affected members. [10, 18]

Lioresal See *baclofen*. [8]

lipids Fatty molecules in the body. Lipids are a major component of cell membranes, and some of them also act as neurotransmitters. [3]

lithium carbonate Drug that stabilizes moods, preventing episodes of mania and depression, in people with bipolar disorder. [18]

local potentials Small localized short-lived change in voltage across the cell membrane following the opening of ligand-gated channels. [2]

loci (sing. locus) The location of genes on a chromosome. [19]

locus coeruleus (LC) Collection of noradrenergic neurons in the reticular formation of the pons that supplies most of the NE to the cortex, limbic system, thalamus, and hypothalamus. These cells cause arousal and increased attention when active. [2, 5]

lofexidine (Lucemyra) Selective α2-adrenergic receptor agonist that stimulates autoreceptors and inhibits noradrenergic cell firing. It is used to reduce symptoms of opioid withdrawal. [5]

long-term depression (LTD) Type of synaptic plasticity resulting in weakening of synaptic connections. [8]

long-term potentiation (LTP) Phenomenon whereby synaptic connections are strengthened for a period of at least an hour. It requires activation of NMDA receptors for its induction and AMPA receptors for its expression. [8]

Lopressor See *metoprolol*. [5]

lorcaserin (Belviq) Selective 5-HT$_{2C}$ receptor agonist. It is used in the treatment of obesity. [6]

Lotronex See *alosetron*. [6]

LSD See *lysergic acid diethylamide*. [6, 15]

LTD See *long-term depression*. [8]

LTP See *long-term potentiation*. [8]

Lucemyra See *lofexidine*. [5]

luteinizing hormone (LH) Hormone secreted by the anterior pituitary that stimulates gonadal growth and function, including increased estrogen and androgen secretion. [3]

lysergic acid Core structural unit of all ergot alkaloids. [15]

lysergic acid diethylamide (LSD) Psychedelic/hallucinogenic drug that is synthesized from lysergic acid and based on alkaloids found in ergot fungus. It is thought to produce its effects mainly by stimulating 5-HT$_{2A}$ receptors in the brain. [6, 15]

lysis Bursting of a cell. [8]

M

macroelectrode Device used to electrically stimulate deep brain regions while monitoring behavior or recording the summated electrical response of thousands of neurons. [4]

MAGL See *monoacylglycerol lipase*. [14]

magnetic resonance imaging (MRI) Technique used to visualize in high resolution, detailed slices through the brain or other organ by taking computerized measurements of the signals emitted by atoms in the tissue as they are exposed to a strong magnetic field. Computer technology permits recreation of the structure in 3-dimensions. [4]

magnetic resonance spectroscopy (MRS) Using MRI-generated data, MRS calculates the quantity of brain chemicals such as glutamate. [4]

magnocellular neurons General term for neurons with large cell bodies. Included within this category are neurosecretory neurons located in the paraventricular and supraoptic nuclei of the hypothalamus that project their axons to the posterior pituitary gland where they release vasopressin and oxytocin into the bloodstream to act as hormones. [3]

major depression Type of affective disorder characterized by extreme recurring episodes of dysphoria and negative thinking that are reflected in behavior. [18]

male hypogonadism Condition involving deficient functioning of the testes, abnormally low secretion of testosterone, and reduced sperm production. [16]

MAO See *monoamine oxidase*. [5]

MAO inhibitors (MAOIs) Class of drugs that inhibit monoamine oxidase (MAO), thereby causing an accumulation of catecholamines and serotonin in the brain. They are often used to treat clinical depression. [18]

MAOIs See *MAO inhibitors*. [18, 20]

marble burying task See *defensive burying*. [4]

marijuana Crude mixture of dried and crumbled leaves, small stems, and flowering tops of the cannabis plant. Commonly smoked for recreational purposes but can also be used for medicinal purposes where permitted legally. [14]

Marinol See *dronabinol*. [14]

maternal separation Technique used to test the role of early-life stress as a factor in the development of depression, substance misuse, and other psychopathology. Week-old animals are separated from their mothers for brief periods daily. [4]

mavoglurant Selective mGluR5 antagonist that was developed and clinically tested for the treatment of fragile X syndrome. [8]

MDMA See *3,4-methylenedioxymethamphetamine*. [6]

MDPV Cathinone derivative (3,4-methylenedioxypyrovalerone) that is a misused stimulant drug. Common street names are "Vanilla Sky," "Ivory Wave," and "Energy-1." [12]

mecamylamine (Inversine) Antagonist at nicotinic ACh receptors, particularly at autonomic ganglia. It can be used clinically to treat hypertension. [7, 13]

medial Located near the center or midline of the body or brain. [2]

median eminence Area in the hypothalamus that is not isolated from chemicals in the blood and where hypothalamic-releasing hormones are secreted for transport to the anterior pituitary gland. [3]

median raphe nuclei (sing. nucleus) (MRN) Structure located in the area of the caudal midbrain and rostral pons that contains a large number of serotonergic neurons. In conjunction with the dorsal raphe nucleus, it is responsible for most of the serotonergic fibers in the forebrain. Together they regulate many functions, including sleep, aggression, impulsiveness, and emotions. [2, 6]

medical model See *disease model*. [9]

medication-assisted treatment Treatment modality for opioid use disorder that combines detoxification, pharmacological support, and counseling. [11]

medulla Structure located in the caudal brain stem responsible for regulating heart rate, digestion, respiration, blood pressure, coughing, and vomiting. [2]

melanocortin receptor neurons Group of neurons within the paraventricular nucleus of the hypothalamus that express MC_3 and MC_4 melanocortin receptors and participate in the regulation of hunger and eating behavior. [6]

melatonin Hormone that regulates rhythmic functions in the body. It is secreted by the pineal gland. [3]

memantine (Namenda) Uncompetitive NMDA receptor antagonist that binds to a site within the receptor channel. It is used to treat moderate to severe Alzheimer's disease. [8, 20]

meninges Layers of protective tissue located between the bones of the skull and vertebrae and the tissue of the brain and spinal cord. [2]

5-MeO-DMT See *5-methoxy-dimethyltryptamine*. [15]

MEOS See *microsomal ethanol oxidizing system*. [10]

mephedrone Cathinone derivative (4-methylmethcathinone) that is a misused stimulant drug. Common street names are "meow meow," "M-Cat," "Meph," "bounce," "bubbles," and "Neodove." [12]

3-mercaptopropionic acid Drug that blocks GABA synthesis, inducing convulsions. [8]

mescal button Crown of the peyote cactus, *Lophophora williamsii*, which can be dried and ingested to obtain the hallucinogenic drug mescaline. [15]

mescaline Psychedelic/hallucinogenic drug produced by several cacti species, especially the peyote cactus, *Lophophora williamsii*. [15]

mesocortical dopamine pathway Group of dopaminergic axons that originates in the VTA and travels to the cerebral cortex, including the prefrontal, cingulate, and entorhinal cortices. It may also be called the mesocortical tract. [5]

mesolimbic dopamine pathway Group of dopaminergic axons that originates in the VTA and travels to structures of the limbic system, including the nucleus accumbens, septum, amygdala, and hippocampus. It may also be called the mesolimbic tract. [5]

Mestinon See *pyridostigmine*. [7]

metabolic tolerance Type of tolerance to a drug that is characterized by a reduced amount of drug available at the target tissue, often as a result of more-rapid drug metabolism. It is sometimes also called drug disposition tolerance. [1, 10]

metabolites Byproducts of biochemical pathways, such as those involved in neurotransmitter or drug inactivation. [5]

metabotropic glutamate receptor theory Theory that loss of FMRP causes exaggerated group I mGluR-related functions, resulting in the characteristics of fragile X syndrome. [8]

metabotropic receptor Slow-acting receptor type composed of a single large protein in the cell membrane that activates G proteins. It may also be called a G protein–coupled receptor. [3]

metaraminol (Aramine) Selective α_1-adrenergic receptor agonist used to treat hypotension. [5]

methadone A long-acting opioid drug that may be substituted for other opioids in order to prevent withdrawal symptoms. [11]

methadone maintenance program Most effective treatment program for opioid addicts that involves the substitution of the opioid with methadone to prevent withdrawal symptoms and craving to avoid a relapse. [11]

methamphetamine Psychostimulant that acts by increasing catecholamine release from nerve terminals. It can also cause neurotoxicity at high doses. [5, 12]

5-methoxy-dimethyltryptamine (5-MeO-DMT) Psychedelic/hallucinogenic drug found in certain South American plants. Its street name is "foxy" or "foxy methoxy." [15]

3-methoxy-4-hydroxy-phenylglycol (MHPG) Metabolite of NE, formed primarily as a result of NE breakdown in the brain. [5]

3,4-methylenedioxymethamphetamine (MDMA) Drug similar in structure to amphetamine that stimulates 5-HT release and is neurotoxic at high doses. It is a recreational drug that can be misused but also has therapeutic potential for treating severe cases of post-traumatic stress disorders. [6]

1-methyl-4-phenyl-1,2,3,6-tetrahydropyridine (MPTP) Dopamine neurotoxin sometimes used to produce an animal model of Parkinson's disease. [5]

methyllycaconitine (MLA) Blocks low-affinity nAChRs consisting only of α7 subunits. [13]

methylone Cathinone derivative (3,4-methylenedioxy-*N*-methylcathinone) that is a misusedstimulant drug. Common street names are "Explosion," "Neocor," and "Room Odorizer." [12]

methylphenidate (Ritalin) Synthetic psychostimulant that blocks catecholamine and serotonin reuptake and is used to treat ADHD. [5, 12]

methylxanthines Class of naturally occurring chemicals that include caffeine and theophylline. [13]

metoprolol (Lopressor) Selective β_1-adrenergic receptor antagonist. It limits the force of contraction of the heart muscles and is used for treating hypertension. [5]

Metrazol See *pentylenetetrazol*. [8]

mGluR1–mGluR8 Eight metabotropic glutamate receptors of the nervous system. They can inhibit cyclic adenosine monophosphate synthesis, activate the phosphoinositide second-messenger system, or inhibit glutamate release into the synaptic cleft. [8]

MHPG See *3-methoxy-4-hydroxy-phenylglycol*. [5]

microdialysis Technique used to measure neurotransmitter release in the brain of an awake, freely moving animal by collecting samples of extracellular fluid and then analyzing the samples biochemically using sensitive methods such as HPLC. Chemicals can also be applied to precise brain sites with the same technique. [4]

microelectrode Device used to electrically stimulate or record the response of a single cell intracellularly or extracellularly. [4]

microglia Small nonneuronal cells in the CNS that collect at points of cell damage or inflammation and demonstrate phagocytic behavior. [2]

microsomal enzymes Enzymes in liver cells responsible for metabolizing exogenous substances such as drugs. [1]

microsomal ethanol oxidizing system (MEOS) The cytochrome P450 enzyme CYP 2E1 that metabolizes ethanol and many other drugs. [10]

midodrine (ProAmatine) Selective α_1-adrenergic receptor agonist used to treat hypotension. [5]

midsagittal Section taken of the brain that divides it into left and right symmetrical pieces. [2]

mini-mental state exam (MMSE) Cognitive test for measuring the severity of dementia. [20]

Minipress See *prazosin*. [5]

Mirapex See *pramipexole*. [5]

mitochondria (sing. mitochrondrion) Organelles of the cell that produce energy, in the form of ATP, from glucose. [2]

mixed synapses Synapses at which both chemical and electrical communication occur. [3]

MK-801 (dizocilpine) Uncompetitive antagonist of the NMDA receptor that binds to a site within the receptor channel. [8]

MLA See *methyllycaconitine*. [13]

MMSE See *Mini-Mental State Examination*. [20]

moclobemide Selective MAO-A inhibitor approved in several countries outside of the United States for the treatment of depression and social anxiety. [5]

modafinil (Provigil) Synthetic psychostimulant that is used to treat patients with narcolepsy who exhibit excessive daytime sleepiness, people with obstructive sleep apnea, and people with disordered sleep due to shift work. [12]

monoacyl-glycerol lipase (MAGL) Enzyme primarily responsible for metabolism of the endocannabinoid 2-arachidonoylglycerol. [14]

monoamine Refers to a compound or transmitter that contains a single amine group. [3, 5]

monoamine hypothesis Theory that a reduced level of monoamines in the CNS will cause depressed moods, including clinical depression. [18]

monoamine oxidase (MAO) Enzyme responsible for metabolic breakdown of catecholamines and serotonin. [5]

monoamine oxidase inhibitors (MAOIs) See *MAO inhibitors*. [20]

monosodium glutamate (MSG) Sodium salt of glutamic acid. It is sometimes used as a flavor enhancer in food, and it exerts toxic effects on nerve cells when infused directly into the brain. [8]

moral model Model of addiction that treats addiction as a personal and moral problem. [9]

Morris water maze Maze type that involves repeatedly placing the animal in a pool of opaque water and testing its ability to use visual cues from outside the pool to find the escape platform. It is used to test spatial learning. [4]

motor efferents Nerve fibers originating in the CNS and traveling to the skeletal muscles, controlling voluntary movements. [2]

motor neurons Nerve cells that transmit electrical signals from the CNS to muscles. [2]

MPTP See *1-methyl-4-phenyl-1,2,3,6-tetrahydropyridine*. [5, 20]

MRI See *magnetic resonance imaging*. [4]

MRN See *median raphe nucleus*. [6]

MRS See *magnetic resonance spectroscopy*. [4]

MS See *multiple sclerosis*. [20]

MSG See *monosodium glutamate*. [8]

multiple sclerosis (MS)   Disorder caused by autoimmune destruction of the myelin covering neurons in the brain and spinal cord. MS affects movement, sensation, and bodily functions. [20]

multiple T-maze   Maze type that contains many alleys ending in a "T" shape, which gives the animal two possible directions at each choice point. [4]

μ-receptor   Subtype of opioid receptor located in the brain and spinal cord that has a high affinity for morphine and certain other opiate drugs. [11]

muscarinic receptors   Family of metabotropic cholinergic receptors that are selectively stimulated by muscarine. [7]

muscimol   Drug found in the mushroom *Amanita muscaria* that is an agonist for the $GABA_A$ receptor. [8]

muscle dysmorphia   Psychological disorder characterized by a false perception that the sufferer is weak and small, constant checking of one's appearance, concealing one's body shape, and a preoccupation with working out and using steroids to enhance muscle growth. [16]

muscle relaxants   Drugs, such as benzodiazepines, that reduce muscle tension in a patient. [17]

mutant mice   Genetically modified mice produced by gene disruptions: knockout, knockin, or transgenic manipulations. They are used to study genetic disorders. [18]

myasthenia gravis   Neuromuscular disorder involving an attack on the muscle cholinergic receptors by one's own immune system and leading to overall muscular weakness. [7]

myasthenic syndromes   Congenital neuromuscular disorders caused by mutations in either the ChAT or AChE gene and resulting in symptoms similar to myasthenia gravis. [7]

myelin   A fatty insulating sheath surrounding many axons that increases the speed of nerve conduction. It is produced by oligodendrocytes in the CNS and by Schwann cells in the peripheral nervous system. [2]

N

***N*-benzylphenethylamines (NBOMes)**   Relatively new class of potent synthetic hallucinogens. [15]

N-methyl-ᴅ-aspartate (NMDA)   Exogenous amino acid derivative that has high affinity for a specific subtype of ionotropic glutamate receptors. [20]

Na+–K+ pump   Enzyme (Na+-K+ ATPase) that helps to maintain the resting membrane potential by removing Na+ from inside the cell. Three Na+ ions are exchanged for two K+ ions, maintaining a negative charge inside the cell and transporting the ions against their concentration gradients following an action potential. [2]

nabilone (Cesamet)   Synthetic cannabinoid used to treat appetite and weight loss in patients with HIV/AIDS and to suppress nausea and vomiting in cancer patients receiving chemotherapy. [14]

nabiximols (Sativex)   Cannabis extract containing a mixture of THC and CBD that is administered as an oral spray and is currently licensed in several countries for the treatment of neuropathic pain and spasticity in patients with multiple sclerosis. [14]

NAcc   See *nucleus accumbens*. [2]

nAChRs   See *nicotinic acetylcholine receptors*. [13]

nalmefene   A dual κ/μ-opioid antagonist effective in reducing lever pressing for alcohol in rodent studies, particularly in alcohol-dependent animals. [10]

naltrexone   Long-acting μ-opioid receptor antagonist. It is used clinically in the treatment of opioid use disorder, and it also reduces consumption and craving in some alcoholic individuals, perhaps by reducing the positive feeling caused by alcohol. [10]

Namenda   See *memantine*. [8, 20]

narcolepsy   Sleep disorder characterized by repeated bouts of extreme sleepiness during the daytime. Symptoms include sudden cataplexy, sleep paralysis, and dream-like hallucinations. [3]

narcotic analgesics   Class of drugs originally derived from the opium poppy that reduce pain but do not cause unconsciousness. They create a feeling of relaxation and sleep in an individual, but in high doses can cause coma or death. [11]

Nardil   See *phenelzine*. [5]

naratriptan (Amerge) $5-HT_{1B/1D}$ receptor agonist that causes constriction of cerebral blood vessels. It is used to treat migraine headaches. [6]

natural recovery   Recovery from drug addiction without the aid of treatment. [9]

NBOMes   See *N-benzylphenethylamines*. [15]

NBQX   Antagonist that blocks both AMPA and kainate receptors but has no effect on NMDA receptors. [8]

NE   See *norepinephrine*. [3, 5]

NE transporter   Protein in the membrane of noradrenergic neurons that is responsible for NE reuptake from the extracellular fluid. [5]

necroptosis   See *programmed necrosis*. [8]

necrosis   Cell death resulting from exposure to a chemical agent (such as glutamate), disease, or other injury. It differs in several important ways from apoptosis (programmed cell death). [8]

negative control   Experimental control procedure in which a neutral or inactive treatment is compared to an experimental treatment, whereby the comparison indicates if the experimental treatment yields an effect. See also *placebo*. [4]

negative symptoms   Characteristics of schizophrenia that are observed as a decline in normal function, such as reduced speech, loss of motivation, social withdrawal, and anhedonia. [19]

neonatal ventral hippocampal lesion model (NVHL)   Neurodevelopmental model of schizophrenia that relies on early damage to the hippocampus in rodents. Hippocampal lesioning leads to some behaviors analogous to the early negative symptoms of schizophrenia. Behaviors similar to the positive symptoms of psychosis appear only at post-adolescence. [19]

neonicotinoids   Nicotinic receptor agonists that are relatively selective for insect nAChRs. They are widely used as insecticides. [7]

neostigmine (Prostigmin)   Synthetic analog of the drug physostigmine that cannot cross the blood–brain barrier. It is used to treat myasthenia gravis due to its ability to block AChE activity in muscle tissue. [7]

nerves   Bundles of neurons outside the CNS that transmit electrical signals for nervous system function. [2]

Neupro   See *rotigotine*. [5]

neuraxis   Imposed line through the body that starts at the base of the spinal cord and ends at the front of the brain. [2]

neuroactive steroids   Family of substances that are synthesized in the brain from cholesterol and that have a steroid structure. They act as local signaling agents. [8]

neuroadaptations   Changes in brain functioning that attempt to compensate for the effects of repeated substance use. [9]

neurodevelopmental model   Theory that genetic vulnerability in combination with environmental stressors alters the trajectory of brain development resulting in the symptoms observed in schizophrenics. [19]

neurofibrillary tangles (NFTs)   Abnormal fibrous inclusions, composed primarily of highly phosphorylated tau protein, that are located in the cytoplasm of neurons and are considered one of the characteristic histopathological markers of Alzheimer's disease. Pyramidal neurons are particularly susceptible to NFTs. [20]

neuroleptic malignant syndrome (NMS)   Undesired response to antipsychotic drugs characterized by fever, instability of the autonomic nervous system, rigidity, and altered consciousness. [19]

neuroleptics   Drugs useful in treating schizophrenia; an older term that refers to their ability to selectively reduce emotionality and psychomotor activity. Now more often called antipsychotics. [19]

neuromodulators   Chemicals that don't follow the typical neurotransmitter model. They may regulate neurotransmitter activity or act at distant sites from their point of release. [3]

neuromuscular junction   Connection point between neurons and muscle cells that has some of the characteristics of a synapse. [3, 7]

neurons   Nerve cells that form the brain, spinal cord, and nerves that transmit electrical signals throughout the body. [2]

neuropathic pain   Chronic pain caused by nerve tissue damage. Produced within the nervous system itself, not in response to a nociceptive stimulus like a stab wound or burn. [14]

neuropeptide Y (NPY)   Neuropeptide synthesized by neurons in the arcuate nucleus that stimulates hunger and eating behavior when released onto postsynaptic cells in the paraventricular nucleus. [6]

neuropeptides   Small proteins (3 to 40 amino acids long) in the nervous system that act as neurotransmitters or neuromodulators. [3]

neuropharmacology   Area of pharmacology specializing in drug-induced changes to the function of cells in the nervous system. [1]

neuropsychopharmacology   Area of pharmacology focusing on chemical substances that interact with the nervous system to alter behavior, emotions, and cognition. [1]

neurosteroids   See *neuroactive steroids.* [8]

neurotoxin   Chemical that damages or kills nerve cells and/or their fibers and synapses. [4, 5]

neurotransmitters   Chemical substances packaged in synaptic vesicles and released by neurons to communicate across synapses with other neurons, muscle cells, secretory cells, or cells comprising other tissues/organs. [2, 3]

neurotrophic factors   Proteins that encourage the growth, development, and survival of neurons. They are also involved in neuronal signaling. [3]

neurotrophic hypothesis   Theory that low BDNF is responsible for the loss of dendritic branches and spines and reduced volume of brain areas responsible for clinical depression. [18]

neutral antagonists   Drug that produces no pharmacological activity (i.e., no efficacy) and that can prevent or reverse the effects of a drug agonist by occupying the receptor site. [11]

NFTs   See *neurofibrillary tangles.* [20]

nicotine replacement therapy (NRT)   Method to stop smoking that involves giving the smoker a safer nicotine source, thereby maintaining a level of nicotine in the body and reducing nicotine withdrawal symptoms. [13]

nicotine resource model   Theory that smoking is maintained due to positive effects of nicotine such as increased concentration and greater mood control. [13]

nicotinic acetylcholine receptors (nAChRs)   Family of ionotropic receptors that are activated by ACh and selectively stimulated by nicotine. They may also be called nicotinic receptors. [13]

nicotinic receptors   Family of ionotropic receptors that are activated by ACh and selectively stimulated by nicotine. They may also be called nicotinic cholinergic receptors. [7]

nigrostriatal tract   Dopaminergic nerve tract originating at the substantia nigra and terminating in the stratum. It is important for regulation of movement and is severely damaged in Parkinson's disease. [5]

nitrites   Class of inhalants that are characterized by the presence of an NO_2 group and that heighten sexual arousal and pleasure. [16]

NMDA   See *N-methyl-D-aspartate.* [20]

NMDA receptor   Ionotropic glutamate receptor selective for the agonist NMDA. [8]

NMS   See *neuroleptic malignant syndrome.* [19]

nocebo   Substance that is pharmacologically inert yet can produce negative therapeutic outcomes. [1]

nodes of Ranvier   Gaps in the myelin sheath that expose the axon to the extracellular fluid. [2]

noncompetitive antagonists   Drugs that reduce the effect of an agonist, but do not compete at the receptor site. The drug may bind to an inactive portion of the receptor, disturb the cell membrane around the receptor, or interrupt the intercellular processes initiated by the agonist–receptor association. [1]

nonselective MAO inhibitors   Drugs that block both MAO-A and MAO-B. [5]

nonspecific drug effects   Physical or behavioral changes not associated with the chemical activity of the drug–receptor interaction but with certain unique characteristics of the individual such as present mood or expectations of drug effects. [1]

nonsteroidal anti-inflammatory drugs (NSAIDs)   COX-2 inhibitors such as ibuprofen. [14]

nootropics   Drugs that enhance cognitive function, especially memory. [8]

NOP-R   One of the four opioid receptors. It is widely distributed in the CNS and the peripheral nervous system and is activated by the neuropeptide nociceptin/orphanin FQ. [11]

noradrenergic   Adjectival form of noradrenaline (norepinephrine). [5]

norepinephrine (NE)   Neurotransmitter related to DA that belongs to a group called catecholamines. It also functions as a hormone secreted by the chromaffin cells of the adrenal medulla. Also known as noradrenaline. [3, 5]

Norflex See *orphenadrine*. [7]

novelty suppressed feeding paradigm Experimental technique to evaluate anxiety that measures the latency to eat novel foods in a familiar environment or usual foods in a novel environment. [4]

NPY See *neuropeptide Y*. [6]

NRT See *nicotine replacement therapy*. [13]

NSAIDs See *nonsteroidal anti-inflammatory drugs*. [14]

nuclei Localized cluster of nerve cell bodies in the brain or spinal cord. [2]

nucleus accumbens (NAcc) Structure of the limbic system that mediates the reinforcing and incentive salience effects of many activities, including recreational drug use. Also a major component of the ventral striatum. [2]

Nuedexta Dextromethorphan-containing medication prescribed for the treatment of pseudobulbar affect. [15]

NVHL See *neonatal ventral hippocampal lesion model*. [19]

O

obsessions Worrying thoughts or ideas that an individual cannot easily ignore. [17]

obsessive-compulsive disorder (OCD) Psychiatric anxiety disorder characterized by persistent thoughts of contamination, violence, sex, or religion that the individual cannot easily ignore, and that cause the individual anxiety, guilt, or shame, etc. and may be accompanied by compulsive repetitive behaviors. [17]

occipital lobe One of four lobes of the cerebral cortex. It contains the visual cortex and helps integrate visual information. [2]

OCD See *obsessive-compulsive disorder*. [17]

6-OHDA See *6-hydroxydopamine*. [5]

8-OH-DPAT See *8-hydroxy-2-(di-n-propylamino) tetralin*. [6]

oligoclonal bands Immunoglobins that indicate inflammatory processes within the central nervous system. [20]

oligodendrocytes Glial cells that myelinate nerve axons of the CNS. Also known as oligodendroglia. [20]

oligodendroglia Glial cells that myelinate nerve axons of the CNS. Also known as oligodendrocytes. [2]

ondansetron (Zofran) 5-HT$_3$ receptor antagonist used to treat the nausea and vomiting side effects of cancer chemotherapy. [6]

one-chamber social interaction test Test used to measure the level of anxiety in rodents by recording the time spent investigating other animals. [4]

Ongentys See *opicapone*. [5]

open State of a receptor channel in which the channel pore is open, thereby permitting ion flow across the cell membrane. [7]

open field test Technique used to measure locomotor activity and exploratory behavior by placing the animal on a grid and recording the number of squares traversed in a unit of time. [4]

operant analgesia testing Technique used to test analgesic drugs. Once an animal is trained to lever press to terminate foot shock, the researchers gradually increase shock stimulation from very low levels until the animal responds by lever pressing, to indicate threshold. Analgesic drugs would be expected to raise that threshold. [4]

operant conditioning Type of learning in which animals learn to respond to obtain rewards and avoid punishment. It explains drug tolerance when an animal learns to engage in behaviors when under the influence of a drug. [1]

opicapone (Ongentys) COMT inhibitor used to enhance L-DOPA availability in patients with Parkinson's disease. [5]

optogenetics Neurobiological technique based on the ability of certain light-sensitive proteins, when expressed in a specific subset of neurons, to either excite or inhibit the cells when exposed to light of the appropriate wavelength. [4]

oral administration (PO) Method that involves administering a drug through the mouth. [1]

orexigenic Something that has the property of stimulating appetite. [6]

organophosphorus compounds General name for organic chemicals containing phosphorus, but sometimes applied more specifically to esters of phosphoric acid. OPs are the basis for many insecticides, herbicides, and nerve gases. [7]

orphenadrine (Norflex) Anticholinergic drug used to treat early symptoms of Parkinson's disease. [7]

osmotic minipump Device placed just under the skin of an animal that allows a drug to be administered continuously over a specified period of time. [13]

OT See *oxytocin*. [3]

other hallucinogen use disorder *DSM-5* diagnostic category that defines a psychiatric disorder involving use of hallucinogenic drugs other than PCP and related substances. [15]

ovaries Female-specific gonads that secrete estrogens and progesterone. [3]

oxytocin (OT) Peptide hormone synthesized by certain hypothalamic neurons and secreted into the bloodstream at the posterior lobe of the pituitary gland. Circulating oxytocin induces uterine contractions during childbirth and milk letdown during lactation. Other oxytocin neurons form synapses within the brain and play an important role in social, including maternal, behaviors in some species. [3]

P

PAG See *periaqueductal gray*. [2]

palonosetron (Aloxi) 5-HT$_3$ receptor antagonist used to treat the nausea and vomiting side effects of cancer chemotherapy. [6]

panic attack Feeling of extreme fear that was not preceded by a threatening stimulus. [17]

panic disorder Disease involving repeated attacks of extreme fear, occurring either without warning or in an environment similar to where previous panic attacks occurred. [17]

para-chloroamphetamine Drug similar in structure to amphetamine that stimulates 5-HT release. It is also neurotoxic at high doses. [6]

para-chlorophenylalanine (PCPA) Drug that irreversibly inhibits tryptophan hydroxylase, blocking 5-HT synthesis. [6]

parasympathetic Division of the autonomic nervous system responsible for conserving energy, digestion, glucose and nutrient storage, slowing the heart rate, and decreasing respiration. [2]

parasympatholytic agents Drugs that block muscarinic receptors, inhibiting the parasympathetic system. They are deadly at high doses, but at low doses they are used medicinally to dilate pupils, relax airways, counteract cholinergic agonists, and induce drowsiness. [7]

parasympathomimetic agents Drugs that stimulate muscarinic receptors, thereby mimicking the effects of parasympathetic system activation. [7]

paraventricular nucleus (PVN) Hypothalamic nucleus located adjacent to the 3rd ventricle that contains vasopressin- and oxytocin-secreting neurons. Other neurons with this nucleus participate in the neural circuit that regulates hunger and eating behavior. [3, 6]

paraxanthine Biologically active caffeine metabolite that exerts CNS stimulant activity like the parent compound. [13]

parenteral Methods of drug administration that do not use the gastrointestinal system, such as intravenous, inhalation, intramuscular, transdermal, etc. [1]

parietal lobe One of four lobes of the cerebral cortex. It contains the somatosensory cortex and helps integrate information about body senses. [2]

Parkinson's disease (PD) Chronic, progressive, neurodegenerative disorder characterized by tremor, rigidity, difficulty in initiating movement, slowing of movement, and postural instability. [20]

Parkinson's disease dementia (PDD) Condition in which one or more cognitive functions are impaired to the point of interfering with the ability of the individual to navigate everyday life. [20]

parkinsonian symptoms Undesired response to anti-psychotic drugs that resembles Parkinson's disease, including tremors, akinesia, muscle rigidity, akathesia, and lack of facial expression. [19]

Parlodel See *bromocriptine*. [5]

Parnate See *tranylcypromine*. [5]

partial agonists Drugs that bind to a receptor but have low efficacy, producing weaker biological effects than a full agonist. Hence, they act as agonists at some receptors and antagonists at others, depending on the regional concentration of full agonist. These were previously called mixed agonist-antagonists. [1, 11]

parts per million (ppm) Number of molecules of a gaseous substance per million molecules of air. When applied to an inhaled substance, it is used to describe the amount of exposure to the substance (i.e., dose). [16]

parvocellular neurons General term for neurons with small cell bodies. Included within this category are neurons located in the paraventricular nucleus of the hypothalamus that project their axons to several different brain areas where they release vasopressin and oxytocin to act as neurotransmitters/neuromodulators. [3]

passive avoidance learning Type of learning task in rats and mice in which the animal is trained to avoid a location that it would normally enter (e.g., going into a dark compartment from one that is brightly lit) by administration of a brief electric footshock when it enters the location. The word "passive" in the name of the task reflects the fact that the animal must withhold its usual response of moving into the dark compartment. [5]

passive diffusion Movement of lipid-soluble materials across a biological barrier without assistance based on its concentration gradient, from higher to lower concentration. [1]

patch clamp electrophysiology Technique used to measure the function of a single ion channel by using a micropipette to isolate the ion channel and obtain an electrical recording. [4]

Pavlovian conditioning See *classical conditioning*. [1]

PCP See *phencyclidine*. [8, 15]

PCPA See *para-chlorophenylalanine*. [6]

PD See *Parkinson's disease*. [20]

PDD See *Parkinson's disease dementia*. [20]

peak experience Intense psychedelic state experienced during a hallucinogenic drug-assisted therapeutic session that is hypothesized to be an important contributor to the therapeutic benefit. [15]

pedunculopontine tegmental nuclei (PPTg) Structure within the dorsal lateral pons containing cholinergic neurons that project to the substantia nigra (important for stimulating nigral dopamine neurons) and others that project to the brainstem and thalamus (important for behavioral arousal, sensory processing, and initiation of rapid-eye-movement sleep). [7]

penetrance Frequency with which a particular gene produces its main effect. [20]

pentylenetetrazol (Metrazol) Convulsant drug that acts by blocking the function of $GABA_A$ receptors. [8]

periaqueductal gray (PAG) Structure of the tegmentum located around the cerebral aqueduct that connects the third and fourth ventricles. It is important for regulating pain; stimulation produces an analgesic effect. [2]

PET See *positron emission tomography*. [4]

peyote button Crown of the peyote cactus, *Lophophora williamsii*, that can be dried and ingested to obtain the psychedelic/hallucinogenic drug mescaline. [15]

peyote cactus Species of cactus, *Lophophora williamsii*, that produces mescaline. [15]

pharmacodynamic tolerance Type of tolerance formed by changes in nerve cell functions in response to the continued presence of a drug. [1, 10]

pharmacodynamics Study of physiological and biochemical interactions of a drug with the target tissue responsible for the drug's effects. [1]

pharmacoepigenetics Study of the role of epigenetic modifications in individual variation in response to drug effects. [1]

pharmacogenetics Study of the genetic basis for variability in drug response among individuals (sometimes called pharmacogenomics). [1, 4]

pharmacokinetic Factors that contribute to bioavailability: the administration, absorption, distribution, binding, inactivation, and excretion of a drug. [1]

pharmacological MRI (phMRI) Spin-off of functional MRI (fMRI), it is a technique used to investigate the mechanism of drug action by visualizing changes in brain function following drug administration. [4]

pharmacology Study of the actions of drugs and their effects on living organisms. [1]

pharmacotherapeutic treatment Method of disease treatment that uses drugs to modify a clinical condition. [10]

phasic release Irregularly timed and larger amounts of neurotransmitter release than occurs in the case of tonic release. It is typically associated with the burst mode of cell firing and produces surges in extracellular levels of the transmitter. [5]

phencyclidine (PCP) Uncompetitive antagonist of the NMDA receptor that binds to a site within the receptor channel. It is a dissociative anesthetic that was once used medicinally but is now only taken recreationally. [8, 15]

phenelzine (Nardil) MAO inhibitor used to treat clinical depression. [5]

phenethylamine Class of drugs that includes mescaline as well as NE- and amphetamine-related substances. [15]

phenylephrine α_1-adrenergic receptor agonist that causes behavioral stimulation. It is also used as a decongestant. [5]

phMRI See *pharmacological MRI*. [4]

phobias Fears of specific objects or situations that are recognized as irrational. [17]

phosphodiesterase (PDE) Class of enzymes that degrades cyclic nucleotides. For example, phosphodiesterases break down cAMP to 5'-AMP. [18]

phosphoinositide second-messenger system Neurotransmitter signaling mechanism that activates PKC and is controlled by a variety of different neurotransmitter receptors. [3]

phospholipids Lipid molecules that are major constituents of the cell membrane. They are composed of a polar phosphate-containing head and two lipid tails. [1]

phosphorylate Add a phosphate group to a molecule by means of an enzymatic reaction. [3]

physical dependence Developed need for a drug, such as alcohol or opioids, by the body as a result of prolonged drug use. Termination of drug use will lead to withdrawal symptoms (abstinence). [1, 10, 11]

physiological antagonism Drug interaction characterized by two drugs that act in distinct ways and reduce each other's effectiveness in the body. [1]

physostigmine (eserine) Drug isolated from Calabar beans that blocks AChE activity. Its symptoms include slurred speech, mental confusion, hallucinations, loss of reflexes, convulsions, coma, and death. [7]

phytocannabinoids Compounds with a cannabinoid structure that are found in the cannabis plant. [14]

pia mater Innermost of the meninges consisting of a thin tissue immediately surrounding the brain and spinal cord. [2]

picrotoxin Convulsant drug that acts by blocking the function of $GABA_A$ receptors. [8]

pilocarpine Extract of the shrub *Pilocarpus jaborandi* known for its ability to stimulate muscarinic receptors. [7]

pineal gland Endocrine gland that secretes the sleep-promoting hormone melatonin. It is located above the brain stem and covered by the cerebral hemispheres. [3]

pinocytotic vesicles Type of vesicles that envelop and transport large molecules across the capillary wall. [1]

pituitary gland Endocrine gland that secretes the hormones TSH, ACTH, FSH, LH, GH, PRL, vasopressin, and oxytocin. It is located under the hypothalamus and connects to the brain by a thin stalk. [3]

PKA See *protein kinase A*. [3]

PKC See *protein kinase C*. [3]

PKG See *protein kinase G*. [3]

placebo Substance that is pharmacologically inert, yet in many instances produces both therapeutic and side effects. [1]

PO See *oral administration*. [1]

polarized Possessing an electrical charge. [2]

polypharmacy Use of multiple pharmacological agents at the same time. [16]

POMC See *pro-opiomelanocortin*. [11]

positive control Experimental control procedure in which a well-characterized, active treatment is compared to an experimental treatment [4]

positive reinforcers Something (e.g., a recreational drug) that, when provided to an organism, increases the strength of the response that was used to obtain the item. In studies of addiction, the positive reinforcing quality of a drug is usually measured by means of a self-administration procedure. [9]

positive symptoms Characteristics of schizophrenia that include delusions, hallucinations, disorganized speech, and bizarre behavior. They are often the more dramatic symptoms. [19]

positron emission tomography (PET) Imaging technique used to determine the distribution of a radioactively labeled substance in the body. It can be used to measure drug binding to neurotransmitter receptors or transporters in the brain as well as measuring changes in metabolic activity reflecting neuron function. [4]

post-traumatic stress disorder (PTSD) Emotional disorder that develops in response to a traumatic event, leaving the individual feeling a sense of fear, helplessness, and terror. Symptoms include sleep disturbances, avoidance of stimuli associated with the trauma, intrusive thoughts reliving the event, and a numbing of general emotional responses. An increase in suicidal thoughts has also been observed. [17]

posterior Located near the back or rear of the nervous system. [2]

posterior pituitary Lobe of the pituitary gland from which vasopressin and oxytocin are secreted. [3]

postsynaptic cell Neuron at a synapse that receives a signal from the presynaptic cell. [3]

postsynaptic density Protein-rich structure associated with the postsynaptic membrane of many dendrites that contains a high density of neurotransmitter receptors along with other proteins that anchor the receptors to the postsynaptic area near the presynaptic sites of transmitter release. [3]

postural instability Impaired balance and coordination. In Parkinson's disease, manifests as a pronounced forward or backward lean in upright position. [20]

potency Measure of the amount of drug necessary to produce a specific response. It is dependent on the affinity of the drug for the receptor and the strength of the signaling mechanism elicited by the drug-receptor complex. [1]

potentiation Drug interaction characterized by an increase in effectiveness greater than the collective sum of the individual drugs. [1]

PPI See *prepulse inhibition of startle*. [4, 19]

PPM See *parts per million*. [16]

PPTg See *pedunculopontine tegmental nucleus*. [7]

pramipexole (Mirapex) D_2/D_3 agonist used to treat Parkinson's disease and restless legs syndrome. [5]

prazosin (Minipress) α_1-adrenergic receptor antagonist that causes dilation of blood vessels and is used to treat hypertension. [5]

Precedex See *dexmedetomidine*. [5]

precipitated withdrawal Method used to test drug dependence and withdrawal by administering an antagonist to block drug effects rapidly. [14]

precursor Chemical that is used to make the product formed in a biochemical pathway (e.g., tyrosine is the precursor of DOPA in the pathway for catecholamine synthesis). [3]

predictive validity   Measure of how closely the results from animal tests predict clinically useful effects in humans. [4]

prenatal inflammation   After administration of pro-inflammatory agents to pregnant rodents, neurodevelopmental and behavioral outcomes are evaluated in the offspring. [19]

prepulse inhibition of startle (PPI)   Method to study the ability of an individual to filter out sensory stimuli by applying a weak "prepulse" stimulus shortly before the startle-inducing stimulus. Well validated model of information-processing deficits in schizophrenia. [4, 19]

presenilin-1 (PS-1)   Protein involved in the processing of APP. [20]

presenilin-2 (PS-2)   Protein involved in the processing of APP. [20]

presurgical anesthesics   Drugs used to decrease preoperative anxiety to make administration of the surgical anesthesia less distressing and quicker. [17]

presynaptic cell   Neuron at a synapse that transmits a signal to the postsynaptic cell. [3]

presynaptic facilitation   Signaling by the presynaptic cell to increase neurotransmitter release by the axon terminal of the postsynaptic cell. [3]

presynaptic inhibition   Signaling by the presynaptic cell to reduce neurotransmitter release by the axon terminal of the postsynaptic cell. [3]

primary cortex   The part of each lobe of the cortex that provides conscious awareness of sensory experience and the initial cortical processing of sensory qualities. [2]

primary hypogonadism   Type of hypogonadism caused by lack of responsiveness of the testes to LH and FSH. [16]

PRL   See *prolactin*. [3]

pro-opiomelanocortin (POMC)   One of the four large opioid propeptide precursors that are broken down by proteases to form smaller active opioids (endorphins) in the brain. [11]

ProAmatine   See *midodrine*. [5]

procyclidine (Kemadrin)   Anticholinergic drug used to treat Parkinson's disease. [7]

prodynorphin   One of the four large opioid propeptide precursors that are broken down by proteases to form smaller active opioids (dynorphins) in the brain. [11]

proenkephalin   One of the four large opioid propeptide precursors that are broken down by proteases to form smaller active opioids (enkephalins) in the brain. [11]

progesterone   Female sex hormone secreted by the ovaries that is present at high levels during pregnancy. [3]

progestins   Group of female sex hormones that are important for the maintenance of pregnancy. The principal naturally occurring progestin is progesterone. [3]

programmed cell death   Cell death resulting from the triggering of a genetically programmed series of biochemical events in the cell. There are two types of programmed cell death: apoptosis and necroptosis. [8]

programmed necrosis (necroptosis)   Type of programmed cell death provoked by excitotoxic treatment of adult animals in which the appearance of the dying neurons is different from the appearance of neurons undergoing apoptosis. Also called *necroptosis*. [8]

progressive-ratio procedure   Method used to measure the relative strength of drug reinforcement by steadily increasing the response to reward ratio. [9]

prolactin (PRL)   Hormone secreted by the anterior pituitary that promotes milk production by the mammary glands. [3]

promoter region   Section of a gene, adjacent to the coding region, that controls the rate of transcription as directed by the binding of transcription factors. [2]

pronociceptin/orphanin FQ   One of the four large opioid propeptide precursors, that is broken down by proteases to form smaller active opioids (nociceptin, orphanin FQ) in the brain. [11]

propofol (Diprivan)   Positive allosteric modulator of the $GABA_A$ receptor that is used as a surgical anaesthetic agent. [8]

propranolol (Inderal)   β-Adrenergic receptor antagonist. It is used to treat hypertension due to its ability to block β-receptors in the heart, thereby limiting contraction of the heart muscles. [5]

Prostigmin   See *neostigmine*. [7]

protein kinase A (PKA)   Enzyme that is stimulated by cAMP and that phosphorylates specific proteins as part of a neurotransmitter signaling pathway. [3]

protein kinase C (PKC)   Enzyme that is stimulated by diacylglycerol and Ca^{2+} and that phosphorylates specific proteins as part of a neurotransmitter signaling pathway. [3]

protein kinase G (PKG)   Enzyme that is stimulated by cGMP and that phosphorylates specific proteins, including proteins involved in cell growth and differentiation. [3]

protein kinases   Enzymes that catalyze the phosphorylation of other proteins. [3]

Provigil   See *modafinil*. [12]

Prozac   See *fluoxetine*. [6]

prucalopride (Motegrity) $5-HT_4$ receptor agonist used to treat the constipation-predominant form of irritable bowel syndrome (IBS-C). [6]

PS-1   See *presenilin-1*. [20]

PS-2   See *presenilin-2*. [20]

pseudobulbar affect   Rare neurological disorder seen in a small percentage of patients with brain injury or disease that is characterized by frequent, uncontrollable episodes of laughing or crying that are incongruent with the person's emotional state. [15]

psilocin   Bioactive metabolite of the psychedelic/hallucinogenic drug psilocybin that is responsible for psilocybin's psychological and physiological effects. [15]

psilocybin   Psychedelic/hallucinogenic drug found in several mushroom species. [15]

psychedelic   Substance that causes perceptual changes, visual hallucinations, altered awareness of the mind and body, and cognitive distortions without producing a state of toxic delirium. [15]

psychedelic therapy   Method in which a psychedelic drug such as psilocybin is combined with psychotherapy to augment the therapeutic benefits of the treatment. The term also refers to an earlier procedure that involved giving patients a single high dose of LSD to help them understand their problems by reaching a drug-induced spiritual state. [15]

psychoactive drugs   Those drugs that have an effect on thinking, mood, or behavior. [1]

psycholytic therapy   Therapeutic method that employed LSD in low doses, gradually increasing the dose, in attempts to recover repressed memories or increase communication with the therapist. [15]

psychomotor stimulants Class of drugs that produce strong sensorimotor activation characterized by increased alertness, heightened arousal, and behavioral excitation. Also called *psychostimulants*. [12]

psychopharmacology Area of pharmacology specializing in drug-induced changes in mood, thinking, and behavior. [1]

psychosocial rehabilitation Counseling programs that involve educating the user, promoting behavioral change and alleviating problems caused by drug use. [10]

psychosocial treatment programs Counseling programs that involve educating the user, promoting behavioral change and alleviating problems caused by drug use. [12]

psychotomimetic Substance that mimics psychosis in a subject, such as by inducing hallucinations or delusions. [15]

PTSD See *post-traumatic stress disorder*. [17]

PVN See *paraventricular nucleus*. [6]

pyramidal neuron Neuron with a roughly pyramidal shape that serves as the principal type of output neuron in several brain areas, notably the cerebral cortex, hippocampus, and amygdala. [3]

pyramiding Pattern of steroid use characterized by gradually increasing the drug dose until the middle of the cycle, then gradually decreasing the drug dose until the cycle is complete. [16]

pyridostigmine (Mestinon) Synthetic analog of physostigmine that cannot cross the blood–brain barrier. It is used to treat myasthenia gravis due to its ability to block AChE activity in muscle tissue. [7]

Q

quantitative EEG (qEEG) Computer-assisted evaluation of EEG data, used to monitor brain function and cognitive processing. [4]

quinpirole D_2 and D_3 dopamine receptor agonist. Primarily used in animal research. [5]

R

radial arm maze Maze type composed of multiple arms leading from a central choice point. Radial arm mazes are used to test spatial learning. [4]

radioimmunoassay (RIA) A very sensitive analytical method that uses antibodies to quantify the amount of a substance (antigen) in bodily fluids or tissue extracts. The method typically depends on competitive binding of the antigen to the antibody. [4]

radioligand binding Technique that uses a radioactively labeled ligand to measure the affinity of the ligand (e.g., a drug, neurotransmitter, or hormone) for a binding site on a receptor or transporter as well as the relative density of the receptor or transporter in a particular area of the brain or other tissue. [4]

raphe nuclei Network of cell clusters in the CNS that contain the cell bodies of serotonergic neurons. They are found almost exclusively along the midline of the brainstem. [6]

rasagiline (Azilect) Selective MAO-B inhibitor used clinically to elevate brain DA levels in Parkinson's disease. [5]

rate-limiting enzyme Enzyme that catalyzes the slowest step in a biochemical pathway. It determines the overall rate of product formation. [5]

reactive depression State of sadness that is appropriate and of a reasonable level in response to a given aversive situation. Not usually considered a clinical condition. [18]

readily releasable pool Pool of synaptic vesicles located at presynaptic release sites and capable of rapid release of their neurotransmitter contents. [3]

reboxetine (Edronax) Member of the class of NE reuptake inhibitors. It is used as an antidepressant. [5]

receptor agonists Neurochemicals or drugs that can bind to a particular receptor protein and alter the shape of the receptor to initiate a cellular response. [1]

receptor antagonists Molecules that interact with a receptor protein and produce no cellular effect after binding, and also prevent an "active" ligand from binding. [1]

receptor binding studies Studies that use a radioactively labeled ligand to measure the affinity of the ligand for a binding site on a receptor as well as the relative density of the receptor in a particular area of the brain or other tissue. Such studies are common examples of the more general technique called *radioligand binding*. [18]

receptor cloning Process used to produce large amounts of identical receptor proteins in a cell line. [11]

receptor subtypes Group of receptors that respond to the same neurotransmitter but that differ from each other to varying degrees with respect to their structure, signaling mechanisms, and pharmacology. [1, 3]

receptor trafficking Normal process in which the receptors for a particular neurotransmitter are shuttled into and out of the cell membrane to regulate sensitivity of the cell to that transmitter. [8]

receptor up-regulation Increase in the number of receptors produced and maintained in a target cell. [5]

receptors Proteins located on the surface of or within cells that bind to specific ligands to initiate biological changes within the cell. [1, 2, 3]

rectal administration Drug delivery method requiring placement of the drug (sometimes in the form of a suppository) into the rectum. [1]

reinstatement of drug-seeking behavior Restoration of a behavior (e.g., an operant response) previously used to obtain a drug after that behavior had been extinguished. It is an animal model for relapse to drug use after a period of abstinence in chronic drug users. [9]

relapse prevention therapy Treatment program for drug-addicted people that teaches the individual how to avoid and cope with high-risk situations. [12]

relapses Recurrences of drug use following a period of abstinence. [9]

relative refractory period Short hyperpolarizing phase after an action potential during which a more intense excitatory stimulus is necessary to obtain an action potential. [2]

reliability Term used to indicate how dependable test results are and how likely the same test results will be found in subsequent trials. [4]

Reminyl See *galantamine*. [7]

remissions Periods during which an addict is drug free. [9]

repetitive transcranial magnetic stimulation (rTMS) Method of brain stimulation involving placing an electromagnetic coil on a selected area of the scalp, after which repeated electrical pulses are passed through the coil. This procedure generates magnetic pulses that induce electrical responses within the underlying brain tissue. Primarily used for treating major depression but is also being tested for possible treatment of substance use disorders. [12]

Requip See *ropinirole*. [5]

resensitization Process by which a previously desensitized receptor returns to its normal functional state, as shown by a normal response to agonist stimulation. [7]

reserpine Drug extracted from the roots of *Rauwolfia serpentina* (snakeroot). It inhibits vesicular monoamine uptake by VMAT, thereby reducing monoamine levels in the central and peripheral nervous system. [5]

reserve pool Pool of synaptic vesicles located at some distance from presynaptic release sites. These vesicles must be mobilized (moved to release sites and docked) before they can release their neurotransmitter contents. [3]

resident–intruder test Test of aggressive behavior involving attack by a resident adult male rat or mouse against a strange intruder male. [6]

resting membrane potential The difference in the electrical charge inside a neuron at rest compared to the outside. The inside of the cell is more negative, and that potential is −70 mV. [2]

resting tremor Tremor that is present when the limb is relaxed. Can be present in the hand, foot, jaw or face. Generally disappears with intentional movement. [20]

resting-state fMRI (rs-fMRI) This technique is a variation of fMRI that visualizes brain activity and connectivity in individuals when they are not actively engaged in a task that requires attention or task performance. [4]

restless legs syndrome Neurological disorder characterized by an irresistible urge to move one's legs, usually occurring at night or at other occasions when the legs have not moved for a long period of time. Other symptoms may include feelings of tingling, itching, burning, cramping, pain, and numbness in the legs. [5]

reticular formation Collection of nuclei within the core of the pons forming a network that extends into the mid-brain and medulla. These nuclei are important for arousal, attention, sleep, muscle tone, and some cardiac and respiratory reflexes. [2]

retrograde messengers Chemicals synthesized and released by a postsynaptic cell that diffuse into the nerve terminal of the presynaptic cell, often for the purpose of altering neurotransmitter release by the terminal. [3]

retrograde signaling Mechanism of signaling by a retrograde messenger. One example is the postsynaptic release of an endocannabinoid that subsequently activates CB_1 receptors on nearby nerve terminals. [14]

retropulsion The need to take a step backward when starting to walk. [20]

reuptake Process that involves transport of a neurotransmitter from the extracellular fluid back into the same cell that released it. [3, 5]

reverse tolerance Enhanced response to a particular drug after repeated drug exposure. Also called *sensitization*. [12]

reversible inhibitor Inhibitor of a protein such as an enzyme, receptor, or transporter that permits renewed activity of the protein after dissociation of the inhibitor. [5]

reward circuit Neuronal circuit that, when activated, mediates the rewarding effects of both natural rewards (e.g., food, water, sex) and recreational drugs. [9]

reward-prediction error Discrepancy between a predicted reward and the reward that was actually received. [9]

Reyvow See *Lasmiditan*. [6]

RIA See *radioimmunoassay*. [4]

ribosomes Organelles in the cytoplasm that decode the nucleotide sequence provided by mRNA and link the appropriate amino acids together to form a protein. [2]

rigidity Stiffness and inflexibility in the joints. Two types are present in Parkinson's disease: "lead-pipe" rigidity, which is characterized by maintenance of inflexibility of the joint through the entire range of movement, and "cog-wheel" rigidity, which is characterized by a ratchet-like interruption in movement. [20]

rimonabant CB_1 receptor inverse agonist that is used mainly for its antagonist activity. It is also called SR 141716. [14]

Ritalin See *methylphenidate*. [5, 12]

ritanserin $5-HT_{2A}$ receptor antagonist. [6]

rivastigmine (Exelon) AChE inhibitor. It is used in the treatment of Alzheimer's disease. [7]

ropinirole (Requip) D_2/D_3 agonist used to treat Parkinson's disease and restless legs syndrome. [5]

rostral Located near the front or head end of the nervous system. [2]

rotarod Rodent behavioral test consisting of a horizontally-oriented cylinder that is mechanically rotated at set speeds. Latency to fall off the rod provides a measure of balance and coordination. [4]

rotigotine (Neupro) D_2/D_3 agonist used to treat Parkinson's disease and restless legs syndrome. It is delivered to the patient by means of a transdermal patch. [5]

rsfMRI See *resting-state fMRI*. [4]

rTMS See *repetitive transcranial magnetic stimulation*. [12]

S

Sabril See *vigabatrin*. [8]

saclofen Chemical analog of baclofen that is a competitive antagonist at the $GABA_B$ receptor. [8]

sagittal Section that is taken parallel to the plane bisecting the nervous system into right and left halves. [2]

saltatory conduction Mode of action potential conduction along a myelinated neuron characterized by jumps from one node of Ranvier to the next. [2]

salvinorin A κ-opioid receptor agonist that is the active compound in the psychedelic/hallucinogenic plant *Salvia divinorum*. [15]

sarcopenia Skeletal muscle loss related to aging or to certain diseases. [16]

sarin Irreversible AChE inhibitor that is used as a nerve agent (neurotoxin) for chemical warfare. [7]

Sativex See *nabiximols*. [14]

SC See *subcutaneous*. [1]

SCH 23390 D_1 receptor antagonist that may induce catalepsy when administered in high doses. [5]

Schedule of Controlled Substances System established by the Controlled Substances Act in 1970 that classifies most substances with addictive potential into one of five schedules. Schedules I and II have the strictest guidelines. [9]

schedule of reinforcement Predetermined schedule used to determine when an animal will be rewarded for performing a specific behavior. A fixed ratio (FR) schedule refers to rewards given after a set number of responses; a fixed interval (FI) schedule refers to rewards given to the first response that occurs after a set amount of time has elapsed. [4]

Schwann cells Glial cells that myelinate peripheral nerve axons. [2, 20]

scopolamine Muscarinic receptor antagonist. It is found in nightshade, *Atropa belladonna*, and in henbane, *Hyoscyamus niger*. [7]

second messenger Substance that, when activated by signaling molecules bound to receptors in the cell membrane, will initiate biochemical processes within the cell. [3]

second-messenger systems Biochemical pathways that use second messengers to mediate intercellular signaling. [3]

secondary cortex Section of the cerebral cortex containing the neuronal circuits responsible for analyzing and recognizing information from the primary cortex, and for memory storage. [2]

secondary hypogonadism Type of hypogonadism caused by a decline in LH and FSH secretion. [16]

section Tissue slice showing structures of the nervous system or other organs. [2]

sedative–hypnotics Class of drugs that depress nervous system activity. They are used to produce relaxation, reduce anxiety, and induce sleep. [17]

selective D$_2$ receptor antagonists Drugs that selectively block D$_2$ receptors, including sulpiride, raclopride, and remoxipride. [19]

selective serotonin reuptake inhibitors (SSRIs) Drugs that block the presynaptic membrane transporter for 5-HT. They are used to treat major depression, panic and anxiety disorders, obsessive-compulsive disorder, obesity, and alcoholism. [6, 18, 20]

selegiline (Eldepryl) Selective MAO-B inhibitor used clinically to elevate brain DA levels in Parkinson's disease. [5]

self-administration method Procedure used to measure the addictive potential of a drug by allowing an animal to give itself doses of the drug. [4]

self-medication hypothesis Theory that addiction is based on an effort by the individual to treat themself for mood or other ill feelings. [9]

sensitization Enhanced response to a particular drug after repeated drug exposure. Also called *reverse tolerance*. [1, 11, 12]

sensory afferents Neurons carrying sensory information from the body surface or internal organs into the CNS. [2]

sensory neurons Nerve cells that are sensitive to environmental stimuli and convert the physical stimuli into electrical signals that are sent to the CNS. [2]

serenics Class of drugs capable of inducing a state of calmness, thereby reducing aggressive behaviors. [6]

serotonergic neurons Neurons that use serotonin as their transmitter. [6]

serotonin (5-hydroxytryptamine, 5-HT) Neurotransmitter found in the central and peripheral nervous system and synthesized by serotonergic neurons. [6]

serotonin deficiency hypothesis of aggression Hypothesis that low serotonergic activity in the CNS is associated with hyperaggressiveness. [6]

serotonin reuptake transporter (SERT) Protein in the membrane that is responsible for serotonin (5-HT) reuptake from the extracellular fluid. [18]

serotonin syndrome Cluster of symptoms produced by excessive serotonergic activation produced either by an overdose with one particular serotonergic drug or by the interaction of multiple such drugs. Symptoms include severe agitation, disorientation, confusion, ataxia, muscle spasms, fever, shivering, chills, diarrhea, elevated blood pressure, and increased heart rate. [6, 18]

SERT See *5-HT transporter* and *serotonin reuptake transporter*. [6, 18]

shared etiology Situation in which multiple disorders are caused by the same set of factors. [9]

side effects Undesired physical or behavioral changes associated with a particular drug. [1]

SIDS See *sudden infant death syndrome*. [6]

silent receptors See *drug depots*. [1]

single-photon emission computerized tomography (SPECT) Imaging technique used to view changes in regional blood flow or drug binding by using radioactively labeled compounds injected or inhaled into the body. [4]

single-spiking mode Mode of neuronal cell firing characterized by the production of single action potentials at intervals that may be regular or irregular, depending on the cell type. For midbrain DA neurons, the intervals are irregular. [5]

SKF 38393 Selective D$_1$ receptor agonist. [5]

sleep deprivation Lack of proper sleep, either unintentional (e.g., jet lag), or intentional (such as all-night studying). [18]

SNRIs See *dual NE/5-HT modulators*. [18]

social behavioral neural network Network within the brain that regulates a variety of social behavioral processes. [3]

social cognition Processing of social cues to determine the appropriate behavioral responses to these cues. [3]

sodium oxybate (Xyrem) Sodium salt of γ-hydroxybutyrate (GHB). It is used as a treatment for narcolepsy. [16]

soma Cell body of a neuron, containing all of the organelles needed to maintain the cell. [2]

soman Irreversible AChE inhibitor. It is used as a nerve agent (neurotoxin) for chemical warfare. [7]

somatic genetic engineering Application of gene editing whereby the genome of somatic cells, but not gametes, is affected. See also *human germline engineering*. [4]

somatodendritic autoreceptors Autoreceptors located on the dendrites or cell body that slow the rate of cell firing when activated. [3]

spasticity Constant unwanted contraction of one or more muscle groups. [20]

specific drug effects Physical or behavioral changes associated with biochemical interactions of a drug with the target site. [1]

specific neurotoxins Chemical that damages a specific neural pathway leaving others intact. [4]

SPECT See *single-photon emission computerized tomography*. [4]

spinal interneurons Nerve cells with short axons within the spinal cord. [11]

spinocerebellar ataxias Group of neurological disorders in which rare genetic mutations cause degeneration and death of the cerebellar Purkinje cells. Symptoms include ataxia, impaired balance, poor motor coordination, and in some cases visual dysfunction and cognitive deficits. [8]

SR 141716A   See *rimonabant*. [14]

SSRIs   See *selective serotonin reuptake inhibitors*. [6, 18, 20]

stacking   Pattern of anabolic steroid use characterized by the simultaneous use of multiple steroids, such as a short- and a long-acting steroid. [16]

state-dependent learning   Condition characterized by better performance of a particular task that was learned in a drugged state in the same drugged state, rather than in a nondrugged state. Tasks learned in a nondrugged state are likewise performed better in a nondrugged state. [1]

status epilepticus   Dangerous condition characterized either by continuous epileptic seizures or a sufficiently short period between seizures so that the patient has insufficient time to recover. [8]

steady state plasma level   The desired blood concentration of drug achieved when the absorption/distribution phase is equal to the metabolism/excretion phase. [1]

stereotyped behaviors   Repeated, relatively invariant behaviors associated with a particular situation or drug treatment. They often occur following a high dose of a psychostimulant such as cocaine or amphetamine. [5]

steroids   Class of hormones that are derived from cholesterol and regulate a variety of biochemical pathways. Members of the class include cortisol, estradiol, testosterone, and progesterone. [3]

stop-signal task   Test used to evaluate impulsivity (e.g., lack of behavior control). It requires the human or animal (e.g., nonhuman primate) subject to rapidly press one button or lever when a specific geometric symbol (e.g., a square) is displayed, and the other button or lever when any other shape appears. Periodically, a tone, which is the "stop" signal, is sounded following the visual presentation. The tone indicates that the subject should withhold responding. [4]

Strattera   See *atomoxetine*. [5]

subcutaneous (SC)   Method that involves injection of a drug just below the skin. [1]

sublingual administration   Method of drug administration that requires placing the drug under the tongue in contact with the mucous membrane, which has a rich capillary network for rapid absorption into the blood. [1]

substance use disorders   *DSM-5* classification of psychiatric disorders that involve clinically significant substance misuse. Severe cases of such disorders have features typically associated with addiction. This designation replaced both substance abuse and substance dependence categories in *DSM-IV*. [9]

substance-induced disorders   *DSM-5* classification of disorders pertaining to reversible substance-specific syndromes caused by recent ingestion of the substance. [9]

substance-related disorders   *DSM-5* classification that encompasses both substance use disorders and substance-induced disorders. [9]

substantia nigra   Collection of dopaminergic cell bodies within the tegmentum of the mesencephalon that innervate the dorsal striatum by way of the nigrostriatal tract. Damage to cells in this region leads to Parkinson's disease. [2, 5, 20]

subunits   Individual protein components that must join in the cell membrane to form a complete receptor. [3, 7]

succinylcholine (suxamethonium)   ACh analog that is resistant to metabolism by AChE. It is used as a muscle relaxant during some surgical procedures. [7]

sucrose preference test   Test of hedonic function dependent on rodents' natural preference for sweet solutions. Failure to prefer a sucrose solution over water is an indication of anhedonia, a symptom of clinical depressive disorder in humans. [4]

sudden infant death syndrome (SIDS)   Sudden, unexpected death of an infant under 1 year of age, occurring during sleep, and medically unexplained. [6]

sudden sniffing death syndrome   Fatal cardiac arrhythmia associated with inhalant use. [16]

sulci (sing. sulcus)   Small grooves of the cerebral cortex. [2]

sumatriptan (Imitrex, Zecuity) $5\text{-HT}_{1B/1D}$ receptor agonist that causes constriction of cerebral blood vessels. It is used to treat migraine headaches. Zecuity is the transdermal (patch) form of sumatriptan. [6]

superior Located near the top of the brain in humans. [2]

suppressor T cell   Type of T cell that reduces or suppresses the immune response of other T cells (or B cells) to an antigen. [20]

supraoptic nucleus   Hypothalamic nucleus located above the optic nerves that contains vasopressin- and oxytocin-secreting neurons. [3]

supraspinal   Located above the spinal cord or spine. [11]

suxamethonium   See *succinylcholine*. [7]

swimming performance   A rodent test of coordination used in the study of motor deficit diseases. [4]

sympathetic   Division of the autonomic nervous system responsible for providing energy expenditure to deal with a challenge by triggering the "fight-or-flight" response: increasing heart rate, increasing blood pressure, stimulating adrenaline secretion, and increasing blood flow to skeletal muscles. [2]

sympathomimetic   Substance that produces symptoms of sympathetic nervous system activation. [12]

synapse   Structural unit of information transmission between two nerve cells. It consists of the presynaptic nerve terminal, the synaptic cleft, and a small area of the postsynaptic cell (typically associated with a dendrite or region of the cell body) that receives the incoming signal. [2, 3]

synaptic cleft   Small gap, about 20 nm wide, between the presynaptic and postsynaptic cells. [3]

synaptic plasticity   Ability of synapses to change structurally (i.e., growth of new synapses or loss of existing ones) and functionally (i.e., increased or decreased strength of existing synapses). In the adult nervous system, synaptic plasticity is particularly important for learning and memory and for the development of addiction following repeated exposure to many recreational drugs. [3]

synaptic vesicles   Sac-like structures located in the axon terminal that are filled with molecules of neurotransmitter. [2, 3]

synaptobrevin   Small protein located in synaptic vesicle membranes that plays a critical role in exocytotic fusion of vesicles with the axon terminal membrane. [3]

synaptotagmin-1   Calcium-sensitive protein located within the synaptic vesicle membrane that helps trigger exocytosis in response to calcium influx into the nerve terminal. [3]

synesthesia   Mixing of sensations such that one kind of sensory stimulus creates a different kind of sensation, such as a color producing the sensation of sound. [15]

synthetic cathinones   Synthetic derivatives of the naturally occurring stimulant cathinone. Members of this class include mephedrone, methylone, MDPV, and α-PVP. [12]

systemic Routes of administration in which drugs distribute throughout the entire body, reaching the target tissue through general circulation. [1]

T

T cells A type of white blood cell. [20]

T-maze Maze type that involves an alley ending in a "T" shape, giving the animal two path choices to reach food in goal box. [4]

T3 See *triiodothyronine*. [3]

T4 See *thyroxine*. [3]

tachyphylaxis Form of rapid tolerance involving diminished responses following repeated drug dosing. [5]

tail suspension test Behavioral test in which mice are suspended by the tail from a horizontal rod and the duration of active struggling until the animal becomes immobile is measured. It is used for studying animal models of affective disorders. Antidepressant drugs prolong the active struggling. [4]

tail-flick test Behavioral test in which a beam of light is placed on a rodent's tail to produce increasing heat. The latency for the animal to move its tail out of the light is an index of pain sensitivity. [4]

tar Fine particles present in cigarette smoke that are produced by combustion of the tobacco leaves. It contains a complex mixture of hydrocarbons, some of which are known to be carcinogenic. [13]

tardive dyskinesia (TD) Undesired response to antipsychotic drugs characterized by involuntary muscle movements, particularly of the face, head, and neck, that may be irreversible in some patients. [19]

Tasmar See *tolcapone*. [5]

tau Protein that is the primary constituent of NFTs. [20]

TCA See *tricyclic antidepressant*. [18, 20]

tDCS See *transcranial direct current stimulation*. [12]

tegaserod (Zelnorm) 5-HT$_4$ receptor agonist used to treat the constipation-predominant form of irritable bowel syndrome (IBS-C). [6]

tegmentum Division of the midbrain. The tegmentum is composed of several important structures including the PAG, substantia nigra, and the VTA. [2]

Tegretol See *carbamazepine*. [18]

telotristat (Xermelo) TPH inhibitor that depletes only peripheral 5-HT because it does not cross the blood–brain barrier. It is used to treat carcinoid syndrome. [6]

temporal lobe One of four lobes of the cerebral cortex. It contains the auditory cortex and helps integrate auditory information. [2]

teratogen Any agent including a virus, drug, environmental pollutant, or radiation that induces abnormal fetal development, causing birth defects. [1]

terminal autoreceptors Autoreceptors that are located on axon terminals and that inhibit neurotransmitter release. [3]

terminal buttons Small enlargements at the axon terminal, in close proximity to the postsynaptic cell, containing synaptic vesicles. Also known as boutons. [2]

tertiary association areas Section of the cerebral cortex where the three sensory lobes can interact, providing a higher order of perception and memory. [2]

testes Male-specific gonads that secrete androgens. [3]

testosterone The principal androgen (male sex steroid) secreted by the testes. [3]

tetanic stimulus (tetanus) Electrical stimulus consisting of a brief train of high-frequency impulses, used experimentally to induce LTP. Also referred to as tetanus. [8]

tetanus See *tetanic stimulus*. [8]

tetrabenazine (Xenazine) Reversible VMAT2 inhibitor used to reduce uncontrolled movements associated with Huntington's disease and tardive dyskinesia. [5]

tetrahydrobiopterin Co-factor for TH that is required for catecholamine synthesis. [5]

TH See *tyrosine hydroxylase*. [5]

thalamus Structure of the diencephalon that is responsible for processing and distributing sensory and motor signals to the appropriate section of the cerebral cortex. [2]

THC See Δ^9-*tetrahydrocannabinol*. [14]

theophylline Stimulant drug similar to caffeine that is found naturally in tea. [13]

therapeutic drug monitoring Taking multiple blood samples to directly measure plasma levels of a drug after administration, to identify the optimum dosage for maximum therapeutic potential and minimal side effects. [1]

therapeutic effects Desired physical or behavioral changes associated with a particular drug. [1]

therapeutic index (TI) The relationship between the drug dose that results in a toxic response and the dose required for the desired biological response. It is represented by the equation $TI = TD_{50}/ED_{50}$ where TD_{50} is the dose that is toxic for 50% of the population and ED_{50} is the effective dose for 50%. [1]

thiosemicarbazide Glutamic acid decarboxylase (GAD) inhibitor that blocks GABA synthesis, inducing convulsions. [8]

threshold Membrane potential, typically –50 mV, at which voltage-gated Na$^+$ channels will open, generating an action potential. [2]

thyroid gland Endocrine gland that is located in the throat and secretes T3 and T4. [3]

thyroid-stimulating hormone (TSH) Hormone secreted by the anterior pituitary that stimulates the thyroid gland. [3]

thyrotropin-releasing hormone (TRH) Hormone synthesized by neurons of the hypothalamus that stimulates TSH release [3]

thyroxine (T4) Hormone synthesized from tyrosine and secreted by the thyroid gland. It helps control energy metabolism. [3]

TI See *therapeutic index*. [1]

tiagabine (Gabitril) Selective GAT-1 inhibitor. It is used to treat patients with partial seizures who are resistant to standard antiepileptic drugs. [8]

tianeptine Tricyclic antidepressant (TCA) that modulates glutamate function. [18]

tight junctions Connection between cells characterized by a fusing of adjoining cell membranes. In cerebral capillaries, the lack of small gaps prevents the movement of molecules across the capillary wall unless the molecules are lipid soluble. [1]

tolcapone (Tasmar) COMT inhibitor used in conjunction with L-DOPA to treat Parkinson's disease. [5]

tolerance Decreased response to a drug as a direct result of repeated drug exposure. [1, 10, 11, 12]

tonic release   Slow, consistent release of neurotransmitter that is typically associated with single-spiking mode of cell firing. It maintains low but relatively constant extracellular transmitter levels. [5]

topical   Method that involves administration of a drug directly on a specific body surface such as the skin or a mucous membrane. [1]

TPH   See *tryptophan hydroxylase*. [6]

tracts   Bundles of nerve axons in the CNS sharing a common origin and target. [2]

transcranial direct current stimulation (tDCS)   Method of brain stimulation in which two or more electrodes are placed on the scalp and used to pass a constant direct current at low intensity. [12]

transcription   Process whereby mRNA produces a complementary copy of an active gene. [2]

transcription factors   Nuclear proteins that regulate the rate of gene transcription within a cell. [2, 3]

transdermal   Method that involves administration of a drug through the skin (e.g., with a patch). [1]

transfection   Process used to introduce genetic material into a cell by injecting it with a DNA sequence coding for the desired protein product. [11]

transgenic mice   Mice bred to contain a foreign gene, including a mutant form of a mouse gene or a gene from a different species. They are used to study genetic disorders and to ascertain the functional role of the modified gene. [4]

translation   Process whereby proteins are produced using the nucleotide sequence carried by mRNA to direct the amino acid sequence. Translation is performed by ribosomes. [2]

translational medicine   Process by which basic scientific findings (e.g., using animal models) increase the understanding of important disease processes and aid the development of new medical therapies. [8]

transporters   Cell membrane proteins that transport molecules into and out of the cell (e.g., proteins that remove neurotransmitters from the extracellular fluid following their release). [3]

tranylcypromine (Parnate)   MAO inhibitor used to treat clinical depression. [5]

TRH   See *thyrotropin-releasing hormone*. [3]

tricyclic antidepressants (TCAs)   Class of antidepressants characterized by a three-ring structure. They block reuptake of NE and 5-HT, thereby increasing their concentration in the synaptic cleft. [5, 18, 20]

triggers   Classically conditioned cues associated with drug taking that cause craving. [11]

trihexyphenidyl (Artane)   Anticholinergic drug used to treat early symptoms of Parkinson's disease. [7]

triiodothyronine (T3)   Hormone synthesized from tyrosine and secreted by the thyroid gland. It helps control energy metabolism. [3]

trinucleotide repeat   Type of genetic structure characterized by a stretch of three nucleotides (a codon) repeated in multiple times in the DNA sequence. [20]

TRPV1   Nonspecific cation channel receptor that was first discovered in sensory neurons where it plays a key role in the heat and pain sensations produced by capsaicin. Within the brain, TRPV1 receptors can be activated by anandamide. [14]

tryptophan   Amino acid characterized by the presence of an indole group. It is a precursor to 5-HT. [6]

tryptophan depletion challenge   Research method in which subjects consume a tryptophan-deficient amino acid cocktail that transiently reduces 5-HT levels in the brain. It is used to investigate the role of 5-HT in depressive disorders. [18]

tryptophan hydroxylase (TPH)   Enzyme that catalyzes the conversion of tryptophan into 5-HTP. It is the rate-limiting enzyme in 5-HT synthesis. [6]

tryptophan loading   Administration of pure tryptophan for the purpose of elevating blood tryptophan concentrations. [6]

TSH   See *thyroid-stimulating hormone*. [3]

tuberohypophyseal dopamine pathway   Pathway that controls secretion of the hormone prolactin by the pituitary gland. [5]

twin studies   Studies used to understand how heredity contributes to a disorder by comparing the concordance rate for the disorder in pairs of monozygotic and dizygotic twins. [18]

tyrosine   Amino acid characterized by a phenol group. It is necessary for the synthesis of the catecholamine neurotransmitters. [5]

tyrosine hydroxylase (TH)   Enzyme that catalyzes the conversion of tyrosine to DOPA. It is the first and rate-limiting step in catecholamine synthesis. [5]

tyrosine kinase receptors   Family of receptors that mediate neurotrophic factor signaling. [3]

U

ultrafast endocytosis   Mechanism for extremely rapid retrieval of synaptic vesicle membrane components from the membrane of the axon terminal. [3]

ultrasonic vocalizations   Calls emitted by rats and mice that are above the range of human hearing and are thought to communicate the animals' emotional state. They are produced in both positive and negative social contexts, such as when pups are distressed from being separated from their mothers. [4]

uncompetitive antagonists   Ligand-gated channel receptor antagonists that block the channel by binding to a site within the channel pore. They require the channel to open in order to access the antagonist binding site. [8]

up-regulation   Increase in the number of receptors, which may be a consequence of denervation or of chronic antagonist treatment. [1]

Uprima   See *apomorphine*. [5]

V

VaChT   See *vesicular ACh transporter*. [7]

vacuous chewing movements test   Behavioral test used to evaluate the potential motor side effects of antipsychotic drugs. [19]

valbenazine (Ingrezza)   Reversible VMAT2 inhibitor used to reduce uncontrolled movements associated with Huntington's disease and tardive dyskinesia. [5]

VALI   See *vaping-associated lung injury*. [13]

Valium   See *diazepam*. [8]

valproate (Depakote)   Simple branched-chain fatty acid that was the first anticonvulsant approved by the U.S. FDA for treatment of acute mania. [18]

vanillylmandelic acid (VMA)   Metabolite of NE, formed primarily by NE breakdown in the peripheral nervous system. [5]

vaping-associated lung injury (VALI)   Syndrome that can be produced by vaping and that has the following features:

dyspnea, nonproductive cough, chest pain, nausea and vomiting, abdominal pain, diarrhea, fever, and an unusual lung pathology shown by the appearance of "ground-glass opacities" in CT scans. [13]

varenicline (Chantix) Partial agonist at high affinity $\alpha 4\beta 2$ nAChRs. It is used for treating nicotine dependence. [13]

varicosities Repeated swellings of nerve fibers that contain large numbers of synaptic vesicles and that serve as sites of neurotransmitter release. The fibers of dopaminergic and noradrenergic neurons characteristically show varicosities in the brain areas or (in the case of norepinephrine) peripheral organs that they innervate. [5]

vasopressin (VP) Peptide hormone secreted by the posterior pituitary that increases water retention by the kidneys. [3]

vehicle solution Physiological saline or other biocompatible solvent that a drug is dissolved in. [4]

Ventolin See *albuterol*. [5]

ventral Located toward the underside of the brain or front of the body in humans. [2]

ventral tegmental area (VTA) Region containing dopaminergic cell bodies within the tegmentum of the mesencephalon (midbrain) that form the mesolimbic and mesocortical tracts. [2, 5]

vesamicol Vesicular ACh transporter (VAChT) blocker. [7]

vesicle recycling Multi-step process consisting of removal of synaptic vesicle membrane components from the membrane of the axon terminal after exocytosis, followed by formation of new vesicles. [3]

vesicular ACh transporter (VAChT) Vesicle membrane protein that transports ACh into synaptic vesicles. [7]

vesicular GABA transporter (VGAT) Vesicle membrane protein that transports both GABA and glycine into synaptic vesicles; also known as VIAAT. [8]

vesicular glutamate transporter (VGLUT) Vesicle membrane protein that transports glutamate into synaptic vesicles. There are three such proteins, designated VGLUT1 to VGLUT3, which differ in their location within the brain. [8]

vesicular inhibitory amino acid transporter (VIAAT) See *vesicular GABA transporter*. [8]

vesicular monoamine transporter (VMAT) Vesicle membrane protein that transports monoamines (i.e., catecholamines and 5-HT) into synaptic vesicles. Monoamine neurons express a particular form of VMAT called VMAT2, whereas the epinephrine- and norepinephrine-secreting chromaffin cells of the adrenal medulla express a different form called VMAT1. [5]

VGAT See *vesicular GABA transporter*. [8]

VGLUT See *vesicular glutamate transporter*. [8]

VIAAT See *vesicular GABA transporter*. [8]

vigabatrin (Sabril) Irreversible GABA-T inhibitor that is used to treat epilepsy. [8]

vilazodone (Viibryd) Dual 5-HT transporter inhibitor 5-HT$_{1A}$ receptor partial agonist. It is used to treat anxiety disorders and depression. [6]

viral vectors Use of viruses as a delivery system (called a vector) to carry a gene into the nuclei of target cells. [1]

VMA See *vanillylmandelic acid*. [5]

VMAT See *vesicular monoamine transporter*. [5]

Vogel test See *water-lick suppression test*. [4]

volatile solvents Class of inhalants characterized by chemicals, such as adhesives, ink, and paint thinner, that are liquid at room temperature, but readily give off fumes that can be easily inhaled. [16]

voltage-gated channels Type of ion channels that are regulated by voltage differences across the membrane. [2]

volume transmission Phenomenon characterized by the diffusion of a chemical signal (e.g., a neurotransmitter) through the extracellular fluid to reach target cells at some distance from the point of release. [3]

VP See *vasopressin*. [3]

VTA See *ventral tegmental area*. [2, 5]

W

water-lick suppression test Behavioral test used to measure anxiety in rodents by recording their propensity to lick a drinking spout that will also deliver a mild electric shock. Also called *Vogel test*. [4]

WAY 100635 5-HT$_{1A}$ receptor antagonist. [6]

Western blot Research method that uses antibodies to quantify a specific protein in a tissue homogenate. [4]

wiring transmission Point-to-point communication between neurons in which the neurotransmitter acts locally within the synapse to affect the target cell. The opposite of wiring transmission is volume transmission. [3]

withdrawal syndrome Rebound physiological state that occurs at drug cessation in an individual following chronic drug use. It is the defining element of physical dependence. [1]

withdrawal See *abstinence syndrome*. [11]

X

Xenazine See *tetrabenazine*. [5]

Xermelo See *telotristat*. [6]

Xopenex See *levalbuterol*. [5]

Xyrem See *sodium oxybate*. [16]

Y

Yocon See *yohimbine*. [5]

yohimbine (Yocon) α_2-receptor antagonist that blocks noradrenergic autoreceptors and increases noradrenergic cell firing. It has anxiogenic effects and enhances symptoms of opioid withdrawal. [5]

Z

Zecuity See *sumatriptan*. [6]

Zelnorm See *tegaserod*. [6]

zero maze Elevated circular platform containing two open and two closed quadrants. It is used to measure anxiety in rodents. [4]

zero-order kinetics Process of drug elimination characterized by a constant rate of drug removal from the body, regardless of drug concentration in the blood. [1]

Zofron See *ondansetron*. [6]

zolmitriptan (Zomig) 5-HT$_{1B/1D}$ receptor agonist that causes constriction of cerebral blood vessels. It is used to treat migraine headaches. [6]

Zyban See *bupropion*. [13]

References

A

aan het Rot, M., Mathew, S. J., and Charney, D. S. (2009). Neurobiological mechanisms in major depressive disorder. *CMAJ.*, 180, 305–313.

Abanades, S., Farré, M., Segura, M., Pichini, S., Barral, D., Pacifici, R., et al. (2006). γ-Hydroxybutyrate (GHB) in humans: Pharmacodynamics and pharmacokinetics. *Ann. N. Y. Acad. Sci.*, 1074, 559–576.

Abbott, S. A. (2010). Diagnostic challenge: Myasthenia gravis in the emergency department. *Am. Acad. Nurse Pract.*, 22, 46/1–/273.

Abdel-Hady, H., Nasef, N., Shabaan, A. E., and Nour, I. (2015). Caffeine therapy in preterm infants. *World J. Clin. Pediatr.*, 4, 81–93.

Abelaira, H. M., Réus, G. Z., and Quevedo, J. (2013). Animal models as tools to study the pathophysiology of depression. *Rev. Bras. Psiquiatr.*, 35 (Suppl. 2), S112–120.

Acioglu, C., Li, L., and Elkabes, S. (2021). Contribution of astrocytes to neuropathology of neurodegenerative diseases. *Brain Res.*, 1758, 147291. https://doi.org/10.1016/j.brainres.2021.147291

Adams, R. C., Sedgmond, J., Maizey, L., Chambers, C. D., and Lawrence, N. S. (2019). Food addiction: Implications for the diagnosis and treatment of overeating. *Nutrients*, 11, 2086. doi: 10.3390/nu11092086.

Aday, J. S., Mitzkovitz, C. M., Bloesch, E. K., Davoli, C. C., and Davis, A. K. (2020). Long-term effects of psychedelic drugs: A systematic review. *Neurosci. Biobehav. Rev.*, 113, 179–189.

Addicott, M. A. (2014). Caffeine use disorder: A review of the evidence and future implications. *Curr. Addict. Rep.*, 1, 186–192.

Adel, Y., and Alexander, S.P.H. (2021). Neuromolecular mechanisms of cannabis action. *Adv. Exp. Med. Biol.*, 1264, 15–28.

Adinoff, B., and Cooper, Z. D. (2019). Cannabis legalization: progress in harm reduction approaches to substance use and misuse. *Am. J. Drug Alcohol Abuse*, 45, 707–712.

Adolfsson, O., Pihlgren, M., Toni, N., Varisco, Y., Buccarello, A. L., Antoniello, K., et al. (2012). An effector-reduced anti-β-amyloid (Aβ) antibody with unique Aβ binding properties promotes neuroprotection and glial engulfment of Aβ. *Neurobiol. Dis.*, 32, 9677–9689.

Agabio, R., and Colombo, G. (2014). GABA$_B$ receptor ligands for the treatment of alcohol use disorder: Preclinical and clinical evidence. *Front. Neurosci.*, 8, Article 140. doi: 10.3389/fnins.2014.00140.

Agrawal, A., Verweij, K. J. H., Gillespie, N. A., Heath, A. C., Lessov-Schlaggar, C. N., Martin, N. G., et al. (2012). The genetics of addiction: A translational perspective. *Transl. Psychiatry*, 2, e140. doi: 10.1038/tp.2012.54.

Aguiar Jr., A. S., Speck, A. E., Canas, P. M., and Cunha, R. A. (2020). Neuronal adenosine A1 receptors signal ergogenic effects of caffeine. *Sci. Rep.*, 10, 13414. doi: 10.1038/s41598-020-69660-1.

Aguilar, M. A., García-Pardo, M. P., and Parrott, A. C. (2020). Of mice and men on MDMA: A translational comparison of the neuropsychobiological effects of 3,4-methylenedioxymethamphetamine ("Ecstasy"). *Brain Res.*, 1727, 146556. doi:10.1016/j.brainres.2019.146556.

Agurell, S., Halldin, M., Lindgren, J.-E., Ohlsson, A., Widman, M., Gillespie, H., et al. (1986). Pharmacokinetics and metabolism of Δ9-tetrahydrocannabinol and other cannabinoids with emphasis on man. *Pharmacol. Rev.*, 38, 21–43. Republished with permission of American Society for Pharmacology and Experimental Therapeutics; permission conveyed through Copyright Clearance Center, Inc.

Ahlquist, R. P. (1979). Adrenoreceptors. *Trends Pharmacol. Sci.*, 1, 16–17.

Ahmari, S. E. (2016). Using mice to model obsessive compulsive disorder: From genetics to circuits. *Neuroscience*, 321, 121–137.

Ahmari, S. E., Spellman, T., Douglass, N. L., Kheirbek, M. A., Simpson, H. B., Deisseroth, K., et al. (2013). Repeated cortico-striatal stimulation generates persistent OCD-like behavior. *Science*, 340, 1234–1239.

Ahmed, S. H. (2010). Validation crisis in animal models of drug addiction: Beyond non-disordered drug use toward drug addiction. *Neurosci. Biobehav. Rev.*, 35, 172–184.

Ahmed, S. H. (2012). The science of making drug-addicted animals. *Neuroscience*, 211, 107–125.

Ahmed, S. H., Lenoir, M., and Guillem, K. (2013). Neurobiology of addiction versus drug use driven by lack of choice. *Curr. Opin. Neurobiol.*, 23, 581–587.

Ahmed, S. H., Badiani, A., Miczek, K. A., and Müller, C. P. (2020). Non-pharmacological factors that determine drug use and addiction. *Neurosci. Biobehav. Rev.*, 110, 3–27.

Aigner, T. G., and Balster, R. L. (1978). Choice behavior in rhesus monkeys: Cocaine versus food. *Science*, 201, 534–535.

Akimova, E., Lanzenberger, R., and Kasper, S. (2009). The serotonin-1A receptor in anxiety disorders. *Biol. Psychiatry*, 66, 627–635.

Albano, G. D., Amico, F., Cocimano, G., Liberto, A., Maglietta, F., Esposito, M., Rosi, G. L., et al. (2021). Adverse effects of anabolic-androgenic steroids: A literature review. *Healthcare (Basel)*, 9(1), 97. doi: 10.3390/healthcare9010097.

Albertson, D. N., and Grubbs, L. E. (2009). Subjective effects of Salvia divinorum: LSD- or marijuana-like? *J. Psychoactive Drugs*, 41, 213–217.

Alboni, S., van Dijk, R. M., Poggini, S., Milior, G., Perrotta, M., Drenth, T., et al. (2017). Fluoxetine effects on molecular, cellular and behavioral endophenotypes of depression are driven by the living environment. *Mol. Psychiatry*, 22, 552–561.

Albuquerque, E. X., Pereira, E. F. R., Alkondon, M., and Rogers, S. W. (2009). Mammalian nicotinic acetylcholine receptors: From structure to function. *Physiol. Rev.*, 89, 73–120.

Alcantara, A. A., Chen, V., Herring, B. E., Mendenhall, J. M., and Berlanga, M. L. (2003). Localization of dopamine D2 receptors on cholinergic interneurons of the dorsal striatum and nucleus accumbens of the rat. *Brain Res.*, 986, 2/1–/29.

Alemu, W., Zeleke, T. A., Takele, W. W., and Mekonnen, S. S. (2020). Prevalence and risk factors for khat use among youth students in Ethiopia: systematic review and meta-analysis, 2018. *Ann. Gen. Psychiatry*, 19, 16. doi: 10.1186/s12991-020-00265-8.

Alenina, N., Kikic, D., Todiras, M., Mosienko, V., Qadri, F., Plehm, R., et al. (2009). Growth retardation and altered autonomic control in mice lacking brain serotonin. *Proc. Natl. Acad. Sci. USA*, 106, 10332–10337.

Alexander, B. K. (2010). Addiction: The View from Rat Park. Available at www.brucekalexander.com/articles-speeches/rat-park/148-addiction-the-viewfrom-rat-park.

Alexander, G. C., Emerson, S., and Kesselheim, A. S. (2021). Evaluation of aducanumab for Alzheimer disease: Scientific evidence and regulatory review involving efficacy, safety, and futility. *JAMA*, published online March 30, 2021.

Alexandre, C., Andermann, M. L., and Scammell, T. E. (2013). Control of arousal by the orexin neurons. *Curr. Opin. Neurobiol.*, 23, 752–759.

Alford, C., Cox, H., and Wescott, R. (2001). The effects of Red Bull Energy Drink on human performance and mood. *Amino Acids*, 21, 139–150.

Alkam, T., and Nabeshima, T. (2019). Molecular mechanisms for nicotine intoxication. *Neurochem. Int.*, 125, 117–126.

Allain, F., Minogianis, E.-A., Roberts, D. C. S., and Samaha, A.-N. (2015). How fast and how often: The pharmacokinetics of drug use are decisive in addiction. *Neurosci. Biobehav. Rev.*, 56, 166–179.

Allied Market Research (2019). Energy Drinks Market by Type (Alcoholic and Nonalcoholic) and End User (kids, Adults, and Teenagers): Global Opportunity Analysis and Industry Forecast, 2019–2026. Available at https://www.alliedmarketresearch.com/energy-drink-market (accessed 2/1/21).

Allsop, D. J., Copeland, J., Lintzeris, N., Dunlop, A. J., Montebello, M., Sadler, C., et al. (2014). Nabiximols as an agonist replacement therapy during cannabis withdrawal: A randomized clinical trial. *JAMA Psychiatry*, 71, 281–291.

Allsop, D. J., Lintzeris, N., Copeland, J., Dunlop, A., and McGregor, I. S. (2015). Cannabinoid replacement therapy (CRT): Nabiximols (Sativex) as a novel treatment for cannabis withdrawal. *Clin. Pharmacol. Ther.*, 97, 571–574.

Almeida, L., Andreu-Fernández, V., Navarro-Tapia, E., Aras-López, R., Serra-Delgado, M., Martínez, L., García-Algar, O., et al. (2020). Murine Models for the Study of Fetal Alcohol Spectrum Disorders: An Overview. *Front. Pediatr.*, 8, 359. https://doi.org/10.3389/fped.2020.00359

Almey, A., Milner, T. A., and Brake, W. G. (2015). Estrogen receptors in the central nervous system and their implication for dopamine-dependent cognition in females. *Horm. Behav.*, 74, 125–138.

Alper, K. R. (2001). Ibogaine: A review. In K. R Alper and S. D. Glick (Eds.), *Ibogaine: Proceedings from the First International Conference* (The Alkaloids, Volume 56), pp. 1–38. Academic Press: San Diego.

Alper, K. R., and Lotsof, H. S. (2007). The use of ibogaine in the treatment of addictions. In M. J. Winkelman and T. B. Roberts (Eds.), *Psychedelic Medicine: New Evidence for Hallucinogenic Substances as Treatments*, pp. 43–66. Westport, CT: Praeger/Greenwood Publishing Group.

Alquraini, H., and Auchus, R. J. (2017). Strategies that athletes use to avoid detection of androgenic-anabolic steroid doping and sanctions. *Mol. Cell. Endocrinol.*, doi: 10.1016/j.mce.2017.01.028.

Alquraini, H., and Auchus, R. J. (2018). Strategies that athletes use to avoid detection of androgenic-anabolic steroid doping and sanctions. *Mol. Cell. Endocrinol.*, 464, 28–33.

Alshammari T. K. (2020). The Ketamine antidepressant story: New insights. *Molecules*, 25(23), 5777.

Altemus M., Sarvaiya N., and Neill E. C. (2014). Sex differences in anxiety and depression clinical perspectives. *Front. Neuroendocrinol.*, 35(3), 320–330.

Altemus, M. (2006). Sex differences in depression and anxiety

disorders: Potential biological determinants. *Horm. Behav.*, 50, 534–538.

Alusik, S., Kalatova, D., and Paluch, Z. (2014). Serotonin syndrome. *Neuroendocrinol. Lett.*, 35, 265–273.

Alvarez, A.V.G., Rubin D., Pina, P., and Velasquez, M. S. (2018). Neurodevelopmental outcomes and prenatal exposure to marijuana. *Pediatrics*, 142(1 Meeting Abstract), 787. doi: 10.1542/peds.142.1_MeetingAbstract.787.

Alvarez, J. A., and Emory, E. (2006). Executive function and the frontal lobes: A meta-analytic review. *Neuropsychol. Rev.*, 16, 17–42.

Alvarez, J. I., Katayama, T., and Prat, A. (2013). Glial influence on the blood brain barrier. *Glia*, 61, 1939–1958.

Alzado, L. (1991). I'm sick and I'm scared. Sports Illustrated. Available at www.si.com/vault/1991/07/08/124507/im-sick-and-im-scared-the-author-aformer-nfl-star-has-a-dread-diseasethat-he-blames-on-his-use-of-performance-enhancing-drugs%255D.

Amaladoss, A., and O'Brien, S. (2011). Cough syrup psychosis. *CJEM*, 13, 53–56.

Amantea, D., and Bagetta, G. (2017). Excitatory and inhibitory amino acid neurotransmitters in stroke: from neurotoxicity to ischemic tolerance. *Curr. Opin. Pharmacol.*, 35, 111–119.

Ambre, J. J., Belknap, S. M., Nelson, J., Ruo, T. I., Shin, S. G., and Atkinson, A. J. Jr. (1988). Acute tolerance to cocaine in humans. *Clin. Pharmacol. Ther.*, 44, /1–/2.

American Academy of Pediatrics. (2015). Aap Says No Amount of Alcohol Should Be Considered Safe During Pregnancy. Available at www.aap.org/en-us/aboutthe-aap/aap-press-room/Pages/ AAP-Says-No-Amount-of-AlcoholShould-be-Considered-Safe-DuringPregnancy.aspx.

American Academy of Pediatrics. (2018). Where We Stand: Alcohol During Pregnancy. https://www.healthychildren.org/English/ages-stages/prenatal/Pages/Where-We-Stand-Alcohol-During-Pregnacy.aspx.

American Association for Clinical Chemistry. (2011). Therapeutic Drug Monitoring. Available at www.labtestsonline.org/ understanding/analytes/therapeutic_drug/glance.html.

American College of Obstetricians and Gynecologists (2017). Marijuana use during pregnancy and lactation. Committee Opinion No. 722. *Obstet. Gynecol.*, 130, e205–e209.

American Psychiatric Association. (2013). *Diagnostic and Statistical Manual of Mental Disorders* (5th ed.). Arlington, VA: American Psychiatric Association.

Amireault, P., Sibon, D., and Côté, F. (2013). Life without peripheral serotonin: Insights from tryptophan hydroxylase 1 knockout mice reveal the existence of paracrine/autocrine serotonergic networks. *ACS Chem. Neurosci.*, 4, 64–71.

Amoroso, T., and Workman, M. (2016). Treating posttraumatic stress disorder with MDMA-assisted psychotherapy: A preliminary meta-analysis and comparison to prolonged exposure therapy. *J. Psychopharmacol.*, 30, 595–600.

Anawalt B.D. (2019). Diagnosis and management of anabolic androgenic steroid use. *J. Clin. Endocrinol. Metab.*, 104, 2490–2500.

Andari, E., Duhamel, J. R., Zalla, T., Herbrecht, E., Leboyer, M., and Sirigu A. (2010). Promoting social behavior with oxytocin in high-functioning autism spectrum disorders. *Proc. Natl. Acad. Sci. USA*, 107, 4389–4394.

Andersen, S. L., Tomada, A., Vincow, E. S., Valente, E., Polcari, A., and Teicher, M. H. (2008). Preliminary evidence for sensitive periods in the effect of childhood sexual abuse on regional brain development. *J. Neuropsychiatry Clin. Neurosci.*, 20, 292–301.

Anderson, E., and Hearing, M. (2019). Neural circuit plasticity in addiction. In M. Torregrossa (Ed.), *Neural Mechanisms in Addiction*, pp. 35–60. San Diego: Academic Press.

Anderson, L. J., Flynn, A., and Pilgrim, J. L. (2017). A global epidemiological perspective on the toxicology of drug-facilitated sexual assault: A systematic review. *J. Forensic Legal Med.*, 47, 46–54.

Andrade, A. K., Renda, B., and Murray, J. E. (2019). Cannabinoids, interoception, and anxiety. *Pharmacol. Biochem. Behav.*, 180, 60–73.

Andrade, R., Huereca, D., Lyons, J. G., Andrade, E. M., and McGregor, K. M. (2015). 5-HT1A receptor-mediated autoinhibition and the control of serotonergic cell firing. *ACS Chem. Neurosci.*, 6, 1110–1115.

Andre, C. M., Hausman, J.-F., and Guerriero, G. (2016). Cannabis sativa: The plant of the thousand and one molecules. *Front. Plant Sci.*, 7, 19. doi: 10.3389/fpls.2016.00019.

Andreasen, N. C. (1990). Positive and negative symptoms: Historical and conceptual aspects. In T. A. Ban, A. M. Freedman, C. G. Gottfries, R. Levy, P. Pinchot, and W. Poldinger (Eds.), *Modern Problems of Pharmacopsychiatry*, pp. 1–42. Basel, Switzerland: Karger.

Andreassen, C. S., Pallesen, S., Griffiths, M. D., Torsheim, T., and Sinha, R. (2018). The development and validation of the Bergen-Yale Sex Addiction Scale

with a large national sample. *Front. Psychol.*, 9, 144. doi: 10.3389/fpsyg.2018.00144.

Andreassen, O. A., Wang, Y., Mäki-Marttunen, T., Smeland, O. B., Fan, C. C., et al. (2017). Genetic evidence for role of integration of fast and slow neurotransmission in schizophrenia. *Mol. Psychiatry*, 22, 792–801.

Andresen, H., Aydin, B. E., Mueller, A., and Iwersen-Bergmann, S. (2011). An overview of gamma-hydroxybutyric acid: Pharmacodynamics, pharmacokinetics, toxic effects, addiction, analytical methods, and interpretation of results. *Drug Test Anal.*, 3, 560–568.

Andrews, M. A., Magee, C. D., Combest, T. M., Allard, R. J., and Douglas, K. M. (2018). Physical effects of anabolic-androgenic steroids in healthy exercising adults: A systematic review and meta-analysis. *Curr. Sports Med. Rep.*, 17, 232–241.

Angoa-Pérez, M., Anneken, J. H., and Kuhn, D. M. (2017). Neurotoxicology of synthetic cathinone analogs. *Curr. Topics Behav. Neurosci.*, 32, 209–230.

Angoa-Pérez, M., Kane, M. J., Briggs, D. I., Sykes, C. E., Shah, M. M., Francescutti, D. M., et al. (2012). Genetic depletion of brain 5-HT reveals a common molecular pathway mediating compulsivity and impulsivity. *J. Neurochem.*, 121, 974–984.

Angoa-Pérez, M., Kane, M. J., Sykes, C. E., Perrine, S. A., Church, M. W., and Kuhn, D. M. (2014). Brain serotonin determines maternal behavioral and offspring survival. *Genes Brain Behav.*, 13, 579–591.

Anthony, J. C., Lopez-Quintero, C., and Alshaarawy, O. (2016). Cannabis epidemiology: A selective review. *Curr. Pharm. Des.*, 22, 1–13.

Antkowiak, B., and Rudolph, U. (2016). New insights in the systemic and molecular underpinnings of general anesthetic actions mediated by $GABA_A$ receptors. *Curr. Opin. Anesthesiol.*, 29, 447–453.

Antolin-Fontes, B., Ables, J. L., Görlich, A., and Ibañez-Tallon, I. (2015). The habenulo-interpeduncular pathway in nicotine aversion and withdrawal. *Neuropharmacology*, 96, 213–222.

Anton, R. F., O'Malley, S. S., Ciraulo, D. A., Cisler, R. A., Couper, D., Donovan, D. M., et al. (2006). Combined pharmacotherapies and behavioral interventions for alcohol dependence: The COMBINE study: A randomized controlled trial. *JAMA*, 295, 2003–2017.

Apawu, A. K., Callan, S P., Mathews, T. A., and Bowen, S. E. (2020). Repeated toluene exposure leads to neuroadaptation in dopamine release mechanisms within the nucleus accumbens core. *Toxicol. Appl. Pharmacol.*, 408, 115260. doi: 10.1016/j. taap.2020.115260.

Applegate, M. (1999). Cytochrome P450 isoenzymes: Nursing considerations. *Am. Psychiatr. Nurs. Assoc.*, 5, 15–22.

Apter, A., van Praag, H. M., Plutchik, R., Sevy, S., Korn, M., and Brown, S. L. (1990). Interrelationships among anxiety, aggression, impulsivity, and mood: A serotonergically linked cluster? *Psychiatry Res.*, 32, 191–199.

Aragi, N. and Lesch, K.-P. (2013). Serotonin (5-HT) in the regulation of depression-related emotionality: Insight from 5-HT transporter and tryptophan hydroxylase-2 knockout mouse models. *Curr. Drug Targets*, 14, 549–570.

Arai, A. C. and Kessler, M. (2007). Pharmacology of ampakine modulators: From AMPA receptors to synapses and behavior. *Curr. Drug Targets*, 8, 583–602.

Araque, A., Carmignoto, G., Haydon, P. G., Oliet, S. H. R., Robitaille, R., and Volterra, A. (2014). Gliotransmitters travel in time and space. *Neuron*, 81, 728–739.

Araújo, A. M., Carvalho, F., de Lourdes Bastos, M., de Pinho, P. G., and Carvalho, M. (2015). The hallucinogenic world of tryptamines: An updated review. *Arch. Toxicol.*, 89, 1151–1173.

Archie, S. R., and Cucullo, L. (2019). Harmful effects of smoking cannabis: A cerebrovascular and neurological perspective. *Front. Pharmacol.*, 10, 1481. doi: 10.3389/fphar.2019.01481.

Argilli, E., Sibley, D. R., Malenka, R. C., England, P. M., and Bonci, A. (2008). Mechanism and time course of cocaine-induced long-term potentiation in the ventral tegmental area. *J. Neurosci.*, 28, 909/1–/2100.

Arican, P., Gencpinar, P., Cavusoglu, D., and Dundar, N. O. (2018). Clinical and genetic features of congenital myasthenic syndromes due to CHAT mutations: Case report and literature review. *Neuropediatrics*, 49, 28/1–/288.

Armada-Moreira, A., Gomes, J. I., Pina, C. C., Savchak, O. K., Gonçalves-Ribeiro, J., Rei, N., Pinto, S., et al. (2020). Going the extra (synaptic) mile: Excitotoxicity as the road toward neurodegenerative diseases. *Front. Cell. Neurosci.*, 14, 90. doi: 10.3389/fncel.2020.00090.

Armstrong, F., McCurdy, M. T., and Heavner, M. S. (2019). Synthetic cannabinoid-associated multiple organ failure: Case series and literature review. *Pharmacotherapy*, 39, 50/1–/213.

Arnold, J. C. (2005). The role of endocannabinoid transmission in cocaine addiction. *Pharmacol. Biochem. Behav.*, 81, 396–406.

Arnone, D., Saraykar, S., Salem, H., Teixeira, A. L., Dantzer, R.,

and Selvaraj, S. (2018). Role of Kynurenine pathway and its metabolites in mood disorders: A systematic review and meta-analysis of clinical studies. *Neurosci. Biobehav. Rev.*, 92, 47/1–/285.

Arns, M., and Olbrich, S. (2014). Personalized medicine in ADHD and depression: Use of pharmaco-EEG. In V. Kumari, P. Bob, and N. Boutros (Eds.), *Electrophysiology and Psychophysiology in Psychiatry and Psychopharmacology*, pp. 345–370. New York: Springer.

Arnsten, A. F. T. (2009). Toward a new understanding of attention-deficit hyperactivity disorder pathophysiology: An important role for prefrontal cortex dysfunction. *CNS Drugs*, 23(Suppl. 1), 33–41. doi.org/10.2165/00023210-200923000-00005

Arnsten, A. F. T. (2011). Catecholamine influences on dorsolateral prefrontal cortical networks. *Biol. Psychiatry*, 69, e89–e99.

Arnsten, A. F. T., and Jin, L. E. (2012). Guanfacine for the treatment of cognitive disorders: A century of discoveries at Yale. *Yale J. Biol. Med.*, 85, 45–58.

Arnsten, A. F., Girgis, R. R., Gray, D. L., and Mailman, R. B. (2017). Novel dopamine therapeutics for cognitive deficits in schizophrenia. *Biol. Psychiatry*, 81, 67–77.

Arnsten, A.F.T. (2020). Guanfacine's mechanism of action in treating prefrontal cortical disorders: Successful translation across species. *Neurobiol. Learn. Mem.*, 176, 107237. doi: 10.1016/j. nlm.2020.107237.

Arps, K. (2018). Spotlighting the Effects and Dangers of K2, or Synthetic Marijuana. Available at https://abcnews.go.com/ Health/spotlighting-effects-dangers-k2-synthetic-marijuana/ story?id=54206649 (accessed 2/12/21).

Arranz, M. J., and Kapur, S. (2008). Pharmacogenetics in psychiatry: Are we ready for widespread clinical use? *Schizophr. Bull.*, 34, 1130–1144.

Arria, A. M., Caldeira, K. M., Vincent, K. B., O'Grady, K. E., Cimini, M. D., Geisner, I. M., et al. (2017). Do college students improve their grades by using prescription stimulants nonmedically? *Addict. Behav.*, 65, 245–249.

Arria, A. M., Geisner, I. M., Cimini, M. D., Kilmer, J. R., Caldeira, K. M., Barrall, A. L., Vincent, K. B., et al. (2018). Perceived academic benefit is associated with nonmedical prescription stimulant use among college students. *Addict. Behav.*, 76, 27–35.

Arrigoni, E., Chee, M.J.S., and Fuller, P. M. (2019). To eat or to sleep: That is a lateral hypothalamic question. *Neuropharmacology*, 154, 34–49.

Ashok, A. H., Mizuno, Y., Volkow, N. D., and Howes, O. D. (2017). Association of stimulant use with dopaminergic alterations in users of cocaine, amphetamine, or methamphetamine. A systematic review and meta-analysis. *JAMA Psychiatry*, 74, 511–519.

Ashrafioun, L., Bonadio, F. A., Baik, K. D., Bradbury, S. L., Carhart, V. L., Cross, N. A., Davis, A. K., et al. (2016). Patterns of use, acute subjective experiences, and motivations for using synthetic cathinones ("bath salts") in recreational users. *J. Psychoactive Drugs*, 48, 336–343.

Aso, E., and Ferrer, I. (2014). Cannabinoids for treatment of Alzheimer's disease: Moving toward the clinic. *Front. Pharmacol.*, 5, 37. doi: 10.3389/fphar.2014.00037.

Aso, E., and Ferrer, I. (2016). CB_2 cannabinoid receptor as potential target against Alzheimer's disease. *Front. Neurosci.*, 10, 243. doi: 10.3389/fnins.2016.00243.

Aston-Jones, G., and Waterhouse, B. (2016). Locus coeruleus: From global projection system to adaptive regulation of behavior. *Brain Res.*, 1645, 75–78.

Astorino, T. A., and Roberson, D. W. (2010). Efficacy of acute caffeine ingestion for short-term high-intensity exercise performance: A systematic review. *J. Strength Cond. Res.*, 24, 257–265.

Atroszko, P. A., Andreassen, C. S., Griffiths, M. D., and Pallesen, S. (2015). Study addiction: A new area of psychological study: Conceptualization, assessment, and preliminary empirical findings. *J. Behav. Addict.*, 4, 75–84.

Atsak, P., Roozendaal, B., and Campolongo, P. (2012). Role of the endocannabinoid system in regulating glucocorticoid effects on memory for emotional experiences. *Neuroscience*, 204, 104–116.

Atwood, B. K., and Mackie, K. (2010). CB_2, A cannabinoid receptor with an identity crisis. *Br. J. Pharmacol.*, 160, 467–479.

Aubrey, K. R. (2016). Presynaptic control of inhibitory neurotransmitter content in VIAAT containing synaptic vesicles. *Neurochem. Int.*, 98, 94–102.

Audrain-McGovern, J., and Benowitz, N. L. (2011). Cigarette smoking, nicotine, and body weight. *Clin. Pharmacol. Ther.*, 90, 164–168.

Auer, T., Schreppel, P., Erker, T., and Schwarzer, C. (2020). Impaired chloride homeostasis in epilepsy: Molecular basis, impact on treatment, and current treatment approaches. *Pharmacol. Ther.*, 205, 107422, doi: 10.1016/j. pharmthera.2019.107422.

Augustin, S. M., and Lovinger, D. M. (2018). Functional relevance of endocannabinoid-dependent synaptic plasticity in the central nervous system. *ACS Chem. Neurosci.*, 9, 214/1–/2161.

Auluck, P. K., Caraveo, G., and Lindquist, S. (2010). α-Synuclein: Membrane interactions and toxicity in Parkinson's disease. *Annu. Rev. Cell Dev. Biol.*, 26, 211–233.

Azam, A., Manchanda, S., Thotapalli, S., and Kotha, S. B. (2015). Botox therapy in dentistry: A review. *J. Int. Oral Health*, 7(Suppl. 2), 103–105.

B

Babenko, O., Kovalchuk, I., and Metz, G. A. (2015). Stress-induced perinatal and transgenerational epigenetic programming of brain development and mental health. *Neurosci. Biobehav. Rev.*, 48, 70–91.

Babic, T., and Browning, K. N. (2014). The role of vagal neurocircuits in the regulation of nausea and vomiting. *Eur. J. Pharmacol.*, 722, 38–47.

Babor, T. F, Hofmann, M., DelBoca, F. K., Hesselbrock, V., Meyer, R. E., Dolinsky, Z. S., and Rounsaville, B. (1992). Types of alcoholics, I. Evidence for an empirically derived typology based on indicators of vulnerability and severity. *Arch. Gen. Psychiatry*, 49, 599–608.

Bachner-Melman, R., and Ebstein, R. P. (2014). The role of oxytocin and vasopressin in emotional and social behaviors. *Handb. Clin. Neurol.*, 124, 53–68.

Bachtell, R. K., Whisler, K., Karanian, D., and Self, D. W. (2005). Effects of intranucleus accumbens shell administration of dopamine agonists and antagonists on cocaine-taking and cocaine-seeking behaviors in the rat. *Psychopharmacology*, 183, 41–53.

Badiani A. (2013). Substance-specific environmental influences on drug use and drug preference in animals and humans. *Curr. Opin. Neurobiol.*, 23, 588–596.

Badiani, A., Belin, D., Epstein, D., Calu, D., and Shaham, Y. (2011). Opiate versus psychostimulant addiction: The differences do matter. *Nat. Rev. Neurosci.*, 12, 685–700.

Bagni, C., and Zukin, R. S. (2019). A synaptic perspective of fragile X syndrome and autism spectrum disorders. *Neuron*, 101, 107/1–/2088.

Bailey, D. B., Jr., Berry-Kravis, E., Wheeler, A., Raspa, M., Merrien, F., Ricart, J., et al. (2016). Mavoglurant in adolescents with fragile X syndrome: Analysis of Clinical Global Impression-Improvement source data from a double-blind therapeutic study followed by an open-label, long-term extension study. *J. Neurodev. Disorders*, 8, 1. doi: 10.1186/s11689-015-9134-5.

Baker, L. B., Nuccio, R. P., and Jeukendrup, A. E. (2014). Acute effects of dietary constituents on motor skill and cognitive performance in athletes. *Nutr. Rev.*, 72, 790–802.

Bale, T. L., Abel, T., Akil, H., Carlezon, W. A. Jr., Moghaddam, B., Nestler, E. J., Ressler, K. J., et al. (2019). The critical importance of basic animal research for neuropsychiatric disorders. *Neuropsychopharmacology*, 44(8), 1349–1353. https://doi.org/10.1038/s41386-019-0405-9

Balendra, R., and Patani, R. (2016). Quo vadis motor neuron disease? *World J. Methodol.*, 6, 56–64.

Bales, R. F. (1946). Cultural differences in rates of alcoholism. *Q. J. Studies Alcohol*, 6, 480–499.

Ballard, C. L., and Wood, R. I. (2005). Intracerebroventricular self-administration of commonly abused anabolic–androgenic steroids in male hamsters (*Mesocricetus auratus*): Nandrolone, drostanolone, oxymetholone, and stanozolol. *Behav. Neurosci.*, 119, 752–758.

Ballinger, E. C., Ananth, M., Talmage, D. A., and Role, L. W. (2016). Basal forebrain cholinergic circuits and signaling in cognition and cognitive decline. *Neuron*, 91, 1199–1218.

Balster, R. L., and Woolverton, W. L. (1980). Continuous-access phencyclidine self-administration by rhesus monkeys leading to physical dependence. *Psychopharmacology*, 70, 5–10.

Balster, R. L., and Woolverton, W. L. (1981). Tolerance and dependence to phencyclidine. In E. F. Domino (Ed.), *PCP (Phencyclidine): Historical and Current Perspectives*, pp. 293–306. Ann Arbor, MI: NPP.

Baltimore, D., Berg, P., Botchan, M., Carroll, D., Charo, R. A., Church, G., Corn, J. E., et al. (2015). A prudent path forward for genomic engineering and germline gene modification. *Science*, 348(6230), 36–38. https://doi.org/10.1126/science.aab1028

Balu, D. T., and Coyle, J. T. (2015). The NMDA receptor "glycine modulatory site" in schizophrenia: D-serine, glycine, and beyond. *Curr. Opin. Pharmacol.*, 20, 109–115.

Balu, D. T., and Lucki, I. (2009). Adult hippocampal neurogenesis: Regulation, functional implications, and contribution to disease pathology. *Neurosci. Biobehav. Rev.*, 33, 232–252.

Balzer, N., McLeod, S. L., Walsh, C., and Grewal, K. (2021). Low-dose ketamine for acute pain control in the emergency department: A systematic review and meta-analysis. *Acad. Emerg. Med.*, 28, 444–454.

Bamberger, M., and Yaeger, D. (1997). Over the Edge: Aware That Drug Testing Is a Sham, Athletes To Rely More Than Ever On Banned Performance Enhancers. Sports Illustrated. Available at www.si.com/vault/1997/04/14/225484/over-the-edge-aware-that-drug-testingis-a-sham-athletes-to-rely-more-thanever-on-bannedperformance-enhancers.

Banga, A. K. (2009). Microporation applications for enhancing drug delivery. *Expert Opin. Drug Deliv.*, 6, 343–354.

Banken, J. A., and Foster, H. (2008). Dextromethorphan: An emerging drug of abuse. *Ann. N. Y. Acad. Sci.*, 1139, 402–411.

Banks, M. L., and Negus, S. S. (2017). Insights from preclinical choice models on treating drug addiction. *Trends Pharmacol. Sci.*, 38, 181–194.

Baptiste-Roberts, K., and Leviton, A. (2020). Caffeine exposure during pregnancy: Is it safe? *Semin. Fetal Neonatal Med.*, 25(6), 101174. doi: 10.1016/j.siny.2020.101174.

Barbano, M. F., and Cador, M. (2007). Opioids for hedonic experience and dopamine to get ready for it. *Psychopharmacology*, 191, 497–506.

Barch, D. M., Carter, C. S., Arnsten, A., Buchanan, R. W., Cohen, J. D., Geyer, M., et al. (2009). Selecting paradigms from cognitive neuroscience for translation into use in clinical trials: Proceedings of the third CNTRICS meeting. *Schizophr. Bull.*, 35, 109–114.

Bardo, M. T., Donohew, R. L., and Harrington, N. G. (1996). Psychobiology of novelty seeking and drug seeking behavior. *Behav. Brain Res.*, 77, 23–43.

Bargu, S., Silver, M. W., Ohman, M. D., Benitez-Nelson, C. R., and Garrison, D. L. (2012). Mystery behind Hitchcock's birds. *Nat. Geosci.*, 2–3.

Baribeau, D. A., and Anagnostou, E. (2015). Oxytocin and vasopression: Linking pituitary neuropeptides and their receptors to social neurocircuits. *Front. Neurosci.*, 9, 335. doi: 10.3389/fnins.2015.00335.

Barlow, D. H., and Durand, V. M. (1995). *Abnormal Psychology: An Integrative Approach*. New York: Brooks/Cole.

Barnes, R. K. (2020). "Pediatric anesthetic neurotoxicity": Time to stop! *Anesth. Analg.*, 131, 73/1–/237.

Barnett, G., Chiang, C.-W. N., Perez-Reyes, M., and Owens, S. M. (1982). Kinetic study of smoking marijuana. *J. Pharmacokinet. Biopharm.*, 10, 495–506. doi.org/10.1007/BF01059033

Barnett, M. L., Olenski, A. R., and Jena, A. B. (2017). Opioid-prescribing patterns of emergency physicians and risk of long-term use. *N. Engl. J. Med.*, 376, 663–673.

Baron, E. P. (2015). Comprehensive review of medicinal marijuana, cannabinoids, and therapeutic implications in medicine and headache: What a long strange trip it's been …. *Headache*, 55, 885–916.

Barrera-Algarín, E., and Vázquez-Fernández, M. J. (2021). The rise of online sports betting, its fallout, and the onset of a new profile in gambling disorder: young people. *J. Addict. Dis.*, 39(3), 363–372.

Barrington-Trimis, J. L., Kong, G., Leventhal, A. M., Liu, F., Mayer, M., Cruz, T. B., Krishnan-Sarin, S., et al. (2018). E-cigarette use and subsequent smoking frequency among adolescents. *Pediatrics*, 142(6), e20180486. doi: 10.1542/peds.2018.0486.

Bartus, R. T., Dean, R. L., III, Beer, B., and Lippa, A. S. (1982). The cholinergic hypothesis of geriatric memory dysfunction. *Science*, 217, 408–414.

Basaria, S. (2014). Male hypogonadism. *Lancet*, 383, 1250–1263.

Basaria, S. (2018). Use of performance-enhancing (and image-enhancing) drugs: A growing problem in need of a solution. *Mol. Cell. Endocrinol.*, 464, 1–3.

Basile, A. S., Fedorova, I., Zapata, A., Liu, X., Shippenberg, T., Duttaroy, A., et al. (2002). Deletion of the M5 muscarinic acetylcholine receptor attenuates morphine reinforcement and withdrawal but not morphine analgesia. *Proc. Natl. Acad. Sci. USA*, 99, 11452–11457.

Bass M. (1970). Sudden sniffing death. *J. Amer. Med. Assoc.*, 212, 2075–2079.

Bass, C. E., Grinevich, V. P., Gioia, D., Day-Brown, J. D., Bonin, K. D., Stuber, G. D., Weiner, J. L., et al. (2013). Optogenetic stimulation of VTA dopamine neurons reveals that tonic but not phasic patterns of dopamine transmission reduce ethanol self-administration. *Front. Behav. Neurosci.*, 7, Article 173.

Bassetti, C.L.A., Adamantidis, A., Burdakov, D., Han, F., Gay, S., Kallweit, U., et al. (2019). Narcolepsy – clinical spectrum, aetiopathophysiology, diagnosis and treatment. *Nat. Rev. Neurol.*, 15, 519–539.

Bastiaanssen, T.F.S., Cowan, C.S.M., Claesson, M. J., Dinan, T. G., and Cryan, J. F. (2019). Making sense of … the microbiome in psychiatry. *Int. J. Neuropsychopharmacol.*, 22, 37–52.

Batalia, A., Bos, J., Postma, A., and Bossong, M. G. (2021). The impact of cannabidiol on human brain function: A systematic review. *Front. Pharmacol.*, 11, 618184. doi: 10.3389/fphar.2020.618184.

Bates, G., Van Hout, M. C., Teck, J., and McVeigh, J. (2019). Treatments for people who use anabolic androgenic steroids: a scoping review. *Harm Reduct. J.*, 16(1), 75. doi: 10.1186/s12954-019-0343-1.

Bates, M. L., and Trujillo, K. A. (2021). Use and abuse of dissociative and psychedelic drugs in adolescence. *Pharmacol. Biochem. Behav.*, 203, 173129. doi: 10.1016/j.pbb.2021.173129.

Bates, S. S., Hubbard, K. A., Lundholm, N., Montresor, M., and Leaw, C. P. (2018). *Pseudonitzschia, Nitzschia*, and domoic acid: New research since 2011. *Harmful Algae*, 79, 3–43.

Batista, E. M. L., Doria, J. G., Ferreira-Vieira, T. H., Alves-Silva, J., Ferguson, S. S. G., Moreira, F. A., et al. (2016). Orchestrated activation of mGluR5 and CB₁ promotes neuroprotection. *Mol. Brain*, 9, 80. doi: 10.1186/s13041-016-0259-6.

Battaglia, G., and Bruno, V. (2018). Metabotropic glutamate receptor involvement in the pathophysiology of amyotrophic lateral sclerosis: New potential drug targets for therapeutic applications. *Curr. Opin. Pharmacol.*, 38, 65–71.

Battleday, R. M., and Brem, A.-K. (2015). Modafinil for cognitive neuroenhancement in healthy non-sleep-deprived subjects: A systematic review. *Eur. Neuropsychopharmacol.*, 25, 1865–1881.

Bauer, E. P. (2015). Serotonin in fear conditioning processes. *Behav. Brain Res.*, 277, 68–77.

Bauer, I. (2019). Travel medicine, coca and cocaine: demystifying and rehabilitating Erythroxylum—A comprehensive review. *Trop. Dis. Travel Med. Vaccines*, 5, 20. doi: 10.1186/s40794-019-0095-7.

Bauer, I. E., Soares, J. C., and Nielsen, D. A. (2015). The role of opioidergic genes in the treatment outcome of drug addiction pharmacotherapy: A systematic review. *Am. J. Addict.*, 24, 15–23.

Bauersfeld, K.-H., Olek, J., Meißner, H., Hannemann, D., Spenke, J. (1973). Analyse des Einsatzes u. M. in den leichtathletischen Wurf-/Stoß-disziplinen und Versuch trainingsmethodischer Abteilungen und Verallgemeinerungen [Scientific Report. German Athletic Association (DVfL) of the GDR]. Science Center of the DVfL. 41 pp.

Baumann, M. H., Solis, E., Jr., Watterson, L. R., Marusich, J. A., Fantegrossi, W. E., and Wiley, J. L. (2014). Bath salts, spice, and related designer drugs: The science behind the headlines. *J. Neurosci.*, 34, 15150–15158.

Baumann, M. H., Walters, H. M., Niello, M., and Sitte, H. H. (2018). Neuropharmacology of synthetic cathinones. *Handb. Exp. Pharmacol.*, 252, 113–142.

Bava, S., and Tapert, S. F. (2010). Adolescent brain development and the risk for alcohol and other drug problems. *Neuropsychol. Rev.*, 20, 398–413.

Baxter, L. R., Jr., Schwartz, J. M., Bergman, K. S., Szuba, M. P., Guze, B. H., Mazziotta, J. C., et al. (1992). Caudate glucose metabolic rate changes with both drug and behavior therapy for obsessive-compulsive disorder. *Arch. Gen. Psychiatry,* 49, 681–689.

Baxter, M. G. (2001). Effects of selective immunotoxic lesions on learning and memory. In W. A. Hall (Ed.), *Methods in Molecular Biology,* Volume 166, Immunotoxin Methods and Protocols (pp. 249– 265). Totowa, NJ: Humana.

Bay, T., Eghorn, L. F., Klein, A. B., and Wellendorph, P. (2014). GHB receptor targets in the CNS: focus on high-affinity binding sites. Biochem. Pharmacol., 87, 220–228.

Bazazi, A. R., Zaller, N. D., Fu, J. J., and Rich, J. D. (2010). Preventing opiate overdose deaths: Examining objections to take-home naloxone. J. Health Care Poor Underserved, 21, 1108–1113.

BBC News (2020). Reynhard Sinaga: 'Evil sexual predator' jailed for life for 136 rapes. Available at https://www.bbc.com/news/uk-50987823. Accessed 6/29/21.

Bear, M. F., Connors, B. W., and Paradiso, M. A. (2016). *Neuroscience: Exploring the Brain* (4th ed.). Philadelphia: Lippincott, Williams, and Wilkins.

Bear, M. F., Huber, K. M., and Warren, S. T. (2004). The mGluR theory of fragile X mental retardation. *Trends Neurosci.,* 27, 370–377.

Beaver, K. M., Vaughn, M. G., DeLisi, M., and Wright, J. P. (2008). Anabolic–androgenic steroid use and involvement in violent behavior in a nationally representative sample of young adult males in the United States. Am. J. Pub. Health, 98, 2185–2187.

Becker, H. C., and Mulholland, P. J. (2014). Neurochemical mechanisms of alcohol withdrawal. Handbook of Clinical Neurology, 125, 133–156. https://doi.org/10.1016/B978-0-444-62619-6.00009-4

Becker, J. B., and Hu, M. (2008). Sex differences in drug abuse. *Front. Neuroendocrinol.,* 29, 36–47.

Beckley, J. T., and Woodward, J. J. (2013). Volatile solvents as drugs of abuse: Focus on the corticomesolimbic circuitry. *Neuropsychopharmacology,* 38, 2555–2567.

Befort, K. (2015). Interactions of the opioid and cannabinoid systems in reward: Insights from knockout studies. *Front. Pharmacol.,* 6, 6. doi: 10.3389/fphar.2015.00006.

Beis, D., Holzwarth, K., Flinders, M., Bader, M., Wöhr, M., and Alenina, N. (2015). Brain serotonin deficiency leads to social communication deficits in mice. *Biol. Lett.,* 11(3), 20150057.

Belelli, D., and Lambert, J. J. (2005). Neurosteroids: Endogenous regulators of the GABA$_A$ receptor. *Nat. Rev. Neurosci.,* 6, 56/1–/275.

Belelli, D., Harrison, N. L., Maguire, J., Macdonald, R. L., Walker, M. C., and Cope, D. W. (2009). Extrasynaptic GABA$_A$ receptors: Form, pharmacology, and function. J. Neurosci., 29, 12757–12763.

Bell, K., and Keane, H. (2014). All gates lead to smoking: The "gateway theory," e-cigarettes and the remaking of nicotine. *Soc. Sci. Med.,* 119, 45–52.

Bell, R. L., McKinzie, D. L., Murphy, J. M., and McBride, W. J. (2000). Sensitivity and tolerance to the motor impairing effects of moderate doses of ethanol. *Pharmacol. Biochem. Behav.,* 67, 583–586.

Bello, E. P., Mateo, Y., Gelman, D. M., Noaín, D., Shin, J. H., Low, M. J., et al. (2011). Cocaine supersensitivity and enhanced motivation for reward in mice lacking dopamine D2 autoreceptors. *Nat. Neurosci.,* 14, 1033–1038.

Bello, E. P., Casas-Cordero, R., Galiñanes, G. L., Belluscio, M. A., Rodriguez, V., Noaín, D., et al. (2017). Inducible ablation of dopamine D2 receptors in adult mice impairs locomotion, motor skill learning and leads to severe parkinsonism. *Mol. Psychiatry,* 22, 59/1–/204.

Belmaker, R. H., and Agam, G. (2008). Major depressive disorder. *N. Engl. J. Med.,* 358, 55–68.

Belzer, K., and Schneier, F. R. (2004). Comorbidity of anxiety and depressive disorders: Issues in conceptualization, assessment, and treatment. J. Psychiatr. Pract., 10, 296–306.

Ben-Ari, Y., Khalilov, I., Kahle, K. T., and Cherubini, E. (2012). The GABA excitatory/inhibitory shift in brain maturation and neurological disorders. *Neuroscientist,* 18, 467–486.

Benedetti, F., Carlino, E., and Pollo, A. (2011). How placebos change the patient's brain. *Neuropsychopharmacol.,* 36, 339–354.

Benhamú, B., Martín-Fontecha, M., Vázquez-Villa, H., Pardo, L., and López-Rodríguez, M. L. (2014). Serotonin 5-HT6 receptor antagonists for the treatment of cognitive deficiency in Alzheimer's disease. J. Med. Chem., 57, 7160–7181.

Benko, J., and Vranková, S. (2020). Natural psychoplastogens as antidepressant agents. *Molecules,* 25, 1172. doi: 10.3390/molecules25051172.

Bennett, T., Bray, D., and Neville, M. W. (2014). Suvorexant, a dual orexin receptor antagonist for the management of insomnia. *Pharm. Ther.,* 39, 264–266.

Benowitz, N. L. (1992). Cigarette smoking and nicotine addiction. Med. Clin. North Am., 76, 415–437. © 2014. Reprinted with permission from Elsevier

Benowitz, N. L. (2010). Nicotine addiction. *N. Engl. J. Med.,* 362, 2295–2303.

Benowitz, N. L., and Burbank, A. D. (2016). Cardiovascular toxicity of nicotine: Implications for electronic cigarette use. *Trends Cardiovasc. Med.,* 26, 515–523.

Benson, S., Verster, J. C., Alford, C., and Scholey, A. (2014). Effects of mixing alcohol with caffeinated beverages on subjective intoxication: A systematic review and meta-analysis. *Neurosci. Biobehav. Rev.,* 47, 16–21.

Benzenhöfer, U., and Passie, T. (2010). Rediscovering MDMA (ecstasy): The role of the American chemist Alexander T. Shulgin. *Addiction,* 105, 1355–1361.

Benzer, T. I. (2015). Tetrodotoxin Toxicity Clinical Presentation. Medscape. emedicine.medscape.com/article/818763clinical#b5.

Beoris, M., Wilson, J. A., Garces, J. A., and Lukowiak, A. A. (2016). CYP2D6 copy number distribution in the US population. *Pharmacogenet. Genomics,* 26, 96–99.

Berar, A., Allain, J.-S., Allard, S., Lefevre, C., Baert, A., Morel, I., Bouvet, R., et al. (2019). Intoxication with 3-MeO-PCP alone. A case report and literature review. *Medicine,* 98, 52(e18295). doi: 10.1097/MD.0000000000018295.

Berardi, A., Schelling, G., and Campolongo, P. (2016). The endocannabinoid system and Post Traumatic Stress Disorder (PTSD): From preclinical findings to innovative therapeutic approaches in clinical settings. *Pharmacol. Res.,* 111, 668–678.

Berczik, K., Szabó, A., Griffiths, M. D., Kurimay, T., Kun, B., Urbán, R., and Demetrovics, Z. (2012). Exercise addiction: Symptoms, diagnosis, epidemiology, and etiology. *Subst. Use Misuse,* 47, 403–417.

Berg, K. A., and Clarke, W. P. (2018). Making sense of pharmacology: Inverse agonism and functional selectivity. *Int. J. Neuropsychopharmacol.,* 21(10), 962–977. https://doi.org/10.1093/ijnp/pyy071

Bergman, J., and Paronis, C. A. (2006). Measuring the reinforcing strength of abused drugs. *Mol. Interv.,* 6, 273–283.

Bergman, J., Kamien, J. B., and Spealman, R. D. (1990). Antagonism of cocaine self-administration by selective dopamine D1 and D2 antagonists. *Behav. Pharmacol.,* 1, 355–363.

Berizzi, A. E., Perry, C. J., Shackleford, D. M., Lindsley, C. W., Jones, C. K., Chen, N. A., Sexton, P. M., et al. (2018). Muscarinic M5 receptors modulate ethanol seeking in rats. *Neuropsychopharmacology,* 43, 151/1–/2517.

Berkel, T. D., and Pandey, S. C. (2017). Emerging role of epigenetic mechanisms in alcohol addiction. *Alcohol. Clin. Exp. Res.,* 41, 666–680.

Bermon S. (2017). Androgens and athletic performance of elite female athletes. *Curr. Opin. Endocrinol. Diabetes Obes.,* 24, 246–251.

Berridge, C. W., and Arnsten, A. F. T. (2013). Psychostimulants and motivated behavior: Arousal and cognition. *Neurosci. Biobehav. Rev.,* 37, 1976–1984.

Berridge, C. W., and Arnsten, A. F. T. (2015). Catecholamine mechanisms in the prefrontal cortex: Proven strategies for enhancing higher cognitive function. *Curr. Opin. Behav. Sci.,* 4, 33–40.

Berridge, C. W., and Spencer, R. C. (2016). Differential cognitive actions of norepinephrine α2 and α1 receptor signaling in the prefrontal cortex. *Brain Res.,* 1641, 189–196.

Berridge, C. W., Schmeichel, B. E., and España, R. A. (2012b). Noradrenergic modulation of wakefulness/arousal. *Sleep Med. Rev.,* 16, 187–197.

Berridge, C., Devilbiss, D., Spencer, R., Schmeichel, B., Arnsten, A., and Schmeichel, B. (2012a). Attention deficit hyperactivity disorder. In J. E. Barrett, J. T. Coyle, and M. Williams (Eds), *Translational Neuroscience: Applications in Psychiatry, Neurology and Neurodevelopmental Disorders,* pp. 303–320. Cambridge, UK: Cambridge University Press.

Berridge, K. C., and Kringelbach, M. L. (2008). Affective neuroscience of pleasure: Reward in humans and animals. *Psychopharmacology,* 199, 457–480.

Berridge, K. C., and Kringelbach, M. L. (2015). Pleasure systems in the brain. *Neuron,* 86, 646–664.

Berridge, K. C., and Robinson, T. E. (2003). Parsing reward. *Trends Neurosci.,* 26, 507–513.

Berridge, K. C., Robinson, T. E., and Aldridge, J. W. (2009). Dissecting components of reward: "Liking," "wanting," and learning. *Curr. Opin. Pharmacol.,* 9, 65–73.

Berridge, K. C., and Robinson, T. E. (2016). Liking, wanting, and the incentive-sensitization theory of addiction. *Am. Psychol.,* 71, 670–679.

Berry-Kravis, E., Des Portes, V., Hagerman, R., Jacquemont, S., Charles, P., Visootsak, J., et al. (2016). Mavoglurant in fragile X syndrome: Results of two randomized, double-blind, placebo-controlled trials. *Sci. Transl. Med.,* 8, 321ra5. doi: 10.11126/scitranslmed.aab4109.

Bertelsen, A., Harvald, B., and Hauge, M. (1977). A Danish twin study of manic-depressive disorders. *Br. J. Psychiatry,* 130, 330–351.

Bertozzi, G., Sessa, F., Albano, G. D., Sani, G., Maglietta, F., Roshan, M. H. K., et al. (2017). The role of anabolic androgenic steroids in disruption of the physiological function in discrete areas of the central nervous system. *Mol. Neurobiol.,* 55(7), 5548–5556. doi: 10.1007/s12035-0170774-1.

Bertrand, D., Lee, C.-H. L., Flood, D., Marger, F., and Donnelly-Roberts, D. (2015). Therapeutic potential of α7 nicotinic acetylcholine receptors. *Pharmacol. Rev.*, 67, 1025–1073.

Bertron, J. L., Seto, M., and Lindsley, C. W. (2018). DARK classics in chemical neuroscience: Phencyclidine (PCP). *ACS Chem. Neurosci.*, 9, 2459–2474.

Bertschy, G. (1995). Methadone maintenance treatment: An update. *Eur. Arch. Psychiatr. Clin. Neurosci.*, 245, 114–124.

Bettler, B. and Tiao, J. Y-H. (2006). Molecular diversity, trafficking and subcellular localization of GABA$_B$ receptors. *Pharmacol. Ther.*, 110, 533–543.

Beurmanjer, H., Kamal, R. M., de Jong, C., Dijkstra, B., and Schellekens, A. (2018). Baclofen to prevent relapse in gamma-hydroxybutyrate (GHB)-dependent patients: A multicentre, open-label, non-randomized, controlled trial. *CNS Drugs*, 32, 437–442.

Beveridge, T. J. R., Gill, K. E., Hanlon, C. A., and Porrino, L. J. (2008). Parallel studies of cocaine-related neural and cognitive impairment in humans and monkeys. *Philos. Trans. R. Soc. Lond. B Biol. Sci.*, 363, 3257–3266.

Beynon, S. J., and Chaturvedi, S. (2018). Datura intoxication in an adolescent male: A challenge in the Internet era. *J. Paediatr. Child Health*, 54(1), 84–87. https://doi.org/10.1111/jpc.13726

Bhalerao, A., Sivandzade, F., Archie, S. R., and Cucullo, L. (2019). Public health policies on e-cigarettes. *Curr. Cardiol. Rep.*, 21, 111. doi: 10.1007/s11886-019-1204-y.

Bhasin, S., Storer, T. W., Berman, N., Callegari, C., Clevenger, B. A., Phillips, J., et al. (1996). The effects of supraphysiological doses of testosterone on muscle size and strength in men. *New Engl. J. Med.*, 335, 1–7.

Bhasin, S., Woodhouse, L., Casaburi, R., Singh, A. B., Bhasin, D., Berman, N., et al. (2001). Testosterone dose-response relationships in healthy young men. *Am. J. Physiol. Endocrinol. Metab.*, 281, E1172–E1181. © 2001 American Physiological Society. doi.org/10.1152/ajpendo.2001.281.6.E1172.

Biederer, T., Kaeser, P. S., and Blanpied, T. A. (2017). Transcellular nanoalignment of synaptic function. *Neuron*, 96, 680–696.

Biedermann, S. V., Biedermann, D. G., Wenzlaff, F., Kujak, T., Nouri, S., Auer, M. K., et al. (2017). An elevated plus-maze in mixed reality for studying human anxiety-related behavior. *BMC Biology*, 15, 125. doi: 10.1186/s12915-017-0463-6.

Bierut, L. J. (2020). 2018 Langley Award for basic research on nicotine and tobacco: Bringing precision medicine to smoking cessation. *Nicotine Tob. Res.*, 22, 147–151.

Biezonski, D. K., and Meyer, J. S. (2011). The nature of 3,4-methylenedioxy-methamphetamine (MDMA)-induced serotonergic dysfunction: Evidence for and against the neurodegeneration hypothesis. *Curr. Neuropharmacol.*, 9, 84–90.

Billard, J.-M. (2018). Changes in serine racemase-dependent modulation of NMDA receptor: Impact on physiological and pathological brain aging. *Front. Mol. Biosci.*, 5, 106. doi: 10.3389/fmolb.2018.2018.00106.

Billieux, J., Maurage, P., Lopez-Fernandez, O., Kuss, D. J., and Griffiths, M. D. (2015a). Can disordered mobile phone use be considered a behavioral addiction? An update on current evidence and a comprehensive model for future practice. *Curr. Addict. Rep.*, 2, 156–162.

Billieux, J., Schimmenti, A., Khazaal, Y., Maurage, P., and Heeren, A. (2015b). Are we overpathologizing everyday life? A tenable blueprint for behavioral addiction research. *J. Behav. Addict.*, 4, 119–123.

Binienda, A., Storr, M., Fichna, J., and Salaga, M. (2018). Efficacy and safety of serotonin receptor ligands in the treatment of irritable bowel syndrome: A review. *Curr. Drug Targets*, 19, 177/1–/2781.

Binienda, Z. K., Beaudoin, M. A., Thorn, B. T., and Ali, S. F. (2011). Analysis of electrical brain waves in neurotoxicology: Gamma-hydroxybutyrate. *Curr. Neuropharmacol.*, 9, 236–239.

Binks, H., Vincent, G. E., Gupta, C., Irwin, C., and Khalesi, S. (2020). Effects of diet on sleep: A narrative review. *Nutrients*, 12, 936. doi:10.3390/nu12040936.

Bird, C. M., and Burgess, N. (2008). The hippocampus and memory: insights from spatial processing. *Nat. Rev. Neurosci.*, 9, 182–194.

Bird, S. R., Goebel, C., Burke, L. M., and Greaves, R. F. (2016). Doping in sport and exercise: Anabolic, ergogenic, health and clinical issues. *Ann. Clin. Biochem.*, 53, 196–221.

Birnbaum, S., Sharshar, T., Eymard, B., Theaudin, M., Portero, P., and Hogel, J.-Y. (2018). Marathons and myasthenia gravis: A case report. *BMC Neurol.*, 18, 145. doi: 10.1186/s12883-018-1150-0.

Birrell, J. M., and Brown, V. J. (2000). Medial frontal cortex mediates perceptual attentional set shifting in the rat. *J. Neurosci.*, 20(11), 4320–4324.

Bischof, G., Rumpf, H.-J., Hapke, U., Meyer, C., and John, U. (2001). Factors influencing remission from alcohol dependence without formal help in a representative population sample. *Addiction*, 96, 1327–1336.

Bjørnebekk, A., Kaufmann, T., Hauger, L. E., Klonteig, S., Hullstein, I. R., and Westlye, L. T. (2021). Long-term anabolic-androgenic steroid use is associated with deviant brain aging. *Biol. Psychiatry Cogn. Neurosci. Neuroimaging*, 6, 579–589.

Bjørnebekk, A., Walhovd, K. B., Jørstad, M L., Due-Tønnessen, P., Hullstein, I. R., and Fjell, A. M. (2017). Structural brain imaging of long-term anabolic-androgenic steroid users and nonusing weightlifters. *Biol. Psychiatry*, 82, 294–302.

Black, S. W., Yamanaka, A., and Kilduff, T. S. (2017). Challenges in the development of therapeutics for narcolepsy. *Prog. Neurobiol.*, 152, 89–113.

Blair, R.J.R. (2012). Considering anger from a cognitive neuroscience perspective. *Rev. Cogn. Sci.*, 3, 6/1–/24.

Blanco, M.-J., La, D., Coughlin, Q., Newman, C. A., Griffin, A. M., Harrison, B. L., and Salituro, F. G. (2018). Breakthroughs in neuroactive drug discovery. *Bioorg. Med. Chem. Lett.*, 28, 61–70.

Blanco-Centurion, C., Liu, M., Konoadhode, R., Pelluru, D., and Shiromani, P. J. (2013). Effects of orexin gene transfer in the dorsolateral pons in orexin knockout mice. *Sleep*, 36, 31–40.

Blanpied, T. (2016). Nanocolumn: The Trans-Synaptic Nanocolumn. Available at www.youtube.com/watch?v=PNhUqhwHDaQ.

Blasco, H., Mavel, S., Corcia, P., and Gordon, P. H. (2014). The glutamate hypothesis in ALS: Pathophysiology and drug develoment. *Curr. Med. Chem.*, 21, 3551–3575.

Blauwblomme, T., Jiruska, P., and Huberfeld, G. (2014). Mechanisms of ictogenesis. *Int. Rev. Neurobiol.*, 114, 155–185.

Blessing, E. M., Steenkamp, M. M., Manzanares, J., and Marmar, C. R. (2015). Cannabidiol as a potential treatment for anxiety disorders. *Neurotherapeutics*, 12, 825–836.

Blier, P., de Montigny, C., and Chaput, Y. (1990). A role for the serotonin system in the mechanism of action of antidepressant treatments: Preclinical evidence. *J. Clin. Psychiatry*, 51(Suppl. 4), 4–20.

Bliss, T. V. P., and Lømo, T. (1973). Long-lasting potentiation of synaptic transmission in the dentate area of the anaesthetized rabbit following stimulation of the perforant path. *J. Physiol.*, 232, 331–356.

Bliss, T. V. P., and Collingridge, G. L. (2013). Expression of NMDA receptor-dependent LTP in the hippocampus: Bridging the divide. *Mol. Brain*, 6, 5. doi: 10.1186/1756-6606-6-5.

Bloomfield, M.A.P., Morgan, C.J.A., Egerton, A., Kapur, S., Curran, H. V., and Howes, O. D. (2014a). Dopaminergic function in cannabis users and its relationship to cannabis-induced psychotic symptoms. *Biol. Psychiatry*, 75, 470–478.

Bloomfield, M.A.P., Morgan, C.J.A., Kapur, S., Curran, H. V., and Howes, O. D. (2014b). The link between dopamine function and apathy in cannabis users: An [18F]-DOPA PET imaging study. *Psychopharmacology*, 231, 2551–2259.

Bloomfield, M.A.P., Ashok, A. H., Volkow, N. D., and Howes, O. D. (2016). The effects of Δ⁹-tetrahydrocannabinol on the dopamine system. *Nature*, 369–377.

Bloomfield, M.A.P., Hindocha, C., Green, L.S.F., Wall, M .B., Lees, R., Petrilli, K., et al. (2019). The neuropsychopharmacology of cannabis: A review of human imaging studies. *Pharmacol. Ther.*, 195, 132–161. doi.org/10.1016/j.pharmthera.2018.10.006. CC BY 4.0, https://creativecommons.org/licenses/by/4.0/

Bloomfield, P. S., Selvaraj, S., Veronese, M., Rizzo, G., Bertoldo, A., Owen, D. R., et al. (2016). Microglial activity in people at ultra high risk of psychosis and in schizophrenia: An [(11)C] PBR28 PET brain imaging study. *Am. J. Psychiatry*, 173, 44–52.

Bluett, R. J., Báldi, R., Haymer, A., Gaulden, A. D., Hartley, N. D., Parrish, W. P., Baechle, L., et al. (2017). Endocannabinoid signalling modulates susceptibility to traumatic stress exposure. *Nat. Commun.*, 8, 14782. doi: 10.1038/ncomms14782.

Blume, S. (1991). Sexuality and stigma. National Institute on Alcohol Abuse and Alcoholism. *Alcohol Health Res. World*, 15, 139–145.

Blumenfeld, H. (2014). *Neuroanatomy through Clinical Cases* (2nd ed.) Sunderland, MA: Sinauer.

Bobak, M. J., Weber, M. W., Doellman, M. A., Schuweiler, D. R., Athens, J. M., Juliano, S. A., and Garris, P. A. (2016). Modafinil activates phasic dopamine signaling in dorsal and ventral striata. *J. Pharmacol. Exp. Ther.*, 359, 460–470.

Bock, A., Schrage, R., and Mohr, K. (2018). Allosteric modulators targeting CNS muscarinic receptors. *Neuropharmacology*, 136, 427–437.

Bock, N., Gerlach, M., and Rothenberger, (2010). Postnatal brain development and psychotropic drugs: Effects on animals and animal models of depression and attention-deficit/hyperactivity disorder. *Curr. Pharm. Des.*, 16, 2474–2483.

Bodnar, R. J. (2017). Endogenous opiates and behavior: 2015. *Peptides*, 88, 126–188.

Bodnar, R. J. (2021). Endogenous opiates and behavior: 2019. *Peptides*, 141, 170547. https://doi.org/10.1016/j.peptides.2021.170547

Boehnke, K. F., Gangopadhyay, S., Clauw, D. J., and Haffajee, R. L. (2019). Qualifying conditions of medical cannabis license holders in the United States. *Health Affairs*, 38, 295–302. Republished with permission of Project Hope/Health Affairs Journal; permission conveyed through Copyright Clearance Center, Inc.

Bogenschutz, M. P., and Johnson, M. W. (2016). Classic hallucinogens in the treatment of addictions. *Prog. NeuroPsychopharmacol. Biol. Psychiatry*, 64, 250–258.

Boggs, D. L., Carlson, J., Cortes-Briones, J., Krystal, J. H., and D'Souza, D. C. (2014). Going up in smoke? A review of nAChRs-based treatment strategies for improving cognition in schizophrenia. *Curr. Pharm. Des.*, 20, 5077–5092.

Boggs, D. L., Nguyen, J. D., Mogenson, D., Taffe, M. A., and Ranganathan, M. (2018). Clinical and preclinical evidence for functional interactions of cannabidiol and Δ⁹-tetrahydrocannabinol. *Neuropsychopharmacology*, 43, 142–154.

Bogle, K. E., and Smith, B. H. (2009). Illicit methylphenidate use: A review of prevalence, availability, pharmacology, and consequences. *Curr. Drug Abuse Rev.*, 2, 157–176.

Boileau, I., Dagher, A., Leyton, M., Gunn, R. N., Baker, G. B., Diksic, M., et al. (2006). Modeling sensitization to stimulants in humans. An [11C]raclopride/ positron emission tomography study in healthy men. *Arch. Gen. Psychiatry*, 63, 1386–1395.

Boison, D., Chen, J. F., and Fredholm, B. B. (2010). Adenosine signaling and function in glial cells. *Cell Death Differ.*, 17, 1071–1082.

Bokor, G., and Anderson, P. D. (2014). Ketamine: An update on its abuse. *J. Pharmacy Prac.*, 27, 582–586.

Bolger, G. B. (2017). The PDE4 cAMP-specific phosphodiesterases: Targets for drugs with antidepressant and memory-enhancing action. *Adv. Pharmacol.*, 17, 63–102.

Bolin, B. L., Alcorn, J. L., Reynolds, A. R., Lile, J. A., and Rush, C. R. (2016). Human drug discrimination: A primer and methodological review. *Exp. Clin. Psychopharmacol.*, 24, 214–228.

Bonaz, B., Bazin, T., and Pellissier, S. (2018). The vagus nerve at the interface of the microbiota-gut-brain axis. *Front. Neurosci.*, 12, 49. doi: 10.3389/fnins.2018.00049.

Bondallaz, P., Favrat, B., Chtioui, H., Fornari, E., Maeder, P., and Giroud, C. (2016). Cannabis and its effects on driving skills. *Forensic Sci. Int.*, 268, 92–102.

Bonini, S. A., Premoli, M., Tambaro, S., Kumar, A., Maccarinelli, G., Memo, M., and Mastinu, A. (2018). Cannabis sativa:

A comprehensive ethnopharmacological review of a medicinal plant with a long history. *J. Ethnopharmacol.*, 227, 300–315.

Bontempi, L., and Bonci, A. (2020). μ-Opioid receptor-induced synaptic plasticity in dopamine neurons mediates the rewarding properties of anabolic androgenic steroids. *Sci. Signal.*, 13(647), eaba1169. doi: 10.1126/scisignal.aba1169.

Booij, L., Van der Does, A. J. W., and Riedel, W. J. (2003). Monoamine depletion in psychiatric and healthy populations: Review. *Mol. Psychiatry*, 8, 951–973.

Boonstra, E., de Kleijn, R., Colzato, L. S., Alkemade, A., Forstmann, B. U., and Nieuwenhuis, S. (2015). Neurotransmitters as food supplements: the effects of GABA on brain and behavior. *Front Psychol.*, 6, 1520.

Borgkvist, A., Malmlöf, T., Feltmann, K., Lindskog, M., and Schilström, B. (2012). Dopamine in the hippocampus is cleared by the norepinephrine transporter. *Int. J. Neuropsychopharmacol.*, 15, 531–540.

Börjesson, A., Möller, C., Hagelin, A., Vicente, V., Rane, A., Lehtihet, M., Dahl, M.-L., et al. (2020). Male anabolid androgenic steroid users with personality disorders report more aggressive feelings, suicidal thoughts, and criminality. *Medicina*, 56, 265. doi: 10.3390/medicina56060265.

Borota, D., Murray, E., Keceli, G., Chang, A., Watabe, J. M., Ly, M., et al. (2014). Post-study caffeine administration enhances memory consolidation in humans. *Nat. Neurosci.*, 17, 201–203.

Bosch, M., and Hayashi, Y. (2012). Structural plasticity of dendritic spines. *Curr. Opin. Neurobiol.*, 22, 383–388.

Bosch, O. G., and Seifritz, E. (2016). The behavioural profile of gamma-hydroxybutyrate, gamma-butyrolactone and 1,4-butanediol in humans. *Brain Res. Bull.*, 126, 47–60.

Bosch, O. G., Eisenegger, C., Gertsch, J., von Rotz, R., Dornbierer, D., Gachet, M. S., Heinrichs, M., et al. (2015). Gamma-hydroxybutyrate enhances mood and prosocial behavior without affecting plasma oxytocin and testosterone. *Psychoneuroendocrinology*, 62, 1–10.

Boscolo-Berto, R., Viel, G., Montagnese, S., Raduazo, D. I., Ferrara, S. D., and Dauvillers, Y. (2012). Narcolepsy and effectiveness of gamma-hydroxybutyrate (GHB): A systematic review and metaanalysis of randomized controlled trials. *Sleep Med. Rev.*, 16, 431–443.

Bossong, M. G., Mehta, M. A., van Berckel, N. M., Howes, O. D., Kahn, R. S., and Stokes, P. R. A. (2015). Further human evidence for striatal dopamine release induced by administration of

Δ⁹-tetrahydrocannabinol (THC): Selectivity to limbic striatum. *Psychopharmacology*, 232, 2723–2729.

Botanas, C. J., de la Peña, J. B., Dela Peña, I. J., Tampus, R., Yoon, R., Kim, H. J., et al. (2015). Methoxetamine, a ketamine derivative, produced conditioned place preference and was self-administered by rats: Evidence of its abuse potential. *Pharmacol. Biochem. Behav.*, 133, 31–36.

Botanas, C. J., de la Peña, J. B., Kim, H. J., Lee, Y. S., and Cheong, J. H. (2019). Methoxetamine: A foe or friend? *Neurochem. Int.*, 122, 1–7.

Bouchery, E. E., Henrick, M. S., Harwood, J., Sacks, J. J., Simon, C. J., Brewer, R. D. (2011). Economic Costs of Excessive Alcohol Consumption in the U.S., 2006. *Am. J. Prev. Med.*, 41, 516–524. © 2011 American Journal of Preventive Medicine. Reprinted with permission from Elsevier.

Bowdle, T. A., Radant, A. D., Cowley, D. S., Kharasch, E. D., Strassman, R. J., and Roy-Byrne, P. P. (1998). Psychedelic effects of ketamine in healthy volunteers: relationship to steady-state plasma concentrations. *Anesthesiology*, 88, 82–88.

Bowen, S. E. (2011). Two serious and challenging medical complications associated with volatile substance misuse: Sudden sniffing death and fetal solvent syndrome. *Subst. Use Misuse*, 46, 68–72.

Bowers, M. E., and Yehuda, R. (2016). Intergenerational transmission of stress in humans. *Neuropsychopharmacology.*, 41, 232–244.

Braak, H., and Braak, E. (1995). Staging of Alzheimer's disease-related neurofibrillary changes. *Neurobiol. Aging*, 16, 271–278.

Braak, H., Del Tredici, K., Rub, U., de Vos, R.A.I., Jansen Steur, E.N.H., and Braak, E. (2003). Staging of brain pathology related to sporadic Parkinson's disease. *Neurobiol. Aging*, 24, 197–211.

Bradley, C. (1937). The behavior of children receiving benzedrine. *Am. J. Psychiatry*, 94, 577–585.

Brady, K. T. and Sonne, S. C. (1999). The role of stress in alcohol use, alcoholism treatment, and relapse. *Alcohol Res. Health*, 23, 263–271.

Braestrup, C., and Squires, R. F. (1978). Pharmacological characterization of benzodiazepine receptors in the brain. *Eur. J. Pharmacol.* 48, 263–270.

Bramwell, B. (1886). *Diseases of the Spinal Cord*. Edinburgh: Young J. Pentland.

Branco, T., and Staras, K. (2009). The probability of neurotransmitter release: variability and feedback control at single synapses. *Nat. Rev. Neurosci.*, 10, 37/1–/282.

Brand, M., Rumpf, H. J., Demetrovics, Z., Müller, A., Stark, R., King, D. L., et al. (2020). Which conditions should be considered as disorders in the International Classification of Diseases (ICD-11) designation of "other specified disorders due to addictive behaviors"? *J. Behav. Addict.*, in press.

Brandt, L., Chao, T., Comer, S. D., and Levin, F. R. (2020). Pharmacotherapeutic strategies for treating cocaine use disorder—What do we have to offer? *Addiction*, 116(4), 694–710.

Braunscheidel, K. M., Wayman, W. N., Okas, M. P., and Woodward, J. J. (2020). Self-administration of toluene vapor in rats. *Front. Neurosci.*, 14, 880. doi: 10.3389/fnins.2020.00880. CC BY 4.0, creativecommons.org/licenses/by/4.0/

Breedlove, S. M. and Watson, N. V. (2017). *Behavioral Neuroscience* (8th ed.). Sunderland, MA: Sinauer.

Breivogel, C. S., Childers, S. R., Deadwyler, S. A., Hampson, R. E., Vogt, L. J., and Sim-Selley, L. J. (1999). Chronic Δ⁹-tetrahydrocannabinol treatment produces a time-dependent loss of cannabinoid receptors and cannabinoid receptor–activated G proteins in rat brain. *J. Neurochem.*, 73, 2447–2459.

Brennan, K. A., Laugesen, M., and Truman, P. (2014). Whole tobacco smoke extracts to model tobacco dependence in animals. *Neurosci. Biobehav. Rev.*, 47, 53–69.

Brennan, R., and Van Hout, M. C. (2014). Gamma-hydroxybutyrate (GHB): A scoping review of pharmacology, toxicology, motives for use, and user groups. *J. Psychoactive Drugs*, 46, 243–251.

Brennenstuhl, H., Jung-Klawitter, S., Assmann, B., and Opladen, T. (2019). Inherited disorders of neurotransmitters: Classification and practical approaches for diagnosis and treatment. *Neuropediatrics*, 50, 2–14.

Brenner, D. M., and Sayuk, G. S. (2020). Current US Food and Drug Administration-approved pharmacologic therapies for the treatment of irritable bowel syndrome with diarrhea. *Adv. Ther.*, 37, 83–96.

Brents, L. K. (2016). Marijuana, the endocannabinoid system and the female reproductive system. *Yale J. Biol. Med.*, 89, 175–191.

Bresnahan, R., Gianatsi, M., Maguire, M. J., Smith, C. T., and Marson, A. G. (2020). Vigabatrin add-on therapy for drug resistant focal epilepsy. *Cochrane Database Syst. Rev.*, 7, CD007302. doi: 10.1002/14651858.CD007302.pub3.

Bresnahan, R., Martin-McGill, K. J., Hutton, J. L., and Marson, A. G. (2018). Tiagabine add-on therapy for drug-resistant focal epilepsy. *Cochrane Database Syst. Rev.*, 10(10), CD001908. doi: 10.1002/14651858.CD001908.pub4.

Brewer, J. A., Worhunsky, P. D., Gray, J. R., Tang, Y.-Y., Weber, J., and Kober, H. (2011). Meditation experience is associated with differences in default mode network activity and connectivity. *Proc. Natl. Acad. Sci. USA*, 108, 20254–20259.

Briars, L., and Todd, T. (2016). A review of pharmacological management of attention-deficit/hyperactivity disorder. *J. Pediatr. Pharmacol. Ther.*, 21, 192–206.

Brickley, S. G., and Mody, I. (2012). Extrasynaptic $GABA_A$ receptors: Their function in the CNS and implications for disease. *Neuron*, 73, 23–34.

Bright, F. M., Vink, R., and Byard, R. W. (2018). Neuropathological developments in sudden infant death syndrome. *Pediatr. Dev. Pathol.*, 21, 515–521.

Britch, S. C., Babalonis, S., and Walsh, S. L. (2021). Cannabidiol: pharmacology and therapeutic targets. *Psychopharmacology*, 238, 9–28.

Brody, A. L., Mandelkern, M. A., Costello, M. R., Abrams, A. L., Scheibel, D., Farah, J., et al. (2009). Brain nicotinic acetylcholine receptor occupancy: effect of smoking a denicotinized cigarette. *Int. J. Neuropsychopharmacol.*, 12, 305–316.

Brody, A. L., Mandelkern, M. A., London, E. D., Olmstead, R. E., Farahi, J., Scheibal, D., et al. (2006). Cigarette smoking saturates brain $α4β2$ nicotinic acetylcholine receptors. *Arch. Gen. Psychiatry*, 63, 907–915.

Brody, A. L., Mukhin, A. G., La Charite, J., Farahi, J., Sugar, C. A., Mamoun, M. S., et al. (2013). Up-regulation of nicotinic acetylcholine receptors in menthol cigarette smokers. *Int. J. Neuropsychopharmacol.*, 16, 957–966.

Brook, J. S., Kessler, R. C., and Cohen, P. (1999). The onset of marijuana use from preadolescence and early adolescence to young adulthood. *Dev. Psychopathol.*, 11, 901–914.

Brook, J. S., Stimmel, M. A., Zhang, C., and Brook, D. W. (2008). The association between earlier marijuana use and subsequent academic achievement and health problems: A longitudinal study. *Am. J. Addict.*, 17, 155–160.

Brook, J. S., Zhang, C., Leukefeld, C. G., and Brook, D. W. (2016). Marijuana use from adolescence to adulthood: Developmental trajectories and their outcomes. *Soc. Psychiatry Psychiatr. Epidemiol.*, 51, 1405–1415.

Brooks, J., Erickson, T. B., Kayden, S., Ruiz, R., Wilkinson, S., and Burkle, F. M. Jr. (2018). Responding to chemical weapons violations in Syria: legal, health, and humanitarian recommendations.

Conflict Health, 12, 12. doi: 10.1186/s13031-018-0143-3.

Brower, K. J. (2009). Anabolic steroid abuse and dependence in clinical practice. *Phys. Sportsmed.*, 37, 131–140.

Brower, K. J., Blow, F. C., Young, J. P., and Hill, E. M. (1991). Symptoms and correlates of anabolic–androgenic steroid dependence. *Br. J. Addict.*, 86, 759–768.

Brower, K. J., Eliopulos, G. A., Blow, F. C., Catlin, D. H., and Beresford, T. P. (1990). Evidence for physical and psychological dependence on anabolic androgenic steroids in eight weight lifters. *Am. J. Psychiatry*, 147, 510–512.

Brown, D. A. (2019). Acetylcholine and cholinergic receptors. *Brain Neurosci. Adv.*, 3, 1–10.

Brown, J. D., Bonin, K. D., Stuber, G. D., et al. (2013). Optogenetic stimulation of VTA dopamine neurons reveals that tonic but not phasic patterns of dopamine transmission reduce ethanol self-administration. *Front. Behav. Neurosci.*, 7, 173.

Brown, S. J., Brown, J., and Foskett, A. (2013). The effects of caffeine on repeated sprint performance in team sport athletes—A meta-analysis. *Sport Sci. Rev.*, 22, 25–32.

Brown, V. J., and Tait, D. S. (2016). Attentional set-shifting across species. *Curr. Top. Behav. Neurosci.*, 28, 363–395. https://doi.org/10.1007/7854_2015_5002

Brown, W. A. (1998). The placebo effect. *Sci. Am.*, 278, 90–95.

Browne, C. A., and Lucki, I. (2013). Antidepressant effects of ketamine: Mechanisms underlying fast-acting novel antidepressants. *Front. Pharmacol.*, 4, Article161.

Browne, C. J., Godino, A., Salery, M., and Nestler, E. J. (2020). Epigenetic mechanisms of opioid addiction. *Biol. Psychiatry*, 87, 22–33.

Browne, T. R. and Holme, G. L. (2008). *Handbook of Epilepsy* (3rd ed.). Philadelphia: Wolters Kluwer.

Broyd, S. J., van Hell, H. H., Beale, C., Yücel, M., and Solowij, N. (2016). Acute and chronic effects of cannabinoids on human cognition: A systematic review. *Biol. Psychiatry*, 79, 557–567. Copyright 2016. Reprinted with permission from Society of Biological Psychiatry, via Elsevier.

Bruehl, S., Apkarian, A. V., Ballantyne, J. C., Berger, A., Borsook, D., Chen, G., et al. (2013). Personalized medicine and opioid analgesic prescribing for chronic pain: Opportunities and challenges. *J. Pain*, 14, 103–113.

Bruhn, J. G., De Smet, P. A. G. M., El-Seedi, H. R., and Beck, O. (2002). Mescaline use for 5700 years. *Lancet*, 359, 1866.

Bruin, J. E., Gerstein, H. C., and Holloway, A. C. (2010).

Long-term consequences of fetal and neonatal nicotine exposure: A critical review. *Toxicol. Sci.*, 116, 364–374.

Brun, A., and Englund, E. (1981). Regional pattern of degeneration in Alzheimer's disease: neuronal loss and histopathological grading. *Histopathology*, 5, 549–564.

Bruns, R. F., Mitchell, S. N., Wafford, K. A., Harper, A. J., Shanks, E. A., Carter, G., O'Neill, M. J., et al. (2018). Preclinical profile of a dopamine D1 potentiator suggests therapeutic utility in neurological and psychiatric disorders. *Neuropharmacology*, 128, 351–365.

Brunt, T. M., van Amsterdam, J. G. C., and van den Brink, W. (2014). GHB, GBL and 1,4-BD addiction. *Curr. Pharm. Des.*, 20, 4076–4085.

Brunzell, D. H., Stafford, A. M., and Dixon, C. I. (2015). Nicotinic receptor contributions to smoking: Insights from human studies and animal models. *Curr. Addict. Rep.*, 2, 33–46.

Brüstle, O., Jones, K. N., Learish, R. D., Karram, K., Choudhary, K., Wiestler, O. D., et al. (1999). Embryonic stem cell-derived glial precursors: A source of myelinating transplants. *Science*, 285, 754–756.

Bubser, M., Byun, N., Wood, M. R., and Jones, C. K. (2012). Muscarinic receptor pharmacology and circuitry for the modulation of cognition. In A. D. Fryer, A. Christopoulos, and N. M. Nathanson (Eds.), *Muscarinic Receptors*, Volume 208, Handbook of Experimental Pharmacology (pp. 121–166). Berlin: Springer-Verlag.

Buchanan, G. F., Smith, H. R., MacAskill, A., and Richerson, G. B. (2015). 5-HT2A receptor activation is necessary for CO_2-induced arousal. *J. Neurophysiol.*, 114, 233–243.

Buchanan, R. W., Freedman, R., Javitt, D. C., Abi-Dargham, A., and Lieberman, J. A. (2007). Recent advances in the development of novel pharmacological agents for the treatment of cognitive impairments in schizophrenia. *Schizophr. Bull.*, 33, 1120–1130.

Buchsbaum, M. S. (1990). The frontal lobes, basal ganglia, and temporal lobes as sites for schizophrenia. *Schizophr. Bull.*, 16, 379–390.

Buckingham-Howes, S., Berger, S. S., Scaletti, L. A., and Black, M. M. (2013). Systematic review of prenatal cocaine exposure and adolescent development. *Pediatrics*, 131, e1917–e1936.

Buckley, N. E. (2008). The peripheral cannabinoid receptor knockout mice: An update. *Br. J. Pharmacol.*, 153, 309–318.

Budney, A. J., Lee, D. C., and Juliano, L. M. (2015). Evaluating the validity of caffeine use disorder. *Curr. Psychiatry Rep.*, 17, 74. doi: 10.1007/s11920–015–0611-z.

Budney, A. J., Moore, B. A., Vandrey, R. G., and Hughes, J. R. (2003). The time course and significance of cannabis withdrawal. *J. Abnorm. Psychol.*, 112, 393–402.

Budney, A. J., Roffman, R., Stephens, R. S., and Walker, D. (2007). Marijuana dependence and its treatment. *Addict. Sci. Clin. Pract.*, 4, 4–16.

Bühler, K.-M., Giné, E., Echeverry-Alzate, V., Calleja-Conde, J., de Fonseca, F. R., and López-Moreno, J. A. (2015). Common single nucleotide variants underlying drug addiction: More than a decade of research. *Addict. Biol.*, 20, 845–871.

Burgess, A., Dubey, S., Yeung S., Hough, Ol, Eterman, N. Aubert, I., and Hynynen, K. (2014) Alzheimer disease in a mouse model: MR imaging-guided focused ultrasound targeted to the hippocampus opens the blood-brain barrier and improves pathologic abnormalities and behavior. *Radiology*, 273, 736–745

Burglass, M. E., and Shaffer, H. (1984). Diagnosis in the addictions I: Conceptual problems. *Adv. Alcohol Subst. Abuse*, 3, 19–34.

Burguière, E., Monteiro, P., Mallet, L., Feng, G., and Graybiel, A. M. (2015). Striatal circuits, habits, and implications for obsessive compulsive disorder. *Curr. Opin. Neurobiol.*, 30, 59–65.

Burke, L. K., and Heisler, L. K. (2015). 5-Hydroxytryptamine medications for the treatment of obesity. *J. Neuroendocrinol.*, 27, 389–398.

Burke, L. M. (2008). Caffeine and sports performance. *Appl. Physiol. Nutr. Metab.*, 33, 1319–1334.

Burns, C. J., McIntosh, L. J., Mink, P. J., Jurek, A. M., and Li, A. A. (2013). Pesticide exposure and neurodevelopmental outcomes: Review of the epidemiologic and animal studies. *J. Toxicol. Environ. Health B*, 16, 127–283.

Burns, E. (2007). *The Smoke of the Gods. A Social History of Tobacco*. Philadelphia: Temple University Press.

Burns, J. M., and Boyer, E. W. (2013). Antitussives and substance abuse. *Subst. Abuse Rehabil.*, 4, 75–82.

Burnstock, G. (2012). Purinergic signalling: Its unpopular beginning, its acceptance and its exciting future. *Bioessays*, 34, 218–225.

Burnstock, G. (2016). Purinergic signalling in the gut. *Adv. Exp. Med. Biol.*, 891, 91–112.

Burnstock, G. (2017). Purinergic signaling in the cardiovascular system. *Circ. Res.*, 120, 207–228.

Burnstock, G. (2020). Introduction to purinergic signalling in the brain. *Adv. Exp. Med. Biol.*, 1202, 1–12.

Busardò, F. P., and Jones, A. W. (2014). GHB pharmacology and toxicology: Acute intoxication, concentrations in blood and urine in forensic cases and treatment of the withdrawal syndrome. *Curr. Neuropharmacol.*, 13, 47–70.

Busardò, F. P., Kyriakou, C., Napoletano, S., Marinelli, E., and Zaami, S. (2015). Mephedrone related fatalities: A review. *Eur. Rev. Med. Pharmacol. Sci.*, 19, 3777–3790.

Busardò, F. P., Gottardi, M., Tini, A., Minutillo, A., Sirignano, A., Marinelli, E., and Zaami, S. (2018). Replacing GHB with GBL in recreational settings: A new trend in chemsex. *Curr. Drug Metab.*, 19, 1080–1085.

Buu, A., Hu, Y.-H., Wong, S.-W., and Lin, H.-C. (2020). Internalizing and externalizing problems as risk factors for initiation and progression of e-cigarette and combustible cigarette use in the US youth population. *Int. J. Ment. Health Addiction.* doi: 10.1007/s11469-020-00261-9.

Byck, R. (Ed.). (1974). *The Cocaine Papers by Sigmund Freud.* New York: Stonehill.

Bymaster, F. P., Katner, J. S., Nelson, D. L., Hemrick-Luecke, S. K., Threlkeld, P. G., Heiligenstein, J. H., Morin, S. M., et al. (2002). Atomoxetine increases extracellular levels of norepinephrine and dopamine in prefrontal cortex of rat: A potential mechanism for efficacy in attention deficit/hyperactivity disorder. *Neuropsychopharmacology*, 27(5), 699–711. https://doi.org/10.1016/S0893-133X(02)00346-9

Byrne, J. H. (2014). Postsynaptic potentials and synaptic integration. In J.H. Byrne, R. Heidelberger, and M.N. Waxham (Eds.), *From Molecules to Networks*, 3rd edition. An Introduction to Cellular and Molecular Neuroscience, pp. 489–507. San Diego: Academic Press.

C

C'olovic´, M. B., Krstic´, D. Z., Lazarevic´-Pašti, T. D., Bondžic´, A. M., and Vasic´, V. M. (2013). Acetylcholinesterase inhibitors: Pharmacology and toxicology. *Curr. Neuropharmacol.*, 11, 315–335.

Caballero, A., Granberg, R., and Tseng, K. Y. (2016). Mechanisms contributing to prefrontal cortex maturation during adolescence. *Neurosci. Biobehav. Rev.*, 70, 4–12.

Cabýoglu, M. T., Ergene, N., and Tan, U. (2006). The mechanism of acupuncture and clinical applications. *Int. J. Neurosci.*, 116, 115–125.

Cadet, J. L. (2016). Epigenetics of stress, addiction, and resilience: Therapeutic implications. *Mol. Neurobiol.*, 53, 545–560.

Cadet, J. L., McCoy, M. T., and Jayanthi, S. (2016). Epigenetics and addiction. *Clin. Pharmacol. Ther.*, 99, 502–511.

Cahill, E., Salery, M., Vanhoutte, P., and Caboche, J. (2014). Convergence of dopamine and glutamate signaling onto striatal ERK activation in response to drugs of abuse. *Front. Pharmacol.*, 4, 172. doi: 10.3389/fphar.2013.00172.

Cahill, K., Stevens, S., Perera, R., and Lancaster, T. (2013). Pharmacological interventions for smoking cessation: An overview and network meta-analysis. *Cochrane Database Syst. Rev.*, Issue 5, Article CD009329. doi: 10.1002/14651858. CD009329.pub2.

Caille, S., Clemens, K., Stinus, L., and Cador, M. (2012). Modeling nicotine addiction in rats. *Methods Mol. Biol.*, 829, 243–256.

Cain, M. A., Bornick, P., and Whiteman, V. (2013). The maternal, fetal, and neonatal effects of cocaine exposure in pregnancy. *Clin. Obstet. Gynecol.*, 56, 124–132.

Caine, S. B., Negus, S. S., Mello, N. K., Patel, S., Bristow, L., Kulagowski, J., et al. (2002). Role of dopamine D2-like receptors in cocaine self-administration: Studies with D2 receptor mutant mice and novel D2 receptor antagonists. *J. Neurosci.*, 22, 2977–2988.

Caine, S. B., Thomsen, M., Barrett, A. C., Collins, G. T., Butler, P., Grundt, P., et al. (2012). Cocaine self-administration in dopamine D3 receptor knockout mice. *Exp. Clin. Psychopharmacol.*, 20, 352–363.

Caine, S. B., Thomsen, M., Gabriel, K. I., Berkowitz, J. S., Gold, L. H., Koob, G. F., et al. (2007). Lack of self-administration of cocaine in dopamine D1 receptor knock-out mice. *J. Neurosci.*, 27, 13140–13150.

Cairney, S., O'Connor, N., Dingwall, K. M., Maruff, P., Shafiq-Antonacci, R., Currie, J., et al. (2013). A prospective study of neurocognitive changes 15 years after chronic inhalant abuse. *Addiction*, 108, 1107–1114.

Calabrese J.R., Bowden C.L., Sachs G., Yatham L.N., Behnke K., Mehtonen O.P., et al. (2003) A placebo-controlled 18-month trial of lamotrigine and lithium maintenance treatment in recently depressed patients with bipolar I disorder. *J. Clin. Psychiatry*, 64(9), 1013–1024.

Calabrese, J. R., Bowden, C., and Woyshville, M. J. (1995). Lithium and the anticonvulsants in the treatment of bipolar disorder. In F. E. Bloom and D. J. Kupfer (Eds.), *Psychopharmacology: The Fourth Generation of Progress*, pp. 1099– 1111. New York: Raven.

Calarco, C. A., and Picciotto, M. R. (2020). Nicotinic acetylcholine receptor signaling in the hypothalamus: Mechanisms related to nicotine's effects on food intake. *Nicotine Tob. Res.*, 22, 15/1–/263.

Caldwell, H. K. (2017). Oxytocin and vasopressin: Powerful regulators of social behavior. The *Neuroscientist*, 23, 517–528.

California Society of Addiction Medicine. (2011). Methadone Treatment Issues. California Society of Addiction Medicine. Available at www.csam-asam.org/methadone-treatment-issues.

Calignano, A., La Rana, G., Giuffrida, A., and Piomelli, D. (1998). Control of pain initiation by endogenous cannabinoids. *Nature*, 394, 277–281.

Calipari, E. S., Bagot, R. C., Purushothaman, I., Davidson, T. J., Yorgason, J. T., Peña, C. J., et al. (2016). In vivo imaging identifies temporal signature of D1 and D2 medium spiny neurons in cocaine reward. *Proc. Natl. Acad. Sci. USA*, 113, 2726–2731.

Calipari, E. S., Ferris, M. J., and Jones, S. R. (2014a). Extended access of cocaine self-administration results in tolerance to the dopamine-elevating and locomotor-stimulating effects of cocaine. *J. Neurochem.*, 128, 224–232.

Calipari, E. S., Ferris, M. J., Siciliano, C. A., Zimmer, B., and Jones, S. R. (2014b). Intermittent cocaine self-administration produces sensitization of stimulant effects at the dopamine transporter. *J. Pharmacol. Exp. Ther.*, 349, 192–198.

Calipari, E. S., Siciliano, C. A., Zimmer, B. Z., and Jones, S. R. (2015). Brief intermittent cocaine self-administration and abstinence sensitizes cocaine effects on the dopamine transporter and increases drug seeking. *Neuropsychopharmacology*, 40, 728–735.

Calixto, E. (2016). GABA withdrawal syndrome: GABA$_A$ receptor, synapse, neurobiological implications and analogies with other abstinences. *Neuroscience*, 313, 57–72.

Calpe-López, C., García-Pardo, M. P., and Aguilar, M. A. (2019). Cannabidiol treatment might promote resilience to cocaine and methamphetamine use disorders: A review of possible mechanisms. *Molecules*, 24, 2583. doi: 10.3390/molecules24142583.

Calvey, T., and Howells, F. M. (2018). An introduction to psychedelic neuroscience. *Prog. Brain Res.*, 242, 1–/23.

Calvigioni, D., Hurd, Y. L., Harkany, T., and Keimpema, E. (2014). Neuronal substrates and functional consequences of prenatal cannabis exposure. *Eur. Child Adolesc. Psychiatry*, 23, 931–941.

Cameron, L. P., Tombari, R. J., Lu, J., Pell, A. J., Hurley, Z. Q., Ehinger, Y., Vargas, M. V., et al. (2021). A non-hallucinogenic psychedelic analogue with therapeutic potential. *Nature*, 589, 47/1–/279.

Campbell, A., Villavicencio, A. T., Yeghiayan, S. K., Balikian, R., and Baldessarini, R. J. (1997). Mapping of locomotor behavioral arousal induced by microinjections of dopamine within nucleus accumbens septi of rat forebrain. *Brain Res.*, 771, 55–62.

Campbell, U. C., Rodefer, J. S., and Carroll, M. E. (1999). Effects of dopamine receptor antagonists (D1 and D2) on the demand for smoked cocaine base in rhesus monkeys. *Psychopharmacology*, 144, 381–388.

Campbell, W. G. and Hodgins, D. C. (1993). Alcohol-related blackouts in a medical practice. *Am. J. Drug Alcohol Abuse*, 19, 369–376.

Campeny, E., López-Pelayo, H., Nutt, D., Blithikioti, C., Oliveras, C., Nuño, L., Maldonado, R., et al. (2020). The blind men and the elephant: Systematic review of systematic reviews of cannabis use related health harms. *Eur. Neuropsychopharmacol.*, 33, /1–/25.

Cannon, M. E., Cooke, C. T., and McCarthy, J. S. (2001). Caffeine-induced cardiac arrhythmia: An unrecognised danger of health-food products. *Med. J. Aust.*, 174, 520–521.

Cannon, W. B. (1922). Bodily Changes in Pain, Hunger, Fear and Rage. New York: Appleton.

Cano, M., Oh, S., Salas-Wright, C. P., and Vaughn, M. G. (2020). Cocaine use and overdose mortality in the United States: Evidence from two national data sources, 200/1–/2018. *Drug Alcohol Depend.*, 214, 108148. doi: 10.1016/j.drugalcdep.2020.108148.

Cantin, L., Lenoir, M., Augier, E., Vanhille, N., Dubreucq, S., Serre, F., et al. (2010). Cocaine is low on the value ladder of rats: Possible evidence for resilience to addiction. *PLOS ONE*, 5, e11592. doi: 10.1371/journal.pone.0011592.

Cappelletti, S., Daria, P., Sani, G., and Aromatario, M. (2015). Caffeine: Cognitive and physical performance enhancer or psychoactive drug? *Curr. Neuropharmacol.*, 13, 71–88.

Cappelletti, S., Piacentino, D., Fineschi, V., Frati, P., Cipolloni, L., and Aromatario, M. (2018). Caffeine-related deaths: Manner of death and categories of risk. *Nutrients*, 10, 611. doi: 10.3390/nu10050611.

Caputo, F., Vignoli, T., Tarli, C., Domenicali, M., Zoli, G., Bernardi, M., et al. (2016). A brief up-date of the use of sodium oxybate for the treatment of alcohol use disorder. *Int. J. Environ. Res. Public Health*, 13, 290. doi: 10.3390/ijerph13030290.

Caraci, F., Nicoletti, F., and Copani, A. (2018). Metabotropic glutamate receptors: the potential for therapeutic applications in Alzheimer's disease. *Curr. Opin. Pharmacol.*, 38, /1–/2.

Carbonaro, T. M., Johnson, M. W., and Griffiths, R. R. (2020). Subjective features of the psilocybin experience that may account for its self-administration by humans: a double-blind comparison of psilocybin and dextromethorphan. *Psychopharmacology*, 237, 229/1–/2304.

Carbonaro, T. M., Johnson, M. W., Hurwitz, E., and Griffiths, R. R. (2018). Double-blind comparison of the two hallucinogens psilocybin and dextromethorphan: similarities and differences in subjective experiences. *Psychopharmacology*, 235, 52/1–/234.

Carboni, E., Spielewoy, C., Vacca, C., Nosten-Bertrand, M., Giros, B., and Di Chiara, G. (2001). Cocaine and amphetamine increase extracellular dopamine in the nucleus accumbens of mice lacking the dopamine transporter gene. *J. Neurosci.*, 21, RC141 (1–4).

Carhart-Harris, R. L., Muthukumaraswamy, S., Roseman, L., Kaelen, M., Droog, W., Murphy, K., et al. (2016). Neural correlates of the LSD experience revealed by multimodal neuroimaging. *Proc. Natl. Acad. Sci. USA*, 113, 4853–4858.

Carhart-Harris, R. L., Erritzoe, D., Williams, T., Stone, J. M., Reed, L. J., Colasanti, A., Tyacke, R. J., et al. (2012). Neural correlates of the psychedelic state as determined by fMRI studies with psilocybin. *Proc. Natl. Acad. Sci. USA*, 109, 213/1–/2143.

Carlezon, W. A., Jr., and Wise, R. A. (1996). Rewarding actions of phencyclidine and related drugs in nucleus accumbens shell and frontal cortex. *J. Neurosci.*, 16, 3112–3122.

Carli, M., Robbins, T. W., Evenden, J. L., Everitt, B. J. (1983). Effects of lesions to ascending noradrenergic neurones on performance of a 5-choice serial reaction task in rats; implications for theories of dorsal noradrenergic bundle function based on selective attention and arousal. *Behav. Brain Res.*, 9, 361– 380.

Carlino, E., Piedimonte, A., and Benedetti, F. (2016). Nature of the placebo and nocebo effect in relation to functional neurologic disorders. *Handb. Clin. Neurol.*, 139, 597–606.

Carlsson, A. (1960). On the problem of the mechanism of action of psychopharmaca. *Psychiatr. Neurol.* 140, 220.

Carlsson, A. (2001). A paradigm shift in brain research. *Science*, 294, 1021–1024.

Carlsson, A., Lindqvist, M., and Magnusson, T. (1957). 3,4-Dihydrozypheylalanine and 5-hydroxytryptophan as reserpine antagonists. *Nature*, 180, 1200.

Carlton, P. L. (1983). *A Primer of Behavioral Pharmacology*. New York: Freeman.

Carmack, S. A., Koob, G. F., and Anagnostaras, S. G. (2017). Learning and memory in addiction. In J.H. Byrne (Ed.), *Learning and Memory: A Comprehensive Reference*, 2nd edition, Volume 4, pp. 52/1–/238. San Diego: Academic Press.

Carod-Artal, F. J. (2015). Hallucinogenic drugs in pre-Columbian Mesoamerican cultures. *Neurologia*, 30, 42–49.

Carpenter, C. M., Wayne, G. F., and Connolly, G. N. (2007). The role of sensory perception in the development and targeting of tobacco products. *Addiction*, 102, 136–147.

Carrillo, M., Ricci, L. A., Coppersmith, G. A., and Melloni, R. H., Jr. (2009). The effect of increased serotonergic neurotransmission on aggression: A critical meta-analytical review of preclinical studies. *Psychopharmacology*, 205, 349–368.

Carroll, C. R. (1996). *Drugs in Modern Society* (4th ed.). Guilford, CT: Brown and Benchmark.

Carroll, K. M., Nich, C., Petry, N. M., Eagan, D. A., Shi, J. M., and Ball, S. A. (2016). A randomized factorial trial of disulfiram and contingency management to enhance cognitive behavioral therapy for cocaine dependence. *Drug Alcohol Depend.*, 160, 135–142.

Carroll, M. E., Krattiger, K. L., Gieske, D., and Sadoff, D. A. (1990). Cocaine-base smoking in rhesus monkeys: Reinforcing and physiological effects. *Psychopharmacology*, 102, 443–450.

Carter, L. P., Koek, W., and France, C. P. (2009a). Behavioral analyses of GHB: Receptor mechanisms. *Pharmacol. Ther.*, 121, 100–114.

Carter, L. P., Pardi, D., Gorsline, J., and Griffiths, R. R. (2009b). Illicit gammahydroxybutyrate (GHB) and pharmaceutical sodium oxybate (Xyrem): Differences in characteristics and misuse. *Drug Alcohol Depend.*, 104, 1–10.

Carter, L. P., Richards, B. D., Mintzer, M. Z., and Griffiths, R. R. (2006). Relative abuse liability of GHB in humans: A comparison of psychomotor, subjective, and cognitive effects of supratherapeutic doses of triazolam, pentobarbital, and GHB. *Neuropsychopharmacology*, 31, 2537–2551.

Carter, M. E., de Lecea, L., and Adamantidis, A. (2013). Functional wiring of hypocretin and LC-NE neurons: Implications for arousal. *Front. Behav. Neurosci.*, 7, 43. doi: 10.3389/fnbeh.2013.00043.

Carter, M. E., Yizhar, O., Chikahisa, S., Nguyen, H., Adamantidis, A., Nishimo, S., et al. (2010). Tuning arousal with optogenetic modulation of locus coeruleus neurons. *Nat. Neurosci.*, 13, 1526–1533.

Carter, R. J., Lione, L. A., Humby, T., Mangiarini, L., Mahal, A., Bates, G. P., et al. (1999).

Characterization of progressive motor deficits in mice transgenic for the human Huntington's disease mutation. *J. Neurosci.*, 19, 3248–3257.

Carucci, S., Balia, C., Gagliano, A., Lampis, A., Buitelaar, J. K., Danckaerts, M., Dittman, R. W., et al. (2020). Long term methylphenidate exposure and growth in children and adolescents with ADHD. A systematic review and meta-analysis. *Neurosci. Biobehav. Rev.*, 120, 509–525.

Carvey, P. M. (1998). *Drug Action in the Central Nervous System*. New York: Oxford University Press.

Casadeus, G. (Ed.). (2011). *Handbook of Animal Models in Alzheimer's Disease*. Amsterdam, Netherlands: IOS.

Casadó-Anguero, V., Bonaventura, J., Moreno, E., Navarro, G., Cortés, A., Ferré, S., et al. (2016). Evidence for the heterotetrameric structure of the adenosine A2A–dopamine D2 receptor complex. *Biochem. Soc. Trans.*, 44, 595–600.

Casey, D. E. (2004). Pathophysiology of antipsychotic drug-induced movement disorders. *J. Clin. Psychiatry*, 65 (Suppl. 9), 25–28.

Casoni, F., Galbiati, A., and Ferini-Strambi, L. (2019). D3 receptor agonist efficacy in restless legs syndrome. *Adv. Pharmacol.*, 84, 2/1–/25.

Caspi, A., Sugden, K., Moffitt, T. E., Taylor, A., Craig, I. W., Harrington, H., et al. (2003). Influence of life stress on depression: Moderation by a polymorphism in the 5-HTT gene. *Science*, 301, 386–389.

Casselman, I., Nock, C. J., Wohlmuth, H., Weatherby, R. P., and Heinrich, M. (2014). From local to global: Fifty years of research on *Salvia divinorum*. *J. Ethnopharmacol.*, 151, 768–783.

Castaldelli-Maia, J. M., Ventriglio, A., and Bhugra, D. (2016). Tobacco smoking: From "glamour" to "stigma": A comprehensive review. *Psychiatry Clin. Neurosci.*, 70, 24–33.

Castañé, A., Berrendero, F., and Maldonado, R. (2005). The role of the cannabinoid system in nicotine addiction. *Pharmacol. Biochem. Behav.*, 81, 381–386.

Castaneto, M. S., Gorelick, D. A., Desrosiers, N. A., Hartman, R. L., Pirard, S., and Huestis, M. A. (2014). Synthetic cannabinoids: Epidemiology, pharmacodynamics, and clinical implications. *Drug Alcohol Depend.*, 144, 12–41.

Castelli, M. P., Pibiri, F., Carboni, G., and Piras, A. P. (2004). A review of pharmacology of NCS-382, a putative antagonist of γ-hydroxybutyric acid (GHB) receptor. *CNS Drug Rev.*, 10, 243–260.

Castells, X., Cunill, R., Pérez-Mañá, C., Vidal, X., and

Capellà, D. (2016). Psychostimulant drugs for cocaine dependence. *Cochrane Database Syst. Rev.*, 9, CD007380. doi: 10.1002/14651858. CD007380. pub4.

Castillo, P. E., Younts, T. J., Chávez, A. E., and Hashimotodani, Y. (2012). Endocannabinoid signaling and synaptic function. *Neuron*, 76, 70–81. © 2012. Reprinted with permission from Elsevier.

Castrén E., Hen R.. (2013) Neuronal plasticity and antidepressant actions. *Trends Neurosci.*, 36(5), 259–267.

Castro, D. C., and Berridge, K. C. (2014a). Advances in the neurobiological bases for food "liking" versus "wanting." *Physiol. Behav.*, 136, 22–30.

Castro, D. C., and Berridge, K. C. (2014b). Opioid hedonic hotspot in nucleus accumbens shell: mu, delta, and kappa maps for enhancement of sweetness "liking" and "wanting." *J. Neurosci.*, 34, 4239–4250.

Ceccarini, J., Kuepper, R., Kemels, D., van Os, J., Henquet, C., and Van Laere, K. (2015). [18F] MK-9470 PET measurement of cannabinoid CB1 receptor availability in chronic cannabis users. *Addict. Biol.*, 20, 357–367.

Celada, P., Bortolozzi, A., and Artigas, F. (2013). Serotonin 5-HT1A receptors as targets for agents to treat psychiatric disorders: Rationale and current status of research. *CNS Drugs*, 27, 703–716.

Celli, R., Santolini, I., Van Luijtelaar, G., Ngomba, R., Bruno, V., and Nicoletti, F. (2019). Targeting metabotropic glutamate receptors in the treatment of epilepsy: rationale and current status. *Expert Opin. Ther. Targets*, 23, 34/1–/251.

Cendes, F., Sakamoto, A. C., Spreafico, R., Bingaman, W., and Becker, A. J. (2014). Epilepsies associated with hippocampal sclerosis. *Acta Neuropathol.*, 128, 21–37.

Cengel, H. Y., Bozkurt, M., Evren, C., Umut, G., Keskinkilic, C., and Agachanli, R. (2018). Evaluation of cognitive functions in individuals with synthetic cannabinoid use disorder and comparison to individuals with cannabis use disorder. *Psychiatry Res.*, 262, 4/1–/24.

Center for Behavioral Health Statistics and Quality. (2015). 2014 National Survey on Drug Use and Health: Detailed Tables. Rockville, MD: Substance Abuse and Mental Health Services Administration. Available at www.samhsa.gov/ data/sites/default/ files/NSDUH-DetTabs2014/ NSDUH-DetTabs2014.htm.

Center for Behavioral Health Statistics and Quality. (2016). 2015 National Survey on Drug Use and Health: Detailed Tables. Rockville, MD: Substance Use and Mental Health Services

Administration. Available at www.samhsa.gov/data/sites/default/files/NSDUHDetTabs-2015/NSDUH-DetTabs-2015/NSDUH-DetTabs-2015.pdf.

Center for Behavioral Health Statistics and Quality. (2016). Key Substance Use and Mental Health Indicators in the United States: Results from the 2015 National Survey on Drug Use and Health. (HHS Publication No. SMA 16-4984, NSDUH Series H-51). Available at www.samhsa.gov/data/.

Center for Behavioral Health Statistics and Quality. (2017). 2016 National Survey on Drug Use and Health: Detailed Tables. Rockville, MD: Substance Use and Mental Health Services Administration. Available at www.samhsa.gov/ data/sites/default/files/NSDUH-DetTabs-2016/NSDUH-DetTabs-2016.pdf.

Center for Behavioral Health Statistics and Quality. (2020). Results from the 2019 National Survey on Drug Use and Health: Detailed tables. Rockville, MD: Substance Abuse and Mental Health Services Administration. Retrieved from https://www.samhsa.gov/data/.

Centers for Disease Control (2019). https://www.cdc.gov/media/releases/2019/1205-nyts-2019.html, accessed 12/18/20.

Centers for Disease Control and Prevention (2019). Data from Table 2 in National Youth Tobacco Survey, 2019; https://www.cdc.gov/mmwr/volumes/68/ss/ss6812a1.html.

Centers for Disease Control and Prevention (CDC), U.S. Department of Health and Human Services. (2015a). Fetal Alcohol Spectrum Disorders. Available at www.cdc.gov/ncbddd/fasd/data. html.

Centers for Disease Control and Prevention (CDC), U.S. Department of Health and Human Services. (2015b). Facts about FASDs. Available at www.cdc.gov/ncbddd/fasd/facts.html.

Centers for Disease Control and Prevention (CDC), U.S. Department of Health and Human Services. (2016). Impaired Driving: Get the Facts. Available at www.cdc.gov/motorvehiclesafety/impaired_driving/impaired-drv_factsheet.html.

Centers for Disease Control and Prevention (CDC), U.S. Department of Health and Human Services. (2016a). Drug Overdose Death Data. Available at www.cdc.gov/drugoverdose/data/statedeaths.html.

Centers for Disease Control and Prevention (CDC), U.S. Department of Health and Human Services. (2016b). Increases in drug and opioid overdose deaths: United States 2000–2014. Morbidity and Mortality Weekly Report (MMWR), 64, 1378–1382.

Available at www.cdc. gov/mmwr/preview/mmwrhtml/mm6450a3.htm.

Centers for Disease Control and Prevention (2020). Sudden Unexpected Infant Death and Sudden Infant Death Syndrome. Data and Statistics. https://www.cdc.gov/sids/data.htm, accessed July 9, 2020.

Centers for Disease Control and Prevention (CDC), U.S. Department of Health and Human Services. (2019). Alcohol Related Disease Impact (ARDI). https://nccd.cdc.gov/DPH_ARDI/Default/Default.aspx.

Centers for Disease Control and Prevention (CDC), U.S. Department of Health and Human Services. (2020). Opioid Data Analysis and Resources | Drug Overdose | CDC Injury Center. https://www.cdc.gov/drugoverdose/data/analysis.html.

Centers for Disease Control and Prevention (CDC), U.S. Department of Health and Human Services. (2020). Basics about FASDs. https://www.cdc.gov/ncbddd/fasd/facts.html.

Centers for Disease Control and Prevention (CDC), U.S. Department of Health and Human Services. (2021). Data & Statistics. https://www.cdc.gov/ncbddd/fasd/data.html.

Centola, C., Giorgetti, A., Zaami, S., and Giorgetti, R. (2018). Effects of GHB on psychomotor and driving performance. Curr. Drug Metab., 19, 1065–1072.

Cerdá, M., Mauro, C., Hamilton, A., Levy, N. S., Santaella-Tenorio, J., Hasin, D., Wall, M. M., et al. (2020). Association between recreational marijuana legalization in the United States and changes in marijuana use and cannabis use disorder from 2008 to 2016. JAMA Psychiatry, 77, 16/1–/271.

Cerniglia, L., Zoratto, F., Cimino, S., Laviola, G., Ammaniti, M., and Adriani, W. (2017). Internet addiction in adolescence: Neurobiological, psychosocial and clinical issues. Neurosci. Biobehav. Rev., 76, 174–184.

CESAR (Center for Substance Abuse Research). (2013). Ritalin. Available at www.cesar.umd.edu/cesar/drugs/ritalin.asp.

Chadi, N., Minato, C., and Stanwick, R. (2020). Cannabis vaping: Understanding the health risks of a rapidly emerging trend. Paediatr. Child Health, 25(Suppl. 1), S16-S20.

Chaffee, B. W., Watkins, S. L., and Glantz, S. A. (2018). Electronic cigarette use and progression from experimentation to established smoking. Pediatrics, 141(4), e20173594. doi: 10.1542/peds.2017-3594.

Chait, L. D. (1994). Reinforcing and subjective effects of methylphenidate in humans. Behav. Pharmacol., 5, 281–288.

Chait, L. D., and Burke, K. A. (1994). Preference for high- versus low-potency marijuana. Pharmacol. Biochem. Behav., 49, 643–647.

Chait, L. D., and Zacny, J. P. (1992). Reinforcing and subjective effects of oral Δ^9-THC and smoked marijuana in humans. Psychopharmacology, 107, 255–262.

Chaki, S., Koike, H., and Fukumoto, K. (2019). Targeting of metabotropic glutamate receptors for the development of novel antidepressants. Chronic Stress, 3, 2470547019837712. doi: 10.1177/2470547019837712.

Challman, T. D., and Lipsky, J. J. (2000). Methylphenidate: Its pharmacology and uses. Mayo Clin. Proc., 75, 711–721.

Chamberlain, S. R., and Robbins, T. W. (2013). Noradrenergic modulation of cognition: Therapeutic implications. J. Psychopharmacol., 27, 694–718.

Chamorro, A. J., Marcos, M., Mirón-Canelo, J. A., Pastor, I., González-Sarmiento, R., and Laso, F. J. (2012). Association of μ-opioid receptor (OPRM1) gene polymorphism with response to naltrexone in alcohol dependence: A systematic review and meta-analysis. Addict. Biol., 17, 505–512.

Chamorro, A., Dirnagl, U., Urra, X., and Planas, A. M. (2016). Neuroprotection in acute stroke: Targeting excitotoxicity, oxidative and nitrosative stress, and inflammation. Lancet Neurol., 15, 869–881.

Chan, B., Kondo, K., Freeman, M., Ayers, C., Montgomery, J., and Kansagara, D. (2019). Pharmacotherapy for cocaine use disorder—a systematic review and meta-analysis. J. Gen. Intern. Med., 34, 285/1–/2873.

Chan, K. (2002). Jimson Weed Poisoning—A Case Report. Perm. J., 6(4), 28–30.

Chan, K. W. S., Lee, T. M. C., Siu, A. M. H., Wong, D. P. L., Kam, C.-M., Tsang, S. K. M., et al. (2013). Effects of chronic ketamine use on frontal and medial temporal cognition. Addict. Behav., 38, 2128–2132.

Chan, S. (2016). 6 Hospitalized, one of them brain-dead, after drug trial in France. New York Times. Available at https://www.nytimes.com/2016/01/16/world/europe/french-drug-trial-hospitalization.html.

Chanaday, N. L., and Kavalali, E. T. (2017). How do you recognize and reconstitute a synaptic vesicle after fusion? [version 1; peer review: 3 approved]. F1000Research, 6(F1000 Faculty Rev), 1734. doi: 10.12688/f1000research.12072.1.

Chand, G. B., Dwyer, D. B., Erus, G., Sotiras, A., Varol, E., Srinivasan, D., Doshi, J., et al. (2020). Two distinct neuroanatomical subtypes of schizophrenia

revealed using machine learning. Brain, 143(3), 1027–1038. https://doi.org/10.1093/brain/awaa025

Chandler, D. J., Waterhouse, B. D., and Gao, W.-J. (2014). New perspectives on catecholaminergic regulation of executive circuits: Evidence for independent modulation of prefrontal functions by midbrain dopaminergic and noradrenergic neurons. Front. Neural Circuits, 8, 53. doi: 10.3389/fncir.2014.00053.

Chandra, M., and Anthony, J. C. (2020). Cocaine dependence: "Side effects" and syndrome formation within /1–/22 months after first cocaine use. Drug Alcohol Depend., 206, 107717. doi: 10.1016/j.drugalcdep.2019.107717.

Chang, P. K.-Y., Verbich, D., and McKinney, R. A. (2012). AMPA receptors as drug targets in neurological disease: Advantages, caveats, and future outlook. Eur. J. Neurosci., 35, 1908–1916.

Changeux, J.-P. (2013). The concept of allosteric modulation: An overview. Drug Discov. Today Technol., 10, e223–e228.

Changeux, J.-P. (2020). Discovery of the first neurotransmitter receptor: The acetylcholine nicotinic receptor. Biomolecules, 10, 547. doi: 10.3390/biom10040547.

Changeux, J. P., and Christopoulos, A. (2016). Allosteric modulation as a unifying mechanism for receptor function and regulation. Cell, 165, 108/1–/2102.

Chapman, S., Bareham, D., and Maziak, W. (2018). The gateway effect of e-cigarettes: Reflections on main criticisms. Nicotine Tob. Res., 21, 69/1–/298.

Charney, D. S., Grillon, C.C.G., and Bremner, J. D. (1998). The neurobiological basis of anxiety and fear: Circuits, mechanisms, and neurochemical interactions (part II). Neuroscientist, 4, 122–132.

Chartier, K. G., Hesselbrock, M. N., and Hesselbrock, V. M. (2010). Development and vulnerability factors in adolescent alcohol use. Child Adolesc. Psychiatr. Clin. N. Am., 19, 493–504.

Chatterjee, K., Alzghoul, B., Innabi, A., and Meena, N. (2018). Is vaping a gateway to smoking? A review of longitudinal studies. Int. J. Adolesc. Med. Health, 30(3).

Chaudhury, D., Walsh, J. J., Friedman, A. K., Juarez, B., Ku, S. M., Koo, J. W., et al. (2013). Rapid regulation of depression-related behaviors by control of midbrain dopamine neurons. Nature, 493, 532–536.

Chausmer, A. L., Elmer, G. I., Rubinstein, M., Low, M. J., Grandy, D. K., and Katz, J. I. (2002). Cocaine-induced locomotor activity and cocaine discrimination in dopamine D2 receptor mutant mice. Psychopharmacology, 163, 54–61.

Chegeni, R., Pallesen, S., McVeigh, J., and Sagoe, D. (2021). Anabolic-androgenic steroid administration increases self-reported aggression in healthy males: a systematic review and meta-analysis of experimental studies. *Psychopharmacology*, 238, 1911–1922.

Chemali, J. J., Van Dort, C. J., Brown, E. N., and Solt, K. (2012). Active emergence from propofol general anesthesia is induced by methylphenidate. *Anesthesiology*, 116, 998–1005.

Chemelli, R. M., Willie, J. T., Sinton, C. M., Elmquist, J. K., Scammell, T., Lee, C., et al. (1999). Narcolepsy in orexin knockout mice: Molecular genetics of sleep regulation. *Cell*, 98, 437–451.

Chen, B. T., Yau, H.-J., Hatch, C., Kusumoto-Yoshida, I., Cho, S. L., Hopf, F. W., et al. (2013). Rescuing cocaine-induced prefrontal cortex hypoactivity prevents compulsive cocaine seeking. *Nature*, 496, 359–362.

Chen, J., Cheuk, I.W.Y., Shin, V. Y., and Kwong, A. (2019). Acetylcholine receptors: Key players in cancer development. *Surg. Oncol.*, 31, 4/1–/23.

Chen, J.-F., and Schwarzschild, M. A. (2020). Do caffeine and more selective adenosine A2A receptor antagonists protect against dopaminergic neurodegeneration in Parkinson's disease? *Parkinsonism Relat. Disord.*, 80 (Suppl. 1), S45-S53.

Chen, J. Q., Scheltens, P., Groot, C., and Ossenkoppele, R. (2020). Associations between caffeine consumption, cognitive decline, and dementia: A systematic review. *J. Alzheimers Dis.*, 78, 1519–1546.

Chen, K., and Kandel, D. B. (1995). The natural history of drug use from adolescence to the mid-thirties in a general population sample. *Am. J. Public Health*, 85, 41–47.

Chen, L.-Y., Chen, C.-K., Chen, C.-H., Chang, H.-M., Huang, M.-C., and Xu, K. (2020). Association of craving and depressive symptoms in ketamine-dependent patients undergoing withdrawal treatment. *Am. J. Addict.*, 29, 4/1–/20.

Chen, P., Lin J. J., Lu, C. S., Ong, C. T., Hsieh, P. F., Yang, C. C., et al. (2011). Carbamazepine-induced toxic effects and HLA-B*1502 screening in Taiwan. *N. Engl. J. Med.*, 364, 1126–1133.

Chen, Q., and Tesmer, J. J. G. (2017). A receptor on acid. *Cell*, 168, 339–341.

Cheng, T., Wallace, D. M., and Tuli, M. (2018). Valium without dependence? Individual GABA$_A$ receptor subtype contribution to benzodiazepine addiction, tolerance, and therapeutic effects. *Neuropsychiatr. Dis. Treat.*, 14, 135/1–/2361.

Cheng, W.-J., Chen, C.-H., Chen, C.-K., Huang, M.-C., Pietrzak, R. H., Krystal, J. H., and Xu, K. (2018). Similar psychotic and cognitive profile between ketamine dependence with persistent psychosis and schizophrenia. *Schizophr. Res.*, 199, 31/1–/218.

Cherblanc, F., Chapman-Rothe, N., Brown, R., and Fuchter, M. J. (2012). Current limitations and future opportunities for epigenetic therapies. *Future Med. Chem.*, 4, 425–446.

Chergui, K., Suaud-Chagny, M. F., and Gonon, F. (1994). Nonlinear relationship between impulse flow, dopamine release and dopamine elimination in the rat brain in vivo. *Neuroscience*, 62, 641–645.

Chesney, E., McGuire, P., Freeman, T. P., Strang, J., and Englund, A. (2020). Lack of evidence for the effectiveness or safety of over-the-counter cannabidiol products. *Ther. Adv. Psychopharmacol.*, 10, /1–/23.

Cheung, A. S., and Grossmann, M. (2018). Physiological basis behind ergogenic effects of anabolic androgens. *Mol. Cell. Endocrinol.*, 464, 14–20.

Cheung, H. M., and Yew, D.T.W. (2019). Effects of perinatal exposure to ketamine on the developing brain. *Front. Neurosci.*, 13, 138. doi: 10.3389/fnins.2019.00138.

Chiamulera, C., Padovani, L., and Corsi, M. (2017). Drug discovery for the treatment of substance use disorders: novel targets, repurposing, and the need for new paradigms. *Curr. Opin. Pharmacol.*, 35, 12/1–/224.

Chiang, M., Lombardi, D., Du, J., Makrum, U., Sitthichai, R., Harrington, A., Shukair, N., et al. (2018). Methamphetamine-associated psychosis: Clinical presentation, biological basis, and treatment options. *Hum. Psychopharmacol. Clin. Exp.*, 34, e2710. doi: 10.1002/hup.2710.

Chiao, S., and Zuo, Z. (2014). A double-edged sword: Volatile anesthetic effects on the neonatal brain. *Brain Sci.*, 4, 27/1–/294.

Chiappini, S., Claridge, H., Corkery, J. M., Goodair, C., Loi, B., and Schifano, F. (2015). Methoxetamine-related deaths in the UK: An overview. *Hum. Psychopharmacol.*, 30, 244–248.

Chiarlone, A., Bellocchio, L., Blázquez, C., Resel, E., Soria-Gómez, E., Cannich, A., et al. (2014). A restricted population of CB$_1$ cannabinoid receptors with neuroprotective activity. *Proc. Natl. Acad. Sci. USA*, 111, 8257–8262.

Childers, S. R., and Breivogel, C. S. (1998). Cannabis and endogenous cannabinoid systems. *Drug Alcohol Depend.*, 51, 173–187. © 1998 Elsevier Science Ireland Ltd. Reprinted with permission from Elsevier.

Childress, A. R., McLellan, T., and O'Brien, C. P. (1986). Abstinent opiate abusers exhibit conditioned craving, conditioned withdrawal and reductions in both through extinction. *Br. J. Addict.*, 81, 655–660.

Childress, A. R., Mozley, P. D., McElgin, W., Fitzgerald, J., Reivich, M., and O'Brien, C. P. (1999). Limbic activation during cue-induced cocaine craving. *Am. J. Psychiatry*, 156, 11–18.

Childs, E. (2014). Influence of energy drink ingredients on mood and cognitive performance. *Nutr. Rev.*, 72(Suppl. 1), 48–59.

Chiron, C. (2016). Stiripentol and vigabatrin current roles in the treatment of epilepsy. *Expert Opin. Pharmacother.*, 17, 109/1–/2101.

Chklovskii, D. B., Mel, B. W., and Svoboda, K. (2004). Cortical rewiring and information storage. *Nature*, 431, 782–788.

Choi, Y. M., and Kim, K. H. (2015). Etifoxine for pain patients with anxiety. *Korean J. Pain*, 28, 4–10.

Chomchai, C., and Chomchai, S. (2015). Global patterns of methamphetamine use. *Curr. Opin. Psychiatry*, 28, 269–274.

Chou, N.-H., Huang, Y.-J., and Jiann, B.-P. (2015). The impact of illicit use of amphetamine on male sexual functions. *J. Sex. Med.*, 12, 169/1–/2702.

Chowdhary, S., Bhattacharya, R., and Banerjee, D. (2014). Acute organophosphorus poisoning. *Clin. Chim. Acta*, 431, 66–76.

Christie, N., and Meier, C. A. (2015). Hypotestosteronaemia in the aging male: Should we treat it? *Swiss Med. Wkly.*, 145, w14216. doi: 10.4414/ smw.2015.14216.

Christou, M. A., Christou, P. A., Markozannes, G., Tsatsoulis, A., Mastorakos, G., and Tigas, S. (2017). Effects of anabolic androgenic steroids on the reproductive system of athletes and recreational users: A systematic review and meta-analysis. *Sports Med.*, 47(9), 1869–1883. doi: 10.1007/s40279-017-0709-z.

Chu Sin Chung, P., and Kieffer, B. L. (2013). Delta opioid receptors in brain function and diseases. *Pharmacol. Ther.*, 140, 112–120.

Chu, P. S.-K., Ma, W.-K., Wong, S. C.-W., Cu, R. W.-H., Cheng, C.-H., Wong, S., et al. (2008). The destruction of the lower urinary tract by ketamine abuse: A new syndrome? *BJU Int.*, 102, 1616–1622.

Chua, H. C., and Chebib, M. (2017). GABA$_A$ receptors and the diversity in their structure and pharmacology. *Adv. Pharmacol.*, 79, /1–/24.

Chuang, S.-H., and Reddy, D. S. (2018). Genetic and molecular regulation of extrasynaptic GABA-A receptors in the brain: Therapeutic insights for epilepsy. *J. Pharmacol. Exp. Ther.*, 364, 18/1–/297.

Chung, W. H., Hung, S. I., Hong, H. S., Hsih, M. S., Yang, L. C., Ho, H. C., et al. (2004). Medical genetics: A marker for Stevens-Johnson syndrome. *Nature*, 428, 486.

Ciccocioppo, R. (2013). Genetically selected alcohol preferring rats to model human alcoholism. *Curr. Top. Behav. Neurosci.*, 13, 25/1–/269.

Cisneros-Mejorado, A., Pérez-Samartin, A., Gottlieb, M., and Matute, C. (2015). ATP signaling in brain: Release, excitotoxicity and potential therapeutic targets. *Cell. Mol. Neurobiol.*, 35, 1–6.

Claeysen, S., Bockaert, J., and Giannoni, P. (2015). Serotonin: A new hope in Alzheimer's disease? *ACS Chem. Neurosci.*, 6, 940–943.

Clapcote, S. J. (2017). Phosphodiesterase-4B as a therapeutic target for cognitive impairment and obesity-related metabolic diseases. *Adv. Neurobiol.*, 17, 10/1–/231.

Clark, I., and Landolt, H. P. (2017). Coffee, caffeine, and sleep: A systematic review of epidemiological studies and randomized controlled trials. *Sleep Med. Rev.*, 31, 70–78.

Clark, K. L., and Noudoost, B. (2014). The role of prefrontal catecholamines in attention and working memory. *Front. Neural Circuits*, 8, 33. doi: 10.3389/fncir.2014.00033.

Clark, L. (2014). Disordered gambling: The evolving concept of behavioral addiction. *Ann. N. Y. Acad. Sci.*, 1327, 46–61.

Clark, L., Boileau, I., and Zack, M. (2019). Neuroimaging of reward mechanisms in Gambling disorder: an integrative review. *Mol. Psychiatry*, 24, 674–693.

Clarke, T. K. and Schumann, G. (2009). Gene-environment interactions resulting in risky alcohol drinking behavior are mediated by CRF and CRF1. *Pharmacol. Biochem. Behav.*, 93, 230–236.

Clemow, D. B. (2017). Misuse of methylphenidate. *Curr. Top. Behav. Neurosci.*, 34, 99–124.

Clemow, D. B., Johnson, K. W., Hochstetler, H. M., Ossipov, M. H., Hake, A. M., and Blumenfeld, A. M. (2020). Lasmiditan mechanism of action – review of a selective 5–HT1F agonist. *J. Headache Pain*, 21, 71. doi: 10.1186/s10194-020-01132-3.

Clewitt, D., and Murty, V. P. (2019). Echoes of emotions past: How neuromodulators determine what we recollect. *eNeuro*, 6(2), e0108–18.2019, 1–19.

Cloninger, C. R. (1987). Neurogenetic adaptive mechanisms in alcoholism. *Science*, 236, 410–416.

Cloutier, M., Aigbogun, M. S., Guerin, A., Nitulescu, R., Ramanakumar, A. V., Kamat, S. A., et al. (2016). The economic burden of schizophrenia in the United States in 2013. *J. Clin. Psychiatry*, 77, 764–771.

Cobb, C. O., Hendricks, P. S., and Eissenberg, T. (2015). Electronic cigarettes and nicotine dependence: Evolving products, evolving problems. *BMC Med.*, 13, 119. doi: 10.1186/s12916-015-0355-y.

Coccaro, E. F., and Kavoussi, R. J. (1997). Fluoxetine and impulsive aggressive behavior in personality-disordered subjects. *Arch. Gen. Psychiatry*, 54, 1081–1088.

Coccaro, E. F., Fanning, J. R., Phan, K. L., and Lee, R. (2015). Serotonin and impulsive aggression. *CNS Spectr.*, 20, 295–302.

Coccaro, E. F., and Lee, R. J. (2019). 5-HT2C agonist, lorcaserin, reduces aggressive responding in intermittent explosive disorder: A pilot study. *Hum. Psychopharmacol. Clin. Exp.*, 34, e2714. doi: 10.1002/hup.2714.

Coffey, C., and Patton, G. C. (2016). Cannabis use in adolescence and young adulthood: A review of findings from the Victorian Adolescent Health Cohort Study. *Can. J. Psychiatry*, 61, 318–327.

Cogan, P. S. (2020). The 'entourage effect' or 'hodge-podge hashish': the questionable rebranding, marketing, and expectations of cannabis polypharmacy. *Expert Rev. Clin. Pharmacol.*, 13, 835–845.

Cohen, I., Navarro, V., Clemenceau, S., Baulac, M., and Miles, R. (2002). On the origin of interictal activity in human temporal lobe epilepsy in vitro. *Science*, 298, 1418–1421.

Cohen, J. Y., Amoroso, M. W., and Uchida, N. (2015). Serotonergic neurons signal reward and punishment on multiple timescales. *eLife*, 4, e06346. doi: 10.7554/eLife.06346.

Cohen, S. M., Tsien, R. W., Goff, D. C., and Halassa, M. M. (2015). The impact of NMDA receptor hypofunction on GABAergic neurons in the pathophysiology of schizophrenia. *Schizophr. Res.*, 167, 98–107.

Colagiuri, B., Schenk, L. A., Kessler, M. D., Dorsey, S. G., and Colloca, L. (2015). The placebo effect: From concepts to genes. *Neuroscience*, 307, 171–190.

Colby, S. M., Tiffany, S. T., Shiffman, S., and Niaura, R. S. (2000). Are adolescent smokers dependent on nicotine? A review of the evidence. *Drug Alc. Depend.*, 59(Suppl. 1), S83–S95.

Coles, A. S., Kozak, K., and George, T. P. (2018). A review of brain stimulation methods to treat substance use disorders. *Am. J. Addict.*, 27, 71–91.

Colizzi, M., and Bhattacharyya, S. (2018). Cannabis use and the development of tolerance: a systematic review of human evidence. *Neurosci. Biobehav. Rev.*, 93, 1–25.

Collins, E. D., Vosburg, S. K., Hart, C. L., Haney, M., and Foltin, R. W. (2003). Amantadine does not modulate reinforcing, subjective, or cardiovascular effects of cocaine in humans. *Pharmacol. Biochem. Behav.*, 76, 401–407.

Collins, G. T., Sulima, A., Rice, K. C., and France, C. P. (2019). Self-administration of the synthetic cathinones 3,4-methylenedioxypyrovalerone (MDPV) and α-pyrrolidinopentiophenone (α-PVP) in rhesus monkeys. *Psychopharmacology*, 236, 3677–3685.

Collins, M. A., Neafsey, E. J., Mukamal, K. J., Gray, M. O., Parks, D. A., Das, D. K., and Korthuis, R. J. (2009). Alcohol in moderation, cardioprotection, and neuroprotection: Epidemiological considerations and mechanistic studies. *Alcohol. Clin. Exp. Res.*, 33(2), 206–219. https://doi.org/10.1111/j.1530-0277.2008.00828.x.

Collo, G., Cavaalleri, L., and Spano, P. F (2014). Structural plasticity in mesencephalic dopaminergic neurons produced by drugs of abuse: critical role of BDNF and dopamine. *Front. Pharmacol.*, 5, 259. doi: 10.3389/fphar.2014.00259

Colombo, G., Serra, S., Vacca, G., Carai, M. A. M., and Gessa, G. L. (2005). Endocannabinoid system and alcohol addiction: Pharmacological studies. *Pharmacol. Biochem. Behav.*, 81, 369–380.

Colver, A., and Longwell, S. (2013). New understanding of adolescent brain development: Relevance to transitional healthcare for young people with long-term conditions. *Arch. Dis. Child*, 98, 902–907.

Comer, S. D., Ashworth, J. B., Foltin, R. W., Johanson, C. E., Zacny, J. P., and Walsh, S. L. (2008). The role of human drug self-administration procedures in the development of medications. *Drug Alcohol Depend.*, 96, 1–15.

Committee on Nutrition and the Council on Sports Medicine and Fitness. (2011). Sports drinks and energy drinks for children and adolescents: Are they appropriate? *Pediatrics*, 127, 1182–1189.

Commons, K. G., Cholanians, A. B., Babb, J. A., and Ehlinger, D. G. (2017). The Rodent Forced Swim Test Measures Stress-Coping Strategy, Not Depression-like Behavior. *ACS Chem. Neurosci.*, 8(5), 955–960. https://doi.org/10.1021/acschemneuro.7b00042

Compton, W. M., Dawson, D. A., Conway, K. P., Brodsky, M., and Grant, B. F. (2013). Transitions in illicit drug use status over 3 years: a prospective analysis of a general population sample. *Am. J. Psychiatry*, 170, 660–670.

Conner, S. N., Bedell, V., Lipsey, K., Macones, G. A., Cahill, A. G., and Tuuli, M. G. (2016). Maternal marijuana use and averse neonatal outcomes. A systematic review and meta-analysis. *Obstet. Gynecol.*, 128, 713–723.

Connery, H. S. (2015). Medication-assisted treatment of opioid use disorder: Review of the evidence and future directions. *Harv. Rev. Psychiatry*, 23, 63–75.

Connolly, C. G., Bell, R. P., Foxe, J. J., and Garavan, H. (2013). Dissociated grey matter changes with prolonged addiction and extended abstinence in cocaine users. *PLOS ONE*, 8(3), e59645. doi: 10.1371/journal.pone.0059645.

Connolly, E., and O'Callaghan, G. (1999). MDMA toxicity presenting with severe hyperpyrexia: A case report. *Crit. Care Resusc.*, 1, 368–370.

Connor, D. F., Arnsten, A. F., Pearson, G. S., and Greco, G. F. (2014). Guanfacine extended release for the treatment of attention-deficit/hyperactivity disorder in children and adolescents. *Expert Opin. Pharmacother.*, 15, 1601–1610.

Connor, J. P., Stjepanović, D., Le Foll, B., Hoch, E., Budney, A. J., and Hall, W. D. (2021). Cannabis use and cannabis use disorder. *Nat. Rev. Dis. Primers*, 7(1), 16. doi: 10.1038/s41572-021-00247-4.

Connors, B. W., and Long, M. A. (2004). Electrical synapses in the mammalian brain. *Annu. Rev. Neurosci.*, 27, 393–418.

Conradt, E., Adkins, D., Crowell, S. E., Raby, K. L., Diamond, L. M., and Ellis, B. (2018). Incorporating epigenetic mechanisms to advance fetal programming theories. *Dev. Psychopathol.*, 30, 807–824.

Conti, A. A. (2010). Doping in sports in ancient and recent times. *Med. Secoli*, 22, 181–190.

Conti, A. A., Tolomeo, S., Steele, J. D., and Baldacchino, A. M. (2020). Severity of negative mood and anxiety symptoms occurring during acute abstinence from tobacco: A systematic review and meta-analysis. *Neurosci. Biobehav. Rev.*, 115, 48–63.

Cook, J., and Sepinwall, J. (1975). Behavior analysis of the effects and mechanisms of action of benzodiazepines. *Psychopharmacol. Bull.* 11, 53–55.

Cook, P. J. (2007). *Paying the Tab: The Costs and Benefits of Alcohol Control*. Princeton, NJ: Princeton University Press.

Cools, R., Roberts, A. C., and Robbins, T. W. (2007). Serotoninergic regulation of emotional and behavioural control processes. *Trends Cogn. Sci.*, 12, 31–40.

Cooper, A. (2013). An anxious history of Valium. Online essay. Wall Street Journal. Available at www.wsj.com/articles/an-anxious-history-of-valium1384547451?tesla=y.

Cooper, A. J. L. (2012). The role of glutamine synthetase and glutamate dehydrogenase in cerebral ammonia homeostasis. *Neurochem. Res.*, 37, 2439–2455.

Cooper, Z. D. (2016). Adverse effects of synthetic cannabinoids: Management of acute toxicity and withdrawal. *Curr. Psychiatry Rep.*, 18, 52. doi: 10.1007/s11920-016-0694-1.

Cooper, Z. D., and Haney, M. (2008). Cannabis reinforcement and dependence: Role of the cannabinoid CB$_1$ receptor. *Addict. Biol.*, 13, 188–195.

Cooper, Z. D., and Haney, M. (2009). Actions of delta-9-tetrahydrocannabinol in cannabis: Relation to use, abuse, dependence. *Int. Rev. Psychiatry*, 21, 104–112.

Copeland, J., and Pokorski, I. (2016). Progress toward pharmacotherapies for cannabis-use disorder: An evidence-based review. *Subst. Abuse Rehabil.*, 7, 41–53.

Copeland, J., and Swift, W. (2009). Cannabis use disorder: Epidemiology and management. *Int. Rev. Psychiatry*, 21, 96–103.

Corazza, O., Assi, S., and Schifano, F. (2013). From "special K" to "special M": The evolution of the recreational use of ketamine and methoxetamine. *CNS Neurosci. Ther.*, 19, 454–460.

Corbit V.L., Manning E.E., Gittis A.H., and Ahmari S.E. (2019). Strengthened inputs from secondary motor cortex to striatum in a mouse model of compulsive behavior. *J Neurosci.*, 39(15), 2965–2975.

Corcoran, A. E., Hodges, M. R., Wu, Y., Wang, W., Wylie, C. J., Deneris, E. S., and Richerson, G. B. (2009). Medullary serotonin neurons and central CO$_2$ chemoreception. *Respir. Physiol. Neurobiol.*, 168, 49–58.

Córdoba-Montoya, D. A., Albert, J., and López-Martín, S. (2010). All together now: Long term potentiation in the human cortex. *Rev. Neurol.*, 51, 367–374.

Corkery, J. M. (2018). Ibogaine as a treatment for substance misuse: Potential benefits and practical dangers. *Prog. Brain Res.*, 242, 217–257.

Cornelius, M. E., Wang, T. W., Jamal, A., Loretan, C. G., and Neff, L. J. (2020). Tobacco product use among adults—United States, 2019. *MMWR Morb. Mortal. Wkly. Rep.*, 69, 1736–1742.

Corona, G., Sansone, A., Pallotti, F., Ferlin, A., Pivonello, R., Isidori, A. M., Maggi, M., et al. (2020). People smoke for nicotine, but lose sexual and reproductive health for tar: a narrative review on the effect of cigarette smoking on male sexuality and reproduction. *J. Endocrinol. Invest.*, 43, 1391–1408.

Correll, C. U., and Schenk, E. M. (2008). Tardive dyskinesia and new antipsychotics. *Curr. Opin. Psychiatry*, 21(2), 151–156. https://doi.org/10.1097/YCO.0b013e3282f53132

Corrigall, W. A., Franklin, K. B., Coen, K. M., and Clarke, P. B. (1992). The mesolimbic dopaminergic system is implicated in the reinforcing effects of nicotine. *Psychopharmacology*, 107, 285–289.

Cortès-Saladelafont, E., Lipstein, N., and García-Cazorla, A. (2018). Presynaptic disorders: a clinical and pathophysiological approach focused on the synaptic vesicle. *J. Inherit. Metab. Dis.*, 41, 1131–1145.

Cosgrove, K. P., Esterlis, I., Sandiego, C., Petrulli, R., and Morris, E. D. (2015). Imaging tobacco smoking with PET and SPECT. *Curr. Top. Behav. Neurosci.*, 24, 1–17.

Costall, B., and Naylor, R. J. (1991). Anxiolytic effects of 5-H3 antagonists in animals. In R. J. Rodgers and S. J. Cooper (Eds.), *5-HT1A Agonists, 5-HT3 Antagonists and Benzodiazepines: Their Comparative Behavioral Pharmacology*, pp. 133–157. New York: Wiley.

Costantino, C. M., Gomes, I., Stockton, S. D., Lim, M. P., and Devi, L. A. (2012). Opioid receptor heteromers in analgesia. *Expert Rev. Mol. Med.*, 14, e9.

Counotte, D. S., Smit, A. B., Pattij, T., and Spijker, S. (2011). Development of the motivational system during adolescence, and its sensitivity to disruption by nicotine. *Dev. Cogn. Neurosci.*, 1, 430–443.

Covarrubias, M., Barber, A. F., Carnevale, V., Treptow, W., and Eckenhoff, R. G. (2015). Mechanistic insights into the modulation of voltage-gated ion channels by inhalational anesthetics. *Biophys. J.*, 109, 2003–2011.

Covey, D. P., Roitman, M. F., and Garris, P. A. (2014). Illicit dopamine transients: Reconciling actions of abused drugs. *Trends Neurosci.*, 37, 200–210.

Covey, D. P., Wenzel, J. M., and Cheer, J. F. (2015). Cannabinoid modulation of drug reward and the implications of marijuana legalization. *Brain Res.*, 1628, 233–243.

Cox, B. M. (2013). Recent developments in the study of opioid receptors. *Mol. Pharmacol.*, 83, 723–728.

Cox, F. (Ed.). (2009). Perioperative Pain Management. Wiley-Blackwell. https://www.wiley.com/en-us/Perioperative+Pain+Management-p-9781444309591

Cox, S.M.L., Yau, Y., Larcher, K., Durand, F., Kolivakis, T., Delaney, J. S., Dagher, A., et al. (2017). Cocaine cue-induced dopamine release in recreational cocaine users. *Sci. Rep.*, 7, 46665. doi: 10.1038/srep46665.

Coyle, C. M., and Laws, K. R. (2015). The use of ketamine as an antidepressant: A systematic review and meta-analysis. *Hum. Psychopharmacol.*, 30, 152–163.

Coyle, J. T., and Konopaske, G. (2016). Glutamatergic dysfunction in schizophrenia evaluated

with magnetic resonance spectroscopy. *JAMA Psychiatry*, 73, 649–650.

Coyle, M. G., Salisbury, A. L., Lester, B. M., Jones, H. E., Lin, H., Graf-Rohrmeister, K., and Fischer, G. (2012). Neonatal neurobehavior effects following buprenorphine versus methadone exposure. *Addiction*, 107(Suppl. 1), 63–73.

Crabbe, J. C., Phillips, T. J., and Belknap, J. K. (2010). The complexity of alcohol drinking: Studies in rodent genetic models. *Behav. Genet.*, 40, 737–750.

Crane, E. H. (2015). The CBHSQ Report: Emergency Department Visits Involving Narcotic Pain Relievers. Rockville, MD: Substance Abuse and Mental Health Services Administration, Center for Behavioral Health Statistics and Quality. Available at www.samhsa.gov/data/sites/default/files/report_2083/ShortReport-2083.html.

Crawford, C., Teo, L., Lafferty, L., Drake, A., Bingham, J. J., Gallon, M. D., O'Connell, M. L., et al. (2017). Caffeine to optimize cognitive function for military mission-readiness: a systematic review and recommendations for the field. *Nutr. Rev.*, 75, 17–35.

Crawford, P., and Gosliner, W. (2017). Energy drinks are killing young people. It's time to stop that. Washington Post, available at https://www.washingtonpost.com/opinions/energy-drinks-are-killing-young-people-its-time-to-stop-that/2017/05/25/6343be9c-3ff8-11e7-9869-bac8b446820a_story.html. Accessed 2/1/21.

Crawley, J. N. (1996). Unusual behavioral phenotypes of inbred mouse strains. *Trends Neurosci.*, 19, 181–182.

Crawley, J. N. (2004). Designing mouse behavioral tasks relevant to autisticlike behaviors. *MRDD Res. Rev.*, 10, 248–258.

Crean, R. D., Crane, N. A., and Mason, B. J. (2011). An evidence-based review of acute and long-term effects of cannabis use on executive cognitive functions. *J. Addict. Med.*, 5, 1–8.

Creed, M. C. (2017). Toward a targeted treatment for addiction. *Science*, 357, 464–465.

Crestani, F., Keist, R., Fritschy, J.-M., Benke, D., Vogt, K., Prut, L., et al. (2002). Trace fear conditioning involves hippocampal α5 GABAₐ receptors. *Proc. Natl. Acad. Sci. USA*, 99, 8980–8985.

Crist, R. C., Clarke, T.-K., and Berrettini, W. H. (2018). Pharmacogenetics of Opioid Use Disorder Treatment. *CNS Drugs*, 32(4), 305–320. https://doi.org/10.1007/s40263-018-0513-9

Cristino, L., Palomba, L., and Di Marzo, V. (2014). New horizons on the role of cannabinoid CB₁ receptors in palatable food

intake, obesity and related dysmetabolism. *Int. J. Obesity Suppl.*, 4, S26–S30.

Crockett, M. J., Clark, L, Roiser, J. P., Robinson, O. J., Cools, R., Chase, H. W., den Ouden, H., et al. (2012). Converging evidence for central 5-HT effects in acute tryptophan depletion. *Mol. Psychiatry*, 17, 121–123.

Crombag, H. S., Bossert, J. M., Koya, E., and Shaham, Y. (2008). Review. Context-induced relapse to drug seeking: A review. *Philos. Trans. R. Soc. Lond. B Biol. Sci.*, 363, 3233–3243.

Cropper, E. C., Jing, J., Vilim, F. S., and Weiss, K. R. (2018). Peptide cotransmitters as dynamic, intrinsic modulators of network activity. *Front. Neural Circuits*, 12, 78. doi: 10.3389/fncir.2018.00078

Crossin, R., and Arunogiri, S. (2020). Harms associated with inhalant misuse in adolescent females a review of the pre-clinical and clinical evidence. *Drug Alcohol Depend.*, 216, 108232. doi: 10.1016/j.drugalcdep.2020.108232.

Crossin, R., Cairney, S., Lawrence, A. J., and Duncan, J. R. (2017). Adolescent inhalant abuse leads to other drug use and impaired growth: Implications for diagnosis. *Aust. N. Z. J. Public Health*, 41, 99–104.

Crossin, R., Lawrence, A. J., Andrews, Z. B., Churilov, L., and Duncan, J. R. (2019). Growth changes after inhalant abuse and toluene exposure: A systematic review and meta-analysis of human and animal studies. *Hum. Exp. Toxicol.*, 38, 157–172.

Crossin, R., Qama, A., Andrews, Z. B., Lawrence, A. J., and Duncan, J. R. (2019). The effect of adolescent inhalant abuse on energy balance and growth. *Pharmacol. Res. Perspect.*, 7(4), e00498. doi: 10.1002/prp2.498.

Crow, T. J. (1980). Molecular pathology of schizophrenia: More than one disease process? *Br. Med. J.*, 280, 66–68.

Crow, T. J. (2008). The emperors of the schizophrenia polygene have no clothes. *Psychol. Med.*, 38, 1681–1685.

Crowe, T. P., Greenlee, M. H. W., Kanthasamy, A. G., and Hsu, W. H. (2018). Mechanism of intranasal drug delivery directly to the brain. *Life Sciences*, 195, 44–52. https://doi.org/10.1016/j.lfs.2017.12.025

Cruickshank, C. C., and Dyer, K. R. (2009). A review of the clinical pharmacology of methamphetamine. *Addiction*, 104, 1085–1099.

Crumb, M. W., Bryant, C., and Atkinson, T. J. (2018). Emerging trends in pain medication management: Back to the future: A focus on ketamine. *Am. J. Med.*, 131, 883–886.

Crunelle, C. L., Veltman, D. J., Booij, J., van Emmerik-van Oortmerssen, K., and van den

Brink, W. (2012). Substrates of neuropsychological functioning in stimulant dependence: A review of functional neuroimaging research. *Brain Behav.*, 2, 499–523.

Cruz, S. L., and Domínguez, M. (2011). Misusing volatile substances for their hallucinatory effects: A qualitative pilot study with Mexican teenagers and a pharmacological discussion of their hallucinations. *Subst. Use Misuse*, 46, 84–94.

Cruz, S. L., Rivera-Garcia, M. T., and Woodward, J. J. (2014). Review of toluene action: Clinical evidence, animal studies and molecular targets. *J. Drug Alcohol Res.*, 3, 235840. doi: 10.4303/jdar/235840.

Cryan, J. F., and O'Leary, O. F. (2010). Neuroscience: A glutamate pathway to faster-acting antidepressants? *Science*, 329, 913–914. Reprinted with permission from AAAS.

Cryan, J. F., and Sweeney, F. F. (2011). The age of anxiety: Role of animal models of anxiolytic action in drug discovery. *Br. J. Pharmacol.*, 164, 1129–1161.

Cryan, J. F., and Dinan, T. G. (2012). Mind-altering microorganisms: the impact of the gut microbiota on brain and behavior. *Nat. Rev. Neurosci.*, 13, 701–712.

Cryan, J. F., O'Riordan, K. J., Sandhu, K., Peterson, V., and Dinan, T. J. (2020). The gut microbiome in neuro–logical disorders. *Lancet Neurol.*, 19, 179–194.

Csengeri, D., Sprünker, N.-A., Di Castelnuovo, A., Niiranen, T., Vishram-Nielsen, J. K., Costanzo, S., Söderberg, et al. (2021). Alcohol consumption, cardiac biomarkers, and risk of atrial fibrillation and adverse outcomes. *European Heart Journal*, 42(12), 1170–1177. https://doi.org/10.1093/eurheartj/ehaa953

Cui, C. L., Wu, L. Z., and Luo, F. (2008). Acupuncture for the treatment of drug addiction. *Neurochem. Res.*, 33, 2013–2022.

Culp, C., Kim, H. K., and Abdi, S. (2021). Ketamine use for cancer and chronic pain management. *Front. Pharmacol.*, 11, 599721. doi: 10.3389/fphar.2020.599721.

Culverhouse, R. C., Saccone, N. L., Horton, A. C., Ma, Y., Anstey, K. J., Banaschewski, T. et al. (2017). Collaborative meta-analysis finds no evidence of a strong interaction between stress and 5-HTTLPR genotype contributing to the development of depression. *Mol. Psychiatry*, April 4 Epub ahead of print. doi: 10.1038/mp.2017.44.

Cummings, J. L. (2004). Alzheimer's disease. *N. Engl. J. Med.*, 351, 56–67.

Cummings, J., Lee, G., Ritter, A., Sabbagh, M., Zhong, K. Alzheimer's disease drug pipeline: 2020. *Alzheimer's Diment.* 6, e12050, 1–29.

Cummings, K. J., and Hodges, M. R. (2019). The serotonergic system and the control of breathing during development. *Respir. Physiol. Neurobiol.*, 270, 103255. doi: 10.1016/j.resp.2019.103255.

Cummings, K. J., Hewitt, J. C., Li, A., Daubenspeck, J. A., and Nattie, E. E. (2011). Postnatal loss of brain serotonin neurones compromises the ability of neonatal rats to survive episodic severe hypoxia. *J. Physiol.*, 589, 5247–5256.

Cunningham, C. W., Rothman, R. B., and Prisinzano, T. E. (2011). Neuropharmacology of the naturally occurring κ-opioid hallucinogen salvinorin A. *Pharmacol. Rev.*, 63, 316–347.

Cunningham, J. A. (1999). Resolving alcohol-related problems with and without treatment: The effects of different problem criteria. *J. Stud. Alcohol*, 60, 463–466.

Cunningham, R. L., Lumia, A. R., and McGinnis, M. Y. (2013). Androgenic anabolic steroid exposure during adolescence: Ramifications for brain development and behavior. *Horm. Behav.*, 64, 350–356.

Curran, G., Ravindran A. (2014) Lithium for bipolar disorder: a review of the recent literature. *Expert Rev. Neurother.*, 14(9), 1079–1098.

Curran, H. V., Brignell, C., Fletcher, S., Middleton, P., and Henry, J. (2002). Cognitive and subjective dose–response effects of acute oral Δ⁹tetrahydrocannabinol (THC) in infrequent cannabis users. *Psychopharmacology*, 164, 61–70.

Curtin, K., Fleckenstein, A. E., Robison, R. J., Crookston, M. J., Smith, K. R., and Hanson, G. R. (2015). Methamphetamine/amphetamine abuse and risk of Parkinson's disease in Utah: A population-based assessment. *Drug Alcohol Depend.*, 146, 30–38.

Cussotto, S., Clarke, G., Dinan, T. G., and Cryan, J. F. (2019). Psychotropics and the microbiome: a chamber of secrets. *Psychopharmacology*, 236, 1411–1432.

Cyrus, E., Coudray, M. S., Kiplagat, S., Mariano, Y., Noel, I., Galea, J. T., Hadley, D., et al. (2021). A review investigating the relationship between cannabis use and adolescent cognitive functioning. *Curr. Opin. Psychol.*, 38, 38–48.

Czoty, P. W., Stoops, W. W., and Rush, C. R. (2016). Evaluation of the "pipeline" for development of medications for cocaine use disorder: A review of translational preclinical, human laboratory, and clinical trial research. *Pharmacol. Rev.*, 68, 533–562.

D

D'Souza, D. C., Cortes-Briones, J. A., Ranganathan, M., Thurnauer, H., Creatura, G., Surti, T., et al. (2016). Rapid changes in cannabinoid 1 receptor availability in cannabis-dependent male subjects after abstinence from cannabis. *Biol. Psychiatry Cogn. Neurosci. Neuroimaging*, 1, 60–67.

D'Souza, M. S., and Markou, A. (2012). Schizophrenia and tobacco smoking comorbidity: nAChR agonists in the treatment of schizophrenia-associated cognitive deficits. *Neuropharmacology*, 62, 1564–1573.

D'Souza, M. S., and Markou, A. (2013). The "stop" and "go" of nicotine dependence: Role of GABA and glutamate. *Cold Spring Harb. Perspect. Med.*, 3, a012146. doi: 10.1101/cshperspect. a012146.

Dacarett-Galeano, D. J., and Diao, X. Y. (2019) Brexanolone: A novel therapeutic in the treatment of postpartum depression. *Am. J. Psychiatry*, 15, 2–4.

Dackis, C. A., and Gold, M. S. (1985). New concepts in cocaine addiction: the dopamine depletion hypothesis. *Neurosci. Biobehav. Rev.*, 9, 469–477.

Dahan, L., Astier, B., Vautrelle, N., Urbain, N., Kocsis, B., and Chouvet, G. (2007). Prominent burst firing of dopaminergic neurons in the ventral tegmental area during paradoxical sleep. *Neuropsychopharmacology*, 32, 1232–1241.

Dahchour, A., and DeWitte, P. (2000). Ethanol and amino acids in the central nervous system: Assessment of the pharmacological actions of acamprosate. *Prog. Neurobiol.*, 60, 343–362.

Dahlström, A., and Fuxe, K. (1964). Evidence for the existence of monoaminecontaining neurons in the central nervous system. I. Demonstration of monoamines in the cell bodies of brainstem neurons. *Acta Physiol. Scand.*, 62 (Suppl. 232), 1–55.

Dalgarno, P. (2007). Subjective effects of Salvia divinorum. *J. Psychoactive Drugs*, 39, 143–149.

Dalgarno, P. J., and Shewan, D. (1996). Illicit use of ketamine in Scotland. *J. Psychoactive Drugs*, 28, 191–199.

Dallaspezia, S., and Benedetti, F. (2015). Chronobiology of bipolar disorder: Therapeutic implication. *Curr. Psychiat. Rep.*, 17, 606–616.

Dallery, J., Defulio, A., and Meredith, S. E. (2015). Contingency management to promote drug abstinence. In H.S. Roane, J. E. Ringdahl, and T.S. Falcomata (Eds.), *Clinical and Organizational Applications of Applied Behavior Analysis*, pp. 395–424. San Diego: Academic Press.

Dalley, J. W., Cardinal, R. N., Robbins, T. W. (2004). Prefrontal executive and cognitive functions in rodents: neural and neurochemical substrates. *Neurosci. Biobehav. Rev.*, 28, 771–784.

Dalton, A., Mermier, C., and Zuhl, M. (2019). Exercise influence on the microbiome-gut-brain axis. *Gut Microbes*, 10, 555–568.

Daly, J. W., and Fredholm, B. B. (1998). Caffeine: An atypical drug of dependence. *Drug Alcohol Depend.*, 51, 199–206.

Dam, S. A., Mostert, J. C., Szopinska-Tokov, J. W., Bloemendaal, M., Amato, M., and Arias-Vasquez, A. (2019). The role of the gut-brain axis in attention-deficit/hyperactivity disorder. *Gastroenterol. Clin. North Am.*, 48, 407–431.

Dani, J. A. (2015). Neuronal nicotinic acetylcholine receptor structure and function and response to nicotine. *Int. Rev. Neurobiol.*, 124, 3–19.

Dani, J. A., and De Biasi, M. (2013). Mesolimbic dopamine and habenulo-interpeduncular pathways in nicotine withdrawal. *Cold Spring Harb. Perspect. Med.*, 3, a012138. doi: 10.1101/cshperspect. a012138.

Daniulaityte, R., Nahhas, R. W., Wijeratne, S., Carlson, R. G., Lamy, F. R., Martins, S. S., et al. (2015). "Time for dabs": Analyzing Twitter data on marijuana concentrates across the U.S. *Drug Alcohol Depend.*, 155, 307–311.

Darke, S., Kaye, S., McKetin, R., and Duflou, J. (2008). Major physical and psychological harms of methamphetamine use. *Drug Alcohol Rev.*, 27, 253–262.

Darvas, M., and Palmiter, R. D. (2009). Restriction of dopamine signaling to the dorsolateral striatum is sufficient for many cognitive behaviors. *Proc. Natl. Acad. Sci. USA*, 106, 14664–14669.

Daskalakis, N. P., McGill, M. A., Lehrner, M. A., and Yehuda, R. (2015). Endocrine aspects of PTSD: Hypothalamic–pituitary–adrenal (HPA) axis and beyond. In C. R. Martin, V. R. Preedy, and V. B. Patel (Eds.), *Comprehensive Guide to Post-Traumatic Stress Disorder*, pp. 1–14. Basel, Switzerland: Springer International.

Davani-Davari, D., Karimzadeh, I., and Khalili, H. (2019). The potential effects of anabolic-androgenic steroids and growth hormone as commonly used sport supplements on the kidney: a systematic review. *BMC Nephrol.*, 20(1), 198. doi: 10.1186/s12882-019-1384-0.

Davidson, A. J., and Sun, L. S. (2018). Clinical evidence for any effect of anesthesia on the developing brain. *Anesthesiology*, 128, 840–853.

Davidson, L. (2015). Vaping takes off as e-cigarette sales break through $6bn. The Telegraph. Available at www.telegraph.co.uk/finance/newsbysector/retailandconsumer/11692435/Vapingtakes-off-as-e-cigarette-sales-breakthrough-6bn.html.

Davidson, R. J., Jackson, D. C., and Kalin, N. H. (2000). Emotion, plasticity, context, and regulation: Perspectives from affective neuroscience. *Psychol. Bull.*, 126, 890–909.

Davie, C. A. (2008). A review of Parkinson's disease. *Br. Med. Bull.*, 86, 109–127.

Davies, N., English, W., and Grundlingh, J. (2018). MDMA toxicity: Management of acute and life–threatening presentations. *Br. J. Nurs.*, 27, 616–622.

Davis, K. L., Kahn, R. S., Ko, G., and Davidson, M. (1991). Dopamine in schizophrenia: A review and reconceptualization. *Am. J. Psychiatry*, 148, 1474–1486.

Davis, M. (1997). Neurobiology of fear responses: The role of the amygdala. *J. Neuropsychiatry Clin. Neurosci.*, 9, 382–402.

Davis, M. (2006). Neural systems involved in fear and anxiety measured with fear-potentiated startle. *Am. Psychol.*, 61, 741–756.

Davis, S. R., and Wahlin-Jacobsen, S. (2015). Testosterone in women: The clinical significance. *Lancet Diabetes Endocrinol.*, 3, 980–992.

Davis, S. R., Worsley, R., Miller, K. K., Parish, S. J., and Santoro, N. (2016). Androgens and female sexual function and dysfunction: Findings from the Fourth International Consultation of Sexual Medicine. *J. Sex. Med.*, 13, 168–178.

Davis, W. (1985). *The Serpent and the Rainbow*. New York: Warner.

Dawkins, L., and Corcoran, O. (2014). Acute electronic cigarette use: Nicotine delivery and subjective effects in regular users. *Psychopharmacology*, 231, 401–407.

Dawkins, L., Kimber, C. F., Doig, M., Feyerabend, C., and Corcoran, O. (2016). Self-titration by experienced e-cigarette users: Blood nicotine delivery and subjective effects. *Psychopharmacology*, 233, 2933–2941.

Dawson, D. A., Grant, B. F., Stinson, F. S., and Chou, P. S. (2006). Maturing out of alcohol dependence: The impact of transitional life events. *J. Stud. Alcohol*, 67, 195–203.

Dawson, D. A., Grant, B. F., Stinson, F. S., Chou, P. S., Huang, B., and Ruan, W. J. (2005). Recovery from DSM-IV alcohol dependence: United States, 2001–2002. *Addiction*, 100, 281–292.

Dayan, P., and Huys, Q. (2015). Serotonin's many meanings elude simple theories. *eLife*, 4, e07390. doi: 10.7554/ eLife.07390.

de Alarcón, R., de la Iglesia, J. I., Casado, N. M., and Montejo, A. L. (2019). Online porn addiction: What we know and what we don't. A systematic review. *J. Clin. Med.*, 8(1), 91. doi: 10.3390/jcm8010091.

de Araujo, D. B., Ribeiro, S., Cecchi, G. A., Carvalho, F. M., Sanchez, T. A., Pinto, J. P., et al. (2012). Seeing with the eyes shut: Neural basis of enhanced imagery following ayahuasca ingestion. *Hum. Brain Mapp.*, 33, 2550–2560.

de Azua, I. R., and Lutz, B. (2019). Multiple endocannabinoid-mediated mechanisms in the regulation of energy homeostasis in brain and peripheral tissues. *Cell. Mol., Life Sci.*, 76, 1341–1363.

de Beaurepaire, R., Sinclair, J.M.A., Heydtmann, M., Addolorato, G., Aubin, H.-J., Beraha, E. M., Caputo, F., et al. (2019). The use of baclofen as a treatment for alcohol use disorder: A clinical practice perspective. *Front. Psychiatry*, 9, 708. doi: 10.3389/fpsyt.2018.00708.

de Boer, S. F., and Koolhaas, J. M. (2003). Defensive burying in rodents: Ethology, neurobiology and psychopharmacology. *Eur. J. Pharmacol.*, 463(1), 145–161. https://doi.org/10.1016/S0014-2999(03)01278-0

de Boer, S. F., and Koolhaas, J. M. (2005). 5-HT1A and 5-HT1B receptor agonists and aggression: A pharmacological challenge of the serotonin deficiency hypothesis. *Eur. J. Pharmacol.*, 526, 125–139.

de Brouwer, G., Fick, A., Harvey, B. H., and Wolmarans, D. W. (2019). A critical inquiry into marble-burying as a preclinical screening paradigm of relevance for anxiety and obsessive–compulsive disorder: Mapping the way forward. *Cogn. Affect. Behav. Neurosci.*, 19(1), 1–39. https://doi.org/10.3758/s13415-018-00653-4

De Crescenzo, F., Ciabattini, M., D'Alo, G. L., De Giorgi, R., Del Giovane, C., Cassar, S., Janiri, L., et al. (2018). Comparative efficacy and acceptability of psychosocial interventions for individuals with cocaine and amphetamine addiction: A systematic review and network meta-analysis. *PLoS Med.*, 15(12), e1002715. doi: 10.1371/journal.pmed.1002715.

De Dreu, C.K.W. (2012). Oxytocin modulates cooperation within and competition between groups: An inte-grative review and research agenda. *Horm. Behav.*, 61, 419–428.

De Gregorio, D., Comai, S., Posa, L., and Gobbi, G. (2016). d-Lysergic acid diethylamide (LSD) as a model of psychosis: Mechanism of action and pharmacology. *Int. J. Mol. Sci.*, 17, 1953. doi: 10.3390/ijms17111953.

de Kloet, S. F., Mansvelder, H. D., and De Vries, T. J. (2015). Cholinergic modulation of dopamine pathways through nicotinic acetylcholinergic receptors. *Biochem. Pharmacol.*, 97, 425–438.

de Kruif, P. (1945). *The Male Hormone*. New York: Harcourt, Brace and Company.

de la Mora, M. P., Gallegos-Cari, A., Arizmendi-García, Y., Marcellino, D., and Fuxe, K. (2010). Role of dopamine receptor mechanisms in the amygdaloid modulation of fear and anxiety: Structural and functional analysis. *Prog. Neurobiol.*, 90, 198–216.

de Lecea, L. (2015). Optogenetic control of hypocretin (orexin) neurons and arousal circuits. *Curr. Top. Behav. Neurosci.*, 25, 367–378.

de Lecea, L., and Huerta, R. (2014). Hypocretin (orexin) regulation of sleep-to-wake transitions. *Front. Pharmacol.*, 5, 16. doi: 10.3389/fphar.2014.00016.

de Lecea, L., Kilduff, T. S., Peyron, C., Gao, X.-B., Foye, P. E., Danielson, P. E., et al. (1998). The hypocretins: Hypothalamus-specific peptides with neuroexcitatory activity. *Proc. Natl. Acad. Sci. USA*, 95, 322–327.

De Luca, M. A., Valentini, V., Bimpisidis, Z., Cacciapaglia, F., Caboni, P., and Di Chiara, G. (2014). Endocannabinoid 2-arachidonoylglycerol self-administration by Sprague-Dawley rats and the stimulation of in vivo dopamine transmission in the nucleus accumbens shell. *Front. Psychiatry*, 5, 140. doi: 10.3389/fpsyt.2014.00140.

De Luca, M. T., Meringolo, M., Spagnolo, P. A., and Badiani, A. (2012). The role of setting for ketamine abuse: Clinical and preclinical evidence. *Rev. Neurosci.*, 23, 769–780.

De Roo, M., Klauser, P., Mendez Garcia, P., Poglia, L., and Muller, D. (2008). Spine dynamics and synapse remodeling during LTP and memory processes. *Prog. Brain Res.*, 169, 199–207.

Deakin, J. F. W., Lees, J., McKie, S., Hallak, J. E. C., Williams, S. R., and Dursun, S. M. (2008). Glutamate and the neural basis of the subjective effects of ketamine. *Arch. Gen. Psychiatry*, 65, 154–164.

Dean, A. C., Groman, S. M., Morales, A. M., and London, E. D. (2013). An evaluation of the evidence that methamphetamine abuse causes cognitive decline in humans. *Neuropsychopharmacology*, 38, 259–274.

Debnam, K. J., Saha, S., and Bradshaw, C. P. (2018). Synthetic and other drug use among high school students: The role of perceived prevalence, access, and harms. *Subst. Use Misuse*, 53, 2069–2076.

Debruyne, D., and Le Boisselier, R. (2015). Emerging drugs of abuse: Current perspectives on synthetic cannabinoids. *Subst. Abuse Rehabil.*, 6, 113–129.

De-Carolis, C., Boyd, G.-A., Mancinelli, L., Pagano, S., and Eramo, S. (2015). Methamphetamine abuse and "meth mouth" in Europe. *Med. Oral Patol. Oral. Cir. Bucal.*, 20, e205–e210.

Deeb, T. Z., Maguire, J., and Moss, S. J. (2012). Possible alterations in GABA$_A$ receptor signaling that underlie benzodiazepine-resistant seizures. *Epilepsia*, 53(Suppl. 9), 79–88.

Degenhardt, L., Singleton, J., Calabria, B., McLaren, J., Kerr, T., Mehta, S., et al. (2011). Mortality among cocaine users: A systematic review of cohort studies. *Drug Alcohol Depend.*, 113, 88–95.

Deisseroth, K. (2015). Optogenetics: 10 years of microbial opsins in neuroscience. *Nat. Neurosci.*, 18, 1213–1225.

dela Peña, I., Gevorkiana, R., and Shi, W.-X. (2015). Psychostimulants affect dopamine transmission through both dopamine transporter-dependent and independent mechanisms. *Eur. J. Pharmacol.*, 764, 562–570.

DeLisi, L. E., Hoff, A. L., Schwartz, J. E., Shields, G. W., Halthore, S. N., Gupta, S. M., et al. (1991). Brain morphology in first-episode schizophrenic-like psychotic patients: A quantitative magnetic resonance imaging study. *Biol. Psychiatry*, 29, 159–175.

Dell, C. A., Dell, D. A., and Hopkins, C. (2005). Resiliency and holistic inhalant abuse treatment. *J. Aboriginal Health*, March, 4–12.

DeLong, M. R. (1990). Primate models of movement disorders of basal ganglia origin. *Trends Neurosci.* 13, 281–285.

DeMaagd, G., and Philip, A. (2015). Parkinson's disease and its management. Part 3, Nondopaminergic and nonpharmacological treatment options. *PT*, 40, 668–679.

Demick, B. (2009). A high-tech approach to getting a nicotine fix. Los Angeles Times. Available at www.articles.latimes.com/2009/apr/25/world/fg-chinacigarettes25.

Deroche-Gamonet, V., Darnaudéry, M., Bruins-Slot, L., Piat, F., Le Moal, M., and Piazza, P. V. (2002). Study of the addictive potential of modafinil in naïve and cocaine–experienced rats. *Psychopharmacology*, 161, 387–395.

deRoux, S. J., and Dunn, W. A. (2017). "Bath salts" the New York City medical examiner experience: A 3-year retrospective review. *J. Forensic Sci.*, 62, 695–699.

De-Sola Gutiérrez, J., Rodriguez de Fonseca, F., and Rubio, G. (2016). Cell-phone addiction: A review. *Front. Psychiatry*, 7, 175. doi: 10.3389/fpsyt.2016.00175.

Devane, W. A., Dysarz, F. A., III, Johnson, M. R., Melvin, L. S., and Howlett, A. C. (1988). Determination and characterization of a cannabinoid receptor in rat brain. *Mol. Pharmacol.*, 34, 605–613.

Devane, W. A., Hanus, L., Breuer, A., Pertwee, R. G., Stevenson, L. A., Griffin, G., et al. (1992). Isolation and structure of a brain constituent that binds to the cannabinoid receptor. *Science*, 258, 1946–1949.

DeVito, E., Herman, A. I., Waters, A. J., Valentine, G. W., and Sofuoglu, M. (2014). Subjective, physiological, and cognitive responses to intravenous nicotine: Effects of sex and menstrual cycle phase. *Neuropsychopharmacology*, 39, 1431–1440.

DeVito, E., Herman, A. I., Waters, A. J., Valentine, G. W., and Sofuoglu, M. (2014). Subjective, physiological, and cognitive responses to intravenous nicotine: Effects of sex and menstrual cycle phase. *Neuropsychopharmacologyogy*, 39, 1431–1440.

Devor, A., Andreassen, O. A., Wang, Y. Maki-Marttunen, T., Smeland, O. B., Fan, C.-C., et al. (2017). Genetic evidence for role of integration of fast and slow neurotransmission in schizophrenia. *Mol. Psychiatry*, 22, 792–801.

Dews, P. B. (1982). Caffeine. *Ann. Rev. Nutr.*, 2, 323–341.

D'Haese, P. F., Ranjan, M., Song, A., Haut, M. W., Carpenter, J., Dieb, G., Najib, U., et al. (2020). β-Amyloid plaque reduction in the hippocampus after focused ultrasound-induced blood-brain barrier opening in Alzheimer's disease. *Front. Hum. Neurosci.*, 14, 1–5.

Dhawan, A., Chopra, A., Ambekar, A., and Ray, R. (2015). Treatment seeking behavior of inhalant using street children: Are we prepared to meet their treatment needs. *Indian J. Psychol. Med.*, 37, 282–287.

Dhoble, P. L. and Bibra M. (2013). Phenomenology of inhalant abuse among adolescents in urban India. *Int. J. Res. Health Sci.*, 2, 540–544.

Di Forti, M., Marconi, A., Carra, E., Fraietta, S., Trotta, A., Bonoma, M., et al. (2015). Proportion of patients in south London with first-episode psychosis attributable to use of high potency cannabis: a case-control study. *Lancet Psychiatry*, 2, 233–238.

Di Marzo, V., and De Petrocellis, L. (2012). Why do cannabinoid receptors have more than one endogenous ligand? *Philos. Trans. R. Soc. Lond. B Biol. Sci.*, 367, 3216–3228.

Di Pilato, P., Niso, M., Adriani, W., Romano, E., Travaglini, D., Berardi, F., et al. (2014). Selective agonists for serotonin 7 (5-HT7) receptor and their applications in preclinical models: An overview. *Rev. Neurosci.*, 25, 401–415.

Diamond, I. and Gordon, A. (1997). Cellular and molecular neuroscience of alcoholism. *Physiol. Rev.*, 77, 1–20.

Diana, M., Pistis, M., Carboni, S., Gessa, G. L., and Rossetti, Z. L. (1993). Profound decrement of mesolimbic dopaminergic neuronal activity during ethanol withdrawal syndrome in rats: Electrophysiological and biochemical evidence. *Proc. Natl. Acad. Sci. USA*, 90, 7966–7969.

Dias, B. G., and Ressler, K. J. (2014). Parental olfactory experience influences behavior and neural structure in subsequent generations. *Nat. Neurosci.*, 17, 89–96.

DiChiara, G. (1997). Alcohol and dopamine. *Alcohol Health Res. World*, 21, 108–114.

DiChiara, G., and North, R. A. (1992). Neurobiology of opiate abuse. *Trends Pharmacol. Sci.*, 13, 185–193.

Dichter, G. S., Gibbs, D., and Smoski, M. J. (2015). A systematic review of relations between resting-state functional-MRI and treatment response in major depressive disorder. *J. Affective Dis.*, 172, 8–17.

Didato, G., and Nobili, L. (2009). Treatment of narcolepsy. *Expert Rev. Neurother.*, 9, 897–910.

Diederen, K.M.J., and Fletcher, P. C. (2021). Dopamine, prediction error and beyond. *The Neuroscientist*, 27, 30–46.

Diel, P. (2020). Caffeine and doping—What have we learned since 2004. *Nutrients*, 12, 2167. doi: 10.3390/nu12082167.

DiFranza, J. R. (2015). A 2015 update on the natural history and diagnosis of nicotine addiction. *Curr. Pediatr. Res.*, 11, 43–55.

DiFranza, J. R., Sanouri Ursprung, W. W., and Carson, A. (2010). New insights into the compulsion to use tobacco from an adolescent case-series. *J. Adolesc.*, 33, 209–214.

DiFranza, J. R., Savageau, J. A., Fletcher, K., Ockene, J. K., Rigotti, N. A., McNeill, A. D., et al. (2002). Measuring the loss of autonomy over nicotine use in adolescents: The DANDY (Development and Assessment of Nicotine Dependence in Youths) study. *Arch. Pediatr. Adolesc. Med.*, 156, 397–403.

DiFranza, J. R., Wellman, R. J., Mermelstein, R., Pbert, L., Klein, J. D., Sargent, J. D., et al. (2011). The natural history and diagnosis of nicotine addiction. *Curr. Pediatr. Rev.*, 7, 88–96.

Ding, H., Czoty, P. W., Kiguchi, N., CamiKobeci, G., Sukhtankar, D. D., Nader, M. A., et al. (2016). A novel orvinol analog, BU08028, as a safe opioid analgesic without abuse liability in primates. *Proc. Natl. Acad. Sci. USA*, 113, E5511– E5518.

Dingwall, K. M., and Cairney, S. (2011). Recovery from central nervous system changes following volatile substance misuse. *Subst. Use Misuse*, 46, 73–83.

Dinis-Oliveira, R. J. (2015). Metabolomics of cocaine: Implications in toxicity. *Toxicol. Mech. Methods*, 25, 494–500.

Dinis-Oliveira, R. J. (2016). Metabolomics of Δ⁹-tetrahydrocannabinol: Implications in toxicity. *Drug Metab. Rev.*, 48, 80–87.

Dinis-Oliveira, R. J., Pereira, C. L., and da Silva, D. D. (2019). Pharmacokinetic and pharmacodynamics aspects of peyote and mescaline: Clinical and forensic repercussions. *Curr. Mol. Pharmacol.*, 12, 184–194.

Dionisi-Vici, C., Hoffmann, G. F., Leuzzi, V., Hoffken, H., Bräutigam, C., Rizzo, C., Steebergen-Spanjers, G.C.H., et al. (2000). Tyrosine hydroxylase deficiency with severe clinical course: Clinical and biochemical investigations and optimization of therapy. *J. Pediatr.*, 136, 560–562.

DiPatrizio, N. V. (2016). Endocannabinoids in the gut. *Cannabis Cannabinoid Res.*, 1, 67–77.

Disney, A. A., and Higley, M. J. (2020). Diverse spatiotemporal scales of cholinergic signaling in the neocortex. *J. Neurosci.*, 40, 720–725.

Dittrich, A. (1998). The standardized psychometric assessment of altered states of consciousness (ASCs) in humans. Pharmacopsychiatry, 31 (Suppl.), 80–84.

Divito, C. B., and Underhill, S. M. (2014). Excitatory amino acid transporters: Roles in glutamatergic neurotransmission. *Neurochem. Int.*, 73, 172–180.

Dixit, P. V., Sahu, R., and Mishra, D. K. (2020). Marble-burying behavior test as a murine model of compulsive-like behavior. *J Pharmacological Toxicol Methods*, 102, 106676. https://doi.org/10.1016/j.vascn.2020.106676

Dluzen, D. E., and Liu, B. (2008). Gender differences in methamphetamine use and responses: A review. *Gender Med.*, 5, 24–35.

Doble, A. (1996). The pharmacology and mechanism of action of riluzole. *Neurology*, 47 (Suppl 4), 233S–241S.

Dodge, N. C., Jacobson, J. L., and Jacobson, S. W. (2019). Effects of fetal substance exposure on offspring substance use. *Pediatr. Clin. North Am.*, 66, 1149–1161.

Doepker, C., Lieberman, H. R., Smith, A. P., Peck, J. D., El-Sohemy, A., and Welsh, B. T. (2016). Caffeine: Friend or foe? *Annu. Rev. Food Sci. Technol.*, 7, 117–137.

Doherty, M., and Smith, P. M. (2005). Effects of caffeine ingestion on rating of perceived exertion during and after exercise: a meta-analysis. Scand. J. Med. Sci. Sports, 15, 69–78.

Dolder, P. C., Müller, F., Schmid, Y., Borgwardt, S. J., and Liechti, M. E. (2018). Direct comparison of the acute subjective, emotional, autonomic, and endocrine effects of MDMA, methylphenidate, and modafinil in healthy subjects. *Psychopharmacology*, 235, 467–479.

Dole, V. P., and Nyswander, M. E. (1965). A medical treatment for diacetylmorphine (heroin) addiction. *JAMA*, 193, 646–650.

Dölen, G., and Bear, M. F. (2009). Fragile x syndrome and autism: from disease model to therapeutic targets. *J. Neurodev. Disord.*, 1, 133–140. doi: 10.1007/ s11689-009-9015-x.

Dolphin, A. C., and Lee, A. (2020). Presynaptic calcium channels: specialized control of synaptic neurotrans-mitter release. *Nat. Rev. Neurosci.*, 21, 213–229.

Dombroski, Y., O'Hagan, T., Dittmer, M., Penalva, R., Mayoral, S. R., Bankhead, P., et al. (2017). Regulatory T cells promote myelin regeneration in the central nervous system. *Nat. Neurosci.*, 20, 674–680.

Domino, E. F., and Luby, E. D. (2012). Phencyclidine/schizophrenia: One view toward the past, the other to the future. *Schizophr. Bull.*, 38, 914–919.

Dong, C., and Anand, K.J.S. (2013). Developmental neurotoxicity of ketamine in pediatric clinical use. *Toxicol. Lett.*, 220, 53–60.

Dong, Z., Han, H., Li, H., Bai, Y., Wang, W., Tu, M., et al. (2015). Long-term potentiation decay and memory loss are mediated by AMPAR endocytosis. *J. Clin. Invest.*, 125, 234–247.

Donny, E. C., Brasser, S. M., Bigelow, G E., Stitzer, M. L. , and Walsh, S. L. (2005). Methadone doses of 100 mg or greater are more effective than lower doses at suppressing heroin self-administration in opioid-dependent volunteers. *Addiction* 100, 1496–1509.

Donovan, S. L., Mamounas, L. A., Andrews, A. M., Blue, M. E., and McCasland, J. S. (2002). GAP-43 is critical for normal development of the serotonergic innervation in forebrain. *J. Neurosci.*, 22, 3543–3552.

Dorst, J., Ludolph, A. C., and Huebers, A. (2018). Disease-modifying and symptomatic treatment of amyotrophic lateral sclerosis. *Ther. Adv. Neurol. Disord.*, 11, 1–16.

dos Santos, R. G., Balthazar, F. M., Bouso, J. C., and Hallak, J. E. C. (2016a). The current state of research on ayahuasca: A systematic review of human studies assessing psychiatric symptoms, neuropsychological functioning, and neuroimaging. *J. Psychopharmacol.*, 30, 1230–1247.

dos Santos, R. G., Osório, F. L., Crippa, J. A. S., and Hallak, J. E. C. (2016b). Classical hallucinogens and neuroimaging: A systematic review of human studies. *Neurosci. Biobehav. Rev.*, 71, 715–728.

dos Santos, R. G., Bouso, J. C., Rocha, J. M., Rossi, G. N., and Hallak, J. E. (2021). The use of classic hallucinogens/psychedelics in a therapeutic context: Healthcare policy opportunities and challenges. *Risk Manag. Healthc. Policy*, 145, 901–910.

Dosumu-Johnson, R. T., Corcoran, A. E., Chang, Y, Nattie, E., and Dymecki, S. M. (2018). Acute perturbation of Pet1-neuron activity in neonatal mice impairs cardiorespiratory homeostatic recovery. *eLife*, 7, e37857. doi: 10.7554/ eLife.37857.

Doty, T. J., and Collen, J. F. (2020). Buzzed before bedtime: hidden harms of late day caffeine consumption. *J. Clin. Sleep Med.*, 16(Suppl. 1), 23S–24S.

Doudna, J. (2019). CRISPR's unwanted anniversary. *Science*, 366(6467), 777–777. https://doi.org/10.1126/science.aba1751

Drake, C., Roehrs, T., Shambroom, J., and Roth, T. (2013). Caffeine effects on sleep taken 0, 3, or 6 hours before going to bed. *J. Clin. Sleep Med.*, 9, 1195–1200.

Drake, L. R., and Scott, P.J.H. (2018). DARK classics in chemical neuroscience: Cocaine. *ACS Chem. Neurosci.*, 9, 2358–2372

Drasbek, K. R., Christensen, J., and Jensen, J. (2006). Gamma-hydroxybutyrate: A drug of abuse. *Acta Neurol. Scand.*, 114, 145–156.

W. C. Drevets. (1998). *Annu Rev Med* 49: 341-361. Republished with permission of Annual Reviews, Inc.; permission conveyed through Copyright Clearance Center, Inc.; Courtesy of Wayne C. Drevets.

Drevets, W. C., Gautier, C., Price, J. C., Kupfer, D. J., Kinahan, P. E., Grace, A. A., et al. (2001). Amphetamine-induced dopamine release in human ventral striatum correlates with euphoria. *Biol. Psychiatry*, 49, 81–96.

Drevin, G., Rossi, L. H., Férec, S., Briet, M., and Abbara, C. (2021). Chemsex/slamsex-related intoxications: A case report involving gamma-hydroxybutyrate (GHB) and 3-methylmethcathinone (3-MMC) and a review of the literature. *Forensic Sci. Int.*, 321, 110743. doi: 10.1016/j.forsciint.2021.110743.

Drug Enforcement Administration (2019). National Drug Threat Assessment. DEA-DCT-DIR-007-20.

Drummer, O. H., Gerostamoulos, J., Batziris, H., Chu, M., Caplehorn, J., Robertson, M. D., and Swann, P. (2004). The involvement of drugs in drivers of motor vehicles killed in Australian road traffic crashes. *Accident Analysis & Prevention* 36(2): 239–248, © 2007 The Authors. Journal compilation © 2007 Society for the Study of Addiction.

du Plessis, S. S., Agarwal, A., and Syriac, A. (2015). Marijuana, phytocannabinoids, the endocannabinoid system, and male fertility. *J. Assist. Reprod. Genet.*, 32, 1575–1588.

Duarte-Silva, E., Filho, A.J.M.C., Barichello, T., Quevedo, J., Macedo, D., and Peixoto, C. (2020). Phos-phodiesterase-5 inhibitors: Shedding new light on the darkness of depression. *J. Affect. Disord.*, 264, 138–149.

Dubois, V., Laurent, M., Bioonen, S., Vanderschueren, D., and Claessens, F. (2012). Androgens and skeletal muscle: Cellular and molecular action mechanisms underlying the anabolic actions. *Cell. Mol. Life Sci.*, 69, 1651–1667.

Duchaine, D. (1989). *Underground Steroid Handbook II*. Venice, CA: HLR Technical Books.

Dudok, B., Barna, L., Ledri, M., Szabó, S. I., Szabadits, E., Pintér, B., et al. (2015). Cell-specific STORM super-resolution imaging reveals nanoscale organization of cannabinoid signaling. *Nat. Neurosci.*, 18, 75–86.

Duffy, A., Dawson, D. L., and das Nair, R. (2016). Pornography addiction in adults: A systematic review of definitions and reported impact. *J. Sex. Med.*, 13, 760–777.

Duke, A. A., Bègue, L., Bell, R., and Eisenlohr-Moul, T. (2013). Revisiting the serotonin-aggression relation in humans: A meta-analysis. *Psychol. Bull.*, 139, 1148–1172.

Duke, A. N., Johnson, M. W., Reissig, C. J., and Griffiths, R. R. (2015). Nicotine reinforcement in never-smokers. *Psychopharmacology*, 232, 4243–4252.

Duman, C. H., and Duman, R. S. (2015). Spine synapse remodeling in the pathophysiology and treatment of depression. *Neurosci. Lett.*, 601, 20–29.

Duman, R. S. (2012). New Mechanisms Elicited with Ketamine in Treatment-Resistant Depression. Yale Psychiatry. Published October 3, 2012. Available at www.youtube.com/watch?v=hNsIiq-5354.

Duman, R. S., Heninger, G. R., and Nestler, E. J. (1997). A molecular and cellular theory of depression. *Arch. Gen. Psychiatry*, 54, 597–606.

Duman, R. S., Malberg, J., and Thome, J. (1999). Neural plasticity to stress and antidepressant treatment. *Biol. Psychiatry*, 46, 1181–1191.

Dumontheil, I., Kilford, E. J., and Blakemore, S.-J. (2020). Development of dopaminergic genetic associations with visuospatial, verbal and social working memory. *Dev. Sci.*, 23, e12889. doi: 10.1111/desc.12889.

Dunant, Y., and Gisiger, V. (2017). Ultrafast and slow cholinergic transmission. Different involvement of acetylcholinesterase molecular forms. *Molecules*, 22, 1300. doi: 10.3390/molecules22081300.

Duncan, J. R., and Lawrence, A. J. (2013). Conventional concepts and new perspectives for understanding the addictive properties of inhalants. *J. Pharmacol. Sci.*, 122, 237–243.

Dunkley, P. R., and Dickson, P. W. (2019). Tyrosine hydroxylase phosphorylation in vivo. *J. Neurochem.*, 149, 706–728.

Dunn, M. (2015). Commentary on Lundholm et al. (2015): What came first, the steroids or the violence? *Addiction*, 110, 109–110.

Dürsteler, K. M., Berger, E.-M., Strasser, J., Caflisch, C., Mutschler, J., Herdener, M., et al. (2015). Clinical potential of methylphenidate in the treatment of cocaine addiction: A review of the current evidence. *Subst. Abuse Rehabil.*, 6, 61–74.

Dutta, A., McKie, S., and Deakin, J. F. W. (2014). Resting state networks in major depressive disorder. *Psychiatry Res.*, 224, 139–151.

Dybdal-Hargreaves, N. F., Holder, N. D., Ottoson, P. E., Sweeney, M. D., and Williams, T. (2013). Mephedrone: Public health risk, mechanisms of action, and behavioral effects. *Eur. J. Pharmacol.*, 714, 32–40.

Dyck, E. (2005). Flashback: Psychiatric experimentation with LSD in historical perspective. *Can. J. Psychiatry*, 50, 381–388.

Dyer, J. E. (1991). γ-Hydroxybutyrate: A health-food product producing coma and seizure-like activity. *Am. J. Emerg. Med.*, 9, 321–324.

E

Eagle, D. M., Bari, A., and Robbins, T. W. (2008). The neuropsychopharmacology of action inhibition: Cross-species translation of the stop-signal and go/ no-go tasks. *Psychopharmacology*, 199, 439–456.

Ebert, U., and Kirch, W. (1998). Scopolamine model of dementia: electroencephalogram findings and cognitive performance. *Eur. J. Clin. Invest.*, 28, 944–949.

Eddleston, M. (2019). Novel clinical toxicology and pharmacology of organophosphorus insecticide self-poisoning. *Annu. Rev. Pharmacol. Toxicol.*, 59, 341–360.

Eddleston, M., Buckley, N. A., Eyer, P., and Dawson, A. H. (2008). Management of acute organophosphorus pesticide poisoning. *Lancet*, 371, 597–607.

Edwards, S. A., Bondy, S. J., Callaghan, R. C., and Mann, R. E. (2014). Prevalence of unassisted quit attempts in population-based studies: A systematic review of the literature. *Addict. Behav.*, 39, 512–519.

Einöther, S.J.L., and Giesbrecht, T. (2013). Caffeine as an attention enhancer: reviewing existing assumptions. *Psychopharmacology*, 225, 251–274.

Eisenstein, T. K., and Meissler, J. J. (2015). Effects of cannabinoids on T-cell function and resistance to infection. *J. Neuroimmune Pharmacol.*, 10, 204–216.

El Mestikawy, S., Wallén-Mackenzie, Å., Fortin, G. M., Descarries, L., and Trudeau, L.-E. (2011). From glutamate co-release to vesicular synergy: Vesicular glutamate transporters. *Nat. Rev. Neurosci.*, 12, 204–216.

Elder, L. (2019). Gender and the politics of marijuana. *Soc. Sci. Q.*, 100, 109–122.

Eldridge, W. B., Foster, C., and Wyble, L. (2018). Neonatal Abstinence Syndrome Due to Maternal Kratom Use. *Pediatrics*, 142(6). https://doi.org/10.1542/peds.2018-1839

el-Guebaly, N., Mudry, T., Zohar, J., Tavares, H., and Potenza, M. N. (2012). Compulsive features in behavioural addictions: The case of pathological gambling. *Addiction*, 107, 1726–1734.

Elhaj, H. M., Imam, O., Page, B. W., Vitale, J. M., and Malek, M. H. (2020). Perceived consumption of a high-dose caffeine drink delays neuromuscular fatigue. *J. Strength Cond. Res.*, in press.

Elkins, R. L., King, K., Nabors, L., and Vidourek, R. (2017). Steroid use and school violence, school violent victimization, and suicidal ideation among adolescents. *J. School Violence*, 16, 399–410.

Elliot, D. L., Goldberg, L., Moe, E. L., Defrancesco, C. A., Durham, M. B., and Hix–Small, H. (2004). Preventing substance use and disordered eating: initial outcomes of the ATHENA (Athletes Targeting Healthy Exercise and Nutrition Alternatives) program. *Arch. Pediatr. Adolesc. Med.*, 158, 104/1–/2049.

El-Menyar, A., Mekkodathil, A., Al-Thani, H., and Al-Motarreb, A. (2015). Khat use: History and heart failure. *Oman Med. J.*, 30, 77–82.

ElSohly, M. A., and Slade, D. (2005). Chemical constituents of marijuana: The complex mixture of natural cannabinoids. *Life Sci.*, 78, 539–548.

ElSohly, M. A., Mehmedic, Z., Foster, S., Gon, C., Chandra, S., and Church, J. C. (2016). Changes in cannabis potency over the last 2 decades (1995–2014): Analysis of current data in the United States. *Biol. Psychiatry*, 79, 613–619

ElSohly, M. A., Chandra, S., Radwan, M., Gon, C., and Church, J. C. (2021). A comprehensive review of cannabis potency in the USA in the last decade. *Biol. Psychiatry Cogn. Neurosci. Neuroimaging*, 6(6), 603–606. © 2021. Reprinted with permission from Society of Biological Psychiatry, via Elsevier.

Elsworth, J. D., Hajszan, T., Leranth, C., and Roth, R. H. (2011a). Loss of asymmetric spine synapses in dorsolateral prefrontal cortex of cognitively impaired phencyclidine-treated monkeys. *Int. J. Neuropsychopharmacol.*, 14, 1411–1415.

Elsworth, J. D., Morrow, B. A., Hajszan, T., Leranth, C., and Roth, R. H. (2011b). Phencyclidine-induced loss of asymmetric spine synapses in rodent prefrontal cortex is reversed by acute and chronic treatment with olanzapine. *Neuropsychopharmacology*, 36, 2054–2061.

Embleton, L., Mwangi, A., Vreeman, R., Ayuku, D., and Braitstein, P. (2013). The epidemiology of substance use among street children in resourceconstrained settings: A systematic review and meta-analysis. *Addiction*, 108, 1722–1733.

Emre, M., Aarsland, D., Albanese, A., Byrne, E. J., Deuschl, G., De Deyn, P. P., et al. (2004). Rivastigmine for dementia associated with Parkinson's disease. *N. Engl. J. Med.*, 351, 2509–2518.

Endocrine Society. (2008). Steroid Abuse. Position Statement. Available at https://www.endocrine.org/~/media/endosociety/files/advocacy%20and%20outreach/position%20statements/all/steroidabusepositionstatement wheader.pdf. Accessed 6/23/21.

Engidawork, E. (2017). Pharmacological and toxicological effects of *Catha edulis* F. (Khat). *Phyther. Res.*, 31, 1019–1028.

Engin, E., Benham, R. S., and Rudolph, U. (2018). An emerging circuit pharmacology of $GABA_A$ receptors. *Trends Pharmacol. Sci.*, 39, 710–732.

England, L. J., Aagaard, K., Bloch, M., Conway, K., Cosgrove, K., Grana, R., Gould, T. J., et al. (2017). Developmental toxicity of nicotine: A transdisciplinary synthesis and implications for emerging tobacco products. *Neurosci. Biobehav. Rev.*, 72, 176–189.

Ennaceur, A. (2014). Tests of unconditioned anxiety: Pitfalls and disappointments. *Physiol. Behav.*, 135, 55–71.

Epilepsy Foundation. (n.d.). An Introduction to Epilepsy (website). Available at www.epilepsy.com/start-here/introduction-epilepsy.

Epilepsy Foundation. https://www.epilepsy.com/, accessed 10/12/20.

Epping-Jordan, M. P., Watkins, S. S., Koob, G. F., and Markou, A. (1998). Dramatic decreases in brain reward function during nicotine withdrawal. *Nature*, 393, 76–79.

Equihua, A. C., De La Herrán-Arita, A. K., and Drucker-Colin, R. (2013). Orexin receptor antagonists as therapeutic agents for insomnia. *Front. Pharmacol.*, 4, 163. doi: 10.3389/fphar.2013.00163.

Erdozain, A. M., and Peñagarikano, O. (2020). Oxytocin as treatment for social cognition, not there yet. *Front. Psychiatry*, 10, 930. doi: 10.3389/fpsyt.2019.00930.

Eriksson, J. G. (2016). Developmental Origins of Health and Disease: From a small body size at birth to epigenetics. *Ann. Med.*, 48, 456–467.

Erol, A., and Karpyak, V. M. (2015). Sex and gender-related differences in alcohol use and its consequences: Contemporary knowledge and future research considerations. *Drug Alcohol Depend.*, 156, 1–13.

Erowid.org. (2012). Yikes: The end of all existence: An experience with *Salvia divinorum*. Available at www.erowid. org/experiences/exp.php?ID=89145.

Ersche, K. D., Barnes, A., Jones, P. S., Morein-Zamir, S., Robbins, T. W., and Bullmore, E. T. (2011). Abnormal structure of frontostriatal brain systems is associated with aspects of impulsivity and compulsivity in cocaine dependence. *Brain*, 134, 2013–2024.

Ersche, K. D., Jones, P. S., Williams, G. B., Robbins, T. W., and Bullmore, E. T. (2013). Cocaine dependence: a fast-track for brain ageing? *Mol. Psychiatry*, 18, 134–135.

Escartin, C., Galea, E., Lakatos, A., O'Callaghan, J. P., Petzold, G. C., Serrano-Pozo, A., Steinhäuser, C., et al. (2021). Reactive astrocyte nomenclature, definitions, and future directions. *Nat. Neurosci.*, 24(3), 312–325. https://doi.org/10.1038/s41593-020-00783-4

España, R. A., Schmeichel, B. E., and Berridge, C. W. (2016). Norepinephrine at the nexus of arousal, motivation and relapse. *Brain Res.*, 1641, 207–216.

Esposito, R. U., Porrino, L. J., and Seeger, T. F. (1989). Brain stimulation reward measurement and mapping by psychophysical techniques and quantitative 2-(14C)deoxyglucose autoradiography. In M. A. Bozartth (Ed.), *Methods of Assessing the Reinforcing Properties of Abused Drugs*, pp. 421–447. New York: Springer-Verlag.

Etkin, A. (2009). Functional neuroanatomy of anxiety: A neural circuit perspective. *Curr. Top. Behav. Neurosci.*, 2, 251–277.

Etter, J.-F. (2008). Comparing the validity of the Cigarette Dependence Scale and the Fagerström Test for Nicotine Dependence. *Drug Alcohol Depend.*, 95, 152–159.

Etter, J.-F., and Eissenberg, T. (2015). Dependence levels in users of electronic cigarettes, nicotine gums and tobacco cigarettes. *Drug Alcohol Depend.*, 147, 68–75.

Evans, A. C., and Raistrick, D. (1987). Phenomenology of intoxication with toluene-based adhesives and butane gas. *Br. J. Psychiatry*, 150, 769–773.

Evans, C. J., Keith, D. E., Jr., Morrison, H., Magendzo, K., and Edwards, R. H. (1992). Cloning of a delta opioid receptor by functional expression. *Science,* 258, 1952–1955.

Evans, D. E., and Drobes, D. J. (2008). Nicotine self-medication of cognitive-attentional processing. *Addict. Biol.*, 14, 32–42.

Evans, S. M., and Foltin, R. W. (2010). Does the response to cocaine differ as a function of sex or hormonal status in human and nonhuman primates? *Horm. Behav.*, 58, 13–21.

Everitt, B. J., and Robbins, T. W. (2013). From the ventral to the dorsal striatum: Devolving views of their roles in drug addiction. *Neurosci. Biobehav. Rev.*, 37, 1946–1954.

Everitt, B. J., Belin, D., Economidou, D., Pelloux, Y., Dalley, J. W., and Robbins, T. W. (2008). Neural mechanisms underlying the vulnerability to develop compulsive drug-seeking habits and addiction. *Philos. Trans. R. Soc. Lond. B Biol. Sci.*, 363, 3125–3135.

Ezquerra-Romano, I. I., Lawn, W., Krupitsky, E., and Morgan, C.J.A. (2018). Ketamine for the treatment of addiction: Evidence and potential mechanisms. *Neuropharmacology*, 142, 72–82.

F

Fadda, F., and Rossetti, Z. (1998). Chronic ethanol consumption: From neuroadaptation to neurodegeneration. *Prog. Neurobiol.*, 56, 385–431.

Fakhoury, M. (2017). Role of the endocannabinoid system in the pathophysiology of schizophrenia. *Mol. Neurobiol.*, 54, 768–778.

Falcone, M., Lee, B., Lerman, C., and Blendy, J. A. (2016). Translational research on nicotine dependence. *Curr. Top. Behav. Neurosci.*, 28, 121–150.

Falls, B. J., Wish, E. D., Garnier, L. M., Caldeira, K., O'Grady, K. E., Vincent, K. B., et al. (2011). The association between early conduct problems and early marijuana use in college students. *J. Child Adolesc. Subst. Abuse*, 20, 221–236.

Falqueto, H., Júnior, J., Silvério, M., Farias, J., Schoenfeld, B. J., and Manfredi, L. H. (2021). Can conditions of skeletal muscle loss be improved by combining exercise with anabolic-androgenic steroids? A systematic review and meta-analysis of testosterone-based interventions. *Rev. Endocr. Metab. Disord.*, 22, 161–178.

Fan, A. Z., Chou, S. P., Zhang, H., Jung, J., and Grant, B. F. (2019). Prevalence and correlates of past-year recovery from DSM-5 alcohol use disorder: Results from National Epidemiologic Survey on Alcohol and Related Conditions-III. *Alcohol., Clin. Exp. Res.*, 43, 2406–2420.

Fantegrossi, W. E., Moran, J. H., Radominska-Pandya, A., and Prather, P. L. (2014). Distinct pharmacology and metabolism of K2 synthetic cannabinoids compared to Δ^9-THC: Mechanism underlying greater toxicity? *Life Sci.*, 97, 45–54.

Fantegrossi, W. E., Murnane, K. S., and Reissig, C. J. (2008). The behavioral pharmacology of hallucinogens. *Biochem. Pharmacol.*, 75, 17–33.

Faraone, S. V. (2018). The pharmacology of amphetamine and methylphenidate: Relevance to the neurobiology of attention-deficit/hyperactivity disorder and other psychiatric comorbidities. *Neurosci. Biobehav. Rev.*, 87, 255–270.

Farb, D. H., and Ratner, M. H. (2014). Targeting the modulation of neural circuitry for the treatment of anxiety disorders. *Pharmacol. Rev.*, 66,1002–1032.

Farde, L. (1996). The advantage of using positron emission tomography in drug research. *Trends Neurosci.*, 19, 211–214.

Farde, L., Nordstrom, A.-L., Wiesel, F.-A., Pauli, S., Halldin, C., and Sedvall, G. (1992). Positron emission tomographic analysis of central D1 and D2 dopamine receptor occupancy in patients treated with classical neuroleptics and clozapine. *Arch. Gen. Psychiatry*, 49, 538–544.

Farkas, G., and Rosen, R. C. (1976). The effects of ethanol on male sexual arousal. *J. Stud. Alcohol*, 37, 265–272. Reproduced with permission of the Alcohol Research Documentation, Inc., publisher of the Journal of Studies on Alcohol, now the Journal of Studies on Alcohol and Drugs (www.jsad.com).

Farmer, R. F., Kosty, D. B., Seeley, J. R., Duncan, S. C., Lynskey, M. T., Rohde, P., et al. (2015). Natural course of cannabis use disorders. *Psychol. Med.*, 45, 63–72.

Farquhar-Smith, P., and Chapman, S. (2012). Neuraxial (epidural and intrathecal) opioids for intractable pain. *Br. J. Pain*, 6(1), 25–35. https://doi.org/10.1177/2049463712439256

Farronato, N. S., Dürsteler-Macfarland, K. M., Wiesbeck, G. A., and Petitjean, S. A. (2013). A systematic review comparing cognitive-behavioral therapy and contingency management for cocaine dependence. *J. Addict. Dis.*, 32, 274–287.

Fasinu, P. S., Phillips, S., ElSohly, M. A., and Walker, L. A. (2016). Current status and prospects for cannabidiol preparations as new therapeutic agents. *Pharmacotherapy*, 36, 781–796.

Fattore, L. (2016). Synthetic cannabinoids: Further evidence supporting the relationship between cannabinoids and psychosis. *Biol. Psychiatry*, 79, 539–548.

Faulkner, J. M. (1933). Nicotine poisoning by absorption through the skin. *JAMA*, 100, 1664–1665.

Faure, P., Tolu, S., Valverde, S., and Naudé, J. (2014). Role of nicotinic acetylcholine receptors in regulating dopamine neuron activity. *Neuroscience*, 282, 86–100.

Fayaz, S. M., Suvanish Kumar, V. S., and Rajanikant, G. K. (2014). Necroptosis: Who knew there were so many interesting ways to die? *CNS Neurol. Dis. Drug Targets*, 13, 42–51.

Fearon, I. M., Eldridge, A. C., Gale, N., McEwan, M., Stiles, M. F., and Round, E. K. (2018). Nicotine pharmacokinetics of electronic cigarettes: A review of the literature. *Regul. Toxicol. Pharmacol.*, 100, 25–34.

Featherstone, R. E., and Siegel, S. J. (2015). The role of nicotine in schizophrenia. *Int. Rev. Neurobiol.*, 124, 23–78.

Feder, A., Rutter, S. B., Schiller, D., and Charney, D. S. (2020). The emergence of ketamine as a novel treatment for posttraumatic stress disorder. *Adv. Pharmacol.*, 89, 26/1–/286.

Feduccia, A. A., and Mithoefer, M. C. (2018). MDMA-assisted psychotherapy for PTSD: Are memory reconsolidation and fear extinction underlying mechanisms? *Prog. Neuropsychopharmacol. Biol. Psychiatry*, 84, 221–228.

Feduccia, A. A., Jerome, L., Yazar-Klosinski, B., Emerson, A., Mithoefer, M. C., and Doblin, R. (2019). Breakthrough for trauma treatment: Safety and efficacy of MDMA-assisted psychotherapy compared to paroxetine and sertraline. *Front. Psychiatry*, 10, 650. doi/10.3389/fpsyt.2019.00650.

Felder, C. C., and Glass, M. (1998). Cannabinoid receptors and their endogenous agonists. *Annu. Rev. Pharmacol.*, 38, 179–200.

Felder, C. C. (2019). GPCR drug discovery – moving beyond the orthosteric to the allosteric domain. *Adv. Pharmacol.*, 86, 1–20.

Felmlee, M. A., Morse, B. L., and Morris, M. E. (2021). γ-Hydroxybutyric acid: Pharmacokinetics, pharmacodynamics, and toxicology. *AAPS J.*, 23(1), 22. doi: 10.1208/s12248-020-00543-z.

Feng, Q., Lu, S. J., Klimanskaya, I., Gomes, I., Kim, D., Chung, Y., et al. (2010). Hemangioblastic derivatives from human induced pluripotent stem cells exhibit limited expansion and early senescence. *Stem Cells*, 28, 704–712.

Ferber, S. G., Namdar, D., Hen-Shoval, D., Eger, G., Koltai, H., Shoval, G., Shbiro, L., et al. (2020). The "entourage effect": Terpenes coupled with cannabinoids for the treatment of mood disorders and anxiety disorders. *Curr. Neuropharmacol.*, 18, 87–96.

Ferdman, R. A. (2014). The American Energy Drink Craze in Two Highly Caffeinated Charts. *Quartz.* qz.com/192038/the-american-energy-drink-craze-in-two-highly-caffeinatedcharts/#/h/56821,2/.

Ferguson, S. M., Bazalakova, M., Savchenko, V., Tapia, J. C., Wright, J., and Blakely, R. D. (2004). Lethal impairment of cholinergic neurotransmission in hemicholinium-3-sensitive choline transporter knockout mice. *Proc. Natl. Acad. Sci. USA*, 101, 8762–8767.

Fergusson, D. M., Horwood, L. J., and Beautrais, A. L. (2003a). Cannabis and educational achievement. *Addiction*, 98, 1681–1692.

Fergusson, D. M., Horwood, L. J., Lynskey, M. T., and Madden, P. A. F. (2003b). Early reactions to cannabis predict later dependence. *Arch. Gen. Psychiatry*, 60, 1033–1039.

Ferland, J.-M.N., and Hurd, Y. L. (2020). Deconstructing the neurobiology of cannabis use disorder. *Nat. Neurosci.*, 23, 600–610. doi.org/10.1038/s41593-020-0611-0.

Fern, R., and Matute, C. (2019). Glutamate receptors and white matter stroke. *Neurosci. Lett.*, 694, 86–92.

Fernandez, D. P., Kuss, D. J., and Griffiths, M. D. (2020). Short-term abstinence effects across potential behavioral addictions: A systematic review. *Clin. Psychol. Rev.*, 76, 101828. doi: 10.1016/j.cpr.2020.101828.

Fernández, E., Rajan, N., and Bagni, C. (2013). The FMRP regulon: From targets to disease convergence. *Front. Neurosci.*, 7, 191. doi: 10.3389/fnins.2013.00191.

Fernandez, S. P., and Gaspar, P. (2012). Investigating anxiety and depressive-like phenotypes in genetic mouse models of serotonin depletion. *Neuropharmacology*, 62, 144–154.

Fernández-Ruiz, J., Moro, M. A., and Martinez-Orgado, J. (2015). Cannabinoids in neurodegenerative disorders and stroke/brain trauma: From preclinical models to clinical applications. *Neurotherapeutics*, 12, 795–806.

Fernandez-Twinn, D. S., Constância, M., and Ozanne, S. E. (2015). Intergenerational epigenetic inheritance in models of developmental programming of adult disease. *Semin. Cell Dev. Biol.*, 43, 85–95.

Fernstrom, J. D., and Wurtman, R. J. (1972). Brain serotonin content: Physiological regulation by plasma neutral amino acids. *Science*, 178, 149–152.

Fernstrom, J. D. (2018). Monosodium glutamate in the diet does not raise brain glutamate concentrations or disrupt brain functions. *Ann. Nutr. Metab.*, 73(Suppl. 5), 43–52.

Ferraguti, F. (2018). Metabotropic glutamate receptors as targets for novel anxiolytics. *Curr. Opin. Pharmacol.*, 38, 37–42.

Ferrari, P., Palanza, P., Parmigiani, S., de Almeida, R. M. M., and Miczek, K. A. (2005). Serotonin and aggressive behavior in rodents and nonhuman primates: Predispositions and plasticity. *Eur. J. Pharmacol.*, 526, 259–273.

Ferré, S. (2016). Mechanisms of the psychostimulant effects of caffeine: Implications for substance use disorders. *Psychopharmacology*, 233, 1963–1979.

Ferré, S., Ciruela, F., Woods, A. S., Lluis, C., and Franco, R. (2007). Functional relevance of neurotransmitter receptor heteromers in the central nervous system. *Trends Neurosci.*, 30, 440–446. © 2007. Reprinted with permission from Elsevier.

Ferreira, L. (2017). The Man Who Quit Heroin and Became a Fruit Juice Millionaire. BBC. Available at www.bbc.com/news/business-39339036.

Ferreira-Vieira, T. H., Guimaraes, I. M., Silva, F. R., and Ribeiro, F. M. (2016). Alzheimer's disease: Targeting the cholinergic system. *Curr. Neuropharmacol.*, 14, 101–115.

Ferrés-Coy, A., Santana, N., Castañé, A., Cortés, R., Carmona, M. C., Toth, M., et al. (2013). Acute 5-HT1A autoreceptor knockdown increases antidepressant responses and serotonin release in stressful conditions. *Psychopharmacology*, 225, 61–74.

Fibiger, H. C., Phillips, A. G., and Brown, E. E. (1992). The neurobiology of cocaine induced reinforcement. *Ciba Found. Symp.*, 166, 96–111.

Figueiredo, M. (2021). Dosing Stopped in Phase 3 Trial of Tominersen for Huntington's. https://huntintonsdiseasenews.com. March 2021.

File, S. E., and Seth, P. (2003). A review of 25 years of the social interaction test. *Eur. J. Pharmacol.*, 463, 35–53.

Filiano, J. J., and Kinney, H. C. (1994). A perspective on neuropathologic findings in victims of the sudden infant death syndrome: The triple-risk model. *Biol. Neonate*, 65, 19/1–/297.

Filley, C. M. (2013). Toluene abuse and white matter: A model of toxic leukoencephalopathy. *Psychiatr. Clin. N. Am.*, 36, 293–302. © 2013. Reprinted with permission from Elsevier.

Filley, C. M., McConnell, B. V., and Anderson, C. A. (2017). The expanding prominence of toxic leukoencephalopathy. *J. Neuropsychiatry Clin. Neurosci.*, 29, 308–318.

Fillon, M. (2015). Electronic cigarettes may lead to nicotine addiction. *J. Natl. Cancer Inst.*, 107, djv070. doi: 10.1093/jnci/djv070.

Filosa, J. A., Morrison, H. W., Iddings, J. A., Du, W., and Kim, K. J. (2016). Beyond neurovascular coupling, role of astrocytes in the regulation of vascular tone. *Neuroscience*, 323, 96–109. https://doi.org/10.1016/j.neuroscience.2015.03.064

Finberg, J. P. M. (2014). Update on the pharmacology of the selective inhibitors of MAO-A and MAO-B: Focus on modulation of CNS monoamine neurotransmitter release. *Pharmacol. Ther.*, 143, 133–152.

Finberg, J.P.M. (2019). Inhibitors of MAO-B and COMT: their effects on brain dopamine levels and uses in Parkinson's disease. *J. Neural Transm.*, 126, 43/1–/248.

Finegersh, A., Rompala, G. R., Martin, D. I. K., and Homanics, G. E. (2015). Drinking beyond a lifetime: New and emerging insights into paternal alcohol exposure on subsequent generations. *Alcohol*, 49, 461–470.

Fink, D. J., Wechuck, J., Mata, M., Glorioso, J. C., Goss, J., Krisky, D., et al. (2011). Gene therapy for pain: Results of a phase I clinical trial. *Ann. Neurol.*, 70, 207–212.

Fink, J., Schoenfeld, B. J., Hackney, A. C., Matsumoto, M., Maekawa, T., Nakazato, K., and Horie, S. (2019). Anabolic-androgenic steroids: procurement and administration practices of doping athletes. *Phys. Sportsmed.*, 47, 10–14.,.

Fiorentin, T. R., and Logan, B. K. (2019). Toxicological findings in 1000 cases of suspected drug facilitated sexual assault in the United States. *J. Forensic Legal Med.*, 61, 56–64.

Fiorillo, C. D., Song, M. R., and Yun, S. R. (2013). Multiphasic temporal dynamics in responses of midbrain dopamine neurons to appetitive and aversive stimuli. *J. Neurosci.* 33, 4710–4725.

Fischer, B. D., Platt, D. M., Rallapalli, S. K., Namjoshi, O. A., Cook, J. M., and Rowlett, J. K. (2016). Antagonism of triazolam self-administration in rhesus monkeys responding under a progressive-ratio schedule: In vivo apparent pA2 analysis. *Drug Alcohol Depend.*, 158, 22–29.

Fischer, M., Kaech, S., Knutti, D., and Matus, A. (1998). Rapid actin-based plasticity in dendritic spines. *Neuron*, 20, 847–854.

Fitzgerald, P., and Dinan, T. G. (2008). Prolactin and dopamine: What is the connection? A review article. *J. Psychopharmacol.*, 22(2 Suppl), 12–19. https://doi.org/10.1177/0269216307087148

Flores, R. J., Uribe, K. P., Swalve, N., and O'Dell, L. E. (2019). Sex differences in nicotine intravenous self-administration: A meta-analytic review. *Physiol. Behav.*, 203, 42–50.

Floyd, C. N., Wood, D. M., and Dargan, P. I. (2018). Baclofen in gamma-hydroxybutyrate withdrawal: patterns of use and online availability. *Eur. J. Clin. Pharmacol.*, 74, 349–356.

Fluharty, M., Taylor, A. E., Grabski, M., and Munafò, M. R. (2017). The association of cigarette smoking with depression and anxiety: A systematic review. *Nicotine Tob. Res.*, 19, 3–13.

Folch, J., Busquets, O., Ettcheto, M., Sánchez-López, E., Castro-Torres, R. D., Verdaguer, E., Garcia, M. L., et al. (2018). Memantine for the treatment of dementia: A review on its current and future applications. *J. Alzheimers Dis.*, 62, 1223–1240.

Foltin, R. W., Fischman, M. W., and Byrne, M. F. (1988). Effects of smoked marijuana on food intake and body weight of humans living in a residential laboratory. *Appetite*, 11, 1–14.

Foltin, R. W., and Haney, M. (2004). Intranasal cocaine in humans: acute tolerance, cardiovascular and subjective effects. *Pharmacol. Biochem. Behav.*, 78, 93–101.

Fond, G., Hamdani, N., Kapczinski, F., Boukouaci, W., Drancourt, N., Dargel, A., et al. (2014). Effectiveness and tolerance of anti-inflammatory drugs' addon therapy in major mental disorders: A systematic qualitative review. *Acta Psychiatr. Scand.*, 129, 163–179.

Fonnum, F. (1987). Biochemistry, anatomy, and pharmacology of GABA neurons. In H. Y. Meltzer (Ed.), *Psychopharmacology: The Third Generation of Progress*, pp. 173–182. New York: Raven.

Fontana, A. C. K. (2015). Current approaches to enhance glutamate transporter function and expression. *J. Neurochem.*, 134, 982–1007.

Food and Drug Administration (FDA), U.S. Department of Health and Human Services. (2018) Statement from FDA Commissioner Scott Gottlieb, M.D., on the agency's scientific evidence on the presence of opioid compounds in kratom, underscoring its potential for abuse. https://www.fda.gov/news-events/press-announcements/statement-fda-commissioner-scott-gottlieb-md-agencys-scientific-evidence-presence-opioid-compounds.

Food and Drug Administration (FDA), U.S. Department of Health and Human Services. (2019) Statement from FDA Commissioner Scott Gottlieb, M.D., on unprecedented new efforts to support development of over-the-counter naloxone to help reduce opioid overdose deaths. https://www.fda.gov/news-events/press-announcements/statement-fda-commissioner-scott-gottlieb-md-unprecedented-new-efforts-support-development-over.

Food and Drug Administration (FDA). (2008). FDA Issues Public Health Advisory for Antipsychotic Drugs Used for Treatment of Behavioral Disorders in Elderly Patients. FDA Talk Paper. Rockville, MD: U.S. Food and Drug Administration. Available at www.fda.gov/Drugs/DrugSafety/PostmarketDrugSafetyInformationforPatientsandProviders/DrugSafetyInformationforHeathcareProfessionals/PublicHealthAdvisories/ucm053171.htm

Food and Drug Administration (FDA). (2016). Extending Authorities to All Tobacco Products, Including E-Cigarettes, Cigars, and Hookah. Available at www.fda.gov/TobaccoProducts/Labeling/

RulesRegulationsGuidance/ucm388395.htm.

Food and Drug Administration (FDA). (2016). FDA Approves First Buprenorphine Implant for Treatment of Opioid Dependence. FDA Newsroom. Available at www.fda.gov/NewsEvents/ Newsroom/PressAnnouncements/ ucm503719.htm.

Ford, C. P. (2014). The role of D2-autoreceptors in regulating dopamine neuron activity and transmission. *Neuroscience, 282,* 13–22.

Ford, J. B., Sutter, M. E., Owen, K. P., and Albertson, T. E. (2014). Volatile substance misuse: An updated review of toxicity and treatment. *Clinic. Rev. Allerg. Immunol.,* 46, 19–33.

Forey, B. A., Thornton, A. J., and Lee, P. N. (2011). Systematic review with meta-analysis of the epidemiological evidence relating smoking to COPD, chronic bronchitis, and emphysema. *BMC Pulmonary Med.,* 11, 36. doi: 10.1186/1471-2466-11-36.

Forman, H. (2015). The Dangers of Synthetic Marijuana. U.S. News and World Report. health.usnews.com/health-news/ patient-advice/articles/2015/08/18/ the-dangers-of-synthetic-marijuana.

Forman, S. A., and Miller, K. W. (2011). Anesthetic sites and allosteric mechanisms of action on Cys-loop ligand-gated ion channels. *Can. J. Anaesth.,* 58, 191–205.

Foroozan, R. (2018). Vigabatrin: Lessons learned from the United States experience. *J. Neuroophthalmol.,* 38, 442–450.

Förstera, B., Castro, P. A., Moraga-Cid, G., and Aguayo, L. G. (2016). Potentiation of gamma aminobutyric acid receptors (GABA$_A$R) by ethanol: How are inhibitory receptors affected? *Front. Cell. Neurosci.,* 10, 114. doi: 10.3389/fncel.2016.00114.

Foster J.A., McVey Neufeld K.A. (2013) Gut-brain axis: how the microbiome influences anxiety and depression. *Trends Neurosci.,* 36(5), 305–312.

Foster, A. C., Shorter, G. W., and Griffiths, M. D. (2015). Muscle dysmorphia: Could it be classified as an addiction to body image? *J. Behav. Addict.,* 4, 1–5.

Foster, D. J., Gentry, P. R., Lizard-Ortiz, J. E., Bridges, T. M., Wood, M. R., Niswender, C. M., et al. (2014). M5 receptor activation produces opposing physiological outcomes in dopamine neurons depending on the receptor's location. *J. Neurosci.,* 34, 3253–3262.

Foster, D. J., and Conn, P. J. (2017). Allosteric modulation of GPCRs: New insights and potential utility for treatment of schizophrenia and other CNS disorders. *Neuron,* 94, 431–446.

Fotros, A., Casey, K. F., Larcher, K., Verhaeghe, J. A. J., Cox, S. M. L., Gravel, P., et al. (2013). Cocaine cue-induced dopamine release in amygdala and hippocampus: A high-resolution PET [18F] fallypride study in cocaine dependent participants. *Neuropsychopharmacology,* 38, 1760–1788.

Foulds, J., Stapleton, J. A., Bell, N., Swettenham, J., Jarvis, M. J., and Russell, M. A. H. (1997). Mood and physiological effects of subcutaneous nicotine in smokers and never-smokers. *Drug Alcohol Depend.,* 44, 105–115.

Foulds, J., Veldheer, S., Yingst, J., Hrabovsky, S., Wilson, S. J., Nichols, T. T., et al. (2015). Development of a questionnaire for assessing dependence on electronic cigarettes among a large sample of ex-smoking e-cigarette users. *Nicotine Tob. Res.,* 17, 186–192.

Fowler, C. D., and Kenny, P. J. (2014). Nicotine aversion: Neurobiological mechanisms and relevance to tobacco dependence vulnerability. *Neuropharmacology,* 76, 533–544.

Fowler, C. D., Lu, Q., Johnson, P. M., Marks, M. J., and Kenny, P. J. (2011). Habenular α5 nicotinic receptor subunit signalling controls nicotine intake. *Nature,* 471, 597–601.

Fowler, C. J. (2013). Transport of endocannabinoids across the plasma membrane and within the cell. *FEBS J.,* 280, 1895–1904.

Fowler, J. S., Logan, J., Wang, G. J., Volkow, N. D., Telang, F., Zhu, W., et al. (2003). Low monoamine oxidase B in peripheral organs in smokers. *Proc. Natl. Acad. Sci. USA,* 100, 11600–11605. © 2003 National Academy of Sciences U.S.A.

Frahm, S., Antolin-Fontes, B., Görlich, A., Zander, J.-F., Ahnert-Hilger, G., and Ibañez-Tallon, I. (2015). An essential role of acetylcholine-glutamate synergy at habenular synapses in nicotine dependence. *eLife;* 4, e11396. doi: 10.7554/eLife.11396.

Frahm, S., S'limak, M. A., Ferrarese, L., Santos-Torres, J., Antolin-Fontes, B., Auer, S., et al. (2011). Aversion to nicotine is regulated by the balanced activity of β4 and α5 nicotinic receptor subunits in the medial habenula. *Neuron,* 70, 522–535.

Fraigne, J. J., Torontali, Z. A., Snow, M. B., and Peever, J. H. (2015). REM sleep at its core—Circuits, neurotransmitters, and pathophysiology. *Front. Neurol.,* 6, 123. doi: 10.3389/fneur.2015.00123.

Francis, S. H., Blount, M. A., and Corbin, J. D. (2011). Mammalian cyclic nucleotide phosphodiesterases: Molecular mechanisms and physiological functions. *Physiol. Rev.,* 91, 651–690.

Franco, V., Bialer, M., and Perucca, E. (2021). Cannabidiol in the treatment of epilepsy: Current evidence and perspectives for further research. *Neuropharmacology,* 185, 108442. doi: 10.1016/j.neuropharm.2020/108442.

Franke, A. G., Gränsmark, P., Agricola, A., Schüle, K., Rommel, T., Sebastian, A., et al. (2017). Methylphenidate, modafinil, and caffeine for cognitive enhancement in chess: A double-blind, randomised controlled trial. *Eur. Neuropsychopharmacol.,* 27, 248–260.

Franke, W. W., and Berendonk, B. (1997). Hormonal doping and androgenization of athletes: A secret program of the German Democratic Republic government. *Clin. Chem.,* 43, 1262–1279. By permission of American Association of Clinical Chemistry, via Oxford University Press.

Franklin, R. J. M., and Ffrench-Constant, C. (2017). Regenerating CNS myelin—From mechanisms to experimental medicines. *Nat. Rev. Neurosci.,* 18, 753–769.

Franz, C. A., and Frishman, W. H. (2016). Marijuana use and cardiovascular disease. *Cardiol. Rev.,* 24, 158–162.

Frati, P., Busardò, F. P., Cipolloni, L., De Dominicis, E., and Fineschi, V. (2015). Anabolic androgenic steroid (AAS) related deaths: Autoptic, histopathological and toxicological findings. *Curr. Neuropharmacol.,* 13, 146–159.

Frati, P., Kyriakou, C., Del Rio, A., Marinelli, E., Vergallo, G. M., Zaami, S., et al. (2015). Smart drugs and synthetic androgens for cognitive and physical enhancement: Revolving doors of cosmetic neurology. *Curr. Neuropharmacol.,* 13, 5–11.

Frayer, N. C., and Kim, Y. (2020). Caffeine intake during pregnancy and risk of childhood obesity: A systematic review. *Int. J. MCH AIDS,* 9, 364–380.

Frazer, K. M., Richards, Q., and Keith, D. R. (2018). The long-term effects of cocaine use on cognitive functioning: A systematic critical review. *Behav. Brain Res.,* 348, 241–262.

Fredholm, B. B., Yang, J., and Wang, Y. (2017). Low, but not high, dose caffeine is a readily available probe for adenosine actions. *Mol. Aspects Med.,* 55, 20–25.

Freeman, T. P., Craft, S., Wilson, J., Stylianou, S., ElSohly, M., Di Forti, M., and Lynskey, M. T. (2020). Changes in delta-9-tetrahydrocannabinol (THC) and cannabidiol (CBD) concentrations in cannabis over time: systematic review and meta-analysis. *Addiction,* 116(5), 1000-1010.

Freeza, M., Padova, C., Terpin, M., Baranona, E., and Lieber, C. (1990). High blood alcohol levels in women: The role of decreased gastric alcohol dehydrogenase activity and first-pass metabolism. *N. Engl. J. Med.,* 322, 95–99.

Freudenmann, R. W., Öxler, F., and Bernschneider-Reif, S. (2006).

The origin of MDMA (ecstasy) revisited: The true story reconstructed from the original documents. *Addiction,* 101, 1241–1245.

Friedhoff, A. J., and Silva, R. R. (1995). The effects of neuroleptics on plasma homovanillic acid. In F. E. Bloom and D. J. Kupfer (Eds.), *Psychopharmacology: The Fourth Generation of Progress,* pp. 1229– 1234. New York: Raven Press.

Friedman, D., and Devinsky, O. (2015). Cannabinoids in the treatment of epilepsy. *New Engl. J. Med.,* 373, 1048–1058.

Friedman, D., and Devinsky, O. (2015). Cannabinoids in the treatment of epilepsy. *New Engl. J. Med.,* 373, 1048–1058.

Fritze, S., Spanagel, R., and Noori, H. R. (2017). Adaptive dynamics of the 5-HT systems following chronic administration of selective serotonin reuptake inhibitors: A meta-analysis. *J. Neurochem.,* June 27 Epub ahead of print. doi: 10.1111/jnc.14114.

Fritzius, T., and Bettler, B. (2020). The organizing principle of GABA$_B$ receptor complexes: Physiological and pharmacological implications. *Basic Clin. Pharmacol. Toxicol.,* 126 (Suppl. 6), 25–34.

Froelich, J. C. (1997). Opioid peptides. *Alcohol Health Res. World,* 21, 132–143.

Frohlich, J., and Van Horn, J. D. (2014). Reviewing the ketamine model for schizophrenia. *J. Psychopharmacol.,* 28, 287–302.

Fuenzalida, M., Pérez, M. A., and Arias, H. R. (2016). Role of nicotinic and muscarinic receptors on synaptic plasticity and neurological diseases. *Curr. Pharm. Des.,* 22, 2004–2014.

Fuhrmann, D., Knoll, L. J., and Blakemore, S.-J. (2015). Adolescence as a sensitive period of brain development. *Trends Cogn. Sci.,* 19, 558–566.

Fujikawa, D. G. (2015). The role of excitotoxic programmed necrosis in acute brain injury. *Comput. Struct. Biotech. J.,* 13, 212–221.

Fuller, R. K. and Hiller-Sturmhofel, S. (1999). Alcoholism treatment in the United States. *Alcohol Health Res. World,* 23, 69–77.

Funada, M., Sato, M., Makino, Y., and Wada, K. (2002). Evaluation of rewarding effect of toluene by the conditioned place preference procedure in mice. *Brain Res. Protocols,* 10, 47–54.

Furey, M. L., Pietrini, P., Haxby, J. V., and Drevets, W. C. (2008). Selective effects of cholinergic modulation on task performance during selective attention. *Neuropsychopharmacology,* 33, 913–923.

Furmark, T., Tillfors, M., Garpenstrand, H., Marteinsdottir, I., Långström, B., Oreland, L., et al. (2004). Serotonin transporter polymorphism related to amygdala excitability and symptom severity in patients with social phobia. *Neurosci. Lett.*, 362, 189–192.

Fusar-Poli, P., Borgwardt, S., Bechdolf, A., Addington, J., Riecher-Rössier, A., Schultze-Lutter, F., et al. (2013) The psychosis high-risk state: A comprehensive state-of-the-art review. *JAMA Psychiatry*, 70, 107–120.

Fuxe, K., and Borroto-Escuela, D. O. (2016). Volume transmission and receptor-receptor interactions in het-eroreceptor complexes: understanding the role of new concepts for brain communication. *Neural Regen. Res.*, 11, 1220–1223.

Fuxe, K., Borroto-Escuela, D. O., RomeroFernandez, W., Zhang, W. B., and Agnati, L. F. (2013). Volume transmission and its different forms in the central nervous system. *Clin. J. Integr. Med.*, 19, 323–329.

G

Gado, F., Meini, S., Bertini, S., Digiacomo, M., Macchia, M., and Manera, C. (2019). Allosteric modulators targeting cannabinoid CB_1 and CB_2 receptors: Implications for drug discovery. *Future Med. Chem.*, 11, 2019–2037.

Gage, S. H., Jones, H. J., Burgess, S., Bowden, J., Davey Smith, G., Zammit, S., and Munafò, M. R. (2017). Assessing causality in associations between cannabis use and schizophrenia risk: a two-sample Mendelian randomization study. *Psychol. Med.*, 47, 971–980.

Gagne, J. J., and Power, M. C. (2010). Antiinflammatory drugs and risk of Parkinson disease: A meta-analysis. *Neurology*, 74, 995–1002.

Gahr, M. (2014). Agomelatine in the treatment of major depressive disorder: An assessment of benefits and risks. *Curr. Neuropharmacol.*, 12, 287–398.

Galatzer-Levy, I. R., Steenkamp, M. M., Brown, A. D., Qian, M., Inslicht, S., Henn-Haase, C., et al. (2014). Cortisol response to an experimental stress paradigm prospectively predicts long-term distress and resilience trajectories in response to active police service. *J. Psychiatr. Res.*, 56, 36–42.

Galicia, M., Dargan, P. I., Dines, A. M., Yates, C., Heyerdahl, F., Hovda, K. E., Giraudon, I., et al. (2019). Clinical relevance of ethanol coingestion in patients with GHB/GBL intoxication. *Toxicol. Lett.*, 314, 37–42.

Gallagher, M., Wysocki, C. J., Leyden, J. J., Spielman, A. I., Sun, X., and Preti, G. (2008). Analyses of volatile organic compounds from human skin. *Br. J. Dermatol*, 159, 780–791.

Gallezot, J.-D., Kloczynski, T., Weinzimmer, D., Labaree, D., Zheng, M.-Q., Lim, K., et al. (2014). Imaging nicotineand amphetamine-induced dopamine release in rhesus monkeys with [11C]PHNO vs [11C]raclopride PET. *Neuropsychopharmacology*, 39, 866–874.

Gallo, E. F., and Posner, J. (2016). Moving towards causality in attention-deficit hyperactivity disorder: Overview of neural and genetic mechanisms. *Lancet Psychiatry*, 3, 555–567.

Galvão-Coelho, N. L., Marx, W., Gonzalez, M., Sinclair, J., de Manincor, M., Perkins, D., and Sarris, J. (2021). Classic serotonergic psychedelics for mood and depressive symptoms: a meta-analysis of mood disorder patients and healthy participants. *Psychopharmacology*, 238, 341–354.

Gan, Q., and Watanabe, S. (2018). Synaptic vesicle endocytosis in different model systems. *Front. Cell. Neurosci.*, 12, 171. doi: 10.3389/fncel.2018.00171.

Ganio, M. S., Klau, J. F., Casa, D. J., Armstrong, L. E., and Maresh, C. M. (2009). Effect of caffeine on sport-specific endurance performance: A systematic review. *J. Strength Cond. Res.*, 23, 315–324.

Ganson, K. T., and Cadet, T. J. (2019). Exploring anabolic-androgenic steroid use and teen dating violence among adolescent males. *Subst. Use Misuse*, 54, 779–785.

Ganzer, F., Bröning, S., Kraft, S., Sack, P. M., and Thomasius, R. (2016). Weighing the evidence: A systematic review on long-term neurocognitive effects of cannabis use in abstinent adolescents and adults. *Neuropsychol. Res.*, 26, 186–222.

Garbutt, J. C., West, S. L., Carey, T. S., Lohr, K. N., and Crews, F. T. (1999). Pharmacological treatment of alcohol dependence: A review of the evidence. *JAMA*, 281, 1318–1325.

Garcia, F. D., and Thibaut, F. (2010). Sexual addictions. *Am. J. Drug Alcohol Abuse*, 36, 254–260.

Garcia-Garcia, A., Newman-Tancredi, A., and Leonardo, E. D. (2014). 5-HT1A receptors in mood and anxiety: Recent insights into autoreceptor versus heteroreceptor function. *Psychopharmacology*, 231, 623–636.

Garcia-Garcia, A. L., Canetta, S., Stujenske, J. M., Burghardt, N. S., Ansorge, M. S., Dranovsky, A., and Leonardo, E. D. (2018). Serotonin inputs to the dorsal BNST modulate anxiety in a 5-HT1A receptor-dependent manner. *Mol. Psychiatry*, 23, 1990–1997.

Garcia-Rivas, V., and Deroche-Gamonet, V. (2019). Not all smokers appear to seek nicotine for the same reasons: implications for preclinical research in nicotine dependence. *Addict. Biol.*, 24, 317–334.

Garcia-Romeu, A., Kersgaard, B., and Addy, P. H. (2016). Clinical applications of hallucinogens: A review. *Exp. Clin. Psychopharmacol.*, 24, 229–268.

Gardner, D. M., Baldessarini, R. J., and Waraich, P. (2005). Modern antipsychotic drugs: A critical overview. *CMAJ*, 172, 1703–1711.

Garland, E. L., and Howard, M. O. (2010). Phenomenology of adolescent inhalant intoxication. *Exp. Clin. Psychopharmacol.*, 18, 498–509.

Garnier-Dykstra, L. M., Caldeira, K. M., Vincent, K. B., O'Grady, K. E., and Arria, A. M. (2012). Nonmedical use of prescription stimulants during college: Four-year trends in exposure opportunity, use, motives, and sources. *J. Am. Coll. Health*, 60, 226–234.

Garnock-Jones, K. P. (2013). Sumatriptan iontophoretic transdermal system: A review of its use in patients with acute migraine. *Drugs*, 73, 1483–1490.

Garrett, B. E., and Griffiths, R. R. (1998). Physical dependence increases the relative reinforcing effects of caffeine versus placebo. *Psychopharmacology*, 139, 195–202.

Garthwaite, J. (2016). From synaptically localized to volume transmission by nitric oxide. *J. Physiol.*, 594, 9–18.

Gataullina, S., Bienvenu, T., Nabbout, R., Huberfeld, G., and Dulac, O. (2019). Gene mutations in paediatric epilepsies cause NMDA-pathy, and phasic and tonic GABA-pathy. *Dev. Med., Child Neurol.*, 61, 891–898.

Gawin, F. H., and Kleber, H. D. (1986). Abstinence symptomatology and psychiatric diagnosis in cocaine abusers: Clinical observations. *Arch. Gen. Psychiatry*, 43, 107–113.

Gawin, F. H., and Kleber, H. D. (1988). Evolving conceptualizations of cocaine dependence. *Yale J. Biol. Med.*, 61, 123–136.

Gaziano, J. M. and Hennekens, C. (1995). Moderate alcohol intake, increased levels of high density lipoprotein and its subfractions, and decreased risk of myocardial infarction. *N. Engl. J. Med.*, 329, 1829–1834.

Ge, Y., Chen, W., Axerio-Cilies, P., and Want, Y. T. (2020). NMDARs in cell survival and death: Implications in stroke pathogenesis and treatment. *Trends Mol. Med.*, 26, 533–551.

Gearhardt, A. N., and Hebebrand, J. (2021). The concept of "food addiction" helps inform the understanding of overeating and obesity: YES. *Am. J. Clin. Nutr.*, 113, 263–267.

Gebrie, A., Alebel, A., Zegeye, A., and Tesfaye, B. (2018). Prevalence and predictors of khat chewing among Ethiopian university students: A systematic review and meta-analysis. *PLOS ONE*, 13(4), e0195718. doi: 10.1371/journal.pone.0195718.

Geevasinga, N., Menon, P., Özdinler, P. H., Kiernan, M. C., and Vucic, S. (2016). Pathophysiological and diagnostic implications of cortical dysfunction in ALS. *Nat. Rev. Neurol.*, 12, 651–661.

Gehlbach, S. H., Williams, W. A., Perry, L. D., and Woodall, J. S. (1974). Greentobacco sickness. An illness of tobacco harvesters. *JAMA*, 229, 1880–1883.

Gelernter, J., Kranzler, H. R., Sherva, R., Almasy, L., Koesterer, R., Smith, A. H., Anton, R., et al. (2014). Genome-wide association study of alcohol dependence: significant findings in Africanand European-Americans including novel risk loci. *Mol. Psychiatry*, 19, 41–49.

Geller, M. (2015). E-cigs a 'Consumer-Driven' Revolution Born from a Bad Dream. Reuters. Available at https://www.reuters.com/article/us-ecigarettes-inventor/e-cigs-a-consumer-driven-revolution-born-from-a-bad-dream-idUSKBN0OP1YV20150609.

Genetic Science Learning Center. (2013). The Epigenome at a Glance. Available at www.learn.genetics.utah.edu/content/epigenetics/intro/.

Geoffroy P.A., Scott J., Boudebesse C., Lajnef M., Henry C., Leboyer M., et al. (2015) Sleep in patients with remitted bipolar disorders: a meta-analysis of actigraphy studies. *Acta Psychiatr. Scand.*, 131(2), 89–99.

George, O., and Koob, G. F. (2017). Individual differences in the neuropsychopathology of addiction. *Dialogues Clin. Neurosci.*, 19, 217–228.

George, W. H. and Norris, J. (1991). Alcohol, disinhibition, sexual arousal, and deviant sexual behavior. *Alcohol Health Res. World*, 15, 133–138.

Gerasimov, M. R., Ferrieri, R. A., Schiffer, W. K., Logan, J., Gatley, S. J., Gifford, A. N., et al. (2002). Study of brain uptake and biodistribution of [11C]toluene in non-human primates and mice. *Life Sci.*, 70, 2811–2828.

Gerlai, R. (1996). Gene-targeting studies of mammalian behavior: Is it the mutation or the background genotype? *Trends Neurosci.*, 19, 177–181.

German, C. L., Fleckenstein, A. E., and Hanson, G. R. (2014). Bath salts and synthetic cathinones: An emerging designer drug phenomenon. *Life Sci.*, 97, 2–8.

Gerrits, M., and Vanree, J. (1996). Effects of nucleus accumbens dopamine depletion on motivational aspects involved in initiation of cocaine and heroin self administration in rats. *Brain Res.*, 713, 114–124.

Gershon, M. D. (2013). 5-Hydroxytryptamine (serotonin) in the gastrointestinal tract. *Curr. Opin. Endocrinol. Diabetes Obes.*, 20, 14–21.

Gervais, A., O'Loughlin, J., Meshefedjian, G., Bancej, C., and Tremblay, M. (2006). Milestones in the natural course of onset of cigarettes use among adolescents. *CMAJ*, 175, 255–261.

Geta, T. G., Woldeamanuel, G. G., Hailemariam, B. Z., and Bedada, D. T. (2019). Association of chronic khat chewing with blood pressure and predictors of hypertension among adults in Gurage zone, southern Ethiopa: A comparative study. *Integr. Blood Press. Control*, 12, 33–42.

Geuze, E., van Berckel, B.N.M., Lammertsma, A. A., Boellaard, R., de Kloet, C. S., Vermetten, E., and Westenberg, H.G.M. (2008). Reduced GABA$_A$ benzodiazepine receptor binding in veterans with post-traumatic stress disorder. *Mol. Psychiatry.*, 13, 74–83.

Gibbons, A., and Dean, B. (2016). The cholinergic system: An emerging drug target for schizophrenia. *Clin. Pharm. Des.*, 22, 2124–2133.

Gibbons, D., Morrissey, C., and Mineau, P. (2015). A review of the direct and indirect effects of neonicotinoids and fipronil on vertebrate wildlife. *Environ. Sci. Pollut. Res.*, 22, 103–118.

Gigengack, R. (2014a). The chemo and the mona: Inhalants, devotion and street youth in Mexico City. *Int. J. Drug Policy*, 25, 61–70.

Gigengack, R. (2014b). "My body breaks. I take solution." Inhalant use in Delhi as pleasure seeking at a cost. *Int. J. Drug Policy*, 25, 810–818.

Gilbert, J. A., Blaser, M. J., Caporaso, J. G., Jansson, J. K., Lynch, S. V., and Knight, R. (2018). Current under-standing of the human microbiome. *Nat. Med.*, 24, 392–400.

Gilbertson, M. W., Shenton, M. E., Ciszewski, A., Kasai, K., Lasko, N. B., Orr, S. P., et al. (2002). Smaller hippocampal volume predicts pathologic vulnerability to psychological trauma. *Nat. Neurosci.*, 5, 1242–1247.

Gilhus, N. E., Tzartos, S., Evoli, A., Palace, J., Burns, T. M., and Vershuuren, J.J.G.M. (2019). Myasthenia gravis. *Nat. Rev. Dis. Primers*, 5(1), 30. doi: 10.1038/s41572-019-0079-y.

Gilpin,, N. W., Herman, M. A., and Roberto, M. (2014). The central amygdala as an integrative hub for anxiety and alcohol use disorders. *Biol. Psychiatry*, 77, 859–869.

Gingrich J.A., Malm H., Ansorge M.S., Brown A., Sourander A., Suri D., et al. (2017). New insights into how serotonin selective reuptake inhibitors shape the developing brain. *Birth Defects Res.*, 109(12), 924–932.

Giorgetti, R., Tagliabracci, A., Schifano, F., Zaami, S., Marinelli, E., and Busardò, F. P. (2017). When "Chems" meet sex: A rising

phenomenon called "ChemSex". *Curr. Neuropharmacol.*, 15, 762–770.

Giovanoli, S., Engler, H., Engler, A., Richetto, J., Voget, M., Willi, R., et al. (2013). Stress in puberty unmasks latent neuropathological consequences of prenatal immune activation in mice. *Science*, 339, 1095–1099.

Gipson, C. D., and Fowler, C. D. (2020). Nicotinic receptors underlying nicotine dependence: Evidence from transgenic mouse models. *Curr. Top. Behav. Neurosci.*, 45, 101–121.

Girgis, R. R., Kumar, S. S., and Brown, A. S. (2014). The cytokine model of schizophrenia: Emerging therapeutic strategies. *Biol. Psychiatry*, 75, 292–299.

Giros, B., Jaber, M., Jones, S. R., Wightman, R. M., and Caron, M. G. (1996). Hyperlocomotion and indifference to cocaine and amphetamine in mice lacking the dopamine transporter. *Nature*, 379, 606–612.

Giroud, C., de Cesare, M., Berthet, A., Varlet, V., Concha-Lozano, N., and Favrat, B. (2015). E-cigarettes: A review of new trends in cannabis use. *Int. J. Environ. Res. Public Health*, 12, 9988–10008.

Giv, M. J. (2017). Exposure to amphetamines leads to development of amphetamine type stimulants associated cardiomyopathy (ATSAC). *Cardiovasc. Toxicol.*, 17, 13–24.

Gkioka, E., Korou, L. M., Daskalopoulou, A., Misitzi, A., Batsidis, E., Bakoyiannis, I., et al. (2016). Prenatal cocaine exposure and its impact on cognitive functions of offspring: A pathophysiological insight. *Rev. Neurosci.*, 27, 523–534.

Gladding, C. M., Fitzjohn, S. M., and Molnar, E. (2009). Metabotropic glutamate receptor-mediated long-term depression: Molecular mechanisms. *Pharmacol. Rev.*, 61, 395–412.

Glade, M. J. (2010). Caffeine: Not just a stimulant. Nutrition, 26, 932–938.

Glasner-Edwards, S., and Mooney, L. J. (2014). Methamphetamine psychosis: Epidemiology and management. *CNS Drugs*, 28, 1115–1126.

Glatstein, M. M., Alabdulrazzaq, F., Garcia-Bournissen, F., and Scolnik, D. (2012). Use of physostigmine for hallucinogenic plant poisoning in a teenager: Case report and review of the literature. *Am. J. Ther.*, 19(5), 384–388. https://doi.org/10.1097/MJT.0b013e3181f0cbb4

Glausier, J. R., and Lewis, D. A. (2013). Dendritic spine pathology in schizophrenia. *Neuroscience*, 251, 90–107.

Glazer, W. M., Morgenstern, H., and Doucette, J. T. (1993). Predicting the long-term risk of tardive dyskinesia in outpatients maintained on neuroleptic

medications. *J. Clin. Psychiat*, 54, 133–139.

Glenza, J. (2016). Spice: Americans Turn to Dangerous "Synthetic" Marijuana to Evade Drug Tests. The Guardian. Available at www.theguardian.com/society/2016/may/08/spice-syntheticmarijuana-drug-screenings-tests.

Glikmann-Johnston, Y., Saling, M. M., Reutens, D. C., and Stout, J. C. (2015). Hippocampal 5-HT1A receptor and spatial learning and memory. *Front. Pharmacol.*, 6, 289. doi: 10.3389/fphar.2015.00289.

Gluskin, B. S., and Mickey, B. J. (2016). Genetic variation and dopamine D2 receptor availability: A systematic review and meta-analysis of human in vivo molecular imaging studies. *Transl. Psychiatry*, 6, e747. doi: 10.1038/tp2016.22.

Gobbi, LG., Atkin, T., Zytynski, T., Wang, S., Askari, S., Boruff, J., Ware, M., et al. (2019). Association of cannabis use in adolescence and risk of depression, anxiety, and suicidality in young adulthood. A systematic review and meta-analysis. *JAMA Psychiatry*, 76, 426–434.

Godar, S. C., and Bortolato, M. (2014). Gene-sex interactions in schizophrenia: Focus on dopamine neurotransmission. *Front. Behav. Neurosci.*, 8, Article 71.

Godbout, R., Jelenic, P., Labrie, C., Schmitt, M., and Bourguignon, J. J. (1995). Effect of gamma-hydroxybutyrate and its antagonist NCS-382 on spontaneous cell firing in the prefrontal cortex of the rat. *Brain Res.*, 673, 157–160.

Goedert, M., and Spillantini, M. S. (2006). A century of Alzheimer's disease. *Science*, 314, 777–781.

Goertz, R. B., Wanat, M. J., Gomez, J. A., Brown, Z. J., Phillips, P.E.M., and Paladini, C. A. (2015). Cocaine increases dopaminergic neuron and motor activity via midbrain α1 signaling. *Neuropsychopharmacology*, 40, 1151–1162.

Gökcen, B. B., and Şanlier, N. (2019). Coffee consumption and disease correlations. *Crit. Rev. Food Sci. Nutr.*, 59, 336–348.

Gold, L. H., Geyer, M. A., and Koob, G. F. (1989). Neurochemical mechanisms involved in behavioral effects of amphetamines and related designer drugs. *NIDA Res. Monogr.*, 104, 101–126.

Gold, L. H., and Balster, R. L. (1996). Evaluation of the cocaine-like discriminative stimulus effects and reinforcing effects of modafinil. *Psychopharmacology*, 126, 286–292.

Gold, M. S. (1989). Opiates. In A. J. Giannini and A. E. Slaby (Eds.), *Drugs of Abuse*, pp. 127–145. Oradell, NJ: Medical Economics Books.

Gold, P. E. (2014). Regulation of memory: From the adrenal medulla to liver to astrocytes to neurons. *Brain Res. Bull.*, 105, 25–35.

Gold, P. E., and Korol, D. L. (2014). Forgetfulness during aging: An integrated biology. *Neurobiol. Learn. Mem.*, 112, 130–138.

Goldberg, L., Elliot, D. L., Clarke, G. N., MacKinnon, D. P., Zoref, L., Moe, E., Green, C., et al. (1996). The Adolescents Training and Learning to Avoid Steroids (ATLAS) prevention program. Background and results of a model intervention. *Arch. Pediatr. Adolesc. Med.*, 150, 713–721.

Goldberg, S. B., Pace, B. T., Nicholas, C. R., Raison, C. L., and Hutson, P. R. (2020). The experimental effects of psilocybin on symptoms of anxiety and depression: A meta-analysis. *Psychiatry Res.*, 284, 112749. doi: 10.1016/j.psychres.2020.112749.

Goldman-Rakic, P. S. (1987). Circuitry of primate prefrontal cortex and regulation of behavior by representational memory. In F. Plum (Ed.), *Handbook of Physiology*, Section 1, The Nervous System, Volume. 5, Higher Functions of the Brain, Part I (pp. 373–417). Bethesda, MD: American Physiological Society.

Goldstein, D. B. (1972). Relationship of alcohol dose to intensity of withdrawal signs in mice. *J. Pharmacol. Exp. Ther.*, 180, 203–210.

Goldstein, J. M., Jerram, M., Abbs, B., Whitfield-Gabrieli, S., and Makris, N. (2010). Sex differences in stress response circuitry activation dependent on female hormonal cycle. *J. Neurosci.*, 30, 431–438.

Goldstein, M. J. (1995). Psychoeducation and relapse prevention: An update. In N. Brunello, G. Racagni, S. Z. Langer, and J. Mendlewicz (Eds.), *Critical Issues in the Treatment of Schizophrenia*, pp. 134–141. New York: Karger.

Goldstein, R. Z., and Volkow, N. D. (2011). Dysfunction of the prefrontal cortex in addiction: Neuroimaging findings and clinical implications. *Nat. Rev. Neurosci.*, 12, 652–669.

Goltseker, K., Hopf, F. W., and Barak, S. (2019). Advances in behavioral animal models of alcohol use disorder. *Alcohol*, 74, 73–82. https://doi.org/10.1016/j.alcohol.2018.05.014

Golubeva, A. V., Moloney, R. D., O'Connor, R. M., Dinan, T. G., and Cryan, J. F. (2015). Metabotropic glutamate receptors in central nervous system diseases. *Curr. Drug Targets*, 16, 1–80.

Gomez-Mancilla, B., Berry-Kravis, E., Hagerman, R., von Raison, F., Apostol, G., Ufer, M., et al. (2014). Development of mavoglurant and its potential for the treatment of fragile X syndrome.

Expert Opin. Investig. Drugs, 23, 125–134.

Gonglach, A. R., Ade, C. J., Bemben, M. G., Larson, R. D., and Black, C. D. (2016). Muscle pain as a regulator of cycling intensity: Effect of caffeine ingestion. *Med. Sci. Sports Exerc.*, 48, 287–296.

Goniewicz, M. L., Knysak, J., Gawron, M., Kosmider, L., Sobczak, A., Kurek, J., et al. (2014). Levels of selected carcinogens and toxicants in vapour from electronic cigarettes. *Tob. Control*, 23, 133–139.

Goniewicz, M. L., Kuma, T., Gawron, M., Knysak, J., and Kosmider, L. (2013). Nicotine levels in electronic cigarettes. *Nicotine Tob. Res.*, 15, 158–166.

Goniewicz, M. L., Miller, C. R., Sutanto, E., and Li, D. (2020). How effective are electronic cigarettes for reducing respiratory and cardiovascular risk in smokers? A systematic review. *Harm Reduct. J.*, 17, 91. doi: 10.1186/ s12954-020-00440-w.

Gonzales, R., Mooney, L., and Rawson, R. A. (2010). The methamphetamine problem in the United States. *Annu. Rev. Public Health*, 31, 385–398.

Gonzalez de Mejia, E., and RamirezMares, M. V. (2014). Impact of caffeine and coffee on our health. *Trends Endocrinol. Metab.*, 25, 489–492.

González, D., Riba, J., Bouso, J. C., GómezJarabo, G., and Barbanoj, M. J. (2006). Pattern of use and subjective effects of Salvia divinorum among recreational users. *Drug Alcohol Depend.*, 85, 157–162.

González, S., Cebeira, M., and FernándezRuiz, J. (2005). Cannabinoid tolerance and dependence: A review of studies in laboratory animals. *Pharmacol. Biochem. Behav.*, 81, 300–318.

González-Alzaga, B., Lacasaña, M., Aguilar-Garduño, C., Rodríguez-Barranco, M., Ballester, F., et al. (2014). A systemic review of neurodevelopmental effects of prenatal and postnatal organophosphate pesticide exposure. *Toxicol. Lett.*, 230, 104–121.

González-Maeso, J., Ang, R. L., Yuen, T., Chan, P., Weisstaub, N. V., López-Giménez, J. F., Zhou, M., et al. (2008). Identification of a serotonin/glutamate receptor complex implicated in psychosis. *Nature*, 452, 93–97.

González-Maeso, J., Weisstaub, N. V., Zhou, M., Chan, P., Ivic, L., Ang, R., Lira, A., et al. (2007). Hallucinogens recruit specific cortical 5-HT2A receptor-mediated signaling pathways to affect behavior. *Neuron*, 53, 439–452.

Goode, E. (1993). *Drugs in American Society*. New York: McGraw-Hill.

Goodkin, H. P., and Kapur, J. (2009). The impact of diazepam's discovery on the treatment and understanding of

status epilepticus. *Epilepsia*, 50, 2011–2018.

Goodwin, A. K., Hiranita, T., and Paule, M. G. (2015). The reinforcing effects of nicotine in humans and nonhuman primates: A review of intravenous self-administration evidence and future directions for research. *Nicotine Tob. Res.*, 17, 1297–1310.

Goodwin, A. K., Kaminski, B. J., and Weerts, E. M. (2013). Self-administration of gamma-hydroxybutyric acid (GHB) precursors gamma-butyrolactone (GBL) and 1,4-butanediol (1,4-BD) in baboons. *Psychopharmacology*, 225, 637–646.

Goodwin, A. K., Kaminski, B. J., Griffiths, R. R., Ator, N. A., and Weerts, E. M. (2011). Intravenous self-administration of gamma-hydroxybutyrate (GHB) in baboons. *Drug Alcohol Depend.*, 114, 217–224. © 2010 Elsevier Ireland Ltd. Reprinted with permission from Elsevier.

Gordon, N. (2007). Segawa's disease: Dopa-responsive dystonia. *Int. J. Clin. Pract.*, 62, 943–946.

Gorelick, D. A., and Heishman, S. J. (2006). Methods for clinical research involving cannabis administration. In E. S. Onavi (Ed.), *Methods in Molecular Medicine: Marijuana and Cannabinoid Research: Methods and Protocols*, pp. 235–253. Totowa, NJ: Humana.

Gorelick, D. A., Goodwin, R. S., Schwilke, E., Schwope, D. M., Darwin, W. D., Kelly, D. L., et al. (2013). Tolerance to effects of high-dose oral Δ9tetrahydrocannabinol and plasma cannabinoid concentrations in male daily cannabis smokers. *J. Anal. Toxicol.*, 37, 11–16.

Gori, A., Topino, E., Craparo, G., Bagnoli, I., Caretti, V., and Schimmenti, A. (2021). A comprehensive model for gambling behaviors: Assessment of the factors that can contribute to the vulnerability and maintenance of gambling disorder. *J. Gambl. Stud.*, https://doi.org/10.1007/ s10899-021-10024-3.

Gorlin, A. W., Rosenfeld, D. M., and Ramakrishna, H. (2016). Intravenous subanesthetic ketamine for perioperative analgesia. *J. Anaesthesiol. Clin. Pharmacol.*, 32, 160–167.

Göthert, M. (2013). Serotonin discovery and stepwise disclosure of 5-HT receptor complexity over four decades. Part I. General background and discovery of serotonin as a basis for 5-HT receptor identification. *Pharmacol. Rep.*, 65, 771–786.

Gottesman, I. I. (1991). *Schizophrenia Genesis*. New York: W. H. Freeman.

Gounder, K., Dunuwille, J., Dunne, J., Lee, J., Silbert, P., and Lawn, N. (2020). The other side of the leaf: Seizures associated with synthetic cannabinoid

use. *Epilepsy Behav.*, 104(Pt A), 106901. doi: 10.1016/j. yebeh.2020.106901.

Goyal, D., Limesand, S. W., and Goyal, R. (2019). Epigenetic responses and the developmental origins of health and disease. *J. Endocrinol.*, 242, T105–T119.

Grace, A. A. (1992). The depolarization block hypothesis of neuroleptic action: Implications for the etiology and treatment of schizophrenia. *J. Neural Transm.*, 36(Suppl.), 91–131.

Grace, A. A., Floresco, S. B., Goto, Y., and Lodge, D. J. (2007). Regulation of firing of dopaminergic neurons and control of goal-oriented behaviors. *Trends Neurosci.*, 30, 220–227.

Grace, K. P., and Horner, R. L. (2015). Evaluating the evidence surrounding pontine cholinergic involvement in REM sleep generation. *Front. Neurol.*, 6, 190. doi: 10.3389/fneur.2015.00190.

Grall-Bronnec, M., Bulteau, S., Victorri-Vigneau, C., Bouju, G., and Sauvaget, A. (2015). Fortune telling addiction: Unfortunately a serious topic. About a case report. *J. Behav. Addict.*, 4, 27–31.

Grandjean E.M., Aubry J.M. (2009) Lithium: updated human knowledge using an evidence-based approach: Part I: Clinical efficacy in bipolar disorder. *CNS Drugs*, 23(3), 225–240.

Granger, A. J., and Nicoll, R. A. (2014). Expression mechanisms underlying long-term potentiation: A postsynaptic view, 10 years on. *Philos. Trans. R. Soc. Lond. B Biol. Sci.*, 369, 20130136. doi: 10.1098/ rstb.2013.0136.

Granger, A. J., Wallace, M. L., and Sabatini, B. L. (2017). Multitransmitter neurons in the mammalian central nervous system. *Curr. Opin. Neurobiol.*, 45, 85–91.

Grant, J. E., and Chamberlain, S. R. (2016). Expanding the definition of addiction: DSM-5 vs. ICD-11. *CNS Spectr.*, 21, 300–303.

Granziol, U., Zorzi, A., Cardaioli, F., Cipriani, A., D'Ascenzi, F., Firth, J., Stubbs, B., et al. (2021). Exercise addiction in athletes: Comparing two assessment instruments and willingness to stop exercise after medical advice. *Psychol. Assess.*, 33, 326–337.

Grattan, L. M., Boushey, C. J., Liang, Y., Lefebvre, K. A., Castellon, L. J., Roberts, K. A., et al. (2018). Repeated dietary exposure to low levels of domoic and problems with everyday memory: Research to public health outreach. *Toxins*, 10, 103. doi: 10.3390/toxins10030103.

Gravielle, M. C. (2016). Activation-induced regulation of GABA$_A$ receptors: Is there a link with the molecular basis of benzodiazepine tolerance? *Pharmacol. Res.*, 109, 92–100.

Gravielle, M. C. (2018). Regulation of GABA$_A$ receptors by prolonged exposure to endogenous

and exogenous ligands. *Neurochem. Int.*, 118, 96–104.

Grayson, B., Barnes, S. A., Markou, A., Piercy, C., Podda, G., and Neill, J. C. (2015). Postnatal phencyclidine (PCP) as a neurodevelopmental animal model of schizophrenia pathophysiology and symptomatology: A review. *Curr. Topics Behav. Neurosci.*, 29, 403–428.

Greaves, L., and Hemsing, N. (2020). Sex and gender interactions on the use and impact of recreational cannabis. *Int. J. Environ. Res. Public Health*, 17, 509. doi: 10.3390/ijerph17020509.

Green, A. I., and Brown, W. A. (1988). Prolactin and neuroleptic drugs. *Neurol. Clin.*, 6, 213–223.

Green, B., Kavanagh, D., and Young, R. (2003). Being stoned: A review of self-reported cannabis effects. *Drug Alcohol Rev.*, 22, 453–460.

Green, T. A., and Bardo, M. T. (2020). Opposite regulation of conditioned place preference and intravenous drug self-administration in rodent models: Motivational and non-motivational examples. *Neurosci. Biobehav. Rev.*, 116, 89–98. https://doi.org/10.1016/j. neubiorev.2020.06.006

Greenwood, D. C., Thatcher, N. J., Ye, J., Garrard, L., Keogh, G., King, L. G., and Cade, J. E. (2014). Caffeine intake during pregnancy and adverse birth outcomes: A systematic review and dose-response meta-analysis. *Eur. J. Epidemiol.*, 29, 725–734.

Grela, A., Gautam, L., and Cole, M. D. (2018). A multifactorial critical appraisal of substances found in drug facilitated sexual assault cases. *Forensic Sci. Int.*, 292, 50–60.

Grgic, J., Grgic, I., Pickering, C., Schoenfeld, B., Bishop, D. J., and Pedisic, Z. (2020). Wake up and smell the coffee: caffeine supplementation and exercise performance – an umbrella review of 21 published meta-analyses. *Br. J. Sports Med.*, 54, 681–688.

Grgic, J., Mikulic, P., Schoenfeld, B. J., Bishop, D. J., and Pedisic, Z. (2019). The influence of caffeine supplementation on resistance exercise: A review. *Sports Med.*, 49, 17–30.

Grgic, J., Trexler, E. T., Lazinica, B., and Pedisic, Z. (2018). Effects of caffeine intake on muscle strength and power: a systematic review and meta-analysis. *J. Int. Soc. Sports Nutr.*, 15, 11. doi: 10.1186/s12970-018-0216-0.

Griebel, G., and Holmes, A. (2013). 50 years of hurdles and hope in anxiolytic drug discovery. *Nat. Rev. Drug Discov.*, 12, 667–687.

Griffiths, R. R., and Mumford, G. K. (1995). Caffeine: A drug of abuse? In F. E. Bloom and D. J. Kupfer (Eds.),

Psychopharmacology: The Fourth Generation of Progress, pp. 1699–1713. New York: Raven.

Griffiths, R. R., and Weerts, E. M. (1997). Benzodiazepine self-administration in humans and laboratory animals: Implications for problems of long-term use and abuse. *Psychopharmacology*, 134, 1–37.

Griffiths, R. R., Evans, S. M., Heishman, S. J., Preston, K. L., Sannerud, C. A., Wolf, B., et al. (1990). Low-dose caffeine physical dependence in humans. *J. Pharmacol. Exp. Ther.*, 255, 1123–1132.

Griffiths, R. R., Lamb, R. J., Sannerud, C. A., Ator, N., and Brady, J. V. (1991). Self-injection of barbiturates and benzodiazepines. *Psychopharmacology*, 103, 154–161.

Griffiths, R. R., Richards, W. A., Johnson, M. W., McCann, U. D., and Jesse, R. (2008). Mystical-type experiences occasioned by psilocybin mediate the attribution of personal meaning and spiritual significance 14 months later. *J. Psychopharmacol.*, 22, 621–632.

Grigg, J., Manning, V., Arunogiri, S., and Lubman, D. I. (2019). Synthetic cannabinoid use disorder: an update for general psychiatrists. *Australas. Psychiatry*, 27, 279–283.

Grigioni, G., Saleh, C., Jaszczuk, P., Wand, D., Wilmes, S., and Hund-Georgiadis, M. (2020). Fragile-X-Associated Tremor/Ataxia Syndrome or Alcohol-Induced Cerebellar Degeneration? A Case Report. *Case Rep. Neurol.*, 12(3), 466–471. https://doi.org/10.1159/000511954

Grillon C., Levenson J., and Pine D.S. (2007). A single dose of the selective serotonin reuptake inhibitor citalopram exacerbates anxiety in humans: a fear-potentiated startle study. *Neuropsychopharmacology*, 32(1), 225–231.

Grinspoon, L., and Bakalar, J. B. (1979). *Psychedelic Drugs Reconsidered*. New York: Basic Books.

Griswold, M. G., Fullman, N., Hawley, C., Arian, N., Zimsen, S.R.M., Tymeson, H. D., Venkateswaran, V., et al. (2018). Alcohol use and burden for 195 countries and territories, 1990–2016, A systematic analysis for the Global Burden of Disease Study 2016. *Lancet*, 392(10152), 1015–1035. https://doi.org/10.1016/S0140-6736(18)31310-2

Gritton, H. J., Howe, W. M., Mallory, C. S., Hetrick, V. L., Berke, J. D., and Sarter, M. (2016). Cortical cholinergic signaling controls the detection of cues. *Proc. Natl. Acad. Sci. USA*, 113, E1089-E1097.

Grobin, A. C., Matthews, D. B., Devaud, L. L., and Morrow, A. L. (1998). The role of GABA$_A$ receptors in the acute and chronic effects of ethanol. *Psychopharmacology*, 139, 2–19.

Gröger, N., Matas, E., Gos, T., Lesse, A., Poeggel, G., Braun, K., et al. (2016). The transgenerational transmission of childhood adversity: Behavioral, cellular, and epigenetic correlates. *J. Neural Transm.*, 123, 1037–1052.

Grönbladh, A., Nylander, E., and Hallberg, M. (2016). The neurobiology and addiction potential of anabolic androgenic steroids and the effects of growth hormone. *Brain Res. Bull.*, 126, 127–137.

Gross, C., and Hen, R. (2004). The developmental origins of anxiety. *Nat. Rev. Neurosci.*, 5, 545–552.

Gross, C., Zhuang, X., Stark, K., Ramboz, S., Oosting, R., Kirby, L., et al. (2002). Serotonin1A receptor acts during development to establish normal anxiety-like behaviour in the adult. *Nature*, 416, 396–400.

Grosso, G., Godos, J., Galvano, F., and Giovannucci, E. L. (2017). Coffee, caffeine, and health outcomes: An umbrella review. *Annu. Rev. Nutr.*, 37, 131–156.

Grotenhermen, F., Leson, G., Berghaus, G., Drummer, O. H., Krüger, H.-P., Longo, M., Moskowitz, H., et al. (2007). Developing limits for driving under cannabis. *Addiction*, 102, 1910–1917.

Grubbs, J. B., Hoagland, K. C., Lee, B. N., Grant, J. T., Davison, P., Reid, R. C., and Kraus, S. W. (2020). Sexual addiction 25 years on: A systematic and methodological review of empirical literature and an agenda for future research. *Clin. Psychol. Rev.*, 82, 101925. doi: 10.1016/j.cpr.2020.101925.

Grubbs, J. B., Kraus, S. W., and Perry, S. L. (2019). Self-reported addiction to pornography in a nationally representative sample: The roles of use habits, religiousness, and moral incongruence. *J. Behav. Addict.*, 8, 88–93.

Gruber, A. J., and Pope, H. G., Jr. (2002). Marijuana use among adolescents. *Pediatr. Clin. North Am.*, 49, 389–413.

Grünewald, B., and Siefert, P. (2019). Acetylcholine and its receptors in honeybees: Involvement in development and impairments by neonicotinoids. *Insects*, 10, 420. doi: 10.3390/insects10120420.

Gu, X., Lohrenz, T., Salas, R., Baldwin, P. R., Soltani, A., Kirk, U., Cinciripini, P. M., et al. (2016). Belief about nicotine modulates subjective craving and insula activity in deprived smokers. *Front. Psychiatry*, 7, 126. doi: 10.3389/fpsyt.2016.00126.

Gualtieri, F. (2016). Unifi nootropics from the lab to the web: a story of academic (and industrial) shortcomings. *J. Enz. Inhib. Med. Chem.*, 31, 187–194.

Guay, D. R. (1995). The emerging role of valproate in bipolar disorder and other psychiatric disorders. *Pharmacotherapy*, 15, 631–647.

Guha, P., Harraz, M. M., and Snyder, S. H. (2016). Cocaine elicits autophagic cytotoxicity via a nitric oxide-GAPDH signaling cascade. *Proc. Natl. Acad. Sci. USA*, 113, 1417–1422.

Guidotti, A., and Grayson, D. R. (2011). A neurochemical basis for an epigenetic vision of psychiatric disorders (1994– 2009). *Pharmacol. Res.*, 64, 344–349.

Guidotti, A., Auta, J., Chen, Y., Davis, J. M., Dong, E., Gavin, D. P., et al. (2011). Epigenetic GABAergic targets in schizophrenia and bipolar disorder. *Neuropharmacology*, 60, 1007–1016.

Guidotti, A., Grayson, D. R., and Caruncho, H. J. (2016). Epigenetic RELN dysfunction in schizophrenia and related neuropsychiatric disorders. *Front. Cell. Neurosci.*, 10, Article 89.

Guillem, K., Bloem, B., Poorthuis, R. B., Loos, M., Smit, A. B., Maskos, U., Spijker, S., et al. (2011). Nicotinic acetylcholine receptor β2 subunits in the medial prefrontal cortex control attention. *Science*, 333, 888–891.

Gulliver, D., Werry, E., Reekie, T. A., Katte, T. A., Jorgensen, W., and Kassiou, M. (2019). Targeting the oxytocin system: New pharmacotherapeutic approaches. *Trends Pharmacol. Sci.*, 40, 22–37.

Gunasekera, B., Davies, C., Martin-Santos, R., and Bhattacharyya, S. (2021). The yin and yang of cannabis: A systematic review of human neuroimaging evidence of the differential effects of Δ^9-tetrahydrocannabinol and cannabidiol. *Biol. Psychiatry Cogn. Neurosci. Neuroimaging*, 6(6), 636-645.

Gunduz-Bruce, H. (2009). The acute effects of NMDA antagonism: From the rodent to the human brain. *Brain Res. Rev.*, 279–286.

Gunduz-Cinar, O. (2021). The endocannabinoid system in the amygdala and modulation of fear. *Prog. NeuroPsychopharmacol. Biol. Psychiatry*, 105, 110116. doi: 10.1016/j.pnpbp.2020.110116.

Gunja, N., and Brown, J. A. (2012). Energy drinks: Health risks and toxicity. *Med. J. Aust.*, 196, 46–49.

Gunn, J. K., Rosales, C. B., Center, K. E., Nuñez, A., Gibson, S. J., Christ, C., and Ehiri, J. E. (2016). Prenatal exposure to cannabis and maternal and child health outcomes: A systematic review and meta-analysis. *BMJ Open*, 6, e009986. doi: 10.1136/bmjopen-2015-009986.

Gupta, M., Kaur, H., Jajodia, A., Jain, S., Satyamoorthy, K., Mukerji, M., et al. (2011). Diverse facets of COMT: From a plausible predictive marker to a potential drug target for schizophrenia. *Curr. Mol. Med.*, 11, 732–743.

Gur, R. E. (1995). Functional brain-imaging studies in schizophrenia. In F. E. Bloom and D. J. Kupfer (Eds.), *Psychopharmacology: The Fourth Generation of Progress*, pp. 1185–1192. New York: Raven.

Guru, A., Post, R. J., Ho, Y.-Y., and Warden, M. R. (2015). Making sense of optogenetics. *Int. J. Neuropsychopharmacol.*, 18, pyv079. doi: 10.1093/ijnp/pyv079.

Guyatt, G. H., Oxman, A. D., Vist, G. E., Kunz, R., Falck-Ytter, Y., Alonso-Coello, P., et al. (2008). GRADE: An emerging consensus on rating quality of evidence and strength of recommendations. *BMJ*, 336, 924. doi: 10.1136/bmj.39489.470347. AD.

H

Haam, J., and Yakel, J. L. (2017). Cholinergic modulation of the hippocampal region and memory function. *J. Neurochem.*, 142(Suppl. 2), 111–121.

Haavik, J., Blau, N., and Thöny, B. (2008). Mutations in human monoamine-related neurotransmitter pathway genes. *Hum. Mutat.*, 29, 891–902.

Haber, S. N., and Knutson, B. (2010). The reward circuit: Linking primate anatomy and human imaging. *Neuropsychopharmacology*, 35, 4–26.

Habibian, S., Ahamad, K., McLean, M., and Socias, M. E. (2019). Successful management of gamma-hydroxybutyrate (GHB) withdrawal using baclofen as a standalone therapy: A case report. *J. Addict. Med.*, 13, 415–417.

Haddad, P. M., Das, A., Ashfaq, M., and Wieck, A. (2009). A review of valproate in psychiatric practice. *Expert Opin. Drug Metab. Toxicol.*, 5, 539–551.

Haghparast, A., Fatahi, Z., Arezoomandan, R., Karimi, S., Taslimi, Z., and Zarrabian, S. (2017). Functional roles of orexin/hypocretin receptors in reward circuit. *Prog. Brain Res.*, 235, 139–154.

Hahn, B. (2015). Nicotinic receptors and attention. *Curr. Top. Behav. Neurosci.*, 23, 103–135.

Hahn, B., and Stolerman, I. P. (2005). Modulation of nicotine-induced attentional enhancement in rats by adrenoceptor antagonists. *Psychopharmacology*, 177, 438–447.

Haijma, S. V., Haren, N. V., Cahn, W., Koolschijn, P. C. M. P., Pol, H. E. H., and Kahn, R. S. (2013). Brain Volumes in Schizophrenia: A Meta-Analysis in Over 18 000 Subjects. *Schizophr. Bull.*, 39(5), 1129. https://doi.org/10.1093/schbul/sbs118

Haines, D. D., and Fox, S. C. (2014). Acute and long-term impact of chemical weapons: Lessons from the Iran-Iraq war. *Forensic Sci. Rev.*, 26, 97–114.

Hajek, P., Pittaccio, K., Pesola, F., Smith, K. M., Phillips-Waller, A., and Przulj, D. (2020). Nicotine delivery and users' reactions to Juul compared with cigarettes and other e-cigarette products. *Addiction*, 115, 1141–1148.

Hajek, P., Przulj, D., Phillips, A., Anderson, R., and McRobbie, H. (2017). Nicotine delivery to users from cigarettes and from different types of e-cigarettes. *Psychopharmacology*, 234, 773–779.

Halberstadt, A. L. (2015). Recent advances in the neuropsychopharmacology of serotonergic hallucinogens. *Behav. Brain Res.*, 277, 99–120.

Halberstadt, A. L. (2017). Pharmacology and toxicology of N-benzylphenethylamine ("NBOMe") hallucinogens, In *Neuropharmacology of New Psychoactive Substances (NPS)*, M. Baumann, R. Glennon, and J. Wiley [Eds.], *Curr. Topics Behav. Neurosci* 32, pp. 283–311. Springer: Cham. doi.org/10.1007/7854_2016_64

Halberstadt, A. L., and Geyer, M. A. (2014). Effects of the hallucinogen 2,5-dimethoxy-4-iodophenethylamine (2C-I) and superpotent N-benzyl derivatives on the head twitch response. *Neuropharmacology*, 77, 200–207.

Hall, F. S., Der-Avakian, A., Gould, T. J., Markou, A., Shoaib, M., and Young, J. W. (2015). Negative affective states and cognitive impairments in nicotine dependence. *Neurosci. Biobehav. Rev.*, 58, 168–185.

Hall, F. S., Drgonova, J., Jain, S., and Uhl, G. R. (2013). Implications of genome wide association studies for addiction: Are our a priori assumptions wrong? *Pharmacol. Ther.*, 140, 267–279.

Hall, F. S., Chen, Y., and Resendiz-Gutierrez, F. (2020). The streetlight effect: Reappraising the study of addiction in light of the findings of genome-wide association studies. *Brain Behav. Evol.*, 95, 230–246.

Hall, W. (2015). What has research over the past two decades revealed about the adverse health effects of recreational cannabis use? *Addiction*, 110, 19–35.

Hall, W., and Weier, M. (2017). Lee Robins' studies of heroin use among US Vietnam veterans. *Addiction*, 112, 176–180.

Hall, W., Carter, A., and Forlini, C. (2015). The brain disease model of addiction: Is it supported by the evidence and has it delivered on its promises? *Lancet Psychiatry*, 2, 105–110.

Halldner, L., Ádén, U., Dahlberg, V., Johansson, B., Ledent, C., and Fredholm, B. B. (2004). The adenosine A1 receptor contributes to the stimulatory, but not the inhibitory effect of caffeine on locomotion: a study in mice lacking adenosine A1 and/or A2A receptors. *Neuropharmacology*, 46, 1008–1017.

Haller, J. (2013). The neurobiology of abnormal manifestations of aggression: A review of hypothalamic mechanisms in cats, rodents and humans. *Brain Res. Bull.*, 93, 97–109.

Halpern, J. H., Lerner, A. G., and Passie, T. (2016). A review of hallucinogen persisting perception disorder (HPPD) and an exploratory study of subjects claiming symptoms of HPPD. *Curr. Topics Behav. Neurosci.*, doi: 10.1007/7854_2016_457.

Halpin, L. E., Collins, S. A., and Yamamoto, B. K. (2014). Neurotoxicity of methamphetamine and 3,4-methylenedioxymethamphetamine. *Life Sci.*, 97, 37–44.

Ham, S., Kim, T. K., Chung, S., and Im, H.-I. (2017). Drug abuse and psychosis: New insights into drug-induced psychosis. *Exp. Neurobiol.*, 26, 11–24.

Hamilton, D. A., and Kolb, B. (2005). Differential effects of nicotine and complex housing on subsequent experience-dependent structural plasticity in the nucleus accumbens. *Behav. Neurosci.*, 119, 355–365. © 2005 by American Psychological Association.

Hamilton, L. W., and Timmons, C. R. (1990). *Principles of Behavioral Pharmacology: A Biopsychological Perspective*. Englewood Cliffs, NJ: Prentice Hall.

Hamilton, P. J., and Nestler, E. J. (2019). Epigenetics and addiction. *Curr. Opin. Neurobiol.*, 59, 128–136.

Hamner, M. (2002). The effects of atypical antipsychotics on serum prolactin levels. *Ann. Clin. Psychiatry*, 14, 163–173.

Han, J. S. (2004). Acupuncture and endorphins. *Neurosci. Lett.*, 361, 258–261.

Han, J., Kesner, P., Metna-Laurent, M., Duan, T., Xu, L., Georges, F., et al. (2012). Acute cannabinoids impair working memory through astroglial CB$_1$ receptor modulation of hippocampal LTD. *Cell*, 148, 1039–1050.

Handelsman, D. J. (2020). Performance enhancing hormone doping in sport. In K.R. Feingold, B. Anawalt, A. Boyce, G. Chrousos, W. W. de Herder, K. Dhatariya, K. Dungan, et al. (Eds.), *Endotext [Internet]*. South Yarmouth, MA: MDText.com Inc. Available at https://www.ncbi.nlm.nih.gov/books/NBK305894/. Accessed 6/22/21.

Haney, M. (2009). Self-administration of cocaine, cannabis and heroin in the human laboratory: Benefits and pitfalls. *Addict. Biol.*, 14, 9–21.

Haney, M., Ward, A. S., Comer, S. D., Foltin, R. W., and Fischman, M. W. (1999a). Abstinence symptoms following smoked marijuana in humans. *Psychopharmacology*, 141, 395–404.

Haney, M., Ward, A. S., Comer, S. D., Foltin, R. W., and Fischman, M. W. (1999b). Abstinence symptoms following oral THC administration to humans. *Psychopharmacology*, 141, 385–394.

Hanks, J. B., and González-Maeso, J. (2013). Animal models of serotonergic psychedelics. *ACS Chem. Neurosci.*, 4, 33–42.

Hanlon, C. A., and Canterberry, M. (2012). The use of brain imaging to elucidate neural circuit changes in cocaine addiction. *Subst. Abuse Rehabil.*, 3, 115–128.

Hanlon, C. A., Dowdle, L. T., Gibson, N. B., Li, X., Hamilton, S., Canterberry, M., and Hoffman, M. (2018). Cortical substrates of cue-reactivity in multiple substance dependent populations: transdiagnostic relevance of the medial prefrontal cortex. *Transl. Psychiatry*, 8, 186, doi: 10.1038/s41398-018-0220-9.

Hanlon, C. A., Dufault, D. L., Wesley, M. J., and Poerrino, L. J. (2011). Elevated gray and white matter densities in cocaine abstainers compared to current users. *Psychopharmacology*, 218, 681–692.

Hannestad, J., Gallezot, J.-D., PlanetaWilson, B., Lin, S.-F., Williams, W. A., van Dyck, C. H., et al. (2010). Clinically relevant doses of methylphenidate significantly occupy norepinephrine transporters in humans in vivo. *Biol. Psychiatry*, 68, 854–860.

Hannigan, J. H., and Bowen, S. E. (2010). Reproductive toxicology and teratology of abused toluene. *Syst. Biol. Reprod. Med.*, 56, 184–200.

Hansen, F. H., Skjørringe, T., Yasmeen, S., Arends, N. V., Sahai, M. A., Erreger, K., et al. (2014). Missense dopamine transporter mutations associate with adult Parkinsonism and ADHD. *J. Clin. Invest.*, 124, 3107–3210.

Hansen, R. T. 3rd, and Zhang, H. T. (2017). The past, present, and future of phosphodiesterase-4 modulation of age-induced memory loss. *Adv. Neurobiol.*, 17, 169–199.

Harada, K., Kamiya, T., and Tsuboi, T. (2016). Gliotransmitter release from astrocytes: Functional, developmental, and pathological implications in the brain. *Front. Neurosci.*, 9, 499. doi: 10.3389/fnins.2015.00499.

Hardaway, R., Schweitzer, J., and Suzuki, J. (2016). Hallucinogen use disorders. *Child Adolesc. Psychiatric Clin. N. Am.*, 25, 489–496.

Hardiman, O., van den Berg, L. H., and Kiernan, M. C. (2011). Clinical diagnosis and management of amyotrophic lateral sclerosis. *Nat. Rev. Neurol.*, 7, 639–649.

Harris, J. L., and Munsell, C. R. (2015). Energy drinks and adolescents: What's the harm? *Nutr. Rev.*, 73, 247–257.

Harris, R., and Gurel, L. (2012). A study of ayahuasca use in North America. *J. Psychoactive Drugs*, 44, 209–215.

Hart, C. L., van Gorp, W., Haney, M., Foltin, R. W., and Fischman, M. W. (2001). Effects of acute smoked marijuana on complex cognitive performance. *Neuropsychopharmacology*, 25, 757–765.

Hartmann-Boyce, J., Chepkin, S. C., Ye, W., Bullen, C., and Lancaster, T. (2018). Nicotine replacement therapy versus control for smoking cessation. *Cochrane Database Syst. Rev.*, 5(5), CD000146. doi: 10.1002/14651858.CD000146.pub5.

Hartung D.M. (2017) Economics and Cost-effectiveness of multiple sclerosis therapies in the USA. *Neurotherapeutics*, 14, 1018–1026.

Hartwell, E. E., and Kranzler, H. R. (2019). Pharmacogenetics of alcohol use disorder treatments: An update. *Expert Opin. Drug Metab. Toxicol.*, 15(7), 553–564. https://doi.org/10.1080/17425255.2019.1628218

Harun, N., Johari, I. S., Mansor, S. M., and Shoaib, M. (2020). Assessing physiological dependence and withdrawal potential of mitragynine using schedule-controlled behaviour in rats. *Psychopharmacology*, 237(3), 855–867. https://doi.org/10.1007/s00213-019-05418-6

Harvey, K. V., and Balon, R. (1995). Augmentation with buspirone: A review. *Ann. Clin. Psychiatry*, 7, 143–147.

Hase, A., Jung, S. E., and aan het Rot, M. (2015). Behavioral and cognitive effects of tyrosine intake in healthy human adults. *Pharmacol. Biochem. Behav.*, 133, 1–6.

Hasin, D. S., and Grant, B. F. (2015). The National Epidemiologic Survey on Alcohol and Related Conditions (NESARC) Waves 1 and 2, Review and summary of findings. *Soc. Psychiatry Psychiatr. Epidemiol.*, 50, 1609–1640.

Hasin, D. S., Kerridge, B. T., Saha, T. D., Huang, B., Pickering, R., Smith, S. M., Jung, J., et al. (2016). Prevalence and correlates of DSM-5 cannabis use disorder, 2012–2013, Findings from the National Epidemiologic Survey on Alcohol and Related Conditions – III. *Am. J. Psychiatry*, 173, 588–599.

Hasler, G., Fromm, S., Carlson, P. J., Luckenbaugh, D. A., Waldeck, T., Geraci, M., et al. (2008). Neural response to catecholamine depletion in unmedicated subjects with major depressive disorder in remission and healthy subjects. *Arch. Gen. Psychiatry*, 65, 521–531.

Hasselmo, M. E., and Sarter, M. (2011). Modes and models of forebrain cholinergic neuromodulation of cognition. *Neuropsychopharmacology*, 36, 52–73.

Hasselmo, M. E. (2006). The role of acetylcholine in learning and memory. *Curr. Opin. Neurobiol.*, 16, 710–715.

Hatzidimitriou, G., McCann, U. D., and Ricaurte, G. A. (1999). Altered serotonin innervation patterns in the forebrain of monkeys treated with (±)3,4-methylenedioxymethamphetamine seven years previously: Factors influencing abnormal recovery. *J. Neurosci.*, 19, 5096–5107.

Hauger, L. E., Havnes, I. A., Jørstad, M. L., and Bjørnebekk, A. (2021). Anabolic androgenic steroids, antisocial personality personality traits, aggression and violence. *Drug Alcohol Depend.*, 221, 108604. doi: 10.1016/j.drugalcdep.2021.108604.

Hauger, L. E., Westlye, L. T., and Bjørnebekk, A. (2020). Anabolic androgenic steroid dependence is associated with executive dysfunction. *Drug Alcohol Depend.*, 208, 107874. doi: 10.1016/j.drugalcdep.2020.107874.

Hauser, R. A., Factor, S. A., Marder, S. R., Knesevich, M. A., Ramirez, P. M., Jimenez, R., Burke, J., et al. (2017). KINECT 3, A phase 3 randomized, double-blind, placebo-controlled trial of Valbenazine for tardive dyskinesia. *Am. J. Psychiatry*, 174(5), 476–484. Reprinted with permission from the American Journal of Psychiatry, © 2017. American Psychiatric Association. All Rights Reserved.

Haussmann R., Bauer M., von Bonin S., Grof P., Lewitzka U. (2015) Treatment of lithium intoxication: facing the need for evidence. *Int. J. Bipolar Disord.*, 3(1), 23.

Havakuk, O., Rezkalla, S. H., and Kloner, R. A. (2017). The cardiovascular effects of cocaine. *J. Am. Coll. Cardiol.*, 70, 101–113.

Hays, S. R., and Deshpande, J. K. (2011). Newly postulated neurodevelopmental risks of pediatric anesthesia. *Curr. Neurol. Neurosci. Rep.*, 11, 205–210.

Hayward, A., Adamson, L., and Neill, J. C. (2017). Partial agonism at the α7 nicotinic acetylcholine receptor improves attention, impulsive action and vigilance in low attentive rats. *Eur. Neuropsychopharmacol.*, 27, 325–335.

Heal, D. J., Cheetham, S. C., and Smith, S. L. (2009). The neuropharmacology of ADHD drugs in vivo: Insights on efficacy and safety. *Neuropharmacology*, 57, 608–618.

Heal, D. J., Gosden, J., and Smith, S. L. (2014). Dopamine reuptake transporter (DAT) "inverse agonist": A novel hypothesis to explain the enigmatic pharmacology of cocaine. *Neuropharmacology*, 87, 19–40.

Heaney, C. F., and Kinney, J. W. (2016). Role of GABA$_B$ receptors in learning and memory and neurological disorders. *Neurosci. Biobehav. Rev.*, 63, 1–28.

Heather, N. (2017). Q: Is addiction a brain disease or a moral failing? A: Neither. *Neuroethics*, 10, 115–124.

Heatherton, T. F., Kozlowski, L. T., Frecker, R. C., and Fagerström, K. O. (1991). The Fagerström Test for Nicotine Dependence: A revision of the Fagerström Tolerance Questionnaire. *Br. J. Addict.*, 86, 1119–1127.

Heckman, P. R., Wouters, C., and Prickaerts, J. (2015). Phosphodiesterase inhibitors as a target for cognition enhancement in aging and Alzheimer's disease: A translational overview. *Curr. Pharm. Des.*, 21, 317–331.

Heckman, P.R.A., Blokland, A., Bollen, E.P.P., and Prickaerts, J. (2018). Phosphodiesterase inhibition and modulation of corticostriatal and hippocampal circuits: Clinical overview and translational considerations. *Neurosci. Biobehav. Rev.*, 87, 233–254.

Hedegaard, H., Spencer, M. R., and Garnett, M. F. (2020). Increase in Drug Overdose Deaths Involving Cocaine: United States, 2009–2018. NCHS Data Brief, no. 384. Hyattsville, MD: National Center for Health Statistics.

Heekin, R. D., Shorter, D., and Kosten, T. R. (2017). Current status and future prospects for the development of substance abuse vaccines. *Expert Rev. Vaccines*, 16, 1067–1077.

Hefendehl, J. K., LeDue, J., Ko, R. W. Y., Mahler, J., Murphy, T. H., and MacVicar, B. A. (2016). Mapping synaptic glutamate transporter dysfunction in vivo to regions surrounding Aβ plaques by iGluSnFR two-photon imaging. *Nat. Comm.*, 7, 13441.

Heidbreder, C. A., and Newman, A. H. (2010). Current perspectives on selective dopamine D3 receptor antagonists as pharmacotherapeutics for addictions and related disorders. *Ann. N.Y. Acad. Sci.*, 1187, 4–34.

Heilig, M., and Koob, G. F. (2007). A key role for corticotropin-releasing factor in alcohol dependence. *Trends Neurosci.*, 30, 399–406.

Heilig, M., MacKillop, J., Martinez, D., Rehm, J., Leggio, L., and Vanderschuren, L.J.M.J. (2021). Addiction as a brain disease revised: why it still matters, and the need for consilience. *Neuropsychopharmacology*, 46, 1715–1723.

Heilig, M., Thorsell, A., Sommer, W. H., Hansson, A. C., Ramchandani, V. A., George, D. T., et al. (2010). Translating the neuroscience of alcoholism into clinical treatments: From blocking the buzz to curing the blues. *Neurosci. Biobehav. Rev.*, 35, 334–344.

Heinz, A., Reimold, M., Wrase, J., Hermann, D., Croissant, B., Mundle, G., et al. (2005). Correlation of stable elevations in striatal mu-opioid receptor availability in detoxified alcoholic patients with alcohol craving: A positron emission tomography study using carbon 11-labeled carfentanil. *Arch. Gen. Psychiatry*, 62, 57–64.

Heishman, S. J., Kleykamp, B. A., and Singleton, E. G. (2010). Meta-analysis of the acute effects of nicotine and smoking on human performance. *Psychopharmacology*, 210, 453–469.

Heisler, L. K., Chu, H.-M., Brennan, T. J., Danao, J. A., Bajwa, P., Parsons, L. H., et al. (1998). Elevated anxiety and antidepressant-like responses in serotonin 5-HT1A receptor mutant mice. *Proc. Natl. Acad. Sci. USA*, 95, 15049–15054.

Heisler, L. K., Zhou, L., Bajwa, P., Hsu, J., and Tecott, L. H. (2007). Serotonin 5-HT2C receptors regulate anxiety-like behavior. *Genes Brain Behav.*, 6, 491–496.

Heldt, N. A., Reichenbach, N., McGary, H. M., and Persidsky, Y. (2020). Effects of electronic nicotine delivery systems and cigarettes on systemic circulation and blood-brain barrier. Implications for cognitive decline. *Am. J. Pathol.*, 191(2), 243–255.

Helton, D. R., Modlin, D. L., Tizzano, J. P., and Rasmussen, K. (1993). Nicotine withdrawal: A behavioral assessment using schedule controlled responding, locomotor activity, and sensorimotor reactivity. *Psychopharmacology*, 113, 205–210.

Hemby, S. E., McIntosh, S., Leon, F., Cutler, S. J., and McCurdy, C. R. (2019). Abuse liability and therapeutic potential of the *Mitragyna speciosa* (kratom) alkaloids mitragynine and 7-hydroxymitragynine. *Addict. Biol.*, 24(5), 874–885. https://doi.org/10.1111/adb.12639

Henckens, M. J., Klumpers, F., Everaerd, D., Kooijman, S. C., van Wingen, G. A., and Fernández, G. (2016). Interindividual differences in stress sensitivity: Basal and stress-induced cortisol levels differentially predict neural vigilance processing under stress. *Soc. Cogn. Affect. Neurosci.*, 11, 663–673.

Henden, E., Melberg, H. O., and Regberg, O. J. (2013). Addiction: Choice or compulsion? *Front. Psychiatry*, 4, 77. doi: 10.3389/fpsyt.2013.00077.

Hendershott, J. (1969). Steroids: Breakfast of Champions. Track and Field News, I April, 3.

Hendrickson, R. G., and Cloutier, R. L. (2007). "Crystal Dex": Free-base dextromethorphan. *J. Emerg. Med.*, 32, 393–396.

Henningfield, J. E., Smith, T. T., Kleykamp, B. A., Fant, R. V., and Donny, E. C. (2016). Nicotine self-administration research: the legacy of Steven R. Goldberg and implications for regulation, health policy, and research. *Psychopharmacology*, 233, 3829–3848.

Henry-Unaeze, H. N. (2017). Update on food safety of monosodium l-glutamate (MSG). *Pathophysiology*, 24, 243–249.

Heo, Y.-A., and Scott, L. J. (2017). Deutetrabenazine: A review in chorea associated with Huntington's disease. *Drugs*, 77, 1857–1864.

Hering-Hanit, R., and Gadoth, N. (2003). Caffeine-induced headache in children and adolescents. *Cephalagia*, 23, 332–335.

Herman, A. M., Ortiz-Guzman, J., Kochukov, M., Herman, I., Quast, K. B., Patel, J. M., et al. (2016). A cholinergic basal forebrain feeding circuit modulates appetite suppression. *Nature*, 538, 253–256.

Hernandez, C. C., and Macdonald, R. L. (2019). A structural look at GABA$_A$ receptor mutations linked to epilepsy syndromes. *Brain Res.*, 1714, 234–247.

Hernández-Alvarado, R. B., Madariaga-Mazón, A., Ortega, A., and Martinez-Mayorga, K. (2020). DARK classics in chemical neuroscience: Salvinorin A. *ACS Chem. Neurosci.*, 11, 3979–3992.

Hernandez-Lopez, S., Garduño, J., and Mihailescu, S. (2013). Nicotinic modulation of serotonergic activity in the dorsal raphe nucleus. *Rev. Neurosci.*, 24, 455–469.

Herring, B. E., and Nicoll, R. A. (2016). Long-term potentiation from CaMKII to AMPA receptor trafficking. *Annu. Rev. Physiol.*, 78, 351–365.

Hertel, P., Mathé, J. M., Nomikos, G. G., Iurlo, M., Mathé, LA.A., and Svensson, T. H. (1995). Effects of D-amphetamine and phencyclidine on behavior and extracellular concentrations of neurotensin and dopamine in the ventral striatum and the medial prefrontal cortex of the rat. *Behav. Brain Res.*, 72, 103–114.

Herz, A. (1997). Endogenous opioid systems and alcohol addiction. *Psychopharmacology*, 129, 99–111.

Het, S., Schoofs, D., Rohleder, N., and Wolf, O. T. (2012). Stress-induced cortisol level elevations are associated with reduced negative affect after stress: Indications for a mood-buffering cortisol effect. *Psychosomatic Med.*, 74, 23–32.

Heyman, G. M. (2013). Addiction and choice: Theory and new data. *Front. Psychiatry*, 4, 31. doi: 10.3389/ fpsyt.2013.00031.

Heyman, G. M. (2021). How individuals make choices explains addiction's distinctive non-eliminable features. *Behav. Brain Res.*, 397, 112899. doi: 10.1016/j.bbr.2020.112899.

Hidese, S., Hattori, K., Sasayama, D., Tsumagari, T., Miyakawa, T., Matsumura, R., Yokota, Y., et al. (2021). Cerebrospinal fluid inflammatory cytokine levels in patients with major psychiatric disorders: A multiplex immunoassay study. *Front. Pharmacol.*, 11. https://doi.org/10.3389/ fphar.2020.594394

Higgins, S. T., Bickel, W. K., and Hughes, J. R. (1994). Influence of an alternative reinforcer on human cocaine self-administration. *Life Sci.*, 55, 179–197.

Higgins, S. T., Delaney, D. D., Budney, A. J., Bickel, W. K., Hughes, J. R., Foerg, F., et al. (1991). A behavioral approach to achieving initial cocaine abstinence. *Am. J. Psychiatry*, 148, 1218–1224.

Higgins, S., Straight, C. R., and Lewis, R. D. (2016). The effects of preexercise caffeinated coffee ingestion on endurance performance: An evidence-based review. *Int. J. Sport Nutr. Exerc. Metab.*, 26, 221–239.

Hilbert, K., Lueken, U., and Beesdo-Baum, K. (2014). Neural structures, functioning and connectivity in Generalized Anxiety Disorder and interaction with neuroendocrine systems: A systematic review. *J. Affect. Dis.*, 158, 114–126.

Hildebrand, B. E., Nomikos, G. G., Bondjers, C., Nisell, M., and Svensson, T. H. (1997). Behavioral manifestations of the nicotine abstinence syndrome in the rat: Peripheral versus central mechanisms. *Psychopharmacology*, 129, 348–356.

Hill, M. N., Campolongo, P., Yehuda, R., and Patel, S. (2018). Integrating endocannabinoid signaling and cannabinoids into the biology and treatment of posttraumatic stress disorder. *Neuropsychopharmacology*, 43, 80–102.

Hilt, S., Altman, R., Kalai, T., Maezawa, I., Gong, Q., Wachsmann-Hogiu, S., Jin, L-W., and Voss, J. C. (2018). A bifunctional anti-amyloid blocks oxidative stress and the accumulation of intraneuronal amyloid-beta. *Molecules*, 23, 2010, 1–22.

Himmelsbach, C. K. (1943). Can the euphoric, analgesic and physical dependence effects of drugs be separated? With reference to physical dependence. *Fed. Proc.*, 2, 201–203.

Hingson, R. W., and Zha, W. (2009). Age of drinking onset, alcohol use disorders, frequent heavy drinking, and unintentionally injuring oneself and others after drinking. *Pediatrics*, 123, 1477–1484.

Hingson, R. W., Zha, W., and Weitzman, E. R. (2009). Magnitude of and trends in alcohol-related mortality and morbidity among U.S. college students ages 18–24, 1998–2005. *J. Stud. Alcohol Drugs Suppl.*, 16, 12–20.

Hirose, S. (2014). Mutant GABA$_A$ receptor subunits in genetic (idiopathic) epilepsy. *Prog. Brain Res.*, 213, 55–85.

Hirrlinger, J., Marx, G., Besser, S., Sicker, M., Köhler, S., Hirrlinger, P. G., Wojcik, S. M., et al. (2019). GABA-glycine cotransmitting neurons in the ventrolateral medulla: Development and functional relevance for breathing. *Front. Cell. Neurosci.*, 13, 517. doi: 10.3389/fncel.2019.00517.

Hirsiger, S., Hänggi, J., Germann, J., Vonmoos, M., Preller, K. H., Engeli, E.J.E., Kirschner, M., et al. (2019). Longitudinal changes in cocaine intake and cognition are linked to cortical thickness adaptations in cocaine users. *Neuroimage Clin.*, 21, 101652. doi: 10.1016/j.nicl.2019.101652.

Hirvonen, J., Goodwin, R. S., Li, C.-T., Terry, G. E., Zoghbi, S. S., Morse, C., et al. (2012). Reversible and regionally selective downregulation of brain cannabinoid CB_1 receptors in chronic daily cannabis smokers. *Mol. Psychiatry*, 17, 642–649.

Hitti F.L., Yang A.I., Cristancho M.A., Baltuch G.H. (2020) Deep brain stimulation is effective for treatment-resistant depression: A meta-analysis and meta-regression. *J. Clin. Med.*, 9(9), 2796

Hobbs, W. R., Rall, T. W., and Verdoorn, T. A. (1996). Hypnotics and sedatives: Ethanol. In A. G. Gilman, L. S. Goodman, J. G. Hardman, L. E. Limbird, P. B. Molinoff, and R. W. Rudon (Eds.), *The Pharmacological Basis of Therapeutics*, pp. 361–396. New York: McGraw-Hill.

Hodges, H., Fealko, C., and Soares, N. (2020). Autism spectrum disorder: definition, epidemiology, causes, and clinical evaluation. *Transl. Pediatr.*, 9(Suppl. 1), S55-S65.

Hodges, M. R., and Richerson, G. B. (2010). The role of medullary serotonin (5-HT) neurons in respiratory control: Contributions to eupneic ventilation, CO_2 chemoreception, and thermoregulation. *J. Appl. Physiol.*, 108, 1425–1432.

Hodges, M. R., Wehner, M., Aungst, J., Smith, J. C., and Richerson, G. B. (2009). Transgenic mice lacking serotonin neurons have severe apnea and high mortality during development. *J. Neurosci.*, 29, 10341–10349.

Hodgins, D. C., and Stea, J. N. (2018). Insights from individuals successfully recovered from cannabis use disorder: natural versus treatment-assisted recoveries and abstinent versus moderation outcomes. *Addict. Sci. Clin. Pract.*, 13(1), 16. doi: 10.1186/s13722-018-0118-0.

Hofer, S. B. (2010). Structural traces of past experience in the cerebral cortex. *J. Mol. Med.* (Berl.), 88, 235–239.

Hogg, R. C. (2016). Contribution of monoamine oxidase inhibition to tobacco dependence: A review of the evidence. *Nicotine Tob. Res.*, 18, 509–523.

Hökfelt T., Barde S., Xu Z.D., Kuteeva E., Rüegg J., Le Maitre E., et al. (2018) Neuropeptide and small transmitter coexistence: fundamental studies and relevance to mental illness. *Front. Neural Circuits*, 12, 106.

Hökfelt, T., Barde, S., Xu, Z-Q. D., Kuteeva, E., Rüegg, J., Le Maitre, E., et al. (2018). Neuropeptide and small transmitter coexistence: Fundamental studies and relevance to mental illness. *Front. Neural Circuits*, 12, 106. doi: 10.3389/fncir.2018.00106.

Holden C. (2001). 'Behavioral' addictions: do they exist? *Science*, 294, 980–982.

Holderith, N., Németh, B., Papp, O. I., Veres, J. M., Nagy, G. A., and Hájos, N. (2011). Cannabinoids attenuate hippocampal gamma oscillations by suppressing excitatory synaptic input onto CA3 pyramidal neurons and fast spiking basket cells. *J. Physiol.*, 589, 4921– 4934.

Holliday, E., and Gould, T. J. (2016). Nicotine, adolescence, and stress: A review of how stress can modulate the negative consequences of adolescent nicotine abuse. *Neurosci. Biobehav. Rev.*, 65, 173–184.

Hollinger, M. A. (1995). The criminalization of drug use in the United States. *Res. Commun. Alcohol Subst. Abuse*, 16, 1–23.

Hollinger, M. A. (2008). Animals in research. In *Introduction to Pharmacology* (3rd ed.), pp. 333–353. New York: CRC Press.

Holmes, A., Lachowicz, J. E., and Sibley, D. R. (2004). Phenotypic analysis of dopamine receptor knockout mice; recent insights into the functional specificity of dopamine receptor subtypes. *Neuropharmacology*, 47, 1117–1134.

Holmes, A., Murphy, D. L., and Crawley, J. N. (2002). Reduced aggression in mice lacking the serotonin transporter. *Psychopharmacology*, 161, 160–167.

Holsboer F., Ising M. (2008) Central CRH system in depression and anxiety--evidence from clinical studies with CRH1 receptor antagonists. *Eur. J. Pharmacol.*, 583(2–3), 35–57.

Holtmaat, A., and Svoboda, K. (2009). Experience-dependent structural synaptic plasticity in the mammalian brain. *Nat. Rev. Neurosci.*, 10, 647–658.

Homan, P., Neumeister, A., Nugent, A. C., Charney, D. S., Drevets, W. C., and Hasler, G. (2015). Serotonin versus catecholamine deficiency: behavioral and neural effects of experimental depletion in remitted depression. *Transl. Psychiatry*, 5, e532. doi:10.1038/tp.2015.25.

Hong, C. T., Chan, L., and Bai, C.-H. (2020). The effect of caffeine on the risk and progression of Parkinson's disease: A meta-analysis. *Nutrients*, 12, 1860. doi: 10.3390/nu12061860.

Hood, R. W. Jr. (1975). The construction and preliminary validation of a measure of reported mystical experience. *J. Scient. Study Religion*, 14, 29–41.

Hooper, M. (2015). Hyperbaric Oxygenation Impacts Stroke and Other Traumatic Brain Disorders. OxyMed Australia. Available at www.linkedin.com/pulse/hyperbaric-oxygenation-impacts-stroke-othertraumatic-mal-hooper/.

Hopf, F. W. (2020). Recent perspectives on orexin/hypocretin promotion of addiction-related behaviors. *Neuropharmacology*, 168, epub ahead of print.

Hoque, A., Hossain, M. I., Ameen, S. S., Ang, C.-S., Williamson, N., Ng, D. C. H., et al. (2016). A beacon of hope in stroke therapy: Blockade of pathologically activated cellular events in excitotoxic neuronal death as potential neuroprotective strategies. *Pharmacol. Ther.*, 160, 159–179.

Horne, R.S.C. (2019). Sudden infant death syndrome: current perspectives. *Int. Med. J.*, 49, 433–438.

Hornung, J.-P., and De Tribolet, N. (1994). Distribution of GABA-containing neurons in human frontal cortex: a quantitative immunocytochemical study. *Anat. Embryol.*, 189, 139–145.

Hoskin, J. L., Al-Hasan, Y., and Sabbagh, M. N. (2019). Nicotinic acetylcholine receptor agonists for the treatment of Alzheimer's dementia: An update. *Nicotine Tob. Res.*, 21, 370–376.

Houston, S. M., Herting, M. M., and Sowell, E. R. (2014). The neurobiology of childhood structural brain development: Conception through adulthood. *Curr. Top. Behav. Neurosci.*, 16, 3–17.

Howard, M. O., and Garland, E. L. (2013). Volatile substance misuse: Toward a research agenda. *Am. J. Drug Alcohol Abuse*, 39, 3–7.

Howard, M. O., Bowen, S. E., Garland, E. L., Perron, B. E., and Vaughn, M. G. (2011). Inhalant use and inhalant use disorders in the United States. *Addict. Sci. Clin. Pract.*, 6, 18–31.

Howard, R., Castle, D., Wessely, S., and Murray, R. (1993). A comparative study of 470 cases of early-onset and late-onset schizophrenia. *Br. J. Psychiatry*, 163, 352–357.

Howarth, C. (2014). The contribution of astrocytes to the regulation of cerebral blood flow. *Front. Neurosci.*, 8, Article 103, 1–9.

Howe, M. W., and Dombeck, D. A. (2016). Rapid signalling in distinct dopaminergic axons during locomotion and reward. *Nature*, 535, 505–510.

Howes, O. D., McCutcheon, R., Owen, M. J., and Murray, R. M. (2017). The role of genes, stress, and dopamine in the development of schizophrenia. *Biol. Psychiatry*, 81, 9–20.

Howlett, A. C. (2005). Cannabinoid receptor signaling. *Handb. Exp. Pharmacol.*, 168, 53–79.

Howlett, A. C., and Abood, M. E. (2017). CB_1 and CB_2 receptor pharmacology. *Adv. Pharmacol.*, 80, 169–206.

Hoyle, E., Genn, R. F., Fernandes, C., and Stolerman, I. P. (2006). Impaired performance of alpha7 nicotinic receptor knockout mice in the five-choice serial reaction time task. *Psychopharmacology*, 189, 211–223.

HRB National Drugs Library. (2017). Alcohol: The Irish situation. Dublin: Health Research Board National Drugs Library. Available at www.drugsandalcohol.ie/24954.

Hsu, G., Sun, J. Y., and Zhu, S.-H. (2018). Evolution of electronic cigarette brands from 2013–2014 to 2016–2017, Analysis of brand websites. *J. Med. Internet Res.*, 20(3), e80. doi: 10.2196/jmir.8550.

Hu, S. S.-J., and Mackie, K. (2015). Distribution of the endocannabinoid system in the central nervous system. *Handb. Exp. Pharmacol.*, 231, 59–93.

Hu, X., Primack, B. A., Barnett, T. E., and Cook, R. L. (2011). College students and use of K2, An emerging drug of abuse in young persons. *Subst. Abuse Treat. Prev. Policy*, 6, 16. doi: 10.1186/1747–597X-6–16.

Huang, F., Tang, B., and Jiang, H. (2013). Optogenetic investigation of neuropsychiatric diseases. *Int. J. Neurosci.*, 123, 7–16.

Huang, G., and Basaria, S. (2018). Do anabolic-androgenic steroids have performance-enhancing effects in female athletes? *Mol. Cell. Endocrinol.*, 464, 56–64.

Huang, J., Duan, Z., Kwok, J., Binns, S., Vera, L. E., Kim, Y., Szczypka, G., et al. (2019). Vaping versus JUULing: How the extraordinary growth and marketing of JUUL transformed the US retail e-cigarette market. *Tob. Control*, 28, 146–151.

Huang, K. W., Ochandarena, N. E., Philson, A. C., Hyun, M., Birnbaum, J. E., Cicconet, M., and Sabatini, B. L. (2019). Molecular and anatomical organization of the dorsal raphe nucleus. *eLife*, 8, e46464. doi: 10.7554/eLife.46464.

Huang, Z.-L., Qu, W.-M., Eguchi, N., Chen, J.-F., Schwarzschild, M. A., Fredholm, B. B., et al. (2005). Adenosine A2A, but not A1A, receptors mediate arousal effect of caffeine. *Nat. Neurosci.*, 8, 858–859.

Huberfeld, G., Wittner, L., Clemenceau, S., Baulac, M., Kaila, K., Miles, R., et al. (2007). Perturbed chloride homeostasis and GABAergic signaling in human temporal lobe epilepsy. *J. Neurosci.*, 27, 9866–9873.

Huestis, M. A., Boyd, S. J., Heishman, S. J., Preston, K. L., Bonnet, D., Le Fur, G., et al. (2007). Single and multiple doses of rimonabant antagonize acute effects of smoked cannabis in male cannabis users. *Psychopharmacology*, 194, 505–515.

Huestis, M. A., Gorelick, D. A., Heishman, S. J., Preston, K. L., Nelson, R. A., Moolchan, E. T., et al. (2001). Blockade of effects of smoked marijuana by the CB_1-selective cannabinoid receptor antagonist SR141716. *Arch. Gen. Psychiatry*, 58, 322–328.

Hughes, J. (1975). Search for the endogenous ligand of the opiate receptor. *Neurosci. Res. Prog. Bull.*, 13, 55–58.

Hughes, J. R., Fingar, J. R., Budney, A. J., Naud, S., Helzer, J. E., and Callas, P. W. (2014). Marijuana use and intoxication among daily users: An intensive longitudinal study. *Addict. Behav.*, 39, 1464–1470.

Hughes, J. R., Gust, S. W., Skoog, K., Keenan, R. M., and Fenwick, J. W. (1991). Symptoms of tobacco withdrawal: A replication and extension. *Arch. Gen. Psychiatry*, 48, 52–59.

Hulsken, S., Märtin, A., Mohajeri, M. H., and Homberg, J. R. (2013). Food-derived serotonergic modulators: Effects on mood and cognition. *Nutr. Res. Rev.*, 26, 223–234.

Humphreys, K. (2015). Addiction treatment professionals are not the gate-keepers of recovery. *Subst. Use Misuse*, 50, 1024–1027.

Humphreys, K. (2020). Will hope triumph over experience in pharmacotherapy research on cocaine use disorder? *Addiction*, 116(4), 712-714.

Hung, C. J., Wu, C. C., Chen, W. Y., Chang, C. Y., Kuan, Y. H., Pan, H. C., et al. (2013). Depression-like effect of prenatal buprenorphine exposure in rats. *PLOS ONE*, 8, e82262. doi: 10.1371/journal.pone.0082262. eCollection 2013.

Hung, C.-C., Liu, Y.-H., Huang, C.-C., Chou, C.-Y., Chen, C.-M., Duann, J.-R., Li, C.-S. R., et al. (2020). Effects of early ketamine exposure on cerebral gray matter volume and functional connectivity. *Sci. Rep.*, 10, 15488. doi: 10.1038/s41598-020-72320-z.

Hunt, G. M., and Azrin, N. H. (1973). A community-reinforcement approach to alcoholism. *Behav. Res. Ther.*, 11, 91–104.

Hurd, Y. L., Yoon, M., Manini, A. F., Hernandez, S., Olmedo, R., Ostman, M., et al. (2015). Early phase in the development of cannabidiol as a treatment for addiction: Opioid relapse takes initial center stage. *Neurotherapeutics*, 12, 807–815.

Hurd, Y. L., Manzoni, O. J., Pletnikov, M. V., Lee, F. S., Bhattacharyya, S., and Melis, M. (2019). Cannabis and the developing brain: Insights into its long-lasting effects. *J. Neurosci.*, 39, 8250–8258.

Hussain, A., Tabrez, E. S., Mavrych, V., Bolgova, O., and Peela, J. R. (2018). Caffeine: A potential protective agent against cognitive decline in Alzheimer's disease.

Crit. Rev. Eukaryot. Gene Exp., 28, 67–72.

Huynh, C., Fam, J., Ahmed, S. H., and Clemens, K. J. (2016). Rats quit nicotine for a sweet reward following an extensive history of nicotine use. *Addict. Biol.*, 22, 142–151.

Hydrocephalus Fact Sheet | National Institute of Neurological Disorders and Stroke. (n.d.). Retrieved March 22, 2021, from https://www.ninds.nih.gov/Disorders/Patient-Caregiver-Education/Fact-Sheets/Hydrocephalus-Fact-Sheet.

I

Ibrahim, S., Habiballah, M., and El Sayed, I. (2020). Efficacy of electronic cigarettes for smoking cessation: A systematic review and meta-analysis. *Am. J. Health Promot.*, 35(3), 442–455.

Ikonomidou, C., Bittigau, P., Ishimaru, M., Wozniak, D., Koch, C., Genz, K., et al. (2000). Ethanol-induced apoptotic neurodegeneration and fetal alcohol syndrome. *Science*, 287, 1056–1060.

Ilango, A., Kesner, A. J., Broker, C. J., Wang, D. V., and Ikemoto, S. (2014). Phasic excitation of ventral tegmental dopamine neurons potentiates the initiation of conditioned approach behavior: Parametric and reinforcement-schedule analyses. *Front. Behav. Neurosci.*, 8, 155. doi: 10.3389/fnbeh.2014.00155.

Inada, T., Polk, K., Purser, C., Hume, A., Hoskins, B., Ho, I. K., et al. (1992). Behavioral and neurochemical effects of continuous infusion of cocaine in rats. *Neuropharmacology*, 31, 701–708.

Insel, N., and Takehara-Nishiuchi, K. (2013). The cortical structure of consolidated memory: A hypothesis on the role of the cingulate-entorhinal cortical connection. *Neurobiol. Learn. Mem.*, 106, 343–350.

Inturrisi, C. E. (1997). Preclinical evidence for a role of glutamatergic systems in opioid tolerance and dependence. *Semin. Neurosci.*, 9, 110–119.

Ip, E. J., Barnett, M. J., Tenerowicz, M. J., and Perry, P. J. (2011). The anabolic 500 survey: Characteristics of male users versus non-users of anabolic–androgenic steroids for strength training. *Pharmacotherapy*, 31, 757–766.

Irwin, C., Khalesi, S., Desbrow, B., and McCartney, D. (2020). Effects of acute caffeine consumption following sleep loss on cognitive, physical, and occupational and driving performance: A systematic review and meta-analysis. *Neurosci. Biobehav. Rev.*, 108, 877–888.

Irwin, S. A., Galvez, R., and Greenough, W. T. (2000). Dendritic spine structural anomalies in fragile-X mental retardation syndrome. *Cereb. Cortex*, 10, 1038–1044.

Iseger, T. A., and Bossong, M. G. (2015). A systematic review of the antipsychotic properties of cannabidiol in humans. *Schizophr. Res.*, 182, 153–161.

Ishizuka, T., Murotani, T., and Yamatodani, A. (2012). Action of modafinil through histaminergic and orexinergic neurons. *Vit. Horm.*, 89, 259–278.

Islam, F., Men, X., Yoshida, K., Zai, C. C., and Müller, D. J. (2021). Pharmacogenetics-guided advances in antipsychotic treatment. *Clinical Pharmacology and Therapeutics*. https://doi.org/10.1002/cpt.2339

Itzhak, Y., and Ali, S. F. (2002). Repeated administration of gamma-hydroxybutyric acid (GHB) to mice: Assessment of the sedative and rewarding effects of GHB. *Ann. N. Y. Acad. Sci.*, 965, 451–460. © 2002 New York Academy of Sciences.

Ivarsson, T., Skarphedinsson, G., Kornør, H., Axelsdottir, B., Biedilæ, S., Heyman, I., et al. (2015). The place of and evidence for serotonin reuptake inhibitors (SRIs) for obsessive compulsive disorder (OCD) in children and adolescents: Views based on a systematic review and meta-analysis. *Psychiatr. Res.*, 227, 93–103.

Iversen, L. L. (2000). *The Science of Marijuana*. New York: Oxford University Press.

Iversen, L. L. (2003). Cannabis and the brain. *Brain*, 126, 1252–1270.

J

Jaboinski, J., Cabral, J. C., Campos, R., and Barros, D. M. (2015). Exposure to methylphenidate during infancy and adolescence in non-human animals and sensitization to abuse of psychostimulants later in life: A systematic review. *Trends Psychiatry Psychother.*, 37, 107–117.

Jackson, N. J., Isen, J. D., Khoddam, R., Irons, D., Tuvblad, C., Iacono, W. G., et al. (2016). Impact of adolescent marijuana use on intelligence: Results from two longitudinal twin studies. *Proc. Natl. Acad. Sci. USA*, 113, E500–E508.

Jacobs, B. L., and Fornal, C. A. (1999). Activity of serotonergic neurons in behaving animals. *Neuropsychopharmacology*, 21 (Suppl. 2), 9S–15S.

Jacobs, I. G., Roszler, M. H., Kelly, J. K., Klein, M. A., and Kling, G. A. (1989). Cocaine abuse: Neurovascular complications. *Radiology*, 170, 223–227.

Jacobus, J., and Tapert, S. F. (2014). Effects of cannabis on the adolescent brain. *Curr. Pharm. Des.*, 20, 2186–2193.

Jacobus, J., Bava, S., Cohen-Zion, M., Mahmood, O., and Tapert, S. F. (2009). Functional consequences of marijuana use in adolescents. *Pharmacol. Biochem. Behav.*, 92, 559–565.

Jager, G., and Witkamp, R. F. (2014). The endocannabinoid system and appetite: Relevance for food reward. *Nutr. Res. Rev.*, 27, 172–185.

Jalil, S. J., Sacktor, T. C., and Shouval, H. Z. (2015). Atypical PKCs in memory maintenance: The roles of feedback and redundancy. *Learn. Mem.*, 22, 344–353.

Jamain, S., Radyushkin, K., Hammerschmidt, K., Granon, S., Boretius, S., Varoqueaux, F., et al. (2008). Reduced social interaction and ultrasonic communication in a mouse model of monogenic heritable autism. *Proc. Natl. Acad. Sci. USA*, 105, 1710–1715.

Jamal, A., Gentzke, A., Hu, S. S., Cullen, K. A., Apelberg, B. J., Homa, D. M., and King, D. A. (2017). Tobacco use among middle and high school students—United States, 2011–2016. Morbidity and Mortality Weekly Report (MMWR)., 66. Available at https://www.cdc.gov/ mmwr/volumes/66/wr/mm6623a1. htm.

James, J. E. (2014). Caffeine and cognitive performance: Persistent methodological challenges in caffeine research. *Pharmacol. Biochem. Behav.*, 124, 117–122.

James, J. E. (2020). Maternal caffeine consumption and pregnancy outcomes: a narrative review with implications for advice to mothers and mothers-to-be. *BMJ Evid. Based Med.*, in press.

Jamison, R. N., and Mao, J. (2015). Opioid analgesics. *Mayo Clin. Proc.*, 90, 957–968.

Jamshed, L., Perono, G. A., Jamshed, S., and Holloway, A. C. (2020). Early life exposure to nicotine: Postnatal metabolic, neurobehavioral and respiratory outcomes and the development of childhood cancers. *Toxicol. Sci.*, 178, 3–15.

Janhunen, S. K., Svärd, H., Talpos, J., Kumar, G., Steckler, T., Plath, N., et al. (2015). The subchronic phencyclidine rat model: Relevance for the assessment of novel therapeutics for cognitive impairment associated with schizophrenia. *Psychopharmacology*, 232, 4059–4083.

Jansen, K. L. R. (2000). A review of the nonmedical use of ketamine: Use, users and consequences. *J. Psychoactive Drugs*, 32, 419–433.

Jansen, K. L. R. (2001). *Ketamine: Dreams and Realities*. Sarasota, FL: Multidisciplinary Association for Psychedelic Studies.

Jansen, K. L. R., and Darracot-Cankovic, R. (2001). The nonmedical use of ketamine, part two: A review of problem use and dependence. *J. Psychoactive Drugs*, 33, 151–158.

Jansson, L. M., Velez, M., and Harrow, C. (2009). The opioid exposed newborn: Assessment and pharmacologic management. *J. Opioid Manag.*, 5(1), 47–55.

Jaques, S. C., Kingsbury, A., Henshcke, P., Chomchai, C., Clews, S., Falconer, J., et al. (2014). Cannabis, the pregnant woman and her child: Weeding out the myths. *J. Perinatol.*, 34, 417–424.

Järbe, T. U. C., and Raghav, J. G. (2017). Tripping with synthetic cannabinoids ("Spice"): Anecdotal and experimental observations in animals and man. *Curr. Topics Behav. Neurosci.*, 32, 263–281.

Järbe, T. U. C., Gifford, R. S., Zvonok, A., and Makriyannis, A. (2016). Δ⁹-Tetrahydrocannabinol discriminative stimulus effects of AM2201 and related aminoalkylindole analogues in rats. *Behav. Pharmacol.*, 27, 211–214. © 2016 Wolters Kluwer Health, Inc. All rights reserved. doi.org/10.1097/FBP.0000000000000196

Jasinska, A. J., Stein, E. A., Kaiser, J., Naumer, M. J., and Yalachkov, Y. (2014). Factors modulating neural reactivity to drug cues in addiction: A survey of human neuroimaging studies. *Neurosci. Biobehav. Rev.*, 38, 1–16.

Jasinska, A. J., Zorick, T., Brody, A. L., and Stein, E. A. (2014). Dual role of nicotine in addiction and cognition: A review of neuroimaging studies in humans. *Neuropharmacology*, 84, 111–122.

Jastrzebska-Wiesek, M., Siwek, A., Partyka, A., Kubacka, M., Mogilski, S., Wasik, A., et al. (2014). Pharmacological evaluation of the anxiolytic-like effects of EMD 386088, a partial 5-HT6 receptor agonist, in the rat elevated plus-maze and Vogel conflict tests. *Neuropharmacology*, 85, 253–262.

Jastrzembski, B., Locke, J., and Wan, M. J. (2020). Clinical implications and cost of electroretinography screening for vigabatrin toxicity. *Can. J. Ophthalmol.*, 55, e98-e100.

Jedema, H. P., Song, X., Aizenstein, H. J., Bonner, A. R., Stein, E. A., Yang, Y., and Bradberry, C. W. (2021). Long-term cocaine self-administration produces structural brain changes that correlate with altered cognition. *Biol. Psychiatry*, 89(4), 376–385.

Jellinek, E. M. (1960). *The Disease Concept of Alcoholism*. New Haven, CT: Hillhouse.

Jembrek, M. J., and Vlainic´, J. (2015). GABA receptors: Pharmacological potential and pitfalls. *Curr. Pharm. Des.*, 21, 4943– 4959.

Jensen, K. P. (2016). A review of genomewide association studies of stimulant and opioid use disorders. *Mol. Neuropsychiatry*, 2, 37–45.

Jensen, K. P., DeVito, E., Heman, A. I., Valentine, G. W., Gelernter, J., and Sofuoglu, M. (2015). A CHRNA5 smoking risk variant decreases the aversive effects of nicotine in humans.

Neuropsychopharmacology, 40, 2813–2821.

Jensen, T. S., and Finnerup, N. B. (2014). Allodynia and hyperalgesia in neuropathic pain: Clinical manifestations and mechanisms. *Lancet Neurol.*, 13, 924–935.

Jeppesen, R., Christensen, R.H.B., Pedersen, E.M.J., Nordentoft, M., Hjorthøj, C., Köhler-Forsberg, O., and Benros, M. E. (2020). Efficacy and safety of anti-inflammatory agents in treatment of psychotic disorders—A comprehensive systematic review and meta-analysis. *Brain Behav. Immun.*, 90, 364–380. https://doi.org/10.1016/j.bbi.2020.08.028

Jerome, L., Feduccia, A. A., Wang, J. B., Hamilton, S., Yazar-Klosinski, B., Emerson, A., Mithoefer, M. C., et al. (2020). Long-term follow-up outcomes of MDMA-assisted psychotherapy for treatment of PTSD: A longitudinal pooled analysis of six phase 2 trials. *Psychopharmacology*, in press.

Jeschke, P., and Nauen, R. (2008). Neonicotinoids—From zero to hero in insecticide chemistry. *Pest Manag. Sci.*, 64, 1084–1098.

Jeste, S. S., and Geschwind, D. H. (2016). Clinical trials for neurodevelopmental disorders: At a therapeutic frontier. *Sci. Transl. Med.*, 8, 321fs1. doi: 10.1126/scitranslmed.aad9874.

Jhanjee, S. (2014). Evidence based psychosocial interventions in substance use. *Indian J. Psychol. Med.*, 36,112–118. doi: 10.4103/0253-7176.130960.

Ji, C. (2014). New insights into the pathogenesis of alcohol-induced ER stress and liver diseases. *Int. J. Hepatol.*, 2014, 513787. doi: 10.1155/2014/513787.

Jin, F., and Qiao, C. (2021). Association of maternal caffeine intake during pregnancy with low birth weight, childhood overweight, and obesity: a meta-analysis of cohort studies. *Int. J. Obes.*, 45, 279–287.

Joehanes, R., Just, A. C., Marioni, R. E., Pilling, L. C., Reynolds, L. M., Mandaviya, P. R., et al. (2016). Epigenetic signatures of cigarette smoking. *Circ. Cardiovasc. Genet.*, 9, 436–447.

Joels, M. (2011). Impact of glucocorticoids on brain function: Relevance for mood disorders. *Psychoneuroendocrinology*, 36, 406–414.

Joels, M., Fernandez, G., and Roozendaal, B. (2011). Stress and emotional memory: A matter of timing. *Trends Cogn. Sci.*, 15, 280–288.

Joëls, M., Pasricha, N., and Karst, H. (2013). The interplay between rapid and slow corticosteroid actions in brain. *Eur. J. Pharmacol.*, 719, 44–52.

Johansson, A., Lindstedt, D., Roman, M., Thelander, G., Nielsen, E. I., Lennborn, U., Sandler, H., et al. (2017). A non-fatal

intoxication and seven deaths involving the dissociative drug 3-MeO-PCP. *Forensic Sci. Int.*, 275, 76–82.

Johnson & Johnson. (2011). Pediatric OCD (Obsessive-Compulsive Disorder). Available at www.youtube.com/watch?v=3lvbcShuz14.

Johnson, J. W., and Kotermanski, S. E. (2006). Mechanism of action of memantine. *Curr. Opin. Pharmacol.*, 6, 61–67.

Johnson, J. W., Glasgow, N. G., and Povysheva, N. V. (2015). Recent insights into the mode of action of memantine and ketamine. *Curr. Opin. Pharmacol.*, 20, 54–63.

Johnson, M. W., and Griffiths, R. R. (2013). Comparative abuse liability of GHB and ethanol in humans. *Exp. Clin. Psychopharmacol.*, 21, 112–123.

Johnson, M. W., MacLean, K. A., Reissig, C. J., Prisinzano, T. E., and Griffiths, R. R. (2011). Human psychopharmacology and dose-effects of salvinorin A, a kappa opioid agonist hallucinogen present in the plant Salvia divinorum. *Drug Alcohol Depend.*, 115, 150–155.

Johnson, M. W., Griffiths, R. R., Hendricks, P. S., and Henningfield, J. E. (2018). The abuse potential of medical psilocybin according to the 8 factors of the Controlled Substances Act. *Neuropharmacology*, 142, 143–166.

Johnston, L. D., O'Malley, P. M., Miech, R. A., Bachman, J. G., and Schulenberg, J. E. (2016). *Monitoring the Future, National Survey Results on Drug Use: 1975–2014, Overview, Key Findings on Adolescent Drug Use*. Ann Arbor: Institute for Social Research, University of Michigan.

Johnstone, W. M. 3rd, Honeycutt, J. L., Deck, C. A., and Borski, R. J. (2019). Nongenomic glucocorticoid effects and their mechanisms of action in vertebrates. *Int. Rev. Cell. Mol. Biol.*, 346, 51–96.

Jokanović, M. (2018). Neurotoxic effects of organophosphorus pesticides and possible association with neurodegenerative diseases in man: A review. *Toxicology*, 410, 125–131.

Jonas, D. E., Amick, H. R., Feltner, C., Bobashev, G., Thomas, K., Wines, R., et al. (2014). Pharmacotherapy for Adults with Alcohol Use Disorders in Outpatient Settings. Comparative Effectiveness Review No. 134. AHRQ Publication No. 134-EHC029-EF. Rockville, MD: Agency for Healthcare Research and Quality. Available at www.ncbi.nlm.nih.gov/ books/NBK208590/.

Jones, I. W., and Wonnacott, S. (2004). Precise localization of α7 nicotinic acetylcholine receptors on glutamatergic axon terminals in the rat ventral tegmental area. *J. Neurosci.*, 24, 11244–11252.

Jones, J. D., and Comer, S. D. (2013). A review of human drug self-administration procedures. *Behav. Pharmacol.*, 24, 384–395.

Jones, N. A., Glyn, S. E., Akiyama, S., Hill, T. D., Hill, A. J., Weston, S. E., Burnett, M. D., et al. (2012). Cannabidiol exerts anti-convulsant effects in animal models of temporal lobe and partial seizures. *Seizure*, 21, 344–352.

Jones, N. A., Hill, A. J., Smith, I., Bevan, S. A., Williams, C. M., Whalley, B. J., et al. (2010). Cannabidiol displays antiepileptiform and antiseizure properties in vitro and in vivo. *J. Pharmacol. Exp. Ther.*, 332, 569–577.

Jones, R. T. (1990). The pharmacology of cocaine smoking in humans. *NIDA Res. Monogr.*, 99, 30–41.

Jones, R., Woods, C., and Usher, K. (2018). Rates and features of methamphetamine-related presentations to emergency departments: An integrative literature review. *J. Clin. Nurs.*, 27, 2569–2582.

Jongkees, B. J., Hommel, B., Kühn, S., and Colzato, L. S. (2015). Effect of tyrosine supplementation on clinical and healthy populations under stress or cognitive demands: A review. *J. Psychiatric Res.*, 70, 50–57.

Joshi, S., and Kapur, J. (2019). Neurosteroid regulation of GABA$_A$ receptors: A role in catamenial epilepsy. *Brain Res.*, 1703, 31–40.

Joyce, M. R., and Holton, K. F. (2020). Neurotoxicity in Gulf War Illness and the potential role of glutamate. *Neurotoxicology*, 80, 60–70.

Joyce, P. I., Fratta, P., Fisher, E. M., and Acevedo-Arozena, A. (2011). SOD1 and TDP-43 animal models of amyotrophic lateral sclerosis: Recent advances in understanding disease toward the development of clinical treatments. *Mamm. Genome*, 22, 420–448.

Juliano, L. M., and Griffiths, R. R. (2004). A critical review of caffeine withdrawal: Empirical validation of symptoms and signs, incidence, severity, and associated features. *Psychopharmacology*, 176, 1–29.

Jung, J. (2001). Psychology of Alcohol and Other Drugs: A Research Perspective. London: Sage.

Jung, K.-M., Lin, L., and Piomelli, D. (2021). The endocannabinoid system in the adipose organ. *Rev. Endocr. Metab. Disord.*, in press.

Jung, M. W., Baeg, E. H., Kim, M. J., Kim, Y. B., and Kim, J. J. (2008). Plasticity and memory in the prefrontal cortex. *Rev. Neurosci.*, 19, 29–46.

Jung-Klawitter, S., and Hübschmann, O. K. (2019). Analysis of catecholamines and pterins in inborn errors of monoamine neurotransmitter metabolism—From past to future. *Cells*, 8, 867. doi: 10.3390/cells8080867.

Jurado, S. (2014). The dendritic SNARE fusion machinery involved in AMPARs insertion during long-term potentiation. *Front. Cell. Neurosci.*, 8, 407. doi: 10.3389/fncel.2014.00407.

Justinová, Z., Munzar, P., Panlilio, L. V., Yasar, S., Redhi, G. H., Tanda, G., et al. (2008). Blockade of THC-seeking behavior and relapse in monkeys by the cannabinoid CB$_1$-receptor antagonist rimonabant. *Neuropsychopharmacology*, 33, 2870–2877.

Justinová, Z., Yasar, S., Redhi, G. H., and Goldberg, S. R. (2011). The endogenous cannabinoid 2-arachidonoylglycerol is intravenously self-administered by squirrel monkeys. *J. Neurosci.*, 31, 7043–7048.

K

Kaati, G., Bygren, L. O., Pembrey, M., and Sjöström, M. (2007). Transgenerational response to nutrition, early life circumstances and longevity. *Eur. J. Hum. Genet.*, 15, 784–790.

Kabbani, N. (2013). Not so cool? Menthol's discovered actions on the nicotinic receptor and its implications for nicotine addiction. *Front. Pharmacol.*, 4, 95. doi: 10.3389/fphar.2013.00095.

Käenmäki, M., Tammimäki, A., Myöhänen, T., Pakarinen, K., Amberg, C., Karayiorgou, M., Gogos, J. A., et al. (2010). Quantitative role of COMT in dopamine clearance in the prefrontal cortex of freely moving mice. *J. Neurochem.*, 114(6), 1745–1755. https://doi.org/10.1111/j.1471-4159.2010.06889.x.

Kahn, R. S., and Davis, K. L. (1995). New developments in dopamine and schizophrenia. In F. E. Bloom and D. J. Kupfer (Eds.), *Psychopharmacology: The Fourth Generation of Progress*, pp. 1193–1204. New York: Raven.

Kaidanovich-Beilin, O., Lipina, T., Vukobradovic, I., Roder, J., and Woodgett, J. R. (2011). Assessment of social interaction behaviors. *J. Vis. Exp.*, 48, e2473.

Kaila, K., Ruusuvuori, E., Seja, P., Voipio, J., and Puskarjov, M. (2014). GABA actions and ionic plasticity in epilepsy. *Curr. Opin. Neurobiol.*, 26, 34–41.

Kalakonda, B., Al-Maweri, S.-A., Al-Shamiri, H.-M., Iijaz, A., Gamal, S., and Dhaifullah, E. (2017). Is khat (Catha edulis) chewing a risk factor for periodontal diseases? A systematic review. *J. Clin. Exp. Dent.*, 9(10), e1264-e1270. doi: 10.4317/jced.54163.

Kalant, H. (2009). What neurobiology cannot tell us about addiction. *Addiction*, 105, 780–789.

Kalivas, B. C., and Kalivas, P. W. (2016). Corticostriatal circuitry in regulating diseases characterized by intrusive thinking. *Dialogues Clin. Neurosci.*, 18, 65–76.

Kalivas, P. W., and O'Brien, C. (2008). Drug addiction as a pathology of staged neuroplasticity. *Neuropsychopharmacology*, 33, 166–180.

Kalivas, P. W., Peters, J., and Knackstedt, L. (2006). Animal models and brain circuits in drug addiction. *Mol. Interv.*, 6, 339–344.

Kalman, D. (2002). The subjective effects of nicotine: Methodological issues, a review of experimental studies, and recommendations for future research. *Nicotine Tobacco Res.*, 4, 25–70.

Kalueff, A. V., Olivier, J.D.A., Nonkes, L.J.P., and Homberg, J. R. (2010). Conserved role for the serotonin transporter gene in rat and mouse neurobehavioral endophenotypes. *Neurosci. Biobehav. Rev.*, 373–386.

Kamal, R. M., van Noorden, M. S., Franzek, E., Dijkstra, B. A. G., Loonen, A. J. M., and De Jong, C. A. J. (2016). The neurobiological mechanisms of gamma-hydroxybutyrate dependence and withdrawal and their clinical relevance: A review. *Neuropsychobiology*, 73, 65–80.

Kampman, K. M. (2019). The treatment of cocaine use disorder. *Sci. Adv.*, 5(10), eaax1532. doi: 10.1126/sciadv.aax1532.

Kanayama, G., and Pope, H. G., Jr. (2018). History and epidemiology of anabolic androgens in athletes and non-athletes. *Mol. Cell. Endocrinol.*, 464, 4–13.

Kanayama, G., Brower, K. J., Wood, R. I., Hudson, J. I., and Pope, H. G., Jr. (2009). Anabolic–androgenic steroid dependence: An emerging disorder. *Addiction*, 104, 1966–1978.

Kanayama, G., Brower, K. J., Wood, R. I., Hudson, J. I., and Pope, H. G., Jr. (2010). Treatment of anabolic–androgenic steroid dependence: Emerging evidence and its implications. *Drug Alcohol Depend.*, 109, 6–13.

Kanayama, G., Hudson, J. I., and Pope, H. G., Jr. (2008). Long-term psychiatric and medical consequences of anabolic– androgenic steroid abuse: A looming public health concern? *Drug Alcohol Depend.*, 98, 1–12.

Kanayama, G., Hudson, J. I., DeLuca, J., Isaacs, S., Baggish, A., Weiner, R., Bhasin, S., et al. (2015). Prolonged hypogonadism in males following withdrawal from anabolic-androgenic steroids an under-recognized problem. *Addiction* ,110, 823–831.

Kandel, D., and Kandel, E. (2015). The gateway hypothesis of substance abuse: Developmental, biological and societal perspectives. *Acta Paed.*, 104, 130–137.

Kandel, E. R. (2000). Disorders of mood: Depression, mania, and anxiety disorders. In E. R. Kandel, J. H. Schwartz, and T. M. Jessell (Eds.), *Principles of Neural Science* (4th ed.), pp. 1209–1226. New York: McGraw-Hill.

Kane, M. J., Angoa-Pérez, M., Briggs, D. I., Sykes, C. E., Francescutti, D. M., Rosenberg, D. R., et al. (2012). Mice genetically depleted of brain serotonin display social impairments, communication deficits and repetitive behaviors: Possible relevance to autism. *PLOS ONE*, 7, e48975. doi: 10.1371/journal.pone.0048975.

Kaneda, K. (2019). Neuroplasticity in cholinergic neurons of the laterodorsal tegmental nucleus contributes to the development of cocaine addiction. *Eur. J. Neurosci.*, 50, 2239–2246.

Kaneyuki, H., Yokoo, H., Tsuda, A., Yoskida, M., Mizuki, Y., Yamada, M., et al. (1991). Psychological stress increases dopamine turnover selectively in mesoprefrontal dopamine neurons of rats: Reversal by diazepine. *Brain Res.*, 557, 154–161.

Kannan, G., Sawa, A., and Pletnikov, M. V. (2013). Mouse models of gene-environment interactions in schizophrenia. *Neurobiol. Dis.*, 57, 5–11.

Kanny, D., Brewer, R. D., Mesnick, J. B., Paulozzi, L. J., Naimi, T. S., and Lu, H. (2015). Vital signs: Alcohol poisoning deaths— United States, 2010–2012. Morbidity and Mortality Weekly Report (MMWR), 63, 1238–1242. Available at www.cdc.gov/mmwr/preview/ mmwrhtml/mm6353a2.htm.

Kantor, S., Mochizuki, T., Lops, S. N., Ko, B., Clain, E., Clark, E., et al. (2013). Orexin gene therapy restores the timing and maintenance of wakefulness in narcoleptic mice. *Sleep*, 36, 1129–1138.

Kaplan J. S., Arnkoff D. B., Glass C. R., Tinsley R., Geraci M., Hernandez E., et al. (2012). Avoidant coping in panic disorder: A yohimbine biological challenge study. *Anxiety Stress Coping*, 4, 425–442.

Kaplan, G., and Newcorn, J. H. (2011). Pharmacotherapy for child and adolescent attention-deficit hyperactivity disorder. *Pediatr. Clin. North Am.*, 58, 99–120.

Kapur, A. (2020). Is methylphenidate beneficial and safe in pharmacological cognitive enhancement? *CNS Drugs*, 34, 1045–1062.

Karam, C. S., and Javitch, J. A. (2018). Phosphorylation of the amino terminus of the dopamine transporter: Regulatory mechanisms and implications for amphetamine action. *In Apprentices to genius: A tribute to Solomon H. Snyder*, G. W. Pasternak and J. T. Coyle [Eds.], *Adv. Pharmacol.*, 82, 205–234. Academic Press: San Diego. © 2018. Reprinted with permission from Elsevier.

Karasinska, J. M., George, S. R., Cheng, R., and O'Dowd, B. F. (2005). Deletion of dopamine D1 and D3 receptors differentially affects spontaneous behavior and cocaine-induced locomotor activity, reward and CREB phosphorylation. *Eur. J. Neurosci.*, 22, 1741–1750.

Karila, L., Benyamina, A., Blecha, L., Cottencin, O., and Billieux, J. (2016a). The synthetic cannabinoid phenomenon. *Curr. Pharm. Des.*, 22, 1–6.

Karila, L., Billieux, J., Benyamina, A., Lançon, C., and Cottencin, O. (2016b). The effects and risks associated to mephedrone and methylone in humans: A review of preliminary evidences. *Brain Res. Bull.*, 126, 61–67.

Karila, L., Megarbane, B., Cottencin, O., and Lejoyeux, M. (2015). Synthetic cathinones: A new public health problem. *Curr. Neuropharmacol.*, 13, 12–20.

Karila, L., Wéry, A., Weinstein, A., Cottencin, O., Petit, A., Reynaud, M., et al. (2014). Sexual addiction or hypersexual disorder: Different terms for the same problem? A review of the literature. *Curr. Pharm. Des.*, 20, 4012–4020.

Karlsson, P., Smith, L., Farde, L., Härnryd, C., Sedvall, G., and Wiesel, F. A. (1995). Lack of apparent antipsychotic effect of the D1-dopamine receptor antagonist SCH39166 in acutely ill schizophrenic patients. *Psychopharmacology*, 121(3), 309–316. https://doi.org/10.1007/BF02246068

Kasai, H., Fukuda, M., Watanabe, S., Hayashi-Takagi, A., and Noguchi, J. (2010). Structural dynamics of dendritic spines in memory and cognition. *Trends Neurosci.*, 33, 121–129.

Kasten, C. R., and Boehm, S. L., II. (2015). Identifying the role of pre- and postsynaptic GABA$_B$ receptors in behavior. *Neurosci. Biobehav. Rev.*, 57, 70–87.

Kästner, N., Richter, S. H., Urbanik, S., Kunert, J., Walder, J., Lesch, K-P., Kaiser, S., et al. (2019). Brain serotonin deficiency affects female aggression. *Sci. Rep.*, 9, 1366. doi: 10.1038/s41598-018-37613-4.

Katselou, M., Papoutsis, I., Nikolaou, P., Spiliopoulou, C., and Athanaselis, S. (2016). α-PVP ("flakka"): A new synthetic cathinone invades the drug arena. *Forensic Toxicol.*, 34, 41–50.

Katz, D. L., and Pope, H. G., Jr. (1990). Anabolic–androgenic steroid-induced mental status changes. *NIDA Res. Monogr.*, 102, 215–223.

Kaupmann, K., Cryan, J. F., Wellendorph, P., Mombereau, C., Sansig, G., Klebs, K., et al. (2003). Specific γ-hydroxybutyrate-binding sites but loss of pharmacological effects of γ-hydroxybutyrate in GABA$_B$(1)-deficient mice. *Eur. J. Neurosci.*, 18, 2722–2730. © Federation of European Neuroscience Societies.

Kaur, R., Sidhu, P., and Singh, S. (2016). What failed BIA 10–2474 Phase I clinical trial? Global speculations and recommendations for future Phase I trials. *J. Pharmacol. Pharmacother.*, 7, 120–126.

Kavuluru, R., Han, S., and Hahn, E. J. (2019). On the popularity of the USB flash drive-shaped electronic cigarette Juul. *Tob. Control*, 28, 110–112.

Kazdoba, T. M., Leach, P. T., Silverman, J. L., and Crawley, J. N. (2014). Modeling fragile X syndrome in the Fmr1 knockout mouse. *Intractable Rare Dis. Res.*, 3, 118–133.

Keating, G. M. (2014). Sodium oxybate: A review of its use in alcohol withdrawal syndrome and in the maintenance of abstinence in alcohol dependence. *Clin. Drug Investig.*, 34, 63–80.

Kebabian, J. W., and Calne, D. B. (1979). Multiple receptors for dopamine. *Nature*, 277, 93–96.

Keech, B., Crowe, S., and Hocking, D. R. (2018). Intranasal oxytocin, social cognition and neurodevelopmen-tal disorders: A meta-analysis. *Psychoneuroendocrinology*, 87, 9–19.

Kehr, J., and Yoshitake, T. (2013). Monitoring molecules in neuroscience: Historical overview and current advancements. *Front. Biosci.* (Elite Edition), 5, 947–954. https://doi.org/10.2741/e674

Keith, D. R., Kurti, A. N., Davis, D. R., Zvorsky, I. A., and Higgins, S. T. (2017). A review of the effects of very low nicotine content cigarettes on behavioral and cognitive performance. *Prev. Med.*, 104, 110–116.

Kelly J.R., Borre Y., O' Brien C., Patterson E., El Aidy S., Deane J., et al. (2016) Transferring the blues: Depression-associated gut microbiota induces neurobehavioural changes in the rat. *J Psychiatr Res.*, 82, 109–118.

Kelly, J. R., Keane, V. O., Cryan, J. F., Clarke, G., and Dinan, T. G. (2019). Mood and microbes: Gut to brain communication in depression. *Gastroenterol. Clin. North Am.*, 48, 389–405.

Kelly, J. R., Minuto, C., Cryan, J. F., Clarke, G., and Dinan, T. G. (2020). The role of the gut microbiome in the development of schizophrenia. *Schizophr. Res.*, in press.

Kelly, K. (2001). The Little Book of Ketamine. Berkeley, CA: Ronin Publishing.

Kema, V. H., Mojerla, N. R., Khan, I., and Mandal, P. (2015). Effect of alcohol on adipose tissue: A review on ethanol mediated adipose tissue injury. *Adipocyte*, 4, 225–231.

Kendrick, K. M., Guastella, A. J., and Becker, B. (2018). Overview of human oxytocin research.

Curr. Top. Behav. Neurosci., 35, 321–348.

Kendriks, K. D.W., Maassen, H., van Dijk, P. R., Henning, R. H., van Goor, H., and Hillebrands, J.-L. (2019). Gasotransmitters in health and disease: a mitochondria-centered view. *Curr. Opin. Pharmacol.*, 45, 87–93.

Kennedy, C. (2015). ATP as a co-transmitter in the autonomic nervous system. *Auton. Neurosci.*, 191, 2–15.

Kent, C. N., Park, C., and Lindsley, C. W. (2020). Classics in chemical neuroscience: Baclofen. *ACS Chem. Neurosci.*, 11, 1740–1755.

Kerchner, G. A., and Nicoll, R. A. (2008). Silent synapses and the emergence of a postsynaptic mechanism for LTP. *Nat. Rev. Neurosci.*, 9, 813–825.

Keriotis, A. A., and Upadhyaya, H. P. (2000). Inhalant dependence and withdrawal symptoms. *J. Am. Acad. Child Adolesc. Psychiatry*, 39, 679–680.

Keshavan, M. S., Anderson, S., and Pettegrew, J. W. (1994). Is schizophrenia due to excessive synaptic pruning in the prefrontal cortex? The Feinberg hypothesis revisited. *J. Psychiatr. Res.*, 28, 239–265.

Ketchum, J. S. (2006). *Chemical Warfare: Secrets Almost Forgotten.* Santa Rosa, CA: ChemBooks.

Khandaker, G. M., and Dantzer, R. (2016). Is there a role for immune-to-brain communication in schizophrenia? *Psychopharmacology*, 233, 1559–1573.

Khatri, N., Thakur, M., Pareek, V., Kumar, S., Sharma, S., and Datusalia, A. (2018). Oxidative stress: Major threat in traumatic brain injury. *CNS Neurol. Disord. Drug Targets*, 17, 689–695.

Kheirbek, M. A., Drew, L. J., Burghardt, N. S., Costantini, D. O., Tannenholz, L., Ahmari, S. E., et al. (2013). Differential control of learning and anxiety along the dorsoventral axis of the dentate gyrus. *Neuron*, 77(5), 955–968.

Khoudigian, S., Devji, T., Lytvyn, L., Campbell, K., Hopkins, R., and O'Reilly, D. (2016). The efficacy and short-term effects of electronic cigarettes as a method for smoking cessation: A systematic review and a meta-analysis. *Int. J. Public Health*, 61, 257–267.

Kibaly, C., Alderete, J. A., Liu, S. H., Nasef, H. S., Law, P.-Y., Evans, C. J., and Cahill, C. M. (2021). Oxycodone in the opioid epidemic: High 'liking', 'wanting', and abuse liability. *Cell. Mol. Neurobiol.*, 41(5), 899–926. https://doi.org/10.1007/s10571-020-01013-y.

Kieffer, B. L., Befort, K., Gaveriaux-Ruff, C., and Hirth, C. G. (1992). The delta-opioid receptor: Isolation of a cDNA by expression cloning and pharmacological characterization. *Proc. Natl. Acad. Sci. USA*, 89, 12048–12052.

Kiguchi, N., Ding, H., and Ko, M. C. (2016). Central N/OFQ-NOP receptor system in pain modulation. *Adv. Pharmacol.*, 75, 217–243.

Kikuchi, A. M., Tanabe, A., and Iwahori, Y. (2020). A systematic review of the effect of L-tryptophan supplementation on mood and emotional functioning. *J. Diet. Suppl.*, in press.

Kikuchi, T., Maeda, K., Suzuki, M., Hirose, T., Futamura, T., and McQuade, R. D. (2021). Discovery research and development history of the dopamine D2 receptor partial agonists, aripiprazole and brexpiprazole. *Neuropsychopharmacology Reports*, 41(2), 134–143. https://doi.org/10.1002/npr2.12180

Kikuchi, T., Morizane, A., Doi, D., Magotani, H., Onoe, H., Hayashi, T., Mizuma, H., et al. (2017). Human iPS cell-derived dopaminergic neurons function in a primate Parkinson's disease model. *Nature*, 548(7669), 592–596. https://doi.org/10.1038/nature23664

Kilaru, A., and Chapman, K. D. (2020). The endocannabinoid system. *Essays Biochem.*, EBC20190086. doi: 10.1042/EBC20190086.

Kim Y.K., Shin C. (2018) The microbiota-gut-brain axis in neuropsychiatric disorders: pathophysiological mechanisms and novel treatments. *Curr. Neuropharmacol.*, 16(5), 559–573.

Kim, J. J., and Khan, W. I. (2014). 5-HT7 receptor signaling: Improved therapeutic strategy in gut disorders. *Front. Behav. Neurosci.*, 8, 396. doi: 10.3389/fnbeh.2014.00396.

Kim, S. Y., Adhikari, A., Lee, S. Y., Marshel, J. H., Kim, C. K., Mallory, C. S., et al. (2013). Diverging neural pathways assemble a behavioural state from separable features in anxiety. *Nature*, 496, 219–223.

Kim, S. T., and Park, T. (2019). Acute and chronic effects of cocaine on cardiovascular health. *Int. J. Mol. Sci.*, 20, 584. doi: 10.3390/ijms20030584.

Kimelberg, H. K., and Nedergaard, M. (2010). Functions of astrocytes and their potential as therapeutic targets. *Neurotherapeutics*, 7, 338–353.

Kimura, H. (2015). Signaling molecules: Hydrogen sulfide and polysulfide. *Antioxid. Redox Signal.*, 22, 362–376.

King, A. E., Woodhouse, A., Kirkcaldie, M. T. K., and Vickers, J. C. (2016). Excitotoxicity in ALS: Overstimulation, or overreaction? *Exp. Neurol.*, 275, 162–171.

King, D. L., and Delfabbro, P. H. (2014). Internet gaming disorder treatment: a review of definitions of diagnosis and treatment outcome. *J. Clin. Psychol.*, 70, 942–955.

King, H. E., and Riley, A. L. (2017). The affective properties of synthetic cathinones: Role of reward and aversion in their abuse. *Curr. Top. Behav. Neurosci., 32,* 165–181.

King, J. (2016). Fentanyl-Tainted Pills Wreaking Havoc in Sacramento. AOL News. Available at www.aol.com/article/2016/04/07/fentanyl-taintedpills-wreaking-havoc-in-sacramento/21340032/.

King, M. V., Marsden, C. A., and Fone, K. C. F. (2008). A role for the 5-HT1A, 5-HT4, and 5-HT6 receptors in learning and memory. *Trends Pharmacol. Sci., 29,* 482–492.

Kinney, H. C., and Haynes, R. L. (2019). The serotonin brainstem hypothesis for the sudden infant death syndrome. *J. Neuropathol. Exp. Neurol., 78,* 765–779.

Kinzer, S. (2019). Poisoner in Chief: Sidney Gottlieb and the CIA Search for Mind Control. New York: Henry Holt and Company.

Kirchheiner, J., and Seeringer, A. (2007). Clinical implications of pharmacogenetics of cytochrome P450 drug metabolizing enzymes. *Biochim. Biophys. Acta, 1770,* 489–494.

Kirk, J. M., and de Wit, H. (1999). Responses to oral Δ^9-tetrahydrocannabinol in frequent and infrequent marijuana users. *Pharmacol. Biochem. Behav., 63,* 137–142.

Kirk, J. M., Doty, P., and de Wit, H. (1998). Effects of expectancies on subjective responses to oral Δ^9-tetrahydrocannabinol. *Pharmacol. Biochem. Behav., 59,* 287–293.

Kirkham, T. C. (2009). Cannabinoids and appetite: Food craving and food pleasure. *Int. Rev. Psychiatry, 21,* 163–171.

Kirkpatrick, M. G., Gunderson, E. W., Johanson, C. E., Levin, F. R., Foltin, R. W., and Hart, C. L. (2012). Comparison of intranasal methamphetamine and d-amphetamine self-administration by humans. *Addiction, 107,* 783–791.

Kish, S. J., Boileau, I., Callaghan, R. C., and Tong, J. (2017). Brain dopamine neurone "damage": Methamphetamine users vs. Parkinson's disease—A critical assessment of the evidence. *Eur. J. Neurosci., 45,* 58–66.

Kish, S. J., Morito, C., and Hornykiewicz, O. (1985). Glutathione peroxidase activity in Parkinson's disease brain. *Neurosci. Lett., 58,* 343–346.

Kittirattanapaiboon, P., Srikosai, S., and Wittayanookulluk, A. (2017). Methamphetamine use and dependence in vulnerable female populations. *Curr. Opin. Psychiatry, 30,* 247–252.

Kiyasova, V., Bonnavion, P., Scotto-Lomassese, S., Fabre, V., Sahly, I., Tronche, F., Deneris, E., et al. (2013). A subpopulation of serotonergic neurons that do not express the 5-HT1A autoreceptor. *ACS Chem. Neurosci., 4,* 89–95.

Kjellgren, A., and Jonsson, K. (2013). Methoxetamine (MXE): A phenomenological study of experiences induced by a "legal high" from the Internet. *J. Psychoactive Drugs, 45,* 276–286.

Klein, S. B. (2000). *Biological Psychology.* Upper Saddle River, NJ: Prentice-Hall.

Klenowski, P. M., Fogarty, M. J., Shariff, M., Belmer, A., Bellingham, M. C., and Bartlett, S. E. (2016). In-creased synaptic excitation and abnormal dendritic structure of prefrontal cortex layer V pyramidal neurons following prolonged binge-like consumption of ethanol. *eNeuro, 3(6)* e0248-16.2016.

Klingemann, H., Sobell, M. B., and Sobell, L. C. (2009). Continuities and changes in self-change research. *Addiction, 105,* 1510–1518.

Kloner, R. A., Carson, C. C., III, Dobs, A., Kopecky, S., and Mohler, E. R., III. (2016). Testosterone and cardiovascular disease. *J. Am. Coll. Cardiol., 67,* 545–557. © 2016. Reprinted with permission from American College of Cardiology Foundation, via Elsevier.

Kluger, B., Triolo, P., Jones, W., and Jankovic, J. (2015). The therapeutic potential of cannabinoids for movement disorders. *Mov. Dis., 30,* 313–327.

Klus, H., Scherer, G., and Müller, L. (2012). Influence of additives on cigarette related health risks. *Tab. Int. Contrib. Tob. Res., 25,* 412–493.

Kneeland, R. E., and Fatemi, S. H. (2012). Viral infection, inflammation and schizophrenia. *Prog. Neuropsychopharmacol. Biol. Psychiatry, 42,* 35–48.

Knight, L. K., and Depue, B. E. (2019). New frontiers in anxiety research: The translational potential of the bed nucleus of the stria terminalis. *Front. Psychiatry, 10,* 510. doi: 10.3389/fpsyt.2019.00510.

Knight, R., Khondoker, M., Magill, N., Stewart, R., and Landau, S. (2018). A systematic review and meta-analysis of the effectiveness of acetylcholinesterase inhibitors and memantine in treating the cognitive symptoms of dementia. *Dement. Geriatr. Cogn. Disord., 45,* 131–151.

Knouse, L. E., and Safren, S. A. (2010). Current status of cognitive behavioral therapy for adult attention-deficit hyperactivity disorder. *Psychiatr. Clin. N. Am., 33,* 3497–3509.

Knutson, B., Taylor, J., Kaufman, M., Peterson, R., and Glover, G. (2005). Distributed neural representation of expected value. *J. Neurosci., 25,* 4806–4812.

Ko, C.-H. (2014). Internet gaming disorder. *Curr. Addict. Rep., 1,* 177–185.

Kobayashi, K., and Nagatsu, T. (2005). Molecular genetics of tyrosine 3-monooxygenase and

inherited diseases. *Biochem. Biophys. Res. Commun., 338,* 267–270.

Kobayashi, K., Morita, S., Sawada, H., Mizuguchi, T., Yamada, K., Nagatsu, I., et al. (1995). Targeted disruption of the tyrosine hydroxylase locus results in severe catecholamine depletion and perinatal lethality in mice. *J. Biol. Chem., 270,* 27235–27243.

Kobayashi, M., Iaccarino, C., Saiardi, A., Heidt, V., Bozzi, Y., Picetti, R., et al. (2004). Simultaneous absence of dopamine D1 and D2 receptor-mediated signaling is lethal in mice. *Proc. Natl. Acad. Sci. USA, 101,* 11465–11470.

Kobayashi, Y., and Isa, T. (2002). Sensorimotor gating and cognitive control by the brainstem cholinergic system. *Neural Netw., 15,* 731–741.

Kober, H., Mende-Siedlecki, M., Kross, E. F., Weber, J., Mischel, W., Hart, C. L., et al. (2010). Prefrontal-striatal pathway underlies cognitive regulation of craving. *Proc. Natl. Acad. Sci. USA, 107,* 14811–14816.

Koek, W. (2011). Drug-induced state-dependent learning: Review of an operant procedure in rats. *Behav. Pharmacol., 22,* 430–440.

Kohtala, S. (2021). Ketamine – 50 years in use: from anesthesia to rapid antidepressant effects and neurobiological mechanisms. *Pharmacol. Rep., 73,* 323–345.

Kohtz, A. S., and Frye, C. A. (2012). Dissociating behavioral, autonomic, and neuroendocrine effects of androgen steroids in animal models. In F. H. Kobeissy (Ed.), *Methods in Molecular Biology,* Volume 829, Psychiatric Disorders: Methods and Protocols (pp. 397–431). New York: Humana.

Kokkinou, M., Ashok, A. H., and Howes, O. D. (2018). The effects of ketamine on dopaminergic function: meta-analysis and review of the implications for neuropsychiatric disorders. *Mol. Psychiatry, 23,* 59–69.

Kolb, B., and Whishaw, I. Q. (1989). Plasticity in the neocortex: Mechanisms underlying recovery from early brain damage. *Prog. Neurobiol., 32,* 242.

Kolesnikova, T. O., Khatsko, S. L., Demin, K. A., Shevyrin, V. A., and Kalueff, A. V. (2019). DARK classics in chemical neuroscience: α-Pyrrolidinovalerophenone ("flakka"). *ACS Chem. Neurosci., 10,* 168–174.

Kolisnyk, B., Al-Onaizi, M. A., Prado, V. E., and Prado, M.A.M. (2015). α7 nicotinic ACh receptor-deficient mice exhibit sustained attention impairments that are reversed by β2 nicotinic ACh receptor activation. *Br. J. Pharmacol., 172,* 4919–4931.

Kollins, S. H., English, J., Robinson, R., Hallyburton, M., and

Chrisman, A. K. (2009). Reinforcing and subjective effects of methylphenidate in adults with and without attention deficit hyperactivity disorder (ADHD). *Psychopharmacology, 204,* 73–83.

Kollins, S. H., MacDonald, E. K., and Rush, C. R. (2001). Assessing the abuse potential of methylphenidate in nonhuman and human subjects: A review. *Pharmacol. Biochem. Behav., 68,* 611–627.

Koltai, H., and Namdar, D. (2020). Cannabis phytomolecule 'entourage': From domestication to medical use. *Trends Plant Sci., 25,* 976–984.

Kong, Q., Chang, L.-C., Takahashi, K., Liu, Q., Schulte, D. A., Lai, L., et al. (2014). Small-molecule activator of glutamate transporter EAAT2 translation provides neuroprotection. *J. Clin. Invest., 124,* 1255–1267.

Konghom, S., Verachai, V., Srisurapanont, M., Suwanmajo, S., Ranuwattananon, A., Kimsongneun, N., et al. (2010). Treatment for inhalant dependence and abuse. *Cochrane Database Syst. Rev.,* Issue 12, Article CD007537.

Kononenko, N. L., and Haucke, V. (2015). Molecular mechanisms of presynaptic membrane retrieval and synaptic vesicle reformation. *Neuron, 85,* 484–496.

Koob, G. F. (2005). The neurocircuitry of addiction: implications for treatment. *Clin. Neurosci. Res., 5,* 89–101.

Koob, G. F. (2009). Dynamics of neuronal circuits in addiction: Reward, antireward, and emotional memory. *Pharmacopsychiatry, 42*(Suppl. 1), S32–S41.

Koob, G. F. (2015). The dark side of emotion: The addiction perspective. *Eur. J. Pharmacol., 753,* 73–87.

Koob, G. F., and Le Moal, M. (1997). Drug abuse: Hedonic homeostatic dysregulation. *Science, 278,* 52–58.

Koob, G. F., and Le Moal, M. (2001). Drug addiction, dysregulation of reward, and allostasis. *Neuropsychopharmacology, 24,* 97–129.

Koob, G. F., and Le Moal, M. (2005). Plasticity of reward neurocircuitry and the "dark side" of drug addiction. *Nat. Neurosci., 8,* 1442–1444.

Koob, G. F., and Le Moal, M. (2006). *Neurobiology of Addiction.* London: Academic.

Koob, G. F., and Le Moal, M. (2008a). Addiction and the brain antireward system. *Annu. Rev. Psychol., 59,* 29–53.

Koob, G. F., and Le Moal, M. (2008b). Neurobiological mechanisms for opponent motivational processes in addiction. *Philos. Trans. R. Soc. Lond. B Biol. Sci., 363,* 3113–3123.

Koob, G. F., and Volkow, N. D. (2010). Neurocircuitry of addiction. *Neuropsychopharmacology, 35,* 217–238.

Koob, G. F., and Volkow, N. D. (2016). Neurobiology of addiction: A neurocircuitry analysis. *Lancet Psychiatry*, 3, 760–773.

Koob, G. F., Maldonado, R., and Stinus, L. (1992). Neural substrates of opiate withdrawal. *Trends Neurosci.*, 15, 186–191.

Koob, G. F. (2021). Drug addiction: Hyperkatifeia/negative reinforcement as a framework for medications development. *Pharmacol. Rev.*, 73, 163–201.

Koob, G. F., and Le Moal, M. (2008). Neurobiological mechanisms for opponent motivational processes in addiction. *Phil. Trans. R. Soc. B*, 363, 3113–3123.

Kopera, D. (2012). Excess hair growth. In V. R. Preedy (Ed.) *Handbook of Hair in Health and Disease*. Human Health Handbooks No. 1, Vol 1. Wageningen, Holland: Wageningen Academic Publishers.

Korem, N., Zer-Aviv, T. M., Ganon-Elazar, E., Abush, H., and Akirav, I. (2016). Targeting the endocannabinoid system to treat anxiety-related disorders. *J. Basic Clin. Physiol. Pharmacol.*, 27, 193–202.

Kort, A. (2016, August 6). Major Misnomer: Synthetic Marijuana's Dangerous Highs. Newsweek Special Edition. Available at www.newsweek.com/majormisnomer-synthetic-marijuana-dangerous-highs-marijuana-486667.

Kosten, T., Domingo, C., Orson, F., and Kinsey, B. (2014). Vaccines against stimulants: Cocaine and MA. *Br. J. Clin. Pharmacol.*, 77, 368–374.

Koukkou, M., and Lehmann, D. (1976). Human EEG spectra before and during cannabis hallucinations. *Biol. Psychiatry*, 11, 663–677.

Koukouli, F., and Changeux, J.-P. (2020). Do nicotinic receptors modulate high-order cognitive processing? *Trends Neurosci.*, 43, 550–564.

Kourosh, A. S., Harrington, C. R., and Adinoff, B. (2010). Tanning as a behavioral addiction. *Am. J. Drug Alcohol Abuse*, 36, 284–290.

Kourouni, I., Mourad, B., Khouli, H., Shapiro, J. M., and Mathew, J. P. (2020). Critical illness secondary to synthetic cannabinoid ingestion. *JAMA Netw. Open*, 3, e208516. doi: 10.1001/jamanetworkopen.2020.8516.

Koutsilieri, E., and Riederer, P. (2007). Excitotoxicity and new antiglutamatergic strategies in Parkinson's disease and Alzheimer's disease. *Parkinsonism Relat. Disord.*, 13, S329–S331.

Kovelman, J. A., and Scheibel, A. B. (1984). A neurohistologic correlate of schizophrenia. *Biol. Psychiatry*, 19, 1601–1621.

Kozlowski, L. T., Porter, C. Q., Orleans, C. T., Pope, M. A., and Heatherton, T. (1994). Predicting smoking cessation with self-reported measures of nicotine dependence: FTQ, FTND, and HSI. *Drug Alcohol Depend.*, 34, 211–216.

Kraemer, M., Boehmer, A., Madea, B., and Maas, A. (2019). Death cases involving certain new psychoactive substances: A review of the literature. *Forensic Sci. Int.*, 298, 186–267.

Krakowski, M., and Czobor, P. (1997). Violence in psychiatric patients: The role of psychosis, frontal lobe impairment, and ward turmoil. *Compr. Psychiatry*, 38, 230–236.

Krauss, B., and Green, S. M. (2000). Sedation and analgesia for procedures in children. *N. Engl. J. Med.*, 342, 938–945.

Krauss, M. J., Sowles, S. J., Mylvaganam, S., Zewdie, K., Bierut, L. J., and Cavazos-Rehg, P. A. (2015). Displays of dabbing marijuana extracts on YouTube. *Drug Alcohol Depend.*, 155, 45–51.

Krebs, T. S., and Johansen, P.-Ø. (2012). Lysergic acid diethylamide (LSD) for alcoholism: meta-analysis of randomized controlled trials. *J. Psychopharmacol.*, 26, 994–1002.

Kredlow, M. A., Keshishian, A., Oppenheimer, S., and Otto, M. W. (2019). The efficacy of modafinil as a cognitive enhancer: A systematic review and meta-analysis. *J. Clin. Psychopharmacol.*, 39, 455–461.

Krieger, M. S., Yedinak, J. L., Buxton, J. A., Lysyshyn, M., Bernstein, E., Rich, J. D., Green, T. C., Hadland, S. E., and Marshall, B. D. L. (2018). High willingness to use rapid fentanyl test strips among young people who use drugs. *Harm Reduction Journal*, 15(1), 7. https://doi.org/10.1186/s12954-018-0213-2

Krishnan V., Nestler E.J. (2011) Animal models of depression: molecular perspectives. *Curr. Top. Behav. Neurosci.*, 7, 121–147.

Krishnan, V., and Nestler, E. J. (2010). Linking molecules to mood: New insight into the biology of depression. *Am. J. Psychiatry*, 167, 1305–1320.

Kroll, D. (2016a). Scientists Speculate on What Caused the Bial Drug Testing Tragedy in France. Forbes. Available at www.forbes.com/sites/davidk-roll/2016/01/18/scientists-speculateon-what-caused-the-bial-drug-testingtragedy-in-france/#274bd8d25404.

Kroll, D. (2016b). Why Synthetic Marijuana Is More Dangerous Than Ever. Forbes. Available at www.forbes.com/sites/ davidk-roll/2016/07/19/why-synthetic-marijuana-is-more-dangerous-thanever/#4035cdc2e767.

Kroon, E., Kuhns, L., and Cousijn, J. (2021). The short-term and long-term effects of cannabis on cognition: recent advances in the field. *Curr. Opin. Psychol.*, in press.

Kroska, E. B., and Stowe, Z. N. (2020). Postpartum depression. Identification and treatment in the clinic setting. *Obstet. Gynecol. Clin. N. Am.*, 47, 409–419.

Krotulski, A. J., Cannaert, A., Stove, C., and Logan, B. K. (2021). The next generation of synthetic cannabinoids: Detection, activity, and potential toxicity of pent-4en and but-3en analogues including MDMB-4en-PINACA. *Drug Test Anal* 13: 427– 438. © 2020 John Wiley & Sons Ltd.

Kruk-Slomka, M., Dzik, A., Budzynska, B., and Biala, G. (2017). Endocannabinoid system: The direct and indirect involvement in the memory and learning processes–A short review. *Mol. Neurobiol.*, 54, 8332–8347.

Kruse, A. C., Kobilka, B. K., Gautam, D., Sexton, P. M., Christopoulos, A., and Wess, J. (2014). Muscarinic acetylcholine receptors: Novel opportunities for drug development. *Nat. Rev. Drug Discov.*, 13, 549–560.

Kryst J., Kawalec P., Mitoraj A.M., Pilc A., Lasoń W., Brzostek T. (2020) Efficacy of single and repeated administration of ketamine in unipolar and bipolar depression: A meta-analysis of randomized clinical trials. *Pharmacol Rep.*, 72(3), 543–562.

Krzyz̆anowska, W., Pomierny, B., Filip, M., and Pera, J. (2014). Glutamate transporters in brain ischemia: To modulate or not? *Acta Pharmacol. Sin.*, 35, 444–462.

Kubota, T., Miyake, K., Hariya, N., and Mochizuki, K. (2015). Understanding the epigenetics of neurodevelopmental disorders and DOHaD. *J. Dev. Orig. Health Dis.*, 6, 96–104.

Kuboyama, K., Fujikawa, A., Suzuki, R., and Noda, M. (2015). Inactivation of protein tyrosine phosphatases receptor type z by pleiotrophin promotes remyelination through activation of differentiation of oligodendrocyte precursor cells. *J. Neurosci.*, 35, 12162–12171.

Kudlacek, O., Hofmaier, T., Luf, A., Mayer, F. P., Stockner, T., Nagy, C., Holy, M., et al. (2017). Cocaine adulteration. *J. Chem. Neuroanat.*, 83–84, 75–81.

Kuhn, B. N., Kalivas, P. W., and Bobadilla, A. C. (2019). Understanding addiction using animal models. *Front. Behav. Neurosci.*, 13, 262. doi: 10.3389/fnbeh.2019.00262.

Kühn, S., Düzel, S., Colzato, L., Norman, K., Gallinat, J., Brandmaier, A. M., et al. (2019). Food for thought: association between dietary tyrosine and cognitive performance in younger and older adults. *Psych. Res.*, 83, 1097–1106.

Kulshreshtha, A., and Piplani, P. (2016). Current pharmacotherapy and putative disease-modifying therapy for Alzheimer's disease. *Neurol. Sci.*, 37, 1403–1435.

Kumar, R. (2008). Approved and investigational uses of modafinil: An evidence based review. *Drugs*, 68, 1803–1839.

Kumar, S., and Sagili, H. (2014). Etiopathogenesis and neurobiology of narcolepsy: A review. *J. Clin. Diag. Res.*, 8, 190–195.

Kumari, D., Gazy, I., and Usdin, K. (2019). Pharmacological reactivation of the silenced FMR1 gene as a targeted therapeutic approach for fragile X syndrome. *Brain Sci.*, 9, 39. doi: 10.3390/brainsci9020039.

Kummer, K. K., Hofhansel, L., Barwitz, C. M., Schardl, A., Prast, J. M., Salti, A., et al. (2014). Differences in social interactionvs. cocaine reward in mouse vs. rat. *Front. Behav. Neurosci.*, 8, 363. doi: 10.3389/fnbeh.2014.00363.

Kun, B., Takacs, Z. K., Richman, M. J., Griffiths, M. D., and Demetrovics, Z. (2021). Work addiction and personality: A meta-analytic study. *J. Behav. Addict.*, 9, 945–966,

Kurian, M. A., Zhen, J., Cheng, S.-Y., Li, Y., Mordekar, S. R., Jardine, P., et al. (2009). Homozygous loss-of-function mutations in the gene encoding the dopamine transporter are associated with infantile parkinsonismdystonia. *J. Clin. Invest.*, 119, 1595–1603.

Kuteeva, E., Hökfelt, T., Wardi, T., and Ogren, S. O. (2008). Galanin, galanin receptor subtypes and depression-like behaviour. *Cell Mol. Life Sci.*, 65, 1854– 1863.

Kutlu, M. G., and Gould, T. J. (2015). Nicotinic receptors, memory, and hippocampus. *Curr. Top. Behav. Neurosci.*, 23, 137–163.

Kutlu, M. G., Parikh, V., and Gould, T. J. (2015). Nicotine addiction and psychiatric disorders. *Int. Rev. Neurobiol.*, 124, 171–208.

Kuypers, K.P.C. (2020). The therapeutic potential of microdosing psychedelics in depression. *Ther. Adv. Psychopharmacol.*, 10, 1–15.

Kuypers, K.P.C., Ng, L., Erritzoe, D., Knudsen, G. M., Nichols, C. D., Nichols, D. E., Pani, L., et al. (2019). Microdosing psychedelics: More questions than answers? An overview and suggestions for future research. *J. Psychopharmacol.*, 33, 1039–1057.

Kwako, L. E., Momenan, R., Litten, R. Z., Koob, G. F., and Goldman, D. (2016). Addictions neuroclinical assessment: A neuroscience-based framework for addictive disorders. *Biol. Psychiatry*, 80, 179–189.

Kwako, L. E., Schwandt, M. L., Ramchandani, V. A., Diazgranados, N., Koob, G. F., Volkow, N. D., Blanco, C., et al. (2019). Neurofunctional domains derived from deep behavioral phenotyping in alcohol use disorder. *Am. J. Psychiatry*, 176, 744–753

Kyriakou, C., Marinelli, E., Frati, P., Santurro, A., Afxentiou, M., Zaami, S., et al. (2015). NBOMe: New potent hallucinogens—Pharmacology, analytical methods, toxicities, fatalities: A review. *Eur. Rev. Med. Pharmacol. Sci.*, 19, 3270–3281.

Kyzar, E. J., and Pandey, S. C. (2015). Molecular mechanisms of synaptic remodeling in alcoholism. *Neurosci. Lett.*, 601, 11–19.

Kyzar, E. J., Nichols, C. D., Gainetdinov, R. R., Nichols, D. E., and Kalueff, A. V. (2017). Psychedelic drugs in biomedicine. *Trends Pharmacol. Sci.*, 38, 992–1005.

L

Lowe, H., Steele, B., Bryant, J., Toyang, N., and Ngwa, W. (2021). Non-cannabinoid metabolites of *Cannabis sativa* L. with therapeutic potential. *Plants*, 10, 400. doi: 10.3390/plants10020400.

Lac, A., and Luk, J. W. (2018). Testing the amotivational syndrome: Marijuana use longitudinally predicts lower self-efficacy even after controlling for demographics, personality, and alcohol and cigarette use. *Prev. Sci.*, 19, 117–126.

Lachenmeier, D. W., Habel, S., Fischer, B., Herbi, F., Zerbe, Y., Bock, V., Rajcic de Rezende, T., et al. (2019). Are side effects of cannabidiol (CBD) products caused by tetrahydrocannabinol (THC) contamination? *F1000Res*, 8, 1394. doi: 10.12688/f1000research.19931.3.

Lachman, H. M., Papolos, D. F., Saito, T., Yu, Y. M., Szumlanski, C. L., and Weinshilboum, R. M. (1996) Human catechol-O-methyltransferase pharmacogenetics: Description of a functional polymorphism and its potential application to neuropsychiatric disorders. *Pharmacogenetics*, 6, 243–250.

Lai, T. W., Zhang, S., and Wang, Y. T. (2014). Excitotoxicity and stroke: Identifying novel targets for neuroprotection. *Prog. Neurobiol.*, 115, 157–168.

LaLumiere, R. T., McGaugh, J. L., and McIntyre, C. K. (2017). Emotional modulation of learning and memory: Pharmacological implications. *Pharmacol. Rev.*, 69, 236–255.

Lam, C., and West, A. (2015). Are electronic nicotine delivery systems an effective smoking cessation tool? *Can. J. Respir. Ther.*, 51, 93–98.

Lambert, B. L., and Bauer, C. R. (2012). Developmental and behavioral consequences of prenatal cocaine exposure: A review. *J. Perinatol.*, 32, 819–828.

Lammell, S., Lim, B. K., and Malenka, R. C. (2014). Reward and aversion in a heterogeneous midbrain dopamine system. *Neuropharmacology*, 76, 351–359.

Landgraf, D., McCarthy, M. J., and Welsh, D. K. (2014a). The role of the circadian clock in animal models of mood disorders. *Behav. Neurosci.*, 128, 344–359.

Landgraf, D., McCarthy, M. J., and Welsh, D. K. (2014b). Circadian clock and stress interactions in the molecular biology of psychiatric disorders. *Curr. Psychiat. Rep.*, 16, Article 483.

Landry M., Moreno A., Patry S., Potvin S., and Lemasson M. (2020) Current practices of electroconvulsive therapy in mental disorders: A systematic review and meta-analysis of short and long-term cognitive effects. *J ECT.*, ahead of print.

Lane, H. Y., Lin, C. H., Huang, Y. J., Liao, C. H., Chang, Y. C., and Tsai, G. E. (2010). A randomized, double-blind, placebo-controlled comparison study of sarcosine (N-methylglycine) and D-serine add-on treatment for schizophrenia. *Int. J. Neuropsychopharmacol.*, 13, 451–460.

Lane, R., and Baldwin, D. (1997). Selective serotonin reuptake inhibitor-induced serotonin syndrome: Review. *J. Clin. Psychopharmacol.*, 17, 208–221.

Lange, K. W., Reichl, S., Lange, K. M., Tucha, L., and Tucha, O. (2010). The history of attention deficit hyperactivity disorder. *ADHD Atten. Def. Hyp. Disord.*, 2, 241–255.

Langer, R. (2003). Where a pill won't reach. *Sci. Am.*, 288, 50–57.

Langer, S. Z. (2015). α2-Adrenoceptors in the treatment of major neuropsychiatric disorders. *Trends Pharmacol. Sci.*, 36, 196–202.

Langlais, P. J., and Savage, L. M. (1995). Thiamine deficiency in rats produces cognitive and memory deficits on spatial tasks correlated with tissue loss in diencephalon, cortex and white matter. *Behav. Brain Res.*, 68, 75–89.

Lappin, J. M., Darke, S., and Farrell, M. (2017). Stroke and methamphetamine use in young adults: a review. *J. Neurol. Neurosurg. Psychiatry*, 88, 1079–1091.

Lappin, J. M., Darke, S., and Farrell, M. (2018). Methamphetamine use and future risk for Parkinson's disease: Evidence and clinical implications. *Drug Alcohol Depend.*, 187, 134–140.

Larance, B., Degenhardt, L., Dillon, P., and Copeland, J. (2005). Rapid Assessment of Performance and Image Enhancing Drugs (PIEDs) in New South Wales: Feasibility Study. Sydney, Australia: National Drug and Alcohol Research Centre.

Larson, J., and Munkácsy, E. (2015). Thetaburst LTP. *Brain Res.*, 1621, 38–50.

Laruelle, M., Abi-Dargham, A., Gile, R., Kegeles, L., and Innis, R. (1999). Increased dopamine transmission in schizophrenia: Relationship to illness phases. *Biol. Psychiatry*, 46, 56–72.

Laskaris, L. E., Di Biase, M. A., Everall, I., Chana, G., Christopoulos, A., Skafidas, E., et al. (2016). Microglial activation and progressive brain changes in schizophrenia. *Br. J. Pharmacol.*, 173, 666–680.

Lassi, G., Taylor, A. E., Timpson, N. J., Kenny, P. J., Mather, R. J., Eisen, T., and Munafò, M. R. (2016). The CHRNA5-A3-B4 gene cluster and smoking: From discovery to therapeutics. *Trends Neurosci.*, 39, 851–861.

Lathe, R. (1996). Mice, gene targeting and behaviour: More than just genetic background. *Trends Neurosci.*, 19, 183–186.

Latif, Z., and Garg, N. (2020). The impact of marijuana on the cardiovascular system: A review of the most common cardiovascular events associated with marijuana use. *J. Clin. Med.*, 9, 1925. doi: 10.3390/jcm9061925.

Latsari, M., Antonopoulos, J., Dori, I., Chiotelli, M., and Dinopoulos, A. (2004). Postnatal development of the noradrenergic system in the dorsal lateral geniculate nucleus of the rat. *Dev. Brain Res.*, 149, 79–83.

Lau, A., and Tymianski, M. (2010). Glutamate receptors, neurotoxicity and neurodegeneration. *Pflugers Arch.*, 460, 525–542.

Lau, B. K., Cota, D., Cristino, L., and Borgland, S. L. (2017). Endocannabinoid modulation of homeostatic and non-homeostatic feeding circuits. *Neuropharmacology*, 124, 38–51.

Lau, J., and Herzog, H. (2014). CART in the regulation of appetite and energy homeostasis. *Front. Neurosci.*, 8, 313. doi: 10.3389/fnins.2014.00313.

Laufer, B. I., Mantha, K., Kleiber, M. L., Diehl, E. J., Addison, S. M., and Singh, S. M. (2013). Long-lasting alterations to DNA methylation and ncRNAs could underlie the effects of fetal alcohol exposure in mice. *Dis. Model Mech.*, 6, 977–992.

Lauterborn, J. C., Palmer, L. C., Jia, Y., Pham, D. T., Hou, B., Wang, W., et al. (2016). Chronic ampakine treatments stimulate dendritic growth and promote learning in middle-aged rats. *J. Neurosci.*, 36, 1636–1646.

Laviolette, S. R. (2021). Molecular and neuronal mechanisms underlying the effects of adolescent nicotine exposure on anxiety and mood disorders. *Neuropharmacology*, in press.

Layden, J. E., Ghinai, I., Pray, I., Kimball, A., Layer, M., Tenforde, M. W., Navon, L., et al. (2020). Pulmonary illness related to e-cigarette use in Illinois and Wisconsin—Final report. *N. Engl. J. Med.*, 382, 903–916.

Layman, D. K., Lönnerdal, B., and Fernstrom, J. D. (2018). Applications for α-lactalbumin in human nutrition. *Nutr. Rev.*, 76, 444–460.

Lazarus, M., Chen, J.-F., Huang, Z.-L., Urade, Y., and Fredholm, B. B. (2019). Adenosine and sleep. *Handb. Exp. Pharmacol.*, 253, 359–381.

Le Foll, B., and Goldberg, S. R. (2009). Effects of nicotine in experimental animals and humans: An update on addictive properties. *Handb. Exp. Pharmacol.*, 192, 335–367.

Le Gall, L., Anakor, E., Connolly, O., Vijayakumar, U. G., Duddy, W. J., and Duguez, S. (2020). Molecular and cellular mechanisms affected in ALS. *J. Pers. Med.*, 10, 101. doi: 10.3390/jpm10030101.

Le, A. D., Poulos, C. X., and Cappell, H. (1979). Conditioned tolerance to the hypothermic effect of ethyl alcohol. *Science*, 206, 1109–1110.

Lea, T., Amada, N., Jungaberle, H., Schecke, H., and Klein, M. (2020). Microdosing psychedelics: Motivations, subjective effects and harm reduction. *Int. J. Drug Policy*, 75, 102600. doi: 10.1016/j.drugpo.2019.11.008.

Leal, G., Afonso, P. M., Salazar, I. L., and Duarte, C. B. (2015). Regulation of hippocampal synaptic plasticity by BNDF. *Brain Res.*, 1621, 82–101.

Leal, G., Bramham, C. R., and Duarte, C. B. (2017). BDNF and hippocampal synaptic plasticity. *Vitam. Horm.*, 104, 153–195.

Leary, T. (1984). Personal computers/personal freedom. In S. Ditlea (Ed.), *Digital Deli*, pp. 359–361. New York: Workman.

Leas, E. C., Hendrickson, E. M., Nobles, A. L., Todd, R., Smith, D. M., Dredze, M., and Ayers, J. W. (2020). Self-reported cannabidiol (CBD) use for conditions with proven therapies. *JAMA Netw. Open*, 3, e2020977. doi: 10.1001/jamanetworkopen.2020.20977.

LeBlanc, A. E., Lalant, H., and Gibbins, R. J. (1975). Acute tolerance to ethanol in the rat. *Psychopharmacologia*, 41, 43–46.

LeBlanc, A. E., Lalant, H., and Gibbins, R. J. (1976). Acquisition and loss of behaviorally augmented tolerance to ethanol in the rat. *Psychopharmacology*, 48, 153–158.

LeClerc, S., and Easley, D. (2015). Pharmacological therapies for autism spectrum disorder: A review. *PT*, 40, 389–397.

Ledford, H. (2016). CRISPR: Gene editing is just the beginning. *Nature*, 531, 156–159.

Ledford, H. (2020b). CRISPR gene editing in human embryos wreaks chromosomal mayhem. *Nature*, 583(7814), 17–18. https://doi.org/10.1038/d41586-020-01906-4

LeDoux, J. E. (1996). *The Emotional Brain*. New York: Simon and Schuster.

Lee, A. W., Ventola, P., Budimirovic, D., Berry-Kravis, E., and Visootsak, J. (2018). Clinical development of targeted fragile X syndrome treatments: An industry perspective. *Brain Sci.*, 8, 214. doi: 10.3390/brainsci8120214.

Lee, C. H., Lu, W., Michel, J. C., Goehring, A., Du, J., Song, X., and Gouaux, E. (2014). NMDA receptor structures reveal subunit arrangement and pore architecture. *Nature*, 511, 191–197

Lee, D. E., Gerasimov, M. R., Schiffer, W. K., and Gifford, A. N. (2006). Concentration-dependent conditioned place preference to inhaled toluene vapors in rats. *Drug Alcohol Depend.*, 85, 87–90.

Lee, G., and Zhou, Y. (2019). NMDAR hypofunction animal models of schizophrenia. *Front. Mol. Neurosci.*, 12, 185. doi: 10.3389/fnmol.2019.00185.

Lee, J. H., Ribeiro, E. A., Kim, J., Ko, B., Kronman, H., Jeong, Y. H., Kim, J. K., et al. (2020). Dopaminergic regulation of nucleus accumbens cholinergic interneurons demarcates susceptibility to cocaine addiction. *Biol. Psychiatry*, 88, 746–757.

Lee, M. A., and Shlain, B. (1992). Acid Dreams: The Complete Social History of LSD: The CIA, the Sixties, and Beyond. New York: Grove.

Lee, S. H., Ahn, W. Y., Seweryn, M., and Sadee, W. (2018). Combined genetic influence of the nicotinic receptor gene cluster CHRNA5/A3/B4 on nicotine dependence. *BMC Genomics*, 19(1), 826. doi: 10.1186/s12864-018-5219-3.

Lee, T. J., Zanello, A. F., Morrison, T. R., Ricci, L. A., and Melloni Jr., R. H. (2021). Valproate selectively suppresses adolescent anabolic/androgenic steroid-induced aggressive behavior: implications for a role of hypothalamic γ-aminobutyric acid neural signaling. *Behav. Pharmacol.*, 32, 295–307.

Lee, V. R., Vera, A., Alexander, A., Ruck, B., Nelson, L. S., Wax, P., Campleman, S., et al. (2019). Loperamide misuse to avoid opioid withdrawal and to achieve a euphoric effect: High doses and high risk. *Clin. Toxicol. (Phila.)*, 57(3), 175–180. https://doi.org/10.1080/15563650.2018.1510128

Lefebvre, K. A., and Robertson, A. (2010). Domoic acid and human exposure risks: A review. *Toxicon*, 56, 218–230.

Legay, C. (2018). Congenital myasthenic syndromes with acetylcholinesterase deficiency, the pathophysiological mechanisms. *Ann. N.Y. Acad. Sci.*, 1413, 104–110.

Lehrner, A., Bierer, L. M., Passarelli, V., Pratchett, L. C., Flory, J. D., Bader, H., et al. (2014). Maternal PTSD associates with greater glucocorticoid sensitivity in offspring of Holocaust survivors. *Psychoneuroendocrinology*, 40, 213–220.

Leigh, S. J., and Morris, M. J. (2018). The role of reward circuitry and food addiction in the obesity epidemic: An update. *Biol. Psychol.*, 131, 31–42.

Lemyre, A., Poliakova, N., and Belanger, R. E. (2019). The relationship between tobacco and cannabis use: A review. *Subst. Use Misuse*, 54, 130–145.

Lenoir, M., Cantin, L., Vanhille, N., Serre, F., and Ahmed, S. H. (2013). Extended heroin access increases heroin choices over a potent nondrug alternative. *Neuropsychopharmacology*, 38, 1209–1220.

Lenoir, M., Serre, F., Cantin, L., and Ahmed, S. H. (2007). Intense sweetness surpasses cocaine reward. *PLOS ONE*, 2, e698. doi: 10.1371/journal. pone.0000698.

Leo, D., and Gainetdinov, R. R. (2013). Transgenic mouse models for ADHD. *Cell Tissue Res.*, 354, 259–271.

Leo, D., Sukhanov, I., Zoratto, F., Illiano, P., Caffino, L., Sanna, F., Messa, G., et al. (2018). Pronounced hyperactivity, cognitive dysfunctions, and BDNF dysregulation in dopamine transporter knock-out rats. *J. Neurosci.*, 38, 1959–1972.

Leonard, H. L., Swedo, S. E., Rapoport, J. L., Koby, E. V., Lenane, M. C., Cheslow, D. L., et al. (1989). Treatment of obsessive-compulsive disorder with clomipramine and desipramine in children and adolescents: A double blind crossover comparison. *Arch. Gen. Psychiatry*, 46, 1088–1092.

Leprun, P.M.B., and Clarke, G. (2019). The gut microbiome and pharmacology: a prescription for therapeutic targeting of the gut-brain axis. *Curr. Opin. Pharmacol.*, 49, 17–23.

Lerner, A. G., Rudinski, D., Bor, O., and Goodman, C. (2014). Flashbacks and HPPD: A clinical-oriented concise review. *Isr. J. Psychiatry Relat. Sci.*, 51, 296–302.

Lerner, A., and Klein, M. (2019). Dependence, withdrawal and rebound of CNS drugs: an update and regulatory considerations for new drugs development. *Brain Commun.*, 1(1), fcz025. doi: 10.1093/braincomms/fcz025.

Lesch, K.-P., Araragi, N., Waider, J., van den Hove, D., and Gutknecht, L. (2012). Targeting brain serotonin synthesis: Insights into neurodevelopmental disorders with long-term outcomes related to negative emotionality, aggression and antisocial behaviour. *Philos. Trans. R. Soc. Lond. B Biol. Sci.*, 367, 2426–2443.

Leschziner, G. (2014). Narcolepsy: A clinical review. *Pract. Neurol.*, 14, 323–331.

Leshner, A. I. (1997). Addiction is a brain disease, and it matters. *Science*, 278, 45–47.

Leslie, F. M. (2020). Unique, long-term effects of nicotine on adolescent brain. *Pharmacol. Biochem.*

Behav., 197, 173010. doi: 10.016/j. pbb.2020.173010.

Leuner, B., and Shors, T. J. (2013). Stress, anxiety, and dendritic spines: What are the connections? *Neuroscience*, 251, 108–119.

Leung, A. K. C., and Hon, K. L. (2016). Attention-deficit/hyperactivity disorder. *Adv. Pediatr.*, 63, 255–280.

Leung, J., Chan, G.C.K., Hides, L., and Hall, W. D. (2020). What is the prevalence and risk of cannabis use disorders among people who use cannabis? a systematic review and meta-analysis. *Addict. Behav.*, 109, 106479. doi: 10.1016/j.addbeh.2020.106479.

Levenson, J. M., and Sweatt, J. D. (2005). Epigenetic mechanisms in memory formation. *Nat. Rev. Neurosci.*, 6, 108–118.

Lévesque, A., and Le Foll, B. (2018). When and how to treat possible cannabis use disorder. *Med. Clin. North Am.*, 102, 667–681.

Levine, R. R. (1973). *Pharmacology: Drug Actions and Reactions.* Boston: Little, Brown, and Co.

Levitt, D. G., and Levitt, M. D. (2015). Carbon monoxide: A critical quantitative analysis and review of the extent and limitations of its second messenger function. *Clin. Pharmacol.*, 7, 37–56.

Levy, N. (2013). Addiction is not a brain disease (and it matters). *Front. Psychiatry*, 4, 24. doi: 10.3389/fpsyt.2013.00024.

Lewerenz, J., and Maher, P. (2015). Chronic glutamate toxicity in neurodegenerative diseases: What is the evidence? *Front. Neurosci.*, 9, 469. doi: 10.3389/fnins.2015.00469.

Lewis, D. A., and Levitt, P. (2002). Schizophrenia as a disorder of neurodevelopment. *Annu. Rev. Neurosci.*, 25, 409–432.

Lewis, M. (2015). The Biology of Desire. Why Addiction Is Not a Disease. New York: PublicAffairs.

Lewis, M. (2018). Brain change in addiction as learning, not disease. *N. Engl. J. Med.*, 379, 1551–1560.

Lewis, R. G., and Borrelli, E. (2020). A mechanism of cocaine addiction susceptibility through D2 receptor-mediated regulation of nucleus accumbens cholinergic interneurons. *Biol. Psychiatry*, 88, 738–740.

Lewis, R. G., Serra, M., Radl, D., Gori, M., Tran, C., Michalak, S. E., Vanderwal, C. D., et al. (2020). Dopaminergic control of striatal cholinergic interneurons underlies cocaine-induced psychostimulation. *Cell Rep.*, 31, 107257. doi: 10.1016/celrep.2020.107527.

Lewis, S., and Lieberman, J. (2008). CATIE and CUtLASS: Can we handle the truth? *Br. J. Psychiatry*, 192, 161–163.

Leyton, M., Casey, K. F., Delaney, J. S., Kolivakis, T., and Benkelfat,

C. (2005). Cocaine craving, euphoria, and self-administration: A preliminary study of the effect of catecholamine precursor depletion. *Behav. Neurosci.*, 119, 1619–1627.

Li, H., Pullmann, D., and Jhou, T. C. (2019). Valence-encoding in the lateral habenula arises from the entopeduncular region. *eLife*, 8, e41223. doi: 10.7554/eLife.41223.

Li, J. Y., Popovic, N., and Brundin, P. (2005). The use of the R6 transgenic mouse models of Huntington's disease in attempts to develop novel therapeutic strategies. *NeuroRx*, 2, 447–464.

Li, L., and Vlisides, P. E. (2016). Ketamine: 50 years of modulating the mind. *Front. Hum. Neurosci.*, 10, 612. doi: 10.3389/fnhum.2016.00612.

Li, N., Lee, B., Liu, R. J., Banasr, M., Dwyer, J. M., Iwata, M., et al. (2010). mTORdependent synapse formation underlies the rapid antidepressant effects of NMDA antagonists. *Science*, 329, 959–964.

Li, N., Ragheb, K., Lawler, G., Sturgis, J., Rajwa, B., Melendez, J. A., et al. (2003). Mitochondrial complex I inhibitor rotenone induces apoptosis through enhancing mitochondrial reactive oxygen species production. *J. Biol. Chem.*, 278, 8516–8525.

Li, P., Snyder, G. L., and Vanover, K. E. (2016a). Dopamine targeting drugs for the treatment of schizophrenia: Past, present and future. *Curr. Top. Med. Chem.* 16, 3385–3403. doi: 10.2174/1568026616666160608084834.

Li, V., and Wang, Y. T. (2016). Molecular mechanisms of NMDA receptor-mediated excitotoxicity: implications for neuroprotective therapeutics for stroke. *Neural Regen. Res.*, 11, 1752–1753.

Li, X., Caprioli, D., and Marchant, N. J. (2015). Recent updates on incubation of drug craving: a mini-review. *Addict. Biol.*, 20, 872–876.

Li, Y., Zhong, W., Wang, D., Feng, Q., Liu, Z., Zhou, J., et al. (2016b). Serotonin neurons in the dorsal raphe nucleus encode reward signals. *Nat. Commun.*, 7, 10503. doi: 10.1038/ncomms10503.

Liakoni, E., Dempsey, D. A., Meyers, M., Murphy, N. G., Fiorentino, D., Havel, C., Haller, C., et al. (2018). Effect of γ-hydroxybutyrate (GHB) on driving as measured by a driving simulator. *Psychopharmacology*, 235, 3223–3232.

Liao, Y., Tang, J., Corlett, P. R., Wang, X., Yang, M., Chen, H., et al. (2011). Reduced dorsal prefrontal gray matter after chronic ketamine use. *Biol. Psychiatry*, 69, 42–48.

Liao, Y., Tang, J., Liu, J., Xie, A., Yang, M., Johnson, M., Wang, X., et al. (2016). Decreased thalamocortical connectivity in chronic ketamine users. *PLOS ONE*, 11(12), e0167381. doi: 10.1371/journal.pone.0167381.

Liao, Y., Tang, J., Ma, M., Wu, Z., Yang, M., Wang, X., et al. (2010). Frontal white matter abnormalities following chronic ketamine use: A diffusion tensor imaging study. *Brain*, 133, 2115–2122.

Liberzon, I., Phan, K. L., Khan, S., and Abelson, J. L. (2003). Role of the GABA$_A$ receptor in anxiety: Evidence from animal models, molecular and clinical psychopharmacology, and brain imaging studies. *Curr. Neuropharmacol.*, 1, 267–283.

Liblau, R. S., Vassalli, A., Seifinejad, A., and Tafti, M. (2015). Hypocretin (orexin) biology and the pathophysiology of narcolepsy with cataplexy. *Lancet Neurol.*, 14, 318–328.

Licata, S. C., and Renshaw, P. F. (2010). Neurochemistry of drug action: Insights from proton magnetic resonance spectroscopic imaging and their relevance to addiction. *Ann. N. Y. Acad. Sci.*, 1187, 148–171.

Licata, S. C., and Rowlett, J. K. (2008). Abuse and dependence liability of benzodiazepine-type drugs: GABA$_A$ receptor modulation and beyond. *Pharmacol. Biochem. Behav.*, 90, 74–89.

Lickey, M. E., and Gordon, B. (1991). Medicine and Mental Illness. New York: W. H. Freeman.

Lieberman, J. A., and Stroup, T. S. (2011). The NIMH-CATIE Schizophrenia Study: What did we learn? *Am. J. Psychiatry*, 168, 770–775.

Lieberman, J. A., Stroup, T. S., McEvoy, J. P., Swartz, M. S., Rosenheck, R. A., Perkins, D. O., et al. Clinical Antipsychotic Trials of Intervention Effectiveness (CATIE) Investigators. (2005). Effectiveness of antipsychotic drugs in patients with chronic schizophrenia. *N. Engl. J. Med.*, 353, 1209–1223.

Liechti, M. E., Kunz, I., Greminger, P., Speich, R., and Kupferschmidt, H. (2006). Clinical features of gamma-hydroxybutyrate and gamma-butyrolactone toxicity and concomitant drug and alcohol use. *Drug Alcohol Depend.*, 81, 323–326.

Liggins, J., Pihl, R. O., Benkelfat, C., and Leyton, M. (2012). The dopamine augmenter L-DOPA does not affect positive mood in healthy human volunteers. *PLOS ONE*, 7(1), e23870. doi: 10.1371/journal.pone.0028370.

Ligresti, A., De Petrocellis, L., and Di Marzo, V. (2016). From phytocannabinoids to cannabinoid receptors and endocannabinoids: Pleiotropic physiological and pathological roles through complex pharmacology. *Physiol. Rev.*, 96, 1593–1659.

Lile, J. A., Kelly, T. H., and Hays, L. R. (2012). Separate and combined effects of the GABA$_B$ agonist baclofen and Δ^9-THC in humans discriminating Δ^9-THC. *Drug Alcohol Depend.*, 126, 216–223.

Lim, L., Mi, D., Llorca, A., and Marin, O. (2018). Development and functional diversification of cortical interneurons. *Neuron*, 100, 294–313.

Lim, S. T., Airavaara, M., and Harvey, B. K. (2010). Viral vectors for neurotrophic factor delivery: A gene therapy approach for neurodegenerative diseases of the CNS. *Pharmacol. Res.*, 61, 14–26.

Lin, C. H., Lane, H. Y., and Tsai, G. E. (2012). Glutamate signaling in the pathophysiology and therapy of schizophrenia. *Pharmacol. Biochem. Behav.*, 100, 665–677.

Lin, L., Faraco, J., Li, R., Kadotani, H., Rogers, W., Lin, X., et al. (1999). The sleep disorder canine narcolepsy is caused by a mutation in the hypocretin (orexin) receptor 2 gene. *Cell*, 98, 365–376.

Lin, M. T., and Beal, M. F. (2006). Mitochondrial dysfunction and oxidative stress in neurodegenerative diseases. *Nature*, 443, 787–795.

Lindgren, J. E., Ohlsson, A., Agurell, S., Hollister, L., and Gillespie, H. (1981). Clinical effects and plasma levels of Δ^9-tetrahydrocannabinol (Δ^9-THC) in heavy and light users of cannabis. *Psychopharmacology*, 74, 208–212.

Ling, W., Shoptaw, S., and Goodman-Meza, D. (2019). Depot buprenorphine injection in the management of opioid use disorder: From development to implementation. *Subst. Abuse Rehabil.*, 10, 69–78. https://doi.org/10.2147/SAR.S155843

Lingford-Hughes, A., Potokar, J., and Nutt, D. (2002). Treating anxiety complicated by substance misuse. *Adv. Psychiatric Treat.*, 8, 107–116.

Linssen, A. M. W., Sambeth, A., Vuurman, E. F. P. M., and Riedel, W. J. (2014). Cognitive effects of methylphenidate in healthy volunteers: A review of single dose studies. *Int. J. Neuropsychopharmacol.*, 17, 961–977.

Lipsman, N., Meng, Y., Bethune, A. J., Huang, Y., Lam, B., Masellis, M., Hermann, N., Heyn, C., Aubert, I., Boutet, A., Smith, G. S., Hynynen, K., Black, S. E. (2018). *Nature* Communications, 9, 2236, 1–8.

Lisko, J. G., Tran, H., Stanfill, S. B., Blount, B. C., and Watson, C. H. (2015). Chemical composition and evaluation of nicotine, tobacco alkaloids, pH, and selected flavors in e-cigarette cartridges and refill solutions. *Nicotine Tob. Res.*, 17, 1270–1278.

Lisman, J., Schulman, H., and Cline, H. (2002). The molecular basis of CaMKII function in synaptic and behavioural memory. *Nat. Rev. Neurosci.*, 3, 175–190.

Lisoway, A. J., Chen, C. C., Zai, C. C., Tiwari, A. K., and Kennedy, J. L. (2021). Toward personalized medicine in schizophrenia: Genetics and epigenetics of antipsychotic treatment. *Schizophr. Res.*, 232, 112–124. https://doi.org/10.1016/j.schres.2021.05.010

Litjens, R. P. W., Brunt, T. M., Alderliefste, G.-J., and Westerink, R. H. S. (2014). Hallucinogen persisting perception disorder and the serotonergic system: A comprehensive review including new MDMA-related clinical cases. *Eur. Neuropsychopharmacol.*, 24, 1309–1323.

Liu, C., and Kaeser, P. S. (2019). Mechanisms and regulation of dopamine release. *Curr. Opin. Neurobiol.*, 57, 46–53.

Liu, L., Xu, H., Ding, S., Wang, D., Song, G., and Huang, X. (2019). Phosphodiesterase 5 inhibitors as novel agents for the treatment of Alzheimer's disease. *Brain Res. Bull.*, 153, 223–231.

Liu, L., Zhang, C., Chen, J., and Li, X. (2020). Rediscovery of caffeine: an excellent drug for improving patient outcomes while fighting WARS. *Curr. Med. Chem.*, in press.

Liu, Q.-R., Canseco-Alba, A., Zhang, H.-Y., Tagliaferro, P., Chung, M., Dennis, E., Sanabria, B., et al. (2017). Cannabinoid type 2 receptors in dopamine neurons inhibits psychomotor behaviors, alters anxiety, depression, and alcohol preference. *Sci. Rep.*, 7(1), 17410. doi: 10.1038/s41598-017-17796-y.

Liu, Y., Sun, Y., Zhao, X., Kim, J.-Y., Luo, L., Wang, Q., Meng, X., et al. (2019). Enhancement of aggression induced by isolation rearing is associated with a lack of central serotonin. *Neurosci. Bull.*, 35. 84/1–/252.

Liu, Y., Vaddiparti, K., Cheong, J., and Cottler, L. B. (2020). Identification of typologies of cocaine use based on quantity, frequency, and duration of use: A latent profile analysis. *J. Addict. Med.*, in press.

Liu, Z., Zhou, J., Li, Y., Hu, F., Lu, Y., Ma, M., et al. (2014). Dorsal raphe neurons signal reward through 5-HT and glutamate. *Neuron*, 81, 1360–1374.

Livingstone, N., Hanratty, J., McShane, R., and Macdonald, G. (2015). Pharmacological interventions for cognitive decline in people with Down syndrome. *Cochrane Database Syst. Rev.*, 10, CD011546. doi: 10.1002/14651858. CD011546.pub2.

Livingstone-Banks, J., Ordóñez-Mena, J. M., and Hartmann-Boyce, J. (2019). Print-based self-help interventions for smoking cessation. *Cochrane Database Syst. Rev.*, 1(1), CD001118.

Lo, P. S., Wu, C. Y., Sue, H. Z., and Chen, H. H. (2009). Acute neurobehavioral effects of toluene: involvement of dopamine and NMDA receptors. *Toxicology*, 265, 34–40.

Lochhead, J. J., and Thorne, R. G. (2012). Intranasal delivery of biologics to the central nervous system. *Adv. Drug Deliv. Rev.*, 64, 614–628.

Loflin, M., and Earleywine, M. (2014). A new method of cannabis ingestion: The dangers of dabs? *Addict. Behav.*, 39, 1430–1433.

Logan, B. K., Goldfogel, G., Hamilton, R., and Kuhlman, J. (2009). Five deaths resulting from abuse of dextromethorphan sold over the internet. *J. Anal. Toxicol.*, 33, 99–103.

Logan, B. K., Yeakel, J. K., Goldfogel, G., Frost, M. P., Sandstrom, G., and Wickham, D. J. (2012). Dextromethorphan abuse leading to assault, suicide, or homicide. *J. Forensic Sci.*, 57, 1388–1394.

Logan, R. W., and McClung, C. A. (2016). Animal models of bipolar mania: The past, present and future. *Neuroscience*, 321, 163–188.

Loland, C. J., Mereu, M., Okunola, O. M., Cao, J., Prisinzano, T. E., Mazier, S., et al. (2012). R-Modafinil (armodafinil): A unique dopamine uptake inhibitor and potential medication for psychostimulant abuse. *Biol. Psychiatry*, 72, 405–413.

Long, X., Ye, J., Zhao, D., and Zhang, S.-J. (2015). Magnetogenetics: Remote noninvasive magnetic activation of neuronal activity with a magnetoreceptor. *Sci. Bull.*, 60, 2107–2119.

López-Álvarez, J., Sevilla-Llewellyn-Jones, J., and Agüera-Ortiz, L. (2019). Anticholinergic drugs in geriatric psychopharmacology. *Front. Neurosci.*, 13, 1309. doi: 10.3389/fnins.2019.01309.

López-Giménez, J. F., and González-Maeso, J. (2018). Hallucinogens and serotonin 5-HT2A receptor-mediated signaling pathways. *Curr. Top. Behav. Neurosci.*, 36, 45–73.

Lopez-Leon, S., González-Giraldo, Y., Wegman-Ostrosky, T., and Forero, D. A. (2021). Molecular genetics of substance use disorders: An umbrella review. *Neurosci. Biobehav. Rev.*, 124, 358–369.

López-Pelayo, H., Batalla, A., Balcells, M. M., Colom, J., and Gual, A. (2015). Assessment of cannabis use disorders: A systematic review of screening and diagnostic instruments. *Psychol. Med.*, 45, 1121–1133.

Lopez-Quintero, C., de los Cobos, J. P., Hasin, D. S., Okuda, M., Wang, S., Grant, B. F., et al. (2011a). Probability and predictors of transition from first use to dependence on nicotine, alcohol, cannabis, and cocaine: Results of the National Epidemiologic Survey on Alcohol and Related

Conditions (NESARC). *Drug Alcohol Depend.*, 115, 120–130.

Lopez-Quintero, C., Hasin, D. S., de los Cobos, J. P., Pines, A., Wang, S., Grant, B. F., et al. (2011b). Probability and predictors of remission from lifetime nicotine, alcohol, cannabis, or cocaine dependence: Results from the National Epidemiologic Survey on Alcohol and Related Conditions. *Addiction*, 106, 657–669.

Lorenzetti, V., Solowij, N., Fornito, A., Lubman, D., and Yücel, M. (2014). The association between regular cannabis exposure and alterations of human brain morphology: An updated review of the literature. *Curr. Pharm. Des.*, 20, 2138–2167.

Lou, X. (2018). Sensing exocytosis and triggering endocytosis at synapses: Synaptic vesicle exocytosis-endocytosis coupling. *Front. Cell. Neurosci.*, 12, 66. doi: 10.3389/fncel.2018.00066.

Louhiala, P. (2009). The ethics of the placebo in clinical trials revisited. *J. Med. Ethics*, 35, 407–409.

Loureiro-Vieira, S., Costa, V. M., Bastos, M.D.L., Carvalho, F., and Capela, J. P. (2017). Methylphenidate effects in the young brain: friend or foe? *Int. J. Dev. Neurosci.*, 60, 34–47.

Love, P. R., and Communications, London. (2012). Crystal Meth Case Study: Chris Thrall, Author of "Eating Smoke." Available at www.pressreleases.responsesource.com/news/72465/crystal-meth-case-study-chris-thrall-author-of-eating/.

Love, T., Laier, C., Brand, M., Hatch, L., and Hajela, R. (2015). Neuroscience of internet pornography addiction: A review and update. *Behav. Sci.*, 5, 388–433.

Lovinger, D. M. (2008). Presynaptic modulation by endocannabinoids. *Handb. Exp. Pharmacol.*, 184, 435–477.

Lovinger, D. M. (2018). Presynaptic ethanol actions: Potential roles in ethanol seeking. *Handb. Exp. Pharmacol.*, 248, 29–54.

Lovinger, D. M., and Roberto, M. (2013). Synaptic effects induced by alcohol. *Curr. Top. Behav. Neurosci.*, 13, 31–86.

Loweth, J. A., Tseng, K. Y., and Wolf, M. E. (2014). Adaptations in AMPA receptor transmission in the nucleus accumbens contributing to incubation of cocaine craving. *Neuropharmacology*, 76, 287–300

Lowry C.A., Hale M.W., Evans A.K., Heerkens J., Staub D.R., Gasser P.J., et al. (2008). Serotonergic systems, anxiety, and affective disorder: focus on the dorsomedial part of the dorsal raphe nucleus. *Ann. N. Y. Acad. Sci.*, 1148, 86–94.

Loyo, M., and Kontis, T. C. (2013). Cosmetic botulinum toxin: Has it replaced more invasive facial

procedures? *Facial Plast. Surg. Clin. North Am.*, 21, 285–298.

Lu, H.-C., and Mackie, K. (2016). An introduction to the endogenous cannabinoid system. *Biol. Psychiatry*, 79, 516–525.

Lu, H.-C., and Mackie, K. (2020). Review of the endocannabinoid system. *Biol. Psychiatry Cogn. Neurosci. Neuroimaging*, in press.

Lu, L., Grimm, J. W., Hope, B. T., and Shaham, Y. (2004). Incubation of cocaine craving after withdrawal: A review of preclinical data. *Neuropharmacology*, 47 (Suppl. 1), 214–226.

Lu, X., Barr, A. M., Kinney, J. W., Sanna, P., Conti, B., Behrens, M. M., et al. (2005). A role for galanin in antidepressant actions with a focus on the dorsal raphe nucleus. *Proc. Natl. Acad. Sci. USA*, 102, 874–879.

Lubman, D. I., Cheetham, A., and Yücel, M. (2015). Cannabis and adolescent brain development. *Pharmacol. Ther.*, 148, 1–16.

Lucas, D. R., and Newhouse, J. P. (1957). The toxic effect of sodium L-glutamate on the inner layers of the retina. *Arch. Ophthalmol.*, 58, 193–201.

Luna, L. E. (2011). Indigenous and mestizo use of ayahuasca: An overview. In R. G. dos Santos (Ed.), *The Ethnopharmacology of Ayahuasca*, pp. 1–21. Kerala, India: Transworld Research Network.

Lundholm, L., Frisell, T., Lichtenstein, P., and Långström, N. (2015). Anabolic androgenic steroids and violent offending: Confounding by polysubstance abuse among 10365 general population men. *Addiction*, 110, 100–108.

Luo, Z., and Geschwind, D. (2001). Microarray applications in neuroscience. *Neurobiol. Dis.*, 8, 183–193.

Luoma, J. B., Chwyl, C., Bathje, G. J., Davis, A. K., and Lancelotta, R. (2020). A meta-analysis of placebo-controlled trials of psychedelic-assisted therapy. *J. Psychoactive Drugs*, 52, 289–299.

Lupien, S. J., Juster, R. P., Raymond, C., and Marin, M. F. (2018). The effects of chronic stress on the human brain: From neurotoxicity, to vulnerability, to opportunity. *Front. Neuroendocrinol.*, 49, 91–105.

Lüscher, C., Robbins, T. W., and Everitt, B. J. (2020). The transition to compulsion in addiction. *Nat. Rev. Neurosci.*, 21, 247–263.

Lutz, B., Marsicano, G., Maldonado, R., and Hillard, C. J. (2015). The endocannabinoid system in guarding against fear, anxiety and stress. *Nat. Rev. Neurosci.*, 16, 705–718.

Ly, C., Greb, A. C., Cameron, L. P., Wong, J. M., Barragan, E. V., Wilson, P. C., Burbach, K. F., et al. (2018). Psychedelics promote structural and functional

neural plasticity. *Cell Rep.*, 23, 3170–3182.

Lydon, D. M., Wilson, S. J., Child, A., and Geier, C. F. (2014). Adolescent brain maturation and smoking: What we know and where we're headed. *Neurosci. Biobehav. Rev.*, 45, 323–342.

Lynch, G., Cox, C. D., and Gall, C. M. (2014). Pharmacological enhancement of memory or cognition in normal subjects. *Front. Syst. Neurosci.*, 8, 90. doi: 10.3389/fnsys.2014.00090.

Lynskey, M. T., Coffey, C., Degenhardt, L., Carlin, J. B., and Patton, G. (2003). A longitudinal study of the effects of adolescent cannabis use on high school completion. *Addiction*, 98, 685–692.

Lynskey, M., and Hall, W. (2000). The effects of adolescent cannabis use on educational attainment: A review. *Addiction*, 95, 1621–1630.

Lyon, J. (2017). Chess study revives debate over cognition-enhancing drugs. *JAMA*, 318, 784–786. doi: 10.1001/ jama.2017.8114.

M

Ma, T., Sun, Y., and Ku, Y. (2019). Effects of non-invasive brain stimulation on stimulant craving in users of cocaine, amphetamine, or methamphetamine: A systematic review and meta-analysis. *Front. Neurosci.*, 13, 1095. doi: 10.3389/fnins.2019.01095.

MacAndrew, C., and Edgerton, R. B. (1969). *Drunken Comportment: A Social Explanation*. Chicago: Aldine.

Maccarrone, M., and Wenger, T. (2005). Effects of cannabinoids on hypothalamic and reproductive function. *Handb. Exp. Pharmacol.*, 168, 555–571.

Maccarrone, M., Bab, I., Bíro, T., Cabral, G. A., Dey, S. K., Di Marzo, V., et al. (2015). Endocannabinoid signaling at the periphery: 50 years after THC. *Trends Pharmacol. Sci.*, 36, 277–296.

Maccarrone, M., Rapino, C., Francavilla, F., and Barbonetti, A. (2021). Cannabinoid signalling and effects of cannabis on the male reproductive system. *Nat. Rev. Urol.*, 18, 19–32.

Maccioni, P., and Colombo, G. (2019). Potential of GABA_B receptor positive allosteric modulators in the treatment of alcohol use disorder. *CNS Drugs*, 33(2), 107–123. https://doi.org/10.1007/s40263-018-0596-3

Macdonald, K., and Macdonald, T. M. (2010). The peptide that binds: A systematic review of oxytocin and its prosocial effects in humans. *Harv. Rev. Psychiatry*, 18, 1–21.

Macfarlane, V., and Christie, G. (2015). Synthetic cannabinoid withdrawal: A new demand on detoxification services. *Drug Alcohol Rev.*, 34, 147–153.

Machado-Vieira, R., Ibrahim, L., and Zarate, C. A., Jr. (2010). Histone deacetylases and mood disorders: Epigenetic programming in gene-environment interactions. *CNS Neurosci. Ther.*, 17, 699–704.

Machelska, H., and Celik, M. Ö. (2018). Advances in achieving opioid analgesia without side effects. *Front. Pharm.*, 9, 1388. https://doi.org/10.3389/fphar.2018.01388

Mackie, C. J., Wilson, J., Freeman, T. P., Craft, S., Escamilla De La Torre, T., and Lynskey, M. T. (2021). A latent class analysis of cannabis use products in a general population sample of adolescents and their association with paranoia, hallucinations, cognitive disorganisation and grandiosity. *Addict. Behav.*, 117, 106837. doi: 10.1016/j.addbeh.2021.106837.

Mackie, K. (2007). From active ingredients to the discovery of the targets: The cannabinoid receptors. *Chem. Biodiversity*, 4, 1693–1706.

MacLean, K. A., Johnson, M. W., Reissig, C. J., Prisinzano, T. E., and Griffiths, R. R. (2013). Dose-related effects of salvinorin A in humans: Dissociative, hallucinogenic, and memory effects. *Psychopharmacology*, 226, 381–392.

Macleod, J., Oakes, R., Copello, A., Crome, I., Egger, M., Hickman, M., Oppenkowski, T. et al. (2004). Psychological and social sequelae of cannabis and other illicit drug use by young people: a systematic review of longitudinal, general population studies. *Lancet*, 363, 1579–1588.

Maddux, J. F., and Desmond, D. P. (1981). *Careers of Opioid Users*. New York: Praeger.

Madhusoodanan, S., Parida, S., and Jimenez, C. (2010). Hyperprolactinemia associated with psychotropics: A review. *Hum. Psychopharmacol. Clin. Exp.*, 25, 281–297.

Madsen, H. B., and Ahmed, S. H. (2015). Drug versus sweet reward: Greater attraction to and preference for sweet versus drug cues. *Addict. Biol.*, 20, 433–444.

Madsen, M. K., Fisher, P. M., Burmester, D., Dyssegaard, A., Stenbæk, D. S., Kristiansen, S., Johansen, S. S., et al. (2019). Psychedelic effects of psilocybin correlate with serotonin 2A receptor occupancy and plasma psilocin levels. *Neuropsychopharmacology*, 44, 1328–1334.

Maejima, T., Masseck, O. A., Mark, M. D., and Herlitze, S. (2013). Modulation of firing and synaptic transmission of serotonergic neurons by intrinsic G protein-coupled receptors and ion channels. *Front. Integr. Neurosci.*, 7, 40. doi: 10.3389/fnint.2013.00040.

Maeng L.Y. and Milad M.R. (2015). Sex differences in anxiety disorders: Interactions between fear, stress, and gonadal hormones. *Horm. Behav.*, 76, 106–117.

Maessen, G. C., Wijnhoven, A. M., Neijzen, R. L., Paulus, M. C., van Heel, D.A.M., Bomers, B.H.A., Boersma, L. E., et al. Nicotine intoxication by e-cigarette liquids: a study of case reports and pathophysiology. *Clin. Toxicol.*, 58, 1–8.

Mahabir, V. K., Merchant, J. J., Smith, C., and Garibaldi, A. (2020). Medical cannabis use in the United States: a retrospective database study. *J. Cannabis Res.*, 2, 32. doi: 10.1186/s42238-020-00038-w.

Mahler, S. V., Moorman, D. E., Smith, R. J., James, M. H., and Aston-Jones, G. (2014). Motivational activation: A unifying hypothesis of orexin/hypocretin function. *Nat. Neurosci.*, 17, 1298–1303.

Mahoney, C. E., Cogswell, A., Koralnik, I. J., and Scammell, T. E. (2019). The neurobiological basis of narco-lepsy. *Nat. Rev. Neurosci.*, 20, 83–93.

Mahoney, J. J., III, Kalechstein, A. D., De La Garza, R., II, and Newton, T. F. (2007). A qualitative and quantitative review of cocaine-induced craving: The phenomenon of priming. *Prog. Neuropsychopharmacol. Biol. Psychiatry*, 31, 593–599.

Maier, S. F., and Watkins, L. R. (2010). Role of the medial prefrontal cortex in coping and resilience. *Brain Res.*, 1355, 52–60.

Maiti, P., Manna, J., Ilavazhagan, G., Rossignol, J., and Dunbar, G. L. (2015). Molecular regulation of dendritic spine dynamics and their potential impact on synaptic plasticity and neurological diseases. *Neurosci. Biobehav. Rev.*, 59, 208–237.

Maitre, M., Klein, C., and Mensah-Nyagan, A. G. (2016). Mechanisms for the specific properties of γ-hydroxybutyrate in brain. *Med. Res. Rev.*, 36, 363–388.

Majeed, A., Xiong, J., Teopiz, K. M., Ng, J., Ho, R., Rosenblat, J. D., Phan, L., et al. (2021). Efficacy of dextromethorphan for the treatment of depression: a systematic review of preclinical and clinical trials. *Expert Opin. Emerg. Drugs*, 26, 63–74.

Majic´, T., Schmidt, T. T., and Gallinat, J. (2015). Peak experiences and the afterglow phenomenon: When and how do therapeutic effects of hallucinogens depend on psychedelic experiences? *J. Psychopharmacol.*, 29, 241–253.

Maksymetz, J., Moran, S. P., and Conn, P. J. (2017). Targeting metabotropic glutamate receptors for novel treatments of schizophrenia. *Mol. Brain*, 10, 15. doi: 10.1186/s13041-017-0293-z.

Malas, M., van der Tempel, J., Schwartz, R., Minichiello, A., Lightfoot, C., Noormohamed, A., et al. (2016). Electronic cigarettes for smoking cessation: A systematic review. *Nicotine Tob. Res.*, 18, 1926–1936.

Malcolm, R., Myrick, H., Li, X., Henderson, S., Brady, K. T., George, M. S., et al. (2016). Regional brain activity in abstinent methamphetamine dependent males following cue exposure. *J. Drug Abuse*, 2, 1. doi: 10.21767/2471853X.100016.

Maldonado, R., and Berrendero, F. (2010). Endogenous cannabinoid and opioid systems and their role in nicotine addiction. *Curr. Drug Targ.*, 11, 440–449.

Maldonado, R., Baños, J. E., and Cabañero, D. (2016). The endocannabinoid system and neuropathic pain. *Pain*, 157(Suppl. 1), S23–S32.

Maldonado, R., Calvé, P., García-Blanco, A., Domingo-Rodriguez, L., Senabre, E., and Martín-García, E. (2021). Genomics and epigenomics of addiction. *Am. J. Med. Genet. B, Neuropsychiatr. Genet.*, 186, 128–139.

Maletic, V., and Raison, C. L. (2009). Neurobiology of depression, fibromyalgia and neuropathic pain. *Front. Biosci.*, 14, 5291–5338.

Malfitano, A. M., Basu, S., Maresz, K., Bifulco, M., and Dittel, B. N. (2014). What we know and do not know about the cannabinoid receptor 2 (CB$_2$). *Semin. Immunol.*, 26, 369–379.

Malik, A. R., and Willnow, T. E. (2019). Excitatory amino acid transporters in physiology and disorders of the central nervous system. *Int. J. Mol. Sci.*, 20, 5671. doi: 10.3390/ijms20225671.

Malinauskas, B. M., Aeby, V. G., Overton, R. F., Carpenter-Aeby, T., and BarberHeidal, K. (2007). A survey of energy drink consumption patterns among college students. *Nutr. J.*, 6, 35. doi: 10.1186/1475-2891-6-35.

Malizia, A. L., Cunningham, V. J., Bell, C. J., Liddle, P. F., Jones, T., et al (1998). Decreased brain GABA(A)-benzodiazepine receptor binding in panic disorder: Preliminary results from a quantitative PET study. *Arch. Gen. Psychiatry*, 55, 715–720.

Mallette, J. R., Casale, J. F., Jordan, J., Morello, D. R., and Beyer, P. M. (2016). Geographically sourcing cocaine's origin – Delineation of the nineteen major coca growing regions of South America. *Sci. Rep.*, 6, 23520. doi: 10.1038/srep23520.

Malone, T. C., Mennenga, S. E., Guss, J., Podrebarac, S. K., Owens, L. T., Bossis, A. P., Belser, A. B., et al. (2018). Individual experiences in four cancer patients following psilocybin-assisted psychotherapy. *Front. Pharmacol.*, 9, 256. doi: 10.3389/fphar.2018.00256.

Malvaez, M., Sanchis-Segura, C., Vo, D., Lattal, K. M., and Wood, M. A. (2010). Modulation of chromatin modification facilitates extinction of cocaine-induced conditioned place preference. *Biol. Psychiatry*, 67, 36–43.

Manglik, A., Lin, H., Aryal, D. K., McCorvy, J. D., Dengler, D., Corder, G., et al. (2016). Structure-based discovery of opioid analgesics with reduced side effects. *Nature*, 537, 185–190. doi. org/10.1038/nature19112.

Mann, J. (2000). *Murder, Magic & Medicine* (2nd ed.). Oxford: Oxford University Press.

Mann, K., Torup, L., Sørensen, P., Gual, A., Swift, R., Walker, B., and van den Brink, W. (2016). Nalmefene for the management of alcohol dependence: Review on its pharmacology, mechanism of action and meta-analysis on its clinical efficacy. *Eur. Neuropsychopharmacol.*, 26, 1941–1949.

Mann, R. E., Smart, R. G., and Govoni, R. (2004). The Epidemiology of Alcoholic Liver Disease. National Institute on Alcohol Abuse and Alcoholism. Available at www.pubs.niaaa.nih.gov/publications/arh27–3/209–219.htm.

Manna, S.S.S., and Umathe, S. N. (2012). Involvement of transient receptor potential vanilloid type 1 channels in the pro-convulsant effect of anandamide in pentyltetrazole-induced seizures. *Epilepsy Res.*, 100, 113–124.

Mansour, A., and Watson, S. J. (1993). Anatomical distribution of opioid receptors in mammalians: An overview. In A. Herz (Ed.), *Opioids I*, Volume 104, Handbook of Experimental Pharmacology (pp. 79–106). New York: SpringerVerlag.

Mansour, A., Khachaturian, H., Lewis, M. E., Akil, H., and Watson, S. J. (1988). Anatomy of CNS opioid receptors. *Trends Neurosci.*, 7, 308–314.

Mantsch, J. R., Vranjkovic, O., Twining, R. C., Gasser, P. J., McReynolds, J. R., and Blacktop, J. M. (2014). Neurobiological mechanisms that contribute to stressrelated cocaine use. *Neuropharmacology*, 76, 383–394.

Manvich, D. F., Petko, A. K., Branco, R. C., Foster, S. L., Porter-Stansky, K. A., Stout, K. A., Newman, A. H., et al. (2019). Selective D2 and D3 receptor antagonists oppositely modulate cocaine responses in mice via distinct postsynaptic mechanisms in nucleus accumbens. *Neuropsychopharmacology*, 44, 1445–1455.

Mao, J., Price, D. D., Phillips, L. L., Lu, J., and Mayer, D. J. (1995). Increases in protein kinase C immunoreactivity in the spinal cord of rats associated with tolerance to the analgesic effects of morphine. *Brain Res.*, 677, 257–267.

Mao, L.-M., and Wang, J. Q. (2016). Synaptically localized mitogen-activated protein kinases: Local substrates and regulation. *Mol. Neurobiol.*, 53, 6309–6315.

Maqueda, A. E., Valle, M., Addy, P. H., Antonijoan, R. M., Puntes, M., Coimbra, J., et al. (2015). Salvinorin-A induces intense dissociative effects, blocking external sensory perception and modulating interoception and sense of body ownership in humans. *Int. J. Neuropsychopharmacol.*, 18, 1–14.

Maqueda, A. E., Valle, M., Addy, P. H., Antonijoan, R. M., Puntes, M., Coimbra, J., et al. (2016). Naltrexone but not ketanserin antagonizes the subjective, cardiovascular, and neuroendocrine effects of salvinorin-A in humans. *Int. J. Neuropsychopharmacol.*, 19, 1–13.

Maraz, A., Griffiths, M. D., and Demetrovics, Z. (2016). The prevalence of compulsive buying: A meta-analysis. *Addiction*, 111, 408–419.

Maraz, A., Urbán, R., Griffiths, M. D., and Demetrovics, Z. (2015). An empirical investigation of dance addiction. *PLOS ONE*, 10, e0125988.

Marcellino, D., Kehr, J., Agnati, L. F., and Fuxe, K. (2012). Increased affinity of dopamine for D2-like versus D1-like receptors: Relevance for volume transmission in interpreting PET findings. *Synapse*, 66, 196–203.

Marco, E. M., Adriani, W., Ruocco, L. A., Canese, R., Sadile, A. G., and Laviola, G. (2011). Neurobehavioral adaptations to methylphenidate: The issue of early adolescent exposure. *Neurosci. Biobehav. Rev.*, 35, 1722–1739.

Marconi, A., Di Forti, M., Lewis, C. M., Murray, R. M., and Vassos, E. (2016). Meta-analysis of the association between the level of cannabis use and risk of psychosis. *Schiz. Bull.*, 42, 1262–1269.

Marcotte, E., Srivastava, L., and Quirion, R. (2001). DNA microarrays in neuropsychopharmacology. *Trends Pharmacol. Sci.*, 22, 426–436.

Marczinski, C. A., and Fillmore, M. T. (2009). Acute alcohol tolerance on subjective intoxication and simulated driving performance in binge drinkers. *Psychol. Addict. Behav.*, 23, 238–247.

Marichal-Cancino, B. A., Fajardo-Valdez, A., Ruiz-Contreras, A. E., Méndez-Diaz, M., and Prospéro-García, O. (2016). Advances in the physiology of GPR55 in the central nervous system. *Curr. Neuropharmacol.*, 15, 771–778.

Marinelli, S., Pacioni, S., Cannich, A., Marsicano, G., and Bacci, A. (2009). Selfmodulation of neocortical pyramidal neurons by endocannabinoids. *Nat. Neurosci.*, 12, 1488–1490.

Markou, A., Chiamulera, C., Geyer, M. A., Tricklebank, M., and Steckler, T. (2009). Removing Obstacles in Neuroscience Drug Discovery: The Future Path for Animal Models. *Neuropsychopharmacology*, 34(1),

74–89. https://doi.org/10.1038/npp.2008.173

Markram, H., Toledo-Rodriguez, M., Wang, Y., Gupta, A., Silberberg, G., and Wu, C. (2004). Interneurons of the neocortical inhibitory system. Nat. Rev. Neurosci., 5, 793–807.

Marks, I. (1990). Behavioural (non-chemical) addictions. Br. J. Addict., 85, 1389–1394.

Markus, C. R., Olivier, B., Panhuysen, G. E. M., Van der Gugten, J., Alles, M. S., Tuiten, A., et al. (2000). The bovine protein α-lactalbumin increases the plasma ratio of tryptophan to the other large neutral amino acids, and in vulnerable subjects raises brain serotonin activity, reduces cortisol concentration, and improves mood under stress. Am. J. Clin. Nutr., 71, 1536–1544.

Marlatt, G. A., and Rohsenow, D. J. (1980). Cognitive processes in alcohol use: Expectancy and the balanced placebo design. In N. K. Mello (Ed.), Advances in Substance Abuse: Behavioral and Biological Research, pp. 159–199. Greenwich, CT: JAI.

Marom-Haham, L., and Shulman, A. (2016). Cigarette smoking and hormones. Curr. Opin. Obstet. Gynecol., 28, 230–235.

Marona-Lewicka, D., Thisted, R. A., and Nichols, D. E. (2005). Distinct temporal phases in the behavioral pharmacology of LSD: dopamine D2 receptor-mediated effects in the rat and implications for psychosis. Psychopharmacology, 180, 427–435.

Marsh, D. F. (1951). Outlines of Fundamental Pharmacology. Springfield, IL: Charles C. Thomas.

Marshall, B. D. L., and Werb, D. (2010). Health outcomes associated with methamphetamine use among young people: A systematic review. Addiction, 105, 991–1002.

Marshall, Jr., E. K., and Fritz, W. F. (1953). The metabolism of ethyl alcohol. J. Pharmacol. Exp. Ther., 109, 431.

Marsicano, G., and Lafenêtre, P. (2009). Roles of the endocannabinoid system in learning and memory. Curr. Top. Behav. Neurosci., 1, 201–230.

Marsiglia, F. F., Ayers, S. L., and Kiehne, E. (2019). Reducing inhalant use in Latino adolescents through synchronized parent-adolescent interventions. J. Prev. Interv. Community, 47, 182–197.

Marsit, C. J. (2016). Placental epigenetics in children's environmental health. Semin. Reprod. Med., 34, 36–41.

Martell, B. A., O'Connor, P. G., Kerns, R. D., Becker, W. C., Morales, K. H., Kosten, T. R., and Fiellin, D. A. (2007). Systematic review: Opioid treatment for chronic back pain: prevalence, efficacy, and association with addiction. Ann. Intern. Med., 146(2), 116–127. https://doi.org/10.7326/0003-4819-146-2-200701160-00006

Martin, E. I., Ressler, K. J., Binder, E., and Nemeroff, C. B. (2010). The neurobiology of anxiety disorders: Brain imaging, genetics, and psychoneuroendocrinology. Clin. Lab. Med., 30, 865–891.

Martin, H. L., and Teismann, P. (2009). Glutathione: A review on its role and significance in Parkinson's disease. FASEB J., 23, 3263–3272.

Martin, L. M., and Sayette, M. A. (2018). A review of the effects of nicotine on social functioning. Exp. Clin. Psychopharmacol., 26, 425–434.

Martin, M. M., Graham, D. L., McCarthy, D. M., Bhide, P. G., and Stanwood, G. D. (2016). Cocaine-induced neurodevelopmental deficits and underlying mechanisms. Birth Defects Res. C Embryo Today, 108, 147–173.

Martin, W. R. (1967). Opioid Antagonists. Pharmacol. Rev., 19(4), 463–521.

Martin, W. R., Eades, C. G., Thompson, J. A., Huppler, R. E., and Gilbert, P. E. (1976). The effects of morphine and naloxone-like drugs in the non-dependent and morphine dependent chronic spinal dog. J. Pharmacol. Exp. Ther., 197, 517–532.

Martinak, B., Bolis, R. A., Black, J. R., Fargason, R. E., and Birur, B. (2017). Dextromethorphan in cough syrup: The poor man's psychosis. Psychopharmacol. Bull., 47, 59–63.

Martinasek, M. P., McGrogan, J. B., and Maysonet, A. (2016). A systematic review of the respiratory effects of inhalational marijuana. Respir. Care, 61, 1543–1551.

Martínez-Lozada, Z., and Ortega, A. (2015). Glutamatergic transmission: A matter of three. Neural Plast., 2015, 787396. doi: 10.1155/2015/787396.

Martinotti, G., Santacroce, R., Pettorruso, M., Montemitro, C., Spano, M. C., Lorusso, M., di Giannantonio, M., et al. (2018). Hallucinogen persisting perception disorder: Etiology, clinical features, and therapeutic perspectives. Brain Sci., 8, 47. doi: 10.3390/brainsci8030047.

Martins, D., Tavares, I., and Morgado, C. (2014). "Hotheaded": The role of TRPV1 in brain functions. Neuropharmacology, 85, 151–157.

Martins, S. S., Fenton, M. C., Keyes, K. M., Blanco, C., Zhu, H., and Storr, C. L. (2012). Mood and anxiety disorders and their association with nonmedical prescription opioid use and prescription opioid-use disorder: Longitudinal evidence from the National Epidemiologic Study on Alcohol and Related Conditions. Psychol. Med., 42, 1261–1272.

Martuza, R. L., Chiocca, E. A., Jenike, M. A., Giriunas, I. E., and Ballantine, H. T. (1990). Stereotactic radiofrequency thermal cingulotomy for obsessive compulsive disorder. J. Neuropsychiatry Clin. Neurosci., 2, 331–336.

Marx, M.-C., Billups, D., and Billups, B. (2015). Maintaining the presynaptic glutamate supply for excitatory neurotransmission. J. Neurosci. Res., 93, 1031–1044.

Mash, D. C., Duque, L., Page, B., and Allen-Ferdinand, K. (2018). Ibogaine detoxification transitions opioid and cocaine abusers between dependence and abstinence: Clinical observations and treatment outcomes. Front. Pharmacol., 9, 529. doi: 10.3389/fphar.2018.00529.

Maskos, U. (2008). The cholinergic mesopontine tegmentum is a relatively neglected nicotinic master modulator of the dopaminergic system: Relevance to drugs of abuse and pathology. Br. J. Pharmacol., 153, S438–S445.

Matak, I., Bölcskei, K., Bach-Rojecky, L., and Helyes, Z. (2019). Mechanisms of botulinum toxin type A action on pain. Toxins, 11, 459. doi: 10.3390/toxins11080459.

Mathee, K., Cickovski, T., Deoraj, A., Stollstorff, M., and Narasimhan, G. (2020). The gut microbiome and neuropsychiatric disorders: implications for attention deficit hyperactivity disorder (ADHD). J. Med. Microbiol., 69, 14–24.

Mathew, S. J., Price, R. B., and Charney, D. S. (2008). Recent advances in the neurobiology of anxiety disorders: Implications for novel therapeutics. Am. J. Med. Genet. C Semin. Med. Genet., 148C, 89–98.

Mathis, A., Mamidanna, P., Cury, K. M., Abe, T., Murthy, V. N., Mathis, M. W., and Bethge, M. (2018). DeepLabCut: Markerless pose estimation of user-defined body parts with deep learning. Nat. Neurosci., 21(9), 1281–1289. https://doi.org/10.1038/s41593-018-0209-y

Matson, J. L., and Burns, C. O. (2019). Pharmacological treatment of autism spectrum disorder. In S.M. Evans and K.M. Carpenter (Eds.), APA Handbook of Psychopharmacology, pp. 373–396. Washington, DC: American Psychological Association.

Matsuda, L. A., Lolait, S. J., Brownstein, M. J., Young, A. C., and Bonner, T. I. (1990). Structure of a cannabinoid receptor and functional expression of the cloned cDNA. Nature, 346, 561–564.

Matsumoto, T., Sakari, M., Okada, M., Yokoyama, A., Takahashi, S., Kouzmenko, A., et al. (2013). The androgen receptor in health and disease. Annu. Rev. Physiol., 75, 201–224.

Mattei, D., Schweibold, R., and Wolf, S. A. (2015). Brain in flames: Animal models of psychosis: Utility and limitations. Neuropsychiat. Dis. Treat., 11, 1313–1329.

Matthes, S., and Bader, M. (2018). Peripheral serotonin synthesis as a new drug target. Trends Pharmacol. Sci., 39, 560–572.

Mattson, C. L. (2021). Trends and Geographic Patterns in Drug and Synthetic Opioid Overdose Deaths—United States, 2013–2019. MMWR. Morbidity and Mortality Weekly Report, 70. https://doi.org/10.15585/mmwr.mm7006a4

Maurice, N., Liberge, M., Jaouen, F., Ztaou, S., Hanini, M., Camon, J., Deisseroth, K., et al. (2015). Striatal cholinergic interneurons control motor behavior and basal ganglia function in experimental parkinsonism. Cell Rep., 13, 657–666.

Mawe, G. M., and Hoffman, J. M. (2013). Serotonin signaling in the gastrointestinal tract: Functions, dysfunctions, and therapeutic targets. Nat. Rev. Gastroenterol. Hepatol., 10, 473–486.

Maxwell, J. C., and Rutkowski, B. A. (2008). The prevalence of methamphetamine and amphetamine abuse in North America: A review of the indicators, 1992–2007. Drug Alcohol Rev., 27, 229–235.

May, M. B., and Glode, A. E. (2016). Dronabinol for chemotherapy-induced nausea and vomiting unresponsive to antiemetics. Cancer Manag. Res., 8, 49–55.

Mayberg, H. S., and Frost, J. J. (1990). Opiate receptors. In J. J. Frost and H. N. Wagner, Jr. (Eds.), Quantitative Imaging: Neuroreceptors, Neurotransmitters, and Enzymes, pp. 81–95. New York: Raven.

Maycox, P. R., Kelly, F., Tayor, A., Bates, S., Reid, J., Logendra, R., et al. (2009). Analysis of gene expression in two large schizophrenia cohorts identifies multiple changes associated with nerve terminal function. Mol. Psychiatry, 14, 1083–1094. doi: 10.1038/mp.2009.18.

Mayer, B. (2014). How much nicotine kills a human? Tracing back the generally accepted lethal dose to dubious self-experiments in the nineteenth century. Arch. Toxicol., 88, 5–7.

Mayet, A., Legleye, S., Falissard, B., and Chau, N. (2012). Cannabis use stages as predictors of subsequent initiation with other illicit drugs among French adolescents: Use of a multistate model. Addict. Behav., 37, 160–166.

Mayhew, K. P., Flay, B. R., and Mott, J. A. (2000). Stages in the development of adolescent smoking. Drug Alcohol Depend., 59 (Suppl. 1), S61–S81.

Mayor, D., and Tymianski, M. (2018). Neurotransmitters in the mediation of cerebral ischemic injury. *Neuropharmacology*, 134, 178–188.

Mazier, W., Saucisse, N., Gatta-Cherifi, B., and Cota, D. (2015). The endocannabinoid system: Pivotal orchestrator of obesity and metabolic disease. *Trends Endocrinol. Metab.*, 26, 524–537.

McAlinden, K. D., Eapen, M. S., Lu, W., Sharma, P., and Sohal, S. S. (2020). The rise of electronic nicotine delivery systems and the emergence of electronic-cigarette-driven disease. *Am. J. Physiol. Lung Cell. Mol. Physiol.*, 319, L585–L595.

McAlpine, D. (1965). Multiple Sclerosis: A Reappraisal by Douglas McAlpine. Edinburgh: Livingstone.

McBride, W. J., Rodd, Z. A., Bell, R. L., Lumeng, L., and Li, T. K. (2014). The alcohol-preferring (P) and high-alcoholdrinking (HAD) rats: Animal models of alcoholism. *Alcohol*, 48, 209–215.

McCabe, S. E., and West, B. T. (2013). Medical and nonmedical use of prescription stimulants: Results from a national multicohort study. *J. Am. Acad. Child Adolesc. Psychiatry*, 52, 1272–1280.

McCall, C., and Singer, T. (2012). The animal and human neuroendocrinology of social cognition, motivation and behavior. *Nat. Neurosci.*, 15, 681–688.

McCall, J. G., Al-Hasani, R., Siuda, E. R., Hong, D. Y., Norris, A. J., Ford, C. P., and Bruchas, M. R. (2015). CRH engagement of the locus coeruleus noradrenergic system mediates stress-induced anxiety. *Neuron*, 87, 605–620.

McCall, J. G., Siuda, E. R., Bhatti, D. L., Lawson, L. A., McElligott, Z. A., Stuber, G. D., et al. (2017). Locus coeruleus to basolateral amygdala noradrenergic projections promote anxiety-like behavior. *eLife*, 6, 1–23.

McCann, M. E., and Soriano, S. G. (2019). Does general anesthesia affect neurodevelopment in infants and children? *BMJ*, 367, l6459. doi: 10.1136/bmj.l6459.

McCarley, R. W. (2007). Neurobiology of REM and NREM sleep. *Sleep Med.*, 8, 302–330.

McClernon, F. J., Addicott, M. A., and Sweitzer, M. M. (2015). Smoking abstinence and neurocognition: Implications for cessation and relapse. *Curr. Top. Behav. Neurosci.*, 23, 193–227.

McClernon, F. J., and Kollins, S. H. (2008). ADHD and smoking: From genes to brain to behavior. *Ann. N. Y. Acad. Sci.*, 1141, 131–147.

McClung, C. A. (2007). Circadian genes, rhythms and the biology of mood disorders. *Pharmacol. Ther.*, 114, 222–232.

McEwen B.S., Nasca C., and Gray J.D. (2016). Stress effects on neuronal structure: hippocampus, amygdala, and prefrontal cortex. *Neuropsychopharmacology*, 41(1), 3–23.

McEwen, B. S. (2008). Central effects of stress hormones in health and disease: Understanding the protective and damaging effects of stress and stress mediators. *Eur. J. Pharmacol.*, 583, 174–185.

McEwen, B. S. (2010). Stress, sex, and neural adaptation to a changing environment: Mechanisms of neuronal remodeling. *Ann. N. Y. Acad. Sci.*, 1204 (Suppl. E), 38–59.

McEwen, B. S. (2012). Brain on stress: How the social environment gets under the skin. *Proc. Natl. Acad. Sci. USA*, 109 (Suppl. 2), 17180–17185.

McEwen, B. S., Chattarji, S., Diamond, D. M., Jay, T. M., Reagan, L. P., Svenningsson, P., et al. (2010). The neurobiological properties of tianeptine (Stablon): From monoamine hypothesis to glutamatergic modulation. *Mol. Psychiatry*, 15, 237–249.

McEwen, B. S. and Akil, H. (2020). Revisiting the stress concept: Implications for affective disorders. *J. Neurosci.*, 40(1), 12–21.

McEwen, B. S., Bowles, N. P., Gray, J. D., Hill, M. N., Hunter, R. G., Karatsoreos, I. N., et al. (2015). Mechanisms of stress in the brain. *Nat. Neurosci.*, 18, 1353–1363.

McGaughy, J., Dalley, J. W., Morrison, C. H., Everitt, B. J., and Robbins, T. W. (2002). Selective behavioral and neurochemical effects of cholinergic lesions produced by intrabasalis infusions of 192 IgG-saporin on attentional performance in a five-choice serial reaction time task. *J. Neurosci.*, 22, 1905–1913.

McGlothlin, W. H., and West, L. J. (1968). The marihuana problem: An overview. *Am. J. Psychiatry*, 125, 370–378.

McGonigle, P. (2014). Animal models of CNS disorders. *Biochem. Pharmacol.*, 87, 140–149.

McGonigle, P., and Ruggeri, B. (2014). Animal models of human disease: Challenges in enabling translation. *Biochem. Pharmacol.*, 87, 162–171.

McGrath-Morrow, S. A., Gorzkowski, J., Groner, J. A., Rule, A. M., Wilson, K., Tanski, S. E., Collaco, J. M., et al. (2020). The effects of nicotine on development. *Pediatrics*, 145(3), e20191346. doi: 10.1542/peds.2019-1346.

McKay, J. R., Van Horn, D., Rennert, L., Drapkin, M., Ivey, M., and Koppenhaver, J. (2013). Factors in sustained recovery from cocaine dependence. *J. Subst. Abuse Treat.*, 45, 163–172.

McKetin, R. (2018). Methamphetamine psychosis: insights from the past. *Addiction*, 113, 1522–1527.

McKetin, R., Coen, A., and Kaye, S. (2015). A comprehensive review of the effects of mixing caffeinated energy drinks with alcohol. *Drug Alcohol Depend.*, 151, 15–30.

McLaughlin, I., Dani, J. A., and De Biasi, M. (2015). Nicotine withdrawal. *Curr. Top. Behav. Neurosci.*, 24, 99–123.

McLaughlin, K. J., Baran, S. E., and Conrad, C. D. (2009). Chronic stressand sex-specific neuromorphological and functional change in limbic structures. *Mol. Neurobiol.*, 40, 166–182.

McLaughlin, R. J., and Gobbi, G. (2012). Cannabinoids and emotionality: A neuroanatomical perspective. *Neuroscience, 204,* 134–144.

McLean, C. P., Asnaani, A., Litz, B. T., and Hofmann, S. G. (2011). Gender differences in anxiety disorders: Prevalence, course of illness, comorbidity and burden of illness. *J. Psychiatr. Res.*, 45, 1027–1035.

McLean, P. G., Borman, R. A., and Lee, K. (2006). 5-HT in the enteric nervous system: Gut function and neuropharmacology. *Trends Neurosci.*, 30, 9–13.

McLellan, A. T., Lewis, D. C., O'Brien, C. P., and Kleber, H. D. (2000). Drug dependence, a chronic medical illness: Implications for treatment, insurance, and outcomes evaluation. *JAMA*, 284, 1689–1695.

McLellan, T. M., Caldwell, J. A., and Lieberman, H. R. (2016). A review of caffeine's effects on cognitive, physical and occupational performance. *Neurosci. Biobehav. Rev.*, 71, 294–312.

McMahon L.R. (2015). The rise (and fall?) of drug discrimination research. *Drug Alcohol Depend.*, 151, 284–288.

McMahon, L. R. (2019). Perspective green tobacco sickness: Mecamylamine, varenicline, and nicotine vaccine as clinical research tools and potential therapeutics. *Expert Rev. Clin. Pharmacol.*, 12, 189–195.

McMillan, R., and Muthukumaraswamy, S. D. (2020). The neurophysiology of ketamine: an integrative review. *Rev. Neurosci.*, 31, 457–503. Republished with permission of Walter de Gruyter and Co.; permission conveyed through Copyright Clearance Center, Inc.

McNeece, C. A., and DiNitto, D. M. (1998). *Chemical Dependency*. Boston: Allyn and Bacon.

McPherson, S. M., Burduli, E., Smith, C. L., Herron, J., Oluwoye, O., Hirchak, K., Orr, M. F., et al. (2018). A review of contingency management for the treatment of substance-use disorders: adaptation for underserved populations, use of experimental technologies, and personalized optimization strategies. *Subst. Abuse Rehabil.*, 9, 43–57.

McQuown, S. C., and Wood, M. A. (2010). Epigenetic regulation in substance use disorders. *Curr. Psychiatry Rep.*, 12, 145–153.

Meade, C. S., Bell, R. P., Towe, S. L., and Hall, S. A. (2020). Cocaine-related alterations in fronto-parietal gray matter volume correlate with train and behavioral impulsivity. *Drug Alcohol Depend.*, 206, 107757. doi: 10.1016/j.drugalcdep.2019.107757.

Meckel, K. R., and Kiraly, D. D. (2019). A potential role for the gut microbiome in substance use disorders. *Psychopharmacology*, 236, 1513–1530.

Mędraś, M., Brona, A., and Jóźków, P. (2018). The central effects of androgenic-anabolic steroid use. *J. Addict. Med.*, 12, 184–192.

Mega, T. A., and Dabe, N. E. (2017). Khat (Catha edulis) as a risk factor for cardiovascular disorders: Systematic review and meta-analysis. *Open Cardiovasc. Med. J.*, 11, 146–155.

Mehta, R. I., Carpenter, J. S., Mehta, R. I., Haut, M. W., Ranjan, M., Murano, G., Lockman, P., et al. (2021) MRI-guided focused ultrasound-induced blood-brain barrier opening in humans with early Alzheimer disease: A phase II clinical trial. *Radiology*, 289, 654–662.

Meier, D. S., Balashov, K. E., Healy, B., Weiner, H. L., and Guttman, C.R.G. (2010). Seasonal prevalence of MS disease activity. *Neurology*, 75, 799–806.

Meier, E., and Hatsukami, D. K. (2016). A review of the additive health risk of cannabis and tobacco co-use. *Drug Alcohol Depend.*, 166, 6–12.

Meier, M. H., Caspi, A., Ambler, A., Harrington, H., Houts, R., Keefe, R. S. E., et al. (2012). Persistent cannabis users show neuropsychological decline from childhood to midlife. *Proc. Natl. Acad. Sci. USA*, 109, E2657–E2664.

Mekuriaw, B., Zegeye, A., Molla, A., Hussen, R., Yimer, S., and Belayneh, Z. (2020). Prevalence of common mental disorder and its association with khat chewing among Ethiopian college students: A systematic review and meta-analysis. *Psychiatry J.*, 2, 1462141. doi: 10.1155/2020/1462141.

Melancon, B. J., Hopkins, C. R., Wood, M. R., Emmitte, K. A., Niswender, C. M., Christopoulos, A., et al. (2012). Allosteric modulation of seven transmembrane spanning receptors: Theory, practice, and opportunities for central nervous system drug discovery. *J. Med. Chem.*, 55, 1445–1464.

Melichar, J. K., Daglish, M. R. C., and Nutt, D. J. (2001). Addiction and withdrawal: Current views. *Curr. Opin. Pharmacol.*, 1, 84–90.

Melloni, R. H., Jr., and Ricci, L. A. (2010). Adolescent exposure to anabolic/androgenic steroids and the neurobiology of offensive aggression: A hypothalamic neural model based on findings in pubertal Syrian hamsters. *Horm. Behav.*, 58, 177–191.

Melnik, B., Jansen, T., and Grabbe, S. (2007). Abuse of anabolic–androgenic steroids and body-building acne: An underestimated health problem. *J. Dtsch. Dermatol. Ges.*, 5, 110–117.

Melroy-Greif, W. E., Stitzel, J. A., and Ehringer, M. A. (2016). Nicotinic acetylcholine receptors: Upregulation, age-related effects and associations with drug use. *Genes Brain Behav.*, 15, 89–107.

Meltzer, H. Y., and Massey, B. W. (2011). The role of serotonin receptors in the action of atypical antipsychotic drugs. *Curr. Opin. Pharmacol.*, 11, 59–67.

Meltzer-Brody, S., and Kanes, S. J. (2020). Allopregnanolone in postpartum depression: Role in pathophysiology and treatment. *Neurobiol. Stress*, 12, 100212. doi: 10.116/j.ynstr.2020.100212.

Mena-Segovia, J., and Bolam, J. P. (2017). Rethinking the pedunculopontine nucleus: From cellular organization to function. *Neuron*, 94, 7–18.

Mendelsohn, D., Riedel, W. J., and Sambeth, A. (2009). Effects of acute tryptophan depletion on memory, attention, and executive function. *Neurosci. Biobehav. Rev.*, 33, 926–952.

Mendelson, J. H., Stein, S., Melload, N. K. (1965). Effects of experimentally induced intoxication on metabolism of ethanol-l-C14 in alcoholic subjects. *Metabolism*, 14, 1255–1266. Copyright 1965. Reprinted with permission from Elsevier.

Menkes, D., Bosanac, P., and Castle, D. (2016). MAOIs—Does evidence warrant their resurrection? *Australas. Psychiatry*, 24, 371–373.

Meredith, S. E., Juliano, L. M., Hughes, J. R., and Griffiths, R. R. (2013). Caffeine use disorder: A comprehensive review and research agenda. *J. Caffeine Res.*, 3, 114–130.

Mereu, M., Chun, L. E., Prisinzano, T. E., Newman, A. H., Katz, J. L., and Tanda, G. (2017). The unique psychostimulant profile of (±)-modafinil: investigation of behavioral and neurochemical effects in mice. *Eur. J. Neurosci.*, 45. 167–174.

Mergy, M. A., Gowrishankar, R., Davis, G. L., Jessen, T. N., Wright, J., Stanwood, G. D., et al. (2014). Genetic targeting of the amphetamine and methylphenidate-sensitive dopamine transporter: On the path to an animal model of attention-deficit hyperactivity disorder. *Neurochem. Int.*, 73, 56–70.

Merritt, D. H., and Snyder, S. M. (2019). Inhalant use among child welfare-involved adolescents. *J. Child Adolesc. Subs. Abuse*, 28, 45–54.

Messier, C. (2004). Glucose improvement of memory: A review. *Eur. J. Pharmacol.*, 490, 33–57.

Metna-Laurent, M., and Marsicano, G. (2015). Rising starts: Modulation of brain functions by astroglial type-1 cannabinoid receptors. *Glia*, 63, 353–364.

Meyer, J. S. (2013). 3,4-methylenedioxy-methamphetamine (MDMA): Current perspectives. *Subst. Abuse Rehabil.*, 4, 83–99.

Meyer, J. M., Cummings, M. A., Proctor, G., and Stahl, S. M. (2016). Psychopharmacology of persistent violence and aggression. *Psychiatr. Clin. North Am.*, 39, 541–556.

Meyer, R. E. (1996). The disease called addiction: Emerging evidence in a 200-year debate. *Lancet*, 347, 162–166.

Meyer, U. (2013). Developmental neuroinflammation and schizophrenia. *Prog. Neuropsychopharmacol. Biol. Psychiatry*, 42, 20–34.

Meyers, J. E., and Almirall, J. R. (2004). A study of the effectiveness of commercially available drink test coasters for the detection of "date rape" drugs in beverages. *J. Anal. Toxicol.*, 28, 685–688.

Mhillaj, E., Morgese, M. G., Tucci, P., Bove, M., Schiavone, S., and Trabace, L. (2015). Effects of anabolic–androgens on brain reward function. *Front. Neurosci.*, 9, 295. doi: 10.3389/fnins.2015.00295.

Michalovicz, L. T., Kelly, K. A., Sullivan, K., and O'Callaghan, J. P. (2020). Acetylcholinesterase inhibitor exposures as an initiating factor in the development of Gulf War Illness, a chronic neuroimmune disorder in deployed veterans. *Neuropharmacology*, 171, 108073. doi: 10.1016/j.neuropharm.2020.108073.

Miczek, K. A., and de Wit, H. (2008). Challenges for translational psychopharmacology research: Some basic principles. *Psychopharmacology*, 199, 291–301.

Middlekauff, H. R., Park, J., and Moheimani, R. S. (2014). Adverse effects of cigarette and noncigarette smoke exposure on the autonomic nervous system: Mechanisms and implications for cardiovascular risk. *J. Am. Coll. Cardiol.*, 64, 1740–1750.

Middleton, F. A., and Strick, P. L. (2000). Basal ganglia and cerebellar loops: Motor and cognitive circuits. *Brain Res. Rev.*, 31, 236–250.

Migliarini, S., Pacini, G., Pelosi, B., Lunardi, G., and Pasqualetti, M. (2013). Lack of brain serotonin affects postnatal development and serotonergic neuronal circuitry formation. *Mol. Psychiatry*, 18, 1106–1118.

Mihic, S. J., and Harris, R. A. (1997). GABA and the GABA$_A$ receptor.

Alcohol Health Res. World, 21, 127–131.

Mihordin, R. (2012). Behavioral addiction: Quo vadis? *J. Nerv. Ment. Dis.*, 200, 489–491.

Mihov, Y., and Hasler, G. (2016). Negative allosteric modulators of metabotropic glutamate receptors subtype 5 in addiction: a therapeutic window. *Int. J. Neuropsychopharmacol.*, 19, pyw002. doi: 10.1093/ijnp/pyw002.

Milbank, E., and López, M. (2019). Orexins/hypocretins: Key regulators of energy homeostasis. *Front. Endocrinol. (Lausanne)*, 10, 803. doi: 10.3389/fendo.2019.00830.

Milella, M. S., Fotros, A., Gravel, P., Casey, K. F., Larcher, K., Verhaeghe, J. A. J., et al. (2016). Cocaine cue-induced dopamine release in the human prefrontal cortex. *J. Psychiatry Neurosci.*, 41, 322–330.

Miles, O., and Maren, S. (2019). Role of the bed nucleus of the stria terminalis in PTSD: Insights from preclinical models. *Front. Behav. Neurosci.*, 13, 68, 1–14.

Miller, A. M., and Stella, N. (2008). CB$_2$ receptor-mediated migration of immune cells: It can go either way. *Br. J. Pharmacol.*, 153, 299–308.

Miller, B. J., Culpepper, N., Rapaport, M. H., and Buckley, P. (2013). Prenatal inflammation and neurodevelopment in schizophrenia: A review of human studies. *Prog. NeuroPsychopharmacol. Biol. Psychiatry*, 42, 92–100.

Miller, B. L., Stogner, J. M., and Miller, J. M. (2016). Exploring butane hash oil use: A research note. *J. Psychoact. Drugs*, 48, 44–49.

Miller, D. R., Buettner-Schmidt, K., Orr, M., Rykal, K., and Niewojna, E. (2020). A systematic review of refillable e-liquid nicotine content accuracy. *J. Am. Pharm. Assoc.*, in press.

Miller, G. (2010). Is pharma running out of brainy ideas? *Science*, 329(5991), 502–504

Miller, K. E., Dermen, K. H., and Lucke, J. F. (2018). Caffeinated energy drink use by U.S. adolescents aged 13–17, A national profile. *Psychol. Addict. Behav.*, 32, 647–659.

Miller, N. S., Ipeku, R., and Oberbarnscheidt, T. (2020). A review of cases of marijuana and violence. *Int. J. Environ. Res. Public Health*, 17(5), 1578. doi: 10.3390/ijerph17051578.

Miller, S. C. (2005). Dextromethorphan psychosis, dependence and physical withdrawal. *Addict. Biol.*, 10, 325–327.

Milosavljevic, F., Bukvic, N., Pavlovic, Z., Miljevic, C., Pešic, V., Molden, E., Ingelman-Sundberg, M., et al. (2021). Association of CYP2C19 and CYP2D6 poor and intermediate metabolizer status with antidepressant and antipsychotic exposure: A systematic

review and meta-analysis. *JAMA Psychiatry*, 78(3), 270–280. https://doi.org/10.1001/jamapsychiatry.2020.3643

Mimics, K., Middleton, F. A., Marquez, A., Lewis, D. A., and Levitt, P. (2000). Molecular characterization of schizophrenia viewed by microarray analysis of gene expression in prefrontal cortex. *Neuron*, 28, 53–67.

Mindus, P., Rasmussen, S. A., and Lindquist, C. (1994). Neurosurgical treatment for refractory obsessivecompulsive disorder: Implications for understanding frontal lobe function. *J. Neuropsychiatry*, 6, 467–477.

Minichino, A., Senior, M., Brondino, N., Zhang, S. H., Godwlewska, B. R., Burnet, P., Cipriani, A., et al. (2019). Measuring disturbance of the endocannabinoid system in psychosis: A systematic review and meta-analysis. *JAMA Psychiatry*, 76, 914–923.

Minogianis, E.-A., Shams, W. M., Mabrouk, O. S., Wong, J.-M. T., Brake, W. G., Kennedy, R. T., de Souich, P., et al. (2019). Varying the rate of intravenous cocaine infusion influences the temporal dynamics of both drug and dopamine concentrations in the striatum. *Eur. J. Neurosci.*, 50, 2054–2064.

Minozzi, S., Saulle, R., De Crescenzo, F., and Amato, L. (2016). Psychosocial interventions for psychostimulant misuse. *Cochrane Database Syst. Rev.*, 9(9), CD011866. doi: 10.1002/14651858.CD011866.pub2.

Minter, M. R., Zhang, C., Leone, V., Ringus, D. L., Zhang, X., Oyler-Castrill0, P., et al. (2016). Antibiotic-induced perturbations in gut microbial diversity influences neuro-inflammation and amyloidosis in a murine model of Alzheimer's disease. *Sci. Rep.*, 6, 30038.

Minzenberg, M. J., and Carter, C. S. (2008). Modafinil: A review of neurochemical actions and effects of cognition. *Neuropsychopharmacology*, 33, 1477–1502.

Minzenberg, M. J., Laird, A. R., Thelen, S., Carter, C. S., and Glahn, D. C. (2009). Meta-analysis of 41 functional neuroimaging studies of executive function in schizophrenia. *Arch. Gen. Psychiatry*, 66, 811–822.

Miotto, K., Darakjian, J., Basch, J., Murray, S., Zogg, J., and Rawson, R. (2001). Gamma-hydroxybutyric acid: Patterns of use, effects and withdrawal. *Am. J. Addict.*, 10, 232–241.

Miranda, R. A., Agostinho, A. R., Trevenzoli, I. H., Barella, L. F., Franco, C. C. S., Trombini, A. B., et al. (2014). Insulin oversecretion in MSG-obese rats is related to alterations in cholinergic muscarinic receptor subtypes in pancreatic islets. *Cell. Physiol. Biochem.*, 33, 1075–1086.

Mirnics, K., Middleton, F. A., Marquez, A., Lewis, D. A., and Levitt, P. (2000). Molecular characterization of schizophrenia viewed by microarray analysis of gene expression in prefrontal cortex. *Neuron*, 28, 53–67.

Mirsky, I. E., Piker, P., Rosenbaum, M., and Lederer, H. (1941). "Adaptation" of the central nervous system to various concentrations of alcohol in the blood. *Q. J. Studies Alcohol*, 2, 35–45. Reproduced with permission of Alcohol Research Documentation, Inc., publisher of *the Journal of Studies on Alcohol*, now the *Journal of Studies on Alcohol and Drugs* (www.jsad.com).

Misztak P., Pańczyszyn-Trzewik P., Sowa-Kućma M. (2018) Histone deacetylases (HDACs) as therapeutic target for depressive disorders. *Pharmacol Rep.*, 70(2), 398–408.

Mitchell, D. C., Knight, C. A., Hockenberry, J., Teplansky, R., and Hartman, T. J. (2014). Beverage caffeine intakes in the U.S. *Food Chem. Toxicol.*, 63, 136–142.

Mitchell, L., Murray, S. B., Cobley, S., Hackett, D., Gifford, J., Capling, L., et al. (2017). Muscle dysmorphia symptomatology and associated psychological features in bodybuilders and non-bodybuilder resistance trainers: A systematic review and meta-analysis. *Sports Med.*, 47, 233–259.

Mitchell-Mata, C., Thomas, B., Peterson, B., and Couper, F. (2017). Two fatal intoxications involving 3-methoxyphencyclidine. *J. Anal. Toxicol.*, 41, 503–507.

Mithoefer, M. C., Feduccia, A. A., Jerome, L., Mithoefer, A., Wagner, M., Walsh, Z., Hamilton, S., et al. (2019). MDMA-assisted psychotherapy for treatment of PTSD: study design and rationale for phase 3 trials based on pooled analysis of six phase 2 randomized controlled trials. *Psychopharmacology*, 236, 2735–2745.

Mitrano, D. A., Schroeder, J. P., Smith, Y., Cortright, J. J., Bubula, N., Vezina, P., and Weinshenker, D. (2012). Alpha-1 adrenergic receptors are localized on presynaptic elements in the nucleus accumbens and regulate mesolimbic dopamine transmission. *Neuropsychopharmacology*, 37, 2161–2172.

Miyamoto, S., Duncan, G. E., Marx, C. E., and Lieberman, J. A. (2005). Treatments for schizophrenia: A critical review of pharmacology and mechanisms of action of antipsychotic drugs. *Mol. Psychiatry*, 10, 79–104.

Miyashita, L., and Foley, G. (2020). E-cigarettes and respiratory health: the latest evidence. *J. Physiol.*, 598, 5027–5038.

Mochizuki, K., Imai, C., Sato, N., and Kubota, T. (2017). The role of epigenetics in developmental programming and the developmental origins of health and disease. *OBM Genetics*, 1(4), 008. doi: 10.21926/obm.genet.1704008.

Moeller, S. J., and Stoops, W. W. (2015). Cocaine choice procedures in animals, humans, and treatment-seekers: Can we bridge the divide? *Pharmacol. Biochem. Behav.*, 138, 133–141.

Moghaddam, B., and Javitt, D. (2012). From revolution to evolution: The glutamate hypothesis of schizophrenia and its implication for treatment. *Neuropsychopharmacology*, 37, 4–15.

Möhler, H., and Rudolph, U. (2017). Disinhibition, an emerging pharmacology of learning and memory [version 1; peer review: 3 approved]. *F1000Research*, 6(F1000 Faculty Rev), 101. doi: 10.12688/f1000research.9947.1.

Molas, S., DeGroot, S. R., Zhao-Shea, R., and Tapper, A. R. (2017). Anxiety and nicotine dependence: Emerging role of the habenula-interpeduncular axis. *Trends Pharmacol. Sci.*, 38, 169–180.

Molendijk, M. L., and de Kloet, E. R. (2019). Coping with the forced swim stressor: Current state-of-the-art. Behavioural *Brain Res.*, 364, 1–10. https://doi.org/10.1016/j.bbr.2019.02.005

Molina-Torres, G., Rodriguez-Arrastia, M., Roman, P., Sanchez-Labraca, N., and Cardona, D. (2019). Stress and the gut microbiota-brain axis. *Behav. Pharmacol.*, 30, 187–200.

Molla, H. M., and Tseng, K. Y. (2020). Neural substrates underlying the negative impact of cannabinoid exposure during adolescence. *Pharmacol. Biochem. Behav.*, 195, 172965. doi: 10.1016/j.pbb.2020.172965

Monory, K., Blaudzun, H., Massa, F., Kaiser, N., Lemberger, T., Schütz, G., et al. (2007). Genetic dissection of behavioural and autonomic effects of Δ9tetrahydrocannabinol in mice. *PLOS Biol.*, 5, e269. doi: 10.1371/journal. pbio.0050269.

Mons, N., and Beracochea, D. (2016). Behavioral neuroadaptation to alcohol: From glucocorticoids to histone acetylation. *Front. Psychiatry*, 7, 165.

Monte, A. S., de Souza, G. C., McIntyre, R. S., Soczynska, J. K., dos Santos, J. V., Cordeiro, R. C., et al. (2013). Prevention and reversal of ketamine-induced schizophrenia related behavior by minocycline in mice: Possible involvement of antioxidant and nitrergic pathways. *J. Psychopharmacol.*, 27, 1032–1043.

Monteggia, L. M., and Zarate, C., Jr. (2015). Antidepressant actions of ketamine: From molecular mechanisms to clinical practice. *Curr. Opin. Neurobiol.*, 30, 139–143.

Moore, C. F., Sabino, V., Koob, G. F., and Cottone, P. (2017). Pathological overeating: Emerging evidence for a compulsivity construct. *Neuropsychopharmacology*, 42, 1375–1389.

Moore, K., and Measham, F. (2008). "It's the most fun you can have for twenty quid": Motivations, consequences and meanings of British ketamine use. *Addict. Res. Theory*, 16, 231–244.

Moore, N. A., Sargent, B. J., Manning, D. D., and Guzzo, P. R. (2013). Partial agonism of 5-HT3 receptors: A novel approach to the symptomatic treatment of IBS-D. *ACS Chem. Neurosci.*, 4, 43–47.

Moore, S. R., Gresham, L. S., Bromberg, M. B., Kasarkis, E. J., and Smith, R. A. (1997). A self report measure of affective lability. *J. Neurol. Neurosurg. Psychiatry*, 63, 89–93.

Moore, T. M., Scarpa, A., and Raine, A. (2002). A meta-analysis of serotonin metabolite 5-HIAA and antisocial behavior. *Aggress. Behav.*, 28, 299–316.

Moos, R. H., and Moos, B. S. (2006). Rates and predictors of relapse after natural and treated remission from alcohol use disorders. *Addiction*, 101, 212–222.

Morales, P., Goya, P., and Jagerovic, N. (2018). Emerging strategies targeting CB2 cannabinoid receptor: Biased agonism and allosterism. *Biochem. Pharmacol.*, 157, 8–17.

Morales, P., Hurst, D. P., and Reggio, P. H. (2017). Molecular targets of the phytocannabinoids—A complex picture. *Prog. Chem. Org. Nat. Prod.*, 103, 103–131.

Moran, P. M., O'Tuathaigh, C. M. P., Papaleo, F., and Waddington, J. L. (2014). Dopaminergic function in relation to genes associated with risk for schizophrenia: Translational mutant mouse models. *Progr. Brain Res.*, 211, 79–112.

Moran, S. P., Maksymetz, J., and Conn, P. J. (2019). Targeting muscarinic acetylcholine receptors for the treatment of psychiatric and neurological disorders. *Trends Pharmacol. Sci.*, 40, 1006–1020.

Moratalla, R., Khairnar, A., Simola, N., Granado, N., García-Montes, J. R., Porceddu, P. F., et al. (2017). Amphetamine-related drugs neurotoxicity in humans and in experimental animals: Main mechanisms. *Prog. Neurobiol.*, 155, 149–170.

Moreira J., Geoffroy P.A. (2016) Lithium and bipolar disorder: Impacts from molecular to behavioural circadian rhythms. *Chronobiol Int.*, 33(4), 351–373

Morel, C., Fattore, L., Pons, S., Hay, Y. A., Marti, F., Lambolez, B., et al. (2014). Nicotine consumption is regulated by a human polymorphism in dopamine neurons. *Mol. Psychiatry*, 19, 930–936.

Moreno, J., Holloway, T., Albizu, L., Sealfon, S. C., and González-Maeso, J. (2011). Metabotropic glutamate mGlu2 receptor is necessary for the pharmacological and behavioral effects induced by hallucinogenic 5-HT2A receptor agonists. *Neurosci. Lett.*, 493, 76–79.

Morgan, C. J. A., and Curran, H. V. (2006). Acute and chronic effects of ketamine upon human memory: A review. *Psychopharmacology*, 188, 408–424.

Morgan, C. J. A., Mofeez, A., Brandner, B., Bromley, L., and Curran, H. V. (2004). Ketamine impairs response inhibition and is positively reinforcing in healthy volunteers: a dose–response study. *Psychopharmacology* 172, 298–308. doi:10.1007/s00213-003-1656-y.

Morgan, C.J.A., and Curran, H. V. On behalf of the Independent Scientific Committee on Drugs (ICSD). (2012). Ketamine use: a review. *Addiction*, 107, 27–38.

Morgan, H. W. (1981). *Drugs in America: A Social History, 1800–1980*. Syracuse, NY: Syracuse University Press.

Morgan, J. P., and Kagan, D. (1980). The dusting of America: The image of phencyclidine (PCP) in the popular media. *J. Psychedelic Drugs*, 12, 195–204.

Moriya, R., Kanamaru, M., Ookuma, N., Tanaka, K. F., Izumizaki, M., Onimaru, H., Yoshikawa, A., et al. (2017). The effect of activating serotonergic neurons in the dorsal raphe nucleus on control of vigilance state. *Eur. Resp. J.*, 50, Suppl. 61, OA1753. doi: 10.1183/1393003.congress-2017.OA1753.

Morón, J. A., Brockington, A., Wise, R. A., Rocha, B. A., and Hope, B. T. (2002). Dopamine uptake through the norepinephrine transporter in brain regions with low levels of the dopamine transporter: Evidence from knock-out mouse lines. *J. Neurosci.*, 22, 389–395.

Morris, H., and Wallach, J. (2014). From PCP to MXE: A comprehensive review of the non-medical use of dissociative drugs. *Drug Test. Anal.*, 6, 614–632.

Morris, K. A., Chang, Q., Mohler, E. G., and Gold, P. E. (2010). Age-related memory impairments due to reduced blood glucose responses to epinephrine. *Neurobiol. Aging*, 31, 2136–2145.

Morris, R.G.M. (2013). NMDA receptors and memory encoding. *Neuropharmacology*, 74, 32–40.

Morrison, T. R., Sikes, R. W., and Melloni, R. H., Jr. (2016). Anabolic steroids alter the physiological activity of aggression circuits in the lateral anterior hypothalamus. *Neuroscience*, 315, 1–17.

Morrison, T. R., Ricci, L. A., Puckett, A. S., Joyce, J., Curran, R., Davis, C., and Melloni Jr., R. H.

(2020). Serotonin type-3 receptors differentially modulate anxiety and aggression during withdrawal from adolescent anabolic steroid exposure. *Horm. Behav.*, 119, 104650. doi: 10.1016/j.yhbeh.2019.104650.

Moschino, L., Zivanovic, S., Hartley, C., Trevisanuto, D., Baraldi, E., and Roehr, C. C. (2020). Caffeine in preterm infants: where are we in 2020? *ERJ Open Res.*, 6, 00330–2019. doi: 10.1183/23120541.00330-2019.

Mosienko, V., Beis, D., Pasqualetti, M., Waider, J., Matthes, S., Qadri, F., et al. (2015). Life without brain serotonin: Reevaluation of serotonin function with mice deficient in brain serotonin synthesis. *Behav. Brain Res.*, 277, 78–88.

Most, D., Ferguson, L., and Harris, R. A. (2014). Molecular basis of alcoholism. *Handb. Clin. Neurol.*, 125, 89–111.

Mothet, J.-P., Le Bail, M., and Billard, J. M. (2015). Time and space profiling of NMDA receptor co-agonist functions. *J. Neurochem.*, 135, 210–225.

Mottram, D. R., and George, A. J. (2000). Anabolic steroids. *Baillieres Best Pract. Res. Clin. Endocrinol. Metab.*, 14, 55–69.

Moyer, K. E. (1968). Kinds of aggression and their physiological basis. *Commun. Behav. Biol. A*, 2, 65–87.

Mucchietto, V., Crespi, A., Fasoli, F., Clementi, F., and Gotti, C. (2016). Neuronal acetylcholine nicotinic receptors as new targets for lung cancer treatment. *Curr. Pharm. Des.*, 22, 2160–2169.

Mueller, B. R., and Bale, T. L. (2008). Sexspecific programming of offspring emotionality after stress early in pregnancy. *J. Neurosci.*, 28, 9055–9065.

Mueller, F., Lenz, C., Steiner, M., Dolder, P. C., Walter, M., Lang, U. E., et al. (2016). Neuroimaging of moderate MDMA use: A systematic review. *Neurosci. Biobehav. Rev.*, 62, 21–34.

Mueser, K. T., Penn, D. L., Addington, J., Brunette, M. F., Gingerich, S., Glynn, S. M., et al. (2015). The NAVIGATE program for first-episode psychosis: Rationale, overview, and description of psychosocial components. *Psychiatr. Serv.*, 66, 680–690.

Muglia, P. (2011). From genes to therapeutic targets for psychiatric disorders: What to expect? *Curr. Opin. Pharmacol.*, 11, 563–571.

Mulcahey, M. K, Schiller, J. R., and Hulstyn, M. J. (2010). Anabolic steroid use in adolescents: Identification of those at risk and strategies for prevention. *Phys. Sportsmed.*, 38, 105–113.

Mullane, K., and Williams, M. (2019). Preclinical models of Alzheimer's disease: Relevance and translational validity. *Curr. Protoc. Pharmacol.*, 84(1), e57. https://doi.org/10.1002/cpph.57

Müller, A., Brand, M., Claes, L., Demetrovics, Z., de Zwaan, M., Fernández-Aranda, F., Frost, R. O., et al. (2019). Buying-shopping disorder—Is there enough evidence to support its inclusion in ICD-11? *CNS Spectr.*, 24, 374–379.

Müller, A., Laskowski, N. M., Trotzke, P., Ali, K., Fassnacht, D. B., de Zwaan, M., Brand, M., et al. (2021). Proposed diagnostic criteria for compulsive buying-shopping disorder: A Delphi expert consensus study. *J. Behav. Addict.*, in press.

Muller, C. L., Anacker, A. M., and VeenstraVanderWeele, J. (2016). The serotonin system in autism spectrum disorder: From biomarker to animal models. *Neuroscience*, 321, 24–41.

Müller, C. P., and Huston, J. P. (2006). Determining the region-specific contributions of 5-HT receptors to the psychostimulant effects of cocaine. *Trends Pharmacol. Sci.*, 27, 105–112.

Müller, F., and Borgwardt, S. (2019). Acute effects of lysergic acid diethylamide (LSD) on resting brain function. *Swiss Med. Wkly.*, 149, w20124. doi: 10.4414/smw.2019.20124.

Müller, F., Brändle, R., Liechti, M. E., and Borgwardt, S. (2019). Neuroimaging of chronic MDMA ("ecstasy") effects: A meta-analysis. *Neurosci. Biobehav. Rev.*, 96, 10–20.

Müller, F., Dolder, P. C., Schmidt, A., Liechti, M. E., and Borgwardt, S. (2018). Altered network hub connectivity after acute LSD administration. *Neuroimage. Clin.*, 18, 694–701.

Munawar, K., Choudhry, F. R., Hadi, M. A., and Khan, T. M. (2020). Prevalence of and factors contributing to glue sniffing in the South Asian Association for Regional Cooperation (SAARC) Region: A Scoping review and meta-analysis. *Subst. Use Misuse*, 55, 752–762.

Munir, V. L., Hutton, J. E., Harney, J. P., Buykx, P., Weiland, T. J., and Dent, A. W. (2008). Gamma-hydroxybutyrate: A 30 month emergency department review. *Emerg. Med. Australas.*, 20, 521–530.

Muñoz-Quezada, M. T., Lucero, B. A., Barr, D. B., Steenland, K., Levy, K., Ryan, P. B., et al. (2013). Neurodevelopmental effects in children associated with exposure to organophosphate pesticides: A systematic review. *Neurotoxicology*, 39, 158–168.

Muñoz-Quezada, M. T., Lucero, B. A., Iglesias, V. P., Muñoz, M. P., Cornejo, C. A., Achu, E., Baumert, B., et al. (2016). Chronic exposure to organophosphate (OP) pesticides and neuropsychological functioning in farm workers: a review. *Int. J. Occup. Environ. Health*, 22, 68–79.

Munro, B. A., Weyandt, L. L., Marraccini, M. E., and Oster, D. R. (2017). The relationship between nonmedical use of prescription stimulants, executive functioning and academic outcomes. *Addict. Behav.*, 65, 250–257.

Münster-Wandowski, A., Zander, J.-F., Richter, K., and Ahnert-Hilger, G. (2016). Co-existence of functionally different vesicular neurotransmitter transporters. *Front. Synaptic Neurosci.*, 8, 4. doi: 10.3389/fnsyn.2016.00004.

Murillo-Rodríguez, E., Veras, A. B., Rocha, N. B., Budde, H., and Machado, S. (2018). An overview of the clinical uses, pharmacology, and safety of modafinil. *ACS Chem. Neurosci.*, 9, 151–158.

Murphy, D. L., and Lesch, K.-P. (2008). Targeting the murine serotonin transporter: Insights into human neurobiology. *Nat. Rev. Neurosci.*, 9, 85–96.

Murphy, P. B., Bechmann, S., and Barrett, M. J. (2021). *Morphine*. In StatPearls [Internet]. Treasure Island (FL): StatPearls Publishing. http://www.ncbi.nlm.nih.gov/books/NBK526115/

Murray, C. H., Loweth, J. A., Milovanovic, M., Stefanik, M. T., Caccamise, A. J., Dolubizno, H., Funke, J. R., et al. (2019). AMPA receptor and metabotropic glutamate receptor 1 adaptations in the nucleus accumbens core during incubation of methamphetamine craving. *Neuropsychopharmacology*, 44, 1534–1541.

Murray, D., and Stoessl, A. J. (2013). Mechanisms and therapeutic implications of the placebo effect in neurological and psychiatric conditions. *Pharmacol. Ther.*, 140, 306–318.

Murray, R. M., Englund, A., Abi-Dargham, A., Lewis, D. A., Di Forti, M., Davies, C., et al. (2017). Cannabis-associated psychosis: Neural substrate and clinical impact. *Neuropharmacology*, 124, 89–104.

Murrough, J. W. (2012). Ketamine as a novel antidepressant: From synapse to behavior. *Clin. Pharmacol. Ther.*, 91, 303–309.

Musial, F. (2019). Acupuncture for the treatment of pain—A mega-placebo? *Front. Neurosci.*, 13. https://doi.org/10.3389/fnins.2019.01110

Muskiewicz, D. E., Uhl, G. R., and Hall, F. S. (2018). The role of cell adhesion molecule genes regulating neuroplasticity in addiction. *Neural Plast.*, 2018, 9803764. doi: 10.1155/2018/9803764.

Mustafa, A. K., Gadalla, M. M., and Snyder, S. H. (2009). Signaling by gasotransmitters. *Sci. Signal.*, 2, re2. doi: 10.1126/scisignal.268re2.

Muthukumaraswamy, S. D., CarhartHarris, R. L., Moran, R. J., Brookes, M. J., Williams, T. M., Errtizoe, D., et al. (2013). Broadband cortical desynchronization underlies the human psychedelic state. *J. Neurosci.*, 33, 15171–15183.

Mutti, A., Aroni, S., Fadda, P., Padovani, L., Mancini, L., Collu, R., et al. (2016). The ketamine-like compound methoxetamine substitutes for ketamine in the self-administration paradigm and enhances mesolimbic dopaminergic transmission. *Psychopharmacology*, 233, 2241–2251.

Muzar, Z., Adams, P. E., Schneider, A., Hagerman, R. J., and Lozano, R. (2014). Addictive substances may induce a rapid neurological deterioration in fragile X-associated tremor ataxia syndrome: A report of two cases. *Intractable Rare Dis. Res.*, 3(4), 162–165. https://doi.org/10.5582/irdr.2014.01023

Myers, F. A., Bluth, M. H., and Cheung, W. W. (2016). Ketamine. A cause of urinary tract dysfunction. *Clin. Lab. Med.*, 36, 721–74.

N

Nadeem, I. M., Shanmugaraj, A., Sakha, S., Homer, N. S., Ayeni, O. R., and Khan, M. (2021). Energy drinks and their adverse health effects: A systematic review and meta-analysis. *Sports Health*, 13, 265–277.

Nahas, G. G. (1975). Marijuana: Deceptive Weed. New York: Raven.

Naik, A., Kalia, Y. N., Guy, R. H. (2000). Transdermal drug delivery: Overcoming the skin's barrier function. *Pharm. Sci. Technol. Today*, 3, 318–326.

Nakajima, K., Jain, S., Ruiz de Azua, I., McMillin, S. M., Rossi, M., and Wess, J. (2013). Minireview: Novel aspects of M3 muscarinic receptor signaling in pancreatic β-cells. *Mol. Endocrinol.*, 27, 1208–1216.

Nakakubo, Y., Abe, S., Yoshida, T., Takami, C., Isa, M., Wojcik, S. M., Brose, N., et al. (2020). Vesicular glutamate transporter expression ensures high-fidelity synaptic transmission at the calyx of Held synapses. *Cell Rep.*, 32, 10840. doi: 10.1016/j.celrep.2020.108040.

Nakamura, T., Sato, A., Kitsukawa, T., Momiyama, T., Yamamori, T., and Sasaoka, T. L. (2014). Distinct motor impairments of dopamine D1 and D2 receptor knockout mice revealed by three types of motor behavior. *Front. Integr. Neurosci.*, 8, 56. doi: 10.3389/fnint.2014.00056.

Nakao, T., Okada, K., and Kanba, S. (2014). Neurobiological model of obsessive–compulsive disorder: Evidence from recent neuropsychological and neuroimaging findings. *Psychiatr. Clin. Neurosci.*, 68, 587–605.

Napolitano, A., Cesura, A. M., and Da Prada, M. (1995). The role of monoamine oxidase and catechol O-methyltransferase in dopaminergic transmission. *J. Neural Transm. Suppl.*, 45, 35–45.

Naqvi, N. H., and Bechara, A. (2010). The insula and drug addiction: An interoceptive view of pleasure, urges, and decision-making. *Brain Struct. Funct.*, 214, 435–450.

Naqvi, N. H., Gaznick, N., Tranel, D., and Bechara, A. (2014). The insula: A critical neural substrate for craving and drug seeking under conflict and risk. *Ann. N. Y. Acad. Sci.*, 1316, 53–70.

Naqvi, N. H., Rudrauf, D., Damasio, H., and Bechara, A. (2007). Damage to the insula disrupts addiction to cigarette smoking. *Science*, 315, 531–534.

Naranjo, C., Shulgin, A. T., and Sargent, T. (1967). Evaluation of 3,4-methylenedioxy-amphetamine (MDA) as an adjunct to psychotherapy. *Med. Pharmacol. Exp.*, 17, 359–364.

Narendran, R., and Martinez, D. (2008). Cocaine abuse and sensitization of striatal dopamine transmission: A critical review of the preclinical and clinical imaging literature. *Synapse*, 62, 851–869.

Narendran, R., Frankle, W. G., Keefe, R., Gil, R., Martinez, D., Slifstein, M., et al. (2005). Altered prefrontal dopaminergic function in chronic recreational ketamine users. *Am. J. Psychiatry*, 162, 2352–2359.

Narendran, R., Mason, N. S., Himes, M. L., and Frankle, W. G. (2020). Imaging cortical dopamine transmission in cocaine dependence: A [11C]FLB 457-amphetamine positron emission tomography study. *Biol. Psychiatry*, 88, 788–796.

Nascimento, J. H. M., and Medei, E. (2011). Cardiac effects of anabolic steroids: Hypertrophy, ischemia and electrical remodelling as potential triggers of sudden death. *Mini Rev. Med. Chem.*, 11, 425–429.

Nathan, P. E., Conrad, M., and Skinstad, A. H. (2016). History of the concept of addiction. *Annu. Rev. Clin. Psychol.*, 12, 29–51.

National Academies of Sciences, Engineering, and Medicine. (2017). The Health Effects of Cannabis and Cannabinoids: The Current State of Evidence and Recommendations for Research. Washington, DC: The National Academies Press. doi: 10.17226/24625.

National Conference of State Legislatures. (2016). State Medical Marijuana Laws. Available at www.ncsl.org/research/health/state-medical-marijuana-laws. aspx.

National Highway Traffic Safety Administration (NHTSA), U.S. Department of Transportation. (2019). Alcohol-Impaired Driving. https://crashstats.nhtsa.dot.gov/Api/Public/ViewPublication/812864

National Institute on Alcohol Abuse and Alcoholism (NIAAA). (1983). Fifth Special Report to the U.S. Congress on Alcohol and Health. Washington, DC: Government Printing Office.

National Institute on Drug Abuse (2020). Common Comorbidities with Substance Use Disorders Research Report. Available at https://www.drugabuse.gov/publications/research-reports/common-comorbidities-substance-use-disorders/. Accessed May 15, 2021.

National Institute on Drug Abuse (NIDA) (2012). Stress Receptor Mediates Lifelong Consequences of Early Trauma. Available at www.drugabuse.gov/news-events/ nida-notes/2012/11/stress-receptormediates-lifelong-consequences-earlytrauma.

National Institutes of Health (NIH). (2017). Bench-to-Bedside Program (website). Available at clinicalcenter.nih.gov/ccc/ btb/

National Institutes of Health (NIH) (2020). Bench-to-Bedside and Back Program (BtB) (website). Available at https://ocr.od.nih. gov/btb/btb_program.html.

National Institute on Alcohol Abuse and Alcoholism (NIAAA). (2021). Understanding the Dangers of Alcohol Overdose. https://www.niaaa.nih. gov/sites/default/files/publications/Alcohol_overdose_0.pdf

Navarra, R. L., and Waterhouse, B. D. (2019). Considering noradrenergically mediated facilitation of sensory signal processing as a component of psychostimulant-induced performance enhancement. *Brain Res.*, 1709, 67–80.

Navarrete, F., García-Gutiérrez, M. S., Gasparyan, A., Austrich-Olivares, A., Femenía, T., and Manzanares, J. (2020). Cannabis use in pregnant and breastfeeding women: Behavioral and neurobiological consequences. *Front. Psychiatry*, 11, 586447. doi: 10.3389/fpsyt.2020.586447.

Navarro, G., Morales, P., Rodriguez-Cueto, C., Fernández-Ruiz, J., Jagerovic, N., and Franco, R. (2016). Targeting cannabinoid CB$_2$ receptors in the central nervous system: Medicinal chemistry approaches with focus on neurodegenerative disorders. *Front. Neurosci.*, 10, 406. doi: 10.3389/fnins.2016.00406.

Nayyar, P., Kumar, N., Nayyar, P. V., and Singh, A. (2014). BOTOX: Broadening the horizon of dentistry. *J. Clin. Diag. Res.*, 8, ZE25–ZE29.

Nealey, K. A., Smith, A. W., Davis, S. M., Smith, D. G., and Walker, B. M. (2011). μ-Opioid receptors are implicated in the increased potency of intra-accumbens nalmefene in ethanol-dependent rats. *Neuropharmacology*, 61, 35–42.

Nees, F., Tzschoppe, J., Patrick, C. J., Vollstädt-Klein, S., Steiner, S., Poustka, L., et al. (2012). Determinants of early alcohol use in healthy adolescents: The differential contribution of neuroimaging and psychological factors. *Neuropsychopharmacology*, 37, 986–995.

Negrón-Oyarzo, I., Lara-Vásquez, A., Palacios-García, I., Fuentealba, P., and Aboitiz, F. (2016). Schizophrenia and reelin: A model based on prenatal stress to study epigenetics, brain development and behavior. *Biol. Res.*, 49, Article 16.

Negus, S. S., and Henningfield, J. (2015). Agonist medications for the treatment of cocaine use disorder. *Neuropsychopharmacology*, 40, 1815–1825.

Negus, S. S., and Banks, M. L. (2018). Modulation of drug choice by extended drug access and withdrawal in rhesus monkeys: Implications for negative reinforcement as a driver of addiction and target for medications development. *Pharmacol., Biochem. Behav.*, 164, 32–39.

Negus, S. S., and Banks, M. L. (2020). Learning from lorcaserin: lessons from the negative clinical trial of lorcaserin to treat cocaine use disorder. *Neuropsychopharmacology*, 45, 1967–1973.

Negus, S. S., and Mello, N. K. (2003). Effects of chronic d-amphetamine treatment on cocaineand food-maintained responding under a progressive-ratio schedule in rhesus monkeys. *Psychopharmacology*, 167, 324–332.

Negus, S. S., and Miller, L. L. (2014). Intracranial self-stimulation to evaluate abuse potential of drugs. *Pharmacol. Rev.*, 66, 869–917.

Nehlig, A. (2010). Is caffeine a cognitive enhancer? *J. Alzheimers Dis.*, 20(Suppl. 1), S85–S94.

Nehlig, A. (2016). Effects of coffee/caffeine on brain health and disease: What should I tell my patients? *Pract. Neurol.*, 16, 89–95.

Nehlig, A. (2018). Interindividual differences in caffeine metabolism and factors driving caffeine consumption. *Pharmacol. Rev.*, 70, 384–411.

Nelson, K. M., Bisson, J., Singh, G., Graham, J. G., Chen, S. N., Friesen, J. B., Dahlin, J. L., et al. (2020). The essential medicinal chemistry of cannabidiol (CBD). *J. Med. Chem.*, 63, 12137–12155.

Nelson, R. J., and Chiavegatto, S. (2001). Molecular basis of aggression. *Trends Neurosci.*, 24, 713–719.

Nemergut, M. E., Aganga, D., and Flick, R. P. (2014). Anesthetic neurotoxicity: what to tell the parents? *Pediatr. Anesth.*, 24, 120–126.

Nemeroff, C. B. (1998). The neurobiology of depression. *Sci. Am.*, 278, 42–49.

Németh, Z., Kun, B., and Demetrovics, Z. (2010). The involvement of gammahydroxybutyrate in reported sexual assaults: A systematic review. *J. Psychopharmacol.*, 24, 1281–1287.

Nestler E.J., Peña C.J., Kundakovic M., Mitchell A., Akbarian S. (2016) Epigenetic basis of mental illness. *Neuroscientist*, 22(5), 447–463.

Nestler, E. J. (2008). Transcriptional mechanisms of addiction: Role of ΔFosB. *Philos. Trans. R. Soc. Lond. B Biol. Sci.*, 363, 3425–3255.

Nestler, E. J. (2014). Epigenetic mechanisms of drug addiction. *Neuropharmacology*, 76, 259–268.

Nestler, E. J., Alreja, M., and Aghajanian, G. K. (1994). Molecular and cellular mechanisms of opiate action: Studies in the rat locus coeruleus. *Brain Res. Bull.*, 35, 521–528.

Nestler, E. J., and Hyman, S. E. (2010). Animal models of neuropsychiatric disorders. *Nat. Neurosci.*, 13, 1161–1169.

Neubig, R. R., Spedding, M., Kenakin, T., and Christopoulos, A. (2003). International Union of Pharmacology Committee on Receptor Nomenclature and Drug Classification. XXXVIII. Update on terms and symbols in quantitative pharmacology. *Pharmacological Reviews*, 55(4), 597–606. https://doi. org/10.1124/pr.55.4.4

Neufeld, K.-A. M., Bienenstock, J., Bharwani, A., Champagne-Jorgensen, K., Mao, Y., West, C., Liu, Y., et al. (2019). Oral selective serotonin reuptake inhibitors activate vagus nerve dependent gut-brain signalling. *Sci. Rep.*, 9, 14290. doi: 10.1038/s41598-019-50807-8.

Neural mechanisms of aggression. *Nat. Rev. Neurosci.*, 8, 536–546.

Newcombe, R. (2008). Ketamine case study: The phenomenology of a ketamine experience. *Addict. Res. Theory*, 16, 209–215.

Newell, K. A., Zavitsanou, K., and Huang, X.-F. (2007). Short and long term changes in NMDA receptor binding in mouse brain following chronic phencyclidine treatment. *J. Neural Transm.*, 114, 995–1001.

Newhouse, P. A., Potter, A., and Singh, A. (2004). Effects of nicotinic stimulation on cognitive performance. *Curr. Opin. Pharmacol.*, 4, 36–46.

Newton, T. F., De La Garza, R., Kalechstein, A. D., Tziortzis, D., and Jacobsen, C. A. (2009). Theories of addiction: Methamphetamine users' explanations for continuing drug use and relapse. *Am. J. Addict.*, 18, 294–300.

Ng, J., Heales, S. J. R., and Kurian, M. A. (2014a). Clinical features and pharmacotherapy of childhood monoamine neurotransmitter disorders. *Pediatr. Drugs*, 16, 275–291.

Ng, J., Papandreou, A., Heales, S. J., and Kurian, M. A. (2015). Monoamine neurotransmitter disorders: Clinical advances and future perspectives. *Nat. Rev. Neurol.*, 11, 567–584.

Ng, J., Zhen, J., Meyer, E., Erreger, K., Li, Y., Kakar, N., et al. (2014b). Dopamine transporter deficiency syndrome: Phenotypic spectrum from infancy to adulthood. *Brain*, 137, 1107–1119. doi: 10.1093/brain/awu022.

Ng, P. C., Banerji, S., Graham, J., Leonard, J., and Wang, G. S. (2019). Adolescent exposures to traditional and novel psychoactive drugs, reported to National Poison Data System (NPDS), 2007–2017. *Drug Alcohol Depend.*, 202, 1–5.

Nguyen, J., O'Brien, C., and Schapp, S. (2016). Adolescent inhalant use prevention, assessment, and treatment: A literature synthesis. Int. J. Drug Policy, 31, 15–24.

Nguyen, J. D., Grant, Y., Kerr, T. M., Gutierrez, A., Cole, M., and Taffe, M. A. (2018). Tolerance to hypothermic and antinoceptive effects of Δ^9-tetrahydrocannabinol (THC) vapor inhalation in rats. *Pharmacol. Biochem. Behav.*, 172, 33–38.

Nicholls, A. R., Cope, E., Bailey, R., Koenen, K., Dumon, D., Theodorou, N. C., et al. (2017). Children's first experience of taking anabolic–androgenic steroids can occur before their 10th birthday: A systematic review identifying 9 factors that predicted doping among young people. *Front. Psychol.*, 8, 1015. doi: 10.3389/fpsyg.2017.01015.

Nichols, D. E. (1997). Role of serotoninergic neurons and 5-HT receptors in the action of hallucinogens. In H. G. Baumgarten and M. Göthert (Eds.), Serotoninergic Neurons and 5-HT Receptors in the CNS, Volume 129, Handbook of Experimental Pharmacology (pp. 563–585). Berlin: Springer-Verlag.

Nichols, D. E. (2004). Hallucinogens. *Pharmacol. Ther.*, 101, 131–181.

Nichols, D. E. (2016). Psychedelics. *Pharmacol. Rev.*, 68, 264–355.

Nichols, D. E. (1986). Differences between the mechanism of action of MDMA, MBDB, and the classic hallucinogens. Identification of a new therapeutic class: Entactogens. *J. Psychoactive Drugs*, 18, 305–313.

Nicholson, K. L., and Balster, R. L. (2001). GHB: A new and novel drug of abuse. *Drug Alcohol Depend.*, 63, 1–22.

Nickols, H. H., and Conn, P. J. (2014). Development of allosteric modulators of GPCRs for treatment of CNS disorders. *Neurobiol. Dis.*, 61, 55–71.

Nicoll, R. A., and Roche, K. W. (2013). Long-term potentiation: Peeling the onion. *Neuropharmacology*, 74, 18–22.

Nicoll, R. A. (2017). A brief history of long-term potentiation. *Neuron*, 93, 281–290.

Nicoll, R. A., and Schmitz, D. (2005). Synaptic plasticity at hippocampal mossy fibre synapses. *Nat. Rev. Neurosci.*, 6, 863–876.

NIDA (National Institute of Drug Abuse). (2016). Cocaine. Available at www.drugabuse.gov/publications/research-reports/cocaine/what-cocaine.

NIDA (National Institute of Drug Abuse). (2020). Substance Use in Women. Retrieved from https://www.drugabuse.gov/publications/research-reports/substance-use-in-women on April 26, 2020.

Nie, H., Rewal, M., Gill, T. M., Ron, D., and Janak, P. H. (2011). Extrasynaptic delta-containing GABA$_A$ receptors in the nucleus accumbens dorsomedial shell contribute to alcohol intake. *Proc. Natl. Acad. Sci. USA*, 108, 4459–4464.

Nielsen, D. A., Nielsen, E. M., Dasari, T., and Spellicy, C. J. (2014). Pharmacogenetics of addiction therapy. *Methods Mol. Biol.*, 1175, 589–624.

Nielsen, S., Larance, B., and Lintzeris, N. (2017). Opioid agonist treatment for patients with dependence on prescription opioids. *JAMA*, 317, 967–968.

Niemann, N., and Jankovic, J. (2018). Treatment of tardive dyskinesia: A general overview with focus on the vesicular monoamine transporter 2 inhibitors. *Drugs*, 78, 525–541.

Nieschlag, E., and Vorona, E. (2015a). Doping with anabolic androgenic steroids (AAS): Adverse effects on non-reproductive organs and functions. *Rev. Endocr. Metab. Disord.*, 16, 199–211.

Nieschlag, E., and Vorona, E. (2015b). Medical consequences of doping with anabolic androgenic steroids: Effects on reproductive functions. *Eur. J. Endocrinol.*, 173, R47–R58.

Niesink, R. J., and van Laar, M. W. (2013). Does cannabidiol protect against adverse psychological effects of THC? *Front. Psychiatry*, 4, 130. doi: 10.3389/fpsyt.2013.00130.

Nigro, S. C., Luon, D., and Baker, W. L. (2013). Lorcaserin: A novel serotonin 2C agonist for the treatment of obesity. *Curr. Med. Res. Opin.*, 29, 839–848.

Nigussie, T., Gobena, T., and Mossie, A. (2013). Association between khat chewing and gastrointestinal disorders: A cross sectional study. *Ethiop. J. Health Sci.*, 23, 123–130.

NIH (National Institutes of Health), U.S. Department of Health and Human Services. (2013). Hydrocephalus Fact Sheet. National Institute of Neurological Disorders and Stroke. NIH Publication No. 08-385. Available at www.ninds.nih.gov/Disorders/Patient-Caregiver-Education/Fact-Sheets/Hydrocephalus-Fact-Sheet.

NIH (National Institutes of Health), U.S. Department of Health and Human Services. (n.d.). What Are the Potential Uses of Human Stem Cells and the Obstacles That Must Be Overcome Before These Potential Uses Will Be Realized? Stem Cell Basics. Stem Cell Information (website). Available at www.stemcells.nih.gov/ info/basics/pages/basics6.aspx.

Nikiforuk, A., Kos, T., and Wesolowska, A. (2011). The 5-HT6 receptor agonist EMD 386088 produces antidepressant and anxiolytic effects in rats after intrahippocampal administration. *Psychopharmacology*, 217, 411–418.

Nikiforuk, A., Kos, T., Hołuj, M., Potasiewicz, A., and Popik, P. (2016). Positive allosteric modulators of alpha 7 nicotinic acetylcholine receptors reverse ketamine-induced schizophrenia-like deficits in rats. *Neuropharmacology*, 101, 389–400. © 2015. Reprinted with permission from Elsevier.

Nikolaou, P., Papoutsis, I., Stefanidou, M., Spillopoulou, C., and Athanaselis, S. (2015). 2C-I-NBOMe, an "N-bomb" that kills with "Smiles": Toxicological and legislative aspects. *Drug Chem. Toxicol.*, 38, 113–119.

Ninan, P. T. (1999). The functional anatomy, neurochemistry, and pharmacology of anxiety. *J. Clin. Psychiatry*, 60(Suppl. 22), 12–17.

Ninnemann, A. L., Jeong Choi, H., Stuart, G. L., and Temple, J. R. (2017). Longitudinal predictors of synthetic cannabinoid use in adolescents. *Pediatrics*, 139(4), e20163009. doi: 10.1542/peds.2016-3009.

Nirmay, S. M. (2016). Chasing Bigger High, Marijuana Users Turn To "Dabbing." New York Times. Available at www.nytimes.com/2016/05/13/nyregion/chasingbigger-high-marijuana-users-turn-todabbing.html.

Nishiyama, J. (2019). Plasticity of dendritic spines: Molecular function and dysfunction in neurodevelopmental disorders. *Psychiatry Clin. Neurosci.*, 73, 541–550.

Nobelprize.org. (2014). The Nobel Prize in Chemistry 2012, Popular Information. Nobelprize.org. Nobel Media AB. Available at www.nobelprize.org/nobel_prizes/chemistry/laureates/2012/ popular.html.

Noble, F., and Roques, B. P. (2007). Protection of endogenous enkephalin catabolism as natural approach to novel analgesic and antidepressant drugs. *Expert Opin. Ther. Targets*, 11, 145–159.

Noble, M. J., Hedberg, K., and Hendrickson, R. G. (2019). Acute cannabis toxicity. *Clin. Toxicol.*, 57, 735–742.

Nonnemaker, J. M., Crankshaw, E. C., Shive, D. R., Hussin, A. H., and Farrelly, M. C. (2011). Inhalant use initiation among U.S. adolescents: Evidence from the National Survey of Parents and Youth using discrete-time survival analysis. *Addict. Behav.*, 36, 878–881.

Norberg, M. M., Kavanagh, D. J., Olivier, J., and Lyras, S. (2016). Craving cannabis: A meta-analysis of self-report and psychophysiological cue-reactivity studies. *Addiction*, 11, 1923–1934.

Nordquist, N., and Oreland, L. (2010). Serotonin, genetic variability, behaviour, and psychiatric disorders: A review. *Ups. J. Med. Sci.*, 115, 2–10.

Nordstrom, A.-L., and Farde, L. (1998). Plasma prolactin and central D2 receptor occupancy in antipsychotic drug–treated patients. *J. Clin. Psychopharmacol.*, 18, 305–310.

Nothdurfter, C., Rammes, G., Baghai, T. C., Schüle, C., Schumacher, M., Papadopoulos, V., and Rupprecht, R. (2012a). Translocator protein (18 kDa) as a target for novel anxiolytics with a favourable side-effect profile. *J. Neuroendocrinol.*, 24, 82–92.

Nothdurfter, C., Rupprecht, R., Rammes, G. (2012b). Recent developments in potential anxiolytic agents targeting GABA$_A$/BzR complex or the translocator protein (18kDa) (TSPO). *Curr. Top. Med. Chem.*, 12, 360–70.

Novack, G. D. (2016). Cannabinoids for treatment of glaucoma. *Curr. Opin. Ophthalmol.*, 27, 146–150.

Novak, M. J., and Tabrizi, S. J. (2011). Huntington's disease: Clinical presentation and treatment. *Int. Rev. Neurobiol.*, 98, 297–323.

Nunez, J. (2014). Morris Water Maze Experiment. Published on Mar 3, 2014. Available at www.youtube.com/watch?v=leHLL4vcbCc.

Nuss, P. (2015). Anxiety disorders and GABA neurotransmission: A disturbance of modulation. *Neuropsychiatr. Dis. Treat.*, 11, 165–175.

Nutt, D. (2019). Psychedelic drugs—A new era in psychiatry? *Dialogues Clin. Neurosci.*, 21, 139–147.

Nutt, D. J., Bell, C. J., and Malizia, A. L. (1998). Brain mechanisms of social anxiety disorder. *J. Clin. Psychiatry*, 59 (Suppl. 17), 4–9.

Nutt, D. J., Lingford-Hughes, A., Erritzoe, D., and Stokes, P. R. A. (2015). The dopamine theory of addiction: 40 years of highs and lows. *Nat. Rev. Neurosci.*, 16, 305–312.

Nyhus, E., and Curran, T. (2010). Functional role of gamma and theta oscillations in episodic memory. *Neurosci. Biobehav. Rev.*, 34, 1023–1035.

O

O'Brien, C. P. (1993). Opioid addiction. In A. Herz (Ed.), Opioids II, Volume 104, *Handbook of Experimental Pharmacology* (pp. 803–824). New York: SpringerVerlag.

O'Brien, C. P. (1994). Treatment of alcoholism as a chronic disorder. In B. Jansson, H. Jönvall, U. Rydberg, L. Terenius, and B. L. Vallee (Eds.), *Toward a Molecular Basis of Alcohol Use and Abuse*, pp. 349–359. Basel, Switzerland: Birkhäuser.

O'Brien, C. P., and Gardner, E. L. (2005). Critical assessment of how to study addiction and its treatment: Human and non-human animal models. *Pharmacol. Ther.*, 108, 18–58.

O'Brien, M. S., and Anthony, J. C. (2005). Risk of becoming cocaine dependent: Epidemiological estimates for the United States, 2000–2001. *Neuropsychopharmacology*, 30, 1006–1018.

O'Callaghan, F., Muurlink, O., and Reid, N. (2018). Effects of caffeine on sleep quality and daytime functioning. *Risk Manag. Healthc. Policy*, 11, 263–271.

O'Dell, L. E., and Torres, O. V. (2014). A mechanistic hypothesis of the factors that enhance vulnerability to nicotine use in females. *Neuropharmacology*, 76, 566–580.

O'Farrell, K., and Harkin, A. (2017). Stress-related regulation of the kynurenine pathway: Relevance to neuropsychiatric and degenerative disorders. *Neuropharmacology*, 112, 307–323.

O'Tuathaigh, C. M. P., Desbonnet, L., and Waddington, J. L. (2014). Genetically modified mice related to schizophrenia and other psychoses: Seeking phenotypic insights into the pathobiology and treatment of negative symptoms. *Eur. Neuropsychopharmacol.*, 24, 800–821.

Oberlander, J. G., and Henderson, L. P. (2012). The Sturm und Drang of anabolic steroid use: Angst, anxiety, and aggression. *Trends Neurosci.*, 35, 382–392.

Oberlander, J. G., Porter, D. M., Penatti, C. A. A., and Henderson, L. P. (2012). Anabolic androgenic steroid abuse: Multiple mechanisms of regulation of GABAergic synapses in neuroendocrine control regions of the rodent forebrain. *J. Neuroendocrinol.*, 24, 202–214.

Obeso, J. A., Rodriguez-Oroz, M. C., Goetz, C. G., Marin, C., Kordower, J. H., Rodriguez, M., et al. (2010). Missing pieces in the Parkinson's disease puzzle. *Nat. Med.*, 16, 653–661.

Oddy, W. H., and O'Sullivan, T. A. (2010). Energy drinks for children and adolescents: Erring on the side of caution may reduce long term health risks. *BMJ*, 339, b5268.

Odenwald, M., and al'Absi, M. (2017). Khat use and related addiction, mental health and physical disorders: the need to address a growing risk. *East Mediterr. Health J.*, 23, 236–244.

OECD (Organization for Economic Cooperation and Development). (1978). Road Research: New Research on the Role of Alcohol and Drugs in Road Accidents (a report). Washington, D.C: OECD Publications Center.

Ogawa, S., and Kunugi, H. (2015). Inhibitors of fatty acid amide hydrolase and monoacylglycerol lipase: New targets for future antidepressants. *Curr. Neuropharmacol.*, 13, 760–775.

Ogino, S., Miyamoto, S., Miyake, N., and Yamaguchi, N. (2014). Benefits and limits of anticholinergic use in schizophrenia: Focusing on its effect on cognitive function. *Psychiatry Clin. Neurosci.*, 68(1), 37–49. https://doi.org/10.1111/pcn.12088

Ögren, S. O., Eriksson, T. M., ElvanderTottie, E., D'Addario, C., Ekström, J. C., Svenningsson, P., et al. (2008). The role of 5-HT1A receptors in learning and memory. *Behav. Brain Res.*, 195, 54–77.

Ohlsson, A., Lindgren, J.-E., Wahlen, A., Agurell, S., Hollister, L. E., and Gillespie H. K. (1980). Plasma delta-9-tetrahydrocannabinol concentrations and clinical effects after oral and intravenous administration and smoking. *Clin. Pharmacol. Ther.*, 28, 409–416. doi: 10.1038/clpt.1980.181, PMID: 6250760.

Oikonomou, G., Altermatt, M., Zhang, R.-W., Coughlin, G. M., Montz, C., Gradinaru, V., and Prober, D. A. (2019). The serotonergic raphe promote sleep in zebrafish and mice. *Neuron*, 103, 686–701.

Okada, M., Yamashita, S., Ueyama, H., Ishizaki, M., Maeda, Y., and Ando, Y. (2018). Long-term effects of edaravone on survival of patients with amyotrophic lateral sclerosis. *eNeurologicalSci*, 11, 11–14.

Okubo, T., Sato, A., Okamoto, H., Sato, T., and Sasaoka, T. (2018). Differential behavioral phenotypes of dopamine D1 receptor knockdown mice at the embryonic, postnatal, and adult stages. *Int. J. Dev. Neurosci.*, 66, 1–8.

Oldendorf, W. H. (1977). The blood–brain barrier. *Exp. Eye Res.* 25, 177–190.

Oliveira T., Marinho V., Carvalho V., Magalhães F., Rocha K., Ayres C., et al. (2018) Genetic polymorphisms associated with circadian rhythm dysregulation provide new perspectives on bipolar disorder. *Bipolar Disord.*, 20(6), 515–522.

Olives, T. D., Boley, S. P., LeRoy, J. M., and Stellpflug, S. J. (2019). Ten years of robotripping: Evidence of tolerance to dextromethorphan hydrobromide in a long-term user. *J. Med. Toxicol.*, 15, 192–197.

Olivier, J.D.A., and Olivier, B. (2020). Translational studies in the complex role of neurotransmitter systems in anxiety and anxiety disorders. *Adv. Exp. Med. Biol.*, 1191, 121–140.

Olloquequi, J., Cornejo-Córdova, E., Verdaguer, E., Soriano, F. X., Binvignat, O., Auladell, C., and Camins, A. (2018). Excitotoxicity in the pathogenesis of neurological and psychiatric disorders: Therapeutic implications. *J. Psychopharmacol.*, 32, 265–275.

Olmo, I. G., Ferreira-Vieira, T. H., and Ribeiro, F. M. (2016). Dissecting the signaling pathways involved in the crosstalk between metabotropic glutamate 5 and cannabinoid type 1 receptors. *Mol. Pharmacol.*, 90, 609–619.

Olney, J. W. (1969). Brain lesions, obesity, and other disturbances in mice treated with monosodium glutamate. *Science*, 164, 719–721.

Olney, J. J., Warlow, S. M., Naffziger, E. E., and Berridge, K. C. (2018). Current perspectives on incentive salience and applications to clinical disorders. *Curr. Opin. Behav. Sci.*, 22, 59–69.

Olszewski, D. (2009). Sexual assaults facilitated by drugs or alcohol. *Drugs: Educ. Prev. Policy*, 16, 39–52.

Olszewski, P. K., Wood, E. L., Klockars, A., and Levine, A. S. (2019). Excessive consumption of sugar: an insatiable drive for reward. *Curr. Nutr. Rep.*, 8, 120–128.

Omori, S., Isose, S., Otsuru, N., Nishihara, M., Kuwabara, S., Inui, K., and Kakigi, R. (2013). Somatotopic representation of pain in the primary somatosensory cortex (S1) in humans. *Clin. Neurophysiol.*, 124(7), 1422–1430. https://doi.org/10.1016/j.clinph.2013.01.006

Onakomaiya, M. M., and Henderson, L. P. (2016). Mad men, women and steroid cocktails: A review of the impact of sex and other factors on anabolic androgenic steroids effects on affective behaviors. *Psychopharmacology*, 233, 549–569.

Onaolapo, A. Y., and Onaolapo, O. J. (2020). Dietary glutamate and the brain: In the footprints of a Jekyll and Hyde molecule. *Neurotoxicology*, 80, 93–104.

Oñatibia-Astibia, A., Martínez-Pinilla, E., and Franco, R. (2016). The potential of methylxanthine-based therapies in pediatric respiratory tract diseases. *Respir. Med.*, 112, 1–9.

Ong, W.-Y., Tanaka, K., Dawe, G. S., Ittner, L. M., and Farooqui, A. A. (2013). Slow excitotoxicity in Alzheimer's disease. *J. Alzheimers Dis.*, 35, 643–668.

Ooi, Y. P., Weng, S. J., Kossowsky, J., Gerger, H., and Sung, M. (2017). Oxytocin and autism spectrum disorders: A systematic review and meta-analysis of randomized controlled trials. *Pharmacopsychiatry*, 50, 5–13.

Ordean, A., and Kim, G. (2020). Cannabis use during lactation: Literature review and clinical recommendations. *J. Obstet. Gynaecol Can.*, 42, 1248–1253.

Ordway, G. A., Klimek, V., and Mann, J. J. (2002). Neurocircuitry of mood disorders. In K. L. Davis, D. Charney, J. T. Coyle, and C. Nemeroff (Eds.), *Neuropsychopharmacology: The Fifth Generation of Progress*, pp. 1051–1064. New York: Lippincot Williams & Wilkins.

Orsolini, L., Papanti, G. D., De Berardis, D., Guirguis, A., Corkery, J. M., and Schifano, F. (2017). The "endless trip" among the NPS users: Psychopathology and psychopharmacology in the hallucinogen-persisting perception disorder. A systematic review. *Front. Psychiatry*, 8, 240. doi: 10.3389/fpsyt.2017.00240.

Orson, F. M., Wang, R., Brimijoin, S., Kinsey, B. M., Singh, R. A. K., Ramakrishnan, M., et al. (2014). The future potential for cocaine vaccines. *Expert Opin. Biol. Ther.*, 14, 1271–1283.

Osborn, E., Grey, C., and Reznikoff, M. (1986). Psychosocial adjustment, modality choice, and outcome in naltrexone versus methadone treatment. *Am. J. Drug Alcohol Abuse*, 12, 383–388.

Oswald, L. M., Dunn, K. E., Seminowicz, D. A., and Storr, C. L. (2021). Early life stress and risks for opioid misuse: Review of data supporting neurobiological underpinnings. *J. Pers. Med.*, 11(4). https://doi.org/10.3390/jpm11040315.

Ota, M., Ogawa, S., Kato, K., Masuda, C., and Kunugi, H. (2015). Striatal and extrastriatal dopamine release in the common marmoset brain measured by positron emission tomogrphy and [18F] fallypride. *Neurosci. Res.*, 101, 1–5.

Owotomo, O., Stritzel, H., McCabe, S. E., Boyd, C. J., and Maslowsky, J. (2020). Smoking intention and progression from e-cigarette use to cigarette smoking. *Pediatrics*, 146(6), e2020002881. doi: 10.1542/peds.2020-002881.

Oxymed Australia. (2017). Hyperbaric Oxygen. Stroke (website). Available at www.oxymed.com.au/stroke.

Ozdemir, E. (2020). The role of the cannabinoid system in opioid analgesia and tolerance. *Mini Rev. Med. Chem.*, 20, 875–885.

Ozgen, M. H., and Blume, S. (2019). The continuing search for an addiction vaccine. *Vaccine*, 37, 5485–5490.

P

Padamsey, Z., and Emptage, N. (2014). Two sides to long-term potentiation: A view towards reconciliation. *Philos. Trans. R. Soc. Lond. B Biol. Sci.*, 369, 20130154. doi: 10.1098/rstb.2013.0154.

Pagonis, T. A., Angelopoulos, N. V., Koukoulis, G. N., and Hadjichristodoulou, C. S. (2006a). Psychiatric side effects induced by supraphysiological doses of combinations of anabolic steroids correlate to the severity of abuse. *Eur. Psychiatry*, 21, 551–562.

Pagonis, T. A., Angelopoulos, N. V., Koukoulis, G. N., Hadjichristodoulou, C. S., and Toli, P. N. (2006b). Psychiatric and hostility factors related to use of anabolic steroids in monozygotic twins. *Eur. Psychiatry*, 21, 563–569.

Pahnke, W. N., Kurland, A. A., Unger, S., Savage, C., and Grof, S. (1970). The experimental use of psychedelic (LSD) psychotherapy. *JAMA*, 212, 1856–1863.

Pakkenberg, B., and Gundersen, H.J.G. (1997). Neocortical neurone number in humans: effects of sex and age. *J. Comp. Neurol.*, 384, 312–320.

Palacios-García, I., Lara-Vásquez, A., Montiel, J. F., Díaz-Véliz, G. F., Sepúlveda, H., Utreras, E., et al. (2015). Prenatal stress downregulates Reelin expression by methylation of its promoter and induces adult behavioral impairments in rats. *PLOS ONE*, 10, e0117680.

Palamar, J. J., Barratt, M. J., Coney, L., and Martins, S. S. (2017). Synthetic cannabinoid use among high school seniors. *Pediatrics*, 140(4), e20171330. doi: 10.1542/peds.2017-1330.

Palhano-Fontes, F., Andrade, K. C., Tofoli, L. F., Santos, A. C., Crippa, J.A.S., Hallak, J.E.C., Ribeiro, S. (2015). The psychedelic state induced by ayahuasca modulates the activity and connectivity of the default mode network. *PLOS ONE*, 10(2), e0118143. doi: 10.1371/journal.pone.0118143.

Palmiter, R. D. (2008). Dopamine signaling in the dorsal striatum is essential for motivated behaviors: Lessons from dopamine-deficient mice. *Ann. N. Y. Acad. Sci.*, 1129, 35–46.

Panczyk, K., Gołda, S., Waszkielewicz, A., Zelaszczyk, D., Gunia-Krzyzak, A., and Marona, H. (2015). Serotonergic system and its role in epilepsy and neuropathic pain treatment: A review based on receptor ligands. *Curr. Pharm. Des.*, 21, 1723–1740.

Panagis, G., Vlachou, S., and Nomikos, G. G. (2008). Behavioral pharmacology of cannabinoids with a focus on preclinical models for studying reinforcing and dependence-producing

properties. *Curr. Drug Abuse Rev.*, 1, 350–374.

Panenka, W. J., Procyshyn, R. M., Lecomte, T., MacEwan, G. W., Flynn, S. W., Honer, W. G., and Barr, A. M. (2013). Methamphetamine use: a comprehensive review of molecular, preclinical and clinical findings. *Drug Alcohol Depend.*, 129, 167–179.

Pani, L., Pira, L., and Marchese, G. (2007). Antipsychotic efficacy: Relationship to optimal D2-receptor occupancy. *Eur. Psychiatry*, 22(5), 267–275. https://doi.org/10.1016/j.eurpsy.2007.02.005

Panja, D., and Bramham, C. R. (2014). BDNF mechanisms in late LTP formation: A synthesis and breakdown. *Neuropharmacology*, 76, 664–676.

Panlilio, L. V., Goldberg, S. R., and Justinova, Z. (2015). Cannabinoid abuse and addiction: Clinical and preclinical findings. *Clin. Pharmacol. Ther.*, 97, 616–627.

Panlilio, L. V., Justinova, Z., and Goldberg, S. R. (2010). Animal models of cannabinoid reward. *Br. J. Pharmacol.*, 160, 499–510.

Panza, F., Solfrizzi, V., Barulli, M. R., Bonfiglio, C., Guerra, V., Osella, A., et al. (2015). Coffee, tea, and caffeine consumption and prevention of late-life cognitive decline and dementia: A systematic review. *J. Nutr. Health Aging*, 19, 313–328.

Papanti, D., Orsolini, L., Francesconi, G., and Schifano, F. (2014). "Noids" in a nutshell: Everything you (don't) want to know about synthetic cannabinoids. *Adv. Dual Diagn.*, 7, 137–148.

Pardiñas, A. F., Holmans, P., Pocklington, A. J., Escott-Price, V., Ripke, S., Carrera, N., Legge, S. E., et al. (2018). Common schizophrenia alleles are enriched in mutation-intolerant genes and in regions under strong background selection. *Nat. Genet.*, 50(3), 381. https://doi.org/10.1038/s41588-018-0059-2

Pardini, D., White, H. R., Xiong, S., Bechtold, J., Chung, T., Loeber, R., et al. (2015). Unfazed or dazed and confused: Does early adolescent marijuana use cause sustained impairments in attention and academic functioning? *J. Abnorm. Child Psychol.*, 43, 1203–1217.

Park, L. T., Falodun, T. B., and Zarate, C. A. Jr. (2019) Ketamine for treatment-resistant mood disorders. *Focus*, 17(1), 8–12.

Park, P., Volianskis, A., Sanderson, T. M., Bortolotto, Z. A., Jane, D. E., Zhuo, M., et al. (2014). NMDA receptor-dependent long-term potentiation comprises a family of temporally overlapping forms of synaptic plasticity that are induced by different patterns of stimulation. *Philos. Trans. R. Soc. Lond. B Biol. Sci.*, 369, 20130131. doi: 10.1098/rstb.2013.0131.

Park, S.-J., Yi, B., Lee, H.-S., Oh, W.-Y., Na, H.-K., Lee, M., et al. (2016). To quit or not: Vulnerability of women to smoking tobacco. *J. Environ. Sci. Health C Environ. Carcinog. Ecotoxicol. Rev.*, 34, 33–56.

Park, Y., and Ryu, J.-K. (2018). Models of synaptotagmin-1 to trigger Ca^{2+}-dependent vesicle fusion. *FEBS Lett.*, 592, 3480–3492.

Parker, D. A., Harford, T. C., and Rosenstock, I. M. (1994). Alcohol, other drugs, and sexual risk-taking among young adults. *J. Subst. Abuse*, 6, 87–93.

Parkinson Study Group. (1993). Effects of tocopherol and deprenyl on the progression of disability in early Parkinson's disease. *N. Engl. J. Med.*, 328, 176–183.

Parks, C., Jones, B. C., Moore, B. M., and Mulligan, M. K. (2020). Sex and strain variation in initial sensitivity and rapid tolerance to Δ^9-tetrahydrocannabinol. *Cannabis Cannabinoid Res.*, 5, 231–245.

Parrott, A. C. (2013). MDMA, serotonergic neurotoxicity, and the diverse functional deficits of recreational "Ecstasy" users. *Neurosci. Biobehav. Rev.*, 37, 1466–1484.

Parsons, R. L., Calupca, M. A., Merriam, L. A., and Prior, C. (1999). Empty synaptic vesicles recycle and undergo exocytosis at vesamicol-treated motor nerve terminals. *J. Neurophysiol.*, 81, 2696–2700.

Partin, K. M. (2015). AMPA receptor potentiators: From drug design to cognitive enhancement. *Curr. Opin. Pharmacol.*, 20, 46–53.

Parvaz, M. A., Moeller, S. J., Uquillas, F. D., Pflumm, A., Maloney, T., Alia-Klein, N., and Goldstein, R. Z. (2017). Prefrontal gray matter volume recovery in treatment-seeking cocaine-addicted individuals: A longitudinal study. *Addict. Biol.*, 22, 1391–1401.

Pascale, A., and Laborde, A. (2020). Impact of pesticide exposure in childhood. *Rev. Environ. Health*, 35, 221–227.

Pascoli, V., Cahill, E., Bellivier, F., Caboche, J., and Vanhoutte, P. (2014). Extracellular signal-regulated protein kinases 1 and 2 activation by addictive drugs: A signal toward pathological adaptation. *Biol. Psychiatry*, 76, 917–926.

Pasman, J. A., Verweij, K., Gerring, Z., Stringer, S., Sanchez-Roige, S., Treur, J. L., Abdellaoui, A., et al. (2018). GWAS of lifetime cannabis use reveals new risk loci, genetic overlap with psychiatric traits, and a causal influence of schizophrenia. *Nat. Neurosci.*, 21, 1161–1170.

Passie, T., and Benzenhöfer, U. (2018). MDA, MDMA, and other "mescaline-like" substances in the US military's search for a truth drug (1940s to 1960s). *Drug Test. Anal.*, 10, 72–80.

Patel, N. B. (2019). Khat (Catha edulis Forsk)—And now there are three. *Brain Res. Bull.*, 145, 92–96.

Patel, R.A.G., and McMullen, P. W. (2017). Neuroprotection in the treatment of acute ischemic stroke. *Prog. Cardiovasc. Dis.*, 59, 542–548.

Paterniti, I., Esposito, E., and Cuzzocrea, S. (2014). Phosphodiesterase as a new therapeutic target for the treatment of spinal cord injury and neurodegenerative diseases. *Curr. Med. Chem.*, 21, 2830–2838.

Patil, S. T., Zhang, L., Martenyi, F., Lowe, S. L., Jackson, K. A., Andreev, B. V., et al. (2007). Activation of mGlu2/3 receptors as a new approach to treat schizophrenia: A randomized Phase 2 clinical trial. *Nat. Med.*, 13, 1102–1107.

Patil, S., Arakeri, G., Patil, S., Baeshen, H. A., Raj, T., Sarode, S. C., Sarode, G. S., et al. (2020). Are electronic nicotine delivery systems (ENDs) helping cigarette smokers quit?—Current evidence. *J. Oral Pathol. Med.*, 49, 181–189.

Patrick, M. E., Miech, R. A., Carlier, C., O'Malley, P. M., Johnston, L. D., and Schulenberg, J. E. (2016). Self-reported reasons for vaping among 8th, 10th, and 12th graders in the US: Nationally-representative results. *Drug Alcohol Depend.*, 165, 275–278.

Patrick, S. W., Barfield, W. D., Poindexter, B. B., and Committee on Fetus and Newborn, C. on S. U. and P. (2020). Neonatal Opioid Withdrawal Syndrome. *Pediatrics*, 146(5). https://doi.org/10.1542/peds.2020-029074

Patten S. B. (2020). Cannabis and non-psychotic mental disorders. *Curr. Opin. Psychol.*, 38, 61–66.

Patten, T., and De Biasi, M. (2020). History repeats itself: Role of characterizing flavors on nicotine use and abuse. *Neuropharmacology*, 177, 108162. doi: 10.1016/j.neuropharm.2020.108162.

Paul, B. D., and Snyder, S. H. (2018). Gasotransmitter hydrogen sulfide signaling in neuronal health and disease. *Biochem. Pharmacol.*, 149, 101–109.

Paulson, P. E., Camp, D. M., and Robinson, T. E. (1991). Time course of transient behavioral depression and persistent behavioral sensitization in relation to regional brain monoamine concentrations during amphetamine withdrawal in rats. *Psychopharmacology*, 103, 480–492.

Paulus, F. W., Ohmann, S., von Gontard, A., and Popow, C. (2018). Internet gaming disorder in children and adolescents: a systematic review. *Dev. Med. Child Neurol.*, 60, 645–659.

Peciña, S., and Berridge, K. C. (2005). Hedonic hot spot in nucleus accumbens shell: Where do mu-opioids cause increased hedonic impact of sweetness? *J. Neurosci.*, 25, 1177–1186.

Peciña, S., and Smith, K. S. (2010). Hedonic and motivational roles of opioids in food reward: Implications for overeating disorders. *Pharmacol. Biochem. Behav.*, 97, 34–46.

Pedraza, C., García, F. B., and Navarro, J. F. (2009). Neurotoxic effects induced by gammahydroxybutyric acid (GHB) in male rats. *Int. J. Neuropsychopharmacol.*, 12, 1165–1177.

Peele, S. (2016). People control their addictions. No matter how much the "chronic" brain disease model of addiction indicates otherwise, we know that people can quit addictions with special reference to harm reduction and mindfulness. *Addict. Behav. Rep.*, 4, 97–101.

Peltier, M. R., and Sofuoglu, M. (2018). The role of exogenous progesterone in the treatment of males and females with substance use disorders: A narrative review. *CNS Drugs*, 32, 421–435.

Penberthy, J. K., Ait-Daoud, N., Vaughan, M., and Fanning, T. (2010). Review of treatments for cocaine dependence. *Curr. Drug Abuse Rev.*, 3, 49–62.

Pennsylvania Liquor Control Board. (1995). Responsible Alcohol Management Program (RAMP). Available at www.lcb.pa.gov/.

Pentney, A. R. (2001). An exploration of the history and controversies surrounding MDMA and MDA. *J. Psychoactive Drugs*, 33, 213–221.

Pereda, A. E. (2014). Electrical synapses and their functional interactions with chemical synapses. *Nat. Rev. Neurosci.*, 15, 250–263.

Pereira, T. D., Shaevitz, J. W., and Murthy, M. (2020). Quantifying behavior to understand the brain. *Nat. Neurosci.*, 1–13. https://doi.org/10.1038/s41593-020-00734-z.

Pereira, V., and Goudet, C. (2019). Emerging trends in pain modulation by metabotropic glutamate receptors. *Front. Mol. Neurosci.*, 11, 464. doi: 10.3389/fnmol.2018.00464.

Perez-Paramo, Y. X., and Lazarus, P. (2020). Pharmacogenetics factors influencing smoking cessation success; the importance of nicotine metabolism. *Expert Opin. Drug Metab. Toxicol.*, in press.

Perkins, K. A. (2002). Chronic tolerance to nicotine in humans and its relationship to tobacco dependence. *Nicotine Tob. Res.*, 4, 405–422.

Perkins, K. A., Karelitz, J. L., Conklin, C. A., Sayette, M. A., and Giedgowd, G. E. (2010). Acute negative affect relief from smoking depends on the affect situation and measure, but not on nicotine. *Biol. Psych.*, 67, 707–714.

Perl, D. P. (2010). Neuropathology of Alzheimer's disease. *Mt. Sinai J. Med.*, 77, 32–42.

Perlman, B. (2017). Promising Advances in the Search for Safer Opioids. National Institute of Drug Abuse. NIDA Notes. Available at www. drugabuse.gov/news-events/nida-notes/2017/02/promising-advances-in-search-saferopioids?utm_source=NNEblast&utm_medium=email&utm_term=FeedSubscribers&utm_content=ArticleSaferOpi&utm_campaign=Mar2017.

Perouansky, M., and Pearce, R. A. (2011). How we recall (or don't): The hippocampal memory machine and anesthetic amnesia. *Can. J. Anesth.*, 58, 157–166.

Perron, B. E., Glass, J. E., Ahmedani, B. K., Vaughn, M. G., Roberts, D. E., and Wu, L.-T. (2011). The prevalence and clinical significance of inhalant withdrawal symptoms among a national sample. *Subst. Abuse Rehabil.*, 2011, 69–76.

Perron, B. E., Howard, M. O., Maitra, S., and Vaughn, M. G. (2009a). Prevalence, timing, and predictors of transition from inhalant use to inhalant use disorders. *Drug Alcohol Depend.*, 100, 277–284.

Perron, B. E., Howard, M. O., Vaughn, M. G., and Jarman, C. N. (2009b). Inhalant withdrawal as a clinically significant feature of inhalant dependence disorder. *Med. Hypotheses*, 73, 935–937.

Perry, D. C., Dávila-Garcia, M. I., Stockmeier, C. A., and Kellar, K. J. (1999). Increased nicotinic receptors in brains from smokers: Membrane binding and autoradiography studies. *J. Pharmacol. Exp. Ther.*, 289, 1545–1552.

Pert, C. B., and Snyder, S. H. (1973). Properties of opiate receptor binding in rat brain. *Proc. Natl. Acad. Sci. USA*, 70, 2243–2247.

Pertwee, R. G. (2008). The diverse CB_1 and CB_2 receptor pharmacology of three plant cannabinoids: Δ^9-tetrahydrocannabinol, cannabidiol and Δ^9-tetrahydrocannabivarin. *Br. J. Pharmacol.*, 153, 199–215.

Peters, A., Palay, S. L., and Webster, H. deF. (1991). *The Fine Structure of the Nervous System: Neurons and Their Supporting Cells* (3rd ed.). New York: Oxford University Press.

Peters, K. Z., Oleson, E. B., and Cheer, J. F. (2021). A brain on cannabinoids: The role of dopamine release in reward seeking and addiction. *Cold Spring Harb. Perspect. Med.*, 11(1), a039305. doi: 10.1101/cshperspect.a039305.

Peters, R. J., Jr., Williams, M., Ross, M. W., Atkinson, J., and McCurdy, S. A. (2008). The use of fry (embalming fluid and PCP-laced cigarettes or marijuana sticks) among crack cocaine smokers. *J. Drug Educ.*, 38, 285–295.

Peterson, A. R., and Binder, D. K. (2020). Astrocyte glutamate uptake and signaling as novel targets for antiepileptogenic therapy. *Front. Neurol.*, 11, 1006. https://doi.org/10.3389/fneur.2020.01006

Peterson, T., Rentmeester, L., Judge, B. S., Cohle, S. D., and Jones, J. S. (2014). Self-administered ethanol enema causing accidental death. *Case Rep. Emerg. Med.*, 2014, 1–3. https://doi.org/10.1155/2014/191237

Petrlova, J., Kalai, T., Maezawa, I., Altman, R., Harishchandra, G., Hong, H.-S., et al. (2012). The influence of spin-labeled fluorene compounds on the assembly and toxicity of the Aβ peptide. *PLOS ONE*, 7, 1–10.

Petry, N. M. (2010). Contingency management treatments: Controversies and challenges. *Addiction*, 105, 1507–1509.

Petry, N. M., Alessi, S. M., Olmstead, T. A., Rash, C. J., and Zajac, K. (2017). Contingency management treatment for substance use disorders: How far has it come, and where does it need to go? *Psychol. Addict. Behav.*, 31, 897–906.

Petry, N. M., Zajac, K., and Ginley, M. K. (2018). Behavioral addictions as mental disorders: To be or not to be? *Annu. Rev. Clin. Psychol.*, 14, 399–423.

Pettersson, R., Näslund, J., Nilsson, S., Eriksson, E., and Hagsäter, S. M. (2015). Acute escitalopram but not contextual conditioning exerts a stronger "anxiogenic" effect in rats with high baseline "anxiety" in the acoustic startle paradigm. *Psychopharmacology*, 232, 1461–1469.

Pew Research Center. (2015). In Debate Over Legalizing Marijuana, Disagreement Over Drug's Dangers. Available at https://www.pewresearch.org/politics/2015/04/14/in-debate-over-legalizing-marijuana-disagreement-over-drugs-dangers/. Accessed 3/13/21.

Peyron, C., Faraco, J., Rogers, W., Ripley, B., Overeem, S., Charnay, Y., et al. (2000). A mutation in a case of early onset narcolepsy and a generalized absence of hypocretin peptides in human narcoleptic brains. *Nat. Med.*, 6, 991–997.

Pfefferbaum, A., and Sullivan, E. V. (2004). Diffusion MR imaging in psychiatry and ageing. In J. Gillard, A. Waldman, and P. Barker (Eds.), *Physiological Magnetic Resonance in Clinical Neuroscience*, Chapter 33. Cambridge: Cambridge University Press.

Phatak, D. R., and Walterscheid, J. (2012). Huffing air conditioner fluid: A cool way to die? *Am. J. Forensic Med. Pathol.*, 33, 64–67.

Philippu, A. (1984). Use of push–pull cannulae to determine the release of endogenous neurotransmitters in distinct brain areas of anaesthetized and freely moving animals. In C. A. Marsden (Ed.), *Measurement of Neurotransmitter Release in Vivo*, pp. 3–38. New York: Wiley.

Phillips, C. V. (2015). Gateway effects: Why the cited evidence does not support their existence for low-risk tobacco products (and what evidence would). *Int. J. Environ. Res. Public Health*, 12, 5439–5464.

Phillips, T. J., and Reed, C. (2014). Targeting $GABA_B$ receptors for anti-abuse drug discovery. *Expert Opin. Drug Discov.*, 9, 1307–1317.

Piacentino, D., Kotzalidis, G. D., del Casale, A., Aromatario, M. R., Pomara, C., Girardi, P., et al. (2015). Anabolic–androgenic steroid use and psychopathology in athletes. A systematic review. *Curr. Neuropharmacol.*, 13, 101–121.

Picciotto, M. R., Addy, N. A., Mineur, Y. S., and Brunzell, D. H. (2008). It is not "either/or": Activation and desensitization of nicotinic acetylcholine receptors both contribute to behaviors related to nicotine addiction and mood. *Prog. Neurobiol.*, 84, 329–342.

Pickard, H. (2012). The purpose in chronic addiction. *AJOB Neurosci.*, 3, 40–49.

Pickens, C. L., Airavaara, M., Theberge, F., Fanous, S., Hope, B. T., and Shaham, Y. (2011). Neurobiology of the incubation of drug craving. *Trends Neurosci.*, 34, 411–420.

Pickering, C., and Grgic, J. (2020). Is coffee a useful source of caffeine preexercise? *Int. J. Sport Nutr. Exerc. Metab.*, 30, 69–82.

Picón-Pagès, P., Garcia-Puendia, J., and Muñoz, F. J. (2019). Functions and dysfunctions of nitric oxide in brain. *Biochim. Biophys. Acta Mol. Basis Dis.*, 1865, 1949–1967.

Pidoplichko, V. I., DeBiasi, M., Williams, J. T., and Dani, J. A. (1997). Nicotine activates and desensitizes midbrain dopamine neurons. *Nature*, 390, 401–404.

Pidoplichko, V. I., Noguchi, J., Areola, O. O., Liang, Y., Peterson, J., Zhang, T., et al. (2004). Nicotinic cholinergic synaptic mechanisms in the ventral tegmental area contribute to nicotine addiction. *Learn. Mem.*, 11, 60–69.

Pieprzyca, E., Skowronek, R., Nižnanský, L., and Czekaj, P. (2020). Synthetic cathinones – From natural plant stimulant to new drug of abuse. *Eur. J. Pharmacol.*, 875, 173012. doi: 10.1016/j.ejphar.2020.173012.

Piña, J. A., Namba, M. D., Leyrer-Jackson, J. M., Cabrera-Brown, G., and Gipson, C. D. (2018). Social influences on nicotine-related behaviors. *Int. Rev. Neurobiol.*, 140, 1–32.

Pinky, P. D., Bloemer, J., Smith, W. D., Moore, T., Hong, H., Suppiramaniam, V., and Reed, M. N. (2019). Prenatal cannabinoid exposure and altered neurotransmission. *Neuropharmacology*, 149, 181–194.

Pinna, G., and Rasmusso, A. M. (2014). Ganaxolone improves behavioral deficits in a mouse model of post-traumatic stress disorder. *Front. Cell. Neurosci.*, 8, Article 256, 1–11.

Piontkewitz, Y., Arad, M., and Weiner, I. (2011). Abnormal trajectories of neurodevelopment and behavior following in utero insult in the rat. *Biol. Psychiatry*, 70, 842–851. © 2011. Reprinted with permission from Society of Biological Psychiatry, via Elsevier.

Piper, M. E., Drobes, D. J., and Walker, N. (2019). Behavioral and subjective effects of reducing nicotine in cigarettes: A cessation commentary. *Nicotine Tob. Res.*, 21 (Suppl. 1), S19–S21.

Pisanti, S., and Bifulco, M. (2019). Medical cannabis: A plurimillennial history of an evergreen. *J. Cell. Physiol.*, 234, 8342–8351.

Placzek, M. S., Van de Bittner, G. C., Wey, H.-Y., Lukas, S. E., and Hooker, J. M. (2015). Immediate and persistent effects of salvinorin A on the kappa opioid receptor in rodents, monitored in vivo with PET. *Neuropsychopharmacology*, 40, 2865–2872.

Plante, D. T., and Winkelman, J. W. (2008). Sleep disturbance in bipolar disorder: Therapeutic implications. *Am. J. Psychiatry*, 165, 830–843.

Platt, D. M., Rowlett, J. K., and Spealman, R. D. (2002). Behavioral effects of cocaine and dopaminergic strategies for preclinical medication development. *Psychopharmacology*, 163, 265–282.

Ploner, M., Gross, J., Timmermann, L., and Schnitzler, A. (2002). Cortical representation of first and second pain sensation in humans. *Proc. Natl. Acad. Sci. USA*, 99, 12444–12448.

Plush, T., Shakespeare, W., Jacobs, D., Ladi, L., Sethi, S., and Gasperino, J. (2015). Cocaine-induced agitated delirium: a case report and review. *J. Intensive Care Med.*, 30, 49–57.

Poels, E. M., Kegeles, L. S., Kantrowitz, J. T., Javitt, D. C., Lieberman, J. A., AbiDargham, A., and Girgis, R. R. (2014). Glutamatergic abnormalities in schizophrenia: A review of proton MRS findings. *Schizophr. Res.*, 152, 325–332.

Poewe, W., Antonini, A., Zijlmans, J. C. M., Burkhard, P. R., and Vingerhoets, F. (2010). Levodopa in the treatment of Parkinson's disease: An old drug still going

strong. *Clin. Interv. Aging*, 5, 229–238.

Poltavski, D. V., and Petros, T. (2006). Effects of transdermal nicotine on attention in adult non-smokers with and without attentional deficits. *Physiol. Behav.*, 87, 614–624.

Pop, A. S., Gomez-Mancilla, B., Neri, G., Willemsen, R., and Gasparini, F. (2014). Fragile X syndrome: A preclinical review on metabotropic glutamate receptor 5 (mGluR5) antagonists and drug development. *Psychopharmacology*, 231, 1217–1226.

Pope, H. G., Jr., Kanayama, G., Athey, A., Ryan, E., Hudson, J. I., and Baggish, A. (2014a). The lifetime prevalence of anabolic–androgenic steroid use and dependence in Americans: Current best estimates. *Am. J. Addict.*, 23, 371–377.

Pope, H. G., Jr., Wood, R. I., Rogol, A., Nyberg, F., Bowers, L., and Bhasin, S. (2014b). Adverse health consequences of performance-enhancing drugs: An Endocrine Society scientific statement. *Endocr. Rev.*, 35, 341–375.

Pope, H. G. Jr. Kanayama, G., Hudson, J. I., and Kaufman, M. J. (2021). Review article: Anabolic-androgenic steroids, violence, and crime: Two cases and literature review. *Am. J. Addict.*, in press.

Pope, H. G., Jr, Kanayama, G., Athey, A., Ryan, E., Hudson, J. I., and Baggish, A. (2014). The lifetime prevalence of anabolic-androgenic steroid use and dependence in Americans: current best estimates. *Am. J. Addict.*, 23, 371–377.

Porcu, P., Barron, A. M., Frye, C. A., Walf, A. A., Yang, S. Y., He, X. Y., et al. (2016). Neurosteroidogenesis today: Novel targets for neuroactive steroid synthesis and action and their relevance for translational research. *J. Neuroendocrinol.*, 28, 1–19.

Porrino, L. J., Daunais, J. B., Rogers, G. A., Hampson, R. E., and Deadwyler, S. A. (2005). Facilitation of task performance and removal of the effects of sleep deprivation by an ampakine (CX717) in nonhuman primates. *PLOS Biol.*, 3, e299. doi: 10.1371/journal. pbio.0030299.

Porter, B. E., and Jacobson, C. (2013). Report of a parent survey of cannabidiol-enriched cannabis in pediatric treatment-resistant epilepsy. *Epilepsy Behav.*, 29, 574–577.

Porter, J. H., Prus, A. J., and Overton, D. A. (2018). Drug discrimination: Historical origins, important concepts, and principles. *Curr. Top. Behav. Neurosci.*, 39, 3–26.

Posner, M. I., and Raichle, M. E. (1994). *Images of Mind*. New York: Freeman.

Post, R. M. and Weiss, S. R. B. (1988). Psychomotor stimulant vs. local anesthetic effects of cocaine: Role of behavioral sensitization and kindling. *NIDA Res. Monogr.*, 88, 217–238.

Post, R. M., and Contel, N. R. (1983). Human and animal studies of cocaine: Implications for the development of behavioral pathology. In I. Creese (Ed.), *Stimulants: Neurochemical, Behavioral, and Clinical Perspectives*, pp. 169–203. New York: Raven.

Post, R. M., Ballenger, J. C., Uhde, T., and Bunney, W. (1984). Efficacy of carbamazepine in manic-depressive illness: Implications for underlying mechanisms. In R. M. Post and J. C. Ballenger (Eds.), *Neurobiology of Mood Disorders*, pp. 777–816. Baltimore, MD: Williams and Wilkins.

Potenza, M. (2015). Behavioural addictions matter. *Nature*, 522, S62.

Potvin, S., Pelletier, J., Grot, S., Hébert, C., Barr, A. M., and Lecomte, T. (2018). Cognitive deficits in individuals with methamphetamine use disorder: A meta-analysis. *Addict. Behav.*, 80, 154–160.

Potvin, S., Stavro, K., Rizkallah, E., and Pelletier, J. (2014). Cocaine and cognition: A systematic quantitative review. *J. Addict. Med.*, 8, 368–376.

Powell, J. G., Garland, S., Preston, K., and Piszczatoski, C. (2020). Brexanolone (Zulresso): Finally, an FDA-approved treatment for postpartum depression. *Ann. Pharmacother.*, 54, 157–163.

Prakash, M. D., Tangalakis, K., Antonipillai, J., Stojanovska, L., Nurgali, K., and Apostolopoulos, V. (2017). Methamphetamine: Effects on the brain, gut and immune system. *Pharmacol. Res.*, 120, 60–67.

Preller, K. H., and Vollenweider, F. X. (2016). Phenomenology, structure, and dynamic of psychedelic states. *Curr. Topics Behav. Neurosci.*, doi: 10.1007/7854_2016_459.

Prescott, F., Organe, G., and Rowbotham, S. (1946). Tubocurarine chloride as an adjunct to anesthesia. *Lancet*, 248, 80–84.

PRN Newswire. (2015). Global E Cigarette & Vaporizer Market 2015–2025, Analysis & Forecasts for the $50 Billion Industry. Available at www.prnewswire.com/ news-releases/ global-e-cigarette--vaporizer-market-2015–2025---analysis--forecasts-for-the-50-billion-industry-300124050.html.

Price, L. R., and Martinez, J. (2020). Cardiovascular, carcinogenic and reproductive effects of nicotine exposure: A narrative review of the scientific literature [version 2; peer review: 2 approved, 1 not approved] *F1000Research*, 8, 1586. doi: 10.12688/f1000research.20062.1.

Prini, P., Zamberletti, E., Manenti, C., Gabaglio, M., Parolaro, D., and Rubino, T. (2020). Neurobiological mechanisms underlying cannabis-induced memory impairment. *Eur. Neuropsychopharmacol.*, 36, 181–190.

Prochaska, J. J., and Benowitz, N. L. (2016). The past, present, and future of nicotine addiction therapy. *Annu. Rev. Med.*, 67, 467–486.

Prochaska, J. J., and Benowitz, N. L. (2019). Current advances in research in treatment and recovery: Nicotine addiction. *Sci. Adv.*, 5(10), eaay9763. doi: 10.1126/sciadv.aay9763.

Proebstl, L., Kamp, F., Koller, G., and Soyka, M. (2018). Cognitive deficits in methamphetamine users: How strong is the evidence? *Pharmacopsychiatry*, 51, 243–250.

Proulx, E., Piva, M., Tian, M. K., Bailey, C.D.C., and Lambe, E. K. (2014). Nicotinic acetylcholine receptors in attention circuitry: the role of layer VI neurons of prefrontal cortex. *Cell Mol. Life Sci.*, 71, 1225–1244.

Prozialeck, W. C., Avery, B. A., Boyer, E. W., Grundmann, O., Henningfield, J. E., Kruegel, A. C., McMahon, L. R., McCurdy, C. R., Swogger, M. T., Veltri, C. A., & Singh, D. (2019). Kratom policy: The challenge of balancing therapeutic potential with public safety. *Int. J. Drug Policy*, 70, 70–77. https://doi.org/10.1016/j.drugpo.2019.05.003

Psychiatric GWAS Consortium Coordinating Committee. (2009). Genomewide association studies: History, rationale, and prospects for psychiatric disorders. *Am. J. Psychiatry*, 166, 540–556.

Puighermanal, E., Busquets-Garcia, A., Maldanado, R., and Ozaita, A. (2012). Cellular and intracellular mechanisms involved in the cognitive impairment of cannabinoids. *Philos. Trans. R. Soc. Lond. B Biol. Sci.*, 267, 3254–3263.

Puighermanal, E., Marsicano, G., Busquets-Garcia, A., Lutz, B., Maldanado, R., and Ozaita, A. (2009). Cannabinoid modulation of hippocampal long-term memory is mediated by mTOR signaling. *Nat. Neurosci.*, 12, 1152–1158.

Pulikkan, J., Mazumder, A., and Grace, T. (2019). Role of the gut microbiome in autism spectrum disorders. *Adv. Exp. Med. Biol.*, 1118, 253–269.

Punch, L. J., Self, D. W., Nestler, E. J., and Taylor, J. R. (1997). Opposite modulation of opiate withdrawal behaviors on microinfusion of a protein kinase A inhibitor versus activator into the locus coeruleus or periaqueductal gray. *J. Neurosci.*, 17, 8520–8527.

Purves K. L., Coleman J. R. I., Meier S. M., Rayner C., Davis K. A. S., Cheesman R., et al. (2020). A major role for common genetic variation in anxiety disorders. *Mol Psychiatry.*, 25: 3292–3303.

Purves, D., Augustine, G. J., Fitzpatrick, D., Hall, W. C., LaMantia, A.-S., and White, L. E. (2018). *Neuroscience* (6th ed.). Sunderland, MA: Sinauer.

Q

Qian, J., Chen, Q., Ward, S. M., Duan, E., and Zhang, Y. (2020). Impacts of caffeine during pregnancy. *Trends Endocrinol. Metab.*, 31, 218–227.

Quarta, C., Mazza, R., Obici, S., Pasquali, R., and Pagotto, U. (2011). Energy balance regulation by endocannabinoids at central and peripheral levels. *Trends Mol. Med.*, 17, 518–526.

Quello, S. B., Brady, K. T., and Sonne, S. C. (2005). Mood disorders and substance use disorder: A complex comorbidity. *Sci. Pract. Perspect.*, 3, 13–21.

Quest, D. W., and Horsley, J. (2007). Field-test of a date-rape drug detection device. *J. Anal. Toxicol.*, 31, 354–357.

Qui, C., Kivipelto, M., and von Strauss, E. (2009). Epidemiology of Alzheimer's disease: Occurrence, determinants, and strategies toward intervention. *Dialogues Clin. Neurosci.*, 11, 111–128.

Quiedeville, A., Boulouard, M., Da Silva Costa-Aze, V., Dauphin, F., Bouet, V., and Freret, T. (2014). 5-HT6 receptor antagonists as treatment for age-related cognitive decline. *Rev. Neurosci.*, 25, 417–427.

Quigley, J. A., Logsdon, M. K., Turner, C. A., Gonzalez, I. L., Leonardo, N. B., and Becker, J. B. (2021). Sex differences in vulnerability to addiction. *Neuropharmacology*, 187, 108491. doi: 10.1016/j.neuropharm.2021.108491.

Quinn, V. P., Hollis, J. F., Smith, K. S., Rigotti, N. A., Solberg, L. I., Hu, W., and Stevens, V. J. (2009). Effectiveness of the 5-As tobacco cessation treatments in nine HMOs. *J. Gen. Intern. Med.*, 24, 149–154.

Quinones, C., and Griffiths, M. D. (2015). Addiction to work: A critical review of the workaholism construct and recommendations for assessment. *J. Psychosoc. Nurs. Ment. Health Serv.*, 53, 48–59.

Quintana, D. S., Smerud, K. T., Andreassen, O. A., and Djupesland, P. G. (2018). Evidence for intranasal oxytocin delivery to the brain: recent advances and future perspectives. *Ther. Deliv.*, 9, 515–525.

Quirion, R., and Pilapil, C. (1991). Distribution of multiple opioid receptors in the human brain. In F. A. O. Mendelsohn (Ed.), *Receptors in the Human Nervous System*, pp. 103–121. New York: Academic.

R

Rabin, R. A., and George, T. P. (2017). Understanding the link between cannabinoids and psychosis. *Clin. Pharmacol. Ther.*, 101, 197–199.

Rainville, P. (2002). Brain mechanisms of pain affect and pain modulation. *Curr. Opinion Neurobiol.*, 12, 195–204.

Rainville, P., Duncan, G. H., Price, D. D., Carrier, B., and Bushnell, M. C. (1997). Pain affect encoded in human anterior cingulate but not somatosensory cortex. *Science*, 277, 968–971.

Ramaekers, J. G., van Wel, J. H., Spronk, D. B., Toennes, S. W., Kuypers, K. P. C., Theunissen, E. L., et al. (2016). Cannabis and tolerance: Acute drug impairment as a function of cannabis use history. *Sci. Rep.*, 6, 26843. doi: 10.1038/ srep26843.

Ramaekers, J. G., Mason, N. I., and Theunissen, E. L. (2020). Blunted highs: Pharmacodynamic and behavioral models of cannabis tolerance. *Eur. Neuropsychopharmacol.*, 36, 191–205.

Rambert, F., Hermant, J. F., and Schweizer, D. (2006). Modafinil, a unique wakepromoting drug: A serendipitous discovery in search of a mechanism of action. In J. B. Taylor and D. J. Triggle (Eds.), *Comprehensive Medicinal Chemistry II*, Volume 8, Case Histories (pp. 149– 156). Amsterdam: Elsevier.

Ramirez, M. J., Lai, M. K. P., Tordera, R. M., and Francis, P. T. (2014). Serotonergic therapies for cognitive symptoms in Alzheimer's disease: Rationale and current status. *Drugs*, 74, 729–736.

Ramos, B. P., and Arnsten, A. F. T. (2007). Adrenergic pharmacology and cognition: Focus on the prefrontal cortex. *Pharmacol. Ther.*, 113, 523–536.

Ranade, S. P., and Mainen, Z. F. (2009). Transient firing of dorsal raphe neurons encodes diverse and specific sensory, motor, and reward events. *J. Neurophysiol.*, 102, 3026–3037.

Randall, C. L., Ekblad, U., and Anton, R. F. (1990). Perspectives on the pathophysiology of fetal alcohol syndrome. *Alcohol. Clin. Exp. Res.*, 14, 807–812.

Rando, O. J. (2012). Daddy issues: Paternal effects on phenotypes. *Cell*, 151, 702–708.

Rando, O. J. (2015, December 1). Ghosts in the Genome. The Scientist. Available at www.the-scientist.com/?articles.view/ articleNo/44628/title/Ghosts-in-theGenome/.

Ranganath, A., and Jacob, S. N. (2016). Doping the mind: Dopaminergic modulation of prefrontal cortical cognition. *Neuroscientist*, 22, 593–603.

Rao, M. S., Van Vleet, T. R., Ciurlionis, R., Buck, W. R., Mittelstadt, S. W., Blomme, E.A.G., and Liguori, M. J. (2019). Comparison of RNA-Seq and microarray gene expression platforms for the toxicogenomic evaluation of liver from short-term rat toxicity studies. *Front. Genet.*, 9. https://doi.org/10.3389/fgene.2018.00636

Raposo Pereira, F., McMaster, M., Polderman, N., de Vries, Y., van den Brink, W., and van Wingen, G. A. (2018a). Adverse effects of GHB-induced coma on long-term memory and related brain function. *Drug Alcohol Depend.*, 190, 29–36.

Raposo Pereira, F., McMaster, M., Polderman, N., de Vries, Y., van den Brink, W., and van Wingen, G. A. (2018b). Effect of GHB-use and GHB-induced comas on dorsolateral prefrontal cortex functioning in humans. *Neuroimage Clin.*, 20, 923–930.

Rash, C. J., Weinstock, J., and Van Patten, R. (2016). A review of gambling disorder and substance use disorders. *Subst. Abuse Rehabil.*, 7, 3–13.

Rasmussen, J. J., Albrethsen, J., Frandsen, M. N., Jørgensen, N., Juul, A., and Kistorp, C. (2021). Serum insulin-like factor 3 levels are reduced in former androgen users, suggesting impaired Leydig cell capacity. *J. Clin. Endocrinol. Metab.*, 106, e2664–e2672.

Rasmussen, N. (2008). America's first amphetamine epidemic 1929–1971. A quantitative and qualitative retrospective with implications for the present. *Am. J. Public Health*, 98, 974–985.

Rasmussen, N. (2015). Amphetamine-type stimulants: The early history of their medical and nonmedical uses. *Int. Rev. Neurobiol.*, 120, 9–25.

Rasmussen, S. G., DeVree, B. T., Zou, Y., Kruse, A. C., Chung, K. Y., Kobilka, et al. (2011). Crystal structure of the β2 adrenergic receptor-Gs protein complex. *Nature*, 477, 549–555.

Ratner, M. H., Kumaresan, V., and Farb, D. H. (2019). Neurosteroid actions in memory and neurologic/neuropsychiatric disorders. *Front. Endocrinol.*, 10, 169. doi: 10.3389/fendo.2019.00169.

Rayport, S., Sulzer, D., Shi, W.-X., Sawasdikosol, S., Monaco, J., Batson, D., et al. (1992). Identified postnatal mesolimbic dopamine neurons in culture: Morphology and electrophysiology. *J. Neurosci.*, 12, 4264–4280.

Razak, K. A., Dominick, K. C., and Erickson, C. A. (2020). Developmental studies in fragile X syndrome. *J. Neurodev. Disord.*, 12, 13. doi: 10.1186/s11689-020-093120-9.

Razzoli, M., Andreoli, M., Michielin, F., Quarta, D., and Sokal, D. M. (2011). Increased phasic activity of VTA dopamine neurons in mice 3 weeks after repeated social defeat. *Behav. Brain Res.*, 218, 253–257.

Reddy, D. S., and Estes, W. A. (2016). Clinical potential of neurosteroids for CNS disorders. *Trends Pharmacol. Sci.*, 37, 543–561.

Reddy, D. S. (2007). Perimenstrual Catamenial Epilepsy. Women's Health, 3, 195–206.

Reddy, D. S. (2016). Catamenial epilepsy: Discovery of an extrasynaptic molecular mechanism for targeted therapy. *Front. Cell. Neurosci.*, 10, 101. doi: 10.3389/fncel.2016.00101.

Reddy, D. S., and Estes, W. A. (2016). Clinical potential of neurosteroids for CNS disorders. *Trends Pharmacol. Sci.*, 37, 543–561.

Reed, B., Butelman, E. R., Yuferov, V., Randesi, M., and Kreek, M. J. (2014). Genetics of opiate addiction. *Curr. Psychiatry Rep.*, 16, 504. doi: 10.1007/s11920–014–0504–6.

Reed, G. M., First, M. B., Kogan, C. S., Hyman, S. E., Gureje, O., Gaebel, W., Maj, M., et al. (2019). Innovations and changes in the ICD-11 classification of mental, behavioural and neurodevelopmental disorders. *World Psychiatry*, 18, 3–19.

Reeves, S., and Bernstein, I. (2008). Effects of maternal tobacco-smoke exposure on fetal growth and neonatal size. *Expert Rev. Obstet. Gynecol.*, 3, 719–730.

Regalado, A. (2018, November 25). EXCLUSIVE: Chinese scientists are creating CRISPR babies. MIT Technology Review. https://www.technologyreview.com/2018/11/25/138962/exclusive-chinese-scientists-are-creating-crispr-babies/

Regner, M. F., Dalwani, M., Yamamoto, D., Perry, R. I., Sakai, J. T., Honce, J. M., and Tanabe, J. (2015). Sex differences in gray matter changes and brain-behavior relationships in patients with stimulant dependence. *Radiology*, 277, 801–812.

Regner, M. F., Tregallas, J., Kluger, B., Wylie, K., Gowin, J. L., and Tanabe, J. (2019). The insula in nicotine use disorder: Functional neuroimaging and implications for neuromodulation. *Neurosci. Biobehav. Rev.*, 103, 414–424.

Reilly, M. T., Noronha, A., Goldman, D., and Koob, G. F. (2017). Genetic studies of alcohol dependence in the context of the addiction cycle. *Neuropharmacology*, 122, 3–21.

Reinecke, H., Weber, C., Lange, K., Simon, M., Stein, C., and Sorgatz, H. (2015). Analgesic efficacy of opioids in chronic pain: Recent meta-analyses. *Br. J. Pharmacol.*, 172, 324–333.

Reissig, C. J., Carter, L. P., Johnson, M. W., Mintzer, M. Z., Klinedinst, M. A., and Griffiths, R. R. (2012). High doses of dextromethorphan, an NMDA antagonist, produce effects similar to classic hallucinogens. *Psychopharmacology*, 223, 1–15.

Reissig, C. J., Strain, E. C., and Griffiths, R. R. (2009). Caffeinated energy drinks: A growing problem. *Drug Alcohol Depend.*, 99, 1–10.

Reith, M. E. A., Bough, B. E., Hong, W. C., Jones, K. T., Schmitt, K. C., Baumann, M. H., et al. (2015). Behavioral, biological, and chemical perspectives on atypical agents targeting the dopamine transporter. *Drug Alcohol Depend.*, 147, 1–19.

Ren, H., Du, C., Yuan, Z., Park, K., Volkow, N. D., and Pan, Y. (2012). Cocaine-induced cortical microischemia in the rodent brain: Clinical implications. *Mol. Psychiatry*, 17, 1017–1025.

Ren, J., Friedmann, D., Xiong, J., Liu, C. D., Ferguson, B. R., Weerakkody, T., DeLoach, K. E., et al. (2018). Anatomically defined and functionally distinct dorsal raphe serotonin sub-systems. *Cell*, 175, 472–487.

Ren, M., Tang, Z., Wu, X., Spengler, R., Jiang, H., Yang, Y., and Boivin, N. (2019). The origins of cannabis smoking: Chemical residue evidence from the first millennium BCE in the Pamirs. *Sci. Adv.*, 5, eaaw1391. doi: 10.1126/sciadv.aaw1391.

Ren, S. Y., Wang, Z. Z., Zhang, Y., and Chen, N. H. (2020). Potential application of endocannabinoid system agents in neuropsychiatric and neurodegenerative diseases-focusing on FAAH/MAGL inhibitors. *Acta Pharmacol. Sin.*, 41, 1263–1271.

Renard, J., Rushlow, W. J., and Laviolette, S. R. (2016a). What can rats tell us about adolescent cannabis exposure? Insights from preclinical research. *Can. J. Psychiatry*, 61, 328–334.

Renard, J., Vitalis, T., Rame, M., Krebs, M. O., Lenkei, Z., Le Pen, G., et al. (2016b). Chronic cannabinoid exposure during adolescence leads to long-term structural and functional changes in the prefrontal cortex. *Eur. Neuropsychopharmacol.*, 26, 55–64. Copyright 2015. Reprinted with permission from Elsevier.

Rendell, M. S. (2019). The journey from gene knockout to clinical medicine: Telotristat and sotagliflozin. *Drug Des. Devel. Ther.*, 13, 817–824.

Research Advisory Committee on Gulf War Veterans' Illnesses. (2008). Gulf War Illness and the Health of Gulf War Veterans: Scientific Findings and Recommendations. Washington, DC: U.S. Government Printing Office.

Research Advisory Committee on Gulf War Veterans' Illnesses. (2014). Gulf War Illness and the Health of Gulf War Veterans: Research Update and Recommendations, 2009–2013. Washington, DC: U. S. Government Printing Office.

Research Society on Alcoholism. (2015). Impact of Alcoholism and Alcohol Induced Disease and Disorders on America. Available at archive.rsoa.org/RSA2014WhitePaperFinalVersionVH.pdf.

Rewal, M., Donahue, R., Gill, T. M., Nie, H., Ron, D., and Janak, P. H. (2012). Alpha4 subunit-containing $GABA_A$ receptors in the accumbens shell contribute to the reinforcing effects of alcohol. *Addict. Biol.*, 17, 309–321.

Rey, A. A., Purrio, M., Viveros, M.-P., and Lutz, B. (2012). Biphasic effects of cannabinoids in anxiety responses: CB_1 and $GABA_B$ receptors in the balance of GABAergic and glutamatergic neurotransmission. *Neuropsychopharmacology*, 37, 2624–2634.

Rezai, A. R., Ranjan, M., D'haese, P. F., Haut, M. W., Carpenter, J. S., Najib, U., Mehta, R. I., et al. (2020) Noninvasive hippocampal blood-brain barrier opening in Alzheimer's disease with focused ultrasound. *Proc. Natl. Acad. Sci. USA* 117(17), 9180–9182.

Rezkalla, S., and Kloner, R. A. (2019). Cardiovascular effects of marijuana. *Trends Cardiovasc. Med.*, 29, 403–407.

Ribeiro, J. A., and Sebastião, A. M. (2010). Caffeine and adenosine. *J. Alzheimers Dis.*, 20, S3–S15.

Ribeiro, J. A., Sebastião, A. M., and de Mendonça, A. (2003). Adenosine receptors in the nervous system: Pathophysiological implications. *Prog. Neurobiol.*, 68, 377–392.

Ribeiro, M.-J., Vidailhet, M., Loc'h, C., Dupel, C., Nguyen, J. P., Ponchant, M., et al. (2002). Dopaminergic function and dopamine transporter binding assessed with positron emission tomography in Parkinson disease. *Arch. Neurol.*, 59, 580–586.

Ricci, L. A., Morrison, T. R., and Melloni, R. H., Jr. (2012). Serotonin modulates anxiety-like behaviors during withdrawal from adolescent anabolic–androgenic steroid exposure in Syrian hamsters. *Horm. Behav.*, 62, 569–576.

Richards, J. G., Schoch, P., and Jenck, F. (1991). Benzodiazepine receptors and their ligands. In R. J. Rogers and S. J. Cooper (Eds.), *5-HT1A Agonists, 5-HT3 Antagonists and Benzodiazepines: Their Comparative Behavioural Pharmacology*, pp. 1–30. New York: Wiley.

Richardson, G. A., Goldschmidt, L., Larkby, C., and Day, N. L. (2015). Effects of prenatal cocaine exposure on adolescent development. *Neurotoxicol. Teratol.*, 49, 41–48.

Richardson, K. A, Hester, A. K., and McLemore, G. L. (2016). Prenatal cannabis exposure: The "first hit" to the endocannabinoid system. *Neurotoxicol. Teratol.*, 58, 5–14.

Richardson-Jones, J. W., Craige, C. P., Guiard, B. P., Stephen, A.,

Metzger, K. L., Kung, H. F., et al. (2010). 5-HT1A autoreceptor levels determine vulnerability to stress and response to antidepressants. *Neuron*, 65, 40–52.

Richerson, G. B. (2013). Serotonin: The Anti-SuddenDeathAmine. *Epilepsy Curr.*, 13, 241–244.

Ridley, M. (2015). 'Quitting Is Suffering.' The Spectator. Available at https://www.spectator.co.uk/article/-quitting-is-suffering-

Riebe, C. J., Pamplona, F., Kamprath, K., and Wotjak, C. T. (2012). Fear relief: Toward a new conceptual frame work and what endocannabinoids gotta do with it. *Neuroscience*, 204, 159–185.

Riedel, G., and Davies, S. N. (2005). Cannabinoid function in learning, memory and plasticity. *Handb. Exp. Pharmacol.*, 168, 445–477.

Riegel, A. C., Ali, S. F., and French, E. D. (2003). Toluene-induced locomotor activity is blocked by 6-hydroxydopamine lesions of the nucleus accumbens and the mGluR2/3 agonist LY379268. *Neuropsychopharmacology*, 28, 1440–1447.

Riegel, A. C., Zapata, A., Shippenberg, T. S., and French, E. D. (2007). The abused inhalant toluene increases dopamine release in the nucleus accumbens by directly stimulating ventral tegmental area neurons. *Neuropsychopharmacology*, 32, 1558–1569.

Rietschel, M., and Treutlein, J. (2013). The genetics of alcohol dependence. *Ann. N. Y. Acad. Sci.*, 1282, 39–70.

Rigotti, N. A. (2020). Randomized trials of e-cigarettes for smoking cessation. *JAMA*, 324, 1835–1837.

Ripke, S., Neale, B. M., Corvin, A., Walters, J. T. R., Farh, K.-H., Holmans, P. A., Lee, P., et al. (2014). Biological insights from 108 schizophrenia-associated genetic loci. *Nature*, 511(7510), 421–427. https://doi.org/10.1038/nature13595

Ripley, T. L., and Stephens, D. N. (2011). Critical thoughts on current rodent models for evaluating potential treatments of alcohol addiction and withdrawal. *Br. J. Pharmacol.*, 164, 1335–1356.

Risch, N., Herrell, R., Lehner, T., Liang, K. Y., Eaves, L., Hoh, J., et al. (2009). Interaction between the serotonin transporter gene (5-HTTLPR), stressful life events, and risk of depression: A meta-analysis. *JAMA*, 301, 2462–2471.

Risher, M. L., Fleming, R. L., Risher, W. C., Miller, K. M., Klein, R. C., Wills, T., et al. (2015). Adolescent intermittent alcohol exposure: Persistence of structural and functional hippocampal abnormalities into adulthood. *Alcohol Clin. Exp. Res.*, 39, 989–997.

Risinger, R. C., Salmeron, B. J., Ross, T. J., Amen, S. L., Sanfilipo, M., Hoffmann, R. G., et al. (2005). Neural correlates of

high and craving during cocaine self-administration using BOLD fMRI. *NeuroImage*, 26, 1097–1108.

Ritchie, J. M. (1975). Central nervous system stimulants. In L. Goodman and A. Gilman (Eds.), *The Pharmacological Basis of Therapeutics* (5th ed.), pp. 367–378. New York: Macmillan.

Rivero, G., Gabilondo, A. M., García-Sevilla, J. A., La Harpe, R., Callado, L. F., and Meana, J. J. (2014). Increased α2 and β1-adrenoceptor densities in postmortem brain of subjects with depression: Differential effect of antidepressant treatment. *J. Affect. Disord.*, 167, 343–50.

Roberts, A. J., McDonald, J. S., Heyser, C. J., Kieffer, B. L., Matthes, H. W. D., Koob, G. F., et al. (2000). μ-Opioid receptor knockout mice do not self-administer alcohol. *J. Pharmacol. Exp. Ther.*, 293, 1002–1008.

Roberts, C. A., Jones, A., Sumnall, H., Gage, S. H., and Montgomery, C. (2020). How effective are pharmaceuticals for cognitive enhancement in healthy adults? A series of meta-analyses of cognitive performance during acute administration of modafinil, methylphenidate, and D-amphetamine. *Eur. Neuropsychopharmacol.*, 38, 40–62.

Roberts, C. A., Quednow, B. B., Montgomery, C., and Parrott, A. C. (2018). MDMA and brain activity during neurocognitive performance: An overview of neuroimaging studies with abstinent 'Ecstasy' users. *Neurosci. Biobehav. Rev.*, 84, 470–482.

Roberts, L. J. and B.S. McCrady. (2003). Alcohol Problems in Intimate Relationships: Identification and Intervention, A Guide for Marriage and Family Therapists. National Institute on Alcohol Abuse and Alcoholism (NIAAA): Washington, D.C.; adapted from BAC Charts produced by the National Clearinghouse of Alcohol and Drug Information.

Robertson, S. D., Matthies, H. J. G., and Galli, A. (2009). A closer look at amphetamine-induced reverse transport and trafficking of the dopamine and norepinephrine transporters. *Mol. Neurobiol.*, 39, 73–80.

Robinson, D. M., and Keating, G. M. (2007). Sodium oxybate: A review of its use in the management of narcolepsy. *CNS Drugs*, 21, 337–354.

Robinson, K. J., Watchon, M., and Laird, A. S. (2020). Aberrant cerebellar circuitry in the spinocerebellar ataxias. *Front. Neurosci.*, 14, 707. doi: 10.3389/fnins.2020.00707.

Robinson, M. B., and Jackson, J. G. (2016). Astroglial glutamate transporters coordinate excitatory signaling and brain energetics. *Neurochem. Int.*, 98, 56–71.

Robinson, T. E., and Berridge, K. C. (1993). The neural basis of drug craving: An incentive-sensitization theory of addiction. *Brain Res. Rev.*, 18, 247–291.

Robinson, T. E., and Berridge, K. C. (2000). The psychology and neurobiology of addiction: An incentive-sensitization view. *Addiction*, 95(Suppl. 2), S91–S117.

Robinson, T. E., and Berridge, K. C. (2001). Incentive-sensitization and addiction. *Addiction*, 96, 103–114.

Robinson, T. E., and Berridge, K. C. (2008). The incentive sensitization theory of addiction: Some current issues. *Philos. Trans. R. Soc. Lond. B Biol. Sci.*, 363, 3137–3146.

Robison, A. J., and Nestler, E. J. (2011). Transcriptional and epigenetic mechanisms in addiction. *Nat. Rev. Neurosci.*, 12, 623–637.

Rocha, B. A., Fumagalli, F., Gainetdinov, R. R., Jones, S. R., Ator, R., Giros, B., et al. (1998). Cocaine self-administration in dopamine-transporter knockout mice. *Nat. Neurosci.*, 1, 132–137.

Rocky Mountain High Intensity Drug Trafficking Area. (2019). The Legalization of Marijuana in Colorado: The Impact, Vol. 6. Available at https://www.rm-hidta.org/strategic/. Accessed 3/15/21.

Rodd-Henricks, Z. A., McKinzie, D. L., Li, T.-K., Murphy, J. M., and McBride, W. J. (2002). Cocaine is self-administered into the shell but not the core of the nucleus accumbens of Wistar rats. *J. Pharmacol. Exp. Ther.*, 303, 1216–1226.

Rodgman, A., and Perfetti, T. A. (2013). *The Chemical Components of Tobacco and Tobacco Smoke* (2nd ed.). Boca Raton, FL: CRC.

Rodrigues, L. A., Caroba, M.E.S., Taba, F. K., Filev, R., and Gallassi, A. D. (2020). Evaluation of the potential use of cannabidiol in the treatment of cocaine use disorder: A systematic review. *Pharmacol. Biochem. Behav.*, 196, 172982. doi: 10.1016/j.pbb.2020.172982.

Roepke, T. A., Ronnekleiv, O. K., and Kelly, M. J. (2011). Physiological consequences of membrane-initiated estrogen signaling in the brain. *Front. Biosci.*, 15, 1560–1573.

Rogaeva, E., Meng, Y., Lee, J. H., Gu1, Y., Kawarai, T., Zou, F., et al. (2007). The neuronal sortilin-related receptor SORL1 is genetically associated with Alzheimer disease. *Nat. Genet.*, 39, 168–177. doi.org/10.1038/ng1943

Rogeberg, O., and Elvik, R. (2016). The effects of cannabis intoxication on motor vehicle collision revisited and revised. *Addiction*, 111, 1348–1359.

Rogers, P. J. (2017). Food and drug addictions: Similarities and differences. *Pharmacol. Biochem. Behav.*, 153, 182–190.

Rogge, G., Jones, D., Hubert, G. W., Lin, Y., and Kuhar, M. J. (2008). CART peptides: Regulators of body weight, reward and other functions. *Nat. Rev. Neurosci.*, 9, 747–758.

Rohani, D. A., Faurholt-Jepsen, M., Kessing, L. V., and Bardram, J. E. (2018). Correlations Between Objective Behavioral Features Collected From Mobile and Wearable Devices and Depressive Mood Symptoms in Patients With Affective Disorders: Systematic Review. JMIR MHealth and UHealth, 6(8), e165. https://doi.org/10.2196/mhealth.9691

Rohman, L. (2009). The relationship between anabolic androgenic steroids and muscle dysmorphia: A review. *Eat. Disord.*, 17, 187–199.

Rohsenow, D. J., and Howland, J. (2010). The role of beverage congeners in hangover and other residual effects of alcohol intoxication: A review. *Curr. Drug Abuse Rev.*, 3(2), 76–79. https://doi.org/10.2174/1874473711003020076

Roine, R., Gentry, T., Hernandez-Munoz, R., Baraona, E., and Lieber, C. (1990). Aspirin increases blood alcohol concentrations in humans after ingestion of ethanol. *JAMA*, 264, 2406–2408.

Romanelli, F., and Smith, K. M. (2009). Dextromethorphan abuse: Clinical effects and management. *Pharmacy Today*, 15, 48–55.

Romeo, B., Hermand, M., Pétillion, A., Karila, L., and Benyamina, A. (2021). Clinical and biological predictors of psychedelic response in the treatment of psychiatric and addictive disorders: A systematic review. *J. Psychiatr. Res.*, 137, 273–282.

Romero-Martinez, A., Murciano-Marti, S., and Moya-Albiol, L. (2019). Is sertraline a good pharmacological strategy to control anger? Results of a systematic review. *Behav. Sci.*, 9, 57. doi: 10.3390/bs9050057.

Ronan, P. J., Wongngamnit, N., and Beresford, T. P. (2016). Molecular mechanisms of cannabis signaling in the brain. *Prog. Mol. Biol. Transl. Sci.*, 137, 123–147.

Roncero, C., Diagre, C., Grau-López, L., Barral, C., Pérez-Pazos, J., MartinezLuna, N., et al. (2014). An international perspective and review of cocaine-induced psychosis: A call to action. *Subst. Abuse*, 35, 321–327.

Roncero, C., Valriberas-Herrero, I., Mezzatesta-Gava, M., Villegas, J. L., Aguilar, L., and Grau-López, L. (2020). Cannabis use during pregnancy and its relationship with fetal developmental outcomes and psychiatric disorders. A systematic review. *Reprod. Health*, 17(1), 25. doi: 10.1186/s12978-020-0880-9.

Root, D. H., Zhang, S., Barker, D. J., Miranda-Barrientos, J., Liu, B., Wang, H.-L., and Morales, M. (2018). Selective brain distribution and distinctive synaptic architecture of dual glutamatergic-GABAergic neurons. *Cell Rep.*, 23, 3465–3479.

Roozen, H. G., Boulogne, J. J., van Tulder, M. W., van den Brink, W., De Jong, C. A., and Kerkhof, A. J. (2004). A systematic review of the effectiveness of the community reinforcement approach in alcohol, cocaine and opioid addiction. *Drug Alcohol Depend.*, 74, 1–13.

Rose, C. F., Verkhratsky, A., and Parpura, V. (2013). Astrocyte glutamine synthetase: Pivotal in health and disease. *Biochem. Soc. Trans.*, 41, 1518–1524.

Rose, C. R., Ziemens, D., Untiet, V., and Fahlke, C. (2018). Molecular and cellular physiology of sodium-dependent glutamate transporters. *Brain Res. Bull.*, 36, 3–16.

Rose, J. E. (2006). Nicotine and nonnicotine factors in cigarette addiction. *Psychopharmacology*, 184, 274–285.

Rose, J. E., Mukhin, A. G., Lokitz, S. J., Turkington, T. G., Herskovic, J., Behm, F. M., et al. (2010). Kinetics of brain nicotine accumulation in dependent and nondependent smokers assessed with PET and cigarettes containing ^{11}C-nicotine. *Proc. Natl. Acad. Sci. USA*, 107, 5190–5195.

Rose, J. W., Houtchens, M., and Lynch, S. G. (2000). Multiple Sclerosis. Knowledge Weavers. Spencer S. Eccles Health Sciences Library. University of Utah. Available at www.library.med.utah.edu/kw/ms/mml/ms_worldmap.html.

Rose, S., and Dhandayudham, A. (2014). Towards an understanding of Internetbased problem shopping behaviour: The concept of online shopping addiction and its proposed predictors. *J. Behav. Addict.*, 3, 83–89.

Rosell, D. R., and Siever, L. J. (2015). The neurobiology of aggression and violence. *CNS Spectr.*, 20, 254–279.

Rosenbaum, M. (2002). Ecstasy: America's new "reefer madness." *J. Psychoactive Drugs*, 34, 137–142.

Rosenberg, E. C., Tsien, R. W., Whalley, B. J., and Devinsky, O. (2015). Cannabinoids and epilepsy. *Neurotherapeutics*, 12, 747–768.

Rosenthal, R. N. (2019). Novel formulations of buprenorphine for treatment of opioid use disorder. *Focus (Am. Psychiatr. Publ.)*, 17(2), 104–109. https://doi.org/10.1176/appi.focus.20180043

Rosenthal, T. L., and Rosenthal, R. (1980). The Vicious Cycle of Stress Reaction. Memphis: Stress Management Clinic, Department of Psychiatry, University of Tennessee College of Medicine, Memphis, Tennessee.

Roses, A. D. (1995). Alzheimer's disease as a model of molecular gerontology. *J. Natl. Inst. Health Res.*, 7, 51–57.

Rossen, L. M., Bastian, B., Warner, M., Khan, D., and Chong, Y. (2017). Drug Poisoning Mortality in the United States, 1999–2015. Centers for Disease Control and Preventiom. National Center for Health Statistics. Available at www.cdc.gov/nchs/data-visualization/drug-poisoning-mortality/.

Rossetti, Z. L and Carboni, S. (1995). Ethanol withdrawal is associated with increased extracellular glutamate in the rat striatum. *Eur. J. Pharmacol.* 283, 177–183. Copyright 1995. Reprinted with permission from Elsevier.

Rossi, S., De Chiara, V., Musella, A., Sacchetti, L., Cantarella, C., Castelli, M., et al. (2010). Preservation of striatal cannabinoid CB_1 receptor function correlates with the antianxiety effects of fatty acid amide hydrolase inhibition. *Mol. Pharmacol.*, 78, 260–268.

Rottlaender, D., Motloch, L. J., Reda, S., Larbig, R., and Hoppe, U. C. (2012). Cardiac arrest due to long QT syndrome associated with excessive consumption of energy drinks. *Int. J. Cardiol.*, 158, e51–e52.

Rotundo, R. L. (2020). The NMJ as a model synapse: New perspectives on formation, synaptic transmission and maintenance. *Neurosci. Lett.*, 735, 135157.

Roux, P. P., and Blenis, J. (2004). ERK and p38 MAPK-activated protein kinases: A family of protein kinases with diverse biological functions. *Microbiol. Mol. Biol. Rev.*, 68, 320–344.

Roy, A. (2012). How the FDA Stifles New Cures, Part I: The Rising Cost of Clinical Trials. Forbes. Available at www.forbes.com/sites/aroy/2012/04/24/how-thefda-stifles-new-cures-part-i-the-risingcost-of-clinical-trials/.

Roybal, K., Theobold, D., Graham, A., DiNieri, J. A., Russo, S. J., Krishnan, V., et al. (2007). Mania-like behavior induced by disruption of CLOCK. *Proc. Natl. Acad. Sci. USA*, 104, 6406–6411.

Rozeske, R. R., Evans, A. K., Frank, M. G., Watkins, L. R., Lowry, C. A., and Maier, S. F. (2011). Uncontrollable, but not controllable, stress desensitizes 5-HT1A receptors in the dorsal raphe nucleus. *J. Neurosci.*, 31, 14107–14115.

Rubino, T., and Parolaro, D. (2015). Sex-dependent vulnerability to Cannabis abuse in adolescence. *Front. Psychiatry*, 6, 56. doi: 10.3389/fpsyt.2015.00056.

Rubino, T., and Parolaro, D. (2016). The impact of exposure to cannabinoids in adolescence:

Insights from animal models. *Biol. Psychiatry*, 79, 578–585.

Rucker, J. J. H., Jelen, L. A., Flynn, S., Frowde, K. D., and Young, A. H. (2016). Psychedelics in the treatment of unipolar mood disorders: A systematic review. *J. Psychopharmacol.*, 30, 1220–1229.

Rucker, J.J.H., Iliff, J., and Nutt, D. J. (2018). Psychiatry & the psychedelic drugs. Past, present & future. *Neuropharmacology*, 142, 200–218.

Rudan, I. (2010). New technologies provide insights into genetic basis of psychiatric disorders and explain their co-morbidity. *Psychiatr. Danub.*, 22, 190–192.

Rudd, R. A., Aleshire, N., Zibbell, J. E., and Gladden, R. M. (2016). Increases in Drug and Opioid Overdose Deaths: United States, 2000–2014. Morbidity and Mortality Weekly Report (MMWR), 64, 1378–1382. Available at www.cdc. gov/mmwr/preview/mmwrhtml/ mm6450a3. htm.

Rudgley, R. (1999). *The Encyclopaedia of Psychoactive Substances*. New York: St. Martin's.

Rudolph, U., and Knoflach, F. (2011). Beyond classical benzodiazepines: Novel therapeutic potential of GABA$_A$ receptor subtypes. *Nat. Rev. Drug Discov.*, 10, 685–697.

Rudolph, U., and Möhler, H. (2014). GABA$_A$ receptor subtypes: Therapeutic potential in Down syndrome, affective disorders, schizophrenia, and autism. *Annu. Rev. Pharmacol. Toxicol.*, 54, 483–507.

Rudy, C. C., Hunsberger, H. C., Weitzner, D. S., and Reed, M. N. (2015). The role of the tripartite glutamatergic synapse in the pathophysiology of Alzheimer's disease. *Aging Dis.*, 6, 131–148.

Rudy, J. W. (2008). The Neurobiology of Learning and Memory. Sunderland, MA: Sinauer.

Ruffle, J. K. (2014). Molecular neurobiology of addiction: What's all the (Δ)FosB about? *Am. J. Drug Alcohol Abuse*, 40, 428–437.

Ruhé, H. G., Mason, N. S., and Schene, A. H. (2007). Mood is indirectly related to serotonin, norepinephrine and dopamine levels in humans: A meta-analysis of monoamine depletion studies. *Mol. Psychiatry*, 12, 331–359.

Ruisoto, P., and Contador, I. (2019). The role of stress in drug addiction. An integrative review. *Physiol. Behav.*, 202, 62–68.

Ruiz de Azua, I., Gautam, D., Guettier, J. M., and Wess, J. (2011). Novel insights into the function of β-cell M3 muscarinic acetylcholine receptors: Therapeutic implications. *Trends Endocrinol. Metab.*, 22, 74–80.

Runge, K., Cardoso, C., and de Chevigny, A. (2020). Dendritic Spine Plasticity: Function and Mechanisms. *Front.*

Synap. Neurosci., 12. https://doi.org/10.3389/fnsyn.2020.00036.

Rupprecht, L. E., Smith, T. T., Schassburger, R. L., Buffalari, D. M., Sved, A. F., and Donny, E. C. (2015). Behavioral mechanisms underlying nicotine reinforcement. *Curr. Top. Behav. Neurosci.*, 24, 19–53.

Rupprecht, R., Papadopoulos, V., Rammes, G., Baghai, T. C., Fan, J., Akula, N., et al. (2010). Translocator protein (18 kDa) (TSPO) as a therapeutic target for neurological and psychiatric disorders. *Nat. Rev. Drug Discov.*, 9, 971–988. doi.org/10.1038/ nrd3295

Ruscio A .M., Hallion L. S., Lim C.C.W., Aguilar-Gaxiola S., Al-Hamzawi A., Alonso J., et al. (2017). Cross-sectional comparison of the epidemiology of DSM-5 generalized anxiety disorder across the globe. *JAMA Psychiatry*, 74(5), 465–475.

Russell, M.A.H. (1976). Low-tar medium-nicotine cigarettes: A new approach to safer smoking. *Br. Med. J.*, 1(6023), 1430–1433.

Russo, E. B. (2007). History of cannabis and its preparations in saga, science, and sobriquet. *Chem. Biodiversity*, 4, 1614–1648.

Russo, E. B. (2016). Current therapeutic cannabis controversies and clinical trial design issues. *Front. Pharmacol.*, 7, 309. doi: 10.3389/fphar.2016.00309.

Russo, P., Bonassi, S., Giaconni, R., Malavolta, M., Tomino, C., and Maggi, F. (2020). COVID-19 and smoking: is nicotine the hidden link? *Eur. Respir. J.*, 55(6), 2001116. doi: 10.1183/13993003.01116-2020.

S

Sabbagh, M. N. (2020) Alzheimer's disease drug development pipeline 2020. *J. Prev. Alzheimers Dis.*, 7(2), 66–67.

Sabet, K. (2020). Lessons learned in several states eight years after states legalized marijuana. *Curr. Opin. Psychol.*, 38, 25–30.

Saddoris, M. P., Cacciapaglia, F., Wightman, R. M., and Carelli, R. M. (2015). Differential dopamine release dynamics in the nucleus accumbens core and shell reveal complementary signals for error prediction and incentive motivation. *J. Neurosci.*, 35, 11572–11582.

Sadee, W., Oberdick, J., and Wang, Z. (2020). Biased opioid antagonists as modulators of opioid dependence: opportunities to improve pain therapy and opioid use management. *Molecules*, 25(18). https://doi.org/10.3390/ molecules25184163

Saeed, A. F., Awan, S. A., Ling, S., Wang, R., and Wang, S. (2017). Domoic acid: Attributes, exposure risks, innovative detection techniques and therapeutics. *Algal Res.*, 24, 97–110.

Sagar, K. A., and Gruber, S. A. (2019). Interactions between

recreational cannabis use and cognitive function: lessons from functional magnetic resonance imaging. *Ann. N.Y. Acad. Sci.*, 145, 42–70.

Sagoe, D., Mentzoni, R. A., Hanss, D., and Pallesen, S. (2016). Aggression is associated with increased anabolic-androgenic steroid use contemplation among adolescents. *Subst. Use Misuse*, 51, 1462–1469.

Sah, S. K., Neupane, N., Pradhan Thaiba, A., Shah, S., and Sharma, A. (2019). Prevalence of glue-sniffing among street children. *Nurs. Open*, 7, 206–211

Sahlender, D. A., Savtchouk, J., and Volterra, A. (2014). What do we know about gliotransmitter release from astrocytes? *Philos. Trans. R. Soc. Lond. B Biol. Sci.*, 369, 20130592. doi: 10.1098/ rstb.2013.0592.

Sahli, Z. T., Banerjee, P., and Tarazia, F. I. (2016). The preclinical and clinical effects of vilazodone for the treatment of major depressive disorder. *Expert Opin. Drug Dis.*, 11, 515–523.

Sahu, M., Gandhi, S., and Sharma, M. K. (2019). Mobile phone addiction among children and adolescents: A systematic review. *J. Addict. Nurs.*, 30, 261–268.

Saint Louis, C. (2016). Addicts Who Can't Find Painkillers Turn To Anti-Diarrhea Drugs. New York Times. Available at www.ny-times.com/2016/05/11/ health/ imodium-opioid-addiction.html.

Sakmann, B., and Neher, E. (1976). Single-channel currents recorded from membrane of denervated frog muscle fibres. *Nature* 260, 799–802.

Sakurai, T. (2014). The role of orexin in motivated behaviours. *Nat. Rev. Neurosci.*, 15, 719–731.

Sakurai, T., Amemiya, A., Ishii, M., Matsuzaki, I., Williams, S. C., Richardson, J. A., et al. (1998). Orexins and orexin receptors: A family of hypothalamic neuropeptides and G protein-coupled receptors that regulate feeding behavior. *Cell*, 92, 573–585.

Salahpour, A., Ramsey, A. J., Medvedev, I. O., Kile, B., Sotnikova, T. D., Holmstrand, E., et al. (2008). Increased amphetamine-induced hyperactivity and reward in mice overexpressing the dopamine transporter. *Proc. Natl. Acad. Sci. USA*, 105, 4405–4410.

Salahudeen M. S., Wright C. M., Peterson G. M. (2020) Esketamine: new hope for the treatment of treatment-resistant depression? A narrative review. *Ther Adv Drug Saf.*, 11, 1–23.

Salamone, J. D., Pardo, M., Yohn, S. E., López-Cruz, L., SanMiguel, N., and Correa, M. (2016). Mesolimbic dopamine and the regulation of motivated behavior. *Curr. Topics Behav. Neurosci.*, 27, 231–257.

Salerno, M., Villano, I., Nicolosi, D., Longhitano, L., Loreto, C.,

Iovino, A., Sessa, F., et al. (2019). Modafinil and orexin system: interactions and medico-legal considerations. *Front. Biosci. (Landmark Ed.)*, 24, 563–575.

Salling, M. C., and Martinez, D. (2016). Brain stimulation in addiction. *Neuropsychopharmacology*, 41, 2798–2809.

Sallustio, F., and Studer, V. (2016). Targeting new pharmacological approaches for Alzheimer's disease: Potential for statins and phosphodiesterase inhibitors. *CNS Neurol. Disord. Drug Targets*, 15, 647–659.

Samartzis, L., Dima, D., Fusar-Poli, P., and Kyriakopoulos, M. (2014). White matter alterations in early stages of schizophrenia: A systematic review of diffusion tensor imaging studies. *J. Neuroimaging*, 24, 101–110.

Sami, M. B., Rabiner, E. A., and Bhattacharyya, S. (2015). Does cannabis affect dopaminergic signaling in the human brain? A systematic review of evidence to date. *Eur. Neuropsychopharmacol.*, 25, 1201–1224.

Samson, H. H. (1986). Initiation of ethanol reinforcement using a sucrose-substitution procedure in food- and water-sated rats. *Alcohol Clin. Exp. Res.*, 10, 436–442.

Samuels, E. R., and Szabadi, E. (2008). Functional neuroanatomy of the noradrenergic locus coeruleus: Its roles in the regulation of arousal and autonomic fuction. Part II: Physiological and pharmacological manipulations and pathological alterations of locus coeruleus activity in humans. *Curr. Neuropharmacol.*, 6, 254–285.

Sanacora, G., and Schatzberg, A. F. (2015). Ketamine: Promising path or false prophecy in the development of novel therapeutics for mood disorders? *Neuropsychopharmacology*, 40, 259–267.

Sanchez, E. S., Bigbee, J. W., Fobbs, W., Robinson, S. E., and Sato-Bigbee, C. (2008). Opioid addiction and pregnancy: Perinatal exposure to buprenorphine affects myelination in the developing brain. *Glia*, 56, 1017–1027.

Sanchez-Roige, S., Palmer, A. A., and Clarke, T.-K. (2020). Recent efforts to dissect the genetic basis of alcohol use and abuse. *Biol. Psychiatry*, 87(7), 609–618. https://doi.org/10.1016/j. biopsych.2019.09.011

Sanders, B., and Brula, A. Q. (2021). Intranasal esketamine: From origins to future implications in treatment-resistant depression. *J. Psychiatr. Res.*, 137, 29–35.

Sanders, S. K., and Shekhar, A. (1995). Anxiolytic effects of chlordiazepoxide blocked by injection of GABA$_A$ and benzodiazepine receptor antagonists in the region of the anterior basolateral amygdala of rats. *Biol. Psychiatry*, 37, 473–476.

Saniotis, A. (2020). After more than sixty years we are still unclear whether LSD has a place in clinical psychiatry. *Res. Psychother. Psychopathol. Process Outcome*, 23, 197–198.

Sansone, R. A., and Sansone, L. A. (2011). Agomelatine: A novel antidepressant. *Innov. Clin. Neurosci.*, 8, 10–14.

Santarelli, L., Saxe, M., Gross, C., Surget, A., Battaglia, F., Dulawa, S., et al. (2003). Requirement of hippocampal neurogenesis for the behavioral effects of antidepressants. *Science*, 301, 805–809.

Santos, R. M. M., and Lima, D. R. A. (2016). Coffee consumption, obesity and type 2 diabetes: A mini-review. *Eur. J. Nutr.*, 55, 1345–1358.

Sarkar, A., Lehto, S. M., Harty, S., Dinan, T. G., Cryan, J. F., and Burnet, P. W. J. (2016). Psychobiotics and the manipulation of bacteria-gut-brain signals. *Trends Neurosci.*, 39, 763–781.

Sarter, M., and Lustig, C. (2020). Forebrain cholinergic signaling: Wired and phasic, not tonic, and causing behavior. *J. Neurosci.*, 40, 712–719.

Sarter, M., Lustig, C., Berry, A. S., Gritton, H., Howe, W. M., and Parikh, V. (2016). What do phasic cholinergic signals do? *Neurobiol. Learn. Mem.*, 130, 135–141.

Satel, S. (2006). Is caffeine addictive? A review of the literature. *Am. J. Drug Alcohol Abuse*, 32, 493–502.

Satel, S., and Lillienfeld, S. O. (2014). Addiction and the brain-disease fallacy. *Front. Psychiatry*, 4, 141. doi: 10.3389/fpsyt.2013.00141.

Sato, S. M., Johansen, J. A., Jordan, C. L., and Wood, R. I. (2010). Membrane androgen receptors may mediate androgen reinforcement. *Psychoneuroendocrinology*, 35, 1063–1073.

Sato, S. M., Schulz, K. M., Sisk, C. L., and Wood, R. I. (2008). Adolescents and androgens, receptors and rewards. *Horm. Behav.* 53, 647–658.

Satriyasa, B. K. (2019). Botulinum toxin (Botox) A for reducing the appearance of facial wrinkles: a literature review of clinical use and pharmacological aspect. *Clin. Cosmet. Investig. Dermatol.*, 12, 223–228.

Saunders, A., Grander, A. J., and Sabatini, B. L. (2015). Corelease of acetylcholine and GABA from cholinergic forebrain neurons. *eLife*, 4, e06412. doi: 10.7554/eLife.06412.

Saunders, B. T., Yager, L. M., and Robinson, T. E. (2013). Cue-evoked cocaine "craving": Role of dopamine in the accumbens core. *J. Neurosci.*, 33, 13989–14000.

Saunders, J. B., Conigrave, K. M., Latt, N. C. et al. [Eds.]. (2016). *Addiction Medicine*, 2nd ed. Oxford University Press: Oxford.

Savitz, J. (2020). The kynurenine pathway: a finger in every pie. *Mol. Psychiatry*, 25, 131–147.

Saxena, S., and Rauch, S. L. (2000). Functional neuroimaging and the neuroanatomy of obsessive-compulsive disorder. *Psychiatr. Clin. North Am.*, 23, 563–586.

Saxena, S., Brody, A. L., Ho, M. L., Alborzian, S., Maidment, K. M., Zohrabi, N., et al. (2002). Differential cerebral metabolic changes with paroxetine treatment of obsessive-compulsive disorder vs. major depression. *Arch. Gen. Psychiatry*, 59, 250–261.

Scammell, T. E. (2015). Narcolepsy. *N. Engl. J. Med.*, 373, 2654–2662.

Scarpino, M., Rosso, T., Lanzo, G., Lolli, F., Bonizzoli, M., Lazzeri, C., Mannaioni, G., et al. (2020). Severe neurological nicotine intoxication by e-cigarette liquids: Systematic literature review. *Acta Neurol. Scand.*, 143, 121–130.

Schaffer Library of Drug Policy. The Marihuana Tax Act of 1937. Available at www.druglibrary.org/schaffer/hemp/taxact/t10a.htm.

Schauer, G. L., Rosenberry, Z. R., and Peters, E. N. (2017). Marijuana and tobacco co-administration in blunts, spliffs, and mulled cigarettes. *Addict. Behav.*, 64, 200–211.

Scheibein, F., Wells, J., Henriques, S., and Van Hout, M. C. (2020). "Slam sex" Sexualized injecting drug Use ("SIDU") amongst men who have sex with men (MSM) A scoping review. *J. Homosex.*, in press.

Schenberg, E. E. (2018). psychedelic-assisted psychotherapy: a paradigm shift in psychiatric research and development. *Front. Pharmacol.*, 9 (733), 1–11.

Schenberg, E. E., de Castro Comis, M. A., Chaves, B. R., and da Silveira, D. X. (2014). Treating drug dependence with the aid of ibogaine: A retrospective study. *J. Psychopharmacol.*, 28, 993–1000.

Scheyer, A. Prenatal exposure to cannabis affects the developing brain. *The Scientist*, 33(1), 36–41.

Scheyer, A. F., Loweth, J. A., Christian, D. T., Uejima, J., Rabei, R., Le, T., Dolubizno, H., et al. (2016). AMPA Receptor plasticity in accumbens core contributes to incubation of methamphetamine craving. *Biol. Psychiatry*, 80, 661–670.

Schierenberg, A., van Amsterdam, J., van den Brink, W., and Goudriaan, A. E. (2012). Efficacy of contingency management for cocaine dependence treatment: A review of the evidence. *Curr. Drug Abuse Rev.*, 5, 320–331.

Schifano, F., Napoletano, F., Arillotta, D., Zangani, C., Gilgar, L., Guirguis, A., Corkery, J. M., et al. (2020). The clinical challenges of synthetic cathinones. *Br. J. Clin. Pharmacol.*, 86, 410–419.

Schildkraut, J. J. (1965). The catecholamine hypothesis of

affective disorders: A review of supporting evidence. *Am. J. Psychiatry*, 122, 509–522.

Schipper, S., Aalbers, M. W., Rijkers, K., Swijsen, A., Rigo, J. M., Hoogland, G., et al. (2015). Tonic GABA$_A$ receptors as potential target for the treatment of temporal lobe epilepsy. *Mol. Neurobiol.*, 53, 5252–5265.

Schlagintweit, H. E., Perry, R. N., Darredeau, C., and Barrett, S. P. (2020). Non-pharmacological considerations in human research on nicotine and tobacco effects: A review. *Nicotine Tob. Res.*, 22, 1260–1266.

Schlossarek, S., Kempkensteffen, J., Reimer, J., and Verthein, U. (2016). Psychosocial determinants of cannabis dependence: A systematic review of the literature. *Eur. Addict. Res.*, 22, 131–144.

Schmeichel, B. E., and Berridge, C. W. (2013). Wake-promoting actions of noradrenergic $\alpha_1$and β-receptors within the lateral hypothalamic area. *Eur. J. Neurosci.*, 37, 891–900.

Schmid, B., Blomeyer, D., Treutlein, J., Zimmermann, U. S., Buchmann, A. F., Schmidt, et al. (2010). Interacting effects of CRHR1 gene and stressful life events on drinking initiation and progression among 19-year-olds. *Int. J. Neuropsychopharmacol.*, 13, 703–714.

Schmidt, H. D., Anderson, S. M., and Pierce, R. C. (2006). Stimulation of D1-like or D2 dopamine receptors in the shell, but not the core, of the nucleus accumbens reinstates cocaine-seeking behaviour in the rat. *Eur. J. Neurosci.*, 23, 219–228.

Schmidt, K. T., and Weinshenker, D. (2014). Adrenaline rush: The role of adrenergic receptors in stimulant-induced behaviors. *Mol. Pharmacol.*, 85, 640–650.

Schmitt, K. C., Rothman, R. B., and Reith, M. E. A. (2013). Nonclassical pharmacology of the dopamine transporter: Atypical inhibitors, allosteric modulators, and partial substrates. *J. Pharmacol. Exp. Ther.*, 346, 2–10.

Schmitt, L. M., Shaffer, R. C., Hessl, D., and Erickson, C. (2019). Executive function in fragile X syndrome: A systematic review. *Brain Sci.*, 9, 15. doi: 10.3390/brainsci9010015.

Schneider, L. S. (2014). Idalopirdine for Alzheimer's disease: Written in the starts. *Lancet Neurol.*, 13, 1063–1065.

Schneider, M. L., Moore, C. F., Kraemer, G. W., Roberts, A. D., and DeJesus, O. T. (2002). The impact of prenatal stress, fetal alcohol exposure, or both on development: Perspectives from a primate model. *Psychoneuroendocrinology*, 27, 285–298.

Schneider, S., and Diehl, K. (2016). Vaping as a catalyst for smoking? An initial model on the

initiation of electronic cigarette use and the transition to tobacco smoking among adolescents. *Nicotine Tob. Res.*, 18, 647–653. By permission of Oxford University Press.

Schoeler, T., and Bhattacharya, S. (2013). The effect of cannabis use on memory function: An update. *Subst. Abuse Rehabil.*, 4, 11–27.

Schoeler, T., Monk, A., Sami, M. B., Klamerus, E., Foglia, E., Brown, R., et al. (2016). Continued versus discontinued cannabis use in patients with psychosis: a systematic review and meta-analysis. *Lancet Psychiatry*, 3, 215–225.

Schoenborn, C. A., and Gindi, R. M. (2015). Electronic Cigarette Use among Adults: United States, 2014. NCHS data brief, no. 217. Hyattsville, MD: National Center for Health Statistics.

Scholey, A. B., and Kennedy, D. O. (2004). Cognitive and physiological effects of an "energy drink": An evaluation of the whole drink and of glucose, caffeine and herbal flavouring fractions. *Psychopharmacology*, 176, 320–330.

Schosser, A., and Kasper, S. (2009). The role of pharmacogenetics in the treatment of depression and anxiety disorders. *Int. Clin. Psychopharmacol.*, 24, 277–288.

Schrantee, A., Váckavu, L., Heijtel, D. F. R., Caan, M. W. A., Gsell, W., Lucassen, P. J., et al. (2015). Dopaminergic system dysfunction in recreational dexamphetamine users. *Neuropsychopharmacology*, 40, 1172–1180.

Schreier, L. M., and Griffin, K. W. (2021). Youth marijuana use: a review of causes and consequences. *Curr. Opin. Psychol.*, 38, 11–18.

Schreiner, A. M., and Dunn, M. E. (2012). Residual effects of cannabis use on neurocognitive performance after prolonged abstinence: A meta-analysis. *Exp. Clin. Psychopharmacol.*, 20, 420–429.

Schroeder, S. A. (2005). What to do with a patient who smokes. *JAMA*, 294, 482–487.

Schuckit, M. A. (1994). Low level of response to alcohol as predictor of alcoholism. *Am. J. Psychol.*, 151, 184–189.

Schuckit, M. A. (2000). Genetics of the risk for alcoholism. *Am. J. Addict.*, 9, 103–112.

Schule, C., Nothdurfter, C., and Rupprecht, R. (2014). The role of allopregnanolone in depression and anxiety. *Prog. Neurobiol.*, 113, 79–87. © 2013. Reprinted with permission from Elsevier.

Schulteis, G., Markou, A., Cole, M., and Koob, G. F. (1995). Decreased brain reward produced by ethanol withdrawal. *Proc. Natl. Acad. Sci. USA*, 92, 5880–5884.

Schultz, W. (2010). Dopamine signals for reward value and

risk: basic and recent data. *Behav. Brain Funct.*, 6, 24. doi: 10.1186/1744-9081-6-24.

Schultz, W. (2016a). Dopamine reward prediction error coding. *Dialogues Clin. Neurosci.*, 18, 23–32.

Schultz, W. (2016b). Dopamine reward prediction-error signalling: A two-component response. *Nat. Rev. Neurosci.*, 17, 183–195.

Schwartz, R. H. (2005). Adolescent abuse of dextromethorphan. *Clin. Pediatr.*, 44, 565–568.

Schwartz, R. H., Milteer, R., and LeBeau, M. A. (2000). Drug-facilitated sexual assault ("date rape"). *South. Med. J.*, 93, 558–561.

Schwarzbach, V., Lenk, K., and Laufs, U. (2020). Methamphetamine-related cardiovascular diseases. *ESC Heart Fail.*, 7, 407–414.

Scoriels, L., Jones, P. B., and Sahakian, B. J. (2013). Modafinil effects on cognition and emotion in schizophrenia and its neurochemical modulation in the brain. *Neuropharmacology*, 64, 168–184.

Scoville, W. B., and Milner, B. (1957). Loss of recent memory after bilateral hippocampal lesions. *J. Neurol. Neurosurg. Psychiatry*, 20, 11–21.

Seal, R. P., Akil, O., Yi, E., Weber, C. M., Grant, L., Yoo, J., et al. (2008). Sensorineural deafness and seizures in mice lacking vesicular glutamate transporter 3. *Neuron*, 57, 263–275.

Seeman, P. (2002). Atypical antipsychotics: Mechanism of action. *Can. J. Psychiatry*, 47, 27–38.

Segawa, M. (2010). Hereditary progressive dystonia with marked diurnal fluctuation. *Brain Dev.*, 33, 195–201.

Segawa, M., Hosaka, A., Miyagawa, F., Nomura, Y., and Imai, H. (1976). Hereditary progressive dystonia with marked diurnal fluctuation. *Adv. Neurol.*, 14, 215–233.

Sehatzadeh, S., Daskalakis, Z. J., Yap, B., Tu, H. A., Palimaka, S., Bowen, J. M., and O'Reilly, D. J. (2019) Unilateral and bilateral repetitive transcranial magnetic stimulation for treatment-resistant depression: a meta-analysis of randomized controlled trials over 2 decades. *J Psychiatry Neurosci.*, 44(3), 151–163.

Seibyl, J., Russel, D., Jennings, D., and Marek, K. (2012). Neuroimaging over the course of Parkinson's disease: From early detection of the at-risk patient to improving pharmacotherapy of later-stage disease. *Semin. Nucl. Med.*, 42, 406–414.

Seifert, S. M., Schaechter, J. L., Hershorin, E. R., and Lipshultz, S. E. (2011). Health effects of energy drinks on children, adolescents, and young adults. *Pediatrics*, 127, 511–528.

Self, D. W., and Nestler, E. J. (1995). Molecular mechanisms of drug reinforcement and addiction. *Annu. Rev. Neurosci.*, 18, 463–495.

Self, D. W., Barnhart, W. J., Lehman, D. A., and Nestler, E. J. (1996). Opposite modulation of cocaine-seeking behavior by D1- and D2-like dopamine receptor agonists. *Science*, 271, 1586–1589.

Sellings, L.H.L., and Clarke, P.B.S. (2003). Segregation of amphetamine reward and locomotor stimulation between nucleus accumbens medial shell and core. *J. Neurosci.*, 23, 6295–6303.

Sellström, A., Cairns, S., and Barbeschi, M. (2013). Report of the United Nations Mission to Investigate Allegations of the Use of Chemical Weapons in the Syrian Arab Republic on the Alleged Use of Chemical Weapons in the Ghouta Area of Damascus on 21 August 2013. United Nations. Available at disarmament-library. un.org/UNODA/Library.nsf/780cfafd472b047785257b1000501037/e4d4477c9b67de9085257bf800694bd2/$FILE/A%2067%20997-S%202013%20553.pdf.

Selvaraj, B. T., Livesey, M. R., Zhao, C., Gregory, J. M., James, O. T., Cleary, E. M., Chouha, A. K., et al. (2018). C9ORF72 repeat expansion causes vulnerability of motor neurons to Ca^{2+}-permeable AMPA receptor-mediated excitotoxicity. *Nat. Commun.*, 9, 347. doi: 10.1038/s41467-017-02729-0.

Sener, S., Yamanel, L., and Comert, B. (2005). A fatal case of severe serotonin syndrome accompanied by moclobemide and paroxetine overdose. *Indian J. Crit. Care Med.*, 9, 173–175.

Seoane-Collazo, P., Diéguez, C., Nogueiras, R., Rahmouni, K., Fernández-Real, J. M., and López, M. (2020). Nicotine' action on energy balance: Friend or foe? *Pharmacol. Ther.*, 219, 107693.

Serafine, K. M., O'Dell, L. E., and Zorilla, E. P. (2021). Converging vulnerability factors for compulsive food and drug use. *Neuropharmacology*, 196, 108556.

Seritan, A. L., Ortigas, M., Seritan, S., Bourgeois, J. A., and Hagerman, R. J. (2013). Psychiatric disorders associated with FXTAS. *Curr. Psychiatry Rev.*, 9(1), 59–64. https://doi.org/10.2174/157340013805289699

Servonnet, A., and Samaha, A.-N. (2020). Antipsychotic-evoked dopamine supersensitivity. *Neuropharmacology*, 163, 107630. doi: 10.1016/j.neuropharm.2019.05.007.

Sesack, S. R. (2014). Prefrontal cortical dopamine transmission: Ultrastructural studies and their functional implications. In V. Pickel and M. Segal (Eds.), *The Synapse*, pp. 467–501. San Diego, CA: Academic.

Sessa, B. (2018). Why MDMA therapy for alcohol use disorder? And why now? *Neuropharmacology*, 142, 83–88.

Sessa, B., Higbed, L., and Nutt, D. (2019). A review of 3,4-methylenedioxy-methamphetamine (MDMA)-assisted psychotherapy. *Front. Psychiatry*, 10, 138. doi: 10.3389/f.psyt.2019.00138.

Seth, R., Kuppalli, S. S., Nadav, D., Chen, G., and Gulati, A. (2021). Recent advances in peripheral opioid receptor therapeutics. *Curr. Pain Headache Rep.*, 25(7), 46. https://doi.org/10.1007/s11916-021-00951-6

Sewalia, K., Watterson, L. R., Hryciw, A., Belloc, A., Ortiz, J. B., and Olive, M. F. (2018). Neurocognitive dysfunction following repeated binge-like self-administration of the synthetic cathinone 3,4-methylenedioxy-pyrovalerone (MDPV). *Neuropharmacology*, 134, 36–45.

Sewell, R. A., and Petrakis, I. L. (2011). Does gamma-hydroxybutyrate (GHB) have a role in the treatment of alcoholism? *Alcohol Alcohol.*, 46, 1–2.

Sewell, R. A., Ranganathan, M., and D'Souza, D. C. (2009). Cannabinoids and psychosis. *Int. Rev. Psychiatry*, 21, 152–162.

Sezgin, B., Sibar, S., Bulam, H., Findikcioglu, K., Tuncer, S., and Dogan, B. (2014). Disulfiram implantation for the treatment of alcoholism: Clinical experiences from the plastic surgeon's point of view. *Arch. Plast. Surg.*, 41(5), 571–575. https://doi.org/10.5999/aps.2014.41.5.571

Shabir, A., Hooton, A., Tallis, J., and Higgins, M. F. (2018). The influence of caffeine expectancies on sport, exercise, and cognitive performance. *Nutrients*, 10, 1528. doi: 10.3390/nu10101528.

Shackman, A. J., and Fox, A. S. (2016). Contributions of the central extended amygdala to fear and anxiety. *J. Neurosci.*, 36, 8050–8063.

Shad, M. U., Suris, A. M., and North, C. S. (2011). Novel combination strategy to optimize treatment for PTSD. Hum. Psychopharmacol., 26, 4–11.

Shah, R. S., and Cole, J. W. (2010). Smoking and stroke: The more you smoke the more you stroke. *Expert Rev. Cardiovasc. Ther.*, 8, 917–932.

Shallie, P. D., and Naicker, T. (2019). The placenta as a window to the brain: A review on the role of placental markers in prenatal programming of neurodevelopment. *Int. J. Dev. Neurosci.*, 73, 41–49.

Shamay-Tsoory, S. G., and Abu-Akel, (2016). The social salience hypothesis of oxytocin. *Biol. Psychiatry*, 79, 194–202.

Shang, Y., and Filizola, M. (2015). Opioid receptors: Structural and mechanistic insights into pharmacology and signaling. *Eur. J. Pharmacol.*, 763 (Pt. B), 206–213.

Shannon, J. R., Flattem, N. L., Jordan, J., Jacob, G., Black, B. K., Biaggioni, I., et al. (2000). Orthostatic intolerance and tachycardia associated with norepinephrine transporter deficiency. *N. Engl. J. Med.*, 342, 541–549.

Shapiro, R. E. (2008). Caffeine and headaches. *Curr. Pain Headache Rep.*, 12, 311–315.

Sharkey, K. A., and Wiley, J. W. (2016). The role of the endocannabinoid system in the brain–gut axis. *Gastroenterology*, 151, 252–266.

Sharma, S. K., Klee, W. A., and Nirenberg, M. (1975). Dual regulation of adenylate cyclase accounts for narcotic dependence and tolerance. *Proc. Natl. Acad. Sci. USA*, 72, 3092–3096.

Sharma, V., and McNeill, J. H. (2009). To scale or not to scale: The principles of dose extrapolation. *Br. J. Pharmacol.*, 157, 907–921.

Sharma, Y., Xu, T., Graf, W. M., Fobbs, A., Sherwood, C. C., Hof, P. R., et al. (2010). Comparative anatomy of the locus coeruleus in humans and non-human primates. *J. Comp. Neurol.*, 518, 963–971.

Sharpe, L., Sinclair, J., Kramer, A., de Manincor, M., and Sarris, J. (2020). Cannabis, a cause for anxiety? A critical appraisal of the anxiogenic and anxiolytic properties. *J. Transl. Med.*, 18, 374. doi: 10.1186/s12967-020-02518-2.

Shaw, G. K., Waller, S., Majumdar, S. K., Alberts, J. L., Latham, C. J., and Dunn, G. (1994). Tiapride in the prevention of relapse in recently detoxified alcoholics. *Br. J. Psychiatry*, 165, 515–523.

Shefner, J., Heiman-Patterson, T., Pioro, E. P., Wiedau-Pazos, M., Liu, S., Zhang, J., Agnese, W., Apple, S. (2019). Long-term edaravone efficacy in amyotrophic lateral sclerosis: Post-hoc analyses of Study 19 (MCI186-19). *Muscle Nerve*, 61, 218–242.

Shekhar, A., Truitt, W., Rainnie, D., and Sajdyk, T. (2005). Role of stress, corticotrophin releasing factor (CRF) and amygdala plasticity in chronic anxiety. *Stress*, 8(4), 209–219.

Shelton, K. L. (2018). Discriminative stimulus effects of abused inhalants. *Curr. Top. Behav. Neurosci.*, 39, 113–139.

Shenk, J. W. (2005). Lincoln's Melancholy: How Depression Challenged a President and Fueled His Greatness. Boston: Houghton Mifflin Harcourt.

Sheridan, D. C., Hendrickson, R. G., Beauchamp, G., Laurie, A., Fu, R., and Horowitz, B. Z. (2016). Adolescent intentional abuse ingestions: Overall 10-year trends and regional variation. *Pediatr. Emerg. Care*, Oct.

Sherman, B. J., and McRae-Clark, A. L. (2016). Treatment of cannabis use disorder: Current science and future outlook. *Pharmacotherapy*, 36, 511–535.

Sherwood, N. (1993). Effects of nicotine on human psychomotor performance. *Hum. Psychopharmacol.*, 8, 155–184.

Shi, Y., Hung, S.-T., Rocha, G., Lin, S., Linares, G. R., Staats, K. A., Seah, C., et al. (2019). Identification and therapeutic rescue of autophagosome and glutamate receptor defects in C9ORF72 and sporadic ALS neurons. *JCI Insight*, 4(15), e127736. doi: 10.1172/jci.insight.127736.

Shields, B. C., Kahuno, E., Kim, C., Apostolides, P. F., Brown, J., Lindo, S., et al. (2017). Deconstructing behavioral neuropharmacology with cellular specificity. *Science*, 356, pii: eaaj2161.

Shiffman, S., and Paty, J. (2006). Smoking patterns and dependence: Contrasting chippers and heavy smokers. *J. Abn. Psychol.*, 115, 509–523.

Shiffman, S., Dunbar, M. S., Li, X., Scholl, S. M., Tindle, H. A., Anderson, S. J., and Ferguson, S. G. (2014). Smoking patterns and stimulus control in intermittent and daily smokers. *PLOS ONE*, 9(3), e89911. doi: 10.1371/journal.pone.0089911.

Shiffman, S., Waters, A. J., and Hickox, M. (2004). The nicotine dependence syndrome scale: A multidimensional measure of nicotine dependence. *Nicotine Tob. Res.*, 6, 327–348.

Shippenberg, T. S. (1993). Motivational effects of opioids. In A. Herz (Ed.), *Opioids II*, Volume 104, Handbook of Behavioral Neurology (pp. 633–650). New York: Springer-Verlag.

Shippenberg, T. S., Herz, A., Spanagel, R., and Bals-Kubik, R. (1991). Neural substrates mediating the motivational effects of opioids. *Biol. Psychiatry*, 2, 33–35.

Shirayama, Y., Chen, A. C.-H., Nakagawa, S., Russell, D. S., and Duman, R. S. (2002). Brain derived neurotrophic factor produces antidepressant effects in behavioral models of depression. *J. Neurosci.*, 22, 3251–3261.

Shitik, E. M., Velmiskina, A. A., Dolskiy, A. A., and Yudkin, D. V. (2020). Reactivation of FMR1 gene expression is a promising strategy for fragile X syndrome therapy. *Gene Ther.*, 27, 247–253.

Sholler, D. J., Schoene, L., and Spindle, T. R. (2020). Therapeutic efficacy of cannabidiol (CBD): A review of the evidence from clinical trials and human laboratory studies. *Curr. Addict. Rep.*, 7, 405–412.

Shonesy, B. C., Bluett, R. J., Ramikie, T. S., Báldi, R., Hermanson, D. J., Kingsley, P. J., et al. (2014). Genetic disruption of 2-arachidonoylglycerol synthesis reveals a key role for endocannabinoid signaling in anxiety modulation. *Cell Rep.*, 9, 1644–1653.

Shorter, D., Domingo, C. B., and Kosten, T. R. (2015). Emerging drugs for the treatment of cocaine use disorder: A review of neurobiological targets and pharmacotherapy. *Expert Opin. Emerging Drugs*, 20, 15–29.

Shover, C. L., and Humphreys, K. (2019). Six policy lessons relevant to cannabis legalization. *Am. J. Drug Alcohol Abuse*, 45, 698–706.

Shulgin, A. T., and Nichols, D. E. (1978). Characterization of three new psychotomimetics. In R. C. Stillman and R. E. Willette (Eds.), *The Psychopharmacology of Hallucinogens*, pp. 74–83. Pergamon, New York.

Shults, C. W., Oakes, D., Kieburtz, K., Beal, M. F., Haas, R., Plumb, S., et al. (2002). Effects of coenzyme Q10 in early Parkinson disease: Evidence of slowing of the functional decline. *Arch. Neurol.*, 59, 1541–1550.

Shuster, S. (2013). The World's Deadliest Drug: Inside a Krokodil Cookhouse. Time. time. com/3398086/the-worlds-deadliest-drug-inside-a-krokodil-cookhouse/.

Sial, O. K., Parise, E. M., Parise, L. F., Gnecco, T., and Bolaños-Guzmán, C.A. (2020) Ketamine: The final frontier or another depressing end? *Behavioural Brain Res.*, 383, 112508.

Siciliano, C. A., Calipari, E. S., Ferris, M. J., and Jones, S. R. (2015). Adaptations of presynaptic dopamine terminals induced by psychostimulant self-administration. *ACS Chem. Neurosci.*, 6, 27–36. doi: 10.1021/cn5002705.

Sidorov, M. S., Auerbach, B. D., and Bear, M. F. (2013). Fragile X mental retardation protein and synaptic plasticity. *Mol. Brain*, 6, 15. doi: 10.1186/1756-6606-6-15.

Siebert, D. (2015). The Legal Status of *Salvia divinorum*. Salvia divinorum Research and Information Center. Available at www.sagewisdom.org/legalstatus.html.

Siebert, D. J. (1994). *Salvia divinorum* and Salvinorin A new pharmacologic findings. *J. Ethnopharmacol.*, 43, 53–56.

Siegel, R. L., Jacobs, E. J., Newton, C. C., Feskanich, D., Freedman, N. D., Prentice, R. L., et al. (2015). Deaths due to cigarette smoking for 12 smoking-related cancers in the United States. *JAMA Intern. Med.*, 175, 1574–1576.

Siegel, S. (1978). A pavlovian conditioning analysis of morphine tolerance. In N. A. Krasnegor (Ed.), *Behavioral Tolerance: Research and Treatment Implications*. NIDA Research Monograph 18, U.S. Department of Health, Education and Welfare, Public Health Service, National Institute of Drug Abuse, Washington, D.C.

Siegel, S. (1985). Drug-anticipatory responses in animals. In L. White, B. Tursky, and B. Schwartz (Eds.), *Placebo: Theory, Research and Mechanisms*, pp. 288–305. New York: Guilford Press.

Siegel, S., and Ramos, B. M. C. (2002). Applying laboratory research: Drug anticipation and the treatment of drug addiction. *Exp. Clin. Psychopharmacol.*, 10, 162–183.

Siegelbaum, S. A., and Koester, J. (1991). Ion channels. In E. R. Kandel, J. H. Schwartz, and T. M. Jessell (Eds.), *Principles of Neural Science* (3rd ed.), pp. 66–79. New York: Elsevier.

Siegelbaum, S. A., and Koester, J. (2000). Ion channels. In E. R. Kandel, J. H. Schwartz, and T. M. Jessell (Eds.), *Principles of Neural Science* (4th ed.), pp.105–124. New York: McGraw-Hill.

Siegert, R. J., and Abernethy, D. A. (2005). Depression in multiple sclerosis: A review. *J. Neurol. Neurosurg. Psychiatry*, 76, 469–475.

Sieghart, W. (2015). Allosteric modulation of $GABA_A$ receptors via multiple drug-binding sites. *Adv. Pharmacol.*, 72, 53–96.

Sieghart, W., and Sperk, G. (2002). Subunit composition, distribution and function of $GABA_A$ receptor subtypes. *Curr. Top. Med. Chem.*, 2, 795–816.

Siever, L. J. (2008). Neurobiology of aggression and violence. *Am. J. Psychiatry*, 165, 429–442.

Sifar, A. E., Nozohouri, S., Villalba, H., Vaidya, B., and Abbruscato, T. J. (2020). The role of smoking and nicotine in the transmission and pathogenesis of COVID-19. *J. Pharmacol. Exp. Ther.*, 375, 498–509.

Sigel, E., and Ernst, M. (2018). The benzodiazepine binding sites of $GABA_A$ receptors. *Trends Pharmacol. Sci.*, 39, 659–671.

Sigel, E., and Steinmann, M. E. (2012). Structure, function, and modulation of $GABA_A$ receptors. *J. Biol. Chem.*, 287, 40224–40231.

Silber, B. Y., and Schmitt, J. A. J. (2010). Effects of tryptophan loading on human cognition, mood, and sleep. *Neurosci. Biobehav. Rev.*, 34, 387–407.

Simmler, L. D., and Blakely, R. D. (2019). The SERT Met172 mouse: An engineered model to elucidate the contributions of serotonin signaling to cocaine action. *ACS Chem. Neurosci.*, 10, 3053–3060.

Simmons, S. J., Leyrer-Jackson, J. M., Oliver, C. F., Hicks, C., Muschamp, J. W., Rawls, S. M., and Olive, M. F. (2018). DARK classics in chemical neuroscience: Cathinone-derived psychostimulants. *ACS Chem. Neurosci.*, 9, 2379–2394.

Simon, E. J. (1991). Opioid receptors and endogenous opioid peptides. *Med. Res. Rev.*, 11, 357–374.

Simon, P., Kong, G., Cavallo, D. A., and Krishnan-Sarin, S. (2015). Update of adolescent smoking cessation interventions: 2009–2014. *Curr. Addict. Rep.*, 2, 15–23.

Simon-Delso, N., Amaral-Rogers, V., Belzunces, L. P., Bonmatin, J. M., Chagnon, M., Downs, C., et al. (2015). Systemic insecticides (neonicotinoids and fipronil): trends, uses, mode of action and metabolites. *Environ. Sci. Pollut. Res.*, 22, 5–34.

Simpson, A. K., and Magid, V. (2016). Cannabis use disorder in adolescence. *Child Adolesc. Psychiatric Clin. N. Am.*, 25, 431–443.

Simpson, S., Jr., Blizzard, L., Otahal, P., Vander Mei, I., and Taylor, B. (2011). Latitude is significantly associated with the prevalence of multiple sclerosis: A meta-analysis. *J. Neurol. Neurosurg. Psychiatry*, 82, 1132–1141.

Sinclair, E., Trivedi, D. K., Sarkar, D., Walton-Doyle, C., Milne, J., Kunath, T., Rijs, A. M., et al. (2021) *Nat. Commun.*, 12, 1592, 1–9.

Singer, B. F., Bryan, M. A., Popov, P., Robinson, T. E., and Aragona, B. J. (2017). Rapid induction of dopamine sensitization in the nucleus accumbens shell induced by a single injection of cocaine. *Behav. Brain Res.*, 324, 66–70.

Sinha, R. (2008). Chronic stress, drug use, and vulnerability to addiction. *Ann. N. Y. Acad. Sci.*, 1141, 105–130.

Sinha-Hikim, I., Artaza, J., Woodhouse, L., Gonzalez-Cadavid, N., Singh, A. B., Lee, M. I., et al. (2002). Testosteroneinduced increase in muscle size in healthy young men is associated with muscle fiber hypertrophy. *Am. J. Physiol. Endocrinol. Metab.*, 283, E154–E164.

Siniscalchi, A., Bonci, A., Mercuri, N. G., De Siena, A., De Sarro, G., Malferrari, G., et al. (2015). Cocaine dependence and stroke: Pathogenesis and management. *Curr. Neurovasc. Res.*, 112, 163–172.

Sircar, R., Basak, A., Sircar, D., and Wu, L. C. (2010). Effects of γ-hydroxybutyric acid on spatial learning and memory in adolescent and adult female rats. *Pharmacol. Biochem. Behav.*, 96, 187–193.

Sircar, R., Wu, L.-C., Reddy, K., Sircar, D., and Basak, A. K. (2011). GHB-induced cognitive deficits during adolescence and the role of NMDA receptor. *Curr. Neuropharmacol.*, 9, 240–243.

Sitek, E. J., Thompson, J. C., Craufurd, D., and Snowden, J. S. (2014). Unawareness of deficits in Huntington's Disease. *J. Huntington's Disease*, 3, 125–135.

Skewes, M. C., and Gonzalez, V. M. (2013). The biopsychosocial model of addiction. In P. Miller

(Ed.), *Principles of Addiction. Comprehensive Addictive Behaviors and Disorders*, Vol. 1, pp. 61–70. San Diego: Academic Press.

Skolnick, P. (2012). Anxioselective anxiolytics: On a quest for the Holy Grail. *Trends Pharmacol. Sci.*, 33, 611–620.

Skryabin, V. Y., and Vinnikova, M. A. (2019). Psychotic disorders in patients who use synthetic cannabinoids. *J. Psychiatr. Pract.*, 25, 485–490.

Sleigh, J., Harvey, M., Voss, L., and Denny, B. (2014). Ketamine—More mechanisms of action than just NMDA blockade. *Trends Anaesth. Crit. Care*, 4, 76–81.

Slifstein, M., Kegeles, L. S., Xu, X., Thompson, J. L., Urban, N., Castrillon, J., et al. (2010). Striatal and extrastriatal dopamine release measured with PET and [18F]fallypride. *Synapse*, 64, 350–362.

Slotkin, T. A. (2002). Nicotine and the adolescent brain: Insights from an animal model. *Neurotoxicol. Teratol.*, 24, 369–384.

Slotkin, T. A. (2008). If nicotine is a developmental neurotoxicant in animal studies, dare we recommend nicotine replacement therapy in pregnant women and adolescents? *Neurotoxicol. Teratol.*, 30, 1–19.

Small, A. C., Kampman, K. M., Plebani, J., De Jesus Quinn, M., Peoples, L., and Lynch, K. G. (2009). Tolerance and sensitization to the effects of cocaine use in humans: A retrospective study of longterm cocaine users in Philadelphia. *Subst. Use Misuse*, 44, 1888–1898.

Smart, R., and Pacula, R. L. (2019). Early evidence of the impact of cannabis legalization on cannabis use, cannabis use disorder, and the use of other substances: Findings from state policy evaluations. *Am. J. Drug Alcohol Abuse*, 45, 644–663.

Smigielski, L., Jagannath, V., Rössler, W., Walitza, S., and Grünblatt, E. (2020). Epigenetic mechanisms in schizophrenia and other psychotic disorders: A systematic review of empirical human findings. *Mol. Psychiatry*, 25(8), 1718–1748. https://doi.org/10.1038/s41380-019-0601-3

Smit, H. J., Cotton, J. R., Hughes, S. C., and Rogers, P. J. (2004). Mood and cognitive performance effects of "energy" drink constituents: Caffeine, glucose and carbonation. *Nutr. Neurosci.*, 7, 127–139.

Smith, A. L., Carter, S. M., Chapman, S., Dunlop, S. M., and Freeman, B. (2015). Why do smokers try to quit without medication or counselling? A qualitative study with ex-smokers. *BMJ Open*, 5, e007301. doi: 10.1136/bmjopen-2014-007301.

Smith, A. P., Christopher, G., and Sutherland, D. (2006). Effects of caffeine in overnight-withdrawn consumers and non-consumers. *Nutr. Neurosci.*, 9, 63–71.

Smith, D. A., Blough, B. E., and Banks, M. L. (2017). Cocaine-like discriminative stimulus effects of amphetamine, cathinone, methamphetamine, and their 3,4-methylenedioxy analogs in male rhesus monkeys. *Psychopharmacology*, 234, 117–127.

Smith, D. E., Raswyck, G. E., and Davidson, L. D. (2014). From Hofmann to the Haight Ashbury, and into the future: The past and potential of lysergic acid diethylamide. *J. Psychoactive Drugs*, 46, 3–10.

Smith, H. R., Leibold, N. K., Rapoport, D. A., Ginapp, C. M., Purnell, B. S., Bode, N. M., Alberico, S. I., et al. (2018). Dorsal raphe serotonin neurons mediate CO2-induced arousal from sleep. *J. Neurosci.*, 38, 1915–1925.

Smith, J., Connell, P., Evans, R. H., Gellene, A. G., Howard, M.D.A., Jones, B. H., Kaveggia, S., et al. (2018). A decade and a half of Pseudo-nitzschia spp. and domoic acid along the coast of southern California. *Harmful Algae*, 79, 87–104.

Smith, K. S., Greene, M. W., Babu, J. R., and Frugé, A. D. (2020). Psychobiotics as treatment for anxiety, de-pression, and related symptoms: a systematic review. *Nutr. Neurosci.*, 24, 963–967.

Smith, L. M., and Santos, L. S. (2016). Prenatal exposure: The effects of prenatal cocaine and methamphetamine exposure on the developing child. *Birth Defects Res. (Part C)*, 108, 142–146.

Smith, R. F., McDonald, C. G., Bergstrom, H. C., Ehlinger, D. G., and Brielmaier, J. M. (2015). Adolescent nicotine induces persisting changes in development of neural connectivity. *Neurosci. Biobehav. Rev.*, 55, 432–443.

Smith, S. M., Brown, H. O., Toman, E. P., and Goodman, L. S. (1947). The lack of cerebral effects of d-tubocurarine. *Anesthesiology*, 8, 1–14.

Smith, T. T., Rupprecht, L. E., Cwalina, S. N., Onoimus, M. J., Murphy, S. E., Donny, E. C., et al. (2016). Effects of monoamine oxidase inhibition on the reinforcing properties of low-dose nicotine. *Neuropsychopharmacology*, 41, 2335–2343.

Smoller, J. W., Block, S. R., and Young, M. M. (2009). Genetics of anxiety disorders: The complex road from DSM to DNA. *Depress. Anxiety*, 26, 965–975.

Snoek, A. (2017). How to recover from a brain disease: Is addiction a disease, or is there a disease-like stage in addiction? *Neuroethics*, 10, 185–194.

Snyder, S. H. (1977). Opiate receptors and internal opiates. *Sci. Am.*, 236, 44–56.

Snyder, S. H. (1996). *Drugs and the Brain*, p. 80. New York: Scientific American Library.

Sofroniew, M. V., and Vinters, H. V. (2010). Astrocytes: Biology and pathology. *Acta Neuropathol.*, 119, 7–35.

Sofuoglu, M., and Sewell, R. A. (2009). Norepinephrine and stimulant addiction. *Addict. Biol.*, 14, 119–129.

Sofuoglu, M., Babb, D. A., and Hatsukami, D. K. (2001). Progesterone treatment during the early follicular phase of the menstrual cycle: Effects on smoking behavior in women. *Pharmacol. Biochem. Behav.*, 69, 299–304.

Sofuoglu, M., Mitchell, E., and Kosten, T. R. (2004). Effects of progesterone treatment on cocaine responses in male and female cocaine users. *Pharmacol. Biochem. Behav.*, 78, 699–705.

Sofuoglu, M., Mitchell, E., and Mooney, M. (2009). Progesterone effects on subjective and physiological responses to intravenous nicotine in male and female smokers. *Hum. Psychopharmacol.*, 24, 559–564.

Solé, B., Jiménez, E., Martinez-Aran, A., and Vieta, E. (2015). Cognition as a target in major depression: New developments. *Eur. Neuropsychopharmacol.*, 25, 231–247.

Solimini, R., Rotolo, M. C., Mastrobattista, L., Mortali, C., Minutillo, A., Pichini, S., Pacifici, R., et al. (2017). Hepatotoxicity associated with illicit use of anabolic androgenic steroids in doping. *Eur. Rev. Med. Pharmacol. Sci.*, 21(Suppl. 1), 7–16.

Solinas, M., Goldberg, S. R., and Piomelli, D. (2008). The endocannabinoid system in brain reward processes. *Br. J. Pharmacol.*, 154, 369–383.

Solinas, M., Panlilio, L. V., Justinova, Z., Yasar, S., and Goldberg, S. R. (2006). Using drug-discrimination techniques to study the abuse-related effects of psychoactive drugs in rats. *Nat. Protoc.*, 1, 1194–1206.

Solis, O., Garcia-Sanz, P., Martin, A. B., Granado, N., Sanz-Magro, A., Podlesniy, P., et al. (2019). Behavioral sensitization and cellular responses to psychostimulants are reduced in D2R knockout mice. *Addict. Biol.*, e12840. doi: 10.1111/adb.12840.

Solmi, M., Fornaro, M., Toyoshima, K., Carvalho, A. F., Köhler, C. A., Veronese, N., Stubbs, B., et al. (2019). Systematic review and exploratory meta-analysis of the efficacy, safety, and biological effects of psychostimulants and atomoxetine in patients with schizophrenia or schizoaffective disorder. *CNS Spectrums*, 24(5), 479–495. https://doi.org/10.1017/S1092852918001050

Solomon, R. L. (1977). An opponent-process theory of acquired motivation: The affective dynamics of addiction. In J. D. Maser and M. E. P. Seligman (Eds.), *Psychopathology: Experimental Models*, pp. 66–103. San Francisco, CA: W. H. Freeman.

Solomon, R. L., and Corbit, J. D. (1974). An opponent-process theory of motivation. I. Temporal dynamics of affect. *Psych. Rev.*, 81, 119–145.

Solt, K., Cotten, J. F., Cimenser, A., Wong, K. F. K., Chemali, J. J., and Brown, E. N. (2011). Methylphenidate actively induces emergence from general anesthesia. *Anesthesiology*, 115, 791–803.

Somers, K. R., and Svatikova, A. (2020). Cardiovascular and autonomic responses to energy drinks – clinical implications. *J. Clin. Med.*, 9, 431. doi: 10.3390/jcm9020431.

Sommer, I. E., Tiihonen, J., van Mourik, A., Tanskanen, A., and Taipale, H. (2020). The clinical course of schizophrenia in women and men—A nationwide cohort study. *Npj Schizophrenia*, 6(1), 1–7. https://doi.org/10.1038/s41537-020-0102-z.

Soneji, S., Barrington-Trimis, J. L., Wills, T. A., Leventhal, A. M., Unger, J. B., Gibson, L. A., Yang, JW., et al. (2017). Association between initial use of e-cigarettes and subsequent cigarette smoking among adolescents and young adults. A systematic review and meta-analysis. *JAMA Pediatr.*, 171, 788–797.

Sonntag, K.-C., Song, B., Lee, N., Jung, J. H., Cha, Y., Leblanc, P., Neff, C., et al. (2018). Pluripotent Stem Cell-based therapy for Parkinson's disease: Current status and future prospects. *Prog. Neurobiol.*, 168, 1–20. https://doi.org/10.1016/j.pneurobio.2018.04.005

Sonon, K., Richardson, G. A., Cornelius, J., Kim, K. H., and Day, N. L. (2016). Developmental pathways from prenatal marijuana exposure to Cannabis Use Disorder in young adulthood. *Neurotoxicol. Teratol.*, 58, 46–52.

Sora, I., Wichems, C., Takahashi, N., Li, X.-F., Zeng, Z., Revay, R., et al. (1998). Cocaine reward models: Conditioned place preference can be established in dopamine- and in serotonin-transporter knockout mice. *Proc. Natl. Acad. Sci. USA*, 95, 7699–7704.

Sorensen, L., Ekstrand, M., Silva, J. P., Lindqvist, E., Xu, B., Rustin, P., et al. (2001). Late-onset corticohippocampal neurodepletion attributable to catastrophic failure of oxidative phosphorylation in MILON mice. *J. Neurosci.*, 21, 8082–8090.

Soria-Gomez, E., Bellocchio, L., and Marsicano, G. (2014). New insights on food intake control by olfactory processes: The emerging role of the endocannabinoid system. *Mol. Cell. Endocrinol.*, 397, 59–66.

Soriano, D., Brusco, A., and Caltana, L. (2021). Further evidence of anxietyand depression-like behaviour for total genetic ablation of cannabinoid receptor type 1. *Behav. Brain Res.*, 400, 113007. doi: 10.1016/j.bbr.2020.113007.

Souiza-Reilly, M., and Commons, K. G. (2014). Unraveling the architecture of the dorsal raphe synaptic neuropil using high-resolution neuroanatomy. *Front. Neural Circuits*, 8, 105. doi: 10.3389/fncir.2014.00105.

Southward, K., Rutherfurd-Markwick, K. J., and Ajmol, A. (2018). The effect of acute caffeine ingestion on endurance performance: A systematic review and meta-analysis. *Sports Med.*, 48, 2425–2441.

Souto, E. B., Lima, B., Campos, J. R., Martins-Gomes, C., Souto, S. B., and Silva, A. M. (2019). Myasthenia gravis: State of the art and new therapeutic strategies. *J. Neuroimmunol.*, 337, 577080. doi: 10.1016/j.neuroim.2019.577080.

Sowers, L. P., Massey, C. A., Gehlbach, B. K., Granner, M. A., and Richerson, G. B. (2013). Sudden unexpected death in epilepsy: Fatal post-ictal respiratory and arousal mechanisms. *Respir. Physiol. Neurobiol.*, 189, 315–323.

Spanagel, R., Noori, H. R., and Heilig, M. (2014). Stress and alcohol interactions: Animal studies and clinical significance. *Trends Neurosci.*, 37, 219–227.

Sparks, D. W., Proulx, E., and Lambe, E. K. (2018). Ready, set, go: the bridging of attention to action by acetylcholine in prefrontal cortex. *J. Physiol.*, 596, 1539–1540.

Spear, L. P. (2014). Adolescents and alcohol: Acute sensitivities, enhanced intake, and later consequences. *Neurotoxicol. Teratol.*, 41, 51–59.

Spears, C. A., Hedeker, D., Li, L., Wu, C., Anderson, N. K., Houchins, S. C., Vinci, C., et al. (2017). Mechanisms underlying mindfulness-based addiction treatment versus cognitive behavioral therapy and usual care for smoking cessation. *J. Consult. Clin. Psychol.*, 85, 1029–1040.

Spencer, R. C., Devilbiss, D. M., and Berridge, C. W. (2015). The cognition-enhancing effects of psychostimulants involve direct action in the prefrontal cortex. *Biol. Psychiatry*, 77, 940–950.

Sperk, G., Furtinger, S., Schwarzer, C., and Pirker, S. (2004). GABA and its receptors in epilepsy. In D. K. Binder and H. E. Scharfman (Eds.), *Advances in Experimental Medicine and Biology*, Volume 548, Recent Advances in Epilepsy Research (pp. 92–103). New York: Kluwer/Plenum.

Sperner-Unterweger, B., and Fuchs, D. (2015). Schizophrenia and psychoneuroimmunology: An integrative view. *Curr. Opin. Psychiat.*, 28, 201–206.

Spiegel, A., and Renken, E. (2020). Her Incredible Sense of Smell Is Helping Scientists Find New Ways to Diagnose Disease. National Public Radio. March 2020.

Spiga, S., Mulas, G., Piras, F., and Diana, M. (2014). The "addicted" spine. *Front. Neuroanat.*, 8, 110. doi: 10.3389/ fnana.2014.00110.

Spriet, L. L. (2014). Exercise and sport performance with low doses of caffeine. *Sports Med.*, 44(Suppl. 2), S175-S184.

Spronk, D. B., van Wel, J. H. P., Ramaekers, J. G., and Verkes, R. J. (2013). Characterizing the cognitive effects of cocaine: A comprehensive review. *Neurosci. Biobehav. Rev.*, 37, 1838–1859.

Sprow, G. M., and Thiele, T. E. (2012). The neurobiology of binge-like ethanol drinking: Evidence from rodent models. *Physiol. Behav.*, 106, 325–331.

St. Clair, D., Blackwood, D., Muir, W., Carothers, A., Walker, M., Spowart, G., et al. (1990). Association within a family of a balanced autosomal translocation with major mental illness. *Lancet*, 336, 13–16.

St. Helen, G., Havel, C., Dempsey, D. A., Jacob, P., III, and Benowitz, N. L. (2016). Nicotine delivery, retention and pharmacokinetics from various electronic cigarettes. *Addiction*, 111, 535–544.

St. Helen, G., Liakoni, E., Nardone, N., Addo, N. Jacob, P. III, and Benowitz, N. L. (2020). Comparison of systemic exposure to toxic and/or carcinogenic volatile organic compounds (VOCs) during vaping, smoking, and abstention. *Cancer Prev. Res.*, 13, 153–162.

St. John, A. L., Choi, H. W., Walker, Q. D., Blough, B., Kuhn, C. M., Abraham, S. N., and Staats, H. F. (2020). Novel mucosal adjuvant, mastoparan-7, improves cocaine vaccine efficacy. *NPJ Vaccines*, 5, 12. doi: 10.1038/ s41541-020-0161-1.

Stahl, S. M. (2019). Dextromethorphan/bupropion: A novel oral NMDA (N-methyl-d-aspartate) receptor antagonist with multimodal activity. *CNS Spectr.*, 24, 461–466.

Stanciu, C. N., Penders, T. M., and Rouse, E. M. (2016). Recreational use of dextromethorphan, "Robotripping": A brief review. *Am. J. Addict.*, 25, 374–377.

Staras, S. A., Livingston, M. D., and Wagenaar, A. C. (2016). Maryland alcohol sales tax and sexually transmitted infections: A natural experiment. *Am. J. Prev. Med.*, 50, e73–80.

Starcevic, V. (2014). The reappraisal of benzodiazepines in the treatment of anxiety and related disorders. Expert Rev. *Neurotherapeut.*, 14, 1275–1286,

Stasi, C., Bellini, M., Bassotti, G., Blandizzi, C., and Milani, S. (2014). Serotonin receptors and

their role in the pathophysiology and therapy of irritable bowel syndrome. *Tech. Coloproctol.*, 18, 613–621.

Stead, L. F., Koilpillai, P., and Lancaster, T. (2015). Additional behavioural support as an adjunct to pharmacotherapy for smoking cessation. *Cochrane Database Syst. Rev.*, Issue 10, Article CD009670. doi: 10.1002/14651858.CD009670. pub3.

Stead, L. F., Koilpillai, P., Fanshawe, T. R., and Lancaster, T. (2016). Combined pharmacotherapy and behavioural interventions for smoking cessation. *Cochrane Database Syst. Rev.*, Issue 3, Article CD008286. doi: 10.1002/14651858. CD008286. pub3.

Steeds, H., Carhart-Harris, R. L., and Stone, J. M. (2015). Drug models of schizophrenia. *Ther. Adv. Psychopharmacol.*, 5, 43–58.

Steen, R. G., Mull, C., McClure, R., Hamer, R. M., and Lieberman, J. A. (2006). Brain volume in first-episode schizophrenia: Systematic review and meta-analysis of magnetic resonance imaging studies. *J. Ment. Sci.*, 188, 510–518. https://doi.org/10.1192/ bjp.188.6.510

Steidl, S., Miller, A. D., Blaha, C. D., and Yeomans, J. S. (2011). M_5 muscarinic receptors mediate striatal dopamine activation by ventral tegmental morphine and pedunculopontine stimulation in mice. *PLOS ONE*, 6, e27538. doi: 10.1371/journal. pone.0027538.

Steidl, S., Wasserman, D. I., Blaha, C. D., and Yeomans, J. S. (2017). Opioid-induced rewards, locomotion, and dopamine activation: A proposed model for control by meopontine and rostromedial tegmental neurons. *Neurosci. Biobehav. Rev.*, 83, 72–82.

Stein, C. (2016). Opioid receptors. *Annu. Rev. Med.*, 67, 433–451.

Steinberg, E. E., Boivin, J. R., Saunders, B. T., Witten, I. B., Deisseroth, K., and Janak, P. H. (2014). Positive reinforcement mediated by midbrain dopamine neurons requires D1 and D2 receptor activation in the nucleus accumbens. *PLOS ONE*, 9, e94771.

Steinberg, E. E., Keiflin, R., Boivin, J. R., Witten, I. B., Deisseroth, K., and Janak, P. H. (2013). A causal link between prediction errors, dopamine neurons and learning. *Nat. Neurosci.*, 16, 966–973.

Sterling, P., and Eyer, J. (1988). Allostasis: A new paradigm to explain arousal pathology. In S. Fisher and J. Reason (Eds.), *Handbook of Life Stress, Cognition and Health*, pp. 629–649. New York: Wiley.

Stewart, J. (2000). Pathways to relapse: The neurobiology of drug- and stress-induced relapse

to drug-taking. *J. Psychiatry Neurosci.*, 25, 125–136.

Stewart, R. B., and Li, T.-K. (1997). The neurobiology of alcoholism in genetically selected rat models. *Alcohol Health Res. World*, 21, 169–176.

Stice, E., Figlewicz, D. P., Gosnell, B. A., Levine, A. S., and Pratt, W. E. (2013). The contribution of brain reward circuits to the obesity epidemic. *Neurosci. Biobehav. Rev.*, 37(9, P.t A), 2047–2058.

Stilby, A. I., Hickman, M., Munafò, M. R., Heron, J., Yip, V. L., and Macleod, J. (2015). Adolescent cannabis and tobacco use and educational outcomes at age 16, Birth cohort study. *Addiction*, 110, 658–668.

Stilling, R. M., Bordenstein, S. R., Dinan, T. G., and Cryan, J. F. (2014). Friends with social benefits: Host-microbe interactions as a driver of brain evolution and development? *Front. Cell. Infect. Microbiol.*, 4, 147. doi: 10.3389/ fcimb.2014.00147

Stine, S. M., Southwick, S. M., Petrakis, I. L., Kosten, T. R., Charney, D. S., and Krystal, J. H. (2002). Yohimbine-induced withdrawal and anxiety symptoms in opioid-dependent patients. *Biol. Psychiatry*, 51, 642–651.

Stitzer, M., and Petry, N. (2006). Contingency management for treatment of substance abuse. *Annu. Rev. Clin. Psychol.*, 2, 411–434.

Stoessl, A. J. (2012). Neuroimaging in the early diagnosis of neurodegenerative disease. *Transl. Neurodegener.*, 1, 1–6.

Stolerman, I. (1992). Drugs of abuse: Behavioural principles, methods and terms. *Trends Pharmacol. Sci.*, 13, 170–176.

Stone, A. L., O'Brien, M. S., de la Torre, A., and Anthony, J. C. (2007). Who is becoming hallucinogen dependent soon after hallucinogen use starts? *Drug Alcohol Depend.*, 87, 153–163.

Stone, A. L., Storr, C. L., and Anthony, J. C. (2006). Evidence for a hallucinogen dependence syndrome developing soon after onset of hallucinogen use during adolescence. *Int. J. Methods Psychiatr. Res.*, 15, 116–130.

Stone, J. M., Dietrich, C., Edden, R., Mehta, M. A., De Simoni, S., Reed, L. J., et al. (2012). Ketamine effects on brain GABA and glutamate levels with 1HMRS: Relationship to ketamine-induced psychopathology. *Mol. Psychiatry*, 17, 664–668.

Storch, A., Jost, W. H., Vieregge, P., Spiegel, J., Greulich, W., Durner, J., et al. (2007). Randomized, double-blind, placebo-controlled trial on symptomatic effects of coenzyme Q10 in Parkinson disease. *Arch. Neurol.*, 64, 938–944.

Stowe, G. N., Vendruscolo, L. F., Edwards, S., Schlosburg, J. E., Misra, K. K., Schulteis, G., et al. (2011). A vaccine strategy that induces protective immunity against heroin. *J. Med. Chem.*, 54, 5195–5204.

Strandwitz, P. (2018). Neurotransmitter modulation by the gut microbiota. *Brain Res.*, 1693, 128–133.

Strasburger, S. E., Bhimani, P. M., Kaabe, J. H., Krysiak, J. T., Nanchanatt, D. L., Nguyen, T. N., et al. (2017). What is the mechanism of ketamine's rapid-onset antidepressant effect? A concise overview of the surprisingly large number of possibilities. *J. Clin. Pharm. Ther.*, 42, 147–154.

Strassman, R. J., Qualls, C. R., Uhlenhuth, E. H., and Kellner, R. (1994). Dose-response study of N,N-dimethyltryptamine in humans. II. Subjective effects and preliminary results of a new rating scale. *Arch. Gen. Psychiatry*, 51, 98–108.

Streetz, V. N., Gildon, B. L., and Thompson, D. F. (2016). Role of clonidine in neonatal abstinence syndrome: A systematic review. *Ann. Pharmacother.*, 50(4), 301–310. https://doi.org/10.1177/1060028015626438

Strehl, C., and Buttgereit, F. (2014). Unraveling the functions of the membranebound glucocorticoid receptors: First clues on origin and functional activity. *Ann. N.Y. Acad. Sci.*, 1318, 1–6.

Striepens, N., Kendrick, K. M., Hanking, V., Landgraf, R., Wüllner, U., Maier, W., et al. (2013). Elevated cerebrospinal fluid and blood concentrations of oxytocin following its intranasal administration in humans. *Sci. Rep.*, 3, 3440. doi: 10.1038/srep.03440.

Striley, C. L. W., Griffiths, R. R., and Cottler, L. B. (2011). Evaluating dependence criteria for caffeine. *J. Caffeine Res.*, 1, 219–225.

Striley, C. W., and Khan, S. R. (2014). Review of the energy drink literature from 2013, Findings continue to support most risk from mixing with alcohol. *Curr. Opin. Psychiatry*, 27, 263–268.

Strongin, R. M. (2019). E-cigarette chemistry and analytical detection. *Annu. Rev. Anal. Chem.*, 12, 23–39.

Struble, C. A., Ellis, J. D., and Lundahl, L. H. (2019). Beyond the bud. Emerging methods of cannabis consumption for youth. *Pediatr. Clin. N. Am.*, 66, 1087–1097.

Struchal, L. D., Grattan, L. M., Portier, K. M., Kilmon, K. A., Manahan, L. M., Roberts, S. M., and Morris, J. G. Jr. (2020). Dose-response assessment for impaired memory from chronic exposure to domoic acid among native American consumers of razor clams. *Regul. Toxicol. Pharmacol.*, 117, 104759.

Stuber, G. D., Roitman, M. F., Phillips, P. E. M., Carelli, R. M., and Wightman, R. M. (2005). Rapid dopamine signaling in the nucleus accumbens during contingent and noncontingent cocaine administration. *Neuropsychopharmacology*, 30, 853–863.

Subramaniyan, M., and Dani, J. A. (2015). Dopaminergic and cholinergic learning mechanisms in nicotine addiction. *Ann. N. Y. Acad. Sci.*, 1349, 46–63. © 2015 The Authors.

Substance Abuse and Mental Health Services Administration (SAMHSA). (2011). Results from the 2010 National Survey on Drug Use and Health: Summary of National Findings. NSDUH Series H-41, HHS Publication No. (SMA) 11–4658. Rockville, MD: Substance Abuse and Mental Health Services Administration.

Substance Abuse and Mental Health Services Administration (SAMHSA). (2012). Results from the 2011 National Survey on Drug Use and Health: Summary of National Findings. NSDUH Series H-44, HHS Publication No. (SMA) 12–4713. Rockville, MD: Substance Abuse and Mental Health Services Administration.

Substance Abuse and Mental Health Services Administration (SAMHSA). (2013). Update on emergency department visits involving energy drinks: A continuing public health concern. SAMHSA. Available at www.archive.samhsa.gov/ data/2k13/DAWN126/sr126-energydrinks-use.htm.

Substance Abuse and Mental Health Services Administration (SAMHSA). (2016a). Buprenorphine. SAMHSA. Available at www.samhsa.gov/medication-assisted-treatment/treatment/buprenorphine.

Substance Abuse and Mental Health Services Administration. (SAMHSA). (2016b). Key substance use and mental health indicators in the United States: Results from the 2015 National Survey on Drug Use and Health (HHS Publication No. SMA 16–4984, NSDUH Series H-51). Available at www.samhsa.gov/ data/sites/default/files/NSDUHFFR1-2015/NSDUH-FFR1-2015/NSDUH-FFR1-2015.pdf.

Substance Abuse and Mental Health Services Administration (SAMHSA). (2017). Key substance use and mental health indicators in the United States: Results from the 2016 National Survey on Drug Use and Health (HHS Publication No. SMA 17-5044, NSDUH Series H-52). Rockville, MD: Center for Behavioral Health Statistics and Quality, Substance Abuse and Mental Health Services Administration. Available at www.samhsa.gov/data/.

Substance Abuse and Mental Health Services Administration (SAMHSA). (2019). Results from the 2018 National Survey on Drug Use and Health: Detailed tables. Rockville, MD: Center for Behavioral Health Statistics and Quality, Substance Abuse and Mental Health Services Administration. Retrieved from https://www.samhsa.gov/data/ on April 26, 2020.

Substance Abuse and Mental Health Services Administration (SAMHSA). (2020). Results from the 2019 National Survey on Drug Use and Health. Available at https://www.samhsa.gov/data/report/2019-nsduh-detailed-tables.

Substance Abuse and Mental Health Services Administration. (2020). Key substance use and mental Health indicators in the United States: Results from the 2019 National Survey on Drug Use and Health (HHS Publication No. PEP20-07-01-001, NSDUH Series H-55). Rockville, MD: Center for Behavioral Health Statistics and Quality, Substance Abuse and Mental Health Services Administration. Retrieved from https://www.samhsa.gov/data/

Sugiura, T. (2009). Physiological roles of 2-arachidonoylglycerol, an endogenous cannabinoid receptor ligand. *BioFactors*, 35, 88–97.

Sulik, K. K., Johnston, M. C., and Webb, M. A. (1981). Fetal alcohol syndrome: Embryogenesis in a mouse model. *Science*, 214, 936–938.

Sullivan, E. V. (2000). Human brain vulnerability to alcoholism: Evidence from neuroimaging studies. *NIAAA Res. Monogr.*, 34, 477–508.

Sullivan, G. M., Coplan, J. D., Kent, J. M., and Gorman, J. M. (1999). The noradrenergic system in pathological anxiety: A focus on panic with relevance to generalized anxiety and phobias. *Biol. Psychiatry*, 46, 1205–1218.

Sullivan, L. C., Clarke, W. P., and Berg, K. A. (2015). Atypical antipsychotics and inverse agonism at 5-HT2 receptors. *Curr. Pharm. Des.*, 21, 3732–3738.

Sullivan, P. F., Agrawal, A., Bulik, C. M., Andreassen, O. A., Børglum, A. D., Breen, G., Cichon, S., et al. (2018). Psychiatric genomics: An update and an agenda. *Am. J. Psychiatry*, 175(1), 15. https://doi.org/10.1176/appi.ajp.2017.17030283

Sulser, F. (1989). New perspectives on the molecular pharmacology of affective disorders. *Eur. Arch. Psychiatry Neurol. Sci.*, 238, 231–239.

Sulzer, D., Cragg, S. J., and Rice, M. E. (2016). Striatal dopamine neurotransmission: Regulation of release and uptake. *Basal Ganglia*, 6, 123–148.

Sun, X., Xu, C. S., Chadha, N., Chen, A., and Liu, J. (2015). Marijuana for glaucoma: A recipe for disaster or treatment? *Yale J. Biol. Med.*, 88, 265–269.

Sun, Z., Ma, Y., Xie, L., Huang, J., Duan, S., Guo, R., Xie, Y., et al. (2019). Behavioral changes and neuronal damage in rhesus monkeys after 10 weeks of ketamine administration involve prefrontal cortex dopamine D2 receptor and dopamine transporter. *Neuroscience*, 415, 97–106.

Suppa, A., Huang, Y.-Z., Funke, K., Ridding, M. C., Cheeran, B., Di Lazzaro, V., et al. (2016). Ten years of theta burst stimulation in humans: Established knowledge, unknowns and prospects. *Brain Stimul.*, 9, 323–335.

Suratman, S., Edwards, J. W., and Babina, K. (2015). Organophosphate pesticides exposure among farmworkers: Pathways and risk of adverse health effects. *Rev. Environ. Health*, 30, 65–79.

Suvarna, Y., Maity, N., and Shivamurthy, M. C. (2016). Emerging trends in retrograde signaling. *Mol. Neurobiol.*, 53, 2572–2578.

Suzuki, J., Dekker, M. A., Valenti, E. S., Arbelo Cruz, F. A., Correa, A. M., Poklis, J. L., et al. (2015). Toxicities associated with NBOMe ingestion: A novel class of potent hallucinogens: A review of the literature. *Psychosomatics*, 56, 129–139.

Svensson, K. A., Hao, J., and Bruns, R. F. (2019). Positive allosteric modulators of the dopamine D1 receptor: A new mechanism for the treatment of neuropsychiatric disorders. *Adv. Pharmacol.*, 86, 273–305.

Svensson, K. A., Heinz, B. A., Schaus, J. M., Beck, J. P., Hao, J., Krushinski, J. H., et al. (2017). An allosteric potentiator of the dopamine D1 receptor increases locomotor activity in human D1 knock-in mice without causing stereotypy or tachyphylaxis. *J. Pharmacol. Exp. Ther.*, 360, 117–128.

Svíženská, I., Dubový, P., and Šulcová, A. (2008). Cannabinoid receptors 1 and 2 (CB$_1$ and CB$_2$), their distribution, ligands and functional involvement in nervous system structures: A short review. *Pharmacol. Biochem. Behav.*, 90, 501–511.

Sweatt, J. D. (2001). The neuronal MAP kinase cascade: A biochemical signal integration system subserving synaptic plasticity and memory. *J. Neurochem.*, 76, 1–10.

Sweatt, J. D. (2013). The emerging field of neuroepigenetics. *Neuron*, 80, 624–632.

Sweeney, M. M., Weaver, D. C., Vincent, K. B., Arria, A. M., and Griffiths, R. R. (2020). Prevalence and correlates of caffeine use disorder symptoms among a

United States sample. *J. Caffeine Adenosine Res.*, 10, 4–11.

Swendsen, J., and Le Moal, M. (2011). Individual vulnerability to addiction. *Ann. N. Y. Acad. Sci.*, 1216, 73–85.

Swendsen, J., Conway, K. P., Degenhardt, L., Dierker, L., Glantz, M., Jin, R., et al. (2009). Socio-demographic risk factors for alcohol and drug dependence: The 10-year follow-up of the national comorbidity survey. *Addiction*, 104, 1346–1355.

Swerdlow, N. R., Braff, D. L., and Geyer, M. A. (2016). Sensorimotor gating of the startle reflex: What we said 25 years ago, what has happened since then, and what comes next. *J. Psychopharmacology*, 30, 1072–1081.

Swift, R. M. (1999). Drug therapy for alcohol dependence. *N. Engl. J. Med.*, 340, 1482–1490.

Szechtman, H., Ahmari, S. E., Beninger, R. J., Eilamd, D., Harveye, B. H., Edemann-Callesenf, H., and Winter, C. (2017). Obsessive-compulsive disorder: Insights from animal models. *Neurosci. Biobehav. Rev.*, 76, 254–279.

Szutorisz, H., and Hurd, Y. L. (2016). Epigenetic effects of cannabis exposure. *Biol. Psychiatry*, 79, 586–594.

T

Tafelski, S., Häuser, W., and Schäfer, M. (2016). Efficacy, tolerability, and safety of cannabinoids for chemotherapy-induced nausea and vomiting: A systematic review of systematic reviews. *Schmerz*, 30, 14–24.

Tait, R. J., Caldicott, D., Mountain, D., Hill, S. L., and Lenton, S. (2016). A systematic review of adverse events arising from the use of synthetic cannabinoids and their associated treatment. *Clin. Toxicol.*, 54, 1–13.

Takács, V. T., Cserép, C., Schlingloff, D., Pósfai, B., Szönyi, A., Sos, K. E., Környei, Z., et al. (2018). Co-transmission of acetylcholine and GABA regulates hippocampal states. *Nat. Commun.*, 9, 2848. doi: 10.1038/s41467-018-05136-1.

Takagi, M., Lubman, D. I., and Yücel, M. (2011). Solvent-induced leukoencephalopathy: A disorder of adolescence? *Subst. Use Misuse*, 46, 95–98.

Takamori, S., Holt, M., Stenius, K., Lemke, E. A., Grønborg, M., Riedel, D., et al. (2006). Molecular anatomy of a trafficking organelle. *Cell*, 127, 831–846.

Takeuchi, T., Duszkiewicz, A. J., and Morris, R. G. M. (2014). The synaptic plasticity and memory hypothesis: Encoding, storage and persistence. *Philos. Trans. R. Soc. Lond. B Biol. Sci.*, 369, 20130288. doi: 10.1098/rstb.2013.0288.

Takezawa, K., Kondo, M., Nonomura, N., and Shimada, S. (2017). Urothelial ATP signaling:

what is its role in bladder sensation? *Neurourol. Urodyn.*, 36, 966–972.

Talpos, S. (2019). The Dangers of Energy Drinks Can Be Fatal—Especially for Teens. Quartz, available at https://qz.com/1661390/how-bad-are-energy-drinks-like-red-bull-for-teens/. Accessed 2/1/21.

Tam, T. W., Mulia, N., and Schmidt, L. A. (2014). Applicability of type A/B alcohol dependence in the general population. *Drug Alcohol Depend.*, 138, 169–176.

Tamnes, C. K., and Agartz, I. (2016). White Matter Microstructure in Early-Onset Schizophrenia: A Systematic Review of Diffusion Tensor Imaging Studies. *J. Am. Acad. Child Adolesc. Psychiatry*, 55(4), 269–279. https://doi.org/10.1016/j.jaac.2016.01.004

Tan, H., Ahmad, T., Loureiro, M., Zunder, J., and Laviolette, S. R. (2014). The role of cannabinoid transmission in emotional memory formation: Implications for addiction and schizophrenia. *Front. Psychiatry*, 5, 73. doi: 10.3389/fpsyt.2014.00073.

Tanaka, K., Watase, K., Manabe, T., Yamada, K., Watanabe, M., Takahashi, K., et al. (1997). Epilepsy and exacerbation of brain injury in mice lacking the glutamate transporter GLT-1. *Science*, 276, 1699–1702.

Tanasescu, R., and Constantinescu, C. S. (2010). Cannabinoids and the immune system: An overview. *Immunobiology*, 215, 588–597.

Tanda, G. (2016). Preclinical studies on the reinforcing effects of cannabinoids. A tribute to the scientific research of Dr. Steve Goldberg. *Psychopharmacology*, 233, 1845–1866.

Tanda, G., Hersey, M., Hempel, B., Xi, Z.-X., and Newman, A. H. (2021). Modafinil and its structural analogs as atypical dopamine uptake inhibitors and potential medications for psychostimulant use disorder. *Curr. Opin. Pharmacol.*, 56, 13–21.

Tanda, G., Munzar, P., and Goldberg, S. R. (2000). Self-administration behavior is maintained by the psychoactive ingredient of marijuana in squirrel monkeys. *Nat. Neurosci.*, 3, 1073–1074.

Tang, A.-H., Chen, H., Li, T. P., Metzbower, S. R., MacGillavry, H. D., and Blanpied, T. A. (2016). A trans-synaptic nanocolumn aligns neurotransmitter release to receptors. *Nature*, 536, 210–214.

Tang, M.H.Y., Chong, Y. K., Chan, C. Y., Ching, C. K., Lai, C. K., Li, Y. K., and Mak, T.W.L. (2018). Cluster of acute poisonings associated with an emerging ketamine analogue, 2-oxo-PCE. *Forensic Sci. Int.*, 290, 238–243.

Tang, X., Yang, J., Wang, W., Zeng, Y., Li, J., Lin, S., Nandakumar, K.

S., et al. (2020). Immunotherapy for treating methamphetamine, heroin and cocaine use disorders. *Drug Discov. Today*, 25, 610–619.

Tang, Y., Martin, N. L., and Cotes, R. O. (2014). Cocaine-induced psychotic disorders: Presentation, mechanism, and management. *J. Dual Diagn.*, 10, 98–105.

Tang, Y., Nyengaard, J. R., de Groot, D.M.G., and Gundersen, H.J.G. (2001). Total regional and global num-ber of synapses in the human brain neocortex. *Synapse*, 41, 258–273.

Tanimura, A., Pancani, T., Lim, S.A.O., Tubert, C., Melendez, A. E., Shen, W., and Surmeier, D. J. (2018). Striatal cholinergic interneurons and Parkinson's disease. *Eur. J. Neurosci.*, 47, 1148–1158.

Tank, A. W., and Wong, D. L. (2015). Peripheral and central effects of circulating catecholamines. *Compr. Physiol.*, 5, 1–15.

Tanner, C. M., Kamel, F., Ross, G. W., Hoppin, J. A., Goldman, S. M., Korell, M., et al. (2011). Rotenone, paraquat and Parkinson's disease. *Environ. Health Perspect.*, 119, 866–872.

Tanner, J.-A., and Tyndale, R. F. (2017). Variation in CYP2A6 activity and personalized medicine. *J. Pers. Med.*, 7, 18. doi: 10.3390/jpm7040018.

Tanner, J.-A., Chenoweth, M. J., and Tyndale, R. F. (2015). Pharmacogenetics of nicotine and associated smoking behaviors. *Curr. Top. Behav. Neurosci.*, 23, 37–86.

Tardelli, V. S., Bisaga, A., Arcadepani, F. B., Gerra, G., Levin, F. R., and Fidalgo, T. M. (2020). Prescription psychostimulants for the treatment of stimulant use disorder: a systematic review and meta-analysis. *Psychopharmacology*, 237, 2233–2255.

Targhetta, R., Nalpas, B., and Perney, P. (2013). Argentine tango: Another behavioral addiction? *J. Behav. Addict.*, 2, 179–186.

Tarnopolsky, M. A. (2008). Effect of caffeine on the neuromuscular system: Potential as an ergogenic aid. *Appl. Physiol. Nutr. Metab.*, 33, 1284–1289.

Tart, C. T. (1970). Marijuana intoxication: Common experiences. *Nature*, 226, 701–704.

Tashkin, D. P., and Roth, M. D. (2019). Pulmonary effects of inhaled cannabis smoke. *Am. J. Drug Alcohol Abuse*, 45, 596–609.

Taylor, A. M., Bus, T., Sprengel, R., Seeburg, P. H., Rawlins, J. N. P., and Bannerman, D. M. (2014). Hippocampal NMDA receptors are important for behavioral inhibition but not for encoding associative spatial memories. *Philos. Trans. R. Soc. Lond. B Biol. Sci.*, 369, 20130149. doi: 10.1098/rstb.2013.0149.

Taylor, C. P., Traynelis, S. F., Siffert, J., Pope, L. E., and Matsumoto, R. R. (2016). Pharmacology of

dextromethorphan: Relevance to dextromethorphan/quinidine (Nuedexta) clinical use. *Pharmacol. Ther.*, 164, 170–182.

Taylor, N. E., Chemali, J. J., Brown, E. N., and Solt, K. (2013). Activation of D1 dopamine receptors induces emergence from isoflurane general anesthesia. *Anesthesiology*, 118, 30–39.

Taylor, N. E., Van Dort, C. J., Kenny, J. D., Pei, J., Guidera, J. A., Vlasov, K. Y., et al. (2016). Optogenetic activation of dopamine neurons in the ventral tegmental area induces reanimation from general anesthesia. *Proc. Natl. Acad. Sci. USA*, 113, 12826–12831.

Taylor, S. B., Lewis, C. R., and Olive, M. F. (2013). The neurocircuitry of illicit psychostimulant addiction: Acute and chronic effects in humans. *Subst. Abuse Rehabil.*, 4, 29–43.

Tchang, B. G., Abel, B., Zecca, C., Saunders, K. H., and Shukla, A. P. (2020). An up-to-date evaluation of lorcaserin hydrochloride for the treatment of obesity. *Expert Opin. Pharmacother.*, 21, 21–28.

Tebo, C., Mazer-Amirshahi, M., Wax, P., Campleman, S., Boyer, E., Brent, J., Sheth, A., et al. (2020). Characterizing trends in synthetic cannabinoid receptor agonist use from patient clinical evaluations during medical toxicology consultation. *J. Psychoactive Drugs*, in press.

Tekin, I., Roskoski, R., Jr., Carkaci-Salli, N., and Vrana, K. E. (2014). Complex molecular regulation of tyrosine hydroxylase. *J. Neural Trans.*, 1221, 1451–1481.

Teodorini, R. D., Rycroft, N., and Smith-Spark, J. H. (2020). The off-prescription use of modafinil: An online survey of perceived risks and benefits. *PLOS ONE*, 15(2), e0227818. doi: 10.1371/journal.pone.0227818.

Terenius, L., and Wahlstrom, A. (1974). Inhibitor(s) of narcotic receptor binding in brain extracts and cerebrospinal fluid [Abstract]. *Acta Pharmacol. Toxicol.*, 35(Suppl. 1), 87.

Terner, J. M., and de Wit, H. (2006). Menstrual cycle phase and responses to drugs of abuse in humans. *Drug Alcohol Depend.*, 84, 1–13.

Terry, A. V., Jr., Callahan, P. M., and Hernandez, C. M. (2015). Nicotinic ligands as multifunctional agents for the treatment of neuropsychiatric disorders. *Biochem. Pharmacol.*, 97, 388–398.

Tetel, M. J., de Vries, G. J., Melcangi, R. C., Panzica, G., and O'Mahony, S. M. (2018). Steroids, stress and the gut microbiome-brain axis. *J. Neuroendocrinol.*, 30, e12548. doi: 10.1111/jne.12548.

Tham, M., Yilmaz, O., Alaver-dashvili, M., Kelly, M.E.M., Denovan-Wright, E. M., and Laprairie, R. B. (2019). Allosteric and orthosteric pharmacology of cannabidiol and cannabidiol-dimethylheptyl at the type 1 and type 2 cannabinoid receptors. *Br. J. Pharmacol.*, 176, 1455–1469.

Thannickal, T. C., Moore, R. Y., Nienhuis, R., Ramanathan, L., Gulyani, S., Aldrich, M., et al. (2000). Reduced number of hypocretin neurons in human narcolepsy. *Neuron*, 27, 469–474.

Thase, M. E., Chen, D., Edwards, J., and Ruth, A. (2014). Efficacy of vilazodone on anxiety symptoms in patients with major depressive disorder. *Int. Clin. Psychopharmacol.*, 29, 351–356.

The Sun (2012). Serving in the Royal Marines Was Easy Compared With Being a Crystal Meth Addict. https://www.thesun.co.uk/archives/news/593745/serving-in-the-marines-was-easy-compared-with-being-crystal-meth-addict/. Accessed 10/26/20.

Therapeutic Drug Monitoring | Lab Tests Online. (n.d.). Retrieved January 18, 2021, from https://labtestsonline.org/tests/therapeutic-drug-monitoring.

Theunissen, E. L., Reckweg, J. T., Hutten, N., Kuypers, K., Toennes, S. W., Neukamm, M. A., Halter, S., et al. (2021a). Intoxication by a synthetic cannabinoid (JWH-018) causes cognitive and psychomotor impairment in recreational cannabis users. *Pharmacol. Biochem. Behav.*, 202, 173118. doi: 10.1016/j.pbb.2021.173118.

Theunissen, E. L., Reckweg, J. T., Hutten, N., Kuypers, K., Toennes, S. W., Neukamm, M. A., Halter, S., et al. (2021b). Psychotomimetic symptoms after a moderate dose of a synthetic cannabinoid (JWH-018): implications for psychosis. *Psychopharmacology*, in press.

Thom, M. (2014). Review: Hippocampal sclerosis in epilepsy: A neuropathology review. *Neuropathol. Appl. Neurobiol.*, 40, 520–543.

Thomas, G., Kloner, R. A., and Rezkalla, S. (2014). Adverse cardiovascular, cerebrovascular, and peripheral vascular effects of marijuana inhalation: What cardiologists need to know. *Am. J. Cardiol.*, 113, 187–190.

Thomas, P. (2019). Membrane androgen receptors unrelated to nuclear steroid receptors. *Endocrinology*, 160, 772–781.

Thomas, S. A., Matsumoto, A. M., and Palmiter, R. D. (1995). Noradrenaline is essential for mouse fetal development. *Nature*, 374, 643–646.

Thombs, D. L. (1999). *Introduction to Addictive Behaviors* (2nd ed.). New York: Guilford.

Thompson, A. J., Barnwell, B. L., Barkhof, F., Carroll, W. M., Coetzee, T., Comi, G., Correale, J., Fazekas, F., et al. (2018). Diagnosis of multiple sclerosis: 2017 revisions of the McDonald criteria. *Lancet Neurol.*, 17, 162–173.

Thompson, K., Leadbeater, B., Ames, M., and Merrin, G. J. (2019). Associations between marijuana use trajectories and educational and occupational success in young adulthood. *Prev. Sci.*, 20, 257–269.

Thompson, P. M., Vidal, C., Giedd, J. N., Gochman, P., Blumenthal, J., Nicolson, R., et al. (2001). Mapping adolescent brain change reveals dynamic wave of accelerated gray matter loss in very early-onset schizophrenia. *Proc. Natl. Acad. Sci. USA*, 98, 11650–11655.

Thomsen, M., Han, D. D., Gu, H. H., and Caine, S. B. (2009). Lack of cocaine self-administration in mice expressing a cocaine-insensitive dopamine transporter. *J. Pharmacol. Exp. Ther.*, 331, 204–211.

Thomsen, M., Sørensen, G., and Dencker, D. (2018). Physiological roles of CNS muscarinic receptors gained from knockout mice. *Neuropharmacology*, 136, 411–420.

Thorpe, H.H.A., Talhat, M. A., and Khokhar, J. Y. (2021). High genes: Genetic underpinnings of cannabis use phenotypes. *Prog. NeuroPsychopharmacol. Biol. Psychiatry*, 106, 110164. doi: 10.1016/j.pnpbp.2020.110164.

Thorpy, M. J., and Bogan, R. K. (2020). Update on the pharmacologic management of narcolepsy: mechanisms of action and clinical implications. *Sleep Med.*, 68, 97–109.

Tiffany, S. T., Drobes, D. J., and CepedaBenito, A. (1992). Contribution of associative and nonassociative processes to the development of morphine tolerance. *Psychopharmacology*, 109, 185–190.

Timpone, J. G., Wright, D. J., Li, N., Egorin, M. J., Enama, M. E., Mayers, J., et al. (1997). The safety and pharmacokinetics of single-agent and combination therapy with megestrol acetate and dronabinol for the treatment of HIV wasting syndrome. The DATRI 004 Study Group. Division of AIDS Treatment Research Initiative. *AIDS Res. Hum. Retroviruses*, 13, 305–315.

Ting, P. T., and Freiman, A. (2004). The story of Clostridium botulinum: From food poisoning to Botox. *Clin. Med.*, 4, 258–261.

Tirrell, M. (2017). As Opioid Epidemic Worsens, the Cost of Waking Up From an Overdose Soars. CNBC, Aired January 4, 2017.

Titus, D. J., Oliva, A. A., Wilson, N. M., and Atkins, C. M. (2015). Phosphodiesterase inhibitors as therapeutics for traumatic brain injury. *Curr. Pharm. Des.*, 21, 332–342.

Toczek, M., and Malinowska, B. (2018). Enhanced endocannabinoid tone as a potential target of pharmacotherapy. *Life Sci.*, 204, 20–45.

Tod, D., Edwards, C., and Cranswick, I. (2016). Muscle dysmorphia: Current insights. *Psychol. Res. Behav. Management*, 9, 179–188.

Todorow, M., Moore, T. E., and Koren, G. (2010). Investigating the effects of low to moderate levels of prenatal alcohol exposure on child behaviour: A critical review. *J. Popul. Ther. Clin. Pharmacol.*, 17, e323–330.

Toll, L., Cippitelli, A., and Ozawa, A. (2021). The NOP Receptor System in Neurological and Psychiatric Disorders: Discrepancies, Peculiarities and Clinical Progress in Developing Targeted Therapies. *CNS Drugs*. https://doi.org/10.1007/s40263-021-00821-0

Tolu, S., Eddine, R., Marti, F., David, V., Graupner, M., Pons, S., et al. (2013). Coactivation of VTA DA and GABA neurons mediates nicotine reinforcement. *Mol. Psychiatry*, 18, 382–393.

Tork, I. (1990). Anatomy of the serotonergic system. *Ann. N. Y. Acad. Sci.*, 600, 9–34.

Torres, O. V., and O'Dell, L. E. (2016). Stress is a principal factor that promotes tobacco use in females. *Prog. Neuropsychopharmacol. Biol. Psychiatry*, 65, 260–268.

Torrisi, M., Pennisi, G., Russo, I., Amico, F., Esposito, M., Liberto, A., Cocimano, G., et al. (2020). Sudden cardiac death in anabolic-androgenic steroid users: A literature review. *Medicina (Kaunas)*, 56(11), 587. doi: 10.3390/medicina56110587.

Torten, M., Miller, C. H., Eisele, J. H., Henderson, G. L., and Benjamini, E. (1975). Prevention of the effects of fentanyl by immunological means. *Nature*, 253(5492), 565–566. https://doi.org/10.1038/253565a0

Tóth, A., Blumberg, P. M., and Boczán, J. (2009). Anandamide and the vanilloid receptor (TRPV1). *Vitam. Horm.*, 81, 389–419.

Toufexis, D. (2007). Regionand sex-specific modulation of anxiety behaviours in the rat. *J. Neuroendocrinol.*, 19, 461–473.

Towns, S., DiFranza, J. R., Jayasuriya, G., Marshall, T., and Shah, S. (2017). Smoking cessation in adolescents: Targeted approaches that work. *Paed. Resp. Rev.*, 22, 11–22.

Townsend, L., Flisher, A. J., and King, G. (2007). A systemic review of the relationship between high school dropout and substance use. *Clin. Child Fam. Psychol.*, 10, 295–317.

Treadwell, S. D., and Robinson, T. G. (2007). Cocaine use and stroke. *Postgrad. Med. J.*, 83, 389–394.

Trecki, J., Gerona, R. R., and Schwartz, M. D. (2015). Synthetic cannabinoid-related illnesses and deaths. *New Engl. J. Med.*, 373, 103–107.

Treit, D. (1985). Animal models for the study of anti-anxiety agents: A review. *Neurosci. Biochem. Rev.*, 9, 203–222.

Trenton, A. J., and Currier, G. W. (2005). Behavioural manifestations of anabolic steroid use. *CNS Drugs*, 19, 571–596.

Trifilieff, P., and Martinez, D. (2014). Imaging addiction: D2 receptors and dopamine signaling in the striatum as biomarkers for impulsivity. *Neuropharmacology*, 76, 498–509.

Trifilieff, P., Ducrocq, F., van der Veldt, S., and Martinez, D. (2017). Blunted dopamine transmission in addiction: Potential mechanisms and implications for behavior. *Semin. Nucl. Med.*, 47, 64–74.

Trigo, J. M., Martin-García, E., Berrendero, F., Robledo, P., and Maldonado, R. (2010). The endogenous opioid system: A common substrate in drug addiction. *Drug Alcohol Depend.*, 108, 183–194.

Tritsch, N. X., Granger, A. J., and Sabatini, B. L. (2016). Mechanisms and functions of GABA co-release. *Nat. Rev. Neurosci.*, 17, 139–145.

Trivedi, D. K., Sinclair, E., Xu, Y., Sarkar, D., Walton-Doyle, C., Liscio, C., Banks, P., et al. (2019) Discovery of volatile biomarkers of Parkinson's disease from sebum. *ACS Cent. Sci.* 2019, 5, 599–606.

Trombley, T. A., Capstick, R. A., and Lindsley, C. W. (2019). DARK classics in chemical neuroscience: Gamma-hydroxybutyrate (GHB). *ACS Chem. Neurosci.*, 11, 3850–3859.

Trott, M., Jackson, S. E., Firth, J., Jacob, L., Grabovac, I., Mistry, A., Stubbs, B., et al. (2021). A comparative meta-analysis of the prevalence of exercise addiction in adults with and without indicated eating disorders. *Eat. Weight Disord.*, 26, 37–46.

Trouth, A. J., Dabi, A., Solieman, N., Kurukumbi, M., and Kalyanam, J. (2012). Myasthenia gravis: A review. *Autoimmune Dis.*, 2012, 874680. doi: 10.1155/2012/874680.

Trucco E.M. (2020). A review of psychosocial factors linked to adolescent substance use. *Pharmacol. Biochem. Behav.*, 196, 172969. doi: 10.1016/j.pbb.2020.172969.

Trudeau, L.-E., and Gutiérrez, R. (2007). On cotransmission & neurotransmitter phenotype plasticity. *Mol. Interv.*, 7, 137–146.

Trudeau, L.-E., Hnasko, T. S., WalénMackenzie, A., Morales, M., Sayport, S., and Sulzer, D. (2014). The multilingual nature of dopamine neurons. *Prog. Brain Res.*, 211, 141–164.

Trujillo, K. A. (2000). Are NMDA receptors involved in

opiate-induced neural and behavioral plasticity? *Psychopharmacology*, 151, 121–141.

Truman, P., Stanfill, S., Heydari, A., Silver, E., and Fowles, J. (2019). Monoamine oxidase inhibitory activity of flavoured e-cigarette liquids. *Neurotoxicology*, 75, 123–128.

Tsai, M., Byun, M. K., Shin, J., and Alexander, L.E.C. (2020). Effects of e-cigarettes and vaping devices on cardiac and pulmonary physiology. *J. Physiol.*, 598, 5039–5062. © 2020 The Authors. *The Journal of Physiology* © 2020 The Physiological Society.

Tsankova, N., Renthal, W., Kumar, A., and Nestler, E. J. (2007). Epigenetic regulation in psychiatric disorders. *Nat. Rev. Neurosci.*, 8, 355–367.

Tseng, K. Y., Chambers, R. A., and Lipska, B. K. (2009). The neonatal ventral hippocampal lesion as a heuristic neurodevelopmental model of schizophrenia. *Behav. Brain Res.*, 204, 295–305.

Tuem, K., and Atey, T. M. (2017). Neuroactive steroids: Receptor interactions and responses. *Front. Neurol.*, 8, 442. doi: 10.3389/fneur.2017.00442.

Tupper, K. W., Wood, E., Yensen, R., and Johnson, M. W. (2015). Psychedelic medicine: A re-emerging therapeutic paradigm. *CMAJ*, 187, 14. doi: 10.1503/cmaj.141124.

Tyree, S. M., Borniger, J. C., and de Lecea, L. (2018). Hypocretin as a hub for arousal and motivation. *Front. Neurol.*, 9, 413. doi: 10.3389/fneur.2018.00413.

Tzschentke T.M. (2007). Measuring reward with the conditioned place preference (CPP) paradigm: update of the last decade. *Addict. Biol.*, 12, 227–462.

U

Uhart, M., and Wand, G. S. (2009). Stress, alcohol and drug interaction: An update of human research. *Addict. Biol.*, 14, 43–64.

Ulas, J., and Cotman, C. W. (1993). Excitatory amino acid receptors in schizophrenia. *Schizophr. Bull.*, 19, 105–117.

Umukoro, S., Aladeokin, A. C., and Eduviere, A. T. (2013). Aggressive behavior: A comprehensive review of its neurochemical mechanisms and management. *Aggress. Violent Behav.*, 18, 195–203.

Underwood, M. S., Bright, S. J., and Lancaster, B. L. (2021). A narrative review of the pharmacological, cultural and psychological literature on ibogaine. *J. Psychedelic Studies*, in press.

Ungerstedt, U. (1984). Measurement of neurotransmitter release by intracranial dialysis. In C. A. Marsden (Ed.), *Measurement of Neurotransmitter Release in Vivo*, pp. 81–106. New York: Wiley.

United Nations Office on Drugs and Crime. (2016). World Drug Report 2016. United Nations publication, Sales No. E.16.XI.7. Available at http://www.unodc.org/wdr2016/.

United Nations Office On Drugs And Labor. (2021). World Drug Report 2020 (set of 6 booklets). United Nations. www.unodc.org/wdr2020

United States Department of Health and Human Services (USDHHS) and U.S. Department of Agriculture. (2015). 2015–2020 Dietary Guidelines for Americans (8th ed.). Washington, DC: U.S. Government Printing Office. Available at health.gov/dietaryguidelines/2015/guidelines/.

United States Department of Health and Human Services. (2014). The Health Consequences of Smoking: 50 Years of Progress. A Report of the Surgeon General. Atlanta, GA: U.S. Department of Health and Human Services, Centers for Disease Control and Prevention, National Center for Chronic Disease Prevention and Health Promotion, Office on Smoking and Health. Printed with corrections, January 2014.

United States Department of Health and Human Services. (2016). HHS Takes Additional Steps to Expand Access to Opioid Treatment. Available at wayback. archive-it.org/3926/20170129114910/www.hhs.gov/about/news/2016/11/16/additional-stepsexpand-opioid-treatment.html.

U.S. Department of Health and Human Services (2016). E-Cigarette Use Among Youth and Young Adults. A Report of the Surgeon General. Atlanta, GA: U.S. Department of Health and Human Services, Centers for Disease Control and Prevention, National Center for Chronic Disease Prevention and Health Promotion, Office on Smoking and Health.

U.S. Department of Health and Human Services (2020). Smoking Cessation. A Report of the Surgeon General. Atlanta, GA: U.S. Department of Health and Human Services, Centers for Disease Control and Prevention, National Center for Chronic Disease Prevention and Health Promotion, Office on Smoking and Health.

United States Department of Health, Education, and Welfare. (1968). 1943–1966 Bibliography on Psychotomimetics. Public Health Service. National Institute of Mental Health. Washington, DC: U.S. Government Printing Office.

United States Environmental Protection Agency (2012). Inhalation Health Effect Reference Values for Toluene (CASRN 108-88-3).

Available at https://ofmpub.epa.gov/eims/eimscomm.getfile?p_download_id=512650. Accessed 6/6/21.

United States Federal Emergency Management Agency. (2017). Electronic Cigarette Fires and Explosions in the United States 2009–2016. Lawrence, A. McKenna Jr. Research Group, National Fire Data Center, U.S. Fire Administration. Available at www.usfa.fema.gov/downloads/pdf/publications/electronic_cigarettes.pdf.

University of Nottingham. (2012). Psychiatric Interviews for Teaching: Mania. Published on January 31, 2012. Available at www.youtube.com/watch?v=zAfqvC02oM.

Uno, Y., and Coyle, J. T. (2019). Glutamate hypothesis in schizophrenia. *Psychiatr. Clin. Neurosci.*, 73, 204–215.

Urban, D. J., and Roth, B. L. (2015). DRE-ADDs (Designer Receptors Exclusively Activated by Designer Drugs): Chemogenetic tools with therapeutic utility. *Annu. Rev. Pharmacol. Toxicol.*, 55, 399–417.

Urban, K. R., and Gao, W.-J. (2014). Performance enhancement at the cost of potential brain plasticity: Neural ramifications of nootropic drugs in the healthy developing brain. *Front. Syst. Neurosci.*, 8, 38. doi: 10.3389/fnsys.2014.00038.

Urban, K. R., and Gao, W.-J. (2017). Psychostimulants as cognitive enhancers in adolescents: More risk than reward? *Front. Public Health*, 5, 260. doi: 10.3389/fpubh.2017.00260.

Urban, N. B., Kegeles, L. S., Slifstein, M., Xu, X., Martinez, D., Sakr, E., et al. (2010). Sex differences in striatal dopamine release in young adults after oral alcohol challenge: A positron emission tomography imaging study with [11C] raclopride. *Biol. Psychiatry*, 68, 689–696.

Urbán, R., Kun, B., Mózes, T., Soltész, P., Paksi, B., Farkas, J., Kökönyei, G., et al. (2019). A four-factor model of work addiction: The development of the work addiction risk test revised. *Eur. Addict. Res.*, 25(3), 145–160.

Urban, T. J., and Goldstein, D. B. (2014). Pharmacogenetics at 50, Genomic personalization comes of age. *Sci. Transl. Med.*, 6, 220ps1. doi: 10.1126/scitranslmed.3005237.

Urbanoski, K. A., and Kelly, J. F. (2012). Understanding genetic risk for substance use and addiction: A guide for non-geneticists. *Clin. Psychol. Rev.*, 32, 60–70.

Uteshev, V. V. (2016). Allosteric modulation of nicotinic acetylcholine receptors: The concept and therapeutic trends. *Curr. Pharm. Des.*, 22, 1986–1997.

V

Vadivelu, N., Schermer, E., Kodumudi, V., Belani, K., Urman, R. D., and Kaye, A. D. (2016). Role of ketamine for analgesia in adults and children. *J. Anaesthesiol. Clin. Pharmacol.*, 32, 298–306.

Vaghi, M. M., Vértes, P. E., Kitzbichler, M. G., Apergis-Schoute, A. M., van der Flier, F. E., Fineberg, N. A., et al., (2017). Specific frontostriatal circuits for impaired cognitive flexibility and goal-directed planning in obsessive-compulsive disorder: evidence from resting-state functional connectivity. *Biol Psychiatry*, 81(8), 708–717.

Vail, G., and Roepke, T. A. (2019). Membrane-initiated estrogen signaling via Gq-coupled GPCR in the central nervous system. *Steroids*, 142, 77–83.

Vaiva, G., Ducrocq, F., Jezequel, K., Averland, B., Lestavel, P., Brunet, A., et al. (2003). Immediate treatment with propranolol decreases posttraumatic stress disorder two months after trauma. *Biol. Psychiatry*, 54, 947–949.

Vajaria, R., and Vasudevan, N. (2018). Is the membrane estrogen receptor, GPER1, a promiscuous receptor that modulates nuclear estrogen receptor-mediated functions in the brain? *Horm. Behav.*, 104, 165–172.

Valente, M. J., de Lourdes Bastos, M., Fernandes, E., Carvalho, F., de Pinho, P. G., and Varvalho, M. (2017). Neurotoxicity of β-keto amphetamines: Deathly mechanisms elicited by methylone and MDPV in human dopaminergic SH-SY5Y cells. *ACS Chem. Neurosci.*, 8, 850–859.

Valente, M. J., de Pinho, P. G., de Lourdes Bastos, M., Carvalho, F., and Carvalho, M. (2014). Khat and synthetic cathinones: A review. *Arch. Toxicol.*, 88, 15–45.

Valentine, G., and Sofuoglu, M. (2018). Cognitive effects of nicotine: Recent progress. *Curr. Neuropharmacol.*, 16, 403–414.

Valentino, R. J., and Van Bockstaele, E. (2008). Convergent regulation of locus coeruleus activity as an adaptive response to stress. *Eur. J. Pharmacol.*, 583,194–203.

Valentino, R. M., and Foldvary-Schaefer, N. (2007). Modafinil in the treatment of excessive daytime sleepiness. *Cleve. Clin. J. Med.*, 74, 561–571.

Vallersnes, O. M., Dines, A. M., Wood, D. M., Yates, C., Heyerdahl, F., Hovda, K. E., et al. (2016). Psychosis associated with acute recreational drug toxicity: A European case series. *BMC Psychiatry*, 16, 293. doi: 10.1186/s12888–016–1002–7.

Valmaggia, L. R., Day, F. L., Jones, C., Bissoli, S., Pugh, C., Hall, D., et al. (2014). Cannabis use and transition to psychosis in people at ultra-high risk. *Psychol. Med.*, 44, 2503–2512.

Valverde, O., Karsak, M., and Zimmer, A. (2005). Analysis of the endocannabinoid system by using CB$_1$ cannabinoid receptor knockout mice. *Handb. Exp. Pharmacol.*, 168, 117–145.

van Amsterdam, J. G. C., Brunt, T. M., McMaster, M. T. B., and Niesink, R. J. M. (2012). Possible long-term effects of γ-hydroxybutyric acid (GHB) due to neurotoxicity and overdose. *Neurosci. Biobehav. Rev.*, 36, 1217–1227.

van Amsterdam, J., Brunt, T., and van den Brink, W. (2015a). The adverse health effects of synthetic cannabinoids with emphasis on psychosis-like effects. *J. Psychopharmacol.*, 29, 254–263.

van Amsterdam, J., Nabben, T., and van den Brink, W. (2015b). Recreational nitrous oxide use: Prevalence and risks. *Regul. Toxicol. Pharmacol.*, 73, 790–796.

van Dam, R. M., Hu, F. B., and Willett, W. C. (2020). Coffee, caffeine, and health. *N. Engl. J. Med.*, 383, 369–378.

van de Giessen, E., Weinstein, J. J., Cassidy, C. M., Haney, M., Dong, Z., Ghazzaoui, R. et al. (2016). Deficits in striatal dopamine release in cannabis dependence. *Mol. Psychiatry*, 22, 68–75.

van de Nobelen, S., Kienhuis, A. S., and Talhout, R. (2016). An inventory of methods for the assessment of additive increased addictiveness of tobacco products. *Nicotine Tob. Res.*, 18, 1546–1555.

van de Rest, O, Bloemendaal, M., de Heus, R., and Aarts, E. (2017). Dose-dependent effects of oral tyrosine administration on plasma tyrosine levels and cognition in aging. *Nutrients*, 9, 1279. doi: 10.3390/nu9121279.

van den Bos, M.A.J., Geevasinga, N., Higashihara, M., Menon, P., and Vucic, S. (2019). Pathophysiology and diagnosis of ALS: Insights from advances in neurophysiological techniques. *Int. J. Mol. Sci.*, 20, 2818. doi: 10.3390/ijms.20112818.

van den Heuvel, M. P., and Fornito, A. (2014). Brain networks in schizophrenia. *Neuropsychol. Rev.*, 24, 32–48.

van den Pol, A. N. (2012). Neuropeptide transmission in brain circuits. *Neuron*, 76, 98–115.

van der Steur, S. J., Batalla, A., and Bossong, M. G. (2020). Factors moderating the association between cannabis use and psychosis risk: A systematic review. *Brain Sci.*, 10(2), 97. doi: 10.3390/brainsci10020097.

van Donkelaar, E. L., Blokland, A., Ferrington, L., Kelly, P.A.T., Steinbusch, H.W.M., and Prickaerts, J. (2011). Mechanism of acute tryptophan depletion: Is it only serotonin? *Mol. Psychiatry*, 16, 695–713.

Van Dyke, C., and Byck, R. (1982). Cocaine. *Sci. Am.*, 246, 128–141.

van Leeuwen, A. P., Verhuist, F. C., Reijneveld, S. A., Vollebergh, W. A. M., Ormel, J., and Huizink, A. C. (2011). Can the gateway hypothesis, the common liability model and/or the route of administration model predict initiation of cannabis use during adolescence? A survival analysis: The TRAILS study. *J. Adolesc. Health*, 48, 73–78.

van Marle, H. J. F., Hermans, E. J., Qin, S., and Fernández, G. (2010). Enhanced resting-state connectivity of amygdala in the immediate aftermath of acute psychological stress. *NeuroImage*, 53, 348–354.

van Schayck, O. C. P., Horstman, K., Vuurman, E., de Wert, G., and Kotz, D. (2014). Nicotine vaccination: Does it have a future? *Addiction*, 109, 1223–1225.

Van Timmeren, T., Daams, J. G., van Holst, R. J., and Goudriaan, A. E. (2018). Compulsivity-related neurocognitive performance deficits in gambling disorder: A systematic review and meta-analysis. *Neurosci. Biobehav. Rev.*, 84, 204–217.

Van Zee, A. (2009). The Promotion and Marketing of OxyContin: Commercial Triumph, Public Health Tragedy. *Am. J. Public Health*, 99(2), 221–227. https://doi.org/10.2105/AJPH.2007.131714

Vandaele, Y., Cantin, L., Serre, F., VouillacMendoza, C., and Ahmed, S. H. (2016). Choosing under the influence: A drug-specific mechanism by which the setting controls drug choices in rats. *Neuropsychopharmacology*, 41, 646–657.

Vanderschuren, L. J. M. J., and Ahmed, S. H. (2013). Animal studies of addictive behavior. *Cold Spring Harb. Perspect. Med.*, 3, a011932.

VanPett, K., Viau, V., Bittencourt, J. C., Chan, R. K., Li, H. Y., Arias, C. et al. (2000). Distribution of mRNAs encoding CRF receptors in brain and pituitary of rat and mouse. *J. Comp. Neurol.*, 428, 191–212.

Vargas, A. S., Luis, A., Barroso, M., Gallardo, E., and Pereira, L. (2020). Psilocybin as a new approach to treat depression and anxiety in the context of life-threatening diseases—A systematic review and meta-analysis of clinical trials. *Biomedicines*, 8, 331. doi: 10.3390/biomedicines8090331.

Varlet, V., Concha-Lozano, N., Berthet, A., Plateel, G., Favrat, B., De Cesare, M., et al. (2016). Drug vaping applied to cannabis: Is "cannavaping" a therapeutic alternative to marijuana? *Sci. Rep.*, 6, 25599. doi: 10.1038/srep25599.

Varlet, V., Concha-Lozano, N., Berthet, A., Plateel, G., Favrat, B., De Cesare, M., et al. (2016). Drug vaping applied to cannabis: Is "cannavaping" a therapeutic alternative to marijuana? *Sci. Rep.*, 6, 25599. doi: 10.1038/srep25599.

Varvel, S. A., and Lichtman, A. H. (2002). Evaluation of CB$_1$ receptor knockout mice in the Morris water maze. *J. Pharmacol. Exp. Ther.*, 301, 915–924.

Varvel, S. A., Anum, E. A., and Lichtman, A. H. (2005). Disruption of CB$_1$ receptor signaling impairs extinction of spatial memory in mice. *Psychopharmacology*, 179, 863–872.

Varvel, S. A., Wise, L. E., Niyuhire, F., Cravatt, B. F., and Lichtman, A. H. (2007). Inhibition of fatty-acide amide hydrolase accelerates acquisition and extinction rates in a spatial memory task. *Neuropsychopharmacology*, 32, 1032–1041.

Vassoler, F. M., Byrnes, E. M., and Pierce, R. C. (2014). The impact of exposure to addictive drugs on future generations: Physiological and behavioral effects. *Neuropharmacology*, 76, 269–275.

Vaucher, J., Keating, B. J., Lasserre, A. M., Gan, W., Lyall, D. M., Ward, J., Smith, D. J., et al. (2018). Cannabis use and risk of schizophrenia: a Mendelian randomization study. *Mol. Psychiatry*, 23, 1287–1292.

Vearrier, D., and Greenberg, M. I. (2010). Anticholinergic delirium following Datura stramonium ingestion: Implications for the Internet age. *J. Emerg. Trauma Shock*, 3(3), 303. https://doi.org/10.4103/0974-2700.66565

Vegting, Y., Reneman, L., and Booij, J. (2016). The effects of ecstasy on neurotransmitter systems: A review on the findings of molecular imaging studies. *Psychopharmacology*, 233, 3473–3501.

Velasquez, S., and Eugenin, E. A. (2014). Role of pannexin-1 hemichannels and purinergic receptors in the pathogenesis of human diseases. *Front. Physiol.*, 5, 96. doi: 10.3389/fphys.2014.00096.

Velotti, P., Rogier, G., Beomonte Zobel, S., and Billieux, J. (2021). Association between gambling disorder and emotion (dys)regulation: A systematic review and meta-analysis. *Clin. Psychol. Rev.*, 87, 102437. doi.org/10.1016/j.cpr.2021.102037.

Vendruscolo, L. F., Estey, D., Goodell, V., Macshane, L. G., Logrip, M. L., Schlosburg, J. E., et al. (2015). Glucocorticoid receptor antagonism decreases alcohol seeking in alcohol-dependent individuals. *J. Clin. Invest.*, 125, 3193–3197.

Vengeliene, V., Bilbao, A., and Spanagel, R. (2014). The alcohol deprivation effect model for studying relapse behavior: A comparison between rats and mice. *Alcohol*, 48, 313–320.

Venios, K., and Kelly, J. F. (2010). The rise, risks, and realities of methamphetamine use among women: Implications for research, prevention and treatment. *J. Addict. Nursing*, 21, 14–21.

Venniro, M., Banks, M. L., Heilig, M., Epstein, D. H., and Shaham, Y. (2020). Improving translation of animal models of addiction and relapse by reverse translation. *Nat. Rev. Neurosci.*, 21, 625–643.

Venzi, M., Di Giovanni, G., and Crunelli, V. (2015). A critical evaluation of the gamma-hydroxybutyrate (GHB) model of absence seizures. *CNS Neurosci. Ther.*, 21, 123–140.

Verendeev, A., and Riley, A. L. (2013). The role of the aversive effects of drugs in self-administration: assessing the balance of reward and aversion in drug-taking behavior. *Behav. Pharmacol.*, 24, 363–374.

Verharen, J.P.H., Zhu, Y., and Lammel, S. (2020). Aversion hot spots in the dopamine system. *Curr. Opin. Neurobiol.*, 64, 46–52.

Verheul, R., and van den Brink, W. (2000). The role of personality pathology in the aetiology and treatment of substance use disorders. *Curr. Opin. Psychiatry*, 13, 163–169.

Verster, J. C., Aufricht, C., and Alford, C. (2012). Energy drinks mixed with alcohol: Misconceptions, myths, and facts. *Int. J. Gen. Med.*, 5, 187–198.

Verweij, K. J. H., Zietsch, B. P., Lynskey, M. T., Medland, S. E., Neale, M. C., Martin, N. G., et al. (2010). Genetic and environmental influences on cannabis use initiation and problematic use: A meta-analysis of twin studies. *Addiction*, 105, 417–430.

Vigneault, É., Poirel, O., Riad, M., Prud'homme, J., Dumas, S., Turecki, G., et al. (2015). Distribution of vesicular glutamate transporters in the human brain. *Front. Neuroanat.*, 9, 23. doi: 10.3389/fnana.2015.00023.

Viguier, F., Michot, B., Hamon, M., and Bourgoin, S. (2013). Multiple roles of serotonin in pain control mechanisms: Implications of 5-HT7 and other 5-HT receptor subtypes. *Eur. J. Pharmacol.*, 716, 8–16.

Vikelis, M., Spingos, K. C., and Rapoport, A. M. (2015). The iontophoretic transdermal system formulation of sumatriptan as a new option in the acute treatment of migraine: A perspective. *Ther. Adv. Neurol. Dis.*, 8, 160–165.

Vilarim, M. M., Rocha Araujo, D. M., and Nardi, A. E. (2011). Caffeine challenge test and panic disorder: A systematic literature review. *Expert Rev. Neurother.*, 11, 1185–1195.

Vlachou, S., and Panagis, G. (2014). Regulation of brain reward by the endocannabinoid system: A critical review of behavioral studies in animals. *Curr. Pharm. Des.*, 20, 2072–2088.

Vlisides, P. E., Bel-Bahar, T., Nelson, A., Chilton, K., Smith, E., Janke, E., Tarnal, V., et al. (2018). Subanaesthetic ketamine and altered states of consciousness in humans. *Br. J. Anaesth.*, 121, 249–259.

Vogel, E. A., Prochaska, J. J., Ramo, D. E., Andres, J., and Rubinstein, M. L. (2019). Adolescents' e-cigarette use: Increases in frequency, dependence, and nicotine exposure over 12 months. *J. Adolesc. Health*, 64, 770–775.

Vogel-Sprott, M. (1997). Is behavioral tolerance learned? *Alc. Health Res. World*, 21, 161–168.

Vogt, N. M., Kerby, R. L., Dill-McFarland, K. A., Harding, S. J., Merluzzi, A. P., Johnson, S. C., et al. (2017). Cut microbiome alterations in Alzheimer's Disease. *Sci. Rep.*, 7, 13537–13547.

Voigt, J.-P., and Fink, H. (2015). Serotonin controlling feeding and satiety. *Behav. Brain Res.*, 277, 14–31.

Voisin, A. N., Mnie-Filali, O., Giguére, N., Fortin, G. M., Vigneault, E., El Mestikawy, S., Descarrier, L., et al. (2016). Axonal segregation and role of the vesicular glutamate transporter VLUT3 in serotonin neurons. *Front. Neuroanat.*, 10, 39. doi: 10.3389/fnana.2016.00039.

Volk, L, Chiu, S.-L., Sharma, K., and Huganir, R. L. (2015). Glutamate synapses in human cognitive disorders. *Annu. Rev. Neurosci.*, 38, 127–149.

Volkow, N. D., and Koob, G. (2015). Brain disease model of addiction: Why is it so controversial? *Lancet Psychiatry*, 2, 677–679.

Volkow, N. D., and Morales, M. (2015). The brain on drugs: From reward to addiction. *Cell*, 162, 712–725.

Volkow, N. D., Baler, R. D., Compton, W. M., and Weiss, S. R. B. (2014a). Adverse health effects of marijuana use. *N. Engl. J. Med.*, 370, 2219–2227.

Volkow, N. D., Compton, W. M., and Wargo, E. M. (2017). The risks of marijuana use during pregnancy. *JAMA*, 317, 129–130.

Volkow, N. D., Fowler, J. S., and Wang, G. J. (1999a). Imaging studies on the role of dopamine in cocaine reinforcement and addiction in humans. *J. Psychopharmacol.*, 13, 337–345.

Volkow, N. D., Fowler, J. S., Logan, J., Alexoff, D., Zhu, W., Telang, F., et al. (2009). Effects of modafinil on dopamine and dopamine transporters in the male human brain: Clinical implications. *JAMA*, 301, 1148–1154.

Volkow, N. D., Fowler, J. S., Wang, G. J., Baler, R., and Telang, F. (2009). Imaging dopamine's role in drug abuse and addiction. *Neuropharmacology*, 56, 3–8.

Volkow, N. D., Fowler, J. S., Wang, G. J., Telang, F., Logan, J.,

Jayne, M., et al. (2010). Cognitive control of drug craving inhibits brain reward regions in cocaine abusers. *NeuroImage*, 49, 2536–2543.

Volkow, N. D., Koob, G. F., and McLellan, A. T. (2016). Neurobiologic advances from the brain disease model of addiction. *N. Engl. J. Med.*, 374, 363–371.

Volkow, N. D., Michaelides, M., and Baler, R. (2019). The neuroscience of drug reward and addiction. *Physiol. Rev.*, 99, 2115–2140.

Volkow, N. D., Tomasi, D., Wang, G.-J., Logan, J., Alexoff, D. L., Jayne, M., et al. (2014b). Stimulant-induced dopamine increases are markedly blunted in active cocaine abusers. *Mol. Psychiatry*, 19, 1037–1043.

Volkow, N. D., Wang, G.-J., Fischman, M. W., Foltin, R., Fowler, J. S., Franceschi, D., et al. (2000). Effects of route of administration on cocaine induced dopamine transporter blockade in the human brain. *Life Sci.*, 67, 1507–1515.

Volkow, N. D., Wang, G.-J., Fowler, J. S., and Tomasi, D. (2012). Addiction circuitry in the human brain. *Annu. Rev. Pharmacol. Toxicol.*, 52, 321–336.

Volkow, N. D., Wang, G.-J., Fowler, J. S., Gatley, S. J., Logan, J., Ding, Y.-S., et al. (1998). Dopamine transporter occupancies in the human brain induced by therapeutic doses of oral methylphenidate. *Am. J. Psychiatry*, 155, 1325–1331.

Volkow, N. D., Wang, G.-J., Fowler, J. S., Gatley, S. J., Logan, J., Ding, Y.-S., et al. (1999b). Blockade of striatal dopamine transporters by intravenous methylphenidate is not sufficient to induce self-reports of "high." *J. Pharmacol. Exp. Ther.*, 288, 14–20.

Volkow, N. D., Wang, G.-J., Fowler, J. S., Logan, J., Gatley, S. J., Gifford, A., et al. (1999c). Prediction of reinforcing responses to psychostimulants in humans by brain dopamine D2 receptor levels. *Am. J. Psychiatry*, 156, 1440–1443.

Volkow, N. D., Wang, G.-J., Fowler, J. S., Logan, J., Gatley, S. J., Hitzemann, R., et al. (1997). Decreased striatal dopaminergic responsiveness in detoxified cocaine-dependent subjects. *Nature*, 386, 830–833.

Volkow, N. D., Wang, G.-J., Smith, L., Fowler, J. S., Telang, F., Logan, J., et al. (2015). Recovery of dopamine transporters with methamphetamine detoxification is not linked to changes in dopamine release. *NeuroImage*, 121, 20–28.

Volkow, N. D., Wang, G.-J., Telang, F., Fowler, J. S., Alexoff, D., Logan, J., et al. (2014c). Decreased dopamine brain reactivity in marijuana abusers is associated with negative emotionality

and addiction severity. *Proc. Natl. Acad. Sci. USA*, 111, E3149–E3156.

Volkow, N. D., Wang, G.-J., Telang, F., Fowler, J. S., Logan, J., Childress, A.-R., et al. (2006). Cocaine cues and dopamine in dorsal striatum: Mechanism of craving in cocaine addiction. *J. Neurosci.*, 26, 6583–6588.

Vollenweider, F. X., and Kometer, M. (2010). The neurobiology of psychedelic drugs: Implications for the treatment of mood disorders. *Nat. Rev. Neurosci.*, 11, 642–651.

Vollenweider, F. X., and Preller, K. H. (2020). Psychedelic drugs: neurobiology and potential for treatment of psychiatric disorders. *Nat. Rev. Neurosci.*, 21, 611–624.

Volpicelli, J. R, Alterman, A. I., Hayashida, M., and O'Brien, C. P. (1992). Naltrexone in the treatment of alcohol dependence. *Arch. Gen. Psych.*, 49, 876–880.

Vreeker, A., van Bergen, A. H., and Kahn, R. S. (2015). Cognitive enhancing agents in schizophrenia and bipolar disorder. *Eur. Neuropsychopharmacol.*, 25, 969–1002.

Vucic, S., Rothstein, J. D., and Kiernan, M. C. (2014). Advances in treating amyotrophic lateral sclerosis: Insights from pathophysiological studies. *Trends Neurosci.*, 37, 433–442.

Vyas, A., Mitra, R., Rao, B. B. S., and Chattarji, S. (2002). Chronic stress induces contrasting patterns of dendritic remodeling in hippocampal and amygdaloid neurons. *J. Neurosci.*, 22, 6810–6818. © 2002 Society for Neuroscience.

W

Wacker, D., Wang, S., McCorvy, J. D., Betz, R. M., Venkatakrishnan, A. J., Levit, A., et al. (2017). Crystal structure of an LSD-bound human serotonin receptor. *Cell*, 168, 377–389.

Wadha, P. D., Buss, C., Entringer, S., and Swanson, J. M. (2009). Developmental origins of health and disease: Brief history of the approach and current focus on epigenetic mechanisms. *Semin. Reprod. Med.*, 27, 358–368.

Waghule, T., Singhvi, G., Dubey, S. K., Pandey, M. M., Gupta, G., Singh, M., and Dua, K. (2019). Microneedles: A smart approach and increasing potential for transdermal drug delivery system. *Biomed. Pharmacother.*, 109, 1249–1258. https://doi.org/10.1016/j.biopha.2018.10.078

Wahlstrom, D., Collins, P., White, T., and Luciana, M. (2010). Developmental changes in dopamine neurotransmission in adolescence: Behavioral implications and issues in assessment. *Brain Cogn.*, 72, 146–159.

Waldorf, D. (1983). Natural recovery from opiate addiction: Some

social-psychological processes of untreated recovery. *J. Drug Issues*, 13, 237–280.

Walker, B. M., and Koob, G. F. (2008). Pharmacological evidence for a motivational role of kappa-opioid systems in ethanol dependence. *Neuropsychopharmacology*, 33, 643–652.

Walker, D. L., Miles, L. A., and Davis, M. (2009). Selective participation of the bed nucleus of the stria terminalis and CRF in sustained anxiety-like versus phasic fear-like responses. *Prog. NeuroPsychopharmacol. Biol. Psychiatry*, 33, 1291–1308.

Walker, L. C., and Lawrence, A. J. (2020). Allosteric modulation of muscarinic receptors in alcohol and substance use disorders. *Adv. Pharmacol.*, 88, 233–275.

Walker, M. C. (2015). Hippocampal sclerosis: Causes and prevention. *Semin. Neurol.*, 35, 193–200.

Wall, T. L., and Ehlers, C. L. (1995). Genetic influences affecting alcohol use among Asians. *Alcohol Health Res. World*, 19, 184–189.

Wallén-Mackenzie, Å., Wootz, H., and Englund, H. (2010). Genetic inactivation of the vesicular glutamate transporter 2 (VGLUT2) in the mouse: What have we learnt about functional glutamatergic neurotransmission? *Ups. J. Med. Sci.*, 115, 11–20.

Walley, S. C., Wilson, K. M., Winickoff, J. P., and Groner, J. (2019). A public health crisis: Electronic cigarettes, vape, and JUUL. *Pediatrics*, 143(6), e20182741. doi: 10.1542/peds.2018-2741.

Walters, G. D. (2000). Spontaneous remission from alcohol, tobacco, and other drug abuse: Seeking quantitative answers to qualitative questions. *Am. J. Drug Alcohol Abuse*, 26, 443–460.

Walters, G. D., and Gilbert, A. (2000). Defining addiction: Contrasting views of clients and experts. *Addiction Res.*, 8, 211–220.

Wang P., Liang Y., Chen K., Yau S.Y., Sun X., Cheng K.K., et al. (2020) Potential involvement of adiponectin signaling in regulating physical exercise-elicited hippocampal neurogenesis and dendritic morphology in stressed mice. *Front Cell Neurosci.*, 14, 189.

Wang, G.-B., Wu, L.-Z., Yu, P., Li, Y.-J., Ping, X. J., and Cui, C.-L. (2011). Multiple 100 Hz electroacupuncture treatments produced cumulative effect on the suppression of morphine withdrawal syndrome: Central preprodynorphin mRNA and p-CREB implicated. *Peptides*, 32, 713–721.

Wang, H., Gaur, U., Xiao, J., Xu, B., Xu, J., and Zheng, W. (2018). Targeting phosphodiesterase 4 as a po-tential therapeutic strategy for enhancing neuroplasticity following ischemic stroke. *Int. J. Biol. Sci.*, 14, 1745–1754.

Wang, J.-W., Cao, S.-S., and Hu, R.-Y. (2018). Smoking by family members and friends and electronic cigarette use in adolescence: A systematic review and meta analysis. *Tob. Induc. Dis.*, 16, 5. doi: 10.18332/tid/84864.

Wang, Q., Yan, J., Chen, X., Li, J., Yang, Y., Weng, J.-P., et al. (2011). Statins: Multiple neuroprotective mechanisms in neurodegenerative diseases. *Exp. Neurol.*, 230, 27–34.

Wang, R. (2014). Gasotransmitters: Growing pains and joys. *Trends Biochem. Sci.*, 39, 227–232.

Wang, S.-H., and Morris, R. G. M. (2010). Hippocampal-neocortical interactions in memory formation, consolidation, and reconsolidation. *Annu. Rev. Psychol.*, 61, 49–79.

Wang, T. R., Moosa, S., Dallapiazza, R. F., Elias, W. J., and Lynch, W. J. (2018). Deep brain stimulation for the treatment of drug addiction. *Neurosurg. Focus*, 45(2), E11. doi: 10.3171/2018.5.FOCUS18163.

Wang, X., Derakhshandeh, R., Liu, J., Narayan, S., Nabavizadeh, P., Le, S., et al. (2016). One minute of marijuana secondhand smoke exposure substantially impairs vascular endothelial function. *J. Am. Heart Assoc.*, 5, e003858. doi: 10.1161/JAHA.116.003858.

Wang, Y., and Harvey, B. K. (2016). Reducing excitotoxicity with glutamate transporter-1 to treat stroke. *Brain Circ.*, 2, 118–120.

Wang, Y., Fathali, H., Mishra, D., Olsson, T., Keighron, J. D., Skibicka, K. P., and Cans, A.-S. (2019). Counting the number of glutamate molecules in single synaptic vesicles. *J. Am. Chem. Soc.*, 141, 17507–17511.

Wang, Z. Z., Zhang, Y., Zhang, H.-T., and Li, Y.-F. (2015). Phosphodiesterase: An interface connecting cognitive deficits to neuropsychiatric and neurodegenerative diseases. *Curr. Pharm. Des.*, 21, 303–316.

Ward, A. M., Yaman, R., and Ebbert, J. O. (2020). Electronic nicotine delivery system design and aerosol toxicants: A systematic review. *PLOS ONE*, 15(6), e0234189. doi: 10.1371/journal.pone.0234189.

Warf, B. (2011). Hydrocephalus and Its Treatment. Boston Children's Hospital. Published on February 24, 2011. Available at www.youtube.com/watch?v=bHD8zYImKqA.

Warner, D. O. (2018). Anesthesia and neurodevelopment in children. Perhaps the end of the beginning. *Anesthesiology*, 128, 700–703.

Warner, J. J. (2001). Atlas of Neuroanatomy: With Systems Organization and Case Correlations (1e). Boston: ButterworthHeinemann.

Warner, K. E. (1977). The effects of the anti-smoking campaign on cigarette consumption. *Am. J. Public Health*, 67, 645–650.

Warner, K. E. (1981). Cigarette smoking in the 1970's: the impact of the antismoking campaign on consumption. *Science*, 211, 729–731. Reprinted with permission from AAAS and the author.

Warner, K. E. (1985). Cigarette advertising and media coverage of smoking and health. *NEJM*, 312, 384–388.

Wasko, M. J., Witt-Enderby, P. A., and Surratt, C. K. (2018). DARK classics in chemical neuroscience: Ibogaine. *ACS Chem. Neurosci.*, 9. 2475–2483.

Wasson, R. G. (1957). Seeking the magic mushroom. *Life*, 42, 100–115.

Watanabe, S. (2015). Slow or fast? A tale of synaptic vesicle recycling. *Science*, 350, 46–47.

Waterhouse, B. D., and Navarra, R. L. (2019). The locus coeruleus-norepinephrine system and sensory signal processing: A historical review and current perspectives. *Brain Res.*, 1709, 1–15.

Watson, J., Guzzetti, S., Franchi, C., Di Clemente, A., Burbassi, S., Emri, Z., et al. (2010). Gamma-hydroxybutyrate does not maintain self-administration but induces conditioned place preference when injected in the ventral tegmental area. *Int. J. Neuropsychopharmacol.*, 13, 143–153.

Watterson, L. R., and Oive, M. F. (2014). Synthetic cathinones and their rewarding and reinforcing effects in rodents. *Adv. Neurosci.*, 2014, Article 209875. doi: 10.1155/2014/209875.

Watterson, L. R., and Olive, M. F. (2017). Reinforcing effects of cathinone NPS in the intravenous drug self-administration paradigm. *Curr. Top. Behav. Neurosci.*, 32, 133–144.

Wearne, T. A., and Cornish, J. L. (2018). A comparison of methamphetamine-induced psychosis and schizophrenia: A review of positive, negative, and cognitive symptomatology. *Front. Psychiatry*, 9, 491. doi: 10.3389/fpsyt.2018.00491.

Webling, K., Groves-Chapman, J. L., Runesson, J., Saar, I., Lang, A., Sillard, R., et al. (2016). Pharmacological stimulation of GAL1R but not GAL2R attenuates kainic acid-induced neuronal cell death in the rat hippocampus. *Neuropeptides*, 58, 83–92.

Wechsler, H., Dowdall, G. W., Davenport, A., and Castillo, S. (1995a). Correlates of college student binge drinking. *Am. J. Public Health*, 85, 921–926.

Weeks, J. R., and Collins, R. J. (1987). Screening for drug reinforcement using intravenous self-administration in the rat. In M. A. Bozarth (Ed.), *Methods of Assessing the Reinforcing Properties of Abused Drugs*, pp. 35–43. New York: Springer-Verlag.

Weinberger, A. H., Kashan, R. S., Shpigel, D. M., Esan, H., Taha, F., Lee, C. J., et al. (2017). Depression and cigarette smoking behavior: A critical review of population-based studies. *Am. J. Drug Alcohol Abuse*, 43, 416–431.

Weinberger, D. R. (1995). Neurodevelopmental perspectives on schizophrenia. In F. E. Bloom and D. J. Kupfer (Eds.), *Psychopharmacology: The Fourth Generation of Progress*, pp. 1171–1183. New York: Raven.

Weinhold, S. L., Seeck-Hirschner, M., Nowak, A., Hallschmid, M., Göder, R., and Baier, P. C. (2014). The effect of intranasal orexin-A (hypocretin-1) on sleep, wakefulness and attention in narcolepsy with cataplexy. *Behav. Brain Res.*, 262, 8–13.

Weinshenker, N. J., and Siegel, A. (2002). Bimodal classification of aggression: Affective defense and predatory attack. *Aggress. Violent Behav.*, 7, 237–250.

Weinstein, A., and Weinstein, Y. (2014). Exercise addiction: Diagnosis, bio-psychological mechanisms and treatment issues. *Curr. Pharm. Des.*, 20, 4062–4069.

Weir, C. J., Mitchell, S. J., and Lambert, J. J. (2017). Role of $GABA_A$ receptor subtypes in the behavioral effects of intravenous general anesthetics. *Br. J. Anesth.*, 119(S1), i167-i175.

Weisstaub, N. V., Zhou, M., Lira, A., Lambe, E., Gonález-Maeso, J., Hornung, J. P., et al. (2006). Cortical 5HT2A receptor signaling modulates anxiety-like behaviors in mice. *Science*, 313, 536–540.

Wellman, R. J., DiFranza, J. R., and Wood, C. (2006). Tobacco chippers report diminished autonomy over smoking. *Addict. Behav.*, 31, 717–721.

Wellman, R. J., Dugas, E. N., Dutczak, H., O'Loughlin, E. K., Datta, G. D., Lauzon, B., et al. (2016). Predictors of the onset of cigarette smoking: A systematic review of longitudinal population-based studies in youth. *Am. J. Prev. Med.*, 51, 767–778.

Wenger, J. R., Tiffany, T. M., Bombardier, C., Nicoins, K., and Woods, S. C. (1981). Ethanol tolerance in the rat is learned. *Science*, 213, 575–576.

Wennogle, L. P., Hoxie, H., Peng, Y., and Hendrick, J. P. (2017). Phosphodiesterase 1, A unique drug target for degenerative diseases and cognitive dysfunction. *Adv. Neurobiol.*, 17, 349–384.

Wenthur, C. J. (2016). Classics in chemical neuroscience: Methylphenidate. *ACS Chem. Neurosci.*, 7, 1030–1040.

Wenzel, J. M., and Cheer, J. F. (2014). Endocannabinoid-dependent modulation of phasic dopamine signaling encodes external and internal reward-predictive cues. *Front. Psychiatry*, 5, 118. doi: 10.3389/fpsyt.2014.00118.

Wenzel, J. M., and Cheer, J. F. (2018). Endocannabinoid regulation of reward and reinforcement through interaction with dopamine and endogenous opioid signaling. *Neuropsychopharmacology*, 43, 103–115.

Werneck, M. A., Kortas, G. T., de Andrade, A. G., and Castaldelli-Maia, J. M. (2018). A systematic review of the efficacy of cannabinoid agonist replacement therapy for cannabis withdrawal symptoms. *CNS Drugs*, 32, 1113–1129.

Werner, C. T., Altshuler, R. D., Shaham, Y., and Li, X. (2021). Epigenetic mechanisms in drug relapse. *Biol. Psychiatry*, 89(4), 331–338. https://doi.org/10.1016/j.biopsych.2020.08.005

Wesensten, N. J. (2014). Legitimacy of concerns about caffeine and energy drink consumption. *Nutr. Rev.*, 72 (Suppl. 1), 78–86.

Wess, J., Eglen, R. M., and Gautam, D. (2007). Muscarinic acetylcholine receptors: Mutant mice provide new insights for drug development. *Nat. Rev. Drug Discov.*, 6, 721–733.

West, L. J., Pierce, C. M., and Thomas, W. D. (1962). Lysergic acid diethylamide: Its effects on a male Asiatic elephant. *Science*, 138, 1100–1103.

Westlye, L. T., Kaufmann, T., Alnæs, D., Hullstein, I. R., and Bjørnebekk, A. (2016). Brain connectivity aberrations in anabolic-androgenic steroid users. *NeuroImage Clin.*, 13, 62–69.

Weston-Green, K., Huang, X.-F., and Deng, C. (2013). Second generation antipsychotic-induced type 2 diabetes: A role for the muscarinic M3 receptor. *CNS Drugs*, 27, 1069–1080.

Westwater, M. L., Fletcher, P. C., and Ziauddeen, H. (2016). Sugar addiction: The state of the science. *Eur. J. Nutr.*, 55(Suppl. 2), S55–S69.

Whayne, T. F. (2015). Coffee: A selected overview of beneficial or harmful effects on the cardiovascular system? *Curr. Vasc. Pharmacol.*, 13, 637–648.

Wheeler, M. A., Smith, C. J., Ottolini, M., Barker, B. S., Purohit, A. M., Grippo, R. M., et al. (2016). Genetically targeted magnetic control of the nervous system. *Nat. Neurosci.*, 19, 756–761.

Whetstine, L. M. (2015). Cognitive enhancement: Treating or cheating? *Semin. Pediatr. Neurol.*, 22, 172–176.

Whitaker-Azmitia, P. M. (1999). The discovery of serotonin and its role in neuroscience. *Neuropsychopharmacology*, 21, 2S–8S.

White, A. M., MacInnes, E., Hingson, R. W., and Pan, I. J. (2013). Hospitalizations for suicide-related drug poisonings and co-occurring alcohol overdoses in adolescents (ages 12–17) and young adults (ages 18–24) in the United States, 1999– 2008, Results from the Nationwide Inpatient Sample. *Suicide Life Threat Behav.*, 43, 198–212.

White, C. M. (2016). The pharmacologic and clinical effects of illicit synthetic cannabinoids. *J. Clin. Pharmacol.*, 57, 297–304.

White, C. M. (2018). Why Synthetic Marijuana Is So Risky. Available at https://www.inquirer.com/philly/health/why-synthetic-marijuana-is-so-risky-20181016.html (accessed 2/12/21).

Whitesell, M., Bachand, A., Peel, J., and Brown, M. (2013). Familial, social, and individual factors contributing to risk for adolescent substance use. *J. Addict.*, 2013, 579310. doi: 10.1155/2013/579310.

Whiting, P. F., Wolff, R. F., Deshpande, S., Di Nisio, M., Duffy, S., Hernandez, A. V., et al. (2015). Cannabinoids for medical use: A systematic review and metaanalysis. *JAMA*, 313, 2456–2473.

Wibawa, P., Zombor, R., Dragovic, M., Hayhow, B., Lee, J., Panegyres, P. K., Rock, D., and Starkstein, S. E. (2020) Anosognosia is associated with greater caregiver burden and poorer executive function in Huntington Disease. *J. Geriatric Psychiatry*, 33(1), 52–58.

Wichterle, H., Lieberam, I., Porter, J. A., and Jessell, T. M. (2002). Directed differentiation of embryonic stem cells into motor neurons. *Cell*, 110, 385–397.

Wickham, R. J. (2015). How menthol alters tobacco-smoking behavior: A biological perspective. *Yale J. Biol. Med.*, 88, 279–287.

Wielenga, V., and Gilchrist, D. (2013). From gold-medal glory to prohibition: The early evolution of cocaine in the United Kingdom and the United States. *J. R. Soc. Med. Open.* doi: 10.1177/2042533313478324.

Wikler, A. (1980). *Opioid Dependence.* New York: Plenum Press.

Wilder, R. T. (2010). Is there any relationship between long-term behavior disturbance and early exposure to anesthesia? *Curr. Opin. Anaesthesiol.*, 23, 332–336.

Wilkinson, D., Windfeld, K., and ColdingJørgensen, E. (2014). Safety and efficacy of idalopirdine, a 5-HT6 receptor antagonist, in patients with moderate Alzheimer's disease (LADDER): A randomised, double-blind, placebo-controlled phase 2 trial. *Lancet Neurol.*, 13, 1092–1099.

Willard, S. S., and Koochekpour, S. (2013). Glutamate, glutamate receptors, and downstream signaling pathways. *Int. J. Biol. Sci.*, 9, 948–959.

Williams, C. M., Rogers, P. J., and Kirkham, T. C. (1998). Hyperphagia in pre-fed rats following oral Δ^9-THC. *Physiol. Behav.*, 65, 343–346.

Williams, J. T., Ingram, S. L., Henderson, G., Chavkin, C., von Zastrow, M., Schulz, S., et al. (2013). Regulation of μ-opioid receptors: Desensitization, phosphorylation, internalization, and tolerance. *Pharmacol. Rev.*, 65, 223–254.

Williams, M., and Talbot, P. (2019). Design features in multiple generations of electronic cigarette atomizers. *Int. J. Environ. Res. Public Health*, 16, 2904. doi: 10.3390/ijerph.16162904.

Williams, R. H., and Erickson, T. (2000). Evaluating hallucinogenic or psychedelic drug intoxication in an emergency setting. *Lab. Med.*, 31, 394–401.

Willner, P. (1985). Antidepressants and serotonergic neurotransmission: an integrative review. *Psychopharmacology*, 85, 387–404.

Wills, T. A., Knight, R., Williams, R. J., Pagano, I., and Sargent, J. D. (2015). Risk factors for exclusive e-cigarette use and dual e-cigarette use and tobacco use in adolescents. *Pediatrics*, 135, e43. doi: 10.1542/peds.2014–0760.

Wills, T. A., Soneji, S. S., Choi, K., Jaspers, I., and Tam, E. K. (2020). E-cigarette use and respiratory disorder: An integrative review of converging evidence from epidemiological and laboratory studies. *Eur. Respir. J.*, in press.

Willson, C. (2018). The clinical toxicology of caffeine: A review and case study. *Toxicol. Rep.*, 5, 1140–1152.

Wilson, G. T., and Lawson, D. W. (1976). The effects of alcohol on sexual arousal in women. *J. Abnorm. Psychol.*, 85, 489–497.

Wilson, L. S., and Brandon, N. J. (2015). Emerging biology of PDE10A. *Curr. Pharm. Des.*, 21, 378–388.

Wilson, N., and Gartner, C. (2016). Brief Technical Report. Potential Range of Relative Harm from E-cigarettes for Major Health Conditions for Use in Modelling Work: Based on Recent Biomarker Studies. Available at tobacco.ucsf.edu/sites/ tobacco.ucsf.edu/files/u9/Wilson-Estimates%20of%20e-cig%20impacts%20 for%20Potential%20Modelling%20 29%20June.pdf.

Wiltschko, A. B., Tsukahara, T., Zeine, A., Anyoha, R., Gillis, W. F., Markowitz, J. E., Peterson, R. E., et al. (2020). Revealing the structure of pharmacobehavioral space through motion sequencing. *Nat. Neurosci.*, 23(11), 1433–1443. https://doi.org/10.1038/ s41593-020-00706-3145–160.

Wimmer, M. E., Briand, L. A., Fant, B., Guercio, L. A., Arreola, A. C., Schmidt, H. D., et al. (2017). Paternal cocaine taking elicits epigenetic remodeling and memory deficits in male progeny. *Mol. Psychiatry*, 22, 1641–1650.

Windle, M., and Davies, P. T. (1999). Developmental theory and research. In K. E. Leonard and H. T. Blane (Eds.), *Psychological Theories of Drinking and Alcoholism* (2nd ed.), pp. 164–202. New York: Guilford.

Winstock, A. R., and Barratt, M. J. (2013). Synthetic cannabis: A comparison of patterns of use and effect profile with natural cannabis in a large global sample. *Drug Alcohol Depend.*, 131, 106–111.

Winstock, A., Lynskey, M., Borschmann, R., and Waldron, J. (2015). Risk of emergency medical treatment following consumption of cannabis or synthetic cannabinoids in a large global sample. *J. Psychopharmacol.*, 29, 698–703.

Winterer, G., and Weinberger, D. R. (2004). Genes, dopamine and cortical signal-to-noise ratio in schizophrenia. *Trends Neurosci.*, 27, 683–690.

Winters, K. C., Mader, J., Budney, A. J., Stanger, C., Knapp, A. A., and Walker, D. D. (2020). Interventions for cannabis use disorder. *Curr. Opin. Psychol.*, 38, 67–74.

Winzer-Serhan, U. H. (2008). Long-term consequences of maternal smoking and developmental chronic nicotine exposure. *Front. Biosci.*, 13, 636–649.

Wise, L. E., Thorpe, A. J., and Lichtman, A. H. (2009). Hippocampal CB_1 receptors mediate the memory impairing effects of Δ^9-tetrahydrocannabinol. *Neuropsychopharmacology*, 34, 2072–2080. doi.org/10.1038/npp.2009.31.

Wise, R. A. (1980). The dopamine synapse and the notion of "pleasure centers" in the brain. *Trends Neurosci.*, 3, 91–95.

Wise. J. (2020). Government Orders Urgent Review of Date Rape Drugs. *BMJ*, 368, m51. doi: 10.1136/bmj.m51.

Wiskerke, J., Pattij, T., Schoffelmeer, A.N.M., and De Vries, T. J. (2008). The role of CB_1 receptors in psychostimulant addiction. *Addict. Biol.*, 13, 225–238.

Wisor, J. (2013). Modafinil as a catecholaminergic agent: Empirical evidence and unanswered questions. *Front. Neurol.*, 4, 139. doi: 10.3389/ fneur.2013.00139.

Witkin, J. M., Statnick, M. A., Rorick-Kehn, L. M., Pintar, J. E., Ansonoff, M., Chen, Y., Tucker, R. C., et al. (2014). The biology of Nociceptin/Orphanin FQ (N/OFQ) related to obesity, stress, anxiety, mood, and drug dependence. *Pharmacol. Therapeutics*, 141(3), 283–299. https://doi.org/10.1016/j. pharmthera.2013.10.011

Wittchen, H.-U., Zhao, S., Kessler, R. C., and Eaton, W. W. (1994). DSM-III-R generalized anxiety disorder in the National Comorbidity Survey. *Arch. Gen. Psychiatry*, 51, 355–364.

Witte, A. V., and Flöel, A. (2012). Effects of COMT polymorphisms on brain function and behavior in health and disease. *Brain Res. Bull.*, 88, 418–428.

Wittenberg, R. E., Wolfman, S. L., De Biasi, M., and Dani, J. A. (2020). Nicotinic acetylcholine receptors and nicotine addiction: A brief introduction. *Neuropharmacology*, 177, 108256. doi: 10.1016/j. neuropharm.2020.108256.

Wolf, D., Klasen, M., Eisner, P., Zepf, F. D., Zvyagintsev, M., Palomero-Gallagher, N., Weber, R., et al. (2018). Central serotonin modulates neural responses to virtual violent actions in emotion regulation networks. *Brain Struct. Funct.*, 223, 3327–3345.

Wolf, J., Urits, I., Orhurhu, V., Peck, J., Orhurhu, M. S., Giacomazzi, S., Smoots, D., et al. (2020). The role of the cannabinoid system in pain control: Basic and clinical implications. *Curr. Pain Headache Rep.*, 24(7), 35. doi: 10.1007/ s11916-020-00873-9.

Wolf, M. E., and Tseng, K. Y. (2012). Calcium-permeable AMPA receptors in the VTA and nucleus accumbens after cocaine exposure: When, how, and why? *Front. Mol. Neurosci.*, 5, 72. doi: 10.3389/fnmol.2012.00072.

Wolf, M. E. (2016). Synaptic mechanisms underlying persistent cocaine craving. *Nat. Rev. Neurosci.*, 17, 351–365.

Wolff, K., and Winstock, A. R. (2006). Ketamine: From medicine to misuse. *CNS Drugs*, 20, 199–218.

Wolfman, S. L., Gill, D. F., Bogdanic, F., Long, K., Al-Hasani, R., McCall, J. G., Bruchas, M. R., et al. (2018). Nicotine aversion is mediated by GABAergic interpeduncular nucleus inputs to laterodorsal tegmentum. *Nat. Commun.*, 9, 2710. doi: 10.1038/ s41467-018-04654-2.

Wolfrum, L. A., Nordmeyer, A. S., Racine, C. W., and Nichols, S. D. (2019). Loperamide-associated opioid use disorder and proposal of an alternative treatment with buprenorphine. *J. Addict. Med.*, 13(3), 245–247. https://doi.org/10.1097/ ADM.0000000000000472

Wolk, D. A., Price, J. C., Saxton, J. A., Snitz, B. E., James, J. A., Lopez, O. L., et al. (2009). Amyloid imaging in mild cognitive impairment subtypes. *Ann. Neurol.*, 65, 557–568.

Wong, C. C. Y., Mill, J., and Fernandes, C. (2011). Drugs and addiction: An introduction to epigenetics. *Addiction*, 106, 480–489.

Wong, D. F., Kuwabara, H., Schretlen, D. J., Bonson, K. R., Zhou, Y., Nandi, A., et al. (2006). Increased occupancy of dopamine receptors in human striatum during cue-elicited cocaine craving.

Neuropsychopharmacology, 31, 2716–2727.

Wood, D. M., Brailsford, A. D., and Dargan, P. I. (2011a). Acute toxicity and withdrawal syndromes related to gamma-hydroxybutyrate (GHB) and its analogues gamma-butyrolactone (GBL) and 1,4-butanediol (1,4-BD). *Drug Test. Analysis*, 3, 417–425.

Wood, D. M., Green, S. I., and Dargan, P. I. (2011b). Clinical pattern of toxicity associated with the novel synthetic cathinone mephedrone. *Emerg. Med. J.*, 28, 280–282.

Wood, R. I. (2008). Anabolic–androgenic steroid dependence? Insights from animals and humans. *Front. Neuroendocrinol.*, 29, 490–506.

Wood, R. I., Johnson, L. R., Chu, L., Schad, C., and Self, D. W. (2004). Testosterone reinforcement: Intravenous and intracerebroventricular self-administration in male rats and hamsters. *Psychopharmacology*, 171, 298–305.

Wood, R. I., and Stanton, S. J. (2012). Testosterone and sport: current perspectives. *Horm. Behav.*, 61, 147–155.

Woodman, G. F. (2010). A brief introduction to the use of event-related potentials (erps) in studies of perception and attention. *Atten. Percept. Psychophys.*, 72, 2031–2046.

Woods, J. H., France, C. P., Winger, G., Bertalmio, A. J., and Schwarz-Stevens, K. (1993). Opioid abuse liability assessment in rhesus monkeys. In A. Herz (Ed.), Opioids II, Volume 104, *Handbook of Experimental Pharmacology*, (pp. 609– 632). New York: Springer-Verlag.

Woods, J. H., Katz, J. L., and Winger, G. (1995). Abuse and therapeutic use of benzodiazepines and benzodiazepinelike drugs. In F. E. Bloom and D. J. Kupfer (Eds.), *Psychopharmacology: The Fourth Generation of Progress*, pp. 1777– 1789. New York: Raven.

Woodward, J. J., and Beckley, J. (2014). Effects of the abused inhalant toluene on the mesolimbic dopamine system. *J. Drug Alcohol Res.*, 3, 235838. doi: 10.4303/jdar/235858.

Wootten, D., Christopoulos, A., and Sexton, P. M. (2013). Emerging paradigms in GPCR allostery: Implications for drug discovery. *Nat. Rev. Drug Discov.*, 12, 630–644.

World Drug Report 2020. United Nations publications, Sales No. E.20.XI.6.

World Health Organization (2020). Tobacco. https://www.who.int/news-room/fact-sheets/detail/tobacco. Accessed 1/14/21.

World Health Organization (WHO). (2016a). Tobacco. WHO Media Centre. Fact Sheets. Available at www.who.int/mediacentre/factsheets/fs339/ en/.

World Health Organization (WHO). (2016b). ICD-10 Version:2016. WHO.apps.who.int/classifications/icd10/browse/2016/en#/.

Worob, A., and Wenthur, C. (2020). DARK classics in chemical neuroscience: Synthetic cannabinoids (Spice/K2). *ACS Chem. Neurosci.*,11, 3881–3892.

Worrell, S. D., and Gould, T. J. (2021). Therapeutic potential of ketamine for alcohol use disorder. *Neurosci. Biobehav. Rev.*, 126, 573–589. https://doi.org/10.1016/j.neubiorev.2021.05.006

Wrenn, C. C., and Wiley, R. G. (1998). The behavioral functions of the cholinergic basal forebrain: Lessons from 192 IgG-saporin. *Int. J. Dev. Neurosci.*, 16, 595–602.

Wright, M. E., Ginsberg, C., Parkison, A. M., Dubose, M., and Shores, E. (2021). Outcomes of mothers and newborns to prenatal exposure to kratom: A systematic review. *J. Perinatol.*, 1–8. https://doi.org/10.1038/s41372-021-00952-8

Wu, G. D., Chen, J., Hoffmann, C., Bittinger, K., Chen, Y.-Y., Keilbaugh, S. A., et al. (2011). Linking long-term dietary patterns with gut microbial enterotypes. *Science*, 334, 105–108.

Wu, L.-G., Hamid, E., Shin, W., and Chiang, H.-C. (2014). Exocytosis and endocytosis: Modes, functions, and coupling mechanisms. *Annu. Rev. Physiol.*, 76, 301–331.

Wu, Q. J., and Tymianski, M. (2018). Targeting NMDA receptors in stroke: new hope in neuroprotection. *Mol. Brain*, 11, 15. doi: 10.1186/s13041-018-0357-8.

Wu, T.-C., Tashkin, D. P., Djahed, B., and Rose, J. E. (1988). Pulmonary hazards of smoking marijuana as compared with tobacco. *New Engl. J. Med.*, 318, 347–351.

Wu, Z.-S., Cheng, H., Jiang, Y., Melcher, K., and Xu, H. E. (2015). Ion channels gated by acetylcholine and serotonin: Structures, biology and drug discovery. *Acta Pharmacol. Sin.*, 36, 895–907.

Wuo-Silva, R., Fukushiro, D. F., Borçoi, A. R., Fernandes, H. A., Procópio-Souza, R., Hollais, A. W., Santos, R., et al. (2011). Addictive potential of modafinil and cross-sensitization with cocaine: a pre-clinical study. *Addict. Biol.*, 16, 566–579.

Wyler, S. C., Lord, C. C., Lee, S., Elmquist, J. K., and Liu, C. (2017). Serotonergic control of metabolic homeostasis. *Front. Cell. Neurosci.*, 11, 277. doi: 10.3389/fncel.2017.00277.

X

Xiang, Y., Li, L., Ma, X., Li, S., Xue, Y., Yan, P., Chen, M., et al. (2021). Recreational nitrous oxide abuse: Prevalence, neurotoxicity, and treatment. *Neurotox. Res.*, 39, 975–985.

Xiao, C., Zhou, C.-Y., Jiang, J.-H., and Yin, C. (2020). Neural circuits and nicotinic acetylcholine receptors mediate the cholinergic regulation of midbrain dopaminergic neurons and nicotine dependence. *Acta Pharmacol. Sin.*, 41, 1–9.

Xie, W., Kathuria, H., Galiatsatos, P., Blaha, M. J., Hamburg, N. M., Robertson, R. M., Bhatnagar, A., et al. (2020). Association of electronic cigarette use with incident respiratory conditions among US adults from 2013 to 2018. *JAMA Network Open*, 3(11), e2020816. doi: 10.1001/jamanetworkopen.2020.20816.

Xu, F., Gainetdinov, R. R., Wetsel, W. C., Jones, S. R., Bohn, L. M., Miller, G. W., et al. (2000). Mice lacking the norepinephrine transporter are supersensitive to psychostimulants. *Nat. Neurosci.*, 3, 465–471.

Xu, J., Ou, H., Sun, P., Qin, S., and Yuan, T.-F (2021). Brief report: Predictors of relapse for patients with dextromethorphan dependence. *Am. J. Addict.*, 30, 192–194.

Xu, K., and Lipsky, R. H. (2015). Repeated ketamine administration alters N-methyl-D-aspartic acid receptor subunit gene expression: Implication of genetic vulnerability for ketamine abuse and ketamine psychosis in humans. *Exp. Biol. Med.*, 240, 145–155.

Xu, M., Guo, Y., Vorhees, C. V., and Zhang, J. (2000). Behavioral responses to cocaine and amphetamine administration in mice lacking the dopamine D1 receptor. *Brain Res.*, 852, 198–207.

Xu, M., Hu, X.-T., Cooper, D. C., Moratalla, R., Graybiel, A. M., White, F. J., et al. (1994). Elimination of cocaine-induced hyperactivity and dopamine-mediated neurophysiological effects in dopamine D1 receptor mutant mice. *Cell*, 79, 945–955.

Xu, W., Li, H., Wang, L., Zhang, J., Liu, C., Wan, X., Liu, X., et al. (2020). Endocannabinoid signaling regulates the reinforcing and psychostimulant effects of ketamine in mice. *Nat. Commun.*, 11, 5962. doi: 10.1038/s41467-020-19780-z.

Xu, X. M., Wei, Y. D., Liu, Y., and Li, Z. X. (2019). Gamma-hydroxybutyrate (GHB) for narcolepsy in adults: an updated systematic review and meta-analysis. *Sleep Med.*, 64, 62–70.

Y

Yalcin, E., and de la Monte, S. (2016). Tobacco nitrosamines as culprits in disease: Mechanisms reviewed. *J. Physiol. Biochem.*, 72, 107–120.

Yamaguchi, T. (2021). Neural circuit mechanisms of sex and fighting in males. *Neurosci. Res.*, in press.

Yamamoto, D. J., Nelson, A. M., Mandt, B. H., Larson, G. A.,

Rorabaugh, J. M., Ng, C. M. C., et al. (2013). Rats classified as low or high cocaine locomotor responders: A unique model involving striatal dopamine transporters that predicts cocaine addiction-like behaviors. *Neurosci. Biobehav. Rev.*, 37, 1738–1753.

Yan, J., and Jiang, H. (2014). Dual effects of ketamine: Neurotoxicity versus neuroprotection in anesthesia for the developing brain. *J. Neurosurg. Anesthesiol.*, 26, 155–160.

Yan, Y., Peng, C., Arvin, M. C., Jin, X.-T., Kim, V. J., Ramsey, M. D., Wang, Y., et al. (2018). Nicotinic cholinergic receptors in VTA glutamate neurons modulate excitatory transmission. *Cell Rep.*, 23, 2236–2244.

Yang, C. R., and Chen, L. (2005). Targeting prefrontal cortical dopamine D1 and N-methyl-d-aspartate receptor interactions in schizophrenia treatment. *Neuroscientist*, 11, 452–470.

Yang, X. W., and Lu, X.-H. (2011). Molecular and cellular basis of obsessive-compulsive disorder-like behaviors: Emerging view from mouse models. *Curr. Opin. Neurol.*, 24, 114–118.

Yang, X., Wang, Y., Li, Q., Zhong, Y., Chen, L., Du, Y., He, J., et al. (2018). The main molecular mechanisms underlying methamphetamine-induced neurotoxicity and implications for pharmacological treatment. *Front. Mol. Neurosci.*, 11, 186. doi: 10.3389/fnmol.2018.00186.

Yang, Z., Li, J., Gui, X., Shi, X., Bao, Z., Han, H., and Li, M. D. (2020). Updated review of research on the gut microbiota and their relation to depression in animals and human beings. *Mol. Psychiatry*, in press.

Yarnell, S. (2015). The use of medicinal marijuana for posttraumatic stress disorder: A review of the current literature. *Prim. Care Companion CNS Disord.*, 17, 3. doi: 10.4088/PCC.15r01786.

Yau, S.-Y., Lau, B. W.-M., Tong, J.-B., Wong, R., Ching, Y.-P., Qiu, G., et al. (2011). Hippocampal neurogenesis and dendritic plasticity support running-improved spatial learning and depression-like behaviour in stressed rats. *PLOS ONE*, 6, e24263. doi: 10.1371/journal. pone.0024263.

Yau, S.-Y., Li, A., Zhang, E. D., Christie, B. R., Xu, A., Lee, T. M., and So, K. F. (2014). Sustained running in rats administered corticosterone prevents the development of depressive behaviors and enhances hippocampal neurogenesis and synaptic plasticity without increasing neurotrophic factor levels. *Cell Transplant.*, 23, 481–492.

Yehuda, R., Bierer, L. M., Schmeidler, J., Aferiat, D. H., Breslau, I., and Dolan, S. (2000). Low cortisol and risk for PTSD in adult offspring of holocaust survivors. *Am. J. Psychiatry*, 157, 1252–1259.

Yehuda, R., Marshall, R., and Giller, E. L. (1998). Psychopharmacological treatment of post-traumatic stress disorder. In P. E. Nathan and J. M. Gorman (Eds.), *A Guide to Treatments That Work*, pp. 377–407. New York: Oxford University Press.

Yehuda, R., Pratchett, L. C., Elmes, M. W., Lehrner, A., Daskalakis, N. P., Koch, E., et al. (2014). Glucocorticoid-related predictors and correlates of post-traumatic stress disorder treatment response in combat veterans. *Interface Focus*, 4, 20140048. doi: dx.doi.org/10.1098/rsfs.2014.0048.

Yeomans, J., Forster, G., and Blaha, C. (2001). M5 muscarinic receptors are needed for slow activation of dopamine neurons and for rewarding brain stimulation. *Life Sci.*, 68, 2449–2456.

Yogaratnam, J., Biswas, N., Vadivel, R., and Jacob, R. (2013). Metabolic complications of schizophrenia and antipsychotic medications—An updated review. *East Asian Arch. Psychiatry.*, 23, 21–28.

Yorgason, J. T., Jones, S. R., and España, R. A. (2011). Low and high affinity dopamine transporter inhibitors block dopamine uptake within 5 sec of intravenous injection. *Neuroscience,* 182, 125–132.

Young, A. M., and Goudie, A. J. (1995). Adaptive processes regulating tolerance to behavioral effects of drugs. In F. E. Bloom and D. J. Kupfer (Eds.), *Psychopharmacology: The Fourth Generation of Progress*, pp. 733–742. New York: Raven Press.

Young, E. A. (1993). Induction of the intermediate lobe POMC system with chronic swim stress and β-adrenergic modulation of this induction. *Neuroendocrinology*, 52, 405–411.

Young, J. W., Henry, B. L., and Geyer, M. A. (2011). Predictive animal models of mania: Hits, misses and future directions. *Br. J. Pharmacol.*, 164, 1263–1284.

Young, S. (2013). Marijuana Stops Child's Severe Seizures. CNN. Available at www.cnn.com/2013/08/07/health/charlotte-child-medical-marijuana/.

Youssef, E. A., Berry-Kravis, E., Czech, C., Hagerman, R. J., Hessl, D., Wong, C. Y., Rabbia, M., et al. (2018). Effect of the mGluR5-NAM basimglurant on behavior in adolescents and adults with fragile X syndrome in a randomized, double-blind, placebo-controlled trial: FragXis phase 2 results. *Neuropsychopharmacology*, 43, 503–512.

Yu, C., and McClellan, J. (2016). Genetics of substance use disorders. *Child Adolesc. Psychiatr. Clin. N. Am.*, 25, 377–385.

Yu, D. (2011). Translational research: current status, challenges and future strategies. *Am. J. Transl. Res.*, 3, 422–433.

Yu, H., Li, Q., Wang, D., Shi, L., Lu, G., Sun, L., et al. (2012). Mapping the central effects of chronic ketamine administration in an adolescent primate model by functional magnetic resonance imaging (fMRI). *Neurotoxicology*, 33, 70–77.

Yuan, B. W., Yang, I., Simmons, D. J., O'Leary, J., Lei, J., Brunetti, L., Asal, N., et al. (2019). Evaluation of nonmedical use of prescription stimulants by college students at three northeastern pharmacy schools. *J. Am. Coll. Clin. Pharm.*, 2, 525–530.

Yuan, M., Cross, S. J., Loughlin, S. E., and Leslie, F. M. (2015). Nicotine and the adolescent brain. *J. Physiol.*, 593, 339–3412.

Yuste, R. (2010). *Dendritic Spines*. Cambridge, MA: MIT Press.

Z

Zaami, S., Giorgetti, R., Pichini, S., Pantano, F., Marinelli, E., and Busardo, F. P. (2018). Synthetic cathinones related fatalities: an update. *Eur. Rev. Med. Pharmacol. Sci.*, 22, 268–274.

Zadina, J. E., Martin-Schild, S., Gerall, A. A., Kastin, A. J., Hackler, L., Ge, L. J., et al. (1999). Endomorphins: Novel endogenous mu-opiate receptor agonists in regions of high mu-opiate receptor density. *Ann. N. Y. Acad. Sci.*, 897, 136–144.

Zajecka, J. (1993). Pharmacology, pharmacokinetics, and safety issues of mood-stabilizing agents. *Psychiatr. Ann.*, 23, 79–85.

Zajecka, J., Tracy, K. A., and Mitchell, S. (1997). Discontinuation symptoms after treatment with serotonin reuptake inhibitors: A literature review. *J. Clin. Psychiatry*, 58, 291–297.

Zalcman, G., Federman, N., and Romano, A. (2018). CaMKII isoforms in learning and memory: Localization and function. *Front. Mol. Neurosci.*, 11, 445. doi: 10.3389/fnmol.2018.00445.

Zalewska-Kaszubska, J. (2015). Is immunotherapy an opportunity for effective treatment of drug addiction? *Vaccine*, 33, 6545–6551.

Zamberletti, E., and Rubino, T. (2020). Impact of endocannabinoid system manipulation on neurodevelopmental processes relevant to schizophrenia. *Biol. Psychiatry Cogn. Neurosci. Neuroimaging*, in press.

Zamberlin, F., Sanz, C., Vivot, R. M., Pallavicini, C., Erowid, F., Erowid, E., and Tagliazucchi, E. (2018). The varieties of the psychedelic experience: A preliminary study of the association between the reported subjective effects and the binding affinity profiles of substituted phenethylamines

and tryptamines. *Front. Integr. Neurosci.*, 12, 54. doi: 10.3389/fnint.2018.00054.

Zamora, E. R., and Edwards, S. (2014). Neuronal extracellular signal-regulated kinase (ERK) activity as marker and mediator of alcohol and opioid dependence. *Front. Integr. Neurosci.*, 8, 24. doi: 10.3389/fnint.2014.00024.

Zanda, M. T., Fadda, P., Chiamulera, C., Fratta, W., and Fattore, L. (2016). Methoxetamine, a novel psychoactive substance with serious adverse pharmacological effects: A review of case reports and preclinical findings. *Behav. Pharmacol.*, 27, 489–496.

Zanfirescu, A., Ungurianu, A., Tsatsakis, A. M., Niţulescu, G. M., Kouretas, D., Veskoukis, A., Tsoukalas, D., et al. (2019). A review of the alleged health hazards of monosodium glutamate. *Compr. Rev. Food Sci. Food Safety*, 18, 1111–1134.

Zanos P., Gould T.D. (2018) Mechanisms of ketamine action as an antidepressant. *Mol Psychiatry*, 23(4), 801–811.

Zanos, P., Moaddel, R., Morris, P. J., Georgiou, P., Fischell, J., Elmer, G. I., et al. (2016). NMDAR inhibition-independent antidepressant actions of ketamine metabolites. *Nature*, 533, 481–486.

Zare, S., Nemati, M., and Zheng, Y. (2018). A systematic review of consumer preference for e-cigarette attributers: Flavor, nicotine strength, and type. *PLoS ONE*, 13(3), e0194145. doi: 10.1371/journal.pone.0194145.

Zarei, S., Carr, K., Reiley, L., Diaz, K., Guerra, O., Altamirano, P. F., et al. (2015). A comprehensive review of amyotrophic lateral sclerosis. *Surg. Neurol. Int.*, 6, 171. doi: 10.4103/2152-7806.169561.

Zawilska, J. B. (2014). Methoxetamine a novel recreational drug with potent hallucinogenic properties. *Toxicol. Lett.*, 230, 402–407.

Zawilska, J. B., and Wojcieszak, J. (2013). *Salvia divinorum*: From Mazatec medicinal and hallucinogenic plant to emerging recreational drug. *Hum. Psychopharmacol.*, 28, 403–412.

Zdanowicz, M. M., and Adams, P. W. (2014). The pharmacogenetics of nicotine dependence and smoking cessation therapies. *J. Pharmacogenetics Pharmacoproteomics*, 5, 138. doi: 10.4172/2153-0645.1000138.

Zedler, B. K., Mann, A. L., Kim, M. M., Amick, H. R., Joyce, A. R., Murrelle, E. L., and Jones, H. E. (2016). Buprenorphine compared with methadone to treat pregnant women with opioid use disorder: A systematic review and meta-analysis of safety in the mother, fetus and child. *Addiction*, 111, 2115–2128.

Zeidler, S., de Boer, H., Hukema, R. K., and Willemsen, R. (2017).

Combination therapy in fragile X syndrome: Possibilities and pitfalls illustrated by targeting the mGluR5 and GABA pathway simultaneously. *Front. Mol. Neurosci.*, 10, 368. doi: 10.3389/fnmol.2017.00368.

Zernig, G., and Pinheiro, B. S. (2015). Dyadic social interaction inhibits cocaine-conditioned place preference and the associated activation of the accumbens corridor. *Behav. Pharmacol.*, 26, 580–594.

Zernig, G., Kummer, K. K., and Prast, J. M. (2013). Dyadic social interaction as an alternative reward to cocaine. *Front. Psychiatry*, 4, 100. doi: 10.3389/fpsyt.2013.00100.

Zetzsche, T., Rujescu, D., Hardy, J., and Hampel, H. (2010). Advances and perspectives from genetic research: Development of biological markers in Alzheimer's disease. *Expert Rev. Mol. Diagn.*, 10, 667–690.

Zhang, B., Carroll, J., Trojanowski, J. Q., Yao, Y., Iba, M., Potuzak, J. S., et al. (2012). The microtubule-stabilizing agent, epothilone D, reduces axonal dysfunction, neurotoxicity, cognitive deficits and Alzheimer-like pathology in an interventional study with aged tau transgenic mice. *Neurobiol. Dis.*, 32, 3601–3611.

Zhang, H.-Y., Gao, M., Liu, Q.-R., Bi, G.-H., Li, X., Yang, H.-J., Gardner, E. L., et al. (2014). Cannabinoid CB$_2$ receptors modulate midbrain dopamine neuronal activity and dopamine-related behavior in mice. *Proc. Natl. Acad. Sci. USA*, 111, E5007-E5015.

Zhang, L., and Zhao, J. (2014). Profile of minocycline and its potential in the treatment of schizophrenia. *Neuropsychiatr. Dis. Treat.*, 10, 1103–1111.

Zhang, S., Zhornitsky, S., Angarita, G. A., and Li, C.-S. R. (2020). Hypothalamic response to cocaine cues and cocaine addiction severity. *Addict. Biol.*, 25, e12682. doi: 10.1111/adb.12682.

Zhang, S., Zhornitsky, S., Le, T. M., and Li, C.-S. R. (2019). Hypothalamic responses to cocaine and food cues in individuals with cocaine dependence. *Int. J. Neuropsychopharmacol.*, 22, 754–764.

Zhang, T., Zhang, L., Liang, Y., Siapas, A. G., Zhou, F.-M., and Dani, J. A. (2009). Dopamine signaling differences in the nucleus accumbens and dorsal striatum exploited by nicotine. *J. Neurosci.*, 29, 4035–4043. © 2009 Society for Neuroscience. doi.org/10.1523/JNEUROSCI.0261-09.2009

Zhang, Y., Thompson, R., Zhang, H., and Xu, H. (2011). APP processing in Alzheimer's disease. *Mol. Brain*, 4, 1–13.

Zhang, Y.-Y., Zhou, R., and Gu, W.-J. (2021). Efficacy and Safety of Methylnaltrexone for the

Treatment of Opioid-Induced Constipation: A Meta-analysis of Randomized Controlled Trials. *Pain Therapy*, 10(1), 165–179. https://doi.org/10.1007/s40122-021-00237-0

Zhao, D., Aravindakshan, A., Hilpert, M., Olmedo, P., Rule, A. M., Navas-Acien, A., and Aherrera, A. (2020). Metal/metalloid levels in electronic cigarette liquids, aerosols, and human biosamples: A systematic review. *Environ. Health Perspect.*, 128(3), 36001. doi: 10.1289/EHP5686.

Zhou, Q.-Y., and Palmiter, R. D. (1995). Dopamine-deficient mice are severely hypoactive, adipsic, and aphagic. *Cell*, 83, 1197–1209.

Zhou, Q.-Y., Qualfe, C. J., and Palmiter, R. D. (1995). Targeted disruption of the tyrosine hydroxylase gene reveals that catecholamines are required for mouse fetal development. *Nature*, 374, 640–643.

Zhou, Y., Eid, T., Hassel, B., and Danbolt, N. C. (2020). Novel aspects of glutamine synthetase in ammonia homeostasis. *Neurochem. Int.*, in press.

Zhou, Z., Karlsson, C., Liang, T., Xiong, W., Kimura, M., Tapocik, J. D., et al. (2013). Loss of metabotropic glutamate receptor 2 escalates alcohol consumption. *Proc. Natl. Acad. Sci. USA*, 110, 16963–16968.

Zhu, J., and Reith, M. E. A. (2008). Role of the dopamine transporter in the action of psychostimulants, nicotine, and other drugs of abuse. *CNS Neurol. Disord. Drug Targets*, 7, 393–409.

Zhu, S., and Paoletti, P. (2015). Allosteric modulators of NMDA receptors: Multiple sites and mechanisms. *Curr. Opin. Pharmacol.*, 20, 14–23.

Zhu, S.-H., Sun, J. Y., Bonnevie, E., Cummins, S. E., Gamst, A., Yin, L., et al. (2014). Four hundred and sixty brands of e-cigarettes and counting: Implications for product registration. *Tob. Control*, 23, iii3–iii9.

Zilles, K. 1985. In *The Cortex of the Rat -- A Stereotaxic Atlas*, p. 17. Springer-Verlag: Berlin, Germany. © Springer-Verlag Berlin Heidelberg 1985. doi. org/10.1007/978-3-642-70573-1_3

Zimmer, L. (2017). Contribution of clinical neuroimaging to the understanding of the pharmacology of methylphenidate. *Trends Pharmacol. Sci.*, 38, 608–620.

Zimmerman, J. L. (2012). Cocaine intoxication. *Crit. Care Clin.*, 28, 517–526.

Zimmerman, L., Kilwein, T. M., Beyer, D., Marks, C., and Looby, A. (2019). "Not for human consumption": A descriptive investigation into user characteristics, motives, and consequences associated with bath salt use. *J. Psychoactive Drugs*, 51, 218–224.

Zimmerman-Peruzzato, J. M., Lazzari, V. M., de Moura, A. C., Almeida, S., and Giovenardi, M. (2015). Examining the role of vasopressin in the modulation of parental and sexual behaviors. *Front. Psychiatry*, 6, 130. doi: 10.3389/fpsyt.2015.00130.

Zivin, J. A. (2000). Understanding clinical trials. *Sci. Am.*, 282, 69–75.

Zlebnik, N. E., and Cheer, J. F. (2016). Beyond the CB_1 receptor: Is cannabidiol the answer for disorders of motivation? *Annu. Rev. Neurosci.*, 39, 1–17.

Żmudzka, E., Sałaciak, K., Sapa, J., and Pytka, K. (2018). Serotonin receptors in depression and anxiety: Insights from animal studies. *Life Sci.*, 210, 106–124.

Zobel, A. W., Nickel, T., Kunzel, H. E., Ackl, N., Sonntag, A., Ising, M., et al. (2000). Effects of the high-affinity corticotropin-releasing hormone receptor 1 antagonist R121919 in major depression: The first 20 patients treated. *J. Psychiatr. Res.*, 34, 171–181.

Zoli, M., Pistillo, F., and Gotti, C. (2015). Diversity of native nicotinic receptor subtypes in mammalian brain. *Neuropharmacology*, 96, 302–311.

Zoli, M., Pucci, S., Vilella, A., and Gotti, C. (2018). Neuronal and extra-neuronal nicotinic acetylcholine receptors. *Curr. Neuropharmacol.*, 16, 338–349.

Zorumski, C. F., Izumi, Y., and Mennerick, S. (2016). Ketamine: NMDA receptors and beyond. *J. Neurosci.*, 36, 11158–11164.

Zou, X., Patterson, T. A., Sadovova, N., Twaddle, N. C., Doerge, D. R., Zhang, X., et al. (2009). Potential neurotoxicity of ketamine in the developing rat brain. *Toxicol. Sci.*, 108, 149–158.

Ztaou, S., and Amalric, M. (2019). Contribution of cholinergic interneurons to striatal pathophysiology in Parkinson's disease. *Neurochem. Int.*, 126, 1–10.

Zubieta, J. K., Smith, Y. R., Bueller, J. A., Xu, Y., Kilbourn, M. R., Jewett, D. M., et al. (2001). Regional mu opioid receptor regulation of sensory and affective dimensions of pain. *Science*, 293, 311–315.

Zulli, A., Smith, R. M., Kubatka, P., Novak, J., Uehara, Y., Loftus, H., et al. (2016). Caffeine and cardiovascular diseases: Critical review of current research. *Eur. J. Nutr.*, 55, 1331–1343.

Zunszain, P. A., Horowitz, M. A., Cattaneo, A., Lupi, M. M, and Pariante, C. M. (2013). Ketamine: Synaptogenesis, immunomodulation and glycogen synthase kinase-3 as underlying mechanisms of its antidepressant properties. *Mol. Psychiat.*, 18, 1236–1241.

Zvosec, D. L., Smith, S. W., Porrata, T., Strobl, A. Q., and Dyer, J. E. (2011). Case series of 226 γ-hydroxybutyrate associated deaths: Lethal toxicity and trauma. *Am. J. Emerg. Med.*, 29, 319–332.

Index

Page numbers in *italic* type indicate the information will be found in an illustration.